FLORA

FLORA

VOLUME I

A–K

THE GARDENER'S BIBLE

CHIEF CONSULTANT: TONY LORD

More than 20,000 garden plants
from around the world

CASSELL

Publisher	Gordon Cheers
Associate publisher	Margaret Olds
Art director	Stan Lamond
Project manager	Kate Etherington
Chief consultant	Tony Lord
Senior consultant	Tony Rodd
Contributors	David Austin, David Banks, Cathy Wilkinson Barash, Matthew Biggs, Don Blaxell, David Bond, Peter Brownless, Geoff Bryant, Kate Bryant, Cole Burrell, Derek Butcher, Jerry Coleby-Williams, Ian Connor, Penny Dunn, Lorraine Flanigan, Jim Folsom, Richard Francis, Jo Ann Gardner, William Grant, Ken Grapes, Sarah Guest, Keith Hammett, Patricia Hanbidge, Ian Hay, Terry Hewitt, Sean Hogan, Geoff Hodge, Mark Kane, Ruth Kiew, Melanie Kinsey, Isobyl la Croix, Todd Lasseigne, David Mabberley, Lawrie Metcalf, Valda Paddison, Helene Pizzi, Lee Reich, Martyn Rix, Tony Rodd, Bruce Rutherford, Stephen Ryan, Donald Schnell, Patrick Seymour, Julie Silk, Geoff Stebbings, Wendy Thomas, David Tomlinson, John Trager, R. G. Turner Jr., Marion Tyree, Rachel Vogan, Scott Williams
Hardiness zone maps	John Frith
Illustrations	Spike Wademan
Managing editors	Janet Parker, Margaret Malone
Editors	Loretta Barnard, Annette Carter, Lynn Cole, Dannielle Doggett, Fiona Doig, Alan Edwards, Janet Healey, Carol Jacobson, Erin King, Scott Lumsden, Heather McNamara, Joy Misrachi, Rob Paratore, Anne Savage, Judith Simpson, Julie Stanton, Marie-Louise Taylor, Michael Wall
Picture research	Gordon Cheers
Photo library	Alan Edwards
Cover design	Stan Lamond
Designer	Joy Eckermann
Picture sizing	Kathy Lamond, Suzanne Potma
Typesetting	Dee Rogers
Index	Loretta Barnard, Scott Lumsden, Heather McNamara, Jan Watson
Production	Bernard Roberts
Publishing assistant	Erin King
Foreign rights	Sarah Minns
Photographers	James Young, David Banks, Chris Bell, Rob Blakers, Lorraine Blyth, Greg Bourke, Ken Brass, Geoff Bryant, Derek Butcher, Claver Carroll, Anna Cheifetz, Leigh Clapp, David Austin Roses, Grant Dixon, Heather Donovan, e-garden Ltd, Bruce Elder, Katie Fallows, Stuart Owen Fox, Richard Francis, Robert Gibson, William Grant, Denise Greig, Barry Griffith, Barry Grossman, Gil Hanly, Ivy Hansen, Dennis Harding, Jack Hobbs, Neil Holmes, Paul Huntley, Richard I'Anson, Ionas Kaltenbach, David Keith Jones, Willie Kempen, Colin Kerr, Robert M. Knight, Carol Knoll, Albert Kuhnigk, Mike Langford, Gary Lewis, Geoff Longford, Stirling Macoboy, John McCann, David McGonigal, Richard McKenna, Ron Moon, Eberhard Morell, Barry Myers-Rice, Steve Newall, Connall Oosterbroek, Larry Pitt, Craig Potton, Janet Price, Geof Prigge, Nick Rains, Christo Reid, Howard Rice, Jamie Robertson, Tony Rodd, Rolf-Ulrich Roesler, Luke Saffigna, Don Skirrow, Raoul Slater, Peter Solness, Ken Stepnell, Warren Steptoe, Oliver Strewe, J. Peter Thoeming, David Titmuss, Wayne Turville, Georg Uebelhart, Sharyn Vanderhorst, Kim Westerskov, Murray White, Vic Widman, Brent Wilson, Geoff Woods, Grant Young

This edition published in 2003 by Cassell,
an imprint of Weidenfeld & Nicolson
Wellington House
125 Strand
London WC2R 0BB

Produced by Global Book Publishing Pty Ltd
Unit 1/181 High Street, Willoughby, NSW 2068, Australia
Ph +61 2 9967 3100 Fax +61 2 9967 5891
Email rightsmanager@globalpub.com.au

All rights reserved. No part of this publication may be reproduced, stored in a retrieval system, or transmitted in any form of by any means, electronic, mechanical, photocopying, recording or otherwise, without the prior written permission of the Publisher.

Photos and illustrations from the Global Photo Library
© Global Book Publishing Pty Ltd 2003
Text © Global Book Publishing Pty Ltd 2003

The Publisher would like to thank Duncan Baird Publishers, London, for permission to re-create in this book the map on page 11 of *The History of the Countryside* by Oliver Rackham.
Thanks also to The Art Archive for use of the following pictures: page 16 (above right), page 19 (below right), page 46 (top centre), page 47 (top right), page 48 (below left), and page 51 (both)

The moral rights of all contributors have been asserted

ISBN 0 30436 435 5

British Library Cataloguing in Publication Data
A catalogue record for this book is available from the British Library

Photographers: The publisher would be pleased to hear from photographers interested in supplying photographs that could be included in new editions of *Flora*. Email photoeditor@globalpub.com.au

Suggestions: The editors would be pleased to hear from plant nurseries, general gardeners, and specialty groups about any plants they feel should be added to future editions of *Flora*. Email editor@globalpub.com.au

Printed in Hong Kong by Sing Cheong Printing Co. Ltd
Film separation Pica Digital Pte Ltd, Singapore

VOLUME I
Page i: *Malus* 'Red Sentinel'
Pages ii–iii: *Magnolia* 'Betty'
Page v: Cobweb in conifer, in the snow
Pages vi–vii: Creative plant combinations offer color and fragrance
Pages viii–ix: *Galanthus nivalis*
Pages xii–xiii: A variety of trees and shrubs provide structure to a garden
Pages 64–65: Aster *novi-belgii* cultivar
Pages 212–213: *Banksia ericifolia*
Pages 274-275: *Camellia reticulata* 'Dali Cha'
Pages 462–463: *Dahlia* 'Tout à Toi'
Pages 520–521: *Echinacea purpurea*
Pages 594–595: *Fritillaria imperialis*
Pages 620–621: *Gaillardia* species
Pages 664–665: *Helianthus annuus*
Pages 724–725: *Iris* 'Marie Caillet'
Pages 762–763: *Kalmia latifolia* 'Ostbo Red'

VOLUME II
Page i: *Bellis perennis* Pomponette Series
Page ii–iii: *Leucospermum* species
Page v: *Lantana* species
Pages vi–vii: *Cotinus coggygria* 'Purpureus'
Pages 784–785: *Lilium* 'Barbaresco'
Pages 846–847: *Moraea villosa*
Pages 910–911: *Narcissus* 'Palmares'
Pages 940–941: *Oenothera* species
Pages 968–969: *Paphiopedilum* species with frog
Pages 1120–1121: *Rosa* 'Cathedral'
Pages 1290–1291: *Sarracenia* × *exornata*
Pages 1394–1395: *Telopea speciosissima* cultivar
Pages 1446–1447: *Vanda* 'Pat Delight'
Pages 1480–1481: *Zinnia elegans* 'Oklahoma Pink'

Contributors

Tony Lord was Gardens Adviser for the National Trust until 1989, when he began freelance work as a horticultural author and photographer. He also acts as technical consultant and editor, dealing with books on plants and gardens for numerous publishers. He was sole editor of *The Plant Finder* for its first ten editions (1987–96) and is now Principal Editor in its current incarnation as *The RHS Plant Finder*.

Tony is the author of numerous books, including *The Encyclopedia of Planting Combinations, Designing with Roses,* and *Sissinghurst: Classic Garden Inspiration.*

His committee memberships include: RHS Floral A; RHS Trials Committee; RHS Reginald Cory Memorial Cup Committee; RHS Advisory Panel on Nomenclature and Taxonomy (Chairman); UK Plant Breeders' Rights Controller's Advisory Panel for Herbaceous Plants (Plant Variety Rights Office); and Gardens Panel, National Trust. He is currently based in Tewkesbury, Gloucestershire.

David Austin is the founder of David Austin Roses, one of the world's leading rose nurseries specializing in the breeding of David Austin's English Roses and also the production of the complete range of roses. Born in 1926, he was a passionate gardener and plantsman from an early age. He started his working life on the family farm and during that time started breeding roses primarily as a hobby, introducing three varieties before launching David Austin Roses in 1969. Today, he is still very active in the nursery and is responsible for one of the world's largest rose breeding programs. His books, *Heritage of the Rose* (1988) and *David Austin's English Roses* (1993), are widely acclaimed.

In 1995, David was awarded both the Royal National Rose Society's Award for Innovation in rose breeding, and the Royal Horticultural Society Gold Veitch Memorial Medal. Other awards include the University of East London's Honorary Degree of Master of Science, 1997; the Royal National Rose Society's Dean Hole Medal, 2000; and the Royal National Rose Society Victoria Medal of Honour, 2002.

Matthew Biggs has been a professional gardener for over 20 years. He trained at Pershore College of Horticulture and the Royal Botanic Gardens, Kew, where he also worked as a Guide Lecturer and Staff Training Officer. With this experience, he became a freelance horticulturist, running a landscaping and maintenance company, lecturing to gardening societies and teaching in adult education.

His television and radio career began with the popular Channel 4 series *Garden Club* and continued with appearances on the BBC's *How Does Your Garden Grow?*, among others. He was also a program director and guest expert on Meridian's *Grass Roots.* A seasoned radio presenter, Matthew is a panellist on Radio Four's *Gardener's Question Time,* LBC Radio's *Gardening Phone-in,* BBC Radio Five, and BBC Three Counties Radio.

His writing credits include regular contributions to numerous gardening magazines, among them BBC *Gardener's World Magazine, The Garden,* and *Amateur Gardening,* as well as several books including *A Practical Guide to Growing Healthy Houseplants, Matthew Biggs' Complete Book of Vegetables,* and *What Houseplant Where?,* with Roy Lancaster.

A plant enthusiast, Matthew has traveled extensively worldwide, leading specialist gardening tours to Europe, the Mediterranean, Southeast Asia, South America, Africa, and Australasia. He lives in Flamstead, Hertsfordshire.

Peter Brownless is Garden Supervisor at the Royal Botanic Garden, Edinburgh, Scotland. He gained his qualifications in Horticulture from Writtle Agricultural College before working in a variety of landscaping and horticultural positions throughout the UK.

Currently, Peter supervizes and curates the Edinburgh Garden's nursery, responsible for the temperate nursery and helping to curate the Garden's main collection. As well, he supervizes the department's record keeping; seed and specimen collection; garden and outstations labeling; oversees the horticultural content of the Garden's web site; and represents the Garden on the Members (Friends) committee at lectures, plant sales, and auctions.

Peter contributes articles for various publications, including *Botanics* magazine, *Amateur Gardener,* and *Specialist's Corner.* His own garden has been featured in *The Sunday Times* by Suki Urquhart. Peter has participated in botanical expeditions to Chile and China.

Ian Connor is an experienced lecturer and consultant on ornamental bamboos. His involvement in all things bamboo is extensive: he is the President of the American Bamboo Society; Editor of *Bamboo: The Magazine of the American Bamboo Society;* and Representative for Oregon on the ABS Board of Directors. As well, Ian is the Bamboo Consultant at the Classical Chinese Garden in Portland, Oregon.

Born in England, Ian worked for ten years in the role of Skilled Horticulturist at the Hillier Arboretum, Hampshire, before moving to the United States, where he is currently the Horticultural Manager at the Bamboo Garden, Portland, Oregon. Ian is also a freelance writer and photographer, and is the author of *A Cultivation Guide For Bamboo.*

Isobyl la Croix studied Botany at the University of Edinburgh, Scotland and, after graduation, worked for two years in the Agriculture Department of the University of Aberdeen. After marrying an entomologist, she lived for four years in Ghana, and three in Kenya, in Africa. After a spell back in Britain, the pair returned to Malawi in 1978, where they lived for ten years. It was here that Isobyl's latent interest in orchids developed strongly, and all her spare time was spent orchid-hunting. With some friends, Isobyl and her husband wrote a small book on the epiphytic orchids of Malawi, which was published locally, and they then started collecting material for a book on all the Malawi orchids. This book, *Orchids of Malawi,* was published by A.A. Balkema in 1991, with photographs by her husband, Eric.

After returning to Britain at the end of 1987, Isobyl worked on a two-volume account of Orchidaceae for the *Flora Zambesiaca,* produced by the Royal Botanic Gardens, Kew. She has also published several other books on orchids and runs a small mail-order business selling African and Madagascan orchids, in the hope that the more widespread they are in cultivation, the less likely they are to become extinct. For the past two years she has been editor of *The Orchid Review,* the orchid journal of the RHS and the longest running orchid journal in the world, now in Volume 111.

Ken Grapes was born and brought up in Norfolk and acquired his love of gardening from his mother. He served in the British Army for nearly 30 years. For the past 15 years he has been Secretary General of the Royal National Rose Society. He has in his care the world famous "Gardens of the Rose" at St Albans where international trials for new roses are held, together with practical tests aimed at assessing the validity of many widely held perceptions about rose cultivation. In 1998 he was awarded the Society's highest honor, the Dean Hole Medal.

Terry Hewitt has been an ardent cacti hobbyist for over 40 years. Like most collectors, he started with a few plants on the window ledge, but as his enthusiasm and collection developed, he had the opportunity to grow cacti plants commercially. Today, he is the owner of the Holly Gate Cactus Nursery and Cactus Garden at Ashington, Sussex, which grows thousands of plants for sale each year and also maintains an extensive private collection that is open to the public.

Terry is still a keen hobbyist and has great problems deciding whether he is working or playing. He devotes his spare time to the British Cactus Society, lecturing and talking to interested groups of people. He has also contributed to, or written, several books on cacti and succulents, and has contributed to a number of gardening encyclopaedias.

Geoff Hodge is the Web Editor for the Royal Horticultural Society, Chairman of the Garden Writers' Guild, and all-round gardening correspondent for BBC Radio Cambridgeshire. Geoff graduated from Reading University with a degree in Botany and has been a gardening journalist for the past 12 years, previously working as Gardening Editor of *Garden News* and *Garden Answers.* Before that he managed a garden centre. Geoff is based in Peterborough, Cambridgeshire.

Ruth Kiew holds a PhD in Tropical Botany from Cambridge University. She lectured at the University of Agriculture in Malaysia for 25 years before becoming Professor of Botany. In 1997, she moved to the Singapore Botanic Gardens as the Keeper of the Herbarium and Library.

Ruth is active in botanical exploration in the region, specializing in the taxonomy of rainforest herbs and limestone flora, which has led to the discovery of many new species. She is also active in Malaysian conservation. In 2002 she was awarded the prestigious David Fairchild Award for Botanical Exploration.

Ruth is the author of more than a hundred scientific papers, and her books include *The Pollen Atlas of Malaysian Bee Plants* and *The Seed Plant Flora of Fraser's Hill, Peninsular Malaysia.* She is currently writing a book on the begonias of Peninsular Malaysia.

David Mabberley is Leids Universiteits Fonds Professor at the University of Leiden, The Netherlands, and Honorary Research Associate at the Royal Botanic Gardens, Sydney, Australia. His research interests center on the systematics and ecology of tropical fruit- and timber-trees, economic botany, botanical art, and the history of biology.

David has over 250 publications on botanical and horticultural topics to his name. Among these are 14 books including *The Plant-book, a portable dictionary of the vascular plants* (2nd ed., 1997), *Ferdinand Bauer: The Nature of Discovery* (1999), and *Arthur Harry Church: The Anatomy of Flowers* (2000).

Martyn Rix is a botanist, plant collector, and gardener. He studied botany at Trinity College, Dublin, and at Cambridge, where he wrote his doctoral thesis. After working as botanist at the Royal Horticultural Society's Garden at Wisley, he became an independent botanical advisor and writer and has since produced 17 books and numerous scientific papers, as well as 23 illustrated books with Roger Phillips. He is on the Picture Committee of the Royal Horticultural Society and has been awarded the Gold Veitch Memorial Medal by the Royal Horticultural Society for his services to horticulture.

Along with Roger Phillips, Martyn is a pioneer in the use of photography in plant illustration. Their books, *The Botanical Garden I* and *II,* are exciting and thoroughly modern renditions of illustrated botany books. Ten years in the making, these books combine the finest in photography with up-to-date, expert commentary on flora, and seek to bridge the gap between gardener-friendly books and scientific texts.

Geoff Stebbings discovered the joy of gardening as a child when some privet shoots, destined to feed stick insects, rooted in water. He trained at the Royal Botanic Gardens, Kew, and briefly worked at a garden centre and bromeliad nursery. He became Head Gardener at Myddelton House, Enfield, Middlesex, responsible for the restoration of the garden established by the plantsman E. A. Bowles. Here, Geoff established the National Collection of Award-winning irises and was, for many years, Chairman of the National Council for the Conservation of Plants and Gardens (London Group).

Geoff's first position as a gardening writer was on *Garden News,* later moving to *Practical Gardening* and *Garden Answers.* He then became Features Editor of *The Garden,* the Royal Horticultural Society's journal. Now a freelance writer, Geoff has written three books and contributed to many others. He is also a radio broadcaster and lecturer.

When not writing and researching, Geoff spends time on his own small garden and greenhouse in Peterborough, Cambridgeshire, which are packed with unusual plants. He has a special interest in bulbs, both tender and hardy.

Contents

How This Book Works

Flora provides a wealth of up-to-date information on over 20,000 plants. Selection has been based on those most significant in horticulture, food crops, forestry, and those used for products such as drugs, fibers, and dyes. It is expected that most readers will be interested in the plants found and grown in gardens and parks rather than in the wild. And because the great majority of garden enthusiasts live in the temperate zones, there is proportionately a more complete coverage of temperate plants than of tropical species. But it is not only garden plants that are described here. Many other plants have attracted

notice because they are significant for other reasons—for example the beauty and fame of their wild habitat, their unique evolutionary position, or their adaptation to extreme environments.

The book is composed of three sections. The first section introduces the book and looks at plants in general terms: how they differ from each other and from other types of plants, environmental factors that affect their growth, classification, human uses, cultivation, and native plants. A color-coded map showing plant hardiness zones, and an explanation of the zones, is also included.

Genus entry

Family name

Species entry

Cultivation

Synonym

Flora award

Common name

Symbols
(see listings at right)

Place of origin

Forms
(variants, subspecies
or cultivars)

Hardiness zones

CHAMAEDOREA

Chamaedorea, belonging to the family Arecaceae, is of the larger genera of palms with over 100 species. They are attractive, small, understory palms which adapt to cultivation, especially as indoor plants. Native to tropical America, they include both single-stemmed and clumping palms. Fronds are either pinnate (feather palms) or undivided. Flowers are of different sexes on different plants, very small and fleshy, and borne on spikes. As small single-seeded fruits ripen, fruit color contrasts with that of the spike.
CULTIVATION: Although tropical palms, they adapt well to frost-free warm-temperate climates. Some species are quite sun-hardy, in a humid climate, but most grow best in filtered light in a sheltered spot. Soil should be moderately fertile with a high organic content and the surface mulched with leaves. If grown indoors they need good light, though not direct sunlight. They need regular summer feeding with a dilute high-nitrogen fertilizer. Propagation is normally from seed.

Chamaedorea elegans ★
syns *Collinia elegans, Neanthe bella*
PARLOR PALM
☀ ⌇ ↔ 36 in (90 cm) ↑ 6 ft (1.8 m)
From highland rainforests of southern Mexico and Guatemala. Stems single with knobbly protuberances. Short deep green fronds, crowded. Small yellow flowers, on panicles. Female panicles turn orange-red. Pea-sized black fruit. 'Bella' ★, crown of fronds only 12 in (30 cm) wide. Zones 10–12.

Chamaedorea ernesti-augusti

Chamaedorea ernesti-augusti
☀ ⌇ ↔ 18 in (45 cm) ↑ 3 ft (0.9 m)
From southern Mexico to Honduras. Single-stemmed, wedge-shaped fronds, undivided, with a broad notch at the apex. The male plants have tiny red flowers, the females a spike of greenish flowers, turning bright orange. Small black fruit. Zones 10–12.

Chamaedorea linearis
syns *Chamaedorea megaphylla, C. poeppigiana, C. polyclada*
☀ ⌇ ↔ 7 ft (2 m) ↑ 8–20 ft (2.4–6 m)
Native to the Andes at both low and high altitudes. Single pale green trunk. Spreading dark green fronds with drooping leaflets. Multi-branched inflorescence of white flowers. Red fruits to 1 in (25 mm) on female plants. Zones 10–12.

Chamaedorea microspadix
☀ ⌇ ↔ 10 ft (3 m) ↑ 8 ft (2.4 m)
From southeastern Mexico. Clump of spreading, thin, bamboo-like stems. Fronds crowded, matt green broad leaflets. Flower panicles, females green, bearing bright scarlet fruits to ½ in (12 mm) in diameter. One of the most sun-hardy species. Zones 10–12.

Chamaedorea plumosa ★
☀/☀ ⌇ ↔ 5–8 ft (1.5–2.4 m)
↑ 10–12 ft (3–3.5 m)

Chamaedo...

Chamaedo...

straight ...
minal leaf...
ate male ...
stalks, w...
Round ...

Cham...
syn. *Cham...*
☀ ⌇ ...
Native ...
stemmed ...
regularly ...
short fl...
the fro...
sized b...
Zones 1...

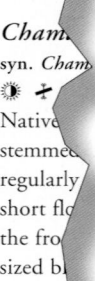

CH...

the Flora award

full sun

half sun

shade

fully hardy

frost hardy

half hardy

frost tender

height

spread

PAGE HEADINGS

help you locate a particular plant. Headings on each double-page spread name the first genus described on the left-hand page, and the last genus described on the right-hand page.

CAPTIONS

indicate the plant's botanical name.

THUMB TABS

are colored alphabetical tabs in the margin that help you find the plant you are looking for.

GENUS ENTRY

contains information about the group as a whole, including geographical range, and cultivation and propagation requirements.

SPECIES ENTRY

contains detailed information on particular species and forms, and includes hardiness rating by zones.

SEASONAL PHOTOGRAPHS

show how the appearance of a plant can change over the course of a year.

"IN THE WILD" PHOTOGRAPHS

show plants in their natural habitat.

CLOSE-UP PHOTOGRAPHS

zoom in on a leaf, flower, fruit, or bark to help you appreciate the plant's unique qualities.

Malus × purpurea cultivar, in autumn

Malus × purpurea cultivar, in winter

Malus × purpurea 'Aldenhamensis'

Malus × purpurea 'Lemoinei'

Malus sargentii
SARGENT'S CRABAPPLE
This is a very small, densely branched crabapple. The leaves are broadly oval, sharp-tipped, heavy, bright green, and lobed, with serrated edges. The

Malus sieboldii
This slow-growing, small- to medium-size, rounded tree comes from Japan. Lobed or simple leaves. Buds red to

Malus × purpurea cultivar, in spring

'Aldenhamensis' blooms u— per season, leaves red-gree— green, buds bright carmin— semi-double pinkish red —
'Eleyi', deep red-purple — to red flowers, subject t—
'Lemoinei', a popular — crabapple. Zones 4–9.

Malus × robusta
Conical-crowned la— tree, an *M. baccata* hybrid. Bright gree— (10 cm) long, scall— white to pink, in — spring. Long-stem— fruits. 'Erecta', l— with pink edges,

Malus × purpurea
A very early flowering crabapple, this is a hybrid of *M.* × *atrosanguinea* and *M. pumila* 'Niedzwetzkyana'. It has deep green leaves, and dark flowers that fade to pale mauve, in late spring.

Malus × robusta 'Erecta'

Malus sar—

CALLIANDRA
This genus in the mimosa subfamily of legume (Fabaceae) family consists of around 200 species, the majority occurring in South and Central America and the West Indies. Mostly shrubs or small trees, they have bipinnate leaves, long-stamened flowers in globular heads or elongated spikes. Flower colors range from white and pink to deep crimson, attracting hummingbirds which pollinate these plants in the wild. Seed pods are rigid and flattened. Most calliandras come from regions that are warm but dry, or at least with a pronounced dry season. Many species are frost tender. Calliandras are useful landscape subjects, providing year-round color as well as a screen of feathery foliage.
CULTIVATION: Tough adaptable shrubs where climate is suitable, tolerating hard dry soils and moderately exposed positions. Most species adapt well to clipping into compact forms and can be used for hedges. Propagate from seed, or from cuttings taken in winter from short lateral branches.

Calliandra haematocephala

Calliandra surinamensis

Calliandra tweedii

Calliandra californica
A native of Baja California, Mexico, this plant is often used in desert style gardens. The tough wiry branches are dotted for much of the year with small tassel-like heads of bright crimson flowers. Zones 10–12.

Calliandra emarginata
Native of southern Mexico and Central America, often confused with the better known *C. haematocephala*. Semi-scrambling habit, large leaflets,

large 'powderpuff' heads of pink to crimson flowers. Semi-prostrate when planted in an open area. Zones 10–12.

Calliandra eriophylla
FAIRY DUSTER, ROCK MESQUITE
Extending from Mexico to the far south of western USA. Crooked prickly branches, fine feathery leaves, profuse wispy heads of pale red flowers in late winter–early spring. Used in desert style gardens. Zones 9–11.

Calliandra haematocephala
BLOOD-RED TASSEL FLOWER, POWDERPUFF TREE
From northern South America. Flowers pink to scarlet or deep red, densely crowded into globular heads at branch tips, most of the year, autumn–winter in cooler areas. Shelter from strong winds. Zones 10–12.

Calliandra houstoniana
From southern Mexico and adjacent Central America. Open habit, leaves bipinnate, numerous tiny bright green leaflets. Flowers in terminal spike-like clusters, with showy red stamens, from summer–autumn. Zones 10–12.

Calliandra surinamensis
PINK-AND-WHITE POWDERPUFF
From northern South America. Showy powderpuff flowerheads, white to pale mauve, most of the year. Vase-shaped habit, with arching branches, and small clustered leaves. Drought tolerant. Zones 10–12.

Calliandra tweedii ★
syn. *Inga pulcherrima*
RED TASSEL FLOWER
This native of Uruguay and southern Brazil grows best in a warm-temperate climate without seasonal rainfall. Multi-stemmed fresh green foliage has tiny crowded leaflets. The deep scarlet flowerheads appear in spring–autumn. Can be cut back hard, or trimmed to a dense hedge. Zones 9–11.

CALLICARPA
BEAUTY BUSH
This genus has about 140 species of trees and shrubs, both deciduous and evergreen, belonging to the mint (Lamiaceae) family. They occur from the tropics to warm-temperate regions around much of the globe. They are close allies of the verbenas, which shows in their simple conspicuously veined and toothed leaves and their

Calliandra californica

Calliandra emarginata

Calliandra eriophylla

Calliandra houstoniana, Plaine du Champ de Bataille, New Caledonia

The second section, the major part of the book, is arranged in alphabetical order according to genus. The symbol × before a genus or species name usually indicates a hybrid genus or species. This convention is not always followed for orchid genera but has been used here for consistency. The genus entries give the family to which the plant belongs, as well as geographical range, number of species, distinguishing features, commercial uses, and propagation and cultivation requirements of the genus as a whole. Under every genus entry are a number of species entries (including synonym and common name, if applicable), each containing the growth habit, flowering season, flower color, forms, and hardiness zones, with symbols denoting aspect, hardiness, width, and height. The width and height given apply to a mature plant in cultivation. The hardiness zones show the climatic areas in which plants can be grown. However, for annuals the minimum zone is that in which the plant can be raised and planted out over the spring to autumn period, disregarding winter hardiness.

Most plant entries have a photograph—each one is captioned with its botanical name. In genera in which many cultivars have been developed, such as *Camellia*, *Rhododendron*, and *Rosa*, there may be a picture without accompanying text; for ease of reference, these cultivars are all included in the index. The color of flowers in cultivation can vary significantly, depending on the soil, the climate, and even the age of the bloom. Many bluish or lavender flowers appear more pink when photographed.

Flora awards, indicated with a star, show the plants recommended by our consultants as outstanding in their group. Usually the award appears next to the plant name; occasionally cultivars not discussed in the text will have the award star with their caption.

The third section includes five pages of color illustrations, depicting flower and leaf structure, shape, and arrangement, and fruit types; a comprehensive glossary; and finally an index that lists botanical names, common names, and synonyms.

The
World
of
Plants

Gardening in the British Isles

Natural habitat is so rare in Great Britain, and only slightly more common in Ireland, that most residents do not see any within the average year. Such areas are mainly restricted to some wetlands and coastal areas, mountaintops, and the far north of Scotland. The climax vegetation natural to most of the British Isles is oak with hazel understory, but with beech on alkaline soils in southern England, and Scots pine with heather in the highlands of Scotland. However, ancient woodland has almost always been managed in some way and can only extremely rarely be considered natural. The flora, much reduced as a result of the Devensian Age (the last Ice Age) is predominantly of species that are commonly found throughout Europe. What ecological richness there is in the British Isles lies very largely in the ancient ecosystems created by humans, based on agriculture (especially grazing) or forestry (including coppicing). In many cases, these have survived for a large part of the life of the current British flora, that is, since the ice retreated some 14,000 years ago.

Right: Pulsatilla vulgaris has long been a popular garden plant in the British Isles and Europe. Its 6-petalled silky purple flowers appear in spring. A hardy plant, it grows best in rocky crevices; it will also perform well in woodland conditions.

Formation of the landmass of the British Isles

Below: The flora of the British Isles cannot claim to be distinctive except in its meager number of species. However, its beauty is undeniable, and derives mainly from the involvement of humans over long periods.

The British Isles were formed over hundreds of millions of years from fragments split off from various landmasses and brought together by the shifting of tectonic plates. It is believed that about 545 million years ago, what is now England and Wales broke away from the supercontinent of Gondwanaland, then at the South Pole, and started to drift northwards. Scotland originated as part of Laurentia, most of which is now North America, and collided with what is now England and Wales around

430 million years ago, thrusting up the Caledonian Mountains where the two landmasses join. By the time a 10-mile wide comet collided with Earth 66 million years ago—causing climatic changes that killed the dinosaurs— the British Isles, as well as Europe, were quite separate from North America and Greenland. For much of this time, the part of the Earth's crust that corresponds to the British Isles was below the oceans but the formation of polar icecaps about 20 million years ago brought what are now the British Isles above sea level and linked them to Europe, allowing the flora to start to develop. However, when the last Ice Age was at its most severe, about 18,000 years ago, the glaciation extended deep into southern England. Even south of this, many native species would have been lost through their inability to adapt to the colder climate.

This checkered history of this part of the earth's crust, derived from different tectonic plates, folding, pushing into, over, and below each other, has made for a very complex pattern of underlying rocks, with equally varied soils above them. Up to about 30 different geological strata are recognized for the British Isles, each with a soil derived from it.

Ecological zones

Historical ecologist Oliver Rackham has classified the British Isles into various zones, each comprising a recognizably distinct type of habitat (see map, facing page, above). In Scotland, the lowland area includes major cities such as Edinburgh, Glasgow, and Dundee; more lowland lies around the northeast coast, via Aberdeen as far as the Moray Firth. North and west of these lowlands are the Highlands of Scotland, with the Grampians separated from the North West Highlands by the Great Glen. The far north of the mainland consists of treeless landscape, as do the Shetland, Hebrides, and Orkney Islands. The southern part of Scotland, stretching from the Mull of Galloway in the west to Berwickshire in the east, is classed as the Southern Uplands.

In England, the Highland Zone stretches south of Scotland from the Lake District and the Pennines, with further enclaves of highland area in the North York Moors and along the Welsh border, Shropshire, and Herefordshire. In southwest England, Cornwall and most of Devon are also classed as belonging to the Highland Zone. Most of the remainder is classed as Ancient Countryside to the west and southeast, with a band of Planned Countryside running south of the North York Moors via the Vale of Pickering, Yorkshire Wolds, and Vale of York, Lincolnshire, the east and south Midlands and central southern England to Dorset.

The differences between these two might seem subtle but they are sometimes absolutely clear-cut. In Ancient Countryside, the product of at least a thousand years of continuity and little-changed since 1700, the settlements tend to be hamlets and small towns. The isolated farms are usually ancient, hedges are mainly mixed and not straight, roads many and not straight, often sunken. Planned Countryside is the result of the Enclosure Acts in the eighteenth and nineteenth centuries when land was hurriedly parcelled out parish by parish to give a "mass-produced, drawing–board landscape." Settlements are villages, the few farms are mainly eighteenth- or nineteenth-century, hedges are mostly straight and of hawthorn, and roads are straight and on the surface.

In Wales, most of the landscape is classed as Highland, with some Ancient Countryside in the Dee Estuary, Anglesey, and the Vale of Glamorgan.

Climate of the British Isles since the Devensian Ice Age

Since the end of the last Ice Age, the Gulf Stream has been the dominant force in determining the climate of the British Isles, as it remains today. Originating in the Gulf of Mexico and driven parallel to the eastern seaboard of North America by the northeast trade winds on to the northwestern shores of Europe, it causes the greatest temperature anomaly in the world, with parts of northwest Europe having temperatures 68°F (20°C) or more warmer than average for their latitude. When the surface waters reach the Arctic Ocean, their salinity increased by the drying winds, some remain as surface currents, circling around Greenland before returning south along North America's eastern seaboard. The remainder sink to form a southward-bound undercurrent, forming along with the surface Gulf Stream the system called the "North Atlantic Conveyor." It is believed that disruptions to this system have brought about past Ice Ages and this could happen again even in the fairly near future: if the salty water did not become cold enough to sink, due to global warming, or was diluted with too much freshwater, the North Atlantic Conveyor would halt. Northwest Europe would become much colder and the Arctic polar icecap would again extend southward.

Since the last Ice Age, the climate of the British Isles has been subject to periodic changes, becoming warmer or cooler, sometimes for merely a few decades, on other occasions for a millennium or more. For instance, the climate was rather warmer than at present between the ninth and fourteenth centuries; the years between 1550 and 1850, during which the River Thames froze over 14 times and "Frost Fairs" were held on it, were known as the "Little Ice Age." Relative to temperatures since the last Ice Age, the climate is currently warm, with most areas matching Zone 8 according to the United States Department of Agriculture system (see map, right),

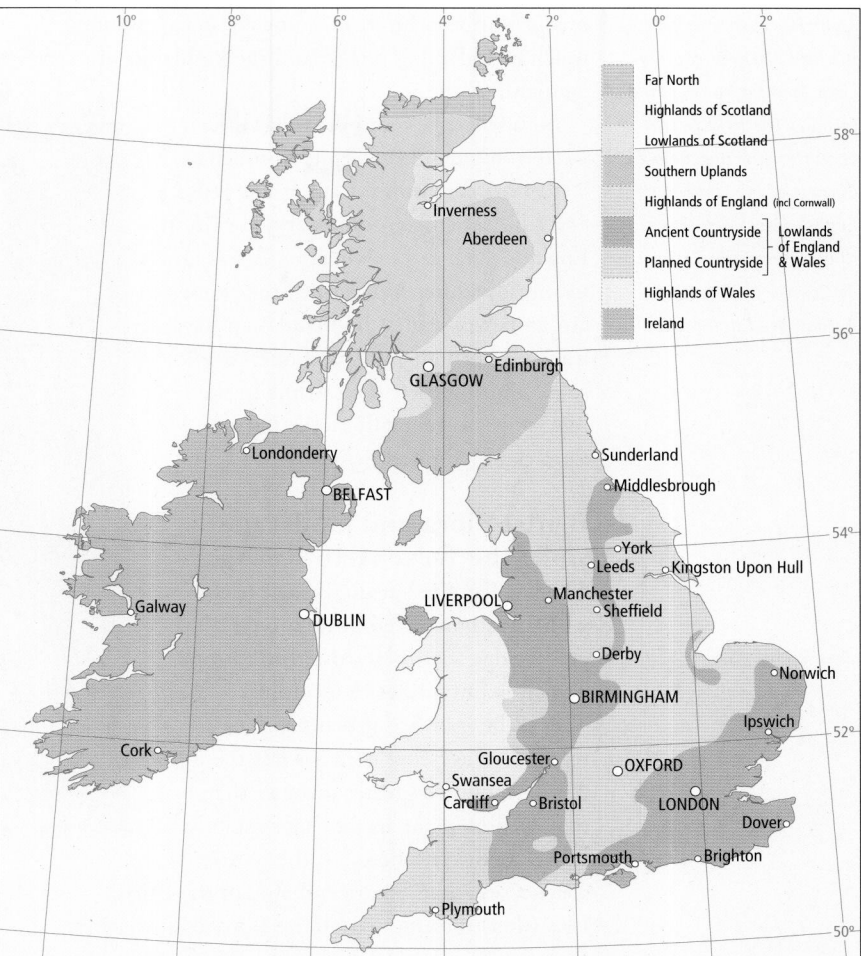

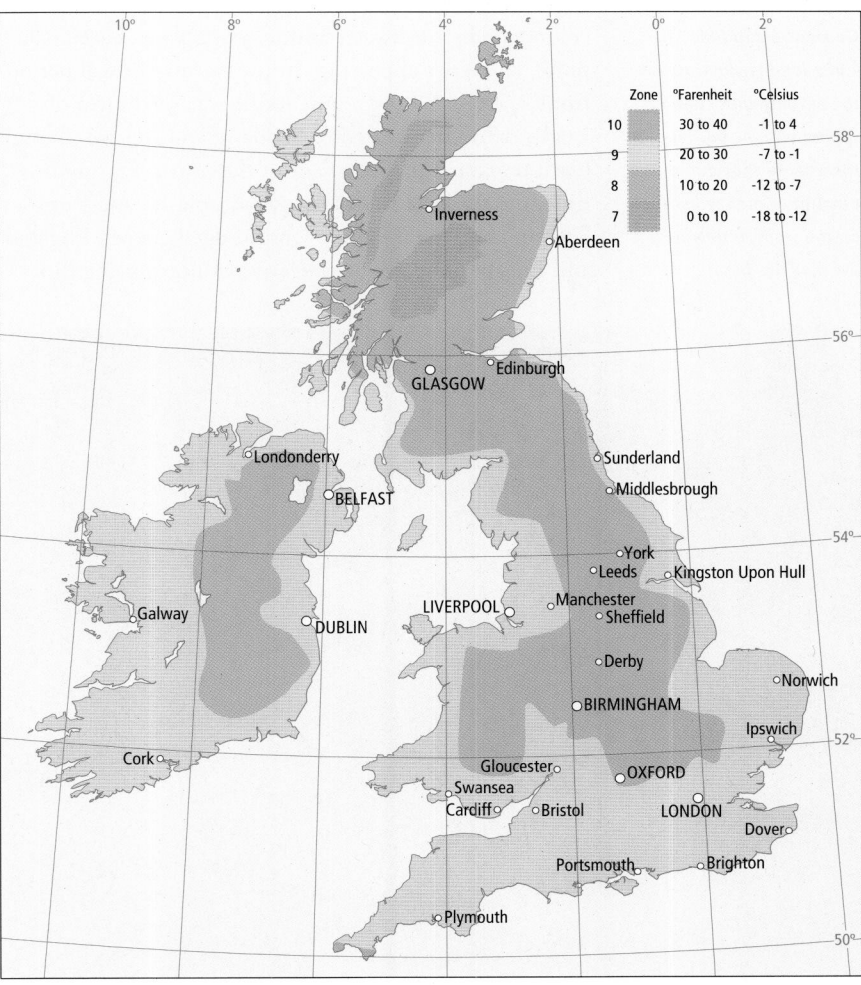

except southern England, some coastal areas, and
much of Ireland (Zone 9) and the highlands of
Scotland (Zone 7).

Rainfall varies considerably, with
western highlands receiving as much as
9 ft (3 m) per annum but with as little
as 24 in (60 cm) in some parts of eastern
England such as Lincolnshire, Essex, and
Cambridgeshire. As a result, some western and even central highlands can have
leached, nutrient-poor, and often acidic
soils, limiting their flora, while in the
east, soils are generally fertile but the
flora can be limited by drought.

British flora and landscape since the Devensian Ice Age

The last Ice Age left the British Isles
with a vastly reduced flora, though the
land bridge that then existed to Europe
helped many species to recolonize.
Today, the number of plant species
recognized as being native is less than
2,000, though a greater number than
that of alien plant species have established themselves here. Of the native
species, less than 50 are endemic to the British
Isles (that is, found wild in no other countries).

In the Post-glacial Age from about 10,000 BC, plants
such as birch and grasses predominated, with willows
colonizing by freshwater and in some places hazel, oak,
pines, and alder appearing. In the warmer Boreal period
from 7,500–5,500 BC, pine forest occupied most of
England and penetrated to Scotland and Ireland, though
birch remained predominant in the north. During this
time, the sea level was rising, separating Ireland from
Scotland and breaking the land bridge between England
and Europe. The population were hunters, using flint

implements, but having little effect on the vegetation. By
the end of the Boreal period, oak had come to predominate, as it still does today, with elm and hazel becoming
more common.

The following Atlantic period lasted until 3,000 BC
and was characterized by a moist mild climate. Alder
and lime became abundant, while pine diminished
in favor of oak, with hazel as the predominant understory. The sinking of the land relative to the sea caused
the formation of the East Anglian Fens and the flooding
of the Somerset Levels. But the most significant change
as far as the flora was concerned was that the Neolithic
peoples had, by about 3,500 BC, come to rely on
agriculture, keeping sheep and cattle and growing
wheat and barley. Within 1,000 years agriculture had
spread to all parts of the British Isles as far north as
the Shetland Islands.

From then on, the influence of humns on the ecosystems of the British Isles was profound, starting with
the clearing of trees from chalk and limestone areas and
accelerating with the introduction of the plow by the
Celts, the Belgic race who invaded in the first century
BC. Successive invading races mostly brought with them
further improvements in agricultural technique. After
the Norman Conquest, the Domesday Book of 1086,
covering England except the northernmost counties,
shows that woodland (including wood pasture) covered
only about 15 percent of the area surveyed, with 35 percent arable, 30 percent pasture, and 1 percent meadow.
The remaining 20 percent included mountains, heaths,
moorlands, fens, houses, and gardens.

The agriculture of this period was subsistence farming, with equilibrium between arable, pasture, and

woodland. From the Middle Ages onwards, farming for profit became more common and the relative proportions of each of these three uses fluctuated with demand. In the mid-fourteenth century, the demand for wool was so great that there were eight million sheep in England and only two million people. The high demand for timber for smelting and glass-making in the sixteenth and seventeenth centuries saw the effective removal of the last English forest reserves, even the high forests, though some of this woodland was converted to coppice. In Scotland, the woods of the Highland glens started to be exploited from the beginning of the seventeenth century and the expansion of sheep farming saw the removal of most of the remainder in the late eighteenth and nineteenth centuries. The enclosure of farming land was a feature of farming for profit, the first enclosures being organized in the twelfth century, continuing gradually until accelerating in the eighteenth century and culminating in the General Enclosure Act of 1801 and the Enclosure Act of 1845.

The scale of agriculture and its impact on the ecosystems of the British Isles continued to increase in the twentieth century, with further advances in mechanization, use of mineral fertilizers, and synthetic pesticides. The Second World War saw a vast increase in arable farming so that, for instance, between 1939 and 1944, the arable acreage of Leicestershire had increased from 58,000 to 191,000. This involved using a considerable area of what had been relatively natural habitat, though some such areas were returned to their former state after the war, especially in Wales and the west of England. The second half of the twentieth century saw the scale of agriculture increase further, with larger combine harvesters and more powerful tractors, resulting in larger fields and the removal of many hedgerows, creating almost a prairie landscape in some counties.

Global warming

Global warming caused by the "greenhouse effect" is now predicted by the UK Government's Department for Environment, Food, and Rural Affairs and the Environment Agency to make very significant changes to the ecology of the British Isles over the rest of this century. Predictions are given region by region and for Southwest England are: winter precipitation will increase by 7 to 15 percent by the 2050s, while summer rainfall, which has fallen by up to 20 percent since the late nineteenth century, will decrease; the climate will get hotter by 1.0 to 2.9°C each century; there will be a rise of sea level of up to 32 in (80 cm) by the 2050s; a growing season that is 5 to 20 days longer is expected by the 2050s; there will be a northward shift of natural habitats by 31–50 miles (50–80 km) per decade; wetland habitats will dry out; more intense winter storms will increase the likelihood of flooding; an increase in the number of frost-free winters may signifi-

cantly change land-use patterns and increase the occurrence of exotic pests and diseases (and alien plant species such as eucalypts). Southwesterly gales, funnelling the sea up the Bristol Channel, are likely to cause flooding of many low-lying areas, the salination making them unsuitable for agriculture or, if they are semi-natural, changing their flora. The effects of climate change are already apparent and generally accepted not to be a statistical freak, though many dispute that change will continue at the same rate. Already, beech populations in southeast England have suffered heavy losses from summer drought (and sycamore, though it is not native); beech might now be more viable further north. For gardeners, flowering seasons quoted in standard reference works, mostly derived from early twentieth century texts, are often a month or more later than currently observed.

More changes might be caused by the current unprofitability of agriculture, with prices paid to farmers by supermarkets often below the cost of production. Whether this results in land being taken out of current agricultural use and allowed to return to scrub and eventually climax flora or leads to a return to forestry or some other land use is still uncertain.

With so little natural habitat remaining, it is the long-established, human-made, but unfertilized ecosystems that are perhaps most treasured for their relatively rich diversity of species. Instances might include water meadows where meadow saxifrage *(Saxifraga granulata)* or snake's-head fritillaries *(Fritillaria meleagris)* flourish or chalk pastures where Pasque flowers *(Pulsatilla vulgaris)* still thrive. But even though most of the countryside is devoted to relatively species-poor agricultural land, hedgerows and roadsides usually show a good range of native flora, often with an interesting and colorful range of local variants.

Gardening in the British Isles

For over 300 years, gardening has been an obsession for the peoples of these islands. When London's National Portrait Gallery decided to start photographing people of the professions that most typify the British way of life, they started with gardeners. It is perhaps because of our relative lack of native species that plant hunters from these islands have so assiduously sought out species from the rest of the world and because of the gentle climate that so many of them thrive here, making gardening a perennially popular pastime. The known history of gardening in the British Isles begins with the Romans, who planted ornamental parterres of box, for instance at Fishbourne Palace in Hampshire. After their departure, the monas-

> *On looking on a meadow, yellow with buttercups I have seen one flower—one flower amongst a thousand thousand flowers, all alike.*
>
> WILLIAM HENRY HUDSON 1841–1922

Below: Common to much of the British Isles and Europe, snake's head fritillary, Fritillaria meleagris, is highly valued for its maroon, green, or purple flowers, checkered with purple. Frost-hardy, it grows well in rockeries.

Above: Narcissus 'Quail' in full bloom at Wisley Gardens, London. Garden visiting is a popular pastime in the British Isles and can only encourage greater appreciation for the world's flora. It has also, however, led to the public's expectation of constant display whenever they visit.

Far right: With very little natural countryside left in the British Isles, relatively informal arrangements are the preferred choice of many gardeners. Color, shape of plants, and water features can all contribute to this end.

Right: Collections of exotic plants have been are part of British horticulture for centuries. Liriodendron tulipifera is naturally found east of the Mississippi River, USA, though this particular specimen can be seen at Kew Gardens, England.

Below: Buxus species and Rhododendron cultivars combine in a grid-based arrangement. Such formal design has fallen in and out of favor more than once in the past, as much due to having to pay gardeners a decent salary as to new horticultural ideas.

teries became the focus for growing and exchanging plants other than agricultural staples, including a handful of ornamentals.

The late seventeenth century saw an extraordinary mania for gardening, especially in England, that was influenced not merely by Italy and France, the predominant influences for the previous millennium, but also the Netherlands, through Dutch-born William III and his consort Queen Mary II, both passionate gardeners. The planting style, "sparse planting," had remained much the same over the previous centuries, with plants set at regular intervals in formal rectilinear beds and borders and in parterres, grown for the beauty of their flowers, without any significant interest in foliage and with relatively few flowers for late summer or autumn. It could be said that until this time, gardens had been designed to express man's dominion over nature, through their rigid formality and intolerance of disorder. All this was to change in the coming century.

The complex labor-intensive gardens of the late seventeenth century had by the eighteenth century come to be seen as a burden by their owners who, from Queen Anne down, sought to reduce maintenance and costs by simplification. There was also a trend towards less rigidly formal, more naturalistic elements in the design. Designers such as Lancelot 'Capability' Brown (1716–83) capitalized on this by combining the two trends, sweeping away almost all formality and maintenance and replacing fiddly beds and parterres with the productive pasture and forestry of the landscape garden and tucking the flowers away in kitchen gardens or walled flower gardens. Growing tired of this severely simple style, dubbed the Beautiful, the artist and writer the Reverend William Gilpin (1724–1804) championed a more rugged, naturalistic style, the Picturesque. The Beautiful and the Picturesque, along with the more awe-inspiring Sublime, were the three principal styles used for the "English landscape garden" (a misnomer because many of its leading proponents were Scots), sometimes, perhaps with tongue in cheek, said to be Britain's only original contribution to world culture.

The Enlightenment saw a fascination with all aspects of the arts and sciences, including botany. Captain Cook's three journeys between 1768 and 1779 and the collections of Francis Masson, Kew's first plant hunter, gathered from the Cape of Good Hope (1772–74), fuelled the interest for more collecting from around the world, so that plant collections became a mania for many,

even the middle classes, for whom the first affordable gardening encyclopedias had appeared. The work of Robert Bakewell (1725–95) and others in improving livestock by hybridization and selection led by the closing years of the century to the application of comparable techniques to the breeding of roses by French nurserymen and ultimately throughout Europe to other flowers, fruit, vegetables, and crops. There were soon enough roses to plant a garden entirely with them, the first example of such specialization. Thus plants, both cultivars and wild species, led garden design. Leading members of the Whigs, almost as much a gardening club as a political party, including Charles James Fox (1749–1806) and Georgiana, Duchess of Devonshire (1757–1806) seem to have created the earliest examples, probably with plants from Lewis Kennedy (c. 1721–82), whose son John (1759–1842) supplied most of the roses for the Empress Josephine's later rose garden at Malmaison, just outside of Paris.

Meanwhile, lovers of gardens were becoming pretty tired of the hike to the distant walled flower gardens where their burgeoning collections grew. They wanted to see flowers from within the house and to be able to fling open the French doors and walk straight into the garden. The designs of Humphry Repton (1752–1818) accommodated these desires, bringing the flower garden back around the house and allowing once again an element of formality in rosaries and parterres.

Throughout the nineteenth century, the flood of new plant introductions continued. Phases of introduction of plant from overseas, first largely from North America, latter on from China and Japan, had an immense effect on garden design, particularly on woodland planting, allowing the style loosely called the "Cornish garden" to proliferate (though it is found throughout Ireland and the south and west of Great Britain), relying mostly on rhododendrons, camellias, and magnolias. The grid planting of borders, with uniformly widely spaced flowers in regularly alternated colors, was replaced by the end of the century by the more informal, closer planting familiar today, though color-scheming was fairly rare until championed by Miss Gertrude Jekyll (1843–1932). Foliage and architectural plants had also come to be appreciated by the likes of Shirley Hibberd (1825–90) and William Robinson (1838–1935) before they were incorporated into Miss Jekyll's symphonic planting as essential elements of the design and ideal foils for flowers.

The twentieth century saw a decline in the great estates, through the effects of two World Wars, death duties, and larger and fairer wages for gardeners; some gardens survived but many were simplified to the point of non-existence, while others were passed to the National Trust or similar bodies.

The growing awareness of environmental matters is to be welcomed. However, some gardeners believe that all synthetic and mineral chemicals are harmful if used in the garden, whereas all extracted from plants are beneficial. This is a fallacy: many pesticides obtained from plants can have disastrous environmental consequences if used carelessly, whereas some synthetic ones can cause less collateral damage and persist for a shorter time. Plant extracts contain a cocktail of chemicals, only one of which is likely to have the desired effect; the rest may cause harm to plants, beneficial insects, or even humans. Environmentally aware gardeners know that there is an ecological consequence for every task, whether it is controlling pests and diseases or improving the soil, whether by chemical or physical means; the benefits of any of these need to be weighed against any possible environmental impact. In the UK, recent legislation has banned the use of any pesticides and herbicides that are not both safe and effective. Many pesticides are now illegal, including, one suspects, most of those still lurking in potting sheds. To check which pesticides remain approved for particular uses, consult the Pesticides Safety Directorate in the UK or the Pesticide Control Service website of the Irish Department of Agriculture and Food.

The climate change of recent decades has caused gardeners, particularly in southeast England, to look for other sorts of planting rather than the traditional lawns and borders. Thus gravel gardens, as championed by Beth Chatto, have become popular, as has the steppe style of planting, deriving from German and Dutch

examples, using herbaceous perennials such as achilleas, artemisias, salvias, and grasses, on well-drained soils that are dry in summer. This latter style has a wildness and informality that appeal to many modern gardeners, the antithesis of the order sought by gardeners of the seventeenth and earlier centuries, though it needs sun and is difficult to adapt to the small rectangular gardens of the towns and suburbs. Now that we have so little natural countryside, gardeners crave for the most natural effect they can achieve; wildflower meadows are another currently popular manifestation of this trend.

Above: Hare St after its transformation, from Fragments on the Theory & Practice of Landscape Gardening *by Humphrey Repton, published 1816. Repton's designs sought to combine garden and home, as well as to reintroduce a sense of formality to gardens.*

Hardiness Zones

Each region of the world has its own set of physical conditions. Topography, the levels of precipitation and evaporation, amount and arrival of heat and cold, days of frost, and length of growing season are all factors that help create our individual climates. Ways of quantifying and charting the weather has been the preoccupation of scientists, farmers, and zealous gardeners down the centuries and, with exploration and technical advances, many countries have developed detailed and accurate mapping systems that categorize conditions, based primarily on temperature, into climate zones.

The system employed in *Flora* follows the map developed in the 1960s by the United States Department of Agriculture (USDA), which divides the country into twelve designated hardiness zones. Each zone is separated by 10°F (5.5°C), beginning with the Arctic at -50°F (45°C) and ending in the equatorial tropics at +50°F (10°C). These average minimum temperatures for each hardiness zone are based on the minimum temperature recorded each winter season over a period of 20 years. The original USDA map has since been expanded to cover much of the rest of the world.

The zones are not uniform. There are cooler and warmer areas within a zone depending on its most northerly or southerly part. Topographical features such as mountain ranges, plains, and proximity to the coast all affect temperature, and therefore, whether that area falls in one zone or another. For this reason, a zone on a map may suddenly dip into an area surrounded by a warmer zone, or curve up in a thin line along a coast.

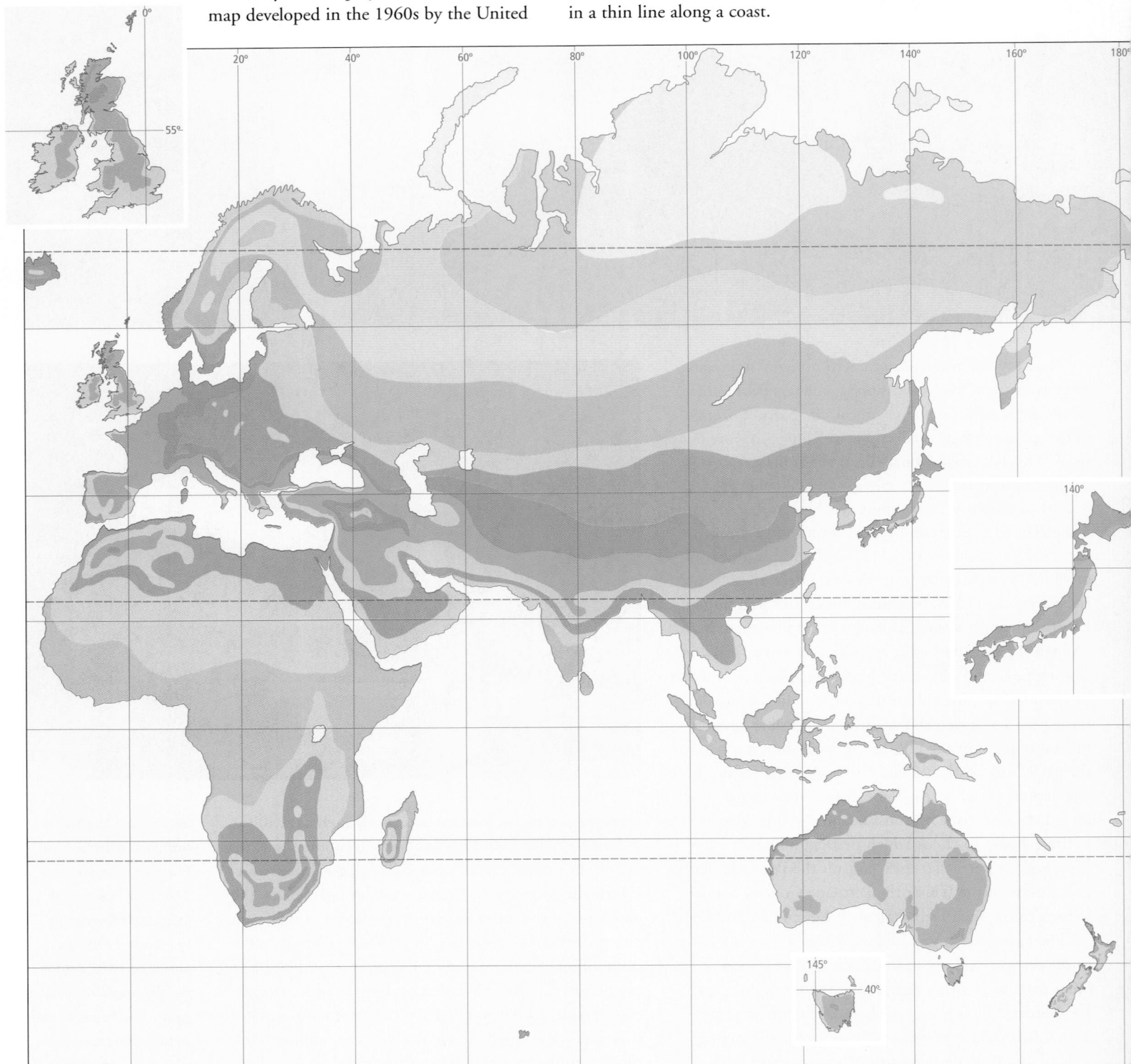

The main purpose of the USDA map is to tell us what zone we are in, and therefore indicate what plants can be grown in our part of the world. Secondly, it allows us to look at other regions or countries in the same zone, and also surrounding zones, and see what plants do well in those areas. Essentially, climate zones provide an indication of a plant's "hardiness", that is, its ability to survive cold weather, including frost and ice.

The zones are based on average low temperatures only, and do not provide additional information about extremes and variations in low temperatures for a region. In some regions temperatures can be much warmer and much colder than the average from year to year. Other factors also need to be considered. For example, if a garden is in or near an urban center, situated on a hillside above a valley floor where cold air is likely to settle, or tends to experience breezes when other areas are still, winter minimums are likely to be a bit warmer than surrounding areas. The opposite is true if a garden is situated at a valley bottom out of the wind. Here, temperatures are likely to fall during the night. These are all characteristics of what is called a microclimate and can be taken advantage of.

It is important to reiterate that the zone maps only indicate the average lowest temperatures. When a plant in this book is rated to a specific zone, it means that horticulturists have succeeded in that zone, even with the reasonable yearly fluctuations in winter lows.

Factors to consider

People garden for the future, but, of course, they also garden for the moment. On occasion, a winter cold spell brings temperatures well below the zone's averages, damaging or even killing a plant normally expected to perform well. Reaction to these possibilities should be reserved to the nature of the individual gardener. Those liking to live life a bit on the wild side might acquire plants knowing they will not be permanent but might try to minimize risk by planting in an area where they can be protected from full sun or frost.

Caution might be best employed where the size and structure of the plant is a consideration. To ensure a long life, a tree or any other anchoring plant could be chosen from a colder zone than the garden it is to be planted in, thereby overcoming the rigors of cold it may experience as a sapling.

Other factors to consider when choosing plants are: length of the frost-free season; whether cold lasts for weeks or months, and, in colder zones, the amount of snowfall, which can act as an insulating blanket for roots.

Another factor is the amount of heat received over the warm season. Areas of high summer temperatures, especially when combined with humidity, are best suited to heat-loving plants that need to reach full maturity quickly, in preparation for possibly lower temperatures in the winter. Areas receiving warmth accompanied by cool summer nights are better off with Mediterranean and Southern Hemisphere treasures that would otherwise melt in high summer heat. Soil conditions and rainfall must be taken into consideration as well, along with the need for mulching, or less water, or drier air.

The more knowledge we have about what kinds of temperatures and other conditions our plants are likely to tolerate, the more our gardens will flourish. The more, also, we can then keep our special needs plants and proclaim with satisfaction to an envious neighbor that this supposed tender creature has been in our garden for years.

Zone	°Farenheit	°Celsius
12	50 to 60	10 to 16
11	40 to 50	4 to 10
10	30 to 40	-1 to 4
9	20 to 30	-7 to -1
8	10 to 20	-12 to -7
7	0 to 10	-18 to -12
6	-10 to 0	-23 to -18
5	-20 to -10	-29 to -23
4	-30 to -20	-34 to -29
3	-40 to -30	-40 to -34
2	-50 to -40	-46 to -40
1	-60 to -50	-51 to -46

Arctic Circle
Tropic of Cancer
Equator
Tropic of Capricorn

Zone 1 -60 to -50°F (-51 to -46°C)

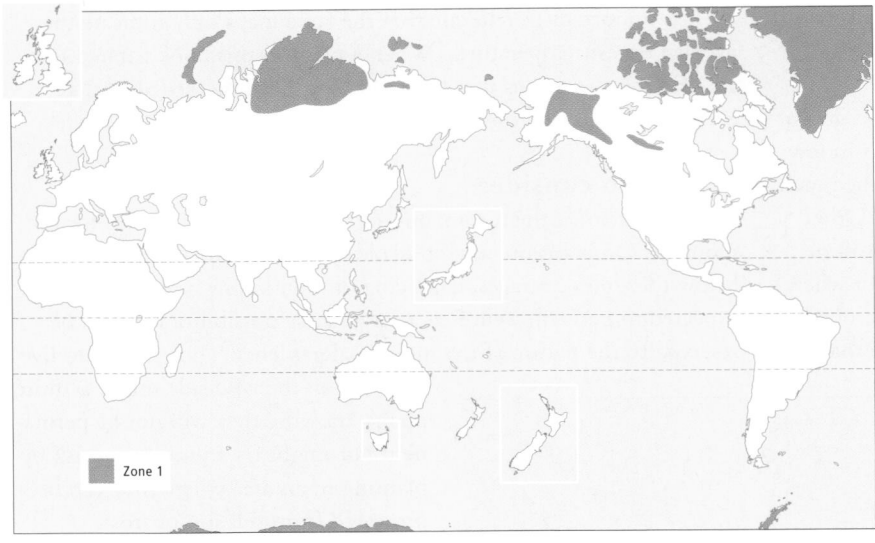

Zone 1

Far right: The Arctic contains the largest areas of remaining wilderness in the Northern Hemisphere. The Svalbard Islands, north of Norway, feature mostly sparse tundra and large caribou populations.

Below: In the northern tundra, a smooth carpet of plant growth is usually a collection of lichens and mosses, and a few tiny and hardy plants like sedge and cotton grass.

It is no small matter to say that the flora of Zone 1 is shaped by the patterns and variations of the climate. The climate is characterized by severity, seasonality, and unpredictable variability. Winter temperatures of -50°F (-46°C) and less—the coldest temperature ever recorded was -87°F (-66°C)—coupled with cool summers, challenge even the hardiest plant material. The summers, lasting for just two brief months from July to August, are so cool that the determining factor behind differing vegetative regions within the zone is not the extreme cold of winter but the amount of warmth received during summer. Precipitation is also limited, with some areas receiving less than 2 in (50 mm) per year. The long days at this time (24 hours of daylight) compensate for the rigors of the short summers and cold conditions.

In the Southern Hemisphere, Zone 1 includes only the Antarctic continent, which is uninhabited and has very few species of flowering plant. These are confined to the Antarctic peninsula. In the remaining area, there are only lichens and mosses. There is greater diversity in the Northern Hemisphere, where the Arctic landscapes range from bare rock to swamp, glacier to meadow, and mountain to lowland plain. The key feature of most land areas in this zone is permafrost. This permanently frozen ground reaches depths of 1,640 yards (1,500 m) in Siberia, and extends under most land areas. Because of the permafrost, plant roots are closer to the surface and are exposed to more severe cold. Plants need to be able to withstand solid freezing for many months. For 7 to 10 months every year, plants are in a state of quasi-

We need a wilderness whether or not we ever set foot in it. I may never in my life get to Alaska but I am grateful that it's there.
EDWARD ABBEY, 1927–1982

hibernation. During the remaining couple of months, they run through their entire growth cycle.

Zone 1 plants survive these extreme conditions in many ways. The severity of the climate means that the major biomass of the plants exists below ground. This reduces the desiccation (drying out) due to prevalent strong winds that result in much sand/soil abrasion. The reproductive cycle of the vascular plants is often carried out over a period of years. For example, buds formed one year will be generally covered in hair to increase insulation, and then will often lie beneath the soil surface until the following year when they complete their reproductive cycle. This survival mechanism also allows plants to miraculously bloom within hours of the snow cover melting. Many plants use unique means to ensure survival. *Dryas integrifolia*, a dwarf, creeping, slightly woody shrub of the rose family which also grows in Zone 2, has flowers in the shape of a curved reflector. This allows them to follow the sun and to focus the sun's rays on their reproductive structures to raise the temperature of these organs several degrees on a sunny day. Many Zone 1 plants will retain dense mats of dead or persistent leaves that can produce a rise of as much as 30°F (as much as 16°C).

Survival in the tundra

The landmass known as the tundra is a true indicator of a Zone 1 climate. It is a treeless barren area occurring south of the polar ice cap worldwide. The tundra flora becomes progressively impoverished (sparser) the closer it is to the ice cap, creating bands of differing vegetation. The tundra "trees" consist of dwarf willow *(Salix)*, birch *(Betula)*, and heaths. The heath (Ericaceae) family—which includes familiar plants like rhododendrons, azaleas, heather, and mountain laurel *(Kalmia latifolia)*—is represented in this zone by dwarf shrubs such as labrador tea *(Ledum)*. They are characterized by small, thick, evergreen leaves and shallow root systems that are particularly well adapted to the acidic, boggy conditions of low Arctic tundra. Some *Vaccinium* species occur throughout the Arctic Circle (the circumpolar north) in all but the highest Arctic areas, including lingonberry *(V. vitis-idaea)*, blueberry *(V. angustifolium)*, and cranberry *(V. macrocarpon)*.

As elevation or latitude increases, the scrub brush peters out and the flora now consists of sedges, grasses, and herbs. This vegetative zone is considered to be sedge meadows. The flora in these meadows belongs to two major genera only, *Eriophorum* and *Carex*, and they are very variable in species: cotton grass *(Eriophorum vaginatum)* is the major, single most abundant plant in the low Arctic, closely followed by a true sedge, *Carex aquatilis.* As climatic conditions vary, as one moves away from the Arctic, the genus remains the same with only the species changing.

A wildflower wonderland

Areas within the sedge meadows can experience slightly different climatic conditions, which produce a different type of vegetation, termed the mesic tundra. The mesic (not too wet and not too dry) tundra is the rock garden of this climatic zone. Grasses are common but the most conspicuous feature of the mesic or grassy tundra is the wild flowers. Nothing on earth compares seeing over 100 species in flower simultaneously along a short walk.

Snowbeds are a particular type of mesic tundra where snow drifts deeply into a hollow. The snow lies late in the spring, which shortens the growing season for the plants under and around it, but also provides a steady source of moisture throughout the growing season. The snow also provides a comparatively warm, moist, protected environment for over wintering plants. Many snowbed species burst into flower within hours of being freed from the drifted snow. Some of our early flowering spring bulbs are derived from snowbed species with this habit. Examples include Siberian fritillary *(Fritillaria pallidiflora)* and Siberian squill *(Scilla siberica).*

Plants of mesic tundra areas are not circumpolar in their distribution patterns. They often appear to have originated in alpine areas and to have migrated into the Arctic secondarily and locally. Therefore, while some

tundra plants may be indistinguishable by locality, the mesic tundra plants will vary with the region.

As the latitude or elevation continues to increase, the last vegetation zone found is the polar desert. This area is largely bare ground or rock, with the last vestiges of plant life being mostly lichens. The polar desert dominates most of the high Arctic areas.

Zone 1 flora consists of distinctive and highly adaptive species. Plants must eke out an existence in a few meager inches of earth, their roots confined by unwieldy bedrock or permafrost that is never far from the surface. Plants are mostly small, prostrate, and always straddling the tenuous line between wakefulness and dormancy. It is not uncommon to find woody plant material that is hundreds of years old yet no thicker than a person's thumb. While hardy species in more temperate latitudes easily succumb to freak frosts, the flora of Zone 1 can be completely frozen one minute and thawed the next. This physiological ability of Arctic plants to be able to freeze with impunity is still a mystery to scientists.

Below: As one moves closer to the pole, the terrain is known as polar desert. These areas lack sufficient moisture and warmth to sustain any significant amount of higher plant life.

Zone 2 -50 to -40°F (-46 to -40°C)

Zone 2

Zone 2 is the world's largest hardiness zone and extends in a band across the Northern Hemisphere, just south of the Artic Circle. It covers a vast area of sparsely populated, predominantly cool, coniferous woodland which is replaced by swamp and then tundra further north. In North America this woodland area is ecologically described as boreal forest while in northern Europe and across Asiatic Russia this area is known as taiga.

The zone has a cold but not arctic climate, with an average minimum winter temperature of -50 to -40°F (-46 to 40°C) with over 40 in (100 cm) of precipitation in a wet year and 20 in (50 cm) in a dry year. The ground is snow covered for eight months of the year and evaporation is slow, creating a cool moist climate. As the land nears the Arctic Ocean, precipitation diminishes, the summers become shorter, cooler, drier and the winters longer and colder.

The southernmost section of this zone is largely timbered, but as the forest progresses northward the trees gradually reduce in size and thin out. The ground progressively becomes more waterlogged and the tree cover declines and is replaced by an almost continuous band of swamp, known as "muskeg" in North America. This ground supports only limited tree growth. Moving further northward, approaching the Arctic Ocean, the ground becomes drier and the subsoil becomes permanently frozen, forming a layer of permafrost that can be several feet deep. Here the muskeg is in its turn replaced by stony barren ground and treeless tundra.

North of this lies Zone 1, which has a uniform cold dry climate. Winters are colder than in Zone 2 and annual precipitation is often as low as 5–10 in (12–25 cm) a year and summer temperatures rarely exceed 50°F (10°C). Plants found in Zone 1 are sparsely distributed, xerophytic in habit (adapted to low levels of water), low growing, and are mainly found on sheltered slopes or in depressions where snow accumulates in winter.

Effects of climate on plant life

The boreal forest and taiga are mainly coniferous, how-ever, they do support some deciduous trees. Evergreens dominate because they do not renew their foliage an-nually and are more efficient in utilizing scarce nutrients and minerals on infertile soils. Due to its northern lo-cation diversity within the forest is restricted to less than a dozen tree species. In the Canadian boreal forest conif-erous trees include tamarack *(Larix laricina)*, white spruce *(Picea glauca)*, black spruce *(Picea mariana)*, and jack pine *(Pinus banksiana)*. Deciduous species such as white birch *(Betula papyrifera)*, trembling aspen *(Populus tremuloides)*, and balsam poplar *(P. balsamifera)* also occur. A similar group of related tree species inhabit Alaska and the taiga of Northern Europe and Siberia.

Many of these tree species are widely distributed and can be grown much further south. This also applies to some of the boreal forest shrubs and herbaceous peren-nial plants that are found in the zone. Most successful are those that grow in profusion following a forest fire: choke cherry *(Prunus virginiana)*, pin cherry *(P. pensylvanica)*, red osier dogwood *(Cornus sericea)*, and herbaeous perennials like fireweed *(Epilobium angustifolium)*, though fireweed can become a major thug in the garden. More desirable, delicate shade plants like twin flower *(Linnaea borealis)* are challeng-ing to horticulturists further south due to the difficulty of re-creating their cool mossy habitat. Twin flower, like most Zone 2 plants, is best grown from seed that requires a 6 to 8 week cold period at 40°F (4°C) to ensure germination.

As the forest nears the tree line, generally defined by the 50°F (10°C) isotherm in mid-July, the trees thin and open lichen-rich wood-land dominates dry sites. These are interspersed by vast areas of muskeg bog and fen (marsh). These poorly drained, peaty wetlands often sup-port continuous sheets of sphagnum moss, with scattered black spruce and a heath layer that includes Labrador tea *(Ledum groenlandicum)* and bog blueberry *(Vaccinium uliginosum)*. On less acid fens, tamarack replaces the black spruce and the shrub layer is mainly willow *(Salix species)*, speckled alder *(Alnus rugosa)*, and bog myrtle *(Myrica gale)* with an herbaceous ground cover of mainly sedges *(Carex species)*. Even in impoverished wetlands such as these, plants will adapt and this area supports several species of insectivorous plants, including northern pitcher plant *(Sarracenia purpurea)*, butterwort *(Pinguicula vulgaris)*, and round-leafed sundew *(Drosera rotundifolia)*. These and other plant species from muskeg bogs can be grown in semi-shade as far south as Zone 7, in 18 in (45 cm) deep beds lined with a rubber pond liner, filled with a mixture of 50 percent sphag-num peat and 50 percent sand.

Closer to the Arctic Ocean, even when the surface of the per-mafrost thaws, this thawing often reaches only a few inches deep by mid-August, and the remaining permafrost layer prevents the rain-fall and melting snow from drain-ing. However, if it were not for this trapped moisture, flowering plants would be rare in the near desert-like conditions of the Arctic. As a result of low tempera-tures and few nutrients, stony bar-rens and tundra, plants are dwarf in size and starved, and frequently drought-tolerant in habit. Vegetation in the far north of the zone is confined to a few tough plants such as alpine bearberry *(Arctostaphylos alpina)*, mountain cranberry *(Vaccinium vitis-idaea)*, Lapland rosebay *(Rhododendron lapponicum)*, and *Dryas integrifolia*.

On moist tundra the vegetation often forms a continuous low mat of sedges such as cotton grass *(Eriophorum angustifolium)*, grasses, and dwarf shrub willow, with unusual plants like *Cassiope tetragona*, lousewort *(Pedicularis lapponica)*, and the pink-flowered tufted moss campion *(Silene acaulis)*. Some of these tundra plants, particularly those from dry gravel or rocky locations, can be grown in a traditional rock-garden alpine scree, as long as these are constructed with an infertile fast-draining gravel soil. Most of the more unusual tundra plants are notoriously difficult to grow successfully further south where high soil tempera-tures are usually fatal. Perhaps the only way to succeed with these plants is grow them in an alpine house in a refrigerated planting bed.

There is no tree but knows a thing or two. Every kind has a wisdom of its own.
BRADFORD TORREY, 1843–1912

Gardening in the zone

Owing to lack of extensive urban settlement in the north of Zone 2, little is known regarding the growing of plants from zones further south. The soils in the north are so infertile that the prospect of establish-ing a successful garden is daunting, but there are some clues as to how this might be done. When a small boy, the doyen of arctic and subarctic botany, A. E. Porsild, lived in the Arctic and planted a small botanic garden. Later he revisited the area and was surprised to see the out-line of his garden still visible. He noticed close by a patch of lush green grass and realized this was on the very spot where he had spilled a wheelbarrow of goat manure intended for his botanic garden. The effects of the manure were still apparent 34 years later.

Provided the garden is placed in a sheltered location, has good snow cover, and the ground is manured, fertil-ized, and limed, there is no reason why some perennial plants from Zones 3 and 4 could not be grown.

Above: Betula papyrifera *is found throughout the Canadian boreal forest. In warmer zones, it is valued for its elegant habit, but this apparent fragility belies its ability to with-stand the cold and even drought of Zone 2.*

Left: Mendenhall Glacier near Juneau, Alaska. Most of Alaska is wilderness. Due to its northern location, only a limited range of coniferous and deciduous trees thrive.

Above: Dryas integrifolia *is a dwarf creeping shrub at home in the harsh condi-tions of the northern parts of Zone 2 and into Zone 1. Its large white flowers often dominate the bleak landscape in July.*

Zone 3

-40 to -30°F (-40 to -34°C)

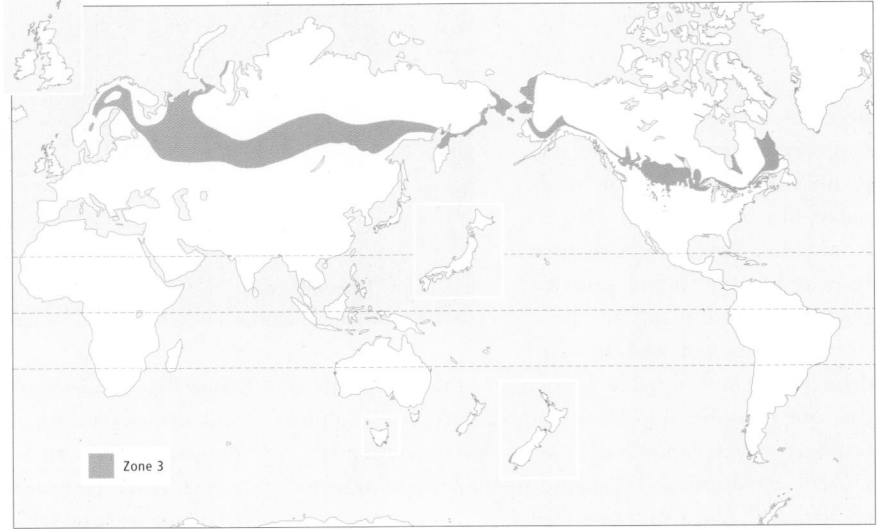

Zone 3

Long cold winters are the foremost characteristic of this climatic zone which forms an arc of varying width around the Northern Hemisphere. In North America, from as far north as Point Hope on the Arctic Ocean in Alaska, well above the Arctic Circle, this zone swings south to the center of the continent. Here it straddles the Canadian/US border and dips as far south as a few isolated mountain ranges in Colorado and New Mexico in the mid 30s latitude. The zone then rises northward again as it approaches the Atlantic Ocean and eventually reaches Ungava Bay in northern Quebec. Zone 3 forms a similar arc in Eurasia and due largely to the influence of the Gulf Stream, it extends far into northern Scandinavia than would perhaps be expected. As the distance from the ocean increases, winter temperatures become colder and summer temperatures become warmer. In climatic terms, this effect is known as continentality, and it plays a major role in shaping the climate of these large continents and explains why Zone 3 reaches so far south into both these landmasses.

Below: Arctostaphylos uva-ursi, bearberry—also known as kinnikinick—is hardy in areas where snow cover offers protection. White flowers, flushed pink, are followed by bright red fruit.

Temperatures and rainfall

Zone 3 is a typical continental climate and the average annual lowest temperature ranges between -40 to -30°F (-40 to -34°C), while the average summer highs can range between 86 to 100°F (30 to 38°C). This climate evokes images of blizzards and frostbite, blowing snow and whiteouts, but this tells only half the story. It is actually a place with dramatically different seasons. Summer can be quite

It is not the strongest of the species that survives, nor the most intelligent that survives. It is the one that is the most adaptable to change.

CHARLES DARWIN, 1809–1882

pleasant and often the majority of the precipitation falls at this time during thunderstorms, promoting a rich growing season. Spring and fall are typically short and often variable. Often, one week in either of these seasons can experience extreme temperature swings. The growing season (frost-free days) varies from under 60 days to more than 120 days. Precipitation in Zone 3 varies. Mountainous regions of British Columbia can experience above 80 in (200 cm) of rainfall per year whereas the driest areas of the prairies receive well under 20 in (50 cm). The amount roughly determines the type of flora present in an area. In very general terms, areas that receive over 25 in (62 cm) annually are forested; those with less are grassland.

Landscape and soil

In North America, Zone 3 includes varying terrain. In the west, moist conifer-covered mountains with thin, acidic soil are prevalent. From the mountains it spills out onto the vast drier prairies where it widens, encompassing the northern regions of this rich rolling prairie, skirting along the southern extent of the boreal forest. It then swings north again through the boreal forest of central Canada north of the Great Lakes where the ground is smooth glaciated bedrock supporting only thin acidic soil again. In winter, the ground freezes solid in all areas of Zone 3 to at least 24 in (60 cm) below the soil surface and often to 36 in (90 cm).

Effects of climate on plant life

Despite the cold winters, many plants are well adapted to the conditions. Plants that thrive in the zone are able to completely freeze (roots and all) and stay dormant for several months with little or no long-term damage. Snow cover is an important factor for plant hardiness as it is excellent insulation for root systems below the ground as well as for the branches above. Areas with reliably heavy snow cover usually have a higher diversity of plants compared to areas with unreliable snow cover as it protects plants from the harsh cold temperatures and desiccating winds.

Despite harsh winters, Zone 3 regions can be rich in flora and many well-known genera are represented by their hardier species. In general, broadleaf evergreen trees or shrubs cannot survive here as they do not grow higher than the usual snow cover. However, low-growing evergreens like mosses such as *Pleurozium schreberi*, clubmoss (*Lycopodium clavatum*), and wintergreen (*Gaultheria procumbens*) that are covered by winter snow are prevalent. These blanket the ground along with deciduous shrubs and perennials including raspberries (*Rubus* species), blueberries (*Vaccinium myrtilloides*), scarlet sumac (*Rhus glabra*), bog myrtle (*Myrica gale*), red osier dogwood (*Cornus sericea*), and alum root (*Heuchera* species), and evening primrose (*Oenothera biennis*) in the glades of the boreal forest floor surrounded by endless stands of primarily conifers.

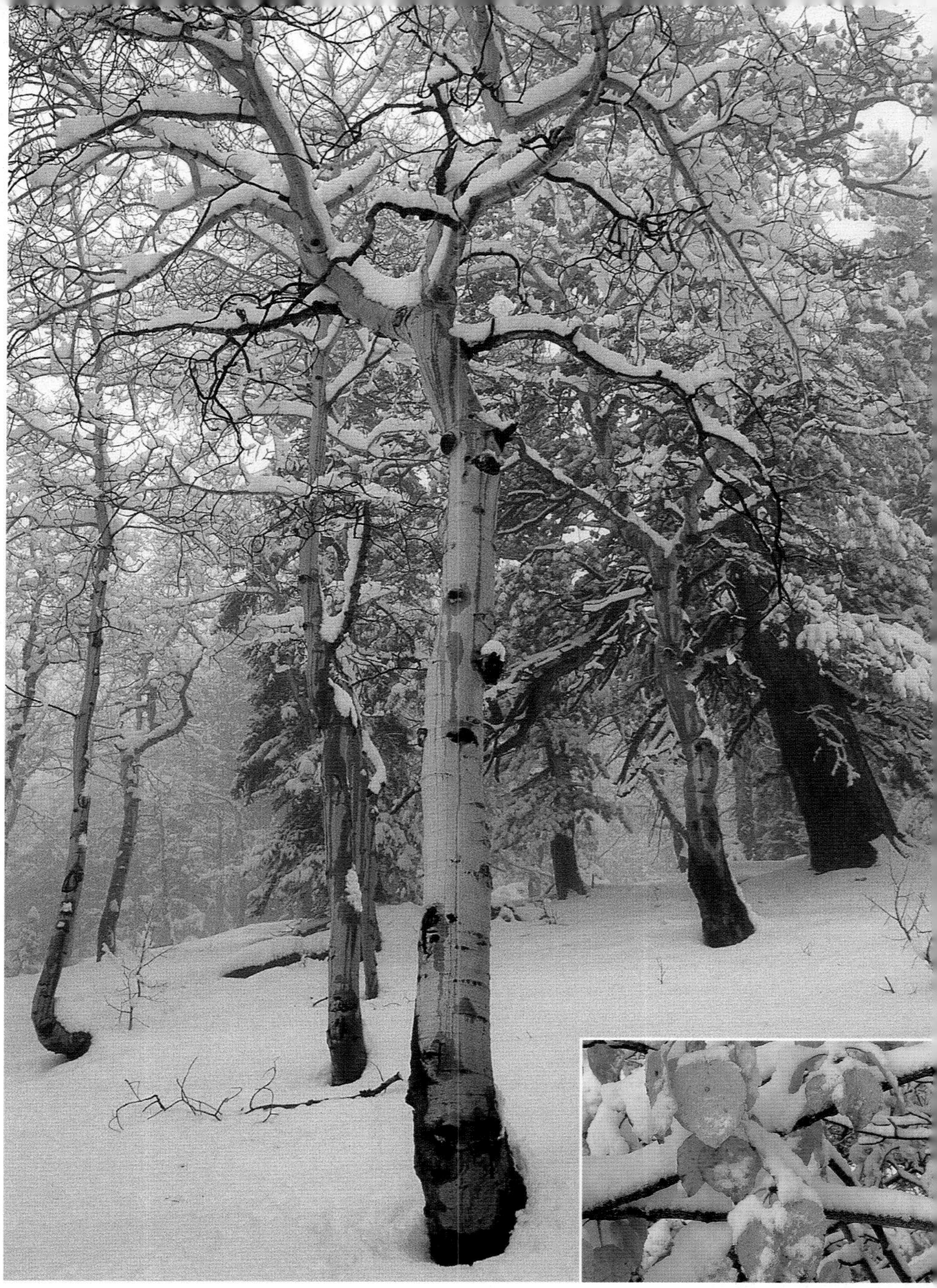

Right: Populus tremuloides *is an extremely hardy North American tree. It reaches near-dominance in Zones 4 and 5 but can be found in areas as cold as Zone 1.*

In the drier areas where prairies dominate the landscape, small deciduous forests appear like scattered islands in an endless sea of grasses, perennials, and annuals. The flora here is very different than that of the boreal forest due to richer deeper soil and less precipitation. The diminutive, slow-growing forest dwellers can't compete against the faster-growing deciduous plants of the prairie. Few conifers are seen in the prairies, instead, deciduous species such as maple *(Acer* species*)*, willows *(Salix)*, Saskatoon *(Amelanchier alnifolia)*, white birch *(Betula papyrifera)*, ninebark *(Physocarpus opulifolius)*, aspen *(Populus tremuloides)*, choke cherry *(Prunus virginiana)*, oak *(Quercus rubra)*, and mountain ash *(Sorbus* species*)* provide a brief but spectacular fall color display. During the short growing season, these small trees and shrubs rush to flower and bear fruit and, in the spring and summer, the prairie forests are alive with their modest blooms and they provide a feast for birds and animals that rely on them to carry them through the long cold winters.

Cacti may not initially come to mind, but ball cactus *(Escobaria vivipara)* and plains prickly pear *(Opuntia polyacantha)*, as well as other desert plants, are native to the driest prairie areas and do extend into this region.

Areas within Zone 3 with warm summers and reasonably long growing seasons are able to produce excellent cereal, vegetable, and fruit crops. In Canada and Russia, the so-called "bread basket" regions envelop Zone 3. Much of their domestic and export crops are grown in these rich fertile plains. Wheat *(Triticum)*, barley *(Hordeum vulgare)*, canola *(Brassica)*, flax *(Linum usitatissimum)*, and sunflower *(Helianthus)* all grow very well in this climate. Similarly, carrots *(Daucus carota* subsp. *sativus)*, beets *(Beta)*, spinach *(Spinacia)*, even tomatoes *(Lycopersicon)* and other vegetable crops thrive.

Gardening in the zone

The gardening season is short as the only time when the ground is not frozen is generally from May to October. It can be very expensive to heat greenhouses, so few operate all winter long. Annual growers begin production in early March, six to eight weeks before the last frosts. Nurseries are usually closed in winter and stock is often imported from warmer climates in April. Summer annuals are widely used and bulbs and tuberous plants such as canna, gladiola, and dahlia are planted in spring then dug up in autumn (to protect them from the cold and kept in frost-free conditions for replanting the following spring). Indoor plants are popular, but low winter humidity is a problem, so plants suited to dry conditions are successful. This includes varieties of *Dieffenbachia, Monstera, Philodendron, Crassula (C. arborescens)*, and *Ficus benjamina*, as well as African violets *(Saintpaulia* cultivars*)* and begonias.

Perennials are often overlooked in Zone 3. Many perennials listed in nursery catalogues as Zone 4 and 5 have never been tried in Zone 3. This zone is home to many wonderful species—too numerous to list—but it is fair to say that many genera familiar to horticulture have representative species native to Zone 3 and many other non-native varieties will grow here, as well. For example, species of lily (such as *Lilium columbianum*), most hostas, and daylilies *(Hemerocallis)* survive and even flourish in Zone 3.

The zone is home to highly acclaimed plants such as sought-after delicate orchids like pink and yellow lady slippers *(Cypripedium aucale* and *C. parviflorum)*, as well as the dainty fairy slipper *(Calypso bulbosa)*.

There are many plants no one has ever attempted to grow here. It is a horticultural frontier as plants are always being introduced and bred for hardiness. There will always be new plants that will thrive in Zone 3.

Above: Salix reptans *is native to the far north of Asia and European Russia. It is a small shrub with green to red branchlets that are covered in dense hairs. The erect catkins, also covered in long hairs, grow to 2 in (5 cm) long.*

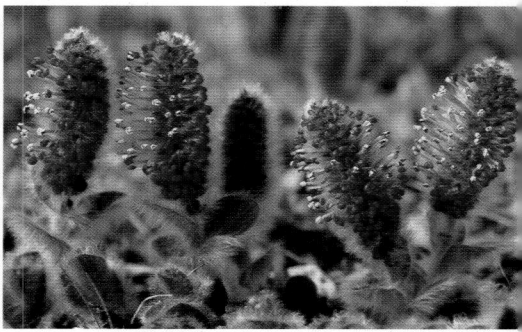

Zone 4 -30 to -20°F (-34 to -29°C)

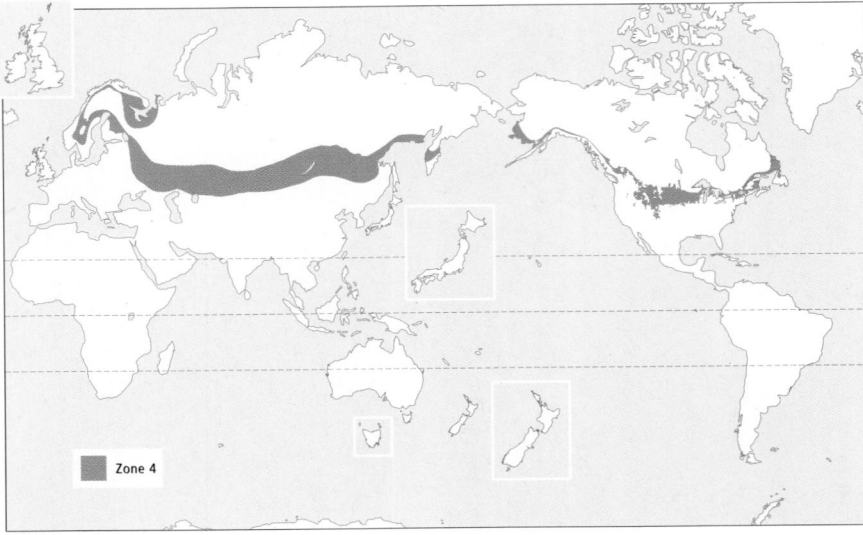

Zone 4

Top right: Willow trees (Salix species) cover vast areas of North America. This genus is a large and varied one, consisting of around 400 species, with the majority occurring in cold and temperate areas.

Right: Native to southern Scandinavia and other parts of Europe, Picea abies is the most commonly cultivated spruce in Europe. It has thick reddish brown bark, dark green leaves, and long, slender, light brown cones.

The geographic regions and plant communities covered by Zone 4 are many and varied, however, they have one thing in common: cold winters that make selection of hardy plants a challenge for gardeners. Most areas within the zone were subject to the effects of glaciers in the most recent, or Pleistocene glaciation. When the glaciers retreated to the polar regions some 10,000 to 12,000 years ago, they left behind a clean slate of mostly deep, rich till (post-glacial) soils. In many places, however, bare bedrock was left exposed. By 4,000 to 6,000 years ago, the post-glacial soils were stabilized, and the broad vegetation patterns that persist to this day were established.

The zone covers a vast area of the Northern Hemisphere (moving in a wide band across the top of the United States and around the Great Lakes, through China and Russia, and over to the Scandinavian countries). The climate is one of extremes. The winter temperature can drop to -30°F (-34°C) for weeks on end. Polar blasts as cold as -45°F (-43°C) are possible. Summer temperatures may soar to around 95°F (35°C), pushed by dry breezes that gain heat over large continental landmasses. Mean annual rainfall can range from 10 to 40 in (250 to 1,000 mm). Where rainfall exceeds evapotranspiration, forests dominate. Grasslands occupy areas where there is insufficient summer moisture for trees.

Dilettante gardeners love the spring and summer; real gardeners also love the winter.
ANNE SCOTT-JAMES, 1913–

Colder regions of the zone

Forests in the colder reaches of the zone are predominately a mix of deciduous and coniferous trees. These forests are mostly composed of aspen *(Populus)* when young, and maples *(Acer)*, linden *(Tilia)*, fir *(Abies)*, and spruce *(Picea)* at maturity. At higher altitudes, hardy deciduous species like aspen are the pioneers that make up the young plant community before conifers become established. On poor or thin mineral soils over bedrock, pine *(Pinus)*, fir, and spruce usually dominate.

In the rain shadows of mountain ranges, such as the Rockies, herbaceous grasslands dominate. Excessive summer heat, persistent winds, and low average precipitation, along with fire, make it difficult for trees to thrive in these areas. The nature of these herbaceous grasslands differs from more familiar woodland landscapes in several significant ways. Grasses have extensive underground networks of fibrous roots that probe deeply and thoroughly for moisture. In fact, most of the body (biomass) of both grasses and prairie wildflowers is below the ground. In times of plenty, growth is lush and flowers are exuberant. During drought cycles, plants may remain in a semi-dormant condition during the growing season to conserve resources. Trees, with their comparatively massive bodies, are not as flexible, and therefore most trees do not survive in this part of the zone.

Warmer regions of the zone

In the warmer reaches of Zone 4, deciduous forests dominate in areas where there is sufficient rainfall. This is a vast area with a variety of soils, and a topography that varies dramatically from ancient mountains and foothills to gently undulating plains. This diverse landscape hosts many plant associations, which will also change over time. In the Northern Hemisphere, moist soils support forests of mixed oak *(Quercus)* and ash *(Fraxinus)* when young, and later beech *(Fagus)*, maple or linden communities. The drier sites with leaner soils support communities of oak and hickory *(Carya)*, or pines. Floodplains have a distinctive association of flood and drought-tolerant species such as silver maple *(Acer saccharinum)* in North America, and aspen *(Populus)* and willow *(Salix)* throughout the Northern Hemisphere.

The forest floor is carpeted with showy herbaceous plants such as bellwort *(Uvularia)*, Solomon's plume *(Smilacina)*, and liverleaf *(Hepatica)*.

Deciduous plants with bloom cycles tied to the availability of light and moisture put on brief but dazzling displays of spring wildflowers. As warm spring sunshine pours through the bare branches of the trees and the days lengthen, tree buds break and the burst of leaf growth begins to form a veil of shade on the forest floor. Within a few short weeks the canopy provides cooling shade. Woodland plants grow and bloom early in the spring to take advantage of this brief contact with the sun's rays. For gardeners, this means a glorious, though short-lived, flower display.

Many species of the zone are hardy plants adapted to cold temperatures, and many also tolerate periods of summer drought by becoming dormant and relying on their specialized water-storage organs, such as bulbs and fleshy underground stems, until the dry period passes. There are a number of exceptions, however: wildflowers such as wood lilies *(Trillium)*, bloodroot *(Sanguinaria)*, and cranesbill *(Geranium)* spread wide foliage to absorb summer's light, instead of becoming dormant. Late blooming plants like asters and goldenrods *(Solidago)* produce a flush of lush foliage early in the year, but flower in the autumn. These varied blooming times are useful to gardeners for year-round interest.

Grassland such as the North American prairie and the European steppe are dominated by grasses and a number of colorful wildflowers, in particular legumes and daisies. Dozens of popular perennial plants originate in the North American prairies, such as *Liatris*, coneflower *(Echinacea)*, and sunflower *(Helianthus)*. The steppes give us peony *(Paeonia)* and *Perovskia*.

Wetlands are common in the zone, especially on areas of shallow bedrock such as found on the Canadian Shield, and in grasslands such as the North American prairies. Forested wetlands include swamps and bogs, and are filled in with sphagnum mosses, heath-like shrubs, and grasses. Prairie potholes and other marshes are shallow and broad and are dominated by sedges *(Carex)*. Wetlands offer gardeners a variety of ornamental plants including the familiar iris and marsh marigold *(Caltha palustris)*.

The zone produces wheat *(Triticum)*, oats *(Avena)*, and other cereal crops; a variety of vegetables such as beets *(Beta)* and potatoes *(Solanum tuberosum)*; and fruits such as apples *(Malus)* and cherries *(Prunus)*.

Gardening in the zone

Gardening in the zone can be a challenge. The intense winter cold, often high summer heat, and periodic drought produce stressful conditions for plants.

However, winters in the northern reaches of the region generally have consistent snow cover that makes gardening with herbaceous plants easier than for more southern neighbors in Zone 5. Consistent winter snows protect plants from the worst of the cold, so perennial and vegetable gardeners are happy, especially in areas where it is moister and the soil is richer. On the down side, the growing season is shorter, on average 160 to 180 days. The number of woody ornamental species, especially flowering trees and shrubs, is dramatically less than that available in warmer zones. But what must be given up in woody species, can often be gained in herbaceous plants. Many plants thrive in the cooler conditions, especially cooler night temperatures, and in the reduced humidity. Insect and disease problems are fewer than in warmer zones. Lilacs *(Syringa)*, viburnums, crabapples *(Malus)*, iris, daylilies *(Hemerocallis)*, and hostas are just a few of the plants that are popular in Zone 4.

Above: Wildflowers form a vibrant, if brief, carpet of color across the prairie landscape. This scene features red-flowering Castilleja *species, cream-flowered* Persicaria bistorta, *and* Pedicularis groenlandica *with its maroon flower heads.*

Zone 5
-20 to -10°F (-29 to -23°C)

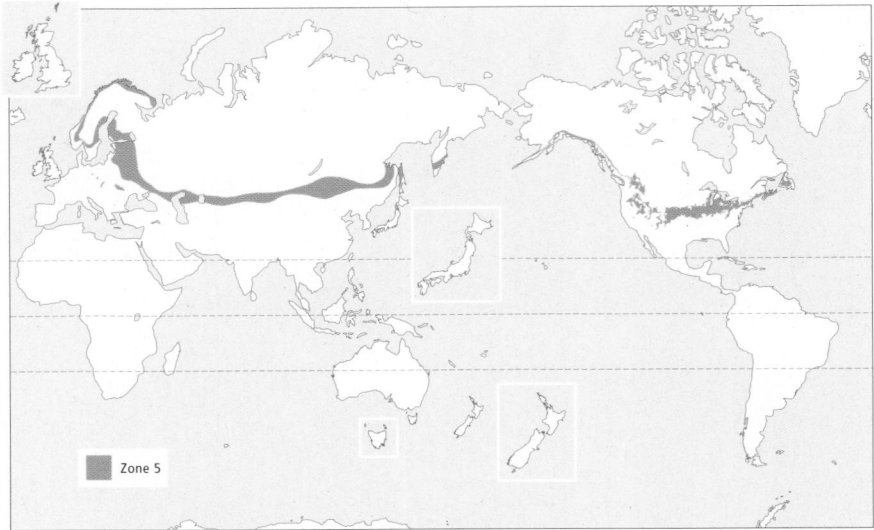

Zone 5

The many climates—wet, dry, maritime, continental, and alpine—of Zone 5 worldwide have in common their position between vast regions of much colder and much warmer temperatures. In short, Zone 5 is in the middle.

Nominally, the climates of this zone are united by low average winter temperatures in the range of -20 to -10°F (-29 to -23°C), but this masks the extremes. The greater portion of the zone runs east-west across the continents of Russia, Asia, and North America at roughly 40 degrees latitude. On these continental landmasses, away from maritime influences, waves of polar air frequently rush southward to the zone with little high ground to hinder them, sometimes driving the temperature well below -20°F (-29°C). During such episodes of deep cold, even hardy plants suffer severe damage and sometimes death.

Rainfall, snow, and soils vary widely across Zone 5. In North America the western plains are dry, with 12–20 in (30–50 cm) of rain a year and snowfalls that do not provide winter-long cover. Unleached by rain, the soils tend to be alkaline. Eastward, rainfall increases, the soils turn neutral or basic, and the prairie ecology of the plains gives way to forest. In Europe, the rainfall is highest in the west and declines to the east, with similar changes in the soils.

Winter varies widely in intensity. Some years temperatures can linger for a month or more at below freezing. Other years, the entire winter passes without dropping this low. In times of protracted cold, the weather is typically dry and windy; a combination that desiccates even tough needle-leafed evergreens such as spruce (*Picea*), and leaves them brown in spring, while broad-leafed evergreens such as rhododendrons may lose leaves, buds, and twigs.

Below: Ulmus × hollandica has given rise to a wide range of cultivars, including 'Modolina', shown here, which is a tall and vigorous-growing tree. It makes a suitable landscape subject in Zone 5 and warmer.

Right: This deciduous tree, Fagus sylvatica, is native to Europe and southern England. It is a valued garden tree, both for its ornamental uses and its capacity to conserve the productiveness of the soil.

To me a lush carpet of pine needles or spongy grass is more welcome than the most luxurious Persian rug.

HELEN KELLER 1880–1968

In eastern North America, winter vagaries are followed by vagaries of heat and humidity when warm moist air from southern regions spreads northward in the summer. Conifers such as larch (*Larix*), hemlock (*Tsuga*), and fir (*Abies*) from colder zones do not tolerate this heat and grow poorly. Instead, southern conifers such as shortleaf pine (*Pinus echinata*) and pitch pine (*P. rigida*) take their place.

Zone 5 is also found running in thin bands at elevations of roughly 5,000 to 8,000 ft (1,525 to 2,440 m). All plants in these high grounds must endure rapid and severe changes of temperature in summer and winter, as well as intense sunlight. Here, penstemons are common perennials, while spruce and pines are familiar trees.

Long cold spells and occasional polar weather limit the viability of broad-leafed evergreens in this zone. *Pieris, Leucothoe,* and even *Kalmia,* among others, do not thrive unless trees shelter them. Other plants, such as heaths (*Erica*) and heathers (*Calluna*), thrive only in the maritime climates of the zone, where the sea buffers outbreaks of polar air and provides moisture. Only a few rhododendron cultivars, such as *Rhododendron* 'Nova Zembla' and *R.* 'PJM', and the hardier species like *R. yakushimanum, R. maximum,* and *R. viscosum,* are reliable. However, even the toughest rhododendrons may suffer damage in this zone. Their performance in spring is acceptable, not perfect. Only the deciduous azaleas reliably escape damage.

Needle-leafed evergreens, such as white pine (*Pinus strobus*) for example, are prominent only where summers are moist and cool, and scarce where the summers are hot and humid, or hot and arid. In the west of North America, native spruces like *Picea pungens,* junipers (*Juniperus*), and pinyon (*Pinus edulis*) are the common evergreens, adapted to alkaline soils and aridity.

Sudden cold snaps and late freezes

On average, the first hard freeze of autumn arrives in mid-October, but it can come a month earlier or later. An early hard freeze, with temperatures at 27°F (-3°C), will burn the still-green leaves of woody and herbaceous perennials, and even damage the twigs of shrubs and trees that have not yet begun hardening. The last hard freeze of winter falls in mid-May, but some years it arrives as early as March and other years as late as June.

Furthermore, false springs and tardy winters bracket the growing season. Surges of southern air can arrive anytime from mid-winter to spring, lulling shrubs, trees, and herbaceous perennials partially out of dormancy. Once started, they lose hardiness. When a new wave of cold arrives, as it usually does, it can kill plants outright. Even temperatures considerably warmer than the average low for the zone can cause damage. In areas where snow is heavy, herbaceous perennials are usually spared from premature awakenings. Where snow is sparse, as it often is on the plains, exotic species such as daffodils *(Narcissus)* that are not adapted to false springs often emerge too soon and are burned by the return of deep cold.

In the areas of Zone 5 with adequate rainfall, the main crops are soybeans, corn, wheat, and oil seeds such as sunflowers. The hardier tree fruits such as apples and pears are grown, but require frequent spraying for the insects and disease that can thrive.

Gardening in the zone

Many plants are adapted to winters in the zone. Among trees and shrubs, some of the toughest are blueberry *(Vaccinium)*, hawthorn *(Crataegus)*, and apple *(Malus)*. Areas with dependable summer rainfall support deciduous shrubs and trees, including maples *(Acer)*, oaks *(Quercus)*, beeches *(Fagus)*, elms *(Ulmus)*, locusts *(Gleditsia)*, ashes *(Fraxinus)*, cherries *(Prunus)*, and more. Some exotics do well. The Chinese dawn redwood *(Metasequoia glyptostroboides)* is hardy in the wetter parts of the zone in North America, as is *Parrotia persica* in areas with cooler summers. Smoke bush *(Cotinus)* is widely adapted and so are the dogwoods, such as *Cornus alternifolia, C. kousa,* and *C. mas.* Daphnes are hardy, as are many species of honeysuckle, like *Lonicera × heckrottii,* some so rampant they are pests.

Among herbaceous perennials, the plains, steppes, and low mountains of the zone offer exceedingly tough species, adapted to cold and heat, drought and downpour. They include coreopsis *(Coreopsis),* black-eyed Susans *(Rudbeckia),* sunflowers *(Helianthus),* cup plant *(Silphium perfoliatum),* species of stachys, and succulents such as sedums, as well as a large group of grasses such as the graceful pennisetums, short fescues *(Festuca),* and hair grasses *(Deschampsia).* In areas with rainfall of 24 in (600 mm) or more, the hostas, the low pachysandras, lobelias, asters, thistley eryngiums, violets, astilbes, and epimediums, notable for their ability to grow in dry shade will all do well.

Though much prized, English ivy and boxwood are ill adapted to Zone 5. English yew *(Taxus baccata)* is also not entirely suitable. However, yews such as *T. canadensis* and *T. media* are fully hardy.

Magnolia × soulangeana is fairly hardy, but in central North America may fail to open its chalice-like flowers three years in five if late cold spells nip the opening buds. Many other magnolias are hardy but unreliable bloomers.

Although the climate can be testing, gardeners of Zone 5 nonetheless have a wide choice of dependable, desirable plants, both woody and herbaceous, and the pleasure of three seasons in the garden. Spring is sudden and intense. Crabapples cover themselves in white and daffodils flower yellow at their feet, while the herbaceous perennials burst from the ground and race into bloom. Within two months the show segues into the summer display of sunflowers and grasses. Autumn bloomers like anemone cannot match the paintbox of spring, but then the maples turn red and the garden season ends ablaze.

Above: Witch hazel, Hamamelis virginiana, is one of the earliest to flower of the trees and shrubs in the zone, but is almost never harmed by the cold. The serviceberries (Amelanchier spp.) are another early-bloomer.

Zone 6 -10 to 0°F (-23 to -18°C)

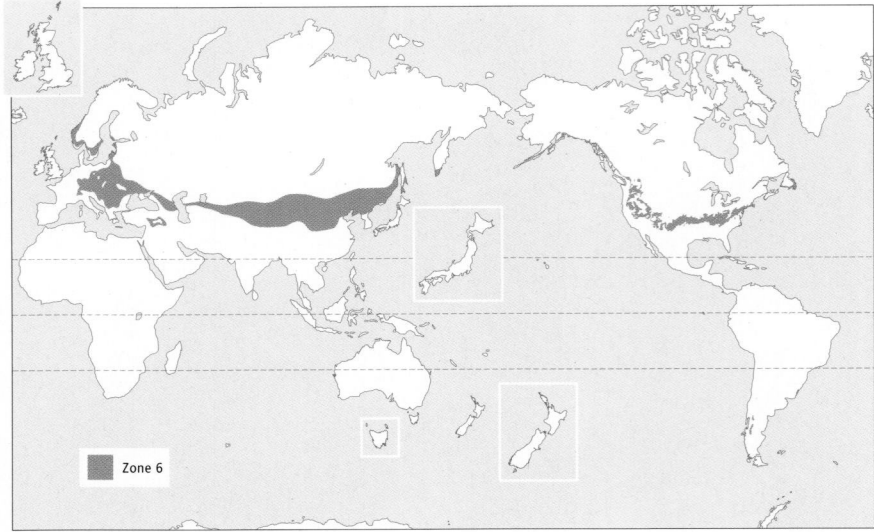

Zone 6

In Zone 6, the average low temperature in winter ranges from -10 to 0°F (-23 to -18°C). It ranges throughout the Northern Hemisphere, making a wide U-shaped curve through the USA from New York City on the east, down through the Midwest and Southwest, and up to Washington and parts of British Columbia. Off the northeastern coast of North America, the warming effects of the Gulf Stream place unlikely areas such as parts of Newfoundland in the zone. Also in this zone's northern tier are areas of Norway, Sweden, Denmark, and Finland.

Zone 6 cuts a path through much of central and eastern Europe, from Germany to Greece and northern Croatia; moving into Asia via the Caspian Sea, and narrowing into a small swathe through Afghanistan and into China. Its sole presence in the Southern Hemisphere is two small regions in Argentina.

Topographically, Zone 6 covers many landscapes: coastal regions, flood plains, lowlands, mountains, prairies, plains, and even some high desert, and the vegetation varies accordingly. Among plants that will grow in wet coastal areas, along riversides and marshes, are giant reed plants *(Phragmites australis)* and cat tail *(Typha latifolia)*. The dry sandy Pine Barrens of New Jersey, USA, support plants that need fire to survive, such as scrub pine *(Pinus virginiana)*, northern pitch pine *(Pinus rigida)*, bearberry *(Arctostaphylos uva-ursi)*, and sweet pepper bush *(Clethra alnifolia)*.

Lowland mountain ranges, such as the Blue Ridge Mountains of USA, and some of the mountains in Europe give rise to dogwoods: among them, the green osier *(Cornus alternifolia)*, the native American flowering dogwood *(C. florida)*, the European and

Below: Bulbs are a favorite of gardeners throughout Zone 6. Colchicum autumnale and Crocus speciosus, below, offer welcome color in autumn.

western Asian Cornelian cherry *(C. mas)*, and the giant dogwood *(C. controversa)*.

The plains and prairies of Zone 6 are home to plants that not only survive winter cold, but also often heat and drought (but flooding some years) over summer. These plants include the coneflowers *(Echinacea)* and sunflowers *(Helianthus)*. The genus *Leucanthemum* (shasta and ox-eye daisies) straddles Zone 6, growing in grasslands, rocky meadows, and wastelands of Europe and temperate Asia.

Seasonal displays

Spring can be beautifully long (and moist in places), arriving early and staying late—especially in the warmer ranges of the zone. Snowdrops *(Galanthus nivalis)* and *Crocus tommasinianus* can put on a spring preview in late winter. Adding to the show are some deciduous shrubs such as forsythia, Chinese witch hazel *(Hamamelis mollis)*, and winter hazels *(Corylopsis)*, as these can shed the snow and keep on blooming. Other woodland and scrub region shrubs and small trees, such as firethorn *(Pyracantha)* and Japanese flowering crab-apples *(Malus floribunda)*, retain colorful berries from autumn. In moist regions of northwestern North America and northeastern Asia, skunk cabbage *(Lysichiton* species*)* actually creates heat as it rises up from the earth in early spring, melting any snow around it. However, early blooming trees, especially magnolias—*Magnolia denudata* from China, the Japanese *Magnolia kobus*, and others—are often hit with a late blast of cold or snow that browns out their blossoms. Shrubs are more forgiving, and it is common to see hardy shrubs such as Korean rhododendron *(Rhododendron mucronulatum)* unaffected by late chills and snows.

Within weeks, spring brings a riot of colors from bulbs, many of which many originated in western Asia and southeastern Europe, such as tulips *(Tulipa)*, daffodils *(Narcissus)*, squill *(Scilla)*, and grape hyacinths *(Muscari)*. Dozens of woodland wildflowers add to the beauty: European forget-me-nots *(Myosotis sylvatica)* and lungwort *(Pulmonaria)*, mayapple *(Podophyllum)*, and columbine *(Aquilegia canadensis)*. Not to be forgotten are the perennials such as lupins *(Lupinus)*, bleeding heart *(Dicentra spectabilis)*,and peonies *(Paeonia)*. Acid-loving woodland shrubs abound, adding to the colors of late spring: rhododendrons and azaleas from around the world, hollies *(Ilex)*, mountain laurel *(Kalmia latifolia)*, viburnums *(Viburnum)*, and blueberries *(Vaccinium)*.

Summer brings another burst of color from daylilies *(Hemerocallis)*, which seemingly defy nature by growing anywhere, lilies that originated in Asia, and perennials such as native American prairie plants: bee balm *(Monarda didyma)*, black-eyed Susan *(Rudbeckia)*, and purple coneflower *(Echinacea purpurea)*. The tough shrubs of summer include shrubby cinquefoil *(Potentilla fruticosa)*, butterfly bush *(Buddleja davidii)*, and the hardy cluster-flowered (floribunda) roses.

Autumn is a second spring when every leaf a flower.
ALBERT CAMUS, 1913–1960

Woodland areas contribute to summer beauty. Even without its airy blooms, purple smokebush (*Cotinus coggyria* 'Purpureus') adds a bold note to the garden with its deep burgundy leaves. Trees such as dove tree (*Davidia involucrata*), sweetspire (*Itea virginica*), and sorrel tree (*Oxydendron arboreum*), with its white blooms, add to the delight of summer.

For many, autumn is a favorite season as Zone 6 is favored with a last burst of color before trees shed their leaves. Maples abound, from the sugar maple (*Acer saccharum*) to red maple (*A. rubrum*) and the numerous Japanese maples (*A. palmatum, A. japonicum,* and cultivars) with their foliage ranging in color from yellow to orange, crimson to burgundy, and almost everything in between. Sweet gum (*Liquidambar styraciflua*) and burning bush (*Euonymus alatus*) are stunning as their leaves turn flaming red, while the eastern North American staghorn sumac (*Rhus typhina*) turns yellow to orange. Sweet autumn clematis (*Clematis ternifolia*) lives up to its name with fragrant white blooms that evolve into magnificent daintily twirled seed heads that often last through the winter. Even autumn bulbs put on a show, for example, the large lavender autumn crocus native to Europe (*Colchicum autumnale*) and autumn daffodil (*Sternbergia lutea*). In acidic areas, hollies (*Ilex* species and cultivars) are king of the broadleaf evergreens. Their berries color in autumn and persist through winter.

Above: Zone 6 is particularly blessed with an abundance of deciduous trees and shrubs, which mark autumn in reds and golds.

Growing in the zone

Zone 6 could be considered a crossover zone, and as such it is able to sustain a larger range of woody plants of varying hardiness than most other zones. Many gardeners use

Above: Acer species are valued throughout the Northern Hemisphere for their beautiful autumn colors. This, combined with their elegant foliage and growth habit, make them very useful to gardeners.

this to their advantage, especially within microclimates in their own properties, growing Zone 7 plants along the south side of the house or in a protected area, and growing plants from cooler zones, in more exposed or north-facing spaces. The range of plants to grow in Zone 6 seems limitless, and includes many trees, shrubs, woody and herbaceous perennials and annuals. If you also make use of the microclimates around your property, you will find thousands of plants suitable for your garden. The choices are up to you.

Zone 7 0 to 10°F (-18 to -12°C)

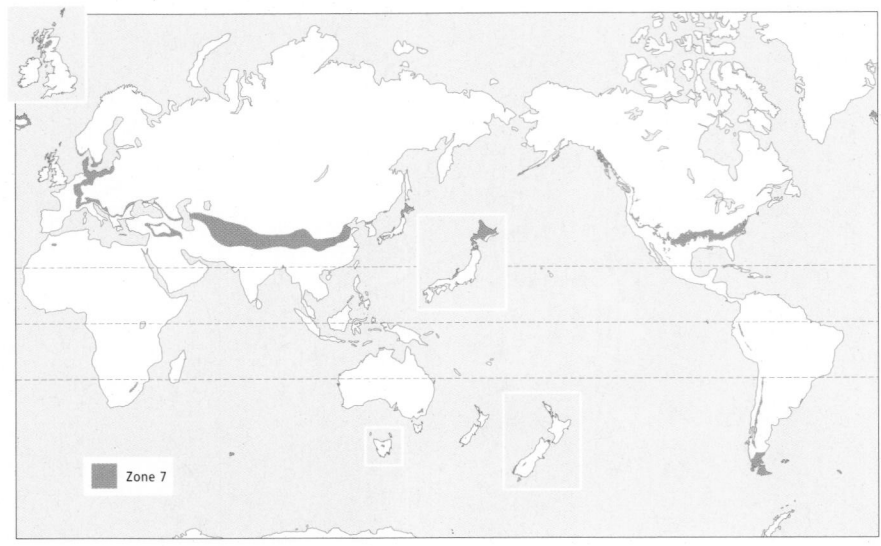

Zone 7

Below: Pinus strobus, Populus tremuloides, Betula, *and* Acer *species combine to beautiful effect in New York State, USA.*

Zone 7 is found mainly across the middle lattitudes of the Northern Hemisphere temperate regions, with only odd patches in the Southern Hemisphere, in mountain areas. In North America, the zone runs in an arc across the southern states of USA, from Virginia through northern Texas, Arizona, and the mountains of California, coming to a northern-most tail in the maritime region of western Canada and the Alaskan Panhandle. In Europe it occupies a north-south belt through central Europe, from Denmark to the Balkans, and also occurs in the Scottish Highlands. From the eastern Mediterranean, it runs in a broad belt through parts of the Caucasus and Turkey and through much of the Himalayas and northern China. Northern Japan is also in this zone. In the Southern Hemisphere, the largest occurrences of Zone 7 are in the higher Andes of South America—dropping almost to sea level in the far south—in the Drakensberg of eastern South Africa, and in the higher mountains of New Zealand's South Island.

A zone of diverse climates

Most parts of this zone experience medium to high rainfall, without any severe dry season. In the continental interiors, for example in central Asia and the American southwest, this zone is pushed towards lower lattitudes by cold air masses expanding from the north in winter. As a result, summers are long and hot and humidity is low for much of the year. These continental climates have more sharply defined seasons and more predictable winter temperatures than those of regions bordering the oceans, where, generally speaking, summers are milder and more humid. Zone 7 is the highest zone in which the soil is likely to be frozen for any length of time in winter, which precludes the growth of many sub-tropical plants, most notably palms (family Arecaceae).

A point worth considering is that climates change and plants may be caught in a climate warmer or colder than the one in which they originally evolved. It often happens that plants can

...the best kind of garden should arise out of its site and conditions.
WILLIAM ROBINSON, 1848–1935

tolerate more cold or heat than is now recorded in their native homes. Recent winters have been warmer than in the past 10,000 years, so plants found wild in Zone 7 can generally grow in Zones 5 or 6.

Flora of the Northern Hemisphere

Woody plants are more sensitive indicators of this zone than herbaceous plants, being less easily protected from heavy frost by soil or snow cover. Unlike their deciduous counterparts, many temperate evergreens have their cold limit at or around Zone 7. One such is *Magnolia grandiflora*, a typical Zone 7 tree from the southern USA, and widely planted elsewhere in the world. Similarly, many of the Chinese evergreen *Rhododendron* species are not hardy below Zone 7.

Certain plants are readily grown right across the zone, others are much more sensitive to climatic factors such as summer temperatures, rainfall, and humidity. For example, some plants that are hardy down to Zone 6 or even Zone 5 in hot dry continental regions will hardly cope with winter in oceanic climates of Zone 7, such as those of southwestern Canada and Scotland, because they enter the winter with their aerial growth less hardened and their root systems wetter. Rose of Sharon *(Hibiscus syriacus)* is one such example.

For the same reason, the Scottish Highlands and the Pacific Northwest (of North America) are excellent for trees and shrubs from the cold wet parts of Chile and New Zealand, or from Himalayan areas with wet summers. The British horticulturist Ken Beckett, who has made several studies of plant hardiness, considers that gardeners in British Isles should choose plants rated to one zone more hardy than that in which they garden.

The greatest horticultural wealth for the zone is to be found in the plants from the mountains of Japan, China, and the Himalayas. Native to this region are the many hardy rhododendron species, which have given rise to a multitude of hybrids, and the magnificent flowering cherries *(Prunus),* developed mainly in Japan although some of their wild progenitors may have come from China.

In the southern interior of the USA, there is a wealth of native plant life for gardeners, in particular, annuals and perennials of the daisy family. Examples include *Helianthus, Rudbeckia, Cosmos,* and *Coreopsis.* Some of the many colorful perennials and sub-shrubs in the genus *Penstemon* are also centered in Zone 7.

Alpine plants from the south

In the Southern Hemisphere, with its stronger oceanic influence on climates, Zone 7 is restricted to mountainous areas. In Australia, the hardy snow gum *(Eucalyptus pauciflora* subsp. *niphophila)* and cider gum *(E. gunnii),* as well as shrubs such as the candle heath *(Richea continentis),* which will survive in warmer parts of Zone 7 in Europe, are only found above 5,000 ft (1,500 m) in New South Wales, Victoria, and Tasmania.

In Africa, only the highlands of Lesotho above 6,500 ft (2,000 m) have Zone 7 winters. Garden plants from this area are mostly bulbs or corms. They are tolerant of fire, which means they can lose their tops to frost and still survive. *Moraea alticola, Kniphofia caulescens,* and the deciduous *Agapanthus campanulatus* subsp. *patens* can grow at altitudes of 8,200 ft (2,500 m).

Zone 7 covers extensive areas of the mountains in the South Island of New Zealand where there is a distinct lack of summer heat. The evergreen *Celmisia* species, from the alpine grasslands, thrive on sandy acid soil with good drainage and the cool summers of eastern Scotland.

Commercial crops

Crops in this zone depend mainly on summer temperatures: maize *(Zea mays)* is grown in warm wet areas, and wheat *(Triticum)* where summers are drier. Few places in Zone 7 have a long enough growing season to produce two crops in a year. In the coldest areas of the Himalayas above 6,560 ft (2,000 m), buckwheat *(Fragopyrum esculentum)* is grown as a grain in place of wheat.

Most fruit trees thrive, and the rather delicate Japanese apricot *(Prunus mume)* can be grown. Figs *(Ficus carica)* will need wall protection and will lose their fruit buds in the coldest winters. Grape vines will survive in many parts of Zone 7 but for high-quality wine they require warm sunny microclimates, such as in the valleys of the Rhine and the Moselle in Germany.

Above: This yellow-flowering Senecio species, with the brown-red flowers of a Buddleja species peeping through, is at home in the temperate conditions of Central Sichuan, China.

Top: A native of China, Lagerstroemia indica makes a highly attractive tree for gardeners in Zones 7 and 8. It has a widespreading habit; white, pink, or purple flowers; and dark green leaves that turn orange-red in autumn.

Zone 8 10 to 20°F (-12 to -7°C)

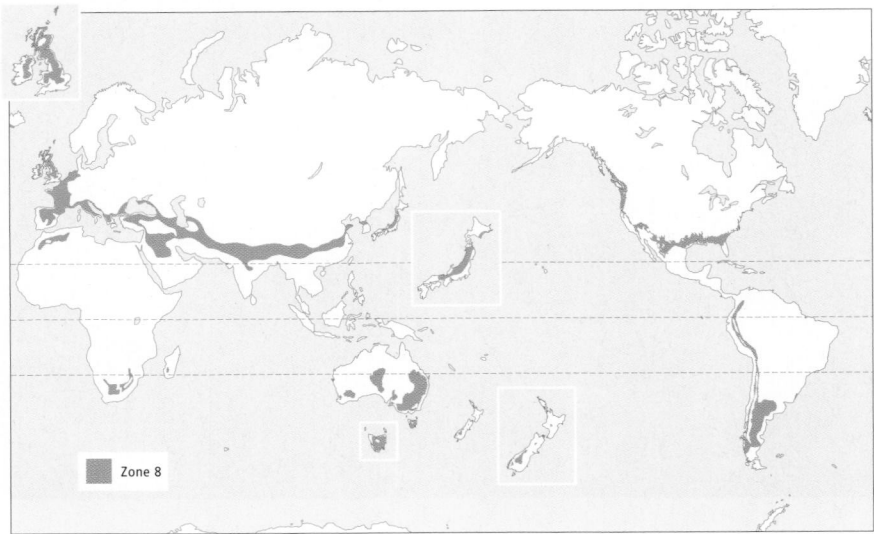

Zone 8

Mother Nature has provided a vast selection of plants hardy to Zone 8, and humans have done a mostly admirable job of carting them all over the world, adding, swapping, and enriching the panorama of flora available.

Characterized by four definite seasons, Zone 8 has mild winters with a sporadic snowfall that doesn't last. Temperatures can plunge from 20 to 10°F (-7 to -12°C). The first frosts begin in November and end in March in the Northern Hemisphere, whereas in the Southern Hemisphere frosts can last from April to as late as November.

Some of the world's most spectacular gardens can be found in this favorable zone. Most of the British Isles and central Ireland lies within the zone. A good part of France, and a large portion of Spain, are also Zone 8. The vast rich agriculture area of the Po River Valley in northern Italy, famous for its many Renaissance gardens is also in this hardiness zone. North America's Zone 8, on the other hand, sweeps across the southern part of the USA, taking in the Californian foothill regions of the Sierra and the northwest coast. South of the equator, Zone 8 moves inland, down the coast of Peru and Chile, and covers much of inland Argentina, part of the Tierra del Fuego, and the Falkland Islands.

On the opposite side of the world, eastern Australia, most of Tasmania, and some of New Zealand lie in Zone 8. In Asia, the zone includes large areas of Japan, and parts of China and Myanmar. The only region of Africa that lies in the zone is at the far south, in a small crescent shaped area that touches Lesotho.

Summer makes a silence after spring.
VITA SACKVILLE-WEST, 1892–1962

Zone 8 worldwide is temperate, with long summer daylight hours that guarantee plants at least six hours of sun per day. As "hardiness" describes places, not plants, variations do occur. Continental regions of this zone have long hot summers that help the plants to mature and tolerate cold better, with some rain. Heavy winter rainfalls follow summer, along with some snow in winter. Maritime regions have mostly cool wet summers, with winters bringing more rain. Mediterranean climates have hot dry summers that are followed by winter rains.

Winter dormancy across the zone lasts three to four months, and in this favorable mild climate plants may bloom for up to ten months. In hot dry places, some plants will have summer dormancy as well.

Common methods of propagation apply in the zone: budding, grafting, and cuttings. Some plants normally tender to Zone 8 may be successfully grown in micro-climate situations. Perfect examples of this are the olive (*Olea europaea*) and citrus trees that grow in the open on the south side of the Alps, protected from the icy north winds by the mountains.

Rosemary (*Rosmarinus*) and lavender (*Lavandula*), natives to the Mediterranean and spread by the Romans, are intolerant to excessive winter wet yet thrive in the British Isles in soil with good drainage. Often, keeping tender plants in place and dry during winter improves their chances for survival. Lavender cotton (*Santolina*), lavender, and butcher's broom (*Ruscus*)—called *pungitopo*, "pricks mice" in Italy—are all Zone 8 plants.

Plants are amazingly adaptable, even to different elevations. English walnuts (*Juglans regia*) will grow to elevations of 4,920 ft (1,500 m), and yet the plants—the famous *noce di Sorrento* of Italy—hug the Tyrrhenian coast. The common bearded iris (*Iris germanica*) will grow from sea level to 3,940 ft (1,200 m). Grapes (*Vitis vinifera*) grow from 0 to 2,620 ft (800 m). Microclimates within Zone 8, influenced by elevation, a diversity of soil, and local climatic conditions, will determine what plant will grow where. A more tender plant, ideal for Zone 9, may thrive in a protected spot in Zone 8, whereas in a windy area, perhaps with poor drainage, a plant usually hardy to this zone may die. Observation is a good garden tool.

Indicator plants

Most roses thrive in Zone 8, requiring a mild winter to perform best. Tender roses, however, such as the double white banksia rose (*Rosa banksiae banksiae*), Teas, and Noisettes may need to be planted in sheltered spots. Hardy plants such as stonecrop (*Sedum*), iris, columbine (*Aquilegia*), bugle (*Ajuga*), some pinks (*Dianthus*), and other cold climate plants, grow at a leisurely pace, almost doubling their leafed-out period in a Zone 8 climate.

The wonderful trees of this zone include one of the oldest and tallest trees on earth; the Californian redwood (*Sequoia sempervirens*). The magnificent giant sequoias (*Sequoiadendron*), also from California, have larger trunks but do not grow as tall.

Below: Parts of New Zealand's South Island boast a mild Zone 8 climate. Conditions are ideal for commercial grape cultivation, and numerous vineyards exist.

Nearly 2,000 years ago, Pliny described the oriental plane tree *(Platanus orientalis)* growing in one of his Tuscany gardens with ivy *(Hedera)* entwining the trunks for contrasting foliage. These plants are still familiar features of the zone. From China and Japan the crape myrtle *(Lagerstroemia indica),* has migrated worldwide, has been overloved, overgrown, and is now overshunned as being common. Little do those in Zone 8 know how cold climate gardeners envy and covet this beautiful elegant little tree.

Apples, a favorite fruit crop today, have been discovered in Swiss and Austrian Stone Age dwellings. Nut crops include chestnut *(Castanea sativa),* grown in southern Europe, and the much sought after pine nut produced from the Mediterranean umbrella pine *(Pinus pinea).* Hazelnuts *(Corylus avellana)* have been grown since humans can remember, and the walnut is also grown for oil. Olives are commercially grown in some warmer protected areas of the zone. Grape crops are grown across Europe—curiously, over the same area that the Roman Empire occupied in the second century AD—and in California, Australia, and New Zealand.

Some problem plants

Humans have caused the spread of some very invasive weeds. The noxious free-floating aquatic fern *Salvinia molesta* has recently invaded areas of Zone 8 worldwide. Faithful to its name *molesta,* this native of southeastern Brazil grows vigorously from sea level to 1,000 ft (300 m), multiplies rapidly, and has already clogged major waterways everywhere, causing serious problems.

Rosa multiflora, introduced into the USA from Japan and China, has "escaped" and is now considered a noxious weed, as pasturing cows eat this rose and the prickles rip their intestines. Yellow wood sorrel *(Oxalis exilis),* from New Zealand and Australia, has become a farmer's nightmare in many places and it is almost impossible to remove. On the other hand, nettle *(Urtica dioica),* might be considered a friendly weed as it enriches the soil and can be harvested to eat. Everyone (except farmers) loves the red Flanders poppy *(Papaver rhoeas),* which regularly survives the crop weed killers by growing along field edges, and in unsprayed areas.

True floral globalization has made hundreds of good (and bad, alas) "discovered" treasures from around the world available in this zone.

Gardening in the zone

With the mild winter temperatures, Zone 8 gardeners have paradise at their fingertips and can choose from a vast selection of plants. Stately fragrant *Magnolia grandiflora* can share garden space with richly perfumed Mexican orange *(Choisya ternata),* Japanese pittosporum *(Pittosporum tobira),* and flowering trees such as flowering dogwood *(Cornus florida)* and the elegant lacy silk tree *(Albizia julibrissin).* The stunning evergreen shrub Oregon holly grape *(Mahonia aquifolium)* and the deciduous flowering-quince *(Chaenomeles speciosa)* bloom in the winter, alongside the cheerful yellow winter jasmine *(Jasminum nudiflorum).* The superb ground covers lily-turf *(Liriope spicata)* and mondo grass *(Ophiopogon japonicus)* grow well in Zone 8. Gardeners in Zone 8 are destined to suffer great temptations (there is always that plant you don't have) and great satisfactions.

Above: In ideal conditions —which include fog, rain, and cool summer winds— Sequoia sempervirens can reach 360 ft (110 m).

Left: Roses should abound in Zone 8 gardens, as almost every type of rose can be grown, including those that can only survive mild winters, and tender classics like 'Mutabilis', 'Lady Hillingdon', and 'Mme Alfred Carrière', left.

Zone 9 20 to 30°F (-7 to -1°C)

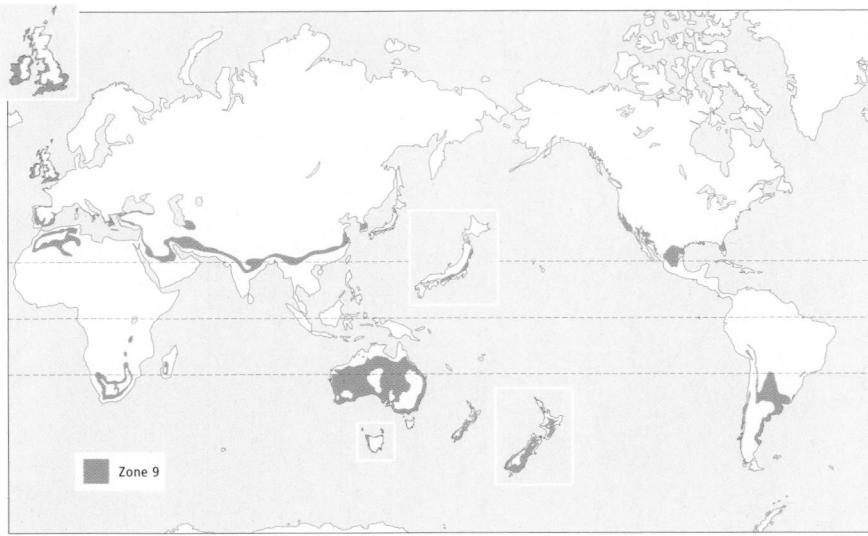

The minimum winter temperature in Zone 9 ranges between 20 and 30°F (-7 to -1°C) and the bulk of the garden plants are from the Mediterranean basin, the Cape region of South Africa, the California/Arizona area in North America, Chile in South America, and central and parts of southern Australia and neighboring areas. Although hardiness zones relate to areas with similarities of climate rather than to plants that are similar biologically, plants from different regions in the same zone frequently share common characteristics. As plants share features and climate, cultivation of the plants also has many similarities. In the main, the native vegetation in these parts of the world is grouped under the name "Mediterranean," from the vegetation found in southern Europe, Turkey, Lebanon, Israel, and North Africa. This vegetation was the subject of the earliest Western study of plants, and many of them are familiar from the Bible. Plants with a true Mediterranean distribution include rosemary *(Rosmarinus officinalis),* strawberry tree *(Arbutus unedo),* and the rock-rose (Cistaceae) family.

Above: Protea cynaroides, *known as king protea, is the floral emblem of South Africa, and is native to the lower mountain slopes and heathlands of the Cape region. Its striking flowers appear from mid-winter to early summer.*

Adaptations to fire and drought

The Mediterranean climate is characterized by mild wet winters and long dry summers, summer being defined as the three months when the days are the longest, hottest, and driest. Plants have become adapted to these hot dry summers in several ways. Some avoid the dry weather by being short lived and surviving as seeds (annuals), others die down to below ground level and survive as corms, bulbs, or fleshy stems: tulips do this. Woody plants such as kermes oak *(Quercus coccifera)* in the Mediterranean tend to have tough leathery leaves, or, as with many ice plants (family Aizoaceae) from southern Africa, succulent leaves or stems. These features help the plant withstand water stress during the summer.

All such plants that have parts aboveground in the hottest time of the year have adaptations to deter grazing animals. These adaptations can be in the form of tough leaves and stems, spines and thorns (such as many legume species like gorse, *Ulex europaeus,* in the Mediterranean), or leaves that are foul smelling or tasting (such as many pelargonium), or through camouflage, so that the plant resembles little stones (like the "living stones," *Lithops*).

Many Mediterranean regions are prone to fires, both natural and induced by humans, and so many of the plants are also adapted to fire. Some, such as cork oak *(Quercus suber),* have thick burn-tolerant bark, while others, like *Cistus salviifolius,* sucker from the base once the existing shoot structure has been killed. Others, as is the case with many Australian plants like banksias and hakeas, will only germinate after fire has cleared an area of competing plants.

The horticultural significance of these features is that the great majority of succulent plants, many "bulbs," and many plants with spines and strong aromatic leaves turn out to be Zone 9 plants. The trees, which formerly dominated much of these Zone 9 ecosystems, were some of the first evergreens brought into cultivation.

The first Mediterranean plants grown as ornamentals were from southern Europe and, in northern countries, they had to be overwintered in buildings called orangeries. Later, plants of the eastern Mediterranean and the North African coast were introduced.

An extensive floral kingdom

Most significant, though, was the bringing into cultivation of the Cape region flora of South Africa. Although grouped under "Mediterranean," it is botanically so distinctive as to be considered one of the world's six floral kingdoms, with some 9,000 species of seed plants and plants that are without seeds and flowers (pteridophytes), of which 69 percent are found only there. It has provided many of the world's most important ornamentals for Zone 9, and accommodating them in the horticulture of northern Europe led to improved greenhouse design, allowing the cultivation of many succulents and winter-flowering heaths *(Erica)*. The introduction of Cape plants also led to the increased use of outside "summer" bulbs in the form of gladioli *(Gladiolus)*, corn lily *(Ixia)*, montbretia *(Crocosmia)*, harlequin flower *(Sparaxis)*, and freesias. Also important was the introduction of half-hardy annuals, such as lobelia, nemesia, and Livingstone daisies *(Dorotheanthus)*, used in summer bedding. The beds often included South African "geraniums" (pelargoniums) that had been overwintered indoors. These species of pelargonium, like many succulent plants from the Cape, were to become some of the most widely grown pot plants and were seen decorating windowsills of even the humblest cottages in northern Europe.

*Here is this land,
where nature unconfined
Taunts the great desert of
the human mind*
ROY CAMPBELL, 1901–1957

Later, other floras in the zone were explored and their plants introduced into other countries. These included California poppy *(Eschscholzia californica)* and species of *Clarkia,* to be grown as half-hardy annuals. From South America came the slipper flower *(Calceolaria),* and from southern Australia came golden everlastings *(Xerochrysum bracteatum)* and, more importantly, hordes of species of wattle *(Acacia)* and gum *(Eucalyptus).* Plantations of both have transformed the landscape of many parts of Zone 9 throughout the world.

Because of their native climate regimes, many plants in this zone are dormant in the hot summer months. Many of them require a baking to flower the following season and will rot if moistened during this time. This means that many of the succulent plants such as those from the Cape region must be grown in greenhouses even in warm climates, merely to keep off rain. Other perennial plants from the zone would die if left outside in cooler climates and are often treated as annuals, though in mild winters some, such as gazanias, will survive to flower the next year. Most of the evergreen trees will not stand the cool dank winters of the north, though in sheltered urban spots, such as at the Chelsea Physic Garden in London, even olive trees *(Olea europaea)* grow unprotected.

Many Zone 9 plants are important to the cut flower industry in this zone and in other warm and temperate countries. Other commercial crops grown include citrus, peaches *(Prunus persica)* and other stone fruit, melons and other cucurbits, strawberries *(Fragaria)*, figs *(Ficus)*, avocados *(Persea americana),* olives, and wine grapes *(Vitis vinifera).* In plastic greenhouses with little other protection, tropical crops can also be grown successfully: papayas *(Carica)*, bananas *(Musa)*, and custard apples *(Annona squamosa).*

Introducing Zone 9 plants to other parts of the world has led to major weed problems in several areas. South African Cape dandelion *(Arctotheca calendula)*, pigface *(Carpobrotus)*, gladioli, and *Watsonia* are weeds in the Mediterranean, California, and Australia. On the other hand, species of wattle *(Acacia)* and *Hakea* from Australia are pests in the Mediterranean and in South Africa, though some of them are now being kept in check using biological control measures.

Below: The red flowers of the candelabra flower, Brunsvigia orientalis, brighten the southern African landscape, where it is endemic, in autumn. When the flowerhead dries out, the seeds are dispersed across the land.

Left: From southeastern Australia, Xanthorrhoea australis has a dense rosette of long, narrow, arching leaves, with sweetly fragrant spring flowers clustered on long "spears."

Zone 10

30 to 40°F (-1 to 4°C)

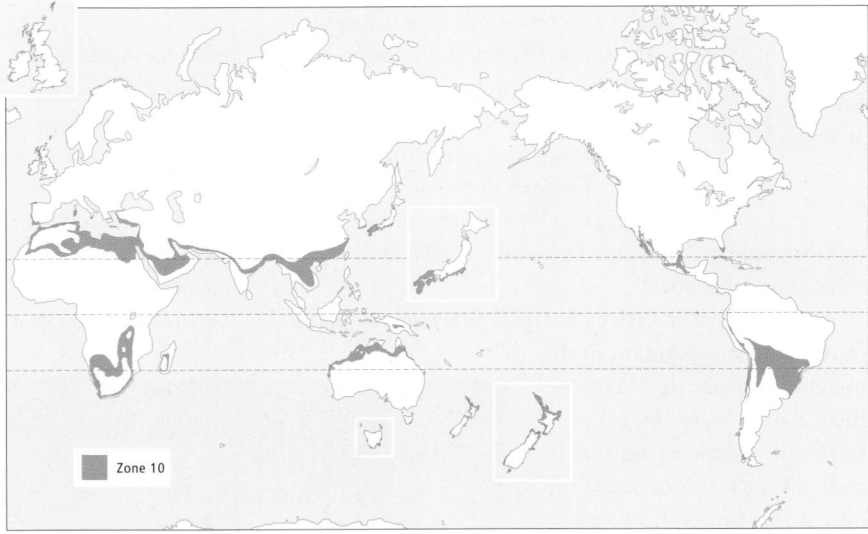

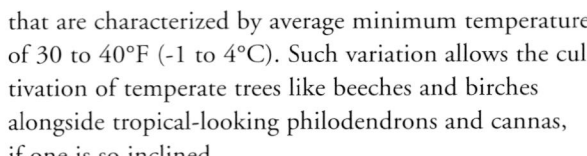

Zone 10 offers the adventurous horticulturist great possibilities. To many gardeners it is horticultural Mecca. The mild climate is influenced both by moist maritime air and dry continental air, resulting in a complex patchwork of microclimates that support a remarkable diversity of plants. Everything seems to grow here with ease.

This zone is characterized by cool wet winters and hot dry summers. It is the climate found around parts of the Mediterranean Sea in Europe and North Africa, and four other regions of the world: southern California in the USA, central Chile in South America, northwestern Australia, and southern areas of South Africa. Mountains provide a buffer from the cold continental air of Zone 9, and distance from the equator diminishes the moist tropical air that brings summer storms to Zone 11. Nevertheless, Zone 10, if based strictly on minimum winter temperatures, does includes some regions with summer monsoons: southern Florida in the USA, northern Australia, eastern South Africa, and parts of South America and Mexico.

Right: The many-petalled red flowers of Opuntia ficus-indica *appear all year round, making this an attractive species, as well as useful; its fruit are an important source of food in some African countries.*

Below: Cistus ladanifer *is native to the southwestern Mediterranean region and North Africa. Ladanum is exuded through the leaves, leaving them sticky; hence its name gum cistus.*

A remarkable variety of plants

There are a number of reasons for the staggering variety of Zone 10 plants. The major factor is climate, an understanding of which can be invaluable in their successful cultivation in the garden. The climate of this zone is far from homogeneous. Diverse topography interacting with latitude and elevation, as well as varying degrees of maritime or continental influence, result in a multitude of climate variations that are characterized by average minimum temperatures of 30 to 40°F (-1 to 4°C). Such variation allows the cultivation of temperate trees like beeches and birches alongside tropical-looking philodendrons and cannas, if one is so inclined.

Along the coast and in isolated thermal belts (that is, neither in the cold sinks of the valleys nor the exposed higher elevations) frost is rare, restricted to cold spells in cycles of ten, twenty, or even fifty years. Further inland, even just ten or fifteen miles (16 or 24 km), several light frosts a year may be typical. However, these are rarely below 30°F (-1°C) and don't last more than an hour or two in the predawn. Along the coast, summer temperatures normally peak between 70 and 86°F (21 and 30°C). In the inland valleys, highs of more than 95°F (35°C) or 100°F (38°C) are not uncommon. Rare heat spells bring temperatures of 113°F (45°C) or higher.

Rainfall in the zone varies from desert levels (under 5 in/12 cm per year) in the shadow of coastal mountain ranges to coastal areas that receive about 15 in (38 cm) per year. Parts of northern Australia and South America in this zone can receive considerably more than this. Humidity decreases with distance from the coast, though fingers of fog can creep many miles inland and can be a vital source of moisture. Cool drizzly days can be followed by scorching ones, with high atmospheric pressure, dry winds, and temperatures of 90°F (32°C) or more. Clearly, plants that demand more uniform conditions are not happy outside of protective greenhouses or shade structures.

Predominant growth forms

The range of possible adaptations for survival in Zone 10 is manifest in four predominant growth forms: annuals, geophytes, xeromorphic woody plants, and succulents. There are thousands of species of annuals native to the zone, and the California poppy (*Eschscholzia californica*) is a well known representative of Zones 9 and 10. As an ecological strategy, annuals are masters of avoidance, surviving the characteristic long dry season of most Zone 10 climates in the form of seed. This seed easily endures a few months of drought until rains return. In some cases, seeds can survive for years to outlive longer cycles of drought. African daisies (*Dimorphotheca*), godetias (*Clarkia*), *Nemesia*, and *Schizanthus* include some of the loveliest examples of the annual strategy.

Geophytes are a group of plants that survive prolonged drought by means of perennial underground bulbs, tubers, or fleshy stems. This group reaches the zenith of its diversity in Zone 10. An example is the iris (Iridaceae) family, especially diverse in South Africa, which is spectacular in its variety of form and color. This family includes some of the most distinctive floral forms in the plant kingdom: irises, moraeas, gladioli, and more.

An ubiquitous plant from this zone is the oleander (*Nerium*). Native to a broad range of regions from the Mediterranean to Japan, *Nerium oleander* is representa-

tive of the dominant growth form of Zone 10: that is, a woody shrub with one or more water-conserving (xeromorphic) adaptations that aid in surviving drought. Some trees also have these adaptations. Other distinctive examples of Zone 10 shrubs include *Ceanothus, Alyogyne* and rosemary.

Other woody plants display different designs for reducing water loss: felty or waxy leaves, water-storing spongy wood, prickly armature for protection, photosynthetic stems, or thick corky bark—an adaptation taken to the extreme in the cork oak, *Quercus suber.*

A fourth universally known Zone 10 growth form is the succulent. Succulents represent a conspicuously different variation on the theme of drought adaptation. The jade plant *(Crassula ovata)* is much loved by windowsill gardeners throughout the temperate Northern Hemisphere, but it is native to Zone 10 in South Africa. There, and in similar climates, the jade plant can grow as tall as a person. Other familiar succulents include the aeoniums and the kalanchoes.

Among succulents, too, adaptations are often combined for best advantage. Succulent leaves with a thick waxy cuticle give some echeverias a magical quality when they capture mercurial-looking droplets of water in their waxy-leafed rosettes. Other species display various protective coverings of hairs or spines and photosynthetic stems (the universally recognized cacti and their look-alike convergent euphorbias); tuberous roots and swollen stems (caudiciforms from more than a dozen different plant families); and a specialized physiology that allows them to keep their pores closed during the heat of the day to avoid water loss found in all succulents including the bromeliads and many orchids.

Gardening in the zone

Soils are as diverse as topography and rock types, but are typically neutral to basic in pH. This means soils may require acidification for plants such as azaleas. Neutral to basic soils can pose a problem for some Australian species which are, paradoxically, adapted to acid soils *and* drought. However,

normal soil-building practices using organic matter are usually ample for most plants.

Careful microclimate selection can afford success with some of the more challenging plants for this zone, such as *Lithodora diffusa* from North Africa and Mediterranean Europe with its gentian-blue star-shaped flowers. Members of the Proteaceae family from South Africa and western Australia may require generous application of iron sulfate or other acidifying measures in the garden. Plant pests and diseases are rarely a problem these days given proper culture and selection of appropriate disease-resistant varieties.

Earth here is so kind,
that just tickle her with a hoe and
she laughs with a harvest.
DOUGLAS JENBOLD, 1803–1857

Zone 11
40 to 50°F (4 to 10°C)

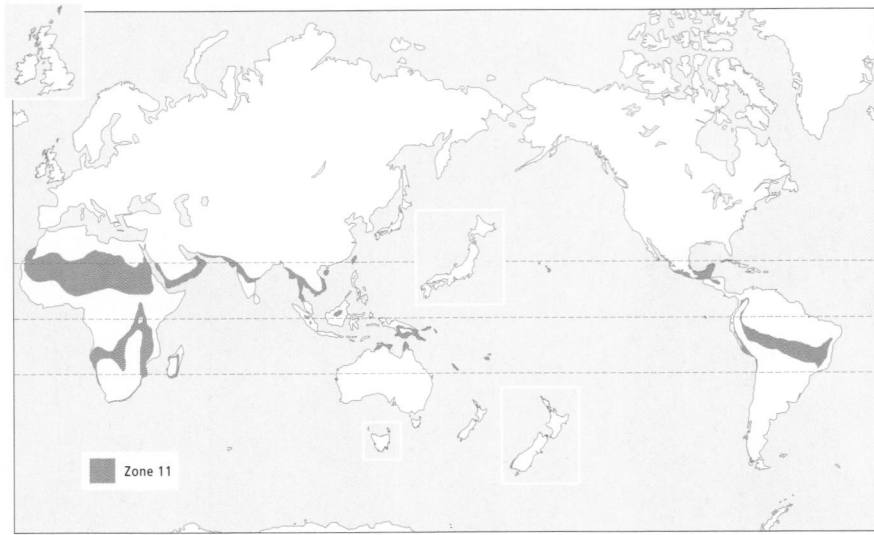

Zone 11

Below: This remarkable plant is a member of the Nepenthes genus, commonly known as pitcher plants. These carnivorous plants have large specialized leaves, "pitchers", whose rim is covered with slippery wax.

Of the twelve hardiness zones, Zones 11 and 12 represent tropical areas where frost, or even severe chilling, are never issues. Zone 11 is distinguished from its warmer counterpart, however, by the potential for very cool weather, where it is not astonishing for temperatures to fall below 50°F (10°C).

As this zone covers the transition from warm temperate and subtropical climates to tropical equatorial, its climate and plant life are far from uniform. Zone 11 includes three distinct regional types: cooler montane areas near the equator; cool tropical lowlands more distant from the equator (nearer the Tropic of Capricorn in the South and the Tropic of Cancer in the North); and certain oceanic islands outside the tropics. Consequently, vegetation native to Zone 11 has many biogeographic

The forest is not merely trees and shrubs. It is not land. It is another element.

H. M. TOMLINSON, 1873–1958

affinities, and varies greatly: from plants characteristic of wet tropical rainforest found near the equator, to those more at home in desert and scrub, such as is found along the twentieth parallel of Africa.

Mountainous tropics

In equatorial mountain areas such as Nairobi, Kenya and Caracas, Venezuela, the day to night temperature differential will be significant; as much as 18 to 22°F (10 to 12°C). For example, in Caracas, the January average daily maximum of 75°F (24°C) yields to an average daily minimum of 56°F (13°C); in Nairobi the difference is equally as marked. The average high for January is 77°F (25°C), while the average low is 54°F (12°C). However, the temperature tends to be moderate throughout the year. In many equatorial mountain areas, rainfall may be high, but in many places patterns of rainfall will often create a distinct "summer"– that is, dry season.

If accompanied by high rainfall throughout the year, such as in the sub-mountain and mountainous areas of Central and South America, the vegetation can be rife with epiphytic orchids such as *Miltoniopsis, Sobralia,* and *Odontoglossum,* as well as bromeliads such as *Guzmania* and *Aechmea.* These habitats frequently involve cloud forest (areas drenched by mist and condensation from low clouds), which further increases the density of epiphytes. Cloud forests also occur in limited areas of Africa, though epiphytes are less evident. In Tanzania for example, the African violet is a native of the mountain regions of the zone. Though not as moist, the high ground of Ethiopia is the native habitat for coffee *(Coffea arabica),* the cultivation or which characterizes both Zones 10 and 11 today.

Cool tropical lowlands

On the non-equatorial edges of the zone, the climate is subtropical and warm-temperate. Unlike the mountain equatorial zones that have a moderate climate and moisture regimen, the cooler temperatures near the Tropic of Cancer or the Tropic of Capricorn arrive seasonally. This cooler tropical climate also occurs away from the equator where maritime influence is great, especially on islands, such as Malta (35°N), and Bermuda and Madeira (32°N).

Areas of the zone closer to the cooler tropics are often characterized by marked dry seasons, as in Calcutta in India. One expects seasonal forest to be less layered and not as tall as wet forest, with a higher presence of deciduous material.

Many locations classified as Zone 11 receive sparse or no rainfall and are desert, as in parts of tropical Africa, such as Faya-Largeau in Chad, and Khartoum in Sudan, Namibia in southwest Africa, or Antofagasto in Chile. From the desert of southern Saudi Arabia come frankincense *(Boswellia sacra)* and myrrh *(Commiphora myrrha),* and one encounters the fabulous *Welwitschia mirabilis* in Namibia, along the southwestern coast of Africa where the heat of this zone is cooled by ocean currents.

Gardening in the zone

Horticulturally (as contrasted with the warmer Zone 12), one recognizes wet areas of Zone 11 for their ability to support cultivation of some temperate garden plants. Roses, evergreen azaleas *(Rhodendron* spp.*)*, and hydrangeas survive but are not at their best, while nasturtiums *(Tropaeolum)* and impatiens, which do not thrive in Zone 12, will perform well. Cool-crop vegetable production and cut flower production begin in Zone 11, both industries developing yet more thoroughly in cooler zones at yet higher altitudes. Dry climates in Zone 11 will support a Mediterranean plant palette, or succulent plants and dryland gardening such as one encounters in more subtropical areas.

Being transitional, Zone 11 is best identified in contrast with Zones 10 and 12. Tropical plants that can be cultivated successfully in Zone 10 (at the risk of an occasional killing frost) should thrive in Zone 11. Plants from dry tropical and subtropical climates will likely thrive in this zone as compared to Zone 12.

However, the most cool-sensitive of lowland tropical plants, especially plants that benefit from warm nights, like cocoa *(Theobroma cacao)* or breadfruit *(Artocarpus)*, or even vanilla *(Vanilla planifolia)* and the various spice trees, are not at their best in this zone. One would not plan to grow true Zone 12 plants such as sealing-wax palm *(Cyrtostachys renda)* or pride of Burma *(Amherstia nobilis)* in the landscape. On the other hand, Zone 11 gardeners can bask in the glory of fuchsias and sensational aroids, such as the *Anthurium veitchii* and *A. warocqueanum,* sometimes referred to as the king and queen anthuriums, respectively, due to their magnificent foliage.

For those who have a moist climate, this is truly the orchid and epiphyte zone, where thousands of species and cultivars of orchids and bromeliads can be grown with modest effort. Gardeners in drier areas can enjoy the pleasure of growing many succulents and honorary succulents that are problematic in more temperate climates, such as *Adansonia.* Landscapes with good rainfall, but a strong dry season, would well support material from the seasonal savannas of Africa (such as *Cussonia* species and *Coccinea*) and South America *(Tabebuia, Jacaranda),* as well as Mexico and into Central America *(Cochlospermum)*—much of which is easily found in the trade.

Even though an incredibly wide range of plant material exists that is completely appropriate for Zone 11, comparatively little effort has been dedicated to "bringing plants into cultivation." It would be exciting and practical to see more work dedicated to the logical and sensitive development of a variety of appropriate plant palates and horticultural techniques for this zone.

Zone 12 50 to 60°F (10 to 16°C)

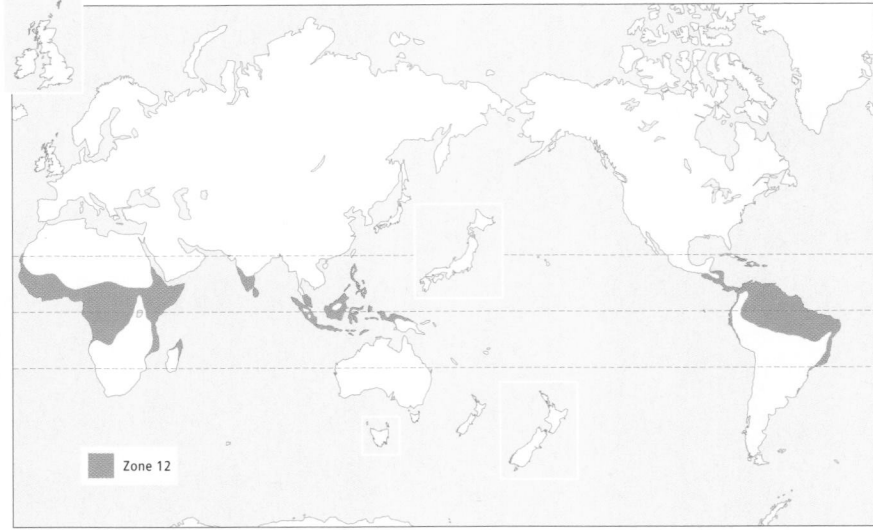

Zone 12

Zone 12 covers much of the area north and south of the equator to latitude 20°. It includes vast regions in the tropical lowlands of South America, the Caribbean, Africa, northern Madagascar, tropical Asia, and Hawaii. Of all the zones, it is the most conducive to plant growth, experiencing neither frosts nor severe dry seasons. Maximum temperature ranges from 79 to 100°F (26 to 38°C) and minimum temperature ranges from a pleasant 50 to 60°F (10 to 16°C). Relative humidity averages at about 80 percent, dropping to around 60 percent in the drier months during the day. Night temperatures often remain above 50°F (10°C) in the lowlands, but drop below this in mountainous regions, which thus are rated Zone 11.

Annual rainfall in the ever-wet tropics exceeds 80 in (200 cm). Although monthly averages vary from year to year, the driest months have not less than 24 in (60 cm) of rain and the dry season usually does not persist for more than three or four consecutive months. Rainfall patterns vary with topography, prevailing winds, and distance from the coast, as well as yearly fluctuations.

Below: This bromeliad Tillandsia lieboldiana, produces purple and red flowers. It is shown here at the Jardîn Botânico Lankester, near Cartago, Costa Rica.

A combination of high rainfall and high temperatures results in heavily weathered soils (frequently red earth laterites) with low fertility. The exception is volcanic soils, which, for example, support intensive wet rice culture in Java and the Philippines.

A vibrant and rich ecosystem

The forests in Zone 12 are some of the most species-rich ecosystems in the world, being home to an estimated one-third of the world's 249,500 species of flowering plants, with many species yet to be found. Vegetation types are primarily determined by water regime and soil and can vary from swamp forests and rainforest in areas of year-round rain, to more open semi-deciduous forest in areas with a pronounced dry season.

Most plants are evergreen but few plants are truly aseasonal, that is, grow at a continuous rate, exceptions being papaya *(Carica papaya),* pineapple *(Ananas comosus),* and banana *(Musa* cultivars*),* among the tropical fruits. Even for herbs, perennial rather than annual is the norm. The exception are weeds, some of which are super-annuals with life cycles as short as eight weeks, so six to seven generations exist in a year. Weeds, however, depend on humans to create ephemeral disturbed conditions. Only a handful can compete in the rainforest.

Although there are broad similarities between the plant families of South America, Africa, and tropical Asia, at the genus and particularly at the species level there are more differences than similarities. The mahogany, the rubber tree, sapodillas, and fig families are found in tropical rainforests across the zone, as are the myrtle, laurel, and nutmeg families, although Africa has less of these last three families. Shrubs belonging to the acanthus and tibouchina families and herbs like the aroid, African violet, orchids, fern, and spikemoss families also grow across the zone. Each continent has more of some families than others: for example, South America has more bromeliads and heliconias; Asia is noted for dipterocarps and gingers, and Africa for the cacao family.

[The] countryside is rather like a rich feast, with a little too much of everything good.
GEORGE WOODCOCK 1912–1995

Reaching for the light

Most of the plants above grow in the multi-layered tropical rainforests. The topmost layer is formed of scattered giant emergent trees, such as the dipterocarps, which grow 100–165 ft (30–50 m) tall. Underneath is the continuous high to middle tree-canopy layer with trees of 35–80 ft (10–24 m) tall, which include fruit and nut trees like durian, rambutan, and the brazil nut, followed by a third canopy layer of smaller and immature trees of the upper canopy. Characteristic of these rainforest trees are giant buttress roots that anchor them to the ground and those that flower and fruit from the trunk, such as the jackfruit and cannonball tree, which have weighty fruits too heavy to be borne on twigs.

Conditions below the tree canopy are extremely uniform for the shrub and herb layers. Here temperatures are about five degrees lower than outside the forest, and the relative humidity is frequently 100 percent. Little wind and only about 1 to 3 percent of sunlight penetrates to the forest floor. Hundreds of species with brilliantly colored or variegated leaves, like begonias, calatheas, and peperomias, thrive in the damp and deep shade.

Large woody climbers (lianas), such as the jade vine or garlic vine, whose thick woody vine-like stems carry photosynthesizing leaf growth up into the canopy, and strangler figs, add to the complexity. So do the epiphytes, which includes many orchids (a large tropical family that comprises about 10 percent of all flowering plant species) and ferns growing in the high canopy. Characteristic, too, are the giant monocots, such as the palms, pandangs *(Pandanus),* bananas, and heliconias.

In semi-deciduous forest, the emergent trees are smaller (up to 100 ft/30 m tall) and less frequent than in rainforest. About a quarter of them are decidous for periods of a few weeks. In some areas, the canopy is open with grasses and herbs in the ground layer. Several tree species, like teak and *Albizia,* also grow in monsoon regions.

Many plantation crops of the zone are grown outside their native regions to escape indigenous pests and diseases. For example, the major world production of oil palm *(Elaeis guineensis),* a native of West Africa, and rubber *(Hevea brasiliensis),* a native from South America, is in Asia. Bananas and cloves *(Syzygium aromaticum)* from Asia are more widely grown in the Caribbean and Zanzibar, respectively.

Above: Dipterocarp trees, in the wild, Borneo. Some of these remarkable trees can grow to 200 ft (60 m) in the wild. They are important in Malaysia, where they provide the country's main source of timber.

Left: Plumeria rubra is native to Central America, Mexico, and Venezuela. It makes a lovely specimen tree in tropical zones, and there are numerous cultivars. 'Rosy Dawn', shown here, bears yellow flowers flushed with pink.

A zone to think big

Gardeners in Zone 12 can think big with majestic flowering trees, massive climbers, giant palms, and a superb display of herbs. Plants from South America such as the rain tree *(Albizia saman)* and royal palms *(Roystonea)* are grown across the zone. So, too, are the African tulip tree *(Spathodea campanulata)* from Africa, the yellow flame tree *(Peltophorum pterocarpum)* and queen crape myrtle *(Lagerstroemia speciosa)* from Asia, and the royal poinciana *(Delonix regia)* from Madagascar.

Canopy plants such as orchids can be grown in shade houses. Most understory forest plants, such as aroids, need deep shade. Provided understory plants adapt to low humidity, they also make ideal house plants and the spectacular foliage of begonias and monsteras, for example, provide year-round interest.

Heavy rain and high temperatures can lead to heavy nutrient-depleted soil. Trees help to mitigate the beating of raindrops on the soil and so reduce run off. Organic fertilizers and mulch also help to maintain soil fertility. Plants that require a distinct dry season, such as jacaranda *(Jacaranda mimosifolia)* and Indian senna *(Cassia fistula)* will not give a showy flowering display. Hybridization has overcome this in bougainvilleas. Plants that require a dry resting season, such as *Curcuma* species, may not flower or even survive beyond the first season. For cacti, a clear roof and free draining soil is necessary to prevent their roots rotting in high rainfall conditions.

Outside the zone, greenhouses are needed in frost regions, as well as lighting to compensate for shorter daylight hours, the lack of which accounts for the spindly growth of some tropical plants, such as papaya.

Plant Nomenclature

It is remarkable that a naming system devised over 250 years ago should still be the best way for people around the world to talk about a plant, confident in the knowledge that everyone will know exactly which plant is being discussed. Common names, though often very evocative, are not reliable as they vary from place to place, country to country, and language to language. For example, in the British Isles, the plant called the bluebell in Scotland is not the same as the bluebell of England. The only unambiguous and reliable name for any plant is its Latin-based botanical name.

The history of botanical nomenclature

Early in human history it was found useful to know which plants were good for food, which were poisonous, and so on. And it was soon noticed that these plants possessed certain consistent features by which they could be recognised. To begin with this information was passed on by word of mouth but eventually began to be written down. When the first printed books appeared in Europe Latin was the international language used by scholars. By the eighteenth century the Latin names of plants had generally become short descriptions that enabled people to

Right: Carolus Linnaeus, 1707–1792, Swedish botanist, naturalist, and explorer. His Species Plantarium established the use of a binomial naming system that could be applied to all species, including humans. Portrait by Johan Henrik Scheffel, 1690–1781.

Below: The conventions of the binomial system are simple and few: Rosa banksiae, the parent of this cultivar 'Lutea', was named after Lady Banks, the wife of Sir Joseph Banks. Though a proper noun, the specific epithet is always in lower case.

recognise plants and distinguish one from another. For instance, the famous Swedish biologist Carolus Linnaeus gave a *Gladiolus* species the name *Gladiolus foliis linearibus, floribus distantibus, coroallarum tubo limbis longiore* (Gladiolus with very narrow leaves, flowers widely spaced, and the tube of the corolla longer than the width of the upper spreading part). At the time this brief description was sufficient to distinguish this plant from all other known species of *Gladiolus*. However, even Linnaeus soon found this convention cumbersome when speaking about plants and also very awkward when compiling indices to his books. In an attempt to simplify the matter he gave each plant a number, so that students, scientists, and others could refer to it simply. For instance, the *Gladiolus* mentioned above became '*Gladiolus* no. 4', but numbers in general are harder to remember than words and, in any case, the scheme was of no use to anyone who did not have Linnaeus's book. His next step was to add a second word instead of a number, often taking the word from the Latin descriptive phrase. In the case of *Gladiolus* no. 4 it was *angustus*, a Latin word meaning narrow in reference to its leaves. Thus '*Gladiolus*' is the name of the genus and '*angustus*,' is known as the 'specific' epithet.

The plant thus acquired a two-word or binomial name, *Gladiolus angustus*, and although he was not the first to use such binomials, Linnaeus used them from 1745 onwards, before applying them consistently to the whole of the plant kingdom known to him in his *Species Plantarium* of 1753. The principal object of this book, however, was not to introduce binomial nomenclature but to provide a concise useable survey of all known plants. By writing in Latin he made his work known immediately to the whole learned world of his day. Had he written in Swedish his work would probably have passed unnoticed.

And a success his system proved to be. In the tenth edition of his *Systema Naturae*, published in 1758, he gave binomials to all known animal species including us, *Homo sapiens*, 'man the wise'.

Botanical names of plants are printed in italics or at least in a typeface different from that of the rest of the text. Also, if there is no chance of confusion, the name of the genus is abbreviated to the initial letter the second and subsequent times the name is used. The name of the genus should always have a capital initial letter and that of the specific epithet should be in lower case, even when derived from a proper noun or a person's name.

Linnaeus worked at a time when exploration and colonialism had made it possible for him to examine plants and animals from many parts of the world. Even then the task was immense and, in all, he coined Latin or Latin-form names for roughly 4,400 species of animals and 7,700 species of plants. Had he lived today, when over 800,000 animal species and more than 260,000 vascular plants (plants with internal conducting systems) have been described and named in accordance with his unambiguous and internationally understandable system, the whole enterprise would have been impossible for one man to complete. As it was, he had planned to share the task of making known what he considered all the works of the Maker in an orderly manner with his friend Petrus Artede. They divided up the work, entering into a pact that if one died the other would finish the task. As it turned out Artede fell into a canal in Amsterdam in 1736 and drowned, with only a book on the fishes published, leaving Linnaeus to deal with everything else.

How the naming system works

Linnaeus's writings are therefore the starting point for the nomenclature of many groups of organisms, plants being just one. As well as establishing the recognized system for naming and describing them, Linnaeus also discussed a hierarchy of groups or ranks that share common characters, but he never really used them. Subsequently naturalists have not only grouped the species into genera, but also the genera into families, the families into orders, the orders into classes, and the classes into kingdoms. More categories have been inter-polated into this hierarchy as is shown below for the classification of a well-known *Rhododendron* species.

Not surprisingly, considering the scientific advances of the past 250 years, the vascular plants are now

Kingdom	Plantae
Division	Angiospermae
Class	Dicotyledonae
Subclass	Dilleniidae
Order	Ericales
Family	Ericaceae
Subfamily	Rhododendroideae
Tribe	Rhododendreae
Genus	*Rhododendron*
Subgenus	Hymenanthes
Section	Ponticum
Subsection	Arborea
Species	*Rhododendron arboreum*
Subspecies	*Rhododendron arboreum* subsp. *delavayi*
Variety	*Rhododendron arboreum* subsp. *delavayi* var. *delavayi*

Below: Rhododendron arboreum *subsp.* delavayi

classified on the basis of characteristics very different from those employed by Linnaeus. They are divided into two major groups, the Spermatophyta, the seed plants, and the Pteridophyta, plants that reproduce by means of spores. The Spermatophyta in turn are divided into two, the Angiospermae (usually loosely referred to as flowering plants), with 249,500 species in over 13,100 genera in 405 families, and the Gymnospermae, containing some 840 species in 86 genera in 17 families. The Gymnospermae, a diverse group of plants whose seeds are not enclosed in carpels and thus do not produce flowers, are divided into 4 groups: the Pinopsida (conifers), Cycadopsida (cycads), Ginkgoopsida *(Ginkgo)* and the Gnetopsida *(Ephedra, Gnetum,* and *Welwitschia).* The Pteridophyta—spore-producing plants—with 9,800 species in 230 or so genera in 38 families include the Filicopsida (ferns), Lycopsida (clubmosses), Psilotopsida (psilophytes), and Equisetopsida (horsetails).

Above: Though Linnaeus aspired to classify all living things, the task was done by many—with inevitable overlaps. For 100 years this plant was known as Rhododendron aucklandii, the name given it by J. D. Hooker in his Rhododendrons of the Sikkim Himalayas, published in 1851. It was later discovered, however, that a surgeon in India, Robert Wight, published a description of the plant in 1847, and named it R. griffithianum, by which it is now known.

there can never be any doubt as to the plant to which the name applies. The type specimens of plants are therefore almost invariably dried specimens kept in a herbarium. This is why taxonomic botanists often have to spend more time with dead dried specimens than with living plants.

Horticulturalists, gardeners, and others are disturbed upon discovering that the name by which they have known a plant for years has been changed. The naming of plants is governed by *The International Code of Botanical Nomenclature*, the aim of which is to provide a stable method of naming plant groups, avoiding and rejecting the use of names which may cause error and ambiguity. Among the principles of the *Code* are those which state that each plant or group of plants may have only one correct name and that where more than one botanical name has been applied, it is the earliest to have been published in print which is correct.

Botanical names may appear to change if it turns out that a plant in cultivation has been misidentified. As an example, for many years a South African composite grown in European rock gardens was called *Euryops evansii*. But when it was examined critically it was found not to be that species at all, but really *Euryops acraeus*, which is the name used for it today. Names also change when research reveals that plants should be classified differently. For example, names change if a species is moved from the genus in which it was originally placed, or when two formerly recognized species are shown not to be sufficiently distinct and are merged, or when it has been shown that one species should be split into two or more. Recent work on the iris family has shown that species of *Acidanthera* are really species of *Gladiolus* and that species of *Anomatheca* belong in *Freesia*. Nowadays the use of DNA sequencing is giving taxonomic botanists a more reliable picture of the relationships between plants and will undoubtedly have a major effect on the future naming of plants.

In the case of the well-known plant names which have been widely and unambiguously used for many years, such that changing of them would be costly as well as destabilizing, exceptions can be made, and a name conserved. For example, a striking example of where international agreement has had happy consequences concerns plants originally placed in the genus *Chrysanthemum,* which have been undergone various classifications and names since the time of Linnaeus. The most confronting of these changes came from the discovery 30 or so years ago that the perennial garden chrysanthemums did not belong in the same genus as the cultivated annual species. This meant that if the

On the whole it is only the names of genera, species, and sometimes the families that are of interest to most horticulturalists. At times, though, the ranks below that of species are of significance from a horticultural point of view. A species may be divided into subspecies when its characters vary noticeably across a wide geographic range, as in the case of *Rhododendron arboreum* given previously. Likewise, a variety differs in a minor but distinct way from the typical species. The lowest rank of all is that known as "form." It is rarely used nowadays but in the past has been applied to plants showing very minor differences from the typical species, such as variations in flower or leaf color.

Cumbersome though it might appear, it sometimes, though mercifully rarely, happens that names in all three of these minor categories are used in order of rank in the name of a plant.

In order for a plant name to be accepted it must be of Latin form and be published in a recognized journal or book along with a description in Latin based on a particular specimen, known as the type specimen, which must be preserved in a recognized museum or herbarium. This ensures that

A plant is completely named when it is furnished with a generic and a specific name.

LINNAEUS, 1707–1778

annuals were still to be called *Chrysanthemum*, then the perennials would have to be placed in a separate genus, for which the earliest correct name is *Dendranthema*. Reflecting widespread concern over this, the committee accepted that the name *Chrysanthemum* should accommodate the perennial garden plants, much to the relief of gardeners everywhere. But the unavoidable consequence of this is that the annual species, which still have to be put in a separate genus, have to be renamed *Xanthophthalmum,* the earliest name for them outside *Chrysanthemum.*

Naming hybrids and cultivars

The names of hybrid plants in the wild or in cultivation (where their parentage is known), have an '×' inserted between the generic and specific epithets. For example, the oranges and grapefruits are hybrids between the shaddock or pomelo *(Citrus maxima)* and the mandarin *(Citrus reticulata)* and are included under the hybrid name, *Citrus × aurantium.* There are other conventions for the names of plants found only in cultivation. These plants are variants of wild species or plants of hybrid origin and are known collectively as cultivated varieties or cultivars. The use of the word "variety" for these plants must be avoided as this is used for a category in the accepted hierarchy of botanical classification outlined above.

To avoid confusion in the naming of cultivars, any person thinking of giving a name to a new cultivar should consult the *International Code for the Nomenclature of Cultivated Plants,* a set of recommendations along the lines of the *International Code of Botanical Nomenclature.* Under the rules of this *Code,* the full name of a cultivar is the accepted Latin botanical name of the plant followed by what is known as the cultivar epithet. To distinguish them from botanical names, cultivar epithets are not written in italics and are enclosed within single quotation marks, for example *Gardenia augusta* 'Magnifica'. Double quotation marks or the abbreviations "cv." and "var." should not be used to distinguish cultivar names. It is usual for all words, with the exception of articles or prepositions, in the cultivar name to have an initial capital letter, for example *Rhododendron* 'Beauty of Littleworth'. Amongst its other recommendations, the *Code* also proposes that new cultivar names should consist of no more than ten syllables and no more than thirty characters overall, excluding spaces and demarcation marks.

These simple practices can be used by breeders everywhere. Unfortunately, some nurserymen tend not to use recognized cultivar names when they consider them to be unsuitable for selling purposes and give trade names to their plants instead. While these trade names may help with sales, they can also be confusing. There are many instances of the same plant appearing in different catalogs under several names, as unsatisfactory as using common names outside of anything but a small area. Hopefully, with increased awareness of the work of Linnaeus and the *International Code for the Nomenclature of Cultivated Plants,* greater appreciation will develop for this remarkable system.

Left: Tulipa, *Lily-flowered Group,* 'Queen of Sheba'. *Owing to the thousands of cultivars now available, tulips are divided into 15 broad groups, such as Lily-flowered, as well as given a specific cultivar name.*

Below: Gardenia augusta 'Magnifica'. *The cultivar name differs from a botanical epithet in its style of printing. It has initial capitals, is in a different typeface, and is usually enclosed in single quotation marks.*

Plant Geography, Discovery, and Classification

Right: In Medieval times, inconsistencies such as the problem of "extinct" plants and animals known only from fossils were explained away by suggestions that they had merely changed their distribution and would be found alive again once the world had been fully explored.

Below: Spore-producing plants include horsetails like Equisetum arvense, *ferns, and club mosses.*

In Medieval times it was widely thought that the world's animals and plants were stable entities, unchanging over time and place. Many attempts were made to match local European plants with those in the Bible, for example. With greater traveling, however, it was found that no such homogeneity existed. Since that time, evolutionary theories, allowing for change in time and space, have been proposed. Darwin's theory of evolution by Natural Selection, formulated in the 1850s, is now accepted so that, although there is still much to learn, we can now interpret fossils and modern plant distributions to explain the history of groups of plants.

Origin of ferns and seed plants

The oldest known land plants with vascular systems are fossils from the Devonian period (some 370 million years ago). Traces of their form can still be seen in some modern ferns, notably species of *Psilotum* found in tropical and other warm parts of the world. Today's ferns, like those ancient plants, still reproduce by spores spread by wind. It was not the ferns that were to form the ecosystems in which humans evolved, however, but those plants derived from ancient fern-like groups: the seed-producing plants.

A seed, in essence, is a tiny plant in suspended animation sealed up in an environment-proof coat. It is formed from fertilization of an egg in an ovule held on an adult plant. In contrast, fertilization of the egg of a spore plant takes place in the open and requires water for the sperms to travel to it. This crucial evolutionary difference gave seed plants the edge. Though many seed plant groups have died out, modern seed plants appear to be more closely related to one another than they are to modern spore plants. Today, the most significant, both ecologically and economically, of the seed plants are the conifers and, above all, the angiosperms, or the "flowering plants."

Left: The genus Liriodendron *has only two species. L. tulipifera, left, is found east of the Mississippi River, USA, while L. chinense is native to China.*

Plant distribution

The shearing apart in the Cretaceous Period (about 100 million years ago) of what are now the continents of Australia and Antarctica and what was to become India and finally Africa, from South America, coincided with the divergence of the angiosperms away from other seed plants and into a number of lineages. From this time, there are fossils of plants, which, if they occurred today, could be put in families we now recognize in the world's flora. The effect of these continental movements on plant distribution is only now being fully assessed, but it is clear that, despite their seed-dispersal mechanisms, some groups of plants failed to reach some of the receding continents. Certain families are found, for example, only in the Americas or with very few recent extensions to Africa, as is the case with Cactaceae and Bromeliaceae. Even very widespread families like Asteraceae have scarcely reached New Caledonia.

On to these basic patterns is superimposed the effects of climatic change of more recent times, notably those of the advancing and contracting ice sheets. These have pushed apart, and then allowed to come back together again in some cases, whole assemblages of plants. The apparent similarity of species of *Liriodendron* and *Magnolia* in the floras of the eastern USA and of East Asia can be explained in this way.

Classification

To comprehend the great diversity of the world's flora, past and present, a system of classification is essential. The great age of cataloging the world's animals and plants was during the eighteenth century, which saw, among other things, the publication of Linnaeus's great system of binomial plant classification, *Species Plantarium*, in 1753.

The system of classification established by Linnaeus hinged on the numbers of stamens and pistils in the flowers. It contains several groupings of plants we recognize today, for example, most temperate legumes (Fabaceae) fall into Decandria Monogynia (ten stamens and one pistil). However, also in that group are many other plants we would not now consider closely allied. The reason is that this "artificial" system is based on the overriding importance of two basic features of the plants and, at this level of classification, ignores all other evidence. This system was never fully acceptable to the French school of science, which maintained "natural" systems invented before Linnaeus's time.

These natural systems attempted to assess all features of the plants. For example, many tropical plants in the family Fabaceae have different numbers of stamens but the "look" of the plants strongly suggests they belong together. Michel Adanson (1727–1806), and his fellow countryman, Adrien de Jussieu, based in Paris, established improved natural systems. By this time, most of the northern European flora had been discovered and named. From the sixteenth century onward, plants had been preserved as herbarium specimens and, therefore, it was no longer necessary to have to describe a new species from a living plant. The number of descriptions grew: from dried and living plants from the Mediterranean, Caribbean and North America, the Near East, Russia, and North and South Africa. In fact, European herbaria contained materials from tropical Southeast Asia and China, and even Australia, before 1700.

Plant introductions

People were interested in importing plants to grow as well as to classify. As living plants of the new species were introduced throughout the nineteenth century, there were horticultural fashions for North American plants, for Cape plants, Australian and, later, Chinese. By the end of that century, plants from almost every country in the world were being grown commercially in North America and Europe.

The First World War brought an end to this great accumulation. Introductions were now concentrated on hardy plants and more focused on the mass market rather than the exclusive connoisseur. Nonetheless, the rich and vainglorious, as well as public institutions, continued to support horticultural expeditions, especially to China and the Himalayas, the Andes, and the Near East.

Hybridization

Throughout the great period of introductions, gardeners were selecting forms of plants with bigger or more brightly colored flowers or for larger or better-flavored fruits and so on. Although considered to be tampering with the work of the Maker, hybridization was championed by the Reverend William Herbert, Dean of Manchester, UK. He was an important influence on the young Charles Darwin who made many hybrids himself and wrote about them at length in his *Origin of Species* (1859). In fact, Darwin's discussions with breeders gave him much evidence for his theory of Natural Selection, and he considered "artificial" selection as merely an extension of an all-pervading phenomenon.

What remains to be done?

Despite all this botanical and horticultural effort, new plants are still being introduced into horticulture all the time. But there are also plants not only to be introduced but also to be found. In developing countries, there are thousands of species of angiosperms still to be described. Many are known just as herbarium specimens and, no doubt, some of them will become extinct due to clearing of their native habitats before they are even named.

Botanists, skilled horticulturists, patrons, and gardeners are needed to help collect, describe, and thereby preserve, the world's plants for the benefit of all.

Above: Charles Darwin, 1809–1882, English naturalist and author of Origin of Species, *which established the theory of Natural Selection. (Painting, 1858.)*

Top: Improved greenhouse technology in the nineteenth century led to the scouring of tropical regions for orchids, ferns, and other exotica. This engraving from that century is of The Victoria Glasshouse, Van Houtte Gardens, Netherlands.

Plant Groups

Over 20,000 plants are included in this book, choice enough for a lifetime. The following pages introduce all the major plant groups, from trees to carnivorous plants, defining the characteristics of each group, and exploring their potential value in the garden.

TREES AND SHRUBS

Throughout much of the world, trees surround us. They populate forests, dot woodlands, and cover stream banks and mountainsides alike. Only in the most arid and coldest of climates do trees disappear from the landscape, due to insufficient water or warmth for adequate growth and metabolism. Trees vary remarkably—not only in the various kinds that populate the planet, but also in their shapes, sizes, and habitats.

Right: A deciduous tree, Magnolia × loebneri is a prolific flowerer, adaptable to a wide range of soils. The cultivar 'Leonard Messel' is especially valued for its winter deep rose lilac buds and pink narrow-petaled flowers.

Trees are defined as woody perennial plants that are distinguished from other woody plants, such as shrubs, by the presence of usually, but not always, a single woody stem—the trunk. Most trees are long lived, with some living for many centuries, such as the bristlecone pines (*Pinus longaeva*) of California that reach ages of 4,500 years or more. Some trees attain great heights (reaching over 100 meters tall), such as the redwoods (*Sequoia sempervirens*) of California and the Australian mountain ashes (*Eucalyptus regnans*); other trees might grow to only 3 ft (0.9 m) tall due to harsh climates.

Below: This rhododendron shrub makes a dramatic impact in a garden. Both species and hybrids are cultivated as ornamental plants, valued for their masses of colorful flowers.

Trees inhabit virtually all climates and soils known. From the Australian eucalypts that can tolerate the most nutrient-poor of soils to conifers such as Monterey cypress (*Cupressus macrocarpa*) and Japanese black pine (*Pinus thunbergii*) that can tolerate ocean salt-spray, there is a tree for every garden setting. Tolerances of soil pH vary with species too. In the USA, eastern red cedar (*Juniperus virginiana*) grows on soils ranging from highly acidic (pH 4.0 or less) to alkaline (pH 8.0 and above). Other trees are less forgiving, and will tolerate only a narrow range in soil pH. In the temperate zone, cold hardiness dictates which trees can be grown, while in the tropics, daily and seasonal heat loads are the main factors when selecting trees. For every environmental stress or limitation (heat, cold, drought, pH, barren soils, fire, salinity, air pollution, limited space, bright or dim light), there is a tree that is adapted to this condition.

Trees can be deciduous (dropping leaves in autumn, or in response to drought) or evergreen (holding leaves year-round, or nearly so). They can bear exquisitely beautiful flowers, as do the magnolias, cherries, and dogwoods familiar to cool-climate gardeners, and the orchid trees, trumpet trees, and wattles of the tropics and subtropics. At the other end of the spectrum, are trees whose value resides in their shade and architectural form, rather than showy flowers. These include the oaks, beeches, birches, conifers, and maples of the temperate zones to mahoganies, banyan tree, Norfolk Island pine, and rubber trees of tropical latitudes. It is hard to imagine a world without such beautiful flowering trees as southern magnolia (*Magnolia grandiflora*), Japanese flowering cherry (*Prunus serrulata*), flowering dogwood (*Cornus florida*), Hong Kong orchid tree (*Bauhinia blakeana*), golden trumpet tree (*Tabebuia chrysantha*), and silver wattle (*Acacia dealbata*). In autumn, trees such as sugar maple (*Acer saccharum*) and sweet gum (*Liquidambar styraciflua*) bring burnished golds and reds to the garden. Similarly, there is little that can match the beauty of the bark of trees like paperbark maple (*Acer griseum*), snow gum (*Eucalyptus pauciflora*), crape myrtle (*Lagerstroemia indica*), Japanese stewartia (*Stewartia pseudocamellia*), lacebark pine (*Pinus bungeana*), and Persian ironwood (*Parrotia persica*). Other trees provide a unique place for solace and reflection, such as live oak (*Quercus virginiana*), European beech (*Fagus sylvatica*), Himalayan birch (*Betula utilis*), maidenhair tree (*Ginkgo biloba*), Japanese maple (*Acer palmatum*), West Indies mahogany (*Swietenia mahagoni*), silver tree fern (*Cyathea dealbata*), banyan (*Ficus benghalensis*), Norfolk Island pine (*Araucaria heterophylla*), and para rubber tree (*Hevea brasiliensis*).

Right: Careful selection of trees and shrubs of differing stature, as well as those with novel growth forms, can create beautiful gardens filled with showy woody plants.

Equalling trees in their variation in form, adaptability, and stress tolerance, are the shrubs. Defined as woody perennial plants that possess multiple stems arising from a common point (this point is known as the crown), shrubs can range in size from less than 12 in (30 cm) to 20 ft (6 m) tall. Not merely existing as "miniature trees," shrubs instead display completely different growth habits—some can "creep" or "sucker", such as *Deutzia* and *Viburnum tinus*, while others rarely or never spread in this fashion. Many shrubs, such as *Choisya,* are very tolerant of harsh pruning, wherein the entire crown can be cut back to ground level—a natural adaptation to fire or browsing by animals.

A garden is incomplete without the woody backbone afforded by shrubs. From broadleaf evergreens to deciduous shrubs, from flowering shrubs to those valued chiefly for their foliage or twigs, the diversity among shrubs is immense. Cool and warm temperate-climate gardeners only have to think of the viburnums, weigelas, forsythias, roses, hydrangeas, rhododendrons, and spireas; while those from warmer climates recall the gardenias, camellias, azaleas, daphnes, sun roses *(Helianthemum),* rock roses *(Cistus),* bottlebrushes *(Callistemon)* and aucubas. Gardens of the tropics have an even larger selection of shrubs from which to choose—Natal plum *(Carissa macrocarpa),* flame of the woods *(Ixora coccinea),* tropical banksias, tea-trees *(Leptospermum),* proteas, and daisy bushes *(Olearia)* to name a scarce few.

An unlimited palette awaits the gardener daring enough to seek out the unusual and lesser grown shrubs. From the winter twigs of *Cornus sanguinea* 'Winter Beauty' to the bold flowers of king protea *(Protea cynaroides),* a garden cannot exist without shrubs.

Although today's gardens exist mostly within small spaces, there are many trees that are suited to these sites, and thoughtful selection will help ensure beautiful results. Given the multitude of selected and hybridized forms of trees that are now available, there is practically a limitless range of trees that we can use to beautify our gardens, local environment, and places in which we live.

ROSES IN THE GARDEN

ROSES are a very diverse group that include the Old Roses, mainly from the nineteenth century and before, and the more modern varieties from the last century. The bulk of Old Roses are summer flowering only and so are less popular than the more modern, often repeat flowering, roses. The latter will provide color for 4 to 5 months of the year in the UK, more in warmer areas. The Hybrid Musks, Rugosas, and the English Roses, which are hybrids between Old Roses and modern varieties, are especially valued for their long blooming season.

Traditionally, roses were planted in formal rose gardens, but gardeners are increasingly planting them in the less formal parts of the garden. They are more likely to plant roses either in rose borders or in mixed borders and, as long as fairly healthy varieties are planted, mixing the roses up with other plants will help to reduce or even eliminate the need to spray.

Another development is a new-found appreciation of the value of fragrance. Breeders have largely ignored fragrance for many decades but many gardeners are now seeking varieties specifically for their perfume, and many of the Old Roses and notably David Austin's English Roses among the Modern Roses are extremely fragrant.

Many people regard roses as needing a high level of care and attention, however they are generally extremely tough, reliable, and easy to grow. The most crucial requirement is a moist humus-rich soil. It is therefore sensible to incorporate a generous quantity of well-rotted manure or garden compost both before planting and as annual mulch each spring. Watering is particularly important in warm climates and will make all the difference between an average display and a very good one. Pruning is simple. Large-flowered (Hybrid Tea) Roses should be pruned hard but most others can be encouraged to form natural shrubby growth. It is a good idea to reduce their height by one-half to one-third. Having done this, it is then only necessary to remove dead or diseased stems or any old growth that is lacking in vigor.

If you haven't planted any roses in your garden then do try some. They have a natural charm and grace, are very versatile, and will give you a great deal of pleasure.

Above: 'Happy Child' is an English Rose, just one of the many Modern Shrub Roses.

ANNUALS AND PERENNIALS

At the heart of many garden displays are annuals, biennials, and perennials, which collectively offer an almost unrivaled choice of brilliantly colored blooms, across a wide range of garden situations.

At the height of summer, as myriad flowers jostle for light and space, the differences between annuals and perennials are not always obvious and plants such as poppies, delphiniums, and gypsophila have a foot in both camps. Their cultivation and life cycles, however, are very different. Annual plants have a frenetic life with only a short time to grow, flower, and set seed to ensure the next generation. They have no means of living through hard times, except as seed, so they must complete their life in a single season. Some flower, set seed, and die in just a few months—such flowers, known as ephemerals, include *Limnanthes* and *Malcolmia,* and are perfect for impatient gardeners.

There are annual representatives in most plant families and there is almost no limit to the range of colors and plant forms. While bright orange and yellow daisies may seem to predominate, seed catalogs will reveal pastel colors and many unusual flower forms. While marigolds and sunflowers seem homely and familiar, spidery cleomes (*Cleome hassleriana*) and azure blue heliophila (*Heliophila coronopifolia*) will satisfy even the most sophisticated of tastes. There are even annual climbers, such as sweet peas and morning glory.

Annuals are divided by gardeners into two categories: hardy and half-hardy. Hardy annuals tolerate frost, though severe cold may kill them. In regions with cold winters, they are usually sown in late spring straight into the ground where they are to bloom. Hardy annuals include calendula, larkspur, and Californian poppy (*Eschscholzia californica*). These provide one of the cheapest and quickest ways to fill the garden with color. Half-hardy annuals are usually raised from seed, with artificial heat in cold areas, and planted out when the danger of frost has passed. They may then continue flowering until the first frost of autumn cuts them down. Examples include marigolds, annual asters, and nemesia.

Not all plants we treat as annuals are strictly annuals. Many are tender perennials but because they flower so quickly from seed we tend not to keep them for longer. Among these are many familiar choices: petunias, bedding salvias, impatiens, and begonias. Because these perennials do not have an inbuilt desire to set seed in the first season, something that can always be prevented by deadheading, they often have a longer flowering season in the garden, which adds to their usefulness. They also encompass a wide range of plants, including some that will tolerate shade.

Perennials, or herbaceous perennials as they should really be called to differentiate them from woody perennials such as trees, are in less of a rush than annuals. They typically take more than a year to reach flowering size, but once they have, they bloom every year. There are exceptions and many seed catalogs promote first-year-flowering perennials, which are as easy to grow as half-hardy annuals and, if sown in early spring, will bloom the same season and every year after. At the other extreme are monocarpic perennials, which gradually build up the strength to flower, only to then die, having set thousands of seeds. The South American puyas such as *Puya mirabilis* function in this way.

Herbaceous perennials are found throughout the world and, though many are evergreen and not strictly herbaceous, they all protect their growing buds at or below soil level. They are most common in cool temperate regions where cold limits year-round growth: in arid areas, bulbs and tubers take their place. All perennials can be raised from seed but they are mostly propagated by dividing the plants when dormant or by taking basal cuttings. This ensures that all the plants are identical.

The rootstock of herbaceous plants, often called the crown, is where roots meet shoots, and is remarkably varied. In the case of bearded iris, it is a creeping stem, and stores water and some food during drier periods. In the case of peonies, the roots are also slightly swollen, to sustain vigorous growth in spring. But in others, such as some asters, bergamot, and daylilies, the clumps expand quickly, colonizing new ground. These need regular dividing.

The traditional herbaceous border was a joy to behold, but its short season has been its demise. Today's range of herbaceous plants means that, from hellebores flowering from late winter to early spring, bergenias during spring, through to the last flowers of Japanese anemones, *Liriope,* and *Schizostylis* in autumn, herbaceous perennials can enhance our gardens throughout much of the year.

BULBS, CORMS, AND TUBERS

Plants that produce underground organs such as bulbs, corms, or tubers are known as geophytes. This varied and large group includes many of the world's favorite ornamental garden plants and cut flowers, as well as being a source of food in many parts of the world.

Bulbs, corms, and tubers are adaptations that enable the plants to survive times of the year unfavorable to aerial growth. In some cases, this may be the cold of winter, while in others it may be a dry season. Plants in many families have developed these underground organs. Though fulfilling the same function, they vary from each other in the degree to which different parts of the plant have been modified to different extents.

A bulb is a modified bud borne on a short thickened stem. There are two main types of bulb: naked and tunicated. Naked bulbs are made up solely of scaly but fleshy modified leaves surrounding the central developing flower stem, as with *Lilium*. On tunicated bulbs, the fleshy inner scales (tunica) are covered with thin membranous scales, such as seen on daffodils and tulips.

Corms are similar to bulbs, but instead of the scales of the underground bud forming the bulk of the organ, the thickened stem is the biggest part. Like tunicated bulbs, corms are covered by a tunica, which in many cases is more fibrous than that of bulbs. Examples of corms are *Freesia* and *Watsonia* plants.

Tubers can be formed from both underground stems and swollen roots. The potato is the best-known example of a tuber that has evolved from a stem; sweet potato (*Ipomoea batatas*), Jerusalem artichoke (*Helianthus tuberosus*), and various yams (*Dioscorea* spp.) are other examples. The buds or eyes from which the aerial shoots develop occur over the surface of the tuber. In contrast, root tubers are formed from roots and the buds for aerial shoots are confined to the stem bases at or near the surface of the soil. Dahlias have root tubers.

Rhizomes are a form of stem tuber, but can be slender as well as swollen and can occur beneath the ground, at ground level, and can even climb other plants as in some epiphytes or the aggressive kikuyu grass (*Pennisetum clandestinum*).

The many types of bulbous plants can be dramatically beautiful, especially when the flowers emerge quickly after autumn rain, often appearing before the leaves do, such as can happen with *Amaryllis belladonna*. In cold climates, in particular, bulbous plants are deservedly popular: the emergence of early spring bulbs such as snowdrops and crocus are welcomed as harbingers of spring, while daffodils bring the promise of warmer weather.

As well as beautiful flowers, scent is an important feature of some bulbs. Hyacinths and some lilies have incomparable fragrance and make ideal pot plants.

Today, the bulb industry worldwide is large and much research has been carried out that enables bulbs to be forced into bloom out of season. The trade supports some gardens such as Keukenhof in the Netherlands and Springfields in Britain as showcases for the industry, and in Germany the garden at Mainau is devoted to dahlias.

Below: Tulipa 'Ballerina'. Tulips are perhaps the most famous bulbs, renowned for the "Tulipomania" seen in the Netherlands in the seventeenth century, when fortunes were made and lost from speculating in bulbs.

Below: Today, bulbs and tubers are used in large quantities to decorate public parks and private gardens. Here, a stunning result is achieved by planting Lilium, Asiatic Hybrid 'Connecticut King' with elegant delphiniums.

Above: Many fruit trees, such as this *Malus pumila 'Shakespeare'*, can be very ornamental. *Malus* species and cultivars have long been valued for their spring blossom.

FRUIT AND NUT PLANTS

Botanically, a fruit is a mature ovary, a home for the seed inside. It is also, of course, a delicious form of food. The two go hand in hand: as we or other animals enjoy and are nourished by succulent fruits, we incidentally help disperse their seeds. A fruit ripens along with its enclosed seeds, usually remaining inconspicuously green and harshly flavored until the time is right for eating.

Not all botanical fruits function in the same way. Nuts are fruits whose mature ovaries are hard shells. In this case, the ovary provides protection. Still other fruits ripen without any seeds at all. The seeds might be absent because they abort, as is the case with seedless grapes, or because the ovary is able to swell and develop without any stimulus of seed development, as is the case with seedless persimmons. These examples have been bred to be seedless.

Climate is an important consideration for fruit growing: not only the minimum winter temperature but also the length of winter and the length and warmth of the growing season. Many temperate climate fruits need an annual period of cool weather to grow well. Late spring frosts can eliminate the year's harvest of temperate fruits.

Right: Fruit and nut plants can be decorative as well as functional. Mostly, though, fruits and nuts are for eating; they are nature's desserts.

For best quality yields, most fruit plants need a helping hand. Fruiting demands considerable energy, so plants need to be positioned in full sunlight for maximum yields, even fruits, like blueberry, that naturally inhabit shaded sites. A few fruits, including currants and gooseberries, bear well in partial shade.

With most cultivated fruits and nuts, annual pruning is essential. Pruning helps expose branches to sun and air, thus avoiding the dank conditions that promote disease while at the same time maximizing photosynthesis and, hence, the harvest's quantity and quality. Pruning also balances stem growth against fruiting, so that the plant has a sufficient but not an excess number of stems, from which hang the fruit. By removing some potential fruits, pruning helps a plant channel more resources into fully developing those fruit that remain. Fruit thinning—the pinching off of excess fruits—further maintains that balance, and ensures good annual crops as heavy fruiting one year leads to reduced yield the next.

"Fruits and nuts" encompasses a broad spectrum of plants, but like most traditionally cultivated plants, they all generally enjoy well-drained moist soils that are slightly acidic and reasonably fertile and high in humus. Blueberry, cranberry, and lingonberry are notable exceptions, requiring soils that are relatively infertile yet are very acidic and very high in humus.

Compared with the array of tree and bush fruit plants, there are comparatively few climbing fruit plants, also referred to as vines. Climbers not only offer tasty fruit, but are also often highly ornamental. Draped over a pergola or fence as with passionfruit (*Passiflora edulis*) or Chinese gooseberry (*Actinidia deliciosa*), or clinging to walls or damp trees as does the split-leaf philodendron (*Monstera deliciosa*), the climbing fruit plants are a splendid and productive addition to the garden.

Climbing fruits vary greatly in their habitats, growth patterns, fruit type, and gardening needs. Local climatic conditions will have a much greater impact on a plant's successful growth than any broad zone category.

VEGETABLES

Comprising a diverse range of plants, with a wide range of uses in the kitchen, vegetables can be defined as any of various herbaceous plants that have edible parts.

Most vegetables are annuals, or are biennials and perennials grown as annuals, cropping in the same year as they are sown or planted. A few, such as asparagus, are perennials remaining in the ground for years. Vegetables can, for ease, be divided into a number of groups: root crops; brassicas and leafy crops; legumes; salad crops; and vegetables with edible fruit. Apart from brassicas and legumes, which are botanical classifications, these groupings are man-made and merely indicate which part of the plant is eaten, or how the crop is cultivated.

Root crops include beetroot, carrot, onion, parsnip, radish, potato (actually an edible tuber), and salsify. These are all biennials and perennials, storing food in their swollen roots, which, in nature, would be used to enhance flowering. Brassicas include broccoli, Brussels sprouts, calabrese, cabbage, cauliflower, swede, and turnip. Within just this one group the range of botanical characteristics used is great. Broccoli and cauliflower are grown for their immature flower heads, cabbages for their succulent leaves, Brussels sprouts for their young sideshoots of tightly folded leaves, and turnips and swedes for their swollen roots. Also included in this leafy group are leeks and spinach.

Legumes include peas and beans: French (variously called dwarf bean, kidney bean, string bean, snap bean, haricot vert, and flageolet); runner (stick or pole bean);

fava (broad bean); soya; and lima (butter or Madagascan bean). Their seeds are enclosed within a pod and it is either the seed (lima and butter beans) or the seed and pod that are eaten (French and runner beans).

Salad crops are similar in growth to many of the leafy vegetables, but this classification includes vegetables that are eaten raw. Although most salad crops—including radicchio (chicory), corn salad, lettuce, and arugula (rocket)—are grown for their leaves, celery is grown for its succulent stems, and celeriac for its swollen stem.

The final group contains vegetables that are grown for their fruit, such as eggplant (aubergine), capsicum, cucumber, marrow (such as pumpkin, and squash) and tomato. Sweetcorn is also included in this group, but in this instance it is the seeds that are eaten.

Growing your own vegetables is hugely satisfying and brings with it the opportunity to grow organically or free from artificial chemicals. Most importantly, vegetables are fresh and tender and have a much better flavor and taste.

HERBS

Herbs can be defined as plants with a significant history of use. For millennia, they have been valued for their useful properties in flavoring foods and beverages, for imparting aromas, for dyeing yarns and fabrics, and, most importantly, for curing or alleviating the various ills of humankind. The epithet *officinalis,* which appears in many Latin herb names, means "from the apothecary," or drugstore, and indicates that the herb was approved for use.

Botanically, herbs include annuals, biennials, and perennials. True annuals include herbs like cilantro (coriander) that complete their entire life cycle within a single growing season. Biennials, such as *Salvia sclarea,* establish their roots in the first season and send up a flowering stalk the second. Perennial herbs are of several types: hardy herbaceous perennials, like tansy *(Tanacetum vulgare),* which die back after blooming, but send up renewed growth from the roots for at least three more seasons; short-lived ones, like lemon balm, which may last for only two seasons, but self-seeds; tender perennials from hot climates, such as pineapple sage *(Salvia elegans),* which are overwintered indoors in cool climates; and shrubby perennials, such as wormwood, which maintain aboveground hardwood.

Among the many herbs easily available, certain families are very important: in the Lamiaceae (mint) family alone there are about 221 genera and more than 3,000 species. Besides true mint *(Mentha),* this family includes the Mediterranean herbs lavender, thyme, and rosemary.

Herb forms range from ground-hugging creeping thyme to robust comfreys *(Symphytum);* contain the comfreys as they can become invasive in the garden. The foliage is typically aromatic and can be smooth and glossy, as with the basils, or furry and silvery, as with many artemisias. The flowers, even when small, as in oregano, are nectar-rich, thus attracting butterflies, bees, and hummingbirds; their visits for food deep in the plant's blossom aid pollination.

The versatility of herbs means there is a plant for every garden. They can be grown as row crops in the kitchen garden; in pots tucked in by the kitchen door; in a formal herb garden; or incorporated into a perennial border or cottage garden. Basils—green and purple, ruffled and plain—are stunning in containers, as are nasturtiums (their flowers are delicious in salads); and Mediterranean herbs thrive when planted in a rock garden or rocky outcrop, or even in the chinks of a wall (try woolly thyme). Woodland herbs such as sweet wood-ruff *(Galium odoratum)* flourish in damp shade.

Many herbs can be raised from seed, either by direct sowing in prepared ground, or by sowing indoors, then planted out after all danger of frost has passed (heat-loving herbs such as basils should be started indoors in cold climates). Herbs such as cilantro (coriander), which quickly bolts, should be sown successively at 2 to 4 week intervals. Others, like the mints, do not come true from seed and should be bought as named cultivars, then propagated from cuttings or by division. Grow woody herbs, except for cultivars, from seed.

Herbs are easily maintained in good health: harvest them for use, cut them for bouquets, or trim back after flowering to encourage fresh foliage. Cut shrubby herbs back to growing points in spring to initiate new growth.

Above: Corn (Zea mays) has a long history, being an important food crop for ancient Central and South American civilizations. Today, a diverse array of products—from breakfast cereal to fuel—are derived from it.

Left: Countless herbs, such as familiar lavender, once again are being cultivated for their therapeutic or medicinal properties, led by a renewed interest in herbal remedies.

Right: Traditionally, herbs were used in raised beds and were spaced apart to produce a formal effect. Today, herbs like Salvia nemorosa 'Mainacht' are valued for the bold impact they can have in gardens.

Left: The Cyathea *genus contains over 600 species of tree ferns.*
C. medullaris *has a graceful habit, with large, soft, arching fronds.*

Fronds appear in a wonderful variety of textures, sizes, shapes, and a lush palette of greens, and are of great value to gardeners. Ferns play important roles in naturalistic garden designs, growing in the dappled shade of a woodland stream or covering the banks of a shady slope. Mixed with spring-blooming wildflowers, fronds unfurl to fill in gaps just as flowers go dormant. They can also be planted with spring bulbs, thereby helping to hide the browning leaves of bulbs such as daffodils.

Ferns are just as attractive grown indoors as they are in the landscape. In pots and planters, hart's-tongue fern *(Asplenium scolopendrium),* holly fern *(Cyrtomium falcatum),* and rabbit's foot fern *(Davallia fejeensis),* make fine specimens. Most ferns grown indoors are native to tropical woodlands where they enjoy ample indirect sunlight and high humidity. Indoors, a spot near a window facing towards the sun will provide them with the bright indirect light needed. Frequent misting, along with regular watering, will create good growing conditions.

Outdoors, most ferns grow best in shade or filtered light in moist (but not soggy) well-aerated soil. Although some prefer an acidic soil and others like alkaline conditions, drainage is usually more important than the soil pH. A soil mix of good loam combined with at least 50 percent humus in the form of leaf mold, or compost dug to a depth of 10 in (25 cm)—just deep enough to accommodate the shallow roots of ferns—should provide adequate drainage but sufficient moisture. Ferns rarely require fertilizing; use slow-release organic fertilizers when performance declines. Seldom bothered by disease, slugs and snails are the most common pests.

PALMS AND CYCADS

Although they look similar, palms and cycads are actually quite different. They both produce rosettes of leaves at the end of a woody trunk, though cycad leaves are tough and leathery, while palms are softer, flexible, and often longer. They both develop single stems or form clumps, and are mostly predictable in size and shape—handy for gardeners. But that's largely where the similarity ends.

Cycads are believed to have been prominent during the Jurassic period 250 million years ago, and are more like conifers than palms (palms produce flowers, cycads do not). Scientists have identified over 180 species of cycads but numbers are increasing with time. They're found in warm-temperate to tropical regions of the world, from rainforest to desert, and are particularly prominent in Africa, Australia, and South America, with the greatest variety occurring in Central America.

Both male and female cycads have a single central cone, which is often an ornamental feature. Some of them also have highly specialized feeding roots, known as "coralloid" roots. These contain algae that allow them to extract nitrogen from the atmosphere. Such cycads are the only cone-bearing plants to do this.

Above: The tremendous paddle-shaped leaves of Johannesteijsmannia magnifica *can stretch up to 15 ft (4.5 m) high and 6 ft (1.8 m) wide.*

FERNS

Constituting one of the most primitive of plants, ferns, along with horsetails and club mosses, belong to a group of plants known as pteridophytes. Unlike most other vascular plants, ferns bear no flowers, fruit, or seeds, but instead reproduce by means of spores. They grow in a great variety of sizes, forms, and habits, but all ferns comprise three parts: a leaf (commonly called a frond), a rhizome or stem, and roots.

There are over 200 genera and about 8,500 species. Ferns may be terrestrial, epiphytic, or aquatic; evergreen or deciduous; and they may hug the ground or grow as tall as 50 ft (15 m). Ferns range far and wide, growing from the Arctic Circle to the tropics, in deserts and in swamps. With such great variety, it is odd that ferns remained unfamiliar to gardeners until the Victorian era, when filmy ferns suddenly became fashionable specimens for Wardian cases. Since then, Boston ferns *(Nephrolepis exaltata* 'Bostoniensis'*)* have become popular indoor plants; tree ferns such as dicksonias and the Australian native, straw tree fern *(Cyathea cooperi),* soar above gardens in tropical, subtropical, and mild-temperate climates; while maidenhair ferns *(Adiantum)* accent woodland gardens with their elegant graceful fronds.

For gardeners wishing to grow cycads indoors, *Cycas revoluta* and *Cycas circinalis* make excellent houseplants; avoid those with large spines on the leaves. One myth is that cycads are slow growing. In fact, cycads have regular bursts of growth, then rest and many, given good growing conditions with regular feeding and mulching, grow rapidly. They prefer neutral to slightly acid soils, including sand, but can suffer in clay soils with poor drainage. Propagation is from seed, or stem or leaf cuttings.

Palms are more numerous than cycads; there are about 2,300 species, mostly in the tropics and subtropics. *Rhopalostylis sapida* from New Zealand is the world's most southerly palm and there are as many palm species on the island of Singapore alone as there are in mainland Africa. Many are economically important, providing oils, fiber, waxes, food, drugs, and furniture (rattan).

Palms are plants of extremes: the leaves range from 12 in (30 cm) to 35 ft (10 m) long, and are either feather- or fan-like. The flowers are equally as spectacular: in some, the plants die soon after flowering, such as the talipot palm (*Corypha umbraculifera*), which boasts the largest flower spike in the world, reaching 25 ft (8 m) tall. Others, like a mature gebang palm (*Corypha utan*) may have up to 15 million flowers, and the double coconut (*Lodoicea*) produces the world's largest seeds.

Many species of palms have been cultivated for so long that their origins are unknown. They are used to line streets, in parks, and as houseplants. When planting in gardens, grow palms as single specimens or in small groups, preferably of the same species and remembering their potential height. Most need moist soil and humidity, with an annual mulch and regular feeding. Indoor palms need bright light. They dislike waterlogging and need regular feeding; don't overfeed those in pots.

CLIMBERS AND CREEPERS

Plants that need a supporting structure to grow upon, such as a wall, trellis, or another plant, are known as climbers, creepers, ramblers, and scramblers. They come from many genera, and are found around the world.

There are two main types of climbing plants: those that have active mechanisms to help them cling and those that have a passive climbing mechanism. Active mechanisms include a number of types: some plants, such as clematis, have tendrils that attach themselves to something, such as branches or wires, while others, like *Pandorea pandorana,* attach themselves by twining up and around the support device, their stems circling thin trees and shrubs or trellis-type structures. Suckers are a third group which attach themselves to surfaces with adventitious roots. Members of the ivy (Araliaceae) family have such roots.

Plants with a passive climbing system can have spines or stiff emergences (hook-shaped spikelets), which they use to attach themselves to other plants. Hooks are especially common in dense stands, where plants come in close contact with one other. The hooks help the plant tangle itself with other plants, gaining more support for itself than by just relying on freestanding shoots.

Scrambling plants fit into this category, with their stiff branches and hooks. Many roses are climbers and are armed with strong backward-pointing stem emergences, which are also found on the backs of leaves. As well, spines make the plant unappealing to feeding herbivores.

For the gardener, climbers and creepers have many uses. They cover a fence or trellis, hide walls, provide color and softness, release fragrance, provide shade, and reduce wind and noise.

The care and cultivation of climbers depends greatly on the species. Some climbers prefer shade and others prefer sun, as do many bougainvillea species. Some like cool soils and roots zones; the warmer the soil gets the slower the roots are to develop. Many disperse fertile seed after flowering, others are rhizomatous and spread along the ground, while others spread by adventitious roots. Many evergreen perennials propagate readily by cuttings in summer and autumn. Provide adequate moisture, depending on the species, and fertilizer as required.

Left: A native of China, Jasminum nudiflorum is valued for its winter flowers, its bright yellow blooms appearing when all else is bare.

Below: Deciduous climbers, such as Campsis grandiflora, *the Chinese trumpet creeper, provide shade and wind protection in summer. Then when the leaves fall, they let in the gentle warmth and light of the winter sun.*

Above: For the gardener, grasses provide interesting forms, subtlety of color, and movement. As well, many, like Festuca glauca, *may grow in situations where other plants fail.*

Right: Bamboo are actually giant grasses, though their size and woody hollow stems distinguish them from most grasses. Bambusa vulgaris 'Vittata' is striking for its thick golden yellow stems with green stripes.

Below: Grasses are prized around the world for their usefulness as lawn cover, and help define areas of the garden.

GRASSES

The grass family features around 635 genera and more than 9,000 different species. They are some of the most adaptable plants on Earth, occurring in almost all regions and on all continents, from the Arctic to the Antarctic peninsular.

When discussing "grasses" it is necessary to distinguish between the true grasses (that is, members of the family Poaceae, also known to some botanists as the Gramineae) and all other grass-like plants that are commonly and broadly referred to as grasses. These include rushes, sedges, and cat tails (bulrushes). True grasses are mainly herbs, either annual or perennial, and have hollow or solid stems. Their root systems may be tufted so that they form single clumps, sometimes quite densely bunched to form tussocks, or they may form quite extensive patches or colonies due to their rhizomatous stems, which either creep along the surface of the ground and root-in or grow below the surface. Generally, their long and narrow leaves are in two rows and arise from a sheath that is usually open down its front and clasps the stem quite tightly. The flowers of grasses are, on the whole, rather small and may be bisexual or unisexual. They are produced in small spikelets of three or more overlapping scales. The stamens hang out on delicate stalks so that they move freely in any breeze and thus disperse the pollen.

There are many familiar plants that people often do not recognize as grasses. The bamboos, for example, are actually giant grasses. Some species of bamboo are quite small, while others, such as *Dendrocalamus giganteus* from Southeast Asia, are veritable giants.

Grasses that live in open country, especially those species that inhabit plains, steppe lands, hill country, and similar areas, often have to endure severe extremes of climate and conditions. *Chionochloa* species are typical of these conditions and are often well adapted for growing in dry and windy areas.

Grasses are some of the most important plants on Earth and it is safe to say that without them civilization, as we know it today, would not exist. All of our grains and cereals such as wheat, oats, barley, maize, rice, and rye, have been derived from wild grasses. For the gardener, grasses are important because of their ornamental uses. Around the world, of course, they feature as the most suitable plants for lawns and sports fields. With careful selection, grasses are a reliable choice for bringing long-term value to the garden.

BAMBOOS

These familiar woody plants are members of the grass (Poaceae) family, and range from dwarfs and shrubs through to giant specimens. Bamboos are native to every continent except Antarctica and Europe, and include 100 genera and 1,500 species, with over 500 ornamental forms in cultivation.

The form of bamboos is highly distinctive: they have woody canes (culms), which are usually hollow; leaf stalks (pseudopetioles), separating leaf from branch; and underground stems (rhizomes), which may be clumping (remaining in tight thickets of canes) or spreading, the canes often emerging in straight lines.

Bamboos can be ground covers (growing up to waist high); shrubs (growing up to 15 ft/4.5 m); cold hardy clumpers (from 10–20 ft/3–6 m); temperate timbers (from 15 ft/4.5 m to over 70 ft/21 m tall); or tropical clumpers (which grow from shrub height to over 100 ft/30 m). There are also temperate and tropical climbers and even herbaceous species.

Being a grass, bamboos are wind pollinated and have a long juvenile vegetative period (from 7 to 100 years). Upon maturity, they flower seasonally for several years, often gregariously, though many subsequently die, especially the clumping type. Bamboos also flower sporadically as individual plants, often through stress, but usually survive. Gardeners are wise to choose species that are not at risk of flowering.

In the home garden, bamboos are greatly neglected, due to misplaced concerns of uncontrollable spread, lack of cold tolerance, and exotic appearance. Hence, they are often segregated, and used solely as windbreaks, screens, or partitions, especially in urban gardens. However, this

is to ignore the immense value they can play in the contemporary landscape: as dwarf hedges; knot gardens and labyrinths; specimens; groves; embankments for soil stabilization; alternative lawns; abstract mounds; textural contrasts in island beds; for trapping the scent of shrubs; and even supporting climbers (annual, herbaceous, or arborescent types). For the timid, bamboo can also be used in myriad locations as containerized specimens on decks, patios, courtyards, conservatories (heated and unheated), atriums (for example the black bamboo *Phyllostachys nigra*) and interiors *(Bambusa multiplex* and its cultivars, Buddha's belly *B. ventricosa,* and arrow bamboo *Pseudosasa japonica).* These examples are selected for their admirable ornamental qualities.

The selection process is vital, however. Consider whether a species has a spreading or clumping habit, what its function and eventual height will be, and its light, temperature, and exposure tolerances. Bamboos are best planted in spring, and will thrive in any humus-rich free-draining soil, especially if fertilized. Water as required throughout the growing season.

Bamboos do not require much maintenance. Remove weak, old, and dead culms by a third annually when bamboos are not shooting (in autumn), clear-cut ground covers at the end of winter, and remove obvious dead culms from cold hardy clumpers as required. Never prune or thin bamboos during active growth. Saw potbound bamboos in two and repot in fresh potting soil that is moisture retentive but free draining. Never allow pots to stand in water, as the plants rot easily.

As you browse through the species descriptions, you will soon discover that bamboos deserve more prominent roles in the contemporary landscape design, adding qualities unmatched by any other plant.

SUCCULENTS AND CACTI

These beautiful and fascinating plants are wonderful examples of the adaptability of nature. In many parts of the world there is either too little rainfall or long periods of drought, conditions that most perennial plants would not be able to survive. Slow-growing cacti and succulent plants have adapted in order to be able to grow in these areas, taking advantage of the minimal competition from faster growing plants.

Succulent plants, as the name suggests, store moisture, which they then slowly use in order to survive until the next rain comes. Water may be stored in thick fleshy leaves, such as seen on the jade tree *(Crassula ovata)* and also on the living stone plants *(Lithops),* whose small swollen leaves are united into a single body. Other plants, like *Stapelia* species, have thick swollen stems, and a third group has swollen roots, such as many members of the cucumber family *(Kedrostris).*

One particular group of stem succulents is the cacti. In order to be classified as a cactus, the plant must have several botanical characteristics, one of which is peculiar to the cactus family. This is called an areole. It is a modi-

fied auxiliary bud from which all the spines, branches, and flowers arise. Only if a succulent has this characteristic, is it classified in the botanical family Cactaceae. So, whilst all cacti are succulents, not all succulents are cacti.

The typical globular shape of cacti and some succulents is designed to maximize bulk but minimize surface area, and hence aid moisture conservation. In order to expand and contract, many also have ribs, which in turn cast shadows on the plant body and retain a microclimate between them. Many cacti and some succulents also have spines or thorns. Whilst they are often thought to be some form of protection from animals, this is probably their least significant function. In dry areas, precious moisture can be gained from the often nightly precipitation of fogs and dews. The spines act as catching points for the dewdrops, which run down the plant body, to be taken up by the normally shallow root system.

Dense spination also helps to shade the plant and create a more humid microclimate, as is the case with Old Man of the Andes *(Oreocereus celsianus).* Although cacti are native to the Americas, the other succulents can come from almost anywhere in the world, mostly from warmer areas. Most of those that come from colder climates (such as *Pediocactus)* have a dry continental winter, and cultivating these plants is often very difficult, as damp winters can be even more detrimental than the cold.

Cacti and succulents generally prefer a bright situation, with a minimum temperature of about 40–50°F (5–10°C). During the summer months, plants should be allowed to dry between waterings. Ideally, give sufficient water at a time so that plants will dry out within ten days. In winter, they should be kept more or less dry, dependent upon temperature. A well-balanced cactus food should be given at regular intervals to encourage sturdy growth and plenty of flowers.

Above: While many succulents are cold-sensitive, there some that can tolerate temperatures as low as 20°F (-7°C). This includes plants commonly grown in temperate gardens such as Sedum spathulifolium.

Left: Native to Mexico and southwestern USA, the low-growing Echinocereus triglochidiatus var. melanacanthus *is popular for its spectacular orange-red flowers, which open during the day.*

Above: Bromeliads are an increasingly popular group of perennial herbs known for their stiff rosettes of foliage and brightly colored unusually shaped flowers. Most Guzmania species are native to tropical areas, though they make superb houseplants.

BROMELIADS

The pineapple, the most famous of the bromeliads, has been popular with gardeners ever since Christopher Columbus first happened upon cultivations of the plant in the West Indies in 1493. However, it represents only the tip of the bromeliad family, which includes over 50 genera and more than 2,000 species and is distributed throughout the tropical and warm-temperate parts of the southern USA, through Central America, and much of South America.

Right: Except for the pineapple fruit, bromeliads are grown today as ornamentals, valued for the great range of flower and leaf shape and color. Popular genera include Aechmea, Billbergia, and Vriesea, as well as cultivars like V. 'Mariae'.

Taxonomically, all members of the bromeliad family follow the pineapple mode. They are perennials, usually consisting of a thickened compressed stem, very densely surrounded with a rosette of stiff strap-shaped leaves. These are so densely packed that they form a central cup, which in many species forms a water-holding urn. The edges of most leaves are armored with spines or hooks and need to be handled with care or they can inflict serious injury. Flowering occurs from the center of the rosette. While the flowers are attractive, they are eclipsed by the coloration of the surrounding bracts (modified leaves) and other foliage, as is the case with the colorful bracts and leaves of *Billbergia amoena*.

The family as a whole has adapted to extreme conditions. Most bromeliads are xerophytes; the name given to plants that have adapted to growing in regions with unreliable rainfall. Many are also epiphytic, giving rise to the Spanish common name "parasitos", though they are not parasites: they only use trees for support, growing in minimal humus on the branches.

The varied habitats of the bromeliads demonstrate they have much to offer the gardener, many able to survive some neglect. Gardeners in (USDA hardiness) zone 6 and warmer can enjoy a range of outdoor species, while those in colder regions will find many rewarding houseplants. For zones 6 and 7, plants from southern Chile and the Mediterranean-type zones of North and South America are best. *Puya berteroniana,* for example, needs only a sheltered site and free-draining soil to make a magnificent specimen plant. Its spires of translucent turquoise blue flowers grow to 6–10 ft (1.8–3 m) tall, and can attract humming birds for pollination. In contrast, *Fascicularia bicolor* grows to only 12 in (30 cm), its

Right: In temperate areas most orchids are grown in greenhouses. The night temperatures needed range from warm to cool but, as most greenhouses have cooler and warmer areas, the majority of species will be fine in an intermediate greenhouse.

rosettes turning fiery red when in flower. In zone 8 and above, the epiphytic species can provide a spectacular display attached to trees or even contemporary man-made art structures. Variegated red and white *Neoregelia carolinae* f. *tricolor,* the zebra patterned *Vriesea splendens,* and tiger striped *Aechmea orlandiana* look like exotic fireworks exploding. Those in cooler climes with conservatories can grow the rather sinister-looking, rock-like *Tillandsia pruinosa* or *Cryptanthus fosterianus,* so often seen glued to a shell or ornament.

Provided bromeliads receive similar conditions to those in which they grow in the wild (good light but not too much direct sun, a little diluted nutrient, and humidity for epiphytic species), most will be happy. Propagation can be easily achieved using division or by raising from seed. Next time you sip a piña colada, while perusing a nurseryman's catalogue for plants to furnish your garden or windowsill, spare bromeliads a thought.

ORCHIDS

Orchids form one of the largest of all plant families, with over 20,000 species in about 800 genera, and can be found in all continents except Antarctica.

Orchids are diverse in size, growth habit, and color and shape of flower, but all share a particular flower formation. They have three sepals, sometimes like the petals, sometimes different, and three petals, one of which differs from the other two and is called the labellum or lip. It is often larger and different in color, with various markings, and sometimes with a nectar-bearing spur at the base. The lip usually lies at the bottom of the flower and may act as a landing platform for pollinating insects. The most distinctive feature of an orchid flower

is the reproductive organs. Here, the stamens, style, and stigmas, separate in most plants, are joined to form a structure called the column. As well, the pollen, instead of being loose, is in masses called pollinia. Pollination mechanisms are often complex, not to say bizarre.

Orchid seeds are minute and are dispersed on the wind, sometimes traveling for long distances. They are so small that they have no food reserves and to grow must come into contact with a fungus, through which it obtains nutrients for the developing seedlings. This link with a fungus was discovered in the late nineteenth century. Now, the necessary nutrients can be supplied in the form of chemicals and, provided the procedure is carried out in a sterile environment, it is relatively straightforward to grow orchids from seed.

Orchids may be either terrestrial or epiphytic. Terrestrial orchids, such as *Disa uniflora*, grow in the soil, while epiphytic orchids, like *Dendrobium speciosum,* grow on trees or shrubs or on rocks, and are known as lithophytes. Over half of all orchids are epiphytes and this includes most that are widely cultivated. Many epiphytes, such as *Vanda coerulea*, have thick fleshy roots with an outer layer that can absorb moisture and many, such as the bulbophyllums, have leathery leaves and swollen stem bases called pseudobulbs. Epiphytic orchids are found in the tropics and subtropics; as you move away from the Equator, the terrestrial orchids increase. Most terrestrial orchids have underground storage organs such as tubers, or fleshy roots and are dormant for a period, usually in the winter or the dry season.

Most widely cultivated orchids are hybrids; well over 100,000 have been registered. In tropical and subtropical parts of the world, epiphytic orchids can be grown out of doors, usually in a shade house or tied on to, or suspended from, trees, to ensure protection from direct sunlight. In temperate regions orchids are mostly grown in greenhouses; intermediate night temperatures of 55–59°F (13–15°C) will generally suffice for most orchids.

CARNIVOROUS PLANTS

Green seed plants rely on photosynthesis for energy production, with acquisition by root absorption of certain basic minerals essential for the process. A group of approximately 450 species of such plants grow in conditions sufficiently moist and sunny but in soils that are deficient in nutrients; they have adapted to obtain these essential minerals by entrapping prey. These are the carnivorous plants. They are found on every continent and large island of the world, with the exception of Antarctica. The usual prey consists of insects and other small arthropods such as spiders, but animals to the size of rats have been recorded.

The traps are modified leaves, which serve to attract prey, entrap the insects or small animal, digest its soft parts, and absorb useful nutrient compounds and minerals. The digestive process is very similar to that of animals; that is, glands in the linings of the trap leaves produce certain chemicals called enzymes, which act to reduce complex chemical compounds in preparation for absorption. Some carnivorous plants do not produce enzymes but rely on bacteria growing in the trap to break down the prey.

The leaf modifications of carnivorous plants are quite attractive, having usually bright red colors and novel configurations. The most famous plant and trap type of this group is the Venus flytrap *(Dionaea muscipula)* which has a bivalved trap up to 2 in (5 cm) in length and bright red lining, the color presumably to attract prey. The trap is remarkably sophisticated and has been the subject of learned studies for decades. Special trigger hairs on the trap lining must be touched, one hair twice or two hairs in succession, and in a specific time sequence to cause the trap to close quite rapidly. The entrapped prey is now in a closed chamber for digestion and absorption over a period of three to five days.

The sundews *(Drosera)* have linear to paddle-shaped leaves and are generally smaller rosetted plants. They are characterized by stalked and unstalked small glands on the upper leaf surface, each gland bearing a drop of mucus to entrap and hold prey. Often, stalk movement slowly occurs to place the prey into the center of the leaf for digestion and absorption in the open, although in some species the leaf also folds over. Sunlight glistening on the surface glands is the reason for the common name, sundew.

Certainly, the most spectacular traps in terms of appearance are the pitcher plants *(Sarracenia)*. In these plants, the leaf has rolled into a trap tube, usually with some sort of lid partially over the opening. Entrapment is not by the lid flapping up and down but by the prey landing on the margins of the tube's opening, to partake of nectar secretions, and then tumbling into the trap interior. The trap lining has slippery surfaces and downward pointing hairs in different zones to prevent escape. The rare waterwheel plant *(Aldrovanda)* grows in water and has quite similar but smaller traps.

Many carnivorous plant species are under various assaults, mainly related to land development, pollution, and unregulated lumber activities. Some of the species numbers have been reduced to the extent that they are endangered, and in these cases collection of the plants by people can be significant in further reducing numbers. If you purchase carnivorous plants to grow, do so only from nurseries that have propagated plants.

Left: The *Paphiopedilum* orchids are distinctive for their large pouched lip, which comes in a wide range of shapes and colors. P. hirsutissimum has a greenish brown pouch, complemented by dark pink petals.

Above: The pitcher plants of the southeastern USA grow up to 3 ft (0.9 m) tall. Sarracenia leucophylla has slender white modified leaves, with purple-red markings, fading to green bases.

A

A

ABELIA

This decorative genus from the woodbine (Caprifoliaceae) family has about 30 ornamental shrubs, both evergreen and deciduous, and occurs across the Northern Hemisphere from eastern Asia to Mexico. Named after Dr Clarke Abel, a British physician and plant collector, the main features are glossy opposite leaves and funnelform or tubular flowers, white or pinkish, sometimes with orange blotches, through summer. Some species also have persistent reddish sepals which provide an additional ornamental feature after the flowers have faded. In the garden they can be planted singly in a shrub border or as a low informal hedge.
CULTIVATION: Propagate by soft-tip cuttings in spring or summer, or half-hardened cuttings in late autumn or winter. Plant in any well-drained, moderately fertile soil, in a sunny spot. Moderately frost hardy, prune in winter, removing some of the basal shoots to make room for new growth, plus the cane ends. Care should be taken to preserve the plant's naturally arching habit.

Abelia biflora
syns *Abelia davidii, A. shikokiana, Linnaea biflora, Zabelia biflora*
☀ ❄ ↔ 3–7 ft (0.9–2 m)
↑ 7–10 ft (2–3 m)
Medium-sized shrub of the dry gullies and hilly regions of northern China

and Mongolia. Leaves narrow, toothed near the base. Pale pink to white flowers are borne in pairs in the upper axils. Rare in cultivation because its other relatives are more striking. Zones 7–8.

Abelia chinensis
☀ ❄ ↔ 8 ft (2.4 m) ↑ 6 ft (1.8 m)
From central and eastern China, a medium deciduous shrub with glossy green leaves. Moderately fragrant white flowers, tinted with rose, in late summer–autumn. Similar to the commonly grown *A.* × *grandiflora*. Zones 8–10.

Abelia 'Edward Goucher'
☀ ❄ ↔ 6 ft (1.8 m) ↑ 5 ft (1.5 m)
Raised in 1911, this hybrid between *A.* × *grandiflora* and *A. schumannii* is from USA. It is a small semi-evergreen shrub with bright glossy leaves, bronzed tinged when young. Lilac-pink flowers appear in summer–autumn. Pink calyces, 2-lobed. Zones 8–10.

Abelia engleriana
☀ ❄ ↔ 4–6 ft (1.2–1.8 m)
↑ 4–6 ft (1.2–1.8 m)
Evergreen shrub from China with glossy bark eventually peeling. Smooth, fine-toothed, oval to elliptical leaves, ¾–1½ in (18–35 mm) long. Pairs of flowers with 2 sepals, rose pink corolla to ¾ in (18 mm) wide. Zones 3–9.

Abelia chinensis

Abelia floribunda
☀ ❀ ↔ 6 ft (1.8 m) ↑ 6 ft (1.8 m)
From Mexico. This abelia is generally evergreen with an open habit. Leaves are smaller and less glossy than *A.* × *grandiflora*. Pendulous clusters of pale rose to deep red flowers in summer–autumn. Persistent sepals. Zones 9–11.

Abelia × *grandiflora* ★
GLOSSY ABELIA
☀ ❄ ↔ 6 ft (1.8 m) ↑ 6 ft (1.8 m)
Evergreen shrub with arching canes, a hybrid between *A. chinensis* and *A. uniflora*. Reddish brown stems. Leaves dark green, turning red to orange in winter. Perfumed flowers flushed mauve-pink. '**Francis Mason**', leaves heavily margined and suffused with yellow; '**Prostrata**', low growing, to 24 in (60 cm) high; '**Sherwoodii**', compact habit, to 3–4 ft (0.9–1.2 m) high; '**Sunrise**', to 6 ft (1.8 m) tall, attractive autumn foliage color. Zones 7–10.

Abelia schumannii
syn. *Abelia longituba*
SCHUMANN'S ABELIA
☀ ❄ ↔ 8 ft (2.4 m) ↑ 4 ft (1.2 m)
From China, this nearly evergreen shrub has pale green to dull green leaves, and pale rosy mauve flowers in clusters, with a broad white

Abelia engleriana

stripe and some orange spots on the lower lobe, produced summer–autumn. Zones 7–10.

Abelia triflora
☀ ❄ ↔ 10 ft (3 m) ↑ 7 ft (2 m)
A deciduous to semi-evergreen shrub from the Himalayas. Introduced into cultivation in 1847. Leaves are narrower than other species. Pale pink flowers are quite fragrant, tubular, and are borne in clusters. Zones 8–10.

ABELIOPHYLLUM

The name of this genus, of the olive (Oleaceae) family, is derived from *Abelia*, which it is said to resemble. It contains just one species of small deciduous shrub, closely related to *Forsythia*, bearing similar flowers in

Abelia × *grandiflora,* in summer

Abelia × *grandiflora,* in spring

Abelia × *grandiflora,* in autumn

Abeliophyllum distichum

Abelmoschus esculentus 'Cajun Delight'

Abelmoschus moschatus, Pacific Series cultivar

Abelmoschus moschatus 'Mischief'

Abelmoschus moschatus 'Oriental Pink'

white. The shrub is native to the mountains of Korea, where it is becoming scarce.
CULTIVATION: The species will grow in a range of soil conditions but in cool temperate climates should be given a warm site. It can be trained against a wall if desired. Less vigorous old canes should be cut out. Prune every 2 to 3 years to maintain shape. Propagation is usually by half-hardened cuttings taken in summer or by layering in spring or autumn.

Abeliophyllum distichum
WHITE FORSYTHIA
☀ ❈ ↔ 6 ft (1.8 m) ↕ 3 ft (0.9 m)
This arching, straggly, deciduous shrub from Korea can be trained up a wall. Late winter, bare branches are smothered in fragrant, white, forsythia-like flowers that burst from pink-tinged buds. In some forms buds are a deeper shade with flowers emerging pale pink. Zones 5–10.

ABELMOSCHUS
This genus in the mallow (Malvaceae) family consists of about 15 species of annuals, perennials, and soft-wooded shrubs native to warmer parts of Asia and Africa. Closely allied to *Hibiscus*, it is distinguished by having flowers with a single bract wrapping around the base of the sepals, splitting down one side as the flower expands. Leaves usually maple-like or divided into finger-like lobes. Flowers often showy, in shades of pink, red, or yellow, and followed by elongated pods. An annual species grown as a vegetable is okra (or gumbo) *(A. esculentus).* Leafy young shoots of most *Abelmoschus* species can also be used as pot greens.
CULTIVATION: They like a sunny position sheltered from strong winds, and well-drained soil, fertilized in summer. Propagation is possible from

basal cuttings as well as from seed sown as soon as weather is warm enough in late spring.

Abelmoschus esculentus
GUMBO, LADY'S FINGER, OKRA
☀ ❈ ↔ 18–24 in (45–60 cm)
↕ 30–48 in (75–120 cm)
Widely naturalized tropical annual, grown extensively as a vegetable. Serrated leaves, 5 to 7 lobes. Solitary flowers, white or yellow marked with red or purple toward the base. Fleshy pod-like fruit, green or red skin. 'Cajun Delight' is a heavy-cropping early-fruiting variety with dark green pods. Zones 7–9.

Abelmoschus manihot
syn. *Hibiscus manihot*
AIBIKA
☀ ❂ ↔ 3 ft (0.9 m) ↕ 3–6 ft (0.9–1.8 m)
Shrubby Southeast Asian perennial. Large, deeply lobed leaves. Pale yellow flowers with a dark purplish eye at the branch tips in summer. Zones 10–12.

Abelmoschus moschatus
syn. *Hibiscus abelmoschus*
MUSKMALLOW
☀ ❂ ↔ 30 in (75 cm) ↕ 4–6 ft (1.2–1.8 m)
Variable species from tropical Asia to northern Australia. Stems and leaves

bear bristly hairs; leaf lobes triangular. Flowers white, pink, or yellow, with a dark eye, in summer. Ornamental strains grown as annuals. Abundant seeds yield the musky perfume, ambrette. Colorful cultivars include **'Mischief'** and **'Oriental Pink'**. The **Pacific Series** comprises scarlet- and pink-flowered cultivars. Zones 10–12.

ABIES
This genus in the pine (Pinaceae) family consists of about 50 species, occurring in the northern temperate zones of Europe, North Africa, Asia, and North America. Mostly long lived

and medium to very tall, these evergreen conifers have long, narrow, smooth leaves in whorls on the branches. Leaves are mid- to dark green, often with a grayish white band. Female cones are carried erect on upper branches, while the hanging male cones grow throughout the crown. Fully hardy, although frost damage can occur on juvenile foliage.
CULTIVATION: Best in neutral to acid, moist, fertile soil with good drainage in full sun; most tolerate some shade. Some, including *A. pinsapo*, tolerate alkaline soils. Some juvenile trees need shelter from cold winds. Adelgids and honey fungus can be a problem. Sow seed as it ripens, but needs to be stratified for 3 weeks for better germination. Graft cultivars in winter.

Abies alba
syn. *Abies pectinata*
EUROPEAN SILVER FIR
☀ ❈ ↔ 20 ft (6 m) ↕ 200 ft (60 m)
Native to mountainous areas of central and southeast Europe, this species produces Europe's tallest tree. Upper leaves dark green, with silver undersides. Cones brown and cylindrical. **'Compacta'** is dwarf form. Zones 6–9.

Abies alba

Abies amabilis, in the wild, in North Cascades National Park, Washington State, USA

Abies balsamea, Hudsonia Group cultivar

Abies amabilis

BEAUTIFUL FIR, PACIFIC FIR

☀ ❄ ↔ 12–20 ft (3.5–6 m) ↑ 100 ft (30 m)

This conifer has glossy green leaves with grayish white stripes beneath, to 1 in (25 mm) long. Cones are egg-shaped, red to deep purple ripening to brown. Grows best in a cool moist climate and acid soil. Zones 5–9.

Abies balsamea

BALSAM FIR, DWARF BALSAM FIR

☀ ❄ ↔ 15 ft (4.5 m) ↑ 50 ft (15 m)

Conical tree with sleek gray bark and fragrant resin. Leaves dark green with whitish undersides. Cones cylindrical,

purplish blue in color. A source of wood pulp in Canada, it is fairly short lived in gardens. Dwarf cultivars include '**Nana**' and the members of the **Hudsonia Group**. Zones 3–8.

Abies bracteata

syn. *Abies venusta*

BRISTLE CONE FIR, SANTA LUCIA FIR

☀ ❄ ↔ 20 ft (6 m) ↑ 80 ft (24 m)

From Santa Lucia Mountains, California, USA. Leaves dark green, silvery green below. Cones egg-shaped, golden brown when ripe, exude resin. Rare in cultivation. Zones 7–10.

Abies cephalonica

syn. *Abies apollinis*

GREEK FIR

☀ ❄ ↔ 25 ft (8 m) ↑ 100 ft (30 m)

Native to central and southern Greece, this pyramidal tree has dark green, rigid, slightly curved leaves with greenish white undersides. Cylindrical greenish brown cones are resinous. '**Meyer's Dwarf**', with shorter leaves, forms a mound, only 20 in (50 cm) high, with a diameter to 10 ft (3 m). Zones 7–10.

Abies balsamea

Abies cilicica

☀ ❄ ↔ 20 ft (6 m) ↑ 100 ft (30 m)

This columnar tree, native to North Africa, has bright green leaves with grayish white undersides. Cones are cylindrical, greenish brown, with hidden bracts and nodular tips. Zones 7–10.

Abies concolor

BLUE FIR, COLORADO WHITE FIR, SILVER FIR, WHITE FIR

☀ ❄ ↔ 25 ft (8 m) ↑ 120 ft (36 m)

Growing in western USA down to northern Mexico, this statuesque tree with a pyramidal crown has dull greenish gray leaves with mid-green to brown cylindrical cones. Cultivars include '**Compacta**', '**Masonic Broom**', and **Violacea Group** ★. Dwarf cultivars grow no more than 30 in (75 cm) in height and spread. Zones 5–9.

Abies fargesii

syn. *Abies sutchuenensis*

☀ ❄ ↔ 12 ft (3.5 m) ↑ 60 ft (18 m)

This statuesque tree comes from central China. Leaves are dark green

Abies bracteata

Abies concolor, in the wild, Nevada, USA

with silver-striped undersides. The egg-shaped cones are violet-purple in color, with protruding, slightly resinous bracts. Zones 7–9.

Abies firma

syn. *Abies bifida*

JAPANESE FIR

☀ ❄ ↔ 20 ft (6 m) ↑ 100 ft (30 m)

Originally from southern Japan, this fir has shiny deep green leaves, and bears brown egg-shaped cones which are up to 6 in (15 cm) long. Susceptible to spring frost damage. Zones 6–9.

Abies firma

Abies fargesii

Abies homolepis

Abies fraseri, in the wild, in Great Smoky Mountains National Park, Tennessee, USA

Abies forrestii

FORREST FIR

☼ ❋ ↔ 20 ft (6 m) ↑ 70 ft (21 m)

Native to northwestern Yunnan and southeastern Tibet, this pyramid-shaped tree has dark green leaves which are silvery white underneath. Cones are egg-shaped, purplish violet in color, ripening to deep brown. Zones 7–9.

Abies fraseri

☼ ❋ ↔ 20 ft (6 m) ↑ 60 ft (18 m)

Pyramidal tree, native to southwestern Virginia, western North Carolina, and eastern Tennessee, USA. Leaves are 1 in (25 mm) long, mid- to dark green with a silvery to greenish white band on the underside. Cylindrical cones are green to dark purple, ripening to brown, pronounced bracts. Zones 6–9.

Abies grandis

GIANT FIR

☼ ❋ ↔ 25 ft (8 m) ↑ 300 ft (90 m)

This giant conical to columnar tree from western North America has dark

green, soft, shiny leaves, with whitish banding on the undersides. Cones are smallish, ripening to gray-brown. The timber of this tree is used in construction work. 'Johnsonii' reaches a height of 60–70 ft (18–21 m). Zones 6–9.

Abies homolepis

syn. *Abies brachyphylla*

MANCHURIAN FIR, NIKKO FIR

☼ ❋ ↔ 25 ft (8 m) ↑ 80 ft (24 m)

A conical tree that is native to southern and central Japan. Leaves are dull grayish green with silver banding.

Abies koreana 'Compact Dwarf'

Branches are tiered up the trunk. Cones are cylindrical and violet-blue, turning brown with age. This species is tolerant of urban pollution. Zones 5–9.

Abies koreana ★

KOREAN FIR

☼ ❋ ↔ 5 ft (1.5 m) ↑ 50 ft (15 m)

From the mountains of South Korea, this fir is a formal, narrow, pyramid-shaped, slow-growing tree with striking purple cones. Leaves are dark green above and shiny white beneath. Cultivars include '**Flava**'; '**Compact Dwarf**', a popular bonsai subject; and '**Silberlocke**' (syn. 'Horstmann's Silberlocke'), a compact tree, new growth white beneath. Zones 5–8.

Abies lasiocarpa

ALPINE FIR, ROCKY MOUNTAIN FIR, SUBALPINE FIR

☼ ❋ ↔ 12 ft (3.5 m) ↑ 60 ft (18 m)

Conical tree found up to the tree line in the Rocky Mountains, North America. Gray-green leaves dense and spiky with bluish stripes on both sides. Oblong cylindrical cones turn from dark purple to brown as they ripen. *A. l.* var. *arizonica*, silver-gray leaves. '**Compacta**' is a popular cultivar to 10 ft (3 m) high. Zones 4–9.

Abies koreana

Abies koreana 'Silberlocke'

Abies lasiocarpa, in the wild, in Grand Teton National Park, Wyoming, USA

Abies nordmanniana 'Golden Spreader'

Abies pinsapo

Abies procera, Glauca Group cultivar

Abies pinsapo 'Glauca'

Abies religiosa

Abies veitchii var. *sikokiana*

Abies nordmanniana
CAUCASIAN FIR

☼ ❄ ↔ 20 ft (6 m) ↑ 180 ft (55 m)

This species is found in mountain forests in the western Caucasus. The tree forms an elegant conical spire, with foliage that is deep glossy green in distinct rows with 2 white bands underneath. Cones are cylindrical in shape and green in color, ripening to purple-brown. '**Golden Spreader**' ★ is a handsome cultivar. Zones 4–8.

Abies pindrow
WEST HIMALAYAN FIR

☼ ❄ ↔ 20 ft (6 m) ↑ 120 ft (36 m)

Native to the Himalayas from Afghanistan to Nepal, this species has glossy green leaves with 2 narrow whitish bands underneath. Cylindrical cones are violet-blue in color, ripening to brown. In cultivation, juvenile trees need to be protected from spring frost. Zones 7–9.

Abies pinsapo
SPANISH FIR

☼ ❄ ↔ 15 ft (4.5 m) ↑ 80 ft (24 m)

From the dry mountain slopes of southern Spain, this tree adds distinction to a garden. Foliage is a series of rigid, short, linear, dark green leaves. The cylindrical cones are purplish brown. Cultivars include: '**Glauca**', with gray-blue leaves; and '**Kelleriis**', a robust dwarf. Zones 6–8.

Abies procera
syn. *Abies nobilis*
NOBLE FIR

☼ ❄ ↔ 30 ft (9 m) ↑ 150 (45 m)

Native to the high rainfall areas of western USA, this pyramidal tree becomes broader with age. Leaves gray-green to blue-silver, banded gray underneath. Barrel-shaped green cones ripen to brown. The **Glauca Group** features cultivars (including '**Glauca Prostrata**'), with blue leaves. Zones 4–9.

Abies religiosa
syn. *Abies hirtella*
MEXICAN FIR

☼ ❄ ↔ 20 ft (6 m) ↑ 100 ft (30 m)

A central Mexican tree with leaves dull green above, whitish green bands underneath. Cones have projecting bracts and are green or purple, ripening to brown. This fir is not as hardy as most other *Abies*. Zones 8–10.

Abies veitchii

☼ ❄ ↔ 20 ft (6 m) ↑ 60 ft (18 m)

This fast-growing pyramidal tree native to Japan has smooth dark green leaves with silvery undersides. Bright gray-blue cylindrical cones ripen to a brown color. *A. v.* **var.** *sikokiana* has smaller leaves. Zones 6–9.

ABRONIA
SAND VERBENA

Although it is known as verbena, this genus is in the four-o'clock (Nyctaginaceae) family and not in the family to which the true verbenas belong. There are 33 species of annuals and perennials occurring in southwestern USA and northern Mexico, from sandy seashores to sandy and gravelly habitats further inland. All the species have terminal heads of small tubular flowers, ranging in color from pale pink to yellow, and tend to be prostrate, sprawling, or scrambling plants. The dried and powdered roots of some species were eaten by the indigenous people.
CULTIVATION: Propagate from seed and cuttings, preferably using new growth from the stem tips after flowering. Full sun in well-draining sandy or gravelly soils gives best results. Some of the species are tolerant of salt-affected coastal locations.

Abronia umbellata
BEACH SAND VERBENA

☼ ❄ ↔ 8–36 in (20–90 cm) ↑ up to 36 in (90 cm)

Native to the North American west coast, from Washington, USA, south to Baja California, Mexico, along the coastal fringe, occasionally further inland. A prostrate perennial with succulent leaves and showy, rose-colored, fragrant flowers. Can be deciduous under stress. Zones 8–10.

ABRUS

This genus is a member of the pea-flower subfamily of the large legume family (Fabaceae). Its 17 species are pantropical, consisting of climbers and creepers, occurring in various open habitats, usually at low altitudes. Plants have compound leaves and numerous small pinkish flowers in dense racemes, followed by flattish pods. One widespread species, *A. precatorius,* produces colorful red and black seeds that are used in some Asian countries as beads and weights; however, they contain a toxic glycoprotein, of which as little as 0.5 gram is fatal to humans.
CULTIVATION: Propagate from seeds, which need to be treated with boiling water or scarified before sowing. A tropical to subtropical climate is essential for success, the plants being susceptible to low temperatures and not at all frost hardy. Greenhouse culture is required in all other regions.

Abronia umbellata

Abutilon × *hybridum* 'Cannington Skies'

Abutilon × *hybridum* 'Canary Bird'

Abutilon × *hybridum* 'Nabob'

Abutilon × *hybridum* 'Summer Sherbet'

Abutilon × *hybridum* 'Boule de Neige'

Abrus precatorius

CORAL PEA, CRAB'S EYES,
PATERNOSTER BEANS

☼/◐ ◊ ↔ 3 ft (0.9 m) ↕ 35 ft (10 m)

Widespread, vigorous, woody climber. White to mauve flowers borne in 4 in (10 cm) long racemes, in autumn–spring (dry season). Flat brown pods, up to 2 in (5 cm) long, remain on the plant into the next flowering, and contain the hard, round, red and black seeds. Zones 10-12.

ABUTILON

CHINESE LANTERN

This genus of the mallow (Malvaceae) family is represented in warmer parts of the world. Species come from South or Central America, Australia, and Africa. Most are shrubs with slen-der tough-barked twigs but a few are annuals, perennials, or even small trees. Leaves vary from heart-shaped to jaggedly lobed with toothed margins. The common name alludes to the pendent bell-shaped flowers with 5 petals. Colors range from white through pink, and from yellow and orange to deep bronzy red. Fruit is a capsule. In mild climates they flower almost throughout the year, in cooler climates from spring to autumn. CULTIVATION: Plant in well-drained moderately fertile soil, in light shade or bright sun. Extra water is needed if in an exposed position. In cool climates keep indoors until the worst frosts are past, then plant out for summer display; newer dwarf cultivars are suitable for this purpose. Prune leading shoots in late winter for a compact form, although some cultivars display their blooms best on long arching branches. Propagate from tip cuttings in late summer.

Abutilon × hybridum

CHINESE LANTERN, GARDEN ABUTILON

☼/◐ ❄ ↔ 5–10 ft (1.5–3 m)
↕ 6–15 ft (1.8–4.5 m)

This is a wide-ranging group of hybrids with unclear origins, although most show *A. pictum* influence. Leaves are usually dark green, smooth, 3–6 in (8–15 cm) long, toothed or with up to 5 lobes. Flowers to 3 in (8 cm) wide, one per leaf axil, mainly yellow, orange, and red shades, appear most of the year. Popular hybrids include: '**Apricot**', open habit, terracotta flowers; '**Ashford Red**', brilliant red flowers; '**Bartley Schwartz**', drooping growth with golden to orange-yellow flowers; '**Boule de Neige**', an older cultivar, flowers white flushed pink; '**Canary Bird**', bright yellow flowers; '**Cannington Carol**', dwarf, dense variegated foliage, flowers bright orange; '**Cannington Skies**', similar to 'Cannington Carol', red flowers; '**Cerise Queen**', flowers dark pink; '**Clementine**', compact plant with bright red flowers; '**Crimson Belle**', bright sealing wax red flowers; '**Dwarf Red**', upright and bushy, small leaves, massed small bright red flowers; '**Kentish Belle**', glowing orange flowers; '**Linda Vista Peach**', upright, peach pink flowers with bronze calyces; '**Mobile Pink**', large downy leaves and wide open soft pink flowers; '**Moonchimes**', compact habit, pale yellow flowers; '**Moritz**', very dark leaves and pendulous orange flowers; '**Nabob**' ★, tall, flowers dark purple-red, leaves purple-tinged; '**Souvenir de Bonn**', tall, narrow leaf lobes edged cream, pendulous orange bells; '**Summer Sherbet**', compact seedling strain for summer bedding, wide color range; and '**Wakehurst**' (syn. 'Wisley Red'), dark red bell-shaped flowers. Zones 8–11.

Abutilon × *hybridum* 'Apricot'

A

Abutilon megapotamicum

syn. *Abutilon vexillarum*

CHINESE LANTERN, TRAILING ABUTILON

↔ 8 ft (2.4 m) ↑ 8 ft (2.4 m)

A native of southern Brazil. Has several forms, from an erect shrub with arching branches to an almost prostrate form. Flowers bell-shaped with red calyx contrasting with pale yellow petals. '**Marianne**', vividly colored flowers; '**Variegatum**', yellow mottled leaves; '**Victory**' ★, smaller, with darker yellow leaves. Zones 8–10.

Abutilon × *milleri*

↔ 8 ft (2.4 m) ↑ 8 ft (2.4 m)

This is a compact shrub with flowers similar to *A. megapotamicum*. The calyx is a dull greenish purple, the petals golden yellow with darker veining. '**Variegatum**', leaves richly mottled with dull gold. Zones 8–10.

Abutilon megapotamicum

Abutilon × *suntense*

Abutilon ochsenii

↔ 10 ft (3 m) ↑ 12 ft (3.5 m)

A shrubby Chilean species resembling the more common *A. vitifolium* but smaller with less downy, 3-lobed, 3 in (8 cm) long leaves. Darker-spotted mauve, 2 in (5 cm) wide flowers in groups of 1 to 3 in the leaf axils in summer. Zones 8–10.

Abutilon pictum

CHINESE LANTERN

↔ 8 ft (2.4 m) ↑ 15 ft (4.5 m)

A native of southern Brazil, this evergreen species is the most important parent of hybrid abutilons. This lanky shrub has scrambling branches, deeply divided dark green leaves, and flowers with orange petals netted with dark red veins. '**Thompsonii**', leaves spattered with pale yellow (a virus variegation), and larger flowers. Zones 9–12.

Abutilon × *milleri*

Abutilon × *suntense*

↔ 8 ft (2.4 m) ↑ 12 ft (3.5 m)

This attractive deciduous shrub has bright green leaves with violet flowers. Several cultivars are available, including: '**Gorer's White**', large pure white flowers; and '**Jermyns**', the best known cultivar, with clear mauve-purple flowers. Zones 8–9.

Abutilon vitifolium

syn. *Corynabutilon vitifolium*

↔ 8 ft (2.4 m) ↑ 15 ft (4.5 m)

This species from Chile is one of a group of abutilons with pink or mauve flowers. A weak-branched deciduous shrub, it has maple-like toothed leaves. Flowers saucer-shaped, white to violet-purple, in spring–summer. '**Veronica Tennant**', slightly larger pale mauve-pink flowers. Zones 8–9.

ACACIA

From the mimosa subfamily of legumes, *Acacia* consists of at least 1,200 species. It comes mainly from Australia, but is also found in Africa, tropical Americas, Asia, and islands of the Pacific and Indian Oceans. There are shrubs, small to medium-sized trees, a few large forest trees, and climbers. Flowers densely crowded into spikes or globular heads in colors of yellow, cream, or white. Leaf structure is basically bipinnate—but in many species the leaves change to phyllodes. The acacia fruit is a typical legume pod, splitting open when ripe to reveal a row of hard seeds. African species form an important part of the scenery over large areas. These are the "thorn trees" with their characteristic flat-topped crowns, fine leaves, and branches armed with sharp spines. Fast-growing acacias enrich the soils by converting nitrogen from the air into soil nitrogen.

CULTIVATION: Most acacias require well-drained soil and full sun. In mild climates they can become environmental weeds. They are often

Acacia acinacea

short-lived. Propagate from seeds, treated to soften the hard case. Give a light prune after flowering.

Acacia acanthoclada

HARROW WATTLE

↔ 3 ft (0.9 m) ↑ 6 ft (1.8 m)

Native to dry inland regions of southern Australia. Small rigid shrub. Short, spiny branchlets, tiny hairy phyllodes. Solitary bright yellow flowerheads, on slender stalks, in late winter–spring. Useful for barrier planting and low windbreaks in semi-arid areas. Zones 8–10.

Acacia acinacea

GOLD-DUST WATTLE

↔ 8 ft (2.4 m) ↑ 8 ft (2.4 m)

From semi-arid regions of southern Australia, this shapely shrub has long arching branches with oval to oblong phyllodes. Flowers form golden yellow globular heads, borne in late winter–spring. Pod is curved, spirally coiled, or twisted. '**Ruby Tips**' (syn. '**Red Tips**') is distinguished from the species by the bright red color of the new growth. Zones 8–10.

Acacia adunca

WALLANGARRA WATTLE

↔ 12 ft (3.5 m) ↑ 20 ft (6 m)

A bushy shrub or small tree from dry woodlands of southeastern Australia. Phyllodes narrow, light green. Long sprays of ball-shaped, sweetly scented, golden yellow flowers in late winter and spring. Prefers well-drained soil. Zones 9–11.

Abutilon ochsenii

Abutilon vitifolium

Acacia baileyana

Acacia aneura

MULGA

☼ ⚘ ↔ 12 ft (3.5 m) ↑ 10–30 ft (3–9 m)

Shrubby tree from dry inland Australia, thrives in arid gardens. Phyllodes gray-green. Golden yellow flowers in winter–spring after good rain. Mulga is the Aboriginal Australian word for the long narrow shield made from the wood. Zones 9–10.

Acacia aulacocarpa

BRUSH IRONBARK WATTLE

☼ ⚘ ↔ 6–10 ft (1.8–3 m)
↑ 15–50 ft (4.5–15 m)

From near coastal tropical Australia. Variable species, requires summer rainfall. Large gray-green phyllodes to 8 in (20 cm) long. Cylindrical golden yellow flowers, summer–autumn. Suits large gardens and parks. Zones 10–12.

Acacia ausfeldii

☼ ⚘ ↔ 8 ft (2.4 m) ↑ 6–12 ft (1.8–3.5 m)

Native to eastern Australia, growing in eucalypt woodland. Resinous branchlets, slightly drooping habit. Narrow phyllodes; large, golden yellow, fluffy flowers in pairs. Grows well under established tall trees. Zones 9–11.

Acacia baileyana

COOTAMUNDRA WATTLE

☼ ❄ ↔ 20 ft (6 m) ↑ 6–20 ft (1.8–6 m)

Widely naturalized in most Australia States, this small elegant tree occurs naturally around Cootamundra, New South Wales. Leaves feathery silver-gray. Flowers bright yellow, globular, in racemes, winter–spring. '**Purpurea**' has attractive purplish foliage and new growth. Zones 8–10.

Acacia berlandieri

BERLANDIER'S ACACIA, GUAJILLO, PLAINS ACACIA

☼/☼ ❄ ↔ 10–17 ft (3–5 m)
↑ 10–17 ft (3–5 m)

Large shrub or small tree from Texas and New Mexico, USA, and northern Mexico. Fine, bright green, fern-like leaves. Cream-colored fragrant balls of flowers, early spring. Elongated, dark brown, broad seed pods. Zones 8–9.

Acacia adunca

Acacia boormanii

Acacia aneura (trees), in the wild, Docker River, Western Australia

Acacia binervia

COAST MYALL

☼ ⚘ ↔ 35 ft (10 m) ↑ 50 ft (15 m)

A handsome tree from the tablelands and slopes of eastern Australia. Large compact crown of silvery gray curved phyllodes. Masses of bright yellow flower spikes in early spring. Young foliage may be poisonous to stock. Zones 9–11.

Acacia boormanii

☼ ❄ ↔ 7 ft (2 m) ↑ 6–12 ft (1.8–3.5 m)

From the Snowy River region of southeastern Australia. Erect bushy shrub, slender branches, dark green narrow phyllodes. Bright yellow ball-shaped flowerheads, axillary racemes, late winter–early spring. Zones 8–11.

Acacia brachybotrya

GRAY MULGA

☼ ❄ ↔ 7–17 ft (2–5 m) ↑ 10–17 ft (3–5 m)

Much-branched, dense, medium to tall shrub from inland regions of all mainland Australia States except Western Australia and Northern Territory. Thick, gray-green, oval phyllodes, ½–1½ in (12–35 mm) long. Flowers in bright yellow balls, each of 20 to 30 tiny flowers in spring–early summer. Pods dark brown. Zones 8–9.

Acacia binervia

Acacia buxifolia

Acacia burkittii

Acacia cavenia

Acacia burkittii
PINBUSH WATTLE

☼ ❈ ↔ 15 ft (4.5 m)
↕ 3–15 ft (0.9–4.5 m)

Tall spreading shrub, occurs naturally in semi-arid regions of southern Australia. Phyllodes long and fine. Bright yellow flowers, in short oblong spikes, late winter–spring. Zones 8–10.

Acacia buxifolia
BOX-LEAF WATTLE

☼ ❈ ↔ 3–8 ft (0.9–2.4 m)
↕ 3–10 ft (0.9–3 m)

Occurring naturally along eastern Australian coast, tablelands, and slopes. Short, leathery, gray-green phyllodes. Profuse, golden yellow, ball-shaped flowerheads appear in winter–spring. Zones 8–10.

Acacia caffra
COMMON HOOK-THORN

☼ ⬦ ↔ 15 ft (4.5 m) ↕ 30 ft (9 m)
Deciduous shrub or tree widespread in South Africa. Branches have pairs of small hooked thorns. In spring has large, pale green, bipinnate leaves and creamy white flower spikes. Foliage used as cattle fodder. Zones 9–11.

Acacia calamifolia
WALLOWA

☼ ❈ ↔ 10 ft (3 m) ↕ 6–12 ft (1.8–3.5 m)
Widespread in dry inland areas of Australia. Erect or spreading shrub, slender wiry stems, narrow hooked phyllodes. Golden yellow flower balls, late winter–late spring. Withstands quite dry conditions. Endangered mallee fowl feed on seed. Zones 8–9.

Acacia cardiophylla
WYALONG WATTLE

☼ ❈ ↔ 5–8 ft (1.5–2.4 m)
↕ 3–10 ft (0.9–3 m)

Beautiful free-flowering shrub from mallee country of inland New South Wales, Australia. Leaves bipinnate with tiny heart-shaped leaflets on long arching branches. Panicles of small, sweetly scented, bright yellow, ball-shaped flowers. 'Gold Lace' (syn. 'Kuranga Gold Lace') differs from the species by its prostrate and trailing habit and an earlier flowering time (late winter–early spring). Stems become twisted with age. Zones 8–11.

Acacia cavenia
CAVAN, ESPINO

☼ ⬦ ↔ 12 ft (3.5 m) ↕ 20 ft (6 m)
From Argentina and Chile, this attractive small tree has flexible spiny branches and ferny bipinnate leaves. Yellow flowers in globular heads in spring. Large seed pods. Good hedging plant. Zones 9–11.

Acacia cognata
NARROW-LEAF BOWER WATTLE

☼ ⬦ ↔ 8 ft (2.4 m) ↕ 10–25 ft (3–8 m)
Small resinous tree, native of coastal southeastern Australia. Has pendulous branches and bright green narrow phyllodes. Shortly stalked, golden yellow, ball-shaped flowers in late winter–spring. Prefers moist conditions. Zones 9–11.

Acacia complanata
FLAT-STEMMED WATTLE

☼ ⬦ ↔ 10 ft (3 m) ↕ 6–15 ft (1.8–4.5 m)
Subtropical species from eastern Australia. Spreading shrub, flattened zigzagging branchlets. Broad lanceolate phyllodes, conspicuous veins. Golden yellow flower balls, in clusters, in late spring–early autumn. Trim annually to maintain shape. Zones 9–11.

Acacia covenyi
BLUE BUSH

☼ ⬦ ↔ 10 ft (3 m) ↕ 20 ft (6 m)
Rare species from the southern tablelands of New South Wales, Australia.

Large shrub or small tree. Narrow blue-green phyllodes. Clusters of small heads of bright yellow flowers in spring. Seed pods up to 3 in (8 cm) long. Zones 9–11.

Acacia crassa

☼ ⬦ ↔ 35 ft (10 m) ↕ 40 ft (12 m)
This woodland species from eastern Australia is often found in dense stands. It has spreading branches and large curved phyllodes. Golden yellow flower spikes are borne in pairs in late winter–early spring. Zones 9–11.

Acacia crassicarpa
WOODYPOD WATTLE

☼ ⬦ ↔ 35 ft (10 m) ↕ 40 ft (12 m)
Native of far northeastern Australia and New Guinea. Large grayish phyllodes. Woody, large, flattish pods up to 1½ in (35 mm) wide. Glossy black seeds. Vigorous long-lived tree for a sheltered position. Zones 10–12.

Acacia cultriformis
KNIFE-LEAF WATTLE, PLOUGHSHARE WATTLE

☼ ❈ ↔ 6–10 ft (1.8–3 m)
↕ 6–10 ft (1.8–3 m)

This widely cultivated tall shrub comes from eastern Australia. Drooping branches with blue-gray almost triangular phyllodes. Perfumed, bright yellow, globular flowers on long sprays. Excellent for hedging. 'Cascade' (syn. 'Austraflora Cascade'), prostrate habit, flowers similar in size and color to the species. Zones 8–11.

Acacia cyclops
ROOIKRANS, WESTERN COASTAL WATTLE

☼ ❈ ↔ 7–15 ft (2–4.5 m)
↕ 7–15 ft (2–4.5 m)

Occurs along the coastal fringe of southern and southwestern Australia. Dense shrub, spreading, branching near ground level. Has thick, slightly curved phyllodes that are 1½–4 in (3.5–10 cm) long, with 3 to 5 prominent veins. Heads of about 40 lemon yellow flowers during spring–autumn. Grayish brown

Acacia complanata

Acacia crassa

Acacia cultriformis

A

Acacia elata

Acacia farnesiana

Acacia giraffae, in the wild, in Namib Naukluft Park, Namibia

leathery pods. Has naturalized in southern Africa and is a serious environmental weed. Zones 8–11.

Acacia dealbata ★
MIMOSA, SILVER WATTLE

☼ ❄ ↔ 25 ft (8 m) ↑ 50 ft (15 m)

From Tasmania, Australia. Trunk has dark gray to black bark, silvery branchlets, gray-green bipinnate leaves. In late winter–spring has pale lemon to bright yellow globular flowers on extended racemes. Known in Europe as mimosa. Cultivars include: 'Gaulois Astier', deep green foliage; 'Kambah Karpet', dense, prostrate habit. Drought tolerant. Zones 8–10.

Acacia decora
SHOWY WATTLE, WESTERN GOLDEN WATTLE

☼ ❄ ↔ 5 ft (1.5 m) ↑ 6–15 ft (1.8–4.5 m)

This spreading dense shrub is widespread in dry inland areas of eastern Australia. Bluish green gently curving phyllodes. Racemes of bright yellow flower balls in winter–spring. Spectacular in flower. Zones 8–11.

Acacia decurrens
BLACK WATTLE

☼ ❄ ↔ 15 ft (4.5 m)
↑ 15–50 ft (4.5–15 m)

This erect tree comes from the coast and tablelands of New South Wales, Australia. Dark gray furrowed bark, deep green bipinnate leaves with widely spaced leaflets. Fragrant, brilliant yellow, ball-shaped flowers in winter–early spring. Zones 9–10.

Acacia drummondii
DRUMMOND'S WATTLE

☼❄❄ ↔ 3–6 ft (0.9–1.8 m)
↑ 3–6 ft (0.9–1.8 m)

An understory shrub of the southwest forests of Western Australia. Has gray-green bipinnate leaves. Golden yellow spike-like flowers on slender stalks are seen in winter–spring. A variable species, it has been divided into 4 subspecies. *A. d.* subsp. *elegans* has large flowerheads up to 2 in (5 cm) long. Zones 9–11.

Acacia dunnii
ELEPHANT-EAR WATTLE

☼ ❄ ↔ 8 ft (2.4 m) ↑ 6–15 ft (1.8–4.5 m)

Single-stemmed shrub or small tree from northern tropical Australia. Much of the plant is covered with a whitish bloom. Very large, broad, gray-green phyllodes. Showy, bright yellow, ball-shaped flowers, in large terminal racemes, up to 20 in (50 cm) long, in late autumn–early winter. Zones 9–11.

Acacia elata
CEDAR WATTLE

☼ ❄ ↔ 40 ft (12 m) ↑ 60 ft (18 m)

From moist sheltered forests in coastal eastern Australia, this is one of the tallest of the wattles. Dark green bipinnate leaves have long individual leaflets. Clusters of fluffy, pale yellow, ball-shaped flowers appear in summer. Useful ornamental. Zones 9–11.

Acacia estrophiolata
IRONWOOD

☼ ❄ ↔ 10–35 ft (3–10 m)
↑ 17–70 ft (5–21 m)

Found in woodlands and shrublands of inland Australia. Spreading light green crown, smooth silvery gray bark. Phyllodes narrow with 3 obvious longitudinal veins. Flowerheads pale yellow, produced irregularly, but particularly after good rains. Zones 9–10.

Acacia decora

Acacia farnesiana
MIMOSA BUSH

☼ ✈ ↔ 15 ft (4.5 m) ↑ 15 ft (4.5 m)

Spreading shrub or small tree, native of tropical Americas. Bipinnate leaves with strong spines in the leaf axils. Golden, sweetly scented, globular flowers in winter–spring. Oil from flowers used in perfumes. Zones 11–12.

Acacia fimbriata
FRINGED WATTLE

☼ ❄ ↔ 20 ft (6 m) ↑ 20 ft (6 m)

Bushy shrub or small low-branching tree from coastal eastern Australia. Dark green linear phyllodes. Dense clusters of perfumed, bright yellow, ball-shaped flowers, late winter–spring. Effective hedge. Zones 9–11.

Acacia floribunda
SALLY WATTLE

☼ ❄ ↔ 15 ft (4.5 m) ↑ 20 ft (6 m)

Tall dense shrub or small tree, coastal eastern Australia. Pendulous branches with crowded narrow phyllodes. Scented pale yellow flowers, in loose spikes, in winter–spring. Zones 9–11.

Acacia giraffae
syn. *Acacia erioloba*
CAMEL THORN

☼ ❄ ↔ 40 ft (12 m) ↑ 40–60 ft (12–18 m)

Shapely tree with wide-spreading crown, widespread in southern Africa. Straight thorns, bipinnate leaves. Sweetly scented, yellow, ball-shaped flowers late winter–early spring. Sickle-shaped pod. Good shade. Zones 9–11.

Acacia estrophiolata

Acacia glaucoptera

CLAY-BUSH WATTLE

☀ ✤ ↔ 10 ft (3 m) ↑ 5 ft (1.5 m)

From Western Australia, this attractive dome-shaped shrub has unusual, flat, gray-green phyllodes overlapping along zigzagging stems. The tree has large deep yellow flower balls in winter–spring. Needs good drainage. Zones 9–11.

Acacia hakeoides

WESTERN BLACK WATTLE

☀ ✤ ↔ 15 ft (4.5 m) ↑ 6–20 ft (1.8–6 m)

From drier parts of Australia, this multi-branched shrub has thick oblong phyllodes and dense bright yellow flower balls, in showy racemes, from winter to spring. Adaptable and drought tolerant. Zones 8–11.

Acacia harpophylla

BRIGALOW

☀ ✤ ↔ 20 ft (6 m) ↑ 30–50 ft (9–15 m)

A native of the semi-arid regions of eastern Australia, this erect densely crowned tree is valued as a shade tree for hot areas. Has dark furrowed bark,

Acacia karroo

Acacia glaucoptera

Acacia implexa

Acacia leptostachya

and phyllodes that are curved and silvery gray. Yellow globular flower-heads in winter–early spring. Seeds soft coated. Zones 9–11.

Acacia havilandiorum

syn. Acacia havilandii

NEEDLE WATTLE

☀ ✤ ↔ 12 ft (3.5 m) ↑ 12 ft (3.5 m)

From the arid stony hills and plains of inland southeastern Australia, this decorative vase-shaped shrub has fine needle-like phyllodes. In late winter–spring its branches are laden with bright yellow globular flowerheads. Zones 9–11.

Acacia howittii

HOWITT'S WATTLE

☀ ✤ ↔ 10 ft (3 m) ↑ 25 ft (8 m)

From southeastern Australia, this attractive small tree has a dense weeping habit. It has sticky dark green phyllodes, and in spring displays masses of scented lemon flower balls. It makes a very good hedge plant. A low spreading form is in cultivation. Zones 9–11.

Acacia lanigera

Acacia implexa

HICKORY, LIGHTWOOD

☀ ✤ ↔ 12 ft (3.5 m) ↑ 15–50 ft (4.5–15 m)

From coastal eastern Australia and slightly inland. Long-lived erect tree, fairly open crown. Green curved phyllodes. Pale creamy yellow flower balls, summer–early autumn. Zones 8–11.

Acacia karroo

KARROO THORN, SWEET THORN

☀ ✤ ↔ 25 ft (8 m) ↑ 25 ft (8 m)

From southern Africa, this common and widespread tree has a spreading rounded crown of deciduous, dark green, bipinnate leaves. It has smooth brownish gray bark and paired straight thorns. Dark yellow, sweetly scented, globular flowers are displayed in summer–autumn. Zones 9–11.

Acacia lanigera

WOOLLY WATTLE

☀ ✤ ↔ 10 ft (3 m) ↑ 10 ft (3 m)

From southern Australia, this hairy woolly shrub has a spreading rounded shape and rigid narrow phyllodes. Bright yellow flowerheads appear in late winter–early spring. The curled brown pods are densely hairy. Zones 8–11.

Acacia leptostachya

☀ ✦ ↔ 12 ft (3.5 m) ↑ 15 ft (4.5 m)

A shapely, rounded, small tree that comes from northern Queensland, Australia. It has a grayish appearance, with gray-green to silvery lance-shaped phyllodes. Its cylindrical flowers are strongly perfumed and bright yellow in color; they grow to 2 in (5 cm) long. Zones 11–12.

Acacia harpophylla

Acacia havilandiorum

Acacia longifolia

Acacia mangium

Acacia leucoclada
NORTHERN SILVER WATTLE

☼ ❄ ↔ 12 ft (3.5 m) ↑ 30 ft (9 m)

Occurs in dryish hills of southeastern Australia's Great Dividing Range. Bipinnate leaves, silvery blue-green cast. Branchlets whitish from a dense coating of hairs. Sprays of globular yellow flowerheads, late winter–spring. *A. l.* subsp. *argentifolia* has foliage of a silvery-pale bluish shade. Zones 9–11.

Acacia longifolia
SYDNEY GOLDEN WATTLE

☼ ❄ ↔ 15 ft (4.5 m) ↑ 6–25 ft (1.8–8 m)

From eastern Australia, this mostly small bushy tree has low spreading branches. Bright green thick phyllodes. Bright yellow flower spikes along branches, winter–spring. Useful as a hedge or windbreak. Zones 9–11.

Acacia mangium
WATTLE

☼ ✤ ↔ 40 ft (12 m)
↑ 50–80 ft (15–24 m)

This spreading tree comes from coastal districts in northern Australia.

Acacia leucoclada subsp. *argentifolia*

Acacia myrtifolia

Has large, veined, lanceolate phyllodes, and white rod-like flowers in summer–autumn. Clusters of twisted woody pods. Excellent shade tree. Zones 11–12.

Acacia mearnsii
LATE BLACK WATTLE

☼ ❄ ↔ 25 ft (8 m) ↑ 30 ft (9 m)

Upright spreading tree from southeastern Australia. Short trunk, blackish bark, and a wide leafy crown of shiny, dark green, bipinnate leaves. Pale yellow ball-shaped flowers in loose clusters, late spring–early summer. Good shade tree. Zones 8–11.

Acacia melanoxylon
BLACKWOOD

☼ ❄ ↔ 20 ft (6 m) ↑ 100 ft (30 m)

From mainland eastern Australia and Tasmania. Spreading bushy crown of dull green phyllodes with longitudinal veins. Clusters of pale yellow globular flowers, late winter–early spring. Best in a moist sheltered situation. A weed in South Africa. Zones 8–11.

Acacia mellifera
SWARTHAAK

☼ ❄ ↔ 15 ft (4.5 m) ↑ 25 ft (8 m)

From southern Africa. Deciduous shrub or small tree, spreading rounded to flat crown. Armed with pairs of sharply curved thorns. Bipinnate leaves. Sweetly scented creamy white flowers in late winter–early spring, before the new leaves. Drought tolerant. Zones 9–11.

Acacia melanoxylon

Acacia mearnsii, in the wild, Upper Brogo, New South Wales, Australia

Acacia muelleriana
MUELLER'S WATTLE

☼ ❄ ↔ 20 ft (6 m) ↑ 6–25 ft (1.8–8 m)

This species from the Australian States of New South Wales and Queensland has dark green pinnate leaves and produces heads of cream to pale yellow flowers in spring–summer, followed by narrow seed pods. Zones 9–11.

Acacia myrtifolia
MYRTLE WATTLE

☼ ❄ ↔ 8 ft (2.4 m) ↑ 8 ft (2.4 m)

This abundant flowering shrub from southern Australia has reddish stems and dark green lanceolate phyllodes. Fluffy pale yellow to creamy white flowers are seen in winter–spring. New growth has an attractive reddish color. Zones 8–11.

Acacia oxycedrus
SPIKE WATTLE

☼ ❄ ↔ 7 ft (2 m) ↑ 3–10 ft

Indigenous to mainland southern Australia, this species is usually a stiff prickly shrub with flat, rigid, sharply pointed phyllodes. Lemon yellow flower spikes appear in winter–spring. It is popular as a barrier plant. Zones 8–10.

Acacia papyrocarpa, in the wild, Madura, Western Australia

Acacia paradoxa

Acacia podalyriifolia

Acacia pravissima

Acacia papyrocarpa

WESTERN MYALL

☼ ❄ ↔ 10–20 ft (3–6 m)
↕ 10–35 ft (3–10 m)

A tall shrub to small tree occurring in arid to semi-arid regions of South Australia and Western Australia. Has drooping branchlets, thick bark, and narrow silver to gray-green phyllodes, 1½–3 in (3.5–8 cm) long. Golden, globular flowerheads are seen in early–late spring. Pods thin, papery. Zones 8–10.

Acacia paradoxa

syn. *Acacia armata*

KANGAROO THORN

☼ ❄ ↔ 10–12 ft (3–3.5 m)
↕ 10–12 ft (3–3.5 m)

Widespread from the coast to semi-arid regions of mainland Australia, this many-branched shrub is armed with needle-like spines. It has wavy oblong phyllodes, and produces large

golden yellow flower balls in late winter–spring. Useful as a barrier hedge. Zones 8–11.

Acacia pendula

BOREE, WEEPING MYALL

☼ ❄ ↔ 20 ft (6 m) ↕ 40 ft (12 m)

This beautiful weeping tree is widespread in low-rainfall areas of eastern Australia. Narrow silvery phyllodes. Small lemon yellow flower balls are inconspicuous. Timber used for wood-turning and small ornamental articles. Zones 9–11.

Acacia podalyriifolia

QUEENSLAND WATTLE

☼ ❄ ↔ 15 ft (4.5 m) ↕ 10–15 ft (3–4.5 m)

Native to coastal areas of southern Queensland, Australia. This large

Acacia pycnantha

shrub or slender small tree is widely cultivated for its decorative, rounded, silvery phyllodes and profuse, fragrant, golden flower balls, in clusters, in early winter–spring. Zones 9–11.

Acacia pravissima ★

OVENS WATTLE, WEDGE-LEAFED WATTLE

☼ ❄ ↔ 10 ft (3 m) ↕ 10–25 ft (3–8 m)

Native to hilly country in southeastern Australia. Spreading shrub or small tree, drooping branches and small, roughly triangular, olive green phyllodes. Profuse, golden yellow, globular flowers in extended racemes, in spring. The prostrate form, 'Golden Carpet', spreads to 15 ft (4.5 m). Zones 8–10.

Acacia prominens

GOSFORD WATTLE

☼ ❄ ↔ 10–12 ft (3–3.5 m)
↕ 12–60 ft (3.5–18 m)

From central coast of New South Wales, Australia. Attractive low-branching tree with narrow blue-green phyllodes. Profuse clusters of sweetly scented pale yellow flower balls in winter–early spring. Zones 9–11.

Acacia pubescens

DOWNY WATTLE

☼ ❄ ↔ 10 ft (3 m) ↕ 3–12 ft (0.9–3.5 m)

This beautiful spreading shrub from coastal New South Wales, Australia, is endangered in its natural habitat. Pendulous branches have bright green bipinnate leaves. Masses of bright yellow flower balls in late winter–spring. Cut flowers last well. Zones 9–11.

Acacia pulchella

WESTERN PRICKLY MOSES

☼ ❄ ↔ 7 ft (2 m) ↕ 5 ft (1.5 m)

From Western Australia. Attractive, multi-branched shrub. Bipinnate leaves, small spines at the base. Single golden flower balls on stalks, longer than the leaves, in late winter–spring. Zones 9–11.

Acacia pycnantha

GOLDEN WATTLE

☼ ❄ ↔ 15 ft (4.5 m) ↕ 10–25 ft (3–8 m)

This tall shrub or small open-branched tree is Australia's national floral emblem. Pendulous branches, bright green phyllodes. Racemes of large, perfumed, golden yellow, ball-shaped flowers in late winter–spring. Zones 9–11.

Acacia redolens

☼ ❄ ↔ 10–25 ft (3–8 m)
↕ 3–15 ft (0.9–4.5 m)

Small spreading shrub with gray-green or bluish green phyllodes with 3 to 4 prominent longitudinal veins, sweetly scented. Yellow flowerheads are borne in spring. Pods narrow. Occurs in southwestern Australia. Zones 8–9.

Acacia retinodes

SILVER WATTLE, SWAMP WATTLE, WIRILDA

☼ ❄ ↔ 10 ft (3 m) ↕ 10–25 ft (3–8 m)

Shrub or small tree native to southeastern Australia. Will withstand short periods of boggy conditions in the garden. Bluish green narrow phyllodes. Lemon yellow globular flowers, in short racemes, in late spring–summer. Zones 8–10.

Acacia pubescens

Acacia rubida

Acacia ulicifolia

Acacia riceana

RICE'S WATTLE

☼ ❄ ↔ 10 ft (3 m) ↑ 10–20 ft (3–6 m)

Native to Tasmania, Australia. Prickly shrub or small tree, often with drooping branches. Narrow, dark green, sharply pointed phyllodes. Profuse pale yellow flower balls, in loose sprays, in early spring. Zones 8–10.

Acacia rigens

NEEDLE WATTLE

☼ ❄ ↔ 12 ft (3.5 m) ↑ 12 ft (3.5 m)

Widespread in arid and semi-arid regions of mainland Australia, this dense rounded shrub is an attractive ornamental. Silver-gray, stiff, narrow, sharply pointed phyllodes. Profuse clusters of golden flower balls in winter–spring. Zones 8–10.

Acacia rubida

RED-STEMMED WATTLE

☼ ❄ ↔ 6–10 ft (1.8–3 m)
↑ 10–30 ft (3–9 m)

Widely distributed in eastern Australia. Bushy shrub or small tree, deep red angular stems, reddish foliage in winter, narrow leathery phyllodes. Bright yellow flower balls, in small clusters, late winter–spring. Zones 8–10.

Acacia salicina

COOBA, COOBAH, NATIVE WILLOW

☼ ❄ ↔ 10–17 ft (3–5 m)
↑ 15–35 ft (4.5–10 m)

Occurs along inland streams of all mainland States of Australia. Tall spreading tree, branches pendulous, often suckering. Phyllodes pendulous, thick, brittle, green to blue-green. Pale yellow flowers during most months, peaking in autumn–winter. Pods light brown, thick, woody. Zones 8–9.

Acacia saligna

syn. *Acacia cyanophylla*

GOLDEN WREATH WATTLE, ORANGE WATTLE, PORT JACKSON WILLOW, WESTERN AUSTRALIAN GOLDEN WATTLE

☼ ❄ ↔ 10–20 ft (3–6 m)
↑ 7–35 ft (2–10 m)

Occurs along the southwest corner of Australia, mainly in coastal areas.

Fast-growing small tree, spreading crown, pendulous reddish branches. Phyllodes green or blue-green, often curved. Bright yellow to orange flowerheads in late winter–early summer. Long flat pods. Zones 9–10.

Acacia spectabilis

MUDGEE WATTLE

☼ ❄ ↔ 10 ft (3 m) ↑ 8–10 ft (2.4–3 m)

From the inland slopes of eastern Australia. Tall slender shrub with pendulous branches, and soft, blue-green, bipinnate leaves. Very showy, golden yellow, ball-shaped flowers in late winter–spring. Zones 9–11.

Acacia stenophylla

EUMONG, NATIVE WILLOW, RIVER COOBA

☼ ❄ ↔ 10–20 ft (3–6 m)
↑ 15–50 ft (4.5–15 m)

Found along inland streams of all mainland States of Australia, this is a dense tree, often weeping, with rough dark bark. The tree has thick, pendulous, gray-green phyllodes, up to 16 in (40 cm) long, with many longitudinal veins. Clusters of creamy colored flowerheads appear in autumn–winter. Pods are straight but wrinkled. Zones 8–10.

Acacia suaveolens

SWEET WATTLE

☼ ❄ ↔ 5 ft (1.5 m) ↑ 8 ft (2.4 m)

Widespread from the coast to the ranges in eastern Australia, this species has narrow blue-green phyllodes. Perfumed pale yellow flower balls are produced through winter–spring. Flattened bluish pods. Advisable to prune after flowering to encourage compact shape. Zones 9–11.

Acacia tenuinervis

☼ ❄ ↔ 12 ft (3.5 m) ↑ 30 ft (9 m)

Occurring on low scrub-covered ranges in southeastern Queensland, Australia, this is an attractive long-lived species that sometimes suckers from the roots. Phyllodes extend to 4 in (10 cm) long and have fine parallel veins. In spring, long spikes of flowers in the leaf axils. Zones 9–12.

Acacia tortilis

UMBRELLA THORN

☼ ❄ ↔ 20–30 ft (6–9 m) ↑ 30 ft (9 m)

From most parts of Africa and the Arabian Peninsula, this tree has an umbrella-shaped crown. Sharp spines, small bipinnate leaves with minute leaflets. Scented, white to pale yellow flowers in mid-summer. Twisted pale brown pods. *A. t.* **subsp.** *heteracantha* is the most widely distributed of the species in southern Africa. Zones 9–11.

Acacia triptera

SPURWING WATTLE

☼ ❄ ↔ 15 ft (4.5 m) ↑ 12 ft (3.5 m)

Native to semi-arid eastern Australia. Densely branched, spreading. Stiff, curved, pointed phyllodes. Golden, rod-like flowers in late winter–spring. Excellent protective hedge. Zones 9–11.

Acacia ulicifolia

PRICKLY MOSES, PRICKLY WATTLE

☼ ❄ ↔ 5 ft (1.5 m) ↑ 6 ft (1.8 m)

Widespread in eastern Australia. Small shrub, spreading or arching wiry branches. Crowded prickly phyllodes. Single, pale yellow, globular flowers, on slender stalks extending beyond the phyllodes, in winter–spring. Good as a low barrier hedge. Zones 9–11.

Acacia triptera

Acacia tortilis with weaver bird nests, in the wild, in Samburu National Park, Kenya

A

Acacia verticillata var. *latifolia*

Acacia verticillata

PRICKLY MOSES

☀ ❄ ↔ 7 ft (2 m) ↑ 10 ft (3 m)

Attractive shrub from southeastern mainland Australia and Tasmania. May be low and spreading or upright with arching branches. Very sharp needle-like phyllodes. Bright yellow flower spikes in late winter–spring. *A. v.* var. *latifolia* covers a range of forms with broader, flatter, and often blunt-tipped phyllodes. Zones 9–11.

Acacia vestita

WEEPING BOREE

☀ ❄ ↔ 6–15 ft (1.8–4.5 m)
↑ 6–15 ft (1.8–4.5 m)

From eastern Australia. Dense shrub, widely cultivated, attractive pendulous branches, green phyllodes. Masses of golden yellow ball-shaped flowers, in clusters, in spring. Good screen, hedge, or low windbreak. Prune after flowering to maintain shape. Zones 9–11.

Acacia victoriae

BRAMBLE WATTLE, GUNDABLUEY

☀ ❄ ↔ 10 ft (3 m) ↑ 6–25 ft (1.8–8 m)

Widespread in inland mainland Australia, this spreading shrub or small tree is useful as a large hedge in areas with low rainfall. Gray-green phyllodes, with strong spines at the base. Fragrant, creamy yellow, ball-shaped flowers in late winter–early summer. Zones 8–11.

Acacia xanthophloea

FEVER TREE

☀ ❄ ↔ 20–40 ft (6–12 m) ↑ 50 ft (15 m)

Native to southeastern Africa, this deciduous tree has a somewhat sparse wide-spreading crown. Bark smooth, powdery, yellow-green, straight sharp thorns and small bipinnate leaves. Fragrant, golden yellow, rounded flowers are seen in spring. This is the fever tree of Kipling's story, 'The Elephant's Child'. Zones 9–11.

ACAENA

BIDDY BIDDY, NEW ZEALAND BURR,
SHEEP'S BURRS

This genus of creeping perennials and evergreen subshrubs is a member of the rose (Rosaceae) family. It contains about 100 species native to California and Hawaii, USA, South America, Australia, and New Zealand where they grow in dry mountainous areas. The leaves are small and often fern-like, their color ranging from bright green to grayish blues and bronze-purple. Tiny spherical flowerheads are held above the foliage and the spiny burrs that follow are very ornamental in some species. Their prostrate stems root freely, making them ideal ground cover plants and for growing over walls.
CULTIVATION: *Acaena* species grow readily in poor soil but must be well drained. They prefer full sun but will tolerate light shade. Most species are hardy but they may be deciduous where prolonged frosts are experienced. Propagate from rooted stem pieces or seed in autumn and spring.

Acaena anserinifolia

☀ ❄ ↔ 32 in (80 cm) ↑ 4 in (10 cm)

From Australia and New Zealand, this species has dull green fern-like foliage, flushed brown at the base. Insignificant flowers are followed by red spiny seed heads held above the foliage from summer to autumn. Zones 6–10.

Acaena anserinifolia

Acaena microphylla

Acaena novae-zelandiae

Acaena microphylla 'Kupferteppich'

Acaena caesiiglauca

☀ ❄ ↔ 32 in (80 cm) ↑ 2 in (5 cm)

A New Zealand species with small pinnately divided leaves of bluish gray, silky beneath. Its small white flowerheads are held well above the foliage and are followed by brown spiny burrs. Zones 6–10.

Acaena microphylla

☀ ❄ ↔ 20 in (50 cm) ↑ 2 in (5 cm)

From New Zealand's North Island, this is a ground-hugging species with fine ferny foliage of green or bronze. The tiny cream flowers are followed by eye-catching, spiny, red burrs in late summer. 'Kupferteppich' (syn. *A. m.* 'Copper Carpet') has green to bronze leaves. Zones 6–10.

Acaena montana

ALPINE BURR

☀ ❄ ↔ 12 in (30 cm) ↑ 2 in (5 cm)

This Australian native is a ground-hugging alpine plant. It has finely divided green leaves and tiny flowerheads held above the foliage. The seed heads have short brownish spines. Zones 6–9.

Acaena novae-zelandiae

BIDDY BIDDY, BIDGEE-WIDGEE, PIRRI-PIRRI

☀ ❄ ↔ 40 in (100 cm) ↑ 6 in (15 cm)

A vigorous species from New Zealand, New Guinea, and southeastern Australia. Naturalized in parts of Britain and a noxious weed in California, USA. Vivid green leaves, finely divided. Spiny red seed heads are borne in late summer. Zones 6–10.

Acacia xanthophloea, in the wild, in Africa

Acaena saccaticupula

☀ ❋ ↔ 3 ft (0.9 m) ↑ 4–8 in (10–20 cm)

From subalpine and alpine New Zealand. Pinnate bronze to red-green leaves to 5 in (12 cm) long, with 9 to 15 toothed leaflets. Purple-red flower-heads with conspicuous, hooked, red spines. 'Blue Haze' has red-tinted blue-green foliage. Zones 6–10.

ACALYPHA

This pantropical genus of the spurge or euphorbia (Euphorbiaceae) family contains over 400 species of perennials, shrubs, and trees best known for their long catkins or spikes of flowers, often bright magenta to red shades. Their leaves are simple, fairly large, oval-shaped with toothed edges. The foliage of *A. amentacea* subsp. *wilkesiana* has showy variegations, though mostly the plants are grown for their flowers. Individually these are minute, but those of female plants form dense-ly packed catkins that in some species can be up to 18 in (45 cm) long. CULTIVATION: Warm, almost frost-free conditions are essential as is plenty of moisture during the growing season. Plant in moist, humus-rich, well-drained soil, and feed well to keep the foliage lush and the plants flowering freely. Pinch back the young shoots and deadhead the flowers to keep the growth compact; otherwise little pruning is required. Propagate from cuttings and, if growing indoors, watch for mealybugs and white flies.

Acalypha amentacea subsp. *wilkesiana*

syn. *Acalypha wilkesiana*

COPPERLEAF, FIJIAN FIRE PLANT, JACOB'S COAT

☀ ⚘ ↔ 10 ft (3 m) ↑ 10 ft (3 m)

From Fiji and nearby Pacific islands. Shrub with striking foliage colors and patterns. Colors range from green to bronze, and in tapestries of pink, rosy red, cream, or yellow, sometimes with contrasting margins that are coarsely serrated. Flowers in summer–autumn are upstaged by the foliage. 'Ceylon', bronze-purple leaves, edged in pink or white; 'Marginata', coppery leaves edged in red. Zones 10–12.

Acalypha hispida

CHENILLE PLANT, RED-HOT CAT-TAIL

☀ ✴ ↔ 5 ft (1.5 m) ↑ 12 ft (3.5 m)

Famed for its long tassels of blood red flowers, this species is most likely a native of tropical East Asia. Leaves are bright green, with toothed edges, and covered in fine hairs. Excellent in hanging baskets where the tassels can be seen from below. Zones 11–12.

Acalypha reptans

Acalypha reptans

RED CAT-TAILS

☀ ⚘ ↔ 12 in (30 cm) ↑ 12 in (30 cm)

Often grown as a hanging basket plant, this native of Florida, USA, and nearby Caribbean islands has soft light to mid-green leaves. Its flower catkins are deep pink to pale red in summer, spot flowering at other times. Zones 10–12.

ACANTHOLIMON

PRICKLY THRIFT

This genus of around 120 species of small tufted or cushion-forming perennials and subshrubs is a member of the leadwort (Plumbaginaceae) family. These species are found from the Mediterranean to central Asia, often in mountain areas. As the common name suggests, they

resemble thrift (*Armeria*) but with rather stiff spine-tipped leaves. Some species have two types of foliage: broad fleshy spring leaves, followed by narrow needle-like summer leaves. The flowers are around ½ in (12 mm) wide, have 5–10 petals and a funnel-shaped calyx, and are borne in small open heads on wiry stems or among the foliage, usually in late spring and summer. CULTIVATION: Most species need perfect drainage and are therefore best suited to rockery, trough, or cool greenhouse cultivation. Plant in gritty free-draining soil in full sun. They can withstand extremes of summer heat and winter cold but will not tolerate being wet and cold. Propagate from seed or small base cuttings.

Acalypha amentacea subsp. *wilkesiana*

Acantholimon avenaceum

☀ ❋ ↔ 4–8 in (10–20 cm)
↑ 8–12 in (20–30 cm)

From central Asia. Forms a dense cushion of light green linear leaves. Long-flowering with open sprays of pink flowers and dark-veined off-white calyces on upright wiry stems. Zones 3–9.

Acantholimon glumaceum ★

☀ ❋ ↔ 12 in (30 cm)
↑ 4–6 in (10–15 cm)

Found from the Caucasus to western Asia. Narrow dark green leaves to 1¼ in (30 mm) long. Stems to 6 in (15 cm) long carry 6–8 small deep pink flowers backed by downy white calyces. Zones 3–9.

Acantholimon hohenackeri

☀ ❋ ↔ 8–16 in (20–40 cm)
↑ 4–6 in (10–15 cm)

Found from the Caucasus to northern Iran, this species has large, spiny, blue-gray cushions on a woody base, and stiff linear leaves. Open sprays of soft pink flowers. Zones 3–9.

Acantholimon hohenackeri

A

Acanthus dioscoridis

Acanthus hirsutus

Acanthus spinosus 'Lady Moore'

Acanthus mollis

ACANTHUS

BEAR'S BREECHES

From the acanthus (Acanthaceae) family, this genus includes 30 species of perennials and subshrubs from the temperate and tropical Old World regions. Cultivated species are valued for their bold, often near-evergreen foliage and upright flower spikes. The leaves, which form a basal clump, are usually large, glossy, and pinnately lobed, the lobes being toothed or spiny. The flowers are tubular, tend to be mauve and white, and are partially enclosed within conspicuous bracts. May self-sow freely and can sucker. Large, but not especially attractive, seed pods follow. The acanthus leaf is the basis for many classical Greek and Roman designs, often featured atop columns and along friezes. It can also be found in Coptic, Byzantine, Celtic, and Baroque art. Early Christians adopted the leaf as a symbol of heaven. CULTIVATION: Species mostly cold tolerant but prefer mild winters. Plant in moist, well-drained, humus-rich soil in sun or half-sun. Many have heavy roots and divide easily, otherwise raise from spring-sown seed.

Acanthus dioscoridis

☼ ❄ ↔ 30–60 in (75–150 cm) ↑ 24–36 in (60–90 cm)

Found from Turkey to Iran. Clump-forming foliage rosettes on spreading roots. Leaves to 2 in (5 cm) wide, silver-green, entire, finely cut or lobed with few spines. Flowers in summer, mauve-pink to 2 in (5 cm) wide within toothed bracts on 16 in (40 cm) inflorescences. *A. d.* var. *laciniatus* has leaves more finely and deeply cut, often to near the midrib. Zones 8–10.

Acanthus hirsutus

☼ ❄ ↔ 24–30 in (60–75 cm) ↑ 18 in (45 cm)

From Turkey, this rosette-forming plant has deeply lobed leaves that have soft spiny tips. The hairy flowering stems bear fewer flowers than other species. Flowers have a yellowish green tubular calyx with protruding off-white to yellow petals. Zones 7–10.

Acanthus mollis

BEAR'S BREECHES

☼/☀ ❄ ↔ 40–60 in (100–150 cm) ↑ 7 ft (2 m)

Deep lustrous green, deeply toothed, soft-spined, pinnate or doubly pinnate leaves up to 36 in (90 cm) long. White flowers flushed pale purple in toothed mauve bracts on stems up to 2 m (7 ft) tall. Found in southern Europe and northwest Africa. 'Candelabrus' has large-lobed flowers on sometimes branching flower stems. Zones 6–10.

Acanthus montanus

MOUNTAIN THISTLE

☼/☀ ❄ ↔ 3–7 ft (0.9–2 m) ↑ 7 ft (2 m)

Shrubby species found at moderate to high altitudes in tropical West Africa. Small, stiff, dark green leaves with a silvery sheen, deeply lobed, thistle-like, harsh spines. Short terminal flower stems with white flowers, can be pink- or mauve-tinted. Zones 10–11.

Acanthus spinosus

☼/☀ ❄ ↔ 40–60 in (100–150 cm) ↑ 36 in (90 cm)

Found around the Mediterranean. Similar to *A. mollis* but with leaves more deeply divided, broader and spinier. White, sometimes mauve-tinted flowers in spiny bracts. 'Lady Moore' (Spinosissimus Group), variegated leaves and purple and white flowers. Zones 6–10.

ACCA

syn. *Feijoa*

This South American genus of the myrtle (Myrtaceae) family consists of 6 species of evergreen shrubs and small trees that bear a guava-like fruit. Simple, smooth-edged leaves are paler on the underside. The attractive single flowers have fleshy petals and conspicuous stamens. Only one species, *A. sellowiana* (syn. *Feijoa sellowiana*), is commonly cultivated, for its tasty fruit or for ornament, and is grown in the same kinds of warm-temperate climates that suit oranges. CULTIVATION: The feijoa likes a sunny position and well-drained soil of moderate fertility. It is tolerant of exposure and even salt-laden winds, and can be clipped to form a dense hedge. Mature plants tolerate moderate winter frosts but in cooler climates will thrive better against a wall that traps the sun's heat. Cross-pollination, preferably by another plant not of the same clone, is needed for good fruit production. Named varieties are propagated from cuttings or grafting, but seed-raised plants are just as ornamental, if lacking fruit quality, and are more reliable pollinators.

Acca sellowiana ★

syn. *Feijoa sellowiana*

FEIJOA, PINEAPPLE GUAVA

☼ ❄ ↔ 10 ft (3 m) ↑ 10 ft (3 m)

Native from southern Brazil to northern Argentina, the feijoa has leathery, oval, glossy green leaves, whitish beneath. Flowers have cupped petals, pale carmine, with dark crimson stamens. Fruit is elliptical with sweet, aromatic, cream flesh. Cultivars include: 'Beechwood', with smooth-skinned fruit; 'Coolidge', bearing abundant fruit; 'Mammoth',

Acca sellowiana

bearing large wrinkled-skinned fruit; '**Nazemetz**', bearing large fruit to 4 in (10 cm) long; and '**Trask**', with thick-skinned fruit. Zones 8–10.

ACER

MAPLE

This mostly deciduous tree genus of the maple (Aceraceae) family has many species valued for their ornamental qualities. It consists of around 120 species, most from the Northern Hemisphere. Maples are forest or woodland trees of moist climates. The majority have simple leaves, mostly toothed or lobed, borne on slender leaf stalks attached to the twigs in opposite pairs. A small number have compound leaves with 3, 5, or 7 leaflets. Flowers are small, in clusters or dense spikes. Fruits consists of two small nuts (samaras), joined where attached to the flower stalk, each terminating in an elongated wing. CULTIVATION: Maples thrive best in cooler temperate climates with adequate rainfall, aided by warm humid summers and sharply demarcated winters. Best in deep well-drained soil with permanent subsoil moisture. Some need dappled shade to preserve their foliage from summer scorching, but some can tolerate exposure to drying winds. Propagation of species is from seed, cultivars by grafting.

Acer buergerianum

TRIDENT MAPLE

☼ ❄ ↔ 25 ft (8 m) ↑ 30 ft (9 m)

From eastern China and Korea. Usually seen as a sturdy small tree, and a popular bonsai subject. Leaves have 3 short lobes, turning yellowish often flushed with red in autumn. Bark flaky, pale gray. Winged fruits persist through winter. Zones 6–8.

Acer campbellii

syns *Acer sinense, A. wilsonii*

☼ ❄ ↔ 8–15 ft (2.4–4.5 m) ↑ 15–40 ft (4.5–12 m)

From China, Indochina, and the eastern Himalayas, this is a variable

Acer campestre, in summer

species divided into 4 subspecies. Leaves have 5 to 7 lobes. New foliage is bronzy red, and autumn color is golden yellow to brilliant red. *A. c.* subsp. *flabellatum* is a smaller hardier tree with a twiggy habit and large shiny leaves, while *A. c.* subsp. *wilsonii* has smaller, 3-lobed leaves. Zones 7–10.

Acer campestre

FIELD MAPLE, HEDGE MAPLE

☼ ❄ ↔ 12 ft (3.5 m) ↑ 30 ft (9 m)

This is a spreading tree from western Asia, Europe, and North Africa that is commonly seen in English country hedges. Its leaves turn clear golden yellow in autumn and its bark becomes thick and furrowed with age. *A. c.* subsp. *tauricum* has smaller leaves, with downy undersides. Cultivars include: *A. c.* '**Carnival**', a slow-growing clone that grows to 10 ft (3 m) high and wide, with leaves heavily margined white; '**Elsrijk**', with rich dark green foliage and conical habit; '**Queen Elizabeth**' ★, with erect habit and lustrous foliage; and '**Schwerinii**', with reddish foliage, turning purple. Zones 3–8.

Acer capillipes

RED SNAKEBARK MAPLE

☼ ❄ ↔ 35 ft (10 m) ↑ 40 ft (12 m)

This species from Japan has interesting bark and attractive foliage. Its young stems are bright pinkish red ageing to white-striped green-brown bark. Leaves are dark green with serrated edges and prominent red stalks. Zones 5–9.

Acer campestre, in winter

Acer cappadocicum 'Aureum'

Acer cappadocicum

CAPPADOCIAN MAPLE

☼ ❄ ↔ 50 ft (15 m) ↑ 60 ft (18 m)

From the highlands of Turkey and southwest Asia to the Himalayas, this fast-growing species has leaves with 5 or 7 very regular, triangular lobes and a flat base. Unfolding leaves may be reddish, and turn butter yellow in autumn. Forms and cultivars include: *A. c.* subsp. *lobelii*, a columnar form; *A. c.* subsp. *sinicum*, which has

more sharply pointed leaf lobes and rougher bark; *A. c.* '**Aureum**', which has golden new foliage in spring; and '**Rubrum**', a cultivar with deep red young foliage. Zones 5–8.

Acer carpinifolium

HORNBEAM MAPLE

☼ ❄ ↔ 30 ft (9 m) ↑ 30 ft (9 m)

From the mountain forests of Japan. Either a tree or large shrub. Densely branched. Unlobed corrugated leaves with serrated margins, turning gold in autumn. Winged fruits are curved. A slow-growing plant. Zones 4–8.

Acer caudatum

☼ ❄ ↔ 15–30 ft (4.5–9 m) ↑ 40 ft (12 m)

From the eastern Himalayas, northeastern China, upper Myanmar and northern Japan. Leaves have 5 triangular lobes and coarsely serrated margins. Bark dark brown, fissured. Winged fruits in clusters. *A. c.* subsp. *ukurunduense* has 5- to 7-lobed leaves with serrated edges. Zones 4–9.

Acer campbellii subsp. *flabellatum*

Acer carpinifolium

Acer caudatum subsp. *ukurunduense*

A

Acer circinnatum

VINE MAPLE

☀ ❄ ↔ 15 ft (4.5 m) ↕ 15 ft (4.5 m)

From western North America, this shrub or low-branching tree is noted for its spectacular color. Leaves rounded with 7 to 9 lobes turn orange-scarlet to deep red in autumn. Purple flowers. Red horizontal winged fruits. 'Monroe' has deeply cut leaves. Zones 4–8.

Acer cissifolium

VINE-LEAF MAPLE

☀ ❄ ↔ 35 ft (10 m) ↕ 30 ft (9 m)

From Japan, this small tree or shrub has a spreading crown, smooth gray bark, and compound leaves. The 3 bronze-tinted leaflets with serrated margins turn yellow, orange, or red in autumn. Seeds in clusters. Needs acid soils. Zones 5–8.

Acer × conspicuum

☀ ❄ ↔ 20–30 ft (6–9 m) ↕ 30 ft (9 m)

This is a hybrid between the 2 snakebark maples *A. davidii* and *A. pensylvanicum*, first found in England in the 1960s. A vigorous tree, it has leaves with 3 or 5 lobes. The original clone is 'Silver Vein', with very large leaves and bark more conspicuously striped than any other maple. Zones 5–9.

Acer crataegifolium

☀ ❄ ↔ 25 ft (8 m) ↕ 25 ft (8 m)

From Japan. Leaves resemble hawthorn *(Crataegus)*. Leaves 3-lobed or almost unlobed, to 3 in (8 cm) long, dark green to bluish green, wavy margins, purplish stalks. Small winged fruits, ¾ in (18 mm) across. Needs summer moisture. Zones 6–8.

Acer davidii ★

PERE DAVID'S MAPLE

☀ ❄ ↔ 25 ft (8 m) ↕ 30 ft (9 m)

Elegant fast-growing tree from central and western China. Open habit with arching branches, striped greenish bark. Leaves pointed, toothed, some with small lobes near base. Small reddish fruits in long pendent spikes. Cultivars include: 'Ernest Wilson', a compact tree with narrow orange leaves; 'George Forrest', with dark red young foliage, almost unlobed leaves; and 'Serpentine', smaller-leafed than the species. Zones 5–9.

Acer forrestii

syn. *Acer pectinatum* subsp. *forrestii*

☀ ❄ ↔ 20–30 ft (6–9 m)
↕ 25–40 ft (8–12 m)

From western China, a medium-sized tree with spreading branches, bark reddish or purplish on young branches, striped with white. Leaves dull

Acer × freemanii 'Armstrong'

Acer × freemanii Celebration/'Celzam'

dark green, long-pointed, with 2 to 4 lateral lobes. 'Alice' is shrubby, with large strongly veined leaves variegated pinkish in summer. Zones 5–9.

Acer × freemanii

☀ ❄ ↔ 20–40 ft (6–12 m) ↕ 50 ft (15 m)

This cross between *A. rubrum* and *A. saccharinum* was raised at the US National Arboretum in 1930, and the two species frequently interbreed in the wild. The resultant plants are quick-growing round-topped trees with 5-lobed leaves. The foliage often develops brilliant autumn colors. Cultivars include: 'Armstrong', with orange-yellow autumn color; Autumn Blaze/'Jeffersred' ★ (syn. *A. rubrum* 'Autumn Blaze'), with intense orange and red autumn foliage; Celebration/'Celzam', fairly compact, with red and gold autumn color; and 'Marmo', with an oval-shaped foliage head and red to maroon autumn color. Zones 5–9.

Acer griseum

CHINESE PAPERBARK MAPLE,
PAPERBARK MAPLE

☀ ❄ ↔ 35 ft (10 m) ↕ 40 ft (12 m)

From central and western China, this species is an attractive slender tree. Its outstanding feature is the texture and color of the bark. Leaves

Acer griseum

turn orange, scarlet, and crimson in autumn. The tree's winged fruits have large seeds. Zones 4–8.

Acer grosseri

syn. *Acer davidii* subsp. *grosseri*

☀ ❄ ↔ 20 ft (6 m) ↕ 15–30 ft (4.5–9 m)

Very similar to *A. davidii*, coming from more northerly regions of central China. Bark more conspicuously white-striped. Leaves almost triangular with broad pointed basal lobes, coloring red in autumn. *A. g.* var. *hersii* has leaves 3-lobed toward their apex. Zones 5–9.

Acer davidii

Acer davidii 'George Forrest'

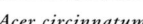

Acer circinnatum

Acer grosseri

Acer japonicum

Acer heldreichii

Acer heldreichii
GREEK MAPLE, HELDREICH'S MAPLE
☼ ❄ ↔ 60 ft (18 m) ↑ 60 ft (18 m)
Native to Greece and the Balkans.
Attractive tree with 3-lobed papery
leaves, turning yellow and sometimes
red in autumn. Smooth bark with
buds almost black. Winged fruits.
A. h. subsp. *trautvetteri*, the red bud
maple, comes from the Caucasus and
northern Turkey. Zones 5–8.

Acer henryi
☼ ❄ ↔ 30 ft (9 m) ↑ 30 ft (9 m)
From mountain forests in central
China, this spreading dome-shaped
tree has bluish olive green, 3-part,
compound leaves, and bark with
bluish striations. Yellow flowers.
Clusters of winged fruits. Zones 6–8.

Acer japonicum
FULL-MOON MAPLE
☼ ❄ ↔ 30 ft (9 m) ↑ 30 ft (9 m)
A broadly spreading small tree from
the mostly dry and sunny mountain
forests of Japan. Leaves are rounded
with 7 to 11 sharply toothed, pointed
lobes turning yellow, orange and
crimson in autumn. Cultivars include:
'Aconitifolium', leaves deeply dissected and toothed turning crimson in
autumn; and 'Vitifolium', large
leaves, bronzy when young. Zones 6–8.

Acer longipes subsp. *amplum*

Acer macrophyllum

Acer 'Keithsform'
syn. *Acer* Norwegian Sunset
☼ ❄ ↔ 25 ft (8 m) ↑ 40 ft (12 m)
This hybrid between *A. platanoides*
and *A. truncatum* is intermediate
in its leaf shape. In comparison to
A. platanoides, it tolerates drought and
heat well. Autumn colors are gold to
red. Zones 4–9.

Acer longipes
☼ ❄ ↔ 15–30 ft (4.5–9 m) ↑ 40 ft (12 m)
From China, this tree is likely to
be smaller in cultivation than it is
in its natural habitat. There are 3
subspecies, including **A. l. subsp.
*amplum***. The leaves are glossy green,
5-lobed, and variable in size. Flowers
form a yellow cluster, but few seeds
are set; therefore the tree is uncommon. Zones 6–8.

Acer macrophyllum
OREGON MAPLE
☼ ❄ ↔ 80 ft (24 m) ↑ 80 ft (24 m)
From western North America this
striking species has the largest leaves
of all maples. Tall broadly columnar
tree. Leaves 5-lobed, dark green,

Acer 'Keithsform'

glossy, turning bright orange in
autumn. Large pendulous fruit clusters. Zones 6–8.

Acer mandshuricum
MANCHURIAN MAPLE
☼ ❄ ↔ 10 ft (3 m) ↑ 30 ft (9 m)
Native to northeastern China, Korea,
and Russia. Superb, if uncommon,
species. Narrow tree, rich color
in autumn. Leaves are 3-part, with
serrated margins and smooth red

stalks. Winged fruits 1 in (25 mm)
long, paired horizontally. Rarely seen
in gardens. Zones 5–8.

Acer maximowiczianum ★
syn. *Acer nikoense*
NIKKO MAPLE
☼ ❄ ↔ 40 ft (12 m) ↑ 60 ft (18 m)
Broadly spreading tree from China
and Japan; 3-part dark green leaves,
brilliant red in autumn. Green winged
fruits in spreading pairs. Zones 4–8.

Acer negundo 'Aureovariegatum'

Acer negundo 'Flamingo'

Acer monspessulanum

Acer negundo var. *violaceum*

Acer mono

Acer mono

☼ ❄ ↔ 50 ft (15 m) ↕ 50 ft (15 m)

From central and northern China to Mongolia, eastern Siberia, Korea, and Japan. Variable species, often found as a spreading dome-shaped tree, but can be shrub-like. Leaves 5- or 7-lobed, turn yellow to orange in autumn. Variegated cultivars can revert. Zones 5–8.

Acer monspessulanum

MONTPELIER MAPLE

☼ ❄ ↔ 35 ft (10 m) ↕ 40 ft (12 m)

Sometimes confused with *A. campestre,* this species from the Mediterranean region is a small tidy tree or large shrub with smooth gray bark and 3-lobed, smooth, leathery leaves. Pendulous clusters of winged fruits. Zones 6–8.

Acer negundo

BOX ELDER, BOX ELDER MAPLE, MANITOBA MAPLE

☼ ❄ ↔ 30 ft (9 m) ↕ 60 ft (18 m)

From eastern North America. This fast-growing hardy tree has several popular variegated forms. The green species is a rounded to broadly

columnar tree. Colored forms are smaller and less vigorous. All have compound leaves with 3 to 5 or 7 large leaflets. **A. n. var.** *violaceum* bears red to purple flowers on dark colored branches. Cultivars include: **A. n.** '**Aureovariegatum**', gold-edged leaflets; '**Elegans**', broad gold margin, male clone; '**Flamingo**', pink-margined in early spring, fading to white; '**Sensation**', rich pink autumn color; and '**Variegatum**' ★, a white-margined, sterile, female clone. Zones 5–9.

Acer palmatum

GREENLEAF JAPANESE MAPLE, JAPANESE MAPLE

☼ ❄ ↔ 25 ft (8 m) ↕ 20 ft (6 m)

With its species name alluding to the lobed leaves resembling a hand, this tree from Japan, Korea, and China has produced more than 1,000 cultivars; it is by far the most prolific of all maples. Best in rich, moist, well-drained loams, sheltered from drying or freezing winds. The 5- to 7-lobed leaves turn yellow, amber, crimson, and purple. Cultivars must be propagated by grafting or cuttings to be true to type. **A. p. var.** *coreanum* '**Korean Gem**' has black bark and spectacular autumn foliage.

Many cultivars belong to **A. p. var.** *dissectum* (syns *A. p.* 'Dissectum' and *A. p.* Dissectum Group), which consists of shrubs with narrow leaf lobes, which themselves are strongly lobed. Most are low growing with cascading branches, giving mature plants an umbrella-like or dome-like form. Further subdivisions of this variety are the **Dissectum Viride Group** with mid-green foliage, and the **Dissectum Atropurpureum Group** with deep

Acer palmatum var. *dissectum*

Acer palmatum var. *dissectum* 'Ornatum'

Acer palmatum var. *dissectum*

Acer palmatum 'Atrolineare'

Acer palmatum 'Nicholsonii'

Acer palmatum, in autumn

purple-red spring foliage that becomes more greenish in summer and often takes on yellow tones in autumn; '**Crimson Queen**', vigorous growth, bright red autumn foliage; '**Dissectum Nigrum**' (syn. 'Ever Red'), bright red in autumn; '**Inabe-shidare**', burgundy foliage; '**Ornatum**', deeply dissected leaves, turning red, amber, and gold in autumn.

Cultivars include: *A. p.* '**Akaji-nishiki**' (syn. 'Bonfire'), pinkish foliage in spring and autumn; '**Atrolineare**' (syns 'Filiferum Purpureum', 'Linearilobium Rubrum'), with 5-lobed red leaves, becoming greenish in summer; '**Atropurpureum**', leaves of 5 to 7 lobes, vibrant red in autumn; '**Bloodgood**', dark red leaves of 5 to 7 lobes, vibrant red in autumn; '**Burgundy Lace**', purple-bronze deeply cut leaves; '**Butterfly**', vase-shaped with cream-white margined 5-lobed leaves; '**Chishio**', spring foliage shrimp pink becoming greenish; '**Chitoseyama**', purple-red 7-lobed leaves; '**Garnet**', deep red spring foliage turning fiery red in

Acer palmatum, in winter

autumn; '**Heptalobum Rubrum**', wine purple spring foliage; '**Higasayama**', cream and pink variegated leaves; '**Katsura**', a spectacular shrubby tree; '**Kotohime**', dwarf to 5 ft (1.5 m) high, green-brown leaves turning golden in autumn; '**Linearilobum**', also known as 'Scolopendrifolium'; '**Moonfire**', claret-colored 7-lobed leaves that

Acer palmatum, in spring

mature to purple; '**Nicholsonii**', a much-branched shrub with leaves olive-bronze in spring, coloring brilliant gold to brilliant crimson; '**Nigrum**', a very dark purple shrub with light green winged fruits; '**Osakazuki**', 7-lobed brown-green leaves, turning russet in autumn; '**Red Dragon**', rich purple foliage; '**Red Filigree Lace**', with the most finely divided leaves of all maples of this type; '**Red Pygmy**', 5-lobed purple-brown leaves; '**Shigitatsu-sawa**' ('Reticulatum'), 7-lobed leaves green with a white net-like patterning;

'**Sango-kaku**', remarkable for its glowing red bark in winter; '**Seiryu**', distinctive vigorous growth and upright habit; '**Shindeshojo**', fresh spring growth an eye-catching scarlet; '**Shishigashira**', known as the "lion's head maple," good for seaside gardens; '**Suminagashi**', 7-lobed purplish leaves cut almost to the midrib, turning crimson in autumn; '**Trompenburg**', unique among maples for its mature foliage; '**Villa Taranto**', vase shaped; and '**Waterfall**', a classic, cascading, dome-shaped shrub. Zones 6–9.

Acer palmatum 'Sango-kaku'

Acer palmatum 'Shishigashira'

Acer pensylvanicum

GOOSEFOOT, MAPLE, MOOSEWOOD, STRIPED MAPLE

☀ ❄ ↔ 35 ft (10 m) ↑ 30 ft (9 m)

The only North American snakebark maple, with branches marked like markings found on the garter snake. From moist woodlands, it is a broadly columnar tree. White and red-brown stripes pattern green bark on the species. '**Erythrocladum**', winter bark is coral to salmon red, striped white. Leaves turn golden amber. Zones 4–8.

Acer pentaphyllum

☀ ❄ ↔ 25 ft (8 m) ↑ 30 ft (9 m)

Native to southern Sichuan Province in China, this striking and elegant

Acer pensylvanicum

small tree is believed to be extinct in the wild. Uncommon in cultivation, the green leaves have 5 narrow lobes turning yellow-amber in autumn. Zones 7–9.

Acer platanoides

NORWAY MAPLE

☀ ❄ ↔ 50 ft (15 m) ↑ 80 ft (24 m)

This fast-growing broadly columnar tree has elegant, 5-lobed, bright green leaves on long slender stalks that color clear yellow in autumn. Yellow-green flower clusters. Large winged fruits. Cultivars include: '**Cavalier**', compact growth habit, to 30 ft (9 m) tall; '**Cleveland**', red-tinged young foliage; '**Columnare**', slow-growing, to 50 ft (15 m) high; '**Crimson King**', deep red spring foliage, reddish green in summer, orange and crimson in autumn; '**Drummondii**', a variegated form, with a broad gold leaf margin maturing to creamy white; '**Laciniatum**', the "eagle's claw maple," an erect tree with wedge-shaped leaves; and '**Palmatifidum**' (syn. 'Lorbergii'), leaves deeply dissected into 5 sculptured lobes. Other popular cultivars include '**Deborah**', '**Emerald Queen**',

Acer platanoides 'Rubrum'

A. p. 'Walderseei'

A. p. 'Goldsworth Purple'

'**Faassen's Black**', '**Globe**', '**Goldsworth Purple**', '**Green Lace**', '**Jade Gem**', '**Rubrum**', '**Schwedleri**', '**Undulatum**', and '**Walderseei**'. Zones 4–8.

Acer pseudoplatanus

SYCAMORE MAPLE

☀ ❄ ↔ 80 ft (24 m) ↑ 100 ft (30 m)

This large-domed tree, native to central and southern Europe is valued for shade, and is tolerant of city air pollution and salt-laden winds. Leaves, mid-green with 5 rounded lobes, turn burnt yellow in autumn. Greenish yellow flowers. Large winged fruit. Seeds prolifically. '**Atropurpureum**', leaves dark green above and reddish purple on the underside; '**Brilliantissimum**', striking salmon pink spring foliage; '**Erectum**', upright branches; '**Leopoldii**', a scene-stealer with gold-flecked and speckled leaves; and

Acer platanoides 'Palmatifidum'

'**Prinz Handjery**', similar to '**Brilliantissimum**', has a purplish reverse to the leaves. Zones 4–8.

Acer rubrum

CANADIAN MAPLE, RED MAPLE, SCARLET MAPLE, SWAMP MAPLE

☀ ❄ ↔ 35 ft (10 m) ↑ 100 ft (30 m)

A native of eastern North America, this large tree is appreciated for its

Acer pensylvanicum 'Erythrocladum'

Acer pseudoplatanus

Acer pseudoplatanus 'Brilliantissimum'

Acer platanoides 'Crimson King'

Acer platanoides 'Drummondii'

Acer saccharum 'Green Mountain'

Acer saccharum subsp. *grandidentum,* in the wild, Utah, USA

Acer saccharum subsp. *nigrum*

A. s. subsp. *nigrum* 'Temple's Upright'

fast growth, spectacular autumn color, and tolerance of wet soils and atmospheric pollution. Its leaves are 3- to 5-lobed, dark green in color, bluish beneath, changing to yellow, amber, or fiery red. Dense red flower clusters are formed. Red winged fruit. *A. r.* var. *drummondii* varies from the typical species in that it has larger flowers and thicker leaves, whitish beneath. Cultivars and hybrids include: *A. r.* '**Autumn Flame**', with a dense rounded crown and crimson autumn foliage; '**Gerling**', with a broad conical shape and fiery red autumn color; '**October Glory**', a spectacular 'Lipstick' tree; '**Scanlon**', with leaves turning gold-orange and speckled crimson in autumn; '**Scarsen**', with an upright habit and yellow-orange to vivid red color in autumn; and '**Sunshine**'. Zones 4–8.

Acer rubrum 'Gerling'

Acer saccharinum 'Beebe's Cutleaf Weeping'

Acer rufinerve

GRAY-BUDDED SNAKEBARK MAPLE, RED-VEIN MAPLE

☼ ✱ ↔ 35 ft (10 m) ↑ 40 ft (12 m)

This tree from Japan has bark that matures from bluish green with white stripes and distinctive diamond-shaped marks, to gray, becoming fissured with age. Leaves are 3- or 5-lobed turning orange, yellow, and scarlet in autumn. The bark of '**Winter Gold**', the goldtwig red-vein maple, turns a lustrous golden yellow color in winter. Zones 5–8.

Acer rufinerve

Acer saccharum, in the wild, in New Hampshire, USA

Acer saccharinum

RIVER MAPLE, SILVER MAPLE, SOFT MAPLE, WHITE MAPLE

☼ ✱ ↔ 80 ft (24 m) ↑ 100 ft (30 m)

From eastern North America, a majestic tree growing on moist riverbanks. Deep angularly lobed leaves, with a silvery reverse, turn clear yellow in

Acer rufinerve 'Winter Gold'

autumn. Coppery green winged fruits fall early. *A. s.* f. *lutescens*, yellow spring foliage turning light green then yellow in autumn; *A. s.* f. *pyramidale*, a narrower form with deeply cut leaves, excellent street tree. Cultivars include: *A. s.* '**Beebe's Cutleaf Weeping**' and '**Skinneri**'. Zones 4–8.

Acer saccharum

HARD MAPLE, ROCK MAPLE, SUGAR MAPLE

☼ ✱ ↔ 40 ft (12 m) ↑ 100 ft (30 m)

This species produces the best sap, which is extracted to make maple syrup. The tree and foliage resemble *A. platanoides*. In autumn individual trees turn yellow-orange and crimson. A stylized interpretation of the leaf is the national symbol of Canada. *A. s.* subsp. *grandidentum* (syn. *A. grandidentum*) reaches a height of 35–40 ft (10–12 m); *A. s.* subsp. *leucoderme* (syn. *A. leucoderme*) grows to 25 ft (8 m) high; and *A. s.* subsp. *nigrum* (syn. *A. nigrum*) is known as the black maple for its black bark; '**Green Column**', light green foliage turning yellow to apricot orange in autumn; '**Temple's Upright**' is a narrow upright form. Cultivars include: *A. s.* '**Flax Hill Majesty**', '**Green Mountain**', '**Legacy**', and '**Seneca Chief**'. Zones 4–8.

Acer rubrum

Acer rubrum 'Autumn Flame'

Acer rubrum 'Scarsen'

Acer rubrum 'Sunshine'

Acer tegmentosum

Acer shirasawanum 'Aureum'

Acer shirasawanum 'Microphyllum'

Acer shirasawanum

☀ ❄ ↔ 20 ft (6 m) ↕ 20 ft (6 m)
Leaves 9- to 13-lobed, lime green spring foliage, turns yellowish, then crimson in autumn. Red winged fruits. **'Aureum'** (syn. *A. japonicum* 'Aureum'), a popular cultivar; **'Microphyllum'** (syn. *A. japonicum* 'Microphyllum'), slightly smaller leaves. Zones 6–8.

Acer sikkimense

syn. *Acer hookeri*
☀ ❄ ↔ 10–20 ft (3–6 m) ↕ 40 ft (12 m)
Native to Sikkim and Assam in India, Bhutan, Myanmar, and Yunnan Province in China. Much smaller in cultivation, semi-deciduous in cold climates. Leaves are dark green, ovate, leathery, and lustrous. Young shoots are reddish. Zones 8–9.

Acer 'Silver Cardinal'

☀ ❄ ↔ 10–20 ft (3–6 m)
↕ 10–25 ft (3–8 m)
Previously thought to be a form of *A. × conspicuum*. Silver-striped maroon bark. Mottled green and cream leaves, pink veins, red leaf stalks. Zones 5–9.

Acer spicatum

MOUNTAIN MAPLE
☀ ❄ ↔ 15 ft (4.5 m) ↕ 30 ft (9 m)
From central and eastern North America, this is usually a large shrub

Acer truncatum

Acer velutinum

and occasionally a spreading tree with dense branch structure and greenish bark. The 3- to 5-lobed leaves are sharply serrated turning amber color in autumn. Zones 4–8.

Acer tataricum

AMUR MAPLE, TATARIAN MAPLE
☀ ❄ ↔ 25 ft (8 m) ↕ 35 ft (10 m)
From China, Japan, and Korea, this is a small, fast-growing, broadly spreading tree or shrub. Its leaves have 3 glossy toothed lobes, and color brilliantly amber and crimson in autumn. Fruits have broad red wings. ***A. t.* subsp. *ginnala*** (syn. *A. ginnala*), the most commonly seen subspecies, has given risen to several cultivars, including: **'Burgundy'**, rich autumn color; **'Compactum'**, to 8 ft (2.4 m) tall, vivid red autumn color; and **'Durand Dwarf'**, to 24 in (60 cm) tall. Zones 4–8.

Acer tegmentosum

☀ ❄ ↔ 35 ft (10 m) ↕ 30 ft (9 m)
From moist soils in Russia, North Korea, and northeastern China, this shrub or tree is appreciated for its

green bark, distinctly striped white. Foliage and young shoots are bluish; autumn foliage is gold. Flowers and fruits hang in pendulous clusters. Zones 5–8.

Acer triflorum

THREE-FLOWER MAPLE
☀/◐ ❄ ↔ 20–30 ft (6–9 m)
↕ 20–30 ft (6–9 m)
A small, upright tree from northeastern China and Korea. Its dark green trifoliate leaves become rich yellow or red in autumn. Flaking bark gives winter interest. This maple has greenish yellow flowers in clusters of 3, giving rise to its common name. Zones 5–7.

Acer truncatum

SHANTUNG MAPLE
☀ ❄ ↔ 18–25 ft (6–8 m)
↕ 25–35 ft (8–10 m)
Upright oval-shaped tree from northern and northeastern China and Korea. Smooth branches tinged with purple when young. Bright green deeply lobed leaves to 4 in (10 cm) long. Zones 5–8.

Acer velutinum

VELVET MAPLE
☀ ❄ ↔ 50 ft (15 m) ↕ 50 ft (15 m)
From the Caucasus and northern Iran, this tree resembles *A. pseudoplatanus*. Leaves are 5-lobed and coarsely serrated, light green and downy on the undersides. Abundant clusters of flowers and large spreading pairs of winged fruits. Zones 5–8.

Acer tataricum subsp. *ginnala* 'Burgundy'

Acer sikkimense

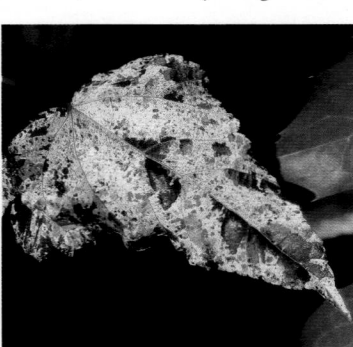

Acer 'Silver Cardinal'

Acer tataricum

A. t. subsp. *ginnala* 'Compactum'

Achillea clypeolata 'Coronation Gold'

ACHILLEA
MILFOIL, YARROW

This genus of about 100 species of clumping or mat-forming perennial plants is a member of the large daisy (Asteraceae) family. They grow throughout Europe and northern and western Asia in a range of habitats, including alpine. Some species can be invasive. The foliage is usually finely divided with a fern-like appearance and is often aromatic. The flowerheads are flattened or umbel-like, comprising numerous small flowers in white and pale cream, lemon, and pink. Numerous cultivars are available in brighter shades and these make excellent border plants. The genus is named after Achilles, the hero of Greek mythology, who is said to have known of its wound-healing qualities. CULTIVATION: Most species of this genus can easily be grown in well-drained soil in full sun. They can tolerate quite poor conditions and are frost hardy to 5°F (–15°C). Alpine species require perfect drainage and protection from winter rain if downy-leafed. Propagation is by division or from seed.

Achillea ageratifolia
☼ ❈ ↔ 18 in (45 cm) ↑ 6 in (15 cm)
A slow-growing alpine species from the Balkans. Downy silver foliage. Smothered in small white flowers in late spring. Zones 3–9.

Achillea clavennae
☼ ❈ ↔ 18 in (45 cm)
↑ 4–12 in (10–30cm)
Alpine species from central and eastern Europe. Silky gray foliage. Small tiny white flowerheads with pale yellow centers in summer. Zones 3–9.

Achillea clypeolata
☼ ❈ ↔ 12–18 in (30–45 cm)
↑ 18–24 in (45–60 cm)
From eastern Europe. A mat-forming species with grayish green foliage. Flowerheads 2–3 in (5–8 cm) across are crowded with small bright yellow flowers in summer. Cultivars include:

Achillea × *kellereri*

'Coronation Gold', a cross with *A. filipendulina*, growing to 40 in (100 cm) high with bright yellow flowers in heads up to 4 in (10 cm) across; and 'Moonshine', a cross with *A. millefolium* 'Taygetea' that has bright yellow flowerheads over silvery foliage. Zones 6–10.

Achillea coarctata
☼ ❈ ↔ 18–24 in (45–60 cm)
↑ 12–24 in (30–60 cm)
A native of eastern Europe. Silky finely divided foliage. Small yellow flowers in crowded heads, 1½–3 in (3.5–8 cm) across, are borne in spring–summer. Zones 6–10.

Achillea filipendulina
☼ ❈ ↔ 24–48 in (60–120 cm)
↑ 24–48 in (60–120 cm)
From central and western Asia, this robust species has divided, hairy, aromatic leaves up to 8 in (20 cm) long. Tiny gold flowers are crowded in flattened flowerheads, up to 4 in (10 cm) across, in summer. 'Cloth of Gold', 'Gold Plate', and 'Parker's Variety' are improved cultivars growing 4–6 ft (1.2–1.8 m) high with bright golden flowerheads up to 6 in (15 cm) across. 'Schwellenburg' grows to about 18 in (45 cm) high and has lemon yellow flowers. Zones 5–10.

Achillea × kellereri
☼ ❈ ↔ 10 in (25 cm) ↑ 6 in (15 cm)
Garden hybrid of *A. clypeolata* and *A. ageratifolia*. Mats of ferny gray foliage. Small creamy white daisy-like flowerheads, pale yellow centers, in summer. Suits rock garden. Zones 5–10.

Achillea 'King Edward'
☼ ❈ ↔ 10 in (25 cm) ↑ 4 in (10 cm)
Garden hybrid of *A. clavennae* and *A. clypeolata*. Feathery silvery gray foliage in tight clumps. Small flat heads of pale yellow flowers in summer. Suits rock garden. Zones 5–10.

Achillea millefolium
MILFOIL, YARROW
☼ ❈ ↔ 18–30 in (45–75 cm)
↑ 12–30 in (30–75 cm)
Weedy species from Europe and western Asia. Naturalized in temperate regions. Fern-like leaves. Flat heads of small dull white flowers summer–autumn. Herbal anti-inflammatory. Too invasive for most gardens but its many worthy cultivars include: 'Anthea'

(syn. 'Anblo'), pale yellow flowers, silvery foliage; 'Apple Blossom' (syn. 'Apfelblute'), rose pink; 'Cerise Queen', cherry red, vigorous; 'Fanal' (syn. 'The Beacon'), crimson-red, yellow centers; 'Heidi', bright salmon, yellow centers; 'Paprika', bright red, yellow centers; and 'Lachsschönheit', salmon fading to pale pink. Quick to flower from seed are 'Taygetea', gray foliage, lemon yellow flowers; 'Terracotta', rusty orange; 'Walther Funcke', red with yellow centers; 'Wesersandstein', salmon fading to cream. Zones 3–10.

Achillea 'King Edward'

Achillea millefolium 'Paprika'

Achillea millefolium

Achillea millefolium 'Fanal'

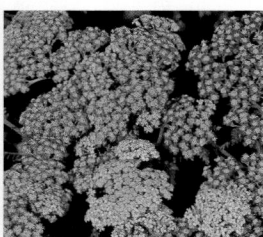

Achillea millefolium 'Taygetea'

A. m. 'Walther Funcke'

A. millefolium 'Apple Blossom'

Achillea millefolium 'Heidi'

A. millefolium 'Terracotta'

A. millefolium 'Wesersandstein'

Achillea ptarmica

SNEEZEWORT

☼ ❋ ↔ 30 in (75 cm) ↑ 30 in (75 cm)

From Europe. Vigorous spreading mats of dark green, narrow, serrated leaves. Loose heads of small white flowers are borne in summer. Tolerant of damp sites. The common name refers to its usage as snuff. '**The Pearl**' (syns 'Boule de Neige', 'Schneeball') bears double white flowers in profusion. Zones 6–10.

Achillea sibirica

☼ ❋ ↔ 24 in (60 cm) ↑ 24 in (60 cm)

From northeastern Asia. Shiny, leathery, dark green, serrated leaves. Small white flowers are borne in summer. *A. s.* var. *camschatica* 'Love Parade' is an attractive variety with soft pink, lemon-centered flowers. Zones 3–9.

Achillea tomentosa

☼ ❋ ↔ 12–18 in (30–45 cm)
↑ 6–10 in (15–25 cm)

Native to central Europe. This mat-forming alpine species has soft woolly foliage, and produces bright yellow flowers in summer. It is suitable for

the rock garden. '**King George**' produces lemon yellow flowers in spring. Zones 3–9.

Achillea umbellata

☼ ❋ ↔ 8 in (20 cm) ↑ 8 in (20 cm)

Native to southern Greece. Low-growing perennial for the rock garden. Very finely divided aromatic leaves are hairy and grayish white. The tiny white flowers have brownish centers and are borne in small umbels in summer. Zones 6–9.

ACHIMENES

HOT WATER PLANT

Found in tropical Americas, including the West Indies, this genus of the African violet (Gesneriaceae) family comprises some 25 species of winter-dormant fleshy-stemmed perennials ranging from ground covers, usually cultivated in hanging baskets, to shrubby species 24–36 in (60–90 cm) tall. Lush deep green, somewhat fleshy, simple elliptical to lance-shaped, tooth-edged leaves are covered with fine downy hair. The flowers are long-tubed with 5 lobes on 2 lips—2 lobes

Achillea umbellata

Achimenes, Hybrid Cultivar, 'Endeavour'

Achimenes, Hybrid Cultivar, 'Lach's Charm'

above, 3 below—which are more or less apparent depending on the species. Flowers appear in the leaf axils, either singly or in small groups.

CULTIVATION: Some species are grown as house or greenhouse plants, others are treated as annuals. All thrive outdoors in tropical and sub-tropical gardens. Plant rhizomes in spring in moist, humus-rich, well-drained soil in a bright but not too hot position. Feed and water well while in growth; dry off in autumn. Propagate by division.

Achimenes erecta

☀ ❦ ↔ 12 in (30 cm)
↑ 12–18 in (30–45 cm)

Found from Mexico to Panama and Jamaica. Upright habit with abruptly pointed, 2½ in (6 cm) long, toothed leaves. Vivid red flowers to 2 in (5 cm) wide, with well-defined lobes. Zones 10–12.

Achimenes longiflora

☀ ❦ ↔ 12–20 in (30–50 cm)
↑ 20–24 in (50–60 cm)

Found from Mexico to Panama. Shrubby with deep green, serrated, lance-shaped leaves to 3 in (8 cm) long. White, mauve, purple to maroon flowers to 2½ in (6 cm) wide, borne singly. Zones 10–12.

Achimenes Hybrid Cultivars

☀ ❦ ↔ 10–15 in (25–38 cm)
↑ 3–6 in (8–15 cm)

Achimenes hybrids vary in size, growth habit, and flower color depending on their parentage. Popular hybrids include: '**Endeavour**', deep orchid pink flowers, leaves bronzy; '**Glacier**', 24 in (60 cm) tall, upright, white flowers tinted blue; '**Lach's Charm**', bright reddish pink flowers, small purple blotch at mouth of tube; '**Peach Blossom**', a trailer with salmon pink flowers; '**Pendent Purple**', vigorous trailer with bright purple-blue flowers; '**Ruby**', 12 in (30 cm) tall, bushy with masses of deep purple-red

Acinos alpinus

flowers; and '**Show Off**', 12–16 in (30–40 cm) tall, bushy, heavy crop of lavender-pink flowers. Zones 10–12.

ACINOS

BASIL THYME, CALAMINTHA, SATUREJA

This Eurasian genus of 10 species of annuals and perennials belongs to the mint (Lamiaceae) family. They may be low and spreading or more upright and bushy. The leaves, opposite on the stems, are simple pointed ellipses, sometimes toothed and/or downy. Flower stems with whorls of simple, small, 2-lipped, tubular, pale mauve to purple-pink flowers appear in summer. Interestingly, the common names reflect some confusion—basil thyme suggests a strongly aromatic culinary herb, which it is not, though it can be used as a garnish, while *Satureja* and *Calamintha* are the proper names for two closely related herb genera: savory and calamint, a genus in which some species were formerly included.

CULTIVATION: Easily grown in any temperate climate that is not extremely hot and dry in summer. Plant in moist, humus-rich, well-drained soil in part shade. Remove spent flower-heads to keep compact and tidy. Propagate from seed or base cuttings.

Acinos alpinus

ALPINE CALAMINT

☀ ❋ ↔ 8–12 in (20–30 cm)
↑ 4–8 in (10–20 cm)

Found in southern and central European mountains. Compact, bushy, downy-leafed perennial. Toothed leaves around ½ in (12 mm) long. Heads of ½ in (12 mm) long violet flowers marked white on the lower lip. Zones 5–9.

ACIPHYLLA

BAYONET PLANT, SPANIARD

Found in New Zealand and Australia, the 40 sometimes aromatic evergreen perennials in this genus are members of the carrot (Apiaceae) family, known

A

for their fierce spine-tipped leaves, which are pinnate, often with long leaflets, resembling fan palm fronds. Forms clumps of varying size ranging from small, dwarf, and tufting to over 4 ft (1.2 m) wide and high, developing from a long tap root. Large, long-stemmed, branching heads of tiny white to cream flowers in summer. CULTIVATION: Some are alpine and not easily cultivated but most grow freely in well-drained gritty soil, preferring a generally cool but not too wet climate. Propagate by division or from spring-sown seed.

Aciphylla aurea
GOLDEN SPANIARD, TARAMEA
☼ ❋ ↔ 4–6 ft (1.2–1.8 m)
↑ 3–4 ft (0.9–1.2 m)

From northeast South Island of New Zealand. Large clumps of doubly pinnate leaves to 30 in (75 cm) long with stiff, narrow, 4–8 in (10–20 cm) long leaflets. Two large leaflets (stipules) at the leaf base are pungent. Cream flowers, male flowerheads paler and broader. **Zones 5–9.**

Aciphylla colensoi
COLENSO'S SPANIARD, WILD SPANIARD
☼ ❋ ↔ 4–6 ft (1.2–1.8 m)
↑ 3–8 ft (0.9–2.4 m)

Found on New Zealand's North and South Islands. Leaves up to 20 in (50 cm) long, usually pinnate with ½ in (12 mm) wide, 8 in (20 cm) long leaflets, sometimes sword-shaped. Orange-gold to red midribs and stiletto-like stipules. Narrow flower stems up to 8 ft (2.4 m) tall with cream flowers. **Zones 5–9.**

Aciphylla congesta
SNOWBALL SPANIARD
☼ ❋ ↔ 12–24 in (30–60 cm)
↑ 8–12 in (20–30 cm)

Found in damp areas in the extreme southwest of New Zealand's South Island. A spreading mat of rosettes, leaves each with 3 to 6, soft, 2–3 in (5–8 cm) long leaflets. Short strong flower stems, rounded heads of white to cream flowers. **Zones 5–9.**

Aciphylla congesta, in the wild, Kepler Track, New Zealand

Aciphylla horrida
HORRID SPANIARD
☼ ❋ ↔ 4–7 ft (1.2–2 m)
↑ 4–5 ft (1.2–1.5 m)

From New Zealand's South Island. Large dense clump of pungent foliage. Leaves to 30 in (75 cm) long with 5–7 leaflets and large stipules. Flower stems to 5 ft (1.5 m) tall with thickened base, greenish cream flowers, and fierce spiny bracts. **Zones 5–9.**

Aciphylla monroi
☼ ❋ ↔ 6 in (15 cm) ↑ 6–8 in (15–20 cm)
Small mounding species from northeast South Island, New Zealand. Yellow-green, tufted, pinnate leaves with up to 8 paired leaflets. Cream flowerheads. Prefers gritty well-drained soil. **Zones 5–9.**

Aciphylla simplicifolia
MOUNTAIN ACIPHYLL
☼ ❋ ↔ 24–36 in (60–90 cm)
↑ 24 in (60 cm)

Found in southeast Australia. Open tufted mound of long, simple, linear, blunt-tipped leaves. Cream flowers widely spaced on stems. **Zones 7–9.**

Aciphylla squarrosa
BAYONET PLANT, SPEARGRASS
☼ ❋ ↔ 40–48 in (100–120 cm)
↑ 24–36 in (60–90 cm)

This species has finely divided leaves, 18–24 in (45–60 cm) long, with very

Aciphylla squarrosa, in the wild, Mt Cook, New Zealand

narrow leaflets and stipules. Heads of greenish cream flowers on stems to 3 ft (0.9 m) high. **Zones 5–9.**

ACMENA

Fifteen species make up this genus from the myrtle (Myrtaceae) family of evergreen rainforest trees, native to eastern Australia and New Guinea. All *Acmena* species were once included in *Eugenia*, but that name is now restricted almost entirely to the American species. Acmenas have simple smooth-edged leaves. Small white flowers are borne in panicles terminating the branches. They are followed by globular fruit. A cavity at the fruit apex has a sharp circular rim, a feature that distinguishes the genus from *Syzygium*. *Acmena* fruits are edible.
CULTIVATION: Only the three most southerly *Acmena* species are widely cultivated, valued for their display of fruit and glossy foliage. They prefer a mild humid climate, a sheltered but sunny position, and deep well-drained soil. Sooty mould can sometimes be a problem. Propagation

is normally from seed, but some selected forms of *A. smithii* are perpetuated from cuttings.

Acmena ingens
syns *Acmena australis, Eugenia brachyandra*
RED APPLE
☼ ⊰ ↔ 15–30 ft (4.5–9 m) ↑ 100 ft (30 m)
From northeastern New South Wales to southeastern Queensland, Australia. In cultivation this tree seldom reaches 50 ft (15 m) high. Narrow pointed leaves. White flowers in summer. Magenta or crimson fruit. **Zones 9–11.**

Acmena smithii
syn. *Eugenia smithii*
LILLYPILLY
☼ ⊰ ↔ 35 ft (10 m) ↑ 60 ft (18 m)
This species is found along the whole length of the east Australian coast and ranges. This medium-sized tree has a dense bushy crown, glossy green leaves, and tiny white flowers in summer. White-mauve fruit, which are edible, ripen in winter. **Zones 9–12.**

Acmena ingens

Acmena smithii

Aconitum napellus

Aconitum carmichaelii

ACOKANTHERA

There are 7 species in this genus of evergreen shrubs and small trees, generally occurring in open forest and scrub from southeastern Africa to southern Arabia. The genus belongs to the dogbane (Apocynaceae) family and has similar poisonous properties—an extract of the wood and bark was traditionally used as an arrow poison and for purposes of murder. However, *Acokanthera* has been widely cultivated for ornament, with accidental poisoning being rare. Leaves are smooth, leathery, in opposite pairs or whorls of three. Sweet-scented, tubular, white flowers in the leaf axils are followed by fruit the shape and size of olives. Fruit, leaves, and bark all bleed a thick white sap.
CULTIVATION: These are tough shrubs and trees that are adapted to growing in exposed positions, and they are fairly drought and salt tolerant. In the garden they tolerate neglect as long as they are not too shaded by other trees or shrubs. Heavy pruning results in vigorous resprouting. Propagate from seed or soft tip cuttings.

Acokanthera oblongifolia
syn. *Carissa spectabilis*
DUNE POISON BUSH, WINTERSWEET
☼ ❀ ↔ 5–8 ft (1.5–2.4 m) ↑ 10 ft (3 m)
Native to the coastal zone of eastern South Africa and adjacent Mozambique, this shrub has foliage often tinged purple, coloring more deeply in winter. Clusters of sweet-scented flowers, pink in bud, opening white. Fruit reddish, ripening black. 'Variegata' has leaves marbled in white and gray-green, flushed pink. Zones 9–11.

Acokanthera schimperi
☼ ❀ ↔ 10–15 ft (3–4.5 m)
↑ 20–25 ft (6–8 m)
ROUND-LEAFED POISON-BUSH
Shrub or small tree with rough gray-brown bark, a component of dry woodland in eastern southern Africa. Leaves almost circular, leathery, shiny dark green above, paler below. Tubular flowers produced in autumn are white, pink, or red, sweetly scented, in dense clusters. Fruits are ripe in spring, fleshy, globular, bright red, maturing to purple. All parts of the plant are poisonous. Zones 9–11.

ACONITUM
BADGER'S BANE, MONKSHOOD, WOLFSBANE
This buttercup (Ranunculaceae) family genus of around 100 species of often tuberous biennials and perennials is found in northern temperate zones. Completely dormant over winter, they quickly develop a clump of deeply lobed fan-shaped leaves from which emerge erect stems bearing clusters of pendulous, hooded or helmet-shaped flowers, usually white, creamy yellow, or mauve-blue to purple in color. Summer to autumn is the main flowering season. Monkshood sap contains several highly toxic alkaloids, principally aconitine, and has a long history of use as a poison, especially in animal traps, hence its common names wolfsbane and badger's bane. Aconitine causes paralysis of the nerves and eventually the heart, and is used medicinally in controlled doses to slow the heart rate.
CULTIVATION: Mostly very hardy and easily grown in full or half-sun in moist, humus-rich, well-drained soil. Propagate by division when dormant or raise from seed.

Aconitum carmichaelii
☼/❂ ❀ ↔ 24–36 in (60–90 cm)
↑ 7 ft (2 m)
From China. Upright growth with dark green, 3- to 5-lobed, toothed, leathery leaves with pale undersides. Dense spikes of white to mauve helmet-shaped flowers that are deep purple inside. Popular cultivars include: 'Arendsii', deep blue flowers; and 'Kelmscott' (Wilsonii Group) ★, light purple-blue flowers. Zones 3–9.

Aconitum lycoctonum
syn. *Aconitum septentrionale*
BADGER'S BANE, WOLFSBANE
☼/❂ ❀ ↔ 2–3 ft (0.6–0.9 m)
↑ 5–7 ft (1.5–2 m)
Found in Europe and into North Africa. Erect perennial with rounded often hairy leaves divided into 5 to 7 toothed lobes. Flowers are white, yellow, or purple, and may be downy. Zones 3–9.

Aconitum napellus
FRIAR'S CAP, HELMET FLOWER, MONKSHOOD
☼/❂ ❀ ↔ 24–32 in (60–80 cm)
↑ 5–6 ft (1.5–1.8 m)
Found in Europe, Asia, and North America. Upright perennial with dark green slightly hairy leaves with 5 to 7 toothed lobes. Bright purple-blue helmet-shaped flowers in dense heads atop tall stems, late summer–autumn. Zones 5–9.

Aconitum Hybrid Cultivars
☼/❂ ❀ ↔ 24 in (60 cm) ↑ 4 ft (1.2 m)
Several hybrid monkshoods, varying in size, color, and flowering season, are sometimes listed under the name *A.* × *cammarum* (*A. variegatum* × *A. napellus*), but as they are not all of this parentage this grouping seems inappropriate. Popular hybrids

Acokanthera oblongifolia

Acokanthera oblongifolia 'Variegata'

Acorus gramineus 'Hakuro-Nishiki'

include: '**Bressingham Spire**', strongly upright with long spikes of purple-blue flowers; '**Grandiflorum Album**', large heads of white flowers; '**Ivorine**', with creamy white flowers; '**Spark's Variety**', tall, non-twining, open plant with bright purple-blue flowers; and '**Stainless Steel**', gray-green foliage and white-centered metallic blue flowers. Zones 4–9.

ACORUS

SWEET FLAG

In the arum (Araceae) family but rather sedge-like in appearance, this genus of 2 evergreen perennial species occurs around pond margins in temperate East Asia and southeast USA. The narrow iris-like leaves in fans are often variegated in the cultivated forms. In summer they produce flowers in which the typically showy arum spathe is leaf-like and inconspicuous. The flowerhead (spadix) is pronounced but not a feature. The stout, aromatic rhizomes contain compounds sometimes used in perfumes or to make a digestive tonic. Extracts or candied fleshy stems of *A. calamus* are used widely in herbal medicines.
CULTIVATION: Tough and easily grown. Plant in damp or boggy soil, preferably by a pond, and cut back or divide occasionally to encourage fresh young leaves. Propagate by division or from seed if available.

Acorus calamus

CALAMUS, FLAGROOT, MYRTLE FLAG, SWEET CALAMUS, SWEET FLAG

☼/◐ ❄ ↔ 3–7 ft (0.9–2 m) ↑ 4 ft (1.2 m)
Originally from temperate Asia and southeast USA but now widely naturalized in Northern Hemisphere. Has iris-like leaves to 5 ft (1.5 m) long and a narrow yellow-green spadix to 4 in (10 cm) long. '**Variegatus**' ★ has cream and yellow variegated leaves. Zones 3–10.

Acorus gramineus

☼/◐ ❄ ↔ 18–36 in (45–90 cm) ↑ 16 in (40 cm)
From Japan and possibly nearby mainland Asia, very similar to *A. calamus* but smaller grassy leaves, to 18 in (45 cm) long. Spadix broad and up to 3 in (8 cm) long. Several foliage cultivars, including: '**Hakuro-Nishiki**', compact, yellow-green foliage; '**Ôgon**' (syn. '**Wogon**'), bright yellow-green and cream variegation; '**Pusillus**', dwarf, leaves 3 in (8 cm) long; and '**Variegatus**' (syn. '**Aureovariegatus**'), golden yellow and cream variegation. Zones 5–10.

ACRADENIA

Members of the rue (Rutaceae) family and closely related to the better known *Boronia,* the 2 species in this genus are large evergreen shrubs or small trees, one from Australia's east coast, the other from Tasmania. Aromatic, deep green, trifoliate leaves with a grainy leathery texture. White flowers are borne in small panicles, and though small, can be quite showy and contrast well with the dark foliage.
CULTIVATION: While the mainland species requires mild conditions and tolerates very little frost, the Tasmanian native *A. frankliniae* is far tougher and generally adapts well to cultivation, though it still needs protection from hard frosts. It thrives in any neutral to slightly acidic soil that is well drained

and humus-rich, and that remains moist through summer. Propagate from half-hardened cuttings.

Acradenia frankliniae ★

WHITEY WOOD

☼ ❄ ↔ 5 ft (1.5 m) ↑ 20 ft (6 m)
Cultivated specimens of this native of Tasmania, Australia, usually remain shrubby and under 12 ft (3.5 m) high. Leaves dark green with three leaflets. Flowers small and clustered, in early summer. Lightly trim to keep natural conical shape. Zones 8–10.

ACTAEA

With 8 species, this is a genus of the buttercup (Ranunculaceae) family, and occurs in temperate regions of the Northern Hemisphere as fleshy-stemmed woodland perennials with divided toothed leaves. Terminal heads of white flowers are followed by white, red, or black poisonous berries.
CULTIVATION: Propagate from seed or by division. Full to part-shade in a friable loamy soil will give good results.

Acradenia frankliniae

Actaea alba

syn. *Actaea pachypoda*
DOLL'S EYES, WHITE BANEBERRY

◐/◐ ❄ ↔ 20–24 in (50–60 cm) ↑ 36 in (90 cm)
From woodlands of eastern North America. Divided leaves, up to 24 in (60 cm) long, composed of 3 to 12 leaflets, arise from the fleshy stem. In late spring–early summer, white flowers are produced in terminal heads, 1–2 in (2.5–5 cm) long. Tiny, globular, white berries. Each berry has a black "eye," hence the common name. Zones 5–7.

Actaea rubra

RED BANEBERRY, RED COHOSH, SNAKEBERRY

☼ ❄ ↔ 24–36 in (60–90 cm) ↑ 12–24 in (30–60 cm)
From North America, this is a bushy perennial for woodland settings. Dark green divided leaves. Clusters of small white flowers in spring. Round red berries appear in summer. All parts, including berries, poisonous if eaten. Zones 3–7.

Aconitum, Hybrid Cultivar, 'Stainless Steel'

A

Actinidia kolomikta

Actinidia deliciosa 'Hayward'

ACTINIDIA

This genus of about 60 species of evergreen and deciduous twining climbers from East Asia belongs to the family Actinidiaceae. The species are grown for their handsome foliage and often scented creamy white flowers in spring. The fruit of some is edible, but both male and female plants are needed to produce these. As decorative climbers, they can be used to cover walls, pergolas and dead or unattractive trees. The name *Actinidia* comes from the Greek *aktin* (ray), alluding to the rayed stigmas of the female flowers. The most famous is *A. deliciosa,* the Chinese gooseberry or kiwi fruit, which isn't a gooseberry nor does it come from New Zealand! CULTIVATION: Plant in full sun to partial shade in any well-drained loamy soil that should not dry out. Prune in winter as necessary. Vigor suggests strong support needed as vines become heavy, with little need for fertilizer. Propagate from seed sown in spring or autumn, from half-hardened cuttings, or by layering in late autumn or winter. Vines of both sexes are required for fruiting of most varieties.

Actinidia arguta
BOWER ACTINIDIA, BOWER VINE, COCKTAIL KIWI, DESSERT KIWI, HARDY KIWI, KOKUWA, SIBERIAN GOOSEBERRY, TARA VINE, YANG-TAO

☼ ❀ ↔ 20–30 ft (6–9 m)
↕ 20–30 ft (6–9 m)

This is a vigorous twining vine of variable habit that comes from Japan, Korea, and northeastern China. It has fragrant white flowers that are tinged with green, with purple anthers, from mid- to late summer. Leaves to 6 in (15 cm) long, oval, smooth and serrated. Abundant yellow-green, hairless fruit that has a slightly acid flavor. 'Ananasnaya' (syn. 'Anna') is a vigorous female cultivar that has large clusters of small sweet-smelling flowers; 'Issai' is a self-pollinating form. Zones 4–9.

Actinidia chinensis
CHINESE GOOSEBERRY

☼ ❀ ↔ 15–30 ft (4.5–9 m)
↕ 10–20 ft (3–6 m)

Long cultivated in southern China, native region uncertain. Resembles the better known *A. deliciosa* in habit, foliage, and flowers but fruit is smaller, tapering more to a point, almost hairless when ripe, with bright yellow to reddish flesh of a rich, sweet aromatic flavor. Zones 7–10.

Actinidia deliciosa ★
syn. *Actinidia chinensis* of gardens
CHINESE GOOSEBERRY, KIWI FRUIT, YANTAO

☼ ❀ ↔ 35 ft (10 m) ↕ 35 ft (10 m)
Vigorous climber from China. Large, furry, green leaves to 8 in (20 cm) long. Scented cream flowers in spring are followed by tasty, brown, fuzzy fruit with green flesh and black seeds

that ripen in early winter. 'Hayward', large-fruited commercial form bred in New Zealand. Zones 7–10.

Actinidia kolomikta
syn. *Trochostigma kolomikta*

☼ ❀ ↔ 17–20 ft (5–6 m)
↕ 20–35 ft (6–10 m)

A climber from East Asia. Grown for its handsome leaves, green or tipped with white or pink. This strange variegation develops as the plant grows, rarely evident in very young plants. Not produced commercially but, if both male and female plants present, fruit is edible. 'September Sun', richer variegated foliage. Zones 4–9.

Actinidia polygama
SILVER VINE

☼ ❀ ↔ 8 ft (2.4 m) ↕ 6–8 ft (1.8–2.4 m)
Climber from eastern Asia. White flowers with yellow anthers and decorative pale silver or gold leaves, to 6 in (15 cm) long. Edible fruit, to 1 in (25 mm) diameter, is regarded as a delicacy in Japan when salted. Zones 4–9.

ACTINOTUS
FLANNEL FLOWER

This genus in the carrot (Apiaceae) family consists of 16 species, 15 of which occur in Australia and 1 in New Zealand. All are herbaceous annuals or perennials, growing in many different soil types, habitats, and climates. Many small flowers are borne in terminal heads surrounded by much larger, sterile, woolly, white, gray, or pinkish bracts, giving a daisy-like appearance.
CULTIVATION: Most species of this genus can be propagated from cuttings and seeds. Germination can be quite erratic if conventional methods are used, but with the advent of "smoke germination" techniques, success is almost assured. Current breeding and selecting programs are producing cultivars suitable for various horticultural purposes, including cut flowers for export.

Actinotus helianthi
☼ ❀ ↔ 20–40 in (50–100 cm)
↕ 20–60 in (50–150 cm)

A somewhat woody, short-lived, Australian perennial, occurring on the shallow, sandy, acid soils of the Sydney region and on deep coastal sand dunes further north, in low sclerophyllous heaths, shrublands, and woodlands. Flowerheads 2–4 in (5–10 cm) in diameter, on long leaf-less stalks, from late winter–summer. Creamy white to gray, felty bracts are sometimes green-tipped. Zones 8–9.

Actinotus minor
LESSER FLANNEL FLOWER

☼ ❀ ↔ to 5 ft (1.5 m) ↕ to 20 in (50 cm)
Spreading, short-lived perennial, occurring on acid, sandy soils in heaths, woodlands, and open forests of coastal eastern Australia. Leaves are variably divided, ½ in (12 mm) long, densely hairy on the undersurface. Flowerheads ½ in (12 mm) in diameter, white to creamy gray, from late winter to summer. Zones 8–9.

Actinotus helianthi cultivar

Adenandra uniflora

ADANSONIA

Eight species make up this remarkable genus of the kapok (Bombaceae) family from North Africa, Madagascar, and Australia. The most famous, the African baobab *(A. digitata),* is famous for its huge girth. The swollen trunks contain soft spongy wood, saturated with water. Leaves are divided into a number of leaflets and are usually deciduous in the tropical dry season. Flowers are large, upright or pendulous, with fleshy white petals, and a dense brush of long white stamens; they are pollinated by animals. Fruit is globular to oval. Leaves are used as a green vegetable or stockfeed; fruit pulp is edible, and is used for refreshing drinks or for medicinal purposes. CULTIVATION: They thrive only in the tropics or warmer subtropics; if winters are too cool and damp, young plants soon rot. Best suited to deep alluvial soils. Propagation is normally from seed, or cuttings of half-hardened wood can also be struck.

Adansonia digitata ★
BAOBAB
☼ ✣ ↔ 90 ft (27 m) ↑ 50 ft (15 m)
Baobab trunks can reach an extraordinary thickness—diameters of almost 30 ft (9 m) have been recorded. The leaves consist of 3 to 9 leaflets. Flowers waxy white in late spring–

Adenanthos sericeus, in the wild, Misery Beach near Albany, Western Australia

early summer. Hard-shelled fruits ripen in autumn, eaten by elephants and baboons. Zones 11–12.

Adansonia gibbosa
syns *Adansonia gregorii, A. rupestris*
BAOBAB, BOTTLE TREE
☼ ✳ ↔ 3–7 ft (0.9–2 m)
↑ 20–40 ft (6–12 m)
Rarely cultivated tree from northwestern Australia. Irregularly shaped, with swollen trunk and smooth bark. Like *A. digitata* but smaller, with erect flowers. Leaves smooth, palmate, 5 to 7 leaflets, no stalk, elliptic, 2½–5 in (5–12 cm) long. Flowers single, erect, strap-like, petals white, many stamens. Seed pods spherical to barrel-shaped, brownish black. Zones 8–10.

ADENANDRA

This rue (Rutaceae) family genus consists of 18 species of small evergreen shrubs native to South Africa, growing on rocky mountainsides and sea

cliffs. Up to 3 ft (0.9 m) in height, they have gland-dotted branches, often sticky. Small aromatic leaves are a feature they share with the related *Coleonema* genus. The 5-petalled flowers are usually white or pink and are fragrant in some species. CULTIVATION: Require deeply worked, free-draining, gritty soil in a sunny open position, ideal for rock gardens and containers. In cooler climates they can be wintered in a greenhouse. Apply fertilizer sparingly. Propagate from seed sown in early summer or half-hardened cuttings in late summer.

Adenandra uniflora
CHINA FLOWER, ENAMEL FLOWER
☼ ✳ ↔ 3 ft (0.9 m) ↑ 2 ft (0.6 m)
Dense twiggy plant with small, narrow, aromatic leaves. Forms a small shrub. In spring and summer it is covered in delicate, porcelain-like, single, white, unscented flowers that show a hint of pink. Zones 8–10.

ADENANTHOS

This southern and western Australian genus belonging to the protea (Proteaceae) family includes around 30 species, many endangered in the wild. Leaves are often densely hairy and variably shaped, being simple, divided, lobed, or toothed edged. Those with hairy gray foliage are known as woollybushes. The others are called jugflowers or basket flowers because they resemble a long-necked cup or urn, containing nectar that is attractive to birds in spring–summer. CULTIVATION: Tolerate only light frosts, but, if the protea family rules are followed—light, well-drained soil, good ventilation, sunshine, little or no

Adenanthos detmoldii

phosphate—are not too hard to cultivate. Most respond to pruning, thinning and shaping, and both flowers and foliage last well in water when cut. Propagation is usually from seed.

Adenanthos detmoldii
SCOTT RIVER JUGFLOWER, YELLOW JUGFLOWER
☼ ✦ ↔ 8 ft (2.4 m) ↑ 10 ft (3 m)
Western Australian native. Very upright shrub with narrow, slightly hairy leaves and golden yellow to light orange flowers that develop in the leaf axils near the branch tips. Zones 9–10.

Adenanthos sericeus
ALBANY WOOLLYBUSH, COASTAL WOOLLYBUSH
☼ ✦ ↔ 10 ft (3 m) ↑ 8 ft (2.4 m)
This native of Western Australia can reach 15 ft (4.5 m) high in the wild. Ferny silver-gray foliage covered in silky hairs. Flowers red and largely hidden among leaves. Zones 9–10.

Adansonia digitata, in the wild, in Africa

Adansonia gibbosa, Western Australia

ADENIA

Adenia species are members of the passionfruit (Passifloraceae) family (and should not be confused with *Adenium* species, which are members of the Apocynaceae family). The genus *Adenia* contains about 90 caudex-forming species, of which about 60 come from South Africa, with the rest from East Africa and Madagascar. (A caudex is a swollen stem or root that persists after the annual branches or vines have died down.) Some adenias grow up to 8 ft (2.4 m) tall and at least 10 species are considered ornamental and are sought by collectors. Lacking the showy flowers of some members of the Passifloraceae family, the appeal of adenias lies in their interesting body shapes and the annual production of branches and vines, which may need to be trimmed or supported by a trellis. In some species in the genus, part of the thickened root system is raised above the soil for added visual impact. The flowers are dioecious (meaning that male and female flowers occur on separate plants). Most species contain toxins or poisons.

CULTIVATION: *Adenia* species are usually grown from seed because plants propagated from cuttings do not always produce a typical caudex, which is the main attraction. They need frost protection, a rich well-drained soil, and plenty of water during the summer. Mature specimens may need to be cut back each season or even root pruned.

Adenia digitata

☀ ⊰ ↔ 40 in (100 cm) ↑ 40 in (100 cm)
From South Africa. Usually grown with its smooth, green, thickened root, or caudex, exposed. This species contains 2 deadly toxins, glucoside and toxalbumin. The leaves resemble those of the oak. Zones 10–11.

Adenia globosa

☀ ⊰ ↔ 8 ft (2.4 m) ↑ 8 ft (2.4 m)
From Tanzania, Kenya, and Somalia. Despite its rarity, this is one of the most popular species because of its large, dark green, warty-skinned caudex, from which scores of very heavily thorned branches arise. Can be grown from a cutting that has been dried out for a week or two. Zones 10–11.

Adenia globosa

Adenium obesum subsp. *swazicum*

Adenium obesum subsp. *somaliense,* in the wild, Samburu National Park, Kenya

Adenocarpus decorticans

Adenia spinosa

☀ ⊰ ↔ 8 ft (2.4 m) ↑ 5 ft (1.5 m)
From South Africa. This popular species produces a fast-growing, symmetrical, green caudex, densely covered during the growing period by leafy spiny branches that may need support. These may be cut back after the leaves fall or before new growth commences in spring. Zones 10–11.

ADENIUM

The current view is that this genus, which belongs to the dogbane (Apocynaceae) family, consists of a single variable species ranging from southern Arabia through eastern and central Africa to northeastern South Africa. There are many subspecies, some with extremely swollen succulent stems. The less succulent forms are popular ornamentals in tropical gardens around the world, displaying their striking trumpet-shaped blooms. When cut or broken, the milky sap is believed to be poisonous. The fleshy leaves, widest toward the apex, are spirally arranged rather than opposite or whorled.

CULTIVATION: Adeniums are grown outdoors in the tropics, in containers or well-drained garden beds. In warm-temperate climates they can be grown against a hot sunny wall but in cool climates they require a greenhouse or conservatory with high light levels. They are very drought and heat tolerant. Watering through summer and autumn promotes leaf growth and prolongs flowering. Propagation is from seed (if obtainable) or cuttings allowed to callus before planting.

Adenium obesum

syn. *Adenium multiflorum*
DESERT ROSE, IMPALA LILY, SABI STAR
☀ ⊰ ↔ 5 ft (1.5 m) ↑ 5 ft (1.5 m)
Usually a shrub, branching into multiple stems with age, the impala lily can be more tree-like, reaching a height of 15 ft (4.5 m) or more.

Growing on sunny rock outcrops, roots are swollen and succulent, as are the stem bases. The forms grown for showy flowers all belong to *A. o.* subsp. *obesum* ★; flower color of cultivars varies from pink to deep crimson, commonly with a white or paler zone, late summer–autumn. *A. o.* subsp. *oleifolium*, tuberous and largely underground; *A. o.* subsp. *somaliense*, small tree, smooth hairless leaves; *A. o.* subsp. *swazicum*, also largely underground. Zones 10–12.

ADENOCARPUS

A genus of the broom tribe of pea-flowered legumes, *Adenocarpus* consists of 15 or so species of deciduous and evergreen shrubs. Many are found in the western Mediterranean region, but a few are native to the Canary Islands and Madeira and as far east as Turkey. They resemble *Genista* in having smallish leaves divided into 3 leaflets, and yellow pea-flowers in terminal spikes. Distinctive features are bark that becomes rough or flaky with age, leaves clustered in crowded short shoots, and sticky seed pods. Some species have proved attractive garden plants, suited to mild climates but often short lived.

CULTIVATION: Most of the species are not very frost hardy and in cool climates are best planted against a sunny wall. Soil should be very open, well drained, and on the dry side. Like most brooms, they adapt poorly to warmer climates with a long wet summer. Propagate from seed or half-hardened tip cuttings.

Adenocarpus decorticans

☀ ❋ ↔ 7 ft (2 m) ↑ 8 ft (2.4 m)
A native of Spain, this deciduous member of the genus has flaky whitish bark, with stiffly spreading branches. Leaves crowded with narrow, almost needle-like leaflets. Golden yellow flowers in late spring–early summer. Zones 8–10.

ADENOPHORA

GARLAND FLOWER, LADYBELLS

Found from Europe to Japan, this genus of around 40 species of perennials is closely related to the bellflowers (*Campanula*) and is included in that family (Campanulaceae). They have fleshy roots and may colonize freely in loose open soil in partial shade. Whorls of oblong to pointed oval leaves form at the base of the plants, from which emerge upright flower stems, usually quite narrow and wiry, around which are tiers of tubular to bell-shaped, blue, violet, or pink flowers, opening mainly in summer and autumn.
CULTIVATION: Plant in cool, moist, humus-rich, well-drained soil with shade from the hottest summer sun. Water and feed well during the growing season. Propagate from seed or by division when dormant.

Adenophora liliifolia

syns *Adenophora communis, A. stylosa*
LADYBELLS, LILYLEAF LADYBELLS
☀/☼ ❄ ↔ 24 in (60 cm)
↑ 18–24 in (45–60 cm)

From East Asia and central Europe. Erect perennial. Rounded green foliage. Fragrant, pale blue, bell-shaped flowers hang downward along the stem; resemble campanula flower; blooms appear early–mid-summer. Zones 4–8.

Adenophora polyantha

☼ ❄ ↔ 12–16 in (30–40 cm)
↑ 36 in (90 cm)

Native to Korea and nearby parts of China. Leaves and flowers in whorls. The flowers are bright blue and closely clustered. Zones 7–9.

ADIANTUM

MAIDENHAIR FERN

Large genus of about 200 terrestrial fern species distributed worldwide; members of the maidenhair-fern (Adiantaceae) family. From the Greek word *adiantos* (dry, unmoistened, or

Adiantum capillus-veneris

unwettable), because the leaflets appear to be waterproof. Wide range of frond colors: pink and red new fronds, changing to shades of green, including variegated types, on maturity. Pinnules borne on thin, shiny, black or brown stems, with oblong or fan-shaped leaflets.
CULTIVATION: Organically rich loams, kept moist but not soggy, with surface mulching in humid semi-shaded situations. Soil pH varies according to species. Protect from wind. Allow abundant light but shelter from hot sun. Propagate from spores or by division.

Adiantum aethiopicum

COMMON MAIDENHAIR FERN
☀/☼ ❄ ↔ 10–36 in (25–90 cm)
↑ 8–32 in (20–80 cm)

Widely distributed clumping fern from a range of climates in Africa, Australia, and New Zealand. Creeping rhizomes produce clusters of spreading, pinnate, lacy, light green fronds on shiny black stems. Many cultivars. Zones 7–9.

Adiantum capillus-veneris

COMMON MAIDENHAIR, SOUTHERN MAIDENHAIR, TRUE MAIDENHAIR, VENUS MAIDENHAIR, VENUS-HAIR FERN, VENUS'S HAIR
☀/☼ ❄ ↔ 12–24 in (30–60 cm)
↑ 12–24 in (30–60 cm)

Robust wiry fern found worldwide in warm-temperate to tropical climates. Creeping rhizomes produce clusters of

Adenophora polyantha

many fronds on circular black stems. Deeply dissected triangular blades give a lacy appearance. Bronze pink new growth. Zones 8–11.

Adiantum concinnum

BRITTLE MAIDENHAIR
☀/☼ ❄ ↔ 12–32 in (30–80 cm)
↑ 12–32 in (30–80 cm)

Clump-forming fern from tropical and subtropical Central America. Neat habit; yellowish green fronds, to 32 in (80 cm) long, with narrowly triangular blade and pinnules to ½ in (12 mm) long. Grows naturally in exposed rocky situations. '**Edwinii**', tall erect fronds with broader segments than the species; '**Noaksii**', compact with arching fronds; '**Upright Noaksii**', similar but with erect fronds. Zones 10–12.

Adiantum excisum ★

CHILEAN MAIDENHAIR
☀/☼ ❄ ↔ 12–20 in (30–50 cm)
↑ 12–20 in (30–50 cm)

Small clump-forming fern from Chile, Panama, Mexico, and Bolivia, named for the deeply cut margins of its densely tufted fronds. Triangular blades, to 16 in (40 cm) long, have many short pinnules and wiry stems. Needs neutral to alkaline soils. '**Rubrum**', dark reddish brown fronds, new growth pale yellow. Zones 9–12.

Adiantum formosum

AUSTRALIAN MAIDENHAIR, BLACK STEM, GIANT MAIDENHAIR, PLUMED MAIDENHAIR
☀/☼ ❄ ↔ 9–48 in (22–120 cm)
↑ 9–48 in (22–120 cm)

Vigorous fern from temperate to subtropical East Asia, Australia, and New

Adiantum concinnum

Zealand. Large, erect, dark green, triangular fronds borne on shiny, black, circular stems, have triangular blades with rectangular segments. Creeping underground rhizomes. Zones 9–11.

Adiantum hispidulum

☀/☼ ❄ ↔ 12–20 in (30–50 cm)
↑ 12–20 in (30–50 cm)

ROUGH MAIDENHAIR FERN, ROSY MAIDENHAIR FERN, FIVE-FINGERED JACK

Small, clump-forming fern from Africa, south India, Malaysia, Australia and the south Pacific. Fronds have pinkish bronze new growth and overlapping pinnules. Creeping rhizomes. Young fronds red becoming light green, then dark green with maturity. Zones 9–12.

Adiantum jordanii

CALIFORNIAN MAIDENHAIR
☀/☼ ❄ ↔ 12–24 in (30–60 cm)
↑ 12–24 in (30–60 cm)

Clump-forming fern from Mexico and west coast USA. Fronds have triangular pinnate blades of finely toothed pinnules. Flushes of new growth in early spring and again in autumn. Zones 8–10.

Adiantum hispidulum

Adiantum pedatum 'Imbricatum'

Adiantum pedatum var. *subpumilum*

Adiantum peruvianum

Adiantum macrophyllum

Adiantum macrophyllum

LARGE-LEAFED MAIDENHAIR

☼/☀ ⧓ ↔ 8–20 in (20–50 cm)
↑ 8–20 in (20–50 cm)

This species of fern comes from the tropical regions of the West Indies, Central America, Brazil, Bolivia and the Galapagos Islands. It grows in upright tussocks of fronds up to 27 in (70 cm) in length, with large triangular leaflets reaching 4 in (10 cm) across. It has a creeping to semi-erect rhizome. Its stems are smooth and black, with new growth that is reddish pink in coloration. Zones 10–12.

Adiantum pedatum

AMERICAN MAIDENHAIR FERN, EASTERN MAIDENHAIR, FIVE-FINGERED MAIDENHAIR FERN

☀ ✳ ↔ 12–24 in (30–60 cm)
↑ 12–24 in (30–60 cm)

Fern from temperate North America and East Asia. Bears pinnate fronds, with leaflets to 12 in (30 cm) across and green triangular or oblong pinnules. Deciduous in cooler climates. *A. p.* subsp. *calderi*, small, clump-forming, upright form from northwestern North America with bluish green fronds and small pinnules. *A. p.* var. *aleuticum*, deciduous and clump-forming variety from Alaska, USA, Canada, and the Aleutian Islands with pale green fronds, new fronds occasionally flushed with pink. *A. p.* var. *subpumilum*, wind-tolerant dwarf variety from northwestern North America, bluish green fronds and overlapping pinnules, yellowish green new growth. *A. p.* 'Asiaticum', drooping fronds; 'Imbricatum', crowded, stiffly erect, green fronds; 'Japonicum', pinkish bronze new growth;

'Laceratum', deeply cut pinnules; 'Miss Sharples', golden green lobed fronds; 'Montanum', compact form. Zones 4–9.

Adiantum peruvianum

PERUVIAN MAIDENHAIR FERN, SILVER DOLLAR MAIDENHAIR FERN

☀/☀ ⧓ ↔ 32–40 in (80–100 cm)
↑ 32–40 in (80–100 cm)

From Ecuador, Peru, and Bolivia, this species has clusters of triangular, pinnate, green fronds borne on slender black stalks from a short-creeping to clump-forming rhizome. New growth is silvery rose in color with a metallic sheen. Zones 10–12.

Adiantum raddianum

DELTA MAIDENHAIR FERN

☀/☀ ✦ ↔ 18–24 in (45–60 cm)
↑ 18–24 in (45–60 cm)

This is a widely cultivated clump-forming fern that comes from tropical regions of Uruguay, Brazil, and

Paraguay. Clusters of green pinnate fronds with triangular blades and wedge-shaped pinnules are borne on purplish black stalks. This species has numerous cultivars, including: 'Bridal Veil', with drooping fronds with small tear-drop segments; 'Deflexum', hardy more open form with black stems, triangular fronds, segments smaller than species; 'Elegans', with hardy, triangular fronds with heart-shaped segments; 'Fragrantissimum', vigorous form with deep green fronds and toothed segments; 'Fritz Luth', with triangular, bright green, erect fronds with overlapping segments; 'Gracillimum', has pendulous divided fronds with pink new growth; 'Lawsonianum', a strong grower with delicate lacy fronds; 'Tinctum', from the Andes, with triangular fronds and large, overlapping, wedge-shaped pinnules; and 'Waltonii', considered by some to be a cultivar of *Adiantum excisum*. Zones 11–12.

Adiantum reniforme

☀/☀ ⧓ ↔ 2–8 in (5–20 cm)
↑ 2–8 in (5–20 cm)

Unusual, small, colonizing maidenhair fern from Kenya, Tenerife, Madeira, and the Canary and Comoros Islands. Short-creeping rhizome. Tough, simple, undivided fronds are rounded to kidney-shaped, on wiry black stems. Zones 10–12.

Adiantum raddianum 'Deflexum'

Adiantum raddianum 'Waltonii'

Adonis annua

Adiantum tenerum

BRITTLE MAIDENHAIR FERN,
FAN MAIDENHAIR FERN

↔ 12–36 in (30–90 cm)
↑ 12–36 in (30–90 cm)

This species of fern is found in
tropical to subtropical regions of
southwestern USA, the West Indies,
and Central America. It has a
creeping rhizome and clusters of
pinnate fronds with rounded or
diamond-shaped blades, borne on
glossy maroon-black stems. Cultivars
of this species include: 'Farleyense',
arching or drooping pinnate fronds,
to 36 in (90 cm) long, with large
ruffled segments and sharp edges;
'Gloriosum Roseum', arching or
pendulous fronds with wavy segments
and pink new growth; 'Japonicum',
fronds 6–8 in (15–20 cm) long, with
large, deeply lobed, overlapping
pinnules on thin wiry stalks; and
'Lady M. Lyalle', pale green fronds
12–24 in (30–60 cm) long, with large,
deeply incised, fan-like segments.
Zones 11–12.

Adiantum tetraphyllum

FOUR-LEAFED MAIDENHAIR

↔ 40–60 in (100–150 cm)
↑ 30–40 in (75–100 cm)

A species of fern from the West
Indies and tropical Americas. It has a
creeping rhizome with pinnate fronds
to 40 in (100 cm) long, with oval to
triangular blades and rectangular pinnules. Zones 10–12.

Adiantum trapeziforme

DIAMOND MAIDENHAIR, GIANT
MAIDENHAIR

↔ 24–100 in (60–250 cm)
↑ 20–80 in (50–200 cm)

This large maidenhair fern, with a
creeping rhizome, comes from the
West Indies and tropical Americas.
Clusters of pinnate fronds, up to
7 ft (2 m) long, with triangular
blades, are borne on stems up to
20 in (50 cm) long. Because of its
large size, it is best grown in the
ground. Zones 10–12.

Adiantum venustum

EVERGREEN MAIDENHAIR, HIMALAYAN
MAIDENHAIR

↔ 12–48 in (30–120 cm)
↑ 8–32 in (20–80 cm)

Native to high altitudes of Afghanistan,
the Himalayas, India, and Canada.
Deciduous in cooler climates. It
has a creeping rhizome, and fronds
up to 32 in (80 cm) long with
triangular blades and toothed pinnules borne on stems that extend to
10 in (25 cm) long. Zones 4–8.

ADONIS

This genus, which is a member of
the buttercup (Ranunculaceae) family,
consists of about 20 species of annual
and perennial herbs. It is found
in mountain meadows in Europe
and Asia. Plants grow to about 16 in
(40 cm) with pinnately divided
foliage that is feathery in some
species. The white, yellow, or red
flowers provide a bright splash in
spring. They are up to 3 in (8 cm)
across and have 3 to 30 petals. The
genus is named after the beautiful
youth of Greek mythology who was
killed by a wild boar and changed
into a flower by Aphrodite.
CULTIVATION: These are plants for
the rock garden or front of border,
where they require moist but well-
drained soil in a sunny or partially
shaded site. They are best suited
to cooler climates. Propagation
can be from fresh seed in summer
or by divisions, which may be quite
difficult to re-establish, in early spring
or autumn.

Adonis aestivalis

PHEASANT'S EYE

↔ 12 in (30 cm) ↑ 18 in (45 cm)
From Europe, this is an annual
species with finely divided foliage.
Solitary terminal flowers are about

1 in (25 mm) across with 5 to 8 deep
blood-red petals with a black base
or "eye." Zones 5–9.

Adonis amurensis

PHEASANT'S EYE

↔ 12 in (30 cm) ↑ 12 in (30 cm)
From Asia. Perennial for use in borders, open woodland, and rock gardens. Green, ferny, deeply dissected
leaves. Yellow flowers similar to
buttercups appear in early spring.
'Sandanzaki', a rare and expensive
cultivar, grows in deep shade, deep
yellow and green petals. Zones 3–9.

Adonis annua

syn. *Adonis autumnalis*
PHEASANT'S EYE

↔ 12 in (30 cm) ↑ 16 in (40 cm)
Found from southern Europe to
southwestern Asia and naturalized in

the UK and northern Europe. A
summer-flowering annual very similar
to *A. aestivalis*. Has fine ferny foliage
on upright branching stems. Flowers
are blood red in color with a black
base. Zones 3–9.

Adonis cyllenea

↔ 8–15 in (20–38 cm)
↑ 8–15 in (20–38 cm)

Native to Greece. A very rare species
thought to be extinct until rediscov-
ered in 1976. Ferny foliage and clear
yellow flowers. Zones 6–9.

Adonis vernalis

↔ 10 in (25 cm) ↑ 16 in (40 cm)
A perennial European species. Basal
leaves are oval while stem leaves are
feathery. The bright yellow flowers are
up to 3 in (8 cm) across with 12 to 20
petals. Zones 3–9.

Adiantum venustum

Adiantum reniforme

Adiantum tenerum

AECHMEA

This is a member of the pineapple (Bromeliaceae) family and is so called because of its spear-like flowerhead ("aichme" being the Greek word for spear-point). This genus is one of the largest, containing plants that do not fit comfortably in the other genera. All species come from the humid regions of Central America, ranging from the upper reaches of the Amazon and the hot dry areas of Bahia in Brazil to cooler areas in the southern parts of Brazil and Argentina. There are 240 species, ranging in size from 4 in (10 cm) to 7 ft (2 m) in diameter, and over 500 cultivars. All grow on trees in their natural environment, though some grow on rocks. Edges of leaves have teeth, ranging from very fine to most vicious. Flowerheads vary from short to elongated cones. Many have bright red banner-like primary bracts under the flower branches,

Aechmea bromeliifolia

Aechmea fasciata

which attract hummingbirds. The small-petalled flowers come in various colors. Fruit can be brightly colored, from yellow to red to blue to purple.
CULTIVATION: Recommended for indoor culture if in flower; for greenhouse or conservatory in cool-temperate areas; or outdoors, with protection from direct continuous sunlight and extremes of rain, in warm-temperate, subtropical, and tropical areas. Water when potting mix is dry. No extra fertilizer needed if potting mix is of good quality. Propagate from seed or by offset.

Aechmea bromeliifolia
☀ ❄ ↔ 12 in (30 cm) ↑ 40 in (100 cm)
Found from Central America to Argentina, this species tolerates a wide range of climates. Flowering to 40 in (100 cm) high. Leaves to 4 ft (1.2m) long, form a tight urn. Flowerhead like a felty corn cob, with yellow flowers soon turning black. Zones 9–10.

Aechmea caudata
☀ ❄ ↔ 24 in (60 cm) ↑ 36 in (90 cm)
Originates in the southern part of Brazil and is hardier than most other

Aechmea caudata var. *variegata*

Aechmea gamosepala

species. Leaves, to 40 in (100 cm) long, form an open funnel-shaped rosette. Flowering to 36 in (90 cm) high; flowerhead erect, to 10 in (25 cm) long, with side spikes at the base, yellow petals. *A. c.* var. *variegata*, a variegated form, more robust than the species. Zones 9–10.

Aechmea chantinii
☀ ❄ ↔ 20 in (50 cm) ↑ 40 in (100 cm)
This species originates in the upper reaches of the Amazon and likes hot humid conditions. Leaves to 40 in (100 cm) long, with strong white cross-banding, forming a loose funnel-shaped rosette. Flowering to 40 in (100 cm) high; flowerhead open, with mainly yellow side spikes on long stems; orange flowers. Lower side spikes have large bright red primary bracts that hang down. This species has numerous cultivars, usually describing the leaf color, for example, '**Ash Blond**', '**Black Goddess**', and '**Green Ice**'. Variegated cultivars include: '**Samurai**', yellow-striped variegation central to the green leaves; and '**Shogun**', with the yellow stripe on the outside. Zones 9–10.

Aechmea dichlamydea
☀ ❄ ↔ 32 in (80 cm) ↑ 40 in (100 cm)
Native of Trinidad, a very popular plant in tropical gardens. Leaves to 20 in (50 cm) long, forming an open almost erect rosette. Flowering to over 40 in (100 cm) high; cylindrical flowerhead to 20 in (50 cm) long, with many pink and blue side branches. Flowers with mostly white petals, contrasting with the red stems. Zones 9–10.

Aechmea distichantha
☀ ❄ ↔ 36 in (90 cm) ↑ 36 in (90 cm)
From southern Brazil, Paraguay and north Argentina. Flowering to 3 ft (0.9 m) high. Leaves stiff, to 5 ft (1.5m) long, forming an open rosette. Pyramidal flowerhead with many side branches of bright red. Blue petals. Zones 9–10.

Aechmea mariae-reginae, in the wild, Monumento Nacional Guayabo, Costa Rica

Aechmea fasciata
☀ ❄ ↔ 16 in (40 cm) ↑ 27 in (70 cm)
From southern parts of Brazil. Leaves to 3 ft (0.9m) long, forming a slender funnel-shaped rosette. Leaves strongly cross-banded in white and in some forms almost totally covered with white scales. Flowering to 27 in (70 cm) high. Flowerhead conical, bracts pink with a light covering of white scales. Flowers blue, ageing to red. There are now variegated forms of this species and non-spined forms such as '**Morgana**', with extra-wide leaves, and '**Kiwi**', with reddish striped leaves. Zones 9–10.

Aechmea fulgens
☀ ❄ ↔ 20 in (50 cm) ↔ 20 in (50 cm)
From eastern Brazil. Leaves 16 in (40 cm) long, forming a dense funnel-shaped rosette. Flowering to 20 in (50 cm) high. Flowerhead to 8 in (20 cm) high, narrowly pyramidal with a few red side branches at the base. Dark red flowers scattered along branches, blue petals soon changing to red. A parent of *A.* '**Maginali**'. Zones 9–10.

Aechmea gamosepala
MATCHSTICK PLANT
☀ ❄ ↔ 10 in (25 cm) ↑ 30 in (75 cm)
From southern parts of Brazil. Leaves to 22 in (55 cm) long, forming a dense funnel-form rosette. Flowering to 30 in (75 cm) high. Flowerhead a narrow cylinder to 10 in (25 cm) long, with flowers standing at right angles from the center stem like matches, red with blue petals. Zones 8–10.

Aechmea mariae-reginae
☀ ❄ ↔ 36 in (90 cm) ↑ 36 in (90 cm)
From Costa Rica. Leaves to 36 in (90 cm) long, forming a spreading rosette. Flowering to 36 in (90 cm) high. Flowerhead a dense cone to 8 in (20 cm) long, flowers yellow with bluish petals. Drooping banner-like scape bracts beneath the flowerhead. This species has male and female plants. Zones 9–10.

Aechmea miniata

☀ ⧢ ↔20 in (50 cm) ↑20 in (50 cm)

From eastern Brazil. Leaves to 20 in (50 cm) long, forming a dense funnel-shaped rosette. Flowering to 20 in (50 cm) high. Flowerhead almost globular, with red side branches to near apex. Red flowers, blue petals. *A. m.* var. *discolor*, leaves red to red-purple on undersides. Zones 9–10.

Aechmea nudicaulis

☀ ⧢ ↔8 in (20 cm) ↑27 in (70 cm)

From southeast Brazil and the countries surrounding the Caribbean. Variable in size, up to 27 in (70 cm) high. Leaves 36 in (90 cm) long, green through to reddish, commonly with white bands, forming a tight tube with a pinched-in look near the base. Flowerhead cylindrical with many flowers sticking out horizontally from the center stem. Mass of erect bright red bracts under flowerhead. Flowers mainly yellow. Zones 9–10.

Aechmea orlandiana

☀ ⧢ ↔16 in (40 cm) ↑16 in (40 cm)

From Espirito Santo, Brazil. Leaves 12 in (30 cm) long, forming a funnelform rosette, strongly marked with large purple-brown blotches and bands. Flowering to 16 in (40 cm) high. Flowerhead egg-shaped, 3 in (8 cm) long, with short dullish yellow side spikes. Zones 9–10.

Aechmea ornata

☀ ⧢ ↔7 ft (2 m) ↑36 in (90 cm)

From the southern part of Brazil. Plant to 7 ft (2 m) in diameter,

Aechmea miniata var. *discolor*

Aechmea pineliana

Aechmea, Hybrid Cultivar, 'Fascini'

flowering to 36 in (90 cm) high. Leaves green, strap-like, 36 in (90 cm) long, with small teeth, forming open rosette. Stout flower stem. Flowerhead a short cylinder with bristles and many flowers on all sides. Petals red or blue. Large red erect bracts under flowerhead. *A. o.* var. *hoehneana*, blue-petalled form. *A. o.* var. *nationalis*, variegated form. Zones 9–10.

Aechmea phanerophlebia

☀ ⧢ ↔20 in (50 cm) ↑30 in (75 cm)

From southern Brazil. Leaves rather spiny, with whitish bands, 40 in (100 cm) long, forming an erect funnel-like rosette. Flowering to 30 in (75 cm) high; flowerhead red, cylindrical with many short side branches, petals blue. Zones 9–10.

Aechmea pineliana

☀ ⧢ ↔20 in (50 cm) ↑36 in (90 cm)

From southern Brazil. Leaves rather spiny, green; can become red in good light, forming a funnel-shaped rosette. Flowering to 36 in (90 cm) high; flowerhead a bristly cylinder, mainly yellow with bright red erect bracts just below. Zones 9–10.

Aechmea recurvata

☀ ❈ ↔8 in (20 cm) ↑8 in (20 cm)

From southern Brazil. Leaves green, to 16 in (40 cm) long, moderately spined, forming an open rosette from a bulbose base. Flowering to 8 in (20 cm) high. Flowerhead almost globular, red bracts on the outside with reddish purple petals. 'Aztec Gold' is a variegated form. Zones 8–10.

Aechmea weilbachii

Aechmea recurvata 'Aztec Gold'

Aechmea phanerophlebia

Aechmea ornata var. *hoehneana*

Aechmea weilbachii

☀ ⧢ ↔20 in (50 cm) ↑20 in (50 cm)

From Southern Brazil. Leaves flexible, 20 in (50 cm) long, green, forming an open rosette. Flowering to 20 in (50 cm) high. Flowerhead cylindrical, to 6 in (15 cm) long, with short side spikes, all predominantly red. Globular blue-purple flowers, pale purple petals. Zones 9–10.

Aechmea Hybrid Cultivars

☀ ⧢ ↔12–24 in (30–60 cm) ↑12–36 in (30–90 cm)

Nearly all the more popular *Aechmea* species have been used in the breeding of hybrids, the aims of breeders being more vigorous plants with year-round blooms of richer color, and foliage in stronger bronze shades. 'Ares', a large plant better suited to outside plantings in semi-tropical areas; 'Bastantha', leaves light yellowish green above and a rich lightly scurfed red below; 'Burning Bush', bright red flower stem and branches, cream flowers; 'Fascini', large green rosette to 32 in (80 cm) tall with branched

Aechmea ornata var. *nationalis*

long-lasting carmine flowerhead; 'Fia', gray-green leaves, red bracts, flowers with contrasting yellow ovaries and red sepals; 'Foster's Favorite', shiny deep red-black leaves, pendent flowerhead, coral petals tipped blue; 'Friederike', a spineless form of 'Fascini'; 'J C Superstar', open funnel-shaped rosette, red bracts, pale petals; 'Royal Wine', rosette of glossy light green leaves, maroon undersides, orange and blue flowers; 'Shelldancer', leaves apple green with red tips, side spikes, flowers white at base, petals blue. Zones 9–10.

Aeonium arboreum

Aeonium glandulosum

Aeonium lindleyi

Aegopodium podagraria

AEGOPODIUM

Native to Europe and western Asia, this genus of 5 perennial herbs, which grows from creeping rhizomes, belongs to the carrot (Apiaceae) family. Flowers are compound, umbels appearing in spring–summer. Fruit consist of 2-winged or ribbed nuts that separate on ripening. CULTIVATION: Frost hardy but drought tender, preferring moist well-drained soil in an open sunny position. Propagate from seed.

Aegopodium podagraria
ASH WEED, BISHOP'S WEED, GOUTWEED, GROUND ASH, GROUND ELDER, HERB GERARD

☼ ❋ ↔ 10–36 in (25–90 cm)
↑ 10–36 in (25–90 cm)

From Europe, naturalized in North America. Leaves usually with 3 oval lobes. Creeping, branching, aromatic, rhizomes and fibrous roots. Large compound umbels of numerous white, pink, or cream flowers in early summer. Oval ribbed fruit. This species was introduced into England during the Norman Conquest and was used as a cure for gout. Young leaves contain high amounts of vitamin C and can be used in salads. 'Variegatum' has off-white splotches on the edges and surface of its leaves. Zones 3–9.

AEONIUM

This genus, a member of the stonecrop (Crassulaceae) family, consists of around 30 species of often shrubby and woody-stemmed succulents with terminal rosettes of fleshy leaves. Mainly from the Canary Islands and Madeira, they can also be found in eastern and northern Africa and the Middle East. Their branches, often arranged rather like a multi-headed candlestick, are brittle and covered with a papery bark. Pyramidal inflorescences of tiny flowers, usually yellow but sometimes pink, red, or white, develop in the centers of the rosettes, followed by brown seed heads.
CULTIVATION: As with most succulents, aeoniums are very drought tolerant once established. They demand full sun and perfect drainage, and in the wild can often be found on precipitous slopes with their roots anchored in the crevices between rocks. They are easily propagated by removing rooted basal suckers, by treating the rosettes as cuttings, or by raising from seed.

Aeonium arboreum
☼ ❄ ↔ 4 ft (1.2 m) ↑ 6 ft (1.8 m)
From the west coast of Morocco, this heavily branching species has bright green sometimes red tinted leaves in rosettes 6–8 in (15–20 cm) wide. Large conical heads of yellow flowers in spring. *A. a.* var. *holochrysum*, 7 ft (2 m) tall, very showy sprays of yellow flowers in summer; *A. a.* 'Atropurpureum' ★, deep purple-bronze leaves; and the cream-variegated 'Variegatum'. Zones 9–11.

Aeonium canariense
CANARY ISLANDS AEONIUM, GIANT VELVET ROSE, VELVET ROSE

☼ ❄ ↔ 20–48 in (50–120 cm)
↑ 8–24 in (20–60 cm)

Canary Islands native with short-stemmed rosettes up to 18 in (45 cm) across. Individual leaflets spoon-shaped, downy, gray-green, with red or yellow edges. Stems multiple but usually unbranched. Yellow-green flowerheads in spring, at 2–3 years. Whole plant monocarpic (dies after flowering), not just stems. Zones 9–11.

Aeonium decorum ★
☼ ❄ ↔ 12–36 in (30–90 cm)
↑ 16–24 in (40–60 cm)

Shrubby and branching. Relatively small rosettes with glossy blue-green leaves to 2 in (5 cm) long, often brown-marked and red-edged. Yellow flowers from mid-spring to mid-summer. *A. d.* var. *mascaense* (syn. *A. mascaense*) is a compact densely

Aeonium haworthii 'Variegatum'

branching plant with succulent, red-marked, bright green leaves. *A. d.* 'Tricolor' ★ has green, cream, and pink variegated foliage. Zones 9–11.

Aeonium glandulosum
☼ ❄ ↔ 32 in (80 cm) ↑ 20 in (50 cm)
Biennial or perennial from Madeira. Shrubby habit with flat wide rosettes of aromatic light green leaves to 5 in (12 cm) long. Yellow or white flower sprays, up to 12 in (30 cm) long, in summer. Often monocarpic (dies after flowering). Zones 9–11.

Aeonium haworthii
PINWHEEL

☼ ❄ ↔ 32 in (80 cm) ↑ 24 in (60 cm)
Mounding perennial, occasionally branching stems with aerial roots, from the Canary Islands. Small rosettes with red-edged blue-green leaves to slightly over 2 in (5 cm) long. Pink-flushed pale yellow flowers from spring. Drops much foliage while flowering. 'Variegatum' ★ has cream variegated foliage that develops pink tints. Zones 9–11.

Aeonium lindleyi
☼ ❄ ↔ 27 in (70 cm) ↑ 20 in (50 cm)
Spreading subshrub from the Canary Islands. Small rosettes of aromatic, thickly succulent, broad leaves to around 2 in (5 cm) long. Leaves have fine hairs and are sticky. Yellow flowers from spring. Rosette dies after flowering. Zones 10–11.

Aeonium nobile
☼ ❄ ↔ 36 in (90 cm) ↑ 24 in (60 cm)
Canary Islands perennial with erect unbranched stems, each bearing a cup-shaped rosette to 20 in (50 cm) wide. Brown-tinted leaves to 12 in (30 cm) long, edged with fine hairs, sticky when young. Tiny yellow flowers in dome-shaped inflorescences. Zones 9–11.

Aeonium sedifolium
☼ ❄ ↔ 16 in (40 cm) ↑ 16 in (40 cm)
Small shrubby perennial from the Canary Islands. Branching stems and

Aeonium sedifolium

Aeonium, Hybrid Cultivar, 'Zwartkop'

Aeonium tabuliforme

small rosettes of a few thickly succulent mid-green leaves, sometimes with red to brown stripes, each less than 1 in (25 mm) long. Leaves sticky when young. Zones 9–11.

Aeonium spathulatum

☀ ✂ ↔ 24 in (60 cm) ↑ 24 in (60 cm)

From the Canary Islands, Madeira, and nearby Atlantic Islands. Has branching upright stems with 2 in (5 cm) wide rosettes of bright green to gray-green, 1 in (25 mm) long leaves with a brown mid-stripe. Small sprays of yellow flowers from spring. Zones 9–11.

Aeonium tabuliforme ★

☀ ✂ ↔ 24 in (60 cm) ↑ 12 in (30 cm)

Low spreading biennial or perennial from the Canary Islands. Has flat rosettes to 16 in (40 cm) wide, densely packed with spirals of pale green. Leaves are often red-tinted and hair-fringed, to 8 in (20 cm) long. Flower stems tall and branching, with yellow flowers. Usually monocarpic (dies after flowering). Zones 9–11.

Aeonium undulatum

SAUCER PLANT

☀ ✂ ↔ 24 in (60 cm) ↑ 12 in (30 cm)

From the Canary Islands, this plant forms clumps of usually unbranched upright stems bearing huge cup-shaped rosettes of deep green brown-edged leaves, around 6 in

(15 cm) long but sometimes larger, curved inward. Yellow flowers in spring. Zones 9–11.

Aeonium urbicum

☀ ✂ ↔ 3–6 ft (0.9–1.8 m) ↑ 3–6 ft (0.9–1.8 m)

From the Canary Islands. Strongly upright unbranched stems with densely foliaged cup-shaped rosettes of blue-green leaves to 6 in (15 cm) long, fleshy at the base. Creamy yellow flowers through the warmer months. Usually monocarpic (dies after flowering). Zones 9–11.

Aeonium Hybrid Cultivars

☀/☀ ✂ ↔ 8–24 in (20–60 cm) ↑ 12–24 in (30–60 cm)

A number of cultivars have arisen from either deliberate or accidental crosses between *Aeonium* species. They feature more colorful foliage (bronze or variegated), or larger, more brightly colored flowers. Cultivars include: '**Plum Purdy**', rosettes of maroon leaves; '**Sunburst**' ★, symmetrical rosettes of pale green leaves with clearly defined creamy yellow edges that often develop pink tints; '**Zwartkop**' ★, rosettes of shiny reddish black leaves. Zones 9–11.

Aeonium urbicum

AERANGIS

This genus of the orchid (Orchidaceae) family consists of about 60 miniature-growing epiphytic orchids from Madagascar and tropical Africa with flattish channelled leaves in two rows and short to long inflorescences of disproportionately large white to cream flowers. These monopodial plants are related to *Angraecum* and are one of the genera known as angraecoids. Various species bloom throughout the year, with the greatest concentration in the warmer months. The flowers, with long nectar-filled spurs, are highly fragrant in the evening and are moth pollinated.
CULTIVATION: Best grown on cork or treefern slabs (either vertical or horizontal), as few like their roots covered. Keep moist year round. Larger specimens can be grown in small baskets. They enjoy semi-shade to strong light and are best suited to greenhouse culture in all but tropical climates. They require warm conditions throughout the year, disliking temperatures that drop below 10°C.

Aeonium undulatum

Aerangis citrata

☀ ✈ ↔ 5–12 in (12–30 cm) ↑ 2½–5 in (6–12 cm)

From Madagascar. Grows well in either pots or slabs. Is unusual in that it has up to 30 pale yellow to creamy white blooms, ¾ in (18 mm) across, which are neatly arranged in two rows on pendent sprays, produced in winter. Zones 11–12.

Aerangis citrata

Aeonium, Hybrid Cultivar, 'Plum Purdy'

Aeonium, Hybrid Cultivar, 'Sunburst'

A

Aerangis cryptodon

☀ ✛ ↔ 6–15 in (15–38 cm)
↑ 6–15 in (15–38 cm)

From Madagascar. Grows well in pots with bark-based mix. In profile, the flowers look rather like white birds in flight. Produces 2-ranked upright sprays of up to 16 white, 2 in (5 cm) wide blooms in autumn. Zones 11–12.

AESCHYNANTHUS

BASKET PLANT, BLUSH WORT

Found in the tropics from India to New Guinea, mainly in Malaysia, this genus of around 100 species of often epiphytic perennials and sub-shrubs belongs in the African violet (Gesneriaceae) family. Often sprawling, with overarching stems, species tend to have simple, fleshy, pointed, elliptical leaves in opposite pairs. Flowers are curved tubes clustered at the stem tips, and are often brightly colored, frequently in orange and red shades, with an upper and lower lip, the lower with 3 small lobes.
CULTIVATION: Prefer even warm temperatures and ample moisture year

Aerangis cryptodon

round. Often grown as house or greenhouse plants, they are mainly cultivated in hanging baskets and prefer a free-draining, humus-rich soil. The creeping species can be good ground cover in tropical gardens. Water and feed well in growing season. Propagate from cuttings or seed if available.

Aeschynanthus hildebrandii

☀/☀ ✛ ↔ 12–24 in (30–60 cm)
↑ 6 in (15 cm)

Native to Myanmar, this is a low, spreading shrub with 1 in (25 mm)

Aeschynanthus radicans

long, finely hairy, red-edged leaves and orange-red, 1 in (25 mm) long flowers in clusters of 1 to 3. It is usually cultivated in hanging baskets. 'Topaz' is a variety with yellow flowers. Zones 11–12.

Aeschynanthus longicaulis

syn. *Aeschynanthus marmoratus*

☀ ✛ ↔ 36 in (90 cm)
↑ 18–24 in (45–60 cm)

From Malaysia, this evergreen trailing perennial has tubular yellowish green to greenish flowers, marked dark brown, in terminal clusters, in summer. Its leaves are oval and waxy, with mottled light and dark green above and purplish red below. Zones 11–12.

Aeschynanthus radicans

LIPSTICK PLANT

☀ ✛ ↔ 18–36 in (45–90 cm)
↑ 5–6 ft (1.5–1.8 m)

This species is an epiphytic evergreen vine from Malaysia with slender trailing and arching stems originating in tree branches. It has long, red, tubular flowers in dense terminal clusters. Its leaves are dark green, elliptical, fleshy and smooth-edged. Fruit grows to 1½ in (35 mm) long. Zones 11–12.

Aeschynanthus speciosus

☀/☀ ✛ ↔ 3 ft (0.9 m) ↑ 3 ft (0.9 m)

This epiphytic evergreen vine from Malaysia and Borneo has slender trailing and arching stems. Terminal clusters of tubular orange flowers, 4 in (10 cm) long × 1 in (2.5 cm) wide, yellow in the centre and scarlet on the edges, with red-dotted lobes. Smooth, dark green, lance-shaped leaves, 2½–4 in (6–10 cm) long, in pairs or whorls, terminating in a rosette surrounding a cluster of flowers. Zones 11–12.

AESCULUS

BUCKEYE, HORSE CHESTNUT

There are about 15 species of deciduous shrubs to tall trees in this genus, a member of the horse-chestnut (Hippocastanaceae) family. Half are native to North America, commonly called buckeye; the remainder spread from Asia to southeastern Europe. Growing in sheltered valleys they have large compound leaves of 5 to 11 leaflets palmately arranged, and in spring to summer showy upright panicles of cream to reddish flowers are borne. The inedible fruits are held in big seed capsules that vary from smooth to spiny and give rise to the other common name, horse chestnut.
CULTIVATION: These trees do best in cool-temperate climates with marked differences in summer and winter temperatures. The larger species suit parks and open landscapes where their pyramidal crowns can develop fully. They need a deep, fertile, and moisture-retentive soil. Propagation is by seed, which is best sown fresh, and cultivars are grafted in late winter.

Aesculus californica

CALIFORNIA BUCKEYE

☼ ❄ ↔ 30 ft (9 m) ↑ 15 ft (4.5 m)

Native to California, USA. Spreading shrub with grayish green leaves. Cylindrical panicles of creamy white flowers, pink tinged, in summer, followed by fig-shaped fruit. Can stand hot dry summers. Zones 7–10.

Aesculus × *carnea*

syn. *Aesculus rubicunda*
RED HORSE CHESTNUT

☼ ❄ ↔ 15 ft (4.5 m) ↑ 30 ft (9 m)

This hybrid of *A. hippocastanum* and *A. pavia* is thought to have originated in Germany. Erect panicles of deep reddish pink flowers with yellow blotches in spring. Better suited to warm climates than other species. 'Briotii' (syn. *A. hippocastanum* 'Briotii') has bigger and darker flowers. Zones 6–9.

Aesculus × *carnea*

Aesculus × *carnea* 'Briotii'

Aesculus hippocastanum

Aesculus 'Dallimorei'

Aesculus hippocastanum 'Pyramidalis'

Aesculus × mutabilis 'Induta'

Aesculus flava

Aesculus chinensis

CHINESE HORSE CHESTNUT

☼ ❋ ↔ 35 ft (10 m) ↑ 90 ft (27 m)

Native to northern China, common tree in temple grounds. Cylindrical panicles of white flowers, up to 18 in (45 cm) long, in summer. Quite slow growing in cultivation, best suited to areas with hot summers and cold dry winters. Zones 6–9.

Aesculus indica

Aesculus indica 'Sydney Pearce'

Aesculus 'Dallimorei'

☼ ❋ ↔ 25 ft (8 m) ↑ 40 ft (12 m)

A graft hybrid of *A. hippocastanum* and *A. flava*, with dark green leaves, downy beneath. Flowers in summer, on erect panicles, up to 8 in (20 cm) long, white to cream with a maroon spot. Zones 5–9.

Aesculus flava

syn. *Aesculus octandra*

SWEET BUCKEYE, YELLOW BUCKEYE

☼ ❋ ↔ 35 ft (10 m) ↑ 90 ft (27 m)

An attractive species that is native to central and eastern USA. Leaflets, which have downy veins, color yellow and orange shades in autumn. Erect panicles of yellow flowers are seen in summer. Hybrids of the species can occur in a variety of colors. *A. f.* f. *vestita* has downy young twigs and undersides of leaves. Zones 4–9.

Aesculus hippocastanum

COMMON HORSE CHESTNUT, EUROPEAN HORSE CHESTNUT, HORSE CHESTNUT

☼ ❋ ↔ 70 ft (21 m) ↑ 100 ft (30 m)

This handsome spreading tree is best suited to parks and large gardens. It has erect panicles of white flowers with yellow to red basal blotches in late spring, followed by round prickly fruits known commonly as conkers. Is tolerant of pollution. Of the cultivars, '**Baumannii**' has a rounded crown and showy white flowers; and '**Pyramidalis**' has a pyramidal growth habit. Zones 6–9.

Aesculus indica

INDIAN HORSE CHESTNUT

☼ ❋ ↔ 70 ft (21 m) ↑ 100 ft (30 m)

This tree, which is native to the northwestern Himalayas, tends to be low-branching or even multi-stemmed. Young leaves are bronze-pink. Flowers are white, tinged yellow-red, in pyramidal panicles up to 15 in (38 cm) long, in early to mid-summer. '**Sydney Pearce**' is a sturdy cultivar. Zones 6–9.

Aesculus flava f. *vestita*

Aesculus × mutabilis

☼ ❋ ↔ 15 ft (4.5 m) ↑ 15 ft (4.5 m)

Hybrid between *A. pavia* and *A. sylvatica*. Upright panicles of yellow and red flowers in summer. '**Induta**', yellow flowers flushed with pink. Zones 5–9.

Aesculus × neglecta

☼ ❋ ↔ ↑ 30 ft (9 m) 50 ft (15 m)

Natural hybrid between *A. pavia* and *A. sylvatica*, found on coastal plains of southeastern USA. New leaves bright pink, becoming light green. Erect panicles of yellow flowers in summer. '**Erythroblastos**', redder spring foliage, flowers peach to pink. Zones 5–9.

A

Aesculus pavia

Aesculus pavia 'Atrosanguinea'

densely crowded blue-green leaves. Dark-veined soft pink flowers from late spring. Protect from wet winter conditions. Zones 7–9.

Aethionema 'Warley Rose'

☼ ✽ ↔ 12 in (30 cm) ↑ 6 in (15 cm)

Most widely grown *Aethionema*, believed to be a hybrid between *A. armenum* and *A. grandiflorum*. Blue-green foliage. Flowers bright rosy red borne profusely from late spring to summer's end. Inclined to be short lived. Zones 6–9.

AFROCARPUS

The 6 or so species of this African genus of conifers, of the podocarp or plum-pine (Podocarpaceae) family, were formerly included in *Podocarpus*. In their native habitats they are tall forest trees with massive trunks, seen in mountainous regions of central, eastern, and southern Africa. At up to 250 ft (75 m) high, *A. usambarensis* is thought to be Africa's tallest tree. All have attractive bark that peels off in flakes or strips. Leaves are leathery and narrow. Male (pollen) and female (seed) organs are on different trees; female cones have a relatively thin stalk with a single, usually larger seed with a thick juicy outer layer. CULTIVATION: These slow-growing trees suit parks and avenues in warm-temperate and subtropical climates with adequate rainfall. Plant in deep, well-drained, reasonably fertile soil. They are affected by few pests or diseases and require little shaping. Propagation normally from seed, sown fresh after removing the fleshy coating.

Afrocarpus falcatus

syns *Nageia falcata*, *Podocarpus falcatus*
OUTENIQUA YELLOWWOOD

☼ ❀ ↔ 25–50 ft (8–15 m)
↑ 60–200 ft (18–60 m)

One of South Africa's largest trees. In cultivation reaches 30–50 ft (9–15 m). Peeling and flaky bark, purplish brown to paler red-brown. Fine dense foliage, drab green. Female trees covered in pale yellow "fruit" in summer–autumn. Zones 9–11.

Afrocarpus falcatus

Aesculus parryi, in the wild, in Ensenada, Baja California, Mexico

Aesculus parryi

PARRY'S BUCKEYE

☼ ❀ ↔ 3–10 ft (0.9–3 m)
↑ 3–10 ft (0.9–3 m)

Xerophytic shrub from the dry hills of northern Baja California, Mexico. Thick branches, sparse small leaves, short sprays of flowers after leaves fall as summer dry season sets in. Only North American west coast species apart from *A. californica*. Zones 9–11.

Aesculus parviflora

BOTTLEBRUSH BUCKEYE

☼ ✽ ↔ 15 ft (4.5 m) ↑ 10 ft (3 m)

A graceful shrub growing in woodland areas of southeastern USA. Leaves

Aesculus parviflora

downy beneath, buff-colored when young. Slender panicles of white summer flowers with protruding pink stamens. Best in areas with hot humid summers. *A. p.* f. *serotina*, leaves less downy, bluish green. Zones 6–10.

Aesculus pavia

syn. *Aesculus splendens*
RED BUCKEYE

☼ ✽ ↔ 10 ft (3 m) ↑ 15 ft (4.5 m)

From woodlands on coastal plains of eastern USA. Shrub or small tree. Leaves reddish in autumn. Crimson flowers on short erect panicles in early summer. 'Atrosanguinea', deep red flowers. Zones 6–10.

AETHIONEMA

STONE CRESS

The 40-odd species in this genus, of the cabbage (Brassicaceae) family, are annuals and perennials distributed from Europe and the Mediterranean to southwest Asia. Most are low, spreading, or mounding plants that thrive in rockery conditions. They have simple, small, fleshy leaves on wiry stems that can become a tangled mass of branches and foliage tufts. In spring and summer flowerheads form at stem tips, bearing dense clusters of tiny 4-petalled flowers. Well-grown plants are smothered in bloom. CULTIVATION: Hardy to repeated frosts but perhaps a little tender for the harsh continental winters. Plant in full sun in gritty well-drained soil with extra humus for moisture retention. Many appreciate a light dressing of dolomite. Water if necessary when flowering but otherwise keep dry. Propagate from seed or cuttings or by layering. May self-sow, though cultivars will not be true to type.

Aethionema grandiflorum

☼ ✽ ↔ 12–24 in (30–60 cm)
↑ 8–18 in (20–45 cm)

Found in the Caucasus and nearby parts of Iran and Iraq. Can mound up to form a moderately sized shrub. Blue-green foliage and bright pink flowers, each slightly over ½ in (12 mm) wide. Zones 7–9.

Aethionema pseudarmenum

☼ ✽ ↔ 6–12 in (15–30 cm)
↑ 4 in (10 cm)

From the Caucasus and western Asia. Compact mounding plant with

Aethionema pseudarmenum

Agapanthus africanus

Agapanthus inapertus

AGAPANTHUS

AFRICAN LILY, LILY-OF-THE-NILE

This southern African genus consists of 10 species of fleshy-rooted perennials of the onion (Alliaceae) family. Long, strappy, fleshy leaves form dense clumps of evergreen or deciduous foliage. Tall flower stems with heads of tubular to bell-shaped flowers, usually blue, are held above the foliage. Flowers of evergreens appear over a long season in frost-free climates, and in summer elsewhere. Their narrow, rather upright habit makes them ideal border plants, but old yellowing foliage should be removed. Dwarf forms are superb in large rockeries or containers. The name agapanthus is derived from the Greek *agape*, meaning love, and *anthos*, meaning flower. Agapanthus is therefore the flower of love, though the reason for the name is unclear—perhaps one needs to grow it to know?

CULTIVATION: Easily grown in any well-drained soil in sun or half-sun. Will withstand drought and poor soil but better flower production with good conditions. Slugs and snails often damage young foliage. Propagate by division in winter or raise from seed.

Agapanthus africanus

syn. *Agapanthus umbellatus*

AFRICAN LILY, BLUE AFRICAN LILY, LILY-OF-THE-NILE

☀ ❅ ↔ 24–36 in (60–90 cm)
↑ 18–24 in (45–60 cm)

A compact species from Western Cape in South Africa. Leaves are evergreen, 12–15 in (30–38 cm) long. Flower stems extend to 24 in (60 cm) with 1–2 in (2.5–5 cm) long, purple-blue, tubular flowers. Of the cultivars, 'Albus' has white flowers; and 'Sapphire' has deep blue flowers. Zones 9–11.

Agapanthus campanulatus ★

☀/❂ ❅ ↔ 40–48 in (100–120 cm)
↑ 30–40 in (75–100 cm)

Vigorous grower from South Africa's KwaZulu-Natal, forms large clumps. Leaves 12–18 in (30–45 cm) long, light green, deciduous. Bell-shaped 2 in (5 cm) flowers from white to mid-blue, rounded heads on stems to 40 in (100 cm). *A. c.* subsp. *patens* is smaller with graceful narrow-stemmed flowerheads. *A. c.* 'Royal Blue' has dark blue flowers. Zones 7–10.

Agapanthus caulescens

☀ ❅ ↔ 4–5 ft (1.2–1.5 m)
↑ 40–48 in (100–120 cm)

Deciduous leaves up to 24 in (60 cm) long emerge from a heavy base, sometimes forming a short trunk. Tall flower stems with 2 in (5 cm), bright blue, tubular flowers with protruding stamens. Zones 7–10.

Agapanthus, Hybrid Cultivar, 'Lilliput'

Agapanthus, Hybrid Cultivar, 'Storm Cloud'

Agapanthus inapertus

DRAKENSBERG AGAPANTHUS, DROOPING AGAPANTHUS

☀ ❅ ↔ 40–50 in (100–130 cm)
↑ 40–50 in (100–130 cm)

Deciduous species from southeastern South Africa forming dense clumps of blue-tinted leaves up to 27 in (70 cm) long. Pendulous, bright purple-blue, sometimes white, tubular flowers on stems to 5 ft (1.5 m) tall. *A. i.* subsp. *hollandii*, especially tall stems and flared flowers. Zones 7–10.

Agapanthus pendulus

☀ ❅ ↔ 36 in (90 cm)
↑ 24–36 in (60–90 cm)

Deciduous, bluish green to grayish leaves. Flower stems to 36 in (90 cm). Pendulous, tubular, light blue flowers with protruding stamens. Zones 7–10.

Agapanthus praecox

☀ ❅ ↔ 40–50 in (100–130 cm)
↑ 40 in (100 cm)

Evergreen, fleshy, bright green leaves to 27 in (70 cm) long. Wide-opening pale to mid-blue flowers on stems to 36 in (90 cm) tall. Most widely cultivated species in warm-temperate gardens. *A. p.* subsp. *orientalis*, smaller than the species, forms dense foliage clumps with tightly packed heads of small bright blue flowers. Zones 9–11.

Agapanthus Hybrid Cultivars

☀ ❅ ↔ 12–30 in (30–75 cm)
↑ 15–48 in (38–120 cm)

Variable group of largely undetermined parentage, ranging from plants suitable for large gardens to those for rockeries or tubs. Mainly easily grown in areas with not too severe winters. Cultivars include: 'Baby Blue', a dwarf cultivar with bright blue flowers on 12–16 in (30–40 cm) tall stems; 'Elaine', upright, vigorous, deep purple-blue flowers on 4 ft (1.2 m) high stems; 'Ellamae', bright violet-blue flowers on stems to 5 ft (1.5 m) tall; 'Henryi', dwarf, narrow leaves, white flowers on 18 in (45 cm) tall stems; 'Lilliput', dwarf, dark blue flowers on 18 in (45 cm) tall stems; 'Loch Hope', large heads of dark blue flowers, 4 ft (1.2 m) high stems, late-flowering; Midnight Blue/'Monmid', compact, deep purple-blue flowers on 16 in (40 cm) tall stems; 'Peter Pan', dwarf, mid-blue flowers on 12 in (30 cm) high stems; 'Queen Anne', bright blue flowers on 24 in (60 cm) tall stems; 'Rancho White', white tubular flowers on stems to 18 in (45 cm) tall; 'Storm Cloud', intense purple-blue flowers on 4 ft (1.2 m) high stems; and 'Tinkerbell', leaves edged cream, pale blue flowers on 16 in (40 cm) tall stems. Zones 7–11.

Agapanthus praecox

Agapanthus praecox cultivar

A

AGAPETES

syn. *Pentapterygium*

Allied to *Vaccinium* in the heath (Ericaceae) family, this genus consists of over 90 species of low, often creeping or scrambling shrubs native to tropical and subtropical Asia, the Malay Archipelago, Pacific islands, and Australia. Found in mountain rainforests, many grow as epiphytes. Leaves are mostly leathery and new growth is colored pink, red, or orange. Emerging singly or in small sprays, flowers are tubular and rather waxy, often 5-angled or 5-ribbed. CULTIVATION: Most can be grown outdoors in sheltered positions in a mild frost-free climate. Some of the Himalayan species will cope with

Agapetes 'Ludgvan Cross'

some frost, but are best planted under trees. Plant in a well-drained spot in acidic humus-rich soil. Conservatory plants prefer a peaty medium in a large pot or hanging basket, and good light with regular watering and misting. Propagation is easiest by layering, although cuttings can also be used.

Agapetes 'Ludgvan Cross'

☀ ❄ ↔ 5 ft (1.5 m) ↑ 3 ft (0.9 m)

Hybrid of *A. incurvata* and *A. serpens*. Leaves to 1½ in (35 mm) long. Pink flowers with darker chevron markings and red calyces. Generally similar to *A. serpens* but with larger leaves and lighter-colored flowers. Zones 9–11.

Agapetes meiniana

☀ ❄ ↔ unlimited ↑ unlimited

This Australian species is a climber that can be trimmed and grown as a shrub. New growth occurs in various shades of pink to red. Flowers are tubular with slightly flared throats, occurring at the stem tips. Zones 9–11.

Agapetes serpens

☀ ❄ ↔ 7 ft (2 m) ↑ 3 ft (0.9 m)

Widely cultivated, this evergreen shrub has arching reddish stems

Agapetes meiniana

arising from a central rootstock. Along the stems 5-sided, tubular, red flowers with darker chevron markings open late winter. Often grown in hanging baskets. Zones 9–10.

AGASTACHE

GIANT HYSSOP, MEXICAN HYSSOP

There are 20 species of very aromatic perennials in this genus, which belongs to the mint (Lamiaceae) family. They are native to North America, China, and Japan where they grow in dry scrub and fields. Leaf shape varies from pointed oval to almost triangular or lance shaped, the margins being shallowly to finely toothed. Flowers may be red, orange, rose, violet, blue, or white, typically tubular with two lips. They are borne in densely packed whorls on spikes or narrow panicles in summer and are very popular with bees. Some species are used in herbal medicines and teas. CULTIVATION: Grow in a well-drained soil in a sunny position. Most species tolerate some frost but the more tender ones should be given a warm sheltered site in cooler climates or be grown as annuals. Can be susceptible to fungal diseases in summer. Propagate from seed or cuttings.

Agastache aurantiaca

ORANGE HUMMINGBIRD MINT

☀ ❄ ↔ 24 in (60 cm)
↑ 18–30 in (45–75 cm)

Found from southern USA to Mexico. Bushy perennial with grayish green, pointed, oval to lance-shaped leaves.

Whorls of orangey pink tubular flowers, borne on spikes, from summer to autumn. Zones 7–10.

Agastache barberi

syn. *Agastache pallida*

GIANT HUMMINGBIRD'S MINT, GIANT HYSSOP

☀ ❄ ↔ 12–18 in (30–45 cm)
↑ 24 in (60 cm)

Found from Arizona, USA, to Mexico. Woody-based perennial. Leaves triangular to pointed oval with coarsely toothed margins. Flower spikes, 6–12 in (15–30 cm) long, bear crowded whorls of tubular flowers with reddish purple calyces and rose-colored petals. Zones 8–10.

Agastache cana

HUMMINGBIRD PLANT, MOSQUITO PLANT

☀ ❄ ↔ 12–18 in (30–45 cm)
↑ 20–24 in (50–60 cm)

From southern USA. Woody-based perennial with slightly downy triangular or pointed oval leaves. The crushed foliage is said to repel insects. Flower spikes, to 12 in (30 cm) long, bear whorls of rose-colored tubular flowers. 'Heather Queen' ★ has bright pink flowers. Zones 9–10.

Agastache foeniculum

syns *Agastache anethiodora*, *A. anisata*

ANISE HYSSOP

☀ ❄ ↔ 18–24 in (45–60 cm)
↑ 20–32 in (50–80 cm)

From North America. Very aromatic plant smelling of aniseed when foliage is brushed or crushed. Leaves triangular to pointed oval with toothed margins, downy beneath. Short, densely packed flower spikes bear small violet-blue flowers. Zones 8–10.

Agastache mexicana

MEXICAN GIANT HYSSOP, MEXICAN HYSSOP

☀ ❄ ↔ 18 in (45 cm) ↑ 24 in (60 cm)

From Mexico. Upright perennial with creeping roots. Lance-shaped, serrated edged leaves. Flower spikes, to 12 in (30 cm) long, bear deep pink to crimson flowers. Can be grown

Agastache foeniculum

Agapetes serpens

as an annual. The **Honeybee Series**, which offers compact plants in selected color strains, includes 'Honeybee White' and 'Honeybee Blue'. Zones 9–11.

Agastache rugosa
HUO XIANG, KOREAN MINT, WRINKLED GIANT HYSSOP

☀ ❄ ↔ 24 in (60 cm)
↕ 24–48 in (60–120 cm)

From China and Japan, this erect perennial has coarsely toothed ovate leaves that are hairy beneath. Used for seasoning meat, as a tea, and in Eastern medicine. Short compact spikes bear small tubular flowers of violet to rose. Zones 7–11.

Agastache rupestris
LICORICE MINT, SUNSET HYSSOP, THREADLEAF GIANT HYSSOP

☀ ❄ ↔ 18 in (45 cm)
↕ 18–36 in (45–90 cm)

From southwestern USA to northern Mexico. A very aromatic species with grayish green thread-like leaves that give the plant a feathery look. Leaves may be used in tea. Orange flowers with lavender calyces, creating the "sunset" effect of its common name. 'Sunset' is a slightly shorter cultivar. Zones 5–9.

Agastache Hybrid Cultivars
☀ ❄ ↔ 1–3 ft (0.3–0.9 m)
↕ 2–6 ft (0.6–1.8 m)

The crossing of several species has resulted in a range of hybrid cultivars of varying heights and colors, including: 'Apricot Sunrise', grayish green foliage and spikes of orange flowers; 'Blue Fortune', bluish purple flowers; 'Firebird', flowers of coppery orange tones; 'Tangerine Dreams', similar to 'Apricot Sunrise' but a taller plant; and 'Tutti Frutti', with grayish green leaves and flowers of raspberry red. Zones 7–10.

Agathis australis

AGATHIS
KAURI

These conifers, which grow into massive trees, are from the araucaria (Araucariaceae) family. This genus is of great evolutionary interest because it dates back to the temperate rainforests that covered much of the southern supercontinent of Gondwana. The species are scattered from Sumatra in the northwest to New Zealand and Fiji in the south-east. Kauri trees have a straight smooth trunk, developing massive ascending limbs with age. Peeling bark produces distinctive patterns. Broad leathery leaves, with no midrib, are arranged in almost opposite pairs. Cones are almost globular with tightly packed scales.
CULTIVATION: *Agathis* grow readily in the wet tropics and in warmer temperate climates. They prefer deep soil with reliable subsoil moisture and are known to reach very large sizes on deep coastal sands. Height growth may be quite fast, but a large trunk diameter takes many decades to achieve. Propagation only from seed, gathered as soon as it falls and sown immediately.

Agathis macrophylla

Agathis australis
NEW ZEALAND KAURI

☀ ❄ ↔ 50 ft (15 m) ↕ 150 ft (45 m)

Famous as New Zealand's largest native tree. Found in swampy lowland forests in the North Island. Small leaves, 1½ in (35 mm) long, closely crowded on adult branches. Slow growing, dense conical or columnar form. Source of the resin copal. Bark dappled gray and brown with small thick scales detaching. Bluish cones in summer. Zones 8–10.

Agathis corbassonii
CORBASSON'S KAURI

☀ ❄ ↔ 25 ft (8 m) ↕ 130 ft (40 m)

Only occurs on the northern half of New Caledonia, at 1,000–2,300 ft (300–700 m) altitude, on soils that are not ultrabasic, in scattered populations in lowland moist forest. Logging is depleting its numbers to a dangerous level. Bark scaly, resinous, and reddish brown. Adult leaves narrow and willow-like, and bluish green on the undersurface. Female cones are egg-shaped, male cones are cylindrical. Zones 10–12.

Agathis labillardierei
WESTERN NEW GUINEA KAURI

☀ ❄ ↔ 40 ft (12 m) ↕ to 200 ft (60 m)

Tall tree, branches of crown at about 45° to trunk, which can be up to 7 ft (2 m) in diameter. Occurs at 660–5,580 ft (200–1,700 m) altitude in the mountains of central New Guinea. Bark dark brown, adult leaves oblong to elliptical, shiny on the undersurface. Female cones globular. Seeds with a small wing. Zones 9–12.

Agathis macrophylla
syn. *Agathis vitiensis*
DAKUA, PACIFIC ISLANDS KAURI, VANIKORO KAURI

☀ ❄ ↔ 40 ft (12 m) ↕ 150 ft (45 m)

Tree with wide-spreading branches, trunk to 17 ft (5 m) in girth, bark whitish and scaly, occurring as emergents in the rainforests of Fiji, Vanuatu, and Solomon Islands at altitudes of 660–3,000 ft (200–900 m). Stout, straight, lower trunk and widely branched crown. Blackish bark peels in broad thin flakes leaving a striking pattern of bands and blotches. Large bluish cones dot canopy. Zones 10–12.

Agastache mexicana 'Honeybee Blue'

Agastache, Hybrid Cultivar, 'Blue Fortune'

Agathis ovata, in the wild, Col de Yaté, New Caledonia

Agathis robusta

Agathis montana

MT PANIE KAURI

☼ ❄ ↔ 40 ft (12 m) ↑ 50–70 ft (15–21 m)

Common species of the high altitude rainforests on Mt Panie in New Caledonia, at 3,280–5,250 ft (1,000–1,600 m). The tree has a flat crown, with a brownish bark shedding in patches and exposing a dark brown underbark. Adult leaves are lance-shaped to elliptical, 2½–3 in (6–8 cm). Female cones globular. Seeds are round with a wing on one side. Zones 10–12.

Agathis ovata

SCRUB KAURI

☼ ❄ ↔ 12 ft (3.5 m) ↑ 20 ft (6 m)

Flat-crowned species from New Caledonia, found in small stands. Can reach 75 ft (23 m), also found as a small tree or shrub. Light tan or whitish bark, with reddish underbark,

fissured. Variable-sized leaves, dark on the upper surface, paler beneath. Growth is slow. Zones 9–12.

Agathis robusta

QUEENSLAND KAURI

☼ ❄ ↔ 40 ft (12 m) ↑ 180 ft (55 m)

The Queensland kauri becomes a huge tree with orange-tan bark finely dappled with gray, becoming flaky with age. In cultivation it is fast growing with a pole-like trunk and short side-branches. At full size stem diameter increases rapidly. Zones 9–12.

AGATHOSMA

These 135 heather-like shrubs and subshrubs belong to the rue (Rutaceae) family, and are native to the southwestern Cape in South Africa. They are 15–24 in (38–60 cm) tall and slightly less in spread. The plant is densely covered with small narrow leaves, often rolled at the edges. The small 5-petalled flowers are in axillary clusters or umbels, ranging from white through to red-mauve and occasionally yellow. The whole plant is aromatic.

CULTIVATION: These plants thrive in neutral to acid, humus-rich, sandy soil with added grit in full sun. In cool-temperate regions grow in containers, putting outdoors in summer. Need moderate watering in the growing season and feeding with a balanced fertilizer once a month. Reduce watering as the weather becomes colder. Overwinter in frost-free conditions. Propagation is from seed in spring, in lime-free compost with added grit, or from ripe cuttings in summer.

Agathosma ovata

OVAL-LEAF BUCHU

☼ ❄ ↔ 18 in (45 cm) ↑ 18 in (45 cm)

From the Cape region of South Africa. Leaves ½ in (12 mm) long. Small pinkish lilac flowers in small clusters in leaf axils on the newer wood of branch tips. Zones 9–10.

AGAVE

CENTURY PLANT

A genus containing about 225 species, 50 subspecies, and varieties of rosette-shaped, succulent, monocarpic plants in the agave or sisal (Agavaceae) family. They are found from southwest USA to Mexico, Central America and the Caribbean, into Colombia and Venezuela. The genus name comes from the Greek *agavos* (stately or noble). Most species take decades to bloom, hence the common name, though many flower within 8–25 years in ideal conditions. After blooming they usually set seeds and some produce offsets or bulbils on the

inflorescence. The leaves usually terminate in a strong sharp spike, and mostly have spiny teeth on the margins. Most species produce basal offsets to ensure survival when the mother plant dies after flowering. Native American peoples have long used agaves for food, fibers, soap, beverages, and medicines. In many tropical areas they are grown to produce sisal for rope, twine, and bags. In Mexico, they are used to make the popular beverages pulque and tequila.

CULTIVATION: Grow in rich well-drained soil. Propagate from seed, offsets, or bulbils. Most benefit from a rest in winter; many need protection from frost.

Agave americana

☼ ❄ ↔ 7–15 ft (2–4.5 m) ↑ 17–50 ft (5–15 m)

From northeastern Mexico. Highly variable, medium to large, hardy species with curving blue-gray leaves. Have 10–20 leaves, 5–8 ft (1.5–2.4 m) long, lance-shaped, toothed, flat to guttered, hard, often turned down with age. Inflorescence 17–50 ft (5–15 m) long with 15 to 35 branches. Numerous, yellow, funnel-shaped flowers. *A. a.* var. *marginata* has yellow or white variegated stripes on the leaf margins. *A. a.* 'Cornelius', compact form with broad yellow margins on leaves; '**Mediopicta**' ★, yellow variegated mid-stripe on leaves; '**Mediopicta Alba**' ★, white variegated mid-stripe on the leaves. Zones 8–11.

Agave americana 'Cornelius'

Agave americana 'Mediopicta Alba'

Agave deserti, in the wild, in Catavina, Baja California, Mexico

Agave angustifolia

☼ ❄ ↔ 7–8 ft (2–2.4 m)
↑ 10–17 ft (3–5 m)

Highly variable species, widespread from Mexico through to Costa Rica. Almost spherical to cylindrical growth habit. Numerous, straight, rigid leaves, tapering toward the tip, 20–60 in (50–150 cm) long, light green to gray-green, toothed. Inflorescence 10–17 ft (3–5 m) long, branched, producing bulbils. Flowers green to yellow. *A. angustifolia* **var.** *marginata* is a variegated form. Zones 9–11.

Agave attenuata ★

☼ ❄ ↔ 24–60 in (60–150 cm)
↑ 3–7 ft (0.9–2 m)

From just a few habitats in Mexico. Brittle, almost flat, rounded, lime-green to bluish green leaves, 10–28 in (25–70 cm) long, lacking teeth and terminal spine. Inflorescence an arching spike, 7–15 ft (2–4.5 m) long. Displays pale yellow flowers and offsets. '**Boutin Blue**' ★ is a distinctly blue-gray cultivar. Zones 9–11.

Agave celsii

syn. *Agave mitis*

☼ ❄ ↔ 28 in (70 cm) ↑ 5–8 ft (1.5–2.4 m)

From eastern Mexico. Medium to large species forming large clumps with age. Leaves apple green to blue-gray, 12–24 in (30–60 cm) long, soft, succulent, curving upward. Margins slightly wavy, with small reddish brown teeth, closely spaced. Inflorescence a spike, 5–8 ft (1.5–2.4 m) long. Flowers greenish with tinge of lilac. Zones 9–11.

Agave chiapensis

☼ ❄ ↔ 20–40 in (50–100 cm) ↑ 7 ft (2 m)

From Chiapas, Mexico. A medium rosette, solitary to clustering, making a short stem. Leaves dark green, 14–20 in (35–50 cm) long, thick, smooth, flat to slightly concave. Margins slightly wavy, with small dark brown teeth. Inflorescence a spike, 7 ft (2 m) tall. Flowers yellow, tinged red. Zones 9–11.

Agave colorata ★

☼ ❄ ↔ 4–6 ft (1.2–1.8 m)
↑ 7–10 ft (2–3 m)

An attractive small plant from Sonora, Mexico. Leaves with wavy edges, prominent cross-bands of color, 10–24 in (25–60 cm) long, gray-blue, rough, with strong bud imprints on both sides of the leaves. Leaf margins are indented between strong brown teeth. Inflorescence is 7–10 ft (2–3 m) long, often arched, with 15–20 branches. Flowers are bright yellow. Zones 9–11.

Agave dasylirioides

☼ ❄ ↔ 24–36 in (60–90 cm)
↑ 5–7 ft (1.5–2 m)

From Morales, Mexico. Small, usually solitary, species with atypically thin, scarcely succulent leaves. Leaves 16–24 in (40–60 cm) long, bluish green, lacking teeth, with 1 mm wide yellow-green margin. Inflorescence an arching spike, 5–7 ft (1.5–2 m) tall. Flowers greenish yellow with pink filaments and yellow anthers. Zones 9–11.

Agave deserti

☼ ❄ ↔ 16–24 in (40–60 cm)
↑ 8–15 ft (2.4–4.5 m)

From southern California and southwestern Arizona, USA, and northern Sonoran Desert areas of Mexico. Simple to clumping, with narrow bluish green to gray leaves, 6–16 in (15–40 cm) long. Small, sharp, marginal teeth. Inflorescence 8–15 ft (2.4–4.5 m) tall, branched. Flowers bright yellow. Zones 9–11.

Agave attenuata 'Boutin Blue'

Agave desmettiana

☼ ❄ ↔ 24–32 in (60–80 cm)
↑ 7–10 ft (2–3 m)

From Cuba. Urn-shaped plant with smooth, arched, toothless leaves, 20–24 in (50–60 cm) long. Inflorescence 7–10 ft (2–3 m) tall, with 20–25 compact branches. Flowers pale yellow. Zones 9–11.

Agave filifera ★

☼ ❄ ↔ 28 in (70 cm) ↑ 7–8 ft (2–2.4 m)

This densely clumping species is from central southern Mexico. Numerous leaves, dark to mid-green, with clear white leaf bud imprints, margins lacking teeth but bearing many white

Agave chiapensis, in Costa Rica

Agave colorata

hairs or filaments. Leaves straight to incurving, 6–8 in (15–20 cm) long. Inflorescence a spike, 7–8 ft (2–2.4 m) tall. Flowers greenish with purple tinge. Zones 8–11.

Agave geminiflora

☼ ❄ ↔ 24–32 in (60–80 cm)
↑ 10–15 ft (3–4.5 m)

From a restricted area of Nayarit State in Mexico. Large solitary species with 100 to 200 long, thin, flexible, dark green leaves, 20 in (50 cm) long, bearing white filaments on margins lacking teeth. Inflorescence a spike, 10–15 ft (3–4.5 m) tall. Flowers in pairs, yellow, tinged red. Zones 9–11.

Agave attenuata

Agave ghiesbreghtii

☀ ✽ ↔ 20–28 in (50–70 cm)
↕ 10–15 ft (3–4.5 m)

Suckering species found from southern Mexico to Guatemala. Leaves dark green, 12–16 in (30–40 cm) long, stout, half-rounded, curving upward. Thick white to gray leaf margins bearing many straight to curved teeth. Inflorescence is a spike, 10–15 ft (3–4.5 m) tall. Flowers are greenish purple. Zones 9–11.

Agave 'Kichiokan'

☀ ✽ ↔ 24 in (60 cm) ↕ 10 ft (3 m)

A neat, symmetrical, slowly offsetting cultivar, possibly of *A. potatorum*, but with shorter more compact leaves and larger more brightly colored teeth on leaf margins. 'Kichiokan Variegated' is a variegated form with ½–¾ in (12–18 mm) wide bands of yellow on the leaf margins. Zones 9–11.

Agave lechuguilla

SHIN DAGGER

☀ ✳ ↔ 8–12 in (20–30 cm)
↕ 8–17 ft (2.4–5 m)

Widespread, low-growing, densely clumping species from southern New Mexico and Texas, USA, and Chihuahua Desert areas of Mexico south to Hidalgo State. Leaves light to yellowish green with darker striations, straight, upright, concaved, 10–20 in (25–50 cm) long, forming a narrow rosette. Thin, gray, horny leaf margins bear irregularly spaced, downward-pointing teeth. Inflorescence a spike, 8–17 ft (2.4–5 m) tall. Flowers yellow with tinges of purple. Zones 8–11.

Agave macroacantha ★

☀ ✽ ↔ 12–24 in (30–60 cm) ↕ 6 ft (1.8 m)

From Oaxaca and Puebla, Mexico. Small, symmetrical, clustering species with stout blue-gray leaves, 10–15 in

Agave ocahui

(25–38 cm) long, flat on upper surface, convexed below. Teeth 3–6 mm long, irregularly spaced along margin. Inflorescence upright, 10 to 14 branches. Flowers green to purple. Zones 9–11.

Agave mckelveyana

☀ ✳ ↔ 12–20 in (30–50 cm)
↕ 7–10 ft (2–3 m)

From central western Arizona, USA. Small, narrow-leafed, heavily toothed, dull gray-green species. Leaves straight or slightly wavy, margins with low tubercles. Teeth widely spaced, to ¼ in (6 mm) long, downward-pointing with red tips. Inflorescence 7–10 ft (2–3 m) tall, 10 to 20 branches. Flowers yellow. Zones 7–11.

Agave murpheyi

☀ ✳ ↔ 27–32 in (70–80 cm)
↕ 10–15 ft (3–4.5 m)

From central Arizona, USA. Medium-sized gray-green to yellow-green species. Leaves have some cross-banding, strong leaf bud imprints, flat at base, concaved at tips, 20–28 in (50–70 cm) long. Teeth small, brown, regularly spaced. Inflorescence

Agave 'Kichiokan'

branched, 10–15 ft (3–4.5 m) tall, usually producing a few seed pods and many bulbils. Flowers yellow-green with purple tinge. Zones 8–11.

Agave neomexicana

MESCAL

☀ ✳ ↔ 12–28 in (30–70 cm)
↕ 10–15 ft (3–4.5 m)

From New Mexico and western Texas, USA. Small to medium-sized, compact, offsetting species with blue-gray to gray-green leaves, 10–18 in (25–45 cm) long, deeply incurving. Teeth dark brown to grayish, ¼–⅓ in (6–8 mm) long, spaced about 1¼ in (30 mm) apart along margin. Inflorescence 10–15 ft (3–4.5 m) tall with 10 to 18 branches. Flowers yellow to orange, opening yellow. Zones 8–11.

Agave ocahui

☀ ✽ ↔ 20–40 in (50–100 cm) ↕ 10 ft (3 m)

From Sonora, Mexico. Solitary highly prized species, rarely producing offsets or bulbils, usually grown from seeds.

Agave neomexicana, in the wild, in Guadalupe Mountains National Park, Texas, USA

Agave murpheyi

Agave macroacantha

A

Agave parviflora

Agave parryi var. *truncata*

Symmetrical rosette of small, smooth, dark green, dagger-shaped leaves with narrow brownish red to gray margins that detach from the older leaves. Leaves 10–20 in (25–50 cm) long. Inflorescence a 10 ft (3 m) tall spike. Flowers yellow. Zones 9–11.

Agave palmeri
☀ ❉ ↔ 40–48 in (100–120 cm)
↑ 10–17 ft (3–5 m)

From southeast Arizona and southwest New Mexico, USA, and Sonora and Chihuahua, Mexico. Usually solitary medium-sized species, variable size and leaf form. Leaves bluish green to pale green, long, tapering to a point, stiff, incurving, 14–30 in (35–75 cm) long, toothed margins. Inflorescence 10–17 ft (3–5 m) tall, 8 to 12 branches. Flowers white, reddish bud. Zones 8–11.

Agave parryi ★
syn. *Agave patonii*
☀ ❉ ↔ 20–28 in (50–70 cm)
↑ 12–20 ft (3.5–6 m)

Compact solitary to suckering species from southeastern Arizona and southwestern New Mexico, USA, and Durango and Chihuahua, Mexico. Tight rosette of 100 to 150 leaves, 10–16 in (25–40 cm) long, straight to slightly rounded, ending in a distinctly sharp tip. Leaves smooth, rigid, flat to slightly concave, overlapping, light-gray to blue-green, toothed margins. Inflorescence 12–20 ft (3.5–6 m) tall,

20 to 30 branches. Flowers yellow, tinged red. *A. p.* var. *huachucensis* ★, larger and more compact than the type, growing to 5 ft (1.5 m) wide. *A. p.* var. *truncata* ★, most attractive form of this species with particularly short, rounded leaves. Zones 8–11.

Agave parviflora
☀ ❊ ↔ 6–8 in (15–20 cm)
↑ 3–7 ft (0.9–2 m)

From southern Arizona, USA, and the northern Sonoran Desert regions of Mexico. Neat symmetrical species, solitary or with few offsets. Leaves marked with thick white leaf bud imprints, filaments on margins. Leaves 2–4 in (5–10 cm) long. Inflorescence a spike, 3–7 ft (0.9–2 m) tall. Flowers yellow. Zones 8–11.

Agave potatorum
☀ ⧓ ↔ 3–8 ft (0.9–2.4 m) ↑ 15 ft (4.5 m)

From Puebla and Oaxaca, Mexico. Symmetrical plant with whitish gray-green leaves, deeply indented along margins, bearing large tubercles from which widely spaced, hooked, red-brown teeth arise. *A. p.* var. *verschaffeltii* ★ is distinguished by its whiter color and bigger tubercles on the leaf margins. Zones 9–11.

Agave pygmae
☀ ⧓ ↔ 10–12 in (25–30 cm)
↑ 7–10 ft (2–3 m)

From the border region between the Mexican State of Chiapas and

Agave schidigera

Guatemala. Tiny neat rosette species with oval to truncated, gray-green to blue-green leaves, 6–12 in (15–30 cm) long, with warty margins. Teeth ¼ in (6 mm) long, widely spaced. Inflorescence 7–10 ft (2–3 m) tall, branched. Flowers yellow. Zones 9–11.

Agave salmiana
MAGUEY DE PULQUE
☀ ⧓ ↔ 10–15 ft (3–4.5 m)
↑ 15–35 ft (4.5–10 m)

A very large, variable, offsetting species, widespread in central Mexico, especially in the States of San Luis Potosi, Hidalgo, and Michoacan. Strong, wide, gray-green, upwardly curving leaves, 3–7 ft (0.9–2 m) long, strongly keeled at the ends, toothed margins. *A. s.* var. *ferox* ★ (syn. *A. ferox*), graceful urn shape; leaves thick, shiny, green, with strong leaf bud imprints and wavy warty margins. Zones 9–11.

Agave schidigera
☀ ⧓ ↔ 40–60 in (100–150 cm)
↑ 7–12 ft (2–3.5 m)

From Chihuahua, Durango, Hidalgo, Zacatecas, San Luis Potosi, and smaller adjacent Mexican States. A solitary to non-suckering species. Leaves 12–20 in (30–50 cm) long, lacking teeth, straight to slightly incurving. Inflorescence is a spike, 7–12 ft (2–3.5 m) tall. Flowers greenish yellow with a tinge of purple. Zones 9–11.

Agave schottii
SHIN DAGGER
☀ ❊ ↔ 40–60 in (100–150 cm)
↑ 5–8 ft (1.5–2.4 m)

From southern Arizona and southwestern New Mexico, USA, and

Sonoran Desert States of Mexico. Small profusely clumping species. Leaves few, narrow, straight to slightly incurving, 8–16 in (20–40 cm) long, yellow-green, occasionally filamented. Marginal teeth absent. Inflorescence a spike, 5–8 ft (1.5–2.4 m) tall. Flowers yellow, fragrant. Zones 8–11.

Agave shawii
☀ ⧓ ↔ 40–60 in (100–150 cm)
↑ 7–15 ft (2–4.5 m)

From the coastal areas of northwestern Baja California, Mexico. It is occasionally solitary but usually clustering. Leaves light to dark green, slightly rough, flat to concave. Margins wavy to warty, smooth or bearing a thick horny edge. Teeth straight to hooked, red-brown, ¼–¾ in (6–18 mm) long. Inflorescence 7–15 ft (2–4.5 m) tall, 10 to 15 branches. Flowers greenish with a purple calyx. Zones 9–11.

Agave shawii, in Baja California, Mexico

Agave parryi

Agave vilmoriniana, in the wild, Sierra Madre Occidental, Sinaloa, Mexico

Agave victoria-reginae

Agave sisalana ★

☀ ❄ ↔ 10–20 ft (3–6 m)
↕ 17–20 ft (5–6 m)

This profusely offsetting sterile hybrid, of cultivated origins, is thought to have originated in Mexico. Leaves gray-green, stiff, sword-like, 36–60 in (90–150 cm) long, lacking marginal teeth. Leaves terminate in a stout reddish brown spine. Inflorescence 17–20 ft (5–6 m) tall, with 10 to 15 branches, producing many bulbils after flowering. Flowers greenish yellow with an unpleasant odor. Zones 9–11.

Agave stricta

☀ ❄ ↔ 40 in (100 cm) ↕ 5–8 ft (1.5–2.4 m)
From Tehuacan, Mexico. Attractive clustering species. Produces hundreds of pencil-thick, straight to upward-curving, dark green, toothless leaves,

Agave victoria-reginae 'Variegata'

10–20 in (25–50 cm) long, tipped with a very sharp, sturdy terminal spine. Inflorescence a spike, 5–8 ft (1.5–2.4 m) tall. Flowers red to purplish. *A. s.* f. *nana* is a dwarf, with heads rarely reaching more than 8–12 in (20–30 cm) in diameter. Zones 9–11.

Agave toumeyana ★

☀ ❄ ↔ 24–32 in (60–80 cm)
↕ 5–8 ft (1.5–2.4 m)

Limited habitat in central Arizona, USA. Small clustering rosette, 40 to 70 stiff thin leaves, 8–12 in (20–30 cm) long, lacking teeth, but with attractive white leaf bud imprints on both surfaces. Leaf margins bear white to gray hairs or filaments. Inflorescence a spike, 5–8 ft (1.5–2.4 m) tall. Flowers yellowish green. *A. t.* subsp. *bella* has more leaves, up to 100, and grows to only half the size. Zones 8–11.

Agave utahensis

☀ ❄ ↔ 10–16 in (25–40 cm)
↕ 5–8 ft (1.5–2.4 m)

Variable in size and color throughout its habitat, which includes Utah,

Arizona, Nevada, and California, USA. Usually small and clumping, with gray-green leaves, 6–12 in (15–30 cm) long. Marginal teeth, hooked, weak, gray, with distinctive ring at base. Inflorescence 5–8 ft (1.5–2.4 m) tall, branched or a spike. Flowers yellow. *A. u.* subsp. *kaibabensis,* attractive solitary form with bright green leaves and gray-white teeth; *A. u.* var. *eborispina,* long, cream-colored, wavy, papery terminal spine; *A. u.* var. *nevadensis,* smaller than type, bluish green to blue-gray leaves, with larger teeth and longer terminal spine. Zones 7–11.

Agave victoria-reginae ★

☀ ❄ ↔ 20–28 in (50–70 cm)
↕ 10–15 ft (3–4.5 m)

Easily recognized, small to medium-sized, solitary species from Coahuila, Durango, and Nuevo Leon, Mexico. Has a dense, symmetrical, tightly packed rosette of hard, dark green, triangular leaves, 6–8 in (15–20 cm) long, marked with thick white lines or leaf bud imprints. 'Variegata', with distinctive yellow leaf margins, has recently been renamed as 'Golden Princess'. Zones 9–11.

Agave vilmoriniana

OCTOPUS AGAVE

☀ ❄ ↔ 5 ft (1.5 m) ↕ 10–17 ft (3–5 m)
From southern Sonora, Sinaloa, Durango, Jalisco, and Aguascalientes, Mexico, where it forms dense colonies on canyon walls. Never offsetting, this species is usually propagated from bulbils. It has many long, incurving, light green to pale green, almost

Agave utahensis subsp. *kaibabensis*

cylindrical leaves which lack marginal teeth and taper evenly to a point bearing a flexible terminal spine. Inflorescence a raceme, 10–17 ft (3–5 m) tall, with yellow to white flowers and bulbils. Zones 9–11.

Agave xylonacantha

☀ ❄ ↔ 4 ft (1.2 m) ↕ 10–20 ft (3–6 m)
From the Sierra Madre Mountains of Nuevo Leon, Tamaulipas, San Luis Potosi, and Hidalgo, Mexico. Flat to incurving, sword-shaped, green to yellow-green leaves with a pale mid-stripe, 14–24 in (35–60 cm) long. Leaf margins brownish white, highly irregular, scalloped or wavy, warty, bearing up to 3 sharp, hooked, or straight teeth. Inflorescence a spike, 10–20 ft (3–6 m) tall. Flowers yellow-green to pale yellow. Zones 9–11.

AGERATUM

FLOSS FLOWER

Found in tropical Americas, including the West Indies, this genus of 43 species of annuals, perennials, and shrubs is a member of the daisy (Asteraceae) family. Best known for the annual bedding species, *A. houstonianum,* the genus is characterized by flowerheads in which the ray florets are tubular filaments rather than petal-like, creating a fine

Ageratum houstonianum

A. h., Hawaii Series, 'Hawaii Pink Shell'

A. h., Hawaii Series, 'Hawaii Royal'

feathery effect. Size varies considerably with the species, but most of the garden forms are compact and have hairy or felted leaves, often with toothed edges. The name *Ageratum* comes from the Greek *a* (without) and *geras* (age), and refers to the long-lasting qualities of the flowers. CULTIVATION: Plant in full sun in gritty well-drained soil that remains moist during the flowering season. Most perennial and shrubby species can tolerate only light frosts and may be grown outdoors only in very mild areas. Raise annuals from seed, usually sown in spring; propagate perennials from half-hardened cuttings.

Ageratum houstonianum

↔ 6–20 in (15–50 cm)
↑ 6–30 in (15–75 cm)

Annuals from Central America and West Indies. Pointed oval to poplar-shaped, downy, tooth-edged, dull green leaves to nearly 4 in (10 cm) long. Large dense or open heads of blue or lavender flowers. Garden forms include pink and white flowers. Popular cultivars include: '**Azure Pearl**', 12 in (30 cm) tall mid-blue flowers; '**Blue Danube**', up to 6 in (15 cm) tall mound forming blue flowers; '**Blue Horizon**', 24–30 in (60–75 cm) tall purple-blue flowers; '**Blue Lagoon**', 8 in (20 cm) tall neat rounded blue flowers; '**Blue Mink**' ★, 12 in (30 cm) tall light dusky blue flowers; '**Pacific**', 8 in (20 cm) tall purple-blue flowers; and '**Red Top**', 24–28 in (60–70 cm) tall bushy purple-red flowers. Among several seedling strains of uniform size but varying flower, one of the best is the **Hawaii Series**—neat rounded plants around 8 in (20 cm) tall— which includes: '**Hawaii Blue**', bright blue; '**Hawaii Pink Shell**', soft mid-pink; '**Hawaii Royal**', deep purple; and '**Hawaii White**', pure white. Zones 10–12.

AGLAIA

This genus in the mahogany (Meliaceae) family contains over 100 species, found from southern Asia to northern Australia and islands of the west Pacific. They are mostly evergreen with pinnate leaves, the leaflets are not very numerous, and the young growths are often covered in small whitish or brownish scales. Flowers are small but numerous, in loose panicles, and are followed by globular fruits with a tough skin and one or two large seeds. Only one species, *A. odorata*, is grown as a garden plant for its sweet-scented flowers and attractive foliage, and even this is little known outside East Asia.
CULTIVATION: Tough, fairly long-lived plants, they are easily grown in tropical and subtropical climates, preferring a sunny but sheltered position and a plentiful supply of water through summer. *A. odorata* is frequently grown in pots or tubs, flowering freely at a small size. Can propagate from cuttings, or fresh seed if available.

Aglaia odorata

MOCK LIME, RICEGRAIN FLOWER
☀ ☷ ↔ 8 ft (2.4 m) ↑ 6–10 ft (1.8–3 m)
An evergreen shrub that is native to Southeast Asia. Spreading, multi-stemmed habit. Glossy foliage, each leaf consisting of 5 leaflets. Pale yellow, fragrant flowers. Plants may bear male or female flowers or both together, so fruits are not always produced. Zones 10–12.

AGLAOMORPHA

This is a genus of large, epiphytic, tropical Asian ferns from the polypody (Polypodiaceae) family. A nest-like spreading cluster of smooth-edged or coarsely cut fronds, lobed at the base, arises from creeping rhizomes.
CULTIVATION: For plants of this genus it is best to use very coarse well-drained potting mix, including bark, gravel, fern fiber, and charcoal. They can be grown in a container or mounted on a wooden slab, and will need plenty of water, but less during winter. Apply fertilizers only during the growing months. They prefer a humid brightly lit situation, but must be protected from hot direct sun. Propagate from spores or by division during active growth in spring or early summer.

Aglaomorpha meyeniana

BEAR'S-PAW FERN
☀/☷ ↔ 32–48 in (80–120 cm)
↑ 20–32 in (50–80 cm)

This epiphytic fern comes from Taiwan and the Philippines. It has a branched creeping rhizome with orange scales. Fronds are lobed, dark green, and leathery, to 32 in (80 cm) long, rather papery and brown at their base. The fertile section in the fertile fronds is a series of bead-like lobes. Zones 11–12.

Aglaia odorata

Ageratum houstonianum 'Azure Pearl'

Ageratum houstonianum 'Red Top'

Ageratum houstonianum 'Blue Lagoon'

Ageratum houstonianum 'Blue Horizon'

AGLAONEMA

This arum (Araceae) family genus consists of about 25 species of herbaceous evergreens, occurring wild from eastern India to southern China and southward to Indonesia and the Philippines. Clustered fleshy stems short, or may grow slowly to over 3 ft (0.9 m) long. Leaves crowded at stem tips are mostly ovate or elliptical, somewhat leathery, and often patterned in gray or cream. Flower spikes project from among the leaf bases. Berry-like red or yellow fruits. Used indoors, or outdoors under trees in tropical gardens. CULTIVATION: Require a humid, virtually frost-free environment and grow best in filtered light, although some tolerate quite deep shade. Pot in an open free-draining medium and feed regularly through summer; remove longer stems. Propagate from stem cuttings or by division.

Aglaonema commutatum
☼/☀ ❀ ↔ 24 in (60 cm)
↑ 24–36 in (60–90 cm)

Most widely cultivated species, from the Philippines and eastern Indonesia.

Agrimonia eupatoria

Stems sprawl as they elongate. Leaves narrowly ovate, dull dark green with feather-like gray markings. *A. c.* **var. maculatum**, leaves highlighted with light green markings. *A. c.* '**Pseudo-bracteatum**', larger areas of white and pale green along veins; '**Treubii**', narrower leaves, contrasting deep green and pale gray pattern; '**White Rajah**', erect thin leaves, much more white and cream than green. Zones 10–12.

Aglaonema costatum
☼/☀ ❀ ↔ 24 in (60 cm) ↑ 12 in (30 cm)

From the Malay Peninsula, a low-growing plant with short, trailing stems and short dark green leaves with paler midrib; flower spikes few, with white spathe, to 1½ in (35 mm) long, in summer. '**Foxii**', scattered, small, white spots, white midrib. Zones 10–12.

Aglaonema crispum
syn. *Aglaonema robelinii*
PAINTED DROP-TONGUE
☼/☀ ❀ ↔ 18–30 in (45–75 cm)
↑ 24–48 in (60–120 cm)

Robust clumping plant with erect stems, from Philippines. Elliptical leaves to 12 in (30 cm) long, gray with dark green zone along midrib. Flower spikes clustered, spathe yellowish to 3 in (8 cm) long. Zones 10–12.

AGONIS

This small genus consists of 12 evergreen species growing naturally in temperate regions of southwest Western Australia. The most widely grown, *A. flexuosa*, is the only tree, but it is the lower-growing cultivars of this species that are more popular for

Aglaonema costatum

gardens. All have white or pink flowers. Like other members of the myrtle (Myrtaceae) family, the leaves contain aromatic oil, released when the leaves are crushed. The fibrous bark is a feature of the genus. CULTIVATION: An adaptable, almost pest-free genus, suited to full sun in a wide range of well-drained soils and climates, although some species can be damaged by frost. While tip pruning can be done at any time for bushier growth, the trees will also respond to pruning after flowering. Propagate by seed or cuttings, though cultivars only come true if cuttings are taken.

Agonis flexuosa ★
PEPPERMINT TREE, WILLOW MYRTLE
☼ ❀ ↔ 15 ft (4.5 m) ↑ 30 ft (9 m)

The mature willow myrtle has a graceful dome shape and weeping habit. Attractive white flowers resemble the tea-tree. Cultivars are more popular for garden use, including '**Nana**', to around 10 ft (3 m); and dwarf form

Aglaonema commutatum var. *maculatum*

'**Weeping Wonder**', to 3 ft (0.9 m). '**Belbra Gold**' and '**Variegata**', dainty variegated foliage forms. Zones 9–11.

AGRIMONIA

AGRIMONY, COCKLEBUR, STICKLEWORT
Found throughout northern temperate zones, this rose (Rosaceae) family genus has 15 species of summer-flowering, fleshy-stemmed, herbaceous perennials. They form clumps of strongly upright stems bearing irregularly pinnate, faintly aromatic leaves with coarsely toothed leaflets. Their yellow flowers are minute but showy, massed in plume-like racemes. Burr-bearing seedheads follow. Agrimony has astringent and diuretic properties, and has long been used in herbal medicines, mainly as an infusion. It is also the source of a yellow dye. CULTIVATION: Easily grown in any temperate climate. Not fussy about soil type if well-drained, and not drying out in summer. Plant in full or half-sun. May self-sow in situ but the seed does not germinate well in cultivation and is prone to damping off. Usually propagated by division.

Agrimonia eupatoria
HEMP AGRIMONY
☼/☀ ❀ ↔ 20–40 in (50–100 cm)
↑ 24–48 in (60–120 cm)

Found from Britain to Iran and North Africa. Leaves to 8 in (20 cm) long, with up to 14 pairs of leaflets with bristly undersides. Open flowerheads to 15 in (38 cm) long. Zones 6–10.

Agonis flexuosa, in the wild, Walpole, Western Australia

AGROSTIS

BENT GRASS, BROWN TOP

A cosmopolitan genus of some 120 species of evergreen annuals and perennials of the grass (Poaceae) family, many spread by runners (stolons). While hardiness varies, the few cultivated species are mostly frost hardy and valued as lawn grasses. Untrimmed, they develop into dense mounds of very fine leaves and from late summer produce numerous inflorescences. CULTIVATION: When cultivated as lawn, bent grass needs to be kept growing steadily with frequent watering and feeding. It is prone to fungal diseases and will suffer if the soil is alkaline. Annual aeration and dethatching is recommended.

Agrostis nebulosa
CLOUD GRASS

☼ ❄ ↔ 12 in (30 cm)
↑ 12–18 in (30–45 cm)

Drought-tolerant annual from Spain. Loosely tufted grass grown for white to tan finely textured flower clusters, open from summer to early autumn. Flowers can be dried. Zones 7–9.

Agrostis stolonifera
CREEPING BENT GRASS

☼ ❄ ↔ 12–24 in (30–60 cm)
↑ 8–16 in (20–40 cm)

Gray-green foliage and short feathery inflorescence. Spreads by runners. Good for golf courses but too high-maintenance for domestic lawns. May be mown short. Considered a weed in many areas. Zones 3–10.

Aichryson bollei

Aichryson × *domesticum* 'Variegatum'

Ailanthus altissima, in Great Smoky Mountains National Park, North Carolina, USA

AICHRYSON

Found on both sides of the Straits of Gibraltar and the Azores, Canary Islands, and Madeira, this stonecrop (Crassulaceae) family genus comprises 15 species of annuals, perennials, and subshrubs that are often monocarpic (die after flowering). Their stems are branched and carry a scattering of leaves along the branches, as well as loose rosettes at the tips. Some species have rather succulent leaves, while those of others are thin. Sprays of small, yellow-green, starry, 7 to 12-petalled flowers appear during the warmer month, the season varying with the species. CULTIVATION: Tolerant of only light frosts, but otherwise easily grown in a bright sunny position with gritty well-drained soil. Although succulent, they appreciate water during the growing season but may be dried off entirely for winter. Provide some shade in very hot summer areas. Propagate from seed or cuttings, depending on the plant type.

Aichryson bollei

☼/◐ ⬩ ↔ 8–12 in (20–30 cm)
↑ 12 in (30 cm)

This is a summer-flowering annual or biennial from the Canary Islands. Upright unbranched stems with fine white hairs and 1¾ in (40 mm) long spoon-shaped leaves covered with fine hairs, toothed or smooth-edged. Zones 9–10.

Aichryson × domesticum
YOUTH AND OLD AGE

☼/◐ ⬩ ↔ 12–20 in (30–50 cm)
↑ 12 in (30 cm)

Naturally occurring *A. tortuosum* × *A. punctatum* hybrid. Bushy perennial or subshrub from the Canary Islands. Upright, branching, brittle, red-brown stems with broad, rounded, ½ in (12 mm) long, bright green leaves, often with fine white hairs. Bright yellow flowers in early summer. 'Variegatum' ★ has leaves with broad white edges. Zones 9–10.

Aichryson laxum

Aichryson laxum

☼/◐ ⬩ ↔ 20 in (50 cm) ↑ 12 in (30 cm)

Annual or biennial from the Canary Islands. Upright branching stem with ½ in (12 mm) long, pale to dark green, sometimes purple-marked leaves irregularly along the stems and in terminal rosettes. Flowers in summer. Zones 9–10.

AILANTHUS

There are 5 or 6 species of medium-sized to large trees in this genus, in the quassia (Simaroubaceae) family, occurring from India to northern China and Australia. They include both evergreen tropical and deciduous cold-hardy species. Leaves are pinnate, mostly with a long midrib and many leaflets arranged in 2 regular rows. Flowers, of different sexes on different trees, small and greenish yellow, in large stalked clusters in leaf axils toward tips of branches, followed by clusters of flat elongated fruits. CULTIVATION: Easily cultivated if their respective climatic requirements are met, they make fast growth when young. Propagate from seed (may need cold stratification) or root cuttings.

Ailanthus altissima
syn. *Ailanthus glandulosa*
TREE OF HEAVEN

☼ ❄ ↔ 40 ft (12 m) ↑ 40 ft (12 m)

From China, deciduous tree with long pinnate leaves with unpleasant smell. Female trees flower in mid-summer, fruit in early autumn. Profuse suckers; a weed in many areas. Zones 5–10.

A

Aiphanes caryotifolia

Ajuga genevensis

Ajuga pyramidalis 'Metallica Crispa'

AIPHANES

Some beautiful palms belong to this tropical American genus of about 30 species from northern South America and the West Indies. Of the palm (Arecaceae) family, they are small to medium-sized feather-leafed palms of the rainforest undergrowth, armed with extremely sharp, needle-like, black spines that project from the trunk, frond stalks, and even leaflets. Leaflets widen toward their tips, which are truncated, toothed, and often frilled. Flowers are small and yellow or cream, in narrow panicles, followed by decorative, globular, bright red fruit. CULTIVATION: The 3 to 4 species usually found in palm collections are easily grown outdoors in the tropics and warmer subtropics, in a sheltered position in partial shade and watered

liberally in dry periods. Fertile well-drained soil is desirable. In cooler climates they need a heated conservatory or greenhouse, and can be kept in pots or tubs for a number of years before growing too large. Propagate from seed after removing fruit flesh.

Aiphanes caryotifolia
RUFFLE PALM

☀ ✈ ↔ 8 ft (2.4 m) ↕ 20 ft (6 m)

Generally considered the most decorative of the species, native to Venezuela, Colombia, and Ecuador. Straight trunk, about 4 in (10 cm) in diameter, with spines to 4 in (10 cm) long. Trunk crowned by a few elegantly arching fronds about 6 ft (1.8 m) long. Leaflets fresh green, in groups along whitish stalk, broadened apical edge strongly frilled, several radiating long

Aira elegantissima

teeth. Adult specimens produce short sprays of yellow flowers and brilliant red fruit. Zones 11–12.

AIRA
HAIR GRASS

Found from Northern Europe to Asia and through Africa to Mauritius, this genus of 9 species of annual grasses (family Poaceae) is related to the bent grasses *(Agrostis)*. They have fine leaves, hair-like in some species. Foliage usually bright green. Flowering stems in summer, with panicles of 2-flowered structures known as spikelets. In some species spikelets are close together like an ear of wheat; in others they are more widely spaced as in a string of beads. Hair grasses are seen in fields and sometimes lawns, but as annuals they are not cultivated for lawns. CULTIVATION: Easily grown in temperate climates. May become slightly invasive. Some species are considered minor weeds. Grow best in full sun with dry light soil that holds moisture in spring when they are becoming established. Can be left to dry after flowering. Propagate from seed.

Aira elegantissima

☀ ✽ ↔ 6 in (15 cm) ↕ 4–12 in (10–30 cm)

Native to the Mediterranean but widely naturalized in temperate zones. Tufts of 2 in (5 cm) long leaves. Flower stems may be upright to near-flat, with panicles 1–4 in (2.5–10 cm) long. Zones 6–10.

AJANIA

A genus of 30 perennial herbs or shrubs from the daisy (Asteraceae) family, native to central and eastern Asia. Racemes of daisy-like flowers, in a radial pattern, appear in autumn. Spread by underground rhizomes. CULTIVATION: Hardy plants that adapt to exposed positions or partial shade. Need well-drained, moderately fertile soil, which should be kept moist. Propagate from seed or by division.

Ajania pacifica
syn. *Chrysanthemum pacificum*
PACIFIC GOLD AND SILVER CHRYSANTHEMUM

☼/◑ ✽ ↔ 8–12 in (20–30 cm)
↕ 12–18 in (30–45 cm)

Drought-tolerant perennial from far-eastern Russia and northern Japan, with clusters of yellow daisy-like flowers. Scalloped felt-like leaves with silver undersides. Zones 5–9.

AJUGA
BUGLE

Members of the mint (Lamiaceae) family, the 40-odd, low, spreading annuals and perennials in this genus occur throughout temperate Eurasia, Africa, and Australia, and are widely naturalized elsewhere. Many spread by fleshy stems, others self-layer as they grow. Leaves are in whorls on narrow angular stems. Conical, short-stemmed, upright flowerheads with small, often purple-blue flowers appearing from axils of leaf bracts, bloom mainly from late spring into summer. Use as a quick ground cover around small shrubs or in containers, but take care to control their spread. The common bugle *(A. reptans)* has had several uses in herbal medicine, including as an astringent and to stop blood flow from injuries. CULTIVATION: Most grow very freely in any well-drained soil and are excellent ground covers for harsh conditions. Some are rather invasive and need to be cut back routinely.

Ajania pacifica

Propagation of the perennials is usually by division or from self-rooted layers; annuals from seed.

Ajuga genevensis

BLUE BUGLE, UPRIGHT BUGLE

☀ ❄ ↔ 12–16 in (30–40 cm)
↑ 12–16 in (30–40 cm)

Native to Europe. Creeping perennial with oblong leaves on long stalks. Upper leaves tinged with blue. Bright blue flowers, borne on leafy spikes, in spring–summer. Zones 6–9.

Ajuga pyramidalis

PYRAMID BUGLE

☀/◑ ❄ ↔ 12–24 in (30–60 cm)
↑ 6–8 in (15–20 cm)

Mat-forming European perennial with rosettes of dark green, finely toothed leaves to 4 in (10 cm) long. Leafy pyramidal flowerheads with mauve-blue flowers backed by purple-bronze bracts. 'Metallica Crispa' has wavy-edged purple-bronze foliage with a metallic sheen. Zones 6–10.

Ajuga reptans

☀/◑ ❄ ↔ 12–48 in (30–120 cm) or more
↑ 4–8 in (10–20 cm)

A temperate Eurasian native. Vigorous, sometimes invasive, forms a carpet, spreading by runners. Foliage often purple tinted. Flowers in blue to purple shades, sometimes pink. Cultivars include: 'Atropurpurea', deep purple-bronze foliage, dark flowers; 'Braunherz', very dark and glossy purple-bronze leaves; 'Burgundy Glow', gray-green leaves with reddish markings; 'Burgundy Lace', purple-bronze, cream and green variegated

Akebia quinata

Alangium chinense

foliage; 'Catlin's Giant', large bronze-green leaves and tall flower spikes; 'Jungle Beauty', vigorous with large deep green leaves, bright purple-blue flowers; 'Jungle Bronze', vigorous upright grower with large, wavy-edged, bronze leaves; 'Pink Elf', compact plant with deep pink flowers; 'Pink Surprise', bronze, gray, and green variegated foliage, bronze in winter, pink flowers; 'Purple Torch', bronze foliage, pink flowers; and 'Multicolor' (syns 'Rainbow', 'Tricolor'), cream, pink, and green foliage. Zones 5–10.

AKEBIA

CHOCOLATE VINE

Found in the small chocolate-vine (Lardizabalaceae) family, which includes some rather unusual plants, this genus from temperate East Asia is composed of just 4 species of evergreen and deciduous twining vines. The extent of foliage loss depends on the degree of winter cold. Leaves are composed of several oval leaflets, the number varying with species. Flowers open in spring, are unisexual, and, while not showy, are distinctive as they occur in panicles and for their color, which ranges from bright maroon to purple-brown. If cross-pollinated, pulpy, sausage-like, blue to purple fruits follow the flowers and are edible, though insipid.
CULTIVATION: Preferring cool shaded conditions with moist humus-rich soil, *Akebia* species are undemanding and in suitable conditions can be vigorous growers that need frequent trimming. Propagate from seed that has been stratified for about 4 weeks or from softwood to half-hardened summer cuttings.

Akebia quinata

☀ ❄ ↔ 20 ft (6 m) ↑ 10 ft (3 m)

From Korea, Japan, and nearby parts of China. Leaves with 5 leaflets to 2 in (5 cm) long. Vanilla-scented, maroon flowers; males very small, females about 1 in (25 mm) wide. Plants that fruit well need support to hold the weight. Zones 5–10.

Alangium platanifolium

Ajuga reptans 'Catlin's Giant'

Ajuga reptans 'Pink Surprise'

ALANGIUM

This genus consists of about 20 species of small to large trees, shrubs and a few climbers ranging from Japan and China through Southeast Asia to eastern Australia and Fiji, outlying occurrence in tropical Africa. It is in a family of its own (Alangiaceae), though allied to the dogwood and tupelo families. Most species are evergreen but a few East Asian species are deciduous, with foliage coloring in autumn. Leaves are arranged spirally on slender twigs and strongly veined. Rather inconspicuous white flowers with narrow recurving petals and hang in small clusters from leaf axils. Fruits are small olive-shaped drupes.
CULTIVATION: The deciduous species are frost hardy to varying degrees and like much the same conditions as the smaller maples (*Acer*). The evergreen species are rainforest plants and enjoy moist, sheltered, frost-free locations. Propagate from seed, sown fresh after removing fruit flesh.

Alangium chinense

☀ ◑ ↔ 20 ft (6 m) ↑ 60 ft (18 m)

Evergreen tree or large shrub, with horizontally spreading branches and heart-shaped leathery leaves with margins that are smooth, toothed, or deeply lobed. Flowers in clusters have white petals, orange stamens. Purple to black fruit. Zones 9–12.

Ajuga reptans 'Purple Torch'

Alangium platanifolium

☀ ❄ ↔ 6 ft (1.8 m) ↑ 15 ft (4.5 m)

A deciduous species from Japan and Korea, with a low-branching habit. Leaves similar to *Platanus*, with 3 to 5 shallow lobes, turn yellow in autumn. Late spring flowers and fruit similar to those of *A. chinense*. Zones 8–10.

ALBERTA

This genus, of the madder or gardenia (Rubiaceae) family, was named after the thirteenth-century German saint, scholar, and scientist, Albertus Magnus, teacher of Thomas Aquinas. It includes 3 species of tropical evergreen trees: 2 from Madagascar and the other from South Africa. They have lush leathery leaves and vibrantly colored tubular flowers clustered at the branch tips. The flowers are backed by 5 conspicuous sepals, 2 of which develop into the conspicuous colored wings of the fruit that follows the flowers.
CULTIVATION: This genus tolerates only light frosts, and does best in warm moist climates. In cooler areas it will often grow well in sheltered coastal locations. The soil should be rich and well drained and should not be allowed to dry out, especially during the growing season. Plants may be raised from half-hardened stem or root cuttings, or from seed.

A

Alberta magna
NATAL FLAME BUSH

☀ ☘ ↔ 7 ft (2 m) ↕ 15 ft (4.5 m)

From South Africa. Usually a large shrub in cultivation. Leaves leathery deep green. For up to 9 months of year—autumn to summer—produces heads of bright red flowers, each backed by a lighter calyx. Zones 10–12.

ALBIZIA
This genus contains trees, shrubs, and vines in the mimosa subfamily of the legumes. Most have attractive feathery foliage of bipinnate compound leaves and showy flowerheads of prominent stamens in pink, cream, or white. Flowers are followed by flattened pods. Species are fast growing but

Alberta magna

Alcea rosea 'Nigra'

Alcea rosea

generally short lived, often attacked by borers, and can become weedy. Most are reasonably drought and cold tolerant. Foliage and seed pods are nutritious fodder and the powdered bark has been used as soap.

CULTIVATION: Tolerant of poor soils but perform best on well-drained loam in a sheltered position, requiring moisture and warmth in summer. As seeds have impermeable coats, soak in sulfuric acid for half an hour, then wash thoroughly prior to sowing. In early spring, root cuttings of at least ½ in (12 mm) diameter, and planted immediately, are also successful.

Albizia julibrissin
PERSIAN SILK TREE, PINK SIRIS, SILK TREE

☀ ❄ ↔ 15–20 ft (4.5–6 m) ↕ 20–40 ft (6–12 m)

Deciduous tree from Japan and western Asia. Pinkish inflorescences with silky stamens in summer. Feathery compound leaves dark green, paler beneath, yellowish in autumn. Zones 8–12.

Albizia saman
MONKEY POD, RAIN TREE, SAMAN

☀/☀ ☘ ↔ 50–100 ft (15–30 m) ↕ 100 ft (30 m)

Evergreen or briefly deciduous tree found from Caribbean and Central America to Brazil. Broad spreading crown of pinnate leaves with fine leaflets. Pink flowerheads, clustered, followed by edible black-brown seed pods. Zones 10–12.

ALBUCA
Most of the 30 species of bulbous plants in this genus, a member of the lily (Liliaceae) family, are native to southern Africa. Only a few are suit-

Albizia saman

Albizia julibrissin

able for cultivation. Leaves range in length from 3 in (8 cm) to 4 ft (1.2 m) and may be flat or keeled. Flowers, 6-petalled, are yellow or greenish white, in loose racemes on tall stems. Fruiting capsule has many black seeds.

CULTIVATION: Suitable for outdoor cultivation only where frosts are light, but can be grown in a conservatory or greenhouse. Grow in full sun in light free-draining soil, in a sheltered position if light frosts might occur. Under glass maintain at 45°F (7°C), keep moist, and provide weak liquid fertilizer regularly when in full growth. Propagate from offsets or seed.

Albuca humilis
☀ ☘ ↔ 4 in (10 cm) ↕ 4–8 in (10–20 cm)

From South Africa. Narrow channelled leaves to 6 in (15 cm) long. Small white flowers, 1 to 3 to a stem, with green stripes. The inner petals are often tipped with yellow. Zones 9–11.

Albuca nelsonii
☀ ☘ ↔ 3 ft (0.9 m) ↕ 2–5 ft (0.6–1.5 m)

An attractive South African species. Pointed bright green leaves to 4 ft (1.2 m) long. Tall stems carry slightly scented white flowers with a green or reddish median stripe on each petal. Zones 9–11.

ALCEA
HOLLYHOCK

A member of the mallow (Malvaceae) family, this genus contains about 60 species of biennials and short-lived perennial herbs native to central and southwestern Asia, where they grow in sunny well-drained areas. Some are naturalized around the Mediterranean. Flowers, to 4 in (10 cm) across and borne on stems to 7 ft (2 m) tall in summer, have 5 petals and may be pink, purple, yellow, or white. Stamens form a prominent central column, usually yellow. A quintessential English cottage garden style plant.

CULTIVATION: Grow in a sunny position in rich soil, moist but well drained. Stake plants on exposed sites and water in dry spells. Rust is a problem, and it is best to renew plants each year. Propagate from seed sown in late summer or early spring.

Alcea ficifolia
ANTWERP HOLLYHOCK

☀ ❄ ↔ 24–36 in (60–90 cm) ↕ 6–8 ft (1.8–2.4 m)

From Siberia. A perennial or biennial species. Large lobed leaves have irregularly toothed margins. Spikes of single or double yellow or orange flowers in summer. Zones 3–10.

Alcea rosea

syn. *Althaea rosea*

HOLLYHOCK

🌣 ❄ ↔ 2–3 ft (0.6–0.9 m)
↕ 2–8 ft (0.6–2.4 m)

Cultivated and naturalized in many places but thought to originate from Turkey or Asia. Rounded leaves have 3 to 7 lobes. Flowers single or double, to 4 in (10 cm) across, shades of pink, purple, yellow, and white. Wide range of cultivars and seed lines. 'Nigra', dark maroon single flowers. Zones 3–10.

ALCHEMILLA

BEAR'S FOOT, LADY'S MANTLE, LION'S FOOT

A widespread Eurasian rose (Rosaceae) family genus of around 300 species of clump-forming soft-stemmed perennials. Foliage, on fine stems that often self-layer, is hand-shaped with rounded lobes, covered in fine hairs. Sprays of tiny yellow-green flowers from late spring. *Alchemilla* comes, via the Arabic name *alkemelych*, from *alchimia* (alchemy), a reference to the fanciful idea that the silvery dewdrops that form on the leaves might be added to recipes for gold. It has featured in herbal medicine, mainly to encourage healing but also in "elixirs of youth."
CULTIVATION: Cultivated species are temperate-zone plants that prefer cool, moist, well-drained conditions with shade from the hottest sun. Good in perennial borders or large rockeries. Propagation usually by division when dormant, but can be raised from seed.

Alchemilla conjuncta

LADY'S MANTLE

🌣/🌣 ❄ ↔ 10 in (25 cm) ↕ 6 in (15 cm)

Sprawling alpine perennial from Europe. Small, serrated, green leaves with silvery edge. Small yellowish green to chartreuse flowers, similar to *A. mollis* but less ornamental. Blooms late spring–early summer. Zones 5–9.

Alchemilla erythropoda

🌣/🌣 ❄ ↔ 12–24 in (30–60 cm)
↕ 8 in (20 cm)

Spreading plant found in the Balkans, Carpathians, and Caucasus. Leaves hairy, deeply cut, toothed, gray-green, 7 to 9 lobes. Pale green flowers, on sometimes purple-red stems, to 8 in (20 cm) long, in summer. Zones 4–9.

Alchemilla glaucescens

🌣/🌣 ❄ ↔ 12–24 in (30–60 cm)
↕ 8 in (20 cm)

Low spreading plant, found from Ireland to western Russia. Rounded, hairy, 7- to 9-lobed, toothed, blue-green leaves. Pale green flowers in summer. Zones 4–9.

Alchemilla erythropoda

Alchemilla lapeyrousei

🌣/🌣 ❄ ↔ 12–24 in (30–60 cm)
↕ 10 in (25 cm)

Mounding Pyrenean species with hairy, kidney-shaped, toothed leaves with 7 to 9 lobes. Airy heads of light green flowers, stems to 10 in (25 cm) long, in summer. Zones 5–9.

Alchemilla mollis ★

LADY'S MANTLE

🌣/🌣 ❄ ↔ 12–32 in (30–80 cm)
↕ 12–20 in (30–50 cm)

Mounding spreading species found from Romania to Greece and Iran. Toothed leaves, finely hairy above, densely hairy below. Sprays of yellow-green flowers in summer. Zones 4–9.

Alchemilla speciosa

🌣/🌣 ❄ ↔ 12–32 in (30–80 cm)
↕ 12–20 in (30–50 cm)

From the Caucasus. Like *A. mollis* but leaves are more deeply lobed and flower stems are hairy. Zones 4–9.

Alchemilla xanthochlora

🌣 ❄ ↔ 16–24 in (40–60 cm)
↕ 12–20 in (30–50 cm)

Mounding and spreading European species. Yellow-green, kidney-shaped, toothed, 9- to 11-lobed leaves, hairless above, hairy below. Yellow-green flowers in summer. Zones 5–9.

Alchemilla speciosa

Alchemilla lapeyrousei

ALDROVANDA

Consisting of only one species, this genus in the sundew (Droseraceae) family is a rootless aquatic occurring in freshwater lakes and ponds in central and southern Europe, western Asia, tropical Africa, and northern Australia. It traps small aquatic animals by means of its whorls of leaves that have modifications similar to the those of the Venus flytrap.
CULTIVATION: The species is best propagated by division.

Aldrovanda vesiculosa

WATERWHEEL PLANT

🌣 ❄ ↔ 8 in (20 cm) ↕ 4 in (10 cm)

Can have branched or single stems, leaves in whorls of 5 to 10, each up to ½ in (12 mm) long with leaf stalks modified to trap small animals. White flowers, ½ in (12 mm) across, are produced during the warmer months. In cultivation, the water needs to be of acid pH, and not to fall below 50°F (10°C). Zones 8–9.

Alchemilla xanthochlora

Aleurites fordii

ALEURITES

Of the 5 species in this Asian-Australasian genus of the spurge (Euphorbiaceae) family, at least 3 are important for the oils obtained from their large seeds. The genus includes evergreen and deciduous species. They are medium-sized to large trees with a straight central trunk and tiered branches. Leaves are large and heart-shaped. Flowers are mostly funnel-shaped with 5 white or cream petals, in large clusters at branch tips. Fruits are globular, the husk enclosing 2 to 5 large nut-like seeds, which may cause violent vomiting if eaten.
CULTIVATION: Best in climates with long humid summers. Thrive in deep fertile soils but will grow well in poorer soils. Deciduous species tolerate moderate winter frosts. Propagate from fresh seed in autumn, or from hardwood cuttings for deciduous species.

Aleurites fordii

syn. *Vernicia fordii*

TUNG-OIL TREE

🌣 ❄ ↔ 10 ft (3 m) ↕ 25 ft (8 m)

Deciduous tree from China, cultivated for seed oil. Compact crown, broad heart-shaped leaves. White flowers with red centers in spring. Fruit green, ripening black, in summer. Zones 8–11.

Allamanda cathartica

Allamanda blanchetii

Aleurites moluccana

syn. *Aleurites triloba*

CANDLENUT TREE

☼ ◈ ↔35 ft (10 m) ↕80 ft (24 m)

From tropical Asia to islands of the western Pacific, this evergreen forest tree can thrive on poor shallow hill soils, and will grow in warm-temperate regions. Glossy heart-shaped leaves. Small cream flowers in spring. Green fruit in summer. Oil content in seeds is so high that they will support a flame if cut open. Zones 10–12.

ALKANNA

This is a genus of about 30 frost-hardy annuals and perennials found from southern Europe to Iran, and belonging to the borage or forget-me-not (Boraginaceae) family. Has branching terminal inflorescences with a long tubular corolla and a downy ring in the centre, and smooth-edged, hairy leaves. Fruits are elongated calyces.
CULTIVATION: Prefer rich warm soil in an open sunny position. Propagate from seed.

Alkanna orientalis

☼ ❊ ↔8–12 in (20–30 cm)
↕8–12 in (20–30 cm)

Annual found from southwest Europe to southwest Asia. White or yellow scented flowers to ½ in (12 mm) wide. Hairy green to whitish green leaves to 3 in (8 cm) long, lance-shaped or narrowly egg-shaped. Zones 6–9.

Alkanna tinctoria

ALKANET, DYER'S BUGLOSS

☼ ❊ ↔12–36 in (30–90 cm)
↕12–36 in (30–90 cm)

Perennial from central and southern Europe. Bright purplish blue flowers to ½ in (12 mm) wide with funnel-shaped corolla. Bristly, smooth-edged, linear to egg-shaped leaves to 3 in (8 cm) long. Extensive root system and a hairy angular stem. Zones 5–8.

ALLAGOPTERA

syn. *Diplothemium*

This genus of the palm (Arecaceae) family contains 5 species, occurring in South America, generally in open habitats, not in forests. They are small feather-leafed palms, with most or all of their stems below ground. Leaves have numerous narrow leaflets

Allamanda schottii

arranged in planes around the leaf axis. Inflorescences are formed among the leaf bases, and consist of male and female flowers on the same stalk, but with a larger number of males than females. Fruits are egg-shaped, with a fleshy fibrous outer covering.
CULTIVATION: Propagate from seed, which can take up to 3 to 4 months to germinate.

Allagoptera arenaria

syn. *Diplothemium maritimum*

BRAZILIAN SAND PALM

☼ ⅓ ↔7–10 ft (2–3 m)
↕40–60 in (100–150 cm)

Occurring as dense thickets on the sand dunes along the east coast of Brazil. Leaves to 4 ft (1.2 m) long, composed of narrow leaflets, dark green on the uppersurface, whitish on the undersurface, in clusters of 2 to 3 along the midrib. Inflorescences, 24 in (60 cm) long, emerge from a woody persistent bract, exposing yellow flowers densely clustered on the flower spike. Fruits ½ in (12 mm) long, egg-shaped, and greenish yellow. Zones 10–12.

ALLAMANDA

This genus, a member of the dogbane (Apocynaceae) family, consists of around 12 evergreen shrubs, including both upright and semi-climbing species. They are tropical American natives and are lush, colorful, and flamboyant. The large, glossy, deep green leaves are the perfect foil to the flowers, usually a deep golden yellow.

The flowers appear mainly in summer and autumn and are trumpet-shaped with a widely flared throat of 5 large, overlapping petals.
CULTIVATION: Protection from frost is paramount and a moist subtropical to tropical climate is best, though it is possible to grow allamandas in very sheltered areas in cooler zones. For a prolific flower display give them rich well-drained soil and plenty of summer moisture. They also do well in conservatories but watch out for mealy bugs, scale insects, and mites. Propagation is usually by half-hardened cuttings.

Allamanda blanchetii

PURPLE ALLAMANDA

☼ ✦ ↔6–8 ft (1.8–2.4 m)
↕6–8 ft (1.8–2.4 m)

This purple-flowered species with an indeterminate South American origin is inclined to twine. Regular trimming will keep it in check. The flowers, while unusually colored and of a heavy texture, are rather a dull shade. Zones 11–12.

Allamanda cathartica

CLIMBING ALLAMANDA, COMMON ALLAMANDA, GOLDEN TRUMPET

☼ ⅓ ↔10 ft (3 m) ↕17 ft (5 m)

From South America. A vigorous climber with whorls of glossy leathery leaves. Bears bright yellow trumpet-shaped flowers, up to 5 in (12 cm) across, in summer. The seed capsules are prickly. '**Grandiflora**', very large flowers in profusion; '**Hendersonii**', smaller flowers with orange markings in throat; and '**Nobilis**', larger, more flaring flowers. Zones 10–12.

Allamanda schottii

BUSH ALLAMANDA

☼ ✦ ↔6 ft (1.8 m) ↕6 ft (1.8 m)

This South American species can be kept neat with regular pinching back and an annual spring trim. It has glossy deep green leaves and bright golden yellow flowers streaked with light orange, followed by large green seed pods. Zones 11–12.

Aleurites moluccana

Alkanna orientalis

Allium cepa

ALLIUM

CHIVE, GARLIC, LEEK, ONION,
ORNAMENTAL ONION

A genus of around 700 species of bulbous perennials and biennials, and the
type genus for the onion (Alliaceae)
family. Famous for their taste and
pungency, many are vital ingredients
in the world's cuisine. Some, especially
garlic, have a long history in herbal
medicine and folklore, and the ornamental species are not without an air
of mystery too. In Europe, *A. moly*
was thought to be protection against
demons, and Homer's Ulysses used its
"magical properties" to enter Circe's
lair. Foliage may be fine and grassy,
strappy or hollow and tubular. Flowers,
often brightly colored, are usually
borne in rounded heads on long stems.
CULTIVATION: Most thrive in fairly
light soil in a sunny well-drained position. Ample water is needed during
foliage growth and flowering, but
then they can dry off. Propagate using
offsets and bulbils, or from seed.

Allium carinatum subsp. *pulchellum*

A. ampeloprasum, Porrum Group, 'Colossal'

Allium cepa, Cepa Group, 'Superstar'

Allium acuminatum

HOOKER'S ONION, ORNAMENTAL ONION,
PINK WILD ONION, TAPERTIP ONION

☼ ❄ ↔ 3 in (8 cm) ↑ 4–12 in (10–30 cm)
From the Rocky Mountains, USA.
Perennial herb. The ½ in (12 mm)
long green leaves wither before flowers
bloom in late spring–early summer.
Flowers are pinkish purple and urn-
shaped. Zones 4–9.

Allium aflatunense

☼ ❄ ↔ 12–24 in (30–60 cm)
↑ 3–5 ft (0.9–1.5 m)

Chinese species with 6 to 8, short,
faintly aromatic, blue-green, tubular
leaves per bulb. Foliage dies before the
flower stems develop in late summer,
carrying 4 in (10 cm) wide spherical
heads of massed, tiny, dark-veined,
violet flowers. Zones 8–10.

Allium ampeloprasum

KURRANT, LEVANT GARLIC, WILD LEEK

☼ ❄ ↔ 12–24 in (30–60 cm)
↑ 2–6 ft (0.6–1.8 m)

Occurs in various forms from Ireland
and southern England to Iran and
North Africa. Flat, rough-edged, gray-
green leaves to 20 in (50 cm) long,

A. ampeloprasum, Porrum Group, 'Unique'

Allium cepa, Cepa Group, 'Aristocrat'

4–10 per bulb. Spherical 2–4 in
(5–10 cm) wide heads of hundreds of
pink to red flowers, initially enclosed
by papery bracts. The **Porrum Group**
(syn. *A. porrum*) comprises the leeks,
of which there are numerous cultivars.
'**Colossal**' and '**Unique**' are long-
stemmed, self-blanching, quick-
maturing cultivars typical of garden
leeks. Zones 6–9.

Allium caeruleum

☼ ❄ ↔ 6–12 in (15–30 cm)
↑ 8–24 in (20–60 cm)

Found from central Asia to southern
Siberia. Grassy, 3-angled, blue-green
leaves to 3 in (8 cm) long, 2 to 4
per bulb. Tiny blue to light purple
flowers in spherical heads around 1 in
(25 mm) wide. Zones 6–9.

Allium carinatum

KEELED GARLIC

☼ ❄ ↔ 6–12 in (15–30 cm)
↑ 12–24 in (30–60 cm)

Found from central and southern
Europe to Russia and Turkey. Grassy
leaves to 8 in (20 cm) long, 2 to 4 per
bulb. Up to 30 purple-pink flowers in
heads 1–2 in (25–50 mm) wide.
Small bulbils develop around the
flowerhead. *A. c.* **subsp.** *pulchellum*
has purplish flower stems and does
not produce bulbils. Zones 7–10.

Allium ampeloprasum, Porrum Group cv

Allium cepa, Cepa Group, 'Kelsae'

Allium cepa

ONION, SCALLION, SPRING ONION

☼ ❄ ↔ 4–8 in (10–20 cm)
↑ 12–24 in (30–60 cm)

Biennial bulb that appears to be a true
species but is not known in the wild.
Cultivated widely as a vegetable. Blue-
green, flattened, cylindrical leaves to
16 in (40 cm) long, up to 10 per bulb.
In summer, strong, tall, sometimes
bulbil-bearing flower stems with heads
of green-veined white flowers. Many
cultivars in 3 groups. The **Aggregatum
Group** (scallions, spring onions) produces clustered bulbs, with no bulbil
on the flowerhead. The **Cepa Group**
(brown, white and red onions) has
single bulbs, with no bulbils on the
flower stem: '**Aristocrat**', good crop of
relatively large bulbs; '**Kelsae**', large,
soft onions; '**Kelsae Giant**', very large
bulbs; '**Red Baron**', large, red-skinned,
near-spherical onions; '**Tough Ball**',
round medium-sized bulbs that keep
well; '**Paris Silver Skin**', a small onion
often used for pickling; and '**Superstar**'
is especially heavy-cropping. The
Proliferum Group produces single
bulbs and clusters of bulbils around
the flowerhead. Zones 5–10.

A

Allium cernuum

LADY'S LEEK, NODDING ONION,
WILD ONION

☼ ❄ ↔ 6–12 in (15–30 cm)
↕ 12–27 in (30–70 cm)

Found from southern Canada to
northern Mexico. Grassy, flattened,
bright green leaves to 8 in (20 cm)
long, 4 to 6 per bulb. In summer,
heads of 30 to 40 white, pink, or
purple-red flowers. '**Hidcote**' is a cultivar with 18 in (45 cm) tall flower
stems and heads of nodding purple-
pink flowers. Zones 6–10.

Allium cratericola

CASCADE ONION, CRATER ONION,
VOLCANIC ONION, WILD GARLIC

☼◐ ❄ ↔ 8–12 in (20–30 cm)
↕ 6–8 in (15–20 cm)

Native to volcanic screes of western
USA. Narrow to strappy, sometimes
red-tinted leaves, 2 per bulb. In
summer, heads of white to pale pink
flowers, deeper pink in bud. Zones 7–9.

Allium cristophii ★

STAR OF PERSIA

☼ ❄ ↔ 8–12 in (20–30 cm)
↕ 8–20 in (20–50 cm)

Found in central Asia and parts of
Iran and Turkey. Narrow to broad

Allium cratericola

blue-green leaves, downy undersides,
2 to 7 per bulb. Strong-ribbed flower
stem with rounded head of small,
starry, purple flowers. Zones 7–10.

Allium cyaneum

☼ ❄ ↔ 5–10 in (12–25 cm)
↕ 5–10 in (12–25 cm)

A perennial clump-forming bulb
from China. Grassy foliage with very
narrow leaves, 2 mm wide. Clusters
of 10 to 12 small blue or purplish
flowers, nodding, appear in late
spring. Zones 5–9.

Allium cyathophorum

☼ ❄ ↔ 12 in (30 cm)
↕ 10–15 in (25–38 cm)

Perennial clump-forming bulb from
northwestern China. Leaves 12–15 in
(30–38 cm) long, bell-shaped.
Purplish red flowers bloom in a loose
umbel in late spring. Zones 5–9.

Allium fistulosum

JAPANESE BUNCHING ONION, JAPANESE LEEK,
WELSH ONION

☼ ❄ ↔ 8–12 in (20–30 cm)
↕ 20–24 in (50–60 cm)

Unknown in the wild. Hollow leaves
to 12 in (30 cm) long, 2 to 6 per
bulb, used in salads or cooked. In

Allium cristophii

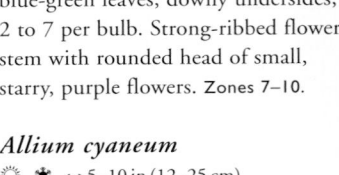

Allium hyalinum

summer, small heads of green flowers
on tall stems, sometimes forming
bulbils. Zones 5–9.

Allium flavum

SMALL YELLOW ONION

☼ ❄ ↔ 4–6 in (10–15 cm)
↕ 8–12 in (20–30 cm)

Found in southern Europe from
France to Greece. Fine, cylindrical,
blue-green leaves to 8 in (20 cm)
long, few per bulb, often drying
before flowering. Heads of scented
bright yellow flowers in summer.
Zones 7–10.

Allium geyeri

GEYER'S ONION

☼ ❄ ↔ 4–6 in (10–15 cm)
↕ 8–20 in (20–50 cm)

Native to western USA. Fine, chive-
like, grassy leaves to 8 in (20 cm)
long. In spring, heads of 10 to 15,
white to soft pink, bell-shaped
flowers. Zones 5–10.

Allium giganteum

GIANT ALLIUM

☼◐ ❄ ↔ 12–20 in (30–50 cm)
↕ 3–6 ft (0.9–1.8 m)

From central Asia. Strappy gray-green
leaves to 3 ft (0.9 m) long and 4 in
(10 cm) wide at the base. In spring,
large near-spherical heads of many
tiny purple-pink flowers, less commonly pale pink or white. Zones 7–9.

Allium hollandicum

☼ ❄ ↔ 8–12 in (20–30 cm)
↕ 32–40 in (80–100 cm)

East Asian species often confused with
A. aflatunense in cultivation. Faintly
aromatic, tubular, blue-green leaves,

Allium fistulosum

Allium karataviense 'Ivory Queen'

usually dried off by the time the dense
rounded heads of starry purple-pink
flowers appear. '**Purple Sensation**' has
near-spherical heads of deep purple
flowers. Zones 7–9.

Allium howellii

☼ ❄ ↔ 6–8 in (15–20 cm)
↕ 12–20 in (30–50 cm)

Species from California, USA, with
few grassy blue-green leaves that
wither before the wiry flower stems
develop fully. White to cream flowers
edged with pink, in loose heads.
Drought and heat tolerant. Zones 8–10.

Allium hyalinum

GLASSY ONION

☼ ❄ ↔ 6–10 in (15–25 cm)
↕ 8–20 in (20–50 cm)

Species from California, USA, with
flat narrow leaves, 8–20 in (10–50 cm)
long. From late spring it bears heads
of 10 to 30 starry flowers, usually
white, sometimes pale pink. The plant
commonly cultivated as *A. h.* var.
praecox is now classified as *A. praecox*.
Zones 8–10.

Allium karataviense

☼◐ ❄ ↔ 8–20 in (20–50 cm)
↕ 4–12 in (10–30 cm)

Central Asian species with broad,
strappy, gray-green leaves, often with
a metallic purple sheen. Short sturdy
stems with large heads of tiny, starry,
white to pale mauve flowers with

Allium geyeri

Allium howellii

darker mid-veins. **'Ivory Queen'** has short stems with pale green to cream flowers. Zones 7–9.

Allium macranthum

☀/◐ ❉ ↔ 12 in (30 cm)
↕ 10–12 in (25–30 cm)

A clump-forming perennial bulb from China and Tibet. Mid-green strap-shaped leaves. Deep bell-shaped plum-purple flowers appear throughout summer. As many as 20 flowers per umbel. Zones 4–6.

Allium moly

GOLDEN GARLIC

☀/◐ ❉ ↔ 8–12 in (20–30 cm)
↕ 8–12 in (20–30 cm)

European species with strappy blue-green leaves, 1 to 3 per bulb. Flower stems fairly short and sturdy with heads of loosely clustered golden yellow flowers from late spring. **'Jeannine'**, slightly larger heads of especially bright flowers. Zones 7–9.

Allium narcissiflorum

☀/◐ ❉ ↔ 4–8 in (10–20 cm)
↕ 6–15 in (15–38 cm)

Found around the French Maritime Alps. Narrow, flat, grassy, gray-green leaves to 6 in (15 cm) long, 3 to 5 per bulb. In summer, loose heads of 5 to 8 nodding, bell-shaped, pale pink to purple flowers. Zones 8–9.

Allium neapolitanum

DAFFODIL GARLIC, FLOWERING ONION, NAPLES GARLIC

☀ ❉ ↔ 6–12 in (15–30 cm)
↕ 8–20 in (20–50 cm)

Found around the Mediterranean, North Africa, and into western Asia.

Allium moly 'Jeannine'

Allium paradoxum var. *normale*

Allium platycaule

Allium regelii

Narrow, blue-green, grassy leaves to 12 in (30 cm) long, 2 per bulb. Leaves are usually withered by the time the flowers open in late spring. The plant has pure white flowers in loose heads around 3 in (8 cm) wide. Zones 8–10.

Allium nigrum

☀ ❉ ↔ 4 in (10 cm) ↕ 36 in (90 cm)

A Mediterranean bulb with broad, strap-shaped, shiny leaves. Flowers are curved and white with a green stripe that gives a green cast to the broad umbel, open in early summer. There is a black ovary in the center of each flower. Zones 7–9.

Allium oreophilum

☀ ❉ ↔ 6–8 in (15–20 cm)
↕ 4–8 in (10–20 cm)

Found in the Caucasus region and Central Asia. Has narrow blue-green leaves that extend beyond the height of the flower stem. Bright pink to purple bell-shaped flowers, in loose heads, are seen in spring–early summer. Zones 7–9.

Allium paradoxum

FEW-FLOWERED LEEK

☀ ❉ ↔ 4–8 in (10–20 cm)
↕ 6–12 in (15–30 cm)

Found from the Caucasus to Iran. Each bulb has a single leaf, 8–12 in (20–30 cm) long × 1 in (25 mm) wide, with a prominent keeled midrib. In early spring white flowers open, 1 to 10 per head, followed by prolific bulbils. *A. p.* var. *normale* grows to 12 in (30 cm) tall, with heads of around 10 white flowers and no bulbils. Zones 7–9.

Allium rosenbachianum 'Purple King'

Allium rosenbachianum 'Michael Hoog'

Allium platycaule

☀ ❉ ↔ 8–12 in (20–30 cm)
↕ 4–6 in (10–15 cm)

Native to mountains of western USA. Leaves are blue-green, usually flat to the ground, growing to 8 in (20 cm) long, 2 per bulb. Showy short-stemmed heads of tiny, starry, deep pink flowers are seen in spring–summer. Zones 6–9.

Allium regelii

☀/◐ ❉ ↔ 12–20 in (30–50 cm)
↕ 32–40 in (80–100 cm)

Found in semi-desert areas of central Asia. Broad, strappy, coarse-edged, green leaves to 20 in (50 cm) long,

2 to 4 per bulb. Stems with up to 6 whorls of pale pink, sometimes purple flowers. Zones 7–10.

Allium rosenbachianum

☀ ❉ ↔ 12–20 in (30–50 cm)
↕ 24–40 in (60–100 cm)

Central Asian species with broad-based, strappy, blue-green leaves to 12 in (30 cm) long, 2 to 4 per bulb. In spring, strong-ribbed flower stems with 4 in (10 cm) wide heads of purple, rarely white, flowers. **'Michael Hoog'** has large heads of purple flowers; **'Purple King'** has blue-green leaves and dark purple flowers with white stamens. Zones 7–10.

Allium sphaerocephalon

Allium schoenoprasum 'Silver Chimes'

Allium schoenoprasum

Allium senescens var. *calcareum*

Allium roseum

ROSY GARLIC

☀ ❄ ↔ 3 in (8 cm) ↕ 24 in (60 cm)

From Southern Europe, North Africa, and Asia Minor. Perennial bulb. Leaves thin, similar to chives. Rose-white flowers in spring. Multiplies quickly from bulbils. Zones 5–9.

Allium sativum

GARLIC

☀ ❄ ↔ 12–16 in (30–40 cm) ↕ 12–32 in (30–80 cm)

Strongly aromatic bulbs widely culti-vated for culinary use but unknown in the wild. Narrow blue-green leaves to 24 in (60 cm) long, often shorter.

Flowers sporadically with few white to pale pink flowers in heads to 2 in (5 cm) wide. Bulbils follow. Zones 8–10.

Allium schoenoprasum

CHIVES

☀/☀ ❄ ↔ 4–12 in (10–30 cm) ↕ 6–20 in (15–50 cm)

Widespread in northern temperate zones. Fine, grassy, hollow foliage is aromatic and a popular culinary gar-nish. Rounded heads of small, bell-shaped, pink flowers in summer. 'Black Isle Blush', up to 12 in (30 cm) tall, with mauve flowers that are deep blush pink at the center; 'Forescate', strong grower to 20 in (50 cm) tall, with gray-green leaves and deep purple-pink flowers; 'Pink Perfection', up to 12 in (30 cm) tall, with many heads of bright pink flowers; and 'Silver Chimes', gray-green foliage and white flowers. Zones 5–10.

Allium scorodoprasum

GIANT GARLIC, SAND LEEK, SPANISH GARLIC

☀ ❄ ↔ 6–16 in (15–40 cm) ↕ 12–36 in (30–90 cm)

Found from southern Europe to west-ern Asia and Russia. Grassy leaves to

10 in (25 cm) long, 2 to 5 per bulb, often withered by summer when the small rounded heads of tiny lilac to purple-red flowers open. Purple-red bulbils follow. Zones 7–9.

Allium senescens

GERMAN GARLIC

☀/☀ ❄ ↔ 12–20 in (30–50 cm) ↕ 8–24 in (20–60 cm)

This native of temperate Eurasia has broad-based gray-green leaves, 8–12 in (20–30 cm) long, 4 to 9 per bulb. In summer and autumn it displays many-flowered heads to 2 in (5 cm) wide with cup-shaped lavender-pink flowers. *A. s.* var. *calcareum* has blue-green leaves and long-petalled flowers. Zones 5–9.

Allium siskiyouense

SISKIYOU ONION

☀/☀ ❄ ↔ 8–12 in (20–30 cm) ↕ 6–8 in (15–20 cm)

Western North American native. Fleshy, fairly broad, green, grassy leaves to 8 in (20 cm) long. In summer, short-stemmed heads of rela-tively large purple flowers. Zones 8–10.

Allium sphaerocephalon

ROUND-HEADED LEEK

☀/☀ ❄ ↔ 12–20 in (30–50 cm) ↕ 24–36 in (60–90 cm)

Found through Europe from England to the Caucasus, in North Africa, and the Middle East. Hollow leaves to slightly over 12 in (30 cm) long, 2 to 6 per bulb. In summer, cone-shaped flowerheads with many tiny purple-red flowers, sometimes followed by bulbils. Zones 5–9.

Allium stellatum

GLADE ONION, PRAIRIE ONION

☀/☀ ❄ ↔ 1–2 in (2.5–5 cm) ↕ 18 in (45 cm)

Perennial from central North America. Its 2 to 6 green flat leaves die back at flowering time. Blooms summer–autumn; flowers pinkish rose. *Stellatum* means starry and describes the flowers. Naturalizes easily. Zones 5–9.

Allium subhirsutum

☀/☀ ❄ ↔ 8–16 in (20–40 cm) ↕ 8–12 in (20–30 cm)

Found around the Mediterranean. Flattened, fairly broad, grassy green leaves with fine hairs on the edges, 10–20 in (25–50 cm) long, 2 to 3 per bulb. In summer, pure white flowers in loose heads. Zones 9–10.

Allium tuberosum ★

CHINESE CHIVES, GARLIC CHIVES

☀/☀ ❄ ↔ 8–12 in (20–30 cm) ↕ 20 in (50 cm)

Southeast Asian species widely culti-vated for garlic-flavored, narrow, grassy, angled stems, used as a vegetable and in salads. Blue-green leaves to 12 in (30 cm) long, 4 to 9 per bulb. In late summer, scented white flowers in small heads on long stems. Zones 7–10.

Allium unifolium

☀ ❄ ↔ 8–12 in (20–30 cm) ↕ 16–24 in (40–60 cm)

Native to western USA. Narrow, flat-tened, blue-green leaves with a con-spicuous central channel/midrib.

Allium subhirsutum

Allium unifolium

Leaves to 12 in (30 cm) long, 1 per bulb. In spring and summer, rounded heads of pink to deep lavender-pink bell-shaped flowers. Zones 8–10.

Allium Hybrid Cultivars

☼ ❄ ↔6–12 in (15–30 cm)
↑18–36 in (45–90 cm)

Among the best of many cultivated hybrids are: '**Beau Regard**', flower stems to 3 ft (0.9 m) tall, large near-spherical heads of starry steel blue to purple flowers; '**Gladiator**', large rounded heads of lilac to purple flowers on stems to 4 ft (1.2 m) tall; and '**Globemaster**', gray-green leaves, 24–36 in (60–90 cm) stems with large heads of violet-blue flowers, excellent cut flower. Zones 7–9.

ALLOCASUARINA

SHE-OAK

Allocasuarina, part of the she-oak (Casuarinaceae) family, has 59 species entirely confined to Australia, all trees or shrubs with a pine-like appearance. The fine twigs appear leafless, but in fact have whorls of narrow leaves fused flat against their surfaces, with only tips remaining free and appearing as rings of minute teeth at regular intervals along the twig. The number of teeth per ring is a characteristic feature of each species. Flowers are mostly of different sexes on different plants. Fruits are cone-like, splitting apart to release the "seeds." These trees make good screens and windbreaks.
CULTIVATION: Most species are adapted to poor sandy or stony soils, low in essential plant nutrients; however the taller tree species adapt to more fertile soils. They make fast growth in the garden and require little maintenance. Propagation is always from seed, which quickly falls out of gathered cones and germinates readily.

Allocasuarina decussata

✻ ❄ ↔15 ft (4.5 m) ↑30 ft (9 m)
From southwest Western Australia. Low-branching bushy habit with slender branches and fine-textured rich green branchlets. Male flowers in

winter covering the tips with reddish brown anthers. Seed cones are rounded with a flat top. Zones 9–10.

Allocasuarina inophloia

syn. *Casuarina inophloia*
THREADY-BARKED SHE-OAK
☼ ❄ ↔10 ft (3 m) ↑20 ft (6 m)
From western Queensland, Australia. Highly distinctive bark, flaking off in long fine strips, with paler reddish brown underbark. Branchlets fine and pendulous. "Cones" of female plants are small, purplish brown. Zones 9–11.

Allocasuarina littoralis

BLACK SHE-OAK
☼ ❄ ↔15 ft (4.5 m) ↑30 ft (9 m)
Widespread along eastern Australian coast. Erect conical tree, dark gray fissured bark, very fine dark green branchlets. Rusty brown male flowers in autumn followed by small red female flowers. Salt tolerant. Zones 9–11.

Allocasuarina torulosa

syn. *Casuarina torulosa*
FOREST OAK, FOREST SHE-OAK
☼/❂ ❄ ↔20 ft (6 m)
↑40–50 ft (12–15 m)
Native to eastern Australian coast. Often grows as an understory tree in open forests. Coppery drooping branches and branchlets in winter. Corky light brown bark. Male flowers golden orange in autumn. Rounded warty cones. Zones 8–11.

Allocasuarina verticillata

DROOPING SHE-OAK
☼ ❄ ↔20 ft (6 m) ↑30 ft (9 m)
Occurring in southeastern Australia, often on coastal cliffs. Small bushy tree, short trunk, rounded weeping crown. Golden brown male flowers appear at end of branchlets from winter to early spring. Female flowers borne on separate trees; cones to 1½ in (35 mm) long. Zones 8–10.

Allocasuarina decussata

ALLOSYNCARPIA

This is the genus of a single species of evergreen tree in the myrtle (Myrtaceae) family, confined to a small area of Australia's Northern Territory, in sandstone gorges of Kakadu National Park. Botanically named only in 1977, its name indicates a resemblance to the genus *Syncarpia*, but later studies have shown they are not closely related. Narrow leathery leaves taper to a point and are arranged in whorls of 3 on the twigs, which terminate in panicles of

small cream flowers with numerous stamens. Fruits are woody capsules.
CULTIVATION: Little planted as yet but makes a fine shade tree for tropical regions with a marked dry season. Propagate from seed.

Allosyncarpia ternata

☼/❂ ✦ ↔30 ft (9 m)
↑40–80 ft (12–24 m)

Large spreading tree, fibrous to flaky brown bark, dense glossy green foliage. Flowers late spring–early summer. Rather slow-growing. Zones 11–12.

Allocasuarina inophloia

Allocasuarina littoralis

Allosyncarpia ternata, in the wild, in Kakadu National Park, Northern Territory, Australia

A

ALLOXYLON

Belonging to the protea (Proteaceae) family, *Alloxylon* comprises 4 species of evergreen rainforest trees native to tropical and subtropical eastern Australia and New Guinea. Among Australian Proteaceae, *Alloxylon* is closely related to the waratah genus *Telopea*, and its species are similarly prized as ornamentals, with conspicuous red or pinkish flowers in large terminal clusters attracting nectar-feeding birds. The leaves are irregularly lobed or pinnate, though tending to become unlobed and simple on flowering branches. The fruit is a large follicle that splits to release winged seeds.

CULTIVATION: They are demanding, requiring a subtropical climate with year-round rainfall, or tropical hill conditions with a not too severe dry season. Soil must be well drained and moderately fertile, and the trees sheltered from strong winds. Young plants are prone to sudden wilting and death, but once above a height of 10–15 ft (3–4.5 m) they usually remain healthy. Propagation is from seed, sown as soon as collected.

Alloxylon flammeum

syn. *Oreocallis wickhamii* of gardens

WARATAH TREE

☼ ❄ ↔ 20 ft (6 m) ↑ 60 ft (18 m)

From the Atherton Tableland of far northeastern Queensland, Australia. Dark green sapling leaves to 18 in (45 cm) long with 3 to 7 large lobes, smaller on flowering shoots. Bright scarlet flower clusters in late winter–spring. Zones 10–11.

Alloxylon pinnatum

syns *Embothrium pinnatum, Oreocallis pinnata*

DORRIGO WARATAH

☼ ❄ ↔ 30 ft (9 m) ↑ 60 ft (18 m)

Found in hill rainforests of the New South Wales–Queensland border region in Australia. Compound leaves of up to 11 pointed leaflets. Dull crimson flowers, on long single stalks, in spring–mid-summer. Zones 9–11.

Alloxylon pinnatum

Alloxylon flammeum

ALLUAUDIA

All 8 species of *Alluaudia* are endemic to the arid southern and southwestern tip of Madagascar. They are members of the Didiereaceae family. All the species are sought-after collector plants and are still rare in cultivation. In habitat they start life as small xerophytic shrubs but most species eventually become tree-like, forming dense forests in which lemurs are often found. Because of their heavily spined bodies, alluaudias resemble cacti and are in fact distant relatives. Unlike most cacti, however, alluaudias are covered in small fleshy deciduous leaves during their growing period. The local habitats of many *Alluaudia* species are currently threatened by subsistence farming, and the spread of sisal plantations (for rope and twine) and eucalypt plantations (for wood products). Both male and female flowers appear on the same plant and are often borne in huge numbers from the ends of mature branches.

CULTIVATION: *Alluaudia* species are easily grown from seeds but are more usually raised from cuttings that have been dried out for a week or two. They thrive in a rich well-drained soil and may grow rapidly when planted in the ground.

Alluaudia humbertii

☼ ❄ ↔ 20–25 ft (6–8 m) ↑ 17–20 ft (5–6 m)

A rather untidy shrub to small tree consisting of many gray-brown, pencil-thin, flexible, intertwining branches that are covered in spines

Alluaudia procera

and pairs of small, round, green leaves. The red stamens of the flowers on male plants contrast with the all-white flowers on female plants. Zones 9–11.

Alluaudia montagnacii

☼ ❄ ↔ 20–40 in (50–100 cm) ↑ 35–50 ft (10–15 m)

This species is the rarest and perhaps the most sought-after species of *Alluaudia*, and has a very limited natural distribution area. It has long stout spines, a shiny silvery stem, and attractive dark green leaves. Flowers resemble those of *A. procera*. Zones 9–11.

Alluaudia procera ★

☼ ❄ ↔ 7–10 ft (2–3 m) ↑ 35–50 ft (10–15 m)

This is the most common species of *Alluaudia* in cultivation. Wood from this tree-like species is used for housing, fencing, boxes, and firewood. The greenish yellow flowers are produced on massive racemes bearing hundreds of blooms. Zones 9–11.

ALNUS

ALDER

Alnus, of the birch (Betulaceae) family, is an essentially Northern Hemisphere genus. Of the 25 alder species only 2 extend across the equator. All are deciduous or semi-evergreen. In the wild, alders are fast-growing pioneer trees of disturbed ground. Alders mostly have darker brownish or blackish bark, with leaves usually larger and slightly thicker than birches; leaf margins vary from smooth and wavy to jaggedly toothed, winter buds sticky and aromatic. The flowers are tiny and arranged in catkins; the male is long and thin, while the female is short and barrel-shaped.

Alnus cordata

Alnus hirsuta

Alnus incana subsp. *tenuifolia*

CULTIVATION: The various species in the genus are easily grown in their appropriate climate. Sapling growth is often very fast but they mature early and are sometimes not very long lived. Many are able to thrive in soils of low fertility and poor drainage, aided by nitrogen-fixing fungi in the roots. Propagation is normally from seed, which may need stratification over winter and should not be covered, as germination is stimulated by light. Some cultivars require grafting.

Alnus acuminata

syn. *Alnus jorullensis* of gardens
EVERGREEN ALDER, MEXICAN ALDER
☼ ❄ ↔ 20 ft (6 m) ↑ 40 ft (12 m)
Often misidentified as *A. jorullensis,* a close relation. In warm climates this broad-crowned tree remains evergreen. Narrow drooping leaves tapering to long points, jaggedly toothed. Brownish yellow male catkins. *A. a.* subsp. *glabrata* is an attractive form. Zones 9–11.

Alnus acuminata subsp. *glabrata*

Alnus cordata

ITALIAN ALDER
☼ ❄ ↔ 20 ft (6 m) ↑ 50 ft (15 m)
From southern Italy, Sardinia, and Corsica. A vigorous, narrow tree which has deep green, broadly rounded, shiny leaves that are held horizontally. Male catkins are yellowish, found on branch ends. Female seed cones follow, in groups of three. Tolerant of all soils, and at home even in boggy conditions. Can be invasive in cold moist climates. Zones 9–10.

Alnus firma

JAPANESE ALDER
☼ ❄ ↔ 25 ft (8 m) ↑ 30 ft (9 m)
The foliage of this species from Japan is particularly attractive, with deep green pointed leaves that have prominent parallel veins. It bears numerous bright gold catkins and grows into a graceful tree. Zones 6–9.

Alnus glutinosa

BLACK ALDER, COMMON ALDER
☼ ❄ ↔ 35 ft (10 m) ↑ 60 ft (18 m)
From Europe to Siberia and North Africa. Deciduous tree, may reach 30 ft (9 m) in cultivation. Leaves dark green, rounded, shallowly toothed. Buds and twigs sticky. Male catkins dull purple to yellow. Female catkins purple to burgundy to green to brown. Cultivars include: 'Imperialis', with an open habit; and 'Laciniata', vigorous with dissected leaves. Zones 4–8.

Alnus hirsuta

MANCHURIAN ALDER
☼ ❄ ↔ 30 ft (9 m) ↑ 70 ft (21 m)
This alder from Japan and northeastern Asia grows in rich moist soil. Deeply lobed leaves are dull green above and reddish brown beneath. Similar to *A. incana*, but has larger leaves and fruit. Zones 4–8.

Alnus firma

Alnus incana

GRAY ALDER
☼ ❄ ↔ 30 ft (9 m) ↑ 70 ft (21 m)
Found in the Caucasus and the mountains of Europe. Hardy and vigorous, well suited to cold wet conditions. Bark smooth gray. Young shoots and undersides of leaves covered in gray down. *A. i.* subsp. *tenuifolia* (syn. *A. tenuifolia*), from British Columbia, Canada, to California, USA, is smaller with red and downy young shoots that are soon smooth; buds also downy, leaves dark green, downy veins and undersides. Cultivars include: *A. i.* 'Aurea', foliage and branches yellowish; 'Laciniata', leaves divided in narrow lobes; and 'Pendula', attractive weeping form. Zones 3–9.

Alnus glutinosa

Alocasia × *amazonica*

Alocasia brisbanensis

Alnus japonica
JAPANESE ALDER

☼ ❄ ↔ 25 ft (8 m) ↑ 80 ft (24 m)

Native to Japan and eastern Asia. Densely leafy tree. Narrow pointed leaves, dark glossy green, finely toothed. Male catkins erect. Zones 4–9.

Alnus maritima
syn. *Alnus oblongata*
SEASIDE ALDER

☼ ❄ ↔ 20 ft (6 m) ↑ 30 ft (9 m)

A native of Delaware and Maryland, USA. Usually of shrubby habit but can be a small tree. Glossy dark green leaves. One of a small group of alders that flower in autumn. Zones 7–10.

Alnus rhombifolia
WHITE ALDER

☼ ❄ ↔ 35 ft (10 m) ↑ 50 ft (15 m)

In western USA this species is found along sides of streams. Spreading rounded crown, branches have pendulous tips. Leaves diamond-shaped, dark shiny green, downy yellow green beneath. Rare in cultivation. Zones 6–9.

Alnus rubra
syn. *Alnus oregona*
OREGON ALDER, RED ALDER

☼ ❄ ↔ 30 ft (9 m) ↑ 50 ft (15 m)

From the canyons and riverbanks of North America. Fast growing tree, pyramidal crown, somewhat pendulous habit. Young shoots dark red, new leaves have reddish brown down, turning dark green above and blue-gray beneath. Zones 6–9.

Alnus serrulata
HAZEL ALDER, SMOOTH ALDER

☼ ❄ ↔ 8 ft (2.4 m) ↑ 12 ft (3.5 m)

Shrubby species from eastern USA. Closely related to *A. incana*. Sticky buds, blunt-ended, finely toothed oval leaves. Zones 3–9.

Alnus subcordata
CAUCASIAN ALDER

☼ ❄ ↔ 20 ft (6 m) ↑ 50 ft (15 m)

Vigorous species native to the Caucasus region. Handsome tree closely related to *A. cordata*. Young shoots downy, finely toothed dark green leaves, heart-shaped bases. Long slender male catkins appear in early winter. Zones 5–9.

ALOCASIA

Comprising 70 species, this genus of the arum (Araceae) family occurs in a variety of habitats, from lowland rainforests to swamps, roadsides, and mountain regions from tropical southern Asia, Indonesia, Malaysia, New Guinea, and Australia, to islands of the Pacific. The species are perennial, evergreen, very small to massive herbs, even tree-like, with corms, runners, or aboveground stems. Leaves are several with sheathing leaf stalk, simple, broadly or narrowly arrowhead-shaped, with entire or deeply lobed margins, but usually heart-shaped at the base. The major veins are often strikingly prominent in some species. Inflorescences are borne at or near the apex of the leafy plant, 2 or more together, the spathes constricted, the spadix in 4 parts, lowermost female, then sterile, then male, then a sterile appendage. The female flower has no petals or sepals, consisting only of the single-celled ovary and stigma. Male flowers consist of 3 to 8, stalkless, narrow anthers united into a pyramid shape. Fruit is a globular berry containing several seeds.

CULTIVATION: Propagate from seed and stem cuttings or by division of fleshy stem. All species require warm moist conditions in shady sheltered locations, and are grown in greenhouses and conservatories in all regions but the tropics.

Alocasia × amazonica
☀ ⚥ ↔ 20–40 in (50–100 cm) ↑ 40–60 in (100–150 cm)

A hybrid of *A. lowii* and *A. sanderiana*, its origins are unknown. Leaves to 24 in (60 cm) long × 12 in (30 cm) wide, arrowhead-shaped, upperside dark green, midrib yellow-greenish white, other veins silvery white. Underside dull purple, major veins green-white. Leaf stalk green, 45 cm long. '**Magnifica**', more intensely silver coloration on uppersurface, all purple below; '**Randall**', larger in all parts. Zones 11–12.

Alocasia brisbanensis
CUNJEVOI, SPOON LILY

☀ ⚥ ↔ 40–60 in (100–150 cm) ↑ 3–7 ft (0.9–2 m)

Formerly included in *A. macrorrhizos*, this stout, fleshy, perennial herb has stems to 20–40 in (50–100 cm) tall, leaves to 7 ft (2 m) long, light green, shiny, fleshy. Leaf blade to 20 in (50 cm) wide, heart-shaped, main veins prominent. Spathe greenish yellow, boat-shaped, spadix with small yellow flowers in summer. Red berries. Occurs in rainforests and other moist habitats of eastern coastal Australia. Zones 10–12.

Alocasia cuprea
☀ ⚥ ↔ 30 in (75 cm) ↑ to 40 in (100 cm)

Perennial herb, fleshy-stemmed, leaf stalks 24 in (60 cm) long, leaf blades oblong to oval, somewhat arrowhead-shaped, surface raised between the lateral veins giving a quilted appearance, upperside with dark green and copper-colored areas, underside reddish purple. Spathes purple, to 6 in (15 cm) long. Flowers in summer. Occurs in forests of Malaysia and Borneo. Zones 11–12.

Alnus maritima

Alnus rhombifolia

Aloe brevifolia

Aloe broomii

Alocasia macrorrhizos

syns *Alocasia indica, A. macrorrhiza*
GIANT TARO

☀ ⚘ ↔ 7–8 ft (2–2.4 m)
↑ 15–17 ft (4.5–5 m)

Massive, fleshy-stemmed, perennial herb with stout trunk to 15 ft (4.5 m) tall, occurring naturally in Sri Lanka, India, and western tropical Asia, widely cultivated in many other tropical regions. Leaf stalks to 7 ft (2 m) long, green, blades broadly arrowhead-shaped, 40–50 in (100–130 cm) long, almost as wide, main veins not as prominent as in other species. Spathes yellow-green, fruiting spathe green. Zones 11–12.

Alocasia sanderiana

syns *Alocasia sanderana, A. sanderi, Schizocasia sanderiana*

◑/☀ ⚘ ↔ 20–36 in (50–90 cm)
↑ 40–60 in (100–150 cm)

Common in cultivation but endangered in the wild; its only known habitat is the moist forests of Mindanao in the Philippines. Leaves broadly arrowhead-shaped, shiny, blackish green on the upperside, main veins and margins silvery white, underside green, 20 in (50 cm) long × 6 in (15 cm) wide, leaf stalks 24 in (60 cm) long. Spathe greenish, shorter than leaves, flowering intermittent. Two cultivars: '**Nobilis**', with leaves more black than green, less silvery white coloration and about twice the size of the species; and '**Van Houtte**', smaller than the species, with broader leaves and more grayish than silvery coloration. Zones 11–12.

ALOE

This genus, of the lily (Liliaceae) family, comprises about 330 species of evergreen succulent plants found through southern and tropical Africa to Madagascar and the Arabian Peninsula. They range from low-growing grass-like perennials to trees, shrubs, and climbers. Succulent leaves grow in rosettes or spirals at the stem or branch tips, usually toothed or spiny and lance-shaped. Red or yellow tubular flowers are produced on spikes in late winter or spring. With striking form and brilliant flowers, aloes are popular landscaping plants in warm dry areas and many can be grown to good effect in containers.
CULTIVATION: Aloes require warm, dry, and well-drained conditions. They can tolerate soils of low fertility. Most prefer full sun although some smaller species do well in partially shaded situations. In cool-temperate climates they are suitable for greenhouse culture, and potted plants can be moved outdoors during the summer months. Propagation is by seed or, more easily, from stem cuttings or offsets.

Aloe arborescens ★

KRANTZ ALOE

☀ ⚘ ↔ 6 ft (1.8 m) ↑ 10 ft (3 m)

From the bush and open forest in southern Africa. Leaves toothed, blue-green, curved and tapering, up to 2 ft (0.6 m) long, in rosettes at the branch ends. Spikes of orange to red flowers are seen in winter. This species is suitable for growing in coastal areas. Zones 9–11.

Aloe aristata ★

LACE ALOE, TORCH PLANT

☀ ⚘ ↔ unlimited ↑ 5 in (12 cm)

From southern Africa. Dense clusters of stemless rosettes with incurved, 4 in (10 cm) long, white-spotted

Aloe capitata

green leaves tapering to a filament-like tip. White spines and soft white teeth. Inflorescences to 20 in (50 cm) tall, often branched. Red 1½ in (35 mm) long flowers from late spring. Zones 9–11.

Aloe brevifolia ★

☀ ⚘ ↔ 20–32 in (50–80 cm)
↑ 20 in (50 cm)

Native to South Africa. Dense clusters of 8 in (20 cm) wide rosettes of short, tightly packed, blue-green, soft-spined leaves. From early summer, unbranched, 16 in (40 cm) tall inflorescences of short, green-tipped, red flowers. Zones 9–11.

Aloe broomii

BERGAALWYN

☀ ⚘ ↔ 3 ft (0.9 m) ↑ 5 ft (1.5 m)

From South Africa. Solitary rosette to 40 in (100 cm) wide with broad-based, upright, red-tinted olive green leaves to 18 in (45 cm) long, edged with prominent red-brown teeth. Unbranched inflorescences to 5 ft (1.5 m) tall. Yellow flowers with cream bracts, 1 in (25 mm) long, in spring. Zones 9–11

Aloe capitata

☀/◑ ⚘ ↔ 40–48 in (100–120 cm)
↑ 24–40 in (60–100 cm)

From Madagascar. Single rosette of red-tinted leaves to 20 in (50 cm) long, edged with red teeth. Inflorescences branched, with bell-shaped yellow flowers. Zones 10–12.

Aloe chabaudii

☀ ⚘ ↔ 3–5 ft (0.9–1.5 m)
↑ 2–5 ft (0.6–1.5 m)

From South Africa to Zambia. Rosettes of thick, fleshy green leaves, red-brown edges and teeth. May have short trunk. Inflorescences with red-brown flowers in winter. Zones 9–11.

Aloe chabaudii

Aloe arborescens

A

Aloe claviflora
CANNON ALOE, KRAALAALWYN

☼ ⚘ ↔ 3–7 ft (0.9–2 m) ↥ 5 ft (1.5 m)

From South Africa. Rosettes clustered, up to 24 in (60 cm) wide, with upright gray-green leaves to 18 in (45 cm) long, edged with widely spaced large teeth. Horizontal inflorescences to 24 in (60 cm) tall, branched, with pinkish red to orange flowers, in spring–summer. Zones 9–11.

Aloe 'Commutata'

☼/◐ ⚘ ↔ 24–60 in (60–150 cm) ↥ 40 in (100 cm)

Of southern African origin. Clustered rosettes of thick, fleshy, pale-spotted, green to blue-green leaves up to 18 in (45 cm) long. Upright inflorescences to 40 in (100 cm) high with tubular dull red flowers in spring. Zones 10–12.

Aloe conifera

☼/◐ ⚘ ↔ 40 in (100 cm) ↥ 40 in (100 cm)

From Madagascar. Sparsely foliaged rosettes of fleshy purple-tinted leaves that often split along the midrib. Leaves to 16 in (40 cm) long with coarse red-brown to purple teeth. Unusual kniphofia-like, yellow-flowered, cone-shaped inflorescences on long stems. Zones 9–11.

Aloe cryptopoda

☼/◐ ⚘ ↔ 3–5 ft (0.9–2 m) ↥ 5–7 ft (1.5–2 m)

Found from South Africa to Zambia. Clusters of a few rosettes, sometimes with short stems. Dark green leaves, sometimes red- or blue-tinted, to 36 in (90 cm) long, edged with very small red-brown teeth. Inflorescences branched, to 6 ft (1.8 m) high, with 1½ in (35 mm) long, green-tipped, red flowers in winter. Zones 9–11.

Aloe debrana
syn. *Aloe berhana*

☼/◐ ⚘ ↔ 3–4 ft (0.9–1.2 m) ↥ 4 ft (1.2 m)

Native of Ethiopia. Solitary stemless rosette of broad, upright, green leaves edged with strong green to brown teeth. Branching inflorescences with yellow orange-red flowers in spring. Zones 9–11.

Aloe claviflora

Aloe descoingsii

☼/◐ ⚘ ↔ 16–24 in (40–60 cm) ↥ 12 in (30 cm)

From Madagascar. Regarded as the smallest *Aloe*, with clustered rosettes around 2 in (5 cm) wide, made up of 1¼ in (30 mm) long, soft brown to olive green, white-spotted leaves edged with very fine white teeth. Inflorescences 6 in (15 cm) tall, unbranched, with ½ in (12 mm) long, red-tipped, orange flowers in winter. Zones 10–12.

Aloe dichotoma

☼ ⚘ ↔ 12 ft (3.5 m) ↥ 30 ft (9 m)

From Namibia and the Cape region of South Africa, this species is a branching flat-topped tree. Leaves relatively short, 15 in (38 cm) long, with yellow-brown margins and tiny inoffensive teeth. Bright yellow flowers, to 12 in (30 cm) long, in winter. Zones 9–11.

Aloe conifera

Aloe distans
JEWELED ALOE

☼/◐ ⚘ ↔ 7–20 ft (2–6 m) ↥ 24–40 in (60–100 cm)

Native of South Africa. Spreading stems that strike root and grow to around 10 ft (3 m) long. Tight rosettes of short, broad, fleshy, blue-green leaves with prominent yellowish teeth. Branched, 24 in (60 cm) high inflorescences in summer with golden to red flowers. Zones 9–11.

Aloe dorotheae ★

☼/◐ ⚘ ↔ 3–7 ft (0.9–2 m) ↥ 20–32 in (50–80 cm)

From Tanzania. Clump-forming species with short suckering stems and loose rosettes of narrow, red-brown, fiercely toothed leaves to 10 in (25 cm) long. In winter, usually unbranched upright inflorescences with 1¼ in (30 mm) long, green-tipped, yellow to red flowers. Zones 10–11.

Aloe excelsa

☼ ⚘ ↔ 3 ft (0.9 m) ↥ 30 ft (9 m)

From southeastern areas of Africa, this aloe forms a single trunked tree, often clothed with dead leaves, topped by a large rosette of broad, channelled leaves. Spikes of orange to deep red flowers, on stems up to 3 ft (0.9 m) long, in late winter. Zones 9–11.

Aloe dichotoma with weaver bird nests, in the wild, in South Africa

Aloe debrana

Aloe 'Commutata'

Aloe cryptopoda

Aloe lateritia var. *graminicola*

Aloe longibracteata

Aloe marlothii, in the wild, Chipinge, Zimbabwe

Aloe ferox ★

BITTER ALOE, CAPE ALOE

☀ ⧆ ↔ 5–10 ft (1.5–3 m) ↑ 7–17 ft (2–5 m)

From South Africa's Cape region, this aloe is tree-like, with heads of broad, fleshy, red-tinted, sometimes spiny leaves to 40 in (100 cm) long, edged with strong red-brown teeth. Branched inflorescences with spikes of orange-red and golden yellow flowers, 1½ in (35 mm) long, are seen from late winter. *A. f.* var. *candelabrum* (syn. *A. candelabrum*) has neatly branched stems, inflorescences that are more heavily branched, and leaf tips that are slightly rolled. Zones 9–11.

Aloe globuligemma

☀ ⧆ ↔ 3–5 ft (0.9–1.5 m) ↑ 3 ft (0.9 m)

From southern Africa. Clumps of a few stemless or short-stemmed rosettes with brown-toothed, white-edged, blue-green leaves to 20 in (50 cm) long. Upright, branching inflorescences, flowerheads held horizontally. Flowers 1 in (25 mm) long, yellow to cream with red base, opening from red buds, in winter. Zones 9–11.

Aloe grandidentata

☀/◑ ⧆ ↔ 3–7 ft (0.9–2 m) ↑ 3 ft (0.9 m)

A native of South Africa. With stems that are short or absent, this species has a suckering habit, forming clumps

of small rosettes with brown-tinted, lance-shaped, white-spotted leaves to 8 in (20 cm) long, edged with red-brown teeth. Its branched inflorescences grow to 3 ft (0.9 m) tall, with white-marked red, 1¼ in (30 mm) long flowers from late winter. Zones 9–11.

Aloe greatheadii

☀ ⧆ ↔ 20–48 in (50–120 cm) ↑ 40 in (100 cm)

Found from South Africa to Zambia. Rosettes solitary or in small clumps. Pale-green-spotted olive green to bronze leaves to 12 in (30 cm) long with prominent teeth. Orange-pink flowers on branching upright inflorescences to 40 in (100 cm) tall from early to mid-winter. *A. g.* var. *davyana* is a slightly hardier South African variety with smaller greener leaves. Zones 10–11.

Aloe haworthioides

☀ ⧆ ↔ 24–40 in (60–100 cm) ↑ 20 in (50 cm)

From Madagascar, this species has clusters of stemless, sometimes suckering rosettes tightly packed with small, narrow, fleshy leaves up to 2 in (5 cm) long, edged with white teeth. Unbranched inflorescences to 12 in (30 cm) tall with ½ in (12 mm) long, white to pale pink flowers. Zones 10–12.

Aloe lateritia

☀/◑ ⧆ ↔ 24–48 in (60–120 cm) ↑ 30 in (75 cm)

Native of east Africa. Clumps of starry rosettes of flattened, pale-spotted, bronze-green leaves to 10 in (25 cm) long with toothed edges. Branched upright inflorescences with pale pink or pink-tipped cream flowers in early summer. *A. l.* var. *graminicola* (syn. *A. graminicola*) has plain green leaves, sometimes red-tinted. Zones 10–12.

Aloe littoralis

☀ ⧆ ↔ 6 ft (1.8 m) ↑ 17 ft (5 m)

Found from South Africa to Angola. Tree-like with unbranched stem to over 12 ft (3.5 m) tall with head of thick gray- to blue-green leaves, up to 24 in (60 cm) long, edged with fierce brown teeth. Branched inflorescences up to 5 ft (1.5 m) high, with 1½ in (35 mm) long pink to orange-red flowers from autumn. Zones 9–12.

Aloe longibracteata

☀/◑ ⧆ ↔ 24–40 in (60–100 cm) ↑ 5 ft (1.5 m)

Native of South Africa. Small clumps of rosettes to 24 in (60 cm) wide with sparsely spotted, fleshy, green leaves, to 12 in (30 cm) long, with toothed edges. Upright branching inflorescences with orange-red tubular flowers from late winter. Zones 9–11.

Aloe grandidentata

Aloe maculata ★

syn. *Aloe saponaria*

SOAP ALOE, ZEBRA ALOE

☀/◑ ⧆ ↔ 24–60 in (60–150 cm) ↑ 40 in (100 cm)

From southern Africa. Clumps of short-stemmed rosettes with fleshy green leaves, light-spotted in bands. Teeth green to brown. Orange flowers on branching inflorescences in spring and summer. Zones 9–11.

Aloe marlothii ★

BERGAALWYN

☀ ⧆ ↔ 7–10 ft (2–3 m) ↑ 12–15 ft (3.5–4.5 m)

Of southern African origin. Tree-like, stem clothed with old leaves. Spine-studded and toothed green to gray-green leaves, 24–60 in (60–150 cm) long. Branching inflorescences to 32 in (80 cm) high, with orange to golden flowers in winter. Zones 9–11.

Aloe dorotheae

Aloe excelsa

Aloe polyphylla

Aloe microstigma

Aloe plicatilis

Aloe melanacantha

KLEINBERGAALWYN

☀/◐ ⬧ ↔40–60 in (100–150 cm)
↕27 in (70 cm)

From South Africa. Mounding clusters of upright or spreading stems to 20 in (50 cm) long, covered with old leaves and topped with rosettes of spiny-toothed dark green leaves to 18 in (45 cm) long. Unbranched inflorescences with long orange-red to yellow flowers in winter. Zones 9–11.

Aloe microstigma

☀/◐ ⬧ ↔20–24 in (50–60 cm)
↕32 in (80 cm)

From South Africa. Short-stemmed, usually solitary rosettes of strongly upcurved narrow leaves to 12 in (30 cm) long, often spotted and red-tinted, with brown teeth. Unbranched, upright inflorescences to 32 in (80 cm) tall with orange-red flowers ageing yellow-green in winter. Zones 9–11.

Aloe mitriformis ★

GOLD-TOOTH ALOE, KRANS AALWYN

☀/◐ ⬧ ↔3–7 ft (0.9–2 m) ↕30 in (75 cm)

A South African species. Sprawling branching stems with ends ascending,

with rosettes of yellow-toothed green to blue-green leaves to 8 in (20 cm) long, sometimes white-spotted. Branched inflorescences to 24 in (60 cm) tall, with tubular scarlet flowers in summer. Zones 9–11.

Aloe peglerae

☀ ⬧ ↔15 in (40 cm) ↕24 in (60 cm)

From near Pretoria in northern South Africa; rare in the wild. Often solitary rosette with overlapping bluish gray leaves, reddish in winter. Flowers dull red in dense cylindrical erect spikes, mid-winter–early spring. Zones 9–10.

Aloe peglerae, in Mont Sare Park, South Africa

Aloe reynoldsii

Aloe plicatilis ★

FAN ALOE

☀ ⬧ ↔7 ft (2 m) ↕15 ft (4.5 m)

From the Cape region in South Africa. Grows into a well-branched shrub to 5 ft (1.5 m) tall in cultivation. Terminal leaves, arranged in 2 ranks of 12 to 16, dull green, flat, with rounded tips and minute teeth. Red flowers in winter. Zones 9–11.

Aloe pluridens

☀ ⬧ ↔4–10 ft (1.2–3 m)
↕10–20 ft (3–6 m)

From South Africa. Winter-flowering tree-like species with sometimes branching trunk and white-toothed yellow-green leaves to 27 in (70 cm) long. Branched 40 in (100 cm) high inflorescences with pink flowers to nearly 2 in (5 cm) long. Zones 9–11.

Aloe polyphylla ★

☀ ❄ ↔16–32 in (40–80 cm)
↕30 in (75 cm)

Native of Lesotho. Short-stemmed rosettes with spirals of light-toothed, purple-edged, gray-green leaves to 12 in (30 cm) long. Branched inflorescences to 24 in (60 cm) high, with 2 in (5 cm) long, red to orange-pink flowers, in spring. Very hardy. Zones 8–10.

Aloe rauhii

☀/◐ ⬧ ↔20–32 in (50–80 cm)
↕16–20 in (40–50 cm)

From Madagascar. Clumps of short-stemmed 5 in (12 cm) wide rosettes

with 4 in (10 cm) long, triangular, pale-spotted, gray-green, finely toothed leaves that redden in drought. Simple inflorescences to 12 in (30 cm) tall, with 1 in (25 mm) long red-pink flowers in summer. Zones 10–11.

Aloe reynoldsii

☀ ⬧ ↔24 in (60 cm) ↕24 in (60 cm)

Rare stemless species from South Africa's Eastern Cape; like *A. striata*. Solitary or clumping, lemon to orange flowers in spring. Zones 9–11.

Aloe speciosa

TILT-HEAD ALOE

☀/◐ ⬧ ↔3–10 ft (0.9–3 m)
↕7–15 ft (2–4.5 m)

From South Africa. Shrubby or tree-like. Branched or unbranched trunk and terminal rosettes of red-brown-toothed, fleshy, blue-green leaves up to 32 in (80 cm) long. Unbranched 20 in (50 cm) high inflorescences of striking 1¼ in (30 mm) long greenish white flowers with protruding red stamens, opening from red buds, in winter. Zones 9–11.

Aloe spicata

☀/◐ ⬧ ↔4 ft (1.2 m) ↕5 ft (1.5 m)

From South Africa. Often solitary rosettes with a stem up to 40 in (100 cm) tall with unmarked green leaves to 24 in (60 cm) long, edged with green or brown teeth. Tall, unbranched, upright inflorescences with kniphofia-like head of yellow and orange flowers in winter. Zones 9–11.

Aloe × spinosissima ★

☀/◐ ⬧ ↔24–48 in (60–120 cm)
↕40 in (100 cm)

This is a hybrid of *A. humilis* and *A. arborescens*. It forms clumps of stemless or short-stemmed rosettes of narrow, recurved, soft-toothed, green leaves. Unbranched, upright inflorescences of orange-red flowers in winter. Zones 9–11.

Aloe striata ★

CORAL ALOE

☀/◐ ⬧ ↔4–7 ft (1.2–2 m) ↕3 ft (0.9 m)

A native of South Africa's Cape region. Spreading branching stems with rosettes of broad, flat, toothless leaves, usually blue-gray with faint longitudinal stripes and reddish edges, to 20 in (50 cm) long. Branching inflorescences to 40 in (100 cm) tall with dull to bright red flowers from winter. *A. s.* subsp. *karasbergensis* has green-veined, white-edged leaves and many-branched inflorescences of green-tipped pink flowers. Zones 9–11.

Aloe striata

Aloe striatula

Aloe vera

Aloe striatula

BASUTO KRAAL ALOE

☼ ❄ ↔ 3 ft (0.9 m) ↑ 6 ft (1.8 m)

Species found in rocky places in Eastern Cape and Lesotho in southern Africa. Well-branched, terminal rosettes, downward curving, bright green, glossy leaves with white toothed edges. Conical flowerheads red to yellow in summer. Zones 9–11.

Aloe variegata ★

PARTRIDGE BREAST ALOE, TIGER ALOE

☼/❄ ❄ ↔ 20–32 in (50–80 cm) ↑ 20 in (50 cm)

This native of western southern Africa has clumps of stemless or short-stemmed rosettes of 4–6 in (10–15 cm) long, broad-based, triangular leaves, with white spots in bands, white edges, and white-striped undersides. Pink to dull red flowers, 1½ in (35 mm) long, are seen in winter on few-branched inflorescences. Zones 9–11.

Aloe vera ★

syn. *Aloe barbadensis*

☼/❄ ❄ ↔ 24–48 in (60–120 cm) ↑ 32 in (80 cm)

Believed to be originally native to southern Arabia or nearby parts of Africa, this well-known species has become widely naturalized in the Mediterranean and tropical Africa. Forms clumps of stemless or suckering rosettes of light-spotted, narrow,

fleshy, dark green leaves up to 12 in (30 cm) long. Yellow 1¼ in (30 mm) long flowers on few-branched inflorescences in summer. Valued for its sap's medicinal properties. Zones 9–12.

Aloe virens

☼/❄ ❄ ↔ 20–32 in (50–80 cm) ↑ 20 in (50 cm)

From southern Africa. Clumps of stemless rosettes. Dark green fleshy leaves to 8 in (20 cm) long, edged with fierce teeth. Red flowers on branching inflorescences to 16 in (40 cm) high. Zones 10–11.

ALOINOPSIS

An attractive genus of 14 dwarf, succulent, rosette-forming, mimicry plants from South Africa that belong to the iceplant (Aizoceae) family. It is named for a resemblance of some species to certain aloes. Attractive, free-flowering plants, they are suitable for small containers and are popular with growers because of their large flowers. They grow in small clusters or mounds that rarely exceed 2 in (5 cm) in height or 20 in (50 cm) across. The thickened, more or less spoon-shaped leaves vary from smooth to rough. Most species have distinct tap roots. Flower colours include white, cream, pink, yellow, and striped combinations. CULTIVATION: Fairly easy to grow in a well-drained soil with a little organic matter and moderate watering at all times, with a distinct rest in winter. Propagation is from seed or by dividing the clusters of rosettes.

Aloinopsis malherbei

☼/❄ ❄ ↔ 16 in (40 cm) ↑ 2 in (5 cm)

Attractive blue-gray leaves, bearing prominent white tubercles on their backs and the tips. Lustrous, yellow flowers, ¾ in (18 mm) wide, appear in late winter or spring. Zones 8–10.

Aloinopsis schooneesii ★

MOUND OF PEBBLES

☼/❄ ❄ ↔ 8 in (20 cm) ↑ 2 in (5 cm)

The leaves of this species are short, round, tightly packed, ½–¾ in

(12–18 mm) long, deep green with dark green spots. When dry and exposed to sufficient sunlight, the leaves turn reddish brown, mimicking the surrounding stones found in the plant's habitat. Flowers yellow with a deep red mid-stripe, ½–¾ in (12–18 mm) wide, in late winter or spring. Zones 8–10.

ALONSOA

MASK FLOWER

A genus of 12 perennial herbs or shrubs, members of the figwort or foxglove (Scrophulariaceae) family and native to the western tropical Americas. Flowers are on terminal racemes, each flower composed of 5 petals and a short tube, held on a long stalk. Fruit is in the form of a capsule containing many small seeds. CULTIVATION: These species prefer rich well-drained soil. Pinch growing

shoots to encourage bushy growth. Make sure to protect from aphids. Propagate from seed in spring.

Alonsoa meridionalis

☼ ❄ ↔ 24–36 in (60–90 cm) ↑ 18–24 in (45–60 cm)

Herb or shrub from Peru which has orange to red flowers and ovate, serrated leaves, 1¼–2 in (30–50 mm) long. Zones 9–11.

Alonsoa warscewiczii

MASK FLOWER

☼ ❄ ↔ 24–36 in (60–90 cm) ↑ 18–24 in (45–60 cm)

Perennial herb or shrub from Peru; may be grown as an annual. Bright red, sometimes white, flowers, through summer–autumn. Slender, branching, red stems, and oval-shaped, toothed, reddish green leaves. Zones 9–11.

Aloe × spinosissima

Aloe virens

Aloinopsis malherbei

ALOPECURUS

FOXTAIL GRASS

Found throughout northern temperate zones, this genus of 25 species of annual and perennial grasses (family Poaceae) is known for its long, soft, plume-like flower panicles. Leaves range from linear and hair-like to flat and quite broad. In summer, flowering stems bear cylindrical plumes of tiny bristled spikelets. Dying flowers are replaced by conspicuous seed heads. Cultivated forms often have larger flowerheads or variegated foliage. CULTIVATION: Mostly very hardy and easily cultivated in temperate climates. Plant in moist well-drained soil in full or half-sun. Some species are somewhat invasive but are rarely serious weeds. Occasionally used as a meadow grass but too coarse for lawns. Propagate annuals from seed and perennials or cultivars by division.

Aloysia citriodora

Alopecurus pratensis

MEADOW FOXTAIL

☀/❂ ❄ ↔ 12–16 in (30–40 cm) ↑ 40–48 in (100–120 cm)

A species that is widespread throughout Eurasia and also found in northeastern Africa. Long, relatively broad, smooth-surfaced leaves. Pale green flower panicles, to 4 in (10 cm) long, are often purple-tinted. Cultivars include: 'Aureomarginatus' (syn. 'Aureovariegatus'), which has leaves with gold edging and longitudinal stripes; and 'Aureus' ★, with golden yellow leaves. Zones 5–10.

ALOYSIA

Mostly from South America in subtropical and temperate climates, this genus of tender shrubs and perennials belongs in the vervain (Verbenaceae) family. All the species contain volatile oils in their foliage, with fragrances resembling citrus, lavender, camphor, and mint, utilized in perfumery and traditional medicine, commonly for respiratory conditions. One species is a substitute for oregano. Another Brazilian species was used as a tea substitute, and its fruit are also eaten. The species with widest appeal is, undoubtedly, *A. citriodora*. Small flowers in clusters at the ends of branches (on current season's wood) can be abundant. CULTIVATION: These plants prefer well-drained loam and summer rainfall or irrigation. They will tolerate only light frosts so require a warm and sheltered position. Straggly growth should be regularly trimmed to encourage new wood and maintain foliage density. Propagate by cuttings which strike readily in summer.

Aloysia citriodora

syn. *Aloysia triphylla*

LEMON-SCENTED VERBENA

☀ ❄ ↔ 10 ft (3 m) ↑ 10 ft (3 m)

From Argentina, Uruguay, and Chile. Semi-deciduous shrub. Lemon-scented foliage, rough textured leaves in whorls of three, used for flavorings, herbal teas, and potpourri. Flowers very pale lavender to white, from summer to autumn. Zones 8–12.

Aloysia wrightii

☀ ❄ ↔ 5 ft (1.5 m) ↑ 5 ft (1.5 m)

From southern areas of North America. Small, rounded to oval, aromatic leaves covered in gray or yellow hairs. The small spikes of tiny, fragrant, white, tubular flowers are also hairy. Zones 8–11.

Alphitonia excelsa

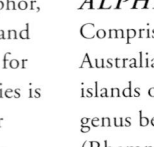

ALPHITONIA

Comprising 6 species of trees in Australia, the Malay Archipelago, and islands of the western Pacific, this genus belongs to the buckthorn (Rhamnaceae) family. Some members, such as the pink ash (*A. petriei*), are rapid-growing pioneer plants that rival wattles, producing abundant long-lived seeds. In Queensland and northern New South Wales, Australia, it is commonly found on disturbed rainforest sites. Other members such as *A. excelsa* are valued timber trees with the unusual characteristic of the pale milled timber darkening with age to bright red—thus the name red ash. The young foliage is strongly aromatic when bruised. CULTIVATION: These trees are hardy to a wide range of soils, with best results achieved using regular applications of fertilizer. They need abundant summer moisture in a warm open position. Propagate from seed.

Alphitonia excelsa

RED ASH

☀ ❄ ↔ 20 ft (6 m) ↑ 60 ft (18 m)

Found in temperate and subtropical rainforests of New South Wales and Queensland, Australia, and also occurs as a much smaller tree on rocky ridges in drier western districts. Leaves elliptical, ovate, white undersides. Fragrant, small, cream flowers. Fleshy blue-black fruits. The straight-grained and easily worked timber which darkens with age to bright red is useful for cabinetwork. Zones 9–10.

ALPINIA

GINGER LILY

The 200 species of fleshy-stemmed perennials in this genus, which belongs to the ginger (Zingiberaceae) family, are native to tropical regions of Asia, Australia, and some Pacific islands where they grow on forest margins. Lance-shaped leaves are arranged in 2 ranks along reed-like stems from 3–12 ft (0.9–3.5 m) tall depending on the species. The usually showy and long-lasting inflorescences range from pale to brilliant colors. The true flowers are often enclosed at first within colorful bracts. Although generally grown for their flowers or foliage, some species are used in cooking and for their essential oils. CULTIVATION: In warm climates grow in sun or half-sun in fertile moist soil. Most species will withstand a little frost but must have 4 to 5 months of uninterrupted growth to flower, so in cool climates start earlier indoors or grow under glass in bright

Alopecurus pratensis 'Aureomarginatus'

filtered light, water plentifully and maintain high humidity. Propagate from seed or by division.

Alpinia calcarata
INDIAN GINGER, SNAP GINGER
☀/◐ ✣ ↔ 2–3 ft (0.6–0.9 m)
↕ 3–6 ft (0.9–1.8 m)

Native to China and India. Glossy narrow leaves to 12 in × 1 in (30 cm × 2.5 cm). The horizontal inflorescence is about 4 in (10 cm) long. White flowers have yellow interiors heavily veined with reddish maroon. Autumn-flowering. Zones 9–11.

Alpinia coerulea
☀/◐ ✣ ↔ 8 ft (2.4 m) ↕ 4–7 ft (1.2–2 m)
Most widespread of the 6 *Alpinia* species native to Australia, on the east coast from Torres Strait Islands almost to Sydney. Spreading habit, leaves rather narrow. Erect panicles of many small white to purplish flowers in spring. Globular china blue fruit, summer–autumn. Zones 10–12.

Alpinia galanga
GALANGAL, SIAMESE GINGER
☀/◐ ✣ ↔ 2–3 ft (0.6–0.9 m)
↕ 4–6 ft (1.2–1.8 m)

From southeastern Asia. Large leaves to 20 in (50 cm) long. In summer the branching inflorescence bears flowers of pale green and white with pink markings. The fleshy rhizome is used in cooking and in eastern herbal remedies. Zones 9–11.

Alpinia purpurata
RED GINGER
☀/◐ ✣ ↔ 2–4 ft (0.6–1.2 m)
↕ 4–12 ft (1.2–3.5 m)

From Melanesia. Large leaves, up to 32 in × 6 in (80 cm × 15 cm), prominent midribs. The long-lasting rich red flowers are borne on upright inflorescences for much of the year. Zones 10–11.

Alpinia coerulea growing along the riverbank, in the wild, Millaa Millaa, Queensland, Australia

Alpinia zerumbet
syn. *Alpinia nutans, A. speciosa*
PINK PORCELAIN LILY, SHELL GINGER
☀/◐ ✣ ↔ 2–3 ft (0.6–0.9 m)
↕ 4–10 ft (1.2–3 m)

From eastern Asia and New Guinea. Most widely grown species. Glossy leathery leaves. Pendulous inflorescence to 16 in (40 cm) long. Pale pink or white bracts at first enclose yellow and red flowers borne in spring and summer. '**Variegata**', leaves variegated with pale yellow stripes. Zones 9–11.

ALSTONIA
There are about 40 species in this dogbane (Apocynaceae) family genus of evergreen trees and shrubs, related to frangipani *(Plumeria).* Most are native to tropical Asia and Australasia, some occur in tropical America and Africa. All parts bleed a milky caustic sap when cut. Bark and roots are very

Alpinia zerumbet

Alpinia purpurata, Hilo, Hawaii, USA

bitter and probably poisonous. Local medicinal and pesticidal uses have been recorded. Smooth-edged leaves are in whorls of up to 7, and sapling branches are also whorled. Flowers are in clusters terminating in branchlets, mostly small with 5 white petals arranged propellor-like. Fruit slender and bean-like, splitting when ripe to release seeds into the wind.

CULTIVATION: Most are frost tender. Some thrive only in tropics and subtropics. In fertile soil and a sheltered position they grow fast, preferring full sun. Propagation is normally from seed, though cuttings can be struck.

Alstonia scholaris
DEVIL TREE, DITA BARK, WHITE CHEESEWOOD
☀ ✦ ↔ 35 ft (10 m) ↕ 100 ft (30 m)
Widely distributed species from India, Southeast Asia, northeastern Australia, and west Pacific. Glossy green leaves to 8 in (20 cm) long, pale beneath. Creamy white flowers, in clusters, in spring–early summer. String-like fruits, 12 in (30 cm) long. Zones 11–12.

Alstonia venenata
☀ ✣ ↔ 10 ft (3 m) ↕ 12 ft (3.5 m)
From the Nilgiri Hills of southern India, this shrub branches into an umbrella-like form. Leaves narrow with wavy margins and drawn-out apex. Clusters of pure white flowers, about 1 in (25 mm) wide, cover the plant throughout summer–autumn. Zones 10–12.

Alstonia venenata

Alstonia scholaris

Alstroemeria ligtu

ALSTROEMERIA

LILY OF THE INCAS, PERUVIAN LILY

A genus of around 50 species of fleshy-rooted perennials, the type genus for the Alstroemeriaceae family. Found in South America, often at altitude, they are known for their long-lasting beautifully marked flowers but notorious for their vigorous roots and self-sowing. At least one of the species, *A. psitticana*, is considered a weed in some areas. Foliage is mid-green, usually lance-shaped, and slightly twisted. It is carried on tall stems that terminate in many flowered heads of 6-petalled lily-like blooms that occur in many shades. The genus was named by Linnaeus after one of his pupils, Claus von Alstroemer (1736–1794), who

around 1753 sent seeds of the plant to Linnaeus from Spain, where it had recently been introduced.
CULTIVATION: Though rather frost tender—the roots should be insulated with mulch—these species are easily grown in any sunny position with moderately fertile well-drained soil that can be kept moist during the flowering season. Propagate by division when dormant, or from seed.

Alstroemeria ligtu

ST MARTIN'S FLOWER

☀/☀ ❄ ↔ 16 in (40 cm) ↕ 24 in (60 cm)
Summer-flowering species from Chile and Argentina. Leaves to 3 in (8 cm) long. Flowers white through creamy yellow and lavender to magenta, usually with yellow throat and darker flecks. Flower clusters of 2 to 3 blooms in heads of up to 8 clusters. Zones 8–10.

Alstroemeria pelegrina

☀/☀ ❄ ↔ 8–16 in (20–40 cm)
↕ 12–24 in (30–60 cm)

Peruvian species with 3 in (8 cm) long leaves and small clusters of white through mauve to pink flowers with yellow center and purple-red flecks. Blooms summer–autumn. Zones 9–10.

Alstroemeria psittacina

syn. *Alstroemeria pulchella*

☀/☀ ❄ ↔ 16–20 in (40–50 cm)
↕ 28–36 in (70–90 cm)

This Brazilian species has leaves up to 3 in (8 cm) long, and heads of red-flushed green flowers with maroon flecks, borne in summer. 'Royal Star' (syn. 'Variegata') is a cultivar with cream edged and/or striped leaves. Zones 8–10.

Alstroemeria Hybrid Cultivars

☀ ❄ ↔ 12–24 in (30–60 cm)
↕ 18–30 in (45–75 cm)

Alstroemerias hybridize freely, and in recent years the range has increased enormously as plant breeders around the world have capitalized on these easily grown plants' use as cut flowers. Many of these cultivars are hybrids between *A. ligtu*, *A. haemantha* and *A. aurea*. Popular hybrids include: 'Aimi', 24 in (60 cm) tall, pink-blushed pale creamy yellow flowers with deep brown flecks; 'Amanda', white-flushed pink flowers with green petal tips and dark flecks; 'Apollo', 3 ft (0.9 m) tall, white flowers with deep yellow center and brown flecks; 'Belinda', soft yellow flowers with darker center and brown flecks; 'Blue Heaven', 3–4 ft (1–1.2 m) tall, lavender blue flowers with pale center and red-brown flecks; 'Blushing Bride', 3 ft (0.9 m) tall, white flowers with faint pink blush; 'Evening Song', 3 ft (0.9 m) tall, deep magenta flowers with yellow throat and dark flecks; 'Friendship', 3 ft (0.9 m) tall, soft yellow flowers with deep brown markings and a darker center, and hint of

Alstroemeria, Hybrid Cultivar, 'Amanda'

Alstroemeria, Hybrid Cultivar, 'Aimi'

Alstroemeria, Hybrid Cultivar, 'Apollo'

purple at the petal tips; **'Fuego'** ★, 5–6 ft (1.5–1.8 m) tall, fiery red flowers with small yellow throat; Ilona/**'Stalona'**, soft orange-red flowers with creamy yellow throat and dark flecks; Irena/**'Statiren'**, white-flushed pink flowers with near-red mid-stripe and dark flecks; **'Marina'**, 20–30 in (50–75 cm) tall, magenta-pink flowers with small yellow throat and dark flecks; **'Marissa'**, 3 ft (0.9 m) tall, rose pink flowers lightening to cream mid-petal with yellow throat and dark flecks; **'Napoli'**, magenta-purple flowers with faint yellow throat and dark flecks; **'Odessa'**, 3–4 ft (1–1.2 m) tall, white flowers flushed and tipped deep red-pink, with yellow throat and red flecks; Olga/**'Stalog'**, white flowers with yellow center and red flecks; **'Orange Gem'**, 3 ft (0.9 m) tall, orange flowers with golden yellow throat and dark flecks; **'Orange Glory'**, 3 ft (0.9 m) tall, deep orange flowers with dark markings and golden throat; Queen Elizabeth The Queen Mother/**'Stamoli'**, brown-marked cream flowers flushed with pink; Rebecca/**'Stabec'**, 3 ft (0.9 m) tall, cream flowers with deep pink blotches, yellow center and dark flecks; **'Red Beauty'**, 3 ft (0.9 m) tall, with black-flecked, red-orange flowers with yellow-throats, **'Romy'**, 4–5 ft (1.2–1.5 m) tall, white flowers with yellow center and red flecks; **'Tessa'**, 30 in (75 cm) tall, brown-flecked red flowers with small yellow center; **'Yellow Friendship'**, black-flecked bright yellow flowers.

The **Little Miss Series** are dwarf plants, 6–12 in (15–30 cm) tall, with large flowers, strong stems and a long

Alstroemeria, Hybrid Cultivar, 'Belinda'

Alstroemeria, Hybrid Cultivar, 'Blue Heaven'

Alstroemeria, Hybrid Cultivar, 'Blue Sky'

Alstroemeria, Hybrid Cultivar, 'Blushing Bride'\

A., HC, 'Butterfly'

A., HC, 'Evening Song'

A., HC, 'Friendship'

A., HC, 'Fuego'

A., HC, Ilona/'Stalona'

A., HC, Irena/'Statiren'

A., HC, 'Marina'

A., HC, 'Napoli'

A., HC, 'Odessa'

A., HC, Olga/'Stalog'

A., HC, 'Orange Gem'

A., HC, 'Orange Glory'

A., HC, Princess Sophia/'Stajello'

A., HC, Queen Elizabeth the Queen Mother/'Stamoli'

A., HC, Rebecca/'Stabec'

A., HC, 'Red Beauty'

A., HC, Princess Alexandra/ 'Zelblanca'

A., HC, 'Princess Syringa'

A., HC, 'Yellow Friendship'

A., HC, 'Little Miss Olivia'

A., HC, 'Little Miss Tara'

A., HC, 'Romy'

A

Alstroemeria, Hybrid Cultivar, HRH Princess Alice/'Staverpi'

A., HC, Diana Princess of Wales/'Stablaco'

A., HC, Princess Daniela/ 'Stapridani'

A., HC, 'Princess Freckles'

A., HC, Princess Grace/'Starodo'

A., HC, Princess Ileana/'Stalvir'

A., HC, Princess Ivana/ 'Staprivane'

A., HC, Princess Marie Louise/'Zelanon'

A., HC, Princess Monica/ 'Staprimon'

A., HC, Princess Morana/ 'Staprirana'

A., HC, Princess Oxana/ 'Staprioxa'

A., HC, Princess Pamela/ 'Stapripame'

flowering period. They include: **'Little Miss Olivia'**, soft cream with pale yellow throat and red-brown flecks; **'Little Miss Roselind'**, deep pink with yellow center; **'Little Miss Sophie'**, cream with red markings and broad pink mid-stripe; and **'Little Miss Tara'**, deep pinkish red with small golden center and dark flecks.

The Dutch-raised **Princess Series** is a range of compact hybrids that grow 12–18 in (30–45 cm) tall and are long flowering because they are sterile. They are ideal as potted plants. This series includes: Princess Daniela/ **'Stapridani'**, pale yellow in color with dark flecks; Princess Ivana/**'Staprivane'**, deep rose pink; Princess Monica/ **'Staprimon'**, red-throated, pink-marked, cream flowers; Princess Morana/**'Staprirana'**, pale cream with orange markings; Princess Oxana/**'Staprioxa'**, magenta pink; Princess Pamela/**'Stapripame'**, mauve-pink; Princess Sissi/**'Staprisis'**, deep pink with yellow markings; and Princess Zavina/**'Staprivina'**, salmon pink with yellow throat and dark flecks. Zones 7–10.

ALTERNANTHERA

CHAFF FLOWER, COPPERLEAF, JOYWEED

A genus of about 200 low, compact, trailing or erect, aquatic, annual or perennial herbs from tropical to subtropical Americas belonging to the amaranth (Amaranthaceae) family. Spikes of small flowers with bracts but no petals. Often grown for their brightly colored foliage, which is smooth-edged or densely toothed. Named for their alternate infertile anthers.

CULTIVATION: Adaptable to most soils, they do best in a protected, warm, sunny position in rich soil with frequent watering. Regularly clip plants to a height of 2½–4 in (6–10 cm) for border displays. In cooler climates plants should be lifted after first frosts. Propagate by division or from cuttings taken in late summer or spring.

Althaea officinalis

Alternanthera bettzichiana

CALICO PLANT

☼ ⬡ ↔ 2–3 ft (0.6–0.9 m)
↑ 2–3 ft (0.6–0.9 m)

An annual or short-lived perennial from Brazil. Erect habit, narrow spoon-shaped leaves of khaki to yellow, with red to purple markings. **'Brilliantissima'** is a variety with vivid red leaves. Zones 10–12.

ALTHAEA

This genus is a member of the mallow (Malvaceae) family and contains 12 species of annual and perennial herbs native to western Europe and central Asia. They grow in moist or marshy ground at low altitudes. The rounded leaves are lobed to varying degrees. The 5-petalled flowers are no bigger than 1½ in (35 mm) across and have prominent tubes of fused stamens. They are borne in racemes or panicles in summer. *Althaea* is closely related to the true hollyhock, *Alcea*, but is much less showy.

CULTIVATION: Well suited to "wild" gardens. Grow in rich moist soil in a sunny position. Propagate by division or from seed in spring.

Althaea armeniaca

☼ ❋ ↔ 40 in (100 cm)
↑ 4–6 ft (1.2–1.8 m)

From eastern Europe and central and southwestern Asia. Leaves are 3- to 5-lobed on slightly hairy stems. Small pink flowers in clusters at the leaf axils. Zones 6–10.

Althaea officinalis

MARSH MALLOW, WHITE MALLOW

☼ ❋ ↔ 4 ft (1.2 m) ↑ 4–7 ft (1.2–2 m)

From Europe, naturalized in eastern USA. A rather lax plant with hairy, grayish, 3- to 5-lobed leaves. The small flowers are pale pink or white with purplish red tubes of fused stamens. The popular confectionery marshmallow was originally made from the roots of this plant. Zones 3–10.

ALYOGYNE

Once included within the genus *Hibiscus*, the 4 species that make up this genus, of the mallow (Malvaceae) family, are distinctive, evergreen, Australian shrubs which, despite their delicate silky blooms, are native to the drier regions of the western half of the continent. Leaves are variable; in some species they are entire, in others palmately lobed. They are fast growing and, as though to make up for their short-lived single blooms, usually in pinks or mauves, they flower profusely over a long period.

Alyssum condensatum

Alyssum spinosum

Alyssum montanum 'Berggold'

Alyssum wulfenianum

CULTIVATION: These are hardy plants for non-humid areas. Most are able to survive frost. They do best planted in full sun and can survive in all soil types but appreciate good drainage. Pruning is sometimes necessary to control shape. Propagation is from easily struck cuttings or by seed.

Alyogyne huegelii ★
BLUE HIBISCUS
☼ ⌘ ↔ 3–6 ft (0.9–1.8 m)
↕ 3–6 ft (0.9 m–1.8 m)

Popular species, hardy and fast growing. Flowers, pale mauve to purplish with overlapping petals set against pale green, slightly felty, and deeply lobed leaves. Prune late summer after flowering. '**Monterey Bay**' and '**Santa Cruz**' are popular cultivars. Zones 9–10.

ALYSSUM
MADWORT

A cabbage (Brassicaceae) family genus of around 170 species of annuals, perennials, and subshrubs found in Eurasia and North Africa. Not to be confused with the bedding annuals

known as alyssum, which were once included in the genus but are now classified as *Lobularia*, nor with the *Aurinia*, also known as alyssum. Most are small mounding plants with simple leaves often covered with fine hairs that give a white or silvery sheen. In summer they produce racemes of tiny 4-petalled flowers, usually white or yellow, above the foliage. The common name comes from an old belief that the plant could cure madness.

CULTIVATION: Most are spreading crevice plants ideal in rockeries, stone walls, or cascading over banks. Prefer light, gritty, well-drained soil in full sun. Drought tolerant once established, they benefit from occasional deep watering. Propagate from seed or base cuttings depending on growth form.

Alyssum condensatum
☼ ❄ ↔ 20 in (50 cm) ↕ 8 in (20 cm)

Perennial found from the Middle East to Iran, becoming woody-based with age. Silvery leaves to ¾ in (18 mm) long. Large racemes of tiny yellow flowers, notched petals. Zones 7–10.

Alyssum montanum
☼ ❄ ↔ 8–16 in (20–40 cm)
↕ 4–8 in (10–20 cm)

Usually prostrate, spreading, European alpine perennial. Downy pale gray leaves in rosettes. Sprays of small, honey-scented, yellow flowers with notched petals. '**Berggold**' (syn. 'Mountain Gold'), low spreading cultivar, golden yellow flowers. Zones 6–9.

Alyssum spinosum ★
☼ ❄ ↔ 16–24 in (40–60 cm)
↕ 16–24 in (40–60 cm)

From southern France and Spain. Small, densely branched, rounded shrub becoming spiny with age. Tiny silvery leaves with persistent stalks that eventually become fine spines. Clusters of white flowers, often pink tinted. Zones 8–10.

Alyssum wulfenianum
☼ ❄ ↔ 8–24 in (20–60 cm)
↕ 4–12 in (10–30 cm)

Western Asian perennial, upright or prostrate. Small silvery white leaves—those on non-flowering stems are in rosettes. Sprays of pale yellow flowers, each to ¼ in (6 mm) wide. Zones 7–10.

ALYXIA

A genus of the dogbane (Apocynaceae) family consisting of some 70 species of mainly coastal evergreen shrubs, noted for their 5-petalled white flowers that are often scented, and their colorful but poisonous fruits. The leaves are usually small and often have a glossy waxy coating that is typical of salt-tolerant seaside plants. The genus

is perhaps centered on Australia, though representatives are found through much of the warm-temperate and tropical Asian-Pacific region. The Hawaiian species, *A. olivaeformis*, is used for producing leis and has a strong fragrance reminiscent of frangipani *(Plumeria)*, to which it is related.

CULTIVATION: Hardiness and adaptability varies among species. Those from the tropics generally prefer warm moist conditions and fairly rich soil, while *A. buxifolia* is a very tough shrub that can tolerate most conditions, with the exception of extreme cold. Most species can be propagated by seed or half-hardened cuttings.

Alyxia buxifolia
SEA BOX
☼ ⌘ ↔ 6 ft (1.8 m) ↕ 5 ft (1.5 m)

This shrub has small leaves reminiscent of box *(Buxus)* foliage. Clusters of small, white, orange-tubed flowers develop at the branch tips, followed by orange berries that blacken with age. Tolerant of dry sandy soils and salt winds. Zones 9–11.

Alyxia buxifolia

Alyogyne huegelii 'Santa Cruz'

Alyogyne huegelii

A

Amaranthus cruentus

A. hypochondriacus 'Pygmy Torch'

Amaranthus tricolor 'Joseph's Coat'

Alyxia ruscifolia

CHAIN FRUIT, PRICKLY ALYXIA

☼ ❀ ↔ 5 ft (1.5 m) ↑ 10 ft (3 m)

This shrub is native to northern New South Wales and southeastern Queensland, Australia. Its sweetly scented white flowers open in summer, followed by clusters of orange berries. Can tolerate coastal conditions. Zones 10–11.

AMARANTHUS

There are about 60 species of weedy annuals and short-lived perennials in this genus, which is a member of the amaranth (Amaranthaceae) family. They have a worldwide distribution, often being found in wasteland areas. Species range from tall to prostrate, with long, often drooping, tassels of small red or green flowers. Individual flowers are either male or female and may be borne on separate plants.

Some species are cultivated as leaf or grain crops in tropical areas, while those with dramatic flowers or colorful foliage are popular in the ornamental garden and for floristry.

CULTIVATION: Easily grown in well-drained fertile soil in full sun. Protect tall varieties from strong wind. In cooler climates sow seed under glass in early spring and plant out after danger of frosts has passed. In warmer areas seed can be sown outdoors later in the season.

Amaranthus caudatus

LOVE-LIES-BLEEDING, TASSEL FLOWER, VELVET FLOWER

☼ ❀ ↔ 24 in (60 cm) ↑ 36–48 in (90–120 cm)

Native to Peru, Africa, and India, this annual or short-lived perennial has dull green leaves, as well as drooping crimson-purple tassels, up

Amaranthus caudatus 'Green Tails'

to 12 in (30 cm) long, in summer. 'Green Tails' has long greenish yellow tassels; 'Viridis' (syn. 'Green Thumb') has long-lasting vivid green tassels. Zones 8–11.

Amaranthus cruentus

syn. *Amaranthus paniculatus*

PRINCE'S FEATHER, PURPLE AMARANTH, RED AMARANTH

☼ ❀ ↔ 30 in (75 cm) ↑ 36–60 in (90–150 cm)

An annual species native to the Americas, with oval to lance-shaped leaves, that can be used as a vegetable. It has greenish to red tassels, erect or drooping, up to 24 in (60 cm) long. The seeds are reddish brown to black. 'Golden Giant' has golden seed heads. Zones 8–11.

Amaranthus hypochondriacus

CEREAL GRAIN AMARANTH

☼ ❀ ↔ 24 in (60 cm) ↑ 4 ft (1.2 m)

From southern USA, Mexico, India, and China. An annual species with green to purplish leaves and erect spikes of tiny deep crimson flowers. Grown as a cereal crop in South America. 'Green Thumb' has upright spikes of green flowers. 'Pygmy Torch' grows to 12 in (30 cm) high, with densely packed crimson flowerheads. Zones 8–11.

Amaranthus tricolor

CHINESE SPINACH, JOSEPH'S COAT, TAMPALA

☼ ❀ ↔ 30 in (75 cm) ↑ 24–36 in (60–90 cm)

From Africa and Asia, this bushy annual is grown as a leaf vegetable or, in varieties which have colorful foliage, for its ornamental value. Flower spikes are green or red. There are several varieties that have colored top growth, the best known being 'Joseph's Coat', with red and gold upper leaves. Zones 8–11.

AMARYLLIS

BELLADONNA LILY, JERSEY LILY, MARCH LILY, NAKED LADIES

This once large genus has now been reduced to just one species, an autumn-flowering bulb native to South Africa. It is the type genus for the amaryllis (Amaryllidaceae) family. Belladonna means "beautiful lady" and is a reference to the legend of Amaryllis, a beautiful shepherdess who appeared in the works of Virgil. Dormant for most of the warmer months, sturdy red-tinted flower stems begin to appear from late summer and grow quickly to as much as 24 in (60 cm) tall. They are topped with heads of flowers in shades from very pale pink to deep magenta. Long strappy leaves soon follow.

CULTIVATION: Plant the bulbs with their tops exposed in a warm sunny location and water well from late summer to encourage good flower production. Like most of the summer-dormant African bulbs, belladonna lily can withstand considerable drought when the foliage is absent. Propagation is usually by division of established clumps once the foliage dies back.

Amaryllis belladonna

☼ ❀ ↔ 12–20 in (30–50 cm) ↑ 24 in (60 cm)

From South Africa's Cape region, this species forms clumps of glossy mid-green leaves to 20 in (50 cm) long. Foliage dies back from spring. In late summer mildly scented, funnel-shaped, 4 in (10 cm) long flowers in heads of 6 or more start to open. Cultivars include: 'Capetown', deep pink; 'Johannesburg', pale pink, white center; 'Major', deep pink, fragrant; and 'Purpurea', purple-pink. Zones 8–10.

Amaryllis belladonna

Amelanchier canadensis

Amelanchier canadensis 'Glenn Form'

Amelanchier laevis

AMELANCHIER

SERVICEBERRY

Amelanchier, a member of the rose (Rosaceae) family, consists of 30 or so species of deciduous shrubs and small trees from North America (including Mexico), with one species in China, and another in Europe and Turkey. All have smallish oval or elliptical leaves with finely toothed margins. Flowers, each with 5 white narrow petals, are borne in small sprays; the small hawthorn-like fruit have sepals at the apex. The fruits ripen to blue-black and are edible. Some make attractive ornamentals.
CULTIVATION: These are mostly woodland plants preferring moist sheltered sites, while some species do well at the edge of a pond or stream. Effective planted against a backdrop

of darker foliage. Prone to the same pests and diseases as apples, pears, and hawthorns, including the dreaded fireblight. Propagation normally from seed, germination being aided by cold-stratification, or by layering of low branches or suckers. Cultivars are often grafted.

Amelanchier alnifolia
syn. *Amelanchier florida*
ALDERLEAF SERVICEBERRY, JUNEBERRY, SASKATOON SERVICEBERRY
☀ ❋ ↔ 12 ft (3.5 m) ↕ 3–6 ft (0.9–1.8 m)
North American species found on banks of rivulets or on sheltered mountainsides. Leaves rounded, toothed mainly in the upper half, around 1 in (25 mm) long. Flowers in late spring–early summer, dark purple edible fruit. *A. a.* var. *semiintegrifolia* (syn. *A. florida*), thicket-forming deciduous shrub or small tree from southern Alaska to northern California. Zones 3–9.

Amelanchier arborea
syn. *Amelanchier canadensis* of gardens
DOWNY SERVICEBERRY
☀ ❋ ↔ 30 ft (9 m) ↕ 60 ft (18 m)
From eastern USA, the tallest-growing species, smaller in cultivation. Narrow rounded crown. Silver-gray smooth bark, rougher with age. Leaves

abruptly pointed, turn red or yellow in autumn. Flowers in early spring. Small purple-black fruit. Zones 4–9.

Amelanchier asiatica
☀/◑ ❋ ↔ 10–20 ft (3–6 m) ↕ 20–40 ft (6–12 m)
From Japan, Korea and China, similar to *A. arborea*. New leaves with coating of fluffy white hairs, soon quite hairless. Late spring flowers in erect sprays, fragrant, petals narrow. Zones 5–9.

Amelanchier canadensis
syn. *Amelanchier oblongifolia*
JUNEBERRY, SERVICEBERRY, SHADBLOW SERVICEBERRY
☀ ❋ ↔ 10 ft (3 m) ↕ 25 ft (8 m)
This eastern North American species is an upright suckering shrub or small tree mainly from boggy ground. Woolly new leaves, spring flowers in upright sprays, juicy blue-black fruits are about ½ in (12 mm) in diameter. Cultivars include 'Glenn Form' and 'Sprizam'. Zones 5–9.

Amelanchier × grandiflora
APPLE SERVICEBERRY, SERVICEBERRY
☀ ❋ ↔ 35 ft (10 m) ↕ 25 ft (8 m)
This hybrid between *A. arborea* and *A. laevis*, the two tallest North

American species, has given rise to several ornamental cultivars: 'Ballerina' ★ (syn. *A. lamarckii* 'Ballerina'), spreading, up to 20 ft (6 m) tall, with bronze new leaves, masses of large flowers; and 'Rubescens', flowers flushed with pink, opening from darker pink buds. Zones 4–9.

Amelanchier laevis
syn. *Amelanchier canadensis* of gardens
ALLEGHENY SERVICEBERRY, SARVIS TREE
☀ ❋ ↔ 25 ft (8 m) ↕ 25 ft (8 m)
Found mainly in the Appalachian mountains of eastern USA, extending into Canada. Bronzy purple slightly downy new leaves, and sweet, juicy, blue-black fruit. It flowers as the leaves unfold in late spring. Zones 4–9.

Amelanchier × *grandiflora*

A. × *grandiflora* 'Rubescens', in summer

A. × *grandiflora* 'Rubescens', in winter

Amelanchier × *grandiflora* 'Rubescens', in spring

A

Amelanchier lamarckii

Amelanchier spicata

Amelanchier lamarckii
LAMARCK SERVICEBERRY

☀ ❄ ↔ 35 ft (10 m) ↑ 30 ft (9 m)

From eastern Canada, now naturalized in northwestern Europe. Small tree with spreading branches, leaves silky-haired, bronzy red when new. Loose sprays of flowers open with the new leaves. Fruit purple-black. Zones 4–9.

Amelanchier spicata

☀ ❄ ↔ 10 ft (3 m) ↑ 8 ft (2.4 m)

From southeastern Canada and eastern USA. A freely suckering shrub or small tree. New leaves downy at first, spring flowers sometimes slightly pinkish. Purplish black fruit, sweet and juicy. Zones 4–9.

Amelanchier stolonifera
RUNNING JUNEBERRY, RUNNING SERVICEBERRY

☀/❄ ❄ ↔ 4–7 ft (1.2–2 m) ↑ 4–7 ft (1.2–2 m)

Found in northeastern USA and far southeastern Canada. Thicket-forming deciduous shrub. Stiff erect stems. Five-petalled white flowers in spring, followed by finely toothed, rounded, medium to dark green leaves. Small, round, green berries become dark purplish black, sweet, juicy, and flavorful in mid-summer. Zones 4–8.

Amelanchier utahensis
UTAH SERVICEBERRY

☀ ❄ ↔ 3–12 ft (0.9–3.5 m) ↑ 3–12 ft (0.9–3.5 m)

Shrub, allied to *A. alnifolia*, from western North American mountain areas. Leaves, wedge-shaped bases, fruit slightly smaller. Native Americans dried and ground up fruit with dried meat to make pemmican. Zones 5–9.

AMHERSTIA

The 1 species of this genus, of the cassia subfamily of legumes (Fabaceae), is beautiful in flower. Related to the poinciana (*Delonix*), it is from the lowlands of southern Myanmar, now almost unknown in the wild. It has long pinnate leaves with glossy leaflets and may be briefly deciduous. At the start of the wet season pale bronzy pink new leaves emerge, changing through brown to green. On long stalks, flowers are orchid-like with a pair of large pink bracts at the base, up to 4 in (10 cm) across, pinkish red with darker red and yellow markings. Rarely produced are the curved woody pods, deep red when immature. CULTIVATION: *Amherstia* has been successfully cultivated only in the lowland wet tropics. Its growth is fairly slow, and it needs a sheltered but sunny situation and deep moist soil. Propagation is ideally from seed but this is very seldom set on cultivated trees. An alternative is layering of low branches.

Amherstia nobilis
PRIDE OF BURMA

☀ ✈ ↔ 50 ft (15 m) ↑ 40 ft (12 m)

Lovely tree with broad low-branching canopy of foliage. Mature specimens may flower for much of the year, but flowering season is spring–early summer. Red orchid-like flowers are best appreciated close up. Zone 12.

AMICIA

A member of the pea-flower subfamily of the legumes (Fabaceae), this genus of 7 perennial herbs or shrubs with tuberous roots comes from the Andes and Mexico. Racemes of pea-like flowers appear at the leaf axils from spring to autumn. The leaves grow on long stalks, in pairs of leaflets that are smooth-edged, triangular, heart-shaped or notched, with a leaf-like bract. Fruit is a pea-like pod. CULTIVATION: Adaptable to most well-drained garden soils in an open sunny position. Propagate from seed. The seeds are retained in the pods, which do not split open.

Amicia zygomeris

☀ ❄ ↔ 2–4 ft (0.6–1.2 m) ↑ 3–6 ft (0.9–1.8 m)

Perennial herb with tuberous roots, from eastern Mexico. Racemes, to 5 in (12 cm) long, of 3 to 10, greenish yellow, pea-like flowers marked with purple, to 1¼ in (30 mm) wide. Leaflets to 3 in (8 cm) long, heart-shaped, on downy leaf stalks to 4 in (10 cm) long. Zones 7–10.

AMMI

A genus of 6 species of annuals and perennials in the carrot (Apiaceae) family. The annuals sometimes behave as short-lived perennials in mild climates. Found through much of the western temperate Eurasian region, they have very finely divided pinnate leaves and in summer produce rounded heads of tiny white flowers, sometimes with bracts, on wiry stems. Flower sprays are dainty and often used cut in the manner of gypsophila. CULTIVATION: Best grown in a warm sunny position with free-draining, rather gritty soil that can be kept moist. Inclined to be top-heavy, so staking and shelter from strong winds are important. Propagate from seed.

Ammi majus
FALSE BISHOP'S WEED

☀ ❄ ↔ 5 ft (1.5 m) ↑ 40 in (100 cm)

Annual species from southern Europe to western Asia. Large sprays of white flowers that last well when cut. Popular with florists. Zones 6–10.

Ammi visnaga
BISNAGA, TOOTHPICK WEED

☀ ❄ ↔ 4 ft (1.2 m) ↑ 32 in (80 cm)

Mediterranean annual or biennial. Greenish white flowers that last well when cut. Dried stems used as toothpicks. Essential oil has many herbal uses, especially for bronchial troubles. Sap can cause contact dermatitis or other sensitivities. Zones 8–11.

Ammi visnaga

Amherstia nobilis

Amicia zygomeris

Ammi majus, seedheads

Amorpha fruticosa

AMORPHA

A genus of 15 species of deciduous shrubs, of the pea-flower subfamily of the legumes (Fabaceae), native to North America. The name is derived from *amorphos* (deformed), and refers to the single-petalled flowers. These are crowded into one-sided racemes, usually in shades of pink, mauve, purple, or white. Foliage is pinnate and composed, in some species, of over 40 elliptical leaflets. Plant size varies considerably, with some less than 3 ft (0.9 m) tall and others over 12 ft (3.5 m). Flowers tend to be short lived but are followed by seed pods that usually remain until leaf-fall.
CULTIVATION: Most are frost hardy and easily grown in average garden conditions. A sunny or partly shaded location with well-drained soil and summer moisture is fine. Propagate by summer half-hardened cuttings, winter hardwood cuttings, or by seed.

Amorpha canescens
syn. *Amorpha brachycarpa*
LEADPLANT
☀ ❄ ↔ 36 in (90 cm) ↑ 36 in (90 cm)
From central Canada and USA. Small, dense, fine-textured, deciduous shrub. Leaves gray-green, twigs hairy. Purple-blue flowers are carried on cylindrical panicles in summer. Zones 2–9.

Amorpha fruticosa
BASTARD INDIGO, FALSE INDIGO
☀ ❄ ↔ 10 ft (3 m) ↑ 12 ft (3.5 m)
From prairies and river valleys of North America. Shrub with pinnate leaves, bright mid-green leaflets. Panicles of small, deep reddish purple, tubular flowers with conspicuous protruding stamens, in spring–summer. Cultivars include the weeping to prostrate 'Pendula'. Zones 4–9.

AMORPHOPHALLUS

This fascinating genus of the arum (Araceae) family of some 170 species occurs in tropical regions from West Africa eastwards to Polynesia. Most species are found in disturbed vegetation, in open savannahs, and limestone outcrops, very few in dense forests. Altitude ranges from sea level to 9,840 ft (3,000 m), and they flower with the onset of the wet season. All are terrestrial herbaceous perennials with underground tubers or fleshy stems. Plants may be small to massive, with a single leaf, rarely 2, produced from the stem and usually lasting only one season. The leaf stalk is generally cylindrical, ranging from green to purple, or blotchy. Inflorescences vary in shape, size, and color, but are composed of a spadix encircled by a spathe. Being pollinated by various bees or flies, the inflorescences emit odors that can be pleasant or disgusting to the human nose.
CULTIVATION: Propagate from seed or by division of fleshy stems or branching tubers. Some succeed in temperate climates but most require warmth and regulated wet and dry periods to flower. Too much moisture in the leafless stage can cause rotting.

Amorphophallus bulbifer ★
☀ ❀ ↔ 5 ft (1.5 m) ↑ 3 ft (0.9 m)
Occurs in India, Bangladesh, Bhutan, and Nepal. Has a tuber to 6 in (15 cm) in diameter, producing 1 to 2 leaves, leaf stalk smooth, fleshy, dark green, mottled with whitish pink spots. Inflorescence stalk 4–27 in (10–70 cm) long, spathe oval to boat-shaped, 12 in (30 cm) long, outside grayish green with blackish green spots, inside at base dark pink, paler towards the top. Spadix about the same length as spathe. Zone 12.

Amorphophallus konjac
syns *Amorphophallus rivieri, Hydrosme rivieri*
DEVIL'S TONGUE, SNAKE PALM, UMBRELLA ARUM
☀ ❂ ↔ 7 ft (2 m) ↑ 36–50 in (90–130 cm)
Produces a tuber to 12 in (30 cm) in diameter. Leaf to 3 ft (0.9 m) tall, dirty whitish pink, with dark green and whitish spots, dull green on uppersurface. Inflorescence long-stalked. Spathe broadly triangular, to 24 in (60 cm) long, whitish purple to blackish purple with blackish green spots. Spadix 6–44 in (15–110 cm) long. Occurs in southern and southeastern China and Vietnam in forest margins and open areas, to 9,840 ft (3,000 m) altitude. Zones 10–12.

Amorphophallus lambii
☀ ❀ ↔ 18 in (45 cm) ↑ 36 in (90 cm)
From Borneo's Sabah and Kalimantan; inflorescence short-stalked, spathe fleshy, green on outside, pale reddish to purplish markings inside; spadix with sterile portion large, tapering, cream aging purplish-gray. Zones 11–12.

Amorphophallus titanum
syn. *Amorphophallus selebicus*
TITAN ARUM
☀ ❂ ↔ 25 ft (8 m) ↑ 17–20 ft (5–6 m)
A huge species, tuber weighing up to 165 lb (75 kg), to 26 in (65 cm) in diameter, occurring in secondary forests in open situations, on hillsides and other aspects, up to 3,940 ft (1,200 m) altitude, on Sumatra. Leaf stalk up to 17 ft (5 m) tall, leaf blade up to 25 ft (8 m) across, divided, glossy green, leathery. Inflorescence short-stalked. Spathe vase-shaped to 6 ft (1.8 m) long, margin serrated and pleated, pale green outside, purplish brown inside. Spadix 3–10 ft (0.9–3 m) long. Berries large, 2 in (5 cm) in diameter. Zones 10–12.

Amorphophallus titanum

Amorphophallus bulbifer

Amorphophallus lambii, in the wild, Sabah, Borneo

A

AMPELOPSIS

A genus of 25 species of deciduous shrubs and tendril-bearing vines of the grape (Vitaceae) family. Native to North America and temperate Asia. Main features are the attractive grape-like fruit and colorful autumn foliage. Leaves are usually large, often toothed, and may be simple or deeply lobed. Sprays of tiny yellow-green flowers open in spring, followed by berries, often dark blue when ripe. CULTIVATION: Prefer humid climate, cool winters, no clear dry period. Plant in deep, humus-rich, well-drained soil. Water well when growing. Can be invasive, so trim often. Propagate from half-hardened summer cuttings, winter hardwood cuttings, or layers.

Ampelopsis glandulosa

☼/◐ ❄ ↔ 17 ft (5 m) or more
↕ 17 ft (5 m) or more

Strong-growing climber from Japan, Korea, and nearby China. Stems hairy

Anacardium occidentale

when young. Leaves 3- to 5-lobed, toothed, to 6 in (15 cm) long. Foliage reddens in autumn. Clusters of ¼ in (6 mm) wide purple to blue fruit. In gardens mainly as *A. g.* var. *brevipedunculata* (syn. *A. brevipedunculata*). 'Elegans' (syn. 'Tricolor'), deeply lobed leaves mottled with white, pink patches in autumn; rather frost tender and easily sun- or wind-burnt. Seldom fruits. Zones 4–10.

AMSONIA

BLUE STAR

Found from southern Europe, through temperate Asia including Japan, and in North America, this genus of the dogbane (Apocynaceae) family has some 20 species of perennials and subshrubs characterized by milky sap and simple narrow leaves. Flowers, though small, are an unusual shade of blue and mass in heads above the foliage. While not spectacular, most species are distinctive, adding something different to the perennial border. CULTIVATION: Prefer a climate with distinct seasons. Most are easily cultivated in a quite sunny position with well-drained soil kept moist in growing season. Propagate perennials by division during dormancy or as growth starts. Those with firmer stems will also grow from summer cuttings.

Amsonia ciliata

☼/◐ ❄ ↔ 30–48 in (75–120 cm)
↕ 12–36 in (30–90 cm)

From southeast USA. Clumps of upright stems, downy when young. Leaves narrow, lance-shaped, 1–2 in (25–50 mm) long. Heads of mid-blue flowers through summer. Zones 7–10.

Ampelopsis glandulosa var. *brevipedunculata* 'Elegans'

Amsonia tabernaemontana

BLUE DOGBANE; BLUE STAR

☼/◐ ❄ ↔ 36–48 in (90–120 cm)
↕ 36 in (90 cm)

Clump-forming perennial of eastern USA. Upright green stems, simple lance-shaped leaves to 3 in (8 cm) long. Heads of pale blue flowers in mid-spring–late summer. Zones 4–9.

ANACARDIUM

A tropical American genus of the cashew (Anarcardiaceae) family, made up of 11 species of evergreen or semi-deciduous small to medium trees with simple, smooth-edged, leathery leaves. Flowers are small in large panicles. Fruit, on fleshy (and edible) stems, is small, and curved like the enclosed seed, which is covered by a thin flesh containing a dangerously caustic juice. CULTIVATION: The cashew is successfully grown in a tropical monsoonal climate with a long dry season; it is prone to pests and diseases in wetter tropics. Intolerant of frost, it prefers well-drained, sandy, moderately fertile soils. It is tolerant of fierce sun or coastal salt spray. Propagate

from seed. The best cultivars can be increased by grafting, cuttings, or air-layering.

Anacardium occidentale

ACAJOU, CASHEW

☼ ✈ ↔ 25 ft (8 m) ↕ 40 ft (12 m)

Origin uncertain, though southern India is the largest supplier of the nuts. The stalk—"cashew apple"—is used for a refreshing drink. Zones 11–12.

ANAGALLIS

PIMPERNEL

This primrose (Primulaceae) family genus includes 20 species, over much of the globe, especially temperate zones. Soft-stemmed, low, spreading plants, mostly biennials or perennials, behaving as annuals in cold climates. Leaves small and simple. Small brightly colored flowers, pink, red, or blue. Some may be weeds, but are not invasive. Scarlet pimpernel (*A. arvensis*) is famous for inspiring Baroness Orczy's novel of the French Revolution. CULTIVATION: Grow in a sunny spot with moist well-drained soil. Cultivated species easily maintained by pinching to shape; not invasive. Propagate from seed, base cuttings, or by layers.

Anagallis monellii

BLUE PIMPERNEL

☼/◐ ❄ ↔ 12–20 in (30–50 cm)
↕ 12–20 in (30–50 cm)

Mediterranean native, small shrub. Dark green leaves. Flowers single but abundant, bright blue, red-tinted undersides. 'Pacific Blue' ★, compact, dark blue flowers; 'Phillipii', low grower, bright blue flowers. Zones 7–10.

Anagallis tenella

BOG PIMPERNEL

☼/◐ ❄ ↔ 8–16 in (20–40 cm)
↕ 2–4 in (5–10 cm)

Low spreading perennial native to western Europe. Paired elliptical leaves on soft stems that strike root as they spread. Flowers small, pink, rarely white. 'Studland', fragrant, pink flowers. Zones 7–10.

Anagallis tenella 'Studland'

A

ANANAS
PINEAPPLE

The pineapple was the first bromeliad known to the Europeans and goes back to Christopher Columbus. Currently there are 7 species in this genus of the pineapple (Bromeliaceae) family, but research by the pineapple industry has shown that there is very little difference between them. In nature they are prickly plants with many seeds in the fruit. Indigenous populations in Central America and northern South America selected the better plants over hundreds of years, resulting in the seedless fruit we enjoy today. Even the leaves are without teeth on the edges in some cultivars. Known as *Ananas* in its native region for thousands of years, how it came to be called "pineapple" is not recorded. CULTIVATION: Good for greenhouse or conservatory in cool-temperate areas, or outdoors in warm-temperate, subtropical and tropical areas. Water before potting mix is totally dry. If good quality potting mix is to be used, extra fertilizer is not necessary. Propagation mainly by basal offset.

Ananas bracteatus
☀ ❄ ↔ 3 ft (0.9 m) ↑ 3 ft (0.9 m)
The variegated form of this species is hardier than the variegated form of *A. comosus* and may be more common in tropical and sub-tropical gardens around the world. The basic difference is that it is spinier in all respects, including the fruit! 'Tricolor', leaves have yellowish markings and are edged with red spines. Zones 9–10.

Ananas comosus
PINEAPPLE
☀ ❄ ↔ 30 in (75 cm) ↑ 30 in (75 cm)
Variable in size but grows to 30 in (75 cm) high. Leaves narrow, triangular, gray-green, to 30 in (75 cm) long, with strong teeth on the edges (some forms are spineless), forming an open rosette. Flower stem short and stout. Flowerhead globular to cylindrical with many small flowers. Petals blue-

Anaphalis triplinervis 'Sommerschnee'

Ananas comosus

lavender. Cultivars include: 'Abacaxi', 'Queen', 'Red Spanish', and 'Smooth Cayenne'. Zones 9–10.

Ananas nanus
☀ ❄ ↔ 12 in (30 cm) ↑ 20 in (50 cm)
Leaves spiny, to 20 in (50 cm) long, thin, forming open rosette. Flower stems to 20 in (50 cm) high. Petals mauve-lavender. Fruit 2 in (5 cm) long, on long stem. Zones 9–10.

ANAPHALIS
PEARLY EVERLASTING

This daisy (Asteraceae) family genus consists of around 100 species of perennials that may be upright, low and bushy, or trailing. Though found across northern temperate zones and on tropical mountains, a feature common to all is that the foliage and stems are covered with a fine white to gray hair. Leaves are simple, linear to lance-shaped, attached to stems without stalks. Flowerheads form dense downy heads, and while they lack ray florets, papery white bracts create a similar effect. Cut flowers last well but are not that attractive, the plants being grown as much for their foliage. CULTIVATION: Mostly very hardy. Plant in full sun with gritty well-drained soil kept moist in summer. Dry winter conditions are preferable. Cut back hard in spring to encourage strong new growth. Propagate from seed, base cuttings, or by division.

Anaphalis margaritacea
PEARLY EVERLASTING
☀ ❄ ↔ 16–24 in (40–60 cm)
↑ 32–40 in (80–100 cm)
Widespread in northern temperate areas. Leaves gray-green above with white hair below. In summer, flowers are clustered in corymbs up to 6 in (15 cm) wide with opalescent bracts. Zones 3–9.

Ananas bracteatus 'Tricolor'

Ananas nanus

Anaphalis triplinervis
☀ ❄ ↔ 16–20 in (40–50 cm)
↑ 32–36 in (80–90 cm)
This is a central Asian species, found from Afghanistan to southwest China, which has spatula-shaped gray-green leaves that grow to 4 in (10 cm) long.

It has dome-shaped heads of white flowers in summer. Valuable in a herb or mixed border, forming clumps quickly. One cultivar, 'Sommerschnee', grows up to 30 in (75 cm) in length and has bright silvery white flowers. Zones 5–9.

Androlepis skinneri

Andromeda polifolia

Andromeda polifolia 'Compacta'

ANCHUSA

ALKANET, BUGLOSS

Classified in the borage or forget-me-not (Boraginaceae) family, this genus includes some 35 species of biennials and perennials from Europe, western Asia, and Africa. They are strong growers, usually clump-forming, with upright stems and simple, pointed, elliptical leaves that can be quite large at the base of the clump. Heads of small 5-petalled flowers in shades from pale blue to purple open through late spring and summer. Some species were once used in herbal medicines but are now largely out of favour. Likewise, the red dye that can be extracted, formerly used as a hair coloring, is now seldom seen.
CULTIVATION: Species thrive in most conditions except very poor soil, deep shade, or drought. Ample feeding and mulching in winter and water in the growing season promotes flowering. Perennials may be divided in winter or very early spring; annuals or biennials must be raised from seed, preferably sown in autumn so young plants can start growth early in spring.

Anchusa azurea

syn. *Anchusa italica*

☼/◐ ❄ ↔ 32 in (80 cm) ↑ 4 ft (1.2 m)
Perennial native to the Mediterranean region and western Asia. Bristly red-tinted stems with lower leaves to 12 in (30 cm) long. Flowers blue to purple, ½ in (12 mm) wide. Cultivars include: 'Dropmore', tall, deep purple-blue flowers; 'Loddon Royalist' ★, compact and bushy, large deep blue flowers; and 'Opal', compact, grayish foliage, light blue flowers. Zones 3–9.

Anchusa caespitosa

☼ ❄ ↔ 8 in (20 cm) ↑ 4 in (10 cm)
Dwarf, tufting, hairy perennial from Crete. Usually a rockery plant. Very narrow 2 in (5 cm) long leaves and bright, deep blue flowers. Zones 5–10.

Anchusa capensis

☼ ⚘ ↔ 16 in (40 cm) ↑ 20 in (50 cm)
Hairy biennial from South Africa with narrow lance-shaped leaves to 5 in (12 cm) long. White-centered bright blue flowers through summer. Treated as a spring-sown annual where summers are long. Zones 9–11.

ANDROLEPIS

From Central America, this unusual genus of the pineapple (Bromeliaceae) family has only one species. The anthers have odd appendages in the male plant. It is impossible to tell the sex of the plant unless in flower, but unless you want to set seed the sex is unimportant because the flowerhead is just as spectacular. The tall, almost white, cylindrical flowerhead stands out in a garden setting. This plant features in tropical gardens or places where extra warmth can be given.
CULTIVATION: Recommended for the large greenhouse or conservatory in cool-temperate areas, or outdoors if given protection from direct continuous sunlight and extremes of rain in warm-temperate, subtropical, and tropical areas. Propagation is by seed or offset.

Androlepis skinneri

☼ ⚘ ↔ 40 in (100 cm) ↑ 5 ft (1.5 m)
Flowering to about 5 ft (1.5 m) high, leaves to 3 ft (0.9 m) long, forming an open rosette, green but often a pale reddish color. Flowerhead is whitish cream, to 3 ft (0.9 m) long, with very short side spikes and many white flowers very close together. Zones 9–10.

ANDROMEDA

Two fully hardy, low-growing, evergreen species make up this genus of the heath or erica (Ericaceae) family, found growing in the acid peat bogs of the Northern Hemisphere. The somewhat leathery, smooth-edged, small oblong leaves form a deep green background to the white or tiny, pink, bell-like flowers held in terminal clusters during spring.
CULTIVATION: *Andromeda* species require an acid soil where constant moisture is assured, and are best grown in peat beds, shady woodlands, or rock gardens. They can be propagated by suckers, layering, or from softwood cuttings.

Andromeda glaucophylla

BOG ROSEMARY

☼/◐ ❄ ↔ 30 in (75 cm)
↑ 4–18 in (10–45 cm)

Low, wiry shrub from the Arctic region and Canada. Narrow oblong leaves, densely covered in spring or early summer with white or pink, tightly closed bell-shaped flowers. Zones 2–9.

Andromeda polifolia

BOG ROSEMARY, MARSH ANDROMEDA

◐ ❄ ↔ 22 in (55 cm)
↑ 4–18 in (10–45 cm)

A variable growing shrub, either erect or prostrate, it has small, pointed, oblong leaves with clusters of bell-like flowers in spring or early summer. Cultivars include: 'Alba', a low-growing prostrate shrub with pure white flowers; 'Compacta', compact growth habit, pink flowers; and 'Macrophylla', with larger leaves and pink flowers. Zones 2–9.

Anchusa azurea

Anchusa azurea 'Loddon Royalist'

Androsace bulleyana

ANDROSACE

ROCK JASMINE

This genus of 100 species of annual, biennial, and perennial herbs belongs to the primrose (Primulaceae) family. They are alpine plants from northern temperate regions, growing in scree at high altitudes and in turf at lower altitudes. The dainty flowers, usually less than ½ in (12 mm) across, have short tubular bases flaring to flat open-faced petals. They are white, pink, or red with a central eye, yellow or orange. CULTIVATION: These plants need perfect drainage, good air circulation, and careful watering. Grow in a cool greenhouse or outdoors in troughs in a low-fertility gritty mix. Prevent collar rot with a gritty mulch on the soil surface and water from beneath. Cover outdoor troughs with glass in winter to protect from rain. Propagate from seed (germination may take 2 years), or cuttings or runners of some species.

Androsace bulleyana

☀ ❀ ↔ 12 in (30 cm) ↑ 4–8 in (10–20 cm)
From the Himalayas and northwestern China. Biennial with rosettes of small spoon-shaped leaves. Small flowerheads of red, yellow-eyed flowers in summer. Zones 6–9.

Androsace carnea

☀ ❀ ↔ 8 in (20 cm) ↑ 3 in (8 cm)
From western Europe. Tufted perennial with dark green, sometimes fleshy leaves. Flowers white or pale pink with a yellow eye, in early summer. *A. c.* subsp. *laggeri* is smaller, more compact, with pink flowers. Zones 5–9.

Androsace geraniifolia

☀ ❀ ↔ 8 in (20 cm) ↑ 3 in (8 cm)
From the Himalayas and western China. Perennial species, spreading by runners, lobed heart-shaped leaves to 2 in (5 cm) long. Pink to white flowers are carried in heads of 6 or more, in late spring. Zones 6–9.

Androsace lanuginosa ★

☀ ❀ ↔ 12–18 in (30–45 cm) ↑ 3 in (8 cm)
From the Himalayas. Prostrate perennial forming a mat of foliage covered in silvery hairs. Small dense heads of pale pink, darker-eyed flowers in summer–early autumn. 'Leichtlinii' has deeper pink flowers. Zones 6–9.

Androsace muscoidea

☀ ❀ ↔ 8 in (20 cm) ↑ 2 in (5 cm)
From the Himalayas. Compact perennial with rosettes of small, silvery green, hairy leaves. The white flowers are borne in spring and early summer. Zones 5–9.

Androsace rotundifolia

☀ ❀ ↔ 8 in (20 cm) ↑ 4–6 in (10–15 cm)
From northern India. Hairy perennial forming rosettes of small, round, lobed leaves. Pale pink flowers, densely packed, are borne in spring–early summer. Zones 4–9.

Androsace sarmentosa

☀ ❀ ↔ 24 in (60 cm) ↑ 4 in (10 cm)
From the Himalayas. Perennial species spread by runners, forming rosettes of narrow leaves, silver-haired at first. Packed flowerheads of deep pink flowers are borne in spring. Zones 4–9.

Androsace sempervivoides

☀ ❀ ↔ 12 in (30 cm) ↑ 2 in (5 cm)
Perennial species from Kashmir and Tibet. Spreads by runners. Tiny bright green leaves form small rosettes. The bright mid-pink flowers have a yellow eye and are borne in spring. Zones 5–9.

Androsace villosa

☀ ❀ ↔ 10 in (25 cm) ↑ 2–3 in (5–8 cm)
A species from Europe and Asia. This mat-forming perennial has small rosettes of hairy grayish green leaves. Its fragrant, white to pale pink flowers, which are yellow-eyed, are ½ in (12 mm) across and are borne on small umbels, in late spring–summer. Zones 4–9.

ANEMIA

This genus is a member of the comb-fern (Schizaeaceae) family and contains over 100 species, occurring in tropical and warm-temperate regions of the Americas (most species), Africa, Madagascar, and India (one species). Its fronds are erect, arising from a creeping, hairy, fleshy stem. Frond blades are pinnate or pinnately compound, with the 2 lower segments only being fertile. Spore-bearing organs are borne in a single row on both sides of the leaflets.
CULTIVATION: Propagate species of this genus from spores or by division.

Anemia mexicana

syn. *Ornithopteris mexicana*

◐ ❧ ↔ 24 in (60 cm) ↑ to 20 in (50 cm)
Wiry, creeping, fleshy stem, 2–3 mm in diameter, covered with coarse blackish hairs, fronds scattered along it, stalks to 12 in (30 cm) long, blades to 10 in (25 cm) long × 6 in (15 cm) wide, lower pair of segments fertile, elongated, sterile segments in 4 to 6 pairs. Occurs on limestone cliffs, in canyons, and other limestone regions of Texas, USA, and northern Mexico. Spores in winter–spring. Zones 9–11.

Anemia mexicana

Androsace muscoidea

Androsace rotundifolia

Androsace geraniifolia

ANEMONE

WINDFLOWER

Widespread in temperate regions of both hemispheres, this buttercup (Ranunculaceae) family genus encompasses some 120 species of perennials. Their roots may be tuberous, fleshy-stemmed or fibrous, and develop into

Anemone coronaria

Anemone coronaria, Mona Lisa Series, cv

clumps of finely divided foliage. Bowl-shaped flowers, single or in small clusters, sit on wiry stems well above the foliage. Most species flower in spring shortly after the foliage appears, but some continue into early summer and a few bloom in autumn. The name is derived most likely from the Greek *anemos* (wind), though some say it comes from Naamen, a variation on Adonis. Legend says it was his blood that gave *A. coronaria* its red flowers.
CULTIVATION: The wood anemones prefer woodland conditions with dappled shade, but most species thrive in a sunny border with moist well-drained soil. Propagation is by division in winter when dormant, or from seed in the case of strains grown as annuals.

Anemone blanda

�/☀ ❄ ↔ 6–12 in (15–30 cm)
↑ 4–8 in (10–20 cm)

Found from southeastern Europe to the Caucasus region. Strong fleshy

Anemone hupehensis var. *japonica*

stems and ferny base leaves. From late winter, 1–1¾ in (25–40 mm) wide white, blue, mauve, or pink flowers. 'Atrocaerulea' (syn. 'Ingramii'), deep blue flowers; 'Radar', white-centered deep magenta-pink flowers; 'White Splendour', tall grower, large white flowers, pink-tinted inside. Zones 5–9.

Anemone canadensis

☼/☀ ❄ ↔ 12–16 in (30–40 cm)
↑ 12–16 in (30–40 cm)

Summer-flowering North American species with woody rootstock. Finely cut pinnate foliage and simple, often green-tinted, creamy white flowers to 1 in (25 mm) wide. Zones 3–9.

Anemone coronaria

FLORIST'S ANEMONE, WIND POPPY, WINDFLOWER

☼/☀ ❄ ↔ 8–16 in (20–40 cm)
↑ 16–24 in (40–60 cm)

Tuberous-rooted native of southeastern Europe and northern Mediterranean. Finely divided ferny base foliage and simple leaves on flower stems. Large spring flowers in most shades except yellow. Parent of many cultivars and a large range of garden hybrids, such as the **Mona Lisa Series**, which grow to 24 in (60 cm) tall with flowers to 4 in (10 cm) wide in all colors. Zones 8–10.

Anemone flaccida

☼/☀ ❄ ↔ 8–16 in (20–40 cm)
↑ 4–8 in (10–20 cm)

Clump-forming, fleshy-stemmed, temperate East Asian species with

Anemone blanda

Anemone blanda 'Radar'

light green ferny foliage. In spring to early summer, 1 in (25 mm) wide cream flowers, sometimes pink-tinted, are seen. Zones 6–9.

Anemone × fulgens

☼/☀ ❄ ↔ 8–16 in (20–40 cm)
↑ 12 in (30 cm)

From Mediterranean France. Clump-forming, tuberous-rooted, natural hybrid of *A. pavonina* and *A. hortensis*. Base clump of finely cut, bright green, ferny foliage and long-stemmed spring flowers, often red but also in a range of forms and colors. Zones 8–10.

Anemone hupehensis

☼/☀ ❄ ↔ 16–40 in (40–100 cm)
↑ 20–36 in (50–90 cm)

Fibrous-rooted, late summer- to autumn-flowering species from China and Japan. Coarsely toothed, lightly downy, 3-part foliage. Upright branching flower stems with large flowers, usually white but often in pink shades. Fluffy seedheads follow. *A. h.* var. *japonica* has stocky flower stems and many-petalled flowers. **'Prinz Heinrich'** is an *A. h.* var. *japonica* cultivar around 32 in (80 cm) tall, forming large clumps with deep pink flowers. *A. h.* 'Hadspen Abundance' is a popular cultivar, to 24 in (60 cm) tall, flowers with alternating light and dark pink petals. Zones 6–9.

Anemone × hybrida

☼/☀ ❄ ↔ 20–48 in (50–120 cm)
↑ 32–60 in (80–150 cm)

Garden hybrids of uncertain origin but certainly with *A. vitifolia* and

Anemone blanda 'White Splendour'

A

A. hupehensis var. *japonica* in their background. Similar to *A. hupehensis* but capable of growing to 5 ft (1.5 m) tall and with infertile flowers. **'Géantes des Blanches'**, 4 ft (1.2 m) tall, large, white, semi-double flowers; **'Honorine Jobert'** ★, 4 ft (1.2 m) tall, large, white, single flowers with pale pink reverse; and **'Margarete'**, 3 ft (0.9 m) tall, pale pink double flowers. **'September Charm'** (syn. *A. hupehensis* 'September Charm'), 30 in (75 cm) high, has tall, pale pink flowers, often drooping. Zones 6–9.

Anemone multifida

☀ ❄ ↔ 8–16 in (20–40 cm)
↑ 6–24 in (15–60 cm)

North American species with woody rootstock and 3- to 5-part downy leaves divided into narrow lobes. Flowers white, cream, or red, up to ¾ in (18 mm) wide, throughout the warmer months. Formerly misidentified as *A. magellanica*. Zones 3–9.

Anemone narcissiflora

☀/☀ ❄ ↔ 8–16 in (20–40 cm)
↑ 12–16 in (30–40 cm)

Found across the temperate Northern Hemisphere. Finely divided, downy, 5-part base leaves and simpler foliage on flower stems. Flowers are around 1 in (25 mm) wide in heads of up to 8, usually white but variably colored. Zones 3–9.

Anemone nemorosa

WINDFLOWER, WOOD ANEMONE

☀/◑ ❄ ↔ 6–16 in (15–40 cm)
↑ 4–12 in (10–30 cm)

This is a fleshy-stemmed, spring-flowering, European native usually found in woodlands. Leaflets are in threes, coarsely toothed, and/or finely divided. Flowers are around 1 in (25 mm) wide, usually white in the wild but garden forms come in a range of mauve and pink shades. **'Allenii'**, 8 in (20 cm) tall, nodding dusky blue flowers with purplish reverse; **'Pallida'**, 6 in (15 cm) tall, pale creamy yellow flowers and dark foliage; **'Robinsoniana'**, 8 in (20 cm)

Anemone nemorosa 'Robinsoniana'

Anemone pavonina

tall, lavendar flowers with pale reverse; **'Vestal'**, 6 in (15 cm) tall, with small, white, double flowers. Zones 5–9.

Anemone pavonina

ANEMONE OF GREECE

☀/☀ ❄ ↔ 12–16 in (30–40 cm)
↑ 12 in (30 cm)

Clump-forming tuberous species native to the Mediterranean region. Three-part base foliage deeply divided and ferny, bright green. In spring, 2–4 in (5–10 cm) wide flowers in a range of colors. Allow to dry off after flowering. Parent of several cultivars and hybrids. Zones 8–10.

Anemone ranunculoides

BUTTERCUP ANEMONE

◑/☀ ❄ ↔ 6–12 in (15–30 cm)
↑ 6 in (15 cm)

Fleshy-stemmed European woodland species that flowers in late winter to early spring. Its leaves are trifoliate, deeply cut and divided, often deep green. Flowers are bright yellow and not more than ¾ in (18 mm) wide. Zones 4–9.

Anemone rivularis

☀ ❄ ↔ 12–20 in (30–50 cm)
↑ 27–36 in (70–90 cm)

Fibrous-rooted Himalayan species that forms clumps of short-stemmed, trifoliate, toothed base leaves up to 6 in (15 cm) wide. In late spring–summer, it bears heads of white flowers on long stems. Petals are blue-tinted on the reverse side. Likes damp soil. Zones 7–9.

Anemone nemorosa 'Vestal'

Anemone sylvestris

Anemone multifida

Anemone trullifolia

Anemone sylvestris

SNOWDROP ANEMONE, SNOWDROP WINDFLOWER

☀ ❄ ↔ 6–20 in (15–50 cm)
↑ 6–12 in (15–30 cm)

A spreading fleshy-stemmed European species that is found to occur in a range of conditions from lowland woods to subalpine regions. The species has deeply divided, deep green, hand-shaped leaves and, appearing from late spring, scented white flowers that are up to 3 in (8 cm) wide, often slightly drooping. These are followed by fluffy seed-heads. Cultivars include: **'Elise Fellman'** (syn. 'Flore Pleno'), a compact plant with double flowers; and **'Grandiflora'**, which has large pendulous flowers. Zones 4–9.

Anemone tomentosa

GRAPELEAF ANEMONE

☀ ❄ ↔ 20–32 in (50–80 cm)
↑ 3 ft (0.9 m)

This woody-rooted Chinese species is similar to *A. hupehensis*. It has large leaves, usually trifoliate but sometimes

entire, with coarsely toothed edges and downy undersides. Flowers, which appear in early summer, are white or pale pink and mildly scented. They are borne singly or in pairs. Zones 3–9.

Anemone trullifolia

☀ ❄ ↔ 12–16 in (30–40 cm)
↑ 12 in (30 cm)

A woody-rooted species from the Himalayas. It features rounded toothed base leaves, as well as upper leaves that often have shallow lobes. Small heads of graceful soft mauve-blue or white flowers are seen in summer. Zones 5–9.

Anemone virginiana

☀/☀ ❄ ↔ 12–20 in (30–50 cm)
↑ 12–24 in (30–60 cm)

This woody-rooted species comes from central and eastern USA. Base leaves with 3 to 5 parts, deeply divided, and ferny. From late spring, sprays of 1 in (25 mm) wide green-tinted white flowers appear on branching stems. Zones 4–9.

Anemonella thalictroides

Anemonella thalictroides 'Betty Blake'

Anemonella thalictroides 'Oscar Schoaff'

ANEMONELLA

Native to eastern North America, the single species in this genus, of the buttercup (Ranunculaceae) family, is a perennial herb with smooth tuberous roots. In spring, 2 to 5 flowers appear on thin stalks, with 5 to 10 sepals and numerous spreading, petal-like, white stamens but no corolla.
CULTIVATION: Heat tolerant but hardy to cold temperatures, preferring shade. Soil should be humus-rich and moist. Plant from containers in early spring, and water until established. Requires little maintenance thereafter and can be cut to ground level in winter. Propagate from seed when fresh or by division every 3 to 5 years in autumn.

Anemonella thalictroides

CROWFOOT, RUE ANENOME
☀ ❄ ↔ 3–6 in (8–15 cm)
↑ 4–10 in (10–25 cm)

This tuberous-rooted perennial comes from eastern North America. It has delicate 3-lobed leaflets and single white to pale pink flowers. Cultivars include: 'Betty Blake', with cream flowers; 'Oscar Schoaff' (syns 'Rosea

Plena', 'Schoaff's Double Pink') with pale pink flowers; and 'Rosea', also with pale pink flowers. Zones 4–8.

ANEMONOPSIS

This genus of a single species in the buttercup (Ranunculaceae) family comes from Japan. A plant for collectors of rarities who can supply its cool, moist, woodland needs, or has a shadehouse in which to grow it.
CULTIVATION: Needs a cool moist spot sheltered from wind. Propagation is usually from fresh seed, although division can be attempted with care.

Anemonopsis macrophylla

☀ ❄ ↔ 20–24 in (50–60 cm)
↑ 24–32 in (60–80 cm)

Herbaceous perennial. Large, soft, compound leaves topped by sprays of soft mauve nodding flowers to 1½ in (35 mm) across with purple center and almost black stems. Zones 4–8.

ANEMOPSIS

This genus in the little-known lizard's tail (Saururaceae) family consists of just one species, formerly classified in

Houttuynia. Native to southwestern USA and nearby parts of Mexico, it is a swamp, marsh, or wet meadow plant with strong deep green leaves. The unusual flowerheads create an effect fancied to resemble an anemone flower by the botanist who named the genus.
CULTIVATION: Not widely cultivated but quite hardy, suited to mild temperate climates with warm summers. Plant around pond margins or wet areas along the banks of slow-moving streams. In suitable conditions it is a vigorous grower, potentially invasive. Propagate by division, late winter.

Anemopsis californica

YERBA MANSA
☀/◑ ❄ ↔ 3–10 ft (0.9–3 m)
↑ 20 in (50 cm)

Perennial that quickly spreads to cover a large area. Upright stems in clumps, bearing long-stemmed, deep-green, elliptical to spatula-shaped leaves. In summer, erect flower spikes with heads of small greenish white flowers coming from large white bracts. Zones 8–11.

ANETHUM

DILL
A genus of 2 species of annual or biennial herbs of the carrot (Apiaceae) family. Only *A. graveolens* is commonly cultivated and is used (foliage and seeds) as a garnish or as flavoring. It is similar in appearance to its close relative, fennel. Dill flowers attract many species of butterflies and can be used in wildflower gardens. Dill is used medicinally for indigestion or flatulence, often given to babies with colic.
CULTIVATION: Easily grown in a sunny well-drained position that is not too dry in summer. Though plants can be raised from seed and then transplanted, it may be easier to prepare a patch of soil and cast seed over it, lightly raking it in afterwards.

Anethum graveolens

☀/◑ ❄ ↔ 12–20 in (30–50 cm)
↑ 24–32 in (60–80 cm)

Strongly aromatic southwest Asian annual with long, finely divided, ferny leaves, the individual leaflets being almost hair-like. Summer-borne heads of tiny yellow flowers are followed by the well-known seeds. Zones 8–10.

ANGELICA

A genus of about 50 species belonging to the carrot (Apiaceae) family, occurring over much of the temperate Northern Hemisphere; some biennial, some perennial, including monocarpic species. Most are grown as ornamentals for their bold foliage, but others are cultivated for herbal uses. Large, often pinnate leaves, deeply divided, sometimes glossy, and usually with toothed edges. Foliage grows from a stout rootstock. In summer compound flowerheads (umbels) of tiny white, cream, green, pink, or red flowers appear. Angelica has had many uses: as a vegetable, for making herbal tonics and medicines, and candied.
CULTIVATION: Plant in deep humus-rich soil with ample moisture. Will grow well in full sun but foliage is usually lusher with some shade. True perennial species may be divided but annual and monocarpic species are raised from seed, best very fresh.

Angelica archangelica

Anemopsis californica

Angelica pachycarpa

Angelica razulii

Angelica archangelica

☼/◐ ❋ ↔ 5 ft (1.5 m) ↑ 6 ft (1.8 m)

Monocarpic perennial found from Greenland through Europe to central Asia. Pinnate leaves to 24 in (60 cm) long. Greenish white to cream flowers. Used in herbal medicine. Young stems are often candied. Zones 4–9.

Angelica gigas

☼ ❋ ↔ 7 ft (2 m) ↑ 3–7 ft (0.9–2 m)

Strong-stemmed biennial from Korea, Japan, and northern China. Very large red-tinted leaves. Purple-red stems topped with red flowerheads from late summer. Zones 5–9.

Angelica pachycarpa

◐ ❋ ↔ 4 ft (1.2 m) ↑ 24 in (60 cm)

A near-evergreen perennial that is often confused with *A. angelica* but is very different and purely ornamental. Very glossy pinnate leaves to over 12 in (30 cm) long with toothed leaflets. Small green flowers quickly turn to seed heads that are best removed to encourage lush foliage. Zones 8–10.

Angelica razulii

☼ ❋ ↔ 36 in (90 cm) ↑ 36 in (90 cm)

Perennial from Pyrenees Mountains. Deeply divided glossy leaves. Pink-flushed cream flowers. Zones 7–9.

ANGELONIA

There are about 30 species of sub-shrubs or perennials in this figwort or foxglove (Scrophulariaceae) family genus. Native to central and southern America, they grow in damp open spaces. Leaves are usually small and simple. The short, 5-lobed, tubular flowers are mauve, blue, or white and are produced for much of the year. In cool and temperate climates these plants are usually treated as annuals. CULTIVATION: Grow in a sunny position in a moist but well-drained light soil. Indoors they require bright filtered light in a potting mix with added organic matter and should be kept moist. Propagate from seed or softwood cuttings, or by division.

Angelonia angustifolia

☼ ❀ ↔ 12 in (30 cm) ↑ 18 in (45 cm)

From Mexico and West Indies, this species has small pointed leaves with serrated edges, and racemes of mauve to violet flowers in summer. 'Alba', white flowers; 'Purple', 'Purple and White', and 'Rose Pink' indicate color strains. Zones 9–11.

ANGIOPTERIS

GIANT FERN, KING FERN, MULE'S FOOT FERN, TURNIP FERN

Genus of 2 huge evergreen ferns from the Marattiaceae family, found in the tropical Pacific. They feature a large, erect, woody rhizome with a wide base supported by thick roots. The fronds are deltoid, pinnate, 17–25 ft (5–8 m) long, with spreading leaflets. CULTIVATION: Easily grown in containers, adaptable in cultivation. Allow ample room to spread. They require shade, moisture, and well-drained acidic soil. Easily grown in damp ground in sheltered humid conditions. Propagate from offsets or from ears at base of frond stalks.

Angiopteris evecta

GIANT FERN, KING FERN, MULE'S FOOT FERN, TURNIP FERN

☼ ❀ ↔ 17–35 ft (5–10 m)
↑ 10–20 ft (3–6 m)

Massive fern from tropical to temperate Malaysia, Polynesia, New Guinea,

Angelonia angustifolia 'Rose Pink'

and Australia. Huge, arching, whorled fronds and erect, stout, rounded, fleshy trunk. Zones 10–12.

ANGOPHORA

This eastern Australian genus of the myrtle (Myrtaceae) family is closely allied to *Eucalyptus* and *Corymbia*. Its 15 species of evergreen trees have separate sepals and petals enclosing the buds. Most are medium to large trees of open forest, woodland, and heath. Bark is usually rough, rather corky or flaky, though smooth in some species. Leaves, in opposite pairs, vary from narrow pointed to broad heart-shaped. Flowers have masses of white to cream stamens, in terminal clusters at the branch tips attractive to insects, birds, and even mammals. Flowers are followed by ribbed woody capsules. CULTIVATION: These trees are light-loving and fast growing, preferring sandy moderately fertile soils and shelter from strong winds. Most tolerate a degree or two of overnight frost

as long as days are warm and sunny. Propagate from seed, to be collected just as capsules discharge.

Angophora bakeri

NARROW-LEAFED APPLE, SMALL-LEAFED APPLE

☼ ❀ ↔ 25 ft (8 m) ↑ 50 ft (15 m)

Localized in the coastal plains and low hills near Sydney, Australia. Grows in open forest on poor soils. Rough closely fissured bark. Dull gray-green leaves to 3 in (8 cm) long. White flowers in mid-summer. Zones 9–11.

Angiopteris evecta

Angophora bakeri

A

Angophora costata

syn. *Angophora lanceolata*

ANGOPHORA, RUSTY GUM, SYDNEY RED GUM

☼ ❄ ↔ 80 ft (24 m) ↑ 100 ft (30 m)

Abundant on rocky sandstone ridges in Sydney, Australia. Bark, pinkish gray, sheds in early summer to bright orange-brown. Clusters of white flowers in spring–early summer. Deep wine red new foliage. **Zones 9–11.**

Angophora floribunda

ROUGH-BARKED APPLE

☼ ❄ ↔ 60 ft (18 m) ↑ 60 ft (18 m)

From the east coast of Australia. Like *A. costata*, but differs in its rough, furrowed, grayish bark. Has contorted low-sweeping boughs and massed, late spring, white blossom. **Zones 9–11.**

Angophora hispida

syn. *Angophora cordifolia*

DWARF APPLE

☼ ❄ ↔ 12 ft (3.5 m) ↑ 10 ft (3 m)

Localized to rocky sandstone ridges around Sydney, Australia. Broad,

Angophora floribunda

Angophora hispida

harsh-textured leaves, with flowers in large heads, mid spring–summer. New leafy shoots and flower buds have deep red bristles. In cultivation can grow to 30 ft (9 m). **Zones 10–11.**

ANGRAECUM

COMET ORCHID

A large orchid genus of the orchid (Orchidaceae) family with over 140 species, ranging from warm- to cool-growing, large to miniature plants, and neat clump-forming to rambling species. The monopodials have leathery, channelled, dark green leaves in two rows and short to long inflorescences of large white to cream flowers. In the wild, they often grow on rocks and trees, exposed to drying winds and strong light. Most species have white and green perfumed flowers, with a long nectar-filled spur. The majority are highly fragrant at night, to attract the moths that pollinate them in their native Madagascar and Africa. The famous naturalist Charles

Angraecum didieri

Darwin accurately predicted the pollination of *A. sesquipedale* by a giant hawk moth, found some fifty years after his death.

CULTIVATION: These are epiphytic orchids for the greenhouse or conservatory, as few species will survive temperatures down to frost level. Most species prefer a temperature range of between 10°C and 30°C. The larger growing species need plenty of room to grow, and like to be grown in pots in a well-drained, open, bark-based medium or can be incorporated into gardens in tropical climates.

Angraecum didieri

☼ ❄ ↔ 4–6 in (10–15 cm) ↑ 4–6 in (10–15 cm)

From Madagascar. Often hidden, the pure white, 2½ in (6 cm) wide, summertime blooms are borne on very short single-flowered inflorescences.

Angraecum Veitchii

Thick warty roots are silvery white. Prefers to be kept cooler and slightly drier in winter. **Zones 10–12.**

Angraecum scottianum

☼ ❄ ↔ 3–6 in (8–15 cm) ↑ 3–12 in (8–30 cm)

From Madagascar. Slender plant with thin stems and semi-terete leaves. White flowers, 2 in (5 cm) wide. Seedlings are quick to mature and will take quite shaded and moist conditions. **Zones 10–12.**

Angraecum Veitchii

☼ ❄ ↔ 12–24 in (30–60 cm) ↑ 8–40 in (20–100 cm)

Primary hybrid between *A. sesquipedale* and *A. eburneum*. It is a popular and robust plant, with up to 8 blooms, 4 in (10 cm) wide. **Zones 10–12.**

ANGULOA

TULIP ORCHID

These orchids (family Orchidaceae) come from mountainous regions of Venezuela, Colombia, Ecuador, Peru, and Bolivia, and are closely related to *Lycaste*, with fat pseudobulbs and large, thin, pleated leaves. The waxy, 3–4 in (8–10 cm) wide, tulip-shaped flowers do not open fully and are solitary on erect stalks from the base of the pseudobulb in spring and summer, coinciding with new growth.

CULTIVATION: These plants require a cool to intermediate growing environment. Because their roots must not

Angophora costata, in the wild, in Watagans National Park, New South Wales, Australia

dry out during the growing season, they are best suited to containers. Water well when in active growth.

Anguloa clowesii

☀ ❄ ↔ 12–24 in (30–60 cm)
↕ 16–24 in (40–60 cm)

Native to Colombia and Venezuela. Arguably the most popular species in cultivation. It has bright lemon to golden yellow highly perfumed flowers. Zones 10–11.

Anguloa hohenlohii

☀ ❄ ↔ 12–24 in (30–60 cm)
↕ 16–24 in (40–60 cm)

From Venezuela. Often seen incorrectly labelled in collections as *A. ruckeri*. The blooms are deep bronzered on the inside and pale greenish brown on the outside. Zones 10–12.

Anguloa uniflora

☀ ❄ ↔ 12–24 in (30–60 cm)
↕ 16–24 in (40–60 cm)

From Venezuela, Colombia, Ecuador, Peru, and Bolivia. Somewhat variable in color, with a white to creamy base, finely to coarsely spotted in pink. Some clones appear dark pink. Often confused with the closely related *A. virginalis*. Zones 10–11.

× *Angulocaste* Jupiter × *Anguloa hohenlohii*

× ANGULOCASTE

A hybrid between the sympodial orchid genera *Anguloa* and *Lycaste*, and likewise a member of the orchid (Orchidaceae) family. Species have fat pseudobulbs and large, thin, pleated leaves. The waxy flowers are solitary on erect stalks from the base of the pseudobulb in spring and summer, coinciding with new growth. The color and shape of the blooms can vary considerably, depending on the genetic makeup of the hybrid. CULTIVATION: They are cool- to intermediate-growing epiphytes or semi-terrestrials best grown in pots, as roots must not dry out in the growing season. Heavy feeders when in active growth, they need copious watering.

× Angulocaste Jupiter × Anguloa hohenlohii

☀ ❄ ↔ 24–36 in (60–90 cm)
↕ 16–24 in (40–60 cm)

An unregistered hybrid that shows the heavy *Anguloa* influence with its upward-facing tulip-shaped blooms. Zones 10–11.

× Angulocaste Rosemary

☀ ❄ ↔ 24–36 in (60–90 cm)
↕ 16–24 in (40–60 cm)

Hybrid between *A.* Sanderae and *Lycaste* Balliae. It has a strong *Lycaste skinneri* influence, with *Lycaste macrophylla* and *Anguloa clowesii* also in its ancestry. Zones 10–11.

ANIGOZANTHOS
KANGAROO PAW

This genus contains 11 species of evergreen sword-leafed perennials of the bloodroot (Haemodoraceae) family, all of which are confined naturally to southwestern Australia. The

Anguloa uniflora

foliage is dark green and varies from grassy to iris-like. Heads of intriguingly furry tubular blooms are borne on branching stems 1–6 ft (0.3–1.8 m) tall, usually in warmer months. Flowers are around 1¼ in (30mm) long and occur in green and warm shades of gold, pink, red, and russet brown, depending on the species. The flower stems last well when cut and many new varieties have been developed with the florist trade in mind. CULTIVATION: Plant in a sunny position with perfect drainage. Better if watered well in the growing season but will tolerate drought. Blackened foliage signals ink disease, which can be very damaging, as can slugs and snails. Propagation in gardens is mostly by careful division. Species may be raised from seed.

Anigozanthos flavidus
EVERGREEN KANGAROO PAW,
TALL KANGAROO PAW

☀ ❄ ↔ 3 ft (0.9 m) ↕ 10 ft (3 m)
Summer-flowering perennial with green leaves to 3 ft (0.9 m) long.

Anigozanthos flavidus, in the wild, Walpole, Western Australia

Flowering stems smooth, green, to 10 ft (3 m). Hairy, tubular flowers are green or yellow-green, with red, orange, or pink populations or individuals in a few locations. Its habitat is moist stream banks, edges of wetlands, and roadside drains in wooded and forested regions of southern and southwestern Australia on sandy and gravelly soils. Zones 8–9.

× *Angulocaste* Rosemary

A

Anigozanthos manglesii

Anigozanthos humilis

CAT'S PAW

☼ ✣ ↔ 20–40 in (50–100 cm)
↕ 8–40 in (20–100 cm)

A winter- to spring-flowering, deciduous perennial with leaves 6–8 in (15–20 cm) long, partly or fully hairy, or hairy only on the margins. Flower stems hairy, not branched, with 10 to 20 flowers in yellow, red, orange, or pink. Occurs on the western and southern coastal regions of Western Australia. Zones 9–10.

Anigozanthos manglesii

MANGLES' KANGAROO PAW, RED AND GREEN KANGAROO PAW

☼ ✣ ↔ 36 in (90 cm)
↕ 12–20 in (30–50 cm)

Leaves flat, smooth, gray-green. Flower stems red, woolly, hairy, rarely branched. Flowers green, red at base, in late winter–early summer. Usually a short-lived perennial, this species occurs on well-drained sandy soils in heaths, woodland, and forests, sometimes on limestone, along the western coast of Western Australia. Zones 9–10.

Anigozanthos rufus

RED KANGAROO PAW

☼ ✣ ↔ to 20 in (50 cm)
↕ 20–40 in (50–100 cm)

Leaves green, 8–16 in (20–40 cm) long, smooth, margins rough. Flowering stems branched, densely woolly-hairy, red, flowers similar.

Flowering spring–summer. Occurs in seasonally wet sandy soils along south coast of Western Australia. Zone 9.

Anigozanthos viridis

GREEN KANGAROO PAW

☼ ✣ ↔ 20 in (50 cm) ↕ to 32 in (80 cm)
Leaves almost cylindrical, ¼–20 in (6 mm–50 cm) long, smooth, gray-green. Flower stems to 34 in (85 cm), with red-brown hairs, unbranched. Flowers with green or yellow-green hairs, in spring. Occurs on the Australian west coast. Zones 9–10.

Anigozanthos Hybrid Cultivars

☼/☀ ✣ ↔ 8–30 in (20–75 cm)
↕ 1–6 ft (0.3–1.8 m)

Many of the 12 species of kangaroo paw have been used in deliberate breeding programs since the 1970s, and there are now many attractive cultivars being offered to the gardening public, that are easy to grow, and

Anigozanthus Hybrid Cultivar

in a wide range of climates. The species most commonly used in hybridizing has been *A. flavidus,* a species that occurs in moist conditions along stream banks and in cultivation is tolerant of "wet feet." Cultivars include: 'Autumn Sunrise' ★, orange flowers in late spring–summer; 'Big Red', many red flowers; 'Copper Charm', tall scapes of orange flowers in spring; 'Dwarf Delight', red hairs on yellow-green flowers; 'Hickman's Delight', dark green leaves, dark red flowers; 'Little Jewel', glossy green evergreen leaves, red flowers in spring; 'Mini Red', compact plant, dense clusters of red flowers; 'Patricia', red-brown flowers in spring; 'Pink Joey', pale, purplish pink flowers; 'Red Cross', large deep burgundy-colored flowers with a yellow spot at the base; 'Regal Claw', red to orange flowers over most of the year; 'Ruby Jools', leaves semi-deciduous, flowers red-green; 'Space Age', red flowers; 'Spence's Spectacular', red-brown flowers, deciduous leaves; 'Sue Dixon', flowers red near base merging to yellow-green near lobes; 'Velvet Harmony', very dark, woolly, purplish flowers. The **Bush Gems Series** comes in a wide variety of colors: 'Bush Haze', tall, hairy stems, bright yellow flowers; 'Bush Heritage', green

flowers, densely covered in reddish brown hairs; 'Bush Nugget', golden yellow flowers; 'Bush Ruby', red flowers. Zones 9–11.

ANISACANTHUS

This genus of 8 subshrubs or shrubs from southwestern USA and Mexico is part of the acanthus (Acanthaceae) family. Flowers in spikes or racemes, with short-lived bracts and funnel-shaped corollas in summer and autumn. Leaves are 4-lobed, opposite, and smooth-edged. Fruit is a capsule containing 4 or more carpels, each containing 2 to 10 seeds.
CULTIVATION: Species prefer well-drained soil with limited water and full sun for best flowers. Prune hard in spring every few years to renew growth and encourage flowering. Propagate from seed or cuttings.

Anisacanthus thurberi

CHUPAROSA, DESERT HONEYSUCKLE, MUICLE

☼/☀ ❄ ↔ 4–6 ft (1.2–1.8 m)
↕ 4–6 ft (1.2–1.8 m)

Heat-tolerant deciduous shrub from southwestern USA and Mexico. New stems are erect, becoming sprawling with age. Rust-red to gold tubular flowers over a long period. Zones 7–9.

ANISODONTEA

Belonging to the mallow (Malvaceae) family, this genus of 20 species of shrubs and subshrubs is native to South Africa. They are evergreen with mostly toothed leaves that can be either lobed, palmate, or elliptic. Flowers 5-petalled with shallow cups. Plants are classed as half-hardy. In cool-temperate climates used as summer bedding and in mild coastal areas may be grown as border plants.
CULTIVATION: Seeds should be sown in spring. Half-hardened cuttings

A., HC, Bush Gem Series, 'Bush Nugget'

A., HC, Bush Gem Series, 'Bush Ruby'

A., HC, Bush Gem Series, 'Bush Haze'

Annona muricata

taken in summer but need bottom heat. Do best in loam-based gritty compost. Grown indoors, they need maximum light. Outdoors they need full sun and should be fed in spring. Pot-grown specimens should receive a balanced fertilizer once a month. In winter, watering should be reduced and feeding stopped. New plants can be tip pruned for bushiness, pruning old wood in spring. Pot plants prone to red spider mite and white fly.

Anisodontea 'African Queen'

☀ ❄ ↔ 30 in (75 cm) ↑ 3 ft (0.9 m)
Cultivar reported to have originated from a cross between *A.* × *hypomadara* and *A. scabrosa*. Forms compact shrub with deep green foliage. Pale pink flowers, 1 in (25 mm) in diameter, late spring–early autumn. Zones 9–11.

Anisodontea capensis

syn. *Malvastrum capensis*
☀ ❄ ↔ 30 in (75 cm) ↑ 3 ft (0.9 m)
Erect shrub with hairy stems and ovate to triangular leaves, 1 in (25 mm) long. Flowers pale red to deep red-purple, up to 1 in (25 mm) across, most of the year in warm climates, all summer in cool-temperate. Zones 9–11.

ANNONA

Widespread in the tropics of Africa and America, this genus of the custard-apple (Annonaceae) family includes some 100 species of evergreen or semi-deciduous shrubs and trees. Several are important either commercially or locally, particularly the cherimoya and the custard apple. Most of the common species have aromatic, simple, oblong leaves with pronounced veins. Flowers are unusual, having 6 thick fleshy petals and a central mass of densely packed stamens and pistils. These develop into a fruit with a pulpy center and a sometimes spiny exterior. CULTIVATION: Species need warm subtropical or tropical conditions, and prefer shelter from strong winds. Best in a sunny position with moist, well-drained, humus-rich soil. Flowering and fruiting can occur any time, and

the plants should not dry out too much or fruit quality will suffer. Propagate from seed or by grafting.

Annona, Atemoya Group

ATEMOYA, CUSTARD APPLE
☀ ❄ ↔ 6–9 ft (1.8–2.7 m)
↑ 10–15 ft (3–4.5 m)
Hybrids between *A. cherimola* and *A. squamosa*, these spreading trees have large drooping leaves and many large, trumpet-shaped, yellow flowers. Fruits with few seeds, flesh free from grainy texture. '**African Pride**', dwarf form, yields fruit about 1–1½ lb (454–680 g) twice annually; '**Pink's Mammoth**', large sweet fruit weighing up to 6½ lb (3 kg). Zones 10–12.

Annona cherimola

CHERIMOYA, CUSTARD APPLE
☀ ❄ ↔ 10 ft (3 m) ↑ 20 ft (6 m)
Evergreen tree, native to Peru and Ecuador. Leaves deep green, oval to lance-shaped, velvety beneath. Flowers fragrant, yellowish, purple spotting inside, covered in fine brown hairs. Fruit rounded, with delicious fleshy pulp. '**El Bumpo**', soft-skinned, sweet flesh; '**Honeyhart**', mid-sized, yellow-green; '**McPherson**', mid-sized, dark green; '**Pierce**', mid-sized, smooth-skinned; '**Sabor**', highly flavored; '**Spain**', abundant fruit, delicate pine-apple flavor. Zones 10–12.

Annona muricata

GUANABANA, SOURSOP
☀ ❄ ↔ 10 ft (3 m) ↑ 20 ft (6 m)
Evergreen tree from Central America and the West Indies. Leaves glossy with age. Flowers yellow-green.

Surface of the ovoid dark green fruit has soft curved spines with meltingly smooth white flesh. Zones 10–12.

Annona squamosa

CUSTARD APPLE, SWEETSOP
☀ ❄ ↔ 10 ft (3 m) ↑ 25 ft (8 m)
Evergreen tree, native to tropical America. Scented leaves, narrow, lance-shaped. Yellowish flowers with purple-spotted interiors. Fruit spherical, light green outside, custard-like creamy white pulp inside. Zones 10–12.

ANOPTERUS

A genus with 2 species, from Tasmania and mainland eastern Australia. Both trees grow in high-rainfall mountain and foothill regions. The genus, of the gooseberry (Grossulariaeceae) family, belongs to a group of flowering plant families that includes the saxifrages and hydrangeas. Species have erect branches on which long leathery leaves crowd at the ends. Short spikes of funnel-shaped white flowers terminate the shoots, new leafy shoots emerging from below these. The fruit, a leathery capsule, splits to release winged seeds.

Anisodontea 'African Queen'

CULTIVATION: These species need a mild humid climate. *A. glandulosus* will tolerate moderate frosts while the mainland species is less frost hardy but more heat tolerant. A sheltered, slightly shaded situation and moist but well-drained soil is best. Attractive conservatory plants in cooler climates, worth growing for the foliage alone. Propagate from seed or cuttings; plants from cuttings flower much smaller.

Anopterus glandulosus ★

TASMANIAN LAUREL
☀ ❄ ↔ 10 ft (3 m) ↑ 10 ft (3 m)
Found throughout Tasmania, Australia. Usually a stiff-branched shrub, but can become a tree to 30 ft (9 m) high. Leaves very leathery, bluntly toothed. Pure white 6-petalled flowers on spikes in spring. '**Woodbank Pink**' has pink petals, almost white on the insides. Zones 8–9.

Anisodontea capensis

Anopterus glandulosus 'Woodbank Pink'

A

ANTENNARIA
CAT'S EARS, EVERLASTING, LADIES' TOBACCO, PUSSY-TOES

Found in the northern temperate zone, especially in Asia and North America, this daisy (Asteraceae) family genus includes some 45 species of near-evergreen perennials characterized by a low, spreading habit and densely felted foliage. Flowerheads, on felted stems well above the foliage, are small, lack ray florets (petals), and are held within dry bracts. They are usually white, cream or pink, the foliage and growth habit perhaps being more important than the flowers.
CULTIVATION: Used mainly as small-scale ground covers for rockeries and alpine troughs and to provide a foliage color contrast for showier plants. Grow in a sunny position with well-drained, somewhat gritty soil that can be kept moist in summer. Established plants can be divided or will self-layer, or fresh stocks can be raised from seed.

Anthemis tinctoria

Anthemis tinctoria 'Wargrave Variety'

Antennaria dioica
CATSFOOT

☼ ❄ ↔ 24–36 in (60–90 cm)
↑ 8 in (20 cm)

Widespread in northern temperate zone. Mat-forming with felted, silver-gray, spatula-shaped, 1½ in (35 mm) long leaves. White, cream, pink, or red flowerheads, on sturdy stems, in summer. Zones 5–9.

Antennaria microphylla
LITTLELEAF PUSSYTOES, PINK PUSSYTOES

☼ ❄ ↔ 20 in (50 cm)
↑ 12–16 in (30–40 cm)

From central and western North America. Mat-forming with rosettes of white-haired, rounded, spoon-shaped, ½ in (12 mm) long leaves. Greenish cream to pink flowerheads, up to 15 per stem. Zones 3–9.

Antennaria parvifolia
☼ ❄ ↔ 20 in (50 cm) ↑ 10 in (25 cm)

Mat-forming species from western USA and nearby parts of Canada. Small, near-white, spatula-shaped leaves. White to mid-pink flowerheads from late spring. Zones 3–9.

ANTHEMIS
DOG FENNEL

Although this genus, along with many others in the daisy (Asteraceae) family, has been revised, it still contains around 100 species. These aromatic perennials and small shrubs are found mainly in the Mediterranean region and western Asia. Their leaves are usually very finely divided, sometimes gray-green or silvery, and form a base foliage clump with the yellow or white, rarely mauve, daisy flowers held above it. Most cultivated species are now grown purely as ornamentals, but the flowers of *A. tinctoria* were once used to make dye and some species are being investigated for the medicinal properties of their essential oils and other extracts.
CULTIVATION: Hardy, easily grown in moist, fertile, well-drained soil in full sun. Cut back after flowering for bushiness. May be short-lived but easily propagated from cuttings and seed; some perennials may be divided.

Anthemis marschalliana
☼ ❄ ↔ 12–20 in (30–50 cm)
↑ 12 in (30 cm)

From northeast Turkey and the Caucasus. Ground-covering perennial with silky, ferny, gray-green leaves. In summer it is covered with small lemon yellow daisies. Zones 7–9.

Anthemis punctata
☼ ❄ ↔ 12–20 in (30–50 cm)
↑ 16–24 in (40–60 cm)

Found in Europe, the Mediterranean islands, and North Africa. Woody-based perennial with silky, white, pin-nate leaves to around 4 in (10 cm) long. Abundant white flowers in summer. *A. p.* **subsp.** *cupaniana* ★ from Sicily has silver-gray foliage and is a vigorous grower. Zones 7–9.

Anthemis tinctoria 'Golden Rays'

Anthemis sancti-johannis
☼ ❄ ↔ 24 in (60 cm)
↑ 18–30 in (45–75 cm)

Upright shrubby perennial from Bulgaria. Both the gray-green pinnate leaves and stems carry sparse downy tufts. Flowers golden yellow to orange. Zones 4–9.

Anthemis tinctoria
DYER'S CHAMOMILE, YELLOW CHAMOMILE

☼ ❄ ↔ 20–40 in (50–100 cm)
↑ 24–36 in (60–90 cm)

A shrubby perennial found from Europe to western Asia. Short finely divided leaves, usually light green and faintly hairy, sometimes downy. Masses of small flowers throughout the warmer months. 'E. C. Buxton' (syn. 'Mrs E. C. Buxton'), 18 in (45 cm) tall with soft yellow daises; 'Golden Rays', 24 in (60 cm) tall with bright yellow flowers; 'Sauce Hollandaise', 24 in (60 cm) tall, vigorous and shrubby with masses of yellow-centered cream daises; 'Wargrave Variety' (syn. 'Wargrave'), stems to 3 ft (0.9 m) tall with dark green leaves and lemon yellow flowers. Zones 6–9.

ANTHERICUM

There are over 50 species of perennial herbs in this genus which belongs to Anthericaceae, one of the lily group of families. They are found in southern Europe, Turkey, and Africa growing in dry meadows and open scrub. They have short fleshy stems and fleshy roots and form clumps of narrow grass-like leaves. The flowering stems are tall and slender and bear airy sprays of white starry flowers in late spring and early summer.
CULTIVATION: Grow in full sun in a fertile well-drained soil. Most species prefer alkaline conditions. Do not allow to dry out during the growth period. Propagate from seed or by division.

Antennaria parvifolia

Anthericum liliago
ST BERNARD'S LILY

☼ ❄ ↔ 12 in (30 cm)
↕ 24–36 in (60–90 cm)

Native to alpine meadows of southern Europe. The most commonly grown species. Grass-like leaves to 16 in (40 cm) long. Starry white flowers, 1 in (2.5 cm) wide, borne on slender stems, in late spring. *A. l.* var. *major* has taller flowering stems and somewhat bigger flowers. Zones 7–9.

Anthericum ramosum

☼ ❄ ↔ 12 in (30 cm)
↕ 24–36 in (60–90 cm)

From southern Europe. Grows at lower altitudes than the similar *A. liliago*. Differs mainly in that flowering stems are branched and the individual flowers are smaller. Zones 7–9.

ANTHOCLEISTA

With 14 species of evergreen trees from tropical Africa and islands of the Indian Ocean, this genus belonging to the logania (Loganiaceae) family is remarkable for the huge size of the sapling leaves, up to 8 ft (2.4 m) long and 2 ft (0.6 m) wide in some species. Fast growing, they often do not branch until the stem is 15 ft (4.5 m), during which time it maintains a cabbage-like crown of enormous paddle-shaped leaves. Flowers have a basal tube and 5 recurved petals, borne in much-branched panicles among the leaves. Fruits are many-seeded berries. CULTIVATION: Dramatic landscape subjects, best planted in well spaced groups. They require a frost-free climate but can be grown in a sheltered sunny spot in warm-temperate coastal climates. A deep, well-drained, fertile soil is preferred and plants should be watered freely. In cool climates they make impressive conservatory plants when young. Propagation is from freshly gathered seed.

Anthocleista grandiflora

Anthurium andraeanum

Anthocleista grandiflora
☼ ✶ ↔ 12 ft (3.5 m) ↕ 30 ft (9 m)

This species is widely distributed through tropical Africa. Striking tree, leaves on unbranched saplings to 4 ft (1.2 m) long and 18 in (45 cm) wide, rounded tips, prominent veining. Panicles of creamy white flowers in spring–summer. Being high up, the flowers are not noticeable. Zones 11–12.

ANTHRISCUS

A genus of about 12 species consisting of annuals, biennials, and herbaceous perennials from Europe, North Africa, and Asia, some of which have become weedy in other countries. They have soft feathery foliage and the flat heads of tiny white flowers typical of the carrot (Apiaceae) family. Some species have marginal ornamental value in the wild type garden, but because of their self-sowing tendencies they need to be planted with discretion. CULTIVATION: Any well-drained but moisture-retentive soil in sun or half-sun will suit. Propagation is from fresh seed, usually self-sown.

Anthriscus cerefolium
CHERVIL

☼ ❄ ↔ 10–12 in (25–30 cm)
↕ 20–24 in (50–60 cm)

This annual plant from Europe and western Asia is grown as a food flavouring and tends to bolt in hot dry weather. Sow seed every few weeks to ensure continuous crops and expect it to germinate in 2 to 3 weeks, and be ready to harvest in about 6 weeks. Zones 7–10.

Anthericum liliago

Anthurium andraeanum

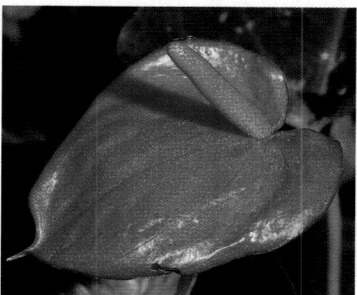

Anthurium andraeanum 'Lady Ruth'

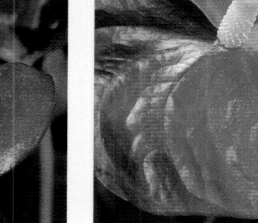

Anthurium andraeanum 'Rhodochlorum'

Anthriscus sylvestris
COW PARSLEY, KECK

☼/◑ ❄ ↔ 16–24 in (40–60 cm)
↕ 24–60 in (60–150 cm)

A wild plant from Europe, North Africa, and Asia. Can be weedy, though attractive with its fine, ferny, rich green foliage and flat heads of tiny white flowers in spring and early summer. 'Ravenswing', purple black foliage; remove any green or poorly colored seedlings. Zones 4–9.

ANTHURIUM

Widely grown as houseplants but also grown outdoors in the tropics, this arum (Araceae) family genus from the tropical Americas encompasses around 900 species of evergreen perennials. The large, elliptical, lance- or arrow-shaped leaves are usually held upright on stiff stems that emerge from a stout rootstock that may also produce aerial roots. The flowerheads consist of a shield-shaped spathe surrounding a protruding spadix. The spathe and spadix tend to be the same colour, often bright red. Anthuriums last well as cut flowers and are an important industry in Hawaii. CULTIVATION: Mainly epiphytes in the wild, they adapt well to container and garden cultivation, thriving in bright humid conditions with moist humus-rich soil. Completely intoler-

Anthurium andraeanum 'Small Talk Pink'

ant of frost, they cope with cool conditions quite well, though prolonged warmth is required for flowering.

Anthurium andraeanum
FLAMINGO FLOWER

◑/☀ ✶ ↔ 12–24 in (30–60 cm)
↕ 20–48 in (50–120 cm)

From Colombia and Ecuador. Dark green arrowhead-shaped leaves up to 20 in (50 cm) long on equally long stalks. Bright, deep red, glossy, heavily veined, heart-shaped spathe with white to cream spadix and red fruit. Cultivars include: 'Lady Ruth', probably of hybrid origin, spathe a brilliant glossy scarlet; 'Rhodochlorum' spathes partly red, partly green; 'Rubrum', very like the species but spathe a lighter brighter red; and 'Small Talk Pink', low grower with large bright pink spathes, pink-tinted cream spadix. Zones 11–12.

A

Antigonon leptopus

Anthyllis vulneraria

Anthurium scandens

☼/☀ ✧ ↔ 3 ft (0.9 m) ↑ 10 ft (3 m)

Climber found from Mexico to Peru,
Guyana, and West Indies. Short-
stemmed leaves to 6 in (15 cm) long.
Small, purple-tinted, green spathes on
2–3 in (5–8 cm) stems. Green spadix
and white fruit, both often mauve-
tinted. Zones 11–12.

Anthurium scherzerianum ★

☼/☀ ✧ ↔ 12–20 in (30–50 cm)
↑ 24–30 in (60–75 cm)

Compact terrestrial species from Costa
Rica. Popular house plant. Narrow
elliptical to lance-shaped leaves to
10 in (25 cm) long on slightly shorter
stems. Stems extend beyond foliage,
often red. Spathes bright red, broad.
Spadix orange to red, twisted. Fruit
red. Zones 11–12.

Anthurium upalaense

☀ ✧ ↔ 3–5 ft (0.9–1.5 m)
↑ 18–30 in (45–75 cm)

Epiphyte from lowland, wet forest
areas of Costa Rica and Nicaragua.
Long narrow leaves to 3 ft (0.9 m) on
shorter stalks. Spathes yellow-green,
often purple-tinted, to 8 in (20 cm)
long on stems to 18 in (45 cm). Red
berries. Zone 12.

Anthurium warocqueanum

QUEEN ANTHURIUM

☼/☀ ✧ ↔ 3–10 ft (0.9–3 m)
↑ 24–60 in (60–150 cm)

From Colombia. Spreading ground
cover sometimes climbing to over 5 ft
(1.5 m) supported by strong roots.
Stunning pendent, elongated, heart-
shaped leaves to 3 ft (0.9 m) long,
dark green with velvety texture and
large pale-green veins. Flowers on
short stems among foliage. Spathe
green and spadix yellow green. Zone 12.

ANTHYLLIS

This genus has about 20 species of
annuals, perennials, and small shrubs
native to the Mediterranean region
and belongs to the pea-flower subfamily of legumes (Fabaceae). Leaves
are palmate or pinnate and flowers
grow in racemes, mainly pink and yellow. They thrive in areas with hot dry
summers and tolerate poor stony soils.
CULTIVATION: Seed needs to be sown
in a sandy medium as soon as the
plant is ripe. Seed can be overwintered
in pots. Half-hardened cuttings
should be taken in summer. Some
species are suitable for rock gardens
and all like free-draining soil. Most
species are hardy and it is often waterlogging combined with frost that kills
the plant, rather than frost alone.

Anthyllis vulneraria

KIDNEY VETCH

☀ ❄ ↔ 24 in (60 cm) ↑ 10 in (25 cm)

Native to Europe, western Asia, and
North Africa. Leaves green, divided
into oblong or elliptical leaflets.
Flowers cream, yellow, orange, red to
purple. Suitable for the rock garden
and wildflower meadow. Zones 7–9.

ANTIDESMA

This mainly tropical genus of the
spurge or euphorbia (Euphorbiaceae)
family includes some 170 species of
trees and shrubs from Africa, Asia,
and Australasia. Its edible berry-like
fruits are arranged in dense spikes at
the branch tips. Simple, smooth-edged
leaves are often deciduous in climates
with a severe dry season. Flowers, of
different sexes on different trees, are
small and greenish and lack petals. The
more or less globular fruits have only
1 or 2 large seeds. Some species are
able to set fruit on the female plant
without a male plant being present.
CULTIVATION: They require a tropical
or subtropical climate with ample rain
in summer. Deep, well-drained, alluvial
soils are preferred, as well as a sheltered spot with adequate sunlight. In
cool climates they can be grown in
heated conservatories. Propagate from
seed, extracted from fully ripe fruit, or
from cuttings or air layers.

Antidesma bunius

BIGNAY, CHINESE LAUREL

☀ ✧ ↔ 15 ft (4.5 m) ↑ 30–40 ft (9–12 m)

Evergreen tree, native to India and
the Malay Peninsula. Glossy, dark
green, elliptical to oblong leaves, to

6 in (15 cm) long. Small yellow-green
flowers. Showy clusters of edible red
fruit. Zones 10–12.

ANTIGONON

A Mexican and Central American
genus comprising 3 species of quick-
growing perennial vines of the
knotweed (Polygonaceae) family.
Evergreen in mild climates if the roots
can be insulated with mulch. Can be
grown in areas with light frosts that
do not freeze the soil to any depth.
Forming a dense canopy, the vines are
smothered throughout the warmer
months in floral racemes that derive
most of their color, usually bright
pink, from the sepals that surround
the tiny flowers. The racemes terminate in a tendril that aids climbing.
Three-angled fruits follow the flowers.
CULTIVATION: Plant in a sunny well-
drained position and water well
during summer. Frequent feeding
encourages strong growth and heavy
flowering. Pinch back to keep compact and remove spent flowers to
prolong blooming. Propagate from
seed or summer base cuttings, or by
division of the tubers in early spring.

Antigonon leptopus

CHAIN OF LOVE, CONFEDERATE VINE,
CORAL VINE, MEXICAN CREEPER

☀ ✧ ↔ 20 ft (6 m) ↑ 15 ft (4.5 m)

Strong-growing tuberous-rooted
Mexican climber that will cover
almost any support. Pointed, heavily
veined, elongated, heart-shaped
leaves around 4 in (10 cm) long,
with strongly frilled margins. Minute
flowers enclosed by coral pink to red
heart-shaped sepals. Zones 10–12.

Anthurium scherzerianum

Anthurium scandens

Anthurium upalaense, in Costa Rica

A. majus, Chimes Series, 'Chimes Pink'

A. majus, Chimes Series, 'Chimes Red'

A. majus, Sonnet Series, 'Sonnet White'

A. majus, Sonnet Series, 'Sonnet Pink'

ANTIRRHINUM

SNAPDRAGON

Found in temperate Northern Hemisphere areas, this genus of around 40 species of annuals, perennials, and subshrubs belongs to the figwort or foxglove (Scrophulariaceae) family. The best known are the garden annuals, beloved of children for the way the mouth of the flower opens and closes with squeezing, hence the common name. Most species are compact, forming a low mound of simple rounded to lance-shaped leaves, sometimes with a gray-green tint. Flowering stems develop from late spring and carry heads of the familiar lobed blooms. Snapdragon seed is rich in oil, which in former times was extracted and used like olive oil. CULTIVATION: These species grow best in a fertile, moist, humus-rich soil in full sun. The Mediterranean species are reasonably drought tolerant but need moisture to flower well. Rust diseases can cause problems in humid conditions. Propagation is from seed, though the perennial species will grow from cuttings of non-flowering stems.

Antirrhinum grosii

☼/◐ ❄ ↔4–8 in (10–20 cm) ↑4–12 in (10–30 cm)

Found in low alpine areas of the western Mediterranean, especially Spain. Sticky dull green leaves around 1 in (25 mm) long. Flowers are yellow or white with yellow throat, often marked pale purple, 1¼ in (30 mm) long. Thrives in hotter, drier conditions than most snapdragons. Zones 7–10.

Antirrhinum majus

☼/◐ ❄ ↔6–20 in (15–50 cm) ↑12–60 in (30–150 cm)

Southwest European perennial, usually treated as an annual. Upright bushy habit, dark green, elliptical leaves. Flowers in upright racemes, usually pink in wild but cultivated in most colors except blue. Popular seedling series include the dwarf **Candelabra Series** and **Chimes Series,** particularly 'Chimes Red' ★, the mid-height **Sonnet Series**, and the slightly taller, often double-flowered **Liberty Series**. Zones 7–10.

Antirrhinum molle

☼/◐ ❄ ↔6–8 in (15–20 cm) ↑8–16 in (20–40 cm)

Native to Portugal and northeastern Spain. Downy elliptical leaves, flowers pale pink or white with yellow throat and downy exterior. 'Avalanche' is a white-flowered cultivar with a small yellow patch on lower lip. Zones 7–10.

Antirrhinum sempervirens

☼/◐ ❄ ↔6–8 in (15–20 cm) ↑8–16 in (20–40 cm)

A Pyrenean native with 1–3 in (2.5–8 cm) long, often downy leaves.

Antirrhinum grosii

Small flowers, usually under 1 in (25 mm) long, white or cream with yellow throat and small mauve patch on upper lip, often purple-veined. Zones 7–10.

APERA

SILKY BENT

The 3 species of annual grasses in this genus, which belongs to the grass (Poaceae) family, are native to Europe and northern Asia where they grow in light sandy soils. Two are naturalized in North America. The leaves are flat or have somewhat rough rolled edges. The tiny flowers are borne in large delicate plumes, often tinted purple. CULTIVATION: Grow in a warm sunny position in light well-drained soil. Propagate from seed. Plants self-sow freely.

Apera spica-venti

LOOSE SILKY BENT

☼ ❄ ↔12–24 in (30–60 cm) ↑24–36 in (60–90 cm)

Native to Europe and widespread in the USA. An ornamental species with flat leaves coloring to chestnut red in winter. The flowering panicles are up to 10 in (25 cm) long and often tinged with purple. Zones 6–9.

APHELANDRA

This genus, a member of the acanthus (Acanthaceae) family, consists of about 170 species of shrubs and subshrubs cultivated for their attractive flowerheads. Short-lived red and yellow flowers appear year-round. Native to tropical North, Central, and South America, all species are frost tender and live in the wild as understory plants in moist woodland. CULTIVATION: To grow in pots, combine loam-based compost in ratio 2:1, with one part of leaf mold. These plants thrive when watered with rainwater (soft water). Should be fed regularly through growing season, with food and water reduced throughout dormancy. Avoid drafts and direct sun. After flowering, cut back plants to encourage side shoots, which can be used for propagation. Spider mite, aphids, and scale insects can be a problem under glass. In the wild, they are pollinated by hummingbirds.

Aphelandra aurantiaca

syn. *Aphelandra fascinator*

☼ ✦ ↔4 ft (1.2 m) ↑4 ft (1.2 m)

Native to tropical Central American countries. Elliptical dark green leaves, flecked silver, 6 in (15 cm) long. Flower spikes to 18 in (45 cm) in length. Flowers protrude from dense bracts; yellow, orange, or reddish brown. 'Roezlii', flowers orange-red, leaves silver-marked. Zones 11–12.

Apera spica-venti

Aphelandra aurantiaca

A

Aphelandra sinclairiana

↔10 ft (3 m) ↑15 ft (4.5 m)

Central America species, often grown as house plant. Attractive deep pink flowers opening from candle-like, orange-pink-bracted flower spikes at stem tips. Leaves bright mid-green, covering of fine hairs. Zones 10–12.

Aphelandra squarrosa

SAFFRON SPIKE, ZEBRA PLANT

↔5 ft (1.5 m) ↑6 ft (1.8 m)

Native to Brazil, this species has 12 in (30 cm) long leaves with heavy cream veining and pronounced midrib. Flower spikes generally yellow with cream, yellow, or maroon bracts and yellow flowers. Good cultivars are: **'Claire'**, similar to 'Louisae' but with broader cream zones along leaf veins; **'Dania'**, which does not flower so freely; **'Leopoldii'**, yellow or orange flowers; **'Louisae'**, white veins against dark green background; and **'Snow Queen'**, more silvery white veins and lemon flowers. Zones 11–12.

Aphelandra tetragona

Aphelandra tetragona

↔4 ft (1.2 m) ↑4 ft (1.2 m)

Native to West Indies, Costa Rica, and northern South America. Leaves dark green, broadly ovate, to 9 in (22 cm) long. Axillary and terminal flower spikes, orange bracts, bright red hooded flowers. Zones 11–12.

APIUM

CELERIAC, CELERY

A member of the carrot (Apiaceae) family, this genus of 20 biennial plants with fleshy bulbous roots originates from Europe and temperate Asia. Pinnate leaves and white flowers in compound short-stalked or stalkless umbels. Fruits are small, ribbed, elliptical to oval seeds.

CULTIVATION: Frost tolerant, drought tender. Plant seedlings 10–12 in (25–30 cm) apart in light, moist, well-drained soil enriched with organic matter, in a protected sunny position. Propagate from seed.

Aphelandra sinclairiana

Apium graveolens

CELERY, WILD CELERY

↔12–18 in (30–45 cm)
↑24–36 in (60–90 cm)

Strongly aromatic perennial from southern Europe. Whitish flowers, in compound umbels arranged in panicles, in summer–autumn. Fruits small, ribbed, elliptical to oval seeds. Leaf segments, to ½–2 in (12–50 mm) long, lance-shaped, and toothed or lobed, on thick, long, grooved stalks. ***A. g.* var. *dulce*** (celery), erect leaves with closely overlapping enlarged leaf stalks, popular garden vegetable; ***A. g.* var. *rapaceum*** (celeriac), grossly swollen taproot, shortened edible leaves; **'Brilliant'**, European, early maturing; ***A. g.* var. *secalinum*** (leaf celery), strong-flavored fragrant leaves on thin rounded stalks, used in soups and stews. ***A. g.* 'Tricolor'** has glossy green leaves tinted bronze at first, edged with cream and a silver central stripe; Zones 5–8.

APOCYNUM

DOGBANE

This genus of 4 to 9 species of perennial herbs belongs to the oleander or dogbane (Apocynaceae) family. They are native to North America, eastern Europe, and Asia where they grow in grassland and open forested areas.

Aphelandra squarrosa 'Claire'

Apium graveolens

Plants have a milky sap and, like most members of the family, are poisonous. The thin textured leaves may be opposite or alternate. Sprays of small, bell-shaped, pink or white flowers are borne terminally in summer. The common name of the genus comes from a belief that one of the species was poisonous to dogs. The fibrous stems of some species are used by Native Americans as a substitute for hemp. Also used in herbal medicine as a diuretic and emetic and to slow the pulse, but the toxicity of the plants means extreme care is required.

CULTIVATION: Seldom cultivated but suitable for naturalizing in the wild garden. Can be invasive. Grow in moisture-retentive well-drained soil in full or half-sun. Propagate from seed or by division.

Apocynum androsaemifolium

COMMON DOGBANE, SPREADING DOGBANE

↔2–3 ft (0.6–0.9 m)
↑2–6 ft (0.6–1.8 m)

From North America. Invasive in some States. Bushy perennial with pointed oval leaves. Small white to pale pink flowers in terminal sprays during summer. Reddish, narrow, bean-like seed pods to 8 in (20 cm) long. Zones 4–9.

APODYTES

This genus of the Icacinaceae family consists of 3 species of evergreen trees, from tropical northeastern Australia, New Caledonia, Africa, and Asia. It belongs to the Icacinaceae family. *Apodytes* species have simple, smooth-edged, leathery leaves and much-branched panicles of small white flowers with recurving petals and conspicuous stamens. The fruits are small drupes with a fleshy appendage on one side attached to the fruit, termed a pseudoaril. Grown in southern Africa for ornament and timber, and a bark preparation is used to drive out intestinal parasites.

CULTIVATION: The African species is grown for its display of white blossom and red and black fruit, as well as for

shade, screening, and hedges. It adapts readily to gardens in warm-temperate to tropical climates, though growth is not particularly fast and it can be kept to large shrub size. A deep fertile soil suits it best but it will grow in poorer soils. Propagate from fresh seed.

Apodytes dimidiata

BIRD'S-EYE, SOUTH AFRICAN WHITE PEAR

☀ ❄ ↔ 6–25 ft (1.8–8 m)
↕ 12–60 ft (3.5–18 m)

A widespread species that is variable in size. It features masses of white flowers in spring–early autumn. Decorative black berries, deep red basal appendages. Valued for its strong heavy timber and traditional medicinal uses, it also contains a powerful molluscicide, killing aquatic snails. Zones 9–11.

APONOGETON

This genus, a member of the family Aponogetonaceae, consists of some 44 species of aquatic herbaceous perennials from many tropical and subtropical areas, some of which have become weedy in areas where they are not native. The foliage can be submerged or floating, rather like that of a waterlily. The flowers are produced in a compound panicle that sits above the water. These species can make attractive pond plants, and the more tropical species among them are often used to good effect in indoor heated aquariums.
CULTIVATION: Plant in mud in the bottom of a pond in sun or half-sun. Propagation is from fresh seed that often sows itself, or by division.

Aponogeton distachyos

CAPE POND WEED, WATER HAWTHORN

☀/❄ ❄ ↔ 32–40 in (80–100 cm)
↕ 24–32 in (60–80 cm)

From South Africa, this species is naturalized in parts of Australia. It has oblong floating leaves. Its white and purple scented flowers are seen, in a forked spike just above water level, during summer. The flowers are edible. Zones 9–11.

Apodytes dimidiata

APOROCACTUS

RAT'S TAIL CACTUS

Pencil-thin, long, graceful, cascading branches covered with short golden brown spines and many flowers have long made this cactus a popular subject for hanging baskets. This genus of the cactus (Cactaceae) family comes from the Mexican States of Oaxaca and Hidalgo. The name comes from the Greek *aporos,* meaning tangled, and refers to the plant's habit of branching profusely from the base. *Aporocactus* has been hybridized with several related epiphytic cactus genera to produce a variety of flower sizes and shapes in shades of pink, red, purple, orange, and yellow. The spherical seed pods may be spiny and are green to red and ½ in (12 mm) in diameter. Some botanists now regard *Aporocactus* as a synonym of *Disocactus* (not to be confused with *Discocactus*) but this is not universally accepted.
CULTIVATION: May be grown from seed but more usually raised from cuttings dried out for a week or more before planting. Usually grown in hanging baskets, they need a well-drained humus-rich soil, moderate watering, some shade, and protection from frost. Give a short rest after flowering when cuttings, 4–8 in (10–20 cm) long, can be taken.

Aponogeton distachyos, in the wild, Cederburg, South Africa

Aporocactus flagelliformis ★

syn. *Disocactus flagelliformis*

RAT'S TAIL CACTUS

☀ ❄ ↔ 20 in (50 cm) ↕ 3–7 ft (0.9–2 m)
From Oaxaca and Hidalgo, Mexico, this old favorite has many, 3- to 8-ribbed, pendulous branches to 7 ft (2 m) long, arising profusely from the base. Spines ¾ in (18 mm), yellow to brown, in dense clusters along stems. Many flowers, pink to red, 2½–3 in (6–8 cm) long. Zones 9–11.

APTENIA

HEARTLEAF ICEPLANT, HEARTS AND FLOWERS

This South African genus in the ice-plant (Aizoaceae) family contains just 2 species—both small, spreading, branching shrubs with fleshy succulent leaves covered in minute protuberances that give the leaves a texture as though they were dusted with fine sugar crystals. The bright light green leaves are rounded to heart-shaped, tapering to a broad point. Established plants may have a wide spread but are easily controlled. Small, purple-pink,

daisy-like flowers, solitary or in 3s, appear at the stem tips in summer. The small, green, fleshy fruits redden as they mature.
CULTIVATION: Surprisingly hardy if kept dry in winter, these little succulents make a bold splash of color and thrive in any sunny well-drained position. Their spreading habit makes them ideal for rockeries, as small-scale ground covers, or in hanging baskets. Will withstand prolonged drought but will not flower until watered. Propagate from seed or cuttings; may self-layer.

Aptenia cordifolia ★

☀/❄ ❄ ↔ 16–40 in (40–100 cm)
↕ 2 in (5 cm)

Native to the Eastern Cape region of South Africa. Heart-shaped leaves to 1 in (25 mm) long and wide. Intense magenta flowers. 'Red Apple' is an especially vigorous form, possibly a hybrid, that can be invasive; 'Variegata' has small cream-edged leaves. Zones 9–11.

Aptenia cordifolia 'Red Apple'

Aporocactus hybrid

Aquilegia caerulea, in the wild, in Juan National Forest, Colorado, USA

Aquilegia canadensis

AQUILEGIA

COLUMBINE, GRANNY'S BONNET

This buttercup (Ranunculaceae) family genus is made up of about 70 species found over much of the temperate and subarctic Northern Hemisphere. Fine-stemmed, often blue-green foliage reminiscent of maidenhair fern fronds emerges from a woody rootstock. Flowering stems usually reach above the foliage and carry spurred, bell-shaped, often pendulous flowers. Some are short-flowering, others bloom through much of late spring and summer. Various species were used medicinally by Native North Americans. The name aquilegia is derived from the Latin *aquila* (eagle) and *lego* (to gather), suggesting that the curved nectaries or spurs resemble the closing talons of an eagle.
CULTIVATION: An adaptable genus, with species suitable for woodland, rockeries, and perennial borders. The general preference is for a cool-winter climate and a place in half-sun with cool, moist, humus-rich, well-drained soil. Often attracts aphids. Some species can be divided when dormant but propagation is usually from seed. May self-sow, can be invasive.

Aquilegia alpina
ALPINE COLUMBINE
☀ ❄ ↔ 6–18 in (15–45 cm)
↑ 8–30 in (20–75 cm)
Very variable European alpine species. Flowers are straight-spurred, pendulous, usually blue-tipped with white. Cultivars in shades from white through blue to purple. Suitable for rockeries. Zones 5–9.

Aquilegia atrata
BLACK COLUMBINE
☀ ❄ ↔ 12 in (30 cm) ↑ 18 in (45 cm)
Southern European alpine with sticky foliage. Small nodding flowers, maroon to almost black with golden stamens and hooked spurs. Zones 4–9.

Aquilegia dichroa

Aquilegia caerulea
BLUE COLUMBINE, ROCKY MOUNTAIN COLUMBINE
☀/☀ ❄ ↔ 8–16 in (20–40 cm)
↑ 8–24 in (20–60 cm)
From high woodlands and mountains of western USA. Large, spreading flowers. White to cream petals, blue or pink sepals, long spurs. Zones 3–9.

Aquilegia canadensis
CANADA COLUMBINE, MEETING HOUSES, ROCK BELLS, WILD COLUMBINE
☀ ❄ ↔ 12–20 in (30–50 cm)
↑ 12–30 in (30–75 cm)
Found over much of eastern North America. Soft yellow, red-spurred flowers on many-branched, wiry stems. Prefers rockery or woodland conditions. Flowers popular with hummingbirds. Zones 2–10.

Aquilegia chrysantha
GOLDEN COLUMBINE
☀ ❄ ↔ 12–32 in (30–80 cm)
↑ 32–36 in (80–90 cm)
Found in southern USA. Vigorous tall stems and large bright yellow flowers with long curved spurs, slightly paler in color. Several cultivars available, including double-flowered, white, and very tall. Zones 3–10.

Aquilegia dichroa
☀ ❄ ↔ 8–20 in (20–50 cm)
↑ 12–30 in (30–75 cm)
Native to Portugal and neighboring northwestern Spain. Paired trifoliate leaves with divided and toothed leaflets. The hook-spurred flowers, appearing in spring and summer, are soft purple-blue all over except for white petal tips. Zones 7–9.

Aquilegia chrysantha

Aquilegia olympica

Aquilegia flabellata

☀ ❋ ↔ 6–12 in (15–30 cm)
↕ 8–18 in (20–45 cm)

This species comes from Japan and nearby temperate Asia. It is a small compact plant with pronounced blue-green leaves and 1 or 2 flowers per stem. Petals white to cream; sepals and short, curved spurs, soft mauve-blue. Makes a superb rockery plant. Zones 3–9.

Aquilegia formosa

WESTERN COLUMBINE
☀ ❋ ↔ 12–20 in (30–50 cm)
↕ 20–36 in (50–90 cm)

From western USA, this species has a graceful open habit with many small, orange-red, short-spurred flowers on each of its stems. A number of cultivars are available, including dwarf, and widely hybridized. Zones 3–9.

Aquilegia longissima

☀ ❋ ↔ 8–10 in (20–25 cm)
↕ 30–36 in (75–90 cm)

A narrow upright plant from New Mexico and western Texas, USA. It displays upward-facing bright yellow flowers, with sepals lighter in color and sometimes red-tinted. Long narrow spurs are evident. Zones 8–10.

A. v., Flore Pleno Group, 'Graeme Iddon Blue'

Aquilegia, McKana Group

☀/☀ ❋ ↔ 12–20 in (30–50 cm)
↕ 32–48 in (80–120 cm)

Hybrids between several North American species covering a wide color range. Most of the hybrids in the group are tall upright plants with long-spurred flowers and contrasting colors of corolla and sepals. Zones 3–10.

Aquilegia olympica

☀ ❋ ↔ 8–12 in (20–30 cm)
↕ 12–24 in (30–60 cm)

From the Caucasus and western Asia. Nodding flower with white petals and blue to pink or pale purple sepals with curved spurs. Zones 5–9.

Aquilegia saximontana

☀ ❋ ↔ 4–8 in (10–20 cm)
↕ 4–8 in (10–20 cm)

A small species from the Rocky Mountains region of Colorado and Utah, USA. Nodding yellow-petalled flowers with blue sepals and curved spurs. Zones 4–9.

A. vulgaris, Stellata Group, 'Blue Barlow'

Aquilegia vulgaris

☀/☀ ❋ ↔ 8–18 in (20–45 cm)
↕ 12–36 in (30–90 cm)

This much-cultivated species is found over most of Europe. It has ferny foliage and flowers with hooked spurs in white and shades of blue, mauve, and red, including double-flowered forms. The wild species is seldom seen in gardens but there are many cultivars. Single-flowered cultivars include: 'Heidi', 24 in (60 cm) tall, purple-red-stemmed, nodding, soft pink flowers; 'Hensol Harebell', 24 in (60 cm) tall with short-spurred, mauve-blue flowers; and 'Nivea' (syn. 'Munstead White'), 36 in (90 cm) tall with foliage that is gray-green and flowers of pure white. Double-flowered cultivars can be divided into the following groups. **Flore Pleno Group** has elongated flowers with rounded petals, and includes: 'Graeme Iddon', a tall cultivar with white flowers which has spawned a range of double-flowered forms; 'Rougham Star', 24 in (60 cm) tall flowers, white inner petals, mauve-

A. vulgaris, Stellata Group, 'Black Barlow'

blue outer petals and sepals. **Stellata Group** has star-shaped double flowers with radiating pointed petals, and includes 'Black Barlow', 24 in (60 cm) tall with deep purple to near black flowers; 'Blue Barlow', 30 in (75 cm) tall with double blue flowers; 'Nora Barlow' ★, 32 in (80 cm) tall with soft green, white, and pink pompon-like flowers; 'Rose Barlow', 32 in (80 cm) tall with mid-pink and cream flowers. **Vervaeneana Group**, marbled green and gold foliage and variable flower color. Zones 3–10.

A. v., Flore Pleno Group, 'Rougham Star'

A. vulgaris, Stellata Group, 'Rose Barlow'

Aquilegia vulgaris, Flore Pleno Group, 'Graeme Iddon Red and White'

A

Aquilegia Hybrid Cultivars

☼/◐ ❄ ↔ 12–24 in (30–60 cm)
↑ 18–36 in (45–90 cm)

Aquilegias have been so widely hybridized, particularly among the American species, that there are now hybrids in almost any conceivable size and flower color. *A.* 'Crimson Star' has large, red-spurred cream flowers, 24 in (60 cm) tall. The **Butterfly Series**, includes **'Brimstone'**, cream and soft yellow, and **'Holly Blue'**, white to pale mauve petals, powder blue sepals. The **Songbird Series** has a compact foliage clump, 24 in (60 cm) flower stems with large flowers in many shades, including: **'Bluebird'**, very large flowers, white petals, soft blue sepals; **'Cardinal'**, white petals with pink markings, dark red sepals; **'Dove'**, pure white; **'Goldfinch'**, bright yellow; **'Redwing'**, white to cream petals, deep red sepals; and **'Robin'**, white to pale pink petals, dusky deep pink sepals. The **State Series** includes **'Alaska'**, pure white flowers; **'Colorado'**, semi-double, mauve and white petals with purple sepals; **'Florida'**, yellow petals, creamy white sepals; **'Kansas'**, bright yellow petals, vivid red sepals; and **'Louisiana'**, creamy white petals, deep red sepals. Zones 4–10.

Aquilegia, HC, State Series, 'Alaska'

Aquilegia, Hybrid Cultivars, Butterfly Series, mixed cultivars

A., HC, Butterfly Series, 'Brimstone'

A., HC, Butterfly Series, 'Holly Blue'

A. HC, 'Crimson Star'

Aquilegia, HC, State Series, 'Colorado'

Aquilegia, HC, State Series, 'Florida'

Aquilegia, HC, State Series, 'Louisiana'

Aquilegia, Hybrid Cultivars, State Series, mixed cultivars

Aquilegia, Hybrid Cultivars, Songbird Series, mixed cultivars

A., HC, Songbird Series, 'Bluebird'

A., HC, Songbird Series, 'Cardinal'

A., HC, Songbird Series, 'Dove'

A., HC, Songbird Series, 'Goldfinch'

A., HC, Songbird Series, 'Redwing'

A., HC, Songbird Series, 'Robin'

ARABIS
ROCK CRESS

A cabbage (Brassicaceae) family genus of around 120 species of annuals and perennials, mainly evergreen and sometimes woody-stemmed. Widespread in the northern temperate zones, especially Eurasia and western North America, they tend to be small plants that are often most at home in rock crevices. Their leaves are simple, sometimes downy or gray-green, and are often borne in tufted rosettes. In spring and early summer they carry upright sprays of small 4-petalled flowers, usually white or purple.
CULTIVATION: Most are hardy and easily grown in any temperate climate. Plant in a sunny position with well-drained soil that remains moist in summer. Ideal in rockeries or spilling over banks. Many species appreciate a light dressing of lime. Remove spent flowerheads to keep tidy and encourage continued blooming. Propagation is mainly from seed, though perennials will grow from base cuttings and a few species can be divided with care.

Arabis alpina
☼/◗ ❄ ↔ 8–20 in (20–50 cm)
↕ 4–12 in (10–30 cm)

This is a small, slowly spreading perennial from the mountains of Europe. Simple leaves made slightly silver by fine hairs. Downy racemes of white flowers, rarely pale pink. *A. a.* subsp. *caucasica* 'Schneehaube' (syn. *A. caucasica* 'Snowcap') is low and spreading with white flowers. Zones 5–9.

Arabis × arendsii
☼/◗ ❄ ↔ 12–24 in (30–60 cm)
↕ 4–8 in (10–20 cm)

This is a garden hybrid between *A. aubrietoides* and *A. caucasica*. It is usually low and spreading, this species forms tufted foliage clumps. Flower stems up to 6 in (15 cm) high, with deep pink flowers. Several selections have been made, including 'Compinkie' (syn. *A. caucasica* 'Compinkie'), a neat compact plant

Arabis × *arendsii* 'Compinkie'

with bright pink flowers; 'Monte Rosa', maroon flowers; and 'Rubin', wine red flowers. Zones 5–9.

Arabis blepharophylla
☼/◗ ❄ ↔ 6–8 in (15–20 cm)
↕ 4–6 in (10–15 cm)

Californian perennial with small rosettes of deep to bright green leaves. Flowers deep pink to purple-red. 'Frühlingszauber' (syn. 'Spring Charm') is a compact cultivar with bright magenta flowers. Zones 7–9.

Arabis breweri
☼/◗ ❄ ↔ 8–12 in (20–30 cm)
↕ 6–8 in (15–20 cm)

Tufting perennial from western USA. Dark green leaves, often grayish. Pink to purple-red flowers with narrow reflexed petals. Zones 7–9.

Arabis caucasica
☼/◗ ❄ ↔ 8–20 in (20–50 cm)
↕ 6–12 in (15–30 cm)

Perennial from southern European mountains. Gray-green leaves, white flowers, rarely pink. Like *A. alpina*, the two sometimes being confused in cultivation. 'Pinkie', bright pink flowers; 'Flore Pleno', more upright growth habit, white double flowers; 'Variegata', white-edged leaves, masses of white flowers. Zones 4–9.

Arabis procurrens
☼/◗ ❄ ↔ 8–24 in (20–60 cm)
↕ 6–12 in (15–30 cm)

Perennial from the Carpathians and Balkans. Dark green leaves and white flowers. Spreads slowly by

Arabis blepharophylla 'Frühlingszauber'

A. alpina subsp. *caucasica* 'Schneehaube'

Arabis soyeri subsp. *jacquinii*

runners. 'Variegata' has white-mottled foliage and racemes to around 10 in (25 cm) high. Zones 5–9.

Arabis soyeri
☼/◗ ❄ ↔ 8–16 in (20–40 cm)
↕ 6–12 in (15–30 cm)

Perennial from the mountains of southern Europe. Dark green leaves contrast well with showy sprays of white flowers. *A. s.* subsp. *jacquinii* has fleshy, rather succulent foliage. Zones 5–9.

ARACHIS

The peanut or groundnut, valued as an oilseed as well as for its high-protein "nuts," is one member of this genus of pea-flower subfamily of the legumes (Fabaceae), and includes about 75 species of annuals and perennials. All are native to South America, the largest number occurring in Peru, Bolivia, and adjacent parts of Brazil and Argentina. Low growing and many stemmed, they have pinnate leaves with few leaflets, and flowers arising from lower leaf axils. The seed pod is remarkable for the way it develops below the soil surface, thrust under by its elongating stalk. Peanuts (*Arachis hypogaea*) were cultivated in Brazil and Peru from ancient times and subsequently taken to Africa, Asia and North America, becoming an important food and oil crop in some regions.
CULTIVATION: Peanuts can be grown in the tropics wherever plentiful moisture is available in the summer growing season, but also adapt to cooler climates as long as summers are hot and sufficiently long. Sow seeds in rows into well-tilled soil (limed if acid) when soil temperature is 59°F (15°C) or above. Raw peanuts from healthfood shops are a source of seed. Feed regularly and water as for green beans; lift plants and harvest nuts when foliage yellows.

Arabis breweri

Arabis caucasica 'Variegata'

Arabis procurrens 'Variegata'

A

Aralia elata

Arachis pintoi

Araiostegia hymenophylloides

Arachis hypogaea

GOOBER, GROUNDNUT, PEANUT

☼ ❄ ↔ 24–36 in (60–90 cm)
↑ 8–12 in (20–30 cm)

Possibly of ancient hybrid origin, the peanut is an annual with a mass of soft spreading stems. Leaves each with 4 rounded leaflets. Small yellowish flowers in spring–summer are self-pollinating, soon developing into pods pushed deep into the soil. Zones 8–12.

Arachis pintoi

FORAGE PEANUT, PINTO PEANUT

☼ ❄ ↔ 36 in (90 cm) ↑ 3–8 in (8–20 cm)

From eastern Brazil, this useful plant has been spread throughout the wet tropics in recent times. Mat-forming perennial with stems rooting at nodes. Bright yellow flowers borne on slender stalks most of the year. Valued as nutritious pasture, soil binder, and weed-suppressing ground cover. Floriferous **'Golden Glory'** is a popular landscape plant. Zones 10–12.

ARACHNIODES

Genus of about 40 ferns from the shield-fern (Dryopteridaceae) family, closely related to *Polystichum* and *Dryopteris*, and native to East Asia, Malaysia, and New Zealand. These plants have a short- to long-creeping scaly rhizome and the fronds are deltoid or ovoid, often leathery, widened at the base, with bipinnate or more divided pinnules. The name comes from the Greek *arachnion,* meaning spider's web.
CULTIVATION: Easily grown in semi-shaded situations in well-drained loamy soil with plenty of moisture. Propagate from spores or by division of rhizomes.

Arachniodes simplicior ★

syn. *Arachniodes aristata* 'Variegata'
EAST INDIAN HOLLY FERN, VARIEGATED SHIELD FERN

❂/☼ ❄ ↔ 18–48 in (45–120 cm)
↑ 12–32 in (30–80 cm)

This slow-growing fern with long-creeping rhizomes comes from subtropical to temperate Japan and China. Glossy, green, pinnate, evergreen fronds are triangular, with a prominent yellowish streak on each side of the midrib. Zones 6–9.

ARAIOSTEGIA

A genus of 12 epiphytic or terrestrial ferns from tropical Asia belonging to the hares-foot fern (Davalliaceae) family. It has finely pinnate thinly textured fronds arising from long scaly stalks joined to creeping rhizomes.
CULTIVATION: Grow in moist organically rich soil in a sheltered shady spot. Propagate from spores or by division.

Araiostegia hymenophylloides

☼ ❄ 12–20 in (30–50 cm)
↑ 12–20 in (30–50 cm)

Found from India to Malaysia and the Philippines, this deciduous fern grows from brown rhizomes with scales tapering to points. Stems to 16 in (40 cm) long; lacy, membranous, pinnate fronds, with oval to lance-shaped leaflets, segments egg-shaped to oblong with ragged lower lobes, diamond-shaped to oblong. Zones 10–12.

ARALIA

From the ivy (Araliaceae) family, this genus of trees, shrubs, and herbaceous perennials consists of around 40 species mostly from Southeast Asia and North, Central, and South America. Most are deciduous and nearly all have compound leaves. Flowers are small, numerous, usually cream, carried in umbels arranged in panicles terminating the branches, followed by black fruits. Some species have prickly stems, and suckering can occur. Roots and bark of several species are used in traditional medicine, and young *A. cordata* shoots are an important vegetable (udo) in Japan, used like celery.
CULTIVATION: All species known in cultivation will tolerate at least light frosts, but most need a warm humid summer for best growth. Prefer deep reasonably fertile soil and shelter from strong winds. Though shade tolerant, they grow and flower better in sun.

Propagate from seed, which for tree species may need cold stratification, or from root cuttings or basal suckers.

Aralia californica ★

ELK CLOVER, SPIKENARD

☼/❂ ❄ ↔ 6–8 ft (1.8–2.4 m) ↑ 10 ft (3 m)

Herbaceous perennial native to California and Oregon. Thornless stems grow very quickly in spring. Deeply divided leaves with toothed leaflets to 12 in (30 cm) long. Large greenish flowered inflorescence with inconspicuous fruit. Zones 8–10.

Aralia chinensis

CHINESE ANGELICA TREE

☼ ❄ ↔ 30 ft (9 m) ↑ 30 ft (9 m)

From northeastern Asia. Doubly pinnate leaves to 3 ft (0.9 m) long and 2 ft (0.6 m) wide. Small off-white flowers, in very large panicles, in summer–early autumn. Some botanists class this as a form of the deciduous *A. elata*. Zones 7–10.

Aralia cordata

JAPANESE SPIKENARD, UDO

☼/❂ ❄ ↔ 8 ft (2.4 m) ↑ 8 ft (2.4 m)

Vigorous herbaceous perennial from Japan, Korea, and nearby parts of China. Huge compound leaves with rounded, finely toothed, 6 in (15 cm) long leaflets. Blanched young stems used as a vegetable in Japan. Large panicles of cream flowers in summer; black fruit. Zones 8–10.

Aralia elata

JAPANESE ANGELICA TREE

☼ ❄ ↔ 30 ft (9 m) ↑ 40 ft (12 m)

Native to Japan, often tall shrub spread by root suckers, with prickly corky trunk. Bipinnate leaves, to 4 ft (1.2 m) long, yellow-purplish in autumn. Large panicles of near-white flowers in late summer. **'Aureomarginata'**, yellow leaf margins, turning to creamy white; **'Variegata'** ★ (syn. 'Albomarginata'), white leaf margins. Zones 4–9.

Aralia spinosa

Araucaria angustifolia

Aralia spinosa

AMERICAN ANGELICA TREE, DEVIL'S
WALKING-STICK, HERCULES CLUB

☀ ❄ ↔ 15 ft (4.5 m) ↑ 20 ft (6 m)

Occurring wild from Pennsylvania, USA, southward, this well-known *Aralia* is found in thickets on edges of damp woodland. Bipinnate leaves, up to 3 ft (0.9 m) long, turning yellow in autumn. Panicles of flowers in mid–late summer. Zones 5–9.

ARAUCARIA

This ancient conifer genus from the araucaria (Araucariaceae) family consists of 19 species—13 from New Caledonia, 2 from South America, 2 from Australia, 2 from New Guinea (1 also in Australia), and 1 from Norfolk Island. Araucarias have a distinctive growth habit with a straight trunk and usually whorled branches; the spirally arranged leaves are densely crowded and often overlapping on flexible branchlets. Male and female organs are on the same tree, the tassel-like pollen cones on the side branches, and egg-shaped seed cones with spine-tipped scales near the top of the crown. The seeds, which may be quite large and nut-like, are embedded in the tough cone scales, a feature unique to this genus.

CULTIVATION: Cold tolerance varies, and these plants cannot be grown outdoors in severe climates. They are best grown as conservatory plants and may be kept in tubs for many years. In warmer climates araucarias are grown in large gardens, parks, and avenues. Propagation is from fresh seed which germinates readily; cuttings tend to retain sideways growth if taken from lower branches.

Araucaria angustifolia

CANDELABRA TREE, PARANA PINE

☀ ⧓ ↔ 20 ft (6 m) ↑ 100 ft (30 m)

From the plateau of southern Brazil, this tree is distinctive for its long, flat, non-overlapping, sharp pointed leaves up to 2 in (5 cm) long, forming 2 rows on the branchlets. Seed cones to 6 in (15 cm) in diameter, with stiff recurving tips to the scales. Zones 9–12.

Araucaria araucana

syn. *Araucaria imbricata*

MONKEY PUZZLE TREE

☀ ❄ ↔ 35 ft (10 m) ↑ 80 ft (24 m)

From the Andean slopes of south-central Chile, this species is suitable for cool climates. Young trees of the species have a tangle of upcurved branches, developing a broad crown with age. Leaves densely overlapping, rigid, sharp pointed. Globular seed cones are 3–6 in (8–15 cm) in diameter. Zones 7–9.

Araucaria araucana, in the wild, Chile

Araucaria columnaris

Araucaria bidwillii

Araucaria bidwillii

BUNYA BUNYA, BUNYA PINE

☀ ⧓ ↔ 35 ft (10 m) ↑ 150 ft (45 m)

From Queensland, Australia. Sharp-pointed leaves, up to 2 in (5 cm) long, glossy dark green, and arranged on branchlets that are soon shed. Large seed cones up to 12 in (30 cm) in diameter. Zones 9–11.

Araucaria columnaris

syn. *Araucaria cookii*

NEW CALEDONIAN PINE, PIN COLONNAIRE

☀ ⧓ ↔ 15 ft (5 m) ↑ 200 ft (60 m)

From New Caledonia, this species forms narrow dense columns with short side branches, crowded and not whorled. Broad blunt leaves overlap so closely that the branchlets resemble plaited ropes. Bristly seed cones, tennis-ball size. Zones 10–12.

Araucaria cunninghamii
HOOP PINE

↔ 12 ft (3.5 m) ↑ 150 ft (45 m)

Native to eastern Australia. The dark gray bark is often furrowed 'hoops' encircling the trunk. Juvenile foliage prickly. Adult leaves small, densely overlapping, very dark green. Bluish-leafed forms are known. In New Guinea the species is represented by *A. c.* var. *papuana*. Zones 9–12.

Araucaria heterophylla
syn. *Araucaria excelsa*
NORFOLK ISLAND PINE

↔ 25 ft (8 m) ↑ 200 ft (60 m)

From Norfolk Island. This species has a very symmetrical form, with regularly whorled branches on which the branchlets form 2 neat rows with a V-shaped trough between. Best near seashores in subtropical regions; not pollution tolerant. Zones 10–11.

Araucaria rulei
RULE ARAUCARIA

↔ 20–45 ft (6–14 m) ↑ 50–100 ft (15–30 m)

Tree from New Caledonia with pendulous branches. Juvenile leaves dark green. Adult leaves to ¾ in (18 mm) long, oval to elliptic, silvery gray above, glossy green underneath. The male cone is cylindrical, 5 in (12 cm) long, and the female cone also grows to 5 in (12 cm) long. Zones 9–11.

Araucaria scopulorum
ROCK ARAUCARIA

↔ 6–30 ft (1.8–9 m) ↑ 12–65 ft (3.5–19.5 m)

Conifer tree from New Caledonia with oval crown and very pale gray bark that peels in thin strips. Adult branchlets grow in a wide U-shape in one plane. Juvenile leaves curved, needle-like, 7 mm long. Adult leaves scale-like, curved slightly inward, 3–4 mm long. Male cone cylindrical, 12–20 in (30–75 cm) long. Zones 8–11.

ARAUJIA

A genus of 2 to 3 species of climber in the dogbane (Apocynaceae) family, occurring in low rainfall regions of temperate and subtropical South America in scrublands and forest margins. Stems are twining, woody, containing white latex, with opposite, entire, gray-green leaves. Flowers are bell-shaped, 5-petalled, whitish, borne in clusters near the leaf axils. Fruits are somewhat pear-shaped, containing numerous dark-colored seeds with many long silky hairs at one end, aiding in wind dispersal. One species has escaped from cultivation, and is a weed in regions such as Australia, California, and New Zealand.

CULTIVATION: Propagate from seed or cuttings. Plants should be grown in full sun or only part shade, in a well-draining soil in near frost-free regions.

Araujia sericifera
syns *Araujia albens*, *A. hortorum*, *A. sericofera*
CRUEL PLANT, MOTH CATCHER, MOTH VINE

↔ ↑ to 40 ft (12 m)

Slender, woody climber. Leaves opposite, wavy-edged, lance-shaped, 2–5 in (5–12 cm) long × 2–2½ in (5–6 cm) wide, green above, gray-green and hairy beneath. White or pale pink, bell-shaped, fragrant flowers, to 1¼ in (30 mm), in clusters summer–autumn. Fruits pear- to egg-shaped, stalk at larger end, dull, gray-green, 2½–6 in (6–15 cm) long, 1½–3 in (3.5–8 cm) wide. Seeds also egg-shaped, dark colored, with attached silky hairs up to 10 times as long. Zones 9–10.

ARBUTUS

This small genus contains about 8 to 10 species of small evergreen trees belonging to the heath or erica (Ericaeae) family, which are known as strawberry trees due to their strawberry-like fruit. They occur in the Mediterranean region, western Asia, and southwestern USA, with a few species in Central America and Mexico. All have attractive bell-shaped flowers and red or yellow fruit of little economic value, and in some cases have red or cinnamon-colored, stringy, peeling bark. Height varies from about 10 to 20 ft (3–6 m).

CULTIVATION: *Arbutus* like a well-drained soil, preferably free of lime, and an open sunny position protected from cold winds. Most species are tolerant of sustained cold winters. Little pruning is required. Propagation is by half-hardened cuttings taken in autumn or winter; scions can also be top-grafted on seedling understocks. Seeds can be sown in spring.

Arbutus andrachne
GRECIAN STRAWBERRY TREE

↔ 20 ft (6 m) ↑ 20 ft (6 m)

From the eastern Mediterranean. Cinnamon brown bark flakes away to reveal greenish cream bark beneath. White pitcher-shaped flowers, in upright clusters, in spring, followed by orange-red fruit. Protect from frost when young. Zones 6–9.

Arbutus andrachne

Araucaria cunninghamii, in the wild, in Lamington National Park, Queensland, Australia

Araucaria heterophylla

Arbutus menziesii

Arbutus × *andrachnoides*

HYBRID STRAWBERRY TREE

☼ ❄ ↔ 25 ft (8 m) ↑ 25 ft (8 m)

A naturally occurring hybrid between *A. andrachne* and *A. unedo*. It has highly ornamental bark which peels back to reveal new dull crimson bark beneath. Panicles of white flowers in late winter. Leaves are downy beneath. Zones 8–10.

Arbutus canariensis

☼ ❄ ↔ 12 ft (3.5 m) 15 ft (4.5 m)

From the Canary Islands, this species has small greenish white flowers, tinged pale pink, in loose panicles, in summer–early autumn. The strawberry-like fruit ripens green to red. Bark reddish brown and flaking. Zones 8–10.

Arbutus glandulosa

☼ ❄ ↔ 20 ft (6 m) ↑ 40 ft (12 m)

Native of southern Mexico, this species branches low. Pale pinkish brown bark peels annually in summer,

revealing creamy new bark. Dull pinkish flowers appear in winter, followed by small orange fruits. Zones 9–10.

Arbutus 'Marina'

☼ ❄ ↔ 20–40 ft (6–12 m) ↑ 25–50 ft (7–15 m)

Possibly clone of *A.* × *andrachnoides* or with some hybrid influence of *A. canariensis*. Attractive tree, first noticed in a San Francisco garden in 1984 though believed brought from Europe much earlier. Smooth reddish bark, bronze new leaves, pink-flushed flowers nearly all year, profuse yellow fruit ageing red, edible. Zones 8–10.

Arbutus menziesii ★

MADRONA, MADRONE, PACIFIC MADRONE

☼ ❄ ↔ 30 ft (9 m) ↑ 30 ft (9 m)

Native to the Pacific coast of northern USA, this species is spreading, shrubby in form. Bark is bright brick red and peels to reveal a green new layer. Fruit orange-red. White flowers, held in drooping clusters. Zones 7–9.

Arbutus xalapensis

Arbutus unedo

IRISH STRAWBERRY TREE, STRAWBERRY TREE

☼ ❄ ↔ 20 ft (6 m) ↑ 25 ft (8 m)

Occurring in the Mediterranean region, Ireland, and UK, this tree has red stringy bark, often arranged in a spiral fashion. Flowers are white, flushed with pink, in autumn–winter. Fruits, ripening green to orange-red to bright red, are edible though quite bland to the taste. This tree is tolerant of pollution. *A. u.* f. *rubra* grows to 4–6 ft (1.2–1.5 m) tall. *A. u.* 'Compacta' is a smaller form,

'Elfin King' is a small bushy form, and 'Oktoberfest' is a pink-flowered form. Zones 7–10.

Arbutus xalapensis

☼/◖ ❄ ↔ 20 ft (6 m) ↑ 35 ft (10 m)

Large evergreen shrub or small tree, southern USA to Guatemala. Leathery, pointed oval to lance-shaped leaves to 4 in (10 cm) long, smooth or toothed edges, downy brown when young. In summer, small, white or pink, bell-shaped flowers in panicles. Warty red fruit. Zones 8–11.

Arbutus 'Marina'

Arbutus glandulosa

Arbutus unedo 'Compacta'

Arbutus unedo

Archontophoenix cunninghamiana, in the wild, Port Macquarie, New South Wales, Australia

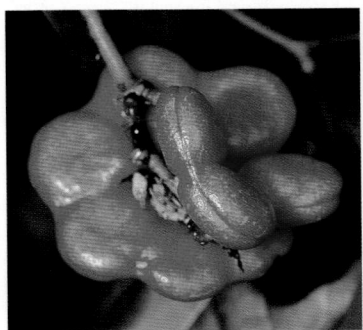

Archidendron lucyi

Archidendron lucyi

ARCHIDENDRON

This is a mainly Australian genus of evergreen and deciduous shrubs and trees. It belongs to the mimosa subfamily of the legumes (Fabaceae). The leaves are usually pinnate, rarely bipinnate, and generally quite a light shade of green. Feathery petal-less flowers that are usually fragrant are followed by seed pods that are often distinctively shaped.
CULTIVATION: Most species are intolerant of frost and need warm-temperate to tropical conditions. Those from areas with a distinct dry season tend to be deciduous at that time, otherwise the general preference is for a moist, humus-rich, well-drained soil and a position in full sun. Propagate from seed, which should be soaked before sowing.

Archidendron lucyi
☼ ⊰ ↔ 10–15 ft (3–4.5 m)
↑ 35–40 ft (10–12 m)
Limited distribution in northeastern Queensland and some islands of the Pacific. Smallish tree, leaves pinnate, 4–6 in (10–15 cm) long, shiny, dark

green, 2 to 3 pairs of leaflets, to 4–6 in (10–15 cm) × 2½–3 in (6–8 cm). Flowers in autumn, white, fluffy, short-lived, borne in dense clusters. Fruits curly, red outside, yellowish inside, seeds shiny black, mature in spring. Zones 10–12.

ARCHONTOPHOENIX

Endemic to eastern Australia, this palm (Arecaceae) family genus consists of 6 species. They have a bare trunk topped by a crownshaft of tightly furled frond bases. Each frond has many leaflets closely spaced in 2 regular rows; from base to tip the frond twists through 90 degrees so that near its outer end leaflets are almost vertical. Flowering branches emerge from the trunk below the crownshaft. Many, star-shaped, cream to pale mauve flowers on pendulous branchlets, and globular red fruit.
CULTIVATION: Popular ornamental palms for frost-free climates, favored by landscapers for their fast early growth and complete shedding of old fronds to give a clean trunk. Although fairly sun hardy, they are shallow

rooted and like well-mulched soil and much water in dry periods. Propagate from freshly fallen and cleaned seed. Protect young plants from strong sun.

Archontophoenix alexandrae
ALEXANDRA PALM
☼ ⊰ ↔ 15 ft (4.5 m) ↑ 50 ft (15 m)
From east coast of Queensland, Australia, this species forms dense stands. Slightly bulbous pale gray trunk, plain green crownshaft, base has stepped rings. Fronds 8–10 ft (2.4–3 m) long, silvery white color beneath. Cream flowers. Zones 10–12.

Archontophoenix cunninghamiana
BANGALOW PALM, PICCABEEN PALM
☼ ⊰ ↔ 15 ft (4.5 m) ↑ 60 ft (18 m)
Found from the Tropic of Capricorn to southern New South Wales, Australia. Grows mainly in moist

forested gullies and stream banks. Similar to *A. alexandrae*, trunk less swollen, fronds droop more, with green undersides. Flowers pale mauve, summer–autumn. Zones 10–11.

Archontophoenix purpurea
MOUNT LEWIS PALM
☼ ⊰ ↔ 15 ft (4.5 m) ↑ 80 ft (24 m)
Recognized only recently, this species is from the high-rainfall mountains of far northern Queensland, Australia. Crownshaft dull purple-gray, new fronds bronze. Large fruit, up to 1 in (25 mm) in diameter. Vigorous in cultivation. Zones 9–12.

ARCTIUM

A small genus of 10 species in the daisy (Asteraceae) family that are erect biennials with large leaves and flower-heads with hooks on them that cling to clothing or fur. Native to parts of Europe and Asia, these bold-looking plants aren't usually grown as ornamentals but are sometimes grown as a vegetable or for medicinal purposes. The leaves are large at the base and reduce in size farther up the stems, and at the top its mauve flowers hide in the green spiked heads. The stalks can be peeled and cooked and very young leaves can be used in salads.
CULTIVATION: Grow in a moist well-enriched soil in half-sun. Propagate from seed sown where it is to grow. Once planted, will self-sow all too well.

Arctium lappa
GREAT BURDOCK
☼ ❄ ↔ 4 ft (1.2 m) ↑ 5–7 ft (1.5–2 m)
Native to most of Europe and a garden escapee in many other places. Large basal leaves to 20 in (50 cm) long, gray-green with a whitish reverse. The burred flowerheads are green with mauve stamens just protruding. Zones 3–10.

Archontophoenix alexandrae

Archontophoenix purpurea

Arctostaphylos canescens ssp. *sonomensis*

Arctostaphylos catalinae

ARCTOSTAPHYLOS

There are about 50 species in this genus of mostly evergreen small shrubs and trees in the heath or erica (Ericaceae) family. The genus is found only in North America, except for 2 species from the alpine-arctic regions of the Northern Hemisphere. They have reddish brown ornamental bark, smooth, or peeling in flakes. Leaves are alternate, smooth, or toothed. Flowers are in terminal racemes or panicles of tiny bells or urn-shaped, white or pink. Fruits spherical. Leaves of *A. uva-ursi* used in Russia as a tea; in the UK has been used as a urinary antiseptic since the thirteenth century. CULTIVATION: They need lime-free soil. In pots water freely and feed in the growing season. Stop feeding and reduce water in the dormant season. Put seed in boiling water for 15–20 seconds before sowing in autumn with protection against frosts. Layer prostrate species in autumn. Plant half-hardened cuttings in summer. Mostly disease-free except for leaf spot.

Arctostaphylos alpina

syn. *Arctostaphylos alpinus*

ARCTIC BEARBERRY, BLACK BEARBERRY

☼/◐ ❄ ↔8 in (20 cm) ↑6 in (15 cm)

Native to Northern Hemisphere heaths. Deciduous creeping shrub, finely serrated, lance-shaped leaves, bright red in autumn. Axillary racemes of flowers, white, flushed pink, in late spring, red-purple berries. Zones 1–8.

Arctostaphylos bakeri

syn. *Arctostaphylos stanfordiana* subsp. *bakeri*

BAKER'S MANZANITA

☼/◐ ❄ ↔3–6 ft (0.9–1.8 m) ↑2–8 ft (0.6–2.4 m)

A rare species from chaparral of Sonoma County, California, USA. Erect to spreading shrub with smooth red bark, small dark green leaves, and small pink flowers in late winter–early spring. '**Louis Edmunds**' is a selected clone of upright form with wine red trunks and dense gray-green foliage. Zones 8–10.

Arctostaphylos canescens

HOARY MANZANITA

☼ ❄ ↔6 ft (1.8 m) ↑6 ft (1.8 m)

Native from southern Oregon to California, USA. Compact shrub with smooth dark red twigs, hairy when young. Oblong to rounded leaves, densely covered in white felty hairs when young. Pink flowers followed by brown fruits. *A. c.* subsp. *sonomensis* is an attractive form. Zones 7–10.

Arctostaphylos catalinae

SANTA CATALINA MANZANITA

☼/◐ ❄ ↔6–10 ft (1.8–3 m) ↑6–15 ft (1.8–4.5 m)

Endemic to Santa Catalina Island off southern California, USA. Spreading shrub or small tree, sinuous trunks. Bark smooth, red. Ovate finely hairy leaves. Clusters of red flowers in autumn–winter. Zones 8–10.

Arctostaphylos columbiana

HAIRY MANZANITA

☼ ❄ ↔6–12 ft (1.8–3.5 m) ↑6–20 ft (1.8–6 m)

Shrub or small tree from northern California, USA, to British Columbia, Canada. Peeling purplish brown bark, white-bristled twigs, ovate leaves to 2 in (5 cm) long. White to pinkish flowers in nodding clusters, in late spring–early summer. Zones 7–9.

Arctostaphylos confertiflora

SANTA ROSA MANZANITA

☼ ❄ ↔4–8 ft (1.2–2.4 m) ↑1–6 ft (0.3–1.8 m)

Endemic to Santa Rosa Island off southern California, USA, growing on

Arctostaphylos confertiflora

sandstone outcrops. Spreading shrub, often with branches semi-prostrate, twigs white-bristled. Leaves crowded, ovate. Clusters of white flowers in spring. Zones 9–11.

Arctostaphylos densiflora

☼/◐ ❄ ↔6 ft (1.8 m) ↑5 ft (1.5 m)

Native to Sonoma County, California, USA. Procumbent shrub with dark red to nearly black, smooth bark. Flowers small short panicles, white with a tinge of pink. Leaves glossy, mid-green, and elliptical. '**Emerald Carpet**', a dense ground cover up to 12 in (30 cm) high; '**Howard McMinn**', denser than the species. Zones 8–10.

Arctostaphylos edmundsii

LITTLE SUR MANZANITA

☼ ❄ ↔4–10 ft (1.2–3 m) ↑6–36 in (15–90 cm)

A rare species from near Monterey on the coast of California, USA. Its mat-like form has made it a popular landscape plant. Some forms mound up with age, others quite prostrate, rooting along branches. Leaves small, rounded, glossy, dark green. Dull pinkish flowers in spring. Brownish fruit in summer. Zones 8–10.

Arctostaphylos glauca

BIGBERRY MANZANITA

☼ ❄ ↔20 ft (6 m) ↑20 ft (6 m)

A large shrub, or small tree, that is native to California, USA. Has red-brown bark, and dull grayish green leaves up to 1½ in (35 mm) long,

elliptic to ovate in shape. Flowers are white or pink, followed by a sticky brown fruit. Zones 8–10.

Arctostaphylos hookeri

MONTEREY MANZANITA

☼ ❄ ↔4–15 ft (1.2–4.5 m) ↑6–48 in (15–120 cm)

This is a coastal species that is found from San Francisco Bay to near Monterey, California, USA, often on dunes. Forms extensive dense mat, mounding with age. Leaves small, shiny green. Flowers white to pink, in winter–spring. Fruit shiny red, in summer. *A. h.* subsp. *franciscana* (Franciscan manzanita), mat-forming, from San Francisco Peninsula, is extinct in the wild but preserved in cultivation; *A. h.* subsp. *hearstiorum* (Hearsts' manzanita), quite prostrate, rooting along stems, leaves under ½ in (12 mm) long; *A. h.* subsp. *montana* (Tamalpais manzanita), more erect or mounding form, to 6 ft (1.8 m) high. *A. h.* '**Monterey Carpet**' is a compact cultivar. Zones 8–10.

Arctostaphylos edmundsii

A. h. subsp. *franciscana*   *A. h.* subsp. *hearstiorum*   *A. h.* subsp. *montana*

Arctostaphylos hookeri

A

Arctostaphylos manzanita
MANZANITA

☀ ❄ ↔ 10 ft (3 m) ↑ 15 ft (4.5 m)

From California, this species forms dense thickets. Its bark is red to brown, tending to peel. Its leaves are leathery, hairy, oval, and green to gray-green in color. Deep pink flowers are seen in early spring. White fruit, ripening to red-brown, is produced in autumn. An attractive addition to a mixed border. 'Doctor Hurd', upright cultivar that reaches 15 ft (4.5 m) in height. Zones 8–10.

Arctostaphylos nummularia

Arctostaphylos pajaroensis

Arctostaphylos × media

☀ ❄ ↔ 8 ft (2.4 m) ↑ 12 in (30 cm)

Natural hybrid between *A. columbiana* and *A. uva-ursi*. Usually prostrate but may send up erect shoots. Leaves to 1 in (25 mm) long. Flowers white or pinkish, in spring. Zones 7–9.

Arctostaphylos nummularia
FORT BRAGG MANZANITA, GLOSSYLEAF MANZANITA

☀/◐ ❄ ↔ 4–8 ft (1.2–2.4 m) ↑ 3–6 ft (0.9–1.8 m)

From the coastal ranges of central California, USA. Spreading or rather mound-like shrub. Smooth red bark, white-bristled twigs. Small, rounded, glossy green leaves. White to pinkish flowers, late winter–spring. Zones 7–10.

Arctostaphylos obispoensis
SERPENTINE MANZANITA

☀ ❄ ↔ 8 ft (2.4 m) ↑ 8–12 ft (2.4–3.5 m)

From California, USA. Distinctive, pointed, gray-green fuzzy leaves on deep red stems. Usually evergreen but can become semi-deciduous during droughts. Flowers are white. It thrives in almost any soil. Zones 8–10.

Arctostaphylos pajaroensis
PAJARO MANZANITA

☀/◐ ❄ ↔ 3–8 ft (0.9–2.4 m) ↑ 3–12 ft (0.9–3.5 m)

Rare, from Pajaro Hills near Monterey, California, USA. Erect shrub, rough gray to reddish bark. Small heart-shaped leaves deep green above, paler bluish below, often red-edged. Pale pink flowers, late winter. Zones 8–10.

Arctostaphylos obispoensis

Arctostaphylos pilosula

Arctostaphylos pilosula
SANTA MARGARITA MANZANITA

☀/◐ ❄ ↔ 4–8 ft (1.2–2.4 m) ↑ 3–6 ft (0.9–1.8 m)

Rarely seen in the wild, this species comes from the chaparral-clad coastal ranges near San Luis Obispo, California, USA. It is a multi-stemmed

Arctostaphylos pumila

erect shrub with dark gray bark and bristly twigs. Its gray-green leaves have pointed tips. White flowers are displayed in late winter. Zones 7–10.

Arctostaphylos pumila
DUNE MANZANITA, SANDMAT MANZANITA

☀ ❄ ↔ 3–10 ft (0.9–3 m) ↑ 1–5 ft (0.3–1.5 m)

From coastal dunes around Monterey Bay, California, USA. Prostrate to mound-forming shrub with ascending branches. Dull green leaves. Small groups of white, sometimes pale pink, flowers in late winter–early spring. Pea-sized, brown fruit in summer. Good as ground cover or for planting in rock gardens. Zones 8–10.

Arctostaphylos manzanita

Arctostaphylos manzanita

Arctostaphylos stanfordiana

A. tomentosa subsp. *bracteosa*

A. tomentosa subsp. *rosei*

Arctostaphylos pungens

MADRESELVA, MANZANILLA, POINTED-LEAF
MANZANITA

☼/◐ ❀ ↔ 3–6 ft (0.9–1.8 m)
↑ 3–10 ft (0.9–3 m)

Wide-ranging over plateaus of
central and northern Mexico and
southwestern USA at up to 9,000 ft
(2,700 m) altitude, this erect shrub
has deep red-brown peeling bark.
Leaves are ovate, gray-green and
mostly sharp-pointed. White to

pink flowers are seen in spring, and
glossy brown fruit is seen in summer–
autumn. Zones 6–10.

Arctostaphylos purissima

LA PURISIMA, MANZANITA

☼ ❀ ↔ 6–15 ft (1.8–4.5 m)
↑ 3–8 ft (0.9–2.4 m)

Rare species from near Santa Barbara,
California, USA. Spreading, mound-
like shrub, dense foliage. Red bark,
twigs white-bristled. Leaves rounded,

glossy green. Nodding clusters of white
flowers in winter–spring. Pinkish fruit
in summer–autumn. Zones 8–10.

Arctostaphylos × *repens*

☼/◐ ❀ ↔ 3–8 ft (0.9–2.4 m)
↑ 3–6 ft (0.9–1.8 m)

Natural hybrid between *A. glandulosa*
and *A. virgata*, occurring where they
grow together north of San Francisco
Bay, California, USA. Zones 7–10.

Arctostaphylos stanfordiana

☼ ❀ ↔ 6 ft (1.8 m) ↑ 6 ft (1.8 m)

Native to California, USA, this erect
shrub has smooth red-brown stems.
Oval, pointed, vivid green leaves.
Pink or pink-white flowers, carried in
racemes, followed by red fruits, in
autumn. Zones 8–10.

Arctostaphylos pungens, in the wild, in Parque Nacional San Pedro Mártir, Mexico

Arctostaphylos tomentosa

DOWNY MANZANITA, WOOLLY MANZANITA

☼/◐ ❀ ↔ 4–10 ft (1.2–3 m)
↑ 3–8 ft (0.9–2.4 m)

From coastal California, USA, divided
into 9 subspecies. Spreading multi-
stemmed habit. Bark smooth, reddish
to gray and rough, twigs and leaves
hairy. White to pinkish flowers in
winter. Red fruits in spring. *A. t.*
subsp. *bracteosa* (syn. *A. bracteosa*),
bristly hairs on twigs and leaf margins;
A. t. **subsp.** *insulicola*, smooth red
bark, occurs on the Channel Islands
off southern California; *A. t.* **subsp.**
rosei (syn. *A. rosei*), rough to peeling
red bark and hairy twigs; *A. t.* **subsp.**
subcordata (syn. *A. subcordata*), also
from Channel Islands, smooth red
bark, densely hairy twigs. Zones 8–10.

Arctostaphylos × *repens*

A

Arctostaphylos uva-ursi

Arctostaphylos uva-ursi

Arctostaphylos uva-ursi 'Vancouver Jade'

Arctostaphylos uva-ursi 'Wood's Red'

Arctostaphylos uva-ursi 'Massachusetts'

Arctostaphylos uva-ursi

BEARBERRY, KINNIKINICK

☼ ❋ ↔ 20 in (50 cm) ↕ 4 in (10 cm)

A native of the cool-temperate regions of the Northern Hemisphere, this species has white flowers flushed pink, followed by red fruit. The leaves form part of a traditional smoking mixture in North America and are often used for herbal tea in Europe. 'Massachusetts' is a vigorous mat-former, building to 12 in (30 cm) high and spreading to as much as 15 ft (4.5 m) across; 'Vancouver Jade' has glossy leaves, a vigorous habit, and good ability to resist diseases; and 'Wood's Red' is a dwarf cultivar with pink flowers, large shiny red fruit, and red young shoots. Zones 4–9.

Arctostaphylos viridissima

MCMINN'S MANZANITA

☼/☼ ❋ ↔ 4–8 ft (1.2–2.4 m) ↕ 6–12 ft (1.8–3.5 m)

Endemic to Santa Cruz Island in the Channel Islands of southern California, USA. Erect to leaning shrub with beautiful, red, shredding bark and hairy twigs. Smallish, shiny, bright green leaves. White flowers in winter–spring. 'White Cloud' is a recent selection. Zones 8–10.

Arctostaphylos wellsii

WELLS'S MANZANITA

☼/☼ ❋ ↔ 6–10 ft (1.8–3 m) ↕ 8–15 ft (2.4–4.5 m)

Known only from the hills southeast of San Luis Obispo, California, USA. Shrub of erect habit with smooth red-brown bark, hairy reddish twigs. Leaves rather narrow and tapering, green to bluish often red-edged, new growths red. White flowers in winter–spring. Tan fruits in summer. Zones 8–10.

Arctostaphylos Hybrid Cultivars

☼/☼ ❋ ↔ 5–15 ft (1.5–4.5 m) ↕ 6 in–10 ft (15 cm–3 m)

Nearly all these hybrids originated in the wild or as accidental crosses in gardens. They range from low mat-forming plants to tall shrubs. 'Indian Hill', possibly a form of *A. edmundsii*, makes an extensive mat of glossy bright green foliage, new shoots an attractive bronze color, white flowers in winter; 'John Dourley' ★, of uncertain classification, mound-forming shrub, foliage dense, bluish green, with bronze new growths, pale pink flowers; 'Pacific Mist', mat-forming to mound-forming shrub with pink young branches, narrow gray-green leaves, white flowers; 'Sunset', densely mounding shrub, dark red branches, deep gray-green foliage, bright new growths, pink flowers. Zones 8–10.

ARCTOTHECA

A genus of 5 species of South African perennial daisies (family Asteraceae) characterized by downy white to silver-gray hair, which occurs on the flower stems and both sides or just on the undersides of the leaves. In species such as *A. populifolia*, which are downy all over, the hair contrasts delightfully with the bright yellow flowerheads. The foliage is mostly basal, in loose rosettes, and the flowerheads, which appear mainly in summer and autumn, are borne singly on short stems. The flowers usually have yellow to golden brown ray florets surrounding yellow disc florets.
CULTIVATION: Apart from being intolerant of repeated frosts, they are easily grown in well-drained soil in a warm sunny position. In mild climates they often naturalize and can be slightly invasive to weedy. *A. calendula*, in particular, has a tendency to colonize lawns. Propagate from seed or by breaking up established clumps.

Arctotheca calendula

CAPE DANDELION, CAPE WEED

☼ ✤ ↔ 6–16 in (15–40 cm) ↕ 4–8 in (10–20 cm)

Dandelion-like rosettes of light green coarsely toothed leaves to 6 in (15 cm) long with downy white undersides. Light yellow flowerheads to 2 in (5 cm) wide through the warmer months. Zones 9–11.

Arctotheca populifolia

☼ ✤ ↔ 8–16 in (20–40 cm) ↕ 8–12 in (20–30 cm)

Occurring on beach dunes, this species forms spreading base clumps or may be upright, developing a woody base with short branches. Leaves white to pale gray, elliptical, rarely lobed, to 3 in (8 cm) long. Flowerheads less than 1 in (25 mm) wide, bright yellow. Zones 9–11.

Arctostaphylos viridissima

Arctostaphylos viridissima 'White Cloud'

ARCTOTIS

AFRICAN DAISY

Found from the southern tip of Africa northward to Angola and sometimes confused with *Gazania*, this daisy (Asteraceae) family genus consists of around 50 species of low spreading annuals and perennials that often produce masses of large and brightly colored flowerheads. The leaves are simple, usually lance-shaped and frequently have felted undersides. For much of the year in mild climates the foliage is topped by 1–4 in (2.5–10 cm) wide flowers in a range of colors. Modern strains cover most of the spectrum except blue. The name *Arctotis* comes from the Greek and means "bear's ear," a rather obscure reference to the resemblance of the flower scales to a bear's ear.

CULTIVATION: They thrive in light well-drained soil and full sun. They are drought tolerant but will flower more heavily if watered well in the growing season. Propagate from seed, though perennial species grow readily from cuttings of non-flowering stems.

Arctotis acaulis

☼ ⁂ ↔ 12–40 in (30–100 cm)
↑ 6–12 in (15–30 cm)

Clumping rosette-forming perennial. Wavy, lobed, or toothed leaves to 8 in (20 cm) long, green above, white hair below. Flowerheads to 4 in (10 cm) wide, ray florets mainly in yellow, orange, or red shades, disc florets deep purple. 'Magenta', long-stemmed purple-red flowers. Zones 9–10.

Arctotis fastuosa

CAPE DAISY, MONARCH OF THE VELDT

☼ ⁂ ↔ 12–16 in (30–40 cm)
↑ 20–28 in (50–70 cm)

Annual or short-lived perennial. Coarsely hairy, deeply lobed, silvery leaves to 6 in (15 cm) long. Orange ray florets, maroon at the base. Deep maroon to brown disc florets. 'Zulu Prince' is a typical garden form with

Arctotis venusta

Arctotis gumbletonii

white ray florets, golden-orange at the base, around purple-blue disc florets. Zones 9–11.

Arctotis gumbletonii

☼ ⁂ ↔ 16–40 in (40–100 cm)
↑ 8–16 in (20–40 cm)

This is a rosette-forming perennial that develops large clumps of lobed silver-gray leaves to 8 in (20 cm) long. Flowerheads to 4 in (10 cm) wide, with orange to red ray florets, yellow to brown at the base, around very dark, almost black, disc florets. Zones 9–10.

Arctotis × hybrida

☼ ⁂ ↔ 8–20 in (20–50 cm)
↑ 8–16 in (20–40 cm)

This species has mainly *A. venusta* × *A. fastuosa* parentage. Compact plants, usually with silvery foliage and often treated as annuals in cool climates. It has many popular named cultivars and seedling strains, including: 'Flame' ★, with bright orange flowers; 'Harlequin Flame', bright orange-red flowers; 'Mahogany', deep red-brown flowers; and 'Red Devil', bright red. Zones 9–11.

Arctotis stoechadifolia

AFRICAN DAISY, BLUE-EYED AFRICA DAISY

☼ ⁂ ↔ 18 in (45 cm)
↑ 18–24 in (45–60 cm)

An annual from South Africa. Gray-green oblong leaves. Daisy-like disk

Ardisia crenata

Arctotis × hybrida 'Red Devil'

Arctotis acaulis

Arctotis × hybrida 'Flame'

flowers, in various bright colors; blooms summer–autumn if dead-headed. Can be used in dry sandy soil, withstands drought. Zones 9–10.

Arctotis venusta

BLUE-EYED AFRICAN DAISY

☼ ⁂ ↔ 8–16 in (20–40 cm)
↑ 16–24 in (40–60 cm)

Annual with deeply lobed to almost pinnate, downy, gray-white leaves and heavily ribbed flower stems. Flowers in cultivation are variably colored but wild plants usually have deep magenta ray florets and purple-blue disc florets. Zones 9–11.

ARDISIA

Over 250 species of evergreen shrubs and small trees make up this Myrsinaceae family genus, occurring in the tropics and subtropics of all continents except Africa. They occur mainly in high-rainfall mountain areas. Leaves are simple with margins sometimes toothed or crinkled, crowded at the ends of branchlets. A common feature is translucent brown-

ish spots or streaks in the leaves, more easily seen in species with thinner leaves. The small flowers are mostly star-shaped, borne in stalked umbels among the outer leaves; the 5 petals are often patterned with tiny spots. Fruits are small one-seeded berries.

CULTIVATION: Most are shade-loving plants and prefer humid conditions protected from the wind. Soil should be well-drained, humus-rich, and moisture-retentive. Indoor plants should be kept away from hot sunny positions. They can be cut back near the base, resulting in renewal by vigorous shoots. Propagation is usually from seed; cuttings can also be used.

Ardisia crenata

CORAL ARDISIA, CORALBERRY

☀ ❄ ↔ 18 in (45 cm)   ↑ 6 ft (1.8 m)

This species occurs wild in southern Japan, China, and the eastern Himalayas. Side branches in tiers form a bushy head of dark green foliage. White starry flowers in umbels, in spring–summer. Coral red fruits persist into winter. Zones 7–11.

Areca ipot

Areca catechu

Ardisia escallonioides

MARLBERRY

☀ ❋ ↔ 12 ft (3.5 m) ↑ 25 ft (8 m)

From Mexico, Guatemala, the northern West Indies, and southern Florida, USA. Yellowish green leaves to 6 in (15 cm) long. White flowers, densely red-dotted, in summer–autumn. Red-brown to black fruit. Zones 9–12.

Ardisia japonica

☀ ❋ ↔ unlimited ↑ 12 in (30 cm)

Native to Japan and China, this groundcover has leaves in whorls of 3 in (8 cm), glossy, dark-green with saw-toothed margins. White to pale pink flowers in summer. Fruits pink to red. '**Nishiki**', a variegated cultivar with irregular cream margins, translucent pink on new leaves. Zones 7–10.

ARECA

From the region between southern India and New Guinea, this palm (Arecaceae) genus of about 60 species is almost exclusively tropical. They are attractive small to medium-sized palms, mostly found in rainforest undergrowth. They vary in growth form with stems solitary or clustered from the base. Larger species have a well-developed crownshaft terminating the trunk. Flowering branches emerge from the top of the trunk just beneath the crownshaft. Flowers are small, mostly cream or yellow, on the branchlets in groups of 3. Red or yellow fruits are egg-shaped. CULTIVATION: Most species thrive outdoors only in the wet tropics, though some from higher altitudes may grow in frost-free climates outside the tropics. They do best in sheltered situations with permanently moist soil. Larger species will tolerate strong sun, but the smaller, more delicate ones need protection. In cooler climates they require a green-

Areca triandra

house with high humidity. Propagate from fresh seed from which the flesh has been stripped away.

Areca catechu

BETEL PALM

☀ ✴ ↔ 12 ft (3.5 m) ↑ 50 ft (15 m)

Single-trunked palm, swollen green crownshaft. Arching feather-like fronds. Flowering branches, short, with stiff branchlets. Yellow to orange-red fruits, up to 3 in (8 cm) long. The chewing of betel nut is a widespread custom throughout the natural distribution region of this species. Zones 11–12.

Areca ipot

☀ ✴ ↔ 10 ft (3 m) ↑ 12 ft (3.5 m)

Native of the the Philippines. The trunk is green and prominently ringed, topped by a smooth green crownshaft. Bright green arching fronds to about 6 ft (1.8 m) long. Short flower clusters. Orange to red egg-shaped fruit. Zones 11–12.

Areca triandra

☀ ✴ ↔ 8 ft (2.4 m) ↑ 10 ft (3 m)

Occurs in mountain rainforest from eastern India to the Philippines. Single-stemmed or multi-stemmed trunk, green, prominently ringed. Smooth green crownshafts, erect fronds, dark green leaflets. Panicles of cream flowers. Bright red fruits. Zones 11–12.

Ardisia escallonioides

ARENARIA

SANDWORT

This genus of about 160 low-growing, largely perennial, woody herbs and some annuals from the pink (Caryophyllaceae) family grows naturally across the temperate Northern Hemisphere. They are ideal as rock-garden plants and compact ground covers. The branching stems bear masses of dense, often hairy, linear to circular foliage that grows in opposite pairs. Abundant, small, star-like flowers, normally white and 5-petalled, grow in cymes or solitary on slender stalks. Their shallow root system can make them drought sensitive. Fruit is a cylindrical or ovoid capsule with 6 lobes. The genus derives its name from the Latin for sand, *arena*, referring to a preference for sandy soils. CULTIVATION: Most of the species in this family need partial shade and protection from hot afternoon sun, especially in hot climates. They will tolerate poor soils, but the soil should be moist, sandy, and well drained. Shallow roots will require mulching or frequent watering around, but not over, the plant. Propagate by division, from seed in autumn or spring, or from softwood cuttings in early summer.

Arenaria montana

☼/☀ ❋ ↔ 9–24 in (23–60 cm) ↑ 4–6 in (10–15 cm)

This vigorous perennial comes from southwestern Europe. It has loose mats of narrow, gray-green, hairy leaves to 1½ in (35 mm) long. White flowers, 15–18 mm across, are solitary or in few-flowered cymes in spring–early summer. '**Avalanche**' is more profuse, with larger white flowers. Zones 4–8.

Arenaria purpurascens

☼/☀ ❋ ↔ 9–24 in (23–60 cm) ↑ 4–6 in (10–15 cm)

Evergreen, tufted, mat-forming perennial with small, sharply pointed, glossy leaves, from mountain areas of

Arenaria montana

Arenga australasica

Arenga porphyrocarpa

northern Spain. Many small clusters of 1 to 4 tiny, star-shaped, pale to deep purplish pink flowers, 5–12 mm across, on stems to 4 in (10 cm) long, early spring–summer. 'Elliot's Variety', abundant pink flowers. Zones 4–8.

ARENGA

An interesting genus of the palm (Arecaceae) family, *Arenga* consists of about 20 species from tropical and subtropical East Asia to northeastern Australia and the Solomon Islands. Variable in size from diminutive palms of rainforest undergrowth to massive solitary trees. *A. pinnata* is a source of palm sugar. Many have trunks sheathed in mats of blackish fibers. The fronds are variable. Flowering branches on single trunked species appear at the top of the fully grown trunk, followed by a succession of flowering branches down the trunk; after the lowest sets fruit the whole tree dies. Flowers, creamy yellow or orange, highly perfumed. Fruits have a gelatinous flesh that is very irritating to the skin and mouth.
CULTIVATION: Arengas are vigorous palms that adapt well to cultivation. They do best in sheltered but sunny situations with ample soil moisture. All the multi-stemmed species will grow readily in pots in a conservatory and take years to outgrow their containers. Propagate from seed, or the clumping species may be divided.

Arenga australasica
☼ ✶ ↔ 15 ft (4.5 m) ↑ 60 ft (18 m)
From far northern Queensland, Australia. A multi-stemmed species where only one or two trunks elongate, rising from a clump of basal shoots. Trunks thick, smooth, and without fibers. Fronds 8–10 ft (2.4–3 m) long, with glossy green leaflets. Zones 11–12.

Arenga engleri
☼ ❧ ↔ 10 ft (3 m) ↑ 12 ft (3.5 m)
Native to Taiwan and Japan's far southern Ryukyu Islands. Makes a dense clump. Fronds have regularly spaced leaflets with toothed edges. Orange flowers in summer. Cherry-sized fruits ripen from yellow to dark red in autumn. Zones 9–12.

Arenga hookeriana
☼ ✶ ↔ 15 in (38 cm) ↑ 18 in (45 cm)
Small Malaysian palm, monocarpic. Leaves 15 in (38 cm) long, may be pinnate or simple and undivided. Grows well as house plant or short-lived garden specimen. Zones 11–12.

Arenga obtusifolia
☼ ✶ ↔ 20–35 ft (6–10 m) ↑ to 40 ft (12 m)
Palm with one or more trunks, to 12 in (30 cm) in diameter. Leaves large, 10–17 ft (3–5 m) long, leaflets narrow, all in the one plane, green above, grayish below. Inflorescences

Arenga hookeriana

40–60 in (100–150 cm) long, flowers brownish. Fruits red, egg-shaped, 1¼–2 in (3–5 cm) long. Occurs in rainforests of mainland Malaysia as well as Sumatra and Java in Indonesia. Zones 11–12.

Arenga pinnata
AREN, GOMUTI PALM, KABONG, SUGAR PALM
☼ ❧ ↔ 40 ft (12 m) ↑ 60 ft (18 m)
From India or Myanmar. Always single-trunked; trunk covered in stiff blackish fibers. Fronds plume-like. The first flowering branch is at 8 years, successive ones emerging over the next 3 to 5 years. Fruits ripen to blackish. Zones 10–12.

Arenga porphyrocarpa
☼ ✶ ↔ 4 ft (1.2 m) ↑ 10 ft (3 m)
This native of Java makes a dense clump of stems. Slender fronds arch outward with widely separated leaflets, to 18 in (45 cm) long. Flowering branches hidden among the leaf bases. Olive-sized purplish fruit. Zones 11–12.

Arenga tremula
☼ ❧ ↔ 10–15 ft (3–4.5 m) ↑ 7–10 ft (2–3 m)
An understory species of tropical lowland rainforests of the Philippines,

Arenga undulatifolia

this short-trunked species of feather-leaf palm grows in large clumps. Trunks green with pale prominent leaf scars. Leaves narrow, green. Inflorescences large, exceeding foliage in length. Zones 10–12.

Arenga undulatifolia
syn. *Arenga ambong*
☼ ✶ ↔ 15 ft (4.5 m) ↑ 20 ft (6 m)
Beautiful species from parts of Borneo and Sulawesi. Makes a clump of stems. Large fronds, fanning out gracefully. Short flowering branches, half-concealed among the frond bases. Fruits are egg-sized. Zones 11–12.

Arenga engleri

A

ARGEMONE

A genus of 23 species of annual or perennial herbs and one shrub, in the poppy (Papaveraceae) family. Occurs in North and South America, West Indies, and Hawaii, in drier plant communities, commonly colonizing. Erect stems are produced from fleshy roots, leaves entire or deeply lobed, prickly or smooth, bluish green. Flowers broad and shallow, white, yellow, or mauve, in clusters or singly, in summer–autumn. Fruits are prickly pods, containing many blackish seeds. Stems contain a yellowish latex. CULTIVATION: Propagate from seed, which germinates readily. Grow in full sun in well-draining gravelly soils. Self-seeding occurs with some species.

Argemone munita

Argyranthemum, HC, 'Donnington Hero'

Argemone mexicana
MEXICAN POPPY, PRICKLY POPPY

☀ ❄ ↔ 12–16 in (30–40 cm)
↑ to 36 in (90 cm)

Erect, spreading annual. Leaves deeply lobed, gray-green with silvery spines, to 5 in (12 cm) long. Yellow flowers, to 3 in (8 cm) across, in summer–autumn. A weed from southern USA to Central America. 'White Lustre', white flowers; 'Yellow Lustre', orange-yellow flowers. Zones 8–10.

Argemone munita
PRICKLY POPPY

☀ ❄ ↔ 12–20 in (30–50 cm)
↑ 24–36 in (60–90 cm)

Multi-stemmed, herbaceous perennial, occurring in chapparal and woodlands of several western USA States. Grows at altitudes from 800 m to 2,500 m, flowering in summer. Leaves deeply lobed, prickly, grayish. White flowers, up to 3 in (8 cm) across, crinkly petals, spiny sepals, up to 250 yellow stamens per flower. Zones 7–9.

Argemone squarrosa
☀ ❄ ↔ to 24 in (60 cm) ↑ to 32 in (80 cm)
Perennial, stems branching, prickly. Leaf margins toothed, prickles on both surfaces. Flowers to ½ in (12 mm)

Argyranthemum, HC, 'Petite Pink'

across, white, stamens pale yellow, in spring–summer. Fruits egg-shaped to cylindrical capsules, prickly, in summer–autumn. Seeds black. Occurs on prairies, arid slopes, foothills, valleys in central-southern USA. Zones 7–9.

ARGYRANTHEMUM

From the Canary Islands and Madeira and often treated as perennials, the 24 members of this genus, of the daisy (Asteraceae) family, are evergreen shrubs. Popular in gardens and as cut flowers, there are numerous cultivars, most with "double" or "semi-double" flowerheads, over a long season. All are shrubs that branch low, with brittle stems and crowded leaves from coarsely toothed to deeply dissected. Leaves have a slightly aromatic, bitter smell when bruised. Long-stalked flowerheads borne in groups of 2 to 5. CULTIVATION: Marginally frost hardy, in cold climates these shrubs need to be brought under shelter in winter. Prefer a temperate climate with a distinct cool winter. Cutting-grown plants can be raised to flowering size in 6 months, so can be treated as annuals. Soil should be very well drained and not too rich, sunny position needed. Pinch out young plants to shape. Propagate from tip cuttings at any time, preferably in autumn for spring and summer display.

Argyranthemum frutescens
syn. *Chrysanthemum frutescens*
MARGUERITE, MARGUERITE DAISY

☀ ✦ ↔ 3 ft (0.9 m) ↑ 3 ft (0.9 m)
The original wild form of this Canary Islands native is a low spreading shrub with leaves dissected into a few narrow segments. Single white flowerheads, golden yellow centers, for much of year. Most recent cultivars have generally been included in this species, but are in fact of hybrid origin, with other species in parentage. Zones 9–10.

Argyranthemum gracile
☀ ✦ ↔ 36 in (90 cm) ↑ 24 in (60 cm)
Endemic to Tenerife in the Canary Islands, growing among rocks close to

Argyranthemum gracile

Argyranthemum gracile 'Chelsea Girl'

the sea. Leaves with very long thin lobes, without teeth, bluish green. Fine-stemmed white flowerheads most of year. 'Chelsea Girl', free-flowering, upright habit. Zones 9–11.

Argyranthemum maderense
YELLOW MARGUERITE

☀ ✦ ↔ 20 in (50 cm) ↑ 18 in (45 cm)
Native of the Canary Islands. Leaves broad, soft, deep green, mostly with coarse blunt teeth toward the tip rather than lobed. Flowerheads have broad pale golden yellow rays, a disc of slightly deeper color. Zones 9–11.

Argyranthemum Hybrid Cultivars
☀◐ ✦ ↔ 18–36 in (45–90 cm)
↑ 12–30 in (30–75 cm)

Though many references have included all *Argyranthemum* cultivars under the species *A. frutescens*, it seems clear that most present-day cultivars are of hybrid origin. Apart from *A. frutescens*, likely parent species include *A. foeniculaceum* and *A. maderense*. Single cultivars include: 'Butterfly', a compact cultivar with rich yellow single flowers; 'California Gold' ★, having a dwarf habit with large golden yellow blooms, with leaf segments few and broad; 'Cornish Gold', yellow flowers, darker centers; 'Donnington Hero', low and spreading with coarsely lobed leaves and neat, single, white flowers; 'Gill's Pink', with pale pink rays, deeper at the base, and broad leaf lobes; 'Jamaica Primrose', a tall cultivar with pale to mid-yellow blooms; and 'Petite Pink', single pink flowers. Doubles include: 'Blizzard', with rather tangled white rays and some disc florets showing. The anemone-form or semi-double group includes: 'Mary Wootton', an older cultivar with a pale pink center; 'Tauranga Star', having white rays, slightly quilled, with a white "button" grading with a pale gold center; and 'Vancouver', similar to 'Mary Wootton' but with a bright pink domed central "button" and paler rays like the spokes of a wheel. Zones 9–10.

Argyranthemum, Hybrid Cultivar, 'Butterfly'

ARGYROCYTISUS

A monotypic genus of the pea-flower subfamily of legumes (Fabaceae), with its sole species an evergreen shrub native to the Rif and Atlas Mountains of Morocco. The name is a combination of *argyros* (silver) and *Cytisus* (the plant's former genus). It refers to the silvery foliage, which derives its coloration from its dense covering of fine silvery hairs that are reflective, giving the plant a metallic sheen. Spikes of bright golden yellow flowers open in late spring and early summer.
CULTIVATION: Left alone, this species can become rather spindly, though it bushes up if trimmed regularly. An alternative is to grow it as an espalier. It is quite hardy and prefers a gritty well-drained soil in full sun. Propagate by seed or half-hardened late summer and autumn cuttings.

Argyrocytisus battandieri
SILVER BROOM
☼ ❄ ↔ 12 ft (3.5 m) ↕ 12 ft (3.5 m)
Widely regarded as the most sophisticated of the brooms. Shrub, with silvery trifoliate foliage. Bright yellow flowers, scented. Pea-pod-like seed capsules, covered with fine silvery hair. 'Yellow Tail', selected for flowers of richer yellow color. Zones 7–9.

ARGYRODERMA

This genus of 10 species of succulents in the iceplant (Aizoaceae) family from South Africa is among those known as "living stones" because their highly succulent, usually stemless, blue-green leaves occur at ground level and can resemble small stones. These distinctive plants form small clumps of a few or many paired, usually cylindrical to egg-shaped leaves that are cleft in the center. Each stem bears just 2 leaves per season but may produce offsets over the years. In some species the old leaves persist and form a short column on which new leaves develop. Solitary daisy-like flowers, usually white, yellow, or purple, appear in the cleft.
CULTIVATION: Like most succulents, they prefer to be kept dry in winter and are also damaged by repeated frosts. To prevent rotting, which can also occur if water collects around the crown, use a mulch of pebbles. Plant in a bright position with gritty free-draining soil. Propagate from seed or careful division of established clumps.

Argyroderma delaetii
☼ ⚘ ↔ 4 in (10 cm) ↕ 2 in (5 cm)
Usually just one pair of egg-shaped blue-green leaves; most of the plant is underground. White, rarely yellow or purple-pink flowers. Zones 9–11.

ARIOCARPUS

Rare, small, slow-growing plants from arid to extreme desert areas of Texas, USA, and Mexico, the 6 species of this genus are members of the cactus (Cactaceae) family. They normally grow as solitary, spineless rosettes with short to quite long tubercles with tufts of wool between them, and in some species a woolly furrow along the upperside of each tubercle. They generally have thick skin and stout turnip-like roots, and may cluster with age. Species are usually wider than they are tall and some even grow flush with the soil. Most mimic their stony habitat, which renders them hard to locate, except when they flower, usually in autumn. Flowers come in shades of white, purple, pink, or yellow, and are mostly self-fertile. Seed pods are hidden in the woolly growing point. All *Ariocarpus* are listed in Appendix I of CITES but illegal collecting has almost eliminated some species in certain habitats. Collected specimens are difficult to re-establish and should not be bought.
CULTIVATION: While habitat collected *Ariocarpus* are difficult to grow, seed-raised plants present few difficulties if grown in a predominantly mineralized soil with a little humus and some gypsum. They should be kept completely dry in summer and winter and watered thoroughly, but not frequently, in spring and autumn. Slow growing, these plants may take decades to fill a 6 in (15 cm) pot.

Ariocarpus fissuratus
☼ ⚘ ↔ 6 in (15 cm) ↕ 1½–4 in (3.5–10 cm)
From southern Texas to northern Mexico. The neat rosettes of this species usually grow flush with the soil. Gray-green triangular tubercles, 15 mm wide, with a distinct furrow. The bulk of the plant consists of a tap

Argyrocytisus battandieri

Argyroderma delaetii

root up to 18 in (45 cm) long. Flowers are pale pink to magenta, 1½–2 in (35–50 mm) wide. Zones 9–11.

Ariocarpus kotschoubeyanus
☼ ⚘ ↔ 2–3 in (5–8 cm)
↕ 1½–2 in (1.2–5 cm)
From central Mexico. Like *A. fissuratus* but narrower, and smooth gray-brown tubercles have no furrows. Just 3 of these plants were found in the 1830s, one of them being sold in Paris for its equivalent weight in gold. Flowers white, pale pink to purple, 1¼–2 in (30–50 mm) wide. Zones 9–11.

Ariocarpus retusus
☼ ⚘ ↔ 15 in (38 cm) ↕ 10 in (25 cm)
Occurs in several central Mexican States. Neat rosette of smooth, gray-green, unfurrowed tubercles pointing upward and outward, covered with thick wool at growing point. Flowers pale pink, 1¼–2 in (30–50 mm) wide. *A. r.* var. *furfuraceus* forms neat rosettes, rock-like in appearance. Zones 9–11.

Ariocarpus retusus var. *furfuraceus*

Ariocarpus kotschoubeyanus

Ariocarpus retusus

Arisaema sikokianum

Arisaema consanguineum

Arisaema kishidae

Arisaema amurense

Arisaema serratum

Arisaema candidissimum

ARISAEMA

Genus of about 150 tuberous perennials in the arum (Araceae) family. Found in Africa, North America, and Asia, usually in shade or woodland. Their ornamental leaves and stems and bizarre flowers make them interesting in gardens. Leaves may be compound or divided and stems are often mottled in pink to purplish shades. Large hooded flower spathes may be yellow, green, brown, red, or pink; striped or mottled. They surround the spadix, a central column of small true flowers from short and club-like to long and drooping. Orange-red berries form on the spadix.
CULTIVATION: Grow frost-tolerant species in shelter, part-shade, or woodland in cool peaty soil. Give protective mulch in winter, guard from slugs. Greenhouse-grown tropical species need a deep pot in a mix of leaf mold, grit, and slightly acid loam. Propagate from seed or by division of tubers.

Arisaema amurense
☀ ❄ ↔ 12 in (30 cm) ↕ 12 in (30 cm)
From northern Asia. One or two leaves with 5 radiating leaflets on dull purple stems. Upright spathe striped purple and green over white. Spring-flowering. Zones 5–9.

Arisaema candidissimum ★
☀ ❄ ↔ 18 in (45 cm) ↕ 12 in (30 cm)
From western China. Single large trifoliate leaf with mottled pinkish brown stem, emerging with or after flower in early summer. Pale pink-striped spathe with long tip. Flowers slightly scented. Zones 6–9.

Arisaema consanguineum
☀ ❄ ↔ 12 in (30 cm) ↕ 36 in (90 cm)
From Himalayas and central China. Single leaf of 11 to 20 radiating leaflets to 16 in (40 cm) long. Spathe has long slightly drooping point, green and purple with narrow stripes. Flowers in early summer. Zones 7–10.

Arisaema dracontium
DRAGONROOT, GREEN DRAGON
◗/☀ ❄ ↔ 12–18 in (30–45 cm) ↕ 30 in (75 cm)
From eastern USA. Herbaceous perennial. Light green spathe in late spring; ends in long projection like a yellow whip. Inedible red-orange berries follow. All parts of the plant are poisonous. Spathe is narrower than that of A. triphyllum. Zones 4–9.

Arisaema kishidae
☀ ❄ ↔ 12 in (30 cm) ↕ 12 in (30 cm)
Native to Japan. Stocky species with 2 leaves of several flaring leaflets, sometimes marked silver. Spathe brownish mauve, striped and hooded. Spring-flowering. Zones 5–9.

Arisaema ringens
syn. Arisaema praecox
☀ ❄ ↔ 12 in (30 cm) ↕ 12 in (30 cm)
From Japan, China, and Korea. Has two leaves each with 3 broad leaflets.

The spathe is small, green and purple with white stripes, and remains in a curled position enclosing the spadix. Flowers are seen in early spring. Zones 7–10.

Arisaema robustum
☀ ❄ ↔ 18 in (45 cm) ↕ 18 in (45 cm)
Native to Japan. Has a single leaf with broad palmate leaflets. The upright spathe is sometimes purple in color but usually green with white stripes. Flowers in early summer. Zones 7–10.

Arisaema serratum
syn. Arisaema japonicum
☀ ❄ ↔ 24 in (60 cm) ↕ 36 in (90 cm)
From northeastern Asia. Two leaves with several leaflets on mottled purple stems. Slender hooded spathe, green or purple, sometimes striped white. Spring-flowering. Zones 5–9.

Arisaema sikokianum
☀ ❄ ↔ 18 in (45 cm) ↕ 18 in (45 cm)
From Japan. Two leaves with 3 to 5 leaflets with toothed margins. Upright spathe has a purple exterior, paler and striped inside. Spadix prominent, white, club-shaped. Flowers in early summer. Zones 5–9.

Arisaema ringens

Arisaema taiwanense

Arisaema speciosum
COBRA LILY

☀ ❄ ↔ 18 in (45 cm)
↑ 24–36 in (60–90 cm)

Native to Nepal and southwestern China. A single leaf with large leaflets flushed red at the margins. Mottled purple stems. Large hooded spathe, dark purple with white stripes. Spadix has a long thread-like appendage. Flowers in early summer. Zones 8–10.

Arisaema taiwanense

☀ ❄ ↔ 18 in (45 cm) ↑ 36 in (90 cm)
From Taiwan. A single leaf with several umbrella-like leaflets and mottled stems. Purplish brown mottled spathe, hooded, with a long thread-like appendage. White spadix, club-shaped. Zones 6–9.

Arisaema tortuosum

☀ ❄ ↔ 18 in (45 cm) ↑ 36 in (90 cm)
Native to the Himalayan region. Two or three leaves with several leaflets. Spathe is green. Spadix with long thread-like twisted appendage. Flowers in early summer. Zones 7–10.

Arisaema triphyllum
INDIAN TURNIP, JACK-IN-THE-PULPIT

☀ ❄ ↔ 18 in (45 cm)
↑ 12–24 in (30–60 cm)

From eastern North America. Has two leaves with 3 pointed leaflets. Spathe hooded, green to purple, striped green or white. Summer-flowering. Zones 4–9.

ARISARUM
This genus of 3 species of tuberous perennials is a member of the arum (Araceae) family and is native to the Mediterranean and Atlantic islands. The arrowhead-shaped leaves are borne on a long stalk. The green or purplish flower spathe is usually level with or just below the foliage and is hooded, enclosing the spadix (central column of true flowers).
CULTIVATION: Grow in a humus-rich moist soil in shade or half-sun. In areas with very heavy frosts give a protective mulch in winter. Propagate by division of tubers when dormant or from seed in spring.

Arisarum proboscideum
MOUSE PLANT

☀ ❄ ↔ 10 in (20 cm) ↑ 8 in (20 cm)
From Italy and Spain. Its glossy arrow-shaped leaves almost conceal the hooded chocolate-brown spathes, which have a curling tail-like appendage, hence the common name. Flowers over a long period in spring. Zones 7–10.

Arisarum vulgare
FRIAR'S COWL

☀ ❄ ↔ 15 in (38 cm) ↑ 10 in (20 cm)
From the Mediterranean and Atlantic islands. Arrowhead-shaped leaves of deep green, often spotted silver. Hooded spathes, purple, striped with silver toward the base, held slightly above the foliage. Flowers late in winter and is summer dormant. Zones 7–10.

ARISTEA
This iris (Iridaceae) family genus is made up of about 50 mainly evergreen species of fleshy-stemmed perennials found in Africa from the tropics to South Africa and Madagascar. They have upright sword-shaped leaves, in some species over 24 in (60 cm) long, in fans resembling those of the irises. The 6-petalled flowers, borne on branching stems with somewhat flattened segments, occur in shades of blue, lavender, and purple, and are short-lived, each bloom lasting only a day or so. The flowering season ranges from late winter to summer, depending on the species.
CULTIVATION: Tolerant of only light frosts, most prefer to grow in sun or half-sun with a light but humus-rich, moist, well-drained soil. Plants can be divided but resent disturbance, so they are usually propagated from seed, which may be sown in autumn in frost-free areas, otherwise in spring.

Aristea africana

☀/◐ ▨ ↔ 8–16 in (20–40 cm)
↑ 8–10 in (20–25 cm)

A fairly small species from South Africa. Narrow leaves about 6 in (15 cm) long. Flowers purplish blue, 1 in (25 mm) wide, relatively few per stem, opening from late winter. Zones 9–11.

Aristea ecklonii

☀/◐ ▨ ↔ 18–32 in (45–80 cm)
↑ 18–32 in (45–80 cm)

A South African species. Arching leaves to 24 in (60 cm) long. Loose open panicles of 1 in (25 mm) wide bright blue to magenta flowers in late spring–summer. Zones 9–11.

Aristea major

☀/◐ ▨ ↔ 24–36 in (60–90 cm)
↑ 3–5 ft (0.9–1.5 m)

A native of the Cape region of South Africa, with blue-green leaves, 3–4 ft (0.9–1.2 m) long. Rootstock can form a short trunk. Densely packed clusters of soft blue flowers, to 1½ in (35 mm) wide, in summer. Zones 9–10.

Aristea major

Arisarum proboscideum

Aristea africana

ARISTOLOCHIA
BIRTHWORT, DUTCHMAN'S PIPE

This genus contains about 300 species ranging from vigorous climbers to perennials, both deciduous and evergreen, found throughout tropical and temperate regions. It is a member of the birthwort (Aristolochiaceae) family. Stems are usually thick and fissured, and leaves vary from entire to lobed, often being heart-shaped. The flowers, which trap pollinating insects, have bladder-like bases and weird, contorted, tubular shapes. They range from 3 in (8 cm) to giants of 20 in (50 cm) and many have an offensive smell. Flowers are mottled in shades of brown, pink, purple, and ivory. The common name, birthwort, comes from the herbal use of some species as an aid to childbirth.
CULTIVATION: Many of the vigorous climbers are hardy only to 23°F (−5°C) and better suit the greenhouse in cooler areas. Where suitable, grow outdoors in sun or half-sun in a rich well-drained soil. Climbers require support and can be pruned in late winter. Propagate from softwood cuttings or seed or by division.

Aristolochia californica
☼/◑ ❋ ↔ 10 ft (3 m) ↑ 15 ft (4.5 m)
Native to California. Deciduous climber with heart-shaped leaves, hairy beneath. Small, contorted, tubular flowers dull red-purple inside, borne along stems in summer. Zones 8–10.

Aristolochia clematitis
BIRTHWORT
☼/◑ ❋ ↔ 24 in (60 cm)
↑ 12–30 in (30–75 cm)
Native to Europe and naturalized in the UK and North America. Herbaceous species with heart-shaped leaves. Small dull greenish yellow flowers appear among the foliage in summer. Zones 6–10.

Aristolochia californica

Aristolochia clematitis

Aristolochia fimbriata

Aristolochia macrophylla

Aristotelia australasica

Aristolochia fimbriata
☼/◑ ⌇ ↔ 10 ft (3 m) ↑ 7–10 ft (2–3 m)
From Brazil, a climber with round to heart-shaped leaves with prominent, pale, netted veining. Small, curving, tubular flowers, fringed edges, greenish brown outside and purplish brown with yellow markings inside. Zones 10–11.

Aristolochia gigantea
☼/◑ ⌇ ↔ 15 ft (4.5 m) ↑ 30 ft (9 m)
From Panama and Brazil. Vigorous climber with triangular leaves, downy below. Very large flowers with bladder-like base and flaring lips of mottled chocolate-purple and ivory can be up to 20 in × 14 in (50 cm × 35 cm). Summer-flowering. Zones 10–11.

Aristolochia grandiflora
PELICAN FLOWER
☼/◑ ⌇ ↔ 6 ft (1.8 m) ↑ 10 ft (3 m)
Native to Central America and West Indies. Deep green heart-shaped leaves. Very large contorted flowers with bladder-like base and lip with long narrow appendage. Mottled in purple, green, and cream. Summer-flowering. Zones 10–11.

Aristolochia labiata
syn. *Aristolochia brasiliensis*
ROOSTER FLOWER
☼/◑ ⌇ ↔ 20 ft (6 m) ↑ 35 ft (10 m)
A South American species with heart-shaped leaves, gray beneath. Flowers mottled red, yellow, green, and purple. They have bladder-like bases with contorted flaring lips. Summer-flowering. Zones 10–11.

Aristolochia littoralis
syn. *Aristolochia elegans*
CALICO FLOWER
☼/◑ ⌇ ↔ 15 ft (4.5 m) ↑ 20 ft (6 m)
Native to Brazil. Naturalized in Central America and southern USA. Can be weedy in warm climates. Vigorous climber with heart-shaped leaves, grayish green beneath. Flowers have bladder-like bases with almost round lips. Mottled in chocolate purple and ivory. Summer-flowering. Zones 9–11.

Aristolochia macrophylla
syns *Aristolochia durior, A. sipho*
DUTCHMAN'S PIPE
☼/◑ ❋ ↔ 20 ft (6 m) ↑ 30 ft (9 m)
From eastern USA. Vigorous climber with very large heart-shaped leaves. Small, tubular, green flowers are mottled with pink, brown, and ivory. Flowers arise from the leaf axils in summer and are hidden by the foliage. Zones 6–9.

ARISTOTELIA
WINEBERRY

Once thought to contain up to 12 species, this Elaeocarpaceae family genus has been revised down to just five. Native to the southern temperate regions, they are large shrubs or small trees that, excepting *A. serrata,* are evergreen. Their flowers, while individually small, are massed in clusters and are followed by colorful berries. The plants are unisexual and both male and female must be grown for fruiting. The leaves are usually rather glossy with toothed edges and the new growth can be very attractive.
CULTIVATION: *Aristotelia* adapts well to cultivation and poses no special problems. It does well in a sunny or

Aristolochia littoralis

semi-shaded position with moist well-drained soil. All the species can withstand light to moderate frosts. Half-hardened cuttings are the preferred method of propagation. Plants can be raised from seed but the sex will be unknown until flowering.

Aristotelia australasica

MOUNTAIN WINEBERRY

☀ ❄ ↔ 6 ft (1.8 m) ↑ 15 ft (4.5 m)

Shrub from mountains of southeastern Australia. Found in forest under-growth. Deep green foliage. Clusters of small white to cream flowers, petals delicately fringed, in spring. Pinkish red fruit darkens with age. Zones 8–10.

Aristotelia chilensis

☀ ❄ ↔ 15 ft (4.5 m) ↑ 15 ft (4.5 m)

Chilean species. Leathery leaves to 4 in (10 cm) long, reddish stems, clusters of tiny green-white flowers. Purple berries ripen to black. Grown mainly as a foliage filler. Gardeners may prefer the white-variegated cultivar, 'Variegata'. Zones 8–10.

Aristotelia serrata

MAKOMAKO, WINEBERRY

☀ ❄ ↔ 12 ft (3.5 m) ↑ 20 ft (6 m)

Unique in the genus and rare among New Zealand plants in being decidu-ous. Flowers tiny, purple-pink to red shade, massed in 4 in (10 cm) long panicles, resembling lilac (*Syringa*) flowers. Appear in spring with the new foliage. Fruit is red. Zones 8–10.

ARMERIA

SEA PINK, THRIFT

Armeria was the Roman name for *Dianthus* and was given to this genus because of a supposed resemblance, also reflected in the common name, "sea pink." However, *Armeria* comes from a different family, the leadworts (Plumbaginaceae), not the carnations. The genus comprises around 80 species of herbaceous and shrubby perennials found in Eurasia, North Africa, and the American Pacific coast. They form clumps of simple linear leaves, above which rounded

Armeria maritima

heads of tiny flowers with colorful bracts are held in spring and summer. The name "thrift" is applied in the sense of the meaning "to thrive", as the plant grows in harsh conditions. CULTIVATION: They occur in a wide range of environments and are easily cultivated, being especially at home in rockeries. Most are hardy and prefer moist well-drained soil and a position in full or half-sun. Propagate from seed or cuttings, or by the careful division of well-established clumps.

Armeria alliacea

☀/☀ ❄ ↔ 6–8 in (15–20 cm) ↑ 8–18 in (20–45 cm)

Cushion-forming species found from Portugal to southern Germany. Narrow, rather strappy leaves to 6 in (15 cm) long. Flower stems to 18 in (45 cm) tall. White flowerheads, ¾ in (18 mm) wide. Zones 7–10.

Armeria girardii

☀/☀ ❄ ↔ 8–12 in (20–30 cm) ↑ 6–8 in (15–20 cm)

Tufted perennial from southern France. Very small, fine, sometimes

Armeria maritima subsp. *californica*

Armeria maritima 'Bloodstone'

blue-green leaves, under 1 in (25 mm) long around the edge of the clump, nearly 2 in (5 cm) at the center. Flower stems to 6 in (15 cm) long. Pink flowerheads, ½ in (12 mm) wide. Zones 8–10.

Armeria juniperifolia

☀/☀ ❄ ↔ 6–8 in (15–20 cm) ↑ 6 in (15 cm)

Small shrubby species native to Spain. Very short, finely hairy, aromatic, grassy leaves. Flower stems less than 2 in (5 cm) long. Pink to magenta flowerheads, ½ in (12 mm) wide. 'Bevan's Variety' is a compact cultivar with dark foliage and short-stemmed pink flowerheads. Zones 8–10.

Armeria maritima

☀/☀ ❄ ↔ 8–16 in (20–40 cm) ↑ 8–12 in (20–30 cm)

This mounding perennial or subshrub is found across the northern temper-ate zone. It has grassy deep green leaves to 4 in (10 cm) long. Flower stems grow to 12 in (30 cm) tall with 1 in (25 mm) wide heads of white, pink, or red flowers. *A. m.*

subsp. *californica*, from California, USA, mounds to 6 in (15 cm) high and has lavender-pink flowerheads on short stems. *A. m.* 'Bee's Ruby' has vivid magenta flowers; 'Bloodstone' ★ has 8 in (20 cm) stems with deep magenta to red flowers; 'Corsica' has a dense clumping habit and small heads of brick red flowers; 'Isobel Burdett' has deep pink flowerheads on 8 in (20 cm) stems; 'Rubrifolia' has very dark black-red leaves and deep magenta flowers; 'Vindictive', has deep pink flowers on 6 in (15 cm) stems. Zones 4–10.

Armeria pseudarmeria

☀ ❄ ↔ 16–40 in (40–100 cm) ↑ 8–16 in (20–40 cm)

This dwarf subshrub or woody-based perennial is a native of coastal Portugal. Has fine grassy leaves around 1 in (25 mm) long. Flower stems are tall compared to the plant, with white to deep pink flower-heads to 2 in (5 cm) wide. 'Rubra' is a red-flowered cultivar; and 'Westacre Beauty' has soft pink flowers. Zones 8–10.

Armeria alliacea

Armeria juniperifolia

A

Arnica latifolia, in the wild, in Grand Teton National Park, Wyoming, USA

Armoracia rusticana

ARMORACIA

HORSERADISH

A genus of 3 species of perennials of the cabbage (Brassicaceae) family. They have strong deep tap roots from which emerge variably sized leaves, the largest of which can be up to 3 ft (0.9 m) long. The panicles of small white flowers are not a feature, and rather than allowing them to go to seed they are usually removed to encourage stronger foliage growth. In

addition to the common use of the roots to make horseradish sauce, both the foliage and the roots have a long history of medicinal use, especially in relation to their diuretic properties. CULTIVATION: Will grow in any temperate climate. For best root production plant in moist humus-rich soil, but take care as roots can be invasive in loose soil. Propagate by division; any small rooted piece will grow.

Armoracia rusticana

HORSERADISH, RED COLE

☀ ❄ ↔ 3–5 ft (0.9–1.5 m) ↕ 3 ft (0.9 m)

Very vigorous southern European native. Toothed, somewhat puckered leaves to 20 in (50 cm) long, pronounced midrib. Strong, rather invasive rootstock. Stout white roots are made into a very pungent condiment—horseradish sauce. '**Variegata**' is a cultivar with slightly smaller leaves that are variegated with bold white or cream splashes. Zones 5–9.

ARNICA

This genus of 32 species of fleshy-stemmed perennial herbs, native to northern temperate and Arctic regions, belongs to the daisy (Asteraceae) family. Many are found in alpine areas and most grow in moist soils. They have hairy oval to lance-shaped leaves that form basal clumps. Yellow daisies are borne on upright, often leafy, stems in summer. The most commonly grown species, *A. montana*, has been used for centuries in herbal medicine as a remedy for many things, including fever reduction, as a diuretic, circulatory stimulation, and externally as a balm for bruising and sprains. CULTIVATION: Grow in a moist, well-drained, humus-rich soil in the rock garden or border. Add extra grit to the soil for alpine species and ensure drainage is very good. Propagate from seed or by division.

Arnica latifolia

BROAD-LEAFED ARNICA, MOUNTAIN ARNICA

☀ ❄ ↔ 12 in (30 cm) ↕ 24–36 in (60–90 cm)

Found from Alaska to Colorado, USA. Clumps of long, oval to lance-shaped, toothed leaves. Yellow daisies, about 2 in (5 cm) wide, have 8 to 12 rays and greenish yellow centers. Zones 3–9.

ARONIA

CHOKEBERRY

This genus of deciduous shrubs from woodlands of eastern USA contains 2 species and a naturally occurring hybrid. Of the rose (Rosaceae) family, it is closely allied to *Photinia*—in fact current opinion suggests it should be in that genus, though this has not gained wide acceptance. The shrubs are of compact size bearing white or pale pink spring blossoms that are followed by small berry-like fruits of red, purple, or black which give rise to the common name of chokeberry. The foliage colors attractively in autumn in shades of red and crimson. CULTIVATION: These shrubs are well suited to informal plantings and

woodland edges. They need deep, moist, well-drained soil and will grow in semi-shade or sun. Sunnier sites encourage better fruiting and autumn coloring. The shiny black cherry and pear slug can cause unsightly damage to the foliage but can be controlled with a carbaryl or pyrethrin preparation. Propagate from half-hardened cuttings, layering, removal of suckers, or seed sown in autumn.

Aronia arbutifolia

syn. *Photinia arbutifolia*

AMELANCHIER, RED CHOKEBERRY

☀ ❄ ↔ 5 ft (1.5 m) ↕ 6 ft (1.8 m)

This shrub has downy young branches and clusters of small white to pale pink flowers in spring. Berries are bright red, persisting into winter. '**Brilliantissima**' is an aptly named cultivar, with vivid red autumn leaves. Zones 4–9.

Aronia melanocarpa

syn. *Photinia melanocarpa*

BLACK CHOKEBERRY

☀ ❄ ↔ 7 ft (2 m) ↕ 3 ft (0.9 m)

A small shrub, producing suckering growth from its base. Flowers and foliage are similar to *A. arbutifolia* but the leaves are not downy. Berries ripen to shiny black. It is more tolerant of dry soils. '**Autumn Magic**' ★ has crimson-purple autumn foliage. Zones 4–9.

ARPOPHYLLUM

CANDLE ORCHID

A small sympodial genus of the orchid (Orchidaceae) family. Its 5 species always impress with their erect candles of tightly packed pink to purple flowers, particularly when seen on large plants. The pseudobulbs are reduced to thickened stems. They are found throughout Central America, Jamaica, and Colombia. The plants have long-lasting, strong, leathery, upright to arching leaves and can grow into large specimens. CULTIVATION: They perform best if given high light levels and intermediate to warm growing conditions. Shallow pots or saucers filled with a

Aronia arbutifolia

Aronia melanocarpa

Artanema fimbriatum

bark-based orchid medium have provided the greatest success. Plants flower best if somewhat potbound, and should only be divided when absolutely necessary.

Arpophyllum giganteum

☀ ◑ ↔ 12–36 in (30–90 cm)
↑ 16–32 in (40–80 cm)

From Central America. A widespread spring-flowering species, the most frequently seen in cultivation. Often confused with the closely related, but less robust, *A. spicatum*. Cylindrical inflorescences, 1¼ in (30 mm) wide and 8 in (20 cm) tall. Numerous, upside-down, purple-pink flowers. Zones 10–12.

ARRHENATHERUM

OAT GRASS

This genus, a member of the grass (Poaceae) family, consists of 6 perennials native to Europe, northern Africa, and northern and western Asia. The panicles are narrow, with flat 2-flowered spikelets. The stalk bases are sometimes swollen into bulbous or pear-shaped structures. The leaves are flat and strap-like, with usually hairless sheaths.
CULTIVATION: These species grow well in both partial shade and full sun. Soil should be dry to moist. Propagate from seed.

Arrhenatherum elatius

BULBOUS OAT GRASS, FALSE OAT, FRENCH RYE, OAT GRASS, ONION COUCH, STRIPED TUBER OAT GRASS, TUBER OAT GRASS

☼/◑ ❄ ↔ 6–8 in (15–20 cm)
↑ 18–60 in (45–150 cm)

Tussock-forming grass from Europe. The raceme is lance-shaped to oblong, lustrous, tinged with purple, containing spikelets of whitish flowers, in summer. Its finely hairy pale green leaves, up to 16 in (40 cm) long × ½ in (12 mm) wide, turn light tan to brown in winter. *A. e.* **subsp.** **bulbosum** has chains of bulb-like

swellings at the bases of its stems; '**Variegatum**' is a loosely tuft-forming, herbaceous, perennial grass with a swollen basal stem and hairless gray-green leaves with ivory white margins. Zones 4–9.

ARTABOTRYS

This genus of over 100 species of the Old World tropics, with 31 species in Africa, is part of the custard-apple (Annonaceae) family. All are woody small trees or shrubs with recurved hooks with a tendency to climb. Leaves are simple and alternate, without hairs. Bisexual flowers are borne singly or in clusters opposite the leaves, the stalks thick and hooked. The flowers are 6-petalled, scented, with many stamens. Each ovary comprises 6 separate units, each becoming fleshy.
CULTIVATION: Propagate from fresh seeds or half-hardened shoot cuttings taken in spring.

Artabotrys hexapetalus

syns *Artabotrys odoratissimus*, *A. uncinatus*

CLIMBING YLANG-YLANG, TAIL-GRAPE

☀ ◑ ↔ 10 ft (3 m) ↑ 15 ft (4.5 m)

This is a vigorous woody perennial that climbs by means of hooks on its stems. It occurs in southern China, Sri Lanka, and Bangladesh, but has been cultivated throughout the tropics for many years. It has become weedy in many countries. Leaves are smooth, elliptical and green. Flowers are small, greenish yellow to brown, fragrant, produced throughout most of the year. A stimulant beverage is made from the flowers in some countries. Zones 10–12.

ARTANEMA

This genus consists of 4 species of herbs or shrubs in the figwort or foxglove (Scrophulariaceae) family, occurring in the Old World tropics. Its leaves are opposite, not divided,

with entire or slightly toothed margins. The flowers are large and showy, snapdragon-like, borne toward the ends of the stems. The fruit is a small capsule that contains many small seeds.
CULTIVATION: Propagate from seed or stem cuttings. Plants grow well in most soils in full sun or only half-sun.

Artanema fimbriatum

☀ ❄ ↔ 10 in (25 cm) ↑ to 20 in (50 cm)

This is an erect annual or perennial herb that sometimes becomes shrub-like. Its lower leaves are 2½–4 in (6–10 cm) long × ¾–2 in (1.8–5 cm) wide, oval or lance-shaped, with margins toothed. Upper leaves are smaller and not toothed. Deep purplish blue and white tubular flowers, ¾–1¼ in (1.8–3 cm) long, are borne terminally. This species occurs in moist coastal regions of eastern Australia. Will regenerate from the rootstock if killed by frosts. Zones 8–10.

Arrhenatherum elatius

Arpophyllum giganteum

A

ARTEMISIA

This genus of about 300 species of evergreen herbs and shrubs is spread throughout northern temperate regions with some also found in southern Africa and South America. It is a member of the daisy (Asteraceae) family but most species bear small dull white or yellow flowers. The beauty of these plants lies in their attractive foliage, which is well dissected and of palest gray to silver. The plants are frequently aromatic. Tarragon, the popular culinary herb, is a member of this genus.
CULTIVATION: These shrubs are ideal for hot dry areas as most can withstand considerable drought. They

should be grown in full sun in well-drained soil. Their silvery leaves provide an attractive foliage contrast in borders, and when clipped some species can be used as a low hedge. Prune quite hard in spring and lightly clip at flowering time if the flowers are not wanted. Propagation is usually from softwood or half-hardened cuttings in summer.

Artemisia abrotanum
LAD'S LOVE, OLD MAN, SOUTHERNWOOD
☀ ❄ ↔ 4 ft (1.2 m) ↕ 4 ft (1.2 m)
Of uncertain origin but naturalized throughout Europe. Soft-stemmed shrub grown for its aromatic, gray, filigree leaves. Insignificant heads of yellow flowers in summer. Zones 4–10.

Artemisia absinthium
ABSINTHE, COMMON WORMWOOD, OLD MAN
☀ ❄ ↔ 36 in (90 cm) ↕ 36 in (90 cm)
From temperate areas of Europe, Asia, and North America. Shrubby species with finely divided, silky, gray leaves. Aromatic. Insignificant tiny flowers in summer. 'Lambrook Mist', very finely divided silky leaves; 'Lambrook Silver' ★, a more compact shrub. Zones 4–10.

Artemisia alba 'Canescens'

Artemisia californica

Artemisia arborescens

Artemisia alba
☀ ❄ ↔ 24 in (60 cm) ↕ 36 in (90 cm)
Native to southern Europe and northern Africa. Subshrub with white downy stems and aromatic, gray, filigree foliage. 'Canescens' has very fine curly foliage with spiky appearance. Zones 6–10.

Artemisia arborescens
SHRUB WORMWOOD
☀ ❄ ↔ 5 ft (1.5 m) ↕ 5 ft (1.5 m)
Attractive Mediterranean species that grows into a rounded shrub of 5 ft (1.5 m). Finely divided silver foliage, aromatic. More frost tender than most species but its cultivar 'Faith Raven' is much hardier. Zones 8–11.

Artemisia californica
CALIFORNIA SAGEBRUSH
☀ ❄ ↔ 5 ft (1.5 m) ↕ 5 ft (1.5 m)
Native to California, USA. Found in poor and sandy soils. Grows into a densely branched shrub with fine, gray, thread-like leaves. Pleasant aroma. Young branches are white. Zones 4–11.

Artemisia dracunculus
syns *Artemisia dracunculoides, A. dracunculina, A. glauca*
DRAGON SAGEWORT, TARRAGON
☀ ❄ ↔ 3 ft (0.9 m) ↕ 2–5 ft (0.6–1.5 m)
Wild forms of tarragon range from European Russia through Central Asia and across the Pacific to western North America, extending down the Rockies as far as northern Mexico. Erect herbaceous perennial spreading by rhizomes. Leaves narrow, pointed, dull green to somewhat bluish. Flowers in tiny brownish heads in summer. *A. d.* var. *inodora*, Russian tarragon, representative of wild forms,

Artemisia lactiflora, Guizhou Group cv

is a more vigorous grower but has little flavor. It has been misnamed *A. dracunculoides*. *A. d.* 'Sativa', French tarragon, is a clone selected for its intense aromatic flavor, renowned for uses as a culinary herb; must be propagated by cuttings or division. Zones 5–9.

Artemisia lactiflora
WHITE MUGWORT
☀ ❄ ↔ 24 in (60 cm) ↕ 5 ft (1.5 m)
From China. A perennial species forming clumps of green divided leaves. Tall showy plumes of tiny cream flowers in mid-summer. Requires more moisture than most species. Mahogany stems and purplish green foliage are a feature of the **Guizhou Group**. Zones 4–10.

Artemisia ludoviciana
syns *Artemisia gnaphalodes, A. purshiana*
CUDWEED, SILVER WORMWOOD, WESTERN MUGWORT, WHITE SAGE
☀ ❄ ↔ 36 in (90 cm) ↕ 36 in (90 cm)
Native to USA. Perennial herb with white downy stems and narrow, silvery gray, aromatic foliage. Sprays of tiny grayish white flowers in summer. *A. l.* subsp. *mexicana* var. *albula* has lance-shaped leaves, white and hairy. *A. l.* 'Silver Queen', to 18 in (75 cm) with finely cut silvery leaves; 'Valerie Finnis', to 24 in (60 cm), broader leaves, silvery white. Zones 5–10.

Artemisia pontica
ROMAN WORMWOOD
☀ ❄ ↔ 24 in (60 cm) ↕ 32 in (80 cm)
This fleshy-stemmed perennial comes from central and eastern Europe. It has downy, grayish green, feathery foliage and is aromatic. Sprays of tiny yellow flowers in summer. Zones 4–9.

Artemisia absinthium

Artemisia 'Powis Castle' ★

☼ ❄ ↔ 4 ft (1.2 m) ↑ 2 ft (0.6 m)

Similar to *A. arborescens* but its habit is more sprawling, with woody stems usually lying on the ground. Possibly a hybrid between *A. arborescens* and the herbaceous *A. pontica*. Zones 7–10.

Artemisia rupestris

syns *Artemisia dentata, A. viridifolia, A. viridis*

☼ ❄ ↔ 12–24 in (30–60 cm) ↑ 10–36 in (25–90 cm)

From the Baltic region, Russia, and central Asia. Sprawling or carpeting subshrub with very fine grayish green foliage. Erect stems of tiny yellowish brown flowers in autumn. Zones 3–9.

Artemisia schmidtiana

☼ ❄ ↔ 18 in (45 cm) ↑ 12–24 in (30–60 cm)

A Japanese species. Fleshy-stemmed perennial forming clumps of finely cut, silky, silvery foliage. Aromatic. 'Nana' (syn. 'Silver Mound') is a dwarf form to 4 in (10 cm) high × 12 in (30 cm) wide. Zones 4–9.

Artemisia stelleriana

BEACH WORMWOOD, DUSTY MILLER, OLD WOMAN

☼ ❄ ↔ 18 in (45 cm) ↑ 18–24 in (45–60 cm)

From northeastern Asia and eastern USA. Evergreen fleshy-stemmed perennial. Heavily felted gray-white leaves, deeply lobed. Sprays of tiny yellow flowers in summer. 'Boughton Silver' and 'Mori' are white-leafed prostrate forms. Zones 3–9.

Artemisia vulgaris

MUGWORT

☼ ❄ ↔ 4 ft (1.2 m) ↑ 5–8 ft (1.5–2.4 m)

From Europe and northern Africa. Tufted perennial, reddish stems, divided green leaves, lighter and downy on undersides. Sprays of small reddish brown flowers in summer–autumn.

Arthropodium cirratum

Artemisia 'Powis Castle'

Artemisia rupestris

Artemisia schmidtiana 'Nana'

Artemisia vulgaris

Oriental Limelight/'Janlim', to 18 in (45 cm) high and wide, features finely cut leaves that are variegated yellow and green. Zones 3–10.

ARTHROCEREUS

This interesting genus of 4 species of small cacti, with cylindrical stems jointed at regular intervals, comes from Brazil and belongs to the cactus (Cactaceae) family. Ranging in size from just ¾ in (18 mm) tall to 4 ft (1.2 m) tall, they have stout stems, 8 to 18 ribs, and dense spines. Nocturnal, funnel-shaped flowers, 2½–3 in (6–8 cm) long, come in shades of white, pink, or yellow. Green seed pods are spherical to pear-shaped.
CULTIVATION: Easy to grow from seeds, or from cuttings up to 20 in (50 cm) long, dried thoroughly for 1 or 2 weeks before planting. They prefer rich well-drained soil, moderate watering, and a rest in winter.

Arthrocereus melanurus

☼ ❄ ↔ 7 ft (2 m) ↑ 4 ft (1.2 m)

This is the most common species, with branches 1–1½ in (25–35 mm)

wide and up to 4 ft (1.2 m) long, arising from the base. Spines numerous, golden brown to white. Flowers 2½ in (6 cm) long, yellow to white. Zones 9–11.

ARTHROPODIUM

A small genus in the lily (Liliaceae) family of about 12 species of evergreen or deciduous fleshy-stemmed perennials found mostly in Australia and New Zealand. Plants form clumps of linear leaves ranging from small and grass-like to long and strap-shaped. The flowers, ranging from white to pale mauve and violet, have 6 flaring petals with fuzzy yellow and purple stamens. They are borne in panicles.
CULTIVATION: In warm areas grow in well-drained soil in sun or half-sun. Where frosts are worse, choose a warm sheltered site or grow in a greenhouse. Protect from slugs and snails. Propagate from seed or by division.

Arthropodium candidum

☼/◐ ❄ ↔ 10 in (25 cm) ↑ 12 in (30 cm)

From New Zealand. Deciduous species with narrow grass-like leaves.

A. vulgaris Oriental Limelight/'Janlim'

Small, starry, white flowers, held above the foliage, late spring–summer. A variety with mottled purple-brown leaves and pale mauve flowers often available. Zones 8–11.

Arthropodium cirratum

RENGARENGA, ROCK LILY

☼/◐ ❄ ↔ 24 in (60 cm) ↑ 20–30 in (50–75 cm)

Variable evergreen species from New Zealand. Fleshy strap-shaped leaves, to 24 in (60 cm) long, may have bluish green overtones. Flowering stems bear airy panicles of starry white flowers, early–mid-summer. Zones 9–11.

A

Arum maculatum

Arum pictum

Arum palaestinum

☀ ⚘ ↔ 8–18 in (20–45 cm)
↕ 12–18 in (30–45 cm)

Middle Eastern species. Long-stemmed, heavily veined, narrow, arrowhead-shaped leaves. Purple-black spadix. Pale green, 6–8 in (15–20 cm) long spathe, purple-black inside, often with recurved edges. Slightly unpleasantly scented. Zones 9–10.

Arum pictum

☀ ❄ ↔ 8–16 in (20–40 cm)
↕ 8–12 in (20–30 cm)

From the western Mediterranean islands. Summer-dormant with autumn-emergent foliage and flowers. Deep green leaves, 6–12 in (15–30 cm) long. Flowers at ground level. Purple-red spadix largely enclosed by spathe, to 10 in (25 cm) long, greenish white to purple-red with deep purple-red interior. Zones 8–10.

ARUNCUS
GOAT'S BEARD

This genus is a member of the rose (Rosaceae) family and contains 2 or 3 species of deciduous perennials native to northern temperate and subarctic regions. They are grown for their large fern-like leaves and for the plumes of tiny cream flowers held well above the attractive foliage in summer.
CULTIVATION: These fully frost hardy plants are suitable for "wild" gardens and woodland plantings as well as the border, where the larger species makes an imposing clump over time. Grow in a moist soil in half-sun. Propagate by division in autumn or early spring, or from seed sown in autumn.

Aruncus aethusifolius

☀ ❄ ↔ 16 in (40 cm) ↕ 16 in (40 cm)

Native to Korea. Compact-clump forming species with deeply divided pinnate leaves to 10 in (25 cm) long. Airy panicles of tiny cream flowers are borne in summer. Zones 3–9.

Arum alpinum

ARTOCARPUS

This pantropical genus of around 50 species of evergreen and deciduous trees of the mulberry (Moraceae) family includes several commercially important fruits, notably breadfruit and jackfruit. Leaves are large, and may be simple or lobed, with bracts at the base of stalks. Separate male and female flowers; males borne in small catkins, females in large heads. Flowers are tiny but the starchy white-fleshed fruit that follows may be very large. Breadfruit was famous as the crop that led to the mutiny on the *Bounty*.
CULTIVATION: Species require constantly warm moist conditions and prefer well-drained humus-rich soil. Will fruit more reliably and heavily if fed well. Plant in full sun or partial shade with shelter from strong winds. Propagate the species from seed and cultivars from cuttings or aerial layers.

Artocarpus altilis
BREADFRUIT

☀ ✦ ↔ 20 ft (6 m) ↕ 50 ft (15 m)

Of East Asian origin, this tree has a broad crown of 3-lobed leaves up to

30 in (75 cm) long. Breadfruit is an impressive tree even without its spherical, 8 in (20 cm) wide, yellow-green fruit, which is eaten boiled or baked. Zone 12.

Artocarpus heterophyllus
JACKFRUIT

☀ ✦ ↔ 20 ft (6 m) ↕ 30–50 ft (9–15 m)

From India to the Malay Peninsula. Simple, dark green leaves. When ripe the fruit is a mustard shade. Its yellow to pink flesh smells unpleasant but is edible. Zones 11–12.

ARUM

A genus of about 26 species of tuberous-rooted perennials commonly known as lilies but actually of the arum (Araceae) family, of which it is the type genus. Found from western Europe to the Himalayas and centered around the Mediterranean. Lustrous dark green leaves, sometimes with lighter marbling, tend to be arrowhead-shaped and usually die away from autumn. Inflorescence consists of a spathe ranging from green to yellow, dull purple or almost black with a cream to purplish spadix. Clustered berries, usually bright orange-red, follow flowers. The unpleasant scent and dark purple-red color of many arums mimics rotting flesh, attracts pollinating flies—unpleasant but effective.
CULTIVATION: Best grown in half-sun in a temperate climate with cool humus-rich soil that remains moist over summer. Propagate by division when the plants are dormant, though new stocks can be raised from seed.

Arum alpinum

☀ ❄ ↔ 8–12 in (20–30 cm)
↕ 8–12 in (20–30 cm)

Native of Europe, from Sweden to Spain and Crete. Arrowhead-shaped

leaves about 5 in (12 cm) long × 2½ in (6 cm) wide. Pale green spadix enclosed in a 5 in (12 cm) green spathe, purple-tinted within. Flowers early summer. Zones 7–10.

Arum italicum

☀/☀ ❄ ↔ 12–16 in (30–40 cm)
↕ 10–12 in (25–30 cm)

From southern and western Europe and North Africa. Most commonly grown species, often naturalizes. Arrowhead-shaped, glossy, deep green leaves, often lighter marbled, 6–12 in (15–30 cm) long. Large pale green spathe encloses deep cream spadix. 'Marmoratum' ★ has pale leaf veins and gray-green mottling. Zones 6–10.

Arum maculatum
CUCKOO PINT, JACK-IN-THE-PULPIT, LORDS AND LADIES

☀/☀ ❄ ↔ 8–16 in (20–40 cm)
↕ 10 in (25 cm)

A European species with long-stemmed arrowhead-shaped leaves up to 8 in (20 cm) long. Has a purple-pink spadix and a pale green spathe to 10 in (25 cm) long, often becoming purple-tinted with age. Orange-red fruit. Zones 6–9.

Artocarpus altilis

Artocarpus heterophyllus

Asarum caudatum

Aruncus dioicus

syns *Aruncus sylvester, A. vulgarus, Spiraea aruncus*

GOAT'S BEARD

↔ 4 ft (1.2 m) ↑ 2–6 ft (0.6–1.8 m)

From a wide area of Europe and northern Asia. Imposing plant forming large clumps of pinnately divided leaves. Panicles of cream flowers, up to 20 in (50 cm) long, in summer. Weed in much of Australia. Zones 3–9.

ARUNDINA

BAMBOO ORCHID

A small orchid (Orchidaceae) family genus consisting of about 8 terrestrial species with a wide natural distribution from northern India across Asia to the Pacific islands. The flowers only last a day or two, but are in such numbers that large plants are always in bloom. *A. graminifolia* has become a weed in Hawaii, colonizing old lava flows to the extent that many consider it an indigenous plant.

CULTIVATION: All species are terrestrials that will suit the garden in warm climates. If grown in the greenhouse, select a large pot to accommodate the extensive root system and use a well-drained medium such as *Cymbidium* compost. Plants can be propagated from aerial growths produced along the upper nodes of the bamboo-like pseudobulbs, and do well sitting in trays of water to 2 in (5 cm) deep.

Arundina graminifolia

↔ 12–36 in (30–90 cm)
↑ 16–84 in (40–200 cm)

From Southeast Asia. A widespread species with attractive flowers that resemble a small *Cattleya*. They range in color from white to deepest purple, often with contrasting shades on the labellum. Zones 11–12.

ARUNDO

GIANT REED

A genus of 3 species of giant, fleshy-stemmed, perennial grasses (Poaceae family) from the Old World tropics and subtropics. Only one species, *A. donax* from the Mediterranean

Asarum asaroides

region, is widely cultivated and it has become a weed in some areas. Very strongly upright plants reminiscent of bamboo, they soon form a large clump of heavy, somewhat flattened stems with long narrow leaves, the base of which is sheathed around the stem. Large feathery flower panicles appear in autumn and can be attractive, especially when young, when they often have a dusky pink tint. The foliage dies back over winter but does not usually disappear entirely.

CULTIVATION: Although commonly known as reeds, they are really grasses and consequently do not require boggy or poolside conditions. Any well-drained moderately fertile soil that can be kept moist through summer will do. As the plants most often cultivated are variegated forms, propagation is usually by division during the dormant period.

Arundo donax

↔ 7–15 ft (2–4.5 m)
↑ 10–20 ft (3–6 m)

Dense clump of strong stems with 24 in (60 cm) long, gray-green leaves. Flower panicles to 24 in (60 cm) long, pink-tinted when young, maturing to silver-gray. *A. d.* var. *versicolor* ★ has white-striped variegated foliage. There are several other variegated forms of varying patterns. Zones 7–11.

ASARINA

TWINING SNAPDRAGON

There are 16 species of sprawling or twining perennials in this genus, of the figwort or foxglove (Scrophulariaceae) family. Native to Mexico, southwestern USA, and southern Europe. Leaves are often triangular and hairy. Flowers, of varying sizes, resemble snapdragons and may be white, yellow, pink, purple, and shades in between.

CULTIVATION: In cool climates they need a warm sheltered position or can be grown in the conservatory. Grow in any reasonably fertile well-drained soil and water well in summer. Good for spilling over walls and banks. Propagate from seed or cuttings.

Asarina procumbens

syn. *Antirrhinum asarina*

↔ 18 in (45 cm) ↑ 3 in (8 cm)

From southwestern Europe. Rather sticky, hairy, trailing plant with grayish green heart-shaped leaves. White snapdragon flowers, tinted yellow or pink, appear in summer. Zones 7–10.

ASARUM

ASARABACCA, WILD GINGER

A genus of some 100 species of herbaceous and evergreen clumping or running perennials in the birthwort (Aristolochiaceae) family. Most are from East Asia with some in North America and one European species. They all have attractive to stunning foliage with bizarre, starfish-like, fleshy flowers in shades of black and brown that hide below the leaves ready to scare the faint-hearted. New and interesting species are still being discovered in Asia. Many are thought to have medicinal properties.

CULTIVATION: Ground cover for half-sun to heavy shade in moist soil. Keep from slugs and snails. Propagate by division or from freshly sown seed.

Asarum asaroides

syn. *Asarum thunbergii*

↔ 12–16 in (30–40 cm)
↑ 3–4 in (8–10 cm)

From Japan. Clumping species with broad rounded leaves to 5 in (12 cm) long that are rich dark green and hide its tiny dark purple-brown flowers to ¾ in (18 mm) wide. Zones 7–9.

Asarum caudatum

↔ 32–40 in (80–100 cm)
↑ 3–4 in (8–10 cm)

An attractive semi-evergreen species from North America with a creeping ground-covering habit. It has kidney-shaped leaves to 4 in (10 cm) wide that hide its brown flowers. Zones 7–9.

Asarina procumbens

Arundo donax

A

Asarum europaeum
ASARABACCA

☀ ❄ ↔ 40–60 in (100–150 cm)
↑ 3–4 in (8–10 cm)

The only European species in the genus. Lovely, evergreen, glossy, kidney-shaped leaves to 4 in (10 cm) across and strange dull brown flowers hidden by the foliage. Zones 4–9.

Asarum shuttleworthii

☀ ❄ ↔ 40–60 in (100–150 cm)
↑ 3–4 in (8–10 cm)

Spreading evergreen species from southeastern USA with heart-shaped rich green leaves, often silver variegated. The hidden flowers are blood red to black. '**Callaway**', handsomely variegated form. Zones 6–9.

ASCLEPIAS
MILKWEED

This American and African genus of the milkweed (Asclepiadaceae) family comprises over 100 species, including annuals, perennials, subshrubs, and shrubs. The shrubs are usually upright, many-branched plants with simple, narrow, elliptical to lance-shaped leaves. They produce heads of small 5-petalled flowers followed by seed pods, sometimes oddly shaped, tightly packed with small seeds, each with a small parachute of silky down. All parts of the plants exude a milky sap if cut, hence the name. CULTIVATION: Easily grown in light, well-drained soil in full sun, milkweeds will, however, have more luxuriant foliage and will flower more heavily if well-fed and watered. They grow readily and quickly from seed, and can be treated as annuals or short-lived perennials. Trim to shape, not into bare wood, as plants can be slow to recover from harsh pruning.

Asclepias curassavica
BASTARD IPECACUANHA, BLOOD FLOWER, BUTTERFLY WEED, SCARLET MILKWEED, SILKWEED, SWALLOW WORT

☀ ❄ ↔ 24 in (60 cm) ↑ 36 in (90 cm)

Native to South America. Weedy in many areas. Short-lived evergreen

Asclepias curassavica

Asclepias curassavica 'Silky Gold'

subshrub. Narrow leaves to 6 in (15 cm) long. Flowerheads of small bright red flowers with a central yellow ruff. The poisonous sap has an emetic effect. '**Silky Gold**' has deep orange-yellow flowers. Zones 8–11.

Asclepias incarnata

☀ ❄ ↔ 24 in (60 cm) ↑ 4 ft (1.2 m)

From USA. A weedy perennial that can be invasive. Narrow lance-shaped leaves on thick stems. Rose pink flowers in summer. Erect pointed seed heads. Zones 3–9.

Asclepias linaria
PINE-NEEDLE MILKWEED, PINELEAF MILKWEED, THREADLEAF MILKWEED

☀ ❄ ↔ 24–36 in (60–90 cm)
↑ 24–36 in (60–90 cm)

From arid areas of California, Arizona, and Mexico, USA. Shrubby perennial with fine needle-like foliage. Flowers

Asclepias linaria

for long periods with small white flowers in clusters to 2 in (5 cm) wide. Zones 9–11.

Asclepias speciosa
DAVIS MILKWEED, SHOWY MILKWEED

☀ ❄ ↔ 24–36 in (60–90 cm)
↑ 24–36 in (60–90 cm)

From western to central USA, invasive in some States. Bushy hairy perennial with large oval leaves. Small starry flowers, pink to light purple and white, borne in spherical clusters, to 3 in (8 cm) across. Zones 2–9.

Asclepias subulata

☀ ❄ ↔ 4 ft (1.2 m) ↑ 6–8 ft (1.8–2.4 m)

Found in southwestern USA and Mexico. Leafless for most of the year, small narrow leaves form after rain, soon fall from the wiry branches. Flowers, creamy white in color, carried in small heads that develop in the leaf axils. Zones 7–10.

Asclepias tuberosa ★
BUTTERFLY WEED, PLEURISY ROOT

☀ ❄ ↔ 12 in (30 cm)
↑ 24–36 in (60–90 cm)

Native to eastern and southern USA. Woody-based perennial herb. Narrow lance-shaped leaves on crowded stems. Heads of yellow, orange, or vermilion flowers. Pointed seed head to 6 in (15 cm) long. Zones 3–9.

× *ASCOCENDA*

This is arguably one of the most popular of the genera in the orchid (Orchidaceae) family. The species of this genus are man-made hybrids between *Ascocentrum* and *Vanda*. Erect-growing to about 24 in (60 cm) high, these epiphytes have strap-like channelled leaves, thick cord-like roots, and long-lasting flowers. In tropical climates they bloom year round; elsewhere mainly during spring and summer. The influence of *Ascocentrum* has greatly reduced the plant size,

Asclepias tuberosa

× *Ascocenda,* Hybrid, Fuchs Gold

× *Ascocenda,* Hybrid, Fuchs Harvest Moon

× *Ascocenda,* Hybrid, Fuchs Serval

× *Ascocenda,* Hybrid, Kwa Geok Choo

× *Ascocenda,* Hybrid, Pramote

× *Ascocenda,* Hybrid, Princess Mikasa 'Pink'

× *Ascocenda,* Hybrid, Udomchai Beauty

× *A.,* Hybrid, (Fiftieth State Beauty × Guo Chia Long)

× *Ascocenda,* Hybrid, Kathleen

× *Ascocenda,* Hybrid, Wichot

Ascocentrum garayi

× *Ascocenda,* Hybrid, Princess Mikasa

injected a range of vibrant colors, and given the blooms a rounder shape.
CULTIVATION: Ideal plants for bark-filled wooden baskets, enjoying warm conditions and high light levels with their colorful showy blooms being long lived. The thick roots will often venture outside the pot or basket, and this should be encouraged, as the roots need unimpeded air circulation and must dry out quickly after water.

× *Ascocenda* Hybrids

☀ ✥ ↔ 12–24 in (30–60 cm)
↑ 16–48 in (40–120 cm)

× *Ascocenda* hybrids include: **Fuchs Gold**, one of the fine hybrids developed by Robert Fuchs of R. F.

Orchids, Florida, USA; **Fuchs Serval**, an unusual hybrid with bold spotting and mustard colored background; **Kwa Geok Choo**, a hybrid made by the Singapore Botanic Gardens, created using the albino (green and white) form of *Vanda sanderiana*; **Pramote**, which has orange blooms, an influence from *Ascocentrum curvifolium*, that last equally well on the plant or as a cut flower, and mature plants will bloom a number of times during the warmer months; **Princess Mikasa**, which has the shape and color as a legacy from *Vanda coerulea*; **Udomchai Beauty**, which has 4 different *Vanda* species and *Ascocentrum curvifolium* in its

makeup; and **Wichot**, a primary hybrid between *Vanda bensonii* and *Ascocentrum ampullaceum*. Zones 11–12.

ASCOCENTRUM

The monopodial genus *Ascocentrum,* a member of the orchid (Orchidaceae) family, is a group of about 8 small compact species from Southeast Asia. These epiphytes are erect growing, with short strap-like channelled leaves, in two ranks. Larger plants may branch at the base, and have numerous, very thick, cord-like roots. The inflorescences appear from the stem at the base of the leaf. They are mostly spring and summer flowering,

but in the tropics the larger plants can bloom throughout the year. *Ascocentrum* has been bred with members of the genus *Vanda* to create the genus × *Ascocenda*.
CULTIVATION: Best suited to container or basket culture, these species require warm conditions and high light levels. Water and feed well during active growth and throughout the flowering season. Roots need to dry out quickly after watering and do best if allowed to grow beyond the confines of the container.

Ascocentrum garayi

☀ ✥ ↔ 5–10 in (12–25 cm)
↑ 5–12 in (12–30 cm)

The bright orange flowers of this species, which comes from Thailand, have ensured its popularity in cultivation. Nurseries have selected horticulturally superior forms and have propagated these in large numbers from seed. For years this species has been confused with *A. miniatum*, which is a close relative. Zones 10–12.

A

Asparagus officinalis

Asparagus officinalis 'Larac'

ASIMINA

This genus of 7 or 8 evergreen or deciduous shrubs or trees from eastern North America is a member of the custard-apple (Annonaceae) family. Generally frost hardy, most species tolerate temperatures of 5°F (–15°C) or lower. White or purple, nodding, bell-shaped flowers appear in small clusters. The fruit is pleasant tasting. CULTIVATION: They will grow in moist well-drained soil in sun or semi-shade, though affected by long dry periods. Respond well to pruning and shaping and can be used for hedging, though this reduces flowers and fruit.

Asimina triloba

PAWPAW

☀ ❄ ↔ 20 ft (6 m) ↑ 30 ft (9 m)

From eastern and central North America. Leaves oval, pointed, and narrow, up to 10 in (25 cm) long. Reddish brown pendulous flowers, around 2 in (5 cm) wide, in spring. Edible fruits ripen to yellowish brown in autumn. '**Prolific**', heaving fruiting, early ripening; '**Rebecca's Gold**', heavy fruiting, late ripening; '**Sunflower**', large, heavy fruiting, late ripening; '**Taylor**', small fruit, late ripening; and '**Wells**', with golden orange flesh. Zones 5–10.

ASPARAGUS

ASPARAGUS

A genus of about 300 perennial herbs, shrubs, or climbers growing from a tuberous rhizome, members of the asparagus (Asparagaceae) family. The green, yellow, or white flowers are small and inconspicuous. Leaves are small, scaly, and often spiny. Cladophylls (flattened stems that function as a leaf) are green and needle-like. Fruit is a round berry. CULTIVATION: These species prefer rich moist soils in a protected semi-shaded position with filtered sunlight. Propagate by division of crowded roots or from seed. Edible asparagus (*A. officinalis*) is grown from 1-year-old crowns planted in mid- to late winter, spaced 12 in (30 cm) apart, in heavily mulched rows 4–6 ft (1.2–1.8 m) apart. Harvest when spears are 6–10 in (15–25 cm) tall by breaking off at ground level. Full production in 2 to 3 years after planting; plants can produce for up to 25 years.

Asparagus asparagoides

syns *Myrsiphyllum asparagoides, Protasparagus aethiopicus*

FLORIST'S SMILAX

☀ ❄ ↔ 3 ft (0.9 m) ↑ 5–6 ft (1.5–1.8 m)

An evergreen vine that is native to South Africa. Vigorous, wiry stem. Solitary or paired, small, white flowers in leaf axils. Glossy green, alternate, leathery, oval branchlets or cladophylls. Fruits are red berries. '**Myrtifolius**' is a small elegant variety. Zones 7–10.

Asparagus densiflorus

syn. *Protasparagus densiflorus*

ASPARAGUS FERN, EMERALD FERN, FOXTAIL SHRUB, SPRENGER ASPARAGUS

☀ ❄ ↔ 36 in (90 cm) ↑ 30–36 in (75–90 cm)

Evergreen trailing shrub, with thick tuberous roots, native to subtropical South Africa. No leaves but needle-like branchlets or cladophylls on wiry, spiny, green or brown stems. Small white flowers in spring and summer on axillary racemes. Fruits are small bright red berries, in winter. '**Compactus**' (syn. '**Nanus**'), compact form with shorter branches, denser tighter growth; '**Deflexus**', wider cladophylls with metallic tint; '**Myersii**' (foxtail fern), fern-like appearance with dark green cladophylls, upright lateral branches; '**Sprengeri**' (syn. *A. sprengeri*), scrambling woody-stemmed plant, small white flowers, ½ in (12 mm) in diameter, maturing into small red berries. Zones 7–9.

Asparagus macowanii

syns *Asparagus zuluensis, Protasparagus macowanii*

☀/☀ ❄ ↔ 8 ft (2.4 m) ↑ 6 ft (1.8 m)

From the South African provinces of Eastern Cape, KwaZulu-Natal and Mpumalanga. Robust shrub with many stems about 1 in (25 mm) thick, springing like giant asparagus spears from a raised root-mass, each whitish stem living for many years, branched above into dense, fine, pale-green foliage. Profuse pure white flowers in mid-summer. Small blackish berries in winter. Zones 9–11.

Asparagus officinalis

ASPARAGUS

☀ ❄ ↔ 3–5 ft (0.9–1.5 m) ↑ 3–5 ft (0.9–1.5 m)

Herbaceous perennial from Europe, Asia, and North Africa grown widely as a foodcrop. Erect multi-branched stems. Rich green, feathery, almost plume-like cladophylls. Small, drooping, greenish white axillary flowers. Bright red berries. '**Larac**', a French variety noted for its wide adaptability, has white spears. Zones 4–8.

Asparagus setaceus

syns *Asparagus plumosus, Protasparagus plumosus*

ASPARAGUS FERN, PLUMOSA FERN LILY

☀/☀ ❄ ↔ 24 in (60 cm) ↑ 12–48 in (30–120 cm)

This species is a twining climber from southern and eastern Africa. Smooth, woody or wiry, green stems and strong thorns. Small white flowers. Red to black berries. Bright or dark green cladophylls, in clusters of 8–20,

Asimina triloba

Asphodelus aestivus

Asphodelus albus

Asphodelus acaulis

in a single plane, form a flat, triangular spray. Varieties include: 'Cupressoides', compact, pyramid-shaped; 'Nanus', compact, upright habit, shorter crowded cladophylls; 'Pyramidalis', roughly pyramidal in shape; and 'Robustus', strongly growing form. Zones 7–11.

ASPERULA
WOODRUFF

A genus of around 100 species of annuals, perennials, and small shrubs in the madder or gardenia (Rubiaceae) family found from Europe through Asia to Australia. Most are mat-forming, with spreading sometimes bristly stems clothed with whorls of simple, narrow, sometimes faintly downy leaves. Some are more upright, often spreading by runners. Tiny, bell- or funnel-shaped, 4-petalled flowers appear in the leaf axils, or in clusters at the stem tips, from spring through summer. The heavy-flowering species smother themselves in bloom. Several species yield dyes, though many of these have been transferred to the genus *Galium*.
CULTIVATION: These species are variable in their growth habit: the neat compact types are marvellous rockery plants, while the taller growers, with their associations with dyeing and herbalists, are more at home in the herb garden. Plant in a bright position with moist, fertile, well-drained soil and trim after flowering. Propagate from seed, by division, layers, or base cuttings as appropriate.

Asperula gussonei
☼ ❋ ↔ 6–12 in (15–30 cm)
↕ 4 in (10 cm)

Sicilian perennial that forms a mat or tufts of silvery blue-gray whorled leaves around ½ in (12 mm) long. Densely packed heads of up to 15, minute, pale pink to red flowers. Zones 7–10.

Asperula orientalis
syn. *Asperula azurea*
BLUE WOODRUFF
☼/◐ ❋ ↔ 16–24 in (40–60 cm)
↕ 8–12 in (20–30 cm)

Annual from southern Europe, western Asia, and the Middle East. Rangy upright habit with widely spaced whorls of green leaves to 2 in (5 cm) long. Terminal heads of lavender-blue funnel-shaped flowers. Often self-sows. Zones 8–10.

ASPHODELINE

This genus is a member of the lily (Liliaceae) family. It has 18 to 20 species of fleshy-stemmed perennial or biennial herbs native to southern Europe where they grow on rocky slopes and in scrubby areas. They are clump-forming plants with grayish green linear leaves to 12 in (30 cm) long, sometimes with slightly serrated margins. The flowers are about 1¼ in (30 mm) across and are borne in spring and summer. They have 6 flaring petals, yellow or white tinged pink, and are scented in some species.
CULTIVATION: Useful plants for the border, rockery, or for naturalizing. Grow in a moderately fertile soil in full sun. Propagate from seed or by division of clumps.

Asphodeline lutea ★
JACOB'S ROD, KING'S SPEAR, YELLOW ASPHODEL
☼ ❋ ↔ 12 in (30 cm)
↕ 36–48 in (90–120 cm)

From the Mediterranean. Narrow silvery leaves to 12 in (30 cm) long. Fragrant yellow flowers, borne on stiff spikes, in late spring–summer. Decorative seed pods. Zones 7–10.

ASPHODELUS

There are 12 species of clump-forming, swollen-rooted perennials in this genus, which is a member of the lily (Liliaceae) family. The species are found from the Mediterranean to the Himalayas growing in scrub and on rocky slopes. Their leaves are linear, up to 24 in (60 cm) long, and may be flat or cylindrical. The flowers have 6 whorled petals and are white or pink with green or brown veining. Flowering stems vary in length, from 7 ft (2 m) tall in one species, to non-existent in another, which flowers within the basal rosette.
CULTIVATION: *Asphodelus* is best grown in a moderately fertile soil in a position that receives full sun. Some of the species, such as the low-growing *A. acaulis*, are better suited to the rockery as they require sharp drainage. Propagation is from seed or by division.

Asphodelus acaulis
☼ ❄ ↔ 12 in (30 cm) ↕ 8–12 in (20–30 cm)
From northern Africa. Perennial, forming clumps of grass-like leaves to 12 in (30 cm) long. The name *acaulis*, meaning stemless, refers to the short spikes of small pink to white flowers that sit within the clump in spring. Zones 9–11.

Asphodelus aestivus
☼ ❋ ↔ 24 in (60 cm) ↕ 40 in (100 cm)
This species is native to the Canary Islands and Mediterranean regions. It has long, flat, basal leaves, and flowering stems with short side branches. Its flowers are starry white, with a central brown stripe on each petal. It is a spring-flowering species. Zones 7–10.

Asphodelus albus
☼ ❋ ↔ 24 in (60 cm) ↕ 36 in (90 cm)
Native to southern and western Europe and northern Africa, this species has linear leaves that are up to 24 in (60 cm) long. Flowering stems, 12–36 in (30–90 cm) tall, bear white to pale pink flowers, with a pinkish brown stripe on each petal, in spring. Zones 6–10.

Asperula orientalis

Asphodeline lutea

A

ASPIDISTRA

Found from the Himalayas to Japan, the 8 species in this genus are evergreen perennials of the lily-of-the-valley (Convallariaceae) family. Spreading from thick rhizomes, they form clumps of tough, deep green, elliptical to lance-shaped leaves that emerge directly from the ground on a strong leaf stalk, either singly or in small clusters. Small, purple-red to brown, bell- to urn-shaped flowers open from spring. They are stemless and occur near ground level where they often pass unnoticed.
CULTIVATION: Easily grown outdoors in a mild temperate climate, preferring a shady spot with cool, moist, well-drained soil. In suitable conditions they spread well, making an excellent large-scale ground cover.

Aspidistra elatior
BAR ROOM PLANT, CAST-IRON PLANT
☀ ❄ ↔ 16–36 in (40–90 cm)
↑ 16–24 in (40–60 cm)

A Chinese native. Veined overarching leaves to 24 in (60 cm) long emerge singly. Flowers bell-shaped, cream with purple spots to overall purple. Popular house plant. Zones 7–10.

Asplenium scolopendrium

ASPLENIUM
SPLEENWORT

A spleenwort (Aspleniaceae) family genus of over 600 ferns, found in tropical and subtropical climates. Short rhizomes are covered with massed roots, hairs, and scales. Fronds, often leathery, grow from a single crown, forming a fountain-like structure. The name is from the Greek *splen* (spleen), as it was thought to cure diseases of the spleen.
CULTIVATION: Plant in freely draining organically rich soil or potting mix in a moist, shady, humid spot, although some species can stand dry spells. Soil pH varies according to species. Tropical species need frost protection. Apply slow-release and liquid fertilizers when growing. Propagate from spores or by detaching plantlets formed on fronds of some species.

Asplenium bulbiferum
HEN AND CHICKEN FERN, MOTHER SPLEENWORT
☀/☀ ❄ ↔ 24–48 in (60–120 cm)
↑ 24–48 in (60–120 cm)

Terrestrial or epiphytic fern from Australia and New Zealand. Short-creeping to suberect rhizome and

A. scolopendrium 'Crispum Speciosum'

Asplenium trichomanes subsp. *quadrivalens*

arching, membranous, pinnate fronds to 48 in (120 cm) across. Flattened, grooved, green to brown stems, to 12 in (30 cm) long. Zones 9–11.

Asplenium nidus
BIRD'S-NEST FERN
☀/☀ ❄ ↔ 18–60 in (45–150 cm)
↑ 18–60 in (45–150 cm)

Large fern species widely distributed throughout the tropics. Nest-like rosette of simple, erect, sword-shaped fronds to 5 ft (1.5 m) long, on short, scaly, black, suberect stems to 2 in (5 cm) long. Variable, with some lobed forms. *A. n.* var. *plicatum* has narrow, dark green, pleated, convoluted fronds. Zones 10–12.

Asplenium sagittatum
MULE'S FERN
☀/☀ ❄ ↔ 4–6 in (10–15 cm)
↑ 4–6 in (10–15 cm)

Fern from Australia with simple or pinnate fronds to 6 in (15 cm) long on stems to 6 in (15 cm) long. Zones 8–10.

Asplenium scolopendrium
syn. *Phyllitis scolopendrium*
HART'S TONGUE FERN, SCOLLIES
☀/☀ ❄ ↔ 8–24 in (20–60 cm)
↑ 8–24 in (20–60 cm)

Robust clump-forming fern, globally distributed through the subtropics and tropics. Scaly rhizomes. Strap-like fronds, to 24 in (60 cm) long, on short stems. Grows naturally on acid or alkaline soils but prefers lime in cultivation. Hundreds of cultivars, including: 'Crispum Bolton's Nobile', broad fronds to 18 in (45 cm) long; 'Crispum Speciosum', sharply tapered fronds sometimes with yellow stripes; 'Cristatum', fronds divided many times, each ending in a spreading crest; 'Kaye's Lacerated', broad irregularly lobed fronds to 8 in (20 cm) long. Zones 4–10.

Asplenium trichomanes
COMMON SPLEENWORT, MAIDENHAIR SPLEENWORT
☀/☀ ❄ ↔ 3–16 in (8–40 cm)
↑ 3–16 in (8–40 cm)

This species is a small terrestrial fern from mountain areas of the temperate to tropical Northern Hemisphere. Erect rhizomes. Neat rosettes of spreading, leathery, dark green, pinnate fronds, to 16 in (40 cm) long, with spherical leaflets in pairs. Stiff brownish purple or black stems. *A. t.* subsp. *quadrivalens*, larger leaflets than species, almost rectangular, tolerates alkalinity. Zones 2–6.

ASTELIA

This genus, of the lily (Liliaceae) family, contains 25 species of clump-forming evergreen perennials with attractive sword-like leaves. Most species are native to New Zealand with others scattered around Southern Hemisphere islands and Australia. Their natural habitat ranges from alpine areas to lowland forests, and many are epiphytes. They are primarily grown for their foliage,

Asplenium sagittatum

which has a silvery sheen. Species have leaves ranging from 8 in (10 cm) to 7 ft (2 m) long. Flowers are unisexual and insignificant but are followed by red berries.
CULTIVATION: Most are frost hardy and can be grown outdoors in a fertile moisture-retentive soil in sun or half-sun. In very cold areas they need a warm sheltered position, or a green-house. Propagate by division in spring.

Astelia alpina
☼/◐ ✤ ↔ 24 in (60 cm) ↕ 6 in (15 cm)
From eastern mainland Australia and Tasmania. Low-growing plant with silvery sword-like leaves. It has showy red berries that are edible. The mainland form, *A. a.* var. *novae-hollandiae,* is usually smaller than the species. Zones 9–10.

Astelia chathamica
☼/◐ ✤ ↔ 5 ft (1.5 m) ↕ 3–6 ft (0.9–1.8 m)
From New Zealand's Chatham Islands. Ornamental species forming clumps of broad, arching, sword-like leaves with a deep silvery sheen. Zones 9–10.

Astelia neocaledonica
◐ ✤ ↔ 4 ft (1.2 m) ↕ 2 ft (0.6 m)
Endemic to New Caledonia, growing on mossy rocks in misty mountain areas. Spreading by short rhizomes, leaves finely tapering, very silvery from a close mat of silky hairs. Flowers cream, in autumn–winter. Fruit purple-black. Zones 9–10.

Astelia alpina

Astelia neocaledonica, in the wild, Mont Bouo track, Monts Koghis, New Caledonia

Aster × frikartii 'Mönch'

Astelia nervosa
☼ ✤ ↔ 5 ft (1.5 m) ↕ 3–7 ft (0.9–2 m)
A variable species from New Zealand. Foliage ranges from reddish tones through green to silver, leaves 2–7 ft (0.6–2 m) long. Named color forms are often available. Zones 9–10.

ASTER
MICHAELMAS DAISY
Found across the temperate Northern Hemisphere and into South America, this group of 250 species of mainly herbaceous perennials is the type genus for the daisy (Asteraceae) family. Upright plants that often sprawl under the weight of their foliage and flowers, they usually have simple linear to lance-shaped leaves, some-times hairy and/or serrated. A few flower in spring but most in late summer and autumn, with large heads of small to medium-sized daisies in a range of colors. The ancient Greeks believed that asters repelled snakes and were an antidote to their venom.
CULTIVATION: Mostly frost tolerant, preferring well-drained soil that stays

moist in the growing season. A sunny, airy, open position ensures maximum flowering and minimum mildew, a problem in humid condi-tions. Cut back hard after flowering. Propagate by winter division or from spring softwood cuttings.

Aster alpinus
ALPINE ASTER
☼ ✻ ↔ 8–32 in (20–80 cm)
↕ 4–10 in (10–25 cm)
Spreading, sometimes mounding perennial from mountains of south-ern Europe. Simple spatula- to lance-shaped base foliage. In spring and summer, masses of short-stemmed daisies, to slightly under 2 in (5 cm) wide, in white and all shades of pink, mauve, and purple. Zones 3–9.

Aster amellus
☼ ✻ ↔ 12–20 in (30–50 cm)
↕ 24–27 in (60–70 cm)
Upright Eurasian perennial. Faintly downy stems, green lance-shaped leaves around 2 in (5 cm) long. In autumn, terminal clusters of 2 in (5 cm) wide daisies, violet pink in the wild. Cultivars include: '**Framfieldii**', 24 in (60 cm) tall, lilac blue flowers; '**Jacqueline Genebrier**', 12 in (30 cm) tall, small bright pink flowers; '**King George**', 24 in (60 cm) tall, gray-green leaves, purple flowers; '**Sonia**', deep pink flowers; and '**Veilchenkönigin**', 16 in (40 cm) tall, dense heads of small deep violet flowers. Zones 5–9.

Aster divaricatus
☼/◐ ✻ ↔ 12–20 in (30–50 cm)
↕ 24 in (60 cm)
Perennial from eastern USA. Unusual, elongated, heart-shaped leaves to 4 in

Aster alpinus

(10 cm) long. Summer and autumn, sprays of dark-stemmed, small, white daisies held above foliage. Zones 4–9.

Aster ericoides
HEATH ASTER
☼/◐ ✻ ↔ 20–32 in (50–80 cm)
↕ 32–40 in (80–100 cm)
Branching, bushy, North American perennial with narrow leaves to 2½ in (6 cm) long. Blooms in summer and autumn with masses of small daisies on leafy flower stems. Many cultivars, of which '**Pink Cloud**' ★, to 3 ft (0.9 m) tall, with bronze new growth and billows of small pink flowers, is typical. Zones 3–9.

Aster × frikartii
☼/◐ ✻ ↔ 16–24 in (40–60 cm)
↕ 20–30 in (50–75 cm)
Garden hybrid between *A. amellus* and *A. thomsonii*. Upright perennial with dark green, elongated, lance-shaped base leaves. In autumn, branching sprays of 2 in (5 cm) wide daisies in shades of lavender and purple-blue. '**Mönch**', 16 in (40 cm) tall, and '**Wunder von Stäfa**', 30 in (75 cm) tall, are two cultivars with lavender-blue flowers. Zones 4–9.

A

Aster novi-belgii cultivar

Aster himalaicus

A. novae-angliae 'Andenken an Alma Pötschke'

Aster himalaicus

☼/◐ ❄ ↔ 12–24 in (30–60 cm)
↑ 6 in (15 cm)

Evergreen, autumn-flowering, spreading perennial from the Himalayas. Narrow spatula-shaped leaves to 3 in (8 cm) long. Flowerheads solitary, to 1¾ in (40 mm) wide, with lavender-blue ray florets around a yellow-brown disc. Zones 6–9.

Aster laevis

☼/◐ ❄ ↔ 24 in (60 cm)
↑ 3–4 ft (0.9–1.2 m)

This is an upright, autumn-flowering, North American perennial with purple-red stems and blue-green leaves to 5 in (12 cm) long. It has branching sprays of lavender to purple flowers. Zones 4–9.

Aster lateriflorus

☼/◐ ❄ ↔ 24–48 in (60–120 cm)
↑ 3–4 ft (0.9–1.2 m)

This upright to spreading North American perennial has base leaves

to 6 in (15 cm) long, and is autumn-flowering, with sprays of pink-centered white to lavender-pink flowers on downy wiry stems. *A. l.* **var.** *horizontalis* is a spreading variety with brown-centered cream flowers. *A. l.* **'Prince'** ★ is a typical cultivar and grows to 24 in (60 cm) tall, with bronze leaves and pink-centered white flowerheads. Zones 3–9.

Aster novae-angliae

NEW ENGLAND ASTER

☼/◐ ❄ ↔ 24–48 in (60–120 cm)
↑ 4–5 ft (1.2–1.5 m)

A bushy autumn-flowering perennial that comes from eastern North America. It has lance-shaped base leaves up to 5 in (12 cm) long, and dense sprays of yellow-centered soft purple flowerheads up to 1¾ in (40 mm) wide. Cultivars include: **'Andenken an Alma Pötschke'**, 4 ft (1.2 m) tall, cerise pink flowers; **'Barr's Pink'**, 4 ft (1.2 m) tall with small, deep pink, double flowers;

'Harrington's Pink', 5 ft (1.5 m) tall with small, soft pink, semi-double flowers; **'Hella Lacy'**, 4 ft (1.2 m) tall with violet-blue flowers; and **'Purple Dome'**, 18 in (45 cm) tall dwarf covered in purple flowers. Zones 2–9.

Aster novi-belgii

MICHAELMAS DAISY, NEW YORK ASTER

☼/◐ ❄ ↔ 24–32 in (60–80 cm)
↑ 3–4 ft (0.9–1.2 m)

This North American perennial is similar to *A. novae-angliae* except that it is slightly shorter and its leaves are more noticeably toothed. Over 400 cultivars have been raised and include: **'Coombe Violet'**, 30 in (75 cm) tall, deep purple flowers; **'Ernest Ballard'**, 30 in (75 cm) tall, bright pink, named after the famous hybridizer; **'Little Red Boy'**, 24 in (60 cm) tall, masses of bright cerise-red flowers; **'Marie Ballard'**, 3 ft (0.9 m) tall, lavender-blue, very fully double flowers; and **'Professor Anton Kippenberg'**, 15 in (38 cm) tall, lavender-blue flowers. Zones 2–9.

Aster oolentangiensis

syn. *Aster azureus*

☼/◐ ❄ ↔ 24–40 in (60–100 cm)
↑ 5 ft (1.5 m)

Upright summer- to autumn-flowering perennial from eastern North America. Leathery lance- to heart-shaped base leaves, smooth-edged or toothed, to 5 in (12 cm) long. Sprays of small lavender-blue or pink flowers. Zones 5–9.

Aster pilosis var. pringlei

☼/◐ ❄ ↔ 3 ft (0.9 m) ↑ 4 ft (1.2 m)

Autumn-flowering perennial from North America. Closely resembles *Boltonia asteroides,* with fine linear leaves and airy sprays of tiny white daisies. Seldom seen; more commonly grown is the cultivar **'Monte Cassino'**, slightly smaller, heavier flowering, and a popular cut flower. Zones 5–9.

Aster radula

☼/◐ ❄ ↔ 32 in (80 cm) ↑ 4 ft (1.2 m)

Upright summer-flowering perennial from western Canada. Angular stems with pointed elliptical leaves to 4 in (10 cm) long, sometimes toothed, downy undersides. Flowerheads solitary or in small sprays, violet. Zones 5–9.

Aster sedifolius

syn. *Aster trinervius*

☼/◐ ❄ ↔ 20 in (50 cm) ↑ 3 ft (0.9 m)

Upright, bushy, summer-flowering perennial found from Nepal through China to Japan. Irregularly toothed lance-shaped leaves to 4 in (10 cm) long, large branching sprays of 1 in (25 mm) wide white flowers. *A. s.* **subsp.** *ageratoides*, compact subspecies, narrow leaves, several cultivars with lavender-pink flowers. Zones 7–9.

Aster turbinellus

☼/◐ ❄ ↔ 3 ft (0.9 m) ↑ 4 ft (1.2 m)

Branching, multi-stemmed, autumn-flowering perennial from eastern USA. Lance-shaped 3 in (8 cm) long base leaves, fringed with fine hairs. Flowerheads 1 in (25 mm) wide, pink, borne singly on the stems but in large numbers. Zones 5–9.

Aster radula

Aster sedifolius subsp. ageratoides

ASTERANTHERA

There is just one species of evergreen scrambling vine in this genus, which is a member of the african violet (Gesneriaceae) family. It is native to Chile where it grows in forest areas of high humidity.
CULTIVATION: Grow in a warm, sunny, sheltered position in an acidic soil. Provide plenty of moisture and scrambling supports. Propagate from cuttings or by division.

Asteranthera ovata

☼ ⊕ ↔ 4 ft (1.2 m) ↑ 10 ft (3 m)
Small rounded leaves with scalloped margins. Tubular flowers to 2 in (5 cm) long, bright red with white markings in the throat. Fruit a fleshy green capsule with red markings. Zones 9–10.

ASTILBE

FALSE SPIRAEA
Found mainly in temperate East Asia, this perennial genus of the saxifrage (Saxifragaceae) family includes just 12 species which have been extensively selected and hybridized. Their toothed pinnate leaves sprout directly from rhizomes and soon form a large foliage clump. Long-stemmed plumes of tiny flowers appear in spring and summer, in white and all shades of pink, mauve, and red. Though astilbe plumes are thought of as bright and showy, the name actually means "without brilliance," from the Greek *a* (without) and *stilbe* (brilliance). This is because, while the flowerheads are bright, each flower is, on its own, tiny and rather dull.
CULTIVATION: Astilbes are not drought tolerant nor do they thrive in the hot summer sun. Instead they prefer moist, humus-rich, woodland soil and dappled sunlight. They often thrive around pond margins but also tolerate being in well-drained soils.

Astilbe × arendsii

☼ ❄ ↔ 12–32 in (30–80 cm)
↑ 2–6 ft (0.6–1.8 m)
This group of garden hybrids involves several parent species. Both flowers and foliage are highly variable. Popular named forms include: '**Anita Pfeifer**', 24 in (60 cm) tall, finely divided foliage and feathery sprays of pink flowers; '**Brautschleier**' (syn. 'Bridal Veil'), 30 in (75 cm) tall, white flowers, early-flowering; '**Bumalda**', 24 in (60 cm) high, white flowers with a faint pink blush, bronze foliage; '**Fanal**' ★, 24 in (60 cm) tall, dark, red-tinted foliage, deep red flowers; '**Federsee**', sprays of deep pink flowers to 24 in (60 cm) tall; '**Gertrud Brix**', 24 in (60 cm) tall, deep red flowers, bronze foliage; '**Gloria**', 27 in (70 cm) tall, deep pink flowers; '**Hyazinth**', bright green foliage, lilac-pink flower sprays to 36 in (90 cm) high; '**Irrlicht**', purple-tinted foliage and white flower sprays to 24 in (60 cm) high; '**Mainz**', 24 in (60 cm) tall, deep rose-pink flowers; '**Rosa Perle**' (syn. 'Pink Pearl'), 30 in (75 cm) tall, silvery to pink flowers; '**Showstar**', dwarf seedling strain in a mixed color range; '**Spinell**', 36 in (90 cm) tall, orange-red flowers; '**Venus**', bright green foliage, sprays of pink flowers to 36 in (90 cm) high; '**Weisse Gloria**', 36 in (90 cm) tall, sprays of white flowers; and '**William Reeves**', 24 in (60 cm) tall, deep pinkish red flowers. Zones 6–9.

Astilbe chinensis

☼ ❄ ↔ 12–20 in (30–50 cm)
↑ 20–27 in (50–70 cm)
Native to China and Japan. Foliage with large and coarsely toothed leaflets. Flowerheads short-stemmed with strongly upright plumes. Several natural varieties, including: *A. c.* var. *davidii*, bronze young leaves and purple-pink flower plumes to 7 ft (2 m) tall; *A. c.* var. *pumila*, just 10 in (25 cm) tall, with green foliage and dense plumes of deep pink flowers; and *A. c.* var. *taquetti* '**Superba**', with magenta flowers on brown stems to 4 ft (1.2 m) tall. *A. c.* '**Visions**' is a typically compact cultivar with 18 in (45 cm) tall, honey-scented, deep pink to red flower sprays and bronze foliage. Zones 5–9.

Astilbe × *arendsii* 'Gloria'

Astilbe × *arendsii* 'Rosa Perle'

Astilbe chinensis 'Visions'

Astilbe × *arendsii* 'Anita Pfeifer'

Astilbe × *arendsii* 'Brautschleier'

Astilbe × *arendsii* 'Bumalda'

Astilbe × *arendsii* 'Fanal'

Astilbe × *arendsii* 'Gertrud Brix'

Astilbe × *arendsii* 'Hyazinth'

Astilbe × *arendsii* 'Mainz'

Astilbe × *arendsii* 'Showstar'

Astilbe × *arendsii* 'Spinell'

Astilbe × *arendsii* 'Venus'

A

Astilbe, Hybrid Cultivar, 'Red Sentinel'

Astilbe koreana

Astilbe × crispa

☀ ❋ ↔ 8–12 in (20–30 cm)
↕ 8–12 in (20–30 cm)

Hybrid group of uncertain origins established by the German breeder Arends. Mainly dwarf plants with broad deeply cut leaflets, and bronze young foliage. '**Perkeo**' is the common form and has deep pink flowers in plumes to 8 in (20 cm) long. Zones 6–9.

Astilbe × *crispa* 'Perkeo'

Astilbe glaberrima

☀ ❋ ↔ 16–20 in (40–50 cm)
↕ 24 in (60 cm)

Japanese species with broad coarsely toothed foliage and mauve flowers in compact plumes atop long stems. '**Saxatilis**', dwarf cultivar that seldom exceeds 8 in (20 cm) tall, with white-tipped mauve flowers. Zones 6–9.

Astilbe japonica

☀ ❋ ↔ 3 ft (0.9 m) ↕ 2–3 ft (0.6–0.9 m)

Endemic to Japan, known in gardens chiefly by its cultivars and hybrids. Leaves bi- or tripinnate, flowers white, in pyramidal panicles up to 8 in (20 cm) long in late spring–early summer. Zones 5–9.

Astilbe, Hybrid Cultivar, 'Deutschland'

Astilbe, Hybrid Cultivar, 'Montgomery'

Astilbe koreana

☀ ❋ ↔ 16–20 in (40–50 cm)
↕ 24 in (60 cm)

Southern Korean species with finely divided ferny foliage. Bright pink buds open to white or very pale pink flowers borne on airy, arching panicles. Zones 7–9.

Astilbe simplicifolia

☀ ❋ ↔ 8–16 in (20–40 cm)
↕ 12–16 in (30–40 cm)

Compact Japanese species. Foliage often simple, glossy, ovate, and lobed but sometimes more deeply divided. Starry white flowers in narrow upright plumes. Several cultivars, including: '**Bronze Elegance**', 12 in (30 cm) tall, pinkish red flowers on red stems; and '**Hennie Graefland**', 16 in (40 cm) tall, soft pink flowers, bronze foliage. Zones 7–9.

Astilbe thunbergii

☀ ❋ ↔ 12–20 in (30–50 cm)
↕ 20–24 in (50–60 cm)

Early-flowering Japanese species with sharply toothed pinnate foliage, broad olive to bronze-green leaflets, sometimes downy. Flowers small but densely massed, opening white and ageing to pink. Zones 7–9.

Astilbe Hybrid Cultivars

☀ ❋ ↔ 3 ft (0.9 m) ↕ 2–3 ft (0.6–0.9 m)

These cultivars have *A. japonica* as a major part of their heritage. '**Betsy Cuperus**', 36 in (90 cm), tall, arching panicles of soft pink flowers; '**Deutschland**', 20 in (50 cm) tall, bright green foliage, pure white flowers; '**Europa**', 24 in (60 cm) high, pale pink flowers; '**Montgomery**',

30 in (75 cm) tall, red flowers, red-tinted foliage; '**Red Sentinel**', 24–36 in (60–90 cm) high, bronze leaves, open sprays of red flowers on red stems; and '**Straussenfeder**' (syn. 'Ostrich Feather'), 36 in (90 cm) high, salmon pink to soft red flowers in arching sprays. Zones 6–9.

ASTILBOIDES

syn. *Rodgersia*

A genus of the saxifrage (Saxifragaceae) family containing only one species, a herbaceous perennial once included in the genus *Rodgersia*. It comes from China and differs from its former relatives mainly in its leaf shape. It is grown for its huge leaves and racemes of tiny white flowers.
CULTIVATION: It grows best in moist soils in a cool sheltered spot and is usually seen at its best near water. It bears very little resemblance to the genus *Astilbe* after which it was named. Propagation is from seed or by division when dormant.

Astilboides tabularis

syn. *Rodgersia tabularis*

☀ ❋ ↔ 40–60 in (100–150 cm)
↕ 40–60 in (100–150 cm)

This impressive perennial has huge, bright green, circular leaves to 36 in (90 cm) across with the stem attached to the center. Above the foliage are its large fluffy heads of tiny white flowers, produced in summer. Zones 7–10.

ASTRANTIA

MASTERWORT, PINCUSHION FLOWER

Primarily European, this genus of 10 species of perennials also occurs westward to Asia, often in alpine meadows or woodlands. Belonging to the carrot (Apiaceae) family, they bear their small pastel-toned flowers in small dome-shaped heads (umbels). The true flowers are often less showy than the surrounding papery bracts. The foliage, which forms a basal clump and spreads by runners, is hand-shaped, with 3 to 7 toothed lobes. The name *Astrantia* probably comes from the star (aster) shaped flower-heads, but a more fanciful explanation

Astrantia carniolica

A

Astrantia major

Astrantia major subsp. *involucrata* 'Moira Reid'

Astrantia major 'Ruby Wedding'

Astrantia maxima

is that it is derived from *ostrutium*, a corruption of *struthio*, an ostrich. The reference is unclear but perhaps the taxonomist thought the flowerheads resemble ostrich plumes.

CULTIVATION: Apart from an intolerance of prolonged dry conditions, grows freely in any cool-temperate garden with moderately fertile free-draining soil. Foliage may be lusher in shade, a consideration with variegated cultivars, but they usually flower best in at least half-sun. Propagate by division when dormant or from seed, which needs stratification.

Astrantia carniolica

☀ ❄ ↔ 16–24 in (40–60 cm)
↕ 20–24 in (50–60 cm)

Found in the southeastern part of the European Alps. Leaves 5-lobed. Flowerheads with large, lance-shaped bracts, greenish white to pale purple. 'Rubra' has soft pink-tinted inflorescences. Zones 6–9.

Astrantia major

GREATER MASTERWORT

☀ ❄ ↔ 16–24 in (40–60 cm)
↕ 24–32 in (60–80 cm)

From central and eastern Europe. Leaves with 3 to 7, broad, toothed lobes. Floral bracts white through red, often green tinted or veined. *A. m.* subsp. *involucrata*, has long narrow bracts creating a lacy flowerhead; 'Moira Reid', very large green-tipped white bracts, pink-tinted early blooms, 30 in (75 cm) tall; and

'Shaggy', green-tipped white flowers and deeply divided leaves, 30 in (75 cm) tall. *A. m.* var. *rosea* has green-tinted pale pink inflorescences, 30 in (75 cm) tall. *A. m.* 'Rubra' ★, deep purple-red inflorescence, 24 in (60 cm) tall; 'Ruby Wedding', dark wine red flowers through summer, 30 in (75 cm) tall; 'Sunningdale Variegated', variably marked cream and green variegated foliage and pink-flushed white flowerheads, 30 in (75 cm) tall. Zones 6–9.

Astrantia maxima

☀ ❄ ↔ 20–24 in (50–60 cm)
↕ 27–36 in (70–90 cm)

Large leaves with 3 to 5 finely toothed lobes. Pink flowerheads, lighter center, bracts fused to create a ruff rather than "petals." Zones 6–9.

ASTREBLA

MITCHELL GRASS

This genus of perennial grasses (family Poaceae) consists of 4 species, all endemic to Australia where they range through the dry northern interior on the more fertile soils of river floodplains. Regarded as among the most valuable native pasture grasses, they form compact tussocks; flowering after rain, they have narrow erect flower-spikes and somewhat prickly small seedheads. New leaves shoot from the lower nodes of the old flowering stems after rain.

CULTIVATION: Not known to be cultivated. Natural pastures are managed by ensuring that the grasses are not grazed too short, otherwise they will not recover after dry periods. Propagation is from seed.

Astrebla elymoides

HOOP MITCHELL GRASS

☀ ❄ ↔ 24 in (60 cm) ↕ 24 in (60 cm)

Occurs mainly in the interior of Queensland but extends into New South Wales and the Northern Territory, Australia. Erect tussock, leaves long and narrow. Inflorescences very narrow, curling in the form of a hoop especially in seed. Zones 9–11.

ASTROPHYTUM

BISHOP'S CAP, BISHOP'S MITER, GOAT HORN CACTUS, SEA URCHIN CACTUS

Astrophytum is an easily recognised and popular genus of small- to medium-sized members of the cactus (Cactaceae) family from Texas, USA, and Mexico. Usually solitary, with 5 to 8 ribs, they appear star-shaped when viewed from above. The genus name comes from the Greek *astron*, star. Taxonomists have recently reduced the genus to just 4 species, but collectors recognize dozens of subspecies as well as hundreds of varieties and inter-species hybrids. Flowers are 1¼–2½ in (3–6 cm) wide, yellow or yellow with a red center. Astrophytums readily cross-pollinate to produce ¾–1¼ in (18–30 mm), spherical, scaly, dry seed pods that ripen quickly. These split open to reveal hundreds of cowry-shell-shaped, brown to black seeds.

CULTIVATION: Almost invariably grown from seed, astrophytums are easy to grow in a well-drained, moderately rich, preferably mineralized soil and given a distinct winter rest. They are somewhat susceptible to over-watering, especially if the medium is not well drained.

Astrophytum asterias

SEA URCHIN CACTUS

☀ ❄ ↔ 4 in (10 cm) ↕ 2 in (5 cm)

From southern Texas, USA, and the States of Nuevo Leon and Tamaulipas in Mexico. This is the smallest species, with 8 low ribs, spineless, adorned with fine horizontal bands of scurfy hairs. Flowers 2–2½ in (5–6 cm) wide, yellow with a red center. Seed pods, brown, scaly, ½–1 in (12–25 mm) in diameter. Zones 9–11.

Astrophytum asterias

Astrebla elymoides, in the wild, Barkly Tableland, Northern Territory, Australia

Astrophytum capricorne

GOAT HORN CACTUS

☀ ⚘ ↔ 4–6 in (10–15 cm)
↑ 4–10 in (10–25 cm)

From a wide area of the Chihuahua Desert of northern Mexico, this species has 7 or 8 well-defined ribs, is spherical to cylindrical and may grow to 40 in (100 cm) tall. Clusters of 5 to 10 twisted, flexible, 2–3 in (5–8 cm) long, black, brown, yellow, or gray spines along the ribs. Plant body may vary from being very smooth, to having many horizontal bands of whitish scurf, to being fully covered in scurf. Flowers 2–2½ in (5–6 cm) wide, yellow with a red center. Seed pods brown, scaly, ½–1 in (12–25 mm) in diameter. *A. c.* var. *senile* has gray spines. *A. c.* f. *aureum* has golden spines when young. Zones 9–11.

Astrophytum myriostigma ★

BISHOP'S CAP, BISHOP'S MITER

☀ ⚘ ↔ 4–6 in (10–15 cm)
↑ 4–10 in (10–25 cm)

From Central Mexico, this is the archetypical astrophytum, with its 5 well-defined spineless ribs and an even spread of whitish scurf. *A. m.* var. *coahuilense*, lower ribs than the type species, more cylindrical in shape, more densely covered in scurf. Some authorities regard this variety as

a separate species. *A. m.* var. *strongylogonum* is distinguished by its quite rounded ribs, and almost spherical shape. *A. m.* f. *nudum* has a bright green plant body completely devoid of scurf; flowers 1½–2 in (35–50 mm) wide, yellow; seed pods brown, scaly. Zones 9–11.

Astrophytum ornatum ★

☀ ⚘ ↔ 12–40 in (30–100 cm)
↑ 12–40 in (30–100 cm)

From Queretaro and Hidalgo, Mexico, this species, the largest in the genus, is named for the ornate clusters of 5 to 11 sharp, 1¼–2 in (30–50 mm) long, needle-like spines. Spine clusters occur 1¼–2 in (30–50 mm) apart along the 7 to 8 ribs. Whitish scurf may be absent, quite dense, or present in horizontal bands. These variations have given rise to a number of named varieties. Flowers about 2 in (50 mm) wide, yellow. Seed pods, brown, scaly. *A. o.* var. *niveum* is covered in trichomes, *A. o.* f. *mirbelii* has bands of scurf, and *A. o.* f. *nudum* has none. Zones 9–11.

ASYSTASIA

Consisting of around 70 species of evergreen soft-wooded shrubs and subshrubs, *Asystasia* ranges through tropical Asia and Africa, extending as far as northern Australia. It belongs to

Asystasia travancorica 'Violacea'

the acanthus (Acanthaceae) family and has that family's characteristic features: simple leaves in opposite pairs, trumpet-shaped flowers with distinct upper and lower lips, and seeds in small capsules that split open explosively. *Asystasia* bears flowers in terminal sprays that lack the large overlapping bracts that are a feature of many others of the acanthus family; they are mainly in shades from white through pink to rose-purple.

CULTIVATION: They are all frost tender and require a tropical or sub-tropical climate for growing outdoors. In cool climates they are easily grown as conservatory plants, preferring good light and high humidity. They are easily propagated from cuttings or lengths of rooted stem, though seed can also be used.

Asystasia gangetica

☀ ⚘ ↔ 2 ft (0.6 m) ↑ 2 ft (0.6 m)
Widespread species. Scrambling sub-shrub. Stems that root on contact with damp ground. Bright green leaves, broad, rounded, to 3 in (8 cm) long. Flowers 1½ in (35 mm) across, cream to rose purple, in summer. Zones 11–12.

Asystasia travancorica

☀ ⚘ ↔ 3 ft (0.9 m) ↑ 3 ft (0.9 m)
Native to southern India. More upright shrub than *A. gangetica*. Dense mass of stems. Dull green leaves, narrower, more pointed. Mauve flowers slightly smaller, with distinct darker markings around the throat. 'Violacea' has flowers of deeper violet color toward the tips. Zones 11–12.

ATHAMANTA

There are 15 species of perennial herbs in this genus, which is a member of the carrot (Apiaceae) family. They are native to the Mediterranean and temperate Eurasia where they grow in scree and other mountain habitats. They have long tap roots and form clumps of finely divided foliage. Their umbels of small flowers are white, occasionally yellow.

CULTIVATION: The tall species are suitable for the wild garden where they can be grown in any well-drained soil in full sun. They dislike winter wet. The alpine species can be grown in troughs or the cool green-house. Propagate from seed or by division in spring.

Astrophytum myriostigma f. *nudum*

A. myriostigma var. *coahuilense*

Astrophytum myriostigma

Astrophytum ornatum

Astrophytum ornatum f. *mirbelii*

Athamanta turbith

syn. *Athamanta mathioli*

CANDY CARROT

☼ ❄ ↔15 in (38 cm) ↑24 in (60 cm)

From central Europe. Clumps of finely divided fern-like foliage. Umbels of small white flowers in summer. Zones 6–9.

ATHEROSPERMA

The sole species in this genus is a large evergreen tree native to New South Wales, Victoria, and Tasmania, Australia. Although not closely related to the true sassafras *(Sassafras albidum),* the tree yields similar oils, most intensely from the bark. As it is the only member of its genus, this is a tree with few close relatives, and it is among just 12 species spread over the 6 genera in its family (Monimiaceae).

CULTIVATION: Although a little tender when young, *Atherosperma* adapts well to cultivation and seems happy in any well-drained soil with at least half-day sun. For the best results grow it in a moist climate with rich soil. Seedlings are slow to develop but are usually more reliable than cuttings.

Atherosperma moschatum ★

BLACK SASSAFRAS, SOUTHERN SASSAFRAS

☼ ❄ ↔15 ft (4.5 m) ↑100 ft (30 m)

Under cultivation this species rarely reaches 100 ft (30 m) tall. Leathery foliage, deep green above with pale hairs below. Pendulous white flowers open in spring. Female flowers have a covering of silky hairs. Zones 8–10.

ATHROTAXIS

Found only in Tasmania, Australia, this conifer genus of 2 species is both interesting and ornamental. A primitive member of the Taxodiaceae family, it is now part of the cypress

Athrotaxis selaginoides, in the wild, in Walls of Jerusalem National Park, Tasmania, Australia

(Cupressaceae) family, which includes *Sequoia* and *Cryptomeria.* They are long-lived trees of medium size with dense conical crowns; crowded branchlets have spirally arranged, overlapping, small leaves varying from flattened and needle-like to scale-like. Seed cones are small, consisting of a few pointed scales; tiny pollen cones, borne on the same tree, are more profuse.

CULTIVATION: These species are moderately frost hardy and prefer cool moist climates without extremes of temperature. Growth is slow but in 10 years they can make very attractive large shrubs under good conditions, and are suitable for large-scale rock gardens. Soil should be well drained but permanently moist and cool. They are readily propagated from cuttings, or from seed, though this is seldom available.

Athrotaxis cupressoides, in Cradle Mt–Lake St Clair National Park, Tasmania, Australia

Athrotaxis cupressoides

TASMANIAN PENCIL PINE

☼ ❄ ↔20 ft (6 m) ↑40 ft (12 m)

The pencil pine develops a neat conical mass of dense bright green foliage. Leaves are reduced to scales clothing the fairly thick whipcord-like branchlets. It is found in rather bleak mountain areas, often at edges of shallow lakes. Zones 8–9.

Athrotaxis selaginoides

KING BILLY PINE, KING WILLIAM PINE

☼ ❄ ↔25 ft (8 m) ↑100 ft (30 m)

The leaves of this species are longer than those of *A. cupressoides,* and are strongly incurved and overlapping, with two conspicuous white bands on their inner faces. This species grows in sheltered areas. The common name for the species is a reference to King William Range in Tasmania, Australia. Zones 8–9.

ATHYRIUM

A member of the shield-fern family (Dryopteridaceae), this genus comprises more than 100 widely variable terrestrial fern species. They are from temperate to tropical regions, and feature short and erect to creeping rhizomes with scales entire to toothed, and brown to black in color. Their fronds are leathery to membranous, often brittle.

CULTIVATION: Most of the species in this genus prefer well-drained, acidic, organically rich loams, with organic mulch applied, in shade or filtered sun. Tropical species are frost tender. Protect from wind, slugs, and snails. Maintain abundant moisture, including water sprayed on foliage in hot weather. Easily propagated from spores or plantlets. Species with multiple crowns or creeping rhizomes can be divided.

Atherosperma moschatum, in the wild, in Tahune Forest Reserve, Tasmania, Australia

Athyrium otophorum var. *okanum*

Athyrium filix-femina

Athyrium niponicum var. *pictum*

Athyrium filix-femina

LADY FERN

☼◑/☼ ❄ ↔ 3–7 ft (0.9–2 m)
↑ 2–5 ft (0.6–1.5 m)

Graceful, easily grown, clumping fern from northern temperate zones in India, China, Japan, North Africa, Canada, North America, Mexico, and Peru. Short-creeping to erect rhizomes. Spreading or arching pinnate fronds, to 3 ft (0.9 m) long, thin-textured and leathery. Smooth frond stalks are green to purple in color. Deciduous in colder regions. This species has over 300 cultivars, including 'Clarissima', a graceful uncrested fern, to 40 in (100 cm); 'Frizelliae' (tatting fern), with ball-shaped leaflets along the midrib; 'Glomeratum', with curious ball-like masses of leaflets on slender fronds; 'Magnificum Capitatum', frond alone crested, leaflets not crested; 'Minutissimum', dwarf form with fronds 4–6 in (10–15 cm) long;

'Vernoniae', crimson frond stalks, broadly triangular blades with strongly ruffled overlapping leaflets, ending in a tassel; 'Victoriae', crested fronds, to 40 in (100 cm) tall, branched at base to form crosses. Zones 3–6.

Athyrium niponicum

☼◑/☼ ❄ ↔ 20–24 in (50–60 cm)
↑ 12–14 in (30–35 cm)

Fully frost-hardy fern from East Asia with a short-creeping reddish brown rhizome. Arching pinnate fronds with yellow-colored stems. *A. n.* var. *pictum* (Japanese painted fern), new fronds metallic gray suffused with red or blue. *A. n.* 'Pictum Crested' (painted lady fern), purplish red midrib suffusing into a silver gray and aquamarine-green lamina. Zones 3–6.

Athyrium otophorum

☼◑/☼ ❄ ↔ 5–24 in (38–60 cm)
↑ 12–18 in (30–45 cm)

Fern from East Asia (China, Japan, and Korea) with short-creeping, clump-forming, erect rhizomes. Dark green 2-pinnate fronds, to 18 in (45 cm) long, on red to purple stems. Leaflets in 8 to 10 pairs with toothed or lobed pinnules. *A. o.* var. *okanum* has stems and midribs that are purple-red, and fronds that are yellowish green. Zones 4–8.

ATRIPLEX

SALTBUSH

From all continents except Antarctica, there are around 300 species included in this genus in the goosefoot or saltbush (Chenopodiaceae) family. *Atriplex* includes many shrubs as well as annuals and perennials. Multi-branched, with wiry crooked twigs. Leaves fleshy, coarsely toothed, and covered in fine whitish scales giving the foliage a silvery or pale bluish cast. They frequently grow in saline soils and the leaf sap is then salty. Flowers

small, of different sexes often on different plants. Used for fodder, and regenerating saline areas. Several species make attractive ornamentals with their dense whitish foliage. Sheep that feed on saltbush produce meat of a distinctive flavor, prized by some gourmets. CULTIVATION: These plants are suited to hot, dry, or saline environments, including exposed seashores. All require full sun and do best in a well-drained soil of moderate fertility. Can be cut back hard, responding with thicker foliage, and trained into hedges. Propagate from softwood cuttings or seed. Soak seed to simulate the effect of rain needed for these plants to germinate.

Atriplex canescens

CHAMIZO, FOUR-WING SALTBUSH

☼ ❄ ↔ 5 ft (1.5 m) ↑ 5 ft (1.5 m)

From western USA and Mexico. Densely massed stems, and narrow blunt-tipped leaves of mealy whitish appearance. Tiny yellowish flowers give way to 4-winged papery fruit bracts crowded onto short spikes, in late summer. Zones 7–10.

Atriplex cinerea

COAST SALTBUSH, GRAY SALTBUSH

☼ ❄ ↔ 10 ft (3 m) ↑ 5 ft (1.5 m)

From temperate coasts of Australia and southern Africa. Dense shrub, bluish green leaves about 2 in (5 cm) long. Male flowers conspicuous, with spikes of yellowish brown flowers and purplish bracts, in winter. Zones 9–10.

Atriplex halimus ★

TREE PURSLANE

☼ ❄ ↔ 10 ft (3 m) ↑ 6 ft (1.8 m)

From the saltmarshes of southern Europe. Similar to the Southern Hemisphere *A. cinerea*, but has slightly larger, more silvery leaves. Irregular spikes of greenish white flowers in late summer. Zones 8–10.

Atriplex hortensis

FAT HEN, FRENCH SPINACH, MOUNTAIN SPINACH, ORACH, SALTBUSH, SEA PURSLANE

☼ ❄ ↔ 16–20 in (40–50 cm)
↑ 7–8 ft (2–2.4 m)

An erect annual from Asia, with grayish leaves, that has naturalized in most temperate parts of the world. Leaves are heart-shaped to triangular, slightly serrated, 4–6 in (10–15 cm) long, green or purplish brown. Terminal clusters of insignificant green or red flowers, without petals, in summer, are followed by tiny brown plate-like seeds. *A. h.* var. *rubra* is a lovely purple-leafed form. *A. h.* 'Cuptorosea' has stems and leaves that are red with a coppery luster; 'Rosea' has paler leaves, with veins and petioles that are dark red. Zones 6–11.

Atriplex spongiosa

POP SALTBUSH

☼ ❄ ↔ 30–40 in (75–100 cm)
↑ 30–40 in (75–100 cm)

An evergreen shrub that comes from inland Australia. Has low branching stems and small, grayish white, stalkless, oval leaves. Flowers are insignificant. Fruit, small rounded berries, are enclosed within inflated bracts. Zones 6–10.

Atriplex cinerea

Atriplex spongiosa, in the wild, Tanami Desert, Northern Territory, Australia

Aubrieta, Hybrid Cultivar, 'Argenteovariegata'

A., HC, 'Blue Cascade'

A., HC, 'Campbellii'

A., HC, 'Eyrei'

A., HC, 'Lavender Queen'

A., HC, 'Rokey's Purple'

Aubrieta, Hybrid Cultivar, 'Doctor Mules'

ATTALEA

This genus, of the palm (Arecaceae) family, of 22 species of feather palms is closely related to the coconut. It is found in Central America and northern South America, from Panama to Peru and Brazil. The species have narrow trunks and a vase-shaped head of long lush fronds with crowded leaflets. The base of the frond may be hairy to very fibrous depending on the species. The flowers are yellow and are borne on branching panicles that when young are protected by large and conspicuous sheaths. Several species yield useful products such as oil, fiber, and even timber in the form of hard nuts.

CULTIVATION: Very much plants of the tropics, these palms demand warm conditions and fertile, moist, well-drained soil, and are best kept sheltered from strong winds. Young plants have more luxuriant foliage if shaded from the hottest sun. Propagate from seed, which should be soaked before sowing.

Attalea butyracea

syns *Scheelea butyracea, S. zonensis*
COROZO PALM

☼ ⚬ ↔ 25 ft (8 m) ↕ 30–60 ft (9–18 m)
Wide-ranging large palm in tropical America from southern Mexico to Bolivia and Trinidad. Short thick trunk and massive pinnate fronds 20 ft (6 m) or more long. Large panicles of cream flowers among frond bases. Fruit 2–3 in (5–8 cm) long, yellow or orange. Zones 10–12.

AUBRIETA

AUBRETIA

Found from Europe to Central Asia, the 12 evergreen cushion or mat-forming perennials of this genus are members of the cabbage (Brassicaceae) family. Indispensable for rockeries and also a colorful addition to flower borders or spilling over banks, they smother themselves in flower in spring and early summer, becoming carpets of tiny, 4-petalled, purple, mauve, or white blooms. The foliage is small and simple, usually dull gray-green and finely downy, often with small lobes or teeth. Named after Claude Aubriet (1668–1743), a French botanical artist, the name was corrupted to aubretia, which became the common name.

CULTIVATION: Hardy in most temperate zones, aubretias prefer gritty well-drained soil in full or half-sun and, while requiring moisture during the flowering season and appreciative of an occasional light dressing of lime, they are otherwise undemanding. Although perennial, at nurseries aubretias are often sold with the bedding annuals and may be treated as such. However, if left to grow on they become far more impressive plants. Propagate from seed, layers, or small basal cuttings or by division.

Aubrieta deltoidea ★

☼/◐ ❄ ↔ 12 in (30 cm) ↕ 3 in (8 cm)
Found in southwest Europe, especially around the Aegean Sea. Leaves diamond-shaped, smooth edged or with 2 to 6 conspicuous teeth. Pale lavender through magenta to purple flowers up to 1 in (25 mm) in diameter. Zones 7–10.

Aubrieta Hybrid Cultivars

☼ ❄ ↔ 8–24 in (20–60 cm) ↕ 3–6 in (8–15 cm)

Garden hybrids are derived from several species. They are difficult to place regarding parentage, but probably all have *A. deltoidea* in their background. All are mat-forming, but otherwise highly variable. Popular named forms include: **'Argenteovariegata'**, with silver-edged leaves and purple flowers; **'Blue Cascade'**, strongly trailing habit, may mound to 6 in (15 cm) high, purplish blue flowers; **'Blue King'**, mauve-blue flowers in abundance; **'Bressingham Pink'**, clusters of large, pink, double flowers; **'Campbellii'**, mauve-blue double flowers; **'Doctor Mules'**, neat, compact habit with attractive violet-blue flowers; **'Hendersonii'**, low spreader with purple flowers, well suited to rock walls and banks; **'Novalis Blue'**, bright mauve-blue flowers; and **'Rokey's Purple'**, which produces deep purple flowers well into summer. Zones 7–10.

Attalea butyracea palms, in the wild, in Parque Nacional Manuel Antonio, Quepos, Costa Rica

A

AUCUBA

This genus of dioecious plants in the dogwood (Cornaceae) family originates from the Himalayas and eastern Asia. It consists of 3 or 4 species of evergreen shrubs or small trees, frequently used in garden situations, as they tolerate deep shade. Spotted forms most popular. The glossy leaves are lanceolate, smooth or serrate, and grow in an alternate arrangement along the branches. Flowers, either green or maroon, are in leaf axils or at the ends of terminal shoots. Fruit are red, orange, or whitish yellow.
CULTIVATION: *Aucuba* grows best in moist soil. The spotted forms require partial shade, since in sun they can scorch, while in deep shade the spotting fades. Cut back in spring. Seed should be sown in spring. Take half-hardened cuttings in summer. Both male and female plants are required to ensure berries. If grown in containers, use loam-based compost, with monthly feeding during the growing season.

Aucuba himalaica

☀/❄ ❄ ↔ 10 ft (3 m) ↑ 30 ft (9 m)
From the Indian state of Sikkim in the eastern Himalayas. Leaves to 12 in

(30 cm) long, leathery, finely serrated toward the base. Flowers arranged in a pyramidal cluster. Fruit orange when ripe. Zones 6–10.

Aucuba japonica

JAPANESE AUCUBA, JAPANESE LAUREL
☀ ❄ ↔ 6 ft (1.8 m) ↑ 6 ft (1.8 m)
From Japan, this evergreen shrub has purplish flowers and red berries. Cultivars include: '**Crotonifolia**', a strongly gold-variegated cultivar; '**Gold Dust**', female, variegated leaves; '**Rozannie**', a self-fruiting form; '**Salicifolia**', female, narrow long-pointed leaves; and '**Variegata**' ★, gold variegated, preferring deep shade. Zones 7–9.

AULAX

This South African protea (Proteaceae) family genus of just 3 species of evergreen shrubs is unusual among the many South African Proteaceae in having male and female flowers on separate plants. The bushes have fine needle-like foliage. In spring and summer female plants produce funnel-shaped *Leucospermum*-like flowerheads that develop into seed cones. The catkin-like male flowers are yellow.

Aucuba japonica 'Gold Dust'

Aucuba japonica 'Salicifolia'

Aucuba japonica 'Variegata'

Auranticarpa rhombifolia

CULTIVATION: in all respects except frost hardiness, these are tough plants. They tolerate extreme heat, very low humidity, and prolonged drought. Like virtually all protea family plants, they grow best on a light gritty soil with good drainage. Propagate from seed or half-hardened late summer–autumn cuttings.

Aulax cancellata

☀ ❄ ↔ 5 ft (1.5 m) ↑ 5 ft (1.5 m)
Native to the southwest Cape region of South Africa. Leaves needle-shaped, to 4 in (10 cm) long, arranged radially on stiff reddish brown stems. Female plants have golden orange buds, opening to heads of creamy yellow flowers. Red seed cones. Zones 9–10.

Aulax umbellata

☀ ❄ ↔ 4 ft (1.2 m) ↑ 4–6 ft (1.2–1.8 m)
Coastal species, broader leaves than the other species. Clusters of male flowers, deep yellow, surrounded by orange-tinted stem-tip foliage. Female flowers surrounded by light orange bracts, smaller than the male. Zones 9–10.

AURANTICARPA

Close study of the large genus *Pittosporum* by some Australian botanists revealed that a group of northern Australian species is not closely related to the remainder of the

species. As a result they named it as a new genus, Auranticarpa ('gold fruit'), though it is still in the pittosporum (Pittosporaceae) family. It is distinguished by a much-branched inflorescence with small bright orange fruit with blackish seeds. It consists of 6 species of evergreen trees, 3 transferred from *Pittosporum* and 3 new to science. Five of them are confined to the tropical north, while one extends down the east coast and ranges from north Queensland to north-eastern New South Wales.
CULTIVATION: Only *A. rhombifolia* is widely cultivated, popular as a street and park tree and adapting well to drier and cooler regions than its wild habitats. It prefers moderately fertile, moist but well drained soils and tolerates exposure to strong winds as well as partial shade, but full sun is required for a good display of its orange fruit. Propagate from seed.

Auranticarpa rhombifolia

syn. *Pittosporum rhombifolium*
DIAMOND-LEAF LAUREL, HOLLY WOOD
☀/ ❄ ↔ 10–20 ft (3–6 m)
↑ 20–60 ft (6–18 m)
Eastern Australian native, young growth covered in dense rusty hairs. Glossy green leaves, roughly diamond-shaped. Small, sweetly scented, white flowers in summer. Showy orange seed capsules. Zones 9–11.

Aulax cancellata

Aulax umbellata

AURINIA

A genus of 7 species of perennials and biennials of the cabbage (Brassicaceae) family, found in central and southern Europe and eastward to Turkey and the Black Sea region. They are small carpeting plants that form loose basal rosettes of leaves that emerge from a sometimes thickened rootstock. Leaves are often covered with fine hairs, giving them a silver-gray appearance. Heads of small bright yellow or white flowers open from spring, often almost hiding the foliage.
CULTIVATION: Best suited to a cool-temperate climate where frosts are not severe, these are superb plants for rockeries or alpine troughs. They prefer full sun and need perfectly drained gritty soil, kept moist in spring and early summer. All may be propagated from seed, which often self-sows, and the perennials can also be grown from self-layered pieces or by taking small tip cuttings.

Aurinia saxatilis
syn. *Alyssum saxatile*
BASKET OF GOLD, YELLOW ALYSSUM
☀ ❄ ↔ 16–24 in (40–60 cm)
↑ 8–12 in (20–30 cm)

Central and southeastern Europe. Low, carpeting perennial with small silver-gray leaves. Sprays of pale to bright yellow flowers from spring. Hardiest species by far. 'Citrina' is heavy-blooming, bright yellow flowers; and 'Compacta' has golden flowers on 8 in (20 cm) high stems. Zones 3–9.

AUSTROCEDRUS

A conifer genus consisting of a single species belonging to the cypress (Cupressaceae) family, *Austrocedrus* is native to Argentina and southern Chile, where it grows in moist forest. The fine branchlets are arranged in somewhat flattened sprays and bear small scale-leaves that alternate between a wider lateral pair and a small facial pair; all the leaves are marked with small but conspicuous bluish white flecks, giving the foliage a blue-gray cast overall. The seed cones are less than ½ in (12 mm) long and egg-shaped with 2 or 3 pairs of thin scales.
CULTIVATION: It does best in a cool but mild climate with year-round rainfall, though it will cope with occasional dry spells. A sheltered situation with moist but well-drained acid soil is desirable, much the same as for the half-hardy rhododendrons, though ample sun will allow the best form and color to develop. Propagate from cuttings or seed.

Austrostipa stipoides, in the wild, Cape Barren Island, Tasmania, Australia

Austrocedrus chilensis
syn. *Libocedrus chilensis*
CHILEAN INCENSE CEDAR
☀ ❄ ↔ 15 ft (4.5 m) ↑ 50 ft (15 m)
Growth habit is usually columnar until quite old, when the crown may broaden at the top. Bark is orange-brown to darker brown and peels in narrow strips. Zones 8–9.

AUSTROCYLINDROPUNTIA

The 11 species in this exclusively South American genus (from the Latin *austro,* meaning south) belong to the cactus (Cactaceae) family. All have segmented stems. Some are shrubby or tree-like, while others may form a mat. Most produce a few weak fleshy leaves at the growing tips, but these soon die away. They produce small, easily detached, irritating spines from the areoles. Flowers are relatively large and showy, to 3 in (8 cm) long but often only 2–2½ in (5–6 cm) wide, in shades of red, orange, pink, and yellow, spiny on the outer surface.
CULTIVATION: Easily grown in a rich well-drained soil. May be grown from seed but more usually from cuttings that have been dried out for a week or two. Rest in winter.

Austrocylindropuntia subulata
syn. *Opuntia subulata*
☀ ❄ ↔ 10–15 ft (3–4.5 m) ↑ 15 ft (4.5 m)
Native to Peru, now widely distributed beyond its native range because it is

Aurinia saxatilis 'Compacta'

useful as a quick-growing barrier or fence. Stems 20 in (50 cm) long, 4 in (10 cm) thick, attractively patterned, with prominent tubercles and 1 to 4, needle-sharp, yellow spines. The scaly, red, 2½ in (6 cm) long flowers do not open widely. Spineless fruit, 4 in (10 cm) long, club-shaped. Zones 9–11.

AUSTROSTIPA
SPEARGRASS

A genus of 65 species of perennial grasses (family Poaceae), nearly all from temperate Australia, with a few from New Zealand. They have recently been separated from *Stipa,* now regarded as a predominantly Northern Hemisphere genus; the difference is in flower and seed details. All are tufted or tussock-forming grasses, with narrow, harsh leaves. Inflorescences progress rapidly to seed: individual "seeds" (technically fruits) consist of a narrow grain sharply pointed at the

Austrocedrus chilensis

lower end and with a long, bent or curled awn at the upper end. Curling and uncurling of the awn with moisture changes drives fallen seeds into cracks in the soil like a corkscrew, aiding germination.
CULTIVATION: Seldom cultivated but some make fine ornamental grasses—they can however be noxious weeds if introduced to similar climates in other continents. Propagate from seed.

Austrostipa stipoides
syns *Stipa stipoides, S. teretifolia*
COAST SPEARGRASS
☀ ❄ ↔ 3 ft (0.9 m) ↑ 2 ft (0.6 m)
From seashores of southern Australia, including Tasmania. Forms dense floppy tussocks of long fine leaves. Grows in large stands on dunes and headlands, blown by the wind so that the foliage moves in waves. Narrow inflorescences appear in spring–summer. Zones 9–10.

A

Averrhoa carambola

Averrhoa bilimbi

Avicennia alba, gathering honey, Sundarbans, eastern India

AVERRHOA

An East Asian genus of 2 species of evergreen trees, of the wood-sorrel (Oxalidaceae) family. Foliage is pinnate, composed of quite large leaflets. Flowers, white to red or purple with white markings, are carried in short inflorescences, followed by 5-angled edible fruit, to 5 in (12 cm) long. CULTIVATION: Easily cultivated, other than requiring tropical or subtropical conditions. Thrive in warm sheltered positions with moist well-drained soil and high humidity. The plants are attractive ornamentally as well as for their fruit. Propagate from seed, or grow fruiting cultivars from grafts or aerial layers.

Averrhoa bilimbi
BILIMBI, PICKLE FRUIT
☀ ✤ ↔ 15 ft (4.5 m) ↑ 50 ft (15 m)
Leaves composed of up to 40 leaflets, 5 in (12 cm) long. Inflorescences sprout directly from the branches. Flowers purple to orange-red. Yellow-green fruit, shallowly angled, lacks the sweetness of *A. carambola*. Zones 11–12.

Averrhoa carambola ★
CARAMBOLA, FIVE-CORNER, STAR FRUIT
☀ ✤ ↔ 10 ft (3 m) ↑ 20 ft (6 m)
Leaflets blue-green on undersides, to 4 in (10 cm) long. Sensitive to touch and light, folding at night or if handled. Dull red flowers appear much of the year. Edible fruit, yellow-green to orange. Zones 11–12.

AVICENNIA
MANGROVE
Often the dominant plant in coastal areas and brackish estuaries in the tropics and Southern Hemisphere subtropics, mangroves occur as far south as far north New Zealand. The 6 species of small to medium-sized evergreen trees in this genus, of the Avicenniaceae family, are similar, with small, glossy, leathery leaves and bearing clusters of small greenish to orange flowers at the branch tips. Flowers develop into single-seeded fruits that germinate on the tree, growing where they fall or floating away to establish elsewhere. CULTIVATION: Mangroves are rarely cultivated; where they occur naturally they are often the only large plants that will grow in salty tidal areas. Seedlings establish easily if necessary.

Avicennia alba
WHITE MANGROVE
☀ ✈ ↔ 25–40 ft (8–12 m)
↑ 35–60 ft (10–18 m)
Fast-growing mangrove tree or shrub found from western India to Southeast Asia and the western Pacific region. Supported in coastal sand by lateral roots. Smooth dark gray bark appears black when wet. Leaves shiny dark green above, waxy white below. Yellow flowers, about 4 mm wide, in cross-like inflorescences. Fruit dull pale green, flattened, elliptical; seedlings germinating from within. Heartwood is used to make tonics, the bark and seeds as a fish poison, and the resin for birth control. Zones 11–12.

Avicennia marina
GRAY MANGROVE
☀ ✈ ↔ 10 ft (3 m) ↑ 15 ft (4.5 m)
A hardy mangrove. Withstands light frosts. Leaves exude salt, whitish on their undersides. Small pale orange flowers appear late summer in temperate areas or with the first rains of the wet season in the tropics. Zones 10–12.

AZARA
One of temperate South America's most popular gifts to horticulture, this governor's-plum (Flacourtiaceae) family of 10 species of evergreen shrubs and trees has attractive foliage, graceful growth habits, and easy culture. Primarily native to Chile, their foliage varies in size but is generally glossy and leathery. Each main leaf is appended with one or two smaller "accessory leaves" (stipules) that soon fall away. Flowers tend to be golden yellow, small fluffy pompons without petals, followed by fleshy fruits. CULTIVATION: Most species will tolerate repeated light frosts but are damaged by severe cold. They do not tolerate extreme heat and generally prefer a temperate climate with cool moist soil. Otherwise, they are easy-care plants that, while inclined to become rather open and leggy with age, can be kept compact with routine trimming or pinching back. Propagate by seed or half-hardened cuttings.

Azara celastrina
☀ ❉ ↔ 8 ft (2.4 m) ↑ 10 ft (3 m)
Leaves small, smooth-edged or toothed, dull gray-green. Flowers, scentless or slightly scented, in spring. Fruit is black. Relatively drought tolerant. Good foliage plant. Zones 8–10.

Azara dentata
☀ ❉ ↔ 3–6 ft (0.9–1.8 m)
↑ 3–6 ft (0.9–1.8 m)
Shrub with light to mid-green glossy leaves that are noticeably toothed. Its flowers are not very showy but they are followed by conspicuous, small, yellow fruits. Zones 8–10.

Azara lanceolata
☀ ❉ ↔ 20 ft (6 m) ↑ 20 ft (6 m)
Found in Chile and Argentina, this small tree has lance-shaped leaves to 3 in (8 cm) long with toothed edges. Stipules are slow to drop. Attractive, yellow, mid-spring flowers, followed by mauve fruit. Zones 8–10.

Avicennia marina

Azara dentata

Azara lanceolata

Azara microphylla

Azara serrata

Azara microphylla
VANILLA TREE

☀ ❄ ↔ 15 ft (4.5 m) ↑ 25 ft (8 m)

Commonly grown tree from Chile and Argentina. Small leaves on frond-like branches, creating a ferny or pinnate spray. Vanilla-scented, tiny, dull yellow flowers in spring, red fruit. 'Variegata', golden variegated, attractive foliage plant. Zones 8–10.

Azara petiolaris

☀ ❄ ↔ 12 ft (3.5 m) ↑ 15 ft (4.5 m)

Large shrub from Chile. Leaves around 1½ in (35 mm) long, glossy upper surfaces, sharply toothed edges. Flowers are a soft yellow shade. Black fruit. Zones 8–10.

Azara serrata ★

☀ ❄ ↔ 8 ft (2.4 m) ↑ 12 ft (3.5 m)

Chilean shrub. Sharply toothed foliage, golden flowers that open later than the other azaras. With age can become rather sparse, so best to trim and shape when young. Zones 8–10.

AZOLLA

FAIRY MOSS, MOSQUITO FERN, WATER FERN

A genus of 8 species of floating aquatic ferns with a near-worldwide distribution. Allocated their own family, floating-fern (Azollaceae), they are unusual plants quite unlike terres-

trial ferns in general appearance. Rather than having upright fronds, they carpet the water surface, forming new plants by division. Each plant has roots, a minute rhizome, and overlapping scales as foliage. Scales bright green if shaded, often red in full sun. In areas of hard frost they overwinter as submerged fragments.
CULTIVATION: Although it is appealing, think twice before introducing *Azolla* to a pond. It will soon cover the water surface, smothering more desirable plants. It is self-propagating and a small cluster dropped in the water will race away in warm weather.

Azolla filiculoides

☼/◐ ❄ ↔ unlimited ↑ ¼–½ in (6–12 mm)

Found in North and South America. Individual plantlets are of irregular shape, occasionally up to 4 in (10 cm) in length, massing to cover large areas. Purple-red in full sun. Zones 7–11.

AZORELLA

This carrot (Apiaceae) family genus of about 70 species of perennials occurs naturally in South America, New Zealand, and the subantarctic islands. They are cushion-forming evergreen perennials that develop into hummocks of bright green foliage. In spring and early summer, tiny heads of greenish cream to bright yellow, rarely pink, flowers are seen.
CULTIVATION: Although found over a wide latitude range, they tend to prefer a cool-temperate climate where the frosts are not severe, occurring at high altitudes in their northerly range and descending as the latitude rises to

the south. Either full or half-sun will do. Plant in gritty, very free-draining soil, but do not allow to dry out for long periods. Superb plants as ground covers for large rockeries or cascading down banks and stone walls.

Azorella trifurcata
syn. *Azorella nivalis*

☼/◐ ❄ ↔ 2–7 ft (0.6–2 m) ↑ 4 in (10 cm)

From Chile and Argentina. Usually compact mound of gray-green to bright deep green, leathery leaves, but can spread in ideal conditions. Yellow-green to yellow flowerheads from late spring. 'Nana' is very compact with smaller leaves. Zones 6–9.

AZORINA

This monotypic genus is in the bell-flower (Campanulaceae) family. Its 1 species is a small shrubby plant previously of the *Campanula* genus. Extremely rare in the wild, found only in the Azores growing on sea-cliffs.
CULTIVATION: In warm areas grow in a very well-drained soil in a sunny position. In cool climates grow in the greenhouse. Plants are short-lived and dislike humidity, which can cause them to rot. Propagate from seed.

Azorina vidalii
syn. *Campanula vidalii*

☼ ❅ ↔ 12 in (30 cm) ↑ 12–20 in (30–50 cm)

A fleshy evergreen perennial with narrow shiny leaves growing toward the branch tips. In late summer stems of waxy, pale pink, bell-shaped flowers are held above the foliage. Zones 10–11.

AZTEKIUM

This extraordinary genus of 2 dwarf cactus species from Mexico belongs to the cactus (Cactaceae) family. The genus was so named because *A. ritteri* is reminiscent of an Aztec sculpture. The 2 species, the other

being *A. hintonii*, both grow on almost vertical limestone or gypsum cliffs in Nuevo Leon, Mexico, where little else grows. They are usually solitary but *A. ritteri* does cluster with age. Flowers are pink or magenta, ½–1 in (12–25 mm) in diameter. They are produced from the downy, slightly depressed growing tips, which also tend to conceal the small seed pods. The popularity of the species has led to much habitat collecting of plants. *A. ritteri* is listed in Appendix I of CITES.
CULTIVATION: *A. ritteri* has long tested the patience of even the most experienced grower. Seeds are dust-like and a 10-year-old seedling may be the size of a pea. A challenge to grow on its own root, it is often encountered as a grafted plant. Both species need a well-drained mineral soil with a little limestone or gypsum added, moderate watering, and a rest in the winter.

Aztekium ritteri

☼ ⬦ ↔ 1¼–2½ in (30–60 mm) ↑ ½–1¼ in (12–30 mm)

From a single valley in Nuevo Leon, Mexico, this little yellow-green gem commences life as a single plant but with age it may cluster. The 6 to 12 spineless ribs are low and concertina-shaped. Flowers pink to white ¼–½ in (6–12 mm) in diameter. Zones 9–11.

Azorella trifurcata

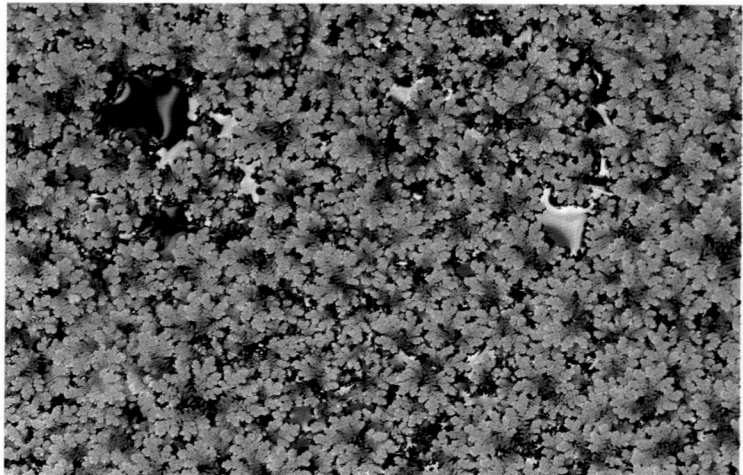

Azolla filiculoides

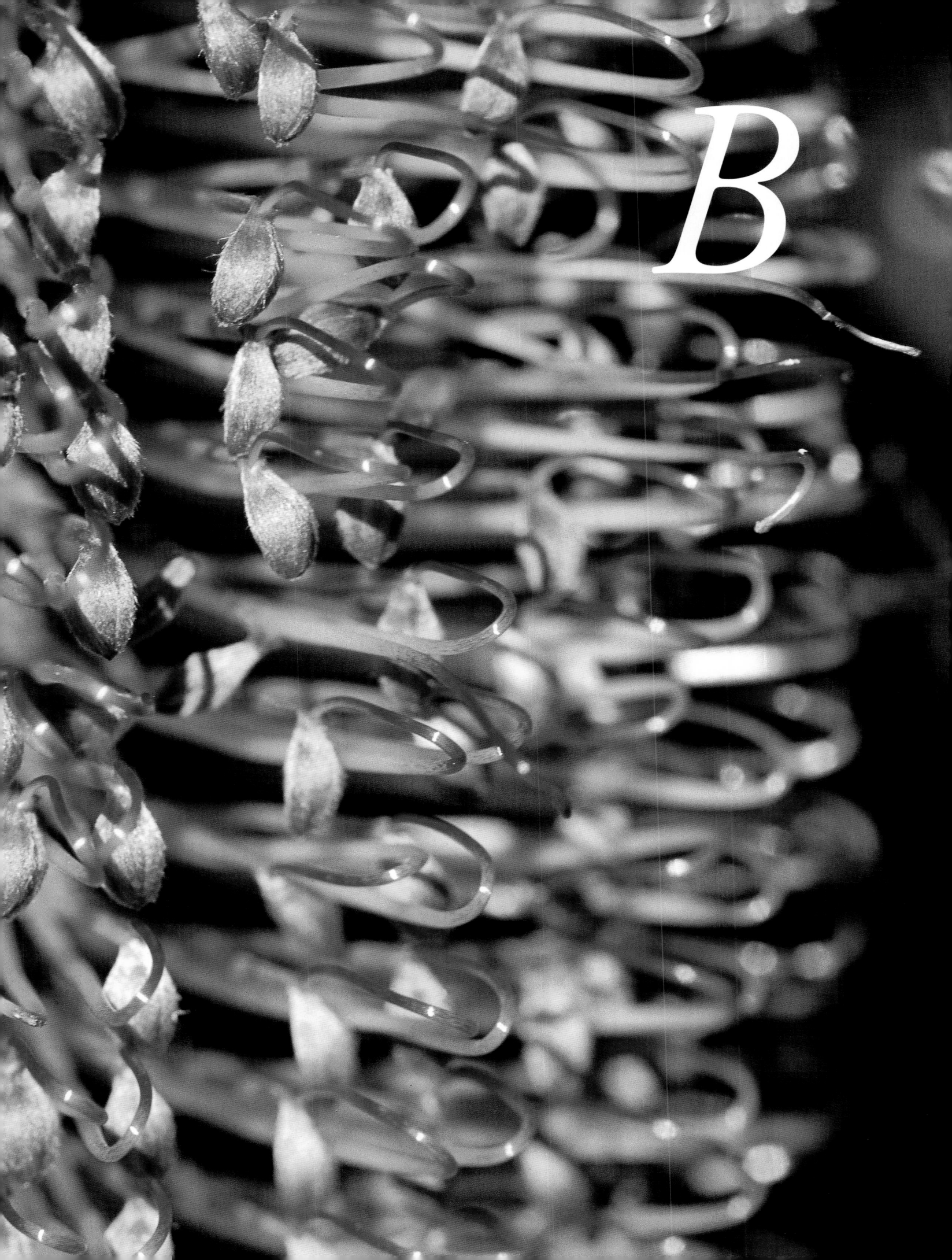

B

B

Babiana rubrocyanea

Babiana ringens

Babiana angustifolia

Babiana stricta

BABIANA

BABOON FLOWER

This genus of about 60 species of brilliant spring-flowering, cormous plants is a member of the iris (Iridaceae) family. Most species are native to southern Africa where they grow in coastal habitats and other dry open areas. They have lance-shaped leaves, ribbed and hairy in some species. The funnel-shaped flowers, some scented, are borne on short spikes and range from white, cream, and yellow to rich pink, red, purple, and blue. Baboons eat the corms of some species. CULTIVATION: These showy plants clump up quickly. Plant corms about 6 in (15 cm) deep in a warm sunny position in light well-drained soil. Increase planting depth in cooler regions and mulch in winter or lift corms in autumn. Propagate from seed or offsets.

Babiana angustifolia
syn. *Babiana pulchra*

☼ ❄ ↔ 4 in (10 cm) ↑ 6–12 in (15–30 cm)
From South Africa. Narrow lance-shaped leaves. Flowers are a deep violet-blue with purple or red markings, darker than in most other species. Best suited to pot culture. Zones 9–11.

Babiana ringens
syn. *Antholyza ringens*

☼ ❄ ↔ 4 in (10 cm) ↑ 6–10 in (15–25 cm)
From Cape Peninsula in South Africa. Narrow lance-shaped leaves. Flowering spikes branched, densely packed with red funnel-shaped flowers with yellow lower lobes in late winter–spring. Zones 9–11.

Babiana rubrocyanea ★
RED-EYED BABOON FLOWER, WINE CUPS

☼ ❄ ↔ 4 in (10 cm) ↑ 6–12 in (15–30 cm)
From Western Cape Province in South Africa. Leaves ribbed, slightly hairy. Spikes of spirally arranged, densely packed, funnel-shaped, blue flowers with dark red throats in late winter–spring. Zones 9–11.

Babiana stricta
BABOON FLOWER

☼ ❄ ↔ 4 in (10 cm) ↑ 6–12 in (15–30 cm)
From southwestern South Africa. The most commonly grown species. Fan of ribbed hairy leaves. Spikes of pink to purplish blue to red cup-shaped flowers, in spirals, sometimes scented, in late spring. '**Purple Star**', dark reddish purple flowers with white stripes; '**White King**', white blooms flushed pale blue; '**Zwanenburg Glory**', violet flowers with pale blotches and darker throat. Zones 9–11.

BACCHARIS

Of the daisy (Asteraceae) family, this genus of about 350 species is native to North, Central, and South America. These shrub or herb perennials are deciduous or evergreen and bear male and female flowers on separate plants. Some species have no leaves, so photosynthesis takes place in the adapted stems. The flowers grow in corymbs or panicles. Some species are used in medicine and to make dye. They are tolerant of salt air in coastal areas. CULTIVATION: Fully frost hardy to frost tender, these plants do best in good soil in full sun. Softwood cuttings can be taken in summer, while seed can be sown in spring. In colder areas plants may behave as perennials.

Baccharis 'Centennial'
COYOTE BRUSH, DESERT BROOM

☼ ❄ ↔ 5 ft (1.5 m) ↑ 3 ft (0.9 m)
Female cultivar from the USA. Cross between *B. pilularis* and *B. sarothroides* resulting in an evergreen sprawling shrub with narrow leaves. Inconspicuous white flowers from winter to spring. Tan seed pods produce white fluffy seeds. Zones 8–10.

Baccharis halimifolia
COTTON-SEED TREE, GROUNDSEL TREE

☼ ❄ ↔ 10 ft (3 m) ↑ 3–10 ft (0.9–3 m)
From the West Indies, southern and eastern USA. Branches sharply angled, with partial downy covering when young. Leaves 2 in (5 cm) long, paddle-shaped, sharply toothed edges. Large clusters of tiny white flowers, followed by downy, white seeds. This species can be invasive. Zones 5–11.

Baccharis magellanica
☼ ❄ ↔ 15 in (38 cm) ↑ 15 in (38 cm)
From the Straits of Magellan and the Falkland Islands. Paddle-shaped leaves to 24 in (60 cm) long, finely toothed edges, sticky coating when young. Small flowerheads of yellow florets, develop into buff-colored seed heads. Zones 8–9.

Baccharis nummularia
☼ ❄ ↔ 2 ft (0.6 m) ↑ 3 ft (0.9 m)
From coast of southern Brazil, in marshy ground; dense shrub, crowded thin branches, leaves around ¼ in (6 mm) long, almost circular (*nummularius* is Latin for coin-like), shiny above, whitish-woolly beneath; terminal clusters of small brownish flowerheads in spring. Zones 10–12.

Baccharis pilularis
CHAPARRAL BROOM

☼ ❄ ↔ 20 in (50 cm) ↑ 20 in (50 cm)
Evergreen shrub native to western USA, mainly California. Leaves broad to ovate, hairless. Flowers white with a green spot, found at branch tips. '**Pigeon Point**', dark green, dense, mounding ground cover; '**Twin Peaks**' ★, fire-retardant properties, to 30 in (75 cm) high, spreading to 10 ft (3 m) across. Zones 8–10.

Baccharis nummularia

Baccharis halimifolia

Baccharis pilularis

Backhousia citriodora

Backhousia myrtifolia

BACKHOUSIA

This genus, a member of the myrtle (Myrtaceae) family, consists of 7 evergreen species of both shrubs and trees, all of which occur in the subtropical and tropical rainforests of east coast Australia. All members of this genus have a neat attractive habit, white or cream flowers that have prominent stamens, and aromatic mid-green foliage. One species, *B. citriodora*, the lemon-scented myrtle, is now being cultivated commercially for culinary purposes.
CULTIVATION: These rainforest plants do best in rich well-composted soil, in which sufficient moisture is retained to be freely available at all times. Although partial shade is appreciated while young, plants often flower more profusely in full sun. Propagation is from cuttings or from fresh seed.

Backhousia citriodora

LEMON-SCENTED MYRTLE, SWEET VERBENA TREE

☼ ❄ ↔ 20–25 ft (6–8 m)
↑ 20–25 ft (6–8 m)

Neat medium-sized shrub with foliage from ground level. Dense dull green leaves scented lemon when crushed. Oil contained in leaves, called citral, used commercially for food flavoring. Flowers strongly lemon scented, creamy white, in summer. Zones 9–10.

Backhousia myrtifolia

GRAY MYRTLE, IRONWOOD

☼ ❄ ↔ 20 ft (6 m) ↑ 20 ft (6 m)

Tall shrub or small tree, with deep green leaves. Trunk and branches make ideal hosts for epiphytic orchids. Fluffy white flowers and persistent greenish sepals in summer. Protect young plants from frost. Zones 9–10.

BACTRIS

There are more than 200 palm species in this genus belonging to the family Arecaceae. Primarily from Central America, only a few are known in cultivation. Two main growth variations: relatively short clump-forming palms with multiple trunks, developing from an underground rhizome; and those with just a few trunks or a single tall trunk, often spiny, ringed with the scars of old fronds. Pinnate leaves are up to 10 ft (3 m) long. Leaflets may be on several planes along the stem, which is often spiny, as is the leaf stalk. Sprays of tiny cream to yellow flowers are followed by edible fruits to more than 2 in (5 cm) long.
CULTIVATION: From the tropics, these palms thrive in well-drained humus-rich soil, with plenty of warmth and water. They can be grown in sun or partial shade. Propagation is from seed, which usually germinates well and develops quickly; or, in the case of the clump-forming species, by division.

Bactris major ★

syn. *Bactris cruegeriana*
BLACK ROSEAU, KAWMAKA, PRICKLY PALM
☼ ✦ ↔ 12 ft (3.5 m) ↑ 15 ft (4.5 m)
Native to Surinam. Clustering stems, initially prickly, becoming smooth and white-ringed. Dull green fronds to 8 ft (2.4 m) long with very prickly stems and up to 30 pairs of leaflets. Purple fruit to 2 in (5 cm) long. Zones 11–12.

Bactris mexicana

☼/◐ ✦ ↔ 5–10 ft (1.5–3 m)
↑ 10–15 ft (3–4.5 m)

From Mexico and neighboring Central American countries. Clusters of narrow trunks, less than 3 in (8 cm) in diameter. Fronds to 7 ft (2 m) long, with leaflets sometimes downy below. Stems can be used as a substitute for rattan. Zones 11–12.

BAECKEA

This genus of evergreen heath-like shrubs is from the myrtle (Myrtaceae) family. Most species are native to Australia, with a few species found in New Caledonia and one extending into Asia. They range in height from tall shrubs to scrambling prostrate species with small neat leaves. The tea-tree-like flowers are small, usually white or pink, produced on thin wiry stems, providing a good display in spring and summer. They make very good cut flowers. The dry seed capsules are tiny and in some species take on reddish tints when ripening.
CULTIVATION: Most species will grow in a well-drained moderately fertile soil free from lime and sheltered from drying winds. They prefer sunny or lightly shaded positions. The shrubs resent root disturbance and will not transplant well at an advanced level. Prune bushes lightly after flowering to maintain compact habit. Propagation is from half-hardened tip cuttings.

Baeckea imbricata

☼ ❄ ↔ 3 ft (0.9 m) ↑ 3 ft (0.9 m)
Compact shrub with erect branches, from coastal areas of eastern Australia. Leaves overlapping, almost circular. Small, white, solitary flowers in upper leaf axils, in spring–summer. Suitable for poorly drained areas. Prune lightly after flowering. Zones 8–10.

Baeckea linifolia

SWAMP BAECKEA
☼ ❄ ↔ 7 ft (2 m) ↑ 8 ft (2.4 m)
From eastern Australia. Small to medium shrub with arching branches. The aromatic linear leaves, to 1 in (25 mm) long, turn bronze in winter.

Tiny white flowers in late summer to autumn. Best in a moist well-drained position. Zones 9–11.

BAILEYA

This small genus from western North America is part of the daisy (Asteraceae) family. It comprises just 3 species of annuals and perennials; one, *B. multiradiata*, is sometimes grown for a bright splash of color in summer and autumn, especially in arid areas.

Baeckea linifolia

Bactris major

Baileya species have opposite pairs of hairy, gray-green, pinnate leaves and have an open habit, rarely growing to more than 12–16 in (30–40 cm) tall. Their cosmos-like yellow flowerheads are held clear of the foliage on long stems, appearing from early summer and continuing until the first frosts. CULTIVATION: *Baileya* plants thrive in semi-desert conditions and, although sometimes considered weeds, they are one of the most reliable and colorful summer annuals for arid gardens. Plant in full sun and water only to get plants established or if dry conditions persist. Remove spent flowerheads to prolong blooming. Propagate from seed, which may be sown in-situ or started under cover and transplanted.

Baileya multiradiata
DESERT BAILEYA, DESERT MARIGOLD, PAPER DAISY, WILD MARIGOLD

☼ ❄ ↔ 4–12 in (10–30 cm)
↑ 8–20 in (20–50 cm)

Native to southern USA and Mexico. Short-lived perennial with grayish green foliage. Bright yellow flowers, 2 in (5 cm) across and resembling marigolds, are borne from spring to autumn. Needs perfect drainage to prevent rotting. Zones 7–10.

BALLOTA
Found from Europe through the Mediterranean region to western Asia, this mint (Lamiaceae) family genus is composed of 35 species of perennials and subshrubs. Bushy and spreading, they are grown primarily for their hairy gray-green stems and foliage, which in the best forms are heavily felted. The leaves may be evergreen or deciduous and are aromatic, oval to heart-shaped, with conspicuously toothed edges. In summer, small upright spikes of white, cream, or lilac-pink flowers appear but they are rarely a feature. The genus has long been used in herbal remedies and was reputed to cure the bite of mad dogs. CULTIVATION: Plants tolerate hardy to moderate frosts and are very easily grown in full or half-sun in a moist well-drained soil. Cut the evergreen types back hard in spring. Will naturalize and can become quite invasive. Propagate by division, or from basal cuttings or seed.

Ballota acetabulosa
☼/◐ ❄ ↔ 24–32 in (60–80 cm)
↑ 40 in (100 cm)

Shrubby semi-evergreen perennial from Greece, Turkey, and eastern Mediterranean islands. Woolly stems and foliage. Leaves heart-shaped, pale green, to 2 in (5 cm) long, with toothed edges. Up to 12 purple-marked white flowers per head, ½ in (12 mm) wide. Zones 8–10.

Ballota nigra
BLACK HOREHOUND

☼ ❄ ↔ 24–60 in (60–150 cm)
↑ 16–40 in (40–100 cm)

Perennial found from southern Europe to North Africa and Iran. Unpleasantly aromatic. Green nettle-like leaves to 3 in (8 cm) long, hairy rather than felted. Mauve flowers in leaf axils. Used in herbal remedies to treat worms. Zones 7–10.

Ballota pseudodictamnus
☼ ❄ ↔ 24–48 in (60–120 cm)
↑ 12–20 in (30–50 cm)

Evergreen subshrub found from Turkey through Crete to North Africa. Rounded, toothed, felted, gray-green leaves to 2 in (5 cm) long. White or mauve flowers with darker spotting, in large green calyces. Zones 8–10.

BALSAMORHIZA
BALSAM ROOT

This small genus in the daisy (Asteraceae) family contains 4 species of perennial herbs native to western North America. Their natural habitat is gravelly slopes and cliffs and other well-drained areas. Plants have long, fleshy, balsam-scented taproots. The leaves grow in basal rosettes and are lance- to arrow-shaped with varying degrees of woolliness. Yellow daisy

Baileya multiradiata, in the wild, Joshua Tree National Park, California, USA

flowers are borne on stems well above the foliage in spring and summer. The seeds, shoots, and roots have all been used medicinally and in cooking by Native Americans. CULTIVATION: Best suited to cooler areas. Grow plants in full sun in deep, fertile, well-drained soil. Winter wet will cause rotting. Propagate from seed.

Balsamorhiza sagittata
ARROWLEAF BALSAMROOT, BALSAMROOT, BREADROOT, GRAY DOCK, SUNFLOWER

☼ ❄ ↔ 12–18 in (30–45 cm)
↑ 8–24 in (20–60 cm)

From western North America. Basal rosettes of coarse arrow-shaped leaves up to 12 in (30 cm) long, downy above and woolly white below. Flowers daisy-like, deep yellow center, paler rays, in summer. Zones 5–9.

BAMBUSA
BAMBOO

This genus in the family Poaceae contains about 120 species of giant grasses from low elevations of tropical and subtropical Asia, tropical America, Africa, and northern Australia. The name comes from the Malay word *bambu*. From 15 ft (4.5 m) to 80 ft (24 m) in height, they have smooth cylindrical stems grown from rhizomes, in loose to dense compact clumps. Stems (called culms) are mostly hollow, except at the nodes (rings). From the higher nodes wiry lateral branches emerge bearing leaves. Large pale scale-leaves sheath young stems, but are cast off as the culms mature. Flowering is rarely seen. The "timber" is used to construct Asian houses, boats, bridges, fences, and furniture. CULTIVATION: Vigorous growers requiring a tropical or subtropical climate. Several species are frost hardy. Plant in deep, fertile, loamy soil with

Ballota acetabulosa

Ballota nigra

Bambusa species

B

Bambusa vulgaris 'Striata'

Banksia attenuata, in the wild, Albany, Western Australia

Banksia baxteri

ample water in summer in a sheltered but sunny position. Propagate from offsets buried in soil; flood, mulch, and feed well when new growth shows.

Bambusa multiplex
syn. *Bambusa glaucescens*
HEDGE BAMBOO
☼ ⌇ ↔ 10 ft (3 m) ↑ 35 ft (10 m)
From southern China. Crowded deep green culms up to 1½ in (35 mm) in diameter, erect then arching at the top. Leaves small, bluish green undersurface. Mature plants produce arching flowering branches every few years. Used in weaving, as windbreak, and as ornamentals. '**Alphonse Karr**' ★, green-striped gold culms forming broad-headed clump; '**Fernleaf**', to 20 ft (6 m) tall; '**Riviereorum**', to 6 ft (1.8 m) tall; '**Silverstripe**', pale stripes on new leaves and stems. Zones 9–12.

Bambusa oldhamii
OLDHAM BAMBOO
☼ ⌇ ↔ 20–40 ft (6–12 m) ↑ 60 ft (18 m)
Native to southern China and Taiwan. Open clump of straight upright culms 24 in (60 cm) thick, bright green with white bloom, ageing to yellow. Grown for edible shoots, hedging, paper pulp, and as ornamental. Zones 9–12.

Bambusa vulgaris
COMMON OR YELLOW-STEMMED BAMBOO
☼ ⌇ ↔ 15–30 ft (4.5–9 m) ↑ 50 ft (15 m)
Grown widely in tropical regions. Open clump of dark green culms 6 in

(15 cm) thick, used for structural purposes, but their high starch content encourages insect and fungal attack. '**Maculata**', culms become blotchy, eventually completely black; '**Striata**' (syn. 'Vittata'), golden yellow culms with green stripes of various thicknesses; '**Wamin**', short wide lower internodes (parts of culm between nodes), to 17 ft (5 m) tall. Zones 9–12.

BANKSIA
From the protea (Proteaceae) family the genus is named for Sir Joseph Banks, British botanist who traveled with Captain Cook in 1770. The 75 or so species are endemic to Australia, with just one, *B. dentata*, extending to New Guinea. They vary from prostrate shrubs to low-branching trees. Thick leathery leaves are variously toothed. Large cylindrical or globular flower spikes are rich in nectar; woody fruiting cones. Species from southwest Western Australian are not always amenable to cultivation, especially in

Banksia 'Giant Candles'

summer-rainfall areas. Species from eastern Australia are more adaptable. CULTIVATION: Most species prefer an open sunny position and well-drained sandy soil low in phosphorus. Some are moderately frost tolerant and, once established, most will withstand dry conditions. Tip prune to maintain shape. Harvest flowers to encourage flower production and foliage density. To propagate, extract seed from cone after it has been heated in a hot oven.

Banksia attenuata
COAST BANKSIA, SLENDER BANKSIA
☼ ⌇ ↔ 17 ft (5 m) ↑ 25–35 ft (8–10 m)
Small tree native to southwestern Western Australia. Leaves narrow, serrated, to 6 in (15 cm) long. Fluffy, cylindrical, soft yellow flower spikes to 10 in (25 cm) long followed by bristly ovoid cones. Zones 9–10.

Banksia baxteri
BAXTER'S BANKSIA
☼ ⌇ ↔ 7 ft (2 m) ↑ 6–10 ft 1.8–3m)
An erect spreading shrub from Western Australia. Triangular-lobed

leaves. Yellowish green dome-shaped flower spikes at branch ends in late spring–early autumn. Suitable for protected coastal gardens with excellent drainage, low summer rainfall. Good cut flower. Zones 9–11.

Banksia ericifolia
HEATH BANKSIA, HEATH-LEAFED BANKSIA
☼ ⌇ ↔ 15 ft (4.5 m) ↑ 20 ft (6 m)
Variable Australian east coast shrub. Narrow linear leaves, bright green above, furry beneath. Flowers to 8 in (20 cm) long, pale yellow to orange-brown with yellow or orange-brown styles, appear in autumn–winter. Zones 9–10.

Banksia 'Giant Candles' ★
HYBRID BANKSIA
☼ ⌇ ↔ 12 ft (3.5 m) ↑ 15 ft (4.5 m)
From eastern Australia, this *B. ericifolia* and *B. spinulosa* hybrid is a shrub branching to near ground level. Bright green foliage. Orange flower spikes to 15 in (38 cm) long, in autumn–winter. Useful as an informal hedge, windbreak, or screen. Zones 9–11.

Banksia ericifolia, in the wild, Blue Mountains, New South Wales, Australia

Banksia integrifolia, in the wild, Bulgo, New South Wales, Australia

Banksia grandis

Banksia menziesii

Banksia media

Banksia grandis

BULL BANKSIA

↔ 10 ft (3 m) ↑ 25 ft (8 m)

Shrub from southwestern Australia. Large, deeply cut, shiny, dark green leaves to 20 in (50 cm) long. Large yellow-green flowers in spring. Thrives in alkaline soil. Zones 9–11.

Banksia integrifolia ★

COAST BANKSIA

↔ 20 ft (6 m) ↑ 80 ft (24 m)

From east coast of Australia, this fast-growing tree has bark with a roughly square pattern. Leaves dull green above, silvery woolly beneath. Flowers pale yellow, in summer–winter. Persistent fruits. Tolerates heavy clay soils. **'Roller Coaster'** has a prostrate form. Zones 8–11.

Banksia marginata ★

SILVER BANKSIA

↔ 15–20 ft (4.5–6 m) ↑ 30 ft (9 m)

From southeast Australia, variable banksia species found as shrub, tree, or prostrate form. Leaves narrow, silvery furry beneath. Flowers short, pale yellow cylinders, in late summer–winter. Hard-prune plants with underground stems, others only lightly shape. Zones 8–10.

Banksia media

SOUTHERN PLAINS BANKSIA

↔ 6 ft (1.8 m) ↑ 6–15 ft (1.8–4.5 m)

A dense shrub with small wedge-shaped leaves from southern coastal districts of Western Australia. Flowers have cylindrical heads to 8 in (20 cm) long, yellow to golden bronze, in autumn–spring. Tolerates quite dry conditions. Zones 10–11.

Banksia petiolaris, bud

Banksia menziesii

FIREWOOD BANKSIA

↔ 15 ft (4.5 m) ↑ 50 ft (15 m)

From Western Australia, this gnarled tree is much smaller and more compact in cultivation. Leaves long and toothed. Flowers silvery pink and gold, acorn-shaped, in autumn to winter. Patterned seed cones. Best in areas with a dry summer. Zones 10–11.

Banksia petiolaris

↔ 7 ft (2 m) ↑ 12 in (30 cm)

A prostrate shrub from Western Australia. Creeping horizontal branches, toothed oblong leaves to 12 in (30 cm) on long stalks. Flowers dull cream in erect oblong spikes to 8 in (20 cm) long, in spring–summer. Zones 9–10.

Banksia praemorsa

↔ 8 ft (2.4 m) ↑ 12 ft (3.5 m)

A strong-growing wind-resistant species from southern Western Australia. Has a dense upright habit with short, wedge-shaped, toothed leaves. Large flower spikes grow up to 12 in (30 cm) long, wine red to greenish yellow, in late winter–spring. Zones 10–11.

Banksia prionotes ★

ACORN BANKSIA

↔ 10 ft (3 m) ↑ 15–30 ft (4.5–9 m)

From Western Australia. Branches covered in dense white hairs; leaves long, narrow, toothed. Flowers large orange spikes in autumn–winter; soft, woolly, white buds. Cultivated for cut-flower market. Thrives in well-drained alkaline soils, best in winter-rainfall areas. Zones 10–11.

Banksia praemorsa

Banksia robur

LARGE-LEAF BANKSIA, SWAMP BANKSIA

↔ 7 ft (2 m) ↑ 10 ft (3 m)

Found on east coast of Australia, usually seen in swampy woodland areas. Leaves stiff, coarsely serrated, smooth above, furry beneath. Persistent golden flowers occur from summer to winter. Prune once established. Fire tolerant. Zones 9–10.

Banksia serrata ★

OLD MAN BANKSIA, SAW BANKSIA

↔ 5–10 ft (1.5–3 m) ↑ 50 ft (15 m)

From Australian east coast. Gnarled trunk and branches. Leaves stiff, coarsely serrated. Flowers large, cylindrical, creamy, in summer–winter. Persistent woody fruits, immortalized by children's author May Gibbs as "big bad Banksia Men." Fire tolerant. **'Pygmy Possum'**, ground cover to 2 ft (0.6 m) tall and 8 ft (2.4 m) wide; **'Superman'**, smaller than species, to 20 ft (6 m) in height. Zones 9–10.

Banksia speciosa

SHOWY BANKSIA

↔ 10–15 ft (3–4.5 m) ↑ 10–15 ft (3–4.5 m)

From the Eyre district of southern Western Australia. Leaves long, narrow, toothed to the midrib,

Banksia prionotes

Banksia robur

Barleria cristata

creating a zigzag effect. Flower spikes to 6 in (15 cm) long, conical, woolly, pale green to light yellow, in summer–autumn. Zones 9–10.

Banksia spinulosa

HAIRPIN BANKSIA

☼/◗ ▨ ↔ 5 ft (1.5 m) ↑ 3 ft (0.9 m)

From east coast of Australia. Branchlets furry. Leaves linear, woolly undersides. Flowers cylindrical to 5 in (12 cm), golden yellow with gold, orange, or red styles, in autumn to winter. Fire tolerant. Under cultivation tolerates pruning. *B. s.* var. *collina* (syn. *B. collina*), bright yellow flowers, yellow to red styles. *B. s.* var. *cunninghamii*, large yellow flowers; 'Lemon Glow', pale yellow-flowered form. *B. s.* 'Honeypots', an open-branched shrub, flowers golden, red styles, in summer–winter. Zones 9–11.

BAPTISIA

FALSE INDIGO, WILD INDIGO

Belonging to the pea-flower subfamily of the legume (Fabaceae) family, this genus contains about 17 species of perennial herbs native to the USA. They grow in sand, gravel, and other poor soils in dry woodlands and open areas. Plants have a shrubby habit, spreading or erect, to 7 ft (2 m) tall, with trifoliate leaves. Spikes of lupin-like flowers are white, yellow, or purplish blue. Once used in dye-making as a substitute for true indigo. CULTIVATION: Grow plants in full sun in deep well-drained, neutral or slightly acidic soil. Most species grow happily in poorly nourished soils. Stake tall plants in exposed positions. Propagate by division or from seed.

Baptisia alba

☼ ✱ ↔ 3 ft (0.9 m) ↑ 2–3 ft (0.6–0.9 m)

Native to central and eastern region of USA. Erect bushy perennial with

Barleria albostellata

bluish green foliage. Upright spikes of pea-like flowers are creamy white, often with purple markings, in summer. The seed pods are erect. 'Pendula', similar to species but with drooping seed pods. Zones 5–9.

Baptisia australis

syn. *Baptisia caerulea*

BLUE FALSE INDIGO

☼ ✱ ↔ 4 ft (1.2 m) ↑ 2–4 ft (0.6–1.2 m)

Native to central and eastern USA, but threatened in some states. Upright or spreading bushy perennial with bluish green foliage. Spikes of purplish blue flowers in summer. Erect, inflated dark gray seed pods can be dried for floral arrangements. Zones 5–9.

Baptisia lactea

syn. *Baptisia leucantha*

ATLANTIC WILD INDIGO, PRAIRIE FALSE INDIGO, WHITE FALSE INDIGO

☼/◗ ✱ ↔ 3 ft (0.9 m) ↑ 3–5 ft (0.9–1.5 m)

Perennial from North America. Blue-green foliage. Spikes of creamy white pea-like flowers in late spring–early summer; attractive seed pods follow. Drought tolerant. Good in wildflower gardens. Zones 3–9.

BARKERIA

This small Central American genus in the family Orchidaceae contains about 15 sun-loving sympodial epiphytes that are allied to *Epidendrum*. The main flower colors range from pale to vivid pink through to a deep magenta; however, there are some species with blooms that are almost white. CULTIVATION: These plants must be kept dry during winter (when most species defoliate, then bloom), so many growers cultivate these showy plants on cork slabs to ensure that the thick roots dry out quickly.

Barkeria scandens

☼/◗ ✿ ↔ 2½–6 in (6–15 cm) ↑ 3–10 in (8–25 cm)

From Mexico, this species has arguably the brightest colored and

most striking flowers of the genus, being an intense magenta-red, up to 1¾ in (40 mm) across. Zones 11–12.

BARLERIA

Barleria belongs to the acanthus (Acanthaceae) family, and consists of around 250 species of shrubs, sub-shrubs, and scrambling climbers. From tropical continents, except Australia, many occur in dry rocky habitats. Leaves are simple and smooth edged, arranged in opposite pairs on the stems. Flowers are more or less trumpet-shaped but distinctly 2-lipped, in shades from white through yellow, orange, pink, mauve, and violet. They emerge from between stiff bracts that are often edged by spiny teeth. Flowers over a long season, followed by club-shaped seed capsules. Only a small number of *Barleria* species are cultivated. CULTIVATION: Easily cultivated in warm climates, fast growing but short lived. Grow in fertile well-drained soil, in a sunny but sheltered position. In cool climates they make good conservatory plants, but need strong light. They can be trimmed as hedges or cut back hard, responding to this treatment with denser, more vigorous foliage. Propagate from cuttings.

Barleria albostellata

GRAY BARLERIA

☼ ▨ ↔ 5 ft (1.5 m) ↑ 5 ft (1.5 m)

From northeastern South Africa, Zimbabwe, and Mozambique. This evergreen shrub has gray foliage due

to a dense coating of hairs on 2–3 in (5–8 cm) long oval leaves. Flowers white, 1 in (25 mm) wide, at branch tips, in spring–summer. Zones 9–12.

Barleria cristata

PHILIPPINE VIOLET

☼ ▨ ↔ 5 ft (1.5 m) ↑ 3 ft (0.9 m)

This widely grown ornamental species originates from Myanmar. Densely branching from ground level with soft deep green foliage. Flowers white, mauve, or violet from bristly edged green bracts, most of the year. Great low hedge. Tip prune to encourage denser growth. Zones 10–12.

Barleria obtusa

BUSH VIOLET

☼ ▨ ↔ 3 ft (0.9 m) ↑ 3 ft (0.9 m)

Native to southern Africa, growing in grassland and among rocks. Spreading shrub, twiggy habit, small silky-haired leaves. Profuse display of white-pink or violet flowers, 1 in (25 mm) wide, emerging from small furry bracts, in autumn. Zones 9–11.

Baptisia australis

Barkeria scandens

B

BARRINGTONIA

This genus, a member of the brazil nut (Lecythidaceae) family, contains about 40 species of small to large evergreen and deciduous trees and occurs in Australia, the Pacific Islands, tropical Asia, East Africa, and Madagascar. Growing mainly at edges of swamps, streams, estuaries, and beaches, these trees have fairly large leaves crowded toward the ends of branchlets. Flowers are usually pendulous spikes, emerging at the branchlet tips, with short petals and a showy "powderpuff" of longer stamens. Largish fruits are hard and usually green. *Barringtonia* plants contain saponins; in most regions the leaves are pounded and then thrown into pools, as the saponins paralyze fish and make them easier to catch.
CULTIVATION: Several species make fine ornamentals in the tropics. The showy flowers attract nectar-feeding birds and bats. They thrive in any situation where soil moisture is fairly constant, tolerating seasonal flooding and brackish groundwater. Propagate from seed, sown when freshly fallen.

Barringtonia asiatica
FISH-KILLER TREE

☼ ✈ ↔ 20 ft (6 m) ↑ 30 ft (9 m)
Evergreen tree with glossy leaves up to 15 in (38 cm) long. Flowers large, with white petals, in late dry or early wet season; stamens to 6 in (15 cm) long, white ageing to red. Fruits up to 4 in (10 cm) long. Zones 11–12.

Barringtonia racemosa
POWDERPUFF TREE

☼ ❄ ↔ 40 ft (12 m) ↑ 60 ft (18 m)
Large shrub or small tree found in tropical Asia, western Pacific, Madagascar, southeastern Africa, northeastern Australia. Leaves broad, to 15 in (38 cm) long. Flower spikes hang from branch ends. Flowers white to red, 1½ in (35 mm) long, in summer–autumn. Zones 10–12.

Barringtonia racemosa

Barringtonia asiatica

Bartlettina sordida

BARTLETTINA

Found in tropical and Central America and Mexico, this daisy (Asteraceae) family genus comprises 23 species of evergreen shrubs and small trees. They form a dense, many-branched crown with young stems that are usually covered with fine hairs. The leaves are lance-shaped to oval, often with toothed edges; the corymbs or panicles of daisy-like flowers, which occur in a variety of shades, appear mainly in summer.
CULTIVATION: Most species grow extremely freely and may be somewhat invasive. Plant in moist well-drained soil with a position in full sun or partial shade. If necessary, trim to shape after flowering. Propagate from seed or half-hardened cuttings.

Bartlettina sordida
syn. *Bartlettina megalophylla*, *Eupatorium megalophyllum*, *E. sordidum*

☼ ❄ ↔ 7 ft (2 m) ↑ 10 ft (3 m)
A very vigorous shrub from Mexico. Young stems covered with red hairs; leaves oval with toothed edges, to 4 in (10 cm) long. Fragrant violet flowers in corymbs that open throughout the warmer months. Zones 10–11.

BASSELINIA

This genus is a member of the palm (Arecaceae) family and contains 11 species of palm, all endemic to New Caledonia. Most have a narrow natural range, preferring specific soil types or habitats. The majority of species are single-trunked, but some have a clumping habit. They have prominent and colorful crownshafts. The flower spikes arise below the crownshaft and bear both male and female flowers.
CULTIVATION: These palms are seldom seen in cultivation as they are difficult to grow, having very specific requirements, depending on the species. However, they all require well-drained soil and at least part-shade. In cool areas grow in the greenhouse or conservatory. Propagation is from seed, which germinates quite easily, but the seedlings can be difficult to handle.

Basselinia gracilis
syn. *Basselinia eriostachys*

☼ ❄ ↔ 7 ft (2 m) ↑ 12 ft (3.5 m)
Colorful clumping species from New Caledonia, where it grows in dense rainforest from sea-level to mountains. Dark green glossy fronds have yellowish green midribs. Sheaths and crownshaft are pink to dark red with purplish tinges. Zones 10–11.

Basselinia pancheri, in the wild, Bois du Sud, New Caledonia

Basselinia pancheri

☼ ❄ ↔ 7 ft (2 m) ↑ 12 ft (3.5 m)
Slender single-trunked palm from New Caledonia, where it grows in drier areas than other species. Crownshaft in shades of orange, red, or purple. Stiffly upright fronds irregularly divided with some leaflets very wide. Black kidney-shaped fruits. Zones 10–11.

BASSIA

A genus of 26 densely branching, shrubby annuals or perennials belonging to the goosefoot (Chenopodaceae) family, *Bassia* plants are found in warm-temperate parts of the Northern Hemisphere. They are grown for their colorful foliage. Leaves are usually narrow and smooth-edged, and the flowers are normally inconspicuous spikes. Fruits are achenes (small, dry, single-seeded fruits). The plants are toxic to livestock and produce allelopathic compounds inhibiting the growth of nearby plants.
CULTIVATION: Sow seed in spring where plants are to grow, in a wide range of soils, including saline. Propagate from seed or cuttings.

Bassia scoparia
syns *Kochia scoparia*, *K. trichophylla*
BELVEDERE, BURNING BUSH, FIREBALL, FIRE-BUSH, FIREWEED, KOCHIA, SUMMER CYPRESS

☼ ❄ ↔ 8–60 in (20–150 cm) ↑ 8–60 in (20–150 cm)
Annual originally from Asia, now naturalized through Europe and North America. Narrow flat leaves, normally mid-green, turning purple-red in late summer. Small inconspicuous flower clusters same color as leaves. With maturity, plant breaks off at base and rolls in tumbleweed fashion, dispersing seed. Zones 8–11.

BAUERA

Bauera is an eastern Australian genus of just 4 species. Named by Sir Joseph Banks in honor of 2 German botanical artists, the genus was among the first group of Australian plants to be described. Once included in the saxifrage (Saxifragaceae) family, these evergreen shrubs are now included among the butterknife bush (Cunoniaceae) family; some botanists name the family after this genus—the Baueraceae. They are characterized as wiry-stemmed shrubs with small leaves, displaying small, colorful flowers in spring and early summer.
CULTIVATION: Apart from being fairly frost tender, *Bauera* plants are easily grown and undemanding. They do best in well-drained, light, sandy soil with added humus for moisture retention. They prefer to avoid extremes of heat and cold, so some shade from the hottest afternoon sun is appreciated, as is winter shelter. Occasional trimming will keep the bushes compact. Propagate from seed or half-hardened cuttings.

Bauera rubioides ★

DOG ROSE, RIVER ROSE

☀ ⬧ ↔ 7 ft (2 m) ↑ 6 ft (1.8 m)
Shrub from moister regions of southeastern Australia. Leaves ½ in (12 mm) long, are often covered in fine hairs. Flowers white or pink, to 1 in (25 mm) wide, with larger lower petals, in late winter–spring. '**Luina Gem**', pale pink double flowers. Zones 9–11.

Bauera sessiliflora

GRAMPIANS BAUERA

☀ ⬧ ↔ 6 ft (1.8 m) ↑ 6 ft (1.8 m)
Native to the Grampians, a mountain range in western Victoria, Australia. Flowers rosy pink to magenta, in late spring–early summer. Best trimmed after flowering to keep shape. Various cultivars are available. Zones 9–10.

BAUHINIA

Bauhinia is a genus of around 300 species, many confined to the tropics. It occurs in all continents (except

Bauera rubioides

Bauhinia carronii, in the wild, near Blackall, Queensland, Australia

Europe) and larger tropical islands. Bauhinias belong to the caesalpinia subfamily of the legume (Fabaceae) family and include shrubs, climbers, and small to medium-sized trees, many deciduous. A characteristic feature is the compound leaf consisting of only 2 broad leaflets. Flowers have 5 petals, borne in the leaf axils or in terminal sprays. Seed pods are slightly woody and flattened. Bauhinias are ornamental trees and shrubs, but some are used in traditional medicine or as a source of fiber; a few have edible seeds.
CULTIVATION: Easily cultivated in warm climates, though often slow growing. Species from tropical climates with a long dry season do not grow or flower well in wetter climates. Deep rooted, they do not like being transplanted, but will often tolerate hot exposed positions and hard dry soils. Few grow well in shade. Propagate from seed; half-hardened cuttings can also be taken.

Bauhinia × blakeana

HONG KONG ORCHID TREE

☀ ⬧ ↔ 15 ft (4.5 m) ↑ 30 ft (9 m)
This hybrid, probably between *B. purpurea* and *B. variegata*, is the floral emblem of Hong Kong. Leaves broad, reliably evergreen. Flowers purple-red, slightly scented, 4–6 in (10–15 cm), in autumn–winter. Zones 10–12.

Bauhinia carronii

QUEENSLAND EBONY

☀/☀ ✤ ↔ 12 ft (3.5 m) ↑ 20 ft (6 m)
Tree native to northeastern Australia. Leaves bifoliate, with leathery leaflets to 1¼ in (30 mm) long. Downy, 2 in (5 cm) wide, white flowers in clusters of 2 or 3. Zones 10–12.

Bauhinia corymbosa

PHANERA

☀ ⬧ ↔ 10 ft (3 m) ↑ 20 ft (6 m)
From southern China. Climbing plant with deeply bilobed rounded leaves. Young shoots reddish brown. Very showy terminal racemes of densely packed, fragrant, pale pink flowers in summer. Zones 10–11.

Bauhinia galpinii

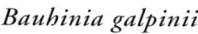

Bauhinia petersiana

Bauhinia × blakeana

Bauhinia galpinii

syn. *Bauhinia punctata*

PRIDE OF DE KAAP, SOUTH AFRICAN ORCHID BUSH

☀ ⬧ ↔ 8 ft (2.4 m) ↑ 10 ft (3 m)
A horizontally branching evergreen shrub from South Africa. Leaves rounded with 2 distinct lobes, paler on undersides. Flowers light to brick red, in summer–autumn. Fruits woody, persistent, flattened, green-brown pods. Lightly prune after flowering. Espaliers well. Zones 9–11.

Bauhinia petersiana

☀ ⬧ ↔ 7 ft (2 m) ↑ 7 ft (2 m)
A low spreading shrub or vine from Africa. Leaves heart-shaped, 2 in (5 cm) long, on narrow stems. Flowers wavy edged, white, up to 6 in (15 cm) wide, carried in racemes of a few blooms in summer. Zones 10–12.

Bauhinia tomentosa

YELLOW BELL BAUHINIA

☀ ⬧ ↔ 10 ft (3 m) ↑ 15 ft (4.5 m)
From tropical Africa and Asia, usually a multi-stemmed evergreen shrub.

Bauhinia tomentosa

Leaves light green, 3 in (8 cm) long, hairy beneath. Flowers bell-shaped, cream to pale yellow throughout the year. Zones 10–12.

Bauhinia variegata

BUTTERFLY BUSH, ORCHID TREE

☀ ⬧ ↔ 25 ft (8 m) ↑ 25 ft (8 m)
From tropical foothills of Himalayas through to Malay Peninsula, small tree with short trunk and spreading canopy. Semi-deciduous in warm areas, fully in cool areas. Orchid-like flowers, pale to deep pink. White form also seen. Zones 9–10.

B

Beallara Marfitch 'Howard's Dream'

Baumea deplanchei

Beallara Tahoma 'Glacier'

BAUMEA

A genus of the sedge (Cyperaceae) family, it includes around 30 species occurring from Madagascar to the Pacific Islands, with 15 species in Australia. All are perennial rhizomatous herbs, with leaves and stems very similar in appearance. The inflorescence is terminal, with the flowers tightly clustered or loosely arranged. The fruits are small nuts. CULTIVATION: Most species occur in open moist habitats; many are found in swamps or seasonally inundated areas. Propagate from transplants, divisions, or from seeds, which germinate readily if sown on damp organic mix and kept moist until shoots appear.

Baumea deplanchei

☼/◐ ❄ ↔ 24–48 in (60–120 cm) ↑ 24–36 in (60–90 cm)

New Caledonian endemic, from moist lowland areas. Attractive sedge with

densely clumped stems clothed in 2 rows of flattened blue-gray leaves and terminated by rusty brown, sometimes drooping, flowering spikelets. Zones 10–12.

BEALLARA

Belonging to the family Orchidaceae, this complex generic orchid hybrid is a combination of *Brassia*, *Cochlioda*, *Miltonia*, and *Odontoglossum*. Generally the crossing of *Miltassia* (*Miltonia × Brassia*) with *Odontodia* (*Odontoglossum × Cochlioda*) is the path used by hybridists to create these members of the *Odontoglossum* alliance. These spidery sympodial hybrids are more tolerant of higher temperatures than most of the pure Odontoglossums, will grow in a wide range of conditions, and have long-lasting flowers that are often fragrant. CULTIVATION: Beallaras have a fine root system, and do not like to dry out throughout the warmer months of the year. They require a drier rest period during winter when they should be watered only sparingly. The plants need to be potted in sphagnum moss or a fine bark mix. They are suitable for cool to intermediate growing conditions, but they should be

grown in a semi-shaded position. They require abundant water throughout the year.

Beallara Marfitch 'Howard's Dream'

☼ ❄ ↔ 12 in (30 cm) ↑ 30 in (75 cm)

Has the strong color inherited from *Miltonia spectabilis* in its background. Up to 10 flowers appear on an upright inflorescence. Flowers in spring. Zones 10–12.

Beallara Tahoma 'Glacier' ★

☼ ❄ ↔ 8–12 in (20–30 cm) ↑ 8–30 in (20–75 cm)

A popular hybrid in the pot plant trade, it is heavily influenced in its color and shape from *Odontoglossum crispum*, *Miltonia spectabilis*, and *Brassia verrucosa*. Flowers in spring and summer. Zones 10–12.

BEAUCARNEA

The 20 species of evergreen trees and shrubs that make up this genus in the dragon-tree (Dracaenaceae) family are found in arid regions ranging from southern USA to Mexico and Guatemala. They are closely related to *Yucca*. The trunks become bulbous and swollen and have thick corky bark. The leaves are long, linear, and often grass-like. It is several years before they commence flowering, when large panicles of tiny white flowers are carried. CULTIVATION: Outdoor cultivation is only possible in warm, dry, and frost-free areas. In cooler areas plants can be grown in greenhouses or as indoor pot plants. Too much water in winter can cause the stem to rot. Propagation is from seed or offsets in spring.

Beaucarnea guatemalensis

syn. *Beaucarnea oedipus*

☼ ❄ ↔ 3–7 ft (0.9–2 m) ↑ 20–40 ft (6–12 m)

Occurs in Guatemalan woodlands at 2,300–5,250 ft (700–1,600 m) altitude. Multi-stemmed, tall, woody

perennial. Narrow leaves 26–40 in (65–100 cm) long, green, slightly rough, in tufts at ends of stems. Inflorescences terminal, in summer. Fruits elliptical to egg-shaped, ¾ in (18 mm) long. Zones 9–10.

Beaucarnea recurvata ★

syn. *Nolina recurvata*

PONYTAIL PALM

☼ ❄ ↔ 6–8 ft (1.8–2.4 m) ↑ 25 ft (8 m)

Native of Mexico. Popular indoor plant and dramatic landscaping feature. Narrow strap-like leaves, up to 3 ft (0.9 m) long, from single bulbous trunk. Slow growing, branching occurs as it ages. Panicles of tiny white flowers, followed by pinkish fruit. Zones 9–11.

Beaucarnea stricta

syn. *Nolina stricta*

☼ ❄ ↔ 6–8 ft (1.8–2.4 m) ↑ 20 ft (6 m)

Native to Mexico, this species has a stout, somewhat branching stem above swollen base. Straight narrow leaves up to 3 ft (0.9 m) long, rigid, channeled, pale green with yellowish margins. Clusters of tiny flowers, secondary to stunning foliage. Zones 10–11.

Beaucarnea stricta

Beaucarnea recurvata

Beaucarnea guatemalensis

Beaufortia sparsa

Beaumontia grandiflora

BEAUFORTIA

From the myrtle (Myrtaceae) family, this genus of around 18 species of evergreen shrubs was named early in the nineteenth century for Mary, Duchess of Beaufort. *Beaufortia* is confined naturally to Western Australia. In many ways the genus can be seen as just another variation on the theme of *Melaleuca, Kunzea,* and *Callistemon,* but the plants tend to be smaller and flower heavily at a younger age. The foliage is often much reduced, making the bushes appear as a cluster of upright wiry stems. The flowerheads are filamentous and may be near spherical or extended and bottlebrush-like.

CULTIVATION: Apart from tolerating only light to moderate frosts, these are fairly easily grown plants that prefer a sunny position with moist well-drained soil. Well-established specimens are drought tolerant, though perhaps not as much as their origins may suggest. For compact growth, trim lightly in spring. Propagate from seed or half-hardened cuttings taken from non-flowering stems.

Beaufortia sparsa
SWAMP BOTTLEBRUSH
☼ ❀ ↔ 5 ft (1.5 m) ↑ 6 ft (1.8 m)
This is the most common species. Leaves roughly diamond-shaped, light green, upward-facing, arranged scale-like on wiry branches. Flowers soft, slightly drooping, bright orange-red, 4 in (10 cm) wide, in late summer to autumn, on year-old wood. Woody seed capsules. Zones 9–10.

BEAUMONTIA

This genus of 9 species of often rampant climbers from tropical Asia belongs to the oleander or dogbane (Apocynaceae) family. They are evergreen, though in subtropical gardens *B. grandiflora* loses many leaves in winter. Leaves are smooth and opposite. The large fragrant flowers are borne in corymbs, terminal and in the leaf axils. The calyx is 5-lobed and the corolla is funnel- or bell-shaped with

5 lobes. Stamens are attached near the base of the corolla tube and have slender filaments with arrow-shaped anthers. The fruit comprises a pair of thick woody follicles.

CULTIVATION: In temperate regions, grow *Beaumontia* plants along walls of greenhouses or conservatories. They require hot moist conditions in the growing season. Propagate from seed or half-hardened cuttings taken with a heel, rooted in sandy soil under mist.

Beaumontia grandiflora
EASTER LILY VINE, HERALD'S TRUMPET
☼ ❀ ↔ 15 ft (4.5 m) ↑ 25 ft (8 m)
Vigorous, woody, evergreen twiner, occurring in moist forests of Southeast Asia from India to Vietnam. Leaves large, oval-shaped, opposite, prominent veins, covered with brown-red hairs when young, glossy green when older. Flowers white, fragrant, trumpet-shaped, to 6 in (15 cm) long, in summer. Zones 10–12.

BECCARIELLA

This is a genus of at least 30 species of evergreen trees in the sapodilla (Sapotaceae) family, found around the

Pacific in the subtropics and tropics, mainly from Indonesia and Malaysia to northern Australia. They have simple leathery leaves, usually elliptical and glossy, that are basically deep green but often suffused with other colors. The flowers are paired or in clusters and are very small; the ovoid fruits that follow are sometimes more conspicuous.

CULTIVATION: Very much plants of the warmer zones, they are intolerant of frost and prefer warm humid conditions with moist soil rich in humus. Propagation is from seed or cuttings; the stems and leaves contain latex that should be allowed to dry before inserting the cuttings. Avoid contact with the latex as it can cause an irritant dermatitis in some people.

Beccariella sebertii
☼/◐ ❀ ↔ 12–17 ft (3.5–5 m)
↑ 35 ft (10 m)
New Caledonian tree with small insignificant flowers but very attractive deep green leaves, around 6 in (15 cm) long, heavily marked in yellow, orange, and red. Small yellow-green fruits. Zones 10–12.

BEDFORDIA

A genus of 3 species of evergreen trees and shrubs from southeastern Australia (including Tasmania), *Bedfordia* is closely allied to *Brachyglottis* and *Senecio* in the daisy (Asteraceae) family. They have erect trunks and thick, somewhat flaky, pale bark, and the younger twigs are coated in a close mat of whitish hairs; the elongated leaves have thick woolly hairs on their undersides. Flowerheads are

small and cylindrical, borne in short clusters among the upper leaves. They lack ray florets but the tubular golden yellow disc florets are quite decorative. *Bedfordia* species grow in cooler mountain and hill regions, usually in tall moist forests.

CULTIVATION: Generally slow growing, they require a cool but mild climate and a humid sheltered situation in semi-shade, with moist but well-drained soil rich in humus. Propagation is possible from either seed or cuttings, though the dense mat of wool on twigs makes the latter method problematic.

Bedfordia arborescens
syn. *Bedfordia salicina*
BLANKET LEAF
☼ ❄ ↔ 6–10 ft (1.8–3 m)
↑ 10–30 ft (3–9 m)
Tree with straight trunk to 8 in (20 cm) diameter, coarse flakes of soft bark, short side branches. Leaves to 10 in (25 cm) long and 2 in (5 cm) wide, woolly hairs beneath. Flowers in spring. Zones 8–9.

Bedfordia arborescens

Beccariella sebertii, in the wild, Mont Bouo, Monts Koghis, New Caledonia

B

Begonia carolineifolia

Begonia aconitifolia

Begonia coccinea

Begonia bowerae 'Tiger'

BEGONIA

Found through the tropics and sub-tropics but most diverse in the Americas, this group of around 900 species of perennials, shrubs, and climbers is the type genus of the family Begoniaceae. Very diverse, they may be fibrous- or rhizome-rooted or tuberous, with foliage emerging from the rootstock or held on cane-like stems. Leaves vary in color, texture, and shape but are often lobed and finely hairy. Flowers are also variable; often a single female flower is surrounded by 2 or more males. CULTIVATION: Mostly frost tender, they are treated as annuals outdoors or grown indoors in cool climates. Plants prefer a bright but not sunny position with fertile, cool, moist, soil rich in humus. Water and feed well. Watch for fungal diseases. Propagate by division or from offsets, leaf cuttings, or seed, depending on type.

Begonia aconitifolia
☼/☀ ⚊ ↔ 24–40 in (60–100 cm)
↑ 40–48 in (100–120 cm)
Fibrous-rooted species from Brazil. Upright canes with glossy, deep green, fan-shaped, maple-like leaves with 4 to 6 fine-toothed lobes. Pendulous white to pale pink flowers, to 2 in (5 cm) wide, in autumn. Zones 10–12.

Begonia bowerae
EYELASH BEGONIA
☼/☀ ⚊ ↔ 16 in (40 cm) ↑ 12 in (30 cm)
Fibrous-rooted Mexican species. Light green leaves with dark bronze marking, asymmetrical, pointed, heart-shaped, to 2 in (5 cm) long, wavy surface, fringed with hairs, undersides red-veined. Upright sprays of small pink flowers in winter–spring. 'Tiger' has small white flowers. Zones 10–12.

Begonia carolineifolia
☼ ⚊ ↔ 24 in (60 cm) ↑ 48 in (120 cm)
Mexican and Guatemalan species with erect, thick, succulent stems and fan-shaped leaves with 6 to 8 lance-shaped toothed leaflets to 6 in (15 cm) long. Small pale pink flowers in branched clusters, in winter. Zones 10–12.

Begonia coccinea
ANGEL-WING BEGONIA
☼/☀ ⚊ ↔ 24 in (60 cm) ↑ 48 in (120 cm)
Fibrous-rooted Brazilian species. Stems sturdy, upright, succulent. Lush green, pointed, wing-shaped leaves, to 6 in (15 cm) long, red undersides. Large racemes of bright red flowers in spring. Zones 10–12.

Begonia crassicaulis
☀ ⚊ ↔ 40 in (100 cm) ↑ 48 in (120 cm)
Thick upright stems. Large angularly lobed leaves drop in winter. Sprays of tiny pink flowers appear in late winter with the new foliage. Zones 10–12.

Begonia dregei
GRAPE-LEAF BEGONIA, MAPLE-LEAF BEGONIA
☼/☀ ⚊ ↔ 20 in (50 cm) ↑ 36 in (90 cm)
Tuberous-rooted South African herbaceous species. Leaves variable, usually pointed oval to rhomboidal with shallow lobes and teeth, light green with purple veining above, red undersides. A few small white flowers appear in summer. Zones 10–12.

Begonia × erythrophylla
BEEFSTEAK BEGONIA
☼/☀ ⚊ ↔ 16–24 in (40–60 cm)
↑ 8–16 in (20–40 cm)
Rhizome-rooted hybrid of *B. hydrocotylifolia* and *B. manicata*. Rounded wavy leaves, deep green above, red below, conspicuous hairs. Small pink flowers in winter–spring. Zones 10–12.

Begonia fuchsioides
FUCHSIA BEGONIA
☼/☀ ⚊ ↔ 20 in (50 cm) ↑ 36 in (90 cm)
Fibrous-rooted Venezuelan species. Succulent upright stems. Toothed, pointed, wing-shaped leaves, to 2 in (5 cm) long, bright green above, red-tinted below. Pendulous sprays of pink to red 1¼ in (30 mm) wide flowers in winter. Zones 10–12.

Begonia gracilis
HOLLYHOCK BEGONIA
☼/☀ ⚊ ↔ 20–24 in (50–60 cm)
↑ 32–36 in (80–90 cm)
Tuberous species from Mexico and Guatemala. Upright succulent stems. Leaves small, fleshy, toothed, rounded to lance-shaped, with leaf axil bulbils. Short sprays of 1¼ in (30 mm) wide pink flowers in summer. Zones 10–12.

Begonia grandis
EVANS' BEGONIA, HARDY BEGONIA
☼/☀ ❄ ↔ 12–18 in (30–45 cm)
↑ 24 in (60 cm)
From China and Japan. Perennial with loose sprays of flower clusters over large clump of leaves. Green leaves heart-shaped, thick, succulent, ruby red veins on lower surfaces. Flowers pink, in drooping cymes, appear in late summer–autumn. 'Heron's Pirouette' starts blooming in early summer and continues to autumn. Zones 6–9.

Begonia listada
☼/☀ ⚊ ↔ 12 in (30 cm) ↑ 12 in (30 cm)
Shrubby fibrous-rooted Brazilian species. Leaves small, downy, asymmetrical, pointed oval, toothed, dark green above with light midrib and edges, red undersides. A few white flowers to 2 in (5 cm) wide, red hairs, in winter. Zones 10–12.

Begonia masoniana
IRON CROSS BEGONIA
☼/☀ ⚊ ↔ 12–16 in (30–40 cm)
↑ 12 in (30 cm)
Rhizome-rooted species from New Guinea. Leaves asymmetrical, pointed, wing- to heart-shaped, to 8 in (20 cm) long, toothed, hairy, with

Begonia gracilis, Chihuahua, Mexico

Begonia venosa

puckered surface, light green with dark central cross pattern. Upright sprays of small pale green flowers in spring–summer. Zones 10–12.

Begonia metallica
METALLIC-LEAF BEGONIA
☀/☀ ❄ ↔ 20–32 in (50–80 cm)
↑ 48 in (120 cm)

Fibrous-rooted Brazilian species. Upright hairy stems. Leaves asymmetrical, pointed oval, to 6 in (15 cm) long, serrated edges, steely purpleblue upper surface veining. Manyflowered sprays of single 1¼ in (30 mm) wide, light to deep pink flowers in summer–autumn. Zones 10–12.

Begonia radicans
syn. *Begonia limmingheiana*
SHRIMP BEGONIA
☀/☀ ❄ ↔ 3–10 ft (0.9–3 m)
↑ 1–3 ft (0.3–0.9 m)

Rhizome-rooted Brazilian species. Long pendulous stems that may scramble up supports. Leaves shortstemmed, wavy, to 3 in (8 cm) long, white-spotted blue-green above, maroon undersides. Short stems with dense clusters of 1 in (25 mm) wide, orange-pink to light red-brown flowers in winter. Zones 10–12.

Begonia schmidtiana
☀/☀ ❄ ↔ 16 in (40 cm) ↑ 12 in (30 cm)

Fibrous-rooted summer-dormant Brazilian species. Leaves lobed, asymmetrical, pointed oval, to 3 in (8 cm) long, toothed, hairy, red undersides. Sprays of many white to pale pink flowers in winter. Zones 10–12.

Begonia solananthera
☀/☀ ❄ ↔ 24–60 in (60–150 cm)
↑ 12–36 in (30–90 cm)

Fibrous-rooted trailing or climbing Brazilian species. Leaves glossy dark green, pointed oval, to 3 in (8 cm) long. Short sprays of scented, redtinted white flowers in winter–spring, females with large, white, winged ovaries. Zones 10–12.

Begonia sutherlandii
☀/☀ ❄ ↔ 20–36 in (50–90 cm)
↑ 8–32 in (20–80 cm)

Tuberous-rooted trailing or semiclimbing herbaceous species from South Africa and Tanzania. Leaves toothed, lance-shaped, to 6 in (15 cm) long; red stems, edges, undersides, and veins. Pendulous clusters of orange to red flowers up to 1 in (25 mm) wide in summer. Zones 9–12.

Begonia venosa
☀/☀ ❄ ↔ 16–24 in (40–60 cm)
↑ 48 in (120 cm)

Fibrous-rooted Brazilian species. Thick upright stems. Leaves large, fleshy, kidney-shaped, dark green, crystalline surface. Arching sprays of a few small, fragrant white or pink flowers, most of year. Zones 10–12.

Begonia Hybrid Cultivars
Begonia is such a large genus and many of the species interbreed so freely that over the years countless hybrids have been introduced. These largely fall into eight quite clear-cut groups. While there are several subgroups, we concentrate here on the main divisions.

CANE-LIKE GROUP
☀ ❄ ↔ 20–32 in (50–80 cm)
↑ 2–6 ft (0.6–1.8 m)

Tall upright stems. Leaves, usually wing-shaped, vary in size, texture, and color; may be deeply lobed, feathery; often silvery or red-tinted. Small red, pink or salmon flowers in sprays. '**Bubbles**', fragrant pink flowers, spotted leaves; '**Honeysuckle**', fragrant pink flowers; '**Irene Nuss**' ★, coral pink flowers, bronze leaves; '**Looking Glass**',

Begonia, Cane-like Group, 'Annan Girl'

Begonia, Cane-like Group, 'Marmaduke'

Begonia, Cane-like Group, 'Annan Style'

Begonia, Cane-like Group, 'Orange Sherbert'

Begonia, Cane-like Group, 'Flamingo Queen'

Begonia, Cane-like Group, 'Pinafore'

Begonia, Cane-like Group, 'Looking Glass'

Begonia, Cane-like Group, 'Sophie Cecile'

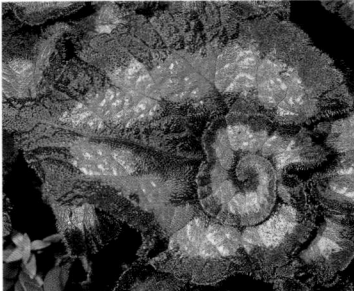

Begonia, Rex Cultorum Group, 'Escargot'

B., Rex Cultorum Group, 'Merry Christmas'

Begonia, Rex Cultorum Group, 'Guinevere'

B., Rex Cultorum Group, 'Silver Horizon'

Begonia, Rex Cultorum Group, 'Tinsel'

pink flowers, leaves silvery above, red underneath; **'Orange Rubra'**, orange flowers, mid-green leaves. Zones 9–11.

REX CULTORUM GROUP

☼/☀ ⚘ ↔ 16–24 in (40–60 cm)
↕ 12–24 in (30–60 cm)

Leaves large, exquisitely colored and marked, heavily veined and textured, velvety, often hairy at edges. Upper surfaces have combinations of bronze-green, bright green, silver, pink, and white; undersides usually purple-red. Clusters of small pink flowers. **'Merry Christmas'**, pink flowers, red leaves; **'Silver Queen'**, pink flowers, silvery leaves. Zones 10–12.

RHIZOMATOUS GROUP

☼/☀ ⚘ ↔ 12–30 in (30–75 cm)
↕ 6–8 in (15–20 cm)

Grow from spreading or upright rhizomes. Short- to long-stemmed, often fleshy leaves, to 12 in (30 cm) wide. Leaf shape, texture, and color variable, often red-tinted undersides and wavy edges. Flowers few to many, mostly pink. Cultivars include **'Munchkin'**, and **'Tiger Paws'**. Zones 9–11.

SEMPERFLORENS GROUP

☼/☀ ⚘ ↔ 12 in (30 cm) ↕ 12 in (30 cm)

Small bushy perennials, usually treated as bedding annuals. Bright green or red, glossy, waxy leaves. Small, white, pink, or red flowers, usually single. Suit cool, fairly moist summers. **All Round**

Series, bronze or green foliage; **Alfa Series**, vigorous plants, bronze foliage, including **'Alfa Pink'**; **Ambassador Series**, compact with mid-green foliage; **Cocktail Series**, single flowers, bronze foliage; **Expresso Series**, bronze foliage, including **'Expresso Scarlet'**; **Inferno Series**, vigorous and resilient, including **'Inferno Apple Blossom'**; **Olympia Series**, green foliage, including **'Olympia White'**; **Prelude Series**, early blooming, rich green foliage; and **Senator Series**, early blooming, bronze foliage. Zones 9–11.

SHRUB-LIKE GROUP

☼/☀ ⚘ ↔ 18–48 in (45–120 cm)
↕ 12–36 in (30–90 cm)

Bushy plants; leaves variably sized, colored, and textured, hairy or smooth, often red-veined. Flowers usually pink or cream, sometimes red or white, usually small and clustered. **'Cockatoo'**,

Begonia, Semperflorens Group cultivars

Begonia, Shrub-like Group, 'Cockatoo'

Begonia, Shrub-like Group, 'Red Amigo'

Begonia, Shrub-like Group, 'Richmondensis'

Begonia, Semperflorens Group, 'Ambassador Blush'

Begonia, Semperflorens Group, 'Prelude Bicolor'

Begonia, Semperflorens Group, 'Prelude Pink'

Begonia, Semperflorens Group, 'Prelude Scarlet'

Begonia, Semperflorens Group, 'Prelude White'

B., Semperflorens Group, 'Rose Pink'

B., Semperflorens Group, 'Rum'

B., Semperflorens, 'Senator Pink'

B., Semperflorens, 'Senator Scarlet'

B., Semperflorens, 'Senator White'

pinkish red flowers; '**Ginny**', dark green leaves, pink flowers; '**Red Amigo**', scarlet flowers; '**Richmondensis**' ★, lush green leaves, pink, red, or white flowers; '**Thurstonii**', green leaves, red undersides, pink flowers. Zones 9–12.

THICK-STEMMED GROUP

☼/☀ ⚘ ↔ 12–18 in (30–45 cm) ↑ 12–18 in ((30–45 cm)

Strong fleshy-stemmed plants, often quite tall. Variably colored leaves, more than 6 in (15 cm) long, deeply toothed, lobed, or smooth-edged. Small flowers, usually white or pink, sometimes scented. '**Boomer**', bronze leaves, white flowers. Zones 9–12.

TRAILING OR SCANDENT GROUP

☼/☀ ⚘ ↔ 18–36 in (45–90 cm) ↑ 6–12 in (15–30 cm)

Low spreading plants with lax stems. Usually grown in hanging baskets but sometimes climbing. Leaves usually small to medium-sized, smooth or hairy, often dark green. Sprays of small flowers are white, pink, or red and often scented. Zones 9–12.

TUBEROUS GROUP

☼/☀ ❄ ↔ 12–20 in (30–50 cm) ↑ 12–32 in (30–80 cm)

This group of plants grow from large flat tubers, producing short, heavy, succulent stems carrying large, often hairy leaves. There is a huge range of flower types and colors, including many that resemble roses. They are suitable for indoor or outdoor cultivation, flowering mainly from midsummer to frost. '**Coppelia**', large crimson-edged white flowers; '**Fairylight**', pink-edged white flowers; '**Roy Hartley**', large salmon pink flowers. The **Non-Stop Series** and **Pin-up Series** ★ include a variety of attractive plants. Zones 8–10.

Begonia, Tuberous Group, 'Apollo'

Begonia, Tuberous Group, 'Apricot Delight'

Begonia, Tuberous Group, 'Coppelia'

B., Tuberous Group, 'Cordelia'

Begonia, Tuberous Group, 'Crimson Scarlet'

Begonia, Tuberous Group, 'Elaine Tarttelin'

B., Tuberous Group, 'Festiva'

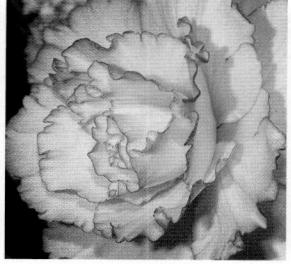

B., Tuberous Group, 'Isabella'

B., Tuberous Group, 'Ivanhoe'

B., Tuberous Group, 'Jessica'

B., Tuberous Group, 'Krakatoa'

B., Tuberous Group, 'Lady Rowena'

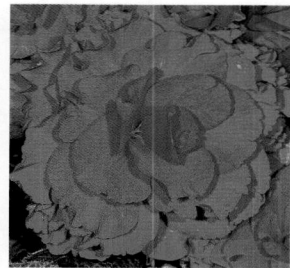

B., Tuberous Group, 'Majesty'

B., Tuberous Group, 'Mardi Gras'

B., Tuberous Group, 'Memories'

B., Tuberous Group, 'Nell Gwynne'

B., Tuberous Group, 'Pin-up Flame'

B., Tuberous Group, 'Pin-up Rose'

B., Tuberous Group, 'Rose Marie'

B., Tuberous Group, 'Roy Hartley'

B., Tuberous Group, 'Royalty'

B., Tuberous Group, 'Saturn'

B., Tuberous Group, 'Sugar Candy'

B., Tuberous Group, 'Tahiti'

Belamcanda chinensis

Bellevalia forniculata

Bellevalia romana

BELAMCANDA

There are 2 species of short-lived rhizomatous perennials in this genus, which is a member of the iris (Iridaceae) family. They are found across a wide area of eastern Europe and Asia. The leaves are sword-like and arranged in fans. Flowers, borne on slender stems, have 6 equal-sized flaring petals and are followed by fruiting capsules that split to reveal large black seeds. Some recent botanical opinion suggests that the species of *Belamcanda* are more appropriately classified in the genus *Iris*.
CULTIVATION: Grow in sun or light shade in a well-drained moderately fertile soil. Water well during the growing period. In cooler climates provide a protective mulch in winter. Propagate from seed, or division in spring or early autumn.

Belamcanda chinensis ★

BLACKBERRY LILY, LEOPARD LILY
☼ ❄ ↔ 12 in (30 cm) ↑ 36 in (90 cm)
From eastern Russia to Japan. Short-lived perennial with deciduous sword-like leaves. Borne on loose spikes in summer, flowers have 6 narrow flaring petals from yellow to orange, usually speckled with crimson. Zones 8–10.

BELLEVALIA

The 45 species of spring-flowering bulbs that make up this hyacinth (Hyacinthaceae) family genus are found from Portugal to northeastern Afghanistan. They are closely related to the grape hyacinths *(Muscari)* and many species could easily be mistaken for them. Foliage ranges from fine and grassy to strappy. Although each bulb produces few leaves, typically 3 to 6, some species that form clusters of bulbs can produce quite large clumps of foliage. The small, tubular, funnel-, bell-, or urn-shaped flowers are borne in heads on upright stems usually held clear of the foliage. Flowers are often in pale blue to purple shades or white.
CULTIVATION: Tolerant of moderate frosts and at home in a mild-temperate climate, these interesting bulbs thrive in rockery conditions and alpine troughs. Plant in a bright but not sunny position with gritty, humus-rich, well-drained soil kept moist in spring. Propagate by root division when dormant.

Bellevalia forniculata

☼ ❄ ↔ 8 in (20 cm) ↑ 12 in (30 cm)
Native to northeastern Turkey where, unlike most species, it grows in permanently damp meadows. Narrow leaves; flower stems to 12 in (30 cm) tall. Purple-blue flowers ¼ in (6 mm) long in early spring. Zones 7–9.

Bellevalia pycnantha

syn. *Muscari paradoxum* of gardens
☼ ❄ ↔ 12 in (30 cm) ↑ 16 in (40 cm)
Found from eastern Turkey to Iran and Armenia. Broad dark green leaves, sometimes blue-tinted, 3 per bulb. Flower stem to 16 in (40 cm) tall, with dense heads of small, dark purple, urn-shaped flowers. Zones 7–9.

Bellevalia romana

syn. *Hyacinthus romanus*
☼ ❄ ↔ 12 in (30 cm) ↑ 12 in (30 cm)
From southern France. Probably the most widely cultivated species. Fleshy bright green leaves to 12 in (30 cm) long. Green- to soft brown-tinted cream flowers slightly more than ¼ in (6 mm) long. Zones 7–9.

Bellis perennis

BELLIS

BELLIS DAISY, BRUISEWORT, LAWN DAISY
This European and Mediterranean genus of 7 species of annual and perennial daisies (family Asteraceae) includes the common bellis daisy *(B. perennis)*, which is the little white flower often seen on lawns. The genus name is derived from the Latin *bellus*, meaning pretty, and although wild species are sometimes weeds, cultivated forms are indeed attractive. They have much larger flowerheads with many more ray florets and a wider color range than wild plants. *Bellis* plants form flat rosettes of spoon- to kidney-shaped leaves and carry their flowerheads on individual stems. The leaves and extracts have been used in herbal medicines to treat wounds and for their anti-inflammatory properties.
CULTIVATION: Best in cool-temperate climates in a sunny or part-shaded open position with good air movement and soil that remains moist during the growing season. White rust and mildew can occur in humid conditions. The fancy cultivars are propagated by division, others from seed.

Bellis perennis

BELLIS DAISY
☼ ❄ ↔ 4–8 in (10–20 cm)
↑ 2–4 in (5–10 cm)
Originally from temperate Eurasia but now naturalized in most temperate zones. Leaves 1–2 in (25–50 mm) long, broad, spatula-shaped. White flowers, sometimes tinted pink, with yellow centers, from late winter. 'Dresden China', very compact, soft pink, double flowers. The **Pomponette Series** was developed from the pink-flowered dwarf '**Pomponette**' to include white and a wide range of pink and red shades. '**Rob Roy**' is a robust plant with tall flower stems and red double flowers. Zones 4–10.

Bellis perennis, **Pomponette Series cultivar**

Berberidopsis corallina

BERBERIDOPSIS

This genus of evergreen climbing shrubs belongs to the family of Flacourtiaceae and consists of one species from eastern Australia and one species from South America, mainly from Chile, that is now very rare in the wild and may even be extinct. The shrubs can be trained to 15 ft (4.5 m) in height, with a similar spread, and are grown for their ornamental foliage and sprays of pendent pink to scarlet flowers, in summer–early autumn.
CULTIVATION: These plants grow best in moist woodland, in acid to neutral soil, preferring a sheltered site in partial shade with root protection in winter. While moisture is essential, good free drainage is also needed. Propagate from seed in spring, half-hardened cuttings in late summer, or layered trailing branches in autumn. Prune only if necessary. In areas prone to frost, grow in a greenhouse.

Berberidopsis corallina
CORAL PLANT
☼ ❄ ↔ Unlimited ↑ 15 ft (4.5 m)
Evergreen climber native to Chile. Heart-shaped to oval dark green leaves sometimes end in tiny spines. Flowers rounded, dark red, ½ in (12 mm) in diameter, on 2 in (5 cm) long scarlet stalks, in summer–autumn. Zones 8–9.

BERBERIS
BARBERRY
This Berberidaceae family genus consists of more than 450 species of deciduous and evergreen shrubs, mainly seen across the Northern Hemisphere. They are variable in size, with spines on their branches. Plants are generally cultivated for the ornamental value of their leaves, flowers, and berries, which are often held until winter. Plants are used to make dye for cloth, leather, wood, and hair. All of the plant parts are supposed to cause mild stomach upsets if eaten. *B.* × *stenophylla* has become a serious pest in New Zealand. Many North American botanists now include all of the *Mahonia* species in *Berberis*.

CULTIVATION: *Berberis* will grow in most well-drained to fairly heavy soils. Tropical African species prefer rocky soil in mountainous areas. Plants can be grown in full sun or partial shade but autumn color is better in full sun. Propagate from softwood cuttings in early summer, or half-hardened cuttings later in summer. Seed will often not come true. Site with care as branch spines can be hazardous.

Berberis × bristolensis
☼ ❄ ↔ 6 ft (1.8 m) ↑ 5 ft (1.5 m)
Evergreen shrub, hybrid of *B. calliantha* and *B. verruculosa*. Leaves elliptical, smooth, shiny dark green upper surface, gray-white underside, some turning red in winter, up to 1½ in (35 mm) long, spiny serrated edges. Flowers yellow, in late spring. Egg-shaped black fruits. Zones 6–9.

Berberis buxifolia
☼ ❄ ↔ 10 ft (3 m) ↑ 8 ft (2.4 m)
Native to Chile and Argentina. Erect evergreen or semi-evergreen species with arching branches. Leaves leathery, dark green, spiny tips. Flowers deep orange-yellow in upper leaf axils, in mid- to late spring. Dark purple fruits. 'Pygmaea' (syn. 'Nana'), dwarf form to 3 ft (0.9 m) tall. Zones 6–9.

Berberis × carminea
☼ ❄ ↔ 8 ft (2.4 m) ↑ 5 ft (1.5 m)
A hybrid of *B. aggregata* and *B. wilsoniae*. Leaves are egg-shaped, dull gray-green. Flowers yellow, arranged in clusters of 10 to 16 blooms per panicle, in late spring–early summer.

Berberis buxifolia

Berberis chingii

Fruits red or orange, in dense clusters. 'Barbarossa', showy bright red fruits; 'Pirate King', dense foliage. Zones 6–9.

Berberis chingii
☼ ❄ ↔ 6 ft (1.8 m) ↑ 6 ft (1.8 m)
Evergreen shrub from Anhui Province, eastern China. Hardly known in cultivation. Clusters of small, white berries in late summer–autumn. Zones 7–10.

Berberis darwinii
DARWIN BARBERRY
☼ ❄ ↔ 10 ft (3 m) ↑ 10 ft (3 m)
Evergreen shrub native to Chile and Argentina. Leaves dark green,

Berberis darwinii

toothed, with spines, pale green beneath. Flowers deep yellow or orange in pendulous racemes. Oblong purplish black fruits with a bloom. 'Flame', grows to half the height of the species. Zones 7–10.

Berberis empetrifolia
☼ ❄ ↔ 12 in (30 cm) ↑ 12 in (30 cm)
Spreading, nearly prostrate evergreen shrub native to Chile and Argentina. Branch spines often longer than the leaves. Leaves dark green, grayish undersides, spiny tips. Flowers deep yellow, in late spring. Fruits blue-black with blue bloom. Zones 7–10.

Berberis empetrifolia

Berberis × *bristolensis*

Berberis henryana

Berberis × frikartii

Berberis 'Georgei'

Berberis × frikartii

☼ ❄ ↔ 5 ft (1.5 m) ↑ 5 ft (1.5 m)

An evergreen hybrid of *B. candidula* and *B. verruculosa*. All cultivars are evergreen. Leaves glossy dark green above, with silvery undersides, coloring red in winter. Flowers yellow, in late spring. Black fruits with blue bloom. '**Amstelveen**', vigorous arching stems to 3 ft (0.9 m) tall; '**Telstar**', similar to 'Amstelveen', with spreading habit; flat top when mature. Zones 6–9.

Berberis gagnepainii

☼ ❄ ↔ 6 ft (1.8 m) ↑ 5 ft (1.5 m)

Originating in western China. Small, dense evergreen shrubs with narrow wavy-edged leaves, yellow flowers, and black berries. The form most often grown is *B. × **hybridogagnepainii*** of garden origin, a cross of *B. verruculosa* and *B. gagnepainii* var. *lanceifolia*. Leaves ovate to lance-shaped, bright green, with reddish or bluish green undersides. Zones 5–9.

Berberis 'Georgei'

☼/❁ ❄ ↔ 10 ft (3 m) ↑ 10 ft (3 m)

Large, bushy, deciduous shrub unknown in the wild but first recorded in China, probably a hybrid with *B. vulgaris* parentage. Forms a thicket of thorny stems with short elliptical leaves. Sprays of small yellow flowers in spring. Red fruit. Zones 3–9.

Berberis × gladwynensis

☼ ❄ ↔ 4 ft (1.2 m) ↑ 3–6 ft (0.9–1.8 m)

Evergreen garden hybrid, hardly known outside the USA. 'William

Berberis julianae

Penn' ★ is the cultivar normally found, forming a broad mound to 4 ft (1.2 m) tall; shiny dark green leaves 1 in (25 mm) long, turn bronzy red in winter. Zones 6–9.

Berberis henryana

☼ ❄ ↔ 5 ft (1.5 m) ↑ 6 ft (1.8 m)

From China, this deciduous shrub has unarmed branches. Leaves 1–2 in (25–50 mm) long, edged with thorny teeth. Flowers yellow, in clusters, followed by red berries. Zones 6–9.

Berberis julianae

WINTERGREEN BARBERRY

☼ ❄ ↔ 10 ft (3 m) ↑ 10 ft (3 m)

Found in western Hubei Province, China. An evergreen shrub, spiny stems, leaves oval shaped with narrow end at base, serrated margins, dark green above, paler undersurface. Juvenile foliage with copper tints. Flowers yellow or tinged red, in clusters, in early spring. Fruits black with white bloom. '**Lombarts Red**' has leaves tinged red underneath. Zones 5–9.

Berberis koreana

KOREAN BARBERRY

☼ ❄ ↔ 5 ft (1.5 m) ↑ 5 ft (1.5 m)

From Korea, a compact deciduous shrub with spines encircling the stem. Leaves oblong to egg-shaped, serrated edges, 2½ in (6 cm) long, color in autumn. Flowers yellow, in clusters; glossy red berries. Zones 4–9.

Berberis linearifolia

☼ ❄ ↔ 5 ft (1.5 m) ↑ 6 ft (1.8 m)

A spiny evergreen shrub from Argentina and the Chilean Andes.

Berberis × macracantha

Leaves dark green, glossy, 2 in (5 cm) long. Flowers reddish yellow to apricot, in clusters, in spring–summer. Fruits black with blue bloom. '**Orange King**', large deep orange flowers. Zones 6–9.

Berberis × macracantha

☼ ❄ ↔ 12 ft (3.5 m) ↑ 12 ft (3.5 m)

Garden hybrid between *B. aristata* and *B. vulgaris*; deciduous shrub. Stems well protected by thorns more than 1 in (25 mm) long. Long racemes of bright yellow flowers, in spring, followed by deep purple-red berries, in autumn. Zones 5–9.

Berberis × ottawensis

HYBRID PURPLE BARBERRY

☼ ❄ ↔ 8 ft (2.4 m) ↑ 8 ft (2.4 m)

A cross between *B. thunbergii* and *B. vulgaris*. Leaves mid-green, egg-shaped. Flowers pale yellow, in clusters, in spring. Fruits egg-shaped red berries. *B. × o.* f. *purpurea*, purple-red foliage; '**Superba**' (syn. 'Purpurea'), new growth almost bronze. *B. × o.* '**Silver Miles**', dark purplish red leaves marked silvery gray. Zones 5–10.

Berberis pruinosa

☼ ❄ ↔ 5 ft (1.5 m) ↑ 5 ft (1.5 m)

Indigenous to Yunnan Province, China, this evergreen shrub has spiny branches. Leaves lance-shaped, mid- to dark green above, white beneath, toothed, tipped with spines. Clusters of pale yellow flowers, in late spring. Fruits black, white bloom. Zones 6–9.

Berberis linearifolia

Berberis × ottawensis f. *purpurea*

Berberis thunbergii f. *atropurpurea*

Berberis thunbergii 'Aurea'

Berberis thunbergii 'Bogozam'

Berberis thunbergii 'Dart's Red Lady'

Berberis thunbergii 'Sparkle'

Berberis × *rubrostilla*

☀ ❄ ↔ 8 ft (2.4 m) ↕ 5 ft (1.5 m)

A deciduous hybrid, possibly from a cross of *B. aggregata* and *B. wilsoniae*. Leaves narrow, egg-shaped, mid-green above, gray undersides, 1¼ in (30 mm) long, with marginal spines. Pale yellow flowers. Egg-shaped, translucent, red fruits. Zones 6–9.

Berberis sargentiana

SARGENT BARBERRY

☀ ❄ ↔ 6 ft (1.8 m) ↕ 6 ft (1.8 m)

An evergreen shrub from western China, densely branching with spines 2½ in (6 cm) long. Elliptic leaves, 4 in (10 cm) long, toothed, spiny, dark green above, yellowish green underneath. Flowers pale yellow,

sometimes tinged with red, in late spring. The fruits are oblong, blue-black. Zones 6–9.

Berberis × *stenophylla*

☀ ❄ ↔ 15 ft (4.5 m) ↕ 10 ft (3 m)

Parents of this vigorous evergreen shrub are *B. darwinii* and *B. empetri-folia*. Leaves narrow, elliptical, ¾ in (18 mm) long, dark green above, bluish green beneath. Flowers deep yellow, in late spring. Fruits black with blue bloom. '**Corallina Compacta**', grows to height and spread of 12 in (30 cm); '**Crawley Gem**', rounded form, red flowers; '**Irwinii**', golden yellow flowers; and '**Lemon Queen**' (syn. 'Cornish Cream'), creamy white flowers. Zones 6–9.

Berberis thunbergii

JAPANESE BARBERRY

☀ ❄ ↔ 8 ft (2.4 m) ↕ 3 ft (0.9 m)

Native to Japan, deciduous shrub with compact foliage and rounded shape. Leaves egg-shaped, smooth, fresh green above, bluish green beneath. Flowers pale yellow, can be tinged red, in racemes, in mid-spring. Fruits glossy red. Often used for hedging. *B. t.* f. *atropurpurea*, purple-red stems and leaves. *B. t.* '**Golden Ring**', red-purple leaves, narrow yellow margins; '**Helmond Pillar**', to 5 ft (1.5 m) tall, dark red foliage; '**Red Chief**', to 6 ft (1.8 m) tall, pink-variegated leaves; '**Rose Glow**' ★, red-purple foliage flecked with white. Zones 4–9.

Berberis valdiviana

☀ ❄ ↔ 15 ft (4.5 m) ↕ 15 ft (4.5 m)

Native to Chile. Leaves 2 in (5 cm) long, elliptical, smooth, dark green above, pale to yellow-green underneath. The saffron yellow flowers

appear in drooping racemes in late spring. The fruits are black with a blue bloom. Zones 8–10.

Berberis vulgaris

BARBERRY

☀ ❄ ↔ 6 ft (1.8 m) ↕ 6 ft (1.8 m)

Native to Europe, the Middle East, North Africa, and temperate Asia. Deciduous shrub, harbors wheat rust. Branches spiny; elliptical to egg-shaped green leaves, margins serrated. Flowers yellow on pendent racemes. Showy red fruits. Zones 3–9.

Berberis wilsoniae

WILSON BARBERRY

☀ ❄ ↔ 6 ft (1.8 m) ↕ 3 ft (0.9 m)

Deciduous or semi-evergreen shrub native to western Sichuan and Yunnan Provinces, China. Branches dense, spiny, arching. Leaves gray-green, egg-shaped to linear, orange-red in autumn. Pale yellow flowers, in summer. Pink to red fruits. Zones 5–10.

Berberis wilsoniae

Berberis pruinosa

Berberis vulgaris

Berberis × *stenophylla* 'Crawley Gem'

B. × *stenophylla* 'Corallina Compacta'

Berberis valdiviana

Bergenia cordifolia 'Perfecta'

Bergenia ciliata

Bergenia emeiensis

BERGENIA
PIGSQUEAK

Found in Asia, from Afghanistan to Mongolia, this genus of the saxifrage (Saxifragaceae) family is made up of 8 species of perennials. Large leathery leaves sprout from tough, woody, fleshy stems. Leaves are broad, often light green, and usually at least 8 in (20 cm) long. They are complemented by long-stemmed heads of 5-petalled flowers in spring. Species most often have pink flowers but garden forms occur in white and shades of pink, red, and mauve. Named for an eighteenth-century German botanist, Karl August von Bergen, the genus is commonly known as pigsqueak because of the sound made when the wet leaves are rubbed between one's fingers.
CULTIVATION: For lush foliage, plant in cool moist conditions in part-shade in soil rich in humus. Plants in full sun often flower well but at the expense of their leaves, which burn. Excellent in large rockeries. Propagate by division after flowering.

Bergenia ciliata
HAIRY BERGENIA, HEARTLEAF
☀ ❄ ↔ 32 in (80 cm) ↕ 12 in (30 cm)
A Himalayan native with densely hairy, dark green, rounded leaves to 12 in (30 cm) long. Pink-tinted white flowers to 2 in (5 cm) wide on 12 in (30 cm) high stems. Damaged by late frosts. Zones 7–10.

Bergenia cordifolia
HEARTLEAF SAXIFRAGE, PIGSQUEAK
☀ ❄ ↔ 48 in (120 cm) ↕ 16 in (40 cm)
Found in the mountains of Siberia and Mongolia. Rounded toothed-edged leaves, to 8 in (20 cm) long, on strong stalks. Bright pink flowers on red stems from late winter. 'Perfecta', red-tinted foliage, very tall flower stems; 'Purpurea', purple-tinted winter foliage and red flowers on tall stems; 'Redstart', bronze leaves and magenta to cerise flowers. Zones 3–10.

Bergenia stracheyi

Bergenia crassifolia
☀ ❄ ↔ 16–32 in (40–80 cm) ↕ 12 in (30 cm)
From Siberia and Mongolia. Shallowly toothed, rounded leaves up to 8 in (20 cm) long, but can be considerably smaller. Magenta to cerise flowers on strong red stems. Zones 3–9.

Bergenia emeiensis
☀ ❄ ↔ 16 in (40 cm) ↕ 8 in (20 cm)
A Chinese species that grows naturally on rocky cliffs. Round leaves, to 6 in (15 cm) long. Large, semi-pendulous, white to pale pink flowers. Zones 7–9.

Bergenia purpurascens
☀ ❄ ↔ 20–48 in (50–120 cm) ↕ 12–18 in (30–45 cm)
An eastern Himalayan species. Purple-tinted leaves to 10 in (25 cm) long, fringed with hairs and often shallowly toothed. Pendulous deep pink to maroon flowers on red stems, stamens sometimes white. Early blooming. Zones 4–9.

Bergenia × schmidtii
☀ ❄ ↔ 24–48 in (60–120 cm) ↕ 12 in (30 cm)
A hybrid, *B. ciliata* × *B. crassifolia*, dating from 1875. Large rounded leaves and deep pink to magenta flowers. Very early blooming; protect the flowers from frost. Zones 5–10.

Bergenia stracheyi
☀ ❄ ↔ 16–24 in (40–60 cm) ↕ 12 in (30 cm)
Native to mountain regions from Afghanistan to Tibet. Serrated oval

Bergenia, Hybrid Cultivar, 'Rosi Klose'

leaves to 8 in (20 cm) long, becoming deep red in winter. In spring each rosette produces several heads of fragrant cream flowers ageing to pink. Zones 6–9.

Bergenia Hybrid Cultivars
☀/☀ ❄ ↔ 16–32 in (40–80 cm) ↕ 8–16 in (20–40 cm)
Mainly derived from *B. cordifolia* and *B. crassifolia* and generally resembling the former in size and leaf shape. Need some sunlight for the best leaf color. Among the most popular are 'Abendglut' (syn. 'Evening Glow'), compact grower with wavy-edged red-tinted foliage, purple-red semi-double flowers; 'Ballawley' (syn. 'Delbees'), glossy leaves, purple-tinted in winter, cup-shaped broad red flowers; 'Bressingham White', pure white flowers; 'Eroica', bronze- to purple-tinted foliage, purple-red flowers; 'Morgenröte' (syn. 'Morning Blush'), large bronze green leaves and deep purple-red flowers; 'Rosi Klose', dark green leaves, pink flowers; 'Silberlicht' (syn. 'Silver Light'), large leaves, white flowers ageing to pink, deep pink calyces; and 'Sunningdale', bronze- to red-tinted winter foliage, deep lavender-pink flowers. Zones 3–9.

BERGEROCACTUS
GOLDEN CEREUS, GOLDEN SPINED CEREUS, SPRAWLING CACTUS

This genus of a single species belongs to the cactus (Cactaceae) family. Found throughout arid parts of southern California, USA, and northern Baja California, Mexico, the attractive yellowish brown spines and the low branching habit of this medium-sized sprawling cactus make it a key element of the landscape. It grows from sea level to an altitude of just 250 ft (76 m), but its original habitat has

Bergenia, Hybrid Cultivar, 'Sunningdale'

Berlandiera lyrata

been reduced by the urban sprawl on both sides of the USA/Mexico border. Despite this, it is so widespread throughout its range that it is not threatened or endangered. The spiny perianth segments of the yellow flowers distinguish the sole species in this genus from plants in genus *Cereus,* which it superficially resembles.
CULTIVATION: Plants are easy to cultivate in a rich, well-drained, but well-watered soil. Propagation can be from seed, but they are usually raised from cuttings that have been dried out completely for a week or two before planting. Plants require a period of rest in winter.

Bergerocactus emoryi

syn. *Cereus emoryi*

☼ ❄ ↔ 10 ft (3 m) ↑ 2 ft (0.6 m)
Stems erect to prostrate, cylindrical, 1½–3 in (3.5–8 cm) in diameter, branching from base to form a wide bushy plant. One central spine, 2 in (5 cm) long, downward facing, surrounded by 20 to 30 radial spines. Flowers yellow, 2½ in (6 cm) in diameter. Seed pods globular, spiny. Zones 9–11.

BERLANDIERA

GREEN EYES

This genus of around 12 species of daisy (Asteraceae) family perennials occurs in southern North America and is known in cultivation through 2 or 3 species with unusually colored or scented flowers. They form dandelion-like basal clumps of bright green to blue-green, deeply lobed, toothed leaves that may die away over winter or simply be reduced to smaller rosettes. Some species develop more upright and woody stems clothed with similar leaves. Summer flowerheads are borne on long, upright, wiry stems and usually have bright yellow ray florets with contrastingly colored disc florets. Flowers sometimes have a scent rather like chocolate.
CULTIVATION: Easily grown, hardy, and drought-tolerant once established,

most species prefer to grow in full sun in light, gritty, free-draining soil with a little extra humus. Water in summer but otherwise keep dry. Propagate from seed or by careful root division in late winter.

Berlandiera lyrata

BROOCH FLOWER, CHOCOLATE FLOWER, LYRE-LEAF GREEN EYES

☼ ❄ ↔ 12 in (30 cm) ↑ 12 in (30 cm)
Native to southern USA and Mexico. Perennial with light green lyre-shaped leaves. Yellow fine-rayed daisies are borne year round. The flowers have dark centers and are heavily scented with a chocolate-like fragrance. Their green cup-like bracts persist after flowering, providing further interest. Zones 8–11.

BERZELIA

This South African genus, a member of the family Bruniaceae, includes some 12 species of upright, wiry-stemmed, evergreen shrubs with a dense covering of small, fine, needle-like leaves. The flowers, which appear in spring and summer, are minute but are packed in spherical clusters, of which there are several per head of bloom. The flowers are white to cream and, because the stamens extend beyond the tiny petals, the flowerheads appear to be studded with protrusions.
CULTIVATION: *Berzelia* is best grown in light well-drained soil with a good supply of summer moisture and a position in full sun. If necessary, trim lightly after flowering to retain a pleasing shape. Most species are easily propagated from seed or from small half-hardened tip cuttings taken from the non-flowering stems.

Berzelia galpinii

BAUBLES

☼/◐ ❄ ↔ 40–48 in (100–120 cm)
↑ 60 in (150 cm)
Strongly upright habit with fine foliage and clearly defined needle-like leaves to around ½ in (12 mm) long. Creamy white flowerheads, after pinkish buds, are spherical and larger than most species. Popular as cut flowers. Zones 9–10.

Berzelia lanuginosa

☼ ❄ ↔ 5 ft (1.5 m) ↑ 6 ft (1.8 m)
Shrub with whippy stems and dense covering of soft, short, needle-like leaves. Tiny button-like cream flowers, in clusters, in summer, after pinkish buds. Trim after flowering for compact growth. Avoid cutting into bare wood as regrowth is slow. Zones 9–11.

BESCHORNERIA

Native to Mexico, the 7 perennial rosette-forming species in this genus resemble agave and belong to the agave (Agavaceae) family. The genus differs from *Agave* in that the stamens are shorter than the perianth segments. Leaves are up to 5 ft (1.5 m) long, lance- to sword-shaped, fleshy

Berzelia galpinii

and bluish green, with rough margins. Surrounded by colorful bracts, flowers are clustered in racemes or panicles to 7 ft (2 m) or more tall. The 6 erect perianth segments are broadest toward the tips and are green tinged red, while the 6 stamens have delicate filaments and versatile anthers. The ovary is inferior, with 3 compartments and a slender style. The fruit is a capsule with many seeds. The leaves provide a soap substitute, and the flowers of some species are edible.
CULTIVATION: Frost tender, requiring full sun and needing greenhouse protection in cool regions. Propagate from seed, from suckers, or by division.

Beschorneria yuccoides

☼ ❄ ↔ 7 ft (2 m) ↑ 4–6 ft (1.2–1.8 m)
Dense clump of gray-green to blue-green sword-shaped leaves to more than 24 in (60 cm) long. Arching deep pink- to red-stemmed inflorescence with green flowers within large pinkish red bracts. Zones 9–11.

Beschorneria yuccoides

Berzelia lanuginosa, Harold Porter National Botanical Garden, South Africa

B

BETA

BEET

A member of the goosefoot (Chenopodiaceae) family, this genus contains one biennial species with 2 main forms. One is grown for its roots (beets), the other for its leaves (chards). Wild forms are often found on the Mediterranean coastline, western Europe, and parts of Asia growing at the high-tide mark. Leaves small and glossy to large and crinkly or puckered. Insignificant flowers are followed by knobbly seeds in profusion. Leaves of both forms are edible. Roots were used as a food source from the sixteenth century. CULTIVATION: Beets favor light well-drained soil, not too rich. Chards prefer rich moist soil. Grow from seed.

Beta vulgaris

BEET

☀ ❄ ↔ 27 in (70 cm) ↕ 27 in (70 cm)
The original wild or sea beet (also classified as *B. v.* subsp. *maritima*) is

Betula albosinensis

Beta vulgaris, Cicla Group, 'Bright Lights'

a perennial growing on seashores of Europe, North Africa, and western Asia. All cultivated beets are believed to be derived from it, including beet-root, sugar beet, fodder beets such as mangel-wurzel, chard, and spinach beet. They have often been treated as all falling within *B. v.* subsp. *vulgaris*, but this is now regarded as a wrong application of the concept of sub-species. Rather they should be divided among the following cultivar groups:

Cicla Group (syn. *B. v.* var. *cicla*, *B. v.* var. *flavescens*): Includes spinach beets, closest to wild beet with slender green leaf stalk and flat blade, but also chards or silver beets with larger leaves puckered to varying degree, stalk and midrib broad, white or colored, root not swollen. **'Bright Lights'** ★ (syns 'Five Colour Mix', 'Rainbow'), stems in shades of red, orange, yellow, pink, and white, or are bicolored; **'Bright Yellow'**, yellow stems and green crinkly leaves; **'Lucullus'**, huge, crinkly or puckered, glossy, green leaves, and wide white midrib and veins; **'Mostruosa'**, refined Italian strain with broad, bright green, puckered leaves; **'Rhubarb Chard'** ★, crimson stalks and dark green crinkly

Beta vulgaris, Cicla Group, 'Lucullus'

Beta vulgaris, Cicla Group, 'Rhubarb Chard'

leaves, midribs can be used as substitute for asparagus or celery.

Conditiva Group (syn. *B. v.* var. *conditiva*): Includes all the root vegetables and crops such as beetroot, sugar beet, fodder beet, mangel-wurzel, and mangold. Root (actually the stem) is swollen, leaf stalk slender, blade flat. Most beetroots have red or yellow roots and leaf stalks. **'Bull's Blood'** (syn. *B. v.* var. *crassa*), dark red leaves, red midrib and veins, striped edible roots; **'Forono'** ★, cylindrical purple beet, sweet and juicy. Zones 8–11.

BETULA

BIRCH

This genus gives its name to the birch family, Betulaceae, and consists of

B. vulgaris, Conditiva Group, 'Bull's Blood'

Betula alleghaniensis, in the wild, Vermont, USA

Beta vulgaris, Cicla Group, 'Bright Yellow'

about 60 deciduous small shrubs or tall trees occurring throughout temperate and arctic zones of the Northern Hemisphere. Tree trunks are often marked in different shades; in many species the outer layer of bark peels off. Wood is used for timber; sap and leaves are used medicinally, as food or drink, or as dye-stuff. Pendulous male catkins and erect female catkins are carried on the same tree in early spring. Leaves are mid- to dark green, ovate in shape, with indented margins. Beautiful ornamental trees. CULTIVATION: Birches are hardy trees, withstanding extreme cold and exposure to wind. Best in well-drained fertile soil, with some moisture and full sun or light shade. Take softwood cuttings in summer, half-hardened cuttings in autumn. Birches are susceptible to fungi such as *Armillaria melea* and *Piptoporus betulinus*; the latter, specific to the birch family, will destroy the tree.

Betula albosinensis

CHINESE RED BIRCH

☀ ❄ ↔ 30 ft (9 m) ↕ 80 ft (24 m)
Native to the Provinces of Sichuan, Gansu, and Shaanxi, southwestern China. New bark gray-cream turning orange or red-brown. Leaves glossy, green above, paler beneath, to 2½ in (6 cm) long, turn yellow in autumn. Showy male catkins. Zones 6–9.

B

Betula alnoides

Betula alleghaniensis ★

syn. *Betula lutea*

YELLOW BIRCH

☼ ❄ ↔ 30 ft (9 m) ↑ 80 ft (24 m)

Native to USA and Canada. Peeling yellow or gray bark; young shoots aromatic. Leaves yellow-green, coarsely toothed, to 6 in (15 cm) long. Male catkins 4 in (10 cm) long, erect female catkins. Zones 4–9.

Betula alnoides

☼ ❄ ↔ 20 ft (6 m) ↑ 100 ft (30 m)

Himalayan region, northeastern India to China. Bark gray and red-brown, peels in horizontal strips. Young twigs downy, purple-red. Tapered leaves 4 in (10 cm) long, serrated, red stalks. Catkins to 3 in (8 cm) long. Zones 8–10.

Betula dahurica

ASIAN BLACK BIRCH

☼ ❄ ↔ 30 ft (9 m) ↑ 40–60 ft (12–18 m)

Native to Korea, northern and northeastern China, and Japan. Bark brown with gray markings and curled fissures. Leaves oval, dark green, slightly hairy beneath, unevenly toothed. Prefers colder climates. Zones 3–9.

Betula ermanii

ERMAN'S BIRCH, GOLD BIRCH, RUSSIAN ROCK BIRCH

☼ ❄ ↔ 40 ft (12 m) ↑ 70 ft (21 m)

Native to Japan and mainland Asia. Bark pink or creamy white turning

Betula kenaica

B. mandschurica var. *japonica,* in spring

B. mandschurica var. *japonica* 'Whitespire'

pinkish. Tapered oval leaves, dark green, margins serrated. Male catkins in groups of 3. Tolerates wet soils but not drought. 'Grayswood Hill' (syn. *B. costata*), very vigorous. Zones 2–8.

Betula grossa

syn. *Betula ulmifolia*

JAPANESE CHERRY BIRCH

☼ ❄ ↔ 30 ft (9 m) ↑ 70 ft (21 m)

Native to Honshu, Kyushu, and Shikoku in Japan. Bark dark gray,

Betula dahurica

peeling in small curls, smooth in young trees. Leaves dull green, serrated, egg-shaped to oblong, tapering to point. Catkins knobbly. Female catkins are upright. Zones 5–9.

Betula kenaica

syn. *Betula papyrifera* var. *kenaica*

ALASKAN PAPER BIRCH, KENAI BIRCH

☼ ❄ ↔ 20–30 ft (6–9 m)
↑ 30–40 ft (9–12 m)

From Alaska and northwestern Canada. Narrow-crowned tree with pinkish to grayish white bark that peels in thin sheets. Like *B. papyrifera* but of smaller size and with smaller leaves, with blunter-tips. The leaves are also more regularly serrated. Zones 1–8.

Betula lenta

Betula mandschurica var. *japonica,* in winter

Betula lenta

BLACK BIRCH, CHERRY BIRCH, SWEET BIRCH

☼ ❄ ↔ 40 ft (12 m) ↑ 50 ft (15 m)

Native to eastern North America. Bark crimson, becomes scaly and gray ageing to black. Leaves egg-shaped, chartreuse, 4 in (10 cm) long, autumn color. Male catkins pendulous 3 in (8 cm). Female catkins erect. Zones 3–9.

Betula litvinovii

☼ ❄ ↔ 35 ft (10 m) ↑ 50 ft (15 m)

Native to Caucasus region to altitudes of 5,900 ft (1,800 m). Similar to *B. pendula,* but bark is not so white. Rare in cultivation. Zones 5–9.

Betula mandschurica

syn. *Betula platyphylla* var. *japonica*

MANCHURIAN BIRCH

☼ ❄ ↔ 30 ft (9 m) ↑ 70 ft (21 m)

Native to northeastern China and southeastern Siberia. Bark dusty milky white. Leaves mid-green, egg-shaped, to 3 in (8 cm) long, deeply indented, heavily veined. Male and female catkins pendulous, 1 in (25 mm) long. *B. m.* var. *japonica,* with white bark, to 80 ft (24 m) tall; 'Whitespire' (syn. *B. platyphylla* 'Whitespire'), narrowly conical habit. Zones 2–9.

B

Betula papyrifera, in the wild, USA

Betula medwedewii

Betula platyphylla

Betula medwedewii

TRANSCAUCASIAN BIRCH

☼ ❄ ↔ 15 ft (4.5 m) ↑ 15 ft (4.5 m)
From the Caucasus mountains of
northwestern Iran and northeastern
Turkey. Erect shrub or small tree.
Bark brown, peels slightly. Leaves
elliptical, deep green, paler green
underneath, deeply serrated edges.
Male catkins pendulous. Female
catkins erect. Zones 5–9.

Betula nana

DWARF BIRCH

☼ ❄ ↔ 4 ft (1.2 m) ↑ 24 in (60 cm)
Native to subarctic areas of Eurasia,
North America, and Greenland.
Leaves are dark green, up to ¾ in
(18 mm) long, kidney-shaped to
rounded, finely toothed, turn yellow
or red in autumn. Grows best in cold
climates. Zones 2–7.

Betula nigra

Betula nigra

RIVER BIRCH, TROPICAL BIRCH

☼ ❄ ↔ 15 ft (4.5 m) ↑ 30 ft (9 m)
Deciduous tree from along rivers in
eastern USA. Bark white, smooth then
thin flaking plates of cream, salmon,
and pale brown. Dark and furrowed

Betula pendula 'Youngii', in summer

Betula nigra 'Little King'

with age. Tolerates heat and dryness.
'**Heritage**', peeling cream to pale
brown bark; '**Little King**', dwarf cultivar, to 10 ft (3 m) tall. Zones 4–9.

Betula papyrifera

CANOE BIRCH, PAPER BIRCH, WHITE BIRCH

☼ ❄ ↔ 30 ft (9 m) ↑ 60 ft (18 m)
North America. Deciduous. White
papery bark peeling to orange-brown.
Light canopy allows sunlight through.
Tolerates cold and drought. Zones 2–8.

Betula pendula 'Youngii', in spring

Betula pendula

EUROPEAN SILVER BIRCH, EUROPEAN
WHITE BIRCH

☼ ❄ ↔ 35 ft (10 m) ↑ 80 ft (24 m)
A deciduous tree that comes from
northern Europe. It is commonly
found on poor soils. The foliage
turns clear yellow in autumn.
Beautiful winter silhouette, arching
habit, and white bark. Trunk blackens
with age. Adaptable to confined
spaces. '**Dalecarlica**' (weeping birch),
with dissected foliage; '**Fastigiata**', an
erect tree to 70 ft (21 m); '**Laciniata**',
loses leaves earlier in autumn than
species; '**Purpurea**', with thin pendulous branches; '**Tristis**', narrowly
conical habit; '**Youngii**' ★, usually
sold as a grafted tree with a strongly
weeping head. Zones 2–8.

Betula platyphylla

☼ ❄ ↔ 40 ft (12 m) ↑ 70 ft (21 m)
Native to Siberia, northeastern China,
Korea, and Japan. Bark pure white.
Leaves chartreuse, 4 in (10 cm) long,
egg-shaped with serrated margins.
Male catkins to 3 in (8 cm) long;
female catkins to 1¼ in (3 cm) long.
Zones 4–9.

Betula pendula 'Youngii', in winter

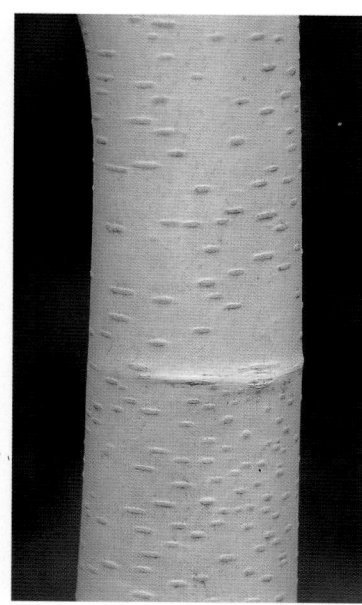

Betula utilis var. *jacquemontii* 'Silver Shadow'

Betula pubescens

syns *Betula glabra*, *B. populifolia*
DOWNY BIRCH

☀ ❄ ↔ 30 ft (9 m) ↑ 70 ft (21 m)

Native to Europe, northern Asia, Greenland, and Iceland. Bark dull white to pale brown, peeling in strips. Leaves mid-green, 2½ in (6 cm) long, elliptic to egg-shaped, unevenly serrated. Male catkins 2½ in (6 cm) long. Female catkins shorter. Zones 2–9.

Betula pumila

AMERICAN DWARF BIRCH

☀ ❄ ↔ 3 ft (0.9 m) ↑ 3 ft (0.9 m)

Erect shrub native to northeastern America. Twigs densely hairy. Leaves green, whitish beneath, roughly serrated, rounded or egg-shaped to 1¼ in (30 mm) long. Catkins to 1 in (25 mm) long, in spring. Zones 2–8.

Betula utilis

HIMALAYAN BIRCH, WHITEBARK

☀ ❄ ↔ 30 ft (9 m) ↑ 60 ft (18 m)

Native to Himalayas and China. Bark pink to orange-brown with white bloom, peels in thin flakes. Leaves dark green, to 5 in (12 cm) long, egg-shaped, unevenly serrated, tapering, turn yellow in autumn. Male catkins 5 in (12 cm) long, female catkins erect. *B. u.* var. *jacquemontii* (syn. *B. jacquemontii*), from Kashmir and Nepal, with white bark; '**Grayswood Ghost**', brilliant white bark, glossy leaves; '**Jermyns**', reddish brown bark, ages to white; '**Silver Shadow**', white bark and deep green leaves. Zones 7–9.

BIDENS

BEGGAR'S TICK, BURR MARIGOLD, PITCHFORKS, SPANISH NEEDLES, STICK TIGHT, TICKSEED

This genus of about 200 annual and perennial species belongs to the daisy

Betula utilis var. *jacquemontii*

(Asteraceae) family. It has a worldwide distribution, with its largest numbers in temperate and tropical Africa and America. The few ornamental forms are used as annual bedding plants. The many common names of the genus come from the sticking hooks on the seeds, which help them to become dispersed over wide areas.
CULTIVATION: These plants require little more than a sunny well-drained site with reasonable moisture-retentive soil. Plant after frosts in very cold climates. Propagate from seed or by division of the perennial forms.

Bidens ferulifolia

APACHE BEGGARTICKS

☀ ❄ ↔ 12–18 in (30–45 cm)
↑ 24–36 in (60–90 cm)

From Arizona (USA), Mexico, and Guatemala. Annual or perennial with ferny foliage. Golden wide-rayed daisies, about 1¼ in (30 mm) across, are borne from late summer to autumn. '**Golden Goddess**' and '**Goldmarie**' are improved selections.

Bikkia campanulata

'**Golden Eye**', Goldie/'**Innbid**', and '**Peters Goldteppich**' ★ are lower trailing cultivars. Zones 8–11.

BIGNONIA

This genus belongs to the trumpet-vine (Bignoniaceae) family. It formerly contained a large number of species but reclassification has reduced it to 1 climbing evergreen vine. Its natural habitat is rich moist woodland areas of southeastern USA.
CULTIVATION: Grow in well-drained fertile soil in full sun or part-shade. In cooler climates grow in the greenhouse, with protection from the hottest summer sun. Cut back previous season's growth by two-thirds in early spring. Mealybugs can be serious pests. Propagate from seed or by layering.

Bignonia capreolata

CROSS-VINE, QUARTER VINE, TRUMPET FLOWER

☀/◐ ❄ ↔ 10 ft (3 m) ↑ 10–30 ft (3–9 m)

From southeastern USA. Vigorous summer-flowering vine, climbs by tendrils. Leaves opposite, deep green. Showy heads of flaring trumpet flowers 2 in (5 cm) long, deep orange to scarlet with darker throat. Flowers most prolifically in full sun. '**Tangerine Beauty**', orange flowers with yellow throats. Zones 7–9.

BIKKIA

Belonging to the madder (Rubiaceae) family, this is a genus of about 20 species of shrubs and small trees from islands of the western Pacific; about half are endemic to New Caledonia.

The leaves are smooth-edged and simple , rather thick and leathery, arranged in opposite pairs or whorls of 3. From axils arise solitary, large, semi-pendulous flowers opening progressively over months; they are bell-shaped to tubular with 4 to 6 prominent angles, each angle ending in a point at the mouth. Colors range from white to yellow, pink, orange, or dark red. Fruits are capsules with 2 compartments containing many small seeds. Bikkias commonly grow in crevices on rock outcrops.
CULTIVATION: Although dramatic in flower, bikkias are seldom cultivated. Unlikely to tolerate any but the lightest frosts, they require humid conditions, a very freely draining soil, and a sheltered but sunny situation. Propagation is from cuttings or seed; seedlings are minute and growth is slow.

Bikkia campanulata

☀/◐ ⬧ ↔ 4 ft (01.2 m) ↑ 8 ft (2.4 m)

New Caledonian shrub of stiff erect habit, narrowly branched. Leaves stiff, leathery, 3–5 in (8–12 cm) long, crowded at branch ends. Flowers 3 in (8 cm) long, orange-red to purple-red, waxy, in autumn–spring. Zones 10–12.

BILLBERGIA

This genus in the bromeliad (Bromeliaceae) family comprises 65 species and some 500 cultivars. It can be divided into 2 main groups: one from the warmer parts of South America and Mexico, the other from Brazil. Leaves form a tubular rosette,

Bidens ferulifolia

B

and come in all colors and markings; colors are more evident when plants are grown in good light. Flowerheads usually vary from spherical to cylindrical and can have a long stem, so the flowerhead hangs outside the leaf tube. Beneath the flowerhead are large, banner-like, red bracts. Flowers are long, thin, and tubular, topped with petals of many different colors in odd combinations.
CULTIVATION: Indoor culture recommended if in flower; in greenhouse in cool-temperate areas; outdoors with protection from direct sunlight and rain in warm-temperate, subtropical, and tropical areas. Water when potting mix is dry. Adding fertilizer to good quality potting mix is not necessary. Propagate from seed or offsets.

Billbergia distachia var. *straussiana* 'Perriam's Pride'

Billbergia pyramidalis

Billbergia amoena
☀ ⚘ ↔ 12 in (30 cm) ↑ 24 in (60 cm)
From southern Brazil. Leaves green to red, sometimes with white spots. Flowerhead erect, mainly green, with up to 20 flowers; petals green, sometimes with blue tips. Beneath flowerhead are 7 or 8 red bracts, erect or drooping. Zones 9–10.

Billbergia distachia
☀ ⚘ ↔ 4 in (10 cm) ↑ 12 in (30 cm)
From southern Brazil. Leaves green to reddish with a hazy coating, sometimes with spots. Flowerhead hanging from almost erect stem, with up to 6 flowers, each about 2½ in (6 cm) long and mainly green. Petals sometimes tipped blue. *B. d.* var. *straussiana*, petals light green; '**Perriam's Pride**', variegated form. Zones 9–10.

Billbergia elegans
☀ ⚘ ↔ 4 in (10 cm) ↑ 12 in (30 cm)
From southern Brazil. Leaves green with white bands, becoming reddish in good light. Flowerhead erect but sometimes slightly bent, salmon pink, up to 8 flowers, blue-tipped green petals. Several salmon pink bracts below flowerhead. Zones 9–10.

Billbergia euphemiae
☀ ⚘ ↔ 8 in (20 cm) ↑ 24 in (60 cm)
From eastern Brazil. Leaves green, sometimes purple. Flower stem erect to slightly bent. Flowerhead mainly yellow, to 6 in (15 cm) long, with up

Billbergia zebrina

to 30 flowers, petals purple. It is not as hardy as some other *Billbergia* species. Zones 9–10.

Billbergia nutans
FRIENDSHIP PLANT, QUEEN'S TEARS, TARTAN FLOWER
☀ ❄ ↔ 6 in (15 cm) ↑ 10 in (25 cm)
From southern Brazil to Uruguay. Leaves green, thin, to 24 in (60 cm) long. Flowerheads nodding, few green and pink flowers, blue-edged petals. Commonly grown bromeliad, but plants may really be the hybrid cultivar 'Albertii'. Zones 8–10.

Billbergia pyramidalis
☀ ⚘ ↔ 6 in (15 cm) ↑ 20 in (50 cm)
From eastern Brazil. Leaves light to dark green, sometimes with narrow white bands, teeth small. Flowerhead erect, mainly red with frosting, pyramidal shape, up to 40 flowers. Many large red bracts beneath flowerhead. Petals red with bluish tips. *B. p.* var. *concolor* (syn. *B. p.* var. *thyrsoidea*), large, wide, pale green leaves and faint blue hue to petal ends. Zones 9–10.

Billbergia nutans

Billbergia, HC, 'Domingos Martins'

Billbergia zebrina
☀ ⚘ ↔ 6 in (15 cm) ↑ 40 in (100 cm)
From southern Brazil and adjacent countries. Leaves to 3 in (8 cm) wide, pale green with white cross-bands. Flowerhead hanging, to 16 in (40 cm) long, felty, yellowish green. Up to 8 large pale pink to rose bracts above flowerhead. Zones 9–10.

Billbergia Hybrid Cultivars
☀ ⚘ ↔ to 8 in (20 cm) ↑ to 24 in (60 cm)
A range of hybrids, flowers often so beautiful that they inspire among enthusiasts a devotion similar to that seen in orchid lovers. '**Afterglow**', green-petalled flowers, large red bracts; '**Albertii**', green-petalled flowers, blue petal edges; '**Breauteana**', drooping flowerhead, mainly light pink with dark blue petals; '**Catherine Wilson**', erect flowerhead, mainly green, with rose-colored bracts below; '**Domingos Martins**', flowerhead to 6 in (15 cm) long, almost totally red, petals blue; '**Euphemie Waterman**', compact flowerhead, leaves maroon with silvery bands; '**Fascinator**', drooping flowerhead comprising about 15 blooms, petals green with blue edges, large red bracts; '**Hallelujah**', flowerhead mainly light green, erect, up to 10 flowers with blue tips; '**Manda's Othello**', flowerhead erect, mainly pale pink with blue-tipped petals, red bracts beneath; '**Muriel Waterman**', flowerhead slightly bent, mainly green to pale pink with blue petals, flowers rarely; '**Platinum**', flowerhead felty, erect, then curved, up to 14 flowers, pale green and pale red with dark blue-tipped petals; '**Poquito Blanco**', flowerhead erect with few flowers, mainly pale pink, petals pale green with purple edges; '**Windii**', large rose red bracts cover hanging flowerhead, mainly green and white, petals green with blue edges. Zones 9–10.

BISCHOFIA

Genus consists of 2 species of large evergreen trees, one widespread in tropical Asia and western Pacific, the other confined to China. Belongs to diverse euphorbia (Euphorbiaceae) family, but is unusual with its truly compound leaves, each with 3 or 5 broad leaflets with bluntly toothed margins. Flowers small, numerous, in panicles at branch tips; male and female flowers usually on different trees. Brownish berries on female trees each contain 6 seeds. *Bischofia* species valued for timber; bark yields a dye. CULTIVATION: They adapt readily to cultivation, growing fast in tropical and subtropical climates. Most at home in wet tropics, but withstand dry spells. Grows best in deep well-drained soil in sheltered, sunny position; can tolerate some exposure. Propagate from seed.

Bischofia javanica
BISHOPWOOD, JAVA CEDAR, TOOG
☀ ⬥ ↔ 80 ft (24 m) ↑ 100 ft (30 m)
Native to Southeast Asia and Pacific Islands. Large tree with thick trunk, pale brown bark. Leaves comprise 3 leaflets about 4 in (10 cm) long. Flowers tiny, greenish, in panicles, in spring. Fruit globular, orange-brown, in autumn. Zones 9–12.

BISMARCKIA

Endemic to Madagascar, this genus in the family Arecaceae has a single species, a fairly large fan palm with a solitary stout trunk topped by a crown of large fronds. These are roughly circular and divided to about half their depth into stiffly radiating segments. Male and female flowers in panicles on separate trees. Tiny male flowers on curving crimson spikes, female flowers on sparser yellowish spikes. Fruits are date-sized, with a single large seed.

Bischofia javanica

CULTIVATION: Widely grown in tropics and subtropics. Best with a distinct dry season, but tolerates cooler and moister regions if planted in a hot sunny position. Propagate from fresh seed with the flesh stripped off; germination requires a container at least 12 in (30 cm) deep to accommodate the downward-growing cotyledon.

Bismarckia nobilis ★
syn. *Medemia nobilis*
☀ ⬥ ↔ 12 ft (3.5 m) ↑ 60 ft (18 m)
Attractive palm, trunk gray, slightly rough. Fronds large, pale bluish green, on a thick stalk about 6 ft (1.8 m) long, split into an inverted Y-shape at the base. Brown fruits. Zones 10–12.

BIXA

Genus of a single species gives its name to family Bixaceae. Sole member is a small tree from tropical South America. Cultivated as an ornamental and also commercially for an orange food and fabric dye, annatto, obtained from its seeds. Pretty flowers, lush foliage, distinctive bristly red seed pods. CULTIVATION: Most at home in moist, humid, tropics, *Bixa* can be grown in frost-free temperate climate if sheltered from cool winds. Prefers year-round moisture, good drainage, and moderately fertile soil in full sun or partial shade. Cutting-grown plants flower at a younger age than seedlings.

Bixa orellana
ANNATTO, LIPSTICK PLANT
☀ ⬥ ↔ 10–15 ft (3–4.5 m) ↑ 30 ft (9 m)
Large shrub or small tree. Leaves oval, leathery, bright green. Pink or pinkish white flowers in panicles. Clusters of red to red-brown spiny seed pods persist after seeds released. Zones 10–12.

BLANDFORDIA
CHRISTMAS BELLS
Blandfordia is a genus of 4 species of erect, perennial, lily-like herbs from eastern Australia in many habitats, often swampy, usually acid and sandy. Originally part of lily (Liliaceae) family, but now in the Blandfordiaceae

Bismarckia nobilis

Blechnum ambiguum, in the wild, in Erinundra National Park, Victoria, Australia

family. Narrow, tough, grass-like leaves. Flowers 6-lobed, tubular, waxy, pendent and bell-like, hence the common name. The fruits are cylindrical and 3-celled, with each containing numerous, small, brown seeds. CULTIVATION: Grow in constantly moist to wet, well-draining, sandy or acid, organic soil. Propagate from seed; often slow to germinate.

Blandfordia grandiflora
CHRISTMAS BELLS
☀ ❄ ↔ 10 in (25 cm) ↑ 32 in (80 cm)
Heathy coastal habitats in eastern Australia. Leaves grass-like, 32 in (80 cm) long, minutely toothed. Flowers to 2½ in (6 cm) long, waxy, red or orange with yellow lobes, in summer. Zones 8–10.

BLECHNUM

A genus of 200 terrestrial or epiphytic ferns in the Blechnaceae family, most native to Australasia and Southeast Asia and from Mexico to southern South America. A single species, *B. spicant*, is widely distributed in cooler parts of Northern Hemisphere. Erect or running fleshy stems covered in glossy brown scales. New fronds often red, bronze, or pink. Upright fronds, glossy and thick, pinnate or

Bixa orellana

deeply and pinnately lobed, dark green in some species, lighter green in softer species. Fertile fronds, carrying continuous linear spore-bodies parallel to midrib, are narrower and more erect than spreading sterile fronds. CULTIVATION: Mostly frost tender or half-hardy only; prefer slightly acidic, moist, humus-rich soil in a protected dense shade. Propagate from spores on constantly moist sphagnum moss.

Blechnum ambiguum
☀ ⬥ ↔ 36 in (90 cm) ↑ 20 in (50 cm)
Evergreen fern from eastern Australia with short- or medium-long creeping rhizome covered with pale brown scales. Dull mid-green pinnate fronds; tapering pointed leaflets, to 5 in (12 cm) long, with finely toothed margins. Zones 9–10.

Blechnum discolor

Blechnum chilense

Blechnum brasiliense

Blechnum brasiliense

BRAZILIAN TREE FERN

☀ ⁍ ↔ 40–60 in (100–150 cm)
↑ 40–60 in (100–150 cm)

Vigorous tree fern from Brazil, Peru, Guatemala, and Ecuador. Frost tender. New spring growth is bronzed-red. Old plants develop a stout erect trunk to 12 in (30 cm) tall, with radiating tussock of coarse crinkled fronds to 36 in (90 cm) long and 12 in (30 cm) wide with closely crowded leaflets. Remove the faded fronds regularly to maintain the plant's tidy appearance. 'Crispum' has slightly ruffled leaflet margins. Zones 9–11.

Blechnum chilense

☀ ❋ ↔ 36–60 in (90–150 cm)
↑ 36–60 in (90–150 cm)

Fern from South America with bold, dark green, deeply and pinnately lobed fronds, up to 60 in (150 cm) long and 8 in (20 cm) wide. Slowly creeping rhizomes form large clump, with outlying crowns up to 6 in (15 cm) from established clumps. Oldest crowns produce short trunks up to 6 in (15 cm) tall. Zones 8–10.

Blechnum discolor

CROWN FERN, NEW ZEALAND WATER FERN

☀ ❋ ↔ 12–18 in (30–45 cm)
↑ 12–20 in (30–50 cm)

Fern from New Zealand. Short stout rhizomatous trunk. Crown of stiff, polished, dark green frond blades, up to 36 in (90 cm) long and 2–6 in (5–15 cm) wide, gradually tapering at both ends. Younger growth densely clothed in bright brown hairs. Zones 8–9.

Blechnum gibbum ★

MINIATURE TREE FERN

☀ ⁍ ↔ 3–5 ft (0.9–1.5 m)
↑ 3–5 ft (0.9–1.5 m)

Vigorous fern native to tropical and subtropical Pacific Islands. Erect, narrow, black, rooting trunk. Deeply divided, spreading sterile fronds, 3 ft (0.9 m) long, 12 in (30 cm) wide. Fertile fronds are erect with numerous narrow leaflets, 4–6 in (10–15 cm) long. Zones 10–11.

Blechnum minus

SOFT WATER FERN

☀ ⁍ ↔ 8–12 in (20–30 cm)
↑ 8–12 in (20–30 cm)

Fern from Australia and New Zealand with short-creeping rhizome. New growth pink. Sterile fronds dark green, deeply and pinnately lobed, 4–26 in (10–65 cm) long, on stalks of similar length, with 5 to 20 pairs of oblong leaflets. Fertile fronds erect and larger than sterile fronds, with narrower leaflets. 'Hellyer Fountain', fronds gracefully arching, leaflets deeply divided into small, almost circular lobes. Zones 9–10.

Blechnum nudum

BLACK-STEM, FISHBONE WATER FERN

☀ ⁍ ↔ 18–30 in (45–75 cm)
↑ 24–30 in (60–75 cm)

Colonizing fern from southeastern Australia. Erect rhizome, can form sturdy slender trunk covered with black shiny leaf bases. Crown of sterile fronds, 16–40 in (40–100 cm) long. Erect fertile fronds, 8–27 in (20–70 cm) long, on short, glossy, black stalks. Tapering leaflets. 'Cristatum', 18 in (45 cm) tall, unusual and rare crested form; 'Forcett Feather', compact form with leaflets deeply lobed, with upright slightly arching habit, 24 in (60 cm) high and wide. Zones 8–10.

Blechnum penna-marina

syn. Blechnum alpinum

☀/❂ ❋ ↔ 3–10 in (8–25 cm)
↑ 3–10 in (8–25 cm)

Dwarf colony-forming fern from temperate and subantarctic South America and Australasia. Rhizome creeping, slender, produces runners. Tufts of spreading, thick, dark green sterile fronds 4–8 in (10–20 cm) long, with numerous linear leaflets. Erect fertile fronds brownish green and longer than sterile fronds. 'Cristatum', frond apex neatly crested. Zones 8–9.

Blechnum spicant

DEER FERN, HARD FERN, LADDER FERN

☀/☀ ❋ ↔ 12–18 in (30–45 cm)
↑ 12–18 in (30–45 cm)

Low-growing tufted fern from North America, Europe, and temperate Asia. Rhizome short-creeping, erect, stout. Spreading, lance-shaped, leathery, dark green sterile fronds, 6–8 in (15–20 cm) long and about 1½ in (35 mm) across, with up to 60 pairs of closely set leaflets. The fertile fronds are taller, up to 30 in (75 cm) long.

'Cristatum', compact form reaching 4–8 in (10–20 cm) high, with crested frond tips. Zones 5–9.

BLETILLA

CHINESE GROUND ORCHID

This genus in the family Orchidaceae contains about 10 species of deciduous sympodial terrestrial orchids from temperate regions of China, Taiwan, and Japan. They are dormant in autumn and winter, blooming with the flush of new growth in early spring. CULTIVATION: They require a well drained, but rich, potting mixture that retains moisture, and also can be grown in the garden. They can be grown in semi-shade to full sun, and appreciate regular watering in spring and summer. Caterpillars can often disfigure the leaves, particularly the young shoots after their dormant period. They will withstand cold winters, however, the new growth needs to be protected from any late heavy frosts.

Bletilla striata

☼/❂ ❋ ↔ 12–48 in (30–120 cm)
↑ 12–24 in (30–60 cm)

A hardy species, frequently grown as a garden plant, often without the owner knowing it is an orchid! Up to eight 2 in (5 cm) wide pale pink to rose-purple (rarely white) blooms that resemble a small Cattleya flower. There is also a form with a variegated leaf. Zones 6–11.

BOCCONIA

This genus of 9 species from subtropical and tropical America is part of the poppy (Papaveraceae) family. The

Blechnum spicant

Blechnum penna-marina

Blechnum spicant 'Cristatum'

Bolusanthus speciosus

Bletilla striata

leaves, while very large, are at least reminiscent of garden poppies, but the flowers are not what would commonly be thought of as poppy-like. They lack petals and are carried in large plume-like terminal racemes. The plants normally start as a single trunk topped with a head of leaves, but with age, side shoots and suckers develop to form multiple trunks. All parts release a yellow latex if cut.
CULTIVATION: *Bocconia* plants can tolerate light frosts but need a mild climate to thrive. They grow best in moist, well-drained, humus-rich soil with a sunny or partly shaded exposure. They are very vigorous plants and care should be taken to plant them only where their seeding and suckering can be controlled.

Bocconia arborea

Found in Central America. Leaves deeply cut and divided, 18 in (45 cm) long, 12 in (30 cm) wide, toothed, often downy on undersides. Flowers in racemes, which are up to 8 in (20 cm) long, in summer. Zones 10–12.

Bocconia frutescens
TREE CELANDINE

Evergreen tree considered a noxious weed in Hawaii. Leaves 15 in (38 cm) long, gray-green, deeply cut almost to midrib, hairy when young. Racemes of flowers in shades of pink, cream, and green, in summer. Zones 9–11.

BOLTONIA
FALSE CHAMOMILE

A genus of about 8 species of tall perennials in the daisy (Asteraceae) family, the plants are found in central and eastern USA and northeastern Asia, where they grow in moist soils.

Their upright leafy stems bear masses of daisy-like flowers in late summer and autumn. The flowers have a yellow eye and are white, pink, mauve, or purple.
CULTIVATION: Showy and easily grown in borders or "wild" gardens, these plants can be cultivated in any moderately fertile soil in full sun or part-shade. Stake in exposed positions. Regular division will maintain vigor. Propagate by division or from seed.

Boltonia asteroides

Clump-forming perennial from eastern USA. Leaves narrow, to 4 in (10 cm) long. Erect leafy stems bear masses of starry white daisies in late summer–autumn. *B. a.* var. *latisquama*, taller plant with large mauve daisies. *B. a.* 'Snowbank', strong grower to 7 ft (2 m) tall, white daisies. Zones 4–10.

BOLUSANTHUS
TREE WISTERIA

This single-species genus belongs to the pea-flower subfamily of the legume (Fabaceae) family. Found in southern Africa, this deciduous large shrub or small tree with long pinnate leaves and drooping racemes of pea-flowers resembles *Wisteria*. An attractive and long-lived plant, it is well suited to the warm-temperate or subtropical garden.
CULTIVATION: Tolerant of very light frost once established, tree wisteria is best grown in a warm climate with ample summer moisture. It prefers soil that is well drained, not too

Bomarea costaricensis, Costa Rica

heavy, and preferably rich in humus. Plant in full sun and, if necessary, trim to shape after flowering. Propagate from seed.

Bolusanthus speciosus
TREE WISTERIA

Slightly weeping branches, upright habit. Winter- or dry-season deciduous, depending on climate. Racemes of violet-blue flowers, on bare wood, in early spring. Pinnate leaves, to 6 in (15 cm) long, covered with fine hairs when young. Zones 9–11.

BOMAREA
CLIMBING ALSTROEMERIA

The South American genus, containing around 100 species, is a member of the alstroemeria (Alstroemeriaceae) family. Tuberous-rooted perennials, many of them climb, usually by twining. Most have elongated, lance-shaped, 4–6 in (10–15 cm) long leaves on wiry stems that grow very quickly. From late spring heads of simple or compound, pendulous, tubular to bell-shaped flowers are produced, in a variety of warm colors often marked with contrasting spots. Flowers have 6 tepals in

Bocconia arborea

Bocconia frutescens

2 whorls. Roasted *Bomarea* tubers often feature in the diet of indigenous South American people.
CULTIVATION: Although nominally evergreen, the tops are frost tender and will die down or become untidy over winter in all but the mildest temperate regions. However, as long as the roots are well insulated with mulch, new shoots will appear in spring. Otherwise, lift the tubers for winter. Plant in moist, humus-rich, well-drained soil with at least half-day sun. Propagate by division or from seed.

Bomarea caldasii

Northern South American species with simple open heads of 2 in (5 cm) long flowers. Outer tepals pinkish red to red-brown, inner tepals yellow to orange with brown, red, or green spotting. Zones 9–11.

Bomarea costaricensis

Costa Rican species with 2 in (5 cm) long flowers in simple heads. Inner and outer tepals are warm red-brown with darker spotting inside. Fruits open to show red seeds. Zones 9–11.

Bomarea caldasii

BOMBAX

This distinctive genus of large tropical deciduous trees, a member of the family Bombacaceae, consists of around 20 species from tropical Africa, southern Asia, and northern Australia. They grow around rock outcrops or along river valleys. Trunks are thick and straight, with tiered branches, often buttressed at the base. Bark is often armed with conical prickles. Leaves are compound with 5 or more leaflets attached to a common stalk. Appearing on leafless branches in the dry season, the large flowers have 5 tongue-shaped red, white, or yellow petals and a central mass of stamens. Large fruits split when ripe to release oily seeds embedded in white hairs. CULTIVATION: Easily grown in the tropics; plants prefer a sheltered site, deep, fertile, well-drained soil, and subsoil moisture. Fast growing when young; can be short lived if attacked by termites and other insects. Propagate from fresh seed or tip cuttings, planted in the wet season.

Bombax ceiba
syn. *Bombax malabaricum*
SILK COTTON TREE
☀ ☘ ↔ 30–40 ft (9–12 m) ↑ 60 ft (18 m)
This widespread Asian species is a broadly spreading, heavy-limbed tree.

Trunk prickly when young. Flowers profuse, deep scarlet, appear in the tropical dry season (spring). In Asia, young leaves and flowers used as vegetables; fiber obtained from the bark. Zones 10–12.

BONGARDIA

This is a monotypic genus in the barberry (Berberidaceae) family. The species is a perennial herb with a large rounded tuber and attractive pinnate leaves. It is native to Greece and Middle Eastern areas.
CULTIVATION: In warm climates grow outdoors in sandy well-drained soil in full sun. It requires hot dry conditions during its summer dormancy and is liable to rot if moisture collects at the neck. In cooler climates it can be grown in a cool greenhouse. Propagate from seed.

Bongardia chrysogonum
☀ ☘ ↔ 12–20 in (30–50 cm)
↑ 12–24 in (30–60 cm)

Pinnately divided leaves 4–10 in (10–25 cm) long arise directly from the tuber. Bluish green foliage often flushed purple-red at base. Lemon yellow flowers on lax panicles held above the foliage in spring. The fruits are oval, and tinged with red. Zones 9–10.

Boophone disticha, in the wild, South Africa

BOOPHONE

From South Africa to eastern Africa, the 6 to 8 species in this genus are bulbs and belong to the amaryllis (Amaryllidaceae) family. The bulbs grow above, rather than below, the ground, and can reach a considerable size—up to 12 in (30 cm) in diameter. Fan-shaped leaves are up to 20 in (50 cm) long; some are a powdery blue color and most have very wavy margins. Produced before the leaves, the inflorescence can be up to 12 in (30 cm) tall, and consists of hundreds of small flowers arranged in a sphere. Indigenous people have used these plants to poison arrows; it also has medicinal uses.
CULTIVATION: These plants are easy to grow in sandy well-drained soil, as long as they are given a rest in the appropriate season. Some are winter dormant, others are summer dormant, so water at the wrong time of year can be fatal. Propagate from seed.

Boophone disticha
BUSHMAN'S POISON BULB, FIRE BALL, OX KILLER FAN, TUMBLE WEED, VELDT FAN
☀ ☘ ↔ 4–8 in (10–20 cm) ↑ 12 in (30 cm)
Summer-growing perennial from South Africa, Botswana, Swaziland, Zimbabwe, Kenya, and Uganda. Fan

of wavy leaves produced after flowering from large bulb. Single inflorescence with hundreds of individual pink flowers in spring. Zones 9–11.

BORAGO
BORAGE, TAILWORT
Part of the borage (Boraginaceae) family, this genus is made up of just 3 species of annuals or short-lived perennials from Europe that are usually used in the herb garden or wilder spots where their self-seeding tendencies won't be a problem. The leaves are rough to touch and the summer flowers are usually a rich blue. The flowers are much loved by bees, and can be eaten in salads. The aromatic young leaves can also be eaten.
CULTIVATION: Any moisture-retentive soil in sun or half-sun will suit. Propagation is from self-sown seed that will need to be thinned out.

Borago officinalis
BORAGE
☀ ✳ ↔ 10–12 in (25–30 cm)
↑ 20–24 in (50–60 cm)

Vigorous, self-seeding, upright annual. rough leaves to 10 in (25 cm) long. Large open heads of rich blue flowers in summer to 1 in (25 mm) across. *B. o.* f. *alba*, white-flowered form that comes true from seed as long as it is not near blue forms. Zones 5–10.

Borago pygmaea
syn. *Borago laxiflora*
☀ ✳ ↔ 10–12 in (25–30 cm)
↑ 10–12 in (25–30 cm)

Short-lived open-growing perennial. Rough leaves to 6 in (15 cm) long. Bright blue flowers in summer. Usually not as invasive as *B. officinalis*. Zones 7–11.

BORASSODENDRON

This genus of 2 species of single-stemmed fan-leafed palms, belonging to the family Arecaceae, occurs in high-rainfall forests of peninsular

Borago officinalis

Borago officinalis f. *alba*

Malaysia, Thailand, and Borneo, often on limestone. The trunks lack a crownshaft, while the leaf stalks are relatively thin and lack spines, but have a hard razorsharp edge. The leaf blade has several segments, separate to near the base. Inflorescences arise from among the leaf bases; male and female flowers appear on separate plants. Male flowers are borne on pendulous branched inflorescences, and the much larger female flowers on unbranched inflorescences. Fruits are large, 3-celled, and more-or-less globular; each cell has 1 seed. In the past, new shoots and fruits have been eaten by indigenous peoples.
CULTIVATION: Requires a wet tropical climate and a sheltered environment; best planted in deep alluvial soils with high water-table. Not well adapted to containers. Propagate from seed, which requires bottom heat for germination.

Borassodendron machadonis ★
☀ ⚓ ↔ 50 ft (15 m) ↑ to 70 ft (21 m)
Now rare in the wild, occurring in northern peninsular Malaysia and southern Thailand. Large shiny green leaves to 20 ft (6 m) long in a dense crown, blades up to 12 ft (3.5 m) wide. Cream flowers. Fruits globular, 4 in (10 cm) in diameter, purplish green. Zones 11–12.

BORASSUS
A genus of massive fan palms in the family Arecaceae, *Borassus* consists of around 10 species ranging through tropical Africa and Asia as far east as New Guinea, growing mainly on open sandy plains and along river banks. The thick solitary trunks are generally covered in the remains of old frond stalks, forming a criss-crossing pattern. The fronds are divided into tapering segments that radiate stiffly or droop. Male and female flowers are borne on

Borassodendron machadonis

Borassus flabellifer

different trees; flowering branches bear small flowers on lateral branches. On the females large fruits with a fibrous husk develop. Some species have a wide range of uses, most notably as sources of palm sugar.
CULTIVATION: Successful cultivation requires a tropical climate. With access to groundwater, they will tolerate a long dry season, but they thrive in the wet tropics. Full sun is essential, and a deep, porous, well-drained soil is preferred. Propagation is from seed only; When seeds sprout, plant out into individual containers.

Borassus aethiopum
☀ ⚓ ↔ 15 ft (4.5 m) ↑ 60 ft (18 m)
Occurs in tropical Africa. Crown of bluish green fronds up to 12 ft (3.5 m) long. Trunk thickened below flower branches. Male flowering branches to 6 ft (1.8 m) long. Edible fruits orange-brown, to 6 in (15 cm). Zones 11–12.

Borassus flabellifer ★
LONTAR PALM, PALMYRA PALM
☀ ⚓ ↔ 15 ft (4.5 m) ↑ 60 ft (18 m)
Ranging from southern India and Sri Lanka to New Guinea and Indochina, similar in size to *B. aethiopum*. Fronds larger, to 10 ft (3 m) across; fruits larger, up to 8 in (20 cm) in diameter. Zones 11–12.

Borassus sundaicus
LONTAR PALM
☀ ⚓ ↔ 15 ft (4.5 m) ↑ 60 ft (18 m)
Hardly distinguishable from *B. flabellifer* and many authorities do not recognize it. Identical in overall appearance to that species, showing only minor differences in structure of

Borassus aethiopum

flowering branchlets and seeds. The name is also applied to southern lontar palms. Zones 11–12.

BORONIA
Noted for its sweet fragrance, early spring blooms, and aromatic foliage, this genus is a member of the rue (Rutaceae) family and consists of approximately 100 species of small to medium-sized, compact, evergreen shrubs, many in Australia. They have simple or pinnate leaves and small 4-petalled flowers that may be open and star-shaped or bell-like with overlapping petals. Flowers come in a range of colors from white, pink, and bluish mauve to red, yellow, yellow-green, and brown. Some species can be short lived.
CULTIVATION: Locate boronias in sheltered positions with the protection of other plants in sun or part-shade. The soil should be well drained with a fairly high organic content; avoid

Borassus sundaicus

drying out. If growing in pots, ensure that the potting mix does not contain added fertilizers with high phosphorus levels. The flowers generally last well when picked. After flowering, up to one half of the plant can be removed to prolong life and improve bushiness. Propagation is from half-hardened tip cuttings.

Boronia ledifolia

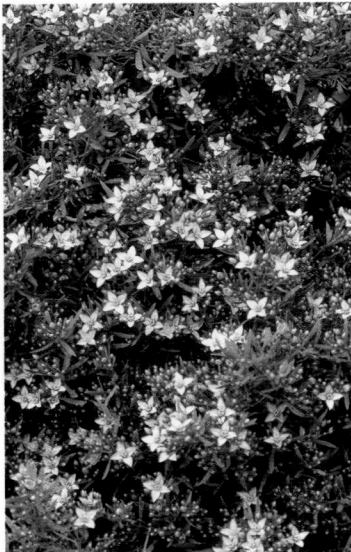

Boronia denticulata

Boronia crenulata

☀ ❧ ↔ 3 ft (0.9 m) ↕ 3 ft (0.9 m)

From Western Australia. Upright
bushy habit. Aromatic leaves. Masses
of pink star-like flowers, in late
winter–summer. Attractive plant for
a rock garden. Grows best in filtered
shade, in a well-drained position
with some moisture. Also useful
for growing beneath taller shrubs.
Zones 9–10.

Boronia denticulata

☀ ❧ ↔ 3 ft (0.9 m) ↕ 4–6 ft (1.2–1.8 m)

From Western Australia. Strong-
growing, bushy, evergreen shrub.
Narrow toothed leaves, strongly aromatic. Pink or mauve starry flowers in
loose clusters appear in late winter–

Boronia crenulata

spring. Adaptable in most soils, but
likes some moisture. Trim lightly after
flowering to retain a pleasing shape.
Zones 9–10.

Boronia heterophylla

KALGAN BORONIA, RED BORONIA

☀ ❧ ↔ 4 ft (1.2 m) ↕ 6 ft (1.8 m)

Evergreen shrub native to southern
Western Australia. Leaves bright
green, aromatic. Flowers fragrant,
deep pink, bell-shaped, in late
winter–early spring. Grown commercially as a cut flower. Prefers partially
shaded, protected position, with a
cool, moist root run. Zones 9–10.

Boronia ledifolia

LEDUM BORONIA, SYDNEY BORONIA

☀ ❧ ↔ 5 ft (1.5 m) ↕ 5 ft (1.5 m)

Erect multi-branched shrub from east
coast of Australia. Leaves dark green,
trifoliate, emit a pungent oil on
crushing. Flowers bright pink, starry,
in late winter–early spring. Great cut
flowers. Best in well-drained moist
situation, dappled shade. Zones 9–11.

Boronia heterophylla

Boronia megastigma ★

BROWN BORONIA

☀ ❧ ↔ 3 ft (0.9 m) ↕ 3 ft (0.9 m)

From southwest Western Australia.
Popular species with light green
foliage, slender stems, spicy aromatic
leaves. Flowers rich yellow and brown,
pendent, bell-like, highly fragrant, in
late winter–early spring. Often short
lived; best in well-drained moist soil.
'Harlequin', yellow and brown
flowers; 'Heaven Scent', compact
dwarf, brown flowers; 'Jack Maguire's
Red', scarlet flowers; 'Lutea', clear

greenish yellow flowers, foliage lighter
green than species; 'Virtuoso', near-
black petals. Zones 9–11.

Boronia molloyae

syn. *Boronia elatior*

TALL BORONIA

☀ ❧ ↔ 4 ft (1.2 m) ↕ 6 ft 1.8 m)

Dense, multi-branched, evergreen
shrub native to Western Australia.
Stems hairy; aromatic divided leaves.
Deep pink bell-like flowers, in
spring–summer. Excellent for cutting.
Add organic matter to keep soil moist
in summer. Zones 9–11.

Boronia muelleri

☀ ❧ ↔ 4 ft (1.2 m) ↕ 5 ft (1.5 m)

An evergreen shrub with aromatic
fern-like foliage, from southeastern
Australia. Flowers pale pink, starry, in
clusters on arching branches, in late
winter–spring. Best in a shady moist
site with good drainage. 'Sunset
Serenade', a compact form, pale pink
flowers turn deep pink with age.
Zones 9–11.

Boronia megastigma cultivar

Boronia megastigma

Bossiaea scolopendria

Bossiaea linophylla

Bossiaea walkeri

Boronia pinnata

PINNATE BORONIA

☀ ❄ ↔5 ft (1.5 m) ↑5 ft (1.5 m)

Erect shrub from temperate east coast Australia. Pinnate leaves, strongly aromatic. Fragrant, mauve to purple, starry flowers, in loose sprays, in late winter–spring. Best in sheltered partially shaded position. Trim lightly after flowering. '**Spring White**', profuse white flowers. Zones 9–11.

Boronia serrulata

NATIVE ROSE

☀ ❄ ↔30 in (75 cm) ↑5 ft (1.5 m)

Evergreen shrub confined to Sydney district in eastern Australia. Leaves rich green, diamond-shaped, finely toothed. Flowers fragrant, vivid pink, cup-shaped, in spring. Excellent as cut flowers. Difficult to cultivate. Zones 10–11.

BOSEA

This genus of evergreen shrubs contains 3 species that are geographically widely separated: one in the Canary Islands, one in Cyprus, and one in the western Himalayas. The genus is of interest as being a woody member of the amaranth (Amaranthaceae) family, which otherwise predominantly consists of annuals and perennials. *Bosea* species have many crowded cane-like stems from ground level, smallish simple leaves with smooth margins, and tiny white or greenish flowers in branched spikes at ends of branches. The fruits are very small berries, which have varied local uses as food

plants and in traditional medicine. CULTIVATION: Although rarely found in cultivation they are easily grown in any well-drained soil, preferring full sun and a warm sheltered position. They resprout vigorously after being cut back and can be grown as an informal kind of hedge. Propagation is easily achieved from cuttings, seed, or root division.

Bosea yervamora

HEDIONDO, HIERBAMORA

☀ ❄ ↔5 ft (1.5 m) ↑8 ft (2.4 m)

From the Canary Islands, a shrub with crowded scrambling stems. Leaves deep green. Flowers tiny, green, in clusters, in winter. Red berries less than ¼ in (6 mm) in diameter. Zones 9–11.

Bosea yervamora

BOSSIAEA

This is an Australian genus of some 40 species of small evergreen shrubs, belonging to the pea-flower subfamily of the legume (Fabaceae) family. They usually have small rounded leaves in pairs. The foliage is often downy when young and occasionally spine-tipped. The pea-flowers are borne singly or in clusters of 2 or 3 blooms, which open from spring to early summer and are often very brightly colored. Generally they open only in sunny conditions. CULTIVATION: Plant in full sun or partial shade with light well-drained soil. Some species occur naturally in marshy areas but in cultivation they are best kept on the dry side. Light feeding and watering will produce more flowers, but if too well cared for the plants will become very leafy and their lives may be shortened. Propagation is from seed, which should be soaked before sowing, or by taking small half-hardened tip cuttings.

Bossiaea linophylla

☀/☀ ❄ ↔4 ft (1.2 m) ↑10 ft (3 m)

Shrub native to Western Australia. Very narrow lance-shaped leaves tipped with a sharp spine. Flowers are small, golden yellow with a red keel, and often continue well into autumn. Zones 9–10.

Bossiaea scolopendria

CENTIPEDE PEA

☀ ❄ ↔27 in (70 cm) ↑36 in (90 cm)

From central coastal region of New South Wales, Australia. Found on

poor sandstone soil. Flattened leathery stems, to ½ in (12 mm) wide; alternating tiny leaves. Flowers golden yellow, red-brown center, at stem tips, in late winter–spring. Zones 9–11.

Bossiaea walkeri

CACTUS PEA

☀ ❄ ↔8 ft (2.4 m) ↑8 ft (2.4 m)

From south of Australia in arid and semi-arid regions. Tangle of flattened, dull blue-green, leafless branches with whitish crust. Pale red pea-flowers, 1 in (25 mm) long, appear in spring–autumn. Zones 9–11.

BOUGAINVILLEA

The 14 species of this South American genus in the four-o'clock (Nyctaginaceae) family, seen in warm-temperate to tropical regions as spectacular climbers, are really scrambling shrubs and usually remain fairly compact or behave as ground covers if left freestanding. Leaves are thin, sometimes downy, and broadly elliptical with pointed tips; stems are protected by long narrow thorns, found at the leaf

Boronia pinnata

Boronia serrulata

Bougainvillea × *buttiana* 'Barbara Karst'

B. × *buttiana* 'Cherry Blossom'

B. × *buttiana* 'Coconut Ice'

B. × *buttiana* 'Enid Lancaster'

B. × *buttiana* 'Lady Mary Baring'

Bougainvillea × *buttiana* 'Mahara'

B. × *buttiana* 'Raspberry Ice'

axils. Foliage is evergreen or deciduous, depending on the species and climate. True flowers, in groups of 1 to 3, are tubular, creamy white to yellow, and around 1 in (25 mm) wide, largely hidden by brightly colored petal-like bracts. The genus is named for the French explorer Louis Antoine de Bougainville (1729–1811).
CULTIVATION: Bougainvilleas will not tolerate heavy or repeated frosts. They prefer light well-drained soil, a sunny position, and will perform better if

watered well in summer but not overfed. Bougainvilleas can withstand the heavy pruning necessary to keep the plants shrub-like. Propagate by taking firm cuttings in summer.

Bougainvillea × *buttiana*
☼ ✤ ↔ 10–20 ft (3–6 m) ↑ 17 ft (5 m)
Hybrid between *B. glabra* and *B. peruviana*. Broad leaves to more than 4 in (10 cm) long with downy midrib. Small bracts but densely packed. Cross originated in Trinidad

around 1900 and is named after the original cultivar 'Mrs Butt'. Popular hybrid cultivars include: '**Afterglow**', 8–15 ft (2.4–4.5 m) high, pink suffused orange, fairly sparse foliage; '**Barbara Karst**', 12–20 ft (3.5–6 m) high, vigorous, red in full sun, deep carmine-pink in part-shade; '**Brilliant Variegated**', 4–6 ft (1.2–1.8 m) tall, mounding shrub, gray-green and silver variegated foliage, red-brown bracts; '**Cherry Blossom**' (syns *B.* 'Bridal Bouquet', 'Limberlost

Beauty'), 7 ft (2 m) tall, compact, slow-growing, white bracts tinted pink, double; '**Coconut Ice**', 12–15 ft (3.5–4.5 m) high, irregularly marked pink and white bracts; '**Enid Lancaster**' (syns *B.* 'California Gold', 'Hawaiian Glow', 'Sunset', *B.* × *b.* 'Golden Glow'), 12–15 ft (3.5–4.5 m) tall, soft yellow bracts ageing to gold; '**Killie Campbell**' (syns *B.* 'Green Light', 'Rose Amber'), 12–15 ft (3.5–4.5 m) tall, trailing habit, long-flowering, large bracts open orange-red and age to magenta; '**Lady Mary Baring**', 12–15 ft (3.5–4.5 m) high, quick-growing, yellow; '**Louise Wathen**' (syn. *B.* 'Orange King'), 15–20 ft (4.5–6 m) high, long stems, copper-orange bracts, tender; '**Mahara**' (syns *B.* 'Manila Red', 'Princess Mahara'), 12–15 ft (3.5–4.5 m) tall, dark green foliage, purple double bracts, '**Mrs Butt**' (syn. *B.* 'Crimson Lake'), 12–15 ft (3.5–4.5 m) high, crimson red, needs heat to flower well; '**Purple Queen**', 4–8 ft (1.2–2.4 m) tall, bushy, deep purple bracts; '**Raspberry Ice**' (syn. *B.* 'Raspberry Ice'), 3–4 ft (0.9–1.2 m) high, bushy, red new growth becomes green with cream to golden edges, vivid magenta bracts, good ground cover or for hanging baskets; '**Rosenka**', 4–8 ft (1.2–2.4 m) high, golden yellow ageing to soft pink, with large papery bracts; '**Tango**' (syn. *B.* 'Miss Manila'), 12–15 ft (3.5–4.5 m) high, pinkish red bracts; and **Texas Dawn**/'**Monas**' (syns *B.* 'Purple King', 'Robyn's Glory'), 12–15 ft (3.5–4.5 m) high, large clusters of purple-pink bracts. Zones 9–12.

Bougainvillea glabra
PAPER FLOWER
☼ ✤ ↔ 15 ft (4.5 m) ↑ 10–12 ft (3–5 m)
Summer-flowering Brazilian native, dark green foliage with few hairs. Leaves to 5 in (12 cm). Trained as a climber, grows to a height or spread of up to 30 ft (9 m). Flower bracts white to magenta. '**Alba**', pure white bracts; '**Cypheri**', deep pink bracts;

Bougainvillea glabra

'Magnifica', masses of short-lived purple bracts; '**Rainbow**', pinkish red bracts that develop various pink tones with age; '**Variegated**', mauve bracts, gray-green and cream variegated foliage. Zones 10–12.

Bougainvillea spectabilis
syn. *Bougainvillea brasiliensis*

↔ 15 ft (4.5 m) ↑ 12 ft (3.5 m)

Vigorous species from Brazil. Velvety leaves up to 4 in (10 cm) long. Flowers mass of panicles of pink to purple bracts, in spring. Stems armed with vicious curved thorns. Zones 10–12.

Bougainvillea **Hybrid Cultivars**

↔ 5–20 ft (1.5–6 m)
↑ 2–20 ft (0.6–6 m)

There are many hybrid bougainvilleas with obscure parentage. As might be expected, they are a variable lot covering most sizes and colors. Popular hybrids include: '**Alexandra**', 15–20 ft (4.5–6 m) high, vigorous, deep magenta-purple; '**Betty Hendry**' (syn. 'Indian Maid'), 8–15 ft (2.4–4.5 m) high, long-flowering, red with occasional purple and yellow flecks; Camarillo Fiesta/'**Monle**', 15–20 ft (4.5–6 m) high, small leaves with magenta and copper bracts; '**Closeburn**' (syns 'Helen Johnson', 'Temple Fire', 'Tom Thumb'), 3–5 ft (0.9–1.5 m) high, spreading shrub, good in containers, coppery red bracts; '**Crimson Jewel**', 2–4 ft (0.6–1.2 m) tall, spreading trailing shrub, ground cover or hanging basket, deep pinkish red; '**Don Mario**', 12–15 ft (3.5–4.5 m) high, purple-red; '**Elizabeth Doxey**' (syns 'Apple Blossom', 'Jamaica White'), 12–15 ft (3.5–4.5 m) tall, white bracts; '**Elsbet**', 8–12 ft (2.4–3.5 m) high, shrubby with dark leaves and small deep purple bracts; '**Hawaiian White**', 15–20 ft (4.5–6 m) high, vigorous, white bracts with green veining; '**Isabel Greensmith**', 12–15 ft (3.5–4.5 m) tall, orange to coppery red; '**James Walker**', 15–20 ft (4.5–6 m) tall, vigorous, deep magenta, large bracts; '**Jamhuri**', 15–20 ft (4.5–6 m) tall, vigorous, purple-red to red bracts; '**Juanita Hatten**', 8–15 ft (2.4–4.5 m) high, deep purple-pink; '**La Jolla**', 3–6 ft (0.9–2 m) high, compact shrub, bright red; '**Lavender Queen**', 12–15 ft (3.5–4.5 m) high, soft purple; '**Mary Palmer Special**', 15–20 ft (4.5–6 m) tall, magenta-pink; '**Mary Palmer's Enchantment**', 15–20 ft (4.5–6 m) tall, very vigorous, pure white bracts; '**Oo-La-La**', 4–8 ft (1.2–2.4 m) high, shrubby growth with deep magenta bracts; '**Pink Tiara**', 8–15 ft (2.4–4.5 m) high, pale pink, long-flowering; '**Purple Robe**', 12–15 ft (3.5–4.5 m) tall, large, bright purple-pink bracts; '**Rubyana**', 15–20 ft (4.5–6 m) tall, vigorous, dark foliage, purple-pink bracts; '**San Diego Red**' (syn. Scarlett O'Hara), 12–15 ft (3.5–4.5 m) high, massed bright scarlet bracts ageing to magenta, bronze young growth; '**Southern Rose**', 12–15 ft (3.5–4.5 m) high, bright pink; '**Tahitian Dawn**', 15–20 ft (4.5–6 m) tall, vigorous, gold bracts ageing to pink; '**Tahitian Maid**', 6–12 ft (1.8–3.5 m) high, deep pink double flowers; '**Thomasii**' (syn. 'Rosea'), 15–20 ft (4.5–6 m) high, vigorous climber, deep reddish pink bracts; '**Torch Glow**', 3–6 ft (0.9–2 m) tall, shrubby, vivid magenta-pink bracts at the stem tips; and '**White Madonna**', 12–15 ft (3.5–4.5 m) tall, pure white bracts. Zones 9–12.

Bougainvillea, Hybrid Cultivar, 'Elizabeth Doxey'

B., HC, 'San Diego Red'

B., Hybrid Cultivar, 'Sundance'

B., HC, 'Hawaiian White'

B., Hybrid Cultivar, 'Sunset'

B., Hybrid Cultivar, 'Alexandra'

B., Hybrid Cultivar, 'Elsbet'

B., Hybrid Cultivar, 'Gold Sun'

B., Hybrid Cultivar, 'Jamhuri'

B., Hybrid Cultivar, 'Zakiriana'

B., HC, 'Mary Palmer Special'

B., Hybrid Cultivar, 'Purple Robe'

B., Hybrid Cultivar, 'Rubyana'

B., HC, 'Juanita Hatten'

B., Hybrid Cultivar, 'Zulu Queen'

Bouvardia ternifolia, in the wild, Vera Cruz, Mexico

Bouteloua gracilis

BOUTELOUA

GRAMA GRASS

Found from southern USA and West Indies to Central and South America, this genus of 39 annual or perennial grasses belongs to the family Poaceae. Features clusters or clumps of stiff slender flower stems. Panicles of flowers have one or many branches of delicate, stalkless, "mosquito-like" spikelets on wiry stems, in summer. Leaves with flat or folded blades arise from a central base.
CULTIVATION: Propagate from seed; any garden soil; open sunny position.

Bouteloua curtipendula

SIDEOATS GRASS

☼ ❅ ↔ 12–18 in (30–45 cm)
↑ 24–32 in (60–80 cm)

Grass native to temperate areas from Canada to Argentina. Panicles of flowers with 30 to 80 branches; 1 to 12 spikelets, each to ½ in (12 mm) long, per branch. Bluish green, rough or slightly hairy leaf blades, to ¼ in (6 mm) wide. Zones 4–9.

Bouteloua gracilis ★

syns *Bouteloua oligostachya, Chondrosum gracile, C. oligostachyum*

BLUE GRAMA, MOSQUITO GRASS, NAVAJITA AZUL, NAVAJITA COMUN

☼ ❅ ↔ 12 in (30 cm) ↑ 24 in (60 cm)

Grass from south and southwestern USA and Mexico. Dense arching

panicles of flowers with 1 to 4 branches; 1 to 12 spikelets, each to ¼ in (6 mm) long, per branch. Narrow, wispy, sometimes hairy leaf blades, rough to touch. '**Lovington**', flowers purple fading to yellow. Zones 8–10.

BOUVARDIA

This genus, reaching from southern North America to northern South America, includes several evergreen shrubs among its 30 or so species, and belongs to the madder (Rubiaceae) family. *Bouvardia* tend to be rather sprawling, weak-stemmed plants that need support to keep them upright. Their leaves are not large but they are a pleasant shade of deep green and are usually glossy. The long-tubed flowers are the main attraction. The brighter colors are visually striking, while those in lighter shades or white are fragrant and popular as cut flowers.
CULTIVATION: *Bouvardia* species tolerate light frost only and need a mild climate with rich well-drained soil to flower well. They are best in partial shade and also perform well as greenhouse and conservatory plants. Although inclined to be straggly, light trimming helps to keep them compact and bushy.

Bouvardia longiflora

SCENTED BOUVARDIA

☼ ☙ ↔ 3 ft (0.9 m) ↑ 3 ft (0.9 m)

From Mexico. A lax shrub with weak stems, easily damaged. Highly fragrant, waxy white, long-tubed, 4-petalled flowers, in autumn–winter. Needs sheltered site. '**Albatross**' (syn. *B. humboldtii* 'Albatross'), larger white flowers. Zones 10–11.

Bouvardia ternifolia

☼ ☙ ↔ 3 ft (0.9 m) ↑ 3 ft (0.9 m)

Soft-stemmed evergreen shrub native to Arizona, Texas, and Mexico. Clustered in corymbs, the tubular

Bouvardia longiflora

flowers are a vivid red. There are several cultivars with flowers in various pink and red shades. Zones 9–11.

BOWENIA

This genus, belonging to the family Boweniaceae, is composed of 2 very similar species of cycads native to the rainforests of coastal northern Queensland, Australia. They have vigorous underground tubers and do not produce a trunk, instead sending up their branched fern-like "fronds" directly from the ground. The separate male and female cones also form at ground level and occur throughout much of the year.
CULTIVATION: These cycads prefer wet tropical conditions and revel in the dripping humidity of the rainforest. In temperate climates they require a heated greenhouse and do not readily adapt to normal indoor conditions and cultivation as house plants. Propagation is from seed or by dividing the rootstock.

Bowenia spectabilis

BYFIELD FERN

☼ ☙ ↔ 5 ft (1.5 m) ↑ 5 ft (1.5 m)

From coastal northern Queensland, Australia. Glossy, deep green, arching leaves, smooth-edged leaflets up to 4 in (10 cm) long. Male cones are dark green and cream. Female cones are pineapple-shaped, yielding purple-green seeds. Zones 11–12.

BOWIEA

This genus of 2 very similar species of perennial, South African succulent plants belongs to the hyacinth (Hyacinthaceae) family. The plants consist of many overlapping scales, which form a tight, pale green, spherical bulb that grows to 8 in (20 cm) above the soil. Dormant in winter, when the outer scales and many of the scale tips dry to a paper-like state, the plants burst into growth in late spring or summer, producing one or more very fast-growing stems that need to be supported by a trellis or stake. The stems are covered with many leafless side branches that may fall off. The genus was named for James Bowie, a nineteenth-century gardener at Kew.
CULTIVATION: *Bowiea* species prefer gritty well-drained soil and a position in full sun. Water rarely, except during the growing season. Propagate from seed.

Bowiea volubilis

☼ ☙ ↔ 8 in (20 cm) ↑ 8–15 ft (2.4–4.5 m)

Outer surface of bulb more or less covered in paper-like remnants of dead or dying scales, especially when dormant. Long vigorous stems bear many inconspicuous greenish white flowers. Zones 9–11.

BOWKERIA

SHELLFLOWER

This South African genus of 5 species of evergreen shrubs and trees in the foxglove (Scrophulariaceae) family was named after Henry Bowker and his sister Mary Elizabeth, nineteenth-century South African botanists. They are generally compact plants with whorls of light to mid-green leaves in groups of three. The flowers resemble those of their relatives, *Calceolaria*, and are pouch-shaped or somewhat like a partly open oyster shell.
CULTIVATION: These plants can be something of a surprise for gardeners

Bowiea volubilis

Brabejum stellatifolium

Bowkeria verticillata

who tend to believe that all South African plants are thoroughly heat and drought tolerant. They prefer cool moist conditions with well-drained humus-enriched soil and partial shade. Their hardiness has not been greatly tested but they are known to tolerate occasional light frosts. New plants may be raised from seed or cuttings.

Bowkeria verticillata
syns *Bowkeria gerrardiana, B. simplici-folia, B. triphylla*

NATAL SHELLFLOWER BUSH

☀ ❄ ↔ 12 ft (3.5 m) ↑ 20 ft (6 m)
From cooler mountain areas of KwaZulu-Natal and Eastern Cape Provinces in South Africa. Bushy shrub or small tree. Leaves dark green, wrinkled above, paler and downy beneath. Flowers waxy, white, ¾ in (18 mm) long, in spring–autumn. Zones 8–10.

BOYKINIA
There are about 9 species of perennial herbs in this genus, which is a member of the saxifrage (Saxifragaceae) family. They are native to North America and Japan, where they grow in moist woodlands. They have creeping rhizomes and form clumps of rounded or kidney-shaped leaves that resemble those of the genera *Heuchera*. The tiny flowers are borne on crowded panicles. They are white, yellowish green, or purple.

CULTIVATION: Best suited to "wild" or woodland gardens, or rockeries. Grow in moist well-drained soil in light shade. Propagate by division.

Boykinia jamesii
syn. *Telesonix jamesii*

☀ ❄ ↔ 6–8 in (15–20 cm)
↑ 2–6 in (5–15 cm)
Compact low-growing species from northwestern USA. Leaves small, toothed, kidney-shaped. Flowers small, purple-red, in early summer. Grow in cool greenhouse or trough. Zones 5–9.

BRABEJUM
A genus of a single species of ever-green tree, *Brabejum* is restricted in the wild to South Africa's Western Cape Province, where it grows in thickets along banks of streams. Belonging to the protea (Proteaceae) family, it is of botanical interest as being Africa's only member of the large grevilleoid subfamily. Leaves appear at intervals along the branches, mostly in whorls of 6, and the plant bears white flowers densely crowded on spikes arising from the leaf axils. The fruits are similar to an almond. The nut is too bitter to eat; however, in earlier times it was boiled, roasted, and ground to make a "coffee" drink. CULTIVATION: Early European settlers at the Cape planted dense hedges of *Brabejum* to protect their livestock, but the tree has otherwise not often

Brachychiton bidwillii

been cultivated. Can be grown in any sheltered position, with moist well-drained soil. Propagate from fresh seed or from cuttings.

Brabejum stellatifolium
SOUTH AFRICAN WILD ALMOND

☀ ❄ ↔ 12 ft (3.5 m) ↑ 25 ft (8 m)
Branches widely at ground level with numerous erect vigorous stems. Leaves to 6 in (15 cm) long, narrow, bluntly toothed. Flowers white, from rusty buds, in summer. Fruits to 2 in (5 cm) long, magenta to reddish brown, in autumn. Zones 8–10.

BRACHYCHITON
This genus in the cacao (Sterculiaceae) family contains around 30 species of evergreen or partially deciduous trees, mostly native to Australia, and found chiefly in northern tropical and sub-tropical regions with a few extending to arid regions. They have large smooth or lobed leaves and showy sprays or clusters of colorful flowers often appearing just ahead of the new foliage in spring and summer. All species have shapely, sometimes swollen trunks and large, boat-shaped, woody seed follicles. Popular shade or ornamental trees, they are often seen in parks, along streets, or on farms. CULTIVATION: Although moderately frost hardy when established, most species are relatively slow growing in the initial stages and require a warm climate to bring out their best display of flowers. They do best in a well-drained acidic soil in full sun. Propagate from fresh seed in spring, or by grafting in the case of hybrid selections.

Brachychiton acerifolius
syn. *Sterculia acerifolia*

FLAME KURRAJONG, ILLAWARRA FLAME TREE

☀ ✤ ↔ 20 ft (6 m) ↑ 40 ft (12 m)
A deciduous tree from the east coast of Australia. Flowers crimson, appear on bare branches. For gardens, grafted trees are desirable because seedlings may take many years to flower. Very drought tolerant. Zones 9–10.

Brachychiton bidwillii
DWARF KURRAJONG

☀ ✤ ↔ 8 ft (2.4 m) ↑ 12 ft (3.5 m)
From the east coast of Queensland, Australia. Small tree, deciduous in dry periods. Leaves deeply lobed, shed when the flowers appear in late spring. Flowers deep pink or red, tubular, compact clusters. Tolerates dry periods. Zones 10–12.

Brachychiton acerifolius

B

Brachychiton discolor
syn. *Sterculia discolor*
LACEBARK KURRAJONG

☼ ❄ ↔30 ft (9 m) ↑80 ft (24 m)

From eastern Australian rainforests, a conical deciduous tree. Leaves dark green, lobed, paler beneath. Bark very green. Flowers pink, velvety, on leafless branches, in early summer. Prefers moist well-drained soils. Zones 9–11.

Brachychiton paradoxus

☼ ✿ ↔10 ft (3 m) ↑10 ft (3 m)

From tropical northern Australia, a straggly, deciduous tree. Leaves large, almost circular, shallowly lobed, slightly hairy, appear in wet season. Clusters of orange-red, bell-shaped-flowers on bare wood. Zones 11–12.

Brachychiton populneus
syn. *Sterculia diversifolia*
KURRAJONG

☼ ❄ ↔15 ft (4.5 m) ↑30 ft (9 m)

One of Australia's favored trees in dry areas, providing summer shade or

Brachyglottis, Dunedin Hybrid, 'Otari Cloud'

emergency stock feed. Semi-deciduous, with greenish bark. Large, simple to deeply lobed leaves. Flowers white, bell-shaped, in spring–early summer. Woody boat-shaped fruits. Zones 8–11.

BRACHYGLOTTIS

This genus of about 30 evergreen trees, shrubs, climbers, and perennials is part of the large daisy (Asteraceae) family. They are found in New Zealand and Tasmania, Australia, in habitats ranging from coastal to alpine. Most were previously included

Brachychiton paradoxus

Brachychiton discolor

Brachyglottis, Dunedin Hybrid, 'Sunshine'

in the genus *Senecio*. They are usually grown for their attractive gray foliage which is covered in white or buff down in varying degrees. Generally the yellow or white daisies are of little significance but in a small number of species they are quite showy.
CULTIVATION: Most species prefer a well-drained soil in a sunny situation and many are tolerant of harsh coastal conditions. In cool-temperate climates the more tender species are cultivated in the greenhouse and the hardier species against a sunny wall. Prune to maintain a compact bushy shape. Flowerheads can be removed if foliage effect is of prime importance. Species are propagated from seed or half-hardened cuttings in autumn, and cultivars from cuttings only.

Brachyglottis compacta
syn. *Senecio compactus*

☼ ❄ ↔7 ft (2 m) ↑3 ft (0.9 m)

From the southeastern coast of New Zealand's North Island. Stout branches. Leaves oblong, slightly wavy margins, downy when young, ageing to smooth and dull. The daisy flowers are small, bright yellow. Zones 9–11.

Brachyglottis compacta

Brachyglottis, Dunedin Hybrids

☼ ❄ ↔6 ft (1.8 m) ↑4–5 ft (1.2–1.5 m)

These hybrids are of 3 species, *B. compacta, B. laxifolia,* and *B. greyi.* They were first recorded at Dunedin Botanic Gardens on New Zealand's South Island. Bushy or somewhat lax; hardier than species. The new growth is covered in white down, which persists on the undersurface. 'Otari Cloud', wide-spreading foliage, bright white to silver-gray shade, flowers semi-soft butter yellow; and 'Sunshine' ★, silvery gray leaves with white down beneath, spreading, small yellow daisies in summer. Zones 8–10.

Brachyglottis greyi
syn. *Senecio greyi*

☼ ❄ ↔10 ft (3 m) ↑5 ft (1.5 m)

From Wellington on New Zealand's North Island, it is widely grown in gardens. Leaves oblong, grayish green, wavy margins, white down beneath. Flowers bright yellow, in summer. Suitable for hedging and coastal planting. Zones 8–10.

Brachyglottis hectoris
syn. *Senecio hectori*

☼ ❄ ↔8 ft (2.4 m) ↑12 ft (3.5 m)

Natural habitat is beside streams and forest margins in the north of the South Island of New Zealand. Large leaves, slightly serrated edges, crowding the branch tips. Clusters of large white daisies in summer. Zones 8–10.

Brachychiton populneus

Brachyglottis laxifolia
syn. *Senecio laxifolius*

☀ ❄ ↔ 7 ft (2 m) ↕ 3 ft (0.9 m)

Found in the mountains of the northern South Island of New Zealand. Lax habit. Leaves narrow, oblong, close set, slightly leathery, covered with dense gray down beneath. Zones 8–10.

Brachyglottis 'Leith's Gold'

☀ ❄ ↔ 5 ft (1.5 m) ↕ 6 ft (1.8 m)

This hybrid is a popular container plant. Leaves large, deep green, dense silver-gray felting on their undersides. Covered in clusters of bright yellow daisy flowers in spring and early summer. Zones 8–10.

Brachyglottis monroi
syn. *Senecio monroi*

☀ ❄ ↔ 6 ft (1.8 m) ↕ 3 ft (0.9 m)

Tough shrub found in mountains of northern South Island of New Zealand. Leaves oblong, crimped margins, downy white beneath. The flowers are small bright yellow daisies, in summer. Not suited to high humidity. Zones 8–10.

Brachyglottis repanda
RANGIORA

☀ ❄ ↔ 10 ft (3 m) ↕ 20 ft (6 m)

Popular garden shrub or small tree. Leaves wide, wavy-edged, to 10 in (25 cm) long, prominent veining, white felted undersides. Flowers tiny, in large showy panicles, in spring. 'Purpurea', excellent foliage plant, leaves deep purple above and downy white beneath. Zones 9–11.

BRACHYLAENA

This genus in the daisy (Asteraceae) family has 23 species of shrubs and trees and is found in Africa from the tropics to South Africa and also in Madagascar and the Mascarene Islands. They have rather leathery, lance-shaped to oblong leaves that some-

Brachyglottis monroi

Brachyglottis laxifolia

times have toothed edges and are often felted on their undersides. The compound flowers are usually white to creamy yellow and are followed by coarsely hairy or spiny seed heads. CULTIVATION: Most species are completely intolerant of frost and demand warm subtropical to tropical conditions. They prefer light well-drained soil with ample moisture during the growing season. Propagation is from seed, cuttings, or by removing the natural layers that sometimes develop.

Brachylaena rotundata
MOUNTAIN OAK, MOUNTAIN SILVER OAK

☀ ❄ ↔ 8 ft (2.4 m) ↕ 25 ft (8 m)

From northern South Africa, Zimbabwe, and Botswana. Semi-deciduous tree; upright bushy habit. Leaves dark green above, gray-haired beneath,

Brachylaena rotundata, Kirstenbosch National Botanical Garden, South Africa

broadest near the tip, wavy edges. Small sprays of deep yellow flower-heads, at branch tips, appear in late winter–early spring. Zones 9–11.

BRACHYPODIUM

A genus of 17 annual or perennial grasses from the Northern Hemisphere, members of the family Poaceae. Flimsy upright stems form tussocks. Flowers appear in compact spike-like racemes with 5 to 25 flowers on each short-stalked spikelet in summer. Leaves are flat or curved. CULTIVATION: Plant in any well-drained garden soil in an open sunny position. Propagate from seed.

Brachypodium pinnatum
TOR GRASS

☀ ❄ ↔ 12–24 in (30–60 cm) ↕ 36–48 in (90–120 cm)

Perennial grass. Erect racemes, to 10 in (25 cm) long, of spikelets to 1½ in (35 mm) long, each with up to 25 flowers. Stiff, narrow, yellowish green to light green leaves, to 18 in (45 cm) long, rough to the touch. Zones 5–9.

Brachypodium pinnatum

BRACHYSCOME
syn. *Brachycome*
DAISY

A popular genus of annuals, perennials, and subshrubs in the daisy (Asteraceae) family. There are 90 to 100 species in the genus, with many cultivars. They occur throughout Australia from coastal to alpine habitats. Leaves are small, bright green, and generally multi-lobed, divided, and/or toothed. Plants can form mats or be suckering or rounded compact bushes. Flowers are a typical daisy type in shades of pink, mauve, blue, purple, lemon, and white, generally

Brachyglottis 'Leith's Gold'

B

Brachyscome iberidifolia 'Blue Star'

Brachyscome iberidifolia 'Blue Mist'

with yellow centers. These daisies are popular in rock gardens, pots, hanging baskets, on banks, and at the front of garden borders. Some cultivars have arisen by chance but others are the result of deliberate breeding programs to improve color selections and the size of the flowers.
CULTIVATION: Any well-drained soil in either full or half-sun will do; some plants are more drought/frost tolerant than others. Propagation is from seed, with named cultivars propagated from cuttings or by division.

Brachyscome angustifolia
STIFF DAISY, GRASSLAND DAISY

☀/◐ ❄ ↔ 16–24 in (40–60 cm)
↑ 15 in (38 cm)

A perennial that is widespread in southeastern Australia, including Tasmania. Spreading mound of wiry stems with linear dark green leaves to 2 in (5 cm) long. Pink, blue, or purple flowerheads around 1 in (25 mm) wide, in spring–early summer. '**Mauve Delight**', strong, spreading, underground runners, mauve flowers. Zones 9–11.

Brachyscome formosa
PILLIGA DAISY

◐ ❄ ↔ 6 in (15 cm) ↑ 2–4 in (5–10 cm)
From the Pilliga region in New South Wales, Australia, this small suckering daisy has toothed, wedge-shaped leaves 1½ in (35 mm) long. Flowers mauve-pink, in spring–summer. '**Happy Face**', fleshier leaves than species, purple-pink flowers; '**Pilliga Posy**', large cerise blooms on short stems. Zones 9–11.

Brachyscome angustifolia 'Mauve Delight'

Brachyscome iberidifolia
SWAN RIVER DAISY

☀ ❄ ↔ 8–12 in (20–30 cm)
↑ 2–16 in (5–40 cm)

Erect annual daisy with pinnate leaves. Flowers 1 in (25 mm) in diameter in blue, purple, or white throughout spring–summer. Can be frost tender. '**Blue Mist**', attractive blue flowers; '**Blue Star**' ★, purple-tinted flowers with quilled petals, lightly scented. Zones 9–11.

Brachyscome multifida
CUT-LEAF DAISY, HAWKESBURY RIVER DAISY

☀ ❄ ↔ 12–40 in (30–100 cm)
↑ 8–16 in (20–40 cm)

Soft, much-divided foliage on a mounding form. Flowers generally purple but can be pink or white. Likes well-drained soil and will tolerate frost. May layer but does not sucker. *B. m.* var. *dilatata*, is a rounded form, leaves more wedge-shaped than species; '**Break O' Day**', hardier and more compact than species, bears deep mauve flowers from spring to autumn. *B. m.* '**Evan**', has cushion-like, deep mauve flowers from spring to autumn; '**White Surprise**', similar to species, except flowers are white. Zones 9–11.

Brachyscome Hybrid Cultivars

☀/◐ ❄ ↔ 18 in (45 cm) ↑ 18 in (45 cm)
These hybrids, mostly of *B. angusti-folia* and *B. iberidifolia*, are compact heavy-flowering plants. '**Blue Haze**', compact, low growing, mauve-blue flowers; '**City Lights**', mounding form with large light lavender-blue flowers; '**Just Jayne**', compact plant that does sucker, bearing white to pale pink flowers in autumn; '**New Amethyst**', fine foliage, small dark purple flowers in spring–autumn; '**Strawberry Mousse**' has reddish mid-green foliage, spoon-shaped lobed leaves, and bright pink flowers; '**Toucan Tango**' (syn. 'Ultra'), lacy foliage, violet-blue flowers year round; '**Valencia**', mauve-pink flowers 1½ in (35 mm) in diameter, year round in tropics. Zones 9–11.

BRACHYSEMA

This genus in the Fabaceae family consists of 16 species, which occur mainly in Western Australia, often on sandy infertile soils. There are 3 species from northern Australia. They are mostly small, spreading shrubs or prostrate creepers with opposite or alternate simple leaves, or with the leaves reduced to small scales on flattened stems. The flowers are pea-shaped and are mainly red in color, although some can be cream, yellow-green, or blackish. The flowers are attractive to nectar-feeding birds. The prostrate species make useful ground covers.
CULTIVATION: Most species grow under a range of soil and climatic conditions, but a sunny position and free-draining soil will suit most. Limited periods of dry soil can be tolerated. Fertilizers high in phosphorus should be avoided as they can kill or injure these plants. Most species respond well to pruning after flowering. Propagate from seed, which has a hard seed coat and needs treatment before it will germinate; cuttings of firm new growth, however, will strike easily. Plants can also be propagated by layering.

Brachysema celsianum
syn. *Brachysema lanceolatum*
SWAN RIVER PEA

☀ ❄ ↔ 10 ft (3 m) ↑ 5 ft (1.5 m)
Variable small shrub or semi-climber native to Western Australia. Leaves large, rounded or lance-shaped, green above, silvery gray and hairy below. Flowers bright red, pea-shaped, appear in winter–spring. A useful plant for growing into low hedges. The flowers attract honey-eating birds. Zones 9–11.

Brachysema celsianum

Brassavola cucullata

BRAHEA

syn. *Erythea*

HESPER PALM

This genus of 12 species of attractive small to medium-sized fan palms in the family Arecaceae is from Mexico and Central America. They are usually grown for their striking appearance and beautiful foliage. Mostly from dry rocky habitats, in open woodland and low scrub, most species have a rough-surfaced single trunk topped by a compact crown of fronds. The flattened frond stalks are often edged with spines. The frond blades are fan-shaped. Flowering branches emerge from the frond bases, gracefully arching. The white to yellowish flowers are tiny, crowded densely onto spike-like branchlets. Olive-shaped fruits ripen to blue-black; some are edible. CULTIVATION: They are sun-loving palms, easily grown in most warm-temperate to subtropical climates, best where summers are hot and dry. Most will tolerate light frosts. Best in well-drained moderately fertile soil with adequate subsoil moisture. Trim away the dead fronds. If left untrimmed the dead fronds form a thatch or "skirt" beneath the crown. Propagate from seed; early growth is often slow but may speed up after a trunk shows beneath the fronds.

Brahea armata ★

syn. *Erythea armata*

BLUE HESPER PALM, HESPER PALM

☼ ⚬ ↔ 10 ft (3 m) ↑ 25 ft (8 m)

From the Baja California peninsula of western Mexico. Fronds stiff, pale blue-gray. Trunk stout. Flowering branches to 15 ft (4.5 m) long, arching in a complete semicircle and held well clear of the foliage. Tiny cream flowers attract numerous insects. Zones 9–11.

Brahea brandegeei

syn. *Erythea brandegeei*

BRANDEGEE HESPER PALM, SAN JOSE HESPER PALM

☼ ⚬ ↔ 15 ft (4.5 m) ↑ 40 ft (12 m)

From steep canyons in southern Baja California, near San Jose del Cabo, Mexico. Trunk brownish, slender, tapering upward. Fronds pale green, drooping, partly hiding the flowering branches. Collected in 1900 by the California botanist Brandegee. 'Elegans' (syn. *Erythea* 'Elegans'), dwarf form, usually under 5 ft (1.5 m) tall. Zones 9–12.

Brahea edulis

syn. *Erythea edulis*

GUADALUPE PALM

☼ ⚬ ↔ 20 ft (6 m) ↑ 30 ft (9 m)

From the remote Mexican island of Guadalupe, growing in steep ravines running up from the seashore. Trunk thick. Fronds pale green with brownish woolly hairs. Shorter flowering branches thick, woolly, bearing greenish white flowers. Edible brown-black fruit. Zones 10–12.

BRASSAVOLA

LADY OF THE NIGHT ORCHID

This genus, belonging to the family Orchidaceae, contains about 25 terete-leafed sympodial epiphytic orchids from Central and South America. They are interesting plants even when not in bloom. The plants are often pendent and produce impressive displays of white to pale green flowers in clusters. These are highly and pleasantly fragrant in the evening. CULTIVATION: They grow well in small pots, baskets, or slabs, as long as they dry out between waterings. They enjoy high light, intermediate to warm temperatures, and can take cool temperatures in winter if kept dry. They have been used in a number of novelty hybrids with related genera in the *Cattleya* alliance.

Brassavola cucullata

☼/◐ ⚬ ↔ 24 in (60 cm) ↑ 12 in (30 cm)

From Central America. Pendulous growth habit, which makes it an ideal candidate for slab culture. The individual flowers are quite large, up to 7 in (18 cm) tall, lax, with yellowish green segments and a white labellum that is partially serrated. Zones 10–12.

BRASSIA

SPIDER ORCHID

Belonging to the family Orchidaceae, this genus of about 20 epiphytic sympodial orchids from tropical America is popular in cultivation due to their large, and often strongly perfumed, spidery blooms. The arching inflorescences display up to a dozen blooms which can reach over 12 in (30 cm) from tip to tip. They are also very amenable to cultivation over a wide range of climatic conditions. *Brassia* has also been used in hybrids with related genera such as *Miltonia*, *Odontoglossum*, and *Oncidium*. CULTIVATION: Many of these species are from the lowlands and like warm, moist, and bright conditions. They grow well in pots in a bark-based medium. Larger plants look good in hanging baskets. In frost-free climates they can also be attached to garden trees that do not shed their bark.

Brahea brandegeei

Brahea armata

Brahea edulis

B

Brassia arcuigera

☀ ✿ ↔ 8–16 in (20–40 cm)
↑ 8–12 in (20–30 cm)

Formerly known as *B. longissima,* this species comes from Costa Rica and Ecuador and has one of the largest flowers in the genus, up to 10 in (25 cm) tall. It has very narrow segments that are yellow, heavily marked rustic brown, giving the flower an overall bronze cast. Zones 11–12,

Brassia glumacea

Brassia glumacea

☀ ✿ ↔ 8–16 in (20–40 cm)
↑ 8–12 in (20–30 cm)

A cool-growing species from Colombia and Venezuela, some botanists classify this species as *Ada glumacea.* Plants can produce 2 inflorescences per pseudobulb. Glossy flowers, up to 5 in (12 cm) tall. Zones 10–11.

Brassia verrucosa

☀ ✿ ↔ 8–24 in (20–60 cm)
↑ 8–12 in (20–30 cm)

From Mexico and Venezuela. A very popular species in cultivation, performing well in shadehouse conditions in frost-free climates, and a reliable late spring bloomer. Large, 8 in (20 cm) wide, spidery, pale green, fragrant flowers, with fine dark green spotting at the base. The smaller flowered *B. brachiata* is now included within this species. Zones 10–12.

Brassia, Hybrid, Rex 'Christine'

Brassia, Hybrid, Spider's Gold

Brassia Hybrids

☀ ✿ ↔ 24 in (60 cm) ↑ 12 in (30 cm)
Brassia hybrids are particularly vigorous and worth cultivating. They bloom best when grown as large, somewhat crowded specimens. Most brassias flower in spring and summer. **Edvah Loo** is a primary hybrid between *B. arcuigera* and *B. gireoudiana,* which are both large-flowered species; **Rex 'Christine'** ★, arguably the most popular *Brassia* hybrid in cultivation, is a primary hybrid between *B. gireoudiana* and *B. verrucosa* and blooms at full potential when grown into a large plant; **Spider's Feast** is an impressive hybrid between *B.* Chieftain and *B. verrucosa,* which has all its blooms out at once and well presented on the flower spike; **Spider's Gold** is the hybrid between *B.* Arania Verde and the large-flowered *B. arcuigera.* Zones 10–12.

Brassia, Hybrid, Edvah Loo

BRASSICA

The cabbage and its relatives are in the Brassicaceae family, which contains only a few species but many subspecies, groups, and cultivars. The cabbages originate from the temperate coastal areas of Europe and North Africa. They are annuals, biennials, and perennials, depending on climate and how they are treated. The brassicas are mainly grown for their leaves (cabbages, kale, Asian greens), their flowering parts (broccoli, cauliflower, brussels sprouts), their seeds (rape/canola), their stems (kohlrabi), or their roots (turnip, swede). The leaves are generally large and waxy with a whitish bloom; flowers are usually yellow but sometimes white. Flowering times depend on the age of the plant and climate. The cabbage family has been utilized by humans for more than 3,000 years.

CULTIVATION: Brassicas like a well-drained moist soil that has been enriched with well-rotted manure. Those grown for their leaves appreciate added nitrogen. Propagate from seed throughout the year, depending on the variety.

Brassia arcuigera, in Jardín Botánico Lankester, Costa Rica

Brassia verrucosa

Brassica napus, canola crop

Brassica juncea

BROWN MUSTARD, CHINESE MUSTARD,
KAI TSOI, MUSTARD GREENS

☀ ❄ ↔ 8–40 in (20–100 cm)
↑ 8–40 in (20–100 cm)

Annual species, native to southern
and eastern Asia, long cultivated as a
leaf vegetable and for mustard seed.
Leaves green, red, or purple, smooth
or puckered, smooth-edged or
toothed. Racemes of light yellow
flowers. Numerous cultivars. '**Red
Giant**' (syn. *B. j.* var. *rugosa*), cool-
season annual, 24 in (60 cm) long
crinkled leaves in shades of green,
purple, and maroon can be cooked
like spinach.

Japonica Group (syn. *B. j.* var.
multiceps): This group is very hardy,
usually growing throughout winter.
The leaves are used raw (especially
when young) or cooked, salted, and
pickled; '**Mizumi**' ★ is a quick-
growing green leaf vegetable, with a
peppery taste. Zones 9–11.

Brassica napus

OIL-SEED RAPE, RUTABAGA, SWEDE,
SWEDISH TURNIP

☀ ❄ ↔ 8–16 in (20–40 cm)
↑ 8–16 in (20–40 cm)

First appearing in medieval times in
Sweden, this species resulted from a
cross between the turnip and the cabbage. It is grown for its storage roots.
Other forms, such as rape and canola,
are grown for their oil-bearing seed.

Napobrassica Group: This group is
hardier and less watery than turnips;
its members have yellowish roots and
blue-gray leaves.

Pabularia Group: Rosetting brassica with smooth purple or white
leaves, eaten raw (when young) or
cooked. Zones 8–11.

Brassica oleracea

WILD CABBAGE

☀ ❄ ↔ 12 in (30 cm) ↑ 16 in (40 cm)

Western European annual or perennial. Ancestor of cabbage, broccoli,

cauliflower, kale, and brussels sprouts.
Forms woody stem with dense head of
overlapping blue-green leaves. Differs
from cultivated types mainly in its
coarsely lyrate or pinnate leaf shape.
Sprays of yellow flowers in summer.

Acephala Group: Non-heading
brassicas, both ornamental and edible;
'**Blue Ridge**', edible kale with dark
blue-green leaves and full curl on all
leaves; '**Red Peacock**', dwarf ornamental kale with pinky red center and
deeply cut leaves; '**Redbor**', hardy,
high-yielding edible kale; '**White
Peacock**', similar to 'Red Peacock' but
white; '**Winterbor**' ★, vigorous edible
kale with finely curled, thick, blue-
green leaves.

Alboglabra Group (syn. *B. o.* var.
alboglabra): Close relative of European
(Calabrese) broccoli, this group produces several small succulent heads
instead of one large head.

Botrytis Group (syn. *B. o.* var.
botrytis): Cauliflower and broccoli,

Brassica juncea, Japonica Group, 'Mizumi'

heads range in color from white
and cream to pink, lime green, and
purple, but color may be lost during
cooking. Calabrese types exhibit a
single head; '**Early Emerald**', blue-
green in color with fine bead and
large, domed, tight head; '**Emperor**',
blue-green broccoli producing high
yields in spring–summer, tolerant
of black rot and downy mildew;
'**Eureka**', late-maturing variety with
small beads and very domed head;
'**Perfection**' ★, mini cauliflower
with a head that grows to about 4 in
(10 cm) in diameter in 2 months;
'**Romanesco**', startling lime green
heads with individual florets in spirals,
can be eaten raw or cooked; '**Shogun**',
Calabrese blue-gray type producing
tall plants with large head 3–5 in
(8–12 cm) in diameter; '**Snowcrown**',
vigorous grower with pure white
round heads 6–8 in (15–20 cm) in
diameter produced in 60 to 70 days.

Brassica oleracea, Acephala Group cultivar

B. oleracea, Acephala Group, 'Blue Ridge'

B. oleracea, Botrytis Group, 'Perfection'

B

Brassica oleracea, Capitata Group cultivar

B. o., Capitata Group cultivar

B. o., Capitata Group, 'Dynamo'

B. o., Capitata Group, 'Primavoy'

B. o., Capitata Group, 'Red Express'

B. o., Capitata Group, 'Savoy King'

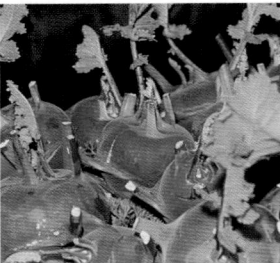

B. o., Gongylodes Group, 'Kolibri'

B. o., Italica Group, 'Emperor'

B. oleracea, Italica Group, 'Eureka'

B. o., Italica Group, 'Shogun'

Brassica oleracea, Capitata Group, 'Alba'

Capitata Group (syn. *B. o.* var. *capitata*): Many forms of cabbage developed in Germany; '**Alba**', large cabbage with flat heavy head and white interior; '**Dynamo**', small head, mild flavor, not prone to splitting; '**Early Curly**', early maturing type with heavily crinkled leaves, small core, sweet flavor; '**Primavoy**' ★, good storage cultivar, compact flattened heads, dark blue-green leaves; '**Primax**', earliest and sweetest variety with round light green heads produced in 60 days; '**Red Express**', small red variety good for the home garden; '**Ruby Ball**' ★, very early, round, solid head medium to dark red in color;

'**Savoy Express**', small heads on compact plants with few wrapper leaves; '**Savoy King**' ★ has large heads, with crinkly leaves and a creamy interior; a fine, subtle flavor.

Gemmifera Group (syn. *B. o.* var. *gemmifera*): First recorded in Belgium about 1750 (hence the common name brussels sprouts), sprouts are compact leaf buds produced directly from the main stem.

Gongylodes Group (syn. *B. o.* var. *gongylodes*): Fast-growing kohlrabi cabbage grown for its swollen stem. It is available in white or purple; '**Kolibri**' ★ has purple skin with sweet, juicy, crunchy white flesh.

Italica Group (syn. *B. o.,* Cymosa Group): Sprouting or Italian broccoli, has many long-stalked heads of green to purplish buds, which mature in

succession. '**Emperor**', mid-sized, high-yielding; '**Eureka**', dark green buds in tightly packed heads. Zones 8–11.

Brassica rapa

syn. *Brassica campestris*

TURNIP

☀ ◈ ↔ 12–20 in (30–50 cm)
↑ 12–20 in (30–50 cm)

This is the species from which today's modern turnip, oil-seed turnip-rape, and Chinese cabbage have been developed. Leaves are green, lobed, and have jagged edges. The roots have yellow or white flesh, with yellow, white, green, or purple skin.

Chinensis Group (syn. *B. chinensis*): Commonly known as bok choy. The prominent white or green stems are spoon shaped with fresh, bright green, glossy leaves.

Pekinensis Group (syn. *B. pekinensis*): Crisp dark or light green leaves often have creamy center, thick white midribs. This is commonly used as salad vegetable.

Rapifera Group: Long and thin (purplish red and white) or small and round (white) turnips. '**Atlantic**' ★, early cropper with purple top, harvest when it reaches the size of a golf-ball; use the leaves in salads. Zones 9–11.

B. o., Capitata Group, 'Savoy Express'

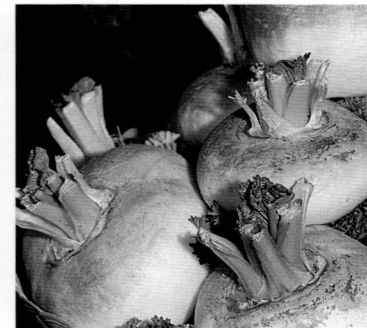

Brassica rapa, Rapifera Group, 'Atlantic'

B

× *Brassidium* Flyaway 'Taida'

× BRASSIDIUM

This man-made bigeneric sympodial orchid hybrid between *Brassia* and *Oncidium* is a member of the family Orchidaceae. The long, upright, sometimes branched inflorescences bear numerous long-lasting flowers. The somewhat spidery blooms are a legacy from the *Brassia* parent.
CULTIVATION: These vigorous hybrids enjoy warm bright conditions. They grow well in pots in a bark-based medium and need frequent watering when in active growth. While they have the potential to bloom at any time, the flowers are more frequently produced in the warmer months.

× *Brassidium* Flyaway 'Taida'

☀ ↔ 8–24 in (20–60 cm) ↕ 8–12 in (20–30 cm)

This hybrid has three species in its background, *Brassia arcuigera*, *Oncidium wentworthianum*, and *Oncidium maculatum*. Zones 10–12.

× *Brassidium* Wild Warrior 'Santa Barbara'

☀ ↔ 8–24 in (20–60 cm) ↕ 8–12 in (20–30 cm)

This is the hybrid between *Oncidium leucochilum* and the large-flowered hybrid *Brassia* Stardust (*gireoudiana × maculata*). Zones 10–12.

× BRASSOCATTLEYA

This man-made bigeneric sympodial orchid hybrid between *Brassavola* and *Cattleya* belongs to the family Orchidaceae. In most cases such hybrids involving *Brassavola* invariably have *Rhyncholaelia digbyana* (previously known as *Brassavola digbyana*) as one of the parents. Hybrids created using the terete-leafed *Brassavola* species, which have predominantly green and white blooms, result in the other parent of the hybrid having a strong

× *Brassidium* Wild Warrior 'Santa Barbara'

influence on the resulting flower color.
CULTIVATION: These orchids have a compact habit and grow well in small terracotta or plastic pots, baskets, or slabs. However, they must be allowed to dry out fully between waterings. They enjoy high light, intermediate to warm temperatures and can take cool temperatures in winter if kept dry. The showy blooms are often produced in large numbers and are quite often pleasantly fragrant.

× *Brassocattleya,* Hybrid, Binosa

× *Brassocattleya* Hybrids

☀/☀ ↔ 12 in (30 cm) ↕ 10 in (25 cm)

These hybrids produce large numbers of showy blooms, often pleasantly fragrant. Hybrids include: **Binosa ★**, hybrid between *Brassavola nodosa* and *Cattleya bicolor*, long-lasting flowers; **Island Charm 'Carmela'**, with *Cattleya intermedia* as one of its parents, producing clusters of blooms in spring; **Maikai**, large plant, spectacular in bloom, floriferous primary hybrid between *Brassavola nodosa* and *Cattleya bowringiana*; **Sunny Delight**, primary hybrid between *Brassavola perrinii* and *Cattleya aurantiaca*, with yellow to orange flowers; and **November Bride 'Santa Clara'**, with large flowers ranging from pink to white. Zones 10–12.

× BRASSOLAELIO-CATTLEYA

Most of the "*Cattleya* orchids" with large single or twin-flowers seen at

× *Brassocattleya,* Hybrid, Island Charm 'Carmela'

florists and orchid shows are actually members of the genus × *Brassolaeliocattleya*, a man-made combination between the sympodial epiphytic orchid genera *Brassavola, Laelia,* and *Cattleya,* and a member of the family Orchidaceae. Many of the registered, intergeneric hybrids listed as involving *Brassavola,* invariably have *Rhyncholaelia digbyana,* previously known as *Brassavola digbyana,* as one of the parents. This species imparts not only

× *Brassocattleya,* Hybrid, Sunny Delight

× *Brassocattleya,* Hybrid, Maikai

× *Brassocattleya,* Hybrid, November Bride 'Santa Clara'

fragrance, but also a large fringed labellum that is a distinctive feature of many of the hybrids. Many of the larger-flowering types are grown commercially for cut flower production. CULTIVATION: These hybrids require semi-shade to strong light, but will burn if exposed to direct sunlight. They grow best in pots incorporating a coarse bark-based medium to ensure unimpeded drainage. Healthy plants will develop an extensive system of thick white roots, which are long-lived and branch freely. The plants require additional warmth on winter evenings, but will tolerate cooler winter temperatures for short periods if kept dry while dormant. The flowers are long lasting and the whole plant can be brought indoors to be enjoyed when in bloom.

× *Brassolaeliocattleya* Hybrids

☀ ❄ ↔ 8–24 in (20–60 cm)
↑ 8–24 in (20–60 cm)

× *Brassolaeliocattleya* hybrids are durable plants with a growth habit very similar to the unifoliate cattleyas. **Alma Kee 'Tipmalee'** has a large genetic influence from the warm-growing species, *Cattleya dowiana* var. *aurea*. Bright yellow petals and sepals, bright red labellum; **Ann Cleo 'Hallona'**, a distinctively colored hybrid with more than a dozen different orchid species in its makeup; **Erin Kobayashi × *Cattleya walkeriana***, an unregistered hybrid back-crossed onto the small-growing Brazilian *Cattleya* species to create a more compact growing plant; **Hawaiian Satisfaction 'Romantic'**, a cultivar propagated using tissue culture to produce large numbers of genetically identical plants—it is rare for seedling orchids to flower with such unusual color combinations; **Lucky 'Golden Ring'**, huge, highly fragrant, long-lasting flowers, large flared labellum with a velvet-like texture, is distinctly lined and blotched with rich color; **(Memoria Benigno Aquino × Golden Embers)**, an unregistered hybrid with gold petals and sepals, dark red labellum; **Memoria Julia Piferrer** is heavily influenced by infusions of *Cattleya dowiana* and *Rhyncholaelia digbyana*, from which it inherits the fringed labellum; **Rosemary Hayden 'Paradise'**, a fine example of one of the traditional colored "Cattleyas," this autumn-flowering hybrid has 9 different species in its background; **(Shades of Jade × Waikiki Gold)** is an example of a "splash-petaled" hybrid—the flower gives the impression of having 3 lips; actually the labellum color has been generically transposed onto the petals of the bloom; **Toshi Aoki 'Blumen Insel'**, bright yellow petals and sepals, bright red labellum, the genetic influence coming from *Cattleya dowiana* var. *aurea*; **Toshi Aoki 'Pokai'** ★, one of the most popular and highly awarded yellow hybrids, bred in Hawaii; **Waianae Leopard**, a cluster-type hybrid that is heavily influenced by the spotted *Cattleya guttata*; and **Williette Wong**, a spectacular orchid, named after a respected member of the Honolulu Orchid Society, Hawaii; an eye-catching plant that gets its distinctive color from *Cattleya dowiana* var. *aurea*. Zones 10–12.

× *Brassolaeliocattleya*, Hybrid, Alma Kee 'Tipmalee'

× *Brassolaeliocattleya*, Hybrid, Ann Cleo 'Hallona'

× *Brassolaeliocattleya*, Hybrid, Erin Kobayashi × *Cattleya walkeriana*

× *Brassolaeliocattleya* Hybrid

× *B.*, Hybrid, Gold Bug

× *B.*, Hybrid, Golden Tang

× *B.*, Hybrid, Hawaiian Satisfaction 'Romantic'

× *B.*, Hybrid, Lucky 'Golden Ring'

× *B.*, Hybrid, (Memoria Benigno Aquino × Golden Embers)

× *B.*, Hybrid, Memoria Julia Piferrer

× *B.*, Hybrid, Rosemary Hayden 'Paradise'

× *B.*, Hybrid, (Shades of Jade × Waikiki Gold)

× *B.*, Hybrid, Sunstate's Easter Parade

× *B.*, Hybrid, Toshi Aoki 'Blumen Insel'

× *B.*, H., (Toshi Aoki × Bryce Canyon)

× *B.*, Hybrid, Toshi Aoki 'Pokai'

× *B.*, H., (Toshi Aoki × Oconee)

× *B.*, Hybrid, Waianae Leopard

× *B.*, Hybrid, Williette Wong

B

BREYNIA

Belonging to the spurge (Euphorbiaceae) family, the 25 or so species in this genus of evergreen shrubs and small trees range from Australia and the Pacific Islands northward to Southeast and East Asia. Often suckering from the roots, they have delicate twigs and small oval leaves arranged alternately and tending to form 2 rows. Leaves often turn black before falling. Inconspicuous greenish flowers, both male and female on the same plant, appear in the leaf axils followed by small, flattened, white, red, or black berries. Few of the species have found their way into home gardens. CULTIVATION: Only the snow bush (*B. disticha*) is grown as an ornamental. Use as a border shrub in tropical and subtropical gardens; in cooler climates, grow indoors in pots or plant out for summer in bedding schemes or patio tubs. Prefers a sunny but sheltered spot and well-drained soil. Propagate from cuttings. Other species may be grown from seed and are used where local native plants are appropriate.

Breynia disticha
syns *Breynia nivosa*, *Phyllanthus nivosus*
SNOW BUSH

☀ ❄ ↔ 3 ft (0.9 m) ↑ 4 ft (1.2 m)
From islands of the western Pacific, sends up additional stems from roots if given enough room. Ovate leaves, 1 in (25 mm) long, spotted white or cream, or some all green, others all white. 'Roseopicta', pink new growth, many leaves pink-flushed, has largely replaced white-spotted form in gardens. Zones 10–12.

BRILLANTAISIA
GIANT SALVIA

This acanthus (Acanthaceae) family genus consists of around 40 species of perennials, subshrubs, and shrubs found in the moist African tropics.

Briza maxima

They range in size from 8 in (20 cm) to 7 ft (2 m) tall and develop rapidly in suitably warm, moist, and humid conditions. Most species have lush, deep green, heavily veined, toothed, heart-shaped leaves and terminal spikes of showy purple flowers with distinct upper and lower lips. Long cylindrical seed pods follow flowers. CULTIVATION: Apart from demanding a warm, moist, tropical or subtropical climate, *Brillantaisia* is easily grown. One species in particular, *B. lamium*, is an extremely vigorous grower that is considered a serious weed in the tropics. Plant in a position shaded from the hottest sun. Water and feed well for lush growth and heavy flowering. Deadhead frequently to encourage continued blooming. Propagate from seed or cuttings, or by division if appropriate.

Brillantaisia lamium

☀ ❄ ↔ 2–4 ft (0.6–1.2 m)
↑ 2–4 ft (0.6–1.2 m)

From central and western Africa. Small shrub capable of quickly forming dense stands. Stems square and hairy. Leaves heart-shaped. Purple flowers to 1¼ in (30 mm) long are followed by cigar-shaped seed pods. Zones 9–12.

BRIZA
QUAKING GRASS, SHIVERGRASS

This genus of 12 annual or perennial grasses belongs to the family Poaceae. The genus name comes from the Greek word *brizo* (to be sleepy or nodding), referring to the delicate nodding panicles of flowers that appear in summer. The leaves are flat and strap-like, while the fruits comprise a single-celled seed known as a caryopsis. *Briza* plants can become invasive in suitable climates. The flowers are ideal for dried arrangements. CULTIVATION: Propagate from seed.

Brillantaisia lamium

Breynia disticha

Breynia disticha 'Roseopicta'

Plant seeds direct where they are to grow, in full sun, in well-drained cultivated soil raked to a fine tilth.

Briza maxima
GREAT QUAKING GRASS

☀ ❄ ↔ 8 in (20 cm) ↑ 24 in (60 cm)
Annual grass from Mediterranean area. Nodding panicles of 7 to 20 heart-shaped flower clusters, light gray or purple, in summer. Strap-shaped leaves up to 8 in (20 cm) long. 'Rubra', flower bracts tinted red-pink, edged with white. Zones 7–10.

Briza media
QUAKING GRASS, TREMBLING GRASS

☀ ❄ ↔ 18 in (45 cm) ↑ 24 in (60 cm)
From Europe and Asia. Ornamental grass with flat mid-green foliage. In early summer tiny light green "spikelets" bloom, shaking in the slightest breeze, hence the common names; turn beige when mature. Does best in poor soils. Zones 7–10.

BRODIAEA

This genus of about 15 species of cormous plants is a member of the onion (Alliaceae) family. Most are native to western North America, where they

grow in grass, scrub, and open forest. Over the years the genus has been extensively revised and several former members are now described under *Triteleia* and *Dichelostemma*. *Brodiaea* species have grass-like foliage, which usually dies back at flowering time. The pink, blue, or purple flowers are borne in loose umbels on stems from 2–30 in (5–75 cm) tall and are bell-shaped or flaring. CULTIVATION: Grow in a light fertile soil in full sun. Plant closely for best flowering display. Keep moist during growth period but allow to dry out when dormant as corms are susceptible to rot. Provide a protective layer of mulch in winter in frosty areas, or grow in pots in the greenhouse. Propagate by division of corms, removal of offsets, or from seed.

Brodiaea coronaria
syns *Brodiaea grandiflora*, *Hookera coronaria*

HARVEST BRODIAEA

☀ ❄ ↔ 4 in (10 cm) ↑ 12 in (30 cm)
From California and northwestern USA. Loose umbels of up to 12 purplish blue starry flowers in late spring or summer. Zones 8–10.

Brownea ariza

Broussonetia papyrifera

BROMELIA

In 1753 Linnaeus named *B. pinguin*, and this genus gave the bromeliad (Bromeliaceae) family its name. From Mexico, the Caribbean islands, and Central America down to Argentina. Leaves up to 40 in (100 cm) long with large curved spines along edges. When flowering the center turns bright red and a club-shaped flowerhead emerges. There are about 50 species, but only 6 are popularly grown. Perhaps the most hardy is *B. serra*, with *B. pinguin* and its variegated form the most common.
CULTIVATION: Recommended for a greenhouse in cool-temperate areas, or outdoors in warm-temperate, subtropical, and tropical areas. Bromelias send out underground fleshy stems, so are best grown in large tubs. Water when potting mix is dry. No extra fertilizer. Propagate from seeds or offsets.

Bromelia pinguin

PINGUIN, PINUELA
☀ ☽ ↔ 7 ft (2 m) ↑ 4 ft (1.2 m)
Clumping species from tropical America. Many rosettes, each with up to 40 spiny leaves to 6 ft (1.8 m) long and 2 in (5 cm) wide, light gray-green flushed with red. Large panicles of white to pink flowers; small, fleshy, yellow fruits. Zones 10–12.

Bromelia serra

☀ ☽ ↔ 7 ft (2 m) ↑ 16 in (40 cm)
From Bolivia to northern Argentina. Leaves green, short spines on edges. Flower stem short. Flowerhead globular, 2½ in (6 cm) wide. Petals blue-purple. Bright red, stiff, spiny bracts up to 8 in (20 cm) long beneath the flowerhead. Zones 9–10.

BROUSSONETIA

From the mulberry (Moraceae) family, *Broussonetia* consists of 8 species of deciduous trees and shrubs with milky sap, from tropical and eastern Asia; 1 species is endemic to Madagascar. Deeply lobed leaves are broad, heart-shaped, with toothed edges. Small male and female flowers are borne on separate trees, males in long catkins, females in globular heads. Male flowers expel pollen explosively, visible as tiny spurts of white dust. Small fleshy fruits are clustered on a globular fruiting head. Inner bark fiber has been used for making paper and cloth.
CULTIVATION: Only the more cold-hardy species from East Asia are known in cultivation. Moderately frost tolerant, they prefer hot humid summers. They adapt to tropical and subtropical climates, as well as inner-urban pollution. Heavy pruning creates vigorous resprouting. Propagate from cuttings of short shoots taken in summer; seed can be used if available.

Broussonetia papyrifera

PAPER MULBERRY
☀ ❋ ↔ 30 ft (9 m) ↑ 50 ft (15 m)
Native to China and Japan. "Tapa" cloth is made from its bark. Young branches softly hairy. Leaves variably lobed or unlobed to 8 in (20 cm). Male catkins whitish, female purplish. Fruiting heads red. Zones 6–12.

BROWNEA

Belonging to the caesalpinia subfamily of the legume (Fabaceae) family, *Brownea* consists of 12 or more species of evergreen trees and shrubs from tropical America. Large pinnate leaves change from bronze when young to cream then deep green when mature. Dense showy heads of red, pink, or orange flowers point downward beneath a group of colored bracts; individual flowers are funnel-shaped with protruding stamens. The fruit is a large, flattened, woody pod.
CULTIVATION: Best in a tropical climate with ample summer rainfall, but are rather slow growing. Grown for the beauty of their flowers and as shade trees, they are best suited to a lawn or courtyard with shelter from strong winds. Lower branches sag toward the ground, and may need to be raised on props to enhance the trees' shade value. Propagation is from seed, if obtainable, from cuttings (though these are slow and difficult to strike), or by air layering.

Brownea ariza

syns *Brownea grandiceps*, *B. princeps*
ROSE OF VENEZUELA
☀ ✛ ↔ 20 ft (6 m) ↑ 30 ft (9 m)
Native to Venezuela and Colombia. Small spreading tree. At onset of tropical wet season (summer) it bears scattered heads of scarlet to pinkish red flowers to 10 in (25 cm) across, surrounded by bracts of a similar color. Zones 11–12.

Brownea capitella

☀ ✛ ↔ 15 ft (4.5 m) ↑ 30 ft (9 m)
From Trinidad and adjacent South American mainland. This attractive species has large head of bright pink flowers with cream stamens. Bases of flowers tightly enclosed in cup of large pink bracts. Zones 11–12.

Brownea coccinea

GUARAMACO
☀ ✛ ↔ 15 ft (4.5 m) ↑ 20 ft (6 m)
Native to Ecuador and Venezuela, this small tree has few leaflets to each leaf. Dramatic pendulous flowerheads have brilliant red flowers, with flaring petals, protruding pink stamens, and conspicuous yellow anthers. Hairy red bracts around the tightly clustered flowers. Zones 11–12.

Brownea capitella

Brownea coccinea

Brugmansia arborea

BRUGMANSIA

This genus in the Solanaceae family contains 5 species of small trees or shrubs native to South America, particularly the Andes. Seeds hallucinogenic. All plant parts poisonous; all have woody stems. Grown for their tubular or funnelform flowers, drooping, not erect as in *Datura*. Flowers fragrant, with 2- to 5-lobed cylindrical calyx. Fruits ovoid or elliptical. CULTIVATION: Brugmansias need a sunny protected position with no more than light frost. Moderately fertile, free-draining soil is suitable. Plants are best trained to a single trunk by removing any competing leaders; branchlets should be shortened annually in late winter or early spring. Propagation is from soft-tip cuttings taken in spring or summer, or hardwood cuttings in autumn or winter; use hormone rooting powder.

Brugmansia arborea
syn. *Brugmansia cornigera*
☀ ❦ ↔ 5–8 ft (1.5–2.4 m) ↑ 15 ft (4.5 m)
Small evergreen tree from Ecuador and northern Chile, seldom seen in gardens. Leaves irregularly alternate.

Flowers white, solitary, with extended green tip, in summer–autumn. Fruits green, ovoid, with numerous seeds. 'Knightii' (syn. *B. × candida* 'Double White'), off-white double flowers, gray-green leaves. Zones 10–12.

Brugmansia aurea
GOLDEN ANGEL'S TRUMPET
☀ ❦ ↔ 15 ft (4.5 m) ↑ 15 ft (4.5 m)
Native to Central Colombia and Ecuador, on Andean Mountains slopes. Small evergreen tree, short trunk, broad leafy crown. Leaves midgreen, paler beneath. Flowers drooping, solitary, yellowish green, in late summer. The fruits are ovoid berries. Zones 10–12.

Brugmansia × candida
ANGEL'S TRUMPET
☀ ❦ ↔ 6 ft (1.8 m) ↑ 10 ft (3 m)
Hybrid between *B. aurea* and *B. versicolor*, sometimes labelled *B. knightii*. Small evergreen tree from Ecuador. Leaves bright green, paler below. Flowers greenish white, fragrant at night, in summer–autumn. Fruit a green capsule. 'Grand Marnier', peach-colored flowers. Zones 10–12.

Brugmansia 'Charles Grimaldi'
☀ ❦ ↔ 4 ft (1.2 m) ↑ 6 ft (1.8 m)
Cross between 'Doctor Seuss' and 'Frosty Pink'. Leaves large. Flowers long, widely flared, fragrant, salmon pink to yellow-orange, in autumn–spring. Compact plant flowers heavily, does well in containers. Zones 10–12.

Brugmansia × insignis
syn. *Brugmania sanguinea* 'Rosea'
☀ ❦ ↔ 8–10 ft (2.4–3 m) ↑ 12 ft (3.5 m)
Developed from crossing *B. suaveolens* and *B. versicolor*, a multi-stemmed shrub resembling *B. suaveolens*. Flowers slender, tubular, flared petals, white ageing to pink or apricot. 'Betty

Marshall', compact growth habit, white flowers; 'Jamaica Yellow', pale yellow blooms. Zones 9–10.

Brugmansia sanguinea ★
RED ANGEL'S TRUMPET
☀ ❦ ↔ 12 ft (3.5 m) ↑ 12 ft (3.5 m)
Small tree native to Colombia, Ecuador, and Peru, often seen as shrub. Leaves long. Flowers solitary, with persistent calyx. Corolla yellowish, turning orange-scarlet. Fruits ovoid,

Brugmansia × insignis

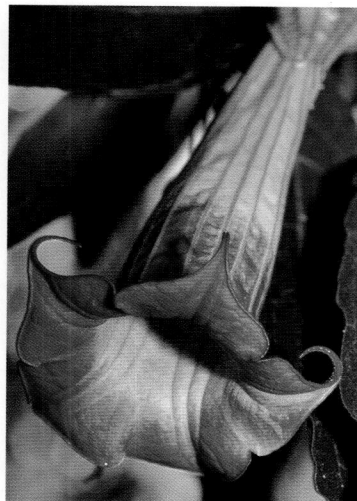

Brugmansia sanguinea

smooth skinned. 'Inca Queen', long orange-red flowers with yellow interior. Zones 9–11.

Brugmansia suaveolens
ANGEL'S TRUMPET
☀ ❦ ↔ 10 ft (3 m) ↑ 15 ft (4.5 m)
Southeastern Brazil. Leaves soft, dark green. Single flowers, calyx green, corolla white, narrowly funnelform, with 3 pale green ribs. Fruits narrowly ellipsoidal, green, smooth. Zones 10–12.

Brugmansia 'Charles Grimaldi'

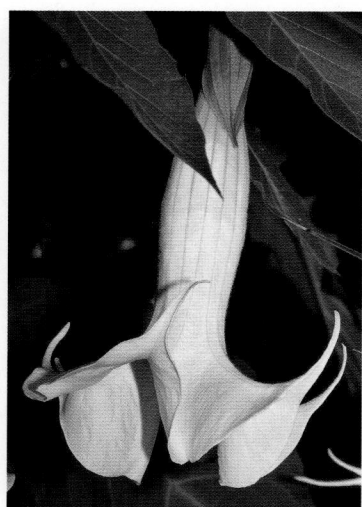

Brugmansia × candida

Brugmansia × candida 'Grand Marnier'

BRUNFELSIA

Found from Central America to sub-tropical South America, this genus in the nightshade (Solanaceae) family includes some 40 species of mainly evergreen shrubs and trees. Most have fragrant, large, simple, long-tubed, 5-petalled flowers, notable for their progression of color changes. White, mauve, and purple are the usual colors. The leaves are usually simple pointed ovals in lush, deep green tones. All species contain potent alkaloids; generally highly toxic, but still used in some local medicines.

CULTIVATION: While very frost tender, *Brunfelsia* presents no cultivation difficulties in suitably mild climates. Any sunny or partly shaded position with moist well-drained soil will do. They are not drought tolerant but grow well in containers if watered routinely. Indoor potted specimens are prone to mites and mealybugs. Propagate from soft or half-hardened tip cuttings.

Brunfelsia americana

LADY OF THE NIGHT

☀ ⚘ ↔ 4–7 ft (1.2–2 m) ↑ 15 ft (4.5 m)

From Central America and the West Indies, this large shrub or small tree

has flowers that are scented at night. White when first open, with a hint of purple, ageing through cream to yellow, in summer. Zones 10–12.

Brunfelsia grandiflora

☀ ⚘ ↔ 7 ft (2 m) ↑ 3–7 ft (0.9–2 m)

Found from Venezuela to Bolivia. Shrub or small tree with slender arching branches. Rather leathery pointed leaves, narrow to oval, dark green above. Clusters of flowers, purple with white centers. Zones 10–12.

Brunfelsia maliformis

☀ ⚘ ↔ 16–32 in (40–80 cm) ↑ 24–40 in (60–100 cm)

Shrubby Jamaican species with light green lance-shaped leaves to 2 in (5 cm) long and long-tubed, soft, creamy yellow flowers. Very distinctive. Zones 10–12.

Brunfelsia pauciflora

syn. *Brunfelsia calycina*

☀/◐ ⚘ ↔ 5 ft (1.5 m) ↑ 8 ft (2.4 m)

Pauciflora means sparsely flowered, inappropriate for this heavy-flowering often semi-deciduous shrub from Brazil and Venezuela. Large flowers open purple-blue then age through pale mauve to white. Dwarf cultivars,

Brunfelsia grandiflora

Brunfelsia maliformis

Brunfelsia pauciflora 'Macrantha'

such as 'Floribunda' ★ and 'Floribunda Compacta', and larger-flowered forms such as 'Macrantha' are widely available. Zones 10–12.

BRUNIA

A genus of 7 shrubs in the brunia (Bruniaceae) family, they are all native to South Africa where they often grow in ground that is boggy in winter. They have small overlapping leaves similar to heather, and terminal clusters of tiny cream or white flowers.

CULTIVATION: In frost-free climates grow outdoors in a moist but well-drained lime-free soil in full sun or part-shade. Prune lightly after flowering. Propagate from seed or cuttings.

Brunia albiflora

STOMPIES

☀ ⚘ ↔ 3 ft (0.9 m) ↑ 4 ft (1.2 m)

From South Africa. Downy branchlets. Leaves are small, and crowded, on short stalks. Flowers small, white, in spherical heads, in spring–summer. Zones 9–11.

Brunia nodiflora

☀/◐ ⚘ ↔ 3 ft (0.9 m) ↑ 3 ft (0.9 m)

Shrubby habit with dense, bright green, conifer-like foliage made up

Brunia albiflora

of tiny, overlapping, bristly leaves. Cream flowerheads to ½ in (12 mm) wide. Zones 9–11.

BRUNNERA

This genus of 3 species of fleshy-stemmed herbaceous perennials of the borage (Boraginaceae) family comes from temperate Eurasia. The species are closely related to the forget-me-nots and resemble them in flower. Sprays of tiny blue or white flowers appear in spring. However, the rounded to heart-shaped leaves of *Brunnera* are far larger than those of the common forget-me-nots and, as the garden forms are often variegated, the foliage is easily as much a feature as the flowers. The genus was named after Samuel Brunner (1790–1844), a Swiss botanist.

CULTIVATION: These plants are most at home in a temperate climate with cool summers. Extremely hardy and easily grown in woodland conditions with dappled sunlight and moist, humus-rich, well-drained soil. Established clumps of cultivars may be divided near the end of the dormant period, otherwise the seed germinates freely. *Brunnera* species often self-sow and naturalize.

Brunfelsia pauciflora

Brunia nodiflora, in the wild, Western Cape, South Africa

Brunnera macrophylla

Brunnera macrophylla 'Hadspen Cream'

Brunnera macrophylla

☼ ❋ ↔ 16–32 in (40–80 cm)
↕ 20 in (50 cm)

A Eastern European perennial with finely hairy, broad, heart-shaped leaves to 6 in (15 cm) long on 8 in (20 cm) stalks. Soft blue flowers are held above the foliage on 20 in (50 cm) stems. 'Hadspen Cream', one of several variegated cultivars, cream-spotted light green leaves, blue flowers. Zones 3–9.

BRUNSVIGIA

There are about 20 species of bulbous plants in this genus, which is a member of the amaryllis (Amaryllidaceae) family. They are native to South Africa, where they grow in a variety of soils but all have a dormant period in summer. They resemble amaryllis plants, to which they are closely related. The leaves are long and strap-like, and in late summer to autumn showy heads of pink to red, funnel-shaped, lily-like flowers are borne on tall stems. The bulbs can grow very large and take several years to flower.
CULTIVATION: In frost-free climates grow in well-drained soil in full sun in a position that is dry during the period of their summer dormancy. In colder areas grow in pots under glass. Bulbs should be planted almost on the soil surface. Water in autumn to bring bulbs into growth. Propagate from offsets in late summer or from seed in autumn.

Brunsvigia josephinae

JOSEPHINE'S LILY

☼ ⚘ ↔ 24 in (60 cm)
↕ 24–48 in (60–120 cm)

From South Africa. Large bulb, up to 12 in (30 cm) across. Heads of 12 to 20 rose pink flowers on tall stems, in late summer. Long strap-like leaves appear after the flowers. Zones 9–11.

Brunsvigia orientalis ★

CANDELABRA FLOWER

☼ ⚘ ↔ 18 in (45 cm) ↕ 20 in (50 cm)

From South Africa. Subterranean bulb producing strap-shaped leaves. Sturdy stems bear large umbels of pink to crimson narrow-petalled flowers. Zones 9–11.

BRYA

Belonging to the pea-flower subfamily of the legume (Fabaceae) family, this genus of evergreen trees from the Caribbean contains just 4 species, 3 of which are endemic to Cuba. Although commonly known as ebony because of their dark heartwood, they are not related to the true ebony, *Diospyros ebenum*. *Brya* leaves are small, and sprout directly from the stems, without stalks. The broom-like flowers, develop in the leaf axils.
CULTIVATION: A tropical climate is vital for these trees, which soon suffer in prolonged cool conditions. Where the climate is suitable, *Brya* can be an attractive tree that flowers heavily, and nursery-grown plants are available in some areas. Propagate from seed,

Brunsvigia orientalis, in the wild, Cape of Good Hope Reserve, Western Cape, South Africa

which should be pre-treated by rubbing on sandpaper and then soaking in cold water.

Brya ebenus

☼ ✿ ↔ 12 ft (3.5 m) ↕ 30 ft (9 m)

COCUS WOOD, GRANADILLA, JAMAICA EBONY, WEST INDIES EBONY

Once widely used for musical instruments, such as flutes and clarinets, and small objects, the timber is still prized although rare. Leaves shiny, 1 in (25 mm) long. Flowers golden yellow, in autumn. Zones 11–12.

BUCHLOE

BUFFALO GRASS

A genus containing 1 species of grass from the family Poaceae, native to North America. The grayish green sparsely hairy leaves arise from a prostrate modified stem or runner, forming tufts. Branched racemes of male flowers, to 8 in (20 cm) long, contain spikelets in 2 rows on 1 side of a central stem. Female flowers appear in short spikes enclosed by leaves.

CULTIVATION: Propagate by division of runners or from seed. Can be planted in any garden soil in an open sunny position.

Buchloe dactyloides

BUFFALO GRASS

☼ ❋ ↔ 3–4 in (8–10 cm)
↕ 4–6 in (10–15 cm)

Low-growing perennial grass from American prairies used widely for ornamental lawns, forming finely textured turf of soft blue-green, which turns gold in autumn. Spreads by surface runners and seed. Zones 3–5.

BUCKINGHAMIA

There are 2 species of this genus in the protea (Proteaceae) family, both from Queensland, Australia. They are fast-growing, tropical rainforest trees that resemble grevilleas in foliage and flower. *B. celsissima* is frequently grown as a street tree and appreciated for its abundant flowers.
CULTIVATION: These plants prefer warm sheltered spots but tolerate cool

Brya ebenus

Buddleja colvilei

Buckinghamia celsissima

Buddleja auriculata

Buddleja alternifolia

Buddleja alternifolia 'Argentea'

frost-free conditions. They prefer moist well-drained loam in full sun or partial shade. Initial directional pruning can be beneficial but pruning is not required once the framework is established. They are propagated from ripe seed in autumn.

Buckinghamia celsissima
IVORY CURL TREE

☼ ❀ ↔ 12 ft (3.5 m) ↕ 30 ft (9 m)
Evergreen tree from northeastern Queensland, Australia. Leaves dark green, shiny, pale beneath, lobed when juvenile. Inflorescences long; creamy recurved flowers on short stems in autumn. Woody fruits follow. Zones 10–12.

BUDDLEJA
The name of this genus of deciduous, semi-deciduous, and evergreen plants from the Americas, Asia, and South Africa can be spelt buddleja or buddleia. The genus, which gives its name to the family Buddlejaceae, consists of about 100 species, of which a few shrubby or tree-like ones are garden grown. There are also some decorative cultivars that are grown for their profuse, small, fragrant flowers that are held in large panicles. The leaves are, with the exception of *B. alternifolia*, paired and opposite. The plants are tough, undemanding, quick growing and salt tolerant. They are also sun loving and vigorous and, if given shelter, can be grown in climates considerably cooler than those found in their native habitats.
CULTIVATION: Basic requirements include sunlight, good drainage, fertile soil, and, from the gardener's point of view, regular pruning. Some plants show a mild preference for chalky and limy soils. Propagate from half-hardened cuttings in summer.

Buddleja alternifolia ★
FOUNTAIN BUDDLEJA

☼ ❀ ↔ 15 ft (4.5 m) ↕ 15 ft (4.5 m)
Deciduous shrub native to northwest China. Leaves small, green above, whitish beneath. Flowers fragrant, misty mauve, attract butterflies, in late spring–early-summer. Remove the flowering stems in summer. 'Argentea', mauve flowers, fine growth of silvery hairs on leaves. Zones 8–10.

Buddleja asiatica

☼ ❀ ↔ 10 ft (3 m) ↕ 10 ft (3 m)
Evergreen tree-like shrub from southeastern Asia. Leaves long, narrow, dark green above, paler undersides. The flowers are very fragrant, long, creamy white, on drooping racemes, and appear on last year's growth, in winter–spring. Zones 8–10.

Buddleja auriculata
WEEPING SAGE

☼ ❀ ↔ 15 ft (4.5 m) ↕ 20 ft (6 m)
Evergreen shrub from rocky riversides of South Africa. Leaves long, crinkled, dark green above, woolly white beneath. Flowers fragrant, creamy white, with yellow or pink centers, in terminal clusters, in winter. Zones 8–10.

Buddleja colvilei
SUMMER LILAC

☼ ❀ ↔ 20 ft (6 m) ↕ 20 ft (6 m)
Large, upright, deciduous or evergreen shrub from eastern Asia. Branches arching. Leaves dark gray-green, long, pointed, heavily veined, white woolly beneath. Flowers large, bell-like, cherry pink to rosy red, terminal pendent panicles, in spring. 'Kewensis', rich raspberry red flowers. Zones 7–9.

Buddleja crispa

☼ ❀ ↔ 15 ft (4.5 m) ↕ 15 ft (4.5 m)
From the Himalayas. A deciduous bushy upright shrub, arching habit. Leaves dark oval, new shoots woolly white. Fragrant mauve flowers in long whorled panicles, in spring–summer. Prune in winter. Zones 7–9.

Buddleja lindleyana

Buddleja madagascariensis

Buddleja globosa

Buddleja fallowiana var. *alba*

green above, wrinkled, woolly white on the undersides; the young stems are silvery white. Flowers are scented, orange-yellow, in clusters, in late spring–early summer. Prune when flowering finishes. Zones 7–9.

Buddleja lindleyana ★

☼ ❄ ↔ 12 ft (3.5 m). ↑ 12 ft (3.5 m). Semi-deciduous shrub from the scrub of eastern Asia. Leaves sage green, pointed, carried on square sage-like stems. Flowers curved, tubular, purple, on long, tapering, upright spikes. Has naturalized in southeast USA. Zones 7–9.

Buddleja 'Lochinch'

☼ ❄ ↔ 8–10 ft (2.4–3 m) ↑ 10–15 ft (3–4.5 m)

A lovely garden hybrid between *B. davidii* and *B. fallowiana,* with gray felted leaves and panicles of summer-blooming, sweetly scented, violet-blue flowers with a tiny orange eye. Zones 6–9.

Buddleja madagascariensis

NICODEMIA

☼ ⧈ ↔ 15 ft (4.5 m) ↑ 20 ft (6 m)

An evergreen, pendulous, scrambling shrub in cold climates, that can be neatly espaliered. Leaves long, large, lance-shaped, mid-green above, woolly white undersides. Flowers small, scented, yellow-orange, in late winter–early spring. Violet berry-like fruits. Zones 9–11.

blue flowers, orange eye; '**Harlequin**', cream-edged leaves; '**Nanho Petite Indigo**', lavender-purple flowers; '**Nanho Petite Purple**', rich purple flowers; '**Royal Red**', purple-red flowers; **White Profusion**', white flowers, golden eye. Zones 4–9.

Buddleja fallowiana

☼ ❄ ↔ 10 ft (3 m) ↑ 10 ft (3 m)

Deciduous Chinese species; arching stems. Leaves lance-shaped, dark gray-green. Flowers fragrant, pale lavender with orange centers, in large panicles, in summer–early autumn. *B. f.* **var. alba**, creamy white flowers with orange eye. Zones 8–9.

Buddleja globosa

ORANGE BALL TREE

☼ ❄ ↔ 10 ft (3 m) ↑ 10 ft (3 m)

Semi-evergreen tree native to Argentina and Chile. The leaves are dark

Buddleja davidii

BUTTERFLY BUSH

☼ ❄ ↔ 17 ft (5 m) ↑ 10–17 ft (3–5 m) Native to rocky riversides in central and western China. Tough deciduous plant with many garden-grown cultivars. Quick vigorous growth, bushy habit, arching stems. Fragrant mauve

flowers in panicles. Long pointed leaves, dark green above, woolly white beneath. Can be invasive. *B. d.* **var. nanhoensis**, to 5 ft (1.5 m) tall and wide. *B. d.* '**Black Knight**', royal purple flowers; '**Dartmoor**', red-purple flowers on fan-like flowering stems ; '**Empire Blue**', steely violet-

Buddleja davidii 'Black Knight'

Buddleja davidii 'Nanho Petite Indigo'

B. d. 'Dart's Ornamental White'

Buddleja davidii 'Fascinating'

Buddleja davidii 'Harlequin'

B. davidii 'Nanho Petite Purple'

B. davidii 'Orchid Beauty'

B

Buddleja nivea

☼ ❄ ↔8ft(2.4m) ↑10ft(3m)
Vigorous, upright, deciduous shrub
from China. Leaves narrow, dark
green above, woolly white down
beneath. Downy panicles of violet-
blue flowers. Zones 7–9.

Buddleja 'Pink Delight'

syn. *Buddleja davidii* 'Pink Delight'
☼ ❄ ↔7ft(2m) ↑5–7ft(1.5–2m)
Grayish green arching foliage. Flowers
are deep pink, fragrant, on racemes
12–15 in (30–38 cm) long, in late
summer–early autumn. Zones 7–10.

Buddleja salviifolia

SOUTH AFRICAN SAGEWOOD,
WINTER BUDDLEJA
☼ ❅ ↔15ft(4.5m) ↑25ft(8m)
Dense shrub or small tree from South
Africa. Leaves long, narrow, pointed,
felted, sage gray, lightly crinkled,
borne on short stalks. Flowers are in
heavy plumes, scented, smoky mauve,
in late autumn–winter. Zones 9–10.

Bulbine frutescens 'Hallmark'

Buddleja 'Wattle Bird'

☼ ❄ ↔6ft(1.8m) ↑10ft(3m)
A relatively recent introduction.
Australian-raised deciduous shrub, a
B. × *weyeriana* (*B. davidii* × *B. globosa*)
hybrid. Long, pointed, lance-shaped
leaves. Instead of spherical flowerheads it bears elongated spikes of
yellow flowers, in late summer–
autumn. Zones 6–10.

Buddleja × *weyeriana*

☼ ❄ ↔12ft(3.5m) ↑15ft(4.5m)
Deciduous hybrid between *B. davidii*
and *B. globosa*. Leaves dark, lance-
shaped. Flowers bobble-like clusters,
scented, orange-yellow shaded with
lilac. '**Golden Glow**', soft purple
buds, profusion of apricot flowers in
open panicles; '**Honeycomb**', pale
yellow flowers; '**Sungold**', dense heads
of bright yellow flowers with orange
centers. Zones 6–9.

BUGLOSSOIDES

This genus of 15 species of annual or
perennial herbs, native to Europe and
Asia, belongs to the borage (Boraginaceae) family. They grow naturally in
habitats ranging from sunny scrub to
rocky slopes and woodland areas.
Plants are covered in fine bristles or
hairs. Stems are upright or sprawling,
branched or unbranched, with simple
oval to lance-shaped leaves. The small
funnel-shaped flowers have flaring
lobes and are usually blue or white.
Perennial species that are rhizomatous
can become invasive and difficult
where conditions are suitable.

Buddleja × *weyeriana*

CULTIVATION: Suitable for "wild" and
woodland gardens, grow these plants
in moist well-drained soil that is neutral to alkaline. Propagate from seed,
from cuttings, or by division.

Buglossoides purpurocaerulea

syn. *Lithospermum purpurocaeruleum*
☼/❖ ❄ ↔24in(60cm) ↑24in(60cm)
Found throughout Europe and central
Asia. Creeping rhizomatous perennial
with narrow pointed leaves. Flowers
reddish purple on opening, becoming
deep blue with age. Zones 6–9.

BULBINE

This diverse group of about 35 species
from South Africa and Australia
belongs to the asphodel (Asphodelaceae) family. While the Latin word
bulbine means a bulb, only a few
species possess this feature. The larger
species have succulent grass-like leaves
and flower spikes that can reach 20 in
(50 cm) or more in height. There are
also several miniature species with

Buddleja salviifolia

attractive leaves; several of these
resemble other succulent genera, such
as *Aloe* and *Haworthia,* and will die
down completely in the dormant
period. Numerous flowers in all
species, yellow or orange, borne on
upright inflorescences. Some species
have healing properties and are used
externally to treat wounds, burns, and
itches, or internally for diarrhea, con-
vulsions, and urinary infections.
CULTIVATION: *Bulbine* species are
easy to cultivate in rich, well-drained,
but well-watered soil. Can be propagated from seed, but usually raised by
dividing old plants.

Bulbine frutescens

syn. *Bulbine caulescens*
☼/❖ ❅ ↔24in(60cm) ↑24in(60cm)
Branching shrub from south coast of
South Africa north into Mozambique.
Leaves light green, linear, semi-cylindrical, 8–10 in (20–25 cm) long.
Inflorescence to 24 in (60 cm), bearing 40 to 50 yellow flowers. '**Hallmark**' (syn. *B. caulescens* 'Hallmark'),
compact form, shorter inflorescence,
orange flowers. Zones 9–11.

Bulbine latifolia

syn. *Bulbine natalensis*
☼/❖ ❅ ↔24in(60cm) ↑24in(60cm)
Clumping rosette-forming succulent
from Eastern Cape and KwaZulu-
Natal Provinces, South Africa. Leaves
triangular, to 15 in (38 cm) long, to
6 in (15 cm) wide at base, strongly
recurved away from growing tip.
Inflorescence to 24 in (60 cm), dense
raceme of yellow flowers. Zones 10-11.

Bulbine latifolia

Bulbophyllum Daisy Chain

Bulbophyllum flaviflorum

Bulbophyllum carunculatum

Bulbine margarethae

☀ ❅ ↔ 2 in (5 cm) ↑ 3 in (8 cm)

From South Africa. Miniature plant with small ½–¾ in (12–18 mm) caudex. Leaves 10–15, cylindrical, resembling a bunch of chives. Flowers yellow, on 2½–3 in (6–8 cm) tall inflorescence. Zones 9–11.

BULBINELLA

This genus of 20 species of fleshy-rooted deciduous perennials is a member of the asphodel (Asphodelaceae) family. The majority of species are native to South Africa, but 6 are found in New Zealand. They form clumps of long somewhat fleshy leaves. Yellow flowers are borne on tall stems in spikes that resemble those of red-hot pokers (*Kniphofia* species.)
CULTIVATION: Grow in sun or part-shade in free-draining but moisture-retentive soil that is neutral or slightly acidic. Also suitable for growing in pots in the greenhouse. They dislike humidity. Propagate from seed or by root division.

Bulbinella hookeri

☀ ❅ ↔ 24 in (60 cm) ↑ 36 in (90 cm)

From alpine areas of New Zealand. Strap-like leaves. Stout stems bear spikes of starry yellow flowers in summer. Winter dormant. Zones 7–9.

Bulbinella latifolia ★

☀ ❅ ↔ 24 in (60 cm) ↑ 36 in (90 cm)

From South Africa. Narrow strappy leaves. Spikes of yellow to deep orange

Bulbinella rossii

flowers from winter to late spring. Summer dormant. Propagate by root division. Zones 7–9.

Bulbinella rossii

☀ ❅ ↔ 12–24 in (30–60 cm) ↑ 24–36 in (60–90 cm)

From Campbell and Auckland Islands south of New Zealand. Bright green stiffly arching leaves. Spikes of densely packed golden-yellow flowers in summer. Winter dormant. Zones 7–9.

BULBOPHYLLUM

This is a huge orchid genus in the family Orchidaceae, with more than 1,500 named species, and many more still being discovered. In this cosmopolitan genus, there are plants with flowers in all shapes, sizes, and colors. These sympodial orchids grow exclusively as epiphytes and lithophytes. The majority of species produce a cylindrical pseudobulb with a single leaf, which develops along a creeping rhizome. There are numerous species, particularly from Africa and Madagascar, that are two-leafed. *Bulbophyllum* includes some of the world's smallest orchids, plus others that form massive plants. Flowers are unlike most orchids; highly specialized to attract specific pollinators. Most species have very mobile lips.
CULTIVATION: Most bulbophyllums are creeping plants that have only a short root system, which rarely branches. In the main, they prefer shaded conditions and constant moisture around the roots. They grow well on tree-fern slabs and rafts, while larger species may be grown in shallow saucers, pots, or baskets. Some species of *Bulbophyllum* only flower in response to wet and dry seasons, while others flower throughout the year.

Bulbophyllum carunculatum

☀ ⚑ ↔ 10 in (25 cm) ↑ 24 in (60 cm)

From Sulawesi and the Philippines, this is an impressive yellowish green-flowered species. Up to five 5 in (12 cm) long widely opening blooms,

Bulbophyllum fletcherianum

produced on an upright inflorescence in summer. Probably pollinated by flies, attracted by its robust odor. Zones 11–12.

Bulbophyllum Daisy Chain

☀ ⚑ ↔ 12 in (30 cm) ↑ 5 in (12 cm)

A popular warm-growing primary hybrid between *B. makoyanum* and *B. amesianum*. The flowers are presented like the spokes of a wheel. Zones 11–12.

Bulbophyllum flaviflorum

☀ ⚑ ↔ 16 in (40 cm) ↑ 3–6 in (8–15 cm)

China, Vietnam, Laos, and Thailand. Up to 10 short sprays of 1¼ in (3 cm)

long blooms. Majority of the flower is comprised of bright yellow, fused, lateral sepals. Zones 11–12.

Bulbophyllum fletcherianum

☀ ⚑ ↔ 10–24 in (24–60 cm) ↑ 12–40 in (30–100 cm)

From New Guinea, this is one of the largest growing plants in the genus. Pendulous, purple stained, wide, leathery leaves up to 40 in (100 cm) in length, coming from pseudobulbs often larger than tennis balls. Clusters of up to 20 smooth but fleshy claret-colored blooms that do not open fully and have a most unpleasant aroma. Zones 11–12.

B

Bulbophyllum graveolens

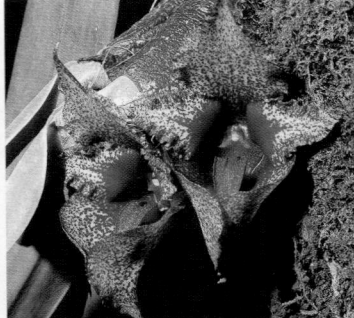

Bulbophyllum macrobulbum, in the wild, New Guinea

Bulbophyllum wendlandianum ★

☀ ⚬ ↔ 12 in (30 cm) ↕ 4–7 in (10–18 cm)
From Thailand and Myanmar. Similar to *B. rothschildianum* but fewer, narrower deep red blooms. Flowers in early summer, inflorescences emerging from new growths. Zones 10–12.

BULNESIA

This tropical American genus in the twinleaf (Zygophyllaceae) family includes at least 11 species of evergreen trees. They have pinnate leaves and showy yellow to orange flowers in terminal clusters. Some species, especially *B. arborea*, are valued for their timber.
CULTIVATION: Apart for the inability to tolerate frost or prolonged cool

Bulbophyllum tridentatum

Bulbophyllum putidum

Bulbophyllum rothschildianum ★

☀ ⚬ ↔ 24 in (60 cm) ↕ 10 in (25 cm)
From India. A member of the *Cirrhopetalum* section of *Bulbophyllum*, which is generally characterized by having flowers in an umbel, lower sepals fused, and filaments and appendages on upper sepal and petals. These "flags" move in the slightest breeze and help attract potential pollinators. This species has clusters of deep maroon blooms. Zones 10–12.

Bulbophyllum tridentatum

☀ ✈ ↔ 12 in (30 cm) ↕ 10 in (25 cm)
From Thailand. Single leathery leaf connected by a rhizome to a round pseudobulb covered in papery scales; plant has a rambling appearance. The small sprays of flowers have an unpleasant aroma. Zones 11–12.

Bulbophyllum unitubum

☀ ✈ ↔ 8 in (20 cm) ↕ 5–8 in (12–20 cm)
An impressive species from New Guinea that has only recently entered general cultivation. Large short-lived flowers, but re-blooms several times throughout the year. Zones 11–12.

Bulbophyllum graveolens

☀ ✈ ↔ 24 in (60 cm) ↕ 20 in (50 cm)
A robust species from New Guinea. Up to a dozen flowers, 3 in (8 cm) long, are arranged on a loose umbel. Petals and sepals pale green to light orange, sometimes finely spotted in dark purple; bright red mobile labellum. Has a rather unpleasant foetid smell. Zones 11–12.

Bulbophyllum guttulatum ★

☀ ⚬ ↔ 10 in (25 cm) ↕ 10 in (25 cm)
Late winter-flowering species from India and Nepal. Small upright inflorescence of up to 8 cream, yellow or greenish flowers, finely spotted with purple. Labellum white with deep pink spots. Zones 10–11.

Bulbophyllum macrobulbum

☀ ✈ ↔ 10–24 in (25–60 cm)
↕ 12–40 in (30–100 cm)
Large-growing species from New Guinea. Pendulous, long and broad, leathery leaves. Flesh-colored blooms,

produced in only small groups, open fully with an unpleasant fragrance. Zones 11–12.

Bulbophyllum putidum

☀ ⚬ ↔ 10 in (25 cm) ↕ 5–8 in (12–20 cm)
A single-flowered species from Southeast Asia. Quite a large bloom considering the compact nature of the plant. Some botanists consider *B. appendiculatum* to be a more appropriate name for this unique orchid. Zones 10–12.

Bulbophyllum wendlandianum

Bulbophyllum guttulatum

Bulbophyllum unitubum, in the wild, New Guinea

Burchellia bubalina

conditions, most species are easily cultivated in any well-drained soil and are drought tolerant once established. Plant in full sun. If necessary, trim after flowering to retain a pleasing shape. Propagation is from seed.

Bulnesia arborea

MARACAIBO LIGNUM-VITAE

☼ ❀ ↔ 20 ft (6 m) ↑ 50 ft (15 m)
Evergreen tree native to Colombia and Venezuela; can reach 100 ft (30 m) in the wild. Finely divided pinnate foliage. Golden yellow flowers with distinctly separate, narrow-based, rounded petals. Commercially significant for its timber. Zones 11–12.

BUPLEURUM

Widely distributed around the temperate Northern Hemisphere and extending to the Canary Islands and South Africa, *Bupleurum* is a genus of the carrot (Apiaceae) family, which includes evergreen shrubs as well as annuals and perennials. Leaves are simple and undivided. The shrubby species are many-stemmed from ground level and have somewhat leathery or succulent foliage. Flowers are small, mostly greenish or yellow, borne in neat compound umbels that may be grouped into larger panicles. The small dry fruits are similar to those of parsnips and hemlock. CULTIVATION: This shrubby species comes from warmer drier regions around the Mediterranean, and the Canary Islands. They grow best in a sunny exposed position in well-drained soil and are tolerant of salt-laden breezes near the seashore. They withstand hard pruning and may be trained into hedges. Propagate from cuttings, root divisions, or seed.

Bupleurum rotundifolium

HARE'S EAR, THOROWAX

☼ ❀ ↔ 24 in (60 cm) ↑ 24 in (60 cm)
Originally from Europe and Russia, but now naturalized in USA. This annual or short-lived perennial has round bluish green leaves that appear to be perforated by their stems. Umbels of tiny greenish yellow flowers surrounded by large green bracts, in summer. Zones 5–9.

Bupleurum salicifolium

HINOJO

☼ ⚘ ↔ 8 ft (2.4 m) ↑ 8 ft (2.4 m)
Native to the Canary Islands and Madeira; rare in cultivation. Grows as densely massed stems with soft bluish foliage. Leaves narrow, tapering to a fine point. Flowers golden yellow in drooping panicles, and appear in late spring–summer. Zones 9–10.

Bupleurum spinosum

☼ ❀ ↔ 12 in (30 cm) ↑ 12 in (30 cm)
Woody-based sparsely branched perennial from southern and eastern Spain. Narrow, lance-shaped, bluish green leaves. Umbels of small yellowish green flowers in summer. Stalks persist for 2 to 3 years, becoming hard and spiny. Zones 7–10.

BURCHELLIA

This genus from South Africa contains a single species in the madder (Rubiaceae) family. It is named for William Burchell, a botanical explorer in South Africa. Not often seen in gardens, despite its attractive foliage and bright flowers.
CULTIVATION: *Burchellia* prefers a light, fertile, and well-drained soil with plenty of summer moisture, in a warm area not subject to heavy frosts. Tolerates full sun and filtered shade. Trim occasionally to maintain shape. A light trimming after flowering will prevent

Bupleurum spinosum

fruit production and so improve flower quality. Propagate from seed sown in late winter or spring or from half-hardened cuttings taken in late summer or autumn.

Burchellia bubalina

syn. *Burchellia capensis*
SOUTH AFRICAN POMEGRANATE

☼ ⚘ ↔ 8 ft (2.4 m) ↑ 10 ft (3 m)
Evergreen shrub found from Cape of Good Hope to Tropic of Capricorn. Leaves simple, dark green and shiny above, bright green beneath. The inflorescence is a terminal umbel, 10 to 12 flowers, bright orange-red to scarlet, in spring–summer. Zones 9–11.

BURRAGEARA

A member of the family Orchidaceae, this is a complex generic orchid hybrid being a combination of *Cochlioda*,

Bupleurum salicifolium

Bulnesia arborea

B

Miltonia, Odontoglossum, and *Oncidium.* Many of these hybrids have rich red colors that can be traced back in part to the *Cochlioda.*
CULTIVATION: Burragearas do not like their roots to dry out, so the plants need to be potted in sphagnum moss or a fine bark mix. They are suitable for cool growing conditions, but need abundant water throughout the year and a semi-shaded position.

Burrageara Hybrids

☀ ❀ ↔ 12 in (30 cm) ↕ 30 in (75 cm)
Among the *Burrageara* hybrids available are: **Living Fire 'Burning Embers'**, a hybrid between

Vuylstekeara Edna and the Central American species *Oncidium maculatum*; **Nelly Isler**, an improvement on its parent *B.* Stefan Isler, has been hybridized with *Miltoniopsis* Kensington; **Stefan Isler**, similar to *B.* Living Fire, is a hybrid between *Vuylstekeara* Edna and *Oncidium leucochilum.* Zones 10–11.

BURRETIOKENTIA

This genus, a member of the family Arecaceae, contains 2 species of single-stemmed palms; both are endemic to the wet rainforests of New Caledonia. The plants have graceful crowns. The pinnate glossy green leaves grow to 8 ft

Burrageara, Hybrid, Living Fire 'Burning Embers'

Burrageara, Hybrid, Nelly Isler

Burrageara, Hybrid, Stefan Isler

(2.4 m) long. Inflorescences consist of striking finger-like stems that are quite thick and densely woolly-hairy.
CULTIVATION: Propagate from seed, which can take many months to germinate. Seedlings have been known to be difficult to keep growing unless given full shade, plenty of water, and high humidity. Once established, older plants will tolerate full sun.

Burretiokentia vieillardii

☀ ✲ ↔ 20 ft (6 m) ↕ 70 ft (21 m)
Occurs only on soils derived from serpentinite (ultramafic) with a high pH. Dull green trunk to 8 in (20 cm) diameter. Crownshaft distinctively marked and colored. Fruits reddish. Difficult to grow, unless given shade, high humidity, plenty of water, and high pH soil. Zones 11–12.

BURSARIA

A genus of the pittosporum (Pittosporaceae) family, *Bursaria* consists of 6 species of evergreen shrubs and small trees native to eastern and southern Australia. Mostly stiff twiggy shrubs with thorny branches and small leaves; in late spring and summer they bear white flowers in small clusters in the leaf axils or in larger panicles at

the branch tips. Each small flower has 5 separate petals alternating with 5 stamens. The fruit is a small flattened capsule. *Bursaria* is derived from Latin *bursa,* "a purse." Relatively unknown outside Australia, they make attractive ornamentals, and are grown as thorny hedges. They can naturalize to become pests in some climates.
CULTIVATION: *Bursaria* species are easily grown in climates in which frosts are not too severe; they are fast growing but not very long lived. A sunny but sheltered position is preferred and soil should be well drained and moderately fertile; the roots can penetrate hard clay. Propagate from cuttings or seed.

Bursaria spinosa

AUSTRALIAN BOXTHORN, BLACKTHORN
☀ ✲ ↔ 7 ft (2 m) ↕ 12 ft (3.5 m)
From coastal eastern Australia and Tasmania. Leaves to 1½ in (35 mm) long, grouped on thorny short shoots. Fragrant white flowers in large panicles, in late spring–early autumn, followed by reddish fruit. Zones 8–11.

BURSERA

Consisting of around 50 species of both evergreen and deciduous trees and shrubs, *Bursera* belongs to the Burseraceae family and is restricted to tropical America and the West Indies, southern Florida, California, and Arizona. Species have smooth or flaky pale bark, pinnate leaves with an odd number of leaflets, and small greenish white to yellow flowers, grouped in short sprays near the branch tips. The

Burretiokentia vieillardii, in the wild, New Caledonia

Bursaria spinosa

fruits are small to large capsules. Some shrubby species from hot dry regions have evolved swollen stems and smaller sparser leaves. *Bursera* plants are best known for their resins, used in varnish, perfume, and incense.
CULTIVATION: The tree species from higher-rainfall areas prefer a sunny but sheltered position and well-drained soil with adequate subsoil moisture. Western Mexican species with swollen stems need a dry atmosphere and open gravelly soil with excellent drainage; in cooler climates they are grown in greenhouses under high light levels. Propagate from seed or cuttings.

Bursera microphylla
ELEPHANT TREE

☼ ❀ ↔ 5 ft (1.5 m) ↑ 12 ft (3.5 m)
Deciduous shrub extending from northwest Mexico to southern California and Arizona. Low branching with swollen stems, pale papery bark. Thick reddish twigs bear leaves at tips, narrow leaflets. Flowers in whitish clusters. Pea-sized fruits. Zones 9–12.

BUTIA
BUTIA PALMS

This genus of small to medium-sized palms in the family Arecaceae comprises 8 species from subtropical and warm-temperate regions of eastern South America. It is characterized by the large spindle-shaped bract around the flowering panicle in bud. Fronds arch from the trunk, consisting of 2 rows of thick narrow leaflets. The stout trunk is clothed by old frond stalks; when shed with age they leave a closely ringed gray surface. Sweet-scented cream to purplish flowers appear on stiff springy spikes; flowering

branch bursts through a slit in the bract before the flowers open. The fruits are edible, and can be fermented to make a kind of wine.
CULTIVATION: Widely grown as landscape subjects in warm-temperate climates, they tolerate hot exposed environments. Deep-rooted, they tolerate dry topsoil, but are readily transplanted at any age. When trimming old fronds, bases should be cut at an even length to preserve the neat pattern on the trunk. Propagation is from seed, but germination may take some months.

Butia capitata ★
BUTIA PALM, JELLY PALM

☼ ❀ ↔ 15 ft (4.5 m) ↑ 20 ft (6 m)
From southern Brazil, Uruguay, and northern Argentina. Fronds recurving, grayish, to 10 ft (3 m) long. Large cream bracts, pale yellow to reddish flowers, in late spring–early summer. Fruits ripen in summer or autumn of the following year. Zones 8–11.

Butia eriospatha
☼ ❀ ↔ 12 ft (3.5 m) ↑ 12 ft (3.5 m)
From southern Brazil; similar to *B. capitata*. Outer surface of large bracts densely coated in brown woolly hairs, look like brown lambskin. Flowers reddish purple on the outside, in early summer. Zones 9–11.

BUTOMUS
FLOWERING RUSH, GRASSY RUSH, WATER GLADIOLUS

A genus containing a single species of aquatic perennial herb from the family Butomaceae, native to Eurasia. The sword-like leaves, to 5 ft (1.5 m) tall, arise from the fleshy stems. Flower

Buxus harlandii

stalk to 3 ft (0.9 m) in height, with terminal umbels of many flowers, often fragrant, with rose-pink tepals (modified sepals and petals), ¼–¾ in (6–18 mm) wide, with 6 to 9 stamens and dark red anthers, in summer.
CULTIVATION: Plant in a warm sunny position in water that does not freeze, up to 6 in (15 cm) deep. Propagate by root division in spring.

Butomus umbellatus
FLOWERING RUSH

☼ ❀ ↔ 30 in (75 cm) ↑ 60 in (150 cm)
Aquatic grass from Europe and Asia. Terminal umbels of rose-pink flowers in summer borne on erect, smooth, leafless stem. Sword-like leaves, bronze-purple when young, maturing to green, arranged in rosette with triangular sheathed base. Zones 5–9.

BUXUS
BOX

A member of the family Buxaceae, the genus *Buxus* has most of its 50 or so

Buxus balearica

species in the West Indies and Central America; there are also species through eastern Asia, the Himalayas, Africa, and Europe. All are evergreen shrubs or small trees with simple smooth-edged leaves arranged in opposite pairs. Small greenish or yellowish flowers are borne in the leaf axils. Fruits are small capsules. Mostly used as garden and landscape plants, the close-grained yellowish wood is also used for wood-cut engraving, and for small turned and carved objects such as buttons and chess pieces. The leaves and twigs are poisonous to livestock.
CULTIVATION: The smaller-leafed species are popular in cool-climate gardens. They are valued for their dense fine-textured foliage, hardiness, and ability to take frequent trimming and shaping. They grow in most soil types, including chalk, as long as there is reasonable drainage. Propagate from cuttings, but seed also germinates readily.

Buxus balearica
BALEARIC BOX

☼ ❀ ↔ 8 ft (2.4 m) ↑ 15 ft (4.5 m)
From the Balearic Islands and nearby parts of Spain and Algeria. It has more erect conical growth habit and larger thicker leaves than *B. sempervirens*. Can grow to 30 ft (9 m) under ideal conditions. Zones 8–11.

Buxus harlandii ★
☼ ❀ ↔ 3 ft (0.9 m) ↑ 3 ft (0.9 m)
Low bushy shrub from southern China. Leaves shiny, dark green, similar size to *B. sempervirens* but narrower in proportion. Many plants grown under this name are in fact forms of *B. microphylla*. Zones 8–11.

Butia capitata

Butia eriospatha

Buxus sempervirens

features that are important. Wild forms have slightly brownish green leaves, ¾ in (18 mm) long. Flowers greenish yellow, in spring. ***B. m.* var. *japonica***, dense upright shrub, slow-growing to 3 ft (0.9 m) high; '**Green Beauty**', deep green foliage; '**Morris Midget**', low-growing with yellow-green leaves. ***B. m.* 'Compacta'**, dwarf with dense foliage; '**Curly Locks**', pale green leaves and twisted shoots; '**Faulkner**', compact with red-brown stems; '**Green Jade**', egg-shaped pale green leaves, grows to 24 in (60 cm) high; '**Green Pillow**', small rounded leaves crowded on dwarf mound to 12 in (30 cm) high. Zones 6–10.

Buxus sempervirens

COMMON BOX, ENGLISH BOX

☼ ❅ ↔ 5–15 ft (1.5–4.5 m)
↑ 5–30 ft (1.5–9 m)

Widespread in Europe, western Asia, and northwestern Africa. Native to British Isles. Leaves to 1 in (25 mm) long; leaf apex may be pointed, blunt, or slightly notched. Greenish cream flower clusters, in late spring. '**Argenteovariegata**' (syn. 'Argentea'), delicate gray-green leaves with narrow cream margin; '**Elegantissima**', mid-green leaves with creamy white margins; '**Graham Blandy**', narrow columnar growth habit; '**Handsworthiensis**', unusually large leaves, good for hedging; '**Latifolia Maculata**', pale gold

Buxus microphylla

CHINESE BOX, JAPANESE BOX, KOREAN BOX

☼ ❅ ↔ 7 ft (2 m) ↑ 8 ft (2.4 m)

East Asian species with a number of forms and cultivars. It is more the differences in frost tolerance than

Buxus sempervirens 'Memorial'

Buxus sempervirens 'Elegantissima'

Buxus sempervirens 'Suffruticosa'

Buxus microphylla var. *japonica* 'Morris Midget'

Buxus microphylla 'Green Pillow'

Buxus sinica var. *insularis* 'Pincushion'

Buxus sinica var. *insularis*

juvenile leaves, yellow-variegated when mature; '**Marginata**', misshapen leaves with yellowish band around upper margin; '**Memorial**', symmetrical form, grows to about 2 ft (0.6 m); '**Suffruticosa**', dense erect habit, small leaves; '**Vardar Valley**' ★, dense mound-forming shrub, mid- to dark green leaves. Zones 5–10.

Buxus, Sheridan Hybrids

☼ ❄ ↔ 18–24 in (45–60 cm)
↕ 18–24 in (45–60 cm)

From North America, these cultivars have originated from crosses between forms of *B. sempervirens* and *B. microphylla* var. *koreana*. They are mostly dense compact shrubs. '**Green Gem**', globular form, with rich green foliage; '**Green Mountain**', conical form, with slightly darker foliage. Zones 5–10.

Buxus sinica

CHINESE BOX, KOREAN BOXWOOD
☼/◑ ❄ ↔ 2–12 ft (0.6–3.5 m)
↕ 3–20 ft (0.9–6 m)

Shrub or small tree from eastern China and Korea and once regarded as variety of *B. microphylla*. Occurs in many varieties covering wide size range. Glossy light green leaves to 1¼ in (30 mm) long. *B. s.* var. *insularis* (syn. *B. microphylla* var. *koreana*), slow-growing, with small but fragrant green-yellow flowers; '**Justin Brouwers**', dense mound with small, narrow, deep green leaves; '**Pincushion**' (syn. *B. microphylla* 'Cushion'), dwarf cushion-forming shrub with dull green rounded leaves; '**Tide Hill**', dwarf to 12 in (30 cm) tall; '**Winter Gem**' (syn. *B. microphylla* 'Winter Gem'), hardy, foliage remains green during winter. Zones 6–10.

Buxus wallichiana

HIMALAYAN BOX
☼ ❄ ↔ 7 ft (2 m) ↕ 6 ft (1.8 m)

From the northwestern Himalayas, rare in cultivation. Dark green leaves,

narrow in proportion to their length, to 2 in (5 cm) long, seldom more than ¼ in (6 mm) wide. Young shoots downy-haired; yellowish flowers in mid-spring. Zones 8–10.

BYSTROPOGON

About 10 species of evergreen shrubs make up this genus in the mint (Lamiaceae) family, occurring in the Canary Islands and Madeira. Allied to *Origanum* and *Thymus*, the genus is characterized by tiny flowers in much-branched clusters, with plume-like sepals that elongate at the fruiting stage, giving the whole tip of each branch a fuzzy appearance. As in other members of the family, stems are square in cross-section and leaves, arranged in opposite pairs, are aromatic when crushed.

CULTIVATION: They make interesting ornamentals and the fruiting branches can be cut for either fresh or dried arrangements indoors. Mild somewhat dry climates suit them best, but in cooler climates it should be possible to raise plants indoors in spring and plant them out for summer display. A sunny position and very well-drained soil are required. Propagate from cuttings or seed.

Bystropogon plumosus

☼ ◑ ↔ 4 ft (1.2 m) ↕ 4 ft (1.2 m)
Branching shrub native to Canary Islands. Stems become woody at base. Leaves small, grayish. Flowers white, in tiny sprays, in early summer. Ripening seed transforms plant into a mass of straw-colored to grayish, fuzzy, fruiting calyces. Zones 9–11.

Bystropogon plumosus

Buxus, Sheridan Hybrid, 'Green Mountain'

C

C

Caesalpinia gilliesii

Caesalpinia ferrea

CACCINIA

This small genus contains 6 species of multi-stemmed herbaceous perennials, placed in the borage (Boraginaceae) family, and found in a wide range of open habitats in mountainous regions of western and central Asia. Hairy stems arise from a stout rootstock, with a base and stem leaves of varying shapes, but usually simple and not hairy. Inflorescences are terminal, with many bluish star-like flowers. CULTIVATION: Not commonly cultivated. Propagate from seed.

Caccinia macranthera
☀ ❄ ↔ 36 in (90 cm) ↑ 24 in (60 cm)
The most widespread and most extensively grown species. Gray-green oblong to lance-shaped leaves closely spaced along the stems. Blue-purple flowers from late spring–summer.

Caesalpinia pulcherrima

Requires a well-drained gritty soil. C. m. var. crassifolia has blue-green leaves. Zones 5–9.

CAESALPINIA

Occurring in the tropics and many warm-temperate regions (mainly in the Americas), Caesalpinia belongs to the cassia subfamily of the legume (Fabaceae) family, and consists of around 150 species of evergreen and deciduous trees, shrubs, and scrambling climbers. Caesalpinia species all have bipinnate leaves, with numerous leaflets. Hooked prickles on branches and leaves are common, mainly on the climbers. Flowers are in spikes, terminating the branches. Many species have yellow flowers; most have 5 petals, and protruding stamens of often contrasting color. The pods can be flattened and smooth, or swollen and spiny, containing hard seeds.
CULTIVATION: These plants are readily cultivated in warm climates. Many caesalpinias tolerate exposed seashores, arid climates, or poorly drained soil. Some of the ornamental shrub and tree species prefer deeper well-drained soils and a sunny but sheltered position.

Caladenia chapmanii, in the wild, Busselton, Western Australia

Propagation is usually from the seed, pre-treated to penetrate the hard coat. C. gilliesii can be grown from cuttings.

Caesalpinia ferrea
BRAZILIAN IRONWOOD, LEOPARD TREE
☀ ❄ ↔ 20 ft (6 m) ↑ 50 ft (15 m)
Native to eastern Brazil. Deciduous, smooth creamy bark dappled with gray. Foliage bright green. Flowers pale gold panicles in summer. Growth is moderately fast, slowing with age; tree is long lived. Zones 10–12.

Caesalpinia gilliesii
syn. Poinciana gilliesii
BIRD-OF-PARADISE SHRUB
☀ ❄ ↔ 4–8 ft (1.2–2.4 m) ↑ 10 ft (3 m)
From northern Argentina and Uruguay. Evergreen or may be deciduous in dry winter climate. Ferny leaves, numerous small leaflets. Flowers are pale yellow, in erect spikes. Showy red stamens to 3 in (8 cm) long. Zones 9–11.

Caesalpinia pulcherrima
syn. Poinciana pulcherrima
BARBADOS PRIDE, PEACOCK FLOWER
☀ ❄ ↔ 6–12 ft (1.8–3.5 m) ↑ 10 ft (3 m)
Of uncertain origin, from tropical America or Asia. Long-stalked showy flowers, varying in color, bright scarlet to pink, gold or pale yellow, or may be red and gold. Stamens like cat's whiskers. Flowers all year. Zones 11–12.

CAJANUS

This genus, which belongs to the pea-flower subfamily of the legumes (family Fabaceae), contains 2 species of shrubby perennials native to the

Old World tropics and naturalized in other warmer regions. They have downy stems and trifoliate leaves. The large yellow and purple pea-flowers are borne in terminal panicles. C. cajan (dahl) is considered to be one of the earliest cultivated food crops. It is grown mainly for its edible pulses but is also used as a fodder crop or green manure, for soil binding, or basketry. CULTIVATION: In tropical and subtropical areas grow in moderately fertile well-drained soil in full sun, sowing seed at 36–48 in (90–120 cm) spacing. In temperate climates plants are sometimes grown for interest. Choose the early maturing cultivars to avoid frost damage, and feed and water regularly. Propagate from seed.

Cajanus cajan
CATJANG PEA, DAHL, PIGEON PEA, RED GRAM
☀ ❄ ↔ 3–7 ft (0.9–2 m) ↑ 7–10 ft (2–3 m)
From tropical regions. This shrubby perennial with downy stems and leaves. Trifoliate leaves are green above and grayish green beneath. The colorful red and yellow flowers are followed by yellow pods to 4 in (10 cm) long. Zones 10–12.

CALADENIA
SPIDER ORCHID

This is a large genus of about 200 terrestrial orchid species belonging to the family Orchidaceae. They are primarily Australian with some smaller populations in New Zealand and New Caledonia. The plants produce a single often hairy leaf and either a single bloom or a small inflorescence with a number of flowers from winter to late spring, depending on the species. The plants are dormant throughout the hot dry Australian summers, where they retreat to underground tubers. The unusual flowers are pollinated by various species of native bee and wasps. There has recently been an upheaval with the naming of many of these orchids, with some botanists splitting the group into a number of smaller genera, although it is too early to tell if this will receive general acceptance.

Caccinia macranthera var. crassifolia

Caccinia macranthera

Calamagrostis foliosa 'Zebrina'

Calamagrostis × *acutiflora* 'Stricta'

CULTIVATION: These spider orchids rely on a mycorrhizal fungus for their survival and have proved very difficult to maintain in cultivation, with the plants annually declining in vigor. Specialist growers of terrestrial orchids have had some success by growing some of the other species in a free-draining sandy mixture containing a small amount of organic matter.

Caladenia chapmanii

⊙ ⚘ ↔ 4–8 in (10–20 cm)
↑ 6–18 in (15–45 cm)

Only known from southwestern Western Australia. Unusual deep pink flowers appear in spring. Recently transferred to new genus *Arachnorchis*, meaning spider orchid, though this new classification is yet to gain wide acceptance. Zones 10–11.

CALADIUM

ANGEL WINGS, ELEPHANT EARS

This genus of 7 species of deciduous tuberous perennials from tropical America belongs to the arum (Araceae) family. They are grown for their stunning leaves, which are attractively splashed or veined with white or brilliant shades of pink and red. These large leaves, up to 18 in (45 cm) long, are arrow- or heart-shaped and are held above the stalks. Although the plants bear arum-like flowers, these are not considered to be of ornamental significance.
CULTIVATION: *Caladium* thrive particularly well in tropical and warm climates. Grow outdoors in a moist but well-drained fertile soil, in a shady position. In colder climates grow in pots indoors or in the conservatory. Use a moist, free-draining, coarse potting mix, and place in bright but not direct sunlight. Maintain a high level of humidity. Water and feed regularly until the leaves fade in autumn, then allow the plants to dry out for dormancy. The first leaves to appear each year do not show the colorful markings.

Caladium bicolor

syn. *Caladium* × *hortulanum*
ANGEL WINGS, ELEPHANT EARS

☀ ⚘ ↔ 12 in (30 cm) ↑ 24 in (60 cm)

From the Amazon region of Brazil. The large green arrow-shaped leaves are irregularly splashed with varying amounts of white, pink, and red. Extensively bred with *C. picturatum* and *C. marmoratum* to produce an extremely wide range of color forms, including: 'Carolyn Whorton', with bright pink blotches, red veining, dark green at edges; 'Festiva', transparent red with green veining; 'Fire Chief', crimson heart, red veining, green margins; 'Kathleen', bright salmon heart, green margins; 'Lord Derby', transparent rose, dark veins, green margins; 'Mrs F. M. Joyner', white flushed with pink, dark red veins, and light green margins; 'Red Flash', bright red heart, red veining, dull green margins; 'Red Frill' ★, deep red center becoming darker red toward the green margins; 'Rosebud', pink heart fading to white, pink veining, green margins; 'Scarlet Pimpernel', red heart, red veining, cream to light green margins; 'White Christmas', white with green veining; and 'White Queen', white with crimson veins. Zones 10–12.

CALAMAGROSTIS

REED GRASS

A genus of around 250 species in the grass (Poaceae) family that is fairly widespread throughout temperate zones of the Northern Hemisphere. Only a few species are of ornamental value and those that are in cultivation are mainly hybrids or selected forms.

Some can be quite invasive. Their upright form and fluffy flowerheads that can be dried make them dramatic feature plants in the garden.
CULTIVATION: They prefer moist to damp soils in a sunny aspect. Propagate from seed; cultivars should be divided at the end of winter.

Calamagrostis × acutiflora

FEATHER REED GRASS

⊙ ❄ ↔ 36–40 in (90–100 cm)
↑ 5–7 ft (1.5–2 m)

Clump-forming herbaceous hybrid between *C. arundinacea* and *C. epigejos* that arose naturally in Europe and is basically sterile. 'Overdam' ★ has variegated silver foliage; 'Stricta' is a vertical form bearing feathery flowers in summer. Zones 4–10.

Calamagrostis brachytricha

⊙/◑ ❄ ↔ 20–40 in (50–100 cm)
↑ 40 in (100 cm)

Found in temperate regions of central to East Asia. Channeled leaves to ½ in (12 mm) in diameter. Panicles from mid-summer, to slightly over 6 in (15 cm) long, tinted purple. Zones 7–9.

Calamagrostis foliosa

FEATHER REED GRASS, LEAFY REED GRASS

⊙/◑ ❄ ↔ 8–20 in (20–50 cm)
↑ 6–16 in (15–40 cm)

Californian species with broad leaves and panicles to 6 in (15 cm) long. Both foliage and flowers light green turning straw colored with purple tints. The young leaves of 'Zebrina' are horizontally banded in green and yellow. Zones 7–9.

Caladium bicolor 'Scarlet Pimpernel'

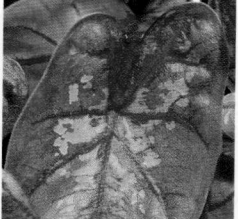

C. bicolor 'Lord Derby'   *C. b.* 'Carolyn Whorton'   *C. bicolor* 'Mrs F. M. Joyner'

Caladium bicolor 'White Christmas'

CALAMINTHA

CALAMINT

This mint (Lamiaceae) family genus is made of 7 species of sometimes shrubby perennials found in the northern temperate zones excluding East Asia. The foliage is evergreen in mild climates but in cool winters plants may die back to a basal clump. Their aromatic pointed oval leaves are often slightly glossy and have toothed edges. Flower stems develop in summer and carry tubular pink to mauve flowers in the leaf axils near their tips. Calamint has had a long history of medicinal use but these days this is usually restricted to just a simple infusion of the leaves, which makes a refreshing tea.

CULTIVATION: Hardiness varies, though most species will tolerate quite severe frosts. Plant in a bright but not baking position with moist, humus-rich, well-drained soil. Some species have vigorous rhizomes and can be slightly invasive. Propagate by division, or from basal cuttings or seed.

Calamus caryotoides

Calamus species, in the wild, Mt Kinabalu, Borneo

Calamintha grandiflora

LARGE-FLOWERED CALAMINT

☼/☀ ❄ ↔ 3–4 ft (0.9–1.2 m) ↕ 2 ft (0.6 m)

Native to southern Europe and North Africa. Bushy plant with spreading rootstock. Dark green, downy, toothed leaves to 3 in (8 cm) long. Flowers are 1½ in (35 mm) long, pink to mauve, and borne singly or up to 5 in a cluster. 'Variegata' (syn. 'Fornsett Form'), compact, rarely exceeds 12 in (30 cm). Zones 5–10.

Calamintha nepeta

LESSER CALAMINT

☼ ❄ ↔ 3–5 ft (0.9–1.5 m) ↕ 32 in (80 cm)

Spreading rhizome-rooted perennial found from Britain to southern Europe. Downy gray-green stems and leaves, to 1¼ in (30 mm) long. They are strongly aromatic. Pink to mauve flowers, ½ in (12 mm) long, with up to 15 in a cluster. Zones 6–10.

Calamintha sylvatica

COMMON CALAMINT

☼ ❄ ↔ 20 in (50 cm) ↕ 24 in (60 cm)

An aromatic, mint-scented native of central and southern Europe. Deep, slightly glossy green, heavily veined, pointed oval leaves to 1½ in (35 mm) long, with shallowly toothed edges. Whorls of ½ in (12 mm) long, pink to purple flowers produced in summer. C. s. subsp. ascendens has strong peppermint aroma, purple flowers, and grows to around 12 in (30 cm) tall. Zones 7–10.

CALAMUS

LAWYER-CANE, RATTAN, ROTANG

The largest palm genus, placed in the Arecaceae family, and consisting of around 400 species, most from the rainforests of Southeast Asia and the Malay Archipelago, with outlying species in eastern Australia and parts of tropical Africa. Most are climbing palms, with long flexible stems. They grapple onto trees with the aid of fierce hooks on various parts of their pinnate fronds. In some these hooks are distributed along a whip-like organ, or cirrus, forming an extension of the frond midrib; in others along a similar organ, called a flagellum, that arises from the sheathing base of the frond. Most species also have needle-like spines on the sheath and blade of the frond. Flowering branches resemble flagella with short lateral branches bearing small yellowish flowers, followed by globular fruits sheathed in overlapping scales and containing sweet white flesh that provides food for monkeys and baboons. Stems of Calamus and allied genera provide the cane used to make cane furniture.

CULTIVATION: Most species need frost-free warm-temperate conditions, preferring a tropical climate. They like high humidity, constant moisture, and a well-drained soil rich in humus. They will tolerate low light levels and can be grown indoors. Propagation of these plants is from seed, which must be fresh to germinate well.

Calamus caryotoides

FISH-TAIL LAWYER CANE

☼ ⚘ ↔ 8 ft (2.4 m) ↕ 17–35 ft (5–10 m)

From northern Queensland. A slender multi-stemmed palm. Leaves are small, to 8–12 in (20–30 cm) long, with 8–10 wedge-shaped leaflets. Leaf sheaths are covered in small sharp spines. Flowers are cream-colored, late spring–summer. Fruit is globular and yellowish, ½ in (12 mm) in diameter. Zones 9–12.

Calamus muelleri

SOUTHERN LAWYER CANE, WAIT-A-WHILE

☼ ⚘ ↔ 10 ft (3 m) ↕ 50 ft (15 m)

Slender, multi-stemmed, scrambling palm found in rainforests from northern New South Wales to northern Queensland, Australia. The leaves are 7–10 ft (2–3 m) long, with 15 to 20 leaflets, sheaths spiny. The flagellum

Calamintha grandiflora 'Variegata'

Calamintha sylvatica subsp. ascendens

Calamintha nepeta

is long and spiny. Cream-colored flowers appear in summer. The fruit is globular, and also cream-colored. Zones 9–12.

Calamus rotang

RATTAN CANE

☼ ⚘ ↔ indefinite ↕ indefinite

Found in Sri Lanka and in parts of southern India. Climbing palm has 30 in (75 cm) long fronds, with drooping 12 in (30 cm) long, glossy, narrow leaflets. Stems are thick and strong. Popular for furniture manufacture. Zones 11–12.

Calamus viminalis

syns Calamus extensus, C. pseudo-rotang

BARA BET, BITTER RATTAN, CHAIR-BOTTOM CANE, KYEIN KA, PEPA

☼ ⚘ ↔ 8 ft (2.4 m) ↕ 80 ft (24 m)

Multi-stemmed climbing palm, widespread in Southeast Asia. Distinctive leaves, with 100 or so leaflets in clusters of 2 to 4 in several planes, giving a feathery effect. Flagellum 7–10 ft (2–3 m) long, spines recurved, yellowish. Fruit globular, and yellow-brown. Zones 11–12.

CALATHEA

Found from Mexico to northern Argentina, this large genus of 300 evergreen, tuberous, or rhizome-rooted perennials belongs in the arrowroot (Marantaceae) family. Although more upright in habit, their bold and often strikingly marked elliptical foliage often resembles that of the marantas, and like their better known cousins they are also commonly grown as house plants. There are 3 basic forms of calatheas: dense clumps of short-stemmed leaves; more open clumps of leaves with long leaf stalks; and those with their foliage on cane-like stems. Leaves can be as much as 3 ft (0.9 m) long, though 6–10 in (15–25 cm) is more common. The flowers, backed by colored bracts, are usually held in a cone-like structure that resembles a rattlesnake's tail.

CULTIVATION: Mainly tropical in origin, calatheas require warm, humid, frost-free conditions. However, they do not need bright light, which makes them good house plants. A draft-free shaded position with moist, humus-rich, well-drained soil is best. Propagate by division.

Calathea burle-marxii

☀ ✤ ↔ 3–5 ft (0.9–1.5 m) ↑ 5 ft (1.5 m)
Upright cane-stemmed Brazilian species with leaves often over 24 in (60 cm) long, and bright green with a yellow-green midrib and gray-green under-sides. Large heads of cream to yellow flowers, which are sometimes tinted blue or purple. Zones 11–12.

Calathea crocata

☀ ✤ ↔ 16–24 in (40–60 cm) ↑ 20 in (50 cm)
From Brazil. Basal clump of simple dark green leaves to 10 in (25 cm) long with slightly darker banding. Bright orange flowers with similarly colored bracts borne on upright stems. Zones 11–12.

Calathea crotalifera

☀/☀ ✤ ↔ 3–5 ft (0.9–1.5 m) ↑ 4 ft (1.2 m)
From Mexico and Central America. Erect, very long-stemmed, plain green leaves to 16 in (40 cm) long. Yellow-green flowers with bronze-gold bracts. Zones 11–12.

Calathea crotalifera, in the wild, Monumento Nacional Guayabo, Costa Rica

Calathea lancifolia

syn. *Calathea insignis*
RATTLESNAKE PLANT
☀ ✤ ↔ 24–32 in (60–80 cm) ↑ 24 in (60 cm)
From Brazil. Long-stemmed, narrow, 12 in (30 cm) long, light green leaves edged and irregularly banded and sectored with darker green, maroon undersides. Zones 11–12.

Calathea lutea

HAVANA CIGAR
☀ ✤ ↔ 3–7 ft (0.9–2 m) ↑ 3–6 ft (0.9–1.8 m)
Found throughout tropical America. Canna-like dark green leaves to over 5 ft (1.5 m) long on narrow stems. Yellow flowers with red-brown bracts. Common name comes from appearance of the furled leaf. Zones 11–12.

Calathea majestica

☀ ✤ ↔ 32–48 in (80–120 cm) ↑ 40 in (100 cm)
From Guyana, Colombia, and Ecuador. Leaves to 24 in (60 cm) long on erect stems, dark green above, maroon below. White, yellow, or violet flowers with dull yellow bracts. Cultivars often have leaves with fine colored lines, such as '**Albolineata**' (white lines) and '**Roseolineata**' (pink lines). Zones 11–12.

Calathea makoyana

CATHEDRAL WINDOWS, PEACOCK PLANT
☀ ✤ ↔ 16–32 in (40–80 cm) ↑ 24–32 in (60–80 cm)
From Brazil. Short-stemmed, 12 in (30 cm) long, translucent light green leaves with midrib and main vein darker green bordered with cream. The pattern is repeated in green and maroon on the undersides. White flowers with green bracts. Zones 11–12.

Calathea picturata

☀ ✤ ↔ 20–27 in (50–70 cm) ↑ 16–24 in (40–60 cm)
From Brazil. Short-stemmed leaves to 10 in (25 cm) long, dark green with white along midrib and inside margin, maroon undersides. The white patches often join to form white-centered leaves. White flowers. Zones 11–12.

Calathea zebrina

ZEBRA PLANT
☀ ✤ ↔ 32–48 in (80–120 cm) ↑ 40 in (100 cm)
From Brazil. Short canes with velvety, light and dark green banded leaves to

Calathea makoyana

27 in (70 cm) long, pale midrib, maroon undersides. White to mauve flowers with purple-brown bracts. Zones 11–12.

CALCEOLARIA

Found from Mexico to southern South America, this genus of 300 species or so in the foxglove (Scrophulariaceae) family includes perennials and shrubs. Leaves tend to be light green and are covered with fine hairs and small glands that make them sticky. Flowers are very distinctive, the general shape common to almost all species. They are 2-lipped with a small hooded upper lip and a large lower lip that is inflated and pouch-like. Yellow, orange, and red shades dominate the flower colors.

Calathea lutea

Calceolaria, Herbeohybrida Group cultivar

Calceolaria, Herbeohybrida Group, Sunset Series

C., Herbeohybrida Group, Sunset Series, 'Sunset Red'

Calceolaria, Herbeohybrida Group cultivar

Calceolaria integrifolia 'Goldbouquet'

CULTIVATION: While calceolarias vary in their frost hardiness and sun tolerance, they prefer cool moist soil conditions. Work in plenty of high-humus compost before planting. The shrubby species become rather untidy after a few years. Pruning rejuvenates them, but replacement with new plants is usually more successful. Seed germinates well, but tip cuttings strike quickly and are the preferred method.

Calceolaria biflora
☀ ❄ ↔ 8–10 in (20–25 cm) ↕ 10–12 in (25–30 cm)

Rosette-forming, stemless, evergreen perennial from Chile and Argentina.

It has oblong hairy leaves, up to 3 in (8 cm) long, and from between which arise fine stems supporting 2 small, pouched, yellow flowers in summer. Zones 6–9.

Calceolaria, Herbeohybrida Group
LADIES' PURSES, POCKETBOOK PLANT, SLIPPER FLOWER
☀ ❄ ↔ 12–16 in (30–40 cm) ↕ 8–20 in (20–50 cm)

Created by hybridization between three South American species, these perennials are treated as annuals. Large winter flowers in shades of reds, oranges and yellows (some speckled or blotched), which have a characteristic pouch-like lip and hairy leaves. **Sunset Series** produces bushy plants and short-stemmed flowers for a long period. Flowers are scarlet, yellow, rich red, and copper-orange. 'Sunset Red' is a selected red form. Zones 9–11.

Calceolaria integrifolia
☀/❄ ❄ ↔ 8–12 in (20–30 cm) ↕ 4 ft (1.2 m)

From Chile. Leaves toothed, light green, sticky, slightly puckered, fine

brown hairs beneath. Flowers yellow or rusty orange, sometimes with contrasting spots, throughout the year, abundant in warmer months. Trim early spring. 'Golden Nugget', bright yellow flowering perennial; 'Kentish Hero' ★, orange-brown pouched flowers; 'Russet', orange-red to brown flowers; 'Goldbouquet', profuse bright yellow flowers. Zones 8–10.

Calceolaria 'John Innes'
☀ ❄ ↔ 12 in (30 cm) ↕ 6 in (15 cm)
This award-winning cultivar bears a rich yellow flower which has faint crimson spots on the middle of the lip. Zones 8–11.

Calceolaria pinifolia
☀ ❄ ↔ 20–27 in (50–70 cm) ↕ 24–40 in (60–100 cm)

Subshrub from the Andes. Yellow pouched flowers. Leaves long, thin, and quite pine-like as species name suggests. Endangered in the wild. Zones 9–11.

Calceolaria uniflora
SAND LADY'S SLIPPER
☀ ❄ ↔ 6–8 in (15–20 cm) ↕ 4–6 in (10–15 cm)

This species, from southern Patagonia, is a rhizomatous rosette-forming perennial. The leaves are hairy, whole to divided. The white and yellow flowers, ¾ in (18 mm) in diameter, often with orange streaks, appear during summer. These plants enjoy a well-drained rocky soil. *C. u.* var. *darwinii*, yellow and white flowers, lower lip darker and spotted with red-brown. Zones 7–9.

CALENDULA
A genus of about 20 species of annual and perennial herbs in the daisy (Asteraceae) family. They are found

around the Mediterranean area and Atlantic Islands where they are often found growing on disturbed ground, particularly *C. officinalis*, which is a widespread garden escapee. All have alternate simple leaves; some of these are aromatic. The cheerful yellow or orange daisies appear for long periods throughout the year. *C. officinalis* has been used for many centuries for a range of culinary and medicinal purposes. The common name marigold is today also associated with some *Tagetes* species.
CULTIVATION: Very easily grown in any well-drained soil in full sun. Sow seed *in situ* or under glass in spring in cooler areas, or earlier in warmer areas. Successive sowings and deadheading will result in a display over many months, from spring to autumn in cooler areas and throughout the year in warm ones.

Calendula arvensis
FIELD MARIGOLD
☀ ❄ ↔ 12 in (30 cm) ↕ 12 in (30 cm)
From southern Europe, a branched annual species with slightly downy oblong leaves. The yellow or orange daisies to 1 in (25 mm) in diameter are carried from spring–autumn. Zones 6–10.

Calceolaria 'John Innes'

Calceolaria uniflora var. *darwinii*

Calendula officinalis

C. o., 'Greenheart Orange'

C. o., Pacific Beauty Series

Calendula officinalis, Fiesta Gitana Group

Calendula officinalis ★

COMMON MARIGOLD, POT MARIGOLD, SCOTCH MARIGOLD

☀ ❄ ↔ 12–18 in (30–45 cm)
↕ 12–24 in (30–60 cm)

Originally from southern Europe but widely naturalized. Bushy annual with slightly downy leaves. Orange or yellow daisies to 3 in (8 cm) diameter from spring–autumn. **Bon Bon Series**, to 12 in (30 cm), a mix of apricot, yellow, and orange; '**Dwarf Gem**', to 12 in (30 cm), double, large, apricot, yellow, and orange daisies; **Fiesta Gitana Group ★**, to 12 in (30 cm), a mix of cream, yellow, orange, and bi-colors; '**Greenheart Orange**', orange petals and a green centre; '**Orange Salad**', petals are a saffron substitute; **Kablouna Series**, short ray florets and prominent quilled centers, mixed yellow, orange, and apricot; **Pacific Beauty Series**, tall-stemmed, yellow, orange, and apricot; '**Radio**', orange flowers, quilled petals resembling cactus-type dahlia. Zones 6–10.

CALIBRACHOA

syn. *Petunia* (in part)
Genus in the nightshade (Solanaceae) family, *Calibrachoa* is closely related

to *Petunia* and its 25 species are found across much the same region of South America, from southern Brazil across to Peru and Chile; one species, *C. parviflora*, extends north to southern USA. Indeed all species were classified under *Petunia* until a Dutch geneticist who was involved in petunia breeding discovered major differences in chromosomes between this group and other *Petunia* species, corresponding to external differences and breeding behavior. The name *Calibrachoa* goes back to 1825 and honors a Mexican professor of pharmacy, Antonio de la Cal y Bracho. They are weak evergreen perennials and subshrubs, mostly sprawling or prostrate with leaves under 1 in (25 mm) long. Flowers are smaller than in most petunias, under 1 in (25 mm) across and short-tubed, arising from leaf axils in continuous succession. In the 1990s the Japanese biotechnology firm Suntory (famous for whiskey) began breeding *Calibrachoa*, though which species they used it is difficult to discover, and released the first of the patented **Million Bells Series**. Many strains followed with a wider range of colors and more compact or trailing habits. All are clonal, produced mainly by tissue culture; they flower almost continuously with adequate light and warmth. CULTIVATION: They will tolerate light frosts and thrive in sun or semi-shade. Mostly grown in pots or baskets; can be treated as annuals or short-lived perennials. Plant in a free-draining medium and apply weak fertilizer at intervals throughout the growing season, pinch back the longer shoots to increase the number of flowers. Water only when the soil is almost dry. Propagate from tip cuttings but be aware that propagation for sale may infringe plant patents.

Calibrachoa Hybrid Cultivars

☀/◐ ❄ ↔ 12–24 in (30–60 cm)
↕ 3–8 in (7–20 cm)

Valued for their low mounding or trailing habit and profusion of small flowers, mid-spring–late autumn or virtually year-round in warm climates. **Million Bells Series** are yellow-throated flowers in shades from white to lemon, pink, red, and purple, mounding to 6 in (15 cm). **Trailing Million Bells Series** are only 3 in (7 cm) or so high, spilling over edges of baskets or planter boxes. Flowers in the **Colorburst Series** come in cherry, red, rose and violet. Flowers of the German-bred **Selecta Series** (syn. Mini-famous Series) are in rich colors, especially oranges, reds, and yellows, and also bicolors. The **Liricashower Series** include strong reds and yellows as well as pastels, with flat open blooms. Zones 8–11.

Calibrachoa, Hybrid Cultivar, Liricashower Series, 'Liricashower Blush'

C., HC, 'Colorburst Violet'

C., HC, 'Million Bells Cherry Pink'

C., HC, 'Million Bells Lemon'

C., HC, 'Million Bells White'

C., HC, 'Million Bells Terra Cotta'

C

CALLIANDRA

This genus in the mimosa subfamily of legume (Fabaceae) family consists of around 200 species, the majority occurring in South and Central America and the West Indies. Mostly shrubs or small trees, they have bipinnate leaves, long-stamened flowers in globular heads or elongated spikes. Flower colors range from white and pink to deep crimson, attracting hummingbirds which pollinate these plants in the wild. Seed pods are rigid and flattened. Most calliandras come from regions that are warm but dry, or at least with a pronounced dry season. Many species are frost tender. Calliandras are useful landscape subjects, providing year-round color as well as a screen of feathery foliage. CULTIVATION: Tough adaptable shrubs where climate is suitable, tolerating hard dry soils and moderately exposed positions. Most species adapt well to clipping into compact forms and can be used for hedges. Propagate from seed, or from cuttings taken in winter from short lateral branches.

Calliandra haematocephala

Calliandra surinamensis

Calliandra tweedii

Calliandra californica

☀ ❦ ↔ 3 ft (0.9 m) ↕ 4 ft (1.2 m)
A native of Baja California, Mexico, this plant is often used in desert style gardens. The tough wiry branches are dotted for much of the year with small tassel-like heads of bright crimson flowers. Zones 9–11.

Calliandra emarginata

☀ ❦ ↔ 20 ft (6 m) ↕ 10 ft (3 m)
Native of southern Mexico and Central America, often confused with the better known *C. haematocephala*. Semi-scrambling habit, large leaflets,

large 'powderpuff' heads of pink to crimson flowers. Semi-prostrate when planted in an open area. Zones 10–12.

Calliandra eriophylla

FAIRY DUSTER, MOCK MESQUITE
☀ ❦ ↔ 36 in (90 cm) ↕ 36 in (90 cm)
Extending from Mexico to the far south of western USA. Crooked prickly branches, fine feathery leaves, profuse wispy heads of pale red flowers in late winter–early spring. Used in desert style gardens. Zones 9–11.

Calliandra haematocephala

BLOOD-RED TASSEL FLOWER, POWDERPUFF TREE
☀/❂ ❦ ↔ 20 ft (6 m) ↕ 10 ft (3 m)
From northern South America. Flowers pink to scarlet or deep red, densely crowded into globular heads at branch tips, most of the year, autumn–winter in cooler areas. Shelter from strong winds. Zones 10–12.

Calliandra houstoniana

☀ ❦ ↔ 7 ft (2 m) ↕ 10 ft (3 m)
From southern Mexico and adjacent Central America. Open habit, leaves bipinnate, numerous tiny bright green leaflets. Flowers in terminal spike-like clusters, with showy red stamens, from summer–autumn. Zones 10–12.

Calliandra surinamensis

PINK-AND-WHITE POWDERPUFF
☀ ❦ ↔ 10 ft (3 m) ↕ 10 ft (3 m)
From northern South America. Showy powderpuff flowerheads, white to pale mauve, most of the year. Vase-shaped habit, with arching branches, and small clustered leaves. Drought tolerant. Zones 10–12.

Calliandra tweedii ★

syn. *Inga pulcherrima*
RED TASSEL FLOWER
☀ ❦ ↔ 6 ft (1.8 m) ↕ 6 ft (1.8 m)
This native of Uruguay and southern Brazil grows best in a warm-temperate climate without seasonal rainfall. Multi-stemmed fresh green foliage has tiny crowded leaflets. The deep scarlet flowerheads appear in spring–autumn. Can be cut back hard, or trimmed to a dense hedge. Zones 9–11.

CALLICARPA

BEAUTY BUSH
This genus has about 140 species of trees and shrubs, both deciduous and evergreen, belonging to the mint (Lamiaceae) family. They occur from the tropics to warm-temperate regions around much of the globe. They are close allies of the verbenas, which shows in their simple conspicuously veined and toothed leaves and their

Calliandra californica

Calliandra emarginata

Calliandra eriophylla

Calliandra houstoniana, Plaine du Champ de Bataille, New Caledonia

Callicarpa americana

Callicarpa japonica

Callicarpa dichotoma 'Purpurea'

Callicarpa rubella

Callicarpa pedunculata

spring-borne heads, or cymes, of tiny flowers. The main attraction of most species, however, is the fruit that ripens in late summer and autumn. Individual drupes are often very small, but massed together create a long-lasting display and are very distinctively colored.
CULTIVATION: Hardiness varies with the species, some tolerate little or no frost, others are very tough. *Callicarpa* seldom has any cultivation difficulties, thriving in any moist well-drained soil in sun or partial shade. Prune after fruit has fallen and propagate from half-hardened cuttings.

Callicarpa americana
AMERICAN BEAUTY BERRY, AMERICAN BEAUTY BUSH
☼/◗ ❄ ↔7 ft (2 m) ↑10 ft (3 m)
Found in southern USA and parts of the West Indies. Leaves to 8 in (20 cm) long, downy undersides. Violet flowers followed by densely clustered bunches of magenta drupes that usually last well into winter. *C. a.* var. *lactea* is a white-fruited cultivar. Zones 6–10.

Callicarpa bodinieri
☼/◗ ❄ ↔8 ft (2.4 m) ↑10 ft (3 m)
From central and western China. Deciduous. Toothed leaves to 8 in (20 cm) long, turn golden in autumn. Flowers lilac. Fruits violet-purple,

small but profuse. The heavy fruiting variety *C. b.* var. *giraldii* and its cultivar, '**Profusion**' ★, are more commonly cultivated. Zones 6–9.

Callicarpa dichotoma
PURPLE BEAUTY BERRY, PURPLE BEAUTY BUSH
☼ ❄ ↔4 ft (1.2 m) ↑4 ft (1.2 m)
From China and Japan, deciduous with toothed oval leaves, pink flowers followed by small violet-purple drupes. Can be temperamental with good and bad years. '**Issai**' and '**Purpurea**' are attractive cultivars. Zones 6–10.

Callicarpa japonica
JAPANESE BEAUTY BERRY, JAPANESE BEAUTY BUSH
☼ ❄ ↔5 ft (1.5 m) ↑6 ft (1.8 m)
Deciduous shrub native to China and Japan. Leaves up to 8 in (20 cm) long, very finely toothed margins, tapering to a point. Flowers pale pink, fruit pink to violet-purple. '**Leucocarpa**' has white fruits. Zones 8–10.

Callicarpa pedunculata
☼ ▤ ↔5 ft (1.5 m) ↑10 ft (3 m)
Found from India to tropical Australia. Evergreen shrub. Leaves up to 6 in (15 cm) long. Flowers pink and the heads have a shaggy covering of fine hairs. Fruit white to deep rosy purple. Zones 10–12.

Callicarpa rubella
BEAUTY BERRY, CHINESE BEAUTY BUSH
☼ ▤ ↔3 ft (1 m) ↑3 ft (1 m)
From tropical and subtropical East Asia. Semi-deciduous shrub. Leaves pale yellowish green to 5 in (12 cm)

long. Flowers are pink, and followed by purple-red drupes. Both flowers and fruiting heads are covered in fine hairs that gradually wear away. Zones 9–11.

CALLICOMA
Found in coastal eastern Australia, usually near streams or rivers, the single species in this genus is a large evergreen tree in the Cunoniaceae family. Although the name wattle has become synonymous with Australian acacias, the early European settlers first gave the name to this tree in a completely different plant family but sharing similar fluffy flowerheads.
CULTIVATION: Apart from intolerance of heavy frosts, black wattle is easily cultivated. It prefers a cool root run with moist, humus-enriched, well-drained soil. Prune to shape when young and thin out any weak branches as tree matures. Propagate from seed.

Callicoma serratifolia
BLACK WATTLE
☼ ▤ ↔10 ft (3 m) ↑30 ft (9 m)
The leaves are glossy, heavily veined, with serrated edges, downy beneath,

to 5 in (12 cm) long. The young stems are also downy. Branch tips studded with round heads of filamentous creamy white flowers, spring–summer. Zones 9–11.

CALLIRHOE
POPPY MALLOWS
A genus of 9 species of deep-rooted annuals and perennials, belonging to the mallow (Malvaceae) family, and found in prairies and grasslands of the USA and Mexico. The leaves are alternate, deeply lobed, green to gray-green, thick to rough textured. The flowers are cup-shaped, and borne singly or in clusters in the upper leaf axils, their colors range from red through to purple and magenta.
CULTIVATION: Well-drained sandy loam produces better growth than heavier soils. They have a good low temperature tolerance, but full sun is required. Both annuals and perennials are propagated from seed, and perennials from softwood cuttings.

Callirhoe involucrata
BUFFALO ROSE, LOW POPPY MALLOW, PRAIRIE POPPY MALLOW, PURPLE POPPY MALLOW, WINE CUPS
☼ ❄ ↔12–24 in (30–60 cm)
↑6–12 in (15–30 cm)
Low-growing sprawling perennial with swollen taproot that comes from inland USA. Naturalized elsewhere. The stems are prostrate, hairy, to 6 in (15 cm) long. Leaves 3 to 7, lobed, 1–2 in (25–50 mm) long. Magenta to cerise flowers with white centers are borne on long erect stems from late spring–summer. Zones 5–8.

Callicoma serratifolia

C

Callistemon citrinus 'Jeffersii'

Callistemon citrinus 'Burgundy'

Callistemon citrinus 'Splendens'

Callistemon citrinus 'White Anzac'

Callisia elegans

CALLISIA

A genus of about 20 species of mostly perennial frost-tender herbs belonging to the spiderwort (Commelinaceae) family. Native to southeastern USA, Mexico, and tropical America. They are closely related to *Tradescantia* and most have a sprawling habit making them useful ground cover plants in warm climates. They are grown as foliage plants, their lance-shaped leaves being succulent to varying degrees, sometimes with light striping or flushed with purple. The delicate 3-petaled flowers are very small and are usually pink or white.
CULTIVATION: Tough plants suitable for growing as ground cover or in hanging baskets in warm areas or as pot plants in cooler regions. Grow

outdoors in half-sun in moist but well-drained soil. Let potted plants rest in winter. Small low-growing species may die back in their dry period.

Callisia elegans
STRIPED INCH PLANT
☀ ⚘ ↔ 18–24 in (45–60 cm)
↑ 3–6 in (8–15 cm)
Sprawling succulent plant from Guatemala and Honduras with velvety dark green leaves with paler stripes above and flushed purple beneath. Small stalkless white flowers. Zones 10–11.

Callisia repens
☀ ⚘ ↔ 12–24 in (30–60 cm)
↑ 6–12 in (15–30 cm)
Native to Texas, the West Indies, and parts of South America. A mat-forming species with creeping stems which root easily. The pointed oval leaves are smooth and green. Tiny white flowers are borne in autumn. Zones 10–11.

CALLISTEMON
BOTTLEBRUSH
This Australian genus of about 30 species of highly ornamental evergreen shrubs and small trees in the myrtle (Myrtaceae) family has a large range

of hybrids and cultivars. They have leathery, linear or lanceolate leaves arranged spirally around the stem. Often new growth is richly colored, usually pink or bronze. Showy flowers massed together in terminal spikes, form cylindrical bottlebrush-like flowers. The flowers open in spring, summer, and autumn. Round woody seed capsules crowd into a cylindrical group along the stem. Nectar-rich flowers attract nectar-feeding birds. The larger species are suitable as small street trees in mild climates.
CULTIVATION: Most callistemons prefer moist, well-drained, slightly acid soil in a sunny position; only marginally frost tolerant. All respond well to pruning in the final days of flowering to promote bushier growth.

Propagate species from the fine seed. Selected forms and cultivars are grown from half-hardened tip cuttings.

Callistemon acuminatus
THIN-LEAFED BOTTLEBRUSH
☀ ⚘ ↔ 7 ft (2 m) ↑ 10 ft (3 m)
From east coast of Australia. Leaves narrow, wavy-edged, to 4 in (10 cm) long. Flowers dense spikes, dark crimson in spring, spot flowering other times. Tolerates dry conditions, a wind-resistant plant suitable for coastal regions. 'Nabiac Red' has larger diameter flower spikes. rich deep red. Zones 9–11.

Callistemon citrinus
SCARLET BOTTLEBRUSH
☀ ❋ ↔ 10 ft (3 m) ↑ 10 ft (3 m)
From eastern Australia. Flowers bright red in spring. Shoots are pink and silky. Tolerate poor drainage and moderate coastal exposure. 'Burgundy', dark red bottlebrush flowers; 'Jeffersii', dwarf to 6 ft (1.8 m) tall, red-purple flowers, lemon-scented leaves; 'Splendens' (syn. 'Endeavour'), broader leaves, masses of large, brilliant red flowers; 'White Anzac', white bottlebrush flowers. Zones 8–11.

Callistemon linearis
NARROW-LEAFED BOTTLEBRUSH
☀ ⚘ ↔ 10 ft (3 m) ↑ 10 ft (3 m)
From temperate eastern Australia. Branching from near ground level, thick narrow leaves. Flowers dense crimson spikes, borne in late spring–early summer. Easily grown, tolerates damp situations, and some coastal exposure. 'Pumilus', dwarf form to around 24 in (60 cm). Zones 9–11.

Callistemon pachyphyllus
WALLUM BOTTLEBRUSH
☀ ⚘ ↔ 5 ft (1.5 m) ↑ 5 ft (1.5 m)
From the coastal heaths of eastern Australia. Evergreen shrub, dull green thick-textured leaves. Flower spikes bright red (occasionally green) in spring–summer, also sporadically through year. Tolerates poor drainage, coastal planting. 'Smoked Salmon', pink-flowered form. Zones 9–11.

Callistemon acuminatus 'Nabiac Red'

C. pachyphyllus 'Smoked Salmon'

Callistemon pallidus, red cultivar

Callistemon pityoides

Callistemon polandii

Callistemon pallidus
LEMON BOTTLEBRUSH

☼ ❄ ↔ 10 ft (3 m) ↑ 10 ft (3 m)

From southeastern Australia. Dense evergreen shrub. Leaves aromatic gray-green, silvery pink and silky when young. Flower spikes pale yellow in late spring or summer; some cultivars have red flowers. 'Candle Glow' is low and spreading, silvery new growth, lemon yellow flowers. Zones 8–11.

Callistemon phoeniceus
LESSER BOTTLEBRUSH

☼ ⚘ ↔ 5 ft (1.5 m) ↑ 10 ft (3 m)

From southern Western Australia. Sturdy, slightly weeping shrub. Leaves narrow, thick, gray-green. Flower spikes bright scarlet in early spring–summer. 'Pink Ice' has pink flowers. Zones 9–11.

Callistemon pinifolius
PINE-LEAFED BOTTLEBRUSH

☼ ⚘ ↔ 5 ft (1.5 m) ↑ 5 ft (1.5 m)

A slightly weeping evergreen shrub from eastern Australia. Leaves narrow, pine-like. Flower spikes large, green (occasionally red), in spring. Trim regularly for compact growth. Zones 9–11.

Callistemon pityoides
MOUNTAIN BOTTLEBRUSH

☼ ❄ ↔ 6 ft (1.8 m) ↑ 7 ft (2 m)

A hardy shrub from higher altitudes of eastern Australia, often in boggy

conditions. Dense, sharply pointed, linear leaves, attractive pinkish new growth. Flower spikes creamy yellow in late spring–mid-summer. Zones 7–10.

Callistemon polandii

☼ ⚘ ↔ 8 ft (2.4 m) ↑ 15 ft (4.5 m)

From coastal central Queensland, Australia. Semi-weeping, large evergreen shrub. Light green leaves, silvery pink and silky when young. Flower spikes large, bright red, with distinct yellow tips in winter–early spring. 'Peak Downs' is notable for its red new growth and slightly smaller leaves. Zones 9–12.

Callistemon recurvus
TINAROO BOTTLEBRUSH

☼ ⚘ ↔ 8 ft (2.4 m) ↑ 20 ft (6 m)

Native to Far North Queensland, Australia. Dark green leaves, prominent oil glands. New foliage bright pink and silky. Dark red flower spikes late winter–spring. Zones 9–12.

Callistemon rigidus
STIFF BOTTLEBRUSH

☼ ⚘ ↔ 7 ft (2 m) ↑ 8 ft (2.4 m)

From damp coastal, temperate, eastern Australia. Erect shrub. Stiff, narrow, pointed leaves with silky new growth. Dense crimson flowers through summer. Good hedging plant. Zones 9–11.

Callistemon salignus
PINK TIPS, WHITE BOTTLEBRUSH

☼ ⚘ ↔ 15–20 ft (4.5–6 m) ↑ 15–30 ft (4.5–9 m)

From moist locations of coastal eastern Australia. Small tree, weeping

Callistemon recurvus

habit, white papery bark. Bright pink silky new foliage. Flower spikes are creamy white, in spring–early summer. Red, pink, and mauve flowering forms available. 'Eureka' ★, an upright bushy form, purplish red new shoots, vivid pink flowers. Zones 9–11.

Callistemon sieberi
RIVER BOTTLEBRUSH

☼ ❄ ↔ 7 ft (2 m) ↑ 15 ft (4.5 m)

Widespread in southeastern Australia, from damp habitats, usually along watercourses. Branches pendulous, silky pink new shoots, small grayish green leaves. Short spikes of creamy yellow flowers in late spring–summer. Suitable for growing in poorly drained situations. Zones 8–11.

Callistemon speciosus
syn. *Callistemon glaucus*
ALBANY BOTTLEBRUSH

☼ ⚘ ↔ 6 ft (1.8 m) ↑ 6 ft (1.8 m)

Thriving in wet or swampy situations in southern Western Australia, this ornamental shrub is perfect for wet problem areas. Upright branches, dull green or grayish leathery leaves, spikes of deep red flowers in spring–summer. Zones 9–11.

Callistemon viminalis 'Wild River'

Callistemon subulatus

☼ ⚘ ↔ 6 ft (1.8 m) ↑ 5 ft (1.5 m)

From eastern Australia. A spreading shrub, arching branches, narrow sharp-pointed leaves. Prolific red bottlebrush flowers, late spring–summer. Tolerates poor drainage. Zones 9–11.

Callestemon teretifolius
NEEDLE-LEAFED BOTTLEBRUSH

☼ ⚘ ↔ 10 ft (3 m) ↑ 8 ft (2.4 m)

South Australian shrub with long, sharply pointed, pine-like foliage. Dense crimson flowers in spring–summer. Spreading habit. Zones 9–10.

Callistemon viminalis
WEEPING BOTTLEBRUSH

☼ ⚘ ↔ 7–10 ft (2–3 m) ↑ 25 ft (8 m)

From coastal eastern Australia, tall shrub or small tree. Heavily weeping crown of light green narrow leaves, brilliant red bottlebrush flowers, in spring–summer. This species tolerates most soils and conditions, including very wet and very dry. The cultivars include: 'Captain Cook', dense shrubby form; 'Dawson River Weeper', slender weeping tree; 'Hannah Ray', vivid red flowers; and 'Wild River', compact form. Zones 9–12.

Callistemon teretifolius

Callistemon viminalis 'Captain Cook'

Callistemon, Hybrid Cultivar, 'Candy Pink'

Callistemon, Hybrid Cultivar, 'Harkness'

Callistemon, Hybrid Cultivar, 'Injune'

Callistemon, Hybrid Cultivar, 'Mauve Mist'

Callistemon, Hybrid Cultivar, 'Old Duninald'

Callistemon, HC, 'Reeve's Pink'

C., HC, 'Demesne Rowena'

Callistemon, HC, 'Running River'

Callistemon, HC, 'Violaceus'

Callistemon, HC, 'Western Glory'

Callistemon viridiflorus

Callistemon viridiflorus

GREEN BOTTLEBRUSH

☼ ❄ ↔ 8 ft (2.4 m) ↑ 8 ft (2.4 m)

Endemic to Tasmania, an erect shrub. Stiff dark green leaves only about 1¼ in (30 mm) long. Greenish yellow bottlebrush flowers in late spring–summer. Can be grown in poorly drained situations. Zones 8–10.

Callistemon Hybrid Cultivars

☼ ❊ ↔ 5–10 ft (1.5–3 m)

↑ 6–20 ft (1.8–6 m)

Callistemons hybridize readily and in recent decades many outstanding hybrid cultivars have been named. All must be propagated from tip cuttings to retain the characteristics of the selected clone. Notable examples include: 'Harkness', light green leaves, brilliant red flowers; 'Injune', gray-green leaves, light pink flowers; 'Little John' ★, dwarf to 3 ft (0.9 m) high, blue-green leaves, dark red flowers; 'Mauve Mist', has narrow leaves, and spikes of mauve-pink flowers; 'Reeve's Pink', grows to 10 ft (3 m) high, with pink flowers. Zones 9–11.

CALLISTEPHUS

CHINA ASTER

The sole species in this genus is an annual daisy (family Asteraceae) from China. However, despite being just one species, it has been developed into an array of garden varieties, which have flowers in white and all shades of pink, mauve-blue, red, and purple in both single- and double-flowered styles, all of which last well when cut.

It is naturally a sturdy upright plant, though dwarf forms are available. The name is from the Greek *kallos* (beautiful) and *stephanus* (crown) and is a reference to the flowers.

CULTIVATION: Plant in the full sun with moist well-drained soil and feed occasionally with liquid fertilizer. Err on the cautious side with feeding or you may produce foliage at the expense of flowers. Raise from seed. Spring sown seed begins flowering by early summer and if the sowing is staggered a succession of bloom results.

Callistephus chinensis

☼ ❄ ↔ 8–12 in (20–30 cm)

↑ 12–36 in (30–90 cm)

Dark green, pointed oval leaves to over 3 in (8 cm) long, with coarsely toothed edges. Flowerheads are 2–4 in (5–10 cm) across, borne singly on long stems. **Milady Series Mixed**, strong-growing and bushy yet compact series growing to around 10 in (25 cm) tall, available in a wide color range. Zones 8–11.

CALLITRIS

AUSTRALIAN CYPRESS PINE

Southern Hemisphere conifer genus consisting of 19 species of small to medium-sized trees, 2 found only in New Caledonia, the 17 remaining species in Australia. This genus belongs to the cypress (Cupressaceae) family. The fine thread-like twigs are clothed in tiny scale-like leaves, arranged in whorls of 3 rather than in opposite pairs as in *Cupressus*. The cones likewise have scales arranged in whorls of three. The pollen cones are tiny, while the seed cones, borne on the same tree, are more or less globular, their gray outer surfaces smooth or dotted with warty resin blisters. *Callitris* species are light-loving, and occur on sandy or stony soils. These trees are used for their timber and resin.

CULTIVATION: Most species adapt very readily to being cultivated in warm-temperate climates; species from semi-arid regions prefer a warm dry summer. Grow in deep well-drained soils. They tolerate trimming and can be grown effectively in groups or closely spaced as hedges. They should be propagated from seed.

Callistephus chinensis

Callistephus chinensis cultivar

Callitris baileyi

Callitris macleayana

Callitris columellaris

Callitris baileyi

☀ ⚘ ↔ 12–15 ft (3.5–4.5 m) ↑ 60 ft (18 m)
From southeastern Queensland and
an adjacent area of New South Wales,
Australia. Smaller in cultivation than
in their natural environment, with a
dense columnar habit. Foliage is dark
green, the almost globular cones only
½ in (12 mm) in diameter, persisting
on the small branches. Zones 9–11.

Callitris columellaris

syn. *Callitris arenosa*
BRIBIE ISLAND PINE, SAND CYPRESS PINE
☀ ⚘ ↔ 15–20 ft (4.5–6 m)
↑ 60–100 ft (18–30 m)
From Brisbane and coastal southeast
Queensland. Conical habit when still
a young tree, but develops spreading
limbs with age. Deeply furrowed, dark
gray bark; fine rich dark green leaves;
small seed cones. Densely columnar in
cultivation, with billowy foliage. These
trees are effective when planted in
groups. Zones 10–12.

Callitris glaucophylla

syns *Callitris columellaris* var. *campestris*,
C. glauca, *C. hugelii*
WHITE CYPRESS PINE
☀ ⚘ ↔ 15 ft (4.5 m) ↑ 70 ft (21 m)
The most abundant of the Australian
species of pine, found south of the
Tropic of Capricorn. The limbs are
spreading and crooked, the fine leaves
from pale green to bluish gray. The
silvery gray globular cones, at the
branch tips, shed their seed annually.
Zones 9–11.

Callitris macleayana

syn. *Octoclinis macleayana*
STRINGYBARK CYPRESS PINE
☀ ⚘ ↔ 12–15 ft (3.5–4.5 m)
↑ 60 ft (18 m)
From the moist eucalypt forest and
subtropical rainforest along areas of
coastal northern New South Wales,
Australia. This tree has a dense columnar habit. Thick, brown, fibrous
bark. Olive green foliage, small needle-
like leaves often in whorls of four. The
cones are long-lived, large, and conical. Zones 9–12.

Callitris rhomboidea

Callitris oblonga

SOUTH ESK PINE
☀ ❄ ↔ 4–6 ft (1.2–1.8 m) ↑ 15 ft (4.5 m)
Thought to be endemic to northeastern Tasmania, Australia, but found
in eastern New South Wales. Densely
columnar, bluish green leaves. Cones
narrowly egg-shaped, and persist in
clusters beneath the foliage. This is
an attractive shrub, suitable for a rock
garden. Zones 8–10.

Callitris rhomboidea

syns *Callitris cupressiformis*, *C. tasmanica*
OYSTER BAY PINE, PORT JACKSON
CYPRESS PINE
☀ ❄ ↔ 10–15 ft (4–4.5 m) ↑ 50 ft (15 m)
A native of mainland southeastern
Australia, Tasmania, and central
Queensland. Variable, sometimes
broadly conical, sometimes columnar.
The leaves are fine, olive green, and
turn brownish in cold winters. Cones
are small and woody, in tight clusters
beneath the leaves. Useful for screens
and hedges. Zones 8–11.

Callitris sulcata

☀/◐ ⚘ ↔ 20 ft (6 m) ↑ 40 ft (12 m)
One of the 2 *Callitris* species native to
New Caledonia, occurring in valleys
close to stream banks, in deep soil.
Dense rounded crown, very fine
foliage drooping at tips; cones only
10 mm diameter. Zones 10–12.

CALLUNA

There is only one species in this genus
belonging to the erica (Ericaceae)
family. Native to north and western
Europe from Siberia to Turkey and
Morocco and the Azores. The height
and spread of this small shrub is 2 ft
(60 cm) on average, but this can vary
greatly in some of the 500 or more
cultivars. The leaves grow in overlapping pairs, arranged oppositely, along
the stems, and look more like scales.
The leaves are dark green, usually

Callitris sulcata, in the wild, near Koh,
New Caledonia

Callitris glaucophylla, in the wild, in Flinders Ranges National Park, South Australia

turning reddish or tinged with purple in winter. *Calluna* differs from *Erica* in that the corolla is hidden by the calyx. Produces pink to purplish pink flowers from summer to late autumn. CULTIVATION: This plant prefers acid soil in an open well-drained position in full sun. Stems can be layered in spring and detached once rooted, or cuttings of half-hardened wood can be taken in mid-summer.

Calluna vulgaris
syn. *Erica vulgaris*
HEATHER, LING

☼ ❄ ↔ 30 in (75 cm) ↑ 24 in (60 cm)
Native to acid heathland. Flowers are tubular or bell-shaped racemes, single or double, ranging from white to pink to purple in mid-summer–late autumn. Leaves of cultivars range from pale yellow to gray-green to dark bottle green. '**Annemarie**', double pink flowers on long racemes; '**Beoley Gold**', yellow foliage, and single white flowers on shorter racemes; '**Blazeaway**' ★, red foliage in winter; '**County Wicklow**', semi-prostrate, with double pale pink flowers in long racemes; '**Dark Beauty**', neat bush, double dark crimson-red flowers; '**Darkness**', dark red flowers; '**Firefly**', rust-colored summer foliage, turning dull dark red in winter, deep mauve flowers; '**Gold Haze**', light gold foliage, white flowers; '**Kinlochruel**', bright green foliage, turning bronze in winter, long racemes of double white flowers; '**Multicolor**', neat bush, copper foliage often tinged red or orange,

mauve flowers; '**Radnor**', bright green foliage, double pink flowers; '**Silver Queen**', silver-gray foliage, pale mauve-tinted white flowers; '**Wickwar Flame**', golden foliage, turning red for the winter months, and mauve-pink flowers. Zones 4–9.

CALOCEDRUS
Genus of 2 or 3 evergreen species, in the cypress (Cupressaceae) family, native to Thailand, Vietnam, Myanmar, southwest China, and western North America. Its name comes from the Greek *kalos* meaning beautiful and *kedros* meaning cedar. A handsome tree; a good ornamental, with the conical form the most popular. The overlapping leaves are arranged in crossed pairs in 2 rows along the stems. Male cones are borne singly and female cones are up to 1 in (25 mm) long, and have 6, sometimes 8, scales in pairs; only the center pair is fertile. The crown shape varies with climatic conditions. The timber is used for shingle tiles. CULTIVATION: These plants are best suited to moderately fertile soil in full sun although they will tolerate partial shade. Half-hardened cuttings can be taken in summer and seed should be grown in containers with protection from winter frosts.

Calocedrus decurrens
INCENSE CEDAR

☼ ❄ ↔ 30 ft (9 m) ↑ 120 ft (36 m)
Native to western North America. Bark flakes off as it ages. Leaves glossy dark

Calocedrus decurrens

Calocedrus decurrens 'Aureovariegata'

green with a triangular tip, are closely pressed to the stem. Cylindrical cones ripen to red-brown. Foliage of cultivar '**Aureovariegata**' is marked with yellow blotches, and smaller than others in the species. '**Compacta**' ★, globe-shaped, sometimes columnar, and very densely branched. In winter its branches turn brown. Zones 5–9.

Calocedrus macrolepis

☼ ❄ ↔ 25 ft (8 m) ↑ 100 ft (30 m)
Native to China. Bark pale gray, scaly. Leaves bright green, triangular, with blue-white undersides. Cones up to ½ in (12 mm) long, elliptical in shape, orange-brown in color, with a purple bloom. Zones 9–11.

CALOCEPHALUS
BILLY BUTTONS
This widespread genus, endemic to Australia, has about 15 species in the daisy (Asteraceae) family. Plants are either annual or perennial herbs and usually have yellow flowers. Their name is from the Greek *kalos* meaning beautiful and *kephalos* meaning head. The flowerheads have no ray florets and are composed of many tiny flowers forming one head. The flowerheads can be conical or flattened and are between ½–1½ in (12–35 mm) wide. CULTIVATION: Billy buttons need a well-drained soil and a position in full sun. Propagation is from seed or half-hardened cuttings.

Calluna vulgaris 'Gold Haze'

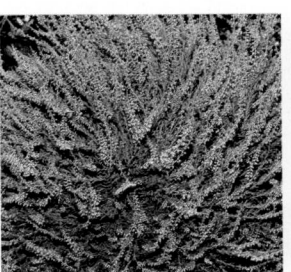

Calluna vulgaris 'Alba Plena'

Calluna vulgaris 'Con Brio'

Calluna vulgaris 'Hibernica'

Calluna vulgaris 'Robert Chapman'

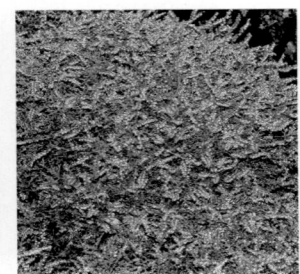

Calluna vulgaris 'Rica'

Calluna vulgaris 'Silver Queen'

Calocephalus platycephalus
YELLOW BILLY BUTTON, YELLOW TOP
☼ ⬧ ↔ 12–18 in (30–45 cm)
↕ 12–18 in (30–45 cm)
From arid and semi-arid areas. Plants have whitish woolly stems and leaves. The leaves are 1¼ in (30 mm) long, and numerous flowers are produced from winter–spring. Zones 9–11.

CALOCHORTUS
CAT'S EAR, FAIRY LANTERNS, MARIPOSA TULIP
This genus of about 60 species of hardy bulbous perennials belongs to the lily (Liliaceae) family. A native of North America, they grow in perfectly drained areas in grassland, scrub, and forest, and from low to high altitudes. The base of the leaves is sword-shaped. The flowers vary greatly—some are dainty, others flamboyant; they may be pendulous and globe-shaped or upright and open. All have 2 distinct whorls of 3 colorful outer sepals and 3 inner petals. At the base of each flower is a nectar gland, which is often prominently displayed. Flowers are colored white, yellow, orange, red, or purple, and are often marked with red or chocolate brown.
CULTIVATION: Cultivation requirements vary due to the different demands of species from a wide variety of habitats. Difficult to grow. In general, they require a sheltered position in full sunlight or half sun and a gritty soil with excellent drainage. They are averse to humidity. The bulbs will rot in winter wet.

Calocephalus platycephalus

Calochortus albus

Calochortus monophyllus

Calochortus albus
WHITE FAIRY LANTERN, WHITE GLOBE LILY
☼ ❄ ↔ 6 in (15 cm) ↕ 6–24 in (15–60 cm)
Native to central California. Small, nodding, goblet-shaped flowers on branching stems. Flowers cream, occasionally flushed pink, with a deep red-brown spot inside, from spring–early summer. Zones 5–9.

Calochortus amabilis
DIOGENES LANTERN, GOLDEN GLOBE TULIP
☼ ❄ ↔ 6 in (15 cm) ↕ 8–12 in (20–30 cm)
Comes from northwestern California. Branching stems of nodding goblet-shaped flowers of deep yellow. Outer petals spreading and triangular, inner petals with fringed edges and folding over each other. Zones 5–9.

Calochortus amoenus
ROSE FAIRY LANTERN, SIERRA GLOBE TULIP
☼ ❄ ↔ 6 in (15 cm) ↕ 18 in (45 cm)
From central and southern California. Similar to *C. albus* but shorter. The nodding flowers of deep rose pink or purple form on slender stems from spring–summer. Flowers narrowly bell-shaped or more globose. Zones 5–9.

Calochortus luteus
GOLD NUGGETS, YELLOW MARIPOSA TULIP
☼ ❄ ↔ 6 in (15 cm) ↕ 8–20 in (20–50 cm)
From central California. Slender stems carry open bell-shaped flowers of clear yellow, up to 3 in (8 cm) wide, usually with a brown spot at the base of each petal. Flowers appear in spring and early summer. Nectar gland is crescent-shaped. Zones 5–9.

Calochortus amoenus

Calochortus luteus

Calochortus splendens

Calochortus umbellatus

Calochortus monophyllus
☼ ❄ ↔ 6 in (15 cm) ↕ 4–8 in (10–20 cm)
Native to northern California and Oregon. A small slender species with branching stems of upright, open, yellow, bell-shaped flowers in spring. The petals are covered in fine hairs. Zones 5–9.

Calochortus splendens
☼ ❄ ↔ 6 in (15 cm) ↕ 8–24 in (20–60 cm)
From western USA. Bears upright bell-shaped flowers on leafy branching stems. The flowers are pale pink, with slightly hairy petals, a purple spot at the base, and contrasting bluish purple anthers. Zones 5–9.

Calochortus superbus
PROUD MARIPOSA
☼/◐ ❄ ↔ 6 in (15 cm) ↕ 16–24 in (40–60 cm)
Native to California. Bears bell-shaped white or cream flowers, streaked with purple, each petal with a maroon spot at the base surrounded by yellow. The outer petals are lance-shaped, the inner petals rounded and slightly hairy. The nectar gland is prominent and V-shaped. Flowering in late spring. Zones 5–9.

Calochortus umbellatus
OAKLAND STAR TULIP
☼ ❄ ↔ 6 in (15 cm) ↕ 4–6 in (10–15 cm)
Rare Californian species. Dainty, upright, open flowers. white or cream, sometimes flushed pink, purple markings on petal bases; carried on umbels for long periods in spring. Zones 5–9.

CALODENDRUM
This genus comprising a single evergreen species in the rue (Rutaceae) family is from the coastal region of South Africa. The name comes from the Greek *kalos*, meaning beautiful, and *dendron*, meaning tree, which aptly describes this majestic tree. It has a spreading crown and is often used in parks and large gardens or as a street tree in the more temperate regions of the Southern Hemisphere and warmer regions of North America.
CULTIVATION: *Calodendrum* prefers an open full sun position where its

Calothamnus gilesii, in the wild, Southern Cross, Western Australia

Calothamnus quadrifidus

crown can develop unhindered. Grow in a reasonably fertile, well-composted and well-drained position where water is assured, especially in its initial growth period. Hardy to light frost when mature, it requires protection in early years when grown in marginal areas.

Calodendrum capense
CAPE CHESTNUT

☼ ❄ ↔ 30 ft (9 m) ↑ 30 ft (9 m)

Bright mid-green leaves dotted with oil glands. Flowers pink clusters, protruding stamens, and recurved petals dotted with oil glands, which reflect the light and make the flowers appear to glow in the sunlight in spring–summer. Zones 9–11.

CALOMERIA
syn. *Humea*

As usually understood, this genus, belonging to the daisy (Asteraceae) family, consists of a single species of tall evergreen biennial or short-lived shrub from the moist forests of south-eastern Australia. It has aromatic foliage and distinctive tiny flowerheads, each consisting of 2 to 4 florets enclosed in reddish bracts. Thousands of flowerheads make up the pendulous inflorescence that terminates the leafy stem. Large leaves have a closely veined upper surface and a coating of cobwebby hairs

beneath. This dramatic plant was first cultivated in Europe from the early nineteenth century.

CULTIVATION: Raise from seed to reach flowering size in its second year. Sow seed in summer and advance seedlings in a rich loamy soil in beds or pots, protecting them from heavy winter frosts under glass if necessary. Feed plants in spring for a late summer to autumn flower display. A sheltered but sunny position suits them best. Cut off the old flowering stems to encourage growth after the second year.

Calomeria amaranthoides
syn. *Humea elegans*
HUMEA, INCENSE BUSH

☼ ❄ ↔ 3 ft (0.9 m) ↑ 10 ft (3 m)

Usually treated as a biennial. Single or multi-stemmed. Leaves highly aromatic, bright green crinkled. Inflorescence rises above the foliage. Tiny pendent flowerheads pinkish bronze, changing to rusty red as seeds mature. Zones 8–11.

CALOPHYLLUM

Almost 200 species make up this genus of evergreen trees, from tropical Asia and the western Pacific region. They belong to the st johns-wort (Clusiaceae) family. Leaves, arranged in opposite pairs on the twigs, are leathery and glossy with closely spaced parallel veins. Panicles of flowers terminate the branchlets or arise from the leaf axils. The flowers have cupped white petals in rows and a central bunch of golden stamens. The fruits are nut-like, with a single seed enclosed in a hard shell covered in a thin flesh. Used for their timber, and the seeds of some species yield a useful oil.

CULTIVATION: Only *C. inophyllum* has been widely cultivated. It is valued for its ability to thrive on tropical seashores as well as for its attractive

Calothamnus validus

shade-giving foliage and its flowers. It prefers deep, well-drained, sandy soils and can grow quickly in first 10 years or so. Easily propagated from the large seeds, which germinate rapidly.

Calophyllum inophyllum
ALEXANDRIAN LAUREL, BEAUTY LEAF, OIL-NUT TREE

☼ ✦ ↔ 20 ft (6 m) ↑ 60 ft (18 m)

Ranging widely from southern India across Asia, tropical Australia, and the Pacific Islands; found in coastal areas. Spreading limbs with a dense rounded canopy. Leaves glossy. Flower clusters, white and gold in summer wet season. Seeds contain fragrant oil. Zones 11–12.

CALOTHAMNUS

NET BUSH, CLAW FLOWER

One of the many Australian myrtle (Myrtaceae) family genera, these 40 species of evergreen shrubs are native to Western Australia. They are notable for the way in which their one-sided flower spikes are formed by the flower filaments being joined. This causes the spikes to fan out and droop at the tips. This has given the genus the common name net bush or, when the filaments are more entirely fused and curved, claw flowers. The flowers usually occur in late winter and spring. The foliage is needle-like, varying in length with the species.

CULTIVATION: Net bushes need a light, gritty, well-drained soil. They are drought tolerant and hardy to light frosts once established, needing moisture and shelter when young. Tip prune as the old wood is slow to

Calomeria amaranthoides

shoot. Propagate by seed or soft to half-hardened tip cuttings, preferably from non-flowering stems.

Calothamnus gilesii
GILES' NET BUSH

☼ ❄ ↔ 7–15 ft (2–4.5 m) ↑ 7–17 ft (2–5 m)

Branches upright, long pointed leaves, round in cross-section, to 8 in (20 cm) long, covered in prominent oil-glands. Clusters of 3 to 4 bright red flowers from winter–summer. Globular fruit, to ½ in (12 mm) long, containing many small seeds, held on stems for many years. Zones 9–10.

Calothamnus quadrifidus
COMMON NET BUSH, ONE-SIDED BOTTLEBRUSH

☼ ❄ ↔ 8 ft (2.4 m) ↑ 8 ft (2.4 m)

Upright, heavily branched shrub. Flattened needle-like leaves to 1¼ in (30 mm) long. Flower spikes bright red, with stamens in bundles of 4, to 8 in (20 cm) long. Cultivars include yellow-flowered, dwarf, and gray-green-foliaged forms. Zones 9–10.

Calothamnus validus
BARRENS CLAW FLOWER

☼ ❄ ↔ 8 ft (2.4 m) ↑ 8 ft (2.4 m)

Easily grown, vigorous, upright or rounded shrub can become a weed. Leaves, narrow, aromatic; the essential

Calophyllum inophyllum

Calodendrum capense

Calotis cuneifolia

Calycanthus floridus

oils used in homeopathy and aroma-therapy. Flowers are large, crimson, and in small clusters below the leaves. Zones 9–11.

CALOTIS
BURR DAISIES

Consisting of 26 species, 2 in southeastern Asia and 24 in Australia, this genus of annual and perennial herbs and small shrubs occurs in a variety of habitats and soils, and is placed in the daisy (Asteraceae) family. The simple or variously divided leaves are smooth, hairy, green, or gray-green. Flowerheads are daisy-like, borne singly or in clusters, terminal or axillary, in white, pink, blue, or yellow colors. The fruits are in globular burr-like heads. *Calotis* is closely related to the genus *Brachyscome*, which is more common in cultivation because its fruiting heads are not burr-like.
CULTIVATION: These plants prefer a sunny position in well-drained soil. They are propagated from seeds and from cuttings, which germinate and strike readily.

Calotis cuneifolia
BINDI-EYE, BLUE BURR DAISY
☼ ❄ ↔ to 3 ft (0.9 m)
↑ 8–16 in (20–40 cm)

Multi-stemmed hairy perennial common across mainland Australia. Leaves wedge-shaped, green, 1¾ in (40 mm) long, with bases sheathing stem. Blue, whitish or mauve flowerheads, ¾–1 in (18–25 mm) in diameter, throughout year, mostly during spring. Reddish fruit. Zones 8–9.

Calycanthus occidentalis

CALTHA

This buttercup (Ranunculaceae) family genus contains 10 species of herbaceous perennials, widespread in temperate regions of both hemispheres. Often very much like buttercups in general appearance, they have fleshy, bright to deep green, kidney- to heart-shaped leaves on sturdy leaf stalks and develop into mounding clumps of foliage. Flowers white to pale yellow or gold; although petal-less, their 5 or more petal-like sepals give them a buttercup-like appearance. Double-flowered forms common. Flowering season varies with species. Once used medicinally—named verrucaria because of supposed ability to cure warts—now considered too toxic for such purposes.
CULTIVATION: They are mostly very frost tolerant with a preference for damp soil and partly shaded conditions, though ordinary well-drained humus-rich garden soil in a woodland environment is perfectly acceptable. Their roots spread readily, though not nearly as aggressively as those of some of their buttercup cousins. Most easily propagated by division.

Caltha leptosepala
☼ ❄ ↔ 12 in (30 cm) ↑ 12 in (30 cm)
Attractive heart-shaped leaves. Silver-white flowers in spring. Zones 6–9.

Caltha palustris
syn. *Caltha polypetala*
KING CUP, MARSH MARIGOLD
☼/☼ ❄ ↔ 16–24 in (40–60 cm)
↑ 12–24 in (30–60 cm)
Widespread in the northern temperate zone. Upright or spreading habit with kidney-shaped leaves, 4–8 in (10–20 cm) wide. Bears bright golden yellow flowerheads on upright stems. Several double-flowered cultivars with rounded heads, including 'Flore Pleno' and the dark-leafed 'Monstrosa'. Zones 3–9.

Caltha scaposa
☼/☼ ❄ ↔ 12 in (30 cm) ↑ 6 in (15 cm)
From the Himalayas and western China. Low spreading habit with

long-stemmed, heart-shaped, deep green leaves to 1½ in (35 mm) long, sometimes finely toothed. Deep yellow flowers in summer. Zones 6–9.

CALYCANTHUS

Resembling magnolias, but in the allspice (Calycanthaceae) family, the aromatic deciduous shrubs of this temperate East Asian and North American genus of up to 6 species have similar characteristics. They grow to around 10 ft (3 m) tall with a considerable spread, have large elliptical leaves and strappy, many-petalled flowers in late spring and summer. Although the flowers are sometimes small and have rather dull colors, they are borne on the new growth and stand out well.
CULTIVATION: Although difficult to propagate from cuttings (layering or seed being preferred), allspice are not difficult to grow. They prefer cool moist soil with ample summer water in sun or half-sun. The flowers do not last well in low humidity.

Calycanthus fertilis
ALLSPICE
☼/☼ ❄ ↔ 7 ft (2 m) ↑ 10 ft (3 m)
Native to southeastern USA. Leaves glossy, deep green, to 6 in (15 cm) long. Mildly fragrant purple-red to brown flowers, to 2 in (5 cm) wide.

Caltha leptosepala, in the wild, USA

Cultivars include the dwarf 'Nanus' and 'Purpureus', which has purple-tinted foliage. Zones 6–10.

Calycanthus floridus
CAROLINA ALLSPICE, STRAWBERRY SHRUB
☼/☼ ❄ ↔ 7 ft (2 m) ↑ 10 ft (3 m)
Native of southeastern USA. Leaves large, oval, dull mid-green. Bright red to dark red-brown fragrant flowers, up to 2 in (5 cm) wide. Zones 5–9.

Calycanthus occidentalis ★
CALIFORNIAN ALLSPICE, SPICE BUSH
☼/☼ ❄ ↔ 7 ft (2 m) ↑ 10 ft (3 m)
From California, similar to *C. fertilis*, with slightly larger leaves, and reddish flowers fading to yellow with age. Large-flowered forms, with blooms up to 3 in (8 cm) wide, most often seen in garden centers. Zones 7–10.

CALYLOPHUS

This genus of 6 species from North America belongs to evening-primrose (Onagraceae) family and is closely allied to *Oenothera*. Herbaceous or subshrubby perennials, rarely annual, flowering in first year from seed. Stems are erect to almost creeping, bearing entire to serrated leaves. Flowers, borne in the upper axils, are hardly different in any obvious way from those of some *Oenothera* species; they open in early morning or from mid-afternoon

Caltha palustris 'Flore Pleno'

Caltha scaposa, in the wild, Tibetan Plateau, Tibet

C

until dusk, wilting after 1½ to 2 hours. The 4 greenish yellow sepals are often marked red or purple; the 4 reflexed yellow petals often redden on withering. Capsules are cylindrical, 4-angled, and contain many seeds in 2 rows in each of the 4 compartments. CULTIVATION: Annuals are propagated from seed, as are perennials, which can also be increased by division of softwood cuttings from spring growths. As they have a tap root, take care when transplanting them to sunny well-drained sites in the garden.

Calylophus serrulatus

syns *Calylophus drummondianus, Oenothera serrulata*

BUSH SUNDROPS, DWARF SUNDROPS, PLAINS YELLOW PRIMROSE

☼ ❄ ↔ 12–24 in (30–60 cm) ↕ 12–24 in (30–60 cm)

Perennial from southern Canada, central and southern USA. Green

Calytrix alpestris

Calytrix exstipulata

Calylophus serrulatus

leaves toothed in upper half. Flowers, opening pale to bright yellow in the morning and fading to apricot by next day, are 1 in (25 mm) across, from late spring–summer. Stamens are two lengths. Zones 3–9.

CALYTRIX

FRINGE MYRTLE, STARFLOWER

This Australian genus of some 75 species of evergreen shrubs, while rather heath-like in appearance, with fine, often needle-like leaves and small, star-shaped, 5-petalled flowers, is actually classed among the myrtles (Myrtaceae). Mainly found in south-western Australia, they rarely exceed 4 ft (1.2 m) tall. Most produce pink-tinted white flowers in spring, though flowers in yellow, pink, purple, and red tones are also common. The foliage contains aromatic oils that can be very pungent.

CULTIVATION: Fringe myrtles prefer gritty well-drained soil that is not too rich, and a position in full sunlight. If they are grown too quickly, they tend to burn out and die at a young age. However, if they are kept on the dry side in a low-nutrient soil and given an annual light trimming, they form neat bushes that will last for a number of years. Propagate by seed or from small tip cuttings, preferably of non-flowering shoots.

Calytrix alpestris

GRAMPIANS FRINGE MYRTLE, SNOW MYRTLE

☼ ❄ ↔ 8 ft (2.4 m) ↕ 8 ft (2.4 m)

Found in the higher altitude areas of South Australia and Victoria. Smaller in cultivation. Graceful open growth. The leaves are variable in shape—some are linear, some rounded. The flowers are white to pale pink, and contrast with pleasing effect against dark foliage. Flowering varies from sparse to extremely profuse. 'Wheeler's Variety', selected as being reliably heavy flowering. Zones 8–9.

Camassia leichtlinii

Calytrix exstipulata

KIMBERLEY HEATH, NORTHERN FRINGE MYRTLE, TURKEY BUSH

☼ ⚘ ↔ 10 ft (3 m) ↕ 15 ft (4.5 m)

From northeastern Australia. Densely packed heads of deep pink flowers. Known as turkey bush because bush (wild) turkeys nest among them. They give essential oil used in homeopathy: said to inspire creativity and renew artistic confidence. Zones 10–12.

CAMASSIA

CAMAS, QUAMASH

This genus consists of 5 species of bulbs in the hyacinth (Hyacinthaceae) family, native mainly to western North America. The name *Camassia* comes from the Native American name, which is usually transliterated as quamash. The meaning of the name is unclear but what is known is that the bulbs are edible and were included in the diet of the native peoples. As garden plants they are tough and adaptable and one species, *C. leichtlinii*, has been extensively developed into garden forms. These plants have long narrow leaves and in late spring and early summer produce heads of 6-petalled flowers atop strong stems, rather reminiscent of some of the *Agapanthus*.

CULTIVATION: Mostly very frost hardy and easily grown in any fertile, well-drained soil that does not dry out. Plant in full or half-sun. May be raised from seed but then take up to 5 years to bloom, and because most garden plants are cultivars, division when dormant during winter is preferred.

Camassia cusickii

☼/◑ ❄ ↔ 24–48 in (60–120 cm) ↕ 24–36 in (60–90 cm)

From northeastern Oregon. Blue-green leaves, 16–32 in (40–80 cm)

Camassia cusickii

Camassia quamash

long. Racemes of pale blue flowers with yellow anthers make up around half the height of the flower stems. Flowers to 2 in (5 cm) wide. Zones 5–9.

Camassia leichtlinii

☼/◑ ❄ ↔ 20–60 in (50–150 cm) ↕ 24–48 in (60–120 cm)

Found from British Columbia in Canada to California, USA. Rather stiff green leaves to 24 in (60 cm) long. Short racemes on tall stems. Flowers creamy white to lavender-blue. 'Semiplena', semi-double cream to yellow flowers. *C. l.* subsp. *suksdorfii* is a widespread blue-flowered subspecies, of which 'Alba' is a white-flowered cultivar and 'Blauwe Donau' ('Blue Danube') has dark blue flowers. Zones 3–9.

Camassia quamash

CAMASH, CAMOSH, SWAMP SEGO

☼/◑ ❄ ↔ 16–40 in (40–100 cm) ↕ 12–32 in (30–80 cm)

Found over much of western USA. Slightly blue-green leaves to 20 in (50 cm) long. Flower racemes about one-third of the flower stem length. Pale blue to deep violet, rarely white flowers to over 2 in (5 cm) wide. Zones 5–9.

Camellia hiemalis 'Bonanza'

Camellia hiemalis 'Chansonette'

CAMELLIA

A member of the Theaceae family, the camellia genus has nearly 300 species, native to the mountainous regions of east Asia. They are evergreen shrubs or small trees, popular in gardens for their ornamental qualities. Camellias are also grown commercially for the teas made from their leaves. There are innumerable cultivars. Camellias bear short-stalked flowers and bloom during the colder months. A number of flower forms, sizes, and subtle and more flamboyant petal markings are recognized. Petal colors range between shades of white, yellow, pink, rose red, dark red, scarlet, purple-red and puce. Camellias are suitable for planting in formal or woodland settings, and for hedging, edging, topiary, and espalier. CULTIVATION: While it is usual to choose and plant camellias in late autumn and winter, it is important to withhold nutrition and additional water during this time. Acid to neutral well-drained soils, shaded or semi-shaded positions, dry winters and wet summers suit the majority. Propagation is by grafting, or from cuttings in late summer to winter.

Camellia crapnelliana

☀ ❄ ↔ 15 ft (4.5 m) ↑ 25 ft (8 m)
Native of southwestern China. Bark is distinctive, smooth, and cinnamon red. Oval leaves glossy, dark green above, pale beneath, and heavily veined. Solitary large flowers with wavy, irregular, white petals, yellow stamens, in autumn. Large, round, brown seed pods. Zones 10–11.

Camellia granthamiana

☀ ❄ ↔ 6 ft (1.8 m) ↑ 12 ft (3.5 m)
From southern China. Buds brown; large, single, creamy, flowers, slightly reflexed petals, in early winter. Long puckered leaves, heavily veined, shiny. Open spreading growth. Zones 8–11.

Camellia grijsi

☀ ❄ ↔ 8 ft (2.4 m) ↑ 10 ft (3 m)
From eastern and central China. Leaves oval, dark green, finely toothed. Flowers fragrant, small, white, lobed petals, yellow stamens. Resembles *C. sasanqua*, but flowers in winter and early spring. Zones 9–10.

Camellia hiemalis

☀ ❄ ↔ 6 ft (1.8 m) ↑ 10 ft (3 m)
Known only in cultivation, may be a hybrid. Leaves dark green, flowers white or pale pink, lobed irregular petals, in winter–spring. 'Bonanza', semi-double peony-form flowers, deep pink to red petals; 'Chansonette', brilliant pink petals with hints of lavender; 'Shishigashira', compact plant, flowers rose pink to red, semi-double, petals slightly fluted; 'Shôwa-no-sakae', Japanese cultivar, semi-double flowers; 'Sparkling Burgundy', peony-formed flowers, dark cerise petals. All suitable for espaliering. Zones 7–10.

Camellia hiemalis 'Shishigashira'

Camellia granthamiana

Camellia japonica
COMMON CAMELLIA

☀ ❄ ↔ 25 ft (8 m) ↑ 30 ft (9 m)

This species, a shrub or small tree, is found on several of the Chinese, Korean, Taiwanese, and Japanese islands. Single flowers, red or puce-pink, mildly scented. Leaves broadly oval, pointed, very glossy above, paler, duller, and lightly spotted beneath. Variable sized fruits. Appearance and tolerance are variable in the wild. Well known variation is *C. j.* **subsp.** ***rusticana***, the snow camellia, found at altitudes where snow protects the slow-growing plant. Another is the apple camellia, *C. j.* **var.** ***macrocarpa***, with large, red, apple-like fruit.

Cultivars of *C. japonica* are most popular; over 2,000 display different flower forms, colors, petal markings, growth habits, preferences, and tolerances. Foliage is glossy, neat, and elliptical. Most grow into neat dense shrubs and, ultimately, small trees. They flourish in suitable climates and soils, in shaded or semi-shaded positions, and sheltered in cold climates. Well-draining neutral to acid soil is essential. '**Adolphe Audusson**', semi-double dark red flowers; '**Alba Plena**', double with snow white, symmetrical, overlapping petals; '**Akashigata**', semi-double rich rose-pink flowers; '**Alexander Hunter**', rich crimson flowers; '**Berenice Boddy**', large, semi-double, pink flowers; '**Bob Hope**', dark red semi-double flowers with yellow stamens; '**Bob's Tinsie**', upright compact growth habit, small, bright red, anemone-form flowers; '**Bokuhan**' (syn. 'Tinsie'), miniature anemone-form flowers, red outer petals, dense boss of white petaloids, small leaves, moderately sun tolerant; '**Brushfield's Yellow**', anemone-form, pale creamish white flowers; '**Coquettii**', formal double, or incomplete double, red flowers; '**Debutante**', large, pale rose, informal double flowers; '**Dona Herzilia de Frietas Magalhaes**', purple-violet flowers; '**Elegans**' (syn. 'Chandleri Elegans'),

pink flowers—has given rise to several breeding programs; '**Elegans Champagne**', big creamy petals; '**Elegans Supreme**', deep pink ruffled flowers; '**Elegans Variegata**', pink flowers with white blotches; '**Gloire de Nantes**', semi-double to incomplete double mid-pink flowers; '**Grand Prix**', semi-double vivid red flowers; '**Janet Waterhouse**', white, double, perfectly symmetrical flowers; '**Jupiter**', formal double red flowers; '**Lady Loch**', veined, whitish pink, peony-form flowers; '**Lavinia Maggi**', white petals, streaked light and dark pinkish red; '**Masayoshi**', rich pinkish red double flowers, whitish blotches on petals; '**Miss Charleston**', upright form, intense red flowers; '**Mrs D. W. Davis Descanso**', upright habit, semi-double flowers of softest pink; '**Nuccio's Cameo**', coral pink flowers; '**Nuccio's Carousel**', medium-sized, semi-double, pink flowers; '**Nuccio's Gem**', early blooming; '**Nuccio's Jewel**', formal double, star-shaped flowers, shaded pink petals; '**Nuccio's Pearl**',

blush white petals tipped in shades of orchid pink; '**Roma Risorta**', flowers with pink and red striped petals; '**Rubescens Major**', glowing rose red, veined petals, dark, glossy leaves; '**Tama-no-ura**', dark red, petals edged in white, upright yellow stamens; '**Tomorrow**', a prize-winning plant bred in America, which has large informal double flowers, pink petals and petaloids with deeper pink markings, and is early blooming (this strong floriferous plant has produced other cultivars, among them '**Tomorrow's Dawn**', an informal double, with deep pink flowers); '**Tricolor**', with semi-double flowers, the petals white with rose-red markings; and '**Twilight**', with large light blush pink flowers that fade to silvery white. The **Higo Group** camellias, a popular Japanese form of *C. japonica*, are not a separate species; they have flat flowers, with profuse flared stamens, gold, pink, or red. Single and semi-double forms. Petals solid, blotched, or striped. Zones 7–10.

Camellia japonica 'Allie Blue'

Camellia japonica 'Althaeiflora'

Camellia japonica 'A. W. Jessep'

Camellia japonica 'Aaron's Ruby'

Camellia japonica 'Ace of Hearts'

Camellia japonica 'Alice Wood'

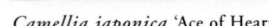

Camellia japonica 'Akashigata'

Camellia japonica 'Alta Gavin'

Camellia japonica 'Alba Plena'

Camellia japonica 'Angela Cocchi' *Camellia japonica* 'Andrea Sebire' *Camellia japonica* 'Anita' *Camellia japonica* 'Anzac' *Camellia japonica* 'Apollo'

Camellia japonica 'Ardoch' *Camellia japonica* 'Arianna Hall' *Camellia japonica* 'Art Howard' *C. japonica* 'Aspasia Macarthur' *Camellia japonica* 'Australis'

Camellia japonica 'Ave Maria' *Camellia japonica* 'Ballet Dancer' *C. japonica* 'Belinda Hackett' *Camellia japonica* 'Belliformis' *Camellia japonica* 'Benten'

C. japonica 'Betty Foy Sanders' *C. j.* 'Betty Sheffield Coral' *C. j.* 'Betty Sheffield Pink' *C. j.* 'Betty Sheffield White' *C. japonica* 'Betty's Beauty'

Camellia japonica 'Bienville' *C. japonica* 'Billie McCaskill' *C. japonica* 'Birthday Girl' *C. japonica* 'Blood of China' *Camellia japonica* 'Bob Hope'

Camellia japonica 'Bokuhan' *Camellia japonica* 'Bronacha' *C. japonica* 'Brushfield's Yellow' *Camellia japonica* 'C. M. Hovey' *C. japonica* 'C. M. Wilson'

C. japonica 'Camden Park'

C. japonica 'Campbell Ashley'

Camellia japonica 'Candy Apple'

C. japonica 'Cardinal's Cap'

C. japonica 'Carolyn Tuttle'

C. japonica 'Carter's Sunburst'

C. j. 'Carter's Sunburst Pink'

Camellia japonica 'Cassandra'

Camellia japonica 'Chandleri'

Camellia japonica 'Chats'

C. japonica 'Cherry's Jubilee'

Camellia japonica 'Cheryll Lynn'

C. japonica 'Chinese Lanterns'

Camellia japonica 'Chô-Chô-san'

C. japonica 'Chow's Han-ling'

Camellia japonica 'Cinderella'

Camellia japonica 'Clark Hubbs'

Camellia japonica 'Colletti'

C. japonica 'Commander Mulroy'

C. japonica 'Confetti Blush'

C. japonica 'Conrad Hilton'

C. japonica 'Contessa Woronzoff'

C. japonica 'Coral Pink Lotus'

Camellia japonica 'Coronation'

C. j. 'Countess of Ellesmere'

C. japonica 'Countess of Orkney'

Camellia japonica 'Cover Girl'

Camellia japonica 'Dahlohnega'

Camellia japonica 'Daikagura'

Camellia japonica 'David Surina'

C. japonica 'Dawn's Early Light' Camellia japonica 'De la Reine' Camellia japonica 'Debutante' Camellia japonica 'Demi-tasse' Camellia japonica 'Desire'

Camellia japonica 'Dewatairin' C. j. 'Diddy's Pink Organdie' Camellia japonica 'Dixie Knight' C. j. 'Doctor Agnew Hilsman' C. japonica 'Doctor Burnside' ★

C. japonica 'Doctor King' C. japonica 'Doctor Tinsley' C. j. 'Dona Herzila de Frietas Magalhaes' C. j. 'Dona Herzila de Frietas Magalhaes Variegated' C. japonica 'Dona Rita de Cassia'

Camellia japonica 'Drama Girl' Camellia japonica 'Easter Morn' Camellia japonica 'Easter Sun' Camellia japonica 'Ecclefield' C. japonica 'Edna Campbell'

Camellia japonica 'El Rojo' C. japonica 'Eleanor Hagood' Camellia japonica 'Elegans' C. japonica 'Elegans Champagne' C. japonica 'Elegans Splendor'

C. japonica, 'Elegans Supreme' C. japonica 'Elegans Variegata' Camellia japonica 'Elena Nobili' C. japonica 'Elsie Ruth Marshall' Camellia japonica 'Emma Grace'

C. japonica 'Emmett Barnes'   *C. japonica* 'Emmett Pfingstl'   *C. japonica* 'Emperor of Russia'   *C. j.* 'Emperor of Russia Variegated'   *C. japonica* 'Enrico Bettoni'

Camellia japonica 'Eric Sievers'   *Camellia japonica* 'Erin Farmer'   *Camellia japonica* 'Eugene Lizé'   *C. japonica* 'Extravaganza'   *Camellia japonica* 'Fashionata'

Camellia japonica 'Fimbriata'   *Camellia japonica* 'Finlandia'   *Camellia japonica* 'Fir Cone'   *Camellia japonica* 'First Prom'   *Camellia japonica* 'Flame'

C. japonica 'Fran Homeyer'   *Camellia japonica* 'Frances Hill'   *Camellia japonica* 'Frank Gibson'   *Camellia japonica* 'Garnet'   *Camellia japonica* 'Gauntlettii'

Camellia japonica 'Gay Marmee'   *C. j.* 'General George Patton'   *C. japonica* 'General Leclerc'   *Camellia japonica* 'Gigantea'   *Camellia japonica* 'Gladys Parks'

Camellia japonica 'Glenwood'   *Camellia japonica* 'Golden Gate'   *Camellia japonica* 'Goshoguruma'   *C. japonica* 'Grace Albritton'   *C. japonica* 'Grand Marshall'

Camellia japonica 'Grand Slam'   *Camellia japonica* 'Grand Sultan'   *Camellia japonica* 'Hagoromo'   *Camellia japonica* 'Hanafûki'   *Camellia japonica* 'Great Eastern'

C. japonica 'Great Western'   *C. japonica* 'Guest of Honor'   *C. japonica* 'Guilio Nuccio'   *C. japonica* 'Gwenneth Morey'   *Camellia japonica* 'Hanasuku'

Camellia japonica 'Happy'   *C. japonica* 'Happy Holidays'   *Camellia japonica* 'Hawaii'   *Camellia japonica* 'Helena'   *Camellia japonica* 'Helenor'

C. japonica 'Henry Turnbull   *C. japonica* 'High Fragrance'   *Camellia japonica* 'High Hat'   *Camellia japonica* 'Hikarugenji'   *C. japonica* 'Hilda Jamison'

Camellia japonica 'Hinomaru'   *Camellia japonica* 'Hishikaraito'   *Camellia japonica* 'Imbricata'   *Camellia japonica* 'Isaribi'   *C. japonica* 'J. J. Pringle Smith'

Camellia japonica 'Jacksonii'   *Camellia japonica* 'Jan's Chance'   *C. japonica* 'Janet Waterhouse'   *Camellia japonica* 'Jean Lyne'   *C. japonica* 'Jeanette Cousins'

Camellia japonica 'John Medley'   *C. japonica* 'Josephine Duell'   *C. japonica* 'Joshua E. Youtz'   *Camellia japonica* 'Julia France'   *C. japonica* 'Katherine Nuccio'

Camellia japonica 'Kimberley'   *C. japonica* 'King's Ransom'   *C. japonica* 'Kingyo-tsubaki'   *Camellia japonica* 'Kitty'   *C. japonica* 'Koshi-no-reijin'

C. japonica 'Kramer's Supreme'   *C. japonica* 'Kumagai Nagoya'   *Camellia japonica* 'Kumasaka'   *Camellia japonica* 'Kuro-tsubaki'   *Camellia japonica* 'Lady Edinger'

Camellia japonica 'Lady Loch'   *C. j.* 'Lady Maude Walpole'   *C. japonica* 'Lady Vansittart'   *C. japonica* 'Lady Winneke'   *Camellia japonica* 'Lalla Rookh'

C. japonica 'Latifolia Variegated'   *Camellia japonica* 'Laura Walker'   *C. j.* 'Laurie Bray Variegated'   *Camellia japonica* 'Lemon Drop'   *Camellia japonica* 'Levertons'

Camellia japonica 'Leviathan'   *Camellia japonica* 'Lipstick'   *Camellia japonica* 'Little Jon'   *Camellia japonica* 'Look Again'   *Camellia japonica* 'Lovelight'

C. japonica 'Madame Lebois'

Camellia japonica 'Magnolia'

Camellia japonica 'Man Size'

Camellia japonica 'Mangetsu'

C. japonica 'Margaret Davis'

C. japonica 'Margarete Hertrich'

Camellia japonica 'Mariana'

Camellia japonica 'Mariann'

Camellia japonica 'Marie Mackall'

Camellia japonica 'Marina'

C. japonica 'Marjorie Huckabee'

C. japonica 'Marjorie Magnificent'

C. j. 'Mark Alan Variegated'

C. japonica 'Maroon and Gold'

Camellia japonica 'Martha Tuck'

C. japonica 'Mary Charlotte'

Camellia japonica 'Mary Paige'

Camellia japonica 'Mathotiana'

C. japonica 'Melbourne White'

Camellia japonica 'Memphis Bell'

Camellia japonica 'Merrillees'

Camellia japonica 'Midnight'

Camellia japonica 'Mikenjaku'

C. japonica 'Minato-no-akebono'

C. japonica 'Minato-no-haru'

Camellia japonica 'Mona Harvey'

Camellia japonica 'Monjusu'

C. japonica 'Moonlight Bay'

Camellia japonica 'Moshio'

C. j. 'Mrs Anne Marie Hovey'

C

C. japonica 'Mrs Beresford'

C. japonica 'Mrs Charles Cobb'

C. j. 'Mrs D. W. Davis Descanso'

C. japonica 'Mrs Freeman Weiss'

Camellia japonica 'Mrs H. Boyce'

Camellia japonica 'Mrs Swan'

C. japonica 'Mrs Tingley' ★

Camellia japonica 'Nancy Bird'

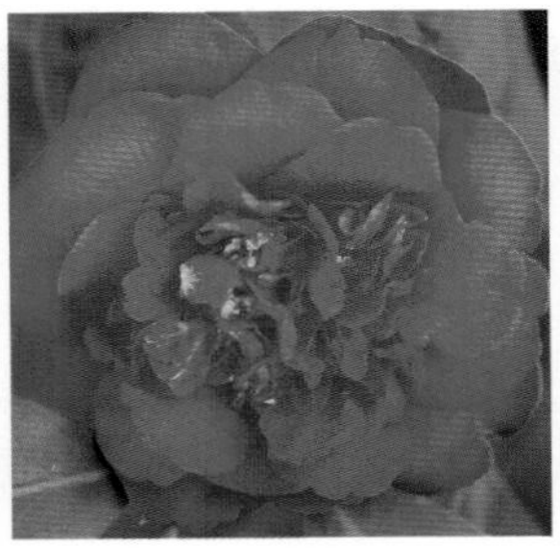

Camellia japonica 'Newington'

C. japonica 'Nuccio's Cameo'

Camellia japonica 'Nuccio's Gem'

C. japonica 'Nuccio's Pink Lace'

Camellia japonica 'Ô-Zora'

Camellia japonica 'Oki-no-nami'

C. japonica 'Otahuhu Beauty'

Camellia japonica 'Owen Henry'

Camellia japonica 'Palmyra'

C. japonica 'Paolina Maggi'

C. japonica 'Paul Sherrington'

Camellia japonica 'Pax'

C. japonica 'Philippa Ifould'

Camellia japonica 'Pink Ball'

Camellia japonica 'Pink Daddy'

Camellia japonica 'Pink Gold'

Camellia japonica 'Pink Pagoda'

Camellia japonica 'Polar Bear'

C. japonica 'Pope John XXIII'

Camellia japonica 'Pope Pius IX'

C. japonica 'Prima Ballerina'

C. j. 'Prince Eugène Napoléon'

C. j. 'Prince Frederick William'

C. japonica 'Princess Mary'

C. japonica 'Professor Sargent'

C. j. 'Professore Giovanni Santarelli'

Camellia japonica 'Pukekura'

Camellia japonica 'Queen Diana'

Camellia japonica 'R. L. Wheeler'

C. j. 'R. L. Wheeler Variegated'

C. j. 'Rachel Tarpy Special'

Camellia japonica 'Rafia'

Camellia japonica 'Ramona'

Camellia japonica 'Red Red Rose'

Camellia japonica 'Red Rogue'

C. japonica 'Regina del Giganti'

Camellia japonica 'Roger Hall'

Camellia japonica 'Roma Risorta'

Camellia japonica 'Rossii'

Camellia japonica 'Rox Cowley'

Camellia japonica 'Royal Velvet'

Camellia japonica 'Ruth Kemp'

Camellia japonica 'Salute'

Camellia japonica 'San Dimas'

Camellia japonica 'Sarasa'

Camellia japonica 'Shiragiku'

Camellia japonica 'Shiranui'

Camellia japonica 'Shiro Chan'

C. japonica 'Sawada's Dream'

Camellia japonica 'Sierra Spring'

C. japonica 'Silver Anniversary'

Camellia japonica 'Silver Waves'

Camellia japonica 'Somersby'

Camellia japonica 'Speciosissima'

Camellia japonica 'Simeon'

C. japonica 'Spencer's Pink'

C. japonica 'Spring Cornets'

C. japonica 'Spring Formal'

C. japonica 'Sugar and Spice'

Camellia japonica 'Susan Stone'

Camellia japonica 'Sweet Olive'

Camellia japonica 'Takanini'

Camellia japonica 'Tama Beauty'

C. japonica 'Tamo-no-ura'

Camellia japonica 'Tamie Fraser'

Camellia japonica 'The Czar'

C. japonica 'The Czar Variegated'

Camellia japonica 'Tick Tock'

Camellia japonica 'Tiffany'

Camellia japonica 'Tom Thumb'

Camellia japonica 'Tomorrow'

C. japonica 'Tomorrow's Dawn'

Camellia japonica 'Tootsie'

C. japonica 'Touch of Class'

Camellia japonica 'Triumphans'

Camellia japonica 'Twilight'

Camellia japonica 'Versicolor'

C. japonica 'Ville de Nantes'

C. j. 'Ville de Nantes Red'

C. japonica 'Violet Bouquet'

Camellia japonica 'Virgin's Blush'

C. japonica 'Virginia Franco'

C. j. 'Virginia Franco Rosea'

Camellia japonica 'Volcano'

C. japonica 'Waiwheto Beauty'

Camellia japonica 'Warrior'

Camellia japonica 'Wellbankiana'

C. japonica 'White Empress'

Camellia japonica 'White Nun'

Camellia japonica 'White Tulip'

Camellia japonica 'Wilamina'

Camellia japonica 'Wildfire'

C. japonica 'William Bartlett'

C. japonica 'William Honey'

Camellia japonica 'Wilson's Red'

Camellia japonica 'Yours Truly' ★

Camellia japonica 'Woodville Red'

Camellia lutchuensis 'Fairy Blush'

Camellia lutchuensis

Camellia nitidissima

Camellia lutchuensis

☀ ❄ ↔ 8 ft (2.4 m) ↕ 8 ft (2.4 m)
From Taiwan and Japan. Open pendulous habit bearing small, scented,
white flowers in winter. The leaves are
small and dark with russet-colored new
growth. Sienna brown buds. Suitable
for a woodland garden. **'Fairy Blush'**,
single, fragrant, pink-toned flowers.
Zones 8–10.

Camellia maliflora

☀ ❄ ↔ 4 ft (1.2 m) ↕ 7 ft (2 m)
Thought to be a Chinese species, now
believed to be of garden origin. Leaves
small, dense, mid-green. Flowers two-
toned, pink, peony-form, appear in
winter. In cold climates espalier against
a sheltered wall. Zones 8–10.

Camellia nitidissima

syn. *Camellia chrysantha*
GOLDEN CAMELLIA
☀ ⚘ ↔ 8 ft (2.4 m) ↕ 10 ft (3 m)
From northern Vietnam and southwestern China. Leaves leathery, large,
conspicuously veined, pale green, with
bronze new growth; pale bark. Flowers
bright yellow, single or semi-double, in
winter–spring. Zones 10–11.

Camellia oleifera

syn. *Camellia drupifera*

OIL CAMELLIA, OIL TEA

☀ ❄ ↔ 12 ft (3.5 m) ↑ 20 ft (6 m)

From southeastern Asia. In China, a clear thin oil is still extracted from its seeds, which is used for cooking and in cosmetics. The flowers are single and scented, their white petals long, lobed, and slightly twisted. Used in the breeding of cold-hardy camellias. **'Lushan Snow'** and **'Snow Flurry'** are attractive cultivars. Zones 7–9.

Camellia pitardii

☀ ❄ ↔ 12 ft (3.5 m) ↑ 20 ft (6 m)

From southern China. The leaves are lance-shaped and saw-toothed. The flowers are shades of delicate pale pink, rose pink, or white, with conspicuous stamens bright red-pink fading to white. This attractive species is used in tubs, mixed shrubberies, bonsai, and breeding programs. Cultivars include **'Adorable'**, with an upright habit and formal double pink flowers; **'Gay Pixie'**, rich pink flowers; **'Moonbeam'**, upright habit, pink flowers; **'Our Melissa'**, anemone-form flowers with soft pink petals; **'Snippet'**, has pale pink notched petals, used as an edging plant and is particularly suitable for bonsai. Zones 9–10.

Camellia purpurea

☀ ❄ ↔ 3–7 ft (0.9–2 m) ↑ 10–17 ft (3–5m)

Small tree from Yunnan Province, China. Thick elliptical leaves, 6–8 in (15–20 cm) long. Closely related to *C. sinensis*. Dark red flowers, 1¾–2½ in (4–6 cm) across. Fruits purple and green. Zones 8–10.

Camellia purpurea

Camellia oleifera 'Lushan Snow'

Camellia oleifera 'Snow Flurry'

Camellia pitardii 'Adorable'

Camellia pitardii 'Snow Storm'

Camellia pitardii 'Our Melissa'

Camellia pitardii

Camellia pitardii 'Fairy Bouquet'

Camellia pitardii 'Gay Pixie'

Camellia pitardii 'Pale Opal'

Camellia pitardii 'Pink Cameo'

Camellia pitardii 'Pink Ruffles'

Camellia pitardii 'Prudence'

C. p. v. *pitardi* 'Moonbeam'

Camellia pitardii 'Snippet'

Camellia pitardii 'Sprite'

C. reticulata 'Arch of Triumph'

C. reticulata 'Barbara Clark'

C. reticulata 'Betty's Delight'

Camellia reticulata 'Black Lace'

C. reticulata 'Blossom Time'

Camellia reticulata 'Bravo'

C. reticulata 'Bright Beauty'

C. reticulata 'Captain Rawes'

Camellia reticulata 'Crinoline'

Camellia reticulata 'Dali Cha'

Camellia reticulata 'Damanao'

Camellia reticulata 'Dark Jewel'

Camellia reticulata 'Dataohong'

C. reticulata 'Eileen Sebire'

C. reticulata 'Hody Wilson'

Camellia reticulata

☼ ½ ↔ 15 ft (4.5 m) ↑ 30 ft (9 m)

Originating in western China. Flowers rose pink, in noticeably velvety bracts. Leaves net-veined and toothed, and duller, darker and narrower than those of *C. japonica*. Today cultivars of *C. reticulata* are sometimes referred to as Yunnan camellias. *C. r.* f. *simplex* is the wild form. *C. r.* 'Captain Rawes', irregular, semi-double, carmine flowers; 'Dayinhong' (syn. 'Shot Silk'), an old Chinese cultivar bearing prolific, large, peony-form flowers composed of wavy ruby pink petals. 'Liue Yinhong' (syn. 'Narrow-leafed Shot Silk') has a somewhat willowy appearance and narrower leaves; 'Mandalay Queen', dark green foliage, pinkish red flowers; 'Zipao' (syn. 'Purple Gown'), an old Chinese cultivar, bears deep purple buds, opening into large wine red flowers, pin-striped in red. Zones 9–10.

Camellia reticulata 'Ellie's Girl'

Camellia reticulata 'Change of Day'

Camellia reticulata 'Margaret Hilford'

C. reticulata, 'John Hunt'

Camellia reticulata 'La Stupenda'

C. reticulata 'Ida Cossom'

Camellia reticulata 'Interval'

Camellia reticulata 'Juban'

Camellia reticulata 'Lila Naff'

Camellia reticulata 'Lady Pamela'

Camellia reticulata 'Lovely Lady'

Camellia reticulata 'Massee Lane'

Camellia reticulata 'Miss Tulare'

C. reticulata 'Nuccio's Ruby'

C. reticulata 'Our Selection'

Camellia reticulata 'Overture'

C. reticulata 'Raspberry Glow'

C. reticulata 'Robert's Jewel'

Camellia reticulata 'S. P. Dunn'

Camellia reticulata 'San Marino'

C. reticulata 'Sir Eric Pearce'

C. reticulata 'Strike it Rich'

C. reticulata 'Suzanne Withers'

C. reticulata 'Winter's Own'

Camellia reticulata 'Zaomudan'

Camellia reticulata f. *simplex*

Camellia rosiflora

☀ ❄ ↔ 2–3 ft (0.6–0.9 m)
↕ 3–7 ft (0.9–2 m)

Spreading evergreen shrub from China.
Soft rose pink to reddish pink, funnel-
shaped flowers with 6 to 9 petals up to
1 in (25 mm) across. Elliptical leaves,
3 in (8 cm) long, dark green above,
paler beneath. '**Mandy**', semi-double
blooms of palest pink. Zones 8–10.

Camellia rusticana

syns *C. decumbens, C. japonica*
subsp. *rusticana*

SNOW CAMELLIA

☀ ❄ ↔ to 2 m ↕ to 4 m

Occurs only in montane forests and
woodlands of western Honshu (Japan)
above 2,300 ft (700 m). It is similar
to *C. japonica*, but its flowers are
pink, not red, and its petiole is shorter
and hairy. Although quite cold-
tolerant, it has not been used much
in breeding programs. '**Botanyuki**',
pale cream flowers; '**Otome**', full pale
pink flowers. Zones 7–9.

Camellia salicifolia

☀ ❄ ↕ 7–10 ft (2–3 m) ↔ 4–7 ft (1.2–2 m)

Small tree from China and Taiwan,
named for similarity of its weeping
habit to willow *(Salix)*. White flowers,
singly or in pairs, with 5 to 6 oval
petals, to ¾ in (18 mm) across. Very
narrow elliptical leaves, 2–4 in
(5–10 cm) long, serrated. Branches
and leaf undersides furry. Zones 9–11.

Camellia saluenensis

☀ ❄ ↔ 4–15 ft (1.2–4.5 m)
↕ 4–15 ft (1.2–4.5 m)

Native to southwestern China. Open,
branching, flowers single, white, sugar
pink, red, wavy lightly lobed petals, in
late–early spring. Crowded, elongate,
oval leaves, dark green with blunt tips.
Used for bonsai, woodlands, breeding
frost-hardy camellias. Zones 7–10.

Camellia rosiflora

Camellia rosiflora 'Mandy'

Camellia rusticana 'Otome'

Camellia saluenensis

Camellia salicifolia

Camellia rusticana 'Botanyuki'

Camellia sasanqua 'Dwarf Shishi'

Camellia sasanqua 'Little Pearl'

Camellia sasanqua

☀ ❄ ↔ 5 ft (1.5 m) ↑ 10 ft (3 m)

From Japan. Straggling, woodland, tree-like shrub. Leaves very shiny, dark green. Flowers scented, single, white or pale pink, in autumn. '**Cotton Candy**' makes a tall, spreading, free-flowering plant with soft, clear pink, semi-double flowers and ruffled petals; '**Crimson King**', blooms early, deep pink-red semi-double flowers; '**Jean May**', upright habit, attractive, double, pink flowers; '**Mikunikô**', is an early bloomer, single rose pink flowers with mauve tonings; '**Mine-no-yuki**', early bloomer, abundant snow white flowers;

'**Misty Moon**', upright habit and large, wavy, rounded petals of pale lavender-pink; '**Narunigata**', white flower petals with curled pinkish red edges. Australia has produced the **Paradise Range** of sasanqua camellias. Their small to medium-sized informal double flowers are profuse and fluffy. Of the cultivars, '**Plantation Pink**' has a tall spreading habit making it especially suitable for hedging or espalier; it bears a profusion of flat, bright pink, single flowers that are beautifully formed. '**Red Willow**' has rose pink petals, muted at the center, with a willowy habit. Zones 9–11.

Camellia sasanqua 'Fuji-no-mine'

Camellia sasanqua 'Agnes O. Solomon'

Camellia sasanqua 'Bert Jones'

Camellia sasanqua 'Cicada'

Camellia sasanqua 'Early Pearly'

Camellia sasanqua 'Edna Butler'

Camellia sasanqua 'Gulf Glory'

Camellia sasanqua 'Hiryû'

Camellia sasanqua 'Jean May'

Camellia sasanqua 'Jennifer Susan'

Camellia sasanqua 'Lucinda'

Camellia sasanqua 'Marge Miller'

Camellia sasanqua 'Mignonne'

Camellia sasanqua 'Mikunikô'

Camellia sasanqua 'Narumigata'

Camellia sasanqua 'Otome-sazanka'

Camellia sasanqua 'Paradise Sayaka'

Camellia sasanqua 'Wahroongah'

Camellia sasanqua 'Russhay'

Camellia sasanqua 'Setsugekka'

Camellia sasanqua 'Shishigashira'

Camellia sasanqua 'Snowcloud'

Camellia sasanqua 'Pure Silk'

Camellia sasanqua 'Paradise Belinda'

Camellia sasanqua 'Paradise Petite'

Camellia sasanqua 'Paradise Blush'

Camellia sasanqua 'Pink Dauphin'

C

Camellia sinensis

syn. *Thea sinensis*

TEA

☀ ☘ ↔ 10 ft (3 m) ↑ 20 ft (6 m)

Probably originating in China, grown commercially for the production of tea for centuries. Flowers small, single, long-stalked, often in pairs, pronounced yellow stamens, usually rounded white petals. Most of the tea drunk in the Western world is made from *C. s.* var. *assamica* (Assam tea), which has smooth-edged, thin, tapering leaves. Grows to 50 ft (15 m) but is usually hedged to a height that is convenient for picking. *C. s.* var. *sinensis* (Chinese tea), from which unfermented green teas are made, has long, narrow, crinkly leaves and a bushy appearance to about 20 ft (6 m). *C. s.* 'Blushing Bride' is an attractive cultivar. Zones 10–12.

Camellia transnokoensis

☀ ❄ ↔ to 7 ft (2 m) ↑ to 25 ft (8 m)

Tall shrub or small tree found on the slopes Mt Noko in Taiwan at an altitude of 7,880 ft (2,400 m) in montane vegetation. Small, white, stalkless flowers, less than 10 mm across, borne singly in the leaf axils. The leaf buds are not hairy, a feature that distinguishes this species from *C. nokoensis*.

Camellia sinensis 'Blushing Bride'

'Sweet Jane' is an attractive cultivar with many overlapping petals in two shades of pink. Zones 8–9.

Camellia tsaii

☀ ☘ ↔ 15 ft (4.5 m) ↑ 30 ft (9 m)

From southern China, Myanmar, and northern Vietnam. Spreading pendulous habit. Prolific, miniature, white flowers in winter. Long, glossy, dark green leaves, paler undersides, wavy margins. Zones 10–11.

Camellia × vernalis

☀ ❄ ↔ 6–12 ft (1.8–3.5 m) ↑ 15 ft (4.5 m)

The derivation of this small group is unclear; it is distinguished from the cultivars of *C. sasanqua*, which it closely resembles, by its tolerance of cold

Camellia vietnamensis

and its mid-winter and mid-spring flowering. 'Egao' has pink semi-double flowers; the blooms of 'Ginryû' have delicate white petals with ruffled edges, sometimes with a pink tinge; 'Shibori-egao' has white-edged pink-petalled flowers; 'Star Above Star', layered reflexed petals arranged in an apparently random manner; 'Yuletide' blooms have clear bright scarlet petals. Zones 7–10.

Camellia vietnamensis

☀ ❄ ↔ to 7 ft (2 m) ↑ to 25 ft (8 m)

Native to Vietnam and neighbouring regions of China, occurring in lightly wooded regions. Small tree, related to *C. sasanqua*. Leaves up to 4 in (10 cm) long. Flowers greenish white, with

Camellia tsaii

5 to 7 petals, up to 1¾–2½ in (4–6 cm) across. Capsules are red to yellow. Zones 8–9.

Camellia × williamsii

☀ ❄ ↔ 4–10 ft (1.2–3 m) ↑ 7–15 ft (2–4.5 m)

These plants, hybrids of *C. japonica* and *C. saluenensis*, were first developed in the UK in the 1930s. Said to be the most easily grown and free flowering of all camellias. They can endure cold climates and winter-wet root runs better than many others. Leaves duller, paler than *C. japonica*. Flowers occur mostly in shades of silvery sugary pink. Award-winner 'Anticipation' has deep pink flowers to 4 in (10 cm) across; 'Brigadoon' has semi-double pink flowers; 'Donation' is light pink with darker pink-veined petals and thrives in cooler climates; 'Elsie Jury', created in New Zealand, is pale pink, producing large frilly blooms to 5 in (12.5 cm) in diameter; 'Francis

Camellia transnokoensis 'Sweet Jane'

Camellia transnokoensis

Camellia × vernalis 'Egao'

Camellia × vernalis 'Ginryû'

C. × vernalis 'Shibori-egao'

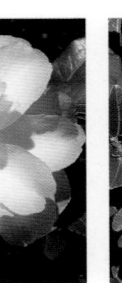

C. × vernalis 'Star Above Star'

Camellia × vernalis 'Yuletide'

Hanger', single white flowers; '**George Blandford**' is early flowering, with semi-double flowers of lavender-pink; '**Golden Spangles**' has single red flowers and variegated leaves; '**J. C. Williams**' produces pink flowers over a flowering season that lasts longer than usual; '**Joan Treharne**' has mid-pink double flowers; '**Jury's Yellow**' has white outer petals around a dense boss of creamy yellow petaloids; '**Margaret Waterhouse**' is a vigorous plant with well-formed, sugar pink, semi-double flowers that have rounded petals; '**Mary Christian**' has rich pink petals surrounding a mass of golden stamens; '**Ole**', dark pink buds opening to salmon pink flowers; '**Saint Ewe**' produces single vivid pink flowers and lustrous leaves; '**Shocking Pink**' is a tall bushy shrub, which bears bright pink, irregular, ruffled petals in an irregular semi-double formation; '**Water Lily**' is an upright shrub, bearing formal double rose pink flowers with pointed petals. Zones 8–10.

Camellia × williamsii 'Anticipation'

Camellia × williamsii 'Barbara Ann'

Camellia × williamsii 'Donation'

C. × williamsii 'Angel Wings'

C. × williamsii 'Ballet Queen'

C. × williamsii 'Beatrice Michael'

C. × williamsii 'Buttons 'n Bows'

C. × williamsii 'Coral Delight'

C. × williamsii 'Cornish Snow'

C. × williamsii 'Daintiness'

C. × williamsii 'Debbie'

C. × williamsii 'Demure'

C. × w. 'E. G. Waterhouse' ★

C

Camellia × *williamsii* 'Elsie Jury'

Camellia × *williamsii* 'Eryldene Excelsis'

Camellia × *williamsii* 'Eryldene Excelsis Variegated'

Camellia × *williamsii* 'Francis Hanger'

Camellia × *williamsii* 'Galaxie'

C. × *williamsii* 'Hari Withers'

C. × *williamsii* 'Hybrid L.'

C. × *williamsii* 'Jamie'

C. × *williamsii* 'Jubilation'

C. × *w.* 'Mary Phoebe Taylor'

C. × *williamsii* 'Mini Mint'

C. × *williamsii* 'Mona Jury'

C. × *williamsii* 'Orchid Princess'

C. × *williamsii* 'Ruby Bells'

C. × *williamsii* 'Sayonara'

C. × *williamsii* 'Tregelan'

C. × *williamsii* 'Softly'

C. × *williamsii* 'Waltz Dream'

C. × *williamsii* 'Winter Gem'

C. × *williamsii* 'Wynne Rayner'

C. × *williamsii* 'Ole'

Camellia yunnanensis

☀ ❋ ↔ 7 ft (2 m) ↕ 20 ft (6 m)

From southern China. Bears prolific, single, white flowers with prominent yellow stamens during late summer–autumn. Leaves dark green on top, paler beneath, smooth and finely toothed. Zones 9–10.

Camellia Hybrid Cultivars

☀ ❋ ↔ 3–20 ft (0.9–6 m) ↕ 3–20 ft (0.9 m–6 m)

Most of the popular hybrids have been bred to withstand particular conditions, notably cold wet winters, exposure to sunlight or marginal soil conditions, as well as for their attractive appearances. **'Fragrant Pink Improved'** has miniature, deep pink, fragrant flowers, open spreading habit, long flowering season, red new growth; **'Francie L.'**, semi-double pink to red flowers; **'Freedom Bell'**, upright habit, semi-double red flowers; **'Inspiration'** has abundant semi-double pink flowers, petals sometimes with ruffled edges; **'Salutation'**, notched silvery pink petals, long yellow stamens, large semi-double flower formation. **'Satan's Robe'**, upright glossy shrub, flowers large, semi-double carmine petals, golden stamens; **'Snow Drop'**, small distinctive gray-green foliage, with miniature white flowers occasionally

Camellia yunnanensis

flushed with pale pink. The camellias of the **Winter Series**, which bloom during the colder months, were bred in Maryland, USA, to withstand the cold conditions and give color to the garden. **'Winter's Charm'**, an upright shrub, has medium-sized, semi-double

flowers composed of orchid pink petals and petaloids. **'Winter's Fire'**, single, open, puce-pink petals surrounding pronounced yellow stamens. **'Winter's Hope'**, white semi-double flowers with uneven lobed petals and pronounced yellow stamens. **'Winter's**

Rose' bears flowers with the palest of pink serrated petals arranged in a semi-double fluffy-looking formation. The Australian-bred **Wirlinga Series** produces an amazing number of miniature, often clustered flowers over quite prolonged periods. **'Wirlinga Belle'**

has single, soft pink, medium-sized flowers, and an open growth habit; **'Wirlinga Cascade'**, a seedling from 'Wirlinga Belle' bears miniature, single, pink flowers; **'Wirlinga Gem'**, abundant tiny pale pink flowers. Zones 8–10.

Camellia, Hybrid Cultivar, 'Alan Raper'

Camellia, Hybrid Cultivar, 'Alaskan Queen'

Camellia, Hybrid Cultivar, 'Alpen Glo'

Camellia, Hybrid Cultivar, 'Arcadia'

Camellia, Hybrid Cultivar, 'Baby Bear'

Camellia, HC, 'Betty Ridley'

Camellia, HC, 'Blondy'

Camellia, HC, 'Bogong Snow'

Camellia, HC, 'Butterfly Girl'

Camellia, HC, 'California Dawn'

Camellia, HC, 'California Sunset'

Camellia, HC, 'Captured Enriches'

Camellia, HC, 'Child of Grace'

Camellia, HC, 'Cinnamon Cindy'

Camellia, HC, 'Contemplation'

Camellia, Hybrid Cultivar, 'Dark Shining Mirror'

Camellia, Hybrid Cultivar, 'Daisy Eagleson'

Camellia, Hybrid Cultivar, 'Debut'

C., HC, 'Doctor Clifford Parks'

C., HC, 'Doctor Robert Withers'

Camellia, HC, 'Elsie Ross'

Camellia, HC, 'Fairy Wand'

Camellia, HC, 'Flower Girl'

Camellia, HC, 'Forty-Niner'

Camellia, HC, 'Fragrant Pink'

Camellia, HC, 'Francie L.'

Camellia, HC, 'Freedom Bell'

Camellia, HC, 'Frosted Pink'

Camellia, HC, 'Golden Glow'

Camellia, HC, 'Happy Days'

Camellia, HC, 'Happy Higo'

Camellia, HC, 'Harold L. Paige'

Camellia, Hybrid Cultivar, 'Fragrant Joy'

Camellia, Hybrid Cultivar, 'Gay Baby'

Camellia, Hybrid Cultivar, 'Dream Baby'

Camellia, HC, 'High Fragrance'

Camellia, HC, 'Highlight'

Camellia, HC, 'Howard Asper'

Camellia, HC, 'Itty Bit'

Camellia, HC, 'Keith Ballard'

Camellia, HC, 'Kono-mon-mani'

Camellia, HC, 'La Petite'

Camellia, HC, 'Lammertsii'

Camellia, HC, 'Lasca Beauty'

Camellia, HC, 'Len Bray'

Camellia, HC, 'Leonard Messel'

Camellia, HC, 'Lois Shinault'

Camellia, HC, 'Milo Rowell'

Camellia, HC, 'Munaroa Road'

Camellia, HC, 'Muriel Tuckfield'

Camellia, HC, 'Nicky Crisp'

Camellia, HC, 'Nonie Haydon'

Camellia, HC, 'Norina'

Camellia, HC, 'Order of St John'

Camellia, HC, 'Otto Hopfer'

Camellia, HC, 'Our Kim'

C., HC, 'Paradise Illumination'

Camellia, HC, 'Peggy Burton'

Camellia, HC, 'Phyl Doak'

Camellia, HC, 'Pink Sparkle'

Camellia, HC, 'Red Crystal'

Camellia, HC, 'Royalty'

Camellia, HC, 'Scented Sun'

C., HC, 'Scented Sun' (white form)

Camellia, HC, 'Scentuous'

C

Camellia, Hybrid Cultivar, 'Spring Mist'

Camellia, Hybrid Cultivar, 'Sweet Jane'

Camellia, HC , 'Silver Mist'

Camellia, HC, 'Sweet Emily Kate'

Camellia, HC, 'Tamzin Coull'

Camellia, HC, 'Temple Mist'

Camellia, HC, 'Terrell Weaver'

Camellia, Hybrid Cultivar, 'Tiny Princess'

Camellia, HC, 'Tom Knudsen'

Camellia, HC, 'Tony Hunt'

Camellia, HC, 'Valentine Day'

C., HC, 'Valentine Day Variegated'

Camellia, HC, 'Valley Knudsen'

Camellia, HC, 'White Retic'

Camellia, HC, 'Wirlinga Bride'

Camellia, HC, 'Wirlinga Gem'

Camellia, Hybrid Cultivar, 'Yoimachi'

Camellia, Hybrid Cultivar, 'Wirlinga Princess'

CAMPANULA

This large genus of about 300 species of hardy annual, biennial, and perennial plants belongs to the bellflower (Campanulaceae) family. It contains a number of popular and beautiful garden plants. Many are native to Mediterranean areas, the Balkans, and Caucasus region. Some are from North America and temperate Asia. Their growth habit is ground-hugging and clump-forming, or erect and branching. A few species are invasive. Leaves are usually alternately arranged. Flowers are in shades of blue, mauve, pale pink, and white. They range from large drooping bells to delicate open stars, and are borne on panicles, spikes, or singly. With such variety there is a *Campanula* that is suitable for any rock garden, border, woodland, or "wild" garden situation.

CULTIVATION: Most species grow easily in any reasonably fertile well-drained soil in sun or half-sun. Some alpine species require grittier soil and dislike winter wet. Propagate from seed, basal cuttings or by division.

Campanula cochlearifolia

Campanula betulifolia

☼/❋ ❄ ↔ 12–16 in (30–40 cm) ↑ 4–12 in (10–30 cm)

From Armenia. A delicate clump-forming perennial with small oval leaves often tinted purple. White or pale pink bell-shaped flowers and are borne in clusters above the foliage. Needs protection from winter wet. Zones 4–9.

Campanula carpatica

syn. *Campanula turbinata*

CARPATHIAN BELLFLOWER, TUSSOCK BELLFLOWER

☼/❋ ❄ ↔ 12–16 in (30–40 cm) ↑ 6–12 in (15–30 cm)

From the Carpathian Mountains. Low-growing perennial forming a thick clump of small bright green leaves. In summer the plant is covered with pale blue or white, upward facing, open cup-shaped flowers, 1–2 in (2.5–5 cm) across: *C. c.* f. *alba* has white flowers. *C. c.* 'Blaue Clips', blue flowers; 'Blue Moonlight', very open flowers,

Campanula carpatica f. *alba*

Campanula betulifolia

light grayish-blue; 'Chewton Joy', light blue petals edged with deeper blue. Zones 3–9.

Campanula chamissonis

☼ ❋ ↔ 8–12 in (10–30 cm) ↑ 2–6 in (5–15 cm)

From eastern Asia, the Aleutian Islands, and Alaska. Low-growing perennial with fleshy stems and small spoon-shaped glossy leaves. Blue bell-shaped flowers are streaked with white and carried on individual stems through summer. 'Superba' has larger flowers. Zones 3–9.

Campanula choruhensis

☼ ❋ ↔ 12 in (30 cm) ↑ 6 in (15 cm)

Native to Turkey. Low-growing perennial with small, deep green, hairy

Campanula carpatica 'Blaue Clips'

Campanula chamissonis 'Superba'

leaves. Large white flowers, occasionally flushed pink, are upward facing and smother the plant during the summer months. It dies back in autumn. Zones 4–9.

Campanula cochlearifolia

syn. *Campanula pusilla*

FAIRIES' THIMBLES

☼ ❋ ↔ 10 in (25 cm) ↑ 3 in (8 cm)

Creeping fleshy-stemmed perennial from the European Alps. Forms tight clumps of small rounded leaves. Bell-shaped pale lavender-blue flowers hang from wiry stems for long periods over summer. *C. c.* var. *alba* has white flowers; the *C. c.* Baby Series includes 'Blue Baby', prolific, pale blue flowers; 'Bavaria Blue', a very compact plant with dark blue flowers; 'Elizabeth Oliver', with double pale blue flowers. Zones 6–9.

Campanula collina

☼ ❋ ↔ 12 in (30 cm) ↑ 12 in (30 cm)

A native plant of the Caucasus, this slowly creeping perennial forms clumps of lance-shaped leaves, that are bigger and broader at the base. The deep purple bell-shaped flowers hang singly or in clusters during the summer. Zones 5–9.

C. cochlearifolia 'Elizabeth Oliver'

Campanula choruhensis

Campanula elatines

ADRIATIC BELLFLOWER

☼ ❋ ↔ 12 in (30 cm) ↑ 2–6 in (5–15 cm)

Native to the Adriatic coast. Compact perennial forming clumps of small rounded leaves on prostrate stems. Blue or white flowers are bell-shaped with flaring lobes, held on lax spikes or panicles. Zones 6–9.

Campanula ephesia

☼ ❋ ↔ 12–18 in (30–45 cm) ↑ 12–18 in (30–45 cm)

From Turkey. Biennial or perennial with thick rootstock. Sprawling white-woolly branches. Lower leaves lyre-shaped to 8 in (20 cm), upper leaves narrower. Broad dark blue bellflowers, with white downy exterior, are borne on spikes in summer. Zones 7–9.

Campanula fenestrellata

Campanula garganica 'Dickson's Gold'

C. latifolia var. *macrantha* 'Alba'

Campanula lactiflora 'Loddon Anna'

Campanula fenestrellata

syn. *Campanula elatines* var. *fenestrellata*
WINDOW BELLFLOWER

☼ ❄ ↔ 8 in (20 cm) ↑ 2–4 in (5–10 cm)
An endangered species from western
Croatia. Low-growing perennial,
forming tight clumps. The starry
flowers are mid-blue with a paler
center. Zones 4–9.

Campanula garganica

syn. *Campanula elatines* var. *garganica*
☼ ❄ ↔ 6–12 in (15–30 cm)
↑ 6 in (15 cm)
Native to Italy. This low-growing
perennial forms tight clumps of small
light green leaves. Bears masses of
small, starry, light blue flowers on lax

panicles, for long periods in summer.
'Dickson's Gold' (syn. 'Aurea') has
golden foliage. Zones 5–9.

Campanula glomerata

CLUSTERED BELLFLOWER
☼ ❄ ↔ 12–24 in (30–60 cm)
↑ 12–36 in (30–90 cm)
Perennial species native to Europe and
Asia, from England to Siberia. Forms
clumps by suckering. Bristly stems,
purplish blue flowers in terminal
spherical heads and also in leaf axils.
Long flowering period over summer.
C. g. var. *acaulis*, very dwarf plants,
stemless flowers at the base of the
rosette. *C. g.* 'Nana' and 'Purple Pixie'
are smaller with deep purple flowers;
'Superba', large robust plant with
deep purple flowers. Zones 4–9.

Campanula isophylla

FALLING STARS, ITALIAN BELLFLOWER, STAR
OF BETHLEHEM
☼ ❄ ↔ 12–18 in (30–45 cm)
↑ 6 in (15 cm)
From northern Italy, trailing perennial
with small heart-shaped leaves. It is
smothered in 1 in (25 mm) wide,
starry, mid-blue flowers in summer.
Suitable for hanging baskets. Protect

Campanula medium

from winter wet. 'Alba', white flowers;
'Stella Blue', mid-blue flowers; 'Stella
White', clear white flowers. Zones 7–9.

Campanula laciniata

☼ ❄ ↔ 12 in (30 cm) ↑ 24 in (60 cm)
From Crete and Greece. Erect branching biennial or perennial with basal
rosettes. Finely cut lance-shaped leaves.
Wide cup-shaped blue flowers, borne
in large crowded racemes in summer.
Zones 8–10.

Campanula lactiflora

MILKY BELLFLOWER
☼ ❄ ↔ 2 ft (0.6 m) ↑ 3–5 ft (0.9–1.5 m)
From the Caucasus region, an upright
perennial with well-branched, leafy,
arching stems. Its milky blue bell-
shaped flowers are borne in wide showy
panicles in summer. 'Alba' bears white
flowers; 'Loddon Anna', soft pinkish
white flowers; 'Macrantha', large
violet-purple flowers; 'Prichard's
Variety', violet-blue flowers on slightly
smaller plant. Zones 5–9.

Campanula lasiocarpa

☼ ❄ ↔ 6–12 in (15–30 cm)
↑ 4–6 in (10–15 cm)
From North America, Siberia, and
Japan. Tufted perennial with small
broad leaves. Upward facing, open,
bell-shaped flowers of violet-blue are
borne singly in summer. Best suited to
rock gardens or pot culture. Zones 4–9.

Campanula glomerata var. *acaulis*

Campanula latifolia

GIANT BELLFLOWER, GREAT BELLFLOWER
☼ ❄ ↔ 2 ft (0.6 m) ↑ 3–5 ft (0.9–1.5 m)
Found throughout Europe and east to
Kashmir. Leafy perennial with stiff
unbranched stems. Slightly velvety,
broad, pointed leaves with serrated
edges. Pale purplish blue, bell-shaped
flowers borne along the stems for long
periods during the summer. *C. l.* var.
macrantha, large flowers of deep
violet-blue. 'Alba', large white flowers.
Zones 4–9.

Campanula latiloba

syn. *Campanula grandis*
☼ ❄ ↔ 18 in (45 cm)
↑ 24–36 in (60–90 cm)
Native to Siberia. Clumping perennial
forms basal rosettes of narrow pointed
leaves. Crowded spikes of open, deep
lavender-blue, cup-shaped flowers in
summer. 'Hidcote Amethyst', lilac-
pink flowers. Zones 4–9.

Campanula longistyla

☼ ❄ ↔ 12–18 in (30–45 cm)
↑ 6–18 in (15–45 cm)
From the Caucasus region. Upright
biennial or perennial. Lower leaves
oval, forming basal rosettes. Upper
leaves lance-shaped, spikes of nodding,
bell-shaped flowers of deep violet in
summer. Zones 5–9.

Campanula medium

CANTERBURY BELLS, CUP AND SAUCER
☼ ❄ ↔ 12 in (30 cm)
↑ 24–36 in (60–90 cm)
Native to southern Europe. Biennial,
with basal rosettes of soft, hairy, lance-
shaped leaves. Showy bell-shaped
flowers, with recurved rims, on leafy
stems in summer, in shades of white,
pink, or blue. Popular for use as cut
flowers. Several seed strains available.
'Calycanthema', calyx is petal-like,
forming "saucer" below cup-shaped
flowers. Zones 8–10.

Campanula laciniata

C. poscharskyana 'Blue Waterfall'

C. poscharskyana 'Lisduggan Variety'

Campanula poscharskyana 'E. H. Frost'

Campanula poscharskyana 'Multiplicity'

Campanula orphanidea

☀ ❁ ↔ 12 in (30 cm) ↑ 6 in (15 cm)

From Bulgaria and northeastern Greece. Low-growing, slightly downy biennial forming basal rosettes of oval to oblong, wavy-edged leaves, upper leaves smaller and broader. Narrow bell-shaped flowers of mauve to violet are borne singly or in racemes in summer. Zones 6–9.

Campanula peregrina

☀ ❁ ↔ 12–16 in (30–40 cm)
↑ 18–27 in (45–70 cm)

From the Mediterranean. Biennial plant with hairy leaves. Broad funnel-shaped flowers are bright to deep blue, borne singly or in clusters during summer. Zones 8–10.

Campanula persicifolia

PEACH-LEAFED BELLFLOWER, WILLOW BELLFLOWER

☀ ❁ ↔ 18 in (45 cm)
↑ 24–36 in (60–90 cm)

Native to Europe, eastern Asia, and northern Africa. Perennial, forming

rosettes of narrow wavy-edged leaves. Open, blue, 2 in (5 cm) wide, bell-shaped flowers, are borne on showy stems in summer. Long-flowering plant with many single and double cultivars: '**Bennet's Blue**' (syn. 'Wortham Belle'), pale blue double flowers; '**Boule de Neige**', large double white flowers; '**Chettle Charm**', single white flowers edged with blue; '**Planiflora**' (syn. 'Nitida'), dwarf form to 8 in (20 cm) high, wide mid-blue flowers; '**White Cup and Saucer**', large white, open, "cup and saucer" flowers. Zones 4–9.

Campanula portenschlagiana

syn. *Campanula muralis*

☀/◐ ❁ ↔ 18–24 in (45–60 cm)
↑ 6 in (15 cm)

From southern Europe. A vigorous alpine perennial with small heart-shaped leaves. It is smothered through the summer months with erect starry flowers of lavender-blue. '**Resholdt's Variety**' produces deep vivid blue flowers. Zones 4–9.

Campanula poscharskyana

SERBIAN BELLFLOWER

☀ ❁ ↔ 18–24 in (45–60 cm)
↑ 6–8 in (15–20 cm)

A native of Croatia. This vigorous alpine perennial is similar to related species, *C. portenschlagiana*, but it has a more refined appearance. Bears starry flowers, lavender to violet, in summer–autumn. Spreads rapidly in rock gardens. '**Blue Gown**', large mid-blue flowers; '**Blue Waterfall**', vigorous and free-flowering, dark blue flowers with lighter centers cascade outward from plant; '**E. H. Frost**' bears milky white starry flowers; '**Erich G. Arends**' has blue flowers; '**Lisduggan Variety**',

lavender-pink flowers; '**Multiplicity**' ★, double lavender-blue flowers; '**Stella**', bright blue flowers. Zones 6–9.

Campanula punctata

syn. *Campanula nobilis*

☀ ❁ ↔ 18 in (45 cm) ↑ 12 in (30 cm)

From Siberia and Japan. A somewhat invasive perennial forming clumps of pointed heart-shaped leaves. Tubular, pendulous, bell-shaped flowers, to 3 in (8 cm) long, cream, flushed with pink and spotted inside with red. *C. p.* f. *rubriflora*, narrow cream flowers tinged pink to purple, heavily spotted with red inside. *C. p.* '**Cherry Bells**', cherry red with paler edging. Zones 6–9.

Campanula pyramidalis

CHIMNEY BELLFLOWER

☀ ❁ ↔ 2 ft (0.6 m) ↑ 4–7 ft (1.2–2 m)

From Europe. Short-lived clumping perennial usually grown as biennial. Broad, pointed, serrated-edged leaves. Tall branching stems of densely packed open bell-shaped flowers in pale blue or white in summer. Best grown in the conservatory in cooler areas. Zones 8–10.

Campanula punctata

Campanula punctata f. *rubriflora*

Campanula orphanidea

Campanula portenschlagiana

C

Campanula raddeana

☀ ❄ ↔ 12 in (30 cm) ↑ 12 in (30 cm)

From the Caucasus region. Tufted perennial with small, glossy, dark green, heart-shaped leaves. Sprays of drooping, violet-purple, bell-shaped flowers on upright stems in summer. Zones 6–9.

Campanula rapunculoides

☀/◑ ❄ ↔ 24 in (60 cm) ↑ 36 in (90 cm)

Native to Europe. Robust, invasive perennial forming large patches of serrated nettle-like leaves. Tall stems of nodding bell-shaped flowers in shades of blue to violet in summer. Best suited to the wild garden. Zones 4–9.

Campanula rapunculus

RAMPION

☀ ❄ ↔ 24 in (60 cm) ↑ 24–36 in (60–90 cm)

A biennial from Europe, northern Africa, and Siberia. The oval leaves are pointed. The small pale blue or white bell-flowers are borne on leafy stems in summer. The thick taproots and leaves can be used as salad vegetables. Zones 4–9.

Campsis grandiflora

Campsis radicans

Campanula rotundifolia

BLUEBELL, HAREBELL

☀ ◑ ❄ ↔ 10–18 in (25–45 cm) ↑ 6–12 in (15–30 cm)

Found throughout much of the Northern Hemisphere, this fleshy-stemmed perennial has heart-shaped leaves forming rosettes. Dainty bell-shaped flowers, white to deep blue, on slender stems during summer. Buds are upright but flowers hang when opened. Zones 3–9.

Campanula speciosa

☀ ❄ ↔ 12 in (30 cm) ↑ 12–18 in (30–45 cm)

A rare species from the Pyrenees. Forms rosettes of small hairy leaves. Bright mauve, bell-shaped flowers with flaring lobes are borne on spikes in summer. Zones 3–9.

Campanula takesimana

◑ ❄ ↔ 18 in (45 cm) ↑ 24 in (60 cm)

This native of Korea is a rather invasive fleshy-stemmed perennial. Forms basal rosettes of large leaves. Bears tall stems of long, drooping, tubular bell-flowers in summer. The flowers are creamy white to lilac-pink on the outside, and spotted maroon inside. 'Beautiful Trust' (syn. 'Beautiful Truth') has drooping spidery petals, pure white; 'Elizabeth' ★, prolific and long flowering. Blooms have a dull purplish pink exterior and maroon spotted interior. Zones 4–9.

Campanula trachelium

COVENTRY BELLS, NETTLE-LEAFED BELLFLOWER, THROATWORT

◑ ❄ ↔ 12 in (30 cm) ↑ 24 in (60 cm)

Native to Europe, northern Africa and Siberia. Bristly perennial with serrated-edged pointed leaves. Fine, hairy, bluish purple, tubular bell-flowers, borne on dense leafy panicles in summer. C. t. subsp. athoa comes

Campanula, Hybrid Cultivar, 'Birch Hybrid'

Campanula takesimana

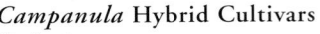

from Greece and Turkey; stalkless flowers. C. t. var. alba produces white flowers. Zones 4–9.

Campanula Hybrid Cultivars

☀/◑ ❄ ↔ 6–36 in (15–90 cm) ↑ 12–48 in (30–120 cm)

Bellflowers are naturally variable. Many hybrids and cultivars have been produced in a range of sizes, colors, and flower forms. 'Birch Hybrid', extremely free-flowering with lavender-blue flowers; 'Blue Wonder', double powder blue flowers in summer; 'Burghaltii', stems of hanging bellflowers turning unusual grayish mauve as they age; 'Joe Elliott', low tufted perennial with large, open, mid-blue flowers; 'Kent Belle', large, hanging, deep violet-blue flowers; 'Mystic Bells', massed mid-blue flowers on erect wiry stems; 'Wonder Bells Blue', lilac-blue double flowers. Zones 5–9.

CAMPSIS

TRUMPET CREEPER, TRUMPET VINE

This genus contains 2 species of flamboyant climbing plants, members of

Campsis radicans 'Flava'

C., Hybrid Cultivar, 'Wonder Bells Blue'

Campanula, Hybrid Cultivar, 'Kent Blue'

the trumpet-vine (Bignoniaceae) family. One is native to China and Japan and the other is native to North America where it is a weed in some places. These vigorous deciduous vines have aerial roots to help them climb and long leaves with 7 to 11 broadly lance-shaped leaflets that are serrated along the margins. The large orange or red trumpet-shaped flowers have widely flaring lobes and are borne in clusters in summer and autumn. CULTIVATION: Grow over walls or fences in a well-drained soil in full sun. In cool climates grow in a warm sheltered position to encourage greater flowering. C. grandiflora should be tied to a sturdy support, as it produces relatively few aerial roots, and C. radicans will also benefit from additional support. Prune hard in late winter–early spring to contain plants within their allotted space. Propagate from cuttings, layering, or seed.

Campsis grandiflora

syns Bignonia grandiflora, B. chinensis, Campsis chinensis, Tecoma grandiflora, T. chinensis

CHINESE TRUMPET CREEPER, CHINESE TRUMPET VINE

☀ ❄ ↔ 8–15 ft (2.4–4.5 m) ↑ 25 ft (8 m)

From Japan and China. Vigorous climber with few aerial roots. Orange to red trumpet-shaped flowers, 3–4 in (8–10 cm) long, borne from summer–autumn on large loose panicles to 20 in (50 cm) long. 'Morning Calm', deep peach with yellow interior. Zones 7–11.

Campsis radicans

syns *Bignonia radicans, Tecoma radicans*
COW-ITCH, TRUMPET CREEPER

☀ ❄ ↔ 8–15 ft (2.4–4.5 m) ↑ 35 ft (10 m)
From southeastern USA. Invasive in
some States. Becomes rampant in rich
soil. Climbs with aerial roots. Orange
or red trumpet-shaped flowers, borne
in terminal clusters during summer,
are a little smaller than those of
C. grandiflora. 'Flava' has deep bright
yellow flowers. Zones 4–10.

Campsis × tagliabuana

syns *Bignonia tagliabuana, Tecoma
hybrida, T. intermedia*

☀ ❄ ↔ 8–15 ft (2.4–4.5 m) ↑ 17 ft (5 m)
This hybrid of *C. grandiflora* and
C. radicans, a robust vine, climbs with
its aerial roots. Bears loose panicles of
orange-scarlet trumpet-shaped flowers,
in summer. 'Madame Galen', large
flaring flowers in rich salmon shades.
Zones 6–10.

CAMPTOTHECA

Sole species in this genus of the dogwood (Cornaceae) family from China's
Sichuan and Yunnan Provinces. A
rather frost-tender deciduous tree, fast
growing when young, it has large, lush,
heavily veined leaves. Small flowers in
spherical heads, followed in autumn
by unusual angular fruit. A cancer-
treating drug, topotecan, is made from
camptothecin, extracted from the bark.

Campsis × tagliabuana

Camptotheca acuminata

CULTIVATION: Intolerant of strong
winds and all but the lightest frosts,
C. acuminata is best grown in a
warm humid climate with moist, well-
drained, humus-rich soil that does not
dry out in summer. Light trimming
when young can improve the shape
of the tree. Propagate from seed.

Camptotheca acuminata

☀ ❧ ↔ 20 ft (6 m) ↑ 40 ft (12 m)
A handsome well-shaped tree, green
leaves over 6 in (15 cm) long. Branched
flower stems with rounded heads of
tiny creamy white flowers in summer.
Zones 10–11.

CANARINA

A genus of 3 species in the bellflower
(Campanulaceae) family, 1 endemic
to the Canary Islands, the other 2
native to tropical East Africa. All
have thick tuberous roots and are
herbaceous climbers, in and near a
range of forest habitats. Leaves are
opposite, smooth or lobed. Pendent
flowers bell-shaped, with 6 reflexed
petal lobes, borne singly or in small
clusters in upper leaf axils.
CULTIVATION: Propagate from seed
and stem cuttings. Allow plants to dry
out after they die down in the summer
months. Water and feed when new
growth appears in autumn.

Canarina canariensis

syn. *Canarina campanula*
BICACARO, CANARY BELLFLOWER

☀ ❧ ↔ 3 ft (0.9 m) ↑ 5 ft (1.5 m)
Canary Islands summer-deciduous
climber with fleshy branching stems.
Leaves arrow-shaped, lobed near base,
green to gray-green, 1¾–3 in (4–8 cm)
long, margins finely serrated. Orange-
red flowers with darker veins, 1¼–½ in
(3–6 cm) long, borne singly in upper
leaf axils from late winter–late spring.
Zones 9–11.

Canarina canariensis

Canarium ovatum

CANARIUM

From the gumbo-limbo (Burseraceae)
family, this genus of around 75 species
of evergreen and deciduous trees
occurs mainly in the Asian tropics,
with some species in tropical Africa,
the Pacific Islands, and northern
Australia. Leaves are pinnate with
very few, fairly large leaflets. Flowers
are of different sexes on different
trees, cream or greenish, borne in
short sprays at branch tips. Fruits are
oval drupes with thin flesh and a hard
stone enclosing a large oily seed. The
nuts of many species are harvested for
food and oil.
CULTIVATION: In urban planting
male trees are preferred, as the fruit
from females is a nuisance on paths
and lawns. Some species tolerant of
seashore conditions but best growth
is on deep well-drained soils with adequate subsoil moisture and a sheltered situation. Propagate from fresh
seed, while air layering can be used to
perpetuate male trees.

Canarium australasicum

CARROT WOOD, MANGO BARK

☀ ❧ ↔ 35–50 ft (10–15 m)
↑ 70–100 ft (21–30 m)

A tall rainforest tree from northeastern Australia. The leaves are pinnate with shiny, green, oval-shaped
leaflets, 3–6 in (8–15 cm) long. The
small red flowers are borne in terminal
or axillary branched inflorescences
during summer. Bluish egg-shaped
fruits ripen from autumn–winter.
Zones 10–12.

Canarium ovatum

PILI NUT

☀ ✈ ↔ 50 ft (15 m) ↑ 100 ft (30 m)
Endemic to the large island of Luzon.
Leaves have up to 20 leaflets, each
up to 8 in (20 cm) long, leathery in
texture. Fruit egg-shaped to 3 in
(8 cm) long, ripens purple to nearly
black. The delicious nut, said to be
the equal in flavor of macadamias
and Brazil nuts, is harvested as a
commercial crop. Zones 11–12.

Canna iridiflora

Canavalia rosea

CANAVALIA

A genus of 51 species of tropical shrubs and climbers placed in the pea-flower subfamily of the legume (Fabaceae) family, with most species occurring in the Americas—the islands of Hawaii have 6 endemic species. The leaves are usually compound with 3 segments (trifoliate), and are smooth in a few species. The flowers are pea-shaped, large and showy in most species, and are borne on an inflorescence longer than the leaves. The fruits are relatively large pods containing many seeds.
CULTIVATION: Several species are used agriculturally for green manures, stock feed and as edible beans. Propagate from seed.

Canavalia rosea
BEACH BEAN
☼ ⬆ ↔ 10–20 ft (3–6 m)
↑ 6–12 in (15–30 cm)
Of pantropical distribution. A creeping seashore perennial sometimes used for sand dune stabilization. This plant has semi-succulent trefoil leaves with

rounded leaflets which fold up in hot sun. Purplish pink pea-flowers are borne on upright stems in summer. Zones 9–12.

CANISTRUM

These bromeliads from the pineapple (Bromeliaceae) family form erect spreading rosettes to 24 in (60 cm) high and 16 in (40 cm) wide. The leaves sometimes have black teeth, are generally narrow and green, and some have dark markings. The flower stem is long and the globular flowerhead is enclosed by mainly red (sometimes orange) bracts, which sometimes spread outward. The flowers appear mainly in the center of the flowerhead. The petals are white to rose to yellow. There are only 7 species and only a few are in general cultivation. Originally from eastern to southeastern Brazil, these plants need extra protection in the winter months.
CULTIVATION: Recommended for indoor culture if in flower, for greenhouse or similar in cool-temperate areas, or outdoors with protection from direct continuous sunlight and extremes of rain in warm-temperate, subtropical, and tropical areas.

Canistrum fosterianum
☀ ⬚ ↔ 8 in (20 cm) ↑ 24 in (60 cm)
A tubular rosette a little flared at the top, leaves green with variable black markings on the outside. The flowerhead, to 4 in (10 cm) in diameter, appears just above the leaf tube and has spreading red bracts. Petals are white. Zones 9–10.

CANNA
CANNA LILY, INDIAN SHOT
Found throughout the New World in tropical and subtropical areas and widely naturalized elsewhere, there are just 9 species making up the type genus for their family, the Cannaceae. They are vigorous plants with strong, upright, reed-like stems that sprout from rhizomes and which bear long lance-shaped leaves. Heads of lily-like flowers—usually in shades of yellow, tangerine, and red, either as solid colors or in patterns—appear throughout the growing season. The common name Indian shot comes from the story that the hard black seeds were sometimes substituted for buckshot. They are certainly hard enough for this but are so light that their range would have been extremely limited.
CULTIVATION: Although they are often tropical in origin most can withstand light frosts as dormant roots if well insulated with mulch. Plant in full sun in moist, humus-rich, well-drained soil and feed well. Propagation of selected forms is by division in early spring. Seeds will often self-sow but rarely result in superior plants.

Canna glauca
☼ ⬚ ↔ 12–36 in (30–90 cm)
↑ 4–6 ft (1.2–1.8 m)
This species, native to tropical America, has bluish green pointed leaves up to 20 in (50 cm) long, and large pale yellow flowers in summer. Zones 9–11.

Canna indica
syn. *Canna edulis*
INDIAN SHOT, QUEENSLAND ARROWROOT
☼/☀ ❄ ↔ 20–32 in (50–80 cm)
↑ 4–7 ft (1.2–2 m)
Widespread in the tropics. Leaves to 20 in (50 cm) long, often purple-tinted. Flowerheads upright, usually simple but sometimes branched. Red to orange flowers, rarely pink, often with contrasting spots, to slightly over 2 in (5 cm) wide. Zones 8–12.

Canna iridiflora
☼/☀ ⬚ ↔ 20–32 in (50–80 cm)
↑ 10 ft (3 m)
Found from Costa Rica to Peru. These plants have banana-like blue-green leaves to 4 ft (1.2 m) long. They bear simple or few-branched heads of semi-pendent, long-tubed, deep pink to orange flowers. Many plants cultivated under this name are now thought to be the hybrid *C. × ehemanii*, of which *C. iridiflora* is one parent. Zones 9–12.

Canna Hybrid Cultivars
☼/☀ ❄ ↔ 3 ft (0.9 m) ↑ 3–7 ft (0.9–2 m)
Large range of garden hybrids with complex and often uncertain parentage. The names *C. × generalis* and *C. × orchioides* have been used for these plants in the past. Ranging in size from 20 in (50 cm) dwarfs to over 7 ft (2 m) tall. Wide range of flower colors and forms. 'Durban', 4 ft (1.2 m) tall, with yellow-striped purple-red leaves, bright red flowers; 'Erebus', 6 ft (1.8 m) tall, silvery blue-green leaves, salmon pink flowers; 'Lucifer' ★, 30 in (75 cm) high, dark foliage and yellow-edged red flowers; 'Minerva', 5 ft (1.5 m) tall, white and green striped foliage, yellow flowers opening from red buds over a long season; 'Pink Sunburst', 3 ft (0.9 m) high, pink-tinted yellow and green striped leave and salmon pink flowers; 'Red King Humbert', 7 ft (2 m) tall, bronze foliage and blood red flowers; 'Roi Humbert', 7–8 ft

Canna, Hybrid Cultivar, 'Erebus'

(2–2.4 m) tall, deep bronze foliage, orange-red flowers, sometimes yellow-marked; 'Tropicanna' (syn. 'Phasion'), 7 ft (2 m) tall, vivid purple-red and yellow-orange striped foliage, bright orange flowers; '**Wyoming**', 6 ft (1.8 m) high, bronze foliage and bright orange flowers. Zones 8–12.

CANTHIUM

Found in tropical areas of Africa, Asia, Australia and the Pacific. At least 50 species of evergreen shrubs, trees, and vines from the madder (Rubiaceae) family. Leaves usually simple, lance-shaped to elliptical, often leathery and heavily veined, and borne on stems sometimes stubbed with rather nasty spines. The 4- to 5-petalled, widely flared flowers, in dense clusters, are the ornamental attraction of the genus.
CULTIVATION: Apart from demanding a warm frost-free climate and soil that remains moist, most *Canthium* are easily cultivated. Most species can be trimmed to keep their shrubbiness or trained to a tree-like single trunk. They like full sun or partial shade and require moderately fertile well-drained soil. Propagation is from seed or half-hardened cuttings.

Canthium coprosmoides
COAST CANTHIUM
☼ ❋ ↔ 12 ft (3.5 m) ↑ 20 ft (6 m)
Large Australian shrub that can become a small tree. Clusters of fragrant white flowers in summer, followed by edible red fruit. Zones 10–12.

CANTUA

South American genus, of the phlox (Polemoniaceae) family, primarily Peruvian. About 6 species of colorful evergreen or semi-deciduous shrubs; all have, at one time or another, been used as garden plants. Their flowers are long tubes with widely flared throats, carried in pendulous clusters, usually at branch tips.

Cantua bicolor

Canna, HC, Island Series, 'Gran Canaria'

CULTIVATION: *Cantua* is best grown in moist, humus-enriched, well-drained soil. A position in full sun will yield the best flower display, though if necessary the shrub will tolerate light shade and still flower satisfactorily. Regular pruning will result in more compact growth. Cutting back main branches and overly long side shoots also encourages flower-bearing new growth, producing heavier flowering and better foliage cover next season. Propagate from tip cuttings or fresh seed, which germinates well at around 65°F (18°C).

Cantua bicolor
☼ ❋ ↔ 5 ft (1.5 m) ↑ 5–8 ft (1.5–2.4 m)
Native to Bolivia. Leaves small, dark green, hairy, young stems as well. Flowers, on individual stalks, massed at branch tips, to 2 in (5 cm) long, yellow-tubed, red at the neck with flared cream lobes. Zones 9–10.

Cantua buxifolia ★
MAGIC FLOWER, SACRED FLOWER OF THE INCAS
☼ ❋ ↔ 8 ft (2.4 m) ↑ 12 ft (3.5 m)
From the mountains of Peru, Bolivia, and northern Chile. Flowers 3 in

Cantua buxifolia

Canna, Hybrid Cultivar, 'Orange Punch'

Canna, Hybrid Cultivar, 'Rosever'

Canna, Hybrid Cultivar, 'Strawberry'

Canna, Hybrid Cultivar, 'Pretoria'

Canna, Hybrid Cultivar, 'Tropicanna'

(8 cm) long, deep pink to purple, early spring or in warm areas year round. The epithet "sacred" comes from its use by Inca priests. '**Hot Pants**' is a popular North American cultivar. Zones 9–11.

CAPPARIS

This genus of around 250 species of shrubs, scrambling climbers, and small trees is from the caper (Capparidaceae) family. It contains both evergreen and deciduous plants, which grow in warm climates around the world. *C. spinosa* is the source of the edible capers used as a condiment and the only species occurring naturally in Europe. The simple leaves have paired and often hooked spines at the base. The flowers have early-shedding petals and long showy stamens. The fruit is berry-like. The species grow in a wide range of habitats, from dry open woodland, vine thickets, and rainforest, to arid rocky seashores. In some regions the foliage is devoured by the larvae of the caper white butterfly.
CULTIVATION: They vary in their needs, but most are sun-loving and prefer a reasonably fertile soil. Few species will tolerate more than very light frosts. *C. spinosa* requires hot dry summers and well-drained open soil; it does best among rocks. Propagate from freshly extracted seed or from half-hardened cuttings in summer.

Capparis mitchellii, in the wild, Mt Painter Sanctuary, South Australia

Capparis arborea

Capparis mitchellii
BUMBIL, NATIVE ORANGE, WILD ORANGE

☼ ❄ ↔ 10 ft (3 m) ↑ 20 ft (6 m)

From the semi-arid inland regions of mainland Australia. Shapely evergreen tree with wide, dense crown of foliage. Fragrant cream flowers in spring–summer. Globular fruits about 2 in (5 cm) in diameter. Zones 9–12.

Capparis spinosa
CAPER BUSH

☼ ❄ ↔ 10 ft (3 m) ↑ 3 ft (0.9 m)

Scrambling shrub, semi-prostrate branches. Leaves very broad, rounded, arranged in 2 rows. Flowers white, pale purple stamens, on slender stalks, in summer–autumn. Unopened buds pickled in brine as capers. Fruits elongated, strongly ribbed. Zones 9–12.

CAPSICUM
PEPPER

This genus of 10 species of which 5, mainly *C. annuum,* are used by people, belongs to the nightshade (Solanaceae) family. Originating in

Capparis spinosa

Mexico and central South America, most capsicums are perennials but are treated as annuals and are grown for their fruit. There are two main types of capsicums—hot or chilli peppers, hot to taste, and sweet or bell peppers, which are not so hot. Some types are also grown for ornamental purposes. Capsicums usually have small white or yellow flowers followed by their hollow fruits, which are full of seeds. They need a long hot summer to fruit well. Capsicums can be eaten fresh, pickled, smoked, dried, tinned or roasted. CULTIVATION: A well-drained moist soil in full sun is best, with fertilizer applied early in the growing season to bulk up plants. Ease this off as they begin to set fruit. Propagate from seed.

Capsicum annuum
syn. *Capsicum annuum* var. *acuminatum*
BELL PEPPER, CHILLI PEPPER, PAPRIKA

☼ ❄ ↔ 8–20 in (20–50 cm)
↑ 8 in–5 ft (20 cm–1.5 m)

Annual or short-lived perennial. Lance-shaped to ovate leaves to 5 in (12 cm) long. Fruits in a range of shapes. Color usually green maturing to red, other colors becoming common. Widely grown. Cultivar groups based on size and shape of the fruit.

Cerasiforme Group: Small, spherical, aromatic fruit. '**Cherry Bomb**', small, globular, bright red, hot fruit, popular for pickling and processing;

'**Guantanamo**', lime green, smooth skin, medium thick walls.

Conioides Group: Small hot chillies, fruit erect, more or less conical in shape. '**Apache**' ★, 18 in (45 cm) tall, fruits small, red, conical and hot; '**Jalapeño**' ★, Mexican variety, dark green fruit ripen to red, very hot; '**Mitla**', an early 'Jalapeño' type, good yielder; '**Shishito**', hot pepper, bright red when mature; '**Tam Vera Cruz**', developed by the Texas A & M University, grows to 3 ft (0.9 m) tall, bears numerous fruit; '**Thai Miniature**' (syn. 'Thai Hot Small'), mounded with showy 1 in (25 mm) long fruit.

Grossum Group: Sweet bell peppers with bell-shaped or blocky fruit, about 4–8 in (10–12 cm) long, that start off green, and ripen to yellow, orange, red, brown, or purple-black; '**Blue Jay**', skin matures from green to lavender-purple and red; '**Blushing Beauty**', sweet crispy fruit, yellow blushed with apricot when mature; '**Giant Marconi**', very sweet and good fried or roasted; '**Jumbo Stuff**', lemon yellow, thick walls; '**Merlin**', early ripening; '**Mohawk**', medium size, very sweet, orange when mature; '**Minibell Yellow**', extremely small yellow to orange bell pepper; '**Super Shepherd**', long, tapered sweet pepper, dark red when mature.

Longum Group: Quite hot fruits, including '**Cayenne**', long, thin, slightly curved fruit, ancient cultivar dried and powdered to make cayenne pepper; '**Sweet Banana**', grows to 20 in (50 cm) tall, pale yellowish fruit matures to red, crisp sweet flesh.

Ornamental Forms: Bred for ornamental purposes. Fruits often held upright, a range of colors. Good short-term house plants or for the greenhouse. Usually edible. '**Nosegay Pepper**', ornamental pepper 6–8 in (15–20 cm) tall, colorful mix of tiny fruits in red, orange, and green.

Capparis arborea
BUSH CAPER BERRY

☼ ❄ ↔ 12 ft (3.5 m) ↑ 25 ft (8 m)

From rainforests of eastern Australia. Deep green adult foliage, with spiny new growths. Pure white flowers, in summer. Edible green fruit in autumn, about 1 in (25 mm) across. Zones 9–12.

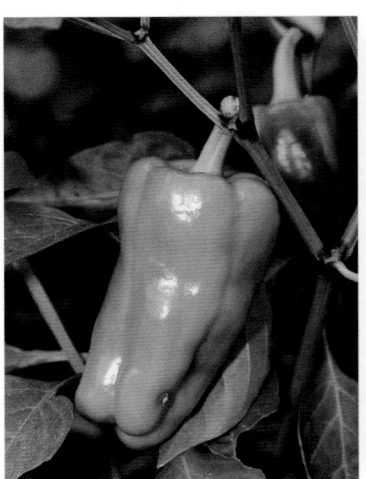

C. a., Cerasiforme Group, 'Guantanamo'

C. annuum, Grossum Group, 'Merlin'

Capsicum annuum, Conioides Group, 'Mitla'

Capsicum annuum, Conioides Group, 'Shishito'

Capsicum annuum, Grossum Group, 'Super Shepherd'

Capsicum annuum, Longum Group, 'Sweet Banana'

Capsicum annuum, Ornamental Group, 'Nosegay Pepper'

Capsicum annuum, Grossum Group, 'Blue Jay'

Capsicum annuum, Grossum Group, 'Blushing Beauty'

Capsicum annuum, Grossum Group, 'Jumbo Stuff'

Capsicum annuum, Grossum Group, 'Minibell Yellow'

Capsicum annuum, Longum Group, 'Cayenne'

C. a., Conioides Group, 'Thai Miniature'

Pimento Group: Original source of Spanish paprika. Heart-shaped fruit to 4 in (10 cm) long. Not as savory as Hungarian paprika. Zones 6–12.

Capsicum chinense

☀ ❄ ↔ 8–20 in (20–50 cm)
↕ 8 in–5 ft (20 cm–1.5 m)

From the Western Amazon Basin. An extra hot species, some golden yellow in color. Cultivars include '**Uvilla Grande**' and '**Rocotillo**'. Best known is '**Habanero**', said to be 1,000 times hotter than '**Jalapeño**'. Zones 10–12.

Capsicum frutescens

CHILLI, GOAT OR SPUR PEPPER

☀ ❄ ↔ 8–20 in (20–50 cm)
↕ 8 in–5 ft (20 cm–1.5 m)

Originally from tropical areas of South America, now widely grown in India and Asia. The best known cultivar is '**Tabasco**', from which tabasco sauce is made, low bushy shrub, upward pointing fruits. Zones 10–12.

Capsicum pubescens

ROCOTO

☀ ❄ ↔ 8–20 in (20–50 cm)
↕ 8 in–5 ft (20 cm–1.5 m)

Tolerates cool humid climates better than some other species and cultivars. Flowers purple, seeds brown. Fruits

Capsicum annuum, Grossum Group, 'Mohawk'

usually round, golf-ball sized, yellow or orange but may be red. Very hot. Zones 10–12.

CARAGANA

PEA SHRUB, PEA TREE

This is a leguminous genus of around 80 species of often extremely hardy deciduous trees and shrubs in the pea-flower subfamily of the legume (Fabaceae) family. They are wiry branched, and sometimes thorny. The pinnate leaves, often clustered near the branch tips, are made up of many tiny leaflets. The small pea-like flowers are nearly always yellow, borne singly or in small clusters in spring and summer. They are followed by small brownish seed pods.

Capsicum annuum, Pimento Group cv.

C. a., Grossum Group, 'Giant Marconi'

CULTIVATION: Naturally adapted to a temperate continental climate with cool to cold winters and hot summers, these are tough, easily grown plants that adapt to most temperate climates with distinct seasons. They are equally unfussy about soil but they generally perform best on neutral to slightly alkaline soils. Trim to shape but avoid hard pruning because the old wood can be slow to reshoot. Propagation is usually from seed; cultivars are cutting-grown or grafted depending on the growth form.

Caragana arborescens
SIBERIAN PEA SHRUB, SIBERIAN PEA TREE

☀ ❄ ↔ 4 ft (1.2 m) ↑ 10 ft (3 m)

Widely cultivated pea tree from Siberia and northeastern China. Leaves have bristle-tipped leaflets, young stems are covered with very fine hairs. Clusters of light yellow flowers in spring. 'Nana', dwarf form, short twisted branches; 'Pendula' ★, weeping growth; 'Sericea', covering of fine silky hairs. Zones 2–9.

Caragana frutex
RUSSIAN PEA SHRUB

☀ ❄ ↔ 8 ft (2.4 m) ↑ 10 ft (3 m)

Found from southern Russia to Siberia, a suckering shrub, thicket-forming with age. Leaves composed of 4 deep green leaflets on a thorny rachis. Yellow flowers, in clusters of 1 to 3 blooms. 'Globosa', a neat compact cultivar with a rounded form; 'Macrantha', large flowers. Zones 2–9.

Caragana sinica
☀ ❄ ↔ 3 ft (1 m) ↑ 3 ft (1 m)

From northern China. Sparsely foliage, with angled branches. Leaves have 4 glossy dark green, 1¼ in (30 mm) long leaflets in 2 distinct pairs. Flowers, borne singly, cream to pale yellow flushed with red, in spring–early summer. Zones 6–9.

CARALLUMA
This genus of around 56 species of clump-forming succulents up to 40 in (100 cm) tall from Asia, northeastern Africa, Micronesia, and Mediterranean belongs to the dogbane (Apocynaceae) family. Stems usually 4-angled, bearing rows of pointed or rounded teeth. Leaves represented by deciduous scales. Inflorescence is an axillary umbel or single flower, sometimes borne near stem tip. Flowers, up to 5 in (12 cm) in diameter, are smelly and largely pollinated by flies. Corolla is bowl- to bell-shaped with 5 lobes. Corona has 2 whorls—outer cup-shaped with 5 free lobes, inner with 5 lobes fused to outer. Fruit is an elongated follicle.
CULTIVATION: Grow outdoors in dry warm areas, or in a cool greenhouse in temperate regions. Species from arid regions need warmer conditions and careful watering. All need gritty soil; should not be overpotted to prevent root rot. Species susceptible to root mealy-bug can be grafted onto *Stapelia* stems or tubers of *Ceropegia linearis*. Propagate from cuttings or seed.

Caralluma burchardii
☀ ❄ ↔ 12–24 in (30–60 cm) ↑ 18 in (45 cm)

From the Canary Islands and Morocco. Stems 4-angled, with downward-facing teeth. Clusters of olive green flowers with yellow outer corona. Zones 9–11.

Caralluma europaea
☀ ❄ ↔ 8–12 in (20–30 cm) ↑ 6 in (15 cm)

From southern Spain, Italy, and western North Africa. Small clumping species with maroon-spotted, 4-angled, gray-green stems. Inflorescences of up to 10 hairy, maroon-banded, yellow flowers. Zones 9–11.

CARDAMINE
BITTER CRESS, CUCKOO FLOWER, LADIES SMOCK, MEADOW CRESS

Genus of about 150 species of annuals and tuberous or fleshy-stemmed herbaceous perennials belonging to the cabbage (Brassicaceae) family, formerly known as Cruciferae. Cosmopolitan in distribution, they are found mainly in the Northern Hemisphere. Some are pernicious weeds, others are dainty woodland and damp meadow plants with attractive foliage and flowers.
CULTIVATION: Most of the ornamental species prefer humus-rich soil shaded by deciduous plants. Propagate from seed or by division of rhizomes when dormant.

Cardamine laciniata
syn. *Dentaria laciniata*
CUT-LEAFED TOOTHWORT, PEPPER ROOT

◐/☀ ❄ ↔ 12 in (30 cm) ↑ 8–12 in (20–30 cm)

Short-lived North American perennial from Quebec south to Florida. Mid-green deeply cut leaves. Flowers appear in early spring in shades of white, lavender, and pink. Zones 3–8.

Cardamine pratensis
CUCKOO FLOWER, LADIES SMOCK, MEADOW CRESS

☀ ❄ ↔ 16–24 in (40–60 cm) ↑ 16–24 in (40–60 cm)

Well-known and loved species found growing in meadowland in many parts of Europe. Forms rosettes of compound leaves topped by spikes of ¾ in (18 mm) wide pure white flowers in spring. 'Flore Pleno', a lilac double-flowered form. Zones 4–9.

CARDIOCRINUM
GIANT LILY

Found from the Himalayas to Japan. This lily (Liliaceae) family genus has just 3 species of bulbs that develop rapidly after winter dormancy, producing a clump of large, fleshy, heart-shaped leaves from which emerge tall flower stems that are usually in bloom before the summer solstice. Flowers are funnel-shaped, sometimes fragrant, and usually clustered near stem tips. Large seed pods follow. Giant lilies are equally impressive as foliage plants.
CULTIVATION: Best suited to woodland conditions in temperate climates where winters are not severe. Plant in fertile, moist, humus-rich, well-drained soil in bright shade or dappled sunlight. The bulb dies after flowering but produces several offsets. These bloom within 3 to 4 years and are a quicker way of securing flowers than raising seedlings, which can take 5 to 7 years to reach flowering age.

Cardiocrinum giganteum ★
HIMALAYAN GIANT LILY

◐/☀ ❄ ↔ 3–5 ft (0.9–1.5 m) ↑ 7–15 ft (2–4.5 m)

From Himalayan region to Myanmar and China. Leaves to 18 in (45 cm) long and nearly as wide. Leafy flower stems, very sturdy at the base, with fragrant, purple-red striped or flecked cream flowers, up to 8 in (20 cm) long. *C. g.* var. *yunnanense* from western and central China has green-tinted flowers. Zones 7–9.

CARDIOSPERMUM
BALLOON VINES

A genus of 14 species of perennial, evergreen, tendril climbers, found in tropical America, Asia, and Africa, particularly on stream banks at edges of rainforest; seeds float after release from the fruits. Placed in the soapberry (Sapindaceae) family, species naturalized in many places are listed as noxious weeds. The leaves are compound, to 4 in (10 cm) long, divided twice into several leaflets. Inflorescences axillary, with tendrils, flowers are small, 5-petalled, cream to pale yellow. The

Caragana frutex

Caragana sinica

Caragana arborescens

Cardiospermum grandiflorum

fruits are inflated (hence the common name), capsular, 2–3 in (5–8 cm) in diameter, and contain large, winged, black seeds. used as beads for ornament and, in some regions, worn for medicinal purposes.
CULTIVATION: These vines do best in fertile, well-drained soil in full sun. Shelter from frosts and drying winds is essential. Propagate from seed and stem cuttings.

Cardiospermum grandiflorum
BALLOON VINE, HEART SEED, LOVE-IN-A-PUFF
☼ ⬧ ↔ 20 ft (6 m) ↑ 17–20 ft (5–6 m)
Thought to be native to tropical America; has become a weed in many tropical regions. Stems hairy, angular; leaflets coarsely lobed, oval, toothed, light green. Flowers cream to pale yellow, fragrant, ½ in (12 mm) across, from spring–summer. Yellowish fruit 2 in (5 cm) in diameter. Zones 9–12.

CARDUNCELLUS
This genus of 29 species from the Mediterranean region belongs to the thistle tribe of the daisy (Asteraceae) family. They are perennials, usually spiny, either rosette-forming or with stems to about 24 in (60 cm) long. The basal leaves are simple to pinnately lobed, the margins often spine-tipped. Flowerheads are disc-like with spiny whorled bracts in many rows, outer ones leaf-like. Florets are blue or purple and, as for all thistles, not differentiated into ray and disc florets.
CULTIVATION: Suitable for rock gardens or raised beds. They grow best in full sun, in gritty soil with good drainage, and most can tolerate temperatures down to 5°F (−15°C) or lower. Propagate from seed or by division.

Carduncellus pinnatus
☼ ❄ ↔ 8–12 in (20–30 cm)
↑ 2–4 in (5–10 cm)
From North Africa, Sicily and central Spain. Leaves usually in a rosette, blue-green, pinnate, with spiny tips. Summer-flowering. Solitary stemless flowerhead, outer bracts spiny-tipped. Florets bluish to mauve. Zones 7–9.

Carduncellus pinnatus

Carex buchananii

Carex comans 'Frosted Curls'

CAREX
SEDGE
A large genus of about 1,000 species of deciduous or evergreen grass-like perennials that belong to the sedge (Cyperaceae) family. They inhabit damp and boggy ground, and are found throughout the world, both indigenously and naturalized. Many are native to northern temperate regions. Plants range from low-growing and tufted to tall and tussock-forming. The grass-like leaves may be flat, folded, or rolled and in various shades of green, red, and brown. They often have sharp cutting edges and some have curling tips. The tiny flowers are insignificant in most species and carried on spikes, with male and female flowers that are borne separately on the same plant.
CULTIVATION: Very easy-care plants that are suitable for growing in problem wet areas, beside ponds, or in other moisture-retentive soils. Some species are invasive. A number are suitable for pot culture. Grow in full sun or half-sun. Propagate by division or seed.

Carex buchananii
☼ ❄ ↔ 18–24 in (45–60 cm)
↑ 24–30 in (60–75 cm)
Native to New Zealand. An upright, rather stiff, tufted plant with narrow, rolled, reddish brown leaves that have curling blond tips. Zones 7–10.

Carex comans
☼ ❄ ↔ 24–30 in (60–75 cm)
↑ 12–16 in (30–40 cm)
Native to New Zealand. A drooping sprawling plant with fine narrow

Carex species, in the wild, Ruby Range, Humboldt National Forest, Nevada, USA

leaves that curl at the tips. The foliage color varies considerably from reddish brown to shades of gray and green. The tips are often blond. **'Frosted Curls'** ★, swirling mound of palest green or straw-colored foliage with curling blond tips. Zones 7–10.

Carex conica
☼ ❄ ↔ 12–22 in (30–55 cm)
↑ 10–20 in (25–50 cm)
From Japan and South Korea. This tufted plant has flat dark green leaves that spill outward from the clump. Blade sheaths are brownish purple. **'Snowline'** (syns 'Hime-kan-sige', 'Variegata'), dark green leaves edged with white. Zones 7–10.

Carex elata
TUFTED SEDGE
☼ ❄ ↔ 3 ft (0.9 m) ↑ 3 ft (0.9 m)
Native to Europe, as far east as the Caucasus, and northern Africa. Dense tussock plant which spreads rapidly in wet places. The leaves are

Carex elata 'Aurea'

folded with a flat tip, and are bluish green with brownish yellow sheaths. **'Aurea'** (syn. 'Bowles Golden Sedge'), golden leaves with green margins. Zones 7–10.

Carex flagellifera
☼ ❄ ↔ 20 in (50 cm) ↑ 20 in (50 cm)
A native of New Zealand, this dense tufted plant, has arching foliage. The narrow leaves with cutting margins, vary in color from shiny green to bronze and brown. The flowering stems elongate across the ground as they mature. Zones 7–10.

Carica quercifolia

Carica × heilbornii

Carica papaya

Carex grayi
MACE SEDGE, MORNING STAR SEDGE

☀ ❄ ↔ 30 in (75 cm) ↑ 30 in (75 cm)

From eastern North America. Upright clump-forming plant with broad flat pale green leaves. The spiky seed heads resemble a mace and are popular in floral decoration. Zones 7–10.

Carex morrowii

☀ ❄ ↔ 30 in (75 cm) ↑ 30 in (75 cm)

Native to Japan. Tufted plant forming an upright clump of rather untidy appearance. The thick, broad, deep green, glossy leaves have rough margins. It is usually seen in one of its cultivated forms such as 'Expallida' (syn. 'Variegata'), leaves striped with white. Zones 8–10.

Carex muskingumensis
PALM SEDGE

☀ ❄ ↔ 24–36 in (60–90 cm) ↑ 24–36 in (60–90 cm)

Native to North America. Dense tufted plant spreading by fleshy stem. Narrow, pointed, light green leaves are slightly arching to sprawling and arise along stems giving a palm-like effect. Zones 7–10.

Carex nigra

☀ ❄ ↔ 12–24 in (30–60 cm) ↑ 8–24 in (20–60 cm)

Found throughout Europe. Tussock-forming plant with narrow bluish green leaves with cutting edges. The dark purplish flower spikes are frequently dried and used in floral arrangements. Zones 5–10.

Carex oshimensis

☀/◑ ❄ ↔ 18 in (45 cm) ↑ 12 in (30 cm)

Tufted evergreen with dark green leaves. 'Evergold' (syn. *C. siderosticha* 'Variegata') has leaves striped in gold and white. Zones 5–10.

Carex pendula

☀ ❄ ↔ 3 ft (0.9 m) ↑ 3–6 ft (0.9–1.8 m)

From Europe. Striking plant forming large clumps of broad bright green leaves. Prominent arching stems bear drooping catkin-like flower spikes to 6 in (15 cm) long. Zones 8–10.

Carex spissa

☀ ❄ ↔ 24 ft (0.6–1.2 m) 3–4 ft (0.9–1.2 m)

Native to southern California. Upright clump of broad bluish gray leaves which intensify in color during summer. The flower spikes turn from gold to tan, providing contrast with the foliage. Zones 6–10.

Carex testacea

☀ ❄ ↔ 24 in (60 cm) ↑ 24 in (60 cm)

From New Zealand. Densely tufted plant with fine, narrow, arching leaves varying in color from green to golden brown, often with orangey green tips. The flowering stem elongates across the ground as it matures. Zones 7–10.

CARICA

The 22 species in this South American and southern Central American genus are thick-stemmed shrubs and trees with large deeply lobed leaves and long, pulpy-fleshed, usually edible fruits; the best known is the common papaya. Foliage is a snowflake shape with a long stem, and leaves a distinct scar on the trunk when falling. Separate male and female flowers are white or cream to green. Larger female flowers quickly develop into fruit once fertilized.

CULTIVATION: Papayas need steady warm temperatures, not necessarily tropical, for the fruit to ripen well. Species from higher altitudes can even withstand very light frosts. Best in rich, moist, well-drained soil with ample humus, in a position that receives at least half-day sun. Papayas fruit heavily from a very young age, but often lose their fruiting vigor just as quickly, so keep a stock of strong young plants to ensure a steady supply of fruit. Propagate from seed, cuttings, or grafts.

Carica × heilbornii
syn. *Carica pentagona*
BABACO, MOUNTAIN PAPAYA

☀ ⚘ ↔ 10 ft (3 m) ↑ 6–12 ft (1.8–3.5 m)

This plant is a natural hybrid between *C. pubescens* and *C. stipulata* that is self-fertile. The large leaves are 18 in (45 cm) wide, and the fruit grows to 12 in (30 cm) long. Fruits are sterile, new plants are raised from cuttings. Zones 10–11.

Carica monoica
syns *Carica boliviana, C. citriformis, C. erythrocarpa, Vasconcella monoica*
PAPAYA, PELADERA, TORONCHE

☀ ⚘ ↔ 5 ft (1.5 m) ↑ 10 ft (3 m)

Native to subtropical parts of eastern Andes. Woody shrub with large palmately lobed leaves. Edible egg-shaped fruit grows to about 3 in (8 cm) long, and ripens to orangey red. Zones 9–11.

Carica papaya
PAPAYA, PAWPAW

☀ ⚘ ↔ 12 ft (3.5 m) ↑ 30 ft (9 m)

Native to lowlands of tropical South America. Single trunk, ringed with leaf scars. Leaves to 24 in (60 cm) wide, stalk to 36 in (90 cm) long. Fruits, mature to orange, contain pinkish flesh, black seeds. Zones 11–12.

Carica parviflora
PAPAYA DE MONTE

☀ ⚘ ↔ 6 ft (1.8 m) ↑ 10 ft (3 m)

This species has shown resistance to a number of diseases, undergoing breeding and development trials. Found in the mountains of Central America. May also be more resistant to cold than current commercial cultivars. Zones 10–12.

Carica quercifolia

☀ ⚘ ↔ 6 ft (1.8 m) ↑ 15 ft (4.5 m)

From South American highlands. The specific name means "oak-leafed," presumably because of the broadly toothed edges of the 3-lobed leaves, to 12 in (30 cm) wide. Fruit, quite bitter, grows to 10 in (25 cm) long. Zones 10–11.

Carex oshimensis 'Evergold'

Carex grayi

Carex nigra

Carex pendula

Carmichaelia odorata

Carmichaelia stevensonii

Carmichaelia williamsii

CARISSA

This genus of around 20 species of evergreen shrubs and small trees, in the dogbane (Apocynaceae) family, is found throughout tropical and subtropical Africa and Asia. Many species are densely branched and spiny, and useful for hedging; they have glossy green foliage, and clusters of fragrant, pure white, 5-petalled, long-tubed flowers. Fruit is edible. A few, small enough for house or greenhouse, may be kept in pots for some years. CULTIVATION: Usually drought tolerant once established, most *Carissa* species prefer to be moist throughout the growing season. They thrive in warm frost-free areas in a position with well-drained soil and full sun. Prune to shape as necessary, or shear hedges after flowering or after fruiting if the fruit is required. Propagate from seed or cuttings. The stems yield a milky sap when cut, and cuttings should be allowed to dry before inserting in the soil mix.

Carissa bispinosa
AMATUNGULA, HEDGE THORN, NUM-NUM
☀ ❧ ↔ 7 ft (2 m) ↑ 10 ft (3 m)
Thorny shrub from southern Africa. Oblong leaves up to 3 in (8 cm) long. Spines 1½ in (30 mm) long, forked and needle-tipped. Flowers long-tubed, petals flaring to ½ in (12 mm) wide. Purple-red berries. Zones 10–11.

Carissa edulis
SMALL NUM-NUM
☀ ❧ ↔ 5 ft (1.5 m) ↑ 5 ft (1.5 m)
Spreading, spiny shrub found in Africa and the Middle East. Leaves rounded, dark green on red stems. Fruit tasty, round, purple-red to black. Pinch back regularly for a thickly foliaged ground cover. Excellent cascading container plant. Zones 10–11.

Carissa lanceolata
CURRANT BUSH, KUNKERBERRY
☀ ⚘ ↔ 3 ft (0.9 m) ↑ 4–6 ft (1.2–1.8 m)
Found over much of subtropical coastal and semi-arid Australia. Thorny sprawling shrub, narrow pointed leaves. Small, highly scented, white flowers in summer. Black berries follow. Can become invasive weed. Zones 11–12.

Carissa macrocarpa
AMATUNGULA, NATAL PLUM
☀ ❧ ↔ 10 ft (3 m) ↑ 7–10 ft (2–3 m)
A widely cultivated species from South Africa with forked spines. Rounded deep glossy green leathery leaves, redden in bright light. Flowers white to 2 in (5 cm) wide. Red to purple-red fruit. 'Boxwood Beauty' ★, compact moulding habit; one form with cream-edged leaves is available. Zones 10–12.

CARMICHAELIA
syns *Chordospartium, Notospartium*
Part of the pea-flower subfamily of the legume (Fabaceae) family, this genus of about 23, almost leafless, small trees and shrubs is native to New Zealand, with a species from Lord Howe Island,

Carissa bispinosa

Australia. They grow in a wide range of habitats, from shaded river valleys to coastal and alpine areas, varying in form from tall to prostrate. Juvenile plants have very small leaves, generally absent in mature specimens. Leafless branchlets are flattened or very slender and reed-like. Many small pea-flowers, often fragrant, are carried on short racemes in shades of pinkish mauve to purple and white in spring or summer. CULTIVATION: Majority of species are only half-hardy, requiring greenhouse protection in cool-temperate areas. They prefer sunny well-drained situations; will tolerate dry and quite poor soils but repay better conditions with profuse flowering. Propagation is best from seed although half-hardened cuttings can be taken in summer.

Carmichaelia australis
syn. *Carmichaelia aligera*
☀ ⚘ ↔ 4 ft (1.2 m) ↑ 10 ft (3 m)
Reclassification of the *Carmichaelia* genus means the name *C. australis* is now used in a rather broad sense to indicate plants that have, at times, been treated as distinct species. Now wide variation in habit. Form previously known as *C. aligera*, larger in the wild. Leafless finely grooved branchlets bear small white and mauve flowers in summer. Zones 9–11.

Carmichaelia enysii
☀ ❄ ↔ 30 in (75 cm) ↑ 12 in (30 cm)
Dwarf shrub from eastern South Island, New Zealand. Found in open, and dry river terraces. Dense branches, thin finely grooved branchlets. Purple flowers in summer. Zones 8–10.

Carmichaelia odorata ★
NEW ZEALAND SCENTED BROOM, SCENTED BROOM
☀ ❄ ↔ 6 ft (1.8 m) ↑ 6 ft (1.8 m)
Scented broom is found along streamsides and forest edges in the North Island. A bushy shrub, with slightly weeping branchlets. White and mauve flowers, lightly scented, in spring–summer. Zones 8–10.

Carmichaelia stevensonii
syn. *Chordospartium stevensonii*
☀ ❄ ↔ 10 ft (3 m) ↑ 12 ft (3.5 m)
From New Zealand's South Island. Graceful weeping branches but can look straw-like and lifeless for several years when young as it has no juvenile leaves. Flowers in summer. Zones 8–10.

Carmichaelia williamsii
☀ ⚘ ↔ 10 ft (3 m) ↑ 12 ft (3.5 m)
From offshore islands and coastal areas of the northern North Island, New Zealand. Distinctive with flattened notched branchlets, large lemony yellow flowers with maroon veining, in spring–early autumn. Zones 9–11.

Carissa edulis

Carissa macrocarpa

C

CARNEGIEA

This genus of a single species belongs to the cactus (Cactaceae) family. Native to northern Mexico and southwestern USA. Slow growing, plants around 50 ft (15 m) in the wild are rare and over 100 years old. It may only flower when it reaches a height of 12 ft (3.5 m); it does not do well in cultivation. Heavy fines and strict regulations have stopped the practice of taking it from the wild for "desert gardens." Used in ceremonies by Native Americans.
CULTIVATION: It is not hardy; in frost areas grow in a warm greenhouse. Grow in full light, but shade from full sun. After winter rest, during which time it must not be watered, mist a few times, then start watering moderately; when in growth, water freely. Feed with a low nitrogen fertilizer

Carpenteria californica

(tomato fertilizer) monthly, reduce water and stop feeding in early autumn. Outdoors in frost-free areas it should be grown in humus-rich, alkaline, well-drained soil.

Carnegiea gigantea
SAGUARO CACTUS
☀ ✦ ↔ 10 ft (3 m) ↑ 50 ft (15 m)
Produces between 12 and 24 ribs, sometimes more; areoles grow from the tops of ribs, non-flowering areoles, with up to 30 spines gray or brown, to 3 in (8 cm) long. White funnel-shaped flowers, followed by egg-shaped fruit in autumn. Zones 9–11.

CARPENTARIA

This single-species genus from the palm (Arecaceae) family consists of a feathery leafed tree native to tropical northern Australia. Panicles of creamy white flowers are produced from spring to summer.
CULTIVATION: This palm grows best in well-drained soil with abundant water during dry periods, especially when young. It is easily propagated from freshly collected seed, germinating in 1 to 3 months. Seedlings resent disturbance and can be difficult to transplant, but they are easier when they are mature.

Carpentaria acuminata ★
CARPENTARIA PALM, THORA, YIRRGI YIRRGI
☀ ✦ ↔ 20–25 ft (6–8 m)
↑ 25–50 ft (8–15 m)
Solitary fast-growing palm, with tall, narrow, erect, smooth, whitish gray trunk, 5–6 in (12–15 cm) across,

Carphalea kirondron

ringed with scars and slightly enlarged at the base. It has a prominent crown of feathery pinnate leaves, to 12 ft (3.5 m) long, with drooping tips. White flowers, oval bright scarlet fruit maturing in summer; the pulp irritates the skin. Australian Aboriginals eat the tender new growth or "cabbage". Zones 11–12.

CARPENTERIA

This genus contains a single species of evergreen shrub from the hydrangea (Hydrangeaceae) family, which has a very limited natural range in central California on rocky mountain slopes. It has narrow glossy green leaves, lightly felted beneath. The fragrant white flowers resemble those of *Philadelphus* (mock orange) to which it is related.
CULTIVATION: *C. californica* requires a sunny site and a light, moisture-retentive, well-drained soil. It can be pruned to maintain a more compact

form. Propagation is by seed sown in spring or autumn, or by cuttings which can be difficult to root.

Carpenteria californica
TREE ANEMONE
☀ ✦ ↔ 8 ft (2.4 m) ↑ 8 ft (2.4 m)
A beautiful shrub. The flowers are pure white with 5 to 7 overlapping petals, prominent yellow stamens, to 2½ in (6 cm) across, in early summer. Zones 11–12.

CARPHALEA

This genus, belonging in the large madder (Rubiaceae) family, contains 10 species of evergreen shrubs, 6 confined to Madagascar, the remainder to tropical Africa, and 1 endemic to the island of Socotra off the Horn of Africa. They have leathery smooth-edged leaves arranged in opposite pairs and colorful flowers in dense terminal panicles. Each flower has 4 large sepals, the much smaller petals are united into a slender tube flaring at the mouth into 4 small lobes. The sepals persist into the fruiting stage and act as wings, enabling the small dry fruits to be carried by the wind.
CULTIVATION: Only one species is in cultivation, becoming popular in tropical and warm-temperate gardens for its colorful flowers or, rarely, grown in heated conservatories in cool climates. It requires a sheltered position, strong light, and fertile well-drained soil. Propagate from cuttings or seed.

Carphalea kirondron
FLAMING BEAUTY
☀ ✦ ↔ 3 ft (0.9 m) ↑ 6 ft (1.8 m)
Native to western Madagascar. Irregular form with glossy dark green foliage. Flowers in dense terminal clusters, brilliant red sepals, 1 longer than the other 3, darker red petal tube, pure white lobes, sepals persist for many months. Zones 10–12.

Carnegiea gigantea, in the wild, Superstition Mountains, near Phoenix, Arizona, USA

CARPINUS
HORNBEAM

This genus in the birch (Betulaceae) family contains about 35 deciduous trees and shrubs found throughout the temperate regions of the Northern Hemisphere. Commonly known as hornbeams, they are appealing trees at all times of year. The leaves have prominent parallel veining and color well in autumn. In spring they bear pendulous yellow male catkins and separate female catkins, which are erect at first. The fruiting clusters in autumn are surrounded by leafy bracts and in winter an attractive branch pattern is revealed.
CULTIVATION: Hornbeams will grow in most soils and are very suitable trees for parks and specimen plantings. *C. betulus* is a popular species for pleaching and hedging. Hornbeams are propagated from seed sown in autumn and cultivars are grafted.

Carpinus betulus
COMMON HORNBEAM, EUROPEAN HORNBEAM

☀ ❄ ↔ 60 ft (18 m) ↕ 80 ft (24 m)
From Turkey, across Europe to southeastern England. Trunk gray, fluted. Pointed oval leaves to 4 in (10 cm) long with serrated margins, prominent veining, turn yellow or orange in autumn. Yellow catkins are borne in spring. **'Fastigiata'** ★, narrowly columnar; **'Fielder's Tabular'**, light green leaves. Zones 5–9.

Carpinus caroliniana
AMERICAN HORNBEAM, BLUE BEECH, IRONWOOD, MUSCLEWOOD

☀ ❄ ↔ 50 ft (12 m) ↕ 40 ft (12 m)
Native to moist woods and riverbanks in eastern North America. Similar to *C. betulus* but often shrubby. Leaves turn to deep shades of orange and scarlet in autumn. Zones 5–9.

Carpinus cordata
☀ ❄ ↔ 50 ft (15 m) ↕ 50 ft (15 m)
Native to Japan. Scaly furrowed bark and broadly columnar shape. The leaves are slightly heart-shaped at base; finely pointed tip, prominent veins. Yellowish catkins in spring. Zones 5–9.

Carpinus japonica
JAPANESE HORNBEAM

☀ ❄ ↔ 50 ft (15 m) ↕ 50 ft (15 m)
From the woods and thickets of Japan. Gray fissured bark. The leaves are irregularly toothed with close-set prominent veins; they color well in autumn. Zones 5–9.

Carpinus orientalis
ORIENTAL HORNBEAM, TURKISH HORNBEAM

☀ ❄ ↔ 15–20 ft (4.5–6 m) ↕ 50 ft (15 m)
Native to southeastern Europe and Turkey. Sometimes a low scrubby bush, generally a small tree or large shrub. Its glossy dark green leaves have doubly toothed margins. Zones 5–9.

Carpinus betulus 'Fastigiata'

Carpinus betulus 'Fielder's Tabular'

Carpinus cordata

Carpinus japonica

Carpobrotus edulis

CARPOBROTUS

This genus of around 25 species from southern Africa and Australia belongs to the iceplant (Aizoaceae) family. Related to *Lampranthus*, *Carpobrotus* is distinctive in having fleshy berries. These plants form large spreading mats with yellow to red stems and long markedly 3-angled leaves. The flowers have purple to white or yellow petals and are borne singly or in groups of 3 on side-branches. The fruits (known as "Hottentot figs" in South Africa) are fleshy-succulent and sometimes edible. *Carpobrotus*, some of the easiest of all succulents to grow, have been used to control sand erosion. All are rampant growers; some species have become naturalized in maritime habitats in North America and Europe, where they are aggressive weeds.
CULTIVATION: Remarkably tough drought-tolerant plants for vegetating bare areas on poor soils, including coastal dunes. *Carpobrotus* species thrive best in milder temperate climates, some species tolerating moderate frosts. Propagate from cuttings or from seed; can be rapidly increased by pulling up the stems of any length and laying them flat under a light covering of sand.

Carpobrotus chilensis 'Doca'

Carpobrotus chilensis
☀/◑ ❄ ↔ 32–60 in (80–150 cm) ↕ 4 in (10 cm)

Disjointed distribution in Chile, southern California, and Baja California, Mexico. Dull green 3-angled leaves with shallow keel. Purple-pink flowers. Can be invasive. Considered by some to be synonymous with *C. aequilateris* and of South African origin, which could explain the unusual distribution. 'Doca', pale yellow flowers. Zones 8–10.

Carpobrotus edulis ★
HOTTENTOT FIG

☀/◑ ❄ ↔ 40–60 in (100–150 cm) ↕ 4–6 in (10–15 cm)

South African native widely naturalized in temperate regions, especially on coastal dunes. Saber-shaped light green leaves to 3 in (8 cm) long, may be red-tinted in sun. Flowers yellow ageing to pink, to over 3 in (8 cm) wide. Fleshy red-tinted edible fruit. Zones 8–10.

Carpinus orientalis

Carthamus tinctorius

Carpodetus serratus

CARPODETUS

A genus of 10 evergreen shrubs and small trees, belonging to the gooseberry (Grossulariaceae) family, 9 of which are found in New Guinea and the other native to New Zealand. The New Zealand species, *C. serratus*, makes an attractive ornamental tree and is the most likely one to be seen in cultivation. They have alternate leaves and bear small panicles of tiny flowers. CULTIVATION: These plants require deep rich soil and ample moisture, and do best in partly shaded situations. Propagation is by seed or from half-hardened cuttings taken in autumn.

Carpodetus serratus

PUTAPUTAWETA

☀ ❄ ↔ 10 ft (3 m) ↕ 30 ft (9 m)

Found throughout New Zealand. Juvenile form, tangled growth, small rounded toothed leaves. Mature form, straighter habit, larger mottled green leaves. Panicles of tiny white flowers in summer, followed by small black pea-sized fruit. Zones 9–11.

CARTHAMUS

A genus of 14 species of thistle-like annuals and perennials of the daisy (Asteraceae) family. Found mainly around the Mediterranean and in western Asia, one species, the common *C. tinctorius*, has a much wider distribution and has long been cultivated as a source of yellow and red dyes. Other species are seldom grown as they tend to become invasive. They are upright plants with stems that branch near the top to make a bushy clump of foliage. The leaves tend to be simple or pinnate with spine-tipped teeth. The whole plant is covered in fine downy hairs. Thistle-like heads with yellow, gold, pink, or violet ray florets appear in summer. Spiny bracts surround the base of the flowerheads. CULTIVATION: They are easily grown in any sunny position with light, gritty, well-drained soil. Sometimes used as a quick filler in annual or perennial borders, they are more likely to be seen as a field-grown commercial crop or as a weed on waste ground.

Carthamus tinctorius

FALSE SAFFRON, SAFFLOWER

☀ ❄ ↔ 16–20 in (40–50 cm) ↕ 24–40 in (60–100 cm)

Lower leaves may be simple or pinnate, sometimes spiny; those on flower stem usually simple and spine-tipped. Flowerheads yellow, gold to orange or red, rarely white. Seeds are an important source of oil used in cooking oils and margarine manufacture. 'Orange Gold' has intensely golden-yellow flowerheads. Zones 4–10.

CARUM

There are about 30 species of biennials and perennials in this genus, which belongs to the carrot (Apiaceae) family. They are found in temperate to subtropical regions. Their finely divided leaves are often aromatic and bear umbels of small white to pink flowers. The most commonly grown species is *C. carvi* (caraway), which grows in meadowland and naturalizes on wasteland. It is usually grown as a flavoring herb but its tap root is sometimes cooked in the manner of parsnips. CULTIVATION: Grow in full sun in deep, fertile, well-drained soil. Propagate from seed sown *in situ* as plants dislike transplanting. Harvest the seed of *C. carvi* as its color begins to darken.

Carum carvi

CARAWAY

☀ ❄ ↔ 12–18 in (30–45 cm) ↕ 24 in (60 cm)

From Europe and western Asia, naturalized in the USA. Attractive biennial with fine feathery foliage. Umbels of small white to pinkish flowers in summer. Primarily grown for its aromatic licorice-flavored seeds. Zones 3–10.

CARYA

syn. *Hicoria*

This genus, belonging to the walnut (Juglandaceae) family, consists of about 25 species, the majority of which come from eastern North America, with some from Vietnam and China. These large deciduous trees have both functional male and female organs present on the one plant. The gray-brown bark becomes scaly with age. The serrated-edged leaves are pinnate or alternate with 3 terminal leaflets. Male inflorescence is a pendent branched catkin; female inflorescence is a terminal spike with up to 20 individual flowers. The fruit is a drupe. Commercially valuable for pecan nuts, and hard wood, used for tools and sports equipment. Transplanting is difficult as they resent disturbance. Most hickories are valuable as ornamentals, making majestic trees, coloring well in autumn. CULTIVATION: Seedlings develop a long tap root very early, so plant when young into deep, fertile, humus-rich but well-drained soil. Sow seed into a seed bed as soon as it is ripe. If growing a species in a pot, use one that is extra deep. Use good loam with added leaf-mold; cultivars require winter grafting.

Carya aquatica

WATER HICKORY

☀ ❄ ↔ 40 ft (12 m) ↕ 70 ft (21 m)

Native to southeastern USA. The bark is light brown and the leaves lance-shaped, 5 in (12 cm) long, with up to 13 individual leaflets. The fruit is egg-shaped. Zones 6–9.

Carya cordiformis

syns *Carya amara, Juglans cordiformis*

BITTERNUT HICKORY, SWAMP HICKORY

☀ ❄ ↔ 50 ft (15 m) ↕ 80 ft (24 m)

From eastern North America. The smooth pale gray bark develops narrow, deep, scaly ridges with age. Buds yellow, flattened, hairy, in winter. Leaves, up to 9 pinnate leaflets, with 5 large terminal leaflets. Grows best in moist ground. Zones 4–9.

Carya floridana

SCRUB HICKORY, SCRUB PECAN

☀/❂ ❄ ↔ 10–17 ft (3–5 m) ↕ 20–25 ft (6–8 m)

Native to southeastern USA. Rather untidy, many-branched, small tree. Pinnate leaves with 5 distinct, finely toothed leaflets. Nuts are edible but not highly prized. Considered a weed in some areas. Zones 7–10.

Carya glabra

HOGNUT BROOM HICKORY, PIGNUT HICKORY

☀ ❄ ↔ 70 ft (21 m) ↕ 80 ft (24 m)

From eastern USA. Bark gray and narrowly ridged. Mid-green leaves lance-shaped with 5 to 7 individual leaflets to 12 in (30 cm) long. Thin-shelled nuts egg-shaped. Zones 4–9.

Carya illinoinensis

syns *Carya olivaeformis, Juglans illinoinensis*

PECAN

☀ ❄ ↔ 70 ft (21 m) ↕ 100 ft (30 m)

Native to the southern and central USA and northern Mexico. Grows best in deep alluvial soil. Scaly gray bark, mid-green leaves, with up to

Carya aquatica

Carya glabra

Caryopteris × *clandonensis*
'Arthur Simmonds'

17 lance-shaped leaflets. Pecan nuts
are an important crop exported
worldwide. Some 500 cultivars are
available: '**Pawnee**' and '**Lucas**' are
early ripeners. Zones 6–11.

Carya laciniosa
BIG SHELLBARK HICKORY
☼ ❄ ↔ 35 ft (10 m) ↑ 100 ft (30 m)
From eastern USA. Bark peels in 3 ft
(0.9 m) long curving plates. Leaves
reach 18 in (45 cm) long with 5 to 7
leaflets. Fruit oval, 2 in (5 cm) long.
Good timber tree. Zones 4–9.

Carya myristiciformis
NUTMEG HICKORY
☼ ✤ ↔ 25 ft (8 m) ↑ 70 ft (21 m)
Native to southern USA and Mexico.
Bark dark brown, new shoots have
glossy yellow scales. Leaves, green
leaflets, broadly oval, white underside,
terminal leaflet larger. Nut egg-shaped,
rust colored with a hard grooved shell.
Zones 9–11.

Carya ovalis
RED HICKORY, SWEET PIGNUT
☼ ❄ ↔ 30 ft (9 m) ↑ 70 ft (21 m)
Originating in eastern USA. Young
downy shoots open to form leaves
consisting of up to 7 leaflets, terminal
leaflet largest at 5 in (12 cm). Fruit
will split at the base when it is ripe.
Zones 6–9.

Carya ovata
syns *Hicoria ovata, Juglans ovata*
LITTLE SHELLBARK HICKORY,
SHAGBARK HICKORY
☼ ❄ ↔ 70 ft (21 m) ↑ 80 ft (24 m)
From eastern USA. Gray to brown
peeling bark. Leaves are mid-green,
with 5 leaflets, turning golden yellow
in autumn. Fruit edible, splitting
when ripe. Cultivars often hybrids
with *C. cathayensis* or *C. laciniosa*.
Zones 4–9.

Carya texana
BLACK HICKORY
☼ ❄ ↔ 25 ft (8 m) ↑ 50 ft (15 m)
This is a native of central USA from
Arkansas to Texas. The furrowed bark

Caryopteris × *clandonensis*
'Worcester Gold'

is dark ginger brown. The leaves are
mid-green and lance-shaped, with up
to 7 leaflets. The fruit is round, and
splits at the base when it is ripe.
Zones 6–9.

CARYOPTERIS
This genus now placed in the mint
(Lamiaceae) family was previously
included in the verbena family. It
occurs in eastern Asia, from the
Himalayas to Japan, and contains
about 6 species of deciduous flowering
shrubs with slender cane-like stems.
The name, derived from the Greek,
refers to the winged nut-like fruit.
Most species have opposite, simple,
toothed leaves, often aromatic and
grayish. Their flowers, borne in late
summer, are mainly blue, mauve, or
white in axillary or terminal panicles.
CULTIVATION: They prefer an open
sunny position and thrive in cool-
temperate regions, ideally in a fibrous
loamy soil with free drainage. They
flower on the current season's growth
and should be pruned moderately in
late winter or early spring to promote
new growth. Propagate by soft-tip
or firm leafy cuttings between spring
and early autumn; dormant hardwood
cuttings from winter prunings can
also be used.

Carya laciniosa

Caryopteris × clandonensis
BLUE MIST SHRUB, BLUE SPIRAEA
☼ ❄ ↔ 5 ft (1.5 m) ↑ 5 ft (1.5 m)
A hybrid species between *C. incana*
and *C. mongolica*. Erect, slender, vase-
shaped stems. Leaves downy, serrated.
Flowers in dense cymes, deep blue
to violet-blue, in late summer. '**Arthur
Simmonds**', purple-blue flowers; '**Dark
Night**' ★, low growing form with dark
blue flowers; '**Worcester Gold**', mauve-
blue flowers. Zones 5–9.

Caryopteris incana
syn. *Caryopteris mastacanthus*
BLUE SPIRAEA, BLUEBEARD
☼ ❄ ↔ 5 ft (1.5 m) ↑ 5 ft (1.5 m)
A native of China and Japan. Small
showy shrub. Grayish, serrated, pointed

Carya ovata

leaves, slender arching stems. Heads
of spiraea-like powder-blue flowers in
tiers along the stems in late summer.
Zones 7–10.

CARYOTA
FISHTAIL PALM
Caryota consists of 12 species, in the
palm (Arecaceae) family, ranging
through tropical Asia. Most species are
single-stemmed; a few multi-stemmed.

Caryopteris incana

Carya illinoinensis

Large bipinnate fronds divide into segments along either side of a midrib, with triangular or wedge-shaped leaflets, reminiscent of a fishtail. Flowering occurs at maximum stem height, the first flowering panicle bursts from the sheathing base of the topmost frond and bears flowers and fruit. Over several years panicles emerge from the stem in lower positions until at the base of the trunk, then with fruiting over, single stemmed plants die. Panicles have cream flowers crowded on drooping spikes. Pink to purple fruits follow. Sugary sap may be fermented for a sort of wine or beer. CULTIVATION: All are fine ornamental palms and most thrive equally well in frost-free climates, with adequate soil moisture. In hot climates growth is very fast, individual stems are short lived, becoming ragged and untidy with age. Propagation is from seed.

Caryota no

Caryota obtusa 'King Kong'

Caryota cumingii

Caryota cumingii

☼ ✿ ↔ 10 ft (3 m) ↑ 30 ft (9 m)

From the Philippines. Single-stemmed trunk 12 in (30 cm) in diameter, marked with prominent rings. Fronds large, with leaflets less drooping than other species. Flowering panicles are massive, sheathed in prominent bracts as they emerge. Zones 11–12.

Caryota mitis ★
CLUSTER FISHTAIL PALM

☼ ❧ ↔ 10 ft (3 m) ↑ 20 ft (6 m)

Widely cultivated. Narrow clump of stems. Fronds 6–10 ft (1.8–3 m) long, crowd together forming a luxuriant crown. Flowering panicles; a mass of scented cream flowers opening from green buds. Fruit dark red. Needs moist fertile soil. Zones 10–12.

Caryota no ★
GIANT FISHTAIL PALM

☼ ❧ ↔ 20 ft (6 m) ↑ 80 ft (24 m)

From Borneo. Fronds up to 15 ft (4.5 m) long and two-thirds as wide, fan out stiffly. Trunk to 24 in (60 cm) in diameter. Flowering panicles to 8 ft (2.4 m) long. Fruit blackish. Zones 10–12.

Caryota obtusa ★
INDIAN FISHTAIL PALM

☼ ❧ ↔ 12–20 ft (3.5–6 m)
↑ 15–20 ft (4.5–6 m)

Clustering palm of open forests from temperate to tropical India and Thailand. Very broad, smooth, grayish, single trunk marked with leaf scars. Large, bipinnate, dark green leaves, up to 10 ft (3 m) long. Cream flowers on a 12 in (30 cm) long stalk, which emerges from leaves. Mature fruit rounded, dull red to black. '**King Kong**', light green leaves. Zones 9–12.

Caryota ochlandra
CHINESE FISHTAIL PALM

☼ ❧ ↔ 10 ft (3 m) ↑ 25 ft (8 m)

Native to southern China. Single-stemmed, trunk 6 in (15 cm) in diameter. Fronds along the trunk. Crowded, drooping, narrow leaflets.

Casearia silvana

Caryota ochlandra

Flowering panicles 6 ft (1.8 m) high or more. Fruit deep red. Will survive light frosts. Zones 9–12.

Caryota urens ★
FISHTAIL PALM, TODDY PALM

☼ ❧ ↔ 15 ft (4.5 m) ↑ 30 ft (9 m)

Cultivated in southern Asia as a source of sugar. Adapts to seasonally dry climates. Trunk 12 in (30 cm) in diameter, chalky white. Fronds with crowded, narrow, drooping leaflets. Flowering panicles 10 ft (3 m) long. Red fruit. Zones 10–12.

CASEARIA

Genus of around 160 species of evergreen or deciduous trees and shrubs in the governor's-plum (Flacourtiaceae) family, widely distributed in tropical and subtropical regions of the world. The leaves are simple and alternate, tending to be arranged in 2 ranks, their margins entire or toothed. Small greenish to reddish flowers are borne in clusters at leaf nodes, often on older wood. The fruit is a yellow or orange capsule that splits into 2 to 4 segments to reveal seeds embedded in arils that are often bright red. CULTIVATION: Rarely grown except in botanical collections, they should present few difficulties in warm-climate gardens if provided with a sheltered position and moist well-drained soil. Propagate from fresh seed.

Casearia silvana

☼ ❧ ↔ 10 ft (3 m) ↑ 20 ft (6 m)

Endemic to New Caledonia, growing in rocky ravines; small tree with somewhat scrambling branches, leathery deep green leaves, tiny green flowers in dense clusters, in autumn–winter. Zones 10–12.

CASIMIROA

This Central American and Mexican genus of 6 species of evergreen trees and shrubs in the rue (Rutaceae) family is best known for the white sapote *(C. edulis)*. *Casimiroa* species have leaves with 3 to 7 lobes and while their flowers are small, they are carried in panicles or corymbs and are fragrant. Fruit is rounded to egg-shaped, containing a sweet edible pulp and is best picked just as the color turns and left to soften for a few days. Fruit is eaten alone, in desserts, or in fruit salads.
CULTIVATION: Most species are frost tender and need a moist subtropical to tropical climate to grow well and crop heavily. They will not tolerate prolonged drought and need a sunny sheltered position with moist well-drained soil. They appreciate added humus and should be fed regularly. Any pruning or trimming can be done as the fruit is harvested. Propagate from seed or by grafting.

Casimiroa edulis
WHITE SAPOTE

☼ ⚘ ↔ 12 ft (4.5 m) ↑ 50 ft (15 m)
Originating in the Mexican highlands. Tolerates light frost but needs warmth to ripen fruit. Drooping branches, palmate leaves with 3 to 5 oval leaflets. Greenish yellow flowers from late spring. Persimmon-shaped fruits to 4 in (10 cm) in diameter. Popular cultivars include: **'Bravo'**, **'Lemon Gold'**, and **'Louise'**. Zones 10–11.

CASSIA

Once a very large genus of perennials, annuals, subshrubs, shrubs, and trees, *Cassia* has been revised in recent years and, while still containing well over 100 species, it is now a far more consistent grouping of plants in the cassia subfamily of the legume (Fabaceae) family. Found in tropical areas of the world, the shrubs and trees in the

Cassia brewsteri

Cassia queenslandica

genus are mainly evergreen. Pinnate, sometimes hairy leaves; bright yellow or pink flowers, borne singly, in small clusters, or in panicles. Flowers often appear over a long season and are followed by bean-like seed pods.
CULTIVATION: Hardiness varies with species, few tolerate repeated frosts. General preference for a mild climate, moist well-drained soil, full or half-sun. Propagation usually from seed, which should be soaked in warm water prior to sowing. Some cassias will grow from half-hardened cuttings.

Cassia brewsteri
LEICHHARDT BEAN

☼ ⚘ ↔ 12 ft (3.5 m) ↑ 40 ft (12 m)
Native to Queensland, Australia. Spreading tree or shrub. Blackish bark. Leaves pinnate, with 4 to 12 lance-shaped leaflets, about 3 in (8 cm) long. Yellow-orange flowers in drooping racemes, in spring. Cylindrical woody pods. Zones 10–12.

Cassia fistula
GOLDEN SHOWER TREE, INDIAN SENNA

☼ ⚘ ↔ 20 ft (6 m) ↑ 60 ft (18 m)
Native to tropical Asia. Deciduous to semi-evergreen. Smooth gray bark, often irregular branching. Leaves pinnate, leaflets in 3 to 8 pairs. Flowers vivid yellow, scented, pendulous racemes, in summer. Dark brown seed pods. Zones 10–12.

Cassia javanica
syn. *Cassia nodosa*
PINK SHOWER, RAINBOW SHOWER

☼ ⚘ ↔ 10 ft (3 m) ↑ 50 ft (15 m)
From Southeast Asia, popular tropical garden, dry-season deciduous tree. Pinnate leaves composed of up to 34 long, narrow, drooping leaflets. Flowers are over 2 in (5 cm) wide in racemes, color variable, buff through pink to crimson. Zones 11–12.

Cassia × *nealiae*

Cassia fistula

Cassia × *nealiae* ★
RAINBOW SHOWER

☼ ⚘ ↔ 20–30 ft (6–9 m)
↑ 25–50 ft (8–15 m)
Handsome deciduous flowering tree, a hybrid between yellow-flowered *C. fistula* and pink-flowered *C. javanica* raised around 1916 in Hawaii. Flowers vary from cream to orange and red. Official tree of the City and County of Honolulu. The commonest cultivars are pale yellow-white **'Queen's**

Hospital White' and **'Wilhelmina Tenney'**, odorless yellow flowers. **'Lunalilo Yellow'**, fragrant yellow flowers. Propagation is from cuttings. Zones 10–12.

Cassia queenslandica

☼ ⚘ ↔ 8 ft (2.4 m) ↑ 20–30 ft (6–9 m)
From Queensland, Australia. Upright tree. Leathery pinnate leaves, golden yellow flowers in pendulous clusters in summer. Zones 10–11.

Cassinia fulvida

Cassinia arcuata

Cassinopsis ilicifolia

CASSINIA

This genus, native to Australia, New Zealand, and South Africa, contains 20 species of evergreen shrubs with alternate smooth-edged leaves. The foliage often shows yellow-green or gray-green tones. *Cassinia* is in the daisy (Asteraceae) family, a fact not readily apparent without inspecting the flowers, which lack ray florets and are massed in terminal heads or corymbs. The flower and foliage colors are often similar and the flowers most often open in summer.
CULTIVATION: *Cassinia* usually does best in relatively harsh conditions. They do not tolerate very heavy frosts and prefer dry, gritty, relatively poor soils with full sun. Rich soils and too much shade will cause them to become soft with elongated stems. Light pruning after flowering keeps them compact. Cuttings strike quickly.

Cassinia arcuata
BIDDY BUSH, CHINESE SHRUB, SIFTON BUSH
☀ ❄ ↔ 4 ft (1.2 m) ↑ 6 ft (1.8 m)
From Australia. Leaves small, narrow, aromatic. Flowerheads of small brownish flowers in spring, spot flowering throughout the year. Can be invasive, declared a weed in New South Wales. Grown for cut foliage. Zones 8–11.

Cassinia fulvida
GOLDEN COTTONWOOD, GOLDEN TAUHINU
☀ ❄ ↔ 4 ft (1.2 m) ↑ 6 ft (1.8 m)
From New Zealand, tough and adaptable. Foliage an unusual greenish yellow shade, more golden in winter. Flowers dull cream. Grown mainly for its foliage. Zones 8–10.

CASSINOPSIS

This genus of 4 species from Africa and Madagascar belongs to the family Icacinaceae. They are evergreen trees or shrubs with simple leaves in opposite pairs on green, zig-zagging twigs, often with a thorn at each node. The small flowers, arising in short cymes from the leaf axils are hermaphrodite with 5 separate petals. The fruit is an orange or red drupe, often asymmetric.
CULTIVATION: They are moderately frost-hardy and make useful screening plants on account of their spreading habit and attractive foliage. Initial growth is quite fast in soils of adequate fertility and moisture content. Propagate from the seed, which germinates readily.

Cassinopsis ilicifolia
syn. *Cassinopsis capensis*
LEMOENDORING, ORANGE-THORN
☀/◑ ❄ ↔ 12–20 ft (3.5–6 m)
↑ 15 ft (4.5 m)
From central to southern Africa. Small tree or scrambling shrub with opposite leaves, often with single thorns between leaf stalks. Leaves glossy green, elliptic-ovate with rolled back toothed margins. Flowers borne in small cymes in leaf axils in autumn, followed by orange berries. Zones 8–11.

CASSIOPE

This genus of 12 species of small evergreen shrubs is closely related to the heaths and heathers (Ericaceae). Found mainly in northern Europe and northern Asia with outliers in the Himalayas and western North America,
they are very much cool-temperate to cold climate plants, with a few species ranging into the Arctic. They seldom exceed 8 in (20 cm) high and have tiny leaves arranged in 4 distinct rows on wiry whipcord stems. The flowers, which appear mainly in spring, are small, usually bell-shaped, and carried singly, though often in large numbers, on fine stems.
CULTIVATION: Cassiopes prefer moist well-drained soil that is rich in humus and slightly acidic. They are not drought tolerant plants and need ample summer moisture. Very frost hardy, they prefer a climate with distinct seasons with a cool moist summer. They are best shaded from the hot summer sun. Trim lightly if necessary. Propa-gate from self-layered stems or by taking cuttings.

Cassiope 'Edinburgh'
☀ ❄ ↔ 8–10 in (20–25 cm)
↑ 10–12 in (25–30 cm)
This hybrid between *C. fastigiata* and *C. tetragona* is a strong upright form with dark scaly foliage and clusters of tiny urn-shaped flowers. Zones 4–8.

Cassiope lycopodioides
☀ ❄ ↔ 10 in (25 cm) ↑ 3 in (8 cm)
A native of the mountains of Japan, northeastern Asia, and Alaska. Resembles a clubmoss (*Lycopodium*). Flat sprawling habit, minute leaves.

Flowers, nodding, around ¼ in (6 mm) wide, carried on 1 in (25 mm) long stems. Zones 3–8.

Cassiope 'Medusa'
☀ ❄ ↔ 8 in (20 cm) ↑ 10 in (25 cm)
This *C. fastigiata* × *C. lycopodioides* hybrid is a very compact plant. It prefers cool moist conditions. Quite vigorous, forms a clump of dark green heather-like foliage. The flowers are white, with red-tinted calyces and leaf stalks. Zones 4–9.

Cassiope mertensiana
☀ ❄ ↔ 10 in (25 cm) ↑ 6–12 in (15–30 cm)
Upright or spreading shrub found in mountainous regions of western North America. Leaves tightly pressed to the stem. Small, white, bell-shaped flowers in spring. 'Gracilis', a mound-forming cultivar. Zones 5–9.

Cassiope 'Muirhead'
☀ ❄ ↔ 8–10 in (20–25 cm)
↑ 6–8 in (15–20 cm)
This cross between *C. wardii* and *C. fastigiata* has a low spreading habit, classical scaly foliage, and masses of tiny white flowers. Zones 4–8.

Cassiope tetragona
☀ ❄ ↔ 8 in (20 cm) ↑ 4–12 in (10–30 cm)
Upright or sprawling shrub from northern Europe and nearby Arctic regions. Tiny downy leaves. Flowers

Cassiope 'Muirhead'

Cassiope lycopodioides

Cassiope 'Medusa'

Castanea sativa

bell-shaped, white, often with a hint of pink, ¼ in (6 mm) long, on ½ in (12 mm) stems. Zones 3–8.

CASTANEA

Belonging to the beech (Fagaceae) family, this is a small genus of about 12 species of sweet chestnuts native to temperate regions of the Northern Hemisphere, from North America across Europe and into eastern Asia. In habit they range from low suckering shrubs to tall trees. Several species are of economic importance, being grown for their sweet-tasting edible nuts, which are enclosed in a spiny whorl of bracts. The taller species are also valued for their use as ornamental trees in parks and large gardens, especially for their spectacular yellowish green drooping catkins.
CULTIVATION: Sweet chestnuts prefer a well-drained and slightly acid soil; adequate rainfall is essential. Most are frost hardy down to Zones 4 or 5. Propagation is usually from seed which should be sown as soon as it is ripe; selected clones can be reproduced by grafts onto 1- or 2-year-old under-stocks, in early spring.

Castanea mollissima

CHINESE CHESTNUT

☼ ❄ ↔ 35 ft (10 m) ↕ 40 ft (12 m)
Native to central and eastern China and Korea. Ovate or oblong, coarsely serrated, short-stalked leaves, coarse white hair beneath. Widely cultivated in China for its edible nuts. Resistant to chestnut blight. Highly valued as an ornamental. 'Pendula', an attractive cultivar. Zones 5–9.

Castanea pumila

ALLEGHENY CHINKAPIN, CHINQUAPIN

☼ ❄ ↔ 20 ft (6 m) ↕ 15 ft (4.5 m)
Large suckering shrub from eastern and southern areas of USA. Downy

Castanea sativa 'Glabra'

young shoots, young leaves white and furry on the undersides. 'Ashei', the coastal chinquapin, has less densely spiny bracts than the species. Zones 6–9.

Castanea sativa

syn. *Castanea vesca*
CHESTNUT, SPANISH CHESTNUT,
SWEET CHESTNUT

☼ ❄ ↔ 40 ft (12 m) ↕ 60 ft (18 m)
Native of the high forest areas of southern Europe and western Asia. Fast-growing deciduous tree. Glossy, dark green, coarsely serrated leaves, lighter and slightly furry beneath. Yellow-green catkins, in mid-summer. Edible nuts are a popular delicacy, "marrons glacés." 'Albomarginata' has creamy white margins to the leaves; 'Glabra', very large dark green leaves; and 'Variegata' (syn. 'Aureomarginata') has yellow borders to the leaves. Zones 5–9.

Castanea Hybrid Cultivars

☼ ❄ ↔ 30 ft (9 m) ↕ 30 ft (9 m)
There are many hybrid chestnuts; they generally have heavier crops of larger nuts than species cultivars. Most of the best forms have *C. sativa* in their parentage. 'Colossal' (*C. sativa* × *C. crenata*) produces 14 to 18 nuts/lb (0.5 kg); 'Nevada' (*C. sativa* × *C. crenata*) has a yield of 15 nuts/lb and is a good pollinator for 'Colossal'; 'Schrader', a good cropper of unknown parentage; and 'Skioka' (*C. mollissima* × *C. sativa*), produces a heavy crop of small nuts, around 35 nuts/lb. Zones 6–9.

CASTANOPSIS

Found in the subtropical and warm-temperate regions of southern and eastern Asia, this genus is comprised of around 110 species of evergreen shrubs and trees in the beech (Fagaceae) family. They have leathery leaves, often serrated, that are usually bronze to dark green above and con-siderably paler below. Upright catkins of small yellow-green flowers appear mainly in spring and early summer. The flowers are followed by hard nuts that are held in a small, prickly,

cup-like structure similar to the acorn cup. Unlike the oak, with its single acorn per cup, *Castanopsis* usually bears 3 nuts in a multi-valved cup. The nuts are edible, though small in some species.
CULTIVATION: Most species will tolerate light to moderate frosts but are most at home in areas with mild winters and warm humid summers. They prefer moist, well-drained, humus-enriched soil, and require ample summer moisture. Trim to shape if required, preferably in the spring; propagation is from seed or half-hardened cuttings.

Castanopsis cuspidata

☼ ❄ ↔ 40 ft (12 m) ↕ 80 ft (24 m)
From southern Japan, South Korea, and southeastern China. Important timber for houses, wharf pilings, and fuel. Leaves narrow, pointed, smooth or slightly toothed edges. Catkins of fragrant yellow-green flowers in late spring–early summer. Edible nuts. Zones 7–10.

Castanea mollissima 'Pendula'

CASTANOSPERMUM

BLACK BEAN, MORETON BAY CHESTNUT
The sole species in this genus in the pea-flower subfamily of the legume (Fabaceae) family is a rainforest tree from northeastern Australia and New Caledonia. Developing slowly into a beautifully shaped tree with a dense rounded crown of lush deep green foliage, it is prized not only as a specimen tree, but also for its timber, which is a warm deep brown color. The summer floral display is also attractive, though the flowers are often largely hidden within the foliage. Very large seed pods follow the flowers in autumn.
CULTIVATION: Considering its origins, the Moreton Bay chestnut is surpris-ingly hardy. Although best grown in warm areas, it does well in any reason-ably mild, frost-free garden and will even tolerate light frosts—with some foliage loss. The soil should be humus rich, moist, and free draining. Young trees will tolerate light shade. Propagation is by seed.

Castanopsis cuspidata

Castanea mollissima

C

Castanospermum australe
MORETON BAY CHESTNUT, QUEENSLAND
BLACK BEAN

☼ ⚘ ↔40 ft (12 m) ↕40 ft (12 m)

Deep green pinnate leaves made up
of 11 to 15 leaflets. Flowers pea-like,
in racemes, yellow, ageing orange-red.
Seed pods to 12 in (30 cm) long,
containing 1 to 5 large black seeds.
Zones 10–12.

CASTANOSPORA

This genus of one species in the soapberry (Sapindaceae) family, occurs as

Castanospora alphandii

single-trunked or occasionally multi-
trunked trees in northeastern Australia's
rainforests from northern New South
Wales to northern Queensland. Leaves
pinnate, with 8 to 10 pairs of leaflets.
Small whitish flowers borne in large
inflorescences during the early part
of the dry season (winter). Fruits produced during the wet season (summer).
CULTIVATION: Young plants require
shelter from winds and frost. They are
not cultivated widely, but some plants
have been grown successfully outside
their native climatic zone. Propagate
from fresh seed.

Castanospora alphandii
BROWN TAMARIND

☼ ⚘ ↔20 ft (6 m) ↕70 ft (21 m)

Trunk 12–16 in (30–40 cm) across,
bark brownish. Leaves to 20 in (50 cm)
long, with oblong leaflets, 4–6 in
(10–15 cm) long, glossy green above,
paler and hairy below. Flowers whitish,
3 mm wide. Fruits 2-celled, each with
a large seed maturing to brown, to
¾ in (18 mm) in diameter. Zones 9–12.

Castilleja angustifolia

CASTILLEJA
INDIAN PAINTBRUSH, PAINTED CUPS,
PRAIRIE FIRE

Named after the eighteenth-century
Spanish botanist Domingo Castillejo,
and well-known as a strikingly vivid
feature of southwest USA, this foxglove (Scrophulariaceae) family genus
of around 200 species of annuals and
perennials is widespread through the
Americas and Eurasia. Usually low
growing but upright in habit, their
foliage tends to be downy and rather
a dull green. Tufted flowerheads appear
in spring and summer and it is not
the flowers that are colorful but their
calyces and the bracts that surround
them. Native American legend says that
the plants are the discarded tools of a
brave warrior who sought painting
guidance from the spirits and was given
brushes loaded with paints colored to
capture the sunset.
CULTIVATION: They are rarely seen in
gardens because they are often semi-
parasitic, taking nourishment via the
roots of certain shrubs and grasses.
Usually left to be appreciated in the
wild, they can be cultivated if the seed
is sown around appropriate host plants,
such as *Alnus*, *Symphoricarpos*, *Festuca*,
and *Aster*.

Castilleja angustifolia
DESERT PAINTBRUSH

☼/◑ ✳ ↔8 in (20 cm) ↕16 in (40 cm)

Perennial from Nevada, Utah, and
Idaho. Small light green to gray-green
leaves, finely hairy. Small yellow
flowers largely enclosed by pink to
red bracts. Zones 4–9.

Castilleja coccinea
INDIAN PAINTBRUSH, SCARLET PAINTBRUSH

☼ ✳ ↔12 in (30 cm)
↕12–14 in (30–35 cm)

From the North American East Coast
to the Rocky Mountains in Canada

Castilleja exserta

Castilleja rhexifolia × *C. sulphurea*, in
San Juan National Forest, Colorado, USA

and USA, south to northern Florida.
Annual or biennial species with basal
rosette leaves and small greenish yellow
flowers. Crimson bracts give good
color and are more prominent than
the flowers. Attracts hummingbirds.
Use in a meadow garden. Zones 4–9.

Castilleja exserta
PURPLE OWL CLOVER

☼/◑ ✳ ↔6–8 in (15–20 cm)
↕8 in (20 cm)

Perennial found from central
California to northern Mexico. Few
hairy basal leaves and upright spikes
with small snapdragon-like cream
to pale yellow flowers almost entirely
enclosed by bright purple-pink bracts.
Zones 7–10.

Castilleja rhexifolia ×
C. sulphurea

☼ ✳ ↔8 in (20 cm) ↕12 in (30 cm)

Where distributions of *C. rhexifolia*
and *C. sulphurea* overlap in the Rocky
Mountains, they often form extensive
hybrid populations. Range of flower
colors from cream to yellow to dusky
pink and deeper mauve. Zones 4–8.

Castanospermum australe

Castilleja talamancensis

☼/◐ ❄ ↔ 6–8 in (15–20 cm)
↑ 12 in (30 cm)

Perennial from the mountains of
Costa Rica where it is found in boggy
conditions at 10,000 ft (3,000 m).
Hairy, dull green leaves and red or
yellow bracts enclosing yellow flowers.
Zones 8–9.

CASUARINA

This is a small genus in the she-oak
(Casuarinaceae) family of shapely
evergreen trees containing approximately 17 species from Australia and
the Pacific Islands. In 1982 the genus
was subdivided into 4 genera, most
Australian species now classified as
Allocasuarina. All species have distinctive, dark green or gray-green, slender,
wiry branchlets, modified to function
as leaves. The true leaves are reduced
to tiny teeth-like scales in whorls at
regular intervals along the branchlets.
The minute, pollen-bearing, rusty red,
male flowers form at tips of branchlets.
Female flowers, small tassel-like, produce the next season's fruiting cones.
Casuarinas are fast-growing and may
be planted singly or grouped for shade,
shelter, and screening purposes. As they
will withstand harsh windy conditions
they are ideal for wind protection.
CULTIVATION: Grow in full sun in
any soil as long as it is well-drained.
Water well during the establishment
period and dry hot weather. Propagate
from seed.

Casuarina collina

☼ ❄ ↔ 15 ft (4.5 m) ↑ 30–50 ft (9–15 m)
A species that is endemic to New
Caledonia in disturbed forest margins
on lower hill slopes and valleys.
Similar to the Australian *C. glauca* but
twigs more slender. Hardly known in
cultivation outside its native land.
Zones 9–12.

Castilleja talamancensis, Costa Rica

Casuarina cunninghamiana

Casuarina collina, in the wild,
Col de Nassirah, New Caledonia

Casuarina cristata

BELAH

☼ ❄ ↔ 25 ft (8 m) ↑ 60 ft (18 m)
Native to the drier areas of eastern
Australia. Hard, dark gray, scaly bark,
drooping gray-green branchlets. This
tree is ideally suited to heavy soils in
low-lying dry situations where it is
able to withstand short periods of
inundation. Zones 9–11.

Casuarina cunninghamiana

RIVER OAK, RIVER SHE-OAK

☼ ❄ ↔ 25 ft (8 m) ↑ 100 ft (30 m)
Stately tree, common on banks of
rivers in eastern Australia. Upright
trunk, dark green, slightly drooping
branchlets occur near ground level.
Useful for windbreaks. Prefers open
moist position. Withstands seasonal
inundation. Zones 9–11.

Casuarina equisetifolia

AUSTRALIAN PINE, BEACH SHE-OAK

☼ ❄ ↔ 20 ft (6 m) ↑ 60 ft (18 m)
From subtropical and tropical eastern
Australia, Pacific Islands, and Malaysia.
Spreading tree, open branching crown,
weeping branchlets. Popular street and
beach tree, which withstands salt-laden
winds. Widely planted for coastal dune
stabilization in Australia. *C. e.* subsp.
incana has weeping silvery green
branchlets. Zones 10–12.

Casuarina equisetifolia subsp. *incana*

Casuarina glauca

Casuarina glauca

SWAMP OAK, SWAMP SHE-OAK

☼ ❄ ↔ 20 ft (6 m) ↑ 70 ft (21 m)
Native to eastern coastal Australia. Upright tree, weeping dark green branchlets with a waxy coating. Forms dense
thickets in saline swamps. Excellent
soil binder. Withstands quite dry conditions and will make a good windbreak. Zones 9–12.

CATALPA

This genus of 11 species of small to
medium deciduous trees, belonging to
the trumpet-vine (Bignoniaceae) family, occurs in North America, Cuba,
and southwestern China. They are
attractive trees, with a tropical appearance from their large long-stalked
leaves. They bear upright panicles of
2 in (5 cm) long, bell-shaped flowers,
followed by hanging bean-like seed
capsules that grow up to 30 in (75 cm)
in length. The genus name is a corruption of the North American Indian
name for the plant.
CULTIVATION: *Catalpa* make excellent
specimen trees and are good for street

Catalpa bignonioides

planting. They should be sheltered
from wind to protect the large leaves.
A sunny site with rich, moist, well-
drained soil provides the most suitable
conditions. Young trees may require
protection from late frosts and should
be trained to a single trunk. The species
are propagated from seed sown in
autumn and the cultivars from softwood cuttings taken in late spring
or early summer.

Catalpa bignonioides

BEAN TREE, INDIAN BEAN TREE,
SOUTHERN CATALPA

☼ ❄ ↔ 40 ft (12 m) ↑ 50 ft (15 m)
Found at streamsides and in low woods
in southeastern USA. The leaves are
large, with heart-shaped bases, and
have an unpleasant smell when they
are crushed. They bear large erect panicles of bell-shaped white flowers,
marked with yellow and purple, in
summer, and large bean-like pods.
'Aurea' ★, a fine form with velvety
golden leaves. 'Nana', a small shrub
to 6 ft (1.8 m) high, seldom bears
flowers. Zones 5–10.

Catalpa bungei

Catalpa longissima

Catalpa fargesii

Catalpa speciosa

Catalpa bungei

☼ ❄ ↔ 25 ft (8 m) ↑ 30 ft (9 m)

Native of northern China. A small tree. Leaves triangular, with a long central tip. Flowers rosy pink to white with purple spots, in summer. Seed capsule may grow up to 20 in (50 cm) in length. Zones 5–10.

Catalpa × erubescens

☼ ❄ ↔ 50 ft (15 m) ↑ 50 ft (15 m)

This is a cultivated hybrid between *C. bignonioides* and *C. ovata*. A broad spreading tree. Large leaves to 12 in (30 cm) long and 10 in (25 cm) across. Fragrant white flowers, purple and white markings, forming dense panicles, in summer. Seed capsules up to 15 in (38 cm) long. '**Purpurea**' has shoots and young leaves that emerge purple-black, becoming dark green. Zones 5–10.

Catalpa fargesii

☼ ❄ ↔ 40 ft (12 m) ↑ 60 ft (18 m)

From open mountain areas of western China. Wide leaves taper to a fine point, bronze when young. Flowers rosy pink, marked with yellow and purple, in dense clusters, in summer. Slender seed pods to 30 in (75 cm) long. Zones 5–10.

Catalpa longissima

BOIS-CHENE, JAMAICAN OAK

☼ ▨ ↔ 60 ft (18 m) ↑ 80 ft (24 m)

Native to Jamaica and Haiti. Leathery leaves shorter and narrower than most species. Loose clusters of pink-tinted white flowers, borne in summer. Seed capsules range up to 26 in (65 cm) in length. Zones 9–10.

Catalpa speciosa

NORTHERN CATALPA, SHAWNEE WOOD, WESTERN CATALPA

☼ ❄ ↔ 90 ft (27 m) ↑ 120 ft (36 m)

From riverbanks, damp woods, and swamps of central southern USA. Rather like *C. bignonioides* but has larger leaves. White flowers are larger, less dense, appearing a few weeks earlier. Considered to be less showy. Zones 5–10.

CATANANCHE

CUPID'S DART

This small genus, belonging to the daisy (Asteraceae) family, contains 5 species of annual or perennial herbs found in countries bordering the Mediterranean. Inhabit dry grassy areas. Leaves usually long and narrow and arise at base of clump. Flowering stems are thin and wiry, bearing cornflower-like flowers of blue, white, or yellow. Bracts below the flowers are transparent and papery, often with a silver tinge. Both common and botanical names refer to the ancient use of the sap in the making of aphrodisiacs.
CULTIVATION: *C. caerulea* is usually the only species seen in cultivation. Grow in full sun in any well-drained soil. It tends to be short-lived as a perennial, especially when grown in heavy clay and can be treated as an annual. Plants propagated from seed will flower in the first year. Propagation can also be by division in winter.

Catananche caerulea

BLUE CUPIDONE, BLUE SUCCORY, CUPID'S DART

☼ ❄ ↔ 12–18 in (30–45 cm)
↑ 24–30 in (60–75 cm)

Native to southwestern Europe and northern Africa. Low clumps of narrow, lance-shaped, grayish green leaves, sometimes with a few long teeth. Delicate stems of blue to mauve flowers, like cornflowers in color and appearance, in summer. '**Major**' has flowers of deep blue. Zones 7–10.

CATHA

The sole species in this genus, in the spindle-tree (Celastraceae) family, is a small to medium-sized evergreen tree, best known as the source of the addictive drug khat, pronounced cot, which is obtained by chewing the young foliage, or by drinking an infusion brewed from the young leaves. This habit is commonplace in the tree's endemic range of tropical and subtropical eastern Africa and has been taken up in other areas where the khat tree can be readily cultivated.
CULTIVATION: Khat is a warm-climate tree that does not tolerate prolonged cold conditions. It occurs naturally in areas that are either arid or have distinct wet and dry seasons. Because of its narcotic effects, khat cultivation is banned in some countries, including the USA. The khat tree prefers relatively dry conditions, especially in winter, and will tolerate the occasional very light frost but does not appreciate excessive humidity. It can be pruned at any time and becomes very bushy with regular trimming. Propagation is from cuttings.

Catha edulis

ARABIAN TEA, CHAT, KHAT, QAT

☼ ▨ ↔ 7 ft (2 m) ↑ 20 ft (6 m)

Usually seen as a large shrub, particularly when routinely harvested for its foliage. Leaves are elliptical with serrated edges. New growth is often red-tinted, foliage resembles the better-known *Photinia*. Clusters of attractive, small, white flowers. Zones 10–12.

Catananche caerulea

Catha edulis

CATHARANTHUS

MADAGASCAR PERIWINKLE, PERIWINKLE, ROSY PERIWINKLE

Although related to the common periwinkle *(Vinca),* the 8 annuals and perennials of this genus, in the dogbane (Apocynaceae) family, are less hardy and tolerate little or no frost. All Madagascan natives, they are bushy plants with simple elliptical leaves on semi-succulent stems. Flat, 5-petalled flowers, mainly in pink and mauve shades, appear at the stem tip and leaf axils. Considered a weed in the tropics and subtropics, the commonly cultivated species *C. roseus* is a perennial often grown as a greenhouse plant or summer bedder in temperate gardens. Naturally highly toxic, it is the source of vinca alkaloids, used to treat lymphocytic leukaemia and Hodgkin's Disease.
CULTIVATION: Very easily grown in sun or part-shade, periwinkles are drought tolerant but flower more heavily with summer moisture. Pinch back to encourage bushiness. In cool areas where winter frost would be fatal, bring indoors or discard and replace in spring. Propagate from seed or half-hardened summer cuttings.

Catharanthus roseus

syn. *Vinca rosea*

MADAGASCAR PERIWINKLE, ROSE PERIWINKLE
☼/◑ ✱ ↔ 16 in (40 cm) ↑ 24 in (60 cm)
Upright perennial from Madagascar. Glossy deep green leaves with pale midrib, to 2 in (5 cm) long. Mauve-throated, soft pink to red, 5-petalled flowers, with red "eye." **'Albus'**, white flowers; **'Blue Pearl'**, 18 in (45 cm) tall, white-centered lavender-blue to mauve flowers; **'Blush Cooler'**, very pale pink flowers, light red center,

one of the compact, 12 in (30 cm) tall, heavy-flowering **Cooler Series**; **'Pacifica Punch'**, deep pink flowers with slightly darker center, one of the 18 in (45 cm) tall **Pacifica Series**; **'Parasol'**, white flowers to 2 in (5 cm) wide, with red "eye"; the very heat-tolerant **Pretty Series**; and **'Stardust Orchid'**, cream-centered deep pink flowers, up to 16 in (40 cm) tall. Zones 11–12.

CATOPSIS

This is probably the most fascinating genus of the bromeliad (Bromeliaceae) family, botanically speaking, and could well be in a separate subfamily. Plants are generally tubular rosettes that retain water and the spineless leaves are often covered with a white wax. They are found mainly growing on trees, but are sometimes found on rocks. Flowerhead is a cluster of small flowers on a longish flower stem, pendent in some species. Petals are white to cream. The flowers can be "perfect," that is with functional male and female parts, or "normal" where only one sexual part is functioning so the plant is basically male or female. Some 20 species make up this genus, coming mainly from southern Florida, Mexico, Guatemala, the Caribbean islands, northern South America, and southern Brazil.

CULTIVATION: Grown mainly by specialists, they can be mounted on pieces of cork or wood or put in small pots with small pieces of bark or rock. Recommended for indoor culture in cool-temperate areas, or outdoors with protection from direct continuous sunlight and extremes of rain in warm-temperate, subtropical, and tropical areas. Water when potting mix is dry. Extra fertilizer is not necess- ary. If mounted, spray at least twice a week in the warmer weather. All species of *Catopsis* have a fleshy stem with off-shoots called "pups" clustered around the main plant. These can be removed and replanted after flowering.

Catharanthus roseus 'Albus'

Catharanthus roseus 'Blue Pearl'

C. roseus Cooler series, 'Blush Cooler'

Catharanthus roseus

Catharanthus roseus 'Stardust Orchid'

C. roseus 'Raspberry Red Cooler'

C. roseus 'Merlot Mix'

C. r. Pacifica Series 'Pacific Punch'

C. r. Pacifica Series, 'Pacifica Red'

C. r. Pacifica Series, 'Pacific White'

Catopsis berteroniana

POWDERY STRAP AIRPLANT

☼ ❄ ↔ 18 in (45 cm)
↑ 18–36 in (45–90 cm)

Only *Catopsis* species known to be carnivorous. Found growing on trees in Florida and Central and South America. Yellow to green leaves 16 in (40 cm) long. Outer surface of leaves covered with waxy powder. Leaves surround a central well in which insects are broken down by bacteria, resulting liquid is absorbed by plant. Small yellow flowers on erect leafless stalk up to 50 in (130 cm) high. Zones 8–11.

CATTLEYA

This tropical American genus is one of the most popular groups of orchids (Orchidaceae) in cultivation, with over 50 species and literally thousands of hybrids. These sympodial rock- and tree-dwellers have showy, colorful,

Cattleya aurantiaca, white form

Cattleya loddigesii 'Blue Sky'

long-lasting, and often highly fragrant flowers produced on stout plants with club-shaped to cylindrical pseudo-bulbs. They are topped with 1 (uni-foliate) or 2 (bifoliate) dull green leathery leaves. There have been thousands of hybrids made within the genus and related members of the *Cattleya* alliance or family, especially *Laelia, Rhyncholaelia* (often credited in hybrid lists under *Brassavola*), and *Sophronitis*, with many of the larger flowering types grown commercially for cut-flower production.

CULTIVATION: They enjoy high light and intermediate to warm tempera-tures, with some taking cooler con-ditions in winter. Most species require warmth in winter, but the Brazilian bifoliate autumn-flowering types will stand cooler winter temperatures for short periods, if kept dry while dor-mant. They must all have unimpeded drainage and a coarse bark-based medium. They grow best in plastic or terracotta pots and must dry out between waterings. Healthy plants will develop an extensive system of thick white roots, which are long-lived and branch freely.

Cattleya aurantiaca

☼/☀ ⚬ ↔ 6–24 in (15–60 cm)
5–24 in (12–60 cm)

From Central America. Smallest flowers of the genus. Up to a dozen glossy,

Cattleya loddigesii 'Bella Vista'

Cattleya intermedia

Cattleya bicolor 'Golden Gate'

2 in (5 cm) wide flowers, ranging from yellow through shades of orange (the most common color) to deep red, occasionally white, are produced in summer. In some clones the flowers do not open fully, whilst inferior forms are self-pollinating. Zones 10–12.

Cattleya bicolor

☼/☀ ⚬ ↔ 8–24 in (20–60 cm)
↑ 8–48 in (20–120 cm)

From Brazil. Tall autumn-flowering species with up to eight, 3 in (8 cm) wide, apple or olive green flowers, sometimes with a coppery cast, and a contrasting purple labellum. *C. b.* var. *braziliensis* has significantly larger but fewer blooms, which often have a stronger color. *C. b.* 'Golden Gate', has striking crimson-cupped flowers. Zones 10–12.

Cattleya bowringiana

☼/☀ ⚬ ↔ 4–24 in (10–60 cm)
↑ 6–36 in (15–90 cm)

From Guatemala and Belize. Strong, easily grown, popular species that grows on rocky cliffs in the wild, in bright humid conditions. Forms large clusters of up to twenty, 3 in (8 cm) wide, rose-purple, fragrant blooms, in autumn. Zones 10–12.

Cattleya intermedia

☀ ⚬ ↔ 4–12 in (10–30 cm)
↑ 6–16 in (15–40 cm)

From Brazil. Variable species, in range of shapes, sizes, and colors—from pure white through shades of pink to deep purple. Up to five 3½ in (9 cm) blooms in spring. Splash-petalled form known as *C. i.* var. *aquinii.* Zones 10–12.

Cattleya loddigesii 'Impassionata'

Cattleya leuddemanniana

Cattleya walkeriana var. *alba*

Cattleya loddigesii

☀ ⚬ ↔ 4–12 in (10–30 cm)
↑ 6–24 in (15–60 cm)

From Brazil and Argentina. Produces up to eight 4 in (10 cm) flowers during the autumn. The petals and sepals are pale pink to purple (rarely white), sometimes finely speckled with darker purple. The labellum is white, yellow, and purple. The color intensity of the blooms can be improved if they are given strong light when in bud. These plants are very similar to and often confused with *C. harrisoniana*. 'Bella Vista', 'Blue Sky', and 'Impassionata' are popular cultivars of *C. loddigesii*. Zones 10–12.

Cattleya leuddemanniana

☀ ✈ ↔ 4–12 in (10–30 cm)
↑ 6–20 in (15–50 cm)

From Venezuela, this is a winter-flowering unifoliate species that in the wild will grow on rocks in quite exposed positions. The shapely white, orchid pink to purple blooms are found up to 8 in (20 cm) in diameter, with as many as 4 on each stalk. Zones 11–12.

Cattleya walkeriana

☀ ⚬ ↔ 4–10 in (10–25 cm)
↑ 3–6 in (8–15 cm)

This species is from Brazil. Its flowering style is unique—a short specialized spike emerges from the rhizome near the base of the previous growth, bear-ing 1 or 2 flat rather than cup-shaped 4 in (10 cm) blooms that are generally lilac-pink to purple. *C. w.* var. *alba* is one of the numerous albino forms bearing flowers of the purest white. Zones 10–12.

Cattleya, Hybrid, Bow Bells July

Cattleya, Hybrid, Bowgata

Cattleya, Hybrid, Eclipse

Cattleya, Hybrid, Frasquita

Cattleya, H, *C.* × *guatemalensis*

Cattleya, Hybrid, Hawaiian Comfort

Cattleya, Hybrid, Humming Bird

Cattleya, Hybrid, Luteous Forb

Cattleya, Hybrid, Penny Kuroda 'Spots'

Cattleya, Hybrid, Purple Glory 'Mori Pride'

Cattleya, Hybrid, Earl 'Imperialis'

Cattleya, Hybrid, (Browniae × *loddigesii*)

Cattleya, Hybrid, Miyuki 'Abe'

Cattleya Hybrids

☀ ◑ ↔ 8–24 in (20–60 cm)
↕ 8–32 in (20–80 cm)

A selection of some popular cultivars and recent seedlings shows the variety of color available. *Cattleya* (Browniae × *loddigesii*) can be grown over a range of climates; protect plants from frosts; **Earl 'Imperialis'**, bred from albino forms of *C. trianaei, C. gaskelliana,* and *C. mossiae,* large, crisp white blooms; **Eclipse**, a primary hybrid between *C. maxima* and *C. skinneri,* clusters of large magenta flowers in spring; **Frasquita**, a tall-growing primary hybrid between *C. bicolor* and

C. velutina, clusters of glossy brown flowers with bright purple labellum; *C.* × *guatemalensis*, a natural hybrid between *C. skinneri* and *C. aurantiaca,* native to Guatemala; **Hawaiian Comfort**, compact growing hybrid with crisp pure white to cream blooms that are excellent as cut flowers and for corsages; **Humming Bird Hybrids**, sprays of up to 8 flowers, often called "cluster cattleyas;" **Luteous Forb**, a primary hybrid between *C. luteola* and *C. forbesii,* clusters of apple green and yellow flowers; **Miyuki 'Abe'**, floriferous hybrid ideal as a specimen plant; **Penny Kuroda 'Spots'**, popular

hybrid used as a parent in many new crosses, distinctive spotting is derived from *C. guttata.* Zones 10–12.

× *CATTLEYTONIA*

× *Cattleytonia* is a genus in the orchid (Orchidaceae) family created by combining members of the sympodial genera *Cattleya* with *Broughtonia*. In most instances the West Indian species *Broughtonia sanguinea* is dominant in their backgrounds. These are often highly colored hybrids with flowers

produced on tall, thin but sturdy inflorescences off compact plants. **CULTIVATION:** They grow well in small pots of a coarse bark-based medium, wooden baskets, or cork or tree-fern slabs, as long as they dry out between waterings. They enjoy high light and intermediate to warm temperatures throughout the year.

× *Cattleytonia* Maui Maid

☀/◑ ✈ ↔ 4–12 in (10–30 cm)
↕ 4–20 in (10–50 cm)

Delightful hybrid created using the white-flowered form of *Broughtonia sanguinea.* Flowers last for over 6 weeks in fine conditions. Zones 11–12.

× *Cattleytonia* Starrlyn

☀/◑ ✈ ↔ 4–12 in (10–30 cm)
↕ 4–20 in (10–50 cm)

Recently registered hybrid. Intense red color with a yellow throat. Four species in its genetic make-up—*Broughtonia sanguinea, Cattleya aurantiaca, C. bicolor,* and *C. intermedia.* Zones 11–12.

× *Cattleytonia* Maui Maid

× *Cattleytonia* Starrlyn

C

Ceanothus × delileanus 'Gloire de Versailles'

Ceanothus gloriosus var. *exaltatus*

Ceanothus gloriosus 'Anchor Bay'

Cavendishia bracteata

CAVENDISHIA

This genus of the erica (Ericaceae) family consists of around 100 species of evergreen shrubs and small trees, native to the Andean region of northern South America, inhabiting mountain cloud-forest, and often growing as epiphytes. They have stiff leathery leaves with smooth margins that are mostly slightly rolled downward. Flowers are tubular and waxy, in shades of pink, orange, or red, and are borne near the branch tips in short sprays, often enclosed in colored leafy bracts when in bud. The fruits are somewhat like blueberries, seldom seen in cultivation. CULTIVATION: The single species in cultivation is fairly adaptable, as long as it is only exposed to the lightest of frosts. It does best in partial shade in similar conditions to those that suit

smaller rhododendrons. In a cold climate grow as a container plant in a cool conservatory in a well-drained peaty compost in filtered light. Propagate from the seed, layers, or half-hardened cuttings.

Cavendishia bracteata
syn. *Cavendishia acuminata*

☀ ❁ ↔ 3 ft (0.9 m) ↑ 2–3 ft (0.6–1 m)
From the mountains of Colombia and Ecuador. Mound-forming shrub, with arching branches. Broad leathery leaves with drawn-out tips, new growth red. Short sprays of glossy deep red flowers, with whitish teeth at the apex, in late spring–autumn. Zones 9–10.

CEANOTHUS
CALIFORNIAN LILAC
This genus of about 50 species of mostly evergreen, ornamental, flowering shrubs is a member of the buckthorn (Rhamnaceae) family. Mainly native to California, some are found in eastern USA, and from Mexico south to Guatemala. They tolerate drought, heat, and cold provided the soil is free draining. In habit they range from low, spreading, ground cover plants to tall shrubs. Most are quick growing but they may also be short lived. The flowers range from powder blue to deep purple, some having white or

cream flowers. The peak flowering season for *Ceanothus* is early in the summer months.
CULTIVATION: *Ceanothus* will grow in most soils, preferring a position in sun with protection from strong winds and an evenly distributed rainfall. Tip prune the young plants; the adult plants require little pruning apart from removing spent flowerheads and wayward shoots. *Ceanothus* resent disturbance. Species can be propagated from the seed, and soft tip or firm hardwood cuttings can be taken between spring and early autumn.

Ceanothus americanus
MOUNTAIN-SWEET, NEW JERSEY TEA
☀ ❁ ↔ 2–3 ft (0.6–0.9 m)
↑ 2–3 ft (0.6–0.9 m)
Small, deciduous shrub, found in eastern and central North America. Slender leaves, believed to have been used as a tea substitute during the American Civil War. Dense panicles of dull white flowers in mid-summer. Zones 7–9.

Ceanothus arboreus
CATALINA MOUNTAIN LILAC,
TREE CEANOTHUS
☀ ❁ ↔ 12 ft (3.5 m) ↑ 20 ft (6 m)
From the southern Californian coast, vigorous, wide-spreading, smaller in cultivation. The ovate leaves are downy beneath, and larger than in other species. The pale blue and fragrant flowers appear in abundant panicles, in spring. 'Mist' ★, paler flowers, gray-blue in color, carried in long spikes. 'Trewithen Blue' is an improved selection, widely planted, which has large panicles of fragrant deep blue flowers. Zones 7–9.

Ceanothus coeruleus
syn. *Ceanothus azureus*
AZURE CEANOTHUS
☀ ❁ ↔ 7 ft (2 m) ↑ 10 ft (3 m)
Medium-sized shrub from Mexico and Guatemala. Semi-evergreen, dark green, roundish leaves, woolly beneath. Panicles of sky blue flowers from summer–autumn. Zones 8–10.

Ceanothus crassifolius
HOARY LEAFED CEANOTHUS
☀ ❁ ↔ 7–12 ft (2–3.5 m)
↑ 7–12 ft (2–3.5 m)
From southern California and Mexico. Evergreen shrub with open branching habit. Pale gray or brown bark, downy twigs. Small leathery leaves with coarsely toothed margins rolled under, olive green above, white hairs below. Umbel-like heads of white flowers in spring. Zones 8–10.

Ceanothus × delileanus
☀ ❁ ↔ 5 ft (1.5 m) ↑ 5 ft (1.5 m)
Strong-growing, deciduous shrub, a hybrid between *C. americanus* and *C. coeruleus*. Broadly oval bright green leaves, panicles of soft blue flowers throughout the summer. One of the parents of the popular "French hybrids." Cultivars include 'Gloire de Versailles' and 'Topaze'. Zones 7–9.

Ceanothus divergens
CALISTOGA CEANOTHUS
☀ ❁ ↔ 4 ft (1.2 m) ↑ 3 ft (0.9 m)
Semi-prostrate evergreen species. Spine-toothed bright green leaves, gray undersides. Rather rigid branches covered with racemes of deep blue flowers in spring. Zones 7–9.

Ceanothus diversifolius
PINE-MAT
☀ ❁ ↔ 3–6 ft (0.9–1.8 m)
↑ 4–12 in (10–30 cm)
From California. Evergreen shrub with long flexible branches forming low clumps. Small pale bluish green leaves, hairy beneath. Tiny heads of white to pale blue flowers from spring–early summer. Zones 8–10.

Ceanothus fendleri
☀ ❁ ↔ 3–6 ft (0.9–1.8 m)
↑ 1–7 ft (0.3–2 m)
From southwestern USA and Mexico. Evergreen shrub, usually prostrate. Densely branched and spiny. Shoots and leaves downy. Small umbel-like clusters of bluish white flowers in early summer. Zones 5–10.

Ceanothus gloriosus
POINT REYES CREEPER
☀ ❁ ↔ 12 ft (3.5 m) ↑ 12 in (30 cm)
Occurring naturally on the central Californian coast. Prostrate shrub with dark green, glossy, toothed leaves. Clusters of lavender-blue

Ceanothus arboreus

Ceanothus griseus var. *horizontalis*
'Yankee Point'

Ceanothus hearstiorum

flowers, in spring. *C. g.* var. *exaltatus*, erect shrub to 6 ft (1.8 m) high; *C. g.* 'Anchor Bay', very dense foliage and mauve-blue flowers. Zones 7–9.

Ceanothus griseus

CARMEL CEANOTHUS

☼ ❋ ↔10 ft (3 m) ↑10 ft (3 m)

Native to hills of central California, shrub, with dark green leaves, gray beneath. Pale lilac-blue flowers in spring. New growth is arching. *C. g.* var. *horizontalis* is a low-growing form with a spreading habit; 'Diamond Heights', a form of 'Yankee Point', produces golden leaves blotched with dark green; 'Hurricane Point' has fast growing, light blue flowers; 'Yankee Point' ★ has bright blue flowers. Another form, *C. g.* 'Kurt Zalnik', discovered clinging precariously to an eroding cliff face, has extremely dark blue blooms, a height to 3 ft (0.9 m), and a spread of 15 ft (4.5 m). 'Santa Ana' has a spreading habit and bears deep blue flowers. Zones 8–10.

Ceanothus hearstiorum

☼ ❋ ↔6 ft (1.8 m) ↑12 in (30 cm)

From California. Previously thought a hybrid, now given species status. Prostrate, spreading, evergreen shrub. Small puckered leaves. Mid- to violet-blue flowers in small clusters from late spring–early summer. Zones 8–10.

C. g. var. *horizontalis* 'Hurricane Point'

Ceanothus impressus

SANTA BARBARA CEANOTHUS

☼ ❋ ↔10 ft (3 m) ↑10 ft (3 m)

Spreading evergreen shrub. The leaves are small, and deeply veined. The flowers are deep blue, and borne in small thin clusters, in spring. One of the hardiest evergreen species. Zones 8–10.

Ceanothus integerrimus

DEER BRUSH

☼ ❋ ↔3–7 ft (0.9–2 m) ↑3–7 ft (0.9–2 m)

Large semi-evergreen shrub with dull sea green leaves. Flowers in pale blue panicles in mid-summer. Zones 7–9.

Ceanothus × lobbianus

☼ ❋ ↔4 ft (1.2 m) ↑4 ft (1.2 m)

A natural hybrid between *C. dentatus* and *C. griseus*. Upright, relatively compact, densely branched, evergreen shrub. Toothed dark green leaves, hairy beneath. Flowers clear bright blue, borne in rounded panicles in late spring. Zones 8–10.

Ceanothus maritimus

MARITIME CEANOTHUS

☼ ❋ ↔36 in (90 cm) ↑12 in (30 cm)

From coastal areas of California. A mat-forming evergreen shrub. Small coarsely toothed leaves with margins rolled under, glossy dark green above,

Ceanothus maritimus

white hairs beneath. Flowers pale mauve to dark blue, in small round clusters, in spring. Zones 8–10.

Ceanothus oliganthus

☼ ❋ ↔3–7 ft (0.9–2 m) ↑3–10 ft (0.9–3 m)

From southern California. Evergreen shrub or small tree. Young branches hairy and tinged red. Leaves dark green and slightly hairy above, paler and hairier beneath. Small loose heads of dark blue to purple flowers in spring. *C. o.* var. *orcuttii* has pale blue flowers; *C. o.* var. *sorediatus* has pale to dark blue flowers. Zones 8–10.

Ceanothus ovatus

INLAND CEANOTHUS, REDROOT

☼/◑ ❋ ↔36 in (90 cm) ↑24–36 in (60–90 cm)

A dense deciduous shrub from New England to central USA. Summer foliage is shiny green, no autumn coloring. Dry seed capsules turn bright red in summer. Small white flowers. Zones 4–9.

Ceanothus papillosus

WART LEAF CEANOTHUS

☼ ❋ ↔3–10 ft (0.9–3 m) ↑3–17 ft (0.9–5 m)

From California. Evergreen shrub with lax downy branches. Narrow,

Ceanothus oliganthus var. *orcuttii*

oblong, dark green leaves, to 2 in (5 cm) long, hairy with prominent wart-like bumps. Pale to dark blue flowers in clusters either terminally or along branches, in spring. *C. p.* var. *roweanus* (Mt Tranquillon ceanothus, Rowe ceanothus) has narrower blunter leaves. Zones 8–10.

Ceanothus prostratus

MAHALA MATS, SQUAW CARPET

☼ ❋ ↔8 ft (2.4 m) ↑3 in (8 cm)

From high mountainous areas of Oregon and California, differing from other ceanothus in being subalpine. Creeping evergreen shrub making a dense mat, stems often rooting as they grow. Leaves toothed, dark green; flowers pale lavender-blue, in spring. *C. p.* var. *occidentalis* has wavy-edged wedge-shaped leaves. Zones 8–10.

Ceanothus prostratus var. *occidentalis*

Ceanothus papillosus var. *roweanus*

Ceanothus × lobbianus

Ceanothus pumilus
SISKIYOU-MAT

☼ ❄ ↔ 7 ft (2 m) ↑ 8 in (20 cm)

From northern California and south-western Oregon. Prostrate evergreen shrub. Hairy twigs. Leaves small, leathery, white hairs beneath. Produces small umbel-like clusters of white, mauve, or blue flowers in spring. Zones 7–10.

Ceanothus rigidus
MONTEREY CEANOTHUS

☼ ❄ ↔ 7 ft (2 m) ↑ 4 ft (1.2 m)

A densely branched spreading shrub. Distinctive, toothed, wedge-shaped, glossy leaves. Produces rather fuzzy

Ceanothus, Hybrid Cultivar, 'Blue Sapphire'

purple-blue flowers, in dense cymes, spring. 'Snowball' ★ bears white flowers and smaller leaves. Zones 8–10.

Ceanothus spinosus
GREEN BARK CEANOTHUS, RED-HEAT

☼ ❄ ↔ 7–12 ft (2–3.5 m) ↑ 7–20 ft (2–6 m)

From California and Mexico. Large evergreen shrub or small tree, smooth olive green bark, ascending spiny branches. Leathery, glossy, green leaves. White to pale blue flower clusters, to 6 in (15 cm) long, spring. Zones 8–10.

Ceanothus thyrsiflorus
BLUE BRUSH, BLUEBLOSSOM, CALIFORNIAN LILAC

☼ ❄ ↔ 20 ft (6 m) ↑ 20 ft (6 m)

Large shrub or small tree, fast growing, evergreen. Leaves dark green; flowers blue in dense clusters in early summer. Prune lightly after flowering. *C. t.* var. *repens*, a prostrate spreading shrub. Zones 7–9.

Ceanothus × veitchianus

☼ ❄ ↔ 10 ft (3 m) ↑ 10 ft (3 m)

From California, a natural hybrid of uncertain origin. Large evergreen

Ceanothus thyrsiflorus

shrub with small, glossy, wedge-shaped leaves with black tips. Lilac-blue flowers in early summer. Hardy and free flowering. Zones 7–9.

Ceanothus Hybrid Cultivars

☼ ❄ ↔ 4–12 ft (1.2–3.5 m) ↑ 6 in–15 ft (15 cm–4.5 m)

Ceanothus species hybridize readily making classification difficult. Almost every ceanothus in cultivation today is of hybrid origin. Various growth habits and flower color, although predominant shade is blue. 'A. T. Johnson', free-flowering, rich blue, fuzzy flowers in spring; 'Autumnal Blue', hardy floriferous evergreen, sky

Ceanothus thyrsiflorus var. *repens*

Ceanothus pumilus

blue flowers in late summer–autumn, leaves bright glossy green; 'Blue Cushion', rich blue flowers; 'Blue Mound', small to medium shrub, glossy green finely toothed leaves, bright blue flowers, late spring–early summer; 'Blue Jeans', shrub to 8 ft × 8 ft (2.4 m × 2.4 m), clips readily for hedging; powder blue flowers; 'Blue Sapphire', small free-flowering shrub, chocolate colored foliage, royal blue flowers; 'Burkwoodii', dense, compact, bushy shrub, bright blue flowers in late summer–autumn; 'Cascade', evergreen, spring flowering, powder blue flower clusters on long stalks; 'Concha', dense medium-sized shrub with arching branches, narrow dark green leaves, deep blue flowers; 'Dark Star', fragrant cobalt blue flowers; 'Delight', exceptionally hardy, with bright blue flowers in long panicles, in spring; 'Edwardsii', fast-growing tall shrub, deep blue flowers in dense clusters, in late spring, leaves glossy deep green, clear green beneath; 'Frosty Blue', dense dark green foliage, spiky clusters of deep blue flowers frosted with white; 'Gentian Plume', large open panicles of dark blue flowers in spring and autumn; 'Italian Skies', vigorous evergreen, deep blue flowers in late spring; 'Joyce Coulter', clusters of blue flowers; 'Julia Phelps' ★, purple-red buds opening to deep mauve flowers; 'Pershore Zanzibar' (syn. 'Zanzibar'), pale gold and dark green variegated foliage; 'Pin Cushion', a compact shrub with an arching habit; 'Puget Blue', an American-raised hybrid, bearing deep blue flowers in late

Ceanothus, Hybrid Cultivar, 'Pin Cushion'

Ceanothus, Hybrid Cultivar, 'Julia Phelps'

Ceanothus, Hybrid Cultivar, 'Blue Cushion'

Ceanothus, Hybrid Cultivar, 'Italian Skies'

spring–summer; '**Ray Hartman**', dark green leaves, hairy gray beneath, clusters of bright blue flowers; '**Snow Flurries**', pure white flowers in late summer–early autumn. Zones 7–10.

CECROPIA

From the Cecropiaceae family this genus of about 75 species of evergreen trees is from tropical America. *Cecropia* includes fast growing trees of the rainforest, with lobed umbrella-like leaves, and smooth, waxy, hollow branches, inhabited by ants. They feed on small nutritious appendages at the leaf bases, and repel the leaf-cutter ants that would otherwise consume the foliage. The flowers are small and of different sexes on different trees, borne on fleshy spikes emerging from the upper branches. Although they are short-lived, *Cecropia* species make a striking ornamental contribution to tropical gardens or large conservatories. Some species have been planted as a wood-pulp crop.
CULTIVATION: *Cecropia* are easily grown in the tropics and subtropics in reasonably fertile well-drained soil. They like a sunny sheltered position. Water well during the growing season. For indoor cultivation they require a large tub and a light open soil mix with frequent feeding. Propagate from seed if it is available, or from soft branch cuttings.

Cecropia peltata
GUAROMO, TRUMPET TREE
☼ ❄ ↔ 30 ft (9 m) ↑ 70 ft (21 m)
A common pioneer tree, with light pale wood. Broad open canopy. Leaves, white beneath, are 12 in (30 cm) across, and lobed to about half their depth. Hollow bluish white branches often inhabited by ants. Zones 10–12.

CEDRELA

This genus consists of 8 species of deciduous trees from tropical America belonging to the mahogany (Meliaceae) family. *Cedrela* members yield an aromatic lightweight timber, renowned for its use in cigar-boxes in Central America and the West Indies—hence they are known as "cigar-box cedars." Asian and Australian species once included in *Cedrela* are now treated as the distinct genus *Toona*. Of vigorous open habit, *Cedrela* trees have pinnate leaves with fairly large leaflets arranged in 2 regular rows. The flowers are small, rather inconspicuous, and borne in large panicles. The fruits are smallish capsules that split open to release winged seeds.
CULTIVATION: They are easily grown in any part of the tropics where rainfall is adequate, or in warm-temperate climates that are frost free. A deep loamy soil and a sheltered position make for best growth. *Cedrela* species provide interest in mixed tree plantings in parks and large gardens. Propagate from seed.

Cedrela odorata
CIGAR-BOX CEDAR
☼ ❄ ↔ 15 ft (4.5 m) ↑ 60 ft (18 m)
A tall fast-growing tree, open canopy and ascending lower limbs. Pinnate leaves are up to 2 ft (0.6 m) long. Zones 10–12.

CEDRONELLA

This genus, a member of the mint (Lamiaceae) family, contains a single species of perennial herb native to the Canary Islands. It is grown primarily for its aromatic foliage, which is used in herbal teas and potpourri. The spiky small pale flowers are of less consequence but nonetheless attractive.

Cecropia peltata

CULTIVATION: In cool areas grow in pots in the conservatory or treat as an annual outdoors. Elsewhere grow in a sunny position in well-drained soil. Propagation of *Cedronella canariensis* is from seed or cuttings.

Cedronella canariensis
syn. *Cedronella triphylla*
BALM OF GILEAD, CANARY BALM
☼ ❄ ↔ 1–3 ft (0.3–0.9 m) ↑ 2–4 ft (0.6–1.2 m)
Found on the Canary Islands. This is a somewhat shrubby perennial with trifoliate leaves comprised of fresh green lance-shaped leaflets. These leaves, when rubbed or crushed, release a strong balsamic scent. The spikes of the small tubular two-lipped flowers are pale pink to lilac. Zones 9–11.

CEDRUS
TRUE CEDAR
The Roman poet Virgil (70–19 BC) said of the cedar, "with the oil whereof the ancients anointed their books, to keep them from being worm-eaten." *Cedrus* come from widely separated regions in northwest Africa, Turkey, Lebanon, and the western Himalayas. They are large long-lived trees from the pine (Pinaceae) family, with needle-like leaves arranged spirally on the leading shoots at the branch tip; crowding on the short lateral shoots to form neat rosettes. Both the male and female cones are large and conspicuous; the seeds have papery wings. All the cedars are somewhat similar in appearnce,

Cedrela odorata

and are sometimes treated as varieties or subspecies of a single species, or 2 species (*C. libani* and *C. deodara*). The classification that is favored by gardeners recognizes the 4 species described here.
CULTIVATION: Cedars are fairly frost hardy but cannot be grown in the more severe northern climates. They adapt to a range of soil types, if the soil is of moderate depth and fertility, and there is subsoil moisture available. These trees do not normally require any pruning to keep them in good shape. Planting out is best done when still at a small size. Propagation is from seed except for the cultivars, which must be grafted.

Cedronella canariensis

Ceiba pentandra

Cedrus deodara

Cedrus atlantica

syn. *Cedrus libani* subsp. *atlantica*
ATLANTIC CEDAR, ATLAS CEDAR
☀ ❄ ↔ 30 ft (9 m) ↕ 80 ft (24 m)

From the Atlas and Rif Mountains of Morocco and Algeria. Young trees are conical with stiff erect leading shoots, ageing to broad-headed. The needles are crowded on the short shoots into tight neat rosettes. Foliage varies from rather bluish to green. '**Aurea**', with distinctive golden yellow-tipped foliage. The **Glauca Group** are particularly blue and are usually grafted trees. '**Glauca Pendula**' ★ has an extraordinary form, requiring support of the long branches from which foliage sweeps to the ground. '**Pendula**' is a striking clone with all growths completely pendulous, forming a curtain of bluish gray foliage, hanging down to 10 ft (3 m) or more. Zones 6–9.

Cedrus brevifolia

syn. *Cedrus libani* subsp. *brevifolia*
CYPRUS CEDAR
☀ ❄ ↔ 20 ft (6 m) ↕ 50 ft (15 m)

Not well known in cultivation, native to the southern mountains of Cyprus. A small tree, very short grayish green needles, mostly under ½ in (12 mm) long. Zones 6–9.

Cedrus deodara

DEODAR, DEODAR CEDAR
☀ ❄ ↔ 30 ft (9 m) ↕ 200 ft (60 m)

Native to the western Himalayas from Afghanistan to western Nepal, this is the largest of the cedars. It has a spire-like crown with lower branches resting on the ground. Leading shoots are drooping with soft green needles. Seed cones are barrel-shaped. '**Aurea**' has pale yellowish new growth, changing to darker lime green. Zones 7–10.

Cedrus libani

CEDAR OF LEBANON
☀ ❄ ↔ 90 ft (27 m) ↕ 150 ft (45 m)

In Lebanon the famous cedars now grow only on Mt Lebanon. Young trees, narrowly conical in form, with stiff leading shoots and grayish green leaves. Old trees have massive horizontally spreading limbs. '**Golden Dwarf**' (syn. 'Aurea-Prostrata') is a dwarf form. Zones 5–9.

CEIBA

syn. *Chorisia*

About 10 species of tropical American deciduous trees make up this genus of the kapok (Bombacaceae) family. *Ceiba* species are tall stout-trunked trees with smooth bark armed with large conical prickles. Leaves are compound with leaflets radiating from the end of leaf stalk. Flowers are cream to yellow, pink, or red, and carried in loose panicles toward branch tips. The fruit is a large green capsule enclosing seeds buried in cottonwool-like hairs called kapok, once used for stuffing pillows.
CULTIVATION: They thrive in lowland tropics or in subtropical regions; best in climates with a summer rainfall and a distinct dry season, in deep, well-drained, alluvial soils and a reasonably sheltered position. Early growth is fast, full height attained in only 10 to 20 years. Propagate from freshly gathered seed or half-hardened cuttings in summer.

Ceiba pentandra

syn. *Chorisia insignis*
KAPOK TREE
☀ ☂ ↔ 80 ft (24 m) ↕ 230 ft (70 m)

Regarded in Africa as the tallest native tree. High open canopy, massive trunk, large buttresses. Cream to dull yellow or pink flowers on pendent stalks from bare branch tips before the new leaves. Elongated pods about 6 in (15 cm) long. Zones 11–12.

Cedrus libani

Cedrus atlantica

Ceiba speciosa

Celmisia prorepens

Ceiba speciosa

syn. *Chorisia speciosa*

PINK FLOSS-SILK TREE

☀ ❋ ↔ 40 ft (12 m) ↑ 60 ft (18 m)

Widespread in tropical South America, where a distinct cool dry season is experienced. It has a highly ornamental, yellowish green trunk, thickest near the ground, and a crown of broadly spreading limbs. Spectacular pink to reddish pink flowers in late summer–winter. Zones 9–11.

CELASTRUS

Although often twining and usually considered as climbers, many of the 30-odd species in this genus, from the spindle-tree (Celastraceae) family, are shrubs that can be grown as free-standing plants or trained against a wall as espaliers. Widespread except in Eurasia, most are deciduous, with rather thin leaves that often have serrated edges. Most species have separate male and female plants; flowers of both sexes are small and cream to green in color occurring in small panicles. Both sexes are required to produce the showy fruit, which is a dry capsule containing a brightly colored fleshy aril, revealed as the capsule splits open.

CULTIVATION: Easily grown in any well-drained soil in sun or half-sun, *Celastrus* species vary in hardiness but are generally tolerant of moderate frosts. They should be cut back immediately after fruiting, or in spring, and can be pruned quite severely if necessary. Propagate from seed, layers, or half-hardened summer cuttings.

Celmisia spectabilis

Celastrus orbiculatus

ORIENTAL BITTERSWEET

☀ ❋ ↔ unlimited ↑ 30 ft (9 m)

From temperate northeastern Asia. Deciduous, needs regular trimming to keep compact. Wiry stems tangled, interwoven, light green leaves. Flowers form in the leaf axils. Colorful fruit, splits open in autumn revealing orange-yellow interior and pink arils. Zones 4–9.

Celastrus scandens

AMERICAN BITTERSWEET

☀ ❋ ↔ unlimited ↑ 20 ft (6 m)

From North America. Spreading as a large-scale ground cover. Leaves 4 in (10 cm) long, serrated, oblong, tapering quickly to a point. Yellow-green flowers in summer. Clusters of fruits open to reveal yellow interior and pinkish red arils. Zones 3–10.

CELMISIA

MOUNTAIN DAISY, SNOW DAISY

Mainly from New Zealand, with a few species in southeastern Australia, this daisy (Asteraceae) family genus encompasses some 60 species of perennials and subshrubs that frequently occur in subalpine and alpine regions where they often dominate the vegetation and may carpet large areas. They form basal rosettes or tufts of simple narrow leaves, sometimes ribbed, often with a covering of downy hair on the undersides. This hair can also cover the upper surfaces of young leaves. Woody stems can develop at the base, especially among the larger spreading species. The flowerheads are simple daisies with white ray florets around a central swelling of golden-yellow disc florets. They are borne one head to a stem and appear mainly around mid-summer.

CULTIVATION: While a few species adapt well to cultivation, many are difficult to grow outside their natural environment. They prefer a cool-summer temperate climate and should be planted in gritty, humus-rich, moist, well-drained soil in full or half-sun. Propagate from seed or by division.

Celmisia incana

☀/◐ ❋ ↔ 24–60 in (60–150 cm) ↑ 4 in (10 cm)

From Canterbury to Coromandel, New Zealand. Spreading woody stems form mats of short white to silver-gray leaves. The 1½ in (35 mm) wide flowerheads are borne on short stems. Zones 7–9.

Celmisia prorepens

☀/◐ ❋ ↔ 8–40 in (20–100 cm) ↑ 4–6 in (10–15 cm)

From southeastern South Island, New Zealand. Forms mats of sometimes widely spaced rosettes of spatula-shaped green leaves, no covering of hair. Small flowerheads on red-tinted stems. Zones 7–9.

Celmisia sessiliflora

WHITE CUSHION DAISY

☀/◐ ❋ ↔ 6–40 in (15–100 cm) ↑ 2–6 in (5–15 cm)

From South and Stewart Islands, New Zealand, common at altitude. Densely branched subshrub forming cushions of stiff, thick, silvery leaves less than 1 in (25 mm) long. Flowerheads abundant, usually at foliage level. Zones 7–9.

Celmisia spectabilis

COTTON DAISY, COTTON PLANT

☀/◐ ❋ ↔ 20–48 in (50–120 cm) ↑ 8–12 in (20–30 cm)

New Zealand species, found from the central North Island southward. The leaves are shining, bright green, 4–6 in (10–15 cm) long with silver to buff-colored hairs, and grow in dense tufts. Can spread with age as a dense ground cover. Flowerheads to 2 in (5 cm) wide, on sturdy downy stems. Zones 7–9.

Celmisia tomentella

syn. *C. asteliifolia* in part

BOG CELMISIA, SILVER SNOW-DAISY

☀ ❋ ↔ 36 in (90 cm) ↑ 12–18 in (30–45 cm)

One of 3 species from the alpine regions of southeastern mainland Australia, and often common in boggy areas. Has a scaly creeping rhizome; narrow pointed leaves to 12 in (30 cm) long, and silvery on both surfaces. Flowerheads up to 2½ in (5 cm) in diameter, in summer–autumn. Prefers a well-drained soil in cultivation. Zones 8–9.

Celmisia tomentella, in the wild, Kosciuszko National Park, New South Wales, Australia

CELOSIA

COCKSCOMB, WOOLFLOWER

Found in the tropics of Asia, Africa, and the Americas, this genus of around 50 species of annuals and perennials belongs to the amaranth (Amaranthaceae) family. The name *Celosia* comes from a Greek word, *keleos*, meaning burning, which is a very appropriate reference to the flame-like color and shape of the flowerhead. *C. argentea* var. *cristata*, an annual, is the only widely cultivated species and it has been developed into many variably flowered and colored seedling strains. Upright plants, some are up to 6 ft (1.8 m) tall, though most are far smaller. They have simple lance-shaped leaves up to 6 in (15 cm) long and tiny vivid yellow, orange, or red flowers massed in upright plumes or combs (cristate).

CULTIVATION: Although as an annual it can be grown far outside its natural tropical range, *Celosia* needs ample warmth to perform well. Plant in fertile well-drained soil in full sun and water well. Raise from seed.

Celosia argentea var. *cristata*, Plumosa Group, Apricot Brandy

Celosia argentea

☼/◐ ✢ ↔ 16–24 in (40–60 cm) ↑ 3–7 ft (0.9–2 m)

Quick-growing annual widespread in the tropics. Leaves lance-shaped to 6 in (15 cm) long. Tiny white flowers in upright spikes to 3 in (8 cm) long. Usually seen as ***C. a.* var. *cristata;*** cultivated forms available with green, purple, or red foliage and many flower colors and styles. Divided into groups: **Childsii Group**, rounded to globose flowerheads; **Cristata** or **Cockscomb Group**, flowerheads terminal, flattened and broad, resembling a rooster's comb; **Plumosa Group**, upright plumes of flowers, not always terminal, though axillary flowerheads usually smaller than terminal; **Apricot Brandy**, 14 in (35 cm) tall, orange plumes, green foliage; **Forest Fire**, 24 in (60 cm) tall, vivid red plumes, red foliage; **Castle Mix**, compact and heavy-flowering, available in wide color range and with green or red-tinted foliage, usually with color name, such as **Pink Castle**, or **Yellow Castle**; **New Look**, 14 in (35 cm) tall, branching habit, red plumes, red foliage; **Venezuela**, crimson flowers; **Pyramidalis Group**, flowerheads broad-based, tapering evenly to a point, often included with Plumosa Group. Zones 11–12.

Celosia spicata

Celosia argentea var. *cristata*, Plumosa Group, Castle Mix

Celosia argentea var. *cristata*, Plumosa Group, Forest Fire

Celosia argentea var. *cristata*

C. a. var. *cristata*, Plumosa, Venezuela

Celosia spicata

☼ ✢ ↔ 12 in (30 cm) ↑ 24–36 in (60–90 cm)

Summer-flowering annual. Narrow upright flowerheads, usually in silvery metallic shades of pink or yellow. Zones 10–12.

CELTIS

Occurring in all continents and many larger islands, the large, mainly tropical and mainly evergreen genus *Celtis*, consists of over 100 species. Belonging to the elm (Ulmaceae) family, the genus has the characteristic leaf shape with usually toothed margins and asymmetric base. Flowers are greenish and inconspicuous, male and female separate on the one tree. Small berry-like fruit with thin but sugary flesh concealing a hard stone; in most species they ripen to black or dark brown, greedily eaten by birds. Some species become troublesome weed trees when cultivated outside their native lands.

CULTIVATION: Vigorous growers, they adapt well to tough environments such as urban streets and parks, tolerating a wide range of soil conditions. The deciduous species make fine shade trees. Propagate from seed, which in the case of temperate species should be cold-stratified for 2 to 3 months before sowing in spring; germination is often erratic.

C. a. var. *cristata*, Plumosa Group, New Look

Celtis australis

EUROPEAN NETTLE-TREE

☼ ❄ ↔ 60 ft (18 m) ↑ 60 ft (18 m)

Found throughout southern Europe, northwest Africa, and the eastern Mediterranean region. Deciduous, rounded canopy, smooth gray-barked trunk. Leaves have saw-toothed edges with a slender point, dense short hairs beneath. Berries ripen bright orange to dark brown, in summer. Can be invasive. Zones 8–11.

Celtis laevigata
syn. *Celtis mississippiensis*
SUGAR HACKBERRY, SUGARBERRY

☼ ❄ ↔ 60 ft (18 m) ↑ 80 ft (24 m)

Native to southeastern USA. Deciduous, smooth dark gray bark. Leaves thin, hairless, very one-sided at base, finely tapered at the apex, with teeth in upper part. Fruit is orange, ripening to purple-black, in autumn. Zones 6–11.

Celtis occidentalis
AMERICAN HACKBERRY

☼ ❄ ↔ 60 ft (18 m) ↑ 60 ft (18 m)

Widely distributed in northern USA. Deciduous, low-branching; smooth, gray, bark, developing rows of corky pustules, becoming dark and closely furrowed with age. Leaves are broad, toothed, pale yellow in autumn. Fruit ripens red to dark purple in autumn. **'Prairie Pride'**, dense bushy crown. Zones 3–10.

Centaurea cyanus

Celtis reticulata
syn. *Celtis douglasii*
NETLEAF HACKBERRY

☼ ❄ ↔ 25 ft (8 m) ↑ 25 ft (8 m)

From the mountains of western USA and Mexico, deciduous species similar to *C. occidentalis*. Pea-sized orange-red fruits. Native Americans mixed the pounded fruit with animal fat and cornmeal as a food item. Zones 6–10.

Celtis sinensis
syn. *Celtis japonica*
CHINESE HACKBERRY, CHINESE NETTLE-TREE

☼ ❄ ↔ 50 ft (15 m) ↑ 60 ft (18 m)

Occurring in eastern Asia. Deciduous or semi-evergreen. Broad irregular canopy. The bark is relatively smooth, leaden gray. The leaves are glossy dark green above, olive green beneath, with toothed edges. Small, globe-shaped, summer fruits ripen from yellow to orange to black. Zones 8–12.

Celtis australis

Celtis reticulata

Celtis occidentalis

Celtis sinensis

Centaurea dealbata

CENTAUREA
CORNFLOWER, KNAPWEED, STAR THISTLE

Widespread in temperate zones, this daisy (Asteraceae) family genus encompasses around 450 species of annuals, perennials, and subshrubs. A variable lot, most readily identifiable by their thistle-like flowerheads, which emerge from an egg-shaped receptacle known as an involucre. Flowerheads often have distinctly different inner and outer florets, with the outer having 5 narrow petals. Flower colors include white, yellow, pink, blue, and mauve. Plant size varies; common features are pinnate foliage, often silver-gray, and an upright habit. Some species have been used to treat wounds; named after the Greek mythological centaur, half-horse, half-man, famed for his healing powers.
CULTIVATION: Plant in full sun, light well-drained soil. Good ventilation will lessen any mildew problems. Annuals like common cornflower (*C. cyanus*) raised from seed; perennials also propagated by division or from softwood cuttings of non-flowering stems.

Centaurea americana

☼ ❄ ↔ 12–20 in (30–50 cm) ↑ 32–40 in (80–100 cm)

Annual from south-central and southeastern USA. Sparsely toothed, lanceshaped, green leaves to 4 in (10 cm) long. Flowerheads white to pale mauve or purple. Zones 4–10.

Centaurea cineraria ★
syn. *Centaurea gymnocarpa*
DUSTY MILLER

☼ ❄ ↔ 12–24 in (30–60 cm) ↑ 20–36 in (50–90 cm)

From western and southern Italy. Perennial sometimes treated as an

Centaurea dealbata 'Steenbergii'

annual. Very decorative silver-gray pinnate leaves, Flowerheads purple-pink. Zones 4–9.

Centaurea cyanus
BACHELOR'S BUTTON, BLUEBOTTLE, CORNFLOWER

☼ ❄ ↔ 8–16 in (20–40 cm) ↑ 12–36 in (30–90 cm)

Annual or biennial from temperate Eurasia. Narrow green to blue-green leaves, sometimes silvery when young. Flowerheads usually blue in species but garden forms include white and wide range of pink and blue shades. Deadheading prolongs flowering. **'Blue Diadem'**, large, ruffled, double, deep blue heads; and the **Florence Series**, dwarf strain, which grows to around 14 in (35 cm) high and covers wide color range. Zones 2–10.

Centaurea dealbata
PERSIAN CORNFLOWER

☼ ❄ ↔ 16–24 in (40–60 cm) ↑ 32–40 in (80–100 cm)

Caucasian and northern Iranian perennial with pinnate leaves, green above, and gray furry below. Pink to purple flowerheads. **'Steenbergii'**, large vigorous cultivar with deep pink flowerheads. Zones 3–9.

C

Centaurea hypoleuca 'John Coutts'

Centaurea macrocephala

Centaurea montana

Centaurea hypoleuca

☼ ❋ ↔ 12–18 in (30–45 cm)
↑ 16–24 in (40–60 cm)

Perennial found from Turkey to northern Iran. Variably shaped foliage, green and sparsely hairy above, grayish covering of hair below. Pink to purple-red flowerheads. 'John Coutts', large deep purple-pink flowerheads. Zones 5–9.

Centaurea macrocephala

GLOBE CORNFLOWER

☼ ❋ ↔ 20–24 in (50–60 cm)
↑ 32–40 in (80–100 cm)

Erect perennial native to the Caucasus region. Green lance-shaped leaves covered with minute silvery hairs. Large yellow flowerheads. Zones 3–9.

Centaurea montana

MOUNTAIN BLUET, PERENNIAL CORNFLOWER

☼ ❋ ↔ 12–40 in (30–100 cm)
↑ 24–32 in (60–80 cm)

Perennial from mountains of Europe. Spreads by rhizomes and may form large clump of broad, green, lance-shaped leaves, sometimes pinnate at base. Flowerheads violet to purple-blue. 'Alba', low-growing, white-flowered cultivar. Zones 3–9.

Centaurea simplicicaulis

☼ ❋ ↔ 12–27 in (30–70 cm)
↑ 12–20 in (30–50 cm)

Low mounding perennial from the Caucasus region and western Asia. Spreads by rhizomes to form a clump of whorls of green to gray-green leaves with silver-gray hairs below. Deep pink flowerheads. Zones 4–9.

CENTELLA

This genus of some 50 species, largely from southern Africa with one widespread in warmer parts of the world, belongs to the carrot (Apiaceae) family. They are creeping or scrambling to erect perennials, sometimes woody at the base. The leaves are simple, linear to broadly kidney-shaped, solitary or grouped. The reddish or dirty white flowers are small, usually hermaphrodite and in simple umbels, sometimes stalked, arising from the nodes.

CULTIVATION: Only *C. asiatica* is in cultivation, as a medicinal plant, but it has no value for ornament. It is easily grown outdoors in moist fertile soil in any warm climate, or as a summer annual in climates with severe winter frost and snow. Spreads rapidly,

Centaurea montana 'Alba'

if left unchecked, and can become invasive. Propagate from rooted runners or from seed.

Centella asiatica

syn. *Hydrocotyle asiatica*

☼/☀ ❖ ↔ 12–36 in (30–90 cm)
↑ 2–12 in (5–30 cm)

Pantropical and Southern Hemisphere. Creeping perennial with prostrate stems rooting at nodes. Leaves of variable size, stalks up to 12 in (30 cm) long and kidney-shaped to rounded blades to 2 in (5 cm) across, notched at base, margins angular-toothed. Flowers tiny, reddish, in summer–autumn. Cultivated for its edible leaves as well as for a cover crop; constituent of western skin ointments promoting rapid healing. Zones 9–12.

CENTRADENIA

There are 4 to 5 species of evergreen perennials or subshrubs in this genus which belongs to the melastoma (Melastomataceae) family. They are native to Central America and Mexico. The leaves are simple and opposite with well-defined veining, somewhat velvety, and often flushed with red on the undersides. The small pink or mauve flowers are borne in panicles either terminally or along the branches.

CULTIVATION: In cool areas grow in the conservatory or greenhouse in filtered light in a well-drained sandy loam. Water well during the growing season. In warm areas grow outdoors in a well-drained soil in sun or half-sun. Pinch out growing tips to maintain a dense habit. Propagate from seed or cuttings.

Centradenia inaequilateralis 'Cascade'

Centradenia inaequilateralis

☼/☀ ❖ ↔ 12 in (30 cm) ↑ 12 in (30 cm)

Native to Mexico. Broadly oval leaves, slightly hairy, tinged with red beneath. Pink flowers in winter. 'Cascade' has a weeping habit. Suitable for pots and hanging baskets. Zones 10–11.

CENTRANTHUS

VALERIAN

This genus consists of 12 species of annual and perennial subshrubs from Europe and the Mediterranean, of which only one, *C. ruber*, is widely cultivated. Forming clumps of upright stems with simple, lance-shaped, blue-green leaves and topped with inflorescences of tiny honey-scented flowers, the species can be 2–5 ft (0.6–1.5 m) tall. The flowers are most often a dusky crimson shade but may be white or pink. Although known as valerian and in the valerian (Valerianaceae) family, none of the species has the medicinal properties found in true valerian (*Valeriana officinalis*).

CULTIVATION: They are very easily grown in any sunny well-drained position. Alkaline soil is preferred but not essential. Plants are drought tolerant and very adaptable. To prevent seeding, cut back flower stems as soon as they fade. *C. ruber* is inclined to self-sow and is considered a weed in parts of New Zealand.

Centranthus angustifolius

NARROW-LEAFED VALERIAN

☼/☀ ❋ ↔ 20–27 in (50–70 cm)
↑ 20–32 in (50–80 cm)

Southern European native with narrow, bright green, lance- to spatula-shaped leaves. Basal leaves are lobed and more rounded. Spring and summer heads of small lavender-pink flowers with conspicuous lower lobes. Zones 7–10.

Centranthus ruber

JUPITER'S BEARD, RED VALERIAN

☼/☀ ❋ ↔ 16–27 in (40–70 cm)
↑ 32–40 in (80–100 cm)

Found in Europe, North Africa, and western Asia. Blue-green oval to lance-shaped leaves, are sometimes finely

Centranthus angustifolius

Centranthus ruber 'Albus'

Centranthus ruber

toothed, to 3 in (8 cm) long. Tiny, fragrant, deep rose pink to red flowers massed in upright heads. 'Albus' has white flowers. Zones 6–10.

CENTROPOGON

Allied to *Lobelia* in the bellflower (Campanulaceae) family, this genus of about 230 species of evergreen shrubs, subshrubs, and perennials is confined to Central and South America and the West Indies; most grow in misty mountain forests, sometimes as epiphytes. The stems are erect, trailing, or scrambling over other vegetation; the simple leaves are toothed or entire, alternate or opposite. Brightly colored flowers arise from upper leaf axils on long stalks; corolla tube often curved downward, lobes hooded or recurved. *Centropogon* differs from *Lobelia* in its long protruding style with fringe of hairs on the stigma (the genus name is the Greek for bearded spur), adapting the flowers to pollination by hummingbirds. The fruit is a fleshy berry, edible in some species.
CULTIVATION: They can be grown outdoors in frost-free climates in sheltered humid situations. Coming from cooler tropical mountains, they may not adapt to the hot lowlands. In cooler climates they have occasionally been grown as conservatory plants in botanical collections. Growing media and other requirements should be similar to those for fuchsias. Propagate from cuttings or from seed.

Centropogon costaricae
☀ ⚘ ↔ 3 ft (0.9 m) ↑ 5 ft (1.5 m)
From the highlands of Costa Rica at elevations of 5,000–10,000 ft (1,500–3,000 m); erect shrub with narrow leaves, their edges and veins on underside red; flowers orange-red, in summer–autumn. Zones 9–11.

Centropogon talamancensis
☀/◑ ⚘ ↔ 5 ft (1.5 m) ↑ 3 ft (0.9 m)
From the mountains of southern Costa Rica at elevations of 8,000–12,000 ft (2,400–3,600 m); soft subshrub with scrambling branches, erect flowering shoots, broad finely toothed leaves; flowers are deep pink to crimson, in summer–autumn. Zones 9–11.

CEPHALANTHUS

This genus, belonging to the madder (Rubiaceae) family, and comprised of only 10 or so species of deciduous or evergreen shrubs and trees has a wide distribution, occurring in temperate to tropical parts of Africa, Asia, and the Americas. They are commonly known as buttonbushes because their very small flowers are borne in rounded button-like heads that are sometimes backed by small bracts. Firm top-shaped fruits follow. The leaves vary in size and shape but are usually a deep

Centropogon talamancensis

green, often tinted with red, especially on the veins, midribs, or stalks.
CULTIVATION: Hardiness varies depending on where the species has come from, with those from the tropics withstanding little or no frost, while the ones that are native to North America are very cold tolerant. All species of *Cephalanthus* adapt well to garden conditions and thrive in any moist well-drained soil with a position in full or half-sun. Trim if necessary and propagate from seed or cuttings.

Cephalanthus occidentalis
BUTTONBUSH
☀ ❄ ↔ 10 ft (3 m) ↑ 20 ft (6 m)
Evergreen or deciduous, depending on winter frosts; shrub or small tree, found in damp soil near lakes or streams. Pointed elliptical to lance-shaped leaves. White to cream lightly scented flowerheads in summer. Zones 5–11.

CEPHALARIA

There are about 65 species of annual and perennial herbs in this genus, belonging to the teasel (Dipsacaceae) family. Found from Europe to central Asia and Africa, they are often called giant scabious because of their resemblance to the closely related *Scabiosa* genus. Plants form clumps of toothed or divided leaves from which arise tall flowering stems. Tight spherical heads open into overlapping ruffs of mostly white to yellow florets reminiscent of daisies. The seed heads are also attractive, being round with soft bristles and a honeycombed appearance.
CULTIVATION: Grow in full sun in moderately fertile, well-drained, but moisture-retentive soil. Most species are suitable for naturalizing in the wild garden. Propagate from seed or by division.

Cephalaria gigantea
GIANT SCABIOUS
☀ ❄ ↔ 24–48 in (60–120 cm)
↑ 4–8 ft (1.2–2.4 m)
From the Caucasus region and Siberia. Robust perennial with large, dark green, pinnate leaves. Tall branching stems of creamy yellow flowers in summer. *Cephalaria gigantea* needs plenty of room to spread in the border. Zones 4–9.

Cephalanthus occidentalis

Centropogon costaricae, in the wild, Cerro de la Muerte, Costa Rica

CEPHALOCEREUS

This genus contains 5 species belonging to the cactus (Cactaceae) family. Many attempts have been made to classify the columnar cacti of Mexico. No doubt further reclassification will occur as research, including DNA testing, throws more light on the true relationship between *Cephalocereus* and related genera, *Carnegia, Lemaireocereus, Mitrocereus, Neobuxbaumia, Neodawsonia, Pachycereus,* and *Pilosocereus*. The International Cactaceae Systemics Group has already recognized 5 species. The genus was established in 1838, its name is derived from the Greek, *cephale* meaning head, with reference to the pseudocephalium—the area of thick wool and bristles normally found on the northern side of mature stems, through which flowers are produced in summer.

CULTIVATION: They are easy to cultivate in a mineral-rich well-drained soil. They may be raised from seed or from cuttings that have been dried out for a week or two. Rest in winter.

Cephalocereus columna-trajani
syn. *Cephalocereus hoppenstedtii*
☀ ❀ ↔16 in (40 cm) ↑25–35 ft (8–10 m)
From Puebla, Mexico. Spectacular columnar cactus, forms large stands

that look like a forest of telegraph poles. Ribs 15 to 25, areoles woolly, especially at the growing tip. Spines 5 to 8 centrals, 2½–3 in (6–8 cm) long, grayish, 15 to 20 white radials. Pseudocephalium is usually about 3 in (8 cm) wide and up to 7–10 ft (2–3 m) long on the northern side of mature stems. Flowers 3 in (8 cm) wide, white to yellow. Zones 9–11.

Cephalocereus senilis
OLD MAN CACTUS, OLD MAN OF MEXICO
☀ ❀ ↔12–16 in (30–40 cm) ↑50 ft (15 m)
From Hidalgo, Guanajuato, and the Metztitlan Valley of Mexico. This is a very popular and easily recognized cactus because of the distinctive long, twisted, gray or white spines that cover the stem of the plant and give it its species name, *senilis* meaning aged, because it looks like a bearded old man. The plants are solitary or branched from the base, slow growing, and can eventually reach over 40 ft (12 m) in the wild. Ribs 20 to 30. Spines strong, 1 to 5 grayish white centrals, 20 to 30 white hair-like radials, thin, twisted. Pseudocephalium on side of mature branches, later covering growing point. Flowers are bell-shaped, apricot, 3–4 in (8–10 cm) wide. The seed pods are oval. Zones 9–11.

CEPHALOPHYLLUM

This genus of about 30 species of leaf-succulents from southern Namibia and surrounding regions belongs to the ice-plant (Aizoaceae) family. Closely related to *Argyroderma*, whose species usually have solitary flowers and differ in the structure of their fruit capsules. The plants are low and creeping, rarely erect and shrubby. In cross-section the leaves are triangular near the tip, rounded near the base. Flowers are rarely solitary and petals are yellow, purple, or white in various combinations, the stamens often of a contrasting color. Capsules (called "tumble fruits") in some species become detached and, as they are blown over the land, disperse the seeds.

CULTIVATION: Grow outside in regions with no winter rainfall, or in a greenhouse in temperate regions. Need full sun, low humidity, and infrequent watering (none at all in winter). Propagate from seed or cuttings allowed to dry before rooting.

Cephalophyllum alstonii
☀/☀ ❀ ↔20 in (50 cm) ↑4 in (10 cm)
From Namibia and Western Cape region of South Africa. Spotted, gray-green, cylindrical leaves to nearly 3 in (8 cm) long. Vivid red flowers with purple-red stamens, to 3 in (8 cm) wide. Zones 9–11.

Cephalophyllum diversiphyllum
syn. *Cephalophyllum loreum*
☀/☀ ❀ ↔20 in (50 cm)
↑4–6 in (10–15 cm)
From Western Cape region. The leaves are green, to 4 in (10 cm) long, roughly cylindrical but with flattened base and tapered, in rosettes. The flowers are yellow with red-tinted undersides, and very large. The seed pods open to reveal an intricate internal structure. Zones 9–11.

Cephalophyllum 'Red Spike'
☀/☀ ❀ ↔20 in (50 cm) ↑6 in (15 cm)
Another species from South Africa's Western Cape region. The narrow, blue-gray, cylindrical leaves grow to over 3 in (8 cm) long. Vivid red-pink flowers, stamens with purple tint. Zones 9–11.

Cephalophyllum subulatoides
☀/☀ ❀ ↔20 in (50 cm) ↑6 in (15 cm)
From southwest Cape region. Leaves tapered, cylindrical, green to gray-green with red spots and becoming red-tinted in sun, especially at the tips, to nearly 3 in (8 cm) long. Purplish to purple-red flowers to 1¾ in (40 mm) in diameter. Zones 9–11.

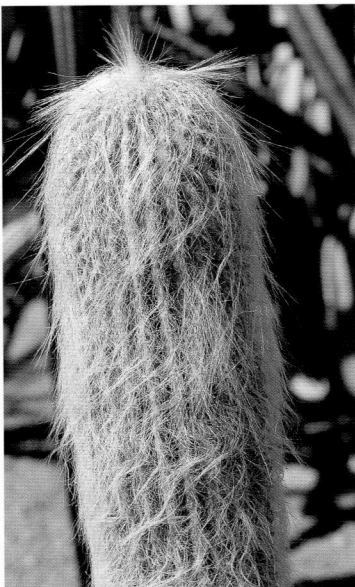

Cephalocereus senilis

Cephalophyllum tricolorum
☀/☀ ❀ ↔20 in (50 cm) ↑6 in (15 cm)
From Western Cape region. Finely spotted, pale green to gray-green, tapered, cylindrical leaves to around 3 in (8 cm) long. Flower petals yellow with purple-red base, stamens and underside of petal tips red, to 2 in (5 cm) wide. Zones 9–11.

CEPHALOTAXUS
PLUM YEW

This interesting genus of conifers consists of 6 or more species, mostly found in China. In foliage features they resemble the yews *(Taxus)* but on female plants the ovules and the plum-like seeds that develop from them are crowded onto stalked head-like cones. On male plants the pollen cones are likewise crowded into small knob-like heads. The genus is now placed in a separate family, Cephalotaxaceae. All species are shrubs or small trees with flaky brown or reddish bark, often multi-stemmed and suckering from ground level.

CULTIVATION: Tough flexible plants that adapt to a wide range of soils and climates, they tolerate exposed positions as well as partial shade, preferring a climate with adequate steady rainfall throughout the year. They are excellent for hedging as they withstand frequent trimming. Propagation is easily achieved from cuttings, preferably taken from leading shoots. Cold stratification is normally used to germinate seed in a nursery.

Cephalotaxus fortunei
FORTUNE'S PLUM YEW
☀ ❄ ↔10 ft (3 m) ↑20 ft (6 m)
Introduced to Britain in 1849 by Scottish plant explorer Robert Fortune.

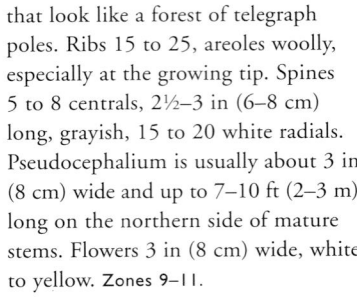

Cephalophyllum alstonii

Cephalotaxus fortunei

Cephalophyllum subulatoides

Whorled branches; linear, gently curved, finely pointed leaves, 2 white bands beneath, arranged in 2 rows. Oval seeds ripen to glossy purplish brown. Zones 7–10.

Cephalotaxus harringtonia
JAPANESE PLUM YEW

☼ ❄ ↔ 10 ft (3 m) ↑ 15 ft (4.5 m)

A spreading shrub, sometimes a small tree. Branches occur alternately, olive green leaves, arranged in 2 rows, narrowed at the tip. Seeds similar to those of *C. fortunei*. *C. h.* var. *drupacea* ★, with short stiff leaves, rows arranged in a neat V-shape. *C. h.* 'Fastigiata' has erect branches densely crowded into a column. Zones 6–10.

CEPHALOTUS
ALBANY PITCHER PLANT, WESTERN AUSTRALIAN PITCHER PLANT

A carnivorous pitcher plant and the only genus in the Cephalotaceae family. It is only found on the southwestern coast of Western Australia in peaty swamps and damp sandy soil. Its small but very strong pitchers resemble little moccasins. Although a perennial, its growth slows and sometimes stops in the cool winters. In spring the plant produces non-carnivorous waxy leaves; as the weather warms, the carnivorous pitchers develop. Formed in a rosette, the outward-facing pitchers are covered in fine white hairs. The pitchers have a central rib and 2 side ribs that slope toward the opening. The rim of the pitcher is also ribbed. In half-sun the pitchers are bright green but in full sun they turn beautiful dark burgundy.

Cerastium arvense

Cerastium boissieri

Insects are attracted to the plant by the bright colors and the nectar just inside the pitcher's rim. Once inside, the insects slide down the slippery surface into a well of digestive liquid.

CULTIVATION: Grow in pots in a mixture of 3 parts peat, 1 part vermiculite and 2 parts sand or in a sunny bog garden. *Cephalotus* are best grown in full sun, the pots can stand in water trays in summer; keep the soil just damp in the cooler months as plants are prone to root rot. Use a soil fungicide every few months. In its natural habitat, temperatures can reach up to 104°F (40°C) in summer but the winter nights are cool to cold. Propagate by division or from stem cuttings in late spring to early summer.

Cephalotus follicularis
ALBANY PITCHER PLANT, WESTERN AUSTRALIAN PITCHER PLANT

☼ ⊕ ↔ 8 in (20 cm) ↑ 15 in (38 cm)

Robust rootstock that produces many short stems bearing 2 different types of leaves: one simple, spoon-shaped, green, fleshy, oval. Other leaves modified to a pitcher-shaped container with a hinged bristled lid, green, brown or red. Flowering stem can be up to 2 ft (0.6 m) high. Zone 9.

CERASTIUM
A genus of about 100 species in the pink (Caryophyllaceae) family. Mostly annuals or perennials, the majority are vigorous carpeting ground covers or tufting plants. Many species in this genus are classed as weeds. *Cerastium* are mainly found throughout Europe and North America, their range is from temperate to arctic zones. Generally the leaves are small and are often hairy giving a silvery appearance. The flowers are usually small and white, and are popular in rock gardens, or confined within troughs, or massed at the front of borders.

CULTIVATION: A well-drained soil in full sun is a must for these plants. Some species can cope with poor or rocky soils. Propagate from seed, division of plants, or from cuttings.

Cephalotus follicularis, in the wild, Denmark, Western Australia

Cerastium arvense
FIELD/LARGE-FLOWERED/MEADOW OR PRAIRIE CHICKWEED, STARRY CERASTIUM

☼ ❄ ↔ 40 in (100 cm) ↑ 6–10 in (15–25 cm)

North American perennial. Large mats of bright white flowers. Linear leaves. Zones 6–11.

Cerastium boissieri
syn. *Cerastium boissierianum*

☼ ❄ ↔ 8–16 in (20–40 cm) ↑ 6–8 in (15–25 cm)

European species found particularly in Spain. Hairy white leaves. White flowers. Does well in sunny dry rock crevices. Zones 6–11.

Cerastium candidissimum
SNOW-IN-SUMMER

☼ ❄ ↔ 40 in (100 cm) ↑ 4–6 in (10–15 cm)

A rampant perennial ground-covering plant. Its narrow silvery leaves are

½–1¼ in (12–30 mm) long. The small white flowers appear in spring–summer. Zones 6–11.

Cerastium macranthum

☼ ❄ ↔ 4–8 in (10–20 cm) ↑ 2–8 in (5–20 cm)

From Turkey. Tufting perennial occurring in grassland. White flowers in spring–summer. Zones 6–11.

CERATONIA
This genus of the cassia subfamily of the legume (Fabaceae) family consists of 2 species of evergreen tree native to the Arabian Peninsula and Somalia, one of them used since biblical times as a food and fodder plant. The leaves are pinnate with large leathery leaflets; the flowers are small and arranged in dense branched spikes emerging from the trunk and branches. The sexes are variably distributed on each tree. The fruits are plump brownish pods with shiny seeds embedded in a sweet, floury, edible pulp.

CULTIVATION: Only *C. siliqua* (carob) is known in cultivation. It prefers a hot dry summer, moderately wet winter, and permanent deep soil moisture. It likes a fertile well-drained soil. If only one tree can be grown it should be of a variety known to bear male and female flowers together. Propagate from seed, or from green branch cuttings planted in late summer.

Cerastium candidissimum

Cerastium macranthum

Ceratonia siliqua

CAROB, ST JOHN'S BREAD

☀ ❄ ↔ 25 ft (8 m) ↑ 40 ft (12 m)

Thick gnarled trunk, broad low canopy casting dense shade. Flowers produced in autumn, pale greenish purple, with a rank smell attracting numerous bees and flies. Abundant curved pods mature early winter. Pulp used as a chocolate substitute. Zones 8–11.

CERATOPETALUM

A genus of 5 evergreen species, in the Cunoniaceae family, from east-coastal Australia and New Guinea. Insignificant flowers followed by swollen reddened calyces lasting for weeks. Leaf size differs with species, some are open lightly foliaged shrubs, others are tall densely clothed trees. Most grow in moist forests or rainforest habitats along eastern coast line. *C. gummiferum* is grown for commercial florist market. CULTIVATION: All species are easy to grow, but require adequate water, well-drained soil, and organic fertilizers in

the form of mulch or compost are to be preferred over chemical fertilizers. Partial shade will suit but better coloring will occur in a full sun position. Propagation is from seed.

Ceratopetalum apetalum

COACHWOOD

☀ ◗ ↔ 30 ft (9 m) ↑ 70 ft (21 m)

From eastern Australian rainforests. Tall slender tree, multi-trunked, with deep green leathery leaves and bright red calyces, often mistaken for the flowers which are insignificant and cream colored. Zones 9–11.

Ceratopetalum gummiferum

NEW SOUTH WALES CHRISTMAS BUSH

☀/◗ ◗ ↔ 6 ft (1.8 m) ↑ 15 ft (4.5 m)

An erect growing shrub, dainty trifoliate leaves, shallow toothed margins. Bright red calyces follow insignificant cream flowers in summer. Popular with florists at Christmas time in New South Wales, Australia. New cultivars continually being developed. Zones 9–11.

Ceratonia siliqua

Ceratostigma plumbaginoides

CERATOSTIGMA

From the leadwort (Plumbaginaceae) family, a genus of 8 species of herbaceous perennials or small evergreen or deciduous shrubs, all but one native to the Himalayas or Southeast Asian regions. Grown for their intense blue, 5-petalled, flat flowers, borne in terminal clusters during summer into autumn, when the small-leafed foliage becomes bronze or red depending on the intensity of the colder weather. CULTIVATION: These low-growing plants are best grown in moist well-

drained soil in full sun. Frost-tender; lightly prune to promote a dense compact bush—but remember that they flower on current season's growth. Will re-shoot if killed back by winter frosts.

Ceratostigma griffithii

☀ ❄ ↔ 7 ft (2 m) ↑ 3 ft (0.9 m)

Evergreen shrub, low multi-branched habit, densely foliaged mounded shape. Terminal clusters of blue flowers in late summer–autumn, when the mid-green leaves turn red. Zones 7–10.

Ceratostigma plumbaginoides ★

syn. *Plumbago larpentiae*

☀ ❄ ↔ 12 in (30 cm) ↑ 18 in (45 cm)

Herbaceous perennial, slender upright stem. Spreading from rhizomes, makes a useful ground cover. Cornflower blue flowers at the ends of red stems, in summer–autumn. Leaves turn red with colder weather. Zones 6–9.

Ceratostigma willmottianum

CHINESE PLUMBAGO

☀ ❄ ↔ 5 ft (1.5 m) ↑ 3 ft (0.9 m)

Deciduous shrub with an open low-branching habit. Mid-green leaves, pale to bright-blue flowers throughout summer–autumn. The foliage turns rich bronze tones in autumn. **Forest Blue**/'**Lice**' has elliptical leaves and deep blue flowers. Zones 7–10.

Ceratostigma griffithii

Ceratostigma willmottianum

C. willmottianum Forest Blue/'Lice'

Ceratopetalum apetalum, in the wild, Blue Mountains, New South Wales, Australia

Ceratopetalum gummiferum

CERATOZAMIA

This genus of 9 to 16 palm-like perennials known as cycads belongs to the zamia (Zamiaceae) family. Native to the mountains of Mexico, Belize, and Guatemala. Develop stout, rounded, and scarred trunks, with whorls of pinnate, erect or arching leaves. Cylindrical, dull green, female cones end in single spine; male cones are narrower and slightly felty. Green or coppery new growth can be smooth or hairy. Named from the Greek *ceras* meaning horn, referring to pairs of horn-like spikes on the male and female cones. CULTIVATION: Suitable for containers or the garden, plant in well-drained, mulched, slightly acid, humus-rich loam. Most prefer high humidity but gentle air movement and light to heavy shade; direct sun causes leaf damage. Protect from frost and lightly fertilize in spring and summer. Propagate from freshly collected seed, which takes 6 to 12 months to germinate. Some species produce offsets and can be divided.

Ceratozamia hildae
☽/☀ ⚘ ↔6–10 ft (1.8–3 m)
↕3–5 ft (0.9–1.5 m)

From Mexico. Trunk small, slender, partly underground, oval shape. Young foliage brown or reddish, hairy. Crown of 5 to 20 erect or spreading, papery, dark green, pinnate leaves, 3–5 ft (0.9–1.5 m) long, with sword-shaped leaflets in alternating clusters of three. Erect, yellow-brown male cones; erect, olive green to brown female cones with smooth whitish seeds. Zones 9–11.

Ceratozamia mexicana
☀ ⚘ ↔4–8 ft (1.2–2.4 m)
↕3–7 ft (0.9–2 m)

Medium-sized Mexican cycad with large, rounded, dark brown trunk.

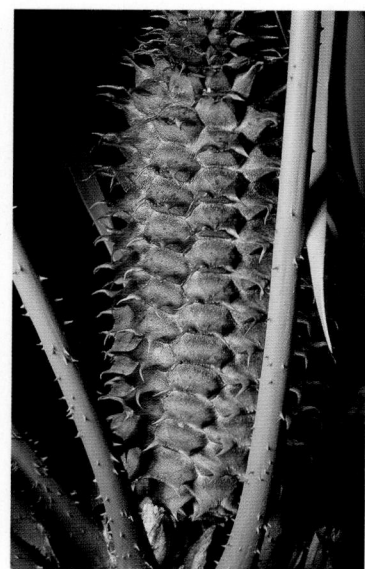

Ceratozamia mexicana

Cercidiphyllum japonicum f. *pendulum*

Young growth light green, hairy. Crown of 12 to 20 arching, erect or spreading, semi-glossy, dark green leaves, 5–8 ft (1.5–2.4 m) long, with up to 150 narrow leaflets, prickles on midribs and leaf stalks. Erect brown male cones. Erect, gray, cylindrical to barrel-shaped female cones. Zones 9–12.

CERCIDIPHYLLUM

Sole member of the Cercidiphyllaceae family, and closely allied to the magnolia family, this genus is represented by 2 species, and includes the largest deciduous native tree species in China and Japan. A distinctive elegant habit of horizontally held branches and heart-shaped leaves that color well—red, pink, and yellow—in autumn are the most notable characteristics of the species. Commonly it is found with the trunks forked low to the ground, which makes it vulnerable to damage in strong winds.
CULTIVATION: A sheltered position is essential to avoid disfigurement from drying winds and late spring frosts. Regular summer moisture is required and preferably rich soils. Propagate from seed after first subjecting to cold. Cuttings are readily struck in the late spring to early summer in cool and moist conditions.

Cercidiphyllum japonicum
KATSURA TREE
☀ ❋ ↔35 ft (10 m) ↕60 ft (18 m)
Elegant horizontal branch structure, vibrant autumn foliage. Smaller in cultivation. Leaves bluish green (reddish when unfolding), change to smoky pink, yellow, red in autumn, exude a pungent aroma reminiscent of burnt sugar. *C. j.* var. *sinense* has velvety hairs beneath the leaves. *C. j.* f. *pendulum* ★ has weeping branches. Zones 6–9.

Cercidiphyllum magnificum
syn. *Cercidiphyllum japonicum* var. *magnificum*
☀ ❋ ↔10–15 ft (3–4.5 m)
↕10–25 ft (3–8 m)

From Japan. Tree are frequently multistemmed, with smooth bark until very mature. Large rounded leaves with

Cercidiphyllum magnificum 'Pendulum'

Cercidiphyllum japonicum

Cercidiphyllum japonicum var. *sinense*

heart-shaped base and toothed margins. Purplish red on opening, becoming darkly bluish green in summer and coloring to a bright gold in autumn. 'Pendulum' has a weeping habit. Zones 6–9.

CERCIS

This small genus of 6 or 7 deciduous trees and shrubs in the cassia subfamily of the legume (Fabaceae) family, found from North America to Southeast Asia, is grown for the showy spring flowers. Leaves are alternate and mostly broadly ovate; the flowers are pea-shaped with 5 petals in a squat calyx, usually borne on bare stems before or with the early leaves. The fruit is a flat legume with a shallow wing along the edge.
CULTIVATION: *Cercis* species prefer a moderately fertile soil that drains well, and exposure to the sun for most of

Cercis canadensis

Cercis canadensis 'Forest Pansy'

Cercis occidentalis

Cercis chinensis

the day. All species frost hardy. Shape to select main leader but little regular pruning required after that. Propagate from fresh seeds; pre-soak in hot water to soften coat. Take half-hardened cuttings in summer or early autumn.

Cercis canadensis
EASTERN REDBUD, REDBUD
☀ ❄ ↔ 30 ft (9 m) ↕ 30 ft (9 m)
Widely distributed in the USA. Variable with short main trunk, or multistemmed, rounded crown. Flowers have dark red-brown sepals, rose pink petals, in late winter–early spring. Fruits reddish brown in summer. '**Alba**,' similar with white flowers. '**Forest Pansy**' has burgundy-colored foliage and pink flowers. Zones 5–9.

Cercis chinensis
CHINESE REDBUD
☀ ❄ ↔ 20 ft (6 m) ↕ 20 ft (6 m)
From central China, and similar to *C. canadensis*, but with shorter leaf

stalks. Flowers deep rosy purple in late winter–early spring. Not suitable for cold areas. Zones 6–9.

Cercis occidentalis
CALIFORNIA REDBUD, WESTERN REDBUD
☀ ❄ ↔ 12 ft (3.5 m) ↕ 15 ft (4.5 m)
Small tree or large shrub from southwestern USA. Leathery rounded leaves, green with paler undersides. Clusters of rose pink flowers in spring. Zones 5–9.

Cercis racemosa
☀ ❄ ↔ 20 ft (6 m) ↕ 30 ft (9 m)
Native to China, flowers pink, drooping clusters, but not on young trees, freely produced in spring. Introduced by E. H. Wilson in 1907. Zones 7–10.

Cercis siliquastrum
JUDAS TREE
☀ ❄ ↔ 35 ft (10 m) ↕ 35 ft (10 m)
Native to the Mediterranean region, flowering ornamental. Heart-shaped to kidney-shaped leaves. Flowers rosy purple, crowding the bare branches, in early spring. Purple-tinted seed pods persist in late summer. *C. s.* f. *albida*, white flowers; '**Bodnant**', deep purple-red flowers. Zones 6–9.

CERCOCARPUS
The 6 species of evergreen or semievergreen shrubs or small trees in this genus belonging to the rose (Rosaceae) family are found in western North

America, often in mountainous areas. Known as mountain mahogany because of their hard red wood. The fairly small leaves, are seldom over 2 in (5 cm) long, and have felted or hairy undersides. Flowers in clusters develop in the leaf axils or branch tips; cup-shaped with 5 greenish to pink-tinted petallike calyx lobes and many stamens. Fruit hard and nut-like, with a silky covering, tipped with a feathery plume. CULTIVATION: Hardiness varies with the species, though all will tolerate some frost. They adapt well to cultivation but are rarely grown outside their native range. Although they do best in moist well-drained soil, they are adaptable and will withstand drought once established. Plant in full sun and propagate from seed, cuttings, or layers, which sometimes form naturally.

Cercocarpus ledifolius
☀ ❄ ↔ 8–12 ft (2.4–3.5 m)
↕ 17–20 ft (5–8 m)
Semi-evergreen shrub or small tree from western USA. Glossy green, lance-shaped to linear leaves to 1½ in (35 mm) long, undersides with silverwhite hair. Very small flowers and plumed fruit in summer. Zones 6–9.

Cercocarpus montanus
HARD-TACK, MOUNTAIN MAHOGANY
☀ ❄ ↔ 4 ft (1.2 m) ↕ 12 ft (3.5 m)
Occurring in several distinct forms in USA. Evergreen shrub to small tree. Sparsely foliaged, small, dark green, rounded leaves, conspicuous veins, downy undersides. Flowers are dull pink, in spring–summer. Long-plumed, small, dry fruit. Zones 7–9.

CEREUS
This genus in the Cactaceae family consists of about 40 species of columnar or tree-like cacti native to South America and the West Indies. The stems are strongly ribbed along their full length, spines short and unyield-

ing. Most nocturnal flowering species are now in the genera *Selenicereus* and *Hylocereus*. The flowers emerging from the ribs are usually white, followed by fruit that is oblong to round or eggshaped, ripening to yellow and red; the fruits split to reveal black shiny seeds in white, pink, or even red pulp. CULTIVATION: Grow in well-drained reasonably fertile soil in full sun and water well in the growing season. Reduce watering in autumn and water in the winter months only if the plant shows signs of shriveling. Propagate from seed during spring or cuttings from large specimens in summer.

Cereus aethiops ★
syns *Cereus azureus*, *C. chalybaeus*, *Piptanthocereus azureus*, *P. chalybaeus*
☀ ✽ ↔ 20 in–3 ft (50 cm–0.9 m) ↕ 7 ft (2 m)
From northern Argentina. Slender, upright columnar, branched, occasionally prostrate. Stems cylindrical, dark blue to dark green, with 7 to 8 ribs. Spines, 2 to 4 black centrals and 9 to 12 radials, gray with black tips. Flowers, funnelform, white to pink. Seedpods oval, red, to 2½ in (6 cm) long. Zones 9–11.

Cereus hildmannianus ★
☀/☀ ✽ ↔ 4–7 ft (1.2–2 m)
↕ 10–17 ft (3–5 m)
Shrub or small tree that comes from eastern Brazil. Strongly upright, with multi-branched, green stems with 5 to 6 ribs. May be spineless or have small

Cereus aethiops

Cercis siliquastrum

Cerinthe major 'Purpurascens'

Cereus horrispinus

white areoles with ¾ in (18 mm) long central spine and up to 12 radial brown spines. The white flowers are up to 4 in (10 cm) in diameter. *C. h.* **subsp.** *uruguayensis* (syns *C. peruvianus* of gardens, *C. uruguayanus*), funnel-shaped flowers, green sepals, tipped red, inner tepals white. *C. h.* '**Monstrosus**' (syn. *C. h.* var. *monstrose*) has twisted and contorted blue-green stems. Zones 10–12.

Cereus horrispinus

syns *Pilocereus wagenaarii*, *Subpilocereus horrispinus*, *S. ottonis*

☼ ❄ ↔ 8 ft (2.4 m) ↑ 17 ft (5 m)

From northern Colombia. Tree-like, sparsely branched. Stems cylindrical, blue-green, becoming olive green with age. Spines, 1 strong straight central, 4 in (10 cm) long, dark at base, becoming gray toward tip, and 6 to 7 dark radials, gray at tips. Flowers funnel-form, white. Seed pods spherical to oval, pink. Zones 8–10.

Cereus jamacaru

☼/◑ ⚘ ↔ 7–15 ft (2–4.5 m)

↑ 17–35 ft (5–10 m)

Impressive tree-sized cactus, native to northeastern Brazil. Short trunk to 24 in (60 cm) diameter topped with multi-branched 4- to 6-ribbed stems, blue-green ageing to gray. Clusters of

9 to 11 spines, short and pale on young growth, dark and nearly 2 in (5 cm) long on mature stems. White and pale green flowers to almost 12 in (30 cm) long. Zones 10–12.

Cereus validus

☼/◑ ⚘ ↔ 5–10 ft (1.5–3 m)

↑ 15–20 ft (4.5–6 m)

Tree-like cactus from Argentina. Stems with 4 to 7 pronounced thin ribs, blue-green ageing to gray. Areole with brown spines, central single spine to nearly 2 in (5 cm) long with 5 radial spines. Magnificent white and deep pink flowers to 10 in (25 cm) long. Zones 9–11.

CERINTHE
HONEYWORT

This genus from the European borage (Boraginaceae) family, has 10 species of small mounding annuals, biennials, and perennials. Most have simple, short-stemmed, elliptical to spatula-shaped leaves, often blue-tinted, sometimes with an oily sheen and/or small glands known as tubercles. Flowers are tubular, 5-lobed, carried in small clusters, usually in spring–early summer. They cover quite a wide color range, including interesting metallic blue to purple shades, and often the bracts that partially enclose them develop similar colors. As the common name honeywort suggests, the flowers are rich in nectar and very popular with bees. CULTIVATION: Hardy and suitable for any temperate climate, honeyworts prefer to be kept dry in winter and should be grown in fairly light well-drained soil, preferably with extra humus. Plant in full or half-sun and deadhead frequently to encourage repeat flowering. Propagate the annuals from seed and the perennials from seed or basal cuttings or by division.

Cerinthe glabra

☼/◑ ⚘ ↔ 12–20 in (30–50 cm)

↑ 20 in (50 cm)

Biennial or perennial from southern and central Europe. Basal foliage long-stemmed and elliptical to 5 in (12 cm) long, upper leaves and those on flower stems smaller, tending to heart-shaped. Flowers to ½ in (12 mm) long, yellow, purple-red base or band. Zones 5–10.

Cerinthe major

☼/◑ ⚘ ↔ 16–24 in (40–60 cm)

↑ 16–24 in (40–60 cm)

Annual to biennial native to southern Europe. Blue-green foliage developing purple tints on flower stems. Basal leaves oval to spatula-shaped to 2 in (5 cm) long, often with tubercles. Purple or maroon flowers, to 1¼ in (30 mm) long, purplish bracts. *C. m.* **var.** *purpurea*, a natural variety, purple-blue bracts. *C. m.* '**Purpurascens**', intense steel blue bracts. Zones 7–10.

CEROCHLAMYS

This genus of 3 species of small succulents from the western Cape region of South Africa belongs to the iceplant (Aizoaceae) family. These are small plants with 3-angled leaves in opposite pairs, joined at the base and rounded at the tips. Flowers are solitary or up to 3 together, the numerous petals pink to purple. Fruit is a capsule with compartments separated by a spongy tissue that swells when wet, causing release of seeds during periods of rain. CULTIVATION: These plants are grown under glass in cool-temperate regions or outside elsewhere but may require protection from winter rainfall. They thrive in full sun and low humidity. They need infrequent watering and none at all in the resting period. If the leaves are wet for too long, they will split. Propagate from seed or cuttings allowed to dry before rooting.

Cerochlamys pachyphylla

☼ ⚘ ↔ 8 in (20 cm) ↑ 4 in (10 cm)

Stemless tufted perennial growing on sandstone rocks in the Little Karoo, South Africa. Leaves in two decussate pairs, to 2½ in (6 cm) long, smooth, waxy, green-brown, united basally. Flowers to 1¼ in (30 mm) across, pink, borne on stalk up to 1¾ in (40 mm) long. Zones 9–11.

CEROPEGIA

A genus of 200-odd often succulent climbers, trailers, or shrubs in the dogbane (Apocynaceae) family. They come mainly from southern Africa but also from elsewhere in Africa, the Canary Islands, Southeast Asia, and northeast Australia. Allied to *Hoya* and *Stapelia*, they have succulent hoya-like foliage and/or stems and unusual 5-lobed lantern-shaped flowers that, as with *Stapelia*, are often rather unpleasantly scented as they are fly-pollinated and may trap visiting insects until pollination is effected. CULTIVATION: All species withstand little, if any, frost. They prefer a light gritty soil and can be allowed to dry out between waterings. The trailing species, such as *C. linearis* subsp. *woodii*, are widely cultivated as indoor hanging basket plants. Outdoors they suit the tropics and subtropics. Propagate from seed or cuttings, or by division. Some species develop small tubers, underground or on the stems, that can be removed and grown on.

Ceropegia dichotoma

☼/◑ ⚘ ↔ 40 in (100 cm)

↑ 40 in (100 cm)

From the Canary Islands. Forms clump of upright, pipe-like, often branching, succulent stems. Leafless or with paired, narrow, gray-green leaves at the stem tips. Clusters of very narrow-tubed yellow flowers. Zones 10–12.

Cerochlamys pachyphylla

C

Ceropegia linearis

☀ ⬥ ↔ unlimited ↑4 in (10 cm)

Southern African trailer. Fine twining stems; small fleshy leaves, triangular to lance-shaped, rounded at base, sometimes linear. Flowers short, broad-based, cream tubes with narrow red-brown lobes fused at tip. *C. l.* subsp. *woodii* ★, "string of hearts", "sweet-heart" vine, heart-shaped leaves, purple-red below. mottled above. Zones 10–12.

Ceropegia sandersonii ★

PARACHUTE PLANT, UMBRELLA FLOWER

☀ ⬥ ↔5 ft (1.5 m) ↑6 ft (1.8 m)

From Mozambique and South Africa. Vigorous twining climber, tuberous

Cestrum elegans 'Smithii'

Cestrum elegans

roots. The heart-shaped leaves are up to 2 in (5 cm) long. The flowers are very distinctive and unusual, they are upward-facing with cream and green vase-shaped tube with lobes united, forming a canopy over the tube. Zones 10–12.

CESTRUM

This genus, belonging to the night-shade (Solanaceae) family, consists of around 180 species all from tropical America. They are evergreen or deciduous woody shrubs or small trees, and have mostly simple alternate leaves, usually narrow with smooth margins. The tubular to funnel-shaped flowers are borne in clusters; and they are often very fragrant and in some species night-scented. The flowers are followed by small mostly blackish or reddish berries, these and all other parts of the plant should be considered poisonous. Some species have been classified as weeds (*C. parqui*). They are mostly frost tender.

CULTIVATION: Most grow easily in full or half-sun and moderately fertile soil with adequate watering in summer.

Cestrum × cultum

Where frosts occur, these plants can be grown against a sunny wall for protection. In colder areas they may be grown in a greenhouse. Plants respond well to pruning; pinch back to encourage bushy growth. Propagation is from soft-tip cuttings.

Cestrum aurantiacum

ORANGE CESTRUM

☀ ⬥ ↔6 ft (1.8 m) ↑10 ft (3 m)

Native to tropical America, an evergreen or semi-deciduous rambling shrub that requires regular pruning. Smooth light green leaves, slightly hairy new growth, unpleasant smell when crushed. The orange flowers, in clusters at the ends of the stems, appear in spring–summer. Fleshy white berries. Zones 10–12.

Cestrum × cultum

PURPLE CESTRUM

☀ ⬥ ↔6 ft (1.8 m) ↑10 ft (3 m)

This is a cross between *C. elegans* and *C. parqui*. Ovate to lance-shaped leaves. Densely flowering terminal panicles, similar to *C. elegans*; single tubular flowers resemble *C. parqui*, although pink to violet in color. Zones 9–11.

Cestrum elegans

syn. *Cestrum purpureum*

☀ ⬥ ↔8 ft (2.4 m) ↑10 ft (3 m)

From Mexico. Strong-growing shrub, arching branches, ovate-oblong to lance-shaped, hairy, olive green leaves give off a disagreeable odor when crushed. Tubular-shaped red to purple

flowers, in dense panicles, in summer–autumn. Succulent, globular, purple-red berries. 'Smithii' has orange-red flowers. Can be invasive. Zones 10–12.

Cestrum 'Newellii'

RED CESTRUM

☀ ⬥ ↔10 ft (3 m) ↑10 ft (3 m)

Arching branches. Dark green leaves, narrowly ovate to elliptical, hairy both sides, emit an unpleasant smell when crushed. The rich crimson unscented flowers are present most of the year. Berries are small, round, and dark red. Zones 9–11.

Cestrum nocturnum

NIGHT-SCENTED JESSAMINE

☀ ⬥ ↔10 ft (3 m) ↑10 ft (3 m)

Evergreen shrub from the West Indies. Pale greenish yellow tubular flowers, which as the species name suggests, give off a strong night fragrance, in summer–late autumn. Flowers have no scent in daylight. Ovoid berries ripen green to white. Leaves are somewhat succulent, and bright green with paler color on the reverse. Zones 10–11.

Cestrum parqui

GREEN CESTRUM

☀ ⬥ ↔10 ft (3 m) ↑10 ft (3 m)

From Chile. Suckering shrub. The leaves are linear, and lance-shaped to elliptic, with an unattractive smell. Large racemes of yellow-green to bright yellow tubular, night-scented flowers, most of the year. Violet-brown berries. This species is considered a troublesome weed in mild areas. Zones 9–11.

Cestrum psittacinum

☀/◐ ⬥ ↔3–6 ft (0.9–1.8 m) ↑3–6 ft (0.9–1.8 m)

From Central America. Semi-climbing evergreen shrub, with soft downy shoots, and oblong leaves. The flowers are narrow, tubular, gold to orange, borne in racemes along the branches, in autumn. Zones 9–11.

Cestrum nocturnum

CHAENOMELES

FLOWERING QUINCE, JAPANESE QUINCE, JAPONICA

This genus, which belongs to the rose (Rosaceae) family, has 3 species of spiny deciduous shrubs, native to the high-altitude woodlands of Japan and China. Their early red, pink, or white flowers appear before the leaves on last year's wood and are highly valued for their beauty. The leaves are alternate, serrate, oval, and deep green. The flowers, which usually have 5 petals, unless double, are cup-shaped and appear from late winter to late spring, singly or in small clusters. The roughly apple-shaped, rounded, green fruit turns yellow when ripe; it is aromatic and used in jams and jellies.
CULTIVATION: Generally, well-drained moderately fertile soil, in sun or half-sun will give best results. Grow against a south wall in colder climates. A good ornamental, it can also be used as a hedging plant. Half-hardened cuttings can be obtained in summer or later in autumn. Seed can be sown

Chaenomeles × superba

C. × superba 'Crimson and Gold'

C. × superba 'Crimson Beauty'

Chaenomeles speciosa 'Nivalis'

in autumn in containers with protection from winter frosts or in a seed bed in the open ground.

Chaenomeles × californica

☀/◐ ❄ ↔ 5 ft (1.5 m) ↑ 6 ft (1.8 m)
A hybrid between *C. cathayensis* and *C. × superba*. Leaves mid-green, lance-shaped, 3 in (8 cm) long. Flowers are 2 in (5 cm) in diameter, pink to pale red, in spring. Fruit 2½ in (6 cm) long. Zones 5–10.

Chaenomeles cathayensis

☀/◐ ❄ ↔ 10 ft (3 m) ↑ 10 ft (3 m)
Native to China. Small tree to large sparsely branched shrub. The branches are spiny, the leaves shiny, mid-green, and lance-shaped, with toothed edges and red velvety undersides. Flowers in clusters, white, pink flushed, in early–mid-spring. Green scented fruit, 6 in (15 cm) long. Zones 5–10.

Chaenomeles 'Hime'

☀/◐ ❄ ↔ 6 ft (1.8 m) ↑ 8 ft (2.4 m)
Vigorous tall hybrid with bright red single flowers that have contrasting golden yellow anthers. Zones 5–9.

Chaenomeles japonica

JAPANESE FLOWERING QUINCE
☀/◐ ❄ ↔ 6 ft (1.8 m) ↑ 3 ft (0.9 m)
From Japan. This species has an uncommon, open twiggy habit with spiny branchlets. Flowers are orange-scarlet, with prominent cream stamens, and appear in late winter–early spring. The fragrant fruit, which turns green-dull yellow when ripe, is used for making jelly. Zones 6–9.

C. × superba 'Glowing Embers'

Chaenomeles japonica

Chaenomeles 'Hime'

Chaenomeles speciosa 'Phylis Moore'

Chaenomeles speciosa

syns *Chaenomeles lagenaria*, *Cydonia speciosa*

CHINESE FLOWERING QUINCE, FLOWERING QUINCE, JAPONICA

☀/◐ ❄ ↔ 15 ft (4.5 m) ↑ 10 ft (3 m)
Native to China. This common shrub has produced numerous cultivars with white, salmon, pink, or red flowers, which can be single, semi-double, or double. It has thicket forming, spiny suckering stems and showy flowers, in winter. The aromatic fruit ripens to a green-yellow. 'Geisha Girl' is an apricot double-flowered form. Some cultivars are hybrids with *C. japonica*, including: 'Nivalis', which has snow white flowers; 'Phylis Moore', which has pale pink flowers; 'Toyo-Nishiki', which has pink and white flowers on the same branch, and sometimes produces a branch of red flowers as well. Zones 6–9.

Chaenomeles cathayensis

Chaenomeles × californica

Chaenomeles × superba

☀/◐ ❄ ↔ 6 ft (1.8 m) ↑ 5 ft (1.5 m)
Hybrid of *C. japonica* and *C. speciosa*, garden origin. Leaves are 2½ in (6 cm) long, oval to oblong-shape, lustrous mid-green. Spring flowers, white, pink, orange to orange-scarlet. Fruit to 3 in (8 cm) long, and aromatic when ripe. 'Cameo' ★ has fleshy pink flowers; 'Crimson and Gold', scarlet blooms with yellow anthers; 'Crimson Beauty', crimson flowers; 'Glowing Embers', orange-red blooms; 'Nicoline', large dark red flowers, 'Rowallane', bright red with yellow anthers. Zones 6–10.

Chaenorhinum origanifolium 'Blue Dream'

Chamaecyparis lawsoniana, in Columbia River Gorge National Scenic Area, Oregon, USA

CHAENORHINUM

DWARF SNAPDRAGON

This genus, which belongs to the fox-glove (Scrophulariaceae) family, contains about 20 species of annual and perennial herbs native to Turkey and the Mediterranean, where they thrive in dry stony areas and scree. They are closely related to *Linaria*. The leaves are linear to oblong or rounded, opposite at the base. The flowers resemble snapdragons, being typically hooded, lobed, and spurred. They are borne in terminal racemes or singly in the leaf axils of the branching stems.

CULTIVATION: Grow in full sun in a well-drained soil. Species from higher altitudes are better grown in a cool greenhouse or trough. Propagate annual species from seed and perennials from seed or by division.

Chaenorhinum origanifolium

☼ ❄ ↔ 6–12 in (15–30 cm)
↑ 6–15 in (15–38 cm)

Native to southern Europe. Perennial with somewhat variable foliage ranging from narrow to almost round. Flowers are violet to white with a pale yellow throat. 'Blue Dream' is a dwarf form with blue-lilac yellow-throated flowers. Zones 6–9.

CHAMAEBATIA

This genus of 2 species from California and Baja California belongs to the rose (Rosaceae) family. They are evergreen erect shrubs with nitrogen-fixing nodules on their roots. The more widespread species, *C. foliolosa* (mountain misery), forms a dense ground cover on parts of the Sierra Nevada. The leaves are fern-like, usually bipinnate with tiny, deeply lobed leaflets, coated in sticky aromatic hairs. The flowers are in terminal corymbs and resemble raspberry flowers with 5 white petals. The fruit contains a single seed.

CULTIVATION: They need full sun and perfect drainage, and sheltered positions in rock gardens, or at the base of sunny walls. They are propagated from seeds or half-hardened cuttings.

Chamaebatia australis

SOUTHERN BEARCLOVER, SOUTHERN
MOUNTAIN MISERY

☼ ❄ ↔ 5 ft (1.5 m) ↑ 7 ft (2 m)

From Southern California and Mexico. Sprawling thicket-forming shrub. The leaves are alternate, finely divided, and highly aromatic. Single white flowers, ¾ in (18 mm) across, appear in early summer. Prefers the dry rocky soil found on mountainous slopes and ridges. Zones 8–10.

CHAMAECYPARIS

Genus in the cypress (Cupressaceae) family consisting of some 8 species from North America and eastern Asia. It is distinguished from true *Cupressus* by its small cones and short branches which have small leaves arranged in pairs and flattened to the stems of the branchlets. Foliage becomes more scale-like as it ages. Pollen and seed cones are borne on the same tree. The rice-grain-sized pollen cones in huge numbers, about ⅓ in (8 mm) or less in diameter, release the small winged seeds as soon as they mature (in contrast to *Cupressus*, in which unopened seed cones may persist for years). Several of the many ornamental cultivars are used for hedging. The timber has many uses including house interiors, fences, and matches. Contact with the foliage can cause skin allergies in some people.

CULTIVATION: This genus is lime and air-pollution tolerant but will grow better in neutral to acid soil. Propagate from half-hardened cuttings taken in summer or seed sown in autumn or spring. Early trimming is necessary. Named cultivars should be grafted in late winter or early spring.

Chamaecyparis lawsoniana

LAWSON CYPRESS, OREGON CEDAR,
PORT ORFORD CEDAR

☼ ❄ ↔ 10–15 ft (3–4.5 m) ↑ 100 ft (30 m)

Native to western North America. The foliage is bright green to blue-green; some cultivars have yellow foliage. Red male flowers in early spring. Grayish cones ripen to rusty brown. 'Chilworth Silver' is a slow growing with bluish gray juvenile foliage; 'Columnaris' has narrow pale gray foliage, and grows to 30 ft (9 m) high; 'Intertexta', with slightly weeping branches and gray-green foliage; 'Nana', yellow foliage to 6 ft (1.8 m); 'Pembury Blue', silver-blue foliage; 'Stardust', medium-sized slow-growing conical tree. Other

Chamaebatia australis

C. lawsoniana 'Aurea Densa'

C. lawsoniana 'Blue Star'

C. lawsoniana 'Chilworth Silver'

C. lawsoniana 'Handcross Park'

C. lawsoniana 'Intertexta'

C. lawsoniana 'Minima Glauca'

popular cultivars include: '**Broomhill Gold**', '**Ellwoodii**' ★, '**Elwood's Pygmy**', '**Gnome**', '**Lanei Aurea**', '**Minima Aurea**', '**Minima Glauca**', '**Stewartii**'. Zones 4–9.

Chamaecyparis obtusa
syn. *Cupressus obtusa*

HINOKI CYPRESS

☼ ❄ ↔ 20 ft (6 m) ↑ 60 ft (18 m)
Native to Japan. A slow-growing tree, larger in the wild. Highly valued for landscaping. Bark thick rusty colored. Leaves opposite, deep green above, striped with silvery white beneath. Foliage aromatic when crushed. Male flowers yellow in the spring. Rounded cones ripen to orange-brown. '**Crippsii**' (syn. 'Crippsii Aurea') has golden-yellow foliage; '**Coralliformis**', to 8 ft (2.4 m) tall, dark green leaves; '**Nana Aurea**', golden foliage; '**Nana Gracilis**', conical tree up to 10 ft (3 m) high; '**Spiralis**', lush bright green foliage. Zones 5–10.

Chamaecyparis lawsoniana 'Lutea'

C. lawsoniana 'Ellwood's Pygmy'

C. lawsoniana 'Forteckensis'

C. lawsoniana 'Gnome'

C. lawsoniana 'Minima Aurea'

C. l. 'President Roosevelt'

C. lawsoniana 'Wisselii'

Chamaecyparis obtusa

C. obtusa 'Coralliformis'

Chamaecyparis obtusa 'Crippsii'

C. obtusa 'Nana Aurea'

Chamaecyparis obtusa 'Spiralis'

Chamaecyparis pisifera
syn. *Cupressus pisifera*
SAWARA CYPRESS

☼ ❋ ↔15 ft (4.5 m) ↑75 ft (23 m)
Native of southern Japan, larger in the
wild. Rusty brown bark. Foliage mid-
green, white markings beneath. Male
flowers very small, tawny; cones round,
black-brown. 'Boulevard', to 30 ft
(9 m) tall, blue-green foliage; 'Filifera
Aurea', golden yellow leaves; 'Filifera
Aurea Nana', a dwarf form; 'Squarrosa'
(syn. 'Squarrosa Veitchii'), soft young
foliage, deep green to blue-green. Other
popular cultivars include: 'Boulevard',
'Gold Spangle', 'Golden Mop', 'Nana
Variegata', 'Plumosa Aurea Nana',
'Plumosa Juniperoides', 'Plumosa
Nana', 'Squarrosa Sulphurea'.
Zones 5–10.

Chamaecyparis thyoides
ATLANTIC WHITE CEDAR, COAST WHITE
CEDAR, WHITE CYPRESS

☼ ❋ ↔12 ft (3.5 m) ↑50 ft (15 m)
East coast USA. Bark gray-brown.
Leaves pointed, dark green, fan-shaped
sprays. Small, yellow, male flowers,
cones purplish black. Tolerates moist
to wet conditions. 'Andelyensis', blue-
green foliage; 'Ericoides', purplish
brown winter foliage; 'Heatherbun' ★,
dwarf form; 'Rubicon' (syn. 'Red Star'),
has feathery frosted green foliage, turning bright to deep purple in winter.
Zones 4–9.

Chamaecytisus purpureus

CHAMAECYTISUS
Chamaecytisus means "false *Cytisus*."
In *Chamaecytisus* most species retain
their foliage, while *Cytisus* remain leafless for much of the year. The genus
includes some 30 species of trees,
shrubs, and subshrubs from Eurasia
and the Canary Islands in the pea-
flower subfamily of the legume
(Fabaceae) family. Some are ornamental, others are cultivated as quick-
growing shelter and fodder or green
manure plants. All have trifoliate
leaves and pea-like flowers, usually in
white, yellow, or pink shades.
CULTIVATION: Although often short-
lived, most species are easily grown
and their ability to use atmospheric
nitrogen allows them to grow in nitro-
gen-poor soils. Good drainage is
important and most prefer to be kept
on the dry side except when in flower.
A full sun position is best. Propagate
from seed or half-hardened cuttings.

Chamaecyparis thyoides

Chamaecytisus albus
PORTUGUESE BROOM

☼ ❋ ↔2 ft (0.6 m) ↑3 ft (0.9 m)
Native of the southwest European
coast to southern Poland. Leaves 1 in
(25 mm) long, leaflets covered in fine
hairs. Flowers are white or pale yellow,
in terminal heads, from summer–
autumn. The low-growing forms make
attractive rock garden plants.
Zones 6–10.

Chamaecytisus purpureus ★

☼ ❋ ↔24 in (60 cm) ↑18 in (45 cm)
Native of southeast Europe and the
Balkans. Deciduous species, densely
branched. The flowers are pale pink to
crimson, with a dark central blotch, in
late summer–spring. Marvellous plants
for large rock gardens. *C. p.* f. *albus*
has white flowers. Zones 6–10.

Chamaecyparis thyoides 'Heatherbun'

Chamaecytisus supinus

Chamaecytisus supinus

☼ ❋ ↔3 ft (0.9 m) ↑3 ft (0.9 m)
Often upright, prostrate forms more
common. Deciduous species, flat to
the ground, densely branched. The
flowers appear in clusters, and are
brown-speckled, yellow-tipped, in
summer. Great spillover plant for rock
gardens. Zones 6–10.

Chamaecyparis pisifera 'Plumosa Nana'

Chamaecyparis pisifera 'Nana Variegata'

Chamaecyparis pisifera 'Snow'

Chamaecyparis pisifera 'Filifera'

C. pisifera 'Filifera Aurea'

C. pisifera 'Gold Spangle'

C. pisifera 'Plumosa'

C. pisifera 'Squarrosa Sulphurea'

CHAMAEDOREA

Chamaedorea, belonging to the family Arecaceae, is of the larger genera of palms with over 100 species. They are attractive, small, understory palms which adapt to cultivation, especially as indoor plants. Native to tropical America, they include both single-stemmed and clumping palms. Fronds are either pinnate (feather palms) or undivided. Flowers are of different sexes on different plants, very small and fleshy, and borne on spikes. As small single-seeded fruits ripen, fruit color contrasts with that of the spike. CULTIVATION: Although tropical palms, they adapt well to frost-free warm-temperate climates. Some species are quite sun-hardy, in a humid climate, but most grow best in filtered light in a sheltered spot. Soil should be moderately fertile with a high organic content and the surface mulched with leaves. If grown indoors they need good light, though not direct sunlight. They need regular summer feeding with a dilute high-nitrogen fertilizer. Propagation is normally from seed.

Chamaedorea elegans ★
syns *Collinia elegans, Neanthe bella*
PARLOR PALM
☀ ⌁ ↔ 36 in (90 cm) ↑ 6 ft (1.8 m)
From highland rainforests of southern Mexico and Guatemala. Stems single with knobbly protuberances. Short deep green fronds, crowded. Small yellow flowers, on panicles. Female panicles turn orange-red. Pea-sized black fruit. 'Bella' ★, crown of fronds only 12 in (30 cm) wide. Zones 10–12.

Chamaedorea plumosa

Chamaedorea seifrizii

Chamaedorea ernesti-augusti

Chamaedorea ernesti-augusti
☀ ⌁ ↔ 18 in (45 cm) ↑ 3 ft (0.9 m)
From southern Mexico to Honduras. Single-stemmed, wedge-shaped fronds, undivided, with a broad notch at the apex. The male plants have tiny red flowers, the females a spike of greenish flowers, turning bright orange. Small black fruit. Zones 10–12.

Chamaedorea linearis
syns *Chamaedorea megaphylla, C. poeppigiana, C. polyclada*
☀ ⌁ ↔ 7 ft (2 m) ↑ 8–20 ft (2.4–6 m)
Native to the Andes at both low and high altitudes. Single pale green trunk. Spreading dark green fronds with drooping leaflets. Multi-branched inflorescence of white flowers. Red fruits to 1 in (25 mm) on female plants. Zones 10–12.

Chamaedorea microspadix
☀ ⌁ ↔ 10 ft (3 m) ↑ 8 ft (2.4 m)
From southeastern Mexico. Clump of spreading, thin, bamboo-like stems. Fronds crowded, matt green broad leaflets. Flower panicles, females green, bearing bright scarlet fruits to ½ in (12 mm) in diameter. One of the most sun-hardy species. Zones 10–12.

Chamaedorea plumosa ★
☀/☀ ⌁ ↔ 5–8 ft (1.5–2.4 m)
↑ 10–12 ft (3–3.5 m)
Medium-sized rainforest palm from southern Mexico, with slender solitary trunk, up to 2½ in (6 cm) thick, and crown of 5 to 9 finely divided feathery leaves with 120 to 170 irregularly arranged, thin leaflets. Separate male and female plants. Round fruit is black when mature. Fresh seed germinates in 2 to 4 months. Zones 9–12.

Chamaedorea radicalis
syn. *Chamaedorea pringlei*
☀ ❉ ↔ 4–6 ft (1.2–1.8 m)
↑ 4–6 ft (1.2–1.8 m)
Widely cultivated slow-growing palm from Mexico. Horizontal, sometimes erect, solitary, suckering trunk, 4 to 8 arched, thick, leathery, deep green leaves, about 36 in (90 cm) long, with

Chamaedorea microspadix

Chamaedorea elegans

Chamaemelum nobile

straight narrow leaflets. Enlarged terminal leaflets resemble fishtails. Separate male and female plants. Erect flower stalks, with yellowish orange flowers. Round orange to red fruit. Zones 8–12.

Chamaedorea seifrizii
syn. *Chamaedorea erumpens*
☀ ✦ ↔ 3 ft (0.9 m) ↑ 10 ft (3 m)
Native to Yucatan, Mexico. Multi-stemmed species, stiff ascending fronds, regularly spaced narrow leaflets. The short flowering branches emerge below the fronds; the female plants bear pea-sized black fruit on orange spikes. Zones 11–12.

CHAMAEMELUM
CHAMOMILE
There are 4 species of annual and perennial herbs in this genus, which belongs to the daisy (Asteraceae) family. They are native to Europe and to the Mediterranean where they grow in light sandy soils. The fern-like foliage is aromatic, having a sharp apple scent when crushed or trodden on. The typical daisy flowers are white with yellow centers. *C. nobile* is the commonly grown species. It is cultivated both for its aromatic foliage and its medicinal qualities. *C. nobile* is often used as a lawn plant and the leaves and flowers have long been made into a tea, taken as a calmative and for complaints such as headache and indigestion.

CULTIVATION: Grow in full sun in well-drained soil. For lawns, place plants about 6 in (15 cm) apart and water them frequently till well established. Cut regularly to maintain a dense cover. Propagate from seed or by rooted divisions.

Chamaemelum nobile
syn. *Anthemis nobile*
CHAMOMILE
☀ ❉ ↔ 12 in (30 cm) ↑ 4–12 in (10–30 cm)
From western Europe. Sprawling perennial with very aromatic fern-like foliage. Small white daisies with yellow centers in summer. 'Treneague' is a non-flowering cultivar particularly suitable for lawns. Zones 4–10.

CHAMAEROPS
There is only a single though rather variable species in this genus of fan palms, from the Arecaceae family, and native to continental Europe. Usually multi-stemmed, single-stemmed forms are known. The trunks of most wild plants are so short that fronds appear to spring from the ground, but in cultivation they may develop trunks of up to 15 ft (4.5 m). Fronds are small, divided into stiffly radiating segments; the stalks are armed with spines. The short flowering branches bear male and female flowers on different plants. male flowers are yellow, conspicuous, and crowded onto flattened spikes.

Chamaerops humilis

Chamaemelum uncinatum

The females are sparser, greenish, and develop dull orange or tan fruits.
CULTIVATION: These plants require a temperate climate with warm summers, and will not thrive in the tropics. Soil should be well-drained, and the plant placed in an open sunny position. It is suited to large pots or tubs for use in sunny conservatories or terraces. Propagation is normally from seed, large clumps can be divided with difficulty, if necessary.

Chamaerops humilis ★
MEDITERRANEAN FAN PALM
☼ ❄ ↔ 12 ft (3.5 m) ↑ 15 ft (4.5 m)
Fronds vary in size, color, and depth of division between segments. Forms with bluish foliage are sometimes found. Zones 8–10.

CHAMELAUCIUM
One of Australia's best known cut flowers, this genus, which belongs to the myrtle (Myrtaceae) family, comprises 23 species, all from the south-western regions of the continent where they can be found growing in well-drained gravelly soil in somewhat dry conditions. They are hardy evergreen shrubs with fine needle-like foliage and masses of white or pink flowers with a wax-like texture that bloom during the winter months.
CULTIVATION: Like many Australian plants, chamelauciums have a reputation for being finicky. However, when

grown in well-drained soil in a sunny situation where water and humidity can be controlled they do well, though they are often short-lived. Propagate from seed or half-hardened cuttings.

Chamelaucium uncinatum
GERALDTON WAX
☼ ❄ ↔ 8 ft (2.4 m) ↑ 8 ft (2.4 m)
From West Australian coast. Species widely grown, in gardens, and for the florists' trade. Flowers pink, purple, or red. Excellent cultivars, including dwarf forms, available. Prune to keep compact. 'University', purple-red flowers; 'Vista' ★, pink flowers. Zones 10–11.

CHAMBEYRONIA
From New Caledonia only 2 species belong to this genus of attractive feather palms in the Arecaceae family. They are medium-sized palms with solitary straight trunks topped by a smooth crownshaft consisting of the sheathing bases of the fronds. The blade of each large frond is composed of broad well-spaced leaflets in 2 rows along a strongly recurved midrib. Short-flowering branches emerge from the trunk just below the crownshaft, bearing fleshy flowers on thick curved spikes. Male and female flowers arranged in groups, female flanked by a pair of males. The fruits are fairly large and egg-shaped.
CULTIVATION: Prized by palm collectors for the striking coloration of the new fronds, they thrive best in humid, subtropical, coastal climates in moist organic soil well mulched with leaf litter. Shelter from strong sun and wind should be provided when young. Propagation is only from fresh seed, which may take some months to germinate.

Chambeyronia macrocarpa
syn. *Chambeyronia hookeri*
☼ ❄ ↔ 10 ft (3 m) ↑ 30 ft (9 m)
Occurring in dense rainforest, with high rainfall. Strongly ringed trunk.

Fronds to 8 ft (2.4 m) long. New fronds, 1 or 2 each year; translucent pale bronze to deep reddish bronze. Spectacular combination. Zones 10–12.

CHAPTALIA
SUNBONNETS
Found from southeastern and south-central USA through Central America and the West Indies to Argentina, this daisy (Asteraceae) family genus includes around 100 species of mainly rosette-forming perennials that commonly occur in woodland clearings and often at high altitudes in the tropics. They have simple, elongated, oval-shaped leaves, often with serrated edges, and their small flowerheads are usually borne singly on long wiry stems.
CULTIVATION: Hardiness varies with origin of species; North American and southern South American examples are generally the most frost tolerant. These small daisies are not spectacular plants; indeed, some are considered weeds, but they can make charming additions to natural gardens and require little or no maintenance. Plant in sun or partial shade with humus-rich soil. Propagate from the seed or by division of established clumps.

Chaptalia nutans
SILVER PUFF
☼ ❄ ↔ 8–12 in (20–30 cm)
↑ 6–8 in (15–20 cm)
Found from Louisiana to Argentina. Small daisy forms clumps of rosettes of dandelion-like, elongated leaves with silvery undersides. Fluffy, often downward-facing flowerheads on stems up to 10 in (25 cm) long. Widely considered a weed. Zones 7–11.

CHASMANTHE
There are 3 species of cormous plants in this genus, which belongs to the iris (Iridaceae) family. Native to South Africa and closely related to *Crocosmia* and *Tritonia*. The sword-shaped leaves are arranged in fans. They flower in late winter to spring, bearing spikes of yellow, orange, or red tubular flowers. May, in sunny well-drained situations, prove moderately frost tolerant.

Chaptalia nutans

CULTIVATION: They are easily grown in warm climates where they clump quickly and can become weedy. Grow in a warm sunny position in a well-drained soil. Propagate from seed or from offsets.

Chasmanthe aethiopica
syn. *Chasmanthe vittigera*
AFRICAN CORN FLAG
☼/❄ ❄ ↔ 5–7 in (12–18 cm)
↑ 16–27 in (40–70 cm)
From coastal South Africa. Grows from large corms that are renewed annually. The bright green lance-like leaves are arranged in fans, forming dense clumps. Bright vermilion-red flowers, held in single file on straight thrusting stems, in winter–early spring. Nectar enjoyed by honey-eating birds. Zones 9–11.

Chasmanthe floribunda
☼ ❄ ↔ 12 in (30 cm) ↑ 2–4 ft (0.6–1.2 m)
From Western Cape, South Africa. A fan of sword-shaped leaves often with a silky sheen. Orangey red flowers with yellow striping, arranged in 2 rows on stems to 4 ft (1.2 m) tall, in winter and spring. Zones 9–11.

CHASMANTHIUM
This genus of 6 usually herbaceous species in the grass (Poaceae) family comes from eastern USA and Mexico. *C. latifolium* is the only species that is usually grown in gardens. It is valued both for its attractive flowerheads, suitable for drying, and for its pleasing bright green foliage that colors well before dying back.
CULTIVATION: Plant in moist soil in full or half-sun. Propagate from seed or by division in late winter.

Chasmanthium latifolium
syn. *Uniola latifolia*
NORTH AMERICAN WILD OATS, SEA OATS, SPANGLE GRASS
☼/❄ ❄ ↔ 12–16 in (30–40 cm)
↑ 36–40 in (90–100 cm)
Does not grow near the sea as one of the common names suggests, but in woodlands and along streams from Texas to New Jersey. Broad bright green

Chasmanthe aethiopica

Cheilanthes fendleri

Cheiridopsis aspera

leaves turn to rich colors in autumn. Drooping heads of oat-like flowers can be dried. Zones 4–11.

CHEILANTHES
CLOAK FERN, LIP FERN

This genus is made up of 180 small, evergreen, terrestrial or rock-inhabiting ferns, all from the maidenhair-fern (Adiantaceae) family, and widely distributed in drier climates and deserts throughout temperate and tropical regions. They are compact, and short- to long-creeping, and produce reclining or erect rhizomes, and wiry brown to black stalks. The rigidly spreading, pinnate, leathery, often heavily scaly fronds have numerous fine divisions. Some species adapt by shrivelling during droughts then expanding when they are rehydrated.
CULTIVATION: They can be difficult to grow and propagate. Minimize damage from moisture fluctuations by planting near large rocks and avoid wetting foliage. Many species prefer full sun (excessive shade causes weak growth); early morning and late afternoon sun are preferable. They have adapted to cold winters. Propagate from spores or by division.

Cheilanthes distans
BRISTLY CLOAK FERN
☀ ❄ ↔ 1–2 in (2.5–5 cm)
↕ 4–8 in (10–20 cm)

Small Australasian fern. Dark brown, scaly stalks, ¾–3 in (1.8–8 cm) long. Pinnate, sword-shaped fronds, 2–6 in (5–15 cm) long, dull green, and scaly above, densely whitish to brown, scaly, hairy below, with roughly triangular to oval-shaped segments. Zones 8–10.

Cheilanthes fendleri
FENDLER'S LIP FERN
☀ ❄ ↔ 1–2 in (2.5–5 cm)
↕ 6–12 in (15–30 cm)

This small fern is an inhabitant of southern USA and Mexico. It grows from a long-creeping rhizome. The arched, scaly, polished, thin, brown stalks can be up to 7 in (18 cm) long. The oval- to sword-shaped, glistening, bright green blades are up to 6 in (15 cm) long, and have narrow, oblong to triangular, bead-like segments with white or brown scales underneath. Zones 5–9.

CHEIRIDOPSIS

This genus of 23 species of succulents from southern Africa belongs to the iceplant (Aizoaceae) family. Most are clump-forming, but a few are shrubby. The leaves are opposite and triangular in section, rarely flattened, the surface more or less velvety, which makes them easy to distinguish from species of the allied genus *Argyroderma*. Each succeeding pair differs from the previous one in form, size, and relative unity of the leaves. Those most united wither in the resting period and form a sheath covering the succeeding pair of leaves. Flowers open during the day, are borne singly, and usually have yellow, rarely purple or red, petals. Named from the Greek, *cheiris* means a sleeve,
CULTIVATION: In warm regions these plants require full sun, low humidity, and protection from the rain in summer when they are resting. Grow in a cool greenhouse in temperate regions, withholding water during the winter. They need rapid-draining soil as the leaves will split open if kept wet too long. Propagation is from seed or from hardened cuttings.

Cheiridopsis aspera
☀/◐ ❅ ↔ 8–12 in (20–30 cm)
↕ 4 in (10 cm)

From Western Cape, South Africa. Forms a dense clump of narrow, pale green to gray-green, rough-textured leaves with minute white dots. It produces small yellow flowers but so infrequently that for many years they were undescribed. Zones 9–11.

Cheiridopsis caroli-schmidtii
☀/◐ ❅ ↔ 6–8 in (15–20 cm)
↕ 2–4 in (5–10 cm)

Native of Namibia. Forms a mound of withered leaves topped with paired, thick, ½ in (12 mm) long, gray-green leaves that are fused for most of their length, forming a wedge or chisel shape. The flowers are golden yellow. Zones 9–11.

Cheiridopsis cigarettifera
☀/◐ ❅ ↔ 6–12 in (15–30 cm)
↕ 4 in (10 cm)

From Western Cape, South Africa. Forms dense circular mats. Narrow, tapering, keeled leaves to slightly over 2 in (5 cm) long. Inner pairs are fused for about a third of their length, and gray-green with a waxy bloom and tiny translucent spots. Flowers in shades of yellow to golden yellow. Zones 9–11.

Cheiridopsis imitans
☀/◐ ❅ ↔ 8–12 in (20–30 cm)
↕ 4 in (10 cm)

From Northern Cape, South Africa. The red-tinted, angled and keeled, gray-green leaves grow to 2 in (5 cm) long. The bright yellow flowers up to 3 in (8 cm) in diameter, are borne on stems long enough to hold the flower clear of the foliage. Zones 9–11.

Cheiridopsis peculiaris
☀/◐ ❅ ↔ 6–8 in (15–20 cm)
↕ 2–4 in (5–10 cm)

From Western Cape, South Africa. Lower leaves lie flat, with flattened upper surface, they dry up to eventually become papery. The upper leaf pairs are entirely united, forming a fleshy, pale gray-green, pointed egg, to 2 in (5 cm) long, with irregular spotting, splitting after winter. Yellow flowers in summer. Zones 9–11.

Cheiridopsis cigarettifera

Cheiridopsis pillansii
☀/◐ ❅ ↔ 8–12 in (20–30 cm)
↕ 4 in (10 cm)

From Western Cape, South Africa. Leaves largely fused, forming small, rounded, pale gray-green to blue-green succulent body, often with darker spotting. Where separate, the lower leaves protrude. Flowers to 3 in (8 cm) wide, cream to straw yellow. Zones 9–11.

CHELIDONIUM
CELANDINE

There is just one species of biennial or perennial herb in this genus of the poppy (Papaveraceae) family. Native to Europe and western Asia and naturalized in the eastern USA, it grows on banks, in hedgerows, and on wasteland. Variable species, branching from the base and with pinnate leaves, often with a 3-lobed terminal leaflet. Golden-yellow flowers, about 1 in (25 mm) wide with 4 petals. They are borne in loose terminal clusters in summer. Although poisonous, the plant has long been used in herbal medicine for a wide range of complaints including jaundice, blindness, and plague. Its orange sap contains a skin irritant that is used to cure warts and ringworm.
CULTIVATION: Suitable for the wild garden and shady corners in a range of soil types. It self-sows readily. Propagate from seed sown *in situ*.

Cheiridopsis caroli-schmidtii

Cheiridopsis pillansii

Chelidonium majus
GREATER CELANDINE

☀/◐ ❄ ↔12–36 in (30–90 cm)
↑12–36 in (30–90 cm)

From Europe, western Asia, naturalized elsewhere. Brittle leafy stems, pinnately divided foliage. Golden-yellow flowers in summer. *C. m.* var. *laciniatum* has deeply cut leaves. *C. m.* 'Flore Pleno' is a double form that is more commonly grown. Zones 6–9.

CHELONE
SHELL FLOWER, TURTLE'S HEAD

This genus which contains 6 species of herbaceous perennials, which are native to North America, belongs to the foxglove (Scrophulariaceae) family. They

Chelidonium majus

Chenopodium botrys

Chenopodium bonus-henricus

have opposite leaves and bear tubular flowers with 2 lips that have suggested the common name turtle's head to some imaginative souls. *Kelone,* from which the genus name comes, is Greek for a turtle or tortoise. Blooms are produced from mid-summer till the cold weather arrives and come in shades of white through to purple. Flowers can be moved sideways on stem and will stay in that position. They are long lasting if cut; seed heads can be dried. CULTIVATION: Although they often grow in swamps in the wild, they are happy in moisture-retentive soil in a half-sun to sunny position. Propagate by division, although they can also be raised from seed.

Chelone glabra
SNAKE HEAD, TURTLE'S HEAD

☀/◐ ❄ ↔16–20 in (40–50 cm)
↑20–32 in (50–80 cm)

A species from eastern and southern North America that has white flowers, often stained pink or purple, to 1 in (25 mm) long, throughout summer and autumn. Zones 3–9.

Chelone lyonii ★

☀/◐ ❄ ↔24–36 in (60–90 cm)
↑40–48 in (100–120 cm)

This tall upright species has deep pink flowers with a yellow beard on the inside lower lip throughout summer and into autumn. Zones 4–9.

Chenopodium giganteum

CHENOPODIUM

One of the most familiar genera in the goosefoot (Chenopodiaceae) family, *Chenopodium* consists of about 100 species of annuals and evergreen or deciduous perennials and shrubs, found in temperate climates around the world including arid regions and saline areas. Some of the annuals are widespread weeds, others are grown as garden flowers, leaf vegetables, herbs or grain crops, or valued as fodder plants. Leaves are alternate, often toothed or lobed, and their surfaces may be covered with minute bladder-like whitish cells that often burst at an early stage giving a mealy appearance; some species also have minute glands that secrete a sticky, pungent-smelling substance. Flowers are tiny and crowded in clusters in the leaf axils or on terminal panicles; grain-like fruits are hardly larger but profuse, developing within the persistent perianth. CULTIVATION: Easily grown in any good garden soil in full sun, they are tough drought-tolerant plants, but if grown as vegetables should be kept well-watered and fertilized to promote leaf growth and delay seeding. Propagate from seed (or division for perennials) in early spring.

Chenopodium bonus-henricus
GOOD KING HENRY

☀ ❄ ↔24 in (60 cm) ↑24 in (60 cm)
Herbaceous perennial from temperate Eurasia, naturalized in North America and the British Isles. The leaves are a deep green, like spinach leaves, to 4 in (10 cm) long; flowers greenish in long terminal spikes, in late spring-summer. Grown as a leaf vegetable or for the tender new shoots used like asparagus. Zones 5–10.

Chenopodium botrys
FEATHER GERANIUM, JERUSALEM OAK

☀ ❄ ↔12 in (30 cm) ↑24 in (60 cm)
Erect annual from southern Europe and western Asia, which is widely naturalized in North America. This plant is occasionally grown as garden annual for its scented greenish yellow summer flowers and attractive deeply lobed leaves. Zones 6–10.

Chenopodium giganteum

☀ ❄ ↔3 ft (0.9 m) ↑4–10 ft (1.2–3 m)
Annual species from northern India. Leaves up to 6 in (15 cm) long. The much-branched growing shoots are purple-tipped. The elongated summer–autumn flower clusters are also purple. Grown as a bedding annual for foliage color; the leaves are edible. Zones 8–11.

Chiastophyllum oppositifolium

Chenopodium quinoa
INCA WHEAT, QUINOA

☀ ❄ ↔2 ft (0.6 m) ↑6 ft (1.8 m)
Once an important grain crop in the highlands of Ecuador, Bolivia and Peru, its wild origin is uncertain. Broad mid-green leaves. Erect stems carry plumes of red to yellow, black, or white seed heads. Now subject of renewed interest; the dehulled grains, high in protein, are tasty in cooked dishes, and a source of edible oil; the green shoots are also eaten. Zones 8–11.

CHIASTOPHYLLUM

The sole species in this crassula (Crassulaceae) family genus is a trailing semi-succulent perennial native to the Caucasus. Its leaves are large and fairly thin, usually with short blunt teeth and from late spring to mid-summer it produces a charmingly delicate flower display. A graceful plant that most of the time hides its succulent origins but which can be relied upon to survive when harsh conditions prevail.
CULTIVATION: Though semi-succulent, it is best grown in a cool rockery or trailing over a moist bank or stone wall. A natural crevice plant that quickly colonizes cracks and gaps in masonry. While preferring moist conditions, it is very drought tolerant once established, shrivelling when dry then growing again when watered. Propagate from seed or by division.

Chiastophyllum oppositifolium

☀/◐ ❄ ↔6–12 in (15–30 cm)
↑6 in (15 cm)

Forms a small clump of rounded, fleshy, finely scalloped, bright green leaves up to 4 in (10 cm) wide, from which emerge flower stems that carry arching sprays of tiny yellow flowers. Zones 7–9.

CHILOPSIS

Belonging to the trumpet-flower (Bignoniaceae) family, in which it is most closely allied to *Catalpa,* this genus consists of a single species of evergreen shrub or small tree native to arid regions of southwestern USA and western Mexico. It has brittle cane-like branches and very narrow leaves. Short sprays of showy trumpet-shaped flowers terminate the branches, each flower somewhat 2-lipped at its mouth. Fruits are pendulous pencil-like capsules packed with very light winged seeds. CULTIVATION: *Chilopsis* comes from a warm climate with a very hot dry atmosphere and although fairly frost hardy, will not thrive in cool humid climates. A warm sunny position and deep, well-drained, sandy soil suit it best. It is readily propagated from cuttings, though seed can also be used.

Chilopsis linearis
DESERT WILLOW

☼ ❄ ↔ 8 ft (2.4 m) ↕ 10 ft (3 m)

Usually a shrub, can become a tree under suitable conditions. Downy twigs, grayish green leaves to 4 in (10 cm) or longer. Flowers 1½ in (35 mm) long, almost as wide, deep rose pink to white, darker spots in the throat. 'Burgundy' ★, deep red-purple flowers; 'Hope', white flowers with light yellow center. Zones 8–11.

CHIMAPHILA
PIPSISSEWA, PRINCE'S PINE

This genus of 4 or 5 species from the temperate Northern Hemisphere extending to the high mountains of tropical America, belongs to the heath (Ericaceae) family. They are evergreen perennials to 12 in (30 cm) tall. The slender, often creeping stems, sometimes branched, bear whorls of leathery toothed leaves. The stalked cluster of pendulous flowers is flat-topped or like a raceme. Flowers have 5 round, hollowed, white or pink to red petals. Fruit is a capsule with 5 compartments, splitting open at top to release seeds. CULTIVATION: These plants are difficult to cultivate, but established plants can be grown in damp, shady, sandy

soils in rock gardens or woodland edges. Damage to the far-spreading root systems can be fatal. They can be propagated by very careful division or from seeds sown on damp sphagnum moss, though germination is erratic and success infrequent. Some are of medicinal significance.

Chimaphila umbellata
PIPSISSEWA, SPOTTED WINTERGREEN

☼/◐ ❄ ↔ 24 in (60 cm) ↕ 5–12 in (12–30 cm)

From cooler regions of Eurasia and North America. Stems branching below ground, shoots erect with whorls of few toothed, obovate leaves. Inflorescence long-stalked with 3 to 10 red or pink to white flowers in summer. Used for treating bladder problems. Zones 5–9.

CHIMONANTHUS
From China. There are 6 species in this deciduous or evergreen genus within the allspice (Calycanthaceae) family. Grown for their ornamental value, their scented flowers can be used dried, like lavender, to fragrance linen. Leaves are arranged opposite in pairs and appear after the flowers in spring. CULTIVATION: In colder areas they benefit from a sheltered position. This may also protect the early flowers from frost damage. In less cold areas they make a good specimen shrub in the open garden and fit in well in a shrub border, needing full sun in fertile free-draining soil. Propagate by cuttings in summer. Sow seed in a position protected from winter frost as soon as it is ripe, but seed-raised plants will take 5 to 10 years or more to flower.

Chimonanthus nitens
☼ ❄ ↔ 8 ft (2.4 m) ↕ 6–10 ft (1.8–3 m)

Native to China, great screening plant. Evergreen shrub. Glossy green leaves,

Chilopsis linearis

opposite, smooth-edged. Solitary, star-like, yellowish white flowers, slightly fragrant, in autumn. Zones 7–9.

Chimonanthus praecox
syns *Chimonanthus fragrans*, *Meratia praecox*

JAPANESE ALLSPICE, WINTERSWEET

☼ ❄ ↔ 10 ft (3 m) ↕ 12 ft (3.5 m)

Native to China. Deciduous shrub. Lance-shaped leaves, glossy green with a rough surface, turn pale yellow in autumn. Fragrant flowers on second-year bare wood, sulfur yellow to pale yellow, purple or brown stain on inner petals, in winter. 'Grandiflorus' ★ has deep yellow flowers, larger than the species, up to 2 in (5 cm) in diameter. 'Parviflorus' has small pale yellow flowers. Zones 6–10.

CHIMONOBAMBUSA
This genus of about 40 species of bamboo from southern and eastern Asia belongs to the grass (Poaceae) family. They are small to medium-sized plants, often quite dense and bushy, with a strongly running habit, making them good for screens and hedges. Although they can be very invasive, they resent and will often fail in dry soils. CULTIVATION: Plant in moist soil in full sun or shade. Prune out old spent canes as needed and put down root barriers or trench around them once a year to control their spread. Propagate by division, which need not mean the complete removal of the clump—just lift a section or use wayward runners.

Chimonobambusa marmorea
KAN-CHIKU, MARBLE SHEATH BAMBOO

☼/◐ ❄ ↔ 10–17 ft (3–5 m) ↕ 7–10 ft (2–3 m)

Introduced from Japan to Europe in 1889. Bushy species, slender black marbled stems that in strong light can

Chimonanthus nitens

completely blacken. Makes fine arching interior plant or ground cover in shady woodland. Fairly rampant. Zones 7–10.

Chimonobambusa quadrangularis
syns *Arundinaria quadrangularis*, *Tetragonocalamus quadrangularis*

SHIKAKUDAKE, SHINO-CHIKU, SQUARE BAMBOO

◐ ❄ ↔ 10–30 ft (3–9 m) ↕ 20–25 ft (6–8 m)

From southeastern China and Taiwan, and naturalized in Japan. Potentially invasive species. Purple new culm sheaths reveal square culms with recurved spines at base. Culm diameter is 2 in (5 cm). 'Suow', pale yellow culm, erratically variegated foliage. Zones 7–10.

Chimonobambusa tumidissinoda
syn. *Qiongzhuea tumidinoda*

CHINESE WALKING STICK

◐ ❄ ↔ 20–40 ft (6–12 m) ↕ 10–20 ft (3–6 m)

Endemic to small region in Yunnan, China, introduced by Peter Addington in 1987. Shoots in late summer, and has rapidly unfurling willow-like foliage; aggressively spreading by rhizomes. Commercially grown for sweet shoots and for walking sticks and tobacco pipes due to disc-like swollen nodes (tumidissinoda). Zones 8–10.

Chimonanthus praecox

Chionochloa rubra, in the wild, Rangipo, New Zealand

Chionochloa conspicua

Chionanthus virginicus

Chionanthus retusus

CHIONANTHUS

This genus in the olive (Oleaceae) family consists of more than 100 species of mostly deciduous trees and shrubs native to eastern Asia, Japan, and the eastern states of the USA. Some of the tropical trees in the genus may be evergreen. Leaves are toothed or smooth and are arranged opposite each other on the branches. The white 4-petalled flowers grow in terminal panicles, and are followed in autumn by a purple-blue fruit with a single seed. The bark is used medicinally. CULTIVATION: Some species tolerate alkaline soil; others prefer a neutral or acid soil and a position in full sunlight. Wood must be ripened by the sun for a good flower set. Sow seed as soon as it is ripe in autumn, ensuring it is protected from winter frosts. Germination is slow, up to 18 months.

Chionanthus retusus ★

CHINESE FRINGE TREE

☼ ❄ ↔ 10 ft (3 m) ↕ 10 ft (3 m)

Native to China and Taiwan. Deciduous shrub or small tree. Bark deeply grooved or peeling. Glossy, bright green, egg-shaped leaves, white downy undersides. Panicles of fragrant white flowers in summer. Blue-black fruit. Grows in alkaline soil. Zones 6–10.

Chionanthus virginicus

FRINGE TREE

☼ ❄ ↔ 10 ft (3 m) ↕ 10 ft (3 m)

Native to eastern USA. Shrub or small tree. Leaves egg-shaped, dark green, glossy, to 8 in (20 cm) long. Fragrant white flowers in pendent panicles. Blue-black fruit about ½ in (12 mm) in size. Needs acid soil, tolerates neutral soil. '**Angustifolius**' ★ has narrower leaves, while the leaves of '**Latifolius**' are broadly egg-shaped. Zones 4–9.

CHIONOCHLOA

SNOW GRASS

Genus containing about 19 species of perennial grasses in the grass (Poaceae) family. Except for one species found in Australia, they are all native to New Zealand where they grow in alpine and subalpine areas. Generally tall tussock-forming plants with arching foliage and graceful flowerheads. CULTIVATION: Easily grown in gritty well-drained soil in full sun. Most species are at least frost hardy but in cool areas some perform better in a hot sheltered position. Propagate by seed or division.

Chionochloa conspicua

HUNANGAMOHO, PLUMED TUSSOCK GRASS

☼ ❄ ↔ 3 ft (0.9 m) ↕ 3–6 ft (0.9–1.8 m)

Found on New Zealand's North and South Islands. Dense tussock-forming grass with broad green leaves. Airy open flowering panicles are carried on slightly arching stems to 6 ft (1.8 m) tall. Resembles a small pampas grass. Zones 7–10.

Chionochloa flavicans

☼ ❄ ↔ 3 ft (0.9 m) ↕ 3–5 ft (0.9–1.5 m)

From coastal areas of the North Island, New Zealand. Attractive clumps of weeping green leaves. Arching flower stems to 5 ft (1.5 m) tall bear silky pale green plumes which age to cream and fawn. Zones 8–10.

Chionochloa rubra

RED TUSSOCK GRASS

☼ ❄ ↔ 3 ft (0.9 m) ↕ 3–5 ft (0.9–1.5 m)

Clumping grass found throughout New Zealand from the central North Island southward. Narrow weeping leaves, up to 6 ft (1.8 m) long, in red shades from brownish green to copper. Loose open flower panicles held above the foliage, initially red-tinted but soon becoming bleached. Zones 7–10.

CHIONODOXA

GLORY OF THE SNOW

These small, bulbous, summer-dormant plants are members of the lily (Liliaceae) family. In their native mountainous habitats of Crete, Cyprus, and western Turkey they bloom in early summer as the last snows melt. In milder climates the display is likely to be in early spring. Either way their clear colors, perky star-shaped flowers, and glossy emerald leaves have great appeal. The bulbs are small and dressed in brown tunics. CULTIVATION: Easily grown in half-sun and at lower altitudes and higher temperatures than those found in their native range. *Chionodoxa* require good drainage, an open situation, and some degree of frost. Divide the established clumps and gather offsets in autumn and plant into gritty soil in a sunny position. Sow the seed during autumn into trays or beds containing a sandy mix. Germination takes place during the winter months.

Chionodoxa forbesii

☼ ❄ ↔ 2–3 in (5–8 cm) ↕ 3–8 in (8–20 cm)

From the mountains of western Turkey. Bears a few sparse leaves that reach 3–10 in (8–25 cm). The erect stems carry up to 12 downturned flowers. Slightly recurved petals, about ¾ in (18 mm) wide, are intensely blue with white central markings. Bulging white tubes. There are several cultivars, including the well-known large but pale '**Pink Giant**' ★. Zones 4–7.

Chionodoxa luciliae

syn. *Chionodoxa gigantea*

☼ ❄ ↔ 2–3 in (5–8 cm) ↕ 4–6 in (10–15 cm)

From mountains of western Turkey. Produces soft violet-blue flowers with small white central zone, 2 to 3 per stem. Production, when climate and season suits, is prolific. The leaves, often slightly recurved, reach 3–8 in (8–20 cm) long. '**Alba**', with white petals; '**Gigantea**', a larger blue form to 8 in (20 cm) high; '**Rosea**' with pinkish petals. Zones 4–7.

Chionodoxa sardensis

☼ ❄ ↔ 2–3 in (5–8 cm) ↕ 4–6 in (10–15 cm)

From the mossy woodlands in western Turkey. Rich blue flowers with small white "eyes." Up to 12 attach to each red-brown stem. Neat, channeled, dark green leaves are erect and spreading. Zones 4–7.

Chionodoxa forbesii

Chionodoxa luciliae

Chironia baccifera

Chironia purpurascens, in Suikerbosrand Nature Reserve, Gauteng, South Africa

CHIRANTHODENDRON

This genus of a single evergreen tree species from southern Mexico and Guatemala is usually referred to the cacao (Sterculiaceae) family, though this classification is under revision. It is closely allied to *Fremontodendron* and hybrids between the 2 genera have been raised (× *Chiranthofremontia*). Broad leaves are cordate and shallowly 3- to 7-lobed. Flowers are borne singly on the branches, each opposite a leaf; they have no petals, only a leathery bell-shaped calyx from which emerges a group of 5 stamens with filaments fused into a tube and extremely large claw-like anthers. Form and position of the flowers adapts them for pollination by perching birds and bats. Resembling human hands, they were held in awe by Mexico's ancient peoples. Capsules contain many back seeds. CULTIVATION: Cultivated in Mexico before the Spanish conquest as objects of religion, elsewhere they have been grown mainly in botanical collections, though becoming more widely grown in California in recent times. Coming from tropical highlands they tolerate very light frosts, but are rather slow-growing. A sheltered but warm position with fertile, well drained soil suits them best. Propagate from freshly gathered seed.

Chiranthodendron pentadactylon
MEXICAN HAND TREE
☼ ❅ ↔ 30 ft (9 m) ↑ 30–50 ft (9–15 m)
Unusual plant, native to Mexico and Guatemala, usually a large shrub or a small tree, smaller in cultivation. Large, 5-lobed, palmate leaves, clusters of red-brown cup-shaped flowers in warmer months. Five-angled seed pods. Zones 10–12.

CHIRONIA

A genus of 15 species of perennials, subshrubs, and shrubs, belonging to the gentian (Gentianaceae) family and found in southern Africa and the island of Madagascar. They have narrow leaves in opposite pairs and in spring produce small starry flowers, usually at the stem tips, that may be carried singly or in small sprays. Small berry-like seed capsules follow the flowers and ripen around Christmas time (Southern Hemisphere), hence the common name, Christmas berry. CULTIVATION: Plant in full sun in well-drained soil that does not become waterlogged in winter. Most tolerate light frosts but rot in constantly cold wet conditions. Other than an occasional trim, pruning should not be needed. Propagate from seed or layers.

Chironia baccifera
CHRISTMAS BERRY
☼ ❅ ↔ 20 in (50 cm) ↑ 20 in (50 cm)
South African native. Wiry-stemmed low shrub. Narrow, 1 in (25 mm) long, gray-green leaves, slightly rolled under at the edges. Deep pink flowers appear at the stem tips, singly or clustered. Fruit orange-red. Zones 9–11.

Chironia purpurascens
☼ ❅ ↔ 6 in (15 cm)
↑ 12–18 in (30–45 cm)
From Zimbabwe to the Eastern Cape. Evergreen biennial, perennial, or sub-shrub. Habit varies from erect to spreading. Sparse narrow leaves. Slender forking inflorescence bearing mauve to deep magenta flowers from late spring–summer. Zones 8–11.

× CHITALPA

The sole species in this genus of the trumpet-vine (Bignoniaceae) family is an intergeneric hybrid of *Catalpa bignonioides* and *Chilopsis linearis*. Although closely related and of North American origin, these 2 species do not meet in the wild, *Catalpa* being found in the moist regions of eastern and southern USA while *Chilopsis* is native to the arid southwestern region of the USA and nearby parts of Mexico. CULTIVATION: In comparison to its *Catalpa* parent, this hybrid is moderately frost tolerant, and is undemanding, thriving in any reasonably deep and fertile well-drained soil that does not dry out entirely in summer. Young

trees can be pruned to shape and established plants benefit from light trimming and thinning in winter or very early spring. Propagate from winter hardwood cuttings, from summer half-hardened cuttings, or by budding onto *Catalpa* rootstocks.

× Chitalpa tashkentensis
☼ ❅ ↔ 20 ft (6 m) ↑ 20–40 ft (6–12 m)
Deciduous tree. Leaves matt mid-green, fuzzy undersides. Flowers bell-shaped, to 1 in (25 mm) long, white or pink, in erect racemes, at branch tips. 'Pink Dawn' ★ is lower, with a spreading crown and pink flowers. Zones 8–10.

CHLOROPHYTUM

This genus in the lily (Liliaceae) family contains about 215 species of fleshy-stemmed perennials native to tropical and subtropical regions of Africa, Asia, South America, and Australia. Range in height from 4–24 in (10–60 cm), with linear to lance-shaped leaves arising from the rootstock. Small white flowers are borne in loose sparse panicles, and in some species the flowering stems form new plantlets. CULTIVATION: A few species are cultivated for their foliage. The most commonly seen is the popular house plant *C. comosum*. In warmer areas where outdoor cultivation is possible grow in light shade in well-drained soil. Can be grown as a ground cover. Indoor plants need bright indirect sunlight and watering well when in full growth.

Chlorophytum comosum
SPIDER PLANT
☼ ❅ ↔ 12–24 in (30–60 cm)
↑ 12–24 in (30–60 cm)
From South Africa. Linear leaves to 16 in (40 cm) long, green or striped white. Flowering stems bear loose panicles of small, white, starry flowers. Plantlets are formed at the flowering nodes. 'Variegatum' has

margins of white or cream. 'Vittatum' has recurved leaves with a central white stripe. Zones 9–11.

Chlorophytum laxum 'Bichetii'
☼ ❅ ↔ 8–12 in (20–30 cm)
↑ 8–12 in (20–30 cm)
Native to Gabon. Fleshy-rooted perennial with linear leaves striped creamy white. Small white flowers are borne in loose panicles. Zones 10–12.

CHOISYA

This genus within the rue (Rutaceae) family has about 8 species of evergreen shrubs that are native to southwest USA and Mexico. These are attractive ornamental shrubs with aromatic palmate foliage and scented, white, star-shaped flowers. CULTIVATION: Most grow well in full sun in fertile well-drained soil. Although *Choisya* are frost hardy, they may suffer some die-back in extreme winters but will regrow. Propagation is from half-hardened cuttings rooted in summer.

Choisya arizonica
☼ ❅ ↔ 3 ft (0.9 m) ↑ 3 ft (0.9 m)
This low-growing, evergreen, multi-branched shrub has 3 or 5 slender, mid-green, gland-edged leaflets, which are aromatic when crushed. Perfumed white flowers in clusters in spring. Grow against a warm wall in cooler climates. Zones 7–10.

Chlorophytum comosum 'Variegatum'

Chiranthodendron pentadactylon

Choisya 'Aztec Pearl'

☀ ❄ ↔8 ft (2.4 m) ↕8 ft (2.4 m)

Hybrid of *C. arizonica* and *C. ternata*. Has fine narrow leaflets of *C. arizonica*, abundant white flowers of *C. ternata*. Strongly aromatic shrub, lush dark green foliage. Flowers open from pale pink buds in spring–early summer. Zones 8–10.

Choisya mollis

syn. *Choisya dumosa* var. *mollis*

ZORILLO

☀/☀ ❄ ↔3–4 ft (0.9–1.2 m) ↕4–5 ft (1.2–1.5 m)

Evergreen shrub from mountain ranges of Arizona and New Mexico known as "sky islands." Leaves with 5 to 10 narrow, leathery, aromatic, deep green leaflets that become gray-green with age. Small, white, mildly scented flowers in clusters at branch tips. Zones 8–10.

Choisya ternata

MEXICAN ORANGE, MEXICAN ORANGE BLOSSOM

☀ ❄ ↔6 ft (1.8 m) ↕6 ft (1.8 m)

Evergreen Mexican shrub. Glossy 3-lobed leaves. White, starry, fragrant flower clusters in spring; second flush in late summer. Lightly prune after flowering. Shelter from winds. Tolerates summer dryness once established. Good drainage essential. **Sundance/ 'Lich'** ★, pale gold foliage, becoming more greenish on ageing, needs light shade. Zones 7–10.

Choisya mollis

Choisya ternata

CHONDROPETALUM

Genus of reeds native to South Africa and closely related to the more widely grown *Restio* (family Restionaceae). They have the typically grassy foliage of most reeds, ranging in size from 8 in (20 cm) to over 7 ft (2 m) tall. The large species have a long history of use as a thatching material. Found mostly in the Western Cape region in damp low-lying areas among proteas, leucospermums, and ericas, they are part of the distinctive vegetation known as "fynbos." Flowers are very small but borne in large, if not especially attractive heads; male and female flowers occur on separate plants. Male flowerheads are open panicles reminiscent of grasses, female flowers are more tightly packed and protected by bracts.
CULTIVATION: Plant in an open position and water and feed well in summer. Although *Chondropetalum* occurs naturally in damp ground, in cultivation well-drained soil is preferable. The plants do not always withstand division and propagation from seed tends to be more successful.

Chondropetalum tectorum

☀/☀ ❄ ↔3–5 ft (0.9–1.5 m) ↕5 ft (1.5 m)

Forms a dense clump of fine, green, grassy stems. Female plants tend to have a more olive coloration, especially in summer when carrying their short bronze flowerheads. Male flowerheads are loose, open, slightly arching, and buff-colored. Zones 9–11.

CHORIZEMA

Genus of 18 species, all but one native to southwest Australia, *Chorizema* consists of evergreen shrubs or twiners, many of which also grow as ground cover. They are members of the pea-flower subfamily of the legume (Fabaceae) family with massed short racemes of pea-like flowers, often in combinations of vividly contrasting

Chondropetalum tectorum

colors. The flowering season varies with the species. The foliage is also variable and may be heart-shaped, narrow or lobed, with or without toothed edges, and sometimes aromatic.
CULTIVATION: Their general preference is for light well-drained soil and a position in full sun or partial shade. While prolonged wet conditions are not tolerated, the plants appreciate an occasional deep watering in summer. Propagation is by seed, which needs to be soaked before sowing, or by half-hardened cuttings.

Chorizema cordatum ★

HEART-LEAFED FLAME PEA

☀/☀ ❄ ↔4 ft (1.2 m) ↕4 ft (1.2 m)

Widely cultivated species from southern Western Australia. Foliage heart-shaped, with small teeth. Flowers orange and yellow standard, deep pink to red keel. Best in well-drained soil, with a little shade, pinch back to keep compact. Zones 9–11.

CHRYSANTHEMOIDES

A genus of only 2 species of evergreen shrubs in the daisy (Asteraceae) family, native to southern and eastern Africa. They are woody toward the base, with weak brittle branches, and strongly ridged twigs. The short broad leaves usually have toothed margins. The yellow flowerheads are daisy-like. The fruit is very unusual for the family, being a small, juicy, black berry, eaten by birds, which are thereby responsible for the distribution of the seeds. In South Africa the fruit is sometimes eaten and the leaves are used medicinally. The plants are short-lived.
CULTIVATION: They can be used to provide shelter and soil protection in exposed situations and can be grown as a hedge. However, they should not be planted in any region of mild-temperate climate outside their native Africa, as they multiply very rapidly from seed and soon become uncontrollable weeds. In cold climates such as northern Europe they can be grown as conservatory plants without risk. Propagate from seed or from half-hardened cuttings.

Chorizema cordatum

Chrysanthemoides monilifera

Chrysanthemoides monilifera

syn. *Osteospermum moniliferum*

BITOU BUSH, BONESEED, BUSH-TICK BERRY

☀ ❄ ↔15 ft (4.5 m) ↕20 ft (6 m)

Young shoots and flower buds variably clothed in white cobwebby hairs. Yellow flowerheads in spring. *C. m.* subsp. *rotundata* is a seashore subspecies, with rounded bright green leaves, tangled white hairs, beneath. Rampant weed in southern Australia, displacing native species. Biological controls introduced. Zones 9–11.

CHRYSANTHEMUM

Although reclassified as *Dendranthema*, the florists' chrysanthemum is now also accepted under its old name. A perennial originally from China where it has been cultivated for over 2,500 years, it rejoins the 5 European and North African annual species left in this once large genus. In China the chrysanthemum was used medicinally and for flavoring, as well as for ornament. The Japanese adopted it and frequently use it in their art as a symbol of longevity and happiness. Annual species are small plants that more closely resemble their daisy (Asteraceae) family relatives and are mainly used for summer bedding or as fillers in borders of perennial flowers.
CULTIVATION: The annuals thrive in a sunny position with light well-drained soil. Florists' chrysanthemums prefer a heavier richer soil and will tolerate some shade. They also need pinching back when young and disbudding to ensure the best flower show. Annual species are raised from seed; the florists' forms by division when dormant or from half-hardened summer cuttings.

Chrysanthemum × *grandiflorum*

FLORISTS' CHRYSANTHEMUM

☼/◐ ❋ ↔ 18–36 in (45–90 cm)
↕ 1–5 ft (0.3–1.5 m)

Large group of hybrids, also known as *Dendranthema* × *grandiflorum*, though generally cultivated under the name *Chrysanthemum*. The names are now recognized as synonymous and equally acceptable when used for garden plants.

Chrysanthemums are available from florists throughout the year; under garden conditions they are autumn-flowering, season ranging from a few weeks before the equinox until the first frosts. Tending to have similar lobed aromatic leaves, yet chrysanthemums occur in wide range of plant sizes and flower types and are classified in groups based on flower characteristics. Categorization varies around the world, but United States National Chrysanthemum Society Standards are probably most straightforward, recognizing the following 13 classes.

1. Irregular incurved: Very large ball-shaped flowers, with incurving florets, the lower ones often loose and irregular, creating a skirt. Popular hybrids include: **'Palisade'**, **'Gold Creamest'**, and **'Shamrock'**.

2. Reflexed: Medium sized to large flowers, regular, downward curving florets, overlap neatly like scales or feathers. Included in this class are **'Euro'**, **'Fiji'**, and Robin/**'Yorobi'**.

3. Regular incurved: Flowers 4–6 in (10–15 cm) wide, near-spherical flowers, neat, regular, upward-curving florets. Includes **'Heather James'**.

4. Decorative: Compact, rather flattened blooms, distinct but short ray florets, no visible disc florets. Includes most of those known as spray chrysanthemums. Usually over 18 in (45 cm) tall. **'Fortune'**, yellow, mid-season; **'Margaret'**, mid-pink with salmon center; **'Salmon Margaret'**, all-over salmon pink; **'Wendy'**, light orange to bronze. Other popular decoratives include: Barbara/**'Yobarsara'**, **'Red Headliner'**, **'Storm King'**, Sundoro/**'Yosuru'**, and **'Wildfire'**.

5. Intermediate incurved: Similar to irregular incurved but with smaller flowerheads, still around 6 in (15 cm) wide. Includes **'Primrose Allouise'** and **'Royal Touch'**.

6. Pompon: Small, densely petalled, spherical blooms ranging from 1–4 in (2.5–10 cm) diameter. Usually under 18 in (45 cm) tall. Popular hybrids include: **'Carillon'**, **'Cheers'**, **'Ping Pong'**.

7. Single and semi-double: Simple flowers, often very large, visible and clearly defined disc florets surrounded by one or more rows of ray florets.

Chrysanthemum × grandiflorum, 1. Irregular incurved, 'Revert'

Chrysanthemum × grandiflorum, 1., 'Gold Creamest'

Singles sometimes known as 'daisies'. **'Amber Enbee Wedding'**, semi-double, soft orange-brown; **'Buckeye'**, single, red, mid-season; **'Golden Megatime'**, bright yellow single to semi-double; **'Tiger'**, single, very small, bronze, mid-season; **'Tracy'**, semi-double, white, mid-season. Other hybrids include: **'Megatime'**, **'Poser'**, and **'Splendor'**.

8. Anemone: Basically semi-double in structure with a clearly defined halo of outer ray florets but smaller ray florets clustered and mounding at the center, and concealing the disc. Includes **'Pennine Marie'**, vivid pink, to 3 ft (0.9 m) tall; **'Pennine Oriel'**, creamy white, to 3 ft (0.9 m) tall; and **'Yellow Pennine Oriel'**, bright yellow,

to 3 ft (0.9 m) tall. Other hybrids include: **'Day's End'**, **'Powder Puff'**, **'Score'**, and **'Sunny Le Mans'**.

9. Spoon: Semi-double flowers, clearly defined disc florets. Ray florets long, narrow, broaden to spoon shape at tips. Cultivars include: **'Citrine'**, yellow flowers, **'Seminole'**, pink flowers.

10. Quill: Large, regularly shaped blooms, long, straight tubular florets open at tips. Includes **'Pennine Flute'**, soft mid-pink.

11. Spider: Long, drooping, tubular florets, either narrow or broad, and often coiled or recurved at the tips. Popular hybrids include: **'Dusky Queen'**, **'Mixed Spider'**, and **'Yellow Knight'** ★.

C. × *g.*, 2. Reflexed, 'Euro'

C. × *g.*, 2. Reflexed, 'Fiji'

C. × *g.*, 7., 'Amber Swingtime'

C. × *g.*, 7. Single, 'Megatime'

C. × *g.*, 7., 'Orange Wimbledon'

C. × *g.*, 7. Single, 'Poser'

C. × *g.*, 7., 'Splendid Reagan'

C. × *g.*, 7. Single, 'Tiger'

C. × *g.*, 8. Anemone, 'Score'

C. × *g.*, 8., 'Sunny Le Mans'

C. × *g.*, 9. Spoon, 'Dublin'

C. × *g.*, 9. Spoon, 'Energy Time'

C. × *g.*, 9., 'Yellow Biarritz'

C. × *g.*, 9. Spider, 'Mixed Spider'

C. × *g.*, 6. Pompon, 'Furore'

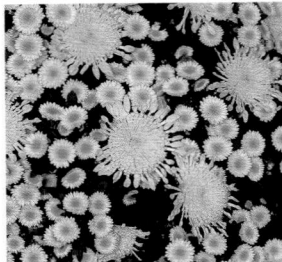

C. × g., 8. Anemone, 'Awesome'

C. × g., 13., 'Harlekijn'

C. × g., 13., 'Lemon Fiji'

C. × g. 8. Anemone, 'Weldon'

Chrysanthemum weyrichii

Chrysanthemum × *grandiflorum*, 8. Anemone, 'Touché'

12. Brush or Thistle: Very narrow, often twisted florets, lower of which stand out at right angles from stem.

13. Unclassified: Catch-all grouping covering blooms yet to be formally classified or not falling into any other categories. **'Max Riley'**, yellow flowers early in the season; **'Pink Gin'**, light pink flowers; **'Roy Coopland'**, bronze blooms; **'Satin Pink Gin'**, pink flowers; **'Yellow John Hughes'**, yellow incurved flowers. Many other cultivars include: **'Amber Yvonne Arnaud'**, **'Angora'**, **'Apricot Shoesmith Salmon'**, **'Beacon'**, **Bravo**/**'Yabravo'**, **'Bronze Cassandra'**, **'Bronze Fairie'**, **'Cherry Nathalie'**, **'Dark Red Mayford Perfection'**, **'Eastleigh'**, **'Flo Cooper'**, **'George Griffiths'**, **'Golden Cassandra'**, **'Harlekijn'**, **'Lemon Fiji'**, **'Madeleine'**, **'Mancetta Bride'**, **'Mavis'**, **'Myss Madi'**, **'Pennine Alfie'**, **'Pennine Lace'**, **'Pennine Signal'**, **'Purple Pennine Wine'**, **'Rose Mayford Perfection'**, **'Rynoon'**, **'Salmon Fairie'**, **'Southway Swan'**, **'Touché'**, **'Weldon'**, and **'Yvonne Arnaud'**. Zones 5–10.

Chrysanthemum weyrichii

MIYABE DAISY

☼/◐ ❄ ↔ 16–24 in (40–60 cm)
↑ 4 in (10 cm)

Spreading ground cover perennial native to Japan. Leaves fleshy, glossy bright green on purple-tinted stems; those near base of stems rounded, 5-lobed, becoming pinnate nearer tips. Short-stemmed 1½ in (40 mm) wide flowerheads with white or pink ray florets in summer–autumn. **'Pink Bomb'** and **'White Bomb'** are heavy-flowering selections with pink and white flowers respectively. Zones 4–9.

Chrysanthemum zawadskii

syn. *Chrysanthemum* × *rubellum*

☼ ❄ ↔ 20–40 in (50–100 cm)
↑ 24 in (60 cm)

Found from the Urals to central and northern Russia. Rhizome-rooted perennial forming clump of densely foliaged upright stems. Leaves finely hairy, pinnate with lobes sometimes toothed, to 1½ in (40 mm) long. Flowerheads white, pink, or purple, to slightly over 2 in (5 cm) wide, borne singly or in groups of up to 5. *C. z.* **var.** *latilobum*, larger in all parts, grows to 3 ft (0.9 m) tall. *C. z.* **'Clara Curtis'** ★ has many bright pink flowerheads; **'Lady Clara'**, deep pink flowers; **'Mary Stoker'**, soft yellow flowers. Zones 3–9.

CHRYSOCEPHALUM

Australian daisy (Asteraceae) family genus established with the breaking up of *Helichrysum, Helipterum,* and *Leptorhynchos,* currently composed of some 6 species of perennials and subshrubs. They are small, spreading plants, which form wide mounds of fine stems with ½–2 in (12–50 mm) long, narrow, finely hairy, gray-green to blue-green leaves. *Chrysocephalum* means yellow head and they do indeed have papery yellow flowerheads, particularly in summer and autumn. The heads, although not large—around ½ in (12 mm) wide—are abundant and quite showy.

CULTIVATION: Hardiness and cultivation requirements vary; most species can be treated as annuals and do best in a bright position with light gritty soil with average summer moisture. They are effective when grown in containers if trimmed and deadheaded routinely. Propagate from seed or from small cuttings; some species produce suckers or natural layers that can be removed and then grown on.

Chrysocephalum semipapposum

syn. *Helichrysum semipapposum*

CLUSTERED EVERLASTING, YELLOW BUTTONS

☼ ❄ ↔ to 5 ft (1.5 m) ↑ to 32 in (80 cm)

Spreading herbaceous to woody perennial, found in a wide variety of habitats in all States of Australia. The woody rootstock produces hairy stems with narrow, clustered, grayish, hairy leaves, up to 2½ in (6 cm) long. The tiny yellow flowers are borne in heads to ½ in (12 mm) in diameter, in terminal clusters of up to 100 heads. Zones 8–10.

CHRYSOGONUM

Part of the daisy (Asteraceae) family, this genus contains only one species—a low perennial herb native to eastern USA. It makes a good ground cover for partly shaded borders and along the edges of woodlands. *C. virginianum* has 2 selections—the northern one is taller and more upright, the southern one is more prostrate. In hot summers, it flowers from mid-spring to early summer. Farther north, flowering occurs from spring to early summer. It also flowers sporadically during the summer months.

CULTIVATION: Moist well-drained soil and partial to full shade are the ideal conditions. Propagate by division in early spring or early autumn; it also self-sows. Self-sown seedlings may be transplanted to desired location. It has no serious insect or disease problems.

Chrysogonum virginianum

GOLDEN STAR, GREEN AND GOLD

☼/◐ ☀ ❄ ↔ 24 in (60 cm)
↑ 6–10 in (15–25 cm)

Coarse hairy leaves have a serrated margin; the flowers are yellow with 5 slightly notched petals, 1–1½ in (25–35 mm) wide. Will grow in colder areas provided it gets good snow cover. Zones 5–9.

CHRYSOLEPIS

CHINQUAPIN, GOLDEN CHESTNUT

This genus, belonging to the beech (Fagaceae) family, is native to the

Chrysocephalum semipapposum, in Grampians National Park, Victoria, Australia

Chrysophyllum cainito

western USA and, depending on current botanical opinion, is composed of 2 species or a single rather variable species. The leaves are leathery ovals with pointed tips. When young the foliage and new growth are covered in fine golden hairs and scales, but these soon wear to a thin surface coating, though the undersides of the leaves retain their hairs. Red-brown bark is also an attraction. Catkins of tiny flowers are followed by clusters of nut cases, each containing an edible nut.
CULTIVATION: Apart from limited frost tolerance, chinquapin is not difficult to cultivate. Provided the drainage is good, these plants are not fussy about the soil type and will grow in sun or partial shade. Pruning is seldom necessary. Propagate by sowing fresh seed, which often germinates better with scarification.

Chrysolepis chrysophylla ★
☀ ❄ ↔ 30 ft (9 m) ↕ 30 ft (9 m)
Yellow-green flowers, summer-borne catkins. Clusters of small warty nut cases. Nuts take about 15 months to ripen, revealing the red-brown nut within. Zones 8–10.

CHRYSOPHYLLUM
This tropical genus from the sapodilla (Sapotaceae) family includes some 80 species of evergreen shrubs and trees. It is widespread in the tropics with the distribution centered on the Americas. They have medium to large-sized smooth-edged leaves, often with brown or golden-yellow hair on the undersides. The flowers are small, white to cream with purple markings, in small clusters that form in the leaf axils or sprout directly from the branches. They are mainly grown for their edible fruits which are large fleshy berries.
CULTIVATION: To grow steadily and fruit reliably these trees need a warm humid climate free of frosts and cold winds. They prefer fertile, moist, well-

drained, humus-enriched soil and regular feeding. Any pruning or trimming can be carried out as the fruit is harvested or, if the fruit is not required, after flowering. Propagate from seed or grafting. Seedlings take 8 to 12 years to fruit, whereas grafted plants will crop well in 4 to 5 years.

Chrysophyllum cainito
STAR APPLE
☀ 🌱 ↔ 15 ft (4.5 m) ↕ 50 ft (15 m)
Native to Central America. Leaves deep green, elliptical, yellow-brown felting beneath. Small, starry, creamy white flowers, in clusters. Rounded, 4 in (10 cm) wide fruit ripening to purple, star-shaped in cross-section. Eat fresh, preserved, or juice. Zones 11–12.

CHRYSOTHAMNUS
RABBIT BRUSH
This genus, which belongs to the daisy (Asteraceae) family, contains around 16 species of shrubs or subshrubs all native to western North America. They grow in very dry conditions in a variety of habitats from plains to canyons and hillsides, and quickly colonize disturbed ground. Plants range from about 12 in (30 cm) to 7 ft (2 m) tall. They are multi-branched and have narrow aromatic leaves. Some species contain rubber sap. Yellow or white flowers small and usually lacking rays. Borne in dense clusters which smother the plants in summer and autumn.
CULTIVATION: Grow in full sun in a light well-drained soil. Propagate from seed or cuttings.

Chrysothamnus nauseosus
syn. *Ericameria nauseosa*
☀ ❄ ↔ 12–36 in (30–90 cm) ↕ 12–60 in (30–150 cm)
Native to western and central USA. Variable well-branched shrub; woolly stems containing a small amount of rubber sap. Narrow grayish green leaves have an unpleasant smell. Smothered

in rayless yellow flowers in summer–autumn. *C. n.* var. *graveolens*, less woolly stems, greener leaves. Zones 6–9.

Chrysothamnus viscidiflorus
STICKY-LEAFED RABBIT BRUSH
☀ ❄ ↔ 12–36 in (30–90 cm) ↕ 12–36 in (30–90 cm)
Found from western USA east to Nebraska. Rounded deciduous shrub with whitish bark. Narrow leaves often twisted in appearance. Plants are covered with rayless yellow daisies in summer–autumn. Zones 6–9.

CHUSQUEA
From Central and South America, the genus *Chusquea*, in the grass (Poaceae) family, has an estimated 200 species of clump-forming bamboos, including a number of species large enough to be treated as shrubs or trees. Though externally similar to other bamboos, except perhaps being longer, with more plumed foliage, they differ internally in having solid pithy-centered stems rather than the hollow stems. *Chusquea* leaf sheaths do not drop and

Chrysolepis chrysophylla

are bristly, with leaf-like outgrowths that are known as auricles.
CULTIVATION: Because many of these bamboos occur at high altitudes in cloud forest, they have a general preference for relatively cool, moist, humid conditions and will not tolerate prolonged dry conditions. Although *Chusquea* bamboos are not huge and do not produce runners, they can be vigorous in suitable climates, so choose a site that allows room for development. Frost hardiness varies, species from southern South America being the hardiest. Propagate by division.

Chusquea culeou
☀ ❄ ↔ 10–20 ft (3–6 m) ↕ 10–20 ft (3–6 m)
Chilean species. Develops into a large clump with tightly packed, solid, erect culms with bottlebrush-like branching. Most widely cultivated of the *Chusquea* species. The stems and leaves are yellowish olive green, the papery leaf sheaths creamy white. The young stems are waxy coated, giving them a bluish appearance. Zones 7–9.

Chusquea culeou

Chrysothamnus nauseosus, in the wild, Grand Canyon, Arizona, USA

Cibotium schiedei

Cichorium endivia 'Green Curled'

CIBOTIUM

This genus of 15 species of the tree fern (Dicksoniaceae) family, allied to *Dicksonia*, has a scattered distribution, occurring in Mexico, Hawaii, India, and parts of tropical and subtropical Asia. The trunk is often upright and tree-like, but in some species may grow horizontally before turning upward. The fronds are very finely divided and the crown and trunk are usually very fibrous and hairy.
CULTIVATION: Some species will tolerate light frosts, but most prefer moist warm-temperate to subtropical conditions. They should be planted in full shade or with shade from the hottest sun in constantly moist humus-enriched soil, and watered well in summer or during dry spells. Propagate by removing basal shoots, from freshly cut lengths of trunk, or from spores.

Cibotium glaucum

HAPU, HAWAIIAN TREE FERN
☀ ❄ ↔ 6–10 ft (1.8–3 m)
↑ 6–15 ft (1.8–4.5 m)

Large slow-growing tree fern from Hawaii. Erect trunk to 15 ft (4.5 m) tall and 12 in (30 cm) thick, covered with lustrous yellowish brown hairs. Arching, oval- to sword-shaped, leathery, slightly glossy fronds, 3–6 ft (0.9–1.8 m) long. Narrow leaflets with long, narrow, serrated tips, on stalks covered with dark hairs. Zones 8–9.

Cibotium schiedei ★

MEXICAN TREE FERN
☀/☀ ❄ ↔ 8 ft (2.4 m) ↑ 15 ft (4.5 m)
From Mexico. Trunk covered with silky golden brown hairs. Mature fronds over 6 ft (1.8 m) long, light green, bluish undersides. Side shoots develop into trunks, forming a clump. Tolerates light frosts. Zones 9–11.

CICER

This genus of 40 species from central and western Asia to Ethiopia, Greece, Morocco, and the Canary Islands belongs to the pea-flower subfamily of the legume (Fabaceae) family. They are erect to creeping annuals or perennials. Leaves are pinnate or have 3 leaflets, sometimes with tendrils. Leaflets are toothed and the stipules are leafy. Its flowers are small, white, or violet, in few-flowered racemes arising in the leaf axils. The pods are oblong to elliptical and burst open at maturity to release 1 to 4 large seeds.
CULTIVATION: The only species that is widely cultivated is *C. arietinum* (chickpea); it is the third most important pulse crop in the world (after beans and peas), and is grown mainly in the Middle East, North Africa, and India. Grown in fields in light, well-drained, fertile soil, they need 4 to 6 months of warm dry conditions to crop satisfactorily. In India seeds are mostly planted in autumn and the peas harvested before the onset of the summer monsoon; in other areas they may be sown in late spring for an autumn harvest.

Cicer arietinum

CHICKPEA, EGYPTIAN PEA, GARBANZO BEAN
☀ ❄ ↔ 10–20 in (25–50 cm)
↑ 8 in–3 ft (20 cm–0.9 m)
Probably derived from *C. reticulatum*, in southeastern Turkey about 4500 BC. Annual, sprawling to erect downy stems, leaves with up to 17 pairs of small leaflets. Flowers white to violet, in spring–early summer, followed by hairy pods to 1½ in (40 mm) long containing globular white, brown, or blackish seeds. Eaten fresh or dried, ground as flour for houmous or as a coffee substitute: it was the 'salted provender' of the Bible. Seedlings, especially of **'Green Seeded'**, eaten as bean-sprouts; **'Kabuli Black'**, drought tolerant and vigorous. Zones 8–11.

CICHORIUM

CHICORY, ENDIVE
A genus of 8 species in the daisy (Asteraceae) family and the tribe Lactuceae. *Cichorium* are annuals or perennials that originate from Europe, especially around the Mediterranean and western Asia, but are now naturalized in parts of North America and Australia. They are grown for their edible roots (chicory) and leaves (endive, witloof, escarole) and come in a range of green or red leaves, either hairy or smooth. Flowers are most often a bright blue but sometimes pink or white, and resemble a dandelion or thistle. Their milky sap may irritate the skin.
CULTIVATION: These plants are generally seed-sown in spring and grown on through summer for a late autumn harvest. A deep, friable, well-fertilized soil with even moisture throughout the growing season is desirable. Some varieties can overwinter in the ground, but the resultant crop is not as good as the initial crop. Watch for slugs and snails and mildew.

Cichorium endivia

ENDIVE, ESCAROLE
☀ ⚘ ↔ 8–20 in (20–50 cm)
↑ 8–20 in (20–50 cm)
Grown for their large slightly bitter leaves for salads, also for cooking. Hearting varieties have outer leaves tied up (or covered with a pot) to blanch hearts and reduce bitterness. **'Batavian Green'** ★, escarole type, mild-flavored creamy centered heart; **'Green Curled'**, green leaves divided and curled; **'Green Curled Ruffec'**, finely cut frilled or ruffled leaves, thick white midribs, slightly bitter, resists cold and wet. Zones 9–11.

Cichorium intybus

CHICORY, RADICCHIO, WITLOOF
☀ ⚘ ↔ 24 in (60 cm)
↑ 20–48 in (50–120 cm)
Roots used for coffee substitute; also grown for blanched forced shoots harvested in autumn–winter. Leaves green or red, blue flowers very ornamental. **'Alouette'**, radicchio type, good flavor, crisp and tender; **'Early Treviso'**, non-heading, slender, tall variety, green leaves change to red as weather cools; **'Giulio'**, compact radicchio resistant to bolting (going to seed early in season); **'Greenlof'**, traditional Dutch cultivar, tall upright heads with green outer leaves, white inside when blanched; **'Long Green'**, green upright leaves, use as for lettuce. **'Magdeburgh'**, grown for white

Cichorium intybus

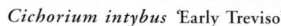
Cichorium intybus 'Early Treviso'

Cichorium intybus 'Long Green'

Cichorium intybus 'Magdeburgh'

Cichorium intybus 'Red Rib'

Cichorium intybus 'Palla Rossa'

Cichorium intybus 'Greenlof'

Cirsium japonicum 'Rose Beauty'

Cinnamomum japonicum

Cineraria saxifraga

tapered root that is dried and powdered as a coffee substitute; **'Palla Rossa'** ★, compact radicchio type; **'Red Rib'**, bright red stems and veins; **'Red Treviso'** (syn. 'Rossa di Treviso'), upright radicchio type, red leaves turn dark purple in winter. **'Red Verona'** ★ (syn. 'Rossa di Verona'), a hardy radicchio type with red leaves and large, tight, round heart; **'Rossana'**, heat resistant; **'Witloof'**, leaves dark green, lobed, upright, produces fat white chicons (forced shoot) when roots are cut and blanched. Zones 9–11.

CINERARIA

This mostly South African genus of around 50 species of evergreen perennials and subshrubs belongs in the daisy (Asteraceae) family. The genus was once the home of the florists' cineraria but that most famous cineraria is now classified under *Pericallis*. Mainly sprawling or straggly plants, their leaves range from small and rounded to pinnate and toothed. Both the stems and the leaves are covered in fine hairs. Sprays of small yellow daisies appear at various times, depending on the species.
CULTIVATION: While not the most spectacular or attractive of plants, these bushy daisies are easily grown and adaptable, preferring cool summers and mild winters. Plant in cool, moist, humus-rich soil with shade from the hottest sun. Propagate by seed, layers, or basal cuttings.

Cineraria saxifraga

☀ ⦂ ↔ 3 ft (0.9 m) ↑ 8 in (20 cm)
Spreading, somewhat mounding, South African subshrub. Strikes root as it spreads. Round to kidney-shaped leaves, coarsely toothed at the tips, to 1½ in (40 mm) long. Short-stemmed yellow flowerheads throughout warmer months. Zones 9–10.

CINNAMOMUM

A genus of about 250 usually evergreen trees and shrubs in the family Lauraceae, with aromatic leaves, wood, and bark. They are native to warm-temperate to subtropical regions from eastern and southeastern Asia to Australia. Panicles of inconspicuous flowers appear in summer. The fleshy berry-like fruit is grown for its spicy flavoring and for use in traditional medicine. The timber is used for making utensils and furniture, for building construction, and as fuel. Oil from the seeds is used for suppositories and in confectionery production. Ornamentally they are valued both for the appearance of their foliage and as shade trees. Cinnamon is derived from the bark of *C. zeylanicum*, which is grown commercially.
CULTIVATION: Best in full sun or part-shade, in well-drained fertile soil, preferably a sandy loam medium. They tolerate regular pruning, and propagation is from seed sown in autumn or from cuttings of half-hardened softwood taken in spring.

Cinnamomum camphora

CAMPHOR LAUREL, CAMPHOR TREE
☀ ⦂ ↔ 30 ft (9 m) ↑ 60 ft (18 m)
From China, Taiwan, and Japan. Evergreen shade and screen tree. Aromatic leaves shiny, pink-red at first, turning light green. Cream flower clusters in spring. Oval, shiny, black berries. Tolerant of poor soils, air pollution. Camphor extracted from timber commercially. Zones 9–11.

Cinnamomum japonicum

YABUNIKKEI
☀ ⦂ ↔ 35 ft (10 m) ↑ 60 ft (18 m)
Native of Korea, Japan, and Taiwan. Evergreen tree. Slender branches, smooth oblong to ovate leaves, 2½ in (6 cm) long. Zones 9–10.

CIRSIUM

With around 250 species this is one of the largest genera in the thistle tribe of the daisy (Asteraceae) family. Most occur in the Mediterranean region and in central and east Asia, but there are also many in North America, principally in the west. Mostly very prickly plants, they include some of the world's most widespread and troublesome weeds, for example *C. vulgare* (spear thistle). Biennials or perennials, in their first season they form a rosette of spreading leaves with marginal teeth tipped by spines, and often with needle-like spines on the leaf surfaces as well. Flowering stems are usually branched into many flowerheads, each consisting of a goblet-shaped receptacle of bristly bracts crowned by a dense group of pink to purple (rarely cream) disk florets. Ray florets are lacking, as in all members of the thistle tribe.
CULTIVATION: A few species have been grown as ornamentals but in most countries the importation of additional species is now prohibited due to the likelihood of their becoming weeds. Easily grown in any good soil in full sun, they are propagated by root division or seed; early sowing can give flowers in the same year.

Cirsium japonicum

JAPANESE THISTLE
☀ ❋ ↔ 2–4 ft (0.6–1.2 m) ↑ 3–5 ft (0.9–1.5 m)
From China, Japan and Korea. Perennial branching into numerous erect, slender stems terminating in 1–2 in (25 mm–5 cm) wide pink to purple flowerheads from late spring–autumn. **Beauty Series** are sold as seed, are less spiny, and good as cut flowers. **'Early Pink Beauty'**, flowers pale pink; **'Rose Beauty'**, reddish pink. Zones 5–9.

Cirsium rivulare

☀ ❋ ↔ 3 ft (0.6 m) ↑ 5 ft (1.5 m)

From central Europe. Perennial with branching rootstock, broad deep green leaves, multiple erect, slender stems terminating in tight clusters of several lilac to purple flowerheads, opening in succession through summer. **'Atropurpureum'**, deep reddish purple heads. Zones 5–9.

Cirsium subcoriaceum

☀ ❋ ↔ 4 ft (1.2 m) ↑ 6–12 ft (1.8–3.6 m)

Giant species from mountains of Central America, from southern Mexico to Panama. Apparently biennial, starting as fountain-like rosette of leaves to 3 ft (0.9 m) long; flowering stem to 3 in (8 cm) thick, branched at top with pendent heads to 4 in (10 cm) wide, florets straw to pinkish orange, in autumn–spring. Zones 8–11.

CISSUS

GRAPE IVY

This genus of around 200 species, mostly vines, found throughout tropical and subtropical parts of the world, belongs to the grape (Vitaceae) family.

Cissus quadrangularis

Some are shrublets and some have succulent or herbaceous stems. Leaves are usually simple, sometimes palmate, rarely with 3 distinct leaflets. They usually have simple or forked tendrils opposite the leaves, sometimes with adhesive discs. Flowers are stalked candelabra-like cymes opposite the leaves, usually on or at the end of lateral tendril-less shoots. They are hermaphroditic, with a cup-shaped calyx, 4 free petals, and 4 stamens. The disc is cup-shaped with a thick margin. The ovary has 2 compartments, each with 2 ovules. The style is round in cross-section, the stigma minute. Berries are spherical to egg-shaped, usually inedible, with 1 seed.
CULTIVATION: Grow outdoors in warmer areas or as shade-tolerant house plants for their glossy foliage or succulent stems in cooler regions. Propagate from stem cuttings, or from seed for the succulent species.

Cissus antarctica

KANGAROO VINE

☀/☀ ⬆ ↔ 3–10 ft (0.9–3 m) ↑ 17–25 ft (5–8 m)

From Australia. Vigorous vine. Branches downy when young. Shiny, dark green, pointed leaves, shallow-toothed margins, to 4 in (10 cm) long. Small green flowers. Edible, black, pea-sized fruit. Popular as a house plant. Zones 10–11.

Cissus hypoglauca

Cistus × aguilarii

Cissus hypoglauca

GIANT WATER VINE, JUNGLE VINE, NATIVE GRAPE

☀ ⬆ ↔ 20 ft (6 m) ↑ 17–35 ft (5–10 m)

From eastern rainforests of Australia. Vigorous climber with compound leaves of 3 to 5 glossy, bluish green, oval leaflets. Clusters of small yellow flowers in early summer. Grape-like fruits, to nearly 1 in (25 mm) across, in late summer–autumn. Zones 10–11.

Cissus quadrangularis

☀ ✛ ↔ 32 in (80 cm) ↑ 60 in (150 cm)

Succulent climber from Africa, southern Asia, and Malaysia. Four-angled stems that are constricted at the nodes. Heart-shaped or 3-lobed leaves to 2 in (5 cm), soon falling. Small greenish flowers. Although poisonous to stock, extracts of *C. quadrangularis* are used medicinally. Zones 10–12.

Cissus rhombifolia

VENEZUELA TREE VINE

☀/☀ ⬆ ↔ 6 ft (1.8 m) ↑ 10 ft (3 m)

Climber native to tropical America, popular as a house plant. Stems and leaves have brownish or silvery down when young. Trifoliate leaves, rhomboid leaflets with serrated margins. **'Ellen Danica'**, larger glossy leaves with deep pointed lobes; **'Mandana'**, erect stems when young, larger more leathery leaves. Zones 10–11.

Cissus trifoliata

MARINE VINE

☀ ⬆ ↔ 15–25 ft (4.5–8 m) ↑ 15–25 ft (4.5–8 m)

From southern USA and Mexico. Woody-stemmed climber with fleshy, semi-succulent, 3-lobed leaves. Foliage

Cistus albidus

falls in drought. Inconspicuous green flowers, followed by small grape-like fruit. Zones 10–11.

CISTUS

A genus of about 20 species in the rock-rose (Cistaceae) family. All are small to medium-sized, evergreen, flowering shrubs found throughout the Mediterranean region. They grow on sun-baked stony hillsides. In cultivation they become very adaptable long-flowering ornamentals, ideal for difficult dry sites. The leaves are opposite, mostly dark green or whitish, and in some species exude a sticky resin called ladanum or labdanum, which is used in the manufacture of incense and perfume. The flowers, which are individually short-lived, have 5 broad petals, white, pink, mauve, or reddish purple, often blotched, and with prominent yellow stamens.
CULTIVATION: All *Cistus* species revel in a hot sunny position and will grow in most soils provided drainage is good. They thrive in all climates of the Mediterranean type. Young plants should be tip pruned; prune older plants after flowering. Seeds can be sown in spring. Short cuttings from non-flowering sideshoots can be taken in autumn.

Cistus × aguilarii

☀ ❋ ↔ 3–5 ft (0.9–1.5 m) ↑ 3–7 ft (0.9–2 m)

Naturally occurring hybrid of *C. ladanifer* and *C. populifolius* found in southwestern Europe and northern Africa. Lance-shaped leaves are bright green with prominent veins. White saucer-shaped flowers, to 1 in (25 mm) across, with fluffy yellow stamens. **'Maculatus'**, maroon blotch at base of each petal. Zones 8–10.

Cistus albidus

☀ ❋ ↔ 8 ft (2.4 m) ↑ 6 ft (1.8 m)

Widely distributed through southwestern Europe and North Africa. Dense shrub. Leaves whitish, white downy twigs. Flowers pale rose-lilac with a yellow center. Zones 7–9.

Cirsium subcoriaceum (foreground), in the wild, Cerro de la Muerte, Costa Rica

Cirsium rivulare 'Atropurpureum'

Cistus × argenteus 'Silver Pink'

Cistus × argenteus

☼/◐ ❋ ↔ 3 ft (0.9 m) ↑ 3 ft (0.9 m)

This is a garden hybrid between *C. laurifolius* and *C. × canescens* (*C. albidus × C. creticus*). The bush is upright-growing, with leaves that are small and gray-green, and it bears white or pink flowers, which open to over 2 in (5 cm) wide. Cultivars include: '**Peggy Sammons**', purple-pink flowers; '**Paper Moon**', pure white flowers; '**Stripy**', white flowers with irregular stripes and sectors colored pink; '**Silver Pink**', pink flowers. Zones 7–10.

Cistus × canescens

☼ ❋ ↔ 8 ft (2.4 m) ↑ 6 ft (1.8 m)

This *C. albidus × C. creticus* hybrid is very similar to *C. albidus*, but its leaves are a slightly darker green and are less hairy and more pointed. Flowers are pink to magenta and do not have the yellow spots characteristic of *C. albidus*. *C. × c.* **f. albus**, grayish foliage, white flowers. Zones 8–10.

Cistus creticus

Cistus creticus subsp. *incanus*

Cistus × canescens f. *albus*

Cistus creticus

syn. *Cistus incanus* subsp. *creticus*
HAIRY ROCK ROSE, ROCK ROSE

☼ ❋ ↔ 3 ft (0.9 m) ↑ 3 ft (0.9 m)

Found in the Mediterranean region. Stems hairy, leaves, wavy margins, whitish green beneath. Flowers purple to crimson, flushed yellow at petal bases. *C. c.* **subsp. *incanus*** (syn. *C. incanus*), less wavy margins, no yellow on petal bases. *C. ×. c.* **var. *tauricus***, purple-pink flowers. Zones 7–9.

Cistus heterophyllus

☼ ❋ ↔ 3 ft (0.9 m) ↑ 3 ft (0.9 m)

From southeastern Europe and northwestern Africa. Erect densely branching shrub. Hairy leaves are dark green above, paler and prominently veined beneath. Purplish pink saucer-shaped flowers, 2–2½ in (5–6 cm) in diameter, yellow basal spot. Zones 8–10.

Cistus × hybridus

syn. *Cistus × corbariensis*

☼ ❋ ↔ 4 ft (1.2 m) ↑ 3 ft (0.9 m)

Hybrid of *C. populifolius* and *C. salviifolius*. Leaves downy, 2 in (5 cm) long, deep green, oval, toothed, pale beneath. Red buds, white flowers, yellow basal spots. Zones 7–10.

Cistus ladanifer

GUM CISTUS, LADANUM

☼ ❋ ↔ 5 ft (1.5 m) ↑ 5 ft (1.5 m)

Native to North Africa and the southwestern Mediterranean. Leaves dark green, whitish, furry beneath, exuding ladanum. Flowers up to 4 in (10 cm) in diameter, white with a brownish

Cistus heterophyllus

Cistus ladanifer

Cistus × hybridus

crimson blotch, bright yellow stamens. *C. l.* **subsp. *sulcatus***, previously called *C. palhinhae*, low-growing, compact, shiny sticky leaves, white flowers. *C. l.* '**Blanche**', deep green glossy leaves, grayish beneath, white flowers; '**Paladin**', glossy green leaves, paler beneath, large white flowers with dark red basal blotches; '**Pat**', large flowers, up to 5 in (12 cm) across, white with maroon basal blotches. Zones 8–10.

Cistus laurifolius

LAUREL-LEAFED ROCK ROSE

☼ ❋ ↔ 6 ft (1.8 m) ↑ 6 ft (1.8 m)

Found naturally in southwestern Europe. Leaves leathery, dark green above, gray to brown, furry beneath.

Cistus heterophyllus

Cistus libanotis

Cistus populifolius

Overlapping petals white, suffused with yellow at the base, stamens dark yellow. Zones 7–9.

Cistus libanotis

☼ ❋ ↔ 15 in (38 cm) ↑ 15 in (38 cm)

Native to southwestern Spain and nearby parts of Portugal. Leaves downy, sticky, to 1 in (25 mm) long, rolled edges. White flowers, 1 in (25 mm) wide. Zones 8–10.

Cistus populifolius

☼ ❋ ↔ 6 ft (1.8 m) ↑ 6 ft (1.8 m)

Distributed over the Mediterranean region. Dark green leaves, small, hairy, heart-shaped. White flowers, yellow basal blotches, in summer. Zones 6–9.

Cistus × *pulverulentus*

Cistus × *purpureus*

Cistus salviifolius

Cistus × pulverulentus

☼ ❋ ↔ 2 ft (0.6 m) ↕ 2 ft (0.6 m)

Hybrid between *C. albidus* and *C. crispus*, often sold in nurseries under the name 'Sunset' ★. Dwarf compact shrub bearing gray-green leaves with undulating margins. Bright pink flowers. Zones 8–10.

Cistus × purpureus

☼ ❋ ↔ 5 ft (1.5 m) ↕ 4 ft (1.2 m)

Parent of several popular cultivars, result of hybridizing between *C. ladanifer* and *C. creticus*. Sticky young stems, dark green leaves, grayish hairs beneath. Flowers pink to magenta, to 2 in (5 cm) wide, conspicuous dark red basal spots. 'Betty Taudevin', dark pink to crimson flowers with maroon basal spots; 'Brilliancy', deep pink flowers

with red-brown basal spots; 'Doris Hibberson', heavy crop of pale pink flowers. Zones 7–10.

Cistus salviifolius

SAGE-LEAFED ROCK ROSE

☼ ❋ ↔ 30 in (75 cm) ↕ 30 in (75 cm)

A species first cultivated in the sixteenth century. Leaves slightly aromatic, wrinkled, rough, downy, dark gray-green upper surface, whitish gray undersurface. Flowers borne singly, with crepe-like white petals, suffused with yellow at their base. 'Prostratus', dwarf form with smaller leaves. Zones 7–9.

Cistus × skanbergii

☼ ❋ ↔ 3 ft (0.9 m) ↕ 3 ft (0.9 m)

Discovered in Greece, a naturally occurring hybrid between *C. mon-*

Cistus × *skanbergii*

Cistus Hybrid Cultivar 'Grayswood Pink'

Cistus Hybrid Cultivar 'Snow Fire'

speliensis and *C. parviflorus*. Light pink flowers in large sprays. Leaves have downy undersides. Zones 8–10.

Cistus Hybrid Cultivars

☼ ❋ ↔ 3–6 ft (0.9–1.8 m)
↕ 2–5 ft (0.6–1.5 m)

Hybrid cultivars that cannot readily be assigned such names as *C.* × *dansereaui, C.* × *pulverulentus,* and *C.* × *purpureus* include: 'Grayswood Pink', pink flowers; 'Snow Fire', vigorous and hardy, with white flowers bearing deep red blotches; 'Victor Reiter', downy reddish stems, large saucer-shaped flowers of medium pink paling to white at the center, prominent yellow stamens. Zones 7–9.

CITRULLUS

An African and Asian pumpkin (Cucurbitaceae) family genus of just 3 species of annual and perennial

trailers and climbers, best known as the home of the watermelon (*C. lanatus*). Their stems are covered with short coarse hairs and bear simple or branched tendrils in the leaf axils. The leaves are oval to palmate but often so deeply lobed that they appear pinnate. Foliage color ranges from blue-gray to deep green, sometimes with small translucent patches. Large, 5-lobed, bell-shaped, yellow flowers appear in the leaf axils and develop into the familiar rounded fruit, usually pale green with dark striping and mottling, and ranging from golf ball to larger than soccer ball size, weighing up to 60 lb (27.25 kg).

CULTIVATION: Melons need a long warm growing season to ripen properly. As with most cucurbits, if the drainage is good and the temperatures warm enough they cannot really be overfed or over-watered. Allow to dry off as the fruit nears ripeness. They are usually propagated from seed, though the perennial *C. colocynthis* will grow from cuttings or layers.

Citrullus lanatus

syn. *Citrullus vulgaris*

WATERMELON

☼/☼ ↝ ↔ 10–20 ft (3–6 m)
↕ 36 in–6 ft (90 cm–1.8 m)

Annual climber or trailer from Namibia, naturalized elsewhere. Of indeterminate size, spreading or climbing throughout growing season.

Citrullus lanatus, in the wild, in Kgalagadi Transfrontier Park, South Africa

Citrullus lanatus 'New Queen'

Citrullus lanatus 'Sweet Favorite'

Oval, lobed, pinnate, green leaves with toothed edges and small translucent patches. Branched tendrils and pink- to red-fleshed, mottled, green fruit to over 20 in (50 cm) long. 'Candy Red', oblong fruit weighing up to 40 lb (18 kg), ripens 85 days after petal fall; 'Dixie Queen', bright red flesh, even round fruit to 50 lb (22.5 kg), 80-day ripening period; 'Fordhook Hybrid', small fruit, deep pink flesh, to 10 lb (4.5 kg), 74-day ripening period; 'Klondike', medium-sized fruit with sweet red flesh, 85-day ripening period; 'New Queen', round fruit; 'Sweet Favorite', oblong, red-fleshed fruit to 20 lb (9 kg), 82-day ripening period; 'Triplesweet Seedless' ★, round fruit with deep pink seedless flesh, to 20 lb (9 kg), 85-day ripening period. Zones 10–12.

CITRUS

syns *Eremocitrus, Fortunella, Microcitrus*
Ranging in the wild from China to India, Southeast Asia, New Guinea, and Australia, this genus comprises about 20 species of evergreen shrubs and small trees and belongs to the family Rutaceae. They are grown in warmer countries for their edible fruits—the oranges, lemons, limes, grapefruit, and mandarins, among others. They are highly ornamental, with dark glossy foliage; fragrant, white, star-shaped flowers appear singly or in clusters at different times of the year. Their unique fruit structure identifies the genus: the tough skin encloses a white pith of greatly varying thickness, inside which are the fruit segments.
CULTIVATION: In frost-free conditions most *Citrus* species flourish in fertile well-drained soil in a sunny position protected from wind. During the growing season they need plenty of water and regular small applications of nitrogenous fertilizer to promote growth and fruit size. They need very little pruning. They are excellent for large pots. Propagation is by budding, or by grafting the desired species onto a suitable rootstock.

Citrus × aurantiifolia

syn. *Limonia aurantiifolia*
LIME
☼ ✦ ↔ 10 ft (3 m) ↑ 8–15 ft (2.4–4.5 m)
Widely cultivated in Mexico, the West Indies, and Florida, USA. Spreading prickly branches. Small, thin-skinned, oval to round, seeded fruit, greenish yellow, acid, juicy, green pulp. Thrives in tropical and subtropical regions. Zones 11–12.

Citrus × aurantium

syns *Citrus × paradisi, C. sinensis, C. × tangelo, C. × tangor*
☼ ❄ ↔ 10 ft (3 m) ↑ 15 ft (4.5 m)
This name has expanded to include the oranges, grapefruits, tangelos, and tangors, all of which are believed to be hybrids between the mandarin (*C. reticulata*) and the shaddock (*C. maxima*). These major citrus types are now treated as cultivar groups.

Grapefruit Group (syn. *C. × paradisi*): Includes many cultivars. Rounded bushy tree to 30 ft (9 m). Large oval leaves, some spines. Large, thin-skinned, yellow fruits, to 4–6 in (10–15 cm) in diameter, ripen late autumn–early spring. Some varieties withstand light frosts. Frost tolerant varieties 'Duncan' and 'Marsh' ★ have pale straw-colored flesh. 'Red Blush' and 'Ruby' have pink flesh and require a hot frost-free climate to develop good color.

Sour Orange Group: The Seville orange is the only widely grown member of this group. Tough spiny tree to 30 ft (9 m), highly perfumed flowers, aromatic thick peel, bitter-tasting

Citrus hystrix

fruit, ripens in autumn, used for marmalade. Withstands light frosts.

Sweet Orange Group (syn. *C. sinensis*): This group comprises the common eating oranges. Attractive, medium-sized, rounded tree to 25 ft (8 m) high. Glossy dark green leaves, beautiful, fragrant, white blossoms. Fruit is deep orange in color, and has sweet juicy flesh. These plants do best in a Mediterranean climate. Some varieties tolerate light frosts. 'Ruby', a popular "blood orange," reddish skin, flesh, and juice, maturing in early spring; 'Valencia' produces abundant fruit, relatively seedless. The navel subgroup of sweet oranges is normally seedless; well known 'Washington Navel' is possibly one of the best eating oranges, large, thick-skinned, sweet fruit, which ripens in winter.

Tangelo Group (syn. *C. × tangelo*): Grows up to 30 ft (9 m), bears reddish orange fruit, pleasant acid-sweet flavor, good for juicing. Frost sensitive, needs a long hot growing season. Most ripen in spring. Best varieties are 'Minneola', 'Orlando', and 'Samson'.

Tangor Group (syn. *C. × tangor*): to 12 ft (3.5 m) high. Fruit is intermediate in flavor and size between orange and mandarin, but more rounded than the latter. 'Honey Murcott', the original cross, has 3 in

Citrus × aurantium 'Washington Navel'

(8 cm) wide, thin-skinned, yellow-orange fruit, juicy, sweet, orange flesh.
'Temple', a deep orange-red easy-to-peel variety with a sweet rich flavor, ripens in spring. Zones 9–11.

Citrus glauca

syn. *Eremocitrus glauca*
DESERT LIME
☼ ❄ ↔ 8 ft (2.4 m) ↑ 6–10 ft (1.8–3 m)
From Australia, drought tolerant. Suckering shrub or rounded, dense, bushy tree. Branches prickly, sometimes almost leafless. Thick gray-green leaves. Small, white, spring flowers. Lemon-yellow, thin-skinned, good flavored, juicy fruit. Zones 9–12.

Citrus hystrix

CAFFRE LIME, LEECH LIME, MAURITIUS PAPEDA
☼ ❄ ↔ 6 ft (1.8 m) ↑ 10 ft (3 m)
Used in Southeast Asian cuisine; aromatic leaves flavor Thai and Malay dishes. Unusual leaves, leaf stalk swells to almost same width as blade. Small, rough, wrinkled fruit, little juice, rind used as flavoring. Zones 10–12.

Citrus glauca

Citrus × aurantium 'Valencia'

Citrus japonica

syns *Fortunella japonica, F. margarita*
CUMQUAT

☀ ❄ ↔ 3 ft (0.9 m) ↑ 6 ft (1.8 m)

Shrub from southern China. Dense branches, oval green leaves, small, round to oval, golden fruit. **Marumi Group**, small leaves, round or flattened fruit: **'Meiwa'**, dwarf form; **'Sunstripe'**, variegated foliage and fruit. **Nagami Group** (syn. *Fortunella margarita*), larger leaves, elongated thin-skinned fruit. Zones 9–10.

Citrus × *latifolia*

TAHITIAN LIME

☀ ❄ ↔ 10 ft (3 m) ↑ 6–15 ft (1.8–4.5 m)

Almost thornless tree of uncertain origin. Large, thin-skinned, yellow fruit, green pulp, few seeds. Harvested autumn–early winter. Zones 10–12.

Citrus limetta

SWEET LEMON, SWEET LIME

☀ ❄ ↔ 6 ft (1.8 m) ↑ 8 ft (2.4 m)

Grown mainly in India, Egypt, and other tropical countries. Medium-sized fruit, rounded base, smooth, thin, green rind, juicy orange flesh with few seeds. Fruit lacks acidity, used as an orange. Zones 10–12.

Citrus × *limon*

LEMON

☀ ❄ ↔ 10 ft (3 m) ↑ 10–15 ft (3–4.5 m)

An ancient hybrid; one parent is *C. medica,* the other uncertain. Smooth-skinned, acidic, yellow fruit, several flushes throughout the year. Best in a Mediterranean climate. Some varieties tolerate light frosts once established. **'Garey's Eureka'**, thornless, fruits year round, mostly in summer. Best variety for temperate climates, including coastal areas; **'Lisbon'**, vigorous thorny variety, winter-bearing, suited to hot areas. Zones 9–11.

Citrus × *limonia*

RANGPUR LIME

☀ ❄ ↔ 12 ft (3.5 m) ↑ 20 ft (6 m)

Lemon/mandarin hybrid, originating in China. Thorny, many branches. Fragrant white flowers, pinkish tinge.

Citrus japonica

Citrus maxima

Rounded fruit, deep yellow-orange, ripen in winter. Used for making marmalade. Zones 10–12.

Citrus maxima

POMELO, SHADDOCK

☀ ❄ ↔ 10 ft (3 m) ↑ 20–40 ft (6–12 m)

Presumed native to Southeast Asia. Dense, large, glossy, oval to oblong leaves. Large pale yellow fruit with yellowish to pink flesh. Zones 10–12.

Citrus medica

CITRON

☀ ❄ ↔ 8 ft (2.4 m) ↑ 6–15 ft (1.8–4.5 m)

From northern India. Shrub or small tree. Short stiff spines, large, oval, serrated leaves, purplish new growth. Large flowers, purplish outside, white within. Large wrinkled fruit, little juice, thick fragrant rind. **'Etrog'**, long-pointed apex. Zones 9–11.

Citrus × *meyeri* 'Meyer'

MEYER LEMON

☀/☀ ❄ ↔ 5–8 ft (1.5–2.4 m) ↑ 7–10 ft (2–3 m)

Lemon/orange (*C. limon* × *C. aurantium*) hybrid. Thorny stems, dark green leaves to 4 in (10 cm) long, clusters of cream flowers, bitter fruit with thin yellow skin. Usually treated as a lemon, but not acidic enough for some uses. Very hardy. Zones 9–11.

Citrus × *microcarpa*

syn. × *Citrofortunella microcarpa*
CALAMONDIN, PANAMA ORANGE

☀ ❄ ↔ 4 ft (1.2 m) ↑ 8 ft (2.4 m)

Hybrid of the cumquat, *C. japonica* (syn. *Fortunella japonica*) and the mandarin (*C. reticulata*). Dense foliage, small, rounded, orange fruit. Popular ornamental. Zones 9–11.

Citrus reticulata

MANDARIN, SATSUMA, TANGERINE

☀/☀ ❄ ↔ 6–10 ft (1.8–3 m) ↑ 10–17 ft (3–5 m)

Thorny small tree from warm-temperate to subtropical East Asia.

Cladrastis kentuckeana

Lance-shaped leaves 2–4 in (5–10 cm) long, petioles with small wings. Small, sweet-scented, white flowers, followed by oval to flattened, sweet-fleshed, golden fruit. **'Clementine'**, large, rather acidic, spherical, orange-red fruit with few seeds; **'Dancy'**, flattened orange-red fruit, good flavor, few to many seeds; **'Encore'**, upright tree, few thorns, rounded orange-yellow fruit with darker spots, good flavor but many seeds; **'Fairchild'**, round deep orange fruit, many seeds, bush near thornless, needs cross-pollination; **'Fremont'**, early fruiting, good flavor, few seeds; **'Kinnow'**, very hardy, thin leaves, flattened, orange-yellow, seedy fruit; **'Page'**, round orange fruit, often very seedy, sometimes sold as an orange; **'Pixie'**, small, very sweet, seedless. Some varieties marketed as mandarins or tangerines are in fact Tangors, which are mandarin/orange hybrids. These are grouped under *C.* × *aurantium*. Zones 9–11.

CLADRASTIS

Native to China, Japan, and eastern USA, these 5 species of deciduous trees in the pea-flower subfamily of the legume (Fabaceae) family are cultivated mainly for their flowers, which are carried in wisteria-like racemes opening from early summer, followed by flat seed pods. The pinnate leaves, around 12 in (30 cm) long, have fine hairs on the undersides of the 4 in (10 cm) long leaflets. They are known as yellow-woods, and the heartwood is used for gunstocks with carved detailing.
CULTIVATION: Yellowwoods tolerate a wide range of soils provided drainage is good. They will not withstand extremes of soil moisture, drought, or waterlogging, but are otherwise easily grown in any sunny position. The branches are narrow-forked and the wood is rather brittle, so shelter from strong winds is advisable and older trees often require corrective pruning or guying to prevent wind damage. Propagate from seed or winter hardwood cuttings.

Citrus × *meyeri* 'Meyer'

Citrus × *microcarpa*

Cladrastis kentuckeana

YELLOWWOOD

☼ ❋ ↔ 30 ft (9 m) ↑ 25–40 ft (8–12 m)

Native to eastern USA. Bright green leaves, 7 to 11 oval leaflets, golden yellow in autumn. Fragrant white flowers, 12 in (30 cm) long racemes, in early summer. Narrow, 3 in (8 cm) long, brown seed pods. Zones 3–9.

CLARKIA

FAREWELL TO SPRING, GODETIA

This genus of 33 species of annual herbs belongs to the evening-primrose (Onagraceae) family. The majority are native to western North America, where they grow in dry open areas in forests. They are cultivated for their showy funnel-shaped flowers, which occur in shades of pink, red, purple, and sometimes yellow and white. The petals are often splashed with red or white. Flowering occurs from late spring to summer. The flowers are long-lasting and are very popular for floral display.

CULTIVATION: Grow in full sun in moderately fertile well-drained soil. All *Clarkia* species dislike hot humid conditions, so in warmer areas seed should be sown in autumn so that the plants will flower before the summer heat becomes intense. In cooler areas sow in early spring.

Clarkia amoena

syns *Clarkia grandiflora*, *Godetia amoena*

SATIN FLOWER

☼ ❋ ↔ 12 in (30 cm) ↑ 24 in (60 cm)

This showy species from northern California bears densely packed spikes of cup-shaped flowers of pink to lavender, sometimes darkening at the base or shading to white, centers usually splashed with dark red. 'Grandiflora' (syn. 'Whitneyi') has flowers up to 4 in (10 cm) across in shades of rose, lavender, pink, red, and white. Zones 7–10.

Clarkia pulchella

☼ ❋ ↔ 12 in (30 cm) ↑ 12–18 in (30–45 cm)

Found from the Rocky Mountains to the Pacific Coast. Compact species

Claytonia perfoliata

Clarkia amoena

bearing frilly funnel-shaped flowers of bright pink to lavender, sometimes with white or purple veining. 'Double Mixed', purple-pink flowers. Zones 7–10.

Clarkia unguiculata

syn. *Clarkia elegans*

☼ ❋ ↔ 12 in (30 cm) ↑ 24–30 in (60–75 cm)

From California. Commonly grown species with many cultivars, often frilly or double. Flowers, about 1 in (25 mm) across, in wide color range extending through pink, purple, and red shades, also yellow and white. Zones 7–10.

CLAYTONIA

PURSLANE, SPRING BEAUTY

Found mainly in the western parts of North America, this genus of the purslane (Portulacaceae) family also includes representatives from South America, Asia, Australia, and New Zealand among its 15 species of succulent perennials. *Claytonia* species are small plants with fleshy tap roots, from which develop basal rosettes of small leaves that sometimes surround the stems, an effect more apparent on the upright flowering stems. The flowers are white, 5-petalled, and usually very small. While sometimes solitary, they usually occur in small clusters but even then are not large enough to be showy. All parts of the plants are edible and are often used as salad vegetables.

CULTIVATION: Very hardy and easily grown in most temperate climates; some species are moderately invasive. While sometimes used as a salad herb, *Claytonia* species are seldom deliberately cultivated but are instead harvested from the wild. Most soils are suitable, and the plants may be raised from seed or by division.

Clarkia pulchella 'Double Mixed'

Claytonia perfoliata

MINER'S LETTUCE

☼/◐ ❋ ↔ 20 in (50 cm) ↑ 12 in (30 cm)

Spreading Californian perennial with fleshy, round, bright green leaves surrounding the stems. Small white flowers appear in spring. Eaten by nineteenth-century Californian gold miners to combat scurvy. Zones 6–9.

Claytonia virginica

FAIRY-SPUDS, SPRING BEAUTY

☀ ❋ ↔ 12 in (30 cm) ↑ 8–12 in (20–30 cm)

From eastern North America. Low-growing, deciduous, perennial herb. Occurs mainly in moist shaded woodland. Narrow succulent leaves up to 6 in (15 cm) long. Racemes of pink-tinged, red-veined, white, 5-petalled flowers appear in early spring. Tubers were once used as a food source by Native Americans. 'Lutea', orangey yellow flowers. Zones 4–8.

CLEISOSTOMA

This genus of about 90 monopodial epiphytic species in the orchid family

Clarkia unguiculata

(Orchidaceae) is found throughout Southeast Asia. Most species are small and of botanical interest. Most have fleshy succulent leaves in 2 ranks along an erect or arching to pendent stem. The flowers are small, but often produced in numbers along a simple or branched inflorescence.

CULTIVATION: *Cleisostoma* species grow well in small pots, baskets, or slabs, and appreciate regular waterings throughout the year. They enjoy humid conditions combined with high light levels and intermediate to warm temperatures.

Cleisostoma weberi

Cleistocactus hyalacanthus

Cleistocactus samaipatanus

Cleistocactus sextonianus

Cleisostoma weberi

☀/☼ ✛ ↔ 4–8 in (10–20 cm)
↑ 6–18 in (15–45 cm)

From the Philippines. Small-growing species, upright habit, and rounded cylindrical leaves. Short inflorescence carries up to 12 brown, white, and purple small blooms. Zones 11–12.

CLEISTOCACTUS

A popular genus of 48 species of upright, sprawling, and even decumbent cacti (family Cactaceae) from southern Ecuador, Peru, Bolivia, western Brazil, Uruguay, Paraguay, and northern Argentina. The genus was named because the long tubular flowers, which are usually pollinated by hummingbirds, appear to be closed even when mature. (The Greek word *kleistos* means closed.) *Cleistocactus* species are popular because they are easy to grow and offer a wide variety of spine and flower colors. The flowers, which are produced along the upper portion of the stems, may be red, maroon, pink, orange, yellow, white, or even a combination of up to 3 colors. There has been, and continues to be, some confusion as to what species should be included in the genus *Cleistocactus*. Currently it includes some or all of the species previously described as *Akersia, Binghamia, Bolivicereus, Borzicactella, Borzicactus, Clistanthocereus, Hildewinteria, Loxanthocereus, Maritimocereus, Seticereus, Seticleistocactus, Winteria,* and *Winterocereus*. More fieldwork and laboratory research is needed in classifying these plants.
CULTIVATION: *Cleistocactus* species are easy to grow in a rich well-drained soil. They may be propagated from seed, or else from cuttings that have been dried out for a week or two. Rest in winter.

Cleistocactus hyalacanthus

syn. *Cleistocactus jujuyensis*

☀ ✳ ↔ 24–48 in (60–120 cm)
↑ 36 in (90 cm)

From northwestern Argentina and southeastern Bolivia; 18 to 22 ribs. Three central spines, yellow to brown, 20 to 30 radials, white to gray, in various lengths, needle-like, bristly. Flowers 1½ in (35 mm) long, purplish pink, outer petals slightly recurved. Seed pods red. Zones 8–12.

Cleistocactus samaipatanus

☀ ✳ ↔ 2 ft (0.6 m) ↑ 3–5 ft (1.2–1.5 m)

From Santa Cruz, Bolivia. Flowers are outstandingly attractive. Plants green, erect, branching from the base. Ribs 14 to 16, low. No central, 12 to 25 radials, needle-like, yellow to gray, ¼–½ in (6–12 mm) long. Flowers distinctly S-shaped, bright red, to 1¼–2 in (30–50 mm) long, outer petals strongly recurved. Flowers bilaterally symmetrical. Seed pods red, spherical. Zones 8–12.

Cleistocactus sextionianus

☀ ✳ ↔ 12 in (30 cm) ↑ 12–24 in (30–60 cm)

Widespread in coastal Peru. Little known species, not very appealing, with decumbent growth habit and woody underground stem segments. Ribs 10 to 14. Spines 1 to 3, pink to yellow to brown, centrals to 1¼ in (30 mm), and 8 to 30 similarly colored radials to ¼ in (6 mm). Seed pods red, spherical. Zones 8–12.

Cleistocactus strausii ★

SILVER TORCH CACTUS

☀ ✳ ↔ 3 ft (0.9 m) ↑ 3–10 ft (0.9–3 m)

From Bolivia and northern Argentina. Its silvery white spines makes this one of the most beautiful of all cacti, even when not in flower. Plants dark green, with 25 to 30 ribs. Spines 4 centrals, creamy white, to ¾ in (18 mm), 30 to 40 radials, hair-like, white, completely obscuring the plant body. Flowers deep maroon, slightly curved, 3–4 in (8–10 cm) long. Seed pods are red, spherical to club-shaped. Zones 8–12.

Cleistocactus tupizensis

☀ ✳ ↔ 3 ft (0.9 m) ↑ 5 ft (1.5 m)

From Tupiza and Potosi, Bolivia. Plants upright, branching from base. Ribs 15 to 25, spines 2 centrals, brown to white, to 2 in (5 cm), 15 to 20 radials, variable in length, dense, white, brittle. Flowers red to whitish, slightly curved, to 3 in (8 cm) long. Zones 8–12.

CLEMATIS

LEATHER VINE, TRAVELLER'S JOY,
VIRGIN'S BOWER

A genus of over 200 species in the buttercup (Ranunculaceae) family genus encompassing a huge range of plants. *Clematis* species are mainly climbing or scrambling but sometimes shrubby or perennial, deciduous or evergreen, flowering at any time in any color, occurring in both northern and southern temperate zones and at higher altitudes in the tropics; there seems to be a clematis for any season and place. Their leaves may be simple or pinnate and their flowers are nearly always showy, with 4 to 8 petal-like sepals. Fluffy seedheads follow. The common name virgin's bower comes from a German legend that Mary and Jesus sheltered under a clematis during their flight into Egypt from the massacre of the innocents.
CULTIVATION: The general rule is that the foliage should be in the sun while the roots are kept cool and moist. Incorporate plenty of humus-rich compost before planting, and water well. Clematis wilt disease is a problem in many areas. Propagate from cuttings or layers. Species may be raised from seed, but sex will be undetermined before flowering.

Cleistocactus strausii

Cleistocactus tupizensis

Clematis aristata

Clematis × aromatica

Clematis chiisanensis 'Love Child'

Clematis × eriostemon

☼/◐ ❄ ↔6 ft (1.8 m) ↑8 ft (2.4 m)

Probably hybrid with *C. viticella*, usually classified under *C. × eriostemon*. Large violet flowers. Zones 6–10.

Clematis florida

☼/◐ ❄ ↔5 ft (1.5 m) ↑15 ft (4.5 m)

Deciduous or part evergreen climber, Japan and China. Paired trifoliate leaves, 2 in (5 cm) leaflets, sometimes toothed. Flowers 3 in (8 cm) wide, often green-tinted, white stamens, violet anthers, in summer. *C. f.* var. *flore-pleno*, double flowers, white, green-striped; *C. f.* var. *sieboldiana* (syn. 'Bicolor'), white flowers, purple-red stamens. Zones 7–10.

Clematis armandii 'Snowdrift'

Clematis alpina ★

☼/◐ ❄ ↔5 ft (1.5 m) ↑8–10 ft (2.4–3 m)

Deciduous early-flowering climber, Europe and northern Asia. Paired trifoliate leaves, serrated, lance-shaped leaflets 2 in (5 cm) long. Flowers blue to mauve, white stamens. 'Frances Rivis' (syn. 'Blue Giant'), blue flowers to 2 in (5 cm) wide; 'Jacqueline du Pré', pink flowers, lighter inside, pink stamens; 'White Columbine', white-flowered cultivar. Zones 5–9.

Clematis aristata

AUSTRALIAN CLEMATIS

☼/◐ ❄ ↔6 ft (1.8 m) ↑10–20 ft (3–6 m)

Evergreen climber native to southeastern Australia. Long-stemmed leaves with 3 leaflets, sometimes toothed. Panicles of 1 in (25 mm) wide, starry, white flowers from late spring to midsummer. Zones 7–10.

Clematis armandii

☼/◐ ❄ ↔7–10 ft (2–3 m) ↑20–30 ft (6–9 m)

Vigorous evergreen climber, central and western China. Leaves with 3 leathery leaflets to 6 in (15 cm) long, bronze-green when young. Clusters of white flowers, sometimes faintly pink-tinted. Flowers may smell slightly of urine. 'Apple Blossom', pink buds opening white; 'Snowdrift' ★, white, waxy, fragrant flowers in cascading panicles. Zones 8–10.

Clematis × aromatica

☼/◐ ❄ ↔3–5 ft (0.9–1.5 m) ↑5–7 ft (1.5–2 m)

Upright deciduous subshrub, a hybrid between *C. flammula* and *C. integri-*

folia. Leaves with 3 to 5 short leaflets. Deep violet flowers with white stamens, from summer–autumn. Despite the name, there is little scent in foliage or flower. Zones 4–9.

Clematis chiisanensis

☼/◐ ❄ ↔5 ft (1.5 m) ↑10 ft (3 m)

Korean deciduous climber. Toothed, heavily veined, trifoliate leaves and simple, nodding, pink-tinted, cream flowers with 4 sepals recurved at tips. 'Lemon Bells', pale yellow flowers; 'Love Child', large cream flowers over a long season (blooms on both old and new wood); 'Monika', deep pink flowers with cream center. Zones 4–9.

Clematis chrysocoma

☼/◐ ❄ ↔4–6 ft (1.2–1.8 m) ↑7–15 ft (2–4.5 m)

Deciduous climber from southwestern China. Trifoliate leaves with 1–2 in (25–50 mm) long, pointed, oval, sometimes serrated leaflets. In summer–autumn 2 in (50 mm) wide, pink-tinted, white flowers on long, downy, brown stems. Zones 7–10.

Clematis cirrhosa ★

☼/◐ ❄ ↔6 ft (1.8 m) ↑10–15 ft (3–4.5 m)

Evergreen climber from southern Europe and Mediterranean region. Paired trifoliate leaves with small lobed leaflets. In winter–early spring, small clusters of pendulous cream flowers, sometimes spotted purple-red. *C. c.* var. *balearica*, flowers always spotted. *C. c.* var. *purpurascens* 'Freckles' ★, large-flowered, long-stemmed. Zones 7–10.

Clematis chrysocoma

Clematis coactilis

☼/◐ ❄ ↔12–32 in (30–80 cm) ↑8–16 in (20–40 cm)

Deciduous shrub from Appalachian Mountains of eastern USA. Green lance-shaped leaves. Small, pendulous, bell-shaped, white flowers, sometimes green- or purple-tinted. Silky hairs on flower stems and buds. Zones 7–10.

Clematis × durandii

☼/◐ ❄ ↔5 ft (1.5 m) ↑6–8 ft (1.8–2.4 m)

Deciduous climber, hybrid between *C. × jackmanii* and *C. integrifolia*. Green, glossy, pointed, oval leaves, to 6 in (15 cm) long. Deep violet-blue flowers, cream to yellow stamens, summer–autumn, usually in groups of three. Zones 5–10.

Clematis coactilis

Clematis florida var. *flore-pleno*

Clematis florida var. *sieboldiana*

Clematis × eriostemon

C

Clematis heracleifolia

☼/◐ ❋ ↔ 2–5 ft (0.6–1.5 m)
↕ 3–6 ft (0.9–1.8 m)

Sprawling, scrambling, woody-based, herbaceous perennial from central and northern China. Lightly downy trifoliate leaves, irregularly toothed leaflets, to 2½ in (6 cm) long. Clusters of dusky, purple-blue, tubular flowers with 4 flared and reflexed sepals, summer–autumn. '**New Love**', very compact with dark purple-blue flowers, lighter inside, fragrant. Zones 3–9.

Clematis integrifolia

☼/◐ ❋ ↔ 3–5 ft (0.9–1.5 m)
↕ 3 ft (0.9 m)

Deciduous perennial or subshrub found from Europe to central Asia. Simple, 3–4 in (8–10 cm) long, lance-shaped leaves with downy undersides. Pendulous, flattened, bell-shaped flowers, to 4 in (10 cm) wide, deep violet-blue. Zones 3–9.

Clematis × jouiniana

☼/◐ ❋ ↔ 7–15 ft (2–4.5 m)
↕ 7–15 ft (2–4.5 m)

Hybrid between *C. tubulosa* and *C. vitalba*. Sprawling, semi-climbing, partly evergreen, woody-based perennial. Compound leaves, 3 to 5 coarsely toothed leaflets. Clusters of fragrant flowers from late summer, opening

Clematis montana var. *rubens* 'Elizabeth'

white, ageing to pale pink or blue. '**Praecox**', vigorous cultivar with pale blue flowers. Zones 4–9.

Clematis lanuginosa

☼/◐ ❋ ↔ 4–8 ft (1.2–2.4 m)
↕ 7–10 ft (2–3 m)

Chinese deciduous climber. Leaves simple or trifoliate, leaflets to 4 in (10 cm) long. Large flowers, white to pale lavender, in groups of up to 3, in warmer months. Zones 6–9.

Clematis lasiantha

CHAPARRAL CLEMATIS, PIPESTEM CLEMATIS

☼/◐ ❋ ↔ 8–15 ft (2.4–4.5 m)
↕ 10–17 ft (3–5 m)

Evergreen climber, western USA. Trifoliate leaves, toothed to lobed leaflets, to 2 in (5 cm) long. Long-stemmed, downy, white flowers, 1 in (25 mm) wide, autumn. Zones 8–10.

Clematis lasiantha

Clematis mandschurica

Clematis macropetala

Clematis macropetala

☼/◐ ❋ ↔ 5–10 ft (1.5–3 m)
↕ 3–10 ft (0.9–3 m)

Deciduous climber from northern temperate Asia. Paired trifoliate leaves, toothed or lobed leaflets, to 1½ in (35 mm) long. Downy dusky blue flowers, spring–early summer; 4 sepals, though cultivars often double-flowered. '**Markham's Pink**' (syn. 'Markhamii'), light pink flowers; '**Snowbird**', white flowers, late; '**White Swan**', large white flowers. Zones 5–9.

Clematis mandschurica

☼/◐ ❋ ↔ 5–10 ft (1.5–3 m)
↕ 3–5 ft (0.9–1.5 m)

Spreading or scrambling herbaceous perennial from Japan and nearby parts of China. Leaves pinnate. Panicles of sweet-scented, starry, white flowers in summer. Zones 7–10.

Clematis montana

☼/◐ ❋ ↔ 10–20 ft (3–6 m)
↕ 15–25 ft (4.5–8 m)

Vigorous, spring-flowering, deciduous climber found from the Himalayas to central China. Deep green trifoliate leaves with toothed leaflets to 4 in (10 cm) long. In spring, massed large sprays of white to pale pink flowers. *C. m.* var. *glabrescens,* very vigorous variety with mauve-pink flowers; *C. m.* var. *grandiflora,* very vigorous variety, to 40 ft (12 m) tall, white flowers. *C. m.* var. *rubens* ★, bronze new growth, large pink flowers: '**Elizabeth**', very pale pink flowers, vanilla scented; '**Marjorie**' ★, semi-double with petal-like stamens, cream over-

Clematis paniculata

Clematis montana var. *rubens* 'Marjorie'

Clematis montana var. *sericea*

Clematis montana var. *wilsonii*

laid with orange-pink and copper; '**Tetrarose**' ★, very large deep pink flowers, strong growing with lush foliage; *C. m.* var. *sericea* (syns *C. chrysocoma* var. *sericea, C. spooneri*), downy young stems and reverse of sepals, white flowers in profusion; *C. m.* var. *wilsonii*, large sprays of tiny white flowers, fragrant; *C. m.* '**Snowflake**', pure white flowers. Zones 6–9.

Clematis orientalis

☼/◐ ❋ ↔ 10–20 ft (3–6 m)
↕ 10–25 ft (3–8 m)

Scrambling deciduous climber, from the Aegean region, Iran, China, and Korea. Leaves pinnate, 3 to 9 elliptical leaflets, sometimes blue-green and/or toothed. Flowers solitary or in panicles, yellow to yellow-green sepals with orange peel texture, bell-shaped, eventually opening wider. Zones 6–9.

Clematis paniculata

☼/◐ ❋ ↔ 10–30 ft (3–9 m)
↕ 17–30 ft (5–9 m)

From New Zealand. Tough climber, dioecious, evergreen, flowering in spring to early summer; large panicles of scented white flowers. Zones 7–10.

Clematis patens

☼/◐ ❋ ↔ 5–10 ft (1.5–3 m)
↕ 10–15 ft (3–4.5 m)

Vigorous climber from Japan and nearby parts of China. Pinnate leaves with 3 to 5 leaflets up to 4 in (10 cm) long. Flowering spring–early summer; white through mauve to blue flowers borne singly at tips of stems, purple-brown stamens. Zones 6–9.

Clematis, Hybrid Cultivar, Florida Group, 'Belle of Woking'

Clematis, Hybrid Cultivar, Florida Group, 'Duchess of Edinburgh'

Clematis, Hybrid Cultivar, Florida Group, 'Louise Rowe'

Clematis, Hybrid Cultivar, Florida Group, Pistachio/'Evirida'

Clematis, Hybrid Cultivar, Florida Group, Arctic Queen/'Evitwo'

Clematis recta

☼/◐ ❋ ↔ 3–4 ft (0.9–1.2 m)
↑ 3–5 ft (0.9–1.5 m)

From southern and central Europe. Summer-flowering erect perennial, sprawls as gains height. Pinnate foliage, 5 to 7 blue-green leaflets. Small white flowers in large panicles. Zones 3–9.

Clematis rehderiana

☼/◐ ❋ ↔ 8–15 ft (2.4–4.5 m)
↑ 17–25 ft (5–8 m)

Strong-growing deciduous climber from western China. Pinnate leaves to over 8 in (20 cm) with 7 to 9 leaflets. Foliage and stems covered with fine golden hairs. Upright panicles of small light yellow to yellowy green flowers in summer–autumn. Young plants frost tender. Zones 7–10.

Clematis patens

Clematis recta

Clematis, HC, Florida Group, 'Proteus'

Clematis tangutica

☼/◐ ❋ ↔ 8–12 ft (2.4–3.5 m)
↑ 7–10 ft (2–3 m)

Climber native to Mongolia and northwestern China. Bright green pinnate leaves, toothed and/or lobed leaflets. Deep yellow bell-shaped flowers from late summer, lantern-shaped if sepals remain unfurled. Zones 5–9.

Clematis terniflora

syn. *Clematis dioscoreifolia*
☼/◐ ❋ ↔ 6–10 ft (1.8–3 m)
↑ 7–15 ft (2–4.5 m)

Japanese perennial that can be upright but usually becomes a mass of tangled scrambling stems. Deep green pinnate leaves with 3 to 5 leaflets to 4 in (10 cm) long, semi-evergreen in mild areas. Panicles of massed greenish white flowers in autumn. Zones 6–10.

Clematis texensis

☼/◐ ❋ ↔ 3–7 ft (0.9–2 m) ↑ 7 ft (2 m)
Scrambling shrubby perennial from southwestern USA. Blue-green pinnate leaves with 4 to 8 rounded leathery leaflets to 3 in (8 cm) long. Unusual, small, urn-shaped flowers on long stems, borne singly, in shades from brick to cherry. Zones 5–10.

Clematis, HC, Florida Group, 'Teshio'

Clematis × triternata

☼/◐ ❋ ↔ 10–15 ft (3–4.5 m)
↑ 10–15 ft (3–4.5 m)

Garden hybrid between *C. flammula* and *C. viticella*. Foliage simple or pinnate, with smooth-edged, lance-shaped leaflets to 3 in (8 cm) long. Masses of small, starry, pale lavender flowers in summer. '**Rubromarginata**', heavy crop of white flowers edged and tipped with soft purple to wine red. Zones 6–9.

Clematis tubulosa

syn. *Clematis heracleifolia* var. *davidiana*
☼/◐ ❋ ↔ 3 ft (0.9 m) ↑ 3 ft (0.9 m)
Clusters of mauve-blue, mildly fragrant flowers. Alan Bloom/'**Alblo**', very compact, light purple-blue flowers, often with 5 sepals. Zones 6–9.

Clematis Hybrid Cultivars

☼/◐ ❋ ↔ 5–15 ft (1.5–4.5 m)
↑ 4–20 ft (1.2–6 m)

The many large-flowered hybrid clematis are broadly classified into 9 groups that vary in growth habit and flowering style depending on their parentage. There is also a large range of ungrouped hybrids of indeterminate parentage. *Clematis* hybrids are now often grouped by flower size and pruning requirements (this varies, as some flower on new growth, others on old wood) rather than on parentage, which is often obscure. Zones 5–9.

DIVERSIFOLIA GROUP

These are hybrids mainly of *C. integrifolia*, *C. viticella*, *C. alpina*, and

C. macropetala, sometimes listed under *C. integrifolia* or in the Viticella Group but meriting a classification of their own. Long-flowering climbers, they usually grow 8–12 ft (2.4–3.5 m tall), but can be low and compact; very hardy, blooming from late spring on new growth, typically with bell-shaped mauve to purple flowers, sometimes with petaloid centers. '**Arabella**', large flowers, deep mauve-blue, variable number of sepals; '**Blue Bird**', long mauve-blue sepals, creamy white double center; '**Blue Boy**', mauve-blue flowers to 3 in (8 cm) wide, will flower in shade; '**Juuli**', mauve-blue flowers, 5 sepals, large broad leaves, low-growing, often under 4 ft (1.2 m) tall.

FLORIDA GROUP

These climbers, 8–12 ft (2.4–3.5 m) tall, flower in spring–summer on previous year's wood. Early flowers are often double or semi-double; later blooms tend to be single, often very large. The group includes: Pistachio/ '**Evirida**', large white flowers sometimes flushed with pale green, cream anthers, dull red stamens.

FORSTERI GROUP

This is a group of evergreen hybrids between several New Zealand species, notably *C. paniculata*, *C. marmoraria*, and *C. forsteri*. Most are low-spreading, though some are more vigorous climbers. Flowers are usually white with hints of green; hardiness varies with parentage, though most survive

Clematis tubulosa Alan Bloom/'Alblo'

Clematis tubulosa

well in zone 8. The group includes: 'Avalanche', over 10 ft (3 m), pure white flowers; 'Early Sensation', around 5 ft (1.5m) high, greenish white flowers; 'Lunar Lass', low spreader, small greenish white flowers, lobed toothed leaves; 'Moonbeam', wiry stems to 5 ft (1.5m) tall, starry, creamy flowers, lobed leaves.

JACKMANII GROUP

These climbers grow up to 6–20 ft (1.8–6 m) tall and produce large flowers with a wide color range and usually with 4 sepals, in summer–autumn on new growth. The group includes: 'Comtesse de Bouchaud', large pink flowers, cream stamens,

very popular; 'Gipsy Queen', 6 in (15 cm) wide with purple flowers striped wine red; 'Jackmanii', semi-pendulous deep purple flowers, 4 widely spaced sepals, cream stamens; 'Jackmanii Superba', deep purple flowers, purple mid-stripe, cream stamens; 'Madame Baron-Veillard', lavender-pink flowers, pointed sepals, white stamens; 'Niobe', deep red flowers, yellow stamens; 'Perle d'Azur', lavender-blue flowers, yellow stamens.

LANUGINOSA GROUP

This group of climbers was formerly known as *C. × lawsoniana*. The plants flower in summer–autumn on side shoots of current season's growth. They

can reach 15 ft (4.5 m) in height, and bear large to very large single or double flowers. The group includes: 'Carnaby', pale mauve with a darker mauve-pink bar; 'Hybrida Sieboldii' (syn. 'Ramona'), large, pale, lavender-blue flowers, purple-red stamens; 'Lawsoniana', large light blue to purplish flowers, pale stamens; 'Marie Boisselot' (syn. 'Madame le Coultre'), vigorous grower, pale pink flowers ageing to white, cream to pale brown stamens; 'Mrs Cholmondeley', large lavender flowers, narrow sepals, light brown stamens; 'Nelly Moser', large lilac-pink flowers with wine red stripes, brown stamens; 'Silver Moon', silvery lilac flowers, yellow stamens; 'Will Goodwin', light lavender-blue flowers, cream to green stamens.

C., HC, Lanuginosa, 'Beauty of Worcester'

PATENS GROUP

These compact climbers seldom grow to more than 12 ft (3.5 m) tall, and flower in spring on previous season's wood. Flowers are usually single and medium to large; sepals often have a darker mid-stripe and may have wavy edges. The group includes: 'Bees' Jubilee', light pink flowers with deep pink markings, yellow stamens; 'Blue Ravine', big mauve-blue flowers with faint purple-

red markings, purple-red stamens; 'Charissima', large cerise flowers, flushed with pale pink, ageing to very pale pink with cerise stripe, cerise stamens; 'Doctor Ruppel', deep pink flowers with carmine markings, yellow stamens; 'Elsa Späth' (syn. 'Xerxes'), blue-purple flowers, purple stamens, red anthers; 'Fireworks', mauve flowers, pink-red markings; 'Gillian Blades', white flowers, may have blue blush, wavy edges; 'Henryi', very large white to cream flowers with up to 8 sepals, brown stamens; 'Lasurstern', large blue flowers, wavy-edged, narrow sepals, cream stamens; 'Lord Nevill', purple-blue flowers, wavy edges, cream stamens, red anthers; 'Miss Bateman', white flowers, red anthers; 'Mrs N. Thompson', purplish flowers with red markings;

Clematis, Hybrid Cultivar, Forsteri Group cultivar

C., HC, Forsteri Group, 'Early Sensation'

Clematis, HC, Forsteri Group, 'Moonbeam'

C., HC, Jackmanii, 'Allanah'

C., HC, Jackmanii, 'Blekitny Aniol'

C., HC, Jackmanii, 'Caroline'

C., HC, Jackmanii Group, 'Comtesse de Bouchaud'

Clematis, HC, Jackmanii Group, 'Hagley Hybrid'

C., HC, Jackmanii Group, 'Niobe'

C., HC, Jackmanii, 'Perle d'Azur'

C., HC, Jackmanii, 'Pink Fantasy'

C., HC, Jackmanii Group, 'Rüütel'

C., HC, Jackmanii Group, 'Sunset'

Clematis, Hybrid Cultivar,
Lanuginosa Group, 'Fuji-musume'

Clematis, Hybrid Cultivar,
Lanuginosa, 'Hybrida Sieboldii'

Clematis, Hybrid Cultivar,
Lanuginosa, 'Lady Caroline Nevill'

Clematis, Hybrid Cultivar,
Lanuginosa Group, 'Lawsoniana'

Clematis, Hybrid Cultivar,
Lanuginosa Group, 'Mrs Bush'

C., HC, Lanuginosa, 'Ruby Glow'

C., HC, Lanuginosa, 'Silver Moon'

C., HC, Patens, 'Asao'

C., HC, Patens, 'Bees' Jubilee'

C., HC, Patens, 'Beth Currie'

C., HC, Patens, 'Daniel Deronda'

C., HC, Patens, 'Doctor Ruppel'

C., HC, Patens, 'Elsa Späth'

C., HC, Patens, 'Fireworks'

C., HC, Patens, 'Gillian Blades'

C., HC, Patens, 'Guernsey Cream'

C., HC, Patens, 'Helen Cropper'

C., HC, Patens, 'Kakio'

C., HC, Patens, 'Miss Bateman'

Clematis, HC, Patens,
'Mrs George Jackman'

C., HC, Patens, 'Mrs N. Thompson'

C., HC, Patens, 'Mrs P. B. Truax'

C., HC, Patens, 'Multi Blue'

C., HC, Patens, 'Rhapsody'

C., HC, Patens, 'Pilu'

C., HC, Patens, 'Richard Pennell'

C., HC, Patens, 'Snow Queen'

C., HC, Patens, 'The President'

C., HC, Patens, 'Vyvyan Pennell'

C., HC, Patens, 'Walter Pennell'

C

Clematis, Hybrid Cultivar, Texensis Group, 'Etoile Rose'

Clematis, Hybrid Cultivar, Texensis Group, 'Princess Diana'

Clematis, Hybrid Cultivar, Viticella Group, 'Madame Julia Correvon'

Clematis, Hybrid Cultivar, Viticella Group, 'Masquerade'

Clematis, Hybrid Cultivar, Viticella Group, 'Perrin's Pride'

C., HC, Viticella, 'Ville de Lyon'

C., HC, Patens, 'Miss Crawshay'

C., HC, Ungrouped, 'Küllus'

C., HC, Ungrouped, 'Pastel Princess'

C., HC, Patens, 'The First Lady'

Clematis, Hybrid Cultivar, Ungrouped, Liberation/'Evifive'

Cleome sesquiorygalis 'Pink Queen'

Cleome sesquiorygalis

'Richard Pennell', purple-blue flowers, red stamens, yellow anthers; '**The President**', purple-blue flowers, reddish stamens.

TEXENSIS GROUP

This is a group of sprawling semi-climbing shrubs that can be trained to climb or left to form bushy mounds. They may also be cut back each year as herbaceous perennials. The flowers, usually bell-shaped, bloom in summer on new growth. The group includes: '**Duchess of Albany**', wide-open bell-shaped to starry flowers, deep pink, lighter at the edges; '**Etoile Rose**', nodding, bell-shaped, rose pink flowers; '**Gravetye Beauty**', upward-facing bell-shaped flowers becoming starry, wine red ageing to soft magenta.

VITICELLA GROUP

These are vigorous climbers that grow 8–20 ft (2.4–6 m) tall. They flower on new growth, but in short intense bursts rather than over a longer season like the Lanuginosa and Jackmanii hybrids. Flowers may be single or double, seldom over 5 in (12 cm) wide, often smaller. Viticella hybrids include: '**Alba Luxurians**', loose open flowers, creamy white, green mid-stripes or patches, dark stamens; '**Etoile Violette**', deep purple flowers, creamy to yellow stamens; '**Lady Betty Balfour**', strong-growing deep violet-blue flowers, creamy yellow stamens; '**Madame Julia Correvon**', large flowers, deep red, sepals slightly twisted, cream stamens; '**Minuet**', creamy white flowers, edged and tipped lavender-pink, cream stamens; '**Polish Spirit**', purple flowers, red anthers; '**Venosa Violacea**', large white flowers, veins and broad edges of deep purple, cream stamens, purple anthers; '**Ville de Lyon**' ★, deep pink flowers, yellow stamens.

UNGROUPED HYBRIDS

Ungrouped *Clematis* hybrids usually result from chance seedlings and display a range of sizes, flower types, and hardiness. All may grow 8–15 ft (2.4–4.5 m) tall, sometimes taller with suitable support. Popular hybrids of this type include: '**Helsingborg**', purple-blue flowers, similarly colored stamens; '**Ivan Olsson**', very pale blue flowers, broad lavender-blue edges, cream stamens, purple-red anthers; '**Pastel Princess**', pastel pink flowers, mauve center; '**Royalty**', dusky deep mauve-pink flowers, double early, single later, pale mid-stripe, cream petal-like stamens.

CLEOME

SPIDER FLOWER

This largely tropical and subtropical genus of around 150 species of annuals and perennials belongs to the small caper (Capparidaceae) family. The commonly grown species are upright summer annuals. Their large palmate leaves have fine-toothed edges and stems that are sometimes spiny. Their 4-petalled flowers have long, protruding, filament-like stamens and are carried in apical heads with the filaments facing outward, hence the name spider flower. Some species, such as *C. lutea* from western North America, yield a yellow dye. In the

USA *Cleome* has long been associated with US president Thomas Jefferson's famous garden at Monticello.
CULTIVATION: In areas with a warm summer the annuals are easily grown in any sheltered sunny position with moist, fertile, free-draining soil. Deadheading the flowers encourages longer blooming. With the exception of a few species, the perennials will not tolerate frost and need at least subtropical conditions. Propagate from spring-sown seed.

Cleome sesquiorygalis
syn. *Cleome spinosa*
SPIDER FLOWER

☼/☀ ☞ ↔ 20 in (50 cm) ↑ 5 ft (1.5 m)
Upright annual from southern Brazil, Paraguay, and northern Argentina. Palmate leaves with 5 to 7 finely toothed hairy leaflets to over 4 in (10 cm) long. Flowers clustered in terminal heads, petals to 1¼ in (30 mm) long with long filaments. In white and many shades of pink to purple. Several seedling strains and named forms, such as '**Helen Campbell**' (syn. 'White Queen'), one of the **Queen Series**, with varieties named after their flower color, such as '**Cherry Queen**', '**Mauve Queen**', '**Pink Queen**', '**Purple Queen**', '**Rose Queen**', '**Ruby Queen**'. Zones 10–12.

CLERODENDRUM

GLORY BOWER

This genus of about 400 evergreen or deciduous small trees, shrubs, and climbers, traditionally placed in the family Verbenaceae, is now assigned to the mint (Lamiaceae) family. They are found mostly in tropical and subtropical regions of Asia and Africa. Their simple leaves are opposite or whorled. They are grown for their summer terminal panicles of showy violet or red flowers. Some species are used in traditional medicine, others make ideal pot plants, and the climbers are ideal for trellis cultivation. The fruit is a drupe or berry.
CULTIVATION: *Clerodendrum* species prefer light to medium well-drained soils, rich in humus, in a protected partly shaded to sunny position. Water freely in the growing season. The stems of young plants may require support, and sucking insects such as mites, mealybugs, or whitefly can pose a problem. Propagation is from seed sown in spring or from cuttings of half-hardened wood taken during winter or summer.

Clerodendrum bungei

GLORY FLOWER

☼/☀ ❄ ↔ 8 ft (2.4 m) ↑ 8 ft (2.4 m)
Found in southern China and northern India. Evergreen aromatic shrub, thicket of suckering stems. Leaves triangular, toothed-edged, dark green with purple overtones. In summer, 6 in (15 cm) wide heads of strongly scented pale pink to purple-red flowers are produced. Zones 8–10.

Clerodendrum bungei

Clerodendrum chinense 'Pleniflorum'

Clerodendrum chinense

syn. *Clerodendrum philippinum*
HONOLULU ROSE, SPANISH JASMINE
☼/☀ ❄ ↔ 7 ft (2 m) ↑ 10 ft (3 m)
Evergreen shrub from southern Japan and China. Angular stems and downy, toothed, pointed, oval to triangular leaves to 10 in (25 cm) long. Flower clusters to 4 in (10 cm) long, blooms white, cream, to red, with 1 in (25 mm) long tube. Considered invasive in Hawaii. The cultivar '**Pleniflorum**' has emphasized, semi-double, rose-like flowers. Zones 10–12.

Clerodendrum floribundum

LOLLY BUSH

☼ ❄ ↔ 10 ft (3 m) ↑ 20 ft (6 m)
Deciduous tree from China. Erect branching habit, smooth oval leaves. Fragrant white flowers with long tubes, 1¼ in (30 mm) long, pinkish calyces, in spikes, blackish purple berries. Zones 10–12.

Clerodendrum glabrum

WHITE CAT'S-WHISKERS

☼ ❄ ↔ 20 ft (6 m) ↑ 40 ft (12 m)
Small tree or shrub from Africa, multi-branched habit. Glossy, dark green, pointed, smooth leaves, opposite or whorled. Scented white or pink flowers, in dense terminal cymes. White to yellow fruit. Zones 10–12.

Clerodendrum minahassae

TUBE FLOWER TREE

☼/☀ ❄ ↔ 10 ft (3 m) ↑ 17 ft (5 m)
Small evergreen tree with deep green, veined, pointed, elliptical leaves to 8 in (20 cm) long. Starry pale pink flowers with long petals and tube to 4 in (10 cm) long. After flowering, calyces turn bright red with small central black fruit. *C. m.* **var. brevitubulosum**, flowers with short tubes about 1 in (25 mm) long. Zones 10–12.

Clerodendrum speciosissimum

JAVA GLORY BEAN, MATA AJAM
☼ ❄ ↔ 4 ft (1.2 m) ↑ 6 ft (1.8 m)
A native of Java. Erect shrub. Large oval leaves to 12 in (30 cm) in length.

Clerodendrum floribundum

Clerodendrum speciosissimum

Clerodendrum trichotomum, in fruit

Vivid red flowers, in panicles to 8 in (20 cm) long. Corolla around 1½ in (35 mm) long, in summer. Purplish blue fruit. Ideal container plant. Zones 10–12.

Clerodendrum splendens

☼/☀ ❄ ↔ 7 ft (2 m) ↑ 7 ft (2 m)
Scrambling or climbing tropical African shrub with lush, dark green, smooth-edged, broad, pointed, oval leaves to over 6 in (15 cm) long and sprays of many bright red flowers. Zones 10–12.

Clerodendrum thomsoniae

BLEEDING HEART VINE

☼/☀/☀ ❄ ↔ 15 ft (4.5 m) ↑ 15 ft (4.5 m)
Vigorous, twining, evergreen climber from tropical West Africa. Smooth-edged, pointed, oval leaves to over 6 in (15 cm) long. Many-bloomed clusters of flowers with white calyces

Clerodendrum glabrum

Clerodendrum splendens

Clerodendrum minahassae var. *brevitubulosum*, in fruit

and dark red corolla, a striking contrast. Red to black fruit follow. Zones 10–12.

Clerodendrum trichotomum

☼ ❄ ↔ 15 ft (4.5 m) ↑ 15 ft (4.5 m)
From Japan. Downy leaves, heads of long-tubed, scented, white flowers in late summer. Flowers backed by pink calyces, darkening as the fruit matures, a contrast against the purplish blue drupes. *C. t.* **var.** *fargesii*, new leaves bronze colored. Zones 8–10.

CLETHRA

This genus of about 60 species of deciduous small trees or shrubs in the family Cyrillaceae is widely distributed from southern USA to Central and South America and Asia, with a few species native to Madeira. They are grown for their white fragrant flowers, often borne in long racemes

Clethra alnifolia

Clethra species, in the wild, in Wolong National Park, Sichuan, China

Clethra arborea

Clethra barbinervis

or panicles, which resemble lily-of-the-valley flowers. Some of the species have attractive peeling bark, and the flowers are followed by numerous tiny seed capsules.

CULTIVATION: Being closely related to the erica family, clethras like a lime-free soil and a moist sheltered spot, with some shade from taller trees. They can be propagated from seed, cuttings, or layers.

Clethra acuminata

CINNAMON CLETHRA, WHITE ALDER

☀ ❄ ↔12 ft (3.5 m) ↑12 ft (3.5 m)
Large shrub from southeastern USA. Racemes of scented creamy white flowers in late summer. Mid-green elliptical leaves have attractive golden tones in autumn. Zones 6–9.

Clethra alnifolia

SUMMERSWEET CLETHRA, SWEET PEPPER BUSH

☀ ❄ ↔6 ft (1.8 m) ↑6 ft (1.8 m)
Species native to eastern North America. Fragrant white flowers, in erect terminal racemes to 6 in (15 cm) long, in late summer. 'Paniculata',

terminal panicles of white flowers; 'Rosea' ★, buds and flowers tinged with pink. Zones 4–9.

Clethra arborea

LILY-OF-THE-VALLEY TREE

☀ ⚘ ↔20 ft (6 m) ↑25 ft (8 m)
From Madeira, densely foliaged. Long terminal panicles of scented white flowers. Needs mild conditions to thrive. 'Flora Plena', double flowers. Zones 9–10.

Clethra barbinervis

JAPANESE CLETHRA

☀ ❄ ↔10 ft (3 m) ↑10 ft (3 m)
From mountainous woodlands of Japan, larger in the wild. Peeling rusty brown bark. Dark green leaves, prominently veined, attractive autumn color. Scented white flowers appear in terminal racemes from summer–autumn. Shoots arch outward. Zones 8–9.

CLIANTHUS

This genus now consists of just one (or possibly two) New Zealand species. (It previously included the Australian

plant known as Sturt's desert pea, now classified in *Swainsona*.) *Clianthus*, a member of the pea-flower subfamily of the legume (Fabaceae) family, grows into a somewhat sprawling evergreen shrub, with pinnate leaves and large red flowers in early summer.

CULTIVATION: When grown in cool-temperate climates *C. puniceus* needs the protection of a sunny wall or greenhouse to prosper. In warmer areas it should be grown in sun or partial shade where protection is available from strong winds and heavy frosts. It requires well-drained soil and should be watered during dry periods. Light pruning will encourage bushier growth. Snails and slugs find the foliage very appealing and are serious pests. Propagation is from seed sown in spring or half-hardened cuttings taken in summer.

Clianthus puniceus ★

KAKA BEAK, PARROT'S BILL

☼/☀ ❄ ↔6 ft (1.8 m) ↑6 ft (1.8 m)
Rare in its native habitat, the northern North Island of New Zealand. Branches clothed with attractive fern-like leaves. Red flowers, shape reminiscent of the beak of the kaka (native parrot). Easy to propagate, fast growing, can be short-lived. 'Albus', attractive white-flowering form that grows true from seed. Zones 8–11.

Clianthus puniceus 'Albus'

CLITORIA

A genus of 60 species of annual and perennial climbers, woody shrubs, and scramblers, placed in the pea-flower subfamily of the legume (Fabaceae) family. All species occur in mostly tropical regions; the Americas have 49, the remainder are from Africa and Asia. A few species are protected by State legislation in parts of the USA. Others have been planted extensively for stock feed and forage crops in many countries, where some have now become naturalized and are trouble-some weeds. All species have pinnate leaves with an uneven number of leaflets, one terminating the leaf. Flowers are pea-shaped, but the largest petal is held downward, in contrast to most other genera in this subfamily, and colors are blue, white, or pinkish.

CULTIVATION: Propagate from seed soaked overnight in water or from cuttings, which strike readily.

Clitoria ternatea

ASIAN PIGEONWINGS, BLUE PEA, BUTTERFLY PEA

☼ ⚘ ↔4 ft (1.2 m) ↑to 70 ft (21 m)
Fast-growing evergreen (deciduous in some climates) climber/scrambler. Leaves pinnate, 5 to 9 oval to oblong leaflets, to 1¼ in (30 mm) long. Solitary flowers on long stalks, largest petal bright blue, whitish, yellowish at base, 1¼–¾ in (30–40 mm) long. Pod flat, to 5 in (12 cm) long, seeds round, flattened. Flowers throughout year. Zones 10–12.

CLIVIA

FIRE LILY

Named not for Robert Clive of Indian fame (or infamy) but instead for his granddaughter, Lady Charlotte Clive, Duchess of Northumberland (died 1868), this amaryllis (Amaryllidaceae) family genus consists of 4 species

Clianthus puniceus

Cloezia buxifolia

Clusia alba

of perennials from southern Africa. Clump-forming with stocky rhizomes, they have long, bright green, strappy leaves and at various times, depending on the species, produce strong flower stems topped with heads of large funnel-shaped flowers in shades of yellow, orange, and red. Red berries follow flowering.

CULTIVATION: Tolerating only light frosts but otherwise easily grown, clivias are superb as greenhouse container plants. Outdoors they are best grown in dappled shade. Water well during the warmer months and allow to dry off for winter. Propagation is usually by division.

Clivia caulescens

☀ ⚘ ↔ 3–7 ft (0.9–2 m) ↕ 24 in (60 cm)

Spring-flowering species with leaves up to 6 ft (1.8 m) long, often drooping under their own weight. Frequently forms a short trunk-like stem. Flowers are pendulous, green and yellow-tipped, salmon pink to soft red, tubular to narrow, funnel-shaped. Zones 10–11.

Clivia gardenii

☀ ⚘ ↔ 24–48 in (60–120 cm) ↕ 16–24 in (40–60 cm)

Autumn- to spring-flowering species with leaves to 30 in (75 cm) long. Heads of tubular to narrow, funnel-shaped, green-tipped, red flowers, sometimes tinted orange or yellow, to 3 in (8 cm) long. Zones 10–11.

Clivia miniata

FIRE LILY

☀ ⚘ ↔ 24–40 in (60–100 cm) ↕ 16–24 in (40–60 cm)

A spring-flowering species with leaves to 24 in (60 cm) long, sometimes quite broad. Heads of wide open, funnel-shaped, yellow-throated, orange to nearly red flowers. *C. m.* var. *citrina*

has primrose yellow flowers. Its cultivars include: '**Kirstenbosch Yellow**', soft pale yellow with darker mid-stripe; and '**Vico Yellow**', probably a hybrid, with beautiful clear yellow flowers. *C. m.* '**Aurea**', golden yellow flowers; '**Flame ★**', very dark foliage, intense orange-red flowers; '**Megen**', bright yellow flowers; '**Striata**', standard orange flowers, white or cream variegated foliage. Zones 9–11.

Clivia nobilis

GREENTIP FIRE LILY

☀ ⚘ ↔ 20–36 in (50–90 cm) ↕ 16–24 in (40–60 cm)

Hardiest and most easily grown *Clivia*. Spring-flowering. Leaves to 18 in (45 cm) long, very finely toothed, producing a rough texture. Heads of green-tipped, yellow to red flowers. Zones 9–11.

CLOEZIA

A genus of 6 species of evergreen shrubs and small trees in the myrtle (Myrtaceae) family, allied to *Metrosideros*. All *Cloezia* species are endemic to New Caledonia. They have small to medium-sized opposite leaves with entire margins, often arranged in 4 ranks; small white or yellow flowers are carried in groups of few to many at branch tips; they have 4 or 5 petals alternating with sepals that in some species are of similar length and color to the petals. Fruits are small capsules. *Cloezia* species grow in open shrublands on poor, often boggy soils.

CULTIVATION: Although *Cloezia* species are found mostly in the wild and are scarcely known in cultivation, they include some species with considerable potential as ornamental shrubs. Acid soils with high organic content should suit them. Propagate from seed.

Cloezia buxifolia

☀ ⚘ ↔ 3 ft (0.9 m) ↕ 5 ft (1.5 m)

Erect bushy shrub found along boggy stream banks among dense sedges and other shrubs. Leaves ¼ in (6 mm) or less long, thick and rounded, in 4 ranks; flowers clustered in upper leaf axils, golden yellow, in autumn–winter. Zones 10–11.

CLUSIA

This genus of over 140 species from the rainforests of the American tropics and subtropics belongs to the St John's wort (Clusiaceae) family. They often start life as epiphytes, but form such a thicket of aerial roots that they eventually swamp or strangle their host tree, grow down to the ground, and form a trunk of their own. Most species have thick, leathery, deep green leaves that are roughly oval in shape. Although both male and female flowers appear on the same

plant, they are separate. Both occur in 3-flowered clusters and have 4 to 9 rounded petals, but the males are larger and have numerous stamens. Near-spherical leathery seed capsules follow the flowers.

CULTIVATION: Most *Clusia* species require tropical warmth. They also need moist, well-drained, humus-rich soil and will not withstand drought, frost, or even prolonged cool conditions. Prune to shape when young. Propagate from cuttings or aerial layers.

Clusia alba

BALSAM TREE

☀/☀ ⚘ ↔ 7–10 ft (2–3 m) ↕ 15–20 ft (4.5–6 m)

Shrub or small tree, usually starting as an epiphyte with aerial roots. Leathery elliptical leaves and attractive though sparse, waxy, white flowers, followed by glossy maroon fruits that burst open when ripe. Zones 11–12.

Clivia caulescens

C. miniata var. *citrina* 'Kirstenbosch Yellow'

Clivia miniata 'Vico Yellow'

Clivia miniata 'Megen'

Clivia miniata 'Striata'

Clivia miniata var. *citrina*

Clusia lanceolata

☼/◑ ✦ ↔3–10 ft (0.9–3 m)
↕7–17 ft (2–5 m)

Shrub or small tree from the coastal mangrove swamps of Brazil. Leathery lance-shaped leaves to 3 in (8 cm) long. Red-centered, waxy, white flowers, to 2 in (5 cm) wide, develop into purple-tinted fruits that open to reveal seeds with orange-red appendages. 'Alba', pure white flowers. Zones 11–12.

Clusia major

COPEY

☼ ✦ ↔50 ft (15 m) ↕50 ft (15 m)

Epiphyte or lithophyte, growing on seemingly barren rock. Shrub or tree with spreading, densely foliaged crown. Several trunks from thickened aerial roots. Flowers, 3 in (8 cm) wide, pale pink with darker markings, in summer. Pale green fruit. Zones 11–12.

CLYTOSTOMA

There are 9 species of evergreen vines in this genus, which belongs to the trumpet-vine (Bignoniaceae) family.

Clytostoma callistegioides

Coccoloba uvifera

They are native to tropical America. The leaves are lobed and divided with 2 leaflets. Clusters of flaring trumpet-shaped flowers, usually pink, are borne terminally or along the branches from spring to summer. The large seed pods are bristly or spiny.

CULTIVATION: In warm climates grow over walls and fences in full sun in well-drained soil and protect from strong winds. In cool climates grow in pots in the glasshouse and protect from direct sun when at its hottest. Propagate from cuttings or seed.

Clytostoma callistegioides

syns *Bignonia callistegioides, B. speciosa, B. violacea*

ARGENTINE TRUMPET VINE, VIOLET TRUMPET

☼ ❧ ↔20 ft (6 m) ↕10 ft (3 m)

Native to Argentina and southern Brazil. Attractive climber with dark green glossy leaves that are bronzed when young. Flaring trumpet-shaped flowers, to 3 in (8 cm) long, are lilac-pink with purple veining and soft creamy centers. Zones 10–11.

CNEORUM

This genus of 2 species, one from Cuba, the second from the western Mediterranean, is now regarded as a member of the rue (Rutaceae) family, though it has often been placed in the small family Cneoraceae, together with another genus from the Canary Islands. The plants are evergreen shrubs or small trees. Leaves are entire, leathery, and spirally arranged. The summer flowers cluster in leaf axils or terminally and have 3 or 4 sepals and 3 or 4 yellow petals. The dry fruit splits at maturity.

Clusia major

CULTIVATION: The plants are grown in full sun in any light well-drained soil and are propagated by half-hardened cuttings rooted under mist.

Cneorum tricoccon

SPURGE OLIVE

☼ ❧ ↔18 in (45 cm) ↕24 in (60 cm)

From the western Mediterranean. Upright shrub with gray-green young shoots. Leaves to 2 in (5 cm) long, glossy gray-green, linear to oblong. Flowers with deep yellow petals, ¼ in (6 mm) long. Fruit bright red, blackening when mature. A violent purgative. Zones 9–11.

COBAEA

About 20 species of perennial climbers belong to this genus of the phlox (Polemoniaceae) family. They are native to Mexico and tropical South America. Plants have alternate lobed leaves and climb with tendrils. Cup-shaped flowers are bright green, violet, or purple, borne singly along the stems. The commonly grown species *C. scandens* has become naturalized in many warm areas.

CULTIVATION: Grow in a moisture-retentive but well-drained soil in a sunny position protected from strong winds. *C. scandens* grows rapidly and can be treated as an annual in cool climates or grown in the conservatory. Propagate from seed or cuttings.

Cobaea scandens

CATHEDRAL BELLS, CUP AND SAUCER VINE, MEXICAN IVY

☼ ❧ ↔unlimited ↕20–25 ft (6–8 m)

From Mexico. Vigorous vine with wide cup-shaped flowers to 2 in (5 cm) long. Color varies from white to deep purple. "Saucer" in the common name refers to the open calyx below the flower; *C. s.* f. *alba* has white or creamy green flowers. Zones 9–11.

Clusia lanceolata

COCCOLOBA

A genus of about 150 mostly evergreen trees, shrubs, or vines in the knotweed (Polygonaceae) family from tropical and subtropical America. They have alternate, entire, leathery leaves, often very large. The immature leaves are normally a different shape to the mature leaves and are larger. Spikes or racemes of small greenish white flowers are followed by a fleshy grape-like fruit, which is technically a small nut enclosed in the swollen floral remains. Some species are grown ornamentally for their foliage. The fruit is used for making jellies.

CULTIVATION: Light or sandy well-drained soils are preferable, in an open sunny position, with ample watering, particularly in dry weather. Pruning is unnecessary except to maintain shape. Propagation is from seed, by cuttings of ripe wood in spring or of half-hardened wood in autumn, or by layering.

Coccoloba uvifera

JAMAICAN KING, PLATTER LEAF, SEA GRAPE

☼ ❧ ↔10 ft (3 m) ↕20 ft (6 m)

Native of tropical America. Erect, branching, evergreen tree. Leaves are mid-green, leathery, and heart-shaped, with reddish veins. Bears racemes of fragrant white flowers in summer, followed by grape-like edible fruit, green, ripening to reddish purple. Zones 10–12.

COCCOTHRINAX

BROOM, SILVER PALM, THATCH PALM

Native to tropical regions of the West Indies and Florida, this genus in the palm (Arecaceae) family consists of 49 graceful, slender, medium-sized palms, normally solitary. Their fan-like palmate fronds have broad blades divided into long radiating segments that are glossy dark green above and silvery beneath. As the fronds die and fall away, they leave behind a layer of fibers that wear away, leaving a ringed trunk exposed. These species are salt and wind tolerant, and are ideal, if slow-growing, ornamental plants for coastal tropical climates; young plants suit cultivation in containers. CULTIVATION: They prefer an open, sunny, or partially protected position in a very well-drained soil, with adequate water in dry periods. Propagate from seed, which germinates within 2 to 6 months, depending on species. Seedling growth is slow.

Coccothrinax argentata ★

syns *Coccothrinax fragrans, C. jamaicensis, C. proctorii, C. readii*

FLORIDA SILVER PALM, SILVER PALM

☀ ⟊ ↔ 8 ft (2.4 m) ↑ 25 ft (8 m)

Native of Florida and the Bahamas. Solitary palm with smooth gray trunk. Small fan-like leaves, glossy light yellow-green above, silvery white beneath. Fragrant white flowers, purplish black fruits. Zones 10–12.

Coccothrinax crinita ★

OLD MAN PALM, THATCH PALM

☀ ⟊ ↔ 7 ft (2 m) ↑ 30 ft (9 m)

From tropical Cuba. Trunk 8 in (20 cm) in diameter, with long, brown, fine, woolly fibers. Fan-like fronds, to 6 ft (1.8 m) across, divided into segments, drooping blades, 30 in (75 cm) long, shiny green above, dull gray beneath. Zones 10–12.

Coccothrinax argentata

Coccothrinax miraguama

syn. *Coccothrinax scoparia*

MIRAGUAMA

☀ ⟊ ↔ 7 ft (2 m) ↑ 15 ft (4.5 m)

Native of Cuba. Elegant palm, trunk 6 in (15 cm) in diameter, covered in long fibers. Glossy, rigid, dark green leaves, silvery and hairy beneath, to 6 ft (1.8 m) across, 28 segments to 24 in (60 cm) long, short slender leaf stalks. Zones 10–12.

Coccothrinax spissa

GUANO, SWOLLEN SILVER THATCH

☀ ⟊ ↔ 10–17 ft (3–5 m)
↑ 15–25 ft (4.5–8 m)

From the island of Hispaniola (Dominican Republic and Haiti). Solitary palm with stout trunk, upper part swollen. Sparse crown with rounded deeply divided leaves on long stalks that arch with age. Small bright purple fruit. Zones 10–12.

COCHEMIEA

The International Cactus Systemics Group has classified the 5 species of *Cochemiea* as *Mammillaria,* but most collectors and taxonomists still classify them as a separate genus belonging to

Coccothrinax spissa

the cactus (Cactaceae) family. They grow to 20 in (50 cm) tall, usually clustering from the base. The spiral ribs of the stems bear prominent tubercles and clusters of stout spines. Narrow red flowers are diurnal, laterally symmetrical, often flared at the ends. Seed pods are spherical or club-shaped, red, about ½–¾ in (12–18 mm) long. CULTIVATION: Reasonably easy to grow in a mineral-rich well-drained soil, *Cochemiea* may be raised from seed or from cuttings that have been dried out for a week or two. They are susceptible to overwatering and to too much organic material in the growing medium. Rest in winter.

Cochemiea maritima

☀ ⟊ ↔ 40 in (100 cm)
↑ 8–12 in (20–30 cm)

From the coast of Baja California, Mexico. Clumping to mat-forming, with cylindrical stems, 1¼–2 in (3–5 cm) in diameter. Spines 4 cetrals, reddish brown, 10 to 15 radals, white with black tips. Flowers 1–1¼ in (2.5–3 cm) long. Seed pods are spherical. Zones 9–11.

Cochemiea setispina

☀ ⟊ ↔ 20 in (50 cm) ↑ 12 in (30 cm)

From the San Borja region, San Julio Canyon, and Angel de la Guarda Island, Baja California, Mexico. Compact clumps of tightly packed

Coccothrinax miraguama

short stems. Spines 1 to 4 centrals, upper ones straight, lower hooked, ¾–2 in (18–50 mm) long, 10 to 12 radials, thin, white, with brown tips. Flowers 2 in (5 cm) long. Seed pods club-shaped. Zones 9–11.

COCHLEANTHES

This is a genus of about 16 sympodial epiphytic species belonging to the family Orchidaceae, found in parts of Central and South America. They lack true pseudobulbs and have thin bright green leaves arranged like a fan. The flowers generally range from white through various pinks to purple. They are produced singly on short spikes from between the leaf axils. CULTIVATION: *Cochleanthes* need high humidity and freely circulating air to avoid fungal spots on the soft leaves. They grow best in small pots in sphagnum moss, as they must be kept moist. If this moss is unavailable, a fine bark mix is a good substitute. They like more shade than most orchids and must not be exposed to direct light. They require intermediate to warm temperatures.

Coccothrinax crinita

Cochemiea setispina

Cochlospermum fraseri, in fruit

Cochleanthes amazonica

Cochleanthes amazonica

☀ ⚘ ↔4–10 in (10–25 cm)
↕4–20 in (10–50 cm)

Found from Brazil to Colombia.
Forms fan-like clumps; large 4 in
(10 cm) blooms produced infrequently at base of plant. Flowers bruise
easily; keep dry to avoid marking,
for example when moving blooming
plants. Zones 11–12.

COCHLOSPERMUM

This genus of 15 deciduous trees
and shrubs in the family Bixaceae
occurs in dry tropical regions of the
Americas, Africa, Asia, and northern
Australia. They have been introduced
widely through other tropical areas.
Some have substantial tuberous root
systems which enable the plants to
resist drought. They have palmate or
divided leaves and racemes or panicles
of showy flowers appearing at the end

of the dry season before the leaves.
Fruit is a capsule which splits into 3
to 5 segments containing cotton-like
seeds, each covered in long silky hairs.
CULTIVATION: *Cochlospermum* species
prefer light to medium soils in an
open sunny position. They can be
pruned to maintain their shape.
Propagation is by seed or by division
of the tubers.

Cochlospermum fraseri
WESTERN KAPOK BUSH, YELLOW KAPOK

☀ ⚘ ↔10 ft (3 m) ↕15 ft (4.5 m)

Native to tropical northern Australia.
Straggling shrub. Attractive yellow
flowers about 3 in (8 cm) in diameter.
Large lobed leaves to 5 in (12 cm)
across. Fruit, ovoid capsule, opening
to release white fluffy seeds. Edible
tuberous roots. Zones 10–12.

COCOS

This genus in the palm (Arecaceae)
family contains just one species,
which is native to coastal regions of
all tropical seas worldwide, growing
to a height of 100 ft (30 m) in good
conditions. The terminal head carries
pinnate fronds. The 3-petalled
flowers, seen only in the tropics, are
produced in panicles from the leaf
axils, followed by the coconuts,
encased in thick fibrous husks. In
tropical islands all parts of this tree
are used: the trunks and fronds for

building and weaving; the fiber for
matting, rope, and soil-less composts;
the flesh of the nut for food and
drink; the endosperm for cosmetics;
the oil for margarine and soap. The
residue is used for cattle feed.
CULTIVATION: Coconuts can be
grown successfully outdoors only in
the tropics. In subtropical conditions
they will not bear fruit. They grow
best in coastal lowlands and on
seashores. Coconuts will thrive if
watered and fed moderately in the
growing season. Grow in moist, well-
drained, humus-rich soil in full sun.
For container growing, provide an
open mixture with coarse sand added.

Cocos nucifera
COCONUT PALM

☀ ⚘ ↔10–20 ft (3–6 m) ↕100 ft (30 m)

Large palm, single trunk swollen at
the base, often leaning away from the
prevailing wind. Bright green pinnate
fronds, 20 ft (6 m) long. Fragrant
yellow flowers. Fruit covered with a
thick husk, green ripening to yellow
or orange-red. '**Malay Dwarf**' ★, a
widely grown strain with heavy crops
of large golden-yellow nuts; '**Nino**',
a dwarf cultivar, will grow to 10 ft
(3 m); '**Panama Tall**', stately tall
cultivar. Zone 12.

CODIAEUM

This genus belonging to the euphorbia (Euphorbiaceae) family consists of
6 species of evergreen perennials,
shrubs, and small trees, native to
tropical Asia and the western Pacific
region. The showy leathery leaves are
often variegated or marked and are
the main ornamental attraction.
Small, star-shaped, usually yellow
flowers, carried in axillary racemes,
appear in spring. They make good
indoor plants. In frost-prone areas
grow in an unheated greenhouse or

conservatory. In subtropical and tropical areas *Codiaeum* species do well in
borders or as specimen plants.
CULTIVATION: They do best in fertile,
well-drained, moist soil, but need to
be fed and misted regularly throughout the growing season. In tropical
areas they can be grown in shade. In
cool climates, where they are grown
under cover, they need maximum
light but can suffer scorching in direct
sunlight through glass. Propagate by
air layering in spring or taking softwood cuttings in summer. Contact
dermatitis may occur as a result of
handling these plants.

Codiaeum variegatum
CROTON

◐/☀ ⚘ ↔2–4 ft (0.6–1.2 m)
↕3–6 ft (0.9–1.8 m)

Native to tropical Asia. Small tree
with numerous cultivars, varying
quite widely in leaf color and pattern.
Leaves may be smooth-edged, lobed,
or twisted into a spiral, and are linear,
egg-shaped, sometimes deeply cut to
the midrib, variegated with white,
red, and yellow on green. '**Elaine**',

Cocos nucifera 'Panama Tall'

Cocos nucifera, Dunk Island, Australia

Cocos nucifera 'Malay Dwarf'

Coelogyne 'Burfordiense'

Coelogyne flaccida 'Dark'

Coelogyne 'Memoria W Micholitz'

stiff erect leaves; '**Grusonii**', narrow greenish yellow leaves, flushed red on the margins; '**Petra**' ★, leaves variously colored yellow, green, and orange; '**Philip Geduldig**', leaves turn rich orange to purple with pinkish veins. '**Evelyn Chilcot**' and '**Lady Balfour**' are also popular. Zones 11–12.

CODONOPSIS

BONNET BELLFLOWER

A bellflower (Campanulaceae) family genus of around 30 species of herbaceous perennials that will climb on structures but prefer to scramble through surrounding vegetation. They have wiry, often twining stems and simple light-textured leaves of variable shape. The flowers are nodding, bell-shaped, with conspicuous calyces, and although fairly large they are often a pale blue-green color that merges well with the foliage, making for a less than showy flower display. These are interesting plants, though not exactly spectacular, and those who pursue that interest and turn the bells upward will often be rewarded by finding brightly colored nectaries and veins within.

CULTIVATION: They are mostly very hardy and easily grown in any temperate climate with reasonable summer rainfall. Bonnet bellflowers prefer woodland conditions with dappled light and cool, moist, humus-rich, well-drained soil. It is best to try to remove the tangle of dry foliage and stems after it has died off, otherwise it may become very untidy. Propagate by division when dormant, or raise from seed.

Codonopsis clematidea

◐ ❀ ↔ 20–60 in (50–150 cm)
↕ 32 in (80 cm)

Perennial from central Asia. Erect when young but eventually sprawling. Slightly downy, 1 in (25 mm) long leaves tinted blue-green. In summer, very pale blue bell-shaped flowers, orange and black markings within. Zones 4–9.

COELOGYNE

This is a large diverse group of sympodial orchids (family Orchidaceae), is of Asian origin. *Coelogyne* species form a distinct pseudobulb that is linked by a woody rhizome. Depending on species, from 1 to 3 leaves are produced on top of the pseudobulb. Most members of this showy genus of epiphytes and lithophytes have white or green flowers, with contrasting labellums displaying profuse brown markings. Flowering often occurs from the developing new growths, or from specialized points at the base of the previous year's pseudobulb. Several of the *Coelogyne* species have pleasantly fragrant blooms.

CULTIVATION: *Coelogyne* species are generally plants from mountainous regions, and about 80 percent of the species are suitable for cultivating in cool to intermediate conditions. However, there are also species from the monsoonal tropical lowlands. They are generally easy to grow and will rapidly build into specimen plants if conditions are favorable. They enjoy being constantly divided, and larger mature plants are the most free-flowering. Most species are grown in pots in a bark-based growing medium, but those with pendulous flower spikes, or rampant growers with long rhizomes, do best in baskets. They enjoy humid conditions and regular watering throughout the year.

Coelogyne 'Burfordiense'

◐ ✣ ↔ 8–32 in (20–80 cm)
↕ 10–36 in (25–90 cm)

A large-growing hybrid between the warm-growing tropical species *C. asperata* and *C. pandurata*, and it is often confused with the latter. Large, 4 in (10 cm), green flowers with a labellum almost black in color,

on long arching inflorescences of about 12 blooms in spring or summer. Zones 11–12.

Coelogyne corymbosa

◐ ✣ ↔ 4–8 in (10–20 cm)
↕ 5–10 in (12–25 cm)

From the Himalayas. White-flowered; requires cool summer evening temperatures to thrive. Best grown in small pots of sphagnum moss. Zones 11–12.

Coelogyne flaccida

◐ ⧈ ↔ 4–27 in (10–70 cm)
↕ 5–15 in (12–38 cm)

From Nepal to China. Variable, cool-growing, fragrant species, blooms in early spring. Most clones have pendulous spikes of up to 14 cream to light bronze flowers. Reliable bloomer, especially fast-growing. '**Dark**', popular cultivar. Zones 9–11.

Coelogyne 'Memoria W Micholitz'

◐ ⧈ ↔ 8–20 in (20–50 cm)
↕ 8–27 in (20–70 cm)

Cool-growing primary hybrid between *C. lawrenceana* and the large white-flowered *C. mooreana*. Flowers at various times throughout the year, primarily in summer. Zones 10–11.

Coelogyne pandurata

◐ ✣ ↔ 8–48 in (20–120 cm)
↕ 8–24 in (20–60 cm)

Robust warm-growing species from Borneo, the Philippines, and Indonesia. Large green flowers, 4 in (10 cm) wide, with an almost black labellum, on long arching inflorescences of about a dozen blooms, in spring or summer. Zones 11–12.

Codiaeum variegatum 'Grusonii'

Codiaeum variegatum 'Evelyn Chilcot'

Codiaeum variegatum 'Petra'

Codiaeum variegatum 'Elaine'

Codiaeum variegatum 'Philip Geduldig'

COFFEA
COFFEE

Renowned as the source of coffee beans, this tropical African and Asian genus in the madder (Rubiaceae) family includes some 40 species of evergreen shrubs and small trees. The species most often grown for commercial coffee production is *C. arabica*, though *C. canephora* is also popular. These are highly ornamental plants with lush deep green foliage. They bear clusters of attractive, white, fragrant flowers in the leaf axils. The flowers are followed by clusters of colorful berries, in which is found the coffee bean.
CULTIVATION: Coffee requires warm temperatures to crop well, but when grown as an ornamental it will survive in most frost-free gardens. It also adapts well to container cultivation and life as a house plant. The soil should be moist, humus enriched, and well drained. A position in light shade is best. Commercial crops are subject to attack by several pests and diseases, but these are seldom a problem in gardens. Propagate from seed, which should be fresh.

Coffea arabica ★
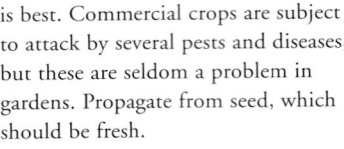
ARABIAN COFFEE

☀/☀ ⚎ ↔ 10 ft (3 m) ↑ 10 ft (3 m)
Widely cultivated commercially. Large shrub or small tree. Lustrous, wavy-edged, glossy, deep green leaves. Clusters of small, fragrant, funnel-shaped, white flowers in autumn. Round berries ½ in (12 mm), ripen to yellow, red, or purple. Zones 10–11.

Coffea liberica
LIBERIAN COFFEE

☀ ⚎ ↔ 10–15 ft (3–4.5 m)
↑ 20–30 ft (6–9 m)
From tropical Africa, Liberia, and the Ivory Coast. Large oblong leaves to 16 in (40 cm) long. Red oval fruits to 1 in (25 mm). Grown commercially but accounts for little of the coffee crop, being considered of inferior flavor. Zones 10–11.

COIX

A small genus consisting of 6 species of annual and perennial plants in the grass (Poaceae) family that come from tropical Asia and are now naturalized in many other parts of the world. They have soft, green, arching leaves, like dwarf sweet corn, and hard black seeds that have been used as rosary beads. The only species with ornamental value is *C. lacryma-jobi*.
CULTIVATION: Grow in moist to damp soil in a sheltered sunny spot and plant out after frosts have finished in areas where these occur. Propagate from seed sown indoors in late winter in frosty areas or from self-sown seedlings elsewhere.

Coix lacryma-jobi
CHRIST'S TEARS, JOB'S TEARS

☀ ⚎ ↔ 36–40 in (90–100 cm)
↑ 40–48 in (100–120 cm)
An annual or short-lived perennial species grown for its drooping stems of hard jet-black seeds, to ½ in (12 mm) in diameter, and lush bright green leaves, to 20 in (50 cm) long. Zones 9–11.

COLCHICUM
AUTUMN CROCUS, MEADOW SAFFRON, NAKED LADIES

A genus of around 45 species of corms that is the type genus for the family Colchicaceae. They are found from eastern Europe to North Africa and eastwards to China. They are not related to the true crocuses, but the name autumn crocus is an apt description of the habit and appearance of many of the species. The plants are dormant and leafless in summer. Their flowers have 6 petals, usually in 2 whorls, and start to appear from early autumn before the foliage develops. Double-flowered forms are available. *Colchicum* species are famous as the source of the cancer treatment drug colchicine, a mutagen that affects cell division. Colchicine is sometimes used to produce new plant cultivars.
CULTIVATION: Hardy, adaptable, and great favorites of rock garden enthusiasts, the autumn crocuses thrive in zones with distinct seasons. Some need a hot dry summer to flower well but most are happy in any fertile well-drained soil in full or half-sun. They also do well in containers.

Colchicum agrippinum
☀/☀ ❋ ↔ 4–8 in (10–20 cm)
↑ 4–6 in (10–15 cm)
From Greece and southwestern Turkey. Possibly a natural *C. variegatum* × *C. autumnale* hybrid. Upright blue-green leaves to 6 in (15 cm) long, sometimes wavy-edged. In autumn, before the foliage, white-tubed purple-pink flowers, mottled white. Purple anthers. Zones 5–9.

Colchicum autumnale
☀/☀ ❋ ↔ 6–16 in (15–40 cm)
↑ 6–10 in (15–25 cm)
Late summer- to autumn-flowering species from western and central Europe. Long, white-tubed, purple-pink flowers, yellow anthers. Later, narrow to broad lance-shaped leaves to 14 in (35 cm) long. **'Alboplenum'**, white double flowers; **'Album'**, small white flowers; **'Plenum'**, lavender-pink double flowers. Zones 5–9.

Colchicum byzantinum
☀/☀ ❋ ↔ 6–16 in (15–40 cm)
↑ 6–12 in (15–30 cm)
From Turkey, Syria, and Lebanon. Lush, bright green, pleated leaves, in spring, to 12 in (30 cm) long. In autumn, soft lavender-pink flowers with long white tubes, pale brown anthers, purple-red stigma. Possibly a natural hybrid. Zones 6–9.

Colchicum cilicicum
☀/☀ ❋ ↔ 6–16 in (15–40 cm)
↑ 6–12 in (15–30 cm)
Native to Turkey, Syria, and Lebanon. Large lavender-pink to purple flowers on strong white stems. Yellow anthers. Bright green leaves to 16 in (40 cm) long emerge in spring. Zones 6–9.

Coffea arabica

Coix lacryma-jobi

Colchicum cilicicum

Colchicum parnassicum

☼/◗ ❄ ↔6–16 in (15–40 cm)
↑6–10 in (15–25 cm)

Native to Greece. Less hardy, but otherwise identical to *C. autumnale,* except for more arching foliage and details of membrane covering the corm. Zones 8–10.

Colchicum speciosum

☼/◗ ❄ ↔6–16 in (15–40 cm)
↑4–8 in (10–20 cm)

Found from northern Turkey westward to Iran and northward to Russia. In autumn, pale-centered bright mauve-pink flowers with sturdy stems. Golden-yellow anthers. In spring, broad, bright green, slightly arched leaves to 10 in (25 cm) long. 'Album', large, green-throated, white flowers. Zones 6–9.

Colchicum 'The Giant'

☼ ❄ ↔8 in (20 cm) ↑10 in (25 cm)

Large white-mottled lilac-pink flowers on strong stems, in autumn. Probably a hybrid with *C. bivonae*. Zones 6–9.

Colchicum 'Waterlily' ★

☼ ❄ ↔8 in (20 cm) ↑8 in (20 cm)

Large and very fully double flowers on fairly short stems. Probably a hybrid with a *C. autumnale* cultivar. Zones 6–9.

COLEONEMA

All of these 8 species of evergreen shrubs in the rue (Rutaceae) family are native to South Africa, most of them confined to Western Cape

Colchicum parnassicum

Colchicum 'The Giant'

Coleonema album

Province. All have small heath-like leaves on fine twigs and small starry flowers in winter and spring, sometimes repeating in summer. The foliage is slightly aromatic. They make useful small hedges if pruned regularly after flowering when young and brought slowly to the required height. They are often referred to as *Diosma,* which is a separate but related genus.
CULTIVATION: A position in full sun is preferred, with a free-draining rather sandy soil. Avoid exposure to strong winds, as they tend to dislodge the surface roots and blow the plants over. These species are not recommended for cold climates. Seeds germinate freely, but may result in plants of uncertain flowering quality; soft-tip cuttings taken in late summer or autumn give true results.

Coleonema album

syn. *Diosma alba*
WHITE BREATH OF HEAVEN, WHITE CONFETTI BUSH

☼ ⚘ ↔6 ft (1.8 m) ↑5 ft (1.5 m)

Densely leafed evergreen shrub, bun-shaped with age. Leaves very small, bright green when young, darker with age; aromatic when bruised. White flowers, solitary or in small clusters, from late winter–early spring. Brown fruit. Prune regularly. Zones 9–10.

Coleonema pulchellum

syn. *Coleonema pulchrum* of gardens

☼ ⚘ ↔36–48 in (90–120 cm)
↑24–60 in (60–150 cm)

From South Africa. Well-foliaged shrub, slender branches, soft, needle-

Colchicum speciosum 'Album'

Colletia paradoxa

Coleonema pulchellum 'Pinkie'

like, aromatic leaves. Masses of tiny, starry, pink flowers in late winter–spring. Number of dwarf forms: 'Pinkie', compact, very floriferous, dark pink flowers, darker pink center stripes on petals; 'Sunset Gold' ★, widely grown dwarf form, pale yellow foliage, intensifies to a deep golden yellow in late summer–autumn if grown in a semi-exposed position. Other dwarf forms include: 'Compactum', 'Nanum' and 'Rubrum'. Zones 9–11.

COLLETIA

ANCHOR PLANT
This genus of 17 thorny shrubs in the buckthorn (Rhamnaceae) family, covered in spines and often with thickened and flattened branches, is native to temperate regions of South America. They are cultivated for their ornamental value, their spines making them particularly useful for boundary

Colchicum speciosum

Coleonema pulchellum

planting. Leaves are non-existent or very small and short-lived, while the small, scented, bell-shaped or tubular, usually yellowish or white flowers, appear singly or in clusters, normally from summer to early autumn. The fruit is a leathery 3-lobed capsule.
CULTIVATION: They prefer light to medium, sandy, well-drained soils in a protected but sunny position. Propagation is from seed or by cuttings of half-hardened wood taken in autumn.

Colletia hystrix

syn. *Colletia armata*

☼ ❄ ↔10–15 ft (3–4.5 m)
↑10–15 ft (3–4.5 m)

Large prickly shrub from Chile. Its tiny inconspicuous leaves are deciduous and its gray-green, rounded, spine-tipped stems do most of the photosynthesis. Produces tiny, scented, tubular, white flowers in late summer–autumn. Zones 8–11.

Colletia paradoxa

syn. *Colletia cruciata*
ANCHOR BUSH

☼ ❄ ↔8 ft (2.4 m) ↑6 ft (1.8 m)

Native of Uruguay and southern Brazil. Slow-growing deciduous shrub. Covered with flattened triangular spines in place of leaves. All plant parts bluish green in appearance. Fragrant yellowish white flowers appear in summer–early autumn. Zones 8–9.

× *Colmanara* Wildcat 'Gemma Webb'

× *Colmanara* Wildcat 'Carmela'

× *Colmanara* Wildcat 'Exile'

COLLINSIA

This genus of 25 species of hardy annuals belongs to the foxglove (Scrophulariaceae) family. They are native to western North America and Mexico, where they grow in rich moisture-retentive soils under trees and on shady slopes. They are grown for their attractive, tubular, 2-lipped flowers that are borne in whorls on slender stems. The flowers are in shades of white, lilac, rose, violet, and blue, and are often bicolored. Flowering is in spring and summer. CULTIVATION: Grow in a rich, moist, but well-drained soil in sun or half-sun. *Collinsia* species can also be grown as pot plants in a conservatory, where plants should be given shade from the hottest sun and a fortnightly dressing of weak liquid fertilizer. Propagate from seed.

Collinsia bicolor
syn. *Collinsia heterophylla*
CHINESE HOUSES, INNOCENCE
☀ ❄ ↔ 6–12 in (15–30 cm)
↑ 12–24 in (30–60 cm)

From California. Slender plants with lance-shaped leaves. Tubular 2-lipped flowers, borne on spikes in whorls of 2 to 7. Upper lip and tube are white, lower lip is rosy purple. Zones 7–10.

Collinsia parviflora
BLUE-EYED MARY
☀/☀ ⚘ ↔ to 16 in (40 cm)
↑ 1¼–6 in (3–15 cm)

From British Columbia to California, eastward to Colorado and eastern Canada. Annual herb with small, tubular, blue flowers with a white lip; green leaves are toothed. Blooms mid-spring to mid-summer. Zones 10–12.

× COLMANARA

This is a tri-generic hybrid in the family Orchidaceae. Many of these hybrids have blooms with rich colors and striking patterns on tall inflorescences. There can be great variation within seedlings derived from the same crossing or seed capsule. The most vigorous and outstanding cultivars have been multiplied through modern tissue culture techniques to satisfy the growing demand for these easily grown plants. CULTIVATION: Colmanaras do not like their roots to dry out, so they need to be potted in sphagnum or a fine bark mix. They are suitable for cool humid growing conditions, and require abundant water throughout the year and a part-shaded position.

× *Colmanara* Hybrids
☀ ⚘ ↔ 8–12 in (20–30 cm)
↑ 8–30 in (20–75 cm)

Hybrids range in color from yellow and brown tones through to deep red-maroon clones, mostly with contrasting labellum colors. Segments often spotted and blotched with darker color. **Wildcat 'Carmela'** ★, very vigorous, wide range of colors; **Wildcat 'Exile'**, orange blooms heavily overlaid with maroon blotching and contrasting white and maroon marked labellum; **Wildcat 'Gemma Webb'**, spectacular deep blood-red variety. Zones 10–11.

COLOBANTHUS

This genus of 15 to 20 seldom cultivated species of low-growing perennials in the pink (Caryophyllaceae) family are Southern Hemisphere plants, the majority found in alpine regions of New Zealand and also in Australia and South America, with one species extending to Antarctica. Identification of the various species is quite difficult. Some are tufted with grassy foliage; others form thick cushions of small, narrow, somewhat fleshy leaves, in overlapping pairs. Small, green, petal-less flowers stud the plants, either within or on the foliage, in summer. CULTIVATION: Very rare in cultivation, these plants are best suited to the alpine enthusiast. Grow in a cool greenhouse in a gritty mix and protect from the hottest sun. Propagate from seed or offsets.

Colobanthus canaliculatus
☀ ❄ ↔ 12 in (30 cm) ↑ 2–4 in (5–10 cm)
From alpine regions of New Zealand's South Island. Dense cushioning plant with tiny channeled leaves and small green flowers. Zones 7–9.

COLOCASIA
COCOYAM, DASHEEN, TARO
A genus of 6 species of tuberous perennials belonging to the arum (Araceae) family. They are native to tropical Asia, where they grow in naturally moist areas. Some are widely naturalized in other tropical and warm-temperate regions. The leaves, which can be very large, are arrow- or heart-shaped with prominent veins. The typical arum flower spike consists of a fleshy spike of minute flowers surrounded by a white to yellow spathe. In tropical areas the roots of *C. esculenta* are a staple food cooked in a variety of ways. Elsewhere they are grown for the ornamental quality of their leaves. CULTIVATION: In suitably warm climates grow in a fertile moisture-retentive soil, watering well in dry spells. If grown as a crop, plant at 24 in (60 cm) spacings and top-dress monthly with a high-potash fertilizer. The tubers are ready for harvesting after about 8 months. In temperate climates grow under glass with high humidity and water well.

Colocasia esculenta
syn. *Colocasia antiquorum*
COCOYAM, TARO
☀ ⚘ ↔ 3–6 ft (0.9–1.8 m)
↑ 3–6 ft (0.9–1.8 m)

From tropical eastern Asia. Widely grown throughout tropical regions as a food crop. Prominently veined dark

Colobanthus canaliculatus, in the wild, South Island, New Zealand

Colocasia esculenta 'Fontanesii'

Colquhounia coccinea var. *vestita*

green leaves to 24 in (60 cm) long, arrow- or heart-shaped, with sturdy stems supporting them from below. Cultivars grown ornamentally include '**Black Magic**', purplish black leaves; '**Fontanesii**', dark purple stems, dark green leaves with purple veins. Zones 9–12.

COLQUHOUNIA

A genus belonging to the mint (Lamiaceae) family, containing 3 to 6 evergreen or semi-evergreen erect or twining shrubs, from the eastern Himalayas to southwestern China. All plant parts have a woolly white covering when young. The scarlet and yellow tubular flowers are borne in leaf axils or terminal racemes. CULTIVATION: *Colquhounia* species prefer well-composted, moist, well-drained soils in a protected partially shaded position. Propagation is from cuttings of growing tips taken in summer and rooted under glass.

Colquhounia coccinea ★

☀ ❅ ↔ 6 ft (1.8 m) ↑ 10 ft (3 m)
Native of northern Asia. Stems square in section. Aromatic, green, oval to spear-shaped leaves, serrated margins, grayish white undersurface. Clusters of scarlet and yellow tubular flowers, 1 in (25 mm) long, late summer–early winter. *C. c.* var. *vestita*, shorter spreading habit, clusters of orange and yellow flowers. Zones 8–9.

COLUBRINA

This genus of 31 species from tropical and other warm parts of the world

Colubrina arborescens

belongs to the buckthorn (Rhamnaceae) family. These evergreen or deciduous trees or shrubs have tough, sometimes spiny, twigs. The leaves are entire and spirally arranged, often 3-veined, with small stipules. The inconspicuous flowers are borne in umbels in the leaf axils. The sepals, usually 5 in number, are joined at the base with an urn-shaped receptacle containing nectar. The petals, also usually 5 in number, are very small and hooded, partly enclosing the 5 stamens. Capsules are usually 3-lobed, each lobe with one seed. Many species are of local medicinal value. CULTIVATION: They are tropical in their requirements but are easily grown in a frost-free climate where the summers are hot and wet. The more widespread species are adapted to seashore environments, often growing on coral sand. Propagate from seed.

Colubrina arborescens

BLACK VELVET, MABIE, SNAKE WOOD
☀ ✤ ↔ 10–20 ft (3–6 m)
↑ 10–40 ft (3–12 m)
Shrub or small tree from Central America and the Caribbean. Rusty reddish young twigs. Leaves to 5 in (12 cm) long, leathery, rusty red beneath. Flowers green, in summer–autumn; 3 glossy black seeds, small blackish capsule. Source of medicinal "snakebark" and timber. Zones 11–12.

COLUMNEA

Named by Linnaeus for Italian botanist Fabius Columna (1567–1640), this mainly epiphytic genus of the African violet family (Gesneriaceae) is made up of around 160 shrubby species native to the New World tropics. They have slightly arching pendulous stems that form a crown of foliage. The leaves are small, oval to lance-shaped, in opposite pairs, and usually downy, as are the stems and calyces of the tubular flowers. Orange and red are the common flower colors, but white, yellow, pink, and maroon also occur. CULTIVATION: Intolerant of frost, these are house or greenhouse plants outside the subtropics. They are nearly always grown in hanging baskets to display their trailing flower stems. They need a steady temperature, not necessarily hot, and dappled light and shelter from cold drafts. Allow to dry in winter. Propagate from semi-ripe tip cuttings.

Columnea 'Early Bird' ★

☀ ✤ ↔ 18 in (45 cm) ↑ 48 in (120 cm)
Easily cultivated, consistent bloomer. Tolerates drought. Bright yellow flowers, red-orange edges, 2 to 3 in (5–8 cm). Small, shiny, mid-green leaves, darker tips. Zones 11–12.

Columnea gloriosa ★

GOLDFISH PLANT
◐/☀ ✤ ↔ 18 in (45 cm) ↑ 12 in (30 cm)
Central American species with stems that arch up before trailing. Hairy, pointed, oval leaves to 1¼ in (30 mm) long. Yellow-throated orange-red flowers borne singly, to 3 in (8 cm) long, of which half is made up of a hooded upper lip. Zones 11–12.

Columnea microphylla

◐/☀ ✤ ↔ 24 in (60 cm) ↑ 6 ft (1.8 m)
Costa Rican species. Long, trailing stems, red-haired rounded leaves less than ½ in (12 mm) long, with red undersides. Flowers borne singly, up to 3 in (8 cm) long, yellow markings, large hooded upper lip. Calyces often red-tinted, finely toothed. Zones 11–12.

Columnea scandens

◐/☀ ✤ ↔ 24 in (60 cm) ↑ 12 in (30 cm)
From the West Indies and Central America. Cascading, sometimes arching stems. Deep green leaves, fine red hairs. Narrow flowers, singly or in pairs, fine-haired, nearly 3½ in (9 cm) long, red or yellow. Zones 11–12.

Columnea microphylla

Columnea scandens

Columnea 'Early Bird'

COLUTEA

The 30-odd species of leguminous deciduous shrubs and small trees in this genus in the pea-flower subfamily of the legume (Fabaceae) family occur naturally in Africa and Europe eastward to Central Asia. They are wiry-stemmed, sometimes spiny, and have pinnate or trifoliate leaves, usually composed of very small leaflets. The small racemes of yellow to orange pea-like flowers appear from spring to autumn and are quite attractive. The pods become very inflated and balloon-like and may be colored, translucent, glossy, or hairy. They are worth growing as novelties; children love the pods because of the noise they make when burst by squeezing.

CULTIVATION: Most *Colutea* species are moderately to very frost hardy and grow in a wide range of soils with good drainage. They thrive in inland gardens and grow well near the coast. Plant in full sun for the best flower

Combretum aubletii

Combretum bracteosum

Colutea arborescens

and pod production. Regular tip pinching and thinning will help to keep plants compact. Propagate from seed or from cuttings taken in summer.

Colutea arborescens
BLADDER SENNA
☀ ❀ ↔ 10 ft (3 m) ↕ 15 ft (4.5 m)
Native to southern Europe. Leaves 6 in (15 cm) long, 5 to 7 pairs of leaflets. Small yellow and orange-red flowers in late spring. Pods to 3 in (8 cm) long, bright green, developing red tints, becoming translucent when mature. 'Bullata', compact form with small puckered leaflets; 'Variegata', cream-edged leaves. Zones 5–10.

Colutea × media
☀ ❀ ↔ 10 ft (3 m) ↕ 10 ft (3 m)
Hybrid between *C. arborescens* and *C. orientalis*. Leaves 2–4 in (5–10 cm) long, composed of 6 to 12 small gray-green leaflets. Flowers light red-brown to orange. Red-tinted 2 in (5 cm) long seed pods. 'Copper Beauty' ★, orange-yellow flowers, red-brown pods. Zones 6–10.

COMBRETUM

Widespread in the tropics, with the exception of Australia, this genus in the family Combretaceae consists of around 250 species of mainly evergreen and a few deciduous trees and shrubs, some of which are scrambling climbers. The paired leaves are usually

Combretum kraussii

a simple, pointed, oval to lance shape. The deciduous species, from South Africa, may have bright foliage in autumn. The flowers are small and may be petal-less, but are brightly colored and carried in racemes or panicles at the stem tips and in the leaf axils. Long-lasting 4- to 5-winged seed pods follow the flowers.

CULTIVATION: Primarily a genus of the seasonal rainfall tropics, most of these species prefer constantly warm conditions. Some of the South African species, however, will tolerate light frosts provided the soil is dry in winter. Soil type is not very important, but it must be well-drained. Plant in full sun and propagate from seed or half-hardened cuttings.

Combretum aubletii
MONKEY'S BRUSH
☀ ✦ ↔ 15–17 ft (4.5–5 m)
↕ 20–35 ft (6–10 m)
Small to medium-sized Brazilian tree with leathery, pointed, elliptical leaves to over 4 in (10 cm) long. One-sided bottlebrush-like flowerheads with red flowers opening from deep pinkish red buds, ageing to golden yellow, very long filaments. Ovoid, 4-winged, golden fruits follow. Zones 11–12.

Combretum bracteosum
HICCUP NUT
☀ ❀ ↔ 7 ft (2 m) ↕ 12 ft (3.5 m)
Evergreen from South Africa. Can be grown as a shrub, as a climber, or espaliered. Oval, dull green, sometimes red-tinted leaves, pale undersides. Mass of orange-red flowerheads in summer. Smooth rounded fruit, local hiccup remedy. Zones 9–11.

Combretum kraussii
☀ ❀ ↔ 15 ft (4.5 m) ↕ 40 ft (12 m)
Deciduous tree from the eastern provinces of South Africa. Leaves elliptical, dark glossy green, silvery white beneath. New leaves change color in spring from green-white to green-red by autumn. Creamy white flowers appear with the new leaves in late winter–late spring. Fruit is 4-winged. Zones 9–11.

Colutea × *media* 'Copper Beauty'

Commelina tuberosa, Coelestis Group

COMMELINA
DAY FLOWER, WIDOW'S TEARS
There are 50 to 100 species of mainly perennial herbs in this genus, which gives its name to the spiderwort (Commelinaceae) family. They are native to mainly tropical and subtropical regions. The roots are often tuberous and the stems are usually slender and sprawling, rooting at the nodes. The flowers are held within spathe-like folded bracts. Commonly grown species have blue flowers, but others are white, yellow, rose, and lilac.

CULTIVATION: Grow in full sun in any well-drained soil. In cooler climates the tuberous species should be lifted in autumn. Propagate from seed or cuttings.

Commelina tuberosa
☀/❂ ❀ ↔ 18–30 in (45–75 cm)
↕ 12–36 in (30–90 cm)
Variable perennial with tuberous roots, occurring from southern Mexico to Peru, in mountains. "Typical" form is low, spreading, and mounding. Brilliant blue flowers open continuously in spring–autumn. Coelestis Group (syn. *Commelina coelestis*) includes taller, more erect forms, larger flowers. Zones 9–12.

COMMERSONIA
A genus in the cacao (Sterculiaceae) family which includes 14 species occurring from Southeast Asia to Australia and New Caledonia; 12 of these *Commersonia* species are endemic to Australia. Those in the eastern states are tall shrubs or trees, while the species from western regions are smaller shrubs. The leaves are simple, hairy, toothed, or lobed. Inflorescences are in the leaf axils or terminal with small flowers, but the calyx is large and conspicuous. The fruit is a capsule, often bristly.

Commiphora woodii

CULTIVATION: Propagated from seed or cuttings, these plants grow readily in sunny positions and in well-drained soils.

Commersonia fraseri
BLACKFELLOWS HEMP, BRUSH KURRAJONG

☀/◐ ❄ ↔ 5 ft (1.5 m) ↕ 12 ft (3.5 m)

Tall shrub from southeastern Queensland to eastern Victoria, Australia. Leaves oval to lance-shaped with toothed margins, dull green, whitish beneath. White flowers in spring–mid-summer. Bristly capsular fruit. Prefers moist situations. Not common in cultivation. Zones 8–10.

COMMIDENDRUM

This genus of 4 (1 already extinct) species, restricted to St Helena in the south Atlantic Ocean, belongs to the daisy (Asteraceae) family. They are small trees or shrubs. Leaves are obovate, entire or with a toothed margin, and bunched at the branch tips. Flowerheads are solitary or in corymbs and have ray- as well as disc-like florets. Fruits are rather compressed and ribbed and have rows of rough bristles. All species have been greatly reduced in numbers through clearing and goat-raising.
CULTIVATION: They are extremely rare in cultivation outside St Helena, where seedlings are being raised in

quantity for restocking of the wild stands. The plants are ornamental, and may eventually be grown in suitably mild, moist climates elsewhere in the world. Propagate from seed.

Commidendrum rugosum
SCRUBWOOD

☀ ⚘ ↔ 5 ft (1.5 m) ↕ 3 ft (0.9 m)

Domed shrub with candelabra-like branching. Leaves to 2 in (5 cm) long, sticky above, hairy below, margins toothed. Flowerheads usually solitary, terminating branchlets; ray florets white to purple-tinged; disk florets green-yellow. Capable of growing on poor saline soil. Zones 9–11.

COMMIPHORA

Known mainly for the aromatic oils and medicinal uses of many of its species, this genus of shrubs and small trees in the family Burseraceae is found in Africa, the Middle East, and western Asia. Apart from such names as balm of Gilead and myrrh, the genus is probably best known for bdellium, a resin from several species, widely used in the perfume industry. The trees have mainly small trifoliate leaves and tiny unisexual flowers.
CULTIVATION: Most do not respond well to cultivation, so their oils tend to be very expensive. They prefer an arid frost-free climate with seasonal

Commiphora wildii, in the wild, Spitzkoppe, Damaraland, Namibia

rains. Plant in light well-drained soil in full sun. Propagate from seed that has been soaked or from cuttings.

Commiphora wildii
OAK-LEAFED CORKWOOD

☀ ⚘ ↔ 17 ft (5 m) ↕ 8 ft (2.4 m)

From Namibia. Spreading shrub with thickened stems. Silver-gray bark peels off in patches to reveal shiny, silky, smooth, greenish brown stems. Leaves glaucous green, resembling oak leaves, with 1 to 4 leaflets. Inflorescences simple or compound. Flowers small, unisexual, bell-shaped, greenish yellow. Seed pods oval, orange to yellow. Zones 8–10.

Commiphora woodii
BOSKANNIEDOOD, FOREST COMMIPHORA

☀ ⚘ ↔ 20–40 ft (6–12 m) ↕ 30–50 ft (9–15 m)

Found in forest areas of southeastern Africa. Medium tree with greenish

gray bark. Pinnate leaves with 7 to 9 large, leathery, oval leaflets. Small creamy green flowers in dense sprays, in late spring–summer. Oval red fruit. Zones 10–11.

COMPTONELLA

A genus of 8 species of evergreen shrubs and small trees in the rue (Rutaceae) family, endemic to New Caledonia. They grow in moist, sheltered situations in rainforest or stunted cloud forest on mountains. Leaves are in opposite pairs, each consisting of 3 smooth-edged leaflets. Flowers are small and white with 4 petals and 4 longer stamens, borne in short dense panicles arising from the lower leaf axils.
CULTIVATION: They are not known to have been cultivated and probably do not adapt well to garden conditions. Propagation from cuttings is more likely to succeed than from seed.

Commersonia fraseri

Commidendrum rugosum

Comptonella oreophila

Comptonia peregrina

Comptonella oreophila

☀/☀ ❄ ↔ 3 ft (0.9 m) ↕ 6 ft (1.8 m)
Erect shrub with tough, woody stem, leaves with glossy obovate leaflets about 2 in (5 cm) long. White flowers under ¼ in (6 mm) long in autumn–winter. Grows on higher mountain slopes, among rocks. Zones 10–11.

COMPTONIA

Native to eastern North America and found from Nova Scotia to Georgia, the sole species in this genus of the wax-myrtle (Myricaceae) family is a small, suckering, deciduous shrub that eventually develops into a many-stemmed thicket. It has pleasantly aromatic foliage which, although more lobed than pinnate, is rather ferny, hence the common name sweet fern. It blooms in spring and early summer, when it produces male and female flowers on separate catkins. The catkins are a red-brown shade, as is the down that coats the young leaves.
CULTIVATION: An inhabitant of fields and woodlands, sweet fern prefers moist, well-drained, humus-enriched, slightly acidic soil and a position in full sun or partial shade. The older wood should be thinned out occasionally to encourage fresh young shoots and maintain the plant's vigor. Propagate by seed, by layering, or by removing rooted suckers.

Comptonia peregrina ★

SWEET FERN
☀/☀ ❄ ↔ 8 ft (2.4 m) ↕ 5 ft (1.5 m)
Leaves 2–4 in (5–10 cm) long, narrow, deeply lobed almost to the midrib. Catkins flower in late spring; male catkins slightly longer than female. Female catkins last longer and enlarge as their seeds ripen. Zones 4–9.

CONGEA

This genus, consisting of about 7 species from Southeast Asia, belongs to the vervain (Verbenaceae) family. They are scrambling shrubs, often forming tangled masses of stems over other shrubs and small trees, with entire, simple, opposite leaves. Flowers are usually borne in a terminal panicle of small condensed cymes, each cyme surrounded by 3 conspicuous colored bracts that can be highly ornamental. The leathery fruit contains a single seed.
CULTIVATION: *Congea* species are grown in full sun and need support and plenty of space. In temperate regions they need to be planted in large pots and kept under glass, or they can be grown in the greenhouse border, requiring a rich loam with additional leafmold. Propagation is best done from seed, or from softwood or half-hardened cuttings.

Congea tomentosa

SHOWER ORCHID
☀ ✈ ↔ 20–40 ft (6–12 m)
↕ 10–30 ft (3–9 m)
From Thailand and Burma. Large shrub with long scrambling branches, densely mounding over fences or trees. Leaves to 8 in (20 cm) long, usually with hairy undersides. Heads of small white flowers, surrounded by woolly-surfaced white to pink or mauve bracts to 1 in (25 mm) long. Zones 11–12.

CONOCLINIUM

MISTFLOWER
A genus of 3 rhizome-rooted perennials of the daisy (Asteraceae) family, found in the eastern USA, the Caribbean, and Mexico. They are low and spreading to shrubby and have fairly large leaves, usually oval and sometimes downy. The flowerheads do not have ray florets but have elongated disc florets that create fluffy *Ageratum*-like flowerheads, usually in shades of powder blue, violet, or white. The hazy effect gives the genus its common name. For much of the growing season the plants make a low spreading foliage mound, but from late summer they produce upright flower stems that bloom until cut back by the first frosts. The flowers are attractive to butterflies.
CULTIVATION: Their hardiness varies with the species, but they are easily grown in sun or partial shade with a preference for moist but well-drained humus-rich soil. They will tolerate drought but do not flower well. Propagate by division when dormant. Seeds germinate freely.

Conoclinium greggii

THOROUGHWORT
☀/☀ ❄ ↔ 36 in (90 cm) ↕ 24 in (60 cm)
Found in Arizona, New Mexico, Texas, and northern Mexico. Leaves elliptical, sometimes downy, textured, veined, to 3 in (8 cm) long. Heads of filamentous, powdery, mauve-blue flowers from late summer. Zones 7–10.

CONOPHYTUM

This genus of around 86 species of small, tufted, stemless succulents from southern Africa belongs to the iceplant (Aizoaceae) family. Each shoot is reduced to 2 leaves fused into a cylindrical body that is flattened, notched or 2-lobed at the apex, with a small mouth-like opening between the lobes. Some species mimic the related *Lithops*, having a green "window" or translucent dots that allow light to penetrate to the green photosynthetic tissue within. New leaf pairs develop inside those of the previous season,

older ones drying as shells that protect new ones in the dry season. Some species are day-blooming, others nocturnal, flowers bursting through the central fissure, with petals white, yellow, purple, or bicolored.
CULTIVATION: These plants require full sun and low humidity all year. They are best grown in pots in sandy or gritty compost, even in warm countries, to control soil moisture. Withhold water from late spring until mid-summer, when new growths are forming inside old sheaths. Propagate from seed or cuttings of leaf pairs with a small amount of stem, allowing to dry before rooting.

Conophytum bilobum

☀/☀ ❄ ↔ 4–6 in (15–30 cm)
↕ 4–6 in (10–15 cm)
From Western Cape. Wedge-shaped, light green, vegetative bodies, often reddening at the edges, sometimes velvety textured. Often blooms profusely; flowers yellow to gold, sometimes red-tipped. Zones 9–10.

Conophytum pillansii

☀ ❄ ↔ 4–8 in (10–20 cm)
↕ 2–4 in (5–10 cm)
From Western Cape. Flat-topped globose bodies, entirely fused or conspicuously divided. Velvety textured, light green to near red with mottled brown markings. Purple-red flowers. Zones 9–11.

Conophytum quaesitum

☀/☀ ❄ ↔ 6–8 in (15–20 cm)
↕ 2–4 in (5–10 cm)
From Namibia and Namaqualand. Round to cylindrical, usually 2-lobed

Conophytum pillansii

Conophytum bilobum

Conophytum quaesitum

Conostylis aculeata

Conradina verticillata

plant bodies, often keeled. Body color pale gray-green to yellow-green, sometimes red-tinted and/or olive- or brown-spotted or mottled. White through cream to pink flowers, fragrant. Zones 10–11.

CONOSPERMUM

This Australian genus in the protea (Proteaceae) family has about 30 species, most from Western Australia, though a few are from the eastern states. They occur on well-drained sandy soils, sometimes on the edges of swamps and usually among plants of their own height, which enables them to receive plenty of sunshine. Most species produce large masses of flowers that have the appearance of smoke, hence the common name smoke bush; the long-lasting flowers are useful for decoration.
CULTIVATION: Smoke bushes are ideal for semi-arid areas but do not appreciate hot and humid climates; most are frost tolerant. A light pruning after flowering helps to produce bushy growth. Propagation from seed has proved difficult; a more reliable method is from cuttings taken from vigorous shoots.

Conospermum burgessiorum
☼ ❄ ↔ 10 ft (3 m) ↕ 12 ft (3.5 m)
From Queensland and New South Wales, Australia. Leaves linear to

narrowly ovate; young branches are hairy at first, then become hairless. Flowers bell-shaped, cream to white, blooming in clusters at ends of branches. Zones 8–11.

Conospermum stoechadis
SMOKE BUSH
☼/❄ ↕ ↔ 2 ft (0.6 m) ↕ 3 ft (0.9 m)
From Western Australia. Small shrub, erect branches. Leaves 6 in (15 cm), with long, sharp tips; juvenile growth silky at first, becoming hairless. Flowers densely woolly, white to gray, in upper axils. Requires well-drained soils. Tolerates extended dry periods. Zones 9–11.

Conospermum teretifolium
SPIDER SMOKEBUSH
☼/❄ ↕ ↔ 2 ft (0.6 m) ↕ 3 ft (0.9 m)
From Western Australia. Hairless branches, rush-like leaves to 12 in (30 cm) long. Flowers white to cream, tubular, with long lobes, in dense terminal panicles. Requires very well-drained soil. Zones 9–11.

CONOSTYLIS

A genus of 45 species of tufted perennial herbs placed in the bloodroot (Haemodoraceae) family. They are found in a variety of habitats in the southwestern corner of Australia. What appear to be individual plants are in fact joined by underground fleshy stems in some species; in others, the clumps are separate from each other. The stems can be short or long, branched or unbranched, on or above the ground. The leaves may be flat or round, generally grass-like, with or without hairs, green, gray-green, or whitish. The tubular bell-shaped flowers are borne in terminal heads and can be various colors. Fruits are 3-celled, containing many small seeds.
CULTIVATION: A few species are in cultivation, but this genus is not as popular as the kangaroo paws (genus *Anigozanthos*), nor has it had the same attention from plant breeders as the latter. Propagate from seed or by division.

Conospermum stoechadis, Western Australia

Conostylis aculeata ★
syns *Conostylis bracteata, C. bromelioides, C. preissii*
PRICKLY CONOSTYLIS
☼ ↕ ↔ to 3 ft (0.9 m) ↕ to 20 in (50 cm)
Variable species from southwestern Australia. Leaves are flat, green or bluish green, 4–24 in (10–60 cm) long, margins bristly. Inflorescence is 1¼–18 in (3–45 cm) long with yellow flowers, ¼–½ in (6–12 mm) long, in spring–summer. Zones 9–10.

Conostylis candicans
syns *Conostylis dealbata, C. propinqua*
GRAY COTTONHEADS
☼ ↕ ↔ 12–20 in (30–50 cm)
↕ 12–20 in (30–50 cm)
Tufted or with prostrate stems, leaves to 16 in (40 cm) long, covered with grayish felt, hence its common name. Flowers golden yellow in spring, ¼–½ in (6–12 mm) long. Zones 9–10.

CONRADINA

There are 7 species of low-growing shrubs in this genus of the mint (Lamiaceae) family. Native to southeastern USA, where they grow in areas with sandy soil. The narrow leaves are opposite and clustered. The 2-lipped tubular flowers are in shades of purple and are borne along the stems.
CULTIVATION: In warm areas grow in a sunny position in well-drained soil. In cooler areas grow in the glasshouse or conservatory in direct sunlight. Propagate from seed or cuttings.

Conradina verticillata
CUMBERLAND FALSE ROSEMARY
☼ ❄ ↔ 18–24 in (45–60 cm)
↕ 6–15 in (15–38 cm)
From Kentucky and Tennessee. Low spreading shrub with branches rooting along ground. Soft, needle-like, aromatic foliage. Tubular flowers, ½ in (12 mm) long, lavender, lower lip spotted with purple. Zones 7–10.

CONSOLIDA
LARKSPUR
A Eurasian buttercup (Ranunculaceae) family genus of around 40 species that are very much the annual cousins of the delphiniums, with which they were once grouped. Larkspurs grow 18–36 in (45–90 cm) tall and have fine feathery foliage, and about half their height is taken up with the upright, sometimes branching heads of their 5-petalled flowers. While most of the myriad many-colored modern strains are developments of *C. ambigua*, the seeds of other species are available. Pretty in the garden, they also make excellent cut flowers. The name comes from the Latin *consolidare*, meaning to make whole, and referring to the medicinal use of the plant to heal wounds. The juice of the leaves has also been used in herbal tonics, but parts of the plant, especially the seeds, are poisonous.
CULTIVATION: Plant in fertile well-drained soil in full sun. *Consolida* species thrive under most conditions and will often self-sow, although the flowers of wild seedlings rarely amount to much. They may need staking. Raise from seed.

Conospermum burgessiorum

Conospermum teretifolium, in the wild, Albany, Western Australia

Consolida ajacis

syns *Consolida ambigua,*
Delphinium ajacis

LARKSPUR

☼/◐ ⚘ ↔ 6–12 in (15–30 cm)
↑ 32–40 in (80–100 cm)

Mediterranean native with lacy finely cut foliage in basal clumps and wiry upright stems carrying heads of many spurred flowers in shades of blue, pink, or white. Garden forms occur in wide color range and include double flowers. **Giant Imperial Series**, including '**Giant Imperial Blue Spire**', '**Giant Imperial Pink Perfection**', and '**Giant Imperial White King**', has double flowers covering the entire color range with long spikes that last

Consolida ajacis 'Giant Imperial Blue Spire'

C. ajacis 'Giant Imperial Pink Perfection'

C. ajacis 'Giant Imperial White King'

Convolvulus cneorum

well and keep their color when dried. The **Dwarf Hyacinth Series** has short tightly packed spikes. Zones 9–11.

Consolida regalis

☼/◐ ⚘ ↔ 8–12 in (20–30 cm)
↑ 20 in (50 cm)

From Europe and the Caucasus. Branching stems, leaves narrowly segmented, hairy. Flowers blue, pink, or white. Used to produce dyes: blue from flowers, green from the foliage. **Cloud Series**, such as white-flowered '**Snow Cloud**', have stocky branching flower stems. Zones 9–11.

CONVALLARIA

LILY-OF-THE-VALLEY

Lily-of-the-valley has been cultivated since at least 1000 BC, which is not surprising considering its unique and intense fragrance and the ease with which it grows. The sole species in the genus, the type for its family, the Convallariaceae, is a low spreading perennial found over much of the northern temperate zone. Its vigorous rhizomes can colonize a large area and in spring produce bright green lance-shaped leaves and short-stemmed

Convallaria majalis

Convallaria majalis 'Hardwick Hall'

white flowerheads of bell-shaped blooms (a form with pale pink flowers is available), followed by red berries. Seventeeth-century herbalists recommended lily-of-the-valley to strengthen the heartbeat, and the plant does indeed contain glycoside compounds used in modern heart medications.
CULTIVATION: Plant in dappled shade in deep, moist, well-drained soil. A cool winter is required for proper dormancy. The rhizomes, known as pips, are somewhat invasive in loose soil. Propagate by division.

Convallaria majalis

◐/● ❄ ↔ 12–40 in (30–100 cm)
↑ 4–8 in (10–20 cm)

Spring–early summer-flowering, fragrant waxy flowers. *C. m.* var. *rosea*, small pale pink flowers, not as vigorous as white-flowered species. *C. m.* cultivars with variegated foliage include: '**Albostriata**', dark leaves with white to cream longitudinal stripes; '**Aureovariegata**' (syn. '**Striata**'), gold stripes; '**Aureomarginata**', cream- to yellow-edged leaves; '**Hardwick Hall**', broad leaves with pale margins; '**Prolificans**', unusually shaped flowers. Zones 3–9.

Convolvulus althaeoides

Convallaria majalis var. *rosea*

Convallaria majalis 'Prolificans'

CONVOLVULUS

This is the name genus of the family Convolvulaceae and comprises around 100 species of twiner climbers, soft-stemmed shrubs, and herbaceous perennials from many temperate regions. The widely flared funnel-shaped flowers bloom in succession over a long period. The leaves are mostly narrow and thin textured; trim shrubby species regularly to encourage density of growth.
CULTIVATION: Most *Convolvulus* species are hardy plants adaptable to a range of soils and situations, but all prefer a sunny position. They are easily propagated from cuttings.

Convolvulus althaeoides

☼ ❄ ↔ 3–5 ft (0.9–1.5 m)
↑ 3–5 ft (0.9–1.5 m)

Perennial trailer or low climber from southern Europe. Gray-green heart- to arrowhead-shaped leaves, often lobed. In summer inflorescences of 1 to 5 funnel-shaped pink to magenta flowers, to 1½ in (35 mm) wide. *C. a.* subsp. *tenuissimus* has covering of fine silvery hairs, narrowly lobed leaves, usually bears flowers singly. Zones 8–10.

Convolvulus cneorum

SILVERBUSH

☼ ❄ ↔ 2 ft (0.6 m) ↑ 2 ft (0.6 m)

From the Mediterranean. Bun-shaped shrub, dense weak stems. Silvery, thin, narrow, silky leaves. White to pale pink flowers, darker pink stripes, flared, funnel-shaped, in spring–summer. Requires free drainage, good air circulation. Suited to coastal gardens, tolerates summer dryness. Zones 8–10.

Convolvulus lineatus

☀/◐ ❄ ↔ 20–40 in (50–100 cm)
↕ 2–10 in (5–25 cm)

Spreading, sometimes mounding
perennial found from France to
southern Russia and Greece. Stems
and narrow elliptical leaves covered
in fine silky hairs. Flowers in leaf
axils, borne singly or in small clusters,
soft pink, in summer. Zones 7–9.

Convolvulus sabatius ★

syn. *Convolvulus mauritanicus*
☀/◐ ❄ ↔ 24–60 in (60–150 cm)
↕ 8–12 in (20–30 cm)

Low spreading perennial or subshrub
from Italy and North Africa. Trailing
stems, fine-haired, gray-green, oval
leaves to 1½ in (35 mm) long. Groups
of 1 to 3 flowers in the leaf axils, pale
mauve to purple, sometimes pink, to
1 in (25 mm) wide. Zones 8–10.

Convolvulus tricolor

☀/◐ ❄ ↔ 12–32 in (30–80 cm)
↕ 20–40 in (50–100 cm)

Found through southern Europe and
in North Africa. Annual or short-lived
perennial shrub or small climber.
Small, pointed, oval leaves. Flowers
up to 2 in (5 cm) wide, borne singly
in the leaf axils, in blue shades, often
with a yellow throat. **Ensign Series**
has brightly colored flowers with

Convolvulus sabatius

contrasting markings, such as '**Blue
Ensign**', white-edged, yellow-throated,
deep blue flowers. Zones 8–10.

COPERNICIA

CARANDA PALM, WAX PALM

Native to tropical and subtropical
regions of the West Indies and South
America, this palm (Arecaceae) family
genus consists of 24 or 25 species.
They may be solitary or clumping,
and may range from dwarf species to
tall spectacular trees. The trunk,
which may be covered with the bases
of old fronds, or scarred, or occasionally bare, is often swollen at its base.
The fan-like palmate fronds are stiff,
deeply divided, and often spiny, the

Convolvulus tricolor

dead fronds remaining on the plant
and creating a "petticoat" below the
living fronds. All species have ornamental value, while one, *C. prunifera*,
is grown commercially for the carnauba wax harvested from the leaves.
CULTIVATION: *Copernicia* species
prefer an open sunny position in well-
drained soil, although they will cope
with half-sun. Propagation is from
seed, which takes 3 to 10 months to
germinate, according to species, but
seedling growth is slow.

Copernicia alba

CARANDA, CARANDAY

☀ ❄ ↔ 12–25 ft (3.5–8 m)
↕ 25–100 ft (8–30 m)

Native to South America. Slender
palm with rounded crown of stiff
palm-shaped leaves. Long leaf stalks
are spiny. Flowering spikes, to 6 ft
(1.8 m) long, arise within the foliage.
Zones 9–11.

Copernicia baileyana ★

YAREY, YAREY HEMBRA

☀/◐ ❄ ↔ 10 ft (3 m) ↕ 40 ft (12 m)
An impressive palm, native of Cuba.
Frond stalks to 4 ft (1.2 m) in length,
covered with spines. Large crowded
crown. Huge, deeply segmented,
bright green, fan-shaped fronds.
Zones 10–12.

Copernicia macroglossa ★

CUBAN PETTICOAT PALM, JATA DE
GUANBOCA

☀/◐ ❄ ↔ 10 ft (3 m) ↕ 20 ft (6 m)
Spectacular palm from Cuba. Spiral
crown, closely packed fronds. In older
plants, a "petticoat" covers the trunk
to ground level. Glossy green fronds,

almost no stalks, deeply divided,
about 64 stiff, pointed, spiny
segments. Zones 10–12.

Copernicia prunifera ★

CARNAUBA

☀/◐ ❄ ↔ 12 ft (3.5 m) ↕ 40 ft (12 m)
From northeastern Brazil. Grown
for its versatile wax. Large rounded
crown, hard patterned trunk, lower
portion covered in persistent leaf
bases. Fan-like fronds divided into
segments hang from deeply toothed
leaf stalks. Zones 10–12.

COPIAPOA

syn. *Pilocopiapoa*

A northern Chilean genus of around
20 species of low, often mounding
cacti (family Cactaceae). The stems,
which may be short and rounded or
longer, tending towards cylindrical,
are ribbed, but seldom heavily, and
are often woolly at the top. The plants
develop from a taproot that may
emerge slightly from the soil, making
the stem appear pinched at the base.
The spines are often large in relation
to plant size and tend to be curved.
The flowers are short and funnel- to
bell-shaped, usually clustered near
the apex of the stems, and are most
commonly yellow, rarely red.
CULTIVATION: Tolerant of only very
light frosts and likely to rot in wet
winter conditions, these cacti are otherwise undemanding plants that are
easily grown in full or half-sun with
gritty very free-draining soil. Water
and feed occasionally in summer,
otherwise keep dry. New plants may
be raised from seed, but offsets and
divisions will establish more quickly.

Copernicia baileyana

Copernicia macroglossa

Copernicia alba

Copernicia prunifera

Copiapoa humilis

Copiapoa cinerea

Copiapoa cinerea var. *columna-alba*

Copiapoa longistaminea

Copiapoa cinerea var. *gigantea*

Copiapoa krainziana

Copiapoa tenuissima

Copiapoa cinerascens

☀/☀ ❄ ↔ 6–24 in (15–60 cm)
↑ 4–8 in (10–20 cm)

Slow to cluster, may for many years be a single stem. Stems gray-green and slightly downy, with 10–17 ribs, up to 4 in (10 cm) in diameter, with the neck of taproot often exposed. Curved gray-brown spines on woolly areoles. Creamy yellow flowers to 2 in (5cm) wide in summer. Zones 10–11.

Copiapoa cinerea

☀/☀ ❄ ↔ 6–16 in (15–40 cm)
↑ 8 in–4 ft (20 cm–1.2 m)

Clustering or mounding, woolly-topped, globose or short cylindrical stems that may reach 10 in (25 cm) in diameter. Up to 45 ribs, studded with areoles bearing short, often very dark spines. Yellow flowers in summer, to 2 in (5 cm) wide. *C. c.* **var.** *columna-alba*, stems to 8 in (20 cm) wide, fewer ribs, flowers often smaller. *C. c.* **var.** *gigantea*, orange-brown wool, ribs with rounded apices, generally spinier than other species. Zones 10–11.

Copiapoa humilis

☀/☀ ❄ ↔ 4–16 in (10–40 cm)
↑ 8 in (20 cm)

Green to deep olive brown stems to 4 in (10 cm) wide, simple or clustered, with 9–17 ribs and partially exposed taproot. Slightly scented yellow-green to yellow flowers, to 1¾ in (40 mm) in diameter, from late spring. Zones 10–11.

Copiapoa krainziana

☀/☀ ❄ ↔ 12–36 in (30–90 cm)
↑ 6–16 in (15–40 cm)

Clusters of wool-topped, globose to short, cylindrical stems to 8 in (20 cm) in diameter, 13 to 24 ribs, covered with clusters of up to 30 white needle-like spines, sometimes curved. Soft yellow flowers, around 1 in (25 mm) wide, in summer. Zones 10–11.

Copiapoa longistaminea

☀/☀ ❄ ↔ 12–36 in (30–90 cm)
↑ 8 in (20 cm)

Clusters of globose to short cylindrical stems to 6 in (15 cm) diameter, topped with buff wool, up to 24 ribs, many short, stiff, dark spines. Yellow flowers from late spring. Zones 10–11.

Copiapoa tenuissima

☀/☀ ❄ ↔ 6–12 in (15–30 cm)
↑ 2–6 in (5–15 cm)

Clusters of globose stems to 2 in (5 cm) in diameter, up to 16 ribs, large tubercles, very short spines, irregular, white, woolly covering. Soft yellow flowers to 1 in (25 mm) diameter from late spring. Zones 10–11.

COPROSMA

This genus belongs to the large family Rubiaceae, which includes *Coffea*, the coffee plant. It comprises about 90 species of evergreen shrubs and small trees from Australia, New Zealand, and Pacific regions. There is a wide variation in habit from erect to creeping; leaves range from minute to large. Inconspicuous male and female flowers grow on separate plants. The berries on the female can give a pretty display in summer and autumn.

CULTIVATION: Adaptable plants tolerating a wide range of situations and soils, *Coprosma* species are usually best in full sun and well-drained conditions. Some are suited to harsh coastal conditions; others are useful for ground cover, hedging, and shelter. In cool-temperate climates they are barely hardy and require overwintering in the greenhouse. If a display of berries is required, male and female plants must be grown together. Propagation is from seed, which is best sown fresh, or from half-hardened cuttings taken in autumn.

Coprosma acerosa

SAND COPROSMA

☀ ❄ ↔ 3 ft (0.9 m) ↑ 3 ft (0.9 m)

Native of New Zealand. Intertwined branches form springy mounds. Leaves small, dark green, needle-like. If both sexes are grown, female bears attractive smoky blue berries. Useful ground cover, excellent coastal plant. 'Lobster', conspicuous pale red stems. Zones 8–11.

Coprosma 'Coppershine'

☀ ❄ ↔ 3–4 ft (0.9–1.2 m)
↑ 3–5 ft (0.9–1.5 m)

New Zealand raised hybrid. Compact shrub, densely foliaged, with small very glossy leaves, green with bronze overtones. Zones 8–10.

Coprosma × kirkii

☀ ❄ ↔ 7 ft (2 m) ↑ 3 ft (0.9 m)

May be a natural hybrid between *C. acerosa* and *C. repens*. Variable plant, mounding or prostrate. Small, narrow, glossy leaves, inconspicuous flowers. Erratic crop of red-flecked, translucent, cream to white berries. Tough ground cover, tolerates coastal gardens. 'Kirkii Variegata', popular cultivar with silvery, cream-edged, sage green leaves. Zones 9–10.

Coprosma × *kirkii* 'Kirkii Variegata'

Coprosma acerosa 'Lobster'

Coprosma rugosa

Coprosma virescens

Coprosma macrocarpa

☼ ⚶ ↔ 8 ft (2.4 m) ↑ 30 ft (9 m)

From New Zealand's North Island. Much smaller in cultivation, to 6 ft (1.8 m) high. Large leaves broadly oval, leathery, wavy margins. Flowers small, inconspicuous; berries orange-red. Zones 9–11.

Coprosma petriei

syn. *Coprosma pumila*

☼ ❄ ↔ 3 ft (0.9 m) ↑ 3 in (8 cm)

Low-growing ground cover shrub, native to alpine areas of New Zealand. Forms a dense cushion. Small, dark green, needle-like leaves, densely crowded on dark brown branchlets. Berries from pale blue to purplish red. Zones 7–10.

Coprosma propinqua

☼ ❄ ↔ 6 ft (1.8 m) ↑ 6 ft (1.8 m)

New Zealand native, larger in the wild. Branching habit, angular, wide-spreading, tangled. Dark green leaves, very small, leathery. Berries attractive, translucent, pale blue. Zones 8–10.

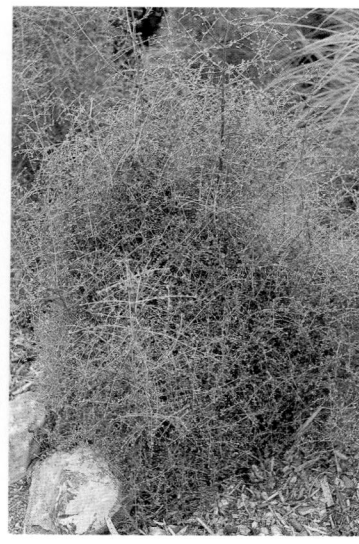

Coprosma rigida

Coprosma repens

MIRROR BUSH, TAUPATA

☼ ⚶ ↔ 12 ft (3.5 m) ↑ 20 ft (6 m)

From New Zealand coastal areas. Very glossy, thick, dark green, oblong leaves. Berries orangey red. Excellent plant for warm coastal gardens. 'Marble Queen' ★, leaves speckled white; 'Painter's Palette', very glossy leaves of red, cream, yellow, green, and chocolate brown; 'Picturata', glossy leaves variegated cream; 'Variegata', cream-edged, shiny green leaves; 'Yvonne', very glossy dark green and chocolate brown leaves, intensifying in color during winter. Zones 9–11.

Coprosma rigida

☼ ❄ ↔ 6 ft (1.8 m) ↑ 6 ft (1.8 m)

Found throughout New Zealand. Erect spreading shrub. Intertangling reddish brown branches. Small, dark green, leathery leaves. Berries orangey yellow or white. Zones 8–10.

Coprosma robusta

KARAMU

☼ ❄ ↔ 10 ft (3 m) ↑ 12 ft (3.5 m)

Common throughout New Zealand. Similar to *C. repens*, but with less glossy leaves, dark orange to yellow berries. Useful shelter when establishing other plants. Prune to keep a compact shape. Zones 8–11.

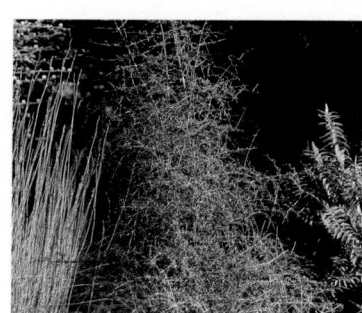

Coprosma propinqua

Coprosma rugosa

☼ ❄ ↔ 6 ft (1.8 m) ↑ 6 ft (1.8 m)

From New Zealand. Reddish brown branches, needle-like leaves. Berries range from pale to dark blue. 'Clearwater Gold', selected male form with attractive golden coloring. Zones 8–10.

Coprosma virescens

☼ ❄ ↔ 8 ft (2.4 m) ↑ 10 ft (3 m)

Spreading New Zealand species. Angled coppery gold branchlets, leaves particularly small. Suitable for informal hedging. Zones 8–10.

CORDIA

This genus in the family Boraginaceae comprises about 300 deciduous or evergreen trees or shrubs that are native to tropical regions of Central and South America, Africa, and Asia. They have terminal flowerheads or spikes of bell-shaped or tubular white or orange flowers, and alternate simple leaves; the fruit is a drupe.
CULTIVATION: They like moist, well-drained, peaty soils, in an open sunny position. Pruning is not usually needed. Propagate in winter to spring from ripe seed, or from cuttings.

Cordia boissieri

TEXAS OLIVE

☼ ❄ ↔ 8 ft (2.4 m) ↑ 8 ft (2.4 m)

Found in Texas and New Mexico, USA, and nearby parts of Mexico.

Coprosma repens 'Variegata'

Evergreen shrub, with leaves that are elliptical to ovate, dull green on the upper surface, downy on the underside. Large, white, yellow-centered flowers bloom in summer. This species will not tolerate prolonged wet, cold conditions. Zones 8–11.

Cordia parvifolia

LITTLE LEAF CORDIA

☼ ⚶ ↔ 3–6 ft (0.9–1.8 m)
↑ 3–10 ft (0.9–3 m)

Semi-deciduous shrub from northern Mexico, with small, grayish, serrated-edged leaves. Bears clusters of crepe-textured white flowers in summer. Zones 9–11.

Cordia boissieri

Coprosma macrocarpa

Coprosma petriei

Cordyline australis, in the wild, New Zealand

Cordyline australis 'Albertii'

Cordyline fruticosa 'Kiwi'

Cordyline fruticosa 'Rubra'

CORDYLINE

A small group of about 15 species of erect, palm-like, evergreen shrubs in the family Dracaenaceae, found in Australasia, the Pacific region, and tropical America. Usually sparingly branched or suckering with fibrous stems tipped with a tuft of strap-like pointed leaves. Masses of small flowers with 6 spreading segments are produced in large panicles, followed by ornamental red, black, or whitish berry-like fruit. Some species are perfect container specimens for indoor decoration; some of the New Zealand species are moderately frost hardy. CULTIVATION: In warmer areas grow in well-drained organically rich soil with regular water during the warmer months. Most prefer a protected partially shaded position, although *C. australis* will thrive in full sun. If multiple trunks and a clumping effect are required, cut the main stem at any height. Propagation is from seed, by division or from stem cuttings.

Cordyline australis
syn. *Dracaena australis*
NEW ZEALAND CABBAGE TREE
☼/◐ ❄ ↔ 8 ft (2.4 m) ↑ 20 ft (6 m)
Erect palm-like tree from New Zealand. Usually an unbranched stem, developing a broad crown of arching, sword-like, pointed leaves. In late spring–summer, mature trees bear broad panicles of sweet-scented, creamy white, starry flowers. Clusters of white or bluish berries. 'Albertii', smaller variegated form; **Purpurea Group ★**, leaves suffused bronze to purple, some forms darker than others. Zones 8–11.

Cordyline fruticosa
syn. *Cordyline terminalis*
◐ ❄ ↔ 4 ft (1.2 m) ↑ 10 ft (3 m)
From Southeast Asia, northern Australia, and many Pacific islands. Erect sparingly branched species, with thin-textured, distinctly stalked, lanceolate leaves. This plant bears white, mauve, or purplish flowers,

and clusters of bright red berries. Colorful foliage forms include '**Kiwi**' and '**Rubra**'. Zones 10–12.

Cordyline glauca
TI PLANT
◐ ❄ ↔ 40 in (100 cm)
↑ 40–60 in (100–150 cm)
Popular, tough, indoor or outdoor (warm to tropical) foliage plant. Slender green leaves with a blackish reverse display a hint of purple on new growth. Small starry flowers in spring. Zones 10–11.

Cordyline indivisa
MOUNTAIN CABBAGE TREE, TOI
◐ ❄ ↔ 8 ft (2.4 m) ↑ 20 ft (6 m)
Originating in New Zealand in cool mountainous regions with high rainfall. Stout and robust trunk, usually with a single stem. Large heads of sword-shaped leaves, often flushed with purple. Bears creamy white flowers on branched panicles reaching 3 ft (0.9 m) long, in spring–early summer, and bluish purple berries. Zones 9–10.

Cordyline petiolaris
BROAD-LEAF PALM LILY
☼ ❄ ↔ 6 ft (1.8 m) ↑ 15 ft (4.5 m)
From subtropical eastern Australia. Rainforest species that develops spreading clumps. Woody fibrous stems, dark green broadly lance-shaped leaves. Long arching panicles of small white or pale purplish flowers in late winter–early spring. Small bright red berries. Attractive house plant. Zones 10–12.

Cordyline rubra
PALM LILY
☼ ❄ ↔ 3–7 ft (0.9–2 m)
↑ 10–15 ft (3–4.5 m)
Of garden origin. Leaves 6–20 in (15–50 cm) long on stalks up to 8 in (20 cm) in length. Lilac flowers in summer, followed by scarlet-red berries. Zones 10–11.

Cordyline stricta ★
SLENDER PALM LILY
☼ ❄ ↔ 3 ft (0.9 m) ↑ 15 ft (4.5 m)
From subtropical rainforests of eastern Australia. Popular in cultivation. Erect multi-stemmed clumps. Leaves narrow, drooping, with toothed margins. Small purple or violet flowers, on branched arching panicles, late spring–summer. Glossy black berries. Zones 10–12.

COREOPSIS
TICKSEED
Found in the Americas, especially in southwestern USA and Mexico, the 80-odd annuals and perennials in this daisy family (Asteraceae) genus are compact plants that flower profusely, providing spectacular summer color. Most are shrubby plants, 2–4 ft (0.6–1.2 m) tall, with narrow sometimes lobed leaves. The flowers are nearly always golden yellow, though garden forms occur in many shades. The tips of the ray florets are often toothed as if cut with pinking shears.

C. petiolaris, Queensland, Australia

Cordyline rubra

Coreopsis lanceolata 'Baby Sun'

Coreopsis lanceolata 'Sterntaler'

Coreopsis gigantea

Coreopsis tinctoria

The flowers of some species yield a golden orange dye. Both the common name tickseed and the Greek word *coreopsis* (bug-like), from which the proper name is derived, refer to the appearance of the small black seeds. CULTIVATION: Plant in a sunny position in light well-drained soil. *Coreopsis* species flower better with summer moisture but are quite drought tolerant. All can be raised from seed, and the perennials will also grow from divisions or small basal cuttings from non-flowering stems.

Coreopsis auriculata

☼/◐ ❄ ↔ 24 in (60 cm) ↑ 5 ft (1.5 m)
Spring-blooming perennial from southeastern USA. Leaves to over 4 in (10 cm) long, entire or with 1 to 2 small lobes. Flowerheads to 2 in (5 cm) wide, yellow, with about 8 ray florets. 'Nana', to around 10 in (25 cm) tall, with dark foliage and orange-gold flowers. Zones 4–10.

Coreopsis gigantea

☼/◐ ❄ ↔ 32 in–4 ft (80 cm–1.2 m) ↑ 7–10 ft (2–3 m)
Vigorous, heavy-stemmed, summer-flowering Californian perennial with doubly pinnate leaves to 8 in (20 cm) and long very narrow leaflets. Long-stemmed yellow flowerheads to over 3 in (7.5 cm) wide. Zones 8–10.

Coreopsis grandiflora

☼/◐ ❄ ↔ 12–20 in (30–50 cm) ↑ 24 in (60 cm)
Bushy perennial from central and southern USA. Leaves to 4 in (10 cm) long; lower leaves often entire, upper tending towards pinnate. From late spring, long-stemmed flowerheads to slightly over 2 in wide, with around 8 ray florets. In the wild, colors range from pale yellow to gold. 'Calypso', 14 in (35 cm) tall, cream variegated foliage, small red spots on ray florets; 'Early Sunrise', 18 in (45 cm) tall, gold double flowers; 'Kelvin Harbutt', up to 36 in (90 cm) tall, golden yellow flowerheads with red-brown disc florets. Zones 7–10.

Coreopsis lanceolata

☼/◐ ❄ ↔ 12–16 in (30–40 cm) ↑ 24 in (60 cm)
Tough perennial from central and southeastern USA. Leaves to 6 in (15 cm) long, usually entire, rarely with shallow basal lobes, lance-shaped to linear. Summer-borne yellow flowerheads to 2½ in (6 cm) wide, usually with around 8 ray florets. 'Baby Gold', 16 in (40 cm) tall, golden flowers; 'Baby Sun' (syn. 'Sonnen-kind'), 12 in (30 cm) tall, gold flowers; 'Sterntaler', 16 in (40 cm) tall, gold flowers, ray florets with bronze-red basal blotch. Zones 3–9.

Coreopsis rosea

☼/◐ ❄ ↔ 12 in (30 cm) ↑ 24 in (60 cm)
Summer- to early autumn-flowering annual or short-lived perennial found in northeastern USA and southeastern

Coreopsis verticillata

Canada. Small compound leaves, sometimes with very narrow lobes. Flowerheads around 1 in (25 mm) wide on 4 in (10 cm) long stems, white to pale red ray florets, yellow disc florets. 'American Dream', to around 12 in (30 cm) tall, many small pink flowerheads. Zones 8–10.

Coreopsis 'Sunray' ★

☼/◐ ❄ ↔ 12–16 in (30–40 cm) ↑ 20 in (50 cm)
Compact bushy plant with entire and pinnate foliage, bright green, leaflets often narrow. Glowing yellow double flowers from late spring. Often listed as a *C. grandiflora* cultivar. Zones 7–10.

Coreopsis tinctoria

☼/◐ ❄ ↔ 16–24 in (40–60 cm) ↑ 4 ft (1.2 m)
Summer-flowering annual found over much of North America. Leaves

Coreopsis verticillata 'Grandiflora'

usually narrow and entire, sometimes pinnate, to 4 in (10 cm) long. Many small flowerheads, ray florets yellow, reddening at base, disc florets red-brown. 'Mahogany Midget', 12 in (30 cm) tall, all-over red-brown flowerheads. Zones 9–10,

Coreopsis verticillata

☼/◐ ❄ ↔ 16 in (40 cm) ↑ 36 in (90 cm)
Upright summer-flowering perennial from southeastern USA. Sticky doubly pinnate leaves, 3 leaflets per section, may be very narrow, to 2½ in (6 cm) long. Bright yellow flowerheads to 2 in (5 cm) wide. 'Golden Gain', 20 in (50 cm), narrow leaf segments, bright yellow flowers; 'Grandiflora' (syn.'Golden Shower'), 24 in (60 cm) tall, large bright yellow flowers; 'Moonbeam', 20 in (50 cm) tall, soft yellow flowers; 'Zagreb', 12 in (30 cm) tall, pale gold flowers. Zones 6–10.

Coreopsis 'Sunray'

Coreopsis verticillata 'Moonbeam'

Coreopsis rosea 'American Dream'

CORIANDRUM

CILANTRO, CORIANDER

Consisting of only 2 species, native to southwestern Asia and parts of North Africa, these slender, erect, annual herbs belong to the carrot (Apiaceae) family. Seeds and leaves are important in many cuisines. Leaves are finely divided to lobed. Flowers appear in umbels, in shades of white to pink, with larger outer petals. Aromatic globular seeds follow the summer flowers. The genus name comes from the Greek word *koriannon,* an insect said to smell like the crushed leaves. CULTIVATION: Plant in sunny well-drained situations when frost risk has passed. Harvest leaves as required. Propagate from seed, harvested when it has ripened to a gray-brown color.

Coriandrum sativum

CHINESE PARSLEY, CILANTRO, CORIANDER

☀ ❄ ↔ 18–24 in (45–60 cm)
↕ 18–24 in (45–60 cm)

Native to eastern Mediterranean and western Asia. Annual herb, strongly aromatic. Parsley-like foliage and seeds are popular flavorings in several cuisines. Umbels of small flowers are white or pale purple. Zones 6–9.

CORIARIA

This name genus of the family Coriariaceae contains 5 to 10 species of perennials, shrubs, and small trees. It has a very wide but scattered distribution, with species from southern Europe, eastern Asia, South America, New Guinea, and New Zealand. Foliage is usually frond-like with a double row of oval leaflets, and the stems often arise from a vigorously spreading somewhat tuberous rootstock with nitrogen-fixing properties like those of the legumes. Small green flowers are carried in racemes that can be showy, and are followed by fleshy fruits of variable coloration. The extremely poisonous fruits are sometimes used in dyes, as are the roots. CULTIVATION: Most are easy to cultivate; some are considered weeds in places. Where frosts are common they may be cut to the ground over winter, but will usually reshoot in spring unless the ground freezes. Partial shade with moist, humus-rich, well-drained soil is best. Propagate from seed or cuttings or by division.

Coriaria japonica

☀ ❄ ↔ 5 ft (1.5 m) ↕ 6 ft (1.8 m)
From Japan. Subshrub with arching stems. Leaves to 4 in (10 cm) long, develop strong red tones in autumn. Inflorescences of green and red flowers in summer. Clusters of deep pink to red fruits that blacken with age. Zones 8–10.

Coriaria myrtifolia

REDOUL

☀ ❄ ↔ 7 ft (2 m) ↕ 10 ft (3 m)
From southwestern Europe and North Africa. Gradually arching branches.

Coriandrum sativum

Whorls of up to 3 in (8 cm) long leaves. Short inflorescences in summer. Red-brown fruit. Zones 8–10.

Coriaria ruscifolia

☀ ❄ ↔ 6–10 ft (1.8–3 m) ↕ 20 ft (6 m)
Found in New Zealand and temperate South America. Leaflets to 3 in (8 cm) long, usually carried in pairs. Long pendulous inflorescences, can exceed 10 in (25 cm) in length. Fruit black when ripe. Zones 8–10.

Coriaria terminalis

☀ ❄ ↔ 7 ft (2 m) ↕ 5 ft (1.5 m)
From the Himalayas and western China. Rhizomatous deciduous subshrub. Leaflets to 3 in (8 cm) long, color well in autumn. Inflorescences at branch tips, 6 in (15 cm) long. Fruit large and black. Has yellow- and red-fruited forms. Zones 8–10.

CORNUS

DOGWOOD

There are about 40 species of deciduous and evergreen trees and shrubs in this genus of the family Cornaceae. A few are ornamental, garden-grown for their autumn leaf color, their colored winter stems, and their branches covered in blankets of "flowers", composed of large petals or wide decorative bracts surrounding small insignificant flowers. The simple oval leaves are usually opposite each other, and the fleshy fruits have stones. CULTIVATION: They need sun or semi-shade, good drainage, and a fertile neutral to acid soil. Those grown for their winter stem color are best grown in full sun and cut back in early spring. Propagate the multi-

Coriaria japonica

stemmed species by layering of sucker growths, from hardwood cuttings taken in summer or autumn, or from seed cleaned and cold-stratified for at least 3 months. The large-bracted species can be raised from seed (also stratified), from half-hardened cuttings in summer, or by grafting.

Cornus alba

RED-BARKED DOGWOOD, TARTARIAN DOGWOOD

☀/◐ ❄ ↔ 10 ft (3 m) ↕ 10 ft (3 m)
Deciduous spreading shrub, native of eastern Asia. Forms dense thickets. Blood red young stems in winter. Dark green oval leaves, orange, red, and brown in autumn. Clusters of creamy flowers in late spring. Small, white, blue-tinted fruits. 'Argenteo-Marginata', cream- to white-edged leaves; 'Aurea', light greenish gold foliage; 'Gouchaltii', white and red variegations; Ivory Halo/'Bailhalo'; 'Kesselringii', black-purple stems, red and purple autumn leaves; 'Sibirica' ★, glowing coral red stems; 'Sibirica Variegata', deep green leaves with creamy white margins. Zones 4–8.

Cornus alternifolia

GREEN OSIER, PAGODA DOGWOOD

☀ ❄ ↔ 20 ft (6 m) ↕ 20 ft (6 m)
A native of eastern North America. Deciduous bushy shrub or small tree. Branches in irregular whorls, forming flat horizontal tiers. The tapering, pointed, mid-green leaves turn red and purple-red in autumn. Star-like whitish cream flowers appear in early summer. Small blue-black fruits. 'Argentea' has white variegations on the leaves. Zones 3–7.

Cornus alternifolia 'Argentea'

Cornus alba 'Argenteo-Marginata'

Cornus alba 'Aurea'

Cornus alba Ivory Halo/'Bailhalo'

Cornus alba 'Sibirica'

Cornus alba 'Sibirica Variegata'

Cornus controversa

Cornus controversa 'Pagoda'

Cornus amomum

Cornus canadensis

Cornus amomum

SILKY DOGWOOD

☀ ❄ ↔ 10 ft (3 m) ↑ 10 ft (3 m)

From North America. Vigorous, compact, deciduous shrub. Dark green leaves, turn red in autumn, reddish brown down on the under-surfaces, hang from purplish stems. Young shoots, purplish, downy. White flowers in late spring. Purplish fruits. **Zones 5–8**.

Cornus canadensis

BUNCHBERRY, CREEPING DOGWOOD

☀ ❄ ↔ unlimited ↑ 4–6 in (10–15 cm)

From Greenland to Alaska. Hardy, low, spreading, deciduous perennial. Whorls of ovate to lance-shaped

Cornus florida

leaves, brilliant red autumn color. Large white bracts around flower-heads. Red edible fruit. Thrives in cool moist conditions. **Zones 2–8**.

Cornus capitata

BENTHAM'S CORNEL, HIMALAYAN DOGWOOD

☀/◑ ❄ ↔ 30 ft (9 m) ↑ 30 ft (9 m)

Bushy evergreen or semi-evergreen tree from China and the Himalayas. Minute flowers, cream to lemon yellow sky-facing bracts in late spring–early summer. Pendent, rose to apricot, pink-tinted fruits. Leathery, oval, gray-green leaves, paler underneath. Tolerates sheltered coastal conditions. **Zones 8–9**.

Cornus controversa

GIANT DOGWOOD, TABLETOP DOGWOOD

☀ ❄ ↔ 50 ft (15 m) ↑ 60 ft (18 m)

Native of Japan and China. Large deciduous tree. Horizontal spreading branches, well-separated tiers. White, upturned, flattish flowers. Fruits blue-black. Oval pointed leaves, glossy dark green above, downy beneath, turn red and purple in autumn. Chalk and lime tolerant. **'Pagoda'**, abundant

Cornus capitata

white flowers; **'Variegata'**, broad, streaked, creamy white margins on drooping leaves. **Zones 5–8**.

Cornus 'Eddie's White Wonder'

☀ ❄ ↔ 15 ft (4.5 m) ↑ 15 ft (4.5 m)

A hybrid between *C. florida* and *C. nuttallii*, deciduous upright tree or shrub, pendulous outer branches.

Dramatic, large, white flowers in spring. Autumn foliage brilliant orange, red, and purple. **Zones 5–8**.

Cornus florida

FLOWERING DOGWOOD

☀/◑ ❄ ↔ 25 ft (8 m) ↑ 30 ft (9 m)

Native to northeastern USA. Highly ornamental spreading tree. Leaves slightly twisted, oval, pointed, dark green, paler undersides, orange, red, yellow, and purple in autumn. Bracts white to pink in late spring–early summer. Berries red, remaining through winter. Does not tolerate inferior or chalky soils. *C. f.* **subsp. urbiniana**, yellow-pink bracts; *C. f.* f. **rubra**, rosy pink bracts. *C. f.* **'Apple Blossom'**, pale pink bracts; **'Cherokee Chief'**, dark rose red bracts; **'Pink Flame'**, pink-edged bracts. **Zones 5–8**.

Cornus florida 'Pink Flame'

Cornus florida f. *rubra*

Cornus florida subsp. *urbiniana*

Cornus mas 'Aureoelegantissima', in spring

Cornus mas 'Aureoelegantissima', in summer

Cornus mas

Cornus mas 'Aurea'

Cornus mas 'Macrocarpa'

Cornus macrophylla

Cornus kousa

CHINESE DOGWOOD, JAPANESE FLOWERING
DOGWOOD, KOUSA DOGWOOD

☼ ❄ ↔ 15 ft (4.5 m) ↑ 25 ft (8 m)
From Japan and Korea. Deciduous.
Glossy wavy-edged leaves, oval and
pointed, turn bronze-crimson in
autumn. Profuse green flowers in
summer. Creamy white bracts, edged
with red. Pink- or red-tinted fruits.
Grows poorly in shallow chalky soils.
C. k. var. *chinensis* ★, paler smooth-
edged leaves. Zones 5–8.

Cornus macrophylla

☼ ❄ ↔ 20 ft (6 m) ↑ 25 ft (8 m)
Deciduous tree from the Himalayas,
China, and Japan. Glossy leaves,
creamy white flowers, late summer.
Blackish blue fruits. Zones 6–9.

Cornus mas

CORNELIAN CHERRY

☼ ❄ ↔ 20 ft (6 m) ↑ 25 ft (8 m)
Native of southern Europe, tolerates
drought and exposure. Short-stemmed

Cornus kousa var. *chinensis*

leaves, oval, pointed, shiny, deeply
veined, mid-green, turn reddish
purple in autumn. Flowers yellow, on
the previous year's bare wood, from
mid-winter to early spring. Kidney-
shaped fruit. **'Aurea'**, yellow juvenile
leaves; **'Aureoelegantissima'**, leaves
with yellow and pink margins;
'Macrocarpa', large, glossy, red fruit;
'Variegata', leaves with white margins.
Zones 5–8.

Cornus nuttallii

CANADIAN DOGWOOD, MOUNTAIN
DOGWOOD

☼ ❄ ↔ 40 ft (12 m) ↑ 60 ft (18 m)
From northwestern USA. Oval leaves,
dark green, turn yellow and scarlet in
autumn. Flowers small; large, flat,
irregular, white bracts, flushed with
pink, in late spring and early autumn.
Orange-red fruits. Grows poorly in
shallow chalky soils. **'Gold Spot'**, as
leaves mature, they become randomly
splotched with patches of yellow.
Zones 7–8.

Cornus kousa

Cornus nuttallii

Cornus pumila

Cornus officinalis

Cornus officinalis

JAPANESE CORNELIAN CHERRY

☼ ❄ ↔ 15 ft (4.5 m) ↕ 15 ft (4.5 m)
Spreading deciduous shrub, similar to
C. mas. Brown flaking bark. Brilliant
yellow flowers, on bare stems, in late
winter. Bright red edible fruits, richly
colored autumn foliage. Zones 6–8.

Cornus pumila

DWARF RED-TIPPED DOGWOOD

☼ ❄ ↔ 7 ft (2 m) ↕ 8 ft (2.4 m)
Deciduous, slow-growing, mound-
forming shrub of unknown origin.
White flowers, borne in large long-
stemmed clusters in summer.
Zones 5–8.

Cornus Rutgers Hybrids

☼ ❄ ↔ 15 ft (4.5 m) ↕ 20 ft (6 m)
This group of *C. kousa* × *C. florida*
hybrids was developed at Rutgers
University in New Jersey, USA.

Deciduous trees bear large flower
bracts in spring, followed by red
fruits. Autumn foliage bright red.
Cultivars include: Aurora/'**Rutban**';
Constellation/'**Rutcan**'; Ruth
Ellen/'**Rutlan**'. Zones 5–9.

Cornus sanguinea

BLOODWING DOGWOOD, COMMON
DOGWOOD, EUROPEAN DOGWOOD

☼ ❄ ↔ 10 ft (3 m) ↕ 15 ft (4.5 m)
A native of northern Europe.
Deciduous shrub. Red-green shoots.
Bears white scented flowers in loose
clusters, blue-black fruit. Red-purple
autumn foliage. '**Midwinter Fire**',

Cornus sericea 'Sunshine'

Cornus, Rutgers Hybrid, Aurora/'Rutban'

Cornus, Rutgers Hybrid, Ruth Ellen/'Rutlan'

bright red winter stems; '**Winter
Beauty**' ★, red shoots in winter.
Zones 6–8.

Cornus sericea

syn. *Cornus stolonifera*
AMERICAN DOGWOOD

☼ ❄ ↔ 7 ft (2 m) ↕ 6 ft (1.8 m)
Native of eastern North America.
Deciduous suckering shrub. Oval
to lance-shaped green leaves turn
orangey red in autumn. White fruit
tinged green. *C. s.* subsp. *baileyi*
(syn. *C. baileyi*), non-suckering
downy shoots, reddish brown in
winter, young leaves and flower stalks
woolly; *C. s.* '**Flaviramea**', white star-
shaped flowers, late spring–early
summer; '**Isanti**', dwarf form, abundant white flowers; '**Sunshine**', striking yellow and green leaves. Zones 2–9.

Cornus sericea 'Flaviramea'

Cornus sericea

Cornus, Rutgers Hybrid, Constellation/'Rutcan'

COROKIA

This is a small genus of 4 evergreen
shrubs in the family Grossulariaceae.
Three are native to New Zealand; the
fourth is a rare Australian species.
The habit and leaf form vary between
the species, but all bear small starry
flowers in early summer, followed by
orange, yellow, or red berries.
CULTIVATION: These shrubs will
grow in sun or semi-shade and in soils
with a reasonable level of fertility.
The site should be well drained. Both
C. cotoneaster and *C. macrocarpa* are
very tolerant of dry conditions. Light
pruning will maintain a compact
shape. Propagation of the species is
from seed, which is best sown fresh,
or from half-hardened cuttings taken
in spring. The cultivars are propagated
from cuttings only.

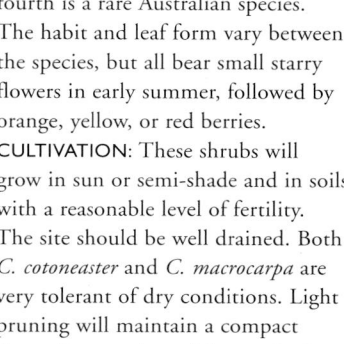

Cornus sanguinea 'Midwinter Fire'

Cornus sericea 'Isanti'

Corokia buddlejoides

KOROKIO

☼/◐ ❄ ↔7ft(2m) ↑10ft(3m)

From the northern North Island of New Zealand. Erect slender habit. Leaves lance-shaped, leathery, olive green above, silvery gray beneath. Small yellow flowers. Berries bright to dark red or almost black. Zones 8–10.

Corokia cotoneaster

WIRE NETTING BUSH

☼/◐ ❄ ↔10ft(3m) ↑10ft(3m)

From New Zealand. Tangled wiry branches, silvery sheen when young. Sparse foliage. Starry yellow flowers. Red to yellow berries. Good hedging plant when clipped. Zones 8–11.

Corokia macrocarpa

☼ ❄ ↔10ft(3m) ↑12ft(3.5m)

Native to the Chatham Islands of New Zealand. Shrub or small tree. Dark green, leathery, lance-shaped leaves, with silvery undersides. Flowers yellow. Red berries. Good for dry sites. Zones 8–10.

Corokia × *virgata*

☼ ❄ ↔6ft(1.8m) ↑6ft(1.8m)

A natural hybrid of *C. buddlejoides* and *C. cotoneaster*. Cultivars form well-branched shrubs, with different leaf colors, more showy displays of berries. 'Bronze King', bronze foliage; 'Cheesemanii', small dark green leaves; 'Frosted Chocolate', chocolate brown leaves; 'Red Wonder' ★ and 'Yellow Wonder', starry yellow flowers and red or yellow berries. Zones 8–10.

CORONILLA

There are about 20 species of annuals, perennials, and shrubs, some evergreen and some deciduous, in this genus in the pea-flower subfamily of the legume (Fabaceae) family. Native to Europe, Africa, and Asia, their habitat ranges from open woodland to dry scrub and grassland. *C. valentina* grows on cliffs, and is useful for erosion control. The leaves of *Coronilla* are usually pinnate; pea-like flowers are borne in umbels, with some species being fragrant. CULTIVATION: They need shelter from cold winds and winter frosts, and do best in full sun in well-drained moderately fertile soil. Propagate by cuttings in summer or autumn, or from freshly ripened seed.

Coronilla valentina

☼ ❁ ↔5ft(1.5m) ↑5ft(1.5m)

Native to southern Portugal, Spain, and southern Europe to Croatia. Evergreen shrub. Bright green leaves, 13 egg-shaped leaflets. Bears bright golden yellow fragrant flowers in late winter–summer, again in autumn. Narrow seed pods about 2 in (5 cm) long. *C. v.* subsp. *glauca,* more compact, leaves more blue-green, flowers may be lighter yellow. 'Citrina', pale yellow blooms. Zones 9–10.

Coronilla valentina

CORREA

A member of the rue (Rutaceae) family, this is an Australian genus of 11 species, all of which hybridize readily. Hybrid cultivars are also available. Often found in cool, moist, shaded positions, some are also able to tolerate coastal situations in full sun. Handsome evergreen shrubs, *Correa* species respond well to cultivation. Most species flower from winter to spring. Some have bell-shaped flowers; others are tubular with protruding stamens. All are favorites of nectar-seeking birds. CULTIVATION: They prefer friable, well-drained, fertile loams. Tip pruning immediately after flowering will improve plant form and density.

Correa alba

☼/◐ ❄ ↔6ft(1.8m) ↑3ft(0.9m)

From coastal southern Australia. Vigorous evergreen shrub. Attractive green leaves, with round, fragrant,

Coronilla valentina subsp. *glauca*

C. valentina subsp. *glauca* 'Citrina'

furry undersurfaces. Small, white, starry flowers from winter–spring. Salt and drought tolerant, this species grows best in well-drained sandy loam. Zones 8–10.

Correa backhouseana

☼ ❄ ↔6ft(1.8m) ↑6ft(1.8m)

From Tasmania, Australia. Dense evergreen shrub. Leaves oval, dark green. Cream-green flowers with golden brown edges, winter–spring. Tolerates front-line coastal situations. Zones 8–9.

Correa baeuerlenii

CHEF'S-CAP CORREA

☼/◐ ❄ ↔6ft(1.8m) ↑6ft(1.8m)

From New South Wales, Australia. Evergreen shrub, pendulous flowers, usually greenish yellow, distinctive "chef's cap," in autumn–spring. Likes cool, moist, protected areas. Zones 8–9.

Correa pulchella ★

☼/◐ ❄ ↔3ft(0.9m) ↑3ft(0.9m)

Small evergreen shrub from South Australia. Leaves smooth, elliptical to lance-shaped. Tubular red, salmon pink, or pink flowers from autumn–spring. Zones 8–9.

Corokia buddlejoides

Corokia × *virgata* 'Yellow Wonder'

Correa backhouseana

Corokia cotoneaster, in the wild, The Tors, near Christchurch, New Zealand

Correa alba

Correa baeuerlenii

Correa reflexa

NATIVE FUCHSIA

☼/◐ ❄ ↔ 7 ft (2 m) ↑ 6 ft (1.8 m)

From Queensland and southern Australia. Tidy but variable shrub. Leaves vary from oval, narrow, or heart-shaped, and from smooth to rough and hairy. Tubular, pendulous, flowers, rich red with green or yellow tips, in spring. '**Fat Fred**' ★, inflated red flowers with greenish yellow tips. Zones 8–10.

Correa Hybrid Cultivars

☼ ⬙ ↔ 2–4 ft (0.6–1.2 m) ↑ 18 in–6 ft (45 cm–1.8 m)

Several cultivars and hybrids of uncertain origin have become popular with gardeners. Compact and heavy flowering. '**Dusky Bells**' ★, deep dusky pink to soft red flowers; '**Ivory Bells**', white to cream flowers; '**Mannii**', long, tubular, red flowers; '**Marian's Marvel**', very pendulous clusters of pink flowers, green at the base. Zones 9–10.

CORTADERIA

PAMPAS GRASS

This genus of about 25 species of grasses belongs to the Poaceae family. With the exception of one New Guinea species, *Cortaderia* are native to South America and New Zealand, where they grow in a range of habitats from grassy plains to mountains. They are dense tussock-forming

Correa reflexa, atypical form

Correa pulchella

Cortaderia richardii, in the wild, Lake Wanaka, Otago, New Zealand

grasses growing to 10 ft (3 m) or more. Their long, stiff, flat leaves are crowded at the base, and the leaf margins range from rough to very sharp. In flower they are a stunning sight, with tall, showy, erect or arching plumes of tiny flowers that are white, pale pink, or pale gold. **CULTIVATION:** Most *Cortaderia* species are at least frost hardy, and can be grown as lawn specimens, in the garden border, by water, and for low shelter or hedging. Grow in a sunny situation in any well-drained reasonably fertile soil. Cut or burn out dead material annually. Propagate from seed or by division.

Cortaderia richardii

TOETOE GRASS, TOITOI

☼ ❄ ↔ 2–3 ft (0.6–0.9 m) ↑ 4–10 ft (1.2–3 m)

Clump-forming tussock-like grass, native to New Zealand. Long, narrow, arching, strap-like, soft green leaves, with sharply serrated edges and shiny undersides. Tall arching plumes of pale yellow-gold, usually drooping flowers, carried on long stalks, up to

10 ft (3 m) long, extending beyond the leaves, from early summer to autumn. Zones 7–9.

Cortaderia selloana

syns *Arundo selloana, Cortaderia argentea*

PAMPAS GRASS

☼ ❄ ↔ 4–6 ft (1.2–1.8 m) ↑ 5–25 ft (1.5–8 m)

Large durable grass from southern South America. Narrow, arching, rough-surfaced leaves, forming dense fountain-like clumps. Silvery white oblong flower panicles, to 4 ft (1.2 m) long, tinged red or purple, in autumn. '**Albolineata**' (syn. 'Silver Stripe'), compact, slow-growing, with leaves edged with white; '**Aureolineata**' (syn. 'Gold Band'), hardy, compact, with leaves broadly edged with rich yellow, later deep gold; '**Bertinii**', dwarf form to 3 ft (0.9 m) high; '**Pumila**' (dwarf pampas grass), dwarf form, up to 3–4 ft (0.9–1.2 m), narrow bluish green foliage, hardier than the species; '**Rosea**', showy with long plumes tinged with pink; '**Sunningdale Silver**', large, sturdy, wind resistant, with

dense white plumes to 12 ft (3.5 m); '**Violacea**', flower panicles tinted violet. Zones 5–10.

CORYBAS

HELMET ORCHID

This deciduous orchid (Orchidaceae) family genus consists of about 100 temperate species from Southeast Asia to Australia, the Pacific Islands, and New Zealand. Many of the Australian representatives are known as helmet orchids, and are pollinated by fungus gnats. Most of these small-flowered single-leafed species occur in heavily shaded moist areas in mountain forests, often in association with sphagnum moss. The solitary flowers are sensitive to minor variations in humidity, and will quickly collapse if the air becomes too dry.
CULTIVATION: There are a number of colony-forming *Corybas* species that are relatively easy to cultivate, bring into flower, and multiply, as long as their basic requirements are met. Two of the most important aspects are high humidity and cool temperatures. They are best grown in a well-drained mix containing a high proportion of peat moss (for moisture) and coarse sand (for drainage). They become dormant in summer and revert to small, white, pea-sized tubers; at this time the pots should be allowed to dry out. They are best repotted every year or two, with the dormant tubers repositioned 1¼ in (30 mm) below the soil surface. Some *Corybas* species can be grown in terrariums. Most flower in autumn and winter.

Correa, Hybrid Cultivar, 'Dusky Bells'

Correa, Hybrid Cultivar, 'Mannii'

Corydalis cheilanthifolia

Corybas pruinosus

Corydalis cava

Corydalis solida

Corybas pruinosus

☀ ⟶ 1–1¼ in (25–30 mm)
↕ ½–1½ in (12–35 mm)

From coastal New South Wales, Australia. Flowers, dark red markings. Blooms in winter only a few weeks after the ground-hugging leaf emerges from dormancy. Zones 10–11.

CORYDALIS

While many of the 300-odd species of annuals and perennials in this poppy (Papaveraceae) family have long been cultivated, *Corydalis* boomed in popularity in the late 1980s, when the blue-flowered *C. flexuosa* and its cultivars became widely available. Mainly confined to the northern temperate zones, the perennials spread by rhizomes or tubers to form clumps of ferny, often blue-green foliage. Their flowers are borne in racemes and are tubular, with 4 tiny petals and a long spur. The flowers are showy, combining well with the delicate foliage. The name comes from the Greek

korudallis (lark), because the spurred flower resembles the bird's foot.
CULTIVATION: Mostly very hardy, preferring temperate climates with distinct seasons. Woodland or rockery conditions are best, with moist, cool, humus-rich, well-drained soil. If soil remains moist, they will grow in full sun, though part-shade is preferable. Propagate by division or from seed.

Corydalis cashmeriana

☀ ❄ ⟶ 12–32 in (30–80 cm)
↕ 10 in (25 cm)

Late spring–summer-flowering perennial from the Himalayas. Bright green ferny foliage with leaflets to 1 in (25 mm) long. Bright blue flowers, conspicuously spurred, ½–1 in (12–25 mm) long, in racemes of up to 8 blooms. Zones 5–9.

Corydalis cava

☀/☀ ❄ ⟶ 6 in (15 cm) ↕ 6 in (15 cm)
Perennial from central Europe. Hollow tuber, and lacks basal foliage. Leaves

dissected, 2 per stem. Violet or white flowers borne in racemes of 10 to 20 in early spring. Zones 6–9.

Corydalis cheilanthifolia

☀ ❄ ⟶ 20–40 in (50–100 cm)
↕ 10 in (25 cm)

Perennial found in central China. Loose rosettes of short-stemmed, ferny, olive green leaves up to 18 in (45 cm) long. In spring, racemes of bright yellow flowers, ½ in (12 mm) long, on stems up to 18 in (45 cm) tall. Zones 6–9.

Corydalis elata

☀ ❄ ⟶ 20–24 in (50–60 cm)
↕ 16–20 in (40–50 cm)

Perennial native to China. Bushy upright habit, blue-green foliage. Blue flowers continue into summer. Flowers mildly fragrant. Zones 5–10.

Corydalis flexuosa

☀/☀ ❄ ⟶ 12–32 in (30–80 cm)
↕ 12 in (30 cm)

Perennial from southwestern China. Blue-green leaves die after flowering. Bright blue flowers, mildly scented, spurred, to 1 in (25 mm) long, spring to early summer. '**Bronze Leaf**', leaves purplish, especially at tips, light blue

Corydalis flexuosa 'Bronze Leaf'

flowers; '**China Blue**', deep blue flowers; '**Père David**', bright blue flowers to 2 in (5 cm) long; '**Purple Leaf**', deep blue flowers, purplish foliage. Zones 5–9.

Corydalis nobilis

☀ ❄ ⟶ 16–32 in (40–80 cm)
↕ 24–32 in (60–80 cm)

Perennial from northern China and Siberia. Coarse, ferny blue-green leaves up to 12 in (30 cm) long. In spring, racemes of short-spurred pale yellow flowers, 1 in (25 mm) long, with purple-brown tips. Zones 5–9.

Corydalis ochroleuca

☀ ❄ ⟶ 12–32 in (30–80 cm)
↕ 8–16 in (20–40 cm)

Southern European perennial. Leaves strongly blue-green, flowers very pale yellow to cream, ½ in (12 mm) long. Zones 5–9.

Corydalis solida

FUMEWORT

☀ ❄ ⟶ 8–12 in (20–30 cm)
↕ 10 in (25 cm)

Perennial originating from temperate Eurasia, with paired, deeply divided, trifoliate leaves. Racemes of up to 20 flowers in spring, graduating in color from lavender through pale red to purple with darker tips. '**George Baker**', deep pink to red flowers. Zones 5–9.

Corydalis flexuosa 'Père David'

Corydalis ochroleuca

Corydalis flexuosa 'China Blue'

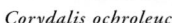

Corydalis flexuosa 'Purple Leaf'

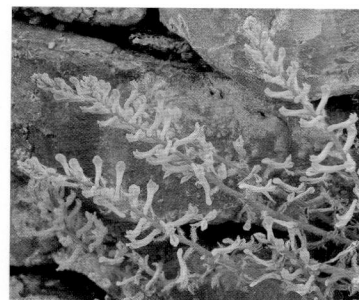

Corydalis tomentella

Corydalis turtschaninovii

Corydalis tomentella

☀ ❄ ↔ 12–20 in (30–50 cm)
↑ 12 in (30 cm)

Chinese perennial with ferny, down-covered, gray-green leaves. In late spring–summer, upright racemes of bright yellow flowers with yellow-green tips. Zones 6–9.

Corydalis turtschaninovii

☀ ❄ ↔ 16–32 in (40–80 cm)
↑ 16–20 in (40–50 cm)

Perennial from northern China and Siberia. Blue-green ferny or aquilegia-like leaves. Bright blue flowers in spring. Extracts of the tubers widely used in herbal remedies, mainly for their analgesic properties. Zones 5–9.

Corydalis wilsonii

☀ ❄ ↔ 12–32 in (30–80 cm)
↑ 12–16 in (30–40 cm)

Chinese perennial with bright green to bronze-green, finely divided, ferny leaves to 4 in (10 cm) long. In spring, small racemes of bright yellow flowers with yellow-green tips. Zones 7–9.

CORYLOPSIS

Native to the eastern Himalayas, China, Taiwan, and Japan, this genus in the family Hamamelidaceae contains about 10 species of deciduous shrubs and small trees. The young branches are downy; the egg-shaped blunt-toothed leaves are light to dark green and appear in spring after the fragrant yellow flowers. The fruit, a woody capsule about ½ in (12 mm) wide, contains 2 shiny black seeds. CULTIVATION: All prefer acid soil and need moist, fertile, well-drained woodland conditions. Propagate from

Corydalis wilsonii

freshly ripened seed in autumn, protected against winter frosts, or take softwood cuttings in summer.

Corylopsis glabrescens

FRAGRANT WINTER-HAZEL

☀ ❄ ↔ 15 ft (4.5 m) ↑ 15 ft (4.5 m)

Native to Korea and Japan. Open spreading shrub. Leaves oval and dark green, heart-shaped base, pointed tip, blue-green undersides, turn yellow in autumn. Pendent racemes of light yellow fragrant flowers, reddish green bracts, in spring. Zones 6–9.

Corylopsis pauciflora

BUTTERCUP WINTER-HAZEL

☀ ❄ ↔ 8 ft (2.4 m) ↑ 8 ft (2.4 m)

Native to Taiwan and Japan. Leaves 3 in (8 cm) long, bronze in spring, maturing to bright green. Pendent racemes of fragrant yellow flowers before foliage in early spring. Hairless fruit in autumn. Zones 7–9.

Corylopsis spicata

Corylopsis glabrescens, in autumn

Corylopsis sinensis ★

syn. *Corylopsis willmottiae*
CHINESE WINTER-HAZEL

☀ ❄ ↔ 15 ft (4.5 m) ↑ 15 ft (4.5 m)

Native to China. Erect spreading shrub. Oblong or slightly egg-shaped leaves, green above, blue-green below, to 5 in (12 cm) long. Pendent racemes of yellow flowers, velvety bracts, in mid-spring–early summer. *C. s.* var. *clavescens* f. *veitchiana* (syn. *C. veitchiana),* more upright than the species, smooth leaf stems, broader pale lemon flowers. Zones 6–9.

Corylopsis spicata

SPIKE WINTER-HAZEL

☀ ❄ ↔ 10 ft (3 m) ↑ 6 ft (1.8 m)

Native to Japan, spreading shrub. Egg-shaped tapering leaves, dark green above, grayish underneath. Pendent racemes of bright yellow flowers, red anthers, felted floral bracts, in spring. Zones 6–9.

CORYLUS

Known as filberts, hazelnuts, cobnuts, and cobs, there are about 15 species of deciduous suckering shrubs and trees in this genus in the birch (Betulaceae) family, some garden grown. The flowers, both the long flouncing male catkins ("lambs' tails") and the inconspicuous female flowers, appear on last year's bare wood, the same plant carrying both sexes.

Corylopsis pauciflora

Corylopsis glabrescens, in spring

Catkins are usually visible by late winter and fluff out in spring, when the female flowers appear. The husked edible nuts ripen in autumn. CULTIVATION: They are easily grown in rich moist soils in full sun or part-shade. Propagate from detached suckers, mounding up soil beforehand to promote root growth. Early summer softwood cuttings are also used, treated with hormone powder. Seeds require cold stratification for about 3 months for germination.

Corylus americana

syn. *Corylus calyculata*
AMERICAN FILBERT, AMERICAN HAZELNUT

☀/☀ ❄ ↔ 10 ft (3 m) ↑ 10 ft (3 m)

Deciduous shrub, native of eastern North America. Similar in habit and form to *C. avellana,* but oval leaves larger. Nuts completely enclosed in long husks. Catkins can be 3 in (8 cm) long. Zones 4–8.

Corylus americana

C. sinensis var. *clavescens* f. *veitchiana*

Corylus avellana

COBNUT, EUROPEAN HAZELNUT, FILBERT

☼/◐ ❄ ↔ 15 ft (4.5 m) ↑ 15 ft (4.5 m)

Native of Europe, western Asia, North
Africa. Thicket-like shrub. Coarse mid-
green leaves turn yellow in autumn.
Long pale yellow catkins in winter
on bare branches; red female flowers
in early spring. Nuts half covered in
ragged husks. '**Aurea**', greenish yellow
leaves; '**Contorta**', dense slow-growing
shrub of twisted branches used for
walking sticks. Zones 4–8.

Corylus colurna

syn. *Corylus byzantina*

TURKISH HAZEL

☼ ❄ ↔ 25 ft (8 m) ↑ 80 ft (24 m)

Native of western Asia. Leaves veined,
bluntly pointed, lightly lobed, turn
yellow in autumn. Yellow catkins in
late winter. Distinctive deeply fringed
husks, cork-like corrugations on bark.
Thrives in continental climates—hot
summers, cold winters. Zones 4–8.

Corylus cornuta

syn. *Corylus rostrata*

BEAKED FILBERT

☼/◐ ❄ ↔ 10 ft (3 m) ↑ 10 ft (3 m)

Deciduous shrub from North
America. Erect stems. Oval, lobed,

Corylus maxima 'Purpurea'

serrated leaves. Catkins reach 1¼ in
(30 mm) in length. Nuts with long
tubular husks. *C. c.* var. *californica*
grows to about 25 ft (8 m) high,
bears shorter husks, longer catkins.
Zones 4–8.

Corylus maxima

FILBERT, PURPLE-LEAF HAZELNUT

☼/◐ ❄ ↔ 15 ft (4.5 m) ↑ 30 ft (9 m)

Native of southern and eastern
Europe and western Asia. Vigorous
bushy shrub or small tree. Leaves
large, heart-shaped, mid-green, new
growth covered in sticky hairs. Large
brown nuts, elongated lobed husks.
'**Purpurea**', young leaves coppery
purple tint, fade to leathery greenish
purple in summer. Zones 5–9.

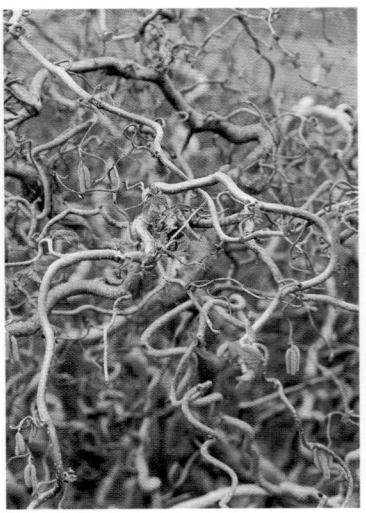

Corylus avellana 'Contorta'

CORYMBIA

This newly named genus of 110 or
more species of evergreen trees
belongs to the myrtle (Myrtaceae)
family. It contains many of the eucalypts (*Eucalyptus* species) traditionally
known as bloodwoods and ghost
gums. Many outstanding flowering
species belong to this group, including the red-flowering gum (*C. ficifolia*
and its close relation, the marri
(*C. calophylla*)). They are grown for
their fine straight trunks and attractive bark. The urn-shaped fruiting
capsules are fairly large and often very
ornamental. The genus occurs mostly
across the northern half of Australia,
from temperate eastern Australia and
southwest Western Australia. A few
species occur in New Guinea.

CULTIVATION: Most are fast-growing
and long-lived, and many are planted
as specimen plants. They are easy to
grow provided the correct species is
chosen for a given area. They prefer
full sun; frost hardiness varies, as does
the preference for moist or dry conditions. Propagation is from seed,
which germinates readily. Flower color
may not always come true from seed.

Corylus colurna

Corylus cornuta

Corymbia aparrerinja

syn. *Eucalyptus aparrerinja*

CENTRAL AUSTRALIAN GHOST GUM

☼ ◹ ↔ 15 ft (4.5 m) ↑ 50 ft (15 m)

Widely distributed in Australia's
arid center. Shapely tree, beautiful,
smooth, intensely white bark.
Drooping glossy foliage. Small clusters
of creamy white flowers. Withstands
drought. Australian Aboriginal name,
Aparrerinja. Zones 10–12.

Corymbia aspera

ROUGH-LEAFED GHOST GUM

☼ ◹ ↔ 17–20 ft (5–6 m)
↑ 17–35 ft (5–10 m)

From Australia and New Guinea.
Single-trunked tree, branching low to
the ground, often twisted or crooked,
bark smooth, powdery white, pink or
gray, flaky near base. Leaves opposite,
short-stalked, oval to heart-shaped,
2½–4 in (6–10 cm) long, light green
to blue-green, rough to the touch.
Compound clusters of white flowers
in groups of 7 to 11 in leaf axils,
produced early in the wet season
(summer). Zones 9–11.

Corymbia calophylla

syn. *Eucalyptus calophylla*

MARRI

☼ ◹ ↔ 20 ft (6 m) ↑ 80 ft (24 m)

Native to southern Western Australia.
Beautiful flowering tree with dense

Corymbia aparrerinja, in the wild, Watarrka National Park, Northern Territory, Australia

C. aspera, in the wild, central Australia

Corymbia watsoniana

Corymbia capricornia, in the wild, Mount Isa, Queensland, Australia

rounded crown. Large clusters of creamy white or—rarely—pink flowers, in summer. Large urn-shaped capsules. Best suited to moist well-drained soil. Zones 9–11.

Corymbia capricornia

syn. *Eucalyptus capricornia*

☼ ❧ ↔ to 17 ft (5 m) ↑ 50 ft (15 m)

Widespread species. Occurs on sandy soils across northern Australia. Single-trunked tree with gray, pink, and white powdery bark and a basal stocking of scaly, flaking, reddish bark on the lower half. Adult leaves lance-shaped, up to 8 in (20 cm) long. Flowers in groups of 7, in late summer–winter (late wet season–early dry season). Mature buds tiny, with rounded cap. Fruits urn-shaped, seeds winged. Zones 10–12.

Corymbia citriodora

syn. *Eucalyptus citriodora*

LEMON-SCENTED GUM

☼ ❧ ↔ 35 ft (10 m) ↑ 100 ft (30 m)

Species native to tropical Queensland, Australia. An attractive deciduous tree with a slender straight trunk and smooth powdery white to gray bark. Long narrow leaves exude a sharp lemony fragrance. Bears white flowers in summer–autumn. Used worldwide for beautifying urban parks and gardens, as well as for

Corymbia citriodora

timber, fuel, and essential oil. *C. c.* subsp. *variegata* is characterised by variegated foliage. Zones 9–12.

Corymbia eximia

syn. *Eucalyptus eximia*

YELLOW BLOODWOOD

☼ ❧ ↔ 30 ft (9 m) ↑ 50 ft (15 m)

Endemic to near-coastal regions of temperate eastern Australia, with scaly

C. c. subsp. *variegata,* in the wild, Carnarvon National Park, Queensland, Australia

yellow-brown bark and curving bluish green leaves, up to 8 in (20 cm) long. Large creamy flowers in spring attract nectar-feeding birds and honey bees. Tolerates dry conditions. Zones 9–11.

Corymbia ficifolia

syn. *Eucalyptus ficifolia*

RED-FLOWERING GUM

☼ ❧ ↔ 15 ft (4.5 m) ↑ 30 ft (9 m)

Native to southern Western Australia. Large densely-foliaged crown, short trunk, dark rough bark. Flowers scarlet, crimson, pink, orange, in terminal clusters, in summer. Urn-shaped fruit to 1½ in (35 mm) long. Zones 9–10.

Corymbia ptychocarpa

syn. *Eucalyptus ptychocarpa*

SWAMP BLOODWOOD

☼ ✈ ↔ 25 ft (8 m) ↑ 50 ft (15 m)

Endemic to tropical northern Australia. Rough fibrous bark.

Corymbia eximia

Large, glossy, dark green leaves. Clusters of white, pink, orange-red, or deep red flowers, appearing throughout the year. Large, barrel-shaped, ribbed fruiting capsules. Zones 11–12.

Corymbia watsoniana

LARGE-FRUITED YELLOWJACKET

☼ ❧ ↔ 10–17 ft (3–5 m)

↑ 50 ft (15 m)

From southeastern Queensland. Trunk straight, bark rough, flaky, and squarely patterned on trunk and larger branches, yellow-brown to grayish yellow; small branches smooth. Adult leaves lance-shaped, alternate, 4–8 in (10–20 cm) in length, dull light green to gray-green. Inflorescences of 3 to 7 flowers on ends of branches, winter–spring. Capsules urn-shaped, seeds glossy reddish brown. Zones 9–11.

Corymbia ficifolia

Corymbia ptychocarpa

CORYNOCARPUS

The 4 species of this genus in the family Corynocarpaceae are tall, evergreen, forest trees. They are found on some western Pacific islands and in New Zealand and Australia. Their simple leathery leaves are arranged alternately on the branches, and they bear tiny flowers in terminal panicles. These are followed by smooth-skinned plum-like fruits. CULTIVATION: The New Zealand *Corynocarpus* species, *C. laevigata*, is the one that is usually seen in cultivation. It requires a warm site in a rich soil with adequate moisture, particularly when it is young. It should be propagated from seed, which is best sown fresh.

Corynocarpus laevigata
KARAKA

☼ ❄ ↔ 25 ft (8 m) ↑ 50 ft (15 m)

Forest tree, found throughout both islands of New Zealand. Densely foliaged, with large, leathery, oblong leaves of a glossy dark green. Oval orange fruits ripen in autumn. The kernels of the fruits are poisonous. Zones 9–11.

Corypha utan

Coryphantha elephantidens

CORYPHA

This group of tall erect members of the palm (Arecaceae) family has stout trunks and very large fan-shaped fronds. It comprises about 6 species, occurring in tropical regions from Asia to Australia. After 30 to 50 years a mature palm produces a burst of millions of individual flowers at the top of the trunk; when the fruits that follow ripen, the whole palm dies. They make outstanding features for large gardens and parks, and in tropical countries the leaves, fruits, and stems have traditional uses. CULTIVATION: In subtropical and tropical climates, grow in well-drained organically rich soil with regular water during the warmer months. Propagate from fresh seed.

Corypha umbraculifera ★
TALIPOT PALM

☼ ❄ ↔ 35–50 ft (10–15 m) ↑ 40–80 ft (12–24 m)

From Sri Lanka and India. Giant palm with fan-shaped fronds to 17 ft (5 m) across. The spectacular flowering stems, 20–25 ft (6–8 m) long, are the largest of any palm. Zones 10–12.

Corypha utan
syn. *Corypha elata*
BURI PALM, FAN-LEAFED CABBAGE PALM

☼ ❄ ↔ 12–15 ft (3.5–4.5 m) ↑ 50–75 ft (15–23 m)

Widely cultivated slow-growing palm from Bengal, Myanmar, the Philippines, Indonesia, and northern Australia. Trunk spirally ringed and furrowed. Crown of massive, rounded, fan-shaped fronds, to 20 ft (6 m), 80 to 100 segments, with black toothed margins. Round fruit, greenish to brown. Huge plume, about 10–25 ft (3–8 m) long, of strong-smelling white flowers. Zones 10–11.

CORYPHANTHA

A genus of small *Mammillaria*-like cacti (family Cactaceae), found in Mexico and nearby parts of the USA. The genus has been revised and is now considered to number around 45 species, some of the former species being combined and others transferred to *Escobaria*. They form clusters of small, sometimes woolly-topped, globose to cylindrical stems, sometimes ribbed but usually with large tubercles instead. Their spines, usually short, may be straight or curved, and frequently overlap and interlace. In some species the spines are modified into colored appendages. The flowers are funnel- to bell-shaped, often yellow or pink, and tend to be large in comparison to the size of the plant. CULTIVATION: Most tolerate light frosts and are easily grown in typical cacti conditions: light, gritty, very free-draining soil, moist in summer but dry in late autumn and winter. Propagate from seed, offsets, or division of large well-established clumps.

Coryphantha elephantidens ★
☼/◐ ❄ ↔ 4–12 in (10–30 cm) ↑ 6–8 in (15–20 cm)

Clustering but sometimes single-stemmed species from southwestern Mexico. Globose stems to around 6 in (15 cm) high and slightly wide. Rows of wool-tipped tubercles with ¾ in (18 mm) long spines held flat, interlacing. Flowers white, flushed pink to near purple, scented. Zones 9–11.

Coryphantha pycnacantha
☼ ❄ ↔ 4–12 in (10–30 cm) ↑ 4–6 in (10–15 cm)

From southern Mexico. Globose to short, cylindrical, dark green, woolly-

Coryphantha pycnacantha

topped stems to 4 in (10 cm) high. Large tubercles with 3 to 4 recurved black central spines to 1 in (25 cm) long and up to 12 radial spines. Many offsets. Yellow flowers in summer. Zones 9–11.

Coryphantha scheeri
☼/◐ ❄ ↔ 12–16 in (30–40 cm) ↑ 8 in (20 cm)

From northern Mexico and southwestern USA. Clusters of elongated ovoid to cylindrical green stems with pronounced tubercles and spines to 1¾ in (40 mm) long, sometimes curved. White, yellow, or pink flowers in summer. *C. s.* var. *robustispina* (syn. *C. robustispina*), tubercles with single spine, usually straight, to 1¾ in (40 mm) long, surrounded by up to 10 short radial spines. Red-striped yellow flowers. Zones 8–10.

COSMOS
MEXICAN ASTER

This genus of the daisy (Asteraceae) family is found in the Americas from the tropics to the warm temperate zones. It comprises 26 species, including both annuals and perennials, of which 3 are commonly grown. The common annual cosmos (*C. bipinnatus*) has fine feathery foliage and showy, large, wide-open flowers with 8 ray florets. It is available in many colors and in varieties, from dwarf to 6 ft (1.8 m) tall. The common perennial species have broader leaves and smaller flowers than the annual *C. bipinnatus*, but are interesting for their colors and scents. Native Americans treated the young tops of *C. sulphureus* as a vegetable. CULTIVATION: Annuals should be planted out only when all danger of frost has past; perennials tolerate occasional moderate frosts. Plant in full sun with moist, well-drained soil. Do not overfeed or the plants may become top-heavy; they may need staking anyway. Propagate the annuals from seed and the perennials from basal cuttings.

Cosmos atrosanguineus ★
CHOCOLATE COSMOS

☼/◐ ❄ ↔ 20–40 in (50–100 cm) ↑ 12–24 in (30–60 cm)

Summer-flowering Mexican perennial. Dark green pinnate leaves to 6 in (15 cm) long, segments sometimes serrated. Long-stemmed, 1–1¾ in (25–40 mm) wide, dark red to almost black flowerheads. As its common name suggests, this species has a distinctive chocolatey fragrance, sometimes varying to vanilla. Zones 8–10.

Corynocarpus laevigata

Cosmos bipinnatus

☼/☀ ❄ ↔ 2–4 ft (0.6–1.2 m)
↕ 4–7 ft (1.2–2 m)

Annual native to Mexico and southern
USA. Ferny pinnate leaves to over
4 in (10 cm) long, with very fine
narrow leaflets. Flowerheads large
and long-stemmed. Pink to lavender
flowers in the wild, but many garden
forms and seedling strains. '**Candy-
stripe**', 24 in (60 cm) tall, white with
red stripes; '**Dazzler**', 4 ft (1.2 m)
tall, bright crimson; '**Picotee**' 30 in
(75 cm) tall, white to pale pink
flushed and edged deep pinkish red;
Sensation Series, 3–4 ft (1–1.2 m)
tall, in wide color range, sold mixed
or in single colors such as the red
'**Sensation Radiance**'; **Sonata Series**,
24–36 in (60–90cm) tall, simple,
daisy-like flowers in pink and white
shades, single colors such as '**Sonata
White**' or mixed; '**Sweet Dreams**',
30–36 in (75–90 cm), soft pink
flowers with darker center. Zones 7–11.

Cosmos sulphureus

☼/☀ ❄ ↔ 32 in–4 ft (80 cm–1.2 m)
↕ 5–7 ft (1.5–2 m)

Annual found from northern South
America to Mexico. Pinnate, sometimes faintly hairy leaves to 14 in
(35 cm) long. Flowerheads deep
yellow through orange to red. Several
seedling strains. '**Bright Lights**', to
4 ft (1.2 m) tall, a mix of yellow,
orange and red shades; '**Cosmic

Cosmos bipinnatus

Yellow', to 24 in (60 cm) tall, bright
yellow single and semi-double flowers;
Ladybird Series, 12–16 in (30–40 cm)
tall, pale yellow to deep red, available
individually or mixed; '**Sunny Red**',
12–16 in (30–40 cm) tall, bright red.
Zones 7–11.

COSTUS

SPIRAL FLAG, SPIRAL GENUS

A ginger (Zingiberaceae) family genus
of some 90 rhizome-rooted perennial
species, found throughout the tropics.
They form clumps of strong cane-like
stems with lance-shaped leaves, usually
around 8–10 in (20–25 cm) long,
spiralling around them. Their spikes
of 3-petalled flowers, subtended by
bracts and sometimes a ruff of leaves,
are bright, flat, and crepe-textured.
They usually bloom in the warmer
months; then the spike develops into
a cone-like fruit, best removed to
encourage repeat flowering.
CULTIVATION: Many are semi-
dormant in winter and can survive
in mild climates if the soil does not
freeze and the summers are warm
enough to encourage strong growth.
Propagate from seed, from spring
basal cuttings, or by dividing clumps
in late winter or very early spring.

Costus scaber

Cosmos bipinnatus, Sonata Series, 'Sonata Pink'

C. b., Sonata Series, 'Sonata Carmine'

C. b., Sonata Series, 'Sonata White'

Costus igneus

FIERY COSTUS

☀ ❦ ↔ 20–40 in (50–100 cm)
↕ 20 in (50 cm)

Brazilian species with purple-tinted
stems and 4–8 in (10–20 cm) long,
dark green leaves with reddish undersides. Bright orange flowers through
winter. Little or no dormant period.
Zones 10–12.

Costus pulverulentus

☀ ❦ ↔ 2–5 ft (0.6–1.5 m)
↕ 5–10 ft (1.5–3 m)

Found from southern Mexico to Peru.
Narrow, velvety, blue-green leaves to
12 in (30 cm) long, with red-tinted
undersides and silvery veins. Upright
inflorescences to 3 in (7.5 cm) long,
with bright red flowers. Zones 10–12.

Costus scaber

☀ ❦ ↔ 3–7 ft (0.9–2 m)
↕ 7–15 ft (2–4.5 m)

From the West Indies, Central, and
northern South America. Pointed
lance-shaped leaves to 8 in (20 cm)
long, sometimes fringed with fine
yellow hairs. Tightly packed showy
red bracts open to reveal white to
yellow flowers. Zones 10–12.

Costus stenophyllus

☀ ❦ ↔ 3–5 ft (0.9–1.5 m)
↕ 3–7 ft (0.9–2 m)

Native to Costa Rica. Stems banded
light and dark brown. Narrow,
velvety, deep green leaves to 8 in
(20 cm) long. Conical inflorescence
on leafless stems, with soft yellow
flowers and red bracts. Zones 10–12.

Cosmos sulphureus 'Cosmic Yellow'

Costus pulverulentus, in the wild, Costa Rica

Costus stenophyllus, in the wild, Costa Rica

Cotinus coggygria 'Royal Purple'

Cotinus coggygria

Cotinus coggygria 'Velvet Cloak'

COTINUS

SMOKE BUSH

This genus contains 3 species of deciduous trees or shrubs found in North America and across southern Europe to central China. It belongs to the same family (Anacardiaceae) as *Rhus* and, like members of that genus, has been known to cause contact dermatitis. *Cotinus* are valuable garden plants, and have a long season of interest. In summer myriads of tiny flowers are borne on long panicles, giving a hazy effect to the plant; hence the common name of smoke bush. In autumn their broadly oval leaves deepen in color to shades of red, yellow, and orange.
CULTIVATION: Smoke bushes will grow in a wide range of soils and climatic conditions but are best in a well-drained site in full sun. As with many trees from cool-temperate climates, richer autumn colors are achieved in areas where winters are cold. Prune to remove dead wood or to shorten long straggly branches. Propagation is from seed sown in autumn or from hardwood cuttings taken in late summer.

Cotinus 'Grace'

Cotinus coggygria

syn. *Rhus cotinus*

EURASIAN SMOKEBUSH, SMOKE BUSH, VENETIAN SUMACH

☼ ❅ ↔ 15 ft (4.5 m) ↑ 15 ft (4.5 m)

Found from southern Europe to central China. A rounded bush with broadly oval leaves. Numerous plume-like panicles, tiny bronze-pink flowers, fading to grayish purple in summer. Cultivars with purplish leaves include: 'Royal Purple' ★, dark red-purple leaves; 'Velvet Cloak', deep reddish purple leaves, turning entirely red in autumn. Zones 5–10.

Cotinus 'Flame'

syn. *Cotinus coggygria* 'Flame'

☼ ❅ ↔ 17–20 ft (5–6 m)
↑ 17–20 ft (5–6 m)

A hybrid cross between *C. coggygria* and *C. obovatus,* resembling the first parent in leaf form but similar to the second in its somewhat tree-like habit. Large, fluffy, gray flowerheads in summer and brilliant scarlet autumn color. Zones 7–10.

Cotinus 'Grace'

☼ ❅ ↔ 15 ft (4.5 m) ↑ 20 ft (6 m)

Hybrid between *C. coggygria* 'Velvet Cloak' and *C. obovatus.* Reddish purple leaves, flower plumes grayish, enhancing the hazy smoke-like effect. Zones 5–10.

Cotinus obovatus

syns *Cotinus americanus, C. cotinoides, Rhus cotinoides*

AMERICAN SMOKE TREE, CHITTAMWOOD

☼ ❅ ↔ 20 ft (6 m) ↑ 30 ft (9 m)

Native to central and southern USA. Foliage colors brilliantly in autumn. Similar to *C. coggygria,* but flowering display less spectacular. Tree-like, broad conical form. Zones 5–10.

COTONEASTER

From the rose (Rosaceae) family, a genus of about 200 species of ever-green, semi-evergreen, or deciduous shrubs and trees from the northern temperate areas. Leaves rounded to lance-shaped, simple, smooth-edged and arranged alternately. Small flowers are white, sometimes flushed pink or red, with 5 petals, and are borne singly or in cymes. They are followed by red-black or red fruits with rather dry flesh and 2 to 5 nutlets. Grown for its profuse flowers and fruit, it can also be used as a hedging plant and as an attractive specimen.
CULTIVATION: Cotoneasters grow well in moderately fertile well-drained soil. Dwarf evergreens and deciduous plants fruit better in full sun, while taller evergreens grow well in part-shade. In exposed situations they may need protection from cold drying winds. Propagate by taking half-hardened cuttings of evergreen species in late summer, and of deciduous species in early summer.

Cotoneaster adpressus

CREEPING COTONEASTER

☼ ❅ ↔ 5 ft (1.5 m) ↑ 12 in (30 cm)

From western China. A low-growing deciduous shrub, which develops roots wherever it touches the ground. Egg-shaped leaves turn red in autumn. White flowers with reddish petal edges. Bright red fruit in autumn. Zones 4–9.

Cotoneaster apiculatus

CRANBERRY COTONEASTER

☼ ❅ ↔ 8 ft (2.4 m) ↑ 3 ft (0.9 m)

Deciduous shrub, native to Sichuan Province in China. Shiny mid-green leaves, rounded, short points, wavy edges, slightly hairy undersurfaces, turn red in autumn. Solitary red to white flowers in summer. Red fruit. Zones 4–9.

Cotoneaster adpressus

Cotoneaster apiculatus

Cotoneaster conspicuus

Cotoneaster dielsianus

Cotoneaster horizontalis

Cotoneaster franchetii

Cotoneaster atropurpureus

☼/❋ ❄ ↔ 8–10 ft (2.4–3 m)
↑ 20–40 in (50–100 cm)

Often confused with *C. horizontalis,* with its similar herringbone branch arrangement and semi-prostrate habit. Small white flowers in spring, followed by little red berries and brightly colored autumn leaves. 'Variegata' has white-edged leaves that turn red and pink in autumn. Zones 4–9.

Cotoneaster conspicuus

syn. *Cotoneaster conspicuus* var. *decorus*

☼ ❋ ↔ 8 ft (2.4 m) ↑ 5 ft (1.5 m)

Native to western China. Densely branched, mound-forming, evergreen or semi-evergreen shrub. Deep green lance-shaped to oblong leaves, spirally arranged. White flowers, sometimes grouped in cymes, in summer. Glossy red fruit. Zones 6–9.

Cotoneaster dammeri

syn. *Cotoneaster humifusus*

☼ ❋ ↔ 6 ft (1.8 m) ↑ 8 in (20 cm)

Native to the Hubei region of coastal eastern China, bordering the Yellow Sea and the East China Sea. Prostrate evergreen shrub. Shiny green leaves, oblong, strongly veined. White flowers, solitary or grouped in cymes, in early summer. Scarlet fruit in autumn. Zones 5–10.

Cotoneaster dielsianus

☼ ❋ ↔ 8 ft (2.4 m) ↑ 8 ft (2.4 m)

Native to China. Loosely branching shrub, semi-evergreen in milder climates but deciduous in colder regions. Leathery egg-shaped leaves, hairy undersides, turn red in autumn. Small cymes of up to 7 pinkish white flowers in summer. Glossy deep red fruit. Zones 5–10.

Cotoneaster frigidus 'Cornubia'

Cotoneaster franchetii

☼ ❋ ↔ 10 ft (3 m) ↑ 10 ft (3 m)

Native to western China. Evergreen, sometimes semi-evergreen, erect shrub. Lustrous, bright green, oval leaves with felty undersides. Generous cymes of pink-tinted white flowers, in summer. Egg-shaped orange-red fruit. Zones 6–10.

Cotoneaster frigidus

HIMALAYAN TREE COTONEASTER

☼ ❋ ↔ 30 ft (9 m) ↑ 30 ft (9 m)

Species native to the Himalayas. Deciduous large shrub or small tree with peeling bark. Egg-shaped dull green leaves have wavy edges. Sprays of profuse white flowers are seen throughout summer. Fruit is red. 'Cornubia' (syn. *C. × watereri* 'Cornubia'), dark green lance-shaped leaves turn rich bronze in winter; 'Fructu

Luteo', creamy yellow fruit; 'Notcutt's Variety', large leaves, dark green in color. Zones 6–9.

Cotoneaster horizontalis

ROCK COTONEASTER, ROCKSPRAY COTONEASTER

☼ ❋ ↔ 5 ft (1.5 m) ↑ 3 ft (0.9 m)

From western China. Deciduous, herringbone-like branching. Elliptical to rounded leaves, dark green, glossy, color in autumn. Flesh pink flowers in late spring. Scarlet fruit. Zones 4–9.

Cotoneaster 'Hybridus Pendulus'

☼ ❋ ↔ 6 ft (1.8 m) ↑ 6 ft (1.8 m)

Of garden origin. Evergreen to semi-evergreen shrub, with elliptical deep green leaves. Cymes of white flowers in summer. Grafted onto an upright stem of tall-growing species, makes a decorative standard; fruits resemble a red waterfall in winter. Zones 6–9.

Cotoneaster lacteus

syn. *Cotoneaster parneyi*

☼ ❋ ↔ 12 ft (3.5 m) ↑ 12 ft (3.5 m)

Native to China. Evergreen shrub, arching branches. Leathery oval leaves, dark green upper surfaces, felty undersides, deep veins. Creamy white flowers in summer. Red fruit persist in winter. Zones 6–11.

Cotoneaster frigidus 'Fructu Luteo'

Cotoneaster lacteus

Cotoneaster linearifolius

syn. *Cotoneaster microphyllus* var. *thymifolius* of gardens

☼ ❄ ↔ 3 ft (0.9 m) ↑ 3 ft (0.9 m)

Native of Nepal. Dwarf evergreen shrub. Tiny, narrow, glossy, dark green leaves with gray undersides. Pink buds open to white flowers in early summer. Dark pink fruit. Zones 6–9.

Cotoneaster lucidus

HEDGE COTONEASTER

☼/◑ ❄ ↔ 6–10 ft (1.8–3 m) ↑ 6–10 ft (1.8–3 m)

Native to Siberia and northern Asia. Upright, round-topped, deciduous shrub, slender spreading branches. Leaves dark green in summer, yellow and red in autumn. Small pink-white flowers in late spring, followed by round blue-black fruit. Zones 3–7.

Cotoneaster microphyllus

☼ ❄ ↔ 3 ft (0.9 m) ↑ 3 ft (0.9 m)

Native to the Himalayas. Prostrate evergreen shrub, dense mound. Thick leaves, egg-shaped, glossy deep green, hairy coating beneath when young. Tiny white flowers in spring–summer. Crimson fruit. Zones 5–10.

Cotoneaster multiflorus

☼ ❄ ↔ 15 ft (4.5 m) ↑ 15 ft (4.5 m)

From northwestern China. Deciduous shrub or small tree. Arching branches

Cotoneaster linearifolius

with weeping tips, relatively thin hairless leaves. White flowers, red fruit. Zones 5–9.

Cotoneaster salicifolius

syn. *Cotoneaster floccosus* of gardens

☼ ❄ ↔ 15 ft (4.5 m) ↑ 15 ft (4.5 m)

Naturally occurring in China. Variable species with slim, graceful, bowed branches. Lance-shaped deeply veined leaves, pointed, white felty undersides. Large corymbs in summer. Round, red, persistent fruit. 'Exburyensis', white flowers in early summer, followed by pinkish yellow fruit in winter; 'Herbstfeuer' (syn. 'Autumn Fire'), low spreading habit, red fruit; 'Repens', a prostrate form; 'Rothschildianus' (syn. *C.* × *watereri* 'Rothschildianus'), vigorous, evergreen, spreading shrub, clusters of white flowers in summer, followed by lemon yellow fruit. Zones 6–10.

Cotoneaster serotinus

syn. *Cotoneaster glaucophyllus* var. *serotinus*

☼ ❄ ↔ 12 ft (3.5 m) ↑ 30 ft (9 m)

Native to western China. Large evergreen shrub or tree. Egg-shaped leaves with dark green upper surfaces and gray felty hairs beneath, becoming hairless with age. White flowers in large corymbs, in summer. Bright red fruit. Zones 6–11.

Cotoneaster multiflorus

Cotoneaster simonsii

☼ ❄ ↔ 6 ft (1.8 m) ↑ 8 ft (2.4 m)

Found naturally in northern India and the eastern Himalayas. Deciduous or semi-evergreen shrub. Egg-shaped deep green leaves, paler with bristly hair on the undersurfaces. Pink-tinged white flowers, single or in cymes, in summer. Orange-red fruit. Zones 5–9.

Cotoneaster sternianus

☼/◑ ❄ ↔ 5–7 ft (1.5–2 m) ↑ 10 ft (3 m)

From Tibet, northeastern India, and Myanmar borders. Semi-evergreen with stiff, upright, fan-shaped growth. Dark green leaves, to 1¾ in (40 mm) long, with downy white undersides. Cluster of 7 to 15 red-tinted white flowers. Pale red fruit. Zones 6–9.

Cotoneaster × *watereri*

☼ ❄ ↔ 15 ft (4.5 m) ↑ 15 ft (4.5 m)

Of garden origin, a 3-way cross between *C. frigidus, C. salicifolius,* and *C. rugosus.* Evergreen shrub or small tree, bowed branches. Leaves egg-shaped, dark green, veined upper surfaces, felty undersides. White flowers in cymes in summer. Round, red, persistent fruit. 'John Waterer' is the original clone, and there are numerous cultivars. Zones 6–10.

COTULA

BRASS BUTTONS

A widespread genus in the daisy (Asteraceae) family of around 80 species of annuals and perennials, many former members of which are now classified under *Leptinella.* Normally spreading by means of rhizomes, they are usually low, compact, mounding or clump-forming plants with ferny, frequently deep bronze-green foliage and flowerheads with ray florets absent or very much reduced. These discoid flowerheads are usually yellow or cream, often with a red or purple tint. The flowers bloom in all seasons, depending on the species. CULTIVATION: *Cotula* species occur in a wide range of conditions, some even growing at the water's edge, sometimes partly submerged. Those most often cultivated tend to be rock garden perennials that prefer to grow in a bright position with well-drained soil that remains moist in summer. Propagation is very straightforward, by seed, by division, or by removing small rooted pieces.

Cotula coronopifolia

☼ ❄ ↔ 12–20 in (30–50 cm) ↑ 6–12 in (15–30 cm)

South African annual or short-lived perennial with spreading or mound-

Cotoneaster salicifolius 'Repens'

Cotoneaster serotinus

ing stems. Leaves to over 4 in (10 cm) long, very narrow, with tiny pinnate lobes, often tooth-like, sometimes absent. Yellow flowerheads in winter. Zones 7–9.

Cotula hispida

☼ ◙ ↔ 8–20 in (20–50 cm) ↑ 2–16 in (5–40 cm)

South African perennial. Usually prostrate and spreading, but stems may be more upright or mounding. Leaves pinnate, to 1¾ in (40 mm) long, on considerably longer petiole. Flowerheads bright yellow, often red-tinted, in winter–spring. Zones 9–10.

COTYLEDON

This formerly large stonecrop (Crassulaceae) family genus of succulents has been extensively revised, and now contains around a dozen species of evergreen, often rather woody-stemmed shrubs from South Africa. The leaves vary widely in shape, from flat and rounded to elongated and cylindrical, but are always fleshy and succulent, sometimes with a powdery white surface bloom of fine hairs. The flowers, usually yellow, orange, or red, have 5 recurved petal-like sepals, are bell-shaped, and are borne in heads on strong stems that hold them well clear of the foliage. Flowers appear throughout the year, most abundantly in late spring.

Cotula hispida

CULTIVATION: Tolerant of light frosts, *Cotyledon* species thrive best in mild climates with relatively dry winters. Plant them in full sun or half-sun with gritty very free-draining soil. Routine deadheading and the removal of old branches and dried leaves will keep the plants tidy and flowering profusely. Propagation is from seed, cuttings, or offsets.

Cotyledon orbiculata ★

☼/◐ ❄ ↔ 20 in–4 ft (50 cm–1.2 m)
↕ 32 in–5 ft (80 cm–1.5 m)

Bushy, often quite densely branched shrub. Leaves rounded, to over 4 in (10 cm) long, seldom hairy, pale green to silver-gray, with a powdery coating. Flowers orange to red, ½ in (12 mm) long, often densely clustered. Can be invasive in favorable climates. *C. o.* f. *variegata,* mid-green leaves with large pale sectors. Zones 9–11.

Cotyledon tomentosa ★

BEAR'S PAW

☼/◐ ❄ ↔ 12–27 in (30–70 cm)
↕ 12–20 in (30–50 cm)

Shrub branching near ground level. Thick, fleshy, 1 in (25 mm) long leaves, with dense silver-gray to gray-green hairs and vestigial brown teeth. Short flower stems. Flowers yellow to orange-red, around ½ in (12 mm) long, often downy. *C. t.* f. *variegata,* cream patches on foliage, usually around edges. Zones 10–11.

Cotyledon orbiculata

Cotyledon undulata ★

syn. *Cotyledon orbiculata* var. *undulata*
SILVER CROWN, SILVER RUFFLES

☼/◐ ❄ ↔ 20 in–4 ft (50 cm–1.2 m)
↕ 32 in–5 ft (80 cm–1.5 m)

Very similar to *C. orbiculata,* except that leaves are always silver-gray with wavy edges. Zones 9–11.

COUROUPITA

From the jungles of tropical South America comes this genus of 4 species of large evergreen trees belonging to the brazilnut (Lecythidaceae) family. Although these trees are fairly rare in cultivation, one species—the cannonball tree, *C. guianensis*—is grown in the USA for its spectacular and remarkable fruits, which emerge and dangle on long stems directly from the tree trunk. The pincushion-like flowers are large and complex in structure, usually with 6 fleshy petals. CULTIVATION: In subtropical and tropical areas *Couroupita* species are grown in well-drained organically rich soil in a sunny position. Propagation is from seed.

Couroupita guianensis

CANNONBALL TREE

☼ ✈ ↔ 15 ft (4.5 m) ↕ 100 ft (30 m)

Smaller in cultivation than the species. Large elliptical leaves grow in rosettes at the branch tips. Large flowers, on long drooping branches that emerge directly from the trunk, are 6 in (15 cm) across, with red spreading petals and hundreds of yellow stamens. Brownish ball-like capsules mature to red pulp; they have a disagreeable odor. Zones 11–12.

CRAMBE

The 20 species of annuals and perennials of this mainly Eurasian genus are classified in the cabbage (Brassicaceae) family, which is quite appropriate, as the name *Crambe* comes from a Greek

Couroupita guianensis

word for cabbage. They are vigorous plants that produce large leaves on fleshy stems, usually in loose rosettes. The foliage varies with the species, and may be dark green and glossy or blue-gray with a powdery bloom. In summer upright sprays of small, honey-scented, 4-petalled, white or yellow flowers appear. The flower stems usually considerably exceed the height of the foliage. CULTIVATION: They are easily grown in any temperate climate that does not experience extremes of winter cold or summer heat. Allow plenty of room for the spread of the foliage and flowerheads. Plant in moist, cool,

well-drained soil in full or half-sun. Water and feed well until after flowering. Propagation is by division or from seed.

Crambe cordifolia ★

COLEWORT

☼/◐ ❄ ↔ 3–7 ft (0.9–2 m)
↕ 5–6 ft (1.5–1.8 m)

Perennial native to the Caucasus region. Leaves heart-shaped to lance-shaped, up to 14 in (35 cm) long, dark glossy green with a puckered surface and toothed edges. Huge billowing inflorescence of tiny white flowers. Zones 6–9.

Crambe maritima

SEA KALE

☼ ❄ ↔ 24–48 in (60–120 cm)
↕ 24–32 in (60–80 cm)

Perennial found around the coasts of northern Europe, the Baltic Sea, and the Black Sea. Fleshy, blue-green, elliptical to rounded leaves, 6–12 in (15–30 cm) long, with toothed edges and a powdery covering. Strong-stemmed heads with massed white to cream flowers. Zones 5–9.

Cotyledon undulata

Crambe cordifolia

Crassula falcata

Crassula capitella 'Campfire'

CRASPEDIA

A genus of about 16 species of annuals and perennials in the daisy (Asteraceae) family. They grow all over Australia, from coastal to alpine regions, in moist grasslands and swamps. Leaves are usually bright green and often covered in hairs, giving a woolly appearance. Flowers bloom in spring or summer and look like small balls on long stems, usually yellow but sometimes orange. Flowers are marble- to golf-ball-sized. They are valued by florists in both dried and fresh arrangements. CULTIVATION: Species from moist to wet areas need extra water; otherwise grow in a well-drained soil in full sun. Propagate from seed or by division.

Craspedia glauca
syn. *Craspedia uniflora*
BILLY BUTTONS
☼ ❄ ↔ 12 in (30 cm)
↑ 12–20 in (30–50 cm)

Woolly light green leaves in a rosette formation. Globular yellow flowers on 12 in (30 cm) long stems in spring–summer. Zones 9–11.

Craspedia globosa
syn. *Pycnosorus globosus*
☼ ❄ ↔ 12–16 in (30–40 cm)
↑ 18–24 in (45–60 cm)

Larger than *C. glauca*; gray grass-like leaves and orangey flowers, ¾–1¼ in (18–30 mm) across, borne on 40 in (100 cm) tall stems. Tolerates water-logging. Zones 9–11.

CRASSULA

This genus in the stonecrop (Crassulaceae) family has some 300 species of annual, biennial, and perennial herbs and small shrubs. A few are found in Asia, Madagascar, and Africa, but most are native to South Africa. Leaves are usually opposite, fleshy, and vary in size, texture, color, and shape. The red, pink, green, or white flowers are star- or funnel-shaped, occasionally tubular, and are sometimes carried as single flowers but more often in cyme-like branches. CULTIVATION: Cultivated as ornamentals, they are best grown in full sun, but will also grow in half-sun. Grow in well-drained average soil with added humus, or in pots in cactus compost. In areas with frost, grow under glass. Water sparingly in winter. Propagate from stem cuttings or set single leaves in soil from spring to mid-summer. Sow seeds in cactus compost with added sharp sand.

Crassula anomala ★
☼/❄ ❄ ↔ 12 in (30 cm) ↑ 12 in (30 cm)
Small, rounded, fleshy leaves, often red-tinted in sun, especially when flowering. Clusters of tiny cream to pale pink flowers. Zones 9–11.

Crassula barklyi
RATTLESNAKE TAIL
☼/❄ ❄ ↔ 8–12 in (20–30 cm)
↑ 2–4 in (5–10 cm)
From South Africa to Namibia. Clustered stems to 3 in (8 cm) long, with ¼ in (6 mm) long olive leaves, overlapping like scales, often edged with hairs. Cream flowers, large in comparison, in small clusters in winter. Zones 9–11.

Crassula capitella
☼/❄ ❄ ↔ 16 in (40 cm)
↑ 8–16 in (20–40 cm)

From coastal southern South Africa. Spirally arranged, red-tinted, sometimes hairy, pointed, lance-shaped leaves from ½–4 in (12 mm–10 cm) long, initially growing in basal rosettes, then elongating into woody stems. Spikes of small, pink-tinted, white flowers appear in late summer. 'Campfire', narrow bright green leaves, broadly edged and flushed vivid red, sprays of minute cream flowers; *C. c.* subsp. *thyrsiflora*, smooth leaves edged with fine hairs, flower sepals sometimes finely toothed. Zones 9–11.

Crassula deceptor
☼/❄ ❄ ↔ 12–20 in (30–50 cm)
↑ 6 in (15 cm)

Low, spreading, branching perennial from South Africa. Thick, fleshy, silver-gray, powder-coated leaves to ½ in (12 mm) long, arranged in 4 rows, pressed tightly into stems. Heads of very small cream to buff flowers in summer. Zones 9–11.

Crassula falcata
syn. *Crassula perfoliata* var. *falcata*
PROPELLER PLANT, SCARLET PAINTBRUSH
☼/❄ ❄ ↔ 12–32 in (30–80 cm)
↑ 20 in–3 ft (50 cm–0.9 m)

From Eastern Cape, South Africa. Slightly twisted, spathulate, gray-green leaves to 4 in (10 cm) long, on strong, upright stems. Leaves broader near base of plant. Heads of massed, vivid, red flowers in summer. Very striking in flower. Zones 9–11.

Crassula hemisphaerica
ARAB'S TURBAN
☼/❄ ❄ ↔ 12–20 in (30–50 cm)
↑ 8 in (20 cm)

Low spreading perennial from South Africa. Rosettes of tightly spiralled, bristle-edged, gray-green to deep green leaves to 2 in (5 cm) long. Rosettes may elongate into short stems. Spikes of tiny cream flowers in spring. Zones 9–11.

Crassula lactea
TAILOR'S PATCH
☼/❄ ❄ ↔ 12–20 in (30–50 cm)
↑ 16–24 in (40–60 cm)

From Eastern Cape, South Africa. Shrubby perennial, spreading or scrambling stems, green, pointed, hard-edged leaves to nearly 3 in (8 cm) long. White flowers, undersides sometimes pink in autumn. Zones 9–11.

Crassula multicava ★
☼/❄ ❄ ↔ 16–20 in (40–50 cm)
↑ 12–16 in (30–40 cm)

From South Africa. Thin, rounded, gray-green leaves to 2½ in (6 cm) long, on short, upright or spreading, sometimes branching stems. Rounded inflorescence of tiny, red-tipped, white to cream flowers, in autumn. Zones 9–11.

Crassula muscosa
MOSS CYPRESS, WATCH-CHAIN CYPRESS
☼/❄ ❄ ↔ 20–40 in (50–100 cm)
↑ 8–32 in (20–80 cm)

From South Africa, Namibia, and Lesotho. Tiny, overlapping, gray-green leaves on short scrambling stems, creating an effect like thickened club-moss or cypress foliage. Inconspicuous inflorescences of up to 8 yellow-green flowers in summer. Zones 9–11.

Crassula namaquaensis
☼/❄/◑ ❄ ↔ 12–24 in (30–60 cm)
↑ 4–6 in (10–15 cm)

Spreading and mat-forming, with small, fleshy, hairy, bead-like, blue-green to grayish leaves. Small terminal heads of cream flowers, black anthers, in summer. *C. n.* subsp. *comptonii*, leaves more pointed in outline, round in section, smaller flowers with yellow anthers. Zones 9–11.

Crassula namaquaensis subsp. *comptonii*

Crassula anomala

Crassula ovata ★

syns *Crassula arborescens* of gardens,
C. argentea of gardens, *C. portulacea*

DOLLAR PLANT, JADE TREE

☼/☀ ❄ ↔ 2–4 ft (0.6–1.2 m)
↑ 6 ft (1.8 m)

Native to most of South Africa.
Upright branching shrub, thick stems
and peeling bark. Fleshy rounded
leaves, usually shiny dark green with
red or pale green edges. Heads of
pink-tinted white flowers. '**Crosby's
Compact**' (syn. 'Crosby's Dwarf'),
low compact habit, rarely exceeding
12 in (30 cm) high, red-tinted foliage;
'**Hobbit**', compact habit with thickened almost cylindrical, to thin slightly
curled leaves, often with red tints;
'**Hummel's Sunset**' ★ (syn. 'Sunset'),
vivid red leaves suffused with yellow
and orange; '**Tricolor**', bold cream-
variegated foliage suffused with bright
pink. Zones 10–11.

Crassula perfoliata

☼/☀ ❄ ↔ 24–40 in (60–100 cm)
↑ 5 ft (1.5 m)

From South Africa. Spathulate gray-
green leaves to 6 in (15 cm) long,
with a powdery coating. Thickened,
sometimes almost flat, usually concave
above, convex below. Leafy thick-
stemmed flowerheads, white through
pink to red. Zones 9–11.

Crassula ovata

Crassula perfoliata

Crassula, Hybrid Cultivar, 'Morgan's Beauty'

Crassula plegmatoides

☼/☀ ❄ ↔ 8–12 in (20–30 cm)
↑ 4–6 in (10–15 cm)

From Namaqualand, South Africa.
Spreading perennial with short stems
densely covered with small, fleshy,
almost globular, gray-green leaves.
Open, somewhat hairy heads of
cream flowers. Zones 9–11.

Crassula pyramidalis

☼/☀ ❄ ↔ 4–8 in (10–20 cm)
↑ 4–10 in (10–25 cm)

Short, sometimes branching stems
with ½ in (12 mm) long, pointed,
oval leaves arranged in groups of
4 and stacked to make a square-
sectioned column. Few-flowered
terminal heads of small white to
cream blooms, in spring. Zones 9–11.

Crassula radicans

RED CARPET

☼/☀ ❄ ↔ 24 in (60 cm)
↑ 4–6 in (10–15 cm)

Prostrate perennial with spreading,
branching stems and lance-shaped,
red-edged, green leaves to over ½ in
(12 mm) long. Small terminal heads
of white flowers, followed by reddish
brown seedheads. Zones 10–11.

Crassula rupestris ★

BEAD VINE, BUTTONS ON A STRING

☼/☀ ❄ ↔ 6–12 in (15–30 cm)
↑ 8–20 in (20–50 cm)

From South Africa and Namibia.
Shrubby perennial with short stems

Crassula plegmatoides

C., Hybrid Cultivar, 'Moonglow'

C., Hybrid Cultivar, 'Buddha's Temple'

bearing slightly overlapping, thick,
red-tinted, olive green, pointed,
oval leaves to ½ in (12 mm) long.
Rounded heads of tiny, red-tinted,
white flowers. *C. r.* subsp. *commutata,*
upright, dense, bushy; *C. r.* subsp.
marnieriana, low, spreading, with
leaves partly fused and larger flower
heads. Zones 9–11.

Crassula schmidtii

☼/☀ ❄ ↔ 6–12 in (15–30 cm)
↑ 6 in (15 cm)

Possibly natural or garden hybrid
between *C. alba* and *C. setulosa.* Wiry
brown-barked stems with 1–2 in
(25–50 mm) long, flattened, cylindrical
leaves, gray-green with faint darker
mottling, edged with fine hairs. Heads
of small pink flowers. Zones 9–11.

Crassula Hybrid Cultivars

☼/☀ ❄ ↔ 2–10 in (5–25 cm)
↑ 2–8 in (5–20 cm)

Grown mostly for their brightly
colored, variably textured and shaped
foliage, and wide range of shapes and
sizes. '**Baby's Necklace**' ★, small, bead-

Crassula radicans

C., Hybrid Cultivar, 'Pink Pagoda'

C., Hybrid Cultivar, 'Polly's Pink'

like, purplish red-edged leaves surrounding upright stems, sprays of tiny
cream flowers; '**Buddha's Temple**' ★,
hybrid of *C. pyramidalis,* rosettes of
thin, upward-curved, gray-green leaves
tiered like a pagoda roof, pale cream
flowers; '**Campfire**', narrow bright
green leaves, broadly edged and flushed
vivid red, sprays of tiny cream flowers;
'**Coralita**', rosettes of fleshy, curly, gray-
green leaves, from center of which
emerge red-tinted stems topped with
heads of pink flowers; '**Fernwood**',
tight rosettes of small bright green
leaves, sprays of light yellow flowers
from late winter; '**Frosty**', small green
leaves edged and highlighted with
silver-gray, sprays of tiny cream
flowers; '**Moonglow**' ★, thick, fleshy,
gray-green leaves on short upright
stems, distinctive soft orange flowers;
'**Morgan's Beauty**' ★ (syn. 'Morgan's
Pink'), mounding rosettes of fleshy,
flat, gray-green leaves to 2 in (5 cm)
long, showy, soft pink flowers opening
from glowing pink buds and ageing to
red; '**Pagoda Village**', clustered upright
stems surrounded by purple-red-edged
bronze-green leaves, tiered like pagoda
roof, sprays of tiny, pink-tinted, cream
flowers; '**Pastel**', small, thick, pale green
leaves clustering around short upright
stems, sprays of tiny, white to pink-
tinted, cream flowers; '**Pink Pagoda**',
thin upright stems, sprays of pale pink
or red flowers, reddish seedheads;
'**Springtime**', broad-based, fleshy,
bright green leaves on short stems in
clusters, sprays of tiny, pink-tinted,
cream flowers in summer. Zones 9–11.

+ CRATAEGOMESPILUS

The + sign indicates that this is a graft hybrid between 2 genera, in this case between *Crataegus*, the hawthorns, and *Mespilus*, the medlars, both members of the rose (Rosaceae) family. A graft hybrid occurs when, for some reason, tissue from the stock grows into and merges with that of the scion, instead of the two retaining their own characteristics. This hybrid from the nursery of a Monsieur Dardar, at Bronvaux, France, in about 1895, gave rise to 2 separate forms. CULTIVATION: This plant will grow in sun or partial shade in most soils, except in very waterlogged areas. It can only be propagated onto a rootstock such as the common hawthorn.

Crataegus laevigata 'Paul's Scarlet', bonsai

Crataegus × *lavalleei*

+ *Crataegomespilus dardarii* 'Jules d'Asnières'

+ *Crataegomespilus dardarii*
BRONVAUX MEDLAR

☼ ❄ ↔ 20 ft (6 m) ↑ 20 ft (6 m)

Wide-spreading small tree. Large white flowers, leaves turn yellow and orange in autumn. Two forms originated from the same graft: 'Bronvaux', shoots occasionally thorny, leaves like those of a medlar but smaller, fruits medlar-like, in clusters; 'Jules d'Asnières', woolly young shoots like a medlar, leaves smooth-edged to deeply lobed, fruits like a hawthorn. Zones 6–9.

CRATAEGUS

HAWTHORN

This genus within the rose (Rosaceae) family contains around 200 species. Most are large spiny shrubs or small trees. The deep green leaves are alternate, simple or lobed, some toothed. The white to pink flowers have 5 sepals and/or petals, depending on the species, and are carried in corymbs or are solitary. Nutlets with a fleshy edible covering follow. The fruit can be black, yellow, or bluish green, but the majority are red. *C. laevigata* and *C. monogyna* have been used as hedging plants for centuries. CULTIVATION: Grow in sun or partial shade in any soil. Bud cultivars in summer or graft them in winter. Sow seeds when ripe in a position that is protected from winter frosts. Germination may take up to 18 months.

Crataegus 'Autumn Glory'

Crataegus arnoldiana
ARNOLD HAWTHORN

☼ ❄ ↔ 30 ft (9 m) ↑ 30 ft (9 m)

Native of northeastern USA. Small tree. Oval, lobed, toothed leaves are dark green above, paler beneath. Scented white flowers in spring. Bright red fruit with 3 to 4 seeds. Zones 5–10.

Crataegus 'Autumn Glory'

☼ ❄ ↔ 10 ft (3 m) ↑ 10 ft (3 m)

Possibly a hybrid of *C. laevigata*. Deciduous shrub. Glossy leaves with 3 to 5 rounded blunt-toothed lobes. Produces clusters of large white flowers in early summer, followed by oval red fruit in autumn, persisting into winter. Zones 5–10.

Crataegus crus-galli
COCKSPUR THORN

☼ ❄ ↔ 35 ft (10 m) ↑ 30 ft (9 m)

Native to eastern USA. Small flat-topped tree with long curved thorns. Shiny, dark green, egg-shaped leaves. Foliage turns red in autumn. Large corymbs of small white flowers appear in spring. Deep red fruit persists throughout winter. *C. c.-g.* var. *salicifolia*, narrow lance-shaped leaves. Zones 5–9.

Crataegus laciniata
syn. *Crataegus orientalis*

☼ ❄ ↔ 20 ft (6 m) ↑ 20 ft (6 m)

Native to southeastern Europe and western Asia. Thorny shrub or tree.

Crataegus × *media* 'Gireoudii'

Crataegus crus-galli var. *salicifolia*

Crataegus crus-galli

Leaves are deeply lobed, dark green, growing to 2 in (5 cm) long, with a covering of silvery white hairs. Clusters of white flowers appear in summer, and are followed by large red fruit. Zones 6–9.

Crataegus laevigata
syn. *Crataegus oxyacantha* of gardens
ENGLISH HAWTHORN, MAY, WHITE THORN

☼ ❄ ↔ 25 ft (8 m) ↑ 25 ft (8 m)

Native to most of Europe and the far northwest of Africa. Thorny tree with egg-shaped leaves that are a glossy mid-green in color, lobed and toothed, with paler green undersides. White or pink flowers appear in corymbs in spring, followed by red fruit. This species is often grown as a hedge, and very ornamental cultivars may be used as specimen trees. 'Paul's Scarlet' ★, double deep pink flowers; 'Plena,' double white flowers, becoming pink-tinged with age; 'Rosea Flore Pleno', double pink flowers. Zones 5–9.

Crataegus × *lavalleei*
LAVELLE HAWTHORN

☼ ❄ ↔ 20 ft (6 m) ↑ 20 ft (6 m)

Of garden origin, from France. Cross between *C. crus-galli* and *C. pubescens*. Semi-evergreen in warmer climates. Leaves are elliptical to oval in shape, toothed, glossy green; they produce a good autumn color. White flowers, red stamens, in early summer. Long-lasting red fruit. Zones 6–10.

Crataegus × *media*

☀/◐ ❄ ↔ 5–7 ft (1.5–2 m)
↑ 8–10 ft (2.4–3 m)

Hybrid between *C. monogyna* and *C. laevigata*. Similar to *C. laevigata*, apart from minor foliage details and slightly flattened spherical rather than ovoid fruit. '**Gireoudii**', spreading tree, broad crown. Zones 5–9.

Crataegus monogyna

HAWTHORN, MAY, QUICKTHORN

☀ ❄ ↔ 25 ft (8 m) ↑ 25 ft (8 m)

Native to Europe. Thorny hawthorn, a common wild hedge. Leaves broadly egg-shaped, dark green upper surface, paler green downy undersides. Small clusters of white flowers, pink-tinged. Dark red, single-seeded fruit. '**Biflora**', the Glastonbury thorn, flowers in mid-winter, a second time in spring; '**Stricta**', columnar habit, spreads to 12 ft (3.5 m). Zones 4–9.

Crataegus nitida

GLOSSY HAWTHORN

☀ ❄ ↔ 25 ft (8 m) ↑ 30 ft (9 m)

A dense, rounded, deciduous shrub from Ohio to Missouri and Arkansas. Leaves dark green, lustrous above, paler below, turning orange to red in autumn. Small white flowers appear in mid-spring, followed by dull red fruit, which may remain until the next spring. Zones 4–6.

Crataegus persimilis '**Prunifolia**'

syn. *Crataegus* × *prunifolia*

☀ ❄ ↔ 25 ft (8 m) ↑ 20 ft (6 m)

Large deciduous shrub or small tree, now considered a cultivar of a distinct species. Dense foliage, thorny branches. Serrated-edged oval leaves to 3 in (8 cm) long, bright red tones in autumn. Flowers white, pink anthers, in corymbs. Red fruit. '**Prunifolia Splendens**', more vigorous, larger leaves and flower clusters. Zones 5–9.

Crataegus phaenopyrum

syn. *Crataegus cordata*

WASHINGTON HAWTHORN,

☀ ❄ ↔ 30 ft (9 m) ↑ 30 ft (9 m)

Native to southeast USA. Thorny tree. Leaves sharply toothed, broadly

Crataegus punctata

Crataegus persimilis '*Prunifolia Splendens*'

egg-shaped, lobed, shiny green, good autumn color. White flowers in summer; glossy, vivid, red fruit, persisting until spring. '**Fastigiata**', narrow upright habit. Zones 5–10.

Crataegus pseudomelanocarpa

syn. *Crataegus pentagyna* subsp. *pseudomelanocarpa*

☀ ❄ ↔ 10–17 ft (3–5 m)
↑ 15–20 ft (4.5–6 m)

Species from the Balkan Peninsula. Source of a herbal medicine. White flowers in summer. Zones 6–11.

Crataegus punctata

DOTTED HAWTHORN

☀ ❄ ↔ 30 ft (9 m) ↑ 30 ft (9 m)

Native to eastern USA. Thorny tree. Broadly egg-shaped, dark green leaves, toothed, downy undersides. White flowers, pale pink anthers, in hairy corymbs. Red fruit with pale speckles. '**Ohio Pioneer**' ★, popular ornamental tree, brick-red fruit. Zones 4–9.

Crataegus schraderiana

☀ ❄ ↔ 20 ft (6 m) ↑ 20 ft (6 m)

Native to Greece and the Crimean Peninsula. Deciduous round-headed tree. Leaves to 2 in (5 cm) long, 5 to 9 deep toothed lobes, deep green, covered by a fine gray down. Flowers in corymbs, white, ½ in (12 mm) wide. Plum-colored fruit. Zones 6–9.

Crataegus schraderiana

Crataegus pseudomelanocarpa

Crescentia cujete

Crinodendron hookerianum

CRESCENTIA

This genus in the trumpet-vine (Bignoniaceae) family has 6 species of evergreen trees and vines, of which one is commonly grown for its decorative fruit. They are found in the Americas from Mexico to Brazil, including the West Indies. They have simple oval to paddle-shaped or trifoliate leaves and tubular flowers with widely flared lobes, usually in shades of yellow to tan. The bat-pollinated flowers grow straight out of the branches, rather than forming in the leaf axils or stem tips. The spherical to ovoid fruit can be very large, with a hard woody shell and a pulpy flesh. CULTIVATION: These plants demand a warm, humid, tropical climate with ample moisture during the fruiting period. They thrive in moist, humus-enriched, well-drained soil in full sun or partial shade, but will tolerate drought and can be grown in the monsoonal tropics. Pruning or trimming is seldom necessary. Propagate from seed or half-hardened cuttings.

Crescentia cujete

CALABASH TREE

☀/◐ ✦ ↔ 20 ft (6 m) ↑ 30 ft (9 m)

Found in Mexico and Central America. Paddle-shaped, deep green leaves to 10 in (25 cm) long. Flowers

single, on old wood, light yellow-brown, purple interior. Yellow-green fruit, to 12 in (30 cm) long, tough shell, often hollowed and used as a gourd. Zones 11–12.

CRINODENDRON

This genus belonging to the family Elaeocarpaceae has 4 South American species; 2 are garden grown for the elegant flowers hanging from long, slender, pendent stalks emerging from the leaf axils. The foliage is dark, glossy, and evergreen. They are usually grown as fairly compact shrubs, but can form upright small trees. CULTIVATION: They require good drainage and year-round moisture, a fertile soil, shelter from wind in cold climates, partial shade or full sun, and a cool root run. Propagate from seed or half-hardened cuttings in a sandy potting mix.

Crinodendron hookerianum ★

syn. *Tricuspidaria lanceolata*

CHILE LANTERN TREE

◐ ❄ ↔ 15 ft (5 m) ↑ 30 ft (9 m)

Stiff, dense, evergreen shrub from Chile, smaller in cultivation. Short-stalked sparse leaves, narrow, dark green, and glossy. Profuse, bright red or carmine, waxy, urn-shaped flowers in early summer. Zones 8–9.

Crinum bulbispermum

Crinum moorei

Crinodendron patagua

☀ ❄ ↔ 10 ft (3 m) ↑ 15 ft (4.5 m)

From Chile, fast-growing evergreen shrub or small upright tree. Glossy, dark green, oval leaves with downy undersides, reddish shoots. White bell-shaped flowers hang below the branches, in mid- to late summer. Tolerates drier conditions than *C. hookerianum*. Zones 8–9.

CRINUM

There are about 130 species of evergreen and deciduous bulbous plants in this genus, which belongs to the amaryllis (Amaryllidaceae) family. They are found in tropical and subtropical zones, usually in coastal areas. The bulbs are large and the leaves broad and long, to 3 ft (0.9 m) or more. Thick flowering stems support large trumpet-shaped flowers with flaring lobes, narrow and spidery in some species. The flowers may be white or in shades of pink or rose, and are often fragrant.

CULTIVATION: In cool areas grow in pots in the conservatory or greenhouse. Elsewhere grow in a sheltered semi-shaded position in well-drained soil. Bulbs dislike being transplanted and take time to become established. Propagate from seed and offsets. Seed-grown plants take 3 years to flower.

Crinum americanum

FLORIDA SWAMP LILY, SOUTHERN SWAMP CRINUM

☀ ⌇ ↔ 24–36 in (60–90 cm) ↑ 18–30 in (45–75 cm)

From southern USA. Large short-necked bulbs. Leaves to 4 ft (1.2 m) long. Flowering stems bear 3 to 6 creamy white flowers tinged with green or purple. Prominent flaring stamens are red or pink. Zones 9–11.

Crinum asiaticum

POISON BULB

☀ ❄ ↔ 3 ft (0.9 m) ↑ 3–5 ft (0.9–1.5 m)

From tropical Asia. Large long-necked bulbs. Very leafy plant with broad bluish green leaves to 4 ft (1.2 m)

Crinum × *powellii* 'Album'

long. Thick flowering stems bear heads of 20 to 30 fragrant white flowers with narrow spidery petals and long red stamens. *C. a.* var. *sinicum* (syn. *C. pedunculatum*), from Australia and some Pacific Islands, has larger leaves and taller flowering stems. Zones 8–11.

Crinum bulbispermum

syn. *Crinum longifolium*

☀ ❄ ↔ 3 ft (0.9 m) ↑ 3 ft (0.9 m)

A South African species. Large long-necked bulb. Tidy, channeled, arching leaves. Large, funnel-shaped, fragrant flowers in white, or in shades of pink, with a red streak on each petal. Zones 7–10.

Crinum erubescens

☀ ⌇ ↔ 3 ft (0.9 m) ↑ 3 ft (0.9 m)

From tropical America. Aquatic species with large bulb. Thick, fleshy, strap-shaped leaves. Large, fragrant, trumpet-shaped flowers with flaring lobes, borne in heads of 4 to 12. Flowers purplish red with a white throat. Zones 10–11.

Crinum 'Ellen Bosanquet'

☀ ⌇ ↔ 2–3 ft (0.6–0.9 m) ↑ 2–3 ft (0.6–0.9 m)

A hybrid of *C. moorei* and *C. zeylanicum*. Tidy foliage with soft slightly

arching leaves. Heads of large, trumpet-shaped, rose red flowers in summer. Zones 9–11.

Crinum moorei

☀ ❄ ↔ 4–5 ft (1.2–1.5 m) ↑ 4–5 ft (1.2–1.5 m)

From South Africa. Extremely large long-necked bulb. Long, broad, rather untidy leaves. Tall flowering stems bear 6 to 12 fragrant, pale pink, trumpet-shaped flowers in summer. Zones 8–11.

Crinum × powellii

☀ ❄ ↔ 4 ft (1.2 m) ↑ 4 ft (1.2 m)

A hybrid of *C. moorei* and *C. bulbispermum*, of garden origin. Large long-necked bulb. Broad, upright, channeled leaves. Trumpet-shaped flowers of pink or white on tall stems in clusters of 8 to 10. 'Album', pure white flowers. Zones 7–10.

CROCOSMIA

FALLING STARS, MONTBRETIA

The iris (Iridaceae) family species in this genus come from the grasslands of South Africa. Their handsome appearance, trouble-free lifestyles, vivid flowers, and erect lance-like leaves make them popular in cultivation. The leaves reach heights of 24–40 in (60–100 cm) and form dense clumps. They can be pleated and/or ribbed, and vary from pale green to mid-green to a brownish shade. The lavish funnel-shaped flowers, which cut well, are held on long, wiry, often branching stems and appear in mid- to late summer. The plants are fully dormant in winter. The corms are disc-like, ivory white, and about 2½ in (6 cm) in diameter.

CULTIVATION: Sun, water, reasonably good drainage, and the regular division of overcrowded corms are the principal requirements of these tough but very attractive plants.

Crinodendron patagua (inset, fruits)

Crocosmia aurea

☼ ❄ ↔ 24–32 in (60–80 cm)
↑ 32–40 in (80–100 cm)

From streambeds, wet woodlands, and shady gorges. Tolerates shade. Flowers, held in double rows on erect sometimes branched spikes, range between burnt orange and chrome yellow. Leaves are papery and pale green. Zones 7–9.

Crocosmia × crocosmiiflora

☼ ❄ ↔ 20–24 in (50–60 cm)
↑ 20–24 in (50–60 cm)

Robust hybrid between *C. aurea* and *C. pottsii*. Pale green leaves, arching branching flower stems. Sunny protected situations suit it best. Invasive in mild wet climates. '**Emily McKenzie**' (syn. 'Lady McKenzie'), grows to 24 in (60 cm), mid-green leaves, generous branched spikes of nodding dark orange flowers splashed with red; '**Solfatarre**' (syn. 'Solphatare'), popular hybrid dating from the 1890s, elegantly branched arching stems, yellow petals, smoky bronze papery leaves. Zones 5–9.

Crocosmia masoniorum

☼ ❄ ↔ 32–40 in (80–100 cm)
↑ 3–4 ft (0.9–1.2 m)

Robust plant from a mountainous habitat. Pleated mid-green leaves and single, spraying, arching stems of red-orange flowers. Best in mild climates and on moist sandy soils. '**Rowallane Yellow**', yellow flowers. Zones 7–9.

Crocosmia pottsii

☼ ❄ ↔ 32–36 in (80–90 cm)
↑ 32–36 in (80–90 cm)

Grows in the wild beside and in streambeds. Needs similarly damp rocky environment in cultivation. Flowers are orange-red. Zones 7–9.

Croscosmia Hybrid Cultivars

☼ ❄ ↔ 12–24 in (30–60 cm)
↑ 18–36 in (45–90 cm)

Many colorful, carefully selected, new and old named cultivars of much mixed parentage. Most bred for cool wet climates. All produce dense

leaf clumps and a generous supply of summer flowers. '**Citronella**' (syn. 'Golden Fleece'), grows to 24 in (60 cm) high, mid-green leaves, yellow flowers with red-brown markings; '**Lucifer**', flowers earlier than most, large rich red flowers; '**Norwich Canary**', orange buds open to bright yellow flowers with orange petal reverse; '**Star of the East**' ★, very large, light-centered, apricot pink to light orange flowers, color more intense at petal tips. Zones 7–10.

CROCUS

A genus of around 80 species of small, herbaceous, lily-like perennials in the iris (Iridaceae) family, found in a range of habitats from sea level to subalpine regions of central and southern Europe, northern Africa, central Asia, and western China. All have subterranean corms, from which inflorescences arise. Leaves are similar in shape but produced at different times: autumn-flowering species are leafless at flowering, growth returning in spring; spring-flowering species have leaves at flowering, and fruit is produced before winter. Flowers have a long tube originating from the top of the corm and terminating in a colorful, tall, 6-segmented "flower." The ovary that forms the fruit is at the base of the floral tube. Seeds develop in the 3-celled capsular fruits. CULTIVATION: Most species grow over some years into compact clumps around 4–6 in (10–15 cm) in diameter. Plant bulbs 4 in (10 cm) apart or in widely spaced groups of more crowded bulbs. Propagate from seed, which germinates readily. Young seedlings should be kept in containers for 2 years before planting out. Soils and aspect vary with the species.

Crocus ancyrensis

☼ ❄ ↔ 3 in (8 cm) ↑ 2 in (5 cm)

Yellow-flowered species found in open rocky places in oak scrub and pine woods in central and northern Turkey at 2,620–5,250 ft (800–1,600 m) altitude. Leaves, 2 to 6, as long as the

Crocosmia masoniorum

1 to 3 flowers. Requires well-drained, alkaline, gritty soil. Flowers from late winter to summer. Zones 6–8.

Crocus angustifolius

syn. *Crocus susianus*

☼ ❄ ↔ 4 in (10 cm) ↑ 2 in (5 cm)

From southwestern Russia. Flowers 1 to 2, yellow, striped or blotched purplish brown on outer floral segments. Leaves 3 to 6, as long as flowers, gray-green. Flowers from late winter–early spring. Cultivated in Europe for over 300 years. Zones 5–7.

Crocus banaticus

syns *Crocus byzantinus*, *C. iridiflorus*

☼ ❄ ↔ 3 in (8 cm) ↑ 4 in (10 cm)

From Romania, northeastern former Yugoslavia, and Ukraine. Flowers solitary, segments lilac to purple, inner ones smaller than outer ones, appearing in autumn; 1 to 3 leaves in spring. Zones 6–7.

Crocus chrysanthus

syns *Crocus annulatus*, *C. croceus*, *C. skorpilii*

☼ ❄ ↔ 4 in (10 cm) ↑ 2 in (5 cm)

Found in a range of habitats from Albania, Bulgaria, Greece, Macedonia, Serbia, Romania, and Turkey. Variable spring-flowering species, flowers fragrant, pale yellow to orange-yellow, sometimes striped bronze or purple on outer segments. Leaves 3 to 7, various lengths, gray-green. Many

C. masoniorum 'Rowallane Yellow'

selections and hybrids, particularly with *C. biflorus*, now in cultivation. '**Blue Pearl**' ★, flowers white, yellow throat, pale lilac-blue outer segments; '**E. A. Bowles**', flowers deep lemon yellow, outer segments with bronze-green bases; '**Ladykiller**', flowers white, deep purple markings on outer segments. Zones 6–8.

Crocus corsicus

syn. *Crocus insularis*

☼ ❄ ↔ 3 in (8 cm) ↑ 3–4 in (8–10 cm)

Found in scrub and rocky hillsides in Corsica, this species has 1 to 2 flowers, sometimes fragrant, lilac inside, outer segments lilac, buff, or yellow, from late winter to early summer. Leaves, 2 to 4 in number, as long as flowers, dark green. Zones 7–9.

Crocosmia × crocosmiiflora

Crocosmia pottsii

Crocus etruscus
☀ ❄ ↔ 3 in (8 cm) ↕ 3 in (8 cm)
From Italy. Flowers 1, rarely 2, from late winter–spring, pale lilac-blue, outer segments creamy to buff. Leaves 2 to 4, shorter than flower, to ¼ in (6 mm) wide, green. Zones 6–8.

Crocus goulimyi
☀ ❄ ↔ 3 in (8 cm) ↕ 4 in (10 cm)
Found in limestone soils in southern Greece. Flowers 1 or 2, fragrant, pale to deep lilac-purple, inner segments paler, throat white, hairy, in autumn. Leaves 4 to 6, shorter than flowers, green. Zones 7–8.

Crocus imperati
syns *Crocus incurvus, C. neapolitanus, C. suaveolens*
☀ ❄ ↔ 3 in (8 cm) ↕ 4 in (10 cm)
From Italy. Flowers 1 or 2, mid- to deep purple inside, outer segments buff-colored on exterior with purple stripes, from late winter–early spring. Leaves 3 to 6, equal to or longer than flowers, glossy green. Zones 7–8.

Crocus kotschyanus
syn. *Crocus zonatus*
☀ ❄ ↔ 4 in (10 cm) ↕ 3 in (8 cm)
Variable species from Russia, Turkey, Syria, and Lebanon. Flowers 1 to 2,

Crocus serotinus subsp. *salzmannii*

Crocus tommasinianus

sometimes fragrant, white or bluish lilac, parallel veins darker, throat white or yellowish, sometimes hairy, in autumn. Leaves 4 to 6, not present at flowering, green. Corms upright or lying on side. Zones 6–7.

Crocus medius
☀ ❄ ↔ 5 in (12 cm) ↕ 3 in (8 cm)
From northern Italy and southeastern France. Flowers 1 to 2, lilac to deep purple, darker veins at base of segments, in autumn. Leaves 2 to 3, well after flowering, green with white stripe. Zones 6–7.

Crocus ochroleucus
☀ ❄ ↔ 3 in (8 cm) ↕ 2 in (5 cm)
From southern Syria, Lebanon, and Israel. Flowers 1 to 5, creamy white, throat, lower part of segments pale to deep yellow, hairy, from late autumn–winter. Leaves 3 to 7, appearing when flowers open, deep green. Zones 7–8.

Crocus pulchellus
☀ ❄ ↔ 4 in (10 cm) ↕ 4–5 in (10–12 cm)
From moist habitats and deciduous oak/pine woodlands and scrub in southern former Yugoslavia, Montenegro, Bulgaria, Greece, and Turkey. Large-flowered species,

Crocus vernus

flowers 1 to 2, fragrant, pale lilac to mid-blue with darker veins, throat deep yellow, from late summer–late autumn. Leaves 3 to 5, form long after flowering, green. Zones 6–7.

Crocus sativus
SAFFRON CROCUS
☀ ❄ ↔ 4 in (10 cm) ↕ 2 in (5 cm)
An ancient source of dye and herbal medicine, saffron has been grown for centuries. A pound (450 g) of dried saffron takes 70,000 flowers, making it the world's most expensive spice. Sterile, it reproduces only by vegetative means. Thought to be a selection from wild populations of *C. cartwrightianus*, a species from Greece. *C. sativus* has larger floral segments and styles, from which dye is produced. Flowers 1 to 5, fragrant, pale to deep lilac-purple or white, veins darker, in autumn. Leaves 7 to 12, normally present at flowering, gray-green. Zones 6–8.

Crocus serotinus
☀ ❄ ↔ 4–6 in (10–15 cm) ↕ 2–4 in (5–10 cm)
From Portugal. Autumn-flowering species, with 3 to 4 grass-like leaves that emerge with flowers. White to mauve flowers, sometimes veined purple, orange stigma. *C. s.* subsp. *salzmannii,* pale lilac flowers with yellow throats. Zones 6–9.

Crocus sieberi
☀ ❄ ↔ 3 in (8 cm) ↕ 2–3 in (5–8 cm)
From the Balkan Peninsula and Crete. Variable species, differences being in flower color and distribution. Hybrids occur where 2 subspecies abut; some have been selected for cultivation. Flowers 1 to 3, fragrant, white, purplish on exterior of outer segments, from spring–summer. Leaves 4 to 7, equal in length to flower, green. 'Bowles White', selection with white flowers, throat golden yellow; 'Hubert Edelsten', inner floral segments white, outer segments lilac-purple; *C. s.* subsp. *sublimis* 'Tricolor', narrow floral segments, each with 3 color bands, yellow throat, then white, then lilac-purple. Zones 6–8.

Crocus speciosus
☀ ❄ ↔ 3 in (8 cm) ↕ 4–6 in (10–15 cm)
From Russia, northern Iran, and Turkey. Widespread variable species. Flowers 1 to 2, fragrant, lilac-blue, darker veins present, exterior of segments often with silvery flush, throat whitish, in autumn. Leaves 3 to 5, emerging long after flowering, dark green. Zones 6–8.

Crocus speciosus

Crocus tommasinianus ★
☀ ❄ ↔ 3 in (8 cm) ↕ 3–4 in (8–10 cm)
From Yugoslavia, Hungary, and Bulgaria. Flowers 1 to 2, in early spring, pale lilac to purple, often silvery or buff-colored on exterior segments, sometimes with darker purple on ends of segments, throat white. Leaves 3 to 4, equal in length to flowers, green with prominent longitudinal stripe. Zones 6–8.

Crocus vernus
DUTCH CROCUS
☀ ❄ ↔ 4 in (10 cm) ↕ 4–5 in (10–12 cm)
Most common *Crocus* species, found over much of Europe from Iberian Peninsula to western Russia. Flowers 1 to 2, in early spring, purple, lilac, white, striped darker in some populations. Leaves 2 to 4, mostly shorter than flowers, green. Many cultivars have been selected. Zones 6–8.

CROSSANDRA
This tropical and subtropical genus of some 50 species of evergreen shrubs and subshrubs in the acanthus (Acanthaceae) family is found in Africa, including Madagascar, and from the Arabian Peninsula to India. Most *Crossandra* species have lush, deep green, lance-shaped leaves in whorls, and terminal heads of brightly colored, large-lobed, tubular flowers for most of the year. The flowerheads also contain leafy bracts, which are usually the same color as the flowers but are often differently textured, being downy or bristly.
CULTIVATION: Often grown as house plants outside the tropics, *Crossandra* species prefer moist, well-drained, humus-enriched soil and a position in full sun or partial shade. The foliage tends to be rather soft and should be protected from strong winds. Pinch the tips back and cut out any weak

stems to keep the plants bushy. Propagation is from seed or half-hardened tip cuttings.

Crossandra guineensis
☼/☀ ✤ ↔ 32 in–5 ft (80 cm–1.5 m)
↑ 6 in (15 cm)

African species. A quick-growing, tropical, tender, perennial ground cover, often treated as an annual. Has whorls of small leaves and displays abundant lilac flowers in summer. Zones 11–12.

Crossandra infundibuliformis
FIRECRACKER FLOWER
☼/☀ ✤ ↔ 26 in (65 cm) ↑ 4 ft (1.2 m)

Native of Sri Lanka and southern India. Downy stems. Deep green, glossy, wavy-edged leaves, 2–5 in (5–12 cm) long. Fan-like flowers in long flower spikes, downy bracts, salmon pink or bright orange-red. Popular in tropical gardens and as a house plant. Zones 11–12.

CROTALARIA
RATTLEBOX

This African tropical and warm-temperate genus in the pea-flower subfamily of the legume (Fabaceae) family contains around 600 species, including many evergreen shrubs notable for their racemes of showy pea-like flowers, often in strong yellow tones. Conspicuous seed pods follow the flowers, and as they ripen the seeds within rattle, hence the common name "rattlebox", and also the scientific name, which comes from *krotalon*, Greek for a castanet. The leaves may be simple or trifoliate, and will vary in texture from soft and pliable to leathery, depending on the species. CULTIVATION: Although some species tolerate light frosts, a warm climate, or at least a good hot summer, is essential to ensure heavy flowering.

Crossandra guineensis

Flowering is mainly in late spring, though trimming after the first flush of flowers can encourage a second crop. Propagate from half-hardened cuttings or by sowing fresh seed, which should be soaked first.

Crotalaria agatiflora ★
BIRD FLOWER
☼ ⚘ ↔ 5 ft (1.5 m) ↑ 10 ft (3 m)

From the higher altitude regions of eastern Africa. Leaves trifoliate, light green, soft-textured leaflets. Flowers in terminal racemes up to 15 in (38 cm) long, bright yellow, but often have a greenish hue. Tolerates light frosts. Can be invasive. Zones 9–11.

Crotalaria mitchellii
RATTLE POD
☼ ❋ ↔ 3 ft (0.9 m) ↑ 3 ft (0.9 m)

Found in the eastern region of Australia, south from Cairns to north of Sydney, on sandy soils in moist sites. Leaves elliptical, smooth, or hairy. Flowerheads terminal, to 8 in (20 cm) long, yellow flowers, early–late spring. Hairy pods to 1 in (25 mm) long. Zones 8–10.

Crotalaria retusa
RATTLEWEED
☼/☀ ⚘ ↔ 24 in (60 cm) ↑ 4 ft (1.2 m)

West Indian perennial. Leaves dull mid-green, simple elongated ellipses to 3 in (8 cm) long. Yellow flowers,

Crossandra infundibuliformis

suffused and marked with red, in terminal racemes. Hard blunt-tipped seedpods. This species is considered invasive and a vector for mosaic viruses. Zones 10–11.

CROTON

Not to be confused with the house plants commonly known as crotons (genus *Codiaeum*), the over 750 species of this genus in the euphorbia (Euphorbiaceae) family include annuals, perennials, shrubs, and trees found mainly in the Americas, especially the tropical and subtropical regions. They are usually densely branched plants with simple, dark green, sometimes downy and/or toothed leaves that are narrow to rhomboidal or heart-shaped. Racemes of tiny buff-colored flowers are followed by seedpods containing bean-like seeds. These plants have a long history of medicinal use. The oil extracted from the seeds of some species has powerful purgative and anti-irritant properties. However, the extracts should be used only under medical supervision, because there is a possibility of severe side-effects. CULTIVATION: Many species are intolerant of frost but are otherwise easily cultivated in warm areas. Others are hardier, or are grown as annuals. Plant in sun or light shade with moist, humus-rich, well-drained soil. *Croton* species are reasonably drought tolerant once established. Propagate by seed, which may need soaking and scarifying before sowing, or by semi-ripe cuttings. Allow the sap to dry before inserting cuttings.

Croton gratissimus
☼ ❋ ↔ 12 ft (3.5 m) ↑ 30 ft (9 m)

Shrub or small tree from Angola, Zambia, and Malawi to northern

Crotalaria mitchellii, in Witjira National Park, South Australia

South Africa. Very attractive foliage, lance-shaped to elliptical leaves, beautiful silvery undersides. Spikes of small creamy colored flowers bloom in spring–early summer. Yellow fruits with 3 lobes. Zones 8–10.

CROWEA

This small Australian genus in the rue (Rutaceae) family is closely related to genus *Eriostemon*. Of its 3 evergreen shrubs, the 2 species from southeastern Australia are the showiest and are the parents of many cultivars. The small rounded shrubs have linear gray-green leaves and star-shaped flowers in white or shades of pink. CULTIVATION: *Crowea* species grow naturally as understory shrubs in light dappled shade, but can withstand full sun provided they are planted in reasonably moist, well-drained, open soil with a mulch of leaf litter or similar organic matter. A light tip prune after flowering will ensure compact growth.

Croton gratissimus, in Kirstenbosch National Botanical Garden, Cape Town, South Africa

C

Cryptanthus × *roseus* 'Marian Oppenheimer'

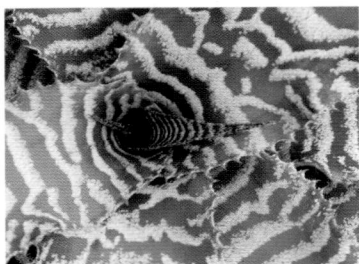

Cryptanthus zonatus

Crowea exalata ★

☀ ❄ ↔ 5 ft (1.5 m) ↑ 3 ft (0.9 m)

Extended flowering period, from spring into winter. Starry 5-petalled flowers, white to deep pink. Many forms selected, hybrids bred for cultivation, including prostrate or low spreading varieties. Zones 9–10.

Crowea saligna

☀ ❄ ↔ 3 ft (0.9 m) ↑ 3 ft (0.9 m)

Rounded shrub, small linear leaves, slightly recurved margins, prominent midrib. Star-like pink flowers, to 1 in (25 mm) across, from autumn–winter. Good cut flower. Zones 9–10.

CRYPTANTHUS

Commonly known as earth stars, these plants are members of the pineapple (Bromeliaceae) family. They are generally small and flattened, with an irregular star shape. The triangular leaves are stiff and broad and of many colors, often with crossbands or longitudinal stripes. There are 2 main groups. One has no flower stem and the flowerhead nestles in the center of the plant; there is male dominance in the flowers in the center but female dominance in the outer flowers. The other group has similar flowers throughout the flowerhead, which is on a short stem. The petals are white for both groups. Found from eastern to southern Brazil, earth stars grow in the ground or on rocks, under the protection of trees or bushes. There are over 50 *Cryptanthus* species, of which only half are generally grown in cultivation. They are propagated from offsets that generally appear on the top of the plant from between the leaves. These usually fall off and are easily rooted. The plants are self-sterile, making it difficult to set seed at species level. However, they are very promiscuous, and there are many hybrids—some 400 to date. Because of the small number of species in the hybridizing program, there are many *Cryptanthus* look-alikes.

CULTIVATION: Earth stars need more moisture than most bromeliads, and protection in the winter. They are best grown in shallow pots, and are recommended for indoor culture and for greenhouse conditions in cool-temperate areas, or outdoors with protection from direct continuous sunlight and extremes of rain in warm-temperate, subtropical, and tropical areas. Water when potting mix is dry. Fertilizer extra to that already incorporated in good quality potting mix is not necessary. Propagate from offsets.

Cryptanthus acaulis

☀ ❄ ↔ 6 in (15 cm) ↑ 2 in (5 cm)

The most common and most hardy of the genus; can survive 32°F (0°C). Plant more circular in general shape than the more usual oval. Leaves triangular, to 4 in (10 cm), a scurfy green, sometimes reddish. Zones 9–10.

Cryptanthus beuckeri

☀ ❄ ↔ 8 in (20 cm) ↑ 2 in (5 cm)

Plant with few radiating leaves, which are of a different type to those of most members of the genus and are best described as paddle-shaped with a long handle. They are whitish but tinged with red and spotted with dark green. Need very warm conditions; can be grown in a terrarium. Zones 9–10.

Cryptanthus bivittatus

☀ ❄ ↔ 10 in (25 cm) ↑ 2 in (5 cm)

Plant is regular in shape, resembling an open star. Leaves dark green with 2 broad, longitudinal, white or pinkish stripes. The center of 'Starlite' (syn. 'Starlight') is cream to light pink instead of dark green; 'Pink Starlite', center stripe dark green, rest of leaf hot pink. These colors will be achieved if the plant is given the best possible planting and growing conditions. Zones 9–10.

Cryptanthus Black Mystic Group

☀ ❄ ↔ 10 in (25 cm) ↑ 2 in (5 cm)

Medium-sized plant, irregular diamond shape. Deep black leaves with silver markings. Grow in low light to achieve the blackness. Zones 9–10.

Cryptanthus fosterianus

☀ ❄ ↔ 16 in (40 cm) ↑ 2 in (5 cm)

Narrow oval plant, irregular in shape. Leaves to 12 in (30 cm) long, thick and fleshy, wavy along the edges, coloring maroon with wavy gray crossbands. Zones 9–10.

Cryptanthus × roseus 'Marian Oppenheimer'

☀ ❄ ↔ 4 in (10 cm) ↑ 2 in (5 cm)

Created by radiation experimentation, probably of *C. acaulis*. Small plant, light gray-green leaves with bright pink edges, sometimes pink stripes. There are wide-leafed and narrow-leafed forms. Zones 9–10.

Cryptanthus 'Rainbow Star'

☀ ❄ ↔ 10 in (25 cm) ↑ 8 in (20 cm)

Named *C. bromelioides* var. *tricolor* in 1953, but in 2001 found to be incorrectly identified; common name, rainbow star, then became official cultivar name. Variegated plant with leaves striped in green, white, and pink. Under optimum conditions can grow up to 16 in (40 cm) high and wide. Two forms, one stiffer leafed than the other; both require similar growing conditions. Best allowed to offset freely; when settled into a large clump it will flower. Zones 9–10.

Cryptanthus zonatus

☀ ❄ ↔ 12 in (30 cm) ↑ 2 in (5 cm)

Oval plant, irregular in shape. Leaves grow to 8 in (20 cm) long and are thick, fleshy, wavy along edges, mainly green, with wavy, shiny, gray crossbands. Zones 9–10.

Cryptanthus 'Rainbow Star'

Cryptocarya laevigata

Cryptocarya murrayi

× *CRYPTBERGIA*

This member of the pineapple (Bromeliaceae) family has attributes inherited from both parents within *Cryptanthus* and *Billbergia*, and each cultivar is unique. Recommended for indoor culture if in flower, for greenhouse or conservatory conditions in cool-temperate areas, or outdoors with protection from direct continuous sunlight and extremes of rain in warm-temperate, subtropical, and tropical areas.
CULTIVATION: Water when potting mix is dry. Fertilizer additional to that already incorporated in good quality potting mix not necessary. Propagation possible only by offset.

× *Cryptbergia* 'Red Burst'

☀ ⚘ ↔ 8 in (20 cm) ↑ 4 in (10 cm)
Narrow, rigid, reddish leaves, bending downward from the center of the plant to form an open rosette. Flowerheads globular, with about 10 flowers pointing upwards. Petals green, blue-edged. Zones 9–10.

CRYPTOCARYA

This largely tropical genus of around 200 species of evergreen shrubs and trees is classified in the laurel (Lauraceae) family. The leaves are typically pointed oval in shape, deep green, and leathery. In spring to summer or at the start of the rainy season, panicles of small yellow flowers appear, followed by hard seed capsules enclosed within the enlarged, now almost nut-like calyx tube of the former flower. These fruits frequently have a peppery flavor, and sometimes have culinary uses in their local area.
CULTIVATION: A few *Cryptocarya* species will tolerate light frosts, but most require constantly warm frost-free conditions with protection from cold winds. Once established they will tolerate drought, but they generally prefer moist, well-drained, humus-enriched soil. Apart from trimming to shape when young, little pruning is necessary. Plant in full sun or partial shade, and propagate from seed or half-hardened cuttings.

Cryptocarya laevigata
syn. *Cryptocarya bowiei*
GLOSSY LAUREL
☀ ⚘ ↔ 15 ft (4.5 m) ↑ 30 ft (9 m)
From subtropical rainforests of eastern Australia and Southeast Asia. Relatively narrow, glossy, deep green leaves, to 3 in (8 cm) long. Yellow flowers in spring, followed by showy red fruit. Zones 10–12.

Cryptocarya murrayi
☀ ⚘ ↔ 35 ft (10 m) ↑ 80 ft (24 m)
From rainforests of northeastern Queensland, Australia. Large leaves, 10 in (25 cm) long, oval to elliptical, glossy above, hairy beneath. Flowers very small, greenish, long brown hairs, in late spring–summer (wet season). Fruits egg-shaped, glossy black. Zones 9–12.

Cryptocarya rubra

Cryptocarya rubra
☀ ⚘ ↔ 30 ft (9 m) ↑ 50 ft (15 m)
From Chile, rarely cultivated. Pointed oval leaves, 2 in (5 cm) long, blue-green below. Small panicles of yellow flowers in late spring. Zones 9–11.

CRYPTOMERIA

This single-species genus belonging to the cypress (Cupressaceae) family has numerous cultivars, which are also prized as garden plants. An evergreen from Japan and China, it is a densely clothed conifer with reddish brown fibrous bark and a straight trunk that forms a buttress as it matures. The pollen-bearing male cones, held in clusters at the tips of the branches, release their pollen in spring, while the persistent female seed-bearing cones, held further along the branches, can take up to 10 months to ripen.
CULTIVATION: This long-lived species prefers deep, moist, rich soil in a full sun position. It can be propagated from fresh seed, but cultivars need to be grown from cuttings.

Cryptomeria japonica

Cryptomeria japonica
JAPANESE CEDAR, SUGI
☀ ❄ ↔ 20 ft (6 m) ↑ 90 ft (27 m)
Narrow, conical shape. Dense adult foliage in forward-growing spirals. Branches tiered, outer branchlets slightly pendulous. 'Araucarioides', dark green leaves; 'Bandaisugu', dwarf form; 'Compressa', dwarf form with purple-brown winter foliage. **Elegans Group:** 'Elegans' ★, fast growing, purplish winter foliage; 'Nana', low growing; 'Vilmoriniana', to 12 in (30 cm) high; 'Yoshino', to 50 ft (15 m) high. Zones 7–11.

Cryptomeria japonica 'Nana'

Cryptomeria japonica 'Yoshino'

Cryptomeria japonica, Elegans Group cultivar

Cryptomeria japonica 'Bandaisugu'

CRYPTOTAENIA

This genus of 6 species from the north temperate zone and the mountains of tropical Africa belongs to the carrot (Apiaceae) family. The plants are perennials with strong taproots or rhizomes. Leaves are pinnate, sometimes reduced to 3 broad leaflets. The erect inflorescences are irregularly branched into loose umbels of tiny flowers, which soon give way to small flattened fruits. *C. japonica* is grown in Japan for its strongly flavored young leaves, which are used as a salad vegetable.

CULTIVATION: *Cryptotaenia* species are easily grown in any good garden soil in full sun; they usually self-seed freely. For the tenderest leaves the plants should be kept well watered and regularly fertilized. Sow seed or plant root divisions in spring.

Cryptotaenia canadensis

Cryptotaenia canadensis
HONEWORT, WHITE CHERVIL

☀ ❄ ↔ 20–27 in (50–70 cm)
↑ 3 ft (0.9 m)

Found in North America, Asia and Europe. Perennial, often short-lived and treated as an annual. Leaves to 4 in (10 cm) long, toothed, lance-shaped leaflets. Loose heads of tiny white flowers in summer. Zones 3–10.

Cryptotaenia japonica
syn. *Cryptotaenia canadensis* subsp. *japonica*
JAPANESE PARSLEY, MITSUBA

☀ ❄ ↔ 16–27 in (40–70 cm)
↑ 24–40 in (60–100 cm)

Perennial, sometimes evergreen, from Japan, where it is used as a vegetable. Very similar to *C. canadensis* (many consider them synonymous), but leaflets usually broader and more closely spaced, plant more compact. *C. j.* f. *atropurpurea*, deep purple-red leaves, stems with pale pink flowers opening from red buds. Zones 4–9.

CTENANTHE

This genus of about 15 species of fleshy-stemmed perennials belongs to the arrowroot (Marantaceae) family. They are native to Costa Rica and Brazil, where they grow on damp forest floors and in scrub. Stems are single or branching, with leaves arising from sheaths at the nodes. Leaves are leathery, oblong, pointed, usually matt, with colored markings. They are grown for their attractive foliage.

CULTIVATION: In suitably warm climates grow in a shady, sheltered position. In temperate climates they are

Ctenanthe oppenheimiana 'Tricolor'

cultivated as indoor plants. Grow in bright filtered light. During active growth, water moderately and apply liquid fertilizer fortnightly. Propagate by division or from cuttings.

Ctenanthe burle-marxii

☀ ❄ ↔ 12–18 in (30–45 cm)
↑ 18 in (45 cm)

From Brazil. Leaves to 6 in (15 cm) long, pale green, with sickle-shaped darker markings above and dark purple beneath. Leaf sheaths also tinged purple. Zones 10–12.

Ctenanthe dasycarpa

☀/☀ ⚘ ↔ 5–10 ft (1.5–3 m)
↑ 3–5 ft (0.9–1.5 m)

From medium-altitude rainforests of Costa Rica, Panama, and Colombia. Spreads by rhizomes forming dense patch. Paddle-shaped glossy green leaves on slender stalks; inflorescences shorter, branched into spikes of white to pale yellow flowers between greenish yellow bracts. Zones 11–12.

Ctenanthe lubbersiana ★

☀ ❄ ↔ 18–24 in (45–60 cm)
↑ 18–24 in (45–60 cm)

From Brazil. Widely branching stems with narrow oblong leaves, deep green with yellow variegation above, pale green beneath. Zones 10–12.

Ctenanthe oppenheimiana
syn. *Maranta lubbersiana*
NEVER NEVER PLANT

☀ ❄ ↔ 24–36 in (60–90 cm)
↑ 36 in (90 cm)

From eastern Brazil. Bushy plant with leathery lance-shaped leaves to 16 in

Ctenanthe dasycarpa

Cucumis melo, Reticulatus Group, 'Ambrosia'

(40 cm) long, green, with silvery marking above and deep red beneath. 'Tricolor', dark green with irregular creamy yellow markings. Zones 10–12.

CUCUMIS
CUCUMBER, MELON

A genus of about 25 species of trailing or climbing annuals in the pumpkin (Cucurbitaceae) family. Originating from warm to tropical areas of Africa and Asia, they are now grown worldwide for their fruit. Their large, often hairy or prickly leaves can be smooth or may be lobed like a grape leaf. Separate male and female flowers are produced on the one plant and are usually yellow or orange. Fruits are generally green and either long and narrow or round, and are best eaten when young, as bitterness often develops as they mature. Skin can be smooth, bumpy, spiny, or ridged. Although refreshing to the palate, the fruits have very little nutritional value, being mostly water, and they can be eaten raw, cooked, or pickled.

CULTIVATION: Cucumbers are grown from seed and appreciate a rich soil with lots of organic matter and a constant supply of moisture during a long warm growing period. Melons are not as demanding as cucumbers. Some varieties need a frame to climb on; others do not. In regions where summers are short they are often grown in greenhouses.

Cucumis anguria
BURR CUCUMBER, JERUSALEM CUCUMBER, WEST INDIAN GHERKIN

☀ ❄ ↔ 7–10 ft (2–3 m)   ↑ 20 in (50 cm)
This species has 5-lobed leaves on a trailing vine. Light green spiny fruits, to 1¼–3 in (3–8 cm) long, picked when young to use for pickling. Grows from seed to harvest in 60 to 75 days. Zones 9–12.

Cucumis melo
CANTALOUPE, HONEYDEW, MELON, MUSKMELON

☀ ❄ ↔ 7–10 ft (2–3 m)
↑ 16–28 in (40–70 cm)

Annual vines found in arid regions of Africa, Arabia, southwest Asia, and

Australia. Wild types may be bitter, but cultivars produce a range of generally round sweet fruit with either smooth or rough skins. **Cantalupensis Group:** Sweet fragrant melons; skin can be smooth, scaly, rough, or grooved, but not netted. Usually round, and about 4–6 in (10–15 cm) in diameter. **Inodorus Group:** Round or oval sweet melons with green, white, orange, pinkish, or yellowish green flesh. **Reticulatus Group:** Netted melons, assorted shapes and sizes. Skins can be ribbed, warty, smooth, or netted. Seed cavity large in old varieties, smaller in newer varieties. Some varieties (muskmelons) have musky aroma. **'Ambrosia'**, firm, luscious, extra sweet, juicy, peach-colored flesh, fragrant aroma when ripe. Zones 9–12.

Cucumis sativus

CUCUMBER, GHERKIN

☼ ◖ ↔ 3–10 ft (0.9–3 m)
↑ 8–20 in (20–50 cm)

There are a great number of different forms in this species, including field, greenhouse, gherkin, Sikkim, apple,

Cucumis sativus 'Spacemaster'

Cucumis sativus 'Muncher'

Cucurbita maxima 'Atlantic Giant'

and snake cucumbers. Some are more tolerant of cold or more "burpless" than others. **'Bush Champion'** ★, compact bush-type, bright green straight fruit, good for slicing; **Beit Alpha Group** (Lebanese cucumbers), thin-skinned glossy fruit, best picked and eaten at 8 in (20 cm) in length; **'Muncher'**, thin smooth skin, easily digestible, tasty when both young and mature; **'Spacemaster'**, disease resistant, compact, slender, dark green fruit, good for pickling when small and for slicing when mature; **'Sunsweet'**, lemon-shaped fruit, cream-colored when young and sweet (eat raw), yellowy orange when mature, with a sharper taste (eat cooked). Zones 9–11.

CUCURBITA

COURGETTE, GOURD, MARROW, PUMPKIN, SQUASH, ZUCCHINI

A trailing or climbing genus of about 27 species of annuals and perennials from North and South America in the pumpkin (Cucurbitaceae) family. *Cucurbita* species are grown for both their edible and their ornamental

Cucumis sativus 'Bush Champion'

fruit. They are generally classified according to when they are harvested (summer or winter) or by their shape. Their leaves are often quite large, sometimes lobed or spotted, and usually rough or prickly, as are their stems. Their flowers are yellow or orange, and are usually separate male or female. Their fruit range in size from tiny to the largest fruit in the world. The fruit can be eaten raw or cooked; it is also a popular and nutritious stock feed. The seeds can also be eaten. *Cucurbita* is believed to have been one of the earliest plants cultivated by humans.
CULTIVATION: A very rich well-drained soil in full sun and a long warm growing season are essential for producing a good crop. Propagate from seed sown in spring.

Cucurbita ficifolia

FIG-LEAFED GOURD, MALABAR GOURD

☼ ❄ ↔ 3–10 ft (0.9–3 m)
↑ 12–20 in (30–50 cm)

A perennial plant in frost-free areas, leaves of this species look just like

Cucurbita maxima 'Autumn Cup'

those of a fig. Widely cultivated from Mexico to Chile and in Asia. The fruit is dark green, round or oval, often striped or blotched, with white flesh. Zones 8–11.

Cucurbita maxima

AUTUMN SQUASH, GOURD, SQUASH, WINTER PUMPKIN, WINTER SQUASH

☼ ❄ ↔ 3–10 ft (0.9–3 m)
↑ 12–20 in (30–50 cm)

A South American species with large round leaves, it is divided into two main groups, the pumpkins and the gourds. A wide range of cultivars of both groups are grown around the world. They are an important food source, and store well. Cultivars include: **'Atlantic Giant'** ★, the largest of the pumpkins and the largest fruit in the world—specimens weighing over 1,000 lb (450 kg) are not uncommon; **'Autumn Cup'**, butternut-type F1 hybrid that produces a dark green squash with fine orange flesh, tasting good steamed, boiled, or baked. Zones 8–11.

Cucurbita moschata

BUTTERNUT, CANADA PUMPKIN, CROOKNECK SQUASH, PUMPKIN, WINTER SQUASH

☼ ❄ ↔ 3–10 ft (0.9–3 m)
↑ 12–20 in (30–50 cm)

Trailing, climbing, or bush species with large leaves. Fruit usually has orange flesh and smooth skin. Stem flares out where it joins the fruit. **'Butternut'** ★, cultivar with bottle-shaped or waisted pumpkin, and smooth skin that is a warm buttery color. Zones 8–11.

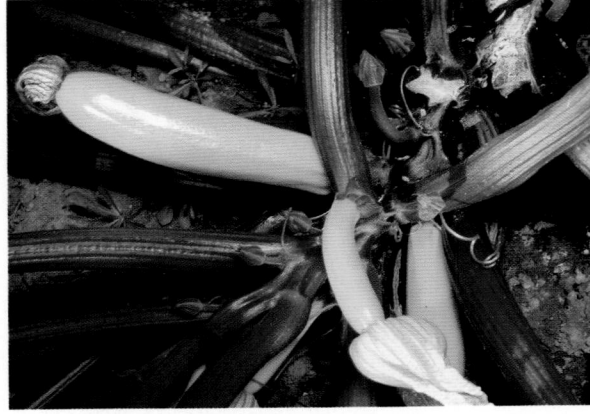

Cucurbita pepo 'Gold Rush'   *Cucurbita pepo* 'Black Beauty'   *Cucurbita pepo* 'Delicata'   *Cucurbita pepo* 'Eightball'

Cucurbita pepo 'Clarimore'

Cucurbita pepo 'Table King'

Cucurbita pepo

COURGETTE, SUMMER SQUASH, VEGETABLE MARROW, ZUCCHINI

☀ ❄ ↔ 3–10 ft (0.9–3 m)
↕ 12–20 in (30–50 cm)

A trailing or bushy species that has many cultivars. Leaves are lobed, triangular, and prickly. Young leaves and flowers can also be eaten. Most varieties are best eaten straight after harvest. '**Black Beauty**', long, straight, smooth, dark green fruit, best eaten when 6–8 in (15–20 cm) long; '**Clarimore**', hybrid Lebanese-type squash with light green, speckled, tapered fruit; '**Delicata**', sweet potato squash with very sweet orange flesh; '**Early White**', creamy white flesh, produced on a bushy plant; '**Eightball**', dark green, speckled, zucchini-type squash, best picked and eaten when the size of a golf-ball; '**Gold Rush**' ★, golden yellow zucchini-type fruit; '**Table King**', dark gray-green fruit, yellow-orange flesh, excellent flavor. Zones 8–11.

CUMINUM

This genus of 4 species of annuals comes from the Mediterranean south to the Sudan and east to central Asia. It belongs to the carrot (Apiaceae) family. The leaves are finely divided and the flowers are in umbels, each umbel with a whorl of unequal bracts. The small notched petals are pink or white. The fruits ("seeds") are elliptical to oblong and flattened.
CULTIVATION: Only one species is known in cultivation: *C. cyminum* (cumin), the source of a major dried herb or spice. Grown in full sun in fertile well-drained soils, cumin needs 3 to 4 warm months to ripen its fruits. In cool countries it is raised under glass and planted out after frosts cease. Propagation is from seed.

Cuminum cyminum

CUMIN

☀ ❄ ↔ 12 in (30 cm) ↕ 12 in (30 cm)
From the Mediterranean. Much-branched annual with leaves to 4 in (10 cm) long, divided into threadlike segments. Numerous, tiny, white flowers in short-stalked umbels about 1 in (25 mm) wide, in early summer. Fruits about ¼ in (6 mm) long. Cultivated since ancient times; fruits used to flavor cheese, cakes, curry powder, and liqueurs. Zones 8–12.

CUNILA

There are 15 species of perennial herbs and shrubs in this genus, which is a member of the mint (Lamiaceae) family. They are native to North and South America. The stems and leaves are aromatic, the leaves sometimes spotted purple. The flowers are tubular and 2-lipped, the lower lip being larger and wider, with 3 lobes.
CULTIVATION: Easily grown in well-drained soil in full sun. Propagate by division or cuttings, or from seed.

Cunila origanoides

DITTANY

☀ ❄ ↔ 9–18 in (23–45 cm)
↕ 9–18 in (23–45 cm)

A somewhat straggly perennial from eastern USA. Square branching stems, small, pointed, oval leaves. Purple or lavender tubular flowers in loose heads. Yields oil of dittany, a fragrant medicinal oil. Zones 6–10.

CUNNINGHAMIA

This genus belonging to the cypress (Cupressaceae) family includes just 2 species, one from central China, the other from Taiwan. They are evergreen conifers that can grow to 150 ft (45 m) tall, though they seldom reach that height in cultivation. The narrow leaves are sharply pointed without really being needle-like. The deep green leaves, with bluish white bands on the undersides, are arranged in irregular whorls of double rows along the stems. The fibrous red-brown bark is reminiscent of the sequoia (*Sequoiadendron giganteum*).
CULTIVATION: Both species are rather frost tender for conifers, *C. lanceolata* being the hardier. They are not fussy about soil type as long as it is reasonably fertile and the drainage is good.

Young plants will tolerate light shade and eventually grow to see the sun. Propagate from seed or cuttings.

Cunninghamia lanceolata

CHINA FIR, CHINESE CEDAR

☀ ❄ ↔ 20 ft (6 m) ↕ 70 ft (20 m)
From central to southern China. Spirally arranged deep green leaves, to 3 in (8 cm) long. Cones, sticky while green, to 1½ in (35 mm) in diameter, carried at the branch tips. '**Glauca**' ★, blue-tinted foliage. Zones 7–10.

CUNONIA

This genus, which is the name genus of the family Cunoniaceae, contains

Cunninghamia lanceolata

Cuphea caeciliae

Cupaniopsis anacardioides

15 species of evergreen shrubs and trees from New Caledonia, and one species in South Africa. They have lustrous, deep green, pinnate leaves, and bear bottlebrush-like racemes of fragrant white to cream flowers, which can turn an unsightly brown as they die, and are best removed. CULTIVATION: Although most species are frost tender, *Cunonia* species are not difficult to grow. They prefer moist, fertile, well-drained soil and a position in full sun. If necessary they will tolerate poor soil and, once established, can withstand considerable periods of drought. Young plants can be pruned to a single trunk to make them tree-like; otherwise, a light trim after flowering will keep them compact. Propagation is from seed or half-hardened tip cuttings.

Cunonia capensis
BUTTERKNIFE BUSH, SPOON BUSH
☼ ❄ ↔ 15 ft (4.5 m) ↑ 50 ft (15 m)
South African species. Smaller in cultivation, often a large shrub. Foliage deep green, bronze-tipped new growth, pinnate leaves of 5 to 7 leaflets, each up to 4 in (10 cm) long. Racemes of cream flowers stand out against the foliage, in late summer–autumn. Zones 9–11.

Cunonia deplanchei
☼ ❄ ↔ 6 ft (1.8 m) ↑ 10–20 ft (3–6 m)
Erect shrub or small tree from poor soils of New Caledonia's nickel-rich southern hills, growing in open shrubland. Leaves of 3 thick oblong leaflets; flowers deep red in short clustered racemes, in winter. Zones 10–11.

Cunonia macrophylla
☼ ❄ ↔ 3 ft (0.9 m) ↑ 8–15 ft (2.4–4.5 m)
Erect shrub of striking appearance, from same habitat as *C. deplanchei*; sometimes grows with only a single unbranched stem, red toward tip; leaves large with 5 thick leaflets, red on midrib and margins. Flowers

are pale lime-green in epaulette-like pairs of racemes, from winter to early summer. Zones 10–11.

CUPANIOPSIS
From Australia, New Guinea, and some Pacific islands, this genus in the soapberry (Sapindaceae) family consists of about 60 species of tropical and subtropical evergreen trees. Many adapt to difficult sites, encompassing poor soils, exposure to salt winds, and pollution-laden air. All have divided leathery leaves, small yellow or greenish flower clusters on the branch ends, and fruit capsules that split into 3 compartments, each with a large seed and a bright fleshy attachment. CULTIVATION: Training to a single stem and early removal of side shoots is desirable for specimen trees. Summer mulching is useful, especially on sandy soils. Regular application of fertilizer promotes much more vigorous growth than is usual under natural conditions. Freshly collected seed germinates readily for propagation.

Cupaniopsis anacardioides
TUCKEROO
☼ ❄ ↔ 15 ft (4.5 m) ↑ 50 ft (15 m)
Occurs along the eastern and northern coasts of Australia. Leathery, shiny, divided leaves. Large clusters of small yellow flowers. In summer, yellow-orange, 3-part, capsular fruits ripen. Tolerant of salt, wind exposure, poor sandy soils, and urban pollution. Zones 9–11.

Cunonia macrophylla

CUPHEA
This large genus in the loosestrife (Lythraceae) family consists of about 250 species of annuals, evergreen perennials, and low-growing shrubs from Central and South America. They have flexible leafy stems and small opposite or whorled leaves. They are grown for their masses of irregularly shaped tubular flowers, produced over a long period—almost the whole year. In warm climates they are easy to grow in average garden conditions, and they make good tub plants. CULTIVATION: *Cuphea* species are fairly frost tender, and do best in full sun or light shade, in well-drained moist soil, with protection from strong winds. Occasional tip pruning from an early age will encourage compact growth. Propagation is from seed or from tip cuttings.

Cuphea caeciliae
☼/◐ ❄ ↔ 12–20 in (30–50 cm)
↑ 12–16 in (30–40 cm)
From Mexico. Spreading or mounding shrub with lax branches. Pointed elliptical leaves, usually with finely serrated edges, 2–3 in (5–8 cm) long.

Tubular flower to over 1 in (25 mm) long, orange at base, orange-red at tips. Zones 10–12.

Cuphea hyssopifolia
FALSE HEATHER, MEXICAN HEATHER
☼ ❄ ↔ 15 in (38 cm) ↑ 18 in (45 cm)
From Mexico and Guatemala. Small rounded shrub. Dark green, narrow, pointed leaves. Purplish pink or white flowers, in small axillary racemes, late spring–summer. Zones 10–12.

Cunonia deplanchei, in the wild, Col de Yaté, New Caledonia

Cunonia capensis

Cuphea micropetala

Cuphea × purpurea

Cuphea ignea

Cuphea ignea
syn. *Cuphea platycentra*
CIGAR FLOWER, CIGARETTE PLANT, FIRECRACKER PLANT

☀ ✤ ↔ 30 in (75 cm) ↑ 24 in (60 cm)

Bushy subshrub from Mexico and Jamaica. Bright green, oval, pointed leaves. Thin, orange-red, tubular flowers, tipped white, touch of black, borne freely almost year-round, mainly late spring–autumn. Zones 10–12.

Cuphea micropetala

☀ ✤ ↔ 30 in (75 cm) ↑ 30 in (75 cm)

From Mexico. Rounded shrub. Dense, flexible, leafy branchlets, bright green lance-shaped leaves. Terminal leafy racemes of narrow tubular flowers, golden yellow to orange-red, tipped with greenish yellow, through summer–autumn. Zones 9–11.

Cuphea × purpurea

☀ ✤ ↔ 18 in (45 cm) ↑ 18 in (45 cm)

Bushy subshrub, garden hybrid between *C. llavea* and *C. procumbens*. Dark green, lance-shaped, pointed leaves. Narrow, tubular, deep pink to purplish red flowers, from late spring–autumn. Zones 9–11.

CUPRESSUS
CYPRESS

Originating in the Northern Hemisphere, this genus in the cypress (Cupressaceae) family comprises about 13 species of evergreen coniferous trees or shrubs. They are cultivated in mild climates for their dense compact crowns and bold symmetrical outlines. The tall, elegant, long-lived *C. sempervirens* is a famous feature of the gardens of Italy. The tiny, scale-like, closely overlapping leaves vary in character and color; they may be soft to the touch or rather coarse, and are often aromatic. They will withstand regular trimming, and are widely planted for large hedges and windbreaks, as ornamental specimens, and as avenue trees. The small female cones have woody scales, are rarely over 1¾ in (4 cm) long, and are usually persistent.
CULTIVATION: These plants grow well in any well-drained fertile soil, preferably in full sun. Place each in a roomy well-spaced position to enable the plant to develop its symmetrical shape naturally and to avoid unsightly fungal disease. Propagate from seed in spring or from cuttings in late summer.

Cupressus arizonica
ARIZONA CYPRESS

☀ ❄ ↔ 15 ft (4.5 m) ↑ 40 ft (12 m)

From Arizona and Mexico. Evergreen conifer, at first densely conical, becomes broadly columnar. Bark gray-brown and stringy. Blue-green foliage, white markings beneath. Cones up to 1 in (25 mm) in diameter. Drought tolerant. *C. a.* var. *glabra,* smooth bark; 'Blue Ice' ★, attractive silvery blue foliage. *C. a.* var. *stephensonii,* smooth, reddish, peeling bark, blue-green foliage. Zones 7–9.

Cupressus cashmeriana
BHUTAN CYPRESS, KASHMIR CYPRESS

☀ ✤ ↔ 20 ft (6 m) ↑ 30 ft (9 m)

Wild stands of this species have been discovered in Bhutan, solving the mystery of its origin. Narrowly

Cupressus arizonica var. *stephensonii*

Cupressus arizonica var. *glabra* 'Blue Ice'

Cupressus arizonica

long, last well when cut and are popular in floristry. Most species have local uses, either medicinally or for the mild ginger flavor of their rhizomes.
CULTIVATION: These plants are easily grown in warm frost-free climates in moist, humus-rich, well-drained soil. Feed and water liberally during the growing season. Rhizomes may be stored dry for short periods. Most species are dormant during the cooler months. Propagate from seed or by division.

Curcuma aromatica
COCHIN TURMERIC
☼/☀ ❧ ↔ 24 in (60 cm) ↕ 3 ft (0.9 m)
From Himalayan eastern India. Strong rhizomes develop flower stems before canna-lily-like leaves to 24 in (60 cm) long. Inflorescence to over 8 in (20 cm) long, lower bracts pale green to white, upper bracts pink to vivid magenta, with yellow and white true flowers. Dormant in winter, tolerates light frosts. Zones 10–12.

Curcuma longa
syn. *Curcuma domestica*
TURMERIC
☼/☀ ❧ ↔ 30 in (75 cm) ↕ 3 ft (0.9 m)
Well-known culinary herb from India. Large aromatic rhizomes, leaves to 20 in (50 cm) long. Flower stems leafy, with inflorescences to 8 in (20 cm) long, white to pale green lower bracts, deep pink or white upper bracts, yellow flowers. Zones 10–11.

Cussonia spicata

Cussonia paniculata

Cyathea australis, in the wild, in Wollemi National Park, New South Wales, Australia

CUSSONIA
Found in southern Africa and the Comoros Islands, this genus in the ivy (Araliaceae) family has 20 species of evergreen and deciduous shrubs and trees. They are characterized by large snowflake-shaped leaves, in spiral rosettes at the branch tips. They produce large candelabra-like heads of small white to yellow blooms and small, soft, red to black drupes.
CULTIVATION: Most need a warm frost-free climate and ample moisture in summer. A sheltered position is essential. Plant in full sun in moist well-drained soil. *Cussonia* species also grow well in containers, but can be very top-heavy and are inclined to tip over. Propagate from seed.

Cussonia paniculata
HIGHVELD CABBAGE TREE
☼ ❧ ↔ 7 ft (2 m) ↕ 12 ft (3.5 m)
Found at moderate altitudes. Large shrub or small tree. Thick corky bark, thin trunk, topped with a head of

Cussonia sphaerocephala

long-stemmed, spine-tipped, blue-green leaves. Many-branched heads of flowers in summer, held well clear of the foliage. Zones 9–11.

Cussonia sphaerocephala
FOREST CABBAGE TREE
☼ ❧ ↔ 12 ft (3.5 m) ↕ 30 ft (9 m)
From the southern African forests of Kwazulu-Natal in South Africa, and Swaziland. Similar to *C. spicata,* but has larger flowerheads and slightly denser foliage rosettes. Withstands very light frosts; not as hardy as *C. spicata.* Zones 9–11.

Cussonia spicata
COMMON CABBAGE TREE
☼ ❧ ↔ 12 ft (3.5 m) ↕ 30 ft (9 m)
Native of southern and eastern Africa and the Comoros Islands. Widely grown species. Thickened rather succulent trunk, develops multiple trunks with age. Much-divided leaves, carried on heavy stems. Large flowerheads in spring–summer. Zones 9–11.

CYANANTHUS
TRAILING BELLFLOWER
There are about 30 species of prostrate alpine perennials in this genus, in the bellflower (Campanulaceae) family. They are native to the Himalayas and China. The leaves are usually simple, sometimes lobed, and alternately arranged. Funnel-shaped flowers of blue, yellow, or white are borne singly on stalks in late summer or autumn.
CULTIVATION: Grow in a rock garden, trough, or cool greenhouse, in deep, gritty, acid soil. Perfect drainage is essential. Propagation is from seed or cuttings.

Cyananthus lobatus
☼ ❄ ↔ 15 in (38 cm) ↕ 4 in (10 cm)
From the Himalayas. Prostrate perennial with lobed leaves. The funnel-shaped flowers have flaring lobes and are deep blue to purple. Zones 5–9.

CYATHEA
Some 600 species of tree ferns with a wide distribution in the tropics and subtropics make up this genus, the second largest among the ferns. Some are among the largest of the tree fern (Cyatheaceae) family, and can grow to as much as 50 ft (15 m) tall, rivaling the palms they resemble. Most have a graceful habit, with large, soft, arching fronds atop a slender trunk. The old frond bases remain for some time but then fall to leave a trunk that though scarred may be quite smooth.
CULTIVATION: Species from furthest southern latitudes may survive temperatures as low as 10°F (–11.5°C), and even some tropical species may tolerate a very light frost. They prefer a constantly moist, humus-rich, fairly fertile soil. They also require atmospheric moisture and need misting and full shade in areas with low humidity or irregular rainfall. Propagate by sowing the abundant spores, or by removing the basal suckers that sometimes form around established plants.

Cyathea australis
ROUGH TREE FERN
☀ ❄ ↔ 20 ft (6 m) ↕ 20 ft (6 m)
Found in the damper parts of eastern Australia, including Tasmania. Height variable. Fronds to 12 ft (3.5 m) long with 40 in (100 cm) long leaflets. Zones 8–11.

Cyathea cooperi (right, foreground), in the wild, Tambourine Mountains National Park, Queensland, Australia

Cyathea brownii

Cyathea brownii

NORFOLK ISLAND TREE FERN

☀ ❋ ↔ 15 ft (4.5 m) ↑15 ft (4.5 m)

Norfolk Island only. Lush bright to deep green fronds, very dark trunk, scarred with old fronds. Zones 9–11.

Cyathea cooperi

SCALY TREE FERN, STRAW TREE FERN

☀ ❋ ↔ 20 ft (6 m) ↑20 ft (6 m)

From Australia. Chaffy straw-colored scales massed around frond bases. Fast growing, more tolerant of dry conditions than most species. Zones 9–11.

Cyathea dealbata

SILVER TREE FERN

☀ ❋ ↔ 20 ft (6 m) ↑30 ft (9 m)

From New Zealand, this species is that country's sporting emblem.

Cyathea dregei

Large fern, fronds up to 12 ft (3.5 m) long. Distinctive, almost metallic, silvery white coloration on their undersides. Fronds soft, easily damaged by strong winds. Shelter is important. Zones 8–11.

Cyathea dregei

CAPE TREE FERN

☀/☀ ❋ ↔ 10 ft (3 m) ↑15 ft (4.5 m)

South African species. Fronds arch downward, then turn up at the tips; relatively short, 6 ft (1.8 m) long, quite broad, light colored undersides. Surprisingly tolerant of both dry and cold conditions. Zones 8–11.

Cyathea intermedia

☀ ❋ ↔ 12–24 ft (4–8 m) ↑10–30 ft (3–10 m)

Large tree fern, native of New Caledonia. Arching, feathery, finely divided fronds, up to 12 ft (4 m) long, with leaflets up to 26 in (65 cm) long and segments 4 in (10 cm) long, carried on stalks covered with pale-colored scales. Zones 8–10.

Cyathea medullaris

BLACK TREE FERN, SILVER TREE FERN

☀ ❋ ↔ 25 ft (8 m) ↑50 ft (15 m)

From Australia, New Zealand, and nearby Pacific Islands. Narrow, almost black trunk, often slightly bent by the weight of head of fronds. Fronds a beautiful fresh green, look very soft, but are quite tough. Zones 9–11.

Cyathea woollsiana

syn. *Alsophila woollsiana*

WOOLLY TREE FERN

☀ ❋ ↔ 15–25 ft (4.5–8 m) ↑15–25 ft (4.5–8 m)

Northeastern Australian cycad. Slender trunk, leaves to 8–12 ft (2.4–3.5 m) long, leaflets to 4 in (10 cm) long, sword-shaped, toothed segments, stalks covered with dark scales, densely hairy midrib. Zones 7–9.

C. intermedia, Isle of Pines, New Caledonia

CYATHODES

Found in Australia, New Zealand, and in higher altitudes of some Pacific Islands, this is a genus in the family Epacridaceae. It contains some 15 species of evergreen heath-like shrubs with small, often needle-like leaves, tiny flowers, and colorful drupes. Among the commoner plants in the mountains of New Zealand and Tasmania, they are also present in lowland areas, but stand out less among the taller vegetation. Lowland species are adaptable to cultivation, but are seldom seen in gardens. CULTIVATION: Best grown in a moist, gritty, well-drained soil with added humus, they generally prefer a cool moist climate. They may need protection from the hottest sun. Light trimming when the fruit is past its best keeps the plants compact. Propagate from seed or by taking small tip cuttings from non-flowering shoots.

Cyathodes glauca

CHEESE BERRY

☀/☀ ❋ ↔ 4 ft (1.2 m) ↑5 ft (1.5 m)

From Tasmania, Australia, this species can develop into a small tree, often regarded as a shrub. Narrow 1¼ in (30 mm) long leaves, bluish beneath. Flowers white, relatively large, quite conspicuous, in late winter–spring. Pink or white fruit. Zones 8–10.

Cyathea medullaris

Cyathea woollsiana, Queensland, Australia

Cycas revoluta

CYCAS

There are about 60 slow-growing woody-stemmed species in this genus of primitive ancient plants in the cycad (Cycadaceae) family. They resemble palms but are not related. Almost all are from tropical and sub-tropical habitats. Male and female cones are found on separate plants. Several species are garden grown. In cooler climates some of the forest dwellers have adapted to conditions in offices, houses, and greenhouses.
CULTIVATION: Full sun and good drainage is required, but cycads can tolerate periods of drought. Propagate from seed or by removing and rooting dormant buds, which can be taken from the mature plant's trunk.

Cycas armstrongii
syn. *Cycas media* var. *inermis*
☼ ✚ ↔ 6 ft (1.8 m) ↑ 15 ft (4.5 m)
From sandy open forests of northern Australia. Trunk dark gray to black, covered in ovate leaf-stem scars. Soft, feathery, glossy leaves, yellowish green, ageing to dark green. Separate male and female cones. Fruits globular, yellowish green, blue powdered. Zones 11–12.

Cycas bougainvilleana
☼ ✚ ↔ 12 ft (3.5 m) ↑ 15 ft (4.5 m)
Found in the Solomon Islands and eastern New Guinea. Broad, 12 in (30 cm) long leaflets, glossy waxy coating. Fronds up to 8 ft (2.4 m) long. *C. bougainvilleana* hybridizes naturally with other species in its native range. Zones 11–12.

Cycas circinalis ★
SAGO CYCAD, SAGO PALM
☼ ✤ ↔ 15 ft (4.5 m) ↑ 15 ft (4.5 m)
Native of southern Asia, India, and the islands of the Pacific. Forms multiple, cylindrical, gray-brown trunks, crowned with bright green glossy fronds to 10 ft (3 m) in length, hooked midrib. Produced large shiny seeds, yellow and mahogany red. Zones 10–12.

Cycas media ★
NUT PALM, ZAMIA PALM
☼ ✤ ↔ 10 ft (3 m) ↑ 15 ft (4.5 m)
Native of northern Australia. Thick trunk, dark, clearly marked with triangular leaf-stem scars. Stiff dark green fronds, bright yellowish green when young, armed with yellow spines. Male cones yellowish brown. Female cones globular. Fruits ripen orange. Zones 10–12.

Cycas revoluta ★
JAPANESE SAGO CYCAD
◑ ✤ ↔ 6 ft (1.8 m) ↑ 10 ft (3 m)
From Japan. Slow-growing, long-lived. Single, straight, cylindrical trunk, several trunks or a branching

Cycas bougainvilleana

Cycas circinalis

trunk. Narrow stiff fronds, narrow, dark, shiny leaflets. Attractive orange fruits in feathery husks. Good indoors or in sheltered courtyards. Zones 9–12.

Cycas rumphii ★
syn. *Cycas thouarsii*
☼ ✤ ↔ 10–12 ft (3–3.5 m)
↑ 20–30 ft (6–9 m)
Cycad from Indonesia, New Guinea, and the Pacific Islands. Arching, glossy, bright green leaves, to 6–8 ft (1.8–2.4 m) long, 150 to 200 narrow sickle-shaped leaflets, to 12 in (30 cm) long, paler beneath, swollen or slightly curved margins, grooved midrib. Cylindrical to oval male cones, yellow to brown. Long, narrow, hairy female cones. Zones 9–11.

Cycas taitungensis
☼ ❄ ↔ 5–10 ft (1.5–3 m)
↑ 10–15 ft (3–4.5 m)
Cycad from Taiwan with occasionally branching trunk. Light green, hairy, young leaves, semi-rounded crown of numerous, spreading, glossy, dark green leaves, 3–6 ft (0.9–1.8 m) in length, growing from spiny stalks, and 200 to 400 narrow leaflets that diminish into spines toward the base of their parent leaf. The male cones are narrow, erect, oval, and orange to brown in color; the female cones are rounded, hairy, and covered with soft spines, with a prominent spine at the top. Zones 8–10.

Cycas media

Cycas armstrongii, in the wild, Litchfield National Park, Northern Territory, Australia

CYCLAMEN

ALPINE VIOLET, PERSIAN VIOLET, SOWBREAD

Distinctive in leaf and flower, the 19 species belonging to this primrose (Primulaceae) family genus are tuberous perennials found in Europe along the shores of the Mediterranean Sea and in western Asia. They vary in size. From their flattened tubers, heart-shaped gray-green to blue-green leaves emerge, often attractively patterned silver-gray. They bear one downward-facing flower per stem, in white or pink through purple to red shades, with large reflexed petals. Dried cyclamen flowers are an ingredient in some strange herbal decoctions: the "love cake" supposedly causes anyone eating it to fall irretrievably in love.
CULTIVATION: The tubers need perfect drainage. Add a little grit and fibrous compost, and plant the tuber with its top at or just above soil level. Raised bed or rockery cultivation also helps to ensure perfect drainage. Most species prefer dappled shade. Propagate from seed, as established clumps flower better if left undivided.

Cyclamen persicum

Cyclamen persicum

Cyclamen africanum

☀ ✂ ↔ 8–12 in (20–30 cm) ↑ 6 in (15 cm)

From Algeria. Kidney- to heart-shaped leaves, with scalloped lobes and toothed edges. Dark green leaves with fine silver and pale green markings above, pale green below. Flowers pale to deep pink, 1 in (25 mm) wide, fragrant, on narrow stems, flowering in autumn. Zones 9–10.

Cyclamen balearicum

☀/☀ ❄ ↔ 6–8 in (15–20 cm) ↑ 3 in (8 cm)

From southern France and the Balearic Islands. Dark green leaves marbled with silver-gray, scalloped shallow-toothed edges, purple-red undersides. Small, fragrant, soft pink or pink-veined white flowers, wavy-edged petals, in spring. Zones 8–10.

Cyclamen cilicium

☀/☀ ❄ ↔ 6–8 in (15–20 cm) ↑ 3–4 in (8–10 cm)

Autumn-flowering species from southwestern Turkey. Forms a neat clump of rounded heart-shaped leaves

Cyclamen africanum

Cyclamen hederifolium

with toothed edges, green with silver-gray markings above, purple-red below. White to pale pink flowers, flushed deep pink. Slightly twisted petals. Zones 7–10.

Cyclamen coum

syn. *Cyclamen atkinsii*

☀/☀ ❄ ↔ 6–12 in (15–30 cm) ↑ 4 in (10 cm)

Native to southeast Europe, the Caucasus, and the Middle East. Silver-gray and dark green-patterned, rounded, heart-shaped leaves, to slightly over 2 in (5 cm) long. Purple-red undersides. Small flowers, white, pink, or purple-pink, darker at base. Blooms mainly late winter–spring. **Pewter Group:** a selection of cultivars with leaves strongly marked with silver-gray. It includes: '**Maurice Dryden**', green-edged silver leaves, white flowers; '**Tilebarn Elizabeth**', light pink flowers, silver leaves with narrow green margins. Zones 6–10.

Cyclamen hederifolium

syn. *Cyclamen neapolitanum*

☀/☀ ❄ ↔ 6–12 in (15–30 cm) ↑ 4 in (10 cm)

Late summer–early winter-flowering species found from southern Europe to Turkey, often flowering with no foliage present. Leaves small to large, 2–6 in (5–15 cm) long, smooth-edged or serrated, overall dark green or

Cyclamen coum

Cyclamen purpurascens

patterned silver-gray, green or purple-red beneath. Small light pink flowers, color deepening at center. Zones 6–9.

Cyclamen persicum

☀/☀ ✂ ↔ 6–12 in (15–30 cm) ↑ 6–8 in (15–20 cm)

Winter–spring-flowering. Native to the eastern Mediterranean, including Crete, Cyprus and other islands, and also Libya. Variably colored and marked, serrated-edged, heart-shaped leaves to over 4 in (10 cm) long. Flowers white, mauve, or pink shades, with darker center. This is the species from which the florists' cyclamen was developed. Zones 9–10.

Cyclamen purpurascens

syn. *Cyclamen europaeum*

☀/☀ ❄ ↔ 6–12 in (15–30 cm) ↑ 4–6 in (10–15 cm)

Central and eastern European species. Round leaves with smooth or finely toothed edges. Bright to deep green, with variable silver-gray markings, red-tinted below. From late summer, small strong-scented flowers in pink shades, rarely white. **Silver Leafed Group** has strongly marked foliage. Zones 6–9.

Cyclamen repandum

☀/☀ ❄ ↔ 6–12 in (15–30 cm) ↑ 4–6 in (10–15 cm)

Found around and on islands of the central and eastern Mediterranean.

Broad heart-shaped leaves, 2–5 in (5–12 cm) long, conspicuously scalloped and toothed, dark green, with variable silver-gray markings above, purple-red below. Fragrant white to magenta flowers, reddening at the center. Zones 7–10.

CYDONIA

The quince, a deciduous tree with a rounded umbrella-like crown, is a member of the rose (Rosaceae) family, and has been cultivated for thousands of years in its area of origin—northern Iran, Armenia, and Turkey. From there it was spread, first throughout the Mediterranean area and then northward through Europe. It was a symbol of love and fertility to the ancient Greeks and Romans, and some believe that it was the "forbidden fruit" in the Garden of Eden. The flowers are self-fertile, so even a single tree is capable of producing fruit.
CULTIVATION: Quinces will grow in a variety of soils. They will weather quite hard frosts but, conversely, will also fruit in subtropical conditions. They like a sunny position, protected from wind. Surplus shoots should be removed in winter. They can be propagated by cutting, but cultivated forms are normally grafted onto cutting-grown quince rootstocks.

Cydonia oblonga
QUINCE

☀ ❄ ↔ 15 ft (4.5 m) ↑ 20 ft (6 m)

Rather crooked tree, producing several shoots from the same branch. Leaves very pale green, hairy beneath. Flowers, on current season's growth, large, upright, white or pink. Fruits vary in size, round or pear-shaped; ripen bright yellow, strong aroma when fully ripe, early–mid-winter. Several selected clones: 'Champion', 'Lusitanica' (syn. 'Portugal'), and 'Smyrna' (a Turkish variety) are two of the best. Zones 6–9.

CYLINDROPUNTIA

This genus of 33 species of shrubby to tree-like opuntias comes from North

Cydonia oblonga

America and belongs to the cactus (Cactaceae) family. The genus name means cylindrical opuntia and refers to the shape of the stems, which are usually cylindrical, occasionally club-shaped. *Cylindropuntia* are a common feature in American deserts, and are usually known by their common name, cholla. *Cylindropuntia* species are distinguished from *Austrocylindropuntia*, their similar looking South American counterparts, by the fact that their spines are always enclosed in a fine papery sheath. The stems vary from being tightly attached to very easily detached, but most have very distinct tubercles on the stems. Flowers are yellow, greenish yellow, magenta, bronze, or red. Seedpods are fleshy or dry, spherical to club-shaped, green, yellow, brown, or red, with or without spines.
CULTIVATION: Cultivation is very easy in any well-drained soil, from seed or from entire seedpods that may be planted as if they were a cutting, and also from stems that have been dried out for a few days. Careful handling is recommended, as they are very irritating. A brief rest from watering in winter is beneficial.

Cylindropuntia bigelovii, in the wild, Joshua Tree National Park, California, USA

C. imbricata, in the wild, Arizona, USA

Cylindropuntia fulgida, in the wild, Superstition Mountains, Arizona, USA

Cylindropuntia acanthocarpa
BUCKTHORN CHOLLA

☀ ❄ ↔ 6–8 ft (1.8–2.4 m) ↑ 15 ft (4.5 m)

From western USA. Shrubby. Cylindrical gray-green segments to 20 in (50 cm) long. Spines dense, including large flat-bladed central spines and broad guard spines around large red flower buds that open in spring into red-tinted golden to orange-red flowers. Spiny brown-tinted fruit. Zones 8–11.

Cylindropuntia bigelovii
JUMPING CHOLLA, TEDDY-BEAR CHOLLA

☀ ❄ ↔ 24–36 in (60–90 cm) ↑ 3–5 ft (1–1.5 m)

Variable in size, this cactus from southwestern USA and northern Mexico can grow to over 8 ft (2.4 m) in height. It has spiny cylindrical stem segments; the spines add considerable color to the plant, being pinkish straw to red-brown, and held in golden yellow sheaths that sprout from prominent tubercles. Clusters of yellow-green to green flowers, sometimes striped with pale mauve, develop into spineless but warty yellow fruits. Zones 9–11.

Cylindropuntia echinocarpa

☀ ❄ ↔ 3 ft (0.9 m) ↑ 5 ft (1.5 m)

From southwest USA and northwest Mexico. Shrubby cylindrical segments to 16 in (40 cm) long, often shorter. Many yellow or silvery spines to 1¾ in (40 mm) long. Yellow-green flowers, spiny green fruit. Zones 9–11.

Cylindropuntia fulgida
SMOOTH CHAIN-FRUIT CHOLLA

☀ ❄ ↔ 6–8 ft (1.8–2.4 m) ↑ 12 ft (3.5 m)

From southwest USA and northwest Mexico. Plant is tree-like, with central "trunk" and drooping branches having cylindrical segments to 6 in (15 cm) long. Spines short and fine but very dense. Flower pink, less commonly white. Many, often seedless, green fruits. Zones 9–11.

Cylindropuntia imbricata

☀ ❄ ↔ 4–7 ft (1.2–2 m) ↑ 10 ft (3 m)

From Mexico and southwest USA. Shrubby, becoming tree-like. Stem segments somewhat flattened, around 12 in (30 cm) long, with tiny leaves and many 1¼ in (30 mm) long spines. Purplish to red or yellowish flowers are followed by spineless yellow fruits 1¼ in (30 mm) long. Zones 9–11.

Cymbalaria muralis

Cylindropuntia spinosior

Cylindropuntia tesajo

C. prolifera, in the wild, near Ensenada, Baja California, Mexico

Cylindropuntia prolifera

COASTAL CHOLLA, JUMPING CHOLLA

☼ ⟨⟩ ↔ 5–6 ft (1.5–1.8 m) ↑ 8 ft (2.4 m)

From the Mexico/California border. Tree-like, with cylindrical to slightly flattened gray-green segments to 6 in (15 cm) long. Spines dense and fine, initially yellow, ageing to red-brown, to 1¾ in (40 mm) long. Purple-red flowers, followed by many fruits, often seedless. Zones 9–11.

Cylindropuntia spinosior

CANE CHOLLA

☼/☀ ⟨⟩ ↔ 3–5 ft (0.9–1.5 m) ↑ 7 ft (2 m)

From southwest USA and northwest Mexico. Shrubby to tree-like, with densely tuberculate cylindrical segments to 12 in (30 cm) long. Pinkish ephemeral leaves, many small pale yellow to white spines. Magenta or red flowers, rarely white or yellow, spineless yellow fruits. Zones 8–11.

Cylindropuntia tesajo

☼ ⟨⟩ ↔ 20–36 in (50–100 cm)
↑ 8–32 in (20–80 cm)

From Baja California, Mexico. Low sprawling shrub with many, slender pale green to brownish green stems, each making 2 or 3 more branches. Tubercles inconspicuous, cream to gray areoles, prominent yellow to orange glochids. Spines sparse: 0 to 1 centrals, sheathed, 0 to 2 radials, not sheathed. Flowers yellow to greenish, seedpods pale brown, dry, spineless. Reddish new growth. Zones 8–10.

Cylindropuntia tunicata

PRICKLY PEAR, TUNA

☼ ⟨⟩ ↔ 4 ft (1.2 m) ↑ 2 ft (0.6 m)

Native to Mexico and southwestern USA, but naturalized in areas of South America. Forms a much-branched shrub. Whorls of blue-green stem segments, and noticeable white areoles with white-sheathed cream or yellowish spines. Yellow flowers from spring–summer, followed by blue-green spineless fruit that persists on shrub for a long time. Zones 9–11.

CYMBALARIA

A western European genus of the fox-glove (Scrophulariaceae) family, made up of 10 species of small ground cover perennials that strike roots as they spread. The leaves are small, kidney-shaped to rounded, often with shallow lobes. Little 5-petalled flowers like tiny violets appear singly in the leaf axils throughout the warmer months. The flowers tend to be mauve to pale purple with darker or yellow throat markings. The common names Coliseum ivy and Kenilworth ivy refer to their habit of growing among the cracks in old buildings such as the Coliseum and Kenilworth Castle.

CULTIVATION: These plants are very easily grown in any soil in sun or shade. They are tolerant of most soils, but capable of growing in crevices between rocks or paving stones. Best with ample moisture but drought tolerant once established, they are very tough and adaptable little plants that can be somewhat invasive, though easily controlled.

Cymbalaria muralis

syn. *Linaria cymbalaria*

COLISEUM IVY, IVY-LEAFED TOAD FLAX, KENILWORTH IVY

☼/☀ ❄ ↔ 8–20 in (20–50 cm)
↑ 2 in (5 cm)

Found from southwest and central Europe and widely naturalized elsewhere. Leaves rounded to kidney-shaped, to ½ in (12 mm) long, with 5 to 9 lobes. Flowers ½ in (12 mm) wide, lavender to purple, with a yellow throat. White-flowered cultivars common. Zones 3–10.

CYMBIDIUM

This genus in the orchid (Orchidaceae) family has 50 or so species, distributed throughout Asia and into Australia. Most of the sympodial species from the mountains are terrestrial, with upright to arching flower spikes, bearing blooms in many colors. They produce a fleshy pseudobulb with many durable, strap-like, long leaves. In the lowlands, most cymbidiums take to the trees as epiphytes, growing in high light. Many have long pendent in-florescences and thick leathery leaves. Over the past century tens of thousands of hybrids have been created, which are often loosely categorized by their flower size: miniature, under 2½ in (6 cm); intermediate, 2½–3½ in (6–9 cm); and standard, over 3½ in (9 cm). These hybrids form the basis of an important pot-plant and cut-flower industry in temperate climates. Traditionally, the main flowering season has been winter to spring, but selective breeding is continually extending this. These orchids have been cultivated for centuries in China and Japan, where they are also valued for spiritual and medicinal purposes. Variegated-leafed and unusual flower forms are also highly prized.

CULTIVATION: Most hybrid species are grown in commercially available "orchid composts," which are usually free-draining but retain some moisture. Other growers prefer fine grade pine bark, while many make up their own combinations to suit their conditions and watering frequency. *Cymbidium* species are remarkably hardy. Epiphytic species prefer a mix incorporating a high percentage of coarse bark. Keep moist year-round, and increase watering and fertilizing from spring to autumn while they are actively growing. Most cool-growing species and complex hybrids need a night-time drop in temperature of at least 18°F (10°C) during summer evenings, to help initiate flowering for the following season. This can be manipulated by giving the plants a regular light misting of water at sunset during the warmer months.

Cymbidium erythrostylum ★

☼/☀ ❄ ↔ 8–24 in (20–60 cm)
↑ 12–27 in (30–70 cm)

From Vietnam. Autumn-flowering species with up to 10, white, 2½ in (6 cm) flowers; labellum has a net-work of thick red-orange veins over a yellow and white base. Petals usually do not open fully, and tend to embrace the column and lip. Zones 8–10.

Cymbidium erythrostylum

Cymbidium suave, New Guinea

Cymbidium lowianum

Cymbidium lowianum

☼/◐ ❋ ↔ 8–36 in (20–90 cm)
↕ 12–48 in (30–120 cm)

From Thailand to China. Hardy terrestrial species, with up to 30 very
long arching spikes, 3½ in (9 cm)
long, bearing olive green flowers with
contrasting cream and red lip. *C.*
(*lowianum* × **Ormoulu**), free-flowering
olive-green hybrid. Zones 7–11.

Cymbidium suave

☼/◐ ❄ ↔ 8–32 in (20–80 cm)
↕ 12–48 in (30–120 cm)

Australian species, with grass-like
leaves and thickened stem instead of
traditional pseudobulb. Late spring-
to summer-flowering epiphyte,
tolerant of wide temperature range
but not of frost. Pendent sprays of
up to 50 apple green to pale yellow-
brown flowers, 1 in (2.5 cm) long,
very fragrant. Zones 9–11.

Cymbidium tracyanum

☼/◐ ❋ ↔ 8–36 in (20–90 cm)
↕ 12–48 in (30–120 cm)

Large cool-growing species, found from
Thailand to China. Flowers strongly

fragrant, 6 in (15 cm) long, light green,
heavily marked, and striped with red-
brown, giving blooms an overall deep
bronze appearance. Zones 7–10.

Cymbidium Hybrids

☼/◐ ❋ ↔ 8–36 in (20–90 cm)
↕ 12–48 in (30–120 cm)

Thousands of *Cymbidium* hybrids
have been registered, varying widely
in shape and color. Many have been
mericloned or tissue cultured to
increase numbers to satisfy demand.
African Adventure 'Sahara Gold', has
new "sunset" tones, some new colors
are being developed; **Bulbarrow 'Friar
Tuck'** ★, popular intermediate-style
cymbidium, gets its distinctive color
combination from *C. devonianum*;
Castle of Mey 'Pinkie', miniature
cymbidium with white flowers, up to
25 cascading blooms on each stem;

Dilly 'Del Mar', rich yellow flowers,
late blooming; **Fanfare 'Spring'**,
flowers vary from yellow green to
deep apple green; **John Woden**, large
salmon pink blooms, deep maroon

spotted labellum, on tall spikes; **Little
Big Horn 'Prairie'** ★, intermediate
hybrid, many upright inflorescences
of mainly green blooms with white
labellums with maroon spots;

Cymbidium, Hybrid, African Adventure 'Sahara Gold'

Cymbidium lowianum 'Tiger' × *C. ormoulu*

Cymbidium tracyanum

C

Cymbidium, Hybrid, Alegria 'Saint Lita'

Cymbidium, Hybrid, Alexfrida 'The Queen'

Cymbidium, Hybrid, Anita 'Pymble'

Cymbidium, Hybrid, Astronaut 'Raja'

Cymbidium, Hybrid, Colina 'Ember'

Cymbidium, Hybrid, Bulbarrow 'Friar Tuck'

Cymbidium, Hybrid, Baldoyle 'Melbury'

Cymbidium, H, Belle Park 'Orange Gleam'

Cymbidium, Hybrid, Bolton Grange

Cymbidium, Hybrid, Cape Crystal

Cymbidium, Hybrid, Castle of Mey 'Pinkie'

Cymbidium, H, Clauboda 'Sydney Rothwell'

Cymbidium, Hybrid, Cranbourne 'Chase'

Cymbidium, Hybrid, Désirée 'Elizabeth A. Logan'

Cymbidium, Hybrid, Dilly 'Del Mar'

Cymbidium, Hybrid, Esmeralda

Cymbidium, Hybrid, Finetta 'Glendessary'

C., Hybrid, Fanfare 'Spring'

C., Hybrid, Fire Wand 'Numan'

C., Hybrid, Gibson Girl 'Mephisto Waltz'

Cymbidium, Hybrid, Highland Advent

Cymbidium, H., Highland Lassie 'Jersey'

Cymbidium, Hybrid, Ice Ranch

Cymbidium, Hybrid, Jeanette 'Enid Haupt'

Cymbidium, Hybrid, Kiri te Kanawa

Cymbidium, Hybrid, John Wooden

Cymbidium, Hybrid, Kiku Ono

Cymbidium, H, Lady McAlpine 'Jersey'

Cymbidium, H, Little Big Horn 'Prairie'

Cymbidium, Hybrid, Lynette Artemis

Cymbidium, Hybrid, Mavourneen 'Jester'

Cymbidium, Hybrid, Rievaulx

Cymbidium, Hybrid, Rosarita 'Stu's Surprise'

Cymbidium, Hybrid, San Francisco

Cymbidium, H, Mini Goddess 'Apricot'

Cymbidium, Hybrid, Pontiac 'Trinity'

Cymbidium, Hybrid, Saint Aubins Bay

Cymbidium, Hybrid, Sumatra 'Astrid'

Cymbidium, H, Sylvia Miller 'Gold Cup'

Cymbidium, Hybrid, Tinsel 'Harriet'

C., Hybrid, Sunshine Falls 'Green Fantasy'

C., Hybrid, Highland Glen 'Cooksbridge'

C., Hybrid, Orchid Conference 'Green Light'

Cymbidium, Hybrid, Mini Verde 'Captain Cook'

Mavourneen 'Jester' ★, unusual standard hybrid with labellum colors transposed onto petals; **Sumatra 'Astrid'**, sprays of dark pink flowers, yellow lip with purple markings; **Sunshine Falls 'Green Fantasy'**, miniature flowered cultivar, highly fragrant and floriferous, inherited from *C. madiddum*. Zones 7–11.

CYMBOPOGON

This genus of 56 species of perennial grasses belongs to the Poaceae family. They are found in tropical Asia and Africa. The plants form into clumps, and have rather coarse leaves. Many *Cymbopogon* species have aromatic foliage. The tiny flowers are borne in airy panicles.
CULTIVATION: Grow in moisture-retentive well-drained soil in full sun. In cooler areas grow indoors in pots, maintaining moderate humidity. Propagate from seed or by division.

Cymbopogon citratus
LEMON GRASS

☼ ⚘ ↔ 1 ft (0.3 m) ↕ 3–5 ft (0.9–1.5 m)
Native to southern India and Ceylon. Clumps of green to bluish green leaves with roughened margins. The strongly lemon-scented foliage is widely used as a flavoring in southeastern Asian cooking. Zones 9–11.

CYNARA

There are 10 species of perennial herbs in this genus, which belongs to the daisy (Asteraceae) family. They are native to the Mediterranean, northwestern Africa, and the Canary Islands. The plants resemble giant thistles; they have large leaves with pointed lobes, sometimes spiny, and tall heads of thistle-like flowers. They are cultivated for their imposing presence in ornamental gardens, and also for the immature flowerheads and young stems of some species, which may be eaten as vegetables.
CULTIVATION: Grow in full sun in a well-drained soil, sheltered from strong winds. Allow plenty of space for the large heavy leaves to develop. Propagate by seed or division.

Cynodon dactylon

Cynara cardunculus
CARDOON

☼ ❄ ↔ 4–8 ft (1.2–2.4 m)
↕ 4–8 ft (1.2–2.4 m)
From Mediterranean regions. Statuesque plant with thick, pointed-lobed, grayish green leaves to 5 ft (1.5 m) long. Large, purple, thistle-like flowers stand above the foliage in summer. Grown ornamentally, young stems can be cooked as a vegetable. Zones 6–10.

Cynara scolymus
GLOBE ARTICHOKE

☼ ❄ ↔ 3–4 ft (0.9–1.2 m)
↕ 2–5 ft (0.6–1.5 m)
From northern Mediterranean regions. Similar to *C. cardunculus*, large grayish green leaves and thistle-like flowers, but a more compact plant. Popularly grown as a vegetable, with the immature flower heads being harvested and cooked. Zones 6–10.

CYNODON

A genus of 8 species of tropical and subtropical grasses in the family Poaceae, well-represented in southern Africa. They have strong stems that strike roots as they spread and can also grow upward. The stems interweave and form a dense thicket, made more impenetrable by their large flat-bladed leaves. Small clusters of flower spikes form at the stems tips, but are not showy and are unlikely to be seen when the grasses are used for lawns or routinely grazed pastures. The vigor of these grasses is both their appeal and their curse, as when they escape from cultivation they can be very invasive. An oft-quoted statistic claims that if the maximum logarithmic growth rates were sustained for a year, a patch measuring 10 feet square (3 meters square) would spread to cover 50 percent of the land surface of the world.
CULTIVATION: Most cultivated species and forms are tolerant of moderate frosts but will suffer in prolonged periods of frost. Plant in full sun to ensure dense growth, and water well in summer. Feed, aerate, and dethatch in spring. The plants are sometimes raised from seed, but more commonly planted as ready-to-lay rolls, or "plugs," of stolons.

Cynodon dactylon
BAHAMA GRASS, BERMUDA GRASS

☼/☀ ❄ ↔ unlimited ↕ 2–6 in (5–15 cm)
Widespread in warm temperate to tropical zones. Vigorous spreading grass forming dense turf. Tough stems up to 12 in (30 cm) long, broad-bladed leaves to 6 in (15 cm) long, often gray-tinted. Dense 2 in (5 cm)

Cymbopogon citratus

long flower spikes from late summer. **'U-3'**, tough, coarse-bladed cultivar, suitable only for high-traffic lawns or pasture, not for fine turf. Zones 7–12.

Cynodon × magennisii
MAGENNIS BERMUDA GRASS

☼/☀ ❄ ↔ unlimited ↕ 2–4 in (5–10 cm)
Natural *C. dactylon* × *C. transvaalensis* hybrid. Similar to *C. dactylon*, slightly less hardy, finer leaf blades, better suited as fine turf grass. **'Santa Ana'**, is popular for tough lawns and sports fields. Many fine-leafed selections have been developed for golf courses: the very fine **'Tifgreen'**, the slightly coarser and more erect **'Tifway'**; and **'Tifdwarf'**, which has dense growth and very short, fine leaves, ideal for greens. Zones 7–12.

CYNOGLOSSUM
HOUND'S TONGUE

A borage (Boraginaceae) family genus of around 55 species of annuals, biennials, and perennials, found mainly in the temperate zones. They have simple, elongated, elliptical to lance-shaped leaves, often densely covered with fine hairs, that form a basal foliage clump from which emerge upright flower stems carrying heads of small 5-petalled flowers, usually in vivid blue shades. The flowers appear mainly in summer. The common name, hound's tongue, refers to the shape and texture of the leaves.
CULTIVATION: Hardiness varies with the species, though most will tolerate quite severe short frosts, if not prolonged freezing. Perfect drainage is essential and summer moisture will improve flowering, so incorporate extra grit and humus. Deadhead the plants frequently to prolong flowering. Taller types may need to be staked or tied back. *Cynoglossum* species can be raised from seed, and the perennials will also grow from basal cuttings.

Cynara cardunculus

Cynoglossum amabile
CHINESE FORGET-ME-NOT

☼/☀ ❄ ↔ 12 in (30 cm)
↕ 20–24 in (50–60 cm)
Biennial from temperate East Asia. Oval to lance-shaped basal leaves to 8 in (20 cm) long, often finely hairy. Sprays of white, pink, or blue flowers, ¼ in (6 mm) wide. **'Firmament'**, dwarf cultivar, gray-green leaves and slightly pendulous bright blue flowers. Zones 7–10.

Cynoglossum grande

☼/☀ ❄ ↔ 12–20 in (30–50 cm)
↕ 24–32 in (60–80 cm)
Perennial native to western North America. Long-stemmed basal leaves to 6 in (15 cm) long, sparsely hairy above, densely hairy below. Showy sprays of deep blue to purple-blue flowers. Zones 8–10.

Cynoglossum nervosum
HAIRY HOUND'S TOOTH

☼/☀ ❄ ↔ 24 in (60 cm)
↕ 24–30 in (60–75 cm)
This bushy upright perennial is native to the Himalayas. The oblong green leaves have short stiff hairs; the flowers are an intense blue, like that of forget-me-nots; they appear in late spring and last for about 4 weeks. Soil must be well drained. This species is highly suitable for a woodland setting, or for a very informal garden. Zones 4–8.

C

Cyperus involucratus

Cyperus involucratus 'Variegata'

CYPERUS

Around 600 species of annual and perennial sedges make up the type genus for the family Cyperaceae. Perhaps best known as the source of our earliest form of paper, papyrus, and also the origin of the word, *Cyperus* includes other locally useful species that provide thatch and fuel, as well as graceful highly ornamental species and several invasive weeds. From a clump of grassy basal foliage, *Cyperus* sedges produce strongly upright flower stems topped with a flowerhead and leafy bracts. Often the bracts also encompass finer, sometimes filament-like leaves. It is this tiered effect and the light airy nature of the foliage and bracts that give the ornamental species their appeal. CULTIVATION: Hardiness varies widely, subtropical and tropical species often being intolerant of frost. Otherwise, cultivation is straightforward. Plant *Cyperus* species in a bright position with moist, humus-rich soil and water well in summer. Many species will grow in damp to boggy conditions, though most are equally at home in well-drained soil. Propagate from seed or by division.

Cyperus albostriatus
☼/◐ ‡ ↔ 12 in (30 cm) ↑ 24 in (60 cm)
South African species with many narrow leaves up to 20 in (50 cm)

long, with 3 conspicuous pale veins. Flower stems, with dense leafy bracts, do not extend much above the height of the foliage. Will grow in wet soil. Zones 9–12.

Cyperus involucratus
☼/◐ ‡ ↔ 24–40 in (60–100 cm) ↑ 3–7 ft (0.9–2 m)
Widespread in Africa. Short basal foliage clump and numerous 3-sided flower stems topped with many bracts to 16 in (40 cm) long, with rays to a little over 4 in (10 cm) long. Considered invasive in some areas. 'Variegatus' ★, foliage with longitudinal cream striping. Zones 9–12.

Cyperus longus
GALINGALE
☼/◐ ✽ ↔ 12–36 in (30–90 cm) ↑ 3–5 ft (0.9–1.5 m)
European and North American native with few glossy basal leaves and strong, stiffly upright, 3-angled, aromatic stems topped with drooping heads of long bracts and attractively contrasting brown flowerheads. Will grow in up to 12 in (30 cm) of water. Zones 6–9.

Cyperus papyrus
EGYPTIAN REED, PAPYRUS
☼/◐ ‡ ↔ 5–10 ft (1.5–3 m) ↑ 7–17 ft (2–5 m)
Vigorous, clump-forming, African species, with few or no basal leaves but many strong, deep green, 3-sided stems topped with long bracts containing both leafy and filamentous foliage. Will grow in water. *C. papyrus* is the "bulrush" of the Old Testament story of Moses. Zones 9–12.

CYPHOSTEMMA

Part of the grape (Vitaceae) family and related to *Cissus*, this genus includes many climbers and vines and a few shrubs among its 150 species.

Cyperus longus

Distribution is centered on southern and eastern Africa, including Madagascar, and the genus includes both evergreen and deciduous species. Many of the African species have a thickened base, swollen succulent stems, and fleshy, often compound leaves; all these features are adaptations to the drought conditions they must frequently endure. Tiny greenish flowers in flat-topped heads are followed by fleshy grape-like berries that are sometimes edible. CULTIVATION: Some species will tolerate light frosts, but most prefer a warm frost-free climate. Like most arid-country plants, they will withstand more cold if kept dry over winter, and may rot if kept cold and damp for prolonged periods. Plant in full sun in light well-drained soil. Propagate from seed.

Cyphostemma bainesii
GOUTY VINE
☼ ‡ ↔ 3 ft (0.9 m) ↑ 6 ft (1.8 m)
From Namibia and Namaqualand. Short but tree-like, with swollen stem, spherical or bottle-shaped, to 24 in (60 cm) tall, dividing at top into

heavy branches. Foliage winter-deciduous, gray-green, coarsely toothed, usually with 3 leaf segments, each to over 4 in (10 cm) long. Flowers small, often insignificant, followed by grape-sized red fruit. Zones 9–12.

Cyphostemma currorii
☼ ✚ ↔ 10–15 ft (3–4.5 m) ↑ 25 ft (8 m)
From South Africa to Angola. Tree, largest species in the genus, with yellowish stems, thickened but not to extreme degree. Free-branching, with light green leaves. Leaflets coarsely toothed and up to 6 in (15 cm) long. Yellow flowers followed by red grape-like fruit. Zones 11–12.

Cyphostemma juttae ★
TREE GRAPE
☼ ‡ ↔ 6 ft (1.8 m) ↑ 6 ft (1.8 m)
From the Namaqualand area of Namibia. Deciduous shrub. Thickened succulent stem. Leaves toothed, 3-part, glossy green, oval leaflet, downy undersides. Stems covered with peeling yellowish bark. Small yellow-green flowers in summer. Grape-like yellow to red-brown berries. Zones 9–11.

Cyphostemma currorii

Cyphostemma juttae

CYPRIPEDIUM

LADY'S SLIPPER

This deciduous genus in the orchid (Orchidaceae) family consists of about 50 sympodial species found in North and Central America, Europe, and Asia. One of the rarest of terrestrial genera, they are protected, and should not be removed from the wild under any circumstances.
CULTIVATION: In cool to temperate climates, these herbaceous perennials can be grown in pots or in the garden, in soils rich in decayed leaf matter. They will not grow in subtropical or tropical climates.

Cypripedium formosanum

☀ ❄ ↔ 4–12 in (10–30 cm)
↑ 4–10 in (10–25 cm)

From Taiwan. Mountainous species, dislikes warm temperatures. Easy to grow in cool climates. Pair of attractive, fan-like, wavy leaves, and single pale pink flower up to 3 in (8 cm) across with darker markings and large inflated lip. Zones 6–9.

CYRILLA

This genus, comprising a single variable species from southeastern USA to northern South America, belongs to

Cyrtanthus falcatus

Cyrilla racemiflora

the family Cyrillaceae, of which the only other genus is *Cliftonia,* from southeastern USA. It is a shrub or small tree, the leaves simple, entire, spirally arranged but tending to be grouped at end of each season's growth. Flowers are in racemes arising from leaf axils and have 5 sepals, 5 petals, and 5 stamens. The fruit is a small capsule with 1 seed in each of its 2 compartments.
CULTIVATION: Grows best in full sun, in rich, moist, slightly acid or neutral soil. Propagate from freshly obtained seed, from softwood or root cuttings in spring, or from half-hardened cuttings in summer.

Cyrilla racemiflora

BLACK TITI, LEATHERWOOD

☼/☀ ❄ ↔ 3–8 ft (1–2.4 m)
↑ 3–30 ft (1–9 m)

Variable shrub or small tree, ranging from Virginia in eastern USA south to the West Indies and eastern South America. Northern forms are deciduous, southern are evergreen. Leaves to 4 in (10 cm) long, leathery, turning orange-crimson. Flowers tiny, white, in whorled racemes to 6 in (15 cm) long, from previous year's wood, in summer. Zones 5–11.

CYRTANTHUS

FIRE LILY

There are 47 evergreen or deciduous bulbous plants in this genus in the amaryllis (Amaryllidaceae) family. They are found in tropical and southern Africa, where they grow in a range of habitats, from damp and bushy to near desert conditions. Leaves form at the base of a loose rosette and are linear or strap-shaped. The flowers, upright or pendulous, are usually borne in umbels on strong stems. They are funnel-shaped with flaring lobes. Some are fragrant. Colors range from red and yellow to white.
CULTIVATION: In warm areas can be grown in a sheltered situation with

Cyrtanthus elatus

Cypripedium formosanum

dappled shade, in well-drained sandy soil, but are best suited to pot culture. In cool areas grow under glass in indirect bright light. Water thoroughly and feed weekly when in growth. Propagate from seed or offsets.

Cyrtanthus brachyscyphus

DOBO LILY

☀ ☽ ↔ 12–18 in (30–45 cm)
↑ 12–18 in (30–45 cm)

Evergreen species from South Africa. Narrow linear leaves. The bright reddish orange tubular flowers are narrow and pendulous, in clusters of 6 to 8. Zones 10–11.

Cyrtanthus elatus ★

syns *Cyrtanthus purpureus, Vallota speciosa*
GEORGE LILY, SCARBOROUGH LILY

☀ ☽ ↔ 12 in (30 cm) ↑ 18 in (45 cm)

An evergreen species from South Africa. Tall flower stems bear heads of 6 to 9 upright trumpet-shaped flowers of brilliant red. A popular cut flower. Zones 10–11.

Cyrtanthus falcatus

☀ ☽ ↔ 12 in (30 cm) ↑ 12 in (30 cm)

From KwaZulu-Natal. Deciduous species, leaves appearing after the flowers in spring. The flowers are pendulous, pinkish red and yellow, blooming in clusters of 6 to 10. Zones 10–11.

Cyrtanthus mackenii

IFAFA LILY

☀ ☽ ↔ 12 in (30 cm) ↑ 12 in (30 cm)

From eastern Cape Province. A dainty plant with grass-like foliage, bearing fragrant, tubular, white or yellow flowers, narrow and curving, to 2 in (5 cm) long. *C. mackenii* blooms for long periods in spring–summer. Zones 10–11.

CYRTOMIUM

This small genus of 15 to 20 fast-growing terrestrial or rock-inhabiting evergreen ferns from Hawaii, East Asia to South Africa, and Central to South America, is part of the shield-fern (Dryopteridaceae) family. The plants produce erect densely scaly rhizomes. Broad, firm, pointed, pinnate fronds, with pointed mostly sickle-shaped leaflets with smooth or irregular margins, appear on short tufted stalks. The genus name comes from the Greek *kyrtoma,* meaning arch, and refers to veins that form arch-like patterns in some species.

CULTIVATION: These ferns are easily grown in light sandy soil or mix that is kept moist to dry. Give them abundant water in summer, less in winter. They tolerate drier air than most ferns. They grow best in medium to high light, but keep them out of direct sunlight in summer. They propagate easily from spores in sandy peat in high humidity.

Cyrtostachys renda

Cyrtomium falcatum

HOLLY FERN

☀/◐ ❄ ↔ 24–36 in (60–90 cm)
↕ 24–36 in (60–90 cm)

Medium-sized fern with erect rhizomes from India to East Asia, naturalized elsewhere in the Northern Hemisphere. Stems to 16 in (40 cm) long, very dark green and glossy pinnate fronds, 8–24 in (20–60 cm) long, usually with 3 to 11 pairs of short-stalked, oval, thick, leathery leaflets, covered with reddish brown scales when young. '**Butterfieldii**' (Butterfield holly fern), margins coarsely serrated; '**Cristatum**' (syn. 'Mayi'), crested frond tips; '**Rochfordianum**' (Rockford holly fern), segment margins deeply etched, like those of a holly leaf. Zones 6–9.

Cyrtomium fortunei

☀ ❄ ↔ 12–24 in (30–60 cm)
↕ 12–24 in (30–60 cm)

Medium-sized highly variable fern from southern and eastern China to

Cyrtomium falcatum

Japan and Korea, with erect rhizomes. Stalks to 12 in (30 cm) long. Broadly sword-shaped fronds with 10 to 26 pairs of narrow pale green to gray-green leaflets with serrated margins, and covered with hair-like scales when young. Zones 5–7.

CYRTOSTACHYS

These 8 to 9 feathery leaved clump-forming palms from New Guinea, the Solomon Islands, Sumatra, Malaysia, and Borneo, are members of the palm (Arecaceae) family. They produce smooth, erect, ringed, often colorful stems with a vase-shaped crown of pinnate leaves on grooved stalks. The rigid leaflets are regularly spaced along a scaly midrib.

CULTIVATION: *Cyrtostachus* species are suited to container growth and light shade in the garden. They need regular watering. Most species are sensitive to cold. Propagate from freshly collected seed (which germinates in 2 weeks to 3 months, depending on species) or by division.

Cyrtostachys renda ★

syn. *Cyrtostachys lakka*

LIPSTICK PALM, MAHARAJAH PALM, SEALING-WAX PALM

☀ ✿ ↔ 7–10 ft (2–3 m)
↕ 15–30 ft (4.5–9 m)

Palm from the Malay Peninsula, Borneo, and Sumatra. The plant forms thick clumps. Slender ringed stems, to 30 ft (9 m) long, and up to 10 stiff dark green leaves, to 3–5 ft (0.9–1.5 m) long, with 50 to 100 leaflets, grayish blue underneath. Brilliant, glossy, scarlet crownshafts and leaf stems. Green male and female flowers on same inflorescence. Oval black fruit contains oval seeds. '**Duvivierana**', bright red crownshaft and stems; '**Orange Crownshaft**', orange crownshafts and crowns of feathery leaves. Zones 11–12.

CYSTOPTERIS

Commonly known as bladder or brittle fern, this member of the shield-fern (Dryopteridaceae) family contains 18 species of delicate deciduous ferns, occurring mostly in the northern temperate zone in rocky situations. Its scientific name comes from the Greek *kustis* (cystis), meaning bladder, and *pteris,* meaning fern; the bladder reference is to the inflated indusium (transparent membrane covering the spores). It is difficult to distinguish between the different species.

CULTIVATION: Grow in shaded moist conditions, such as shady rock gardens or rocky banks. A neutral to slightly alkaline soil is preferred. Propagate from spores or bulblets, or vegetatively by rhizome division. No serious diseases or insect problems.

Cystopteris bulbifera

BERRY BLADDER FERN

☀ ❄ ↔ 24 in (60 cm)
↕ 12–24 in (30–60 cm)

From Newfoundland, Canada, to Georgia, USA. Perennial fern distinguished by hairy lacy fronds, wider at the base than the tip. Reproduces by dropping small bulblets that form on the edges and undersides of the arching fronds. Found in the wild in rocky habitats, often on moist shady rock faces. Zones 3–9.

CYTISUS

BROOM

This genus of about 50 species from the pea-flower subfamily of the legume (Fabaceae) family consists of mainly evergreen shrubs. They are native to Europe, with a few in western Asia and North Africa, and vary from small prostrate shrubs to small trees. All the *Cytisus* species have typical pea-flowers; the main flowering season is late spring or summer. The plant's broom-like twiggy growths are sometimes almost leafless. The fruit is a flattened legume with small hard-coated seeds. These species are highly valued ornamentally for their extreme hardiness and their showy flowers.

CULTIVATION: Brooms need a free-draining soil, slightly acidic, fairly low in fertility. A sunny position gives the best display of flowers. Spent flowers and shoots should be removed after flowering, plus some of the older shoots, to encourage new growth from the base. The typical arching habit of the plant should be maintained. Most *Cytisus* species can be propagated from short-tip cuttings of ripened current year's growth, taken in late autumn or early winter.

Cytisus ardoinoi

※ ❋ ↔ 10–24 in (25–60 cm)
↑ 10–24 in (25–60 cm)

Native of the maritime Alps in southern France. Low, mat-forming, alpine shrub, arching stems, leaves decidu-

Cytisus × *praecox* 'Warminster'

Cytisus × *praecox*

Cytisus supranubius

ous, trifoliate. Bright yellow flowers are produced in leaf axils in spring–summer. Zones 6–9.

Cytisus × beanii

※ ❋ ↔ 30 in (75 cm) ↑ 12 in (30 cm)

A hybrid of garden origin between *C. ardoinoi* and *C. purgans*. Dwarf deciduous shrub. Leaves trifoliate, small, hairy. Arching sprays of golden yellow flowers in spring. Zones 6–9.

Cytisus decumbens

PROSTRATE BROOM

※ ❋ ↔ 30 in (75 cm) ↑ 6 in (15 cm)

Native to southern Europe. Gray-green hairy oval leaves. Covering of bright yellow flowers in mid-spring to early summer. Can also be used in rock gardens. Zones 5–9.

Cytisus × kewensis

※ ❋ ↔ 5 ft (1.5 m) ↑ 18 in (45 cm)

Hybrid between *C. ardoinoi* and *C. multiflorus*. Semi-prostrate habit, trailing stems. Masses of creamy yellow flowers in early summer. Zones 6–9.

Cytisus scoparius, in spring

Cytisus scoparius, in summer

Cytisus multiflorus

syn. *Cytisus albus*

PORTUGUESE BROOM, WHITE SPANISH BROOM

※ ❋ ↔ 8 ft (2.4 m) ↑ 10 ft (3 m)

Erect shrub, native to Spain, Portugal, and parts of North Africa. Leaves simple, narrow in the upper part of the plant, becoming trifoliate lower down. Clusters of white flowers appear along the stems in early to mid-summer. Zones 6–10.

Cytisus × praecox

※ ❋ ↔ 5 ft (1.5 m) ↑ 4 ft (1.2 m)

Group of hybrids between *C. multiflorus* and *C. purgans*. Compact habit, profusion of flowers. 'Albus', white flowers; 'Warminster', grows to about 5 ft (1.5 m) tall, deciduous, stems arching outward, flowers usually held in long sprays on the outer stems, heavily perfumed. Zones 6–9.

Cytisus scoparius

COMMON BROOM, SCOTCH BROOM

※ ❋ ↔ 7 ft (2 m) ↑ 7 ft (2 m)

Widely grown medium-sized shrub. Almost leafless, bears golden yellow flowers, mostly solitary, in the upper leaf axils in early summer. There are brownish streaks on the standards, keels yellow, anthers orange-red. 'Cornish Cream', creamy white flowers. Zones 5–9.

Cytisus × *kewensis*

Cytisus supranubius

TENERIFE BROOM

※ ❋ ↔ 10 ft (3 m) ↑ 10 ft (3 m)

Medium-sized shrub, native to the Canary Islands. Small trifoliate leaves on blue-gray branches. Fragrant flowers in leaf axils, white tinged with rose, in spring. Zones 7–10.

Cytisus Hybrid Varieties

※ ❋ ↔ 3–6 ft (0.9–1.8 m)
↑ 3–8 ft (0.9–2.4 m)

Usually originating from *C.* × *praecox* or *C. scoparius*. Many sizes and flower colors. 'Boskoop Ruby', small rounded shrub, abundant red flowers; 'Burkwoodii' ★, vigorous bushy shrub, pink flowers, crimson wings yellow-edged; 'Firefly', yellow standards, wings stained bronze; 'Fulgens', late flowering, dense compact habit, orange-yellow flowers, deep crimson wings; 'Hollandia', cream flowers, backs of standards and wings pink, late spring–mid-summer; 'Lena', compact free-flowering shrub, red standards, red wings yellow-edged, pale yellow keels; 'Luna', creamy yellow red-tinted flowers, wings yellow, keels lemon yellow; 'Minstead', derived from *C. multiflorus*, mauve-tinged white flowers, wings flushed deeper mauve; 'Porlock', semi-evergreen shrub, racemes of fragrant creamy yellow flowers in spring. Zones 5–9.

D

D

Dacrycarpus dacrydioides, Whirinaki Forest Park, New Zealand

Daboecia cantabrica 'Purpurea'

Daboecia cantabrica 'Creeping White'

Daboecia cantabrica

DABOECIA

There is only 1 species of evergreen, low-growing, spreading shrub in this genus within the heath (Ericaceae) family. Native to western Europe and the Azores, its habitat covers heathland from coastal cliffs to mountains. The roughly egg-shaped leaves are green on the upper surfaces and silver on the undersides. The small urn-shaped flowers are carried in racemes clear of the foliage.

CULTIVATION: If grown indoors, feed and water freely during the growing season; these plants need good light but under glass, in direct sun, young growth can be scorched. Outside they grow well in full sun in lime-free or neutral soil; some cultivars tolerate part-shade. Cut back after flowering. Propagate by sowing seed in spring or take half-hardened cuttings, especially of cultivars, in summer.

Daboecia cantabrica
syn. *Daboecia polifolia*
ST DABEOC'S HEATH

☀ ❄ ↔ 26 in (65 cm) ↑ 15 in (38 cm)
Native to western Europe. Variable habit, erect to very prostrate and straggling. Narrowly elliptic leaves, dark green, shiny. Flowers, pale to pinkish violet in mid-summer–mid-autumn. *D. c.* subsp. *azorica* (syn. *D. azorica*), from the Azores, flowers pale to deep ruby-red, not tolerant of frost. *D. c.* subsp. *scotica*, compact shrub, flowers white to pink and crimson; 'Jack Drake', rich red flowers; 'Silverwells', white flowers, light green foliage; 'William Buchanan' ★, very floriferous with purple-red flowers. *D. c.* 'Alba', white flowers; 'Atropurpurea', deep red-purple flowers; 'Bicolor', mid-green leaves, dark red, pink, and white flowers, sometimes striped, on the same plant or the same raceme; 'Creeping White' has low-growing spreading habit and white flowers; 'Praegerae', mid-green leaves, pinkish red flowers; 'Purpurea', bright purple-pink flowers; 'Snowdrift', white flowers; 'Waley's Red' (syn. 'Whally'), deep magenta flowers. Zones 6–9.

DACRYCARPUS

Found across tropical and temperate Southeast Asia, the Pacific Islands, and New Zealand, this genus of 9 conical evergreen conifers belongs to the plum-pine (Podocarpaceae) family. The trees bear small cones which contain black nut-like seeds. These cones swell into a fleshy berry-like receptacle, providing autumn food for birds. The trees are grown for both their ornamental and timber value.

CULTIVATION: Frost resistant but drought tender, *Dacrycarpus* normally grow well in wet and swampy conditions in deep rich soil. They also tolerate drier conditions, when in a sunny protected position. Propagation is from seed or from cuttings, which are quite easy to strike.

Dacrycarpus dacrydioides
KAHIKATEA, NEW ZEALAND DACRYBERRY, NEW ZEALAND WHITE PINE

☀ ❋ ↔ 20–25 ft (6–8 m) ↑ 200 ft (60 m)
From New Zealand. A large, slow-growing, evergreen tree that reaches 12 ft (3.5 m) in 10 years. It has an elegant, narrow, conical shape. with grayish brown bark, drooping branches. Narrow, bronze-green juvenile leaves, replaced with tiny, shorter, and darker green mature leaves. May develop buttressed trunk with age. Zones 9–11.

DACRYDIUM

Native to subtropical Southeast Asia, the western Pacific, and New Zealand, where most species live still, this genus within the plum-pine (Podocarpaceae) family contains 30 evergreen conifers with scale-like leaves ranges from compact shrubs to substantial trees. The fruit are acorn-like nuts containing 1 to 3 seeds. Valued for their timber as well as their ornamental use.

CULTIVATION: They like cool, moist, deep, rich peaty soils with plenty of moisture, in a protected sunny position. Once planted, they resent root disturbance caused by transplanting. Propagation is from cuttings or from seed sown in autumn.

Dacrydium araucarioides
☀/❂ ❋ ↔ 5–10 ft (1.5–3 m)
↑ 10–20 ft (3–6 m)
Endemic to New Caledonia, growing in poor soils on serpentine rocks in the southern part of the island. Small slow-growing tree, and usually rather crooked; adult leaves are closely overlapping, flattened, incurved, and give branchlets a rat-tail form. Zones 9–11.

Dacrydium beccarii
☀ ❋ ↔ 4 ft (1.2 m) ↑ 12 ft (3.5 m)
From Southeast Asia and the Pacific Islands. Evergreen shrub or can develop into a tree. The branches turn upward, forming dense umbrella-shaped crown. Crowded leaf shoots, juvenile leaves very fine, adult leaves spreading. Cones occur on the ends and along branches. Zones 10–11.

Dacrydium beccarii

Dacrydium araucarioides, in the wild, Chute de la Madeleine, New Caledonia

Dahlia, Hybrid Cultivar, 5. Decorative, 'Arabian Night'

Dahlia, Hybrid Cultivar, 5. Decorative, 'Babylon Paas Violet'

Dahlia, Hybrid Cultivar, 5. Decorative, 'Café au Lait'

Dahlia, Hybrid Cultivar, 5. Decorative, 'Cottbuser Postkutscher'

Dahlia, Hybrid Cultivar, 5. Decorative, 'David Howard'

Dahlia, Hybrid Cultivar, 4. Waterlily, 'Gay Princess'

Dahlia, Hybrid Cultivar, 4. Waterlily, 'Vanessa'

'**Yellow Hammer**', bedding form with yellow flowers and nicely contrasting bronze-green foliage.

2. ANEMONE-FLOWERED

Flowerheads have 1 or 2 rows of outer ray florets, sometimes slightly incurved, with densely packed, similarly colored, tubular disc florets that often give the flowerhead a mounded center. '**Brio**', orange scarlet with large group of disc florets, short reflexed rays; and '**Miss Saigon**', dull orange to pink disc florets, reflexed pale pink rays.

3. COLLARETTE

Collarette flowers have 1 or 2 outer rows of flat ray florets, an inner row of

Dahlia, Hybrid Cultivar, 2. Anemone-flowered, 'Brio'

D., HC, 2. Anemone-flowered, 'Miss Saigon'

short ray-like disc florets called the "collar," and a clear center or anther-bearing disc florets. '**Clair de Lune**', yellow with a pale collar, is typical of the form.

4. WATERLILY

Fully double flowers with relatively few broad ray florets. They may be flat to slightly involute or revolute. (Involute florets are rolled along their length from underside to upperside; revolute florets are rolled the opposite way: upperside to underside.) This produces rather flat blooms lacking the high center that is characteristic of most double dahlias. Popular waterlily cultivars include: '**Fascination**', deep pink, semi-double flowers, dark foliage; '**Fürst Pückler**', deep pinkish red, yellow flushed; '**Gay Princess**', bright pink with yellow center, fringed petal tips; '**Glorie van Heemstede**', bright yellow double flowers; '**Nepos**', white and lavender; and '**Vanessa**', pale to deeper pink.

5. DECORATIVE

Double style, with no central disc, and broad, flat or slightly involute florets making a rounded head. In some classifications this group is subdivided into formal (very even petals that are neatly arranged) and informal (more open and less regular). The flowers are classified as giant, large, medium, small, or miniature depending upon their size. Giant flowers do not, however, necessarily mean giant plants: some of the largest flowers are borne on relatively small plants. Some examples include: '**Akita**', dark red flushed with yellow; '**Arabian Night**', a deep black-red

Dahlia, Hybrid Cultivar, 4. Waterlily, 'Fürst Pückler'

turning red, and lightening with age; '**Audacity**', an unusual combination of maroon with a light golden yellow center; '**Clarion**', bright yellow flowers, with very dark, black-red foliage; '**Doris Duke**', an apricot-pink shade deepening at the center; '**Fiaker**', light purple; '**Formby Perfection**', with magenta to lavender flowers; '**Hamari Gold**', giant flowers of deep golden amber; '**Hamilton Lillian**', yellow- to apricot-pink; '**Hulin's Carnival**', red, splashed white; '**Jennie**', white to cream with a yellow center, flushed and edged with deep pink, fringed

edges; '**Kelvin Floodlight**', enormous bright yellow, fully double flowers; '**My Valentine**', soft light red; '**Pearl of Heenstede**', pale pink, double flowers on thin stems; '**Peter**', deep rose pink; '**Purple Joy**', deep purple-red, darkening at the center; '**Santa Claus**', fire engine red, edged in white; '**Stefan Bergerhof**', bright orange; '**Suffolk Punch**', deep purple; '**Tartan**', white with deep purple markings; '**Ted's Choice**', a deep purple-pink; '**Zingaro**', cream with a yellow center, edged and flushed deep red-pink; and '**Zorro**', huge deep red flowers.

Dahlia, Hybrid Cultivar,
5. Decorative, 'Doris Duke'

Dahlia, Hybrid Cultivar,
5. Decorative, 'Erntedank'

Dahlia, Hybrid Cultivar,
5. Decorative, 'Fiaker'

Dahlia, Hybrid Cultivar, 5. Decorative, 'Englehardt's Matador'

Dahlia, Hybrid Cultivar,
5. Decorative, 'Fire Mountain'

Dahlia, Hybrid Cultivar,
5. Decorative, 'Gitta'

Dahlia, Hybrid Cultivar,
5. Decorative, 'Hamilton Lillian'

Dahlia, Hybrid Cultivar,
5. Decorative, 'Kelvin Floodlight'

Dahlia, Hybrid Cultivar,
5. Decorative, 'Kunterbunt'

Dahlia, Hybrid Cultivar,
5. Decorative, 'Lachsperle'

Dahlia, Hybrid Cultivar,
5. Decorative, 'Mainaugold'

Dahlia, Hybrid Cultivar,
5. Decorative, 'Mexiko'

Dahlia, Hybrid Cultivar,
5. Decorative, 'My Valentine'

Dahlia, Hybrid Cultivar,
5. Decorative, 'Olympia's Jubilee'

Dahlia, Hybrid Cultivar,
5. Decorative, 'Peter'

Dahlia, Hybrid Cultivar,
5. Decorative, 'Purple Joy'

Dahlia, Hybrid Cultivar,
5. Decorative, 'Red Cap'

Dahlia, Hybrid Cultivar,
5. Decorative, 'Schwarze Barbara'

Dahlia, Hybrid Cultivar,
5. Decorative, 'Stefan Bergerhof'

Dahlia, Hybrid Cultivar,
5. Decorative, 'Suffolk Punch'

Dahlia, Hybrid Cultivar,
5. Decorative, 'Sunny Yellow'

Dahlia, Hybrid Cultivar,
5. Decorative, 'Tartan'

D., HC, 5. D, 'Ted's Choice'

D., HC, 5. Decorative, 'Tout à Toi'

D., HC, 5. D, 'Vera Lischke'

D., HC, 5. D, 'Vogtland Echo'

D., HC, 5. Decorative, 'Zingaro'

Dahlia, Hybrid Cultivar, 6. Ball, 'Charles Dickens'

Dahlia, HC, 6. Ball, 'Black Pearl'

Dahlia, HC, 6. Ball, 'Boy Scout'

6. BALL

Ball-shaped flowers are globular but may be slightly flattened on top. The ray florets are broad, rounded at the tips and involute for half their length. They are divided by flower size into miniature, up to 4 in (10 cm) in diameter; small, 4–6 in (10–15 cm) in diameter; medium, 6–8 in (15–20 cm) in diameter; and large, over 8 in (20 cm) across. Popular ball cultivars include: '**Black Pearl**', deep maroon, almost black at center; '**Boy Scout**', deep pink with a darker center; '**Charles Dickens**', small pink flowers;

'**Kathryn's Cupid**', soft orange-pink double flowers; and '**Wootton Cupid**', with dark pink flowers.

7. POMPON

Flowerheads nearly spherical. Similar to the ball style but with smaller flowers that give the impression of more tightly packed florets. Florets are involute for their entire length. Typical pompon cultivars include: '**Aurwen's Violet**', bright purple; '**Bistro**', pink petals marked with yellow at the bases; '**Linos** ', bright yellow almost orange center; '**Lollipop**', pinkish to mauve,

outer ray florets ageing to pale pink; '**Mini Pompon Orange**', orange, turning reddish in center; '**Night Queen**', deepest black-red; and '**White Aster**', evenly shaped, white flowers.

8. CACTUS

Fully double flowers with long quilled ray florets and no central disc. The quilling extends for at least half the length of the floret. Both cactus and semi-cactus forms are further subdivided into large- and small-flowered types and are available in a wide range of colors. Some pop-

ular cultivars include: '**Alfred Grille**', yellow-centered turning deep pink to light red at the tips; '**Border Princess**', with small orange and yellow flowers; '**Feuerwerk**', a bright red with very narrow ray florets like a starburst firework; '**Friquolett**', fiery red with white tips; '**Hillcrest Royal**', intense deep purple-red fully double flowers, strong quilted effect; '**Park Princess**', bright pink with a yellow center, super reliable and often mass planted for effect; and '**Wagschal's Goldkrone**', golden yellow to light orange blooms.

Dahlia, HC, 7. Pompon, 'Night Queen'

Dahlia, HC, 7. Pompon, 'White Aster'

Dahlia, HC, 7. Pompon, 'Bistro'

Dahlia, HC, 7. Pompon, 'Aurwen's Violet'

Dahlia, HC, 7. Pompon, 'Lollipop'

Dahlia, Hybrid Cultivar, 7. Pompon, 'Mini Pompon Orange'

Dahlia, HC, 7. Pompon, 'Linos'

D

Dahlia, Hybrid Cultivar,
8. Cactus, 'Alfred Grille'

Dahlia, Hybrid Cultivar,
8. Cactus, 'Border Princess'

Dahlia, Hybrid Cultivar,
8. Cactus, 'Feuerwerk'

Dahlia, Hybrid Cultivar,
8. Cactus, 'Friedrich Wagschal'

Dahlia, Hybrid Cultivar,
8. Cactus, 'Friquolett'

Dahlia, Hybrid Cultivar, 8. Cactus, 'Lilac Taratahi'

Dahlia, Hybrid Cultivar, 8. Cactus, 'Palmengarten'

Dahlia, Hybrid Cultivar, 8. Cactus,
fringed white cultivar

Dahlia, Hybrid Cultivar, 8. Cactus,
'Henriette'

Dahlia, Hybrid Cultivar, 8. Cactus,
'Isle Werner'

Dahlia, Hybrid Cultivar, 8. Cactus,
'Kleopatra'

Dahlia, Hybrid Cultivar, 8. Cactus,
'Orange Marmalade'

Dahlia, Hybrid Cultivar, 8. Cactus,
yellow cultivar

D., HC, 8. Cactus, 'Park Princess'

D., HC, 8. Cactus, 'Primaner'

D., HC, 8., 'Wagschal's Goldkrone'

D., HC, 8. Cactus, white cultivar

D., HC, 8. Cactus, yellow cultivar

9. SEMI-CACTUS

Not semi-double-flowered cactus forms, but fully double flowers with broad-based ray florets that are quilled for less than half their length. They may be straight or incurving. Popular cultivars include: **'Aspen'**, white, somewhat twisted ray florets, yellowing toward the center; **'Color Magic'**, creamy yellow with irregular sectors, flakes and flecks of deep pink; **'Elga'**, deep mauve with long ray florets; **'Engelhardt's Jubiläum'**, deep golden yellow to light orange; **'Explosion'**, white to cream blooms with purple-red markings and center; **'Fürsten Elizabeth von Bismarck'**, cerise flower-heads; **'Golden Charmer'**, a golden yellow to pale orange; **'Goldener Reiner'**, golden yellow to light orange; **'Hamari Accord'**, a soft but bright yellow; **'Herzdame'**, orange, reddening at the tips, edges and center; **'Magic Moment'**, white, very full flower-heads; **'My Love'**, white blooms with a hint of yellow at the center; **'Royal Wedding'**, orange and yellow; **'So Dainty'**, broad apricot-pink ray florets, with dark edges; **'Vulcan'**, orange-red with lighter tips; **'Wittemann's Best'**, bright red; and **'Wootton Impact'**, which bears flowers that are classic bronze in color.

Dahlia, Hybrid Cultivar, 9. Semi-cactus, 'Aspen'

Dahlia, HC, 9. Semi-cactus, 'Bloemswart'

Dahlia, HC, 9. Semi-cactus, 'Elga'

D., HC, 9. Semi-cactus, 'Engelhardt's Idol'

D., HC, 9. Semi-cactus, 'Engelhardt's Jubiläum'

Dahlia, Hybrid Cultivar, 9. Semi-cactus, 'Explosion'

Dahlia, Hybrid Cultivar, 9. Semi-cactus, 'Gartenfreude'

Dahlia, Hybrid Cultivar, 9. Semi-cactus, 'Golden Charmer'

Dahlia, Hybrid Cultivar, 9. Semi-cactus, 'Goldener Reiner'

Dahlia, Hybrid Cultivar, 9. Semi-cactus, 'Grand Prince'

Dahlia, Hybrid Cultivar, 9. Semi-cactus, 'Heraldine'

Dahlia, Hybrid Cultivar, 9. Semi-cactus, 'Herzdame'

Dahlia, Hybrid Cultivar, 9. Semi-cactus, 'Hibernia'

Dahlia, Hybrid Cultivar, 9. Semi-cactus, 'Katzeldorf'

Dahlia, Hybrid Cultivar, 9. Semi-cactus, 'Magic Moment'

Dahlia, Hybrid Cultivar, 9. Semi-cactus, 'My Love'

Dahlia, Hybrid Cultivar, 9. Semi-cactus, 'Phobos'

Dahlia, Hybrid Cultivar, 9. Semi-cactus, 'Pink Charm'

Dahlia, Hybrid Cultivar, 9. Semi-cactus, 'Piquante'

Dahlia, Hybrid Cultivar, 9. Semi-cactus, 'Pop Stretton'

D., HC, 9. Semi-cactus, 'Red Pygmy'

D., HC, 9. S-c, 'Royal Wedding'

Dahlia, HC, 9. S-c, 'Vulcan'

D., HC, 9. S-c, 'Weston Pinkie'

D., HC, 9. S-c, 'Wittemann's Best'

Dalbergia oliveri

Dahlia, Hybrid Cultivar, 10. Miscellaneous, 'Orange Sun'

Dais cotinifolia

10. MISCELLANEOUS

This is a catch-all group for the left-overs that do not really fit in the other groups, subdivided into several small groups that have too few cultivars to justify a special group of their own. This group includes the very dwarf miniature cultivars. '**Bishop of Llandaff**' is typical, with vivid red *Cosmos*-like flowers and deep red-tinted foliage; '**Gallery Series**' is a continuous flowering dwarf, many colors; '**Jescot Julie**', burnt orange, plum purple, orchid-flowering, miniature; '**Marie Schrugg**', dark red and miniature; '**Nargold**', fimbriated, red, orange, and gold; '**Orange Sun**' has bright orange flowers, flushed with red.

DAIS

This genus consists of 2 species of ever-green or semi-deciduous shrubs or small trees belonging to the daphne (Thymelaeaceae) family. They are from South Africa and Madagascar where they grow in the moist frost-free margins of wooded regions. One species is widely grown in warmer climate gardens as an evergreen; known as the pompon tree for its showy clusters of small pink flowers.
CULTIVATION: Mature plants can withstand light frost, but are best planted in a sunny position with some protection from surrounding shrubs. They thrive in well-drained fertile loam covered with an organic mulch to retain moisture during summer months. Propagate from seed in spring or from half-hardened cuttings.

Dais cotinifolia ★
POMPON TREE
☼ ⚘ ↔ 10 ft (3 m) ↑ 10 ft (3 m)
From South Africa and Madagascar. Compact, rounded, evergreen shrub. Deciduous in cooler situations. Reddish bark, slightly scented pink flowers on tips of branches in summer. Blue-green foliage. Zones 9–11.

DALBERGIA

Tropical genus of 100 species in the pea-flower subfamily of the legume (Fabaceae) family, occurring in forests from Africa through India, southern China, and Central and South America. Apart from trees, genus includes shrubs and woody climbing vines. Leaves alternate and compound. Small pea-flowers borne in terminal or axillary panicles. Fruits are thin flat pods that do not split open to release seeds as in most legumes. Timber of many species has yielded valuable cabinet woods.
CULTIVATION: The genus is not known in cultivation, but, like most of the legumes, it could probably be propagated from seed that has been given some pre-treatment before sowing. The following species could be grown in a range of soils and climates provided shelter from frost is given in their early stages of growth, and adequate water during dry hot periods.

Dalbergia oliveri
TAMALAN
☼ ✷ ↔ 30 ft (9 m) ↑ 50 ft (15 m)
Evergreen tree native to Thailand and Myanmar. Spreading crown of feathery pinnate leaves. Clusters of pink flowers, from lavender buds, fading to white with age, followed by long-stalked narrow seed pods. Zones 11–12.

DALEA
INDIGO BUSH
This genus, comprising about 160 species from North, Central, and South America, most diverse in Mexico and the Andes, is a member of the pea-flower subfamily of the legume (Fabaceae) family. They are small trees, shrubs, or herbs. Shoots, including the flowers, are dotted with tiny glands. The leaves are pinnate, sometimes reduced to only 3 leaflets. Flowers, in terminal racemes or spikes, are yellow, purple, or white, sometimes bicolored with the standard (upper petal) of a color contrasting with that of the wings and keel. Seed pods are egg-shaped in outline, flattened, with 1 or 2 kidney-shaped seeds.
CULTIVATION: Most are best restricted to native plantings and grow well in well-drained soils in full sun. They are propagated from seed. Some species are of local medicinal value.

Dalea frutescens
BLACK DALEA
☼ ❄ ↔ 4 ft (1.2 m) ↑ 3 ft (0.9 m)
From south-central USA, and northern Mexico; spreading semi-deciduous shrub with lower branches resting on ground and taking root. Leaves to 1 in (25 mm) long. Profuse display of bright rose-purple and white flowers, in short spikes, in autumn. Selected forms have been promoted. Zones 7–10.

Dalea greggii
☼ ❄ ↔ 6 ft (1.8 m) ↑ 18 in (45 cm)
Widespread in Mexico, extending into southern Texas and New Mexico, USA. Low mounding subshrub with long trailing and rooting stems, small leaves, spikes of rose-purple flowers, in spring–summer. Zones 8–11.

Dalea purpurea
syn. *Petalostemon purpureum*
PURPLE PRAIRIE CLOVER, VIOLET PRAIRIE CLOVER
☼ ❄ ↔ 18 in (45 cm)
↑ 18–36 in (45–90 cm)
Erect multi-stemmed perennial that is found in drier tall-grass prairie in nearly all interior States of USA and southern Canada. Leaves up to 2 in (5 cm) long, with 5 leaflets. Flowers bright purple, in dense spikes surrounding a cone of buds, in summer. Zones 4–10.

DAMPIERA

Endemic to Australia and named after the seventeenth-century British seafarer William Dampier, this large genus of 66 species is part of the Goodeniaceae family. Most of the species are perennial herbs with a few shrubby species occurring in a range of soil types from pure sand to clay, and in habitats from forests and woodlands to arid parts of the continent, and from sea level to montane. The greater number of species occurs in the southwest of Western Australia. Leaf shape ranges from simple and smooth-edged to lobed or toothed, basal or alternate on the stems, glabrous to densely woolly hairy. Flowers are an irregular shape, borne singly or in terminal or axillary clusters. Color is predominantly blue with some species being mauve to purple, only a couple of species being white, pink, or yellow. A few species produce suckers.
CULTIVATION: Propagation is from stem or leaf cuttings, or by division of the suckering species. Seeds are not easily obtained, but even when available, germination is not assured. Smoke treatment has been successful with germinating some of the western species, but cultivation of most of these has been rather difficult in non-Mediterranean climates of eastern Australia and elsewhere. Several species now commonly cultivated, with a growing number of forms and cultivars being selected. Tissue culture is a propagation method.

Dalea frutescens

Dalea greggii

Dampiera diversifolia

Daphne blagayana

Dampiera diversifolia ★

☼ ❄ ↔40–60 in (100–150 cm)
↑4–20 in (10–50 cm)

A perennial prostrate herb from habitats in southwestern Australia, suckering readily in cultivated forms. Lance-shaped, glabrous, slightly toothed basal leaves. Prostrate stems have smaller leaves, narrow and not toothed. The flowers, purple-blue, are borne in the leaf axils during spring to summer, in great profusion, almost obscuring the rest of the plant. The selection of color forms from the wild has increased the number of shades of blue that are nowadays available commercially, due to successful tissue culture. Zones 8–10.

DANAE

There is just one species of fleshy-stemmed evergreen perennial in this genus, which belongs to the asparagus (Asparagaceae) family. It is found in

Daphne bholua

forests from northern Iran to south-western Asia. Each year new shoots emerge in the manner of asparagus, to which it is related. The plant is primarily grown for its attractive foliage, the tiny cream flowers being of little significance. The flowers are followed by small orange-red berries.
CULTIVATION: This species is easily grown in moisture-retentive soil in sun or part-shade. Propagate by division.

Danae racemosa

syn. *Danae laurus*
ALEXANDRIAN LAUREL
☼/◐ ❄ ↔3–4 ft (0.9–1.2 m)
↑3–4 ft (0.9–1.2 m)

Shrubby perennial annually sending up shoots from rhizomes. The flexible, arching stems are reminiscent of a small bamboo. Pointed oval leaves, attractive glossy green. Zones 6–9.

DAPHNE

Renowned for its fragrance, this genus in the daphne family (Thymelaeaceae) includes 50 or so evergreen and deciduous shrubs, extending from Europe and North Africa to temperate and subtropical Asia. Forming neat compact bushes, many of them make excellent rockery plants. The leaves are usually simple with smooth-edged, blunt-tipped, elongated ovals, either thin and dull green or thick, leathery, and slightly glossy. Individually flowers are small, usually in shades of white, cream, yellow, or pink, and carried in showy rounded heads that are sometimes highly scented. Drupes follow the flowers and are sometimes colorful.
CULTIVATION: Daphnes generally

prefer moist, cool, humus-rich, well-drained, slightly acid soil. If camellias and rhododendrons do well in your garden, so should daphnes. Once established, daphnes resent disturbance, so avoid damaging the surface roots by cultivation. Use mulch to suppress weeds. Small-leafed species prefer bright conditions; those with larger leaves are happier shaded from the hottest sun. Propagate from seed or by cuttings or layers.

Daphne bholua

☼ ❄ ↔4 ft (1.2 m) ↑10 ft (3 m)
Native to the eastern Himalayas. There are deciduous and evergreen forms. Strongly scented white flowers, tinged with pink, develop from deep pink buds, in winter–spring. Drupes ripen to black. They are known as paper daphnes as paper and ropes were once made from the bark. '**Gurkha**' is both hardy and deciduous. Zones 7–10.

Daphne blagayana

☼ ❄ ↔36 in (90 cm) ↑12 in (30 cm)
From the Balkan region. Low-spreading plant with large leaves. Flowers showy, many-flowered heads, fragrant, creamy white, in spring. Will often self-layer if the branches are pegged down. Zones 5–10.

Daphne cneorum

Daphne cneorum 'Ruby Glow'

Daphne × burkwoodii

BURKWOOD DAPHNE
☼ ❄ ↔5 ft (1.5 m) ↑5 ft (1.5 m)
Hybrid between *D. cneorum* and *D. caucasica*. Twiggy, densely foliaged, evergreen or semi-evergreen bush. Matt mid-green foliage. Small, fragrant, pink flowers, in spring. '**Carol Mackie**', variegated foliage form, more colorful when not in flower. Zones 5–9.

Daphne caucasica

☼ ❄ ↔5 ft (1.5 m) ↑6 ft (1.8 m)
Deciduous species from the Caucasus and western Asia. Leaves light green above, glaucous undersides. Flowers, white and fragrant, borne in clusters of around 20, on short lateral shoots. Red or black drupes. Zones 6–9.

Daphne cneorum

GARLAND DAPHNE, GARLAND FLOWER, ROCK DAPHNE, ROSE DAPHNE
☼ ❄ ↔24 in (60 cm) ↑8 in (20 cm)
Near-evergreen Eurasian species. Dense twiggy shrub. Massed heads of small, fragrant, bright pink flowers in spring. Requires excellent drainage, shelter from hot summer sun, and some winter chilling. Worth trying in a rockery or alpine trough. '**Eximia**' ★, sturdier than the species; '**Ruby Glow**', rich red flowers. Zones 4–9.

Daphne caucasica

Daphne × *burkwoodii* 'Carol Mackie'

Daphne × *burkwoodii*

Daphne genkwa
LILAC DAPHNE

☀ ❄ ↔ 5 ft (1.5 m) ↑ 5 ft (1.5 m)

Deciduous shrub from China. The young foliage is coppery with new stems covered in fine down. Bears large, lavender, slightly fragrant, delicate flowers, in spring. Propagation difficulties keep *D. genkwa* a fairly rare plant. Zones 5–9.

Daphne gnidium

☀ ❄ ↔ 4 ft (1.2 m) ↑ 6 ft (1.8 m)

Evergreen shrub from Eurasia, North Africa, and the Canary Islands. Has sparse glossy leaves and small, fragrant, creamy white to pale pink flowers,

Daphne gnidium

Daphne laureola

Daphne genkwa

densely clustered in panicles, during the late spring–early summer. Bears red drupes. Zones 8–10.

Daphne jasminea

☀ ❄ ↔ 12 in (30 cm) ↑ 12 in (30 cm)

From southeastern Greece. Small evergreen shrub with tiny blue-green leaves. Bears very fragrant, small, white flowers with pink to purplish interiors, in clusters of 2 or 3 blooms, in spring. Zones 9–11.

Daphne laureola
SPURGE LAUREL

☀ ❄ ↔ 5 ft (1.5 m) ↑ 5 ft (1.5 m)

Eurasian native, a tough adaptable plant. Dark green, evergreen foliage, tolerates shade. Flowers are fragrant, small, and pale green, in late winter–spring. Zones 7–10.

Daphne × manteniana

☀ ❄ ↔ 27 in (70 cm) ↑ 30 in (75 cm)

Hybrid between *D. × burkwoodii* and *D. tangutica*. Evergreen shrub with dense foliage and glossy dark green leaves. Produces heads of very fragrant purple-pink flowers in spring–autumn Zones 6–9.

Daphne mezereum
FEBRUARY DAPHNE, MEZEREON

☀ ❄ ↔ 3 ft (0.9 m) ↑ 4 ft (1.2 m)

European species, the most common of the deciduous daphnes, similar to *D. × burkwoodii*. The flowers appear on bare wood, in late winter–early

Daphne × napolitana

spring. There are white and pink-flowered, fragrant forms, singles and doubles available. *D. m.* f. *alba*, white flowers, yellow fruit. Zones 4–9.

Daphne × napolitana

☀ ❄ ↔ 30 in (75 cm) ↑ 30 in (75 cm)

Hybrid between *D. sericea* and *D. cneorum*. Dense covering of glossy leaves. Mass of scented, very small, pink flowers, in spring. May also flower in summer and autumn. Zones 8–10.

Daphne odora
WINTER DAPHNE

☀ ❄ ↔ 5 ft (1.5 m) ↑ 5 ft (1.5 m)

Native of China and Japan. Evergreen shrub with deep green leaves. Bears fragrant clusters of small, starry, pale pink flowers, from mid-winter. Not long-lived. Replace every 8 to 10 years. *D. o.* f. *rosacea,* white and pink flowers; 'Rubra', dark reddish pink flowers, less fragrance. *D. o.* 'Variegata' (sometimes called 'Aureomarginata'), yellow-edged leaves, hardier and easier to grow than the species. Zones 8–10.

Daphne pontica

☀ ❄ ↔ 5 ft (1.5 m) ↑ 5 ft (1.5 m)

Native to the Balkans and western Asia. An evergreen shrub with glossy, deep green, leathery leaves. The flowers are fragrant, and sometimes very pale pink to white, but usually light green. Zones 6–10.

Daphne sericea

☀ ❄ ↔ 30 in (75 cm) ↑ 30 in (75 cm)

Found in the eastern Mediterranean region. An evergreen shrub, young branches hairy. The leaves are bright green, glossy and hairy beneath. Bears

Daphne odora

Daphne pontica

Daphne sericea

large, very fragrant, deep rose pink flowers, in clusters, in spring, sporadically in autumn. Orange to red drupes. Zones 8–10.

Daphne tangutica

☀ ❄ ↔ 5 ft (1.5 m) ↑ 6 ft (1.8 m)

Native to northwestern China. Evergreen shrub with small gray-haired leaves. Densely crowded clusters of small, fragrant, rosy purple flowers, reminiscent of lilac *(Syringa)*, in spring–summer. Small red fruits. **Retusa Group**, dark green leaves, small, fragrant, purplish red flowers. Zones 6–9.

DAPHNIPHYLLUM

A native of China, Japan, and Korea, from the family Daphniphyllaceae, this genus of about 15 evergreen shrubs or trees has inconspicuous petal-less flowers borne in clusters in leaf axils, in the late spring or early summer. Members of the genus are dioecious, requiring both male and female plants for reproduction. Male flowers are purplish red, female flowers are green, and leaves are simple and leathery. Fruit is a single-seeded drupe, usually bluish black in color. Valued mostly for their ornamental year-round foliage. **CULTIVATION:** Moist, well-drained, slightly acid, mulched soils are preferred, in a sheltered position with some shade. The plants are relatively free of serious pests. Propagation is from seed.

Daphniphyllum himalaense

☀/☀ ❄ ↔ 10–50 ft (3–15 m) ↑ 10–50 ft (3–15 m)

Shrub or small tree, common in evergreen oak and rhododendron forests of the eastern Himalayas, and western and southern China at elevations of 7,000–10,000 ft (2,000–3,000 m). Bears insignificant flowers without petals in late spring, that emit a pungent odor. Pea-shaped fruit is bluish black. *D. h.* **subsp.** *macropodum* has dark, glossy, leathery, rhododendron-like alternate leaves, with long red stalks. Specimen plant, or suitable for screen or hedge. Zones 6–8.

DARLINGTONIA

syn. *Chrysamphora californica*
CALIFORNIA PITCHER PLANT, COBRA LILY

Single species genus, carnivorous, in the pitcher-plant (Sarraceniaceae) family, which includes *Heliamphora* and *Sarracenia*. Grows in and around springs and streams, in sphagnum bogs, and wherever it has access to cool running water. Found at both high and low altitudes in northern California and southern Oregon, USA. Herbaceous perennial characterized by the cobra-like head of the pitcher, which resembles a snake poised to strike, fangs and all! Insects are attracted by the bright green or dark red pitchers and smell of nectar from around the rim. Nectar lures insect to where it is trapped by downward pointing hairs and dissolved in liquid at base of pitcher. Unlike *Sarracenia,* this liquid does not contain digestive enzymes and the insect is broken down by bacteria.
CULTIVATION: Plant in sphagnum moss, in concrete or terracotta pots standing in a saucer of water, in full or half-sun. Key to growing *Darlingtonia* is to keep roots cool. In warm to hot weather, use chilled water. Propagate by removing the new plantlets that grow on the end of the fleshy stem.

Darlingtonia californica ★
☼/◐ ❄ ↔ 8–10 in (20–25 cm)
↑ 24–40 in (60–100 cm)

Perennial pitcher plant. Slender pitchers have bulbous hood with fishtail or

Darlingtonia californica

Darlingtonia californica

fang-like tongues protruding from the hood's base. Red and green nodding flowers stand singly on a leafless stalk, from spring–late summer. Zones 6–9.

DARMERA

syn. *Peltiphyllum*

A genus of one species from western North America belonging to the saxifrage (Saxifragaceae) family. Large herbaceous perennial, found along stream sides and in damp woods, grown for its dramatic foliage and early flowers. Recommended for bog garden or fernery.
CULTIVATION: Plant in moist to wet soils, rich in organic matter, in a cool sheltered site. Propagate by division of established clumps, although raising from seed is an option if sown fresh.

Darmera peltata

syn. *Peltiphyllum peltatum*
☼ ❄ ↔ 3–10 ft (0.9–3 m)
↑ 5–7 ft (1.5–2 m)

Herbaceous perennial with rounded heads of tiny pink flowers prior to foliage in very early spring. Huge leaves soon follow like bright green umbrellas. Dwarf form also grown. Zones 6–10.

× DARWINARA

Multi-generic orchid (family Orchidaceae), named for naturalist Charles Darwin, and combining 4 monopodial genera—*Ascocentrum, Neofinetia, Rhynchostylis,* and *Vanda.* Erect growing epiphytes, strap-like channeled leaves, in 2 ranks. Larger plants may branch at base; have numerous, very thick, cord-like roots.
CULTIVATION: Prefers intermediate to warm conditions and high light levels. Colorful showy blooms are long lived. Thick roots often venture outside the confines of the pot or basket, and this should be encouraged, as the roots require unimpeded air circulation and must dry out quickly after watering. Propagate by division.

× Darwinara 'Pretty Girl'
☼ ⚘ ↔ 8–15 in (20–38 cm)
↑ 8–24 in (20–60 cm)

This hybrid has the cool-growing, miniature Japanese species *Neofinetia*

Daphniphyllum h. subsp. *macropodum*

× *Darwinara* 'Pretty Girl'

falcata as one of the parents, making it adaptable to a range of climatic conditions and temperatures. Throughout the warmer months, and year-round in the tropics, it bears white to deep purple flowers. Zones 10–12.

DARWINIA

This genus of around 45 species in the myrtle (Myrtaceae) family is endemic to Australia, many are from Western Australia. Most are small evergreen shrubs, with small crowded leaves often marked with numerous oil glands. Tiny tubular flowers have long protruding styles and fall roughly into 2 groups: those clustered into pincushion-like flowers and those enclosed by large colorful bracts giving the flowerhead a bell-like appearance. The flowers of most species are rich in nectar and will attract birds. Some of the highly ornamental, but often unreliable, Western Australian *Darwinia* species are available as grafted plants. They are suited to growing in containers and this is recommended in frost-prone areas.
CULTIVATION: They require a light well-drained soil with some moisture and a little dappled shade. Good mulch around the root area will conserve soil moisture during the summer. Prune lightly after flowering to maintain a compact shape. Propagate from half-hardened tip cuttings at the end of the summer.

Darwinia citriodora

LEMON-SCENTED DARWINIA
☼ ⚘ ↔ 5 ft (1.5 m) ↑ 5 ft (1.5 m)

Widely cultivated, compact, rounded shrub from far southwestern Western Australia. It has small, neatly arranged, blue-green, oblong leaves, sometimes with reddish tints, in autumn–winter, aromatic when crushed. Small clusters

Darwinia citriodora

of flowers, prominent orange and green leaf-like bracts, are seen in winter–summer. Zones 9–11.

DASYLIRION

From southern USA and Mexico, this genus of 18 species is made up of what appear to be shrubs or trees but are in fact very large, woody stemmed, evergreen perennials. *Dasylirion,* in the dragon-tree (Dracaenaceae) family, is closely related to *Agave.* Single trunk topped with a head of spine-edged linear leaves that in some species are over 3 ft (0.9 m) long. From among the foliage emerges a tall spike, bearing bell-shaped creamy white flowers. Male and female flowers occur on separate plants, usually in the summer.
CULTIVATION: As with most dry-country plants, *Dasylirion* species demand good drainage and full sun. They tolerate light to moderate frosts but suffer if kept wet and cold for prolonged periods. Soil should be light and gritty, though a little extra humus is appreciated. Propagate from seed.

Dasylirion acrotriche
☼ ⚘ ↔ 5 ft (1.5 m) ↑ 10–20 ft (3–6 m)

Mexican species. The leaves are light green, very narrow, edges with teeth and hooked spines. Inflorescence usually upright. Zones 9–11.

Dasylirion acrotriche

Datura inoxia 'Evening Fragrance'

Datura stramonium

Dasylirion longissimum
syn. *Dasylirion quadrangulatum*
MEXICAN GRASS TREE, TOOTHLESS SPOON
☀ ❄ ↔ 6–8 ft (1.8–2.4 m)
↑ 5–10 ft (1.5–3 m)

Mounding, grass-like, succulent, ever-green perennial from eastern Mexico. A spray of stiff, arching, narrow, 4-angled, strap-like leaves, forms billowing grassy head. Insignificant white flowers tinged with green, on erect spikes. Grow in sheltered position, with support when in flower. Zones 8–11.

Dasylirion wheeleri ★
DESERT SPOON, SOTOL
☀ ❄ ↔ 3 ft (0.9 m) ↑ 12–25 ft (3.5–8 m)
Found in arid parts of southeastern Arizona and Texas, USA. Leaves blue-green, viciously spiny. Flower spike is very tall. Zones 7–11.

DATURA
This genus of 11 species from southern North America but now widely naturalized in much of the world, belongs to the nightshade (Solanaceae) family. Annual plants with erect flowers and dry capsular fruit, compared with *Brugmansia* (the "daturas" of tropical

horticulture), which have drooping flowers and fleshy fruit. Leaves, simple, smooth-edged, or with wavy margins, are spirally arranged. The short-lived flowers arise from leaf axils or forks in the branches. Flowers are tubular or funnel-shaped, usually white though sometimes blotched purple, occasionally yellow or violet. Fruit is a spiny short-stalked capsule with 2 compartments, splitting irregularly. Like species of *Brugmansia*, they contain powerful alkaloids, which can be highly toxic, though they have been used as hallucinogens by Native Americans.
CULTIVATION: *Datura* demand good drainage and heavy watering rather than light and often. They are ideal in tubs. Propagate from seed in full sun after frost has finished.

Datura inoxia
syn. *Datura meteloides*
ANGEL'S TRUMPET, DOWNY THORN APPLE, INDIAN APPLE
☀ ⁂ ↔ 36 in (90 cm) ↑ 36 in (90 cm)
From Central America. Annual with large, downy, oval leaves. Fragrant flowers, upward-facing, tubular, flaring, white, sometimes flushed pink, and round spiny fruits. 'Evening Fragrance', very fragrant selected form. Zones 9–11.

Datura stramonium
COMMON THORN APPLE, JAMESTOWN WEED, JIMSON'S WEED
☀ ❄ ↔ 3–6 ft (0.9–1.8 m)
↑ 3–6 ft (0.9–1.8 m)
Annual from the Americas, widely naturalized elsewhere. Coarsely toothed leaves with an unpleasant odor when crushed. Tubular flowers, white or

purple. Spiny fruits. This extremely poisonous plant contains a hallucinogen. Zones 7–11.

DAUCUS
This genus of about 22 species from Europe and the Mediterranean to central Asia, tropical Africa, Australasia, and the Americas, belongs to the carrot (Apiaceae) family; in fact the carrot (*D. carota*) is its best known species and the only one widely cultivated. They are annuals or biennials that begin as a rosette of finely divided leaves arising from a taproot, elongating in the first or second year into a flowering stem bearing small white, often purple-flushed, or pale yellow flowers in compound umbels, the flowers are soon followed by small, dry, ribbed fruits, or "seeds." Carrot is Celtic for "red of color"—this refers to edible tap root.
CULTIVATION: Best in well rotted compost to avoid forking. Can remain in ground for several weeks. Water regularly, drying out will cause splitting. Propagate from seed a couple of weeks before end of frost but when soil is dry.

Daucus carota
WILD CARROT
☀ ⁂ ↔ 20 in (50 cm) ↑ 40 in (100 cm)
From Europe, central Asia, Australia, New Zealand, and tropical Africa. Biennial, usually grown as annual, green fern-like foliage. Roots vary from cream to orange and red. Bracts of creamy white flowers in second year, in late summer. *D. c.* subsp. *sativus*, orange root, includes main carrot varieties: 'Canada', disease, heat, and drought tolerant, to deep orange color internally and externally; 'Red Intermediate' ★, dark orange-red color, prefers open soils, sow in summer as can bolt if sown in spring; and 'Topweight', a vigorous sweet-tasting variety, bolt resistant, a good all-purpose carrot, and particularly adaptable to a wide range of soils. Zones 3–9.

DAVALLIA
HARE'S FOOT FERN
A genus of about 40 semi-deciduous terrestrial or epiphytic ferns from

warm-temperate, tropical, and sub-tropical regions that belong to the haresfoot-fern (Davalliaceae) family. Finely divided, triangular, lacy, shiny, pinnate fronds on thick, long, creeping, branching, scaly rhizomes that run along the growing surface. Named for the resemblance of its furry, trailing, aerial rhizomes to animal paws.
CULTIVATION: Well suited to basket cultivation in warm humid spots protected from wind and frost. Grow in shade, in rich, moist, well-drained soil or a potting mix designed for epiphytic plants. Propagate from spore or by division of rhizomes.

Davallia solida
GIANT HARE'S FOOT, POLYNESIAN HARE'S FOOT
☀ ⁑ ↔ 24–36 in (60–90 cm)
↑ 12–18 in (30–45 cm)

Native to Malaysia, Australia, and the South Pacific islands. Fern with hairy, often aerial rhizomes. Tough, shiny, dark green, coarsely cut, bipinnate fronds, on scaly stalks. Leaflets with elliptical notched pinnules. *D. s.* var. *fejeensis* ★, more finely divided fronds, pendulous rhizomes, suitable for basket cultivation. *D. s.* var. *pyxidata*, eastern Australian variety with smaller fronds, hairless on undersides. *D. s.* 'Ornata', broader pinnules with drooping tips; and 'Ruffled Ornata', broader ruffled pinnules. Zones 9–12.

DAVIDIA
The only species in this genus of the dogwood (Cornaceae) family, a deciduous tree, was introduced from China by the French missionary Armand David in the 1890s and the genus was subsequently named after him. *D. involucrata* is native to southwestern China where it grows in damp mountain woods. A handsome tree, with a broadly conical outline and attractive foliage, flowering bracts, and fruit.
CULTIVATION: *D. involucrata* makes an excellent specimen tree although it does have a tendency to branch at a low level so corrective pruning should be carried out to ensure a good straight trunk develops. It requires a deep, rich,

Daucus carota subsp. *s.* 'Red Intermediate'

Daucus carota subsp. *sativus* 'Canada'

Davidia involucrata

Daviesia latifolia

Daviesia mimosoides

Decaisnea fargesii

moist soil and should be given a sheltered site. Flowering occurs when tree is about 10 years old. Propagation best from fresh seed, dry seed has a much reduced germination rate.

Davidia involucrata ★
DOVE TREE, GHOST TREE, HANDKERCHIEF TREE

☀ ❄ ↔30 ft (9 m) ↑60 ft (18 m)
Leaves aromatic, toothed margins, heart-shaped bases, downy beneath, taper to a long point. Tiny true flowers surrounded by 2 large, white ornamental bracts of uneven size, in late spring, with the new leaves. Plum-like fruit ripens to purple-brown. *D. i.* var. *vilmoriniana*, more commonly seen, with leaves smooth beneath. Zones 6–9.

DAVIESIA
Most of the 75 species in this genus in the pea-flower subfamily of the legume (Fabaceae) family are endemic to the southwest of Western Australia, others are found in eastern and southern Australia and the Northern Territory. *Daviesia* is named after Hugh Davies, an eighteenth-century Welsh botanist; comprises dwarf to tall shrubs with simple alternate leaves, branchlets that are sometimes thorny, and, generally, yellow pea-flowers. Grow best in sandy heathland but also understory plants in dry sclerophyll forests.
CULTIVATION: Require well-drained soil and plenty of sunshine. Propagation is quite easy from seed, which ripens quickly in hot weather, although seeds have a hard coat that requires pretreating. Most species flower profusely, and some also have decorative seed pods that change color as they mature.

Daviesia latifolia
syn. *Daviesia horrida*
HOP BITTER PEA

☀ ❄ ↔7 ft (2 m) ↑8 ft (2.4 m)
Found in the eastern states of Australia. Ovate-elliptic or ovate-lanceolate leaves. The yellow and brown, aromatic pea-flowers appear in racemes, in spring. Useful low hedge. The leaves have medicinal properties. Zones 8–11.

Daviesia mimosoides
BLUNT-LEAF BITTER PEA, NARROW-LEAF BITTER PEA

☀ ❄ ↔7 ft (2 m) ↑8 ft (2.4 m)
From Australia's eastern states. Narrow lanceolate to elliptical leaves. Yellow and red perfumed pea-flowers in axillary racemes, in spring to mid-summer. Will grow on stony soil. Zones 8–11.

DECAISNEA
Two species belong to this genus of woodland plants within the chocolate-vine (Lardizabalaceae) family. Its range covers the Himalayas to western China. Both species are deciduous and hardy enough to be made more use of as ornamentals. They are noted for their showy ornamental and edible fruit.

× *Degarmoara* Skywalker 'Red Star'

CULTIVATION: They prefer moist but well-drained fertile soil in sun or partial shade, but need shelter from cold and strong winds, especially when young. Propagate by sowing seed into pots or into a seed bed in autumn, ensuring they are protected against winter frosts. Germination can be erratic.

Decaisnea fargesii
syn. *Decaisnea insignis*

☀ ❄ ↔20 ft (6 m) ↑20 ft (6 m)
Native of western China. Upright deciduous shrub. Egg-shaped, pinnate, dark green leaves, up to 25 leaflets. Pendent racemes with bell-shaped lime green flowers, in early summer. Pod-shaped blue-gray fruit. Black seeds surrounded by white pulp. Zones 5–9.

× *DEGARMOARA*
This tri-generic orchid (family Orchidaceae) hybrid, is a combination of *Brassia*, *Miltonia*, and *Odontoglossum*. These essentially spidery sympodial hybrids, an influence from the *Brassia* parent, are more tolerant of higher temperatures than most pure Odontoglossums. They grow in wide-ranging conditions and have long-lasting often fragrant flowers, making them popular flowering pot plants.
CULTIVATION: These hybrids have a fine root system, and do not like to dry out throughout warmer months of the year. They require a drier rest in the winter when they should only be watered sparingly. The plants need to be potted in sphagnum moss or a fine bark mix. They are suitable for cool to intermediate growing conditions, and require abundant water throughout the year and to be grown in a semi-shaded position. Propagation is by division.

× *Degarmoara* Skywalker 'Red Star'

☀ ✲ ↔8–16 in (20–40 cm)
↑8–32 in (20–80 cm)
Flowers a rich strong color, darker overlay of spotting, contrasting labellum. Up to 6 starry flowers on an upright inflorescence in spring. Zones 10–12.

× *Degarmoara* Starshot 'Fashion'

☀ ✲ ↔8–16 in (20–40 cm)
↑8–32 in (20–80 cm)
Has over 10 different species in its genetic background, with influence of *Brassia verrucosa* prominent. Flowers in spring–early summer. Zones 10–12.

× *Degarmoara* Winter Wonderland 'White Fairy'

☀ ✲ ↔8–16 in (20–40 cm)
↑8–32 in (20–80 cm)
Popular cultivar that has been mass propagated using modern tissue culture techniques for its introduction as a pot plant. Can bloom more than once a year; individual flowers can last for about 6 weeks. Zones 10–12.

× *Degarmoara* Winter Wonderland 'White Fairy'

× *Degarmoara* Starshot 'Fashion'

D

Delonix regia

Delosperma aberdeenense

Delosperma brunnthaleri

Delosperma cooperi

DELONIX

This small genus comprising 10 species of tropical deciduous, semi-evergreen, or evergreen trees in the cassia subfamily of the legume (Fabaceae) family includes the spectacular poinciana, *D. regia*. The wide umbrella-like canopies provide good summer shade. Large, terminal, orchid-like flower clusters almost smother the tree crown, and appear after the deciduous and semi-evergreen species shed their leaves. CULTIVATION: For the first few years, vigorous growth should be promoted in a humus-enriched well-watered soil. A sturdy trunk should be encouraged by removing the side shoots, thus lifting the canopy above head height. These trees require ample space to spread and are tolerant of all soil types except for heavy clay. They are easily propagated from seed or cuttings, but the seedlings take 10 years or longer to flower. The flower color from the seedlings may be disappointing.

Delonix regia

FLAMBOYANT TREE, ROYAL POINCIANA

☀ ✄ ↔ 30 ft (9 m) ↑ 30 ft (9 m)

From Madagascar. This is a deciduous shade tree. The bright green feathery leaves mature to deep green, and are shed prior to flowering. Large orange-scarlet flower clusters form in profusion on the branch ends in summer. The huge flattened pods harden in autumn. Zones 11–12.

DELOSPERMA

Found mainly in southern Africa but also spread through eastern Africa to Saudi Arabia, this genus, a member of the iceplant (Aizoaceae) family, is composed of over 150 species of annuals, biennials, and perennials that often have a low spreading habit and can become shrubby. Most have a thickened, somewhat tuberous, central stem known as a "caudex," from which emerge fine stems clothed in succulent cylindrical leaves. The daisy-like flowers are usually small, but are exceptionally bright and abundant. Most species flower in late spring. CULTIVATION: Intolerant of repeated hard frosts, otherwise undemanding, easily grown in any gritty free-draining soil that can be kept moist during the flowering season. Ideal for covering dry banks and rock walls, often naturalizing in crevices. Propagate from seed, cuttings, or by layering, either natural or deliberately encouraged.

Delosperma aberdeenense

☀/◐ ❄ ↔ 20 in (50 cm)
↑ 4–8 in (10–20 cm)

From South Africa. Small, spreading, slightly mounding, densely branched shrub. Pale pink to magenta flowers. Zones 7–10.

Delosperma ashtonii

☀/◐ ❄ ↔ 20 in (50 cm)
↑ 6–8 in (15–20 cm)

From South Africa. Thick dark green leaves. Clump-forming and slow to spread. Large purple-pink flowers. Zones 8–10.

Delosperma brunnthaleri

☀/◐ ❄ ↔ 20 in (50 cm)
↑ 12–16 in (30–40 cm)

From South Africa. Multi-branched small shrub. Pink or yellow flowers. Zones 8–10.

Delosperma cooperi

☀/◐ ❄ ↔ 24–32 in (60–80 cm)
↑ 6–20 in (15–50 cm)

From South Africa. Densely branched perennial that spreads quickly and may become shrubby. Narrow glandular leaves, sometimes gray-green. Pink to magenta flowers. Zones 7–10.

Delosperma crassuloides

☀ ❧ ↔ 24 in (60 cm) ↑ 2 in (5 cm)

From the Drakensberg mountains of eastern South Africa, this mat-forming plant has densely crowded, oblong, green leaves. Scattered pink flowers. Zones 9–11.

Delosperma lehmannii

☀/◐ ❧ ↔ 20 in (50 cm)
↑ 6–8 in (15–20 cm)

From South Africa. Low spreader with thick, gray-green, keeled leaves reminiscent of *Carpobrotus*. Soft yellow flowers. Zones 9–11.

Delosperma nubigenum

☀/◐ ❄ ↔ 20 in (50 cm)
↑ 2–4 in (5–10 cm)

A native of South Africa, this is the hardiest of the *Delosperma*. It has a prostrate spreading stem with rosettes of short fleshy leaves, which are often red-tinted in sun, and bears flowers that are bright golden yellow to orange-red. Zones 7–10.

Delosperma sutherlandii

☀/◐ ❄ ↔ 24–32 in (60–80 cm)
↑ 6–20 in (15–50 cm)

From South Africa. Low and spreading or shrubby. The leaves are glandular and sometimes edged with fine hairs. The flowers are bright lavender-pink to magenta. Zones 9–11.

Delosperma Hybrid Cultivars

☀ ❧ ↔ 18–36 in (49–90 cm)
↑ 2–4 in (5–10 cm)

Many species hybridize naturally or produce forms with distinctive foliage or flowers. Several have been developed into garden plants, including: **'Album'**, low spreader with incandescent white flowers; **'Oberg'**, prostrate and spreading gray-green foliage, flowers open pale pink from darker buds, ageing to white; **'Ruby Star'**, low spreader with small purple flowers through summer. Zones 9–11.

DELPHINIUM

Sometimes known as larkspur, although that name is best reserved for its relatives in the genus *Consolida*. A member of the buttercup (Ranunculaceae) family, *Delphinium* consists of around 250 species of annuals, biennials and perennials. Most species form a basal clump of finely divided or lobed foliage, from which develops an upright spike bearing long-spurred, 4-petalled flowers backed by 5 sepals that sometimes become bract-like. Plant sizes vary markedly with the species: the smaller species may not

Delosperma sutherlandii

Delosperma lehmannii

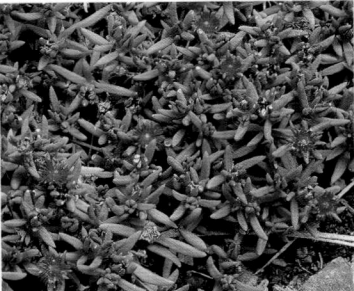

Delosperma, Hybrid Cultivar, 'Ruby Star'

Delphinium, Hybrid Cultivar, 'Albert Shepherd'

Delphinium, Hybrid Cultivar, 'Angela Harbutt'

Delphinium, Hybrid Cultivar, 'Blue Lagoon'

Delphinium, Hybrid Cultivar, 'Bruce'

Delphinium, Hybrid Cultivar, 'Christella'

exceed 12 in (30 cm) tall, while the fancy hybrids can grow to over 7 ft (2 m). Flower colors vary, but *Delphinium* is best known for the intense blue flowers it often produces.
CULTIVATION: Best in an open airy position that lessens the risk of mildew. However, the more exposed the location, the more important it is that the plants are staked to prevent damage from the wind. Plant in moist, humus-rich, fertile soil and water well while in flower. Propagate from seed or basal cuttings, or by division.

Delphinium barbeyi

☼/◐ ❋ ↔ 6–16 in (15–40 cm)
↑ 12–40 in (30–100 cm)

This perennial is native to the Rocky Mountains, USA. Clump of downy basal foliage. Leaves with 5 main lobes further divided or toothed. Strong upright flower stems. Dark blue flowers in summer, yellowish hairs on petals. Zones 5–9.

Delphinium × belladonna

☼/◐ ❋ ↔ 6–20 in (15–50 cm)
↑ 12–40 in (30–100 cm)

Perennial hybrid crosses between *D. elatum* and *D. grandiflorum*. Compact, sometimes dwarf, with finely divided dark green foliage. Flowers to 1¼ in (30 mm) wide. Many selected forms, which include: 'Bellamosum', intensely dark blue flowers; 'Blue Sensation', bright mid-blue flowers; and 'Cliveden Beauty', light sky blue flowers. Zones 3–9.

Delphinium cardinale

☼/◐ ❋ ↔ 8–20 in (20–50 cm)
↑ 3–7 ft (0.9–2 m)

A short-lived perennial, sometimes annual or biennial, from California, USA. It has dark green, finely divided, basal foliage. The wiry upright flower stems hold widely spaced red flowers, with yellow centers, in the summer. Zones 8–10.

Delphinium elatum

☼/◐ ❋ ↔ 8–20 in (20–50 cm)
↑ 2–6 ft (0.6–1.8 m)

Summer-flowering Eurasian perennial. Downy or hairy leaves and 5 to 7 lobes toothed or further divided. Strong upright flower stems, dense racemes of blue flowers, in summer. Zones 3–9.

Delphinium grandiflorum

syn. *Delphinium chinense*

☼/◐ ❋ ↔ 12–24 in (30–60 cm)
↑ 12–40 in (30–100 cm)

Perennial from temperate East Asia. Low bushy foliage clump, very finely divided, bright green leaves. Racemes of vivid blue flowers, sometimes quite tall and upright, usually short and lax. Popular forms include: 'Blue Butterfly', masses of deep blue flowers on short stems; and 'Tom Pouce', with bright gentian blue flowers. Zones 3–9.

Delphinium nudicaule

☼/◐ ❋ ↔ 8–16 in (20–40 cm)
↑ 12–24 in (30–60 cm)

Perennial from California, USA. Short-lived, sometimes annual or biennial.

The leaves are coarsely lobed, secondary divisions fine, downy, dull green. It has wiry flower stems with widely spaced, orange-red flowers marked yellow on upper lips, from late spring. Zones 8–10.

Delphinium semibarbatum

syn. *Delphinium zalil*

☼/◐ ❋ ↔ 6–12 in (15–30 cm)
↑ 20–30 in (50–75 cm)

From Iran and central Asia. Short-lived perennial, sometimes annual or biennial. Forms a small clump of finely cut deep green foliage. Wiry flower stems bear small bright yellow flowers. Zones 6–9.

Delphinium Hybrid Cultivars

☼ ❋ ↔ 1½–3 ft (0.5–0.9 m)
↑ 4–7 ft (1.2–2 m)

Extensively selected and hybridized to produce the Elatum Group, which includes: 'Albert Shepherd', medium height, light blue with pink flush and buff center; 'Angela Harbutt', medium to tall, pinkish mauve; 'Blue Dawn', medium to tall, bright deep blue with white eye; 'Blue Lagoon', medium to tall, pure dark blue with light eye; 'Blue Nile', low-growing, clear mid-blue with contrasting white center; 'Bruce', tall, deep violet-purple with lavender to gray eye; 'Cassius', medium height, mid-blue often suffused with mauve, black center; 'Claire', low-growing, pale pink to nearly white at the center; 'Conspicuous', medium

Delphinium barbeyi, in the wild, Mount Sneffels, Colorado, USA

Delphinium × *belladonna*

Delphinium grandiflorum 'Tom Pouce'

Delphinium, Hybrid Cultivar, 'Clifford Park'

Delphinium, Hybrid Cultivar, 'Cliveden Beauty'

Delphinium, Hybrid Cultivar, 'Cupid'

Delphinium, Hybrid Cultivar, 'Delph Sabrine'

Delphinium, Hybrid Cultivar, 'Harlekijn'

Delphinium, HC, 'Loch Leven'

Delphinium, HC, 'Michael Ayres'

D., HC, New Century hybrid

Delphinium, HC, 'Spindrift'

Delphinium, HC, 'Sungleam'

height, mauve with large brown center; 'Constance Rivett', medium height, pure white; 'Cupid', short, blue with white eye; 'Emily Hawkins', tall and strong-growing, lavender suffused with blue, buff center; 'Fanfare', tall, pale silvery mauve, early flowering; 'Faust', tall, intense almost metallic deep blue with hint of purple; 'Fenella', medium height, bright pure blue with black center; 'Gillian Dallas', medium height, gray-blue with white center, late flowering; 'Giotto', medium height, purple-blue with a mustard center; 'Harlekijn', deep violet, semi-double with blackish center; 'Kathleen Cooke', medium height, mid-blue with white eye; 'Langdon's Royal Flush', medium height, dusky pink with white center; 'Loch Leven', low-growing, light blue with white eye; 'Lord Butler', low-growing, soft mid-blue with white eye, compact and heavy flowering; **Magic Fountain Series** ★, seedling strain, in a wide color range; 'Michael Ayres', medium height, deep pinkish violet with dark center; 'Mighty Atom', short semi-double, deep mauve, late flowering; 'Min', medium height, lavender with dark veining. The **New Century** hybrids, to over 4 ft (1.2 m) tall, come in a wide range of colors. 'Our Deb',

mid-sized, soft pink with a dark eye; 'Rosemary Brock', medium height, soft mid-pink with a buff center; 'Sandpiper' ★, tall, white with black center; 'Spindrift', medium height, flower variable, usually a turquoise shade but sometimes also with blue or pink flowers; 'Sungleam', medium height, creamy yellow with yellow eye; 'Thamesmead', short to medium, gentian blue with black eye; 'Tiddles', medium height, semi-double, dusky mauve; and 'Walton Gemstone', of medium height, pale lavender blue with white eye. Zones 3–9.

DENDROBIUM

The genus *Dendrobium*, of the family Orchidaceae, has always been popular with orchid growers. It enjoys a wide distribution, from India and Sri Lanka, through Southeast Asia to New Guinea, Australia, and the Pacific Islands. They are almost exclusively epiphytes or lithophytes, with a sympodial growth habit. There is an amazing diversity of plant habit, flower form, and color in this large genus. Almost all colors and combinations are represented in the flowers. It contains species whose individual blooms last for only a few hours, to others that can persist for up to 9 months in pristine condition.

Many hybrids have been developed; for both orchid enthusiasts and the important cut-flower industry in tropical countries. The majority of flowers marketed as "Singapore orchids" are actually *Dendrobium* hybrids, which last well as cut flowers. *D. nobile* and related species have been used to create the thousands of colorful and long-lasting "softcane" *Dendrobium* hybrids. Over the past couple of decades, there have been vast inroads made with Australian native *Dendrobium* hybrids. These are very popular and relatively fast growing, incorporating species such as *D. speciosum*, *D. kingianum*, and *D. tetragonum*.

CULTIVATION: Being such a large and varied genus, they also have a range of diverse cultural requirements. Quite a number of species and hybrids produce new plants off the older pseudobulbs. These plants are called aerials or "keikis," a Hawaiian word meaning baby. Once these growths have hardened off and they have produced roots, they can be removed and grown as a new plant. In the dry season, the "softcane" types shed their leaves and are dormant. Once the rains come, the plants burst into flower and produce next season's growth. This deciduous feature is common with many of the

Dendrobium species, which have evolved to adapt to distinct wet and dry seasons. Most dendrobiums can be grown in a bark-based medium with some types performing well on treefern or cork slabs. Some of the smaller growing species from the mountainous regions grow well in sphagnum moss that is kept damp. Propagation is by division.

Dendrobium alexandrae

☀ ⚊ ↔ 8–20 in (20–50 cm)
↕ 8–27 in (20–70 cm)

From New Guinea. Uncommon, only recently entered general cultivation. Yellowish green flowers, often purple spotted, with purple-marked labellum, on inflorescences of up to 8 blooms; the flowers last for a number of weeks in spring. Zones 11–12.

Dendrobium alexandrae

Dendrobium atroviolaceum

☀ ✈ ↔ 8–24 in (20–60 cm)
↑ 8–20 in (20–50 cm)

From New Guinea. Small clusters of long-lasting, nodding, greenish yellow blooms, which are finely spotted with maroon, appear throughout the warmer months, and year-round in the tropics. Zones 10–12.

Dendrobium bigibbum

COOKTOWN ORCHID

☀ ✈ ↔ 8–24 in (20–60 cm)
↑ 4–24 in (10–60 cm)

From Australia, common in the Cape York Peninsula. The spectacular purple blooms, on sprays of up to 20 flowers, appear in autumn. This plant enjoys warm conditions, and must be kept dry in winter when dormant. **D. b. subsp.** *phalaenopsis* has large purple flowers; **D. b. var.** *compactum* ★ is a small-growing form with chunky pseudobulbs up to 5 in (12 cm) tall. Zones 11–12.

Dendrobium bracteosum

☀ ✈ ↔ 5–15 in (12–38 cm)
↑ 6–14 in (15–35 cm)

A native of New Guinea. The long-lasting blooms form in tight clusters, generally off the older leafless pseudo-bulbs, throughout the warmer months, and year-round in the tropics. Flower color varies from white through various shades of pink to deep red-purple. Zones 11–12.

Dendrobium engae

Dendrobium ceraula

Dendrobium bulbophylloides

☀ ✈ ↔ 2–8 in (5–20 cm)
↑ ½–1¼ in (1.2–3 cm)

From New Guinea. Miniature creeping species that hugs its host. Yellow-orange to red-brown blooms, quite large considering the size of the plant, in winter–spring. Performs best when grown on a tree-fern that is kept damp, allowing mosses to also grow on the mount. Zones 10–11.

Dendrobium canaliculatum

ONION ORCHID

☀ ✈ ↔ 4–16 in (10–40 cm)
↑ 4–16 in (10–40 cm)

From Australia. The unique scaly pseudobulbs give it its common name. Up to 40 narrow and twisted flowers, white with yellow to brown tips, white and purple labellum, in spring. Likes warmth and bright light, with a dry rest in winter. Zones 11–12.

Dendrobium ceraula

syn. *Dendrobium gonzalesii*

☀ ✈ ↔ 4–10 in (10–25 cm)
↑ 6–16 in (15–40 cm)

From the Philippines. This species from the mountainous forests, prefers cool, moist, shady conditions. Flowers vary from blue-mauve through pink to white, with flat purple-striped labellum, in winter–spring. Zones 10–11.

Dendrobium chameleon

☀ ✈ ↔ 4–8 in (10–20 cm)
↑ 5–24 in (12–60 cm)

Pendulous growing epiphyte from the Philippines, requiring moist, shady conditions. In autumn and winter, it produces flowers that vary in color from ivory white and creamy yellow to brown. Zones 10–11.

Dendrobium chrysotoxum

☀/☀ ✈ ↔ 8–24 in (20–60 cm)
↑ 8–16 in (20–40 cm)

Robust plant from India to southern China. Swollen pseudobulbs produce sprays of up to 25 golden yellow to orange waxy flowers in late spring. **D. c. var.** *suavissimum* differs in having a dark reddish orange blotch on the labellum. Zones 10–12.

Dendrobium chrysotoxum

Dendrobium bigibbum var. *compactum*

Dendrobium crumenatum

DOVE ORCHID, PIGEON ORCHID

☀/☀ ✈ ↔ 8–24 in (20–60 cm)
↑ 8–24 in (20–60 cm)

From Southeast Asia. This orchid bears white blooms, which last only one day. It needs a sudden drop in temperature, of about 50°F (10°C), to induce flowering. Such an event takes place during tropical storms. Exactly 9 days later the plant, plus any others in the district, will profusely burst into bloom. Zones 11–12.

Dendrobium cuthbertsonii ★

☀ ✈ ↔ 2–8 in (5–20 cm)
↑ 1–3 in (2.5–8 cm)

From New Guinea. One of the gems of the orchid world, with individual blooms that can last up to 9 months under favorable conditions. A cool-growing but frost-tender miniature plant with disproportionately large blooms. Comes in a range of bright colors, including, red, orange, yellow,

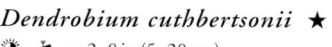

Dendrobium chameleon

Dendrobium bracteosum

Dendrobium bulbophylloides

pink, white, plus bicolor forms utilizing these colors. In cultivation, plants must be kept moist, and sphagnum moss is frequently used for potted plants. Zones 10–11.

Dendrobium discolor

☀ ✈ ↔ 1–4 ft (0.3–1.2 m)
↑ 1–6 ft (0.3–1.8 m)

From Australia and New Guinea. Tall-growing and variable species. Large spikes of undulating brown flowers, most of the year. A coastal species that enjoys strong light and requires a lot of room to reach its full potential. Zones 11–12.

Dendrobium engae

☀ ✈ ↔ 8–20 in (20–50 cm)
↑ 8–27 in (20–70 cm)

Robust epiphytic species from the mountains of Enga Province, New Guinea. Up to 12 large, greenish cream fragrant flowers can last for up to 4 months. Zones 10–11.

Dendrobium cuthbertsonii

Dendrobium fimbriatum

☼/🌣 ✦ ↔ 1–4 ft (0.3–1.2 m)
↑ 1–7 ft (0.3–2 m)

Tall-growing species from Southeast Asia. Bunches of pure yellow to orange flowers, on small spikes, in late spring. *D. f.* var. *oculatum*, more frequently seen in cultivation, orange flowers, deep maroon blotch on the labellum. Zones 10–12.

Dendrobium gibsonii

☼/🌣 ✦ ↔ 12–24 in (30–60 cm)
↑ 12–48 in (30–120 cm)

From Nepal to China. An uncommon summer- to autumn-flowering species. Glossy golden blooms, 2 distinctive deep maroon blotches on labellum. Zones 10–12.

Dendrobium goldschmidtianum

syn. *Dendrobium miyakei*

☼/🌣 ✦ ↔ 8–24 in (20–60 cm)
↑ 8–36 in (20–90 cm)

A showy species from Taiwan. The clusters of up to 20 bright purple

Dendrobium fimbriatum var. *oculatum*

Dendrobium goldschmidtianum

blooms are produced off the leafless pseudobulbs, from late winter to summer. Zones 10–12.

Dendrobium gracilicaule

☼/🌣 ✦ ↔ 8–36 in (20–90 cm)
↑ 8–24 in (20–60 cm)

Epiphyte from Australia. Slender pseudobulbs. Small arching spikes of yellowish green, and sweetly fragrant flowers, heavily blotched with red-brown on the back of the segments, in early spring. Zones 10–11.

Dendrobium harveyanum

🌣 ✦ ↔ 8–16 in (20–40 cm)
↑ 8–16 in (20–40 cm)

This species, native to Thailand and Vietnam, is unique among the genus because of its highly fringed petals and labellum, which are both bright canary yellow. Up to 5 spring blooms are produced on short inflorescences from near the top of the pseudobulb. *Dendrobium harveyanum* grows slowly and particularly resents disturbance. Zones 11–12.

Dendrobium johnsoniae

🌣 ✦ ↔ 8–20 in (20–50 cm)
↑ 8–20 in (20–50 cm)

A native of New Guinea. This species produces clusters of attractive, long-lasting, pure white, fragrant blooms, on short upright spikes, throughout the warmer months of the year. The flower's labellum is striped with purple. Zones 11–12.

Dendrobium johnsoniae

Dendrobium kingianum

Dendrobium laevifolium

Dendrobium lawesii

Dendrobium kingianum ★

🌣 ⚘ ↔ 4–48 in (10–120 cm)
↑ 2–36 in (5–90 cm)

From Australia. Popular and highly variable, spring-flowering, lithophytic species. Produces up to 12 fragrant flowers off compact plants. Colors vary from pure white, through most shades of pink to deep beetroot purple. White labellum, blotched and splashed with purple. Many superior cultivars have been developed through selective line breeding of desirable forms. Zones 9–11.

Dendrobium laevifolium

🌣 ✦ ↔ 2½–8 in (6–20 cm)
↑ 2½–6 in (6–15 cm)

Miniature species from New Guinea. Vibrant purple flowers last for up to 8 weeks. Keep moist all year; blooms off leafless pseudobulbs. Zones 10–12.

Dendrobium lawesii

🌣 ✦ ↔ 4–12 in (10–30 cm)
↑ 6–20 in (15–50 cm)

From New Guinea. Semi-pendent leafy growth habit, attractive even when not in bloom. Bright tubular flowers with an upturned tip to the labellum, probably bird pollinated. Flower color is most variable, with red, orange, yellow, pink, purple, and bicolored forms occurring. Zones 10–12.

Dendrobium lindleyi

syn. *Dendrobium aggregatum*

☼/🌣 ✦ ↔ 8–16 in (20–40 cm)
↑ 8–16 in (20–40 cm)

From India to China. Bears pendent sprays of up to 20 lemon yellow to golden flowers, quite large considering its compact growth habit, in spring–summer. Zones 10–12.

Dendrobium gibsonii

Dendrobium harveyanum

Dendrobium macrophyllum

☀/◐ ♣ ↔ 8–24 in (20–60 cm)
↕ 8–27 in (20–70 cm)

Robust species from New Guinea; often forms huge clumps in the wild. The greenish cream flowers, have contrasting highly detailed labellum with distinctive fine maroon veining. Up to 30 long-lasting blooms per inflorescence, during the warmer months. Backs of sepals and ovary are covered in dense green hairs. Zones 11–12.

Dendrobium masarangense

◐ ♣ ↔ 2–5 in (5–12 cm)
↕ 1–2 in (2.5–5 cm)

Compact-growing, tufted, miniature species from New Guinea. Long-lasting greenish cream blooms, bright orange-red blotch on the labellum, in winter–spring. Dislikes continual warm temperatures and must be kept moist in cultivation. Zones 9–11.

Dendrobium moniliforme

☀/◐ ♣ ↔ 8–24 in (20–60 cm)
↕ 4–10 in (10–25 cm)

From Japan and China. Compact and variable plant; type species of genus *Dendrobium*. Fragrant white to pink blooms, in spring. Variegated leafed forms also in cultivation. Zones 9–11.

Dendrobium nobile

☀/◐ ♣ ↔ 8–24 in (20–60 cm)
↕ 8–24 in (20–60 cm)

From India to China. Highly variable species; a great beginner's orchid; one

Dendrobium pseudoglomeratum

Dendrobium obtusisepalum

Dendrobium macrophyllum

of the "softcanes". Spring flowers from deep purple to pure white, with many shades and bicolored combinations in between. *D. n.* var. *cooksonianum*, unusual, with labellum coloring in the petals; *D. n.* var. *nobilius*, large, deep purple; *D. n.* var. *virginale*, pure white. Zones 9–12.

Dendrobium obtusisepalum

syn. *Dendrobium wentianum*

◐ ♣ ↔ 4–12 in (10–30 cm)
↕ 8–32 in (20–80 cm)

From New Guinea. Stunning species with a pendulous growth habit. Bright orange blooms, waxy texture, in spring. Enjoys cool, moist, humid conditions. Zones 10–11.

Dendrobium pseudoglomeratum

◐ ♣ ↔ 8–20 in (20–50 cm)
↕ 8–27 in (20–70 cm)

From New Guinea. Heads of up to 16 blooms, an unusual and striking color combination of hot pink and orange, appear off the leafless pseudobulbs, in spring. Zones 10–12.

Dendrobium pulchellum

☀/◐ ♣ ↔ 1–3 ft (0.3–0.9 m)
↕ 1–7 ft (0.3–2 m)

Warm-growing species from Nepal to China. Can produce very long cane-like pseudobulbs. Up to a dozen, cream to apricot, fragrant flowers, with a couple of dark maroon blotches on the lip, on pendent spikes off the older leafless stems, in summer. Zones 11–12.

Dendrobium smillieae

Dendrobium masarangense

Dendrobium speciosum

D. speciosum subsp. *capricornicum*

Dendrobium rupestre

◐ ♣ ↔ 2–4 in (5–10 cm)
↕ 1–2 in (2.5–5 cm)

Miniature species from New Guinea. Produces reddish purple blooms in winter and spring. Dislikes continual warm temperatures and must be kept moist in cultivation. Zones 9–11.

Dendrobium smillieae

BOTTLEBRUSH ORCHID

☀/◐ ♣ ↔ 8–27 in (20–70 cm)
↕ 8–48 in (20–120 cm)

Native to Australia and New Guinea. Warm-growing species. Densely packed clusters of blooms from white to pinkish green, with a dark bottle green labellum, throughout the warmer months, and year-round in the tropics. Zones 11–12.

Dendrobium speciosum

KING ORCHID, ROCK LILY

☀/◐ ♣ ↔ 1–10 ft (0.3–3 m)
↕ 4–48 in (10–120 cm)

This is a highly variable orchid, a native of eastern Australia, which has

Dendrobium rupestre

D. speciosum subsp. *curvicaule*, in the wild, Queensland, Australia

D. speciosum subsp. *grandiflorum*

many populations recognized as varieties or subspecies, such as *D. s.* subsp. *capricornicum*, *D. s.* subsp. *curvicaule*, *D. s.* subsp. *grandiflorum*, *D. s.* subsp. *hillii*, and *D. s.* subsp. *pedunculatum*. *D. speciosum* is a popular garden plant, which thrives in frost-free climates, where it blooms from the late winter through to the spring. It produces particularly large inflorescences crowded with white to deep yellow, highly fragrant flowers. It is a most robust plant, with the large specimens becoming massive. *D. speciosum* is unforgettable when seen in full bloom. Zones 9–11.

Dendrobium subclausum, in the wild, New Guinea

Dendrobium sulphureum

Dendrobium tetragonum var. *cacatua*

Dendrobium tapiniense

Dendrobium spectabile

☀/◐ ✿ ↔ 8–24 in (20–60 cm)
↑ 8–32 in (20–80 cm)

From New Guinea. Unique species with twisted and somewhat distorted floral segments, produced on inflorescences of up to 20 blooms, last for a number of weeks, in spring–summer. Zones 11–12.

D. tetragonum var. *melaleucaphilum*

Dendrobium subclausum

☀ ✿ ↔ 4–12 in (10–30 cm)
↑ 6–20 in (15–50 cm)

From New Guinea. Thin upright to flaccid pseudobulbs that frequently branch and produce aerial growths. Bright flowers from red to yellow, bicolored forms also occurring, year-round. Zones 10–12.

Dendrobium sulphureum

☀ ✿ ↔ 2–5 in (5–12 cm)
↑ 1–2 in (2.5–5 cm)

Miniature species from New Guinea. Long-lasting greenish yellow blooms, a bright red blotch on the apex of the

Dendrobium spectabile

labellum, throughout the year. Dislikes continual warm temperatures and must always be kept moist in cultivation. Zones 9–11.

Dendrobium tapiniense

☀/◐ ✿ ↔ 8–24 in (20–60 cm)
↑ 8–32 in (20–80 cm)

Robust species from New Guinea. Spikes of up to a dozen spring and summer blooms that are very thick and can last up to 3 months. Summer-flowering species, which appreciates warm days and cool nights in cultivation. Zones 10–12.

Dendrobium tetragonum

☀ ✿ ↔ 4–20 in (10–50 cm)
↑ 4–27 in (10–70 cm)

Australian species in range of varieties, sizes, and colors. Semi-pendulous pseudobulbs, distinctly 4-angled in cross-section. Spidery blooms, cream to yellow-green, often with dark purple to brown blotches and borders on the floral segments. Labellum can be white or marked with brown to purple spots or striations, in spring–summer. Highly variable, 4 distinct geographical populations recognized as varieties: *D. t.* var. *cacatua*; *D. t.* var. *giganteum*; *D. t.* var. *haysianum*; *D. t.* var. *melaleucaphilum*. Zones 9–12.

Dendrobium thyrsiflorum

☀ ✿ ↔ 8–36 in (20–90 cm)
↑ 8–24 in (20–60 cm)

Found from India to China. Easily grown species, short-lived pendent clusters of flowers, in late spring. Segments are white, sometimes with faint pink flush, bright yellow labellum, resemble a bunch of grapes. Zones 10–12.

Dendrobium victoriae-reginae

Dendrobium thyrsiflorum

Dendrobium vexillarius

☀ ✿ ↔ 2–5 in (5–12 cm)
↑ 1–5 in (2.5–12 cm)

From New Guinea. Miniature species. Bright red, long-lasting flowers. There are also wild populations with other colors present, including orange, yellow, cream, to unusual bluish gray tones. Dislikes continual warm temperatures and must be kept moist in cultivation. Zones 9–11.

Dendrobium victoriae-reginae ★

☀ ✿ ↔ 8–20 in (20–50 cm)
↑ 8–24 in (20–60 cm)

From the Philippines. One of the few "blue" orchids. Up to 4 lilac to dark bluish purple flowers, on short sprays, from nodes along branching pseudobulbs, throughout the year. Prefers cool, moist conditions. Zones 9–11.

Dendrobium wardianum

☀/◐ ✿ ↔ 8–16 in (20–40 cm)
↑ 8–27 in (20–70 cm)

One of the softcane species found from India to China. The waxy, fragrant, tri-colored blooms are produced in late spring, off leafless pseudobulbs. Zones 10–12.

Dendrobium vexillarius

Dendrobium wardianum

Dendrobium williamsonii

☀ ✤ ↔ 8–12 in (20–30 cm)
↑ 8–16 in (20–40 cm)

From India to Thailand. Has fine, short, black hairs along the pseudobulb. One or two, waxy, cream to pale yellow flowers, red blotch on labellum, produced at the top of the mature cane. Must be allowed to dry out between watering and have constant air circulation. Zones 10–12.

Dendrobium Hybrids

The numbers of *Dendrobium* hybrids have greatly increased in recent decades, particularly "hardcane" hybrids for the cut-flower market.

AUSTRALIAN HYBRIDS

☀ ❧ ↔ 8–30 in (20–75 cm)
↑ 4–24 in (10–60 cm)

This is a selection of some Australian hybrids, bred from indigenous species, such as *D. kingianum, D. speciosum,* and *D. tetragonum*. Most of these hybrids are winter and spring blooming, and will bloom off the same pseudobulbs for a number of seasons. They are compact plants that will often produce masses of highly fragrant blooms. **Elegant Heart**, a hybrid betweeen *D. Peewee* and *D. speciosum,* was developed in the 1980s by Walter Upton; **Hilda Poxon ★**, a very popular primary hybrid between *D. speciosum* and *D. tetragonum* that blooms a number of times during the year; **Jonathan's Glory**, one of the newer hybrids, similar to an improved *D. kingianum;* **Kayla**, a slow-growing hybrid with a strong *D. speciosum* influence; **Yondi Brolga**, one of the superb hybrids made by the late Sid Batchelor; and **Zeus**, bearing starry purple flowers that are produced numerous times throughout the year. Zones 9–11.

"HARDCANE" HYBRIDS

☀/☀ ✤ ↔ 8–32 in (20–80 cm)
↑ 8–40 in (20–100 cm)

These hybrids have been derived from many of the lowland tropical *Dendrobium* species such as *D. bigibbum, D. discolor,* and *D. phalaenopsis*. **Chao Praya Rose**, dark magenta blooms that are very long-lived, both on the plant and as a cut flower; **Suzanne Neil**, deep pink-purple flowers; **Thai Pinky**, an important horticultural plant for the florist trade; and **Than-aid Stripes**, heavily veined magenta blooms. Zones 11–12.

"NIGROHIRSUTE" OR BLACK-HAIRED STYLE HYBRIDS

☀/☀ ✤ ↔ 8–16 in (20–40 cm)
↑ 8–16 in (20–40 cm)

These dendrobiums have short black hairs on the pseudobulbs and generally have white to cream blooms with contrasting colors on the labellum. **Frosty Dawn**, a hybrid between *D. Dawn Maree* and *D. Lime Frost,* produces flowers in spring–summer with the blooms lasting about 8 weeks. Zones 10–12.

"SOFTCANE" HYBRIDS

☀/☀ ❧ ↔ 6–16 in (15–40 cm)
↑ 8–24 in (20–60 cm)

Hybrids derived from *D. nobile,* or closely related species. Leaves are short lived, and are shed from the pseudobulbs before flowering. They produce up to 5 flowers from each node along the naked pseudobulb, with potential for many long-lived blooms along the length of the swollen stems. **Golden Blossom 'Kogane'**, yellow flowers, crimson blotched labellum; **Sailor Boy**, pastel colors most popularly with a yellow center, followed by a white band with pale pink tips to the floral

Dendrobium williamsonii

Dendrobium, Australian Hybrid, (Angellene × Ellen Glow)

D., Australian Hybrid, Barry Simpson

D., Australian Hybrid, Brinawa Sunset

D., Australian Hybrid, Bellingen

D., AH, Biddy Genedis

D., AH, (Intense × Rutherford Sunspot)

D., AH, Elegant Heart

D., AH, Elegant Heart 'Blue Tongue'

D., AH, Gillieston Jazz

D., Australian Hybrid, Hilda Poxon

D., AH, Burgundy Cream

D., AH, Jonathon's Glory

D., Australian Hybrid, Kayla

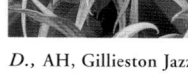

Dendrobium, "Softcane" Hybrid, Kay Lynette

Dendrobium, "Hardcane" Hybrid, Suzanne Neil

Dendrobium, "Hardcane" Hybrid, Thanaid Stripes

D., "Hardcane" Hybrid, Chao Praya Rose

D., "Hardcane" Hybrid, Nagasaki

D., "Softcane" Hybrid, Colorado Springs

D., "Softcane" Hybrid, Golden Blossom 'Kogane'

D., "Softcane" Hybrid, Sailor Boy 'Pinkie' ★

D., "Hardcane" Hybrid, Pua'ala

D., "Hardcane" Hybrid, Sedona

D., "Softcane" Hybrid, Stardust

D., "Softcane" Hybrid, Yellow Ribbon 'Delight'

D., "Softcane" Hybrid, Yukidaruma 'King'

D., "Hardcane" Hybrid, Thai Pinky

D., "Hardcane" Hybrid, White Fairy

D., "Softcane" Hybrid, Lovely Virgin 'Angel'

D., "Softcane" Hybrid, Sailor Boy

Dendrobium, "Nigrohirsute" Hybrid, Frosty Dawn

Dendrochilum cobbianum

Dendrochilum latifolium

segments; **Yukidaruma 'King' ★**, arguably the most popular softcane hybrid in cultivation, an extremely vigorous growing plant and a reliable and prolific bloomer. Zones 9–11.

DENDROCALAMUS

A genus of about 30 giant, clump-forming, perennial bamboos from India, Southeast Asia, China, and Indonesia, that are members of the grass (Poaceae) family. They are mostly restricted to higher rainfall or mountain areas; they grow from short rhizomes. Members form loose to dense clumps with hollow to solid culms. There are numerous branches at a node, one or two larger than the rest. Long, narrow, strap-like, green leaves. Widely grown for construction and craft purposes, as well as for their edible shoots.
CULTIVATION: Plant in spring in light or moderately heavy, slightly acidic, loamy or sandy soil kept moist at all times. Will tolerate full sun but prefer light shade. Cut out oldest shoots in spring. Propagate by division or from stem cuttings.

Dendrocalamus asper
PAI TONG, PRING BETUNG, SWEET BAMBOO
☼ ❄ ↔ 40–80 ft (12–24 m)
↑ 60–100 ft (18–30 m)

From Southeast Asia. Stems 8–12 in (20–30 cm) in diameter, new shoots furry silver-brown, velvety to the touch. This is a most important, large, structural bamboo, with edible shoots. It is used for building, crafts, furniture making, and as a fodder for livestock. 'Hitam', from Indonesia, culms quickly turn black with occasional green stripes; the dark color is retained after harvest, the green stripes becoming tan. Zones 9–12.

DENDROCHILUM
CHAIN ORCHID

Members of this large genus of the orchid (Orchidaceae) family of over 200 sympodial botanicals produce a single leaf per pseudobulb and are related to *Coelogyne*. Most are epiphytes that grow in mossy cloud forests in mountainous regions, where there are rarely significant temperature extremes. Only a few make their homes in the tropical lowlands. The main center of distribution for the genus is the Philippines, with numerous species in Borneo and Sumatra. They bloom once a year, with the developing new growth, and their small but often colorful flowers are arranged in 2 rows and alternately along an inflorescence that is spiraled in some species.
CULTIVATION: Easy to grow, with most being clump-forming and well suited to pot culture. Sphagnum moss may be used solely as a medium for the miniature growers and any plants up to 4 in (10 cm) pot size. Larger plants grow well in a bark-based mix, with a small proportion of gravel, perlite, and chopped moss added. Fresh air and constant high humidity is important and these plants will happily bloom in shaded conditions. They also like to be kept constantly moist. Try to keep these plants as cool as possible during

Dendromecon rigida

hot summer months and protect them from the chill in winter. Propagation is by division.

Dendrochilum cobbianum ★
☼ ✜ ↔ 8–20 in (20–50 cm)
↑ 6–20 in (15–50 cm)

From the Philippines. Arguably the most frequently seen member of the genus in cultivation. Bears spring flowers from white through to yellow and green, and sometimes the labellum is a contrasting color. The nectar gland in the centre of the labellum is a distinctive feature. Zones 10–12.

Dendrochilum glumaceum
HAY-SCENTED ORCHID
☼ ✜ ↔ 8–24 in (20–60 cm)
↑ 8–16 in (20–40 cm)

From the Philippines. Flowers, in winter–early spring, are white to cream, with very pointed sepals and petals. Up to 60 flowers form on the inflorecence, with a wide color range in the labellum, which may be orange, yellow, green, or brown. Zones 10–12.

Dendrochilum latifolium
☼ ✜ ↔ 8–20 in (20–50 cm)
↑ 6–20 in (15–50 cm)

From the Philippines. One of the larger species. A single leaf is up to 16 in (40 cm) long; inflorescence is longer than leaves. Bears up to 60 flowers, scented, creamish green with a brown labellum, in summer. Zones 10–12.

Dendrochilum saccolabium
☼ ✜ ↔ 8–24 in (20–60 cm)
↑ 8–16 in (20–40 cm)

Spectacular and horticulturally attractive species from the Philippines. It bears arching inflorescences, with up to 40 glossy, round, dull to bright red flowers, in winter. Zones 10–11.

Dendrochilum tenellum
☼ ✜ ↔ 8–32 in (20–80 cm)
↑ 8–16 in (20–40 cm)

A native of the Philippines, which forms large clumps on moss-covered rainforest trees. Tiny white to cream flowers appear in late winter–early spring. One of the most "unorchid-like" species in foliage, with very fine, terete, grass-like leaves. A well-grown plant can be likened to the filament lamps that were in vogue years ago. Zones 10–11.

DENDROMECON

This genus contains just one species of evergreen shrub, which is native to California, the USA, and Mexico where it grows on the dry rocky chaparral. It belongs to the poppy (Papaveraceae) family and the relationship can be seen in the single yellow flowers that are borne in summer.
CULTIVATION: These plants require winter protection in climates with severe frosts. When grown outdoors, it will not survive severe winters and must be given a warm sheltered site in a well-drained, gritty soil that is not too rich. The shrub dislikes root disturbance and care should be taken at planting time to reduce transplant shock. Propagation is from half-hardened cuttings taken in summer, but these can be difficult to strike.

Dendromecon rigida
TREE POPPY
☼ ❄ ↔ 10 ft (3 m) ↑ 10 ft (3 m)

Stiff gray-green leaves. which account for its species name. Pure yellow, 4-petalled poppy flowers of a simple beauty, in summer. *D. r.* subsp. *harfordii* has thicker stems and leaves than the species, and slightly smaller yellow flowers. Zones 8–10.

Dendrochilum tenellum

DENDROSENECIO

Giant senecios of east Africa, 11 species of this genus of the daisy (Asteraceae) family were formerly included in the genus *Senecio*. Confined to volcanic massifs, mostly at 9,000–4,000 ft (2,700–4,200 m), characteristic of alpine heaths and some of higher mossy forests. Long-lived evergreen shrubs or small trees reaching heights of up to 25 ft (8 m), usually unbranched when young, with stems terminating in large cabbage-like rosettes of paddle-shaped leaves, woolly on the undersides. Stems below the rosettes remain clothed with dead leaves. Large upright panicles of daisy-like flowers with yellow rays emerge from among the leaves.

CULTIVATION: Doubtful that any have been successfully grown to adult size in gardens. Difficult to predict their needs; their equatorial habitats have almost no seasons, but large variations in temperature and humidity between day and night. Propagate from seed.

Dendrosenecio eric-rosenii

syn. *Senecio eric-rosenii*

☀ ❄ ↔ 3–10 ft (0.9–3 m) ↑ 10–20 ft (3–6 m)

Occurs on Ruwenzori, Virunga, and Kahuzi massifs on borders of Uganda, Zaire, and Rwanda; can form canopy of mossy forest. *D. e-r.* subsp. *alticola* confined to higher parts of Virunga. Zones 9–10.

Dendrosenecio johnstonii

syn. *Senecio johnstonii*

☀ ❄ ↔ 3–10 ft (0.9–3 m) ↑ 10–25 ft (3–8 m)

From Tanzania's Mount Kilimanjaro, in dwarf, moss-shaped, elfin forests and open moorland higher up; becoming tree-like in forest, with a crown of open branches. Zones 8–9.

Dendrosenecio johnstonii, Mt Kenya, Kenya

Dendrosenecio eric-rosenii, in the wild, Ruwenzori Mountains, Uganda

Dennstaedtia punctilobula

DENNSTAEDTIA

CUP FERN

A genus of about 70 medium to large terrestrial or epiphytic ferns in the bracken (Dennstaedtiacae) family, found in most warm-temperate to tropical regions except Europe. Creeping, branching, woody rhizomes; generous, finely divided, triangular foliage.

CULTIVATION: Creeping habit makes *Dennstaedtia* species unsuited to container cultivation. They prefer moist to dry, well-drained, acidic soil, in full to partial shade. Propagate from spore, or by division of rhizomes in spring.

Dennstaedtia punctilobula

HAY-SCENTED FERN

☀ ❄ ↔ 12–24 in (30–60 cm) ↑ 24–36 in (60–90 cm)

Deciduous fern with creeping rhizomes from eastern North America. Large colonies form a carpet. Lacy, triangular or sword-shaped, light green fronds, with notched pinnules, sticky to the touch, and smelling like hay when bruised. Finely downy stalks, with scattered hairs on frond midribs. Zones 3–9.

DEPPEA

This genus of some 25 species from Mexico and Central America to southeastern Brazil belongs to the madder (Rubiaceae) family. They are evergreen shrubs or small trees. Leaves are opposite, rarely in 3s, often unequal in size. Flowers are yellow, less often white, orange, or purple, with a short tube emerging from a large calyx of contrasting color, and 4, usually recurving, lobes. They are borne in cymes arising from the leaf axils or branch tips. Fruit is a small dry capsule.

CULTIVATION: Rarely cultivated, though at least one species is now becoming popular in the gardens of California, USA. They are likely to require a sheltered, humid, frost-free environment and moist well-drained soil. Propagation is from seed or half-hardened cuttings.

Deppea obtusiflora

Deppea obtusiflora

☀ ❄ ↔ 6 ft (1.8 m) ↑ 6–15 ft (1.8–4.5 m)

Shrub from southern Mexican state of Oaxaca, where it grows in cloud forest at around 8,000 ft (2,400 m). Leaves to ¾ in (18 mm) long. Flowers yellow, in clusters of 3 to 17 flowers. Zones 9–12.

DERWENTIA

Small genus of 8 species placed in the foxglove (Scrophulariaceae) family, occurring in subalpine to lower mountain regions of southeastern Australia. Named after the Derwent River in Tasmania, most of the species had previously been placed in the genera *Veronica* and *Parahebe*. Evergreen perennials or subshrubs, with ability to resprout from the rootstock. Leaves are opposite and variously shaped, some species being highly glaucous. White, blue, or mauve flowers are borne in dense clusters in spring and summer.

CULTIVATION: Propagation is from cuttings with most success being from fresh new growth taken from sprouting rootstocks. Seeds are not readily obtained, but if available should be sown when fresh.

Derwentia blakelyi

☀ ❄ ↔ 16–32 in (40–80 cm) ↑ 8–20 in (20–50 cm)

Although first collected in the 1930s by Sydney botanist W. F. Blakely, this species was named only recently. Found only on acid soils in eucalypt woodlands and forests of Central Tablelands of New South Wales, Australia. Small woody shrub, glaucous stems. Leaves oval to lance-shaped, stalkless, with heart-shaped base, margins toothed. Bears terminal clusters of small bluish flowers, in summer. Glaucous capsular fruits. Zones 8–9.

Derwentia perfoliata

syns *Parahebe perfoliata*, *Veronica perfoliata*

DIGGER'S SPEEDWELL

☀ ❄ ↔ 20–60 in (50–150 cm) ↑ 20–60 in (50–150 cm)

Occurs in a range of habitats from central New South Wales, generally above 1,640 ft (500 m) altitude, south to eastern and central western Victoria, Australia. Small shrub with woody rootstock. Stems mostly held erect, glaucous, with finely toothed, oval-shaped, leathery leaves, in 2s or 3s at the nodes. Bluish flowers in terminal and axillary spikes, in spring–summer. Grown in Europe since the early 1800s. Can be grown from both seeds and cuttings. Zones 8–9.

DESCHAMPSIA
HAIR GRASS

Charming genus of about 50 species of grasses in the grass (Poaceae) family. Clump-forming and can be herbaceous or evergreen. Found in temperate to cold regions, and many interesting clones have been selected by growers, mainly in Germany. Grown for their graceful foliage and airy flowerheads. CULTIVATION: Will grow in any good garden soil in sun or light shade. Clean out old spent flower stems in early spring to allow for new growth. Propagate from seed, but named clones must be divided in early spring.

Deschampsia cespitosa
syn. *Aira cespitosa*
TUFTED HAIR GRASS, TUSSOCK GRASS
☼/◐ ❄ ↔4–5 ft (1.2–1.5 m)
↑5–7 ft (1.5–2 m)

An attractive grass native to North America, Asia, and Europe. Fine, rich, evergreen foliage above which billows soft masses of tiny flowers in summer. *D. c.* subsp. *holciformis,* darker green foliage. *D. c.* var. *vivipara*, drooping plants that take root. Numerous clones

Desfontainia spinosa

Deuterocohnia brevifolia

that include: *D. c.* Bronze Veil/ 'Bronzeschleier', bronze flowers and considered a good form; Golden Pendant/'Goldgehänge', slightly pendulous yellow flowers; Gold Dust/'Goldstaub', flowers that open yellow; and Golden Dew/'Goldtau', yellow-green flowers. Zones 5–10.

Deschampsia flexuosa
COMMON HAIR GRASS, CRINKLED HAIR GRASS, WAVY HAIR GRASS
☼/◐ ❄ ↔6–8 in (15–20 cm)
↑27–36 in (70–90 cm)

Found in Eurasia and the Americas. Very fine, wavy, thread-like, green to olive leaves. Fine wiry flower stems with branching, spray-like, pink-tinted inflorescence. Zones 5–9.

DESFONTAINIA

This genus, now regarded as belonging to its own family, Desfontaineaceae, comprises a single species of evergreen shrub, found growing throughout the Andes from Colombia to Tierra del Fuego. In the north it grows in cool mountain forests, while further south it is found at sea level. An attractive shrub with brilliant orange and yellow flowers that stand out against its dark glossy foliage. Well suited to the conditions enjoyed by rhododendrons. CULTIVATION: *Desfontainia* needs a cool moist climate and an acid soil that is moisture retentive and rich in humus. It should have a partially shaded, sheltered position; water well in dry spells. Propagate from seed or half-hardened cuttings in summer.

Desfontainia spinosa ★
☼ ❄ ↔10 ft (3 m) ↑10 ft (3 m)
Bushy slow-growing shrub. Tubular flowers scarlet to orange with yellow tips, in summer–autumn. Cherry-sized fruits. Zones 8–9.

DESMODIUM

A member of the pea-flower subfamily of the legume (Fabaceae) family, this genus from warm-temperate and tropical regions contains about 450 species. Most are scrambling perennials, others

Deuterocohnia lorentziana

Derwentia perfoliata

are deciduous or evergreen shrubs. Genus is characterized by its pink, purple, blue, or white flowers, trifoliate leaves, and fruits that break into single-seeded segments upon maturity. These segments have small hooked bristles that attach them to any passing furry animal or to human clothing, thereby aiding dispersal. Some species from warmer regions are weedy, but some of the shrubby species from cooler origins are attractive garden plants. CULTIVATION: Propagate from seed in spring, or from cuttings. Sunny well-drained sites are preferred, and species from the warmer areas will need greenhouse shelter in cooler locations.

Desmodium canadense
SHOWY TICK-TREFOIL
☼ ❄ ↔12 in (30 cm) ↑4–6 ft (1.2–1.8 m)
From southern Canada to Virginia in the south, and Oklahoma, USA, in the west. Easy to grow perennial with long, oval, green leaves; spikes of pink to lavender, pea-flowers cluster at top of stalk in mid-summer. Spreads quickly and thus can be invasive. Zones 5–9.

DEUTEROCOHNIA
syn. *Abromeitiella*

Mainly from northern Argentina, Peru, and Bolivia, this genus of 15 species is part of the pineapple (Bromeliaceae) family. The plants are sun-loving and prickly, growing in the ground or on rocks and forming large clumps. There are 2 groups of species: one (formerly placed in the genus *Abromeitiella*) consists of low-growing plants that look like cushions in the wild, generally with green tubular flowers; the other group is made up of larger plants with mainly yellow flowers on long stems. The genus is unique among bromeliads in having perennial flowering shoots that produce new branches each year. It is mostly only the smaller species that are cultivated.

Deschampsia cespitosa

CULTIVATION: Smaller species can be grown indoors, larger species are best in greenhouses or conservatories in cool-temperate areas, or outdoors in warm-temperate, subtropical, and tropical areas. Water when dry; do not overfertilize. Propagate from seed or offsets.

Deuterocohnia brevifolia ★
syn. *Abromeitiella brevifolia*
☼/◐ ❄ ↔4–12 in (10 cm)
↑2–4 in (5–10 cm)

From northern Argentina. The plants eventually form broad mounds. Triangular green leaves, with a few spines along edge. Flowers green, tubular, solitary, and stalkless among leaves. *D. b.* subsp. *chlorantha* has more flexible spines on the leaf. Zones 8–10.

Deuterocohnia lorentziana
syn. *Abromeitiella lorentziana*
☼ ❄ ↔4 in (10 cm) ↑4 in (10 cm)
From northern Argentina. Large clump-forming plants formerly known as *Abromeitiella*. Triangular gray-green leaves, with a few spines along edge. Petals tubular, green. Not as popular as *D. brevifolia*. Zones 8–10.

Deutzia compacta

Deutzia crenata

Deutzia × *elegantissima* 'Fasciculata'

DEUTZIA

Widely cultivated for its ornamental members, this genus of the hydrangea (Hydrangeaceae) family contains 60 species of deciduous and evergreen shrubs, mainly from temperate Asia with a toehold in Central America. Most commonly grown deutzias are spring flowering and deciduous. They have pointed oval to lance-shaped leaves in opposite pairs, often with serrated edges, and heads of small, starry, 5-petalled, white, cream, or pink flowers usually held clear of the foliage. CULTIVATION: Most very frost hardy; mainstay of temperate gardens. Shelter from strong winds. Prune and thin after flowering to maintain framework of strong branches. Propagate from seed or half-hardened summer cuttings.

Deutzia compacta
☀ ❄ ↔ 7 ft (2 m) ↑ 6 ft (1.8 m)
Himalayan deciduous species. Narrow, pointed leaves, with fine branches that cascade somewhat. Leaves dark green upper surfaces, pale undersides, toothed edges, covering of fine hairs. Flowers white, in small heads. Zones 6–9.

Deutzia crenata
☀ ❄ ↔ 8 ft (2.4 m) ↑ 8 ft (2.4 m)
Similar to *D. scabra*, deciduous shrub from Japan and southeastern China. Slightly arching stems, hairy leaves, finely toothed edges. White flowers on racemes, in the spring. **D. c. var. nakaiana**, dwarf, to 12 in (30 cm high); 'Nikko', white flowers, dark foliage. Zones 6–9.

Deutzia × elegantissima
☀ ❄ ↔ 5 ft (1.5 m) ↑ 5 ft (1.5 m)
Derived from *D. purpurascens* and *D. sieboldiana,* of garden origin. Ovate to oblong-ovate leaves, uneven sharp teeth. Cymes of pink flowers, in early summer. Cultivars include: 'Fasciculata', with white to pale pink flowers, deep pink in bud; and 'Rosealind' ★, compact white flowers with a pink tinge. Zones 5–9.

Deutzia gracilis
SLENDER DEUTZIA
☀ ❄ ↔ 3–6 ft (0.9–1.8 m) ↑ 3–6 ft (0.9–1.8 m)
One of the main parents of hybrid deutzias, from Japan. Spreading shrub, mounded form. Slender erect shoots arch at the ends. Narrow leaves bright green, ovate to lance-shaped, pointed at the ends. Narrow panicles of pure white flowers, in mid-spring–early summer. Zones 5–9.

Deutzia × kalmiiflora
☀ ❄ ↔ 5 ft (1.5 m) ↑ 5 ft (1.5 m)
Hybrid between *D. parviflora* and *D. purpurascens,* of garden origin. Open shrub with arching branches. Finely toothed, mid-green, narrowly oval leaves. Upright panicles of cup-shaped flowers, deep pink outside, paler inside, early to mid-summer. Zones 5–9.

Deutzia longifolia
☀ ❄ ↔ 7 ft (2 m) ↑ 6 ft (1.8 m)
Deciduous native of western China. Dark green, heavy-textured, lance-shaped leaves, serrated edges, pale hairy undersides. Flowerheads of pale pink flowers, with darker striping, opening from deep pink buds, in early summer. 'Veitchii', narrow leaves, and purplish flowers. Zones 6–9.

Deutzia × magnifica
☀ ❄ ↔ 7 ft (2 m) ↑ 6 ft (1.8 m)
Of uncertain parents, possibly between *D. crenata* and *D. longifolia*, hybrid shrub with strong upright growth. Ovate to oblong-shaped leaves, finely toothed margins, gray and felt-like beneath. Dense panicles of single or double white flowers, in early summer. Zones 5–9.

Deutzia × rosea
☀ ❄ ↔ 3 ft (0.9 m) ↑ 3 ft (0.9 m)
Dwarf shrub, hybrid of *D. gracilis* and *D. purpurascens*. Ovate to oblong lance-shaped, finely serrated, dark green leaves. Short terminal panicles of flowers, pale pink inside, purplish outside. 'Campanulata', white flowers in dense panicles; 'Carminea', pale pink flowers, purplish on outside. Zones 5–9.

Deutzia scabra
FUZZY DEUTZIA
☀ ❄ ↔ 7 ft (2 m) ↑ 10 ft (3 m)
Native to Japan and China. Arching shoots; broadly ovate, rough, dark green leaves. Dense cylindrical panicles of honey-scented, white or pink-tinged, bell-shaped flowers terminate the branches, in early to mid-summer. Attractive peeling brown to orange bark. 'Candidissima', pure white double flowers; 'Pride of Rochester', very large, double white flowers tinged pinkish purple. Zones 5–9.

Deutzia setchuenensis
☀ ❄ ↔ 5 ft (1.5 m) ↑ 6 ft (1.8 m)
From western China. Ovate leaves, densely haired beneath, with fine forward-pointing teeth. Loose clusters of white flowers in summer. More often cultivated is **D. s. var. corymbiflora**, larger flower clusters, peeling pale brown bark with age. Zones 5–9.

DIANELLA

Genus of evergreen perennials comprising some 20 species from Australia, New Zealand, and Pacific Islands. One tropical species *(D. ensifolia)* extends to mainland Asia as far as China, Japan, and India, and to East Africa and Madagascar. Its exact position in the lily group of families is still under investigation; Hemerocallidaceae, Phormiaceae, and Dianellaceae have all been suggested. *Dianella* are herbaceous plants with fibrous roots, often with underground rhizomes. Stems are creeping or erect, bearing terminal fan of leaves. Leaves are grass-like, in 2 ranks, sheathing at the base and often with edges folded and fused together (like an iris leaf) but only in lower part. Inflorescence is a loose panicle with flowers on nodding stalks. Flowers have perianth segments, in 2 whorls of 3, blue to white, sometimes tinged green or purple. Fruit is a pale blue to dark purple-blue, spherical or egg-shaped berry. Seeds are black and shiny.

Deutzia × *magnifica*

Deutzia × *kalmiiflora*

Deutzia longifolia

Deutzia setchuenensis

Dianella tasmanica

CULTIVATION: In warmer regions they are grown in borders or wild plantings; elsewhere best under glass. Some will tolerate temperatures down to 20°F (−7°C) or even lower, others are frost tender. Tolerate light shade. Easily propagated by division or from seed.

Dianella caerulea

BLUE FLAX-LILY, BLUEBERRY LILY

☼ ⊰ ↔ 20–60 in (50–150 cm)
↕ to 7 ft (2 m)

Tufted-forming perennial with much-branched, stout, underground rhizomes. Occurs from New Guinea south to Tasmania, as well as on the eastern side of the Great Dividing Range on mainland Australia. Leaves are flat or with margins slightly re-curved. Inflorescences are longer than leaves, each with 3 to 30 flowers, from deep blue to yellow-green or cream. Each flower with 6 segments, appearing in spring–summer. Fruits globular, blue to purplish berries, each containing many shiny black seeds. There are 8 varieties recognized. **D. c. var. cin-erascens**, gray-green to silvery foliage. Zones 9–12.

Dianella tasmanica

syns *Dianella archeri, D. densa, D. divaricata, D. hookeri*

BLUE FLAX-LILY, TASMANIAN FLAX-LILY

☼ ❄ ↔ 12 in (30 cm) ↕ 40 in (100 cm)

Tufted perennial, rarely forms clumps. Occurs in Australia, in rocky habitats on shallow sandy soils from northern inland New South Wales south to the alpine country and Tasmania, ranging

from sea level to 3,940 ft (1,200 m) altitude. Leaves up to 40 in (100 cm) long, green, inflorescences may exceed the leaves in length. Blue flowers in spring–summer. Globular berries, bluish purple, containing many black shiny seeds. Zones 8–10.

DIANTHUS

CARNATION, PINK

The 300 or so species in this genus are tufting or spreading perennials largely from the Eurasian region. *Dianthus* is type genus for its family, the pink (Caryophyllaceae). Most have narrow, somewhat grassy, blue-green leaves emerging directly from a dense basal clump or on wiry spreading stems. The foliage color is a perfect foil for the flowers, which in the species are simple 5-petalled structures often powerfully fragrant, with a spicy scent. Flower stem length varies greatly. The common flower color is pink, but the common name, pinks, refers to the ragged petal edges, which appear as if cut with pinking shears. Most species flower from late spring.
CULTIVATION: Plant in a bright, open position in moist, well-drained, humus-rich soil. Most appreciate a little lime and need regular feeding to prevent center of clump from dying out. Propagate from seed or small basal cuttings known as "slips," or by division.

Dianthus alpinus

☼/◑ ❄ ↔ 6–12 in (15–30 cm)
↕ 4–6 in (10–15 cm)

Short-lived perennial from European Alps. Leaves are dark green and grassy. Flowers are borne singly, deep pinkish red with darker spots and a white eye, pinked, in late spring. '**Joan's Blood**' are maroon-centered with deep red flowers. Zones 3–9.

Dianthus arenarius

☼/◑ ❄ ↔ 6–12 in (15–30 cm)
↕ 12 in (30 cm)

Northern and eastern European perennial forming a dense tufted mound of short, narrow, green leaves. Flowers on wiry stems, usually borne singly, white to pale pink, pinked. Zones 3–9.

Dianthus barbatus ★

SWEET WILLIAM

☼/◑ ❄ ↔ 6–12 in (15–30 cm)
↕ 12–24 in (30–60 cm)

Short-lived, southern European perennial usually grown as an annual. Makes clump of lance-shaped leaves. Pinked flowers clustered in heads. Seedling strains available in many colors and patterned forms, such as **Auricula-eyed Mixed Group**, which has a contrasting colored ring near the center. Zones 4–9.

Dianthus carthusianorum

syn. *Dianthus tenuifolius*

CARTHUSIAN PINK

☼/◑ ❄ ↔ 6–12 in (15–30 cm)
↕ 16–24 in (40–60 cm)

Mounding tufted perennial of southern and central Europe. Light green grassy foliage sheathed for much of length. Heads of small pink to purple flowers, rarely white, pinked. Zones 3–9.

Dianthus caryophyllus

CARNATION

☼/◑ ❄ ↔ 8–16 in (20–40 cm)
↕ 20–32 in (50–80 cm)

Perennial from Mediterranean region. Leaves sheathed, gray-green to blue-green, on wiry spreading stems. Flower-heads on upright, sometimes spindly stems, strongly fragrant. Wild plants have pink flowers, garden forms many colors. **Knight Series**, named for color: '**Crimson Knight**', '**White Knight**', and '**Yellow Knight**'. Zones 8–10.

Dianthus erinaceus

Dianthus deltoides

MAIDEN PINK

☼/◑ ❄ ↔ 6–12 in (15–30 cm)
↕ 8–16 in (20–40 cm)

Eurasian perennial, forming carpet, sometimes mounding, of small green to blue-green leaves with spreading narrow-leafed stems around the edge. Flowers, usually borne singly, in pink shades, often with dark central spotting, pinked. Cultivars include: '**Albus**', white flowers; and '**Brilliancy**', deep crimson flowers. Zones 3–9.

Dianthus erinaceus

☼/◑ ❄ ↔ 6–12 in (15–30 cm)
↕ 4–6 in (10–15 cm)

A Turkish perennial forming a hard, densely packed, moss-like mat of small green leaves that is studded with small, bright, pink flowers, pinked, in summer. Zones 7–9.

Dianthus gratianopolitanus

syn. *Dianthus caesius*

CHEDDAR PINK

☼/◑ ❄ ↔ 8–16 in (20–40 cm)
↕ 6–8 in (15–20 cm)

A mat-forming perennial native to central and western Europe. The older leaves can be small and very densely packed. The fragrant pink to crimson flowers, are usually borne singly, and are pinked. '**Baker's Variety**' bears semi-double pinkish purple flowers; '**Flore Pleno**' has semi-double pink flowers. Zones 3–9.

Dianthus gratianopolitanus 'Baker's Variety'

Dianthus carthusianorum

Dianthus deltoides

Dianthus barbatus, Auricula-eyed Mixed Group cultivar

Dianthus monspessulanus
syn. *Dianthus sternbergii*
☼/◐ ❄ ↔ 12–20 in (30–50 cm)
↑ 12–24 in (30–60 cm)

Perennial from mountains of eastern and southern Europe. Spreading habit with wiry stems and narrow blue-green to green foliage. Flowers in groups of up to 7, pink or white, fragrant, with deeply cut petals, in summer. Zones 4–9.

Dianthus nitidus
☼/◐ ❄ ↔ 6–10 in (15–25 cm)
↑ 8–12 in (20–30 cm)

Found west of Carpathian Mountains. Small, tufted, summer-flowering perennial, narrow slightly glossy leaves. Pink, often darker, spotted flowers in pairs or small clusters, pinked. Zones 6–9.

Dianthus pavonius
☼/◐ ❄ ↔ 6–12 in (15–30 cm)
↑ 20–30 in (50–75 cm)

Tufting or mat-forming perennial from the European Alps. Leaves gray-green,

Dianthus monspessulanus

Dianthus nitidus

Dianthus pavonius 'Inshriach Dazzler'

narrow. Flowers light pink to crimson, usually borne singly, pinked. '**Inshriach Dazzler**', bright green foliage, intense magenta flowers; '**La Bourboule**' (syn. 'La Bourbille'), blue-gray foliage, pink pinked-edged flowers. Zones 4–9.

Dianthus plumarius
PINK
☼/◐ ❄ ↔ 8–16 in (20–40 cm)
↑ 6–14 in (15–35 cm)

Perennial from eastern and central Europe. Forms loose tuft of blue-green foliage. Flowers pink or white, often with darker markings or center. Parent of most of the garden pinks; crossed with *D. caryophyllus* to produce perpetual-flowering carnations. Zones 3–9.

Dianthus pontederae
☼/◐ ❄ ↔ 8–16 in (20–40 cm)
↑ 6–8 in (15–20 cm)

Perennial found from European Alps to the Balkans. Mat-forming with tiny linear leaves, stems sometimes wiry and spreading. Heads of purple-pink flowers in summer, pinked. Zones 6–9.

Dianthus spiculifolius
☼/◐ ❄ ↔ 6–12 in (15–30 cm)
↑ 8–12 in (20–30 cm)

Mat-forming tufted perennial from the eastern Carpathian Mountains. Narrow basal leaves, upper leaves smaller. Scented, deeply cut, pink flowers (occasionally white), borne singly or in clusters. Zones 6–9.

Dianthus pontederae

Dianthus spiculifolius

Dianthus subacaulis
☼/◐ ❄ ↔ 6–8 in (15–20 cm)
↑ 2–4 in (5–10 cm)

A perennial from the mountains of southwestern Europe. Forms densely tufted clumps of deep green foliage. Deep pink flowers are borne singly, with smooth or pinked edges. *D. s.* subsp. *brachyanthus* develops into a densely foliaged dome. Zones 5–9.

Dianthus superbus
☼/◐ ❄ ↔ 12–20 in (30–50 cm)
↑ 20–30 in (50–75 cm)

Strong-growing Eurasian perennial with spreading stems. The flowers are usually borne singly, with pink to purple-pink, highly scented, deeply cut almost jagged petals. *D. s.* var. *longicalycinus* has mauve to light purple flowers with an elongated calyx. Zones 4–9.

Dianthus turkestanicus
☼/◐ ❄ ↔ 6–12 in (15–30 cm)
↑ 8–16 in (20–40 cm)

Perennial from central Asia. Wiry stems with lower leaves to 2 in (5 cm) long, upper leaves smaller. White to mauve-pink flowers, borne singly or in groups of up to 3, shallowly pinked. Zones 4–9.

Dianthus Hybrid Cultivars
☼/◐ ❄ ↔ 6–12 in (15–30 cm)
↑ 8–15 in (20–28 cm)

Like other genera with a long garden history that have been extensively hybridized, the many carnations and pinks and their cultivars are divided into groups based on growth habit and flower color and style. Zones 8–10.

ANNUAL BEDDING DIANTHUS
Although sometimes really perennial, these small plants are grown as annuals. In many ways they resemble sweet William (*D. barbatus*), but they are available in a wider range of sizes and growth forms, including some suitable for hanging baskets. Popular annual dianthus include: the **First Love Series**; the **Floral Lace Series**, masses of small flowers with pinked edges; and the **Melody Series**, similar to First Love but taller, mainly single-colored in pink shades and white.

Dianthus superbus var. *longicalycinus*

Dianthus turkestanicus

PERENNIAL DIANTHUS
Perennial dianthus were among the first plants to be cultivated in European gardens. In medieval times they were grown for their medicinal and flavoring properties as well as for their scent. Since then, countless hybrids have been raised, either as garden plants or for the cut-flower trade. Today we recognize three main groups of dianthus hybrids that are further divided, primarily by flower type.

BORDER CARNATIONS
Tall growers that are derived from *D. caryophyllus*. Flowers are usually strongly scented, often fully double, with or without pinked edges. They bloom mainly in spring and early summer, and are divided as follows:

Fancies: Flowers are basically one color but with flecks, spots, or small sectors of one other color, such as 'Brookham Fancy', which is yellow with pink flecks.

Selfs: Flowers are all one color, such as the soft pink 'Cathlene Hitchcock'; the vivid red 'Fiery Cross'; the soft yellow 'Golden Cross'; and the dusky mauve 'Grey Dove'.

Clove-scented: Flowers are strongly scented, color may be variable, such as the red-striped white 'Candy Clove'.

Picotees: One base color edged with another color, such as the purple-edged white 'Eva Humphries'. The edging width is variable.

PERPETUAL-FLOWERING CARNATIONS
These are the tallest carnations, often with flower stems that need staking or tying. Not hardy to repeated severe

frosts, and best grown in mild climates for their year-round flowering.

The rare Malmaison carnation is a diploid form with especially strong foliage and flower stems, and very intense clove perfume. '**Duchess of Westminster**', large cream flowers, is the most widely grown Malmaison.

Perpetuals are widely cultivated as greenhouse plants for florists. Popular forms, which are all doubles unless stated otherwise, include:

Fancies: '**Bright Rendez-vous**', a creamy white, with soft pink lacing; '**Cheerio**', pinkish white and red; '**Crimson Tempo**', rich red; '**Havana**', red and yellow; '**Impulse**', creamy white, deep pinkish red; '**New Tempo**', pinkish white and red; '**Rendez-vous**', white laced with deep pink; '**Tempo**', white with fine red lacing, a few red sectors; '**Tundra**', yellow laced with light red; '**Yellow Rendez-vous**', soft yellow laced with deep pink.

Selfs: '**Delphi**', white; '**Mambo**', bright yellow; '**Moutarde**', yellow; '**Pink Dona**', shades of pink ; '**Prado**', creamy pale green; '**Raggio di Sole**', orange.

Spray carnations: These flowers are usually slightly smaller but they have 5 to 6 per stem. '**Fiorella**' is yellow and red; '**Ibiza**', yellow; and '**Kortina**', purple-red.

PINKS

Developed from *D. plumarius* but often crossed with other species and hybrids. The most common cross is with the perpetual-flowering carnations, which gave rise to the Allwoodii Pinks. Their flowers may or may not be fragrant but nearly always have pinked edges.

Fancies: '**Dad's Favourite**' (syn. 'Dad's Favorite'), white flowers with maroon lacing and center, double; '**Gran's Favourite**', white with pinkish red lacing, double; '**Red Ensign**', deep pink with white lacing.

Selfs: '**Becky Robinson**', deep pink; '**Bovey Belle**', purple, double; '**Carmine Letitia Wyatt**', deep pink, semi-double, good scent; '**Devon Pride**', bright pink; '**Dwarf Helen**', pink, double; '**Inglestone**', bright pink; '**Lemsii**', small pink flowers; '**Letitia Wyatt**' ★, bright pink, double, strong scent; '**Lionheart**', red, sometimes lighter edges, single, fragrant; '**Neon Star**', bright purple-pink, single, strong scent; '**Valda Wyatt**', pink, double, fragrant; '**Whatfield Can-can**', soft pink, frilled double flowers, fragrant; '**White Joy**', white, and sometimes flushed pale pink, double.

Allwoodii Pinks: Usually *D. plumarius* × *D. alpinus* hybrids. '**Whatfield Ruby**', vivid crimson flowers.

D

Dianthus, Hybrid Cultivar, Perennial, Pink, Fancy, 'Red Ensign'

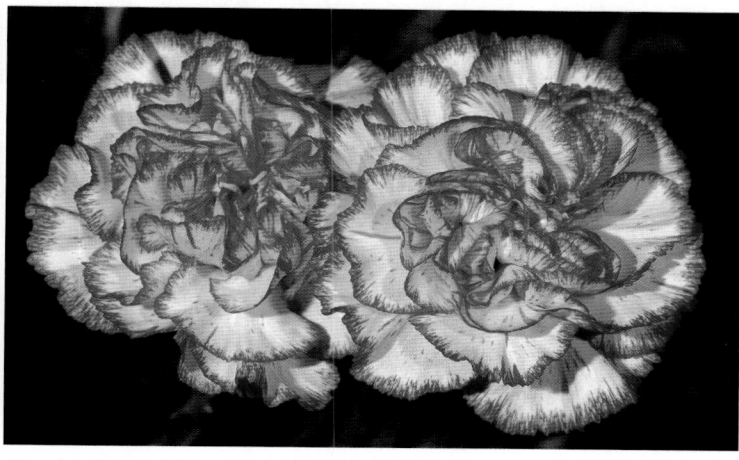

Dianthus, Hybrid Cultivar, Perennial, Perpetual-flowering, Fancy, 'Tundra'

D., HC, Annual Bedding, Floral Lace Series, 'Floral Lace Crimson'

D., HC, Annual Bedding, Floral Lace Series, 'Floral Lace Violet'

D., HC, Annual Bedding, Melody Series, 'Melody Blush Pink'

D., HC, Annual Bedding, Melody Series, 'Melody Pink'

D., HC, Perennial, P-f. Fancy, 'Bright Rendez-vous'

D., HC, Perennial, Perpetual-flowering, Fancy, 'Cheerio'

D., HC, Perennial, Perpetual-flowering, Fancy, 'Crimson Tempo'

D., HC, Perennial, Perpetual-flowering, Fancy, 'Havana'

D., HC, Perennial, Perpetual-flowering, Fancy, 'Hi-lite'

D., HC, Perennial, P-f., Fancy, 'Yellow Rendez-vous'

D., HC, P, P-f, Fancy, 'Lisboa'

D., HC, P, P-f, Fancy, 'New Tempo'

D., HC, P, P-f, Fancy, 'Rendez-vous'

D., HC, P, P-f, Fancy, 'Tempo'

D., HC, P, P-f, Fancy, 'Impulse'

Dianthus, HC, Perennial, Perpetual-flowering, Self, 'Delphi'

Dianthus, HC, Perennial, Perpetual-flowering, Self, 'Mambo'

Dianthus, HC, P, Perpetual-flowering, Self, 'Moutarde'

Dianthus, HC, Perennial, Perpetual-flowering, Self, 'Pink Dona'

Dianthus, HC, Perennial, Perpetual-flowering, Self, 'Prado'

D., HC, P, P-f, Self, 'Raggio di Sole'

Dianthus, HC, P, P-f, Self, 'Reiko'

Dianthus, HC, P, P-f, Self, 'Spirit'

Dianthus, HC, P, P-f, Self, 'Sahara'

Dianthus, HC, P, P-f, Self, 'Terra'

Dianthus, HC, Perennial, Pink, Self, 'Carmine Letitia Wyatt'

Dianthus, HC, Perennial, Pink, Self, 'Charles Edward'

Dianthus, HC, Perennial, Pink, Self, 'Devon General'

Dianthus, HC, Perennial, Pink, Self, 'Dwarf Helen'

Dianthus, HC, Perennial, Pink, Self, 'Haytor White'

D., HC, P, Pink, Self, 'Ingelestone'

D., HC, P, Pink, Self, 'Lemsii'

D., HC, P, Pink, Self, 'Letitia Wyatt'

D., HC, P, Pink, Self, 'Lionheart'

D., HC, P, Pink, Self, 'Neon Star'

Dianthus, HC, Perennial, Pink, Bicolor, 'Cranmere Pool'

Dianthus, HC, Perennial, Pink, Bicolor, 'Rose Monica Wyatt'

Dianthus, HC, Perennial, Pink, Allwoodii, 'Whatfield Ruby'

Dianthus, HC, Perennial, Pink, Self, 'Whatfield Can-can'

Dianthus, HC, Perennial, Pink, Allwoodii cultivar

D., HC, P, Pink, Self, 'Pink Dome'

D., HC, P, P, Bicolor, 'Monica Wyatt'

D., HC, P, P, Bicolor, 'Peach Mambo'

D., HC, P, Pink, Self, 'Pink Pearl'

D., HC, P, Pink, Self, 'Valda Wyatt'

Diasca, Hybrid Cultivar, Coral Belle/ 'Hecbel'

D., Hybrid Cultivar, Redstart/'Hecstart'

D., Hybrid Cultivar, 'Langthorn's Lavender'

Diascia, Hybrid Cultivar, 'Twinkle'

D., Hybrid Cultivar, Little Dancer/'Pendan'

Bicolors: 'Cranmere Pool', white to pale pink, deep red center, double; '**Doris**' ★, light pink with purple-red center, double; '**Houndspool Ruby**' (syn. 'Ruby Doris'), deep pink with crimson center, double, sport of 'Doris'; '**Monica Wyatt**', pink with red center, double; '**Peach Mambo**', cream with soft orange-pink center, double; '**Rose Monica Wyatt**', deep pink with red center, double.

Old-Fashioned Pinks: Usually forms of *D. plumarius* but are sometimes hybrids or just varieties of indeterminate origin that have been so long cultivated that their history is forgotten. '**Earl of Essex**', deep pink, double flowers; the well-known, very fragrant, white double '**Mrs Sinkins**'; and the pink semi-double '**Pike's Pink**' are typical examples.

DIASCIA

TWINSPUR

Until the 1970s few gardeners were aware of *Diascia*, a South African genus of around 50 species of annuals and perennials, belonging to the foxglove (Scrophulariaceae) family. They have since grown enormously in popularity for borders and rockeries, especially in temperate areas where the winters are mild. They are generally low mounding or spreading plants with upright or semi-trailing stems and small oval to elliptical leaves with toothed edges. The flowers, in shades of mauve, pink, and soft orange, are tiny but showy, because they are massed in racemes at the stem tips. The flowers have 4 small lobes, 2 short-spurred nectaries, a large lower lip, and are produced mainly in the summer.

CULTIVATION: Plant in a bright open position with good air movement, and well-drained humus-rich soil that is kept moist throughout the flowering season. Pinch back to keep the plants bushy, and deadhead regularly to encourage continued blooming. Propagate from seed or from cuttings, as appropriate for the growth form.

Diascia barberae

☼/◐ ❄ ↔ 12–16 in (30–40 cm)
↑ 12 in (30 cm)

From the Drakensberg region of South Africa and Lesotho. Perennial with upright or sprawling habit. Flowers are bright pink, with conspicuous spurs and small yellow patch, edged and spotted maroon. '**Blackthorn Apricot**', low growing but spreading, bright, apricot-pink to soft orange flowers; '**Fisher's Flora**', heart-shaped leaves and dark-centered flowers with two yellow spots; '**Ruby Field**', deep pinkish red flowers. Zones 8–10.

Diascia fetcaniensis

☼/◐/☀ ❄ ↔ 40 in (100 cm)
↑ 10 in (25 cm)

Native to Eastern Cape, South Africa, and Lesotho. Compact mounding

Diascia fetcaniensis

perennial with bright green, often downy leaves and small rose to salmon pink flowers. Wonderful rockery plant or for naturalizing in the crevices of dry-stone walls. Zones 8–10.

Diascia integerrima

☼/◐ ❄ ↔ 48 in (120 cm) ↑ 18 in (45 cm)
Spreading perennial, widespread in eastern South Africa. Gray-green leaves, sometimes smooth-edged. Open spikes of dark-centered, mauve-pink flowers with conspicuous downward-curved spurs. '**Coral Canyon**', a more upright habit, more distinctly pink flowers. Zones 8–10.

Diascia rigescens

☼/◐ ❄ ↔ 24 in (60 cm)
↑ 16–20 in (40–50 cm)

From the Drakensberg region of southern Africa. Perennial with sprawling habit. Pointed oval leaves, sometimes with fine red edge. Upright flower spikes, closely spaced flowers, less open heads than other species. The flowers are deep pink with a distinct keel on the lower lobe. Zones 8–10.

Diascia vigilis

☼/◐ ❄ ↔ 48 in (120 cm)
↑ 20 in (50 cm)

Native of the Drakensberg region of southern Africa. Strong-growing perennial with slightly glossy fleshy leaves. Soft pink flowers, small dark spots in the throat. Continues flowering

later than other species. '**Jack Elliott**' produces especially large mid-pink flowers. Zones 8–10.

Diascia Hybrid Cultivars

☼ ❄ ↔ 12–24 in (30–60 cm)
↑ 8–18 in (20–45 cm)

The species tend to interbreed freely, when cultivated and produce many intermediate hybrids. Hybridizers, in particular Hector Harrison of England, have been quick to promote these selected forms. Those that are currently available include: **Coral Belle**/'**Hecbel**', which has narrow, slightly glossy leaves, coral red flowers, and is semi-trailing and good in baskets; '**Joyce's Choice**', with heart-shaped leaves, and apricot-pink flowers; '**Langthorn's Lavender**, with pretty pink-mauve flowers; '**Lilac Belle**', small leaves, and light purple flowers with a conspicuous lower lip; **Little Dancer**/'**Pendan**', small heart-shaped leaves, vivid pink flowers, very good in baskets; **Redstart**/'**Hecstart**', coral pink to red flowers; '**Rupert Lambert**' ★, deep pink, to around 10 in (25 cm) tall and twice as wide, blooms from summer through to autumn; '**Salmon Supreme**', light salmon pink flowers with darker spots; **Sydney Olympics**/ '**Hecsyd**', light salmon pink flowers, compact and heavy-flowering; and '**Twinkle**', dark foliage, purple-pink flowers, trailing habit, good in baskets. Zones 8–10.

Diascia vigilis

Diascia vigilis 'Jack Elliott'

D

DICENTRA
BLEEDING HEART

This genus of around 20 species of annuals and perennials from North America and Asia belongs in the poppy (Papaveraceae) family, though the resemblance may not be obvious. Most have roots adapted as storage organs, as tap roots, rhizomes, or tubers. The foliage, ferny and often finely cut, disappears for winter, but redevelops quickly with the arrival of spring, the larger species often making noticeable daily growth. The flowers have 4 petals, the outer pair creating a pouched structure that largely envelopes the inner pair. The pendulous flowers appear in spring, and are borne in clusters on stems rising above the foliage, mostly in white, pink, or cream shades.
CULTIVATION: These species prefer a cool moist soil that is humus-rich, fertile, and well drained. They thrive in woodlands and perennial borders, and the smaller forms also do well in rockeries. Best lightly shaded from hottest sun. Propagate from seed or basal cuttings, or by division.

Dicentra cucullaria
DUTCHMAN'S BREECHES
☼/◑ ❄ ↔ 20–40 in (50–100 cm)
↕ 12–16 in (30–40 cm)

Perennial from eastern North America. Leaves green, lacy, fern-like, with blue-green undersides, finely divided. Small flowers, heart-shaped but inner petals protruding, white or pink, tipped yellow. Flowers look like upside-down bloomers. May cause dermatitis in some people. Zones 5–9.

Dicentra eximia
STAGGERWEED, TURKEY CORN
☼/◑ ❄ ↔ 20–40 in (50–100 cm)
↕ 12–26 in (30–65 cm)

Perennial found over much of the USA. Blue-green leaves are finely

Dicentra formosa

divided. Sprays of pink or white heart-shaped flowers. The plant is somewhat toxic to stock, hence the common name, staggerweed. Zones 5–9.

Dicentra formosa
syn. *Dicentra eximia* of gardens
WILD BLEEDING HEART
☼/◑ ❄ ↔ 20–40 in (50–100 cm)
↕ 12–26 in (30–65 cm)

A perennial native to western North America. Ferny leaves with blue-green undersides. Panicles up to 30 flowers, most commonly deep pink, sometimes yellow, and rarely white. *D. formosa* and *D. eximia* have been confused in cultivation and it now appears that even in the wild they may be one quite variable species. 'Aurora', gray-green leaves, white flowers; 'Bacchanal', gray-green foliage, pinkish red flowers; 'Bountiful', light blue-green leaves, deep pink flowers; 'Langtrees', very compact, blue-green leaves, pink-tinted cream flowers; 'Luxuriant' ★, blue-green foliage, deep cherry pink to red flowers; 'Stuart Boothman', blue-green leaves with narrow leaflets, deep pink flowers on short stems; and 'Zestful', with light blue-green foliage and deep purple-pink flowers. Zones 4–9.

Dicentra macrocapnos
☼/◑ ❄ ↔ 5 ft (1.5 m) ↕ 7 ft (2 m)
Northern Indian climbing perennial, often evergreen. Leaves light green and

Dichorisandra thyrsiflora

Dicentra formosa 'Aurora'

Dicentra formosa 'Luxuriant'

Dicentra spectabilis, pale pink form

ferny, with oval leaflets. Pendent, narrow heart-shaped, yellow flowers, in summer. Zones 7–10.

Dicentra spectabilis
BLEEDING HEART
☼/◑ ❄ ↔ 20–40 in (50–100 cm)
↕ 40–56 in (100–140 cm)

Perennial from Japan, northeastern China, and Russia's far east. A vigorous grower with leaves coarsely divided. Strongly upright, the often red-tinted flower stems carry up to 15 large, pink, heart-shaped flowers with slightly protruding white inner petals. 'Alba', pure white flowers. Zones 6–9.

DICHORISANDRA

This genus of about 25 species from Central and South America belongs to the spiderwort (Commelinaceae) family that includes the well-known *Tradescantia*. All are perennials, sometimes becoming shrubby, with soft stems and glossy green leaves, sometimes striped with cream or purple. The small flowers are borne in dense terminal spikes and are blue or purple.
CULTIVATION: *Dichorisandra* species are best grown in shady or only partly sunny, sheltered positions in moist

Dicentra formosa 'Bacchanal'

Dicentra spectabilis

Dicentra spectabilis 'Alba'

soil. They are somewhat frost tender but in cold climates plants can be overwintered in a greenhouse. Propagation is from division or from cuttings taken in summer.

Dichorisandra reginae
◑ ⚘ ↔ 12–24 in (30–60 cm)
↕ 12–24 in (30–60 cm)

Native to Peru. Perennial with leaves arranged in 2 ranks along stems. The leaves are often striped with silver and flushed purple beneath. Clusters of small violet-blue flowers are borne in summer–autumn. Zones 9–12.

Dichorisandra thyrsiflora
BLUE GINGER
◑ ⚘ ↔ 3 ft (0.9 m) ↕ 3–10 ft (0.9–3 m)
Native of northern South America. Dark green glossy leaves. Produces terminal clusters of purple-blue flowers, on stems that can reach 10 ft (3 m) high, depending upon the growing conditions. Zones 9–12.

DICHROA

This is a temperate to subtropical Asian genus from the family Hydrangeaceae of possibly 13 species of shrubs, resembling the closely related *Hydrangea*.

The name is derived from *di* (2 or twice) and *chroma* (color), and refers to the often 2-toned flowers. They have bright mid- to deep green leaves, pointed oval in shape with toothed edges. Heads of flowers rather like lacecap hydrangeas appear at various times, depending on the species, and eventually develop into a mass of tiny dry seed capsules.

CULTIVATION: This is an easily grown, adaptable genus for mild-temperate gardens. Most species prefer moist humus-enriched soil in partial shade and are reasonably frost hardy—to around 18°F (–8°C)—but are best with a little overhead protection such as under trees or eaves, which protect winter-flowering species from frost. Propagate from the seed or from half-hardened cuttings taken in summer or early autumn.

Dicksonia squarrosa, in the wild, in beech forest, South Westland, New Zealand

Dichroa febrifuga

◑ ❈ ↔ 5–8 ft (1.5–2.4 m)
↑ 5–8 ft (1.5–2.4 m)

Found from the Himalayas through China to Japan and southward to the mountains of Indonesia. Similar to hydrangea, but evergreen. Lavender to bright blue flowers, from autumn–spring. Wonderful plant for a partly shaded area, winter color. Zones 8–10.

Dichroa versicolor

◑/◑ ❈ ↔ 6 ft (1.8 m) ↑ 7 ft (2 m)

A native of northern Myanmar. Large pointed oval leaves of rich dark green have an almost quilted surface. Heads of small deep blue flowers are produced for long periods. In alkaline soil the flowers will be mauve or pink. Zones 8–10.

DICKSONIA

This genus belonging to the family Dicksoniaceae of tree-ferns consists of around 30 species, occurring in the South Pacific, tropical America, and parts of Southeast Asia. The trunks are covered in the lower part by a dense mass of fibrous roots, and in the upper part by overlapping frond stalks, which persist after the fronds are shed with age. The fronds are large and arching,

and bipinnately divided into narrow, deeply lobed, parallel leaflets. The spore clusters on the undersides of the fronds are protected by a leaf cap, appearing as rows of tiny green balls along leaflet edges.

CULTIVATION: *Dicksonia* is best grown in a moist well-drained soil in part- to full shade with protection from the wind. In cold climates, they grow best in greenhouses and conservatories. Propagation is usually from spores, or from offsets of the trunks. Some species transplant easily, or plants can even be re-established from the cut-off upper half of the trunk, as long as this is well covered by fibrous roots.

Dicksonia antarctica ★

SOFT TREE FERN, TASMANIAN TREE FERN

◑/◉ ❈ ↔ 12 ft (3.5 m) ↑ 20 ft (6 m)

A native of southeastern Australia, from Tasmania north to Queensland, with attractive fronds, tripinnate. The trunk is a dark brown-black, densely fibrous, and upright. This species is an excellent plant for tubs. Shower the trunks to keep them moist in hot dry weather. Zones 8–10.

Dicksonia antarctica, in the wild, Tasmania, Australia

Dicksonia fibrosa

WHEKI-PONGA

◑/◉ ❈ ↔ 10 ft (3 m) ↑ 20 ft (6 m)

From New Zealand. An upright trunk, and brownish red, aerial fibrous rootlets. The fronds are dark green, 2- or 3-pinnate, the leaf stalks are hairy, and dark brown when mature. Grows best in a cool, moist, shaded environment. Zones 8–10.

Dicksonia squarrosa

HARD TREE FERN, WHEKI

◑/◉ ❈ ↔ 10 ft (3 m) ↑ 25 ft (8 m)

Native to New Zealand. Many-branched, dark green fronds, paler green underside, 2- or 3-pinnate, hard texture. Leaf stalks dense brown to black hairs. Zones 8–10.

DICLIPTERA

Genus of about 150 annual and perennial herbs and shrubs, belonging to the acanthus (Acanthaceae) family, and native to tropical and warm-temperate regions. Stems are usually 6-angled. Flowers are borne in terminal clusters with 2-lipped tubular corollas, expanding toward the throat.

Dicksonia fibrosa

Dicliptera suberecta

CULTIVATION: Easily grown in average well-drained soils in full sun and will tolerate some shade and drought. Suited to containers or hanging baskets. Propagate from seed or cuttings.

Dicliptera suberecta

syns *Jacobina suberecta, Justicia suberecta*

HUMMINGBIRD PLANT, KING'S CROWN

◯ ❈ ↔ 18–24 in (45–60 cm)
↑ 18–24 in (45–60 cm)

Perennial subshrub from Uruguay. Slender, velvety, gray foliage on erect or arching stems. Two-lipped, rusty reddish orange, tubular flowers, in summer–autumn. These blooms attract hummingbirds. Zones 7–11.

Dichroa febrifuga

Dichroa versicolor

Dictamnus albus

Dictamnus albus 'Roseus'

DICTAMNUS

BURNING BUSH, DITTANY

This genus in the rue (Rutaceae) family contains only one species, a herbaceous perennial with a woody base found from southwestern Europe through to Asia. The leaves are compound, composed of up to 6 pairs of leaflets, and showy flowers are produced in spikes above the foliage in summer. All parts of the plant can make you ill if ingested, and it exudes a volatile gas that in hot weather can be ignited without harm to the plant, hence one of its common names.

CULTIVATION: This plant likes a sunny aspect in a well-drained but moist humus-rich soil and may take many years to build up into a large flowering clump. Propagate from seed, which takes a long time, or by dividing large established clumps.

Dictamnus albus

☀ ❄ ↔ 20–24 in (50–60 cm)
↑ 16–36 in (40–90 cm)

Clumping plant with spikes of white flowers in summer above bright green foliage. Due to its wide distribution, several variants have been named, though the only one currently recognized is *D. a.* var. *purpureus*, pink flowers veined with purple. *D. a.* 'Roseus', pale pink flowers. Zones 3–10.

DICTYOSPERMA

Although widely grown throughout the tropics for its ornamental value in landscaped gardens and as a container plant, this genus of one palm (family Arecaceae) is close to extinction in its native Mascarene Islands (Mauritius, Réunion, and Rodrigues) in the southern Indian Ocean. The arching pinnate leaves grow to 10 ft (3 m) long. Large fragrant flowers are grouped in large clusters of 3s, with 1 female and 2 male blooms. Fruit are small, purplish black, bullet-shaped berries.

CULTIVATION: This palm can withstand strong winds, but is not drought tolerant and prefers high humidity in moist rich soils. Best suited to warm coastal areas, in bright sunny situations. Propagate from seed, which germinates in 2 to 4 months.

Dictyosperma album ★

HURRICANE PALM, PRINCESS PALM

☀ ✤ ↑ 60 ft (18 m) ↔ 20 ft (6 m)

An attractive tall palm with graceful crown, gray-ringed trunk, and swollen base. Feather-shaped fronds, yellow midrib, flowers reddish. Attractive pot plant when young. *D. a.* var. *aureum*, prominent yellow stripe beneath the leaflets, indistinct veins; *D. a.* var. *conjugatum*, shorter with larger trunk, and long fringes hanging from leaf tips. Zones 10–12.

DIEFFENBACHIA

DUMB CANE, MOTHER-IN-LAW'S TONGUE, TUFTROOT

A genus of about 25 evergreen, erect, perennial herbs from tropical America, members of the arum (Araceae) family, grown for their colorful patterned foliage. Large oval-shaped leaves, spotted or streaked with cream, spread out from a stout central stem. Flowers are borne on long spikes with a green boat-shaped spathe blade. These are very poisonous plants; contact with the sap will cause the tongue to swell, giving rise to the common names.

CULTIVATION: *Dieffenbachia* are ideal as houseplants in bright light and rich moist soil, preferring full sun or partial shade and high humidity. Protect from frost or plant in frost-free areas. Propagate from stem or root cuttings or by division of established clumps.

Dieffenbachia seguine

SPOTTED DUMBCANE

☀/◐ ✤ ↔ 18–24 in (45–60 cm)
↑ 3–6 ft (0.9–1.8 m)

A variable perennial from tropical America. Cane-like stems; and large, leathery, oval-shaped leaves, with pointed tips. 'Amoena' has very robust, thick stems, with large green leaves evenly marked in cream; 'Exotica' is a compact form, with pointed oval-shaped leaves sprinkled with ivory cream; 'Maculata' has bright green leaves spotted with cream; 'Pia' is an offspring of 'Superba'; the leaves of 'Rudolph Roehrs' are mostly yellow, spotted with ivory, and have a ribbed, deep green margin; 'Superba' has fresh green leaves variegated with creamy white; 'Tropic Snow' (syns 'Snow Queen', 'Tropic Topaz', 'Hi-color'), is a dense tall plant, and is known by its heavy cream leaf markings. Zones 10–12.

DIERAMA

AFRICAN HAREBELL, ANGEL'S FISHING ROD, WAND FLOWER

From the high grasslands of southern Africa and Ethiopia, these perennial plants in the iris (Iridaceae) family form almost evergreen clumps of grassy gray-green foliage. Of the 40-plus species only a few are common in cultivation. The pendulous funnel-shaped flowers, in shades of wine red, pink, mauve, purple, and white, are held on long, graceful, arching, wiry stems and appear some time between early and mid-summer. The corms, which are replaced annually, reproduce themselves one on top of another. However, although these multitudinous corms often seem overcrowded, they are best left to sort themselves out as disturbance can be resented.

CULTIVATION: Open sunny sites and deep, rich, moist but well-drained soils suit best, but keep well watered during early growth. Propagate from seed or by division. Some forms of *Dierama* become weedy.

Dierama pulcherrimum

☀ ❄ ↔ 12 in (30 cm) ↑ 5 ft (1.5 m)

Tough, graceful species from South Africa. Flowers bell-shaped, colors variable, commonly magenta pink, madder pink, rich sugary pinks, and deep purples. 'Album', pure white form. Zones 7–10.

DIERVILLA

Native to North America, this genus of 3 species of deciduous shrubs in the woodbine (Caprifoliaceae) family is similar to *Weigela* but have smaller yellow flowers. Their suckering roots are useful for soil stabilization.

CULTIVATION: *Diervilla* species are frost hardy and will grow in full sun or partial shade in a well-drained soil. They should be cut back in late winter or early spring to encourage the new flowering growth. Propagation is best from cuttings.

Dictyosperma album

Dieffenbachia seguine

Digitalis ciliata

Digitalis × fulva

Diervilla rivularis

BUSH HONEYSUCKLE, GEORGIA BUSH
HONEYSUCKLE

☼/◐ ❄ ↔ 36–48 in (90–120 cm)
↑ 24–36 in (60–90 cm)

A spreading, suckering, slow-growing,
deciduous shrub found from southeastern USA. The leaves are dark
green, oval- to sword-shaped, and
slightly hairy; finely hairy branches.
It produces crowded heads of lemon
yellow to reddish yellow trumpet-
shaped flowers, in terminal panicles,
during summer. '**Morton**' (syn.
'Summer Stars'), a densely-branched
dwarf selection. Zones 3–9.

Diervilla sessilifolia ★

SOUTHERN BUSH HONEYSUCKLE

☼ ❄ ↔ 5 ft (1.5 m) ↑ 5 ft (1.5 m)

Found in southeastern USA. Leaves
have reddish veins. Good autumn
foliage color. Sulfur yellow flowers,
generally in pairs, during the summer.
Zones 4–9.

DIETES

A genus consisting of 6 species of evergreen clumping plants, which belongs
to the iris (Iridaceae) family, 5 from
southern Africa and the other from
Lord Howe Island, Australia. The
flowers, produced in summer, are held
above the leaves and are flat, lacking
the upward-pointing petals of an iris.
They make strong bold feature plants.
The flowers individually only last a
day or two, but the flowering season
can last most of the summer.
CULTIVATION: Although these plants
are able to endure only very light frosts,
in all other respects they are very tough,
and will tolerate sun or deep shade,
poor soils, and dry conditions. Propagate from seed. Although *Dietes* can
be divided, they tend to resent disturbance and will need some care to help
them re-establish.

Dietes bicolor

☼/◐ ⚘ ↔ 24–36 in (60–90 cm)
↑ 32–36 in (80–90 cm)

Well-known species from the East
Cape, South Africa. The long, arching,
deep green, strap-like leaves are over-
topped by flat lemon flowers with
contrasting, brown, basal blotches.
Zones 9–11.

Dietes grandiflora

syn. *Dietes iridioides* 'Johnsonii'

WILD IRIS

☀ ⚘ ↔ 20–27 in (50–70 cm)
↑ 20–27 in (50–70 cm)

Found in the forests of South Africa.
Broader leaves than *D. bicolor*, white
flowers marked with yellow and brown
blotches. Zones 9–11.

Dietes Hybrid Cultivars

☼/◐ ❄ ↔ 24 in (60 cm) ↑ 30 in (75 cm)

The most popular hybrids take their
names from their central colors.
'**Lemon Drops**', resembles *D. bicolor*
in habit and size but has darker leaves,
flowers are cream with yellow basal
spot; and '**Orange Drops**', similar to
D. grandiflora, but smaller with narrower leaves, white to cream flowers
have orange basal spot. Zones 8–11.

DIGITALIS

FOXGLOVE

Common in gardens, particularly in
traditional herbaceous borders, and in

Dierama pulcherrimum

the wild, usually as garden escapees,
the genus *Digitalis*, once confined to
Eurasia and North Africa, now occurs
throughout most temperate regions of
the world. It is a member of the foxglove (Scrophulariaceae) family and
is made up of around 20 species of
biennials and perennials that are quite
similar to one another. They form a
basal clump of rather coarse, often elliptical, heavily veined leaves, from the
center of which emerge upright flower
stems carrying smaller leaves, and many
downward-facing, 4-lobed, bell-shaped
flowers that open progressively upwards
along the spike, thus ensuring a long
flowering period. Most flower from
late spring into summer, in pink, lavender, purple, yellow, cream, or white.
All parts of the foxglove are toxic if
swallowed; contact with the leaves
may irritate the skin; deer and rabbits
avoid eating them. Once widely used
in the production of heart stimulant
drugs that are now mostly synthesized.
CULTIVATION: Easily cultivated in
most temperate areas. Plant in moist,
humus-rich soil, water well in spring,
and while in flower. Biennials must be
raised from seed, but perennials will
also grow from basal offshoots.

Diervilla sessilifolia

Digitalis ciliata

☼/◐ ❄ ↔ 12–16 in (30–40 cm)
↑ 24 in (60 cm)

A perennial native to the Caucasus
with hairy leaves and rather stiff spikes
of pink-tinted, cream to pale-yellow
flowers. Yields glycosides that may be
important in the development of new
drugs. Zones 5–9.

Digitalis ferruginea

RUSTY FOXGLOVE

☼/◐ ❄ ↔ 12–20 in (30–50 cm)
↑ 48 in (120 cm)

Biennial or short-lived perennial from
southern Europe and western Asia.
The basal leaves are deep green, sometimes hair-fringed, and narrow. The
flowers that occur along most of the
stem length are golden brown to rusty
red. Zones 7–10.

Digitalis × fulva

☼/◐ ❄ ↔ 20–24 in (50–60 cm)
↑ 40 in (100 cm)

A natural hybrid between *D. grandiflora* and *D. purpurea*, found in southern Europe. Its leaves are finely downy
and toothed. It has narrow spikes of
white to pale yellow-green flowers.
Zones 7–9.

Dietes, Hybrid Cultivar, 'Orange Drops'

Diervilla rivularis 'Morton'

D

Digitalis grandiflora

syn. *Digitalis ambigua*

LARGE YELLOW FOXGLOVE

☼/◐ ❄ ↔ 20–24 in (50–60 cm)
↑ 40 in (100 cm)

European biennial or short-lived perennial. Lush dark green leaves, toothed edges, downy undersides, leafy flower stems. The flowers are pale yellow with darker veining. '**Carillon**', to 24 in (60 cm) tall, primrose yellow flowers. Zones 4–9.

Digitalis grandiflora 'Carillon'

Digitalis grandiflora

Digitalis 'John Innes Tetra'

☼/◐ ❄ ↔ 12–16 in (30–40 cm)
↑ 24 in (60 cm)

Perennial tetraploid hybrid *(D. grandiflora × D. lanata)*; lush foliage, compact stocky growth, large, gold and brown marked yellow flowers. Zones 6–10.

Digitalis laevigata

☼/◐ ❄ ↔ 18 in (45 cm) ↑ 36 in (90 cm)

Southern European perennial. Narrow, leathery, finely toothed leaves. Flowers yellow to pale orange, purplish veining, white lower lip, often sparse. Zones 7–10.

Digitalis lanata

GRECIAN FOXGLOVE

☼/◐ ❄ ↔ 20–24 in (50–60 cm)
↑ 40 in (100 cm)

Biennial or short-lived perennial from Turkey and northeastern Greece. Narrow, downy, lance-shaped leaves. Strong upright flower stems, dull white to buff flowers, brown veining, pale lower lip. Zones 6–9.

Digitalis lutea

STRAW FOXGLOVE

☼/◐ ❄ ↔ 16–24 in (40–60 cm)
↑ 24–40 in (60–100 cm)

A native of Europe and North Africa. The leaves are dark green, hairless,

Digitalis purpurea, Costa Rica

Digitalis obscura

and finely to heavily serrated. Produces abundant flowers of soft yellow or white. Zones 4–9.

Digitalis × mertonensis

STRAWBERRY FOXGLOVE

☼/◐ ❄ ↔ 16–20 in (40–50 cm)
↑ 20–30 in (50–75 cm)

Widely grown perennial garden hybrid *(D. grandiflora × D. purpurea)* providing the best of *D. purpurea*—large, downy, pinkish red to purple-pink flowers—with none of its vices of invasiveness and top-heavy growth. Compact plant with lush foliage and tightly packed flowers. Zones 4–9.

Digitalis obscura

WILLOW-LEAFED FOXGLOVE

☼ ❄ ↔ 16–24 in (40–60 cm)
↑ 24 in (60 cm)

Perennial or woody-based subshrub from Spain, with narrow slightly glossy leaves and flower stems that are wiry

Digitalis parviflora

and not always upright. Flowers are yellow to red-brown with orange to red markings. Zones 7–9.

Digitalis parviflora

CHOCOLATE FOXGLOVE

☼/◐ ❄ ↔ 16–20 in (40–50 cm)
↑ 24–36 in (60–90 cm)

Perennial from northern Spain. Dense foliage rosette of lance-shaped shallowly toothed leaves. Abundant flower spikes and flowers. Deep red-brown flowers with light base, purple-tinted lower lip. Zones 7–9.

Digitalis purpurea

COMMON FOXGLOVE

☼/◐ ❄ ↔ 12–32 in (30–80 cm)
↑ 5–6 ft (1.5–1.8 m)

Biennial from western Europe and now widely naturalized, often considered a weed. Forms dense clump of hairy basal leaves. Strongly upright flower stems with many pink, purple, or white flowers, heavily spotted within. Natural forms include: *D. p.* subsp. *heywoodii*, white flowers, leaves with silvery hairs, perhaps more correctly considered a cultivar, '**Heywoodii**'; *D. p.* subsp. *tomentosa*, densely hairy leaves; *D. p.* f. *albiflora*, flowers often free of throat markings. Several seedling strains, including: *D. p.* **Excelsior Group**, with flowers surrounding the stem, in a mix of colors, such as '**Sutton's Apricot**', creamy salmon pink flowers. Zones 4–9.

Digitalis thapsi

☼/◐ ❄ ↔ 12 in (30 cm)
↑ 16–24 in (40–60 cm)

Perennial found from central Spain to eastern Portugal. Leaves puckered and toothed, covered in fine golden hairs. Downy, pale-throated, red-spotted, purple flowers. '**Spanish Peaks**', soft rose pink flowers. Zones 7–9.

Digitalis purpurea, Excelsior Group

DILLENIA

This genus of about 60 evergreen trees and shrubs of the Dilleniaceae family is distributed throughout tropical Asia, the islands of the Indian Ocean, and Australia. Leaves are large, lustrous and simple; flowers are borne in large terminal panicles, in spring and summer. Fruit, fleshy and star-shaped, with 5 to 8 segments, each containing a seed. CULTIVATION: Drought and frost tender, *Dillenia* prefer well-drained soils with heavy mulching and watering, and a protected sunny position. Propagate from seed or cuttings.

Dillenia alata
QUEENSLAND RED BEECH
☼ ✦ ↔ 12 ft (3.5 m) ↕ 25 ft (8 m)
From Queensland and the Northern Territory, Australia. Broadly spreading tree. Loose, bright reddish brown, papery bark. Thick, glossy, egg-shaped leaves. Large, showy, yellow flowers, in spring–summer. Red fruit, fleshy part edible, used by Aboriginal Australians to stop swelling. Zones 10–12.

Dillenia indica
CHULTA, ELEPHANT APPLE, INDIAN DILLENIA
☼ ✦ ↔ 12 ft (3.5 m) ↕ 30–50 ft (9–15 m)
Widespread from India through to Java. Evergreen shrub or tree, erect stems, roughly textured bark. Large leaves, deeply ribbed. White magnolia-like flowers. Fruit up to 4 in (10 cm) across. Drought tender. Zones 10–12.

DILLWYNIA

A genus of about 40 species of low to medium evergreen shrubs in the pea-flower subfamily of the legume (Fabaceae) family, distributed widely over Australia and named after Lewis Dillwyn, a nineteenth-century English botanist. These plants usually inhabit sandy heath or dry *Eucalyptus* forest.

Dillenia indica

Leaves small, often almost needle-like with a groove on the underside which may spiral through a half-turn. Free-flowering, with flowers in clusters in leaf axils, mostly yellow to brick red, usually with central darker blotch on the standard (upper petal) which is characteristically wider than it is long. CULTIVATION: Well-drained soils and partial sun. Pruning after flowering results in a dense bushy habit. Propagate from seed or cuttings, but, like most members of the pea-flower family, the seeds have a hard coat and need pretreatment before sowing. Cuttings can be taken from firm growth.

Dillwynia retorta
EGGS AND BACON PEA, PARROT PEA
☼ ❄ ↔ 4 ft (1.2 m) ↕ 5 ft (1.5 m)
Native of eastern Australia. Narrow linear leaves. Yellow and red flowers, in terminal or axillary racemes. Tolerates wide range of soils, climatic conditions. Responds well to hard pruning, suitable for containers. Zones 8–11.

DIMOCARPUS
syn. *Euphoria*
This is a small genus of 5 species in the soapberry (Sapindaceae) family closely allied to *Litchi* (lychee), occurring from Southeast Asia to Australia. All are trees with large pinnate leaves, a heavy crown, and small flowers borne in large dense terminal panicles. A characteristic is the fleshy edible aril

Dillwynia retorta, prostrate coastal form

Dimocarpus longan

Dillenia alata

surrounding the seeds inside the almost leathery skin of the fruit, which is smooth by comparison with the rough checkered skin of the lychee fruit. *D. longan* is grown in many countries for its fruit, but in China is grown more for herbal medicine purposes. CULTIVATION: Propagation is from seed sown soon after hardening since the seeds lose viability quite quickly. Rich sandy loams and protection from frost are preferred.

Dimocarpus longan
syn. *Euphoria longan*
LONGAN
☼ ✦ ↔ 20 ft (6 m) ↕ 40 ft (12 m)
Native to Southeast Asia. Cultivated for its fruit. Heavily foliaged branches, alternate pinnate leaves. Flowering in spring, fruit ripens in summer. Longan prefers tropical regions, but can grow where heavy frosts do not occur. *D. l.* subsp. *malesianus* varies little from the typical trees. Zones 11–12.

DINTERANTHUS

This genus of some 5 species from southeastern Namibia and neighboring parts of South Africa belongs to the iceplant (Aizoaceae) family. It is closely allied to *Lithops*, from which most species differ in that plant is clumped above ground and not sunk in it and fruits have 6 to 15 compartments as opposed to 4 to 7 compartments. The plants are small, apparently stemless, and with one or more branches. Leaves semi-spherical and joined for about half their length; the leaf surface is gray. Flowers solitary, terminal, and open in late afternoon; petals are bright yellow.

Dinteranthus microspermus

CULTIVATION: Need full sun and low humidity; can be grown in any low-fertility well-drained compost. Growth period is from mid-summer to early spring and plants must receive no water during their resting period. Therefore, best grown under cover even in warm regions. Propagate from seed or cuttings allowed to dry before rooting.

Dinteranthus microspermus
☼ ⬧ ↔ 2–6 in (5–15 cm) ↕ 2 in (5 cm)
From Namibia. Vegetative bodies, solitary or in small clusters. Leaves largely united but free above halfway to form two distinct sections. Gray, sometimes red-tinted or marked, with fine granular surface. Flowers are yellow. *D. m.* subsp. *puberulus* (syn. *D. puberulus*), velvety surface marked with olive dots and pale mauve flowers. Zones 9–11.

Dinteranthus vanzylii
☼ ⬧ ↔ 2–6 in (5–15 cm) ↕ 2 in (5 cm)
From Western Cape, South Africa. Vegetative bodies in clumps, leaf pairs united to form a single, center-cleft, smooth, gray-brown body with an obscure dark brown patterning. Orange flowers. Zones 9–11.

Dionaea muscipula

Dionaea muscipula 'Akai Ryu'

Dionaea muscipula 'Sawtooth'

DIONAEA

Charles Darwin called the Venus fly-trap "the most wonderful plant in the world," and indeed it is a truly remarkable plant. It was named in 1770 by John Ellis for Dione, the mother of Aphrodite who was the goddess of beauty in Greek mythology. *Dionaea* gains its common name from Venus, the Roman goddess of beauty. This single-species genus belongs to the sundew (Droseraceae) family. The Venus flytrap is found in coastal areas of North and South Carolina, USA, on open grassy plains, in damp acidic soil, and in areas dotted with pine trees. It captures its prey in spring traps that snap shut around the insect when the trap's trigger hairs have been touched more than once in quick succession. As the insect struggles to free itself, digestive enzymes enter the trap and the soft tissue of the insect is dissolved. Eventually the trap reopens and the hard remains blow away in the breeze or are washed away by rain.
CULTIVATION: Grow in pots containing either just peat moss or 1 part sand to 3 parts peat, in full sun to half-sun. Water by tray; when winter dormancy approaches, remove pots from trays and only water once a week. Remove any black leaves or traps. Repot every couple of years. Propagate by division at the end of winter.

Dionaea muscipula ★
VENUS FLYTRAP
☼/◐ ❄ ↔ 8 in (20 cm) ↕ 4 in (10 cm)
Leaves green, each leaf blade having 2 eyelid-shaped fringed lobes. Each lobe has 3 fine trigger hairs. Small white flowers, appear on a leafless stalk, at the end of spring. 'Akai Ryu', in full sun, has bright burgundy traps; 'Fang', and 'Sawtooth', edges of the traps have jagged "teeth" rather than a fringe. Zones 5–9.

DIOON

This genus of tree-like cycads in the zamia (Zamiaceae) family is made up of 10 species found in Mexico and Central America. Palm-like in appearance, with upright trunks, ringed with the scars of old leaf bases, and frond-like leaves, their name is derived from the Greek and means "two eggs," a reference to their paired seeds. Cycads are ancient plants that do not bear true flowers, instead reproducing by means of pollen cones and seed cones, rather like conifers. The female or seed cones are often very large and woolly.
CULTIVATION: Frost tender, not tolerant of prolonged drought, *Dioon* is best grown in moist, well-drained, humus-rich soil in sun or partial shade. Water well during the warmer months. Restrict pruning to removing old trunks with untidy or dead foliage. Propagate from seed or by removing rooted offsets that develop at the base.

Dioon edule ★
MEXICAN FERN PALM
☼/◐ ❄ ↔ 5 ft (1.5 m) ↕ 6 ft (1.8 m)
A commonly cultivated species from Mexico. The fronds are upright, gray-green, and glaucous when young. The female cones contain edible seeds. Zones 10–12.

Dioon edule

Dioon spinulosum ★
☼/◐ ❄ ↔ 10 ft (3 m) ↕ 30 ft (9 m)
From Mexico. Slender trunk. Near-erect to arching fronds, woolly coating on emerging, wearing away with age. Sharp spines tip the aromatic dark green leaflets, which have distinctive blue tint when young. Zones 10–12.

DIOSCOREA
syns *Rajania, Tamus, Testudinaria*
YAM
Principal genus, comprising 850 species in all tropical and subtropical regions, especially in seasonal climates, in the yam (Dioscoreaceae) family of monocots. They are dioecious plants with rhizomes and annual shoots twining to the left or right. Attached to the rhizomes are one or more tubers, sometimes large, and starch-filled. The stems are erect or creeping, round in cross-section or angled, often armed with prickles especially near the base. The leaves are opposite or spirally arranged, smooth-edged to lobed or compound. The inflorescences are racemes or panicles from leaf axils and the flowers are small. Fruit is a 1- or 3-winged capsule, or a berry. These are the true yams (as opposed to the sweet potato that is sometimes called yam) and were domesticated independently in many parts of the tropical world. Many are staple carbohydrate food crops, especially in West Africa (fufu), and their cultivation is intimately associated with the annual cycle of life and ceremony of many peoples. Some important ones are ancient hybrids. These plants are the source of diosgenin, a precursor in the synthesis of the steroidal hormones used in female contraceptive pills. Some species are poisonous.
CULTIVATION: They are grown in rich soils in full sun or light shade and in

Dioon spinulosum

Dioscorea alata

Dioscorea bulbifera

Dioscorea elephantipes

temperate regions may occasionally be grown as ornamentals for their attractively colored foliage, though *D. elephantipes* is to be seen in collections of succulents. They are propagated by division of the dormant tuber or from the seed.

Dioscorea alata
GUYANA ARROWROOT, WATER YAM, WHITE YAM

☼/◐ ✿ ↔ 6 ft (1.8 m) ↑ 10 ft (3 m)

A native of tropical Asia. This is the most widely cultivated species, the tubers reaching occasionally 8 ft (2.4 m) in length and 110 lb (50 kg) in weight. The stem is 4-angled, often with axillary tubers. The leaves are ovate to oblong, with a heart-shaped base. Zones 10–12.

Dioscorea batatas
CHINESE POTATO, CHINESE YAM, CINNAMON VINE

☼/◐ ❄ ↔ 6 ft (1.8 m) ↑ 10 ft (3 m)

From East Asia, and naturalized in USA. The tubers grow up to 36 in (90 cm) long. The stem is angled, twining to the right, with axillary tubers. The leaves are ovate with a heart-shaped base. The white flowers are scented like cinnamon. Zones 8–11.

Dioscorea bulbifera
AERIAL YAM, AIR POTATO, OTAHEITE POTATO, OTAHEITE YAM

☼/◐ ❄ ↔ 10 ft (3 m) ↑ 6–12 ft (1.8–3.5 m)

From tropical Asia. Its underground tubers are small or absent, spherical in shape. The stem grows to 20 ft (6 m) with hard, corky-surfaced tubers in the leaf axils. The leaves are ovate with a heart-shaped base. This plant has become a troublesome weed in some areas. Zones 9–12.

Dioscorea elephantipes
syn. *Testudinaria elephantipes*
ELEPHANT'S FOOT

☼/◐ ❄ ↔ 12 in (30 cm) ↑ 36 in (90 cm)

Found growing on dry rocky slopes in southern Africa. A perennial with an exposed tuber covered in tough armor-like plates and stems twining to the left. Heart-shaped leaves. It bears yellowish green flowers, the males are in the erect inflorescences, the females in the nodding to spreading spiny ones. Zones 9–11.

Dioscorea esculenta
CHINESE YAM, IGNAME, LESSER YAM, POTATO YAM

☼/◐ ❄ ↔ 6 ft (1.8 m) ↑ 4–8 ft (1.2–2.4 m)

From subtropical eastern Asia. The tubers are egg-shaped, developing near the surface of the soil, with sweet white flesh. The stems twine to the left, and are often prickly. The leaves are almost circular, there are 2 spines at the base of the stalk. Flowering is rare in cultivated plants. Zones 9–12.

DIOSPYROS
EBONY, PERSIMMON

This genus in the ebony (Ebenaceae) family of some 475 species of evergreen and deciduous, tender and hardy, tropical and temperate shrubs and trees is a very diverse group of plants. Some have considerable economic importance, either for their timber or their fruit, while others are attractive ornamentals. Their foliage is usually quite simple and the leaves of the deciduous species can be very colorful in autumn.

The flowers are unisexual, and to ensure better fruit production it helps to have several trees for cross-pollination. The fruits range from small fleshy berries to the pear-like persimmons.
CULTIVATION: With such a large and diverse genus it is difficult to generalize about cultivation requirements. What can be said is that only a few species will tolerate prolonged drought and most prefer moist well-drained soil that is reasonably fertile. Propagation is from seed or by root cuttings or grafting.

Diospyros kaki
JAPANESE DATE PLUM, PERSIMMON

☼ ❄ ↔ 25 ft (8 m) ↑ 50 ft (15 m)

Long cultivated in Japan, this species is not known in the wild. It is a deciduous tree with edible fruit. Choose named cultivars for fruit production where warmth is needed. 'Fuyu' ★, a low tannin variety, needs ample warmth; 'Hachiya', produces a large, tender-skinned, conical-shaped, pinkish orange fruit, not sweet, which is unpalatable until fully ripe and soft; and 'Izu', a compact low tannin variety. Zones 8–10.

Diospyros lotus
DATE PLUM, SMALL DATE PLUM

☼ ❄ ↔ 25 ft (8 m) ↑ 50 ft (15 m)

This temperate Asian species is similar to *D. kaki*, but the fruit it produces is considerably smaller. Deciduous, with leaves often dropping while they are still green. The flowers are insignificant. The fruit is yellow, red, to black. Zones 5–9.

Diospyros kaki

Diospyros kaki, with ripe fruit

Diospyros lotus

D

Diospyros virginiana

AMERICAN PERSIMMON, PERSIMMON

☀ ❄ ↔ 10 ft (3 m) ↑ 50 ft (15 m)

Native to eastern USA, deciduous tree, simple oval leaves color well in autumn. Small, edible, yellow fruit. Timber used for making golf woods. '**John Rick**' ★, old-established fruiting cultivar grown for superior eating qualities. Zones 5–9.

DIPELTA

This genus belonging to the woodbine (Caprifoliaceae) family of 4 deciduous shrubs from China is closely related to *Weigela*. Pinkish or purplish, tubular, bell-shaped flowers, in singles or in clusters of up to 8, appear in spring or early summer. Generally grown for their ornamental value, some are also used in traditional Chinese medicine. CULTIVATION: Frost resistant, drought tender, *Dipelta* species are adaptable to a wide range of soils but do better in a protected position. Propagate from softwood cuttings taken in summer, by layering or from seed sown in spring.

Dipelta floribunda ★

ROSY DIPELTA

☀ ❄ ↔ 10 ft (3 m) ↑ 8 ft (2.4 m)

Native of central and western China. Branches, broad spreading, long arching. Hanging clusters of fragrant, tubular, bell-shaped white flowers, flushed with a shell pink, yellow or orange throat, in spring. Zones 6–9.

Dipelta floribunda

Diplazium pseudodoederleinii

Dipelta yunnanensis

☀ ❄ ↔ 12 ft (3.5 m) ↑ 6–12 ft (1.8–3.5 m)

From southwestern China. Spreading shrub, downy shoots, leaves downy beneath. Short clusters of tubular flowers, cream to white, stained pink, with an orange throat, in spring. Zones 6–9.

DIPLARRHENA

BUTTERFLY FLAG

The 2 members of this genus in the iris (Iridaceae) family come from the grassy slopes of southeastern Australia where moisture persists during drier months. Tuft-forming leaves, rising from short fleshy stems and creeping rootstocks, evergreen, narrow, flat, and linear. Honey-scented flowers, in terminal clusters of 2 or 3 on straight stiff stalks, are vaguely iris-like with 3 large petals. Each one is short lived, but healthy established plants bloom abundantly over a prolonged period in spring–summer. Commonly, the white petals unfurl at night and shrivel in the sunlight. CULTIVATION: Trouble-free, grow well in well-drained, neutral to acid soils and in sun or part-shade. Garden forms chosen for their ability to display their flowers by day. Drought tender.

Diplarrhena moraea

☀ ❄ ↔ 16–22 in (40–55 cm) ↑ 24–40 in (60–100 cm)

From southeastern Australia. These plants have wiry narrow leaves. The

Diplarrhena moraea

flowers are held on strong stiff stems in spring and early summer. The petals are lightly suffused or veined at the base in purple or yellow. The fruits are cylindrical, and modestly decorative. The leaves are glossy, graceful, and grasslike. Zones 7–9.

DIPLAZIUM

Genus of around 400 species of mostly tropical ferns, world-wide in their distribution, making up the majority of species in the family Athyriaceae. Some botanists have preferred to merge it with the genus *Athyrium*, in which case all species take that genus name. They are ground-dwelling ferns with short or long rhizomes, sometimes forming a short erect trunk. The frond stalks are usually blackish and the fronds are broad and much divided; ultimate leaflets are toothed. On fertile fronds the dark spore-patches (sori) are linear and follow the veins, often arranged in a fan-like manner. In some species plantlets are produced on the frond tips. CULTIVATION: In the wild these plants grow in moist soil, sometimes in the quite deep shade of the forest understory. They prefer very humid conditions and a spongy growing medium with a high organic content. Some of the species adapt easily to cultivation but others resent disturbance. Propagate from the spores or by division of the rhizomes.

Diplazium doederleinii

☀/◐ ⬩ ↔ 3–6 ft (0.9–1.8 m) ↑ 3 ft (0.9 m)

A native of the islands of Okinawa and Iriomote in Japan's southern Ryukyu Archipelago, where they grow in the mountains. They are creeping rhizomes, with large fronds, that are more or less triangular in outline, and pinnate with their primary leaflets deeply lobed. Zones 9–11.

Diplazium pseudodoederleinii

☀/◐ ⬩ ↔ 3–6 ft (0.9–1.8 m) ↑ 3 ft (0.9 m)

This species is a native of Taiwan. It is closely allied to *D. doederleinii*, but differing in details of frond structure. Zones 9–11.

Diplazium doederleinii

Diospyros virginiana 'John Rick'

Diploglottis campbellii

Diplazium pycnocarpon

syn. *Athyrium pycnocarpon*

GLADE FERN, NARROW-LEAFED SPLEENWORT, SILVERY SPLEENWORT

☀/◐ ❄ ↔ 4 ft (1.2 m) ↑ 24–36 in (60–90 cm)

From eastern Canada to southeastern USA. Deciduous fern. Forms rosettes. Green arching fronds are silvery, light green in spring, darkening in summer then turning russet before dying back. Zones 3–9.

DIPLOGLOTTIS

This genus of 8 species of erect shrubs or small trees belonging to the soapberry (Sapindaceae) family is found in eastern and southern Australia. All have a spreading crown of large pinnate leaves and are useful shelter plants and street trees. The seeds of all species are enclosed in a fleshy pulp, which can be made into jams and drinks. CULTIVATION: Prefer dappled shade, but can be fast growing under suitable conditions in well-drained acid soil containing organic matter. Propagate from seed, sown as soon as it is ripe.

Diploglottis campbellii

SMALL-LEAFED TAMARIND

◐ ⬩ ↔ 15 ft (4.5 m) ↑ 60 ft (18 m)

From southern Australia. Leaves pinnate, broadly lanceolate, dull green, end in a blunt point. Flowers creamy brown, hairy, fragrant, in spring–autumn. Edible red fruits mature in late summer or autumn. Zones 9–11.

DIPTERIS

Consisting of 8 species from tropical Asia and the Pacific region, this is the sole genus of the family Dipteridaceae. They are large ground-dwelling ferns of striking aspect, growing in open, often disturbed habitats in high- rainfall mountain areas. Rhizomes are long-creeping and covered in bristly dark scales; long-stalked fronds are divided into two large fan-shaped leaflets, each of which is further deeply divided into a number of lobes. The undersides of the lobes are sprinkled with large numbers of tiny spore-patches (sori). CULTIVATION: They require a humid tropical or subtropical climate for growing outdoors, or in cooler climates, a heated and well-lit conservatory. They resent disturbance to roots and rhizomes and so can be difficult to establish from divisions. A spongy, acid, organic medium kept permanently moist is most likely to produce success. Propagation from spores may be preferable to division.

Dipteris conjugata
UMBRELLA FERN

☼/◑ ✦ ↔ 10–20 ft (3–6 m)
↑ 4–10 ft (1.2–3 m)

Native habitat ranges from mainland Southeast Asia to Fiji, and tropical Queensland, Australia. This is an impressive fern, carrying widely spaced umbrella-like fronds on erect or arching stalks. It is often seen growing

wild on road and track embankments or beside waterfalls, but the species is rarely cultivated. Zones 11–12.

DIRCA
LEATHERWOOD

This genus in the daphne (Thylemaeaceae) family consists of 2 deciduous shrubs, both native to North America. They have tough flexible branches, simple alternate leaves, and fruit which is a small red or greenish drupe with 4 segments. The insignificant yellow flowers have no petals and open in spring before leaves appear. All parts of the plant are poisonous and if touched may cause skin irritation. The fruit has a narcotic effect. CULTIVATION: Leatherwoods need exposure to full sun to achieve their best habit but will also grow in shade. They are quite hardy and grow best in a well-drained moist soil. Propagation is from seed or by layering.

Dirca occidentalis
WESTERN LEATHERWOOD

☼ ❄ ↔ 4–6 ft (1.2–1.8 m)
↑ 4–6 ft (1.2–1.8 m)

From California, USA. Rare shrub with attractive yellow foliage in autumn. It is similar to D. palustris but has smaller leaves and stalkless flowers. Bears yellow tubular flowers, with long protruding stamens, in groups of 3 to 4, in spring. Zones 7–10.

Dirca palustris
LEATHERWOOD, ROPEBARK, WICOPY

☼/◑ ❄ ↔ 6 ft (1.8 m) ↑ 6 ft (1.8 m)
From east coast USA and Canada, a slow-growing, dense, rounded, deciduous shrub. Yellowish branches, fibrous,

Dipteris conjugata

gray, tough, leathery bark. Leaves 3 in (8 cm) long. Clusters of insignificant flowers in leaf axils, before leaves, in spring. Fruit a green to red oval-shaped drupe, with a single seed. Zones 4–9.

DISA

Primarily a South African terrestrial orchid genus (family Orchidaceae) with over 100 species. While the famous D. uniflora, known colloquially as "The Pride of Table Mountain," is well known to orchid growers, the majority of the species are only of botanical interest and few of these are in cultivation. In the wild, they are often seen growing on the fringes of marshlands or on the banks of flowing streams, in substrates that generally have a poor nitrogen content, and often grow in association with sphagnum moss. There have been numerous attractive hybrids bred, particularly over the past decade. Many of these have a high percentage of D. uniflora in their pedigree, and generally exhibit hybrid vigor. The color range is also expanding with whites, lemons, and pinks now supplementing the reds and oranges. CULTIVATION: Live sphagnum moss has proved the best medium for cultivated plants. They are very particular about water quality, and rainwater is preferable. The plants should be kept moist throughout the year. Do not sit in trays of water for extended periods, otherwise you run the risk of rotting the tubers from which the plant grows. Some growers have had success by using "waterwell" containers, which are often marketed for indoor plants. Mature specimens may produce daughter plants at the edge of the pot (or frustratingly at times through the drainage holes!). These can be potted separately when they are large enough to handle. These plants should be re-potted annually into fresh moss, in the

Disa uniflora

autumn, a few months after the main summer flowering period. They enjoy cool to intermediate conditions. Propagate by division.

Disa uniflora ★

☼/◑ ❄ ↔ 4–10 in (10–25 cm)
↑ 6–32 in (15–80 cm)

One of the most magnificent plant species from South Africa. Despite its specific name, it can produce up to 6 flowers on an erect inflorescence, during the summer. The color of the large flowers varies, from a brilliant scarlet-red through various shades of orange, to rare yellow (lutea) forms. Zones 9–11.

Disa Hybrids

☼/◑ ❄ ↔ 4–10 in (10–25 cm)
↑ 8–32 in (20–80 cm)

The following hybrids have been primarily bred from the popular and award-winning D. uniflora and have the same cultivation requirements. These hybrids have been developed to improve the flower count and quality, as well as to expand the range of colors. **Diores**, a hybrid between D. uniflora and D. Veitchii, long-lasting flowers popular for cutting; **Kewbett**, a hybrid of D. Betty's Bay and D. Kewensis; **Kewensis**, a hybrid between D. uniflora and D. tripetaloides; and **Watsonii**, a hybrid between D. uniflora and D. Kewensis. Zones 9–11.

Disa, Hybrid, Watsonii

Disa, Hybrid, Kewensis

Disa, Hybrid, Diores

Disa, Hybrid, Kewbett

Disanthus cercidifolius

Discaria pubescens

DISANTHUS

This genus belonging to the witch-hazel (Hamamelidaceae) family contains a single deciduous shrub, with alternate leaves and inconspicuous flowers, that is native to China and Japan. The fruit are dehiscent capsules containing several, shiny, black seeds.
CULTIVATION: Frost resistant but drought tender, *Disanthus* species prefer a cool, moist, rich, acid or peaty soil in a protected sunny position, in conditions similar to rhododendrons and azaleas. Propagate from seed, which takes 2 years to germinate, or from cuttings taken in summer and struck under glass, or by layering.

Disanthus cercidifolius ★
☼ ❄ ↔ 10 ft (3 m) ↕ 20 ft (6 m)
From mountainous areas of China and Japan. Long leaf stalks, luxuriant,

heart-shaped, bluish green leaves, turning maroon, red, and orange in autumn. Curious, inconspicuous, deep purple flowers, spidery petals, in late autumn. Zones 7–9.

DISCARIA

This buckthorn (Rhamnaceae) family genus consists of 12 deciduous shrubs or small trees with long thorns, small leaves, and groups of 4 to 5 fragrant petal-less flowers, native to temperate regions of South America, Australia, and New Zealand. They are sometimes cultivated for their ornamental value. The fruit is a leathery drupe or capsule.
CULTIVATION: *Discaria* species are adaptable to most well-drained soils and prefer an open sunny position. They are discouraged by root disturbance and should be pruned to maintain their shape. Propagation is from cuttings or seed.

Discaria pubescens
☼ ❄ ↔ 48–60 in (120–150 cm)
↕ 20–36 in (50–90 cm)
This rigid, spreading, deciduous shrub from northern Australia, is armed with stout spines. The scattered, small, oblong leaves are borne on smooth stems. It has creamy white flowers, in clusters, in spring, and dark reddish brown stipules. Zones 8–10.

Diselma archeri, in the wild, Tasmania, Australia

DISELMA

This genus of a single species of conifer belongs to the cypress (Cupressaceae) family. It is a native of Australia and may be found in the island state of Tasmania, growing in wet subalpine areas in small localized stands. It resembles the related *Libocedrus* but is smaller in all its parts. It is usually of shrubby habit but may develop into a tree of up to 20 ft (6 m) in sheltered locations. The male and female cones are borne on separate plants.
CULTIVATION: Grow in a moist but well-drained soil in sun or part-shade. Protect from drying winds and keep well-watered in summer. Best propagated from cuttings.

Diselma archeri
☼/◐ ❄ ↔ 3–10 ft (0.9–3 m)
↕ 3–20 ft (0.9–6 m)
From Tasmania, Australia. Slow-growing conifer forming mounds of green scale-like foliage. Attractive, arching, drooping habit in juvenile plants, becoming denser with age. Both male and female cones are tiny. Zones 8–10.

DISPORUM
FAIRY-BELLS

This genus, comprising 10 species from Southeast Asia and Japan, belongs to the lily-of-the-valley (Convallariaceae) family. They are perennial plants with

rhizomes, the leaves spiraly arranged, lanceolate to oblong. The usually pendulous flowers occur in few-flowered umbels or solitary. The red or bluish black fruit is a berry. American species, once included here, are now referred to the genus *Prosartes*.
CULTIVATION: They grow best in part-shade in well-drained but moisture-retentive neutral to acid soils with plenty of organic matter. Propagate by division in spring or from fresh seed.

Disporum sessile
JAPANESE FAIRY BELLS
◐ ❄ ↔ 12–24 in (30–60 cm)
↕ 12–24 in (30–60 cm)
Spreading perennial from Japan. Lance-shaped leaves. Small, green to white, drooping, lily-like flowers, tips tinged green, singly or in clusters of 1 to 3, in spring. Bluish black fruit in late summer. 'Variegatum', leaves broadly striped with cream. Zones 4–8.

Disporum uniflorum
syns *Disporum flavens*, *D. flavum*
YELLOW FAIRY BELLS
◐ ❄ ↔ 12–24 in (30–60 cm)
↕ 12–24 in (30–60 cm)
Upright clump-forming perennial from central to northeastern China and Korea. Pale yellow, lily-like flowers, from spring. Dark black berries in late summer. Zones 4–9.

Disporum uniflorum

Disporum sessile

Disporum sessile 'Variegatum'

Dissotis princeps

Distictis buccinatoria

Diuris maculata

DISSOTIS

From tropical and subtropical Africa, this genus of 100 or so species in the melastoma (Melastomataceae) family, is related to the South American *Tibouchina*. Includes small-flowered creepers and taller larger-flowered shrubs. The 5-petalled flowers, ranging from pink to purple, borne in terminal spikes or clusters in leaf axils, appear over long periods depending on rainfall patterns. In winter rainfall areas, flowering tends to be from late spring to autumn. CULTIVATION: *Dissotis* can be grown in a range of garden soils in full sun or part-shade. Propagation is by seeds or cuttings taken in warmer months.

Dissotis princeps
☼ ❄ ↔ 5 ft (1.5 m) ↑ 10 ft (3 m)
From tropical Africa. Large-flowered shrubby species. Flowers purple, in terminal spikes, in summer. Suitable for sheltered positions. Zones 9–11.

DISTICTIS

Genus of 9 evergreen woody-stemmed climbers, from Mexico and the West Indies, belonging to the trumpet-vine (Bignoniaceae) family. Terminal racemes or panicles of colorful, tubular to trumpet-shaped, occasionally scented flowers in spring to summer. Branches are hexagonal with tendrils that cling to surfaces. Fruit is a 2-valved capsule containing winged seeds. CULTIVATION: Ideal for shade under pergolas. Grow in fertile, moist, well-drained soil. Not suited to hot humid conditions or cold or dry inland areas but withstands light frost. Propagate from half-hardened cuttings in growing season or by layering in early spring.

Distictis buccinatoria
syns *Bignonia cherere, Phaedranthus buccinatorius*
MEXICAN BLOOD TRUMPET
☼ ❄ ↔ 10–20 ft (3–6 m)
↑ 6–15 ft (1.8–4.5 m)
Vigorous, evergreen, perennial climber or creeper from Mexico. Fast growing. Purple-red, large, tubular to funnel-shaped flowers, corolla about 3 in (8 cm) long, yellow in the throat and covered with minute yellow hairs. 'Mrs Rivers', late-flowering, dark mauve-pink, golden yellow throat. Zones 9–11.

DIURIS

Genus of Australian deciduous terrestrial orchids (family Orchidaceae) with close to 100 species. Generally grow during autumn and winter, then bloom in spring, reverting to dormant tubers during the hot dry summers. They are commonly known as donkey orchids or doubletails. They produce only a few grass-like leaves, and upright scapes of up to a dozen flowers, depending on the species. They have generally yellow blooms, with other combinations of colors, including browns, purples, and reds. There are also pink- and white-flowered species. Most are pollinated, in the wild, by native bees, which mistake the blooms for superficially similar, (but unrelated) pea-flowers. CULTIVATION: Grow in a well-drained terrestrial mix, with a high proportion (up to 50 percent) of coarse gritty sand. *Diuris* species enjoy bright light and detest stagnant conditions. Repot the dormant tubers in summer. These are orchids for specialist collectors.

Diuris maculata
☼ ❄ ↔ 4–8 in (10–20 cm)
↑ 4–16 in (10–40 cm)
Variable species from Australia. Yellow to orange and brown blooms, heavily spotted, dark brown on outer surface of petals. Up to 8 blooms produced on an erect inflorescence. Zones 8–11.

DOCKRILLIA
PENCIL ORCHID
Dockrillia is essentially an Australian and New Guinean genus consisting of about 30 sympodial orchids (family Orchidaceae), with outlying populations throughout parts of the Pacific Islands. This genus, only recently recognized, loosely accommodates the previously so-called "terete-leafed" *Dendrobium* species. The principal characteristics that separate *Dockrillia* from *Dendrobium* include a lack of pseudobulbs, succulent leaves (which are often terete and circular in cross-section), and flowers that are generally nonresupinate (upside down), with the labellum uppermost. Even novice gardening enthusiasts are readily able to distinguish between the two. The name of this genus commemorates the well-known Australian orchidologist, Alick Dockrill. CULTIVATION: *Dockrillia* species are among the easiest of orchids to cultivate, and may be treated in many ways. The larger growing, pendent species grow well on generous slabs of tree-fern or cork, where they will be happy for many years and will even tolerate a degree of neglect. Some of the species, which clump at the base, may be grown in small pots or wooden baskets, in a bark-based medium. They have a vigorous root system, which prefers not to be disturbed. They grow and bloom in quite strong light, and will be comfortable in a wide range of temperatures. However, some of the mountain species will only grow (and will rarely bloom) in tropical lowland conditions. Propagation of all *Dockrillia* species is by division.

Dockrillia linguiformis
syn. *Dendrobium linguiforme*
THUMBNAIL ORCHID, TONGUE ORCHID
☼/◐ ❄ ↔ 4–24 in (10–60 cm)
↑ 1–5 in (2.5–12 cm)
Australian species. Great creeping foliage plant. Bears short sprays of feathery white blooms in spring. Larger but narrower blooms than the related and rough-leafed *D. nugentii*. Type species for the genus *Dockrillia*. Zones 9–12.

Dockrillia striolata ★
syn. *Dendrobium striolatum*
☼/◐ ❄ ↔ 4–20 in (10–50 cm)
↑ 4–30 in (10–75 cm)
From Australia. Variable, lithophytic, clump-forming species, spring blooms. Flower color from greenish yellow to mushroom pink, darker striations on back of blooms, contrasting pure white labellum with frilled edges. One of the most cold tolerant species, with plants in some locations periodically dusted with snow in winter. Easy to grow, but can be difficult to bloom in subtropical and tropical climates. Zones 9–11.

Dockrillia striolata

Dockrillia linguiformis

Dockrillia teretifolia
syn. *Dendrobium teretifolium*
BRIDAL VEIL ORCHID
☼/◐ ▮ ↔ 1–3 ft (0.3–0.9 m)
↑ 1–10 ft (0.3–3 m)

From Australia, and arguably the most outstanding species in the genus. To see mature plants in full bloom is an unforgettable sight. Masses of white to greenish cream, slender, feathery blooms, in late winter–early spring. Zones 9–12.

Dockrillia wassellii
syn. *Dendrobium wassellii*
☼/◐ ▮ ↔ 2½–8 in (6–20 cm)
↑ 2½–6 in (6–15 cm)

This adaptable species from Australia can be grown in a range of climatic conditions. Attractive, succulent, erect leaves. Up to 50, densely flowered, slender, white blooms, with a yellow labellum, on upright inflorescences. Plants bloom spasmodically during the warmer months. Zones 10–12.

Dockrillia wassellii

Dodecatheon meadia

DODECATHEON
AMERICAN COWSLIP, SHOOTING STARS
A charming genus of some 14 species of small rosette-forming herbaceous perennials belonging to the primrose (Primulaceae) family, native to North America. They produce several flowers per stem, in spring, with fully reflexed petals like those of a cyclamen.
CULTIVATION: Grow naturally in moist meadows and mountain pastures and so need similar garden conditions. Will not thrive in humid or tropical areas. Usually grow best in a cool rock garden or pot. Propagate from freshly sown seed; division in late winter, just before they break dormancy, is also possible.

Dodecatheon dentatum
☼/◐ ❋ ↔ 6–12 in (15–30 cm)
↑ 4–16 in (10–40 cm)

Found from Washington and Oregon through Idaho to Arizona, USA. Leaves oblong to lance-shaped, bright green, sometimes with finely toothed margins. White flowers, turned-back petals, yellow anthers, from spring–early summer. Zones 5–9.

Dodecatheon hendersonii
MOSQUITO-BILLS, SAILOR'S CAP
☼/◐ ❋ ↔ 6–12 in (15–30 cm)
↑ 8–15 in (20–38 cm)

From California, USA. Deep green, fleshy, oval leaves. Flowers in heads of 2 to 3. Pinkish purple turned-back petals, yellow anthers. Zones 6–9.

Dodecatheon meadia
syn. *Dodecatheon pauciflorum*
AMERICAN COWSLIP, EASTERN SHOOTING STAR, SHOOTING STAR
☼/◐ ❋ ↔ 12 in (30 cm)
↑ 8–18 in (20–45 cm)

From eastern USA. Oblong leaves, and flowers in heads of 10 to 20, turned-

Dodonaea angustifolia

Dodonaea viscosa, seed capsules

back petals usually purple, cream to white base, may be pink or white. *D. m.* f. *album*, white-flowers. Zones 3–9.

DODONAEA
A genus in the soapberry (Sapindaceae) family of about 70 species of evergreen shrubs or small trees found in tropical and temperate regions, mostly in Australia, quite often in arid and semi-arid areas. Commonly known as hopbush; early European settlers substituted fruits of some species for hops in brewing. Male and female flowers mostly on separate plants. Flowers small and insignificant; it is the highly colored, inflated, winged capsules that form the attraction of these plants.
CULTIVATION: Frost tender, they do best in a moderately fertile well-drained soil in full sun. Some species withstand extended dry periods. Tip pruning will maintain bushy growth. Propagate from tip cuttings taken in summer.

Dodonaea adenophora
☼ ❋ ↔ 2–7 ft (0.6–2 m)
↑ 20–60 in (50–150 cm)

Medium-sized shrub, branches reddish, occurring in woodlands and mallee scrubs of inland southern Western Australia. Leaves small, pinnate, with 3 to 7 sticky opposite leaflets. Male and female flowers borne on separate plants, winter–spring. Fruits winged, reddish when mature. Zones 8–9.

Dodonaea angustifolia
syn. *Dodonaea viscosa* subsp. *angustifolia*
☼ ▮ ↔ 5–15 ft (1.5–4.5 m)
↑ 5–17 ft (1.5–5 m)

This species is part of the *D. viscosa* complex. Occurs in eastern Australia,

Dodonaea lobulata, seed capsules

Dodonaea viscosa 'Purpurea', seed capsules

Africa, Asia, and the Americas. Forms dense shrub with narrow, lance-shaped leaves, margin slightly wavy. Zones 9–12.

Dodonaea lobulata
LOBED-LEAF HOPBUSH
☼ ▮ ↔ 6 ft (1.8 m) ↑ 10 ft (3 m)
Widespread in semi-arid regions of southern Australia. Open wiry shrub. Sticky linear leaves, small irregular lobes. Masses of attractive, deep pink, 3-winged capsules on pendulous stalks, in winter–spring. Responds well to pruning, attractive hedge in hot dry areas. Zones 9–11.

Dodonaea microzyga
BRILLIANT HOPBUSH
☼ ❋ ↔ 3–6 ft (0.9–1.8 m)
↑ 20–60 in (50–150 cm)

From arid Australia. A small spreading shrub with sticky, reddish, slightly hairy stems. The leaves are small and pinnate with 3 to 11, somewhat oval-shaped, tiny, sticky leaflets, covered in very prominent glands. The male and female flowers are borne on separate plants during winter. Ripe fruits in spring. Zones 8–9.

Dodonaea viscosa
HOPBUSH
☼/◐ ▮ ↔ 5 ft (1.5 m) ↑ 10 ft (3 m)
A fast-growing evergreen tree from Australia, New Zealand, Pacific islands, tropical America, and southern Africa. Shiny, light green, sticky foliage. Bears masses of green winged fruit capsules in summer, hardening to a papery light brown. Best with regular trimming. 'Purpurea' ★, a sought-after form distinguished by its purple-red foliage and capsules. Zones 9–11.

DOMBEYA

This is a large genus of about 225 species occurring from Africa to the Mascarene Islands, with 190 species in Madagascar alone. It is a member of the cacao (Sterculiaceae) family. All are evergreen, deciduous, or semi-deciduous shrubs or trees with simple alternate leaves often with conspicuous stipules at the base of the leaf stalk. The flowers, in axillary or terminal panicles, often densely packed and very showy, are 5-petalled, white, pink, or red in color. The fruits are small, and often hairy, capsules.

CULTIVATION: Only a few species from the summer rainfall regions of southern Africa are cultivated, in warm-temperate and subtropical localities with adequate moisture in summer. A well-drained, fertile soil in full sun or part-shade is required. Some species are only just frost hardy for short periods. Propagate from seed in spring, or by cuttings in summer.

Dombeya burgessiae
PINK DOMBEYA, PINK WILD PEAR

☼ ❄ ↔ 7 ft (2 m) ↑ 10 ft (3 m)

From northeastern South Africa and Zimbabwe. Dense multi-stemmed shrub branching from ground level. Leaves large, hairy, lobed. Pink flowers in late autumn–winter. Fruits mature in winter–spring. Zones 9–12.

Dombeya rotundifolia

Dombeya burgessiae

Dombeya cacuminum

☼ ⚘ ↔ 20 ft (6 m) ↑ 40 ft (12 m)

Upright, evergreen tree native to open woodlands of Madagascar. Large leaves, maple-like, shiny. Flowers in large terminal clusters, deep pink to red. Zones 10–12.

Dombeya rotundifolia
SOUTH AFRICAN WILD PEAR

☼ ❄ ↔ 12 ft (3.5 m) ↑ 15 ft (4.5 m)

From northeastern South Africa, Mozambique, Zimbabwe, Botswana, west to Namibia. Deciduous or semi-deciduous tree. Sweetly scented flowers, white, rarely pink, in dense heads, on bare wood, in late winter–spring. Fruit is a spherical capsule, dark and hairy. Zones 9–10.

Dombeya tiliacea
FOREST DOMBEYA, NATAL WEDDING FLOWER

☼ ❄ ↔ 12 ft (3.5 m) ↑ 25 ft (8 m)

A native of Eastern Cape and KwaZulu Natal in South Africa. Small evergreen tree. Flowers white, in few-flowered pendulous clusters, in late summer–autumn, followed by fruit, in autumn–winter. Zones 9–10.

Dombeya wallichii

☼ ❄ ↔ 10 ft (3 m) ↑ 15 ft (4.5 m)

Evergreen tree originating from East Africa and Madagascar. Leaves large. Large deep pink to red flowers, in dense clusters, in winter–spring. One of the parents of widely grown hybrid *D. × cayeuxii* ★. Zones 9–10.

DOODIA
HACK SAW FERN, RASP FERN

This genus of 12 species of very hardy and adaptable, medium-sized, terres-

Dombeya cacuminum

Dombeya tiliacea

Doodia caudata

trial ferns from Sri Lanka to Polynesia, New Zealand, and Australia, is in the hard-fern (Blechnaceae) family. These long-lived ferns are closely related to *Blechnum* species. *Doodia* is known for its narrow, short, erect fronds, the fertile fronds often taller than the sterile ones and with narrower leaflets. New fronds have a distinctive red color that changes to different shades of green as they mature. The harsh leathery foliage can irritate sensitive skin.

CULTIVATION: Prefer acidic soils in a cool shady position, but will also grow in dry rockery areas. Propagate from spores; offspring may vary in color to parent plant. They are not fully hardy but will grow happily under glass.

Doodia caudata
SMALL RASP FERN

☼/◐ ❄ ↔ 12 in (30 cm)
↑ 8–12 in (20–30 cm)

From New Zealand, Australia, and Polynesia. Forms neat rounded clumps. Lance-shaped fronds are pinkish red when new and change to mid-green as they mature. Excellent plant for pots, containers, and rockeries. Plant in sun or part-shade. Zones 9–11.

DORONICUM
LEOPARD'S BANE

There are about 35 species of perennial herbs, native to Europe, southwestern Asia, and Siberia, in this genus in the daisy (Asteraceae) family. They grow from tubers or rhizomes, producing clumps of oval basal leaves. In spring, brilliant yellow daisies are borne on stems either singly or in small groups. Both rays and central discs are yellow.

CULTIVATION: Grow in part-shade in moderately fertile soil that is moisture retentive but well drained. Suitable for wild and woodland plantings. These plants are not suitable for hot climates. Propagate by division in autumn.

Doronicum orientale

Doronicum columnae

☼/◐ ❄ ↔ 24 in (60 cm) ↑ 12 in (30 cm)

From Europe and western Asia. Woodland perennial. Slightly hairy, heart-shaped leaves, scalloped edges. Yellow, sunflower-like flowers from spring–early summer. May die back in midsummer. Zones 4–8.

Doronicum orientale
syn. *Doronicum caucasicum*

◐ ❄ ↔ 12 in (30 cm)
↑ 12–24 in (30–60 cm)

Native to the Caucasus, Lebanon, and southern Europe. A fleshy-stemmed perennial forming clumps of oval leaves. The bright yellow daisies, finely rayed, are carried singly on tall slender stems, in spring. 'Magnificum' ★, large flowers. Zones 5–9.

DOROTHEANTHUS
LIVINGSTONE DAISY

This genus of 6 species of succulent annuals, belonging to the iceplant (Aizoaceae) family, is confined to South Africa. Spreading or mounding plants with thickened leaves that have a crystalline surface, creating a sugar-coated look. Flowers are daisy-like, often very abundant, in a range of colors, mainly shades of pink or white but also yellow, orange, red, and purple. Mostly ephemeral, these subdesert plants can race into growth with the arrival of rain. In frost-free climates, the plants may

Doryanthes excelsa, in the wild, New South Wales, Australia

Doryanthes palmeri

grow at any time but in temperate areas they are mainly summer-flowering. CULTIVATION: Plant in spring in a bright sunny position to ensure maximum flowering time. Soil should be light, gritty, and well-drained, but the plants do need occasional water when flowering. Deadhead frequently for continued bloom. In cooler climates, sow seed under glass in winter or spring. Propagate from seed.

Dorotheanthus bellidiformis
☀ ❄ ↔ 8–16 in (20–40 cm)
↑ 2–6 in (5–15 cm)

From South Africa. Low spreading plant. Red-tinted stems, fleshy gray-green leaves, rough textured surface.

Daisy-like flowers in mainly pink to purple shades but also white. Garden forms with yellow and multi-colored flowers may be *D. bellidiformis* × *D. gramineus* hybrids. Zones 9–11.

DORSTENIA
A member of the mulberry (Moraceae) family, this genus of around 170 species of fleshy-stemmed perennials, some of which are succulent, occurs mainly in the African and American tropics, with a few species from India. Unusual plants, mostly forming short stems with elliptical to heart-shaped leaves, sometimes toothed, wavy or lobed, they have one very distinctive feature: the way they bear their flowers. These plants

produce stems topped with a flattened spongy structure rather like a thicker more extensively lobed leaf. To the naked eye, the surface of this receptacle is studded with small dots, which are actually minute flowers. They are not followed by any obvious seed pod, the receptacle simply developing small protuberances, then drying and shedding its minute seeds as it breaks up. CULTIVATION: Outside tropics these unusual plants are cultivated indoors. Prefer a bright, but not overly sunny position, even warmth, shelter from cold drafts, fairly high humidity, and moist, humus-rich, well-drained soil. Propagate by division or from seed.

Dorstenia barkeri
☀ ❦ ↔ 24 in (60 cm) ↑ 24 in (60 cm)
Perennial from tropical West Africa. Prominently veined leaves. Slightly convex saucer-like receptacle has narrow thread-like appendages. Tiny male and female flowers at first embedded before opening over the surface. *D. b.* var. *multiradiata*, angular receptacle, narrower appendages. Zones 10–12.

Dorstenia foetida ★
syn. *Dorstenia crispa*
☀ ❦ ↔ 12 in (30 cm) ↑ 6–16 in (15–40 cm)
Found from Saudi Arabia to Kenya. Very distinctive succulent species forming short stems topped with dark green, fleshy, narrow, lance-shaped leaves. Floral receptacles reminiscent of starfish, with central body and long, narrow, radial lobes. Zones 10–12.

DORYANTHES
Genus of 2 species of large perennial herbs, in own family, Doryanthaceae, occurring in woodlands, open forests, and rocky hillsides on sandy or gravelly, well-draining soils in eastern Australia. Leaves are lance-shaped, pointed with an appendage at the apex. Flower stalks can exceed the leaves in length by 2 to 3 times. Flowers are in terminal heads, each large, red, and with 6 equal segments. Fruits are 3-celled capsules. Plants are long-lived in cultivation and were grown in the UK as early as 1800. CULTIVATION: Propagation is usually from seeds, but flowering could be up to 10 years from germination. Division of clumps, or from suckers, will produce flowering plants sooner.

Doryanthes excelsa
GIANT LILY, GYMEA LILY, ILLAWARRA LILY
☀ ❦ ↔ 10 ft (3 m) ↑ 8–20 ft (2.4–6 m)
Found in woodlands on sandy soils in the central coast region of New South Wales, Australia. Leaves are bright or slightly yellowish green, generally stiff

and erect. Flower stalk, up to 20 ft (6 m) long, terminating in a dense head of many red flowers, in spring–summer. Each flower contains large quantities of nectar, presumably as a bird-attractant to effect pollination. Dark colored capsules. Zones 9–11.

Doryanthes palmeri
SPEAR LILY
☀ ❦ ↔ 3–10 ft (0.9–3 m)
↑ 3–10 ft (0.9–3 m)

From northern New South Wales and southern Queensland, Australia, on skeletal soils on rocky hillsides. Leaves long, bright green, lance-shaped, with a cylindrical appendage at apex. Flower stalks up to 17 ft (5 m) long, usually not erect, but tending to arch, with brownish flowers, during spring. Capsules greenish. Zones 10–12.

DOVYALIS
Genus of 15 species in the governor's-plum (Flacourtiaceae) family from warm-temperate regions of Africa and Sri Lanka. Evergreen shrubs or small trees, often spiny, especially young growth. Small, insignificant, greenish or yellow flowers; male and female flowers on separate plants. Fruits spherical, fleshy; sometimes used for pickles and jams. Some species used as hedging; pruning encourages spines. CULTIVATION: Propagated from both seeds and cuttings, these plants prefer a frost-free situation in full sun with rich, fertile, well-drained soil.

Dorstenia foetida

Dorstenia barkeri var. *multiradiata*

Dovyalis caffra

Draba polytricha

Draba bruniifolia

Dovyalis caffra

KEI APPLE

☼ ⚘ ↔ 15 ft (4.5 m) ↑ 15 ft (4.5 m)

Found in grasslands of Eastern Cape, South Africa, north to Mozambique and Malawi. Evergreen shrub or small tree. Branches bear long spines with inconspicuous greenish flowers, in summer. Edible, spherical summer fruits, fleshy, apricot-colored; makes pleasantly flavored jellies and jams. Zones 9–10.

DRABA

WHITLOW GRASS

A large genus in the cabbage family (Brassicaceae) of about 300 species of annuals and more or less cushion-forming perennials. They are mainly plants of the Arctic and mountain regions of Europe and the Americas. The annual species are rarely grown and have little ornamental value. CULTIVATION: The perennial species can make extremely neat tight domes much admired by alpine plant enthusiasts and often are grown in pots for competition. They can be grown in troughs or the rock garden but the best plants are those tended in a cool greenhouse. Propagate from fresh seed or tiny cuttings or by careful division.

Draba aizoides

☼ ❄ ↔ 4–6 in (10–15 cm) ↑ ¾–1¼ in (18–30 mm)

Semi-evergreen mat-forming perennial from central and southern Europe and the UK. Rosettes of lance-shaped stiffly bristled leaves. Bright yellow flowers on erect smooth stems. Zones 3–8.

Draba bruniifolia

☼ ❄ ↔ 6–12 in (15–30 cm) ↑ 2½–4 in (6–10 cm)

Perennial from Mediterranean area. Mat-forming, semi-evergreen. Loose heads of 8 to 16 bright golden yellow flowers on smooth stems. *D. b.* subsp. *olympica*, from Turkey, hairy flowering stems with 3 to 8 flowers. Zones 5–8.

Draba polytricha

☼ ❄ ↔ 4–6 in (10–15 cm) ↑ 1¼–1¾ in (30–40 mm)

Perennial from Armenia and Turkey. Semi-evergreen, mat-forming, heads of 4 to 10 bright yellow flowers, on finely hairy stalks. Zones 5–8.

DRACAENA

A dragon-tree (Dracaenaceae) family genus consisting of about 40 evergreen perennials, shrubs, or trees, mostly from tropical West Africa. Leaves are smooth, glossy, sword-like, often variegated; terminal panicles of short-lived flowers. Some species have spiky growth habit; others are softer and more shrubby. Fruit is a berry. Ornamental as garden or container plants. CULTIVATION: In garden, prefer rich, moist, well-drained soil in a protected sunny position, or a standard potting mix in diffused sunlight or full shade. Propagate from stem or tip cuttings, root cuttings, preferably with bottom heat, or from seed sown in spring.

Dracaena draco ★

DRAGON'S-BLOOD TREE, DRAGON TREE

☼ ⚘ ↔ 12 ft (3.5 m) ↑ 30 ft (9 m)

From Canary Islands. Slow-growing palm-like tree. Trunk upright, multi-stemmed. Canopy of stiff gray leaves bunched at branch ends. Insignificant flowers, orange berries, in summer. Require free-draining soil, warmth, lots of sun. Suitable in containers. Zones 10–12.

Dracaena fragrans

syn. *Pleomele fragrans*

HAPPY PLANT

☼/◐ ⚘ ↔ 6 ft (1.8 m) ↑ 10–30 ft (3–9 m)

Variable species, widespread from tropical West Africa to Malawi. Glossy, sword-like, pale green leaves. Clusters of fragrant yellow flowers. Cultivars belonging to **Deremensis Group** (syn. *D. deremensis*) have dark red flowers: '**Longii**', leaves with broad white central stripe; '**Warneckei**', leaves greenish white with a bright green edging. *D. f.* '**Massangeana**', known as corn plant, bright green leaves striped with cream to yellow down the center. Zones 9–11.

Dracaena marginata ★

☼/◐ ⚘ ↔ 3–10 ft (0.9–3 m) ↑ 7–17 ft (2–5 m)

Upright branching shrub or small tree from Réunion Island, Mauritius. Good structural upright form. Long, lance-shaped, green leaves cover tips of thin erect branches. Adapts well to indoor and outdoor cultivation. Prefers fertile moist soils. Zones 9–11.

Dracaena reflexa

☼ ✈ ↔ 3 ft (0.9 m) ↑ 8 ft (2.4 m)

Native of Madagascar and Mauritius, but now linked with plants from tropical Africa, merged as *D. reflexa*. Tangle of wiry stems, lance-shaped dark green leaves. Flowers cream, sweet-smelling at night, in spring. Pollinated by moths. Bright red berries, early summer. '**Song of India**', variegated, broad creamy white marginal stripes. Zones 10–12.

Dracaena sanderiana

RIBBON PLANT

☼ ⚘ ↔ 16–32 in (40–80 cm) ↑ 5 ft (1.5 m)

From Cameroon. Upright narrow shrub, only few branches from base. Rich dark green, lance-shaped leaves edged in white. Zones 9–11.

Dracaena fragrans 'Massangeana'

Dracaena draco

Dracaena reflexa 'Song of India'

DRACOCEPHALUM

Genus, in mint (Lamiaceae) family, containing about 45 species of annuals, perennials, and dwarf shrubs. Most are found in Europe and Asia, some in northern Africa, and USA. Leaves opposite and simple with toothed or indented margins. Flowers usually deep blue or violet-blue, borne in whorls on spikes, terminally and on branching stems. They are tubular and 2-lipped, lower lip having 3 lobes and upper lip 2 lobes. Some species are aromatic.
CULTIVATION: Full sun, fertile well-drained soil. Grow perennials from cuttings or division, annuals from seed.

Dracocephalum ruyschianum

☼ ❄ ↔ 12–18 in (30–45 cm)
↑ 12–24 in (30–60 cm)

Perennial from central Europe and Russia. Upright stems, narrow leaves. Whorls of 2 to 6 flowers, blue to violet, occasionally pink or white, in dense terminal spikes, in summer. Zones 3–9.

DRACOPHYLLUM

Genus in the epacris (Epacridaceae) family of 48 evergreen trees and erect or prostrate shrubs. Long grass-like

Dracocephalum ruyschianum

leaves that often form dense clusters at branch tips. Tiny 5-petalled flowers are borne singly or in racemes. About 35 species native to New Zealand with the remainder found in Australia and New Caledonia. They grow in forest and scrub, often at high altitudes.
CULTIVATION: The striking form of grass trees makes them an interesting addition to the garden but they are slow-growing and can be very difficult to cultivate. They require a gritty friable soil and perfect drainage. Although they should not be allowed to become too dry, care must be taken not to overwater as they are very susceptible to root rot. In cool temperate climates they are best grown in a greenhouse or conservatory. Propagation is usually by seed sown in autumn as cuttings are difficult to strike.

Dracophyllum traversii

MOUNTAIN NEINEI

☼ ❄ ↔ 7 ft (2 m)   ↑ 30 ft (9 m)

From alpine regions of New Zealand's South Island. Branches are dark brown, erect, with terminal clumps of strap-like leaves. Tiny flowers in crowded panicles, at branch ends, in spring. Difficult to cultivate, extremely slow growing. Zones 7–9.

DRACULA

These are cool-growing sympodial orchids (family Orchidaceae) related to *Masdevallia,* and previously placed within this large diverse genus. The majority, 100 or so species, live in the moist high cloud forests of western Colombia and Ecuador. Being close to the equator, there are no seasons, so plants experience same weather conditions and day length all year. The plant habit is very similar for most of the species, with a single, somewhat fleshy, upright leaf that may be paddle shaped. Blooms are outstanding; you

Dracophyllum traversii, in the wild, New Zealand

Dracula tubeana

can see "faces" in many flowers, with the tiny petals becoming the "eyes." Increasing numbers of *Dracula* hybrids are being produced, which are easier to grow. Combinations with *Masdevallia* have created the genus *Dracuvallia.*
CULTIVATION: Need cool conditions and deteriorate quickly if conditions do not suit. Do not like daytime temperatures rising above 79°F (26°C), and prefer nighttime minimum of 54°F (12°C). This very narrow range must be observed if cultivated plants are to thrive. They also demand constant air movement and high humidity. Most successful growers cultivate plants in live sphagnum moss. Because many species have a descending inflorescence, suspended baskets or mesh pots are used. Seventy per cent shade suits most species; they will not take bright sunlight, particularly in combination with high temperatures. Growers often modify or create new growing enclosures just to house this genus, because of their large, spectacular, bizarre flowers. Blooms collapse in high temperatures but can be re-hydrated by misting with cold water. Propagate by division.

Dracula tubeana

☼ ☂ ↔ 4–16 in (10–40 cm)
↑ 4–16 in (10–40 cm)

From Ecuador. Creamy, medium-sized, white blooms, with distinct red-brown border. Sepals have fine hairs on the edges. Zones 10–11.

Dracula velutina

☼ ☂ ↔ 4–16 in (10–40 cm)
↑ 4–16 in (10–40 cm)

From Colombia. Smaller flowered. White blooms with dark purple tails attached to sepals. Zones 10–11.

DRIMYS

This genus is one of 5 which make up the small family Winteraceae, origins of which date back to earliest evolution of flowering plants in the age of dinosaurs. It consists of 6 species of evergreen shrubs and small trees occurring in South America and higher mountains of Mexico and Central America.

Dracula velutina

Drimys winteri

Another 20 to 40 species from Australasia and Southeast Asia have often been included in *Drimys*, but most recent evidence supports their being separated into the separate genus *Tasmannia*. Simple leathery leaves, without teeth or lobes, arranged spirally and clustered towards end of season's growth, new leaves often red. Star-shaped white or cream flowers are carried in umbel-like clusters in spring. Bark is aromatic with a hot, pepper-like taste. From its first discovery by Europeans it was believed to be an effective treatment for scurvy. It thrives in a sheltered position.
CULTIVATION: Most species are not fully frost hardy and at best tolerate down to 14°F (–10°C) for short spells. Grow in sun or partial shade in moist but well-drained fertile soil. Propagate by taking half-hardened cuttings in summer or sowing seed into pots as soon as it is ripe in autumn, with protection against winter frosts.

Drimys winteri ★

syn. *Wintera aromatica*

WINTER'S BARK

☼/◑ ❄ ↔ 30 ft (9 m)   ↑ 50 ft (15 m)

Aromatic tree, from Mexico, Chile, and Argentina. Lustrous, dark-green, lance-shaped leaves, pale blue-white beneath. Flowers fragrant, creamy white, in umbels of 20 individual blossoms, in spring–early summer. Zones 8–9.

DROSANTHEMUM

Found in South Africa and Namibia, this genus of succulents in the iceplant (Aizoaceae) family is made up of about 90 species of perennials, many trailing,

the others mounding or shrubby. The leaves are succulent, cylindrical in section, covered in tiny protuberances and often small. Attraction lies largely in its dense carpeting habit and weight of bloom. Flowers seldom very large but incredibly abundant, frequently making a solid mass of color, in white or any shade of pink, purple, yellow, orange, or red, usually from late spring.
CULTIVATION: Hardiness varies; mostly intolerant of repeated frosts. Plant in open sunny position in gritty, very free-draining soil with a little extra humus. Water when in flower, otherwise allow to survive on natural rainfall. Propagate from seed or cuttings or by layering.

Drosanthemum speciosum ★
☼ ❄ ↔ 40 in (100 cm) ↑ 24 in (60 cm)
From Cape region, South Africa. Shrub with upright branching stems. Leaves have crystalline surface. Flowers deep orange-red, occasionally purplish, green center, large, many-petalled, plumed effect. Zones 9–11.

DROSERA
SUNDEW

A diverse genus of more than 130 carnivorous plants found on every continent except Antarctica. *Drosera* belongs to the sundew (Droseraceae) family, which also contains the Venus flytrap *(Dionaea muscipula).* Almost half the species are native to Australia but are also found in South America's swamps, the snow-covered alps of New Zealand, and the rainforests of Borneo. Their size and shape is as varied as their habitat. The tentacle-covered leaves can be erect, climbing, fan-leafed, or arranged in a rosette. All species trap prey in the same way. An insect is lured to sticky, dew-like liquid sparkling on the red tentacles on the sundew's leaves. Struggling to free itself, it becomes entrapped when its body touches more sticky tentacles. In some species,

Drosera adelae

the leaf curls around the insect to complete the capture. Over time, digestive enzymes break down the soft parts of the insect's body, the leaf uncurls and the insect's shell is blown away.
CULTIVATION: Growing conditions for *Drosera* vary but they can be roughly divided into the 4 groups below. Some species grow in both tropical and temperate zones. Many species grow easily from leaf cuttings.
Tropical species: Grow in sphagnum moss, in pots in tray of water in shade. Need high humidity. Best if temperature does not fall below 59°F (15°C).
Subtropical species: Many are very easy to grow. Use a soil mix of 3 parts peat and 2 parts sand, keep soil damp. Full sun to part-shade. Some species tolerate light frosts, but are best treated as an annual in colder areas. Grow in a greenhouse or on a sunny windowsill.
Temperate species: Use a soil mix of 3 parts peat to 2 parts sand. Stand containers in water. Full sun in temperate climates, part-shade in warmer areas. Plants usually dormant in winter.
Tuberous species: Use a soil mix of 3 parts peat to 2 parts sand. In native habitat (most tuberous species come from Western Australia) summers are hot and dry and plants experience summer dormancy so pots should be kept dry and out of direct sunlight during this period. Start to water by tray as winter approaches and new growth appears. Protect from frosts.

Drosanthemum speciosum

Drosera adelae
LANCE-LEAFED SUNDEW
☀ ⚓ ↔ 10 in (25 cm) ↑ 8 in (20 cm)
From coast of northern Queensland, Australia. Herbaceous perennial, with narrow lanceolate leaves, sparsely tentacled. Tiny but beautiful red flowers in spring–summer. Tropical (*see* Cultivation). Zones 10–12.

Drosera aliciae
☼ ❄ ↔ 2 in (5 cm) ↑ 1 in (2.5 cm)
From the Cape region of South Africa. A rosette *Drosera*, with spathulate, green leaves densely covered in red tentacles. Pink to purple flowers on leafless stalk. Temperate to subtropical (*see* Cultivation). Zones 9–11.

Drosera binata
FORKED SUNDEW
☼ ❄ ↔ 8 in (20 cm) ↑ 12 in (30 cm)
From east coast of Australia and New Zealand. Many varieties, all have leaf blades that fork into "Y" shape. Slender green to yellow leaves, densely covered with tentacles. Temperate to subtropical (*see* Cultivation). Zones 8–10.

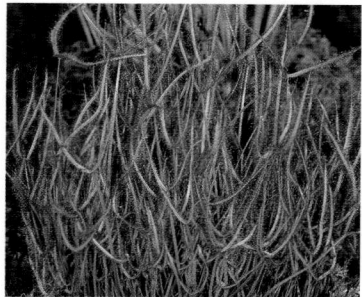

Drosera binata

Drosera capensis
CAPE SUNDEW
☼ ❄ ↔ 6 in (15 cm) ↑ 6 in (15 cm)
One of the easiest sundews to grow. Comes from the Cape region of South Africa where it grows in bogs, marshes, and wet grasslands. The slender green leaves, are covered in fine red tentacles; the ends of leaves are rounded and curl around the trapped prey. Older plants produce a woody trunk with green foliage at top. Pretty pink flowers appear on a leafless stalk in spring. Does not experience dormancy in winter. Temperate to subtropical (*see* Cultivation). Zones 8–11.

Drosera capensis

D

Drosera pulchella

Drosera montana var. *schwackei*

Drosera pygmaea

Drosera schizandra

Drosera capillaris

PINK SUNDEW

☼ ⚘ ↔ 3 in (8 cm) ↑ 2 in (5 cm)

Rosette sundew from southern USA, Central and South America. Spathulate green leaves, covered with red tentacles. Small pale pink flowers in spring. Sub-tropical (*see* Cultivation). Zones 9–12.

Drosera erythrorhiza

REDINK SUNDEW

☼ ⚘ ↔ 4 in (10 cm) ↑ 1 in (2.5 cm)

Rosette *Drosera* in open scrub, south-western Western Australia. Green to red leaves have central depressed valley running from base to tip. Up to 30 white flowers on 4 in (10 cm) stem. Tuberous (*see* Cultivation). Zones 9–11.

Drosera filiformis

THREADLEAF SUNDEW, DEW THREAD

☼/◐ ❋ ↔ 12 in (30 cm) ↑ 20 in (50 cm)

There are 2 main subspecies. **D. f. subsp. *filiformis***, erect species from

east coast USA, short stem, fine leaves that uncurl like fern fronds, 1 to 3 leafless stalks, up to 25 small pink flowers on each stalk. **D. f. subsp. *tracyi***, from Gulf coast of USA, larger leaves, and slightly larger pink flowers, dormant in winter. Temperate to subtropical (*see* Cultivation). Zones 8–11.

Drosera indica

☼ ⚘ ↔ 8 in (20 cm) ↑ 6 in (15 cm)

From Asia, Africa, and Australia. Slender green leaves from a trailing stem. Pink or white flowers on a leafless stalk. Tropical (*see* Cultivation). Zones 9–12.

Drosera intermedia

☼ ❋ ↔ 3 in (8 cm) ↑ 4 in (10 cm)

Found mainly in Europe and North America. Rosette *Drosera*, both temperate and subtropical, depending on its location. In warm climates plants can grow up to 8 in (20 cm) tall and do not experience winter dormancy. Oblong-shaped leaves radiate from central stem. Tiny white flowers. Grows in very moist soil in bogs, and even in shallow water. Temperate (*see* Cultivation). Zones 6–11.

Drosera linearis

☼ ❋ ↔ 2 in (5 cm) ↑ 2 in (5 cm)

Found in alkaline bogs in northern USA and Canada. Very dark green, slender, erect leaves covered in fine red tentacles. Tiny white flowers in sum-

mer. Often found with *D. rotundifolia* and *D. anglica*. Temperate (*see* Cultivation). Zones 6–10.

Drosera montana

MOUNTAIN SUNDEW

☼ ⚘ ↔ 1 in (25 mm) ↑ 1/2 in (12 mm)

Small, pretty, Brazilian rosette *Drosera*. Wedge-shaped green to red leaves covered in bright red tentacles. Small white flowers in spring. **D. m. var. *schwackei*** usually has yellow-green leaves. Subtropical (*see* Cultivation). Zones 9–12.

Drosera petiolaris

WOOLLY SUNDEW

☼/◐ ⚘ ↔ 4 in (10 cm) ↑ 2 1/2 in (6 cm)

Found in northern Australia and New Guinea in very wet soil that dries out during winter when plant goes into dormancy. (In cultivation, plants do not experience winter dormancy if soil is kept moist.) Rosette *Drosera*, peltate leaves on fine green stalks, bright red tentacles around edges. White or dark pink flowers in spring–summer. Tropical (*see* Cultivation). Zones 9–12.

Drosera pulchella

PRETTY SUNDEW

☼ ⚘ ↔ 1 1/4 in (30 mm) ↑ 1/2 in (12 mm)

Found in swamps, wet peat and damp sandy soil in Western Australia. Rosette sundew with round, tentacled, green leaves on broad stalks. Flowers set in spring on 2 or 3 leafless stalks; can be

Drosera spatulata

Drosera indica

white, pink, orange, or dark red with metallic sheen. Dormant in wild in hot dry summer, but not in cultivation if plant is kept moist. Sub-tropical (*see* Cultivation). Zones 9–11.

Drosera pygmaea ★

PYGMY SUNDEW

☼/◐ ❋ ↔ 3/4 in (18 mm) ↑ 1/2 in (12 mm)

From damp sandy soils in Australia and New Zealand. Round, green to red leaves on short stalks in basal rosette. Tiny white flowers, on up to 4 leafless stalks, in spring. Easy to grow. Subtropical (*see* Cultivation). Zones 8–10.

Drosera rotundifolia

ROUND-LEAFED SUNDEW

☼ ❋ ↔ 4 in (10 cm) ↑ 2 in (5 cm)

Most widely distributed of temperate sundews, found in Asia, Europe, and North America in sphagnum bogs. Cup-shaped leaves on a fine stalk. Tiny flowers, white to pink, on a leafless stalk, in spring–summer. Temperate (*see* Cultivation). Zones 3–9.

Drosera schizandra

NOTCHED SUNDEW

◐ ⚘ ↔ 3 in (8 cm) ↑ 4 in (10 cm)

Rosette sundew, from bogs in North Queensland, Australia. Green spoon-shaped leaves, sometimes with notched end, sparse red tentacles. Inconspicuous white flowers, on leafless stalk, a little shorter than leaves. Tropical (*see* Cultivation). Zones 9–12.

Drosera spatulata

☼/◐ ❋ ↔ 2 in (5 cm) ↑ 1 in (2.5 cm)

From Australia, New Zealand, and parts of Asia. Rosette sundew from damp soil in wetlands. Leaves green to red, depending on how much light the plant receives, spoon-shaped, covered in red tentacles. Up to 15 small white to pink flowers on 1 or 2 erect leafless stalks. Temperate to subtropical (*see* Cultivation). Zones 8–10.

Drosera zonaria

PAINTED SUNDEW

☼ ❋ ↔ 3 in (8 cm) ↑ 1 in (2.5 cm)

Sundew from Western Australia. Has rounded leaves with short stems in

Drosera zonaria

Dryandra polycephala

Dryandra quercifolia

overlapping rosette. Green leaves, usually red around the edges. Flowers are white but rare. Tuberous (*see* Cultivation). Zones 8–10.

DROSOPHYLLUM
DEWY PINE, PORTUGUESE SUNDEW

A carnivorous single-species genus of the sundew (Droseraceae) family, the Portuguese sundew is found in Spain, Morocco, and Portugal. A small perennial shrub, it grows in dry sandy soil on coastal hills, often among short fir trees (*Pinus pinaster*). The plant has a dewy appearance, caused by the droplets of sticky mucus on the leaves. The name comes from the Greek, *drosos*, meaning dew and *phyllon*, meaning leaf. Small insects get trapped on the leaves by the very sticky liquid; the leaves then secrete a digestive enzyme which dissolves the prey's soft tissue.
CULTIVATION: Grow in mix of 3 parts sand to 1 part peat, add a teaspoon of limestone or dolomite to a 6 in (15 cm) clay pot. Place the clay pot in a plastic pot containing live sphagnum moss (ensure the plastic pot has a large drainage hole), in full sun. Water by tray, never from above. Allow the pot to dry out for one day each month. Small plantlets frequently appear among the branches, these can be removed and planted once they have 10 or 12 leaves; dip stem in rooting hormone and plant in mix of 1 part sand to 2 parts peat.

Drosophyllum lusitanicum
☼ ❄ ↔ 16 in (40 cm) ↑ 12 in (30 cm)
Woody base. Up to 100 slender green leaves covered in sticky red liquid; leaves uncurl outwardly, unlike *Drosera*, where the leaves curl toward the center of the plant. Bright yellow flowers appear in spring. Zones 8–10.

DRYANDRA

These beautiful flowering, evergreen shrubs, numbering about 60 species, are native to Western Australia. They belong to the protea (Proteaceae) family and are related to banksias, and in many respects closely resemble that genus. They are grown for their highly decorative, lobed or toothed leaves and

richly-colored, yellow, gold, or bronze, rounded flowerheads. Some species flower during the winter months. The flowers are most attractive to nectar-feeding birds and are excellent for indoor arrangements. Dryandras come from warm regions with winter rainfall and a pronounced dry summer season. Many species will grow well in containers. They are frost tender.
CULTIVATION: Excellent drainage is essential, in full sun or part-shade. They prefer dry neutral or acid soil and low levels of nitrates or phosphates. Tip prune while young, and lightly after flowering to promote compact growth. Propagate from seed in spring.

Dryandra formosa
SHOWY DRYANDRA
☼ ❄ ↔ 7 ft (2 m) ↑ 10 ft (3 m)
From far southern coastal regions of Western Australia. Prized for its cut flowers. Slender, dark green leaves, with prickly triangular lobes, whitish undersides. Rounded, almost metallic, golden flowerheads, in winter–spring. The flowers produce large quantities of nectar. Tolerates fairly heavy pruning. Zones 9–11.

Dryandra polycephala
MANY-HEADED DRYANDRA
☼ ❄ ↔ 7 ft (2 m) ↑ 12 ft (3.5 m)
Native of Perth and wheat belt region of Western Australia. The narrow leaves have widely spaced prickly lobes. Lemon yellow flowerheads appear along the branches, in late winter–spring. Cut branches of flowers and foliage excellent for indoor arrangements. Zones 9–11.

Dryandra praemorsa ★
SEA-URCHIN DRYANDRA
☼ ❄ ↔ 10 ft (3 m) ↑ 10 ft (3 m)
A shrub found in the Perth region of Western Australia. Its hairy branches are prickly, almost holly-like, the dark green leaves have whitish undersides. The upper leaves form a collar around the base of each flowerhead. The large golden yellow flowerheads, appear in winter–spring. Requires regular pruning to maintain bushiness. Zones 9–11.

Dryandra quercifolia
OAK-LEAF DRYANDRA
☼ ❄ ↔ 10 ft (3 m) ↑ 10 ft (3 m)
From Esperance region of far southern Western Australia. Felty new growth, dark green leaves prickly lobed. Flowerheads iridescent yellow and green, in winter–spring. Surrounded by a collar of floral leaves. An excellent species for cultivation and cut flowers. Zones 9–11.

DRYAS
MOUNTAIN AVENS

A small genus of 3 species, all evergreen mat-forming shrubs from Arctic and Northern Hemisphere alpine regions, belonging to the rose (Rosaceae) family. They produce comparatively large, white or lemon flowers in summer, well clear of the foliage, followed by large fluffy seed heads. The botanical name comes from that of the Greek mythological wood nymph to whom the oak was sacred, and alludes to the oak-shaped foliage.
CULTIVATION: These shrubs prefer a sunny moist aspect in non-tropical climates in a rock garden or between pavers. Their mat-forming habit and copper-colored leaves in winter make them ideal ground covers over small bulbs. Propagate by division, from cuttings or freshly sown seed.

Dryas octopetala ★
MOUNTAIN AVENS
☼ ❄ ↔ over 40 in (100 cm)
↑ 3–4 in (8–10 cm)
Northern European species. Glossy oak-shaped leaves, white reverse turns coppery in winter. White flowers, in summer. Fluffy seed heads. Zones 3–9.

Dryas × suendermannii
☼ ❄ ↔ over 40 in (100 cm)
↑ 3–5 in (8–15 cm)
Hybrid between *D. drummondii* and *D. octopetala* that arose in cultivation. Pale, creamy yellow, slightly nodding flowers, in summer. Zones 3–9.

DRYOPTERIS
BUCKLER FERN, SHIELD FERN, WOOD FERN

Part of shield-fern (Dryopteridaceae) family, this genus is made up of about 200 species found in temperate forests, fields, and wet areas of the Northern Hemisphere. This genus contains the largest number of good ferns for ornamental gardening. The green foliage looks attractive with its upright arching fronds. These ferns work well when planted in mixed borders with most herbaceous plants. Many species have scaly tips to the fronds that can be dramatically beautiful in the spring as they begin to unravel.
CULTIVATION: Mostly deciduous but in mild areas will retain their foliage. An easy to cultivate, resilient fern group that will grow in poor dry soils, with little natural light. Propagate from spores as soon as they harden.

Dryas octopetala

Dryandra praemorsa

Dryopteris affinis
GOLDEN MALE FERN

☀ ❄ ↔ 27–36 in (70–90 cm)
↕ 36 in (90 cm)

Deciduous fern from Europe, including the UK, and parts of Asia. Very upright fronds appear in spring, initially a brown-green, changing to a lush rich green as the fronds unravel. '**Crispa Gracilis**', dwarf evergreen, fronds have very congested leaflets (tight foliage) with dark green tonings on the tips; '**Cristata Angustata**', elegant fern with slim, graceful, long, arching, crested fronds; '**Pinderi**', uncrested mid-green fronds that narrow to very sharp point. Zones 6–8.

Dryopteris carthusiana
syn. *Dryopteris maderensis*
NARROW BUCKLER FERN

☀ ❄ ↔ 12 in (30 cm) ↕ 24 in (60 cm)

Delicate-looking fern from Europe producing tufts of pale, lime green, lance-shaped fronds. Creeping, ground-covering habit. Enjoys damp, grows well in boggy areas. Zones 6–10.

Dryopteris × complexa

☀ ❄ ↔ 36 in (90 cm) ↕ 36 in (90 cm)

Hybrid of *D. affinis × D. filix-mas*. Medium to large, semi-evergreen fern, similar to *D. affinis*, with upright fronds that reappear in spring, initially brown-green, changing to mid-green as they mature. Winter dormant in cool areas. Zones 4–9.

Dryopteris affinis

Dryopteris carthusiana

Dryopteris × complexa

Dryopteris cristata
COMMON SHIELD FERN, CRESTED WOOD FERN, NARROW SWAMP FERN

☀ ❄ ↔ 36 in (90 cm)
↕ 18–30 in (45–75 cm)

From Europe and northern Asia and eastern North America. Erect fern with green, narrow, lance-shaped fronds with short, widely spaced, tilted leaflets. Spores held on undersides of fronds. Good in very damp areas. Will be evergreen in Zones 6 and 7. Zones 3–7.

Dryopteris cycadina
syn. *Dryopteris atrata*
SHAGGY SHIELD FERN

☀ ❄ ↔ 18 in (45 cm) ↕ 24 in (60 cm)

From Japan, China, Taiwan, and northern India. Long, dark green, distinctive, narrow fronds, serrated margins. Black stems support these in an arching habit. Needs well-drained soil. Zones 8–10.

Dryopteris dilatata
syn. *Dryopteris austriaca*
BROAD BUCKLER FERN

☀ ❄ ↔ 36 in (90 cm) ↕ 48 in (120 cm)

Vigorous fern from northern, western, and central Europe. Forms rosettes of broad dark green fronds. Easily grown, tolerates some sun. '**Crispa Whiteside**' (Whiteside's broad buckler fern), only reaches 24 in (60 cm) high, fronds paler green in color ruffled crispy look. Zones 5–8.

Dryopteris erythrosora
AUTUMN FERN

☀ ❄ ↔ 16 in (40 cm) ↕ 24 in (60 cm)

From Asia. Shiny triangular fronds, rosy pink in spring, changing to bronze and eventually deep green as season progresses. Reliable, striking, and easy to grow. Usually deciduous. Zones 6–9.

Dryopteris filix-mas
MALE FERN

☀ ❄ ↔ 24 in (60 cm) ↕ 48 in (120 cm)

From Europe and North America. Mass of lance-shaped green fronds appear in spring. Spreads along ground with rhizomes. Prefers part-shade and neutral to acid soil. Plant ceases growth in autumn, may become deciduous over winter. '**Barnesii**', a very tall fern with large, sparsely clothed, arching

Dryopteris dilatata 'Crispa Whiteside'

Dryopteris filix-mas 'Crispa Cristata'

Dryopteris cycadina

fronds, prefers a light dry soil, perfect in dry shade; '**Crispa**', dwarf compact plant with sturdy, heavily crested, frilly fronds; '**Crispa Cristata**', crested pale lime green, very frilly fronds; '**Cristata**', foliage lightly crested, frond tips very frilly; '**Depauperata**', compact fern with pretty, ruffled, dense, green foliage along each frond; **Grandiceps Group**, frond tips have a heavy terminal crest, a very vigorous and clumping fern; '**Grandiceps Wills**', a striking plant, frond tips have large fluffy crests, vigorous and tolerant fern once established; '**Linearis Cristata**', dwarf fern, dark green foliage, short narrow fronds, plant has a very delicate appearance but is very tough. Zones 4–8.

Dryopteris marginalis
LEATHER WOOD FERN, MARGINAL WOOD FERN

☀ ❄ ↔ 20 in (50 cm) ↕ 10 in (25 cm)

From Quebec, Canada, to Kansas, USA. A robust evergreen fern. The short rhizomes produce groups of upright, blue-green, lance-shaped fronds. Perfect for shady hillsides. Zones 9–11.

Dryopteris sieboldii
JAPANESE WOOD FERN

☀ ❄ ↔ 20 in (50 cm) ↕ 20 in (50 cm)

From Japan. Distinctive fern with glossy green palmate fronds. Broad lance-shaped leaves; each frond has 5 to 7 leaflets. Reliable once established. Zone 7–10.

Dryopteris wallichiana
WALLICHS WOOD FERN

☀ ❄ ↔ 24–32 in (60–80 cm)
↕ 24–48 in (60–120 cm)

A deciduous fern from the Himalayas. The mature fronds are dark green, yellow-green when young. Produces a strong flush of fronds in the spring. Forms an open tussock-like plant with a small trunk. This species is easy to grow. Zones 8–11.

Dryopteris sieboldii

DUBOISIA

This is a small genus of 3 species, 2 of which are endemic to Australia, with a third extending to New Caledonia. The genus, in the nightshade (Solanaceae) family, is named after Charles du Bois, a London merchant who had a nursery in southern England in the late seventeenth century. They are shrubs or trees with a corky bark, simple alternate leaves, and small tubular flowers. The leaves contain alkaloids that are used in drug manufacture and the plants are grown commercially in Australia for this purpose.

CULTIVATION: *Duboisia* needs sun and well-drained soil; it withstands regular pruning and responds to feeding. Propagation is usually from root cuttings, as seeds are difficult to germinate.

Duboisia hopwoodii

PITCHERI, PITURI

☀ ✤ ↔ 8 ft (2.4 m) ↑ 8 ft (2.4 m)

Widely distributed in Australia's arid interior. Brownish yellow to purplish corky bark. Has dark green linear to lanceolate leaves. The flowers are bell-shaped, white with purplish stripes. The fruit is a black, globular berry. Leaves are highly toxic to cattle, but were chewed by Aboriginal Australians and early settlers for their narcotic effect. Zones 10–12.

Duboisia hopwoodii

Duboisia myoporoides

CORKWOOD, DUBOISIA

☀ ❄ ↔ 10 ft (3 m) ↑ 20 ft (6 m)

A native of coastal New South Wales and Queensland, Australia, and New Caledonia. Gray to yellowish, brown corky bark. Pale green, glabrous, thin-textured, lanceolate leaves. The flowers are white, and sometimes tinted with mauve, bell-shaped, flared tips. Leaves toxic to cattle. Zones 9–12.

DUCHESNEA

INDIAN STRAWBERRY, MOCK STRAWBERRY.

This genus belonging to the rose (Rosaceae) family contains 2 species of perennials native to eastern and southern Asia. The toothed leaves are comprised of 3 to 5 leaflets and the 5-petalled flowers are yellow. They are related to *Fragaria*, strawberry, and their small fruits resemble strawberries, hence their common names. Although there seems little justification for keeping *Duchesnea* and *Fragaria* separate from *Potentilla*, this change has not yet been generally adopted.

CULTIVATION: Grow in full sun, in well-drained soil. Careful placement of *D. indica* is necessary due to its invasive tendencies. Propagate from seed or by division of runners.

Duchesnea indica

☀ ❄ ↔ 6 ft (1.8 m) ↑ 4 in (10 cm)

Found from India to Japan and naturalized elsewhere. Invasive ground-covering plant with long thin runners. Dark green trifoliate leaves. Yellow flowers in spring. Small, dry, red berries of little flavor. Zones 6–11.

DUDLEYA

A genus of some 40 species of rosette-forming perennials from southwestern USA and western Mexico. Members of the stonecrop (Crassulaceae) family, they are closely allied to *Echeveria*, in which genus they were once included. Many have gray or gray-green foliage, often with a powdery white bloom. The foliage withers with age but may remain attached. The flower stems tend to be upright, sometimes branching,

Duchesnea indica

Dudleya candelabrum

Dudleya anthonyii

and carry many small 5-petalled flowers, usually in spring. Old plants often have rosettes that have developed thickened stems or short trunks

CULTIVATION: Although many species tolerate moderate frost, they need mild winters as they tend to grow during the cooler months. Usually do best when placed in full sun but may need a little shade inland. Water in autumn and spring but otherwise keep dry. Rotting is the most common cause of failure, so be sure to plant in gritty free-draining soil. Propagate from seed, or offsets, or by division.

Dudleya anthonyii

☀ ❄ ↔ 32–40 in (80–100 cm) ↑ 40 in (100 cm)

Found in northern Baja California, Mexico, and offshore islands. This species bears red-tinted green leaves with a white bloom turning opaque white in dry season. The flowers are red with a yellow base. Zones 9–12.

Dudleya attenuata

☀ ❄ ↔ 16–24 in (40–60 cm) ↑ 12–16 in (30–40 cm)

Native to California, USA, and Baja California, Mexico. A low-growing

Dudleya attenuata subsp. *orcuttii*, in the wild, Baja California, Mexico

plant with narrow, cylindrical, powdery, gray- to blue-green leaves in open rosettes. Yellow flowers on branching stems. *D. a.* subsp. *orcuttii*, white flowers, tinted with pink. Zones 8–11.

Dudleya caespitosa

☀ ❄ ↔ 16–24 in (40–60 cm) ↑ 24 in (60 cm)

From coastal California as far north as Monterey, USA. Bears gray-green to yellow-green, somewhat keeled leaves in short-stemmed, clumping, rather open rosettes. Yellow to red flowers. Zones 8–11.

Dudleya candelabrum

☀ ❄ ↔ 14 in (35 cm) ↑ 14 in (35 cm)

A native of California, USA, including some of the islands. This plant usually forms a single short-stemmed rosette of powdery gray-green leaves. Many small, soft yellow flowers are borne on stocky flower stems. Zones 8–11.

Duranta erecta

Durio zibethinus

Dyakia hendersoniana

Dudleya farinosa

☀ ❄ ↔ 16–20 in (40–50 cm)
↑ 8–12 in (20–30 cm)

From the coast of California north to Oregon, USA. Branching at base to form a clump of small, powder-coated, blue-green rosettes that develop strong red tints in the sun. Flower stems usually short, with bright yellow flowers. Zones 8–10.

Dudleya greenei ★

☀ ❄ ↔ 16–24 in (40–60 cm)
↑ 12–16 in (30–40 cm)

From California, USA, including some of the islands. Clusters of powdery, bronze-tinted, blue-green rosettes. Flower stems tall compared to rosette size, pale yellow flowers. Zones 8–11.

Dudleya hassei

☀ ❄ ↔ 20–32 in (50–80 cm)
↑ 12 in (30 cm)

A species found on Santa Catalina Island, USA. The distinctive pointed, powdery, gray-green, cylindrical leaves appear in clustered open rosettes that eventually form short stems. The pale green flowers are carried on branching stems. Zones 9–11.

Dudleya pulverulenta

CHALK LETTUCE

☀ ❄ ↔ 20 in (50 cm) ↑ 40 in (100 cm)

Native to California, USA, and Baja California, Mexico. Usually solitary rosette. Leaves broad, yellow-green with powdery white bloom. Sturdy flower stems with branching heads of red flowers. Zones 9–11.

Dudleya viscida

☀ ❄ ↔ 24 in (60 cm) ↑ 24 in (60 cm)

From southern California, USA. Clusters of short-stemmed rosettes with narrow dark green leaves, aromatic, sticky. Pink-tinted white flowers. Zones 9–11.

DURANTA

Genus in the vervain (Verbenaceae) family, 30 species or so of hard-wooded ornamental shrubs from tropical and subtropical regions of the Americas, from southern USA to Mexico and Brazil. Evergreen, except in cold climates, with blue, white, or violet flowers, in terminal or axillary racemes, or panicles. Summer flowers followed by decorative but poisonous fruit in autumn and winter. Only one species commonly grown.

CULTIVATION: Will grow in most subtropical and frost-free temperate areas in fertile well-drained soil and full sun. They can be grown as small trees on a single trunk or pruned to make a small or medium-sized shrub. Propagate from soft-tip cuttings in spring, or from firm-wood leafy cuttings in autumn.

Duranta erecta

syns *Duranta repens*, *Duranta plumieri*
GOLDEN BEAD TREE, GOLDEN DEW DROP, PIGEON BERRY

☀ ❄ ↔ 8 ft (2.4 m) ↑ 15 ft (4.5 m)

A small evergreen tree from tropical America. Drooping branches with sharp spines. The inflorescence consists of 5 to 12 racemes, and carries up to 30 lavender-blue flowers, with purplish calyx, in early mid-autumn. The fruits are enclosed in the persistent calyx, and harden glossy yellow in early autumn. 'Alba', white flowers; 'Variegata', leaf margins creamy yellow. Zones 9–12.

Duranta stenostachya

BRAZILIAN SKY FLOWER

☀ ❄ ↔ 4–5 ft (1.2–1.5 m)
↑ 4–6 ft (1.2–1.8 m)

Evergreen shrub from tropical Brazil. Oblong to sword-shaped leaves, slightly toothed. Clusters of fragrant, tubular, medium, blue-lilac to purple flowers, in summer. Contrasting orange-yellow berries. Zones 9–11.

DURIO

Night-flying bats pollinate flowers of the 28 species of tall evergreen trees in this genus, placed in the kapok (Bombacaceae) family, and found from Myanmar to Malaysia and Indonesia in lowland rainforest. All have simple lance-shaped leaves, shiny on upper surface, lower surface grayish and covered with small scales. Large, creamy white flowers are borne in clusters on the stems and trunks.

CULTIVATION: Like most tropical tree species, propagation is best from fresh seed, since viability is lost quite quickly. Grow in full sun or dappled shade, in a moist humus-rich soil with good drainage. Apart from the durian, members of this genus are seldom grown.

Durio zibethinus

DURIAN

☀ ⚘ ↔ 20 ft (6 m) ↑ 80 ft (24 m)

From Malaysia and Indonesia. Leaves simple, lance-shaped, shining green, grayish beneath. About 50 flowers on short inflorescences, on older wood, creamy white or pink. Fruits large, green to greenish bronze, covered in sharp spines. Zone 12.

DYAKIA

Monotypic monopodial orchid genus (family Orchidaceae) from Borneo that was previously included within genus *Ascocentrum*. It differs by its floral structure, as well as its flat leaves (they are strongly channeled in *Ascocentrum*).

CULTIVATION: These epiphytes are quite compact and need warm to hot, moist conditions throughout the year, and grow best in either small pots or cork mounts. Propagate by division.

Dyakia hendersoniana ★

syn. *Ascocentrum hendersoniana*

☀/◐ ⚘ ↔ 2½–6 in (6–15 cm)
↑ 3–8 in (8–20 cm)

From Borneo. Throughout warmer months, year-round in tropics, this stunning species has upright, densely packed spikes, vivid rose to magenta flowers with a contrasting white labellum. Zones 11–12.

DYCKIA

A genus of over 120 species in the pineapple (Bromeliaceae) family, mostly from Brazil, Argentina, and neighboring countries, with only a few in cultivation. These clump-forming plants grow on rocks or in the ground. Leaves are triangular, usually green and

Dudleya hassei

Dudleya farinosa

Dudleya viscida

Dyckia choristaminea

Dyera costulata

very succulent, with mostly weak teeth on the edges. The generally long flower stems do not emerge from the plant's center, which means the plant does not die after flowering as with most other Bromeliaceae. The flowerhead is sometimes single, sometimes open-branched, each branch having many well-spaced yellow to orange flowers.

CULTIVATION: Grow in well-drained sandy soil mix, in greenhouses or conservatories, in cool-temperate areas, or outdoors in warm-temperate, subtropical, and tropical areas. Water when potting mix is dry. Do not over-fertilize. Propagate from seed or offsets.

Dyckia choristaminea

☀ ❄ ↔ 8 in (20 cm) ↑ 10 in (25 cm)
From southern Brazil. Small clump-forming plant, with small, narrow, light green leaves, with fairly long supple teeth. Flowerhead almost globular, with yellow flowers, pointing upward. Delightfully scented. Ideal size for pot culture. Zones 9–11.

Dyckia remotiflora

☀ ❄ ↔ 16 in (40 cm) ↑ 40 in (100 cm)
From southern Brazil to Argentina. Slow clump-forming plant. Narrow, triangular, dark green leaves. Flowerhead is a single stem with a few yellow flowers scattered on all sides. Mainly grown in open rockeries. Zones 9–11.

DYERA

A tropical genus within the dogbane (Apocynaceae) family of evergreen trees, some of which are important timber sources. They are tall canopy-forming trees, with the type of strong clean trunk more commonly found among temperate climate trees. Have simple, smooth-edged, elliptical leaves and produce rather insignificant inflorescences of small flowers. Exude white latex which has some commercial uses.

CULTIVATION: Seldom grown in gardens but cultivated in some quantity for timber and latex, the genus is only really at home in the tropics and prefers moist, deep, humus-enriched soil with a steady year-round supply of moisture. Young trees should be trimmed of lower branches to establish a strong trunk free of knots. Propagate from seed or half-hardened cuttings, which usually strike better if their exudations are allowed to dry before they are inserted in the cutting mix.

Dyera costulata

JELUTONG TREE

☀ ✾ ↔ 30 ft (9 m) ↑ 200 ft (60 m)
From the Malay Peninsula, Borneo, and Sumatra. An impressive tree with up to 90 ft (27 m) of clean trunk at the base. Highly valued for its timber, which is used for interior joinery and small items, as it lacks durability and strength. Zones 11–12.

DYMONDIA

From South Africa, single species genus in the daisy (Asteraceae) family. Forms a ground-hugging, evergreen mat with large, stemless, yellow flowers summer–autumn. It was named after a South African botanist, Margaret Dymond: her surname was used for the genus, her first name to denote the species.

CULTIVATION: Prefers a sunny aspect in moist to dry soils, and will tolerate only very slight frosts. Ideal ground covers over small bulbs or to grow between pavers. Propagate by division.

Dymondia margaretae

☀ ❄ ↔ 20–40 in (50–100 cm)
↑ 1¼–1¾ in (30–40 mm)
From South Africa. Evergreen, mat-forming plant that roots down as it expands. Narrow, gray-green, scalloped leaves, white reverse, slightly exposed as leaf edges curl in, giving a variegated look. Yellow daisies among the leaves through warmer months. Zones 10–11.

DYPSIS

syns *Chrysalidocarpus, Neodypsis*
This genus of feather-leafed palms in the family Arecaceae consisting of

140 species, all native to Madagascar except for 2 species on the Comoros Islands, and one on Pemba Island, Tanzania. Growth forms range from tiny undergrowth palms with pencil-thick stems and grass-like fronds, to quite massive palms that tower above the forest canopy. Stems solitary or clustered. Fronds are basically of feather type, some species have fronds that fork into two lobes; others a very few broad leaflets, and many plume-like fronds. Usually smooth crownshaft. Flowering panicles, below frond bases, bear small green, cream, or yellow (rarely red) flowers. Fruits are single-seeded drupes.

CULTIVATION: Needs vary greatly; no species is frost tolerant. Some of more robust species thrive outdoors and are very sun hardy; more delicate species require shade and humidity. Most can be grown as indoor plants as long as light levels are not too low. Propagation is normally from seed, although the clumping *D. lutescens* can be divided.

Dypsis decaryi

Dypsis decaryi

syn. *Neodypsis decaryi*
THREE-CORNERED PALM, TRIANGLE PALM
☀ ❄ ↔ 6 ft (1.8 m) ↑ 20 ft (6 m)
From the far south of Madagascar. Fronds arranged in 3 vertical ranks, bluish gray, recurved tips. Sheaths and lower parts of frond stalks coated in rusty brown fur when young, ageing to gray. Thick, closely ringed trunk. Great for patio tubs and planter boxes. Zones 10–12.

Dypsis lutescens

syns *Areca lutescens, Chrysalidocarpus lutescens*
BUTTERFLY PALM, GOLDEN CANE PALM
☀ ❄ ↔ 6 ft (1.8 m) ↑ 20 ft (6 m)
From east coast of Madagascar. Forms compact clumps of yellow-green stems branching above ground, slender crownshaft. Fronds recurved, stalks and midribs, yellow-orange. Branched flowering panicles, tiny yellow flowers. Oval yellow fruit. Zones 10–12.

Dypsis lutescens

Dymondia margaretae

E

Echeveria agavoides

Echeveria colorata

Echeveria chihuahuaensis

Echeveria agavoides var. corderoyi

EBENUS

This small genus in the pea-flower subfamily of the legume (Fabaceae) family comprises 18 species of perennials and small shrubs. From central Asia to the eastern Mediterranean, they grow on cliffs and in rocky habitats. The leaves are trifoliate or pinnate, sometimes finely silken. The typical pea-flowers are pink or purple and the fruit that follows is a 1- to 2-seeded capsule.
CULTIVATION: These seldom grown plants require hot dry conditions. Grow in a warm sunny position in gritty perfectly drained soil in the rock garden or at the front of a border. Where the winters are cold and damp, grow in a greenhouse in a gritty mix. Propagate from seed; scarify before sowing.

Ebenus cretica
☀ ❄ ↔ 24–36 in (60–90 cm)
↕ 24–36 in (60–90 cm)

From Crete. Attractive evergreen subshrub. Silvery trifoliate leaves. Flower spikes, covered in silky hairs, opening to reveal pink pea-flowers. Zones 7–9.

ECBALLIUM

Within the pumpkin (Cucurbitaceae) family, this genus comprises a single

Mediterranean species of trailing herb. The leaves are triangular to ovate, with palmate lobes. The male inflorescences are racemes, the female flowers are solitary, and both have a cup-shaped receptacle. The corolla has a tube at the base and 5 petal lobes. Fruits are ovate to nearly cylindrical and fall when ripe, explosively ejecting the seeds.
CULTIVATION: In temperate areas plant out seedlings in sunny well-drained sites in early summer, but in Mediterranean climates this plant seeds itself rather too freely and can be a nuisance, so it may be best restricted to waste areas. The fruit has been used as a purgative (elaterium).

Ecballium elaterium
SQUIRTING CUCUMBER
☀ ❄ ↔ 3–6 ft (0.9–1.8 m)
↕ 12–18 in (30–45 cm)

Short-lived spreading perennial with hairy stems. Leaves to 6 in (15 cm) across, grayish and bristly above, paler and downy beneath, 5-lobed, with wavy margins. The male inflorescences to 16 in (40 cm) long. The flowers are a washed-out yellow. Ripe fruit bluish-green, and covered in dense, coarse, white bristles. Usually grown from seed as a half-hardy annual. Zones 8–11.

ECCREMOCARPUS
CHILEAN GLORY FLOWER
This genus, comprising 5 species of evergreen or herbaceous tendril

climbers from South America, belongs to the trumpet-vine (Bignoniaceae) family. Grown for their brightly colored lopsided trumpets, produced in abundance throughout the warmer months, and often used as quick cover plants, as they will hide almost anything in one growing season.
CULTIVATION: These plants prefer moist but well-drained soil in a sunny site sheltered from strong winds. Grow on wire-up fences, over arches, or through large shrubs and small trees. Can be treated as annuals in frost-prone areas. Propagate from seed; in frost-prone areas plant out young plants as soon as possible after frosts. In warmer climates they can self-sow and become invasive.

Eccremocarpus scaber
CHILEAN GLORY FLOWER
☀ ❄ ↔ 7–10 ft (2–3 m) ↕ 10–15 ft (3–4.5 m)
From Chile and Peru. Fast-growing climber, and virtually the only species grown. Soft green compound leaves. Clusters of yellow, orange, or red tubular flowers, 1½ in (35 mm) long, in late spring–summer. Orange is the color of the wild form and the color most commonly cultivated. Zones 9–10.

ECHEVERIA
This genus of about 150 species of rosette-forming succulents in the stonecrop (Crassulaceae) family is found mainly in Mexico, with a few from Central America. It was named after Atanasio Echeverria Codoy, an eighteenth-century Spanish botanical artist. Though superficially similar to, and sometimes confused with Sempervivum, Echeveria are generally far less

frost hardy but more drought tolerant than their European cousins. Apart from a few species that are shrubby or more leafy and perennial-like, all form spiraling rosettes of flattened but fleshy, pointed, spoon-shaped leaves. The flowers, usually appearing in spring and early summer, are borne on short stems, either along the stem or in branching heads, and are simple, 5-petalled, bell-shaped structures, often in shades of pink, red, yellow, or orange.
CULTIVATION: Most Echeveria species prefer full sun and mild winters with only light frosts. They may require some shade in very hot inland areas. Plant in light, gritty, very free-draining soil. Water in spring and when they are flowering, but otherwise keep dry, especially in winter. Propagate from seed or offsets, or by division.

Echeveria agavoides ★
☀ ❄ ↔ 8–12 in (20–30 cm)
↕ 6–8 in (15–20 cm)

This species forms clumps of small short-stemmed rosettes with red-edged light gray-green to blue-green leaves, to 3 in (8 cm) long. The forked inflorescence bears ½ in (12 mm) long orange-pink flowers, which are yellow inside. E. a. f. cristata has rosettes with many small leaves in rows across the center; E. a. var. corderoyi (syn. E. a. 'Red Edge') produces rosettes with numerous small leaves and an inflorescence with 3 branches and smaller flowers. Zones 9–11.

Echeveria chihuahuaensis
☀ ❄ ↔ 12 in (30 cm) ↕ 10 in (25 cm)
Forms clusters of many small rosettes. The leaves are blue-green with a white bloom and reddish tips, and are 1¾ in (40 mm) long. The inflorescence can be simple or branched, and up to 8 in (20 cm) tall. It bears yellow-centered red flowers that are ½ in (12 mm) long. Zones 9–11.

Ecballium elaterium

Ebenus cretica

Echeveria elegans

Echeveria elegans 'Kesselringii'

Echeveria gigantea 'Dee'

Echeveria colorata

☼ ❄ ↔ 20 in (50 cm) ↑ 16 in (40 cm)
Rosettes of upright, red-tinted, pale blue-green leaves with a white bloom. Red-orange flowers. Zones 9–11.

Echeveria derenbergii

☼ ❄ ↔ 8–16 in (20–40 cm) ↑ 6 in (15 cm)
Short branching stems carry many small rosettes with red-edged pale blue-green leaves, to just under 2 in (5 cm) long. Inflorescence to 4 in (10 cm) long, with sparse, red-tipped, golden yellow, ½ in (12 mm) long flowers. Zones 9–11.

Echeveria elegans ★

MEXICAN SNOWBALL, WHITE MEXICAN ROSE
☼ ❄ ↔ 12–16 in (30–40 cm)
↑ 6–8 in (15–20 cm)
Forms clusters of short-stemmed densely foliaged rosettes, 4 in (10 cm) in diameter, with pale gray-green leaves, to 2¾ in (65 mm) long, that are coated with a white powder. Simple 4–6 in (10–15 cm) long inflorescence with as many as 10 golden-centered deep

pink flowers. '**Kesselringii**' produces globular rosettes of blue-gray leaves. Zones 9–11.

Echeveria gibbiflora

☼ ❄ ↔ 20 in (50 cm) ↑ 48 in (120 cm)
Forms open rosettes, to 20 in (50 cm) in diameter, on unbranched stems, to 12 in (30 cm) tall. Leaves are broad, purple-tinted, wavy-edged, powdery, pale blue-green, to 14 in (35 cm) long. The branching inflorescence, to 36 in (100 cm) tall, has soft, brown-centered, red flowers that are backed by lavender calyces through the autumn–winter. *E. g.* **var.** *carunculata* has pale leaves, heavily distorted and covered with protuberances; *E. g.* **var.** *metallica* has silvery gray foliage with a metallic sheen. Zones 9–11.

Echeveria gigantea ★

☼ ❄ ↔ 20 in (50 cm) ↑ 5–7 ft (1.5–2 m)
Winter-flowering species with loose open rosettes, to 16 in (40 cm) across, on unbranched stems, to 20 in (50 cm) tall. Leaves purple-edged, pale green, spatula-shaped, to 8 in (20 cm) long. Branching inflorescence, to 7 ft (2 m) tall, with deep pink-red flowers, over ½ in (12 mm) long. '**Dee**', rosettes with broad blue-green leaves ageing red in sun. Zones 10–12.

Echeveria × gilva

GREEN MEXICAN ROSE
☼ ❄ ↔ 12–16 in (30–40 cm)
↑ 14 in (35 cm)
Hybrid of *E. agavoides* and *E. elegans.* Short branching stems with densely foliaged rosettes, to 6 in (15 cm) across. Green leaves, to a little over 3 in (8 cm) long, with crystalline surface and translucent edges. Branching inflorescence, up to 10 in (25 cm) tall, with small yellow-topped pink flowers. Zones 9–11.

Echeveria harmsii

syn. *Oliveranthus elegans*
☼ ❄ ↔ 12 in (30 cm)
↑ 12–16 in (30–40 cm)
Shrubby plant with branching stems and small open rosettes clustered at the tips, finely hairy throughout. Narrow green leaves with red edges, to 2 in (5 cm) long. Produces simple inflorescences, to 8 in (20 cm) long, with few red flowers with yellow tips and interior. Zones 9–11.

Echeveria × imbricata ★

☼ ❄ ↔ 12–16 in (30–40 cm)
↑ 12–16 in (30–40 cm)
Short-stemmed cup-shaped rosettes, to 10 in (20 cm) wide, with broad but thin gray-green to silver-gray leaves. Branching inflorescences with yellow-centered deep pink flowers, to ½ in (12 mm) long. Zones 9–12.

Echeveria leucotricha ★

☼ ❄ ↔ 20–40 in (50–100 cm)
↑ 24 in (60 cm)
Shrubby plant with branching red-tinted stems. Open rosettes with few, finely hairy, red-tipped, broadly strappy, gray-green leaves, to over 24 in (60 cm) long. Simple or slightly branched leafy inflorescence, to 16 in (40 cm) tall, with up to 15 red-edged orange flowers, ¾ in (18 mm) long. Zones 9–11.

Echeveria nodulosa ★

☼ ❄ ↔ 12–20 in (30–50 cm)
↑ 16 in (40 cm)
A shrubby species with leafy branching stems, to 8 in (20 cm) tall. The loose open rosettes have narrow, thickened, red-edged and keeled, light blue-green leaves, up to 2 in (5 cm) long. They produce inflorescences to 12 in (30 cm) long, with up to 12 yellow-centered and edged, orange-red flowers. Zones 9–11.

Echeveria pallida

☼ ❄ ↔ 16–24 in (40–60 cm)
↑ 24–40 in (60–100 cm)
Clusters of short-stemmed, loose, open, 8–10 in (20–25 cm) wide rosettes with broad, spoon-shaped, light-textured, pale green leaves, to 6 in (15 cm) long. Inflorescence, 24–36 in (60–90 cm) tall, with pink flowers during winter. Zones 9–11.

Echeveria pallida

Echeveria × *gilva*

Echeveria leucotricha

Echeveria × *imbricata*, along pathway, Tasmania, Australia

Echeveria peacockii ★

☀ ✥ ↔ 12–24 in (30–60 cm) ↑ 12 in (30 cm)

Clusters of powdery pale blue-gray rosettes, each to 6 in (15 cm) across. Leaves to 2½ in (6 cm) long, red-edged and tipped. Inflorescence to 10 in (25 cm) tall, with up to 20 soft orange to pinkish red flowers. Zones 9–11.

Echeveria potosina

☀ ✥ ↔ 12–16 in (30–40 cm) ↑ 6–8 in (15–20 cm)

Clusters of short-stemmed densely foliaged rosettes, 4 in (10 cm) across. Powdery pale gray-green leaves, often maroon-tinted, to 2¾ in (65 mm) long. Simple 4–6 in (10–15 cm) long inflorescence, up to 10 golden-centered deep pink flowers. Zones 9–11.

Echeveria pulvinata

CHENILLE PLANT, PLUSH PLANT

☀ ✥ ↔ 12–20 in (30–50 cm) ↑ 12–16 in (30–40 cm)

Branching stems forming dense mounding clusters of small rosettes

Echeveria runyonii 'Topsy Turvy'

Echeveria sayulensis

Echeveria, Hybrid Cultivar, 'Dondo'

with many finely downy, red-tinted, green to blue-green leaves, about 2 in (5 cm) long. Inflorescence, 8–12 in (20–30 cm) long, with up to 15 red-edged golden yellow to orange flowers from mid-winter. 'Ruby', velvety-textured red leaves. Zones 9–11.

Echeveria runyonii

☀ ✥ ↔ 12–20 in (30–50 cm) ↑ 12 in (30 cm)

Clusters of usually stemless rosettes, to 8 in (20 cm) across, with spoon-shaped powdery gray-blue leaves, about 3 in (8 cm) long. Short forked inflorescence with ¼ in (18 mm) long coral pink flowers. 'Topsy Turvy' ★, narrow leaves curled downward at the edges and up at the tips. Zones 9–11.

Echeveria sayulensis

☀ ✥ ↔ 16–20 in (40–50 cm) ↑ 12–16 in (30–40 cm)

Shrubby species, low-spreading stems. Densely foliaged, 10 in (25 cm) wide rosettes of pointed blue-green leaves with red edges, to 6 in (15 cm) long.

Echeveria peacockii

Echeveria, Hybrid Cultivar, 'Kirchneriana'

Echeveria, Hybrid Cultivar, 'Fire Light'

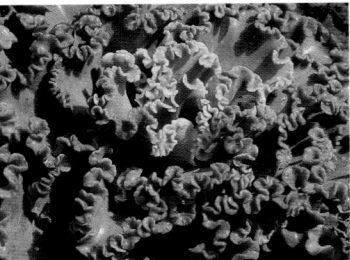

Echeveria, Hybrid Cultivar, 'Lace'

Branched inflorescence, up to 14 in (35 cm) long, up to 30 yellow-centered pink flowers in winter. Zones 9–11.

Echeveria secunda ★

☀ ✥ ↔ 12 in (30 cm) ↑ 12 in (30 cm)

Mounded clusters of densely foliaged short-stemmed rosettes. The leaves are thick, keeled, blue-green with maroon edges, to about 3 in (8 cm) long. The simple inflorescence, to 12 in (30 cm) long, bears up to 15 yellow-centered pale orange to red flowers. *E. s.* var. *glauca*, thin pale blue-gray leaves; *E. s.* var. *pumila*, small narrow leaves. Zones 9–11.

Echeveria setosa

MEXICAN FIRECRACKER

☀ ✥ ↔ 12–16 in (30–40 cm) ↑ 8–12 in (20–30 cm)

Small clumping species, which forms 4–6 in (10–15 cm) wide rosettes of

2 in (5 cm) long green leaves covered with fine white hairs, becoming bristly with age. The inflorescence is 12 in (30 cm) long, with up to 10 red-tipped yellow flowers. Zones 9–11.

Echeveria Hybrid Cultivars

☀ ✥ ↔ 4–18 in (10–45 cm) ↑ 6–24 in (15–60 cm)

Many species hybridize freely, and garden hybrids are available in a wide range of sizes, flower colors, and growth forms. 'Arlie Wright', large gray leaves flushed with pink, heavily crimped edges, and a single rosette, to 16 in (40 cm) across; 'Dondo', an *E. dehren-bergii* × *E. setosa* hybrid, rosettes of gray-blue leaves with scalloped and pointed tips, golden yellow flowers; 'Fire Light' ★, rosette of broad leaves, blue-green rapidly ageing to deep glossy red, with frilled edges; 'Kirchneriana', massed 4 in (10 cm)

Echeveria potosina

Echeveria setosa

Echeveria pulvinata

Echeveria, Hybrid Cultivar, 'Morning Light'

Echeveria, Hybrid Cultivar, 'Powder Blue'

Echeveria, Hybrid Cultivar, 'Princess Lace'

Echeveria, Hybrid Cultivar, 'Pulv-oliver'

Echeveria, Hybrid Cultivar, 'Violet Queen'

Echeveria, HC, Galaxy Series, 'Apollo'

Echeveria, HC, Galaxy Series, 'Fire Storm'

Echeveria, HC, Galaxy Series, 'Nebula'

Echeveria, HC, Galaxy Series, 'Spaceship'

wide pale powdery blue-gray rosettes, narrow leafy stems with small heads of orange-tipped yellow flowers in spring; '**Lace**', similar but with more complexly frilled leaves; '**Morning Light**' ★, clusters of small blue-green rosettes edged with pink; '**Powder Blue**' ★, light blue-green rosettes, to 6 in (15 cm) across, light orange flowers; '**Princess Lace**', pale green rosettes, to 12 in (30 cm) across, with the edges red and heavily crimped; '**Pulv-oliver**', a shrubby *E. pulvinata* × *E. harmsii* hybrid, to 20 in (50 cm) tall, with small open rosettes of red-tinted, downy, light green leaves and soft orange flowers; '**Set-oliver**' ★, an *E. harmsii* × *E. setosa* hybrid with rosettes of downy, thickened, red-tinted, light green leaves and orange-red flowers on 16 in (40 cm) tall inflorescences; '**Violet Queen**' ★, clusters of 6 in (15 cm) wide, pink-edged, pale blue-green rosettes. The **Galaxy Series** are similar to 'Pulv-oliver' and 'Set-oliver', and bear flowers in a range of brilliant orange-reds with varying amounts of yellow on the petal tips. Zones 9–11.

ECHINACEA

CONEFLOWER

This genus, comprising 9 species of summer-flowering perennials, some of which grow as tall as 7 ft (2 m), belongs to the daisy (Asteraceae) family. Found in eastern USA and closely allied to *Rudbeckia* and *Helianthus*, they spread by rhizomes and after a few years can colonize large areas, though they are not difficult to control. The foliage is simple, usually lance-shaped, and sometimes toothed. The flower-heads are large and have relatively few ray florets, often deep purple-pink and downward facing, around a prominent, often dark, central cone of disc florets. The dried rhizomes and roots of cone-flowers are widely used as an ingredient in herbal medicines; they are thought to fortify the immune system's power to ward off infection.

CULTIVATION: Coneflowers grow very freely in temperate gardens, thriving in an open sunny position with well-drained humus-rich soil that is kept moist in summer. Staking is sometimes required, as they can grow quite tall. Propagate from seed or basal cuttings, or by division; they may self-sow.

Echinacea pallida

PALE CONEFLOWER, PALE PURPLE CONEFLOWER

☼/◑ ✽ ↔ 12–24 in (30–60 cm) ↑ 24–36 in (60–90 cm)

From midwestern USA. Easy-to-grow perennial. Narrow dark green leaves with parallel veins. Petals narrower than those of *E. purpurea*. Pale to dark purple ray flowers with dark centers in early spring–mid-summer; attractive to birds and butterflies. These plants are good in a naturalized area or wild garden. *E. p.* **var.** *angustifolia* (syn. *E. angustifolia*) has deep pink to light purple ray florets, often drooping. Zones 3–10.

Echinacea pallida var. *angustifolia*

Echinacea purpurea

syn. *Rudbeckia purpurea*
PURPLE CONEFLOWER

☼/◑ ✽ ↔ 40 in (100 cm) ↑ 60 in (150 cm)

Forms a clump of quick-growing strongly upright stems. The leaves are broad, toothed, deep green, pointed oval to lance-shaped, to 6 in (15 cm) long. The reflexed magenta-purple ray florets, to 3 in (8 cm) long, form around orange-brown disc florets opening from dark buds. *E. purpurea* is the species most widely used in herbal medicines. '**Magnus**' ★, with large, intensely colored flowerheads; '**White Lustre**', about 32 in (80 cm) tall, the white ray florets have dark centers; '**White Swan**' ★, is compact, 20 in (50 cm) tall, with white flower-heads. Zones 3–10.

Echinacea purpurea 'Magnus'

Echinacea purpurea 'White Swan'

Echinacea purpurea

Echinocereus cinerascens

Echinocactus grusonii

Echinocactus platyacanthus

ECHINOCACTUS

This genus in the cactus (Cactaceae) family, as now understood, comprises just 5 species native to Mexico and southwestern USA. Globular in growth habit for many years, with prominent spiny ribs and a woolly crown, most eventually become columnar, though none grow to any great height. In cultivation they are favored for their slow growth and symmetry. The flowers are usually in shades of yellow or pink, and tend to be short and not very spectacular, though they bloom for a long time in summer.
CULTIVATION: Tolerant of occasional light frosts but inclined to rot in damp conditions, especially in winter. Plant in light, very gritty, free-draining soil. Water in summer but otherwise keep dry. Most grow best in full sun but some may need light shade in hot inland areas. Offsets are few but can be propagated; otherwise, raise from seed.

Echinocactus grusonii
GOLDEN BARREL CACTUS, MOTHER-IN-LAW'S CHAIR
☀ ⚡ ↔ 32 in (80 cm) ↑ 50 in (130 cm)
From central Mexico. Stems usually solitary, globular for many years. The crown is very woolly. Offsets rare. Up to 40 ribs with closely spaced areoles bearing many yellow spines, to 2 in (5 cm) long. The flowers are yellow, brown at the tip, a little over 2 in 5 cm) long, and clustered around the crown. Zones 9–12.

Echinocactus platyacanthus
☀ ⚡ ↔ 36 in (90 cm) ↑ 8 ft (2.4 m)
From central and northern Mexico. Solitary stem, spherical when young, becoming columnar and very sturdy. Up to 60 ribs when mature, edged with strong spines, to 3 in (8 cm) long. Yellow-green flowers, 2 in (5 cm) long, 3 in (8 cm) across. Zones 9–11.

Echinocactus polycephalus
☀ ⚡ ↔ 12–24 in (30–60 cm)
↑ 12–24 in (30–60 cm)
From northwestern Mexico and southwestern USA. Clumps of spherical to short cylindrical stems, each to 8 in (20 cm) in diameter, with numerous 2–3 in (5–8 cm) long curved spines interwoven to form a dense matrix. Flowers are 2 in (5 cm) long, 2 in (5 cm) across, and yellow with faint pink stripes. Zones 9–11.

ECHINOCEREUS
HEDGEHOG CACTUS
This genus comprises about 60 species of cacti (family Cactaceae) found in Mexico and southern USA. The name comes from the Greek echinos, a hedgehog, and Latin/Greek cereus, a candle or taper, referring to the commonly occurring combination of densely packed spines and showy flowers. Most form clumps of cylindrical stems, which are sometimes elongated and may spread across the ground or clamber over low objects. The flowers form near the top of the stem, often developing from woolly areoles. Most open in spring or summer, and are usually large in comparison to the plant and often brightly colored or strikingly marked.
CULTIVATION: Hardiness varies, but none will tolerate repeated hard freezes. Plant in light, gritty, very free-draining soil; keep dry in winter. Best grown in full sun, though in inland continental areas they may need shade from the hottest summer sun. Propagate from seed, offsets, or from stem cuttings.

Echinocereus brandegeei
☀ ⚡ ↔ 3–7 ft (0.9–2 m)
↑ 8–12 in (20–30 cm)
From Baja California, USA. Clusters of spreading stems, to 36 in (100 cm) long, 2½ in (6 cm) in diameter. Stems with up to 10 ribs and a dense covering of flattened spines, to 4 in (10 cm) long. Dark-centered magenta flowers, to 3 in (8 cm) long, during the summer. Zones 10–11.

Echinocereus cinerascens
syn. Echinocereus chlorophthalmus
☀ ⚡ ↔ 20–40 in (50–100 cm)
↑ 12–24 in (30–60 cm)
From eastern and northeastern Mexico. A clustering, somewhat spreading, species. Narrow stems, usually about 12 in (30 cm) long, with many fine spines, to over 1¾ in (40 mm) long. The flowers are magenta with a white to yellow-green throat, to 4 in (10 cm) across. Zones 9–11.

Echinocereus engelmannii ★
STRAWBERRY HEDGEHOG CACTUS
☀ ❄ ↔ 12–20 in (30–50 cm)
↑ 12–20 in (30–50 cm)
From the western USA–Mexico border region. Clustering, upright, narrow, cylindrical stems with ribs densely covered with fine spines, to over 2 in (5 cm) long. The flowers are magenta to lavender, to 3½ in (9 cm) across, and appear in summer. Zones 8–11.

Echinocereus fendleri
☀ ⚡ ↔ 8–20 in (20–50 cm)
↑ 8–20 in (20–50 cm)
From the western USA–Mexico border region. Clusters of narrow, upright, cylindrical stems with many ribs and sometimes pronounced tubercles. The spines are short and the areoles widely spaced. Flowers, usually magenta with a darker center, sometimes light pink or white, to 4 in (10 cm) across, in summer. The fruit is red. E. f. var. kuenzleri, stout spines, and very large flowers. Zones 9–11.

Echinocereus knippelianus
PEYOTE VERDE
☀ ⚡ ↔ 4–6 in (10–15 cm)
↑ 4–6 in (10–15 cm)
From the mountains of northeastern Mexico. Short spherical stems, often solitary, with a few broad indistinctly defined ribs and sparse, small, woolly areoles with 3 short spines. Many-petalled flowers, 2½ in (6 cm) across, in white, pink or purple, in spring–early summer. Zones 9–11.

Echinocereus maritimus
☀ ⚡ ↔ 3–7 ft (0.9–2 m)
↑ 8–16 in (20–40 cm)
From northwestern Mexico. Branching spreading stems forming wide mounds. Stem segments, to 12 in (30 cm) long, 2 in (5 cm) in diameter, with up to 10 sharply defined ribs edged with many spines, to 2½ in (6 cm) long. Yellow flowers tinted red, becoming orange, to 2½ in (6 cm) across, in summer. Zones 9–11.

Echinocereus pectinatus ★
☀ ❄ ↔ 6–16 in (15–40 cm)
↑ 14 in (35 cm)
From southwestern USA and northern Mexico. Clusters of spherical to short cylindrical stems, rarely branched, to 5 in (12 cm) in diameter, with 12 or more ribs carrying many light brown interlacing spines, to 1 in (25 mm)

Echinocereus engelmannii

Echinocereus fendleri var. kuenzleri

Echinocereus maritimus

Echinocereus pentalophus

Echinocereus rigidissimus

long. The flowers are green-centered white or pink to red-brown, to about 4 in (10 cm) in diameter, and appear in summer. *E. p.* var. *dasyacanthus* (syn. *E. dasyacanthus*) bears yellow or white flowers. Zones 8–11.

Echinocereus pentalophus ★

LADY FINGER CACTUS

☀ ⚘ ↔ 20 in–7 ft (50 cm–2 m)
↕ 8–12 in (20–30 cm)

Found from eastern Mexico to Texas, USA. Clustering, narrow, sometimes sprawling, cylindrical stems with few ribs and a mix of spines ranging from very short to ½ in (6 cm) long. Stems often red-tinted in sun. Deep pink flowers with a white to yellow-green throat, to 6 in (15 cm) across, in summer. Zones 9–11.

Echinocereus reichenbachii ★

☀ ❄ ↔ 8–20 in (20–50 cm)
↕ 16 in (40 cm)

Found from northeastern Mexico to Texas, USA. Usually clustering spherical to short cylindrical stems with over 10 indistinctly defined ribs bearing many tubercles with short pale spines. Floral tubercles woolly. Many-petalled pink to purple flowers, to over 5 in (12 cm) across. Zones 8–11.

Echinocereus rigidissimus ★

☀ ⚘ ↔ 4 in (10 cm) ↕ 8 in (20 cm)

From northwestern Mexico to Arizona, USA. Solitary cylindrical stem, rarely branched, with 15 or more ribs bearing woolly tubercles, often pink-tinted, with many small spines held flat to the stem. White-centered pink to crimson flowers, to 3 in (8 cm) across, in early summer. Zones 9–11.

Echinocereus stramineus

Echinocereus stramineus

☀ ❄ ↔ 16 in–7 ft (40 cm–2 m)
↕ 12–18 in (30–45 cm)

From the western USA–Mexico border region. Forms dense colonies of up to several hundred narrow cylindrical stems with up to 17 ribs largely hidden below many needle-like spines, some to nearly 4 in (10 cm) long. The bright magenta funnel-shaped flowers, 3–5 in (8–12 cm) across, appear during mid-summer. Zones 8–11.

Echinocereus subinermis

☀ ⚘ ↔ 6–12 in (15–30 cm)
↕ 8–10 in (20–25 cm)

From northwestern Mexico. The stems are solitary or few, clustered, dark gray-green to blue-green, with up to 11 clearly defined ribs bearing starry clusters of usually short stout spines. The yellow flowers, to 4 in (10 cm) long and 5 in (12 cm) across, appear in summer. Zones 9–11.

Echinocereus triglochidiatus ★

CLARET CUP

☀ ❄ ↔ 8–20 in (20–50 cm)
↕ 12–16 in (30–40 cm)

From the western USA–Mexico border region. Stems solitary or clumping, ovate to cylindrical, with about 10 ribs bearing woolly areoles with short radial spines around a central spine to nearly 2¾ in (7 cm) long. Long-tubed bright red flowers, to over 2 in (5 cm) across, in summer. *E. t.* var. *gurneyi*, compact species from the Chihuahuan desert grasslands; *E. t.* var. *melanacanthus* (syn. *E. coccineus*) are found among mountain pines, forming mounds of up to several hundred small stems. Zones 8–11.

E. triglochidiatus var. *melanacanthus*

Echinocereus viereckii

☀ ⚘ ↔ 12–24 in (30–60 cm)
↕ 12 in (30 cm)

Native to Mexico, low alpine species, with clusters of deep green branching stems that are initially upright then spreading, with spiny tubercles. The plants produce many large, deep pink to magenta flowers with pale centers during the summer months. Zones 9–11.

Echinocereus viridiflorus

☀ ❄ ↔ 4–12 in (10–30 cm)
↕ 2–5 in (5–12 cm)

From southwestern USA. Clusters of short ovate to cylindrical stems with up to 12 ribs largely hidden beneath many fine needle-like spines. The many-petalled, yellow-green, citrus-scented flowers, to 1¼ in (30 mm) diameter, appear during the summer. *E. v.* subsp. *davisii*, a dwarf variety, often has solitary, stems, and is only 1 in (25 mm) tall. Zones 8–11.

ECHINOPS

GLOBE THISTLE

This genus, comprising about 120 species of thistle-like perennials found from Europe eastward to central Asia and southward to the mountains of Africa, is from the daisy (Asteraceae) family. The leaves are spine-tipped and usually deeply lobed, and may be simple or have up to 3 large leaflets.

Echinocereus subinermis

The flowers, appearing in summer–early autumn, are small, mostly white to mauve-blue, borne in spherical heads without ray florets, and backed by often spiny basal bracts, which are sometimes colored though smaller and far less colorful than those of the similar-looking but otherwise unrelated *Eryngium*. The flowerheads are sometimes dried but tend to disintegrate rather quickly.

CULTIVATION: These are mostly very hardy plants and easily grown in any temperate climate garden with a moderately fertile, well-drained soil. Best grown in a fairly open position to reduce the risk of mildew. Propagated mainly from seed but easily divided in the late winter.

Echinocereus viridiflorus subsp. *davisii*

Echinocereus viereckii

Echinocereus triglochidiatus

Echinops bannaticus

☼/◐ ❄ ↔ 24 in (60 cm) ↑ 48 in (120 cm)
This species is found from Greece to the Czech Republic. It has an upright stem; finely hairy leaves, which are angularly lobed almost to the midrib, with a few narrow spines; and downy stems. The gray-blue flowerheads, to 2 in (5 cm) across, are lighter in bud. 'Blue Globe', dark blue flowerheads, 2½ in (6 cm) across; 'Taplow Blue', bright steel blue flowerheads. Zones 3–9.

Echinops exaltatus

☼/◐ ❄ ↔ 20–32 in (50–80 cm) ↑ 5–7 ft (1.5–2 m)
Found from Italy to Poland and southwestern Russia. A vigorous plant, which forms a dense basal foliage clump, and produces tall flower stems. The leaves are light green, and deeply angularly

Echinops bannaticus 'Taplow Blue'

Echinops bannaticus 'Blue Globe'

Echinops ritro

lobed, with a few short spines. The white to pale gray flowerheads are 2½ in (6 cm) in diameter. Zones 3–9.

Echinops humilis

☼/◐ ❄ ↔ 12 in (30 cm) ↑ 12 in (30 cm)
Found from central Asia to Siberia and northwestern China. Forms a dense low clump of narrow-lobed spiny leaves, to 3 in (8 cm) long, with fine white hairs. Light steel blue flowerheads, to 1¾ in (40 mm) across. Zones 3–9.

Echinops ritro

☼/◐ ❄ ↔ 16–24 in (40–60 cm) ↑ 12–24 in (30–60 cm)
Eurasian species. The leaves are finely hairy, narrow, triangular, deeply lobed, with small spines. The flowerheads are deep steel blue to purple, rarely white, to nearly 2 in (5 cm) wide. *E. r.* subsp. *ruthenicus* (syn. *E. ruthenicus*), leaves with small spines and white woolly hair on undersides, steel blue flowerheads; *E. r.* 'Blue Glow' bears large light blue flowerheads. Zones 3–9.

Echinops sphaerocephalus

☼/◐ ❄ ↔ 16–32 in (40–80 cm) ↑ 3–7 ft (0.9–2 m)
Native to southern and central Russia. The downy deeply lobed leaves have short spines and white hair on the undersides. Bears white to pale ash gray flowerheads, to over 2 in (5 cm) across. Zones 3–9.

Echinops ritro 'Blue Glow'

Echinopsis backebergii

ECHINOPSIS

syns *Chamaecereus, Helianthocereus, Lobivia, Trichocereus*

EASTER LILY CACTUS, SEA URCHIN CACTUS
The species in this South American cactus genus (family Cactaceae) encompass a wide range of forms, from small, cylindrical, and clustering to tree-like with strong branching trunks. The genus has been expanded in recent years to include the species formerly placed in *Lobivia* and *Trichocereus*, and it now comprises up to 120 species. Most have cylindrical stems with clearly defined ribs, and some also have tubercles bearing areoles with conspicuous and often quite fierce spines. Some species have spectacular, long-tubed, funnel-shaped flowers that are large in comparison to the plant. These are known as Easter lily cacti because they may be in bloom as early as Easter in the Northern Hemisphere, though their main flowering season is early to mid-summer. Some species are night-blooming, with attractive, fragrant, white flowers, while others are day-blooming, with unscented flowers that occur in various shades of red, pink, yellow, or orange.
CULTIVATION: As with most cacti, plant in full sun/half-sun in very free-draining, light, gritty soil and water well in summer but keep dry during the winter months. Most species will tolerate only occasional

Echinops sphaerocephalus

Echinopsis formosa

light frosts. Propagate from offsets where it is appropriate, from stem cuttings of the branching types, or from seed.

Echinopsis backebergii

syns *Echinopsis wrightiana, Lobivia wrightiana*
☼ ⚊ ↔ 4–8 in (10–20 cm) ↑ 6 in (15 cm)
From Peru and Bolivia. Forms clusters of dark gray-green spherical stems with up to 15 ribs bearing short curved spines. Produces pink to violet flowers, to 4 in (10 cm) in diameter, often exceeding the stem width, in summer. Zones 10–12.

Echinopsis chamaecereus

syns *Chamaecereus silvestrii, Lobivia silvestrii*
PEANUT CACTUS
☼ ⚊ ↔ 12 in (30 cm) ↑ 4 in (10 cm)
From Argentina. Mat-forming, with freely branching cylindrical stems, to 12 in (30 cm), and numerous lateral stems, 1–4 in (20–100 mm) long. Low ribs and tiny spines on stems. Orange-red flowers, to 2 in (5 cm) across, in early summer. Zones 9–11.

Echinopsis ferox

syn. *Trichocereus ferox*
☼ ⚊ ↔ 8–12 in (20–30 cm) ↑ 8 in (20 cm)
From Bolivia and northern Argentina. Unbranched stem is usually solitary, and spherical, with up to 30 spiraled ribs. The areoles are slightly over 1 in (25 mm) apart, carrying up to 12 radial spines, 2½ in (60 mm) long, and about 3 to 4 curved central spines, to 6 in (15 cm) long. The white or pale pink flowers are up to 4 in (10 cm) across. Zones 9–11.

Echinopsis formosa ★

syn. *Trichocereus randallii*
☼ ⚊ ↔ 8–16 in (20–40 cm) ↑ 20 in–5 ft (50 cm–1.5 m)
From western Argentina. Stem usually solitary, initially spherical, becoming cylindrical, with up to 35 ribs and central spines to nearly 3 in (8 cm) long. Short-tubed yellow, orange, or red flowers, to about 3 in (8 cm) across. Zones 9–11.

Echinopsis hertrichiana

syns *Lobivia incaiaca, L. hertrichiana*

☀ ⚘ ↔ 6–12 in (15–30 cm)
↑ 6–16 in (15–40 cm)

From Peru. The stems are often solitary, spherical, becoming columnar and clustered with great age. Up to 22 deep ribs with small woolly areoles and few spines to 1¼ in (30 mm) long. Bright red flowers, about 2 in (5 cm) long and across. Zones 10–12.

Echinopsis huascha ★

syns *Lobivia huascha, Trichocereus andalgalensis*

☀ ⚘ ↔ 24 in (60 cm) ↑ 24 in (60 cm)

From Argentina. The stems are clustering, cylindrical, upright, sprawling, branching, to 2 in (5 cm) in diameter. Up to 17 ribs and many fine needlelike spines, to 3 in (8 cm) long. The floral areoles are densely hairy, opening to bright orange-red or yellow flowers, to 4 in (10 cm) long and 3 in (8 cm) across. Zones 9–11.

Echinopsis litoralis

☀ ⚘ ↔ 3–7 ft (0.9–2 m) ↑ 3–7 ft (0.9–2 m)

A native of Chile. This shrubby species forms spreading clumps of upright and sprawling branching stems, to slightly over 4 in (10 cm) in diameter, with 15 or more ribs and spines, to 1 in (25 mm) long. The white flowers are sometimes tinted maroon, to nearly 6 in (15 cm) long. Zones 10–11.

Echinopsis maximiliana

syn. *Lobivia caespitosa*

☀ ⚘ ↔ 6–12 in (15–30 cm) ↑ 4 in (10 cm)

Native to southern Peru and northern Bolivia. Clusters of flat-topped spherical stems, to 2 in (5 cm) wide with up to 17 ribs ridged with tubercles bearing central spines, to nearly 3 in (8 cm) long. Red flowers, to 3 in (8 cm) wide, with orange centers. Zones 10–12.

Echinopsis oxygona ★

syn. *Echinopsis multiplex*

☀ ⚘ ↔ 12–24 in (30–60 cm)
↑ 12 in (30 cm)

From southern Brazil and northern Argentina. Clusters of spherical to short

Echinopsis litoralis

cylindrical stems, to 6 in (15 cm) in diameter, with up to 15 ribs bearing spines to 1 in (25 mm) long. Green-tubed red flowers, to 10 in (25 cm) long and 4 in (10 cm) across, appear in summer. Cristate forms are common. Zones 9–11.

Echinopsis pentlandii

syns *Echinocactus pentlandii, Lobivia boliviensis,* and many others

☀ ⚘ ↔ 12–16 in (30–40 cm)
↑ 6–8 in (15–20 cm)

From southern Peru and northern Bolivia. Clusters of ovoid to spherical stems, to over 4 in (10 cm) in diameter, with about 15 ribs ridged with tubercles bearing 1–4 in (25–100 mm) long central spines. Yellow, orange, red, or magenta flowers, about 2 in (5 cm) long and wide. Zones 10–11.

Echinopsis schickendantzii

syn. *Trichocereus schickendantzii*

☀ ⚘ ↔ 5–10 in (12–25 cm) ↑ 12 in (30 cm)

From western Argentina. Shrubby species forming wide clumps of low-branching cylindrical stems, about 2 in (5 cm) in diameter, 14 to 18 ribs, and small spines. Funnel-shaped white flowers, to about 8 in (20 cm) across. Zones 9–12.

Echinopsis spachiana ★

syn. *Trichocereus spachianus*

GOLDEN TORCH CEREUS

☀ ⚘ ↔ 40 in (100 cm) ↑ 5–7 ft (1.5–2 m)

From Argentina. Shrubby species, tall cylindrical stems, each to 4 in (10 cm)

Echinopsis, Hybrid Cultivar, 'Arizona'

in diameter, branching at the base, and 10 to 15 ribs with sturdy spines, to 2 in (5 cm) long. White flowers, to 10 in (25 cm) long and 6 in (15 cm) across. Zones 9–12.

Echinopsis Hybrid Cultivars

syns × *Chamaelobivia* Hybrid Cultivars, × *Lobivopsis* Hybrid Cultivars

☀ ⚘ ↔ 6–12 in (15–30 cm)
↑ 6–18 in (15–45 cm)

Most *Echinopsis* hybrid cultivars have been bred for their large flowers and glowing colors and are derived from the large-flowered day-blooming species, including some formerly classified under *Lobivia*. Some such hybrids were thus treated as bigeneric hybrids. 'Arizona' produces crowded, large, funnel-shaped flowers, with apricot shading to yellow centers, and ageing dull pinkish; 'Chico Mendes' forms a compact mounding plant, with flowers to 5 in (13 cm) across, opening almost flat; the petals are broad, and pinkish orange with deeper pink at the edges; 'Samantha Smith' has clustering short stems, and bears large flowers of apricot shading to a deeper color in the center. Zones 9–12.

Echinopsis, Hybrid Cultivar, 'Chico Mendes'

E., Hybrid Cultivar, 'Samantha Smith'

ECHIUM

This genus comprises about 60 species in the borage (Boraginaceae) family, a large proportion of which are endemic to the Canary Islands and Madeira. Some of these endemics are shrubs or giant biennials. The remaining species are found in parts of the Mediterranean region, through western Asia, and in parts of Africa. These are nearly all smaller annuals, biennials, or perennials, generally beginning as a rosette of narrow leaves clothed in stiff hairs. Bell-shaped flowers, usually blue, pink, purple, or reddish, are borne in branched, usually erect, spikes in spring and summer.

CULTIVATION: The shrubby species of *Echium* thrive best with only moderate amounts of fertilizer and water. The herbaceous species can be fertilized and watered more liberally. All do best in full sun. The species that are from the Canary Islands are less frost hardy than the European species. They are usually propagated from seed, but cuttings may be taken in spring or summer. These plants have a tendency to self-seed in mild climates, so they must be positioned carefully.

Echinopsis hertrichiana

Echinopsis huascha

Echium plantagineum, Stirling Range, Western Australia

Echium amoenum

Echium amoenum

⬚ ❄ ↔ 12–18 in (30–45 cm)
↑ 12–24 in (30–60 cm)

From Europe. This seldom grown perennial species bears blood red flowers.
Zones 7–9.

Echium candicans ★

syn. Echium fastuosum
PRIDE OF MADEIRA

⬚ ❅ ↔ 6 ft (1.8 m) ↑ 6 ft (1.8 m)
Native to the Canary Islands and
Madeira. A thick-stemmed, soft-
wooded, evergreen shrub, with large
densely hairy leaves, to 10 in (25 cm)
long. Clusters of about 8 blue flowers
with protruding pink to lilac-purple
stamens, are borne in a spiky panicle,
in early spring–early summer. May
naturalize in cool climates. Zones 9–10.

Echium plantagineum 'Blue Bedder'

Echium plantagineum

syn. Echium lycopsis
PATERSON'S CURSE, PURPLE VIPER'S BUGLOSS

⬚ ❄ ↔ 12–18 in (30–45 cm)
↑ 18–36 in (45–90 cm)

Hairy-leafed annual or biennial from
Europe; often weedy elsewhere, and
especially in Australia, where it is
known as Paterson's curse. The pinkish
red buds, are borne in spikes, opening
to intense reddish or violet blue tubular flowers, to 1¼ in (30 mm) long, in
late spring–summer. 'Blue Bedder'
(syn. E. vulgare 'Blue Bedder'), shorter
form. Zones 8–10.

Echium vulgare

BLUE WEED, VIPER'S BUGLOSS

⬚ ❄ ↔ 18–24 in (45–60 cm)
↑ 18–24 in (45–60 cm)

From Europe and western Asia. Biennial usually grown as an annual.
Often confused with E. plantagineum
but bristlier and with smaller flowers.
Branching spikes of intense violet-
blue flowers, to ¾ in (18 mm), in summer. Zones 7–10.

Echium candicans

EDGEWORTHIA

This genus of 2 or 3 rather similar
species in the daphne (Thymelaeaceae)
family is named for Michael Pakenham
Edgeworth (1812–81), a part-time
botanist, plant collector, and employee
of the East India Company. They are
heavily wooded shrubs with large,
elongated oval, mid-green leaves; when
young the leaves have prominent midribs and a felty coating. The bark contains a very strong fiber and is naturally
papery, and has been used for the production of paper pulp. The structure
and fragrance of the flowerheads, which
open in late winter to spring, reveal the
close relationship between this genus
and Daphne.
CULTIVATION: Edgeworthia are best
suited to moist, well-drained, humus-
enriched soil in part-shade. They are
moderately frost hardy plants, but are
likely to be severely damaged if struck
by a late frost after the young foliage
has started to develop. Propagate from
half-hardened cuttings, by air-layering,
or from seed.

Edgeworthia chrysantha ★

PAPER BUSH

⬚ ❄ ↔ 6 ft (1.8 m) ↑ 8 ft (2.4 m)
A native of China. Deciduous shrub
with sparse growth and very heavy
branches, which produces attractive
new foliage. The globose heads of
short, fragrant, tubular flowers are
bright yellow, ageing to creamy white,
at the end of winter, and are followed
by dry drupes. Some botanists regard
E. papyrifera and E. chrysantha as one
species. Zones 8–10.

Edgeworthia chrysantha

EDMONDIA

This small genus, comprising 3 species
of perennials and small shrubs in the
daisy (Asteraceae) family, is confined
to the Cape region of South Africa. It
is closely related to Helichrysum and
was formerly classified under that
genus. The flowerheads are composed
of disc florets only, the daisy appearance is given by the papery bracts surrounding the flowerheads. This latter
feature makes Edmondia species good
"everlastings."
CULTIVATION: Best grown in relatively frost-free regions in well-drained
soil in full sun. Propagate from seed
in the spring or from cuttings during
summer or autumn.

Edmondia pinifolia

⬚ ❄ ↔ 12 in (30 cm) ↑ 12 in (30 cm)
An evergreen subshrub with small narrow leaves; hence the epithet pinifolia.
The flowerheads are surrounded by
crimson bracts, borne at the branch
tips, in spring. Zones 8–9.

EDRAIANTHUS

GRASSY BELLS

This genus of about 24 tuft-forming
perennial herbs belonging to the bellflower (Campanulaceae) family is
found from the Mediterranean to
eastern Europe. All species form small
mats or mounds consisting of crowded
narrow leaves emerging from a central
base. The large, lilac to violet, bell-
shaped flowers are borne from spring
through to summer, either singly or in
tightly clustered heads surrounded by
leafy bracts.
CULTIVATION: Ideal for rock gardens
and containers in a sunny position in
well-drained soil; water regularly in
summer. Propagate from seed in early
summer or from softwood cuttings
taken from side shoots in autumn.

Edmondia pinifolia

Ehretia amoena

Ehretia anacua

Eichhornia crassipes

Edraianthus pumilio

☀ ❄ ↔ 6–10 in (15–25 cm) ↑ 2½–6 in (6–15 cm)

From the Balkans. This dwarf perennial forms rounded mounds of stiff, narrow, grayish to silvery green leaves, which are hidden by the large, solitary, lavender-blue to violet-blue, bell-shaped flowers in early to mid-summer. Zones 4–9.

EHRETIA

This genus belonging to the borage (Boraginaceae) family of 75 species of tall shrubs or trees is found in the tropics and subtropics, principally in Africa and Asia, with 3 species in the Americas and 6 species in Australia. The leaves are simple and alternate, toothed in some species, but smooth in others. Clusters of small white flowers are borne in the leaf axils or at the branch tips, followed by fleshy fruit. Most species flower in spring or summer and fruit in autumn.
CULTIVATION: Growing conditions vary according to the species' origin, but all are somewhat frost tender when young. Watering is essential through prolonged dry periods. Propagate from fresh seed only.

Ehretia amoena

SANDPAPER BUSH

☀ ❄ ↔ 8 ft (2.4 m) ↑ 25 ft (8 m)

Native to northern South Africa, Mozambique, Botswana, Zimbabwe, and Namibia. A shrub or small tree. Leaves almost circular, hairy on both surfaces, with irregularly and coarsely toothed margins. Scented white to mauve flowers in early–late summer. Fleshy fruit ripens to red. Zones 9–11.

Ehretia anacua

☀ ❄ ↔ 25 ft (8 m) ↑ 50 ft (15 m)

From the dry scrublands of northern Mexico and southern Texas. Tough oval-shaped leaves, to 3 in (8 cm) long, with stiff hairs on both surfaces. Bears crowded clusters of fragrant white flowers in spring–autumn. Globular yellow fruit with 4 seeds, ripening in spring–autumn. Zones 9–11.

EICHHORNIA

This genus, comprises 7 species from tropical America, belonging to the pickerelweed (Pontederiaceae) family. The plants are rhizomatous aquatics, usually perennial, with floating or submerged leaves. The stems are short and floating, and may be detaching or rooted in mud. The shiny hairless leaves form either floating or emergent rosettes; when free-floating they have tufts of thread-like roots below. The leaves have either narrow cylindrical stalks or, in floating species, elliptical stalks inflated with air-filled tissue. The inflorescence is a spike or panicle; the outer part has 6 lobes, arises from a tube at the base, and is usually violet to blue with white or yellow markings. The fruit is a many-seeded capsule.
CULTIVATION: These plants do not tolerate frost and generally require water at least 6 in (15 cm) deep. They respond to dissolved nutrients with faster growth; in hotter climates growth is so rapid that planting is not recommended in any but small ponds. Propagate by division.

Eichhornia crassipes

WATER HYACINTH

☀ ❄ ↔ 18 in (45 cm) ↑ 12 in (30 cm)

Usually a free-floating plant with swollen leaf stalks and leaf blades raised above the water that act as sails. Violet-blue flowers in summer; some selections are tinted pink or yellow. It was originally introduced as an ornamental, but has spread to choke many tropical waterways and has become naturalized in many parts of the world, as far north as Portugal. Two parents can give rise to 30 offspring through vegetative budding in just 23 days, and to 1,200 in 4 months. The fiber is used in furniture making and basketry. Regarded as a noxious weed in many countries, its use in others must be carefully planned. Zones 10–12.

ELAEAGNUS

This genus of 30 to 40 species of deciduous and evergreen shrubs or small trees belonging to the oleaster (Elaeagnaceae) family is found in Asia and southern Europe; North America has a single species. They are valuable as hedges and windbreaks, particularly in coastal areas; some species have spiny branches. The leaves may be simple or alternate, green or variegated, often covered beneath with silvery brown scales. Abundant tubular or bell-shaped flowers are borne on the lower side of the upper twigs. The flowers are small, whitish or cream, sometimes strongly fragrant. The red, brown, or yellowish fruit is edible.
CULTIVATION: These plants tolerate a wide range of soil types, the exception is shallow chalk soils, and they like adequate summer water and a position in full sun. They should be pruned lightly to promote a dense leafy habit; hedges should not be close-clipped. Propagate from seed, which germinates readily if sown as soon as ripe, or from soft-tip or semi-hardwood cuttings; cultivars should be grown from cuttings.

Elaeagnus angustifolia

OLEASTER, RUSSIAN OLIVE

☀ ❄ ↔ 20 ft (6 m) ↑ 25 ft (8 m)

From temperate western Asia. Large, spiny, deciduous shrub or small tree. Silvery gray willow-like leaves, similar to those of the willow-leafed pear (*Pyrus salicifolia*); the leaves of young plants are broad and hairy. Fragrant yellowish flowers are borne in mid-summer. *E. a.* var. *caspica,* striking form with tapered leaves and silvery new growth. Zones 2–9.

Elaeagnus commutata

syn. *Elaeagnus argentea*

SILVERBERRY

☀ ❄ ↔ 8 ft (2.4 m) ↑ 15 ft (4.5 m)

Found in North America occurring in poor prairie soils. Suckering shrub with red-brown shoots and silvery leaves. The fragrant flowers, silvery outside, yellow within, are borne in the late spring to early summer. Small, oval, silvery fruit. Zones 2–9.

Elaeagnus commutata

Elaeagnus angustifolia

Elaeagnus × ebbingei

☼ ❄ ↔ 12 ft (3.5 m) ↕ 12 ft (3.5 m)

A hybrid of garden origin between
E. macrophylla and *E. pungens*. This
dense, fast-growing, hardy, evergreen
shrub has glossy dark green leaves, silvery beneath, to 4 in (10 cm) long.
It bears silver-scaled, fragrant, creamy
white flowers in autumn. Orange-red
fruit with silver freckles follow in the
spring. 'Gilt Edge' ★ has deep green
leaves with a bright golden yellow margin; 'Limelight', silvery young leaves
becoming light green with golden yellow variegation in the center, though
many revert as the plant grows older.
Zones 6–9.

Elaeagnus pungens 'Maculata'

Elaeagnus pungens 'Aurea'

Elaeagnus umbellata

Elaeagnus macrophylla

☼ ❄ ↔ 12 ft (3.5 m) ↕ 10 ft (3 m)

From Korea and Japan. Large spreading shrub. Broadly ovate leaves covered
in silvery scales on both surfaces, upper
surface becoming green. Fragrant silvery flowers in autumn. Red scaly fruit.
Zones 7–10.

Elaeagnus multiflora

☼ ❄ ↔ 10 ft (3 m) ↕ 10 ft (3 m)

From China and Japan. An evergreen
wide-spreading shrub. Leaves green on
upper surface, silvery beneath. Fragrant
creamy white flowers, on red-brown
new shoots, in spring. Most attractive
in mid- to late summer when covered
with oblong, oxblood red, edible fruit.
Zones 5–9.

Elaeagnus pungens

SILVERBERRY

☼ ❄ ↔ 20 ft (6 m) ↕ 15 ft (4.5 m)

From Japan. Evergreen shrub suitable
for hedging. Main branches spiny and
horizontal. Leaves oval, glossy green
above, silvery white beneath, with
scattered, brown, glandular dots. Small
clusters of creamy white flowers with
brown dots in autumn. Fruit reddish
brown with silvery white spots. 'Aurea',
leaves with a bright yellow margin of
irregular width; 'Goldrim', deep glossy
leaves with a bright yellow margin;
'Maculata', spectacular form with a
large, yellow, central patch on each

Elaeagnus × *ebbingei* 'Gilt Edge'

leaf and a dark green margin, though
it can revert; 'Variegata', large shrub,
leaves with a thin creamy yellow margin. Zones 7–10.

Elaeagnus umbellata

syn. *Elaeagnus crispa*

AUTUMN OLIVE

☼ ❄ ↔ 30 ft (9 m) ↕ 30 ft (9 m)

From China, Korea, and Japan. Strong-growing shrub. New shoots are golden
brown, thorny. Leaves soft green, wavy-edged, silvery beneath. Fragrant yellow-white flowers are borne in late spring–
early summer. Small, rounded, silvery
bronze fruit ripens to pale red speckled
with white in autumn. Zones 3–9.

ELAEIS

OIL PALM

This tropical palm genus (family
Arecaceae) has 2 species, one is native
to Central and South America and the
other to Africa, where it occurs in open
places, along streams and in swamps,
and occasionally in savannah. Large,
single-stemmed plants with "feather"
fronds. Large inflorescences appear
year-round, with males and females
separate but on the same plant. They
fruit heavily. Seeds and pulp of the
fruit contain large quantities of oils,
used for many purposes, from soap,
margarine, and candle manufacture to,
in some tropical cities, car fuel.

Elaeagnus × *ebbingei* 'Limelight'

Elaeis oleifera

Elaeis guineensis

CULTIVATION: Ideal for tropical coastal
areas, being salt tolerant; growth slower
in subtropical regions. They prefer a
rich, moist, medium loam in a protected sunny position; keep the roots
moist. Propagate from seed; crack open
the hard shell of the large seed, or soak
it in hot water, before germinating.

Elaeis guineensis

AFRICAN OIL PALM, MACAW FAT, OIL PALM

☼ ⚘ ↔ 12 ft (3.5 m) ↕ 60 ft (18 m)

From tropical Africa. Large palm. Solid,
erect, rough trunk marked with scars.
Shiny green fronds, to 15 ft (4.5 m)
long, forming a graceful spreading
crown. Red flowers. Zones 11–12.

Elaeis oleifera

AMERICAN OIL PALM, COROZO PALM

☼ ⚘ ↔ 10 ft (3 m) ↕ 6 ft (1.8 m)

From Central and South America.
Similar to *E. guineensis* but yielding
oil of a lower quality. Rough trunk
growing horizontally before bending
upward. Fronds to 12 ft (3.5 m) long.
Yellowish flowers. Heads of dark orange
fruit. Zones 11–12.

ELAEOCARPUS

Species in this genus of about 60 ever-green shrubs and trees, in the family
Elaeocarpaceae, occur throughout the
Indo-Pacific region, from tropical East
Asia and India to New Zealand. The
leaves are usually simple, deep green,
elongated ovals, often with markedly
serrated edges. The flowers are small,
often white and fragrant, and very
graceful, with fringed edges. They are
carried in small, sometimes rather
pendulous, racemes, and followed by
unusually colored drupes.
CULTIVATION: Hardiness varies, but
most species tolerate only light frosts,
if any. They prefer moist, well-drained,
fairly fertile soil with a position in sun

or part-shade; they are not drought tolerant. Unless complete rejuvenation is required, restrict pruning to trimming to shape. Propagate from half-hardened cuttings or from seed that has been soaked before sowing.

Elaeocarpus grandis
BLUE MARBLE TREE, BLUE QUANDONG

☀ ♦ ↔ 20 ft (6 m) ↑ 30 ft (9 m)

From coastal and mountain rainforests in eastern Australia. The older leaves turn bright red. Bears fimbriated white flowers in summer. Bright blue edible fruit, 1 in (25 mm) in diameter. The blue quandong is also valued for its timber. Zones 9–12.

Elaeocarpus hookerianus
POKAKA

☀ ♦ ↔ 15 ft (4.5 m) ↑ 40 ft (12 m)

From New Zealand. An evergreen tree with densely interwoven branches. The leaves are usually narrow and irregularly lobed when young, and become broader, with toothed edges and a more clearly defined pointed tip, with age. Small sprays of pale green to greenish white flowers in spring–summer. Purple-red drupes. Zones 9–10.

Elaeocarpus obovatus
HARD QUANDONG

☀ ♦ ↔ 15 ft (4.5 m) ↑ 20 ft (6 m)

From eastern Australia. Racemes of fringed, white, bell-shaped flowers in spring. The bright blue fruit is attractive to birds. Zones 9–12.

Elaeocarpus reticulatus
BLUEBERRY ASH

☀ ♦ ↔ 15 ft (4.5 m) ↑ 30 ft (9 m)

From Australia. Usually kept pruned to a shrub in cultivation. Leaves to 6 in (15 cm) long, with toothed edges. Short racemes of creamy white to pale pink flowers in spring–summer. Deep blue drupes. Zones 9–11.

Elaeocarpus sphaericus
INDIAN BEAD TREE

☀ ♦ ↔ 30 ft (9 m) ↑ 50 ft (15 m)

From India, Southeast Asia, and the islands of the Western Pacific. Tree with tiered branches. Leaves to 5 in (12 cm)

Elaeocarpus obovatus

long, with serrated edges, dark green turning bright red with age. The white flowers are borne in racemes in leaf axils. The dull purple-blue drupes are used to make Rudraksha beads, sacred to Hindus. Zones 10–12.

ELEGIA
AFRICAN THATCHING RUSH

An extremely ornamental genus comprising about 35 species of rush-like plants in the family Restionaceae. They are restricted to southern Africa and are evergreen clumping perennials with the foliage reduced to brown bracts and the rich green stems taking over the function of photosynthesis. Tiny coppery-brown flowers are produced in clusters at the top of the stems in summer. The male and female flowers are borne on different plants, which often look quite different. At times. this has led to the two sexes being wrongly classified as different species. Many species resemble horsetails (*Equisetum*) and were classified as such in the past.

CULTIVATION: Accustomed in the wild to poor sandy soils in seasonally flooded areas, these plants prefer similar conditions in cultivation, although any sunny moist to wet aspect in areas with minimal frosts will do. Propagate from seed, which has to be smoke-treated to germinate, or by careful division of young plants.

Elaeocarpus grandis

Elaeocarpus reticulatus

Elegia capensis
FONTEINRIET, FOUNTAIN RUSH

☀ ❄ ↔ 3–7 ft (0.9–2 m) ↑ 7–10 ft (2–3 m)

From the Cape of Good Hope region, South Africa. The largest and most spectacular species, with tall upright stems and clusters of fine secondary stems in fluffy masses at the nodes. Flowers, borne in large clusters, look much the same in both sexes. Popular for cut foliage, which lasts for weeks in water. Zones 8–11.

Elegia filacea

☀ ❄ ↔ 8–12 in (20–30 cm) ↑ 16–20 in (40–50 cm)

Native to regions from Clanwilliam to Port Elizabeth, South Africa. Fine, unbranched, upright stems. Male flowerheads with dark brown narrow bracts, female flowerheads with broader paler bracts. Will grow in moist or dry conditions. Zones 8–11.

ELEOCHARIS
SPIKE RUSH

There are about 150 species of annual or perennial rush-like plants in this genus in the sedge (Cyperaceae) family. Found throughout the world in bogs, shallow water, and damp places. True leaves are reduced or non-existent, and the plants comprise cylindrical stems bearing spikelets of tiny flowers at their tips. Height ranges from a few inches to 5 ft (1.5 m) or more.

Elaeocarpus reticulatus

Elaeocarpus sphaericus

CULTIVATION: Easily grown in bog gardens and shallow ponds, or on pond margins, in sun or part-shade. In Asia, *E. dulcis* (water chestnut) is grown like rice as a crop in flooded fields. Propagate from seed or by division.

Eleocharis acicularis
HAIR GRASS, NEEDLE SPIKE RUSH, SLENDER SPIKE RUSH

☀/☀ ❄ ↔ 6–12 in (15–30 cm) ↑ 2–12 in (5–30 cm)

Found throughout North America, Europe, and Asia. Perennial with thin mat-forming runners. Narrow cylindrical stems bearing compressed pointed spikelets of tiny flowers in late summer–autumn. Zones 7–10.

Elegia filacea

Eleocharis acicularis

E

Eleutherococcus henryi

Eleutherococcus lasiogyne

ELETTARIA

A genus of 7 species found from India to the western Malay Archipelago, belonging to the ginger (Zingiberaceae) family. All are perennial herbs with creeping rhizomes. The leaves are in 2 ranks. Inflorescences are borne on prostrate shoots, with scale leaves arising directly from the rhizomes. Bracts surround several flowers; bracteoles and calyx are tube-shaped. The 3-petalled corolla sometimes forms a hood. Fruit is a spherical to elliptical capsule with a thin smooth or ridged wall.
CULTIVATION: *E. cardamomum* (cardamom) grows in the southern Indian hills under a forest canopy; they need little cultivation once established.

Elettaria cardamomum

CARDAMOM
☀️/☀️ 🌱 ↔ 5–8 ft (1.5–2.4 m)
↑ 5–8 ft (1.5–2.4 m)
From India. Thick rhizome. Leaves to 24 in (60 cm) long, narrowly

lanceolate, hairy beneath. Flower spike to 24 in (60 cm). The flowers have a white corolla with violet or pink stripes on the lip and a yellow margin. In Asia *E. cardamomum* is widely grown for its spicy seeds, which are used in cooking, as a masticatory, and in medicine. The spice was known to the Romans who imported substantial quantities; today it is used in Middle Eastern cuisine, and curries and desserts. Zones 10–12.

ELEUTHEROCOCCUS

This genus of about 30 mostly deciduous prickly shrubs or trees native to southern and eastern Asia belongs to the ivy (Araliaceae) family and sometimes has a sprawling habit. The leaves are pinnate, consisting of 3 to 5 leaflets. Small flowers appear from late spring to autumn in umbels of 5, followed by black or purplish black drupes. They are cultivated mainly for the ornamental value of their foliage and sometimes for use in traditional herbal medicine.
CULTIVATION: A sunny position is preferred, in well-drained sandy or loamy soil. Propagate from seed sown in spring, or divide roots or separate suckers in autumn.

Eleutherococcus henryi

☀️ ❄️ ↔ 6–12 ft (1.8–3.5 m)
↑ 6–12 ft (1.8–3.5 m)
From central China. Sturdy, sprawling, deciduous shrub. The branches have curved prickles. The compound leaves, to 4 in (10 cm) long, are rough to the touch, with 3 to 5 toothed elliptical leaflets. The bluish black fruit ripens in late summer. Tolerates poor soil and air pollution. 'Nanus', more compact. Zones 4–9.

Eleutherococcus lasiogyne

syn. *Acanthopanax lasiogyne*
☀️ ❄️ ↔ 10 ft (3 m) ↑ 20 ft (6 m)
From western China. Large, rounded, deciduous shrub or small tree. Compact umbels of white flowers in late summer–autumn. Black fruit, about ⅓ in (8 mm) long. Zones 6–9.

Eleutherococcus sessiliflorus

WANGRANGKURA
☀️ ❄️ ↔ 12 ft (3.5 m) ↑ 15 ft (4.5 m)
From temperate northeastern Asia. Shrub with a spreading growth habit. Leaves with 3 to 5 serrated-edged leaflets, each to 6 in (15 cm) long; leaf stalks sometimes prickly. Umbel-like heads of purplish flowers in late summer. Black drupes, ½ in (12 mm) long. Zones 4–9.

Eleutherococcus sieboldianus ★

☀️ ❄️ ↔ 8 ft (2.5 m) ↑ 10 ft (3 m)
Native to eastern China. A shrub with slender, arching, cane-like branches. Bears solitary umbels of greenish white flowers in late spring–early summer. The black fruit is ⅓ in (8 mm) in diameter. Zones 4–9.

ELODEA

syn. *Anacharis*
This genus belonging to the frogbit (Hydrocharitaceae) family comprises 12 species. These prolific freshwater plants, native to North and South America, are useful in aquariums,

ponds, and water gardens. Because they are submersed, they provide good protection for spawning and young fish; they also counteract algae build-up. Some species are rooted, some free floating. Even in an aquarium, rooted species can grow to 15 ft (4.5 m).
CULTIVATION: For best results, grow in full sun in slow-moving or still water. Under ideal conditions, *Elodea* can spread rapidly. Reproduce by simply breaking off a section of the plant and either replanting it or allowing it to float freely.

Elodea canadensis

CANADIAN PONDWEED, WATERWEED
☀️ ❄️ ↑ 36 in (90 cm) ↔ indefinite
From North America. Excellent perennial oxygenator for the water garden, but can become invasive. Densely branched stems covered in whorls of dark green pointed leaves, and minute white flowers in summer. Dies back in winter. Zones 3–10.

ELYMUS

WHEAT GRASS, WILD RYE
A genus comprising about 150 species of grasses in the family Poaceae, few of which are usually considered ornamental. They include running and clumping species, and inhabit such diverse habitats as steppes, dunes, and woodland in temperate regions of the Northern and Southern Hemispheres. Most species flower in summer.

Eleutherococcus sessiliflorus

CULTIVATION: All noteworthy species are fully frost hardy and require nothing more than a sunny aspect and a moisture-retentive soil. Propagation is usually by division in early spring.

Elymus canadensis

BLUE WILD RYE, CANADA WILD RYE, MOUNTAIN WILD RYE, WESTERN WILD RYE

↔ 24–36 in (60–90 cm)
↕ 36–60 in (90–150 cm)

Found from North Carolina to Alaska, USA. Drought-tolerant, ornamental, perennial grass. Wheat-like greenish flowerheads; seed plumes turning gold in mid- to late summer. Delicate-looking but tough; good in a wild garden or as a ground cover, providing winter interest. Zones 3–9.

Elymus condensatus

GIANT WILD RYE

↔ 3 ft (0.9 m) ↕ 3–7 ft (0.9–2 m)
From North America. Vigorous, semi-evergreen, upright grass; can be dormant in dry summer climates. The gray-green foliage tones in with the bluish flower stems, which sit 8 in (20 cm) above the foliage in the summer months. Propagate from seed. **'Canyon Prince'** (blue giant wild rye), slow spreading habit, upright bright bluish green foliage, showy creamy blue flowers sitting 24 in (60 cm) above the grass; propagation is by division. Zones 3–9.

Elymus magellanicus

syns *Agropyron magellanicum*, *A. pubiflorum*

BLUE WHEATGRASS, MAGELLAN WHEATGRASS

↔ 36–40 in (90–100 cm)
↕ 40–60 in (100–150 cm)

A native of South America. This spectacular mountain plant is probably the most attractive member of this genus. The semi-evergreen clumps of intense silver-blue foliage are topped

Emmenopterys henryi

with narrow heads of flowers that start out the same color, later turning to a parchment shade. Zones 6–9.

EMBOTHRIUM

This genus in the protea (Proteaceae) family is now considered to be represented by a single species, with regional forms, from Chile and the adjacent Andean region of Argentina. The rather upright tree is spectacular when in flower in late spring and early summer; its profusion of orange-scarlet tubular flowers are best appreciated from above. CULTIVATION: An open sunny position with free-draining soil will reduce this plant's inclination to legginess. Protect from frost. With plentiful moisture, it grows quickly, producing a worthwhile display within a decade, but its life expectancy may not exceed 25 years. Can be propagated from seed, cuttings, or basal suckers.

Embothrium coccineum

CHILEAN FIRE BUSH

↔ 20 ft (6 m) ↕ 40 ft (12 m)
This native of Chile is an upright evergreen tree with glossy leathery leaves. It produces brilliant orange-scarlet flowers. In cultivation, treat as a tall shrub; prune after flowering to encourage flowering at eye level. The hardiest *Embothrium* is reputed to be **'Ñorquincó'** ★, introduced in the 1920s by Harold Comber from the Ñorquincó Valley in the province of Neuquén, Argentina; its flower clusters are closely crowded on branches. Zones 9–10.

EMILIA

There are about 24 species of rather sparse annual herbs in this genus, belonging to the daisy (Asteraceae) family. They are found throughout Polynesia, India, and tropical Africa. Their foliage is reminiscent of sow thistles, and the finely rayed flowers, which are borne singly or in small corymbs, are in bright shades of purple, scarlet, yellow, or orange. CULTIVATION: *Emilia* species are easily grown in most soils in the full sun; plant close together for the best effect. Propagate from seed.

Emilia sonchifolia

FLORA'S PAINTBRUSH, TASSEL FLOWER

↔ 6–10 in (15–25 cm)
↕ 6–20 in (15–50 cm)
From tropical Asia and Africa. This annual produces rosettes of lyre-shaped leaves, sometimes bluish green. The tassel-like flowers bloom in shades of scarlet, brilliant orange, or yellow in summer. Zones 9–11.

Emilia sonchifolia

Elymus condensatus 'Canyon Prince'

Elymus magellanicus

EMMENOPTERYS

A genus of 2 deciduous trees from China and Southeast Asia belonging to the madder (Rubiaceae) family. The oval leaves are opposite and smooth-edged, and the fruit is a winged capsule. Panicles of funnel- or bell-shaped flowers are borne at the branch tips in summer. They are valuable as specimen trees. CULTIVATION: These trees prefer a sunny position in medium loam but will tolerate clay soils. Propagate from seed or from softwood cuttings grown under glass in summer.

Emmenopterys henryi

↔ 40 ft (12 m) ↕ 40–80 ft (12–24 m)
From central and western China, Myanmar, and Thailand. Deciduous tree with rough dark gray bark and gray or purple branchlets. Leaves to 8 in (20 cm) long; young growth reddish bronze. Panicles of white or yellow bell-shaped flowers. Zones 6–9.

EMPETRUM

Exposed windswept sites across the cool-temperate regions of the Northern

Embothrium coccineum

Hemisphere (and also the southern Andes and the Falkland Islands in the South Atlantic) are home to this genus of 2 heath-like, intricately branched, evergreen shrubs belonging to the family Empetraceae. Low growing and carpeting in habit. Very small solitary flowers appear in the leaf axils, and the fruit is a small, juicy, berry-like drupe containing up to 9 hard white seeds. The shrubs are grown for both their ornamental value and their edible fruit. CULTIVATION: They prefer moist lime-free soil in an open sunny position; ideal for the rock garden in cooler climates. Propagate from seed sown in spring or from cuttings.

Empetrum nigrum

BLACK CROWBERRY, CRAKE BERRY, CURLEW BERRY, MONOX

☀ ❋ ↔ 15 in (38 cm) ↑ 12 in (30 cm)

From the USA, northern Europe, and Asia. Spreading, heath-like, evergreen shrub resembling a miniature fir tree. Decumbent branches. Short needle-like leaves on stems with long woolly hairs. Loose clusters of purplish red flowers in late spring–early summer. Edible fruit, glossy, blackish purple. Zones 3–8.

ENCELIA

Genus of about 15 species of perennials and low shrubs, native to arid regions of southwestern USA, Mexico, Peru, and Chile, and belonging to the daisy (Asteraceae) family. Foliage often aromatic; daisies bright orange or yellow.

Encephalartos hildebrandtii

Encephalartos altensteinii

Encephalartos friderici-guilielmi

CULTIVATION: Grow in full sun in deep sharply drained soil. Useful plants for dry areas; they dislike winter wet. In cold climates they can be grown in the greenhouse. Propagate from seed or cuttings.

Encelia farinosa

BRITTLE-BUSH, INCIENSO

☀ ❋ ↔ 36 in (90 cm) ↑ 36 in (90 cm)

From southwestern USA and Mexico. Aromatic shrub with silvery foliage. Bears orange-yellow daisies with yellow or reddish brown centers in spring. Zones 8–11.

ENCEPHALARTOS

This African genus belonging to the zamia (Zamiaceae) family consists of around 100 species of slow-growing cycads, the majority from southern Africa. There are both male and female plants. They prefer dry winters and summer rainfall. The pinnate fronds are often long and straight or arching, the leaflets are without a midrib and often spiny-toothed. Some develop a stout trunk, but suckering is common in those with underground cylindrical stems. Female plants have spectacular large seed cones with colorful fleshy seeds, maturing mostly in summer to

Encephalartos horridus

autumn. Male pollen cones are usually smaller. The name comes from the Greek *en*, within, *cephale*, head, and *artos*, bread, referring to the starchy inner part of the trunk of some species, which is used as a staple food (sago) in some areas.

CULTIVATION: All species require well-drained soil. Species with blue-toned leaves are generally more tolerant of full sun, dry conditions, and heat; those with softer green leaves do best in filtered shade, with more regular watering. Propagate from seed or offsets.

Encephalartos altensteinii ★

PRICKLY CYCAD

☀/◐ ⚹ ↔ 12 ft (3.5 m) ↑ 15 ft (4.5 m)

From South Africa. Very slow-growing cycad. The trunk forms clumps from basal suckers. Stiff, glossy, green leaves; narrow leaflets with 1 to 3 prickles on each margin. Large yellow seed cones with red fruits. The trunks are a source of sago. Zones 10–11.

Encephalartos friderici-guilielmi ★

syn. *Zamia friderici-guilielmi*

WOOLLY CYCAD

☀ ⚹ ↔ 10 ft (3 m) ↑ 17–20 ft (5–6 m)

Native to South Africa's Eastern Cape Province, occurring on rocky sites in grassy and shrubby habitats. Leaves to 5 ft (1.5 m) long; narrow leaflets, not lobed and with a few teeth on lower margin, to 7 in long and ⅓ in wide (18 cm × 8 mm). Male cones, yellow and shaped like elongated egg. Broader female cones and seeds also yellow. Species name is Latinized form of Friedrich Wilhelm, a nineteenth-century king of Prussia. Zones 9–11.

Empetrum nigrum

Encelia farinosa

Encephalartos hildebrandtii

☀/◐ ⚹ ↔ 12 ft (3.5 m) ↑ 12 ft (3.5 m)

Native to East Africa. Large tropical species with glossy dark green leaves, usually 6–10 ft (1.8–3 m) long; narrow lance-shaped leaflets with heavily toothed margins, woolly when young. Yellow seed cones, to 24 in (60 cm) long, with orange, red, or yellow seeds. Zones 10–12.

Encephalartos horridus

EASTERN CAPE BLUE CYCAD

☀/◐ ⚹ ↔ 3 ft (0.9 m) ↑ 3 ft (0.9 m)

From South Africa. Cycad with a very stiff growth habit and distinctly glaucous foliage. Most of the stem grows below ground. Fronds arching, to 3 ft (0.9 m) long; leaflets tipped with fierce spines. Cones are a warm buff shade. Zones 9–11.

Encephalartos natalensis

NATAL CYCAD, THOUSAND HILLS CYCAD

☀/◐ ⚹ ↔ 8 ft (2.4 m) ↑ 20 ft (6 m)

From southern KwaZulu-Natal, South Africa. Sturdy trunk. Glossy light or bright green leaves, to 10 ft (3 m) long; leaflets do not overlap and usually lack prickles. Cones in clusters, and woolly when young. Zones 10–12.

Encephalartos villosus ★

syns *Encephalartos villosus* f. *intermedia*, *E. niveo-lanuginosis*

☀ ⚹ ↔ to 20 ft (6 m) ↑ to 10 ft (3 m)

Native to KwaZulu-Natal and the Cape region in South Africa, and to Swaziland. Occurring in scrubs and forests. No stem is above ground; distinguished by long, glossy, dark green leaves, to 10 ft (3 m), and its woolly crown. Leaflets narrow to lance-shaped, to 10 in (25 cm) long, margins with 1 to 3 teeth. Male cones are elongated ovate, yellow; female cones are ovate, also yellow, shorter and wider than the male. Red seeds. Zones 9–11.

ENCYCLIA

A complex genus of over 200 sympodial orchids (family Orchidaceae) from Central and South America, generally comprising intermediate to warm-growing species. This genus was once

Encephalartos villosus

included within the related *Epidendrum*. Often clumping plants with a distinct pseudobulb, usually topped with 2 or 3 leaves. Recently sections of *Encyclia* have been transferred to separate genera. In 1998 a large group of the "cockleshell" *Encyclia* species was moved into the genus *Prosthechea*. This met with some resistance, even though they are easily recognized by their "upside down" flowers and labellum that displays varying degrees of dark purple striation (most species are also highly fragrant).

CULTIVATION: Readily grown, on cork slabs or potted in a well-drained bark-based medium. Most species have a dormant period from late autumn to early spring. The majority flower in summer and enjoy bright light conditions. Propagate by division.

Encyclia alata
☼/☀ ✛ ↔ 8–20 in (20–50 cm)
↑ 8–36 in (20–90 cm)

From Central America. Numerous forms, varying widely in number of blooms and size. Light brown flowers with a white and yellow labellum with deep purple striations. Zones 10–12.

Encyclia belizensis
☼/☀ ✛ ↔ 8–20 in (20–50 cm)
↑ 8–27 in (20–70 cm)

Found in Central America. Up to 16 fragrant long-lived flowers, mustard yellow with a brown overlay, 1½ in (35 mm) across. Zones 11–12.

Encyclia belizensis

Enkianthus campanulatus

Encyclia hanburyi
☼/☀ ✛ ↔ 8–20 in (20–50 cm)
↑ 8–27 in (20–70 cm)

From Mexico. Clusters of conical pseudobulbs producing upright spikes of brown flowers, 1½ in (35 mm) wide, with a contrasting purple labellum. Zones 10–12.

Encyclia michuacana
☀ ✛ ↔ 8–16 in (20–40 cm)
↑ 8–48 in (20–120 cm)

From Central America. Tall, upright, branched inflorescences bear numerous reddish brown to olive green flowers, 1 in (25 mm) wide, with predominantly white labellum. Zones 10–11.

Encyclia Sunburst
☀ ✛ ↔ 8–20 in (20–50 cm)
↑ 8–20 in (20–50 cm)

A primary hybrid of *E. radiata* (now *Prosthechea radiata*) and *E. vitellina*, with characteristics intermediate between these species. Flowers, about 1¼ in (30 mm) tall, yellow to creamy orange. Zones 10–12.

Encyclia vitellina
☀ ✛ ↔ 8–16 in (20–40 cm)
↑ 8–24 in (20–60 cm)

From Mexico and Guatemala. One of the showiest and most striking members of this genus, unique in having large orange-red blooms with broad segments. Erect inflorescence with up to 12 blooms, 1½ in (35 mm) across, in summer–autumn. Zones 10–11.

ENKIANTHUS
This genus from the heath (Ericaceae) family consists of about 10 species of

Encyclia michuacana

Encyclia hanburyi

mainly deciduous, rarely evergreen, shrubs found from the Himalayas to Japan. The leaves are elliptical or ovate. The plants flower from mid-spring through to early summer, producing umbels or racemes of white, pink, or red urn- or bell-shaped flowers at the ends of the branches.

CULTIVATION: Ornamental shrubs growing on the edge of woodlands or in woodland conditions, preferring full sun or light shade and moist, well-drained, humus-rich, acid to neutral soil. Propagate from half-hardened cuttings taken during summer, by air-layering in autumn, or from seed sown in the winter or early spring. The best propagation medium is peat with lime-free sharp sand.

Enkianthus campanulatus
REDVEIN ENKIANTHUS
☼ ✳ ↔ 15 ft (4.5 m) ↑ 15 ft (4.5 m)

From the mountains of Honshu in Japan. Deciduous species with whorled branches. Leaves dull green and elliptic with a sharp tip and toothed margins, turning deep red in autumn. Flowers in drooping corymb-like racemes of creamy bells with red or pink veining in late spring–early summer. *E. c.* var. *palibinii* has dark red flowers. *E. c.* 'Albiflorus', cream flowers; 'Donardensis', larger red

Encyclia Sunburst

Enkianthus perulatus, left foreground, Lake Wanaka, New Zealand

Enkianthus chinensis

flowers than the species; 'Red Bells' ★, to 10 in (25 cm) tall, with red autumn leaves, and red flowers in pendent clusters. Zones 6–9.

Enkianthus cernuus
☼ ✳ ↔ 8 ft (2.4 m) ↑ 8 ft (2.4 m)

From Honshu in Japan. A deciduous shrub with bright green leaves, ovate to elliptic, with toothed margins, pointed tips, and brown downy veins beneath. Good autumn color. Pendent racemes of white flowers in late spring–summer. *E. c.* f. *rubens* has deep red flowers. Zones 6–9.

Enkianthus chinensis
☼ ✳ ↔ 6 ft (1.8 m) ↑ 12 ft (3.5 m)

A native of northern Myanmar and China. This deciduous shrub has leaves of mid-green, elliptical to oval, with toothed margins, which turn a good autumn color. The racemes of creamy yellow flowers with pink veins and rosy lobes appear in late spring. Zones 6–9.

Enkianthus perulatus
☼ ✳ ↔ 7 ft (2 m) ↑ 7 ft (2 m)

From Japan. Produces attractive shiny red young shoots. Oval, toothed leaves with downy midribs beneath, mid-green, turning bright red in autumn. Small drooping umbels of white flowers, in mid-spring. Zones 6–9.

Epacris impressa

Epacris longiflora

ENSETE

Members of the banana (Musaceae) family, to which this genus belongs, are really giant, tree-like, perennial herbs. *Ensete* is a genus of 7 species of bananas found in tropical Asia and Africa, and is closely related to the banana genus *Musa*. The often heavy trunk or pseudostem is composed of the sheathing bases of the huge leaves, the blades of which are easily frayed by strong winds. Flowers are carried in large pendulous inflorescences on arching stems and develop into small, dry, inedible bananas containing hard seeds. CULTIVATION: All species of *Ensete* are easy to grow; these ornamental forms do not require nearly as much warmth as their edible relatives. The plants will survive all year in a mild frost-free climate; otherwise, treat them as annuals. Plant in moist, rich, well-drained soil in full sun or part-shade. These plants are usually propagated from seed, though it is sometimes possible to remove and strike basal suckers with roots.

Ensete ventricosum
ABYSSINIAN BANANA, ETHIOPIAN BANANA
☼ ⚘ ↔ 15 ft (4.5 m) ↕ 30 ft (9 m)
African species with a huge crown of leaves, up to 20 ft (6 m) long, with a strong purple tint and a purple-red midrib. 'Maurelii', large, broad, red-tinged leaves. Zones 9–12.

ENTELEA

Belonging to the linden (Tiliaceae) family, this genus consists of a single species of small evergreen tree native to New Zealand. It is an attractive plant with large leaves, appealing flowers, and interesting seed pods. Its wood is one of the lightest known, weighing less than cork.
CULTIVATION: Requires greenhouse or conservatory protection in cool-temperate climates. In warmer frost-free areas it will grow in sun or part-sun and does best in good deep soil. Grows rapidly; quite short-lived. Easy to propagate from seed or cuttings.

Entelea arborescens
WHAU
☼ ⚘ ↔ 10 ft (3 m) ↕ 10–20 ft (3–6 m)
Attractive small tree. Leaves large, heart-shaped, soft, drooping, with doubly toothed margins and prominent veins. Clusters of 4- to 5-petalled white flowers, 1 in (25 mm) across, borne near branch tips, in spring. Spiny burr-like fruit. Zones 9–11.

EOMECON

This genus belonging to the poppy (Papaveraceae) family comprises one species of fleshy-stemmed perennial from eastern China. Spreading plant with attractive foliage and flowers. The leaves are thick, dull green, and up to 5 in (12 cm) in diameter. Single white poppy flowers, to 1½ in (4 cm) across, are carried in airy panicles in spring and summer.
CULTIVATION: Grow in well-drained fertile soil in shade or part-shade. This plant makes a good ground cover, as it colonizes readily. Propagate from seed or by division.

Eomecon chionantha
POPPY OF THE DAWN, SNOW POPPY
☼ ❄ ↔ 12–24 in (30–60 cm)
↕ 12–24 in (30–60 cm)
From eastern China. Quick-spreading fleshy-stemmed perennial. Leaves heart- to kidney-shaped, with wavy margins, paler beneath. Clear, white, 4-petalled flowers with a prominent central boss of fluffy yellowish orange stamens. Zones 7–10.

EPACRIS

From the epacris (Epacridaceae) family, this genus comprises approximately 40 species of shrubs or subshrubs. The vast majority are native to heathland or sandy soils in southeastern Australia, including Tasmania, where they do not dry out because of the moisture from creeks or "hanging swamps." Foliage is mostly prickly, gray-green to deep green, with a coarse texture. Many flower for months or in regular flushes all year, but their lifespan is short to medium, even under ideal conditions.
CULTIVATION: Prefer filtered light. To maintain density and improve longevity, trim lightly after flowering. Mulch to retain moisture; gravels are ideal. Propagate from half-hardened cuttings taken in summer. Their fine root systems makes transplanting difficult; buy as small a plant as possible.

Epacris impressa
COMMON HEATH, PINK HEATH
☼ ❄ ↔ 30 in (75 cm) ↕ 3 ft (0.9 m)
Floral emblem of the State of Victoria, Australia. Straggly shrub. Tubular pendulous flowers in colors from white through pink to red. Spot-flowers throughout the year, with a winter–spring flush. Zones 8–10.

Epacris longiflora
FUCHSIA HEATH
☼ ⚘ ↔ 3 ft (0.9 m) ↕ 3 ft (0.9 m)
Found on poor sandstone-derived soils in New South Wales and Queensland, Australia. This straggly but adaptable shrub. flowers sporadically with flushes of tubular flowers, red with white tips, producing a major flush in the spring. Zones 9–10.

EPHEDRA

JOINT FIR, JOINT PINE, MEXICAN TEA
The 40 or so curious shrubs or climbing plants in this genus, the only one of the joint-fir (Ephedraceae) family, have slender, rush-like, jointed, green branches resembling horsetails, becoming woody with age, and very reduced, opposite, scale-like leaves. Small yellow flowers, to ½ in (12 mm) across, appear in cone-like clusters, followed by fleshy, red, berry-like fruit. *Ephedra* is interesting botanically as it is a link between flowering plants and conifers. Species are native to the dry or desert regions across southern Europe, North

Eomecon chionantha

Ensete ventricosum 'Maurelii'

Entelea arborescens

Ephedra distachya

Ephedra viridis

Ephedra gerardiana

Africa, Asia, and the mountains of both North and South America. Native Americans prepare a medicinal tea from the branches; the Chinese stimulant drug ma-huang is *E. sinica,* and ephedrine and its derivatives were developed from *Ephedra* species.
CULTIVATION: These plants prefer sandy soil in a sunny position; they are ideal ground-cover or rock-garden plants in drier areas. Propagate by dividing clumps, separating suckers, or air-layering, or from seed.

Ephedra distachya
EUROPEAN JOINT PINE
☀ ❄ ↔ 3 ft (0.9 m) ↕ 3 ft (0.9 m)
From southern Europe to Siberia; cultivated as early as the sixteenth century. Low evergreen shrub with creeping stems forming mats. Slender erect branches. Scale-like leaves. Red fruit in summer. Zones 4–9.

Ephedra gerardiana
☀ ❄ ↔ 6 ft (1.8 m) ↕ 12 in (30 cm)
From China and the Himalayan mountains. A creeping evergreen shrub with thin dark green branches. It is best suited to growing over rocky banks. Zones 7–10.

Ephedra viridis
GREEN JOINT-FIR, MORMON TEA
☀ ❄ ↔ 3 ft (0.9 m) ↕ 4 ft (1.2 m)
From western USA. Erect evergreen shrub. Thin vivid green branches and awl-like leaves. Zones 6–10.

EPIBLASTUS
This is a small group of about 15 cool- to intermediate-growing, somewhat succulent, sympodial orchids in the family Orchidaceae. They come from higher areas of Sulawesi, New Guinea, and parts of the Pacific Islands. They have branching rhizomes and in the wild produce clusters of brightly colored blooms throughout the cooler months of the year.
CULTIVATION: These uncommon species perform best in pots of sphagnum moss; larger plants can be grown on tree-fern rafts, as long as the substrate is kept moist. They dislike hot dry conditions and must be kept moist in a buoyant atmosphere. In cultivation most species bloom from autumn to early spring. Propagate by division.

Epiblastus basilis
☀ ❄ ↔ 4–12 in (10–30 cm) ↕ 4–12 in (10–30 cm)
A native of New Guinea. The species most frequently seen in cultivation. The small clusters of waxy bright red blooms, just over ½ in (8 mm) in diameter, appear in winter. Zones 10–11.

× *EPICATTLEYA*
Artificial bigeneric sympodial orchid hybrid between *Epidendrum* and *Cattleya,* family Orchidaceae, which has produced a range of novelty hybrids that are often vigorous and free flowering. Many of the registered combinations involve members of the genus *Encyclia,* previously included within *Epidendrum.*

CULTIVATION: These compact-growing orchids grow well in small terracotta or plastic pots, in baskets, or on slabs, but must dry out fully between waterings. They enjoy high light and intermediate to warm temperatures, and can take cool temperatures in winter if kept dry. The showy blooms are often produced in large numbers and are frequently pleasantly fragrant. Propagate by division.

× *Epicattleya* Siam Jade
☀/◐ ❄ ↔ 4–16 in (10–40 cm) ↕ 8–16 in (20–40 cm)
Popular spring-flowering hybrid with green and white flowers that is the result of combining 7 different orchid species. The most prominent are the albino form of *Cattleya guttata* and the green and white *Euchile mariae* (which was previously well known as *Encyclia mariae*). Zones 10–12.

EPIDENDRUM
This is a large sympodial orchid genus from Central and South America, with more than 1,000 recognised species. Many gardeners are familiar with "crucifix" orchids, which are actually "reed-stem" *Epidendrum* species and their hybrids. Many of these species grow as terrestrials among grasses in bright positions, frequently in full sun. The majority of the species, however, occur as lithophytes or epiphytes. *Epidendrum* belong to the same group of genera as *Brassavola, Cattleya, Encyclia, Laelia, Rhyncholaelia,* and *Sophronitis.*
CULTIVATION: As the various species come from a range of altitudes, there would be some to suit most frost-free climates, but most enjoy bright and warm conditions. The "reed-stem" or "crucifix" types may be grown in the ground in frost-free climates. Some species have a dormancy period, while many are in continual growth. Many species may be grown in a free-draining bark-based medium or tied onto slabs of cork or tree-fern. Propagation is by division.

Epidendrum barbeyanum
☀ ❄ ↔ 4–10 in (10–25 cm) ↕ 4–10 in (10–25 cm)
Epidendrum barbeyanum is a native of Central America. This species produces succulent growths that in spring and summer give rise to small showy heads of apple green 2 in (5 cm) flowers with broad labellums. When in cultivation, this orchid is most comfortable with moist conditions throughout the year. Zones 10–12.

Epidendrum barbeyanum

Epiblastus basilis

× *Epicattleya* Siam Jade

E

Epidendrum ciliare

☀/◐ ⚘ ↔ 8–36 in (20–90 cm)
↕ 8–24 in (20–60 cm)

From Central America. Looks like a *Cattleya* in growth habit, but without the telltale floral sheath. A variable species that can produce inflorescences of up to 8 spidery, green, 40 in (10 cm) flowers with a white labellum in summer and autumn. It needs strong light and a dry winter rest to bloom. Zones 10–12.

Epidendrum elongatum

☀/◐ ⚘ ↔ 8–48 in (20–120 cm)
↕ 8–36 in (20–90 cm)

From Central America. Common terrestrial species that comes in a range of colors. It is one of the "reed-stem" epidendrums that produce ¾ in (18 mm) spherical heads of blooms throughout the year. Zones 10–12.

Epidendrum ibaguense

☀/◐ ⚘ ↔ 8–48 in (20–120 cm)
↕ 8–48 in (20–120 cm)

From Central and South America. A common and widespread species, the classic "reed-stem" or "crucifix" orchid that is popular in horticulture. Spherical heads, 1¼ in (30 mm) across, of red to orange blooms with a modified yellowish labellum. It requires strong light, and in favorable conditions will continue to bloom throughout the year. Zones 9–12.

Epidendrum ilense ★

◐ ⚘ ↔ 8–24 in (20–60 cm)
↕ 8–48 in (20–120 cm)

From Ecuador. An amazing species that bears bizarre 1½ in (35 mm) flowers with somewhat bland pinkish green petals and sepals but a highly specialized white labellum fringed with long fine hairs. The flowers are produced in small bunches that hang down from the tall pseudobulbs. This showy species requires consistently warm moist conditions; large plants may flower constantly, as they re-bloom from the same stem for many years. Zones 11–12.

Epidendrum parkinsonianum ★

☀/◐ ⚘ ↔ 8–24 in (20–60 cm)
↕ 1–7 ft (0.3–2 m)

From Central America. A pendulous species that is worth growing just for its succulent purple-stained foliage. Older plants can grow up to 7 ft (2 m) long. In the spring it produces up to 4 large, 5 in (12 cm), greenish flowers with a pure white labellum. Best grown on large slabs of cork or tree-fern, or allowed to hang from small wooden baskets. Zones 10–12.

Epidendrum pseudepidendrum

◐ ⚘ ↔ 4–16 in (10–40 cm)
↕ 8–40 in (20–100 cm)

From Costa Rica and Panama. Warm-growing, tall, "reed-stem" type, producing one of the most spectacular flowers in the genus. Glossy flowers, 3 in (8 cm) tall, with apple green petals and sepals and a broad, protruding, bright orange to red labellum through the summer. The column is green, orange, and pink. Zones 11–12.

Epidendrum Hybrids

☀/◐ ⚘ ↔ 8–48 in (20–120 cm)
↕ 8–48 in (20–120 cm)

The most common types in cultivation are the "reed-stem" hybrid or "crucifix" orchids, which come in a range of colors, with deep reds predominating. All have globular heads of blooms that can re-bloom off the same flowering stem many times. While many of the older hybrids can grow up to 48 in (120 cm) tall, hybridists have been successful in selecting for plants that are more compact growing, up to 24 in (60 cm) tall, with larger and more brightly colored flowers. Of the new cultivars, **Hokulea 'Santa Barbara'** ★ is one of the finest, with a compact growing habit and boldly colored blooms; **Venus Valley 'Lemon'** bears yellow flowers. White-flowering forms have also been developed. Zones 9–12.

Epidendrum ibaguense

Epidendrum elongatum

Epidendrum ilense

Epidendrum parkinsonianum

Epidendrum ciliare

Epidendrum, Hybrid, Eagle Valley 'Naranja' × Star Valley 'Yamada'

Epidendrum, Hybrid, Hokulea 'Santa Barbara'

Epidendrum, Hybrid, Joseph Glow 'Seto Raspberry'

E., Hybrid, Orange Glow 'Fiesta' × Star Valley 'Yamada'

E., Hybrid, Orange Glow 'Dusk' × Star Valley 'Red Rounder'

E., Hybrid, Joseph Lii 'Reiddy'

E., Hybrid, Orange Glow

E., Hybrid, Pele 'Pretty Princess'

Epidendrum, Hybrid, white form

E., Hybrid, Venus Valley 'Lemon'

EPIGAEA

A genus of 3 small, prostrate, evergreen shrubs in the heath (Ericaceae) family. Their distribution is interesting, with one species each from North America, Japan, and Turkey. Among the hardiest broadleaf evergreens, they make charming additions to a rockery in a cool temperate climate. The leaves are pointed oval with a heart-shaped base, usually deep green and glossy, sometimes red-tinted in winter. Clusters of tiny, bell-shaped, erica-like flowers appear in spring at the branch tips and in the leaf axils.
CULTIVATION: Although requiring some sunlight to flower well, these are cool climate plants that appreciate being shaded from the hottest sun and freedom from drought. Plant in cool, moist, humus-rich soil in dappled sunlight and water well in summer. Unless the seed is required, remove the spent flowers and trim any lanky shoots to keep the plant tidy. Propagation can be from the seed, which is very fine, or from small tip cuttings, and also by air-layering.

Epigaea repens
MAYFLOWER, TRAILING ARBUTUS
☼ ❄ ↔ 12–24 in (30–60 cm)
↑ 4–8 in (10–20 cm)

A native of North America, with a low spreading habit. The leaves are 1–3 in (25–75 mm) long and half as wide. The racemes of 4 to 6 sweetly scented white to pale pink flowers are about ½ in (12 mm) long. Zones 2–9.

EPILOBIUM
WILLOW HERB

A genus of about 200 species of perennials, annuals, and subshrubs belongs to the evening-primrose (Onagraceae) family. Many species are invasive, and spread by runners and prolific seeding. Some of the showier species are cultivated and can spread quickly. They are

Epimedium franchetii 'Brimstone Butterfly'

Epilobium angustifolium, in the wild, Grand Teton National Park, Wyoming, USA

found throughout the world in climates ranging from temperate to tropical or polar, varying greatly in habit. The clusters of 4-petalled flowers, in various shades of purple, pink, yellow, and white, are borne in the leaf axils or at the branch tips.
CULTIVATION: Best suited to wild gardens or areas where they can spread freely. Grow in full sun in moisture-retentive soil. Alpine species need perfect drainage and protection from the hottest sun. Propagation is from seed or cuttings.

Epilobium angustifolium
syn. *Chamaenerion angustifolium*
FIREWEED, FRENCH WILLOW, GREAT WILLOW HERB, ROSEBAY WILLOW HERB
☼ ❄ ↔ 3–8 ft (0.9–2.4 m)
↑ 3–8 ft (0.9–2.4 m)

Found throughout the Northern Hemisphere. Invasive vigorous perennial. Willowy stems of narrow alternately arranged leaves. Racemes of pink or purplish pink flowers in summer–early autumn. Zones 3–9.

EPIMEDIUM
BARRENWORT, BISHOP'S HAT, BISHOP'S MITRE, HORNY GOAT WEED

A genus of 44 species at present, and still growing. Of this number, 36 have been discovered since 1975. Both evergreen and deciduous, they are clumping to slightly running perennials in the barberry (Berberidaceae) family that are found mainly in Asia but extend to the Mediterranean. They have attractive foliage, which is often their biggest asset, and the dainty

Epimedium acuminatum

spring flowers occur in a range of colors, often with long curved spurs. In China the dried roots are thought to cure male sexual dysfunction.
CULTIVATION: Most species prefer a cool shaded aspect under deciduous trees in humus-rich soil; many are surprisingly drought tolerant once established. Propagate by division in the late winter.

Epimedium acuminatum
☼ ❄ ↔ 36–40 in (90–100 cm)
↑ 10–18 in (25–45 cm)

From China. Evergreen. Leaves with 3 long tapered leaflets per leaf, bronze brown when young, turning green with age. Flowers with long, spurred, white sepals with purple petals, are ¾ in (18 mm) across, borne on fine arching stems, in spring and often well into the summer. Zones 5–9.

Epimedium alpinum
☼ ❄ ↔ 12–32 in (30–80 cm)
↑ 10–12 in (25–30 cm)

From southern Europe. More or less evergreen, with 5 to 9 spiny-edged leaflets that are bronze in winter. The

Epimedium davidii

flowers are small, spurless, about ½ in (12 mm) across, and dusty cherry red with a cream center. Zones 5–9.

Epimedium × cantabrigiense
☼ ❄ ↔ 12–18 in (30–45 cm)
↑ 12–24 in (30–60 cm)

Of garden origin. Heart-shaped evergreen leaves, downy beneath, with a few marginal spines. Stems of dainty red and pale yellow flowers in spring. Zones 5–9.

Epimedium davidii
☼ ❄ ↔ 16–20 in (40–50 cm)
↑ 10–12 in (25–30 cm)

From western China. Evergreen; the 3 leaflets are bright green in summer. Long-spurred lemon yellow flowers, to ¼ in (18 mm) across. Zones 5–9.

Epimedium franchetii
☼ ❄ ↔ 36–40 in (90–100 cm)
↑ 10–18 in (25–45 cm)

From China. The foliage is very like *E. acuminatum*, but the long spurred flowers are a soft pale yellow throughout. 'Brimstone Butterfly', yellow flowers. Zones 5–9.

Epimedium sempervirens

Epimedium grandiflorum

Epimedium × perralchicum

Epimedium × setosum

Epimedium pinnatum subsp. colchicum

Epimedium grandiflorum

☀ ❄ ↔ 8–12 in (20–30 cm)
↕ 8–12 in (20–30 cm)

From Japan, China, and Northern Korea. Widespread more or less deciduous species with heart-shaped leaves and a clumping habit. Small spurred flowers in shades of white, yellow, pink or purple. More selected clones than any other species. 'Lilacinum', lilac flowers; 'Lilafee', magenta flowers; 'Rose Queen' ★, deep pink flowers with white-tipped spurs. Zones 5–9.

Epimedium × perralchicum

☀ ❄ ↔ 20–24 in (50–60 cm)
↕ 14–16 in (35–40 cm)

Hybrid between E. perralderianum and E. pinnatum subsp. colchicum that was discovered at Wisley Gardens in the UK. Forms large solid clumps of evergreen foliage, bronze when young, and has sprays of bright yellow spurless flowers. 'Frohnleiten', German selection with spikier foliage and larger flowers. Zones 7–9.

Epimedium perralderianum

☀ ❄ ↔ 20–24 in (50–60 cm)
↕ 14–16 in (35–40 cm)

From northern Africa. Slowly spreading evergreen with a slowly spreading habit. Leaves with 3 toothed leaflets, bronze ageing to green. Yellow flowers with short brown spurs. Zones 7–9.

Epimedium pinnatum

☀ ❄ ↔ 8–12 in (20–30 cm) ↕ 8–12 in (20–30 cm)

From northern Iran. Slowly spreading evergreen. Spiny-edged leaves. Yellow flowers, ¾ in (18 mm) across, with tiny brown spurs. E. p. subsp. colchicum, most commonly grown form, with less spiny foliage and a tighter clumping habit. Zones 6–9.

Epimedium × rubrum

☀ ❄ ↔ 10–12 in (25–30 cm)
↕ 10–12 in (25–30 cm)

Clump-forming garden hybrid between E. alpinum and E. grandiflorum with pointed spiny-edged leaves that are reddish when young and also in winter. Crimson and soft lemon flowers with short spurs, ¾ in (18 mm) across. Zones 5–10.

Epimedium sempervirens

☀ ❄ ↔ 10–12 in (25–30 cm)
↕ 10–12 in (25–30 cm)

From Japan and Korea. An evergreen species similar to E. grandiflorum. Rich green leaves, bronze at first. Small, white, spurred flowers. Zones 7–9.

Epimedium × setosum

☀ ❄ ↔ 16–20 in (40–50 cm)
↕ 8–12 in (20–30 cm)

Species native to Japan. The leaves are bronze-tinged, slightly furry to start, when they are young. It bears small white flowers that are more or less spurless. Zones 7–9.

Epimedium × versicolor

☀ ❄ ↔ 10–12 in (25–30 cm)
↕ 10–12 in (25–30 cm)

Range of evergreen clump-forming garden hybrids between E. grandiflorum and E. pinnatum subsp. colchicum. The spiny-edged leaves are often richly colored with bronze when young. The flowers have short spurs that do not exceed the length of the calyx. The cultivar, 'Neosulphureum', produces soft lemon flowers; 'Sulphureum' has bright yellow flowers with slightly longer spurs. Zones 5–9.

Epimedium × warleyense

☀ ❄ ↔ 24–32 in (60–80 cm)
↕ 16–20 in (40–50 cm)

A garden hybrid between E. alpinum and E. pinnatum subsp. colchicum bred by the famous Miss Ellen Willmott in about 1909 at her equally famous property, Warley Place, in Essex, UK. This species forms sizeable open clumps. The flowers, which are spurless, are burnt orange with a yellow center. The new foliage is an attractive bronze color. Zones 5–9.

Epimedium × versicolor

Epimedium × youngianum

☀ ❄ ↔ 10–12 in (25–30 cm)
↕ 8–12 in (20–30 cm)

Hybrids between E. diphyllum and E. grandiflorum with usually spineless leaflets that are attractively bronzed when young. The small spurless flowers can be white through to rose pink. 'Niveum', charming cultivar with white flowers, richly colored new foliage. Zones 5–9.

EPIPHYLLUM

A genus of 19 species of epiphytic and lithophytic cacti (family Cactaceae) from Mexico, Central America, northern South America, and the Caribbean. Named from the Greek epi, upon, and phyllon, leaf, referring to the very large, white, night-blooming flowers, borne on leaf-like stems. While many plants in collections and nurseries are labeled orchid cacti or Epiphyllum hybrids, the term orchid cactus is more correctly applied to hybrids of the genera Selenicereus, Schlumbergera, Disocactus, and Pseudorhipsalis, with flowers that are neither night-blooming nor white. Many so-called Epiphyllum hybrids have no Epiphyllum ancestry at all. Stems of true Epiphyllum species are usually long and bear aerial roots; they are round in cross-section in the lower part but usually flattened and leaf-like toward the tips, with scalloped or toothed margins. The flowers often have very long floral tubes; outer perianth segments are whitish, yellowish, or pinkish, inner petal-like ones are pale yellow or white. Seed pods are oval to ovate, ridged, and spineless.

Epimedium × versicolor 'Sulphureum'

Epimedium × youngianum 'Niveum'

Epiphyllum oxypetalum

CULTIVATION: Easily grown in organic, rich, well-drained soil. Fertilize when the flower buds are forming; they may also be lightly fertilized during the growing period. Withhold water for 1 to 2 weeks after flowering. Propagate from seed or, more usually, from cuttings dried out for a week or two.

Epiphyllum hookeri
syn. *Epiphyllum stenopetalum*

☀ ✲ ↔ 3–5 ft (0.9–1.5 m)
↑ 30 in (75 cm)

From Mexico, Central America, and Venezuela. Bushy plants with arching to pendent branches, 3-angled at the base, becoming flattened, with areoles 2 in (5 cm) apart. Bears white flowers that open widely to 1½ in (3.5 cm) across, with straight narrow petals and tube, to 10 in (25 cm) long, in the summer. The seed pods are purplish to red. Zones 10–12.

Epiphyllum oxypetalum ★

☀ ✲ ↔ 5–10 ft (1.5–4.5 m)
↑ 5–10 ft (1.5–3 m)

From Mexico and Central America. Profuse arching to pendent branches. Main stems flattened at tips, thin, with scalloped wavy margins. White funnel-shaped flowers, 5–7 in (12–17 cm) across, borne on long curved tubes with maroon-colored outer segments, in summer. Crimson-red seed pods, fragrant when ripe. Zones 10–12.

EPIPREMNUM

This genus of some 15 species found from Southeast Asia to the western Pacific belongs to the arum (Araceae) family. They are evergreen climbers with distinct juvenile and mature phases. Adhesive roots emerge from aerial stems. The leaves are ovate to oblong or lanceolate, often pinnately divided or lobed, but entire on young

Epipremnum pinnatum 'Aureum'

plants. The leaf stalks have a "knee" and sheathe the stem at the base. In mature leaves veins are parallel. The inflorescence stalk is solitary. The spathe does not form a tube, and is purple to yellow or green and deciduous; the spadix is short and included within the spathe, and is covered with hermaphrodite flowers. The seeds are kidney-shaped and have tough coats. These climbers closely resemble species of *Monstera*.

CULTIVATION: In tropical regions species of *Epipremnum* are grown as scramblers up trees, but in temperate regions they are usually seen as house plants or trained up sphagnum poles in greenhouses. A number of variegated forms are grown around villages in the western Pacific. The plants need filtered light and high humidity, but often they do not flower in cultivation, as flowering occurs only in the mature phase. Easily propagated from stem cuttings or cuttings made from shoot tips, by air-layering, or, less usually, from fresh seed.

Epipremnum pinnatum
syn. *Rhaphidophora pinnata*
FALSE MONSTERA

☀ ✲ ↔ 6 ft (1.8 m) ↑ 12–20 ft (3.5–6 m)

Found from Southeast Asia to New Guinea and in northern Queensland, Australia. An evergreen climber with a slender twining and branching stem. Downy, oval- to heart-shaped, pinnate leaves grow to 3 ft (0.9 m) long, with holes along the midrib. Cream tubular flowers are marked with purple. 'Aureum' (syns *Pothos aureus, Rhaphidophora aurea, Scindapsus aureus*) (commonly known as devil's ivy, golden pothos, hunter's robe), bright green heart-shaped leaves variegated with yellow or cream; 'Marble Queen', the stems and moss green leaves are streaked with white; 'Tricolor', the off-white stems and leaves are variegated with white. Zones 10–12.

EPISCIA

This genus, comprises 9 species from tropical America, belonging to the African violet (Gesneriaceae) family. They are epiphytic or terrestrial, sometimes subshrubby, herbs and are exceptional in the family in having runners. The leaves are opposite, often colored, and in equal or unequal pairs; when unequal the smaller one is often deciduous. The flowers are borne in stalked racemes in the leaf axils, and may be clustered or solitary. The calyx has 5 green or colored sepals, which are sometimes joined at the base. The corolla is funnel-shaped with 5 spreading lobes, which may be smooth-edged or have fringed margins. The fruit is a 2-valved capsule containing many elliptical seeds.

CULTIVATION: In temperate areas *Episcia* need greenhouse culture and are often grown in hanging baskets, but in the tropics they can be grown as ground cover or used in bedding schemes. These plants are difficult to overwinter in the poor light of temperate regions, but can be readily propagated from cuttings, which root easily, or from seed. Many hybrids have been raised.

Episcia cupreata
CARPET PLANT, FLAME VIOLET

☀/☀ ✲ ↔ 12–24 in (30–60 cm)
↑ 8–12 in (20–30 cm)

Native to Central and South America (southern Mexico to Ecuador). Evergreen creeping perennial. Leaves oval, brown to dark green, wrinkled, downy, to 3½ in (9 cm) long, flecked with copper and purple underneath. Clusters of scarlet flowers with a yellow ring, throat sometimes spotted with purple, in summer. Good plants for hanging baskets. 'Acajou', lighter-colored leaves with silvery markings; 'Chocolate Soldier', very large brown leaves with a silvery gray center band; 'Country Cowgirl', silvery green pebble-textured leaves with copper-green margins; 'Metallica', copper leaves marked with silver, red flowers; 'Silver Sheen', bright copper-green margins, yellow, lilac, or red flowers; 'Tetra', large orange-red flowers with wavy lobes, orange-yellow inside; 'Tropical Topaz', bright yellow flowers. Zones 10–12.

Episcia dianthiflora
syn. *Alsobia dianthiflora*
LACE-FLOWER VINE

☀/☀ ✲ ↔ 18–36 in (60–90 cm)
↑ 8 in (20 cm)

This species is found from southern Mexico to Costa Rica. It is a low-growing evergreen perennial with leaves of dark green, which are toothed, elliptical to oval-shaped, to 1¾ in (40 mm) long, and often veined with purple-red. The solitary, pearly white, tubular flowers, borne in summer, are spotted with purple at the base, with their rounded petals conspicuously fringed. Zones 10–12.

Episcia cupreata

Episcia cupreata 'Acajou'

Episcia Hybrid Cultivars

☼/◐ ⚘ ↔ 32–40 in (80–100 cm)
↕ 8–20 in (20–50 cm)

Episcia species interbreed quite freely, which has resulted in many hybrid cultivars appearing in cultivation. The best of these tend to be compact plants that flower heavily and often have interesting marked foliage. **'Chocolate 'n' Cherries'**, very dark bronze foliage, yellow-dotted bright red flowers; **'Star of Bethlehem'**, dark bronze leaves with red undersides, distinctive bright pink flowers with a broad white margin; **'Toy Silver'**, a very dwarf cultivar, with leaves of dark green, heavily marbled and veined with silver-gray, bright red flowers. Zones 10–12.

EPITHELANTHA

This genus of beautiful diminutive plants in the cactus (Cactaceae) family comprises just 2 species, one of which has 5 subspecies, and is found in the Chihuahua Desert regions of Arizona, New Mexico, and Texas, USA, and Coahuila, San Luis Potosi, and Nuevo Leon, Mexico. They resemble the genus *Mammillaria* but bear flowers on the ends of the tubercles rather than between them. The genus name is derived from two Greek words, *epi* (on) and *thelos* (nipple), referring to the plant's tubercles. The spines and growth habit vary. The plants contain hallucinogenic chemicals and are occasionally ingested by the shamans of native tribes as part of their diagnostic rituals when healing the sick.

CULTIVATION: Not easily grown, because these plants do not like compost or wet feet. They need sandy, loamy, well-drained, mineralized soil. Withhold water in winter and again in midsummer. Propagate from seed or from cuttings that have been dried out for a week or two.

Epithelantha micromeris

☼ ⚘ ↔ 2½ in (6 cm)
↕ ¾–1¾ in (18–40 mm)

From eastern Arizona, New Mexico, and western Texas, USA, and northern Mexico. Small, neat, solitary to clustering, white to grayish white plants with a depressed growing tip. No central spine but 20 to 25 white radial spines, 1/8–½ in (3–12 mm) long.

Equisetum giganteum

Equisetum telmateia

Pink to white flowers in summer. Red seed pods. *E. m.* subsp. *unguispina*, similar to the type species but usually clustering with age and with a distinct, slightly curved, black-tipped central spine. Zones 9–11.

EQUISETUM

HORSETAIL, SCOURING-RUSH

This genus of about 25 unusual, rush-like, flowerless, perennial herbs from the scouring-rush (Equisetaceae) family is found worldwide, except in Australia and New Zealand. All species consist of clumps of erect, cylindrical, jointed, bamboo-like stems. The leaves are minute and are usually reduced to a ring of black or brown teeth at the stem nodes, but are sometimes longer, thin, straggly, and wiry. The spore-bearing cones are located at the tips of the stems. These plants resemble a horse's tail; they are called "scouring-rush" because early American settlers used them for cleaning pots. They are also used in Japanese flower arrangements.

CULTIVATION: Plant around water features such as marshes, using garden soil or potting mix kept moist and well drained; pots may be stood in water. Propagate from spores or by division of rhizomes, burying the stem segments directly in the soil.

Equisetum arvense

COMMON HORSETAIL, FIELD HORSETAIL

☼ ❄ ↔ 12–18 in (30–45 cm)
↕ 16–24 in (40–60 cm)

This species is found across Europe, North America, Asia, and Greenland. A very hardy perennial with irregularly spaced dense whorls of sterile green stems, to 24 in (60 cm) tall, prostrate or erect, slightly rough, and furrowed. Short-lived, light brown, branching stems are smooth and fertile. The fine foliage is feathery and bright green. Zones 2–9.

Equisetum arvense

Equisetum giganteum

GIANT HORSETAIL

☼ ⚘ ↔ 18–24 in (45–60 cm)
↕ 9–12 ft (2.7–3.5 m)

Native to the American tropics. This is a vigorous, colonizing, rush-like perennial. The erect green stems, 1 in (2.5 cm) in diameter, have thin dark brown or black bands at the nodes and lean on surrounding plants for support. Zones 10–12.

Equisetum hyemale

DUTCH RUSH, HORSETAIL RUSH, ROUGH HORSETAIL, SCOURING-RUSH, WINTER SCOURING-RUSH

☼ ❅ ↔ 12–24 in (30–60 cm)
↕ 3–5 ft (0.9–1.5 m)

Found in Eurasia and North America. An evergreen rush-like perennial that forms large colonies. The unbranched stems are rough, broad, rounded, ridged, to 5 ft (1.5 m) tall, with gray and black bands. Cones at the tips of the stems have a minute point at their tip. **'Robustum'**, larger form, to 10 ft (3 m) tall. Zones 3–10.

Equisetum telmateia

GIANT HORSETAIL

☼ ❄ ↔ 12–24 in (30–60 cm)
↕ 20 in–6 ft (0.5–1.8 m)

Native to Eurasia, north Africa, and northern North America. Perennial. Erect, finely grooved, ivory white or

Episcia, HC, 'Chocolate 'n' Cherries'

Episcia, HC, 'Star of Bethlehem'

Episcia, Hybrid Cultivar, 'Toy Silver'

pale green, sterile stems, to 6 ft (1.8 m) tall, with smoothly ridged nodes and whorls of numerous simple, rough, feathery branches. Can be too invasive for domestic gardens. Zones 5–10.

ERAGROSTIS
LOVE GRASS

This genus of about 250 species of clumping annuals or perennials, belonging to the grass (Poaceae) family, is native to tropical and subtropical North and South America, South Africa, and Australia. The leaves are narrow, and can be either rolled or flat, with glandular sheaths. The flowerheads are open or form dense panicles of closely overlapping 2- to many-flowered spikelets. CULTIVATION: These plants are drought tolerant and prefer a sunny position in well-drained sandy soil, but will also tolerate heavy clay. Propagate most species from seed and some by division of the rhizomes.

Eragrostis australasica
BAMBOO GRASS, CANE GRASS
☼ ❄ ↔ 7–15 ft (2–4.5 m)
↑ 3–10 ft (0.9–3 m)

From inland areas in all mainland States of Australia, where it grows around lakes and swamps and in depressions that are flooded in wet periods. Stems branching, bamboo-like,

Eranthis hyemalis

Eranthemum pulchellum

to just under ½ in (1 cm) in diameter; leaves flat or rolled, to 8 in (20 cm) long. Flowering panicles, to 10 in (25 cm) long, with long spikelets, to ½ in (12 mm) long, in spring–summer. Propagate by division of the rhizomes. Zones 9–11.

Eragrostis curvula
AFRICAN LOVE GRASS, WEEPING LOVE GRASS
☼ ❄ ↔ 9–12 in (22–30 cm)
↑ 3–4 ft (0.9–1.2 m)

From South Africa. Clumping, tufted, perennial grass. Simple narrow leaves, to 12 in (30 cm) long, rough to the touch, green in summer, becoming yellow to bronze in winter. Erect flower stalks in summer–autumn. Zones 7–10.

ERANTHEMUM

Native to tropical regions in Asia and within the acanthus (Acanthaceae) family, this genus consists of about 30 shrubby perennial herbs and evergreen shrubs with opposite simple leaves. They produce dense branched spikes or panicles of flowers with slender tubular corollas in the spring. CULTIVATION: All species thrive in light, rich, medium loams in a semi-shaded or protected position provided they have ample moisture. Propagate from cuttings of younger wood taken in the spring.

Eranthemum pulchellum
syn. *Eranthemum nervosum*
BLUE SAGE
☼ ✿ ↔ 3 ft (0.9 m) ↑ 4 ft (1.2 m)
From India. Evergreen shrub. Slightly toothed, prominently veined, glossy, green leaves, 4–8 in (10–20 cm) long. Feathery flower spikes, about 3 in (8 cm) long, bear tubular vivid blue flowers, 1¼ in (30 mm) across, with deep purple throats and green, papery, pointed bracts. Zones 10–12.

Eragrostis australasica, in the wild, Carnegie, Western Australia

ERANTHIS
WINTER ACONITE

In the wild these small tuberous plants from the buttercup (Ranunculaceae) family are found in the damp deciduous woodlands of Europe and Asia, where their golden flowers do much to enliven bleak late-winter landscapes. In similar cool, damp, summer-shady situations they colonize and extend their territory. The cupped flowers, each held on a single stem, are encircled with pronounced green "ruffs." CULTIVATION: Transplant in early spring while the plants are in leaf; they can be temperamental if transplanted when dry during the summer months. Aphids and birds can cause damage. Grow in moisture-retentive soil, with plenty of winter sun. Propagate by dividing the tubers or from seed.

Eranthis hyemalis
☼ ❄ ↔ 3–4 in (8–10 cm)
↑ 3–4 in (8–10 cm)

From southern France to Bulgaria; now naturalized over a far wider range. The brilliant golden flowers, like buttercups, often appearing before snow-melt, held on short curved stems. Stems elongate and straighten as the flower develops from a diameter of ¼ in (6 mm) to about 1 in (25 mm) across. Basal leaves emerge after the flowers fade, and are bright green, lobed, and circular. Plant beneath deciduous trees in alkaline soils. Zones 5–8.

Eranthis × tubergenii 'Guinea Gold'
☼ ❄ ↔ 3–4 in (8–10 cm)
↑ 4–8 in (10–20 cm)

A tough, vigorous, but sterile hybrid, product of *E. hyemalis* and *E. cilicica*. Given the right conditions, it quickly expands into decent-sized clumps. The flamboyant flowers are yellow, large, and held above bronzed "ruffs." Zones 5–8.

Eragrostis curvula

EREMOPHILA

This genus of about 200 species belongs to the boobialla (Myoporaceae) family and is a native of mainland Australia, with most species occurring in semi-arid and arid areas. They are evergreen shrubs or small trees, often with felted or resinous leaves, stems, and floral parts. The 2-lipped tubular flowers, on short to long stalks emerging from the leaf axils, are variously lobed and may be white, yellow, violet, purple, pink, or red, and sometimes have a spotted interior. The fruits are berry-like drupes, the seed enclosed in a tough corky or fibrous layer. Popular as ornamental shrubs in drier regions, and many thrive in alkaline soils. Some are available as grafted plants, making those species from dry areas easier to grow in the higher-rainfall areas. Many *Eremophila* species are attractive to nectar-feeding birds. CULTIVATION: Marginally frost hardy, most species do not like moist humid conditions. They prefer a position with excellent drainage in an open sunny area with plenty of air movement. Regular light pruning encourages vigorous growth. These plants are propagated most readily from half-hardened cuttings; in fact, germination is only practicable if the seed is first extracted from the tough inner fruit layer, and the sowing medium is treated thoroughly with a fungicide.

Eremophila nivea

Eremophila maculata

Eremophila maculata 'Aurea'

Eremophila maculata 'Pink Beauty'

Eremophila glabra
COMMON EMU BUSH, FUCHSIA BUSH

☼ ❄ ↔ 3–10 ft (0.9–3 m) ↕ 5 ft (1.5 m)

Occurring throughout arid and semi-arid regions of Australia. Prostrate or erect evergreen shrub with narrow mid-green to grayish leaves. The orange, yellow, red, or green tubular flowers are borne for much of the year. 'Murchison River' ★, compact plant, soft silvery gray foliage, bright red flowers. Zones 9–11.

Eremophila laanii
EMU BUSH

☼ ❄ ↔ 3 ft (0.9 m) ↕ 5 ft (1.5 m)

This species is restricted to the Carnarvon–Meekatharra region of Australia. Green leaves, to 2 in (5 cm) long. Bears pink tubular flowers in winter–spring. Grows well in heavy soils; wind tolerant. A good plant for

growing in containers. 'Rodger's Pink', compact plant, gray-green foliage, soft pink flowers. Zones 9–11.

Eremophila maculata
SPOTTED EMU BUSH

☼ ❄ ↔ 3–10 ft (0.9–3 m) ↕ 3–8 ft (0.9–2.4 m)

Occurs across the length and breadth of mainland Australia. Compact dense shrub with gray-green leaves, to 2 in (5 cm) long; young leaves often downy. Red, purple, pink, or yellow flowers, often spotted with darker blotches, in autumn–spring. 'Aurea', a compact habit to about 3 ft (100 cm), with light green leaves, yellow flowers; 'Carmine Star', low shrub, to 20 in (50 cm) high, purplish young branches, carmine flowers, the insides paler and with prominent carmine spots; 'Pink Beauty',

Eremophila mitchellii

10–12 ft (3–3.5 m) tall, bears profuse bluish pink flowers, 1½ in (35 mm) across, in late winter. Zones 9–11.

Eremophila mitchellii
BUDDA, FALSE SANDALWOOD

☼ ❄ ↔ 12 ft (3.5 m) ↕ 30 ft (9 m)

Native to inland northern New South Wales and Queensland, Australia. This resinous aromatic shrub or small tree has shiny linear leaves to 2½ in (6 cm) long. The small, lightly perfumed, bell-shaped flowers are white to creamy pink with lightly spotted throats, 2 to 3 in each leaf axil, in spring and again in autumn. Zones 9–11.

Eremophila nivea

☼ ❄ ↔ 5 ft (1.5 m) ↕ 5 ft (1.5 m)

From Western Australia's "wheatbelt," east of Perth. A beautiful silvery gray shrub. Erect stems covered in dense white hairs. Small, velvety gray, linear leaves. Tubular lilac flowers, borne in upper leaf axils, in winter–spring. Dislikes humidity; best in an open sunny position. An excellent container plant. Zones 9–11.

Eremophila polyclada
FLOWERING LIGNUM

☼ ❄ ↔ 3–6 ft (0.9–1.8 m) ↕ 3–6 ft (0.9–1.8 m)

From arid central and eastern Australia. Open mound-like shrub with sprawling branches and thin light green leaves; leafless in drier periods. White or pale pink tubular flowers, 1½ in (35 mm) long, with spreading lobes and conspicuously spotted throats in spring and sporadically throughout the year. Suitable for dry inland gardens, especially in heavy soils. Zones 9–11.

EREMURUS
DESERT CANDLE, FOXTAIL LILY

This genus of 40 to 50 species of fleshy-stemmed perennials belongs to the asphodel (Asphodelaceae) family.

They are native to western and central Asia, where they grow in dry areas among rocks and in grassland. These statuesque plants form basal clumps of strap-shaped leaves and send up flower spikes to 10 ft (3 m) tall. The white, pink, or yellow flowers are borne in tapering spikes and resemble small starry lilies. Their prominently protruding stamens give the spike a soft fluffy appearance.
CULTIVATION: Grow in a rich, well-drained, sandy soil in sheltered position in full sun. Stake taller species. Protect from winter wet with mulch; remove before new growth emerges. Protect new growth from slugs and snails. Propagate from seed or divide carefully, avoiding damage to the fragile roots.

Eremurus himalaicus

☼ ❄ ↔ 30 in (75 cm) ↕ 36–48 in (90–120 cm)

From Afghanistan and northwestern Himalayas. One of the first species to flower in early summer. Narrow strap-shaped leaves. Bears dense heads of white, starry, lily-like flowers with protruding stamens in the late spring–summer. Zones 3–9.

Eremurus robustus

☼ ❄ ↔ 36–48 in (90–120 cm) ↕ 7–10 ft (2–3 m)

Native to Tajikistan, Kyrgyzstan, and Afghanistan. Vigorous species with

Eremophila polyclada

Eremophila laanii 'Rodger's Pink'

Eremurus, Hybrid Cultivar, 'Cleopatra'

Eremurus, Hybrid Cultivar, 'Moneymaker'

leaves to 4 ft (1.2 m) long, often deciduous before flowering. Very showy densely packed spikes of pink flowers marked with brown and green in summer. Zones 6–9.

Eremurus stenophyllus
☼ ❄ ↔ 24–36 in (60–90 cm)
↕ 36–60 in (90–150 cm)

Found in central Asia and the western Himalayas. Bears dense tapering spikes of clear yellow flowers in summer. The flowers fade to orangey brown, giving a two-toned effect. Zones 5–9.

Eremurus Hybrid Cultivars
☼ ❄ ↔ 24–40 in (60–100 cm)
↕ 4–7 ft (1.2–2 m)

Most Eremurus hybrids originate from the cross E. × isabellinus (E. olgae × E. stenophyllus), which has resulted in a number of free-flowering hybrid groups in white and various shades of

pink, amber, orange, and yellow. 'Cleopatra' ★, deep orange flowers; **Erfo Hybrids**, to 5–6 ft (1.5–1.8 m) tall, pastel flowers; **Highdown Hybrids**, richly colored, flower in summer: 'Himrob', pink flowers, late-flowering; **Ruiter Hybrids**, to 7 ft (2 m), brightly colored: 'Moneymaker', yellow flowers ageing to orange; **Shelford Hybrids**, to 4 ft (1.2 m), richly colored flowers in early summer. Zones 5–9.

ERIA

The orchid genus *Eria* (family Orchidaceae) is widespread through tropical Asia, New Guinea, Australia, and Polynesia. Despite having several hundred representatives, only a very small percentage of these are in cultivation. The individual flowers last for less than a week, but plants often bloom a number of times during the year. Some of the species are quite spectacular when in flower, and make up for the small size of their blooms by the large numbers they produce. There is enormous diversity within this sympodial genus, which is related to *Dendrobium*, with a number of distinct plant forms. They generally occur as epiphytes, but some are lithophytes.
CULTIVATION: Most species are easy to cultivate as long as their moisture and temperature requirements are met. They like to grow in dappled light, but many will take strong light for part of the day. Some of the smaller-growing species perform best in pots; grow in a bark-based medium and keep moist while the plants are in active growth. The lowland species require year-round warm conditions, while those from the mountainous regions appreciate cooler temperatures. Propagation is by division.

Eria gigantea
☼ ⚘ ↔ 8–24 in (20–60 cm)
↕ 8–36 in (20–90 cm)

Native to the Philippines. Produces a number of spikes from the top of the matured pseudobulb and flowers sequentially over a couple of months. The ½ in (12 mm) pale yellow flowers that crowd the plant during its flowering period are thickly peppered with very small purple spots. Zones 10–11.

Eria pubescens
syn. *Eria flava*
☼ ⚘ ↔ 4–24 in (10–60 cm)
↕ 4–16 in (10–40 cm)

Found from Nepal to Indochina. This showy epiphyte produces mustard yellow to green blooms with a reddish purple labellum. The backs of the 1¼ in (30 mm) flowers, and the in-

florescence, are covered with white woolly hairs, giving them a felt-like texture. Zones 10–11.

Eria stricta
☼ ⚘ ↔ 4–10 in (10–25 cm) ↕ 4–10 in (10–25 cm)

From India and Nepal. Small tufted plant producing upright spikes of small (5 mm) creamy white flowers that all face the same way. The backs of the flowers are distinctly woolly. Zones 10–12.

ERICA

HEATH, HEATHER

This large genus gives its name to the heath (Ericaceae) family. It consists of about 750 species of evergreen shrubs, ranging from small subshrubs to trees, the great majority endemic to the Cape region of South Africa, the remainder scattered throughout East Africa, Madagascar, the Atlantic Islands, the Mediterranean region, and Europe. Habitats include wet and dry heathland and moorland. Most are only half-hardy; the European species are more frost hardy. The small linear leaves are linear with rolled edges, whorled, rarely opposite. The flowers are bell-shaped or tubular, in all colors except blue. Briar pipes are made from the woody root burls of *E. arborea*. Some species yield a yellow dye.
CULTIVATION: The winter-flowering heathers are lime tolerant and will grow in neutral and alkaline soil, while the summer-flowering ones like acid soil; both grow in neutral soil. Feed container-grown plants monthly during the growing season and give them plenty of water, reducing both feed and water during the dormant season. Propagation is from half-hardened cuttings taken from mid- to late summer or by air-layering in spring. The successful germination of some of the South African Cape heaths is helped by smoke treatment.

Eria gigantea

Erica canaliculata

Erica arborea

Erica capitata

Erica blenna

Erica arborea

BRUYERE, TREE HEATH

☼ ❊ ↔ 10 ft (3 m) ↑ 15 ft (4.5 m)

Native to southwest Europe, through the Mediterranean, and in the higher mountains of east Africa. This upright shrub has dark green leaves, grooved beneath. It bears pyramidal racemes of gray-white, scented, bell-shaped flowers in late spring. *E. a.* var. *alpina*, a smaller shrub, with dense cylindrical racemes of white flowers; *E. a.* 'Albert's Gold', carries golden leaves all year round, white flowers; 'Estrella Gold', compact yellow-green foliage, young growth is bright yellow, white flowers. Zones 7–10.

Erica australis

SOUTHERN HEATH, SPANISH HEATH

☼ ❊ ↔ 3 ft (0.9 m) ↑ 6 ft (1.8 m)

A species native to Portugal, western Spain, and Tangiers. An upright open shrub, with leaves of dark green, linear, and grooved beneath. The reddish pink tubular or bell-shaped flowers, are borne in umbel-like racemes on the previous year's wood, in late spring– early summer. Cultivars bloom in dif-ferent colors: 'Mr Robert' produces white flowers; 'Riverslea', lilac-pink flowers. Zones 8–10.

Erica blenna

CHINESE LANTERN HEATH

☼ ❊ ↔ 24 in (60 cm) ↑ 48 in (120 cm)

Found in the Western Cape region of South Africa. Upright evergreen shrub. Leaves are narrow, to ¾ in (18 mm) long, borne on finely hairy branches. The luminous orange flowers with green markings, form in clusters of 3, in winter–early spring. Zones 8–10.

Erica brachialis

☼ ❊ ↔ 2–4 ft (0.6–1.2 m) ↑ 3–10 ft (0.9–3 m)

From the Western Cape region of South Africa. This erect, very bushy, evergreen shrub has thick branches. The narrow smooth leaves are ¼ in (6 mm) long. Umbels of 1 to 5 short,

Erica carnea 'Foxhollow'

tubular, green to pale ocher-yellow flowers, are borne at the branch tips, in summer. Zones 9–10.

Erica canaliculata

☼ ❊ ↔ 4 ft (1.2 m) ↑ 6 ft (1.8 m)

From Western and Eastern Cape in South Africa. Erect shrub. Mid-green linear leaves in whorls; undersurfaces paler green, hairy. Produces whorls of 3 white to pale pink flowers at the ends of the branchlets in winter– spring. Zones 8–10.

Erica capitata

☼ ❊ ↔ 6–9 in (15–22 cm) ↑ 9–12 in (22–30 cm)

From the area around Cape Town, South Africa; now rare in the wild.

Erect evergreen shrub with ascending branches. Tiny narrow leaves, densely woolly underneath. Heads of up to 3 creamy white flowers, borne at the branch tips, in late spring. Sepals cov-ered with bright green hairs, giving the appearance of green flowers. Zones 8–9.

Erica carnea

syn. *Erica herbacea*

ALPINE HEATH, SNOW HEATH, WINTER HEATH

☼/☀ ❊ ↔ 22 in (55 cm) ↑ 12 in (30 cm)

From the Alps, northwest Italy, the northwest Balkans, and eastern Europe. Low-spreading shrub. Dark green linear leaves in whorls of 4. Bears purple-pink flowers in winter–spring. Tolerates some lime. 'Ann Sparkes', rose pink flowers, golden foliage with bronze tips; 'Challenger', green foliage, magenta flowers; 'December Red', deep pink flowers that turn red; 'Foxhollow', ro-bust shrub, lime green leaves, pinkish

Erica carnea 'Kramer's Rubin'

Erica carnea 'Ann Sparkes'

Erica cinerea 'Atrorubens'

Erica cinerea 'Atrosanguinea'

Erica cinerea 'Alice Ann Davies'

Erica cinerea 'C. D. Eason'

Erica cinerea 'Cindy'

white flowers; '**Kramer's Rubin**', blackish green foliage, flowers a dull deep pink; '**March Seedling**', flowers into late spring; '**Myretoun Ruby**' (syn. 'Myreton Ruby'), pink flowers deepening to crimson; **Pink Spangles**', deep pink flowers; '**Pirbright Rose**', compact form, rose pink flowers; '**R. B. Cooke**', mid-green leaves, pink flowers turning mauve; '**Springwood White**', vigorous, bright green foliage, abundant white flowers; '**Winter Beauty**', compact, masses of deep pink flowers. Zones 5–9.

Erica cerinthoides

☼ ⬗ ↔ 3 ft (0.9 m) ↕ 2–5 ft (0.6–1.5 m)
Species from Limpopo to Eastern Cape in South Africa, also native to Swaziland and Lesotho. The erect, hairy, gray-green leaves form in whorls. The small umbels of tubular flowers, to 1½ in (35 mm) long, are bright scarlet, occasionally pink or white, and borne at the branch tips, in winter–spring. *E. cerinthoides* should be pruned regularly for a denser plant. Zones 9–10.

Erica ciliaris

DORSET HEATH

☼ ❋ ↔ 20 in (50 cm) ↕ 24 in (60 cm)
From Ireland, southwest England, and southwest Europe. A spreading shrub. Whorls of gray to dark green lance-shaped leaves with downturned margins and a silvery undersurface. Racemes of urn-shaped lilac-pink flowers in mid-summer to autumn. '**Corfe Castle**', mid-green winter foliage turning bonze, rose pink flowers; '**David McClintock**', white flowers with pink throats; '**Egdon Heath**', gray-green foliage, pink flowers; '**Stapehill**', long-flowering off-white blooms that turn purple. Zones 7–9.

Erica cinerea

BELL HEATHER

☼ ❋ ↔ 30 in (65 cm) ↕ 24 in (60 cm)
From western Europe. Compact low-growing shrub. Bottle green leaves with rolled-under edges in whorls of 3. Racemes of urn-shaped flowers, at stem tips, in summer–early autumn, colors ranging from white to pink to purple. Cultivars include: '**Alba Major**', mid-green foliage, white flowers; '**Alba Minor**', dense habit, with profuse white blooms; '**Alice Ann Davies**', a vigorous spreader, with long spikes of dark pink blooms; '**Altadena**', chartreuse foliage; '**Atrorubens**', profuse bright rose purple flowers; '**Atrosanguinea**', bright reddish purple flowers; '**C. D. Eason**', broadly spreading low shrub, erect sprays of rose purple flowers; '**Cindy**', dwarf,

Erica carnea 'March Seedling'

Erica carnea 'Pink Spangles'

Erica carnea 'Pirbright Rose'

Erica carnea 'R. B. Cooke'

Erica cerinthoides

almost prostrate, with tight clusters of rose purple flowers; '**Fiddler's Gold**', leaves turning from gold to red in winter, lilac-pink flowers; '**Flamingo**', vigorous, spreading, bright rose pink flowers; '**Golden Drop**', mat-like habit, lilac-pink flowers; '**Katinka**', dark green foliage, black-purple flowers; '**Mrs E. A. Mitchell**', fine dark green foliage, dark red flowers; '**Pink Ice**', dwarf shrub, bearing soft rose pink flowers; '**Plummer's Seedling**', mound-forming, deep pinkish red flowers; '**Prostrate Lavender**', semi-prostrate, compact, lavender-pink flowers fading to white; '**Purple Beauty**', dwarf cultivar, dense heads of rose-purple flowers; '**Startler**', broadly spreading, with erect sprays of

Erica cinerea 'Golden Drop'

Erica cinerea 'Mrs E. A. Mitchell'

Erica × darleyensis 'Darley Dale'

bright rose flowers; '**Vivienne Patricia**', lax spreading habit, and mauve-pink flowers; and '**Wine**', spreading, semi-prostrate, dense spikes of rose pink blooms. Zones 5–9.

Erica cruenta

BLOOD RED HEATH

☼ ❄ ↔ 27 in (70 cm) ↑ 3 ft (0.9 m)
Native to the southwest Cape region of South Africa. This upright sparsely branched shrub carries dark green leaves in whorls of 3. Blood red tubular flowers held on the ends of lateral branches, prolonged flowering period. Hardy species. Prune regularly in first 2 years to promote growth. Zones 9–10.

Erica cinerea 'Plummer's Seedling'

Erica × darleyensis 'Margaret Porter'

Erica cruenta

Erica cubica

☼ ❄ ↔ 18 in (45 cm) ↑ 24 in (60 cm)
From southern South Africa. Erect, woody, evergreen shrub, with smooth branches, and needle-like leaves, ¼ in (6 mm) long. Pink to purple flowers, to ¾ in (18 mm) across, borne at the branch tips, in spring–summer. Zones 8–10.

Erica × darleyensis

DARLEY DALE HEATH

☼ ❄ ↔ 24 in (60 cm) ↑ 12 in (30 cm)
Crosses between *E. carnea* and *E. erigena* of garden origin. Vigorous bushy shrub. Mid-green lance-shaped leaves. Racemes of various-colored flowers,

Erica × darleyensis 'Silberschmelze'

Erica cubica

depending on the cultivar, in winter–early spring. Likes well-drained soil. '**Darley Dale**', pink flowers and cream-tipped leaves in spring; '**Ghost Hills**', light green cream-tipped leaves; '**Jenny Porter**', pinkish white flowers, pale cream-tipped foliage; '**Kramers Rote**', bronze-green foliage, magenta flowers; '**Margaret Porter**', lilac-pink flowers over a long season; '**Silberschmelze**', silver-white flowers, foliage tinged red in winter. Zones 6–9.

Erica densifolia

☼ ❄ ↔ 3 ft (0.9 m) ↑ 5 ft (1.5 m)
From South Africa. An upright shrub. Tiny, deep green, linear leaves. Finely

Erica cinerea 'Flamingo'

Erica cinerea 'Flamingo'

Erica cinerea 'Prostrate Lavender'

Erica cinerea 'Purple Beauty'

Erica cinerea 'Startler'

Erica cinerea 'Vivienne Patricia'

Erica cinerea 'Wine'

hairy young stems. Spike-like heads of tubular, 1 in (25 mm) long, slightly curved, red flowers, greenish yellow at the mouth, in summer. Zones 9–10.

Erica erigena
syns *Erica hibernica, E. mediterranea*
IRISH HEATHER

☼ ❄ ↔ 3 ft (0.9 m) ↑ 8 ft (2.4 m)

Found in Ireland, southwest France, Spain, Portugal, and Tangiers in northwest Africa. An upright shrub with brittle stems. Dark green linear leaves. The racemes of urn-shaped, honey-scented, lilac-pink flowers appear in winter–spring. Cultivars include: 'Golden Lady', golden yellow foliage, white flowers; 'Irish Dusk', gray-green foliage, rose pink flowers in the late autumn–spring; 'Superba' ★ (syn. 'Mediterranea Superba'), mid-green foliage, strongly scented pale pink flowers; 'W. T. Rackliff', mid-green foliage, abundant white flowers in spring. Zones 7–9.

Erica glandulosa
☼ ❋ ↔ 36 in (90 cm) ↑ 24 in (60 cm)

Native to the Cape region of South Africa. Sprawling shrub. Light green linear leaves with glandular hairs in whorls of 4. Clusters of pinky orange tubular flowers, borne at branch tips, in autumn–spring. Zones 9–10.

Erica mammosa

Erica lusitanica

Erica glandulosa

Erica glomiflora
☼ ❋ ↔ 3 ft (0.9 m) ↑ 5 ft (1.5 m)

From the Western Cape, South Africa. Mid-green linear leaves in whorls of 3. Shiny ovate flowers, white with a pink tinge, borne at tips of lateral branches, in spring–early summer. Zones 9–10.

Erica × griffithsii
☼ ❄ ↔ 24 in (60 cm)
↑ 18–36 in (45–90 cm)

Hybrids between *E. manipuliflora* and *E. vagans* come under this name, combining the vigor of the first with the dense growth and early flowering of the second. 'Heaven Scent', compact form, dark gray-green foliage, long sprays of scented lilac flowers in mid-summer–mid-autumn. Zones 6–9.

Erica × hiemalis
FRENCH HEATHER

☼ ❄ ↔ 24 in (60 cm) ↑ 24 in (60 cm)

Parents and origin unknown. Upright, fairly dense. Light green leaves, whorls of 4. Tubular flowers, white with pink shading, in autumn–winter. Zones 8–10.

Erica melanthera

Erica glomiflora, in Kirstenbosch Botanical Garden, South Africa

Erica densifolia

Erica infundibuliformis
☼ ❄ ↔ 18–24 in (45–60 cm)
↑ 24–36 in (60–90 cm)

From South Africa. Erect evergreen shrub. Spreading, smooth, slender branches. Tiny narrow leaves. Clusters of small white, pink, or red flowers with narrowly tubular corollas, borne at the branch tips, in late summer to autumn. Zones 8–9.

Erica lusitanica
syn. *Erica codonodes*
PORTUGUESE HEATH, SPANISH HEATH

☼ ❄ ↔ 3 ft (0.9 m) ↑ 5–10 ft (1.5–3 m)

Native from the west of the Iberian Peninsula to southwest France. Has naturalized in southern England, New Zealand, and Australia. Whorls of 3 or 4 mid-green linear leaves. Racemes of tubular flowers, pink in bud, opening to white, during winter–spring. Grows best in acid soil. Can be invasive. 'George Hunt', yellow leaves, white flowers. Zones 8–10.

Erica mackayana
syns *Erica crawfordii, E. mackaii*

☼ ❄ ↔ 30 in (75 cm) ↑ 20 in (50 cm)

From Spain and Ireland. Erect spreading shrub. Dark green lance-shaped to oblong leaves, margins turned under, hairy at tips. Pink urn-shaped flowers in summer–autumn. Needs moist soil.

Erica infundibuliformis

'Plena', double magenta flowers 6 in (15 cm) long; 'Shining Light', smaller than species, gray-green leaves, white flowers. Zones 5–9.

Erica mammosa
☼ ❋ ↔ 6 ft (1.8 m) ↑ 5 ft (1.5 m)

From the Western Cape, South Africa. Dark green lance-shaped leaves in whorls of 4. Tubular flowers in spring–summer, colors ranging from white or green through to pink and dark red. 'Jubilee', pink flowers. Zones 9–10.

Erica manipuliflora
syn. *Erica verticillata* of gardens

☼ ❄ ↔ 3 ft (0.9 m) ↑ 3 ft (0.9 m)

Found in southeastern Italy and the Balkans. Mid-green, linear, pointed leaves in whorls of 3. Bears rose pink flowers, in irregular racemes on the previous year's wood, in the summer–autumn. 'Aldeburgh', scented lilac-pink flowers; 'Korcula', long sprays of pink-tinged white flowers. Zones 8–10.

Erica melanthera
☼ ❄ ↔ 18 in (45 cm) ↑ 24 in (60 cm)

From the Western Cape, South Africa. Erect shrub. Tiny dark green leaves in whorls of 3. Pendent pale pink to deep red blooms with black anthers extending outside the cup in spring to early summer. Zones 8–10.

Erica regia

Erica patersonia

Erica patersonia

MEALIE HEATH

☼ ⊰ ↔ 24 in (60 cm) ↑ 36 in (90 cm)

From Western Cape in South Africa. Erect shrub. Mid-green linear leaves in whorls of 4, arranged in bunched groups. Small dense spikes of tubular, waxy, golden yellow flowers with darker lobes in the late winter to early spring. Zones 9–11.

Erica perspicua

PRINCE OF WALES HEATH

☼ ⊰ ↔ 3 ft (0.9 m) ↑ 6 ft (1.8 m)

From Western Cape in South Africa. Erect, gray-green, linear, overlapping leaves in whorls of 3 or 4. Pseudo-spikes of translucent, finely hairy, tube-shaped flowers, white or pale pink to deep mauve, with white tips, from autumn to winter. Needs moisture to grow well. Zones 9–10.

Erica plukenetii

Erica plukenetii

☼ ⊰ ↔ 18 in (45 cm) ↑ 24 in (60 cm)

From South Africa's Cape region. An upright, evergreen, woody shrub, with leaves under ¾ in (18 mm) long, borne close together. Flowers in shades ranging from crimson to pale pink, ¾ in (18 mm) long, in the spring–summer. Zones 9–10.

Erica regia

ELIM HEATH

☼ ⊰ ↔ 3 ft (0.9 m) ↑ 3 ft (0.9 m)

From Western Cape in South Africa. Erect much-branched shrub. Gray-green leaves in whorls of 6 on hairy branches. Smooth, waxy, tubular flowers with small spreading lobes in spring. Colors unusual: upper red part is separated from the lower white part by a purple band. Zones 9–10.

Erica retorta

☼ ❊ ↔ 18–24 in (45–60 cm) ↑ 18–24 in (45–60 cm)

From the Cape region of South Africa. A spreading evergreen shrub of variable habit. Leaves crowded, thick, rigid, slightly hairy, tipped with a long

Erica × stuartii 'Irish Orange'

bristle. Produces umbels of 4 to 8 dark to light pink flowers with a bottle-shaped sticky corolla in the spring–autumn. Zones 8–9.

Erica rubens

RED HEATH

☼ ❊ ↔ 3–5 ft (0.9–1.5 m) ↑ 3–5 ft (0.9–1.5 m)

From the Cape region of South Africa. Evergreen shrub. Slender reddish stems. Tiny, dark green, cylindrical leaves in groups of 4. Spikes with masses of tiny, pink to deep red, tubular flowers, borne at stem tips. Zones 7–9.

Erica scoparia

BESOM HEATH

☼ ❊ ↔ 3 ft (0.9 m) ↑ 6 ft (1.8 m)

From southwest France, Spain, the Canary Islands, and north Africa. An erect shrub. Dark green linear leaves in whorls of 3 or 4. Racemes of small bell-shaped flowers, brownish red tinged green, in summer. Zones 8–10.

Erica sessiliflora

☼ ❊ ↔ 28 in (70 cm) ↑ 7 ft (2 m)

From South Africa's southern Cape region, where it occurs largely in warm, dry, well-drained, acid situations. Densely branched evergreen shrub with an upright habit. Fine leaves,

Erica perspicua

¼–¾ in (6–18 mm) long. Soft lime green tubular flowers predominantly in spring. Zones 8–10.

Erica sparrmanii

☼ ❊ ↔ 12–18 in (30–45 cm) ↑ 12–18 in (30–45 cm)

From South Africa. A sparse, erect, evergreen shrub, with straight branches, bearing long stiff hairs and tiny, narrow, overlapping leaves. Clusters of 4 greenish yellow to yellow flowers with tubular corollas, up to ¾ in (18 mm) long, borne at branch tips, in winter–summer. Zones 8–9.

Erica × stuartii

☼ ❊ ↔ 18 in (45 cm) ↑ 10 in (25 cm)

From western Ireland. This is a naturally occurring hybrid of *E. mackayana* and *E. tetralix*. Most forms are very similar to *E. mackayana* except for minor floral details. 'Irish Lemon' has lemon-tipped young foliage, mauve

Erica sessiliflora

Erica rubens

Erica tetralix 'Alba Mollis'

Erica verticillata

Erica versicolor

flowers; '**Irish Orange**' produces orange young foliage maturing to green, and soft pink flowers. Zones 8–10.

Erica tetralix
CROSS-LEAFED HEATH

☀ ❄ ↔ 20 in (50 cm) ↑ 12 in (30 cm)

From the UK, France, and the Iberian Peninsula. Dwarf spreading. Gray-green lance-shaped to linear leaves, silver undersides, whorls of 4. Umbels of pale pink urn-shaped flowers, at stem tips, in summer–autumn. Prefers moist soil. '**Alba Mollis**', silvery foliage, white flowers; '**Con Underwood**', gray-green leaves, purple-red flowers; '**Pink Star**', dark pink upright flowers. Zones 3–9.

Erica vagans
CORNISH HEATH, WANDERING HEATH

☀ ❄ ↔ 30 in (75 cm) ↑ 30 in (75 cm)

From the UK, Ireland, western France, and Spain. Dark to mid-green linear

leaves in whorls of 4 or 5. Racemes of cylindrical or bell-shaped flowers that range from white to pink and mauve, in mid-summer–mid-autumn. Prefers a well-drained soil. '**Lyonesse**', white flowers with light brown anthers, bright green foliage; '**Mrs D. F. Maxwell**', compact habit, vivid rose pink flowers; '**Saint Keverne**', bright pink flowers; '**Valerie Proudley**', yellow foliage, white flowers. Zones 5–9.

Erica × veitchii

☀ ❄ ↔ 26 in (65 cm) ↑ 6 ft (1.8 m)

Of garden origin, this species is a cross between *Erica arborea* and *E. lusitanica*. Linear mid-green leaves. The young branches are covered with downy hairs. Produces racemes of lightly scented white flowers in the spring. '**Exeter**' bears masses of white scented flowers in spring; '**Gold Tips**', golden yellow young shoots maturing to green, tolerates some alkalinity in the soil; '**Pink Joy**', pale pink flowers. Zones 8–10.

Erica ventricosa

☀ ❄ ↔ 20 in (50 cm) ↑ 20 in (50 cm)

From South Africa's Western Cape. Compact shrub. Dark green leaves with dark green hairy margins in whorls of 4. The clusters of pinkish red, waxy, tubular flowers, are borne at the branch tips, in spring. The cultivar, '**Grandiflora**', is larger, with pink-mauve flowers. Zones 9–11.

Erica versicolor

☀ ❄ ↔ 3 ft (0.9 m) ↑ 10 ft (3 m)

From Western Cape in South Africa. Erect shrub. Mid-green linear leaves in whorls of 3. Racemes of tubular flowers, red with green to yellow tips, in whorls of 3 in autumn–winter. Zones 9–11.

Erica verticillata

☀ ❄ ↔ 3 ft (0.9 m) ↑ 3 ft (0.9 m)

From South Africa's Cape Peninsula. A bushy erect shrub, believed to be extinct in the wild. Linear green leaves in whorls of 4 to 6. Clusters of purple-pink, finely hairy, tubular flowers in summer. Zones 9–10.

Erica viridiflora

☀ ❄ ↔ 18–24 in (45–60 cm) ↑ 24–36 in (60–90 cm)

From South Africa. An erect, much-branched, evergreen shrub. Tiny, thick, sticky, oval-shaped leaves. Produces heads of 3 very sticky vivid emerald green flowers with a tubular corolla, turning brown with maturity, borne at the branch tips. Zones 8–9.

Erica × williamsii

☀ ❄ ↔ 18 in (45 cm) ↑ 30 in (75 cm)

This hybrid is a cross between *E. tetralix* and *E. vagans* that occurred in the wild in Cornwall in the UK. It produces racemes of rose pink bell-shaped flowers in the summer to late

Erica viridiflora

autumn. '**P. D. Williams**', with yellow-tipped new growth and pink flowers. Zones 5–9.

ERICAMERIA

This genus of evergreen shrubs and subshrubs comprising some 27 species from southwestern and western North America is from the daisy (Asteraceae) family. The leaves are heath-like and linear, more rarely obovate, and are dotted with resinous glands. The flowerheads are with or without ray florets and borne in branched inflorescences at the stem tips. The bracts surrounding the small flowerheads are papery or leathery, the florets yellow. They have often been included in the genus *Haplopappus*, and some are of medicinal value.

CULTIVATION: *Ericameria* species are easily grown in regions with warm dry summers, preferring well-drained light sandy or gravelly soils of moderate fertility. A position in full sun ensures good flower production; these plants are well suited to placement in a large rock garden. Propagate from seed or half-hardened cuttings.

Erica ventricosa

Erica vagans 'Lyonesse'

Erica vagans 'Mrs D. F. Maxwell'

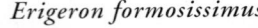

Caption: *Ericameria aborescens* subsp. *peninsularis*, in the wild, Sierra San Pedro Mártir, Baja California, Mexico

Ericameria aborescens

syn. *Haplopappus arborescens*

GOLDENFLEECE

☼ ❄ ↔ 6–10 ft (1.8–3 m)
↑ 5–8 ft (1.5–2.4 m)

Widespread in chaparral vegetation on the dry hills of California, USA. Shrub with erect branches and fine narrow leaves. Dense clusters of small orange-yellow flowerheads with a few narrow ray florets, are borne at the branch tips, in summer–autumn. *E. a.* subsp. *peninsularis* is endemic to the mountains of northern Baja California, Mexico. Zones 8–10.

ERIGERON

FLEABANE

This genus of about 200 species of annuals and perennials belongs to the daisy (Asteraceae) family. They are found throughout temperate regions, particularly in North America, and grow in a variety of habitats. Their daisy flowers usually have numerous narrow rays in shades of white, pink, or lavender, occasionally yellow. Cultivars extend the color range. Plant habits vary from the very low alpine species, suitable for a rock garden, to robust larger-flowered species growing to 30 in (75 cm) or more. They flower profusely, often over a long season. CULTIVATION: Apart from the alpine species, which benefit from protection in winter and need very good drainage, most are easily grown in full sun in any reasonable soil. Propagate from seed or by division.

Erigeron formosissimus

☼ ❄ ↔ 18 in (45 cm) ↑ 18 in (45 cm)

From the Rocky Mountains, USA. Perennial. Clumps of narrow oblong leaves. Heads of blue, pink or white daisies with yellow centers in summer. Zones 6–9.

Erigeron glaucus

BEACH ASTER, SEASIDE DAISY

☼ ❄ ↔ 12–24 in (30–60 cm)
↑ 6–12 in (15–30 cm)

From western USA. A somewhat succulent straggly perennial, with broadly oval leaves. It bears large gold-centered daisies with lilac to violet rays in the late spring to early summer. 'Arthur Menzies', compact form, pink daisies; 'Rose Purple', pink-purple daisies. Zones 3–10.

Erigeron karvinskianus

syn. *Erigeron mucronatus*

MEXICAN DAISY, SANTA BARBARA DAISY

☼ ❄ ↔ 24–60 in (60–150 cm)
↑ 12–24 in (30–60 cm)

From highlands of southern Mexico, Central America, and Venezuela. This perennial forms mounds of small toothed leaves on slender stems. Airy masses of small, white to pink, yellow-centered daisies are produced all year round in frost-free areas, from spring to autumn in colder regions. Popular ground cover, but sometimes a weed. Zones 8–11.

Erigeron glaucus 'Arthur Menzies'

Erigeron formosissimus

Erigeron karvinskianus

Erigeron glaucus

Erigeron glaucus 'Rose Purple'

Erigeron peregrinus

WANDERING DAISY, WANDERING FLEABANE

☀ ❄ ↔ 16–24 in (40–60 cm)
↑ 16–24 in (40–60 cm)

From western North America. This perennial daisy has narrow oblong or spoon-shaped leaves, to 8 in (20 cm) long. White to purple flowers with yellow centers, solitary or in groups, in summer. Zones 2–9.

Erigeron pulchellus

ROBIN'S PLANTAIN

☀ ❄ ↔ 8–16 in (20–40 cm)
↑ 6–16 in (15–40 cm)

This species is a native of North America. It is a biennial or short-lived perennial with creeping rhizomes. The leaves are spoon-shaped leaves. The dainty pale pink or pale purple daisies with yellow centers appear in summer. Zones 4–9.

Erigeron 'Rosa Jewel'

☀ ❄ ↔ 16–24 in (40–60 cm)
↑ 18–30 in (45–75 cm)

An attractive cultivar with bright pink flowers, which is similar to *E. speciosus*. Zones 3–9.

Erinacea anthyllis

Erigeron speciosus

☀ ❄ ↔ 16–24 in (40–60 cm)
↑ 18–30 in (45–75 cm)

From northwestern USA. Popular perennial. Prolific blue daisies with yellow centers in summer. *E. s.* var. *macranthus*, slightly larger flowers. There are many cultivars in shades of pink and blue: '**Rosa Jewel**' ★ (syn. 'Pink Jewel'), bright pink flowers; '**Quakeress**', light mauve-pink flowers. Zones 3–9.

ERINACEA

The sole species in this genus from the pea-flower subfamily of the legume (Fabaceae) family is a small, evergreen shrub found at moderate altitudes in France (the Pyrenees), Spain, and Morocco. The leaves are very small and often hidden within a mound of spiny twigs. When not in flower, hedgehog broom may lack appeal, but from late spring into early summer the bush is smothered in small clusters of showy, pale blue to purple pea-flowers.

CULTIVATION: Although quite frost hardy, it dislikes being cold and wet in winter; in these conditions grow in an alpine house. Superb rockery plant in dry winter areas. Plant in a light, gritty, very well-drained soil in full sun, watering well in spring. Lightly trim after flowering. In a suitable position it is long lived and reliable. Propagate from seed or summer cuttings, which can be reluctant to strike.

Erinacea anthyllis

HEDGEHOG BROOM

☀ ❄ ↔ 3 ft (90 cm) ↑ 12 in (30 cm)
The branches are slow-growing, with rather thorny tips. Tiny dark green leaves composed of 1 to 3 leaflets. Leafless for much of the year, sprouts more foliage in spring. Flowers abundantly. Pods small, seeds often self-sow. Zones 8–10.

Erigeron speciosus 'Quakeress'

Erigeron pulchellus

ERINUS

This genus, comprising just 2 species of perennials from North Africa, the Pyrenees, and the Alps, belongs to the foxglove (Scrophulariaceae) family. They have small, spirally arranged, slightly sticky leaves, and the inflorescences are racemes, borne at the stem tips. The flowers are shortly tubular, expanding at the mouth into 5 spreading petals. The fruit is a capsule with many seeds. Grown as alpines, these perennials are short-lived, but they self-seed in the rock garden.

CULTIVATION: Easily grown in sun or part-shade in well-drained soil in the garden or in troughs, but also on walls or soft porous rock and in cracks in paving. They can be grown from fresh seed sown directly in the ground; protect from winter frosts. Many cultivars breed true from seed; others must be propagated from softwood cuttings taken in spring.

Erinus alpinus

ALPINE BALSAM, FAIRY FOXGLOVE

☀ ❄ ↔ 6 in (15 cm) ↑ 4 in (10 cm)
Cushion-forming herb. Leaves to 1 in (25 mm) long, soft, oblanceolate to wedge-shaped, with toothed or wavy margins, covered with sticky hairs. Abundant purple or white flowers late spring and summer. '**Doktor Hähnle**', deep crimson flowers; '**Mrs Charles Boyle**', pink flowers. Zones 4–9.

Erigeron speciosus var. *macranthus*

ERIOBOTRYA

This genus belonging to the rose (Rosaceae) family consists of about 10 species of evergreen trees and shrubs found from the eastern Himalayas to Southeast Asia and China. They are all tough plants with dull green, leathery, strongly veined leaves, felted underneath. The felted buds held at the branch tips develop into scented creamy flower clusters in the autumn. The showy, fragrant, fleshy, edible fruits are sweet, soft, and juicy at full ripeness. The best known species is the loquat, *E. japonica,* which is both edible and decorative, but attracts birds and fruit fly.

CULTIVATION: These plants prefer subtropical conditions; although they are generally drought-tolerant, they need abundant moisture in winter to produce good fruit. All except strongly alkaline soils are suitable. Seedlings are easily propagated but variable, often producing fruit with large seeds and minimal flesh, but grafted selected varieties are available. Self-sown seedlings are common and the trees survive with little care.

Erinus alpinus

Eriobotrya japonica

Eriogonum fasciculatum

Eriogonum giganteum

Eriobotrya japonica

LOQUAT

☼ ❄ ↔ 15 ft (4.5 m) ↑ 20 ft (6 m)

Long cultivated in Japan but native to central China. The common name derives from the Cantonese name, *lo kwat*. Evergreen tree valued for its luscious fragrant fruit in early spring. The leaves are large, dull green, and lance-shaped, with prominent veins and woolly undersides, occurring mostly at the branch tips. Flowers (usually self-fertile) developing from woolly buds in autumn. Zones 8–11.

ERIOGONUM

WILD BUCKWHEAT

Genus from western North America in the knotweed (Polygonaceae) family, which includes about 150 annuals, perennials, and small evergreen shrubs of varied habit, most of which grow from a basal rosette of leaves. Small flowers appear in dense clusters or umbels, and the fruit is a 3-angled achene. *Eriogonum* species are good rockery or background plants for drier gardens and are also grown for cut and dried flower arrangements.

CULTIVATION: Adaptable to a wide range of climates, they will grow in sun or part-shade in a well-drained, preferably sandy, soil. They require plenty of water in warm conditions but need to be drier in winter. Remove

spent flowerheads. Propagate from seed sown in spring or from cuttings. The root clumps of perennial species may be divided.

Eriogonum arborescens

SANTA CRUZ ISLAND BUCKWHEAT

☼/☽ ❄ ↔ 5 ft (1.5 m) ↑ 5 ft (1.5 m)

From California, USA. Peeling bark. Narrow near-linear leaves with slightly rolled edges and felted undersides. White to pale pink flowers, in downy inflorescences 2–6 in (5–15 cm) wide, in early summer–autumn. Good cut flower. Zones 9–10.

Eriogonum fasciculatum

CALIFORNIA BUCKWHEAT

☼ ❄ ↔ 4 ft (1.2 m) ↑ 3 ft (0.9 m)

From Utah, Nevada, and California, USA, and Baja California, Mexico. Spreading shrub with upright stems at its center. Leaves dark green to gray, hairy on upper surfaces, with white-felted undersides. White to pale pink flowers ageing to red-brown in spring–autumn. 'Theodore Payne' ★, prostrate form. Zones 7–11.

Eriogonum flavum

YELLOW BUCKWHEAT

☼ ❄ ↔ 7–10 in (18–25 cm) ↑ 4–9 in (10–22 cm)

From western Canada and the northern Rocky Mountains region of the USA.

Low-growing perennial herb, woody at base. Mat-forming rosettes of oval-shaped grayish green leaves, to 4 in (10 cm) long, slightly hairy above and densely woolly underneath. Umbels of lemon yellow flowers are sometimes tinged with red, in the early summer. Zones 3–9.

Eriogonum giganteum

SAINT CATHERINE'S LACE

☼ ❄ ↔ 10 ft (3 m) ↑ 8 ft (2.4 m)

From the Santa Barbara Islands off southern California, USA. A rounded evergreen shrub, with a central trunk, and oval, leathery, grayish white leaves. The flat clusters of woolly flowerheads, to 12 in (30 cm) across, appearing in summer, are white slowly fading to rusty red. Zones 9–11.

Eriogonum grande

syn. *Eriogonum latifolium* subsp. *grande*

☼ ❄ ↔ 20–36 in (50–90 cm) ↑ 18–24 in (45–60 cm)

Native to California, USA. Rare, low-growing, shrubby perennial. Curling oblong to oval leaves, to 4 in (10 cm) long, with dense white down underneath. The flat-topped heads of white to pale pink flowers appear in summer–early autumn. 'Rubescens', a lower, more sprawling, form, with large leaves, and big clusters of rose pink flowers. Zones 8–10.

Eriogonum parishii

☼ ❄ ↔ 18–24 in (45–60 cm) ↑ 12–18 in (30–45 cm)

Native to southern California and Arizona, USA, and the mountains of northern Baja California, Mexico, this species grows in denuded areas in gritty soils. It is an annual with a small basal rosette. The inflorescence, a mist-like mass of fine stalks with minute reddish flowers, appears in the late summer–autumn. Zones 8–11.

Eriogonum umbellatum

SULFUR FLOWER

☼ ❄ ↔ 3–4 ft (0.9–1.2 m) ↑ 6–18 in (15–45 cm)

From northwestern USA and southwestern Canada. This variable, low-spreading, perennial herb has rosettes of spatula-shaped, purplish-tinged, stalked leaves, finely hairy underneath, in winter. Bears loose ball-like clusters of bright sulfur yellow or cream flowers in summer. Zones 6–10.

Eriogonum wrightii

BASTARD SAGE, SHRUBBY WILD BUCKWHEAT, WRIGHT'S BUCKWHEAT

☼ ❄ ↔ 1–5 ft (0.3–1.5 m) ↑ 3–24 in (7–60 cm)

From southwestern USA and adjacent Mexico. Low branched perennial or shrub. Small elliptical to sword-shaped leaves with fine white hairs underneath. Tight heads of white or pink flowers, arranged in a spike, on stalks to 10 in (25 cm) tall, in summer. *E. w.* var. *subscaposum*, from dry rocky Californian mountain sites, prostrate, mat-forming. Zones 6–10.

ERIOPHORUM

COTTON GRASS

This genus of about 22 grass-like perennial herbs, native to the cooler regions of Eurasia, North America, and South Africa (one species only), belongs to the sedge (Cyperaceae) family.

Eriogonum parishii

Eriogonum grande 'Rubescens'

Eriogonum wrightii var. *subscaposum*

They are common in bogs, shallow ponds, and other wet areas. The plants spread by rhizomes and have slender flat leaves on tufted, leafy, 3-angled stems. In the spring the stem tips bear dense spikelets of flowers with numerous perianth parts reduced to soft, pale, cotton-like hairs that elongate with age to aid dispersal. The seed heads, which form during the summer, resemble tufts of cottonwool.

CULTIVATION: Plant in full sun in damp garden soil or on the shallow margins of ponds. Propagate from seed or by division.

Eriophorum vaginatum ★
syns *Eriophorum callitrix, E. spissum, Scirpus faurieri*

COTTON GRASS, COTTONSEDGE, TUSSOCK COTTON GRASS, HARE'S TAIL

☼ ❋ ↔ 6–12 in (15–30 cm)
↑ 12–32 in (30–80 cm)

From the Northern Hemisphere's temperate regions. Tussock-forming sedge that dies back to rootstock annually, the basal portions of leaves and stems remaining green. Simple multi-flowered spikelet covered with white hairs, borne at the tips of the 8–28 in (20–71 cm) long stems, in spring. Zones 5–9.

ERIOPHYLLUM
In the daisy (Asteraceae) family, this genus comprises 13 species of annual or perennial herbs or subshrubs from western North America. They usually grow in dry, exposed, rocky regions. Perennial species are generally small, closely branched, and woody at the base. Stems and leaves are often woolly. The cheerful yellow flowers are held above the foliage. Rather short-lived; their hardiness varies with the species. Many are attractive to butterflies.

Eriophorum vaginatum

CULTIVATION: Grow in full sun in well-drained soil and water moderately. Easily propagated from seed or from cuttings, or by division.

Eriophyllum lanatum
GOLDEN YARROW, OREGON SUNSHINE, WOOLLY SUNFLOWER

☼ ❋ ↔ 24 in (60 cm)
↑ 12–24 in (30–60 cm)

From southern California, USA, to northern British Columbia and the Rocky Mountains in Canada. This is a subshrub perennial with blue-gray woolly leaves. The long-lasting, star-shaped, daisy-like flowers appear in mid-spring–late summer; deadhead for a second flowering. Drought tolerant. Zones 5–9.

ERIOSTEMON
As now understood, following a recent revision, this genus of evergreen shrubs in the rue (Rutaceae) family consists of only 2 species from coastal eastern Australia. Other species formerly included in *Eriostemon* have now been reclassified under *Philotheca*. Growing in stunted forest heathland in poor sandy soil, they have simple spirally arranged leaves and rather conspicuous flowers with 5 waxy pink petals, borne singly in leaf axils, in the late winter to spring, giving massed displays for long periods.

CULTIVATION: Prefers light to medium, well-drained, slightly acid to neutral soil in an open position in sun or part-shade. Prune lightly to preserve shape. Propagate from tip cuttings; seed is difficult to germinate.

Eriostemon australasius
syn. *Eriostemon lanceolatus*
PINK WAX FLOWER, WAX PLANT

☼/◐ ❉ ↔ 3 ft (0.9 m) ↑ 6 ft (1.8 m)
From eastern New South Wales and southeastern Queensland, Australia. Erect shrub. Foliage narrow-elliptical. Massed, shell pink, mauve, or white flowers, to 1½ in (35 mm) across. Requires perfect drainage and cool root conditions; mulch with stone. Excellent cut flower. Zones 9–10.

ERIOSYCE
syns *Chileniopsis, Horridocactus, Islaya, Neochilenia, Neoporteria, Pyrrhocactus*

This genus of 35 species of small to dwarf South American cacti in the family Cactaceae is found from sea level to 10,000 ft (3,000 m) on the slopes of the Andes, from central Chile north to southern Peru. Until a botanical study in 1994, this genus was not well understood and many genus names were applied to its species. The genus name comes from 2 Greek words, *erion*, wool, and *sykon*, fig, because of the woolly seed pods all species bear. Usually solitary, and spherical to shortly cylindrical, the plants vary greatly in size and number of ribs; tubercles are always present but vary in structure. Spines range from thin and bristle-like to stiff and needle-like, and vary in number. Flowers appear near stem tips and are funnel-shaped to tubular, white to yellow, pink, or carmine-red. Seeds, loose within spherical pods, burst open at the base.

CULTIVATION: Easily grown in rich well-drained soil; withhold water in winter. Propagate from seed.

Eriosyce crispa
syns *Horridocactus crispus, Neoporteria huascensis, Pyrrhocactus crispus*

☼ ❉ ↔ 2–4 in (5–10 cm)
↑ 2–4 in (5–10 cm)

Native to the coastal Atacama Desert of Chile. The stem is bun-shaped to

Eriosyce crispa var. *huascensis*

shortly cylindrical, blackish gray-green, and has 10 to 16 ribs. The spines are upward-curving, sometimes twisted, sometimes hair-like, black to brown, to 3 in (7 cm) long. The funnel-shaped flowers, to 2 in (5 cm) across, have whitish pink petals with red markings, and appear in late summer–autumn. *E. c.* var. *huascensis* has fewer and needle-like spines than the species, and 10 to 12 ribs. Zones 9–11.

Eriosyce subgibbosa
syns *Neoporteria heteracantha, N. microsperma, N. subgibbosa,*

☼ ❉ ↔ 21/2–10 in (6–25 cm)
↑ 3–40 in (7–100 cm)

Native to the central coastal region of Chile. This species is very variable in form and has been given many names in the past. A yellow-green plant with 16 to 22 deeply notched ribs. The spines are stiff, yellow to brown or black, needle-like, and straight to strongly incurved. The deep pink to carmine-red funnel-shaped flowers are variable in size, appearing in late summer. Zones 9–11.

Eriosyce subgibbosa

Eriostemon australasius, Ku-ring-gai Wildflower Garden, New South Wales, Australia

Erodium corsicum

Erodium corsicum 'Rubrum'

Eriosyce taltalensis

syns *Neoporteria echinus, N. pulchella, N. taltalensis, Pyrrhocactus floccosus*

☼ ⚘ ↔ 1–6 in (2.5–15 cm)
↕ 1–6 in (2.5–15 cm)

From the coastal Atacama Desert, and south to Concepción in Chile, this species, very variable in form, has been given many names. Bluish green plant with 8 to 13 notched ribs. The spines are irregular, dark brown to black, and straight to curved. The narrowly to broadly funnel-shaped flowers, appear in red to pink, pale yellow, or creamy white, to 1½ in (35 mm) across, in late summer–autumn. **Zones 9–11.**

ERODIUM

HERONSBILL, STORKSBILL

Genus in the geranium (Geraniaceae) family, including 60 species of perennials and a few annuals and subshrubs. They are found in sunny rocky areas in mountainous regions of Europe, Asia, Australia, and South America. Some are mat-forming, others are erect, growing to 20 in (50 cm) tall. The leaves are lobed or pinnately divided, often finely and ornately, sometimes silvery gray. The charming 5-petalled flowers resemble cranesbill geraniums but have 5 rather than 10 stamens. Some species carry male and female flowers on separate plants. The flowers are pink, red, purple, blue, yellow, or white, and often veined or stained with darker tones. The common names refer to the elongated tapering seed vessels. **CULTIVATION:** Grow small species in rockeries, pots, or a greenhouse; taller plants are ideal in borders. Heronsbills need full sun and well-drained slightly alkaline soil. Propagate annuals from seed; perennials from seed or cuttings, or by division.

Erodium absinthoides

syns *Erodium armenum, E. haradjianii*
☼ ❋ ↔ 12 in (30 cm) ↕ 8 in (20 cm)
From southeastern Europe and Asia Minor. Perennial. Grayish green ferny foliage. Male and female flowers on separate plants. White, pink, or violet starry flowers, to ¾ in (18 mm) across, in spring–summer. **Zones 6–9.**

Erodium cheilanthifolium

syn. *Erodium petraeum* subsp. *crispum*
☼ ❋ ↔ 12 in (30 cm) ↕ 6 in (15 cm)
From Spain and Morocco. Perennial. Low clumps of finely divided grayish leaves. Flowers are dainty white to pale pink flowers with purplish veins and blotches, to ¾ in (18 mm), in spring–summer. **Zones 6–9.**

Erodium chrysanthum

☼ ❋ ↔ 12–16 in (30–40 cm)
↕ 4–6 in (10–15 cm)

From Greece. Low tufts of ferny silvery leaves. Male and female flowers on separate plants. Saucer-shaped creamy lemon flowers, to ¾ in (18 mm) across, in summer. **Zones 7–10.**

Erodium corsicum

☼ ❋ ↔ 12 in (30 cm) ↕ 8 in (20 cm)
From Corsica and Sardinia. Short-lived mat-forming perennial. Downy silvery gray foliage. Small, crumpled, oval leaves with wavy margins. Flowers rose pink, darker veining, to ¾ in (18 mm) across, late spring–summer. 'Rubrum' deeper pink flowers. **Zones 8–10.**

Erodium cossonii

☼ ❋ ↔ 15 in (38 cm) ↕ 8 in (20 cm)
From Morocco. Perennial with deeply lobed rounded leaves. Starry pale pink flowers marked with purple veining and blotches on the upper petals in spring–summer. **Zones 7–10.**

Erodium 'Eileen Emmett'

☼ ❋ ↔ 12 in (30 cm) ↕ 6 in (15 cm)
May be a selection of *E. foetidum*. Mid-green finely divided foliage. Bears pale pink darker-veined flowers in summer. **Zones 7–10.**

Eriosyce taltalensis

Erodium absinthoides

Erodium 'Eileen Emmett'

Erodium chrysanthum

Erodium cheilanthifolium

Erodium foetidum

syn. *Erodium petraeum*

☼ ❄ ↔ 18 in (45 cm) ↑ 10 in (25 cm)

From France. Perennial with strong-smelling, finely divided, grayish green leaves. The flowers are pink with purplish red veins and blotches, to ¾ in (18 mm) in diameter, during summer. Zones 7–10.

Erodium glandulosum

syns *Erodium macradenum, E. petraeum* subsp. *glandulosum*

☼ ❄ ↔ 12 in (30 cm) ↑ 6–8 in (15–20 cm)

From the Pyrenees. Tufted perennial. Finely divided, aromatic, silvery gray leaves. Pale lilac to white saucer-shaped flowers with purple blotches during summer. Zones 7–10.

Erodium × kolbianum ★

☼ ❄ ↔ 8 in (20 cm) ↑ 6 in (15 cm)

Hybrid of garden origin. Fern-like bluish-gray foliage. The sprays of small flowers, vary in color from white to pale rose. 'Natasha' ★, white flowers, which are heavily veined and marked with maroon. Zones 6–9.

Erodium 'Pickering Pink'

☼ ❄ ↔ 8 in (20 cm) ↑ 4 in (10 cm)

A hybrid cultivar with fern-like slightly silvery foliage. The flowers are two-toned, white beneath and pink above, marked with darker veins and blotches. Zones 7–10.

Eruca vesicaria subsp. *sativa*

Erodium trichomanifolium

Erodium × *kolbianum* cultivar

Erodium reichardii

ALPINE GERANIUM

☼ ❄ ↔ 10 in (25 cm) ↑ 1–2 in (25–50 mm)

From Majorca and Corsica. This mat-forming species has small, crinkled, scallop-edged leaves. It produces delicate white flowers with pink veins, to ½ in (12 mm) across, in summer. 'Charm', white flowers. Zones 7–10.

Erodium rodiei

☼ ❄ ↔ 15 in (38 cm) ↑ 15 in (38 cm)

From southern France. Perennial. Mounds of finely divided light green leaves. Mid- to dark pink flowers, nearly 2 in (5 cm) across. Zones 8–10.

Erodium trichomanifolium

☼ ❄ ↔ 12 in (30 cm) ↑ 8 in (20 cm)

From Syria and Lebanon. Perennial. Mounds of fern-like, hairy, grayish green leaves. Male and female flowers carried on separate plants. Dainty pale pink flowers with purplish veining and blotches in summer. Zones 8–10.

Erodium × variabile

☼ ❄ ↔ 10 in (25 cm) ↑ 6–12 in (15–30 cm)

These hybrids of *E. corsicum* and *E. reichardii* that are intermediate between the parents. 'Bishop's Form', deep pink flowers with reddish veins; 'Derek' (syn. *E. reichardii* 'Derek'), very compact, with deep pink flowers; 'Flora Pleno', small, pale or deep pink, double flowers; 'Roseum', pink flowers veined with crimson. Zones 7–10.

ERUCA

This genus, comprising 3 species of annuals and perennials native to the

Erodium × *variabile* 'Roseum'

Erodium foetidum

Erodium 'Pickering Pink'

Mediterranean region, belongs to the cabbage (Brassicaceae) family. The leaves are pinnately lobed. Violet, yellow, or white 4-petalled flowers veined in contrasting colors are borne in racemes. The narrow seed pod splits into 2 halves, releasing several seeds.

CULTIVATION: Only *E. vesicaria* subsp. *sativa* is cultivated, as a salad green or, in India, as an oilseed. Raise from seed in open ground or, for early harvest in temperate regions, in trays under glass. For a succession of tender young shoots for the table, sow seed fortnightly throughout the season. It does best with added nitrogenous fertilizer and plenty of water; starved old shoots are too strongly flavored for culinary use. After leaves have been harvested, plants can regenerate up to 4 more flushes of leaves. Shade young plants in summer to prevent bolting.

Eruca vesicaria

ARUGULA, ROCKET, ROQUETTE

☼/◐ ❄ ↔ 12–24 in (30–60 cm) ↑ 16–40 in (40–100 cm)

From the Mediterranean region. Short-lived perennial forming a clump of deeply lobed dark green leaves with an erect raceme of pale yellow flowers. The ancestral wild forms are more pungent-tasting than the commonly eaten variety, though still edible. *E. v.* subsp.

Erodium rodiei

Erodium reichardii 'Charm'

sativa (syn. *E. sativa*), known as garden or salad rocket, is the cultivated race: an annual, with deeply divided leaves and 1 in (25 mm) wide pale yellow flowers with violet-veined petals in summer, pods to 1 in (25 mm) long, held erect. This fashionable salad green is also grown as an oilseed. Zones 7–10.

ERYNGIUM

Belonging to the carrot (Apiaceae) family, this genus of well over 200 species of annuals, biennials, and perennials is found throughout most of the temperate world. Although the flower stems often carry rudimentary leaves, the foliage, which can be very spiny, is almost entirely basal, often forming a large clump. Unlike most umbellifers, with their open airy flowerheads, the flowerheads of *Eryngium* are thistle-like,

E

Eryngium amethystinum

Eryngium bourgatii cultivar

Eryngium bourgatii cultivar

with the flowers clustered in a central cone surrounded by spiny bracts, often in shades of metallic blue or silver gray. Flowerheads and foliage last well when cut and have a certain charm when dried. Summer is the main flowering season for this genus.

CULTIVATION: Their hardiness varies with different species, though most will tolerate at least moderate frosts. Although some are drought tolerant, most are comfortable in a moist well-drained soil with regular watering during the growing season. Propagate by division or from the seed, which germinates readily.

Eryngium alpinum

☀/☼ ❄ ↔ 24 in (60 cm) ↑ 24 in (60 cm)
From western France to the Balkans. This perennial has long-stemmed leaves, which are deeply lobed, spiny, triangular to heart-shaped, and up to 6 in (15 cm) long. The purple-blue flowerheads are surrounded by a large feathery ruff of spiny, 2½ in (6 cm) long, metallic purple-blue bracts. The cultivar '**Blue Star**' grows to 30 in (75 cm) tall, and has bracts more blue than purple. Zones 6–9.

Eryngium alternatum

☀/☼ ❄ ↔ 12 in (30 cm) ↑ 18 in (45 cm)
From the central Mexican plateau. A perennial with a rosette of narrow green leaves with round ends and spiny teeth. Flat panicles of flowerheads with neat circles of pure white sharply toothed bracts surrounding blue-gray florets. Zones 7–10.

Eryngium amethystinum

AMETHYST SEA HOLLY
☀/☼ ❄ ↔ 20 in (50 cm) ↑ 28 in (70 cm)
Found around the Adriatic to Sicily. Perennial. Leaves to 6 in (15 cm) long, palmately lobed and further divided into narrow spine-tipped segments.

Eryngium alpinum 'Blue Star'

Eryngium alternatum

Many near-spherical purple-blue flowerheads surrounded by narrow, spiny, purple-tinted bracts, to 2 in (5 cm) long. Zones 7–9.

Eryngium bourgatii

☀/☼ ❄ ↔ 16 in (40 cm) ↑ 16 in (40 cm)
Native to Spain and the Pyrenees. Perennial forming low clump of foliage. Leaves much-divided, spiny, rounded, to 3 in (8 cm) across. Branching inflorescence of many flowerheads, to over ½ in (12 mm) in width, with up to 12 narrow light mauve-blue bracts, not always spiny. '**Oxford Blue**', attractive silver-blue flowerheads and bracts. Zones 5–10.

Eryngium giganteum

MISS WILLMOTT'S GHOST
☀/☼ ❄ ↔ 32 in (80 cm) ↑ 5 ft (1.5 m)
This species is native to the Caucasus. A perennial with long-stemmed leaves that are triangular in shape, up to 6 in (15 cm) long, deeply toothed, and spiny. It produces a green to silvery mauve-blue flowerhead, surrounded by up to 10 large, spiny, silver-white bracts. Zones 6–9.

Eryngium 'Jos Eijking'

☀/☼ ❄ ↔ 16 in (40 cm) ↑ 24–32 in (60–80 cm)
Dutch perennial hybrid of uncertain parentage. It forms a compact clump of deeply lobed spiny basal foliage. Striking bright metallic blue flowerheads and similarly colored, narrow, spiny bracts. Zones 6–9.

Eryngium maritimum

SEA HOLLY
☀/☼ ❄ ↔ 20 in (50 cm) ↑ 24 in (60 cm)
From coastal Europe. This short-lived perennial has rounded silver-gray to blue-gray leaves, to 4 in (10 cm) long, with 5 spine-tipped lobes. Pale lavender blue flowerheads, to 1 in (25 mm) across; green to cream bracts developing lavender tints. Zones 5–9.

Eryngium × oliverianum

☀/☼ ❄ ↔ 20–24 in (50–60 cm) ↑ 24–40 in (60–100 cm)
Garden hybrid between *E. alpinum* and possibly *E. giganteum*. Perennial with long-stemmed, spiny, toothed leaves, rounded to heart-shaped, with 3 lobes on basal leaves. Bright metallic blue flowerheads, to 1¾ in (40 mm) across, with up to 15 narrow, spiny, purple bracts. Zones 5–9.

Eryngium × oliverianum

Eryngium, Hybrid Cultivar, 'Jos Eijking'

Eryngium × tripartitum

Eryngium variifolium

Eryngium pandanifolium
☼/◐ ❄ ↔ 20–24 in (50–60 cm)
↑ 7–8 ft (2–2.4 m)

Native to Brazil, Argentina, Uruguay, and Paraguay. Perennial, which forms a basal clump of narrow serrated leaves and many strongly upright, branching flower stems with many small heads of small-bracted purple flowers. *E. p.* var. *lasseauxii*, white flowerheads, the most commonly grown. Zones 8–10.

Eryngium planum
☼/◐ ❄ ↔ 24 in (60 cm) ↑ 40 in (100 cm)

The native habitat of this species extends from central Europe to central Asia. Perennial. Leaves dark green, oval, with spine-tipped lobes. Many small purple-blue flowerheads with up to 8 spiny narrow bracts, to 1 in (25 mm) long. Zones 4–9.

Eryngium serra
☼/◐ ❄ ↔ 40 in (100 cm) ↑ 7 ft (2 m)

From Brazil and Argentina. Perennial forming a basal clump of spine-edged sword-shaped leaves, to 24 in (60 cm) long. Strongly upright flower stems with many small white flowerheads, each with up to 9 tiny greenish-white bracts. Zones 8–11.

Eryngium × tripartitum
☼/◐ ❄ ↔ 24–32 in (60–80 cm)
↑ 48 in (120 cm)

Natural hybrid perennial of unknown parentage. Leaves dark green, trifoliate, with spine-tipped, coarsely toothed, lance-shaped segments. Blue-green flower stems with metallic blue flowerheads, less than ½ in (12 mm) across, and up to 9 narrow blue-green bracts, to about 1 in (25 mm) long. Zones 5–9.

Eryngium variifolium
☼/◐ ❄ ↔ 16–20 in (40–50 cm)
↑ 20–30 in (50–75 cm)

Native to North Africa. An evergreen perennial forming a thistle-like basal rosette of white-marbled, dark green, toothed leaves. Flowerheads are purple-blue, to 1 in (25 mm) across, with up to 7 narrow, spiny, white-centered bracts. Zones 7–9.

Eryngium yuccifolium
BUTTON SNAKEROO, RATTLESNAKE MASTER
☼/◐ ❄ ↔ 5 ft (1.5 m) ↑ 6 ft (1.8 m)

From eastern and central USA. Perennial species with basal clump of sword-shaped fiercely spiny leaves, to 36 in (100 cm) long. The strong, upright flower stems bear white to blue flowerheads, to 1 in (25 mm) across, and up to 10 bracts, to ½ in (12 mm) long. Zones 4–9.

ERYSIMUM
syn. *Cheiranthus*
WALLFLOWER

A genus in the cabbage (Brassicaceae) family, comprising some 80 species of sometimes shrubby annuals and perennials, now includes many species formerly classified under *Cheiranthus*. The narrow green to blue-green leaves with shallow lobes are unremarkable, but the 4-petalled flowers are brightly colored, often fragrant, and frequently appear over a long season. In mild climates the bushy forms flower all year round. The hybrids come in many colors.

CULTIVATION: Although most species of *Erysimum* are very hardy, they prefer a temperate climate with distinct seasons. Plant in moist humus-rich soil and water well during the flowering period. Often quite drought tolerant, but these plants will flower more abundantly with regular watering, feeding,

Eryngium serra

trimming, and deadheading. Propagate annual species by seed; perennials can be propagated from seed, from small cuttings of non-flowering stems, or sometimes by division.

Erysimum cheiri
syn. *Cheiranthus cheiri*
WALLFLOWER

☼/◐ ❄ ↔ 16 in (40 cm) ↑ 24 in (60 cm)
From southern Europe. This shrubby perennial is usually cultivated as a biennial. The foliage is narrow and deep green; the lower leaves to 8 in (20 cm) long, becoming smaller higher up. Produces large heads of yellow and/or orange flowers. The cultivated forms, which are most likely hybrids, include: 'Cloth of Gold', a deep golden yellow; Fair Lady (quite often called My Fair Lady) Strain, to 18 in (45 cm) tall, offering blooms in a range of pastel shades; 'Fire King Improved', growing to 16 in (40 cm) tall, with brilliant orange-red flowers; 'Harpur Crewe', yellow double flowers; Prince Series, stocky, to 18 in (45 cm) tall, in a wide color range and usually given a color name, for example, 'Prince Primrose Yellow'. Zones 7–9.

Erysimum kotschyanum
☼/◐ ❄ ↔ 6–8 in (15–20 cm)
↑ 2–4 in (5–10 cm)

Native of Turkey. A small tufted perennial, which makes dense mats of narrow, toothed, light green leaves of less than ½ in (12 mm). It produces long, small, yellow to pale orange flowers in summer. Zones 6–10.

Erysimum kotschyanum

Erysimum cheiri, Fair Lady Strain

Erythrina acanthocarpa

Erythrina × *bidwillii*

Erysimum pulchellum

☀/◐ ❄ ↔ 12–16 in (30–40 cm)
↑ 16–24 in (40–60 cm)

From Eurasia. Perennial. Whorls of toothed spatula-shaped leaves. Golden yellow flowers from spring. The cream variegated form '**Variegatum**' is more common than the species. Zones 6–9.

Erysimum Hybrid Cultivars

☀/◐ ❄ ↔ 24 in (60 cm)
↑ 24–36 in (60–90 cm)

These bushy hybrids are of uncertain parentage but may be hybrids between *E. bicolor* and *E. perofskianum*. Though not long-lasting, they are easily propagated and flower virtually continuously. The best known, '**Bowles' Mauve**' ★ (syn. 'E. A. Bowles'), produces masses of small mauve-purple flowers; '**Gold Shot**', 18 in (45 cm) tall, golden yellow flowers; '**Sunlight**', yellow-flowered low spreader, about 4 in (10 cm) tall, and probably with *E. helveticum* and/or *E. kotschyanum* in its background; '**Wenlock Beauty**', with flowers magenta and ageing to mauve; '**Winter Cheer**', two-tone orange and light purple flowers. Zones 7–10.

ERYTHRINA

CORAL TREE

A member of the pea-flower subfamily of the legume (Fabaceae) family this genus of over 100 mainly tropical deciduous or semi-evergreen trees, perennials, and shrubs is distributed globally in warm-temperate to tropical regions. Stems, branches, and even the leaflet midribs may be armed with

Erythrina crista-galli

conical or curved prickles. The compound leaves have 3 broad leaflets and inflorescences are erect to drooping racemes of showy tubular to bell-shaped flowers with the upper petal longer than the other petals. Flowers in deciduous species usually precede leaves. The fruits are elongated pods, narrowed between the seeds. They are grown as an ornamental summer shade tree. Some species have medicinal properties; others may be poisonous. The seeds are used to make necklaces.

CULTIVATION: Species of *Erythrina* prefer a warm dry climate and thrive in sandy, moist, but well-drained soils in sunny exposed positions in coastal environments. They are easily propagated from seed sown in spring and summer, and from cuttings of growing wood; the rootstock of herbaceous species may be divided. While fairly free of pests, mites can be a problem in drier weather.

Erythrina acanthocarpa

TAMBOOKIE THORN

☀ ⚘ ↔ 6 ft (1.8 m) ↑ 6 ft (1.8 m)

From the Cape region of South Africa. A deciduous stiff shrub with many thorny stems with bluish green leaflets arising from a large underground root. The clusters of showy, pea-flower-like, scarlet blooms are tipped with green in late spring–early summer. Prickly bean-like pods. Zones 9–11.

Erythrina × bidwillii ★

HYBRID CORAL TREE

☀ ⚘ ↔ 10 ft (3 m) ↑ 12 ft (3.5 m)

Originated in Australia as a garden hybrid between *E. crista-galli* and

Erysimum, Hybrid Cultivar, '**Gold Shot**'

E. herbacea. A deciduous shrub suited to drier gardens. The pale to mid-green trifoliate leaves, to 4 in (10 cm) long, on prickly stems. Striking dark red flowers with the upper petal to 2 in (5 cm) long, in threes, in spring–early summer. Zones 9–11.

Erythrina caffra

COAST CORAL TREE, KUSKORAALBOOM

☀ ⚘ ↔ 35 ft (10 m) ↑ 50 ft (15 m)

Native to southeastern South Africa. Semi-evergreen tree, sometimes with thorny branches. The compound leaves have 3 leaflets, with the end leaflet larger. It bears dense racemes of pea-flower-like, usually orange-scarlet, blooms, to 6 in (15 cm) long. These appear with the emerging leaves at the tips of the branches in late spring to early summer. Zones 9–11.

Erythrina crista-galli

COCKSPUR CORAL TREE,
COMMON CORAL TREE

☀ ⚘ ↔ 12–40 ft (3.5–12 m) ↑ 30 ft (9 m)

Native to Brazil. A deciduous species sometimes found as a gnarled old tree with considerable character. If lopped annually, very large red flower clusters appear in spring–summer. *E. crista-galli* can be grown as a potted greenhouse plant in cooler climates; it should be pruned heavily in the late autumn. Zones 9–11.

Erysimum, Hybrid Cultivar, '**Bowles' Mauve**'

Erysimum, Hybrid Cultivar, '**Sunlight**'

Erythrina × sykesii

Erythrina zeyheri

Erythrina lysistemon

Erythrina herbacea

CARDINAL SPEAR, CHEROKEE BEAN, CORAL BEAN, EASTERN CORAL BEAN

☼ ❄ ↔ 2–6 ft (0.6–1.8 m) ↑ 4–10 ft (1.2–3 m)

From southeastern USA and Mexico. Perennial herb; sometimes a shrub or small tree. The triangular leaflets are held on prickly leaf stalks. Racemes of deep scarlet flowers with the upper petal to 2 in (5 cm) long in summer–autumn. Leathery pods of scarlet seeds. Zones 8–10.

Erythrina humeana

DWARF ERYTHRINA, NATAL CORAL TREE

☼ ❦ ↔ 7 ft (2 m) ↑ 12 ft (3.5 m)

Native to eastern South Africa and Mozambique. A deciduous shrub or small tree with light gray prickly bark and dark green shiny leaflets. Slender dense racemes, to 20 in (50 cm) long, of scarlet-red, tubular, pea-flower-like blooms, borne at the branch tips, in summer. Bean pods are black or purple. Zones 9–11.

Erythrina lysistemon

LUCKY BEAN TREE, TRANSVAAL CORAL TREE

☼ ❦ ↔ 10–30 ft (3–9 m) ↑ 30 ft (9 m)

Found in southern and eastern Africa. Semi-evergreen tree. Large compound leaves; ovate leaflets with tapering ends. Bears compact racemes of bright scarlet flowers, at the branch tips, in summer. The slender woody pods contain orange-red seeds, which are known as "lucky beans." Zones 9–12.

Erythrina × sykesii

syn. *Erythrina indica* of gardens

CORAL TREE

☼ ❦ ↔ 30 ft (9 m) ↑ 50 ft (15 m)

Deciduous tree of uncertain origin, first appearing in Australia and New Zealand. Squat trunk with ascending branches armed with hooked prickles. Large scarlet pea-flowers, in winter–spring. Very brittle; sheds limbs when windy. Tolerates poor soil and salt-laden air. Easily grown from branches or even wood chips. Zones 9–11.

Erythrina variegata

syn. *Erythrina indica*

CORAL TREE, INDIAN CORAL BEAN, TIGER'S CLAW

☼ ✈ ↔ 30 ft (9 m) ↑ 30–60 ft (9–18 m)

Widespread along coastlines of tropical Asia, the Indian Ocean, and the western Pacific. Deciduous tree with thick large-prickled branches, grayish green furrowed bark. Large heart-shaped leaflets. Dense clusters of scarlet or crimson pea-flowers, occasionally white, borne at branch tips, in winter. 'Parcellii', leaves variegated with light green and yellow. Zones 11–12.

Erythrina zeyheri

PLOUGHBREAKER, PRICKLY CARDINAL

☼ ❄ ↔ 30 in (75 cm) ↑ 3 ft (0.9 m)

From eastern South Africa. Small very prickly shrub, dying back to large, woody, underground rootstock in autumn and winter. Ovate to diamond-shaped leaflets, thorny beneath, noticeably veined. Racemes of tubular red flowers in mid-summer. Non-hairy woody seed pods, red seeds. Zones 8–10.

ERYTHRONIUM

DOGTOOTH VIOLET, TROUT LILY

A member of the lily (Liliaceae) family, this genus of bulbs is found in the wild in North America, Asia, and across Europe, some species growing in a wide variety of habitats. The flowers, held well above the leaves, hang down, with distinctive, recurved, pointed petals. The shiny leaves fan outward and, in many varieties, are mottled, flecked, or spotted with silver, brown, maroon, or bronze. This striking feature begins to fade as the season progresses.

CULTIVATION: Most thrive in cool damp climates and dappled shade, but those from western North America can, if shaded, tolerate hot dry summers. None like humid heat; majority dislike disturbance. Plant in autumn, always keeping bulbs moist, about 2 in (5 cm) below the surface. Protect from slugs. To propagate, divide as leaves wilt, replanting immediately, or sow fresh seed in rich moisture-retentive soil.

Erythronium albidum

BLONDE LILIAN, WHITE DOGTOOTH VIOLET

☼ ❄ ↔ 3–6 in (8–15 cm) ↑ 6–12 in (15–30 cm)

From central North America. Long green leaves, rarely mottled. Flowers 1–2 in (2.5–5 cm) long, gleaming white with some yellow, in mid- to late spring. Plant then goes dormant. Eventually forms drifts. Zones 3–9.

Erythronium americanum

ADDER'S TONGUE, AMBERBELL, AMERICAN TROUT LILY, YELLOW ADDER'S TONGUE

☼/☼ ❄ ↔ 3–6 in (8–15 cm) ↑ 4–10 in (10–25 cm)

From eastern North America. Mottled maroon-purple leaves. Single, nodding, yellow, bell-shaped flowers in

Erythronium americanum

early spring. Plant goes dormant in early summer. Eventually forms drifts. Zones 3–9.

Erythronium californicum

FAWN LILY

☼ ❄ ↔ 6 in (15 cm) ↑ 10 in (25 cm)

From California, USA. Vigorous clump-forming plant found on the north-facing slopes of coastal pine forests. It has mid-green leaves, lightly patterned in purplish green. Flowers, sometimes 3 per stem, appear in spring. The petals are creamy white with brownish to yellow staining on the petal reverse and at the base. Will tolerate some heat. 'White Beauty' (syn. *E. revolutum* 'White Beauty') is easily grown, with glossy lettuce-green leaves marbled with dark green. It puts on a glamorous show during the spring. The flowers have white petals suffused with a clear cream at their center, and the basal ring is flecked with maroon. Zones 4–9.

Erythronium californicum

Erythronium californicum 'White Beauty'

Erythronium dens-canis
DOG'S TOOTH VIOLET

☼ ❋ ↔ 6 in (15 cm) ↕ 6–8 in (15–20 cm)

From cool-temperate Europe and Asia. A variable plant, with white, pale pink, rose pink, or lilac flowers, to 1½ in (35 mm) across, held individually on straight stems, in spring–early summer. These have protruding purple or blue anthers. The leaves are long and mid-green, sometimes mottled or splotched with chocolate brown, purple-green, lettuce green, or silver, and sometimes plain. The common name derives from

Erythronium revolutum

the elongated fang-like shape of the bulb. *E. dens-canis* can be grown through thin grass. Zones 3–9.

Erythronium helenae

☼ ❋ ↔ 4 in (10 cm) ↕ 6–15 in (15–38 cm)

This species is found on wooded, scrub-covered, moist, volcanic slopes in northwestern California and Mt St Helens in Washington, USA. Flowers have white to cream petals, darkening at the center, and cream anthers in the spring. Leaves are green, mottled with chocolate brown. Requires good drainage and a dryish winter. Zones 4–9.

Erythronium hendersonii
TROUT LILY

☼ ❋ ↔ 4 in (10 cm) ↕ 6–15 in (15–38 cm)

From the pine forests of southwestern Oregon and northwestern California, USA. Flowers are several to a single stem, in spring and mid-summer. Petals dark or pale lilac-pink; anthers and flower centers purple. Leaves dark green, marbled. Requires good drainage and a dry summer. Zones 4–9.

Erythronium helenae

Erythronium oregonum

Erythronium oregonum

☼ ❋ ↔ 10 in (25 cm) ↕ 10 in (25 cm)

From North America. This very variable species is similar in appearance to *E. californicum,* but the stamens have thread-like filaments. The dark green leaves are mottled with brown. The petals are creamy white, with yellow at the base, and the anthers a bright yellow. Produces several flowers per stem in spring. Zones 4–9.

Erythronium 'Pagoda'

☼ ❋ ↔ 8 in (20 cm) ↕ 6–12 in (15–30 cm)

This is a vigorous decorative hybrid, with glossy, deep green, mottled leaves. The sulfur yellow flowers have deep yellow anthers emerging from a highly visible dark central ring. Each stem bears 3 to 4 blooms, during the spring. Zones 4–9.

Erythronium revolutum
TROUT LILY

☼ ❋ ↔ 6 in (15 cm) ↕ 6–8 in (15–20 cm)

From North America. A dainty variable species. The flowers, 3 to 4 per stem, appear in spring. The petals are cyclamen pink, the stamens protruding, cream, spreading, and recurved. The leaves are deep green, marbled, and slightly wavy. There are many named selections. 'Pink Beauty' produces deep lavender-pink petals. Zones 4–9.

Erythronium hendersonii

Erythronium 'Pagoda'

Erythronium tuolumnense

Erythronium tuolumnense

☼ ❋ ↔ 8 in (20 cm) ↕ 8–15 in (20–38 cm)

Native to the open evergreen forests of central California, USA. The flower production of *E. tuolumnense* is sometimes sparse, with 3 or 4 small flowers per stem in spring. The bright yellow petals are sometimes veined in green, the anthers are yellow. The leaves are plain, pale to mid-green, and are modestly waved at the margins. This species will tolerate hot dry conditions, but it must have shade throughout the summer months. Zones 4–9.

ERYTHROPHLEUM

There are 9 species in this tropical genus, which is found in Africa, on the offshore island of Madagascar, in Southeast Asia, and parts of northern Australia. The genus is placed in the cassia subfamily of legume (Fabaceae) family, and all are trees. Most parts of the plant are poisonous to some degree. Some of the African species were once used in tribal rituals.
CULTIVATION: These trees can be grown in tropical and subtropical regions, but because of their size, they are really only suitable for large parks and gardens. Propagation is from seed, which requires some pre-treatment before it will germinate.

Erythrophleum chlorostachys

COOKTOWN IRONWOOD

☀ ⚘ ↔ 15 ft (4.5 m) ↕ 50 ft (15 m)

The only species of *Erythrophleum* occurring in Australia, extending across the far north. It is deciduous in the dry season, but with regular water it retains leaves in cultivation. The large bipinnate leaves, even when dead, are extremely poisonous to animals. Panicles of lime green flowers are borne at the branch tips in summer. Blackish seed pods. Zones 11–12.

ESCALLONIA

A genus of about 60 species of mostly evergreen shrubs and small trees in the gooseberry (Grossulariaceae) family, which are native to temperate regions of South America, and found mainly on hill slopes or exposed coasts in the Andes region. Free-flowering over a long season, they bear panicles or racemes of small white to pink or red flowers with 5 separate petals, though these are usually pressed together in the lower half to form an apparent tube. Leaves are usually small and toothed, sometimes glandular and aromatic. The fruits are small globular capsules that shed fine seed.

CULTIVATION: Not all species are hardy in cold inland areas but most can be grown successfully in exposed coastal gardens. These plants are lime tolerant and drought resistant, and they thrive in almost any well-drained soil in full sun. Prune immediately after flowering, but in cold climates delay this until the early spring. Propagation is from soft-tip cuttings taken in the spring or semi-hardwood tips taken in the autumn.

Escallonia × exoniensis

Escallonia rubra

Escallonia virgata

Escallonia bifida

syn. *Escallonia montevidensis*

WHITE ESCALLONIA

☀ ❄ ↔ 10–20 ft (3–6 m)
↕ 15–30 ft (4.5–9 m)

From Uruguay and southern Brazil. Small tree. Leaves finely toothed, larger than most species; dark green and slightly shiny on the upper surface, with a whitish midrib, paler beneath. Panicles of sweetly honey-scented white flowers, borne at branch tips, in early to mid-autumn. Zones 8–10.

Escallonia × exoniensis

☀ ❄ ↔ 12 ft (3.5 m) ↕ 15–20 ft (4.5–6 m)

Hybrid of two Chilean species *E. rosea* and *E. rubra*. Strong erect shoots from the base. Young stems are glandular. The leaves are dark lustrous green above, paler beneath. Loose panicles of blush pink to white flowers appear at the tips of branches, in mid-spring to late autumn. 'Frades', crimson flowers. Zones 8–10.

Escallonia rubra

syns *Escallonia microphylla, E. punctata*

☀ ❄ ↔ 15 ft (4.5 m) ↕ 15 ft (4.5 m)

From Chile. Variable shrub. Parent of many hybrids. Aromatic leaves. Loose panicles of deep pink to red flowers in mid-summer. *E. r.* var. *macrantha*, rose-crimson flowers set among glossy aromatic leaves; 'C. F. Ball', seedling of *E. rubra* var. *macrantha* raised in Scotland, grows to 10 ft (3 m) tall, large aromatic leaves, crimson flowers, excellent for coastal areas; *E. r.* 'Crimson Spire' ★, erect habit and bright crimson flowers; 'Woodside', low-growing, small leaves, good rock-garden plant. Zones 8–10.

Escallonia rubra var. *macrantha*

Erythrophleum chlorostachys, in the wild, Kakadu National Park, Northern Territory, Australia

Escallonia virgata

☀ ❄ ↔ 6 ft (1.8 m) ↕ 6 ft (1.8 m)

From Chile. Small-leafed deciduous shrub. Parent of many hybrids. Arching reddish branches. Bright, glossy, green leaves. Racemes of white flowers, borne in leaf axils, in summer. Dislikes chalk soils. Zones 8–10.

Escallonia Hybrid Cultivars

☀ ❄ ↔ 6–12 ft (1.8–3.5 m)
↕ 5–10 ft (1.5–3 m)

The most popular hybrids are derived mainly from *E. rubra* and *E. virgata* and originated in the UK and Ireland in the first half of the twentieth century. Most were raised in the Slieve Donard Nursery in County Down, Ireland. 'Apple Blossom', attractive cultivar suitable for hedging, to 8 ft (2.4 m), short racemes of pink and white flowers; 'Donard Beauty', rich rose red flowers, free-flowering, large leaves, aromatic when crushed; 'Donard Radiance', bushy plant, rounded, glossy, dark green foliage, to 1¾ in (40 mm) long, and clusters of rich pink tubular flowers throughout summer; 'Donard Seedling', vigorous, slightly arching, with oval, deep green, glossy leaves, to 1 in (25 mm) long, and clusters of pink-stained white flowers

Escallonia, HC, 'Pride of Donard'

all summer; 'Iveyi', handsome upright shrub, one of the best for hedging, very dark green glossy leaves, to 2½ in (6 cm) long, dense clusters of white flowers in summer; 'Langleyensis', large spreading shrub with oval dark green leaves, to 1 in (25 mm) long, and masses of almost flat bright cerise flowers in summer; 'Peach Blossom', medium-sized, and similar in habit to 'Apple Blossom', clear peach pink flowers; 'Pride of Donard', racemes of brilliantly rose-colored, somewhat bell-shaped flowers, larger than those of most other species, borne at the branch tips, from mid-summer onward; and 'Slieve Donard', medium-sized, compact, very hardy, with small leaves and panicles of apple-blossom-pink flowers. Zones 8–10.

E

Eschscholzia californica

Eschscholzia lobbii

Eschscholzia cultivar

ESCHSCHOLZIA
CALIFORNIA POPPY

Native to western North America and now widely naturalized, this genus in the poppy (Papaveraceae) family is made up of about 8 annuals and short-lived perennials. It was named in 1820 for Johann Friedrich Eschscholtz (1793–1831), the leader of the Russian expedition on which it was first collected, in 1816. (The "t" in his name was somehow lost in the transcription.) The seeds were among the many David Douglas took to England. They have fine-feathery foliage, often a rather grayish green, and in summer produce masses of bright golden yellow 4- to 8-petalled poppies that only open on sunny days. Modern seed strains come in many flower colors; the flowers are followed by long seed capsules.
CULTIVATION: Very easily grown in any sunny position with light, gritty, very well-drained soil. Often self-sows and naturalizes, especially in gravel riverbeds. Most are very frost hardy and tolerate poor soil. Propagate from seed, which is best sown directly where it is required to grow.

Eschscholzia caespitosa
TUFTED CALIFORNIA POPPY

☀ ❄ ↔ 10 in (25 cm) ↑ 10 in (25 cm)
From northern California and Oregon, USA. Annual. The leaves are very finely divided, feathery, green to blue-green. Bright yellow flowers, 2 in (5 cm) across. 'Sundew', to 6 in (15 cm) tall, lemon yellow flowers. Zones 7–10.

Eschscholzia californica
CALIFORNIA POPPY

☀ ❄ ↔ 8–16 in (20–40 cm)
↑ 8–24 in (20–60 cm)
From western USA and northern Baja California, Mexico. Now a weed in much of Australia. Annual or short-lived perennial. Leaves variable but usually finely divided, feathery, blue-green. Flowers to over 2 in (5 cm) across, usually orange but often yellow, rarely cream or pink. Seedling strains in many colors and forms, including double flowers. 'Dali', interesting soft apricot-colored form with two rows of petals. Zones 6–10.

Eschscholzia lobbii
FRYING PANS

☀ ❄ ↔ 12 in (30 cm) ↑ 12 in (30 cm)
From California's Central Valley, USA. Annual. Sticky green foliage and stems. Leaves finely divided and grass-like. Bright yellow flowers, to 2 in (5 cm) across. Similar to E. caespitosa; often sold under that name. Zones 7–10.

ESCOBARIA

This genus comprises 23 species of small solitary to clustering cacti (family Cactaceae) found from southwestern Canada through western USA and into northern Mexico, with one species a native of Cuba. It now includes all species formerly belonging to the genus Neobesseya. These plants have a depressed spherical to cylindrical form, with no distinct ribs. Lower tubercles may become corky as they grow older. The spines are usually dense, fine, and short. The flowers, in various shades of pink, have short floral tubes and naked outer segments and often do not fully open owing to the denseness of the spines. Escobaria is a distinct genus but is related to Coryphantha and Mammillaria.
CULTIVATION: All species are easily cultivated in well-drained mineral soil; withhold water through winter. Propagation is from seed, by dividing clumps, or from cuttings dried out for a week or two.

Escobaria vivipara
syn. Coryphantha vivipara
BEEHIVE CACTUS, FOXTAIL CACTUS, SHOWY PINCUSHION, SPINY STAR CACTUS

☀ ✻ ↔ 1¼–2 in (3–5 cm) ↑ 2–3 in (5–8 cm)
Found across a wide area of the USA and Canada, this attractive species is known by at least a dozen common names throughout its extensive range. The plants are usually clumping, with prominent tubercles. The spines, 3 to 7, orange to brown, do not obscure the stems. Pink to violet flowers, to 2 in (5 cm) across. Oval green seed pods. Zones 9–11.

ESPOSTOA

A genus of 16 beautiful columnar cacti from Bolivia, Ecuador, and Peru that belong to the family Cactaceae. The genus was named in honor of the early twentieth century Peruvian botanist, Nicholas Esposto. The plants are shrubby to columnar and bear a long lateral cephalium on mature branches.

Young plants are often clothed in a dense web of white wool, which protects them from their extremely harsh desert environment. The cylindrical branches bear many ribs. The night-blooming flowers are usually creamy white to reddish. The seed pods are spherical, juicy, and red to green, and may be naked or covered in tufts of hair. The genus now includes all former species of Thrixanthocereus and Pseudoespostoa and some species of Facheiroa.
CULTIVATION: Easily grown in rich well-drained soil; withhold water in winter to avoid root rot. Grows faster in open ground than in pots. Propagate either from seed or from cuttings dried out for a week or two.

Espostoa lanata ★
COTTON BALL CACTUS, OLD MAN OF THE ANDES

☀ ✻ ↔ 3–10 ft (0.9–3 m)
↑ 7–25 ft (2–8 m)
Found from southern Ecuador to northern Peru. One of the most popular of all cacti. Columnar to shrubby, the erect stems clothed in pure white wool, especially noticeable on seedlings. Ribs 20 to 25; central spines sparse, to 2 in (50 mm) long, often absent, radials numerous, short. Cephalium of light gray to brown wool, to 15 ft (4.5 m) long; this is used in Peru to stuff pillows. The purple funnel-shaped flowers are 1¼ in (30 mm) across, and the pear-shaped seed pods are plum-colored. Zones 8–11.

Espostoa melanostele

☀ ✻ ↔ 40–60 in (100–150 cm) ↑ 7 ft (2 m)
From northern to central Peru. These shrubby plants branch from the base. Ribs 20 to 35, with dense white to brown hair. Spines white or yellow, the central ones becoming black, to ½ in (12 mm) long. Cephalium white, yellow, or brown, to 28 in (70 cm) long.

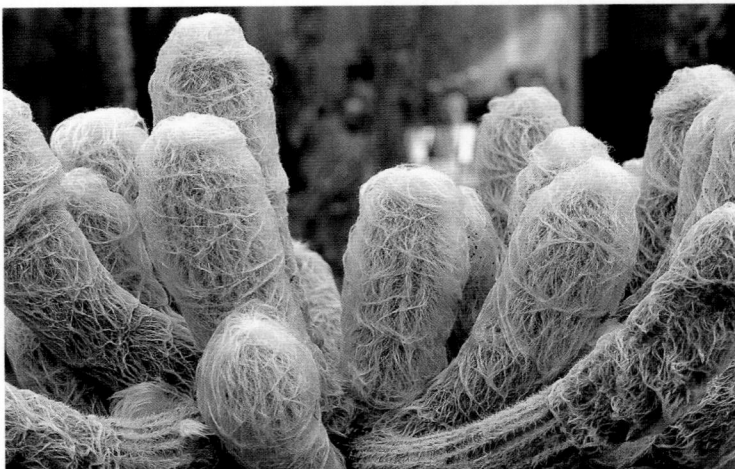

Espostoa melanostele

White bell-shaped flowers, to 2½ in (6 cm) long, 2 in (5 cm) across, appear in summer. Spherical green to red seed pods. Zones 8–11.

Espostoa senilis ★

☼ ❄ ↔ 3–7 ft (0.9–2 m) ↑ 7–15 ft (2–4.5 m)

A native of Ancash in Peru. Shrubby to tree-like plants. The branches are gray-green, covered with brownish white hairs. Ribs 16 to 18. The 1 to 3 central spines are brown, to 1¼ in (30 mm) long; the 60 or more radial spines are white, ½ in (12 mm) long. Purple flowers, to 2½ in (6 cm) long, 1¾ in (40 mm) across. Spherical green seed pods, ¾ in (18 mm) in diameter. Zones 9–11.

ETLINGERA

About 60 species of rhizomatous perennials occur in this genus, which belongs to the ginger (Zingiberaceae) family, and is found from Sri Lanka to New Guinea. The stems are cane-like and the long leaves are borne in 2 ranks. Terminal flowerheads arise from the rhizomes on separate leafless stems; these are made up of small flowers and are surrounded by large, colorful, petal-like bracts.
CULTIVATION: In suitably warm climates grow in sun or part-shade in a moist humus-rich soil. In cool climates grow indoors in bright filtered light and maintain high humidity. Water well and feed regularly during growth periods. Propagation is from seed or by division.

Etlingera elatior

syns *Nicolaia elatior, Phaeomeria speciosa, P. magnifica*

PHILIPPINE WAX FLOWER, TORCH GINGER

☼/◐ ✦ ↔ 5–8 ft (1.5–2.4 m) ↑ 10–20 ft (3–6 m)

From western Indonesia and the Malay Peninsula. A spectacular plant with large linear leaves. Cone-like heads of pink to bright red, densely packed, small flowers and waxy bracts of the same color, the outer bracts large and flaring, in summer–autumn. Young buds are traditionally eaten as a vegetable. Zones 11–12.

EUCALYPTUS

Most of the approximately 800 species of this large genus of evergreen trees are endemic to Australia; a few are found in New Guinea and southeastern Indonesia, with one *(E. deglupta)* restricted to the southern Philippines and eastern New Guinea. This genus belongs to the myrtle (Myrtaceae) family and is noted for its aromatic leaves dotted with oil glands. Species vary in size from immense forest trees to the small multi-stemmed shrubs collectively called mallees. The distinctive bark types of these plants give rise to many of the common names. Most species have 2 distinctive types of foliage: opposite juvenile leaves and alternate adult leaves. The flowers have numerous fluffy stamens, which may be white, cream, yellow, pink, or red; in bud the stamens are enclosed in a cap known as an operculum, which is composed of the fused sepals or petals or both. As the stamens expand, the operculum is forced off, splitting away from the cup-like base of the flower; this is one of the main features that unites the genus. The fruit is a woody capsule. Eucalypts are cultivated in many parts of the world and used for many purposes. Their flowers are rich in nectar; some species are among the world's finest honey plants. In a recent reclassification over 100 species have been split off from *Eucalyptus* to form the genus *Corymbia,* including a few well known as ornamentals, such as the Western Australian red-flowering gum and the lemon-scented gum.
CULTIVATION: The great majority of species are fast growing and long lived, and once established require very little artificial watering or fertilizer. They are best suited to semi-arid or warm-temperate regions. Frost hardiness varies between species, as does the need for moist or dry conditions. Some of the Western Australian mallees dislike summer humidity. Most species can be shaped by pruning or cut back heavily if desired. Propagation is from seed, which germinates readily.

Eucalyptus alba

POPLAR GUM, WHITE GUM

☼ ✦ ↔ 20 ft (6 m) ↑ 60 ft (18 m)

A native of the Northern Territory, Australia. The deciduous tree is noted for its beautiful, smooth, white bark. The adult leaves are dull green. The small clusters of small creamy white flowers appear in late winter–early spring. Suitable for tropical areas; this species is able to withstand seasonal waterlogged conditions. Zones 10–12.

Eucalyptus baileyana

BAILEY'S STRINGYBARK

☼ ❄ ↔ 15 ft (4.5 m) ↑ 80 ft (24 m)

Found in southeastern Queensland and northeastern New South Wales, Australia. Fibrous-barked tree. The adult leaves are dark green. The cream flowers, usually form in heads of 7 blooms. Gumnuts to ½ in (12 mm) wide. This tree is sought after for its good timber. Zones 10–11.

Etlingera elatior

Eucalyptus alba, in the wild, Kakadu National Park, Northern Territory, Australia

Eucalyptus bicostata
syn. *Eucalyptus globulus* subsp. *bicostata*
EURABBIE

☼ ❋ ↔ 25 ft (8 m) ↑ 120 ft (36 m)

From southeastern Australia. Smooth white or blue-gray bark, shedding in long ribbons. Leaves, juvenile, silvery blue, heart-shaped; adult, deep glossy green, to 24 in (60 cm) long. Creamy white flowers in spring–summer. Fruit ribbed and bell-shaped. Fast-growing; tolerates dry conditions. Zones 8–10.

Eucalyptus biturbinata
GRAY GUM

☼ ❄ ↔ 30 ft (9 m) ↑ 70 ft (21 m)

Native to northeastern New South Wales and southeastern Queensland, Australia, where it occurs on reasonably nutrient-rich soils; closely related to *E. punctata.* A tall tree with smooth-ish, mottled, whitish gray bark, shedding annually. Adult leaves glossy and dark green on the uppersurface,

Eucalyptus caesia subsp. *magna*

lighter and duller on the lower. Inflorescences, borne in the leaf axils, with 7 small white flowers in summer–early autumn. Zones 9–11.

Eucalyptus blakelyi
BLAKELY'S RED GUM

☼ ❋ ↔ 20 ft (6 m) ↑ 60 ft (18 m)

Found in eastern Australia. This tree has a short straight trunk with smooth,

Eucalyptus blakelyi

attractively mottled, gray bark, peeling in large irregular flakes. The juvenile leaves are broad and grayish green; the adult leaves are sickle-shaped and pendulous. Bears white or pinkish flowers in late winter–spring, popular with honey-bees. This is an excellent timber tree. Zones 8–11.

Eucalyptus brookeriana
BROOKER'S GUM

☼ ❋ ↔ 20 ft (6 m) ↑ 120 ft (36 m)

From the cooler forests of southeastern mainland Australia and Tasmania. Long straight trunk with persistent gray-brown fibrous bark on lower part of trunk and smooth creamy gray bark above. Creamy white flowers appear, in summer–autumn. Zones 8–9.

Eucalyptus caesia
GUNGURRU

☼ ❄ ↔ 15 ft (4.5 m) ↑ 20 ft (6 m)

From Western Australia. Mallee or small tree with weeping branches and a fairly open crown. Stems, buds, and

Eucalyptus brookeriana

capsules have a powdery white appearance. Smooth reddish brown bark, shedding in long curling strips. Pendent clusters of red or pink flowers in late spring–early autumn. Urn-shaped capsules. *E. c.* subsp. *magna,* sturdier than the species, produces prolific red bell-shaped flowers and waxy, white, bell-shaped fruit. Zones 9–11.

Eucalyptus camaldulensis
RIVER RED GUM

☼ ❄ ↔ 25 ft (8 m) ↑ 150 ft (45 m)

Found along watercourses in inland Australia. Single or multiple, often massive, trunk with smooth attractively mottled bark. Rich green pendent leaves. Profuse white flowers in late

Eucalyptus biturbinata, in the wild, Lamington National Park, Queensland, Australia

Eucalyptus bicostata, in the wild, Kinglake National Park, Victoria, Australia

Eucalyptus camaldulensis, in the wild, Yanga-Nyawi National Park, Victoria, Australia

Eucalyptus coccifera, in the wild, Pelion Plains, Tasmania, Australia

Eucalyptus cinerea

spring–summer. Grown worldwide for its ornamental value, timber and honey, and as fuel wood. Zones 9–12.

Eucalyptus cinerea
ARGYLE APPLE, SILVER DOLLAR TREE

☀ ❄ ↔ 30 ft (9 m) ↑ 50 ft (15 m)
From southeastern Australia. Fairly short trunk. Dense spreading crown. Juvenile foliage circular, silvery gray. Small white flowers in early summer. Moderately fast growing; retains lower branches to near ground level. Ideal for screens or windbreaks. Zones 8–11.

Eucalyptus cladocalyx
SUGAR GUM

☀ ❄ ↔ 20 ft (6 m) ↑ 50–100 ft (15–30 m)
From South Australia. Fairly short stout trunk; smooth, pale gray, mottled bark. Wide dense crown. Dark green glossy leaves. Profuse creamy yellow flowers in summer. Can be invasive. '**Nana**', low-growing bushy form, to about 30 ft (9 m) high, often used for shelterbelts. Zones 8–10.

Eucalyptus coccifera
TASMANIAN SNOW GUM

☀ ❄ ↔ 10 ft (3 m) ↑ 80 ft (24 m)
From Tasmania, Australia. Peeling white and gray bark reveals yellow or pink fresh bark beneath. Juvenile leaves rounded, bluish green; adult leaves gray-green, lanceolate. Creamy white flowers in summer. Zones 8–9.

Eucalyptus coolabah
syn. *Eucalyptus microtheca*, in part
COOLABAH, COOLIBAH

☀ ⦂ ↔ 12 ft (3.5 m) ↑ 60 ft (18 m)
From the dry inland regions of mainland Australia. The trunk is covered with rough gray bark persisting to the larger branches; the upper branches are smooth, whitish gray. The leaves are gray-green and narrow-lanceolate. This tree produces creamy white flowers in summer. Tolerant of drought, waterlogged conditions, and extreme heat. Zones 9–12.

Eucalyptus cordata
SILVER GUM

☀ ❄ ↔ 10 ft (3 m) ↑ 60 ft (18 m)
From Tasmania, Australia. The smooth white bark is mottled with green and purplish patches. The attractive, silvery gray, heart-shaped juvenile leaves, to 4 in (10 cm) long, often persist on more mature trees. A profusion of creamy white flowers is produced in the spring. Fast-growing. Cut foliage from this species is used for floral decoration. Zones 8–9.

Eucalyptus cornuta
YATE

☀ ⦂ ↔ 10 ft (3 m) ↑ 60 ft (18 m)
From Western Australia. Rough dark brown bark persisting to the larger branches; upper branches are smooth, and whitish gray. Shiny, dark green, lanceolate leaves. Bears clusters of pale yellow flowers in spring. Tolerates dry conditions and some coastal exposure. Zones 9–10.

Eucalyptus cosmophylla
CUP GUM

☀ ⦂ ↔ 12 ft (3.5 m) ↑ 25 ft (8 m)
From South Australia. Tall mallee or small tree. Short, often crooked, trunk with deciduous, gray-white, patchy bark. Dense spreading crown of gray-green foliage. The showy creamy white flowers appear in late summer–spring. Zones 9–11.

Eucalyptus cordata

Eucalyptus cosmophylla

E

Eucalyptus delegatensis, in the wild, Brindabella National Park, New South Wales, Australia

Eucalyptus costata

Eucalyptus crebra

Eucalyptus costata

RIDGE-FRUITED MALLEE

☀ ❄ ↔ 12 ft (3.5 m) ↑ 20 ft (6 m)

From semi-arid regions of southeastern Australia. An attractive mallee with smooth gray-brown bark, deciduous in ribbons. Thick, glossy, green leaves. Large clusters of profuse creamy white flowers in spring. Urn-shaped, often ribbed, seed capsules. Zones 9–11.

Eucalyptus crebra

NARROW-LEAFED IRONBARK

☀ ❄ ↔ 20 ft (6 m) ↑ 120 ft (36 m)

From eastern Australia. Long straight trunk with dark gray deeply furrowed bark persisting to the small branches. Narrow gray-green leaves. Small white flowers in spring–summer. Small cup-shaped seed capsules. Valued for strong durable timber and honey. Zones 9–12.

Eucalyptus crenulata

BUXTON GUM

☀ ❄ ↔ 15 ft (4.5 m) ↑ 50 ft (15 m)

From Victoria, Australia, often growing on swampy sites. Conspicuously glaucous new buds and leaves. Adult leaves highly aromatic, gray-green, usually heart-shaped, with shallow-toothed margins; popular for cut foliage. Small white flowers in spring. Zones 8–9.

Eucalyptus crucis

SILVER MALLEE

☀ ❄ ↔ 10 ft (3 m) ↑ 20 ft (6 m)

From Western Australia. All parts have a powdery gray appearance. Smooth red or reddish brown bark shedding in curling strips. Glaucous rounded leaves. Profuse creamy white flowers in spring–autumn. Best in a winter-rainfall climate. Zones 9–11.

Eucalyptus dalrympleana

MOUNTAIN GUM, WHITE GUM

☀ ❄ ↔ 35 ft (10 m) ↑ 120 ft (36 m)

From higher elevations of southeast Australia. Straight trunk, smooth white or reddish bark almost to ground, shed in long ribbons in summer. Fairly dense crown. Thin, glossy, dark green leaves. White flowers in autumn. Zones 8–9.

Eucalyptus delegatensis

syn. *Eucalyptus gigantea*

ALPINE ASH

☀ ❄ ↔ 12 ft (3.5 m) ↑ 150 ft (45 m)

From mountain forests of southeastern Australia. Lower half of trunk has brown fibrous bark; upper trunk and branches have smooth creamy white or blue-gray bark, shedding in long ribbons. Adult leaves curved; juvenile foliage broader and blue-green. White flowers in late summer. Zones 8–9.

Eucalyptus diversicolor

KARRI

☀ ❄ ↔ 25 ft (8 m) ↑ 300 ft (90 m)

Western Australia's tallest tree. Smooth whitish gray or yellowish brown bark,

Eucalyptus crucis

shedding in irregular blotches. The adult leaves are broad-lanceolate, dark green above, and distinctly paler beneath. The creamy white flowers are produced in spring–summer and their nectar makes excellent honey. This tree is also highly valued for its hardwood. Zones 9–10.

Eucalyptus dives

BROAD-LEAFED PEPPERMINT

☀ ❄ ↔ 20 ft (6 m) ↑ 25–100 ft (8–30 m)

From southeastern Australia. A low-branching tree, large open crown, persistent bark covered trunk, and larger branches. The glossy broad-lanceolate leaves are pungently aromatic when crushed. *E. dives* bears a profusion of creamy white flowers in the spring. Zones 8–10.

Eucalyptus elata

RIVER PEPPERMINT

☀ ❄ ↔ 35 ft (10 m) ↑ 100 ft (30 m)

From southeastern Australia. Dark persistent bark on the lower trunk; the upper trunk has smooth white, gray, or yellow bark, shedding in long ribbons. Adult leaves are narrow, sparse, somewhat weeping, and give off a peppermint smell when crushed. The clusters of small creamy white flowers are borne in spring. Zones 9–11.

Eucalyptus erythrocorys ★

ILLYARRIE, RED-CAP GUM

☀ ❄ ↔ 10 ft (3 m) ↑ 25 ft (8 m)

From Western Australia. *E. erythrocorys* is a mallee shrub or small tree with smooth, gray to white, deciduous bark, and bright green leathery leaves. Unusual, large, 4-lobed, scarlet bud caps open to reveal bright yellow flowers in summer–autumn. They are followed by attractive, broad, bell-shaped, woody seed capsules, to 1½ in (35 mm) long. Zones 9–11.

Eucalyptus diversicolor

Eucalyptus microcorys

Eucalyptus marginata, in the wild, Manjimup, Western Australia

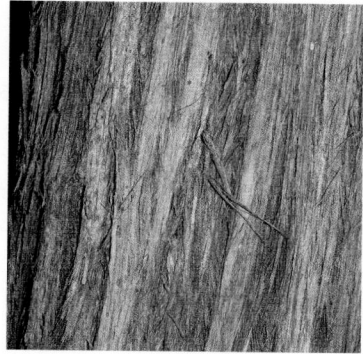

Eucalyptus macrorhyncha, bark

Eucalyptus macrocarpa
MOTTLECAH

☀ ⚘ ↔ 12 ft (3.5 m) ↕ 3–12 ft (0.9–3.5 m)

From Western Australia. Mallee shrub with the largest flowers and fruit of any of the eucalypts. Stems, new bark, and buds powdery gray. Leaves are broadly ovate, silvery gray, thick-textured, and stem-clasping. Showy deep pink to red flowers in late winter–spring. Woody seed capsules, to 4 in (10 cm) wide. Best in winter-rainfall areas. Zones 9–10.

Eucalyptus macrorhyncha
RED STRINGYBARK

☀ ❄ ↔ 20 ft (6 m) ↕ 120 ft (36 m)

From southeastern Australia. Straight-trunked tree with fibrous, reddish brown, stringy bark. Dense rounded crown of dark green lance-shaped adult leaves, to 6 in (15 cm) long. White flowers, in clusters of 7 or more, in summer–early autumn. Zones 8–10.

Eucalyptus mannifera
BRITTLE GUM

☀ ❄ ↔ 15 ft (4.5 m) ↕ 70 ft (21 m)

Widespread in southeastern Australia. Powdery white, cream, or gray bark, smooth to ground level, turning reddish before shedding in short ribbons. Open canopy of narrow, gray-green, drooping leaves. The clusters of small white flowers are borne through summer and autumn. This is an attractive street tree. Zones 8–10.

Eucalyptus marginata
JARRAH

☀ ⚘ ↔ 15 ft (4.5 m) ↕ 120 ft (36 m)

From the southwestern corner of Western Australia. Straight trunk with rough, reddish brown to gray, fibrous bark. Dense canopy of dark green, pointed, lance-shaped leaves, to 5 in (12 cm) long. Showy clusters of nectar-rich creamy white flowers in spring. One of Australia's most important hardwood trees. Zones 9–10.

Eucalyptus megacornuta
WARTY YATE

☀ ⚘ ↔ 10 ft (3 m) ↕ 40 ft (12 m)

From the Ravensthorpe Range in Western Australia. An ornamental tall shrub or a small tree with an open crown and dull green sickle-shaped leaves. Smooth gray bark mottled with red and green. The specific epithet *megacornuta* refers to the large, horn-like, warty bud caps. Showy yellow-green flowers in spring. Zones 9–11.

Eucalyptus melliodora
YELLOW BOX

☀ ⚘ ↔ 35 ft (10 m) ↕ 100 ft (30 m)

From eastern Australia. Bark variable, usually rough and fibrous on trunk and lower branches, smooth and white on upper parts. Adult leaves grayish green, to 6 in (15 cm) long. Profuse sweetly scented, white or, rarely, pink flowers in summer. Valued as an ornamental shade tree and for honey. Zones 9–11.

Eucalyptus microcorys
TALLOWWOOD

☀/◐ ⚘ ↔ 15 ft (4.5 m) ↕ 60 ft (18 m)

From eastern Australia. Distinctive soft, fibrous, reddish brown bark. Dense spreading crown. Thin-textured dark green leaves. Showy clusters of creamy white flowers in winter–early summer. Yields valuable hardwood. Excellent shade and shelter tree for farms, parks and public gardens. Zones 10–12.

Eucalyptus macrocarpa

Eucalyptus mannifera

Eucalyptus megacornuta

Eucalyptus pauciflora, in the wild, Baw Baw National Park, Victoria, Australia

Eucalyptus orbifolia

Eucalyptus nicholii

NARROW-LEAFED BLACK PEPPERMINT

☼ ❄ ↔ 25 ft (8 m) ↑ 50 ft (15 m)

From eastern Australia. Fast-growing. Relatively short trunk, fibrous brown bark. Compact crown. Pendulous, fine, sickle-shaped, blue-green leaves. Small white flowers in autumn. Zones 8–11.

Eucalyptus orbifolia

ROUND-LEAFED MALLEE

☼ ❄ ↔ 7 ft (2 m) ↑ 10 ft (3 m)

From southern Western Australia. This mallee shrub has multiple stems. The smooth reddish brown bark peels, exposing fresh green bark. Gray-green adult leaves, rounded, with indented tip. Stems, buds, and fruit powdery gray. Profuse pale yellow flowers in winter–early spring. Zones 9–11.

Eucalyptus parvifolia

syn. *Eucalyptus parvula*

SMALL-LEAFED GUM

☼ ❄ ↔ 10–20 ft (3–6 m) ↑ 15–25 ft (4.5–8 m)

From southeastern New South Wales, Australia, occurring in a small area of tablelands above 3,000 ft (900 m) on somewhat boggy soils. Small bushy tree, often branching near ground level, with a broad umbrella-shaped crown. Grayish bark, shedding in strips, exposing smooth gray to pinkish surface. Juvenile leaves opposite, stalkless, oval, green, to 1¾ in (4 cm) long, often persisting well into the crown; adult leaves to about 3 in (7 cm) long. The inflorescences, which carry 7 small white flowers, appear in the summer. Zones 7–9.

Eucalyptus pauciflora subsp. *niphophila*, in the wild, Snowy Mountains, Victoria, Australia

Eucalyptus pauciflora

SNOW GUM, WHITE SALLY

☼ ❄ ↔ 20 ft (6 m) ↑ 60 ft (18 m)

From the mountains of southeastern Australia. Short trunk with smooth, mottled, light gray, white, or yellowish bark, shedding in irregular patches. The adult leaves are shiny, leathery, blue-green, to 8 in (20 cm) long. Profuse nectar-rich white blossoms in spring–summer. *E. p.* subsp. *niphophila* (syn. *E. niphophila*), commonly known as the alpine snow gum, occurring above 5,000 ft (1,500 m) in the Snowy Mountains of New South Wales and Victoria; low-branching habit; attractive bark that sheds to leave a smooth white or gray surface with patches of orange, red, yellow, and olive green; shiny blue-green leaves; glaucous buds and fruit. Zones 7–9.

Eucalyptus perriniana

SPINNING GUM

☼ ❄ ↔ 10–20 ft (3–6 m) ↑ 20–40 ft (6–12 m)

From subalpine areas of southeastern Australia. Mallee-like small tree. Bark sheds to leave a smooth whitish gray surface with pale brown and green patches. Juvenile leaves powdery gray, fused into a disk around twig; adult leaves dull gray-green, lance-shaped. Profuse creamy white flowers in the

Eucalyptus pauciflora subsp. *niphophila*, in the wild, Snowy Mountains, Victoria, Australia

Eucalyptus perriniana

Eucalyptus populnea

summer. The juvenile leaves are popular as cut foliage for floral arrangements. Zones 7–9.

Eucalyptus polyanthemos
RED BOX

☀ ❄ ↔ 20 ft (6 m) ↑ 25–80 ft (8–24 m)

From southeastern Australia. Short trunk. Large, often irregular, crown. Oval to almost circular bluish gray leaves, pendent on slender stalks. Bark variable: may be rough, gray, and persistent to the smaller branches or may

shed annually, leaving the tree smooth-barked. The small white flowers occur in spring. Zones 8–11.

Eucalyptus polybractea
BLUE MALLEE

☀ ❄ ↔ 10 ft (3 m) ↑ 30 ft (9 m)

Small tree from southeastern Australia. Rough fibrous bark at base of stems, smooth grayish bark above. Bluish gray leaves. Cream flowers from yellowish buds in autumn–spring. Used for distilling eucalyptus oil. Zones 9–11.

Eucalyptus populnea
BIMBLE BOX, POPLAR BOX

☀ ❄ ↔ 15 ft (4.5 m) ↑ 80 ft (24 m)

From inland eastern Australia. Shortish trunk, persistent finely fibrous bark. Compact crown. Leaves shiny, green, oval. Small white flowers, late summer. Useful for shade and shelter; withstands drought and waterlogging. Zones 9–11.

Eucalyptus preissiana
BELL-FRUITED MALLEE

☀ ❄ ↔ 8 ft (2.4 m) ↑ 15 ft (4.5 m)

From southern districts of Western Australia. Straggling mallee shrub. Gray bark smooth or mottled. Thick, ovate, gray-green leaves. Large, reddish, pear-shaped buds, in clusters of 3, opening to bright yellow flowers in winter–spring. Bell-shaped seed capsules. Best in winter-rainfall climates. Zones 9–10.

Eucalyptus propinqua
SMALL-FRUITED GRAY GUM

☀ ❄ ↔ 20 ft (6 m) ↑ 120 ft (36 m)

From the central coast of Queensland south to just north of Sydney, Australia.

The bark is smooth and light-colored with colored patches ranging from cream to orange, ageing to gray, shedding all year round. The adult leaves are lance-shaped, glossy green, and paler beneath. White flowers appear in summer–autumn. *E. propinqua* is infrequently seen as a cultivated species. Zones 9–10.

Eucalyptus propinqua

Eucalyptus polybractea

Eucalyptus polyanthemos

Eucalyptus pulverulenta

☼ ❋ ↔ 12 ft (3.5 m) ↑ 15–30 ft (4.5–9 m)

From the mountains of southeastern New South Wales, Australia, and rare. Small tree or mallee shrub. This species has circular silvery blue juvenile leaves, and rarely produces adult leaves. The attractive smooth bark, often pale brown or coppery, peels in long strips. The buds and fruit have a silvery waxy bloom. The small white flowers are produced in spring. Popular for cut foliage. Zones 8–10.

Eucalyptus pyriformis

DOWERIN ROSE, PEAR-FRUITED MALLEE

☼ ⚶ ↔ 10 ft (3 m) ↑ 6–20 ft (1.8–6 m)

From Western Australia. Mallee shrub with multiple stems and smooth gray bark. Gray-green thick-textured leaves. The highly ornamental, ribbed, pear-shaped buds open to pendulous red, yellow, or creamy flowers in winter–spring. Large decorative seed capsules. Zones 9–11.

Eucalyptus regnans

MOUNTAIN ASH

☼ ❋ ↔ 15–25 ft (4.5–8 m) ↑ 320 ft (96 m)

From the cool mountain forests in southeastern Australia. Straight trunk with fibrous persistent bark on the lower part; the remainder sheds to reveal a smooth whitish or gray-green surface. Narrow open crown. Lance-shaped leaves. Produces small white flowers in summer. *E. regnans* is the tallest hardwood species in the world. Zones 8–9.

Eucalyptus rhodantha

Eucalyptus rhodantha

ROSE MALLEE

☼ ⚶ ↔ 10 ft (3 m) ↑ 10 ft (3 m)

From southwestern Australia. Spreading mallee. Smooth pale brown bark. Powdery whitish gray branchlets. Juvenile and adult leaves are rounded to heart-shaped, thick-textured, and powdery gray. Solitary red flowers, on pendent stalks, in spring–autumn. Broad seed capsules. Zones 9–11.

Eucalyptus robusta

SWAMP MAHOGANY

☼ ⚶ ↔ 35 ft (10 m) ↑ 80 ft (24 m)

From the coastal swamps of eastern Australia. Reddish brown, deeply furrowed, persistent bark. Dense spreading crown. Large dark green leaves, slightly

Eucalyptus regnans, in the wild, Otway National Park, Victoria, Australia

paler beneath. Bears white flowers that are nectar-rich in spring–autumn. This tree will tolerate coastal exposure and heavy wet soils. Koalas feed on the foliage. Zones 9–11.

Eucalyptus rossii

INLAND SCRIBBLY GUM

☼ ⚶ ↔ 30 ft (9 m) ↑ 60 ft (18 m)

Native to eastern Australia. The attractive, smooth, grayish white trunk is often marked with "scribbles" left by

insect larvae. These trees have a fairly low-branching habit, with a spreading canopy of narrow gray-green leaves. The small white flowers occur in summer, and are followed by tiny seed capsules. Zones 9–11.

Eucalyptus rubida

CANDLEBARK GUM

☼ ❋ ↔ 20–30 ft (6–9 m) ↑ 50–80 ft (15–24 m)

From the cooler regions of southeastern Australia. An attractive smooth-barked tree; the height varies according to its habitat. Creamy white bark develops reddish patches in late summer before shedding. Narrow gray-green leaves. White flowers in late spring–summer. Zones 8–9.

Eucalyptus rossii, in the wild, Goulburn River National Park, New South Wales, Australia

Eucalyptus pyriformis

Eucalyptus saligna
SYDNEY BLUE GUM

☀ ❄ ↔ 35 ft (10 m) ↑ 120 ft (36 m)

From tall open forests of eastern Australia. Ornamental, smooth, bluish white bark, shedding annually in short ribbons. Broad, tapering, dark green leaves. Profuse nectar-rich, white flowers in summer. Excellent timber and honey producer. Koalas feed on the foliage. Zones 9–11.

Eucalyptus scoparia
WALLANGARRA WHITE GUM

☀ ❄ ↔ 20 ft (6 m) ↑ 40 ft (12 m)

Rare in the wild; known only from a small area on the southeastern border of Queensland, Australia. Ornamental species with a straight smooth trunk and graceful weeping branches. New bark is white, turning pale gray with age, then shedding in patches. Narrow, pendulous, shining, green leaves. Small creamy white flowers during spring–summer. Zones 9–11.

Eucalyptus sideroxylon
MUGGA, RED IRONBARK

☀ ❄ ↔ 25 ft (8 m) ↑ 100 ft (30 m)

Widespread in southeastern Australia. Handsome, deeply furrowed, nearly black bark. Drooping, narrow, grayish green to bluish leaves. Showy white, cream, pink, or red flowers, in hanging clusters of 7, in winter–early spring. Important honey source; strong durable timber. Zones 9–11.

Eucalyptus spathulata ★
SWAMP MALLET

☀ ❄ ↔ 20 ft (6 m) ↑ 40 ft (12 m)

From southwestern corner of Australia. Smooth reddish brown bark, ageing to gray before shedding in late summer. Very narrow gray-green leaves. Red bud caps opening to profuse creamy white

Eucalyptus scoparia

flowers in winter–spring. Fast-growing; useful for windbreak planting in low-rainfall areas. Zones 9–11.

Eucalyptus tereticornis
FOREST RED GUM, QUEENSLAND BLUE GUM

☀ ❄ ↔ 25 ft (8 m) ↑ 150 ft (45 m)

From east coast of Australia and into New Guinea. Large shapely tree. Bark sheds in large irregular sheets, revealing smooth surface mottled with shades of cream, bluish gray, and white. Shiny, green, curved leaves. Profuse white flowers in winter–spring. Zones 9–12.

Eucalyptus tetragona
TALLERACK

☀ ❄ ↔ 15 ft (4.5 m) ↑ 25 ft (8 m)

Widespread tree in southern Western Australia. Stems, buds, and capsules covered in a white powdery bloom and highly valued in floral arrangements. Square stems; thick, pale gray-green, oval leaves. Creamy flowers in spring–summer. Withstands very dry conditions. Zones 9–11.

Eucalyptus tetraptera
FOUR-WINGED MALLEE

☀ ❄ ↔ 8 ft (2.4 m) ↑ 10 ft (3 m)

Widespread along the southern coast of Western Australia. A tree with contorted, smooth, gray limbs. Bright green leathery leaves. Conspicuous red

Eucalyptus viminalis, in the wild, Angahook-Lorne State Park, Victoria, Australia

flowers with bright pink stamens, to 1½ in (35 mm) long. Square gray fruit. Can be pruned to shape. Zones 9–11.

Eucalyptus urnigera
URN GUM

☀ ❄ ↔ 15 ft (4.5 m) ↑ 40 ft (12 m)

From Tasmania, Australia. Smooth-barked. Olive green leaves, to 4 in (10 cm). Creamy white flowers, in clusters of 3, in late summer–autumn. Urn-shaped seed capsules. Zones 8–9.

Eucalyptus viminalis
CANDLEBARK, MANNA GUM, RIBBON GUM

☀ ❄ ↔ 35 ft (10 m) ↑ 180 ft (55 m)

From eastern Australia. Tall forest tree. Bark smooth or with stocking of rough bark on lower trunk; upper bark sheds, revealing smooth white bark. Koalas favor dark green leaves. Many small white flowers in summer. Zones 8–10.

Eucalyptus tetragona

EUCOMIS
PINEAPPLE LILY

These plants, which grow from large, ovate, shiny, greenish purple bulbs, gain their common name from the flowering stem's pineapple-like topknot. Mainly from the summer-rainfall eastern parts of southern Africa, they are members of the hyacinth (Hyacinthaceae) family. The broad leaves are glossy and can be plain or flecked; they appear with the flowers and form a basal rosette. Many tiny star-shaped flowers cluster around a single semi-erect stem in cylindrical formation. These striking plants lend themselves to greenhouse culture and are popular in cut-flower arrangements. In consequence, they are seen at many times of the year, but when left to themselves, they bloom in late summer to early autumn. There are numerous strains and cultivars, in a variety of sizes, shapes, and shades, and new ones appear regularly.

CULTIVATION: The major requirements of these plants are rich, well-drained soil, a dry dormancy, and a moist growth period. Propagate from seed sown in spring or from offsets taken during the winter dormancy.

Eucalyptus saligna

Eucalyptus tereticornis

Eucalyptus urnigera

Eucryphia × intermedia

Eucryphia glutinosa

Eucomis autumnalis

WHITE PINEAPPLE LILY

☼/◐ ❄ ↔ 24 in (60 cm)
↑ 10–18 in (25–45 cm)

From eastern South Africa, widespread. Leaves broad, wavy-edged, green, to 18 in (45 cm) long. Flower stems upright, not lax, with 6 in (15 cm) long racemes of white flowers ageing to yellow-green in mid-summer–early autumn. There are several subspecies with widely varying foliage and flowers. Zones 8–11.

Eucomis bicolor

☼ ❄ ↔ 12–24 in (30–60 cm)
↑ 12–24 in (30–60 cm)

From eastern-central South Africa. Grows wild in wet meadows and on stream banks. Bears slightly ragged pendent flowers with green-white petals, sometimes marked with purple, and maroon-flecked stems in late summer. The leaves are undulating and oblong. This plant needs plenty of water during growth. Zones 7–9.

Eucomis comosa

☼ ❄ ↔ 16 in (40 cm)
↑ 12–24 in (30–60 cm)

Highly variable species from Eastern Cape and KwaZulu-Natal, South Africa. The leaves are wavy-edged. The flowers with green or whitish, pink or reddish, brown-purple or deep purple petals appear in late summer–early autumn. Some selections have purple leaves, but mid-green is more common, often with spotted undersides. Zones 8–10.

EUCOMMIA

This genus consists of a single species of deciduous tree from China with simple alternate leaves and petal-less flowers that appear in spring before or with the foliage. The fruit is a winged nutlet, to 1½ in (35 mm) long. A form of rubber can be extracted from the tree, which is also valued in herbal medicine and as a specimen tree in the larger garden. *Eucommia* is the sole

Eucommia ulmoides

member of the family Eucommiaceae, the affinities of which have long been in doubt; current thinking is that its closest allies are *Aucuba* and *Garrya*.
CULTIVATION: Frost resistant and drought tender, it prefers sandy, light to medium, well-drained soil in an open sunny position. Propagate from seed, or from cuttings of young wood under glass.

Eucommia ulmoides

GUTTA-PERCHA TREE

☼ ❄ ↔ 25 ft (8 m) ↑ 60 ft (18 m)

From central China. Broadly domed crown. The leathery, toothed, oval leaves, to 3–6 in (8–15 cm) long, resemble elm leaves. Insignificant solitary flowers appear before or with the new leaves. Zones 5–10.

EUCRYPHIA

Found in Chile, eastern mainland Australia, and Tasmania, this genus includes 7 species of evergreen or semievergreen shrubs and trees, 2 of them recently discovered in Queensland, Australia. Although previously placed in a family (Eucryphiaceae) of its own, *Eucryphia* is now regarded as a member of the family Cunoniaceae. The leaves are simple or pinnate, with oblong to elliptical leaflets. In all species the leaves are dark green above and much lighter below, usually with a fine downy covering which soon wears away from the upper surfaces. The flowers, which

resemble small single rose blossoms, have 4 or 5 petals that are white, cream, or occasionally pale pink. They open from late spring to autumn, and are often slightly scented.
CULTIVATION: These plants tolerate only light to moderate frost but are easily cultivated in a mild climate. The general preference is for a relatively humid atmosphere; a moist, humusenriched, well-drained soil; and a position in sun or partial shade. In areas with hot dry summers, provide shade from the hottest sun.

Eucryphia glutinosa

HARDY EUCRYPHIA, NIRRHE

☼ ❄ ↔ 20 ft (6 m) ↑ 30 ft (9 m)

From the dry mountainous areas in central Chile. May drop foliage in cold winters, coloring well in the process. Leaves pinnate, 2 in (5 cm) long, composed of elliptical leaflets with serrated edges. Large white flowers, 2½ in (6 cm) across, with red-brown anthers in summer. **Plena Group** cultivars have semi-double or double flowers. Zones 8–9.

Eucryphia × intermedia

☼ ❄ ↔ 15 ft (4.5 m) ↑ 30 ft (9 m)

Hybrid between the Chilean species *E. glutinosa* and *E. lucida,* the evergreen from Tasmania, Australia. Carries simple and trifoliate foliage, also a few pinnate leaves. Although evergreen, may drop some foliage over winter. Leaves light green with a hint of blue on undersides. Pure white flowers. 'Rostrevor' ★, named after the Irish garden where the cross originated, is the most common form. Zones 8–9.

Eucryphia lucida

PINKWOOD, TASMANIAN LEATHERWOOD

☼ ❄ ↔ 15 ft (4.5 m) ↑ 25 ft (8 m)

From Tasmania, Australia. Upright tree. Juvenile and adult foliage distinctly different, the trifoliate foliage of young

Eucomis comosa

Eucomis autumnalis

Eucomis bicolor

plants changing to simple, narrow, ob-long leaves with age. Pendulous, and usually white, flowers, to 2 in (5 cm) across, in summer. Famous in Tasmania for its aromatic honey. '**Ballerina**' bears flowers 1¼ in (30 mm) across, with pale pink petals edged with darker pink, and red stamens; '**Leatherwood Cream**', cream-edged leaves. Other pink-flowered forms, such as '**Pink Cloud**', are also grown. Zones 8–9.

Eucryphia milliganii
MOUNTAIN LEATHERWOOD

☼ ❋ ↔ 6 ft (1.8 m) ↑ 20 ft (6 m)

From Tasmania, Australia. Slow-grow-ing tree with a narrow, often columnar, habit. Leaves are small, short, narrow. Creamy white flowers are 1 in (25 mm) across. Its short narrow leaves and massed small flowers differentiate it from the other eucryphias. Zones 8–9.

Eucryphia × nymansensis

☼ ❋ ↔ 15 ft (4.5 m) ↑ 30 ft (9 m)

This hybrid between 2 Chilean species, *E. cordifolia* and *E. glutinosa*, appeared around 1914 at Nymans in Sussex, England. '**Mount Usher**' often has semi-double flowers. The most com-monly grown form, '**Nymansay**', is densely foliaged, strongly upright, and evergreen, bearing both simple, glossy, elliptical leaves and compound leaves with 3 serrated-edged leaflets. White flowers, to 3 in (8 cm) across, with clearly separated petals. Zones 8–9.

Eucryphia lucida

Eucryphia × nymansensis

EUGENIA
STOPPER

This genus in the myrtle (Myrtaceae) family, has about 550 species of ever-green trees or shrubs with firm, opposite, glossy, simple leaves. Widely spread across tropical to subtropical regions in the Americas, with scattered species in Africa, Asia, and the Pacific Islands. Conspicuous flowers, with numerous stamens, may be solitary, in panicles, or in racemes, and usually appear in spring or summer. The fruit is a drupe-like yellow, purple, red, or black berry and is sometimes edible. This genus is grown for the ornamental value of its flowers, fruit, and foliage; for hedging and screening; and some species for their edible fruit. CULTIVATION: Easily grown in tropical and subtropical areas in sun or part-shade. They do best in well-drained sandy loam. Propagate from seed in summer or from cuttings of half-hardened wood in autumn.

Eugenia capensis
DUNE MYRTLE

☼ ❦ ↔ ↑ 3–30 ft (0.9–9 m)

From Cape Town, South Africa, to Mozambique, Botswana, and Malawi. Extremely variable species with 9 rec-ognized subspecies. Leaves oval to al-most circular, shiny dark green above, paler below. White flowers, borne singly or in clusters in leaf axils, in autumn–winter. Ovate, reddish purple, fleshy, edible fruit. *E. c.* subsp. *nata-litia* (syn. *E. natalitia*), many-branched shrub with elliptical purple fruit, ½ in (12 mm) long. Zones 9–12.

Eugenia uniflora
BRAZILIAN CHERRY, FLORIDA CHERRY, PITANGA, SURINAM CHERRY

☼ ❧ ↔ 8 ft (2.4 m) ↑ 10–30 ft (3–9 m)

From Brazil. Shrub or small tree. Dull green narrow leaves, to 2½ in (6 cm) long. Fragrant, fluffy, white flowers,

Eulophia guineensis

Eugenia capensis subsp. *natalitia*

½ in (12 mm) across, solitary or in groups, in summer. Red, 8-ribbed, edible fruit, 1¼ in (30 mm) in diam-eter. Can be invasive. Zones 10–12.

EULOPHIA

This large genus (family Orchidaceae) of some 250 terrestrial orchid species, is distributed throughout the tropics and some warm-temperate regions, with the majority occurring in Africa, followed by Asia and the Americas. Leaves are long, narrow to pleated, and deciduous, retiring to fleshy underground rhizomes when dormant, which is usually in winter. Tall erect spikes of numerous flowers, highly variable in shape and color, are pro-duced in spring or summer. CULTIVATION: These orchids should be potted in a well-drained terrestrial mix and appreciate a high proportion of coarse sand with some organic mat-ter. They require bright light to induce flowering and like to be kept moist when in active growth. The potting medium should be allowed to dry out during the dormant period. Propagate by division.

Eulophia guineensis

☼/❙❦ ❧ ↔ 8–24 in (20–60 cm) ↑ 16–36 in (40–90 cm)

From tropical Africa. Upright spikes of showy, pinkish brown, 3 in (8 cm) wide blooms with a deep lilac flared labellum. Zones 10–12.

EULYCHNIA

A genus of 5 massive, candelabra-shaped cacti (Cactaceae family) from the coastal fog regions of southern Peru and northern Chile, where they form extensive forests. The name comes from 2 Greek words, *eu*, good, and *lychnos*, lamp, referring to the strong straight stems like lamp stands. The plants often have a distinct trunk with many straight to sprawling branches.

Eulychnia breviflora

The prominent areoles usually bear several long stiff spines and, in some species, long hairs and wool. Flowers open in the day and last for one night. They are white to pink, with very short floral tubes, the scaly outsides of which bear wool or bristly spines. The seed pods are spherical, fleshy, scaly, or hairy but rarely spiny. CULTIVATION: Easily cultivated in rich well-drained soil; withhold water in winter. Usually propagated from seed but may be grown from cuttings dried out for a week or two.

Eulychnia breviflora
syns *Eulychnia longispina*, *E. saint-pieana*

☼ ❦ ↔ 3–10 ft (0.9–3 m) ↑ 10–25 ft (3–8 m)

From coastal regions of northern Chile. Tree-like plant usually with mul-tiple erect gray-green or dark green branches. Areoles bearing abundant wool and hairs; spines brownish, be-coming gray with age, the erect cen-tral spines 4–5 in (10–12 cm) long, radial spines much shorter. White to pale rose flowers, 2–3 in (5–8 cm) long, outer segments covered in dense brown to white wool. Zones 9–11.

EUONYMUS

This genus belonging to the spindle-tree (Celastraceae) family consists of over 175 species of evergreen, semi-evergreen, or deciduous shrubs, trees, and climbers native to Asia, Europe, North and Central America, and the island of Madagascar; there is also a single Australian species. Not all are frost hardy. Stems and branches are often 4-sided. The leaves may be toothed or smooth-edged. The small flowers may be yellow, green, white, or red-brown, and are borne singly or in cymes in the leaf axils from late spring to early summer. The fruit is a distinctive capsule with 3, 4, or 5 compartments, each containing one large seed surrounded by a usually red or orange aril. The capsule splits open to reveal a paler, often pink, interior that contrasts with the brightly colored aril. Parts of the plant can cause stomach upsets or even severe poisoning if they are eaten.

CULTIVATION: They tolerate all types of soil, but *E. alatus* is especially good in alkaline soil. Grow in well-drained soil in sun or part-shade. Evergreen species need shelter from drying cold winds and slightly more moisture in the soil. Variegated forms perform better in full sun. Propagation is from seed, or from nodal cuttings taken from deciduous plants in summer or from evergreen plants in early summer to mid-autumn.

Euonymus alatus

BURNING BUSH, CORKBUSH, WINGED SPINDLE TREE

☼ ❄ ↔ 10 ft (3 m) ↕ 6 ft (1.8 m)

Found from northeastern Asia to central China and Japan. Dense, deciduous, bushy shrub with corky wings on branches. Leaves ovate to elliptical, dark green, with toothed margins, turning brilliant red in autumn. Pale green flowers in summer. Fruit is pale red, 4-lobed, and has bright orange seeds. '**Compactus**', a dwarf compact shrub, with winged corky branches, scarlet to purple foliage in winter; '**Nordine**', large orange leaves in winter, abundant fruit; '**Timber Creek**', vigorous, with arching branches and broad recurving leaves that color brilliant scarlet in autumn. Zones 3–9.

Euonymus americanus

STRAWBERRY BUSH, WAHOO

☼ ❄ ↔ 6 ft (1.8 m) ↕ 8 ft (2.4 m)

From eastern USA. Deciduous upright shrub. The deep green ovate to lance-shaped leaves with scalloped margins, are somewhat wrinkly, lasting well into late autumn. The red-tinged green flowers appear in summer. Pink 3- to 5-lobed fruit with yellow-tinged white seeds. Zones 6–9.

Euonymus bungeanus

☼ ❄ ↔ 15 ft (4.5 m) ↕ 20 ft (6 m)

From China and Korea. Deciduous or semi-evergreen shrub or tree. Arching

Euonymus alatus 'Compactus'

Euonymus alatus 'Nordine'

Euonymus alatus 'Timber Creek'

Euonymus fortunei 'Emerald Gaiety'

slender shoots; leaves pale green, ovate to elliptic, with finely toothed margins and pointed tips, turning pink and yellow in autumn. Small cymes of yellow flowers. Pink-tinged yellow fruit with bright orange arils. *E. b.* var. *semipersistens*, semi-evergreen foliage; and *E. b.* 'Pendulus' has elegant pendulous branches. Zones 4–9.

Euonymus europaeus

EUROPEAN EUONYMUS, EUROPEAN SPINDLE TREE, SPINDLE TREE

☼ ❄ ↔ 8 ft (2.4 m) ↕ 20 ft (6 m)

Found from Europe to western Asia. Deciduous shrub or small tree. Green branches; leaves elliptic, scalloped, with pointed tips. Small cymes of 5 to 7 yellow to green flowers in spring. Pink to red 4-lobed fruit with white seeds and orange arils. *E. e.* f. *albus*, white fruit. *E. e.* 'Aucubifolius', white variegated foliage; '**Red Cap**', bright red fruit, persisting on bare winter branches; '**Red Cascade**' ★, often a small tree, good autumn color, persistent orange-red fruit. Zones 3–9.

Euonymus fortunei

syn. *Euonymus radicans*

WINTERCREEPER EUONYMUS

☼ ❄ ↔ 3–10 ft (0.9–3 m) ↕ 1–10 ft (0.3–3 m)

From China. Evergreen ground-cover shrub or root-clinging climber; as a climber, can reach 15 ft (4.5 m) high. Green branches with fine warts. Leaves

Euonymus fortunei 'Canadale Gold'

oval or elliptic, toothed, with pointed tips. Greenish yellow flowers in summer. White fruit, orange arils. *E. f.* var. *vegetus*, spreading, bushy, stiff branches, thick dull green leaves. *E. f.* '**Canadale Gold**', leaves, marginal bands of yellow; '**Coloratus**', green foliage turns purple-red in winter; '**E.T.**', prostrate form, rounded leaves with pinkish cream margins; '**Emerald Gaiety**', green leaves with white margins tinged pink in winter; '**Emerald 'n' Gold**', leaves with yellow margins tinged pink in winter; '**Harlequin**', leaves grayish green, streaked and marbled with cream or white, frequently throwing entirely cream leaves; '**Kewensis**', prostrate form, tiny leaves; '**Minims**', procumbent, rooting along branches, 2 in (5 cm) high; '**Niagara Green**', deep green leaves, new growth lime green; '**Sheridan Gold**', yellowish green young foliage; '**Silver Queen**', bushy shrub or spreading climber,

Euonymus americanus, fruit

Euonymus europaeus, fruit

Euonymus fortunei 'E. T.'

Euonymus fortunei 'Harlequin'

Euonymus fortunei 'Sunspot'

Euonymus myrianthus

leaves, broad white margins tinged pink in winter; '**Sunspot**', semi-prostrate, weak arching branches, leaves with large cream or yellow blotch mainly on basal half. '**Variegatus**' an older variegated cultivar. Zones 5–10.

Euonymus grandiflorus

☀ ❄ ↔ 10 ft (3 m) ↑ 15 ft (4.5 m)
Found in northern India and western China. Semi-evergreen. The leaves are dark green, variable, but usually lance-shaped to elliptic, with pointed tips, finely toothed margins. Bears cymes of green to yellow flowers and light pink fruit with black seeds and scarlet arils. Zones 9–10.

Euonymus hamiltonianus

YEDDO EUONYMUS
☀ ❄ ↔ 20 ft (6 m) ↑ 20 ft (6 m)
Found from the Himalayas to Japan. Deciduous small tree or shrub. Leaves

are oblong to lance-shaped with short pointed tips. Red-tinged white flowers in summer. Pink fruit. *E. h.* subsp. *sieboldianus* (syns. *E. sieboldianus, E. yedoensis*) similar to the species but leaves are longer and pointed, the fruit almost round, 4-lobed, and pink, with blood red seeds and orange arils. *E. h.* '**Red Elf**' fruits well; fruit and seeds dark pink with red arils. Zones 4–9.

Euonymus japonicus

EVERGREEN EUONYMUS
☀ ❄ ↔ 6–12 ft (1.8–3.5 m) ↑ 12 ft (3.5 m)
Found in Korea, China, and Japan. An evergreen, dense, bushy shrub or small tree that grows larger in the wild than in cultivation. Leaves are dark green, oval to oblong, tough, and leathery. Produces flattened cymes of green flowers during summer. Rounded pink fruit contains white seeds and orange arils.

'**Albomarginatus**', dark green leaves with narrow white margins; '**Bravo**', leaves deep green streaked gray-green with broad yellow margins; '**Emerald 'n' Gold**', dwarf form with compact foliage, and pale yellow leaves with green central zone; '**Microphyllus Aureovariegatus**', deep green leaves with narrow yellow margins; '**Ovatus Aureus**', leaves blotched and streaked yellow. Zones 7–10.

Euonymus myrianthus

☀ ❄ ↔ 12 ft (3.5 m) ↑ 10 ft (3 m)
An evergreen shrub originating from western China. Dull green leaves, generally broad, oval to lance-shaped, leathery, sparsely toothed. Clusters of tiny, greenish yellow, star-shaped flowers. Orange-yellow to red 4-ribbed fruit containing seeds with orange arils, from late summer to spring. Zones 9–11.

Euonymus japonicus 'Bravo'

Euonymus japonicus 'Emerald 'n' Gold'

Euonymus japonicus 'Ovatus Aureus'

E. hamiltonianus subsp. *sieboldianus*

Euonymus grandiflorus

Euonymus planipes

Euonymus nanus
DWARF BURNING BUSH, DWARF EUONYMUS,
TURKESTAN BURNING BUSH

☼ ❄ ↔ 3 ft (0.9 m) ↑ 3 ft (0.9 m)

From eastern Europe to western China.
Deciduous shrub with 4-sided angular
branches. Leaves linear, alternate, with
sparsely toothed margins and down-
turning edges. Cymes of pale brown
flowers in spring–summer. Pink to rose
red 4-lobed fruit with brown seeds and
red arils. *E. n.* var. *turkestanicus,* longer
leaves and pink seeds. Zones 2–9.

Euonymus occidentalis
☼ ❄ ↔ 10 ft (3 m) ↑ 15 ft (4.5 m)

From western North America. Deciduous shrub or small tree. Leaves lance-
shaped to ovate, finely toothed, with
pointed tips. Small cymes of purple-
to brown-tinged flowers. Red-purple
fruit. Zones 5–9.

Euonymus phellomanus
☼ ❄ ↔ 10–15 ft (3–4.5 m)
↑ 10–15 ft (3–4.5 m)

From northern and western China.
Deciduous shrub with broad, distinc-

tive, corky wings on 4-sided branches.
The leaves are oval to oblong, and
rough-textured, to 4 in (10 cm) long.
Fragrant yellowish white flowers are
borne in autumn. Dark-colored
4-lobed fruit. Zones 3–9.

Euonymus planipes
syn. *Euonymus sachalinensis* of gardens

☼ ❄ ↔ 10 ft (3 m) ↑ 10 ft (3 m)

From northeastern China to Japan and
far eastern Russia. Deciduous upright
shrub or small tree. The leaves are mid-
green, elliptic, coarsely toothed, and
turn brilliant red in autumn. Small
greenish flowers. Fruit red, almost
spherical, with 4 to 5 lobes and red
seeds with orange arils. Zones 4–9.

EUPATORIUM
In the broadest sense, this is a genus
of more than 450 species, but some
botanists have preferred to split off
several other genera, leaving only about
40 species in a more narrowly defined
Eupatorium. As the genus is traditionally understood, *Eupatorium* includes
annuals, perennials, subshrubs, and

Eupatorium ligustrinum

shrubs within the daisy (Asteraceae)
family, which is native to eastern North
America, Central America and South
America, with a very few species in
Europe and Asia. All the species of
Eupatorium have whorled or opposite
leaves on simple or branched stems,
the stems terminating in corymbs or
panicles of small flowerheads. The fruit
is plumed, like thistledown. The foliage
of some species is still used in traditional herbal remedies, and an infusion made from the leaves and flowers
was once used to treat fevers. The
flowers are attractive to butterflies.
CULTIVATION: These plants require
a sunny position in well-drained but
moist fertile soil. Growing tips can be
pinched back to encourage compact
growth. Propagate in spring from seed
or cuttings of green wood, or by dividing root clumps when the plant is
dormant; protect from frosts.

Eupatorium ligustrinum
syns *Ageratina ligustrina, Eupatorium
micranthum, E. weinmannianum*

☼ ⧫ ↔ 3–6 ft (0.9–1.2 m)
↑ 3–6 ft (0.9–1.2 m)

From Mexico to Costa Rica. A rare,
densely branched, evergreen shrub.
Leaves dark green to bronze green,
slightly toothed. Large, flat, fluffy corymbs of fragrant cream flowerheads
tinged with grayish white or rose pink
in late summer–autumn. Zones 9–11.

Eupatorium perfoliatum
BONESET, THOROUGHWORT

☼ ❄ ↔ 3–5 ft (0.9–1.5 m)
↑ 3–5 ft (0.9–1.5 m)

From southeastern USA. Perennial
herb, with leaves opposite, wrinkled,
toothed, to 8 in (20 cm) long. Large
compound heads of 10 to 40 white
flowers, often tinged with purple, in
late summer–autumn from the second
year. Zones 3–4.

Eupatorium purpureum ★
JOE PYE WEED, TRUMPET WEED

☼/◐ ❄ ❄ ↔ 6–10 ft (1.8–3 m)
↑ 6–10 ft (1.8–3 m)

From eastern USA. Perennial. Large
whorls of elliptical leaves that are finely

toothed, with a purplish tinge. Inflorescence consists of a half-rounded panicle with 5 to 15 flowerheads, purple
or pale pink to greenish yellow or rose-
purple, in late summer–autumn. *E. p.*
subsp. *maculatum* (syn. *E. maculatum*),
smaller, with a flat-topped panicle of
15 pale or rose purple flowerheads.
Zones 3–9.

Eupatorium rugosum
syn. *Ageratina altissima*
FALL POISON, SNOW THOROUGHWORT,
WHITE SNAKEROOT

☼ ❄ ↔ 3–6 ft (0.9–1.8 m)
↑ 3–6 ft (0.9–1.8 m)

From northeastern North America.
Perennial herb with slightly hairy
stems. Leaves opposite, elliptical to
sword-shaped, grayish green to purplish green, slightly hairy, toothed.
Flat-topped rounded clusters of white
flowers, borne at stem tips, in late summer. 'Braunlaub', young foliage tinted
with brown, brown-tinged flowers.
Zones 4–6.

EUPHORBIA
This large genus of about 2,000 species
of annuals, perennials, shrubs, and
trees, both evergreen and deciduous,
is distributed throughout the world.
It gives its name to the large and diverse family Euphorbiaceae. *Euphorbia*
alone takes in a very diverse range of
forms and natural habitats, from spiny
and succulent cactus-like species occurring mainly in hot dry areas to leafy
perennials from cool-temperate climates. All species contain a poisonous
milky sap which can cause severe irritation if it comes in contact with the
skin and, if rubbed into the eyes, will
sometimes bring on temporary blindness. The sap has purgative qualities.
The true flowers are tiny, with separate male and female forms attached
to a smooth cup-like structure, or cy-
athium (plural: cyathia). Cyathia are
generally accompanied by bracts, which
may be larger and are often colored,
such as the scarlet bracts of poinsettia
(*E. pulcherrima*). These cyathia and
bracts may be arranged in repeatedly
branched inflorescences and sometimes form large flowerheads. The
flowering times of many species are
rainfall dependent; in temperate climates with even rainfall, the likely
flowering time is from late spring to
mid-summer.
CULTIVATION: Provide similar growing conditions to the plant's natural
habitat. In cool-temperate climates
most succulent and subtropical species
will require greenhouse protection;
some will grow in dry rock gardens.

Euphorbia balsamifera

Euphorbia candelabrum, center, in the wild, Africa

Avoid the toxic sap when pruning and disposing of branches. Some species can only be propagated from seed, others can be grown from stem-tip cuttings or by division of the plants.

Euphorbia amygdaloides
WOOD SPURGE

☼/☀ ❋ ↔ 24–40 in (60–100 cm) ↑ 20–32 in (50–80 cm)

A native of temperate Eurasia. This species is a spreading, mounding, leafy perennial. The soft stems are densely foliaged with spatula-shaped leaves, to over 3 in (8 cm) long; they are often purple-tinted and have a slight sheen. The sprays of showy yellow-green flowerheads are produced throughout the spring and summer. *E. a.* **var. robbiae**, more robust dark foliage and spreading rosettes. Stems and foliage

of *E. a.* 'Purpurea' are strongly tinted with purple-red, new growth is red-wine colored. Zones 7–10.

Euphorbia antisyphilitica
CANDELLILA

☼/☀ ❋ ↔ 24 in (60 cm) ↑ 40 in (100 cm)

A native from southwestern USA. This is a succulent shrub with many narrow, upright, spineless, gray-green stems, often purple-tinted at the nodes, which in spring–early summer bear short-lived, 2 in (5 cm) long, red leaves and cream flowerheads stained purple to red, the flowers opening from red buds. Zones 8–11.

Euphorbia avasmontana

☼/☀ ⌁ ↔ 40–60 in (100–150 cm) ↑ 7 ft (2 m)

From Namaqualand and Namibia. This succulent shrub has from 5- to 7-angled, upright, sturdy branching stems, the angles edged with opposite pairs of fierce, stiff, ½ in (12 mm) long spines, sometimes red. The yellow-green flowers occur in small heads. This is a rare species in cultivation. Zones 9–11.

Euphorbia balsamifera

☼ ⌁ ↔ 3 ft (0.9 m) ↑ 6 ft (1.8 m)

From cliff tops and dry slopes of north-western Africa and the Canary Islands Semi-succulent. Well branched spine-less stems, turn gray and gnarled with age. Rosettes of pale green glaucous leaves on branch tips. Modest solitary flowers, winter–early spring. Zones 9–11.

Euphorbia burmanii

☼ ⌁ ↔ 5 ft (1.5 m) ↑ 7 ft (2 m)

From South Africa. Succulent shrub. Woody base with branching spineless

Euphorbia burmanii

stems. Leaves tiny, spatula-shaped, often short-lived. Pale green, usually yellow-tinted, flowerheads. Zones 9–11.

Euphorbia candelabrum ★

☼ ⌁ ↔ 8 ft (2.4 m) ↑ 60 ft (18 m)

From southern to northeastern Africa. Succulent species, smaller in cultivation. Diamond-shaped segmented branches arch upward, bearing small rust-colored spines. The leaves are tri-angular and short lived. Golden green flowerheads. Sap has been used to poison tips of arrowheads. Zones 9–11.

Euphorbia avasmontana

Euphorbia amygdaloides 'Purpurea'

Euphorbia antisyphilitica

Euphorbia caput-medusae ★
MEDUSA'S HEAD

☼/◑ ✣ ↔ 48 in (120 cm) ↑ 12 in (30 cm)

From South Africa. Succulent shrub.
Many spreading, tubercle-studded, cylindrical stems radiating from a central
caudex, like the snakes on Medusa's
head. Stems broaden at the tip, bearing
tiny, often short-lived, linear leaves.
Unusual cream flowerheads with fimbriated snowflake-shaped cyathia.
Zones 9–10.

Euphorbia cereiformis
MILK BARREL

☼ ✣ ↔ 40 in (100 cm) ↑ 40 in (100 cm)

South African succulent, unknown in
the wild. Shrubby habit. Stems clustering, cactus-like, ribbed, to 2 in (5 cm)
wide, branching, tubercle-studded,
spine-edged, sometimes topped with
small fleshy leaves. Inconspicuous
yellow-green flowerheads. Zones 9–11.

Euphorbia characias
☼ ❉ ↔ 5 ft (1.5 m) ↑ 6 ft (1.8 m)

Various forms from the Mediterranean
region and southern Europe. Perennial

Euphorbia characias

subshrub or shrub with soft stems. Narrow, elliptical, gray-green leaves. The
heads of up to 20 small purple-green
or yellow flowers, are backed by conspicuous yellow-green whorled bracts,
usually in late winter–early summer.
The yellow-green-flowered *E. c.* subsp.
wulfenii ★, with its various cultivars,
is more widely cultivated than the
species; '**Bosahan**', selected from a
garden in Cornwall, UK, is a vigorous
plant, with pale yellow flowers; '**John
Tomlinson**', has 16 in (40 cm) long
heads of bright yellow-green flowers.
Zones 8–10.

Euphorbia coerulescens ★
NOOR, SWEET NOOR

☼ ✣ ↔ 40 in (100 cm) ↑ 60 in (150 cm)

From South Africa. Succulent shrub.
The stems are branching, segmented,
4- to 6-angled, blue-green, and edged
with paired ½ in (12 mm) long spines.

Euphorbia coerulescens

Euphorbia cornigera

E. characias subsp. *wulfenii* 'Bosahan'

Inconspicuous yellow-green flowerheads usually in spring, followed by
red seed capsules. Zones 9–11.

Euphorbia cooperi ★
TRANSVAAL CANDELABRA TREE

☼ ✣ ↔ 6 ft (1.8 m) ↑ 15 ft (4.5 m)

From southern and eastern Africa.
Succulent tree with upwardly arching
segmented branches, usually pentagonal
in shape. Pairs of buff-colored spines
accentuate margins. Small yellowish
flowers arise between them usually in
autumn–spring. Zones 9–11.

Euphorbia corollata
FLOWERING SPURGE, TRAMP'S SPURGE,
WILD HIPPO, WILD IPECAC

☼/◑ ❉ ↔ 12 in (30 cm)
↑ 12–36 in (30–90 cm)

From eastern North America. An erect
perennial, with alternate oblong leaves,
turning red in autumn. The slender
stem exudes a milky juice, which may
irritate the skin. Its small white flowers
appear in early summer–early autumn.
Zones 4–9.

Euphorbia cornigera
☼/◑ ❉ ↔ 24 in (60 cm) ↑ 30 in (75 cm)

From the Himalayas. Perennial shrub.
Red stems; the red-tinted dark green
leaves have a pale, almost white, midrib.
Showy bright yellow-green flowerheads
in early summer. Zones 6–9.

Euphorbia cyathophora
syn. *Poinsettia cyathophora*

FIRE ON THE MOUNTAIN, MEXICAN FIRE
PLANT, PAINTED LEAF

☼/◑ ✣ ↔ 20 in (50 cm) ↑ 20 in (50 cm)

From southeastern USA and neighboring Mexico. Evergreen shrub, with

E. c. subsp. *wulfenii* 'John Tomlinson'

Euphorbia characias subsp. *wulfenii*

upright stems. Leaves variable, narrow
to spatula-shaped, toothed or smooth-
edged. The bright red flowerheads,
surrounded by leafy bracts, appear
in summer. Zones 9–11.

Euphorbia cyparissias
CYPRESS SPURGE

☼/◑ ❉ ↔ 24 in (60 cm) ↑ 16 in (40 cm)

Widespread in Europe. Perennial,
which spreads by rhizomes, forming
a clump of narrow stems with narrow
green leaves, 1¾ in (40 mm) long,
which sometimes redden in sun or
drought. Yellow-green inflorescence
surrounded by mauve- to red-tinted
feathery bracts in late spring to mid-
summer. '**Fens Ruby**', carries bright
red bracts, near yellow flowerheads,
very compact. Zones 4–9.

Euphorbia dregeana
☼ ✣ ↔ 4 ft (1.2 m) ↑ 7 ft (2 m)

From Namaqualand and Namibia.
Succulent shrub. Stems spineless and

Euphorbia cooperi, in the wild, Karoo National Park, South Africa

Euphorbia cyparissias

Euphorbia dregeana

upright, branching, and pale green.
The leaves are small and short-lived.
It bears inconspicuous inflorescences
of yellow-green flowers. Zones 9–11.

Euphorbia dulcis
PURPLE SPURGE

☼/◐ ❄ ↔ 12 in (30 cm) ↑ 12 in (30 cm)
Found in Europe. *E. dulcis* is a
rhizomatous perennial. The leaves
are narrow, downy, to just under 3 in
(8 cm) long, and often purple-tinted.
The yellow-green, sometimes red-
tinted, inflorescence is surrounded by
feathery purple-red bracts in summer.
The cultivar, '**Chameleon**', has strongly
purple-tinted leaves, and its bracts are
especially colorful and showy in summer. Zones 6–9.

Euphorbia franckiana

Euphorbia gottlebei

Euphorbia echinus

☼ ❄ ↔ 40 in (100 cm) ↑ 60 in (150 cm)
From Morocco. Succulent shrub. Stems
branching, deep green, cactus-like, and
usually 6-angled, with paired pale gray
to dusky red spines on shield-like bases.
The spines often contrast strikingly
with the stem color. The stem tips are
topped with small yellow-green flowers.
Zones 8–11.

Euphorbia franckiana

☼ ◑ ↔ 40 in (100 cm) ↑ 40 in (100 cm)
From South Africa. Succulent shrub.
Stems branching, segmented, usually
acutely 3-angled, blue-green, edged
with paired ½ in (12 mm) long
spines. Yellow-green inflorescences,
inconspicuous except that they occur
between spine pairs, in spring–early
summer. Zones 9–11.

Euphorbia fulgens ★
SCARLET PLUME

☼ ✿ ↔ 30 in (75 cm) ↑ 5 ft (1.5 m)
From Mexico. Arching well-branched
shrub. Leaves deciduous, lance-shaped,

Euphorbia echinus

carried on long stalks. Rounded bright
red floral bracts appear in the winter.
'**Alba**' has cream bracts; '**Albatross**',
bluish green leaves and pure white
bracts; '**Purple Leaf**' is distinguished
by burgundy foliage and bright orange
bracts. Zones 10–11.

Euphorbia gottlebei

☼/◐ ✿ ↔ 4 ft (1.2 m) ↑ 5 ft (1.5 m)
From Madagascar. This very distinctive
perennial shrub has upright densely
thorny stems. The leaves are narrow,
light to deep green, to 4 in (10 cm)
long. The heads of about 8 blooms
have salmon pink to soft red bracts.
Zones 10–12.

Euphorbia grandicornis ★
BIG-HORN EUPHORBIA, COW'S HORN
EUPHORBIA

☼ ❄ ↔ 3 ft (0.9 m) ↑ 6 ft (1.8 m)
From southern Africa. A succulent
species well armed with spines, to 3 in
(8 cm) long, which arise in pairs along
the uneven margins of the upright,
bright green, triangular branches. Its
flowers with very small yellowish green
floral bracts appear between the spines.
Zones 8–11.

Euphorbia grandicornis

Euphorbia griffithii

☼ ❄ ↔ 36 in (90 cm) ↑ 36 in (90 cm)
From the Himalayas. Widely grown
and usually a perennial, it can become
shrubby in mild climates. The leaves
are narrow, to 5 in (12 cm) long, dark
green, and tinted pink to orange. The
flowerheads, with vivid orange-red
bracts in summer, develop coppery
tones with age. '**Fireglow**', vivid red
bracts. Zones 5–10.

Euphorbia griffithii 'Fireglow'

Euphorbia fulgens

Euphorbia ingens

Euphorbia jansenvillensis

Euphorbia horrida var. *noorsveldensis*

Euphorbia horrida ★

AFRICAN MILK BARREL

☀/◐ ⚘ ↔5 ft (1.5 m) ↑5 ft (1.5 m)

From South Africa. Clumps of 7- to 20-angled succulent stems are bright green when young but become dry brown with age, with many spines to 2 in (5 cm) long. The yellow-green flowerheads, on pink stalks at the stem tips, are not showy, and usually appear in the spring–early summer. *E. h.* var. *noorsveldensis*, conspicuously ribbed cactus-like stems and fewer, much

shorter spines; *E. h.* var. *striata*, gray-green striated stems with undulating ribs, short spines. Zones 9–11.

Euphorbia inermis

☀/◐ ⚘ ↔20 in (50 cm) ↑12 in (30 cm)

From South Africa. Small spreading shrub with radiating succulent stems. Tubercle-studded stems, up to 12 in (30 cm) long and a little over ½ in (12 mm) across, with small spines. Leaves are ephemeral. Small white inflorescences on long stalks contrast with the dark stems, and appear in spring–early summer. Zones 9–11.

Euphorbia ingens

NABOOM, TREE EUPHORBIA

☀ ⚘ ↔10 ft (3 m) ↑40 ft (12 m)

From South Africa and Kenya. Very cactus-like. Short trunk, crowded crown of upward angular branches. Leaves seldom seen. Spines usually absent on mature branches. Zones 9–11.

Euphorbia jansenvillensis

☀/◐ ⚘ ↔12 in (30 cm) ↑12 in (30 cm)

From South Africa. Dwarf succulent shrub with a largely subterranean stem. Branches erect, 5-ridged, up to 6 in (15 cm) long and just over ½ in

(12 mm) in diameter, studded with small warty protuberances. Sparse red-tinted green cyathia. Zones 9–11.

Euphorbia keithii

☀ ⚘ ↔3–10 ft (0.9–3 m) ↑7–20 ft (2–6 m)

From Swaziland, southern Africa. Large shrub to small tree. Branching stems, 4- to 5-angled, edged with pairs of dark brown spines, about 1 in (25 mm) long. Leaves small, usually at stem tips. Inconspicuous yellow-green flowerheads usually in spring–early summer. Zones 10–12.

Euphorbia lambii

☀ ⚘ ↔3 ft (0.9 m) ↑5 ft (1.5 m)

From Canary Islands. Round-headed, bushy shrub. Semi-succulent stems, not thorny or angled. Leaves simple, elongated, elliptical, near stem tips. Yellow-green flowerheads with large bracts in spring–early summer. Zones 9–11.

Euphorbia lathyris

CAPER SPURGE, MYRTLE SPURGE

☀/◐ ❄ ↔40 in (100 cm) ↑40–60 in (100–150 cm)

From Europe, northwest Africa, and western Asia. Biennial, which is usually

considered a weed. Upright and fairly weak stems; fleshy blue-green leaves in 4 ranks. Unspectacular, rather open, yellow-green flowerheads in the warmer months, followed by caper-like but poisonous seed heads. Zones 6–10.

Euphorbia ledienii

☀/◐ ⚘ ↔5 ft (1.5 m) ↑7 ft (2 m)

From South Africa. Succulent, often clumping, shrub. The stems are cactus-like, branching, segmented, 4- to 7-angled, blue-green, and edged with paired short spines. The inconspicuous yellow-green flowerheads are most

Euphorbia keithii

Euphorbia lambii

Euphorbia inermis

Euphorbia leucocephala

Euphorbia mauritanica

Euphorbia ledienii

and *E. milii*. It is very like the common crown of thorns, *E. milii*, but generally shorter, with broader stems. Densely prickly; light green leaves, to 6 in (15 cm) long, are red-tinted in the sun. The salmon to red flowerheads and bracts occur at any time except during periods of severe drought. The **Somona Range** includes various flower colors, such as the pale pink '**Merle**' and the cerise '**Rosemarie**'. Zones 10–12.

Euphorbia marginata
GHOST WEED, SNOW ON THE MOUNTAIN

☼/☀ ❋ ↔ 20 in (50 cm) ↕ 40 in (100 cm)
Native to North America. An annual, which is usually cultivated in gardens in low-growing forms. It produces a dense mound of light green, soft, downy leaves, to 3 in (8 cm) long, edged in white, sometimes entirely

white at the top of the plant. White bracts in summer. Contact with the sap can cause severe dermatological problems. Zones 4–10.

Euphorbia × *martinii*
☼ ❋ ↔ 3 ft (0.9 m) ↕ 3 ft (0.9 m)
A hybrid between *E. amygdaloides* and *E. characias*. This variable plant can

closely resemble either of its parents. An unusual plant, less predictable than the parent species. Zones 7–10.

Euphorbia mauritanica
JACKAL'S FOOD, YELLOW MILK BUSH

☼/☀ ꒐ ↔ 20 in (50 cm) ↕ 40 in (100 cm)
From South Africa. Succulent shrub. Stems are narrow, spineless, upright, branching, and yellow-green. Leaves are small and short-lived. Inconspicuous solitary yellow-green cyathia usually appear in spring–early summer. Zones 9–11.

Euphorbia mellifera
HONEY SPURGE

☼ ꒐ ↔ 7 ft (2 m) ↕ 6 ft (1.8 m)
From Madeira. Rare shrubby species. The leaves are multi-stemmed, mid-green, lance-shaped, with prominent whitish central veins. The clusters of tiny greenish flowers with very small bronze-green floral bracts, occur at the ends of the stems, in spring–summer. *Mellifera* means honey-bearing, and refers to the flowers' scent, which is attractive to bees. Zones 9–11.

Euphorbia × *lomii*

Euphorbia × *lomii*

usually seen in spring–early summer and are followed by red seed capsules. Zones 9–11.

Euphorbia leucocephala
PASCUITA, SNOWS OF KILIMANJARO

☼ ꒐ ↔ 6–10 ft (1.8–3 m)
↕ 6–10 ft (1.8–3 m)
From Central America (despite the popular name—snows of Kilimanjaro). Deciduous shrub. Erect habit; widely spaced whorls of up to 10 long-stalked pale green leaves. Profuse panicles of blooms like miniature poinsettia (*E. pulcherrima*); white floral bracts in winter–spring. Zones 9–11.

Euphorbia × *lomii*
GIANT CROWN OF THORNS

☼/☀ ✦ ↔ 40 in (100 cm) ↕ 40 in (100 cm)
This species is a garden hybrid between two Madagascan species, *E. lophogona*

Euphorbia × *martinii*

Euphorbia marginata

Euphorbia misera, in the wild, Baja California, Mexico

Euphorbia milii f. *lutea*

Euphorbia milii ★

CROWN OF THORNS

☼ ❄ ↔2–8 ft (0.6–2.4 m)
↑1–3 ft (0.3–0.9 m)

From Madagascar. Erect or scrambling shrub, sparsely foliaged, bright green leaves near branch tips. Stems prickly. Tiny yellow flowers with bright red floral bracts appearing intermittently for long periods. *E. m.* var. *splendens* (syn. *E. splendens*), commonly cultivated, mound of tangled branches to 2 ft (60 cm), pinkish red bracts; *E. m.* f. *lutea* ★, cream bracts. Zones 9–11.

Euphorbia milii

Euphorbia misera

CLIFF SPURGE

☼/❄ ❄ ↔12–24 in (30–60 cm)
↑40–60 in (100–150 cm)

From southern California, USA, and western Mexican States of Sonora and Baja California. Semi-succulent deciduous shrub. Whorls of small, rounded, fleshy, gray-green or blue-green leaves on similarly colored stems. Pale green flowerheads, marked with cream and mauve, in spring–summer. Zones 9–12.

Euphorbia myrsinites ★

CREEPING SPURGE, DONKEY TAIL

☼ ❄ ↔20 in (50 cm) ↑10 in (25 cm)

From Eurasia. Clump-forming perennial with sprawling stems. Leaves spiraled, finely toothed, pointed, fleshy, blue-green, to 1¾ in (40 mm) long. Bright green cyathia with chrome yellow bracts in spring. Zones 6–10.

Euphorbia nicaeensis

Euphorbia obesa

Euphorbia milii var. *splendens*

Euphorbia neriifolia

HEDGE EUPHORBIA, OLEANDER SPURGE

☼ ✤ ↔4 ft (1.2 m) ↑20 ft (6 m)

From India and Southeast Asia. Semi-succulent shrub or small tree. The whorled fresh green branches carry leathery spoon-like leaves near the tips. The flowerheads, with yellowish green bracts, appear in spring. The sap from this species has been used as a fish poison in India. Zones 10–12.

Euphorbia nicaeensis

☼ ❄ ↔24 in (60 cm) ↑24 in (60 cm)

From Europe. Attractive bushy perennial. Stems often tinged red and well covered with narrow bluish gray leaves. The floral bracts are a contrasting yellow-green. Zones 6–10.

Euphorbia obesa ★

BASEBALL PLANT, GINGHAM GOLF BALL, KLIPNOORS

☼/❄ ❄ ↔6 in (15 cm) ↑8 in (20 cm)

From South Africa. Small succulent. Flat-topped cylindrical stem, near-spherical when young, green with faint purple banding, and tubercle-studded ribbing reminiscent of baseball stitching. Green flowerheads, mainly near stem tips, usually in spring to early summer. Zones 9–11.

Euphorbia palustris

☼ ❄ ↔40 in (100 cm) ↑40 in (100 cm)

From Europe. This clump-forming perennial is very like the better-known *E. polychroma* but is somewhat larger. It has wiry stems, and narrow elliptical leaves, to over 2 in (5 cm) long, often red-tinted in the sunlight. The light green to bright yellow densely clustered flowerheads appear in spring–summer. Zones 6–9.

Euphorbia polychroma

CUSHION SPURGE

☼ ❄ ↔24 in (60 cm) ↑24 in (60 cm)

From Eurasia. Clump-forming perennial. Fine stems, with bright green, elliptical, velvety leaves, to about 2 in (5 cm) long. The bright yellow-green, sometimes red-tinted, flowerheads appear in spring–summer. The cultivar, '**Major**' is a compact form, which produces chrome yellow flowerheads. Zones 6–9.

Euphorbia neriifolia

Euphorbia myrsinites

Euphorbia stolonifera

Euphorbia pontica

☼ ❄ ↔ 20 in (50 cm) ↑ 10 in (25 cm)

From Central Asia and Russia. This perennial shrub is closely allied to *E. myrsinites* but is more compact in form. The leaves are spiraled, finely toothed, pointed, blue-green, and to 1 in (25 mm) long. The bright green cyathia with chrome yellow bracts appear in summer. Zones 6–10.

Euphorbia pulcherrima ★

syn. *Poinsettia pulcherrima*

POINSETTIA

☼ ❋ ↔ 7 ft (2 m) ↑ 10 ft (3 m)

From Mexico. A straggly deciduous shrub, the most widely grown of all shrubby euphorbias. Inconspicuous yellow flowers surrounded by large brilliant red floral bracts in winter–spring. Potted poinsettias have a huge commercial market. 'Henrietta Ecke', double form; 'Rosea', one of a number of named pink varieties. Other forms have cream, white, or marbled floral bracts. Zones 9–11.

Euphorbia pontica

Euphorbia polychroma

Euphorbia tirucalli, Kirstenbosch Botanical Garden, South Africa

Euphorbia rigida

☼/◐ ❄ ↔ 24 in (60 cm) ↑ 16 in (40 cm)

Found from southwestern Europe to the Caucasus. Evergreen perennial. Clustered clumps of upright blue-green stems; similarly colored, fleshy, lance-shaped leaves, notched at the tips. Bright yellow-green flowerheads in summer. Zones 7–10.

Euphorbia schillingii

☼/◐ ❄ ↔ 5 ft (1.5 m) ↑ 4 ft (1.2 m)

From Nepal. Shrubby perennial. Leaves are narrow, bright green, elliptical, and to 3 in (8 cm) long. The showy yellow-green flowerheads with rounded green bracts, borne at stem tips, occur in summer. Zones 7–9.

Euphorbia seguieriana

☼/◐ ❄ ↔ 32 in (80 cm) ↑ 20 in (50 cm)

From central Europe to Pakistan and Siberia. Woody-based perennial. Forms clump of blue-green stems; similarly colored, pointed, linear leaves, up to

Euphorbia pulcherrima

1¾ in (40 mm) long. Large heads of yellow-green cyathia and yellow bracts in summer. *E. s.* subsp. *niciciana* has a slightly more spreading habit and less crowded flowerheads. Zones 5–9.

Euphorbia sikkimensis ★

☼/◐ ❄ ↔ 36 in (90 cm) ↑ 36 in (90 cm)

From the eastern Himalayas. Rhizome-rooted perennial with upright stems and narrow elliptical leaves, up to 4 in (10 cm) long, and often red-tinted. Attractive pink new growth. Showy orange-red flowerheads in summer. Zones 6–9.

Euphorbia spinosa

☼/◐ ❄ ↔ 20 in (50 cm) ↑ 8 in (20 cm)

From the Mediterranean region. Low-mounding shrub. Small blue-green leaves enclosed in an interlaced thicket of wiry branches. Yellow-green flowerheads in spring–summer. Zones 7–10.

Euphorbia schillingii

Euphorbia stolonifera

☼ ❋ ↔ 24 in (60 cm) ↑ 16 in (40 cm)

Spreading, rhizome-rooted, succulent shrub from South Africa. The stem is largely subterranean, producing many dark green, somewhat wrinkled, cylindrical branches less than ½ in (12 mm) in diameter. Solitary yellow-green cyathia in spring–early summer. Zones 9–11.

Euphorbia tirucalli

FINGER TREE, MILK BUSH, PENCIL BUSH, PENCIL TREE, RUBBER HEDGE

☼ ✦ ↔ 7–12 ft (2–3.5 m) ↑ 15–30 ft (4.5–9 m)

From tropical and southern Africa, and India east to Indonesia. A large shrub or small tree with dense crown of succulent, pale green, cylindrical branches. Small, short-lived, lance-shaped leaves. Insignificant flowers. Can be invasive. Zones 10–12.

Euphorbia triangularis, Kirstenbosch Botanical Garden, South Africa

Euphorbia virosa, Spitzkoppe, Damaraland, Namibia

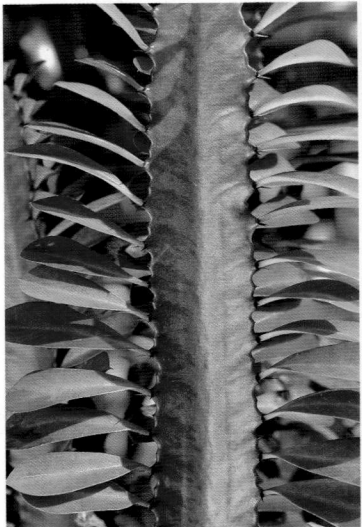

Euphorbia trigona 'Green Angel'

Euphorbia trigona

Euphorbia triangularis

☀ ⚘ ↔ 6 ft (1.8 m) ↑ 60 ft (18 m)

From southern Africa. Large succulent tree. The upright angular branches are ridged and segmented, with extremely thorny margins. The small leaves soon drop from the branches. Zones 9–11.

Euphorbia trigona

☀ ⚘ ↔ 12–24 in (30–60 cm)
↑ 3–8 ft (0.9–2.4 m)

From Namibia. Succulent cactus-like shrub. Branches all erect, 3-cornered, dark green mottled with white, with vertical ranks of spoon-shaped leaves and short reddish brown spines. Often seen as a house plant. 'Green Angel' ★, stems and leaves always plain green; 'Red Devil' ★, attractive cultivar with red leaves. Zones 9–11.

Euphorbia virosa

☀/◐ ⚘ ↔ 4 ft (1.2 m) ↑ 7 ft (2 m)

Found from South Africa's southwestern Cape to Angola. Succulent shrub. Stems upright, branching, and cactus-like, 5- to 8-angled, with many ½ in (12 mm) long spines, red when young.

Ephemeral leaves and inconspicuous yellow-green flowerheads usually in spring–early summer. Zones 9–12.

EUPTELEA

Native to Japan, China, and the eastern Himalayas, this genus consists of only 2 species of smallish deciduous trees, valued in temperate-climate gardens for their sharply toothed leaves, which quiver gracefully on slender stalks in slight breezes and take on pretty tints in autumn. Small bisexual flowers appear in globular clusters along the twigs just before the leaves, followed by small winged fruits. Euptelea, the only genus in the family Eupteleaceae, is one of a group of rather primitive flowering plant families that includes the planes and the beeches.

CULTIVATION: A cool moist climate, a sheltered but sunny position, and deep, moderately fertile soil produce the best growth. Euptelea are useful small trees for overplanting of rhododendrons, azaleas, and other such shrubs. Little maintenance required, apart from trimming away basal

suckers from time to time. Propagate from freshly collected seed or by air-layering of suckers or low branches.

Euptelea pleiosperma

☀ ❄ ↔ 15 ft (4.5 m) ↑ 15–30 ft (4.5–9 m)

Occurs wild from central and western China to far northeastern India and Bhutan. Leaves shallowly toothed, the undersides somewhat whitish, turning red in autumn. Pinkish green flowers with red anthers in spring. Small brown fruit, usually containing more than one seed. Zones 6–9.

Euptelea polyandra

☀ ❄ ↔ 15 ft (4.5 m) ↑ 25 ft (8 m)

From Japan. Heart-shaped leaves with a long tail-like apex and deeply and jaggedly toothed margins. Autumn foliage with yellow and reddish tones. Fruit always one-seeded. Zones 6–9.

EURYA

Allied to camellias (Theaceae family), this genus of about 70 species of evergreen shrubs and trees occurs naturally in southern and eastern Asia and the western Pacific. Leaves usually glossy, pointed, oval, and arranged in herringbone pattern, on slightly arching stems. Leaves are short-stalked, with serrated edges. Small, 5-petalled, downward-facing, unisexual flowers, single or in clusters, develop in the leaf axils, followed by green to purple-black berries.

CULTIVATION: Frost hardiness varies considerably between species, but provided the climate is suitable, the general preference is for cool, moist, well-drained, slightly acidic soil with ample humus. Most species grow in sun or part-shade. Propagate from seed or half-hardened tip cuttings.

Eurya japonica

☀ ❄ ↔ 20 ft (6 m) ↑ 20 ft (6 m)

From Japan and Korea. This is an attractive shrub or small tree with lush foliage. The pink-tinted white to cream flowers produce a rather acrid and unpleasant scent in the spring. These are followed by tiny purple-black berries. 'Aurea', golden foliage. Zones 7–10.

Eurya japonica

Euptelea pleiosperma

Eurya japonica 'Aurea'

Euryops tenuissimus

Euryops acraeus

Euryops pectinatus

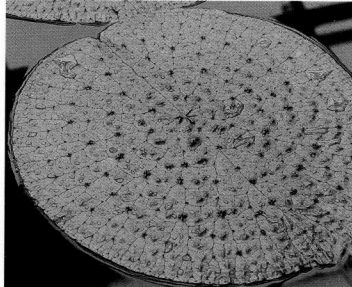
Euryale ferox

EURYALE

This genus, comprising just one species found from northern India to China and Japan, belongs to the waterlily (Nymphaeaceae) family. It is a very large, perennial, aquatic plant with a massive rhizome. The leaves are round, strongly ribbed, and very prickly, with the stalk attached under the middle of the blade. Flowers consist of 4 sepals and numerous petals, which are shorter than the sepals. The fruit is a prickly berry with many seeds. Plants resemble the tropical American *Victoria*, but the leaves have flat, rather than upturned, margins and the flowers are smaller, with all the stamens fertile.
CULTIVATION: Often grown as an annual in tropical greenhouses, where it is raised from seed sown immersed in water at 70–73°F (21–23°C).

Euryale ferox
☀ ❄ ↔ 5 ft (1.5 m) ↕ 3 ft (0.9 m)
Leaves 2–5 ft (0.6–1.5 m) across. Upper surface puckered, dull green, with sparse prickles; lower surface reddish, with prominent spongy veining densely armed with prickles. Summer flowers often do not open, remaining more or less submerged. Flower stalks and calyx prickly. Sepals green; petals red

to purple or lilac. Cultivated for 3,000 years by the Chinese for its edible rhizomes and seeds (fox nuts), now sold in Indian markets roasted and "puffed" like wheat. Zones 8–11.

EURYOPS

There are about 100 species of evergreen shrubs, perennials, and annuals in this genus, a member of the large daisy (Asteraceae) family. The majority are native to South Africa. They are attractive plants with lobed or finely divided green to grayish green leaves and bright yellow daisy flowers borne over a long period. Easily grown in a wide range of conditions, *Euryops* can withstand some frost, are drought tolerant, and suitable for coastal planting.
CULTIVATION: Deep free-draining soil in full sun is best. Grow against a warm wall or in a greenhouse or conservatory in cool-temperate climates. Prune after flowering to maintain a compact form. Propagate from seed or half-hardened or softwood cuttings.

Euryops acraeus
syn. *Euryops evansii*
☀ ❄ ↔ 36 in (90 cm)
↕ 12–36 in (30–90 cm)
Compact plant with small, narrow, silvery gray leaves. Bright yellow daisies, to 1½ in (35 mm) across, in spring–summer. Short-lived in damp climates; requires perfect drainage. Ideal plant for the rock garden. Zones 7–10.

Euryops chrysanthemoides
syn. *Gamolepis chrysanthemoides*
PARIS DAISY
☀ ❄ ↔ 5 ft (1.5 m) ↕ 4 ft (1.2 m)
Popular, easily grown plant, particularly in warm climates. Well foliaged

with deeply lobed dark green leaves. Yellow daisies, 2 in (5 cm) across, borne on slender stalks above the foliage, in winter–spring. Zones 9–11.

Euryops pectinatus
GOLDEN DAISY BUSH, GRAY-HAIRED EURYOPS
☀ ❄ ↔ 5 ft (1.5 m) ↕ 4 ft (1.2 m)
Fern-like foliage, deeply cut, downy, gray leaves. Bright yellow daisies are held well above the foliage, in spring–summer. Seldom without flowers in warm climates. Zones 8–11.

Euryops tenuissimus
☀ ❄ ↔ 4 ft (1.2 m) ↕ 3–6 ft (0.9–1.8 m)
Similar in size, shape, and flower to *E. pectinatus* but with bright green sparsely hairy leaves. Most at home in coastal gardens. Zones 9–10.

EUSTOMA
LISIANTHUS, PRAIRIE GENTIAN, TEXAS BLUEBELL

Formerly classified as *Lisianthus* and still sold under that name, these long-stemmed gentian relatives (family Gentianaceae) are widely cultivated for cut flowers. There are 3 species in the genus, consisting of annuals or short-lived perennials found from southern USA to northern South America.

Form clumps of fleshy oval to narrowly elliptical leaves, in summer producing showy 5- to 6-petalled, funnel- to bell-shaped flowers, up to 2 in (5 cm) wide. Some species carry flowers singly, but the cultivated plants have many-flowered stems up to 24 in (60 cm) long with blooms in a wide range of colors and in double-flowered forms. Lisianthus means bitter flower, and refers to the taste; the flowers were used medicinally by Native Americans.
CULTIVATION: Usually cultivated as annuals. Slow-growing, they need prolonged warm conditions to flower well. Plant in full or half-sun with fertile, moist, well-drained soil. The heavy flower stems are best staked. May be propagated by cuttings but better if raised fresh from seed.

Eustoma grandiflorum ★
syns *Eustoma russellianum*, *Lisianthus grandiflorus*
☀/◐ ❄ ↔ 20 in (50 cm)
↕ 24–32 in (60–80 cm)
Annual or short-lived perennial from southern USA and Mexico. Upright blue-green stems; fleshy, blue-green, pointed oval leaves, to 3 in (8 cm) long. Heads of bell-shaped flowers, to 2½ in (6 cm) across. Many seedling strains, such as the **Echo** mixed color strain, to 24 in (60 cm) tall, in lilac-, blue-, pink-, yellow-, and white-flowered forms as well as picotee-edged; the **Heidi Series**, to 18 in (45 cm) tall, in many colors; the **Mermaid Series**, including the early-flowering dwarf 'Lilac Rose', with light purple-pink single flowers; and individual named varieties, such as 'Forever Blue', to 12 in (30 cm) tall, with large purple-blue flowers. Zones 9–11.

Eustoma grandiflorum 'Forever Blue'

Eustoma grandiflorum 'Lilac Rose'

E. g. 'Echo Pink Picotee'

E. g. 'Echo Pink Picotee'

E. grandiflorum 'Echo Yellow'

E. grandiflorum 'Echo Blue'

E

Euterpe edulis

EUTERPE

ASSAI PALM, MANACO

This genus of feather-leafed palms (family Arecaceae) consists of 7 species from tropical America, though up to 30 species have formerly been distinguished. Single-trunked or clustered, medium to large, with crowns of rather few pinnate fronds, their elongated basal sheaths forming a smooth crownshaft; the leaflets droop gracefully, with finely tapering tips. The inflorescences appear in continuous succession from the trunk below the crownshaft; their branchlets have a dense covering of short soft hairs. The branchlets bear numerous small flowers in groups of one female flanked by two males. The smooth-coated, almost spherical, fruits contain a single seed. The vegetative buds, a single one terminating each

trunk, are the principal source of palm-hearts, sometimes called "millionaire's salad" because their removal kills the trunk; but these palms are now grown rapidly in plantations and canned palm-hearts are sold quite cheaply.
CULTIVATION: These palms are native to lowland rainforests and mountain forests and swamps. Fast growing, but because they require high humidity and temperatures they are really only suitable for tropical gardens, not for greenhouses in temperate regions. Propagate from seed.

Euterpe edulis ★
JUÇARA PALM, PALMITO, YAYIH
☼ ✈ ↔ 12–18 ft (3.5–5.5 m)
↑ 20–40 ft (6–12 m)

From coastal regions of Brazil and adjacent parts of Argentina and Paraguay.

Slender, usually solitary, palm with a smooth green crownshaft. Finely divided fronds with 120 to 150 pendulous leaflets. Purple flowers are followed by clusters of small, round, dark purple fruit. It is generally agreed that *E. edulis* yields the best-tasting palm-hearts. Zones 11–12.

Euterpe oleracea
ASSAI PALM, AÇAÍ, MANAC, NAIDI, PINOT
☼ ✈ ↔ 12–18 ft (3.5–5.5 m)
↑ 20–60 ft (6–8 m)

Native to the lower Amazon region of Brazil and far northern South America and west to Colombia. Clumping palm with several tall slender trunks and a crown of drooping feathery fronds, which emerge from a reddish crownshaft. The juicy blackish-purple fruit is the basic ingredient of the sweet drink açaí, a staple of the Amazon's estuary region, and this species of palm also provides the major source of the palm-hearts used in the canning industry. Zones 11–12.

EVOLVULUS

This genus of about 100 species comes mostly from tropical and other warm parts of the Americas. It belongs to the bindweed (Convolvulaceae) family. These plants are annuals, perennials, or subshrubs, often creeping but never climbing. The leaves are small, simple, and often narrow. The inflorescences are borne in the leaf axils or at the ends of the stems, each with one to several flowers with 5 small sepals. The corolla is funnel-shaped to flat, blue or pink to white, and has a lobed to smooth margin. The dry seed capsule is spherical to ovate in shape and contains 1 to 4 small seeds.
CULTIVATION: These plants thrive in well-drained soil in full sun. Propagate by root division or from cuttings; the shorter-lived species are readily raised from seed.

Evolvulus glomeratus
syn. *Evolvulus pilosus* of gardens
☼ ❀ ↔ 24–36 in (60–90 cm)
↑ 10–18 in (25–45 cm)

From Brazil and some neighboring countries. Evergreen perennial. Dense mound of foliage emerging from mass of rhizomes; leaves gray-green with soft silky hairs. Long succession of brilliant blue flowers with a small white eye, 1 in (25 mm) across, in the spring–autumn, wilting after noon in hot weather. Sold under the names 'Blue Daze', 'Hawaiian Blue Eyes', and 'Sapphire', but these are doubtfully distinct as cultivars. Often grown in hanging baskets. Zones 9–11.

EXACUM

There are about 25 species of tender annuals, biennials, and perennials in this genus, which belongs to the gentian (Gentianaceae) family and is native to the Old World tropics. The leaves are opposite, oval or elliptic, and often stalkless. Clusters of flowers, sometimes fragrant, are borne on leafy stems. The flowers consist of a narrow tube flaring to 5 flattened petal lobes with protruding yellow stamens.
CULTIVATION: Popular in temperate regions as pot plants for the house or conservatory. Grow in well-drained but moist potting mix in a well-lit position. These plants can also be grown outdoors as a bedding annual but they are suitable for permanent outdoor cultivation only in humid tropical and subtropical areas. Propagate from seed.

Exacum affine
GERMAN VIOLET, PERSIAN VIOLET
☼ ✈ ↔ 12 in (30 cm)
↑ 12–18 in (30–45 cm)

A native of the island of Socotra at the mouth of the Red Sea. An annual or short-lived perennial with pointed oval leaves. Small fragrant flowers, ranging

Evolvulus glomeratus

Exochorda giraldii

Exochorda × macrantha

in color from sky blue to pale and deep violet, are borne from spring through to autumn. Zones 10–12.

EXOCARPOS

About half of the 26 species of this genus of shrubs and small trees in the sandalwood (Santalaceae) family are indigenous to Australia, with the rest being distributed from the Philippines and New Zealand to Hawaii. They are semi-parasitic on the roots of other plants. The leaves are alternate, sometimes opposite, and in most species small and scale-like on adult plants. The flowers are tiny, on short spikes, and the fruits are small drupes borne on swollen stalks that become juicy and edible as the fruit matures; these were a source of food for Aboriginal Australians and were also eaten by the early settlers. Once established, many species are quite hardy. Found in a wide range of habitats, from exposed coastal situations to the mountains, and in regions with semi-arid conditions, they are especially admired for their handsome pendulous branches.
CULTIVATION: *Exocarpos* have proved very difficult to grow in gardens. Their

Exocarpos cupressiformis

propagation from seed has not proved easy; root cuttings are more reliable, but most plants are short-lived. A research project aimed at finding ways of growing *E. cupressiformis* is currently being carried out at the University of Melbourne, Australia.

Exocarpos cupressiformis
CHERRY BALLART, NATIVE CHERRY
☀ ❄ ↔ 10 ft (3 m) ↕ 25 ft (8 m)
From southeastern Australia. Upright to spreading tall shrub or small tree with graceful drooping branches. The leaves are reduced to small scales. The short spikes of minute cream-colored flowers appear in summer. The fruit is hard, gray, and nestled in the concave of its succulent red stalk. Zones 8–11.

EXOCHORDA
PEARL BUSH
This genus consists of 4 or 5 species of deciduous shrubs, within the rose (Rosaceae) family, native to northeast and central Asia. Some botanists now prefer to combine these into a single variable species, for which the name *E. racemosa* takes priority. They are all attractive spring-flowering shrubs, many with arching branches that become festooned with waxy white flowers, which are borne in racemes in the leaf axils or at the branch tips. The leaves are simple and alternate.
CULTIVATION: Easy to cultivate, they prefer moderately fertile well-drained

Exacum affine

soil in a cool-temperate climate with well-defined seasons, and a sheltered position in full sun. They may become chlorotic in chalk soils. Prune basal shoots by about one-third in late winter; remove spent flower clusters after flowering. Seeds germinate readily when sown in spring in a warm humid atmosphere. Soft-tip or half-hardened cuttings taken in summer or autumn can be rooted under cover; or use hardwood cuttings from winter pruning.

Exochorda giraldii
☀ ❄ ↔ 10 ft (3 m) ↕ 10 ft (3 m)
From northwestern China. Large freeflowering shrub, arching, spreading habit. Green leaves with red veins. White flowers, in late spring. *E. g.* **var.** *wilsonii* is more upright, with flowers to 2 in (5 cm) in diameter. Zones 5–9.

Exochorda × macrantha
PEARL BUSH
☀ ❄ ↔ 10 ft (3 m) ↕ 7 ft (2 m)
This strong-growing hybrid between *E. korolkowii* and *E. racemosa* closely resembles *E. racemosa*. The abundant

racemes of pure white flowers occur in late spring. 'The Bride' ★, compact shrub, to 6 ft (1.8 m) high, with a slightly weeping habit and arching branches covered with large white flowers in spring. Zones 5–9.

Exochorda racemosa
syn. *Exochorda grandiflora*
COMMON PEARL BUSH, PEARL BUSH
☀ ❄ ↔ 10 ft (3 m) ↕ 10 ft (3 m)
A native shrub of northeastern China. Dense spherical shape when mature, with many erect arching shoots from the base. Flower buds are like miniature white pearls and open to pure white, waxy, slightly fragrant flowers. Zones 4–9.

Exochorda serratifolia
KOREAN PEARL BUSH
☀ ❄ ↔ 7 ft (2 m) ↕ 8 ft (2.4 m)
From Korea and nearby parts of China. A shrub of upright habit. Serrated leaves with downy undersides, 3 in (8 cm) long. Loose racemes of flowers, 1½ in (35 mm) across, in early spring. Zones 5–9.

Exochorda serratifolia

Exochorda racemosa

F

F

Fagus grandifolia

FABIANA

This genus is a member of the potato (Solanaceae) family containing about 25 shrubs found in warm-temperate parts of South America, especially Chile and Argentina. They have small, overlapping, needle-like to narrow, triangular leaves, usually deep green. The light-colored flowers are tubular, rather like those of some of the South African ericas. They open in summer, and are usually white to pale pink.
CULTIVATION: Most species tolerate light to moderate frosts but prefer mild winters. They are not fussy about soil requirements, provided the winter drainage is good. It is surprising that these attractive shrubs, which are easily propagated by half-hardened cuttings, are not more widely grown.

Fabiana imbricata

PICHI

☼ ❀ ↔ 7 ft (2 m) ↑ 8 ft (2.4 m)
Chilean species. Leaves dark green, covered with fine down when young.

Upper third of stems smothered with tubular, white to pale pink flowers, in summer. *F. i.* f. *violacea*, mauve to light purple flowers; *F. i.* 'Prostrata', low-growing cultivar. Zones 8–10.

FAGUS

BEECH

Beech trees have their own family (Fagaceae), native to Europe and the British Isles, and also found through temperate Asia and North America, China, and Japan. The genus consists of about 10 deciduous species with branches to ground level and smooth light green leaves. The horizontally held limbs produce layers of foliage that protect the smooth silvery gray trunks from sunburn. In late autumn to winter, the foliage turns golden brown or coppery red before falling. Buds are distinctly sharp-pointed, held at an angle to the stem. Prickly fruits (masts) release 2 triangular nuts. Some splendid examples of hedged beeches are found throughout Europe.

Fagus orientalis

CULTIVATION: Grow in well-drained reasonably fertile soil in wind-sheltered gardens. Summer moisture is necessary until trees become established. They handle moderate air pollution. Propagate from seed sown when fresh, or use grafted cultivars.

Fagus crenata

JAPANESE BEECH

☼ ❀ ↔ 20 ft (6 m) ↑ 30 ft (9 m)
From Japan, important deciduous tree of temperate areas. Bark gray. Leaves oval, pale green on underside, wavy furry margins when young. Veins beneath, also furry. Zones 6–8.

Fagus grandifolia

AMERICAN BEECH

☼ ❀ ↔ 35 ft (10 m) ↑ 80 ft (24 m)
Originating in Canada, and eastern USA, deciduous straight-trunked tree, which develops a spreading crown in the open. Does not perform well in cooler summers. Often produces suckers. Zones 4–8.

Fagus japonica

JAPANESE BLUE BEECH

☼ ❀ ↔ 25 ft (8 m) ↑ 80 ft (24 m)
From mountains of Honshu, Shikoku, and Kyushu in Japan. Deciduous tree, persistent soft hairs on undersides of the oval leaves. Both surfaces furry when leaves are young. Zones 6–8.

Fagus orientalis

ORIENTAL BEECH

☼ ❀ ↔ 40 ft (12 m) ↑ 100 ft (30 m)
Found naturally in southwest Asia, the Balkans, and the Caucasus. Fast-growing tree, smaller in cultivation. Trunk furrowed, smooth, dark gray bark, numerous narrowly forked branches. Leaves bluntly oval, strongly veined. Buds orange, markedly spreading. Zones 6–8.

Fagus sylvatica

COMMON BEECH, EUROPEAN BEECH

☼ ❀ ↔ 50 ft (15 m) ↑ 100 ft (30 m)
From Europe and southern England. Deciduous tree, elegant, strongly veined foliage, graceful habit, provides dense shade. Trunk straight, smooth gray bark. Autumn foliage gold to orange to brown. Prickly fruits. *F. s.* var. *heterophylla* 'Aspleniifolia', narrow long-pointed leaves; *F. s.* f. *pendula*, weeping beech, pendulous thick branches; *F. s.* f. *tortuosa*, twisted branches. Also *F. s.* 'Albomarginata', variegated leaves; 'Cuprea', copper colored; 'Dawyck', upright tree resembling Lombardy poplar; 'Dawyck Gold', gold-tipped foliage; 'Dawyck Purple', purplish foliage; 'Fastigiata', deep green with gold; 'Purpurea' ★, soft green turning purple; 'Purpurea Pendula', weeping foliage; 'Quercina', prickly pale copper nuts; 'Riversii Purple' ★, color intensifies to almost black; 'Tricolor', slow growing, pink margins, white-blotched green leaves. Zones 5–8.

Fabiana imbricata

Fagus sylvatica 'Purpurea', in winter

F. sylvatica 'Purpurea', in spring

F. sylvatica 'Purpurea', in summer

Fagus sylvatica 'Purpurea Pendula'

Fagus sylvatica 'Dawyck Gold'

Fagus sylvatica 'Quercina'

Fagus sylvatica 'Albomarginata'

Fagus sylvatica f. *tortuosa*

Fagus sylvatica f. *tortuosa*

Fagus sylvatica, in the wild, Sweden

Fagus sylvatica 'Fastigiata'

Fagus sylvatica f. *pendula*

FALLOPIA

syn. *Polygonum*

FLEECE VINE, KNOTWEED, SILVER LACE VINE

This is a genus of about 150 woody-stemmed annual or perennial herbs from the knotweed (Polygonaceae) family, found across almost all Northern Hemisphere temperate regions. Panicles or spikes of small funnel-shaped flowers appear from axils or ends of branches. The fruit is 2- to 3-angled and nut-like.

CULTIVATION: They grow in sun or shade in any well-drained garden soil, but will thrive in damper conditions. Propagate from seed or by division from autumn to spring; propagate climbers from semi-hardened cuttings in summer. Can become invasive.

Fallopia baldschuanica

syns *Bilderdykia baldschuanica, Polygonum baldschuanicum*

MILE-A-MINUTE VINE, RUSSIAN VINE

☼ ❋ ↔ 20–40 ft (6–12 m)
↑ 20–40 ft (6–12 m)

Vigorous, woody, deciduous climber from Iran. Pale green heart-shaped leaves, on long stalks. Broad drooping panicles of white flowers, tinged pink, in summer–autumn. Zones 3–8.

Fallopia japonica

syns *Polygonum japonicum, Reynoutria japonica*

JAPANESE KNOTWEED, MEXICAN BAMBOO

☼ ❋ ↔ 3–7 ft (0.9–2 m) ↑ 3–7 ft (0.9–2 m)

Very vigorous, suckering, rhizomatous perennial from Japan. Very invasive.

Oval leaves, short stalks. Showy panicles of tiny creamy white flowers, late summer–autumn. *F. j.* **var.** *compacta* (syn. *Polygonum reynoutria*), compact form, almost circular leaves, pink to reddish flowers; *F. j.* **'Spectabilis'**, red leaves marbled with yellow. Zones 3–8.

FARFUGIUM

syns *Ligularia, Senecio, Tussilago*

A genus of only 2 species in the daisy (Asteraceae) family, from East Asia. These handsome plants are evergreen perennials with large, deep green, kidney-shaped leaves and clusters of yellow daisies from autumn to winter.

CULTIVATION: Hardy and easily grown in temperate zones in cool, moist, humus-rich soil. Will grow in

Fallopia japonica var. *compacta*

damp areas but prefer woodland conditions with good drainage. Full sun is tolerated, but foliage is lusher in partial shade. Good indoor pot plants in colder climates. Propagate by division in late winter and spring.

Farfugium japonicum
syn. *Ligularia tussilaginea*

☀ ❄ ↔ 24–40 in (60–100 cm)
↑ 24–40 in (60–100 cm)

Native to Japan, evergreen herbaceous perennial. The only species usually cultivated. Large, kidney-shaped, rich green leaves. Yellow flowers, widely spaced rays, in winter. '**Argenteum**', leaves edged with white; '**Aureomaculatum**' ★ (leopard plant), irregular yellow spots on leaf; '**Crispatum**' (syn. 'Cristata'), green leaves, crumpled crested edges. Zones 8–11.

FARGESIA

This Himalayan bamboo genus is a member of the grass (Poaceae) family. It contains just 4 species, but there are also several cultivated varieties. Most species are fairly compact, and are clumping, not running, and hence non-invasive. Stems are fine and well foliaged, forming a dense impenetrable clump, very useful as a screen or barrier. Flowers seldom appear on garden specimens, which is just as well since the plants die after flowering. Of immense ornamental value.

× *Fatshedera lizei*

CULTIVATION: Tolerant of light frosts and easily grown in mild temperate climates in moist, humus-rich, well-drained soil in full sun or shade. The only maintenance required is to thin out old canes as necessary. Propagate by division, or from seed if available.

Fargesia murieliae ★
syns *Sinarundinaria murieliae, Thamnocalamus spathaceus*

UMBRELLA BAMBOO

☼ ❄ ↔ 2–4 ft (0.6–1.2 m)
↑ 10–12 ft (3–3.5 m)

Hardy bamboo from west and central China; important food of the giant panda. Narrow apple green leaves, long-drawn-out apex. Jointed culms, ½ in (12 mm) diameter, yellowish green, fade to yellow. '**Harewood**', dwarf form; '**Jumbo**', taller, wider foliage; '**Simba**', to 6 ft (1.8 m) high; '**Thyme**', 5 ft (1.5 m) high. Zones 4–6.

Fargesia nitida
syn. *Sinarundinaria nitida*

FOUNTAIN BAMBOO

☼ ❄ ↔ 2–4 ft (0.6–1.2 m)
↑ 10–12 ft (3–3.5 m)

From central China. Purplish culms to ½ in (12 mm) wide, branching in 2nd year, persistent purplish green sheaths. Cascades of narrow, rough, dark green, tapered leaves. '**Anceps**', narrower foliage, more open habit; '**De Belder**', shorter, purple culms; '**Eisenae**', upright, purple culms; '**McClure**', reaches 18 ft (5.5 m) high; '**Nymphenburg**', narrow foliage. Zones 3–8.

× *FATSHEDERA*

One of the few examples of a hybrid between two genera. Originally from France and now Europe, this is a cross between Atlantic ivy (*Hedera hibernica*)

Felicia amelloides

and Japanese fatsia (*Fatsia japonica*) and belongs to the ivy (Araliaceae) family. Unusual, sprawling, evergreen climber shrub, or a little of both. Flowers are insignificant and sterile, so it is very much a foliage plant.
CULTIVATION: Easily grown in moist well-drained soil in partial or full shade. Tolerates neglect provided it remains moist. With a somewhat rangy habit, it needs regular pinching back to keep it compact and a support to keep it upright. As it is sterile it must be propagated from cuttings, though it sometimes self-layers.

× *Fatshedera lizei*

◐/☼ ❄ ↔ 8 ft (2.4 m) ↑ 6 ft (1.8 m)

From Europe. Multi-stemmed shrub. Leaves deeply lobed, hand-shaped, bright glossy green. Small heads of greenish white flowers, in autumn; best removed because flies pollinate them. '**Annemeike**', yellow leaves; '**Variegata**', cream-edged leaves. Zones 7–11.

FATSIA

This genus within the ivy (Araliaceae) family contains only 3 evergreen species of thick-leafed small trees and shrubs from moist coastal woodlands of South Korea, Japan, and Taiwan. They tend to sucker from the base, producing a fuller shrub; unwanted stems can be removed. Tolerant of pollution and salt spray and moderately frost hardy. Variegated cultivars are less frost tolerant. Good indoor and conservatory plants with ornamental leaves, and good specimen plants for courtyards and terraces.
CULTIVATION: They like moisture-retentive soil in sun or part shade. In warm climates they can be grown under trees. In shade, they tolerate dry nutrient-deficient soil, but do better in more fertile soil. In colder areas, they need the protection of a wall or similar. Under glass and in

pots, they need a loam-based compost, regular feeding, and watering during growing season. Propagate from seed sown in autumn, from cuttings, or by air-layering.

Fatsia japonica
syns *Aralia japonica, A. sieboldii*

FATSIA, JAPANESE ARALIA

☼/◐ ❄ ↔ 6–12 ft (1.8–3.5 m)
↑ 6–12 ft (1.8–3.5 m)

Native to South Korea and Japan. Leaves dark green, glossy, 7 to 11 lobes, mostly toothed, palmate. Rounded flowerheads of creamy white flowers, in late summer–autumn. Fruit green, ripening black by spring. '**Aurea**', yellow variegations; '**Marginata**', leaves gray-green, white margins, deeply lobed; '**Moseri**' ★, more compact, vigorous, larger leaves; '**Variegata**', leaf lobes deeply edged with cream tips. Zones 8–11.

FELICIA

This is a genus of about 83 species of annuals, perennials, subshrubs, and shrubs in the daisy (Asteraceae) family. The shrubs and subshrubs are evergreens, native to the Arabian Peninsula and tropical and southern Africa. Preferring open, sunny, low-humidity areas, most need frost-free conditions and low rainfall. They are grown for their mainly blue flowers with yellow disc florets. Mauve, pink, and white forms are also available, as are many new cultivars. The shrubby forms are popular as annual container and patio plants, and will overwinter in a greenhouse in colder areas.
CULTIVATION: They grow outdoors in moderately fertile soil, but prolonged damp conditions can kill them. In containers they need a loam-based compost with added grit for drainage. Propagate from seed sown in spring, or by taking stem-tip cuttings in summer and overwintering in frost-free conditions.

Fatsia japonica

Felicia amelloides

syns *Agathaea coelestis, Felicia aethiopica*
BLUE DAISY, BLUE MARGUERITE
☀ ✤ ↔ 24 in (60 cm)
↑ 16–24 in (40–60 cm)

Summer-flowering South African sub-shrub, trailing and/or upright stems. Fine-haired leaves light green. Solitary flowers, vivid yellow disc florets, light to dark blue ray florets. '**Blue Eyes**', deep blue flowers; '**Santa Anita**', heavy flowering, hardier. Zones 9–10.

Felicia filifolia

WILD ASTER
☀ ✤ ↔ 36 in (90 cm) ↑ 36 in (90 cm)
Native to South Africa, evergreen subshrub. Mid-green leaves, linear, needle-like, arranged alternately. Profuse mauve to white flowers with yellow disc florets growing from leaf axils up stems, in spring. Zones 9–11.

Felicia fruticosa

☀ ✤ ↔ 36 in (90 cm) ↑ 36 in (90 cm)
Evergreen shrub, native to South Africa. Linear leaves densely packed. Ray florets pink, purple, or white, with yellow disc. Fruits are hairy. Lengthy flowering season through spring–summer; can be extended by deadheading. Zones 9–11.

FENESTRARIA

This genus, comprising just one species from southern Namibia and neighboring parts of South Africa, belongs to the iceplant (Aizoaceae) family. The plants form subterranean clumps with fleshy leaves, stems, and roots. Leaves are club-shaped, with window-like translucent tips, which, in the wild, are all that is seen above-ground until it flowers. Light is focused through these "lenses" into the internal photosynthetic tissue of the leaves. Flowers are usually borne singly and have yellow or white petals. The capsule has 8 to 16 compart-

ments and becomes detached intact, releasing seeds as it is blown over the land (a "tumble" fruit).
CULTIVATION: This plant requires full sun and low humidity, with no water at all in autumn and winter. Although in the wild the plant is almost subterranean, it can be grown with leaves fully exposed, but is best grown under cover everywhere to prevent dampness and consequent rotting. Propagate from seed or cuttings.

Fenestraria rhopalophylla

BABY'S TOES, WINDOW PLANT
☀ ❄ ↔ 6–10 in (15–25 cm)
↑ 4–6 in (10–15 cm)
Stemless, succulent, mostly subterranean, evergreen perennial from South Africa, forms mats or single clumps. Crowded rosettes of smooth, waxy, opposite, club-shaped leaves, flattened tops, transparent windows. White to yellow flowers, solitary or in threes, on long stalks, many petals and stamens, from mid-winter–early spring. Cone-shaped whitish brown seeds in pods. Zones 8–11.

FEROCACTUS

BARREL CACTUS
This is a genus of 29 species of barrel-shaped cacti (family Cactaceae) from the semi-arid areas of southwestern USA and Mexico, especially Baja California. The name refers to the strong stout spines, which are often savagely hooked. *Ferocactus* is distinguished from the closely related genus *Echinocactus* by the absence of wool at the growing tip. Most are solitary, a few branch, and some form mats and grow to massive proportions. Stems are spherical to columnar to barrel-shaped. Ribs range from few to many, often very deep and prominent. The large areoles usually have glands, which secrete nectar that is attractive to ants and other insects. Flowers

Felicia fruticosa

Felicia filifolia

Fenestraria rhopalophylla

form near the growing tip and are short, funnelform or bell-shaped, with prominent scales. Seed pods are oval to spherical, dry or juicy at maturity.
CULTIVATION: Relatively easy to grow in rich, very well-drained, predominantly mineral soil, with moderate watering in warmer months but a distinct rest in winter. For good spination, full sun and low humidity are essential. Being mainly solitary, they are almost invariably raised from seed.

Ferocactus alamosanus

☀ ✤ ↔ 12 in (30 cm) ↑ 40 in (100 cm)
From Mexico. Usually solitary, densely spined, with 12 to 20 ribs, narrow, sharply pointed, blunt, or rounded. Spines yellow, needle-like, central, 8 to 12 radials. Flowers funnelform,

greenish yellow. Seed pods oval. *F. a.* subsp. *reppenhagenii*, 12 to 18 ribs, merging areoles. Zones 9–11.

Ferocactus cylindraceus

syns *Ferocactus acanthodes, F. lecontei, F. tortulispinus*

CALIFORNIA BARREL CACTUS, COMPASS CACTUS
☀ ✤ ↔ 20 in (50 cm) ↑ 10 ft (3 m)
From southern California, Nevada, Utah, and Arizona, USA, and Baja California and Sonora, Mexico. Solitary, spherical to cylindrical, 20 to 30 ribs with tubercles, slightly wavy ribs with transverse creases. Spines are white, yellow, red, or gray; 10 centrals, 4 to 12 radials. Flowers are bell-shaped, red, yellow, or orange. Seed pods are yellow. *F. c.* subsp. *lecontei*, straight central spines, never hooked, closely pressed against stem. Zones 9–11.

Ferocactus emoryi

syn. *Ferocactus covillei*
☀ ✤ ↔ 3 ft (0.9 m) ↑ 8 ft (2.4 m)
From central Arizona, USA, and Sonora, Sinaloa, and Baja California Sur, Mexico. Solitary, spherical to cylindrical, light to bluish green with 15 to 30 ribs, distinctly tuberculed when young. Spines whitish to reddish; 1 central, 7 to 9 radials. Flowers funnelform, mahogany red to red, tinged with yellow. Seed pods oval. *F. e.* subsp. *rectispinus*, smaller stems, 21 ribs. Zones 9–11.

Ferocactus alamosanus subsp. *reppenhagenii*

Ferocactus cylindraceus

Ferocactus emoryi

Ferocactus histrix

Ferocactus gracilis

Ferocactus herrerae

Ferocactus glaucescens

Ferocactus latispinus

Ferocactus glaucescens ★

☀ ❄ ↔ 20 in (50 cm) ↑ 18 in (45 cm)
From Hidalgo, Mexico. Solitary
to many-stemmed, with slightly
depressed tops, distinctly powdery
pale bluish gray-green, 12 to 17 ribs,
no tubercles, long merging areoles.
Spines awl-shaped, yellow, 1 central,
6 to 7 radials. Flowers bell-shaped,
yellow. Seed pods spherical, whitish
or yellowish. Zones 9–11.

Ferocactus gracilis

FIRE BARREL CACTUS

☀ ❄ ↔ 12 in (30 cm) ↑ 5 ft (1.5 m)
From Baja California, Mexico.
Solitary, spherical to cylindrical, deep
green, 16 to 24 ribs, slightly tuberculed. Spines red with yellow tips; 7 to
13 centrals, 4 main centrals, 8 to 12
radials. Flowers funnelform, red. Seed
pods oval, yellow. *F. g.* subsp. *coloratus,*
rarely reaches 40 in (100 cm), widest
central spine often over ¼ in (6 mm)
in diameter. Zones 9–11.

Ferocactus herrerae

syn. *Ferocactus wislizenii* var. *herrerae*

☀ ❄ ↔ 18 in (45 cm) ↑ 7 ft (2 m)
From Sinaloa, Sonora, and Durango,
Mexico. Solitary, with 13 deep, spiraling, deeply tuberculed ribs. Spines
variable with age; 6 centrals, several
radials. Flowers funnelform, yellow
with red mid-stripes, to 2½ in (6 cm)
long and wide. Seed pods oval,
yellow-green. Zones 9–11.

Ferocactus histrix

☀ ❄ ↔ 32 in (80 cm) ↑ 48 in (120 cm)
From central Mexico. Solitary, flattened spherical to short cylindrical,
with large, depressed, woolly stem tip,
20 to 40 ribs, areoles almost merging.
Spines strong, yellow, becoming gray
with age; 1 to 4 centrals, 6 to 9
radials. Flowers bell-shaped, yellow.
Seed pods fleshy, yellow. Zones 9–11.

Ferocactus latispinus ★

☀ ❄ ↔ 16 in (40 cm) ↑ 12 in (30 cm)
From much of central Mexico.
Solitary, light green, spherical to flattened, 20 or more deep tuberculed
ribs. Spines reddish to yellowish to
white; 4 centrals, 5 to 15 radials.
Flowers funnelform, purplish pink or
yellow, densely overlapping, fringed
bracts. Seed pods oval, covered with
scales. Zones 9–11.

Ferocactus robustus

☀ ❄ ↔ 7 ft (2 m) ↑ 3 ft (0.9 m)
From southeastern Puebla, Mexico.
Distinctive species, usually grows in
large clumps of spherical to club-
shaped deep green stems, about 8
deep tuberculed ribs with widely
spaced areoles. Spines can be reddish,
purplish, or tan, with 4 to 7 centrals,
erect, straight, and 10 to 14 radials,
upper similar to centrals, lower
bristle-like, white. Flowers are yellow,
funnelform. Seed pods are spherical,
yellow, and fleshy. Zones 9–11.

Ferocactus wislizeni ★

ARIZONA BARREL CACTUS,
CANDY BARREL CACTUS

☀ ❄ ↔ 32 in (80 cm) ↑ 10 ft (3 m)
From central and southern Arizona,
southern New Mexico, southwest
Texas, USA, and northwest Mexico.
Solitary giant, 20 to 30 ribs, barely
tuberculed, widely spaced areoles
when young, merging with age.
Spines variable, white to red to gray,
4 centrals; 12 or so radials. Flowers
funnelform, yellow to yellowish
orange. Seed pods oval, green, turning
yellow when ripe. The native Seri
peoples of Mexico have used the
spines as fishhooks, the flesh to make
candies, and the dried floral remains
as a dye for face paint. Zones 9–11.

FESTUCA

FESCUE

A genus of some 300 species in the
grass (Poaceae) family, widespread
throughout the world. Mostly small
unassuming plants, they are valued
ornamentally for their sometimes distinctively colored foliage and showy
flower plumes; and commercially and
practically as some of the finest lawn
grasses available, especially for high-
quality, low-traffic lawns. The leaves
are usually folded around the midrib,
in some species making the foliage
very fine and hair-like. The flowerheads, which usually exceed foliage
in height, are feathery and open.
CULTIVATION: While hardiness varies,
most are at home in temperate zones
and thrive in most soils with minimal
attention, though few will tolerate
prolonged poor drainage. Plant in full
sun or partial shade. As lawn grasses,
they appreciate annual dethatching
and aeration. Green year-round, but
in hot conditions take care to water
well and do not mow too closely.
Propagate by dividing established
clumps, or raise from seed.

Festuca amethystina

LARGE BLUE FESCUE, TUFTED FESCUE

☀/◐ ❄ ↔ 10 in (25 cm)
↑ 18 in (45 cm)

From central and eastern Europe.
Tussock-forming perennial grass with
soft gray-green foliage. Flower spikes
appear, bearing small violet-green
flowers, in early summer. Zones 4–9.

Festuca californica

CALIFORNIA FESCUE

☀ ❄ ↔ 24 in (60 cm)
↑ 24–36 in (60–90 cm)

From California, USA. Foliage green
to bright blue; blue forms take on
purplish tones once frosts commence.
Pale creamy green flower spikes, in
summer. 'Serpentine Blue' ★ (blue
California fescue), rich silvery foliage,
red-purple autumn tones, not good in
shade. Zones 5–9.

Festuca filiformis

FINE-LEAFED SHEEP'S FESCUE, HAIR FESCUE

☀/◐ ❄ ↔ 8 in (20 cm) ↑ 15 in (38 cm)

North American species with short,
very fine, green to blue-green, hair-
like leaves. Panicles of green or light
purple flowers, on wiry stems, in
summer. Zones 4–9.

Festuca californica

Festuca longifolia

Festuca glauca

BLUE FESCUE, GRAY FESCUE

☼ ❄ ↔ 10 in (25 cm) ↕ 12 in (30 cm)

Found throughout Europe. Densely tufted evergreen grass. Smooth blue-green leaves surround crown of plant. Creamy flower spikes appear from mid-summer, sitting well above the foliage. 'Blaufuchs' ★ (syn. Blue Fox), intense powder blue leaves, fade to cream at tips; 'Blauglut' (syn. Blue Glow), clump-forming, intense silver-blue foliage; 'Elijah Blue', soft powdery blue foliage, very compact; 'Seeigel' (syn. Sea Urchin), very fine, upright, spiky, blue-green leaves, very compact. Zones 4–10.

Festuca idahoensis

☼/◗ ❄ ↔ 12 in (30 cm) ↕ 15 in (38 cm)

From western Canada and northwestern USA, densely tufted, longer living species than *F. glauca*. Tends not to die out in center. Foliage blue-green to silver-blue. Creamy flower spikes appear in summer. Tolerant of wet conditions. Zones 3–8.

Festuca longifolia

HARD FESCUE

☼/◗ ❄ ↔ 16 in (40 cm) ↕ 24 in (60 cm)

Widespread in almost all northern temperate zones. Popular pasture and lawn grass. Bright green leaves. Buff-colored panicles of flowers, on tall wiry stems, in summer. Does best in cool climates. Zones 5–9.

Festuca glauca

Festuca pratensis

Festuca ovina

SHEEP'S FESCUE

☼/◗ ❄ ↔ 16 in (40 cm) ↕ 24 in (60 cm)

Tussock-forming species, very widespread in northern temperate zones. Sometimes used in lawns. Fine blue-green leaves with similarly-colored panicles of flowers, on tall wiry stems, in summer. Zones 5–9.

Festuca pratensis

MEADOW FESCUE, WESTERN FESCUE

☼/◗ ❄ ↔ 16 in (40 cm) ↕ 24 in (60 cm)

Quick-growing species, widespread in northern temperate zones, and especially in western North America. Fine foliage and summer-flowering panicles, which are golden brown when dry. Occasionally may be used in pastures, but considered a potentially invasive weed in many areas. Zones 5–10.

Festuca valesiaca

WALLIS FESCUE

☼ ❄ ↔ 6 in (15 cm) ↕ 6 in (15 cm)

This tight, clump-forming, dwarf grass species from central Europe has soft powdery blue foliage. The bluish white flower spikes are held above foliage, in mid-summer. This

Festuca glauca 'Elijah Blue'

Festuca glauca 'Seeigel'

plant needs well-drained soils, and is ideal in rockeries but not in hot situations. Zones 5–9.

Festuca varia

☼/◗ ❄ ↔ 15 in (38 cm) ↕ 22 in (55 cm)

Southern European alpine species, aromatic hair-like foliage and downy, violet-tinted, blue-green panicles of flowers. *F. v.* subsp. *scopari*, downy, blue tips. Zones 5–9.

FICUS

FIG

Although this genus is in the mulberry (Moraceae) family, its flower and fruiting stages differ from those of the rest of this family. Fig species come in many variations, from climbers and creepers to large shrubs and very large trees. Many fig species of tropical forests display the "strangler" growth habit, some also develop "curtains" of aerial roots, or even the "banyan" growth form. *Ficus* species have a milky sap, and a large stipule enclosing the tip of each twig and leaving a ring-like scar when it falls. Leaves vary from tiny to huge, with variable shape. Many species shed their leaves in the tropical dry season. The "fruits" (figs) also vary greatly in size, and can be eaten by birds or mammals.

CULTIVATION: *F. carica* can cope with occasional frosts down to about 21°F (−6°C); other species tolerate light frosts only if protected when small. Figs are vigorous growers, and will quickly outgrow a small garden. Propagate from seed, from cuttings, or by air layering. *F. carica,* the edible fig, is the most easily propagated species.

Festuca varia subsp. *scoparia*

Festuca glauca 'Blauglut'

Ficus aspera
CLOWN FIG, MOSAIC FIG

☼ ✈ ↔ 8 ft (2.4 m) ↑ 20 ft (6 m)

From islands of the southwest Pacific. A non-strangling "sandpaper" fig. Leaves extremely rough, harsh surface. 'Parcellii', highly variable mosaic of paler gray-green, cream, and dull pink, on dark green leaves. Variegation is caused by a virus. Zones 11–12.

Ficus benghalensis
BANYAN

☼ ✈ ↔ 75–400 ft (23–120 m)
↑ 30–40 ft (9–12 m)

Southern Asian fig, widespread in India. Vastly spreading; a single tree may produce hundreds, sometimes thousands, of trunks, creating its own mini forest. Broad, stiff leaves, shiny deep green; stalkless figs, ripen to orange. A sacred tree of Hinduism, special in Indian folklore. 'Krishnae', similar proportions, inrolled cup-shaped leaves. Zones 11–12.

Ficus aspera 'Parcellii'

Ficus brachypoda

Ficus benjamina var. *nuda*

Ficus benghalensis

Ficus benjamina
BENJAMIN FIG, BENJAMIN TREE, WEEPING FIG

☼ ⸙ ↔ 50 ft (15 m) ↑ 80 ft (24 m)

Tropical Asian species, popular foliage plant. Small glossy leaves, pointing downward, narrowing abruptly at apex. Figs deep reddish tan. *F. b.* var. *nuda* (syn. *F. b.* var. *comosa*), robust, broad-spreading limbs, non-drooping branchlets, leaves abruptly narrowed at tip, orange figs. *F. b.* 'Exotica' ★, thinner, more finely pointed leaves; 'Golden Princess', leaves tinged lemon yellow; 'Pandora', small thin leaves, wavy margins; 'Starlight', similar to 'Variegata', leaves cream-edged gray-green flecked. Zones 10–12.

Ficus brachypoda
syn. *Ficus platypoda* var. *lachnocaulon*
ROCK FIG

☼ ⸙ ↔ 10–30 ft (3–9 m)
↑ 10–30 ft (3–9 m)

Widely distributed through central and northern Australia, on rocky

Ficus benjamina 'Starlight'

Ficus carica

Ficus deltoidea

Ficus benjamina

outcrops, often in arid habitats. Thick leaves of variable size. Figs yellow to red, fruiting throughout much of the year. Zones 9–12.

Ficus carica
EDIBLE FIG

☼ ⸙ ↔ 15 ft (4.5 m) ↑ 35 ft (10 m)

Cultivated over 5,000 years ago in western Asia, origins are obscure. Deciduous tree, spreading rounded canopy. Smooth silvery-gray bark. Leaves 3- to 5-lobed, toothed edges. Tiny flowers. Purple-brown fruit. Used for dried figs. Prefers a climate with long warm summers, dry atmosphere, on soils of low to medium fertility. 'Black Genoa' ★, large tree, profuse dull purple fruits, very sweet dark red flesh; 'Brown Turkey', prolific, pink-fleshed, brown-skinned figs, flavor sweet but slightly insipid; 'White Adriatic', tall grower, pale greenish brown figs, tasty deep pink flesh. Zones 10–12.

Ficus destruens

Ficus elastica

Ficus deltoidea
MISTLETOE FIG, TRIANGLE FIG

☼ ✈ ↔ 4–10 ft (1.2–3 m) ↑ 8 ft (2.4 m)

From Southeast Asia. Small, densely massed leaves, broad, blunt apex on adult plants. Leaves narrower, more pointed on young plants. Growing in forks of trees or on cliffs, branching from the base into thick spreading boughs. Small, stalked, dull pink figs. Useful for embankments or rocky outcrops. Zones 11–12.

Ficus destruens
RUSTY FIG

☼ ✈ ↔ 35 ft (10 m) ↑ 50 ft (15 m)

Large strangler fig from rainforests of far northeastern Australia; kills its host tree. Leathery leaves. Young twigs and leaf undersides have a felty coating of rust-colored hairs. Figs are hard and orange-brown, with a distinctive bulge at the apex. Zones 11–12.

Ficus elastica
INDIA-RUBBER TREE, RUBBER TREE

☼ ✈ ↔ 70–200 ft (21–60 m)
↑ 90–200 ft (27–60 m)

Tropical Asian fig, renowned as the principal source of rubber, or "caoutchouc," tapped from trees in Bangladesh and Assam in India. In mid-twentieth century, it became the archetypal indoor plant. Large tree, numerous aerial roots draped from its branches. 'Decora' ★, broad, glossy, bronze-tinted leaves, large reddish buds at apex; 'Doescheri', leaves irregularly edged cream, center marbled gray; 'Schrüveriana', leaves peppered with dark green, new leaves flushed red; 'Variegata', variegated leaves of deep green and cream. Zones 11–12.

Ficus glumosa

BERGVY, MOUNTAIN FIG

☼ ✳ ↔ 25–60 ft (8–18 m)
↑ 17–30 ft (5–9 m)

Slow-growing deciduous tree from
South Africa. Large vigorous root
system, short upright trunk, bark
mottled yellow and gray. Green oval-
shaped foliage. Leaves and branches
covered with yellowish hairs. Figs,
borne in the axils without stems,
turn yellow with age. Zones 7–9.

Ficus lutea

syns *Ficus nekbudu, F. vogelii,
F. zuluensis*

NEKBUDU, VOGEL'S FIG, ZULU FIG

☼ ✦ ↔ 40 ft (12 m) ↑ 60 ft (18 m)

Found throughout most of Africa
south of the Sahara, and on Madagascar and other Indian Ocean
islands. Large strangler fig, very wide
rounded crown. Evergreen leaves;
small orange to red figs, crowded
along branch ends. Zones 11–12.

Ficus lyrata

FIDDLE-LEAF FIG

☼ ⚡ ↔ 30 ft (9 m) ↑ 30 ft (9 m)

From rainforests of central Africa and
tropical west Africa. Bushy-crowned
erect tree; large stiff leaves resemble a
violin body. Green figs, hidden under
the leaves. Popular pot plant in the
1950s and 1960s. Zones 9–12.

Ficus natalensis

Ficus lutea

Ficus macrophylla subsp. *columnaris*

Ficus macrophylla

MORETON BAY FIG

☼ ⚡ ↔ 130 ft (40 m) ↑ 80–100 ft (24–30 m)

From Australia's east coast; rapid
growth, dramatic trunk buttresses,
large canopy. Large dark green leaves,
glossy, thick. Purple figs. *F. m* **subsp.**
columnaris, known as banyan, occurs
offshore on Lord Howe Island, forming subsidiary trunks and a spreading
canopy over endemic palm, *Howea
forsteriana.* Zones 9–11.

Ficus microcarpa

syns *Ficus nitida, F. retusa*

BANYAN FIG, INDIAN LAUREL FIG,

☼ ⚡ ↔ 20–50 ft (6–15 m)
↑ 40–70 ft (12–21 m)

Native to southern China, Southeast
Asia to northern Australia. Evergreen
tree, upright branchlets, often forms
aerial roots. Gray to reddish bark,
small horizontal flecks. Dense foliage
with small, oval, dark green leaves
alternating along stems. *F. m.* **var.**
hillii (syn. *F. hillii*) (Hill's weeping
fig), popular park tree from Australia,
open habit, high sweeping limbs,
drooping branchlets. Zones 10–12.

Ficus natalensis

NATAL FIG

☼ ⚡ ↔ 50 ft (15 m) ↑ 100 ft (30 m)

From tropical and southern Africa.
Epiphytic shrub or tree. Opposite,

Ficus glumosa

Ficus macrophylla subsp. *columnaris,* in the wild, Lord Howe Island, Australia

long, leathery, spatula-shaped leaves.
Aerial roots. Fruits solitary or in pairs.
Suitable for bonsai. Most plants in
cultivation are *F. n.* **subsp.** *leprieurii*.
Zones 10–12.

Ficus palmeri ★

ANABA, BAJA FIG, DESERT FIG

☼ ✦ ↔ 10 ft (3 m) ↑ 12 ft (3.5 m)

Spreading evergreen tree from Baja
California, Mexico. White or yellowish bark. Virtually succulent, drawing
moisture from swollen trunk base in
drought. Young leaves covered in
white hairs, becoming smooth and
prominently veined with age. Small
figs appear in pairs, covered in white
down. Zones 11–12.

Ficus pleurocarpa

BANANA FIG

☼ ✦ ↔ 30 ft (9 m) ↑ 50 ft (15 m)

Species found only in northeastern
Queensland, Australia. Dense spreading canopy; leaves oval-shaped, dark
glossy green. Fruits yellow, banana-
shaped; final ripening stage occurs

Ficus pseudopalma

mid- to late wet season (around late
summer–early autumn). Suitable for
large garden or park. Zones 11–12.

Ficus pseudopalma

DRACAENA FIG, PALM-LIKE FIG,
PHILIPPINE FIG

☼ ✦ ↔ 10 ft (3 m) ↑ 20 ft (6 m)

Unusual, multi-stemmed, palm-like
species, native to the Philippines.
Often has no branches, but has stiff,
long, coarsely notched, thick leaves,
arising from rosettes. Figs are oblong
and ribbed, greenish purple in color,
with raised white flecks. Zones 11–12.

Ficus virens, in the wild, Borneo

Ficus pumila 'Sonny'

Ficus pumila
CREEPING FIG

☀ ✦ ↔unlimited ↑10–15 ft (3–4.5 m)

From China and Japan, self-clinging evergreen climber. Small, flat, heart-shaped leaves. Vigorous, new, non-clinging growth with age, thick-stemmed, with large fleshy leaves. Large, purplish green, barrel-like fruits develop on old plants. 'Dorthe', green leaves, cream centers; 'Minima', smaller leaves; 'Sonny', cream leaves, green centers. Zones 9–11.

Ficus religiosa
BO TREE, PEEPUL TREE, SACRED FIG

☀ ✦ ↔25 ft (8 m) ↑30–40 ft (9–12 m)

Native to the mountains of Southeast Asia and the Himalayan foothills; this species is significant for its rôle in Buddhist philosophy. Strangling fig, normally deciduous in monsoonal climates. Pale gray-barked trunk, spreading branches. Leaves heart-shaped, apex drawn out into a long slender point. Zones 9–12.

Ficus rubiginosa
PORT JACKSON FIG, RUSTY FIG

☀ ✦ ↔35 ft (10 m) ↑60 ft (18 m)

From the east coast of Australia. Evergreen tree, forms a broad dome. Massive buttressed trunk, smooth gray limbs, sprouting aerial roots. Thick, leathery, oval leaves, dark green with rusty or pale olive felted reverse. Figs yellowish green, warty, ripen in autumn. A gold-variegated form is available. Zones 9–11.

Ficus superba
DECIDUOUS FIG, SEA FIG

☀ ✦ ↔35–60 ft (10–18 m) ↑20–70 ft (6–21 m)

Large briefly deciduous tree, some aerial roots, native of Japan, China, and Southeast Asia. Young leaves pink, becoming mid-green with maturity. Flying foxes feed on the dull purple figs, clustered on short stalks.

Ficus superba var. *henneana*

F. s. var. *henneana*, smaller form, native to the northern part of Australia. Zones 9–11.

Ficus sycomorus
EGYPTIAN SYCAMORE, MULBERRY FIG, SYCAMORE

☀ ✦ ↔35 ft (10 m) ↑80 ft (24 m)

From the Arabian Peninsula and north of Sudan, Africa. Briefly decid-uous, thickly branched tree, often buttressed, large spreading crown. Rounded, prominently veined, deep green leaves, paler underneath, like sandpaper. Bears small, spherical, velvety, edible figs, yellow, orange, or red. Zones 10–12.

Ficus thonningii
syn. *Ficus petersii*

COMMON STRANGLER FIG, COMMON WILD FIG, GEWONE WILDEVY

☀ ❊ ↔unlimited ↑10–15 ft (3–4.5 m)

Evergreen climber from South Africa. Variable size and habit, can be free-standing, strangler fig, or rock fig. Vigorous invasive root system. Hairy figs borne in leaf axils, on short stalks or none. Timber used for furniture and implements. Zones 7–9.

Ficus religiosa

Ficus virens
GRAY FIG, JAVA WILLOW, SPOTTED FIG, STRANGLER FIG

☀ ✦ ↔50–100 ft (15–30 m) ↑50–100 ft (15–30 m)

From India through to the Solomon Islands and northern Australia. Briefly deciduous, heavily limbed, spreading tree, drooping branches, aerial and pillar roots. Dark green leaves, promi-nently veined, young foliage scarlet or bronze. Pairs of small, spherical, figs in leaf axils, finely hairy, green becoming white. Zones 10–12.

Ficus watkinsiana
BELLINGER RIVER FIG, WATKINS FIG

☀ ❊ ↔10–17 ft (3–5 m) ↑50–100 ft (15–30 m)

Evergreen tree with buttresses, from the northern regions of Australia. Smooth leaves. Rounded or oblong, velvety, green to rusty figs, with pro-truding apex. Zones 8–10.

Ficus thonningii

Ficus rubiginosa

Filipendula vulgaris

FILIPENDULA
DROPWORT, MEADOWSWEET

This genus of about 10 species of fleshy-stemmed or tuberous clump-forming perennials belongs to the rose (Rosaceae) family. They are native to northern temperate regions, where they are usually found growing in damp habitats. These tall attractive plants have large pinnate and palmate leaves, and bear plumes of tiny white or pink flowers. Some species have been used in herbal medicine for centuries. Salicin, an ingredient in aspirin, was discovered in *F. ulmaria* in 1839. The name aspirin is in part derived from *Spiraea*, the genus in which *Filipendula* was once included. CULTIVATION: Grow in part-shade in moist humus-rich soil that does not dry out in summer. Propagate from seed or by division.

Filipendula camtschatica
syn. *Spiraea kamtschatica*
☼ ❄ ↔ 24 in (60 cm) ↕ 4–8 ft (1.2–2.4 m)
Native to Japan. Large, deeply toothed, divided leaves with rounded terminal leaflets. Tall plumes of small white to pink flowers, in summer–autumn. Zones 3–9.

Filipendula purpurea
☼ ❄ ↔ 18 in (45 cm) ↕ 36–48 in (90–120 cm)
Native to Japan. Stems and leaf stalks often purple. Stiff, palmate, dark green leaves. Plumes of small deep pink to purplish red flowers, in summer. Zones 6–9.

Filipendula rubra
QUEEN OF THE PRAIRIE
☼ ❄ ↔ 2 ft (0.6 m) ↕ 3–7 ft (0.9–2 m)
From eastern USA. Vigorous perennial, forming large clumps of deeply divided foliage. In summer, tall stems of peachy pink flowers are borne in plumes. 'Venusta' ★ (syn. 'Magnifica'), deep rose flowers. Zones 2–9.

Filipendula ulmaria
MEADOWSWEET, QUEEN OF THE MEADOWS
☼ ❄ ↔ 12–18 in (45–60 cm) ↕ 24–48 in (60–120 cm)
From Europe and Western Asia. Large divided leaves, dark green, hairy beneath. Plumes of creamy white fragrant flowers borne in summer. 'Aurea', golden foliage; 'Rosea', soft pink flowers; 'Variegata', leaves with central yellow stripe. Zones 3–9.

Filipendula vulgaris
syn. *Filipendula hexapetala*
DROPWORT
☼ ❄ ↔ 18 in (45 cm) ↕ 24–36 in (60–90 cm)
From Europe and northern and central Asia. Tuberous with deeply cut fern-like leaves. Small white flowers, often tinged reddish purple, borne in feathery heads, in summer. Zones 3–9.

FIRMIANA

This is a genus of 9 mostly deciduous trees or shrubs found in tropical parts of Southeast Asia, with one species occuring in eastern Africa. It is a member of the cacao (Sterculiaceae) family. In warmer climates they are valued as shade trees; these trees have smooth-edged or palmate leaves and racemes or panicles of stalk-like flowers, with no petals but a colored calyx. The curious fruit consists of 4 or 5 papery, leaf-like follicles, each containing round wrinkled seeds on its margins. CULTIVATION: Adaptable to most soil types and easily transplanted, they prefer some protection from wind. Propagation is from seed sown in warmer months, or from cuttings of lateral shoots taken in early spring.

Firmiana simplex ★
CHINESE BOTTLE TREE, JAPANESE VARNISH TREE
☼ ☙ ↔ 35 ft (10 m) ↕ 60 ft (18 m)
Long cultivated in Japan, deciduous tree native to China and eastern Asia, from the Ryukyu Islands to Vietnam. Smooth green bark; large, maple-like, palmate leaves divided into 3 to 7 lobes. Calyx is lemon yellow, seed follicles are hairy. 'Variegata', green leaves mottled with white. Zones 9–10.

FITTONIA

Usually seen as house plants but also well-suited to use as ground covers in tropical gardens, the 2 species of low, spreading, evergreen perennial that make up this tropical South American genus belong in the acanthus (Acanthaceae) family, though the relationship is anything but obvious. The plants form a mat of stems that root as they creep across the ground. Both the stems and the undersides of the oval leaves are downy. Ornamentally speaking, the foliage is the main attraction, rather than the somewhat inconspicuous spikes of tiny creamy white flowers. Leaves are deep green to olive in color, sometimes red-tinted, with very colorful or contrasting veins that may be pink to red, or silvery white.
CULTIVATION: *Fittonia* species are intolerant of prolonged cool conditions, let alone frost; they need a warm, humid, draft-free environment with moist, well-drained, humus-rich soil. They thrive in terrariums and are very easily propagated by removing small rooted pieces.

Fittonia albivenis
MOSAIC PLANT
☼ ✈ ↔ 12–24 in (30–60 cm) ↕ 6 in (15 cm)
From the headwaters of the River Amazon in Ecuador, Peru, and the western edge of Brazil. Mat-forming, with stems rooting at nodes. Leaves broadly rounded at tip, dark green with network of contrasting veins. Flowers small, cream, much of the year. 'Nana', smaller leaves. **Argyroneura Group** (syns *F. argyroneura*, *F. verschaffeltii* var. *argyroneura*), leaves deep green, veined white or faintly pink. **Verschaffeltii Group** (syn. *F. verschaffeltii*), leaves dark bronzy green, veins pink. Zones 11–12.

FITZROYA

This genus consists of a single evergreen conifer from the rainforests of southern South America. It is a member of the cypress (Cupressaceae) family, one in Chile, *F. cuppresoides*, was recorded as reaching an age of 3,622 years. It has an erect branching habit, scale-like leaves in whorls of 3, solitary male cones toward the tips of the branches, and single female cones at the ends of the branches. CULTIVATION: Frost resistant but drought tender, *Fitzroya* prefers moist well-drained soil and an open sunny position. Propagate from seed.

Fitzroya cupressoides
ALERCE
☼ ❄ ↔ 20 ft (6 m) ↕ 100–200 ft (30–60 m)
Native of central Chile and northern Patagonia. Large, evergreen, coniferous tree; rusty red or gray bark. Tiny scale-like leaves, dark green, with paler midrib. Female cones spherical, green when fertilized, hardening to brown. Zones 8–9.

Firmiana simplex, seeds

Fittonia albivenis 'Nana'

FLACOURTIA

A genus in the governor's-plum (Flacourtiaceae) family of 15 mostly deciduous shrubs or small trees native to tropical Africa and Asia, China, and Madagascar. Often spiny, they have alternate, simple, toothed leaves and clusters of small, petal-less, yellow-green to white flowers. Male and female flowers grow on different plants. Fruit is a round, smooth, fleshy, berry-like drupe with 8 to 12 flat seeds in a sweet juicy pulp used in jams and preserves. It can be invasive out of its natural habitat.
CULTIVATION: Although adaptable and undemanding once established, they prefer rich moist soils and do not tolerate frost or drought. Propagate from seed or cuttings, or by budding or separation of root suckers.

Flacourtia jangomas
PANIALA, RUKAM
☼ ❄ ↔ 10 ft (3 m) ↑ 30 ft (9 m)
Deciduous tree, cultivated in India, naturalized on Australian east coast. Erect stem, thin narrow leaves, emerging glossy red, several times yearly, ageing to dark green. Clusters of tiny, white, very fragrant flowers, in spring. Fruit dark brown, pleasant-tasting, yellowish green pulp. Zones 10–12.

Flacourtia rukam
FILIMOTO, GOVERNOR'S PLUM, INDIAN PRUNE
☼ ❄ ↔ 12 ft (3.5 m) ↑ 50 ft (15 m)
From the Philippines and Malaysia. Shrub or small tree, largest of the species. Branches spiny. Thin narrow leaves. Flowers greenish yellow. Juicy edible fruit, pink becoming dark red or purple. Not suitable for home use because of its spines. Zones 10–12.

FLAGELLARIA

Bamboo-like genus of tropical species of climbing and scrambling plants placed in its own family, Flagellariaceae. The smooth stems are jointed, with simple, sheathing, alternate, grass-like leaves with coiled tips, by which the plants climb high into jungle canopy or scramble over other plants in light breaks or other open spaces. Small, creamy, 6-segmented flowers are borne in large terminal bunches, followed by whitish fruits.

CULTIVATION: They need well-drained soils of light texture and moderate fertility. Propagate from seed sown while fresh. Division of new shoots from the base of older plants has had mixed success.

Flagellaria indica
SUPPLEJACK
☼◐ ❄ ↔ 8–15 ft (2.4–4.5 m)
↑ 20–40 ft (6–12 m)
Widespread species occurring in Asia, India, Indonesia, and from northern Australia to Sydney on the east coast. Rampant climber, leaves narrowly tapering to coiled tip, light green, bases sheathing. Inflorescences dense, small white flowers in terminal clusters, in summer. Globular white fruits, in autumn. Young leafy shoots have been cooked and eaten. Zones 9–12.

FLINDERSIA

Genus of 16 species, mostly from humid rainforests of subtropical to tropical east coast Australia; a member of the rue (Rutaceae) family. Often used in parks and as street trees. Some of their common names reflect their foliage likeness to the Northern Hemisphere ash *(Fraxinus)* species; however, all species are evergreen.
CULTIVATION: They prefer relatively high rainfall in reasonably fertile well-drained soil with summer water. Most tolerate frost and in full sun develop a well-rounded, often open habit. Propagate from seed in spring.

Flindersia australis
AUSTRALIAN TEAK, CROW'S ASH
☼ ❄ ↔ 35 ft (10 m) ↑ 120 ft (36 m)
From tropical Australia. Dense crown of large leaves, many leaflets. Profuse, creamy white, individual flowers. Fruit 5-segmented, prickly, used for decoration. Smaller in cultivation. Zones 9–11.

Flindersia australis

Foeniculum vulgare 'Purpureum'

FOENICULUM
FENNEL

A culinary herb, and in many areas a weed of waste ground, fennel belongs to the carrot (Apiaceae) family. It is an aromatic biennial or perennial from Europe and the Mediterranean region. It forms a clump of erect hollow stems with feathery foliage made up of many hair-like deep green to bronze leaflets. Heads of small yellow flowers appear through summer, then dry to become similarly shaped pale brown seed heads. Despite its scent and flavor, it is not a plant for small gardens, as it has invasive tendencies.
CULTIVATION: It will grow in most soils and climates, from cool-temperate to subtropical, in moderately fertile soil and a little summer moisture, but a rich well-drained soil and good water will impart a more delicate flavor. Propagate from seed; perennial forms will also grow from divisions.

Foeniculum vulgare
FENNEL
☼ ❄ ↔ 18–36 in (45–90 cm)
↑ 3–7 ft (0.9–2 m)
From Europe and the Mediterranean region, naturalized elsewhere. Hollow-stemmed aromatic perennial, soft, fine, green, fern-like foliage smelling of aniseed. Umbels of small yellow flowers in summer. *F. v.* var. *azoricum* (Florence fennel, Finocchio), smaller annual grown as a vegetable for its swollen basal stem, eaten fresh or cooked; **'Perfection'** and **'Zefo Fino'**, slow to grow. *F. v.* **'Purpureum'** (syns 'Bronze', 'Purpurascens') has dark purplish maroon to bronze foliage. Zones 5–10.

Flacourtia jangomans

Flacourtia rukam

FONTANESIA

This genus of 1 or 2 deciduous shrubs or sometimes small trees, native to China, is a member of the olive (Oleaceae) family. Panicles or racemes of small flowers bloom terminally or in leaf axils, with a deeply lobed corolla, united only at the base. The thin fruit is flat and winged.
CULTIVATION: *Fontanesia* thrive in any soil type. Propagate from seed, by layering, or from softwood cuttings struck under glass.

Fontanesia phillyreoides

☼ ❋ ↔ 7 ft (2 m) ↑ 10–25 ft (3–8 m)
Native of China. Spreading deciduous shrub, smooth upright branches. Narrow, glossy, dull green, smooth-edged leaves. Many greenish white flowers, in spring–early summer. Yellowish brown winged fruit. *F. p.* subsp. *fortunei*, hardier, more erect habit; 'Titan', selection from subspecies; exceptionally tall, vigorous, with long arching branches. Zones 6–9.

FORESTIERA

A genus of some 15 species from the Americas, especially southwest North America, in the olive (Oleaceae) family. Usually dioecious deciduous small trees or shrubs. Short-stalked leaves are opposite, with smooth to minutely toothed margins. Inflorescences are racemes or clusters in leaf axils on previous season's growth, sometimes maturing before the leaves. Flowers

Fontanesia phillyreoides

Fontanesia phillyreoides subsp. *fortunei* 'Titan'

are small, with green petals or none. Fruit is a single-seeded black drupe.
CULTIVATION: They need full sun and well-drained soil. Propagate from half-hardened cuttings or seed. They have little ornamental value.

Forestiera pubescens ★

syn. *Forestiera neomexicana*
DESERT OLIVE, NEW MEXICAN PRIVET
☼ ❋ ↔ 8 ft (2.4 m) ↑ 10 ft (3 m)
Deciduous shrub from southwestern USA. Small, smooth, green leaves, turn yellow in autumn. Insignificant yellow flowers appear in spring before the leaves. Clusters of small, bluish black fruits. Zones 6–10.

FORSYTHIA

This small genus of about 7 species of deciduous shrubs is a member of the olive (Oleaceae) family. They occur mainly in eastern Asia, with one species in southeastern Europe. The simple opposite leaves color in autumn. The yellow flowers appear before, or with, the new leaves in spring. Those species that are semi-pendulous can be trained over a support as wall plants.
CULTIVATION: They are frost hardy and easy to cultivate in well-drained fertile soil in an open sunny position, with adequate water in summer, and winter temperatures below freezing to induce flowering. Flowers are borne on overwintered year-old shoots; remove older shoots when flowering has finished to make room for new shoots that arise from the base of the plant. Propagate from soft-tip cuttings taken in summer, or hardwood cuttings taken in winter. Some species are self-layering and can be increased in this way in late winter.

Forsythia giraldiana

☼ ❋ ↔ 12 ft (3.5 m) ↑ 12 ft (3.5 m)
From northwestern China. Shrub with open arching habit. One of the

Forsythia × intermedia 'Arnold Giant'

Forsythia × intermedia 'Goldzauber'

Forsythia ovata 'Tetragold'

earliest in this genus to flower. Gray-green leaves. Pale yellow blooms, in late winter. Zones 5–9.

Forsythia × intermedia

BORDER FORSYTHIA
☼ ❋ ↔ 7 ft (2 m) ↑ 15 ft (4.5 m)
This shrub has an erect spreading habit and is a hybrid between *F. suspensa* var. *sieboldii* and *F. viridissima*. It has a single basal trunk, and ascending, arching branches. The leaves are oval-shaped, sharply toothed on the upper half, with reddish stalks. Lemon yellow blooms are solitary or in 2- to 6-flowered racemes and appear on 1- and 2-year-old branches during spring. 'Arnold Giant', large, nodding, rich yellow flowers; 'Goldzauber', brilliant yellow flowers appear before leaves; 'Lynwood', prolific large flowers, broad petals; 'Spectabilis', upright, outwardly arching shrub, flowers large, golden yellow. Zones 5–9.

Forsythia ovata

EARLY FORSYTHIA, KOREAN FORSYTHIA
☼ ❋ ↔ 8 ft (2.4 m) ↑ 5 ft (1.5 m)
Compact, bushy, early-flowering species from Korea. Leaves dark green, ovate. Golden yellow flowers, in early spring. 'Tetragold', raised in Holland, dense habit, larger flowers appear earlier. Zones 5–9.

Forsythia suspensa

Forsythia suspensa

GOLDENBELLS, WEEPING FORSYTHIA
☼ ❋ ↔ 10 ft (3 m) ↑ 12 ft (3.5 m)
From China. Slender drooping branches. Autumn foliage dull yellow. Flowers solitary or in small clusters, golden yellow, in spring. *F. s.* var. *fortunei*, vigorous form, more upright habit; *F. s.* var. *sieboldii*, almost prostrate, rarely taller than 3 ft (0.9 m), spreads by self-layering. Zones 4–9.

Forsythia viridissima

GOLDEN BELLS, GREEN STEM FORSYTHIA
☼ ❋ ↔ 10 ft (3 m) ↑ 10 ft (3 m)
From China. Cane-like branches grow from base into hemispherical bush. Long narrow leaves, smooth, dark green, rather shiny, maroon in autumn. Clusters of yellow flowers in leaf axils appear before leaves, calyx purple shaded. 'Bronxensis', dwarf form, primrose-colored flowers. Zones 5–9.

Forsythia, HC, 'Arnold Dwarf'

Forsythia, HC, 'Happy Centennial'

Forsythia, HC, 'Maluch'

F., HC, Marée d'Or/'Courtasol'

Forsythia, HC, 'Northern Gold'

Forsythia, Hybrid Cultivar, 'Northern Sun'

Forsythia, HC, 'New Hampshire Gold'

Forsythia Hybrid Cultivars

☼ ❄ ↔10 ft (3 m) ↕5–10 ft (1.5–3 m)
Hardy and colorful, they include:
'Arnold Dwarf' ★, light green foliage;
'Happy Centennial', bright yellow
flowers; 'Maluch', profuse flowers
with new leaves; Marée d'Or/'Courtasol', heavily branched dwarf, prolific
yellow-gold flowers; 'Meadow Lark',
heavy flowering, buds very hardy;
'New Hampshire Gold', yellow
flowers, in early spring; 'Northern
Gold', shiny bright green leaves,
golden yellow flowers; 'Northern
Sun', strong-growing shrub, clear
yellow flowers, in spring. Zones 4–9.

FOTHERGILLA

Mainly from southeastern USA, this
genus of 2 deciduous shrubs belongs
to the witchhazel (Hamamelidaceae)
family. Spikes of petal-less flowers
appear in spring before the leaves,
their long white stamens creating a
bottlebrush effect. Autumn foliage is
crimson, orange, and yellow.
CULTIVATION: Slow growing, they
need moist, well-drained, humus-rich
soil. Full sun gives best autumn color.
Propagate from seed, best sown fresh,
from softwood cuttings in summer,
or by layering.

Fothergilla gardenii ★

DWARF FOTHERGILLA
☼ ❄ ↔3 ft (0.9 m) ↕3 ft (0.9 m)
Southeastern USA, from North
Carolina to Alabama. Spreading
shrub, oval leaves, irregularly toothed,
fragrant white flowers. 'Blue Mist',
glaucous blue foliage. Zones 5–9.

Fothergilla major

LARGE FOTHERGILLA
☼ ❄ ↔6 ft (1.8 m) ↕5–10 ft (1.5–3 m)
From the Allegheny Mountains of
eastern USA. Slow growing erect
habit. Leaves dark green above,
glaucous beneath. Good autumn
color. Fragrant white flower spikes,
pinkish tinge, in late spring–early
summer. 'Mount Airy', scented,
white, bottlebrush-like flowers, red
autumn foliage. Zones 5–9.

FOUQUIERIA

This genus of 11 species of woody or
succulent, spiny, deciduous shrubs
and small trees occurs in arid regions
in the southwest of North America,
such as Baja California, Mexico. It is
a member of the ocotillo (Fouquieri-
aceae) family. Small bright green leaves
emerge after the irregular rains of
those regions. All species have spines
along stems and branches. Some grow
as columnar unbranched stems up to
50 ft (15 m) tall. Red, purple, cream,
or yellow tubular flowers are produced
at tips of branches or stems after rain,
usually in spring, followed by capsules
containing winged seeds.
CULTIVATION: They require full sun,
in climates similar to those where they
occur naturally. Too much rain, or
over-watering, can be fatal. Since all
species are frost tender when young,
propagate from seed or cuttings in
late spring to summer.

Fouquieria diguetii

TALL OCOTILLO
☼ ◗ ↔6 ft (1.8 m) ↕7 ft (2 m)
Occurs in the Sonoran Desert of
southern California, USA, and in
Mexico in Baja California and the

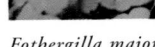

Fothergilla major

Fothergilla gardenii

Fouquieria diguetii

northwest. Short, but definite, trunk, erect branches. Panicles of red tubular flowers, in late winter–early spring. Best in low rainfall areas. Frost tender when young. Zones 9–11.

Fouquieria splendens ★
OCOTILLO

☼ ❄ ↔ 6 ft (1.8 m) ↑ 30 ft (9 m)

Occurs in arid regions of northern Mexico, and southern California, New Mexico, and Texas, USA. Many-branched shrub; long, cylindrical, gray-green, spiny stems. Small green leaves appear after rain, falling during long dry periods. Panicles of bell-shaped bright red flowers, in early spring–summer. Zones 7–11.

FRAGARIA
STRAWBERRY

This genus of 12 perennials, a member of the rose (Rosaceae) family, is found in northern temperate zones and in Chile. Many botanists now believe that the distinction between *Fragaria* and the large, diverse genus *Potentilla* is artificial, and that the strawberries should be included in *Potentilla*. It is likely that this reclassification will be generally accepted in the future. Among the most widely grown of the small fruits, strawberries are tough adaptable plants that spread by runners. The leaves grow in groups of 3, and are heart-shaped to rounded, with toothed edges. Clusters of pretty, white, 5-petalled flowers precede the familiar fruits, which may be red, white, yellow, pink, or orange. The fruits are unusual in that they carry their seeds on the outside.
CULTIVATION: Hardy in temperate zones in all but the coldest winters, strawberries need moist, fertile, well-drained soil, water to swell the fruit, and sun to ripen it. Planting atop mounds ensures good drainage and, combined with mulching, helps to keep the fruit dry. Covers of netting to keep the birds away from the fruit are almost essential. Propagation is usually by layering, using either natural layers or runners, pegged down until the roots establish.

Fragaria chiloensis

Fragaria × ananassa
GARDEN STRAWBERRY

☼ ❄ ↔ 40 in (100 cm) ↑ 6 in (15 cm)

From Holland. Low-growing ground cover; parent of many of the most successful strawberries around the world. Palmate, toothed, green leaves. White flowers with yellow centers in late spring–autumn. Medium-sized dark red fruits, in summer–autumn. 'Cambridge Rival', long picking season, large, firm, sweet fruit, excellent for dessert; 'Earlisweet', popular early fruiting variety, rich flavor, medium-sized fruit; 'Eros', mid-season, large, firm, glossy, red fruit, resistant to red stele; 'Hapil', often used in breeding, reliable cropper; 'Redgauntlet', vigorous growth habit, sweet medium-sized fruit, mid-season; 'Symphony', shiny, medium-sized fruit; 'Tioga', large sweet fruit, heavy cropper, disease resistant; 'Tribute', medium to large, flavorful, firm fruit, one of the most successful varieties in commercial plantings. Zones 3–10.

Fragaria chiloensis
BEACH STRAWBERRY

☼/◐ ❄ ↔ 20 in (50 cm) ↑ 6 in (15 cm)

From North and South America. Short thick leaves, hairy undersides. White flowers, rose-colored edible fruit with white flesh. Called "beach strawberry" because it grows naturally in coastal areas. Zones 4–10.

Fragaria vesca
WILD STRAWBERRY

☼/◐ ❄ ↔ 12 in (30 cm) ↑ 2 in (5 cm)

From European woodland regions. Compact rosettes of dark green leaves on ground-hugging plant. Flowers white; dark red, sweet, edible fruits in summer. 'Alexandra', smaller red berries, very sweet, plant habit slightly smaller than species; 'Fructo Albo' (white wild strawberry), creamy white edible fruits, in summer. Zones 5–9.

Fragaria Hybrid Cultivars
☼/◐ ❄ ↔ 8–60 in (20–150 cm) ↑ 2–6 in (5–15 cm)

These are popular mainly for their ground-covering abilities, although

Fragaria, Hybrid Cultivar, 'Rosie'

Fouquieria splendens, in the wild, Big Bend National Park, Texas, USA

Fragaria × ananassa 'Eros'

Fragaria × ananassa 'Symphony'

Fragaria × ananassa 'Tribute'

some do produce edible fruits. The most popular hybrid cultivars include: 'Darselect', large, firm, bright red berries; 'Lipstick', ornamental variety, dark green leaves, deep pink flowers, small fruit; Pink Panda/'Frel', dark green, heavily veined, palmate foliage, sterile pink flowers, no fruit; 'Rosie', ground-covering habit, sterile variety, rosy red flowers. Zones 5–9.

FRAILEA

This genus of 17 diminutive globular cacti from Argentina, Bolivia, Brazil, Colombia, Paraguay, and Uruguay, belongs to the cactus (Cactaceae) family. They are extremely popular with collectors because of their small size (only *Blossfeldia* are smaller) and their relatively large flowers. *Frailea* are usually solitary to clustering, neat, and spherical, with tiny harmless spines. In some species seed is set without flowers even opening.
CULTIVATION: Easily grown in a rich well-drained soil. Propagate from seed or offsets after the plant has formed a clump. Rest in winter.

Frailea castanea
syn. *Frailea asterioides*

☼ ⬤ ↔ 1¼–1¾ in (30–40 mm) ↑ 1¾ in (40 mm)

From southern Brazil and northern Uruguay. Most sought after because of its solitary growth habit and chestnut

to chocolate color, occasionally in shades of blue-green to gray-green. Low ribs with small areoles. Dark brown to black spines, close to plant body. Comparatively large flowers, bell-shaped, pale yellow. Yellowish green seed pods. Zones 9–11.

FRANCOA
BRIDAL WREATH

This Chilean genus is a member of the saxifrage (Saxifragaceae) family. It is sometimes treated as comprising 5 species, but recent studies treat it as having the single variable species *F. sonchifolia*. These summer-flowering perennials have rosettes of foliage and long-stemmed, many-flowered sprays of small pink and white blooms. Leaves are pointed, oval to lance-shaped in outline, but with large lobes that often effectively make them pinnate. Upper leaf surface is bristly and underside is conspicuously veined.

F

Fraxinus angustifolia

Fraxinus americana 'Autumn Purple'

Francoa sonchifolia

The wiry flower stems, with their tiny 4-petaled flowers, create an airy effect.
CULTIVATION: Hardy in temperate areas where winter frosts are light and infrequent. Easily grown in any well-drained soil that does not dry out in summer. Plant in a bright position, and remove spent flowerheads to keep plants tidy. Most often propagated by division or from small basal cuttings.

Francoa sonchifolia
syns *Francoa glabrata*, *F. ramosa*
☼/◐ ❊ ↔ 18–24 in (45–60 cm)
↕ 24 in (60 cm)
From Chile. Rosettes of soft, hairy, spoon-shaped leaves. Unbranched

flowering stems bear spikes of white or pink flowers with darker spotting, in summer. Zones 7–10.

FRANKLINIA
This is a monotypic genus in the camellia (Theaceae) family. Probably every franklinia in cultivation today is a direct descendant of seeds collected in 1765 in Georgia, USA, and named after Benjamin Franklin. The species has not been seen in the wild for over 200 years. *Franklinia* is closely related to *Gordonia*, with which it is sometimes merged, but differs in being deciduous, and having almost stalkless flowers. Fruit is a large woody capsule containing two flattened seeds.
CULTIVATION: *Franklinia* will tolerate a slightly alkaline soil, but likes plenty of organic material; a sheltered aspect with some morning sun is preferred. Propagate from fresh seed.

Franklinia alatamaha ★
FRANKLIN TREE, FRANKLINIA
◐ ❊ ↔ 12 ft (3.5 m) ↕ 20 ft (6 m)
From the Altahama River region in Georgia, USA. Attractive, small,

upright, deciduous tree. The glossy bright green leaves color scarlet in autumn. The single camellia-like flowers, pure white with a central bunch of yellow stamens, appear in late summer–autumn. Zones 7–10.

FRAXINUS
ASH
This genus in the olive (Oleaceae) family consists of 65 species. Most *Fraxinus* species are deciduous trees, but the genus also includes a few evergreens. They are mainly from temperate Europe, Asia, and North America, although a few species are found in the tropics. Their leaves are opposite and pinnate. Racemes of small, usually insignificant flowers are borne terminally or in the leaf axils, appearing before the leaves, in spring; flowers are unisexual or bisexual. They harden into single-seeded winged fruits. The timber is used for sports equipment and tool handles, and the bark is used medicinally. The foliage is utilized as cattle fodder in Scandinavia. *F. chinensis* is the source of "Chinese insect white wax," and *F. ornus* is cultivated in southern Italy for manna syrup.
CULTIVATION: Most grow well in moist loam and make good specimen trees in large gardens. They tolerate coastal salt air, exposed positions, urban pollution, alkaline soil, and heavy clay. Most species prefer alkaline soil. Propagate by sowing seed after stratifying.

Fraxinus angustifolia subsp. *syriaca*

Cultivars can be grafted in spring, or they may be budded onto seedling stock of the same species in summer.

Fraxinus americana
WHITE ASH
☼ ❊ ↔ 50 ft (15 m) ↕ 80 ft (24 m)
Native to eastern North America, columnar tree with spreading crown. Leaves pinnate, dark green, with 5 to 9 lance-shaped leaflets. 'Autumn Blaze', purple color in autumn; 'Autumn Purple' ★, autumn foliage colored red to deep crimson; 'Rose Hill', dark green leaves, turning bronze-red in autumn. Zones 4–10.

Fraxinus angustifolia
syn. *Fraxinus rotundifolia*
NARROW-LEAFED ASH
☼ ❊ ↔ 40 ft (12 m) ↕ 80 ft (24 m)
Closely allied to *F. excelsior*, occurs wild in Mediterranean region and western Asia. Typical race (*F. a.* subsp. *angustifolia*) is restricted to southern Europe and northwestern Africa. Vigorous tree, ascending branches, darkish furrowed bark. The leaves have 7 to 13 rather narrow leaflets, arranged in whorls of 3. The winter buds are large and dark brown. *F. a.* subsp. *oxycarpa* (syn. *F. oxycarpa*) occurs in southeastern Europe and Caucasus region, only 5 to 7 leaflets per leaf, bands of hairs on undersides; *F. a.* subsp. *syriaca* (syn. *F. syriaca* 'Desert Ash'), occurs in Turkey, Syria, and Iran, smaller bushier tree, blackish bark, very thick knobbly twigs, leaves in whorls of 3 or 4, grows well in semi-arid climates. *F. a.* 'Elegantissima', small tree, light green leaves; 'Lentiscifolia', leaflets more widely spaced on longer common stalk; 'Raywood' (claret ash), vigorous, erect, narrow in habit, dark wine red autumn foliage. Zones 6–10.

Fraxinus bungeana

Fraxinus chinensis

Fraxinus bungeana

☼ ✽ ↔ 10 ft (3 m) ↑ 15 ft (4.5 m)

From northern China. New shoots have a finely hairy appearance. Leaves with up to 7 leaflets, finely scalloped margins. Flowers downy, in showy panicles, in late spring. Fruit winged, narrow, with notch at tip. Zones 5–9.

Fraxinus chinensis

☼ ✽ ↔ 25 ft (8 m) ↑ 80 ft (24 m)

Native to Korea and China. Yellow hairless young growth. Leaves with 8 leaflets, invertly egg-shaped, dark green above, slightly downy underneath. Flowers on new growth in terminal panicles. Winged fruits in summer. Zones 6–9.

Fraxinus dipelta

☼ ✽ ↔ 10 ft (3 m) ↑ 15 ft (4.5 m)

From California, USA. Angular branches, red-tinged new growth, turning gray. Up to 7 pairs of leaflets on leaves, oval, smooth, or scalloped edges, pale green above, reticulate veining below. Showy white flower panicles appear with leaves, in late spring. Zones 8–10.

Fraxinus excelsior

COMMON ASH, EUROPEAN ASH

☼ ✽ ↔ 60 ft (18 m) ↑ 100 ft (30 m)

Native to Europe. Gray branches, prominent black buds, in winter. Dark green leaves with 11 pairs of leaflets, turn bright yellow in autumn. Flower panicles appear before leaves, in spring. Fruits winged, pendent, remaining after leaves fall. *F. e.* f. *diversifolia* (one-leafed ash), leaves usually a single large leaflet; *F. e.* 'Aurea Pendula', pendulous golden branches; 'Eureka', bright green leaves with serrated edges; 'Jaspidea', yellow shoots in winter, yellow new growth, yellow leaves in autumn; 'Pendula', weeping branches. Zones 4–10.

Fraxinus floribunda

HIMALAYAN MANNA ASH

☼ ✽ ↔ 40 ft (12 m) ↑ 120 ft (36 m)

Native to the Himalayas. Mauve young branches. Nine pairs of leaflets, oval, coarsely toothed, hairless above, downy beneath. Showy panicles of white flowers appear in early summer. Winged fruits. Zones 8–10.

Fraxinus greggii

BARRETA, CHINA, DOGLEG ASH, MEXICAN ASH

☼ ✽ ↔ 10–17 ft (3–5 m) ↑ 12–20 ft (3.5–6 m)

Fast growing, multi-stemmed, semi-evergreen shrub or small tree from southwestern USA and Mexico. Bark smooth, dark green, turns light gray with age. Compound pinnate leaves, with 5 to 7 leaflets. Small insignificant flowers in spring. Single, winged, tan-colored seeds. Zones 7–10.

Fraxinus latifolia

syn. *Fraxinus oregona*

OREGON ASH

☼ ✽ ↔ 50 ft (15 m) ↑ 80 ft (24 m)

Valuable timber tree from western North America. Deciduous species. Leaves with 9 leaflets, egg-shaped with pointed tips, dark green above, lighter and downy underneath, turn yellow in autumn. Panicles of flowers on previous year's wood. It is closely related to *F. pennsylvanica*. Zones 5–10.

Fraxinus ornus

Fraxinus excelsior 'Pendula'

Fraxinus nigra

BLACK ASH, SWAMP ASH

☼ ✽ ↔ 25 ft (8 m) ↑ 50 ft (15 m)

Upright deciduous tree, native to North America. Leaves dark green, 11 stalkless leaflets, lance-shaped, small-toothed edges, curved upward, downy brown veins; underside paler green. Fruit oblong, winged. 'Fallgold', vigorous, non-fruiting, good yellow autumn color. Zones 7–10.

Fraxinus ornus

FLOWERING ASH, MANNA ASH

☼ ✽ ↔ 40 ft (12 m) ↑ 50 ft (15 m)

Native to southern Europe and south-western Asia. Leaves with 7 leaflets, paler beneath, rather hairy midribs. Showy, dense panicles of fragrant white flowers, in late spring. Fruit narrow, winged. Sugary substance secreted when bark is damaged. 'Arie Peters', creamy flowers. Zones 6–10.

Fraxinus excelsior, in winter

Fraxinus excelsior, in summer

Fraxinus excelsior, in the wild, Scotland

Fraxinus pennsylvanica

GREEN ASH, RED ASH

☀ ❄ ↔ 70 ft (21 m) ↑ 70 ft (21 m)

Robust tree from North America. Olive green leaves, 9 lance-shaped leaflets, smooth or toothed edges, pointed tips, sunken midrib. Flowers appear on old wood, followed by winged fruit. '**Marshall's Seedless**', vigorous, non-fruiting, dark green leaves; '**Patmore**', strongly erect, glossy leaves, oval crown, does not fruit; '**Summit**' ★, pyramidal when young, becoming upright, autumn leaves deep yellow. Zones 4–10.

Fraxinus spaethiana

☀ ❄ ↔ 20 ft (6 m) ↑ 30 ft (9 m)

From Japan. Light to mid-gray bark, leaf buds very dark brown, almost black. Dark green leaves, 9 large, lance-shaped leaflets, toothed edges,

sparsely hairy undersides. Spring-borne panicles of petal-less white flowers. Winged fruits. Zones 6–9.

Fraxinus uhdei

EVERGREEN ASH, SHAMEL ASH

☀ ❄ ↔ 15 ft (4.5 m) ↑ 25 ft (8 m)

Semi-evergreen to evergreen upright tree from Mexico and Central America. Rounded canopy. Leaves dark green, lance-shaped to oblong, toothed, hairless, 7 leaflets. Flowers in dense panicles. Thrives in warmer moist conditions. '**Tomlinson**', small upright tree, reaches 12 ft (3.5 m) in 10 years. Zones 8–11.

Fraxinus velutina

ARIZONA ASH, DESERT ASH, VELVET ASH

☀ ❄ ↔ 30 ft (9 m) ↑ 30 ft (9 m)

Native to southwestern USA and northwestern Mexico. Dull green

leaves, 7 lance-shaped to oval, toothed leaflets, leathery, hairy felting beneath. *F. v.* var. *coriacea,* from southern California, leaves thicker and almost hairless; *F. v.* var. *glabra*, doubtfully distinct from *F. v.* var. *coriacea*; *F. v.* var. *toumeyi*, longer-stalked, narrower leaflets, gray-green upper surfaces stay velvety until late summer. *F. v.* '**Fan-Tex**', handsome tree, larger dark green leaves, non-fruiting. Zones 7–10.

FREESIA

syn. *Anomatheca*

This genus is a member of the iris (Iridaceae) family and consists of 6 species of corms found in southern and central Africa. They are mainly small plants, forming clumps of simple narrow leaves, usually with a prominent midrib. In the warmer months they produce sprays of small, 6-petalled, sometimes fragrant flowers on wiry, often branching stems, held above the foliage. These plants are not showy, but make an attractive display where left to naturalize.

Fraxinus velutina, in the wild, in Zion National Park, Utah, USA

Fraxinus pennsylvanica

Fraxinus uhdei

Freesia laxa

CULTIVATION: Freesias, which are undemanding plants, are easily grown in any sunny position with moderately fertile well-drained soil. Provided the soil does not freeze to the depth of the corm, they can be left in the ground to overwinter; otherwise store dry in a frost-free place. Propagation is usually by breaking up established clumps while the plants are dormant. Freesias are easily raised from seed, and sometimes they will self-sow.

Freesia alba

syns *Freesia lactea, F. refracta* var. *alba*

☀ ✿ ↔ 3 in (8 cm) ↑ 4–6 in (10–15 cm)

Vigorous old garden inhabitant of confused nomenclature and possibly muddled ancestry. Strongly perfumed, prolific, small flowers. Petals variable; common coloration is cream splashed in onion-skin colors of gold, brown, purple, bronze, and rose. Stems short. Prefers dry summers, sharp drainage, and poor soils. Zones 9–11.

Freesia laxa

syn. *Anomatheca laxa*

SCARLET FREESIA

☀ ❄ ↔ 8–12 in (20–30 cm)
↑ 12–16 in (30–40 cm)

From South Africa and Mozambique. Forms clumps of grassy leaves. Bears flowers in shades of pink to purpled-red, sometimes white or pale blue. Self-sows. '**Joan Evans**', only 6 in (15 cm) tall, with pale-centered pink flowers. Zones 8–11.

Freesia viridis

syn. *Anomatheca viridis*

☀ ❄ ↔ 8 in (20 cm) ↑ 15 in (38 cm)

From the Cape region of South Africa. Narrow grassy leaves. Green flowers, sometimes fragrant, with reflexed petals, in sprays of up to 10 blooms. Zones 8–10.

Freesia Hybrid Cultivars

FLORIST'S FREESIAS

☀/◐ ❄ ↔ 6–12 in (15–30 cm)
↑ 12–20 in (30–50 cm)

This group of cultivars and hybrids has a complex parentage involving several known parents, such as *F. alba, F. corymbosa, F. leichtlinii, F. refracta,* and possibly a few others. They cover a wide range of plant sizes and flower colors, and vary greatly in the intensity of their fragrance. Popular hybrid cultivars in the pink double-flowered range include: '**Aphrodite**'; mixed-color seedling strains such as '**Parego's Blue**', blue tones; '**Parego's Red**', pink to red; **Royal Crown Series**, pink, yellow throats; '**Super Emerald**', shades of green. Zones 8–11.

FREMONTODENDRON
FLANNEL BUSH

There are 3 species of evergreen shrubs in this genus from southwestern North America, which is a member of the cacao (Sterculiaceae) family. Flannel bushes have showy golden yellow to orange blooms of 5 petal-like sepals. The stems, flower buds, and seed capsules, and the undersides of the leaves, are covered with fine bronze bristles that give rise to the common name of flannel bush. CULTIVATION: These shrubs require a warm, sunny, sheltered site, and in cool-temperate climates should be grown under the protection of a wall, although they will withstand some frost. Poor dry soils suit them best, as rich soils produce an excess of foliage rather than flowers and can be a factor in reducing the plant's life span. Too much moisture and root disturbance are other reasons why flannel bush plants are fairly short-lived. Propagate from seed, or from softwood or half-hardened cuttings.

Fremontodendron californicum
FLANNEL BUSH, FREMONTIA

☼ ❄ ↔ 15 ft (4.5 m)
↑ 12–25 ft (3.5–8 m)

Found in the Sierra Nevada range of California, USA. Leaves variable, almost round to a pointed oval shape, dull green, roughened by tiny hairs. Flowers appear in flushes during spring–summer, bright yellow, often with orange tones on their backs. Zones 8–10.

Fremontodendron californicum

Fremontodendron decumbens
syn. *Fremontodendron californicum* subsp. *decumbens*

PINE HILL FLANNEL BUSH

☼ ❄ ↔ 10 ft (3 m) ↑ 2 ft (0.6 m)

Extremely rare and endangered species in the wild, found only within a mile of the summit of one hill in the Sierra Nevada range in southwestern USA. Low spreading shrub, flowers coppery in color, borne up to 9 months of the year. Zones 8–10.

Fremontodendron mexicanum
MEXICAN FLANNEL BUSH, MEXICAN FREMONTIA, SOUTHERN FLANNEL BUSH

☼ ⁑ ↔ 12 ft (3.5 m) ↑ 20 ft (6 m)

Native to Mexico's Baja California Peninsula and the San Diego area, USA; rare. Grows in chaparral and woodland. More tender than *F. californicum*. Golden yellow flowers, partly hidden by foliage, over many months, from spring. Zones 9–11.

Fremontodendron Hybrid Cultivars

☼ ❄ ↔ 10–15 ft (3–4.5 m)
↑ 12–20 ft (3.5–6 m)

Hybrids between *F. californicum* and *F. mexicanum* have largely proved superior to either of their parents, being more vigorous, with a heavier crop of larger flowers. Popular hybrids include: '**California Glory**', vigorous shrub, large yellow flowers; '**Ken**

Fremontodendron, Hybrid Cultivar, 'California Glory'

Fremontodendron mexicanum

Taylor' low grower, bright orange-yellow flowers; '**Pacific Sunset**', vigorous, almost tree-like, bright yellow flowers with elongated petal tips. Zones 8–10.

FREYLINIA

A small genus of 4 species occurring in tropical and southern Africa, this is a member of the foxglove (Scrophulariaceae) family. All are shrubs or small trees with opposite leaves. The flowers are bisexual and funnel-shaped, and the fruit is an egg-shaped capsule. CULTIVATION: A moist, well-drained, sheltered situation is essential. Propagate from seed or cuttings.

Freylinia lanceolata
HONEYBELL BUSH

☼ ⁑ ↔ ↑ 15 ft (4.5 m)

From the extreme tip of South Africa's Cape Provinces. Shrub or small tree.

Freylinia lanceolata

Dull green leaves, narrow, lance-shaped. Flowers whitish, yellow inside, in terminal clusters, throughout the year with fruit. Zones 9–11.

FRITILLARIA
FRITILLARY

This genus of natives from the Mediterranean, Asia, and America contains about 100 species of perennial, herbaceous, bulbous plants that are members of the lily (Liliaceae) family. They are increasingly popular with domestic gardeners, who value them for their unusual coloring, delicate appearance, interesting formations, and odd, almost mechanical markings. The majority bloom in spring. The flowers are usually bell-shaped and somewhat pendent. Their scent is sometimes less than pleasing. The botanical name comes from the Latin *fritillus* (dice box), referring to the neat checked markings that some species bear on their petals and to the shape of the capsules. CULTIVATION: The origin of each individual species is an important pointer. Many are seriously fussy about their needs, and the moisture levels, soil types, climate, and altitude of the original habitat should be taken into account in cultivation. Propagate from purchased bulbs (avoid if dried out), from bulb scales, from basal "rice-grain" bulbets, or from seed.

Freesia, Hybrid Cultivar

Freesia, Hybrid Cultivar, double form

Freesia, Hybrid Cultivar, Royal Crown Series

Fritillaria acmopetala

Fritillaria agrestis

Fritillaria meleagris

Fritillaria meleagris 'Aphrodite'

Fritillaria glauca 'Goldilocks'

Fritillaria imperialis

Fritillaria camschatcensis

Fritillaria acmopetala

☀ ❄ ↔ 1¾–2 in (4–5 cm)
↑ 16–18 in (40–45 cm)

Found in vineyards and grain fields across western Asia and the eastern Mediterranean. Flowers are usually solitary, petals pale, shiny, green-yellow with chocolate-purple blotches. Leaves alternate, linear, gray-green. Prefers fertile well-drained soil. Less demanding than many. Zones 7–10.

Fritillaria agrestis

syn. *Fritillaria biflora* subsp. *agrestis*
STINK BELL

☀ ❄ ↔ 1¾–2 in (4–5 cm)
↑ 12–16 in (30–40 cm)

Found on grassy, lightly treed hills of coastal California, USA. Leaves yellowish green, linear, broad and clustered at base, then fine and alternate. Flowers white with sulfur yellow veining, or murky purple-brown, petals recurved, in spring. Their scent is unpleasant. Prefers a heavy moisture-retentive soil, hot dry summers, winter and spring rainfall; resents disturbance. Zones 6–9.

Fritillaria biflora

BLACK FRITILLARY, MISSION BELLS

☀ ❄ ↔ 1¾–2 in (4–5 cm)
↑ 10–16 in (25–40 cm)

From coastal grasslands of California, USA. Basal leaves are glossy green.

Flowers with variable petals, glossy, commonly dark brown with lime green shading and/or checking, 1 to 6 per stem, appearing from early to mid-spring. Prefers full sun, shelter from rain, sharp drainage, winter and spring rainfall, and hot dry summers. Zones 7–9.

Fritillaria bucharica

☀ ❄ ↔ 1¾–2 in (4–5 cm)
↑ 8–12 in (20–30 cm)

Found on cliffs and rocky slopes at altitude in northeastern Afghanistan and central Asia. Leaves profuse, linear, in basal pairs, then alternate. Stems of 3 to 4 flowers, petals white with hint of green. Prefers good drainage, dry dormancy. Well suited to container culture. Zones 5–9.

Fritillaria camschatcensis

BLACK SARANA, ESKIMO POTATOES

☀/◐ ❄ ↔ 1¾–2 in (4–5 cm)
↑ 8–16 in (20–40 cm)

Widespread through northwestern America and northern Japan, in moist open woods and subalpine meadows. Leaves glossy, light green, lance-like, held in whorls. Stems bear 2 to 3 flowers, grape-like, rich dark purple-brown petals with interior sheen, in late spring–early summer. Prefers humus-rich moisture-retentive soil and cool damp summers. Zones 4–9.

Fritillaria cirrhosa

☀/◐ ❄ ↔ 1¾–2 in (4–5 cm)
↑ 6–16 in (15–40 cm)

Widespread on limestone habitats in the Himalayas. Leaves linear, gray-green, opposite. Stems bear 1 to 4 flowers, petals long, narrow, checked yellow or gray-green over chestnut, in early summer. Requires humus-rich moisture-retentive soil that is not allowed to dry out, and cool damp summers. Zones 4–9.

Fritillaria glauca

SISKIYOU LILY

☀ ❄ ↔ 1¾–2 in (4–5 cm) ↑ 4–6 in (10–15 cm)

Found on rocky screes from California to Oregon, USA. Leaves are mostly basal, widely linear, with bluish bloom. Flowers largish, open bell-shaped, solitary; petals waxen, yellow, sometimes with markings. Stamens protruding, yellow. Prefers deep, moist, stony soil. 'Goldilocks', low-growing selection, golden yellow petals. Zones 6–8.

Fritillaria graeca

☀ ❄ ↔ 1¾–2 in (4–5 cm)
↑ 2½–8 in (6–20 cm)

Found on exposed rocky habitats in southern Greece, Albania, and Yugoslavia. The leaves are broad at the base, mid-green, and clustered around the stem. The flowers are solitary or paired, in broad, heavy, pendent bells, appearing in late spring–early summer; petals slightly incurving, green and red, often with central stripe. Prefers fertile soil, good drainage,

dry dormancy. The robust *F. g.* subsp. *thessala* is the most common form in cultivation. Zones 7–9.

Fritillaria hermonis

☀ ❄ ↔ 2½ in (6 cm) ↑ 4–5 in (10–12 cm)

Found in rocky habitats in southern Turkey and Lebanon; highly variable species. Leaves gray-green, oblong, and alternate. Stems of 2 to 3 flowers, petals elongated, red and green, tinted or checked, appearing in late spring. Prefers sharp drainage, dry dormancy, and fertile soil. *F. h.* subsp. *amana* is the only species that is common in cultivation. Zones 7–9.

Fritillaria imperialis

CROWN IMPERIAL, TEARS OF MARY

☀ ❄ ↔ 16 in (40 cm)
↑ 36–48 in (90–120 cm)

Widespread from southern Turkey to Kashmir. Leaves mid-green, glossy, in whorls. Flowers large, bright, clustered at top of upright stems, appearing in late spring. Scent unpleasant, fox-like. Petals yellow, lemon yellow, orange, or red, commonly orange. Prefers a fertile well-drained soil. 'Aureomarginata', margins of leaves lemon yellow; 'Lutea', yellow petals. Zones 4–7.

Fritillaria meleagris

GUINEA HEN FLOWER, LEPER LILY, SNAKES HEAD FRITILLARY/LILY

☀ ❄ ↔ 1¾–2 in (4–5 cm)
↑ 7–8 in (18–20 cm)

Variable protected species, rare in the wild, found in grassy flood plains from southern England to western Russia. Leaves alternate, long, sharply pointed, gray-green. Flowers square-shouldered bells, sometimes paired, appearing in mid-spring; petal color variable, distinctly checked maroon, dark purple, and/or murky pink. Prefers fertile well-drained soils and damp summers. *F. m.* var. *unicolor* subvar. *alba*, white petals; *F. m.* 'Aphrodite', white petals with green veining. Zones 4–9.

Fritillaria michailovskyi

Fritillaria olivieri

Fritillaria tuntasia

Fritillaria michailovskyi

☀ ❄ ↔ 2 in (5 cm) ↑ 4–8 in (10–20 cm)

From the alpine slopes of Turkey. Leaves alternate, lance-shaped, mid-green. Stems bear 1 to 7 flowers, broadly bell-shaped, appearing in early summer; petals glossy deep purple-brown with distinctive lower band of yellow. Prefers gritty soil, cold winters, cool summers. Zones 7–9.

Fritillaria olivieri

☀ ❄ ↔ 3 in (8 cm)
↑ 12–15 in (30–38 cm)

Found in damp mountain meadows in Iran. Leaves broadly basal, lance-like, alternate on stem, in whorls of 3, growing above the flowers. Flowers square-shouldered, appearing in early summer; petals rusty brown with lime green central stripe. Requires deep root run, summer rest, damp fertile soil. Zones 5–9.

Fritillaria pallidiflora

☀ ❄ ↔ 2½–3 in (6–8 cm)
↑ 4–28 in (10–70 cm)

Variable species from the subalpine slopes of central Asia. Leaves opposite or alternate, broadly lance-like, gray-green. Up to 6 flowers per stem, large, pendent, square-shouldered, appearing in late spring; petals lemon to butter yellow. Scent unpleasant. Prefers rich, well-drained, peaty soil, damp conditions. Zones 3–8.

Fritillaria persica

☀ ❄ ↔ 3 in (8 cm) ↑ 4–36 in (10–90 cm)

Robust variable species with changeable nomenclature. Found in the eastern Mediterranean region and inland, on rocky slopes and along the edges of cornfields. Leaves numerous, gray, alternate, lance-like. Flowers appear in conical raceme of 7 to 20 heads, lasting several weeks, in spring; petals narrow, bell-shaped, plum-purple with gray bloom. Prefers deep, damp, fertile soil, protected from both late frosts and sun. 'Adiyaman', darker petals. Zones 5–9.

Fritillaria tuntasia

☀ ❄ ↔ 2½ in (6 cm) ↑ 4–15 in (10–38 cm)

Found on lower slopes, rocky places, and scrub of the Greek Islands. Leaves clustered and opposite at base, alternate on stem, gray-green. Stems of 1 to 4 flowers, small, appearing in late spring; petals plum-purple, almost black, slightly incurving, anthers yellow. Prefers dry summers, sharp drainage. Zones 8–10.

FUCHSIA

There are about 100 species of small or medium-sized trees and spreading or climbing shrubs in this genus, which is a member of the evening primrose (Onagraceae) family. Almost all species are from South and Central America, but a few are native to New Zealand and Tahiti. They are evergreen or deciduous, with foliage growing in whorls, alternate or opposite. Flowers bloom in terminal clusters or from leaf axils and are usually tubular and pendent, often bicolored. The flowers are followed by edible berries, usually with many seeds. In their native habitat, the American species are pollinated by hummingbirds.
CULTIVATION: Most fuchsias are frost tender, and even the few fully hardy forms may die down to ground level in a severe winter. Fuchsias planted in the garden do best in fairly fertile moist soil with good drainage in full sun or partial shade. Feed regularly during flowering. Propagate species from seed and cuttings; raise cultivars from cuttings only, using softwood cuttings in spring or half-hardened cuttings in late summer.

Fuchsia andrei

☀ ❄ ↔ 2–7 ft (0.6–2 m)
↑ 3–12 ft (0.9–3.5 m)

Shrub from Ecuador and Peru. Opposite, narrow, elliptical leaves with a waxy texture. Terminal racemes of numerous coral red flowers, with narrow tubular corollas, appearing in summer–autumn. Zones 7–9.

Fuchsia arborescens

TREE FUCHSIA

☀/◑ ❄ ↔ 5 ft (1.5 m) ↑ 6 ft (1.8 m)

This species is a native of Mexico and Central America. The leaves are opposite or in whorls of 3 or 4, elliptical in shape with a pointed tip, shiny, dark green upper surface, with paler green underneath. Flowers are in panicles of pink-purple sepals and tubes with a pale mauve corolla, appearing in summer. The fruit is purple and becomes wrinkled when it is ripe. Zones 10–12.

Fuchsia × bacillaris

☀ ❄ ↔ 2–4 ft (0.6–1.2 m)
↑ 3–7 ft (0.9–2 m)

This erect or spreading shrub comes from Mexico and is a hybrid of *F. microphylla* and *F. thymifolia*. The leaves are finely toothed and sword-shaped to oval. The flowers are solitary, with a tube, and have narrow rose pink to red sepals and deep red elliptical petals, appearing in summer–autumn. Rounded, glossy, black fruit. Zones 7–9.

Fuchsia boliviana

☀ ❄ ↔ 3–4 ft (0.9–1.2 m) ↑ 12 ft (3.5 m)

This species occurs naturally in South America from northern Argentina to Peru; it has become naturalized in Colombia and Venezuela. Erect shrub or small tree. Dark green leaves in whorls of 3, pale gray felty veining on undersides. Terminal flowers, tubes pale to dark pink, sepals pale pink to red, scarlet petals, appearing in summer–autumn. Fruit is edible. *F. b.* var. *alba* ★, white tubes, sepals with light red marks at bases. Zones 9–11.

Fuchsia boliviana

Fuchsia boliviana var. *alba*

Fuchsia arborescens

Fuchsia coccinea

☼/◐ ❄ ↔ 4 ft (1.2 m)
↑ 5–20 ft (1.5–6 m)

Native of Brazil, climber or erect shrub. Older branches lose bark in long strips. Leaves in groups of 2, 3, or 4, egg-shaped, pointed tip, matt light green above, paler underneath, hairless or slightly hairy. Deep pink to red flowers grow from leaf axils, appearing in summer. Zones 8–11.

Fuchsia corymbiflora

◐ ⚎ ↔ 3 ft (0.9 m) ↑ 12 ft (3.5 m)
Erect to climbing shrub from Peru. Dark green leaves, usually opposite, oval to oblong, with a pointed base and tip and undersides of a paler green. Pale pink to scarlet-red flowers, blooming in large arching or pendent terminal panicles. Round red fruit. Zones 9–11.

Fuchsia denticulata

syn. *Fuchsia serratifolia*

☼/◐ ⚎ ↔ 3 ft (0.9 m) ↑ 8 ft (2.4 m)
Native to Peru and Bolivia. Peeling bark. Leaves are large, lance-shaped or oval, with toothed edges and a pointed tip and base, shiny or matt dark green above, paler and heavily veined underneath. Flowers are pink to light red, tipped with green and white, petals orange to vermilion. Glossy green to purple-red fruit, in summer. Zones 9–11.

Fuchsia denticulata

Fuchsia magellanica

Fuchsia excorticata

KOTUKUTUKU, NEW ZEALAND TREE FUCHSIA

☼/◐ ❄ ↔ 4 ft (1.2 m) ↑ 15 ft (4.5 m)
Deciduous shrub or small tree, native to New Zealand; larger in the wild. Red-brown peeling bark. Leaves are alternate, egg- to lance-shaped with a slender pointed tip, mid-green above, silver-green underneath. Flowers are green, flushed with maroon, appearing during summer–autumn. Pollen is blue. May be evergreen in warm climates. Zones 8–10.

Fuchsia fulgens ★

☼/◐ ✢ ↔ 30 in (75 cm) ↑ 5 ft (1.5 m)
Native to Mexico. Toothed heart-shaped leaves, red above, undersides paler, flushed with red. Small flowers with red sepals tinged yellow-green towards the tips and a bright red corolla. Fruit oblong, deep purple. Zones 11–12.

Fuchsia procumbens

Fuchsia excorticata, in the wild, in Westland National Park, New Zealand

Fuchsia magellanica var. *gracilis*

Fuchsia lycioides

☼ ⚎ ↔ 4 ft (1.2 m) ↑ 10 ft (3 m)
Native to Chile, deciduous or evergreen shrub. Leaves egg-shaped, less sharply tipped than those of most species. Tube is constricted at base, wider toward sepals. Pink-red petals, deeper color than sepals. Zones 10–11.

Fuchsia magellanica

LADIES' EARDROPS

☼/◐ ❄ ↔ 6 ft (1.8 m) ↑ 10 ft (3 m)
Originating in Chile and Argentina, naturalized elsewhere. Erect vigorous shrub; older branches have flaking bark. Leaves are elliptical to egg-shaped and tinted red underneath. Flowers have red tubes, dark red sepals, a purple corolla, and appear in summer–late autumn. Fruits are oblong and crimson in color. Makes a colorful hedge in mild winter areas; **'Riccartonii'** is commonly used for hedging in Ireland and islands around Britain. *F. m.* **var.** *gracilis* (syn. *F. m.* var. *macrostemma*), small leaves, abundant, very pendent, small flowers, deep scarlet calyx, purple petals; *F. m.* **var.** *molinae*, name used for pale-pink-flowered variants in cultivation; *F. m.* **var.** *pumila*, to 12 in (30 cm) high, red and blue flowers. *F. m.* **'Versicolor'**, gray-green leaves, tinted silver, small deep red flowers. Zones 7–10.

Fuchsia microphylla

SMALL-LEAFED FUCHSIA

☼/◐ ⚎ ↔ 2–5 ft (0.6–1.5 m)
↑ 2–15 ft (0.6–4.5 m)
Bushy shrub or climber found from Mexico to Panama. Leaves opposite,

Fuchsia sanctae-rosae

Fuchsia magellanica var. *molinae*

Fuchsia magellanica 'Versicolor'

lance-shaped, pointed tip and base, toothed or smooth edges. Flowers with white to red-purple tubes, sepals, and petals, in summer. Zones 9–11.

Fuchsia procumbens

TRAILING FUCHSIA

☼/◐ ⚎ ↔ 3 ft (0.9 m) ↑ 6 in (15 cm)
Native to New Zealand. Evergreen, prostrate, spreading shrub. Leaves small, heart-shaped. Small upward-facing flowers, greenish to pale orange tubes, purple-tipped green sepals, no petals, appearing in summer. Fruit bright red, persistent. Good rock-garden plant. Zones 9–11.

Fuchsia ravenii

☼ ❄ ↔ 3–7 ft (0.9–2 m)
↑ 7–12 ft (2–3.5 m)

Upright, tall, vigorous shrub from Mexico. Hairy, mid-green, oval leaves with curled edges. Produces abundant solitary flowers in the leaf axils, both bisexual flowers and smaller male (pistillate) red flowers, with a cylindrical tube, spreading sepals, and rounded spreading petals, in summer–autumn. The fruits contain 14 to 18 seeds. Zones 7–9.

Fuchsia sanctae-rosae

☼ ❄ ↔ 2–8 ft (0.6–2.4 m)
↑ 3–10 ft (0.9–3 m)

Erect or climbing shrub from high altitudes in southern Peru and Bolivia. Very variable, elliptical leaves. Numerous orange-red flowers in leaf axils, with narrow tube, spreading corolla and sepals. Fruit dark reddish purple berry. Zones 7–10.

Fuchsia splendens

☼/◐ ❄ ↔ 2 ft (0.9 m) ↑ 8 ft (2.4 m)

Terrestrial or epiphytic shrub from Mexico to Costa Rica. Leaves heart-shaped, toothed edges, green above, paler, flushed red and veined beneath. Flower tube rose pink, sepals green with red base, petals olive green. Fruit green to purple, warty. Zones 8–11.

Fuchsia thymifolia

☼/◐ ❄ ↔ 20 in (50 cm) ↑ 36 in (90 cm)

From Mexico to northern Guatemala; larger in the wild. Leaves oval to egg-shaped, sometimes with a toothed edge, finely hairy both above and underneath. Flowers solitary, tube green-white to pink, sepals and petals in the same colors, ageing to dark purple, in summer–autumn. Fleshy black-purple fruits. Zones 8–11.

Fuchsia triphylla

HONEYSUCKLE FUCHSIA

☼/◐ ✦ ↔ 2 ft (0.6 m) ↑ 6 ft (1.8 m)

Native to the West Indies; much smaller in cultivation. Leaves oppo-

Fuchsia triphylla 'Billy Green'

Fuchsia splendens

Fuchsia vulcanica

site, in whorls of 3 or 4; oval or lance-shaped, sometimes finely toothed, dull dark green upper surfaces and paler undersurfaces, which are often tinged with silvery purple. Flowers are all-over orange to coral red; fruit is shiny reddish purple. 'Billy Green', rose pink flowers, light green leaves. Zones 11–12.

Fuchsia vulcanica

syn. *Fuchsia canescens*

☼ ❄ ↔ 2–7 ft (0.6–2 m) ↑ 4–12 ft (1.2–3.5 m)

Strong upright shrub from Colombia and Ecuador. Whorls of 3 or 4 narrow elliptical leaves. Flowers at ends of branches with deep scarlet tube, purplish base, scarlet corolla. Zones 8–10.

Fuchsia Hybrid Cultivars

☼/◐ ✤ ↔ 18–36 in (45–90 cm) ↑ 1–7 ft (0.3–2 m)

Over 8,000 fuchsia cultivars have been recorded, with about 2,000 still in cultivation. Most are derived from *F. magellanica*, *F. fulgens*, and *F. triphylla*.

Some cultivars, the "hardy" types, can withstand winter in Zone 7. These

Fuchsia, Hybrid Cultivar, 'Amelie Aubin'

Fuchsia, Hybrid Cultivar, 'Balkon'

Fuchsia, Hybrid Cultivar, 'Beacon Rosa'

Fuchsia, Hybrid Cultivar, 'Cliantha'

Fuchsia, HC, 'Brutus'

Fuchsia, HC, 'Ben Jammin'

Fuchsia, HC, 'Carla Johnston'

Fuchsia, HC, 'Celia Smedley'

F., HC, Charlie Dimmock/'Foncha'

Fuchsia, HC, 'Checkerboard'

Fuchsia, HC, 'Chillerton Beauty'

Fuchsia, HC, 'Corallina'

Fuchsia, HC, 'Deutsche Perle'

Fuchsia, HC, 'Deutsche Perle'

Fuchsia, HC, 'Estelle Marie'

Fuchsia, HC, 'Eva Boerg'

Fuchsia, HC, 'Garden News'

Fuchsia, HC, 'Lord Byron'

Fuchsia, HC, 'Madame Cornelissen'

Fuchsia, HC, 'Coachman'

Fuchsia, HC, 'Fountains Abbey'

F., HC, 'Gartenmeister Bonstedt' ★

Fuchsia, HC, 'Graf Witte'

Fuchsia, HC, 'Joan Goy'

Fuchsia, Hybrid Cultivar, 'Margaret Pilkington'

Fuchsia, Hybrid Cultivar, 'Leonora'

Fuchsia, Hybrid Cultivar, 'Marcus Graham' ★

include: '**Abbé Farges**', semi-double flowers, cherry red tube and sepal, rose-lilac corolla; '**Constance**', bushy, tube pale pink, sepals pale pink, green-tipped corolla, mauve base tinted pink; '**Hawkshead**', tube and sepals white with green, corolla white; '**White Pixie**', yellow red-veined leaves, red tube and sepal, corolla white, veined with deep pink.

Other hybrids include: '**Brookwood Belle**', prolific, double medium-sized flowers, deep cerise tube, sepals and corolla white, flushed pale pink; '**Coachman**', coral pink sepals, reddish orange corolla; '**Display**', large flowers, pink-red calyx, corolla deeper rose pink, long stamens; '**Dollar Princess**', medium-sized double flowers, small cerise tubes, reflexed cerise sepals, small purple corollas, deep pink at base; '**Golden Marinka**', later flowering form, trailing habit, variegated red-veined leaves, medium-sized single blooms, rich red tube and sepals, darker red corolla; '**Graf Witte**', red sepals and reddish mauve tube; '**Heidi Ann**', medium-sized double blooms, crimson-cerise tube and sepals, bright lilac corolla; '**Jack Shahan**', weeping form, large single blooms, pale pink; '**La Campanella**', semi-double, white tube, white sepals tinted pink, corolla imperial purple; '**Lena**', medium-sized semi-double blooms, flesh pink tube, flesh pink sepals shading darker, tipped green, corolla purple, fading toward base; '**Margaret Pilkington**', white sepals, reddish purple tube; '**Pacquesa**', deep green leaves, large single flowers, dark red tube, white corolla, faint red veins; '**Prosperity**', medium-sized double flowers, crimson tube, crimson sepals, pink corolla, veined rose red; '**Rading's Inge**', tiny flowers, rose pink tube, cream sepals, orange corolla; '**Ri Mia**', pale lilac tube, sepals, corolla; Zones 9–11.

FURCRAEA

syn. *Fourcroya*

Up to 20 species have been credited to this genus of evergreen succulents in the agave (Agavaceae) family from Central and South America and the West Indies, but there may be far fewer. Like agaves, they have rosettes of sword-like leaves, ending in a spine and usually with prickly edges. The flowers have a shorter tube and more spreading petals. A trunk may develop below the rosette, and lateral shoots sprout from the plant base or the trunk. An inflorescence ends the life of a rosette, but may take several decades to appear; some are extremely tall. After flowering, the inflorescence usually develops aerial plantlets that eventually fall and take root.

CULTIVATION: These are among the toughest of plants, and in warm climates will grow and multiply with no attention at all. They have become invasive in some tropical countries. In cold climates they can be grown under glass, but they require a lot of space at maturity. Propagate from offsets, aerial plantlets, or seed.

Furcraea bedinghausii
syn. *Furcraea roezlii*

☼ ❄ ↔4–7 ft (1.2–2 m) ↑4–7 ft (1.2–2 m)
Succulent perennial from Mexico. Has rosettes of bluish sword-shaped leaves with soft tips, forming a ball that eventually develops a trunk. Inflorescences of green flowers appear on tall stems. Zones 8–10.

Furcraea selloa

☼ ❄ ↔4–7 ft (1.2–2 m) ↑4–7 ft (1.2–2 m)
Succulent perennial from Mexico and Guatemala. Forms dense rosettes of 30 to 40 bright green leaves, with horny spines along the edges. Faintly scented white flowers flushed with green. *F. s.* f. *marginata*, white or yellow leaf edges. Zones 8–10.

Fuchsia, Hybrid Cultivar, 'Orange Flare'

Fuchsia, Hybrid Cultivar, 'Phyllis'

Fuchsia, Hybrid Cultivar, 'Patio Princess'

Fuchsia, Hybrid Cultivar, 'Windmill'

Fuchsia, HC, 'Santa Cruz'

Fuchsia, HC, 'Natasha Sinton'

Fuchsia, Hybrid Cultivar, 'Pink Fantasia'

Fuchsia, HC, 'Katrina Thompson'

Fuchsia, HC, 'Minirose'

Fuchsia, HC, 'Nancy Lou'

Fuchsia, HC, 'Mrs Popple'

Fuchsia, HC, 'Rufus the Red'

Fuchsia, HC, 'Ruth'

Fuchsia, HC, 'Sylvia Barker'

Fuchsia, HC, 'Tom Thumb'

G

Gahnia sieberiana, in the wild, New Caledonia

Gaiadendron punctatum, in the wild, Cerro de la Muerte, Costa Rica

GAHNIA

This genus of 40 species is placed in the sedge (Cyperaceae) family. Members occur in, generally, wet and boggy habitats in southern Asia, the Malay archipelago, Australia, and the Pacific islands. All species are perennial herbs, clumping or rhizomatous, with long, narrow, grass-like leaves, often with spiky or prickly margins. Small creamy flowers borne in pairs in terminal leafy inflorescences. The fruits are usually dark shiny nuts.
CULTIVATION: *Gahnia* species require an open sunny position and moist acid soil. Some may be intolerant of phosphorus. Propagation is by division or from seed but, although seeds are usually readily obtainable, germination is difficult with some species. Germination of species from drier habitats may be improved by smoke treatments. Some species are quite ornamental in habit, but few species have been cultivated except by avid enthusiasts.

Gahnia sieberiana

RED-FRUITED SAW-SEDGE

☼ ❄ ↔ to 7 ft (2 m) ↑ to 10 ft (3 m)
Large clumping sedge. Widespread in most states of Australia, also in New Guinea and New Caledonia, in a range of habitats and soil types. Stems up to 10 ft (3 m) tall. Rough, often pendulous leaves up to 7 ft (2 m) long. Nuts egg-shaped, red-brown, shiny. Zones 8–9.

GAIADENDRON

A member of the mistletoe (Loranthaceae) family, this genus contains one species only and is what is known as a hemi-parasite. Its roots attach themselves to the stems or roots of other plants, thereby extracting water and nutrients for their own use. Hemi-parasites have green or greenish leaves and so can manufacture some of their nutrient requirements as well as "stealing" from their hosts. It is a shrub, sometimes forming a tree with a trunk to 10 in (25 cm) in diameter, parasitizing other terrestrial plants, but it also can parasitize epiphytic plants high up in the forest canopy.
CULTIVATION: As both host and parasite must be grown together, it can be quite difficult to cultivate this group of plants.

Gaiadendron punctatum

☼ ✿ ↔ 10 ft (3 m) ↑ 15 ft (4.5 m)
Small shrub or tree occurring in the tropical forests of Central and South America. Elliptical green leaves. White to yellow flowers. Fruits berry-like, eaten by birds, principally mistletoe birds; seeds are excreted and germinate on a suitable host plant. Zones 11–12.

GAILLARDIA

BLANKET FLOWER, FIREWHEEL

Discovered in the Rocky Mountains around 1825 by David Douglas and named for a French patron, Gaillard de Charentonneau (sometimes given as Marentonneau), this genus of around 30 species of annual, biennial, and perennial daisies (family Asteraceae) occurs mainly in southern USA and Mexico. The name blanket flower comes from a Native American legend of a blanket maker whom the spirits rewarded with an ever-blooming blanket of flowers on his grave. Appropriately then, the small mounding plants are covered in summer and autumn with 2–4 in (5–10 cm) wide flowerheads. The ray florets are typically red at the center with a yellow outer half. Garden forms occur in a range of warm tones.
CULTIVATION: Hardiness varies, though they are so easily cultivated that replacing any winter casualties is no problem. Plant in a sunny open position with gritty well-drained soil that remains moist during the growing season. Propagate from seed or basal cuttings, or by division.

Gaillardia aristata

☼ ❄ ↔ 32 in (80 cm) ↑ 20 in (50 cm)
Perennial found in North America's Rocky Mountains. Very hairy stems and leaves, with basal leaves to 8 in (20 cm) long. Narrow lance-shaped leaves may have small basal lobes and/or toothed edges. Flowerheads to 4 in (10 cm) wide with ray florets to more than 1 in (25 mm) long, yellow or yellow with red base; disc florets usually same color as base of ray florets. Zones 6–10.

Gaillardia × grandiflora

☼ ❄ ↔ 40 in (100 cm) ↑ 24 in (60 cm)
Garden hybrid between *G. aristata* and *G. pulchella.* Very similar to *G. aristata* but often slightly larger and generally more vigorous, hardier, and heavier flowering. 'Burgunder' (syn. 'Burgundy'), deep red flowers; 'Dazzler', 12 in (30 cm) tall, red ray florets tipped golden yellow; 'Indian Yellow', bright golden yellow flowers; Goblin/'Kobold' ★, 16 in (40 cm) tall, red ray florets with yellow border. Also seedling strains, such as **Gaiety** and **Royal Monarch** hybrids and double-flowered forms in mixed red and gold shades. Zones 5–10.

Gaillardia pulchella

☼ ❄ ↔ 16 in (40 cm) ↑ 24 in (60 cm)
Hairy annual found in northeastern Mexico and neighboring parts of eastern and central USA. Leaves to over 3 in (8 cm) long, sometimes lobed and/or toothed. Flowerheads around 2½ in (6 cm) wide, ray florets yellow, red, or red with yellow tips. Selected forms include: 'Lollipop', to 18 in (45 cm) tall, interesting combination of yellow, red, and orange; 'Red Plume', 12–18 in (30–45 cm) tall, red double flowers; and 'Yellow Plume', 12–18 in (30–45 cm) tall, yellow double flowers. Zones 8–10.

GALACTITES

Found around the Mediterranean and in the Canary Islands, this genus belongs to the daisy (Asteraceae) family and consists of just 3 species of white woolly annuals that thrive in sunny coastal areas. They grow quickly and develop into mounding bushes with pinnate leaves that are toothed and/or spiny and often quite large. The flowerheads are thistle-like, with white, mauve, or purple disc florets, surrounded by a ruff of similarly colored ray florets and silvery spine-tipped bracts known as "phyllaries," sometimes covered with fine cobweb-like filaments. Considered in some areas to be potentially invasive weeds.
CULTIVATION: Plant in a bright sunny position with light, gritty, free-draining soil. Pinch to shape when

Gaillardia × *grandiflora* 'Indian Yellow'

Gaillardia × *grandiflora* 'Burgunder'

Gaillardia × *grandiflora* Goblin/'Kobold'

Gaillardia pulchella, Texas, USA

Galactites tomentosa

young to keep the plants compact, and remove the spent flowers to encourage continued blooming. Propagate from seed sown in late winter, ready for early planting out after the last frosts.

Galactites tomentosa

☼ ❄ ↔ 40 in (100 cm) ↕ 40 in (100 cm)

A Mediterranean native with basal leaves to 8 in (20 cm) long, lobes deep and spine-tipped, upper surfaces green heavily veined white, with white woolly undersides. Flowerheads mauve-purple with white webbing, in summer. Zones 8–11.

GALANTHUS
SNOWDROP

Probably the most welcome harbinger of spring, this normally late winter-flowering Eurasian genus of 15 bulbs in the amaryllis (Amaryllidaceae) family also includes a few species that bloom in autumn. The narrow grassy leaves usually break through shortly after mid-winter and are soon joined by short flower stems, each carrying one mildly scented, pendulous, white, 6-petalled flower. The name *Galanthus* comes from the Greek *gala* (milk) and *anthos* (a flower) and refers to the flower color. The inner 3 petals are short and green-tipped, and double-flowered forms are available. Flowering is often brief but occurs when most welcome. According to Christian legend, the snowdrop first bloomed to coincide with the Feast of Purification on February 2, known as Candlemas Day.

CULTIVATION: Snowdrops grow best in cool-temperate climates and thrive in woodland or rockery conditions, preferring dappled shade and moist humus-rich soil. Can be propagated from seed, but they usually multiply quickly enough so that division after the foliage dies back is more practical. Do not let the bulbs dry out.

Galanthus 'Atkinsii'

☼ ❄ ↔ 7 in (18 cm) ↕ 8 in (20 cm)

Robust plant. Flowers, in winter, to 1¼ in (30 mm) long, with heart-shaped markings. Leaves narrow, gray-green. Zones 4–8.

Galanthus elwesii
GIANT SNOWDROP

☼ ❄ ↔ 4 in (10 cm) ↕ 4–6 in (10–15 cm)

Robust plant with honey-scented winter flowers, to 1¼ in (3 cm) long, with 2 green markings on each inner petal, flaring in sunshine. Broadly oblong gray-green leaves, sometimes twisted. Zones 6–9.

Galanthus gracilis

☼ ❄ ↔ 4 in (10 cm) ↕ 4–6 in (10–15 cm)

Native to Bulgaria, Turkey, and Greece. A dainty little plant, smaller than the common *G. nivalis*. Narrow, twisted, gray-green leaves. Flowers white with green center and petal tips, sometimes faintly scented, in winter. Zones 6–9.

Galanthus ikariae ★

☼ ❄ ↔ 4 in (10 cm) ↕ 4–6 in (10–15 cm)

Highly variable species found from the Aegean to the Caucasus region. Broad, glossy, bright green leaves, up to 6 in (15 cm) long. Flowers to

1¼ in (30 mm) long, with large green marking at petal tips, from late winter–early spring. Zones 6–9.

Galanthus 'Magnet'

☼ ❄ ↔ 7 in (18 cm) ↕ 8 in (20 cm)

Vigorous plant; flowers 1 in (25 mm) long, with inverted "V" markings. Gray-green leaves, to 6 in (15 cm) long, with folded margins. Zones 6–9.

Galanthus nivalis
COMMON SNOWDROP, ENGLISH SNOWDROP

☼ ❄ ↔ 4 in (10 cm) ↕ 6–8 in (15–20 cm)

Small European species with flat, narrow, blue-green leaves to slightly under 4 in (10 cm) long. Flowers small, slightly scented, with green petal tips and central markings. '**Flore Pleno**', very small, with beautiful white double flowers finely detailed in lime green. Zones 4–9.

Galanthus plicatus
CRIMEAN SNOWDROP

☼ ❄ ↔ 6 in (15 cm) ↕ 10 in (25 cm)

Vigorous species found from eastern Europe to Greece. Broad leaves dull green, blue-green central band, up to 4 in (10 cm) long, recurved margins. Strong flower stem with flowers lacking green petal tips. Hybridizes freely with *G. nivalis*. Zones 6–9.

Galanthus 'S. Arnott'

☼ ❄ ↔ 6 in (15 cm) ↕ 8 in (20 cm)

Large, robust, vigorous plant; strongly honey-scented rounded flowers, with

inverted "V" markings, from late winter–early spring. Gray-green leaves, 6 in (15 cm) long. Zones 6–8.

GALEGA
GOAT'S RUE

There are 6 species of perennial herbs in this genus, which belongs to the pea-flower subfamily of the legume (Fabaceae) family. They are found growing in damp ditches and meadows from southern Europe to Turkey, and tropical eastern Africa. Some species have naturalized in other countries. The leaves are pinnately divided. Pea-like flowers of white to bluish violet are borne on racemes in summer. The most commonly grown species, *G. officinalis* has been used for centuries to induce sweating in fever cases, and also as a remedy for worms.

CULTIVATION: Grow in full sun or light shade in a moisture-retentive but well drained soil. Where conditions are to its liking *G. officinalis* can be invasive. Propagate by division or seed which should be soaked for 12 hours before sowing.

Galega officinalis
GOAT'S RUE

☼ ❄ ↔ 2 ft (0.6 m) ↕ 3–5 ft (0.9–1.5 m)

From central and southern Europe and Turkey. Rather lax plant, well foliaged, with mid-green pinnately divided leaves. Flower spikes to 12 in (30 cm) long bear white to lavender pea-flowers in summer. Zones 4–9.

Galanthus nivalis

Galanthus plicatus

Galanthus 'S. Arnott'

Galanthus elwesii

GALIUM

BEDSTRAW, CLEAVERS, WOODRUFF

A widespread madder (Rubiaceae) family genus of around 400 species of often sprawling annuals and perennials. Includes a few useful species and some rather persistent weeds. Plants are characterized by weak angular stems that spread through surrounding growth and adhere to it through sticky coatings and/or fine hooked hairs. The small bright green leaves are sometimes in opposite pairs but more often in distinct whorls at intervals. Tiny white or yellow flowers, either solitary or in small clusters, appear in the leaf axils and at the stem tips. Woodruff (*G. odoratum*), by far the most attractive species, is widely used herbally and as a flavoring. CULTIVATION: Hardiness varies; most thrive in temperate climates. Easily grown in any well-drained soil in full sun or half-sun. Mostly propagated from seed; perennials also by division.

Galium odoratum

SWEET WOODRUFF, WOODRUFF

☀ ❆ ↔ 36 in (90 cm) ↕ 18 in (45 cm)

Carpet-forming perennial from Europe and North Africa, with erect,

Galtonia candicans

Galvezia juncea, in the wild, Baja California, Mexico

square-sectioned stems and all parts aromatic. Stiff, narrow, slightly prickly, elliptic leaves, to 2 in (5 cm) long, and with rough margins, in neat whorls of 6 to 8. Fragrant white flowers, 1½ in (35 mm) across, with deeply lobed corollas, in terminal clusters, in spring–summer. Zones 3–9.

Galium verum

OUR LADY'S BEDSTRAW, YELLOW BEDSTRAW

☀ ❆ ↔ 3 ft (0.9 m) ↕ 3–4 ft (0.9–1.2 m)

Clump-forming perennial from North America, Europe, and Asia. Small narrow leaves, to 1¼ in (30 mm) long, in whorls of 6 or 8, rough margins rolled under and tipped with bristles. Dense spikes of small, star-shaped, bright yellow flowers in summer–autumn. Lax, erect, squarish stems become woody toward the base. Can be invasive and weedy. Zones 2–10.

GALTONIA

This southern African genus, belonging to the lily (Liliaceae) family, contains 3 species of bulbous perennials. They are grown for their tall spires of white bell-shaped flowers, which bloom in late summer. The leaves, which are rather fleshy and strap-shaped, form a basal clump. CULTIVATION: Grow in a sunny sheltered position in a light, fertile, well-drained soil. Plants dislike being disturbed and bulbs will rot in winter

Galium verum

Garcinia livingstonei

in wet ground. Protect new growth from snails. Propagate from seed or careful division of offsets.

Galtonia candicans ★

SUMMER HYACINTH

☀ ❆ ↔ 1 ft (0.3 m) ↕ 4 ft (1.2 m)

From Free State and KwaZulu-Natal, South Africa, and Lesotho. Strap-shaped leaves to 30 in (75 cm) long. Fragrant, drooping, bell-shaped, white flowers, base tinged green. Zones 5–9.

Galtonia viridiflora

☀ ❆ ↔ 12 in (30 cm) ↕ 36 in (90 cm)

From Free State and KwaZulu-Natal, South Africa, and Lesotho. Bluish green leaves to 24 in (60 cm) long. Pale green bell-shaped flowers, flushed white at the petal edges. Zones 8–10.

GALVEZIA

A genus of 6 species of shrubs in the foxglove (Scrophulariaceae) family from the California islands to Peru. These scrambling ground covers have simple elliptical to ovate leaves, rarely more than 2 in (5 cm) long. Flowers, in summer, are reminiscent of those of some of the shrubby sages (*Salvia*), occurring in terminal racemes and with 2 lips that remain almost closed. Hummingbirds have the knack of getting into the blooms and pollinate them while probing for nectar. CULTIVATION: Best in full sun if grown near the coast, but needing some shade in hot inland areas, these are drought-tolerant plants that need little or no additional water once established. They prefer light gritty soil and demand perfect drainage. Versatile plants, they can be grown as ground covers, espaliered against fences, or allowed to trail from hanging baskets. Propagate from seed or by taking half-hardened cuttings from non-flowering stems.

Galvezia juncea

BAJA BUSH SNAPDRAGON

☀ ❅ ↔ 24 in (60 cm) ↕ 36 in (90 cm)

Small evergreen shrub native to Baja California, Mexico. Thin, arching, reed-like stems, small dark green

Garcinia mangostana

leaves. Bright red flowers, 1 in (25 mm) diameter, at tips of branches throughout the year. Zones 9–10.

GARCINIA

This is a genus in the St John's-wort (Clusiaceae) family containing 200 tropical species found particularly in Asia and Africa. They are densely foliaged evergreen trees and shrubs with highly scented flowers that open at night. The fleshy fruits of some are edible, notably those of *G. mangostana,* the mangosteen. The male and female flowers are separate, usually on different plants, sometimes on the same plant. Damaged branches and twigs secrete a yellow sap reputed to have medicinal qualities. CULTIVATION: Require a rich soil and plenty of water and are very frost sensitive, being suitable only for tropical and subtropical regions. Propagation is generally from fresh seed, although some species have been successful using cuttings and air-layering.

Garcinia livingstonei

AFRICAN MANGOSTEEN

☀ ❅ ↔ 15 ft (4.5 m) ↕ 35 ft (10 m)

From Angola to southern Mozambique and northern South Africa. It has acute-angled branches, rough gray bark, and the plant parts contain a sticky yellow sap. Leaves leathery, glossy dark green above, paler beneath, young leaves often bright red. Sweetly scented, greenish yellow-cream flowers, on older wood, in spring. Orange-colored spherical fruits. Zones 9–12.

Garcinia mangostana

MANGOSTEEN

☀ ❧ ↔ 15 ft (4.5 m) ↕ 50 ft (15 m)

Native to Malaysia and Indonesia, slow growing (15 years before fruit),

Garrya elliptica

Garrya veatchii

Garrya elliptica 'James Roof'

evergreen tree cultivated for its delicious fruit. Large glossy leaves, heavy crown. Male and female flowers on separate trees, females generally produce seedless fruits, to 4 in (10 cm) in diameter, thick skin, rich purple color when ripe. Zones 11–12.

GARDENIA

This genus from the madder (Rubiaceae) family consists of around 250 species, from tropical Africa and Asia. Mostly evergreen shrubs or small trees, with opposite or whorled, shiny, simple, deep green leaves. Fragrant large flowers, tubular to funnel-shaped, white or yellow, produced singly or in few-flowered cymes. Fruit is a leathery or fleshy berry. Useful landscape subjects, wonderful container plants. Some species are used to scent tea; others to treat influenza and colds in modern Chinese herbalism. A yellow dye was made from the fruits. CULTIVATION: Most are fairly adaptable shrubs tolerant of sun or semi-shade, and do best in a well-drained, humus-rich, acidic soil. Gardenias are surface rooted, responding well to regular mulching with good quality compost, fertilizer, and adequate summer watering. In cool climates grow in a heated greenhouse, as most gardenias are frost tender. Propagate from seed or leafy tip or half-hardened cuttings in late spring and summer.

Gardenia augusta
syn. *Gardenia jasminoides*
CAPE JASMINE, COMMON GARDENIA
☀/☼ ✦ ↔ 5 ft (1.5 m) ↑ 5 ft (1.5 m)
Native of southeastern China and Japan. Bushy habit; elliptic to obovate, glossy, dark green leaves. Strong fragrance, white, wheel-shaped flowers, in summer. Double-flowered cultivars include: 'August Beauty', lush green foliage, white flowers; 'Florida' ★, to about 3 ft (0.9 m) tall with white flowers; 'Grandiflora', larger leaves and pure white flowers; 'Magnifica', semi-double creamy white flowers; 'Radicans', spreading low growth with rooting stems, smaller foliage, plentiful semi-double white flowers; and 'Veitchii', upright yet compact shrub with small, highly scented, double white flowers. Zones 10–11.

Gardenia thunbergia
STARRY GARDENIA
☀ ❄ ↔ 7 ft (2 m) ↑ 12 ft (3.5 m)
Occurs in the humid forests of South Africa. Upright shrub or small tree. Smooth gray bark. Glossy dark green leaves with wavy margins. Fragrant, white or cream, solitary flowers, spoke-like petals at the end of a long tube, in summer. Zones 9–11.

GARRYA

This genus of about 18 freely flowering, durable, evergreen shrubs or trees belongs to the silk-tassel (Garryaceae) family. They are grown for their tough leathery leaves and distinctive pendulous catkins of inconspicuous flowers without petals. Male and female flowers are borne on separate plants from winter to early summer, while the fruit of the female plant consists of clusters of round, dry, dark, 2-seeded berries, borne from summer to autumn. Native to western North America and the West Indies, they are valued for their ornamental qualities and durability in warmer climates. CULTIVATION: Well suited to salty coastal environments and tolerant of pollution, *Garrya* species prefer a sunny sheltered position but can cope with a wide range of soil types. Avoid transplanting. They are propagated from cuttings of half-hardened wood, or by layering, and from seed.

Garrya elliptica ★
CATKIN BUSH, COAST SILKTASSEL, SILKTASSEL BUSH
☀ ❄ ↔ 6 ft (1.8 m) ↑ 8–12 ft (2.4–3.5 m)
Native of southwestern USA, from Oregon to California. Glossy, oval, gray-green to matt green leaves, undulating margins, dense woolly coating underneath. Long grayish green male catkins, in winter–spring. Smaller female catkins, abundant clusters of oval-shaped dark purple fruit. 'Evie' has catkins up to 12 in (30 cm) long; 'James Roof' is a stronger male form with larger leaves and catkins than the species. Zones 8–9.

Garrya fremontii
FEVER BUSH, FREMONT SILKTASSEL, QUININE BUSH, SKUNK BUSH
☀ ❄ ↔ 6 ft (1.8 m) ↑ 7–10 ft (2–3 m)
Native of western USA, from California to Oregon. Leathery, glossy, hairy, dark green leaves, smooth above, woolly underneath. Terminal clusters of male catkins, to 8 in (20 cm) long, in spring. Woolly female catkins, to 2 in (5 cm) long, in late summer–autumn. Dark purple oval-shaped fruit. Zones 7–9.

Garrya veatchii
☀ ❄ ↔ 7 ft (2 m) ↑ 10 ft (3 m)
Evergreen shrub native to southwest USA. Downy leaves to 3 in (8 cm) long. Male catkins to 4 in (10 cm) long, in spring. Female catkins to 2 in (5 cm) long, in summer. Zones 8–9.

GASTERIA

These 15 or more compact, very short-stemmed, succulent perennials, native to South Africa, belong to the asphodel (Asphodelaceae) family; the genus is closely allied to *Aloe*. The thick, fleshy, dark green leaves are spirally arranged in tight compact rosettes, and the pendulous, pink to vermilion, tubular flowers appear in simple or branched racemes. The fruit is a capsule; seeds are winged to aid dispersal. The genus name comes from the Greek word for stomach. CULTIVATION: Easily grown in light, sandy, well-drained soil in a protected spot with sun or part-shade. Moderate water in summer, keep drier in winter. Propagate by leaf cuttings, or by dividing offsets and plantlets at stem tops.

Gasteria bicolor
DWARF GASTERIA
☀/☼ ❄ ↔ 16 in (40 cm) ↑ 16 in (40 cm)
From Eastern Cape. Tapering, smooth, strap-shaped, dark green leaves, 1¼–9 in (3–22 cm) long, rounded or pointed ends, arise from the base, forming dense groups of up to 10 or more plants. Simple elongated raceme, 6–16 in (15–40 cm) in height, with reddish pink flowers, in spring–summer. Seed capsule contains small black seeds. *G. b.* var. *liliputana* (syn. *G. liliputana*), a dwarf form, leaves spotted with white, to 2½ in (6 cm) long. Zones 9–11.

Gardenia augusta 'Magnifica'

Gardenia thunbergia

G

Gaultheria mucronata 'Coccinea'

Gaultheria depressa var. *novae-zelandiae*

Gaultheria hispida

Gasteria glomerata

Gasteria carinata
RICE GASTERIA

☼/◐ ✿ ↔ 36 in (90 cm) ↑ 36 in (90 cm)

From Eastern Cape and Western Cape, South Africa. Forms rosettes of narrow triangular to sword-shaped leaves, 1¼–5 in (3–12 cm) long, with thickened margins. Flower stalk to 36 in (90 cm) high, with red flowers, 1 in (25 mm) long, in late spring to summer. Zones 9–11.

Gasteria glomerata

☼ ✿ ↔ 3 in (8 cm) ↑ 1½ in (4 cm)

Clump-forming perennial. Rosettes of dark green leaves. Orange-red flowers on spikes. Zones 9–10.

Gasteria obliqua

☼ ✿ ↔ 24–36 in (60–90 cm)
↑ 24–36 in (60–90 cm)

From Eastern Cape, South Africa. Narrow, finely toothed, tapering leaves, 10–15 in (25–38 cm) long, marked with white spots. Branched flowerhead, on leafy stems, to 36 in (90 cm) high, red flowers, in late spring–summer. Zones 9–11.

GAULTHERIA
SNOWBERRY, WINTERGREEN

This genus, named after Canadian botanist Jean-Francois Gaultier, contains some 170 species of evergreen shrubs, ranging from the Americas to Japan and Australasia. Belonging to the heath (Ericaceae) family, these tough bushes have leathery foliage and prefer temperate to cool climates. They are often found in mountainous areas, where their bright, relatively large fruits stand out among the short alpine vegetation. Flowers tend to be bell-shaped and pendulous. Fruit may be small and fairly dry or a fleshy berry, depending on the species. Many species are quite aromatic,

Gaultheria mucronata

often highly so, especially the fruit.
CULTIVATION: Frost hardiness varies with the species, the toughest being among the large broadleafed evergreens. They prefer moist, well-drained, humus-rich, slightly acidic soil with ample summer moisture. The exposure preference also varies with the species, though few do well in full shade. Propagate from seed, or from half-hardened cuttings or layers, which will often form naturally where the stems remain in contact with the ground.

Gaultheria depressa

☼/◐ ❄ ↔ 10 in (25 cm) ↑ 4 in (10 cm)

Near-prostrate, wiry-stemmed shrub from the mountain regions of New Zealand, carpeting patches of rocky or boggy ground. Tiny, leathery, serrated leaves, reddish stems. Small white to pale pink flowers, carried singly, in summer. White to deep pink berries. *G. d.* var. *novae-zelandiae* was first described in 1962. Zones 8–9.

Gaultheria hispida
SNOWBERRY, WAXBERRY

☼/◐ ✿ ↔ 18 in (45 cm) ↑ 15 in (38 cm)

Prostrate to low mounding shrub, native to southeastern Australia, including Tasmania. Leaves to 2 in (5 cm) long, bristly, with serrated edges. White flowers, in racemes to 3 in (8 cm) long, small, urn-shaped, in late summer. Pure white berries, in autumn. Zones 8–10.

Gaultheria mucronata
syn. *Pernettya mucronata*

☼/◐ ❄ ↔ 4 ft (1.2 m)
↑ 18–60 in (45–150 cm)

Native of Argentina and Chile. Strongly branched suckering shrub, young stems often bright pinkish red, densely covered with small deep green leaves, sharp pointed tips. White or pale pink flowers in late spring. Fruit large, white, shades of pink and red. 'Alba', white fruit; 'Bell's Seedling', crimson fruit; 'Coccinea', scarlet fruit; 'Crimsonia', crimson fruit; 'Mulberry Wine', maroon to purple fruit; Snow

White/'Sneeuwwitje', red-speckled white fruit; 'Wintertime', long-lasting white fruit. Zones 6–10.

Gaultheria myrsinoides
syn. *Pernettya prostrata*

☼ ✿ ↔ 18 in (45 cm) ↑ 6 in (15 cm)

Tiny creeping shrub found from Costa Rica to central Chile, at high altitudes in the tropics and subtropics, lower altitudes further south. Very small leaves, sharply tipped. White flowers, in spring–summer. Fruit blue-black, over ½ in (12 mm) wide. *G. m.* subsp. *pentlandii*, bushier plant with purple fruit. Zones 9–10.

Gaultheria nummularioides

☼/◐ ✿ ↔ 10 in (25 cm) ↑ 4 in (10 cm)

Tiny summer-flowering shrub, native of the Himalayan region. Neat hummock of densely interwoven twigs. Small, rounded, somewhat wrinkled leaves, dull green upper surfaces, finely hairy undersides. White to pale pink flowers borne singly, hidden within the foliage. Fruit blue-black in color. Zones 8–10.

Gaultheria procumbens
CHECKERBERRY, TEABERRY, WINTERGREEN

☼/◐ ❄ ↔ 36 in (90 cm) ↑ 6 in (15 cm)

Attractive shrub from eastern North America. Deep green glossy leaves to 2 in (5 cm) long. Racemes of white to pale pink flowers, in summer. Red fruit, to ½ in (12 mm) wide; source of the pungent liniment used for muscle or joint problems. 'Macrocarpa', compact form, abundant fruit. Zones 4–9.

Gaultheria shallon
SALAL, SHALLON

☼/◐ ❄ ↔ 5 ft (1.5 m) ↑ 5 ft (1.5 m)

Found in western North America, from California to Alaska. Spreading shrub takes root along prostrate branches. Broad oval leaves to 4 in

Gaultheria myrsinoides subsp. *pentlandii*

Gaultheria procumbens

Gaultheria × wisleyensis

Gaultheria shallon

(10 cm) long. Tiny white to deep pink flowers, carried in conspicuous red-stemmed racemes near the stem tips, in late spring. Red fruit ripens to black. Zones 5–9.

Gaultheria × wisleyensis

syn. × *Gaulnettya wisleyensis*

☼/◐ ❉ ↔ 3 ft (0.9 m) ↕ 3 ft (0.9 m)

Hybrid between the North American *G. shallon* and *G. mucronata* of South America. Low spreading shrub forms small thickets of suckering stems. Several cultivars with leaves of varying sizes, up to 1½ in (35 mm) long. Flowers white or various shades of pink to light purple. Fruit is purplish red. Zones 6–9.

GAURA

The name *Gaura* comes from the Greek *gauros*, meaning superb, and while not really superb in the sense of being spectacular, the cultivated species of the 21 annuals and perennials in this North American genus are well worth growing. Members of the evening-primrose (Onagraceae) family, they generally form a clump of irregularly shaped basal leaves from which emerge wiry stems bearing graceful, airy, 4-petalled, white and soft pink flowers. The stems are usually more than 36 in (90 cm) tall and appear throughout the warmer months. In recent years *Gaura* has become very popular and various pink-flowered and dwarf cultivars are now available.

CULTIVATION: *Gaura* species prefer full sun with light, gritty, well-drained soil. While drought-tolerant, they flower better with summer moisture. Deadhead routinely and cut back hard after flowering. Propagate from seed in autumn and spring, or from basal cuttings in summer.

Gaura lindheimeri

☼/◐ ❉ ↔ 40 in (100 cm) ↕ 48–60 in (120–150 cm)

Vigorous heavy-flowering perennial from Texas and Louisiana, USA. Forms a clump of upright stems with narrow, elliptical, toothed leaves less than ½ in (12 mm) long. Sprays of pink-tinted white flowers to nearly 1 in (25 mm) wide, upper petals large and wing-like, in spring–summer. 'Corrie's Gold', variegated foliage edged in golden yellow; 'Karalee Petite', 24 in (60 cm) tall, deep pink flowers; 'Siskiyou Pink', bright pink flowers; and 'Whirling Butterflies', 24 in (60 cm) tall, very heavy-blooming, large flowers. Zones 5–9.

GAZANIA

TREASURE FLOWER

The 16 species of annuals and perennials in this daisy (Asteraceae) family genus are found mainly in South Africa, with a few species extending the range to the tropics. They are low, near-evergreen, clump-forming plants with simple, narrow, lance-shaped, sometimes downy leaves with paler undersides. Their flowers, which appear throughout the warmer months, are large, brightly colored, often interestingly marked, and always showy. While the species usually have yellow or orange flowers, garden forms are available in a huge color range. The name *Gazania* comes from Theodore of Gaza (1398–1478), who translated the botanical texts of Theophrastus from Greek into Latin.

CULTIVATION: Apart from being somewhat frost tender and resenting wet winters, they are easily grown in any open sunny position with gritty very free-draining soil. They appreciate additional humus but will grow in poor dry soils. Propagate by division, or from basal cuttings or seed.

Gazania linearis

☼ ❊ ↔ 24 in (60 cm) ↕ 6 in (15 cm)

A tough woody-based perennial, with narrow lance-shaped leaves, smooth or near-pinnately lobed, green above, woolly white beneath. Flowerheads to 3 in (8 cm) wide, ray florets yellow, disc florets brown. 'Colorado Gold' has all-yellow flowerheads. Zones 7–11.

Gazania rigens

TREASURE FLOWER

☼ ⚘ ↔ 40 in (100 cm) ↕ 8 in (20 cm)

Perennial with fleshy stems that strike root as they spread, forming large leafy clump. Leaves to over 4 in (10 cm) long, smooth-edged or near-pinnately lobed, deep green to bronze above, white hair below. Long-stemmed flowerheads to 3 in (8 cm) wide, ray florets orange with black base, disc florets yellow or reddish orange. *G. r.* var. *uniflora*, small flowerheads, yellow ray florets. *G. r.* 'Variegata', foliage variegated with cream or gold, orange flowers. Zones 9–11.

Gazania rigens 'Variegata'

Gazania rigens

Gaura lindheimeri 'Siskiyou Pink'

Gaura lindheimeri 'Whirling Butterflies'

G

Gazania, Hybrid Cultivar, 'Blackberry Ripple'

Gazania, HC, 'Christopher Lloyd'

Gazania, Hybrid Cultivar, 'Bronze Gnome'

Gazania Hybrid Cultivars

☀ ⚘ ↔ 20 in (50 cm) ↑ 4–6 in (10–15 cm)

Gazanias naturally flower in a wide range of colors and hybridize freely, so there is now a wide variety of garden forms, sizes, and flower colors. '**Aztec**', soft silvery gray foliage, white ray florets shading to purple-brown at the center; '**Aztec Queen**', yellow ray florets with red-brown base; '**Blackberry Ripple**', buff ray florets with purple mid-stripe; '**Bronze Gnome**', compact, bronze double flowers; '**Christopher Lloyd**', ray florets light red, darkening near center, green base; '**Cookei**', silvery gray foliage, burnt orange petals shading to taupe toward center; '**Copper King**', large copper-red flowers; '**Cream Dream**', silver-gray foliage, cream ray florets with green base; '**Fiesta Red**', rusty red ray florets with orange base; '**Michael**', dark foliage, yellow ray florets with black base; '**Moonglow**', golden double flowers. Also available as mixed color seedling strains, such as the early-flowering **Chansonette Series**, the compact **Daybreak Series** and **Mini-star Series**, and the gray-leafed **Talent Series**. Zones 9–11.

GEIJERA

A member of the rue (Rutaceae) family, this genus contains 8 species occurring in New Guinea, eastern Australia, and New Caledonia. Of the 5 endemic Australian species, 2 occur in rainforests and the other 3 in various habitats, even relatively arid regions. All are small to medium trees reaching 80 ft (24 m) tall when growing in rainforest. The flowers are small, no more than ¼ in (6 mm) across and they are borne in terminal panicles. They are followed by small brown fruits of 2 to 4 compartments, each containing a glossy black seed.
CULTIVATION: The different species come from natural habitats ranging from semi-arid inland plains to drier types of coastal rainforest, but the inland species adapt well to moister climates. All prefer reasonably fertile soil. Propagation is from fresh seed, which may germinate quite erratically.

Geijera parviflora ★
WILGA

☀ ❅ ↔ 35 ft (10 m) ↑ 40 ft (12 m)

Small tree occurring in drier inland regions of all Australian states except Tasmania and Western Australia.

Pendulous narrow leaves. Creamy white flowers, in spring. Propagation is not easy, as seed is often difficult to obtain. Grown successfully in other countries. Zones 8–11.

GEISSOIS

This is a genus of around 25 species of shrubs and trees placed in the Cunoniaceae family, occurring in Australia, New Caledonia, Vanuatu, Fiji, and South America. The leaves are opposite, simple, or pinnate and with large stipules where the stalks join the stem. The leaflets on the pinnate species are large and toothed. The inflorescence is a spike, either axillary or clustered toward the ends of the branches. Small dull flowers consist of sepals only, petals are absent. The fruits are small capsules.
CULTIVATION: Young plants prefer a sheltered humid situation in filtered sunlight. Soil should be moderately fertile, acid to neutral, and moist but well drained. Propagation is from seed and its freshness is important.

Geissois benthamii
BRUSH MAHOGANY, LEATHER JACKET, RED CARRABEEN

☀ ⚓ ↔ 15–20 ft (4.5–6 m) ↑ 17–35 ft (5–10 m)

Large tree from coastal and near-coastal rainforests of southeastern Queensland and northeastern New South Wales, Australia. Leaves with 3 leaflets, large, up to 8 in (20 cm) long, oval to elliptical, shiny dark green, coarse teeth on margins. Many small flowers, on axillary spikes, in summer. Long hairy capsules in winter. Zones 10–11.

Geissois pruinosa
COMMON GEISSOIS

☀ ⚘ ↔ 7 ft (2 m) ↑ 15 ft (4.5 m)

Tall shrub or small tree, may be multi-stemmed, found in the maquis vegetation of New Caledonia, particularly in the south, on ultrabasic soils. Leaves are trifoliate, somewhat bluish green. Numerous flowers, borne on older and leafless stems, in axillary

spikes, cerise to pale pink, in winter. Fruits cylindrical, pointed, reddish before opening. Zones 9–11.

GELSEMIUM
CAROLINA JASMINE, YELLOW JESSAMINE

Gelsomino is the Italian name for jasmine, and the 3 twining evergreen vines in this genus resemble yellow-flowered jasmines, but they're not even in the same family. *Gelsemium* is in the logania (Loganiaceae) family, while *Jasminum* is related to the olives (Oleaceae). Found in North and Central America and Southeast Asia, they have simple, pointed, oval leaves, around 2 in (5 cm) long, and grow slowly but steadily to cover a large area. The flowers are mildly scented, small, yellow trumpets borne in clusters. As might be expected of a genus related to the strychnine and curare trees, *Gelsemium* is highly poisonous.
CULTIVATION: Suitable as a ground cover and for container cultivation, as well as for training over trellises and walls. While tolerant of moderate frosts, they grow and flower better in a mild climate. Plant in a sunny position with fertile, moist, well-drained soil. Trim back if necessary. Propagate from half-hardened cuttings or seed.

Gelsemium sempervirens ★

☀/◑ ❅ ↔ 20 ft (6 m) ↑ 20 ft (6 m)

Found from southern USA to Guatemala. Jasmine-like, glossy green, 2 in (5 cm) long, pointed elliptical

Geijera parviflora

Geissois benthamii

Geissois pruinosa

Genista tinctoria

Genista tinctoria 'Royal Gold'

leaves. Sprays of scented, 1 in (25 mm) long, yellow flowers followed by dark fruits. **'Pride of Augusta'** has double flowers. Zones 8–11.

GENISTA

syns *Chamaespartium*, *Echinospartium*
About 90 species belong to this genus within the pea-flower subfamily of the legume (Fabaceae) family. Most are deciduous but some appear evergreen because of their flat green branchlets. Native to Europe and the Mediterranean to western Asia, these shrubs or small trees tolerate all types of soils; most grow on rocky hillsides. Leaves are alternate, simple, or consist of 3 leaflets; branches can be nearly leafless. CULTIVATION: Full sun is necessary and not all plants are fully frost hardy. Grow half-hardy plants in a well-ventilated greenhouse. They need a light well-drained soil to flower well. Sow seed in pots as soon as ripe, in autumn or spring, and protect from winter frosts until plants are ready for transplanting. Propagation also from half-hardened cuttings in summer.

Genista aetnensis

MOUNT ETNA BROOM
☼ ❀ ↔ 25 ft (8 m) ↑ 25 ft (8 m)
Native to Sardinia and Sicily, Italy. Upright shrub, weeping branches, narrow leaves only on young shoots,

Genista × spachiana

dropping off as the branches age. Fragrant, yellow, pea-like flowers on the pendent shoots, throughout summer–autumn. Zones 8–10.

Genista hispanica

SPANISH BROOM, SPANISH GORSE
☼ ❀ ↔ 48 in (120 cm) ↑ 30 in (75 cm)
Native to southern France and northern Spain. Deciduous, erect, spiny shrub, forms a dense mound. Oblong to egg-shaped leaves, on flowering branches. Racemes of golden flowers, in late spring–summer. Zones 6–10.

Genista lydia

DWARF GENISTA, GENISTA
☼ ❀ ↔ 36 in (90 cm) ↑ 24 in (60 cm)
Native to the eastern Balkans. Deciduous prostrate shrub, smaller in the wild. Blue-green leaves, long and narrow or elliptic in shape. Short racemes of golden yellow flowers in late spring–early summer. Flat non-hairy fruit. Zones 7–9.

Genista pilosa

GENISTA, SILKY WOADWAXEN, SILKY LEAF WOADWAXEN
☼ ❀ ↔ 15 in (38 cm) ↑ 15 in (38 cm)
Native to western and central Europe. Deciduous shrub, prostrate or erect in habit. Leaves narrow, dark green above, pale undersides. Golden yellow flowers in racemes, in late spring to

Genista aetnensis

early summer. Densely hairy seed pods. **'Goldilocks'**, to 24 in (60 cm) tall and much wider; **'Vancouver Gold'** ★, a spreading mound, dark green leaves, golden flowers. Zones 5–9.

Genista sagittalis

WINGED BROOM
☼ ❀ ↔ 36 in (90 cm) ↑ 6 in (15 cm)
Prostrate shrub, native to southern and central Europe; appears evergreen, but is not. Winged branchlets. Leaves lance-shaped, hairy undersides. Golden flowers in terminal racemes, in late spring–early summer. Silky fruit. Zones 4–9.

Genista × spachiana

syns *Cytisus fragrans*, *C. × spachiana*, *Genista fragrans*
☼ ⊗ ↔ 17 ft (5 m) ↑ 10–20 ft (3–6 m)
Vigorous, evergreen, arching shrub, a cross of *G. stenopetala* and *G. canari-*

Genista sagittalis

Genista hispanica

ensis, often grown as a house plant. Dark green leaves with 3 oval leaflets, ¼–¾ in (6–18 mm) long, silky underneath. Long slender clusters of fragrant golden yellow flowers, ½ in (12 mm) across, in winter–early spring. Zones 9–11.

Genista tinctoria

COMMON WOADWAXEN, DYER'S GREENWEED
☼ ❀ ↔ 3 ft (0.9 m) ↑ 3 ft (0.9 m)
Native to Europe and western Asia. Variable in form and habit, deciduous shrub has no spines, can grow 6 ft (1.8 m) tall. Bright green leaves, elliptic or lance-shaped. Golden flowers on upright racemes, in summer. Used to produce dyes. **'Flore Pleno'**, dwarf form with double flowers; **'Golden Plate'**, clear yellow flowers, spreading compact shape, weeping branches; **'Royal Gold'**, more erect, with flowers carried in panicles. Zones 2–9.

Genista lydia

Genista pilosa

Gelsemium sempervirens

Gentiana makinoi

Genlisea violacea

Gentiana acaulis 'Rannoch'

Gentiana acaulis

GENLISEA

CORKSCREW PLANT

A genus of carnivorous plants, with about 15 species, belonging the bladderwort (Lentibulariaceae) family. They come from Africa, Madagascar, and South America, growing in very wet soils along watercourses and in swampy savannahs. These small perennial plants produce 2 types of leaves: green spoon-shaped or lance-shaped leaves above the ground and carnivorous corkscrew-like leaves below ground. These carnivorous leaves fork into 2 prongs, at the base of which is a mouth in which very small prey are captured. Once inside the mouth, the prey cannot escape because inward-pointing hairs block

their way, forcing them up through the trap into the digestive chamber.
CULTIVATION: These plants do best in tropical conditions. Grow in a greenhouse in cooler climates. Plant in sphagnum moss or a mix of 1 part sand to 1 part peat. Keep soil water-logged and provide filtered light. Propagate from leaf cuttings.

Genlisea violacea

◐ ⧓ ↔2 in (5 cm) ↕1 in (2.5 cm)
Native of Brazil. Dense rosettes of green, 1 in (2.5 cm) long, spoon-shaped leaves. Violet-like flowers on 4 in (10 cm) leafless stalks. Zones 9–12.

GENTIANA

GENTIAN

A genus of around 400 widely distributed species of annuals, biennials and perennials and the type genus for its family, the Gentianaceae. Although ranging from tiny tufted alpine plants to species with 24 in (60 cm) long flower stems, most form a compact clump of simple pointed leaves, sometimes in rosettes. The trumpet- or bell-shaped flowers may be borne singly among the foliage or clustered on upright or overarching stems. Not

Gentiana concinna

all gentians have blue flowers, many are white, cream, yellow, or purple. Some gentians have medicinal uses and the name honors Gentius, King of Illyria, who in 180 BC was cited by Pliny as having discovered these properties. Modern herbalists use root extracts to treat anaemia and some gentians are also used as a flavoring.
CULTIVATION: Gentians prefer a climate with distinct seasons and grow best in full sun/half-sun with moist, well-drained, humus-rich soil, perhaps with a little dolomite lime. The small species thrive in rockeries. Propagate by division or from seed.

Gentiana acaulis

◐ ❋ ↔12 in (30 cm) ↕4 in (10 cm)
Spring- to early summer-flowering perennial found from Spain to the Balkans. Clump of short-stemmed, 1 in (25 mm) long, elliptical leaves in basal rosettes. Solitary, deep blue, green-spotted, flared bell-shaped flowers to 2 in (5 cm) long. 'Rannoch', 2 in (5 cm) tall, dark-centered, deep blue flowers with fine green and/or white stripes. Zones 3–9.

Gentiana asclepiadea

WILLOW GENTIAN
◐ ❋ ↔24–40 in (60–100 cm)
↕16 in (40 cm)
Eurasian summer- to autumn-flowering herbaceous perennial with arching stems to 24 in (60 cm) long. Finely tapering, 2–3 in (5–8 cm) long, oval to lance-shaped leaves. Narrow bell-shaped flowers to 1¼ in (30 mm) long, in clusters of 2 to 3 in leaf axils, mauve to purple-blue with darker spotting. Zones 6–9.

Gentiana clusii

◐ ❋ ↔12 in (30 cm) ↕4 in (10 cm)
Low, tufted, summer-flowering perennial from central and southern Europe. Basal rosettes of leathery, bright green, pointed elliptical leaves, to 1 in (25 mm) long. Bright deep blue, green-spotted, flared trumpet-shaped flowers, to 2 in (5 cm) long. Resembles G. acaulis but is less hardy, though more lime-tolerant. Zones 6–9.

Gentiana concinna

❂ ❋ ↔4–8 in (10–20 cm)
↕3–6 in (8–15 cm)
From the subantarctic to Auckland Islands. Annual with close-set, smooth, narrow, leathery leaves. Small flowers, to ½ in (12 mm) across, vary from white streaked with red or purple to wholly pinkish red. Zones 7–9.

Gentiana cruciata

◐ ❋ ↔12 in (30 cm) ↕16 in (40 cm)
Summer-flowering Eurasian perennial. Short, leafy, upright stems developing from basal rosettes. Glossy lance-shaped leaves, 4–8 in (10–20 cm) long, upper leaves smaller. Terminal and axillary clusters of 1 in (25 mm) long, narrow bell-shaped, azure to purple-blue flowers. Zones 5–9.

Gentiana × macaulayi

◐ ❋ ↔16 in (40 cm) ↕4 in (10 cm)
Summer- to autumn-flowering garden hybrid between G. sino-ornata and G. farreri. Low, spreading, sometimes rooting stems with small rosettes of leaves to over 1¼ in (30 mm) long. Flared funnel-shaped flowers to 2¾ in (65 mm) long, deep blue with faint violet, green, and white markings. 'Kingfisher' is especially vigorous, with dark foliage and conspicuously white-striped flowers. Zones 4–9.

Gentiana makinoi

◐ ❋ ↔16 in (40 cm) ↕24 in (60 cm)
Summer-flowering Japanese species. Basal leaves to around 2 in (5 cm) long. Upright leafy stems bearing 1¼ in (30 mm) long, dark-spotted, blue, bell-shaped flowers at the stem tips and in leaf axils. Zones 6–9.

Gentiana paradoxa

◐ ❋ ↔12 in (30 cm) ↕8 in (20 cm)
Summer- to autumn-flowering Eurasian perennial with wiry stems and narrow foliage, spreading to form a small mounding clump. Long-lobed, bell-shaped, mid-blue to light purple flowers, to more than 1¼ in (30 mm) long. Zones 6–9.

Gentiana punctata

SPOTTED GENTIAN
◐ ❋ ↔12 in (30 cm) ↕24 in (60 cm)
Summer-flowering central European perennial with basal foliage clump and upright stems developing from a stout tap root. Basal leaves elliptical, to 4 in (10 cm) long, stem leaves smaller. Terminal and axillary clusters of purple-spotted pale yellow flowers to more than 1¼ in (30 mm) long. Zones 5–9.

Geranium albanum

Geranium argenteum

Gentiana saxosa

☀ ❄ ↔ 12 in (30 cm) ↑ 8 in (20 cm)
Summer-flowering near-prostrate perennial from New Zealand. Rosettes of purple-tinted, spatula-shaped, basal leaves, to over 1¼ in (30 mm) long. Short upright flower stems with purple-veined, white, open bell-shaped flowers, solitary or in small heads. Zones 8–9.

Gentiana septemfida ★

☀ ❄ ↔ 16 in (40 cm) ↑ 12 in (30 cm)
Summer- to autumn-flowering western and central Asian perennial with spreading sometimes upright stems. Paired pointed oval leaves to nearly 1¾ in (40 mm) long and clusters of light-spotted, bright blue, bell-shaped flowers, to 1¾ in (40 mm) long. *G. s.* var. *lagodechiana*, branching stems, solitary flowers. Zones 3–9.

Gentiana sino-ornata

☀ ❄ ↔ 12 in (30 cm) ↑ 6 in (15 cm)
Autumn-flowering spreading perennial from western China and Tibet. Stems root as they spread. Loose rosettes of narrow lance-shaped leaves to over 1¼ in (30 mm) long. Solitary, vivid blue, funnel-shaped flowers, to over 2 in (5 cm) long, lighter inside, with purple and white bands. Zones 6–9.

Gentiana ternifolia

☀ ❄ ↔ 16 in (40 cm)
↑ 4–8 in (10–20 cm)
Spreading autumn-flowering perennial native to western China. Stems often erect at the tips. Loose basal rosettes of narrow lance-shaped leaves to nearly ¾ in (18 mm) long. Flowers 1¾ in (40 mm) long, mid-blue, marked green and white, funnel-shaped. Zones 8–9.

Gentiana verna

☀ ❄ ↔ 8–12 in (20–30 cm) ↑ 2 in (5 cm)
Prostrate spring- to summer-flowering European perennial. Leaves bright green, oval, to 1 in (25 mm) long. Starry, pale-centered, vivid blue flowers, usually solitary, to around 1 in (25 mm) wide. Zones 5–9.

GENTIANOPSIS

FRINGED GENTIAN

Gentian-like in appearance, these plants are closely related to the true gentians (family Gentianaceae) and were once included in the genus. However, all but 1 of the 25 species that make up this North American and Eurasian genus are summer-flowering annuals and biennials, not perennials like the majority of gentians. They are usually upright, with strong angular stems bearing opposite pairs of variably shaped leaves. The widely flared tubular flowers are 4-petalled, clustered or solitary, frequently with finely fringed edges, usually blue to purple-blue, and often long-stemmed.
CULTIVATION: Hardy and easily grown in most temperate areas that aren't very dry in summer. Although some species are natural bog plants, in cultivation they prefer well-drained, moist, humus-rich soil. Full sun is best in cool climates, otherwise shade from hottest summer sun. Propagate from seed sown in spring; biennials can also be sown in early autumn.

Gentianopsis crinita

syn. *Gentiana crinita*
GREATER FRINGED GENTIAN
☀/◑ ❄ ↔ 18 in (45 cm) ↑ 36 in (90 cm)
Annual or biennial from eastern USA. Erect branching stems; oval to lance-shaped leaves. Fringed flowers, bright blue, up to 2 in (5 cm) across, borne in late summer–autumn. Zones 3–9.

GEOHINTONIA

A minor sensation was created in the cactus world in 1991 when George

Gentiana septemfida

Hinton, a leading Mexican cactus expert, discovered a new single-species genus of cactus in the gypsum hills of the Sierra Madre Oriental region of Mexico. This genus, which belongs to the cactus (Cactaceae) family, was named in his honor. The novelty of this cactus and its unusual appearance sparked a subsequent rash of illegal field collecting. It grows with *Aztekium hintonii*, which was discovered at about the same time.
CULTIVATION: Easily grown in a rich well-drained soil. Propagate from seed or cuttings taken from grafted plants. Rest in winter.

Geohintonia mexicana

☀ ❅ ↔ 4 in (10 cm) ↑ 4 in (10 cm)
From Nuevo Leon, Mexico. Solitary spherical to slightly columnar cactus. High straight ribs may be up to 8 in (20 cm) above the plant body. Areoles continuous along the edges of the ribs. Spines tiny, pale brown, easily detached. Flowers diurnal, funnel-shaped, pink to magenta. Spherical seed pods. Zones 9–11.

GERANIUM

CRANESBILL

The plants often called geraniums in fact belong in the genus *Pelargonium*. While both genera are in the geranium (Geraniaceae) family, true geraniums are a very different group of some 300 species of perennials and subshrubs, sometimes evergreen, that are widespread in temperate zones. Their leaves, usually palmate, with toothed lobes, are often finely hairy. They bloom in summer and have simple, flat, 5-petalled flowers in pink or purple-blue shades, less commonly white or purple-black. The flowers

develop into long narrow fruits. The name *Geranium* comes from the Greek *geranos* (crane), referring to the fruit's resemblance to the shape of a crane's bill. *G. robertianum* (commonly known as Herb Robert) and others have a long history in herbal medicine for a wide range of ailments and uses.
CULTIVATION: Most species are hardy and will grow in a wide range of conditions, preferring full sun or half-sun and moist humus-rich soil. The roots can be invasive. Propagate from seed, cuttings, or by division. May self-sow.

Geranium albanum

☀/◑ ❄ ↔ 20 in (50 cm) ↑ 8 in (20 cm)
From the Caucasus region and Iran. Basal leaves rounded, divided into 7- to 9-toothed palmate lobes, to 2 in (5 cm) wide. Magenta-veined pink flowers to 1 in (25 mm) wide, with blue stigma. Zones 7–9.

Geranium argenteum

☀/◑ ❄ ↔ 12 in (30 cm) ↑ 6 in (15 cm)
Found from the Alps to the Balkans. Rosettes of silver-gray finely hairy leaves to 2 in (5 cm) wide, divided in 7 sections, each 3-lobed. Flowers are ½ in (12 mm) wide, deep pink, dark-veined, indented petal tips, sparse. Zones 6–9.

Gentiana ternifolia

Gentiana paradoxa

Geranium asphodeloides

☼/◑ ❄ ↔ 24 in (60 cm) ↕ 20 in (50 cm)
Found from Italy to northern Iran.
Hairy stems and leaves palmately
lobed, 5 to 7 lobes, to 2 in (5 cm)
wide. Flowers narrow-petalled, starry,
white to pale mauve-pink, dark veins,
to more than 1¼ in (30 mm) wide.
Zones 8–10.

Geranium bohemicum

☼/◑ ❄ ↔ 24 in (60 cm) ↕ 18 in (45 cm)
Freely self-sowing annual to short-
lived perennial from central Europe.
Finely hairy, deeply lobed and cut,
maple-like, palmate leaves. Flowers
small, cup-shaped, light mauve with
purple veins, clustered mainly near
the stem tips. Zones 6–9.

Geranium canariense

☼/◑ ⧫ ↔ 24 in (60 cm) ↕ 20 in (50 cm)
Short-lived evergreen perennial from
the Canary Islands. Rosettes of long-
stemmed leaves, to 10 in (25 cm)

Geranium bohemicum

Geranium × *cantabrigiense*

Geranium × *cantabrigiense* 'Biokovo'

Geranium clarkei

wide, ferny, with 5 finely divided
pinnate lobes. Large terminal heads
of starry mauve-pink flowers to 2 in
(5 cm) wide, from late spring.
Zones 9–11.

Geranium × *cantabrigiense*

☼/◑ ❄ ↔ 24 in (60 cm) ↕ 8 in (20 cm)
A low spreading *G. macrorrhizum* ×
G. dalmaticum hybrid. Aromatic,
bright green, rounded leaves, to 3 in
(8 cm) wide, divided into 7 toothed
lobes. Flowers to 1 in (25 mm) wide,
pink or white with pink center.
'**Biokovo**', pink-flushed white flowers;
'**Cambridge**', deep pink to magenta
flowers. Zones 5–9.

Geranium cinereum

☼/◑ ❄ ↔ 20 in (50 cm) ↕ 6 in (15 cm)
Found in the Balkans and around the
Adriatic. Spreading perennial, rosettes
of 5- to 7-lobed gray-green leaves, to
2 in (5 cm) wide. Small heads of
often dark-veined white to deep pink

Geranium × *cantabrigiense* 'Cambridge'

Geranium dalmaticum

flowers, to 1 in (25 mm) wide. *G. c.*
var. *subcaulescens*, dark green leaves,
large flowers with black central markings. *G. c.* '**Ballerina**', red-veined
purple-pink flowers, notched petal
tips; '**Purple Pillow**', very compact
habit, striking funnel-shaped purple-
red flowers. Zones 5–9.

Geranium clarkei

☼/◑ ❄ ↔ 20 in (50 cm) ↕ 12 in (30 cm)
Spreading perennial from Kashmir.
Mounding habit. Basal leaves to 3 in
(8 cm) wide, 7 deep lobes, toothed.
Open sprays of upward-facing, dark-
veined, purple, white, or pink flowers,
1¾ in (40 mm) wide. '**Kashmir
White**', large white flowers. Zones 7–10.

Geranium dalmaticum

☼/◑ ❄ ↔ 20 in (50 cm) ↕ 6 in (15 cm)
Small spreading native of Albania
and southwest Balkans. Glossy 5- to
7-lobed leaves, to 1¾ in (40 mm) wide.
Airy sprays of bright pink flowers to
over 1¼ in (30 mm) wide. Zones 5–9.

Geranium endressii

☼/◑ ❄ ↔ 24 in (60 cm) ↕ 18 in (45 cm)
Long-flowering evergreen perennial
from the Pyrenees. Basal leaves are

Geranium cinereum

Geranium cinereum 'Ballerina'

Geranium endressii 'Wargrave Pink'

Geranium farreri

5-lobed, to 6 in (15 cm) wide, upper
leaves 3- to 5-lobed and smaller.
Foliage reddens in winter. Heads of
dark-veined bright pink flowers to
1¾ in (40 mm) wide. '**Wargrave
Pink**', a vigorous grower, clusters of
small leaves, many soft orange-pink
flowers. Zones 5–9.

Geranium farreri

☼/◑ ❄ ↔ 16 in (40 cm) ↕ 4 in (10 cm)
Spreading alpine species from western
China. Sprawling stems radiate from
central tap root and take root. Leaves
kidney-shaped, 7 palmate divisions,
lobed and toothed, lower leaves to
2 in (5 cm) wide. Flowers solitary,
rounded, mauve-pink, to more than
1¼ in (30 mm) wide. Zones 4–9.

Geranium gracile

☼/◑ ❄ ↔ 24 in (60 cm) ↕ 16 in (40 cm)
Found in the wild from Turkey to
Iran. Thickened, partly emergent
rootstock. Leaves wrinkled, hairy,
light green, 5- to 7-lobed, toothed, to
4 in (10 cm) wide. Few long-
stemmed, dark-veined, mauve-pink
flowers. Keep dry in winter. Zones 7–9.

Geranium guatemalense

☼/◑ ⧫ ↔ 30 in (75 cm) ↕ 12 in (30 cm)
Evergreen perennial from the cloud
forests of Central America. Heads of
starry mauve-pink flowers, to 1¾ in
(40 mm) wide. Zones 9–11.

Geranium harveyi

syn. *Geranium sericeum*
☼/◑ ❄ ↔ 30 in (75 cm) ↕ 4 in (10 cm)
Spreading ground cover from the
Ecuadorian Andes. Rosettes of finely
hairy silver-gray leaves, 5 deeply

toothed lobes, to 1¾ in (40 mm) wide. Funnel-shaped white to light pink flowers. Zones 7–9.

Geranium himalayense

☀/◐ ❄ ↔ 40 in (100 cm)
↕ 18 in (45 cm)

Found from northern Afghanistan to Nepal. Spreading habit with hairy stems and leaves. Basal leaves to 8 in (20 cm) wide, 7-lobed and toothed, upper leaves considerably smaller. Airy sprays of deep purple-blue flowers, to more than 2 in (5 cm) wide, often pink- or white-centered. '**Baby Blue**', compact habit, vivid bright blue flowers; '**Gravetye**' (syn. 'Alpinum'), intense blue flowers, red-tinted autumn foliage; '**Plenum**' (syn. 'Birch Double'), compact habit, small leaves, purple-blue double flowers. Zones 4–9.

Geranium ibericum

☀/◐ ❄ ↔ 30 in (75 cm) ↕ 16 in (40 cm)
Sprawling perennial from Turkey, the Caucasus region, and northern Iran. Leaves bright green, to 4 in (10 cm) wide, 9- to 11-lobed, toothed. Small heads of dark-veined purple-blue flowers to over 1¾ in

Geranium guatemalense

Geranium ibericum

Geranium macrorrhizum 'Album'

Geranium maculatum

(40 mm) wide. *G. i.* subsp. *jubatum* differs only in having hairs on the flower stems. Zones 6–9.

Geranium incanum

☀/◐ ❄ ↔ 40 in (100 cm) ↕ 40 in (100 cm)
Evergreen South African species, with branching main stems; long-stemmed, aromatic, bright green leaves, sometimes paired, finely cut into 5 narrow toothed lobes, downy white undersides. Airy sprays of long-stemmed, light-centered, magenta flowers to over 1¼ in (30 mm) wide. Zones 8–11.

Geranium lambertii

☀/◐ ❄ ↔ 24 in (60 cm) ↕ 12 in (30 cm)
Trailing Himalayan native. Hairy, kidney-shaped, 5-lobed leaves, to 6 in (15 cm) wide. Open heads of hairy-stemmed white flowers, to 1¾ in (40 mm) wide, black anthers. '**Swansdown**', leaves marbled light green, large nodding flowers with purple-red centers. Zones 8–10.

Geranium macrorrhizum

☀/◐ ❄ ↔ 40 in (100 cm) ↕ 20 in (50 cm)
Spreading perennial native to southern Europe. The leaves are 4–8 in

Geranium ibericum subsp. *jubatum*

Geranium macrorrhizum 'Czakor'

Geranium himalayense

G. himalayense 'Baby Blue'

G. himalayense 'Gravetye'

Geranium himalayense 'Plenum'

(10–20 cm) wide, with 5 to 7 lobes, toothed and further divided. Densely clustered heads of pink to purple-red flowers. '**Album**', white flowers with red-tinted sepals; '**Bevan's Variety**', small leaves, bright magenta flowers; '**Czakor**', low-growing, magenta flowers with dark sepals; '**Ingwersen's Variety**', light glossy green leaves, pale pink flowers. Zones 4–9.

Geranium maculatum

☀/◐ ❄ ↔ 40 in (100 cm) ↕ 27 in (70 cm)
Bushy North American perennial found from Manitoba to Kansas. Basal leaves to 8 in (20 cm) wide, upper leaves to 4 in (10 cm) wide, 5- to 7-lobed, further divided and toothed. Heads of upward-facing deep pink flowers, to 1¾ in (40 mm) wide. Zones 4–9.

Geranium maderense

☀/◐ ❄ ↔ 60 in (150 cm) ↕ 60 in (150 cm)
This native of Madeira is regarded as the largest geranium. Shrubby habit with rosettes of deeply lobed and

G. macrorrhizum 'Ingwersen's Variety'

Geranium maderense

divided leathery leaves, to 12 in (30 cm) wide, long purple-tinted stalks. Large, hairy, purple-stemmed flowerheads with many dark-veined deep pink to magenta flowers, to 1¾ in (40 mm) wide. Zones 9–11.

Geranium × magnificum

☀/◐ ❄ ↔ 40 in (100 cm)
↕ 20 in (50 cm)

Garden hybrid between *G. ibericum* and *G. platypetalum*. Leaves bright green, to 4 in (10 cm) wide, 9- to 11-lobed, toothed; hairy stems. Heads of dark-veined purple flowers to more than 1¾ in (40 mm) wide. Zones 5–9.

Geranium nodosum

☀/◐ ❄ ↔ 32 in (80 cm) ↕ 12 in (30 cm)
Clump-forming perennial native to the mountains of southern Europe. Leaves glossy, with shallow lobes, toothed. Lower leaves to 8 in (20 cm) wide, as small as 2 in (5 cm) wide elsewhere. Upright heads of purple flowers to more than 1 in (25 mm) wide, notched petal tips. Zones 6–9.

G

Geranium × oxonianum 'Rose Clair'

Geranium × oxonianum

Geranium × oxonianum 'Lady Moore'

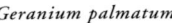

Geranium palmatum

Geranium × oxonianum

☼/◗ ❋ ↔ 48 in (120 cm) ↕ 24 in (60 cm)

Hybrid between *G. endressii* and *G. versicolor*. It spreads to cover a large area. Leaves with 5 fairly shallow lobes, 2–4 in (5–10 cm) wide, sometimes larger. Masses of dark-veined light pink flowers to 1 in (25 mm) wide. **'A. T. Johnson'**, pale silvery pink flowers; **'Claridge Druce'**, vigorous, hairy stems, dark leaves, deep pink flowers; **'Lady Moore'**, purple-veined pink flowers; **'Rose Clair'**, small grower with purple to

Geranium palustre

pink flowers; and **'Sherwood'**, starry flowers with very narrow pale pink petals. Zones 5–9.

Geranium palmatum

☼/◗ ❅ ↔ 24 in (60 cm) ↕ 40 in (100 cm)

Evergreen perennial, sometimes short-lived, native to Madeira. Compact for a while but eventually develops woody stem. Rosettes of long-stemmed, lobed, finely divided leaves, to 14 in (35 cm) wide. Large terminal heads of starry red-pink flowers, to 2 in (5 cm) wide, cream anthers. Zones 9–11.

Geranium phaeum

Geranium palustre

☼/◗ ❋ ↔ 20 in (50 cm) ↕ 12 in (30 cm)

Mounding perennial from central and eastern Europe. Large lower leaves, upper leaves around 3 in (8 cm) wide, with 7 pinnate toothed lobes. Airy sprays of magenta flowers to more than 1¼ in (30 mm) wide. Zones 6–9.

Geranium phaeum
BLACK WIDOW

☼/◗ ❋ ↔ 16 in (40 cm) ↕ 32 in (80 cm)

Upright, bushy, European perennial with 9-lobed leaves, large at the base, much smaller higher up the plant. Heads of 1 in (25 mm) wide flowers, mauve, maroon, to dark purple-red, sometimes near-black. **'Album'** ★, large white flowers; **'Lily Lovell'**, large purple flowers. Zones 5–9.

Geranium platypetalum

☼/◗ ❋ ↔ 16 in (40 cm) ↕ 12 in (30 cm)

A clumping perennial from the Caucasus region, Turkey, and northern Iran. Strong rootstock bearing hairy-stemmed, light green, 7- to 9-lobed and toothed leaves, 4–8 in (10–20 cm) wide. Densely clustered heads of dark-veined deep mauve-pink flowers, to nearly 2 in (5 cm) wide. Zones 6–9.

Geranium pratense
MEADOW CRANESBILL

☼/◗ ❋ ↔ 40 in (100 cm) ↕ 48 in (120 cm)

Sturdy spreading perennial found from central Europe to the western Himalayas. Upright stems, leaves 4–8 in (10–20 cm) wide, 7 to 9 deep pinnate lobes, toothed. Flowerheads crowded to rather open, blue flowers to 2 in (50 mm) wide. **'Mrs Kendall**

Geranium phaeum 'Lily Lovell'

Clark', pale flowers with translucent veins; **'Splish-splash'**, pale flowers randomly sectored and flecked with light purple-blue. Zones 5–9.

Geranium psilostemon

☼/◗ ❋ ↔ 16–24 in (40–60 cm) ↕ 24–40 in (60–100 cm)

Upright slightly spreading perennial from northeastern Turkey. Leaves 2–8 in (5–20 cm) wide, deeply lobed, and further divided. Erect heads of black-centered magenta flowers, to over 1¼ in (30 mm) wide. Zones 6–9.

Geranium pyrenaicum

☼/◗ ❋ ↔ 24 in (60 cm) ↕ 24 in (60 cm)

Evergreen, finely hairy, late-flowering perennial from southern Europe. Rounded 5- to 9-lobed leaves, to 4 in (10 cm) wide. Airy sprays of mauve to purple-pink flowers, to ¾ in (18 mm) across. Zones 7–9.

Geranium regelii

☼/◗ ❋ ↔ 40 in (100 cm) ↕ 48 in (120 cm)

A sturdy spreading perennial that comes from central Asia and northern parts of Afghanistan and Pakistan. Upright stems, leaves around 4 in (10 cm) wide, 7 to 9 broad lobes,

Geranium regelii

Geranium pratense

Geranium pratense 'Mrs Kendall Clark'

Geranium pratense 'Splish-splash'

Geranium pyrenaicum

Geranium renardii

Geranium robustum

G. × riversleaianum 'Mavis Simpson'

toothed. Flowerheads rather open; mauve to blue flowers, to nearly 2 in (50 mm) wide. Zones 6–9.

Geranium renardii

☀/☼ ❄ ↔ 16 in (40 cm) ↑ 8 in (20 cm)
Clump-forming perennial from the Caucasus region. Leaves to 4 in (10 cm) wide, rounded, 5-lobed, further divided and toothed. Heads of flat, ¾ in (18 mm) wide, violet-veined, white to lavender flowers, notched petal tips. Zones 6–9.

Geranium × riversleaianum

☀/☼ ❄ ↔ 24 in (60 cm) ↑ 4 in (10 cm)
Garden hybrid between *G. endressii* and *G. traversii*. Low spreading habit with small, 7-lobed, bronze green leaves. Open heads of dark-veined, funnel-shaped, pink flowers, to more than 1¼ in (30 mm) wide. '**Mavis Simpson**', light-centered flowers; '**Russell Prichard**', deep pink flowers, sharply toothed leaves. Zones 7–10.

Geranium robertianum

HERB ROBERT
☀/☼ ❄ ↔ 20 in (50 cm) ↑ 10 in (25 cm)
Annual or biennial, widespread in the Northern Hemisphere. Rosettes of

aromatic, long-stemmed, finely cut, ferny leaves, somewhat resembling hemlock. Tiny deep pink flowers, borne singly or in clusters. Zones 6–10.

Geranium robustum

☀/☼ ❄ ↔ 24 in (60 cm) ↑ 40 in (100 cm)
South African subshrub with woody base, upright stems and silver-gray, hairy, 2 in (5 cm) wide leaves, 3 to 7 finely cut lobes. Clustered heads of light-centered purple flowers, to more than 1¼ in (30 mm) wide. Zones 8–11.

Geranium rubescens

☀/☼ ⊗ ↔ 32 in (80 cm) ↑ 32 in (80 cm)
Biennial native to Madeira. Rosettes of aromatic, finely cut, toothed leaves, long red-tinted stalks. Many starry bright magenta flowers, to 1½ in (35 mm) wide. Zones 9–10.

Geranium sanguineum

BLOODY CRANESBILL
☀/☼ ❄ ↔ 16 in (40 cm) ↑ 8 in (20 cm)
Low, slowly spreading, bushy Eurasian perennial. Leaves 2–4 in (5–10 cm) wide, 5- to 7-lobed and further divided. Many flowers, borne singly, magenta to purple-red, to over 1¼ in (30 mm) wide. *G. s.* **var.** *striatum* is a

G. sanguineum Alan Bloom/'Bloger'

small plant with dark-veined soft pink flowers, of which '**Splendens**' is a taller form. *G. s.* Alan Bloom/'**Bloger**', small leaves, compact habit, deep magenta flowers; '**Album**', white flowers; and '**Max Frei**', similar to Alan Bloom/'Bloger' but darker foliage and longer flower stems. Zones 5–9.

Geranium sessiliflorum

☀/☼ ❄ ↔ 16 in (40 cm) ↑ 4 in (10 cm)
Prostrate perennial from New Zealand. Leaves to a little over 1 in (25 mm) wide, 5 to 7 shallow lobes. Many tiny white to pale pink flowers, around ¼ in (6 mm) wide. '**Nigricans**' has very deep bronze leaves, turning orange with age. Zones 8–10.

Geranium soboliferum

☀/☼ ❄ ↔ 16 in (40 cm) ↑ 8 in (20 cm)
Perennial; eastern Russia and north-eastern China. Clustered basal leaves, 2 in (5 cm) wide, 7 narrow toothed lobes. Flowers rose-purple, to 1¼ in (30 mm) wide; dense heads. Zones 6–9.

Geranium sylvaticum

☼ ❄ ↔ 40 in (100 cm) ↑ 27 in (70 cm)
Native to Europe and northern Turkey, usually growing in moist

places. Leaves finely hairy, 2–8 in (5–20 cm) wide, 7 to 9 deep lobes, further divided and toothed. Dense heads of usually mauve-blue but sometimes white to magenta flowers, to 1¼ in (30 mm) wide. '**Album**', pure white flowers; '**Mayflower**', purplish blue flowers with pale centers. Zones 4–9.

Geranium traversii

☀/☼ ❄ ↔ 20 in (50 cm) ↑ 4 in (10 cm)
Small spreading perennial from New Zealand's Chatham Islands. Small bronze green leaves with silvery hairs, 5 to 7 broad shallow lobes, sometimes further divided. Flowers solitary or in small heads, dusky pink, around ½ in (12 mm) wide. Zones 8–10.

Geranium sylvaticum

Geranium sessiliflorum 'Nigricans'

Geranium sanguineum var. *striatum*

Geranium soboliferum

Geranium sylvaticum 'Mayflower'

Geranium sanguineum 'Max Frei'

G

Geranium tuberosum

☼/◐ ❄ ↔ 16 in (40 cm) ↑ 16 in (40 cm)

Upright tuberous perennial native to Mediterranean shores. Deeply cut, pinnately lobed and toothed leaves, to 4 in (10 cm) wide. Flowers dark-veined mauve to purple, about 1¼ in (30 mm) in diameter. Zones 8–10.

Geranium versicolor

☼/◐ ❄ ↔ 32 in (80 cm) ↑ 8 in (20 cm)

Mounding and spreading perennial found from Sicily to the Balkans and Greece. Bristly stems and foliage. Leaves to 8 in (20 cm) wide at base, smaller higher up plant, with 5 pinnate toothed lobes. Airy sprays of magenta-veined white flowers. '**Snow White**' has white flowers. Zones 6–9.

Geranium tuberosum

Geranium versicolor

Geranium, Hybrid Cultivar, 'Ann Folkard'

Geranium wallichianum

☼/◐ ❄ ↔ 24 in (60 cm) ↑ 6 in (15 cm)

Spreading mountain perennial found from northeastern Afghanistan to Kashmir. Paired, 3- to 5-lobed, deeply divided and toothed leaves, about 3 in (8 cm) wide, often long-stemmed. Bowl-shaped, light-centered, magenta or light purple flowers, to over 1¼ in (30 mm) wide. '**Buxton's Variety**' ★ (syn. 'Buxton's Blue') has a prostrate habit and light-centered bright mauve-blue flowers. Zones 7–10.

Geranium wlassovianum

☼/◐ ❄ ↔ 20 in (50 cm) ↑ 12 in (30 cm)

Shrubby perennial from northeastern temperate Asia. Leaves rounded,

Geranium versicolor 'Snow White'

Geranium, Hybrid Cultivar, 'Frances Grate'

downy, short-stemmed, divided into 7 coarsely cut pinnate lobes, to 6 in (15 cm) wide at the base, smaller higher up the plant. Airy heads of dark-veined pale magenta to deep purple flowers, to more than 1½ in (35 mm) wide. Zones 3–9.

Geranium Hybrid Cultivars

☼/◐ ❄ ↔ 24–48 in (60–120 cm) ↑ 8–36 in (20–90 cm)

Geraniums tend to sport readily and interbreed freely, so there are many garden forms in assorted sizes and flower colors. Some popular cultivars include: '**Ann Folkard**', trailing habit, yellow-green foliage, magenta flowers with dark-center; '**Frances Grate**', a cross between the South African species *G. incanum* and *G. robustum*, silvery foliage, reddish purple flowers; '**Johnson's Blue**' ★, 18 in (45 cm) tall, bushy to semi-trailing habit, bright blue to purple-blue flowers; '**Nimbus**', 16 in (40 cm) tall, glossy foliage, starry purple flowers; '**Patricia**', spreading, rather open habit with black-centered magenta-pink flowers; '**Philippe Vapelle**', 16 in (40 cm) tall, large leaves, densely foliaged, dark-veined

Geranium, Hybrid Cultivar, 'Patricia'

Geranium, HC, 'Rambling Robin'

Geranium, Hybrid Cultivar, 'Johnson's Blue'

Geranium, Hybrid Cultivar, 'Nimbus'

lavender blue flowers; '**Pink Spice**', trailing, dark bronze foliage, small pink flowers; '**Rambling Robin**', mounding, spreading habit, lavender-blue flowers; **Rozanne/'Gerwat**', to 20 in (50 cm) tall, variegated foliage, large violet-blue flowers; '**Sea Spray**', trailing, bronze foliage, small pink flowers; and '**Sue Crûg**', bushy habit, mauve-pink flowers, with darker centers and veins. Zones 6–9.

GERBERA

BARBERTON DAISY, TRANSVAAL DAISY

Some 40 species of daisy (Asteraceae) family perennials comprise this genus, best known for its winter-flowering South African representatives; other species occur in western and southern Asia. Resembling highly sophisticated dandelions, they have a basal rosette of deeply lobed and softly toothed spatula- to lance-shaped leaves, and from the center of the rosette emerge strong flower stems, each bearing one large daisy head. Available in a wide color range and double flowers. The botanical name honors Traugott Gerber, a German botanist who

Geranium, Hybrid Cultivar, 'Sue Crûg'

Geranium, HC, Rozanne/'Gerwat'

traveled in Russia and died in 1743. CULTIVATION: Gerberas are tender but can tolerate light frosts if kept barely moist in winter. Plant in full sun with deep, light, humus-rich soil with added grit for drainage. Popular as a house plant and cut flower. Propagate from seed or by careful division after flowering.

Gerbera jamesonii ★
BARBERTON DAISY
☀ ❄ ↔ 30 in (75 cm) ↕ 27 in (70 cm)
Native to South Africa and Swaziland. Doubtful if the original wild forms are still in cultivation except in native gardens in South Africa. Long-stemmed, deep green, dandelion-like leaves with coarse lobes and finely hairy undersides. Leaves can be more than 24 in (60 cm) long but usually considerably smaller. Flowerheads long-stemmed, to 4 in (10 cm) wide, usually in yellow, orange, or red shades. Zones 8–11.

Gerbera Hybrid Cultivars
☀ ❄ ↔ 12 in (30 cm) ↕ 8-18 in (20-45 cm)
Breeding of gerberas began at the end of the nineteenth century with the crossing of *G. jamesonii* and *G. viridiflora* in Cambridge, England. Most later cultivars are derived from this cross. Breeding was directed to producing long-stemmed blooms in a range of colors and varying degrees of doubleness, chiefly for the cut-flower industry, until short-stemmed seed-raised strains were developed for sale as flowering pot plants in the 1980s. Such plants produce a long succession of large flowerheads through much of the year, in both pastel and strong

Gerbera Hybrid Cultivar

colors, but they generally do not make satisfactory garden plants. **Dwarf Pandora Series**, large single blooms on short stems, in a mix of reds, oranges, yellows, pinks, and whites, usually 3 to 6 open at any one time. **Fantasia Double Series**, very large double blooms with quilled central florets, in a range of soft colors. **Happipot Series**, large blooms in vivid shades, deep green leaves. Zones 9–11.

GEUM
AVENS
This genus in the rose (Rosaceae) family, consisting of around 40 species and perennials, is widely distributed in the temperate regions. Known as avens, which was the Roman name for the plant, they are either rosette-forming or spread by rhizomes or runners, with their finely hairy pinnate or lobed leaves arising directly from the roots. From late winter to late summer, depending on the species, they produce flower stems bearing showy flowers that resemble tiny single roses, usually in bright shades of yellow, orange, pink, or red.

Gerbera Hybrid Cultivar

Bristly dry fruits follow. Tincture of avens, an ingredient in some herbal medicines, is a mild sedative. CULTIVATION: The small species are popular for rockeries, while larger forms suit perennial borders. Plant in a sunny position with moist well-drained soil that does not become compacted. Propagate by division when dormant, or raise from seed.

Geum aleppicum
YELLOW AVENS
☀/◐ ❄ ↔ 16 in (40 cm) ↕ 20 in (50 cm)
Perennial found over much of the temperate Northern Hemisphere. Leaves with 5 to 11 segments, each to 4 in (10 cm) long, finely toothed. Strongly upright branching flower stem with relatively few yellow to soft orange flowers, to ¾ in (18 mm) wide. Zones 3–9.

Geum chiloense
☀/◐ ❄ ↔ 20 in (50 cm) ↕ 30 in (75 cm)
Heavy-flowering Chilean perennial that has been extensively developed in cultivation. Long leaves divided into many toothed 1 in (25 mm) lobes. Erect flower stems with sprays of bright red flowers. '**Werner Arends**' (syn. '**Borisii**') has many light orange-red semi-double flowers. Zones 5–9.

Geum montanum
ALPINE AVENS
☀/◐ ❄ ↔ 20 in (50 cm) ↕ 12 in (30 cm)
Creeping rhizome-rooted perennial from the mountains of central and southern Europe. Rosettes of bright green pinnate leaves, to 6 in (15 cm) long, large terminal leaflet making up half that length. Small heads of bright yellow flowers, to more than 1 in (25 mm) wide. Zones 6–9.

Geum rivale
INDIAN CHOCOLATE, WATER AVENS
☀/◐ ❄ ↔ 30 in (75 cm) ↕ 12 in (30 cm)
Eurasian and North American native forming a small clump and spreading by rhizomes. Slightly pendulous heads of creamy yellow flowers within downy purple-red calyces. Leaves to 12 in (30 cm) long, pinnate, with 7 to 13 toothed leaflets. '**Leonardii**' (syn. '**Leonard's Variety**'), soft orange-red flowers. Zones 3–9.

Geum triflorum
LION'S BEARD, OLD MAN'S WHISKERS, PRAIRIE SMOKE, PURPLE AVENS
☀/◐ ❄ ↔ 16 in (40 cm) ↕ 16 in (40 cm)
As the common names suggest, the ferny leaves of this North American species, to 6 in (15 cm) long, are gray-green and sometimes very downy. Flower stems to 16 in (40 cm) tall, with clusters of small, maroon-tinted, yellow flowers. Zones 6–9.

Geum Hybrid Cultivars
☀/◐ ❄ ↔ to 36 in (90 cm) ↕ 24 in (90 cm)
Geums hybridize freely, and although many garden forms can be traced to *G. chiloense*, some have more complicated parentage and are classified separately. Popular hybrids include: '**Beech House Apricot**', flower stems to 8 in (20 cm) tall, light yellow to apricot flowers; '**Coppertone**', pale apricot flowers; '**Fire Opal**', 30 in (75 cm), semi-double orange-red flowers; '**Lady Stratheden**', 24 in (60 cm), bright yellow double flowers; '**Mrs J. Bradshaw**' ★, 24 in (60 cm), bright red semi-double flowers; '**Starker's Magnificum**', flower stems to 16 in (40 cm), flowers soft orange-pink; '**Tangerine**', very compact, 5 in (12 cm) flower stems, bright orange flowers. Zones 6–9.

Geum aleppicum

Geum chiloense 'Werner Arends'

Geum, HC, 'Beech House Apricot'

Geum, Hybrid Cultivar, 'Coppertone'

G

Gevuina avellana

Gibbaeum album

GEVUINA

This genus, containing at least one evergreen shrub from Chile, is a member of the protea (Proteaceae) family, and has alternate pinnate leaves and flowers appearing in summer. The fruit is a red drupe, ripening to black, and is edible.
CULTIVATION: *Gevuina* prefers a sheltered woodland environment and should be fertilized sparingly. Propagation is from seed or by cuttings of green wood struck under glass.

Gevuina avellana
CHILE NUT, CHILEAN HAZEL
☼ ⬦ ↔ 25 ft (8 m) ↑ 40 ft (12 m)
Large evergreen shrub or small tree from Chile. Long branches, open habit. Large, shining, pinnate leaves, to 18 in (45 cm) long, 30 leaflets. Panicles of tubular ivory to pale buff flowers, to 1 in (25 mm) long. The coral red fruit has an edible kernel. Zones 9–10.

GIBBAEUM
syns *Imitaria, Muiria*
This genus of 17 species of succulent plants from the Karoo and Western Cape regions in South Africa belongs to the iceplant (Aizoaceae) family. These plants are compact, rarely cushion-forming, with often thickened but rarely fleshy rhizomes and roots. The 3-angled leaves have green to grayish-white surfaces; the long and weakly united leaves found on some species resemble a shark's head. The stalked single flowers come in different shades of purple, pink, or white; the calyx is a 6-lobed tube, in some species united with the 6 petals. Up to 200 to 300 stamens, along with many staminodes, form a central cone in the flower. The capsule usually has 6 compartments.
CULTIVATION: These succulents require full sun and low humidity with no water during the resting period. Best grown under cover even in warm regions. They require very sharply drained compost to minimize the risk of splitting of leaves or root rot. Propagate from seed or from cuttings allowed to dry before rooting.

Gibbaeum album
☼/◐ ⬦ ↔ 8 in (20 cm) ↑ 3–5 in (8–12 cm)
Slow-growing, clump-forming succulent. Sturdy erect stem. The 2 unequal, downy, white leaves form a swollen oval-shaped body. White or pink daisy-like flowers, in winter–spring. Leaves divide after flowering and spread to form a low mound. Zones 9–11.

Gibbaeum dispar
☼/◐ ⬦ ↔ 4–6 in (10–15 cm) ↑ 4–6 in (10–15 cm)
Erect, sturdy, clump-forming stem. Unequal pairs of leaves form a velvety, slightly glossy, egg-shaped body, gray-green tinged with red, with a deep fissure. The open, daisy-like, mauve-red to pink flowers are about ¼ in (6 mm) across. Zones 9–11.

Gibbaeum gibbosum
☼/◐ ⬦ ↔ 4–6 in (10–15 cm) ↑ 4–6 in (10–15 cm)
Branching prostrate stems, forming dense clumps. Unequal pairs of smooth deep green to yellowish green leaves form semi-cylindrical body with flattened top. Reddish to pinkish purple flowers, spring–summer. Zones 9–11.

Gibbaeum heathii
☼/◐ ⬦ ↔ 8 in (20 cm) ↑ 2–4 in (5–10 cm)
Spreading mat-forming species, with a long rootstock. Pairs of unequal leaves form a smooth, spherical, bright green body with a split in the center. Daisy-like flowers, cream to pinkish or purple, appear in winter. Zones 9–11.

Gibbaeum pilosulum
syns *Conophytum pilosulum, Mesembryanthemum pilosulum*
☼/◐ ⬦ ↔ 8 in (20 cm) ↑ 3–5 in (8–12 cm)
Mat-forming, with fused leaves forming slightly glossy, light green, egg-shaped bodies, covered with fine white hairs, with small notch, ½ in (12 mm) long, in the top of each. Small mauve-red flowers in winter. Zones 9–12.

Gibbaeum velutinum
syns *Mentocalyx velutinum, Mesembryanthemum velutinum*
☼/◐ ⬦ ↔ 8–12 in (20–30 cm) ↑ 3–5 in (8–12 cm)
Spreading mat-forming species. Light gray to grayish green, finger-like, velvety leaves, joined at the base, rest on the soil surface. Longer leaf is hooked and ridged, shorter leaf is triangular. White, pink, lilac, or mauve-red, daisy-like flowers, 2 in (5 cm) across, spring–autumn. Zones 9–12.

GILLENIA
A North American genus of 2 species of rhizome-rooted perennials in the rose (Rosaceae) family. They form shrubby clumps of upright, arching, branching stems bearing stemless trifoliate leaves with toothed leaflets that turn orange in autumn. Loose sprays of 5-petaled flowers appear from spring into summer, with calyces that last long after the flowers have fallen, enlarging and reddening as the small seed heads develop. Root extracts are sometimes used medicinally but are potentially dangerous.
CULTIVATION: *Gillenia* species are very hardy but best protected from hot sun. They are easily grown in woodland conditions with dappled light and moist, humus-rich, well-drained soil. Propagate from seed, which should be stratified, or by dividing established clumps as they enter or leave dormancy in autumn or spring.

Gillenia trifoliata
BOWMAN'S ROOT, INDIAN PHYSIC
☼ ✳ ↔ 48 in (120 cm) ↑ 48 in (120 cm)
Found in eastern North America, from Ontario to Georgia. Leaves with serrated pointed oval leaflets to nearly 3 in (8 cm) long. Flowers to 1 in (25 mm) wide, white, sometimes pink- or purple-tinted. Zones 4–9.

GINKGO
A primitive genus containing a single species and given its own family, Ginkgoaceae, *Ginkgo* is quite different from all other conifers. Fossil records show it to be very ancient. Now unknown in the wild, it was certainly grown in China in the eleventh century; some specimens are believed to be well over 1,000 years old. The foliage resembles that of the maidenhair fern, hence the common name. Pollination is achieved by motile spores, a feature unknown among the higher plants, but normal among

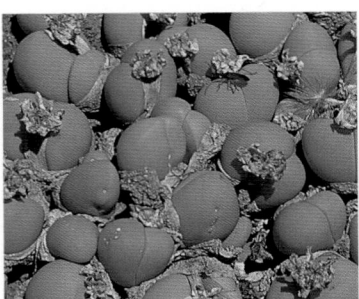

Gibbaeum heathii

Gibbaeum pilosulum

ferns. Male and female flowers are carried on separate trees. The fruits are edible, nutritious, and are a source of various medicinal substances. CULTIVATION: This attractive tree prefers hot summers but tolerates a range of conditions, including atmospheric pollution, giving it potential as a street tree. Plant in well-draining soil in full sun. Propagate from seed or half-hardened summer cuttings.

Ginkgo biloba
GINKGO, MAIDENHAIR TREE

☀ ❄ ↔ 25 ft (8 m) ↑ 100 ft (30 m)
Deciduous, very long lived, crown only developing fully after the first 100 years. Fronds fan-shaped, parallel veins spreading out from the stalk. Male flowers, pendulous short-stalked catkins. Fruit yellow-green, unpleasant odor when decaying. Foliage turns a beautiful golden yellow in autumn. 'Aurea', yellow leaves in summer; 'Autumn Gold' ★, broadly conical in shape, leaves turn gold in autumn; 'Fastigiata', an erect male cultivar that grows to 30 ft (9 m) in height; **Pendula Group** members have nodding branches; 'Tremonia', strongly erect form, very narrow crown; **Variegata Group** members have bold streaks of whitish yellow on the leaves. Zones 3–10.

Ginkgo biloba

Ginkgo biloba 'Fastigiata'

GLADIOLUS
SWORD LILY

Think *Gladiolus,* and large-flowered hybrids, derived mainly from South African species, come to mind. But this genus in the iris (Iridaceae) family includes around 180 species of corms found from Europe to western Asia and South Africa, many quite different from the showy hybrids. Those with less colorful flowers are sometimes scented. The name *Gladiolus* comes from the Latin *gladius* (sword). CULTIVATION: A rule of thumb is to plant the corms at 4 times their own depth. Plant in full sun with light well-drained soil. In cold areas corms will survive outdoors if planted below freezing depth, otherwise lift and store dry for winter. *Gladiolus* produce tiny cormlets and propagation is simply a matter of growing these cormlets on.

Gladiolus callianthus

☀/◐ ✿ ↔ 12 in (30 cm) ↑ 40 in (100 cm)
From tropical East Africa. Narrow leaves, to around 20 in (50 cm) long. Scented, red- or purple-marked, white flowers, to just over 2 in (5 cm) wide, up to 10 per stem, from early autumn. Zones 10–11.

Gladiolus communis

☀/◐ ❄ ↔ 12 in (30 cm) ↑ 40 in (100 cm)
Southern European native. Narrow leaves to around half of the flower stem length. Flowerheads usually with 2 to 3 branches, up to 20 red- or white-marked pink flowers. *G. c.*
subsp. *byzantinus* ★ has long, pink-marked, purple-red flowers on less branching stems. Zones 6–10.

Gladiolus murielae

☀/◐ ❄ ↔ 20 in (50 cm) ↑ 40 in (100 cm)
From Ethiopia. Compact clump of upright, broad, spear-shaped leaves to 20 in (50 cm). Many erect flower stems with solitary or paired, fragrant, white flowers with maroon blotch, in late summer–autumn. Zones 8–10.

Gladiolus tristis
MARSH AFRIKANER

☀/◐ ❄ ↔ 12 in (30 cm) ↑ 24 in (60 cm)
South African species. Narrow leaves, thickened midrib, often twisting at tips. Up to 20 often widely spaced cream to yellow flowers, sometimes marked purple or maroon, on wiry stems. Scented in evening. Zones 7–10.

Gladiolus communis subsp. *byzantinus*

Gladiolus murielae

Gladiolus callianthus

Gladiolus tristis

Gladiolus Hybrid Cultivars

☀ ❄ ↔ 12 in (30 cm) ↑ 2–5 ft (0.6–1.5 m)

It is estimated that some 10,000 *Gladiolus* hybrids have been raised. They are divided into groups with similar characteristics. The classifications vary in different parts of the world but most recognize just 3 main styles. Hardiness varies with the hybrids, though most will withstand overwintering in the ground provided the soil does not freeze to corm depth.

GRANDIFLORUS GROUP

The common gladioli seen in gardens with their showy flowers belong to this group. They are sometimes subdivided by the size of the flower.

Small-flowered: Flowers less than 3 in (8 cm) across, such as 'Goldfinch', 24 in (60 cm) tall, yellow ruffled flowers.

Medium-flowered: Flowers to 3–4 in (8–10 cm) across, such as 'Candyman', 27 in (70 cm) tall, pink flowers; 'Green Woodpecker', soft yellow-green flowers, contrasting red throat; 'Lady Lucille', to 32 in (80 cm) tall, light-centered pink flowers, over 20 blooms per stem; 'Midnight Moon', 32 in (80 cm) tall, dark purple-blue flowers marked with white; 'Shiloh', cream-edged deep pink with red blotch; 'Sundoro', to 30 in (75 cm) high, yellow flowers with red markings; 'Sunsport', 27 in (70 cm) tall, yellow and creamy ivory, more than 20 blooms per stem; and 'Tahiti Sunrise', to 27 in (70 cm) tall, yellow-throated straw-colored flowers, pink-edged.

Large-flowered: Reaching 40–48 in (100–120 cm) tall with flowers to 6 in (15 cm) across, such as 'Doris Darling', with long-stemmed heads of up to 25 ruffled pink flowers; 'Her Majesty', white-throated mauve to lavender flowers; 'Madison Avenue', orange-red flowers; 'Nova Lux', lemon yellow flowers; 'Peerless', intense deep red, regarded as the standard for the color; and 'Saxony', with yellow-throated apricot flowers.

Giant-flowered: Around 48 in (120 cm) tall, flowers more than 6 in (15 cm) across, such as 'Amsterdam', pure white flowers; and 'Dream's End', yellow-centered apricot flowers. Zones 9–11.

NANUS GROUP

Also known as **Miniature Hybrids**. Up to 36 in (90 cm) but often less than 24 in (60 cm) tall, with dense heads of flowers to 2 in (5 cm) across. Popular forms include: 'Charm', pink flowers with chartreuse blotches; and 'Nymph', pale pink flowers with dark edges and cream marks. Zones 9–11.

PRIMULINUS GROUP

Seldom exceed 24 in (60 cm) tall. Very narrow leaves. Single wiry stem of small flowers with a conspicuously hooded upper petal. Forms often seen include: 'Frank's Perfection', spaced bright red flowers; 'Lady Godiva', white flowers; and 'Pegasus', yellow flowers tipped with red. Zones 9–11.

GLAUCIDIUM

This genus in the peony (Paeoniaceae) family contains just 1 species, a rhizome-rooted summer-flowering perennial from Japan. It forms a small clump of stiffly upright stems to around 12 in (30 cm) high that carry pairs of kidney- to heart-shaped leaves with 7 to 11 pointed and toothed palmate lobes. The flowers are borne on separate taller stems, each with 1 flower subtended by 2 small leaves. The flowers occur in pastel shades of mauve and lavender, have 4 petal-like sepals, are around 3 in (8 cm) wide, and open from late spring.

Gladiolus, Hybrid Cultivar, Grandiflorus Group, 'Her Majesty'

G., HC, Grandiflorus Group, 'Nova Lux'

G., HC, Grandiflorus Group, 'Blue Bird'

G., HC, Grandiflorus, 'Eurovision'

G., HC, Grandiflorus, 'Gold Field'

G., HC, Grandiflorus, 'Priscilla'

G., HC, Grandiflorus, 'Saxony'

G., HC, Grandiflorus, 'Amsterdam'

Glaucidium palmatum

Glaucium flavum

CULTIVATION: Hardy and easily grown if given woodland conditions and a moist cool-temperate climate. Intolerant of prolonged heat, drought or low humidity and best sheltered from wind. Propagate from seed sown in spring after stratification or by dividing established clumps in late winter or early spring just before growth recommences.

Glaucidium palmatum

☀/☀ ❄ ↔20 in (50 cm) ↑18 in (45 cm)
Leaves to 8 in (20 cm) wide, deep green, heavily veined, sharply lobed. Cup-shaped flowers on stems to 18 in (45 cm) tall. The white-flowered *G. p.* var. *leucanthemum* (syn. 'Album') is probably more widely cultivated than the species. Zones 6–9.

GLAUCIUM
HORNED POPPY, SEA POPPY

This poppy (Papaveraceae) family genus of around 25 species of annuals, biennials, and perennials is found from Europe to North Africa, central and western Asia, often in coastal areas. Similar in general appearance to poppies but clearly differentiated by the long horn-shaped seed capsules that follow the flowers. Most species have blue-green leaves, toothed and often pinnately lobed, in a basal rosette. Upright, sometimes branching, flower stems with small leaves emerge from the rosette in summer, and carry 4-petalled flowers, usually 2–4 in (5–10 cm) wide, in warm shades of yellow, orange, or red. The stems exude orange latex when cut.
CULTIVATION: These plants are hardy to moderate frosts and very easily grown in any temperate climate with reasonably warm summers. Plant in full sun with light, rather gritty, free-draining soil. Most species, even the perennials, are raised from seed and may self-sow, though rarely invasively.

Glaucium flavum
YELLOW-HORNED POPPY

☀ ❄ ↔16 in (40 cm) ↑40 in (100 cm)
Biennial or short-lived perennial from Europe, North Africa, and the Middle East. Finely hairy, pinnately lobed, toothed, blue-green leaves. Branching stems with bright yellow or orange flowers, to 2 in (5 cm) wide. Very narrow curved seed pods, to 12 in (30 cm) long. Zones 7–10.

GLEDITSIA
LOCUST

There are 14 species of deciduous trees in this genus from the cassia subfamily of the legume (Fabaceae) family, native to North and South America, central and eastern Asia, Iran, and parts of Africa. All have fern-like, pinnately or bipinnately arranged leaves, and stout, sometimes branching, thorns on the trunk and branches. Flowers are insignificant and followed by seed pods of varying lengths. In some species the pods contain a sweet pulp.
CULTIVATION: *Gleditsia* species grow best on a sunny site in moderately fertile soil that is moisture retentive, and may require frost protection when young. However, they are generally very tough, tolerating a range of soils and climates and are pollution resistant. Species are propagated from seed sown in autumn, while cultivars are grafted or budded.

Gleditsia caspica
CASPIAN LOCUST

☀ ❄ ↔35 ft (10 m) ↑40 ft (12 m)
Native to northern Iran near the Caspian Sea. Well armed with branching thorns, 6 in (15 cm) or more long. Tiny greenish flowers densely packed on downy racemes, thin scythe-shaped seed pods to 8 in (20 cm) long. 'Nana' is an interesting cultivar of the species. Zones 6–10.

Gleditsia japonica

Gleditsia japonica
JAPANESE LOCUST

☀ ❄ ↔35 ft (10 m) ↑70 ft (21 m)
Native of Japan and China. Well armed with branching thorns. Seed pods to 12 in (30 cm) long, often twisted at maturity. *G. j.* var. *koraiensis* comes from eastern China. Zones 6–10.

Gleditsia triacanthos
HONEY LOCUST, THORNLESS HONEY LOCUST

☀ ❄ ↔70 ft (21 m) ↑150 ft (45 m)
Common in cultivation. Native of central and eastern USA. Fern-like foliage bright green, turning clear bright yellow in autumn. Thorns up to 12 in (30 cm). *G. t. f. inermis* is thornless—nearly all cultivars of honey locust are derived from it. 'Elegantissima', very compact, almost shrub-like, fine foliage, very slow-growing, rarely exceeds 15 ft (4.5 m) tall; 'Emerald Cascade', weeping tree, dark emerald green foliage turns bright yellow in autumn; 'Halka', fast-growing thornless selection, high, rather narrow crown; fine yellow color in autumn; 'Marando', dwarfed cultivar with spreading twisted branches; 'Moraine' ★, tall, shapely, thornless

tree, broadly spreading lower branches, dense ferny foliage; 'Rubylace', dark red young foliage, bronzing as it ages; 'Shademaster', broad-crowned upright tree, deep green leaves persisting late in autumn; 'Skyline', symmetrical outline, developing a broadly conical crown, dark green leaves, golden yellow in autumn; 'Sunburst', bright yellow young leaves becoming lime green as season progresses. Zones 3–10.

Gleditsia triacanthos f. *inermis* 'Halka'

G. t. f. inermis 'Sunburst', in spring

G. t. f. inermis 'Sunburst', in summer

Gleditsia japonica var. *koraiensis*

Globularia cordifolia

Globularia incanescens

GLEICHENIA

This genus of 10 species of bracken-like ferns found from South Africa to New Zealand, belongs to the coral-fern (Gleicheniaceae) family. The branching, widely creeping rhizomes are clad with hairs and scales. Slender branching fronds grow from the narrow erect stalks.

CULTIVATION: Plant in light moist soil in a protected shady position. Propagate from spores or by division.

Gleichenia microphylla

SCRAMBLING CORAL FERN

☀ ❄ ↔ 3–7 ft (0.9–2 m)
↕ 5–8 ft (1.5–2.4 m)

Freely scrambling fern from New Zealand, Australia, and Malaysia. Flat pale green fronds, up to 10 ft (3 m) long, with a darker midrib, fork repeatedly, on warty reddish stems. Zones 9–11.

GLOBBA

There are about 70 species of tender fleshy-stemmed perennials in this genus, which belongs to the ginger (Zingiberaceae) family. They are native to forested areas of southeastern Asia and northeastern India. The lance-shaped to oblong leaves are carried on reed-like stems to 3 ft (0.9 m) tall. Pendulous terminal racemes bear odd-shaped flowers, often spurred, with protruding stamens and colorful bracts. Bulbils often form on the lower part of the flowering spike.

CULTIVATION: In warm areas grow these plants outdoors in a shady well-drained situation. In cooler climates start plants indoors in spring and place outside after danger of frost has passed, or grow indoors in bright indirect light with high humidity. Propagate from the bulbils produced on the flowering stems.

Globba winitii

☀ ❄ ↔ 24 in (60 cm) ↕ 36 in (90 cm)

From Thailand. The most commonly grown species. Long leaves, heart-shaped bases, hairy beneath. Flowers have magenta bracts with yellow floral parts. Zones 9–11.

GLOBULARIA

There are about 22 species of evergreen herbaceous plants and shrublets in this genus belonging to the globe-daisy (Globulariaceae) family, which is native to Europe, the Cape Verde and Canary Islands, and western Asia. The majority of these species grow in open rocky places, but some are high-altitude or alpine plants. In cultivation they do well in the front of borders but are also useful in troughs, and in alpine and rock gardens.

Globularia nudicaulis

CULTIVATION: These plants need neutral or slightly alkaline soil and grow best in full sun. Good drainage is necessary, especially in wetter areas, and they require protection in winter. Propagate by sowing seed into pots in autumn, as soon as ripe, with protection from winter frosts; by division into individual rosettes in spring or early summer; or from softwood cuttings in spring, or half-hardened cuttings in summer.

Globularia cordifolia

☀ ❄ ↔ 8 in (20 cm) ↕ 2 in (5 cm)

Dwarf evergreen species from southern and central Europe. Shiny dark green leaves, in rosettes that root along the ground. Lavender-blue flowers, nearly stemless, through most of the summer. Less robust than *G. meridionalis*. Zones 6–9.

Globularia incanescens

☀ ❄ ↔ 24–36 in (60–90 cm)
↕ 1¼–4 in (3–10 cm)

Native to northern Italy, this evergreen creeper has a prostrate, mat-forming stem, growing from a tall slender rhizome. The leaves are rounded to sword-shaped, and grayish green. The flowers are small, blue, and daisy-like. The fruit is a narrow capsule. Zones 7–10.

Globularia meridionalis

syns *Globularia bellidifolia*, *G. cordifolia* subsp. *meridionalis*

☀ ❄ ↔ 12 in (30 cm) ↕ 4 in (10 cm)

Mat-forming woody evergreen, native to the mountains of southern Europe. Shiny dark green leaves, shaped like an inverted lance. Globular lavender-purple flowerheads, stand up above the leaves, in summer. Zones 6–9.

Globularia nudicaulis

☀ ❄ ↔ 20 in (50 cm) ↕ 12 in (30 cm)

Native of the Alps and Pyrenees. Leaves erect, massed around the base of the stem, inversely lance- or egg-shaped. Flower stems reach 12 in (30 cm) high. Flowers pale blue to lavender. Zones 5–9.

Globularia repens

☀ ❄ ↔ 6 in (15 cm) ↕ 2 in (5 cm)

Dwarf creeping subshrub from southwestern Europe. Rosettes of folded spatula-shaped leaves. Small, blue, daisy-like flowers, on stalks ½–2 in (12–50 mm) long. Fruit is a narrow capsule. Zones 5–7.

GLOCHIDION

There are 300 species in this genus, part of the euphorbia (Euphorbiaceae) family, occurring in a variety of habitats from Madagascar to Asia, Australia, the western Pacific, and tropical America. All are shrubs or trees, some with male and female flowers on different plants, others with both sexes on the same plant. The leaves are simple and smooth-edged, but are held on the stems in a way that gives the appearance of a compound leaf.

CULTIVATION: The tropical species require well-drained organic soils and year-round water in sheltered positions. Those species from more temperate regions are able to tolerate

Gleichenia microphylla

Glottiphyllym longum

Glottiphyllym linguiforme

somewhat lower temperatures, but still need shelter from hot dry winds. Propagation is by very fresh seed.

Glochidion puberum

☀ ⬧ ↔ 15 ft (4.5 m) ↑ 10–30 ft (3–9 m)
From scrub-covered hills of southern China. Deciduous shrub or small tree noteworthy mainly for its use in Chinese herbal medicine, particularly for the treatment of female infertility. Zones 9–12.

GLORIOSA

CAT'S CLAW, CLIMBING LILY, FLAME LILY, GLORY LILY

This genus from the autumn-crocus (Colchicaceae) family presently consists of a single, highly variable, tuberous, perennial species from tropical Africa and Asia. The climbing scrambling plant ascends by means of glossy emerald leaves that taper into coiling clinging tendrils. The showy single flowers, which appear in late summer and autumn, are held on short stems that emerge from the leaf axils. Petals are recurved, widely separated, and bright yellow, red, or purple. Bicolors are common. All plant parts are toxic.
CULTIVATION: Glory lilies require good drainage and full sun to half-sun. Plant the large, red-brown, fang-shaped tubers in a horizontal position, taking great care as they are dangerously brittle. Water plentifully when in growth and liquid feed with weak solution every 2 weeks.

Gloriosa superba

CLIMBING LILY, CREEPING LILY, GLORY LILY
☀ ⬧ ↔ 12–20 in (30–50 cm)
↑ 6–8 ft (1.8–2.4 m)
Tuberous perennial vine with 1 to 4 slender, scrambling, bright green stems, native to tropical Africa and Asia. Soft, oval- to spear-shaped, glossy, bright green leaves, 2–3 in (5–8 cm) long, with tendrils, 1¼–2 in (3–5 cm) long, at leaf tips. Flowers are solitary, yellow, red, purple, or bicolored, 1¾–4 in (4–10 cm) long, on long stalks, from summer–autumn. Many cultivars including: 'Citrina', with yellow flowers striped with maroon; 'Grandiflora', with large golden yellow flowers; 'Rothschildiana' ★, with bright red or scarlet petals fading to garnet and purple, yellow near the base and at margins, completely recurved, undulating; and 'Simplex', with deep orange and yellow flowers. Zones 9–12.

GLOTTIPHYLLUM

This genus of around 60 species from the Karoo and Cape regions of South Africa belongs to the iceplant (Aizoaceae) family. They are compact succulent plants with semi-prostrate forking stems. Leaves are very fleshy, tongue-shaped or cylindrical, sometimes of different lengths, in 2 or 4 ranks, bright glossy green or whitish, sometimes tinged purple. The single yellow flowers, sometimes stalked, are borne in summer.
CULTIVATION: These succulent plants are easily grown in low-fertility compost as long as it is well drained; little watering is required. Too much water or too many nutrients lead to lush watery leaves that are prone to damage from handling, rots, and winter cold. Plant in full sun and keep completely dry from late summer until spring. Propagate from seed or cuttings, allowing them to dry out well before rooting.

Glottiphyllym linguiforme

syns *Mesembryanthemum linguiforme, M. lucidum, M. scalpratum*
☀ ⬧ ↔ 8 in (20 cm) ↑ 3–5 in (8–12 cm)
Mat-forming perennial with pairs of curved, glossy, fleshy, apple green, unequal leaves, 2–2½ in (5–6 cm) long, with a rounded tip. Golden yellow flowers, 3 in (8 cm) wide, in autumn. Zones 9–11.

Glottiphyllym longum

☀ ⬧ ↔ 8 in (20 cm) ↑ 4–6 in (10–15 cm)
Perennial species. Pairs of fleshy leaves, 3–4 in (8–10 cm) long. Golden yellow flowers, 2½–3 in (6–8 cm) wide, in autumn. Zones 9–11.

Glottiphyllym nelii

syn. *Gibbaeum pygmaeum*
☀ ⬧ ↔ 12 in (30 cm) ↑ 1–6 in (2.5–15 cm)
A rambling perennial that forms rounded clumps. It has unequal, semi-cylindrical, fleshy, light green, erect leaves, 1½–2 in (3.5–5 cm) long, with rounded tips. Daisy-like golden yellow flowers, 1½ in (3.5 cm) across, in spring–summer. Zones 9–11.

GLOXINIA

Not to be confused with *Sinningia*, the genus that includes the florist's gloxinia, this group of some 8 species of perennials and subshrubs in the African violet (Gesneriaceae) family occurs in Central America and tropical South America. Mostly small plants that form bushy clumps of stems bearing opposite pairs of simple pointed oval leaves, often finely toothed. The stems and foliage are usually covered with fine velvety hairs. Single or paired funnel- or bell-shaped flowers appear in the leaf axils and occur throughout most of the year.
CULTIVATION: Attractive plants that adapt well to pot cultivation; outside the tropics usually grown as house or greenhouse plants. They prefer even warm temperatures, freedom from cool drafts, and ample humidity. Plant in half-sun or full shade in moist, humus-rich, free-draining soil. Can be propagated from their very fine seeds or from stem or leaf cuttings.

Gloxinia perennis

◑ ⬧ ↔ 15 in (38 cm) ↑ 24 in (60 cm)
Rhizomatous perennial from Colombia to Peru. Narrow, erect, heart-shaped, hairy, toothed leaves in pairs, to 8 in (20 cm) long, pale red underneath. Solitary lower flowers, upper flowers in racemes with bell-shaped pale purple corollas, to 1½ in (35 mm) long, with purple-blotched throat, late summer–autumn. Zones 10–12.

Glochidion puberum

Gloriosa superba 'Rothschildiana'

Gloxinia sylvatica

☀ ✤ ↔ 24 in (60 cm) ↑ 24 in (60 cm)
Native to Bolivia and Peru. Mounds, then spreads by runners, to become slightly trailing. Lustrous, narrow, lance-shaped leaves, tapering to a long fine point. Throughout the cooler months, orange-red to red bell-shaped flowers, to 1 in (25 mm) long, held clear of the foliage, in terminal clusters. '**Bolivian Sunset**', red flowers with orange interior. Zones 10–12.

GLYCERIA
MANNA GRASS, MEADOW GRASS, SWEET GRASS

A genus of 16 species of perennial marsh grasses (family Poaceae) that will grow in shallow water. Distribution is widespread throughout the northern temperate zones and temperate regions of South America, Australia, and New Zealand. They spread by rhizomes, from which develop reed-like stems bearing long, strappy, succulent leaves. Large flower plumes, often purple-tinted, develop in summer, followed by edible small seeds.
CULTIVATION: Sweet grass species are mostly frost hardy and easily grown in any temperate climate. Plant in full sun with moist humus-rich soil. Although naturally adapted to damp conditions, they will grow well enough in regular garden soils if they are kept moist. Useful as marginal

Gloxinia sylvatica 'Bolivian Sunset'

Gloxinia sylvatica

pond plants and for stabilizing easily eroded stream banks. Propagate from seed or by division.

Glyceria maxima

syns *Glyceria aquatica, Molinia maxima, Poa aquatica*

REED MEADOW GRASS, REED SWEET GRASS
☀ ❄ ↔ unlimited ↑ 1–8 ft (0.3–2.4 m)
Spreading, rhizomatous, perennial grass, native to temperate Europe and Asia, from the British Isles to Japan. Forms large stands of erect stems, unbranched. Narrowly strap-shaped leaves, to 24 in (60 cm) long, with a central ridge. Panicles of creamy greenish flowers, sometimes with purplish or purplish green tones, appear in summer. *G. m.* var. *variegata* (reed manna grass, striped manna grass), cream-striped green leaves tinged with pink toward the base. Zones 3–5.

GLYCINE
SOYA BEAN, SOYBEAN

From Asia and Australia, this genus belongs to the pea-flower subfamily of the legume (Fabaceae) family. Although it includes some 9 to 18 species of perennials, some of them twining semi-climbers, it is known in cultivation for just one, *G. max*, the soya bean, which has been cultivated for more than 5,000 years and is most likely a hybrid. All species have trifoliate leaves but can produce foliage with up to 7 leaflets. The flowers, clustered in small inflorescences, are typically pea-flower-like, usually mauve or pink. They are followed by pods with 2 to 4 seeds: the all-important beans can be used to produce a huge range of products.
CULTIVATION: To thrive, these tender plants must be kept growing steadily and without check. They need hot humid conditions and moist humus-rich soil. Water and feed well. Propagate from seed or cuttings of non-flowering basal shoots.

Glycine canescens

Glycine canescens

syns *Glycine sericea, G. sericea* var. *orthotrica, Leptocyamus sericeus*
☀ ⚘ ↔ 2 ft (0.6 m) ↑ 3–5 ft (0.9–1.5 m)
Widespread variable species, found in all mainland states of Australia, predominantly in regions away from the coasts. Herbaceous perennial twiner, woody rootstock. Leaves with 3 leaflets, each up to 3 in (8 cm) long, linear, hairy, grayish. Flowers pink to purplish, on axillary inflorescences, during winter–summer. Fruits are pods with grayish hairs. Zones 9–10.

Glycine max

syn. *Glycine soja*
MANCHURIAN BEAN, SOJA BEAN, SOYA BEAN, SOYBEAN
☀ ❄ ↔ 3 ft (0.9 m) ↑ 4–7 ft (1.2–2 m)
Erect annual from the northeast of China. Compound leaves with oval leaflets up to 6 in (15 cm) long. Heads of 8 white to violet or pink pea-flowers, to 8 mm long. Hanging pods, to 3 in (8 cm) long, contain 2 to 4 rounded or flattened seeds. All parts are covered with fine reddish brown hairs. One of the world's most important oilseed crops and a staple food in Asia. Zones 7–8.

GLYCYRRHIZA

There are 20 species of perennial herbs in this genus, which belongs to the pea-flower subfamily of the legume (Fabaceae) family. They have pinnate leaves and small pea-like flowers of white, violet, or yellow. Although not common in the garden, one species, *G. glabra*, is grown for its sweet root,

Glyceria maxima var. *variegata*

Glyptostrobus pensilis

licorice. This is used in confectionery making and in medicines that relieve coughs and other cold symptoms.
CULTIVATION: Grow these plants in full sun in rich, deeply cultivated, well-drained soil. Propagate from seed or division.

Glycyrrhiza glabra

LICORICE, LIQUORICE, SWEETWOOD
☀ ❄ ↔ 36 in (90 cm) ↑ 36 in (90 cm)
Found from Mediterranean areas to southwestern Asia. Rather coarse deep-rooting plant with pinnately divided sticky leaves and loose spikes of pale blue to violet pea-flowers in summer. The thick dark reddish brown roots are harvested in autumn. Zones 7–9.

GLYPTOSTROBUS

There is just a single species in this genus, allied to *Taxodium*, within the cypress (Cupressaceae) family. This tree is grown in China and northern Vietnam at the edges of riverbanks and rice paddies to stabilize the banks.
CULTIVATION: Ideal for planting in wet sites, beside water features, and riverbank planting, *Glyptostrobus* needs moist marshy soil and will even grow in shallow water. When green wood is damaged by frost, multiple stems can be produced. In moist warm climates with long, hot, humid summers it can be grown from seed. In acid soil, cuttings can be taken or it should be grafted onto *Taxodium*. The graft should be below water or soil level to encourage root growth.

Glyptostrobus pensilis

CHINESE SWAMP CYPRESS
☀ ❄ ↔ 20 ft (6 m) ↑ 80 ft (24 m)
Originally native to southeastern China and northern Vietnam, probably extinct in the wild. Conical or

Gomphocarpus physocarpus

Gnetum gnemon

columnar in shape, with an irregular open canopy. Deciduous tree; gray bark. Fine, pale green, new spring foliage, turns red-brown in autumn. Male cones form clusters of tassels; female cones erect, pear-shaped. Zones 8–11.

GNETUM

This genus of 28 woody climbing plants and trees or shrubs, gives its name to the family Gnetaceae. It is found in tropical Africa and Southeast Asia. Male and female flowers are on the same or separate plants, with the male flowers carried in distinctive catkins. As well as having ornamental value, *G. gnemon* is cultivated in Indonesia where the seeds are beaten and fried like potato chips.
CULTIVATION: *Gnetum* species prefer rich, moist, well-drained soils in a partially shaded or open position. Propagation is from seed.

Gnetum gnemon

☀ ✤ ↔ 20 ft (6 m) ↕ 60 ft (18 m)
Evergreen tree from tropical Asia. Pyramidal crown, gray bark. Leaves 3–8 in (8–20 cm) long, bronze when young, maturing with age to glossy dark green. Yellow fruit ripens to red tinged with orange. Zones 10–12.

GOMPHOCARPUS

MILKWEED, SWAN PLANT
Consisting of only several species, this small group, native to southern Africa, has often been classified under the genus *Asclepias*. These short-lived perennial shrubs belong to the milk-weed (Asclepiadaceae) family, and are often found growing in disturbed soil as a roadside weed. All species produce an irritating milky sap, which contains toxic cardiac glycosides, known to cause death of livestock. Despite this fact, the genus itself has a history in traditional African medicine, the dried leaves and roots being used to alleviate headache. The genus has also generated some interest in the West as an ornamental due to the butterfly-attracting ability of some species, as well as their decorative seed pods, often floated in bowls in place of flowers.
CULTIVATION: These plants prefer a sunny well-drained situation, in soil that is somewhat deficient in nutrients. Propagate from seed; harvest seed pods for decoration while green, and ripe seed as the pods turn brown in mid-summer.

Gomphocarpus physocarpus

syn. *Asclepias physocarpa*
BALLOON COTTON BUSH, SWAN PLANT, TINDER PLANT
☀ ✤ ↔ 1 ft (0.3 m) ↕ 7 ft (2 m)
Upright perennial shrub, often grown as an annual. Narrow leaves to 4 in (10 cm) long. Cream flowers, to 15 mm wide, borne in clusters during spring, followed by large inflated seed pods to 2½ in (60 mm) long. The decorative seed pods contribute to the popularity of this species as a greenhouse specimen. The fibers contained

within the seed pods were used by Afrikaans settlers as a valuable source of tinder. Zones 9–11.

GOMPHOLOBIUM

This is a genus of about 30 species in the pea-flower subfamily of the legume (Fabaceae) family, all endemic to Australia except for one that occurs in New Guinea. All are small woody shrubs with either narrow simple leaves or compound leaves with 3 leaflets. The flowers are relatively large, up to 1½ in (35 mm) across, and are bright yellow, greenish, or deep pink in color, occurring generally in spring. The fruits are egg-shaped green pods containing several seeds and ripen in summer. Habitats vary from sclerophyllous heaths to woodlands and forest margins on soils ranging from low-nutrient sands to rich loams.
CULTIVATION: Keeping plants of some species growing is a little tricky. Best results seem to come with part-shade, exceedingly well-drained soils, and reasonably dry conditions generally. Propagation is from pre-treated seed, which germinates well.

Gompholobium latifolium

Gompholobium latifolium

GOLDEN GLORY PEA
☀ ✽ ↔ 3 ft (0.9 m) ↕ 7 ft (2 m)
Found in dry sclerophyll forests, on a range of soils, in eastern Australia from Queensland to Victoria. Trifoliate leaves, narrow leaflets, to 2 in (5 cm) long. Yellow pea-flowers, to 2 in (5 cm) across, in terminal and axillary groups of 2 or 3 blossoms. Pods to ¾ in (18 mm) long. Prune after flowering. Zones 8–10.

GOMPHRENA

Native to tropical parts of the Americas and Australia, the 90-odd annuals and perennials in this genus are members of the amaranth

G

Gordonia axillaris

Goodia lotifolia

(Amaranthaceae) family. However, unlike the long pendulous flower tassels of many amaranths, *Gomphrena* flowers are borne in small, usually upright, heads. The cultivated species form bushy mounds with leaves that are simple narrow oblongs in opposite pairs. The stems are finely hairy, the leaves less so. The flowerheads are borne on wiry stems and held just above the foliage. Each head is a short plume of many tiny flowers, usually creamy yellow, mauve, or pink in the species, with cultivated forms available in most colors.
CULTIVATION: Outside the tropics these plants are treated as summer annuals; they need long warm summers to flower well. Plant in moist humus-rich soil and water well, but do not overfeed. Propagate from seed.

Gomphrena globosa
BACHELOR'S BUTTON, GLOBE AMARANTH
☀ ❄ ↔ 18 in (45 cm) ↕ 24 in (60 cm)
From Panama and Guatemala. Bushy annual with slightly hairy pointed leaves. Flowers papery and round, resembling a clover flower, white through to red, purple, and yellow, borne in summer. 'Lavender Lady', lavender-colored flowers; 'Strawberry Fields', flowers of scarlet to crimson. Zones 7–11.

Gomphrena haageana
☀ ❄ ↔ 20 in (50 cm) ↕ 27 in (70 cm)
From southern USA and Mexico. Well-branched perennial, usually grown as an annual. Leaves hairy. Spherical papery flowers, pale rusty red. 'Amber Glow', flowers tending to orange shades; 'Strawberry Fair', redder flowers. Zones 7–11.

GONGORA
The sympodial orchid genus *Gongora* is distributed throughout Central and

South America, from Mexico to Peru and Brazil. They are related to *Stanhopea* and, like that genus, are increasing in popularity. They are best grown in hanging baskets, or in pots that are suspended by hangers, due to the long pendulous inflorescences that are a feature of most of the 80 or so species. The flowers are relatively short-lived, rarely lasting for more than a week. Interestingly, the flowers rarely wither on the spike like most orchids; they drop their blooms when they have had enough. The shapes of the blooms are fairly similar, but the range of colors is significant. Most species flower in spring to summer.
CULTIVATION: Most gongoras like warm humid conditions with plenty of air circulation. They can be grown in a bark-based mix or in sphagnum moss. These plants enjoy being kept moist and relatively shaded, as direct sunlight will scorch the broad thin leaves. Propagate by division.

Gongora histrionica
☀ ✤ ↔ 27 in (70 cm) ↕ 36 in (90 cm)
From Costa Rica to Colombia. Has a long, hanging spike with up to 25 golden yellow blooms, 2 in (5 cm) wide, which are heavily blotched and spotted with dark reddish brown. Zones 11–12.

GOODIA
This is a genus of 2 species in the pea-flower subfamily of the legume (Fabaceae) family, both endemic to Australia, with distribution mainly in coastal regions from southern Queensland to the Yorke and Eyre Peninsulas in South Australia. The genus was named after Peter Good, the English gardener and plant collector who died in Sydney in 1803. Both are small to medium-sized shrubs with pinnate, trifoliate leaves and pea-like flowers.

CULTIVATION: Adapted to a wide range of soils, except alkaline ones, members of this genus prefer a semi-shaded position but will tolerate sun. Usually quick growing and may need regular pruning to maintain a bushy habit. Hardy to most frosts and to long dry periods. Propagation is from seed or stem and root cuttings.

Goodia lotifolia
CLOVER TREE, GOLDEN TIP
☀ ✤ ↔ 10 ft (3 m) ↕ 10 ft (3 m)
Medium shrub, open to dense habit, often suckering. Dull bluish green to gray-green leaves. Flowers conspicuous, yellow with a reddish blotch, in terminal racemes about 4 in (10 cm) long, in autumn–spring. Zones 9–11.

GORDONIA
Found in East Asia and the warmer temperate parts of North America, this genus of some 70 species of evergreen trees and shrubs is from the camellia (Theaceae) family. *Gordonias* are impressive plants with lush deep green foliage and beautiful flowers. Some species provide the added bonus of flowering in winter, though frost may destroy the flowers. Their flowers are usually white or cream with golden stamens and closely resemble the blooms of a single-flowered camellia.
CULTIVATION: The large deep green leaves suggest a preference for shade,

but, as with camellias and rhododendrons, they need some sun to flower well. Shade from the midday summer sun is best. The soil should be humus-rich, friable, slightly acidic, and well drained—in other words, a woodland soil. Gordonias are not drought tolerant and need ample summer moisture. Prune lightly or tip-pinch after flowering. Propagate from seed or half-hardened cuttings.

Gordonia axillaris ★
☀ ❄ ↔ 12 ft (3.5 m) ↕ 12–20 ft (3.5–6 m)
The most widely cultivated species, large shrub or small tree. Leaves are

Gongora histrionica

Gomphrena globosa

Gomphrena globosa 'Lavender Lady'

Graptophyllum ilicifolium

Graptophyllum pictum

leathery, dark green, to 6 in (15 cm) long, smooth-edged, slightly lobed or shallowly toothed. Creamy white flowers, conspicuous stamens, 5 or 6 petals, 4 in (10 cm) wide, from midwinter to spring. Feed regularly to prevent yellowing foliage. Zones 8–10.

Gordonia lasianthus
LOBLOLLY BAY

☼ ❄ ↔ 30 ft (9 m) ↑ 50 ft (15 m)

A native of southeastern USA, it is more commonly around 25 ft (8 m) tall in cultivation. It has a narrow upright habit and shallowly serrated, deep green, glossy leaves. Although evergreen, older leaves develop red tones before finally falling. Flowers white, to 3 in (8 cm) wide, appear in summer. Zones 9–11.

GOSSYPIUM
COTTON

Widely distributed across warm-temperate and tropical regions, this genus from the mallow (Malvaceae) family consists of 39 annual or woody perennial herbs, evergreen shrubs, and small trees with alternate, palmately lobed leaves. The fruit is a capsule or "boll," splitting to release the seed embedded in fine, dense, white fibers of cotton. These fibers, mainly from the commercially grown *G. herbaceum*, are used in the production of cotton for the textile industry.
CULTIVATION: *Gossypium* species prefer a rich moist soil in a protected but sunny position. Will not tolerate frost. Propagation is from seed sown in spring and, in some species, also from cuttings.

Gossypium australe
AUSTRALIAN WILD COTTON

☼ ❄ ↔ 6 ft (1.8 m) ↑ 6 ft (1.8 m)

This erect, branching, evergreen shrub is a native of northern Australia. It has palmately lobed leaves with coarsely serrated margins. The mauve flowers, with 5 petals, are darker colored at the base and look rather like hibiscus flowers. The shrub is drought tolerant. Zones 10–12.

Gossypium sturtianum ★
DESERT ROSE, STURT'S DESERT ROSE

☼ ❄ ↔ 3 ft (0.9 m) ↑ 3–10 ft (0.9–3 m)

Native of tropical northern Australia, drought-tolerant evergreen shrub. Grayish green oval-shaped leaves, on long leaf stalks. Delicate, 5-petalled, hibiscus-like mauve flowers, purple center, in summer. Fruit a black capsule, ½ in (12 mm) long. Zones 10–12.

GRAPTOPETALUM
These 12 species of succulent perennials native to Paraguay and Mexico to Arizona, USA, belong to the stonecrop (Crassulaceae) family. They form rosettes of fleshy leaves. The flowerheads are cymes bearing flowers with 5 spreading petals that are fused toward the base.
CULTIVATION: *Graptopetalum* species are easily grown in light to medium very well-drained soil in an open sunny position. Propagation is from seed, from stem or leaf cuttings, or by division of the offsets.

Graptopetalum amethystinum
LAVENDER PEBBLES

☼ ❄ ↔ 3–5 in (8–12 cm)
↑ 4–6 in (10–15 cm)

Clumping succulent perennial from Mexico. Forms rosettes of thick, blunt, rounded, blue-gray leaves, to 3 in (8 cm) long, with an amethyst tinge. Stout erect stems become prostrate with age. The terminal clusters of creamy white, bell-shaped flowers have red markings, and are ½–1 in (12–25 mm) across, appearing in spring–summer. Zones 9–11.

Graptopetalum paraguayense ★
GHOST PLANT, MOTHER OF PEARL PLANT

☼ ❄ ↔ 5–12 in (12–30 cm)
↑ 4–12 in (10–30 cm)

Small succulent perennial from Mexico. Stout stem forms rosettes, to 6 in (15 cm) across, at stalk ends. Thick, stiff, oval to wedge-shaped, whitish gray leaves, with a pinkish cast, 1½–2 in (3.5–5 cm) long, ridged undersurface. Young leaves pale purple. Terminal flowerhead, to 6 in

(15 cm) tall, with up to 6 white star-shaped flowers, red-spotted, to ¾ in (18 mm) across, appear from late winter–early spring. *G. p.* subsp. **superbum** has succulent leaves with an eye-catching purplish gray bloom. Zones 9–11.

GRAPTOPHYLLUM
Occurring in Australia, New Guinea, and the southwestern Pacific, this is a genus of 10 species of tall shrubs or small trees in the acanthus (Acanthaceae) family, several of which are popular as house plants. It has a tropical and subtropical distribution in a range of habitats from rainforest margins to rocky hillsides. All have curved tubular flowers in various shades of red, as well as opposite and attractive glossy leaves; some species have unfriendly spines on the stems or leaves.
CULTIVATION: These plants will grow in sun or part-shade on a range of well-drained soils, but flower better in full sun. They are mostly frost tender and require a warm climate if they are to be grown outdoors. Propagate from fresh seed, if obtainable, or from cuttings of 2- to 3-year-old shoots.

Graptophyllum ilicifolium
HOLLY-LEAFED FUCHSIA BUSH,
PRICKLY FUCHSIA BUSH

☼ ❄ ↔ 4 ft (1.2 m) ↑ 20 ft (6 m)

More of a medium to tall shrub than a small tree, Australian species from coastal northern and central Queensland. Leaves oval, glossy, leathery, toothed edges. Reddish tubular flowers, 1¼ in (30 mm) long, borne in dense clusters, in leaf axils, from early–late spring. Zones 9–11.

Graptophyllum pictum
CARICATURE PLANT

☼ ✿ ↔ 30 in (75 cm) ↑ 6 ft (1.8 m)

From New Guinea. Leaves elliptical, glossy, deep green. Flowers in terminal spikes of red to purple, in summer. Various color forms include leaves all purple-bronze, others green marked with white, yellow, pink, or purple, in blotches or stripes of many shapes and sizes. Propagate cultivars from cuttings to ensure color. Zones 10–12.

× GRAPTOVERIA
These hybrid succulent perennials are members of the stonecrop (Crassulaceae) family and are the result of crossing species of *Echeveria* with species of *Graptopetalum*. The diversity of growth-form, leaf shape, and coloring found in both parent genera is perpetuated in their hybrids, so it is difficult to generalize about their appearance; most could be mistaken for echeverias. Breeding has mostly been directed toward colorful foliage.
CULTIVATION: Plant these succulents in full sun or light shade in a sandy well-drained soil. Tip prune after flowering. Propagate from stem or leaf cuttings or by division of offsets.

Graptopetalum amethystinum

Gossypium australe

× *Graptoveria* Hybrid Cultivars

☼ ❄ ↔ to 18 in (45 cm) ↑ 12 in (30 cm)

The partnership of *Echeveria* and *Graptopetalum* has given rise to many hybrid cultivars, including: 'Accolade', compact, pale bluish green leaves, edged red; 'Debbi', low-growing, rosette-forming succulent with rich pink paddle-shaped leaves; 'Dusty', long, narrow, dusky pink leaves, forms a stem; 'Fanfare', yellow flowers, rosettes of long narrow leaves with blue-gray bloom; 'Huth's Pink' ★ (syn. 'Douglas Huth'), flat rosette of pink leaves, which forms stems; 'Kameri', short, thick, pointed, pearly pink and white leaves, forms stems; 'Margaret Reppin', compact rosette, dull green with pink blush, edges ending in long points, of clumping habit; 'Nausicaa', very small, green, clumping rosette, red tips; 'Purple Dream', small crowded rosettes, deep purple to red leaves; 'Rapeco', compact rosette, leaves short, pointed, bluish green; 'Rose Queen', compact rosette, leaves short, pointed, dusky pink; and 'Spirit of '76' ★, compact bright powdery pink rosette. Zones 9–11.

GRASTIDIUM

GRASS ORCHID

This orchid (family Orchidaceae) genus is found throughout Southeast Asia, reaching its greatest diversity and concentration of species in New Guinea. The generic name refers to the

Grevillea asteriscosa

grass-like foliage, a feature of many of these sympodial species. They were previously included within *Dendrobium* and are generally lowland orchids, which require warm conditions to thrive. There are some cooler-growing species that come from higher altitudes. The flowers are produced in pairs (often facing), and are short-lived, rarely lasting past daylight hours. Species with spidery blooms twist and become intertwined, and stay this way for another couple of days before withering and falling off. They bloom prolifically about 9 days after a thunderstorm or a significant weather change. All plants in a region flower on the same day and, interestingly, different species (even from different countries) often synchronize their blooming in cultivation. They will repeat this cycle numerous times during the warmer months.

CULTIVATION: Grastidiums can be grown in pots utilizing a bark-based medium. Larger plants perform well on tree-fern slabs, with the thick roots quickly traveling through the fibers. They require warm humid conditions and grow well in shaded to bright situations, as long as the root system is kept relatively moist. They are in active growth throughout the year. Propagate by division.

Grastidium cathcartii

☼ ✿ ↔ 36 in (90 cm) ↑ 48 in (120 cm)

This species from India has yellow-green, 1 in (25 mm) flowers that last for 2 or 3 days. It is one of the few cool-growing members of this genus. Zones 10–12.

Grastidium tozerense

☼ ✿ ↔ 4–24 in (10–60 cm)
↑ 8–36 in (20–90 cm)

From Australia. This is a rare species that has pure white starry flowers that are about 1½ in (35 mm) tall. The

× *Graptoveria*, Hybrid Cultivar, 'Debbi'

individual blooms last for only about 6 hours before twisting and collapsing. Zones 11–12.

GREVILLEA

This genus in the protea (Proteaceae) family is represented by around 340 species. Most are native to Australia, with some from New Guinea, New Caledonia, Vanuatu, and Sulawesi. Naturally occurring Australian forms have been selected and hybrid cultivars developed with huge horticultural potential. They range from prostrate ground covers to tall trees. Distinctive, colorful flower clusters come in 3 basic forms—spider-like, toothbrush-like, and large brushes. Many are rich in nectar, which makes them attractive to insects, birds, and animals (especially Australian marsupials), all of which are pollinators. They are found in a wide climatic range and are tolerant of extremes. Some are short lived but spectacular, others have unique flower clusters, and some have a strong sweet fragrance.

CULTIVATION: Most grevilleas prefer an open sunny position and free-draining loams, and many perform best in phosphorus-deficient soils. Propagate from half-hardened cuttings; seed also germinates well but is often difficult to obtain; some of the species that are difficult to grow have responded well to grafting onto stocks

Grastidium tozerense

of vigorous species such as *G. robusta*; this technique has also been used to produce weeping standard specimens.

Grevillea acanthifolia

☼ ❄ ↔ 5 ft (1.5 m) ↑ 10 ft (3 m)

From New South Wales, Australia, a species represented by 3 subspecies of irregular, prostrate to erect shrubs. Stiff, pointed, deeply divided, glossy, dark green leaves. Long toothbrush flowerheads, pink to purple, in spring to autumn. Tolerates "wet feet" on heavy clay soils. Zones 7–9.

Grevillea aquifolium

HOLLY GREVILLEA

☼ ❄ ↔ 6 ft (1.8 m) ↑ 6 ft (1.8 m)

From southeastern Australia. Variable habit, prostrate and suckering, or rounded dense shrub. Holly-like foliage, thick sharp-pointed lobes, hairy undersides. Toothbrush flowers, red, pink, or dull orange, in winter to summer. Long lived, excellent nectar source. Zones 8–10.

Grevillea aspleniifolia

FERN-LEAF GREVILLEA

☼ ❄ ↔ 15 ft (4.5 m) ↑ 15 ft (4.5 m)

From the Blue Mountains of eastern New South Wales, Australia. Gray felting covers branches. Leaves long, willowy, occasionally toothed, curved outwards; smooth, shiny, olive green above, gray felty beneath. Toothbrush flowers reddish purple, in winter to spring. Zones 8–9.

Grevillea asteriscosa

STAR-LEAF GREVILLEA

☼ ❄ ↔ 6 ft (1.8 m) ↑ 6 ft (1.8 m)

Native to far southwestern Australia. Dense prickly shrub, star-shaped sharp-pointed leaves clasp the stems. New growth velvety red. Sparse spider flowers of glowing red, in winter to spring. Zones 8–9.

Grevillea australis

ALPINE GREVILLEA, SOUTHERN GREVILLEA

☼ ❄ ↔ 5 ft (1.5 m) ↑ 6 ft (1.8 m)

Spiky shrub from southern Australia. Narrow, sharp-pointed, shiny, dark

Grevillea acanthifolia

Grevillea australis

green leaves. Spider flowers small, white, strong honey perfume. Requires well-drained soils and summer watering. Zones 7–10.

Grevillea baileyana
BROWN SILKY OAK, SCRUB BEEFWOOD
☼ ⚘ ↔ 15 ft (4.5 m) ↑ 100 ft (30 m)
Long-lived tree from northern Australia and New Guinea. Scaly, hard, gray bark. Leaves smooth, leathery, and deeply lobed when juvenile, simple oval when mature, with rusty-furry undersides. Creamy white long-brushed flowers, in spring–summer. Prune regularly to encourage juvenile foliage. Zones 10–12.

Grevillea banksii
BANKS'S GREVILLEA, RED SILKY OAK
☼ ⁂ ↔ 7 ft (2 m) ↑ 10–30 ft (3–9 m)
Variable dense shrub or slender tree, native to coastal Queensland, Australia. Long leaves, very deeply divided, smooth, silky both sides, prominent midvein. Large nectar-rich brush flowers, red or white, with pink and apricot forms, long flowering period, spring peak. Annual light pruning, avoid old wood. **G. b. var. forsteri**, silvery leafed shrub to 10 ft (3 m), red or cream flowers over a long period. Zones 9–11.

Grevillea barklyana
GULLY GREVILLEA
☀ ❄ ↔ 20 ft (6 m) ↑ 25 ft (8 m)
Tall shrub or small tree, wide-spreading branches, from Victoria, Australia. Leaves leathery, long oval shape, occasional triangular lobes, furry white beneath. Pale pink-red toothbrush flowers, in spring–summer. Zones 7–8.

Grevillea barklyana

Grevillea curviloba subsp. *incurva*

Grevillea chrysophaea

Grevillea baueri
BAUER'S GREVILLEA
☼ ❄ ↔ 6 ft (1.8 m) ↑ 3 ft (0.9 m)
Sprawling shrub native to New South Wales, Australia. Small oblong leaves smooth, occasionally grainy, sometimes silky, reddish new growth. Spider flower clusters, red and cream, in winter–spring. Hardy plant prefers sandy loam, tolerant of light shade. Zones 8–9.

Grevillea bronwenae
☼ ❄ ↔ 3 ft (0.9 m) ↑ 6 ft (1.8 m)
Erect shrub from Western Australia. Pointed, thin, long leaves, recurved margins. Abundant vibrant scarlet flower clusters with deep blue styles, in autumn–spring, spot flowering in summer. Sometimes grafted to combat its short life. Zones 9–10.

Grevillea buxifolia
GRAY SPIDER FLOWER
☼ ❄ ↔ 7 ft (2 m) ↑ 8 ft (2.4 m)
Native to eastern New South Wales, Australia. Densely hairy branchlets. Small, green, oval leaves, white furry undersides. Erect clusters of woolly spider flowers, gray-brown with pinkish tinges, appearing all year, with a winter–spring flush. Tolerates dryness; does well on the coast. Zones 8–10.

Grevillea chrysophaea
GOLDEN GREVILLEA
☼ ❄ ↔ 4 ft (1.2 m) ↑ 6 ft (1.8 m)
From Victoria, Australia. Soft, oval, green leaves, velvety white undersides. Glowing golden yellow flower clusters, sometimes flushed orange-tan, in winter–early summer. Tip prune regularly. Zones 8–10.

Grevillea dielsiana

Grevillea banksii

Grevillea buxifolia

Grevillea confertifolia
GRAMPIANS GREVILLEA, STRAWBERRY GREVILLEA
☼ ❄ ↔ 10 ft (3 m) ↑ 6 ft (1.8 m)
Native to Victoria, Australia. Spreading shrub, sometimes prostrate, sometimes erect. Narrow pointed leaves. Bright mauve-pink spider flower clusters, in spring–summer. Tolerant of heavy wet soils. Zones 8–10.

Grevillea curviloba
☼ ❄ ↔ 4 ft (1.2 m) ↑ 6 ft (1.8 m)
Spreading informal shrub, native of southwest Western Australia. Leaves rich bright green, deeply lobed. Fragrant white flower clusters, in spring. Long-lived dense ground

Grevillea dimorpha

Grevillea bronwenae

cover. **G. c. subsp. incurva**, form most widely grown, much narrower, slightly curved leaf lobes. Prostrate to more erect, often grown under the wrong name, *G. biternata*. Zones 8–10.

Grevillea dielsiana
☼ ⁂ ↔ 4 ft (1.2 m) ↑ 6 ft (1.8 m)
From Western Australia, compact very prickly shrub. Large spider flower clusters of red or apricot-orange, in winter–spring. Excellent barrier or bird habitat. Extremely prickly foliage renders maintenance hazardous. Zones 9–10.

Grevillea dimorpha
syn. *Grevillea speciosa* subsp. *dimorpha*
FLAME GREVILLEA, OLIVE GREVILLEA
☀ ❄ ↔ 7 ft (2 m) ↑ 10 ft (3 m)
Erect shrub native to western Victoria, Australia. Leaves vary from narrow needle-like to dark green

G

Grevillea eriostachya, in the wild, Uluru–Kata Tjuta National Park, Northern Territory, Australia

Grevillea dryandri

ovals, silky undersides. Flowers bright red spider clusters, in spring–autumn. Long-lived specimen. Zones 8–10.

Grevillea dryanderi
DRYANDER'S GREVILLEA

☼ ✿ ↔ 7 ft (2 m) ↑ 3 ft (0.9 m)

A sprawling shrub from northern Australia. Long brush flower clusters, held above the narrow, deeply lobed foliage. Both red and white forms occur. Flowering in autumn-winter, sometimes into spring. Zones 10–11.

Grevillea erectiloba

☼ ✿ ↔ 12 ft (3.5 m) ↑ 5 ft (1.5 m)

From southern Western Australia. Pale blue-gray leaves, divided into needle-like lobes diverging at very narrow angles, all point upward. Large clusters of glossy flowers appear among

Grevillea erectiloba

the foliage, in spring–summer, a mixture of green buds, orange young flowers, deep red older flowers. Zones 9–11.

Grevillea eriostachya
DESERT GREVILLEA,
YELLOW FLAME GREVILLEA

☼ ✿ ↔ 7 ft (2 m) ↑ 6 ft (1.8 m)

From central and western Australia. Long, showy, nectar-rich flower clusters, green to yellow or orange, held high above the foliage. Leaves with long narrow lobes, silky uppersurface. Under cultivation on well-drained sandy loams and regular moisture, flowering extends all year, peaking in spring. Zones 9–11.

Grevillea floribunda
RUSTY SPIDER FLOWER

☼/◑ ❊ ↔ 6 ft (1.8 m) ↑ 6 ft (1.8 m)

Occurring in New South Wales and Queensland, Australia. Species represented by 2 subspecies, both shrubs, oval to linear silky-covered leaves. Spider flower clusters, yellowish, orange, or rusty brown, in late winter–spring. Prefers dry well-drained loam. Zones 8–10.

Grevillea × gaudichaudii

☼ ❊ ↔ 10 ft (3 m) ↑ 4 in (10 cm)

Naturally occurring hybrid between *G. acanthifolia* and *G. laurifolia.* Vigorous prostrate ground cover. Handsome divided foliage, reddish at tips. clusters of burgundy toothbrush flowers, in spring–summer. Zones 8–10.

Grevillea gillivrayi

☼ ✿ ↔ 4 ft (1.2 m) ↑ 30 ft (9 m)

From New Caledonia. Tree or straggly shrub. Angular branches and new foliage have silky-furry covering. Oval leathery leaves. Long brush flower clusters, held erect, all year, flush in winter–spring, ranging in color from cream through pink to red. Zones 9–12.

Grevillea hookeriana
BLACK TOOTHBRUSHES

☼ ✿ ↔ 8 ft (2.4 m) ↑ 8 ft (2.4 m)

From southwestern Western Australia. Long narrow leaves, simple or divided into long lobes, uppersurface felty. Nectar-rich toothbrush flower clusters, pale to mid-yellow, prominent black or yellow styles, in early winter–early summer. Requires very well-drained soils. Zones 9–10.

Grevillea jephcottii
GREEN GREVILLEA,
PINE MOUNTAIN GREVILLEA

☼ ❊ ↔ 7 ft (2 m) ↑ 10 ft (3 m)

Dense shrub found in southeastern Australia on the upper Murray River. Finely furred, pointed, soft, oval leaves. Young branches also finely furred. Greenish cream flower clusters, in winter–summer. Rich in nectar; prefers a light or gravelly clay loam. Zones 8–10.

Grevillea johnsonii
JOHNSON'S GREVILLEA

☼ ✿ ↔ 7 ft (2 m) ↑ 15 ft (4.5 m)

Single-stemmed spreading shrub from Goulburn River catchment in south-eastern Australia. Long, divided, pine-like foliage, young growth, with rusty felting. Striking red or orange spider flower clusters, suffused with pink and cream, in spring. Likes a cool root run; well-drained loam. Zones 9–11.

Grevillea floribunda

Grevillea gillivrayi

Grevillea jephcottii

Grevillea johnsonii

Grevillea lavandulacea

Grevillea juncifolia

Grevillea juniperina

Grevillea lanigera

Grevillea juncifolia

HONEYSUCKLE SPIDER FLOWER

☀ ❄ ↔ 7 ft (2 m) ↕ 20 ft (6 m)
Grayish erect or spreading shrub, widespread across Australia. Long narrow or divided leaves, leathery, gray furry covering. Long nectar-rich brushes, golden orange, at branch tips, in winter–spring, and sporadically after rain. Prefers sandy loam, thrives under arid conditions. Zones 9–11.

Grevillea juniperina

JUNIPER-LEAF GREVILLEA, PRICKLY SPIDER FLOWER

☀ ❄ ↔ 7 ft (2 m) ↕ 8 ft (2.4 m)
Found in eastern New South Wales, Australia. Dense spreading shrub. Leaves dark green, needle-like. Spider flower clusters, commonly red, but can be yellow, apricot, or orange, in spring–summer. Long-lived hardy plants, providing excellent shelter for small birds. 'Lunar Light' (syn. *G.* 'Australflora Lunar Light'), yellow leaf-margin variegation, orange and pink flowers; 'Molonglo', spreading habit, pale apricot flowers. Zones 8–10.

Grevillea lanigera ★

WOOLLY GREVILLEA

☀ ❄ ↔ 4 ft (1.2 m) ↕ 5 ft (1.5 m)
Native to southeastern Australia. Variable shrub, sometimes prostrate and suckering. Narrow, occasionally fleshy leaves, soft silvery felting.

Flowers all year, with a flush of spider clusters of pink, red, orange, or yellow in winter–spring. Prefers well-drained soils in cooler areas, dislikes humidity. Zones 7–10.

Grevillea lavandulacea

LAVENDER GREVILLEA

☀ ❄ ↔ 3 ft (0.9 m) ↕ 3 ft (0.9 m)
Compact shrub from southern Australia, a parent of several hybrid cultivars. Gray-green needle-like foliage, plentiful spider flower clusters of pink-red. Variations in leaf texture, habit, and flower color common. Do not crowd, avoid summer watering. Zones 8–10.

Grevillea leucopteris

WHITE PLUME GREVILLEA

☀ ❄ ↔ 7 ft (2 m) ↕ 10 ft (3 m)
Attractive species from Western Australia. Arching branches of leathery, gray-green, narrow leaves. Held above the foliage, large brushes of spider

Grevillea linearifolia

flowers which open to cream, in spring–summer. Their scent can be overpowering, especially at night. Zones 9–10.

Grevillea linearifolia

LINEAR-LEAF GREVILLEA

☀ ❄ ↔ 7 ft (2 m) ↕ 12 ft (3.5 m)
From the east coast of New South Wales, Australia. Variable single-stemmed shrub with loose open foliage, or a densely foliaged prostrate specimen to 3 ft (0.9 m). Leaves narrow, linear, silky. Hardy adaptable species. Some color variation, ranging from white to cream to pink. Zones 8–10.

Grevillea neurophylla

☀ ❄ ↔ 5 ft (1.5 m) ↕ 8 ft (2.4 m)
Australian species, occurs on stream banks in the mountains of central Victoria. Bushy shrub with somewhat weeping branches. Narrow sharply pointed leaves, to 2 in (5 cm) long.

Grevillea oleoides

Grevillea leucopteris

Among the foliage, masses of tiny white flowers with pink markings, in late spring–summer. Zones 8–10.

Grevillea obliquistigma

☀ ❄ ↔ to 10 ft (3 m) ↕ to 20 ft (6 m)
Bushy shrub from low-rainfall inland regions of Western Australia. Erect branches can be smooth, silky hairy, or glaucous. Leaves are up to 8 in (20 cm) long, erect, leathery, with margins rolled back almost obscuring the under-surface. Some plants have lobed leaves. Erect, terminal, branched inflorescences, up to 4 in (10 cm) long. Cream flowers in spring–summer. Fruits are slightly flattened oval-shape, sometimes sticky. Zones 9–10.

Grevillea oleoides

☀ ❄ ↔ 6 ft (1.8 m) ↕ 6 ft (1.8 m)
Erect, sometimes suckering shrub, from New South Wales, Australia. Angular branchlets, long oval or linear leaves, silky gray undersides. A number of different forms occur naturally. Red spider flower clusters, produced all year, with a spring flush. Prefers dry sandy or gravelly soils. Zones 8–10.

Grevillea obliquistigma

Grevillea olivacea
OLIVE GREVILLEA
☼ ⚘ ↔ 5 ft (1.5 m) ↑ 12 ft (3.5 m)
Vigorous upright shrub from west coast of Western Australia. Leaves simple, dark green, silky undersides. Spider flower clusters of red, orange, or yellow, in winter, mostly on older wood. Prefers well-drained gravelly or sandy alkaline loam. Zones 9–10.

Grevillea petrophiloides
PINK POKERS
☼ ⚘ ↔ 4 ft (1.2 m) ↑ 10 ft (3 m)
Upright open shrub from southwestern Western Australia. Variable, narrow-lobed, divided leaves. Long spectacular flower brushes, from white through cream to pink, appear above the foliage, in winter–summer. Difficult under cultivation, requiring superb drainage. Zones 9–10.

Grevillea pinaster
☼ ⚘ ↔ 5 ft (1.5 m) ↑ 6 ft (1.8 m)
Single-stemmed sturdy shrub from the west coast of Western Australia. Pine-like leaves, either simple and

Grevillea sericea subsp. *riparia*

narrow-linear or divided. Pink spider flower clusters, in winter–spring. Adaptable to heavy clay or well-drained sandy soils, summer or winter rainfall. Zones 9–11.

Grevillea plurijuga
☼ ⚘ ↔ 10 ft (3 m) ↑ 6 ft (1.8 m)
Hardy prostrate or low-mounding shrub from the south of Western Australia. Gray-green, narrow-linear, lobed leaves. Deep pink brush flower clusters, held above the foliage, in spring and summer. Unusual warty-looking fruits. Zones 9–11.

Grevillea olivacea

Grevillea plurijuga

Grevillea petrophiloides

Grevillea robusta

Grevillea rivularis
CARRINGTON FALLS GREVILLEA
☼ ❄ ↔ 15 ft (4.5 m) ↑ 6 ft (1.8 m)
From a restricted colony in eastern New South Wales, Australia. Dense spreading shrub, reddish angular branches. Narrow, rigid, divided, dark green leaves, sharp-pointed tips. Toothbrush flower clusters, in late winter–spring, varying from cream-mauve to pink. Prefers well-drained but moist loams. Zones 8–11.

Grevillea robusta
SILK OAK, SILKY OAK
☼ ❄ ↔ 30 ft (9 m) ↑ 60 ft (18 m)
Largest of all the grevilleas, semi-deciduous. Valued timber and shade tree from southeastern Queensland, Australia. Large, golden, nectar-laden flower brushes, in spring–summer; fern-like foliage. Rapid growing, deep rooting, prefers a rich, well-drained, heavy loam. Zones 8–12.

Grevillea rosmarinifolia
ROSEMARY GREVILLEA
☼ ❄ ↔ 6 ft (1.8 m) ↑ 6 ft (1.8 m)
From southeastern Australia, variable, dense or open shrub. Dark green needle-like foliage. Abundant spider flower clusters, in winter–summer, from cream to pale or deep pink. Prefers well-drained sandy loams, moisture in winter. Zones 8–10.

Grevillea rosmarinifolia

Grevillea sericea
PINK SPIDER FLOWER, SILKY GREVILLEA
☼ ⚘ ↔ 7 ft (2 m) ↑ 6 ft (1.8 m)
Adaptable species from New South Wales, Australia. Dense shrub; elongated oval leaves, silky reverse. Pink-lilac or white spider-like flower clusters, in winter–spring. *G. s.* subsp. *riparia* has long, narrow, nearly hairless leaves, purple-pink flowers. Zones 9–10.

Grevillea shiressii
MULLET CREEK GREVILLEA
☼ ❄ ↔ 12 ft (3.5 m) ↑ 10 ft (3 m)
Densely foliaged slender shrub from the mid-coastal area of New South Wales, Australia. Long oval leaves, soft, with prominent venation. Unusual green to burgundy spider-like flower clusters, in winter–summer. Excellent, long-lived, hardy screen plant, attractive to nectar-seeking birds. Zones 8–11.

Grevillea speciosa
RED SPIDER FLOWER
◐ ❄ ↔ 5 ft (1.5 m) ↑ 6 ft (1.8 m)
Variable upright shrub, from the mid-coast of New South Wales, Australia. Soft hairy branchlets. Small oval leaves, leathery, sometimes gray-felted. Showy large red spider-like flower clusters appear all year. Well-drained moist soils preferred. Zones 8–10.

Grevillea rivularis

Grevillea wickhamii

Grevillea spinosa

TJILKA-TJILKA

☀ ⚬ ↔ to 10 ft (3 m) ↔ to 10 ft (3 m)

Straggly, spreading, prickly shrub, occurring in remote inland regions of Western Australia. Flaking papery bark. Spiny green leaves, once or twice-divided, occasionally tripartite. Toothbrush-type inflorescences, up to 4 in (10 cm) long, in winter–spring. Flowers green and black in bud, changing to light and dark orange upon opening. Fruits egg-shaped, reddish stripes and blotches. Seeds winged. Zones 9–10.

Grevillea stenobotrya

RATTLE-POD GREVILLEA, SANDHILL SPIDER FLOWER

☀ ⚬ ↔ 8 ft (2.4 m) ↑ 20 ft (6 m)

Widespread across central Australia. Initially smooth, bark becomes fibrous. Leaves long, narrow, bright green. Abundant, strongly fragrant, cream-yellow brushes, rich in nectar, in winter–spring. Seed pods persistent. Tolerant of dry and difficult conditions, requires excellent drainage. Zones 9–12.

Grevillea thelemanniana

HUMMINGBIRD BUSH, SPIDER-NET GREVILLEA

☀ ⚬ ↔ 6 ft (1.8 m) ↑ 3 ft (0.9 m)

Dense shrub from southwestern Western Australia. Leaves linear or divided, dark green. Red spider flower clusters, in winter–spring. Prefers moist but well-drained sandy loam, responds well to hard pruning. Zones 9–11.

Grevillea wilsonii

Grevillea treueriana

☀ ⚬ ↔ to 3 ft (0.9 m) ↑ to 3 ft (0.9 m)

This open prickly shrub is found in inland South Australia on one mountain only, where it grows in crevices on sandstone cliffs. The leaves are divided 2 or 3 times, rigid and spiky, to 1¾ in (40 mm) long. The terminal flower spikes, to 3 in (8 cm) long, have bright red flowers in "toothbrush" inflorescences, appearing in spring. The fruits are egg-shaped and hairy with reddish stripes or blotches. Zones 9–10.

Grevillea tripartita

☀ ⚬ ↔ 10 ft (3 m) ↑ 10 ft (3 m)

Spreading shrub, strongly erect habit, from south coast of Western Australia. Leaves narrow, rigid, sharp-pointed. Clusters of bold scarlet and yellow spider flowers with long styles appear all year, spectacular spring flush. Zones 9–10.

Grevillea victoriae

ROYAL GREVILLEA

☀ ❄ ↔ 6 ft (1.8 m) ↑ 6 ft (1.8 m)

Hardy adaptable shrub from southern Australia. The leaves are simple, oval or narrowly so, with a leathery texture, shiny uppersurface, and silky underside. Pendent spider-like flower

Grevillea stenobotrya

clusters of red, orange, yellow, or pink, in spring–summer. Generally long-lived, reliable feature or screen plant. Zones 8–10.

Grevillea wickhamii

WICKHAM'S GREVILLEA

☀ ⚬ ↔ 7 ft (2 m) ↑ 10 ft (3 m)

A robust variable shrub, from the far north of Western Australia. It has distinctive gray-green lobed leaves, with prominent veins and bristle-tipped lobes. The showy spider-like flower brushes are red, orange, or apricot, in late autumn–early spring. Will not tolerate hard frosts. Zones 10–12.

Grevillea wilsonii

WILSON'S GREVILLEA

☀ ⚬ ↔ 5 ft (1.5 m) ↑ 5 ft (1.5 m)

Spreading shrub from the southwest of Western Australia. Deeply divided, rich green, tangled foliage, soft when young, becoming coarse and prickly as it ages under harsh conditions. Vibrant red spider-like flower clusters, in spring to summer. Prefers well-drained sandy loam; tolerates hard-pruning. Zones 9–11.

Grevillea treueriana

Grevillea Hybrid Cultivars

☀/◐ ⚬ ↔ 4–15 ft (1.2–4.5 m) ↑ 6 in–20 ft (15 cm–6 m)

Most hybrids fall into 3 groups, each derived from a limited range of parent species but with none shared between the groups. A few hybrids can be placed in a "miscellaneous" group.

Grevillea spinosa

Grevillea tripartita

Grevillea, Hybrid Cultivar, Banksii Group, 'Sylvia'

Grevillea, Hybrid Cultivar, Banksii Group, 'Misty Pink'

Grevillea, HC, Banksii Group, 'Honey Gem'

G., HC, Banksii Group, 'Mason's Hybrid'

Grevillea, HC, Banksii Group, 'Moonlight'

G., HC, Banksii Group, 'Robyn Gordon'

BANKSII GROUP

The main parent species of these attractive and very popular hybrids is *G. banksii* from the east coast of Australia, but the cultivars can be subdivided into 2 groups: those whose other parent is *G. bipinnatifida,* and those bred from taller-growing tropical and subtropical species such as *G. pteridifolia* and *G. sessilis.* All have leaves dissected into narrow segments and dense bottlebrush-like spikes of flowers, which are crowded toward the upper side of the spike. '**Coconut Ice**', a shrub to 7 ft (2 m) tall, has bright green foliage, red-pink flowers; '**Honey Gem**', a shrub to 15 ft (4.5 m) has tall, dark green fern-like leaves, prolific orange or yellow flower clusters; '**Mason's Hybrid**' (syn. 'Ned Kelly'), a fast-growing hardy shrub to 6 ft (1.8 m), similar to 'Robyn Gordon', paler orange blooms, ferny light green foliage, orange-red flower clusters all year; '**Misty Pink**', is a silvery shrub to 10 ft (3 m) tall, long pink flower clusters with cream tips; '**Moonlight**', an upright shrub to 10 ft (3 m) tall, has ferny olive green foliage, long creamy flower clusters; '**Parfait Crème**', a dense shrub to 10 ft (3 m) high and wide, has creamy yellow to caramel flowers; '**Robyn Gordon**'—the most widely planted grevillea—is a shrub to 6 ft (1.8 m) tall, with ferny foliage, spectacular clusters of bright pinkish red flowers; '**Sandra Gordon**', a shrub to 15 ft (4.5 m) tall, bright yellow flowers; '**Superb**', similar to 'Robyn Gordon', apricot-pink tint to flowers; '**Sylvia**', a shrub to 10 ft (3 m) tall, has rosy pink flower clusters with cream tips; '**Winter Sparkles**', winter-flowering shrub to 20 ft (6 m) tall, has yellow-orange flowers. Zones 9–12.

ROSMARINIFOLIA GROUP

Most of the earliest hybrids belonged to this group, derived from *G. rosmarinifolia, G. juniperina* and their allies with small smooth-edged leaves and flowers in the characteristic spider flower clusters. It includes most Clear-

Grevillea, Hybrid Cultivar, Banksii Group, 'Superb'

Grevillea, Hybrid Cultivar, Rosmarinifolia Group, 'Canberra Gem'

Grevillea, Hybrid Cultivar, Rosmarinifolia Group, 'Crosbie Morrison'

Grevillea, Hybrid Cultivar, Rosmarinifolia Group, 'Scarlet Sprite'

view and Poorinda hybrids. Some cultivars in this group hybridize freely and their progeny may become invasive. 'Canberra Gem', a 6 ft (1.8 m) tall shrub, dark green needle foliage, cerise flowers; 'Clearview David', a dense shrub to 8 ft (2.4 m) tall, with prickly leaves, and bright red spider flowers; 'Clearview Robyn', a shrub to 6 ft (1.8 m) tall, blue-green needle leaves, vibrant cerise spider flowers; 'Crosbie Morrison', a dense shrub to 5 ft (1.5 m) tall, with gray-green leaves, and pink-red spider flowers; 'Evelyn's Coronet', an erect shrub to 6 ft (1.8 m) tall, with silvery, woolly, pink spider flowers; 'Noellii', may not be a hybrid but merely a compact form of *G. rosmarinifolia* with a neat bushy growth habit; 'Penola', gray leaves and an abundance of red and cream blooms; 'Poorinda Beauty', a 3 ft (0.9 m) tall shrub, with needle foliage, dense clusters of orange-red flowers; 'Poorinda Constance', dense shrub with soft foliage to 8 ft (2.4 m) high, red flowers; 'Poorinda Firebird', a shrub to 6 ft (1.8 m) high, with abundant scarlet spider flower clusters; 'Poorinda Leane', dense soft-foliaged shrub to 8 ft (2.4 m) tall, orange flowers; 'Poorinda Rachel', a shrub

to 3 ft (0.9 m) tall, with oval leaves, and orange-red flowers; 'Poorinda Stephen', a shrub to 3 ft (0.9 m) tall, with silvery oval leaves, and large dark red spider flower clusters; and 'Poorinda Vivacity', a shrub to 3 ft (0.9 m) tall, with broad oval foliage, tight orange-red spider flower clusters. Other cultivars include 'Poorinda Queen', 'Poorinda Rondeau', 'Poorinda Tranquillity', and 'Scarlet Sprite'. Zones 8–12.

G., HC, Toothbrush Group, 'Fanfare'

TOOTHBRUSH GROUP

These hybrid cultivars are derived from a large group of species, mainly from southeastern Australian, with the "toothbrush" type of flower spike, in which the flowers are densely crowded and all turned upward to form an elongated brush; often they are bent sharply backward as well. The leaves of both species and hybrids range from simple and smooth-edged to toothed, lobed, or dissected into narrow segments. The plants range from quite prostrate to tall and erect. 'Boongala Spinebill' ★, very adaptable spreading shrub to 8 ft (2.4 m) tall, cascading branches, new ferny foliage coppery red, deep crimson toothbrush flower clusters; 'Bronze Rambler', vigorous ground cover with a spread of 15 ft (4.5 m), dissected leaves, bronze tint on new growth, purplish flowers; 'Brookvale Letitia', tall shrub to 15 ft (4.5 m) high, orange and red hairy flowers; 'Fanfare' (syn. 'Austraflora Fanfare'), prostrate, spreading to about 17 ft (5 m), spring to summer inflorescences are dark red with pink styles; 'Ivanhoe' ★, dense foliage,

dense habit, and vigorous growth to 10 ft (3 m) tall and 15 ft (4.5 m) across, red flowers. Zones 9–12.

MISCELLANEOUS GROUP

This group includes: 'Granya Glory', to 2 ft (0.6 m) high, creamy and rosy flowers; 'Long John', shrub to 10 ft (3 m) tall, red and pink flowers; 'Merinda Gordon', to 10 ft (3 m) tall, deep pink to red flowers; 'Orange Marmalade', to 8 ft (2.4 m) tall, leaves smooth-edged and silky hairy on the undersurface, flowers orange; 'Pendant Clusters' (syn. 'Austraflora Pendant Clusters'), creamy yellow flowers with deep red styles; 'Poorinda Ensign', less than 3 ft (0.9 m) tall, leaves smooth edged, densely clustered bright pink flowers; 'Sid Reynolds', shrub to 8 ft (2.4 m) tall, pale reddish pink flowers; and 'Winpara Gem', shrub to 7 ft (2 m) tall, reddish flowers. Zones 9–12.

GREWIA

This genus from the linden (Tiliaceae) family encompasses about 150 species of shrubs, trees, and climbers found in

G., HC, Miscellaneous Group, 'Long John'

Grevillea, Hybrid Cultivar, Miscellaneous Group, 'Winpara Gem'

Africa, Asia, and Australia. Although often attractive plants, very few are cultivated and only one species, *G. occidentalis*, is at all common. Most species have oval leaves with finely toothed edges. The flowers are starry, with 5 narrow petals and a conspicuous group of stamens at the center; they are followed by small drupes.
CULTIVATION: Best suited to warm-temperate to subtropical climates, few species will tolerate any but the lightest frosts. They prefer a sunny

Greyia radlkoferi

position with moist well-drained soil and should be pinched back to keep the growth compact. If necessary, old overgrown plants can often be rejuvenated by heavy pruning. Propagate from seed or half-hardened cuttings.

Grewia occidentalis
FOUR CORNERS
☀ ❄ ↔ 10 ft (3 m) ↕ 10 ft (3 m)
Southern African shrub, attractive throughout the year. Bright green foliage. Flowers are around 1½ in (35 mm) wide, mauve to pale purple shade, sepals same length as petals, creating a double-flowered effect, in spring–summer. Purple-red 4-lobed fruit. Zones 9–11.

GREYIA
This South African genus of 3 species of deciduous shrubs gives its name to the family Greyiaceae. Notable for its striking flowers and unusual foliage, the leaves resemble those of a regal pelargonium, being rounded, lobed,

and around 3 in (8 cm) wide. They occur mainly at the tips of heavily wooded branches and redden before dropping in autumn. The flowers are bright red and have an unusual structure: 5 petals fused to a fleshy central disc, from which protrude 10 long stamens. They are clustered in racemes up to 6 in (15 cm) wide.
CULTIVATION: Best grown in a hot sunny position, *Greyia* species prefer mild climates but will tolerate light frosts. Soil should be fairly fertile and well drained. Water well in summer but allow plants to dry off as they approach winter dormancy. Propagate from seed or half-hardened cuttings in late spring or summer.

Greyia radlkoferi
TRANSVAAL BOTTLEBRUSH
☀ ❄ ↔ 6 ft (1.8 m) ↕ 6–10 ft (1.8–3 m)
The young leaves are covered with hair. Red flowers with petals that narrow down where they attach to the central disc, creating a starry effect, in spring. Zones 9–11.

Greyia sutherlandii
NATAL BOTTLEBRUSH
☀ ❄ ↔ 7 ft (2 m) ↕ 15 ft (4.5 m)
Large shrub; branches very heavy at base. Bright red flowerheads at tips of bare branches, in late winter–early spring. Deeply lobed leaves follow, an attractive feature through summer, coloring in autumn. Zones 9–11.

Grindelia stricta

Grewia occidentalis

GRINDELIA
GUM PLANT, ROSIN WEED, TAR WEED
Found in the drier regions of western North America and South America, this daisy (Asteraceae) family genus is made up of some 60 species, mostly annuals and perennials with a few shrubs. They have wiry stems with simple leaves covered with small resin glands that make them sticky to touch. The stems exude resin when cut, which dries to form a white deposit that is often a conspicuous feature on the stems and leaves. Yellow daisy-like flowerheads appear mainly in summer. Extracts of the leaves of some California species have been used medicinally, mainly for bronchial complaints.
CULTIVATION: Hardiness varies considerably with the species, but most are at home in a temperate climate with only light to moderate frosts. Plant in full sun with light, gritty, free-draining soil. They can be propagated from seed or spring to summer cuttings. Because of the woody base, division is seldom practical.

Grindelia camporum
☀ ❄ ↔ 40 in (100 cm) ↕ 60 in (150 cm)
Annual or short-lived perennial from California. Upright quite open growth habit. Very resinous toothed leaves to 3 in (8 cm) long. Flowerheads to over 1½ in (35 mm) wide, with up to 35 recurved ray florets. Zones 8–10.

Greyia sutherlandii

Grindelia camporum, in the wild, Baja California, Mexico

Grindelia squarrosa

☀ ❆ ↔ 32 in (80 cm) ↑ 40 in (100 cm)

Biennial or perennial from western and central regions of North America. Pointed oval leaves, to more than 2 in (5 cm) long, smooth or serrated edges. Flowerheads around 1¼ in (30 mm) wide, with yellow-green disc florets and up to 35 ray florets. **Zones 3–9.**

Grindelia stricta

PACIFIC GRINDELIA

☀ ❆ ↔ 40–60 in (100–150 cm)
↑ 8–36 in (20–90 cm)

Perennial from western North America. Upright or spreading habit. Leaves deep green, oblong to spatula-shaped, usually minutely toothed, around 4 in (10 cm) long. Bright yellow flowerheads to 2 in (5 cm) wide, with up to 35 narrow recurved ray florets. *G. s.* subsp. *venulosa*, low and spreading, 2 in (5 cm) long leaves. **Zones 8–10.**

GRISELINIA

This is a genus of 7 evergreen trees and shrubs from the dogwood (Cornaceae) family, 5 of which are native to Chile and southeastern Brazil and 2 to New Zealand. Generally plants of coastal areas, they have large, glossy, leathery leaves. The tiny yellow-green flowers are unisexual, with male and female flowers borne on separate trees.

CULTIVATION: *Griselinia* species are grown for their attractive shiny foliage and are particularly useful for providing screens, shelter, and hedging. They are invaluable in coastal areas, being very tolerant of salt winds, and will grow in most well-drained soils in sun or part-shade. In very cold areas they are best given a warm sheltered site or grown in a conservatory. Pruning should be carried out in summer. Propagation is easiest from half-hardened cuttings in autumn, as seed can be difficult to germinate.

Griselinia littoralis

Griselinia littoralis

BROADLEAF, KAPUKA, PAPAUMA

☀ ❆ ↔ 15 ft (4.5 m) ↑ 25 ft (8 m)

Found throughout New Zealand. Leathery oval leaves, very glossy, bright green. Panicles of tiny flowers, in spring. Small purplish fruits on female trees. Attractive cultivars, foliage variegated in creamy yellow are often available; these include '**Dixon's Cream**' and '**Variegata**'. **Zones 8–11.**

Griselinia lucida

AKEPUKA, PUKA

☀ ❧ ↔ 15 ft (4.5 m) ↑ 15 ft (4.5 m)

In the wild this New Zealand species starts life as an epiphyte. Puka forms a wide-spreading tree, branches close to the ground. Large oval leaves, uneven sides, to 8 in (20 cm) long, very glossy rich green above, paler undersides. '**Variegata**' ★ has variegated leaves. **Zones 9–11.**

GRUSONIA

A genus of 17 species of *Opuntia*-like cacti from southwestern USA, and Baja California and parts of northern Mexico. The genus belongs to the cactus (Cactaceae) family and now includes all species of the former genera *Corynopuntia*, *Marenopuntia*, and *Micropuntia*. It is distinguished from the genus *Cylindropuntia*, however, on the basis of its spines that are flattened, rough or thickened at the base, with little or no sheath. Plants are low-growing, mat-forming to shrubby or even tree-like with numerous jointed branches, which may be cylindrical to club-shaped. The areoles usually carry hairs, glochids, and spines. Flowers are diurnal, pink, purple, yellow, or white. Seed pods are fleshy, dry, and often sterile.

CULTIVATION: Easily grown in a rich well-drained soil. Propagate from seed or cuttings that have been dried out for a week or two. Rest in winter.

Griselinia littoralis '*Variegata*'

Gunnera manicata

Grusonia clavata

syn. *Opuntia clavata*

CLUB CHOLLA, DAGGER CHOLLA

☀ ❧ ↔ 20–84 in (50–200 cm)
↑ 2–6 in (5–15 cm)

From the Great Plains, USA, to northern central Mexico. Stems club-shaped, 1–3 in (25–80 mm) long, oval tubercles. Areoles with white to gray wool, yellowish to white glochids. The spines are prominent, the upper spines white to creamy brown, lower spines white. Flowers bright yellow, to 1 in (25 mm) long. Seed pods barrel- to egg-shaped, yellow, fleshy. **Zones 9–11.**

Grusonia emoryi

syn. *Opuntia emoryi*

CURSED CHOLLA, DEVIL CHOLLA

☀ ❧ ↔ 40 in (100 cm) ↑ 12 in (30 cm)

From the Sonoran and Chihuahuan Deserts of USA and Mexico. Plants form multi-branched low mats of curved club-shaped stem segments with prominent tubercles, 3–8 in (8–20 cm) long. Areoles with white to gray wool, yellow glochids. Spines yellow, reddish brown to tan. Flowers yellow, to 1¼ in (30 mm) long. Seed pods yellow, cylindrical to egg-shaped, fleshy, spineless but with glochids. **Zones 9–11.**

GUNNERA

There are 40 to 50 species of fleshy stemmed perennials in this genus, which belongs to its self-named family, the Gunneraceae. They are native to Australasia, South Africa, South America, and the Pacific. Species range from tiny ground huggers to spectacular giants of 7 ft (2 m) or more. Grown for their foliage, which may be round to oval, heart-shaped or deeply lobed, with or without toothed margins. Tiny greenish yellow or red flowers are borne on

Gunnera insignis

spikes in summer, and followed by red, orange, yellow, or white berries.

CULTIVATION: Excellent plants for waterside planting, the larger species being quite dramatic. Grow in moisture-retentive soils in full sun. Cover the crowns of large species with a protective mulch in winter. Propagate from seed or by division.

Gunnera insignis

POOR MAN'S UMBRELLA

☀ ❆ ↔ 10 ft (3 m) ↑ 7 ft (2 m)

From Central America. Rounded, rough-textured leaves, 3–5 ft (0.9–1.5 m) across, lobed, spiny beneath. Reddish flowers on tall spikes. **Zones 8–10.**

Gunnera manicata

syn. *Gunnera brasiliensis*

GIANT RHUBARB

☀ ❆ ↔ 10–15 ft (3–4.5 m)
↑ 6–10 ft (1.8–3 m)

Spectacular species from South America. The leaves are rhubarb-like, to 7 ft (2 m) or more across, sharply toothed, spiny beneath. Tiny greenish red flowers on erect spikes 3–6 ft (0.9–1.8 m) tall. **Zones 7–9.**

Gustavia augusta

Gunnera tinctoria

Gunnera prorepens

Gunnera prorepens

☼ ❄ ↔ 12–18 in (30–45 cm)
↕ 2–4 in (5–10 cm)

Mat-forming stoloniferous perennial from New Zealand. Small, round-toothed, ovate leaves, bronze to purplish green. Male and female flowers on separate plants; the female plants bear short spikes of dense red berries after flowering. Zones 8–10.

Gunnera tinctoria

syns *Gunnera chilensis, G. scabra*
☼ ❄ ↔ 8 ft (2.4 m) ↕ 6 ft (1.8 m),
From Chile. Similar to *G. manicata* but of smaller and more compact habit. Leaves up to 5 ft (1.5 m) across. Flowering spikes, with redder flowers and fruit than *G. manicata*, are about 2 ft (0.6 m) tall. Zones 7–9.

GUSTAVIA

This genus of 41 evergreen trees from the brazilnut (Lecythidaceae) family family is native to wet tropical Central and South America. Leaves are clustered at the ends of the branches, and

showy flowers are carried in terminal or axillary racemes. The berry-like fruit contains a nut or kernel.
CULTIVATION: Moist, rich, well-drained soils; hot damp conditions. Propagate from seed or by layering.

Gustavia augusta

syn. *Gustavia marcgraaviana*
☼ ❀ ↔ 7 ft (2 m) ↕ 20 ft (6 m)
Native to northeastern South America. Evergreen shrub or small tree, stiff erect habit. Coarse paddle-shaped leaves, to 18 in (45 cm) long, finely toothed edges. Large showy flowers, 6 in (15 cm) or more in diameter, camellia-like white to pink petals, most of the year. Tolerates quite severe dry seasons. Zones 10–12.

GUZMANIA

This genus of about 200 usually epiphytic species, few of which are in cultivation, and over 200 hybrids

Guzmania lingulata

belongs to the bromeliad (Bromeliaceae) family. These plants are found mainly in the high rainforests of Ecuador and Colombia and also in Central America and the West Indies. They grow up to 40 in (100 cm) high and wide but are mostly smaller, with green, spineless, strap-like leaves, sometimes finely lined or cross-banded on the undersides, forming an open rosette. The flower stem is usually conspicuous and the flowerhead is globular to cylindrical, with side branches and flowers on all sides. Beneath each branch or flower there are generally brilliant colored bracts in yellow to orange to red shades. Petals are white or yellow.
CULTIVATION: Recommended for indoor culture if in flower, for greenhouse or conservatory in cool-temperate areas, or outdoors with protection from continuous sunlight and excessive heat in warm-temperate, subtropical, and tropical areas. Prefers a damp atmosphere and a constant temperature 68–86°F (20–30°C). Water when potting mix is dry. Do not over-fertilize. Propagate from seed or offsets.

Guzmania lingulata

☼ ❀ ↔ 8 in (20 cm) ↕ 12 in (30 cm)
Widespread from the West Indies and Central America to Bolivia and Brazil. Leaves 18 in (45 cm) long, green, fine

Guzmania lingulata var. *cardinalis*

Guzmania lingulata 'Rondo'

reddish longitudinal lines beneath, forming a dense spreading rosette. Flower stem usually shorter than leaves. Flowerhead globular with up to 50 flowers, petals white, nestling in a bed of large red to pink bracts. *G. l.* var. *cardinalis* has bright red hooded bracts, foliage often striped. *G. l.* 'Estrella', orange-red flowerhead; 'Empire', smaller form with orange-red star-shaped flowerhead; 'Fortuna', white-tipped brilliant red bracts; and 'Rondo', similar to 'Empire' but with red-striped leaves. Zones 10–12.

Guzmania monostachia

☼ ❀ ↔ 10 in (25 cm) ↕ 16 in (40 cm)
Found from southern Florida to the West Indies, northern Brazil, and Peru. Leaves 12 in (30 cm) long, green, triangular, forming an open spreading rosette. Flower stem much shorter than leaves. Flowerhead erect, cylindrical, to 6 in (15 cm) long, with flowers in all directions. Below each flower is an erect bract up to 1 in (25 mm) long. Bracts are red at top of flowerhead, grading to pale green with brown stripes at base. Petals white. Zones 10–12.

Guzmania musaica

☼ ❀ ↔ 16 in (40 cm) ↕ 20 in (50 cm)
From Panama and Colombia. Strap-like leaves, to 27 in (70 cm) long, can

Guzmania lingulata 'Empire'

Gymnocalycium bruchii

be totally green on both sides, or green on top and purple beneath, or with fine, dark, irregular, transverse lines, forming an open rosette. Flower stem shorter than leaves. Spherical flowerhead, with up to 25 flowers mainly pointing upward. Below each flower is a small red bract. Petals white. Zones 10–12.

Guzmania sanguinea

☀ ⚘ ↔ 32 in (80 cm) ↑ 16 in (40 cm)

From Costa Rica, Colombia, Ecuador, and the coastal area of Venezuela. Leaves 16 in (40 cm) long, strap-like, green, forming an open rosette; center leaves turn bright red at flowering (sometimes yellowish nearest center). No flower stem. Flowerhead globular, in the center of rosette, with up to 12 flowers. From above flowers appear yellow but with white petals. *G. s.* **var.** *comosa* has a rather odd "false" inflorescence composed entirely of reddish bracts that emerges from the center of the flowerhead. Zones 10–12.

Guzmania wittmackii

☀ ⚘ ↔ 36 in (90 cm) ↑ 30 in (75 cm)

From Colombia and Ecuador. Green strap-like leaves, 32 in (80 cm) long, forming an open funnel-shaped

rosette. Flower stem equal in length to leaves. Flowerhead long and slender with very small branches arranged in all directions and well apart. Below each branch is a long thin bract, to 3 in (8 cm) long, which can be red, orange, white, or even green. Flowers have a long white petal tube, about 3 in (8 cm) long. Zones 10–12.

Guzmania Hybrid Cultivars

☀ ⚘ ↔ 10–24 in (25–60 cm) ↑ 18–36 in (45–90 cm)

Most of these cultivars show a strong influence of *G. lingulata* and have a similar growth habit, but usually with more brilliantly colored and larger inflorescence bracts. 'Amaranth', green leaves with brownish lines on the undersides, intense raspberry-purple flower bracts, petals white; 'Attila', dark green rosette, red bracts, yellow flowers; 'Caroline', bright green rosette, pinkish red bracts; 'Cherry', leaves reddish green with faint striping at the base, vibrant cherry red bracts, yellow flowers. 'Cherry Smash', 'Grand Prix' ★, 'Grapeade', 'Orangeade', and 'Samba' are similar but have different-colored bracts. Some forms also have variegated leaves. Zones 9–12.

GYMNOCALYCIUM

A genus of 71 species of small cacti in the Cactaceae family from the Andes in Bolivia, southern Brazil, Paraguay, Uruguay, and Argentina. The genus name is derived from the Greek *gymnos* (naked) and *calyx* (bud), referring to the smooth flower buds. Many species are solitary, but several offset freely. They feature a depressed spherical to short cylindrical trunk with 4 to 15 fairly rounded ribs. Many species have distinct "chins" below the usually large areoles. Spines are variable from thin and weak to strong and stout. Flowers are diurnal, borne at or near the top of the plant, funnelform to bell-shaped, in shades of white, pink, yellow, or red, with large, broad, naked scales on the calyx. Seed pods are spherical to cylindrical.
CULTIVATION: These cacti are easily grown in a rich well-drained soil. Propagate from seed, offsets, or cuttings that have been dried out for a week or two. May also be grown by

dividing clumps of older plants. Rest in winter when plants often pull into the soil and appear rather shrivelled.

Gymnocalycium andreae

☀ ❄ ↔ 6 in (15 cm) ↑ 2 in (5 cm)

From Cordoba and San Luis provinces, Argentina. Freely offsetting, with spherical stems bearing about 8 low rounded ribs with cross-furrows but no chins. Spines 1 to 3, dark brown, upward-curving centrals, 7 thin, white, spreading radials. Flowers yellow, to 1¼ in (30 mm) long. Pods cylindrical, blue-green. Zones 8–11.

Gymnocalycium bruchii

syns *Gymnocalycium albispinum*, *G. lafaldense*

☀ ❄ ↔ 20 in (50 cm) ↑ 1½ in (35 mm)

From the province of Cordoba, Argentina. Depressed spherical trunk, freely offsetting with age, gray-green stems bearing 12 low, rounded, warty ribs without chins. Spines 1 to 3, dark white or brownish, erect centrals,

Guzmania, Hybrid Cultivar, 'Orangeade'

Guzmania, Hybrid Cultivar, 'Amaranth'

Guzmania, Hybrid Cultivar, 'Caroline'

Guzmania, Hybrid Cultivar, 'Grand Prix'

Gymnocalycium mostii

Gymnocalycium mackieanum

Gymnocalycium hossei

G. monvillei subsp. *horridispinum*

gray with age, 7 to 9 spreading radials, curving backward, brown becoming gray with darker tips. Flowers funnelform to bell-shaped, whitish to deep pink. Zones 8–11.

Gymnocalycium mackieanum
syn. *Gymnocalycium schatzlianum*

☀ ❄ ↔ 3 in (8 cm) ↕ 3 in (8 cm)

From Buenos Aires province, Argentina. Solitary, flattened, spherical trunk bearing 16 to 20 ribs forming weak tubercles without chins. Spines 4 to 7 centrals, sometimes only 1, and 9 to 11 thin pale brown radials. Flowers wide, funnelform, greenish yellow, 2½–3 in (6–8 cm) wide. Seed pods club-shaped, dark green. Zones 8–11.

Gymnocalycium monvillei

☀ ❄ ↔ 8 in (20 cm)
↕ 2½–3 in (6–8 cm)

From San Luis and Cordoba provinces, Argentina. Solitary, spherical to elongated-spherical, dark green trunk bearing 10 to 17 broad strongly tubercled ribs. Spines strong, slightly curved, yellowish with red-brown bases, 1 to 4 centrals, sometimes absent, 7 to 13 radials. Flowers white tinged pink, 2½ in (6 cm) wide. Seed pods spherical, green. *G. m.* **subsp.** *horridispinum* ★, 10 to 12 heavy stiff radial spines. Zones 8–11.

Gymnocalycium mostii

☀ ❄ ↔ 5 in (12 cm) ↕ 2½–3 in (6–8 cm)

From Cordoba province, Argentina. Solitary, flattened spherical, dark green trunk bearing 14 to 16 ribs with prominent tubercles and distinct chins. Spines yellowish brown with dark tips becoming gray with age, strong, curved, 1 to 2 centrals, 7 to 11 radials. Flowers bell-shaped, rose pink, to 3 in (8 cm) wide. Seed pods oval, slate blue. Zones 8–11.

12 to 14 backward-curving radials. Flowers pale mauve-pink to white, 2 in (5 cm) across. Seed pods spherical, bluish to whitish. Zones 8–11.

Gymnocalycium castellanosii

☀ ❄ ↔ 4 in (10 cm) ↕ 6 in (15 cm)

From La Rioja and Cordoba provinces, Argentina. Solitary, spherical

to elongated-spherical trunk bearing 10 to 12 low wide ribs divided into distinct tubercles. Spines 1 central, 5 to 7 radials, all to 1 in (25 mm) long, whitish with dark tips. The flowers are funnelform to bell-shaped, white tinged pink, to ¾ in (40 mm) wide. Seed pods spherical, green. Zones 8–11.

Gymnocalycium hossei
syns *Gymnocalycium mazanensis*, *G. nidulans*, *G. weissianum*

☀ ❄ ↔ 6 in (15 cm) ↕ 4 in (10 cm)

From La Rioja and Catamarca provinces, Argentina. Solitary, flattened, spherical trunk, gray-green to brownish green, with 13 to 19 broad ribs. Spines 1 central, brown becoming

Gymnocalycium castellanosii

Gymnocalycium monvillei

Gymnocalycium pungens

Gymnocalycium ochoterenae ★

☀ ❄ ↔ 4–5 in (10–12 cm)
↑ 2–2½ in (5–6 cm)

From Cordoba, La Rioja, and San Luis provinces, Argentina. Solitary, spherical to flattened-spherical, olive green to brownish trunk bearing 14 to 16 ribs. Spines 1 to 7 radials only, bending backward, sometimes comblike, brownish yellow to whitish yellow with dark tips. Flowers white with pink throats, to 1½ in (35 mm) long. Seed pods barrel-shaped, green to dull red. *G. o.* subsp. *vatteri*, only 1 to 3 recurved spines and *G. o.* subsp. *herbertshofferianum* has 6 to 7 comb-like radial spines. Zones 8–11.

Gymnocalycium pungens

☀ ❄ ↔ 3 in (8 cm) ↑ 4 in (10 cm)

Distribution unknown. Solitary, spherical to barrel-shaped, dark green trunk with 13 ribs. Spines 1 to 2 cen-

trals, 7 radials, all equally thin. Flowers are white, ¾ in (18 mm) long. Seed pods are spherical, light red. Zones 8–11.

Gymnocalycium saglionis ★

☀ ❄ ↔ 12 in (30 cm) ↑ 6 in (15 cm)

From northern Argentina. Solitary, spherical, dull green trunk with 10 to 30 deep ribs and prominent rounded tubercles. Spines yellowish brown to reddish black, becoming gray with age, 1 to 3 straight centrals, 10 to 15 radials. Flowers short, white or pink with a red throat, ¾–1¼ in (18–30 mm) wide. Seed pods are spherical, reddish. Zones 8–11.

Gymnocalycium schicken-dantzii

☀ ❄ ↔ 4 in (10 cm) ↑ 2½–3 in (6–8 cm)

From the provinces of Cordoba to Tucuman, Argentina. Has a solitary,

Gymnocalycium schickendantzii

Gymnocarpium dryopteris

spherical, dark olive green to brownish green trunk with 7 to 14 distinctly tubercled ribs. Spines 6 to 7, not distinguished between centrals and radials, reddish gray to yellowish brown. Flowers with long floral tubes, white to reddish, to 2 in (5 cm) long. Seed pods are oval, green to slate blue. Zones 8–11.

Gymnocalycium stenopleurum

syn. *Gymnocalycium mihanovichii* var. *friederichii*

☀ ❄ ↔ 5 in (12 cm) ↑ 5 in (12 cm)

From Boqueron department, Paraguay. Solitary, flattened spherical, gray-green to brown trunk with 1 to 14 rounded ribs with distinct chins. Spines 3 to 6, radials only, light to dark brown. Flowers white, 2–2½ in (5–6 cm) long. Seed pods cylindrical, gray-green. A red variegated form of this plant has been widely propagated by grafting onto *Hylocereus* stocks and sold worldwide under various names such as 'Moon Cactus', 'Red Star Cactus', and 'Ruby Ball'. Zones 8–11.

Gymnocalycium stenopleurum, red form

GYMNOCARPIUM

These 5 deciduous terrestrial ferns from the shield-fern (Dryopteridaceae) family are native to Europe, North America, and Asia. The slender, creeping, and freely branching rhizomes are covered with scales and bristles. Scales cover the bases of the erect frond stalks, which darken in color toward the base. The thin, papery, pinnate, triangular fronds arise singly or in masses.
CULTIVATION: These plants prefer low to medium light in moist garden soil or potting mix. Propagate by division or from spores.

Gymnocarpium dryopteris

COMMON OAK FERN

☀ ❄ ↔ 9–15 in (22–38 cm)
↑ 9–15 in (22–38 cm)

From Europe, temperate Asia, and North America. Spreading blackish rhizomes with brown fibrous scales. Broadly triangular, chartreuse fronds, on erect, slender, shiny, straw-colored stalks, usually single but often in masses, 3–15 in (8–38 cm) tall. Zones 2–9.

GYMNOCLADUS

A member of the pea-flower subfamily of the legume (Fabaceae) family, this genus of 2 to 5 deciduous trees occurs across warm-temperate regions of North America and eastern Asia. They have bipinnate leaves and separate male and female plants with flowers in short terminal panicles. The fruit is a large woody pod containing flat, hard, glossy seeds. The fruit of *G. dioica* was used by early American settlers as a substitute for coffee. Native Americans cooked and ate the seeds. CULTIVATION: Adaptable to most soil types in an open sunny position, these trees are drought and frost tolerant. Propagation is from seed.

Gymnocladus dioica ★

CHICOT, KENTUCKY COFFEE TREE

☼ ❄ ↔ 12 ft (3.5 m) ↑ 75 ft (23 m)

Native to central and eastern North America. Coarsely textured bark, thick branchlets, young twigs light gray, almost white. Large bipinnate leaves, 8 to 14 oval leaflets, pink, turning yellow in autumn. Dull greenish white flowers, in racemes,

Gymnostoma australianum

in summer. Thick, succulent, reddish brown or maroon fruit. *G. d.* var. *folio-variegata*, variegated foliage; *G. d.* 'Variegata', variegated cream foliage. Zones 4–8.

GYMNOSTOMA

This is a genus in the she-oak (Casuarinaceae) family with 18 species occurring in tropical Malaysia, Indonesia, the Philippines, New Guinea, New Caledonia, Fiji, and Australia. All are trees or tall shrubs. Male and female flowers are borne on the same plant or on different plants. The female flowers form a cone that becomes woody and contains the seeds. The needles of the green "foliage" are actually the stems and branchlets, the true leaves being small scale-like objects at the nodes, not functioning as leaves at all. CULTIVATION: Although not grown to any great extent, they deserve greater recognition for their ornamental qualities. Some species are frost tender. They prefer a deep, humus-rich, moist soil. Propagation is from seed, but some will grow from cuttings.

Gymnostoma australianum

☼ ⚘ ↔ 5 ft (1.5 m) ↑ 25 ft (8 m)

Very attractive small tree occurs in small populations in northern Queensland, Australia. Habitat open scrubland on the summit, along streams that descend from the peak to the west and east. Roots are always in water. In cultivation much

Gymnostoma deplancheanum, in the wild, New Caledonia

further south, grows well without wet feet, tolerates near-freezing temperatures. Zones 10–12.

Gymnostoma deplancheanum

☼ ⚘ ↔ 10 ft (3 m) ↑ 20 ft (6 m)

From the Maquis vegetation of New Caledonia, small tree, more robust in all its parts than *G. australianum*. Not known in cultivation, could be grown in regions with low-nutrient soils. Zones 9–10.

Gymnostoma nodiflorum

☼ ⚘ ↔ 20 ft (6 m) ↑ 50 ft (15 m)

This evergreen tree from New Caledonia has a conical habit. The scale leaves are on needle-like stems. The female flowers form a cone. Zones 10–11.

GYNURA

VELVET PLANT

This genus of some 50 species of perennials and subshrubs belongs in the daisy (Asteraceae) family and comes from the tropics, ranging from Java through Thailand to China all the way to East Africa. Although often brightly colored, the flowers are small. These plants are grown for their handsome velvet-covered foliage. CULTIVATION: Except in the tropics, where they can be grown outside in part-shade, these plants are usually grown in containers indoors. Propagation from cuttings and fresh young stock grown each year is best.

Gynura aurantiaca

PURPLE VELVET PLANT, ROYAL VELVET PLANT, VELVET PLANT

☼ ⚘ ↔ 4 ft (1.2 m) ↑ 7–8 ft (2–2.4 m)

Trailing, soft-wooded, evergreen plant from Java. Rich purple bristles cover the 8 in (20 cm) long, spearhead-shaped, scalloped leaves and stems.

Gymnocladus dioica

Gymnostoma nodiflorum

Gypsophila muralis 'Gypsy'

Small orange flowers, to 1 in (25 mm) wide, in open clusters, in winter. **'Purple Passion'** (syn. *G. sarmentosa* of gardens), somewhat more trailing, stems and leaves heavily covered with purple bristles. **Zones 10–12.**

GYPSOPHILA
BABY'S BREATH

Related to the pink (Caryophyllaceae) family, the 100-odd annuals and perennials in this genus occur naturally in temperate Eurasia. They can be spreading mat-forming plants studded with pink or white blooms, or upright shrubby species with billowing heads of tiny flowers. Leaves simple linear to lance-shaped, sometimes rather fleshy and often blue-green. *G. paniculata* and its cultivars are very popular cut flowers. The common name comes from the sweet scent of the flowers. CULTIVATION: *Gypsophila* means lime-loving, but most species are happy in any neutral to slightly alkaline soil that is fertile, moist, and well-drained. Mat-forming species are superb rockery plants. Plant in full sun. Larger types will often rebloom if cut back after their first flush. Propagate from basal cuttings or seed.

Gypsophila cerastioides
☀/◐ ❄ ↔ 8 in (20 cm) ↑ 3 in (8 cm)
Mat-forming perennial from the Himalayas. Small, downy, gray-green

Gypsophila repens

leaves with small sprays of pink-veined white or mauve flowers to over ½ in (12 mm) wide. **Zones 5–9.**

Gypsophila elegans
☀/◐ ❄ ↔ 24 in (60 cm) ↑ 20 in (50 cm)
Annual species native to the Caucasus region, Ukraine, and western Asia. Small clump of narrow blue- to gray-green leaves topped with panicles of tiny flowers; white in the wild, often pink in cultivation. **Zones 7–11.**

Gypsophila muralis
☀/◐ ❄ ↔ 24 in (60 cm) ↑ 24 in (60 cm)
Low spreading annual from central Europe to Siberia. Narrow green to blue-green leaves. Billowing panicles densely packed with tiny white to mauve flowers. **'Garden Bride'**, 12 in (30 cm) tall, starry white and deep pink flowers; **'Gypsy'**, 12 in

(30 cm) tall, dense mound of billowing sprays of small, soft pink, double flowers. **Zones 5–9.**

Gypsophila paniculata
BABY'S BREATH
☀/◐ ❄ ↔ 48 in (120 cm) ↑ 48 in (120 cm)
Rhizome-rooted perennial found from central Europe to central Asia. Forms a bushy clump of narrow blue-gray leaves to 3 in (8 cm) long, often hidden below billowing panicles massed with tiny white or pink flowers. **'Bristol Fairy'** ★, the most widely grown form, has relatively large white double flowers. **Zones 4–9.**

Gypsophila repens
☀/◐ ❄ ↔ 24 in (60 cm) ↑ 4 in (10 cm)
Mat-forming perennial from the mountains of central and southern Europe. Narrow, pointed oval, blue-green leaves to more than ½ in (12 mm) long. Sprays of up to 25 tiny, white, pink, or mauve flowers. **'Rosa Schönheit'** (syn. 'Rose Beauty'), rose pink flowers. **Zones 4–9.**

Gypsophila 'Rosenschleier'
syn. *Gypsophila* 'Rosy Veil'
☀ ❄ ↔ 36 in (90 cm) ↑ 20 in (50 cm)
A pale pink-flowered 12 in (30 cm) tall hybrid with *G. repens*. **Zones 4–9.**

Gypsophila muralis 'Garden Bride'

Gypsophila repens 'Rosa Schönheit'

H

Haemanthus humilis subsp. *hirsutus*

H

Haemanthus amarylloides, in the wild,
Nieuwoudtville, Northern Cape, South Africa

HABERLEA

A genus of only 2 species of evergreen,
stemless, rosette-forming perennials
from the mountains of the Balkans.
Of the African violet (Gesneriaceae)
family, they are much admired by collectors of alpine plants. The foliage is
scalloped and rich dark green, and the
flowers are trumpet-shaped, borne in
clusters on stems held well above the
foliage in spring and early summer.
CULTIVATION: Usually grown in pots
in a cool greenhouse, in rock crevices
or dry-stone walls in cool aspects in
non-tropical climates. Propagate by
division or from leaf cuttings. Can
raise from seed, but hard to germinate.

Haberlea ferdinandi-coburgii

syn. *Haberlea rhodopensis* var.
ferdinandi-coburgii

☀ ❄ ↔ 8–10 in (20–25 cm)
↑ 5–6 in (12–15 cm)

Bulgarian alpine plant. Produces dense
rosettes of scalloped leaves above which
grow violet flowers to 1 in (25 mm)
across with brown and white throats,
in spring–early summer. Zones 6–9.

Haemanthus humilis

HABRANTHUS

This genus of about 10 bulbous
perennials from Central and South
America belongs to the amaryllis
(Amaryllidaceae) family. The solitary,
trumpet-shaped flowers, which appear
after rain in summer and autumn, are
held at an angle from their straight
stems. The leaves are semi-erect,
narrow, and linear. Some species are
evergreen and some deciduous. The
name comes from the Greek *habros,*
meaning graceful—which they are.
CULTIVATION: Give these plants
sharp drainage and a sandy loam.
Apply a weak liquid feed while in
growth and keep slightly moist while
dormant. Propagation is best done
from offsets or from fresh ripe seeds
kept at 61°F (16°C).

Habranthus robustus ★

syn. *Zephyranthes robusta*

☀ ❄ ↔ 4 in (10 cm)
↑ 8–12 in (20–30 cm)

Robust, invasive in appropriate
conditions. Flowers open funnel-
shaped, solitary or paired, 2½ in
(6 cm) across, in summer. Petals
rose pink fading to almost white.
Leaves deep green, finely linear with
a visible midrib, appearing after
flowers and persisting until late
spring. Zones 8–10.

Habranthus tubispathus

☀ ❄ ↔ 3 in (8 cm) ↑ 6–10 in (15–25 cm)
Robust, invasive in appropriate conditions. Flowers small, funnel-shaped,
produced in succession throughout
summer. Petals coppery red, orange,
or yellow. Leaves appear after flowers
and persist until late spring. '**Rosea**',
dark pink petals. Zones 8–10.

HACQUETIA

This genus of a single species in the
carrot (Apiaceae) family inhabits lowland to alpine woods in Europe. It is a
herbaceous clumping perennial with
cut foliage and clusters of tiny yellow
flowers surrounded by green bracts,
looking like large green-petalled
flowers. This charming plant shows
little obvious connection to the carrot.
CULTIVATION: A moist humus-rich
soil under deciduous trees and shrubs
or in a cool rock garden will suit.
Propagate from seed or root cuttings,
or by careful division.

Hacquetia epipactis

☀ ❄ ↔ 6–12 in (15–30 cm)
↑ 5–6 in (12–15 cm)

Widespread throughout Europe, this
woodlander produces bright green-
bracted flowerheads with tiny yellow
flowers, to 1¾ in (40 mm) across, in
early spring. Glossy green leaves, to
2½ in (6 cm) long, have 3 wedge-
shaped leaflets and only reach maturity after flowering. '**Thor**' is a cream
variegated form whose variegation
extends into floral bracts. Zones 6–9.

HAEMANTHUS

At various times, in various places,
and for various reasons botanists have
moved plants between the *Haemanthus*
and *Scadoxa* genera. From tropical
and southern Africa, this bizarre bulbous perennial group from the
amaryllis (Amaryllidaceae) family
divides into those whose growth and
dormancy coincide with wet winter/
dry summer climates and the evergreens that come from areas where
rainfall is more evenly distributed
throughout the year. Typically numerous small flowers form a dense head

with a surrounding decorative whorl
of brightly colored, waxy spathes.
Often, the huge bulbs produce only
2 huge leaves. The name derives from
the Greek *haema*, blood, and *anthos,*
flower. In cool climates many adapt to
frost-protected container culture.
CULTIVATION: Plant with the neck
protruding from the soil, keep wet
and use weak liquid fertilizer while in
growth; cut back moisture when
leaves turn yellow. Propagate from offsets removed when growth resumes,
or from ripe seed.

Haemanthus albiflos

☀ ❄ ↔ 15 in (38 cm) ↑ 12 in (30 cm)
Evergreen species from South Africa.
Large oblong leaves. Thick green stems
support greenish white flowers crowded with yellow-tipped stamens, creating a shaving-brush effect. Zones 9–11.

Haemanthus amarylloides

☀ ❄ ↔ 12 in (30 cm)
↑ 6–12 in (15–30 cm)

From South Africa. Dark green leaves,
upright to spreading, appear after
flowers. Thick purplish red stems bear
shaving-brush flowers varying from
palest to deeper pink. Zones 9–11.

Haemanthus humilis

☀ ❄ ↔ 6 in (15 cm) ↑ 12 in (30 cm)
Flowers about 120, white to pink, in
loose umbels, in early summer. Leaves
2 or 3, borne with flowers, prostrate
or erect, lance-like. *H. h.* subsp.
hirsutus has a much stiffer, conical
umbel. Zones 9–11.

Haemanthus sanguineus

☀ ❄ ↔ 6 in (15 cm) ↑ 12 in (30 cm)
In summer and autumn, produces
dense umbels of 100 small flowers
in red, salmon-pink, or sugar pink.
Stems dark red. Leaves paired, prostrate, dark green, appear after flowers.
Deciduous. Zones 8–10.

HAKEA

There are about 140 species in this
genus of evergreen Australian plants
of the protea (Proteaceae) family,
mostly shrubs or small trees. Leaves

Habranthus robustus

Hacquetia epipactis 'Thor'

Hakea coriacea

vary in shape. Many are grown for their ornamental foliage, particularly the silky new growth. The nectar-rich bird-attracting flowers are borne in short axillary clusters, tight pincushion-like heads or showy spike-like racemes. Large and decorative woody fruits usually persist on the plant until dried or burnt and then split open into 2 valves to release 2 winged seeds. CULTIVATION: Most species are frost tender, especially when young. Hakeas prefer full sun and good drainage and dislike high phosphorus fertilizers. Many are from Western Australia and can usually tolerate periods of dryness during the summer months. Light or moderate pruning will stimulate a compact shape, healthy regrowth and vigor. Some prickly species will trim into a fine impenetrable hedge. Propagation is from seed.

Hakea bucculenta
RED POKERS

☀ ❦ ↔ 7 ft (2 m) ↑ 8 ft (2.4 m)
From Western Australia. Shrub, erect open habit. Flat, leathery, narrow-linear leaves to 8 in (20 cm) long. Red flowers, spike-like racemes to 6 in (15 cm) long, in late winter–spring. Ornamental, bird-attracting species. Does best away from summer humidity. Zones 9–10.

Hakea cinerea
ASHY HAKEA, GRAY HAKEA

☀ ❦ ↔ 4 ft (1.2 m) ↑ 8 ft (2.4 m)
Common on sand heaths in southern Western Australia. Upright or round-ed shrub, hairy branchlets, stiff, sharply pointed gray-green leaves to 6 in (15 cm) long, giving an ashy look. Attractive greenish yellow flowers in rounded clusters 2 in (5 cm) across, in late winter–spring. Zones 9–10.

Hakea cinerea

Hakea coriacea
PINK SPIKE HAKEA

☀ ❦ ↔ 7 ft (2 m) ↑ 20 ft (6 m)
Beautiful flowering shrub or small tree from semi-arid wheatbelt region of Western Australia. Linear gray-green leaves, fine longitudinal veins. Pale to deep pink flowers in spike-like racemes, in late winter–spring. Best suited to winter-rainfall areas. Zones 9–11.

Hakea cristata

☀ ❦ ↔ 8 ft (2.4 m) ↑ 12 ft (3.5 m)
Medium upright shrub from Western Australia. Gray-green leaves, prickly toothed edges. White flowers in small clusters, upper leaf axils, in winter. Dis-likes excessive humidity. Zones 9–11.

Hakea dactyloides
BROAD-LEAFED HAKEA

☀ ❦ ↔ 8 ft (2.4 m) ↑ 10 ft (3 m)
Widely distributed in temperate eastern Australia. Small to medium rounded shrub. Broad flat leaves, 3 or more prominent veins. Numerous clusters of creamy white flowers, in leaf axils, in spring–summer. Good hedge. Zones 9–11.

Hakea drupacea
syn. *Hakea suaveolens*
SWEET-SCENTED HAKEA

☀ ❦ ↔ 10 ft (3 m) ↑ 10 ft (3 m)
From Western Australia. Rounded shrub. Narrow divided foliage with

Hakea dactyloides

sharp-pointed leaf segments. Small, scented, pink-tipped white flowers, in dense axillary clusters, autumn–winter. Useful for hedges and screens, toler-ates coastal exposure. Zones 9–10.

Hakea epiglottis

☀ ❄ ↔ 8 ft (2.4 m) ↑ 12 ft (3.5 m)
Large shrub indigenous to Tasmania, Australia; inhabits wet heaths. Needle-like leaves 1–4 in (25 mm–10 cm) long. Cream or yellowish flowers in small clusters, upper leaf axils, in spring. Small warty fruit. Zones 8–10.

Hakea eyreana
STRAGGLY CORKBARK

☀ ❦ ↔ 6 ft (1.8 m) ↑ 20 ft (6 m)
Small gnarled tree from inland Australia. Dark gray corky bark, cylindrical, divided, pointed leaves. Nectar-rich yellowish flowers, slightly

Hakea laurina

pendulous racemes to 4 in (10 cm) long, in winter. In traditional Aboriginal medicine, bark used to treat burns. Zones 9–10.

Hakea laurina
PINCUSHION HAKEA, PINCUSHION TREE, SEA URCHIN

☀ ❦ ↔ 8 ft (2.4 m) ↑ 25 ft (8 m)
Ornamental shrub or small tree from southern sandplains of Western Australia. Long, narrow, leathery, prominently veined leaves. Nectar-rich creamy white and bright crimson flowers in ball-like clusters, autumn–winter. Dislikes strong winds, exces-sive humidity. Zones 9–11.

Hakea drupacea

Hakea eyreana

H

Hakea lissocarpha

HONEYBUSH

☼ ❄ ↔ 5 ft (1.5 m) ↑ 5 ft (1.5 m)

Widespread in southern Western Australia. Spreading open shrub. Sharply pointed linear leaves in stiff segments. Sweetly scented white or sometimes pale pink flowers in axillary clusters, winter–spring. Prune for low impenetrable hedge. Zones 9–11.

Hakea lissosperma

MOUNTAIN NEEDLEWOOD, NEEDLE BUSH

☼ ❄ ↔ 6 ft (1.8 m) ↑ 10 ft (3 m)

Tall spreading shrub from mountains of southeastern mainland Australia and Tasmania. Gray-green leaves, needle-shaped, about 4 in (10 cm) long, sharply pointed. Small white flowers in short compact spikes, in spring. Zones 8–10.

Hakea microcarpa

SMALL-FRUITED HAKEA

☼ ❄ ↔ 6 ft (1.8 m) ↑ 6 ft (1.8 m)

Spreading shrub often found in wet areas at higher altitudes of southeastern Australia. Leathery needle-like

leaves. Creamy white flowers in small clusters, in late winter–spring. Small leathery fruits. Zones 8–10.

Hakea myrtoides

MYRTLE HAKEA

☼ ❄ ↔ 15 in (38 cm) ↑ 18 in (45 cm)

Low spreading shrub from Western Australia. Crowded leaves, small, broad with long points. Small clusters of deep pink flowers toward branch ends, winter–early spring. Prefers excellent drainage, low humidity. Zones 9–11.

Hakea plurinervia

☼ ❄ ↔ 5 ft (1.5 m) ↑ 10 ft (3 m)

Widespread on coast and nearby ranges of Queensland, Australia. Attractive open shrub. Leathery sickle-shaped leaves, longitudinal veins. Scented white flowers, in dense rounded clusters along stems, in spring. Zones 9–11.

Hakea purpurea

☼ ❄ ↔ 6–10 ft (1.8–3 m) ↑ 6–10 ft (1.8–3 m)

Eastern Australian shrub. Dark green cylindrical leaves divided into prickly

Hakea myrtoides

Hakea plurinervia

Hakea lissosperma

Hakea scoparia

segments. Showy reddish flowers in clusters along the stems, in winter–spring. Prefers warm dry conditions. Good hedge plant. Zones 9–11.

Hakea salicifolia

syn. *Hakea saligna*

WILLOW HAKEA

☼ ❄ ↔ 12 ft (3.5 m) ↑ 20 ft (6 m)

Eastern Australian shrub or small tree. Flat deep green leaves, may be bronze-colored when young. Masses of creamy white scented flowers in axillary clusters, in spring. Small woody fruit. Adaptable plant, will withstand

Hakea purpurea

Hakea microcarpa

Hakea sericea

dry periods. Tolerates strong winds. Excellent hedge, boundary and screen plant. Zones 8–9.

Hakea scoparia

☼ ❄ ↔ 10 ft (3 m) ↑ 10 ft (3 m)

From drier inland districts of southern Western Australia. Ornamental bushy shrub. Sharply pointed linear to cylindrical leaves. Profuse cream, pink or purplish flowers in rounded axillary clusters, winter–spring. Nectar-rich flowers, highly scented, attract birds. Useful screening plant. Zones 9–10.

Hakea sericea

NEEDLEBUSH, SILKY HAKEA

☼ ❄ ↔ 7 ft (2 m) ↑ 3–10 ft (0.9–3 m)

Spreading eastern Australian shrub. Very prickly needle-like leaves. White, or rarely pink, flowers in axillary clusters, during winter–spring. Attractive deep pink form is in cultivation. Tolerant of dry periods and wide range of soil types. Zones 9–10.

Hakea teretifolia

DAGGER HAKEA, NEEDLEBUSH

☼ ❄ ↔ 8 ft (2.4 m) ↑ 8 ft (2.4 m)

Native to southeastern Australia. Spreading prickly shrub. Extremely sharp needle-like leaves 2 in (5 cm) long. White flowers in small axillary clusters, in spring–summer. Unusual narrow fruits, dagger-shaped. Used as a prickly hedge or screen. Zones 9–11.

Hakea victoria

ROYAL HAKEA

☼ ❄ ↔ 4 ft (1.2 m) ↑ 10 ft (3 m)

From southern Western Australia. Cup-shaped leathery leaves, 6 in (15 cm) across, variegated in cream, yellow and green; upper leaves age orange and bright red. Small creamy white flowers in winter. Good drainage needed, without summer humidity. Zones 9–11.

HAKONECHLOA

A grass (Poaceae) family genus comprising one delightful ornamental species and numerous cultivars. This slow-spreading, rhizomatous, perennial grass is found on wet rocky cliffs in the mountains of the Tokaido district of southeast Honshu, Japan. The linear to lance-shaped blades grow to 12–36 in (30–90 cm) tall, and in mid- to late summer small airy inflorescences appear between the leaves, which turn orange to bronze in autumn. A number of attractive variegated forms exist whose variegation is affected by siting and climatic conditions: in deep shade, yellow variegation is lime green; in partial shade in warm regions, the yellow parts turn a strong gold-yellow; grown in full sun in cool summer climates, yellow variegation bleaches to creamy white.
CULTIVATION: Frost-hardy. Prefers moist, humus-rich, well-drained soil. Grow in full or half-sun, depending on climate. It requires shade in hot dry areas. Generally disease free, it can be propagated by division in spring.

Hakonechloa macra
HAKONE GRASS, JAPANESE FOREST GRASS, URAHAGUSA
☼ ❄ ↔ over 24 in (60 cm)
↑ to 24 in (60 cm)

Slender, arching, green leaves with wiry stems form loose cascading mounds. Provides dramatic textural contrasts, particularly planted in drifts. Orange- to red-flushed autumn foliage persists into winter. Green-leafed form is more cold hardy (Zone 4), sun and drought tolerant, and faster growing than cultivars, which both reach 12 in (30 cm) high. 'Alboaurea', mostly off-white and yellow variegated leaves with green, and red- to pink-flushed autumn foliage; 'Aureola' ★, golden yellow leaves and thin green stripes, pinkish red tints in autumn. Zones 6–11.

HALESIA
SILVERBELL
This is a genus of 4 or 5 species of deciduous shrubs or small trees in the storax (Styracaceae) family, indigenous to China and eastern North America. Predominantly found in moist deciduous woodlands, these plants have graceful and attractive spring flowers. Individually the flowers are simple, small white bells, but massed together, moving on the breeze, they have an instant appeal. Winged fruits appear in autumn. The leaf is usually a simple mid-green ellipse, to 5 in (12 cm) long.
CULTIVATION: At home in a moist humid environment sheltered from strong winds. They are cool-climate plants but need a hot summer for best display of flowers. Soil should be well drained and slightly acidic. Confine pruning to trimming shape. Propagate from seed or summer cuttings.

Halesia carolina
syn. *Halesia tetraptera*
CAROLINA SILVERBELL, SILVERBELL, SNOWDROP TREE
☼ ❄ ↔ 25–30 ft (8–10 m)
↑ 25–40 ft (8–12 m)
From North Carolina, USA. Spreading crown. Most commonly cultivated species. Heavy flowering, in spring, with the tree smothered in pendulous clusters of white or pink-flushed bells which, by autumn, develop into 4-winged fruit. Foliage develops yellow tones, in autumn. Zones 3–9.

Halesia diptera
TWO-WING SILVERBELL
☼ ❄ ↔ 30 ft (9 m) ↑ 20 ft (6 m)
Native to southeastern USA. Most commonly a large shrub, sometimes attains tree-like proportions. Leaves to 4 in (10 cm) long, edged with minute teeth, downy when young. Flowers less than 1 in (25 mm) wide, white with downy calyces, in clusters of 3 to 6, followed by 2-winged fruits. Zones 6–9.

Halesia monticola
syn. *Halesia carolina* subsp. *monticola*
CAROLINA SILVERBELL, MOUNTAIN SILVERBELL, MOUNTAIN SNOWDROP TREE
☼ ❄ ↔ 20 ft (6 m) ↑ 30 ft (9 m)
From North America. Larger in the wild. Wide-spreading crown. White flowers in clusters of 2 to 5 blooms, followed by 4-winged fruit. *H. m.* f.

Halgania cyanea

rosea, pale pink flowers. Some botanists now treat this as a subspecies of *H. carolina*. Zones 4–9.

HALGANIA
This small genus of evergreen shrubs from Australia belongs to the borage (Boraginaceae) family, the majority occurring in Western Australia in poor sandy soils and often rather arid climates. They are low-growing sparse shrubs with small simple leaves that are harsh to the touch and often rather sticky due to a resinous exudation. Flowers are star-shaped, mostly blue or purple, sometimes white or pink, with the stamens grouped in a tight cone in the center.
CULTIVATION: Halganias prefer light to medium alkaline soils in an open sunny position, and are drought and frost resistant. Propagate by tip cuttings taken in early autumn or by division of suckers.

Halgania cyanea
ROUGH HALGANIA
☼ ❄ ↔ 18 in (45 cm) ↑ 12 in (30 cm)
Native of dry central Australia. Drought-resistant evergreen shrub. Erect, branching habit, hairy stems, narrow, blunt dull green leaves, finely toothed margins. Deep blue, tubular star-shaped flowers, 5 petals, in loose heads, in spring–summer. Zones 10–12.

× HALIMIOCISTUS
This grouping of intergeneric hybrids between *Halimium* and *Cistus* includes some that occur naturally in their Mediterranean homelands and others of garden origin. These members of the rock-rose (Cistaceae) family are small evergreen shrubs intermediate in form between the parent genera, with small downy leaves, often gray-green to slightly glaucous, with flowers similar to *Cistus* but smaller and with the addition of yellow to their palette. Most flower in summer.

Hakea victoria

CULTIVATION: Tolerating hardy to moderate frosts and easily grown in any sunny position with light well-drained soil, these are vigorous shrubs well suited to large rock gardens or general planting with other sun-lovers. They can be trimmed after flowering, though tidying is often best left until spring, when any winter damage can also be removed. Propagation is done by taking half-hardened tip cuttings in late summer or autumn.

× Halimiocistus 'Ingwersii'
☼ ❄ ↔ 36 in (90 cm) ↑ 18 in (45 cm)
Found growing in Portugal about 1929; hybrid between *Halimium umbellatum* and *Cistus hirsutus*. Dwarf spreading shrub, narrow, elongated, dark green, hairy leaves. White flowers produced over an extended period through summer. Zones 8–10.

× Halimiocistus sahucii
syn. × *Halimiocistus revolii*
☼ ❄ ↔ 20–36 in (50–90 cm)
↑ 20–24 in (50–60 cm)
From southern France. Naturally occurring hybrid between *Halimium umbellatum* and *Cistus salviifolius*.

Halesia carolina

Halesia diptera

× *Halimiocistus wintonensis* 'Merrist Wood Cream'

× *Halimiocistus sahucii*

Narrow ½–1 in (12–25 mm) long leaves with a covering of fine hairs. Massed 3- to 5-flowered clusters of small white flowers, in spring–summer. Zones 8–10.

× *Halimiocistus wintonensis*
☼ ❄ ↔ 30 in (75 cm) ↑ 24 in (60 cm)
Originating in Hillier's Nursery, this chance hybrid between *Halimium ocymoides* and *Cistus salviifolius* has grayish leaves. Large, 2 in (5 cm) wide flowers, pearly white, feathered zone of crimson-maroon, contrasting with yellow stains at base of petals. 'Merrist Wood Cream', a sport found in 1978, flower color pale milky yellow, with maroon basal spot. Zones 8–9.

HALIMIUM

There are about 12 species of evergreen shrubs and subshrubs in this genus of the rock-rose (Cistaceae) family. They are native to the Mediterranean region and western Asia in dry open forest thickets and sandy and rocky scrubland. These gray-leafed plants resemble *Cistus* (rock rose), for which they are often mistaken.
CULTIVATION: Mild winters and warm summers are the ideal condi-

tions for cultivation. *Halimium* species grow in full sun in sandy, moderately fertile soil with protection from cold and drying winds. For best results, grow in pots or a rock garden border. In areas with wet winters, extra sharp drainage needs to be provided or the plants need to be protected from oversaturation. Grow from seed in spring in a heated tray or take half-hardened cuttings in late summer.

Halimium atriplicifolium
☼ ❄ ↔ 3 ft (0.9 m) ↑ 5 ft (1.5 m)
Upright shrub native to Spain and Morocco. Leaves elliptic with silvery scales, 3 distinctive veins. Bright yellow flowers, with or without a reddish brown spot, in late spring–early summer. Zones 8–9.

Halimium halimifolium
☼ ❄ ↔ 3 ft (0.9 m) ↑ 3 ft (0.9 m)
Erect shrub from southwestern Europe and North Africa. Leaves oblong to lance-shaped, gray-green with silver scales. Panicle-like cymes of yellow flowers, with a red-brown blotch at base of each petal, in late spring–early summer. Zones 8–9.

Halimium lasianthum ★
syn. *Halimium formosum*
☼ ❄ ↔ 4 ft (1.2 m) ↑ 3 ft (0.9 m)
Bushy erect shrub from Spain and Portugal. Gray foliage. Clusters of yellow flowers, with a dark red basal spot, from leaf axils, in spring–early summer. *H. l.* subsp. *alyssoides*, compact shrub, native to southwestern Europe; egg- to lance-shaped leaves, dark green above, white hairy undersides; small yellow flowers, in cymes from the axils or tips of branches,

in late spring–early autumn. *H. l.* subsp. *formosum*, has slightly larger flowers with a distinct rust red basal spot. *H. l.* 'Concolor', no basal spot; 'Sandling', bright maroon basal spot. Zones 8–9.

Halimium ocymoides
syn. *Cistus algarvensis*
☼ ❄ ↔ 3 ft (0.9 m) ↑ 3 ft (0.9 m)
Erect, compact, bushy shrub from southwestern Europe. Leaves are lance- to egg-shaped, gray-green, with white down. Golden yellow flowers, each petal with a deep maroon spot, arise from terminal panicles, in early–late summer. Zones 8–9.

Halimium Hybrid Cultivars
☼ ❄ ↔ 3 ft (0.9 m) ↑ 3 ft (0.9 m)
Shrubs with spreading habit. 'Sarah', bright yellow blooms with brown centers; 'Susan', more compact than *H. ocymoides* with broader leaves, often with semi-double yellow flowers, in summer. Zones 8–9.

HALLERIA

Belonging to the foxglove (Scrophulariaceae) family, this genus contains 4 species occurring in southern Africa and Madagascar. All are evergreen trees or shrubs with curved tubular flowers which are rich in nectar and attract many birds, sunbirds in particular. Fruits are fleshy and black when ripe; the long style persists at maturity.
CULTIVATION: These plants are frost hardy and drought resistant and prefer a fertile light soil and full sun in a warm climate. Propagate from seed or cuttings. The fruits contain a germination inhibitor so the flesh must be removed and the seeds air-dried in shade before sowing. Seedlings take 4 to 8 weeks to appear.

Halleria lucida
TREE FUCHSIA
☼ ❄ ↔ 12 ft (3.5 m) ↑ 35 ft (10 m)
Evergreen tree, larger in wild, from Ethiopia to southern tip of Africa. Leaves glossy green above, paler below, broadly lance-shaped to oval,

tapering tip, finely toothed edges. Flowers tubular, orangey red, in clusters in leaf axils or borne on branches or trunk, stems, in winter–spring. Edible fleshy black fruits. Zones 8–10.

HALOCARPUS

There are 3 species of evergreen coniferous trees or shrubs in this genus, all native to New Zealand. The genus, in the plum-pine (Podocarpaceae) family, is closely related to *Dacrydium*. Juvenile foliage is needle-like and becomes compressed and scale-like on adult plants. The male cones and fruiting structures are very small.
CULTIVATION: All are slow growing and are useful additions to the conifer or rock garden. *H. bidwillii* and *H. biformis* can withstand cold and fairly wet conditions but *H. kirkii* is less hardy. They grow best in a deep, moist but well-drained soil. Propagation is usually from seed but half-hardened cuttings can be taken in summer.

Halocarpus bidwillii
syn. *Dacrydium bidwillii*
BOG PINE
☼ ❄ ↔ 3 ft (0.9 m) ↑ 7 ft (2 m)
From mountainous areas of New Zealand. Spreading shrub, needle-like juvenile leaves, bronze tones in winter, compressed adult foliage deep green. Although called bog pine, it also grows in dry stony ground. Zones 7–10.

Halleria lucida

Halimium lasianthum

Halimium, Hybrid Cultivar, 'Sarah'

Halocarpus biformis

Hamamelis × *intermedia* cultivar

Hamamelis × *intermedia* 'Pallida'

Halocarpus biformis
syn. *Dacrydium biforme*
YELLOW PINE
☼ ❄ ↔ 10 ft (3 m) ↑ 12 ft (3.5 m)
Slow-growing species, found in mountainous regions of New Zealand. Rounded shrub or tree. Needle-like juvenile foliage and scale-like adult foliage sometimes appear together on the same branches. Zones 7–10.

HAMAMELIS
A small genus of 5 or 6 species of deciduous winter-flowering shrubs or small trees in the witch hazel (Hamamelidaceae) family, found in eastern North America and eastern Asia. They are characterized by spider-like, yellow or reddish, perfumed flowers, with crinkled strap-shaped petals, clustered on the bare branches from mid-winter to early spring. Foliage often provides attractive autumn color. Fruit is a horned capsule containing 2 shiny black seeds.
CULTIVATION: Witch hazels grow mainly in the shade of light woodland, prefer some shade from the midday sun, and like a cool moist climate. The best flowers are borne on strong, young, 1 to 3-year-old shoots that

have not been shortened. Cutting for indoor decoration makes way for new shoots. Seeds can be collected before they are discharged and sown at once, but germination may take a year or more. Layers can be put down in winter and lifted the following winter.

Hamamelis 'Brevipetala'
syn. *Hamamelis mollis* 'Brevipetala'
☼/☀ ❄ ↔ 10–15 ft (3–4.5 m)
↑ 10–17 ft (3–5 m)
Probably a hybrid, not a form of *H. mollis*. Has short, curled, rich yellow petals with a brown-red center. Scented blossoms in dense clusters along bare stems in winter. Zones 6–9.

Hamamelis × intermedia
HYBRID WITCH HAZEL
☼ ❄ ↔ 12 ft (3.5 m) ↑ 12 ft (3.5 m)
Hybrid between *H. japonica* and *H. mollis*, large shrub. Leaves, to 6 in (15 cm) long, turn yellow in autumn. Flowers have crimped petals, creamy, red, and apricot. 'Arnold Promise' ★, dense clusters of dark yellow flowers; 'Diane', red flowers, with leaves that color well in autumn; 'Jelena', vigorous spreading habit, large broad leaves, flowers yellow suffused with copper red, foliage turning orange, red and scarlet; 'Pallida', clear sulfur or lemon yellow flowers with no trace of other colors. Zones 4–9.

Hamamelis japonica
JAPANESE WITCH HAZEL
☼ ❄ ↔ 12 ft (3.5 m) ↑ 15 ft (4.5 m)
Large spreading shrub or small tree. Short stout trunk, rigid branches. Leaves become shiny and smooth when mature. Flowers small to medium, with crimpled petals. 'Sulphurea', large spreading shrub, ascending branches, small to medium flowers, pale sulfur yellow in color. Zones 4–9.

Hamamelis mollis
CHINESE WITCH HAZEL, WITCH HAZEL
☼ ❄ ↔ 12 ft (3.5 m) ↑ 15 ft (4.5 m)
Native of central and eastern China. Leaves mid-green, downy above, gray-green beneath, turning deep golden yellow, in autumn. Perfumed flowers in axillary clusters, 1 to 2-year-old wood, golden yellow straight petals; calyx yellow-brown, 4 spreading sepals chocolate brown inside. Zones 4–9.

Hamamelis virginiana ★
syn. *Hamamelis macrophylla*
COMMON WITCH HAZEL, WITCH HAZEL
☼ ❄ ↔ 8–12 ft (2.4–3.5 m)
↑ 12–15 ft (3.5–4.5 m)
Native to northeastern USA down to the Lawrence Valley and into Virginia. Leaves dark green, shiny above, paler beneath. Flowers in small clusters in upper axils, yellow in color, in autumn before leaves fall, sometimes partly obscured. Zones 7–9.

HAPLOPAPPUS
IRONPLANT
This genus contains about 160 annual or perennial herbs, subshrubs and shrubs in the daisy (Asteraceae) family

Hamamelis mollis

Hamamelis virginiana

that come from North and South America. The yellow or sometimes purple daisy-like flowers are borne singly or in clusters of many-flowered heads. The woody tap root can reach depths of 36–48 in (90–120 cm), forming a hard woody base, hence "ironplant." Fruits are tiny achenes (one-seeded fruits), with bristles to aid wind dispersal. The botanical name is from the Greek *haplous* (simple) and *pappos* (down or fluff), referring to the bristles at the base of the flowers. Navajo Indians used the leaves and roots for toothache.
CULTIVATION: Prefer full sun with moist soil, though quite drought tolerant. Propagate from seed.

Haplopappus glutinosus
☼ ⚘ ↔ 4–12 in (10–30 cm)
↑ 4–12 in (10–30 cm)
Perennial from Chile and Argentina. Spreading or erect stems, often forming cushions. Oblong or elliptical lobed leaves, to 1¾ in (40 mm) long, with 1 to 4 narrow segments. Single flowerheads of yellow daisy-like flowers on stalks to 6 in (15 cm) tall, in winter. Zones 9–11.

Hamamelis japonica

HARDENBERGIA
AUSTRALIAN SARSAPARILLA

A member of the pea-flower subfamily of the legume (Fabaceae) family, this genus consists of 3 species of evergreen climbing shrubs or trailers. They are all native to Australia where they often make quite an impact in late winter and early spring when they flower. The spearhead-shaped leaves are glossy and set off the cluster of small usually purple pea-flowers.
CULTIVATION: In the almost frost-free climates in which these species grow best, they are used to cover banks, are trained over fences and arbors, or are used to hide any eyesore in the garden. They can be grown in full sun or light shade in well-drained to dry soils. Propagation is best done from seed soaked in hot water before sowing; selected cultivars are grown from cuttings.

Hardenbergia comptoniana
NATIVE LILAC, WILD SARSAPARILLA, WILD WISTERIA VINE

☼/◐ ⬧ ↔ 3–10 ft (0.9–3 m)
↑ 10–15 ft (3–4.5 m)

Native to Western Australia, from Perth to Albany, this is a vigorous evergreen climbing vine with 3 leaflets per leaf, to 2½ in (6 cm) long. Masses of usually purple-blue flowers, to ½ in (12 mm) across, with green spots at their base, are seen in late winter. Zones 10–11.

Harrisia martinii

Hardenbergia violacea

☼ ⬧ ↔ 3–7 ft (0.9–2 m)
↑ 3–10 ft (0.9–3 m)

From Eastern Australia. Climbing or sprawling plant. Wiry stems with dark green, leathery, lance-shaped leaves. Racemes of deep purple pea-flowers smother the plant in late winter. 'Happy Wanderer' ★, vigorous, free-flowing, climbing form; 'Minihaha', compact dwarf shrub to 6 in (15 cm) tall, with small leaves and deep mauve flowers in spring. Zones 9–11.

HARPEPHYLLUM

One species makes up this genus from South Africa which, though its common name suggests it is a type of plum, is a member of the cashew (Anacardiaceae) family. An evergreen, it is widely planted as a street or park tree in warmer climates or on the west side of houses for shade. However, in a garden situation it may be difficult to grow plants under it due to the dense shade it provides.
CULTIVATION: Although tolerant of a wide range of soils, it needs a frost-free situation where its low branching habit has room to form a dense crown. Propagation is from seed, which is only produced by the female tree if a male tree is nearby.

Harpephyllum caffrum
SOUTH AFRICAN WILD PLUM, WILDEPRUIM

☼ ⬧ ↔ 25 ft (8 m) ↑ 30 ft (9 m)

Densely foliaged tree, broad crown deep green, shiny compound leaves. White flowers insignificant. Plum-sized fruit follows, ripening to orange-red, used for jam. Zones 9–11.

HARPULLIA

This genus in the soapberry family (Sapindaceae), which includes the lychee tree, consists of around 37 species from tropical Asia to Australia and Madagascar. Most are rainforest trees or shrubs and have pinnate

Harpephyllum caffrum

Hardenbergia violacea

leaves. The white to greenish or yellowish flowers have 4 or 5 petals, usually in a raceme or panicle. The fruit is a leathery, inflated, often hairy capsule containing black shiny seeds. Only 1 of the species is commonly cultivated, though all have potential as container plants in a bright spot indoors.
CULTIVATION: These plants require full sun to half-sun, depending on the species; *H. pendula* can be grown in full sun and is used as a street tree in tropical and subtropical regions. A well-drained mulched soil with adequate watering in dry periods is needed and protection from strong winds is best. Propagate from seed sown when fresh.

Harpullia pendula
TULIPWOOD

☼ ⬧ ↔ 15 ft (4.5 m) ↑ 50 ft (15 m)

Native of coastal northeast Australia. Broad crown, straight trunk, suitable shade tree. Compound pinnate leaves, glossy green leaflets, paler beneath. Pendulous panicles, pale greenish yellow, fragrant flowers. Capsules ripen yellow to red, and contain black seeds. Zones 9–11.

HARRISIA

A genus of about 20 species of thin sprawling cacti in the Cactaceae family, widespread in Florida, the Caribbean, Brazil, Bolivia, Paraguay, and Argentina. The genus name commemorates the work of the Jamaican botanist, William Harris. Plants are shrubby to tree-like, clambering or prostrate, with many upright, arching

Harpullia pendula

Hardenbergia violacea 'Minihaha'

or even prostrate branches up to 25 ft (8 m) long. Branches are usually cylindrical, ribbed, not segmented, and do not make aerial roots. Spines vary from a few to numerous. Flowers are funnel-form, nocturnal, white and relatively large, 5–10 in (12–25 cm) long, 3–5 in (8–12 cm) in diameter. Seedpods are spherical, yellow, orange or red, 1¾–2½ in (4–6 cm) in diameter. This genus now includes the former *Eriocereus* and *Roseocereus* species.
CULTIVATION: These species are easily grown in a rich well-drained soil. Propagate from seed or cuttings that have been dried out for a week or two. Rest in winter.

Harrisia 'Jusbertii'
MOON CACTUS

☼ ⬧ ↔ 4–8 ft (1.2–2.4 m)
↑ 7–15 ft (2–4.5 m)

Believed to be from Argentina or Peru but with no natural location established, and now assumed to be a hybrid. Solitary becoming branched from base with solid dark green stems, about 2 in (5 cm) in diameter, bearing 5 to 6 low ribs and clusters of very distinctive spines—1 to 4 centrals and 6 to 7 radials to ¼ in (6 mm) long, black, thick and conical. Flowers white, nocturnal, 6 in (15 cm) long. Seedpods spherical, red. Zones 9–12.

Harrisia martinii
MOON CACTUS

☼ ⬧ ↔ 7–10 ft (2–3 m) ↑ 7 ft (2 m)

From the Gran Chaco region of Argentina. Forms dense thickets of long green to gray-green branches, 4- to 5-ribbed, becoming cylindrical with age. Spines: 1 central, yellow with a dark tip, ¾–1¼ in (18–30 mm) long; 5 to 7 shorter radials. Flowers 6–8 in (15–20 cm) long. Seedpods egg-shaped, red, 1½ in (35 mm) long. Zones 9–12.

HATIORA

A genus of 5 species of epiphytic or lithophytic cacti from Brazil belonging to the Cactaceae family. Several species resemble some members of the genus *Rhipsalis* but are distinguished by their determinate growth habit— that is, each stem segment grows to a predetermined size and shape before producing another segment. The stem shapes are variable, from flattened to cylindrical. The name *Hatiora* is an anagram of the family name of Thomas Hariot, a sixteenth-century Jamaican botanist. Plants are erect at first, then spreading, and in time becoming pendulous. Flowers are diurnal, bell-shaped, yellow, pink or red, and arise only from the terminal stem segments.

CULTIVATION: Easily grown in a rich well-drained soil. Propagate from seed or cuttings that have been dried out for a week or two. Rest in winter.

Hatiora gaertneri ★
syns *Schlumbergera gaertneri,*
Rhipsalis gaertneri
EASTER CACTUS
☀/◑ ❄ ↔ 12–20 in (30–50 cm)
↕ 12–20 in (30–50 cm)

From Parana and Santa Catarina, Brazil. Pendent multi-branched shrub consisting of numerous dull green segments, 1¾–3 in (40 mm–8 cm) long, with brown bristles at the tips, from which 1 to 3 funnel-form red flowers arise. Has been an important parent in many successful hybrids with other species of *Hatiora* and related epiphytic cacti. Zones 9–12.

Hatiora rosea ★
syn. *Rhipsalis rosea*
EASTER CACTUS
☀/◑ ❄ ↔ 8–12 in (20–30 cm)
↕ 12–16 in (30–40 cm)

From Parana to Rio Grande do Sol, Brazil. Erect to sprawling plant. Stem segments are flat to 3-sided, reddish becoming green, ¾–1¼ in (18–40 mm) long, margins with 2 to 3 notches. Areoles from segment

× *Hawkinsara* Keepsake 'Lake View'

tips. Flowers terminal, diurnal, pink, funnel-form, 1¼–1¾ in (30–40 mm) long. Zones 9–12.

× HAWKINSARA
A member of the orchid (Orchidaceae) family, × *Hawkinsara* is a multi-generic artificial orchid genus created by combining members of the sympodial Central and South American genera *Broughtonia, Cattleya, Laelia,* and *Sophronitis.* The use of the miniature *Broughtonia* and *Sophronitis* has significantly reduced the plant size of these hybrids and contributed to the flowers' round shape and bold color. The flowers are often highly colorful and long lasting, with many intense reds, and the blooms are produced on strong stems well clear of the compact foliage.

CULTIVATION: They grow well in small pots of a course bark-based medium or in wooden baskets, as long as they dry out between waterings. They enjoy high light and intermediate to warm temperatures throughout the year. Propagate by division.

× Hawkinsara Keepsake 'Lake View'
☀/◑ ❄ ↔ 4–12 in (10–30 cm)
↕ 4–20 in (10–50 cm)

Compact-growing, brightly colored orange to red hybrid combining 5 species—*Broughtonia sanguinea,*

Hatiora gaertneri

Cattleya aurantiaca, Cattleya aclandiae, Laelia cinnabarina, and *Sophronitis coccinea.* Blooms in summer, individual flowers 2 in (5 cm) across. Zones 10–12.

HAWORTHIA
This genus, grown for its interesting foliage, belongs to the asphodel (Asphodelaceae) family and contains 70 to 160 species of dwarf succulent perennials native to southern Africa. Plants form low spirally arranged rosettes and often resemble in miniature the related *Aloe.* Leaf form varies widely, with shapes ranging from triangular to lance-shaped, margins toothed or even, and leaf tips blunt or sharp. Some have transparent "windows" to allow light into the middle of the plant. The leaf surfaces may be plain or patterned, smooth or roughened with tiny growths called tubercles. Some have a firm consistency while others are soft and juicy. The small 2-lipped flowers, borne on relatively tall stems, are usually white with 6 flaring petals.

CULTIVATION: Grow in a well-drained soil in semi-shade. Water well in summer but keep dry and protect from frosts in winter. Indoor plants will tolerate quite low light levels. Propagate from offsets or seed.

Haworthia arachnoidea
COBWEB ALOE
◑ ❄ ↔ 5 in (12 cm) ↕ 4 in (10 cm)
From South Africa, this species has stemless rounded rosettes and oblong to lance-shaped, soft, juicy, green leaves with semi-transparent flecking. They are edged with fine white to brown teeth that are filament-like in some varieties. Zones 9–11.

Haworthia coarctata
☀ ❄ ↔ 6 in (15 cm) ↕ 8 in (20 cm)
From South Africa. Dense columnar rosettes of overlapping, incurving, triangular, yellowish green leaves can turn reddish brown under hard conditions. Leaf surface covered with white or pale green tubercles. Zones 9–11.

Haworthia cymbiformis
◑ ❄ ↔ 4 in (10 cm) ↕ 2 in (5 cm)
From South Africa. Stemless rosettes which offset freely. Soft, incurving, thick, triangular leaves are translucent pale green with darker lines. *H. c.* var. *variegata* has cream leaves with splashes of green. Zones 9–11.

Haworthia fasciata ★
ZEBRA HAWORTHIA
◑ ❄ ↔ 6 in (15 cm) ↕ 6 in (15 cm)
From South Africa. Stemless rosettes of narrow, sharply pointed, upright leaves, dark green; smoother upper-surface, horizontal striping of white tubercles on undersides. Zones 9–11.

Haworthia pumila
syn. *Haworthia margaritifera*
◑ ❄ ↔ 6 in (15 cm) ↕ 4 in (10 cm)
From South Africa. Rosettes of long, triangular, upright and incurving leaves. Undersides are prominently covered in large white tubercles. Zones 9–11.

Haworthia reinwardtii
◑ ❄ ↔ 3 in (8 cm) ↕ 6 in (15 cm)
From South Africa, this species forms a tight columnar rosette of incurving triangular leaves. Closely resembles *H. coarctata* but leaves are slightly bigger and tubercles larger but less prominent. Zones 9–11.

Haworthia coarctata

HEBE

There are about 100 species of evergreen shrubs in this genus in the figwort or foxglove (Scrophulariaceae) family, most native to New Zealand, others from Australia and South America. The species described below are found in New Zealand. They grow in a wide range of habitats from coastal to alpine regions. There are 2 distinct foliage groups: those with oval to lance-shaped leaves, and the 'whipcord' hebes, which have compressed scale-like leaves resembling conifers. Flower spikes of small tubular flowers range in color from white through pink to deep purple and crimson. Many cultivars and hybrids are available. CULTIVATION: Most hebes prefer a sunny situation, tolerating a wide range of soil conditions. They vary in degree of frost hardiness, bigger-leafed species being more tender. Whipcord species dislike heat and humidity, requiring a gritty well-drained soil. Some are suitable for coastal planting.

Hebe albicans 'Red Edge'

Hebe albicans 'Sussex Carpet'

Hebe cockayneana

Leaf spot and downy mildew can be a problem in humid areas. Prune after flowering to maintain a compact shape. Propagation is from seed or half-hardened cuttings in late summer, cultivars from cuttings only.

Hebe albicans

☼ ❄ ↔ 27 in (70 cm)
↕ 18–24 in (45–60 cm)

Found in rocky mountain areas of northern South Island, New Zealand. Forms a compact shrub. Attractive glaucous leaves, closely packed on stout branchlets. Small white flowers, summer–autumn, crowded on short racemes. 'Red Edge', dark red margins around its grayish green leaves, in winter becoming suffused with maroon; 'Sussex Carpet', opposite pairs of blue-green leaves. Zones 8–10.

Hebe amplexicaulis

☼ ❄ ↔ 24 in (60 cm) ↕ 20 in (50 cm)
Sprawling shrub, grows naturally in a few mountainous locations of central South Island, New Zealand. Thick oval bluish leaves, small white flowers, in summer. *H. a.* var. *hirta*, small pale mauve flowers. Zones 8–10.

Hebe × andersonii ★

☼ ❄ ↔ 4 ft (1.2 m) ↕ 3–7 ft (0.9–2 m)
Hybrid of *H. speciosa* and *H. stricta*. Well-branched shrub, broadly lance-shaped leaves to 4 in (10 cm) long. Violet flowers crowded on spikes to 4 in (10 cm) long, summer–autumn.

Hebe amplexicaulis var. *hirta*

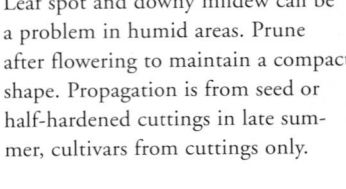

Hebe buchananii

H. × *a.* 'Variegata', attractive foliage, in shades of dark green, grayish green and creamy white. Zones 9–11.

Hebe armstrongii

☼ ❄ ↔ 3 ft (0.9 m) ↕ 3 ft (0.9 m)
Whipcord species, erect well-branched shrub. Very rare in the wild, found in a few mountain areas of central South Island, New Zealand. Yellowish green color of branches intensifies in winter. Small white flowers, secondary to the foliage effect. Zones 8–10.

Hebe buchananii

☼ ❄ ↔ 12 in (30 cm) ↕ 12 in (30 cm)
Alpine species from the South Island, New Zealand. Small, sometimes sprawling shrub, suitable for rock gardens. Well-branched, blackish branches. Small, almost round, dark green leaves become glaucous in full sun. Small white flowers on short spikes, in spring–autumn. 'Minor', low-growing shrub. Zones 8–10.

Hebe carnosula

☼ ❄ ↔ 16 (40 cm) ↕ 8–16 in (20–40 cm)
Variable species or natural hybrid, growing wild from Nelson to Otago, on New Zealand's South Island. Nearly prostrate, with broadly egg-shaped gray-green leaves with a whitish bloom, to 15 mm long. Early summer flowers with pinkish buds open to white. Zones 7–10.

Hebe chathamica

☼ ❄ ↔ 3 ft (0.9 m) ↕ 12 in (30 cm)
Native to the Chatham Islands, growing on seaside cliffs. Prostrate shrub, small shiny green leaves, fleshy, white to pale violet flowers, on short

Hebe × andersonii 'Variegata'

Hebe cheesemanii

Hebe cupressoides 'Boughton Dome'

rounded heads, in summer. Good for trailing over walls, very tolerant of salt spray. Zones 9–11.

Hebe cheesemanii

☼ ❄ ↔ 12 in (30 cm) ↕ 12 in (30 cm)
Compact whipcord hebe from the mountains of eastern South Island, New Zealand. Tiny tightly packed leaves, pale olive to soft gray-green. Wiry stem tips crowned with small clusters of white flowers, pinkish red pollen sacs, in summer. Good rock garden plant, needs cool root run. Zones 8–9.

Hebe cockayneana

☼ ❄ ↔ 3 ft (0.9 m) ↕ 3 ft (0.9 m)
Named after Leonard Cockayne, one of New Zealand's best-known botanists. Found in southern South Island. Leaves small, thick, dark green, elliptical. Terminal heads of loosely clustered small white flowers, with conspicuous purple-red anthers, in summer. Zones 8–9.

Hebe colensoi

☼ ❄ ↔ 18 in (45 cm) ↕ 18 in (45 cm)
Low-growing shrub. Branches and leaves have glaucous coloring. Short crowded racemes of white flowers, in spring–summer. Zones 8–10.

Hebe cupressoides

WHIPCORD HEBE
☼ ❄ ↔ 3 ft (0.9 m) ↕ 3 ft (0.9 m)
Whipcord species native to subalpine regions of South Island, New Zealand. Attractive conifer-like appearance, densely branched. Well-spaced scale-like leaves, branchlets bright green. Pale blue flowers, borne sparingly, are

of secondary importance. **'Boughton Dome'** grows to 30 in (75 cm) tall, gray-green branchlets covered in small scale-like leaves. Zones 8–10.

Hebe diosmifolia

☼ ❄ ↔ 24 in (60 cm) ↑ 3 ft (0.9 m)
Variable species from northern North Island, New Zealand. Well-branched shrub, narrow glossy green leaves. Covered with small flower-heads of tiny white to lavender flowers, in spring. Zones 8–11.

Hebe elliptica

☼ ❄ ↔ 4 ft (1.2 m) ↑ 3–7 ft (0.9–2 m)
Found in southern South America as well as New Zealand. Well-branched, small, leathery, dark green leaves. White to lavender flowers, bigger than most species, in late spring–autumn. Tolerant of salt spray, suitable for sea-side gardens. Zones 8–11.

Hebe epacridea

☼ ❄ ↔ 3 ft (0.9 m) ↑ 6 in (15 cm)
Common plant of alpine areas of the South Island, New Zealand. Similar to *H. haastii*. Small, overlapping, usually blue-green to olive leaves, sometimes purplish tint, reverse and edges. Terminal heads of small white flowers, with purple-red anthers, in summer. Zones 7–9.

Hebe × franciscana

☼ ❄ ↔ 4 ft (1.2 m) ↑ 3 ft (0.9 m)
Older hybrids, cross between *H. elliptica* and *H. speciosa*. Rounded habit, dark green leaves. Pinkish purple flowers on spikes up to 3 in (8 cm) long, in summer–autumn. **'Blue Gem'**, bluish purple flowers, often

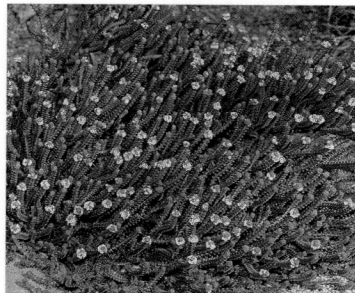

Hebe epacridea

Hebe × franciscana 'Variegata'

Hebe macrantha

seen, useful for coastal areas. **'Variegata'** (syn. *H.* 'Waireka'), mottled leaves with yellow margins. Zones 7–11.

Hebe glaucophylla ★

☼ ❄ ↔ 3 ft (0.9 m) ↑ 3 ft (0.9 m)
Neat bushy shrub from New Zealand's South Island. Attractive small bluish gray leaves and short racemes of white flowers, in summer. Zones 7–10.

Hebe haastii

☼ ❄ ↔ 12 in (30 cm) ↑ 10 in (25 cm)
From the alpine regions of New Zealand's South Island. Low sprawling shrub, twisted branches. Densely packed toward the tips with small fleshy leaves, in 4 distinct rows. Small white flowers, in summer. Suitable for rock gardens. Zones 7–10.

Hebe hectoris

☼ ❄ ↔ 20 in (50 cm)
↑ 4–30 in (10–75 cm)
Whipcord-foliaged shrub found in wet tussocklands of New Zealand's South Island from Mount Cook southward. Minute, overlapping, scale-like leaves, bright green-olive on yellow-brown stems. Flowers white, in small terminal heads. Zones 7–9.

Hebe lycopodioides

☼ ❄ ↔ 26 in (65 cm) ↑ 18 in (45 cm)
Whipcord species, well-branched shrub. Distinctive 4-angled stems, overall yellowish green coloring from close-set compressed leaves. Zones 7–10.

Hebe macrantha

☼ ❄ ↔ 36 in (90 cm) ↑ 2 ft (0.6 m)
From the mountain regions of the South Island of New Zealand. It

Hebe diosmifolia, in spring

Hebe diosmifolia, in winter

has sparingly branched, regularly toothed, leathery, pale green oval leaves. Beautiful white flowers, in groups of 4 to 6 near branch tips, in summer. Prune to encourage bushy habit. Zones 6–9.

Hebe macrocarpa

☼ ❄ ↔ 3 ft (0.9 m) ↑ 7 ft (2 m)
Rather variable species from the northern North Island, New Zealand. Stiff erect habit, relatively large, narrow oval leaves, thick and fleshy. White flowers, on spikes to 6 in (15 cm) long, in autumn–spring. *H. m.* var. *brevifolia*, rich hot pink flowers; *H. m.* var. *latisepala*, deep purple flowers. Zones 9–11.

Hebe menziesii

☼ ❄ ↔ 10 ft (3 m) ↑ 10 ft (3 m)
Probably a form of the highly variable *H. divaricata*, found in the Nelson and Marlborough regions of New Zealand's South Island. Shade-tolerant and bushy, with narrow, bright green,

Hebe macrocarpa var. *brevifolia*

Hebe macrocarpa var. *latisepala*

¾–1¼ in (18–30 mm) long leaves and showy white flowers in early summer. Zones 8–10.

Hebe ochracea

☼ ❄ ↔ 3 ft (0.9 m) ↑ 18 in (45 cm)
Low-growing whipcord species found in the northwestern mountains of New Zealand's South Island. Dense flat-topped shrub. Branches and scale-like leaves, ochre to golden green. **'James Stirling'**, rich golden coloring that intensifies in winter. Zones 6–9.

Hebe odora

syn. *Hebe buxifolia*
☼ ❄ ↔ 4 ft (1.2 m) ↑ 3 ft (0.9 m)
Variable in the wild, in cultivation this is a rounded bush. Small dark green box-like leaves. Conical heads of white flowers at branch tips, from spring to late summer. **'Patty's Purple'** is a popular American cultivar; **'New Zealand Gold'** is a strong grower whose new leaves can be bright yellow. Zones 7–10.

Hebe haastii

Hebe ochracea

Hebe rakaiensis

Hebe parviflora var. *arborea*

Hebe pinguifolia 'Pagei'

Hebe parviflora

☼ ❄ ↔ 4 ft (1.2 m) ↑ 7 ft (2 m)
Variable shrub, well-branched. Light green, narrow lance-shaped leaves. White to pale lilac flowers in racemes near branch tips, in summer. *H. p.* var. *arborea*, spreading branches, lilac-tinted white flowers, suits wide range of conditions. Zones 7–11.

Hebe pimeleoides

☼ ❄ ↔ 26 in (60 cm) ↑ 18 in (45 cm)
From New Zealand's South Island. Attractive plant for rock gardens. Small shrub, dark purplish branchlets, glaucous leaves, red margins. Flowers bluish purple, in summer–autumn. 'County Park', spreading plant with grayish green leaves edged with red and flushing reddish purple in winter; 'Quicksilver', particularly small and very glaucous leaves. Zones 7–10.

Hebe pinguifolia

VERONICA
☼ ❄ ↔ 30 in (75 cm) ↑ 10 in (25 cm)
From the drier eastern ranges of the South Island of New Zealand.

Variable habit in the wild. Cultivated plants are usually low-growing. Stout branches, small thick bluish gray leaves with red margins. Small white flowers rise in dense heads near branch tips, in spring–autumn. 'Pagei' is an excellent rock garden plant, spreading to 3 ft (0.9 m), with very glaucous leaves and dark purplish branchlets. Zones 6–10.

Hebe rakaiensis

☼ ❄ ↔ 4 ft (1.2 m) ↑ 3–7 ft (0.9–2 m)
Bushy shrub from the South Island, New Zealand. Short narrow leaves, glossy bright green. White flowers carried in loose racemes 1½ in (35 mm) long, in spring. Zones 6–9.

Hebe salicifolia

KOROMIKO
☼ ❄ ↔ 7 ft (2 m) ↑ 8 ft (2.4 m)
Found throughout the South Island of New Zealand and also in Chile. Well-branched spreading shrub. Attractive willow-like leaves. Drooping racemes of white to pale lilac flowers, in summer. Zones 7–10.

Hebe salicifolia

Hebe speciosa

SHOWY HEBE
☼ ❄ ↔ 3 ft (0.9 m) ↑ 3 ft (0.9 m)
Rare in wild, in some coastal areas of North Island, New Zealand. Rounded shrub. Glossy dark green leaves, oval, reddish margins, red midrib. Racemes of purplish red flowers, in summer–autumn. Used in breeding programs. 'Variegata', leaves with yellow variegation, reddish margins. Zones 9–11.

Hebe topiaria

☼ ❄ ↔ 3 ft (0.9 m) ↑ 3 ft (0.9 m)
Compact, ball-shaped. Good for foliage contrast. Small, almost overlapping bluish green leaves. Small white flowers between the leaves, in summer. Zones 8–11.

Hebe townsonii

☼ ❄ ↔ 26 in (65 cm) ↑ 3 ft (0.9 m)
Very localized distribution in North and South Islands of New Zealand. Erect habit, leathery leaves, narrow, bright green. White to pale mauve flowers in loose clusters around 4 in (10 cm) long, in summer. Zones 7–10.

Hebe venustula

☼ ❄ ↔ 26 in (65 cm) ↑ 3 ft (0.9 m)
Erect bushy shrub from the mountains of the central North Island, New Zealand. Narrow bright green leaves, flowers, white to pale mauve, in summer. Zones 8–10.

Hebe vernicosa

☼ ❄ ↔ 4 ft (1.2 m) ↑ 3 ft (0.9 m)
Natural habitat New Zealand's South Island beech-forest floor. Small glossy leaves carried on the one plane, along almost horizontal branches. Short spikes of densely packed white to pale lavender flowers borne near branch tips, spring–summer. Zones 7–10.

Hebe Hybrid Cultivars

☼ ❄ ↔ 12 in–5 ft (30 cm–1.5 m) ↑ 12 in–5 ft (30 cm–1.5 m)
The many attractive *Hebe* cultivars available include: 'Alicia Amherst', well-branched shrub to 5 ft (1.5 m) tall, young branchlets, reddish coloring, leaves glossy dark green, deep purple flowers densely packed on spikes up to 2½ in (6 cm) long, from autumn; 'Amy', rounded compact shrub growing to 3–5 ft (1–1.5 m) tall, dark branchlets, leaves deep purplish bronze when young, older foliage flushed purple in winter, erect spikes of purple flowers, late summer; 'Autumn Glory' ★, low bushy shrub to 24 in (60 cm) tall with purplish branchlets, dark green leaves, violet flowers on short crowded spikes, mid-summer–autumn; 'Carnea', old cultivar, dense spreading shrub to 5 ft (1.5 m) tall, leaves lance-shaped, summer flowers on racemes to 3 in (8 cm) long, rosy purple; 'Edinensis', low

Hebe speciosa 'Variegata'

Hebe speciosa

Hebe townsonii

Hebe, Hybrid Cultivar, 'Marjorie'

Hebe, Hybrid Cultivar, 'Pink Elephant'

Hebe, Hybrid Cultivar, 'Wardiensis'

Hebe, Hybrid Cultivar, 'Great Orme'

Hebe, Hybrid Cultivar, 'Fragrant Jewel'

spreading habit, to 12 in (30 cm) high, 18 in (45 cm) wide, tiny vivid green leaves, semi-whipcord appearance, white flowers slightly tinted with mauve; **'Emerald Green'** (syns 'Emerald Gem', 'Green Globe'), natural hybrid, semi-whipcord appearance, fresh green compact bun shape 8–12 in (20–30 cm) high, small white flowers, in summer; **'Fragrant Jewel'**, reaches 5 ft (1.5 m) high, masses of large, fragrant, lavender-purple flowers; **'Inspiration'**, hybrid with *H. speciosa* parentage, grows into neat shrub about 3 ft

(0.9 m) high, dark green shiny leaves, deep purple flowers for long periods, main flush in summer, good shrub for coastal areas; **'Loganioides'** (syn. *H. selaginoides*), 10 in (25 cm) tall heath-like whipcord with white flowers; **'Margret'**, 16 in (40 cm) tall, sky blue flowers fading to white, late spring–early summer; **'Marjorie'**, to 5 ft (1.5 m) tall, yellow-green leaves, large mauve-blue flowers fading to white; **'Midsummer Beauty'** (syn. *H.* × *andersonii* 'Midsummer

Hebe, Hybrid Cultivar, 'La Seduisante'

Beauty'), to 6 ft (1.8 m) tall, plum-colored new growth, lilac-purple flowers fading to white; **'Mrs Winder'** (syns 'Waikiki', 'Warleyensis'), spreading rounded shrub about 3 ft (0.9 m) high, leaves flushed red at base, reddish purple in winter, violet flowers, in summer; **'Orphan Annie'**, to 3 ft (0.9 m) tall, narrow cream and green variegated foliage, new growth pink, pink early summer flowers; **'Pink Elephant'**, 2 ft (0.6 m) tall, yellow-edged pink-tinged new growth, white summer flowers; **'Temptation'**, to 12 in (30 cm) tall, apple-blossom pink flowers fading to white; **'Wardiensis'**, to 8 in (20 cm) tall, gray-green leaves and white summer flowers; **'Youngii'** (syn. 'Carl Teschner'), well-branched spreading shrub, 8 in (20 cm) tall, branchlets purplish, small leaves dark green, leathery, deep violet flowers on short spikes, in summer. Extensive breeding at Auckland's Botanic

Gardens has resulted in the **Wiri Series**, including **'Wiri Charm'**, dense wide shrub 30 in (75 cm) high, rosy purple flowers, in summer; **'Wiri Dawn'**, low spreading plant to 18 in (45 cm) high, light olive green foliage, pale pinkish white flowers; **'Wiri Grace'**, large rounded shrub to 5 ft (1.5 m), long spikes of light purple flowers, in summer; **'Wiri Image'**, vigorous shrub to 3 ft (0.9 m) bears long racemes of violet flowers, in early summer. Zones 8–11.

Hebe, Hybrid Cultivar, 'Margret'

Hebe, Hybrid Cultivar, 'Temptation'

Hebe, Hybrid Cultivar, 'Orphan Annie'

Hebe, Hybrid Cultivar, 'Blue Clouds'

Hebe, HC, Wiri Series, 'Wiri Charm'

Hebe, Hybrid Cultivar, Wiri Series, 'Wiri Grace'

H

HECHTIA

This genus, which belongs to the bromeliad (Bromeliaceae) family, contains some 50 species of sun-loving plants from hot dry areas of southern Texas, Mexico, and Honduras. Individual plants form large clumps 16 in (40 cm) to 7 ft (2 m) in diameter. Their leaves form a dense rosette and are long and mainly narrow, with strong curved teeth on the edges, sometimes green turning red, or green with a hairy covering for protection from the sun. Some leaves are gray without spines. The flower stem is erect and the flowerhead is open with many long branches that bear flowers singly or in clusters. Petals are red or white and flowers are unisexual on different plants. Best grown with cacti and other succulents in rock gardens, or in pots for smaller species.
CULTIVATION: Grow outdoors in warm-temperate and subtropical areas. Water when potting mix is dry. Do not over-fertilize. Propagate from offsets.

Hechtia glomerata

☀ ✂ ↔ 3 ft (0.9 m) ↕ 6 ft (1.8 m)
From southern Texas through Mexico to Guatemala. About 40 leaves, green turning red in strong sunlight, 16 in (40 cm) long by 1¼ in (3 cm) wide, narrow, triangular, with hooked teeth to ¼ in (6 mm) long on the edges, forming a spreading rosette. Flower stem emerges from the side of the plant. Flowerhead to 20 in (50 cm)

Hedera azorica

Hedera colchica 'Dentata'

long composed of side branches to 2½ in (6 cm) long in the female plant and shorter in the male, with dense clusters of white flowers. Zones 9–11.

HEDERA

IVY

A well-known genus of 11 species of evergreen climbers from Europe, Asia, and northern Africa that will cling by aerial roots to almost any surface. These plants, members of the ivy (Araliaceae) family, are used to clothe walls and grow up trees, as well as being efficient ground covers. They will grow in a wide range of soils and climates, and can become quite weedy outside their native habitats. The foliage usually changes shape to an adult form when it can no longer grow any taller, and cuttings taken from this wood will produce a shrubby form. The flowers are small, borne in clusters, and of little interest to all but their fly pollinators. The berries that follow are usually black.
CULTIVATION: Ivy will grow in almost any soil that is not waterlogged, in aspects from heavy shade to full sun, or in pots as indoor plants. Propagate from cuttings, which strike easily at almost any time of the year.

Hedera azorica

syn. *Hedera canariensis* 'Azorica'
☀ ❄ ↔ 20–60 ft (6–18 m)
↕ 17–20 ft (5–6 m)
Native to the Azores. Has 5- to 7-lobed leaves, to 4 in (10 cm) long, slightly hairy and bright mid-green. Not as cold hardy as European ivies, but less somber in color. Zones 8–10.

Hedera canariensis

CANARY ISLAND IVY, NORTH AFRICAN IVY
☀ ❄ ↔ 20–60 ft (6–18 m) ↕ 15–20 ft (4.5–6 m)
From northern Africa and the Canary Islands. Large, leathery, slightly glossy, unlobed to shallowly lobed leaves, to 5

Hedera helix 'Amberwaves'

in (12 cm) long. 'Gloire de Marengo' (syn. *H. c.* 'Variegata'), leaves go from green through silvery-gray to white at the edges; 'Ravensholst', shallowly lobed bright green leaves to 6 in (15 cm) long. Zones 8–10.

Hedera colchica

BULLOCK'S HEART IVY, COLCHIC IVY, PERSIAN IVY

☀/◐ ❄ ↔ 20–60 ft (6–18 m)
↕ 20–35 ft (6–10 m)
Large-leafed species found from northern Iran to the Caucasus. Strong self-clinging climber. Foliage is rich deep green, leathery and generally unlobed, to 5 in (12 cm) long. Cultivars include: 'Dentata', very large unlobed leaves to 9 in (22 cm) long, bright green on purple-flushed stems; 'Dentata Variegata', one of the boldest ivies grown, mottled gray-green leaves with wide, irregular, yellow edges; 'Sulphur Heart' (syn. 'Paddy's Pride'), rich green leaves, irregular yellow and light green central splashes. Zones 6–10.

Hedera helix

COMMON IVY, ENGLISH IVY

☀ ❄ ↔ 20–60 ft (6–18 m)
↕ 35–50 ft (10–15 m)
Well-known species, distributed over most of Europe. The most genetically unstable, there are hundreds of named clones. Typical form has 3- to 5-lobed, dark green, juvenile leaves, 1¾–2½ in (4–6 cm) long. When a plant has grown as tall as it can on its given support, it produces adult non-climbing branches that flower and fruit, and produce unlobed adult leaves. 'Amberwaves', squarish, 5-lobed, overlapping, yellow-green leaves; 'Atropurpurea', classic ivy leaves, green in summer, turning rich dark purple if exposed to light and enough cold; 'Buttercup', strongly climbing, 5-lobed, rounded, bright yellow leaves turn green in the shade; 'Ceridwen', well-branched, ideal for pots, 3-lobed yellow variegated leaves, some of which are completely yellow; 'Cockle Shell', 3- to 5-lobed, round, cupped leaves; 'Glacier', widely grown, will climb or trail,

Hedera helix

Hedera helix 'Cockle Shell'

with 3-lobed, mid gray-green leaves, irregularly edged with creamy white; 'Goldchild', dense form, good in pots, with 3-lobed leaves to 1¾ in (4 cm) long, boldly edged with yellow; 'Green Ripple' ★, shiny green rippled leaves with creamy yellow veins, can be vigorous to invasive; 'Harrison', 3-lobed leaves to 2½ in (6 cm) long, dark green veined white, turning purple with enough winter cold; 'Lalla Rookh', bright green form with 5-lobed leaves, irregularly and deeply toothed, good in pots or as ground cover; 'Manda's Crested', good ground cover, bright green leaves that turn bronze in cold weather, with 5 lobes that curl and twist; 'Misty', miniature, 5-lobed variegated leaves; 'Needlepoint', a dense mat-forming selection with 3 to 5 deep green narrow lobes on leaves to 1 in (25 mm) long; 'Plume d'Or', rich green narrowly lobed leaves, may be a form of *H. h.* 'Irish Lace', which is similar to the better-known 'Needlepoint', all of which are probably confused in the trade; 'Schafer Three' (syn. *H. h.* 'Calico'), a form with 3-lobed leaves splashed with creamy white, to 1¾ in (4 cm) by 1¾ in (4 cm); 'Treetop', adult non-climbing shrubby plant of the type often known as a tree ivy, with unlobed rich green leaves, selected off a plant of *H. h.* 'Pittsburgh'. Zones 5–10.

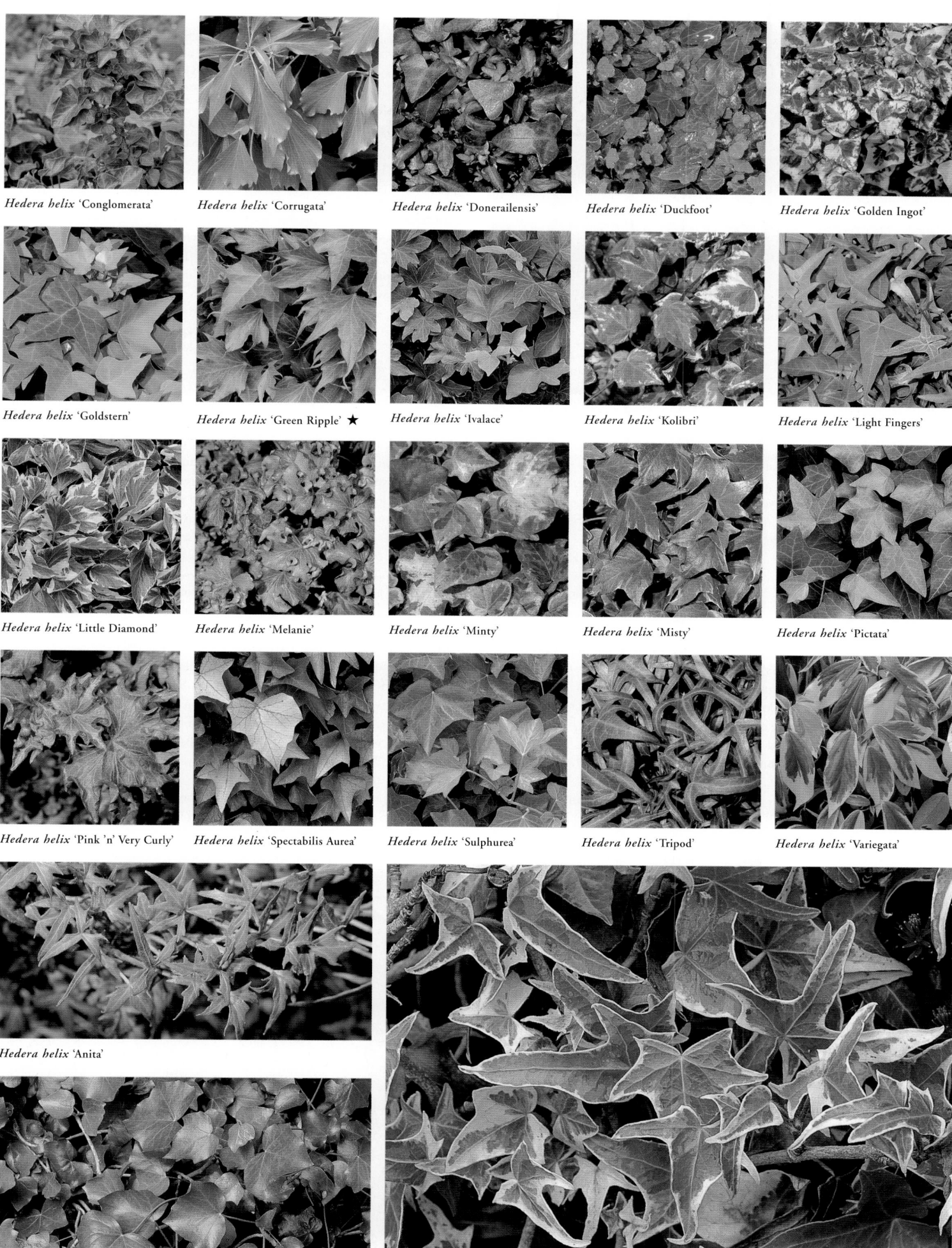

Hedera helix 'Conglomerata'

Hedera helix 'Corrugata'

Hedera helix 'Donerailensis'

Hedera helix 'Duckfoot'

Hedera helix 'Golden Ingot'

Hedera helix 'Goldstern'

Hedera helix 'Green Ripple' ★

Hedera helix 'Ivalace'

Hedera helix 'Kolibri'

Hedera helix 'Light Fingers'

Hedera helix 'Little Diamond'

Hedera helix 'Melanie'

Hedera helix 'Minty'

Hedera helix 'Misty'

Hedera helix 'Pictata'

Hedera helix 'Pink 'n' Very Curly'

Hedera helix 'Spectabilis Aurea'

Hedera helix 'Sulphurea'

Hedera helix 'Tripod'

Hedera helix 'Variegata'

Hedera helix 'Anita'

Hedera helix 'Walthamensis'

Hedera helix 'Sagittifolia Variegata'

Hedychium spicatum

Hedera hibernica

syn. *Hedera helix* subsp. *hibernica*

ATLANTIC IVY, IRISH IVY

☀ ❄ ↔ 20–60 ft (6–18 m)
↑ 25–35 ft (8–10 m)

Not restricted to Ireland but native to much of western Europe. Widely grown as a vigorous ground cover or climber. Differs from *H. helix* in its larger leaves, to 3½ in (9 cm) long, with 5 lobes. Zones 6–10.

Hedera nepalensis

HIMALAYAN IVY, NEPAL IVY

☀ ❄ ↔ 20–60 ft (6–18 m)
↑ 10–17 ft (3–5 m)

Found from Afghanistan east to Assam, India. Rich green, leathery, spearhead-shaped leaves, irregular shallow lobes. Good wall cover with its orange berries, though these are rarely produced in colder climates. '**Marbled Dragon**' has gray-green veins. Zones 6–10.

HEDYCHIUM

GARLAND LILY, GINGER LILY

This genus is a member of the ginger (Zingiberaceae) family and includes some 40 species of perennials with heavy rhizomes from which emerge strong cane-like stems with large leaves reminiscent of those of canna lilies. Found in tropical Asia, the Himalayan region, and Madagascar, they have naturalized elsewhere and have become troublesome at times, one species being a serious pest in New Zealand. Ginger lilies are grown mainly for their colorful and fragrant flowerheads, in which are clustered many slender-tubed flowers with protruding anthers. The flowers appear in summer and are mainly yellow or pink shades. Several of the species are known to be used in Indian Ayurvedic medicines.

CULTIVATION: They are mostly tolerant of very light frosts and capable of reshooting from the rootstock. Plant in sun or shade with fertile, moist, humus-rich, well-drained soil. Cut back the spent flower stems and any old, unproductive canes to encourage fresh growth. Propagate by division or from seed.

Hedychium coccineum

RED GINGER LILY, SCARLET GINGER LILY

☀/◐ ❋ ↔ 2–5 ft (0.6–1.5 m)
↑ 7–10 ft (2–3 m)

An autumn-flowering Himalayan native with very narrow leaves to 20 in (50 cm) long. Heads of pink, orange, or red flowers with similarly colored lower lip and filaments. '**Tara**' has large spikes of orange flowers. Zones 9–11.

Hedychium coronarium

BUTTERFLY LILY, GARLAND FLOWER, WHITE GINGER

☀/◐ ❋ ↔ 2–5 ft (0.6–1.5 m)
↑ 10 ft (3 m)

Spring-flowering Indian species with leaves to 24 in (60 cm) long by a little over 4 in (10 cm) wide. Heads of very fragrant white flowers with yellow-green markings. '**F. W. Moore**' has soft yellow-brown flowers with orange markings. Zones 9–11.

Hedychium densiflorum

☀/◐ ❋ ↔ 3–7 ft (0.9–2 m) ↑ 17 ft (5 m)

Summer-flowering Himalayan native, probably the tallest species in the genus. It has narrow leaves to 16 in (40 cm) long and dense spikes of deep orange flowers with red filaments. '**Assam Orange**' is a small form with very fragrant orange-brown flowers. Zones 8–11.

Hedychium gardnerianum

GINGER LILY, KAHILI GINGER

☀/◐ ❋ ↔ 3–5 ft (0.9–1.5 m)
↑ 8 ft (2.4 m)

This summer- to autumn-flowering northern Indian and Himalayan native has leaves up to 16 in (40 cm)

Hedychium greenei

long. Dense spikes of many cream and yellow flowers with conspicuous red filaments. A very vigorous species. Zones 8–11.

Hedychium greenei

☀/◐ ❋ ↔ 32–48 in (80–120 cm)
↑ 7 ft (2 m)

Summer-flowering native of Bhutan. Very narrow leaves to 10 in (25 cm) long and bright red flowers in 5 in (12 cm) long spikes. Sometimes forms bulbils in the leaf axil near flowerheads. Zones 10–11.

Hedychium horsfieldii

syn. *Brachychilum horsfieldii*

☀/◐ ❋ ↔ 20 in (50 cm) ↑ 7 ft (2 m)

Summer-flowering, slender, upright species from Java. Naturally epiphytic and may have exposed roots. Leaves to over 24 in (60 cm) long. Greenish white flowers with much reduced lower lip and twisted petals. Green fruit splits to reveal orange interior and seed with red arils. Zones 10–12.

Hedychium spicatum

☀/◐ ❋ ↔ 20 in (50 cm) ↑ 40 in (100 cm)

Small, autumn-flowering, Himalayan species with leaves that grow to 16 in (40 cm) long. White to yellow flowers with soft orange lips and pink pro-

truding stamen-like structures. *H. s.* subsp. *acuminatum* has leaves with distinct stalks and its flowers have purple filaments. Zones 9–11.

HEDYSCEPE

UMBRELLA PALM

This genus of a single palm in the Arecaceae family is native to Lord Howe Island in the southwest Pacific Ocean. Its solitary trunk has a prominent crownshaft and distinctive white rings. The pinnate fronds are curved, erect and sword-shaped, smooth above, with slightly hairy margins underneath. Branched clusters of up to 3 egg-yellow flowers are followed by dull red elliptical fruit, to 2 in (5 cm) long, containing a single seed. The botanical name comes from the Greek *hedys*, meaning sweet, and *scepe*, meaning covering.

CULTIVATION: This good wind-resistant coastal and container palm requires well-drained soil with year-round moisture and shelter from full sun for the first 5 years. Propagate from seed, which will germinate erratically from 5 to 19 months.

Hedyscepe canterburyana ★

BIG MOUNTAIN PALM, UMBRELLA PALM

☀ ❄ ↔ 6–8 ft (1.8–2.4 m)
↑ 15–30 ft (4.5–9 m)

Medium-sized, slow-growing, slim palm. Slender gray-ringed trunk, to 5 in (12 cm) in diameter, light bluish green cylindrical crownshaft. Compact dense crown of short, silvery, curved, dark green, arching fronds, 5–7 ft (1.5–2 m) long, divided into numerous erect, stiff, upward-pointing leaflets, densely arranged in a V-shape. Clusters of cream flowers, followed by large, bright red, oval-shaped fruit. Zones 8–10.

Hedychium coccineum

Hedychium gardnerianum

Helenium, Hybrid Cultivar, 'Waldtraut'

Helenium, Hybrid Cultivar, 'Wyndley'

HEIMIA

Found in temperate regions of both North and South America, this is a genus of 2 or 3 small evergreen shrubs or perennials in the loosestrife (Lythraceae) family. Flowers with 5 to 7 petals appear singly or in panicles of 3, with horn-like appendages on a bell-shaped calyx. The fruit is a capsule. CULTIVATION: Suitable for a warm sunny position in a well-drained soil, this genus prefers warm conditions and can be cut back by severe winter cold. Propagate from seed or half-hardened cuttings.

Heimia salicifolia

☀ ❄ ↔ 7 ft (2 m) ↕ 10 ft (3 m)
Deciduous shrub, native to southern USA, Central America, and as far south as Argentina. Small, narrow opposite leaves, to 3 in (8 cm) long. Solitary yellow flowers about ¾ in (18 mm) in diameter. Zones 8–9.

HELENIUM

SNEEZEWEED

These are known as sneezeweed not because they cause allergies, but from the use by Native Americans of the powdered flowers of some species to make snuff. They also used the genus medicinally and an alkaloid extract, helanalin, is part of modern chemo-therapy. This mainly North American genus in the daisy (Asteraceae) family contains about 40 species of annuals, biennials, and perennials. Most form an upright foliage clump and have simple lance-shaped leaves, usually covered with fine hairs. From mid-summer into autumn they produce large flowerheads with a central cone of disc florets and large often slightly drooping ray florets. Yellow and orange to red shades are common. CULTIVATION: Hardiness varies but most are very frost tolerant. Plant in a sunny, open position in moist, well-drained soil. Routine deadheading

prolongs flowering; alternatively use as a cut flower to encourage repeat flowering. Propagate by division, or from basal cuttings or seed.

Helenium autumnale

SNEEZEWEED

☀ ❄ ↔ 3 ft (0.9 m) ↕ 5 ft (1.5 m)
North American perennial making a dense clump of stems with narrow, usually serrated, leaves to 6 in (15 cm) long topped with many 2 in (5 cm) wide, bright yellow to golden flower-heads each with up to 20 reflexed ray florets. '**Sunshine Hybrid**' is a seedling strain with yellow, orange, red-brown, and red flowers in a range of color patterns. Zones 3–9.

Helenium hoopesii

☀ ❄ ↔ 40 in (100 cm) ↕ 40 in (100 cm)
Native to the southwestern quarter of USA. Narrow lower leaves up to 12 in (30 cm), upper leaves lance-shaped and smaller. Flowerheads to 3 in (8 cm) wide with up to 21 orange ray florets held horizontally. Zones 3–9.

Helenium Hybrid Cultivars

☀ ❄ ↔ 40 in (100 cm) ↕ 40 in (100 cm)
These hybrids mostly have *H. autum-nale* somewhere in their parentage. They are heavy-flowering plants usually more compact than the species. Popular forms include: '**Moerheim Beauty**', red-brown to red flowers, strongly downward-angled ray florets; Pipsqueak/'**Blopip**', 18 in (45 cm) tall, yellow ray florets and red-brown disc florets; '**Waldtraut**' ★, burnt orange and gold flowers; '**Wyndley**', gold to tawny brown ray florets, brown disc florets. Zones 5–9.

HELIAMPHORA

SUN PITCHER, MARSH PITCHER

A carnivorous genus of 9 known species in the pitcher plant (Sarraceni-aceae) family, native to the high

sandstone plateaus of Brazil, Guyana, and Venezuela. They have tubular green to red pitchers ranging from 1¾ in (40 mm) to 20 in (50 cm) in height, and most have a small over-hanging cap. The pitchers are arranged in a rosette attached to a stem at the base. Insects are attracted to the plant by the bright colors and nectar under the lid of the pitcher. The upper interior of the pitcher is covered in downward-pointing hairs, and then it becomes smooth and slippery. Insects slide into the well of water and are digested by the plant. The name of

the genus comes from the Greek *helios* (marsh) and *amphora* (pitcher). CULTIVATION: Grow in full sun in sphagnum or a mix of 4 parts peat to 1 part perlite. In very hot weather pots should be placed in the shade or in trays of water. Keep soil moist, water overhead, mist regularly. Use a weak liquid fertilizer every couple of weeks. Ideal temperatures are 65–80°F (18–26°C) during the day and 35–50°F (2–10°C) overnight. These plants do well in a cool or warm greenhouse. Propagate by division in spring.

Helenium autumnale

Helenium, HC, Pipsqueak/'Blopip'

Heimia salicifolia

Heliamphora heterodoxa

☼/◐ ❄ ↔ 12 in (30 cm) ↑ 17 in (45 cm)

Found on Torono, Chimanta, Auyan, and Ptari Tepui Plateaus in Venezuela, this species has lime green pitchers, usually red toward the top. The lid of the pitcher is green on young plants, red on older ones, and the pitcher has a "waist" about a third of the way up. Pink and white flowers in early to mid-winter. One of the easier species to grow. Zones 10–12.

Heliamphora minor

☼/◐ ❄ ↔ 6 in (15 cm) ↑ 3 in (8 cm)

The smallest of the *Heliamphora*, this species comes from Auyan Tepuis and Chimanta Tepuis in Venezuela. Cone-shaped, green to red, 3 in (8 cm) high pitchers. Emerging pitchers are covered in fine white hairs; older pitchers have hairs along central seam and near rim. Pink flowers in spring. *H. m.* × *heterodoxa*, pale pink flowers. Zones 8–10.

Heliamphora heterodoxa

Heliamphora minor × *heterodoxa*

Heliamphora nutans ★

☼/◐ ❄ ↔ 12 in (30 cm) ↑ 10 in (25 cm)

Found on Mt Roraima and Mt Duida in Venezuela. Hourglass-shaped green pitchers, red around the margins, up to 10 in (25 cm) in height. Yellow flowers on a 20 in (50 cm) long scape from late winter to spring. *H. n.* × *heterodoxa* has light green pitchers. Zones 8–10.

HELIANTHEMUM

ROCK ROSE, SUN ROSE

Related to *Cistus*, the 110 or so evergreen and semi-evergreen shrubs and subshrubs in this genus, in the rockrose (Cistaceae) family, are less widely grown but have a wider natural range: Eurasia, North Africa, and the Americas. Relatively low mounding, short-lived plants, foliage is often hairy, giving it a gray-green coloration. Flowers resemble tiny single roses, and are individually short-lived but appear over much of late spring and summer. They are usually in bright shades of yellow, orange, red, or pink, with bright yellow stamens massed at the center. CULTIVATION: They need full sun for their flowers to develop and open properly and suit sunny borders, rock gardens or large containers such as alpine troughs. Soil should be rather gritty and free draining. Keep moist in summer, dry in winter. Trim lightly after flowering to shape and encourage vigor. Propagation is from seed;

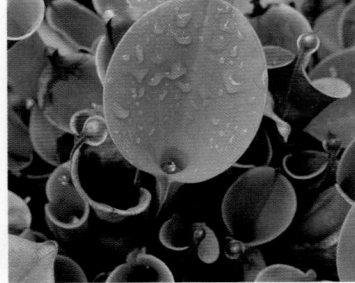

Heliamphora nutans × *heterodoxa*

hybrids and cultivars should be propagated by cuttings or by removing rooted pieces from established plants.

Helianthemum almeriense

syn. *Helianthemum leptophyllum*

☼ ❄ ↔ 12 in (30 cm)
↑ 4–8 in (10–20 cm)

Native to southern Europe from Spain to Italy. Small, erect, shrubby plant with narrow, hairy, grayish green leaves. Yellow flowers, up to ¾ in (18 mm) across, in summer. Zones 7–10.

Helianthemum apenninum

☼ ❄ ↔ 20–24 in (50–60 cm)
↑ 12–16 in (30–40 cm)

Soft-wooded subshrub found from northwestern Italy to Turkey. Gray-green leaves to 1¼ in (30 mm) long and pure white flowers with a boss of yellow stamens to 1¼ in (30 mm) across. Flowers are short-lived, but plant blooms from spring to mid-summer. Zones 6–10.

Helianthemum croceum

☼ ❄ ↔ 16–20 in (40–50 cm)
↑ 12–14 in (30–35 cm)

From southern Europe and northern Africa. Slightly fleshy leaves to ¾ in (18 mm) long. Flowers up to ¾ in (18 mm) wide in shades of yellow, white, or apricot. Zones 7–10.

Helianthemum nummularium

syn. *Helianthemum chamaecistus*

COMMON SUN ROSE, SUN ROSE

☼ ❄ ↔ 24 in (60 cm) ↑ 20 in (50 cm)

Widely cultivated species, parent of many hybrids and cultivars. Leaves dark green above, gray-green, felted below. Flowers bright yellow, orange

Helianthemum apenninum

Helianthemum croceum

Helianthemum Hybrid Cultivars

or red shades, any color except purple or blue, in late spring–summer. *H. n.* subsp. *glabrum* (syn. *H. nitidum*), from central and southwest Europe, fewer foliage hairs, slightly downy margins, orange-yellow flowers. Zones 5–10.

Helianthemum oelandicum

☼ ❄ ↔ 12 in (30 cm) ↑ 8 in (20 cm)

European species. Mounding subshrub with tufts of foliage. Leaves under ½ in (12 mm) long, mid- to deep green, smooth or coated with tiny hairs. Tiny bright yellow flowers appear in late spring–summer. There are 6 subspecies, which are widely scattered throughout Europe, including *H. o.* subsp. *incanum*, from southern Europe and northern Africa, a variable sprawling shrub, gray-green leaves to 1¼ in (30 mm) long; masses of open bright yellow flowers to 1¼ in (30 mm) wide from spring to mid-summer. Zones 6–10.

Helianthemum Hybrid Cultivars

☼ ❄ ↔ 18–36 in (45–90 cm)
↑ 6–12 in (15–30 cm)

Alpine and rock garden enthusiasts have produced many hybrids in a broad color spectrum. Most have *H. nummularium* somewhere in their background. 'Ben Heckla', bronze-gold flowers; 'Ben Hope', light foliage, red flowers with orange centers; 'Ben Ledi', dark green leaves, deep rose flowers; 'Ben Vane', terracotta flowers; 'Ben Vorlich', orange flowers; 'Butter and Eggs', creamy yellow; 'Dazzler', dark green foliage, deep red flowers; 'Fire Dragon', gray-green leaves, orange-red flowers; 'Golden Queen',

Helianthemum, Hybrid Cultivar, 'Ben Heckla'

Helianthemum, Hybrid Cultivar, 'Ben Ledi'

Helianthemum, Hybrid Cultivar, 'Ben Vane'

Helianthemum, HC, 'Butter and Eggs'

Helianthemum, Hybrid Cultivar, 'Henfield Brilliant'

Helianthemum, Hybrid Cultivar, 'Ben Vorlich'

Helianthemum, Hybrid Cultivar, 'Fire Dragon'

Helianthemum, HC, 'Rhodanthe Carneum'

Helianthemum, HC, 'Mrs C. W. Earle'

Helianthemum, HC, 'Sudbury Gem'

Helianthemum, HC, 'Wisley Primrose'

large bright yellow flowers; **'Henfield Brilliant'** ★, gray-green leaves, dark red flowers; **'Jubilee'**, double primrose yellow flowers; **'Mrs C. W. Earle'**, double scarlet flowers; **'Orange Surprise'**, orange flowers; **'Raspberry Ripple'**, deep reddish pink flowers tipped with white; **'Rhodanthe Carneum'**, silvery gray leaves, orange-centered pink flowers; **'Rose Queen'**, rose pink flowers; **'Sudbury Gem'**, grayish green leaves, deep pink flowers with red centers; **'The Bride'**, silver-gray foliage, white flowers; **'Wisley Pink'**, silver-gray foliage with light

pink flowers; **'Wisley Primrose'**, gray-green foliage and primrose yellow flowers; **'Wisley White'**, gray foliage with white flowers. Zones 6–10.

HELIANTHUS
SUNFLOWER

Sunflowers are so called not so much for the shape of the bloom as for the way the flowerhead turns to follow the sun. This genus of 70 annuals and perennials in the daisy (Asteraceae) family is from the Americas and is best known for the common or giant sunflower *(H. annuus)*, an annual

daisy that grows to over 6 ft (1.8 m) tall and which is both popular as an ornamental and widely grown commercially for its seeds and the oil extracted from them. Other species are smaller and tend to have lance-shaped rather than heart-shaped leaves. Most have bristly stems. The flowers are held above the foliage and are nearly always yellow. Double-flowered forms are common.
CULTIVATION: Plant in a sunny, open position with fertile, moist, well-drained soil. Mildew can be a problem but usually only when

the plants are past their best. Propagate annuals from seed and perennials also by division and from basal cuttings.

Helianthus angustifolius
SWAMP SUNFLOWER

☀ ❄ ↔ 2–3 ft (0.6–0.9 m) ↑ 7 ft (2 m)
Biennial or short-lived perennial from eastern USA. Narrow, hairy, lance-shaped leaves to 8 in (20 cm) long. Flowerheads with golden ray florets around a purple-brown disc, to 2 in (5 cm) wide, from early autumn. Zones 6–9.

Helianthus annuus, Provence, France

Helianthus annuus 'Teddy Bear'

Helianthus annuus 'Vanilla Ice'

Helianthus annuus 'Italian White'

Helianthus annuus 'Ruby Eclipse'

Helianthus annuus 'Sunrich Orange'

Helianthus annuus 'Moonshadow'

Helianthus annuus 'Sunbeam'

Helianthus annuus 'Ring of Fire'

Helianthus annuus
COMMON SUNFLOWER

☼ ❄ ↔ 2–4 ft (0.6–1.2 m)
↑ 10–17 ft (3–5 m)

Quick-growing annual that is native to USA. Broad, bristly, toothed, pointed heart-shaped leaves to 16 in (40 cm) long. Flowerheads to 12 in (30 cm) wide from mid-summer, ray florets golden yellow around a purple-brown disc. Many cultivars, including: **'Italian White'**, 5 ft (1.5 m) tall, very pale yellow flowers; **'Moonshadow'**, 4 ft (1.2 m) tall, near-white ray florets; **'Music Box'**, mixed color

seedling strain with 2-tone ray florets, 30 in (75 cm) tall; **'Ring of Fire'**, 5 ft (1.5 m) tall, flower 5 in (12 cm) wide, yellow and red ray florets; **'Ruby Eclipse'**, 6 ft (1.8 m) tall, bright red-tinted ray florets, red at base, no pollen; **'Sunbeam'**, 5 ft (1.5 m) tall, golden yellow ray florets, outer disc florets yellow around a green center; **'Sunrich Orange'**, 5 ft (1.5 m) tall, bright orange ray florets, no pollen; **'Teddy Bear'**, 3 ft (0.9 m) tall, fully double, golden yellow flowers 5 in (12 cm) wide; **'Vanilla Ice'**, 5 ft (1.5 m) tall,

starry, 4 in (10 cm) wide flowerheads, creamy yellow ray florets around a dark disc. Zones 4–11.

Helianthus atrorubens
DARK-EYE SUNFLOWER

☼ ❄ ↔ 2 ft (0.6 m) ↑ 7 ft (2 m)

Perennial native to southeastern USA. Basal clump of broad, hairy, toothed leaves to 12 in (30 cm) long, from which emerge, in summer, upright flower stems with smaller leaves and flowerheads to 4 in (10 cm) wide. Golden to light orange ray florets around purple-brown disc. Zones 7–10.

Helianthus debilis

☼ ❄ ↔ 2 ft (0.6 m) ↑ 7 ft (2 m)

Annual native to the Gulf of Mexico region, USA. Leaves broadly lance-shaped to 6 in (15 cm) long, smooth-edged or deeply toothed, hairy or hairless. Flowerheads to 2½ in (6 cm) wide, yellow ray florets around a maroon disc in summer. Zones 7–11.

Helianthus decapetalus
THIN-LEAF SUNFLOWER

☼ ❄ ↔ 2 ft (0.6 m) ↑ 7 ft (2 m)

Perennial native to south-central and southeastern USA. Forms a bushy clump of coarsely hairy, lance-shaped lower leaves to 8 in (20 cm) long. From mid-summer flowerheads to over 3 in (8 cm) wide. Ray and disc florets yellow. Zones 5–9.

Helianthus giganteus
GIANT SUNFLOWER

☼ ❄ ↔ 3 ft (0.9 m) ↑ 15 ft (4.5 m)

Perennial found from Canada to southern USA. Leaves to 8 in (20 cm) long, shallowly toothed and finely hairy, pointed oval to lance-shaped. From mid-summer, 3 in (8 cm) wide flowerheads with yellow ray florets around yellow-brown disc. Zones 4–9.

Helianthus maximilianii

☼ ❄ ↔ 2–3 ft (0.6–0.9 m)
↑ 7–10 ft (2–3 m)

Perennial found from Texas to southern Canada. Forms a bushy base of 8 in (20 cm) long, often shallowly toothed, blue-green, lance-shaped leaves. Yellow flowerheads to 4 in (10 cm) wide in autumn. Zones 4–9.

Helianthus × *multiflorus* 'Loddon Gold'

Helianthus salicifolius

Helichrysum frigidum

Helianthus, Hybrid Cultivar, 'Newcutt Gold'

Helianthus, Hybrid Cultivar, 'Sunny'

Helianthus × *multiflorus*

☀ ❄ ↔ 2 ft (0.6 m) ↑ 7 ft (2 m)

Garden hybrid between *H. annuus* and *H. decapetalus*. Perennial with coarsely hairy, lance-shaped lower leaves to 8 in (20 cm) long. Flower-heads to nearly 5 in (12 cm) wide, often double, sometimes with no disc florets, from late summer until first frosts. '**Capenoch Star**', 5 ft (1.5 m) tall, soft yellow flowerheads; '**Loddon Gold**', 5 ft (1.5 m) tall, golden yellow, double flowerheads. Zones 5–9.

Helianthus salicifolius

☀ ❄ ↔ 2–4 ft (0.6–1.2 m) ↑ 10 ft (3 m)

Perennial native to south-central USA. Drooping, slightly hairy, narrowly lance-shaped leaves to 8 in (20 cm) long. Flowerheads to 3 in (8 cm) wide, yellow ray florets around a dark disc, in autumn. '**Golden Pyramid**', 5 ft (1.5 m) tall, has a double row of yellow ray florets. Zones 4–9.

Helianthus tuberosus ★

JERUSALEM ARTICHOKE

☀ ❄ ↔ 5 ft (1.5 m) ↑ 10 ft (3 m)

Tuberous perennial found from Canada to southeastern USA. Coarsely hairy, toothed, lance-shaped or pointed oval leaves to 12 in (30 cm) long. Flower-heads yellow, to 4 in (10 cm) wide, in autumn. Edible tubers. Spreading plants, suited to containers. Zones 4–9.

Helianthus Hybrid Cultivars

☀ ❄ ↔ 3–4 ft (0.9–1.2 m) ↑ 4–7 ft (1.2–2 m)

Robust hardy plants popular with gardeners. '**Monarch**', 6 in (15 cm) wide flowerheads, double row of golden ray florets; '**Newcutt Gold**', rich yellow flowers; '**Sunny**', double row of bright yellow blooms. Zones 5–10.

HELICHRYSUM

Revision by botanists in recent years has reduced the number of species in this genus, which once stood at around 500. A member of the daisy (Asteraceae) family, it is perhaps best known for its perennials, though it also includes a few shrubby species. They have simple, often heavily felted leaves, usually in pale green to gray-green shades, and tiny flowers, lacking ray florets or petals but usually quite heavily clustered and conspicuous if not especially showy.

CULTIVATION: Most are drought tolerant once established. Planted in full sun with light, gritty, very well-drained soil. Their frost hardiness varies, but few will tolerate prolonged cold; if wet at the same time, they tend to rot before they are killed by frost. Any trimming or shaping should be done in spring. Propagation is from seed (some species self-sow freely), or layers can be pegged down at any time. Half-hardened tip cuttings strike well in both summer and autumn.

Helichrysum adenophorum

☀ ✤ ↔ 16 in (40 cm) ↑ 20 in (50 cm)

Eastern Australian annual with small, hairy, green leaves and papery, pink-tinted white flowers throughout the warmer months. Zones 9–11.

Helichrysum appendiculatum

SHEEP'S EARS

☀ ✤ ↔ 20 in (50 cm) ↑ 20 in (50 cm)

Summer-flowering South African perennial. Lance-shaped leaves to 3 in (8 cm) long, densely covered with fine white to gray hairs. Clusters of ½ in (12 mm) wide white, yellow, or pink flowerheads. Zones 9–11.

Helichrysum ecklonis

☀ ✤ ↔ 16–24 in (40–60 cm) ↑ 4–16 in (10–40 cm)

Summer-flowering, carpeting South African perennial, sometimes has an upright habit. Rosettes of oblong leaves to 8 in (20 cm) long with patchy covering of down, sometimes cobweb-like. Flowerheads solitary, to 1¼ in (30 mm) wide, white to purple. Zones 9–11.

Helichrysum frigidum

☀ ❄ ↔ 12 in (30 cm) ↑ 4 in (10 cm)

Spring- to summer-flowering, mat-forming subshrub from Sardinia and Corsica. Forms a dense carpet with many narrow, ¼ in (6 mm) long, white to gray downy leaves. White flowerheads to ½ in (12 mm) wide, solitary. Zones 8–10.

Helichrysum italicum

☀ ❄ ↔ 20 in (50 cm) ↑ 16 in (40 cm)

Summer-flowering, bushy, aromatic perennial native to southwestern Europe. Narrow, sparsely downy leaves to 1¼ in (30 mm) long. Tiny dull white to yellow flowerheads in small clusters. *H. i.* subsp. *serotinum* (curry plant) has foliage with a strong curry aroma. Zones 8–10.

Helichrysum appendiculatum

Helichrysum ecklonis

Helichrysum meyeri-johannis

☼ ❄ ↔ 12 in (30 cm) ↑ 6 in (15 cm)

Summer- to autumn-flowering alpine perennial from Kenya, endemic to Kirinyaga (Mt Kenya). Small, lance-shaped, gray-haired leaves and small, rounded, red flowerheads. Zones 9–10.

Helichrysum milfordiae

☼ ❄ ↔ 12 in (30 cm) ↑ 6 in (15 cm)

Spring-flowering, cushion-forming subshrub from South Africa. Densely downy, spatula-shaped leaves to ½ in (12 mm) long. Deep pink to red buds open to white flowerheads, to 1½ in (35 mm) wide. Zones 8–10.

Helichrysum montanum

syn. *Helichrysum splendidum* var. *montanum*

☼ ❄ ↔ 12 in (30 cm) ↑ 12 in (30 cm)

Summer-flowering, carpeting to mounding South African perennial. Narrow, densely downy, white to silver-gray leaves and clusters of small yellow flowerheads. Zones 9–10.

Helichrysum orientale

☼ ❄ ↔ 20 in (50 cm) ↑ 12 in (30 cm)

Summer-flowering subshrub from Greece and around the Aegean Sea.

White downy, narrowly spatula-shaped leaves to over 2 in (5 cm) long, crowded near base. Silvery white to pale yellow flowerheads, less than ½ in (12 mm) wide, in small clusters. Zones 7–10.

Helichrysum petiolare

LICORICE PLANT, LIQUORICE PLANT

☼ ❄ ↔ 5 ft (1.5 m) ↑ 12–18 in (30–45 cm)

This winter-flowering South African native is a spreading shrub that forms a mounding ground cover. It has a long soft stem and rounded leaves to over 1¼ in (30 mm) long. Leaves and stems covered in pale gray down. Small, dull white flowerheads loosely clustered. 'Limelight', distinctive pale yellow-green foliage; 'Variegatum', gray and cream variegated leaves. Zones 9–11.

Helichrysum plicatum

☼ ❄ ↔ 12 in (30 cm) ↑ 20 in (50 cm)

This summer-flowering, upright, perennial from southeastern Europe has hairy narrowly lance- to spatula-shaped leaves, 1½ in (35 mm) long, crowded near base. Yellow flowerheads over ¼ in (6 mm) wide, in dense clusters. Zones 7–9.

Helichrysum rutidolepis

Helichrysum retortoides

☼ ❄ ↔ 12 in (30 cm) ↑ 4 in (10 cm)

Compact mounding subshrub from South Africa. Glossy dark green leaves to 2 in (5 cm) long, silver-gray when young but losing downiness with age. Flowerheads silvery white, often pink-tinted, from late spring to late summer. Zones 9–11.

Helichrysum rutidolepis

PALE EVERLASTING

☼ ❄ ↔ 32 in (80 cm) ↑ 12 in (30 cm)

Autumn-flowering, low, spreading perennial from southeastern Australia. Narrow leaves, downy when young, sparsely so when mature. Bright golden yellow flowerheads. Zones 9–11.

Helichrysum sibthorpii

☼ ❄ ↔ 20 in (50 cm) ↑ 4 in (10 cm)

Small summer-flowering perennial from northern Greece. Low, spreading stems with white downy, spatula-shaped leaves to over 2 in (5 cm) long. Flowerheads ½ in (12 mm) wide, white. Zones 7–10.

Helichrysum splendidum

☼ ❄ ↔ 3 ft (0.9 m) ↑ 5 ft (1.5 m)

Autumn- to winter-flowering shrub from eastern and southern Africa. Narrowly lance-shaped leaves to over 2 in (5 cm) long with a thin covering of down. Tiny yellow to orange flower-heads clustered together. Zones 8–11.

Helichrysum stoechas

☼ ❄ ↔ 20 in (50 cm) ↑ 20 in (50 cm)

Summer-flowering shrubby perennial from southern and western Europe. Narrow white- to gray-felted leaves to 1¼ in (30 mm) long. Very small white flowerheads in clusters. 'White Barn' (syn. 'Elmstead'), 24 in (60 cm) tall, white felted leaves and soft yellow flowerheads. Zones 8–10.

HELICONIA

FALSE BIRD OF PARADISE, LOBSTER CLAW, WILD PLANTAIN

Widespread in the American tropics, southern Asia, and the Pacific Islands, this group of around 100 species of evergreen perennials is

Helichrysum milfordiae

Helichrysum petiolare 'Limelight'

from the banana (Musaceae) family. Ranging from small clumps to tree-like species and with large leaves resembling those of canna lilies or bananas, they are impressive foliage plants but their main feature is the floral inflorescence in which small flowers are each backed by a colorful bract that overlaps with the next flower to form a long spiral; hence the name *Heliconia*, from the Greek word *helix*, meaning spiral. Most bloom continuously.

CULTIVATION: All but a very few species will not do well in prolonged cool conditions. Plant in a part-shaded, warm, sheltered place with moist, humus-rich, well-drained soil. Water and feed well. Remove spent inflorescences to encourage flowering. Propagate by division, or from offsets or seed if available.

Heliconia angusta

☼ ❄ ↔ 7 ft (2 m) ↑ 15 ft (4.5 m)

Southeast Brazilian species with banana-like growth habit. Leaves to 3 ft (0.9 m) long, usually with a sparse brown covering of hair on the undersides. Upright inflorescence with up to 10 large yellow, orange, or red bracts enclosing green-tipped white to pale yellow flowers. 'Holiday', deep pink to red bracts; 'Yellow Christmas', chrome yellow and green bracts. Zones 10–12.

Helichrysum meyeri-johannis

Helichrysum orientale

Helichrysum plicatum

Heliconia aurantiaca

Heliconia caribaea

Heliconia latispatha, in the wild, Monumento Nacional Guayabo, Costa Rica

Heliconia aurantiaca

☀ ⚘ ↔ 3 ft (0.9 m) ↑ 7 ft (2 m)

Found from southern Mexico to Costa Rica. Narrow cane-like stems with narrow elliptical leaves to 14 in (35 cm) long. Upright, spiralling inflorescence, up to 5 bracts, orange to red, sometimes yellow or green. Flowers cream to orange. Zones 10–12.

Heliconia bihai

MACAW FLOWER, WILD PLANTAIN

☀ ⚘ ↔ 2–7 ft (0.6–2 m) ↑ 7–17 ft (2–5 m)

Central and tropical South American species forming a clump of banana-like stems with leaves often red-veined, to 6 ft (1.8 m) long, though usually considerably shorter. Long, upright inflorescence with up to 20 green-

Heliconia psittacorum

edged red bracts enclosing green-tipped white flowers. '**Aurea**', bracts with a broad gold edge; '**Chocolate Dancer**', deep red-brown bracts edged gold; '**Emerald Forest**', narrow bright green bracts; '**Schaefer**', brilliant red bracts edged orange; '**Yellow Dancer**', yellow bracts tipped green. Zones 10–12.

Heliconia caribaea

BALISIER, WILD PLANTAIN

☀ ⚘ ↔ 2–7 ft (0.6–2 m) ↑ 7–17 ft (2–5 m)

West Indian species with banana-like stems bearing pointed elliptical leaves to 4 ft (1.2 m) long. Relatively short, upright inflorescence with 2 overlapping rows of up to 15 triangular golden yellow to red bracts, often green-tipped and with a keel. Flowers white, green-tipped. '**Barbados Flat**', very flat inflorescence, red-brown bracts edged yellow; '**Gold**', deep golden yellow bracts; '**Flash**', bracts with yellow base, red center, and green edges. Zones 10–12.

Heliconia collinsiana

HANGING HELICONIA

☀ ⚘ ↔ 5–7 ft (1.5–2 m)
↑ 15–20 ft (4.5–6 m)

Banana-like species found from southern Mexico to Nicaragua. Leaves

Heliconia longiflora, in the wild, Parque Nacional Manuel Antonio, Costa Rica

3–7 ft (0.9–2 m) long and inflorescence to over 24 in (60 cm) long, pendulous, with up to 18 large, lighter-centered orange to red bracts. Flowers yellow to orange, partly protruding. Zones 10–12.

Heliconia farinosa

syn. *Heliconia brasiliensis*

☀ ⚘ ↔ 3 ft (0.9 m) ↑ 7 ft (2 m)

Southeast Brazilian species, banana-like growth habit. Leaves 32 in (80 cm) long, sometimes with a sparse dusty bloom. Wedge-shaped bristly inflorescence with narrow red bracts enclosing yellow or red flowers. Zones 10–12.

Heliconia latispatha

☀ ⚘ ↔ 3–4 ft (0.9–1.2 m) ↑ 10 ft (3 m)

Species found from southern Mexico to Colombia and Venezuela. Broad, sometimes red-edged leaves to over 5 ft (1.5 m) long. Upright inflorescence with long narrow bracts tapering to a fine point, yellow with a broad red edge. Zones 10–12.

Heliconia longiflora

☀ ⚘ ↔ 2–5 ft (0.6–1.5 m)
↑ 7–17 ft (2–5 m)

Central American native producing many narrow canes with a strongly erect habit bearing narrow, tapering leaves to 3 ft (0.9 m) long. Bracts orange, often suffused yellow, enclosing white flowers. Zones 10–12.

Heliconia bihai 'Yellow Dancer'

Heliconia collinsiana

Heliconia psittacorum

PARAKEET FLOWER, PARROT FLOWER

☀ ⚘ ↔ 20–32 in (50–80 cm)
↑ 2–7 ft (0.6–2 m)

Compact species from eastern Brazil and the southern West Indies. Banana-like growth habit with very slender stems bearing narrow leaves up to 20 in (50 cm) long, edges and stalks often red. Tall, upright inflorescence with few large bracts, pink, orange, or red. Enormous number of cultivars in wide range of colours. One of these, '**Strawberries and Cream**', has creamy yellow bracts suffused pink. Zones 10–12.

Heliconia psittacorum 'Strawberries and Cream'

H

Heliconia stricta 'Iris'

Heliconia rostrata

Heliconia rostrata

☀ ✤ ↔ 20–32 in (50–80 cm)
↑ 3–4 ft (0.9–1.2 m)

Found in the warmer and wetter areas of Peru and Argentina. Leaves 2–4 ft (0.6–1.2 m) long and pendulous inflorescence to 24 in (60 cm) long. Bracts strongly curved, red, edged green, flowers yellow-green. Zones 10–12.

Heliconia schiedeana

☀ ✤ ↔ 32–60 in (80–150 cm)
↑ 7–10 ft (2–3 m)

Southern Mexican species with banana-like growth habit. Leaves to 5 ft (1.5 m) long with web-like hairs on underside midrib. Inflorescence hairy, upright, around 24 in (60 cm) long. Spiralled bracts, variably sized, sometimes large, orange to red. Flowers yellow-green. Zones 10–12.

Heliconia trichocarpa, in the wild,
Monumento Nacional Guayabo, Costa Rica

Heliconia stricta

☀ ✤ ↔ 2–7 ft (0.6–2 m)
↑ 3–15 ft (0.9–4.5 m)

Variably sized banana-like tropical South American species with leaves 1–5 ft (0.3–1.5 m) long. Erect inflorescence to 12 in (30 cm) long. Bracts orange to red with green tip, keel and edges yellow. 'Ali', 20 in (50 cm) tall, red midribs, bracts red, edged green or yellow; 'Iris', vibrant red bracts; 'Iris Bannochie', 5–10 ft (1.5–3 m) tall, pinkish red bracts with green edges; 'Tagami', 10 ft (3 m) tall, red bracts, yellow keel and green edges. Zones 10–12.

Heliconia trichocarpa

☀/☀ ✤ ↔ 6–8 ft (1.8–2.4 m)
↑ 6–12 ft (1.8–3.5 m)

From Costa Rica to Colombia. Erect clump of slender shoots, long-stalked

Heliconia vellerigera

Heliconia wagneriana

leaves; inflorescences pendent, zig-zagging. Bracts spirally arranged, long-pointed, bright red; flowers yellow. Zones 11–12.

Heliconia vellerigera

☀ ✤ ↔ 5–8 ft (1.5–2.4 m)
↑ 15–20 ft (4.5–6 m)

Very large species native to Colombia, Ecuador, and Peru. Leaves 4–10 ft (1.2–3 m) long. Pendent inflorescence around 5 ft (1.5 m) long with stems and bracts covered with brown down. Up to 50 plus bracts, spiralled, red. Flowers yellow. Zones 10–12.

Heliconia wagneriana

☀ ✤ ↔ 4–7 ft (1.2–2 m) ↑ 12 ft (3.5 m)

Banana-like species that is found from Central America to northern Colombia. Has wavy edged leaves to over 6 ft (1.8 m) long. Inflorescence upright, to 18 in (45 cm) long. Bracts deep pink, orange, or red with creamy yellow keel and green edges. Zones 10–12.

HELICTOTRICHON

OAT GRASS

This grass (Poaceae) family genus includes some 60–100 perennial species, mostly native to dry hillside

meadows and woodland margins in temperate Eurasia but also found in other temperate regions. These tussock-forming grasses can reach 3–7 ft (0.9–2 m) in height, with slender culms and flat, folded or rolled-back blades. Erect or nodding panicles of flowers are produced in summer. *H. sempervirens* is the major ornamental species and makes a superb specimen, border mixer and container plant. The name *Helictotrichon* is derived from the Greek *heliktos* (twisted) and *thrix* or *trichos* (hair or bristle), referring to the shape of the awn.
CULTIVATION: Most prefer full sun and well-drained soil and are quite drought tolerant, depending on native habitat. They flower best if springtime conditions are cool and steadily moist, and are sparsely flowering in hot humid climates. Avoid root rot by providing good drainage and mulch in climates where temperatures drop below 5°F (−15°C).

Helictotrichon sempervirens ★

syns *Avena candida, A. sempervirens*
BLUE OAT GRASS

☀ ❄ ↔ 36 in (90 cm) ↑ 24 in (60 cm)
Clump-forming western Mediterranean native found on dry rocky hillsides. Produces dense tufts of erect vivid silver-blue foliage that is evergreen in mild climates. Straw-colored inflorescences on slender, arching, 24 in (60 cm) long stems, late spring. 'Pendula', heavy blooming, inflorescences more nodding; 'Robusta', rust-resistant for humid climates; 'Saphirsprudel', bright steely blue, fairly rust-resistant foliage. Zones 4–9.

HELIOHEBE

This small genus of evergreen shrubs and subshrubs belonging to the foxglove (Scrophulariaceae) family is native to New Zealand and was previously included in *Hebe*. Currently 5 species are contained in the genus, all being found in northeastern and central eastern areas of the South Island. The leaves usually have toothed and reddened margins and the flowers

Helictotrichon sempervirens

Heliohebe 'Hagley Park'

Heliohebe raoulii

are borne on terminal panicles.
CULTIVATION: These shrubs require a light well-drained soil in a sunny position and dislike humidity. Propagation is from seed or cuttings.

Heliohebe 'Hagley Park'

syns *Hebe* 'Hagley Park', *H.* 'Hagleyensis', *H.* 'Lady Hagley', *Veronica* 'Hagleyi'
☀ ❄ ↔ 24 in (60 cm) ↑ 18 in (45 cm)
A chance seedling, probably of *H. raoulii* and *H. hulkeana*. Spreading shrub with fairly glossy ¾–1¼ in (18–30 mm) long leaves with toothed reddish margins. Pinkish lilac flowers in erect terminal panicles are evident from mid-autumn to early winter. Zones 8–10.

Heliohebe hulkeana

syns *Hebe hulkeana*, *Veronica* 'Hailciana', *V.* 'Hulkei', *V.* 'Lawtonii'
NEW ZEALAND LILAC
☀ ❄ ↔ 36 in (90 cm) ↑ 36 in (90 cm)
Grows on banks and rocky bluffs to 3,000 ft (900 m) in Marlborough and Canterbury North, South Island, New Zealand. Leaves 1½ in (35 mm) long, oblong-elliptical, finely toothed, glossy, mid-green, tinged red. Long terminal panicles of lavender to white flowers in early summer. '**Lilac Hint**', rather small leaves and pale lilac flowers; '**Sally Blunt**', larger leaves and wisteria blue flowers. Zones 8–10.

Heliohebe raoulii

syn. *Hebe raoulii*
☀ ❄ ↔ 30 in (75 cm) ↑ 10 in (25 cm)
Found in rocky, drier, mountainous regions of Canterbury, South Island, New Zealand, above 500 ft (150 m). Leaves ½–1 in (12–25 mm) long, serrated, with reddish margins. Flowers, borne in spring in terminal panicles, are pinkish mauve. Zones 7–10.

HELIOPHILA

CAPE STOCK
This genus, native to South Africa, contains 71 species of annuals, perennials, and subshrubs belonging to the cabbage (Brassicaceae) family. They vary from erect to spreading or climb-

ing and the leaves may be entirely, lobed, or pinnately divided; 4-petalled flowers are usually borne on racemes and are white, blue, or pink, making a colorful display in summer.
CULTIVATION: Cultivated plants are usually grown as annuals. In cooler climates sow seed under glass, or *in situ* in warmer areas. Grow in well-drained soil in an open sunny site. Propagate from seed.

Heliophila coronopifolia

☀ ❂ ↔ 12–24 in (30–60 cm) ↑ 12–24 in (30–60 cm)
From South Africa, this annual has simple or pinnate leaves. Airy racemes of small blue flowers create a haze above the foliage in summer months. Zones 9–11.

Heliophila leptophylla

☀ ❂ ↔ 12–18 in (30–45 cm) ↑ 12–18 in (30–45 cm)
From South Africa, this annual has finely divided bluish green foliage. The small flowers are bright blue, characterised by a distinctive yellow eye. Zones 9–11.

HELIOPSIS

FALSE SUNFLOWER, OX-EYE
Native to North America, this genus of 13 species of loosely branched, erect, perennial herbs is a member of the daisy (Asteraceae) family. Flowerheads of bright yellow daisy-like flowers are produced from mid-summer to autumn, over a long period. The name *Heliopsis* means "resembling the sun".

Heliopsis, HC, 'Loraine Sunshine'

CULTIVATION: Fully frost hardy, these plants are ideal for herbaceous borders. They prefer full sun and average soil kept moist throughout summer. Some staking may be needed. Propagate from seed or divide clumps periodically in spring or autumn.

Heliopsis helianthoides

EVERLASTING SUNFLOWER, FALSE SUNFLOWER, SMOOTH OX-EYE
☀ ❄ ↔ 12–24 in (30–60 cm) ↑ 24–60 in (60–150 cm)
Perennial found from Ontario, Canada, to Florida and Mississippi, USA. Smooth, oval- to sword-shaped, coarse-toothed, mid-green leaves, to 6 in (15 cm) long. Numerous terminal flowerheads of yellow daisy-like flowers, to 3 in (8 cm) across, on stems to 10 in (25 cm) long. *H. h.* var. *scabra*, double orange-yellow flowers, very rough stems and leaves; '**Incomparabilis**', single orange-yellow flowers; '**Light of Loddon**', double bright golden orange flowers, to 48 in (120 cm) high. Zones 3–9.

Heliopsis Hybrid Cultivars

☀ ❄ ↔ 12–24 in (30–60 cm) ↑ 4 ft (1.2 m)
These are all perennials with mid-green leaves. '**Goldgefieder**' (ox-eye),

Heliophila coronopifolia

Heliophila leptophylla

Heliopsis helianthoides var. *scabra*

late-flowering, 48–60 in (120–150 cm) tall, with double golden daisy-like flowers; '**Loraine Sunshine**', dwarf, variegated, loosely branched form, 16–30 in (40–75 cm) long, white leaves with green veins and large, golden yellow, daisy-like flowers. Zones 3–9.

HELIOTROPIUM

A member of the borage family (Boraginaceae), this is a genus of about 250 species, mainly evergreen shrubs, from Central America and temperate South America. Some species are locally important for medicinal purposes, and others are significant ornamentals. The fragrant flowers can be white, yellow, blue, or purple.
CULTIVATION: Most of the species prefer fertile free-draining soils, summer moisture and shelter from cold. Full sun to filtered light is their favored habitat. Where frosts occur, the most sheltered position in the garden must be selected. Prune moderately immediately after flowering to encourage new shoots. Propagate from soft-tip cuttings in spring or summer or half-hardened cuttings in autumn to winter in a warm and moist situation.

H

Heliotropium arborescens

CHERRY PIE, COMMON HELIOTROPE

☼ ✣ ↔ 20 in (50 cm) ↑ 3 ft (0.9 m)

From tropical Peru. Spreading, evergreen bun-shaped shrub. Narrow oval leaves dark and shiny above, paler reverse. Abundant sweetly perfumed mauve to purple flowers, from early spring to late summer. Cultivars are good for use in borders or pots, and include: '**Black Beauty**' ★, very dark purple-black flowers; '**Chatsworth**', purple flowers, strongly scented; '**Fragrant Delight**', dark purple flowers, also strongly scented; '**Iowa**', dense, upright habit, purple-tinted foliage, large clusters of fragrant dark purple flowers; '**Lord Roberts**', compact growth, violet flowers; '**Marine**', bushy and compact growth, purple-blue flowers; and '**Princess Marina**', dark violet-blue flowers. Zones 9–12.

Heliotropium curassavicum

☼/☼ ✣ ↔ 24 in (60 cm) ↑ 16 in (40 cm)

Annual to short-lived perennial from the American tropics and subtropics. Forms a mounding and spreading bush with fleshy stems and foliage. Narrow lance-shaped, light green leaves to 2 in (5 cm) long. Terminal inflorescences to 4 in (10 cm) wide, opening cream, ageing to purple. Zones 10–12.

H. arborescens 'Fragrant Delight'

Heliotropium arborescens 'Lord Roberts'

Heliotropium arborescens

Heliotropium indicum

☼/☼ ✣ ↔ 32 in (80 cm) ↑ 40 in (100 cm)

Bushy annual widespread in the tropics. Open habit with bristly stems. Wavy-edged elliptical to lance-shaped leaves up to 6 in (15 cm) long. Spikes of blue, mauve, or white flowers. Zones 10–12.

HELLEBORUS

LENTEN ROSE, WINTER ROSE

This genus of 15 species of buttercup (Ranunculaceae) family perennials was a favorite of Gertrude Jekyll and she used it extensively in her garden at Munstead Wood. Found in the temperate zone from Europe to western China, they are mainly low-growing plants with short-stemmed, often toothed, palmate foliage emerging direct from a rhizome. The simple, 5-petalled, bowl-shaped flowers appear from mid-winter into spring and occur in unusual shades of green, dusky pink, and maroon as well as white. At the center of the flower are prominent greenish nectaries and many yellow stamens.

CULTIVATION: Most prefer woodland conditions with deep, fertile, humus-rich, well-drained soil and dappled shade. Some of the smaller types are well suited to rock gardens. Many are near-evergreen but benefit from having old foliage removed when

dormant. Propagation is by division or from seed, which may require 2 periods of stratification. Naturalizes in suitable climates.

Helleborus argutifolius

☼/☼ ❄ ↔ 24–40 in (60–100 cm) ↑ 40 in (100 cm)

Winter- to spring-flowering native of Corsica, France, and Sardinia, Italy. Evergreen, leathery trifoliate leaves with soft-spined and toothed leaflets to 8 in (20 cm) long, sometimes gray-green. Large heads of green flowers to 2 in (5 cm) wide. '**Janet Starnes**', compact habit with foliage mottled cream; '**Pacific Frost**', mottled cream, pink, and green foliage, narrow leaflets, pale flowers, sometimes maroon-tinted. Zones 7–10.

Helleborus × ballardiae

☼/☼ ❄ ↔ 12–16 in (30–40 cm) ↑ 12 in (30 cm)

Hybrid between *H. niger* and *H. lividus*. Leaves with 3 to 9 segments to 6 in (15 cm) long, blue-green with silvery veins, semi-evergreen. Pale green, white, or pink flowers, to over 2½ in (6 cm) wide, in winter. Zones 5–9.

Helleborus cyclophyllus

☼/☼ ❄ ↔ 24–32 in (60–80 cm) ↑ 16 in (40 cm)

Found from Greece to Albania and Bulgaria. Deciduous leaves with 8 to 11 leaflets, rarely up to 25, largest to 8 in (20 cm) long, hairy undersides. In winter, stems to 20 in (50 cm) long with yellow-green flowers to over 2 in (5 cm) wide. Zones 7–9.

Heliotropium curassavicum

Helleborus argutifolius

Helleborus cyclophyllus

Helleborus foetidus

Helleborus foetidus

BEAR'S FOOT, STINKING HELLEBORE, STINKWORT

☼/☼ ❄ ↔ 24–40 in (60–100 cm) ↑ 24–32 in (60–80 cm)

Evergreen found from Britain to Hungary. Foliage is pungent if crushed. Dark green leaves with 5 to 13 narrow leaflets, longest to 8 in (20 cm), toothed. Green flowers, often red-tinted, bell-shaped, around 1 in (25 mm) wide, on strongly upright stems. '**Green Giant**', very bright green flowers, finely divided foliage; '**Miss Jekyll**', fragrant flowers, intensity varying with the time of day; '**Sierra Nevada Form**', only 12 in (30 cm) high; '**Wester Flisk**', red-tinted stems and leaves, gray-green flowers. Zones 6–9.

Helleborus lividus

☼/☼ ❄ ↔ 24 in (60 cm) ↑ 16 in (40 cm)

Evergreen from Majorca and possibly neighboring Cabrera, Spain. Simple 3-part, deep green, purple-tinted leaves, usually smooth-edged. Flowers from mid-winter, bright green flushed purple to all-over purple, near flat when open. May rot in cold wet winters. Zones 7–10.

Helleborus multifidus

☼/☼ ❄ ↔ 16–32 in (40–80 cm) ↑ 20 in (50 cm)

Winter- to spring-flowering deciduous species from Italy and the Balkans. Leaves much divided. Flowers usually green, to 1½ in (35 mm) wide, but no typical form, instead 3 distinct subspecies: *H. m.* subsp. *bocconei*, with flowers to nearly 3 in (8 cm) wide; *H. m.* **subsp.** *hercegovinus*, with narrow, lacy leaflets, rarely very finely divided into up to 100 leaflets, maximum recorded is 185; and *H. m.* **subsp.** *istriacus*, with strongly purple-tinted flowers. Zones 6–9.

Helleborus niger
CHRISTMAS ROSE

☼/◐ ❄ ↔ 12–20 in (30–50 cm)
↑ 12 in (30 cm)

Winter- to spring-flowering evergreen from northern Italy to southern Germany. Deep green, serrated, leathery leaves with 5 to 9 broad leaflets, to 8 in (20 cm) long. White flowers on strong stems, sometimes flushed pink, opening flat. *H. n.* **subsp.** *macranthus* has large flowers and blue-green leaves with broad, soft-spined leaflets. *H. n.* **'Potter's Wheel'** has pure white flowers to 4 in (10 cm) wide; **'White Magic'** has dark-stemmed pure white flowers, pink-tinted with age. Zones 3–9.

Helleborus × *nigercors*

☼/◐ ❄ ↔ 24 in (60 cm) ↑ 24 in (60 cm)
Hybrid between *H. niger* and *H. argutifolius*. Leaves evergreen, large, gray-green, 3 to 7 leaflets coarsely toothed and often soft-spined. Heads of large blue-green-tinted white flowers from mid-winter. Zones 7–10.

Helleborus orientalis ★
LENTEN ROSE

☼/◐ ❄ ↔ 16–24 in (40–60 cm)
↑ 16 in (40 cm)

Semi-evergreen winter-flowering species from northern Turkey and Greece and around the Black Sea. Leaves with 7 to 9 coarsely serrated leaflets, longest to 10 in (25 cm). Flowers variable, from pure white to red-black forms, often dark-spotted. *H. o.* **subsp.** *orientalis*, white flowers, sometimes green tinted; *H. o.* **subsp.** *abchasicus*, red to purplish flowers, *H. o.* **subsp.** *a.* **'Early Purple'** (syn. *Helleborus atrorubens*), flowers greenish purple, nodding; and *H. o.* **subsp.** *guttatus*, white flowers, usually dark-

H. o. subsp. *abchasicus* 'Early Purple'

spotted. *H. o.* **'Alberich'**, early purple-black flowers; **'Banana Split'**, large creamy yellow flowers; **'Blue Spray'**, dark buds opening to bell-shaped smoky purple flowers; **'Fred Whitsey'**, white flowers with purple spots and streaks; **'Hades'**, dark-speckled gray-blue flowers; **'Mardi Gras'**, red-blotched white flowers; **'Pleiades'**, dwarf with red-flecked white flowers; **'Southern Belle'**, lavender flowers on tall stems; and **'Trotter's Spotted'**, large purple-spotted white flowers. Zones 5–9.

Helleborus purpurascens

☼/◐ ❄ ↔ 16–30 in (40–75 cm)
↑ 12 in (30 cm)

Deciduous species found from Hungary to the Ukraine. Leaves palmate, usually 5 main leaflets in up to 25 segments, undersides hairy. Flowers to nearly 3 in (8 cm) wide, purple or blue-gray with metallic sheen. Zones 6–9.

Helleborus × *sternii*

☼/◐ ❄ ↔ 12–32 in (30–80 cm)
↑ 12–32 in (30–80 cm)

Variably sized semi-evergreen hybrid between *H. argutifolius* and *H. lividus*. Leaves dark gray-green, sometimes lighter veined and/or purple-tinted, smooth-edged or spiny. Heads of green flowers from winter, often flushed pink or purple. Zones 7–9.

Helleborus vesicarius

☼/◐ ❄ ↔ 12–16 in (30–40 cm)
↑ 24 in (60 cm)

Summer-dormant succulent species from Turkey and Syria. It resembles

Helleborus orientalis

Helleborus orientalis subsp. *guttatus*

Helleborus vesicarius

other hellebores only when in flower. Foliage with 5 finely divided, lobed, and toothed leaflets. Leaves appear from late autumn followed by upright flower stems and small green-tinted purple flowers to 1 in (25 mm) wide in spring. Zones 7–10.

Helleborus viridis
GREEN HELLEBORE

☼/◐ ❄ ↔ 24 in (60 cm) ↑ 16 in (40 cm)
Deciduous plant native to western Europe, including Britain. Usually just 2 leaves divided into 7 to 13 toothed leaflets with downy undersides. Bright green, sometimes red-veined flowers, usually carried singly, from late winter. Zones 6–9.

HELONIOPSIS
There are 4 species of rhizomatous perennials in this genus, which belongs to the bunchflower (Melanthiaceae) family. They are native to Japan, Korea, and Taiwan where they grow in mountain woods and meadows. The oblong to lance-shaped leaves form basal rosettes from which stems of nodding flowers arise in spring. Flowers may be solitary or in loose umbels. They are white, pink or yellow.
CULTIVATION: Grow these species in a rich, moisture-retentive soil in light shade. Protect from cold winds to prevent leaf scorch. Propagation is by division or from seed.

Heloniopsis orientalis

Heloniopsis orientalis
syn. *Heloniopsis japonica*

☼ ❄ ↔ 8–12 in (20–30 cm)
↑ 8–12 in (20–30 cm)

From Japan and Korea, this species has oblong leathery leaves that form basal rosettes. The nodding flowers have flaring petals and are borne 2–10 to a stem. They are pink or violet with bluish anthers. *H. o.* **var.** *kawanoi* is a dwarf form, 2–8 in (5–20 cm) high. Zones 7–9.

HELWINGIA
This is a genus in the dogwood (Cornaceae) family consisting of 3 to 5 deciduous shrubs which are native to the Himalayas, Japan, and Taiwan. With separate male and female plants, clusters of unusual flowers appear on the surface of their alternate toothed leaves. The fruit is a fleshy berry-like drupe.

Helleborus multifidus subsp. *bocconei*

Helleborus niger

Hemerocallis minor

Hemerocallis citrina

Hemerocallis lilio-asphodelus

Helwingia japonica

CULTIVATION: *Helwingia* species prefer a position in full sun or semi-shade in moist soil. Propagation is normally from cuttings of green wood struck under glass in summer. They can also be propagated from seeds, although the male and female plants need to be grown in close proximity for successful reproduction.

Helwingia japonica
☼ ❄ ↔ 5 ft (1.5 m) ↑ 5 ft (1.5 m)
From China and southern Japan. Elliptical olive green leaves, with bristle-like teeth, bear 12 tiny, greenish white star-shaped flowers on the male plants. Single female flowers are followed by spherical black fruit, which is also carried on the surface of the leaves. Zones 8–9.

HEMEROCALLIS
DAYLILY
Daylilies are so-named because each of their funnel- to bell-shaped flowers

lasts just one day, though they carry a succession of blooms from late spring until autumn. Once classified with the true lilies, this group of 15 species of rhizome-rooted perennials from temperate East Asia is now the type genus for its own family, the Hemerocallidaceae. They form clumps of grassy or iris-like leaves with sometimes branching racemes of 6-petalled flowers in a range of warm yellow, apricot, and red shades. All parts of the plant, especially the buds and flowers, are edible and may be added to salads or used as a colorful garnish. The stamens can be used as a saffron color substitute.
CULTIVATION: They are hardy and easily grown in a sunny or part-shaded position with fertile, moist, well-drained soil. Slugs and snails often badly disfigure the foliage. Take care when siting as the flowers turn to face the sun. Rust disease is a problem in some areas. Propagation is usually by division.

Hemerocallis citrina
☼/◐ ❄ ↔ 3–7 ft (0.9–2 m) ↑ 5 ft (1.5 m)
Chinese species with narrow leaves to 4 ft (1.2 m) long. Flower stems are upright, branching from above half-height, bearing up to 50 plus fragrant pale yellow flowers to over 4 in (10 cm) wide. Flowers open at night and stay open for most of the next day. Zones 4–9.

Hemerocallis dumortieri
LEMON LILY
☼/◐ ❄ ↔ 16–24 in (40–60 cm)
↑ 16 in (40 cm)
Compact, early-flowering species from Korea and eastern Russia. Very narrow leaves to around 14 in (35 cm) long. Flower stems, red-tinted, unbranched and only slightly exceeding foliage height, bearing just 2 to 4 fragrant golden flowers to a little over 2 in (5 cm) wide, backed by broad bracts. Zones 4–9.

Hemerocallis fulva
☼/◐ ❄ ↔ 4–5 ft (1.2–1.5 m)
↑ 3 ft (0.9 m)
Wild origin uncertain, perhaps China or Japan, but may be a hybrid. Leaves to over 24 in (60 cm) long, strappy. Flower stems usually 2-branched with up to 20, dark-striped, light orange-brown, 3–4 in (8–10 cm) wide flowers. '**Kwanzo**' (syn. 'Kwanzo Flore Pleno'), an early cultivar from 1860, has dark-centered double flowers; '**Kwanzo Variegata**' has the same flowers and creamy white-edged foliage. Zones 4–9.

Hemerocallis lilio-asphodelus
CUSTARD LILY
☼/◐ ❄ ↔ 40–48 in (100–120 cm)
↑ 24–40 in (60–100 cm)
An early-flowering Chinese species characterised by very narrow sickle-

shaped leaves to over 24 in (60 cm) long. Wiry, branching flower stems carry up to 12 night-scented, pale yellow flowers to 3 in (8 cm) wide. Zones 4–9.

Hemerocallis middendorffii
☼/◐ ❄ ↔ 20–24 in (50–60 cm)
↑ 18 in (45 cm)
Native to Japan and nearby parts of mainland northeastern Asia. Leaves strappy, to 12 in (30 cm) long. Flower stems unbranched but extending well beyond the foliage, with few fragrant yellow flowers clustered together. Zones 5–9.

Hemerocallis minor
☼/◐ ❄ ↔ 20–24 in (50–60 cm)
↑ 20 in (50 cm)
From Japan and nearby parts of China. Very narrow leaves to 18 in (45 cm) long. Flower stems with 2 or sometimes more branches bearing up to 5 soft yellow flowers to over 2 in (5 cm) wide. Zones 4–9.

Hemerocallis Hybrid Cultivars
☼/◐ ❄ ↔ unlimited
↑ 12–48 in (30–120 cm)
Daylilies hybridize readily, and with such beautiful flowers it should not come as a surprise to find that there are several hundred hybrids and cultivars covering a wide range of flower colors and plant sizes, from

Hemerocallis, Hybrid Cultivar, 'Anzac'

Hemerocallis, HC, 'Barbary Corsair'

Hemerocallis, Hybrid Cultivar, 'Baby Betsy'

miniatures growing only to around 12 in (30 cm) tall to those with 4 ft (1.2 m) flower stems. Some of the most popular or distinctive of these cultivars include: '**Anzac**', 30 in (75 cm), yellow-centered dark red;

'**Baby Betsy**', 18 in (45 cm), deep cherry red; '**Barbara Mitchell**' ★, 20 in (50 cm), pale creamy apricot pink with yellow-green center; '**Barbary Corsair**', 16 in (40 cm), purple-red; '**Blue Sheen**', 24 in

(60 cm), purplish blue flowers to 4 in (10 cm) wide, prominent yellow center; '**Cartwheels**', 30 in (75 cm), bright yellow, light mid-stripe, large cultivar; '**Charlie Brown**', 20 in (50 cm), pink to orange with yellow

center, large cultivar; '**Cherry Lace**', 20 in (50 cm), pinkish red with yellow centers; '**Corky**', 24 in (60 cm) long wiry stems with yellow flowers and brown buds; '**Etched in Gold**', 24 in (60 cm), apricot with yellowish edging;

Hemerocallis, Hybrid Cultivar, 'Bess Ross'

Hemerocallis, Hybrid Cultivar, 'Bishops Crest'

Hemerocallis, Hybrid Cultivar, 'Blue Sheen'

Hemerocallis, Hybrid Cultivar, 'Bonanza'

Hemerocallis, Hybrid Cultivar, 'Buzz Bomb'

Hemerocallis, Hybrid Cultivar, 'Cartwheels'

Hemerocallis, HC, 'Charlie Brown'

Hemerocallis, HC, 'Cherry Lace'

Hemerocallis, HC, 'Chicago Rosy'

Hemerocallis, Hybrid Cultivar, 'Corky'

Hemerocallis, HC, 'Crimson Icon'

Hemerocallis, HC, 'Double Glamour'

Hemerocallis, HC, 'Dune Buggy'

Hemerocallis, HC, 'Etched in Gold'

Hemerocallis, Hybrid Cultivar, 'Fabulous Favorite'

Hemerocallis, Hybrid Cultivar, 'Flambeau'

Hemerocallis, Hybrid Cultivar, 'Franz Hals'

Hemerocallis, Hybrid Cultivar, 'Hans Hals'

Hemerocallis, Hybrid Cultivar, 'Heather Queen'

Hemerocallis, HC, 'High Lama'

Hemerocallis, HC, 'Jaune d'Or'

H., HC, 'Little Bumble Bee'

Hemerocallis, HC, 'Little Celenna'

H., HC, 'Little Gypsy Vagabond'

Hemerocallis, HC, 'Little Tawny'

H., HC, 'Many Happy Returns'

Hemerocallis, HC, 'May Unger'

H., HC, 'Missouri Beauty'

H., HC, 'Moonlight Mist'

Hemerocallis, HC, 'Pink Dream'

Hemerocallis, HC, 'Pink Sundae'

Hemerocallis, HC, 'Pirate'

H., HC, 'Prairie Blue Eyes'

Hemerocallis, HC, 'Precious'

Hemerocallis, HC, 'Purple Pauper'

Hemerocallis, HC, 'Red Precious'

H., HC, 'Sarah Elizabeth'

Hemerocallis, HC, 'Scarlet Oak'

H., HC, 'Solano Bulls Eye'

H., HC, 'Sounds of Music'

Hemerocallis, HC, 'Stafford'

Hemerocallis, HC, 'Stoke Poges'

Hemerocallis, HC, 'Thumbelina'

Hemerocallis, HC, 'Torpoint'

'Fabulous Favorite', 24 in (60 cm), rusty orange, deep yellow center; '**Franz Hals**', 28 in (70 cm), red-brown and orange flowers with fine cream midstripe; '**Golden Chimes**', branching stems with small gold flowers, brown buds; '**Green Flutter**', 20 in (50 cm), greenish yellow, semi-double, late; '**High Lama**', 36 in (90 cm), large, lavender; '**Hope Diamond**', scented golden yellow flowers, wide; '**Little Bumble Bee**', 20 in (50 cm), many small maroon-centered yellow flowers; '**Little Gypsy Vagabond**', 18 in (45 cm), light yellow with maroon center; '**Little Tawny**', 20 in (50 cm), rusty orange, heavy-flowering; '**Many Happy Returns**' ★, 16 in (40 cm), pale yellow, long-flowering and heat tolerant; '**Midnight Magic**', 28 in (70 cm), very dark red; '**Missouri Beauty**', 36 in (90 cm), green-tinted yellow, ruffled; '**Moonlight Mist**', 20 in (50 cm), very pale apricot pink; '**Neal Berrey**', 18 in (45 cm), deep pink shades; '**Nob Hill**', gold-centered pale pink and lavender flowers; '**Paper Butterfly**', 28 in (70 cm), mauve-pink with purple and yellow center; '**Pink Flirt**', 24 in (60 cm), bright pink; '**Prairie Blue Eyes**', 28 in (70 cm), light purple, large; '**Priscilla's Rainbow**', 24 in (60 cm), pale apricot with purple and pink band around yellow center; '**Purple Pauper**', 20 in (50 cm), purple with yellow-green throat, large; '**Stafford**', 24 in (60 cm), bright red with yellow center, wiry stems; '**Stella d'Oro**' ★, 16 in (40 cm), orange-centered bright yellow flowers over long season; '**Stoke Poges**', 24 in (60 cm), lilac pink shades, orange-yellow center; '**Thumbelina**', 14 in (35 cm), small gold flowers, wiry stems. Zones 4–9.

HEMIANDRA

This small Australian genus of 8 species is placed in the mint (Lamiaceae) family. All the species occur in the southwest of Western Australia in sandy and lateritic gravelly soils in heath and jarrah forest communities. Some are prostrate shrubs, others are more upright, and all have spiky,

Hemigraphis alternata

narrow leaves. The flowers range in color from almost white through to mauve and scarlet.

CULTIVATION: Only a couple of the 8 species are so far in cultivation. An open, sunny and well-drained position is essential. Periods of moist humid weather, particularly in summer, can cause loss from fungal attack. Propagation is from fresh seed or from half-hardened cuttings taken from young growth.

Hemiandra pungens

SNAKEBUSH, SNAKE VINE

☀ ❄ ↔ 8 ft (2.4 m) ↑ 3 ft (0.9 m)

Variable species, prostrate to upright. Leaves are narrow, with a sharp point. Flowers are very showy, 2-lipped, white or pink with purplish spots on throat, year round, peaking in late spring–summer. Fruits are ripe most of the year. Zones 8–9.

HEMIGRAPHIS

This genus, which is a member of the acanthus (Acanthaceae) family, contains about 90 species of annuals, perennials and subshrubs which are native to tropical Asia. They have low-growing slender stems with opposite leaves that usually have toothed or scalloped margins. The small flowers are tubular with 5 petal lobes and have conspicuous bracts. They are carried on terminal spikes, which appear intermittently through the year.

CULTIVATION: In tropical and subtropical regions these plants can be grown as ground cover outdoors in partial shade. Elsewhere they are suitable for indoor plants and as ground cover in the tropical greenhouse. In these situations they require filtered light and plentiful watering during the growing period. Propagate from cuttings.

Hemigraphis alternata

syn. *Hemigraphis colorata*

METAL LEAF, RED IVY

☀ ✢ ↔ 12–18 in (30–45 cm) ↑ 4 in (10 cm)

From India and Java. Prostrate perennial rooting at the nodes. It is grown

Hemiandra pungens

for its attractive, scallop-edged, oval leaves, which are purple beneath and dark bluish green above with a metallic sheen. Flowers are small and white. 'Exotica' has puckered leaves with rolled margins. Zones 11–12.

Hemigraphis repanda

☀ ✢ ↔ 12–18 in (30–45 cm) ↑ 4 in (10 cm)

Native to Malaysia. Prostrate perennial rooting at the nodes. Slender stems flushed with maroon. Lance-shaped leaves with scalloped edges are satiny gray flushed with maroon or purple. Zones 11–12.

HEMIONITIS

This genus of 7 species of evergreen ferns from the American tropics belongs to the maidenhair-fern (Adiantaceae) family. They have short, scaly, almost erect rhizomes and crowded, simple or pinnate, often hairy, rounded, heart-shaped or palm-shaped fronds. The fertile fronds are longer than the sterile fronds. The name *Hemionitis* comes from the Greek *hemionos* (mule), referring to the plant's sterile fronds.

CULTIVATION: These species are suitable for container growth. They should be sheltered from full sun, and prefer a fibrous potting mix that is kept moist. Propagate in spring to early summer from spores or plantlets arising from frond bases, or by dividing the rootball.

Heemionitis arifolia ★

HEART FERN, PIGGY-BACK FERN

☀ ⅊ ↔ 4–12 in (10–30 cm) ↑ 4–12 in (10–30 cm)

Compact evergreen fern from India, Sri Lanka, Myanmar, Taiwan, and the Philippines. Wiry, rich brown to black, hairy stalks with plantlets forming at bases. Simple, mid-green,

Hemionitis arifolia

triangular to heart-shaped fronds, rough to the touch, hairy and scaly underneath. Zones 10–11.

HEPATICA

This is a small genus of 10 species in the ranunculus (Ranunculaceae) family, closely related to *Anemone*. They are native to northern temperate zones in woodland settings. The leaves are basal, usually 3- to 5-lobed, leathery in texture, and often persist throughout winter. The flowers, produced in very early spring, are bowl-shaped and borne one per stem. They are hugely popular, and vast amounts of money are changing hands for unusual colors and forms.

CULTIVATION: As they are woodlanders by nature, a cool aspect in humus-rich soil is best, and as the plants are small in stature, the intimacy of a small pocket in a shaded rock garden makes a good setting. Propagate from freshly sown seed or by division of selected clones, which will take time to re-establish.

Hepatica acutiloba

☀ ❄ ↔ 4–6 in (10–15 cm) ↑ 2½–3 in (6–8 cm)

From eastern USA. Leaves are 3- to 7-lobed, to 3 in (8 cm) long. Slightly cupped flowers to 1 in (25 mm) across in shades of white, pink or blue, in early spring. Zones 4–9.

Hepatica nobilis

☀ ❄ ↔ 4–6 in (10–15 cm) ↑ 3–4 in (8–10 cm)

This European species has mid-green leaves with 3 rounded lobes, and open bowl-shaped flowers, to 1 in (25 mm) across, in shades of white through pink to blue and almost purple. Many selections in a range of colors and with double flowers exist. Zones 5–9.

Heptacodium miconioides

Hereroa tugwelliae

HEPTACODIUM

This genus, in the woodbine (Caprifoliaceae) family and allied to *Abelia* and *Kolkwitzia*, consists of 1 species of deciduous shrub from central and eastern China. It has large glossy leaves with 3 longitudinal veins, in opposite pairs on the twigs. Small white flowers are borne in large panicles at branch ends. As the small dry fruits develop, the sepals, inconspicuous in flower, enlarge and turn deep pink, making a display that lasts several months. The species is little known in cultivation outside northeastern USA.
CULTIVATION: This plant likes woodland conditions with moist acid soil and shelter, though not too much shade. Lower twiggy growth should be thinned out in winter. Propagation should be from hardwood cuttings in autumn or half-hardened tip cuttings in summer, from basal suckers, or from seed.

Heptacodium miconioides ★
syn. *Heptacodium jasminoides*
CHINESE HEPTACODIUM, SEVEN SON FLOWER
☼ ❄ ↔ 7–10 ft (2–3 m)
↑ 10–15 ft (3–4.5 m)
Chinese deciduous shrub or small tree, dark green elliptical leaves. Heads of fragrant white flowers, from late summer to the first frosts. Calyces of flowers remain, turning bright rosy red to purple in autumn. Zones 5–9.

HEREROA

This genus of over 30 species of succulent mat-forming perennials or small shrubs belongs to the iceplant (Aizoaceae) family and is native to South Africa and Namibia. The leaves are arranged in opposite pairs at right angles. They are fleshy and rounded toward the base, becoming flatter or keeled near the tips and often with raised dots. The daisy-like flowers are borne either singly or in clusters and are usually yellow in color, sometimes becoming pink as they age. They open in the afternoon or evening.
CULTIVATION: In warm regions with dry winters grow outdoors in full sun. In temperate climates grow in the greenhouse in pots of very well-drained soil mix. Plants need low humidity. Water carefully from spring to autumn and allow to dry out through winter. Propagate from seed or cuttings.

Hereroa granulata
☼ ❄ ↔ 6 in (15 cm) ↑ 3 in (8 cm)
From South Africa. Mat-forming perennial. Narrow, upright to spreading, keeled leaves to 2½ in (6 cm) long, cylindrical near the base, flatter toward the apex. They are dark green with a rough dotted surface. Yellow flowers. Zones 9–11.

Hereroa tugwelliae
☼ ❄ ↔ 4 in (10 cm) ↑ 4 in (10 cm)
From South Africa. Subshrub with woody roots. Thick, light green, dotted, tapering leaves. Yellow flowers to 2 in (5 cm) across. Zones 9–11.

HERMANNIA
HONEYBELLS

This genus, a member of the cacao (Sterculiaceae) family, consists of about 100 species of evergreen subshrubs and shrubs native to tropical and southern Africa. Their leaves have leafy bracts and produce honey-scented bell-shaped flowers with 5 petals and spirally twisted corollas, borne singly or in cymes of several from the leaf axils. The genus is named after Paul Hermann, a seventeenth-century professor of botany from Leiden, Holland.
CULTIVATION: *Hermannia* species prefer fertile well-drained soil in full sun. Tip-prune to maintain a bushy habit. Propagate from softwood or greenwood cuttings from late spring to summer.

Hermannia incana
HONEYBELLS
☼ ❄ ↔ 18–36 in (45–90 cm)
↑ 3–7 ft (0.9–2 m)
Perennial from South Africa with erect slightly hairy stems and oval-shaped leaves, slightly hairy, ¼–1½ in (6–35 mm) long, with wedge-shaped bases. Leafy panicles of yellow flowers with rounded petals, narrowing into a claw shape. Zones 8–10.

HERMODACTYLUS
SNAKE'S HEAD IRIS

This genus in the iris (Iridaceae) family contains 1 species of tuberous perennial which is so closely related to *Iris* that some botanists consider it should be included in that genus. Native to southern Europe, it grows in scrub and on grassy banks. It has a creeping rootstock of fingerlike tubers. The linear leaves are grayish green. In late winter to early spring it bears unusual, fragrant, iris-like flowers.

CULTIVATION: Grow in sun in any well-drained soil, making sure to give protection from slugs and snails. Propagation is by division.

Hermodactylus tuberosus
SNAKE'S HEAD IRIS, WIDOW IRIS
☼ ❄ ↔ 6 in (15 cm) ↑ 12 in (30 cm)
From southern Europe. Narrow, soft, loose leaves. Flowering stems covered in sheathing leaves, bear solitary iris-like flowers of yellowish green with purplish brown falls. Zones 6–9.

HESPERALOE

This agave (Agavaceae) family genus, which contains 3 species of stemless evergreen perennial herbs that form grass-like clumps, is native to southwestern Texas and the Chihuahuan Desert region of northern Mexico. The species produce spreading rosettes of soft, narrow, strap-like leaves with margins that have thread-like appendages. Narrow bell-shaped flowers are produced in sparsely branched racemes or panicles to 1¼ in (30 mm) in diameter. The fruit is a brown capsule.
CULTIVATION: Plant at any time in full sun or half-sun in well-drained rocky gravel or sandy soil. Removing spent flower stalks will prolong blooming. Propagation is from seed or by division of clumps in winter.

Hermannia incana

Hermodactylus tuberosus

Hesperaloe parviflora

FALSE RED YUCCA

☼/◐ ❄ ↔ 24–48 in (60–120 cm)
↑ 24–48 in (60–120 cm)

Clumping succulent perennial native
to southwestern Texas. Thick, spreading, leathery, tapering, blue-green
leaves, to 48 in (120 cm) long, developing buds at base, margins with fine
white threads. Slender flower stalk, up
to 40 spikes of nodding rose to rich
salmon pink flowers, golden yellow
inside, 1¼ in (30 mm) across, in late
summer. *H. p.* var. *engelmannii*, more
bell-shaped flowers; **'Rubra'**, bright
red flowers. Zones 7–10.

HESPERIS

This cabbage (Brassicaceae) family
genus consists of 60 biennials and
short-lived perennials of upright
habit. Stems are clothed with oblong
leaves and topped with open clusters
of 4-petalled flowers in shades of
yellow, white, or purple, often sweetly
scented, particularly in the evenings.
H. matronalis is food for the orange-tip
butterfly and a good source of nectar.
CULTIVATION: These plants are suitable for the border or wild garden.
They do best in full sun or light shade
and prefer a neutral to alkaline soil.
Although they tolerate poor soils, they
will perform better if the ground is
enriched. Propagate from seed, which
will usually self-sow, or from cuttings
of the sterile double forms.

Heteropappus meyendorfii 'Blue Knoll'

Heteropyxis natalensis

Hesperis matronalis

DAMASK VIOLET, DAMES VIOLET,
SWEET ROCKET

☼/◐ ❄ ↔ 16–20 in (40–50 cm)
↑ 32–36 in (80–90 cm)

Well-known biennial or short-lived
perennial from southern Europe
through to central Asia. Dark green
leaves to 8 in (20 cm) long. Clusters
of scented flowers, 1¾ in (40 mm)
across, late spring–summer. Forms
with both white and lilac, single and
double flowers are grown. Zones 3–10.

HETEROCENTRON

syn. *Heeria*

A basically tropical genus of about
27 species in the meadow-beauty
(Melastomataceae) family from
Central and South America. They
are evergreen perennials and ground
cover plants. The leaves may be heart-
shaped, lance-shaped or pointed oval
and are often prominently veined.
Showy 4-petalled flowers either in
clusters or solitary are produced in
shades of white, pink, and mauve to
purple, from late summer.
CULTIVATION: In frosty climates they
can be grown in a greenhouse and
planted out for summer color when
the danger of frost is over. In warm
regions plant in a moist soil in a
sunny aspect as a ground cover or
rock garden subject. Propagate from
seed or cuttings, or by division.

Heterocentron elegans

syn. *Schizocentron elegans*

CREEPING LASIANDRA, SPANISH SHAWL

☼ ☙ ↔ 18–40 in (45–100 cm)
↑ 3–4 in (8–10 cm)

From Mexico, Guatemala, and
Honduras. Mat-forming showy evergreen subshrub with small, pointed,
downy leaves often stained purple.
Upward-facing, bowl-shaped, magenta
to mauve flowers smother the plant
in a vivid display in late summer–
autumn. Zones 10–12.

HETEROMELES

CALIFORNIA HOLLY, CHRISTMAS BERRY,
TOLLON, TOYON

This genus comprises a single species,
a native of California that is an evergreen shrub closely related to *Photinia*.
Fruit, which may be red or yellow,
small or large, develops from heads
of small creamy white flowers and, as
the name "Christmas berry" suggests,
it ripens around Christmas, or mid-
winter, in its home range.
CULTIVATION: Any well-drained soil
with a sunny or partly shaded aspect
will do. Heat and drought resistant,
this species will tolerate poor soils. The

Heteromeles arbutifolia

bush is usually a neat grower and needs
trimming to shape only occasionally. It
may be propagated from half-hardened
cuttings or seed.

Heteromeles arbutifolia

☼ ❄ ↔ 12 ft (3.5 m) ↑ 12 ft (3.5 m)

Native to the Sierra Nevada foothills
of coastal California, USA, to Baja
California, Mexico. Simple, oval,
mid-green leaves, finely serrated
edges. Flowerheads nectar-rich, with
a honey-like scent, in summer. A
compact, tough plant. Zones 8–10.

HETEROPAPPUS

This genus of 5 biennial or perennial
herbs from temperate eastern Asia
belongs to the daisy (Asteraceae)
family. They are small bushy plants
that look very much like asters. The
simple leaves are alternately arranged
and may have serrated or coarsely
toothed margins. The daisies, which
appear in late summer and autumn,
are borne terminally, either singly or
in loose clusters. They are white to
blue in color, with yellow centers.
CULTIVATION: Grow in full sun in
a rich moisture-retentive soil. Propagation is by division or from seed. If
seed is sown early, plants can flower
in the first year.

Heteropappus hispidus

☼ ❄ ↔ 12 in (30 cm) ↑ 12 in (30 cm)

Perennial from far eastern Russia,
Japan, Korea, China, and Taiwan.
Most often cultivated as *H. h.* var.
meyendorffii, small bushy perennial,
can be grown as annual. Aster-like
daisies in autumn, bluish mauve with
yellow centers. **'Blue Knoll'**, improved
selection. Zones 7–10.

HETEROPYXIS

LAVENDER TREE

This southern African genus of just
2 species is in the myrtle (Myrtaceae)

Heterocentron elegans

family, though sometimes it is classified as the sole member of the family
Heteropyxidaceae. These plants are
medium-sized deciduous trees, usually
with a low-branching trunk, crooked
main stems, and pendulous outer
branches. The foliage is dense and
composed of opposite pairs of large,
deep green, pointed elliptical leaves
that emit a pleasant lavender-like
aroma when crushed. Young leaves
may be downy. Sprays of tiny, sweetly
scented, yellow-green flowers appear
in summer and are followed by small
oval seed capsules that persist long
after releasing their many seeds. The
leaves redden in autumn.
CULTIVATION: Lavender trees tolerate
only very occasional light frosts and
prefer to grow in subtropical or tropical conditions, thriving in humid,
moist conditions with humus-rich,
well-drained soil. They will, however,
withstand dry conditions in winter
when leafless. Plants may be raised
from seeds or cuttings.

Heteropyxis natalensis

LAVENDER TREE

☼ ☙ ↔ 12 ft (3.5 m) ↑ 20 ft (6 m)

Slow-growing tree from southeastern
Africa. Glossy green foliage turns red,
in autumn. Pale gray, almost white
bark, flakes thinly. Small, fragrant
cream to yellow flowers. Fruit is in
the form of tiny, oval, dark brown
capsules. Zones 10–12.

HETEROTHECA
GOLDEN ASTER

This genus of about 30 species of branched annual or perennial herbs from the daisy (Asteraceae) family is native to South America and North America. They produce erect clusters of flowerheads with yellow daisy-like flowers and lance-shaped leaves. The fruit is a scaly and bristly achene (one-seeded fruit).
CULTIVATION: They prefer full sun, light watering and well-drained moist soil. Propagate from seed.

Heterotheca grandiflora
TELEGRAPH WEED

☀ ❋ ↔ 6–12 in (15–30 cm)
↕ 3–6 ft (0.9–1.8 m)

From western USA. Annual or short-lived perennial, hairy in all its parts. Grayish green leaves. Flowerheads smell of camphor. Short-stemmed panicles of clear yellow daisies are borne throughout the year. Zones 5–9.

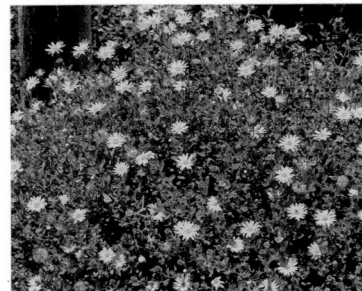

Heterotheca mucronatum

Heuchera americana

Heuchera maxima

Heterotheca mucronatum

☀ ❋ ↔ 8 in (20 cm) ↕ 12 in (30 cm)

From North America. Low-growing species suitable for garden edging. Grayish green leaves. Golden yellow daisies. Zones 5–9.

Heterotheca villosa
GOLDEN ASTER, HAIRY FALSE GOLDEN ASTER, HAIRY GOLDEN ASTER

☀ ❋ ↔ 9–18 in (22–45 cm)
↕ 12–40 in (30–100 cm)

Perennial from USA and Canada. Hairy stems and minutely toothed, hairy, silver-green, narrowly elliptical leaves, to 3 in (8 cm) long, lowest leaves reduced and often deciduous. Several flowerheads with 10–25 yellow rays per head, in early summer. Zones 5–9.

HEUCHERA
ALUM ROOT, CORAL BELLS

This genus, a member of the saxifrage (Saxifragaceae) family, consists of around 55 near-evergreen perennials native to North America. It was named after Johann Heinrich von Heucher (1677–1747), professor of medicine at Wittenburg University. The species form a dense clump of basal foliage with rounded to kidney-shaped, toothed leaves on thin wiry leaf stalks. The branching flower stems are also very fine and from late spring to autumn carry sprays of tiny flowers, usually 5-petalled but sometimes petal-less. Extracts of the root are strongly astringent and often used in herbal medicines.
CULTIVATION: They are mostly very hardy and adaptable and are suitable for perennial borders or rock gardens, depending on size. Plant in full or half-sun with fertile, moist, humus-rich, well-drained soil. Remove flower stems as they fade. Propagate by division or from seed, sown fresh in early autumn.

Heuchera × brizoides, Bressingham Hybrid

Heuchera americana
ROCK GERANIUM

☀/◐ ❋ ↔ 16 in (40 cm) ↕ 18 in (45 cm)

Evergreen North American native with downy, broad, lobed, heart-shaped leaves about 3 in (8 cm) long, sometimes white mottled. Upright flower stems with narrow heads of faintly pink-tinted cream flowers. 'Garnet', leaves which are red when young, turning bronze-veined green, developing a red center in winter; 'Lace Ruffles', ruffled, silver-mottled leaves, white flowers; 'Persian Carpet', silver-marked red to purple-red leaves, buff flowers; 'Pewter Moon', silver-veined deep purple-red foliage; 'Pewter Veil', purple-red foliage overlaid silver-gray; 'Ring of Fire', red-veined green foliage turning pink in winter with pale edges; 'Ruby Veil', deep maroon and silver-gray upper leaves with purple-red undersides; 'Velvet Night', darkest purple-black leaves overlaid metallic purple. Zones 4–10.

Heuchera × brizoides

☀/◐ ❋ ↔ 12–18 in (30–45 cm)
↕ 12–30 in (30–75 cm)

A group of hybrids that share *H. sanguinea* as one parent, the other being *H. micrantha, H. americana* and perhaps others. They are a mixed group, sharing simple green, lobed, heart-shaped leaves and differing mainly in flower color. Popular forms include: **Bressingham Hybrids**, with graceful, airy flowerheads, available in many shades of pink, red, and white; 'Firefly', coral pink, faintly scented; 'Freedom', dwarf form, flowers bright pink; 'June Bride', white flowers; and 'Snowstorm', white-mottled foliage, red flowers. Zones 4–10.

Heuchera hirsutissima

☀/◐ ❋ ↔ 6–8 in (15–20 cm)
↕ 10 in (25 cm)

Evergreen subalpine to alpine species from California. Has a compact habit with rounded, lobed leaves up to 1½ in (35 mm) wide. Stems and leaves are hairy. Flowers cream to pale pink. Zones 6–9.

Heuchera pilosissima

Heuchera pubescens

Heuchera maxima

☀/◐ ❋ ↔ 16–20 in (40–50 cm)
↕ 24 in (60 cm)

Evergreen species from western USA. Rounded, toothed leaves to over 6 in (15 cm) wide, underside veins downy. Pinkish white flowers. Zones 6–10.

Heuchera micrantha

☀/◐ ❋ ↔ 12–16 in (30–40 cm)
↕ 24 in (60 cm)

Western North American species with broad, shallowly lobed, heart-shaped leaves to over 3 in (8 cm) long. Open sprays of small white to cream flowers. *H. m.* var. *diversifolia* 'Palace Purple', deep purple-red leaves and stems, small white flowers. Zones 5–9.

Heuchera pilosissima

☀/◐ ❋ ↔ 12–16 in (30–40 cm)
↕ 24 in (60 cm)

Evergreen species, surprisingly hardy despite being native to coastal California, USA. Roughly diamond-shaped leaves to over 3 in (8 cm) long, covered with fine red-brown hairs, bristly and toothed at the edges. Loose sprays of pinkish white flowers. Zones 6–10.

Heuchera pubescens

☀/◐ ❋ ↔ 16–20 in (40–50 cm)
↕ 40 in (100 cm)

Native to northeastern USA. Pointed oval leaves to nearly 4 in (10 cm) long, with rounded lobes. Flower stems leafy at the base, with open sprays of small white to mauve flowers. Zones 5–9.

Heuchera sanguinea

☼/◐ ❄ ↔ 12–16 in (30–40 cm)
↕ 24 in (60 cm)

Evergreen species native to New Mexico and Arizona, USA. Roughly kidney-shaped leaves to 2 in (5 cm) wide, with irregular lobes and downy undersides. Bright red flowers on stems with a few small leaves. Many former cultivars now listed under *H. × brizoides*; those remaining include: '**Brandon Pink**', bright coral-pink flowers and green and white leaves; '**Northern Fire**', pinkish red flowers, green leaves, vigorous; '**Singham**', bright green leaves, hot pink flowers; '**Splendens**', deep red flowers; and '**Virginalis**', white flowers. Zones 3–9.

Heuchera Hybrid Cultivars

☼/◐ ❄ ↔ 12–18 in (30–45 cm)
↕ 12–36 in (30–90 cm)

In recent years many *Heuchera* hybrids have been introduced. Breeders have concentrated on providing interesting foliage, often seen as a more important feature than the flowers. Popular hybrids include: '**Amber Waves**', late 2002 introduction with light golden bronze foliage and deep pink flowers; '**Autumn Haze**', purple leaves overlaid silver, autumn tones of pink and buff; '**Chocolate Ruffles**' ★, deep bronze-green foliage with purple-brown overtones, white flowers; '**Fireglow**', red blooms; '**Mint Frost**', green leaves overlaid silver, cream flowers;

Heuchera sanguinea 'Singham'

× *Heucherella alba* 'Rosalie'

Heuchera, Hybrid Cultivar, 'Autumn Haze'

Heuchera, Hybrid Cultivar, 'Plum Pudding'

Heuchera, HC, 'Fireglow'

Heuchera, HC, 'Monet'

Heuchera, HC, 'Mint Frost'

H., HC, 'Strawberry Candy'

Heuchera, Hybrid Cultivar, 'Snow Angel'

Heuchera, HC, 'Petite Marble Burgundy'

'**Monet**', white-variegated green foliage, red flowers; '**Petite Marble Burgundy**', compact, silver-marked, purple-red leaves, pinkish flowers; '**Plum Pudding**', purple-brown leaves with red undersides, cream flowers; '**Red Spangles**', plain green leaves, bright red flowers; '**Santa Ana Cardinal**' (*H. maxima × H. sanguinea*), tall, rounded bright green leaves, deep pink to red flowers; '**Snow Angel**', red flowers, white-flecked green foliage; '**Strawberry Candy**', green leaves overlaid silver, pink flowers; '**Wendy**' ★ (*H. maxima × H. sanguinea*), large light green leaves, soft pink flowers.

The **Canyon Series** is a group of compact evergreen hybrids raised by the American breeder Emery. Small, lobed, rounded to heart-shaped leaves, usually deep green, sometimes with a hint of purple. Many tiny flowers in upright, airy sprays. Original varieties include: '**Canyon Delight**', tall, deep pink to red; '**Canyon Pink**', bright pink. The **Canyon Quartet Series** was released in 1993 after Emery's death and includes '**Canyon Bell**', short stems, bright red; '**Canyon Chimes**', tall stems, red; '**Canyon Duet**', bicolor red and white; and '**Canyon Melody**', smaller plant, pink and white. Zones 5–10.

× *HEUCHERELLA*

A group of garden hybrids in the saxifrage (Saxifragaceae) family that are crosses between the genera

Heuchera sanguinea 'Splendens'

Heuchera and *Tiarella*. They are sterile hybrids with evergreen maple-shaped leaves that often color well in winter and sprays of tiny dainty pale pink to white flowers on upright stems in late spring.

CULTIVATION: These hybrids are best grown in humus-rich moist soils in cool woodland-type aspects where they make attractive slow-moving ground covers. Propagation is by division.

× *Heucherella alba*

☼/◐ ❄ ↔ 20 in (50 cm) ↕ 12 in (30 cm)

Mid-green divided leaves form tight compact mounds. Creamy white flower spikes sit 16 in (40 cm) above plant, in mid-summer. In winter leaves shrink in size; flush of new leaves in spring. '**Rosalie**', compact dark green foliage, reddish bronze center, masses of rose pink blooms, for a long time in late spring, ideal woodland plant. Zones 5–9.

× *Heucherella tiarelloides*

☼/◐ ❄ ↔ 18 in (45 cm) ↕ 18 in (45 cm)

Smooth, light green, divided leaves heart-shaped at the base. Each leaf has dark brown marking along the veins when young. Short stems of pink flowers sit above the foliage through spring–summer. Zones 5–9.

Hibbertia miniata

× *Heucherella*, Hybrid Cultivar, 'Kimono'

× *Heucherella*, HC, 'Viking Ship'

× *Heucherella*, HC, 'Dayglo Pink'

× *Heucherella* Hybrid Cultivars

☀/◐ ❄ ↔ 12–16 in (30–40 cm)
↕ 16–20 in (40–50 cm)

Evergreen perennials, striking foliage. **'Bridget Bloom'**, heart-shaped mid-green leaves, heavy brown markings, white flower spikes, spring–autumn; **'Dayglo Pink'**, mid-green leaves, chocolate-colored inlay, purple foliage tones in winter, brilliant pink flowers; **'Kimono'**, tawny flowers, summer–autumn; **'Viking Ship'**, silver leaves in spring, silvery maple-like leaves in summer, coral-pink spires of star-like flowers ascending to 16 in (40 cm). Zones 5–9.

HEXISEA

A small genus of sympodial epiphytic orchid species (family Orchidaceae) from Central and South America, closely related to *Scaphyglottis*. They have clustered pseudobulbs topped with grass-like foliage. Plants shoot from the base of the pseudobulb as well as from the top of the recently matured bulb, and older plants can have a somewhat straggly appearance. Flowers are small but colorful, from pale orange to deep red.
CULTIVATION: Grows readily in pots of a well-drained but moisture-retentive bark-based mixture or on tree-fern slabs. They prefer intermediate growing conditions and regular watering; as they are always growing, they like to be kept moist. Propagate by division.

Hexisea imbricata

☀ ❄ ↔ 4–16 in (10–40 cm)
↕ 4–20 in (10–50 cm)

From Venezuela. Colorful, spring-flowering. Small clusters of bright orange, 1 in (25 mm) blooms from top of pseudobulb. *H. bidentata* is a closely related species. Zones 10–12.

HIBBERTIA
GOLDEN GUINEA FLOWER

This mostly Australian genus in the Dilleniaceae family contains around 120 species of small evergreen shrubby plants or climbers grown for their profuse, usually bright yellow or

Hibbertia aspera

sometimes orange flowers. Flowering is mostly during spring and early summer, though with some species it also occurs sporadically throughout most of the year. Though there is variation in growth habit, it is mostly the low spreading species and climbers that have become well known to horticulture. These make ideal rock garden, container and ground cover subjects.
CULTIVATION: Easy to grow, they enjoy moderately fertile well-drained soil that does not dry out too quickly. In hotter areas partial shade is best. Marginally frost hardy, they need protection in colder regions, especially when young. To keep shape, prune tips from an early age and after flowering. Propagate from half-hardened tip cuttings taken in late summer.

Hibbertia aspera

☀/◐ ❄ ↔ 40 in (100 cm) ↕ 24 in (60 cm)
Eastern and southern Australia native. Spreading plant with small dark green leaves. Bright yellow flowers are about ½ in (12 mm) wide and appear throughout the year. Zones 9–11.

Hibbertia cuneiformis ★
CUTLEAF GUINEA FLOWER

☀ ❄ ↔ 4 ft (1.2 m) ↕ 12 ft (3.5 m)
From coastal districts of southern Western Australia. Erect bushy shrub, tendency to twine. Toothed oblong leaves, deep golden flowers at branch ends in spring–summer and odd times through the year. Zones 9–11.

Hibbertia miniata

☀ ❄ ↔ 8 in (20 cm) ↕ 15 in (38 cm)
Small erect shrub, rare in the wild, confined to the jarrah forests of

Hexisea imbricata, Costa Rica

Western Australia. Broad gray-green linear leaves. Showy orange flowers, dark purple anthers, spring–summer. Ideal rock garden plant. Zones 9–11.

Hibbertia obtusifolia

☀ ❄ ↔ 30 in (75 cm) ↕ 24 in (60 cm)
Small shrub from eastern Australia. Spreading stems, young growth with short grayish hairs. Gray-green leaves, bright yellow flowers, spring–summer. An excellent plant for a rock garden. Zones 9–11.

Hibbertia scandens

☀ ❄ ↔ unlimited ↕ 8 ft (2.4 m)
Found in Queensland and New South Wales, Australia. Twining climber, can be grown as a ground cover. Slightly glossy narrow leaves, developing bronze tints. Flowers bright yellow, slightly unpleasant scent. Zones 10–12.

Hibbertia sericea

☀ ❄ ↔ 3 ft (0.9 m) ↕ 3 ft (0.9 m)
From eastern Australia. Attractive erect or spreading shrub. Silky hairy stems, densely hairy linear leaves to 1 in (25 mm) long. Masses of bright yellow terminal flowers, in late winter–spring. Prefers well-drained, fairly moist position. Zones 9–11.

Hibbertia stellaris
ORANGE STARS

☀ ❄ ↔ 30 in (75 cm) ↕ 30 in (75 cm)
Small dense shrub from coastal areas of Western Australia, growing at the edges of swamps. Soft fine green foliage, red stems. Small starry apricot flowers, from spring to autumn. Is often difficult to grow, and is short-lived. Zones 9–11.

Hibbertia scandens

Hibbertia cuneiformis

Hibiscus arnottianus

Hibiscus elatus

HIBISCUS

GIANT MALLOW, MALLOW, ROSE MALLOW

This genus of over 200 annual or perennial herbs, shrubs or trees in the mallow (Malvaceae) family is widely distributed throughout warm-temperate, subtropical and tropical regions of the world. They are grown mostly for their large dramatic flowers, borne singly or in terminal clusters, usually lasting for just a day. The open bell-shaped flowers appear in a wide variety of colors, and are characterized by a prominent staminal column and a darker coloring in the center. The alternate simple leaves are usually palmate. The fruit is a capsule. **CULTIVATION:** Most species of *Hibiscus* are drought tender and rather frost tender, and prefer a position in full sun in a rich and moist soil. Many will tolerate hard pruning after flowering to maintain shape. Perennials are propagated from seed or by division, while annuals are best grown from seed in the growing position. Shrub types can be propagated from cuttings, by grafting or from seed sown in containers for later transplanting.

Hibiscus × *archeri*

☼ ❄ ↔ 7 ft (2 m) ↑ 15 ft (4.5 m)
Hybrid between *H. rosa-sinensis* and *H. schizopetalus*. Large shrub or small

tree, evergreen in frost-free climates. Closely resembles *H. rosa-sinensis* in habit and flower, though leaves are larger and more roughly serrated, and flowers crimson to red. Popular garden specimen. Zones 9–11.

Hibiscus arnottianus

HAWAIIAN WHITE HIBISCUS

☼ ❄ ↔ 10 ft (3 m) ↑ 25 ft (8 m)
Fast-growing, erect, branching evergreen shrub or small tree, native to the Hawaiian Islands. Dark green, smooth-edged, oval-shaped leaves. Solitary white or yellow flowers, delicately fragrant, red staminal column. Good hedge plant. '**Kona Kai**', attractive cultivar. Zones 10–12.

Hibiscus brackenridgei

☼ ❄ ↔ 8 ft (2.4 m) ↑ 10 ft (3 m)
Native of Hawaiian Islands. Sprawling evergreen shrub or small tree. Leaves have 3 to 7 lobes. Flowers have red to yellow calyx and yellow petals, with maroon spot at base. Zones 10–12.

Hibiscus calyphyllus

☼ ❄ ↔ 3 ft (0.9 m) ↑ 10 ft (3 m)
Native of tropical and southern Africa. Prostrate or straggly, evergreen shrub, fast growing, short-lived. Hairy, roundish, light green leaves, 3 lobes, serrated edges. Large, single,

short-lived sulfur yellow flowers, maroon base and staminal column, in summer–autumn. Zones 10–12.

Hibiscus cannabinus

BIMLI, DECCAN HEMP, INDIAN HEMP, KENAF

☼ ❄ ↔ 6 ft (1.8 m) ↑ 12 ft (3.5 m)
Annual or short-lived, shrubby perennial, thought to be from East Indies. Pale yellow, sometimes pale purple flowers in racemes, reddish purple column and center. Leaves prickly, deeply lobed, serrated. Zones 10–12.

Hibiscus cisplatinus

☼ ❄ ↔ 4 ft (1.2 m) ↑ 10 ft (3 m)
Native of southern Brazil, Paraguay, and Argentina, cultivated in Hawaiian Islands. Stout yellow spines, 6 in (15 cm) long leaves, up to 5 lobes. Solitary rose pink flowers, to 3 in (8 cm) long, purple base. Zones 10–12.

Hibiscus coccineus

SCARLET HIBISCUS, SCARLET ROSE MALLOW, SWAMP HIBISCUS

☼ ❄ ↔ 2–3 ft (0.6–0.9 m) ↑ 7 ft (2 m)
From southern USA. Shrub-like herbaceous perennial with 5-petalled crimson flowers, 6–8 in (15–20 cm) across, that appear in early to mid-summer; followed by attractive papery green fruits. Vigorous grower in good conditions. '**Davis Creek**', robust cultivar. Zones 7–11.

Hibiscus diversifolius

NATIVE HIBISCUS, SWAMP HIBISCUS

☼ ❄ ↔ 3 ft (0.9 m) ↑ 3 ft (0.9 m)
Spreading evergreen shrub, native of tropical Africa, Asia, northern Australia, and tropical Pacific Islands. Stems hairy, serrated palmate leaves. Flowers solitary or in loose terminal

heads, from summer–autumn, pale yellow petals, maroon center, purple staminal column. Zones 10–12.

Hibiscus elatus

CUBAN BAST, MAHOE

☼ ❄ ↔ 15 ft (4.5 m) ↑ 75 ft (23 m)
From Jamaica and Cuba. Erect, sparingly branched evergreen tree, densely textured crown. Open, orange-yellow to orange-red flowers, 5 petals, around 5 in (12 cm) long. Oval leaves with downy undersides. Zones 10–12.

Hibiscus heterophyllus

AUSTRALIAN NATIVE ROSELLA, SCRUB KURRAJONG

☼ ❄ ↔ 6–10 ft (1.8–3 m)
↑ 10–20 ft (3–6 m)
Native to eastern Australia. Evergreen shrub or small tree. Prickly branches, narrow pointed leaves, deeply lobed. Flowers white with purple eye. *H. h.* subsp. *luteus*, yellow flowers usual in northern parts of range. Zones 10–12.

Hibiscus cisplatinus

Hibiscus diversifolius

H. heterophyllus subsp. *luteus*

Hibiscus arnottianus 'Kona Kai'

H

Hibiscus insularis
PHILLIP ISLAND HIBISCUS

☀ ❄ ↔ 6 ft (1.8 m) ↑ 12 ft (3.5 m)

This very rare plant is a native of Phillip Island, off the eastern coast of Australia. It is a dense, bushy, branching evergreen shrub with small smooth-edged leaves. Long-lasting, small, single, pale lemon flowers with a purplish base, fading to mauve with age, in summer–autumn. Zones 10–12.

Hibiscus lasiocarpus
syn. *Hibiscus californicus*
ROSE-MALLOW

☀ ❄ ↔ 3–5 ft (0.9–1.5 m)
↑ 4–7 ft (1.2–2 m)

From southern USA and Mexico, this plant has softly hairy, pointed, oval to heart-shaped leaves. The white to pink flowers are 4–6 in (10–15 cm)

Hibiscus insularis

Hibiscus rosa-sinensis 'Apple Blossom'

wide, often with maroon basal spots, and are borne in leaf axils in late summer. Zones 6–9.

Hibiscus moscheutos
COMMON ROSE MALLOW,
SWAMP ROSE MALLOW

☀ ❄ ↔ 40 in (100 cm) ↑ 8 ft (2.4 m)

From eastern North America, common from Ohio through to Alabama and Florida, USA. Woody perennial shrub. Lobed leaves, 2–6 in (5–15 cm) long. Large trumpet-shaped flowers in pink and white produced from spring to summer. '**Lord Baltimore**', large, single, crimson red flowers, to 12 in (30 cm) across; '**Southern Belle**', compact, to 40 in (100 cm), serrated leaves, deep pink flowers. Zones 5–9.

Hibiscus lasiocarpus

Hibiscus rosa-sinensis cultivar

Hibiscus mutabilis
CONFEDERATE ROSE, COTTON ROSE

☀ ❄ ↔ 6–8 ft (1.8–2.4 m)
↑ 10–15 ft (3–4.5 m)

Native of China. Small, spreading deciduous shrub, or erect, branching small tree. Large palm-shaped leaves, 7 serrated lobes. Double or single flowers, white or pink with darker base and staminal column. '**Plena**', rounded double flowers that open white and turn a deep rose red. Zones 8–9.

Hibiscus pedunculatus
DWARF PINK HIBISCUS

☀ ❄ ↔ 5 ft (1.5 m) ↑ 4–6 ft (1.2–1.8 m)

Southern African native from Mozambique to South Africa. Leaves have 3 to 5 rounded lobes. Nodding solitary flowers, staminal column and 2 in (5 cm) long petals, pale or deep rose purple or lilac. Zones 10–12.

Hibiscus rosa-sinensis
CHINA ROSE, CHINESE HIBISCUS, HAWAIIAN HIBISCUS, ROSE OF CHINA, SHOE BLACK

☀ ❄ ↔ 5 ft (1.5 m) ↑ 8 ft (2.4 m)

Erect, branching evergreen shrub, or small tree to 30 ft (9 m) high. Solitary flowers, variable in color, normally red to dark red, summer–winter. Oval-shaped, serrated, glossy, deep

Hibiscus rosa-sinensis 'Chandleri'

green leaves. Prune straight after winter, before new growth appears. The many hybrid cultivars include: '**Agnes Galt**' ★, tall vigorous shrub, large rose pink flowers; '**Aurora**', blush pink, pompon-shaped flowers; '**Bridal Veil**', large pure white flowers with a crape texture; '**Cooperi**', small, rose pink single flowers, narrow variegated leaves, olive green marbled with red, pink and white, good container plant; '**Crown of Bohemia**', bushy shrub, medium double flowers, gold with bright orange throat; '**D. J. O'Brien**', medium, double orange-apricot flowers; '**Eileen McMullen**', large, deep yellow flowers heavily flushed with crimson; '**Moon Beam**', bright yellow flowers, crimson throat, strongly reflexed petals. Zones 9–11.

Hibiscus moscheutos 'Lord Baltimore'

Hibiscus mutabilis

Hibiscus mutabilis 'Plena'

H. rosa-sinensis 'Dorothy Brady'

H. r-s 'Eileen McMullen'

H. rosa-sinensis 'Evelyn Howard'

H. rosa-sinensis 'Harvest Moon'

H. rosa-sinensis 'I. D. Clare'

H. rosa-sinensis 'Jason Blue'

H. rosa-sinensis 'Mongon'

Hibiscus rosa-sinensis 'Mary Wallace'

H. rosa-sinensis 'Moon Beam'

H. rosa-sinensis 'Nanette Peach'

H. rosa-sinensis 'Persephone'

H. rosa-sinensis 'Picardy'

H. rosa-sinensis 'Rosalind'

H. rosa-sinensis 'Ruby Wedding'

H. rosa-sinensis 'Sweet Violet'

Hibiscus rosa-sinensis 'Tubize'

Hibiscus rosa-sinensis 'Ya-Ya'

Hibiscus schizopetalus

CORAL HIBISCUS, FRINGED HIBISCUS,
JAPANESE HIBISCUS, JAPANESE LANTERN

☼ ❄ ↔6 ft (1.8 m) ↕10 ft (3 m)

Evergreen to semi-deciduous shrub,
native to tropical east Africa. Arching,
slender, weeping habit, clusters of
small, oval-shaped, serrated leaves.
Flowers ragged, deeply fringed margins, petals pink or brilliant red,
long staminal column, from summer
to autumn. Zones 10–12.

Hibiscus schizopetalus

Hibiscus rosa-sinensis 'Whirls-n-Twirls'

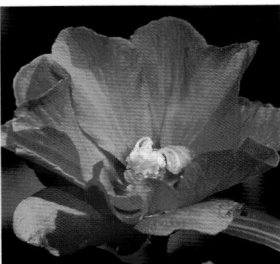

Hibiscus syriacus 'Boule de Feu'

Hibiscus syriacus 'Diana'

Hibiscus syriacus 'Hamabo'

Hibiscus syriacus 'Lady Stanley'

Hibiscus syriacus 'Lady Stanley'

Hibiscus syriacus 'Blue Bird'

Hibiscus syriacus 'Blue Bird'

Hibiscus syriacus 'Lohengrin'

Hibiscus syriacus 'Red Heart'

Hibiscus sinosyriacus

☼ ❄ ↔ 6–10 ft (1.8–3 m)
↑ 8–12 ft (2.4–3.5 m)

Handsome, vigorous, medium-sized shrub, very similar to *H. syriacus* but with broader, sage green leaves and larger flowers with thicker petals, in autumn. Zones 5–9.

Hibiscus syriacus

BLUE HIBISCUS, ROSE OF SHARON,
SHRUB ALTHEA, SYRIAN HIBISCUS

☼ ❄ ↔ 6–10 ft (1.8–3 m)
↑ 8–12 ft (2.4–3.5 m)

Shrub or small tree, native to cool-temperate regions of Asia. Smooth gray branches, leaves with 3 narrow, coarsely toothed triangular lobes. Single or double flowers, petals white, reddish purple or bluish lavender with a crimson base and staminal column. '**Blue Bird**' (syn. 'Oiseau Blue'), gentian blue flowers, lilac-purple centers, grows to about 5 ft (1.5 m); '**Diana**', single pure white flowers, grows to about 5 ft (1.5 m); '**Hamabo**', large, light pink single flowers with a red center that radiates at edges into fine red streaks; '**White Supreme**', semi-double white flowers with a crimson center, rose pink on outside of the petals; '**Wood-**

bridge', wine red flowers with darker center, grows to about 6 ft (1.8 m). Other cultivars include: '**Aphrodite**', '**Boule de Feu**', '**Lady Stanley**', '**Lohengrin**', '**Minerva**', and '**Red Heart**'. Zones 5–9.

Hibiscus tiliaceus

COAST COTTONWOOD, MAHOE,
MANGROVE HIBISCUS, MAU

☼ ◗ ↔ 10 ft (3 m) ↑ 25 ft (8 m)

Widespread across tropical regions of the world. Evergreen shrub or small tree. Smooth gray bark, gnarled picturesque trunk. Rounded, smooth, leathery green leaves, hairy beneath. Solitary yellow or white flowers, with red to brown throat and staminal column, in summer. Salt tolerant and drought resistant. Zones 10–12.

Hibiscus trionum

FLOWER-OF-AN-HOUR

☼ ◗ ↔ 12 in (30 cm)
↑ 12–24 in (30–60 cm)

From Australia, New Zealand, tropical Africa, and Asia. Perennial or annual. Hairy stems and lobed leaves. Yellow flowers, crimson-black eye. Zones 10–12.

Hibiscus trionum

Hibiscus tiliaceus

H., Herbaceous Hybrid, 'Lady Baltimore'

Hibiscus Herbaceous Hybrids

☼ ❄ ↔ 2–4 ft (0.6–1.2 m)
↑ 18 in–5 ft (45 cm–1.5 m)

Perennials derived mainly from *H. moscheutos*. Leaves vary from toothed to deeply lobed. Succession of large, flat to funnel-shaped flowers from upper leaf axils in shades from white or pale pink to dark red, sometimes with darker eye. '**Davis Creek**', pinkish red flowers; '**Lady Baltimore**', pink flowers; '**Miss Kitty**', yellow flowers. Zones 5–10.

HICKSBEACHIA

Endemic to Australia, this rainforest genus in the protea (Proteaceae) family contains 2 species. One occurs in northeastern Queensland, the other in northern New South Wales and

Hibiscus, Herbaceous Hybrid, 'Davis Creek'

Hibiscus, Herbaceous Hybrid, 'Miss Kitty'

Hippeastrum, Hybrid Cultivar, 'Christmas Star'

Hippeastrum, Hybrid Cultivar, 'Las Vegas'

Hippeastrum, Hybrid Cultivar, 'Royal Velvet'

H., HC, 'Flamingo'

H., HC, 'Picotee'

H., HC, 'Pamela'

Hippeastrum papilio

southeastern Queensland. Both are small trees or large shrubs that have a few unbranched stems arising from near the base of the plant, with large pinnate or pinnately lobed leathery leaves to 4 ft (1.2 m) long, toward the upper ends of the stems, and small pinkish purple flowers about ¾ in (18 mm) long on very long pendent spikes. After flowering, orange to red fruits are produced.
CULTIVATION: A well-drained organic soil, with adequate water in dry periods, and only occasional light frost, provide suitable conditions for cultivation. The seeds have a short period of viability, hence must be sown as soon as possible after ripening.

Hicksbeachia pinnatifolia ★

RED BOPPLE NUT

☼ ❄ ↔ 8 ft (2.4 m) ↑ 35 ft (10 m)
Tall shrub or small tree, leaves to 4 ft (1.2 m) long, pinnate, dark shiny

Hicksbeachia pinnatifolia

green, coarsely toothed edges. Strongly scented pinkish purple flowers on pendent spikes, late winter–mid-summer. Almost spherical fruits, orangey red. Successfully cultivated outside its natural distribution. Zones 9–12.

HIPPEASTRUM

AMARYLLIS, KNIGHT'S STAR LILY
From the subtropics of Central and South America these bulbous, deciduous, spring-flowering perennials of the amaryllis (Amaryllidaceae) family are grown as pot plants in cooler climates. In the past, 2 single trumpet-shaped heads per stem and petals in red, white, or pink shades were common. Today the range of robust cultivars includes pale translucent yellows, doubles, and stems carrying up to 5 large, outward-facing heads. Leaves are strap-like and mid-green. Stems are straight, stout, and hollow.
CULTIVATION: Grow outdoors in frost-free areas or as greenhouse plants elsewhere. They are heavy feeders and drinkers while in growth, but prior to a dry winter dormancy reduce their foliage and water. The bulbs are large and should be planted with the necks protruding from the soil. They mildly resent root disturbance. Provide total shelter from frost and rain in winter. Propagate from offsets or from fresh ripe seeds kept at 61°F (16°C).

Hippeastrum papilio

BUTTERFLY AMARYLLIS
☼/◑ ❄ ↔ 12–16 in (30–40 cm)
↑ 24 in (60 cm)
From southern Brazil. Flowers 2 to 3 per stem, large, open, star-like. Usually flowers mid-winter–early spring. Petals flamboyant, striped pale

green-cream, stained reddish chocolate. The 5 distinctive leaves are dark green, purple at base, strap-like. Zones 9–10.

Hippeastrum reticulatum

☼/◑ ❄ ↔ 14–18 in (35–45 cm)
↑ 10–14 in (25–35 cm)
From southern Brazil. Flowers long-tubed, downward-facing, crimson-pink, 3 to 4 per stem, in late summer. Leaves deep green, 2 in (5 cm) wide, with pale central marking. *H. r.* var. *stratifolium* bears up to 5 flowerheads per stem with pale pink petals striped in soft crimson. Zones 9–10.

Hippeastrum vittatum

ST JOSEPH'S LILY
☼ ❄ ↔ 12 in (30 cm) ↑ 36 in (90 cm)
Large, robust plant from the Peruvian Andes. Flowers are wide open stars, 5 to 6 per tall stout stem. Petals in variable arrangement of white with red stripes. Leaves are bright green, and appear after flowers. Likes a crowd, dislikes disturbance. Zones 9–10.

Hippeastrum Hybrid Cultivars

☼/◑ ❄ ↔ 12–16 in (30–40 cm)
↑ 20–36 in (50–90 cm)
When growing *Hippeastrum* hybrid cultivars, the temperature should not be allowed to fall below 55°F (13°C). '**Apple Blossom**', robust bulb, 20 in (50 cm) high, large flowers, petals white tinged with pink; '**Christmas Star**', stems with up to 8 brilliant red and white flowers; '**Flamingo**', large trumpets, red petals; '**Las Vegas**', bright red with white center stripe; '**Pamela**' ★, 20 in (50 cm) high, robust miniature, free-flowering, small and fine blue-green stems, narrow leaves, flowers up to 5 per stem, perfect shape, petals clear bright red; '**Picotee**', spectacular but can prove weak, 20 in (50 cm) high, up to 5 large flowerheads per stem, petals white, finely margined in red, flushed green at the base; '**Royal Velvet**', deep velvety blackcurrant red petals, robust, big firm bulbs and strong stems. Zones 9–12.

HIPPOCREPIS

There are about 21 species of annual and perennial herbs or small shrubs in this genus in the pea-flower subfamily of the legume (Fabaceae) family. Native to Europe and western Asia, they grow in limestone areas of rock and turf. Leaves are pinnately divided and the pea-flowers are yellow. Some species are vigorous and can be a nuisance by self-sowing. Suited to the wild garden. CULTIVATION: Grow in full sun in a light, well-drained, alkaline, low-fertility soil. Propagate annuals from seed and perennials from seed, division or cuttings.

Hippocrepis emerus ★
syn. *Coronilla emerus*
SCORPION SENNA
☼ ❄ ↔ 6 ft (1.8 m) ↑ 6 ft (1.8 m)
Native to southeastern Europe. Pinnate bright green leaves are divided into 9 egg-shaped leaflets. Umbels of light yellow fragrant flowers in late spring–autumn. Narrow seed pods. *H. e.* subsp. *emeroides*, fewer leaflets per leaf, more floriferous. Zones 6–9.

HIPPOPHAE

From Eurasia, the Himalayas, and China, these 3 dioecious species belong to the oleaster (Elaeagnaceae) family, growing in coastal dunes and screes on riverbanks in the mountains. All are deciduous large shrubs or small trees,

used in gardens for their long-lasting berries and good silver foliage, and make useful coastal windbreaks. The berries can be used in sauces and drinks; the wood is suitable for turning and as a source of yellow dye; and the oil from the wood is used in cosmetics. CULTIVATION: Best in full sun in well-drained but moist, alkaline to neutral, preferably sandy soil. In dry areas they grow well in clay soil as this retains moisture. For berry production, male and female plants are needed. Propagate by taking half-hardened cuttings in summer or hardwood cuttings in autumn, or from suckers. Sow fresh seed in autumn or after several months' stratification in spring.

Hippophae rhamnoides
SEA BUCKTHORN
☼ ❄ ↔ 20 ft (6 m) ↑ 20 ft (6 m)
Native to western China. Spiny, deciduous. Leaves narrow, linear, gray-green, rough scaly surfaces. Yellow-green female flowers in small racemes, before the leaves. Male flowers, on previous year's growth, tiny spikes. Orange, oval to round fruit. Zones 2–9.

Hippophae sinensis
CHINESE SEA BUCKTHORN
☼ ❄ ↔ 12 ft (3.5 m)
↑ 15–40 ft (4.5–12 m)
Deciduous tree from temperate East Asia to western China. *H. rhamnoides*

Hippophae sinensis

Hippocrepis emerus

is a close relative. Flowers in spring. Female trees produce edible fruit that yields medicinal oils and is very rich in vitamin C, in autumn. Zones 3–9.

HISTIOPTERIS
BAT FERN, BAT-WINGED FERN
This genus of a single species of evergreen tropical terrestrial fern belongs to the bracken (Dennstaedtiaceae) family. It produces long-creeping rhizomes and lustrous straw-colored to chestnut stipes. Fronds are erect, oval to triangular, pinnate, bracken-like, to 10 ft (3 m) long, with narrowly oval-shaped pinnae, to 16 in (40 cm) long, and notched or lobed segments, to 3 in (8 cm) long. It naturalizes rapidly, self-seeding in the right conditions. The botanical name comes from the Greek *histion* (sail) and *pteris* (fern), referring to shape of the pinnae. CULTIVATION: This plant can be invasive and quite rampant. It prefers moist, well-drained, acid soil in a protected spot in medium to high light. Propagate from spores or by division at any time.

Histiopteris incisa
BAT'S WING FERN, MATA, WATER FERN
☼ ❄ ↔ unlimited ↑ 3–10 ft (0.9–3 m)
Fern from New Zealand and east coast of Australia. Triangular fronds divided into numerous blunt leaflets, soft and pale grayish green when young, red-brown with age. Segments closest to stalk show the characteristic x-pattern bat appearance that gives the fern its name. Zones 7–11.

HOHERIA
LACEBARK, RIBBONWOOD
This New Zealand genus of 5 species of deciduous and evergreen trees is in the mallow (Malvaceae) family. Leaves usually have pointed tips and serrated margins. White 5-petalled flowers are profuse in summer or autumn. The name "lacebark" is due to the lace-like fibrous layer under the surface bark. CULTIVATION: These attractive, graceful trees are suitable for specimen or woodland planting. They are fast growing and most will tolerate a wide range of conditions in sun or part shade. In cold climates they need the protection of a warm wall and in such areas the deciduous species are more hardy. Plants can be pruned if necessary. Propagation is from seed sown in autumn, or half-hardened cuttings.

Hoheria angustifolia
☼/◐ ❄ ↔ 8 ft (2.4 m) ↑ 10–20 ft (3–6 m)
An interesting evergreen species. Distinct juvenile stage, columnar

Histiopteris incisa

Hoheria angustifolia

form, tangled branches, small round leaves. Adult tree becomes slender, with elongated serrated leaves. Starry white flowers smother the tree, in mid-summer. Zones 8–11.

Hoheria lyallii
MOUNTAIN RIBBONWOOD,
NEW ZEALAND LACEBARK
☼ ❄ ↔ 10 ft (3 m) ↑ 7–12 ft (2–3.5 m)
Leaves bright green, often turning yellow in autumn. White flowers. Found on New Zealand's South Island's drier east coast. Tolerates dry conditions. Zones 8–10.

Hoheria populnea
HOUHERE, LACEBARK,
NEW ZEALAND LACEBARK
☼ ❄ ↔ 15 ft (4.5 m) ↑ 15–20 ft (4.5–6 m)
Fast-growing but variable species, evergreen leaves. In late summer–autumn, bears starry white flowers in great profusion. 'Alba Variegata' has dark green leaves with creamy white margins. Zones 8–11.

Hoheria sexstylosa
RIBBONWOOD
☼ ❄ ↑ 15–20 ft (4.5–6 m)
Like *H. populnea*, a variable species. Toothed leaves, longer and narrower. Flowers smaller and scented. Branches tend to weep, giving the tree a graceful appearance. Zones 8–11.

HOLCUS
This grass (Poaceae) family genus contains 8 species of annual or perennial grasses that spread from creeping rhizomes and are native to Europe, temperate Asia and North and South Africa. They have narrow flat or

folded leaf blades. Flowers are borne in panicles with stalked laterally flattened spikelets, each with 2 flowers on erect tufted stems, in summer. They are excellent ground covers.
CULTIVATION: Plant in full sun or partial shade in a moist well-drained soil. Propagate by division.

Holcus mollis
CREEPING FOG, CREEPING SOFT GRASS, CREEPING VELVET GRASS

☀ ❄ ↔unlimited ↕12–40 in (30–100 cm) Mat-forming, semi-evergreen to evergreen, perennial grass from Europe. Flat, strap-like, gray-green, slightly hairy leaves, 24–48 in (60–120 cm) long, with hairy nodes. Spikes of purplish white flowers in narrow, oblong to oval-shaped, densely branched panicles, in spring–summer. 'Variegatus' has white leaves with a narrow green central stripe. Zones 5–9.

HOLMSKIOLDIA
This vervain (Verbenaceae) family genus from the tropics of Africa and Asia is made up of 10 species of sprawling evergreen shrubs that are usually treated as climbers or espaliers when cultivated. Leaves are usually simple pointed ovals with a variable covering of fine hairs, and sometimes finely serrated edges. But it is the flowers that are intriguing. They occur in small panicles or racemes and are very interestingly shaped with a narrow tubular corolla backed by a flattened, widely flared calyx.
CULTIVATION: Quite frost tender, these shrubs are best grown in a light well-drained soil that stays moist through the warmer months. Plant in

Homalocladium platycladium

full sun or partial shade and provide a trellis or other support to keep the growth upright. Regular pinching back will prevent the stems becoming too elongated. Propagate from seed or half-hardened cuttings.

Holmskioldia sanguinea
CHINESE HAT PLANT, CUP AND SAUCER PLANT

☀/◑ ❀ ↔6 ft (1.8 m) ↕3–6 ft (0.9–1.8 m) Found in the Himalayan lowlands. The most widely cultivated species. Shallowly serrated leaves to 3 in (8 cm) long. Flowers are in dense clusters in the warmest months, orange to scarlet with brick red calyces. Zones 10–11.

HOLODISCUS
This genus in the rose (Rosaceae) family consists of 8 species of deciduous shrubs. Growing in dry woodland, they are found in western North America and as far south as Colombia. These plants bear airy panicles of small flowers, sometimes with red buds; flowers open to a creamy white.
CULTIVATION: Tolerant of full sun or part-shade and need moist, fertile, humus-rich soil that does not dry out. Most easily increased by layering. Heel cuttings of half-hardened wood in a peat-sand mixture; may need mist propagation. Can be difficult to root.

Holodiscus discolor
CREAMBUSH, OCEAN SPRAY

☀/◑ ❄ ↔12 ft (3.5 m) ↕12 ft (3.5 m) Native to western North America. Leaves broadly egg-shaped, with 4 to 8 lobes, scalloped margins, deep green above, white felty undersides. Flowers in plume-like creamy panicles, in summer. Zones 4–10.

Homeria flaccida

HOMALOCLADIUM
This genus in the knotweed family (Polygonaceae) consists of one curious evergreen shrub from the Solomon Islands, often grown as a container plant. Leafless at flowering time, it has flat, ribbon-like jointed stems and tiny flowers, in spring. The fruit is enclosed by a fleshy, red to purple berry. Some botanists consider *Homalocladium* to be a bizarre species of *Muehlenbeckia*.
CULTIVATION: Easily grown and tolerant of light frosts, *Homalocladium* prefers a light, rich, moist well-drained soil or a regular potting mix in a protected, partially shaded position. Propagation is either from fresh seed or from cuttings.

Homalocladium platycladum
CENTIPEDE PLANT, RIBBON BUSH, TAPEWORM PLANT

◑ ⚘ ↔6 ft (1.8 m) ↕6–10 ft (1.8–3 m) Unusual evergreen shrub. Distinctive, flat, green, ribbon-like jointed stems. Whitish green flowers in small clusters at joints of branches, in spring; narrow green leaves. Zones 10–12.

HOMERIA
CAPE TULIP

A member of the iris (Iridaceae) family, this genus consists of 30-plus cormous perennials. Natives of South Africa, where they favor sunny sandy habitats, some species have been declared noxious weeds in parts of Australia. Flowers are bowl-shaped, symmetrical with narrow well-separated petals and, although often short-lived, are borne in succession over an extended period. The plants are winter-growing, spring-flowering, and summer-dormant. Colors range

Homeria collina

from pink to yellow, and peach. Recent research shows there is no clear distinction between this genus and *Moraea*, and some botanists now place all *Homeria* species under that name.
CULTIVATION: When grown in containers in colder climates, provide shelter from frost and a fast-draining potting mix. Reduce water and nutrition after flowering and store corms in dry, frost-free conditions. Propagate from offsets or from fresh ripe seeds.

Homeria collina
☀ ⚘ ↔3 in (8 cm) ↕6–14 in (15–35 cm) From southwestern Cape region of South Africa. Robust, potentially weedy. Flowers are scented, upturned, held well above the foliage. Petals pale yellow, peach-pink, bronze-pink, or sugar pink, darker at the base. Leaves linear, grayish green, often trailing, provide little support to flowers. Stems solitary or sparsely branched. All parts toxic to stock. Zones 9–12.

Homeria flaccida
☀ ❄ ↔3 in (8 cm) ↕6–14 in (15–35 cm) Similar to *H. collina*; in fact, sometimes listed as being one and the same plant. Apricot to orange flowers, yellow in the center. Zones 8–10.

Hoheria lyallii

Holcus mollis 'Variegatus'

Holmskioldia sanguinea

Hosta fluctuans 'Variegated'

Hosta decorata

HOMORANTHUS

This Australian genus, a member of the myrtle (Myrtaceae) family, consists of 7 species of erect or spreading shrubs. They are found on a range of soils from northeastern Queensland to central New South Wales, with 1 species on the Eyre Peninsula in South Australia. The leaves are narrow, opposite and aromatic. The flowers are borne on various types of inflorescence, are tubular and produce a nut that is enclosed by the base of the floral tube.
CULTIVATION: All species require a well-drained acid or neutral soil. Some are hardy to frosts, others are tolerant of dry periods. Propagate from cuttings, but seed can be used if available.

Homoranthus darwinioides

☀ ❊ ↔ 5 ft (1.5 m) ↕ 5 ft (1.5 m)
From the central west region of New South Wales, Australia. Small shrub. Gray-green leaves almost circular in cross-section. Pendent flowers ¼ in (6 mm) long, in the leaf axils, cream to green with reddish tinges, most of year. Zones 8–11.

Homoranthus flavescens

☀ ❊ ↔ 4 ft (1.2 m) ↕ 15 in (38 cm)
Popular ground cover in temperate and subtropical regions. Branches are more or less horizontal. Leaves are aromatic, gray-green, narrow cylinders,

to ½ in (12 mm) long. Flowers are yellowish green, in spring–summer. Cuttings root easily. Zones 8–9.

HOODIA

This genus contains about 17 species of unusual succulent perennials in the milkweed (Asclepiadaceae) family. They are found naturally in arid areas among rocks in southern Africa. These leafless plants have robust, angular, usually grayish green stems up to 40 in (100 cm) tall. The stems are covered in small growths, called tubercles, and hard thorny teeth. The large saucer-shaped flowers are borne near the stem tips in groups of 1 to 5. They are in muted shades of yellow to brown and have an unpleasant smell.
CULTIVATION: In temperate climates grow in the greenhouse in a well-drained potting mix with a mulch of gravel to prevent collar rot. Water sparingly and leave dry in winter. Can be grown outdoors in dry, subtropical, and tropical areas. Propagation is from seed.

Hoodia bainii

☀ ⚘ ↔ 12 in (30 cm) ↕ 12 in (30 cm)
Stems, to 1½ in (35 mm) wide, have spirally arranged tubercles with pale brown spines. Flowers range from bell-shaped to almost flat. They are pale yellow to buff colored with darker veining. Zones 10–12.

HORDEUM

BARLEY
This grass (Poaceae) family genus contains about 20 species of annual or short-lived perennial grasses that are native to temperate regions of the Northern Hemisphere and South America. They have long, narrow, flat or rolled, strap-like leaves. Flowers are borne in dense, narrow, cylindrical or flattened, spike-like panicles, appearing in summer.

CULTIVATION: These plants prefer moist well-drained soil in full sun. Sow seed directly in growing position, in early spring.

Hordeum hystrix

MEDITERRANEAN BARLEY
☀ ❊ ↔ 6–12 in (15–30 cm)
↕ 12–16 in (30–40 cm)
Annual grass from the Mediterranean and central Asia. Downy leaves to 3 in (8 cm) long by ¼ in (6 mm) wide. Flowers in narrow, oval-shaped, grayish green spikes, tinged with purple, 2½ in (6 cm) long. Zones 5–7.

Hordeum jubatum

FOXTAIL BARLEY, SQUIRRELTAIL, SQUIRRELTAIL BARLEY
☀ ❊ ↔ 12 in (30 cm)
↕ 18–30 in (45–75 cm)
Northern Hemisphere perennial grass growing in low tufts, with ornamental drooping green or purple spikes. Looks best grown in masses but can become invasive. Zones 5–8.

HOSTA

PLANTAIN LILY
Hosta, from the agave (Agavaceae) family, was named for Dr Nicholaus Host (1761–1834), the physician to the emperor of Austria. Previously called *Funkia*, the genus was first described by Engelbert Kaempfer in 1712, a Dutch East India Company employee who, in exchange for plants, taught Japanese astronomy and mathematics. Hostas are clump-forming and grown primarily for their large, bold, heart-shaped leaves. In addition to green, blue, and grayish tones, there are cultivars variegated or with yellow-green foliage. The flowers are funnel-shaped and borne in small racemes atop stiff stems. They are usually white, mauve, or purple, appear from mid-summer, and are sometimes scented.
CULTIVATION: Although sun-tolerant cultivars have been raised, hostas prefer shaded conditions with moist, cool, humus-rich, well-drained soil. Water and feed well during the growing season. Propagate by dividing

as the first buds show. The young shoots are very vulnerable to slug and snail damage.

Hosta crispula

SAZANAMI GIBOSHI
◐/☀ ❊ ↔ 24 in (60 cm) ↕ 36 in (90 cm)
From Japan, though not known in wild. Deeply veined, pointed oval to lance-shaped leaves to around 10 in (25 cm) long, deep green with white edges, usually twisted with wavy edges rolled around leaf stalk. Pale mauve flowers on tall stem. Zones 6–10.

Hosta decorata

OTAFUKU GIBOSHI
◐/☀ ❊ ↔ 20 in (50 cm) ↕ 20 in (50 cm)
Japanese species. Rounded leathery leaves to near 6 in (15 cm) long, pointed at the tip, deep green with lighter edges. Flowers light purple, less commonly white. Zones 6–10.

Hosta fluctuans

KURONAMI GIBOSHI
◐/☀ ❊ ↔ 24 in (60 cm) ↕ 40 in (100 cm)
Japanese species with heavily veined, narrow, twisted leaves to 10 in (25 cm) long, deep green above, gray-green below. Narrow, pale mauve flowers on tall stem. 'Variegated' has wider leaves with creamy yellow edges. Zones 6–10.

Hosta fortunei

◐/☀ ❊ ↔ 32–48 in (80–120 cm)
↕ 36 in (90 cm)
Wild status uncertain—it is perhaps Japanese but may be a garden hybrid from Europe. Wavy, deep green, heart-to lance-shaped leaves tapering to a fine point, often variegated. Mauve flowers on leafy stems. Cultivars

Homoranthus flavescens

Homoranthus darwinioides

Hordeum jubatum

Hosta hypoleuca

Hosta kikutii 'Green Fountain'

Hosta minor

Hosta lancifolia

☼/◐ ❄ ↔ 16–20 in (40–50 cm)
↕ 18 in (45 cm)

Not known in the wild. Narrow, deep green, lance-shaped leaves to around 6 in (15 cm) long, tapering to a fine point. Flower stems leafy, flowers purple. Zones 6–10.

Hosta longissima

MIZU GIBOSHI

☼/◐ ❄ ↔ 16–20 in (40–50 cm)
↕ 20 in (50 cm)

A Japanese species forming a clump of leaves that is held upright or slightly overarching. Leaves are dark green, narrow, tapering to a fine point and extending to over 6 in (15 cm) in length. Zones 6–10.

Hosta minor

KIRIN GIBOSHI

☼/◐ ❄ ↔ 16 in (40 cm) ↕ 24 in (60 cm)

Korean species long cultivated in Japan. Clump of small, dark green, pointed oval to heart-shaped leaves to 3 in (8 cm) long. Comparatively tall flower stem with deep mauve flowers. Zones 6–10.

include: '**Albomarginata**', large white-edged leaves; '**Albopicta**', large, thin leaves, light green when young, maturing to green with hint of cream; '**Antioch**', dark green leaves, yellow edge turning cream; '**Aurea**', leaves yellow, turning light green; '**Aureo-marginata**', clearly defined gold-edged leaves; '**Elizabeth Campbell**', leaves with broad green edge and light green central zone; '**Francee**', white-edged deep green leaves, slightly puckered; '**Gold Haze**', like 'Aurea' but slower to turn green; '**Gold Standard**', green-gold leaves, clearly defined dark green edge; '**Goldbrook Gold**', yellow-gold leaves; '**Joker**', gray-green to blue-green

leaves; '**Mary Marie Ann**', bright green edges around a broad yellow-green center; '**Minuteman**', bright green leaves, with irregular broad white edge; '**North Hills**', mid-green leaves with an irregular narrow white edge; '**Striptease**', heart-shaped blue-green leaves with a narrow cream and green central zone; '**Whirlwind**', mid-green, broad yellow-gold center. Zones 6–10.

Hosta hypoleuca

URAJIRO GIBOSHI

☼/◐ ❄ ↔ 40 in (100 cm) ↕ 16 in (40 cm)

Japanese species with slightly wavy, pointed oval to heart-shaped leaves to

18 in (45 cm) long, blue-green above, very pale beneath. Flowers lavender to white on short, sometimes leafy stem. Zones 6–10.

Hosta kikutii

HYUGA GIBOSHI

☼/◐ ❄ ↔ 32 in (80 cm) ↕ 16 in (40 cm)

Japanese native with lustrous deep green, arching, deeply veined, pointed oval leaves to 8 in (20 cm) long. Leafy flower stems with bracts partly enclosing white to cream flowers, sometimes mauve-tinted. '**Green Fountain**' has larger leaves with wavy edges and curved flower stems. Zones 6–10.

Hosta fortunei 'Whirlwind'

Hosta fortunei 'Albopicta'

Hosta fortunei 'Joker'

H. fortunei 'Elizabeth Campbell'

Hosta fortunei 'Francee'

Hosta fortunei 'Mary Marie Ann'

Hosta fortunei 'Gold Haze'

Hosta fortunei 'Minuteman'

H. fortunei 'Goldbrook Glimmer'

Hosta fortunei 'Striptease'

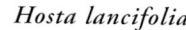

Hosta fortunei 'Antioch'

Hosta fortunei 'Albomarginata'

Hosta montana

OBA GIBOSHI

☼/☀ ❄ ↔ 40 in (100 cm)
↑ 40 in (100 cm)

Wild status uncertain, though probably Japanese. Broad, deep green to blue-green, heavily veined, sometimes undulating oval leaves tapering to fine point, to 12 in (30 cm) long. Flowers lavender-gray to white, stems leafy. **'On Stage'**, bright gold leaves with irregular green margins; **'Yellow River'**, leaves with a sharply defined yellow edge and flower stems to 24 in (60 cm) tall. Zones 6–10.

Hosta nakaiana

KANZASHI GIBOSHI

☼/☀ ❄ ↔ 12–16 in (30–40 cm)
↑ 16 in (40 cm)

Compact low ground cover from Korea and Japan. Long-stemmed, bright green, heavily veined, undulating, heart-shaped leaves to around 2½ in (6 cm) long, pale undersides. Wiry flower stem with bell-shaped mauve flowers. **'Emerald Scepter'**, especially

Hosta nakaiana 'Emerald Scepter'

bright green foliage; **'Golden Scepter'**, golden yellow leaves; **'Golden Tiara'**, gold-edged leaves; **'Grand Tiara'**, sport of 'Golden Tiara' with broader leaves and wider golden edge; **'Platinum Tiara'**, lime green leaves with clearly defined white edge. Zones 6–10.

Hosta nigrescens

KURO GIBOSHI

☼/☀ ❄ ↔ 3–4 ft (0.9–1.2 m)
↑ 3–7 ft (0.9–2 m)

Bushy, late-flowering Japanese species. Tall flower stems. Pointed oval leaves to 10 in (25 cm) long, base rolled

Hosta nakaiana 'Grand Tiara'

over the stalk, blue-gray when young, maturing to dark green. Stems leafy, flowers open white from mauve buds. **'Sum and Substance'**, heavy textured, glossy, golden green leaves. Zones 6–10.

Hosta plantaginea

AUGUST LILY, MARUBA

☼/☀ ❄ ↔ 32 in (80 cm) ↑ 26 in (65 cm)

Native to China and Japan. Unlike most hostas, grown as much for flowers as foliage. Leaves bright green, wavy, deeply veined, lance-shaped tapering to a fine point, to 10 in (25 cm) long. Flowers white, sometimes mauve-tinted, large and pleasantly scented. *H. p.* var. *japonica* (syn. *H. p.* var. *grandiflora*), taller flower stems with larger flowers. *H. p.* **'Honey Bells'**, mauve-tinted flowers; **'Venus'**, double flowers. Zones 8–10.

Hosta pulchella

UBUTAKE GIBOSHI

☼/☀ ❄ ↔ 12 in (30 cm) ↑ 12 in (30 cm)

Compact rock garden-style species from Japan. Bright green, heart-shaped

Hosta nakaiana 'Platinum Tiara'

Hosta plantaginea

leaves to 2 in (5 cm) long. Leafy flower stems with mauve often scented flowers, late. **'Kifukurin'** has yellow-edged leaves and purple flowers. Zones 6–10.

Hosta sieboldiana ★

☼/☀ ❄ ↔ 3–5 ft (0.9–1.5 m)
↑ 20–24 in (50–60 cm)

Japanese species. Large, fine-pointed, heart-shaped leaves to 20 in (50 cm) long. Leaves usually in striking blue-gray tones with a heavily veined and puckered surface. Flowers white to mauve, on leafy stems. *H. s.* var.

Hosta montana 'Yellow River'

Hosta pulchella 'Kifukurin'

Hosta nigrescens

Hosta nigrescens 'Sum and Substance'

Hosta s. 'Birchwood Parky's Gold'

Hosta sieboldiana 'Blue Angel'

Hosta sieboldiana 'Crumples'

Hosta sieboldiana 'Reversed'

Hosta sieboldiana var. *elegans*

elegans, thick, heavily puckered leaves, pearly mauve flowers. *H. s.* **'Aurora Borealis'**, leaves with bright gold edges, white flowers; **'Big Daddy'**, very large, heavy textured, intensely blue-green leaves; **'Birchwood Parky's Gold'**, light yellow-green leaves, mauve flowers; **'Blue Angel'** ★, very vigorous with huge blue-green leaves, white flowers; **'Bressingham Blue'**, large, undulating leaves, white to pale mauve flowers; **'Crumples'**, pale blue-green with incredibly deeply puckered surface; **'Frances Williams'**, leaves with broad green-gold edges; **'Great Expectations'**, gold leaves with blue-green edges; **'Reversed'**, blue-green leaves, broad white center. Zones 6–10.

Hosta sieboldii

KOBA GIBOSHI

☽/☀ ✹ ↔ 32 in (80 cm) ↑ 20 in (50 cm)

Native to Japan and Sakhalin Island. Finely pointed, often undulating and puckered, lance-shaped leaves to 6 in (15 cm) long, deep green with clean white edges. Mauve flowers. *H. s.* f. *kabitan*, small, green-edged golden leaves. *H. s.* **'Krossa Cream Edge'**, narrow, cream-edged leaves; **'Wogon'**, bright lime green leaves. Zones 5–10.

Hosta × tardiana

☽/☀ ✹ ↔ 16–20 in (40–50 cm)
↑ 16 in (40 cm)

Hybrids between *H. sieboldiana* var. *elegans* and *H. tardiflora*. Mainly forming mounding clumps of heavily veined blue-green leaves, sometimes variegated. Flower stems fairly short, flowers cream to pale mauve. **'Brother Ronald'**, dark blue-green leaves to over 6 in (15 cm) long; **'Camelot'**, wide spreading with broad, heart-shaped, intensely blue-green

Hosta tokudama 'Love Pat'

Hosta ventricosa

Hosta sieboldii

Hosta sieboldii f. *kabitan*

Hosta sieboldii 'Krossa Cream Edge'

Hosta × tardiana 'Brother Ronald'

Hosta tardiflora

Hosta undulata var. *albomarginata*

Hosta × tardiana 'Camelot'

Hosta undulata 'White Christmas'

Hosta × tardiana 'Halcyon'

leaves to 8 in (20 cm) long, lavender flowers; **'Devon Blue'**, pointed, gray-marked, blue-green leaves to over 6 in (15 cm) long; **'Halcyon'**, heart-shaped blue-green leaves to 8 in (20 cm) long, many lavender-gray flowers; **'Moody Blues'**, broad, intensely blue-green leaves, pale lavender flowers. Zones 6–10.

Hosta tardiflora

☀/☀ ✹ ↔ 20 in (50 cm) ↑ 12 in (30 cm)

A species unknown in the wild, with prominently veined, glossy, olive green, sometimes undulating, lance-shaped leaves to 6 in (15 cm) long. Flower stem to 14 in (35 cm) long but held at around a 45° angle, flowers mauve within cream to purple bracts. Zones 6–10.

Hosta tokudama

TOKUDAMA GIBOSHI

☀/☀ ✹ ↔ 32–48 in (80–120 cm)
↑ 18 in (45 cm)

Unknown in the wild, long cultivated in Japan. Broad oval to heart-shaped

leaves, puckered surface, bright blue-green, to 10 in (25 cm) long and wide. Flowers lavender-gray to white. *H. t.* f. *aureonebulosa*, leaves irregular, large central yellow-green area. *H. t.* **'Love Pat'**, possibly of hybrid origin, heavily textured, deep blue-green leaves, mauvish white flowers. Zones 6–10.

Hosta undulata

SUJI GIBOSHI

☀/☀ ✹ ↔ 16–20 in (40–50 cm)
↑ 12 in (30 cm)

This species is unknown in the wild, though it has long been cultivated in Japan. Dark green leaves, narrow central band of creamy white, pointed elliptical to lance-shaped, wavy edged with undulating surface, to nearly 6 in (15 cm) long. Flowers pale purple within greenish white bracts. **'Albomarginata'**, leaves with white edges, wavy but not twisted; **'Variegata'** (syn. *H. u.* var. *undulata*), leaves with central area cream and 2-tone green; **'Univittata'**, large leaves with a narrow central creamy white zone;

and **'White Christmas'**, white leaves with narrow irregular green edge. Zones 6–10.

Hosta ventricosa

MURASAKI GIBOSHI

☀/☀ ✹ ↔ 24–32 in (60–80 cm)
↑ 40 in (100 cm)

Chinese species long cultivated in Japan. Deep green, broad, often wavy, heart-shaped leaves to 10 in (25 cm) long. Tall flower stems, light purple flowers. *H. v.* var. *aureomaculata*, young leaves with bright yellow center. *H. v.* **'Peedee Elfin Bells'**, pendulous flowers. Zones 6–10.

Hosta venusta

OTOME GIBOSHI

☀/☀ ✹ ↔ 12 in (30 cm) ↑ 14 in (35 cm)

Low-growing, spreading, late-flowering native of Korea and Japan. Dark green, pointed oval, short-stemmed leaves under 2 in (5 cm) long, sometimes wavy edged. Mauve flowers. Sun-tolerant, good rock garden plant. Zones 6–10.

Hosta, Hybrid Cultivar, 'August Moon'

Hosta, Hybrid Cultivar, 'Blue Arrow'

Hosta, Hybrid Cultivar, 'Candy Hearts'

Hosta, Hybrid Cultivar, 'Cheatin' Heart'

Hosta, Hybrid Cultivar, 'County Park'

Hosta, HC, 'Devon Gold'

Hosta, Hybrid Cultivar, 'Fresh'

Hosta, Hybrid Cultivar, 'Gaiety'

Hosta, HC, 'Gold Edger'

Hosta, HC, 'Green Piecrust'

Hosta, HC, 'Green with Envy'

Hosta, HC, 'Ground Sulphur'

Hosta, HC, 'Hadspen Samphire'

Hosta, HC, 'Iced Lemon'

Hosta, HC, 'Island Charm'

Hosta, Hybrid Cultivar, 'Floradora'

Hosta Hybrid Cultivars

◐/☀ ❋ ↔ 12–60 in (30–150 cm)
↕ 6–36 in (15–90 cm)

In recent decades hostas have been among plant breeders' favorites, and extensive hybridizing has produced a myriad of foliage forms. Although much effort has gone into producing sun-tolerant forms, most are still better with some shade. 'Allan P.

McConnell', medium height, dark green with white edge, purple flowers; 'August Moon', tall, wavy yellow-gold leaves, lavender flowers; 'Blue Moon', low-growing, small blue-green leaves, white flowers; 'Brim Cup', tall, puckered, light yellow-green leaves with irregular green center, mauve flowers; 'Candy Hearts', tall blue-green leaves, pale mauve flowers; 'County Park',

tall, broad, flat, mid-green leaves, white flowers; 'Devon Gold', medium height, small yellow-green leaves, purple flowers; 'Floradora', medium height, neat heart-shaped mid-green leaves, pale mauve flowers; 'Gold Edger', low-growing, golden green leaves, white flowers; 'Green Piecrust', tall, large mid-green wavy-edged leaves, lavender flowers; 'Ground Sulphur', a medium height, low spreader with bright yellow-green leaves; 'Island Charm', medium height, small pink-stemmed bright green heart-shaped leaves with yellow center, lavender flowers; 'Julie Morss', medium height, yellow-gold leaves with green edges, lavender-pink flowers; 'June', medium height, small yellow-centered blue-green leaves, violet flowers; 'King Michael', tall, large lustrous mid-green leaves, white flowers; 'Krossa Regal', tall, long-stemmed blue-green leaves, white to pale mauve flowers; 'Lady Isobel Barnett', tall, very large mid-green leaves with creamy yellow margin, white to pale lavender flowers; 'Medusa', medium height, narrow green-edged cream leaves, purple flowers; 'Midwest Magic', tall, yellow-green leaves with darker edges, lavender flowers; 'Patriot', tall, dark green leaves with broad white edge, violet flowers; 'Paul's Glory', medium height,

heavily puckered yellow-centered blue-green leaves, lavender flowers; 'Pearl Lake', tall, small mid-green leaves, many lavender flowers; 'Pizzazz', medium height, broad blue-green leave with thin irregular yellow edges, pale mauve flowers; 'Radiant Edger', tall, small mid-green leaves with yellow-green edges, mauve flowers; 'Royal Standard', tall, glossy mid-green leaves, fragrant white flowers; 'Ryan's Big One', tall, very large puckered blue-green leaves, pale lavender flowers; 'September Sun', tall, leaves initially yellow-green becoming green-edged, white flowers; 'Shade Fanfare', medium height, puckered white-edged blue-green leaves, pale mauve flowers; 'Summer Music', medium height, slightly twisted dark green leaves with white to cream center, pale mauve flowers; 'Tall Boy', tall, long-stemmed mid-green leaves, purple flowers on tall stems; 'Torchlight', medium height, dark green leaves with broad white edge, lavender flowers; 'Veronica Lake', medium height, blue-green leaves with white to light green edges, pale mauve flowers; 'Wide Brim', tall, blue-green leaves with creamy yellow edge, mauve flowers; 'Yellow Waves', low-growing, small yellow-gold leaves, mauve flowers. Zones 6–10.

Hosta, HC, 'Julie Morss'

Hosta, Hybrid Cultivar, 'Just So'

Hosta, HC, 'Krossa Regal'

Hosta, HC, 'Krossol Royal'

Hosta, HC, 'Lady Isobel Barnett'

Hosta, HC, 'Little Caesar'

Hosta, HC, 'Magic Moments'

Hosta, HC, 'Marble Rim'

Hosta, Hybrid Cultivar, 'Medusa'

Hosta, HC, 'Midwest Magic'

Hosta, HC, 'Neat Splash'

Hosta, Hybrid Cultivar, 'Oriole'

Hosta, HC, 'Paradise Red Delight'

Hosta, HC, 'Paul's Glory'

Hosta, Hybrid Cultivar, 'Pearl Lake'

Hosta, HC, 'Radiant Edger'

Hosta, HC, 'September Sun'

Hosta, HC, 'Shade Fanfare'

Hosta, Hybrid Cultivar, 'Snowcap'

Hosta, HC, 'Summer Music'

Hosta, HC, 'Sunburst'

Hosta, Hybrid Cultivar, 'Sweetie'

Hosta, Hybrid Cultivar, 'Tall Boy'

Hosta, Hybrid Cultivar, 'Torchlight'

Hosta, HC, 'Veronica Lake'

Hosta, HC, 'Wogon's Boy'

Hosta, HC, 'Wrinkles and Crinkles'

Hosta, HC, 'Yellow Waves'

Hosta, Hybrid Cultivar, 'Wagon'

HOUTTUYNIA

A genus of a single species in the lizard's-tail (Saururaceae) family from East Asia. It is a widely spreading herbaceous perennial with heart-shaped leaves and cones of tiny yellow flowers surrounded by 4 white petal-like bracts. Leaves can be eaten raw or cooked and have a peppery taste. CULTIVATION: Grows well in moist to wet soil and even slightly submerged in water, and is happy in full sun or half-sun. Can become quite invasive and hard to remove, although growing them in pots kept off the ground will control them. Propagate by division.

Houttuynia cordata

☼/☀ ❄ ↔ over 40 in (100 cm) ↕ 6–12 in (15–30 cm)

Herbaceous plant from swamps and damp margins of China and Japan. Aromatic heart-shaped leaves to 3½ in (9 cm) long, deep green often stained burgundy. White-bracted flower clusters atop red stems from mid-summer onward. Below ground produces thong-like rhizomes. Usually grown in one of its forms, which include:

'Chameleon' (syns *H. c.* 'Court Jester', *H. c.* 'Tricolor', *H. c.* 'Variegata'), slightly less vigorous, leaves broadly edged in yellow and stained red; 'Flore Pleno', masses of white bracts arranged like little cones and just as vigorous as the species. Zones 5–10.

HOVENIA

The 2 species in this buckthorn (Rhamnaceae) family genus have been cultivated so long their natural range can only be vaguely defined as temperate East Asia. These deciduous shrubs or trees are grown for their graceful habit, attractive heart-shaped leaves, around 6 in (15 cm) long, and fruit massed in large clusters on branched stems. The flowers are not a feature. CULTIVATION: Hardy and adaptable, they will grow with minimal attention in any well-tended garden. All that is required is a sunny position with moist, reasonably fertile well-drained soil. Low humidity, hot dry winds and prolonged drought can cause problems. Propagation is from seed sown as soon as it is ripe or by taking half-hardened summer cuttings.

Hovenia dulcis

Houttuynia cordata 'Chameleon'

Houttuynia cordata 'Chameleon'

Howea forsteriana

Hovenia dulcis ★

JAPANESE RAISIN TREE

☼ ❄ ↔ 20 ft (6 m) ↕ 30 ft (9 m)

Probably from China, long cultivated in Japan. Good shade tree. Sprays of small yellow-green flowers, on thick stalks, in summer. Small red fruit stalks swell and sweeten, becoming edible, after first frosts. Zones 6–9.

HOWEA

The 2 species in this genus of the palm (Arecaceae) family are natives of Lord Howe Island, off the coast of New South Wales, Australia. They are upright, single-trunked palms with lush heads of feather fronds. Flower-heads form near the base of the fronds and develop into red-green fruit. CULTIVATION: Although quite frost tender, they do not need high temperatures or bright light to grow well, so are good house or conservatory plants. They will grow outdoors in frost-free gardens in any area that is not too hot and dry. A lightly shaded spot with moist, humus-rich, well-drained soil is best. Propagate from seed scarified before sowing and kept warm and moist until germination.

Howea belmoreana ★

BELMORE PALM, CURLY PALM, SENTRY PALM

☼ ❧ ↔ 10 ft (3 m) ↕ 25 ft (8 m)

The less commonly grown of the 2 species. Slender trunk ringed with the scar of old frond bases. Deep green fronds arch gracefully, and reach around 7 ft (2 m) long. Zones 10–11.

Howea forsteriana ★

KENTIA PALM, PARADISE PALM

☼ ❧ ↔ 15 ft (4.5 m) ↕ 30–50 ft (9–15 m)

Native to Lord Howe Island, also widely cultivated on nearby Norfolk Island for its seeds, for the nursery trade. Fronds up to 10 ft (3 m) long, usually held quite stiffly. Zones 10–11.

HOYA

WAX FLOWER

This genus, in the milkweed (Asclepiadaceae) family, is native to Polynesia, Asia and Australia. It contains 200 species of mainly climbing, sometimes

Hoya australis

Hoya carnosa

shrubby or succulent, evergreen plants. They are woody-stemmed and some contain milky sap. In the wild, climbers will reach 20 ft (6 m) or more. Foliage is usually dark green and glossy. Their exquisite waxy flowers, often fragrant, look like fine porcelain. The thick petals are usually white or in shades of pink. The center of the flower has a corona that is starry in many species and often brightly colored. CULTIVATION: In warm climates grow outdoors in semi-shade in a moist, rich, free-draining soil. Elsewhere hoyas are popular house plants often grown in hanging baskets. Grow in bright filtered light in a well-drained potting mix. Water and feed regularly and maintain a high level of humidity. Propagate from cuttings.

Hoya australis ★

◗ ❧ ↕ 2–6 ft (0.6–1.8 m)

Twining and rooting Australia climber. Thick, shiny, succulent, dark green leaves. Umbels of small, starry, scented, white to pale pink flowers, with reddish purple coronas, in summer. Zones 10–12.

Hoya carnosa

WAX PLANT

◗ ❧ ↕ 2–6 ft (0.6–1.8 m)

Found from India to southeastern China. Climber widely grown as a house plant. Thick dark green leaves. Umbels of fragrant white to palest pink flowers have starry, white, red-centered coronas: 'Exotica', leaves variegated yellow and pink with green margins; 'Krinkle Kurl', twisted curly leaves; 'Variegata', leaves with a yellow central zone and pinker flowers. Zones 10–12.

HUERNIA
LIFE BUOY PLANT

There are about 70 species of small succulent perennials in this milkweed (Asclepiadaceae) family genus, native to dry areas of Africa. They are leafless plants with fleshy angular stems often with small growths called tubercles, and spines or bristles. The fleshy flowers may be clustered or solitary and emerge from the plant base or stem tips. They are star- or bell-shaped and some species have a prominent fleshy central ring, hence "life buoy plant." They are usually strongly colored and marked in shades of maroon, red, yellow, and green, and have an unpleasant odor of varying intensity.
CULTIVATION: In suitably warm climates grow outdoors in shade in free-draining soil or in a pot. Keep dry in winter. In the greenhouse they need bright shade. Water with care as plants rot easily. They are susceptible to root and stem mealy bugs.

Huernia zebrina ★
LITTLE OWL, OWL-EYES
☀ ❄ ↔ 6 in (15 cm) ↕ 4 in (10 cm)
From South Africa, Botswana, and Namibia. Stems 5-angled with toothed edges. Basal flowers have a prominent raised central ring of maroon, sometimes marked yellow. Surrounding triangular lobes are pale yellow with reddish brown bands. Zones 10–12.

HUMULUS

This genus of 2 species in the hemp (Cannabidaceae) family consists of herbaceous, climbing, and twining perennials from northern temperate regions. The plants naturalize in trees

Huernia zebrina

Hunnemannia fumariifolia

and woodland areas and can grow up to 70 ft (21 m) in a season. Grown primarily for their attractive foliage, many cultivars have been selected for ornamental purposes. *H. lupulus* is grown for its fruits (hops), used to flavor beer. Spreading via underground suckers, they cover large areas quickly.
CULTIVATION: These plants need well-drained, moist, fertile soil. They die back to the ground over winter, and are prone to mildew in the damp. Propagate from semi-hardwood stem cuttings in late summer or by division when plants are dormant.

Humulus lupulus
BINE, COMMON HOP, EUROPEAN HOP
☀ ❄ ↔ 10–30 ft (3–9 m)
↕ 17–20 ft (5–6 m)
Well-known vigorous herbaceous twiner with rough stems. Source of hops, an indispensable ingredient of beer. Suckers far and wide from its questing rhizomes. Leaves 3- to 5-lobed, to 6 in (15 cm) long. Female plants are festooned with bracted hops in summer. Usually grown in its golden-leafed form, 'Aureus', which varies in color depending on how much light it gets. *H. l.* var. *neomexicanus* is a North American form that, apart from its distribution, is almost indistinguishable from the species. Zones 5–10.

HUNNEMANNIA
GOLDEN CUP, MEXICAN TULIP POPPY

This genus belongs to the poppy (Papaveraceae) family and contains one species of perennial that is often grown as an annual. It is native to highland areas of Mexico. Although rather woody at the base, it is of delicate appearance with finely divided bluish gray foliage. The flowers are up to 3 in (8 cm) wide and are clear yellow.
CULTIVATION: Grow in full sun in a well-drained soil. It will not tolerate wet conditions. Care should be taken not to disturb the roots on transplanting. Propagate from seed.

Hunnemannia fumariifolia
☀ ❄ ↔ 10 in (25 cm)
↕ 18–36 in (45–90 cm)
A perennial or annual that has attractive bluish gray filigree leaves. The satiny flowers are clearest yellow and held above the foliage in summer. Zones 8–10.

HYACINTHOIDES
BLUEBELL

From western Europe and northern Africa, these vigorous bulbous plants, members of the hyacinth (Hyacinth-

Hyacinthoides hispanica

Hyacinthoides hispanica 'La Grandesse'

Hyacinthoides italica

aceae) family, are well suited to informal naturalistic plantings. The flowers, in the form of elegant pendent bells attached to a single stem, are commonly an azure blue and appear in spring. Some are sweetly fragrant. The leaves are linear to strap-shaped and fleshy. Hybrids between *H. hispanica* and *H. non-scripta* are as common as they are confusing.
CULTIVATION: They are best grown in the ground in damp-summer climates or in irrigated beds, placed beneath deciduous trees and shrubs and planted deeply in a humus-rich, moisture-retentive, fairly heavy soil. Give them sun in winter and shade in summer, and moisture-retentive conditions throughout the year. The plants are robust and fecund and, in appropriate conditions, have considerable weedy potential. Survival time in a vase is brief and the copious syrupy sap can cause skin irritations. The plants are said to be toxic if ingested. Propagate by division (the bulbs lie deep), or from ripe fresh seed.

Hyacinthoides hispanica ★
syns *Endymion hispanicus,*
Scilla campanulata, S. hispanica
SPANISH BLUEBELL
☽/☀ ❄ ↔ 4–6 in (10–15 cm)
↕ 16–18 in (40–45 cm)
Flowers without fragrance, arranged loosely around a single erect stem, in spring. Petals commonly blue, also

lilac-pink and white; anthers blue. Leaves broad, strap-shaped, glossy emerald green, copious, erect but usually prostrate after rain. Clump-forming. Cultivars include: 'Excelsoir', large-flowered, tall, with violet-blue petals adorned with a stripe; 'La Grandesse', with widely spaced, pure white bells. Zones 6–7.

Hyacinthoides italica
syn. *Scilla italica*
☽/☀ ❄ ↔ 2–6 in (5–15 cm)
↕ 4–8 in (10–20 cm)
Native to southern Europe from Spain to Italy. Bluish violet flowers densely packed, bell-shaped, upward-facing, 6 to 30 per stem, in spring. Leaves linear, dull dark green. Zones 5–9.

Hyacinthoides non-scripta
syns *Endymion non-scriptus,*
Scilla non-scripta
BLUEBELL, ENGLISH BLUEBELL, WILD HYACINTH
☽/☀ ❄ ↔ 2–6 in (5–15 cm)
↕ 8–16 in (20–40 cm)
Clump-forming colonizer of damp oak, beech, and chestnut woodlands. Flowers 6 to 10 per stem, narrow bells, scented, arranged in drooping racemes on a single side of stem, in spring. Petals commonly azure blue; anthers creamy white. Stem bent like a shepherd's crook. Leaves narrow, glossy dark green. 'Alba', common white form; 'Rosea', lilac-pink flowers. Zones 5–10.

Hyacinthus orientalis 'Amethyst'

Hyacinthus orientalis 'Bismarck'

Hyacinthus orientalis 'Blue Jacket'

Hyacinthus orientalis 'Blue Magic'

Hyacinthus orientalis 'Carnegie'

Hyacinthus orientalis 'Jan Bos'

H. orientalis 'King of the Blues'

H. orientalis 'Multiflora Blue'

Hyacinthus orientalis 'Pink Pearl'

H. orientalis 'Violet Pearl'

Hyacinthus orientalis 'City of Haarlem'

Hyacinthus orientalis 'Queen of the Night'

Hyacinthus orientalis 'Queen of the Pinks'

HYACINTHUS

HYACINTH

There are only 3 species in this bulbous perennial genus, which is in the lily (Liliaceae) family and comes from western and central Asia. However, many more have been developed for the cut-flower market and for container culture. Today the most common are the showy cultivars of *H. orientalis*, which can bloom at almost any time of the year. There are 3 basic forms: Dutch hyacinths, which pack their numerous flowerheads tightly around a central stem forming a dense cylinder; Roman hyacinths, which have less numerous flowerheads and a looser arrangement; and the Multiflora Group, which produce several stems of loosely set flowerheads. All are sweetly fragrant and, to greater and lesser extents, lend themselves to container culture and forcing.
CULTIVATION: In gardens, plant in autumn under a light deciduous canopy, in well-drained moderately fertile soil. In containers, use a moisture-retentive mix, plant in autumn,

and keep in a cool dark place until roots are well developed, or suspend over water and keep in a cool dark place until the roots are well developed. Bulbs grown over water should be discarded after flowering. Give them sun in winter and shade in summer. Propagate from offsets or fresh ripe seed. Cultivars are encouraged to form offsets by cutting into the base of the bulb.

Hyacinthus orientalis

COMMON HYACINTH
☼/☀ ❅ ↔ 3 in (8 cm)
↑ 8–12 in (20–30 cm)
Flowers in 6 or 7 heads sparsely arranged at angles around a central stem, smallish, dainty, narrowly bell-shaped, waxy, fragrant. Petals blue, blue-mauve, pink, white, and cream. '**Amethyst**', mauve-violet petals; '**Anna Marie**', light pink; '**Bismarck**', lilac with pale margins; '**Blue Jacket**', navy with purple veins; '**Carnegie**', compact, pure white, late; '**City of Haarlem**', primrose yellow, late; '**Delft Blue**', soft blue flushed with

mauve; '**Gipsy Queen**', salmon orange; '**Hollyhock**', compact, crimson, double; '**Jan Bos**', carmine-red; '**King of the Blues**', rich dark blue; '**Ostara**', large, deep lavender-blue; '**Violet Pearl**', carmine-pink with pale margins.
Zones 5–9.

HYDRANGEA

There are about 100 species of deciduous and evergreen shrubs, trees, and climbers in this Hydrangeaceae family genus, native to eastern Asia, North and South America. Leaves are usually large and oval with serrated edges. Flowerheads are comprised of very small fertile flowers surrounded by larger, 4-petalled sterile florets, conical, flat-topped (lacecap) or rounded (mophead). Colors range from white through to red, purple and blue.
CULTIVATION: Hydrangeas grow in a wide range of conditions. However, they will do better in good soil with compost and light feeding. Grow in sun or dappled shade, ensuring they have ample moisture. Grow *H. macrophylla* cultivars to suit the soil pH. Color can be changed by dressing with aluminium sulphate for blue and with lime for red. Prune in late winter, and remove old wood. Species can be propagated from seed sown in spring as well as from tip cuttings in late spring or hardwood cuttings in winter. Cultivars are propagated from cuttings only.

Hydrangea arborescens

SMOOTH HYDRANGEA
☼/☀ ❅ ↔ 8 ft (2.4 m)
↑ 3–12 ft (0.9–3.5 m)
Native to North America, from moist shady sites. Deciduous shrub, open

Hydrangea arborescens 'Annabelle'

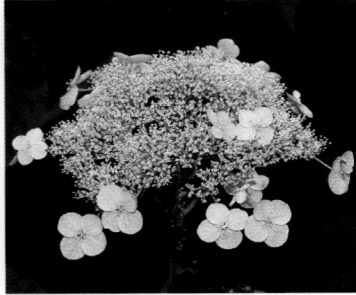

Hydrangea arborescens subsp. *radiata*

Hydrangea macrophylla

Hydrangea macrophylla, Mophead, 'Ami Pasquier'

Hydrangea macrophylla, Mophead, 'Ave Maria'

Hydrangea macrophylla, Mophead, 'Ayesha'

Hydrangea macrophylla, Mophead, 'Enziandom'

H. m., Mophead, 'Freudenstein'

H. m., Mophead, 'Générale Vicomtesse de Vibraye'

H. m., Mophead, 'Hatfield Rose'

H. m., Mophead, 'Hobergine'

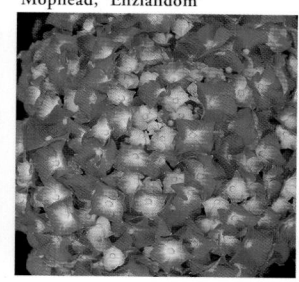

H. macrophylla, Mophead, 'Koningin Wilhelmina'

habit, often spreading from suckers. Flat creamy white flowerheads, in summer, numerous tiny fertile flowers surrounded by a few sterile florets. *H. a.* subsp. *radiata* has deep green leaves. *H. a.* 'Annabelle' ★, extremely large white mophead flowerheads; 'Grandiflora', slightly uneven mopheads of pure white sterile flowers. Zones 3–10.

Hydrangea aspera
syn. *Hydrangea villosa*

☼/◐ ❄ ↔10 ft (3 m) ↑10 ft (3 m)

Native of eastern Asia. Variable deciduous species. Lacecap flowers, held well above foliage, to 10 in (25 cm) wide, pale mauve sterile florets, tiny, bright purplish blue fertile flowers in center. *H. a.* f. *kawakamii*, pink veined leaves. *H. a.* subsp. *sargentiana*, large leaves, velvety above, bristly beneath. Flat-topped flowerheads, pinkish white sterile florets surrounding mauve fertile flowers. *H. a.* 'Mauvette', mauve dome-shaped flowerheads to 6 in (15 cm) across; 'Peter Chappell', large downy leaves, flat-topped flowerheads of white sterile florets surrounding creamy pink fertile flowers. Zones 7–10.

Hydrangea heteromalla

☼/◐ ❄ ↔10 ft (3 m)
↑10–15 ft (3–4.5 m)

Deciduous species from China and the Himalayas. Variable in habit, foliage and flowers. Leaves usually broadly lance-shaped, downy beneath in some forms. Lacecap flowers, white to pink sterile florets surrounding greenish white fertile flowers, in summer. 'Jermyn's Lace', attractive shrub, pink-tinged greenish white flowers. Zones 6–9.

Hydrangea involucrata

☼/◐ ❄ ↔6 ft (1.8 m) ↑3 ft (0.9 m)

From Japan and Taiwan, rare in cultivation. Broadly oblong leaves, rough, bristly margins. Lacecap flowerheads, to 5 in (12 cm) across, a few white sterile florets around mauve fertile flowers, late summer. 'Hortensis', interesting form with showy, double sterile florets of pinkish white, more difficult to cultivate. Zones 7–10.

Hydrangea macrophylla
syn. *Hydrangea hortensis*

BIGLEAF HYDRANGEA, FLORIST'S HYDRANGEA, GARDEN HYDRANGEA, HORTENSIA

☼/◐ ❄ ↔8 ft (2.4 m) ↑10 ft (3 m)

Long-cultivated species from coastal areas of Japan, wild form rare in cultivation. Deciduous shrub, large shiny leaves, pinkish blue flat-topped flowers. Many cultivars are popular garden plants. Cultivars usually grow 3–6 ft (1–1.8 m) high, divided into two groups: mophead (hortensias) and lacecap. There are more than 500 cultivars of the well-known mophead type, with globular heads of showy sterile florets. Mophead cultivars are suitable for coastal gardens. There are about 20 lacecap cultivars, with flat-topped formation of outer sterile florets, central fertile flowers.

Mophead Cultivars: 'Alpenglühen' ★, medium-sized robust plant, maintaining a rosy red color even in slightly acid soil; 'Altona' grows to 6 ft (1.8 m), with pink or blue flowers depending on soil pH; 'Amethyst', semi-double flowers and serrated bracts, lavender in acid soil and pale pink in alkaline soil; 'Ami Pasquier', medium size, producing rich crimson to purple flowers all summer, leaves turn red in autumn; 'Enziandom' (syn. 'Gentian Dome'), compact shrub of 5 ft (1.5 m), needing

acid soil to produce its stunning gentian blue flowers; 'Générale Vicomtesse de Vibraye', medium grower, flowerheads commencing as soft cream, gradually becoming powder blue; 'Hamburg', large serrated petals of deep rose to purple or blue, depending on soil pH; 'Madame Emile Mouillère', growing up to 6 ft (1.8 m), one of the best of the white mopheads; 'Miss Belgium', growing to 3 ft (1 m), small heads of pink flowers when grown in alkaline soil; 'Montgomery', yellow and pink

Hydrangea involucrata

Hydrangea involucrata 'Hortensis'

Hydrangea aspera f. *kawakamii*

Hydrangea heteromalla 'Jermyn's Lace'

Hydrangea macrophylla, Mophead, 'Lavblaa'

H. macrophylla, Mophead, 'Madame Faustin Travouillon'

Hydrangea macrophylla, Mophead, 'Mein Liebling'

Hydrangea macrophylla, Mophead, 'Montgomery'

Hydrangea macrophylla, Mophead, 'Nigra'

H. m., Mophead, 'Nikko Blue'

H. m., Mophead, 'Nikko Rose'

H. m., Mophead, 'Parzifal'

H. macrophylla, Mophead, 'Souvenir de President Doumer'

H. m., Lacecap, 'Blauling'

H. m., Lacecap, 'Blaumeise'

H. m., Lacecap, 'Buchfink'

H. m., Lacecap, 'Fireworks'

H. m., Lacecap, 'Fireworks Pink'

H. m., Lacecap, 'Hobella'

H. m., Lacecap, 'Love You Kiss'

H. m., Lacecap, 'Maculata'

H. m., Lacecap, 'Mariesii'

H. m., Lacecap, 'Mariesii Perfecta'

H. m., Lacecap, 'Zaunkönig'

Hydrangea macrophylla, Lacecap, 'Lilacina'

flowerheads; **'Nigra'**, distinctive black stems, small flowerheads from pink to blue depending on soil pH; **'Nikko Blue'** ★, growing to 5 ft (1.5 m), blue flowers; **'Parzifal'**, flowers from deep pink to deep blue, depending on soil type; **'Pia'**, very dwarf form growing slowly to only 2 ft (0.6 m), flowers ranging from pink to red; **'President Doumer'**, rich cherry red flowers in small clusters on top of small, dark green, serrated leaves; **'Soeur Thérèse'**, growing up to 6 ft (1.8 m) tall, a pure white variety that is best grown in shade in order to prevent scorching.

LACECAP CULTIVARS

'Fireworks Pink', double, star-shaped, pink florets around outer edge of each flowerhead, in autumn new flowers opening while older ones become green; **'Geoffrey Chadbund'**, flowerheads in shades of magenta; **'Hobella'**, soft pink flowers ageing to green, then to cherry red; **'Lanarth White'**, pure white flowers; **'Libelle'**, stunning heads of white sterile florets surrounding deep blue fertile flowers; **'Lilacina'**, lavender-purple flowerheads; **'Love You Kiss'**, large white flowerheads, each petal with a red margin, red-tinted leaves; **'Mariesii'**, pale pink to light blue flowers; **'Sea Foam'**, excellent for coastal planting—flowerheads up to 12 in (30 cm) across, consisting of white sterile florets surrounding mauve to blue fertile flowers. Zones 5–11.

Hydrangea paniculata
PANICLE HYDRANGEA

☼/☀ ✲ ↔ 10 ft (3 m) ↑ 6–20 ft (1.8–6 m)
Deciduous species from Japan and southeastern China. Conical flowerheads, densely packed, creamy white sterile and fertile flowers, often create an arching shape, in late summer–autumn. **'Grandiflora'**, creamy white sterile flowers on panicles up to 18 in (45 cm) long; **'Kyushu'**, smaller bush with dainty airy panicles of creamy white sterile and fertile flowers; **'Praecox'**, early-flowering cultivar; **'Tardiva'**, late-flowering cultivar; **'Unique'**, round-ended panicles larger than those of 'Grandiflora'. Zones 3–10.

Hydrangea paniculata

H. paniculata 'Kyushu'

H. paniculata 'Praecox'

H. paniculata 'Tardiva'

H. paniculata 'Unique'

Hydrangea quercifolia, summer

Hydrangea quercifolia, autumn

Hydrangea serrata 'Bluebird'

Hydrangea petiolaris ★

syn. *Hydrangea anomala* subsp. *petiolaris*

☼ ❄ ↔ 17–35 ft (5–10 m) ↑ 50 ft (15 m)

Climbing hydrangea from Russia, Korea, Taiwan, and Japan. Attractive dark green leaves; flowers with large lacecap blooms at start of the season. May take several years to bear flowers. Do not prune. Often treated as a subspecies of *H. anomala.* Zones 4–9.

Hydrangea quercifolia

OAK-LEAFED HYDRANGEA

☼/◗ ❄ ↔ 8 ft (2.4 m)
↑ 3–8 ft (0.9–2.4 m)

Deciduous shrub, loosely rounded in shape, from southeastern USA. Large, lobed, green leaves turn crimson in

Hydrangea serrata 'Preziosa'

Hydrangea serrata 'Preziosa'

autumn. In summer, creamy white flowers on conical panicles, to 10 in (25 cm) long, take on pinkish shades as autumn approaches. Cultivars include: 'Snow Flake', double flowers; 'Snow Queen', larger sterile florets than the species, exceptional autumn foliage colors. Zones 5–10.

Hydrangea scandens

☼ ❄ ↔ 36–40 in (90–100 cm)
↑ 36–40 in (90–100 cm)

Deciduous arching shrub from East Asia, including Japan. Lance-shaped leaves to 3½ in (9 cm) long and flattish, small, lacecap-style flowerheads with very few bracted flowers. Zones 9–10.

Hydrangea serrata 'Grayswood'

Hydrangea serrata

syn. *Hydrangea macrophylla* subsp. *serrata*

☼/◗ ❄ ↔ 5 ft (1.5 m)
↑ 3–6 ft (0.9–1.8 m)

Deciduous species from Japan and Korea, closely related to *H. macrophylla.* Flat-topped flowerheads, sterile florets of white, pink, or blue surrounding white or blue fertile flowers, in summer, color changing with age. 'Bluebird', neat shrub with lacecap flowers of pale and rich blue, carried for a long time, foliage turning red in autumn; 'Grayswood', attractive flowerheads with bluish purple fertile flowers surrounded by sterile florets, changing color to shades of white, pink and crimson; 'Preziosa', growing up to 5 ft (1.5 m) with distinctive reddish stems, red-flushed leaves, small globular flowerheads changing color from creamy white through shades of pink to reddish purple. Zones 6–10.

Hydrangea serratifolia

syn. *Hydrangea integerrina*

☼/◗ ❄ ↔ 7–17 ft (2–5 m)
↑ up to 35 ft (10 m)

Woody deciduous climber from Chile. Clings to structures with its sticky aerial roots. Dark green serrated leaves in late spring. Clean white flowerheads in masses in mid-summer. Flowers can be tinged pink. Zones 6–9.

HYDRASTIS

This genus, a member of the buttercup (Ranunculaceae) family, contains only 2 species of low-growing perennial herbs, one native to Japan and the other to eastern North America. The North American species is often grown for the medicinal properties of its roots, and Native Americans used it as a dye.

CULTIVATION: It grows best in conditions similar to its natural habitat—the forest floor. Give it a shady position with rich moist soil that has been enriched with leafmold. Add more leafmold or similar organic matter every year. Propagate from seed or by division.

Hydrastis canadensis

EYE ROOT, GOLDENSEAL, GROUND RASPBERRY, INDIAN DYE, JAUNDICE ROOT, ORANGEROOT, TURMERIC, YELLOW PUCCOON

☼ ❄ ↔ 8 in (20 cm) ↑ 12 in (30 cm)

This perennial woodland herb comes from eastern North America. Each of its stems carries 2 large, serrated, 5-lobed, wrinkled leaves; in spring, small white flowers bloom in the middle of the leaves, and raspberry-like fruit, in the form of a cluster of red berries, follows in summer. Listed as an endangered species. All parts are poisonous. Zones 6–8.

Hylocereus undatus, with epiphytic bromeliad on stem, Jardín Botánico Lankester, Costa Rica

HYLOCEREUS

A genus of 18 species of climbing night-flowering cacti, in the Cactaceae family, from southern Mexico, the Caribbean, Central America, and northern South America. These clambering, climbing, or epiphytic plants produce aerial roots and may reach 35 ft (10 m) wide and 7–10 ft (2–3 m) long. Usually stems have only 3 sides, are segmented, green to bluish green, with a horny margin. Spines are absent or few, and always small. Flowers are very large, nocturnal, white, rarely red. Floral tubes are strong with large naked scales. Seedpods are spherical to oval, usually red. CULTIVATION: Easily grown in a compost-rich well-drained soil. May be raised from seed but are usually propagated from cuttings dried out for a week or two. Rest in winter.

Hylocereus undatus ★
DRAGON FRIT, QUEEN OF THE NIGHT
☀ ❄ ↔ 15–25 ft (4.5–8 m) ↑ 17 ft (5 m)
Of uncertain origin, long cultivated as an ornamental for its spectacular flowers and delicious fruits. Sprawling, climbing, producing many stout, 3-angled, jointed stems, with a wavy horny margin. Has 1 to 3 spines, short, conical, brown to gray, 3 mm long. Flowers from sides of stems, white, 10–12 in (25–30 cm) long. Seedpods spherical to oval, bright red, with large often green scales, edible. Zones 10–11.

HYMENOCALLIS
syn. *Ismene*
SACRED LILY OF THE INCAS, SPIDER LILY
Some members of this bulbous, perennial, tropical and semi-tropical genus from Central and South America, in the amaryllis (Amaryllidaceae) family, were once classified as *Ismene*, and the name persists in horticulture. The distinctive and dramatic, well-held flowers have a central narcissus-like

Hymenocallis littoralis, in the wild, Cahuita National Park, Costa Rica

cup encased by long, narrow, recurved, or streamer-like petals. The name comes from the Greek *hymen* (membrane) and *kallos* (beauty), referring to the membrane that unites the stamens. CULTIVATION: The group divides neatly into deciduous and evergreen species. The deciduous ones require a dry dormancy and a sunlit or semi-shaded position, whereas the evergreen species, which have clivia-like leaves, thrive in damp, fertile, shaded soil. Plant with the bulb's neck protruding. Propagation is from offsets or fresh ripe seed. Clumps can be divided in winter.

Hymenocallis × *festalis* ★
☀ ❄ ↔ 12–24 in (30–60 cm)
↑ 24–32 in (60–80 cm)
Common in horticulture. Up to 4 flowers at right angles to the stout stem, pure white, fragrant, cup with spidery swept-back outer segments, in late spring in seasonal climates, otherwise spasmodic. Stamens golden. Leaves clump-forming, deciduous, dark green, long and broad. Give them rich soil, warm humid summers, and a dry dormancy. Zones 9–11.

Hymenocallis littoralis
syn. *Hymenocallis americana*
☀/☀ ❄ ↔ 30–60 in (75–150 cm)
↑ 27–36 in (70–90 cm)
From central South America. Robust. Flowers 4 to 8 borne in umbel; white, long-tapering streamer-like reflexed petals surround a flattened cup. Leaves evergreen, 48 in (120 cm) long, semi-erect, clump-forming, fleshy, tapering at both ends, bright green. 'Variegata', bright green central stripe on leaves margined with cream. Zones 10–12.

Hymenocallis narcissiflora
SACRED LILY OF THE INCAS
☀ ❄ ↔ 12–24 in (30–60 cm)
↑ 20–24 in (50–60 cm)
From the Peruvian Andes, growing in stony fields to 9,840 ft (3,000 m) above sea level. Flower a long daffodil-like cup, filaments stand out like aeroplane propellers, very fragrant, white with touches of green, held well above the foliage. Flower stem emerges from 12 in (30 cm) false stem. Leaves deciduous, strap-like. 'Advance', slightly elongated cup lobes, robust, pure white version of species. Zones 9–11.

Hymenocallis speciosa
☀/☀ ❄ ↔ 12–24 in (30–60 cm)
↑ 18–20 in (45–50 cm)
From the West Indies. Flowers white, fragrant, open umbels, filaments splayed outward. Anthers protruding, golden. Broad leaves evergreen, glossy, to 24 in (60 cm) long. Zones 10–12.

Hymenocallis 'Sulphur Queen'
☀ ❄ ↔ 12–20 in (30–50 cm)
↑ 20–24 in (50–60 cm)
Scented hybrid cultivar. Cross between yellow-flowering Peruvian *H. amancaes* and *H. narcissiflora*. Narrow leaves to 20 in (50 cm) long. Very large primrose yellow cup and white filaments. Zones 8–10.

Hymenosporum flavum

HYMENOSPORUM
Consisting of a single evergreen tree species, this genus in the pittosporum (Pittosporaceae) family is from subtropical areas of Australia's east coast where grows in rainforests. Cultivated for many years for its creamy white flowers, which turn yellow as they age, it is a slender, often open tree with mid-green shiny foliage. CULTIVATION: Though it likes a spot in full sun, it can grow in part-shade but may not flower as profusely. Moist humus-enriched soil will suit this plant as it does not like to be deprived of moisture when conditions are dry. Propagate from seed or cuttings.

Hymenosporum flavum
NATIVE FRANGIPANII
☀ ❄ ↔ 12 ft (3.5 m) ↑ 30 ft (9 m)
Slender tree. Light foliage coverage, widely spaced horizontal branches bearing shiny deep green leaves. Fragrant cream blossoms ageing to yellow, in spring. Zones 9–11.

HYOSCYAMUS
HENBANE
This genus contains 15 species of annual, biennial or perennial, downy, sticky and fetid herbs in the nightshade (Solanaceae) family that are native to western Europe, North Africa, and central and southwestern Asia. Leaves are alternate, gray-green, covered with short glandular hairs, oblong to lance-shaped. Flowers are tubular to bell-shaped, 5-lobed, pale yellowish brown with purple veins and throat, borne in leafy racemes or spikes. The fruit is an egg-shaped 2-chambered capsule with many brown to gray seeds. *H. niger* has been used medicinally for centuries and is commercially cultivated in Europe for its alkaloid compounds. All parts are toxic to humans and animals when ingested. CULTIVATION: Grow in full sun in moist, fertile, well-drained soil. Propagate from seed.

Hyoscyamus niger
BLACK HENBANE, HENBANE, HOG'S BEAN, JUSQUAIME, STINKING NIGHTSHADE
☀ ❄ ↔ 16–36 in (40–90 cm)
↑ 16–36 in (40–90 cm)
Coarse erect or prostrate annual or biennial herb from Europe with alternate, irregularly cut, oval- to sword-shaped leaves to 8 in (20 cm) long. Flower spike with nearly stemless flowers and funnel-shaped corollas to 1¼ in (30 mm) wide, purple-veined olive to green to dull yellow, spring–autumn. Fruit is a black capsule, 12 in (12 mm) in diameter. Zones 3–5.

Hypericum adenotrichum

Hypericum androsaemum

Hypericum ascyron

H. androsaemum 'Dart's Golden Penny'

Hypericum beanii

HYPERICUM

Belonging to the St John's-wort (Clusiaceae) family, this genus has more than 400 species of deciduous, semi-evergreen and evergreen annuals, herbaceous perennials, shrubs and trees. They occur worldwide in various habitats, and have simple smooth-edged leaves in opposite pairs and usually yellow 5-petalled flowers with a central bunch of many stamens. Some are used locally as medicinal plants. CULTIVATION: Most will thrive in sun or partial shade in good garden soil. *H. calycinum* takes root along its prostrate branches in dry shade, but also does well in partial shade. *H. olympicum* is a good rock-garden plant, and needs sharp drainage. Most North American species prefer damper conditions. Evergreen species are best sheltered from cold drying winds. Propagate by sowing seed in autumn, though seed may not come true. Take softwood cuttings in spring, half-hardened cuttings in summer.

Hypericum cerastioides

Hypericum adenotrichum

☀ ❄ ↔ 12–15 in (30–38 cm) ↑ 4–12 in (10–30 cm)

Native to Turkey. Perennial with stems erect to prostrate, sometimes rooting at nodes. Small oblong leaves. Starry golden yellow flowers, to 1 in (25 mm) across, in summer. Zones 7–10.

Hypericum androsaemum
TUTSAN

☀ ❄ ↔ 3 ft (0.9 m) ↑ 30 in (75 cm)

Native to western, southwestern Europe, the Mediterranean to the Caucasus. Deciduous shrub, leaves oblong to broadly egg-shaped, mid-green above, paler below. Star-shaped yellow flowers, mid-summer–autumn. Fruits ripen to red and black. Used for cut flowers. Invasive weed in Australia and New Zealand. *H. a.* f. *variegatum*, variegated pink and white foliage; *H. a.* 'Albury Purple', purple-tinged leaves; 'Dart's Golden Penny', bright yellow flowers, long stamens. Zones 6–9.

Hypericum ascyron
syn. *Hypericum pyramidatum*
GIANT ST JOHN'S WORT, GREAT ST JOHN'S WORT

☀ ❄ ↔ 12–30 in (30–75 cm) ↑ 2–5 ft (0.6–1.5 m)

Native of Asia, Russia, and northeastern North America. Variable perennial

Hypericum forrestii

with shiny pointed leaves, paler beneath. Starry bright yellow flowers, to 3 in (8 cm) wide, have very prominent stamens. Summer flowering. Zones 3–9.

Hypericum balearicum

☀ ❄ ↔ 10 in (25 cm) ↑ 10 in (25 cm)

From the Balearic Islands. Evergreen, densely branched shrub, characterised by its warty glandular stems and leaves. Leaves oblong to egg-shaped, wavy edges. Solitary, star-shaped, golden yellow flowers, in summer. Zones 7–9.

Hypericum beanii

☀ ❄ ↔ 6 ft (1.8 m) ↑ 2–6 ft (0.6–1.8 m)

Native to Yunnan and Guizhou Provinces in China. Vigorous, evergreen bushy shrub. Mid-green leaves, elliptic to lance-shaped, with pale undersides. Golden yellow flowers, bowl- to star-shaped, in summer. Zones 7–10.

Hypericum calycinum
AARON'S BEARD, CREEPING ST JOHN'S WORT, ROSE OF SHARON

☀ ❄ ↔ 5 ft (1.5 m) ↑ 8–24 in (20–60 cm)

Native to parts of Bulgaria and Turkey. Evergreen or semi-evergreen shrub, rooting branches. Elliptic or oblong leaves, dark green above, paler below. Bright yellow flowers, from mid-summer to autumn. Flowers better in light shade—a good ground cover plant for dry shade. Zones 6–9.

Hypericum cerastioides
syn. *Hypericum rhodoppeum*

☀ ❄ ↔ 18 in (45 cm) ↑ 6–12 in (15–30 cm)

From southern Bulgaria, Greece, and Turkey. Variable perennial, erect or

Hypericum calycinum

forming loose mats. Small oblong leaves, slightly hairy. Open golden yellow flowers 1 in (25 mm) wide, in summer. Zones 7–10.

Hypericum empetrifolium

☀ ❄ ↔ 3 ft (0.9 m) ↑ 2 ft (0.6 m)

Native to southeastern Europe, Turkey, and Libya. Dwarf, cushion-forming evergreen shrub. Narrow leaves mid-green in whorls of 3. Cylindrical cymes of up to 40 golden yellow star-shaped flowers, in summer. *H. e.* subsp. *oliganthum* (syn. *H. e.* var. *prostratum* of gardens), 2 in (5 cm) tall with cymes of 4 to 7 deep yellow flowers. Zones 8–9.

Hypericum forrestii
syn. *Hypericum patulum* var. *forrestii*

☀ ❄ ↔ 4 ft (1.2 m) ↑ 1–5 ft (0.3–1.5 m)

Native to northeastern Myanmar, and northwestern Yunnan and southwestern Sichuan Provinces in China. Bushy deciduous shrub. Mid-green leaves, paler green underneath, turning red, in autumn. Cymes of golden yellow bowl-shaped flowers, in summer–autumn. Zones 5–9.

Hypericum 'Hidcote'

☀ ❄ ↔ 4 ft (1.2 m) ↑ 4 ft (1.2 m)

Likely cross between *H.* × *cyathiflorum* 'Gold Cup' and *H. calycinum*. Dense evergreen or semi-evergreen shrub. Leaves dark green, lance-shaped. Large, bowl-shaped, deep yellow flowers, summer–autumn. Zones 7–10.

Hypericum × *inodorum*

☀ ❄ ↔ 4 ft (1.2 m) ↑ 2–7 ft (0.6–2 m)

Natural hybrid between *H. androsaemum* and *H. hircinum* from north-western Mediterranean. Deciduous shrub, 1–4 in (2.5–10 cm) long, ovate to lance-shaped leaves. Scentless flowers to 1 in (25 mm) wide. Zones 8–10.

Hypericum kouytchense

syns *Hypericum grandiflorum*, *H. patulum* var. *grandiflorum*

☀ ❄ ↔ 4 ft (1.2 m) ↑ 6 ft (1.8 m)

From Guizhou Province, China. Semi-evergreen. Leaves dark blue-green. Cymes of up to 11 star-shaped golden yellow flowers, in summer. Red fruit. Showy stamens. Zones 6–10.

Hypericum kouytchense

Hypericum lancasteri

Hypericum orientale

Hypericum 'Hidcote'

Hypericum lancasteri

☀ ❄ ↔ 3 ft (0.9 m) ↑ 3 ft (0.9 m)

Native of northern Yunnan and southern Sichuan in China. Deciduous shrub, purple-red young growth. Leaves oblong to triangular lance-shaped, mid-green in color. Cymes of yellow bowl- or star-shaped flowers, in summer. Zones 7–10.

Hypericum × *moserianum*

☀ ❄ ↔ 24–32 in (60–80 cm) ↑ 12–16 in (30–40 cm)

Attractive, arching, semi-deciduous garden hybrid with lance-shaped leaves to 2 in (5 cm) long and yellow flowers to 2½ in (6 cm) across throughout summer and autumn. Usually grown in variegated form 'Tricolor', which has green leaves broadly edged with yellow and stained pink. Zones 7–10.

Hypericum olympicum

☀ ❄ ↔ 15 in (38 cm) ↑ 10 in (25 cm)

Native to Greece and the southern Balkans. Dwarf deciduous shrub.

Hypericum olympicum

Oblong, elliptic gray-green leaves, glaucous undersides. Cymes of 5 golden yellow star-shaped flowers, in summer. *H. o.* f. *uniflorum* 'Citrinum' has pale citron flowers. Zones 6–10.

Hypericum orientale

☀ ❄ ↔ 18–24 in (45–60 cm) ↑ 10–18 in (25–45 cm)

Variable perennial from Turkey and the Caucasus. Erect or spreading stems, sometimes rooting. Small narrow leaves with golden gland-tipped margins. Starry yellow flowers, to 1 in (25 mm) wide, in summer. Zones 7–10.

Hypericum prolificum

☀ ❄ ↔ 5 ft (1.5 m) ↑ 6 ft (1.8 m)

Loosely branched shrub from central and eastern USA and southern Canada. Leaves narrow, oblong, elliptical or lance-shaped, leaf edges sometimes recurved, undersides, pale waxy bloom. Golden yellow flowers, in summer. Zones 4–9.

Hypericum pseudohenryi

☀ ❄ ↔ 6 ft (1.8 m) ↑ 5 ft (1.5 m)

Native to north Yunnan and central Sichuan Provinces in China. Erect or arching stems. Leaves paler green undersides, with a white bloom. Golden yellow star-shaped flowers, in summer. Young fruit is red. Zones 6–9.

Hypericum 'Rowallane'

☀ ❄ ↔ 4 ft (1.2 m) ↑ 6 ft (1.8 m)

Semi-evergreen shrub, believed to be a chance hybrid between *H. leschenaultii* and *H. hookerianum* 'Charles Rogers'. Leaves egg-shaped, oblong to lance-shaped, dark green above, paler green and crinkly underneath. Rich golden flowers in small cymes, late summer–autumn. Zones 8–10.

Hypericum prolificum

Hypericum × *moserianum*

Hypericum pseudohenryi

Hypericum 'Rowallane'

Hypericum stellatum

Hypericum stellatum

☀ ❄ ↔ 10 ft (3 m) ↑ 3–10 ft (1–3 m)

Native to northeastern Sichuan Province in China. Spreading shrub. Flowers on the tips of branches in lax groups of golden stars, sometimes tinged red, in summer. Zones 6–9.

HYPHAENE

This is a genus of 10 or more shrubby or tree-like solitary palms (family Arecaceae), unusual in that they develop forked trunks. Native to tropical regions around the Indian Ocean, they have fan-shaped leaves and clusters of large, smooth, oval, orange to brown, sweet-smelling, edible fruits.
CULTIVATION: Both drought and frost resistant, they prefer light or sandy well-drained soils, an open sunny spot and hot dry climates. Propagate from seed, which can be hard to germinate.

Hyphaene coriacea

EAST AFRICAN DOUM PALM, ITALA PALM

☀ ❄ ↔ 10 ft (3 m) ↑ 15 ft (4.5 m)

Native of southeastern Africa and Madagascar. Solitary or suckering palm. Roughly scarred trunk branches distinctively grayish green, glaucous, waxy, fan-shaped leaves to 3 ft (1 m) in diameter, spiky leaf stalks. Pear-shaped fruit to 2½ in (6 cm) long. Zones 10–12.

Hyphaene thebaica
EGYPTIAN DOUM PALM, GINGERBREAD PALM
☀ ❄ ↔ 15 ft (4.5 m) ↑ 20–30 ft (6–9 m)
Native of the Nile region of Africa.
Branching stem, rigid erect leaves to
3 ft (1 m) long. Leaves, deeply lobed,
form a fan-like appearance. Pear-
shaped orange-brown fruit, to 3 in
(8 cm) across; edible mealy flesh and
young leaf shoots. Zones 10–12.

HYPOESTES
An acanthus (Acanthaceae) family
genus of 40 perennials, subshrubs and
shrubs from open woodland regions
of South Africa, Madagascar, and
Southeast Asia. Some decoratively
foliaged species are used as indoor
plants or grown as annuals in cooler
areas; others are valued for their
autumn flowers. Evergreen, the leaves
are held opposite on upright stems and
in some species are velvety to touch.
CULTIVATION: Grow in humus-
enriched well-drained soil. Water
freely in summer but keep drier in the
cold months when growth is not
apparent. These half-hardy plants do
well in part-shade with protection
from drying winds. Propagate in
spring from seed, or from stem cuttings taken from spring to summer.

Hypoestes aristata
RIBBON BUSH
☀ ❄ ↔ 26 in (65 cm) ↑ 3 ft (0.9 m)
Evergreen shrubby plant, upright
stems. Downy mid-green leaves.

Hyphaene thebaica

Hyphaene coriacea, in the wild, Kenya

Masses of small purple flowers in
the upper leaf axils, in autumn. Prune
after flowering. Zones 9–11.

Hypoestes phyllostachya
POLKA-DOT PLANT
☀ ❄ ↔ 30 in (75 cm) ↑ 3 ft (0.9 m)
Subshrub grown for its pink-speckled
green leaves, widely used as an indoor
plant in cold areas. Soft tender stems,
becoming woody near the base. Tip
pruning ensures a well-covered bushy
plant. 'Splash', larger pink markings.
Zones 10–12.

HYPOXIS
STAR GRASS, STARFLOWER
With a wide habitat—through North
America, Africa, Australia, and tropical
Asia—only a few of this large (about
150 species) perennial genus of low-
growing cormous plants in the starflower (Hypoxidaceae) family have
been cultivated. The upturned star-
like flowers, which open in sunlight,
are composed of radiating petals, the
outer 6 being wider than the inner
ones. Roots are fibrous and emerge
from an annual corm. Leaves are
linear, grass-like, and often hairy.
CULTIVATION: Grow in light, well-
drained soil and in sunlight. Dry off
after flowering. Root disturbance is
resented, as is frost, but many species
can be grown through fine grass and,
in appropriate climates, be established
in lawns and rock gardens. Propagate
from offsets or fresh ripe seed.

Hypoxis acuminata
☀ ❄ ↔ 12 in (30 cm) ↑ 24 in (60 cm)
Widely distributed through the eastern half of South Africa. Yellow flowers
in spring–summer. Zones 8–11.

Hypoxis capensis
WHITE STAR GRASS
☀ ❄ ↔ 8–24 in (20–60 cm)
↑ 8–24 in (20–60 cm)
Perennial from South Africa. Leaves
4–12 in (10–30 cm) long. Solitary
white or yellow flowers, spotted purple
at center, on stems 2–10 in (5–25 cm)
long, in spring–summer. Zones 9–11.

Hypoxis hirsuta
☀ ❄ ↔ 2 in (5 cm) ↑ 4–8 in (10–20 cm)
From eastern North America. Flowers
up to 7 per stem, yellow with greenish
backs, spring–summer. Leaves basal,
hairy, ribbed, semi-erect. Zones 5–6.

HYSSOPSUS
This genus in the mint (Lamiaceae)
family contains 10 species of perennials or small shrubs. The opposite
leaves are lance-shaped and aromatic.

Hypoestes aristata

Hypoestes phyllostachya

Hypoxis hirsuta

Hypoxis acuminata, in the wild, North
West Province, South Africa

Hyssopsus officinalis 'Sissinghurst'

Rather sparse flower spikes bear the
2-lipped tubular flowers. *H. officinalis*
has in the past been used in asthma
and bronchitis remedies.
CULTIVATION: Grow in well-drained
soil in a sunny situation. *H. officinalis*
can be used as a low hedge. Pinch
growing tips to encourage bushiness.
Propagate from seed or cuttings.

Hyssopsus officinalis
HYSSOP
☀ ❄ ↔ 12 in (30 cm)
↑ 18–24 in (45–60 cm)
From southern and eastern Europe.
Naturalized in USA. Variable shrubby
perennial with aromatic foliage. Violet
to blue flowers carried on thin spikes
in late summer. 'Sissinghurst' has a
dwarf, compact habit. Zones 3–10.

HYSTRIX
This genus, of the grass (Poaceae)
family, has 9 species in Asia, North
America, and New Zealand. These tall
upright grasses adapt to a wide range
of conditions but do best in part to

complete shade. They bloom in
early to late summer, and their straw-
colored seed heads give summer
and autumn interest to a woodland
garden. They also mix well with spring
ephemerals, filling in when they go
dormant. *Hystrix* in Greek means
hedgehog or porcupine—the seed
heads are said to resemble their quills.
CULTIVATION: Grow in dry to
medium moist soil in half-sun to
shade. They prefer a sandy loamy soil,
though will tolerate a wide variety of
soils. They are easily grown from seed
and will self-seed in optimum growing conditions.

Hystrix patula
BOTTLEBRUSH GRASS
☀/❂ ❄ ↔ 12 in (30 cm)
↑ 24–60 in (60–150 cm)
From North America. Perennial
woodland grass that produces lovely
seed heads, which resemble a bottlebrush. Seed heads are green maturing
to brown, and are retained well into
autumn. Zones 3–6.

I

Iberis gibraltarica

Iberis saxatilis subsp. *cinerea*

IBERIS
CANDYTUFT

Popular for the bold effect of their massed heads of white, pink, mauve, or purple flowers, the 30-odd annuals, perennials, and subshrubs in this genus in the cabbage (Brassicaceae) family are found from western and southern Europe to western Asia. They usually have simple, small, narrow leaves; when not flowering they form a rounded bush. Their flowerheads open in summer, on short stems holding them clear of the foliage. *Iberis* refers to Iberia, the Roman name for Spain; candytuft means "the tufted plant

from Candia," a former name for the island of Crete.
CULTIVATION: Plant in a sunny position with light yet moist, well-drained soil. A light dressing of dolomite lime is appreciated. Deadhead regularly to encourage continuous blooming. Propagate the annuals from seed and the perennials and subshrubs from seed or small cuttings.

Iberis amara
☼/◑ ✿ ↔ 12–20 in (30–50 cm) ↕ 12 in (30 cm)
Western European summer-flowering annual. Small, lance-shaped, sometimes toothed leaves often hidden under massed heads of white, pink, or purple flowers. Sow in succession as blooms are not always long-lasting. Zones 10–11.

Iberis gibraltarica
GIBRALTAR CANDYTUFT
☼/◑ ❄ ↔ 20–24 in (50–60 cm) ↕ 12 in (30 cm)
Evergreen summer-flowering subshrub from Gibraltar. Forms a neat mound of narrow stems with rosettes of small

Iberis umbellata, Flash Mixed cultivar

leaves at tips. Heads of white, lavender, or pink-tinted flowers. May be used as annual. Zones 7–10.

Iberis saxatilis
☼/◑ ❄ ↔ 12–20 in (30–50 cm) ↕ 6 in (15 cm)
Small, spreading, evergreen subshrub found from the Pyrenees to Sicily. It has narrow, fleshy, rather succulent leaves, fringed with fine hairs. The heads of white flowers, purple-tinted with age, appear in summer. *I. s.* subsp. *cinerea* has silver-gray foliage and stems. Zones 7–10.

Iberis sempervirens
☼/◑ ❄ ↔ 20–24 in (50–60 cm) ↕ 12 in (30 cm)
Spreading evergreen subshrub from southern Europe with small oblong leaves, mainly clustered at the stem tips. Flowerheads to 2 in (5 cm) wide, usually white, from spring–summer. 'Flore-Plena', compact habit, double flowers; 'Purity', to 8 in (20 cm) high; 'Schneeflocke' ★ (syn. 'Snowflake'), low-growing, dark foliage, glowing silvery white flowers; 'Weisser Zwerg' (syn. 'Little Gem'), compact habit, 6 in (15 cm) high, early white flowers. Zones 7–10.

Iberis umbellata
☼/◑ ❄ ↔ 16 in (40 cm) ↕ 12 in (30 cm)
Annual from southern Europe. The very narrow lance-shaped leaves are sometimes toothed. Produces purple flowers from spring–summer. The flower colors of **Flash Mixed Series** include white, all shades of pink,

mauve, red, and purple. Grow from autumn-sown seed in mild areas; summer annual elsewhere. Zones 7–10.

IBICELLA
DEVIL'S CLAW

Native to South America and introduced to the southern USA, this genus of 3 annual species belongs to the sesame (Pedaliaceae) family. They are spreading plants with rounded, flat, sticky leaves and a spiky "clawed" seed capsule, hence their common name. *I. lutea* was once thought to be carnivorous following experiments conducted in 1916. Later research has shown that although insects do get stuck on the sticky leaves, there is no evidence as yet that the plant actually digests the insects.
CULTIVATION: Grow in full sun/half-sun in the garden in warm climates or in ordinary potting mix with some sand or perlite added to the mix. Water well and let the soil dry out a little before rewatering. Propagate from seed, which may take a while to germinate; pricking the seed assists germination.

Ibicella lutea
☼/◑ ✤ ↔ 4 ft (1.2 m) ↕ 24 in (60 cm)
Scrambler from subtropical South America, with rounded, green, 6 in (15 cm) long leaves, and a thick green stem. Fine sticky hairs on leaves and stem. Bell-shaped yellowish green flowers, 2 in (5 cm), from spring–summer. Zones 9–11.

IDESIA
WONDER TREE

The sole species in this genus in the governor's-plum (Flacourtiaceae) family is a medium-sized deciduous tree found naturally in Japan, Korea, Taiwan, and nearby parts of China. Its large foliage makes it an excellent shade tree. Bright red berries hang in large pendulous clusters long after the foliage has fallen. The flowers are unisexual but the plants are debatably dioecious: so-called female plants often bear fruit without the presence of male plants, though fruiting is better with a cross-pollinator.

Iberis sempervirens 'Purity'

Iberis sempervirens 'Flore-Plena'

Iberis sempervirens

Iberis sempervirens 'Weisser Zwerg'

Idesia polycarpa

Idesia polycarpa

☼ ❀ ↔ 35 ft (10 m) ↑ 50 ft (15 m)

Usually fairly upright tree, with a rounded crown. Deep green leaves, heart-shaped, to 8 in (20 cm) long, red leaf stalks. Flowers tiny, in large sprays, yellow-green, mildly fragrant. Sealing wax red berries on bare branches. Zones 6–10.

ILEX

HOLLY

Widely distributed genus, belonging to the holly (Aquifoliaceae) family, and containing more than 400 species of evergreen or deciduous trees, shrubs, and climbers. Used for its foliage and berries since Roman times, holly has long been associated with Northern Hemisphere festivals celebrating the winter solstice and Christmas. Wood of some species is used for veneers and musical instruments; leaves are used as tea substitutes or in tisanes. Male and female flowers usually grow on separate trees, thus plants of both sexes are required for the production of berries.

CULTIVATION: Although reasonably frost hardy, *Idesia* can be severely damaged by late spring frosts that arrive after the foliage has expanded. It prefers a climate with a warm summer, a long autumn, and a short winter without late frosts. While the soil should be well drained, the tree will cope with most soil types. Prune foliage to shape when young, otherwise trim lightly after the fruit has fallen. Propagate from the seed or from half-hardened cuttings.

CULTIVATION: North American hollies prefer neutral to acid soils, while the Asian and European species will grow in most soils that are moderately fertile, well drained, and humus-rich. Green hollies will also grow in part- or full shade (but not deep shade). Variegated hollies require a position in full sun for best effect. Propagate from half-hardened cuttings in late summer or early autumn. Seed germination may take 2 or 3 years. Tender species need greenhouse protection in winter in colder climates.

Ilex × *altaclerensis*

HIGHCLERE HOLLY

☼ ❀ ↔ 20 ft (6 m) ↑ 70 ft (21 m)

Hybrid group of evergreen trees or shrubs of garden origin, a cross between *I. aquifolium* and *I. perado*. They are more robust than *I. aquifolium*, and their leaves are larger and broader. The berries are mostly red. These hybrids tolerate coastal situations and pollution better than most. They are good shrubs for hedging and windbreaks.

'Camelliifolia' has stems with purple hue, and red berries; 'Golden King', dark green leaves edged in yellow; 'Hendersonii', vigorous tree, with brown-red berries; 'Lawsoniana', female, compact shrub with yellow-streaked stems, gold and green markings in centers of leaves, lighter green background, brownish red berries; 'Platyphylla' with broad, glossy, dark green, spine-toothed leaves; 'Purple Shaft', columnar in habit, vigorous, fruits profusely. Zones 6–10.

Ilex × *altaclerensis* 'Platyphylla'

Ilex × *altaclerensis* 'Camelliifolia'

Ilex × *altaclerensis* 'Lawsoniana'

Ilex aquifolium

COMMON HOLLY, ENGLISH HOLLY

☼ ❄ ↔ 25 ft (8 m) ↑ 40–80 ft (12–24 m)

Occurs over southern and western Europe, North Africa, and western Asia. Glossy dark green leaves, elliptic, spine-toothed edges. The male and female flowers usually borne on separate trees. Berries red, sometimes yellow or orange. The cultivars include: 'Amber', a female cultivar, to 20 ft (6 m) tall, bright green leaves, amber berries; 'Argentea Marginata', a female cultivar, with dark green leaves edged in creamy white; 'Argentea Marginata Pendula' (syn. 'Argentea Pendula'), a weeping female tree with spiny, cream-margined, elliptic leaves; 'Ferox Argentea', spiny leaves with cream margins; 'Handsworth New Silver', a female clone, with elongated, spiny, cream-edged leaves, dark purple stems; 'J. C. van Tol', a broad female tree, with dark green leaves, and scarlet berries; 'Madame Briot', a vigorous female form, which has egg-shaped dark green leaves with gold margins, and vivid red fruit; 'Pyramidalis', a self-fertile cultivar, yellowish green stems, and spiny bright green leaves; 'Pyramidalis Fructu Luteo', a female conical shrub or small tree, with yellow berries; 'Silver Milkmaid', a female cultivar, pale green to yellow stems, spiny mid-green leaves with silver-white markings. Other popular cultivars include: 'Aurifodina', 'Bacciflava', 'Gold Flash', 'Golden Milkboy', and 'Silver Queen'. Zones 6–10.

Ilex × aquipernyi

☼ ❄ ↔ 12 ft (3.5 m) ↑ 20 ft (6 m)

Evergreen tree or shrub of garden origin, hybrid between *I. aquifolium* and *I. pernyi*. Elongated glossy green leaves, strong spines. Red berries. 'San Jose' ★, female form, green leaves with up to 9 spines. Red fruit. Zones 6–10.

Ilex aquifolium

Ilex aquifolium 'Aurifodina'

Ilex aquifolium 'Bacciflava'

I. aquifolium 'Golden Milkboy'

Ilex aquifolium 'Silver Milkmaid'

Ilex aquifolium 'Argentea Marginata Pendula'

Ilex aquifolium 'Ingramii'

Ilex aquifolium 'Madame Briot'

Ilex aquifolium 'Wateriana'

Ilex aquifolium 'Aurea Marginata'

Ilex aquifolium 'Winter Queen'

I. a. 'Handsworth New Silver'

I. a. 'Handsworth New Silver'

I. aquifolium 'Rubricaulis Aurea'

Ilex × *attenuata*

TOPAL HOLLY

☀ ❄ ↔ 6 ft (1.8 m) ↑ 12 ft (3.5 m)

Evergreen conical shrub, natural hybrid between *I. cassine* and *I. opaca*. Light green, egg- to lance-shaped leaves, dark red berries. '**East Palatka**', female tree, pyramidal, light green leaves with single spine at tip, red berries; '**Foster No. 2**', heavy fruiting female, conical habit, small dark green leaves, spine at tip, red berries; '**Sunny Foster**', slow-growing female, narrow in habit, some golden yellow leaves, bright red berries. Zones 7–10.

Ilex cassine

DAHOON HOLLY

☀ ❄ ↔ 15 ft (4.5 m) ↑ 40 ft (12 m)

Evergreen tree, native to Cuba and southeastern USA. Pointed or rounded, glossy, dark green leaves with pronounced midrib, leaf edges smooth or toothed near the apex. Yellow or red berries. Zones 6–10.

Ilex ciliospinosa

☀ ❄ ↔ 12 ft (3.5 m) ↑ 20 ft (6 m)

Evergreen upright shrub, native to western China. Narrow, pointed, dull dark green leaves, weakly spined. Red berries. Zones 5–9.

Ilex cornuta

CHINESE HOLLY, HORNED HOLLY

☀ ❄ ↔ 6–12 ft (1.8–3.5 m) ↑ 6–12 ft (1.8–3.5 m)

Native to China and Korea. A dense, evergreen, rounded shrub. Oblong dark green leaves, variable spines. Large red berries, long-lasting. '**Burfordii**', free-fruiting, female form, red berries, leaves with terminal spines; '**Dwarf Burford**', to 10 ft (3 m) high, dense habit, dark red berries. Zones 6–10.

Ilex crenata

JAPANESE HOLLY

☀ ❄ ↔ 12 ft (3.5 m) ↑ 15 ft (4.5 m)

Evergreen shrub or small tree from Korea, Japan, and Sakhalin Island. Small deep green leaves, minutely scalloped. Flowers white; fruit mainly glossy black, sometimes white or yellow. '**Convexa**' (syn. '**Bullata**'),

Ilex crenata 'Sky Pencil'

female, purple-green stems, abundant black fruit; '**Golden Gem**', compact female, to 3 ft (0.9 m) high, golden yellow leaves, prefers full sun; '**Helleri**', spreading female shrub, dark green leaves, black fruit; '**Ivory Tower**', female, late-ripening white fruit; '**Mariesii**' (syns *I. c.* var. *nummularioides*, *I. mariesii*), very slow growing, dark green leaves, black fruit; '**Shiro Fukurin**' (syns '**Fukarin**', '**Snow Flake**'), upright female, rounded leaves with cream markings, black fruit; and '**Sky Pencil**', narrowly columnar female. Zones 6–10.

Ilex decidua

POSSUMHAW, WINTERBERRY

☀ ❄ ↔ 6–15 ft (1.8–4.5 m) ↑ 6–20 ft (1.8–6 m)

Native to southeastern and central USA. Upright deciduous shrub, rarely a tree. Mid-green leaves, sprout in late spring, oval or egg-shaped, scalloped,

Ilex crenata

crowded on short lateral spurs. Berries orange or red, sometimes yellow, last well into winter. Zones 6–10.

Ilex dimorphophylla

OKINAWAN HOLLY

☀ ❄ ↔ 3 ft (0.9 m) ↑ 5 ft (1.5 m)

Restricted in the wild to the Ryukyu Islands of Japan. Evergreen rounded shrub. Juvenile plant very spiny. Oval, glossy, dark green leaves tipped with a spine when mature. Tiny red berries. Zones 7–10.

Ilex dipyrena

HIMALAYAN HOLLY

☀ ❄ ↔ 35 ft (10 m) ↑ 50 ft (15 m)

Native to the eastern Himalayas and western China, and closely related to *I. aquifolium*. Foliage on young plants and suckers very spiny, less so as the plant matures. Dark green leaves, oblong to elliptic, leathery texture. Red berries. Zones 7–10.

Ilex dipyrena

Ilex cornuta 'Burfordii'

Ilex glabra f. *leucocarpa* 'Ivory Queen'

Ilex glabra

GALLBERRY, INKBERRY

☀ ❄ ↔ 10 ft (3 m) ↑ 10 ft (3 m)

Erect evergreen shrub from eastern North America. Glossy dark green leaves, almost smooth-edged, slightly toothed near the apex. Berries round, black. Shallow rooting. *I. g.* f. *leucocarpa* bears white fruit; '**Ivory Queen**' is a popular form. *I. g.* '**Compacta**' ★, to 4 ft (1.2 m) high, denser foliage than species, black berries. Zones 3–9.

Ilex kingiana

syn. *Ilex insignis*

☀ ❄ ↔ 12 ft (3.5 m) ↑ 15 ft (4.5 m)

Native to the eastern Himalayas and Yunnan Province, China. Silver-gray branches; glossy green leaves, lance- to egg-shaped, smooth-edged, slightly toothed when mature. Suckers and juvenile plants very spiny, waxy foliage. Green-yellow flowers, bright red berries. Zones 8–10.

Ilex × *attenuata* 'Sunny Foster'

Ilex cassine

Ilex decidua

Ilex × *koehneana*

Ilex macropoda

Ilex mitis

Ilex × *meserveae* 'Blue Girl'

Ilex × *koehneana*

☀ ❄ ↔ 12 ft (3.5 m) ↑ 20 ft (6 m)

Evergreen shrub or tree, hybrid between *I. aquifolium* and *I. latifolia*. Strongly resembles *I. latifolia*, but more spiny; sometimes wrongly sold as that plant. Zones 7–10.

Ilex latifolia

TARAJO

☀ ❄ ↔ 12 ft (3.5 m) ↑ 20 ft (6 m)

Evergreen narrow shrub from Japan and China. Glossy dark green leaves, oblong to egg-shaped, smooth-edged or toothed with spines. Flowers greenish yellow, in late spring. Orange-red berries. Zones 7–9.

Ilex macropoda

☀ ❄ ↔ 10–17 ft (3–5 m)
↑ 30–35 ft (9–10 m)

Deciduous tree from Japan, Korea, and China. Serrated leaves to 3 in (8 cm) long. Female trees produce red berries, to ¼ in (6 mm) across, after the tiny white flowers. Closely related to *I. verticillata*. Zones 7–10.

Ilex × *meserveae*

BLUE HOLLY, HYBRID BLUE HOLLY,
MESERVE HOLLY

☀ ❄ ↔ 10 ft (3 m) ↑ 6–15 ft (1.8–4.5 m)

Of garden origin, a hybrid between *I. aquifolium* and *I. rugosa*. The small, often blue-green are leaves similar to those of *I. aquifolium* but smaller. The red berries are borne on female plants. '**Blue Angel**' is a compact female shrub, slow-growing, to 12 ft (3.5 m) high, with royal purple stems, and blue-green leaves; it is least hardy; '**Blue Boy**', male, grows up to 10 ft (3 m) high; '**Blue Girl**' is female and produces red berries; '**Blue Maid**'is a dense female shrub with red berries; '**Blue Prince**', male shrub with lustrous bright green leaves; '**Blue Princess**', female shrub with prolific red berries. Zones 6–10.

Ilex opaca

Ilex mitis

CAPE HOLLY

☀ ❄ ↔ 20 ft (6 m) ↑ 30 ft (9 m)

Thick-trunked evergreen tree from wetter regions of southern and eastern Africa. Smooth-edged leaves, oblong to lance-shaped; juvenile foliage red. White flowers, from spring–summer. Red berries. Zones 8–11.

Ilex montana

☀ ❄ ↔ 10 ft (3 m) ↑ 40 ft (12 m)

Native to eastern USA. Deciduous shrub or small tree. Leaves sharply toothed, lance to egg-shaped. Bears white flowers, red berries. *I. m.* var. *mollis*, leaves with hairy undersides. Zones 5–9.

Ilex opaca

AMERICAN HOLLY

☀ ❄ ↔ 35 ft (10 m) ↑ 50 ft (15 m)

From USA. Leaves oblong to elliptic, smooth-edged or spiny, matt green above, yellow-green beneath. White flowers. Red, orange, or yellow berries. *I. o.* f. *xanthocarpa*, yellow berries. *I. o.* '**Hedgeholly**', hardy, compact; '**Morgan Gold**', golden fruit; '**Old Faithful**', large berries; less hardy. Zones 5–9.

Ilex opaca 'Old Faithful'

Ilex verticillata 'Afterglow'

Ilex serrata

Ilex verticillata

Ilex verticillata 'Nana'

Ilex verticillata f. *aurantiaca*

Ilex pedunculosa

☼ ❋ ↔ 20 ft (6 m) ↑30 ft (9 m)

Evergreen tree found in China, Japan, and Taiwan. The glossy dark green leaves are egg-shaped with pointed tips, smooth-edged and spineless. This species bears white flowers and red fruits. Zones 5–9.

Ilex perado

CANARY ISLAND HOLLY

☼ ❋ ↔ 20 ft (6 m) ↑20–30 ft (6–9 m)

Evergreen upright shrub or small tree native to the Azores and the Canary Islands. It has glossy dark green leaves, oblong or lance-shaped, leathery. The

fruit is red. *I. p.* subsp. *platyphylla* has broad, glossy, dark green, spine-toothed leaves. Zones 7–9.

Ilex pernyi

PERNY'S HOLLY

☼ ❋ ↔ 12 ft (3.5 m) ↑30 ft (9 m)

From Gansu and Hubei Provinces in China. Evergreen shrub, smaller in cultivation. Almost stalkless, dark green leaves, triangular to rectangular. Yellow flowers, in late spring, Red berries. Prefers a moisture-retentive soil. Zones 5–10.

Ilex purpurea

syn. *Ilex chinensis*

☼ ❋ ↔ 12 ft (3.5 m) ↑40 ft (12 m)

Evergreen conical tree, native to Japan and China. The thinly textured dark green leaves, elliptic to lance- or egg-shaped, scalloped edges. Juvenile leaves purplish green. Flowers lavender or red. Glossy scarlet berries. Zones 8–10.

Ilex pernyi

Ilex serrata

FINETOOTH HOLLY, JAPANESE WINTERBERRY

☼ ❋ ↔ 10 ft (3 m) ↑15 ft (4.5 m)

Native to Japan and China. Bushy deciduous shrub, purple new twigs. Finely toothed, oval, dark green leaves, downy coating on both surfaces. Pink flowers, small red berries. Zones 5–10.

Ilex verticillata

BLACK ALDER, WINTERBERRY

☼ ❋ ↔ 15 ft (4.5 m) ↑15 ft (4.5 m)

Deciduous shrub from eastern North America. Bright green leaves, obovate or lance-shaped, toothed, fine downy undersides. White flowers, red, yellow, or orange berries. *I. v.* f. *aurantiaca*,

Ilex pedunculosa

orange berries. *I. v.* '**Afterglow**', female shrub, orange-red berries; '**Nana**' (syn. 'Red Sprite'), female shrub, needs early-flowering male for pollination; '**Winter Red**' ★, female shrub, dark green leaves, red berries. Zones 3–9.

Ilex vomitoria

CAROLINA TEA, YAUPON

☼/◐ ❋ ↔ 12 ft (3.5 m) ↑20 ft (6 m)

Evergreen shrub or small tree, native to southeastern USA and Mexico. Glossy dark green leaves, elliptic to egg-shaped, scalloped edges. White flowers, red berries. '**Nana**', to 3 ft (0.9 m) high; '**Pendula**', lax branches, clear red fruit. Zones 6–10.

Ilex vomitoria 'Pendula'

Ilex perado subsp. *platyphylla*

Ilex Hybrid Cultivars

☀ ❄ ↔ 5–15 ft (1.5–4.5 m)
↕ 8–20 ft (2.4–6 m)

Hollies have been extensively hybridized. Some of the best cultivars are 'China Boy', very hardy male pollinator, grows quickly to 8 ft (2.4 m) tall; 'China Girl', very hardy, female, evergreen shrub, masses of bright red berries; 'Ebony Magic', female clone, evergreen leaves with a wavy margin and up to 22 spines, leaf stems almost black, orange-red berries; 'John T. Morris', male form, dark evergreen foliage, a good pollinator; 'Nellie R. Stevens', evergreen female, orange-red berries; 'September Gem', female evergreen hybrid, narrow dark green leaves, red berries; and 'Sparkleberry', deciduous female shrub, bright red berries. Zones 6–10.

ILLICIUM

This genus of over 40 evergreen shrubs and trees in the star-anise (Illiciaceae) family is found in moist shaded areas of India, East Asia, and the Americas. Leaves and flowers are fragrant, and members of the genus supply aromatic oils used in some perfumes. *I. verum* is the source of the Chinese spice, star-anise. These trees were originally included in the same genus as magnolias because of their resemblance to them. Flowers range in color from cream to reddish purple and are followed by

Ilex, Hybrid Cultivar, 'John T. Morris'

Ilex, Hybrid Cultivar, 'Sparkleberry'

Ilex, Hybrid Cultivar, 'Nellie R. Stevens'

Illicium floridanum, fruit

star-shaped fruit. Leaves are deep green. The genus name comes from the Latin for "allurement," in reference to the perfume of some species. CULTIVATION: *Illicium* species will survive in full sun but do best in a sheltered position out of direct sunlight, in a moist, well-drained, acid soil. Propagate from half-hardened cuttings taken in summer or by layering in autumn.

Illicium anisatum

ANISE SHRUB, JAPANESE ANISE, JAPANESE STAR-ANISE

☀ ❄ ↔ 20 ft (6 m) ↕ 25 ft (8 m)

Conical evergreen shrub from China, Taiwan, and Japan. Aromatic wood, leaves, and bark. Greenish yellow flowers, in mid-spring. Woody fruits are poisonous; the alkaloid concentrated in the seed has been used to kill fish. Variegated form available. Zones 7–11.

Illicium anisatum

Illicium floridanum

FLORIDA ANISE TREE, POLECAT TREE, PURPLE ANISE

☀ ❄ ↔ 8 ft (2.4 m) ↕ 10 ft (3 m)

Aromatic, bushy, evergreen shrub from southeastern States of USA. Slightly furrowed, smooth, dark brown trunk. Slender, leathery, deep green leaves. Showy, star-shaped, reddish purple flowers, from late spring–early summer. 'Album', white flowers; 'Halley's Comet', large red flowers; 'Variegatum', variegated leaves; 'Woodland Ruby' ★, reddish pink flowers. Zones 8–11.

Illicium henryi

☀ ❄ ↔ 10 ft (3 m) ↕ 25 ft (8 m)

Native of central and western China. Evergreen shrub or small tree. Slender leaves, 6 in (15 cm) long. Cupped flowers, copper to dark red, in late spring. Zones 8–11.

Illicium mexicanum

☀ ❄ ↔ 7–8 ft (2–2.4 m) ↕ 7–8 ft (2–2.4 m)

Rare species from Mexico. Very similar to *I. floridanum*, with flowers about twice as large, to 3 in (8 cm) across, with more and narrower petals. Zones 8–10.

Illicium parviflorum

☀ ❄ ↔ 7–10 ft (2–3 m) ↕ 7–10 ft (2–3 m)

North American species. Foliage strongly scented, bright green. Inconspicuous yellow flowers, about ½ in (12 mm) across. Zones 7–10.

Illicium verum

CHINESE ANISE, STAR ANISE

☀ ❄ ↔ 20 ft (6 m) ↕ 60 ft (18 m)

Native of China and North Vietnam, smaller in cultivation. Star-shaped fruits used for spice and medicine. Leaves are lance-shaped, with a prominent midvein. Flowers whitish yellow, turning deep pink or purple-red, in early summer. Glossy brown fruits. Zones 8–11.

Illicium mexicanum

IMPATIENS

BALSAM, BUSY LIZZIE, WATER FUCHSIA

The type genus giving its name to the balsam (Balsaminaceae) family is home to around 850 species of annuals, perennials, and subshrubs found worldwide except in Australasia, South America, and the polar regions. These are generally soft-stemmed plants with simple, pointed, lance-shaped leaves, often with toothed edges. Flowers in many colors appear through the year in mild areas and have 5 petals, an upper standard and the lower 4 fused into 2 pairs, the sepals also partly fused to form a spur. When ripe the seed pods explosively eject their contents at the slightest touch, hence the genus name from the Latin for "impatient." CULTIVATION: Grow the annuals as summer plants in cooler climates outside the recommended zones; perennials need mild winter conditions. Provide shade from the hottest sun and plant in deep, cool, moist, humus-rich soil. Feed well. Propagate annuals from seed, the perennials also by cuttings. Some species self-sow and are slightly invasive.

Impatiens balsamina

BALSAM

☀/☀ ✦ ↔ 12 in (30 cm) ↕ 27 in (70 cm)

Vigorous upright annual from East Asia. Toothed lance-shaped leaves. Flowers to nearly 2 in (5 cm) wide, clustered, in many colors, mainly

Impatiens, New Guinea Hybrid, 'Celebrette Hot Pink'

Impatiens, New Guinea Hybrid, 'Improved Quepos'

Impatiens, New Guinea Hybrid, 'Celebration Light Lavender'

pink, mauve to red shades. Conspicuous seed pods burst when ripe. Garden seedling strains include: **Camellia-flowered Series**, large double flowers; and **Tom Thumb Series**, low-growing double-flowered. Zones 10–12.

Impatiens cristata

☀/☀ ⚘ ↔ 12 in (30 cm) ↑ 24 in (60 cm)
Annual from the Himalayas. Pointed oval leaves, serrated, to 3 in (8 cm) long. Small clusters of yellow and cream flowers spotted with golden brown. Zones 9–11.

Impatiens cristata

Impatiens niamniamensis

Impatiens hawkeri

☀/☀ ⚘ ↔ 16–40 in (40–100 cm)
↑ 3–7 ft (0.9–2 m)
Shrubby, continuous-flowering, evergreen perennial from New Guinea and Solomon Islands. Heavy fleshy stems; pointed oval to lance-shaped leaves, toothed, usually red or red-tinted. Long-spurred flowers to over 3 in (8 cm) wide, white, or pink, red, and purple shades. Zones 10–12.

Impatiens New Guinea Hybrids

☀/☀ ⚘ ↔ 16–40 in (40–100 cm)
↑ 18–48 in (45–120 cm)
These are usually cultivars of *I. hawkeri* or hybrids with *I. linearifolia*. They generally resemble *I. hawkeri* but are available in many striking combinations of flower and foliage, such as: **'Celebration Light Lavender'**, with mauve flowers and mid-green leaves; **'Celebrette Hot Pink'** with vivid magenta flowers and mid-green leaves; **'Improved Quepos'**, bright reddish flowers, dark red-tinted green leaves; **'Pascua'**, deep pink flowers, mid-green leaves; **'Sarchi'**, deep magenta flowers, dark green leaves; **'Tagula'**, pale pink flowers with red upper petal, dark green leaves; **'Tango'** ★, bright orange flowers, bronze-green leaves; **'Timor'**, deep orange-red flowers, red-tinted bright green leaves; and **Velvetea/ 'Secret Love'**, which produces white flowers with orange spotting, the enlarged lower petals have a yellow base, the central petals are edged with an orange-red. Zones 10–12.

Impatiens, New Guinea Hybrid, 'Pascua'

Impatiens, New Guinea Hybrid, 'Sarchi'

Impatiens, New Guinea Hybrid, 'Tagula'

Impatiens, New Guinea Hybrid, 'Timor'

Impatiens niamniamensis

☀/☀ ⚘ ↔ 16 in (40 cm) ↑ 36 in (90 cm)
Continuous-flowering evergreen perennial from tropical east Africa. Deeply toothed leaves. Large, heavy-textured, long-spurred, deep red flowers with yellow upper petal. Zones 10–12.

Impatiens pseudoviola

☀/☀ ⚘ ↔ 24–48 in (60–120 cm)
↑ 12 in (30 cm)
Continuous-flowering, semi-trailing, mounding, evergreen perennial from

Impatiens pseudoviola

tropical east Africa. Leaves small, finely toothed, rounded leaves, under 1 in (25 mm) long. White to bright pink flowers. Zones 10–12.

Impatiens 'Seashell Yellow'

☀/☀ ⚘ ↔ 20 in (50 cm) ↑ 12 in (30 cm)
American-raised, first commercially available yellow-flowered hybrid, between *I. walleriana* and *I. auricoma*. It has a compact bushy habit, bright green lance-shaped leaves, and bright yellow flowers in small clusters. **'African Queen'** is a similar cultivar. Zones 10–12.

Impatiens sodenii

☀/☀ ⚘ ↔ 3–7 ft (0.9–2 m)
↑ 3–7 ft (0.9–2 m)
Shrubby evergreen perennial from tropical east Africa. Whorls of toothed lance-shaped leaves. Long-stemmed flowers to over 2 in (5 cm) wide, in lavender and pink shades or white, in summer. Zones 10–12.

Impatiens sodenii

Imperata cylindrica 'Rubra'

Impatiens walleriana

☀/☀ ✿ ↔ 8–20 in (20–50 cm)
↕ 8–24 in (20–60 cm)

Continuous-flowering, shrubby, ever-green, tropical east African perennial; often treated as annual. Fleshy, succulent stems; toothed lance-shaped leaves, often red-tinted. Spurred flat-faced flowers, evenly sized petals; most colors except yellow and blue. Cultivars and seedling strains include: **'Blackberry Ice'**, double purple-red flowers; **Carousel Mix**, rosebud doubles in wide range of colors; **Dazzler Series**, many single flowers in warm pastel shades; **Deco Series**, spreading, single flowers in all shades; **Fiesta Series**, rosebud double flowers in many shades including bicolors; **Garden Leader Series** comes in a wide range of colors; **Ice Series**, white-marked foliage, rosebud double flowers in all shades; **Merlot Series**, bright green foliage, single flowers in all colors; **Super Elfin Series**, very compact, single flowers in all shades; **Tempo Series**, large flowers, compact evenly sized plants; **'Victorian Rose'**, semi-double deep pink flowers, spreading habit. Zones 10–12.

IMPERATA

This genus in the grass (Poaceae) family, from warmer regions around the world, consists of about 8 species of perennial grasses with deep long-running rhizomes and erect tufts of long flat leaves. Tiny flowers are crowded into a plume-like spike topping a slender stalk; seeds are like thistledown, dispersed by the wind. They can form dense stands after removal of forest cover and often dominate the ground layer after fires; in some areas they are regarded as very troublesome weeds, though at the same time they may stabilize denuded soils on slopes. Some colored-leafed forms of *I. cylindrica* are grown only for ornamental value.
CULTIVATION: The ornamental forms may be grown in containers and are also suitable for waterside planting. Plant in fertile, moist, well-drained soil in full sun. Propagate from seed or by division of rhizomes.

Imperata cylindrica

BLADY GRASS, COGON GRASS, KUNAI GRASS
☀ ✿ ↔ 8–12 in (20–30 cm)
↕ 24–72 in (60–180 cm)

Perennial grass from Japan. Flat, semi-erect, narrow leaves to 20 in (50 cm) long. Silvery white panicles to 8 in (20 cm) long, sword-shaped spikelets. **'Rubra'** ★ (syn. 'Red Baron'), leaves tinted wine red, scarlet in autumn. Zones 8–12.

INCARVILLEA

This group of 14 species from central and eastern Asia includes annuals and perennials, some of which are slightly woody, and belongs in the trumpet-vine (Bignoniaceae) family. Depending on which species you plant, they can make exotic-looking rock-garden or border plants with an almost tropical look that is unusual in such cold-hardy species. The flowers are trumpet-shaped with flared and often undulated edges, and are usually a bright pink to magenta, although yellow forms have been discovered. Most species have a long flowering period, which means that they pay for their space; besides the decorative value of the flowers, the foliage is usually also attractive.

Impatiens walleriana 'Dazzler Merlot Mix'

I. walleriana, Fiesta Series, 'Burgundy Rose'

I. walleriana, Fiesta Series, 'Salmon Sunrise'

I. walleriana, Fiesta Series, 'Salsa Red'

I. walleriana, Fiesta Series, 'Sunrise'

I. walleriana, Garden Leader Series, 'Coral'

I. walleriana, Garden Leader Series, 'Coral'

I. walleriana, Garden Leader Series, 'Fuchsia'

I. walleriana, Super Elfin Series, 'Blue Pearl'

I. walleriana, Super Elfin Series, 'Blush'

Impatiens walleriana, variegated form

Impatiens walleriana 'Victorian Rose'

Incarvillea arguta

CULTIVATION: Grow in moisture-retentive but not wet soils in a position sheltered from the hottest afternoon sun. Propagate from fresh seed or by careful division, although established plants resent disturbance.

Incarvillea arguta

☼ ❋ ↔ 12–16 in (30–40 cm)
↑ 36–40 in (90–100 cm)

Slightly shrubby species from the Himalayas and western China. Compound leaves to 8 in (20 cm) long. The flowers are rich pink, sometimes white, and trumpet-shaped, 1½ in (35 mm) long, and appear in the late spring to autumn. Zones 8–10.

Incarvillea delavayi

☼ ❋ ↔ 12–16 in (30–40 cm)
↑ 20–24 in (50–60 cm)

Rosette-forming species from western China. Long compound leaves. Up to 10 large rich pink trumpets per stem, to 3 in (8 cm) across, with a yellow throat, held above the foliage, in early to mid-summer. 'Snowtop', white with a yellow throat. Zones 6–9.

Incarvillea emodi

☼ ❋ ↔ 12–16 in (30–40 cm)
↑ 16–20 in (40–50 cm)

Rosette-forming perennial from Afghanistan, Pakistan, and into northern India. Large leaves; stems of deep pink trumpets with a yellow throat, each bloom 2½ in (6 cm) long. Spring-flowering. Zones 7–9.

Incarvillea mairei ★

☼ ❋ ↔ 10–12 in (25–30 cm)
↑ 16–20 in (40–50 cm)

Small perennial from China and Nepal. Prominent tap root, wrinkled leaves to 10 in (25 cm) long. Rich deep pink flowers with yellow and white throat, 2½ in (6 cm) across, produced in small numbers per stem. Zones 4–9.

Incarvillea emodi

INDIGOFERA

The source of the purple-blue dye indigo, this genus in the pea-flower subfamily of the legume (Fabaceae) family includes some 700 species of perennials, shrubs, and a few trees that are widespread in the tropics and subtropics. Foliage varies but is typically pinnate, often made up of many small leaflets. The flowers are primarily in pink, mauve, and purple shades, carried in long racemes or spikes. They usually open in summer but may occur year-round in mild climates. Small seed pods follow.
CULTIVATION: The shrubby species are usually neat bushes, often deciduous, that vary in hardiness depending on their origins. They generally grow best in full sun with light well-drained soil and ample summer moisture. If necessary, prune after flowering or in late winter. Propagate from seed or half-hardened cuttings. Many species produce suckers that can be replanted.

Indigofera amblyantha

☼ ❋ ↔ 8 ft (2.4 m) ↑ 6 ft (1.8 m)

Chinese deciduous shrub. Pinnate leaves spread widely on wiry branches, 7–11 leaflets. Racemes of pale pink to red flowers, in the leaf axils, in late spring–autumn. Zones 5–9.

Indigofera australis

AUSTRALIAN INDIGO

☼ ⚘ ↔ 6 ft (1.8 m) ↑ 6 ft (1.8 m)

Evergreen from Australia. Foliage pinnate, 9–21 blue-green leaflets, to 1 in (25 mm) long, hairy undersides. Racemes of mauve-pink to magenta-red flowers, in summer. Brown seed pods. Zones 9–11.

Indigofera australis

Indigofera cylindrica

TREE INDIGO

☼ ⚘ ↔ 6 ft (1.8 m) ↑ 15 ft (4.5 m)

Evergreen shrub or small tree from South Africa. Leaves to 4 in (10 cm) long, 8–14 leaflets, notched at tip. Racemes of small flowers, white, pink, or purple-red. Sometimes confused with *I. frutescens*. Zones 9–11.

Indigofera decora ★

☼ ❋ ↔ 4 ft (1.2 m) ↑ 30 in (75 cm)

Widely cultivated, deciduous, spreading, suckering shrub from China and Japan. Leaves to 8 in (20 cm) long, 25–40 leaflets. Large racemes of light pink flowers, in summer. Zones 6–10.

Indigofera hebepetala

☼ ❋ ↔ 3 ft (0.9 m) ↑ 4 ft (1.2 m)

Native to northwestern Himalayas. Evergreen in mild climates, deciduous to herbaceous if frosted. Leaves to 6–8 in (15–20 cm) long, 5–11 leaflets. Racemes of large pink and red flowers, in summer–autumn. Zones 8–11.

Indigofera heterantha

syn. *Indigofera gerardiana*

☼ ❋ ↔ 8 ft (2.4 m) ↑ 8 ft (2.4 m)

Deciduous shrub from northwestern Himalayas, widely cultivated species, smaller in cultivation. Densely twiggy plant, short pinnate leaves. Massed racemes of bright pink to light red flowers, in summer. Zones 7–10.

Indigofera cylindrica

Indigofera kirilowii

☼ ❋ ↔ 3–6 ft (0.9–1.8 m)
↑ 2–5 ft (0.6–1.5 m)

Deciduous shrub found in Korea, nearby parts of China, and Kyushu, Japan. Pinnate leaves, bright green, 13 leaflets. Smothered in short racemes of rose pink flowers, in spring–early summer. Zones 5–10.

Indigofera potaninii

☼ ❋ ↔ 4 ft (1.2 m) ↑ 3–5 ft (0.9–1.5 m)

Sometimes sold by nurseries as *I. amblyantha*. True species is a deciduous shrub from southwestern China. Differs from *I. amblyantha* in shorter leaves, fewer leaflets, densely hairy below, larger flowers, usually mauve, from summer–autumn. Zones 5–9.

Indigofera tinctoria

☼ ⚘ ↔ 6 ft (1.8 m) ↑ 6 ft (1.8 m)

Most common dye-yielding species, native of Southeast Asia, evergreen shrub. Short pinnate leaves with hairy undersides. Small racemes of pink to light red flowers with a blue keel, through most of the year. Zones 10–12.

Indigofera decora

Indigofera heterantha

INDOCALAMUS

A genus of about 30 species of bamboo in the grass (Poaceae) family, native to China, Japan, and Malaysia. They have thin culms that branch up to 3 times and large leaves that in some species are so heavy as to make the culms arch over towards the ground. Not commonly grown bamboos, these are elegant plants that will give a tropical look to the garden. They make excellent ground covers or fine erect specimens of pillar-like growth for shady courtyards, or understory planting to specimen trees. CULTIVATION: The hardier species usually encountered prefer a position in half-sun with humus-rich moist soil, although they are reasonably drought tolerant once established. They spread by underground runners and can become invasive, so a trench or other root barrier may be desirable; they can also be pot grown by the truly nervous. Propagate by division in early spring.

Inula grandiflora

Indocalamus tessellatus

☀ ❄ ↔ 7–20 ft (2–6 m) ↑ 3–6 ft (0.9–1.8 m)
From central China and Japan. This species has the largest leaves of any hardy bamboo, 24 in (60 cm) wide by 4 in (10 cm) long. Pendulous culms, ½ in (12 mm) in diameter, form mound-like habit. *I. t.* var. *hamada*, from Japan, to 10 ft (3 m) high, thicker foliage. Zones 8–10.

INGA

A member of the pea-flower sub-family of the legume (Fabaceae) family, this genus of over 300 ever-green trees and shrubs is native to tropical and subtropical parts of the Americas. Larger specimens can grow to over 70 ft (21 m) and are valuable shade trees, being used to provide shelter for coffee plantations while maintaining soil fertility and preventing erosion. The flowers, which can be a feature, are white or whitish and are held on heads or stalks. Seeds are produced in pods and in some species are surrounded by a sweet edible pulp. CULTIVATION: If grown in tropical areas, these trees will thrive on benign neglect. They succeed in a variety of soils from acid to alkaline. In cooler temperate areas they require a green-house or conservatory heated in winter. In temperate areas they need plentiful water in summer and a dry winter. Propagate by sowing the seed fresh (within a month of maturity) or from half-hardened cuttings.

Inula helenium

Inga paterno

Inga edulis

ICE-CREAM BEAN

☀ ✿ ↔ 35 ft (10 m) ↑ 60 ft (18 m)
Large quick-growing tree from the West Indies and Mexico through to subtropical South America. Brilliant green leaves; heads of fragrant white flowers, at tips of stems. Long bean-shaped seed pods contain a sweet white pulp, eaten or used as flavoring. Zones 10–12.

Inga paterno

☀/☀ ✿ ↔ 20 ft (6 m) ↑ 35 ft (10 m)
Native to Central America; adapted to seasonally dry conditions. Very finely divided, doubly pinnate leaves, red-tinted when young. White flowers in the dry season in native habitat, late winter elsewhere. Seed pods 6–20 in (15–50 cm) long. Zones 10–12.

INULA

Members of this large genus in the daisy (Asteraceae) family are found in a wide range of habitats, from dry mountainsides to moist shaded sites, from Europe through to subtropical Africa and Asia. Most are herbaceous perennials, with some biennials and annuals, the perennial species being those most commonly grown. Some can be invasive. The basal leaves tend to be largest, the leaves reducing in size towards the top of the stems. All have yellow daisy flowers produced mainly in summer. *I. helenium* is often grown in herb gardens for its medicinal properties. CULTIVATION: Despite the range of habitats from which they originate, most species like a sunny aspect and rich moist soil. The dwarf species are suited to the larger rock garden, while the taller species can be planted in the wilder parts of the garden or amongst other perennials in the border. Propagation is from seed or by division.

Inula ensifolia

☀ ✿ ↔ 10–12 in (25–30 cm) ↑ 16–24 in (40–60 cm)

Bushy, clumping, thin-stemmed perennial from the Caucasus region. Narrow, stalkless, mid-green, bristly leaves, to 4 in (10 cm) long. Masses of yellow daisy flowers. Zones 5–10.

Inula grandiflora

syns *Inula glandulosa*, *I. orientalis*
☀ ✿ ↔ 36–40 in (90–100 cm) ↑ 20–24 in (50–60 cm)

Almost shrubby species from the Caucasus region. Smooth-edged leaves, to 5 in (12 cm) long, yellow to brown hairs, densely covered in minute glands. Yellow daisy flowers, to 3 in (8 cm) across. Zones 6–10.

Inula helenium

ELECAMPANE

☀/☀ ✿ ↔ 3–4 ft (0.9–1.2 m) ↑ 8–10 ft (2.4–3 m)

Tall, robust, somewhat invasive species from temperate Eurasia. Roots used to make an expectorant. Large hairy lower leaves, to 27 in (70 cm) long, serrated and undulating edges. Spikes of yellow daisy flowers. Zones 5–10.

Inula hookeri

☀ ✿ ↔ 20–24 in (50–60 cm) ↑ 24–30 in (60–75 cm)

Clump-forming herbaceous perennial from the Himalayas. Bright green lance-shaped leaves, to 6 in (15 cm) long. Yellow daisy flowers, to 3 in (8 cm) across. Zones 6–10.

Inula magnifica

syn. *Inula afghanica*
☀ ✿ ↔ 3–5 ft (0.9–1.5 m) ↑ 5–6 ft (1.5–1.8 m)

Robust, impressive, herbaceous peren-nial from Caucasus region. Large, deep green, basal leaves, to 10 in (25 cm) long, hairy beneath. Large open clus-ters of yellow daisies. Zones 6–10.

IOCHROMA

These large-leafed evergreen shrubs from Central America and Andean South America have a rather lax habit with long brittle branches. Although there are around 15 species within this genus, only 5 or 6 are generally used in horticulture. The soft foliage of most species is a downy mid-green. In common with other members of the nightshade (Solanaceae) family, the late summer flowers, usually held in clusters of drooping tubular blooms, are in shades of purple, orange, red, and white.

CULTIVATION: These plants need a sunny position with wind protection to ensure their quick-growing soft-stemmed branches are not damaged. Plant in well-drained moisture-retentive soil and ensure they are given ample water during summer. Suitable for pot culture in cooler areas. They can be pruned to shape in early spring without undue loss of blossom. Propagate from cuttings or seed.

Iochroma australe

☀ ❄ ↔ 7–10 ft (2–3 m)
↑ 10–15 ft (3–4.5 m)

More or less evergreen shrub from northern Argentina. Leaves to 4 in

Iochroma australe

Iochroma coccineum

(10 cm) long. Rich purple-blue, drooping, flared, trumpet-shaped flowers, to 2½ in (6 cm) long, throughout summer–autumn. Zones 9–11.

Iochroma coccineum

☀ ❄ ↔ 6 ft (1.8 m) ↑ 10 ft (3 m)

Soft-stemmed shrub from Central America. Soft, gray-green, felty leaves. Produces small clusters of tubular scarlet flowers with a yellow throat, in summer. Zones 9–11.

Iochroma cyaneum

syn. *Iochroma tubulosum*

☀ ❄ ↔ 5 ft (1.5 m) ↑ 10 ft (3 m)

Quick-growing well-clothed shrub from northwestern South America. Large felty leaves, sometimes partly obscuring the purple tubular flowers held in large pendent clusters, in summer. Zones 9–11.

Iochroma grandiflorum

☀ ❄ ↔ 6 ft (1.8 m) ↑ 8 ft (2.4 m)

From Ecuador. Downy green leaves. Large purple flowers, in clusters of 5 or 6, in summer–autumn. Adds an interesting dimension to the warmly sited garden. Zones 9–11.

IPHEION

In the past this genus, a member of the onion (Alliaceae) family, was incorporated in *Brodiaea*, *Triteleia*, and *Milla*, and some confusion remains in common horticulture. Some botanists have proposed *Ipheion* be merged with *Tristogma*. Native to South America, these bulbous perennials give off a strong smell of stale garlic when the leaves are bruised. The starry flowers are upward-facing and prolific.

CULTIVATION: These easy-going lusty plants thrive in well-drained sunny situations in warmer climates, but

Iochroma cyaneum

Ipheion uniflorum 'Wisley Blue'

require protection against frost in colder climates. Keep just moist during dormancy. Propagate from seed in spring or from offsets taken as the foliage dies down.

Ipheion uniflorum

syns *Brodiaea uniflora*, *Tristogma uniflorum*, *Triteleia uniflorum*

SPRING STAR FLOWER

☀ ❄ ↔ 2 in (5 cm) ↑ 6–8 in (15–20 cm)

From Argentina and Uruguay. Robust plant with weedy potential. Leaves mat-forming, linear, grassy, gray-green. Flowers starry, prolific, soap-scented, produced in succession over 6–8 weeks, from mid-winter to mid-spring, opening only during sunlit hours. Petals silvery mauve, palest blue, white, with a pronounced midrib. Summer dormant. 'Alberto Castillo', pleasingly fragrant, large, white flowers; 'Froyle Mill', large deep purple petals; 'Rolf Fiedler', scented flowers, vivid blue, white-throated; 'Wisley Blue', a popular pale blue form, bluish petals, darker midrib. Zones 6–10.

IPOMOEA

This large and variable genus in the bindweed (Convolvulaceae) family, takes its name from the Greek word for a type of worm, because many of

Iochroma grandiflorum

Ipheion uniflorum 'Alberto Castillo'

its members are twining climbers; others are annual or perennial herbs, shrubs, and small trees. Widely cultivated in tropical to warm-temperate areas for their showy flowers and vigorous growth. Some species, including the sweet potato (*I. batatas*), have tuberous roots that are used as food. Flowers appear in the leaf axils and range from bell-shaped to tubular.

CULTIVATION: *Ipomoea* species prefer full sun and plenty of water in the growing season but will make the best of almost any conditions. Species other than annuals may be propagated from softwood or half-hardened cuttings in summer. Seeds are better started under glass. Make sure these plants have plenty of room and cut back after flowering. They may require support.

Ipomoea alba

syns *Calonyction aculeatum*, *Ipomoea bona-nox*

BELLE DE NUIT, MOONFLOWER

☀ ✤ ↔ 20–30 ft (6–9 m)
↑ 10–20 ft (3–6 m)

Found throughout tropical regions. Perennial climber with long-stalked heart-shaped leaves. White saucer-shaped flowers, to 6 in (15 cm) wide, open at night, fragrant. Summer-flowering. Zones 10–12.

Ipomoea horsfalliae

Ipomoea batatas 'Vardaman'

Ipomoea cairica

Ipomoea batatas
KUMARA, SWEET POTATO

☼ ❄ ↔ 10 ft (3 m) ↑ 10 ft (3 m)

Native to tropical regions. Important food crop with edible tubers, usually grown as a prostrate annual. Leaves oval to heart-shaped, lobed or toothed. Tubers have purple, red, or yellow skins, orange or white flesh. '**Blackie**', ornamental variety grown for its purple-black foliage; '**Vardaman**', ornamental dark green foliage, flushed purple when young, orange-fleshed tubers. Zones 9–12.

Ipomoea cairica
syn. *Ipomoea palmata*

☼ ❄ ↔ 10 ft (3 m) ↑ 10 ft (3 m)

From tropical and subtropical regions. Prostrate or climbing plant with tuberous rootstock. Leaves palmately lobed. Funnel-shaped flowers of red, purple, or white, purple interior. Summer-flowering. Zones 9–12.

Ipomoea horsfalliae
CARDINAL CREEPER

☼ ❄ ↔ 5–10 ft (1.5–3 m) ↑ 15–25 ft (4.5–8 m)

Perennial twining climber from the West Indies. The palmate leaves have 3–5 lobes, to 8 in (20 cm) long. Bears large clusters of flared deep pink to purple flowers. Zones 9–12.

Ipomoea indica
syn. *Ipomoea learii*
BLUE DAWN FLOWER, MORNING GLORY

☼ ✦ ↔ 10–30 ft (3–9 m) ↑ 10–30 ft (3–9 m)

Found throughout tropical regions. Vigorous perennial climber regarded

Ipomoea indica

Ipomoea lobata

as a nuisance weed in some areas. Broadly heart-shaped leaves. Funnel-shaped flowers, produced throughout the year, open dark blue or purple, occasionally white, and fade during the day. Zones 10–12.

Ipomoea lobata
syns *Mina lobata*, *Quamoclit lobata*
SPANISH FLAG

☼ ❄ ↔ 3–6 ft (0.9–1.8 m) ↑ 10–15 ft (3–4.5 m)

Native to Mexico. A perennial that is often grown as an annual. Variable smooth or deeply lobed leaves. Produces racemes of small, tubular, scarlet flowers, fade to yellow, giving a two-toned effect. Summer-flowering. Zones 9–12.

Ipomoea mauritiana

☼ ❄ ↔ 6 ft (1.8 m) ↑ 15 ft (4.5 m)

Vigorous perennial woody climber found throughout the tropics. Palmlike leaves, 3–9 lobes. Funnel to bell-shaped pink to maroon flowers, in the leaf axils, darkest in color at base of corolla. Zones 9–12.

Ipomoea × multifida

Ipomoea mauritiana

Ipomoea × multifida
syn. *Ipomoea × sloteri*
CARDINAL FLOWER

☼ ❄ ↔ 3–6 ft (0.9–1.8 m) ↑ 3–10 ft (0.9–3 m)

Of garden origin; hybrid of *I. coccinea* and *I. quamoclit*. Leaves deeply divided, several linear lobes. Funnel-shaped flowers, 1–2 in (25–50 mm) wide, red with white centers, from summer to autumn. Zones 8–12.

Ipomoea nil

☼ ❄ ↔ 2–5 ft (0.6–1.5 m) ↑ 10–15 ft (3–4.5 m)

Found throughout tropical regions. Annual climber with hairy stems. Broadly oval or 3-lobed leaves. Blue funnel-shaped flowers, around 4 in (10 cm) wide, in clusters of 1–5, in summer. '**Chocolate**', pale chocolate brown flowers; '**Scarlett O'Hara**', red flowers. Zones 9–12.

Ipomoea ochracea

☼ ✦ ↔ 5–10 ft (1.5–3 m) ↑ 6–12 ft (1.8–3.5 m)

From the West Indies. Fast-growing perennial climber usually grown as an annual. Heart-shaped leaves. Profuse soft yellow flowers, about 2 in (5 cm) wide, in summer. Zones 10–12.

Ipomoea purpurea
COMMON MORNING GLORY

☼ ❄ ↔ 5–10 ft (1.5–3 m) ↑ 5–10 ft (1.5–3 m)

Vigorous annual climber originally from Mexico, but now naturalized in many countries and often declared as a weed. Stems hairy, leaves whole to

Ipomoea ochracea

lobed, heart-shaped, 4 in (10 cm) wide. Flowers large, trumpet-shaped, in shades ranging from red through to pink, blue, white, and purple, opening in the morning and lasting only a day, from spring–summer. *I. p.* **var.** *diversifolia*, leaves more often 3- to 5-lobed than smooth. Zones 7–11.

Ipomoea tricolor
MORNING GLORY

☼ ❄ ↔ 3 ft (0.9 m) ↑ 10 ft (3 m)

From Mexico and Central America. Annual climber with heart-shaped leaves. Wide funnel-shaped flowers that fade as the day progresses, sky blue, yellow interior base, in summer. **'Heavenly Blue'**, blue flowers, white and yellow throat; **'Minibar Rose'**, rosy crimson, white throat, variegated leaves; **'Tie Dye'**, leaves green, purple, and white. Zones 8–12.

IPOMOPSIS

This genus in the phlox (Polemoniaceae) family, contains 24 species of annuals and perennials that are native to western North America, with outlying species found in Florida and temperate South America. Leaves often form a basal rosette and are either smooth or pinnately divided. The tubular flowers, in shades of red, yellow, pink, white, or violet, are borne in loose racemes in spring and summer. CULTIVATION: In cooler climates they can be grown as temporary summer bedding or in the conservatory or greenhouse. Elsewhere, grow in full sun in fertile well-drained soil. Propagate from seed.

Ipomopsis rubra
syn. *Gilia rubra*
STANDING CYPRESS

☼ ❄ ↔ 18 in (45 cm) ↑ 3–6 ft (0.9–1.8 m)

From South Carolina, Florida and Texas, USA. Erect unbranched perennial or biennial that forms basal rosettes of thread-like leaves. Stems of tubular flowers, scarlet with speckled yellow throats, from summer to autumn. Zones 7–10.

Ipomoea tricolor 'Minibar Rose'

Iresine herbstii 'Brilliantissima'

IRESINE
BLOODLEAF

There are about 80 species of annuals, perennials, and subshrubs in this genus, which belongs to the amaranth (Amaranthaceae) family. They are native to the Americas and Australia. The simple leaves are often brilliantly colored with contrasting veins, and it is for this feature that these plants are cultivated. The spikes of small white or green flowers are of little ornamental significance.
CULTIVATION: Grow outdoors all year round in tropical and subtropical areas. In cooler regions, grow outside in summer. Plant in well-drained moisture-retentive soil in full sun for best leaf coloring. Can be used in summer bedding schemes and in pots, both indoors and outdoors. Pinch growing tips to maintain bushiness. Propagate from cuttings, seed, or by division.

Iresine herbstii
BEEF PLANT, BEEF STEAK PLANT, BLOOD-LEAF

☼ ⚘ ↔ 12–18 in (30–45 cm) ↑ 18–24 in (45–60 cm)

Native to Brazil. Perennial, often renewed annually in cultivation. Green, purple, or red stems. Pointed oval leaves vary in color from deep purple with pink veins to green with yellow veins. **'Aureo-reticulata'**, red stems, green, gold, and red leaves; **'Brilliantissima'**, rich crimson leaves. Zones 9–12.

IRIS

Iris is the type genus for the family Iridaceae, taking its name from the Greek goddess of the rainbow. The

Ipomoea tricolor 'Tie Dye'

Iris afghanica

300-odd species, which are divided into various sections, and scattered over the northern temperate zones, occur in bulbous, rhizomatous, and fibrous-rooted forms. The sword-shaped foliage, often arranged in fans, is sometimes variegated. The flowers have 6 petals, usually in the fleur-de-lis pattern of 3 upright standards and 3 downward-curving falls, which may be bearded, beardless, or crested, and occurring in all colors. Irises have been cultivated for a very long time, since the reign of the Egyptian pharaoh Thutmosis I, around 1500 BC.
CULTIVATION: Bog irises need a sunny position at pond margins or in permanently damp soil. Woodland irises thrive in dappled sunlight with moist well-drained soil. Bearded irises need sun and should be dried off after flowering. Rockery irises require a sunny position in moist, perfectly drained, gritty soil. Propagation is usually by division when dormant, less commonly by seed.

Iris afghanica

☼ ❄ ↔ 6 in (15 cm) ↑ 6–14 in (15–35 cm)

A fleshy-stemmed bearded iris, native to Pakistan and Afghanistan. The leaves are curved. The stems are unbranched, and usually bear solitary flowers. The flowers are creamy white and have purplish brown veins and dark beards. Zones 3–9.

Iris aphylla

☼ ❄ ↔ 6 in (15 cm) ↑ 12 in (30 cm)

Dwarf, bearded, fleshy-stemmed iris, from central and eastern Europe to Russia, with fans of deciduous ribbed leaves. Well-branched flowering stems bear deep purple flowers in spring. Zones 3–9.

Iris bucharica

Iris bracteata

☼ ❄ ↔ 6 in (15 cm) ↑ 8–12 in (20–30 cm)

This fleshy-stemmed beardless iris is native to Oregon and California, USA. It is dormant in winter. The plants are sparsely foliaged with thick stiff leaves. Unbranched flowering spikes with sheathing bracts. The large yellow flowers, veined with reddish maroon, appear in the early summer. Zones 7–9.

Iris brevicaulis
syns *Iris foliosa, I. lamancei*

☼ ❄ ↔ 15–20 in (38–50 cm) ↑ 15–20 in (38–50 cm)

Fleshy-stemmed beardless iris from central USA. Foliage longer than flowering stems. Large blooms, blue to violet; falls have yellow center, usually veined with white and green. Summer-flowering. Zones 7–9.

Iris bucharica
syn. *Iris orhioides*

☼ ❄ ↔ 6 in (15 cm) ↑ 18 in (45 cm)

A native of Russia and Afghanistan. Bulbous iris, which has distinctive, shiny green, channeled leaves that resemble dwarf maize. Creamy flowers, yellow-centered falls, small white standards, in the upper leaf axils, appear in spring. Zones 5–9.

Iris ensata 'Activity'

Iris ensata 'Blue King'

Iris ensata 'Carnival'

Iris ensata 'Dresden Blue'

Iris ensata 'Eden's Blue Pearl'

Iris ensata 'Flying Tiger'

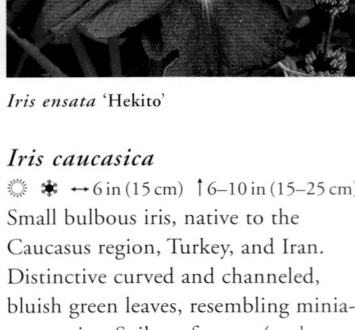
Iris ensata 'Hekito'

Iris ensata 'Iso-no-nami'

Iris ensata 'Rose Queen'

Iris bulleyana

☀ ❄ ↔ 12 in (30 cm)
↕ 15–18 in (38–45 cm)

Fleshy-stemmed beardless iris from western China and northern Myanmar. Glossy foliage. Purple flowers, veined and streaked yellow, maroon, and white, to 3 in (8 cm) wide, 1–2 per stem, in summer. Zones 5–9.

Iris chrysographes 'Black Knight'

Iris caucasica

☀ ❄ ↔ 6 in (15 cm) ↕ 6–10 in (15–25 cm)

Small bulbous iris, native to the Caucasus region, Turkey, and Iran. Distinctive curved and channeled, bluish green leaves, resembling miniature maize. Spikes of up to 4 pale yellow flowers in late winter–spring. *I. c.* subsp. *turcica*, smoother leaf margins. Zones 6–9.

Iris chrysographes

GOLD NET IRIS, GOLD PATTERN IRIS

☀ ❄ ↔ 12 in (30 cm)
↕ 12–20 in (30–50 cm)

Fleshy-stemmed beardless iris from China, Myanmar, and Tibet. Strappy grayish green leaves. Flowers in late spring–summer, color variable to purple-black, varying amounts of gold streaks on falls. '**Black Knight**', purple-black flowers. Zones 7–10.

Iris confusa

☀ ❄ ↔ 24 in (60 cm) ↕ 36 in (90 cm)

Vigorous, clump-forming, crested iris from western China. Fans of flat strap-like leaves on cane-like stems. The branching flower stems bear many small blooms, white, spotted yellow, or mauve, with yellow crests, in spring. '**Martyn Rix**', ruffled blue flowers. Zones 8–11.

Iris cristata

CRESTED IRIS

☀ ❄ ↔ 12–20 in (30–50 cm)
↕ 4–5 in (10–12 cm)

Dainty herbaceous woodlander from eastern USA, with exposed, creeping, fleshy stems, and fans of bright green strappy leaves. Produces blue spring flowers, on stems to height of leaves, with white markings on falls and yellow crests. A white-flowered form is also grown. Zones 6–10.

Iris delavayi

☀ ❄ ↔ 8–12 in (20–30 cm)
↕ 36–40 in (90–100 cm)

This clumping herbaceous species is native to western China, and related to *I. sibirica*. Upright narrow leaves. Elegant rich purple flowers, to 3 in

(8 cm) across, white markings on falls, held above leaves, in late spring. Prefers moist to wet soil. Zones 6–10.

Iris douglasiana

☀ ❄ ↔ 18 in (45 cm)
↕ 20–32 in (50–80 cm)

Fleshy-stemmed beardless iris from California and Oregon, USA. Loose clumps of dark green ribbed leaves. Branching flower stems. Blooms, in summer, vary in color from cream to deep reddish purple, veining usually in darker tones. Zones 7–9.

Iris ensata ★

syn. *Iris kaempferi*

JAPANESE WATER IRIS, WOODLAND IRIS

☀ ❄ ↔ 40 in (100 cm) ↕ 36 in (90 cm)

Native to Europe, Asia, and North America. Tall, dark green, strappy, grass-like foliage. Single, occasionally branched stems of flowers vary in color from red, purple, or blue, held well above foliage, in early summer. Will grow in shallow water. Not tolerant of dry hot conditions. '**Flying Tiger**', white flowers, heavily veined in violet; '**Hekito**', deep blue flowers, yellow signals, white styles, blue-tipped; '**Hue and Cry**', red-veined plum-red flowers, yellow signals with white margins; '**Rose Queen**', soft pink flowers, darker veined falls; '**Variegata**', purple-red flowers, variegated foliage; '**Yaemomiji**', cerise-purple flowers streaked with white, yellow signals. Zones 5–8.

Iris foetidissima

GLADDON, GLADWYN, ROAST BEEF PLANT, STINKING GLADWYN

☀/☀ ❄ ↔ 18–30 in (45–75 cm)
↕ 18–30 in (45–75 cm)

Vigorous, fleshy-stemmed, beardless iris, native to Europe and north Africa.

Iris caucasica subsp. *turcica*

Iris bulleyana

Iris iberica

Iris innominata

Glossy, deep green, sword-shaped leaves, distinctive odor when crushed. Spring flowers unspectacular, buff-yellow and dusty dull purple. Large green seed pods split to expose scarlet seeds. '**Variegata**' has boldly white-striped leaves. **Zones 6–10**.

Iris forrestii

☼ ❀ ↔ 6–8 in (15–20 cm)
↑ 15–16 in (38–40 cm)

Dainty, narrow-leafed, herbaceous species from China and northern Myanmar. Leaves narrow, glossy, gray-green undersides. Bears yellow flowers, spotted all over with brown, to 2½ in (6 cm) across, in early summer. Moist soil required. **Zones 7–10**.

Iris × fulvala

☼ ❀ ↔ 10 in (25 cm)
↑ 18–30 in (45–75 cm)

Hybrid of *I. fulva* and *I. brevicaulis*, both of which are beardless irises from USA. Purplish red flowers, in summer. Plants require a very moist soil. **Zones 7–10**.

Iris germanica

☼ ❀ ↔ 18–24 in (45–60 cm)
↑ 24–48 in (60–120 cm)

Rhizomatous bearded iris. Origin uncertain, widely naturalized; possibly from the Mediterranean or an ancient fertile hybrid. Blue, white, and yellow flowers, to 4 in (10 cm) wide, yellow beards. **Zones 5–9**.

Iris graminea

syn. *Iris colchica*

☼ ❀ ↔ 10 in (25 cm) ↑ 8–18 in (20–45 cm)
Variable, fleshy-stemmed, beardless iris, found from Spain eastwards to Russia. Narrow grassy leaves. Small purple flowers, 1–2 per stem, often hidden within the foliage, distinctive fruity fragrance, in summer. **Zones 5–9**.

Iris iberica

☼ ❀ ↔ 6 in (15 cm) ↑ 8 in (20 cm)
Fleshy-stemmed, dwarf, bearded iris from southwestern Asia. Narrow grayish green leaves. Relatively large white flowers, veined with brown, purplish

beards, in spring. A difficult garden subject requiring perfect drainage. **Zones 6–9**.

Iris innominata

☼/❂ ❀ ↔ 10 in (25 cm)
↑ 8–10 in (20–25 cm)

A fleshy-stemmed beardless iris, native to Oregon and California, USA, with narrow dark green leaves. The slender-petaled flowers vary from cream to purple, with darker veining, and appear in summer. This species is used extensively in breeding the Californian hybrids. **Zones 8–10**.

Iris japonica

syns *Iris chinensis, I. fimbriata*

☼ ❀ ↔ 18–24 in (45–60 cm)
↑ 24–32 in (60–80 cm)

Fleshy-stemmed crested iris from central China and Japan. Shiny dark green leaves in fans. Pale lavender flowers with orange markings, ruffled and fringed at margins, borne on branching airy stems, in spring. **Zones 8–10**.

Iris lactea

☼ ❀ ↔ 10 in (25 cm) ↑ 6–16 in (15–40 cm)
Found from central Asia eastwards to China. Fleshy-stemmed beardless iris. Rather stiff grayish green foliage. Fragrant violet to pale bluish flowers, 1 to 3 per stem, in summer. **Zones 4–9**.

Iris lacustris

☼ ❀ ↔ 4–6 in (10–15 cm)
↑ 2–3 in (5–8 cm)

Native to North America. Very dwarf, fleshy-stemmed, crested iris. Soft bright green leaves, to 3 in (8 cm)

Iris japonica

long. Small sky blue flowers, with frilly gold-tipped crests, from late spring to summer. **Zones 4–9**.

Iris laevigata

JAPANESE WATER IRIS, RABBIT EAR IRIS

☼/❂ ❀ ↔ 5 ft (1.5 m) ↑ 2–5 ft (0.6–1.5 m)

From Japan. These robust upright irises tolerate wet soil, growing in water and boggy areas. They will naturalize on the edges of swamps and ponds. Tall spikes of purple, mauve, and white flowers, held above foliage, in summer. Large floppy petals that hang gracefully toward the ground. '**Variegata**', to 16 in (40 cm) tall, green leaves striped with large white veins, purple-blue flowers, on short stems, in summer. **Zones 3–9**.

Iris lactea

Iris longipetala

Iris lazica

☼/❂ ❀ ↔ 10–12 in (25–30 cm)
↑ 10–12 in (25–30 cm)

From northeastern Turkey and Georgia. This evergreen species is related to *I. unguicularis* but has thicker shorter leaves arranged in fans. Soft lavender-blue flowers, white and yellow falls, in late winter–early spring. **Zones 8–10**.

Iris longipetala

☼ ❀ ↔ 12 in (30 cm)
↑ 12–24 in (30–60 cm)

From western USA. Fleshy-stemmed beardless iris with dark green foliage. Unbranched flower stems carry up to 6 white, blue, or purple blooms; long, narrow, white falls veined with violet, in late spring–summer. **Zones 5–9**.

Iris foetidissima

Iris milesii

Iris magnifica 'Alba'

Iris orientalis

Iris lutescens

syn. *Iris chamaeiris*

☼ ❋ ↔ 8 in (20 cm) ↑ 8 in (20 cm)

Variable, dwarf, bearded iris, native to
Europe. Leaves to 12 in (30 cm) long.
Flowers borne 1–2 per stem, white,
yellow, or shades of bluish purple,
usually with yellow beards, in early
to mid-spring. Zones 5–9.

Iris magnifica

syn. *Iris vicaria*

☼ ❋ ↔ 10 in (25 cm)
↑ 12–24 in (30–60 cm)

Bulbous iris, native to Tajikistan and
northern Afghanistan. Distinctive,
shiny, bluish green, channeled leaves
resembling dwarf maize. Flower spikes
of up to 7 flowers, usually pale lavender with yellow on falls, in spring.
'Alba', white flowers. Zones 5–9.

Iris milesii

☼ ❋ ↔ 10 (25 cm) ↑ 12–36 in (30–90 cm)

Fleshy-stemmed crested iris from the
Himalayas. Bright green ribbed foliage.
Frilly lilac-purple flowers, with darker
markings, on branched stems, in the
summer. Zones 7–9.

Iris missouriensis

☼ ❋ ↔ 12 in (30 cm)
↑ 12–20 in (30–50 cm)

From western North America. This
fleshy-stemmed beardless iris is similar
to *I. longipetala*. Narrow grayish green
leaves. White, blue, or purple flowers,
long narrow falls, in late spring to
summer. Zones 3–8.

Iris orientalis

syn. *Iris ochroleuca*

☼ ❋ ↔ 24 in (60 cm) ↑ 48 in (120 cm)

Native to Greece and Turkey. A fleshy-
stemmed, almost evergreen, beardless
iris with stiff, sword-like, dark green
leaves. The large white flowers, with

Iris pallida

Iris purdyi

gold markings on falls, are carried on
branching stems, through summer.
Zones 4–9.

Iris pallida

syns *Iris glauca, I. odoratissima*

DALMATIAN IRIS

☼ ❋ ↔ 12 in (30 cm)
↑ 36–48 in (90–120 cm)

Fleshy-stemmed bearded iris from
the European Alps. Stiff, sword-like,
bluish green foliage. Large fragrant
flowers, blue with yellow beards, in
early summer. *I. p.* subsp. *cengialti* ★
(syn. *I. cengialti*), greener leaves than
species, dark purple flowers. *I. p.*
'Argentea Variegata', white stripes on
leaf edges; 'Variegata', creamy yellow
leaf markings. Zones 5–9.

Iris prismatica

☼ ❋ ↔ 12 in (30 cm)
↑ 24–32 in (60–80 cm)

Fleshy-stemmed beardless iris, native to
eastern USA. Long, bluish green, grassy
leaves. Flowers pale violet, veined blue,
on wiry stems, in summer. Zones 5–9.

Iris pseudoacorus

YELLOW FLAG

☼ ❋ ↔ 5–7 ft (1.5–2 m)
↑ 4–5 ft (1.2–1.5 m)

Robust, potentially weedy water iris
from Europe, Middle East, and northern Africa. Long, upright, rich green
leaves die down in winter. Bright
yellow flowers with brown markings

Iris pallida subsp. cengialti

on falls, 4 in (10 cm) across, produced
just below the tallest leaves. 'Variegata',
boldly cream-variegated leaves fade to
green after flowering. Zones 6–10.

Iris pumila

DWARF BEARDED IRIS

☼ ❋ ↔ 4–6 in (10–15 cm)
↑ 4–6 in (10–15 cm)

Dainty little rock-garden iris, found
from eastern Europe to the Ural
Mountains of Russia. Solitary flowers,
perfumed, blue, purple, or yellow, in
mid-spring. Zones 5–10.

Iris purdyi

☼ ❋ ↔ 10 in (25 cm)
↑ 12–16 in (30–40 cm)

From California, USA. Fleshy-
stemmed beardless iris. Glossy grayish
green foliage. Unbranched flowering
stems bear 2 blooms with narrow flaring petals. Cream flowers with lavender tints and reddish purple veining.
Summer-flowering. Zones 6–9.

Iris purpureobractea

☼ ❋ ↔ 12 in (30 cm) ↑ 8–20 in (20–50 cm)

Fleshy-stemmed bearded iris, native to
Turkey. Forms clumps of sword-shaped
leaves. Flowers, pale yellow with greenish brown veins, or pale blue with
darker veins, in late spring. Zones 6–9.

Iris purpureobractea

Iris pseudoacorus 'Variegata'

Iris sibirica 'Camberley'

I. sibirica 'Dance Ballerina Dance'

Iris sibirica 'Golden Crimping'

Iris sibirica 'Polly Dodge'

Iris sibirica 'Ruffled Velvet'

Iris sibirica 'Ruffles'

Iris sibirica 'Anniversary'

Iris reichenbachii

syns *Iris balkana, I. bosniaca, I. skorpilii*
☀ ❋ ↔ 8 in (20 cm) ↑ 12 in (30 cm)
Fleshy-stemmed, dwarf, bearded iris from the Balkans region. Slender leaves arranged in fans. Yellow or purple flowers, darker veining, 2 per stem, in spring. Zones 5–9.

Iris reticulata

☀ ❋ ↔ 2 in (5 cm) ↑ 6 in (15 cm)
From the Caucasus region. Variable bulbous iris with very narrow channeled leaves. Solitary stemless flowers, narrow petals, in violet shades with gold markings on falls. **'Blue Veil'** and **'Cantab'** are popular cultivars. Zones 3–9.

Iris × robusta

☀ ❋ ↔ 20 in (50 cm)
↑ 32–40 in (80–100 cm)
This is a hybrid of *I. versicolor* and *I. virginica*, two of the moisture-loving beardless irises from North America, which has characteristics that are intermediate between the parents. The leaves are dark green and ribbed. The flowers are borne in late spring to early summer, in bluish violet shades. **'Gerald Darby'** produces dark violet flowers, on spikes to 40 in (100 cm) tall. Zones 4–9.

Iris sanguinea

☀ ❋ ↔ 12–24 in (30–60 cm)
↑ 24–36 in (60–90 cm)
Native to Siberia, China, Japan, and Korea. Fleshy-stemmed beardless iris similar to *I. sibirica*. Narrow grassy foliage, usually taller than the flowering spike. Unbranched stems bear 2 bluish violet flowers in early summer. *I. s.* var. *violacea*, narrower leaves, darker purple flowers. Zones 4–9.

Iris setosa

☀ ❋ ↔ 18 in (45 cm) ↑ 30 in (75 cm)
Widespread species from Siberia, China, Canada, and Alaska, USA. Fleshy-stemmed beardless iris. Narrow ribbed leaves. Numerous pale bluish purple dark-veined flowers borne on branching spikes, in late spring. Large falls and very small

standards give flowers a 3-petaled appearance. *I. s.* **subsp.** *interior* has narrower leaves. Zones 3–9.

Iris sibirica

☀ ❋ ↔ 8–24 in (20–60 cm)
↑ 18–48 in (45–120 cm)
From Europe and northern Asia. This popular adaptable group of irises is

Iris sanguinea

Iris setosa subsp. *interior*

happy in heavy clay soils. Dark green strappy foliage. The flower spikes are taller than the foliage, producing up to 5 flowers on each stem; the flowers are usually blue-violet or white. The flowers of **'Annemarie Troeger'** are in 2 shades of blue with white signals; **'Anniversary'** produces ruffled white flowers; **'Caesar's Brother'**, bright blue

Iris reichenbachii

Iris × robusta 'Gerald Darby'

Iris reticulata 'Blue Veil'

Iris sanguinea var. *violacea*

Iris sibirica 'Marcus Perry'

Iris sibirica 'Sally Kerlin'

Iris sibirica 'Sea Shadows'

Iris sibirica 'Silver Edge'

Iris sibirica 'Smudger's Gift'

Iris sibirica 'Troika'

Iris sibirica 'Tropic Night'

Iris sibirica 'Weisse Etagen'

Iris sibirica 'White Ruffles'

Iris sibirica 'White Swirl'

Iris tectorum

Iris tenax 'Alba'

Iris tenuis

Iris trojana

Iris tenax

flowers, yellow signals; **'Harpswell Happiness'**, ruffled white flowers; **'Perry's Blue'**, pale lavender-blue flowers, creamy yellow veined eyes; **'Pink Haze'**, lavender-pink flowers, red-violet veins on falls; **'Ruffles'**, ruffled blue-violet flowers, dark styles; **'White Swirl'**, pure white flowers, yel-low blotches at base, rounded flared outer petals. Other popular cultivars include: **'Crème Chantilly'**, **'Dreaming Yellow'**, **'Mikiko'**, **'Oban'**, **'Perfect Vision'**, **'Roisin'**, **'Ruffled Velvet'**, **'Smudger's Gift'**, **'Uber den Wolken'**, and **'Zakopane'**. Zones 4–9.

Iris spuria

☼ ❄ ↔ 3–7 ft (0.9–2 m)
↕ 4–7 ft (1.2–2 m)

From northern and northwestern Iran. Colonizing iris are usually found in damp fields, shallow riverbeds, and even in saline soils. Flowers range in color from pale and dark blues, through to whites, creams, and mauves. Plants need rich warm soils. *I. s.* subsp. *halophila*, pale to deep yellow flowers, dark green strappy foliage. Zones 6–9.

Iris susiana

MOURNING IRIS

☼ ❄ ↔ 12 in (30 cm) ↕ 12–16 in (30–40 cm)
From Lebanon. Iris with soft, curly, green leaves, to 6 in (15 cm). Flowers with gray petals, deep purple veining, purple beards, in late spring. Zones 7–9.

Iris tectorum

ROOF IRIS

◑ ❄ ↔ 12 in (30 cm) ↕ 12–16 in (30–40 cm)
Native to China. Fleshy-stemmed crested iris. Fans of light green leaves. Bluish purple flowers, darker veining appear in early summer. Zones 6–9.

Iris tenax

syn. *Iris gormanii*

◐ ❄ ↔ 12 in (30 cm) ↕ 16 in (40 cm)
From western USA. Fleshy-stemmed beardless iris with deciduous foliage.

Flowers in white, yellow, blue, and purple shades, on unbranched stems, in early summer. **'Alba'** is a white-flowered form. Zones 8–10.

Iris tenuis

◑ ❄ ↔ 6 in (15 cm) ↕ 12 in (30 cm)
Rare native of western USA. Fleshy-stemmed crested iris, like *I. cristata* but taller. Flowers lavender-blue, darker veining, some yellow markings, in late spring. Zones 6–9.

Iris trojana

☼ ❄ ↔ 12 in (30 cm)
↕ 24–36 in (60–90 cm)

From Turkey. Fleshy-stemmed bearded iris. Fans of grayish green leaves. Long pointed flower buds; large, fragrant, purple flowers, white and yellow beards, in summer. Zones 7–10.

Iris unguicularis

syn. *Iris stylosa*

ALGERIAN IRIS, WINTER IRIS

☀/☼ ❄ ↔16–20 in (40–50 cm)
↑12–15 in (30–38cm)

Evergreen species from Greece, Turkey, western Syria, Algeria, and some of the Mediterranean islands. Grows well in hot dry aspects, producing tough grassy leaves and pale lavender to blue flowers, hidden amongst the leaves, in winter–early spring. Many forms have been selected. '**Alba**' has white flowers with yellow on the falls; '**Mary Barnard**' has deep violet-blue flowers; the flowers of '**Starkers Pink**' are a soft mauve-pink; and '**Variegata**' has deep blue blotching and streaking on soft blue flowers. Zones 7–10.

Iris variegata

syns *Iris lepida, I. leucographa, I. reginae, I. virescens*

☀ ❄ ↔6–10 in (15–25 cm)
↑8–20 in (20–50 cm)

Fleshy-stemmed bearded species from central and eastern Europe. The leaves are dark green, ribbed, and sword-shaped. The yellow flowers, marked with variable veining of blue to reddish brown, appear from spring to summer. Zones 6–9.

Iris versicolor

☀ ❄ ↔10 in (25 cm)
↑8–32 in (20–80 cm)

From eastern USA. Vigorous, water-loving, fleshy-stemmed, beardless iris. Broad, ribbed, green foliage. Many small flowers in bluish purple shades, with darker veining, on branching flower spikes, in summer. Zones 4–9.

Iris virginica

☀ ❄ ↔10 in (25 cm)
↑8–32 in (20–80 cm)

From eastern USA. Vigorous water-loving beardless iris. Heavily ribbed dark green foliage. Similar to *I. versicolor*, but with unbranched flower spikes. Bluish purple flowers, larger and longer standards, in summer. Zones 4–9.

Iris Hybrid Cultivars

ARILBRED HYBRIDS

☀ ❄ ↔12 in (30 cm)
↑10–27 in (25–70 cm)

Hybrids of species in the Aril Group and Tall Bearded Iris. Large flowers in a range of purple shades and yellow, with variously colored markings. Flowers in early spring. Require a dry dormant summer season. '**Judean Gem**', 10 in (25 cm) high, bearded,

early season, white flowers, yellow falls with orange-red signals; '**Oyez**', 24 in (60 cm) high, early season, white flowers, dark purple veins on standards and falls. Zones 3–9.

BEARDED HYBRIDS

☀ ❄ ↔12–36 in (30–90 cm)
↑8–40 in (20–100 cm)

These hardy perennials are grown from rhizomes. They will survive in most climates but produce more flowers in cooler climates. The upright pale blue-green foliage sits above the ground, and large heads of flowers appear in late spring, ranging in color from blues, purples, and browns through to oranges, whites, and yellows. Flowers have standards and falls, with a distinctive beard on each fall. Do not cover rhizomes with soil, as they will rot and die. These plants need well-drained and fertile soil in full sun. Divide every 5 to 7 years.

Miniature Dwarf Bearded Hybrids: Reaching to less than 8 in (20 cm) high, these are the smallest and earli-

est-flowering of the bearded hybrids. They produce small flowers, 1½–3 in (35–80 mm) wide, in spring.

Standard Dwarf Bearded Hybrids: These flower well in cool maritime climates. Reach height of 8–15 in (20–38 cm) high. Will form good clumps and are reliable garden plants. Flowers appear in late spring. They need a good cold period through the winter to perform well. '**Bromyard**', early season, blue-gray standards, blue-purple and ocher falls, blue-gray beards; '**Bibury**', white to cream flowers; '**Eyebright**', mid-season, yellow flowers with deep brown lines, creamy yellow beards; '**Flower Shower**', ruffled flowers in violet and white; '**Honington**', cream-yellow flowers; '**Quark**', cream flowers with maroon markings; '**Rain Dance**', early season, violet-blue flowers, matching violet-blue beards; '**Tirra Lirra**', mauve flowers; and '**Wow**', bright yellow flowers with maroon markings.

Intermediate Bearded Hybrids: These hybrids reach 16–27 in

Iris, Hybrid Cultivar, Bearded, Intermediate, 'Cannington Skies'

Iris unguicularis

Iris versicolor

Iris, Hybrid Cultivar, Bearded, Standard Dwarf, 'Bibury'

Iris, Hybrid Cultivar, Bearded, Standard Dwarf, 'Eyebright'

Iris, Hybrid Cultivar, Bearded, Standard Dwarf, 'Flower Shower'

Iris, Hybrid Cultivar, Bearded, Standard Dwarf, 'Tirra Lirra'

Iris, Hybrid Cultivar, Bearded, Standard Dwarf, 'Wow'

Iris, HC, B, I, 'Alienor d'Aquitaine'

Iris, HC, Bearded, I, 'Anlieu Bleue'

Iris, HC, Bearded, I, 'Barocco'

Iris, HC, Bearded, I, 'Blue Boy'

Iris, HC, Bearded, I, 'Candy Walk'

(40–70 cm) high. These medium-sized plants bear blooms that are also medium-sized. They will flower well in most areas, the flowers well able to support themselves on their stems. They do well in wind-prone areas, but need full sun. '**Arctic Fancy**', pure white flowers with purple markings; '**Barocco**', deep pink to maroon flowers; '**Eye Magic**', yellow flowers, with red thumbprint on falls; '**Happy Mood**' ★, creamy flowers edged in lavender; '**Maui Moonlight**', mid-season, rich lemon flowers; '**Mon Ange**', yellow-veined white flowers; '**Sunny Dawn**', bright yellow flowers with red beard. Other popular Intermediate Bearded Hybrids include: '**Katie-Koo**', '**Miss Carla**', '**Sherbet Lemon**', and '**Templecloud**'.

Miniature Tall Bearded Hybrids: Sharing a similar flowering season to the Tall Bearded Hybrids, and reaching a similar height to Border Bearded Hybrids, these hybrids produce smaller flowers on wiry stems. '**Bumblebee Deelite**', flowers have yellow standards, maroon falls edged with yellow; '**Frosted Velvet**', two-tone flowers with white centers, rich velvet purple falls edged in white.

Border Bearded Hybrids: Flowering at the same time as the Tall Bearded Hybrids, but with somewhat smaller flowers held on stalks 16–27 in (40–70 cm) high. '**Apricot Frosty**', white flowers, deep apricot falls, apricot beards; '**Batik**', white-striped purple flowers, yellow beards with white tips; '**Brown Lasso**', deep butterscotch and yellow flowers, petals edged in pale lavender.

Tall Bearded Hybrids: Well-branched spikes of robust large flowers, may be ruffled or smooth-edged. Can reach height of 27–40 in (70–100 cm). Good for cutting. '**Apricorange**', orange flowers; '**Berry Sherbet**', early flowering, pink and violet flowers; '**Blue-Eyed Brunette**', ruffled bronze flowers, blue beards; '**Breakers**', mid-blue ruffled flowers; '**Celebration Song**', late season, pinkish standards, lavender-blue falls; '**Champagne Elegance**' ★, apricot flowers, yellow standards, white falls edged in apricot, with yellow-red beards, large number of blooms; '**Cinderella's Coach**', pumpkin orange flowers, bright red-tangerine beards, ruffled flowers; '**Cupid's Arrow**', pink to maroon flowers; '**Dazzling Gold**', mid-season, yellow and red flowers; '**Designing Woman**', rosy lilac standards and falls, coral beards, very wavy and ruffled blooms; '**Dusky Challenger**', large, ruffled, dark black-purple flowers; '**Early Light**', creamy yellow ruffled flowers; '**Good Morning America**', mid-season, pale blue flowers; '**Hello Darkness**', mid-season, rich velvet black flowers; '**Honky Tonk Blues**', mid-season, blue-violet, heavily washed over a white base, giving a soft blue effect, wide ruffled blooms; '**In Town**', mid-season, lilac blue standards, with slightly ruffled purple falls; '**Incantation**', mid-season, bluish standards, pure white falls; '**Jesse's Song**', white center bleeding into violet, lemon beard, violet edging; '**Joyce Terry**', early mid-season, yellow standards, white falls, yellow beards; '**June Sunset**', mid-season, white standards, soft peach-orange falls; '**Mystique**', early to mid-season, blue standards, purple-blue midribs, deep purple falls, blue beards. '**Silverado**', mid-season, silvery lavender flowers and beards; '**Stepping Out**', similar to 'Jesse's Song'; '**Thornbird**', yellowish standards, greenish brown falls; '**Vanity**', pink flowers, with salmon pink beards. Other attractive Tall Bearded Hybrids include: '**Bewick Swan**', '**Meg's Mantle**', '**Paradise**', '**Paradise Bird**', '**Phil Keen**', '**Precious Heather**', and '**Sun Miracle**'. Zones 3–9.

Iris, Hybrid Cultivar, Bearded, Miniature Tall, 'Bumblebee Deelite'

Iris, Hybrid Cultivar, Bearded, Intermediate, 'Happy Mood'

Iris, Hybrid Cultivar, Bearded, Intermediate, 'Eye Magic'

Iris, Hybrid Cultivar, Bearded, Intermediate, 'Firmament'

Iris, Hybrid Cultivar, Bearded, Intermediate, 'La Poussin'

Iris, Hybrid Cultivar, Bearded, Intermediate, 'Mon Ange'

Iris, Hybrid Cultivar, Bearded, Intermediate, 'Of Course'

Iris, HC, B, I, 'Painter's Hill'

Iris, HC, B, I, 'Short Distance'

Iris, HC, B, I, 'Switchcrozzle'

Iris, HC, B, I, 'Tchin Tchin'

Iris, HC, B, I, 'Three Dollars'

Iris, Hybrid Cultivar, Bearded, Tall, 'Acoma'

Iris, Hybrid Cultivar, Bearded, Tall, 'Allzarine'

Iris, Hybrid Cultivar, Bearded, Tall, 'Ancient Egypt'

Iris, Hybrid Cultivar, Bearded, Tall, 'Andalou'

Iris, Hybrid Cultivar, Bearded, Tall, 'Arpège'

Iris, Hybrid Cultivar, Bearded, Tall, 'Balançoire'

Iris, Hybrid Cultivar, Bearded, Tall, 'Bal Masque'

Iris, Hybrid Cultivar, Bearded, Tall, 'Beach Girl'

Iris, Hybrid Cultivar, Bearded, Tall, 'Berry Sherbet'

Iris, Hybrid Cultivar, Bearded, Tall, 'Amas'

Iris, Hybrid Cultivar, Bearded, Tall, 'Best Bet'

Iris, Hybrid Cultivar, Bearded, Tall, 'Betty Simon'

Iris, Hybrid Cultivar, Bearded, Tall, 'Beyond'

Iris, Hybrid Cultivar, Bearded, Tall, 'Bicentennial'

Iris, Hybrid Cultivar, Bearded, Tall, 'Black and Gold'

Iris, Hybrid Cultivar, Bearded, Tall, 'Black Flag'

Iris, Hybrid Cultivar, Bearded, Tall, 'Blazing Sunrise'

Iris, Hybrid Cultivar, Bearded, Tall, 'Buisson de Roses'

Iris, Hybrid Cultivar, Bearded, Tall, 'Capricious'

Iris, Hybrid Cultivar, Bearded, Tall, 'Caribbean Dream'

Iris, HC, B, T, 'Carriage Trade'

Iris, HC, B, T, 'Celebration Song'

Iris, HC, B, T, 'Champagne Waltz'

Iris, HC, B, T, 'Chapeau'

Iris, HC, B, T, 'Cinderella's Coach'

Iris, Hybrid Cultivar, Bearded, Tall, 'Codicil'

Iris, Hybrid Cultivar, Bearded, Tall, 'Columbia Blue'

Iris, Hybrid Cultivar, Bearded, Tall, 'Con Fuoco'

Iris, Hybrid Cultivar, Bearded, Tall, 'Confetti'

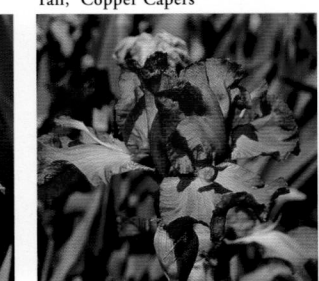

Iris, Hybrid Cultivar, Bearded, Tall, 'Copper Capers'

Iris, Hybrid Cultivar, Bearded, Tall, 'Crème Glacée'

Iris, Hybrid Cultivar, Bearded, Tall, 'Crinoline'

Iris, Hybrid Cultivar, Bearded, Tall, 'Crowd Pleaser'

Iris, Hybrid Cultivar, Bearded, Tall, 'Daisy Powell'

Iris, Hybrid Cultivar, Bearded, Tall, 'Dauber's Delight'

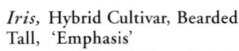

Iris, Hybrid Cultivar, Bearded, Tall, 'Dazzling Gold'

Iris, Hybrid Cultivar, Bearded, Tall, 'Deep Space'

Iris, Hybrid Cultivar, Bearded, Tall, 'Designing Woman'

Iris, Hybrid Cultivar, Bearded, Tall, 'Eco de France'

Iris, Hybrid Cultivar, Bearded, Tall, 'Elysian Fields'

Iris, Hybrid Cultivar, Bearded, Tall, 'Emphasis'

Iris, Hybrid Cultivar, Bearded, Tall, 'Evolution'

Iris, Hybrid Cultivar, Bearded, Tall, 'Exotic Isle'

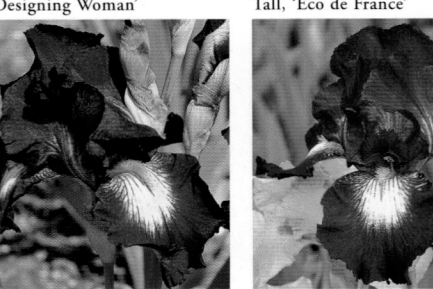

Iris, Hybrid Cultivar, Bearded, Tall, 'Extravagant'

Iris, Hybrid Cultivar, Bearded, Tall, 'Flaming Victory'

Iris, Hybrid Cultivar, Bearded, Tall, 'Cupid's Arrow'

Iris, Hybrid Cultivar, Bearded, Tall, 'Gallant Moment'

Iris, Hybrid Cultivar, Bearded, Tall, 'Gladys Austin'

Iris, HC, B, T, 'Good Guy'

Iris, HC, B, T, 'Goodbye Heart'

Iris, Hybrid Cultivar, Bearded, Tall, 'Great Lakes'

Iris, Hybrid Cultivar, Bearded, Tall, 'Grecian Skies'

Iris, Hybrid Cultivar, Bearded, Tall, 'Handiwork'

Iris, Hybrid Cultivar, Bearded, Tall, 'Hephaistos'

Iris, Hybrid Cultivar, Bearded, Tall, 'Hilow'

Iris, Hybrid Cultivar, Bearded, Tall, 'Hula Girl'

Iris, Hybrid Cultivar, Bearded, Tall, 'Horizon Bleu'

Iris, Hybrid Cultivar, Bearded, Tall, 'Hortense'

Iris, Hybrid Cultivar, Bearded, Tall, 'Imperator'

Iris, Hybrid Cultivar, Bearded, Tall, 'In Town'

Iris, Hybrid Cultivar, Bearded, Tall, 'Incantation'

Iris, HC, B, T, 'Jesse's Song'

Iris, Hybrid Cultivar, Bearded, Tall, 'Island Dancer'

Iris, Hybrid Cultivar, Bearded,
Tall, 'Land o' Lakes'

Iris, Hybrid Cultivar, Bearded,
Tall, 'London Lord'

Iris, Hybrid Cultivar, Bearded,
Tall, 'Lace Jabot'

Iris, Hybrid Cultivar, Bearded,
Tall, 'Lorenzaccio de Medicis'

Iris, Hybrid Cultivar, Bearded, Tall, 'June Sunset'

Iris, Hybrid Cultivar, Bearded, Tall, 'Madame Chereau'

Iris, Hybrid Cultivar, Bearded,
Tall, 'Lord Baltimore'

Iris, Hybrid Cultivar, Bearded,
Tall, 'Loudoun Charmer'

Iris, Hybrid Cultivar, Bearded,
Tall, 'Louis d'Or'

Iris, Hybrid Cultivar, Bearded,
Tall, 'Loyalist'

Iris, Hybrid Cultivar, Bearded,
Tall, 'Lurid'

Iris, Hybrid Cultivar, Bearded,
Tall, 'Mme Louis Auréau'

Iris, Hybrid Cultivar, Bearded, Tall, 'Patina'

Iris, Hybrid Cultivar, Bearded,
Tall, 'Madeira Belle'

Iris, Hybrid Cultivar, Bearded,
Tall, 'Mary Frances'

Iris, HC, B, T, 'Mer du Sud'

Iris, HC, B, T, 'Minnie Colquitt'

Iris, Hybrid Cultivar, Bearded, Tall, 'Memoirs'

Iris, Hybrid Cultivar, Bearded, Tall, 'Mod Mode'

Iris, Hybrid Cultivar, Bearded, Tall, 'Mystique'

Iris, Hybrid Cultivar, Bearded, Tall, 'Navajo Blanket'

Iris, Hybrid Cultivar, Bearded, Tall, 'Night Game'

Iris, Hybrid Cultivar, Bearded, Tall, 'Nightfall'

Iris, Hybrid Cultivar, Bearded, Tall, 'Ovation'

Iris, Hybrid Cultivar, Bearded, Tall, 'Pacific Tide'

Iris, Hybrid Cultivar, Bearded, Tall, 'Palerme'

Iris, Hybrid Cultivar, Bearded, Tall, 'Peach Picotee'

Iris, Hybrid Cultivar, Bearded, Tall, 'Persian Gown'

Iris, Hybrid Cultivar, Bearded, Tall, 'Peppermint Crush'

Iris, Hybrid Cultivar, Bearded, Tall, 'Pink Pussycat'

Iris, Hybrid Cultivar, Bearded, Tall, 'Pirate's Quest'

Iris, Hybrid Cultivar, Bearded, Tall, 'Proud Tradition'

Iris, Hybrid Cultivar, Bearded, Tall, 'Provencal'

Iris, Hybrid Cultivar, Bearded, Tall, 'Raspberry Ribbon'

Iris, HC, B, T, 'Royal Kingdom'

Iris, HC, Bearded, Tall, 'Rustler'

Iris, Hybrid Cultivar, Bearded, Tall, 'Pink Taffeta'

Iris, Hybrid Cultivar, Bearded, Tall, 'Sable'

Iris, Hybrid Cultivar, Bearded, Tall, 'Salonique'

Iris, Hybrid Cultivar, Bearded, Tall, 'Secret Melody'

Iris, Hybrid Cultivar, Bearded, Tall, 'San José'

Iris, Hybrid Cultivar, Bearded, Tall, 'Sapphire Hills'

Iris, Hybrid Cultivar, Bearded, Tall, 'Samsara'

Iris, Hybrid Cultivar, Bearded, Tall, 'Scintillation'

Iris, Hybrid Cultivar, Bearded, Tall, 'Sea Captain'

Iris, Hybrid Cultivar, Bearded, Tall, 'Spreckes'

Iris, Hybrid Cultivar, Bearded, Tall, 'Song of Gold'

Iris, Hybrid Cultivar, Bearded, Tall, 'Souvenir de Mme Gaudichau'

Iris, Hybrid Cultivar, Bearded, Tall, 'Starlette Rose'

Iris, Hybrid Cultivar, Bearded, Tall, 'Soft Caress'

Iris, Hybrid Cultivar, Bearded, Tall, 'Snow Flurry'

Iris, Hybrid Cultivar, Bearded, Tall, 'Space Blazers'

Iris, HC, B, T, 'Stellar Lights'

Iris, HC, B, T, 'Stepping Out'

Iris, Hybrid Cultivar, Bearded, Tall, 'Sultan's Palace'

Iris, Hybrid Cultivar, Bearded, Tall, 'Storm Warning'

Iris, Hybrid Cultivar, Bearded, Tall, 'Swedish Modern'

Iris, Hybrid Cultivar, Bearded, Tall, 'Terre de Feu'

Iris, Hybrid Cultivar, Bearded, Tall, 'Thunder Echo'

Iris, Hybrid Cultivar, Bearded, Tall, 'Tomoko'

Iris, Hybrid Cultivar, Bearded, Tall, 'Ultimatum'

Iris, Hybrid Cultivar, Bearded, Tall, 'Valley Charm'

Iris, Hybrid Cultivar, Bearded, Tall, 'Van Gogh'

Iris, Hybrid Cultivar, Bearded, Tall, 'Vaudeville'

Iris, Hybrid Cultivar, Bearded, Tall, 'Thornbird'

Iris, Hybrid Cultivar, Bearded, Tall, 'Touch of Bronze'

Iris, Hybrid Cultivar, Bearded, Tall, 'Violet Rings'

Iris, Hybrid Cultivar, Bearded, Tall, 'Wedding Vow'

Iris, HC, B, T, 'Welcome Aboard'

Iris, HC, B, T, 'Winner's Circle'

Iris, Hybrid Cultivar, Californian, 'Agnes James'

Iris, Hybrid Cultivar, Californian, mixed

Iris, Hybrid Cultivar, Californian, 'Broadleigh Carolyn'

Iris, Hybrid Cultivar, Californian, 'Broadleigh Emily'

Iris, Hybrid Cultivar, Californian, 'Broadleigh Lavinia'

Iris, Hybrid Cultivar, Californian, 'Broadleigh Clare'

Iris, HC, Californian, 'Broadleigh Nancy'

CALIFORNIAN HYBRIDS

☼/◐ ❁ ↔ 12 in (30 cm)
↕ 10–20 in (25–50 cm)

Hybrids of about 4 species of Californian iris, sometimes known as Pacific Coast Hybrids, with wide color range, from yellow to pink and purple. Long bloom period from spring. **'Broadleigh Carolyn'**, compact

Iris, Hybrid Cultivar, Californian, 'Broadleigh Medusa'

Iris, HC, Californian, 'Broadleigh Rose'

Iris, Hybrid Cultivar, Californian, 'Broadleigh Sybil'

Iris, Hybrid Cultivar, Californian, 'Broadleigh Idylwild'

white flowers, mauve-purple veining and yellow blotches in eye; **'Broadleigh Medusa'**, rich purple flowers, cream and yellow throats; **'Broadleigh Nancy'**, mid-purple flowers, petals edged in white, white and yellow blotch in eye; **'Broadleigh Rose'**, rich rose pink flowers, yellow and cream blotches in eye; **'Broadleigh Sybil'**, creamy apricot standards, deep rose pink falls. Zones 5–9.

DUTCH HYBRIDS

☼ ✱ ↔ 12–18 in (30–45 cm)
↕ 24–36 in (60–90 cm)

Bulbous irises with large spring blooms in shades of blue and purple, yellow

Iris, Hybrid Cultivar, Dutch, 'Blue Magic'

Iris, Hybrid Cultivar, Dutch, 'Blue Diamond'

Iris, Hybrid Cultivar, Dutch, 'Madonna'

Iris, Hybrid Cultivar, Louisiana, 'Marie Caillet'

Iris, Hybrid Cultivar, Louisiana, 'Newsbrief'

and white. Extensively grown for the cut flower trade. '**Blue Diamond**', dark blue buds open to mid-blue flowers, yellow thumbprints at base of petals; '**Blue Magic**', deep blue flowers, yellow thumbprints; '**Cream Beauty**', ivory flowers, gold thumbprints; '**Madonna**', crisp white, yellow thumbprints; '**Telstar**', rich purple-blue flowers, golden yellow thumbprints at base of petals. Zones 5–9.

LOUISIANA HYBRIDS

☼/☀ ❄ ↔ 3–7 ft (0.9–2 m)
↕ 18–60 in (45–150 cm)

Water plants from the swamps of Louisiana. Very adaptable to growing

in water and also on edges of ponds and rivers. Will grow in ordinary garden soil if given plenty of water. Need to be planted in well-prepared soil, with a good amount of humus. Will grow in full sun or part-shade. Flower spikes vary considerably in height from 14 in (35 cm) to 5 ft (1.5 m). Flowers range in color from pinks, yellows, and blues through to oranges, purples, and browns. '**Green Elf**', mid-season, chartreuse-green flowers, ageing to cream; '**Marie Caillet**', ruffled violet-blue flowers, with yellow signals; '**Newsbrief**', purple-red flowers, paler centers; '**President Hedley**', early season, dark buttery yellow flowers, areas of brown shading on falls, with yellow-orange signals. Zones 6–9.

ONCOCYCLUS HYBRIDS

☼ ❄ ↔ 40 in (100 cm)
↕ 4–24 in (10–60 cm)

These are similar in appearance to the bearded iris, but are smaller in size. Only one flower is borne on each flower stem. A large blotch and dark veining on the flowers are characteristics of this group. They are adaptable

Isabelia virginalis

to hot dry climates. The large seed heads are produced in the autumn. Zones 7–9.

SPURIA HYBRIDS

☼ ❄ ↔ 18–24 in (45–60 cm)
↕ 30–48 in (75–120 cm)

Tall plants with large flowers in white and yellow to red and purple shades. Flowering in spring–summer. Dislike being divided and transplanted. '**Shelford Giant**', 4 ft (1.2 m) tall, mid-season, large lemon and white flowers. Zones 4–9.

ISABELIA

A small South American genus of sympodial orchids (family Orchidaceae). Most of the 5 species occur in Brazil. They are miniature-growing epiphytes, with tight clusters of small pseudobulbs topped with a single leaf, and tend to hug the branches on which they grow. They produce short inflorescences with a single flower.
CULTIVATION: Best grown on slabs of cork or tree-fern, or potted in small terracotta pots using sphagnum moss as the growing medium. They prefer humid shaded conditions; do not like to become desiccated. They must have good air circulation to ensure successful cultivation. Propagate by division.

Isabelia virginalis

☼ ✦ ↔ 2–6 in (5–15 cm)
↕ 1½–3 in (35–80 mm)

Delightful species from Brazil; interesting and distinctive growth habit. Pseudobulbs covered in a criss-crossing pattern of fibrous bracts. Individual white to pale mauve-pink blooms, 8 mm wide, in winter. Zones 10–12.

ISATIS

WOAD

Genus of 30 annual, biennial, and perennial herbs, belonging to the cabbage (Brassicaceae) family, native to Europe and the Mediterranean to central Asia. They feature simple leaves and loose racemes of 4 small flowers, usually in yellow shades, in late spring to early summer. The fruit is a flat seed pod containing 1 or 2 seeds. Woad (*I. tinctoria*) was used as a source of blue dye before indigo.
CULTIVATION: These plants thrive best in gravelly soil that is fertile,

Iris, HC, Dutch, 'Cream Beauty'

Iris, Hybrid Cultivar, Dutch, 'Telstar'

Isoplexis canariensis

well-drained, and moist. Place in full sun. Propagate from seed in autumn and spring.

Isatis indigotica

☼ ❄ ↔ 12–24 in (30–60 cm)
↑ 12–24 in (30–60 cm)

Herbaceous perennial. Fleshy leaves, lance-shaped, toothed. Yellow flowers in late spring–early autumn. Black seed pods. Zones 6–9.

Isatis tinctoria

DYER'S WOAD, GUADO
☼ ❄ ↔ 1–2 ft (0.3–0.6 m)
↑ 3–5 ft (0.9–1.5 m)

Vigorous upright biennial or short-lived perennial herb from Europe and southwestern Asia. Freely branching stems, oblong to lance-shaped leaves. Terminal panicles of small, 4-petaled, yellow flowers. Flat seed pods shiny purple-black when mature. Zones 6–8.

ISMELIA

This genus of around 5 species of annuals and short-lived perennials in the daisy (Asteraceae) family, which was established with the break-up of the genus *Chrysanthemum*, may prove to be indistinguishable from *Xanthopthalmum*. Found around the Mediterranean region and on Madeira and the Canary Islands, they are bushy plants with upright stems that sometimes become woody at the base. The foliage is pinnately lobed, sometimes with very narrow lobes, and may be toothed. The daisy-like flowerheads are often brightly colored and appear in abundance.
CULTIVATION: These plants are intolerant of repeated frosts but are otherwise very adaptable in mild climates. Plant in a bright position with light

well-drained soil. Water well when in bud and flower, but otherwise keep rather dry. Usually raised from seed, although perennial species may also be propagated from half-hardened stem cuttings.

Ismelia carinata

syns *Chrysanthemum carinatum, Ismelia versicolor*
☼/◐ ✦ ↔ 12–16 in (30–40 cm)
↑ 32–40 in (80–100 cm)

Annual of obscure origin, probably from Morocco. Upright stems; bright green, fleshy, pinnately lobed leaves. Flowerheads to 4 in (10 cm) diameter, disc florets dark, ray florets multicolored in yellow, orange, and red tones with light base, in summer–early autumn. '**Court Jesters**', popular mixed color strain. Summer annual in cool areas. Zones 10–12.

ISOCHILUS

This is a small genus containing about 8 sympodial orchid species (family Orchidaceae) that are native to Central and South America. These graceful botanical species with grass-like foliage look attractive even when they are not in flower. They flower from the top of the thin matured growth, with the top leaves sometimes changing color, taking on purple tones before blooming commences. The flowers are small and colorful, and in some cases do not open fully and are self-pollinating.
CULTIVATION: With their thick succulent root system, these plants are very readily grown in pots of a well-drained but moisture-retentive bark-based mixture. All species of *Isochilus* prefer intermediate growing conditions and must be watered regularly, as the plants are invariably in constant growth. Propagate by division.

Isochilus linearis

Isochilus aurantiacus

☼ ✦ ↔ 4–20 in (10–50 cm)
↑ 4–16 in (10–40 cm)

Winter-flowering species from Brazil. Small clusters of tiny bright tangerine-orange blooms. Zones 10–12.

Isochilus linearis

☼ ✦ ↔ 4–24 in (10–60 cm)
↑ 4–24 in (10–60 cm)

From central and northern South America; most frequently cultivated species. Pink to purple flowers, tubular, ½ in (12 mm) wide, in spring. Some forms are self-pollinating and rarely open. Zones 10–12.

ISOPLEXIS

Evergreen subshrubs, 3 species, from the Canary Islands and Madeira in the foxglove (Scrophulariaceae) family. Bear upright spikes of flaring tubular flowers in shades of yellow and orange.
CULTIVATION: These showy shrubs grow well in warm-temperate climates;

Ismelia carinata

require protection in colder areas. Need moderately fertile soil, full sun or light shade, and plentiful water in summer. Deadhead regularly. Propagate from seed in spring, from softwood cuttings taken in late summer, or basal suckers.

Isoplexis canariensis ★

☼/◐ ❧ ↔ 3 ft (0.9 m) ↑ 4 ft (1.2 m)
Native to the Canary Islands. Lance-shaped to oblong leaves, toothed

Isatis indigotica

Isopogon cuneatus

Isoplexis sceptrum

margins, slightly downy. Foxglove-like flower spikes to 12 in (30 cm) long; flowers are orangey yellow to yellowish brown, appearing in the summer. Zones 9–11.

Isoplexis sceptrum

☼ ⌇ ↔ 7 ft (2 m) ↕ 6 ft (1.8 m)
This species has slightly glossy foliage, and is a native of Madeira. The flower spikes, held well above the foliage, are shorter than those of *I. canariensis*, but are very showy, being well packed with tawny orange flowers. Zones 9–11.

ISOPOGON

The majority of the 30 or so species in this southern Australian genus of the protea (Proteaceae) family are found in Western Australia. They are attractive evergreen shrubs with tough dissected foliage and showy flowers that form dense globular heads, generally in shades of yellow and pink. The rounded or egg-shaped cone-like fruits are usually borne terminally and persist

for a considerable time, giving some members of the genus the common name of cone bush.
CULTIVATION: These plants like full sun and light well-drained soil. Some species are best suited to winter rainfall areas, especially those from Western Australia. Pruning is not usually necessary, except when young to form the basis of a well-branched shrub. Most species will tolerate occasional light frosts. Propagate from cuttings or from seed, which may be slow to germinate.

Isopogon anemonifolius 'Woorikee 2000'

Isopogon anemonifolius
DRUMSTICKS

☼ ⌇ ↔ 4 ft (1.2 m) ↕ 6 ft (1.8 m)
An erect bushy shrub, which is found in eastern Australia. The flat dull green leaves are divided into 3 segments, and then again divided and lobed, with an attractive purplish tinge. The soft yellow flowers form in terminal rounded heads, 1½ in (35 mm) across, and appear in the late spring to summer. 'Woorikee 2000', dwarf cultivar, with leaves tipped with red, and yellow flowers. Zones 9–11.

Isopogon anethifolius
NARROW-LEAF DRUMSTICKS

☼ ⌇ ↔ 6 ft (1.8 m) ↕ 6 ft (1.8 m)
Shrub native to Eastern Australia, with pinnate leaves, and very narrow linear-like leaflets . Tightly packed flowerheads, deep yellow, appear in summer. Zones 9–10.

Isopogon ceratophyllus

☼ ❊ ↔ 3 ft (0.9 m) ↕ 3 ft (0.9 m)
Occurring in Victoria, Tasmania, and South Australia. Dwarf compact shrub, with deeply divided, green, spiky leaves. The terminal flowerheads, with individual yellow flowers, to 1 in (25 mm) long, appear in spring–early summer. Withstands periods of water-logged soils. Zones 8–9.

Isopogon cuneatus
syn. *Isopogon cuniatus*

☼ ⌇ ↔ 7 ft (2 m) ↕ 8 ft (2.4 m)
From Western Australia. Large shrub with an erect habit, enjoying poor sandy soils but preferring some summer watering. Stiff mid-green leaves, ¾ in (18 mm) long. Flowers in globular heads, usually in shades of pink and soft purple, in spring. Prune well when young to encourage fresh dense growth. This species is sold

Isopogon anemonifolius

Isopogon dubius

Isopogon formosus

central base; 3 oval deeply notched lobes; stems often very dark. White, sometimes pinkish, flowers produced in spring. Single seed with 8 to 10 ribs. Zones 4–6.

ITEA

SWEETSPIRE

Very attractive but not widely culti-vated, the 10 evergreen and deciduous shrubs and small trees in this genus present an interesting combination of foliage and flowers. They are members of the gooseberry (Grossulariaceae) family. Their foliage is often more re-miniscent of holly and their flowers are similar to those of hazel or the tassel tree *(Garrya)*. Found naturally in Asia, with a sole eastern North American representative, the evergreens offer dark lustrous leaves throughout the year, while the deciduous species have brilliant autumn foliage color. The catkin-like racemes are not color-ful and are really more of a novelty for their contrast with the foliage. Named from the Greek, *itea*, meaning willow, on account of their pendulous catkins.
CULTIVATION: Frost hardiness varies, but the commonly grown species are reasonably tough and will thrive in most well-drained soils with a posi-tion in full sun or partial shade. They are, however, not drought tolerant and need ample summer moisture. Propagate from seed or from half-hardened cuttings.

extensively throughout the world as a cut flower, due to its unusual form and lasting qualities. Zones 9–11.

Isopogon dawsonii

◌ ❄ ↔ 5 ft (1.5 m) ↑ 12 ft (3.5 m)
Erect open shrub or small tree from eastern Australia. Tolerant of summer humidity. Narrow linear leaves, to 5 in (12 cm) long, divided into seg-ments. Creamy yellow silky flowers, in terminal heads, in winter–spring. Zones 9–11.

Isopogon dubius

◌ ❄ ↔ 5 ft (1.5 m) ↑ 5 ft (1.5 m)
Bushy upright shrub from Western Australia, well known in cultivation. Flat, grayish green, prickly leaves, divided into 3 segments. Rose pink flowers, in terminal heads, in late winter–spring. Requires excellent drainage, tolerates dry conditions. Zones 9–11.

Isopogon formosus ★

ROSE CONE FLOWER

◌ ❄ ↔ 6 ft (1.8 m) ↑ 6 ft (1.8 m)
Erect or spreading shrub from Western Australia. Narrow prickly leaves divided into short cylindrical segments. Mauve-pink flowers in cone-like heads, about 2½ in (6 cm) across, in winter–spring. Highly orna-mental, requires excellent drainage, dislikes summer humidity. Zones 9–11.

ISOPYRUM

FALSE RUE ANEMONE

This genus of 30 rhizomatous or tuberous perennial herbs, native to North America and temperate

Eurasia, belongs to the buttercup (Ranunculaceae) family. Their thin leaves are deeply divided, each leaflet with up to 3 lobes, giving a feathery fern-like appearance. Cupped, nod-ding, white flowers, in panicles or solitary, with 5 or 6 petal-like sepals and numerous stamens, appear in early spring. The fruit is an achene which may contain numerous seeds. Although some *Isopyrum* species may be toxic, Native Americans used

certain North American species to treat digestive disorders.
CULTIVATION: These plants prefer moist to average soil, rich in organic matter, in full to light shade. Propagate from seed or by division of roots.

Isopyrum thalictroides

◌ ❄ ↔ 3–6 in (8–15 cm)
↑ 4–10 in (10–25 cm)
Herbaceous perennial from Europe; whorls of fern-like leaves arise from

Isopogon dawsonii

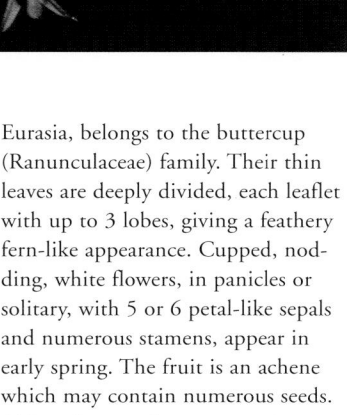

Itea chinensis

CHINESE SWEETSPIRE, SWEETSPIRE

☼ ❄ ↔6–10 ft (1.8–3 m)
↑6–10 ft (1.8–3 m)

Evergreen shrub, native to western China. Arching branches; leaves deep green, serrated edges, rather holly-like. Narrow clusters of tiny white flowers, on 8 in (20 cm) long racemes. Small brown seed capsules. Zones 7–9.

Itea ilicifolia

HOLLYLEAF SWEETSPIRE

☼ ❄ ↔10 ft (3 m) ↑15 ft (4.5 m)

Widely cultivated evergreen shrub from western China. Narrow erect habit. Deep green holly-like leaves, 2–4 in (5–10 cm) long, edged with small spines. Cream to pale yellow flowers, on racemes to 15 in (38 cm) long, honey scented, in summer. Zones 7–10.

Itea japonica

☼◐ ❄ ↔12–16 in (30–40 cm)
↑12–16 in (30–40 cm)

Attractive deciduous shrub of bushy habit from Japan. Leaves to 1¾ in

Ixia curta

(4 cm) long. Upward-pointing 2½ in (6 cm) spikes of tiny, fluffy, white, scented flowers, in summer. Foliage turns brilliant colors in autumn. 'Beppu', particularly rich autumn color. Zones 6–9.

Itea virginica

SWEETSPIRE, VIRGINIA WILLOW

☼ ❄ ↔5 ft (1.5 m) ↑4–10 ft (1.2–3 m)

Deciduous shrub from eastern North America, and the most widely grown species. Forms clump of arching stems, 2–4 in (5–10 cm) long, serrated-edged leaves, develop vivid red and orange

Itea virginica 'Henry's Garnet'

Ixia paniculata

tones in autumn. Racemes of tiny honey-scented cream flowers, 2–6 in (5–15 cm) long, erect rather than pendulous. 'Henry's Garnet' is a well-known cultivar. Zones 5–9.

IXIA

CORN LILY, WAND FLOWER

This South African genus in the iris (Iridaceae) family contains some 50 species of corms with fine grassy foliage, usually quite short in comparison to the wiry, often arching flower stems. The flowers are simple 5- or 6-petaled structures massed in spikes at the stem tips. Often brightly colored, they may also be pale with brighter markings, and occur in some unusual shades including pale blue-green.
CULTIVATION: Plant in a sunny position in light well-drained soil. In hot areas the flowers will last longer with a little shade. Water well in spring but allow to dry off after flowering. Propagation is usually from offsets, less commonly from seed.

Ixia curta

☼/◐ ⚘ ↔6–8 in (15–20 cm)
↑8–16 in (20–40 cm)

Spring-flowering species. Grassy, sometimes twisted leaves, to 10 in (25 cm) long. Short spike of cup-shaped orange flowers with red or green blotch often outlined in red. Zones 9–10.

Ixia maculata

☼ ⚘ ↔6 in (15 cm) ↑8–20 in (20–50 cm)

Variable robust plant with weedy potential. Stems are erect and wiry. Leaves are grassy and untidy, withering quickly after the flowers fade. Numerous large cupped flowers, petals in cream, purple-pink, cherry red, pink, yellow, orange shades, often with a dark eye, as well as stripes and bicolors, spring-flowering. Zones 9–10.

Ixia maculata

Ixia paniculata

syn. *Morphixia paniculata*

☼/◐ ⚘ ↔6 in (15 cm)
↑18–30 in (45–75 cm)

Robust species with weedy potential. Leaves a little broader than most species, to 24 in (60 cm) long. Flower stems long, with heads of white to creamy yellow flowers, often pink- to red-tinted, petals sometimes darker at base, in spring–summer. Zones 9–10.

Ixia viridiflora

☼ ⚘ ↔8 in (20 cm) ↑12–24 in (30–60 cm)

Robust species from southwest Cape region, South Africa. Fine grassy leaves to 20 in (50 cm) long. Variable short-lived flowers in open stars, petals sea-green, turquoise, teal, aqua-blue, duck-egg blue, often with a dark central marking, appear from mid-spring. Zones 9–10.

IXIOLIRION

A genus of 4 bulbous perennial herbs from the family Tecophilaeaceae, originating from southwest and central

Itea ilicifolia

Itea chinensis

Asia. The narrow grassy leaves grow from a central point, forming rosettes. In spring and summer tall slender stems carry umbels or loose racemes of funnel-shaped flowers in blue to violet shades.

CULTIVATION: Plant these bulbs in a sheltered sunny position in light, well-drained, sandy soil, allowed to become hot and dry in summer. Propagate from seed or by dividing the bulbs and removing the offsets in autumn.

Ixiolirion tataricum

SIBERIAN LILY, TARTAR LILY

☼ ❄ ↔ 12–16 in (30–40 cm)
↑ 10–16 in (25–40 cm)

Bulbous perennial from southwest and central Asia. Narrow, semi-erect, grass-like leaves. Abundant clusters of up to 4 flowers, on 16 in (40 cm) tall stems, blue or purple-blue tepals, darker stripe at center, in spring–early summer. Zones 5–9.

IXORA

JUNGLE FLAME

Common throughout the tropics, this genus of about 400 evergreen summer-flowering shrubs and small trees belongs to the madder (Rubiaceae) family. The genus name is from the Portuguese word for the Hindu deity, Siva, to whom the blooms are dedicated. The flowers are usually produced in showy clusters, ranging from scarlet, pink, and yellow to white, and are sometimes fragrant. Attractive glossy leaves and a compact habit makes them suitable for containers or massed plantings. The fruit, a 1- to 2-seeded drupe, mostly red, ripens to black. In addition to the

Ixora casei

species, there are numerous hybrids and varieties that are of uncertain botanical origin.

CULTIVATION: Frost tender, these plants will not tolerate a temperature much below 55°F (13°C), and prefer bright indirect sun. The soil should be friable, with added sharp sand and leaf mold. Pinch out the tips when young to encourage branching, and prune older plants after flowering. Propagate from seed in spring, or from half-hardened cuttings, taken from short-jointed non-flowering shoots, in summer.

Ixora casei

☼ ⚘ ↔ 8 ft (2.4 m) ↑ 12 ft (3.5 m)

Medium evergreen shrub from the Caroline Islands in the tropical Pacific. Large glossy leaves, to 12 in (30 cm) long. Very large compact flowerheads carry numerous, small, orange to red flowers, in summer. 'Super King' bears large vivid red flowers. Zones 10–12.

Ixora chinensis

☼ ⚘ ↔ 5 ft (1.5 m) ↑ 6 ft (1.8 m)

Small, rounded, evergreen shrub originating from tropical parts of East Asia, particularly China and Taiwan. Glossy deep green leaves. Flowers in very large, showy, terminal clusters, to 4 in (10 cm) across, bright orange, in late spring–autumn. Good hedge plant. 'Nora Grant', coral red flowers; 'Prince of Orange' ★, prolific orange-red flowers. Zones 10–12.

Ixora coccinea

FLAME OF THE WOODS

☼ ⚘ ↔ 8 ft (2.4 m) ↑ 8 ft (2.4 m)

Bushy gently rounded shrub from tropical Asia, mainly India and Sri

Lanka. Leaves are glossy, dark green. Small brilliant orange-red flowers, in large round clusters, appear in summer. Zones 11–12.

Ixora javanica

☼ ⚘ ↔ 8 ft (2.4 m) ↑ 15 ft (4.5 m)

This shrub or small tree, from Java and the Malay Peninsula, is smaller in cultivation than in its natural habitat. The flowers are red or, less often, pink or orange, and appear in dense clusters. Zones 11–12.

Ixora Hybrid Cultivars

☼ ⚘ ↔ 12–36 in (30–90 cm)
↑ 1–6 ft (0.3–1.8 m)

There are numerous *Ixora* hybrid cultivars, most of which are derived from *I. coccinea*. They include: 'Exotica', bright red flowers fading to orange, creating a distinctively two-toned flowerhead; 'Frances Perry', deep yellow flowers; 'Fraseri', vivid salmon pink flowers; 'Herrera's White', white flowers; 'Orange Glow', bright orange flowers; 'Pink Delight', pink flowers; 'Rosea', rose pink flowers; 'Sunkist', the most common *Ixora* cultivar, a dwarf shrub to 3 ft (0.9 m), small, slender, glossy leaves, and flowers of apricot-yellow, ageing to brick red; 'Sunny Gold', orange-amber flowers; 'Thai Dwarf', flowers in a range of colors from pink to red, yellow to orange; and 'Thai King', orange-red flowers. Other attractive cultivars include: 'Aurora' and 'Florida Sunset'. Zones 11–12.

Ixora chinensis 'Prince of Orange'

Ixora javanica

Jacaranda mimosifolia

Jaborosa integrifolia

JABOROSA

There are about 20 scrambling, ever-green, perennial herbs from South America in this genus, and they are members of the nightshade (Solan-aceae) family. The leaves arise from a central base. Clusters of 5-lobed, bell-shaped or tubular flowers, are solitary or in few-flowered cymes. Fruits are flat green berries, and the seeds germi-nate in 3 to 6 weeks.
CULTIVATION: These plants prefer rich, moist soil kept drier in winter, in a partly shaded position. Propagate in spring from seed or by division.

Jaborosa integrifolia

☼ ❄ ↔ 8 in (20 cm) ↕ 4–8 in (10–20 cm)
Tuft-forming perennial, native to southern Brazil, Uruguay, and Argen-tina, growing from an underground trailing stem. Narrowly oval-shaped leaves, to 6 in (15 cm) long, are on long stalks. Large, solitary, tubular, green to white, narrow-lobed flowers, to 2½ in (6 cm) in diameter, in summer, fragrant at night. Zones 7–9.

JACARANDA

The genus comprises about 50 species of deciduous and evergreen trees and shrubs belonging to the trumpet-vine (Bignoniaceae) family. They are native to the drier areas of tropical and sub-tropical Central and South America and have elegant, fern-like, bipinnate leaves, some pinnate or simple. Mauve-blue, rarely pink or white, funnel- or bell-shaped flowers in terminal or axillary panicles appear in spring–summer. Widely grown as an avenue tree or lawn specimen. Pretoria, South Africa, is called the jacaranda city.
CULTIVATION: Jacarandas will grow quickly in fertile well-drained soil in full sun. Protect from the wind and frost when young. They are relatively frost hardy once established. Pruning is not necessary for outdoor speci-mens. Water freely in the growing season and sparingly in winter. They are shallow-rooted heavy feeders, and shrubs planted nearby may suffer. Propagation is from seed in late winter or early spring, and from half-hardened cuttings taken in summer.

Jacaranda caerulea

☼ ❄ ↔ 10 ft (3 m) ↕ 40–70 ft (12–21 m)
Native to the West Indies, evergreen tree. Large dense panicles of purple, blue, or white bell-shaped flowers, in late spring. Fern-like leaves bipinnate, with 4 to 13 pairs of tiny leaflets. The fruits are oblong capsules. Zones 10–11.

Jacaranda cuspidifolia

☼ ❄ ↔ 30 ft (9 m) ↕ 15–40 ft (4.5–12 m)
Native of Brazil, Argentina, Bolivia, and Paraguay. Compared with *J. mim-osifolia*, the leaves are larger, with more leaflets (up to 20 pairs on each pinna), and the flowers are larger, brighter blue-violet, with bigger clusters. Fruits nearly spherical, white to pale brown. Zones 10–11.

Jacaranda mimosifolia

BLUE HAZE TREE, BRAZILIAN ROSEWOOD, FERN TREE, JACARANDA
☼ ❄ ↔ 20–35 ft (6–10 m)
↕ 25–50 ft (8–15 m)
This fast-growing deciduous tree comes from drier areas of South America. Elegant, mid-green, bipin-nate foliage, may turn rich yellow in late winter before being shed. From late spring–early summer, produces prolific terminal clusters of hanging, bell-shaped, mauve-blue flowers on leafless branches. Disc-shaped red-brown seed pods. 'Variegata', green and yellow variegated leaves; '**White Christmas**', large clusters of white flowers. Zones 10–11.

JACKSONIA

This genus with 40 species of shrubs or small trees is endemic to parts of Australia and is a member of the pea-flower subfamily of the legume (Fabaceae) family. The pea-flower-like blooms are orange or yellow, occa-sionally red. Habitats vary from coastal heaths to sclerophyll forests on a range of soils. An obvious feature is the general lack of leaves; the green or gray-green stems carry out the func-tions of photosynthesis while the leaves are greatly reduced to small brownish scales or spines.
CULTIVATION: Since the 40 species occur over a wide range of climates and soils, their requirements in culti-vation also vary, from some that will not tolerate high humidity in summer to those that will grow happily with "wet feet." All species can be propa-gated from seed, which requires pre-treatment; some can be propagated from cuttings, from young growth that is not too soft.

Jacksonia scoparia

AUSTRALIAN DOGWOOD
☼ ❄ ↔ 10 ft (3 m) ↕ 15 ft (4.5 m)
Found in Queensland and New South Wales, Australia. Tall shrub, hard gray bark, often occurs in areas of poor drainage. Green-gray branches, leaves small brown scales. Pea-flower-like scented blooms, in terminal clusters, in spring, yellow to orange, with a patch of red. Hairy fruits. Zones 8–10.

JAMESIA

Genus of the hydrangea (Hydrange-aceae) family comprising a single species of deciduous shrub found in the mountains of western USA. Closely

Jacksonia scoparia

Jacaranda caerulea

Jacaranda cuspidifolia

Jamesia americana

related to *Deutzia*, it is named after Dr Edwin James, an early botanical explorer of the Rocky Mountains. This bushy shrub is usually grown for its rough-textured foliage, which colors brilliantly in autumn, and its lightly scented white flowers.
CULTIVATION: This frost-hardy shrub requires moderately fertile well-drained soil and a sunny location for the development of good autumn color. It is suitable for planting in a shrub border or as a specimen in a rock garden. Prune after flowering to remove old or overcrowded growth. Propagate from seed, half-hardened cuttings, or by layering in spring.

Jamesia americana
CLIFFBUSH, WAXFLOWER
☼ ❋ ↔ 8 ft (2.4 m) ↑ 3–8 ft (0.9–2.4 m)
Rounded deciduous shrub, velvety gray-green foliage, colors to a brilliant orange-red, in autumn. Peeling papery bark on older stems. Small terminal clusters of star-shaped, fragrant, white flowers, sometimes tinted pink in bud, in late spring. Small fruits. Zones 6–9.

JASIONE
SHEEP'S BIT
There are about 20 species of annuals, perennials, and biennials in this genus, which belongs to the bellflower (Campanulaceae) family. These plants are native to Europe and regions of the Mediterranean, where they grow in grassland. Plants form tufts of narrow grassy foliage. Their small blue flowers are borne in compact terminal heads reminiscent of scabious, and are surrounded by 1 or more rows of bracts. Flowering occurs in summer.
CULTIVATION: Small species are best grown in the rock garden while taller ones are suitable for the front of the border. Grow in full sun in a well-drained sandy soil. Propagate by division or from seed.

Jasione laevis
syn. *Jasione perennis*
SHEEP'S BIT, SHEPHERD'S SCABIOUS
☼ ❋ ↔ 8–10 in (20–25 cm)
↑ 8–20 in (20–50 cm)
From southern and western Europe. Perennial forming dense tufts of narrow leaves. The blue flowerheads are a little over 1 in (25 mm) wide and have numerous bracts. 'Blaulicht' (syn. 'Blue Light') has globose flowerheads of vivid blue. Zones 5–9.

JASMINUM
JASMINE
Famed for the fragrance of its flowers, this genus, which belongs to the olive (Oleaceae) family, is native to Africa, Europe, and Asia (with a single American species). The genus includes some 200 species of deciduous, semi-deciduous, and evergreen shrubs and woody-stemmed climbers. The foliage is usually pinnate or less commonly trifoliate and varies greatly in color and texture. The flowers, in clusters at the branch tips and leaf axils, are tubular with 5 widely flared lobes. They are most commonly white, white flushed with pink, or yellow, and can be scentless to overpoweringly fragrant.
CULTIVATION: Jasmines vary greatly in their hardiness, depending on their origins, though few will tolerate repeated severe frosts. They are averse to drought, preferring moist, humus-rich, well-drained soil and a position in full sun or partial shade. In suitable climates most species grow rapidly and some can become rather invasive. Readily propagated from seed, cuttings, or layers, which with some low-growing species may form naturally, making them difficult to contain.

Jasminum angulare
syn. *Jasminum capense*
☼/◐ ⚘ ↔ 7–10 ft (2–3 m)
↑ 15–17 ft (4.5–5 m)
From South Africa. Evergreen climber or rambler. Dark green pinnate leaves, 3 to 5 leaflets, with sweetly scented bunches of star-shaped flowers, 1¼ in (30 mm) wide. Flowers cover the plant from mid-summer to late autumn. Zones 10–11.

Jasminum azoricum ★
AZORES JASMINE
☼/◐ ⚘ ↔ 20 ft (6 m) ↑ 20 ft (6 m)
Evergreen climbing shrub from the Azores. Glossy, deep green, leathery leaves, 3 or sometimes 5 lance-shaped leaflets, to 2 in (5 cm) long. Flowers pure white, very scented, in loose panicles, in late summer. Zones 10–11.

Jasminum beesianum
☼/◐ ❋ ↔ 15 ft (4.5 m) ↑ 15 ft (4.5 m)
Scrambling or twining, Chinese, deciduous shrub. Simple, 2 in (5 cm) long, lance-shaped leaves in pairs. Small fragrant blooms in 3-flowered clusters, shades of pink from pale to deep rose, in late spring–autumn. Glossy black fruits. Zones 7–10.

Jasminum fruticans
☼/◐ ❋ ↔ 10 ft (3 m) ↑ 10 ft (3 m)
Native to the Mediterranean region and western Asia. Near-evergreen to evergreen shrub. Foliage trifoliate, leathery deep green leaflets. Clusters of up to 5 unscented flowers, in summer, throughout the year in frost-free climates. Zones 8–10.

Jasminum humile
ITALIAN JASMINE, ITALIAN YELLOW JASMINE
☼/◐ ❋ ↔ 12 ft (3.5 m) ↑ 12 ft (3.5 m)
Evergreen or semi-evergreen shrub found naturally from the Middle East to China. Short pinnate leaves, up to 7 leaflets. Clusters of yellow, variably scented flowers, in summer. 'Revolutum' is a reliably fragrant cultivar with large leaves. Zones 8–10.

Jasminum humile 'Revolutum'

Jasminum mesnyi
PRIMROSE JASMINE, YELLOW JASMINE
☼/◐ ❋ ↔ 10 ft (3 m) ↑ 10 ft (3 m)
Native of western China. Evergreen shrub, sprawling, untidy growth habit, forms a clump of arching cane-like stems. Foliage trifoliate, semi-glossy, bright green shade. Unscented flowers, bright yellow, usually semi-double, in summer. Zones 8–10.

Jasminum nitidum
ANGEL WING JASMINE
☼/◐ ❋ ↔ 3–7 ft (0.9–2 m) ↑ 10 ft (3 m)
Dark green glossy foliage. Twining climbing habit, can be trimmed into a hedge. Fragrant purple-pink buds open to large, star-shaped, white flowers in spring. Flowers until early autumn. Zones 7–9.

Jasminum nudiflorum
WINTER JASMINE
☼/◐ ❋ ↔ 10 ft (3 m) ↑ 10 ft (3 m)
From northern China. Sprawling deciduous shrub. Mass of slightly arched, whippy, green canes, dark green trifoliate leaves. Bright yellow blooms, in winter, when all else is bare. Zones 6–9.

Jasminum mesnyi

Jasminum nudiflorum

Jasminum odoratissimum
CANARY ISLAND JASMINE

☀ ⊱ ↔ 10 ft (3 m) ↑ 10 ft (3 m)

Canary Islands native. Large deciduous shrub. Deep green, glossy, pinnate
leaves. Clusters of very white fragrant
flowers, in summer, essence of which
is used in perfumes. Zones 9–11.

Jasminum officinale
COMMON JASMINE, COMMON WHITE
JASMINE, POETS' JASMINE, TRUE JASMINE

☀/◐ ❄ ↔ 15 ft (4.5 m) ↑ 30 ft (9 m)

Found from the Middle East to
China. Sprawling, somewhat twining,
deciduous shrub, usually trimmed to
8 ft (2.4 m). Slightly downy pinnate
leaves, 5 to 9 leaflets. White or very
pale pink flowers, fragrant, in early
summer–autumn. Several variegated
foliage cultivars, such as cream-edged
'**Argenteovariegatum**' and gold-
blotched '**Aureum**'. Zones 7–10.

Jasminum parkeri
DWARF JASMINE

☀/◐ ❄ ↔ 24 in (60 cm) ↑ 12 in (30 cm)

Small, spreading, evergreen shrub,
native to northwest India. Tiny yellow
unscented flowers, perfect replicas of
those of the larger jasmines. Good for
rock gardens or large containers, produces flowers in summer. Zones 8–10.

Jasminum polyanthum

☀/◐ ❄ ↔ 25 ft (8 m)
↑ 10–17 ft (3–5 m)

Vigorous evergreen climber from
southwestern China that twines and
tangles through trees, trellises, and
other structures. Dark green foliage
consists of 5 to 7 leaflets, can have
bronze tones in winter. Delicate pink
buds appear from late winter and
open to white fragrant flowers, ¾ in
(18 mm) wide, in spring. Flowers
through to mid-autumn. Zones 7–9.

Jasminum sambac
ARABIAN JASMINE, ZAMBAC

☀ ⊱ ↔ 6 ft (1.8 m) ↑ 5–12 ft (1.5–3.5 m)

Woody-stemmed evergreen climber,
can be treated as a lax shrub. Large
simple, not pinnate, leaves, glossy
deep green with a heavy texture.
Clusters of up to 12 fragrant, waxy,
white flowers that age to pale pink,
throughout the year. '**Grand Duke
of Tuscany**', double-flowered cultivar.
Zones 10–11.

Jasminum sambac

Jatropha integerrima

Jatropha cinerea, in the wild, Bahia de los Angeles, Baja California, Mexico

Jatropha multifida

Jatropha podagrica

Jasminum × stephanense

☀ ❄ ↔ 5–10 ft (1.5–3 m) ↑ 17 ft (5 m)

A *J. beesianum* × *J. officinale* hybrid
from southwestern China. Rampant,
woody, twining, deciduous climber
with soft gray-green foliage that has
a dull appearance. Bunches of fragrant
pale pink flowers, ¾ in (18 mm) long,
appear from summer–autumn.
Zones 8–10.

JATROPHA

This variable genus of the euphorbia
(Euphorbiaceae) family comprises some
170 species of succulent perennials and
evergreen or deciduous shrubs, rarely
trees. All species contain a milky latex
that may irritate the skin. They are
found in tropical to warm-temperate
regions of the world, mainly Central
and South America. Leaves are usually
palmately lobed, although some are
lobeless. Small clusters of purple, yellow, scarlet, or red flowers are borne in
summer. All parts of the plant are
mildly poisonous, but they are used
medicinally in the tropics.
CULTIVATION: Used in street plantings, borders, and hedges, these plants
appreciate a fertile, well-drained, sandy
soil and full sun, but most will tolerate part-shade. Frost tender, in temperate zones they can be grown in a
warm greenhouse. Half-hardened cuttings should be placed in cool shade
to allow the ends of the cuttings to
dry before rooting, or propagate from
seed in spring or summer.

Jatropha cinerea

☀ ⊱ ↔ 10 ft (3 m) ↑ 10–25 ft (3–8 m)

From desert areas of western Mexico.
Spreading, multi-stemmed deciduous
shrub or, rarely, small tree with thick
twigs, leaves kidney-shaped, to 4 in
(10 cm) wide. Small panicles of
dull pink bell-shaped flowers, ½ in
(12 mm) long, in spring–summer.
Zones 10–12.

Jatropha integerrima
syns *Jatropha hastata*, *J. pandurifolia*
PEREGRINA, SPICY JATROPHA

☀ ⊱ ↔ 4–8 ft (1.2–2.4 m)
↑ 10–20 ft (3–6 m)

Spreading evergreen tree, native of
Cuba, Hispaniola, and Puerto Rico;
may reach 20 ft (6 m) high. This
species does best in moist tropical
conditions. Leaves variable, ranging
from 3-lobed to fiddle-shaped, rich
green with bronze undersides.
Branched clusters of small, funnel-
shaped, 5-petalled, bright rose red
flowers in terminal clusters, throughout the year, but predominantly in
warmer weather. Seeds and sap are
both poisonous. Zones 10–12.

Jatropha multifida
CORAL PLANT, PHYSIC NUT

☀ ⊱ ↔ 10 ft (3 m) ↑ 12 ft (3.5 m)

Large evergreen shrub or small tree
found from Mexico to Brazil. Rounded
leaves, deeply divided into 7 to
11 blades, dark green above, whitish
underneath. Small scarlet flowers on
green or red stalks, above the foliage,
in summer. Egg-shaped fruit contains
up to 3 seeds. All parts of this plant
are poisonous. Zones 10–12.

Jatropha podagrica ★
GOUT PLANT, GUATEMALA RHUBARB,
TARTOGO

☀ ⊱ ↔ 10–12 in (25–30 cm)
↑ 20–36 in (60–90 cm)

Small succulent shrub from Central
America. The trunk is grotesquely
swollen, becoming knobbly with age,
gray, resembling a miniature baobab
tree (*Adansonia digitata*). Round to
oval 3- to 5-lobed leaves, dark green
uppersurface, glaucous beneath.
Terminal clusters of small brilliant
orange-red to scarlet flowers held
above the foliage on red or green
stalks. Long flowering season, usually
from winter–summer. Zones 10–12.

JEFFERSONIA
syn. *Plagiorhegma*
TWIN LEAF

This genus consists of 2 species of herbaceous perennials in the barberry (Berberidaceae) family, one from North America and the other from northeastern Asia. They are small clump-forming plants with 2-lobed kidney-shaped leaves and dainty cup-shaped flowers in late spring. The genus was named after Thomas Jefferson, third president of the USA.
CULTIVATION: They are woodlanders by nature so like a cool moist aspect under a deciduous canopy in a com-post-enriched soil. As they are small plants, care should be taken in siting them in large woodland areas and they may be better cared for in a slightly shaded rock garden. Propagate from seed sown as soon as ripe, or by dividing established clumps.

Jeffersonia diphylla
RHEUMATISM ROOT

☀ ❄ ↔ 8 in (20 cm) ↑ 6–8 in (15–20 cm)
Found from Ontario, Canada, to Tennessee, USA. Leaves to 6 in (15 cm) wide. Flowers are 1 in (25 mm) across and white. Zones 5–9.

Jeffersonia dubia
syn. *Plagiorhegma dubia*

☀ ❄ ↔ 6–8 in (15–20 cm)
↑ 6–8 in (15–20 cm)
From the woods of northeastern Asia. Blue-green leaves to 4 in (10 cm)

Joinvillea ascendens subsp. *glabra*, in the wild, Le Belvedere track, Monts Koghis, New Caledonia

Johannesteijsmannia magnifica

across. Flowers are pale lavender-blue or rarely white, and 1¼ in (30 mm) across. Zones 5–9.

JOHANNESTEIJSMANNIA
JOEY PALM

This genus of 4 palms in the family Arecaceae is endemic to tropical rainforests of southern Thailand, the Malay Peninsula, and Sumatra. Growing in the dense shade of the jungle canopy, a rosette of huge, simple, paddle-shaped fronds emerges from the subterranean trunk. These fronds collect litter and guide it to the center to cover the developing crown. The roots grow into the litter as it decays. Large fruits are covered with numerous corky warts. They are quite rare in the wild.
CULTIVATION: Truly magnificent, these palms are keenly sought by enthusiasts. They have been success-fully grown in tropical and warm sub-tropical regions but require a moist well-shaded position. In colder areas they can be grown indoors in contain-ers. Seed germinates readily if sown fresh. Joey palms display significant variation, even within individual species. Sow seed that comes from a specimen enjoying conditions similar to those where the palm will grow.

Johannesteijsmannia altifrons ★
☀ ⚘ ↔ 10 ft (3 m) ↑ 15 ft (4.5 m)
From Southeast Asia. Huge paddle-shaped fronds provide excellent shel-ter in a downpour. Simple, pleated, diamond-shaped leaves are used for thatching roofs in Malaysia. Crown has 20 fronds. Fruits covered in corky warts. Zones 11–12.

Johannesteijsmannia magnifica
SILVER JOEY PALM

☀ ⚘ ↔ 10 ft (3 m) ↑ 15 ft (4.5 m)
Rare in cultivation, native to the rain-forests of the Malay Peninsula. Paddle-shaped leaves, underside covered in fine white hairs, which may give a sil-very appearance. Fruits to 2 in (5 cm) wide, covered with numerous corky warts. Adaptable palm. Zones 10–12.

JOINVILLEA
The only genus in the family Joinvil-leaceae, now regarded as one of the closest relatives of the huge grass family (Poaceae), consists of only 2 species of large grass-like perennials from the Pacific Islands and Malay region. The usually leaning stems bear 2 rows of ribbed and pleated leaves and terminate in panicles of small, globular, greenish flowers that are soon followed by dry pea-sized or smaller orange-red to dark brown fruits containing 1 to 3 seeds. They grow in openings in tropical forests, in exposed scrub on ridges, or in moist gullies. The genus was named by botanist-explorer Gaudichaud-Beaupré in honor of Prince François de Joinville of France.
CULTIVATION: As yet seldom culti-vated, these plants have the potential to supply interesting foliage textures for warm-climate gardens. A site that is sheltered and humid but with ample light is their likely preference, together with soil of low to moderate fertility but permanently moist. Propagation is from seed.

Joinvillea ascendens
syn. *Joinvillea gaudichaudiana*

◐/◑ ⚘ ↔ 10 ft (3 m) ↑ 15 ft (4.5 m)
Variable species divided into a num-ber of subspecies distributed over the whole range of the genus. Stems and leaf sheaths strongly compressed, leaves finely bristly. Flowers displaying pale pink stigmas. Fruit to ¼ in (6 mm) in diameter, red-brown. The typical subspecies is endemic to Hawaii.

Juglans ailanthifolia

Jubaea chilensis

J. a. subsp. *glabra* is endemic to New Caledonia, where it may grow beside the only other species, the endemic *J. plicata.* Zones 10–12.

JOVELLANA

There are 6 species of evergreen shrubs and subshrubs in this genus, within the foxglove (Scrophulariaceae) family. Two are native to New Zealand and the remainder to Chile. They are closely related to *Calceolaria* and bear similar flowers with pouched petals. The rather thin leaves have toothed margins and are variable in shape, and both the stems and leaves are slightly downy.
CULTIVATION: In cool-temperate climates these half-hardy plants need the protection of a greenhouse. Outdoors they should be grown in a sheltered shady or semi-shady position in rich well-drained soil. *J. violacea* is a little hardier but may defoliate in winter. Prune regularly to maintain a compact shape. Propagation is from seed or softwood cuttings.

Jovellana sinclairii

☼ ❄ ↔ 22 in (55 cm) ↑ 20 in (50 cm)
Found in New Zealand, growing on forest and stream margins. Subshrub with erect or sprawling habit. Small white flowers, spotted purple inside, are borne in panicles, in summer. Zones 9–11.

Jovellana violacea

☼ ❄ ↔ 3 ft (0.9 m) ↑ 3 ft (0.9 m)
Native to Chile. Dense suckering shrub. Small toothed or lobed leaves. Flowers pale violet, spotted purple, and blotched yellow on the throat, in summer. Zones 9–11.

JOVIBARBA

A small genus of 6 species from the mountains of Europe belonging to the stonecrop (Crassulaceae) family. They are rosetting succulents that are often confused with the better known houseleeks *(Sempervivum)*, which in foliage they resemble. The insignificant flowers are 6-petalled and bell-shaped, whereas those of the houseleeks are star-shaped.
CULTIVATION: These are hardy little succulents, ideal in well-drained poor soil in the rock garden, dry stone walls, troughs, or pots. Remove old rosettes after they have flowered. Propagate by division; some species detach their own rosettes that will then roll away to take root elsewhere.

Jovibarba hirta

☼ ❄ ↔ 10–12 in (25–30 cm)
↑ 4–6 in (10–15 cm)
From the mountains of central and southeastern Europe. Rosettes to 2 in (5 cm) across. Small flat leaves are narrow or broadly lance-shaped, convex below, green with darker colored tips. Branching heads of small pale yellow flowers are produced in summer. *J. h.* var. *neilreichii*, from the

lower Carpathian Mountains, has narrow leaves arranged in open rosettes. Zones 6–10.

JUANULLOA

This genus, which belongs to the nightshade (Solanaceae) family, contains about 10 species of epiphytic or climbing and rooting shrubs. They are native to central and southern America where they grow in forests, often climbing trees and flowering in the tree tops. Leaves are simple, smooth or downy, and leathery. Tubular flowers of yellow, red, or orange are borne in showy clusters.
CULTIVATION: In frost-free zones grow outdoors in fertile soil in full sun. In cool climates grow in a greenhouse or conservatory in free-draining potting mix with medium to low humidity. Propagate from seed or cuttings.

Juanulloa mexicana

☼/❂ ❄ ↔ 6 ft (1.8 m) ↑ 6 ft (1.8 m)
From Mexico and Central America. An epiphytic vine that can be grown as a shrub. Leathery, prominently veined leaves. Long, waxy, orange calyces split to reveal the drooping, tubular, orange flowers. Zones 9–12.

JUBAEA

This genus contains a single species of palm, in the family Arecaceae, native to coastal areas of Chile, where wild populations have been greatly reduced by harvesting. Its tall stout trunk has a dense crown of leaves. The sugary sap is made locally into syrup or alcohol.
CULTIVATION: Tolerates short periods of light frost but grow in a conservatory or greenhouse in cool climates. Grow in any reasonable soil in sun or filtered light and give plenty of water when young. Propagation is from fresh seed but germination is slow.

Jubaea chilensis

syn. *Jubaea spectabilis*
CHILEAN WINE PALM, COQUITO PALM
☼ ❄ ↔ 25 ft (8 m) ↑ 80 ft (24 m)
From Chile. Stout trunk, occasionally swollen in the middle. Dense crown;

fronds to 15 ft (4.5 m) long, arching or rigid, pinnately arranged leaves. Long-stalked flowers hidden within the leaves. Small, egg-shaped, edible yellow fruits, called coquito. Zones 8–10.

JUGLANS

The walnuts, a genus of the Juglandaceae family, comprise about 20 species of deciduous trees. They are distributed over the temperate zones of the Americas, southeastern Europe, and Southeast Asia. They have alternate compound leaves and monoecious flowers, borne in spring. The fruit is a hard-shelled nut enclosed in a fleshy green drupe, the kernels being prized as food. Some species produce hard, beautifully grained wood, valued for furniture making; some produce juglose, which can poison apple trees.
CULTIVATION: Walnuts thrive on deep, alluvial, well-drained soil with a high organic content, and an assured water supply, in a cool humid climate. Plantation trees are often severely pruned after 1 year to force strong single trunk growth, then stopped at 12 ft (3.5 m) or so to induce lateral branches; ornamental trees can be treated the same way. Seeds can be collected as soon as ripe in early autumn and stored in cool conditions until sown in early spring.

Juglans ailanthifolia

syn. *Juglans sieboldiana*
JAPANESE WALNUT
☼ ❄ ↔ 40 ft (12 m) ↑ 50 ft (15 m)
From Japan. Upright tree, attractive leaves, 11 to 17 leaflets, covered in

Juanulloa mexicana

Jovellana violacea

Jovibarba hirta var. *neilreichii*

Juglans cinerea

Juglans cathayensis

dark red fine hairs. Bark striped pale and dark gray. Male catkins 6–12 in (15–30 cm) long, female flowers deep red. Fruits covered in an adhesive down. *J. a.* **var.** *cordiformis* differs only in the shape of the fruits. Zones 4–9.

Juglans californica

☼ ❋ ↔ 30 ft (9 m) ↑ 30 ft (9 m)
Native of southern California, USA. Large shrub or small tree, attractive leaves composed of 11 to 15 lanceolate leaflets. Zones 7–10.

Juglans cathayensis

CHINESE BUTTERNUT, CHINESE WALNUT
☼ ❋ ↔ 50 ft (15 m) ↑ 50–70 ft (15–21 m)
From Taiwan and western and central China. Leaves have finely hairy, tooth-edged leaflets. The fruit, in clusters, encloses sweet and edible nuts. Some botanists believe this species to fall within the ambit of *J. mandshurica*. Zones 5–10.

Juglans cinerea

BUTTERNUT, BUTTERNUT WALNUT, WHITE WALNUT
☼ ❋ ↔ 50 ft (15 m) ↑ 60 ft (18 m)
From New Brunswick, Canada, to Georgia, USA. Fast-growing species, smaller in cultivation. Shoots sticky, leaves oblong, notched edges, hairy, yellow-green. Fruits solitary or in clusters. Can be short-lived. Zones 4–9.

Juglans major

syn. *Juglans elaeopyren*
ARIZONA WALNUT, NOGAL
☼ ⚘ ↔ 30 ft (9 m) ↑ 50 ft (15 m)
New Mexico to Arizona, USA. Single upright trunk, slender crown. Leaves oblong to lance-shaped, 9 to 13 leaflets. Nuts with dark brown shells. Autumn foliage creamy yellow. Zones 9–11.

Juglans nigra

AMERICAN WALNUT, BLACK WALNUT
☼ ❋ ↔ 70 ft (21 m) ↑ 100 ft (30 m)
Native of eastern and central USA and southeastern Canada. Dome-shaped crown, large leaves, 11 to 23 leaflets. Edible nuts dark brown. Grows quickly in warm areas on rich soils, usually slow elsewhere. 'Laciniata' has finely cut leaves. Zones 4–10.

Juglans regia

ENGLISH WALNUT, PERSIAN WALNUT, WALNUT
☼ ❋ ↔ 35 ft (10 m) ↑ 40–60 ft (12–18 m)
Native to southeastern Europe, the Himalayas, and China. Grown for its edible nuts. Bark pale gray. Smooth aromatic leaves, 7 leaflets; young leaves coppery purple turning green as they mature. Cultivars of the **Carpathian Group** are cold hardy, and popular throughout the USA, especially selected commercial clones 'Broadview' and 'Buccaneer'. 'Laciniata' has deeply cut leaflets. Zones 4–10.

JUNCUS

This genus of some 225 species of grass-like plants belongs to the self-named Juncaceae or rush family. Species are of cosmopolitan distribution and are found growing in wet soils such as bogs and water margins. Leaves may be flat, channeled, cylindrical, or reduced to sheaths at the stem bases. The small green or brown flowers are borne in round heads or more open clusters at the stem ends. The plants range from 12 in–5 ft (30 cm–1.5 m) in height. The name *Juncus* is derived from the Latin word meaning to bind, and refers to the use made of the stems for tying.
CULTIVATION: Many species are invasive and few are grown ornamentally. They have some use around large ponds or in wild gardening in wet areas. Grow in full sun or part-shade in heavy wet soil or shallow water. Propagate from seed or by division.

Juncus effusus

COMMON RUSH
☼ ❋ ↔ 30 in (75 cm) ↑ 5 ft (1.5 m)
Stiff, upright, twisted evergreen with rush-like leaves. Stems are rigid but smooth and look like a corkscrew. Tiny brown flowers appear in clusters in autumn, sitting above the foliage. Needs a moist soil. 'Spiralis' (corkscrew rush) has mounding, curly, sometimes upright stems. Zones 6–9.

Juncus effusus

Juncus effusus 'Spiralis'

Juglans regia

Juglans regia 'Laciniata'

Juglans major

Juncus patens
CALIFORNIAN GRAY RUSH

☼/◐ ❉ ↔ 24 in (60 cm) ↑27 in (70 cm)

Steel blue-gray foliage, upright habit. Inconspicuous flowers appear in summer. Very tolerant to dry soils but will grow in shallow water. 'Carman's Gray', silvery gray, stiff, upright foliage and needs little room for roots; will grow in bog-like areas as well as dry areas. 'Elk Blue', intense steely blue foliage, wider leaves than the species. Zones 7–10.

JUNIPERUS

This genus consists of some 60 generally slow-growing evergreen trees and shrubs in the cypress (Cupressaceae) family, occurring naturally in the Northern Hemisphere. The larger trees are valued for their timber and all species are long lived, performing particularly well on alkaline soils. Two foliage types are seen: juvenile, which

Juncus patens

Juniperus chinensis 'Foemina', bonsai

Juniperus chinensis 'Shoosmith'

Juniperus chinensis 'Variegata'

is awl-shaped (curved and needle-like), and adult, which is scale-like and stem-clasping. When crushed, the foliage of most is pungently aromatic. The small, fleshy, berry-like fruits are actually cones that ripen to blue-black or reddish. Usually separate male and female plants are found.

CULTIVATION: Although drought tolerant and tough, these plants are susceptible to fungal attack, needing an open airy situation. Well-drained soils are essential. Regular light pruning maintains shape, but do not cut bare wood. Propagation from fresh seed is best, although named cultivars should be either grafted or grown from a cutting in winter. The new season's terminal growth will also strike readily.

Juniperus ashei

☼ ❉ ↔ 20 ft (6 m) ↑30 ft (9 m)

From southern USA and Mexico. Slow-growing large shrub, sometimes

Juniperus chinensis 'Blaauw', bonsai

Juniperus chinensis var. *sargentii*, bonsai

Juniperus chinensis

a small conical tree. Young awl-shaped foliage is sage green maturing to dark green, scale-like. Small, fleshy, aromatic fruits, deep blue when ripe. Zones 8–10.

Juniperus chinensis
CHINESE JUNIPER

☼ ❉ ↔ 15 ft (4.5 m) ↑30 ft (9 m)

Native to China and Japan. Variable species in habit and size. Blunt-tipped adult foliage, prickly juvenile foliage, both on lower branches and within the tree. Berries small, round, blue-green. *J. c.* var. *sargentii*, low growing, excellent bonsai subject. *J. c.* 'Aurea', golden adult foliage, yellowish green juvenile leaves, narrow, upright or conical habit, to 20 ft (6 m); 'Blaauw', vigorous shrub, to 5 ft (1.5 m) with dense sprays of green to gray-blue scale-like leaves; 'Foemina', good bonsai subject; 'Kaizuka', large upright shrub or small tree, spreading branches densely clustered, scale-like bright green foliage; 'Keteleeri' ★, upright spire of dark green, distinctive spiraled habit of blunt-tipped closely held scales, attractive blue-green berries;

Juniperus chinensis 'Olympia'

Juniperus chinensis 'Pyramidalis'

'Mountbatten', shrub or small tree, dense columnar habit, gray-green awl-shaped leaves; 'Oblonga', rounded shrub, dense branches, inner foliage dark green, awl-shaped and prickly, outer foliage adult and scale-like; 'Olympia', of Japanese origin, a small conical tree; 'Shoosmith', conical tree with bright green foliage; 'Spartan', columnar form, dark green foliage, considered one of the best of this habit; 'Variegata', mostly juvenile foliage on long branchlets when young, then progressively develops adult foliage, at all stages irregularly flecked with creamy yellow or white. Zones 4–9.

Juniperus communis
COMMON JUNIPER

☼ ❉ ↔ 3–15 ft (0.9–4.5 m) ↑20 ft (6 m)

Widespread in the Northern Hemisphere. Variable evergreen shrub or small tree. In mild situations, narrow-columnar, tendency to spread in colder climates. Silver-backed foliage is always juvenile, needle-like, and prickly; fruits (used for flavorings and gin) green ripening to glossy black with a whitish bloom. Numerous

Juniperus communis 'Compressa'

Juniperus communis 'Hibernica'

Juniperus communis 'Pendula'

Juniperus communis 'Depressed Star'

Juniperus communis 'Repanda'

Juniperus communis 'Effusa'

Juniperus communis 'Suecica' ★

cultivars (including prostrate forms) selected for shape, foliage, and color are available. '**Compressa**', compact, narrow and slow-growing column to 3 ft (0.9 m); '**Depressa Aurea**' ★, wide-spreading ground cover to approximately 2 ft (0.6 m) tall, foliage

Juniperus davurica 'Expansa Variegata'

dense, slightly ascending and brownish green, becoming more bronze in winter; '**Depressed Star**', rounded spreading habit, light green foliage; '**Hibernica**' (syn. 'Stricta'), slender column to 10 ft (3 m), dense foliage shows a prominent silvery reverse; '**Nana**', very prostrate, slow-growing ground cover, forms a mat of dark green, excellent choice on embankments and coastal cliffs; '**Pendula**', graceful weeping branches. Zones 2–8.

Juniperus conferta
SHORE JUNIPER

☼ ❈ ↔ 5–8 ft (1.5–2.4 m) ↑ 2 ft (0.6 m)
From Japan. Wide-spreading, fast-growing, prostrate ground cover, salt

tolerant. Light green to blue-green foliage, very prickly and dense. Small berry-like fruits, ripen from green to brown. Excellent for embankments. '**Blue Lagoon**' and '**Blue Pacific**', bluer foliage; '**Emerald Sea**', gray-green foliage; '**Sunsplash**', green and gold variegated foliage. Zones 5–9.

Juniperus davurica

☼ ❈ ↔ 6–10 ft (1.8–3 m) ↑ 2 ft (0.6 m)
Very variable species occurring naturally throughout northern Asia. Gray flaking bark, branches with scale-like leaves. A number of cultivars including '**Expansa**', dwarf shrub, wide-spreading sturdy branches eventually mounding to 3 ft (0.9 m) in the

center, sage-green scale-like leaves, in dense clustered sprays; '**Expansa Variegata**' is similar but flecked with creamy white sprays. Zones 4–8.

Juniperus deppeana
ALLIGATOR JUNIPER,
CHEQUERBOARD JUNIPER

☼ ❈ ↔ 7 ft (2 m) ↑ 20 ft (6 m)
Broad gray-barked tree with blue-green leaves. *J. d.* var. *pachyphlaea*, sometimes sold as '**Conspicua**', conical, coarse-textured, Mexican tree, silvery gray leaves, distinctive red-brown bark in square plates. Foliage is of adult type. Performs best under cool dry conditions. Zones 7–9.

Juniperus drupacea
SYRIAN JUNIPER

☼ ❈ ↔ 8 ft (2.4 m) ↑ 50 ft (15 m)
From the mountain forests of southwest Asia, Syria, and Greece. Distinctive, narrow-columnar, small tree. Bark orange-brown, peels in vertical strips. Awl-shaped leaves prickly, light green, white reverse. Round fruits ripen green to black-purple with a whitish bloom. Zones 5–9.

Juniperus deppeana var. *pachyphlaea*

Juniperus conferta 'Sunsplash'

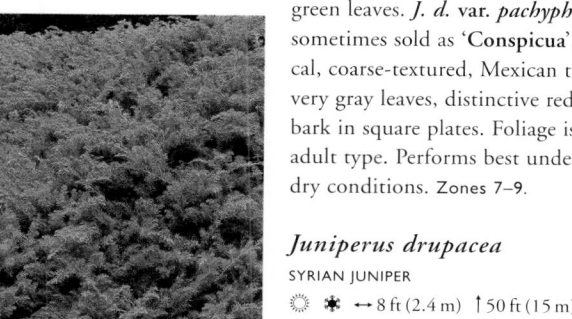

Juniperus conferta

Juniperus osteosperma, in the wild, Island in the Sky Section, Canyonlands National Park, Utah, USA

Juniperus × pfitzeriana 'Golden Sunset'

Juniperus × pfitzeriana 'Pfitzeriana'

Juniperus monosperma

Juniperus flaccida

MEXICAN JUNIPER

☼ ❄ ↔ 20 ft (6 m) ↑ 30 ft (9 m)

From Mexico and Texas, USA. Tree with slender branches weeping at the tips. Bark is scaly. Awl-shaped leaves, gray-green on young plants, becoming brighter, scale-like on mature plants. Small round fruits ripen reddish brown with a white bloom. Zones 5–9.

Juniperus horizontalis

CREEPING JUNIPER, HORIZONTAL JUNIPER

☼ ❄ ↔ 12 ft (3.5 m) ↑ 18 in (45 cm)

From northern North America, found on coastal cliffs and stony hillsides. Vigorous ground-hugging shrub with long trailing branches. Leaves gray-green or bluish, often develop a purplish tinge in winter. '**Bar Harbor**', mat-forming cultivar with blue-green foliage, the tips turning mauve in

winter; '**Blue Chip**', blue-green foliage, variegated with gold; '**Douglasii**', prostrate form to 2 ft (0.6 m) high, displaying blue-green foliage of both juvenile and adult type, turns purplish in autumn–winter; '**Prince of Wales**', mat-forming with deep green foliage; '**Repens**', blue-green foliage; '**Wiltonii**', blue-foliaged, prostrate, trailing cultivar. Zones 4–8.

Juniperus indica

syn. *Juniperus wallichiana*

HIMALAYAN BLACK JUNIPER

☼ ❄ ↔ 20 ft (6 m) ↑ 70 ft (21 m)

From the Himalayas. Large shrub or small tree, ascending branches, narrow-conical habit when young, spreading with age. Foliage consists of green scale-like leaves, most noticeable on young plants. Small oval fruits ripen to black. Zones 6–8.

Juniperus monosperma

CHERRYSTONE JUNIPER, ONE-SEED JUNIPER, REDBERRY JUNIPER

☼ ❄ ↔ 5–10 ft (1.5–3 m) ↑ 30 ft (9 m)

From southwestern USA and northern Mexico. Large shrub or tree, brown-red fibrous bark; gray-green, mostly

adult, scale-like foliage. Small round fruits ripen gray-blue; each contains a single seed. Zones 6–10.

Juniperus occidentalis

WESTERN JUNIPER

☼ ❄ ↔ 30 ft (9 m) ↑ 40 ft (12 m)

From the mountains of California, USA. Often shrubby in the wild, tree in protected gardens. Branches with near-horizontal habit, with drooping tips, blue-green scale-like leaves. Small blue-green cones. Zones 5–9.

Juniperus osteosperma

UTAH JUNIPER

☼ ❄ ↔ 20 ft (6 m) ↑ 12–20 ft (3.5–6 m)

Forms large areas of open woodland from eastern California to Montana,

and New Mexico, USA. Short thick trunk, forking low, broad irregular crown. Dull olive-green foliage, small red-brown cones. Zones 4–9.

Juniperus × pfitzeriana

syn. *Juniperus × media*

☼ ❄ ↔ 5–15 ft (1.5–4.5 m) ↑ 4–10 ft (1.2–3 m)

This name refers to a collection of garden hybrids, derived mainly from *J. chinensis*, which usually have adult and juvenile foliage present simultaneously. Adult foliage is stem-clasping scales, while the juvenile foliage is triangular, sharp, and protruding. The branches are wide spreading and lifted just above the horizontal. Dull green, adult, scale-like leaves release an

Juniperus horizontalis 'Bar Harbor'

Juniperus horizontalis 'Douglasii'

Juniperus horizontalis

Juniperus horizontalis 'Blue Chip'

Juniperus horizontalis 'Repens'

unpleasant scent when crushed. Many have white or blue-black fruits, globular to rounded. Vigorous ground covers. '**Golden Sunset**', low-growing shrub; '**Pfitzeriana**', vigorous, spreading shrub with sturdy ascending branches and pendulous tips, leaves are mostly green and scale-like. Excellent ground cover where space is available, shade tolerant; '**Pfitzeriana Aurea**', greenish yellow foliage, similar in habit to 'Pfitzeriana'. Zones 4–10.

Juniperus pinchotii
PINCHOT JUNIPER

☼ ❄ ↔ 15 ft (4.5 m) ↑ 20 ft (6 m)
From western Texas, USA. An uncommon large shrub, dark yellow-green foliage on widespreading limbs. Leaves awl-shaped on young plants, scale-like on adult plants. Zones 5–9.

Juniperus procumbens
BONIN ISLAND JUNIPER, CREEPING JUNIPER, JAPANESE GARDEN JUNIPER

☼ ❄ ↔ 12 ft (3.5 m) ↑ 30 in (75 cm)
From western China. Prostrate spreading ground cover, stiff and wiry habit, prickly blue-green leaves. Small

Juniperus sabina

berry-like cones, brown-green, each contains 2 to 3 seeds. '**Nana**' has smaller leaves, softer texture, and a more conical habit. Both are excellent for covering embankments. Zones 4–9.

Juniperus recurva
COFFIN JUNIPER, DROOPING JUNIPER, HIMALAYAN JUNIPER

☼ ❄ ↔ 15 ft (4.5 m) ↑ 30 ft (9 m)
From southwestern China, Myanmar, and the Himalayas. Weeping sprays of aromatic foliage, in whorls of 3 needle-like, gray-green leaves. The bark peels off in reddish brown strips. Fruit small, round, fleshy, and berry-like, ripening to glossy blue-black. The timber is used traditionally in

Juniperus sabina 'Tamariscifolia'

Juniperus sabina 'Calgary Carpet'

Juniperus procumbens

China for making coffins. *J. r.* **var.** *coxii* is slow growing, with smaller leaves. Zones 7–9.

Juniperus rigida
NEEDLE JUNIPER

☼ ❄ ↔ 15 ft (4.5 m) ↑ 20 ft (6 m)
From Japan, Korea, and northern China, this is an elegant large shrub or small tree with pendulous branchlets. The leaves are dark, needle-like in whorls of 3, and have a prominent white band on the uppersurface. The fruit ripens to a glossy blue-black. Zones 4–8.

Juniperus sabina
SAVIN JUNIPER

☼ ❄ ↔ 15 ft (4.5 m) ↑ 12 ft (3.5 m)
From southern and central Europe. Variable, spreading, self-layering ground cover, excellent for binding slopes. Dark green foliage with a disagreeable odor when crushed. Leaves awl-shaped on young foliage, scale-like on adult. Fruit is a small, ovoid, blue-black berry with whitish bloom, containing 1 to 3 seeds. '**Calgary Carpet**', bright green foliage, low-growing form; '**Skandia**', mid-green foliage; '**Tamariscifolia**', spreading ground cover, green to blue-green foliage. Zones 4–9.

Juniperus recurva var. *coxii*

Juniperus scopulorum
ROCKY MOUNTAINS JUNIPER

☼ ❄ ↔ 15 ft (4.5 m) ↑ 30 ft (9 m)
Small tree or shrub, from western North America and Texas, USA. Sturdy spreading branches. Tightly held scale-like leaves, light to glaucous green. Small round fruits. '**Blue Heaven**', blue-green foliage; '**Horizontalis**', spreading, blue-green foliage; '**Mountaineer**', bright green foliage; '**Repens**', prostrate, blue-green; '**Table Top**', spreading, blue-

Juniperus indica, in the wild, Karakoram Range, Pakistan

Juniperus scopulorum 'Horizontalis'

Juniperus scopulorum 'Mountaineer'

Juniperus scopulorum, in the wild, North Unit, Theodore Roosevelt National Park, North Dakota, USA

Justicia adhatoda

Juniperus squamata 'Blue Star'

Juniperus squamata 'Blue Carpet'

green foliage; '**Tolleson's Blue Weeping**', pendulous; '**Wichita Blue**', conical, blue-gray foliage. Zones 5–9.

Juniperus squamata

HOLLYWOOD JUNIPER, SINGLESEED JUNIPER, SQUAMATA JUNIPER

☼ ❆ ↔ 15 ft (4.5 m) ↑ 2–20 ft (0.6–6 m)
Extremely variable species from Asia. May be a small shrubby tree, a mound-like shrub, or a prostrate ground cover. Bark red-brown and flaky. Dense, juvenile-type, awl-shaped leaves, grayish green to silvery blue-green, upper-surface marked white or pale green. '**Blue Carpet**', spreading form with

blue-green foliage; '**Blue Star**', very blue, small, dense, and rounded shrub; '**Chinese Silver**', medium to large, dense, multi-stemmed shrub with recurved terminal shoots, leaves strongly silvery blue; '**Meyeri**', open vase shape, several leaders, leaves very blue when young, turning dark green with age. Zones 4–9.

Juniperus taxifolia

RYUKYU JUNIPER

☼ ❆ ↔ 36 in (90 cm) ↑ 12 in (30 cm)
Prostrate ground cover usually found as *J. t.* var. *lutchuensis* and resembling *J. conferta*. Rich green awl-shaped leaves, light brown stems. Excellent on embankments. Zones 5–9.

Juniperus virginiana

EASTERN RED CEDAR, PENCIL CEDAR, RED CEDAR

☼ ❆ ↔ 12–20 ft (3.5–6 m)
↑ 40 ft (12 m)
From central and eastern North America. Upright tree, becoming more open with age. Bark reddish brown, peels in long strips. Small, adult, closely held scale leaves with pointed tips, glaucous green, becoming

Juniperus taxifolia

purplish in winter. Fragrant timber traditionally used for the casings of lead pencils. '**Burkii**' ★, narrowly pyramidal habit, blue-foliaged shrub becoming steel-blue in cold winters; '**Skyrocket**', very narrow columnar form to 10 ft (3 m) tall, silvery blue foliage, arguably the narrowest of all conifers. Two popular pencil-shaped cultivars are '**Blue Arrow**' and '**Manhattan Blue**'. Zones 2–8.

JUSTICIA

syns *Adhatoda, Beloperone, Drejerella, Jacobinia, Libonia*

This largely tropical and subtropical American genus of the acanthus (Acanthaceae) family encompasses more than 400 species of perennials, subshrubs, and shrubs. The shrubby species are evergreen, their leaves usually simple pointed ovals in opposite pairs, sometimes hairy or with a velvety surface. The flowers are clustered, sometimes in upright panicles at the branch tips, or in looser, more open heads. The true flowers are often small, the flowerheads made colorful and showy by the large bracts.
CULTIVATION: A feature of gardens in warm climates and popular house and greenhouse plants elsewhere, most justicias do not tolerate severe frosts. Some tolerate being frosted to the ground, reshooting in spring, but most need mild winter conditions. Justicias prefer moist well-drained soil in sun or partial shade with shelter from strong winds. Water regularly during the growth period. Keep compact by regular tip pinching or a light trimming after flowering. Propagate from seed or half-hardened cuttings.

Justicia adhatoda

syn. *Adhatoda vasica*
ADHATODA, MALABAR NUT, PHYSIC NUT
☼/◐ ↔ 3–5 ft (0.9–1.5 m)
↑ 6–8 ft (1.8–2.4 m)
Evergreen shrub, native to southern India and Sri Lanka. Erect growth habit; mid-green lance-shaped leaves. The flowers are white with red to purple veining, appearing in summer. Powder-coated leaves, flowers, roots, and seed pods are used in Indian medicine. Zones 10–12.

Juniperus virginiana 'Blue Arrow'

Juniperus virginiana 'Manhattan Blue'

Justicia californica

Justicia aurea

☼ ↔3 ft (0.9 m) ↑3–5 ft (0.9–1.5 m)

From Mexico and Central America. Similar to the better-known *J. carnea*, but the foliage is a slightly lighter green; heads of yellow flowers rather than the pink of *J. carnea*. Flowers in late summer–autumn. Often reshoots if the foliage is cut back by frost. Zones 9–12.

Justicia brandegeeana

syns *Beloperone guttata, Drejerella guttata*

SHRIMP PLANT

☼/◐ ↔26 in (65 cm) ↑36 in (90 cm)

From Mexico. Evergreen shrub, curved array of overlapping pink and yellow bracts enclose small white

Justicia rizzinii 'Firefly'

Justicia aurea

flowers with red markings. Elliptical downy leaves, to 3 in (8 cm) long. '**Fruit Cocktail**', yellow-green bracts. Zones 9–11.

Justicia californica

syn. *Beloperone californica*

CHUPAROSA HONEYSUCKLE

☼ ↔4 ft (1.2 m) ↑3–5 ft (0.9–1.5 m)

Found in the deserts of southwestern North America, shrub differs in being nearly leafless. Mounding stems covered in fine silvery hairs for protection from harsh elements. Small leaves, after the spring rains. Narrow, nectar-rich, red flowers. Zones 9–10.

Justicia candicans

syns *Jacobinia ovata, Justicia ovata*

ARIZONA WATER-WILLOW, HUMMINGBIRD BUSH, RED JUSTICIA

☼ ❄ ↑3–6 ft (0.9–1.8 m) ↑2–3 ft (0.6–0.9 m)

Native of Arizona, USA, and adjacent Mexico. Semi-evergreen to evergreen shrub with compact, branching, spreading habit. Bright green heart-shaped leaves. Bright red tubular flowers, 1 in (25 mm) long, attractive to hummingbirds, appear in clusters at branch ends from spring–autumn. Zones 8–10.

Justicia carnea

Justicia carnea

BRAZILIAN PLUME

☼ ↔3 ft (0.9 m) ↑3–6 ft (0.9–1.8 m)

Evergreen shrub from northern South America. Leaves velvet-textured, conspicuously veined. Plume-like spikes of deep pink flowers, at branch tips throughout the year, especially late summer. Pinch back when young to keep compact. Zones 10–12.

Justicia rizzinii

syns *Jacobinia pauciflora, Libonia floribunda*

☼/◐ ↔10–22 in (25–55 cm) ↑10–22 in (25–55 cm)

One of the hardier justicias, from Brazil, densely twiggy shrub. Small, leathery, oval leaves, which often

Justicia spicigera

develop bronze tints in winter, the main flowering season. '**Firefly**', heavier flowering, scarlet red flowers with glowing golden yellow tips, flared tubes, slightly under 1 in (25 mm) long, in small clusters. Zones 9–11.

Justicia spicigera

syn. *Justicia ghiesbreghtiana*

MEXICAN HONEYSUCKLE, MOHINTLI

☼/◐ ↔5 ft (1.5 m) ↑6 ft (1.8 m)

Found from Mexico to Colombia. Upright shrub, deeply veined oval leaves to 6 in (15 cm) long. Leaves with fine down on the underside, smooth uppersurface. Flowers up to 1½ in (35 mm) long, through the warmer months, in bright shades of orange to red. Zones 10–12.

Justicia brandegeeana

Justicia brandegeeana 'Fruit Cocktail'

Kalanchoe blossfeldiana hybrid

Kalanchoe flammea

Kalanchoe pumila

Kalanchoe fedtschenkoi

KADSURA

A genus of 22 species of woody evergreen climbers from Southeast and East Asia in the family Schisandraceae. The leaves are smooth-edged, usually leathery, and the tiny flowers, either male or female, are produced on separate plants. These blossoms are produced singly in the leaf axils and, although not showy, are scented and followed by heads of red berries. CULTIVATION: Best grown up a wall in a sheltered site, these climbers are happy in sun or shade and are not fussy about soil type. Propagate from seed or semi-hardwood cuttings.

Kadsura japonica

☼/◐ ❄ ↔10 ft (3 m) ↑17 ft (5 m)
From China, Japan, Korea, and Taiwan; this is the only species usually grown. Dark green leathery leaves, to

4 in (10 cm) long. Cup-shaped cream flowers followed by red raspberry-like berries. Zones 7–10.

KALANCHOE

This genus belonging to the stonecrop (Crassulaceae) family contains about 125 species of succulent shrubs, herbs, and climbers distributed throughout tropical regions of Africa, Madagascar, and parts of Asia. Usually grown for their interesting foliage forms, although the vibrantly colored flowers of K. blossfeldiana make a popular house plant. Growth habits range from low sprawling subshrubs to tall tree-like plants, with a similar wide variation in leaves, from small to large and glossy to felted.
CULTIVATION: Plants require indoor or greenhouse cultivation in all but the warmest climates; grow in a moderately fertile gritty potting mix. Can be grown outdoors in suitable climates in a sunny sheltered position in well-drained soil; keep fairly dry in winter. Propagation is commonly by stem or leaf cuttings, or seed sown in spring.

Kalanchoe beharensis

FELT PLANT, GIANT KALANCHOE
☼ ❁ ↔3 ft (0.9 m) ↑10 ft (3 m)
Tree-like species from Madagascar, smaller in cultivation. Foliage stunning; large, thick, triangular leaves to 12 in (30 cm), heavily felted, silvery gray, light bronze overtones on uppersurface; wavy, uneven, toothed edges.

Kalanchoe thyrsiflora

Small, tubular, yellowish flowers seen rarely on mature specimens. 'Oak Leaf' ★, greenish yellow flowers. Zones 10–11.

Kalanchoe blossfeldiana

FLAMING KATIE
☼ ❁ ↔16 in (40 cm) ↑16 in (40 cm)
From Madagascar. Bushy perennial succulent with large, round, dark green, fleshy leaves. Spikes of tubular scarlet flowers in clusters from early spring. Free-draining soil. Zones 10–12.

Kalanchoe daigremontiana

syn. Bryophyllum daigremontianum
MEXICAN HAT PLANT
☼ ✦ ↔12 in (30 cm) ↑40 in (100 cm)
From Madagascar. Upright perennial succulent with long, lance-shaped, silver-gray leaves, changing to green as temperatures fall. On leaf edges, plantlets appear that look like "Mexican hats"; these can be separated to produce new plants. Pendulous pale pink flowers in spring. Zones 11–12.

Kalanchoe delagoensis

syn. Kalanchoe tubiflora
CHANDELIER PLANT
☼ ✦ ↔12 in (30 cm) ↑40 in (100 cm)
From Madagascar and South Africa. Upright multi-branched succulent with cylindrical, long, pale green leaves with irregular red spots and small plantlets on the edge. In winter purple, orange, or yellow flowers will appear. Zones 11–12.

Kalanchoe beharensis 'Oak Leaf'

Kalanchoe eriophylla

☼ ✦ ↔8 in (20 cm) ↑8 in (20 cm)
From Madagascar. Low-growing bushy succulent. Slender stems; fluffy mid-green leaves. Some of the young leaves may have red tips. Bell-shaped violet-blue flowers in spring. Zones 11–12.

Kalanchoe fedtschenkoi

☼ ✦ ↔12 in (30 cm) ↑20 in (50 cm)
From Madagascar. Upright spreading succulent with thick, fleshy, blue-green, round leaves with serrated edges. Tubular orange to red flowers in panicles in spring. K. f. var. variegata ★, blue-gray white-edged foliage, new leaves creamy white, changing to blue-green edged in white. Zones 11–12.

Kalanchoe flammea

☼ ❁ ↔12 in (30 cm) ↑12 in (30 cm)
From Somalia. Spreading plant with small, dark green, serrated, glossy leaves. Pendulous, apricot-pink to orange-red flowers in summer. Zones 10–12.

Kalanchoe grandiflora

☼ ✦ ↔16 in (40 cm) ↑32 in (80 cm)
From southern India. Upright succulent with blue-green oval leaves. Panicles of tubular yellow flowers throughout summer. Zones 11–12.

Kalanchoe manginii

☼ ✦ ↔12 in (30 cm) ↑12 in (30 cm)
From Madagascar. Sprawling succulent with notched, furry, green leaves. Groups of bright red flowers cover the plant in spring. Zones 11–12.

Kalanchoe marmorata

syn. Kalanchoe somaliensis
☼ ✦ ↔36 in (90 cm) ↑50 in (130 cm)
From Sudan. Sprawling succulent; branches come from base of plant. Dusty gray leaves have distinctive brown markings. Panicles of white flowers appear in summer. Zones 11–12.

Kalanchoe beharensis

Kalanchoe tomentosa

Kalanchoe pumila

☼ ✧ ↔ 18 in (45 cm) ↑ 8 in (20 cm)

From Madagascar. Low-growing suc-culent ground cover with cream-green leaves frosted with white; serrated edges. Pink flowers sit up on the foliage in spring. Zones 11–12.

Kalanchoe thyrsiflora ★

☼ ✧ ↔ 12 in (30 cm) ↑ 24 in (60 cm)

From southern Africa. Bushy succu-lent with white frosted green leaves. Red margins around edge of leaves. Tubular, fragrant, yellow flowers appear in spring. Zones 11–12.

Kalanchoe tomentosa ★

PANDA PLANT

☼ ✧ ↔ 7 in (18 cm) ↑ 15 in (38 cm)

This small erect shrub is native to Madagascar. Dense rosettes of oblong gray leaves, heavily felted, brown markings near tips. Small yellowish green flowers. Zones 10–12.

KALIMERIS

This genus is made up of 10 perennial herbs native to East Asia; it is part of the daisy (Asteraceae) family. Leaves are alternate and narrowly oval to elliptical. Plants produce clusters of rounded panicles of spreading white ray florets, tinged with purple or violet, and yellow disc florets. CULTIVATION: Plant in full sun to part-shade. Plants tolerate damp soil, and are suitable for bog gardens and water margins. Propagate from seed.

Kalimeris incisa

syn. *Bottonia incisa*

☼ ❄ ↔ 5 ft (1.5 m) ↑ 1–5 ft (0.3–1.5 m)

Perennial from northeastern Asia with oblong to spear-shaped, stalkless,

smooth, toothed leaves with hairy margins, up to 4 in (10 cm) long. Purple to white flowerheads, from summer–autumn. '**Alba**', starry, single, white flowers; '**Blue Star**', starry, single, blue flowers. Zones 3–9.

KALMIA

Genus of 7 species of shrubs in the heath (Ericaceae) family. Most are evergreen. They are native to north-eastern USA, a single species occurs in Cuba. They are grown for their attrac-tive foliage and their showy flowers, ranging in color from pale pink to deep red. Leaves are smooth, opposite or alternate, sometimes found in whorls, deep green on the uppersur-face, paler beneath, occasionally stalk-less. Flowers are generally carried in terminal corymbs. Fruits are small capsules containing very small seeds. CULTIVATION: Kalmias are at home in slightly acid, peaty soil but resent clay and lime in any form. Adequate water is needed on hot summer days. Dappled shade under tall deciduous trees in a cool moist climate is ideal. Little pruning is necessary apart from the removal of spent flowers. Propa-gate from seed. Firm tip-cuttings taken in late summer through to winter may be struck; alternatively, simple layers can be set down in autumn and severed a year later.

Kalmia angustifolia

SHEEP LAUREL

☼ ❄ ↔ 5 ft (1.5 m) ↑ 3 ft (0.9 m)

From northeastern USA. Dwarf shrub, slowly spreading to a dense bush. Smooth leaves ovate-oblong, to ¾ in (18 mm) long. Pinkish red flowers, in mid-summer. All parts of the plant are

poisonous. '**Rubra**', pinkish red flowers, borne over a long period; '**Rubra Nana**', dwarf form with rich garnet red flowers. Zones 2–9.

Kalmia latifolia

CALICO BUSH, MOUNTAIN LAUREL

☼ ❄ ↔ 10 ft (3 m) ↑ 10 ft (3 m)

Dense shrub found from eastern Canada to the Gulf of Mexico. Leaves dark green, smooth above, paler beneath, to ½ in (12 mm) long. Flower buds crimped round the edge; open to shell pink, purplish markings inside. In cultivation a number of clones have different flower colors, otherwise resembling the parent. '**Carousel**', mid-pink flowers; '**Clementine Churchill**', rosy pink flowers; '**Elf**', dwarf with faded pink flowers; '**Minuet**', pink flowers with purplish margins; '**Myrtifolia**', pale pink blooms; '**Nipmuck**', dark red buds open to almost white; '**Olympic Fire**', rich crimson flowers; '**Ostbo Red**' ★, vivid red buds opening to faded pink; '**Pink Charm**', crimson flowers; '**Silver Dollar**', white flowers with red anthers; '**Snow Drift**', white blooms. Zones 3–9.

Kalmia polifolia

EASTERN BOG LAUREL, SWAMP LAUREL

☼ ❄ ↔ 36 in (90 cm) ↑ 24 in (60 cm)

From northeastern America. Dwarf shrub; thin leaves, dark glossy green above, silvery gray beneath. Vivid pinkish purple flowers, in large

terminal clusters, in early spring. The native habitat is in swamps and boggy places. Zones 3–9.

KALMIOPSIS

Named for its resemblance to *Kalmia*, this genus also belongs to the heath (Ericaceae) family. It includes a single species, a small evergreen shrub found in northwestern USA that looks like a small-leafed alpine rhododendron. Oval leaves slightly over 1 in (25 mm) long. Its small showy flowers are bell- to funnel-shaped, in clusters up to 2 in (5 cm) across, with prominent stamens; usually held erect. CULTIVATION: Requires conditions typical of most ericas from the temperate zones: cool, moist, humus-rich, well-drained soil; cool moist atmosphere. Does not tolerate wet winter conditions; add fine grit to soil to improve drainage. This is a superb plant for an alpine house. Propagate from seed, layers, or cuttings under mist.

Kalmia angustifolia

Kalmia latifolia 'Snow Drift'

Kalmia latifolia 'Ostbo Red'

Kalmia latifolia 'Carousel'

Kalmia latifolia 'Minuet'

Kalmia latifolia 'Myrtifolia'

Kalmia latifolia 'Olympic Fire'

Kalmia latifolia 'Pink Charm'

Kalmiopsis leachiana

☀ ❄ ↔ 12 in (30 cm) ↕ 12 in (30 cm)

Neat little bush, smothered in tightly clustered heads of mid-pink to magenta flowers, in spring. Combines well with rhododendrons, heaths, and heathers, wonderful in a well-drained rock garden. 'Glendoick', shiny ever-green foliage and long flowering season; 'Umpqua Valley', vigorous and compact. Zones 7–9.

KALOPANAX

This genus of the ivy (Araliaceae) family contains a lone species of tree native to the cool deciduous forests of eastern Asia. It has scattered stout prickles on the trunk and branches, especially on the young new growth. The leaves are large and palmately lobed. The flowerheads of small white flowers are followed by ornamental clusters of bluish black berries.

Kefersteinia laminata

Kalmiopsis leachiana 'Glendoick'

Kalmiopsis leachiana

Kalmiopsis leachiana 'Umpqua Valley'

CULTIVATION: Despite its tropical appearance, this is a hardy species that should be grown in deep, moist, fertile soil. It will grow in sun or semi-shade and makes an attractive specimen or shade tree. Propagation is from seed or half-hardened cuttings taken in summer.

Kalopanax septemlobus

syn. *Kalopanax pictus*

CASTOR ARALIA, HARA-GIRI, TREE ARALIA

☀ ❄ ↔ 30 ft (9 m) ↕ 60 ft (18 m)

Round-headed, sparingly branched tree. Leaves on long stalks, 5 to 7 pointed palmate lobes, finely toothed margins, dark green above, lighter below. Large rounded clusters of small flowers, in late summer. *K. s.* var. *maximowiczii*, lance-shaped leaves. Zones 5–10.

KECKIELLA

This is a genus of the foxglove (Scrophulariaceae) family comprising 7 species of semi-deciduous perennials, subshrubs, and shrubs from western USA and northwestern Mexico, grow-ing mainly among rocks or in disturbed soil in pine woodland or chaparral. Its species were all formerly included in *Penstemon*, but *Keckiella* was separated as a distinct genus in 1966 on the basis of floral structure, the name honoring Californian botanist David Keck. The plants are generally

Kalopanax septemlobus

K. septemlobus var. *maximowiczii*

multi-stemmed, the somewhat woody branches bearing small leaves in oppo-site pairs or whorls of three. Flowers, borne in terminal racemes, are tubular with a hooded upper lip and strongly diverging lower lip, in shades of yellow, pink, orange, or red.

CULTIVATION: They can be grown in full sun or partial shade, depending on species; some dwarf species can be treated as rock garden plants. Soil type is not critical as long as drainage is perfect; a surface mulch of gravel may be beneficial. Most are not hardy below about 0°F (-18°C). Propagation is generally from seed.

Keckiella ternata

syn. *Penstemon ternatus*

CLIMBING PENSTEMON

☀/☀ ❄ ↔ 10 ft (3 m) ↕ 8 ft (2.4 m)

From southern California, USA, and northern Baja California, Mexico, at up to 9,000 ft (2,700 m). Thin cane-like stems that may scramble over other shrubs. Narrow down-curved leaves in whorls of 3. Bright red flowers to 1¼ in (30 mm) long, in summer–early autumn. Zones 7–10.

KEFERSTEINIA

This is a genus of some 40 sympodial orchid species (family Orchidaceae) from Central and South America. These epiphytes lack true pseudobulbs and have thin narrow leaves in 2 ranks forming a fan-like plant. The single-flowered inflorescences appear from the leaf axils. It is a variable genus, with the individual blooms coming in a wide variety of colors and shapes.

CULTIVATION: These orchids require humid intermediate growing condi-tions and must be kept shaded. Direct sunlight will quickly burn the delicate foliage. Keep plants moist at all times and have ample air circulation, to avoid potential rot problems. Plants are best grown in either sphagnum moss or a bark-based medium that is kept moist. Propagate by division.

Kefersteinia laminata

☀/☀ ❄ ↔ 16 in (40 cm) ↕ 12 in (30 cm)

Uncommon species from Ecuador. Predominantly green, 1¼ in (30 mm)

Keckiella ternata, in the wild, Baja California, Mexico

wide, crystalline blooms, overlaid with light mauve suffusions. The broad labellum is purple with a white mar-gin. *K. gemma* is a closely related species from Colombia. Zones 10–11.

KENNEDIA

CORAL PEA

A genus of 16 species of evergreen climbers and trailers in the pea-flower subfamily of the legume (Fabaceae) family; those in cultivation are native to Australia. The flowers are usually brightly colored and produced in spring and summer, and they usually have a contrasting color on the keel petal. Flowers are followed by flat-tened pea-style pods. The leaves are composed of 3 leaflets.

CULTIVATION: In nature these plants tolerate drought and poor soils and in near frost-free conditions will do so in gardens as well. They make attractive ground covers or can be grown on fences and arches in full to half-sun. They are usually raised from seed that must be soaked in hot water prior to sowing in spring.

Kennedia coccinea

CORAL VINE

☀/☀ ❄ ↔ 10 ft (3 m) ↕ 7–10 ft (2–3 m)

Widely distributed around Australia including Tasmania. Fast-growing twiner or ground cover with leathery, green, wedge-shaped leaflets to ¾ in (18 mm) long. Bright red pea-flowers with yellow blotches, ¾ in (18 mm) wide, in spring–summer. Zones 10–11.

Kennedia macrophylla

☀/◐ ✦ ↔ 10 ft (3 m)
↑ 15–17 ft (4.5–5 m)

Vigorous climber from Western Australia. Leaflets to 2½ in (6 cm) long, Spikes of red to brownish red flowers with yellow blotches, in spring–summer. Zones 10–11.

Kennedia nigricans

BLACK BEAN, BLACK CORAL PEA

☀/◐ ✦ ↔ 10–15 ft (3–4.5 m)
↑ 17–20 ft (5–6 m)

Extremely vigorous climber from Western Australia. Leaflets to 5 in (12 cm) long. Black pea-flowers with yellow patches, to 1½ in (35 mm) long, in spring–summer. Zones 10–11.

Kennedia rubicunda

DUSKY CORAL PEA

☀/◐ ✦ ↔ 15 ft (4.5 m)
↑ 10–15 ft (3–4.5 m)

Strong-growing climber from eastern Australia. Leaflets to 6 in (15 cm) long. Deep red flowers with paler blotches, to 1½ in (35 mm) long, in spring–summer. Zones 10–11.

KERRIA

This genus with a single species in the rose (Rosaceae) family is native to China and Japan. Leaves are 2½ in (6 cm) long, alternate, egg-shaped, and dark green. It is a low, suckering, deciduous shrub with bright yellow cup-shaped flowers, 2 in (5 cm) across, and graceful cane-like stems

Kirengeshoma palmata

Kigelia africana

Kennedia macrophylla

with rather sparse but attractive foliage, and makes an interesting addition to a shrub border.

CULTIVATION: *K. japonica* will grow in any moderately fertile soil with free drainage, preferring a sunny or lightly shaded position and a cool moist climate. Several of the older flowering shoots should be removed at the base after flowering each year to make room for new shoots; no further pruning is necessary. It is easily propagated; soft-tip or half-hardened cuttings taken in spring or summer strike readily, or stems can be layered and lifted a year later.

Kerria japonica

☀/◐ ✿ ↔ 5 ft (1.5 m) ↑ 6 ft (1.8 m)

Found naturally in the mountains of Japan and in southwestern China. Bright green leaves, simple and alternate, to 4 in (10 cm) long, prominent veins, downy beneath, turn yellow in autumn. Deep yellow flowers on short terminal and axillary spurs, in early–late spring. More common form is 'Pleniflora' (syn. 'Flore Plena'), fully double flowers, taller, more vigorous; 'Variegata', creamy white variegated foliage, low-spreading habit, seldom exceeding 5 ft (1.5 m) in height. Zones 5–10.

KIGELIA

This genus within the trumpet-vine (Bignoniaceae) family consists of a lone species. A tropical to subtropical

Kennedia nigricans

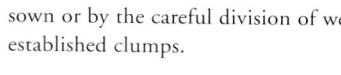

Kerria japonica

Kerria japonica 'Pleniflora'

evergreen tree, it is a native of central and southern Africa. It is characterized by long pendent racemes of striking red to orange flowers, often reaching 6 ft (1.8 m) in length. The flowers are followed by large, brownish gray, woody fruits, up to 18 in (45 cm) in length on very long stalks.

CULTIVATION: *Kigelia* will grow in any rich and well-drained soil, in a warm climate and in a protected sunny position. Water regularly during the growing season. Propagate from seed.

Kigelia africana

syn. *Kigelia pinnata*

SAUSAGE TREE

☀ ✦ ↔ 12 ft (3.5 m) ↑ 40 ft (12 m)

From central and southern Africa. Evergreen tree; pinnate leaves with 7 to 9 leaflets. Reddish orange bell-shaped flowers, in summer, open at night with a disagreeable odor that attracts the bats which pollinate them. The large woody fruits, resembling a sausage, are inedible. Zones 10–12.

KIRENGESHOMA

A genus of a single species in the hydrangea (Hydrangeaceae) family. A woodland perennial from Japan and Korea with large, maple-like, soft green leaves and drooping thick-petalled flowers, shaped like a shuttlecock, in late summer.

CULTIVATION: Give *Kirengeshoma* a cool shaded aspect in moist humus-rich soil that is sheltered from the

wind. Propagation is from seed freshly sown or by the careful division of well established clumps.

Kirengeshoma palmata

☀ ✿ ↔ 30 in (75 cm) ↑ 48 in (120 cm)

Elegant, arching, herbaceous perennial from Japan and Korea. Leaves to 8 in (20 cm) long on black stems. Pale lemon flowers to 1½ in (35 mm) long, in late summer. Zones 5–9.

KLEINIA

This genus of the daisy (Asteraceae) family contains about 40 species of succulent perennials from the drier parts of tropical Africa, the Arabian Peninsula, and India. Their stems can be cylindrical or angular, prostrate or upright. Many of them have tuberous roots. Mauve, red, yellow, or white thistle-like flowers are produced in summer, either singly or on heads. They are closely related to *Senecio*.

CULTIVATION: They are frost tender and if the temperature is going to drop below 50°F (10°C) they should be grown indoors or in a greenhouse. They like full sun and moderate watering during their growing season but keep them dry when dormant. The plants like a gritty, sharply draining soil and will appreciate the occasional application of a balanced liquid fertilizer. Seeds can be sown when the temperature is reliably above 68°F (20°C) for germination, or cuttings can be taken in spring or summer.

Knightia deplanchei

Knightia excelsa

Knautia macedonica

Kleinia stapeliiformis

Kleinia abyssinica

Kleinia abyssinica

☼/☀ ❄ ↔ 3 ft (0.9 m) ↕ 8 ft (2.4 m)
Central and East African species.
Forms clump of succulent, purple-tinted, usually unbranched, 1 in
(25 mm) diameter stems to as much
as 8 ft (2.4 m) tall. Fleshy, pale- to
gray-green, elliptical leaves to 10 in
(25 cm) long. Heads of flowers, up to
¾ in (18 mm) wide, opening pink to
red. Zones 10–12.

Kleinia stapeliiformis

☼/☀ ❄ ↔ 2 ft (0.6 m) ↕ 8 ft (2.4 m)
South African species spreading by
underground stems to form small
clumps of upright, fleshy, angular,
toothed stems resembling those of
Stapelia. Small, thread-like, often
thorn-tipped leaves and solitary, long-stemmed, orange-red flowerheads.
Zones 9–11.

KNAUTIA

A genus of some 60 species of annuals
and herbaceous perennials within the
teasel (Dipsacaceae) family. They can
be found in Europe, the Caucasus
region, Siberia, and the Mediter-ranean in a wide range of habitats,
from woods to meadows and rocky
hillsides. They have flowers very like
those of Scabiosa species, consisting
of a cluster of small flowers that look
like a single bloom. Their open airy
habit makes them useful in the border
or the wild garden. They are loved by
nectar-feeding insects.

CULTIVATION: Grow in any well-drained fertile soil in full sun. Propa-gation is usually from seed and they
will usually self-seed, sometimes to
the extent of weediness.

Knautia arvensis

syn. Scabiosa arvensis
BLUE BUTTONS, FIELD SCABIOUS
☼ ❄ ↔ 12 in (30 cm) ↕ 5 ft (1.5 m)
Upright clumping perennial from
Europe through to Siberia via the
Caucasus, Iran, and central Asia.
Hairy dull green leaves can be smooth-edged through to indented and up to
10 in (25 cm) long. Flowerheads are
1½ in (35 mm) across and usually
a soft lilac-blue. Flowers from mid-summer through to when it becomes
too cold. Zones 6–10.

Knautia macedonica

syn. Scabiosa rumelica
☼ ❄ ↔ 20 in (50 cm) ↕ 32 in (80 cm)
Clumping perennial from central
Europe. Lyre-shaped leaves at the base
to 6 in (15 cm) long; these become
smaller and compound higher on the
stems. Flowerheads are up to 1½ in
(35 mm) across, from mid-summer,
usually a deep purple-red. 'Melton
Pastels', flowers in soft shades of
cream through pale pink to soft
lavender-blue. Zones 6–10.

KNIGHTIA

This genus of the protea (Proteaceae)
family contains 3 species of large
evergreen shrubs or trees, 2 from New
Caledonia and 1 from New Zealand.
They are upright plants with tough
leathery leaves that often have con-spicuously toothed edges. The flowers
are narrow tubes clustered in heads
with long protruding styles. Individu-ally they resemble long-tubed honey-suckle flowers and are rich in nectar,
making wonderful honey. Woody seed
capsules follow the flowers.

CULTIVATION: The New Caledonian
species are rare in cultivation and
require subtropical conditions with
ample summer moisture. The New
Zealand species tolerates regular light
frosts, and is quite widely grown. It
thrives in most well-drained soils but,
like nearly all protea family plants, it
prefers little or no phosphate. Pruning
should be restricted to shaping while
young, as old wood can be reluctant
to reshoot. Propagate from seed,
which should be fresh.

Knightia deplanchei

syn. Eucarpha deplanchei
☼/☀ ❄ ↔ 20 ft (6 m) ↕ 60 ft (18 m)
One of 2 species of Knightia endemic
to New Caledonia. Tall tree in low-land rainforest or stunted shrub in
exposed scrub on mountain ridges.
Leaves very thick, rounded, with scal-loped edges, glossy green. Buds held
in yellow-brown bracts, flowers yellow
to reddish in small hemispherical
heads in autumn–winter. Zones 10–11.

Knightia excelsa

NEW ZEALAND HONEYSUCKLE, REWAREWA
☼ ❄ ↔ 25 ft (8 m) ↕ 50 ft (15 m)
Large forest tree from New Zealand.
Beautifully marked reddish brown
heartwood. Narrow toothed-edged
leaves, to 6 in (15 cm) long.
Unpleasantly scented red flowers open
in spring from felted red-brown buds.
Hard seed pods. Zones 9–10.

KNIPHOFIA

RED-HOT POKER, TORCH LILY
Most of the nearly 70 species in this
genus in the asphodel (Asphodelaceae)
family are South African clump-form-ing perennials with grassy to sword-shaped, often evergreen, foliage that
emerges from vigorous rhizomes.
They are grown for their spikes of
intensely colored, usually orange
and/or yellow, flowers, borne mainly
in autumn to spring in bottlebrush
heads at the top of strong, tall, up-right stems. Excellent cut flowers.
Many hybrids and cultivars in a variety
of sizes and flower colors. Named
after German professor Johann
Hieronymus Kniphof (1704–1763).

CULTIVATION: Hardiness varies,
though none will tolerate repeated
heavy frosts. Plant in an open sunny
position in moist, humus-rich, well-drained soil. Water and feed well
during active growth. Most will toler-ate salt winds and thrive near the
coast. Propagation is usually by
division after flowering or from seed.

Kniphofia caulescens

☼/☀ ❄ ↔ 20 in (50 cm) ↕ 4 ft (1.2 m)
Tough alpine species; evergreen,
narrow but thick blue-green leaves.
Coppery flower stems and densely
packed heads of pink-tinted cream
flowers opening from red buds, in
late summer–autumn. Zones 7–10.

Kniphofia citrina

☼/☀ ❄ ↔ 16 in (40 cm) ↕ 36 in (90 cm)
Evergreen perennial. Thick bright
green leaves with deep central channel.
The flowerheads are rounded, with

Kniphofia caulescens

cream to yellow-green flowers. '**Lime Select**' has bright, very noticeably green-tinted flowers. Zones 8–10.

Kniphofia ensifolia
WINTER POKER

☼/◐ ❄ ↔ 40 in (100 cm) ↑ 7 ft (2 m)

Evergreen perennial. Broad green leaves. Tall spikes, cylindrical heads of often green-tinted white to soft yellow flowers, from late summer–winter. Zones 8–10.

Kniphofia hirsuta

☼/◐ ❄ ↔ 12 in (30 cm) ↑ 16 in (40 cm)

Evergreen perennial. Narrow blue-green leaves. Short-stemmed cylindrical heads of orange-red flowers with lower buds yellow-green. Tolerant of dry conditions; flowers start to open when stem just 4 in (10 cm) tall. '**Traffic Lights**', green, orange, and red flowers. Zones 8–10.

Kniphofia linearifolia

☼/◐ ❄ ↔ 32 in (80 cm) ↑ 4 ft (1.2 m)

Evergreen perennial. Narrow deep green leaves, red buds, large, ovoid yellow-green to orange flowerheads in late summer–autumn. Zones 8–10.

Kniphofia northiae

☼/◐ ❄ ↔ 40 in (100 cm) ↑ 5 ft (1.5 m)

Evergreen perennial. Thick, broader, slightly blue-green leaves with deep

central keel; dense cylindrical heads of yellow flowers opening from red buds, from late spring–autumn. Zones 8–10.

Kniphofia × praecox
RED-HOT POKER

☼/◐ ❄ ↔ 20–40 in (50–100 cm) ↑ 4–5 ft (1.2–1.5 m)

This is a fairly general name for the wild and garden hybrids between *K. uvaria* and/or *K. linearifolia* and *K. bruceae*. Evergreen perennial. The plants have dense basal clumps of narrow leaves that are deeply channeled. The strong upright flower stems bear cylindrical to rounded heads of orange, yellow, or cream flowers, which appear mainly in late summer–winter. Zones 7–10.

Kniphofia pumila

☼/◐ ❅ ↔ 12–20 in (30–50 cm) ↑ 20–32 in (50–80 cm)

This compact summer-flowering species is a native of Ethiopia. Evergreen perennial. Grassy foliage and dense cylindrical heads of small yellow to red flowers on short stems. Zones 9–11.

Kniphofia rooperi

☼/◐ ❄ ↔ 20–24 in (50–60 cm) ↑ 4 ft (1.2 m)

Evergreen perennial. Thick leaves with conspicuous keels. From late summer,

large spherical heads of bright red flowers appear; the lower flowers are often yellow-green. Zones 8–10.

Kniphofia sarmentosa

☼/◐ ❅ ↔ 24 in (60 cm) ↑ 36 in (90 cm)

Evergreen perennial. Blue-green leaves and cylindrical heads of pinkish red to orange-red flowers opening from green buds on stocky stems, from mid-summer to autumn. Zones 8–10.

Kniphofia thomsonii

☼/◐ ❅ ↔ 16–24 in (40–60 cm) ↑ 4 ft (1.2 m)

From Kenya. Usually evergreen. Narrow leaves. Strong flower stems, large cylindrical heads of deep dusky red flowers, yellow-gold at base of head, in mid-summer to autumn. *K. t.* var. *snowdenii* is deciduous. Zones 9–11.

Kniphofia triangularis

☼/◐ ❄ ↔ 16–24 in (40–50 cm) ↑ 36 in (90 cm)

Evergreen perennial. Narrow grassy foliage. Fairly narrow flower stems with small heads of yellow to soft red flowers, from late summer. Zones 8–10.

Kniphofia uvaria

☼/◐ ✽ ↔ 24 in (60 cm) ↑ 4 ft (1.2 m)

Evergreen perennial. Thick, deeply channeled leaves. Strong flower stems

with ovoid heads of yellow-tipped bright orange-red flowers, in late summer–autumn. Parent of many garden hybrids. Zones 5–10.

Kniphofia Hybrid Cultivars

☼/◐ ❄ ↔ 12–20 in (30–50 cm) ↑ 2–5 ft (0.6–1.5 m)

Among the best of the many hybrids are: '**Bees' Sunset**', deciduous, leaves have serrated edges, yellow-orange flowers on dark stems to 3 ft (0.9 m) tall; '**Green Jade**', evergreen, flowers initially pale cream ageing through cream to white, 5 ft (1.5 m) stems; '**Ice Queen**', deciduous, green buds open pale yellow and age to off-white, 5 ft (1.5 m) stems; '**Little Maid**', deciduous, fine grassy leaves, green buds open soft yellow and age to cream, 24 in (60 cm) stems; '**Painted Lady**', dusky red flowers age to orange-pink, 3 ft (0.9 m) stems; '**Primrose Beauty**', fine grassy foliage, bright yellow flowers on 24 in (60 cm) stems; '**Royal Standard**', deciduous, bright yellow flowers open from red buds on stocky 3 ft (0.9 m) stems; '**Sunset**', orange to red flowers; '**Tetbury Torch**', broad, slightly blue-green leaves, golden yellow flowers open from orange buds, 3 ft (0.9 m) stems; '**Yellowhammer**', spring-flowering, bright yellow flowers on 4 ft (1.2 m) stems. Zones 8–10.

Kniphofia ensifolia

Kniphofia linearifolia

Kniphofia northiae

Kniphofia pumila

Kniphofia, HC, 'Little Maid'

Kniphofia sarmentosa

Kniphofia triangularis

Kniphofia, HC, 'Ice Queen'

Kniphofia, HC, 'Primrose Beauty'

Kniphofia, HC, 'Sunset'

KOELERIA

JUNEGRASS

This genus of about 25 to 35 annual and perennial grasses with narrow leaf blades belongs to the grass (Poaceae) family. The species originates from temperate and colder regions of the Northern Hemisphere. The plants produce very dense, cylindrical, spike-like panicles, to 4 in (10 cm) long, each compressed spikelet with 2 to 8 flowers, on flimsy erect stems.
CULTIVATION: Plant in a sunny position in well-drained soil. Propagate by division in spring or autumn.

Koeleria glauca

LARGE BLUE HAIR GRASS

☀ ❊ ↔ 24 in (60 cm) ↕ 24 in (60 cm)
Short-lived, evergreen, herbaceous, tuft-forming, perennial grass from central Europe and Siberia, forming neat low mounds of bright blue ribbed foliage with stems thickened at the base. Panicles of flowers to 4 in (10 cm) long, with spikelets, each up to ¼ in (6 mm) long, in summer. Zones 4–9.

KOELREUTERIA

There are only 3 species of deciduous small trees in this genus within the soapberry (Sapindaceae) family. Their natural habitat is dry woodland in open valleys in China, Korea, and Taiwan. Best suited to dry warm climates with an extended growing season, they are moderately frost

Kolkwitzia amabilis

Kolkwitzia amabilis 'Pink Cloud'

hardy and are widely grown as ornamentals for the beauty of their flowers and seed heads. The flowers are also used medicinally and as a source of yellow dye in China. The seeds are used as beads.
CULTIVATION: Koelreuterias prefer a quite fertile, well-drained soil and thrive in full sun. Propagation is by root cuttings taken in late winter or from seed sown in autumn in sheltered conditions. Seed can also be stratified in the refrigerator and sown in spring. Plants grown from seed are very variable and root cuttings from a good tree are preferable.

Koelreuteria bipinnata

syn. *Koelreuteria integrifolia*

CHINESE FLAME TREE, PRIDE OF CHINA

☀ ❊ ↔ 25 ft (8 m) ↕ 30 ft (9 m)
Native to Yunnan Province in southwestern China. Bipinnate leaves, elliptical to oblong leaflets, finely toothed, mid-green, turning deep gold in autumn. Yellow flowers, red spot at base of petals, borne in large panicles, in summer–autumn. Red seed heads. Zones 8–11.

Koelreuteria paniculata ★

CHINA TREE, GOLDEN RAIN TREE, VARNISH TREE

☀ ❊ ↔ 30 ft (9 m) ↕ 30 ft (9 m)
Spreading tree, originally from China and Korea. Leaves pinnate, sometimes bipinnate, leaflets elliptical-oblong, scalloped edges. Young foliage turns red to green with age, yellows in autumn. Panicles of small yellow flowers, in summer. Fruit capsules rosy pink or red when ripe. *K. p.* var. *apiculata*, bipinnate leaves, light yellow flowers; *K. p.* 'Fastigiata', columnar habit. Zones 6–10.

KOHLERIA

These 50 hairy herbs and shrubs, native to tropical Central and South

Koelreuteria bipinnata

America, are part of the African violet (Gesneriaceae) family, and are often cultivated as house plants. Large rhizomes grow across the soil surface and thick, serrated, hairy or velvety leaves are often mottled with red. Large trumpet-shaped flowers with erect, thick, hairy sepals and tubular corollas, usually in colors ranging from yellow through red to purple, are covered with red hairs and spotted with a contrasting color.
CULTIVATION: They prefer moist, well-drained soil, kept drier in winter, in full sun or part-shade. Propagate in spring by division of rhizomes or from seed sown in spring.

Kohleria digitaliflora

syn. *Kohleria warscewiezii*

◐ ❊ ↔ 12–24 in (30–60 cm) ↕ 12–24 in (30–60 cm)
Erect perennial from Colombia. Hairy white stems and dark green narrowly oval to sword-shaped leaves to 8 in (20 cm) long. Stalked clusters of very hairy flowers with white corolla tubes to 1¼ in (3 cm) long, flushed with deep rose, and green lobes spotted with purple, in summer–autumn. Zones 8–10.

Kohleria eriantha

◐ ❊ ↔ 3–4 ft (0.9–1.2 m) ↕ 3–4 ft (0.9–1.2 m)
Perennial shrub from tropical Colombia. Reddish, densely hairy stems and oval to spear-shaped, deep green, velvety leaves, to 5 in (12 cm) long, with hairy red margins. Clusters of up to 4 huge drooping flowers, fuzzy, with corolla tubes to 2 in (5 cm) long, of scarlet-orange, with lobes ¼ in (6 mm) across, spotted with yellow, in late spring–summer. Zones 8–10.

Kohleria eriantha

Koelreuteria paniculata

Koelreuteria paniculata var. *apiculata*

KOLKWITZIA

There is just one species in this genus within the woodbine (Caprifoliaceae) family—an attractive deciduous shrub occurring in the wild among rocky outcrops in the mountainous areas of Hubei Province, China. It is grown in gardens for its floriferous spring show.
CULTIVATION: *Kolkwitzia* grows in full sun in well-drained fertile soil. When planted in very cold areas it needs protection from cold spring winds, but in general it is frost hardy. Propagation is from cuttings taken from young wood in late spring or early summer or from suckers, which can be removed and grown on. Prune after flowering to retain a tidy shape.

Kolkwitzia amabilis

BEAUTY BUSH

☀ ❊ ↔ 12 ft (3.5 m) ↕ 12 ft (3.5 m)
Bushy deciduous shrub; long, upright or arching shoots. Leaves opposite, broadly egg-shaped, tapered, with rounded tip. Corymbs of bell-shaped flowers, white to pink, yellow-marked throats, late spring–early summer. 'Pink Cloud' ★, slightly larger, deeper pink flowers. Zones 4–9.

KOPSIA

Genus in the dogbane (Apocynaceae) family containing 25 species of evergreen trees and shrubs that are all found in tropical southeastern Asia.

Kunzea ambigua

Kunzea parvifolia

Kunzea ericoides, in the wild, New Zealand

They have a milky sap and smooth leathery leaves arranged oppositely. Clusters of 5-petalled flowers.
CULTIVATION: In warm frost-free areas these plants can be grown outside in a rich moist soil in full sun. In other areas they will need the protection of a greenhouse. Propagation is from seed or half-hardened cuttings rooted in sand.

Kopsia fruticosa
SHRUB VINCA
☀ ✿ ↔ 10 ft (3 m) ↑ 8 ft (2.4 m)
Native to the Malay Peninsula. Thin-textured glossy leaves. Spring flowers pale pink with a crimson throat, tubular with flaring, starry petal ends. Zones 10–12.

KRASCHENINNIKOVIA
syn. *Eurotia*
About 10 deciduous shrubs and sub-shrubs make up this genus in the goosefoot (Chenopodiaceae) family. One of them is widespread in western North America, the remainder are native to temperate Asia and the Mediterranean region. They have dense wiry branches and small, rather fleshy leaves that in most species are covered with white hairs. The inconspicuous flowers are crowded at the branch ends among leaf-like bracts, and they rapidly give way to small dry fruits with fluffy plumes. They grow in semi-arid grasslands and shrub steppes, their succulent foliage providing browse for animals.
CULTIVATION: They are useful garden shrubs for dry regions and poor alkaline soils, their white foliage providing an interesting color contrast. They are

relatively nonflammable and suitable for planting in areas prone to forest fires. Full sun is essential, and a dry exposed position. Propagate from seed or tip cuttings.

Krascheninnikovia ceratoides
PAMIRIAN WINTERFAT
☀ ✳ ↔ 16 in (40 cm) ↑ 36 in (90 cm)
Very hardy and drought-tolerant evergreen perennial widely considered a weed. Found through much of the northern temperate zone. Inconspicuous clusters of tiny, pink-tinted, green flowers develop into fluffy seed heads resembling lambs' tails. Zones 4–9.

KUNZEA
This genus of the myrtle (Myrtaceae) family, containing about 35 species of evergreen shrubs, is endemic to Australia, except for *K. ericoides*, which also occurs in New Zealand. Kunzeas have small, aromatic, heath-like leaves, and are cultivated mainly for their profuse honey-scented flowers with masses of protruding stamens that give them a fluffy appearance. The flowers appear mostly in spring, attracting honey-eaters and insectivorous birds.
CULTIVATION: Prefer a mild winter climate, full sun or part-shade, and a well-drained soil. Prune lightly from an early age and after flowering to encourage compact bushy growth. Propagate from seed or half-hardened tip cuttings taken in early summer.

Kunzea ambigua
TICK-BUSH
☀ ⚘ ↔ 12 ft (3.5 m) ↑ 12 ft (3.5 m)
Evergreen shrub from eastern Australia. Arching branches; small

Kunzea recurva var. *montana*

Kunzea baxteri

crowded leaves, dark green, narrow-linear. Masses of small creamy white flowers, in the upper leaf axils, in spring–early summer. Occurs chiefly in coastal areas, may be grown in protected seaside gardens. Zones 9–11.

Kunzea baxteri
SCARLET KUNZEA
☀ ⚘ ↔ 8 ft (2.4 m) ↑ 8 ft (2.4 m)
Many-stemmed spreading shrub from Western Australia. Crowded linear leaves. Crimson flowers, in dense spikes, in late winter–spring. May be grown in coastal gardens with some protection. Prune after flowering to maintain bushy appearance. Zones 9–11.

Kunzea ericoides
BURGAN, KANUKA
☀ ✳ ↔ 15 ft (4.5 m) ↑ 15 ft (4.5 m)
Tall sometimes pendulous shrub or small tree from southeastern Australia and New Zealand. Narrow dark green leaves. Small white flowers, like tea-tree flowers. Fast growing in cultivation, ideal for regenerating cleared land. Could become a serious weed in temperate areas. Zones 8–11.

Kunzea parvifolia
VIOLET KUNZEA
☀ ✳ ↔ 5 ft (1.5 m) ↑ 5 ft (1.5 m)
An open twiggy shrub from southeastern Australia. Minute, heath-like, downy leaves. Masses of fluffy deep mauve flowers in small terminal clusters, in late spring–early summer. Zones 8–10.

Kunzea pulchella
☀ ⚘ ↔ 6 ft (1.8 m) ↑ 6 ft (1.8 m)
From semi-arid regions in southern Western Australia. Spreading or arching branches. Gray-green, silky hairy leaves. Bright red flowers in terminal spikes. Bird-attracting plant, suited to dry-summer climate. Pinch out the tips lightly after flowering. Zones 9–11.

Kunzea recurva
☀/◐ ⚘ ↔ 6 ft (1.8 m) ↑ 6 ft (1.8 m)
From Western Australia. Erect rounded shrub with small stem-clasping leaves that curve backward. Bright pinkish mauve flowers, in rounded clusters at branch ends, in late winter–spring. *K. r.* var. *montana* has yellow flowers. Zones 9–11.

Krascheninnikovia ceratoides

Kopsia fruticosa

.

Printed in Hong Kong by Sing Cheong Printing Co. Ltd

Film separation Pica Digital Pte Ltd, Singapore